CHILTON'S GUIDE TO
AUTOMATIC TRANSMISSION REPAIR
1984-89 DOMESTIC CARS & LIGHT TRUCKS

D1709010

President, Chilton Enterprises	David S. Loewith
Senior Vice President	Ronald A. Hoxter
Publisher and Editor-In-Chief	Kerry A. Freeman, S.A.E.
Managing Editors	Peter M. Conti, Jr. □ W. Calvin Settle, Jr., S.A.E.
Assistant Managing Editor	Nick D'Andrea
Senior Editors	Debra Gaffney □ Ken Grabowski, A.S.E., S.A.E.
	Michael L. Grady □ Richard J. Rivele, S.A.E.
	Richard T. Smith □ Jim Taylor
	Ron Webb
Director of Manufacturing	Mike D'Imperio

CHILTON BOOK COMPANY

ONE OF THE **ABC PUBLISHING COMPANIES**,
A PART OF **CAPITAL CITIES/ABC, INC.**

Manufactured in USA
© 1990 Chilton Book Company
Chilton Way, Radnor, PA 19089
ISBN 0–8019–8054–2
234567890 9876543

Contents

1 GENERAL INFORMATION

2 AUTOMATIC TRANSAXLE AND TRANSMISSION

3 AUTOMATIC TRANSAXLES

4 AUTOMATIC TRANSMISSIONS

5 OIL FLOW CIRCUITS

Section 1
Automatic Transmissions and Transaxles
General Information

GENERAL INFORMATION

Introduction

With this edition of Chilton's Professional Transmission Manual- domestic vehicles, we continue to assist the professional transmission repair trade to perform quality repairs and adjustments for that "like new" dependability of the transmission/transaxle assemblies.

This concise, but comprehensive service manual places emphasis on diagnosing, troubleshooting, adjustments, testing, disassembly and assembly of the automatic transmission/transaxle.

Metric Fasteners and Inch System Fasterners

Metric bolt sizes and thread pitches are more commonly used for all fasteners on the automatic transmissions/transaxles now being manufactured. The metric bolt sizes and thread pitches are very close to the dimensions of the similar inch system fasteners and for this reason, replacement fasteners must have the same measurement and strength as those removed.

Do not attempt to interchange metric fasteners for inch system fasteners. Mismatched and incorrect fasteners can result in

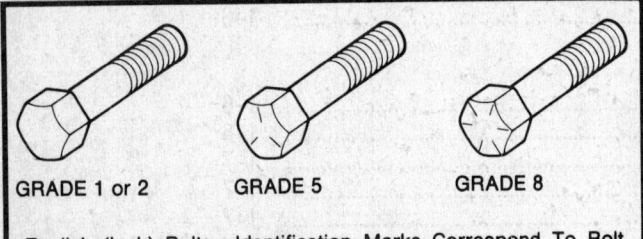

GRADE 1 or 2   GRADE 5   GRADE 8

English (Inch) Bolts—Identification Marks Correspond To Bolt Strength—Increasing Number Of Slashes Represent Increasing Strength.

Typical SAE bolt head identification marks

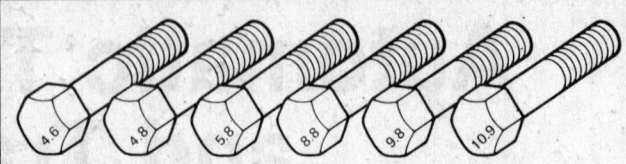

Metric Bolts—Identification Class Numbers Correspond To Bolt Strength—Increasing Numbers Represent Increasing Strength. Common Metric Fastener Bolt Strength Property Are 9.8 And 10.9 With The Class Identification Embossed On The Bolt Head.

Typical metric bolt head identification marks

damage to the transmission/transaxle unit through malfunction, breakage or possible personal injury. Care should be exercised to reuse the fasteners in their same locations as removed when every possible. If any doubt exists in the reuse of fasteners, install new ones.

To avoid stripped threads and to prevent metal warpage, the use of the torque wrench becomes more important, as the gear box assembly and internal components are being manufactured from light weight material. The torque conversion charts should be understood by the repairman, to properly service the requirements of the torquing procedures. When in doubt, refer to the specifications for the transmission/transaxle being serviced or overhauled.

Critical Measurements

With the increase use of transaxles and the close tolerances needed throughout the drive train, more emphasis is placed upon making the critical bearing and gear measurements correctly and being assured that correct preload and turning torque exists before the unit is reinstalled in the vehicle. Should a comeback occur because of the lack of proper clearances or torque, a costly rebuild can result. Rather than rebuilding a unit by "feel", the repairman must rely upon precise measuring

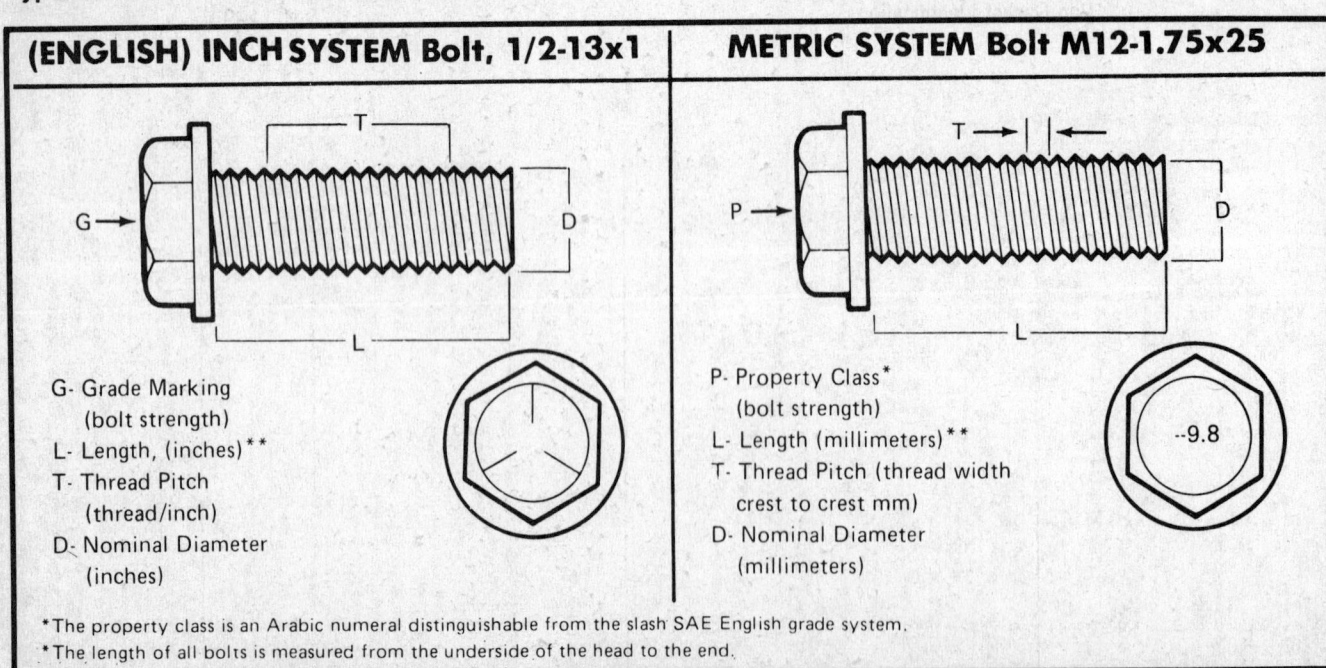

(ENGLISH) INCH SYSTEM Bolt, 1/2-13x1

G- Grade Marking
   (bolt strength)
L- Length, (inches) **
T- Thread Pitch
   (thread/inch)
D- Nominal Diameter
   (inches)

METRIC SYSTEM Bolt M12-1.75x25

P- Property Class*
   (bolt strength)
L- Length (millimeters) **
T- Thread Pitch (thread width
   crest to crest mm)
D- Nominal Diameter
   (millimeters)

--9.8

*The property class is an Arabic numeral distinguishable from the slash SAE English grade system.
*The length of all bolts is measured from the underside of the head to the end.

SAE and metric system bolt and thread nomenclature

(ENGLISH) INCH SYSTEM		METRIC SYSTEM	
Grade	Identification	Class	Identification
Hex Nut Grade 5	3 Dots	Hex Nut Property Class 9	Arabic 9
Hex Nut Grade 8	6 Dots	Hex Nut Property Class 10	Arabic 10
Increasing dots represent increasing strength.		May also have blue finish or paint daub on hex flat. Increasing numbers represent increasing strength.	

SAE and metric system strength identification marks

tools, such as the dial indicator gauge, micrometers, torque wrenches and feeler gauges to insure that correct specifications are adhered to. At the end of each transmission/transaxle section specification data is provided so that the repairman can measure important clearances that will effect the outcome of the transmission/transaxle rebuild.

Electronically Controlled Units

Today transmissions/transaxles are being developed and manufactured with electronically controlled components. The demand for lighter, smaller and more fuel efficient vehicles has resulted in the use of electronics to control both the engine spark and fuel delivery. Certain transmission/transaxle assemblies are a part of the electronic controls, by sending signals of vehicle speed and throttle opening to an on-board computer, which in turn computes these signals, along with others from the engine assembly, to determine if spark occurrence should be changed or the delivery of fuel should be increased or decreased. The computer signals are then sent to their respective controls and/or sensors as required.

Automatic transmissions/transaxles with microcomputers to determine gear selections are now in use. Sensors are used for engine and road speeds, engine load, gear selector lever position, kickdown switch and a status of the driving program to send signals to the microcomputer to determine the optimum gear selection, according to a preset program. The shifting is accomplished by solenoid valves in the hydraulic system. The electronics also control the modulated hydraulic system during shifting, along with regulating engine torque to provide smooth shifts between gear ratio changes. This type of system can be designed for different driving programs, such as giving the operator the choice of operating the vehicle for either economy or performance.

Lockup Torque Converter Units

DESCRIPTION

Most all vehicle transmissions/transaxles are equipped with a lockup torque converter. The lockup torque converter clutch should apply when the engine has reached near normal operating temperature in order to handle the slight extra load and when the vehicle speed is high enough to allow the operation of the clutch to be smooth and the vehicle to be free of engine pulses.

When the converter clutch is coupled to the engine, the engine pulses can be felt through the vehicle in the same manner as if equipped with a clutch and standard transmission. Engine condition, engine load and engine speed determines the severity of the pulsations.

The converter clutch should release when torque multiplication is needed in the converter, when coming to a stop, or when the mechanical connection would affect exhaust emissions during a coasting condition.

The electrical control components consists of the brake release switch, the low vacuum switch and the governor switch. Some transmission/transaxles have a thermal vacuum switch, a relay valve and a delay valve. Diesel engines use a high vacuum switch in addition to certain above listed components. These various components control the flow of current to the apply valve solenoid. By controlling the current flow, these components activate or deactivate the solenoid, which in turn engages or disengages the transmission/transaxle converter clutch, depending upon the driving conditions. The components have 2 basic circuits, electrical and vacuum.

ELECTRICAL CURRENT FLOW

All of the components in the electrical circuit must be closed or grounded before the solenoid can open the hydraulic circuit to engage the converter clutch. The circuit begins at the fuse panel and flows to the brake switch as long as the brake pedal is not depressed. The current will flow to the low vacuum switch on gasoline engines and to the high vacuum switch on diesel engines. These switches open or close the circuit path to the solenoid, dependent upon the engine or pump vacuum. If the low vacuum switch is closed (high switch on diesel engines), the current continues to flow to the transmission/transaxle case connector and then into the solenoid and to the governor pressure switch. When the vehicle speed is approximately 35–50 mph, the governor switch grounds to activate the solenoid. The solenoid, in turn, opens a hydraulic circuit to the converter clutch assembly, engaging the unit.

It should be noted that external vacuum controls include the thermal vacuum valve, the relay valve, the delay valve, the low vacuum switch and a high vacuum switch (used on diesel engines). Keep in mind that all of the electrical or vacuum components may not be used on all engines, at the same time.

VACUUM FLOW

The vacuum relay valve works with the thermal vacuum valve to keep the engine vacuum from reaching the low vacuum valve switch at low engine temperatures. This action prevents the clutch from engaging while the engine is still warming up. The delay valve slows down the response of the low vacuum switch to changes in engine vacuum. This action prevents the low vacuum switch from causing the converter clutch to engage and disengage too rapidly. The low vacuum switch deactivates the converter clutch when engine vacuum drops to a specific low level during moderate acceleration just before a part-throttle transmission downshift. The low vacuum switch also deactivates the clutch while the vehicle is coasting because it receives no vacuum from its ported vacuum source.

The high vacuum switch, on diesel engines, deactivates the converter clutch while the vehicle is coasting. The low vacuum switch used on diesel engines only deactivates the converter clutch during moderate acceleration, just prior to a part-throttle downshift. Because the diesel engine's vacuum source is a vacuum pump, rather than from a carburetor port, diesel engines require both the high and the low vacuum switch to achieve the same results as the low vacuum switch used on gasoline engines.

COMPUTER CONTROLLED CONVERTER CLUTCH

With the use of microcomputers governoring the engine fuel and spark delivery, the converter clutch electronic control has been changed to provide the grounding circuit for the solenoid valve through the microcomputer, rather than the governor pressure switch. Sensors are used in place of the formerly used switches. These sensors send signals back to the microcomputers to indicate if the engine is in its proper mode to accept the mechanical lockup of the converter clutch.

Normally a coolant sensor, a throttle position sensor, an engine vacuum sensor and a vehicle speed sensor are used to signal the microcomputer when the converter clutch can be applied. Should a sensor indicate the need for the converter clutch to be deactivated, the grounding circuit to the transmission/transaxle solenoid valve would be interrupted and the converter clutch would be released.

HYDRAULIC CONVERTER CLUTCH OPERATION

Numerous automatic transmissions/transaxles rely upon hydraulic pressures to sense and determine when to apply the converter clutch function. This type of automatic transmission/transaxle unit is considered to be a self-contained unit with only the shift linkage, throttle cable or modulator valve being external. Specific valves, located within the valve body or oil pump housing, are put into operation when a sequence of events occur within the unit. For example, to engage the converter clutch, most all automatic transmissions require the gear ratio to be in the top gear before the converter clutch control valves can be placed in operation. The governor and throttle pressures must maintain specific fluid pressures at various points within the hydraulic circuits in the engagement or disengagement of the converter clutch. In addition, check valves must properly seal and move the exhaust pressurized fluid at the correct time to avoid "shudders" or "chuckles" during the initial application and engagement of the converter clutch.

CENTRIFUGAL CONVERTER CLUTCH

Transmissions/transaxles also use a torque converter that mechanically locks up centrifugally without the use of electronics or hydraulic pressure. At specific input shaft speeds, brake-like shoes move outward from the rim of the turbine assembly, to

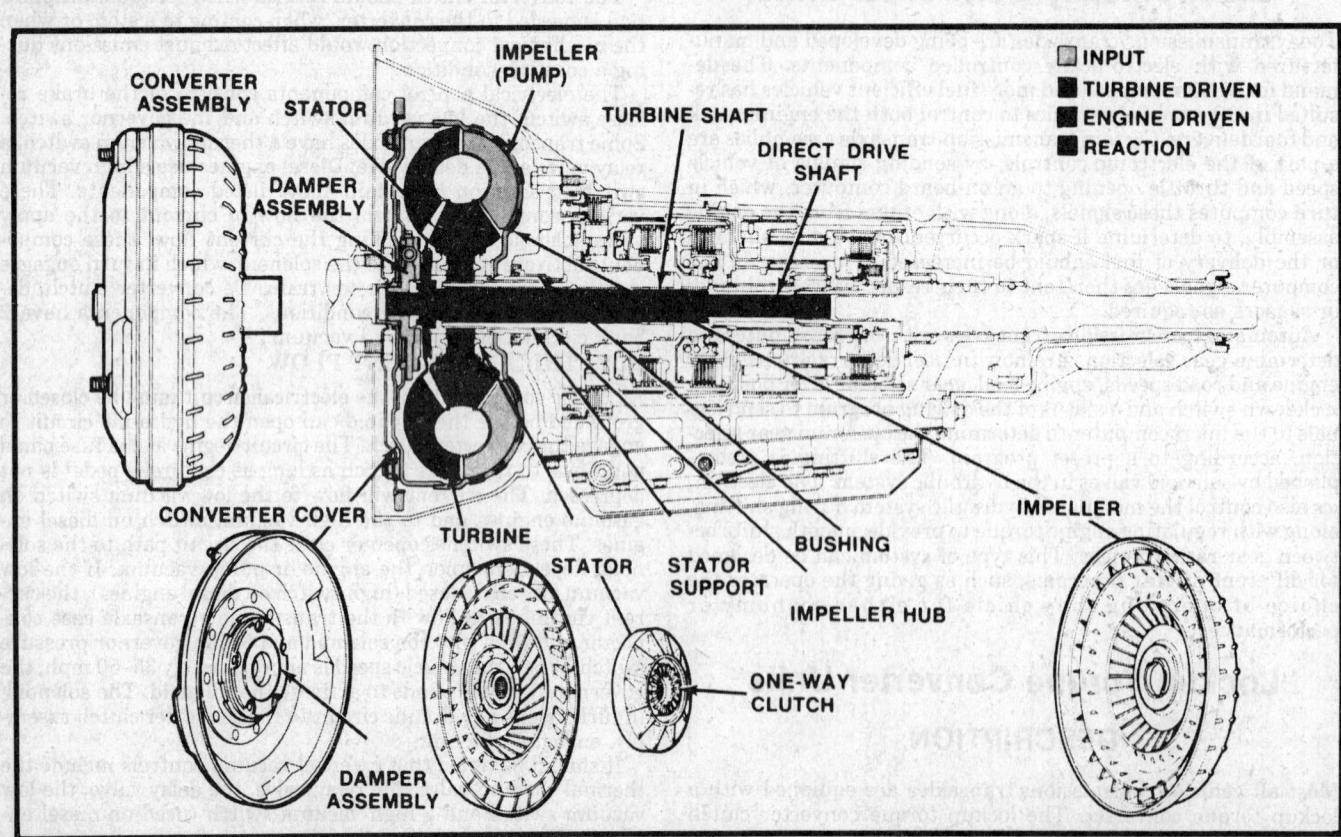

Torque converter and direct driveshaft—AOD transmission

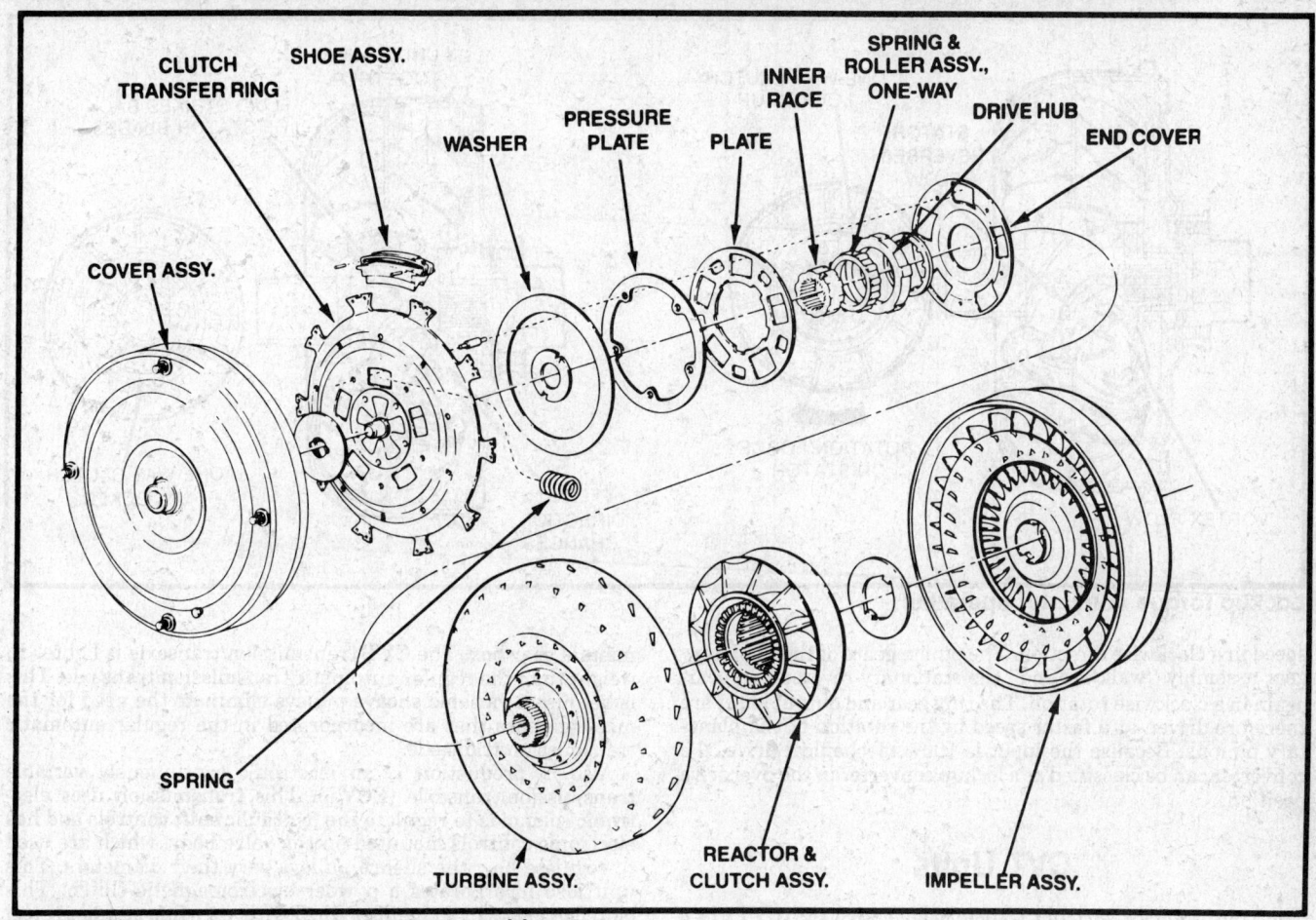

Centrifugal torque converter clutch assembly

engage the converter housing, locking the converter unit mechanically together for a 1:1 ratio. Slight slippage can occur at the low end of the rpm scale, but the greater the rpm, the tighter the lockup. Again, it must be mentioned, that when the converter has locked up, the vehicle may respond in the same manner as driving with a clutch and standard transmission. This is considered normal and does not indicate converter clutch or transmission/transaxle problems. Keep in mind if the engine is in need of a tune-ups or repairs, the lockup "shudder" or "chuckle" feeling may be greater.

MECHANICAL CONVERTER LOCKUP

Another type of converter lockup is the Ford Motor Co. AOD automatic overdrive transmission, which uses a direct drive input shaft splined to the damper assembly of the torque converter cover to the direct clutch,thereby bypassing the torque converter reduction components. A second shaft encloses the direct drive input shaft and is coupled between the converter turbine and the reverse clutch or forward clutch, depending upon their applied phase. With this type of unit, when in third gear, the input shaft torque is split, 30% hydraulic and 70% mechanical. When in the overdrive or fourth gear, the input torque is completely mechanical and the transmission is locked mechanically to the engine.

CONFIRMING CONVERTER LOCKUP

To confirm that the lockup function of the torque converter has occurred, check the engine rpm with a tachometer while the vehicle is being driven. If the torque converter is locked up, the engine rpm will decrease approximately 200–400 rpm, at the time of lockup.

Overdrive Units

With need for greater fuel economy, the automatic transmission/transaxles were among the many vehicle components that have been modified to aid in this quest. Internal changes have been made and in some cases, additions of a fourth gear to provide the overdirect or overdrive gear ratio. The reasoning for adding the overdrive capability is that an overdrive ratio enables the output speed of the transmission/transaxle to be greater than the input speed, allowing the vehicle to maintain a given speed with less engine speed. This results in better fuel economy and a slower running engine.

The automatic overdrive unit usually consists of an overdrive planetary gear set, a roller one-way clutch assembly and 2 friction clutch assemblies, one as an internal clutch pack and the second for a brake clutch pack. The overdrive carrier is splined to the turbine shaft, which in turn, is splined into the converter turbine.

Another type of overdrive assembly is a separation of the overdrive components by having them at various points along the gear transassembly and also utilizing them for other gear ranges. Instead of having a brake clutch pack, an overdrive band is used to lock the planetary sun gear. In this type of transmission, the converter cover drives the direct driveshaft clockwise at engine speed, which in turn drives the direct clutch. The direct clutch then drives the planetary carrier assembly at engine

Lockup torque converter operation

speed in a clockwise direction. The pinion gears of the planetary gear assembly "walk around" the stationary reverse sun gear, again in a clockwise rotation. The ring gear and output shaft are therefore driven at a faster speed by the rotation of the planetary pinions. Because the input is 100% mechanical drive, the converter can be classified as a lockup converter in the overdrive position.

CVT Units

The continuously variable transmission/transaxle (CVT) is a new type of automatic transmission/transaxle. The CVT offers a vehicle drive ratio that is equal to that of a 5 speed (or more)

manual gear box. The CVT transmission/transaxle is lighter in weight than the regular automatic transmission/transaxle. This is because 2 variable sheave pulleys eliminate the need for the mass of gears that are incorporated in the regular automatic transmission/transaxle.

Also in production is an electronic continuously variable transmission/transaxle (ECVT). This transmission uses electronic solenoids to regulate the hydraulic shift controls and has electronic controls mounted on the valve body, which are used to regulate how the sheave pulleys vary their diameters. This unit also incorporates a powder electromagnetic clutch. This clutch consists of a chamber filled with very fine stainless steel powder. The clutch spins free until the coils are energized and in turn magnetize the powder and lockup the clutch.

DIAGNOSING AUTOMATIC TRANSMISSION/TRANSAXLE MALFUNCTIONS

Introduction

Diagnosing automatic transmission/transaxle problems is simplified following a definite procedure and understanding the basic operation of the individual transmission/transaxle that is being inspected or serviced. Do no attempt to short-cut the procedure or take for granted that another technician has performed the adjustments or the critical checks. It may be an easy task to locate a defective or burned-out unit, but the technician must be skilled in locating the primary reason for the unit failure and must repair the malfunction to avoid having the same failure occur again.

Each automatic transmission/transaxle manufacturer has developed a diagnostic procedure for their individual transmissions/transaxles. Although the operation of the units are basically the same, many differences will appear in the construction, method of unit application and the hydraulic control system.

The same model transmission/transaxle can be installed in different makes of vehicles and are designed to operate under different load stresses, engine applications and road conditions. Each make of vehicle will have specific adjustments or use certain outside manual controls to operate the individual unit, but

may not interchange with another transmission/transaxle vehicle application from the same manufacturer.

The identification of the transmission/transaxle is most important so that the proper preliminary inspections and adjustments may be done and if in need of a major overhaul, the correct parts may be obtained and installed to avoid costly delays.

Systematic Diagnosis

Transmission/transaxle manufacturers have compiled diagnostic aids to use when diagnosing malfunctions through oil pressure tests or road test procedures. Diagnostic symptom charts, operational shift speed charts, oil pressure specifications, clutch and band application charts and oil flow schematics are some of the aids available.

Numerous manufacturers and re-manufacturers require a diagnosis check sheet be filled out by the diagnostician, pertaining to the operation, fluid level, oil pressure (idling and at various speeds), verification of adjustments and possible causes and the need correction of the malfunctions. In certain cases, authorization must be obtained before repairs can be done, with the diagnostic check sheet accompanying the request for payment or warranty claim, along with the return of defective parts.

It is a good policy to use the diagnostic check sheet for the evaluation of all transmission/transaxle diagnosis and include the complete check sheet in the owners service file, should future reference be needed.

Many times, a rebuilt unit is exchanged for the defective unit, saving down time for the owner and vehicle. However, if the diagnostic check sheet would accompany the removed unit to the rebuilder, more attention could be directed to verifying and repairing the malfunctioning components to avoid costly comebacks of the rebuilt unit, at a later date. Most large volume rebuilders employ the use of dynamometers, as do the new unit manufacturers, to verify proper build-up of the unit and its correct operation before it is put in service.

General Diagnosis

Should the diagnostician not use a pre-printed check sheet for the diagnosing of the malfunctioning unit, a sequence for diagnosis of the gear box is needed to proceed in an orderly manner. During the road test, use all the selector ranges while noting any differences in operation or changes in oil pressure, so that the defective unit or hydraulic circuit can be isolated and the malfunction corrected. A suggested sequence is as follows:

1. Inspect and correct the fluid level.
2. Inspect and adjust the throttle or kickdown linkage.
3. Inspect and adjust the manual linkage.
4. Be sure to properly install a pressure gauge to the transmission/transaxle as instructed in the individual repair section.
5. Road test the vehicle (with owner if possible).

Road Test Diagnosis

Prior to driving the vehicle on a road test, have the vehicle operator explain the malfunction of the transmission/transaxle as fully and as accurate as possible. Because the operator may not have the same technical knowledge as the diagnostician, ask questions concerning the malfunction in a manner that the operator can understand. It may be necessary to have the operator drive the vehicle, with the technician, on a road test and to identify the problem. The diagnostician can observe the manner in which the transmission/transaxle is being operated and can point out constructive driving habits to the operator to improve operation reliability.

Many times, an actual transmission/transaxle malfunction can occur without the operator's knowledge, due to slight slippages occurring and increasing in duration while the vehicle is being driven. Had the operator realized that a malfunction existed, minor adjustments possibly could have been done to avoid costly repairs.

Be aware of the engine's performance. For example, if a vacuum modulator valve is used to control the throttle pressure, an engine performing poorly cannot send the proper vacuum signals to the transmission/transaxle for proper application of the throttle pressure and control pressure, in the operation of the bands and clutches. Slippages and changes in shift points can occur.

During the road test, the converter operation must be considered. Related converter malfunctions affecting the road test could be that the stator assembly free wheels or the stator assembly remains locked up.

When the stator roller clutch freewheels in both directions, the vehicle will have poor acceleration from a standstill. At speeds above approximately 45 mph, the vehicle will act normally. A check to make on the engine is to accelerate to a high rpm in neutral. If the engine responds properly, this is an indication that the engine is operating satisfactorily and the problem may be with the stator.

When the stator remains locked up, the engine rpm and the vehicle speed will be restricted at higher speeds, although the

vehicle will accelerate from a standstill normally. Engine overheating may be noticed and visual inspection of the converter may reveal a blue color, resulting from converter overheating.

Clutch and Band Application Diagnosis

During the road test, operate the transmission/transaxle in each gear position and observe the shifts for signs of any slippage, variation, sponginess or harshness. Note the speeds at which the upshifts and downshifts occur. If slippage and engine flare-up occurs in any gear, clutch band or overrunning clutch problems are indicated and depending upon the degree of wear, a major overhaul may be indicated.

The clutch and band application chart in each transmission/transaxle section provides a basis for road test analysis to determine the internal units applied or released in a specific gear ratio.

NOTE: Some transmissions/transaxles use brake and clutches in place of bands and are usually indicated at B1 and B2 on the unit application chart. These components are diagnosed in the same manner as one would diagnose a band equipped gearbox.

TRANSMISSION/TRANSAXLE NOISE DIAGNOSIS

In diagnosisng transmission/transaxle noises, the diagnostician must be alert to any abnormal noises from the transmission/transaxle area or any excessive movement of the engine or the transmission/transaxle assembly during torque application or transmission/transaxle shifting.

CAUTION

Before attempting to diagnose automatic transmission/transaxle noises, be sure the noises do not originate from the engine components, such as the water pump, alternator, air conditioner compressor, power steering or the air injection pump. Isolate these components by removing the proper drive belt and operate the engine. Do not operate the engine longer than 2 minutes at a time to avoid overheating.

---

1. Whining or siren type noises can be considered normal if occurring during a stall speed test, due to the fluid flow through the converter.
2. A continual whining noise with the vehicle stationary and if the noise increases and decreases with the engine speed, the following defects could be present:
   a. Oil level low
   b. Air leakage into pump (defective gasket, O-ring or porosity of a part)
   c. Pump gears damaged or worn
   d. Pump gears assembled backward
   e. Pump crescent interference
3. A buzzing noise is normally the result of a pressure regulator valve vibrating or a sealing ring broken or worn out and will usually come and go, depending upon engine and the transmission/transaxle speed.
4. A constant rattling noise that usually occurs at low engine speed can be the result of the vanes stripped from the impeller or turbine face or internal interference of the converter parts.
5. An intermittent rattleing noise reflects a broken flywheel or flex plate and usually occurs at low engine speed with the transmission/transaxle in gear. Placing the transmission/transaxle in N or P will change the rattling noise or stop it for a short time.
6. Gear noise (1 gear range) will normally indicate a defective planetary gear unit. Upon shifting into another gear range, the noise will cease. If the noise carries over to the next gear range, but at a different pitch, defective thrust bearings or bushings are indicated.

7. Engine vibration or excessive movement can be caused by transmission/transaxle filler or cooler lines vibrating due to broken or disconnected brackets. If excessive engine or transmission/transaxle movement is noted, look for broken engine or transmission/transaxle mounts.

CAUTION

When necessary to support an engine equipped with metal safety tabs on the mounts, be sure the metal tabs are not in contact with the mount bracket after the engine or transmission/transaxle assembly is again supported by the mounts. A severe vibration can result.

---

8. Squeal at low vehicle speeds can result from a speedometer driven gear seal, a front pump seal or rear extension seal being dry.

9. The above list of noises can be used as a guide. Noises other than the ones listed can occur around or within the transmission assembly. A logical and common sense approach will normally result in the source of the noise being detected.

Fluid Diagnosis
FLUID INSPECTION AND LEVEL

Most automatic transmissions/transaxles are designed to operate with the fluid level between the **ADD** or **ONE PINT** and **FULL** marks on the dipstick indicator, with the fluid at normal operating temperature. The normal operating temperature is attained by operating the engine assembly for at least 8–15 miles of driving or its equivalent. The fluid temperature should be in the range of 150–200°F when normal operating temperature is attained.

NOTE: If the vehicle has been operated for long periods at high speed or in extended city traffic during hot weather, an accurate fluid level check cannot be made until the fluid cools, normally 30 minutes after the vehicle has been parked, due to fluid heat in excess of 200°F.

The transmission fluid can be checked during 2 ranges of temperatures.
1. Transmission/transaxle at normal operating temperature.
2. Transmission/transaxle at room temperature.

During the checking procedure and adding of fluid to the transmission/transaxle, it is most important not to overfill the reservoir in order to avoid foaming and loss of fluid through the breather, which can cause slippage and transmission/transaxle failure.

Transmission/Transaxle at Room temperature
65–95°F – DIPSTICK COOL TO TOUCH

CAUTION

The automatic transmissions/transaxles are sometimes overfilled because the fluid level is checked when the transmission/transaxle has not been operated and the fluid is cold and contracted. As the transmission/transaxle is warmed to normal operating temperature, the fluid level can change as much as ¾ in.

---

1. With the vehicle on a level surface, engine idling, wheels blocked or parking brake applied, move the selector lever through all the ranges to fill the passages with fluid.
2. Place the selector lever in the **P** position and remove the dipstick from the transmission/transaxle. Wipe clean the re-insert it back into the dipstick tube.
3. Remove the dipstick and observe the fluid level mark on the dipstick stem. The fluid should be directly below the **FULL** indicator.

NOTE: Most dipsticks will have either one mark or two marks, such as dimples or holes in the stem of the dipstick, to indicate the cold level, while others may be marked HOT or COLD levels.

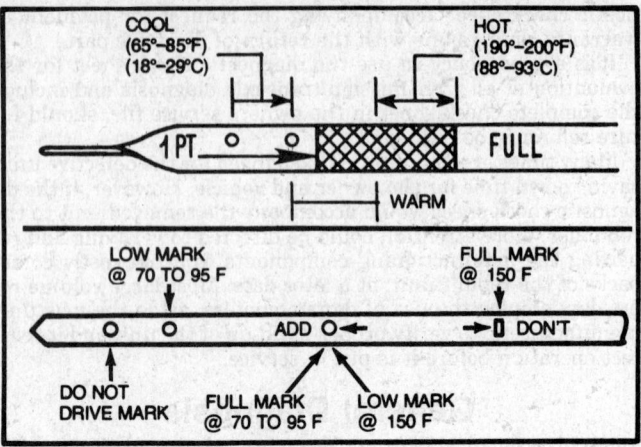

Typical fluid level indicators

4. Add enough fluid, as necessary, to the transmission/transaxle, but do not overfill.

CAUTION

This operation is most critical, due to the expansion of the fluid under heat.

Transmission/Transaxle at Normal Operating Temperature
150–200°F – DIPSTICK HOT TO THE TOUCH

1. With the vehicle on a level surface, engine idling, wheels blocked or parking brake applied, move the gear selector lever through all the ranges to fill the passages with fluid.
2. Place the selector lever in the **P** position and remove the dipstick from the transmission/transaxle. Wipe clean and reinsert and dipstick to its full length into the dipstick tube.
3. Remove the dipstick and observe the fluid level mark on the dipstick stem. The fluid level should be between the **ADD** and the **FULL** marks. If necessary, add fluid through the filler tube to bring the fluid level to its proper height.
4. Reinstall the dipstick and be sure it is sealed to the dipstick filler tube to avoid the entrance of dirt or water.

FLUID TYPE SPECIFICATIONS

The automatic transmission fluid is used for numerous functions such as a power-transmitting fluid in the torque converter, a hydraulic fluid in the hydraulic control system, a lubricating agent for the gears, bearings and bushings, a friction-controlling fluid for the bands and clutches and a heat transfer medium to carry the heat to an air or cooling fan arrangement.

Because of the varied automatic transmission/transaxle designs, different frictional characteristics of the fluids are required so that one fluid cannot assure freedom from chatter or squawking from the bands and clutches. Operating temperatures have increased sharply in many new transmissions/transaxles and the transmission drain intervals have been extended or eliminated completely. It is therefore most important to install the proper automatic transmission fluid into the automatic transmission/tranaxle design for its use.

FLUID CONDITION

During the checking of the fluid level, the fluid condition should be inspected for color and odor. The normal color of the fluid is deep red or orange-red and should not be a burned brown or black color. If the fluid color should turn to a green/brown shade at an early stage of transmission/transaxle operation and have an offensive odor, but not a burned odor, the fluid condition is considered normal and not a positive sign of required maintenance or transmission/transaxle failure.

With the use of absorbent white paper, wipe the dipstick and examine the stain for black, brown or metallic specks, indicating clutch, band or bushing failure, and for gum or varnish on the dipstick or bubbles in the fluid, indicating either water or antifreeze in the fluid.

Should there be evidence of water, antifreeze or specks of residue in the fluid, the oil pan should be removed and the sediment inspected. If the fluid is contaminated or excessive solids are found in the removed oil pan, the transmission/transaxle should be disassembled, completely cleaned and overhauled. In addition to the cleaning of the transmission/transaxle, the converter and transmission/transaxle cooling system should be cleaned and tested.

SYSTEM FLUSHING

Much reference has been made to the importance of flushing the transmission/transaxle fluid coolers and lines during an overhaul. With the increased use of converter clutch units and the necessary changes to the internal fluid routings, the passage of contaminated fluid, sludge or metal particles to the fluid cooler is more predominate. In most cases, the fluid returning from the fluid cooler is directed to the lubrication system and should the system be deprived of lubricating fluid due to blockage premature unit failure will occur.

Procedure

1. Disconnect both fluid lines from the transmission/transaxle assemblies, leaving the lines attached to the cooler.
2. Add a length of hose to the return line and place in a container. Flush both lines and the cooler at the same time.

NOTE: **When flushing the cooling components, use a commercial flushing fluid or its equivalent. Reverse flush the lines and cooler with the flushing fluid and pulsating air pressure. Continue the flushing process until clean flushing fluid appears. Remove the flushing fluid by the addition of transmission fluid through the lines and cooler.**

Special Tools

There are an unlimited amount of special tools and accessories available to the transmission rebuilder to lessen the time and effort required in performing the diagnosing and overhaul of the automatic transmission/transaxles. Specific tools are necessary during the disassembly and assembly of each unit and its subassemblies. Certain tools can be fabricated, but it becomes the responsibility of the repair shop operator to obtain commercially manufactured tools to insure quality rebuilding and to avoid costly "come backs".

The commercial labor saving tools range from puller sets, bushing and seal installer sets, compression tools and presses (both mechanically and hydraulically operated), holding fixtures, oil pump aligning tools, degreaser tanks, steam cleaners, converter flushing machines, transmission/transaxle jacks and lifts, to name a few. For specific information concerning the various tools, a parts and tool supplier should be consulted.

The use of the basic measuring tools has become more critical in the rebuilding process. The increased use of front drive transaxles, in which both the automatic transmission/transaxle and the final drive gears are located, has required the rebuilder to adhere to specifications and tolerances more closely than ever before.

Bearings must be torqued or adjusted to specific preloads in order to meet the rotating torque drag specifications. The end play and backlash of the varied shafts and gears must be measured to avoid excessive tightness or looseness. Critical tensioning bolts must be torqued to specification.

Dial indicators must be protected and used as a delicate measuring instrument. A mutilated or un-calibrated dial indicator invites premature unit failure and destruction. Torque wrenches are available in many forms, some cheaply made and others, accurate and durable under constant use. To obtain accurate readings and properly applied torque, recalibration should be applied to the torque wrenches periodically, regardless of the type used. Micrometers are used as precise measuring tools and should be properly stored when not in use. Instructions on the recalibration of the micrometers and a test bar usually accompany the tool when it is purchased.

Other measuring tools are available to the rebuilder and each in their own way, must be protected when not in use to avoid causing mis-measuring in the fitting of a component to the unit.

Pan Gasket Identification

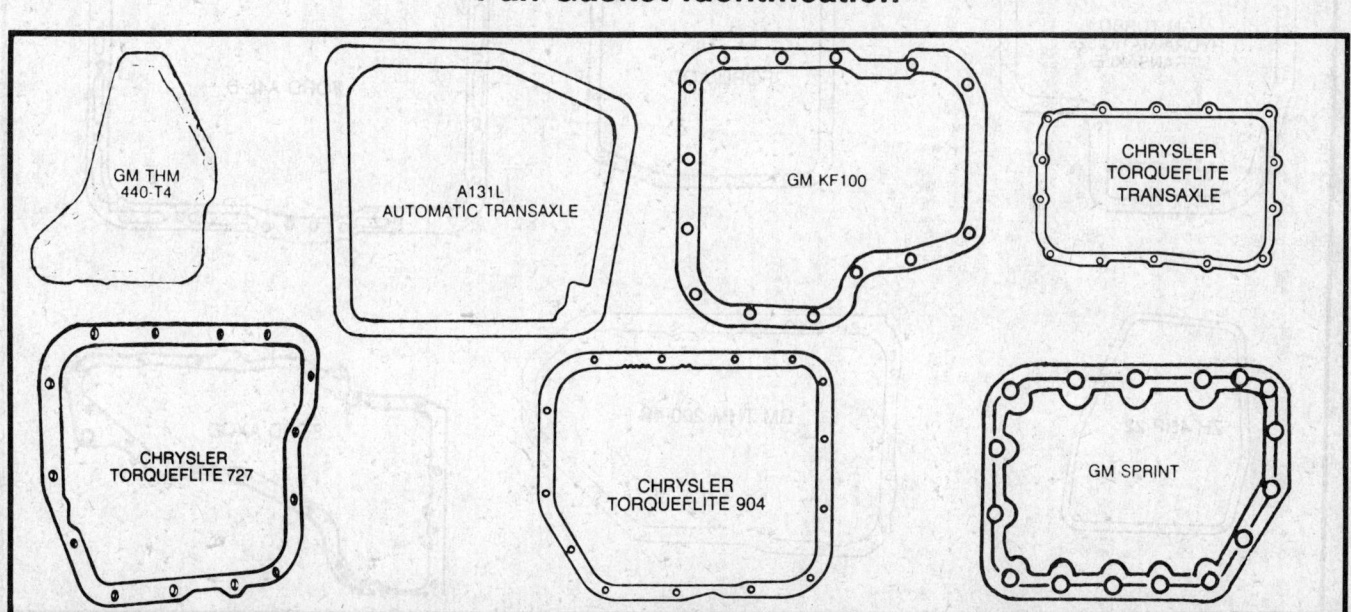

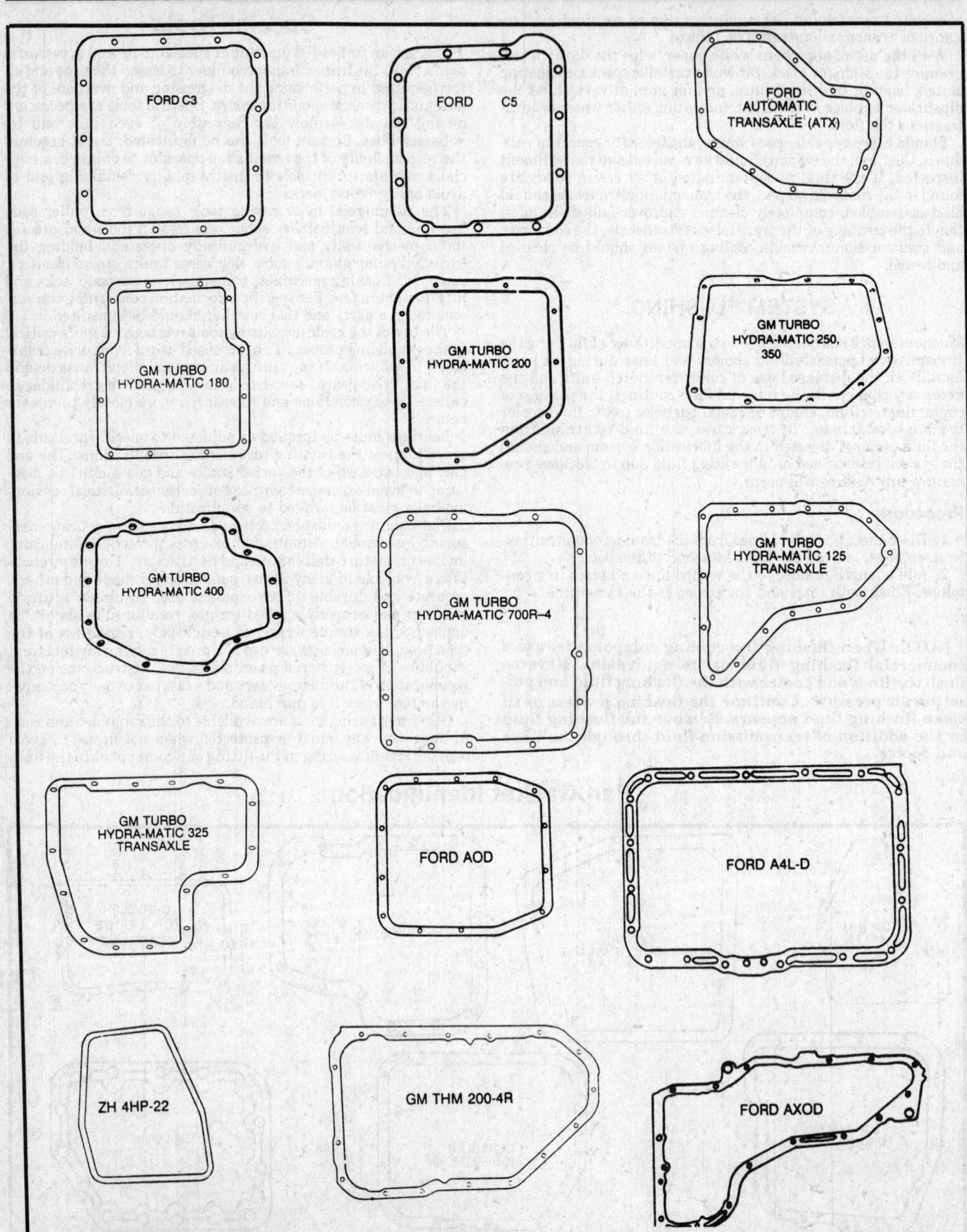

FORD C3

FORD C5

FORD AUTOMATIC TRANSAXLE (ATX)

GM TURBO HYDRA-MATIC 180

GM TURBO HYDRA-MATIC 200

GM TURBO HYDRA-MATIC 250, 350

GM TURBO HYDRA-MATIC 400

GM TURBO HYDRA-MATIC 700R-4

GM TURBO HYDRA-MATIC 125 TRANSAXLE

GM TURBO HYDRA-MATIC 325 TRANSAXLE

FORD AOD

FORD A4L-D

ZH 4HP-22

GM THM 200-4R

FORD AXOD

Section 2
Automatic Transmission/ Transaxle Applications

AMC-JEEP-EAGLE TRANSMISSION APPLICATIONS

Transmission	Year	Engine	Vehicle	Transmission Code
727	1984	2.5L	CJ	89-33-000-914, 89-33-000-915, 89-33-000-918, 89-53-001-836
			Wagoneer	89-33-000-914, 89-33-000-915, 89-33-000-918, 89-53-001-836
		2.8L	Wagoneer	89-33-000-914, 89-33-000-915, 89-33-000-918, 89-53-001-836
		4.2L	CJ	89-33-000-914, 89-33-000-915, 89-33-000-918, 89-53-001-836
			J10	89-33-000-914, 89-33-000-915, 89-33-000-918, 89-53-001-836
		5.9L	Grand Wagoneer	89-33-000-914, 89-33-000-915, 89-33-000-918, 89-53-001-836
			J10	89-33-000-914, 89-33-000-915, 89-33-000-918, 89-53-001-836
			J20	89-33-000-914, 89-33-000-915, 89-33-000-918, 89-53-001-836
727	1985	2.1L	Cherokee	89-33-000-914, 89-33-000-915, 89-33-000-918, 89-53-001-836
		2.5L	CJ	89-33-000-914, 89-33-000-915, 89-33-000-918, 89-53-001-836
		4.2L	CJ	89-33-000-914, 89-33-000-915, 89-33-000-918, 89-53-001-836
			Grand Wagoneer	89-33-000-914, 89-33-000-915, 89-33-000-918, 89-53-001-836
			J10	89-33-000-914, 89-33-000-915, 89-33-000-918, 89-53-001-836
		5.9L	Grand Wagoneer	89-33-000-914, 89-33-000-915, 89-33-000-918, 89-53-001-836
			J10	89-33-000-914, 89-33-000-915, 89-33-000-918, 89-53-001-836
			J20	89-33-000-914, 89-33-000-915, 89-33-000-918, 89-53-001-836
727	1986	2.5L	CJ	89-33-000-914, 89-33-000-915, 89-33-000-918, 89-53-001-836
		4.2L	CJ	89-33-000-914, 89-33-000-915, 89-33-000-918, 89-53-001-836
			Grand Wagoneer	89-33-000-914, 89-33-000-915, 89-33-000-918, 89-53-001-836
			J10	89-33-000-914, 89-33-000-915, 89-33-000-918, 89-53-001-836
		5.9L	Grand Wagoneer	89-33-000-914, 89-33-000-915, 89-33-000-918, 89-53-001-836
			J10	89-33-000-914, 89-33-000-915, 89-33-000-918, 89-53-001-836
			J20	89-33-000-914, 89-33-000-915, 89-33-000-918, 89-53-001-836
727	1987	4.2L	J10	53005-019
		5.9L	Grand Wagoneer	53005-019
			J10	53005-019
			J20	53005-019
727	1988	4.2L	J10	53005-019
		5.9L	J10	53005-019
			J20	53005-019

AMC-JEEP-EAGLE TRANSMISSION APPLICATIONS

Transmission	Year	Engine	Vehicle	Transmission Code
727	1989	5.9L	Grand Wagoneer	53005-019
998	1984	2.5L	Eagle	33000-916
		4.2L	Eagle	33000-916
998	1985	4.2L	Eagle	33002-366
998	1986	4.2L	Eagle	33002-366
998	1987	4.2L	Eagle	33004-126
998	1988	4.2L	Eagle	33004-126 Type I, 83505-566 Type II
999	1984	2.5L	CJ	89-33-000-913, 89-33-000-917
		4.2L	CJ	89-33-000-913, 89-33-000-917
			Grand Wagoneer	89-33-000-913, 89-33-000-917
			J10	89-33-000-913, 89-33-000-917
	1985	2.5L	CJ	89-33-000-913, 89-33-000-917
		4.2L	CJ	89-33-000-913, 89-33-000-917
			Grand Wagoneer	89-33-000-913, 89-33-000-917
			J10	89-33-000-913, 89-33-000-917
	1986	2.5L	CJ	89-33-000-913, 89-33-000-917
		4.2L	CJ	89-33-000-913, 89-33-000-917
			Grand Wagoneer	89-33-000-913, 89-33-000-917
			J10	89-33-000-913, 89-33-000-917
	1987	2.5L	Wrangler	53003-074, 53005-018, 83505-55
		4.2L	Wrangler	53003-074, 53005-018, 83505-55
	1988	2.5L	Wrangler	53003-074, 53005-018, 83505-55
		4.2L	Wrangler	53003-074, 53005-018, 83505-55
	1989	4.2L	Wrangler	53003-074, 53005-018, 83505-55
AR4	1987	2.2L	Medallion	AR4-xxx ①
		2.5L	Premier	AR4-xxx ①
		3.0L	Premier	AR4-xxx ①
AR4	1988	2.2L	Medallion	AR4-xxx ①
		2.5L	Premier	AR4-xxx ①
		3.0L	Premier	AR4-xxx ①
AR4	1989	2.2L	Medallion	AR4-xxx ①
		2.5L	Premier	AR4-xxx ①
		3.0L	Premier	AR4-xxx ①
AW4	1984	2.5L	Cherokee	530001-141, 530001-334, 53002-430
			Wagoneer	530001-141, 530001-334, 53002-430
		2.8L	Cherokee	530001-141, 530001-334, 53002-430
			Wagoneer	530001-141, 530001-334, 53002-430
AW4	1985	2.1L	Cherokee	530001-334
			Wagoneer	530001-334
		2.5L	Cherokee	530001-141, 530001-334, 53002-430
			Wagoneer	530001-141, 530001-334, 53002-430
		2.8L	Cherokee	530001-141, 530001-334, 53002-430
			Wagoneer	530001-141, 530001-334, 53002-430

① Serial numbers in sequence

AMC-JEEP-EAGLE TRANSMISSION APPLICATIONS

Transmission	Year	Engine	Vehicle	Transmission Code
AW4	1986	2.1L	Cherokee	53001-672, 53003-810, 811, JR775-140, 1
			Commanche	53001-672, 53003-810, 811, JR775-140, 141
			Wagoneer	53001-672, 53003-810, 811, JR775-140, 141
		2.5L	Cherokee	53001-672, 53003-810, 811, JR775-140, 141
			Commanche	53001-672, 53003-810, 811, JR775-140, 141
			Wagoneer	53001-672, 53003-810, 811, JR775-140, 141
		2.8L	Cherokee	53002-840, 839, JR775-142, 143
			Commanche	53002-840, 839, JR775-142, 143
			Wagoneer	53002-840, 839, JR775-142, 143
AW4	1987	2.1L	Cherokee	53001-672, 53003-810, 811, JR775-140, 141
			Commanche	53001-672, 53003-810, 811, JR775-140, 141
			Wagoneer	53001-672, 53003-810, 811, JR775-140, 141
		2.5L	Cherokee	53001-672, 53003-810, 811, JR775-140, 141
			Commanche	53001-672, 53003-810, 811, JR775-140, 141
			Wagoneer	53001-672, 53003-810, 811, JR775-140, 141
		2.8L	Cherokee	53002-840, 839, JR775-142, 143
			Commanche	53002-840, 839, JR775-142, 143
		2.8L	Wagoneer	53002-840, 839, JR775-142, 143
		4.0L	Cherokee	53002-840, 839, JR775-142, 143
			Commanche	53002-840, 839, JR775-142, 143
			Wagoneer	53002-840, 839, JR775-142, 143
AW4	1988	2.5L	Cherokee	53001-672, 53003-810, 811, JR775-140, 141
			Commanche	53001-672, 53003-810, 811, JR775-140, 141
			Wagoneer	53001-672, 53003-810, 811, JR775-140, 141
		2.8L	Cherokee	53002-840, 839, JR775-142, 143
			Commanche	53002-840, 839, JR775-142, 143
			Wagoneer	53002-840, 839, JR775-142, 143
		4.0L	Cherokee	53002-840, 839, JR775-142, 143
			Commanche	53002-840, 839, JR775-142, 143
			Wagoneer	53002-840, 839, JR775-142, 143
AW4	1989	2.5L	Cherokee	53001-672, 53003-810, 811, JR775-140, 141
			Commanche	53001-672, 53003-810, 811, JR775-140, 141
			Wagoneer	53001-672, 53003-810, 811, JR775-140, 141
		4.0L	Cherokee	53002-840, 839, JR775-142, 143
			Commanche	53002-840, 839, JR775-142, 143
			Wagoneer	53002-840, 839, JR775-142, 143
MJ3	1987	2.2L	Medallion	MJ3-xxx ①
MJ3	1988	2.2L	Medallion	MJ3-xxx ①
MJ3	1989	2.2L	Medallion	MJ3-xxx ①
ZF-4HP-18	1988	2.5L	Premier	ZF-xxx ①
		3.0L	Premier	ZF-xxx ①
ZF-4HP-18	1989	2.5L	Premier	ZF-xxx ①
		3.0L	Premier	ZF-xxx ①

① Serial numbers in sequence

CHRYSLER-DODGE-PLYMOUTH TRANSMISSION APPLICATIONS

Transmission	Year	Engine	Vehicle	Body Code	Transmission Code
727	1984	3.7L	Pick-Up and Ram	D, W	4058-384, 4295-941, 4329-468, 4329-482, 4329-458, 4329-488
			Van	B	4295-941, 4329-438, 4329-821
		5.2L	Pick-Up and Ram	D, W	4058-384, 4295-941, 4329-468, 4329-482, 4329-458, 4329-488
			Van	B	4295-941, 4329-438, 4329-821
		5.9L	Pick-Up and Ram	D, W	4058-384, 4295-941, 4329-468, 4329-482, 4329-458, 4329-488
			Van	B	4295-941, 4329-438, 4329-821
		7.2L	Pick-Up and Ram	D, W	4058-384, 4295-941, 4329-468, 4329-482, 4329-458, 4329-488
727	1985	3.7L	Pick-Up and Ram	D, W	4058-384, 4295-941, 4329-468, 4329-482, 4329-458, 4329-488
			Van	B	4295-941, 4329-438, 4329-821
		5.2L	Pick-Up and Ram	D, W	4058-384, 4295-941, 4329-468, 4329-482, 4329-458, 4329-488
			Van	B	4295-941, 4329-438, 4329-821
		5.9L	Pick-Up and Ram	D, W	4058-384, 4295-941, 4329-468, 4329-482, 4329-458, 4329-488
			Van	B	4295-941, 4329-438, 4329-821
		7.2L	Pick-Up and Ram	D, W	4058-384, 4295-941, 4329-468, 4329-482, 4329-458, 4329-488
727	1986	3.7L	Pick-Up and Ram	D, W	4377-823, 4331-552, 4377-824, 4431-552, 4348-785, 4348-718
			Van	B	4377-823, 4331-552, 4377-824, 4431-552
		5.2L	Diplomat	M	4412-560
			Fifth Avenue	M	4412-560
			Gran Fury	M	4412-560
			Pick-Up and Ram	D, W	4377-823, 4331-552, 4377-824, 4431-552, 4348-785, 4348-718, 4348-783, 4431-562
			Van	B	4377-823, 4331-552, 4377-824, 4431-552
		5.9L	Pick-Up and Ram	D, W	4377-823, 4331-552, 4377-824, 4431-552, 4348-785, 4348-718, 4348-786
			Van	B	4377-823, 4331-552, 4377-824, 4431-552
727	1987	3.7L	Pick-Up and Ram	D, W	4377-823, 4331-552, 4377-824, 4431-552, 4348-783, 4431-562, 4348-786
			Van	B	4377-823, 4331-552, 4377-824, 4431-552
		5.2L	Diplomat	M	4431-560, 4431-574
			Fifth Avenue	M	4431-560, 4431-574
			Gran Fury	M	4431-560, 4431-574
			Pick-Up and Ram	D, W	4377-823, 4331-552, 4377-824, 4431-552, 4348-783, 4431-562, 4348-786
			Van	B	4377-823, 4331-552, 4377-824, 4431-552
		5.9L	Pick-Up and Ram	D, W	4377-823, 4331-552, 4377-824, 4431-552, 4348-783, 4431-562, 4348-786, 4412-004, 4412-517
			Van	B	4377-823, 4331-552, 4377-824, 4431-552

CHRYSLER-DODGE-PLYMOUTH TRANSMISSION APPLICATIONS

Transmission	Year	Engine	Vehicle	Body Code	Transmission Code
727	1988	3.7L	Pick-Up and Ram	D, W	4431-563, 4431-552, 4471-406
			Van	B	4431-563, 4431-552
		3.9L	Pick-Up and Ram	D, W	4431-563, 4431-552, 4471-406
		5.2L	Diplomat	M	4431-574, 4505-209
			Fifth Avenue	M	4505-209, 4431-574
			Gran Fury	M	4431-574, 4505-209
			Pick-Up and Ram	D, W	4431-563, 4471-406
			Van	B	4431-563, 4431-552
		5.9L	Pick-Up and Ram	D, W	4431-552, 4471-406
			Van	B	4431-563, 4431-552
727	1989	3.7L	Van	B	4431-563, 4431-552
		5.2L	Diplomat	M	4505-209
			Fifth Avenue	M	4505-209
			Pick-Up and Ram	D, W	4431-563, 4471-406
			Van	B	4431-563, 4431-552
		5.9L	Pick-Up and Ram	D, W	4431-552, 4471-406
			Van	B	4431-563, 4431-552
904	1984	3.7L	Pick-Up and Ram	D, W	4058-383
			Van	B	4058-383
		5.2L	Diplomat	M	4058-398, 4329-436, 4295-887, 4329-631
			Fifth Avenue	M	4058-398, 4329-436, 4295-887, 4329-631
			Gran Fury	M	4058-398, 4329-436, 4295-887, 4329-631
904	1985	3.7L	Pick-Up and Ram	D, W	4058-383
			Van	B	4058-383
		5.2L	Diplomat	M	4058-398, 4329-436, 4295-887
			Fifth Avenue	M	4058-398, 4329-436, 4295-887
			Gran Fury	M	4058-398, 4329-436, 4295-887
			Newport	M	4058-398, 4329-436, 4295-887
904	1986	3.7L	Pick-Up and Ram	D, W	4329-633, 4431-566, 4348-782, 4431-555
			Van	B	4329-633, 4431-566, 4348-782, 4431-555
		5.2L	Diplomat	M	4412-001, 4412-002, 4348-703
			Fifth Avenue	M	4412-001, 4412-002, 4348-703
			Gran Fury	M	4412-001, 4412-002, 4348-703
904	1987	3.7L	Pick-Up and Ram	D, W	4329-633, 4431-566, 4348-782, 4431-555
			Van	B	4329-633, 4431-566, 4348-782, 4431-555
904	1988	3.7L	Van	B	4329-633, 4431-566, 4348-782, 4431-555
998	1986	2.2L	Dakota	N	4329-608, 4431-412
		2.6L	Dakota	N	4329-608, 4431-412
998	1987	2.2L	Dakota	N	4446-367
		2.6L	Dakota	N	4446-367
		3.9L	Dakota	N	4446-367

CHRYSLER-DODGE-PLYMOUTH TRANSMISSION APPLICATIONS

Transmission	Year	Engine	Vehicle	Body Code	Transmission Code
998	1988	2.2L	Dakota	N	4446-367, 4431-424, 4429-628
		2.6L	Dakota	N	4446-367, 4431-424, 4429-628
		3.9L	Dakota	N	4446-367, 4431-424, 4429-628
			Pick-Up and Ram	D, W	4471-406, 4431-425
			Van	B	4471-406, 4431-425
998	1989	2.2L	Dakota	N	4446-367, 4431-424, 4429-628
		2.6L	Dakota	N	4446-367, 4431-424, 4429-628
		3.9L	Dakota	N	4446-367, 4431-424, 4429-628
			Pick-Up and Ram	D, W	4471-406, 4431-425
			Van	B	4471-406, 4431-425
999	1984	5.2L	Pick-Up and Ram	D, W	4058-398
			Van	B	4058-398
999	1985	5.2L	Van	B	4058-398
999	1986	5.2L	Pick-Up and Ram	D, W	4348-715, 4431-554, 4329-632, 4431-554
			Van	B	4348-715, 4431-554
999	1987	5.2L	Diplomat	M	4431-501, 4431-572, 4431-503, 4431-573
			Fifth Avenue	M	4431-501, 4431-572, 4431-503, 4431-573
			Gran Fury	M	4431-501, 4431-572, 4431-503, 4431-573
			Pick-Up and Ram	D, W	4348-715, 4431-554, 4329-632, 4431-554
			Van	B	4348-715, 4431-554
999	1988	5.2L	Diplomat	M	4471-529, 4471-533, 4431-572, 4446-365, 4505-207, 4471-537, 4471-531, 4471-535, 4505-171
			Fifth Avenue	M	4471-529, 4471-533, 4431-572, 4446-365, 4505-207, 4471-537, 4471-531, 4471-535, 4505-171
			Gran Fury	M	4471-529, 4471-533, 4431-572, 4446-365, 4505-207, 4471-537, 4471-531, 4471-535, 4505-171
			Pick-Up and Ram	D, W	4431-556, 4431-428, 4431-554, 4431-427, 4431-441
			Van	B	4431-556, 4431-428
999	1989	5.2L	Diplomat	M	4471-533, 4505-207, 4505-171, 4446-368
			Fifth Avenue	M	4471-533, 4505-207, 4505-171, 4446-368
			Gran Fury	M	4471-533, 4505-207, 4505-171, 4446-368
			Pick-Up and Ram	D, W	4431-556, 4431-428, 4431-554, 4431-427, 4431-441
			Van	B	4431-556-4431-428
A413, A470, A670	1984	2.2L	600	K	4295-512, 4295-513
			Aries	K	4295-512, 4295-513
			Caravan	S	4295-763
			Charger	L	4295-512, 4295-513
			Charger Shelby	L	4295-512, 4295-513
			Daytona	G	4295-512, 4295-513
			E-Class	E	4295-512, 4295-513
			Horizon	L	4295-512, 4295-513
			Laser	G	4295-512, 4295-513
			LeBaron	K	4295-512, 4295-513
			Omni	L	4295-512, 4295-513
			Reliant	K	4295-512, 4295-513

CHRYSLER-DODGE-PLYMOUTH TRANSMISSION APPLICATIONS

Transmission	Year	Engine	Vehicle	Body Code	Transmission Code
A413, A470, A670	1984	2.2L	Town and Country	K	4295-512, 4295-513
			Turismo	L	4295-512, 4295-513
			Voyager	S	4295-763
		2.2L ①	600	E	4329-827
			Daytona	G	4329-827
			E-Class	E	4329-827
			Laser	G	4329-827
			Town and Country	K	4329-827
		2.6L	600	E	4295-515, 4329-544, 4295-517, 4329-556, 4329-819
			Aries	K	4295-515, 4329-544, 4295-517, 4329-556, 4329-819
			E-Class	E	4295-515, 4329-544, 4295-517, 4329-556, 4329-819
			LeBaron	K	4295-515, 4329-544, 4295-517, 4329-556, 4329-819
			New Yorker	E	4295-515, 4329-544, 4295-517, 4329-556, 4329-819
			Reliant	K	4295-515, 4329-544, 4295-517, 4329-556, 4329-819
			Town and Country	K	4295-515, 4329-544, 4295-517, 4329-556, 4329-819
			Voyager	S	4295-515, 4329-544, 4295-517, 4329-556, 4329-819
A413, A470, A670	1985	2.2L	600	E, K	4207-905, 4329-506
			Aries	K	4207-905, 4329-506
			Caravan	S	4329-546
			Caravelle	E	4207-905, 4329-506
			Charger	L	4207-905, 4329-506
			Charger Shelby	L	4207-905, 4329-506
			Daytona	G	4207-905, 4329-506
			Horizon	L	4207-905, 4329-506
			Lancer	H	4207-905, 4329-506
			Laser	G	4207-905, 4329-506
			LeBaron	K, H	4207-905, 4329-506
			Omni	L	4207-905, 4329-506
			Reliant	K	4207-905, 4329-506
			Turismo	L	4207-905, 4329-506
			Voyager	S	4329-546
		2.2L ①	600	E, K	4329-538
			Caravelle	E	4329-538
			Charger Shelby	L	4329-538
			Daytona	G	4329-538
			Laser	G	4329-538
			LeBaron	K, H	4329-538
			New Yorker	E	4329-538
			Omni	L	4329-538
			Town and Country	K	4329-538
			Lancer	H	4329-538
		2.6L	600	E, K	4329-547, 4329-564
			Aries	K	4329-547, 4329-564
			Caravan	S	4329-565
			New Yorker	E	4329-547, 4329-564

CHRYSLER-DODGE-PLYMOUTH TRANSMISSION APPLICATIONS

Transmission	Year	Engine	Vehicle	Body Code	Transmission Code
A413, A470, A670	1985	2.6L	Reliant	K	4329-547, 4329-564
			Town and Country	K	4329-547, 4329-564
			Voyager	S	4329-565
A413, A470, A670	1986	2.2L	600	E, K	4377-906, 4377-954, 4446-779, 4377-902, 4377-951, 4446-780, 4377-907, 4377-955, 4446-782
			Aries	K	4377-906, 4377-954, 4446-779, 4377-902, 4377-951, 4446-780, 4377-907, 4377-955, 4446-782
			Caravan	S	4377-903, 4377-952
			Caravelle	E	4377-906, 4377-954, 4446-779, 4377-902, 4377-951, 4446-780, 4377-907, 4377-955, 4446-782
			Charger	L	4377-906, 4377-954, 4446-779, 4377-902, 4377-951, 4446-780, 4377-907, 4377-955, 4446-782
			Daytona	G	4377-906, 4377-954, 4446-779, 4377-902, 4377-951, 4446-780, 4377-907, 4377-955, 4446-782
			Horizon	L	4377-906, 4377-954, 4446-779, 4377-902, 4377-951, 4446-780, 4377-907, 4377-955, 4446-782
			Lancer	H	4377-906, 4377-954, 4446-779, 4377-902, 4377-951, 4446-780, 4377-907, 4377-955, 4446-782
			Laser	G	4377-906, 4377-954, 4446-779, 4377-902, 4377-951, 4446-780, 4377-907, 4377-955, 4446-782
			LeBaron	K, H	4377-906, 4377-954, 4446-779, 4377-902, 4377-951, 4446-780, 4377-907, 4377-955, 4446-782
			Omni	L	4377-906, 4377-954, 4446-779, 4377-902, 4377-951, 4446-780, 4377-907, 4377-955, 4446-782
			Reliant	K	4377-906, 4377-954, 4446-779, 4377-902, 4377-951, 4446-780, 4377-907, 4377-955, 4446-782
			Turismo	L	4377-906, 4377-954, 4446-779, 4377-902, 4377-951, 4446-780, 4377-907, 4377-955, 4446-782
			Voyager	S	4377-903, 4377-952
		2.2L ①	600	E, K	4377-907, 4377-955, 4446-782
			Caravelle	E	4377-907, 4377-955, 4446-782
			Charger Shelby	L	4377-907, 4377-955, 4446-782
			Daytona Shelby	G	4377-907, 4377-955, 4446-782
			Lancer	H	4377-907, 4377-955, 4446-782
			New Yorker	E	4377-907, 4377-955, 4446-782
			Omni	L	4377-907, 4377-955, 4446-782
		2.5L	600	E, K	4377-903, 4377-952, 4377-907, 4377-955, 4377-951, 4446-780
			Aries	K	4377-903, 4377-952, 4377-907, 4377-955, 4377-951, 4446-780
			Caravelle	E	4377-903, 4377-952, 4377-907, 4377-955, 4377-951, 4446-780
			Daytona	G	4377-903, 4377-952, 4377-907, 4377-955, 4377-951, 4446-780
			Lancer	H	4377-903, 4377-952, 4377-907, 4377-955, 4377-951, 4446-780
			Laser	G	4377-903, 4377-952, 4377-907, 4377-955, 4377-951, 4446-780

① Turbocharged engine

CHRYSLER-DODGE-PLYMOUTH TRANSMISSION APPLICATIONS

Transmission	Year	Engine	Vehicle	Body Code	Transmission Code
A413, A470, A670	1986	2.5L	LeBaron	K, H	4377-903, 4377-952, 4377-907, 4377-955, 4377-951, 4446-780
			New Yorker	E	4377-903, 4377-952, 4377-907, 4377-955, 4377-951, 4446-780
			Reliant	K	4377-903, 4377-952, 4377-907, 4377-955, 4377-951, 4446-780
		2.6L	Caravan	S	4377-911, 4377-958, 4446-784
			Voyager	S	4377-911, 4377-958, 4446-784
A413, A470, A670	1987	2.2L	600	E, K	4377-954, 4431-483, 4471-483, 4431-484, 4431-485, 4431-485
			Aries	K	4377-954, 4431-483, 4471-483, 4431-484, 4431-485, 4431-485
			Caravan	S	4431-486, 4471-486
			Caravelle	E	4377-954, 4431-483, 4471-483, 4431-484, 4431-485, 4431-485
			Charger	L	4377-954, 4431-483, 4471-483, 4431-484, 4431-485, 4431-485
			Horizon	L	4377-954, 4431-483, 4471-483, 4431-484, 4431-485, 4431-485
			Lancer	H	4377-954, 4431-483, 4471-483, 4431-484, 4431-485, 4431-485
			LeBaron	K, H	4377-954, 4431-483, 4471-483, 4431-484, 4431-485, 4431-485
			Omni	L	4377-954, 4431-483, 4471-483, 4431-484, 4431-485, 4431-485
			Reliant	K	4377-954, 4431-483, 4471-483, 4431-484, 4431-485, 4431-485
			Shadow	P	4377-954, 4431-483, 4471-483, 4431-484, 4431-485, 4431-485
			Sundance	P	4377-954, 4431-483, 4471-483, 4431-484, 4431-485, 4431-485
			Town and Country	K	4377-954, 4431-483, 4471-483, 4431-484, 4431-485, 4431-485
			Turismo	L	4377-954, 4431-483, 4471-483, 4431-484, 4431-485, 4431-485
			Voyager	S	4431-486, 4471-486
		2.2L ①	600	E, K	4377-955, 4431-485, 4471-485
			Caravelle	E	4377-955, 4431-485, 4471-485
			Charger Shelby	L	4377-955, 4431-485, 4471-485
			Lancer	H	4377-955, 4431-485, 4471-485
			LeBaron	J,K,H	4377-955, 4431-485, 4471-485
			New Yorker	E	4377-955, 4431-485, 4471-485
			Omni	L	4377-955, 4431-485, 4471-485
			Shadow	P	4377-955, 4431-485, 4471-485
			Shadow	P	4377-955, 4431-485, 4471-485
			Sundance	P	4377-955, 4431-485, 4471-485
			Town and Country	K	4377-955, 4431-485, 4471-485
		2.5L	600	E, K	4431-491, 4431-492

① Turbocharged engine

2–9

CHRYSLER-DODGE-PLYMOUTH TRANSMISSION APPLICATIONS

Transmission	Year	Engine	Vehicle	Body Code	Transmission Code
A413, A470, A670	1987	2.5L	Aries	K	4431-491, 4431-492
			Caravan	S	4431-492, 4471-486
			Caravelle	E	4431-491, 4431-492
			Daytona	G	4431-491, 4431-492
			Lancer	H	4431-491, 4431-492
			LeBaron	K, H	4431-491, 4431-492
			New Yorker	E	4431-491, 4431-492
			Reliant	K	4431-491, 4431-492
			Voyager	S	4431-492, 4471-486
		3.0L	Caravan	S	4431-493, 4471-493
			Voyager	S	4431-493, 4471-493
A413, A470, A670	1988	2.2L	600	E	4471-568, 4531-085, 4471-491
			Aries	K	4471-568, 4531-085, 4471-491
			Caravelle	E	4471-568, 4531-085, 4471-491
			Horizon	L	4471-568, 4531-085, 4471-491
			Lancer	H	4471-568, 4531-085, 4471-491
			LeBaron	K, H	4471-568, 4531-085, 4471-491
			Omni	L	4471-568, 4531-085, 4471-491
			Reliant	K	4471-568, 4531-085, 4471-491
			Shadow	P	4471-568, 4531-085, 4471-491
			Sundance	P	4471-568, 4531-085, 4471-491
		2.2L ①	600	E, K	4471-494, 4531-099
			Caravelle	E	4471-494, 4531-099
			Daytona Shelby	G	4471-494, 4531-099
			Lancer	H	4471-494, 4531-099
			LeBaron	J,K,H	4471-494, 4531-099
			New Yorker	E	4471-494, 4531-099
			Omni	L	4471-494, 4531-099
			Shadow	P	4471-494, 4531-099
			Sundance	P	4471-494, 4531-099
			Town and Country	K	4471-494, 4531-099
		2.5L	600	E, K	4531-115, 4471,491
			Aries	K	4531-115, 4471,491
			Caravan	S	4471-486, 4531-087
			Caravelle	E	4531-115, 4471-491
			Daytona	G	4531-115, 4471-491
			Lancer	H	4531-115, 4471-491
			LeBaron	K, H	4531-115, 4471-491
			New Yorker	E	4531-115, 4471-491
			Reliant	K	4531-115, 4471-491
			Sundance	P	4531-115, 4471-491
		2.5L	Voyager	S	4471-486, 4531-087
			Caravan	S	4471-493, 4471-527, 4531-097
			Dynasty	C	4471-569, 4531-027

① Turbocharged engine

CHRYSLER-DODGE-PLYMOUTH TRANSMISSION APPLICATIONS

Transmission	Year	Engine	Vehicle	Body Code	Transmission Code
A413, A470, A670	1988	3.0L	New Yorker	E	4471-569, 4531-027
			Voyager	S	4471-493, 4471-527, 4531-097
A604	1989	2.5L	Caravan	S	4471-895
			Voyager	S	4471-895
		3.0L	Caravan	S	4471-895
			Voyager	S	4471-895
AW372	1987	2.0L	D-50 Pick Up		MD72-4505
		2.6L	D-50 Pick Up 2WD		MD72-4506
AW372	1988	2.0L	D-50 Pick Up		MD72-4505
		2.6L	D-50 Pick Up 2WD		MD72-4506
AW372	1989	2.0L	D-50 Pick Up		MD72-4505
		2.6L	D-50 Pick Up 2WD		MD72-4506
KM148	1987	2.6L	D-50 Pick Up 4WD		MD72-4507
			Raider		MD72-4508
KM148	1988	2.6L	D-50 Pick Up 4WD		MD72-4507
			Raider		MD72-4508
KM148	1989	2.6L	D-50 Pick Up 4WD		MD72-4507
			Raider		MD73-1530
KM171	1985	1.5L	Colt		MD99-6026
KM171	1986	1.5L	Colt		MD99-6026
KM171	1987	1.5L	Colt		MD99-6091
KM171	1988	1.5L	Colt		MD99-6091
KM171	1989	1.5L	Colt		MD99-6183, MD99-6184
KM172	1984	1.6L	Colt		MD70-7058
		2.0L	Colt Vista		MD99-6047, MD70-4959
KM172	1985	1.6L	Colt		MD99-6049
		2.0L	Colt Vista		MD99-6047
KM172	1986	1.6L	Colt		MD99-6049
		2.0L	Colt Vista		MD99-6047
KM172	1987	1.6L	Colt		MD99-6092
		2.0L	Colt Vista		MD99-6047
KM172	1988	1.6L	Colt		MD99-6092
		2.0L	Colt Vista		MD99-6047
KM172	1989	1.6L	Colt		MD99-6161
		2.0L	Colt Vista		MD99-6187, MD99-6186
KM175	1989	2.0L	Summit		MD99-6192

FORD-LINCOLN-MERCURY TRANSMISSION APPLICATIONS

Transmission	Year	Engine	Vehicle	Transmission Code
4EAT	1989	2.2L	Probe	NONE
A4DL	1985	2.3L	Aerostar	85GT-ACA
			Ranger	85GT-ABA
		2.8L	Aerostar	85GT-AMA, BCA
			Bronco II	85GT-AGA, BAA
			Ranger 2WD	85GT-AEA, ALA
			Ranger 4WD	85GT-AGA, BAA
A4DL	1986	2.3L	Aerostar	85GT-ACA
			Ranger	86GT-AAA
		2.8L	Aerostar	85GT-AMA, BCA
		2.9L	Bronco II 2WD	86GT-ABA, ACA
			Bronco II 4WD	86GT-DAA, EAA
			Ranger 2WD	86GT-BAA, CAA
			Ranger 4WD	86GT-DAA, EAA
		3.0L	Aerostar	86GT-KAA, LAA
A4DL	1987	2.3L	Cougar	87GT-AAA, BAA
			Mustang	87GT-ABA
			Ranger	87GT-CAA, CAB
			Thunderbird	87GT-AAA, BAA
		2.9L	Bronco II	87GT-KAA, KAG, LAA, HAE
			Ranger	87GT-DAA, DAC, FAA, FAD, HAA, HAE, KAA, KAG
		3.0L	Aerostar	87GT-MAA, NAA
A4DL	1988	2.3L	Mustang	88GT-HAA, NAA
			Ranger	88GT-ABB
			Thunderbird	88GT-GAA, KAA
		2.9L	Bronco II	88GT-DAA, EAA
			Ranger	88GT-BAA, CAA
		3.0L	Aerostar	88GT-LAA, LAB, MAA, MAB
A4DL	1989	2.3L	Mustang	88GT-HAA, NAA
			Ranger	89GT-AAB, BBB
			Thunderbird	88GT-GAA, KAA
		2.9L	Bronco II	89GT-BAA, BBA, CAA, DAA
			Ranger 2WD	89GT-AAA, BAA
			Ranger 4WD	89GT-CAA, DAA
		3.0L	Aerostar	89GT-EAA, GAA, TAA, TBA
AOD	1984	3.8L	Capri	PKA-BZ1, 2, 3, 4, CD1, 2, 3, 4
			Cougar	PKA-BT6, 7, 8, 9, 10, CB6, 7, 8, 9, 10
			LTD	PKA-BT6, 7, 8, 9, 10, CB6, 7, 8, 9, 10
			Marquis	PKA-BT6, 7, 8, 9, 10, CB6, 7, 8, 9, 10
			Mustang	PKA-BZ1, 2, 3, 4, CD1, 2, 3, 4
			Thunderbird	PKA-BT6, 7, 8, 9, 10, CB6, 7, 8, 9, 10
		4.9L	F-100/250	PKB-E6, E7, E8, E9, E10, F4, F5, F6, F7, F8, F9
		5.0L	Capri	PKA-BW1, 2, 3, 4, BZ1, 2, 3, 4
			Continental	PKA-BD18, 19, 20, 21, 22
			Cougar	PKA-K6, 7, 8, 9, 10

FORD-LINCOLN-MERCURY TRANSMISSION APPLICATIONS

Transmission	Year	Engine	Vehicle	Transmission Code
AOD	1984	5.0L	Crown Victoria	PKA-AG23, 24, 25, 26, 27, AU23, 24, 25, 26, 27, AY18, 19, 20, 21, 22, BB18, 19, 20, 21, 22
			F-150/250	PKB-A26, A27, A28, A29, A30, A31
			Gran Marquis	PKA-AG23, 24, 25, 26, 27, AU23, 24, 25, 26, 27, AY18, 19, 20, 21, 22, BB18, 19, 20, 21, 22
			LTD	PKA-CE1, 2, 3, CF1, 2, 3
			Mark VII	PKA-BV1, 2, 3, 4
			Marquis	PKA-CE1, 2, 3, CF1, 2, 3
			Mustang	PKA-BW1, 2, 3, 4
			Thunderbird	PKA-K6, 7, 8, 9, 10
			Town Car	PKA-M31, 32, 33, 34, 35, BC12, 13, 14, 15, 16
		5.8L	Crown Victoria	PKA-C31, 32, 33, 34, 35, AS23, 24, 25, 26, 27
			Gran Marquis	PKA-C31, 32, 33, 34, 35, AS23, 24, 25, 26, 27
AOD	1985	3.8L	Capri	PKA-CD7
			Cougar	PKA-CB13
			LTD	PKA-CB13
			Marquis	PKA-CB13
			Mustang	PKA-CD7
			Thunderbird	PKA-CB13
		4.9L	E-150/250 Van	PKB-F12
			F-150	PKB-E12, F12
		5.0L	Bronco	PKB-K, M
			Capri	PKA-BW7
			Continental	PKA-BD25
			Cougar	PKA-K13, CJ
			Crown Victoria	PKA-AG30, AY25
			E-150/250 Van	PKB-A33, G
			F-150/250	PKB-A33, J, K, L
			F-150/250 4WD	PKB-M
			Gran Marquis	PKA-AG30, AY25
			LTD	PKA-BW17, CE6, CF6
			Mark VII	PKA-BD25
			Mustang	PKA-BW7
			Thunderbird	PKA-K13, CJ
			Town Car	PKA-M38, BC19
		5.8L	Crown Victoria	PKA-C38
			Gran Marquis	PKA-C38
AOD	1986	2.3L	Capri	PKA-CD9
		3.8L	Cougar	PKA-CB15
			LTD	PKA-CB15
			Marquis	PKA-CB15
			Mustang	PKA-CB15
		4.9L	E-150/250 Van	PKB-F17
			F-150	PKB-E17, E18, F17, F18
		5.0L	Bronco	PKB-K5, K6, K7, M5, M6, M7
			Capri	PKA-CY4

FORD-LINCOLN-MERCURY TRANSMISSION APPLICATIONS

Transmission	Year	Engine	Vehicle	Transmission Code
AOD	1986	5.0L	Continental	PKA-CS4, CT4
			Cougar	PKA-CZ4
			Crown Victoria	PKA-CL4, CM4, DB, CN4
			E-150/250	PKB-J5, J6, J7, N1, N2, N3
			F-150/250	PKB-J5, J6, J7, J8, L5, L6, L7, L8
			F-150/250 4WD	PKB-K5, K6, K7, M5, M6, M7
			Gran Marquis	PKA-CL4, CM4, DB
			Mark VII	PKA-CU4, CV4, CW4
			Mustang	PKA-CY4
			Thunderbird	PKA-CZ4
			Town Car	PKA-CP5, DC2
		5.8L	Crown Victoria	PKA-C38, AS30
			Gran Marquis	PKA-C38
AOD	1987	3.8L	Cougar	PKA-CB15, DK
			Thunderbird	PKA-CB15, DK
		4.9L	E-150 Van	PKB-T2, T3, U2, U3
		5.0L	Bronco	PKB-P2, R2
			Continental	PKA-CS5, CT5
			Cougar	PKA-CZ5, DE1
			Crown Victoria	PKA-CL4, 5, CM4, 5, CN4, 5, DB, 1
			E-150/250 Van	PKB-J10, N5
			F-150/250	PKB-J10, L9, P2, R2, T2, T3
			Gran Marquis	PKA-CL4, 5, CM4, 5, DB, 1
			Mark VII	PKA-CU5, CV4, CW5, DG, DJ
			Mustang	PKA-DL, 1, DD3
			Thunderbird	PKA-CZ5, DE1
			Town Car	PKA-CP5, DC2
		5.8L	Crown Victoria	PKA-C40, AS32
			Gran Marquis	PKA-C40
AOD	1988	3.8L	Cougar	PKA-DK1, 2
			Thunderbird	PKA-DK1, 2
		4.9L	E-150 Van	PKB-AA, AB
			F-150	PKB-AA
		5.0L	Bronco	PKB-Y, Z
			Cougar	PKA-DR2, DS2
			Crown Victoria	PKA-CM8, CN7, CN8, CN9, DB3, DB4, DU, DU1, EM1
			E-150 Van	PKB-N
			F-150/250	PKB-J12, L11
			F-150/250 4WD	PKB-Y, Z
			Gran Marquis	PKA-CM8, DB3, DB4
			Mark VII	PKA-DG4, DG5, DG7, DJ4, DJ6
			Mustang	PKA-DD4, DD5, DL2, DL3
			Thunderbird	PKA-DK1, 2, DR2, DS2
			Town Car	PKA-CP7, CP8, CP9, DC4, DC5
		5.8L	Gran Marquis	PKA-C42, C43

FORD-LINCOLN-MERCURY TRANSMISSION APPLICATIONS

Transmission	Year	Engine	Vehicle	Transmission Code
AOD	1989	3.8L	Thunderbird	PKA-DK1, 2
		4.9L	E-150 Van	PKB-AC, AD
		5.0L	Bronco	PKB-AG, AJ
			Cougar	PKA-DR2, DS2
			Crown Victoria	PKA-CM8, CN7, CN8, CN9, DB3, DB4, DU, DU1, EM1
			E-150 Van	PKB-AF
			F-150/250	PKB-AC, AE, AH
			F-150/250 4WD	PKB-AG, AJ
			Gran Marquis	PKA-CM8, DB3, DB4
			Mark VII	PKA-DG4, DG5, DG7, DJ4, DJ6
			Mustang	PKA-DD4, DD5, DL2, DL3
			Thunderbird	PKA-DK1, 2, DR2, DS2
			Town Car	PKA-CP7, CP8, CP9, DC4, DC5
		5.8L	Gran Marquis	PKA-C42, C43
ATX	1984	1.6L	Escort/EXP	PMA-V3, U1, 2, Z3, PMB-C2, D, R
			Lynx/LN-7	PMA-V3, U1, 2, Z3, PMB-C2, D, R
		2.3L	Tempo	PMA-N1, 2, 3, AA, AA1, 2, 3, AE
			Topaz	PMA-N, N1, 2, 3, AA, AA2, 3, AE
ATX	1985	1.6L	Escort/EXP	PMA-V5, V6, 7, Z6, Z7, Z8, U4, U5, 6
			Lynx/LN-7	PMA-U4, 5, 6, V5, 6, 7, Z6, 7, 8
		1.9L	Lynx	PMA-U4, 5, 6, V5, 6, 7, Z6, 7, 8
			Topaz	PMA-AD
		2.3L	Tempo	PMA-N5, 6, 7, AA5, AA6
			Topaz	PMA-N5, 6, 7, AA5, AA6, AS
ATX	1986	1.9L	Escort/EXP	PMA-AD, AD1, AD2, AM, AP
			Lynx	PMA-AD, AD1, AD2, AM, AP
		2.3L	Tempo	PMA-N8, N8A, N9, 10, AA8, AA8A, AA9, 10
			Topaz	PMA-N8, N8A, N9, 10, AA8, AA8A, AA9, 10
		2.5L	Sable	PMA-AK, 1, 2, 3
			Taurus	PMA-AK, 1, 2, 3
ATX	1987	1.9L	Excort/EXP	PMA-AU, BE, PMP-W, X
			Lynx	PMA-AU, BE, PMB-W, X
		2.3L	Tempo AWD	PMA-AW
			Topaz	PMA-AV, BD
			Topaz AWD	PMA-AW
		2.5L	Sable	PMA-AK, 1, 2, 3
			Taurus	PMA-AK, 1, 2, 3
ATX	1988	1.9L	Escort/EXP	PMA-K3, 4, P, P1
			Escort/EXP	PMA-BR1, BS1, PMB-Y, PMB-Z
		2.3L	Tempo	PMA-BJ, BM, CB
			Tempo AWD	PMA-BX
			Topaz	PMA-BJ, BM, CB
			Topaz AWD	PMA-BX
		2.5L	Sable	PMT-BT

FORD-LINCOLN-MERCURY TRANSMISSION APPLICATIONS

Transmission	Year	Engine	Vehicle	Transmission Code
ATX	1989	1.9L	Escort/EXP	PMA-BR1, BS1, PMB-Y, PMB-Z
		2.3L	Tempo	PMA-BJ, BM, CB
			Tempo AWD	PMA-BX
			Topaz	PMA-BJ, BM, CB
			Topaz AWD	PMA-BX
AXOD	1986	3.0L	Sable	PNA-C
			Taurus	PNA-C
AXOD	1987	3.0L	Sable	PNA-C
			Taurus	PNA-C
AXOD	1988	3.8L	Continental	PNA-V, W
		3.0L	Sable	PNA-W, Y
			Taurus	PNA-W, Y
AXOD	1989	3.8L	Continental	PNA-V, W
		3.0L	Sable	PNA-W, Y
			Taurus	PNA-W, Y
C3	1984	2.3L	Capri	84DT-AAA, ACA, AJA
			Cougar	84DT-AEA, AFA
			LTD	84DT-ADA, AKA
			Marquis	84DT-ADA, AKA
			Mustang	84DT-AAA, ACA, AJA
			Ranger	83DT-ALB, AMB
			Thunderbird	84DT-AEA, AFA
		2.8L	Ranger 2WD	83DT-DLC, DMC
C3	1985	2.3L	Capri	85DT-AAA, EAA, JAA
			Cougar	85DT-KAA, LAA
			LTD	85DT-BAA, DAA, FAA
			Marquis	85DT-BAA, DAA, FAA
			Mustang	85DT-AAA, EAA, JAA
			Thunderbird	85DT-KAA, LAA
C3	1986	2.3L	Capri	86DT-AAA, 85DT-ACA
			Cougar	86DT-AEA, AFA
			LTD	86DT-ABA, ADA
			Marquis	86DT-ABA, ADA
			Mustang	86DT-AAA, 85DT-ACA
			Thunderbird	86DT-AEA, AFA
C5	1984	2.8L	Bronco II	PEJ-AJ
			Ranger 4WD	PEJ-AJ
		3.8L	Capri	PEP-AF
			Cougar	PEP-AD, AE
			LTD	PEP-Z, AC, AE, AK
			Marquis	PEP-Z, AC, AE, AK
			Mustang	PEP-AF
			Thunderbird	PEP-AE, K6, 7, 8, 9, 10
		4.9L	F-150	PEA-CU
		5.0L	F-150	PEA-CW

FORD-LINCOLN-MERCURY TRANSMISSION APPLICATIONS

Transmission	Year	Engine	Vehicle	Transmission Code
C5	1985	3.8L	Capri	PEP-AF1
			Cougar	PEP-AD1, AE1, AN, AP
			LTD	PEP-Z1, AC1, AE1, AL, A
			Marquis	PEP-Z1, AC1, AE1, AL, AM
			Mustang	PEP-AF1
			Thunderbird	PEP-AD1, AE1, AN, AP
		4.9L	F-150	PEA-CU
		5.0L	F-150	PEA-CW
C5	1986	2.3L	Capri	PEP-AF1, AF2
		3.8L	Cougar	PEP-AD1, AP
			LTD	PEP-Z1, AC1, AE1
			Marquis	PEP-Z1, AC1, AE1
			Mustang	PEP-AD1, AP
			Thunderbird	PEP-AD1, AP
		4.9L	F-150	PEA-CU
C6	1984	4.9L	Bronco	PGD-EG2, EG3
			E-100/350	PGD-A32, AW26, EK10, DB17
			F-100/250 4WD	PGD-EA12, EA13, EG2, EG3, EG4
			F-100/350 2WD	PGD-EK10
		5.0L	Bronco	PGD-EA12, EA13
			E-150/250	PGD-BF27, DC18, EP1, EU
			F-150/250	PGD-BF27, EP1
		5.8L	Bronco	PGD-EY1, EY2
			E-150/350 Van	PGD-DK13, DP14, DW11, EC11, EV, EW, EZ, FA
			F-150/350 4WD	PGD-DL13, DL14, DL15, EY, EY1, EY2
		6.9L	F-250/350	PJE-A, B
			F-250/350 4WD	PJE-C, C1
		7.5L	F-250/350	PJD-BB1, BC1
			F-250/350 4WD	PJD-BA3
C6	1985	4.9L	Bronco	PGD-EG4
			E-100/350	PGD-FB, AW27, FC10, F12
			F-100/250 4WD	PGD-EG4
			F-150	PEA-FE, FF
		5.8L	Bronco	PGD-DL15
			E-150/350 Van	PGD-EV1, DW12, FD
			F-150/350	PGD-DW12, EV1, FD
			F-150/350 4WD	PGD-DL15, EY2
		6.9L	E-250/350 Van	PJE-B1
			F-250/350	PJE-A, B1, C1
		7.5L	E-250/350 Van	PJD-BB1, BC2
			F-250/350	PJD-BA3, BA4, BB1, BB2, BC2, BC3
C6	1986	4.9L	Bronco	PGD-EG4
			E-150/350 Van	PGD-AW27, EK10, EK11, FB1, FC1, FC2, FF1
			F-150 4WD	PGD-EG4, EG5
			F-150/250 2WD	PGD-AW27, AW28, EK10, EK11, FE, FE1, FF, FF1

FORD-LINCOLN-MERCURY TRANSMISSION APPLICATIONS

Transmission	Year	Engine	Vehicle	Transmission Code
C6	1986	5.0L	F-150	PGD-FG, FG1
		5.8L	Bronco	PGD-EY2
			E-150/350 Van	PGD-EV1, EV2, FD1, FD2
			F-150/350	PGD-FD, FD1, EV1, EV2
			F-150/350 4WD	PGD-EY2, EY3
		6.9L	E-250/350 Van	PJE-B2, B3, B4
			F-250/350	PJE-A, A1, A2, B2, B3, B4
			F-250/350 4WD	PJE-C2, C3, C4
		7.5L	E-250/350 Van	PJD-BB2, BB3, BC3, BC4
			F-250/350	PJD-BB2, BB3, BC3, BC4
			F-250/350 4WD	PJD-BA4, BA5
C6	1987	4.9L	Bronco	PGD-FR, FU
			E-150/350 Van	PGD-FN, FP, FW, FZ
			F-150/350	PGD-FM, FN, FP, FR, FZ, GD, GD1, GD2
		5.0L	F-150/250 2WD	PGD-FM, GA, GA1
		5.8L	Bronco	PGD-FK, FT
			E-150/350 Van	PGD-FV, FY, FY1
			F-150/350 2WD	PGD-FK, FV, FY, FY1
		6.9L	E-250/350 Van	PJE-G, G1
			F-250/350	PJE-F, G, G1
		7.5L	E-250/350 Van	PJD-BF, BG, BH
			F-250/350	PJD-BE, BF, BF1, BG, BH
C6	1988	4.9L	Bronco	PGD-GN1
			E-150/350 Van	PGD-FN2, FP2
			F-150 4WD	PGD-GM1
			F-150/350 2WD	PGD-FN2, FP2, GD2, GW
		5.0L	Bronco	PGD-GU
			F-150 4WD	PGD-GT
			F-150/250 2WD	PGD-FM1, GA1
		5.8L	Bronco	PGD-GH, GJ
			E-150/350 Van	PGD-GE, GF
			F-150/350	PGD-GE, GF, GY
			F-150/350 4WD	PGD-GG, GR
		7.3L	E-250/350 Van	PJE-G1
			F-250/350	PJE-G1, H, J
		7.5L	E-250/350 Van	PJD-BF1
			F-250/350	PJD-BF1, BR, BT
C6	1989	4.9L	Bronco	PGD-JD, HP
			E-150/350 Van	PGD-HA, HB, HZ
			F-150 4WD	PGD-HN, JC
			F-150/350	PGD-HA, HD, HF, HZ
		5.0L	Bronco	PGD-HV
			F-150 2WD	PGD-GZ, HD
			F-150 4WD	PGD-HU

FORD-LINCOLN-MERCURY TRANSMISSION APPLICATIONS

Transmission	Year	Engine	Vehicle	Transmission Code
C6	1989	5.8L	Bronco	PGD-HL, HM
			E-150/350 Van	PGD-HG, HH, JA, JE
			F-250/350	PGD-HG, HH, HL, HM, HS, JA, JE
			F-250/350 4WD	PGD-HJ
		7.3L	E-250/350 Van	PJE-K, L
			F-250/350	PJE-K, L
			F-250/350 4WD	PJE-M
		7.5L	E-250/350 Van	PJD-BV, CB
			F-250/350 2WD	PJD-BV, CB
			F-250/350 4WD	PJD-BZ
E40D	1989	5.8L	E-250 Van	PRA-E, E1, S
			F-250/350	PRA-E, E1, S
			F-250/350 4WD	PRA-H, H1
		7.3L	E-250 Van	PRA-L, L1, U
			F-250/350	PRA-L, L1, U
			F-250/350 4WD	PRA-G, G1
			F-450 Super Duty	PRA-C, C1
		7.5L	E-250 Van	PRA-J
			F-250/350	PRA-J, T
			F-250/350 4WD	PRA-F
F3A	1987	1.6L	Tracer	NONE
	1988	1.6L	Tracer	NONE
F3A	1989	1.3L	Festiva	NONE
		1.6L	Tracer	NONE
ZF 4 HP-22	1984	2.4L Diesel	Continental	E4LP-CA
			Mark VII	E4LP-CA
ZF 4 HP-22	1985	2.4L Diesel	Continental	E4LP-CA
			Mark VII	E4LP-CA

GENERAL MOTORS TRANSMISSION APPLICATIONS

Transmission	Year	Engine	Engine Code	Vehicle	Body Code	Transmission Code
125C	1984	1.8L	J	Cavalier	J	PE, P4, PR
			J	Firenza	J	PE, P4, PR
			J	Skyhawk	J	PE, P4, PR
			J	Sunbird, J2000	J	PE, P4, PR
		2.0L	B, P	Cavalier	J	HC, HY, CA
			B, P	Cimarron	J	CA, C4, HY, C3, CB, CI, CM
			B, P	Firenza	J	HC, HY, CA
			B, P	Skyhawk	J	HC, HY, CA
			B, P	Sunbird, J2000	J	HC, HY, CA
		2.5L	R	6000	A	PD, PW
			R	Celebrity	A	PD, PW
			R	Century	A	PD, PW
			R	Ciera	A	PD, PW
			R	Citation	X	5PD, 5PW
			R	Fiero	P	6PF
			R	Omega	X	5PD, 5PW
			R	Phoenix	X	5PD, 5PW
			R	Skylark	X	5PD, 5PW
		2.8L	Z	6000	A	CL, CC, HS
			X	6000	A	CL, CC, HS
			Z	Celebrity	A	CL, CC, HS
			X	Celebrity	A	CL, CC, HS
			X	Century	A	CL, CC, HS
			X	Ciera	A	CL, CC, HS
			X, Z	Citation	X	5CE, CC, CT
			Z	Omega	X	5CE, CC, CT
			Z	Phoenix	X	5CE, CC, CT
			X, Z	Skylark	X	5CE, CC, CT
		3.0L	E	Century	A	4BF, 5BF, BBZ
			E	Ciera	A	4BF, 5BF, BBZ
		4.3L	T	6000	A	OP
			T	Celebrity	A	OP
			T	Century	A	OP
			T	Ciera	A	OP
125C	1985	1.8L	J	Cavalier	J	PE, P4, PR, 5P5, 5P2, 5PJ
			J	Cavalier	J	PE, P4, PR, 5P5, 5P2, 5PJ
			J	Firenza	J	PE, P4, PR, 5P5, 5P2, 5PJ
			J	Skyhawk	J	PE, P4, PR, 5P5, 5P2, 5PJ
			J	Skyhawk	J	PE, P4, PR, 5P5, 5P2, 5PJ
			J	Sunbird, J2000	J	PE, P4, PR, 5P5, 5P2, 5PJ
			J	Sunbird, J2000	J	PE, P4, PR, 5P5, 5P2, 5PJ
		2.0L	P	Cavalier	J	6CA, 6CC, CA, MI, CM
			P	Cimarron	J	CA, C4, HY, C3, CB, CI, CM, 5CA, 5CC
			P	Firenza	J	5CA, 5CC, CA, MI, CM
			P	Skyhawk	J	6CA, 6CC, CA, MI, CM

GENERAL MOTORS TRANSMISSION APPLICATIONS

Transmission	Year	Engine	Engine Code	Vehicle	Body Code	Transmission Code
125C	1985		P	Sunbird, J2000	J	6CA, 6CC, CA, MI, CM
		2.5L	R	6000	A	5PD, 5PW
			U	Calais	N	6PN
			R	Celebrity	A	5PD, 5PW
			R	Century	A	5PD, 5PW
			R	Ciera	A	5PD, 5PW
			R	Citation	X	5PD, 5PW
			R	Fiero	P	6PF
			U	Grand Am	N	6PN
			R	Skylark	X	5PD, 5PW
			U	Somerset, Skylark	N	6PN, PN
		2.8L	X	6000	A	HS, 5CT, 5CL
			W	6000	A	HS, 5CT, 5CL
			X	Celebrity	A	HS, 5CT, 5CL
			W	Celebrity	A	HS, 5CT, 5CL
			X	Century	A	HS, 5CT, 5CL
			X	Ciera	A	HS, 5CT, 5CL
			W	Cimarron	J	CJ
			W	Citation	X	5CE, CC, CT
			9	Fiero	P	CD, 6CP
			W	Firenza	J	CJ
			W	Skylark	X	5CE, CC, CT
		3.0L	L	Calais	N	BD, BP
			E	Century	A	4BF, BBZ
			E	Ciera	A	4BF, BBZ
			L	Grand Am	N	BD, BP
			L	Somerset, Skylark	N	BD, BP, 6BA
			L	Somerset, Skylark	N	BD, BP
		4.3L	T	6000	A	50P
			T	Celebrity	A	50P
			T	Century	A	50P
			7	Ciera	A	50P
125C	1986	1.8L	J	Cavalier	J	PE, P4, PR, 5P5, 5P2, 5PJ, 6PA, 6PJ
			J	Cavalier	J	PE, P4, PR, 5P5, 5P2, 5PJ, 6PA, 6PJ
			J	Firenza	J	PE, P4, PR, 5P5, 5P2, 5PJ, 6PA, 6PJ
			J	Firenza	J	PE, P4, PR, 5P5, 5P2, 5PJ, 6PA, 6PJ
			J	Skyhawk	J	PE, P4, PR, 5P5, 5P2, 5PJ, 6PA, 6PJ
			J	Skyhawk	J	PE, P4, PR, 5P5, 5P2, 5PJ, 6PA, 6PJ
			J	Sunbird, J2000	J	PE, P4, PR, 5P5, 5P2, 5PJ, 6PA, 6PJ
		2.0L	P	Cavalier	J	6CA, 6CC, CB, CI, CM
			P	Cimarron	J	6CA, 6CC, CB, CI, CM, CA, C4, NY, CB
			P	Firenza	J	6CA, 6CC, CB, CI, CM
			P	Skyhawk	J	6CA, 6CC, CB, CI, CM
			P	Sunbird, J2000	J	6CA, 6CC, CB, CI, CM

GENERAL MOTORS TRANSMISSION APPLICATIONS

Transmission	Year	Engine	Engine Code	Vehicle	Body Code	Transmission Code
125C	1986	2.5L	R	6000	A	6PD, 6PW
			U	Calais	N	6PN
			R	Celebrity	A	6PD, 6PW
			R	Century	A	6PD, 6PW
			R	Ciera	A	6PD, 6PW
			R	Fiero	P	6PP
			U	Grand Am	N	6PN
			U	Somerset, Skylark	N	6PN
		2.8L	W	6000	A	HS, 6CT, 6CL, 6CU, CX
			X	6000	A	HS, 6CT, 6CL, 6CU, CX
			X	Celebrity	A	HS, 6CT, 6CL, 6CU, CX
			W	Celebrity	A	HS, 6CT, 6CL, 6CU, CX
			X	Century	A	HS, 6CT, 6CL, 6CU, CX
			W	Ciera	A	HS, 6CT, 6CL, 6CU, CX
			X	Ciera	A	HS, 6CT, 6CL, 6CU, CX
			W	Cimarron	J	CJ, 6CJ
			9	Fiero	P	CD, 6CP
			W	Firenza	J	CJ, 6CJ
		3.0L	L	Calais	N	BD, 6BD, 6BP
			L	Grand Am	N	BD, 6BD, 6BP
			L	Somerset, Skylark	N	BD, 6BD, 6BP
			L	Somerset, Skylark	N	BD, BP, 6BA
125C	1987	2.0L	M	Cavalier	J	7PKC, 7PFC, 7PHC, 7PPC
			K	Cavalier	J	7PKC, 7PFC, 7PHC, 7PPC
			1	Corsica, Beretta	L	7CRC, 7C8C
			K	Firenza	J	7PKC, 7PFC, 7PHC, 7PPC, 7CBC
			1	Firenza	J	7PKC, 7PFC, 7PHC, 7PPC, 7CBC
			M	Grand Am	N	7PMC
			1	Skyhawk	J	7PKC, 7PFC, 7PHC, 7PPC
			M	Skyhawk	J	7PKC, 7PFC, 7PHC, 7PPC
			K	Skyhawk	J	7PKC, 7PFC, 7PHC, 7PPC
			M	Sunbird, J2000	J	7PKC, 7PFC, 7PHC, 7PPC
			K	Sunbird, J2000	J	7PKC, 7PFC, 7PHC, 7PPC
		2.3L	D	Calais	N	8KDC
			D	Grand Am	N	8KDC
			D	Somerset, Skylark	N	8KDC
		2.5L	R	6000	A	7PDC
			U	Calais	N	7PNC
			R	Celebrity	A	7PDC
			R	Century	A	7PDC
			R	Ciera	A	7PDC
			R	Fiero	P	7PSC
			U	Grand Am	N	7PNC
			U	Somerset, Skylark	N	7PNC

GENERAL MOTORS TRANSMISSION APPLICATIONS

Transmission	Year	Engine	Engine Code	Vehicle	Body Code	Transmission Code
125C	1987	2.8L	W	6000	A	7CXC, 7CTC
			W	Cavalier	J	7CJC
			W	Celebrity	A	7CXC, 7CTC
			W	Century	A	7CXC, 7CTC
			W	Ciera	A	7CXC, 7CTC
			W	Cimarron	J	7CJC
			W	Corsica, Beretta	L	7CVC
			9	Fiero	P	7CPC
			W	Firenza	J	7CJC
			W	Sunbird	J	7CJC
		3.0L	L	Calais	N	7BPC, 7BDC, 7BHC, 7BJC
			L	Grand Am	N	7BPC, 7BDC, 7BHC, 7BJC
			L	Somerset, Skylark	N	7BPC, 7BDC, 7BHC, 7BJC
			L	Somerset, Skylark	N	7BPC, 7BDC, 7BJC
125C	1988	1.6L	6	Lemans	T	7, 8, 9PTC
		2.0L	K	Cavalier	J	8TRC, 8PPC
			1	Corsica, Beretta	L	8CRC
			1	Firenza	J	8TRC, 8PPC, 8CBC, 8PKC
			K	Firenza	J	8TRC, 8PPC, 8CBC, 8PKC
			M	Grand Am	N	8PMC
			K	Lemans	T	8PRC
			1	Skyhawk	J	8TRC, 8PPC
			K	Skyhawk	J	8TRC, 8PPC
			M	Sunbird, J2000	J	8TRC, 8PPC
			K	Sunbird, J2000	J	8TRC, 8PPC
		2.3L	D	Calais	N	8KDC
			D	Grand Am	N	8KDC
			D	Somerset, Skylark	N	8KDC
			D	Somerset, Skylark	N	8KDC
		2.5L	R	6000	A	8PDC
			U	Calais	N	8PNC
			R	Celebrity	A	8PDC
			R	Ciera	A	8PDC
			R	Fiero	P	7PSC, 8PSC
			U	Grand Am	N	8PNC
			U	Somerset, Skylark	N	8PNC
		2.8L	W	6000	A	8CTC, 8LSC
			W	Cavalier	J	8TNC, 8CJC
			W	Celebrity	A	8CTC, 8LSC
			W	Century	A	8CTC, 8LSC
			W	Ciera	A	8CTC, 8LSC
			W	Cimarron	J	8CTC, 8LSC
			W	Corsica, Beretta	L	8CVC
			9	Fiero	P	8CPC

GENERAL MOTORS TRANSMISSION APPLICATIONS

Transmission	Year	Engine	Engine Code	Vehicle	Body Code	Transmission Code
125C	1988	3.0L	L	Calais	N	8BHC, 8BJC
			L	Somerset, Skylark	N	8BHC, 8BJC
125C	1989	1.6L	6	Lemans	T	7, 8, 9PTC
		2.0L	1	Cavalier	J	9TRC, 9PPC, 9CBC
			K	Cavalier	J	9TRC, 9PPC
			1	Corsica, Beretta	L	9CRC
			1	Firenza	J	9TRC, 9PPC, 9CBC, 9PKC
			M	Grand Am	N	9PMC
			K	Lemans	T	8PRC
			K	Skyhawk	J	9TRC, 9PPC
			1	Skyhawk	J	9TRC, 9PPC, 9CBC
			K	Sunbird, J2000	J	PTRC, 9PPC, PCBC
			M	Sunbird, J2000	J	9TRC, 9PPC, 9CBC
		2.3L	D	Grand Am	N	9KDC, 9KCC
			D	Somerset, Skylark	N	9KDC
		2.5L	R	6000	A	8PDC
			U	Calais	N	9PNC
			R	Celebrity	A	8PDC
			R	Century	A	8PDC
			R	Ciera	A	8PDC
			U	Grand Am	N	9PNC
			U	Somerset, Skylark	N	9PNC
		2.8L	W	6000	A	8CTC, 8LSC
			W	Cavalier	J	9TNC, 9CJC
			W	Celebrity	A	8CTC, 8LSC
			W	Century	A	8CTC, 8LSC
			W	Ciera	A	8CTC, 8LSC
			W	Corsica, Beretta	L	9CVC, 9CRC
		3.1L	T	6000	A	9CTC
			T	Celebrity	A	9CTC
		3.3L	N	Calais	N	9BUC
			N	Somerset, Skylark	N	9BUC
180C	1984	1.6L	C	Chevette	T	PR, TP, TN, VQ, JY
			C	T1000	T	PR, TP, TN, VQ, JY
180C	1985	1.6L	C	Chevette	T	PR
			C	T1000	T	PR
180C	1986	1.6L	C	Chevette	T	PR, UG, UR
			C	T1000	T	PR, UG, UR
180C	1987	1.6L	C	Chevette	T	UG, UR
			C	T1000	T	UG, UR
180C	1989	1.6L		Geo Tracer	J1	None
200-4R	1984	3.8L	A	Cutlass	G	4CH
			A	Grand Prix	G	4CH
			A	Monte Carlo	G	4CH
			9	Regal	G	4CH

GENERAL MOTORS TRANSMISSION APPLICATIONS

Transmission	Year	Engine	Engine Code	Vehicle	Body Code	Transmission Code
200-4R	1984	4.1L		98	D	4AP, 4AA, 4BT
				Electra	D	4AP, 4AA, 4BT
			8	Fleetwood DeVille	D	4AP, 4AA, 4BT
			4	LeSabre, Estate Wagon	B	4BY, 4BT
			4	Regal	G	4GH
		4.3L	V	Regal	G	40F
			V	Regal	G	40F
		5.0L	Y	88, Custom Cruiser	B	4KC, KJ
			Y	98	D	40J, 40G
			Y	Cutlass	G	40Z, 40G
			H	Cutlass	G	4HG, 4CR
			Y	Electra	D	40J, 40G
			H	Grand Prix	G	4HG, 4CR
			Y	LeSabre, Estate Wagon	B	40G
			G	Monte Carlo	G	5CQ
			H	Monte Carlo	G	4HG, 4CR
			H	Regal	G	4HG, 4CR
		5.7L	N	88, Custom Cruiser	B	40M
			N	98	D	40M
			N	Caprice	B	40M
			N	Cutlass	G	40M
			N	Electra	D	40M
			N	Fleetwood DeVille	D	40M
			N	Grand Prix	G	40M
			N	LeSabre, Estate Wagon	B	40M
			N	Monte Carlo	G	40M
			N	Parisienne	B	40M
200-4R	1985	3.8L	A	Cutlass	G	5CH, 50K
			9	Regal	G	5BQ
		4.1L	8	Fleetwood Brgm	D	5AA, 5A0, 6AB, AP
			4	LeSabre, Estate Wagon	B	4BY, 4BT
		5.0L	Y	88, Custom Cruiser	B	50G, 50M
			Y	88, Custom Cruiser	B	50G, 50J
			H	Caprice	B	KC, KJ
			Y	Cutlass	G	6KA, 6KB
			H	Cutlass	G	5HG, 5CR, 6CR
			H	Grand Prix	G	5HG, 5CR, 6CR
			Y	LeSabre, Estate Wagon	B	40G
			H	Monte Carlo	G	5HG, 5CR, 6CR
			H	Parisienne	B	KC, KJ
		5.7L	N	88, Custom Cruiser	B	50M
			N	Caprice	B	50M
			N	Cutlass	G	40M
			N	Fleetwood Brgm	D	40M
			N	LeSabre, Estate Wagon	B	40M

GENERAL MOTORS TRANSMISSION APPLICATIONS

Transmission	Year	Engine	Engine Code	Vehicle	Body Code	Transmission Code
200-4R	1985	5.7L	N	Parisienne	B	50M
200-4R	1986	3.8L	7	Regal	G	6HH
		4.3L	Z	Grand Prix	G	6CH
			Z	Monte Carlo	G	6CH
		5.0L	Y	Caprice	B	6KC, 6KJ
			H	Caprice	B	6CR, 6HC, 6CA
			9	Cutlass	G	6KZ
			Y	Estate Wagon	B	6KC, 6KB
			Y	Fleetwood Brgm	D	5AJ
			H	Parisienne	B	6CR, 6HC, 6CA
			Y	Parisienne	B	6KC, 6KJ
			H	Regal	G	6HL
			Y	Regal	G	6KB, 6KC
200-4R	1987	3.8L	7	Regal	G	7BHB
		4.3L	Z	Grand Prix	G	7CHF, 7CYF
			Z	Monte Carlo	G	7CHF, 7CYF
		5.0L	Y	Caprice	B	7HFF, 7KCF, 7KJF
			Y	Custom Cruiser	B	6KC, 6KY
			H	Cutlass	G	7CRF, 7CCF, 7HTF
			Y	Cutlass	G	7KJF, 8KJF
			Y	Estate Wagon	B	7HFF, 7KCF, 7KJF
			Y	Fleetwood Brgm	D	7KJF, 7KCF
			H	Grand Prix	G	7CRF, 7CCF, 7HTF
			G	Monte Carlo	G	7CZF
			H	Regal	G	7HTF
			Y	Regal	G	7KJF, 7KTF, 8KJF
			Y	Safari	B	7HFF, 7KCF, 7KJF
200-4R	1988	5.0L	H	Caprice	B	8CTF
			Y	Custom Cruiser	B	8KJF, 8KTF
			Y	Cutlass	G	8KJF
			Y	Estate Wagon	B	8KJF, 8KTF
			Y	Fleetwood Brgm	D	8KJF, 8KTF
			H	Safari	B	8CTF
			Y	Safari	B	8KJF, 8KTF
200-4R	1989	3.8L	7	Firebird	F	9TAF
		5.0L	E	Custom Cruiser	B	9CTF, 9CUF
			Y	Custom Cruiser	B	9KJF, 9KTF
			Y	Estate Wagon	B	9KJF, 9KTF
			Y	Fleetwood Brgm	D	9KJF, 9KTF
			Y	Safari	B	9KJF, 9KTF
			E	Safari	B	9CTF, 9CUF
200C	1984	1.6L	C	Chevette	T	JY
			C	T1000	T	JY
		3.8L	A	88, Custom Cruiser	B	4BH
			A	Caprice	B	4BH

GENERAL MOTORS TRANSMISSION APPLICATIONS

Transmission	Year	Engine	Engine Code	Vehicle	Body Code	Transmission Code
200C	1984	1.6L	A	LeSabre, Estate Wagon	B	4BH
			A	Parisienne	B	4BH
			A	Regal	G	4XE, 4WK
		4.3L		Cutlass	G	5C6, 5C5, 5CH, 5CY
		5.0L	Y	88, Custom Cruiser	B	40I
			H	Caprice	B	5HL
			9, Y	Cutlass	G	40I
			Y	LeSabre, Estate Wagon	B	40I
			H	Parisienne	B	5HL
			Y	Parisienne	B	40U
			H	Regal	G	5CO, 5CV, 9CU
		5.7L	N	88, Custom Cruiser	B	40U
			N	Caprice	B	40U
			N	Cutlass	G	40U
			N	Grand Prix	G	40U
			N	LeSabre, Estate Wagon	B	40U
			N	Monte Carlo	G	40U
			N	Parisienne	B	40U
200C	1985	3.8L	A	88, Custom Cruiser	B	5HH, 5BH
			A	Caprice	B	5HH, 5BH
			A	Cutlass	G	6BH
			A	Grand Prix	G	5HH
			A	LeSabre, Estate Wagon	B	4BH
			A	Monte Carlo	G	5HH
			A	Parisienne	B	5HH, 5BH
			A	Regal	G	6BH
		4.3L	Z	Caprice	B	5CS
			V	Cutlass	G	5C6, 5C5, 5CH, 5CY
			V	Monte Carlo	G	5C6, 5C5, 5CH, 5CY
			Z	Parisienne	B	5CS
		5.0L	H	Caprice	B	5HL
			Y	Custom Cruiser	B	50I
			9, Y	Cutlass	G	50I
			H	Cutlass	G	5CO, 5CV, 9CU
			H	Grand Prix	G	5CO, 5CV, 9CU
			Y	LeSabre, Estate Wagon	B	40I
			H	Monte Carlo	G	5CO, 5CV, 9CU
			H	Parisienne	B	5HL
			H	Regal	G	5HL
		5.7L	N	88, Custom Cruiser	B	50U
			N	Caprice	B	50U
			N	Cutlass	G	50U
			N	LeSabre, Estate Wagon	B	40U
			N	Parisienne	B	50U

GENERAL MOTORS TRANSMISSION APPLICATIONS

Transmission	Year	Engine	Engine Code	Vehicle	Body Code	Transmission Code
200C	1986	3.8L	A	Cutlass	G	6HH
			A	Grand Prix	G	6HH
			A	Monte Carlo	G	6HH
			A	Regal	G	6KJ
		4.3L	Z	Caprice	B	6CA
			Z	Parisienne	B	6CA
		5.0L	H	Caprice	B	6HL
			Y	Custom Cruiser	B	50I
			9, Y	Cutlass	G	6KA, 6KB
			H	Cutlass	G	6HL, 6CU
			Y	Estate Wagon	B	6KA, 6KB
			H	Grand Prix	G	6HL, 6CU, 6BR
			H	Monte Carlo	G	6HL, 6CU
			H	Parisienne	B	6HL
			H	Regal	G	6BR
			Y	Regal	G	6HC, 6KA
200C	1987	3.8L	A	Cutlass	G	7HHB
			A	Grand Prix	G	7HHB
			A	Monte Carlo	G	7HHB
			A	Regal	G	7HHB, 7BHB
		4.3L	Z	Grand Prix	G	7CAB
			Z	Monte Carlo	G	7CAB
		5.0L	H	Cutlass	G	7HLB, 7CUB
			H	Grand Prix	G	7HLB, 7CUB
			H	Monte Carlo	G	7HLB, 7CUB
			H	Regal	G	7HLB
			Y	Regal	G	7KBB
			Y	Cutlass	G	8KBB
250C	1984	3.8L	A	88, Custom Cruiser	B	4XP
			A	Caprice	B	4XD
			A	Grand Prix	G	4WK, 4XE
			A	LeSabre, Estate Wagon	B	4XD
			A	Monte Carlo	G	4WK, 4XE
			A	Parisienne	B	4XD
250C	1985	3.8L	A	LeSabre, Estate Wagon	B	4XD
3254L	1984	2.8L	L	Riviera	E	5BJ
		4.1L	8	Eldorado, Seville	E, K	4AJ, 5AB, 4AA, 5AJ
			4	Riviera	E	4BE
			4	Toronado	E	4BE
		5.0L	Y	Riviera	E	50E, 50Q
			Y	Toronado	E	50E, 50Q
		5.7L	N	Riviera	E	50K
			N	Toronado	E	50K

GENERAL MOTORS TRANSMISSION APPLICATIONS

Transmission	Year	Engine	Engine Code	Vehicle	Body Code	Transmission Code
3254L	1985	5.0L	N	Riviera	E	50K
			Y	Riviera	E	50E, 50Q
			Y	Toronado	E	50E, 50Q
		5.7L	N	Toronado	E	50K
3254L	1986	4.1L	8	Eldorado, Seville	E, K	4AJ, 5AB, 4AA, 5AJ
350C	1984	5.0L	H, F	Light Truck	C, K	XX, 5XX
			H	Light Truck	C, K	4MF, 4MD, 4MK, 4TE, 4ME, 4TK
			H	Light Truck	C, K	5MF, 5MD, 4MK, 4MD, 5TE, 5ME, TK, 5TK
			F, H	Van	G	4XX, 5XX, XX
350C	1985	5.0L	H	Light Truck	C, K	5MF, 5MD, 5MK, 5MDM, 5TE, 5ME, 6TKM, 5TK
			F, H	Van	G	6XX, 5XX
350C	1986	5.0L	F, H	Van	G	6XX
400	1984	4.8L	T	Light Truck	C, K	FC
		5.7L	M	Light Truck	C, K	5TH, 5FZ, TH, FZ, FM, 4FA, 5FA
		6.0L		Fleetwood Limo	D	40M
		6.2L	J	Light Truck	C, K	5TZ, 5FX, FD, 5FD, FX
			J	Van	G	FD, 4FD, FX
		7.4L	W	Light Truck	C, K	FJ, 5FJ, FB, 5FB, FK, 5FK, FN, 4FN
400	1985	4.8L	T	Light Truck	C, K	5FC
		5.7L	M	Light Truck	C, K	5VH, 6MDM, 5VH, 6TKM, 5TK, 5TH, 6FMA, 5FM
		6.2L	J	Light Truck	C, K	5T, 5FX, 6FDA, 5FD
			J	Van	G	6FDA, 5FD, 5FX
		7.4L	W	Light Truck	C, K	6FJA, 5FJ, 6FBA, 5FB, 6FKA, 5FK, 6FNA, 5FN
400	1986	4.3L	N	Light Truck	C, K	6LSA
			Z	Van	G	6LSA
		4.8L	T	Light Truck	C, K	6FQA, 6FCA, 5FC
		5.0L	9	Fleetwood Brgm	D	6AH
		5.7L	M	Light Truck	C, K	6FAA, 6FMA, 6FZA, 6FWA
			M	Van	G	6FMA, 6FAA
		6.2L	J	Light Truck	C, K	6FDA, 6FXA, 6FFA
			J	Van	G	6FDA
		7.4L	W	Light Truck	C, K	6FPA, 6FJA, 6FKA, 6FNA, 6FBA
400	1987	4.3L	Z	Light Truck	R, V	7LAA, 7LSA
			Z	Van	G	7LSA
		5.0L	9	Fleetwood Brgm	D	7AH
			H	Light Truck	R, V	7LCA, 7LJA, 7LDA
		5.7L	K	Light Truck	R, V	7FTA, 7TKA
			M	Light Truck	R, V	7FAA
			M	Van	G	7FAA
			K	Van	G	7FTA, 7LTA, 6TKA
		6.2L	J	Light Truck	R, V	7FZA, 7LZA, 8LKA, 7FXA
			J	Van	G	7FZA, 7LZA, 7FXA
		7.4L	W	Light Truck	R, V	7FBA
			N	Light Truck	R, V	7TCA, 7FUA
			N	Van	G	7FYA

GENERAL MOTORS TRANSMISSION APPLICATIONS

Transmission	Year	Engine	Engine Code	Vehicle	Body Code	Transmission Code
400	1988	4.3L	Z	Light Truck	C, K	7LFA, 8LFA, 7LRA, 8LRA, 7FHA, 7FCA, 8FCA
		4.8L	T	Light Truck	R, V	8FQA, 8TLA
		5.0L	9	Fleetwood Brgm	D	8AHA
			H	Light Truck	C, K	7LHA, 8LBA, 7LBA, 8LHA, 7LDA, 8LDA
			H	Van	G	8LJA
		5.7L	K	Light Truck	R, V	7FWA, 8LWA, 7LWA, 7TDA, 8LTA, 8TKA, 8TDA, 8FWA
			M	Light Truck	R, V	7TAA, 8FAA, 8TAA
			K	Light Truck	C, K	7FMA, 8FMA, 7LMA, 8LMA, 87MA, 7TMA, 7FWA, 8FWA, 8LWA, 7LWA, 7TDA, 8TDA
			K	Van	G	8FTA, 8LTA, 8KTA
			M	Van	G	8FAA
		6.2L	J	Light Truck	C, K	7FOA, 8FDA, 7LVA, 8LVA, 7FFA, 8FFA, 8KLA, 7LKA
			J	Light Truck	R, V	7TDA, 7FFA, 7FRA, 7LKA, 8LZA, 8FZA, 8FXA, 8FFA, 8FRA, 8LKA
			J	Van	G	8FZA, 8LZA, 8FXA
		7.4L	N	Light Truck	C, K	7FJA, 8FJA, 8FPA, 7FPA, 8TNA, 7TNA, 8FNA, 7FNA, 8TFA, 7TFA
			N, W	Light Truck	R, V	7TBA, 8FBA, 7FNA, 8FBA, 8TPA, 8FUA, 8TBA, 9FNA, 9TFA
			N	Van	G	9LSA
400	1989	4.3L	Z	Light Truck	C, K	8LFA, 8LRA, 8FCA, 9LFA, 9MXM, 9MFM, 9LRA, 9FCA
		4.8L	T	Light Truck	R, V	9FQA
		5.0L	9	Fleetwood Brgm	D	9AHA
			H	Light Truck	C, K	8LBA, 8LHA, 8LDA, 9LBA, 9LHA, 9LDA
			H	Van	G	9LJA
		5.7L	K	Light Truck	C, K	8FMA, 8LMA, 87MA, 8FWA, 8LWA, 8TDA, 9TMA, 9FMA, 9LMA, 9TDA, 9FWA, 9LWA
			K	Light Truck	R, V	9TUA, 9TYA, 9TKA, 9FAA, 9FWA, 9TDA, 9TAA, 9LWA
			K	Van	G	9LTA, 9TKA, 9TFA
		6.2L	J	Light Truck	C, K	8FDA, 8LVA, 8FFA, 8KLA, 9FDA, 9LVA, 9FFA, 9LKA
			J	Light Truck	R, V	9FZA, 9LZA, 9FXA, 9FFA, 9LKA, 9FRA
			J	Van	G	9FZA, 9LZA, 9FXA
		7.4L	N	Light Truck	C, K	8FJA, 8FPA, 8TNA, 8FNA, 8TFA, 9FJA, 9FPA, PTNA, 9FNA, 9TFA
			N, W	Light Truck	R, V	9FUA, 9FYA, 9TCA, 9TPA, 9TBA
			N	Van	G	9LTA, 9FUA
440T4	1984	2.8L	Z	6000	A	CN, CW
			X	6000	A	CN, CW
			X	Celebrity	A	CN, CW
			Z	Celebrity	A	CN, CW
			X	Century	A	CN, CW
			X	Ciera	A	CN, CW
		3.0L	L	Ciera	A	BS, BU, BV, BN, BV
		3.8L	3	Century	A	BR, BC, BA
		5.7L	N	Eldorado, Seville	E, K	6AA, 6AT, 6ATH, 6ADH, 7AHH, 7ADH

GENERAL MOTORS TRANSMISSION APPLICATIONS

Transmission	Year	Engine	Engine Code	Vehicle	Body Code	Transmission Code
440T4	1985	2.8L	X	6000	A	CN, CWCM, CP, 5HT, HJ
			W	6000	A	CN, CWCM, CP, 5HT, HJ
			W	Celebrity	A	CN, CWCM, CP, 5HT, HJ
			X	Celebrity	A	CN, CWCM, CP, 5HT, HJ
			X	Century	A	CN, CWCM, CP, 5HT, HJ
			X	Ciera	A	CN, CWCM, CP, 5HT, HJ
		3.0L	E	98	C	BS, BU, BV, 5BV, BN, BY, 5BY
			L	Ciera	A	BS, BU, BV, 5BV, BN
			E	Electra	C	BS, BU, BV, 5BV, BN, BY, 5BY
			E	Fleetwood, DeVille FWD	C	BS, BU, BV, 5BV, BN, BY, 5BY
			E	Fleetwood, DeVille FWD	C	BS, BU, BV, 5BV, BN, BY, 5BY
		3.8L	—	98	C	5BA, 5BC, 5BR, 5BW, 5BX
			3	Century	A	BR, BC, BA
			—	Electra	C	5BA, 5BC, 5BR, 5BW, 5BX
			—	Fleetwood, DeVille FWD	C	5BA, 5BC, 5BR, 5BW, 5BX
			—	Fleetwood, DeVille FWD	C	5BA, 5BC, 5BR, 5BW, 5BX
		4.1L	8	Eldorado, Seville	E, K	6AA, 6AT, 6ATH, 6ADH, 7AHH, 7ADH
		4.3L	T	98	C	OY, OB
			T	Electra	C	OY, OB
			T	Fleetwood, DeVille FWD	C	OY, OB
			T	Fleetwood, DeVille FWD	C	OY, OB
		5.7L	N	Eldorado, Seville	E, K	6AA, 6AT, 6ATH, 6ADH, 7AHH, 7ADH
440T4	1986	2.8L	W	6000	A	6CF, 6CM, CN, CF, HJ
			X	6000	A	6CF, 6CM, CN, CF, HJ
			X	Celebrity	A	6CF, 6CM, CN, CF, HJ
			W	Celebrity	A	6CF, 6CM, CN, CF, HJ
			X	Century	A	6CF, 6CM, CN, CF, HJ
			X	Ciera	A	6CF, 6CM, CN, CF, HJ
			W	Ciera	A	6CF, 6CM, CN, CF, HJ
		3.0L	L	Electra	C	BS, BU, BV, 5BV, BN, BY, 5BY
			L	Fleetwood, DeVille FWD	C	BS, BU, BV, 5BV, BN, BY, 5BY
		3.8L	B, 3	6000	A	6BS, 6BAH, 6BC
			3	88 FWD	H	6BHH, 6BB, 6BD, 6BA
			B	88 FWD	H	6BHH, 6BB, 6BD, 6BA
			—	98	C	6BA, BM, BS, 6BAH, 6BL, 6FTH, 6BT, 6BB
			B, 3	Celebrity	A	6BS, 6BAH, 6BC
			3	Century	A	6BS, 6GAH, 6BC
			3	Ciera	A	6BS, 6BAH, 6BC
			B	Ciera	A	6BS, BGAH, 6BC
			—	Electra	C	6BA, BM, BS, 6BAH, 6BL, 6FTH, 6BT, 6BB
			—	Fleetwood, DeVille FWD	C	6BA, BM, BS, 6BAH, 6BL, 6FTH, 6BT, 6BB
			C	LeSabre	H	6BHH, 6BB, 6BD, 6BAHCH
			3	LeSabre	H	6BHH, 6BB, 6BD, 6BA
			B	Riviera	E	6FZH, 6BZ, 6FYH, 6BY
			B	Toronado	E	6FZH, 6BZ, 6FYH, 6BY

GENERAL MOTORS TRANSMISSION APPLICATIONS

Transmission	Year	Engine	Engine Code	Vehicle	Body Code	Transmission Code
440T4	1987	2.8L	W	6000	A	7CAH, 7CBH, 7CAH
			W	Celebrity	A	7CAH, 7CBH, 7CAH
			W	Century	A	7CAH, 7CBH, 7CAH
			W	Ciera	A	7CAH, 7CBH, 7CAH
		3.8L	3	6000	A	7FCH, YFLH, 7FSH
			3	88 FWD	H	7FBH, 7FKH, 7FJH, 7HAH, 7HCH
			—	98	C	7FBH, 7FKH, 7FNH, 7TFH, 7FSH
			3	Bonneville	H	7FBH, 7FKH, 7FHJ, 7HAH, 7HCH
			3	Celebrity	A	7FCH, YFLH, 7FSH
			3	Century	A	7FCH, 7FLH, 7FSH, 7FSH
			3	Ciera	A	7FCH, FFLH, 7FSH, 7FSH
			—	Electra	C	7FBH, 7FKH, 7FNH, 7FTH, 7FSH
			—	Fleetwood, DeVille FWD	C	7FBH, 7FKH, 7FNH, 7FTH, 7FSH
			3	LeSabre	H	7FBH, 7FKH, 7FJH, 7HAH, 7HCH
			C	LeSabre	H	7FBH, 7FKH, 7FHJ, 7HCH
			3	Riviera	E	7FRH, 7FZH
			3	Toronado	E	7FRH, 7FZH
		4.1L	7	Allante	V	7APZ
			8	Eldorado, Seville	E, K	6AA, 6AT, 6ATH, 6ADH, 7AHH, 7ADH
440T4	1988	2.8L	W	Ciera	A	8CFH, 8CMN, 8CWH
			W	Cutlass FWD	W	8CRH
			W	Grand Prix	W	8CRH, 8CTH
			W	Regal	W	8CRH
		3.8L	C	88 FWD	H	8FBH, 8FJH, 8FSH, 8BJH, 8BKH
			3	88 FWD	H	8FBH, 8FJH, 8FSH, 8BJH, 8BKH
			C	98	C	8FBH, 8FJH, 8FSH, 8BJH, 8BKH
			3	Bonneville	H	8FBH, 8FJH, 8FSH, 8BJH, 8BKH
			C	Bonneville	H	8FBH, 8FJH, 8FSH, 8BJH, 8BKH
			3	Century	A	8FCH
			3	Ciera	A	8FCH
			C	Electra	C	8FBH, 8FJH, 8FJH, 8FTH, 8FSH
			3	LeSabre	H	8FBH, 8FJH, 8FSH, 8FJH, 8FKH
			C	LeSabre	H	8FBH, 8FJH, 8FSH, 8FJH, 8FKH
			C	Riviera	E	8BRH, 8BYH
			C	Toronado	E	8BRH, 8BYH
		4.1L	7	Allante	V	8APZ
		4.5L	5	Eldorado, Seville	E, K	8AJH, 8ATH
			5	Fleetwood, DeVille FWD	C	8FBH, 8FKH, 8FJH, 8FTH, 8FSH
440T4	1989	2.8L	W	6000	A	8CHF, 8CMN, 8CWH
			W	Celebrity	A	8CHF, 8CMN, 8CWH
			W	Century	A	8CHF, 8CMN, 8CWH
			W	Ciera	A	8CHF, 8CMN, 8CWH
			W	Cutlass FWD	W	9CDH
			W	Grand Prix	W	9CDH, 9CYH
			W	Regal	W	9CDH

GENERAL MOTORS TRANSMISSION APPLICATIONS

Transmission	Year	Engine	Engine Code	Vehicle	Body Code	Transmission Code
440T4	1989	3.1L	T	Cutlass FWD	W	0CHH
			T	Grand Prix	W	0CJH, 0LAH
			T	Regal	W	0CHH
		3.8L	C	88 FWD	H	9FJH, 9BHH, 9PAH, 9BWH
			C	98	C	9BHH, 9BWH
			C	Bonneville	H	9BJH, 9BHH, 9PAH, 9BWH
			C	Electra	C	9BHH, PBWH
			C	LeSabre	H	9BJH, 9BHH, 9PAH, PBWH
			C	Riviera	E	9BPH, 9BWH
			C	Toronado	E	9BPH, PBWH
		4.5L	—	Allante	V	9AZH
			5	Eldorado, Seville	E, K	9AJH, 9ATH, 9ABH
			5	Fleetwood, DeVille FWD	C	9BHH, 9BWH
700R4	1984	2.0L	Y	S-10, S-15	S, T	T2
		2.5L	2	Camaro	F	PQ, 6PL
			2	Firebird	F	PQ, 6PL
		2.8L	1	Camaro	F	Y7, 4Y7
			1	Firebird	F	Y7, 4Y7
			B	S-10, S-15	S, T	5T7, 4MP, 4ML, 5ML, 5MP, 4MS
		4.3L	N	Light Truck	C, K	5VR, VR, 5MX, VF, VZ, TW, 5TW
		5.0L	G, H	Camaro	F	4YP, Y8, YF, 6YF, 4YG
			H	Caprice	B	4YK, Y6, YL
			G, H	Firebird	F	4YP, Y8, YF, 6YF, 4YG
			F	Light Truck	C, K	5TE, TE
			H	Parisienne	B	4YK, Y6, YL
			F, H	Van	G	5MF, 5ME, MF, ME
		5.7L	8	Corvette	Y	Y9
			M	Van	G	FA, 5FA
			L	Van	G	5MK, 5ME, MD, TE
		6.2L	C	Light Truck	C, K	MH, GH, 5VJ, 5MH, 5MG, 5VJ, 5VE, 5TL, 5T8, 5TM, 5TZ, VJ, VE, TL
			C	Light Truck	C, K	5MH, 5MG, 5VJ, MH, 5MH, 5MG, 5VJ, 5VE, 5TL, 5T8, 5TM, TR, 4TZ
			J	Van	G	5TL, 5VJ, 5VE, TL, VJ, MG, VE
700R4	1985	2.5L	2	Camaro	F	5PQ
			2	Firebird	F	5PQ
			E	S-10, S-15	S, T	6PRM, 5PR, 6MTM, 5MT
			S	Camaro	F	YX, 6YX
			S	Firebird	F	YX, 6YX
			B	S-10, S-15	S, T	5T7, 5ML, 5MP, 5MS
		4.3L	N	Light Truck	C, K	6MMM, 5VR, 6MXM, 5MX, 5VF, 5VZ, 5TW, 6TWM
		4.3L	Z	Caprice	B	5YT
			Z	Parisienne	B	5YT
		5.0L	H	Camaro	F	Y8, YF, 6YF, 5YP
			F	Camaro	F	5YZ, YS, YW, YZ, 6YW

GENERAL MOTORS TRANSMISSION APPLICATIONS

Transmission	Year	Engine	Engine Code	Vehicle	Body Code	Transmission Code
700R4	1985	2.5L	H	Caprice	B	YK, 6YK, 5Y6, 5YK
			F	Firebird	F	5YZ, YS, YW, YZ, 6YW
			H	Firebird	F	Y8, YF, 6YF, 5YP
			F	Light Truck	C, K	5TE, 6TJM
			H	Parisienne	B	YK, 6YK, 5Y6, 5YK
			F, H	Van	G	5MF, 5ME
		5.7L		Caprice	B	5TS
			8	Corvette	Y	Y9
			L	Van	G	5MK, 5ME, 6MDM, 6TJM
			M	Van	G	6FAA, 5FA
		6.2L	C	Light Truck	C, K	5MH, 5MG, 5VJ, 6MHM, 5MH, 5MG, 5VJ, 5VE, 5TL, 5T8, 5TM, 6TRM, 5TZ
			J	Van	G	5TL, 5VJ, 5VE, 6MHM, 5MG, 5VE
700R4	1986	2.5L	2	Camaro	F	YX, 6YX
			2	Firebird	F	YX, 6YX
			E	S-10, S-15	S, T	6PRM, 6MTM
		2.5L	S	Camaro	F	YX, 6YX
			S	Firebird	F	YX, 6YX
			R	S-10, S-15	S, T	6TB, 6TA
		4.3L	Z	Caprice	B	5YT, 6YT, YT
			N	Light Truck	C, K	6MMM, 6MAM, 6MXM, 6MRM, 6TWM
			Z	Parisienne	B	5YT, 6YT, YT
			N	Van	G	6MAM, 6MMM, 6MXM, 6MFM, 6MHM
		5.0L	H	Camaro	F	YPM, 6YP
			H	Caprice	B	YL, Y6, 6YL
				Firebird	F	YPM, 6YP
			F	Light Truck	C, K	6TJM, 6MPM
			H	Light Truck	C, K	6MDM, 6TKM
			H	Parisienne	B	YL, Y6, 6YL
			F, H	Van	G	6TJM, 6MPM, 6MDM, 6MKM
		5.7L	8	Corvette	Y	GYA
			L	Light Truck	C, K	6MDM, 6MKM, 6TJM, 6MPM, 6MWM, 5MW
			L	Van	G	6MDM, 6MKM, 6TJM, 6MPM
		6.2L	C	Light Truck	C, K	6MHM, 6TNM, 6TRM
			C	Van	G	6MHM, 6TNM
700R4	1987	2.5L	E	S-10, S-15	S, T	8PRM, 7PRM, 7MTM
		2.8L	S	Camaro	F	7YXM
			S	Firebird	F	7YXM
			R	S-10, S-15	S, T	7TBM, 7TAM
		4.3L	Z	Light Truck	R, V	7MMM, 8MAM, 7MAM
			Z	Van	G	8MAM, 7MAM
		5.0L	H	Camaro	F	7YFM, 7YPM
			F	Camaro	F	7YSM, Y7WM, 7YZM
			F	Firebird	F	7YSM, Y7WM, 7YZM
			H	Firebird	F	7YFM, 7YPM

GENERAL MOTORS TRANSMISSION APPLICATIONS

Transmission	Year	Engine	Engine Code	Vehicle	Body Code	Transmission Code
700R4	1987	5.0L	H	Light Truck	R, V	7MUM, 8TJM, 7TJM
			H	Van	G	8TUM, 7TUM, 8TJM, 7TJM
		5.7L	8	Camaro	F	7YMM
			8	Corvette	Y	7YAM, 7YCM, 7YDM
			8	Firebird	F	7YMM
			K	Light Truck	R, V	8TUM, 7TUM, 8MWM, 7MWM, 8TXM, 7TXM
		6.2L	C	Light Truck	R, V	7MHM, 7TNM
			C	Van	G	7TNM
700R4	1988	2.5L	E	S-10, S-15	S, T	8PRM, 8MTM
		2.8L	S	Camaro	F	8YXM
			S	Firebird	F	8YXM
			R	S-10, S-15	S, T	8TBM, 8TAM
		4.3L	Z	Caprice	B	8YTM
			Z	Light Truck	C, K	8MXM, 7MXM, 7MFM, 8MFM, 8MRM, 7MRM
			Z	S-10, S-15	S, T	8THM, 9TLM, 8TLM
			Z	Safari	B	8YTM
			Z	Van	G	8LSA
		5.0L	E, F	Camaro	F	8YPM, 8YWM, 8YZM
			H	Caprice	B	8YKM
			E, F	Firebird	F	8YPM, 8YWM, 8YZM
			H	Light Truck	R, V	8TUM
			H	Light Truck	C, K	7MRM, 8MRM, 7MDM, 8MDM, 8MLM, 7MLM, 8TRM
			H	Safari	B	8YKM
			H	Van	G	8MAM, 8TJM
		5.7L	8	Camaro	F	8YMM
			8	Caprice	B	9YNM
			8	Corvette	Y	8YDM
			8	Firebird	F	8YMM
			K	Light Truck	C, K	8MPM, 8MZM, 7MZM, 8TXM, 7TXM, 7FWA
			K	Light Truck	R, V	8TXM, 7TXM, 8MWM
			8	Safari	B	9YNM
		6.2L	C	Light Truck	R, V	8MHN, 8TNM, 9PCM, 8PCM
			C	Light Truck	C, K	7PAM, 8MPM, 7MPM, 7PBM, 8PBM, 8PAM, 7PAM, 7PCM, 8PCM
			C	Van	G	8TNM
700R4	1989	2.5L	E	S-10, S-15	S, T	9PRM
		2.8L	S	Firebird	F	9YPM, 9YWM, 9YZM
		4.3L	Z	Caprice	B	9YTM
			Z	Light Truck	C, K	8MXM, 8MFM, 8MRM, 9MPM
			Z	S-10, S-15	S, T	9THM, 9TLM
			Z	Van	G	9LSA
		5.0L	Y	Caprice	B	9YKM
			H	Caprice	B	9YKM

GENERAL MOTORS TRANSMISSION APPLICATIONS

Transmission	Year	Engine	Engine Code	Vehicle	Body Code	Transmission Code
700R4	1989	5.0L	E, F	Firebird	F	9YPM, 9YZM
			H	Light Truck	C, K	8MRM, 8MDM, 8MLM, 8TRM, 9MLM, 9TRM, 9MKM, 9MDM, 9MLM
			H	Van	G	9TJM
		5.7L	8	Camaro	F	9FKM, 9FXM
			8	Corvette	Y	9YDM
			8	Firebird	F	9FKM, 9FXM
			K	Light Truck	C, K	8MPM, 8MZM, 8TXM, PMZM, 9TXM
			K	Light Truck	R, V	9TUM, 9MWM, 9TXM
		6.2L	C	Light Truck	C, K	8MPM, 8PBM, 8PAM, 8PCM, 9PCM, 9PBM, 9PAM
			C	Light Truck	R, V	9PCM, 9TNM, 9MHM
			C	Van	G	9TNM
A131L	1985	1.6L	4	Nova	S	None
A131L	1986	1.6L	4	Nova	S	None
A131L	1987	1.6L	4	Nova	S	None
A131L	1988	1.6L	4	Nova	S	None
A131L	1989	1.6L	6	Geo Prizm	S	None
A240E	1988	1.6L	5	Nova	S	MS7
KF100	1985	1.5L	K	Spectrum	R	04-260
KF100	1986	1.5L	7	Spectrum	R	04-260
KF100	1987	1.5L	7	Spectrum	R	04-260
KF100	1988	1.5L	7	Spectrum	R	04-260
KF100	1989	1.5L	7	Geo Spectrum	R	04-260
Sprint	1985	1.0L	M	Sprint	M	04-012
Sprint	1986	1.0L	5	Sprint	M	04-012
Sprint	1987	1.0L	5	Sprint	M	04-012
Sprint	1988	1.0L	5	Sprint	M	04-012
Sprint	1989	1.0L	5, 6	Geo Metro	O	04-034

Section 3
MJ3 Transaxle
AMC/Jeep-Eagle

APPLICATION

1987–89 Medallion

GENERAL DESCRIPTION

The MJ3 automatic transaxle enables 3 foward speeds to be engaged one after the other with continous action. There are 3 main components, the torque converter, the differential and the rear case. The transaxle is electronically controlled, with the aid of an electronic microprocessor (computer) that interprets information from the road speed sensor, the engine load potentiometer and the malfunction switch. It then converts the information received from these sensors into electrical instruction (inputs) to the solenoid valves in the valve body assembly to change gears. The solenoid operated ball valves open or close hydraulic channels to change gears. These solenoid valves are controlled by the computer. The governor is small low wattage alternator (appoximately 1 watt). It supplies to the computer an alternating current (AC) which varies according to the vehicle speed and engine load.

The torque converter provides a smooth coupling for transmitting the engine torque to the rear case components with automatic clutch action. Increased torque is provided for moving from a standard position.

The differential transmits power from the rear case components to the wheels. It consists of a step-down gear cluster that lowers the drive centerline and a ring gear and pinion that drive the differential housing.

The rear case components provide 3 reduction ratios for forward movement and 1 for reverse movement. The rear case components include an epicyclic gear train with 3 different control elements; mechanical, hydraulic and electric. The epicyclic gear train is an assembly of helical gears that enable the different ratios to be obtained (3 forward, 1 reverse) depending on the hydraulic pressure to the receivers.

Transaxle and Converter Identification

TRANSAXLE

The transaxle has a stamped identification plate that is located on the top center rear of the transaxle. The identification number is stamped on the plate with the following data, the first part of the number is the transaxle type, the second part of the number is the transaxle model number and the last identification number is the transaxle fabrication number.

CONVERTER

The torque converter is a completely sealed unit and is not equipped with a drain plug and therefore cannot be flushed if contaminated, only replaced. The torque converter may vary depending on the engine and transaxle combination being used. The converter may have an identifying decal attached to the front cover. The decal is circular in shape and states converter type and stall ratio.

Electronic Controls

The transaxle is electronically controlled, with the aid of an elec-

tronic microprocessor (computer) that interprets information from the road speed sensor, the engine load potentiometer and the malfunction switch. It then converts the information received from these sensors into electrical instruction (inputs) to the solenoid valves in the valve body assembly to change gears. The solenoid operated ball valves open or close hydraulic channels to change gears. These solenoid valves are controlled by the computer.

The potentiometer provides variable voltage based on the throttle position. The road speed sensor is a winding located opposite the park ring that senses vehicle speed.

Metric Fasteners

The metric fastener dimensions are very close to the dimensions of the familiar inch system fasteners and for this reason, replacement fasteners must have the same measurement and strength as those removed.

Do not attempt to interchange metric fasteners for inch system fasteners. Mismatched or incorrect fasteners can result in damage to the transaxle unit through malfunctions, breakage or possible personal injury.

Care should be taken to reuse the fasteners in the same locations as removed.

Capacities

Vehicles equipped with extra transaxle coolers will all vary slightly in their capacity. Therefore, check fluid level carefully. The transaxle capacity is 6.4 quarts dry fill capacity and 2.6 quarts refill capacity.

Checking Fluid Level

The dipstick is located on the right side of the vehicle, on top of the transaxle.

1. With the vehicle on a level surface, engine idling, wheels blocked and the parking brake applied, move the selector lever through all the gear positions and return to the **P** position. Allow the engine to idle.

2. Clean the dipstick area of dirt and remove the dipstick from the filler tube. Wipe the dipstick indicator clean and reinsert the dipstick back into the filler tube and seat firmly.

3. Remove the dipstick from the filler tube again and check the fluid level as indicated on the dipstick indicator. The fluid level should be at the between the **ADD** and the **FULL** mark when the vehicle is at 160°–170°F. With the temperature at 100°F the fluid level should be at the **ADD** mark.

4. If necessary, add fluid through the filler tube to bring the fluid level to its proper height.

5. When the fluid level is correct, fully seat the dipstick in the filler tube to avoid entrance of dirt or other foreign matter.

NOTE: It takes only a ½ pint of transmission fluid to raise the level from the ADD mark to the FULL mark. Do not overfill.

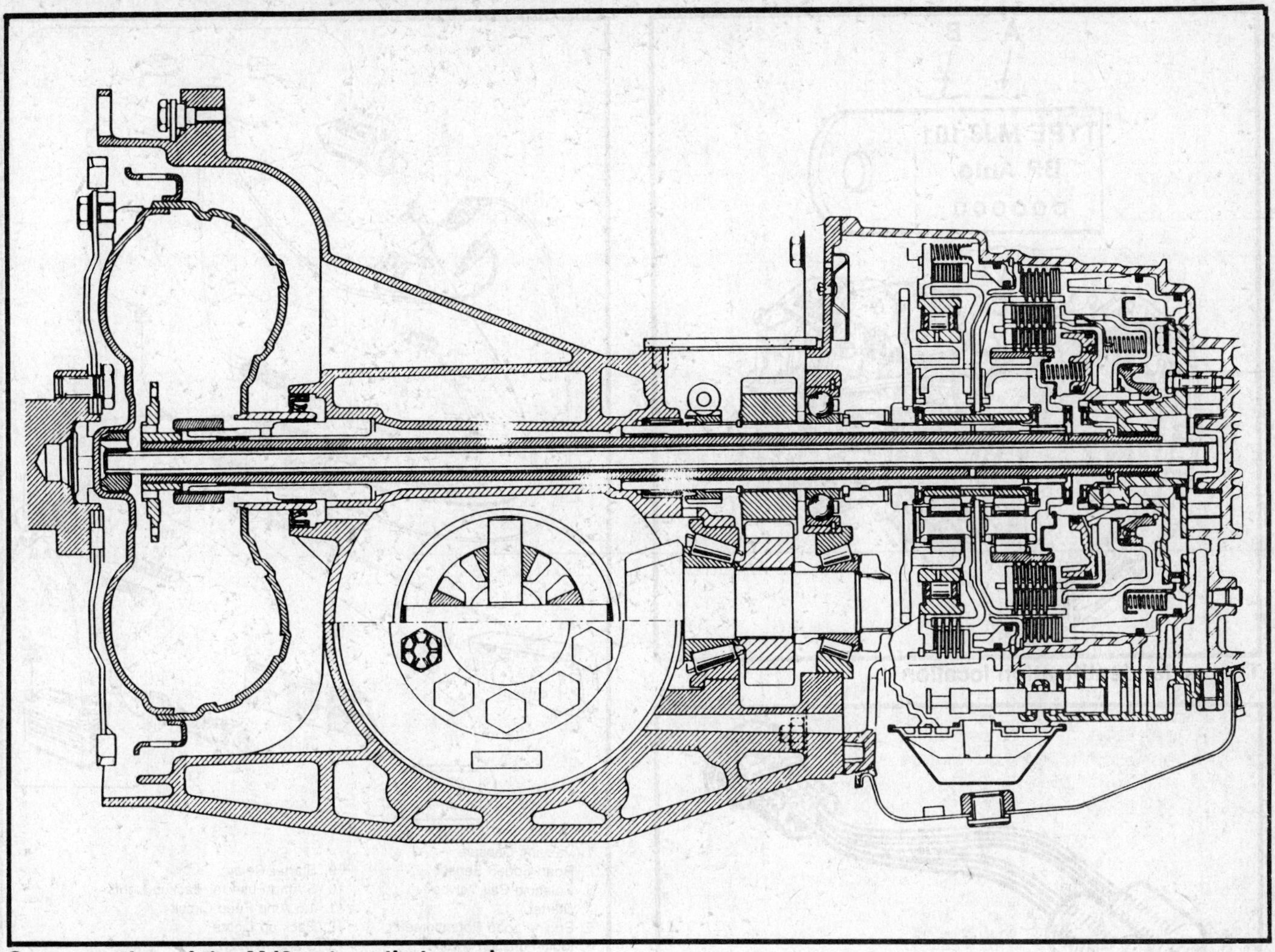

Cross section of the MJ3 automatic tranaxle

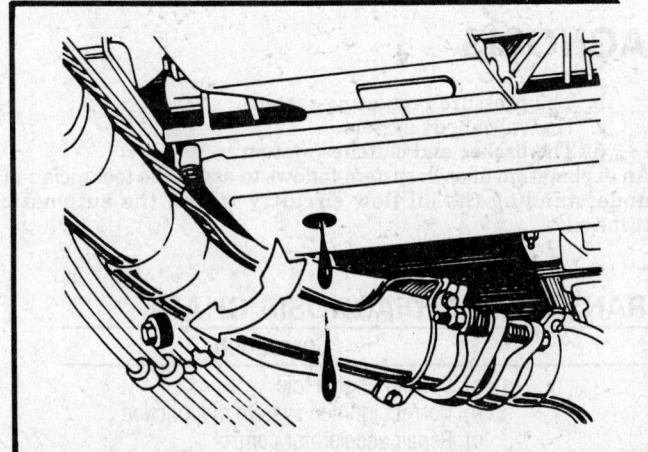

Fluid drain plug location

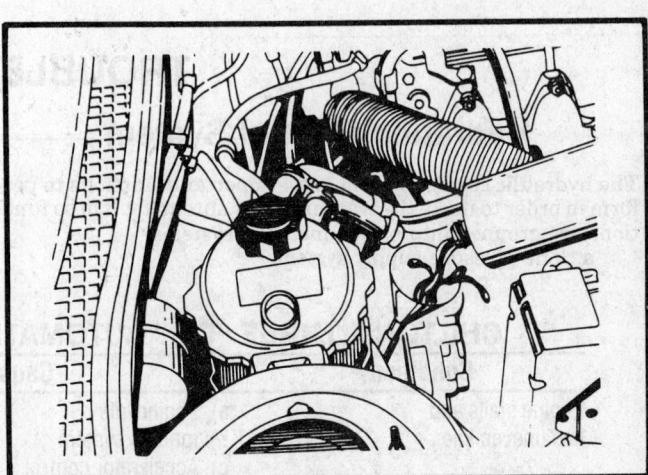

Fluid fill location

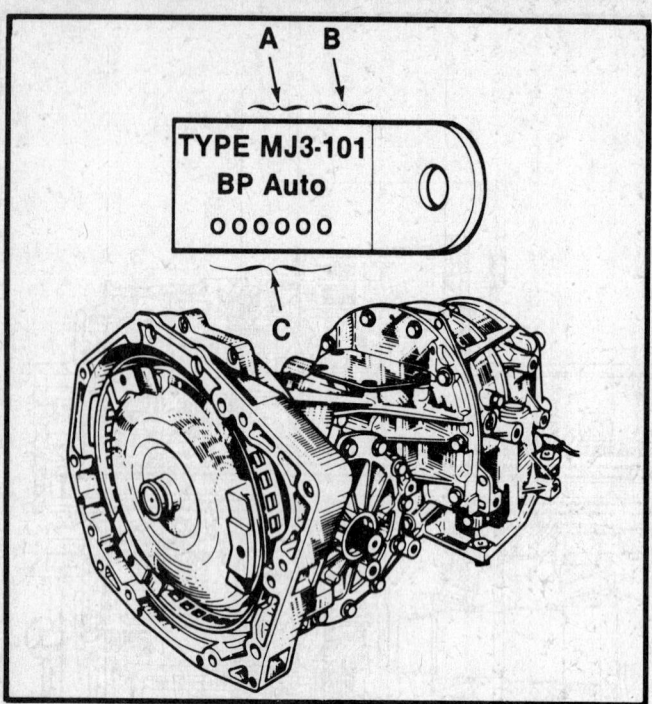

Transaxle identification location

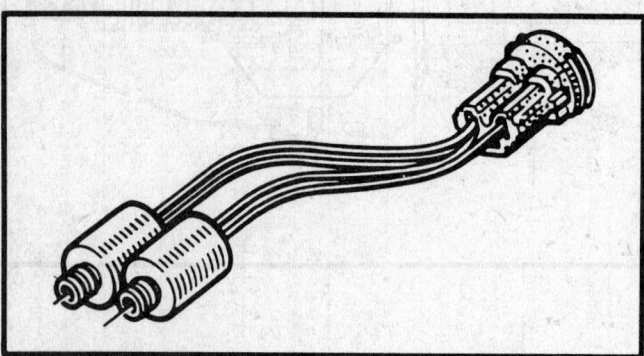

Typical solenoid ball valves

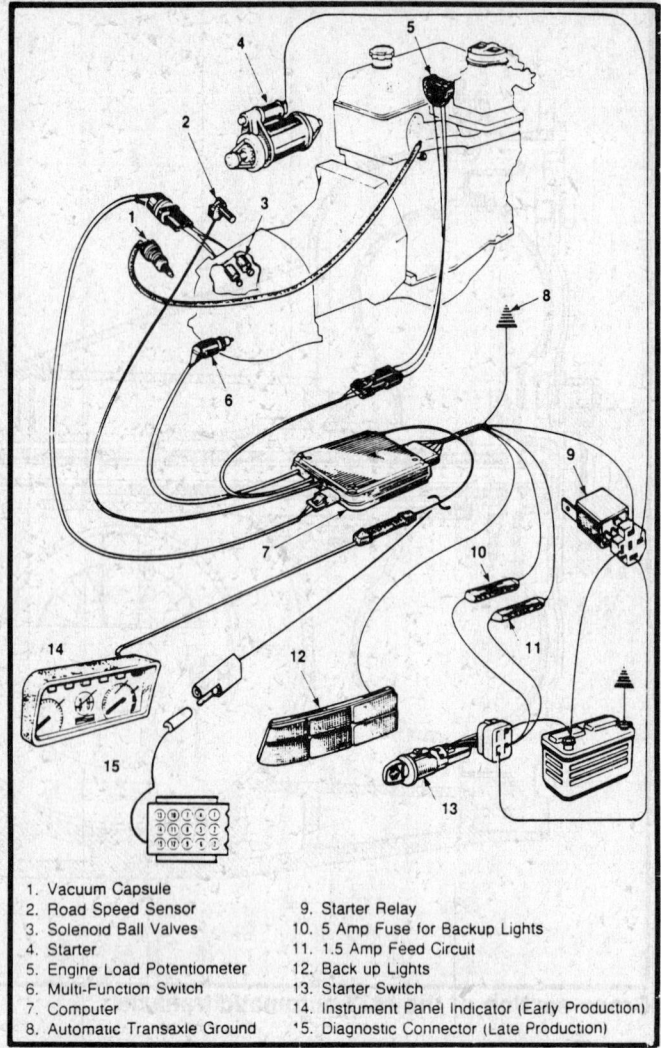

1. Vacuum Capsule
2. Road Speed Sensor
3. Solenoid Ball Valves
4. Starter
5. Engine Load Potentiometer
6. Multi-Function Switch
7. Computer
8. Automatic Transaxle Ground
9. Starter Relay
10. 5 Amp Fuse for Backup Lights
11. 1.5 Amp Feed Circuit
12. Back up Lights
13. Starter Switch
14. Instrument Panel Indicator (Early Production)
15. Diagnostic Connector (Late Production)

Electronic transaxle wire harness and electrical components

TROUBLE DIAGNOSIS

Hydraulic Control System

The hydraulic control system has 4 important functions to perform in order to make the transaxle fully automatic. These functions are grouped into basic functional systems.

    a. The pressure supply system.

    b. The pressure regulating system.
    c. The valve body system.
    d. The brakes and clutches system.

An explanation of each system follows to assist the technician in understanding the oil flow circuitry within the automatic transaxles.

CHILTON'S THREE "C'S" AUTOMATIC TRANSMISSION DIAGNOSIS CHART

Condition	Cause	Correction
Engine stalls and has uneven idle	a) Engine idle b) Ignition system c) Accelerator control d) Vacuum modulator and/or hoses	a) Correct engine idle b) Correct ignition system malfunction c) Repair accelerator control d) Repair or renew vacuum modulator and/or hoses
Creeps in "N" position	a) Gear selector lever b) E-1/E-2 clutches	a) Adjust gear selector lever b) Overhaul as required

CHILTON'S THREE "C'S" AUTOMATIC TRANSMISSION DIAGNOSIS CHART

Condition	Cause	Correction
Excessive creep in "D"	a) Engine Idle b) Accelerator control c) Converter	a) Correct engine idle b) Correct accelerator control c) Renew converter assembly
Slippage when starting in "D" or "R"	a) Fluid level b) Fluid pressure c) Valve body d) Converter	a) Correct fluid level b) Adjust fluid pressure c) Clean, repair or renew valve body assembly d) Renew converter assembly
Slippage when starting off in "D" only	a) Fluid level b) E-1/E-2 clutches c) Overrunning clutch	a) Correct fluid level b) Correct or renew clutches c) Renew overrunning clutch
Slippage during shift	a) Fluid pressure b) Modulator c) Valve body d) Oil pump screen e) E-1/E-2 or overrunning clutches	a) Correct fluid pressure b) Adjust or renew modulator assembly c) Clean, repair or renew valve body d) Clean or renew oil pump screen e) Overhaul and renew as required
No 1st gear hold	a) Selector lever b) Harness, plugs, grounds c) Computer control unit d) Multifunction switch e) Valve body	a) Adjust selector lever b) Clean, repair, or renew components as required c) Test and/or renew computer control unit d) Clean, repair or renew components as required e) Clean, repair or renew valve body assembly
No 2nd gear hold	a) Selector lever b) Harness, plugs, grounds c) Computer control unit d) Multifunction switch e) Valve body	a) Adjust selector lever b) Clean, repair, or renew components as required c) Test and/or renew computer control unit d) Clean, repair or renew components as required e) Clean, repair or renew valve body assembly
Remains in 1st gear when in "D" position	a) Harness, plugs, grounds b) Computer control unit c) Solenoid valves d) Road speed indicator e) Valve body	a) Clean, repair or renew components as required b) Test and/or renew computer control unit c) Clean, repair or renew solenoid valves d) Test, repair or renew indicator assembly e) Clean, repair or renew valve body assembly
Remains in 3rd gear	a) Fuses b) Harness, plugs, grounds c) Computer control assembly d) Oil pump e) Valve body	a) Test circuits and renew fuses b) Clean, repair, or renew components as required c) Test and/or renew computer control unit d) Repair or renew oil pump e) Clean, repair or renew valve body assembly
Some gear ratios unobtainable and selector lever out of position	a) Selector lever b) Selector control c) Manual valve mechanical control	a) Adjust selector lever b) Adjust or repair selector control c) Repair or renew components as required
Park position not operating	a) Selector lever b) Broken or damaged components	a) Adjust selector lever b) Repair or renew components as required
No 1st in "D" position, operates— 2nd to 3rd to 2nd	a) EI-1 solenoid ball valve stays open	a) Test and/or renew EI-1 solenoid ball valve
No 2nd in "D" position, operates— 1st to 3rd to 1st	a) EI-1 solenoid ball valve stays closed b) Solenoid ball valves reversed	a) Test and/or renew EI-1 solenoid ball valve b) Reverse solenoid ball valves

CHILTON'S THREE "C'S" AUTOMATIC TRANSMISSION DIAGNOSIS CHART

Condition	Cause	Correction
Operates in 3rd only	a) El-2 solenoid ball valve stays open	a) Test and/or renew El-2 solenoid ball valve
No 3rd, operates 1st to 2nd to 1st	a) El-2 solenoid ball valve stays closed	a) Test and/or renew El-2 solenoid ball valve
Surge when starting off	a) Idle speed b) Accelerator controls c) Fluid level	a) Correct idle speed b) Correct the accelerator controls c) Correct fluid level
Surge during shifting	a) Modulator valve and/or hoses b) Valve body assembly	a) Adjust or renew modulator assembly and/or hoses b) Clean, repair or renew valve body assembly
Incorrect shifting speeds	a) Accelerator controls b) Load potentiometer setting c) Harness, plugs or grounds d) Kickdown switch e) Computer control units f) Road speed	a) Correct accelerator controls b) Adjust setting of load potentiometer c) Clean, repair or renew components as required d) Adjust or renew kickdown switch e) Test and/or renew computer control f) Bring vehicle to correct road speed
No drive	a) Selector lever ad b) Fluid level c) Valve body d) Oil pump e) Oil pump screen f) Oil pump shaft broken g) Turbine shaft broken h) Final drive i) Converter drive plate broken j) Converter k) E-1/E-2 clutches	a) Adjust selector lever b) Correct fluid level c) Clean, repair or renew valve body assembly d) Repair or renew oil pump e) Clean or renew oil pump screen f) Renew oil pump shaft g) Replace turbine shaft h) Correct final drive malfunction i) Replace converter drive plate j) Renew converter k) Correct or renew clutches
No drive in 1st gear hold or in "D" position	a) Valve body b) E-1/E-2 clutches c) Overrunning clutch	a) Clean, repair or renew valve body assembly b) Correct or renew clutches c) Renew overrunning clutch
No drive in "R" or 3rd gear	a) Valve body b) E-1/E-2 clutches	a) Clean, repair or renew valve body assembly b) Correct or renew clutches
No reverse or engine braking in 1st gear hold	a) Multifunction switch b) Valve body c) F-1 brake	a) Test, repair or renew multifunction switch b) Clean, repair or renew valve body assembly c) Correct or renew brake
No 1st gear in "D" position	a) Harness, plugs or grounds b) Solenoid valves c) Overrunning clutch	a) Clean, repair or renew components as required b) Clean, repair or renew solenoid valves c) Renew overrunning clutch
No 2nd gear in "D" position	a) Harness, plugs or grounds b) Valve body assembly c) F-2 brake	a) Clean, repair or renew components as required b) Clean, repair or renew valve body assembly c) Correct or renew brake
No 3rd gear in "D" position	a) Harness, plugs or grounds b) Computer control unit c) Solenoid valves d) Multifunction switch e) Valve body	a) Clean, repair or renew components as required b) Test and/or renew computer control c) Clean, repair or renew solenoid valves d) Test, repair or renew multifunction switch e) Clean, repair or renew valve body assembly

CLUTCH AND BAND APPLICATION CHART
MJ3 Automatic Transaxle

Lever Position	Free-Wheel	Clutches		Brakes		Solenoid Valves	
		E1	E2	F1	F2	EL1	EL2
P	—	—	—	—	—	—	Applied
R	—	—	Applied	Applied	—	—	Applied
N	—	—	—	—	—	—	Applied
A1	Applied	Applied	—	—	—	—	Applied
A2	—	Applied	—	—	Applied	Applied	Applied
A3	—	Applied	Applied	—	—	—	—
2nd Hold	—	Applied	—	—	Applied	Applied	Applied
1st Hold	—	Applied	—	Applied	—	—	Applied

E1—Clutch 1
E2—Clutch 2
F1—Brake 1
F2—Brake 2
EL1—Solenoid valve 1
EL2—Solenoid valve 2

THE PRESSURE SUPPLY SYSTEM

The pressure supply system consists of the involute oil pump which is located in the back of the rear case. The pump is driven directly by the engine through the torque converter drive plate and supplies pressurized fluid for the converter, gear lubrication and the brakes and clutches.

THE PRESSURE REGULATING SYSTEM

The pressure regulating system consists of the vacuum capsule and pressure regulator which provides pressure that, depending on the engine load, determines the fluid pressure to the receivers and as a result controls the gear change quality.

THE VALVE BODY SYSTEM

The valve body ensures that the fluid pressure regulation is taking into account the engine load. It controls the pressurized fluid supply or release to or from the clutches and brakes. Ratio changes are determined by the operation of the 2 solenoid ball valves (EL1 and EL2). They receive the electrical instructions from the computer.

THE BRAKES AND CLUTCHES

Clutches E1 and E2 and brakes F1 and F2 are the multi-disc oil bath type. They are hydraulic receivers that, depending on their feed, lock or release units in the epicyclic gear train to engage the various forward gear ratios.

Diagnostic Tests

FLUID PRESSURE CHECK AND ADJUSTMENT

This test must be performed when the transaxle is hot and during a road test. The fluid pressure varies with the fluid temperature. Low fluid pressure will cause excessive slip during gear shifting, overheating of the clutches and brakes and eventual damage to the transaxle.

High fluid pressure will cause harsh gear shifting that is harmful to the transaxle. The fluid pressure testing gauge B.Vi. 466.04 or equivalent, must be handled carefully and calibrated regularly.

1. Verify the correct accelerator pedal cable adjustment. Adjust the cable as necessary.
2. Remove the oil pressure test port.
3. Connect pressure test gauge B.Vi.466.07 or equivalent to the pressure test port. Position the gauge inside the vehicle so it can be easily read while the vehicle in in motion.
4. Drive the vehicle a few miles to warm the transaxle fluid to normal operating temperature. Then, check fluid pressure as follows:

    a. Shift the transaxle into 2nd gear.
    b. Simultaneously press the accelerator pedal to the floor and apply the brakes to hold the vehicle speed at 50 mph.
    c. Note the oil pressure. The oil pressure reading should be 66.7 psi (4.6 bars). Release the accelerator pedal and brakes and shift the transaxle into the **D** position. If the pressure is above or below specifications, go on to the next step.
    d. Remove the vacuum capsule retaining bolt and bracket.
    e. Rotate the vacuum capsule clockwise to increase the pressure and counterclockwise to decrease the pressure.

NOTE: The pressure is increased or decreased by 1.2 psi (0.08 bars) for every 2 notches of capsule rotation.

5. Install the bracket and retaining bolt. Place a white paint mark on the vacuum capsule to indicate the pressure has been asjusted correctly.

VACUUM CAPSULE CHECK

1. Apply an extended vacuum of 16 in. Hg. to the vacuum capsule.
2. If the test gauge needle remains steady, check the fluid pressure. If the needle falls, either the capsule or its pipe must be replaced.
3. Make sure that the union on the inlet manifold is sound. Check that the pipe is tight at both capsule and union ends.
4. An air leak into the capsule or into its pipe will cause whistling, unsteady idling and rough gear shifting on a light load.

NOTE: The vacuum capsule should be replaced it it is the cause of a fluid leak. The capsule cannot be repaired.

HYDRAULIC PRESSURE TEST

Before starting the pressure test, make sure the fluid level is correct and linkage is adjusted properly. A good pressure test is an important part of diagnosing transaxle problems. Oil pressure checks are made once it is obvious that the vacuum capsule and vacuum circuit are in good condition. Regulated oil prerssure varies with the ATF fluid temperature. It is therefore normal to find, in the case of a fluid temperature of less than 176°F pressure values higher than the specifications.

1. Check fluid level and linkage adjustments. Remember that fluid must be at operating temperature (176–200°F) during tests.

2. Connect a suitable fluid pressure gauge to the transaxle. Apply the parking brake and block the drive wheels. Connect a suitable tachometer to the engine.

High Pressure Check in Park

1. Move the selector lever to the **P** position.
2. The fluid pressure must be 68 psi (5 bars) minimum at 800 rpm; it should then rise rapidly as the engine rpm is increased until it reaches a maximum pressure of 183–203 psi (13–14 bars).

Light Throttle Pressure Check

1. Disconnect the vacuum capsule.
2. Move the selector lever to the **N** position.
3. The light throttle pressure should be 36–39 psi (2.45–2.7 bars).
4. If necessary, adjust the pressure by turning the vacuum capsule; 1 notch is equal to 1.5 psi (0.1 bar).
5. The pressure will increase as the vacuum capsule is screwed in. The initial adjustment is as follows:
   a. Place the selector lever to the **N** position.
   b. Run the engine at 3800 rpm.
   c. The pressure obtained must be closed to 68 psi (5 bars).
   d. The final test and adjustment must then be made by road testing at 176°F.

ROAD TEST

The road test will be done at full throttle pressure.
1. Be sure to reconnect the vacuum capsule.
2. Drive a few miles to bring the ATF fluid up to operating temperature.
3. With the selector lever in the **D** position, fully depress the accelerator pedal. Just before the transaxle shifts from 1st to 2nd, read the maximum pressure, which should be 68 psi (5 bars).
4. If the pressure is abnormal, check the vacuum capsule and vacuum circuit. Replace the capsule if necessary and adjust the full throttle pressure.
5. If the pressure is still not correct, the pressure regulator or the transaxle is at fault.
6. Too low a pressure produces a considerable slippage during gear shifts, overheating of the clutches and brakes and consequently damage these parts.
7. Too high a pressure causes gear shifts that are too harsh and jerky, both for driver comfort and for the long life of the transaxle.
8. Frequently have the fluid pressure gauge calibration checked, especially in the 68 psi (5 bars) zone and if the gauge has been mistreated.

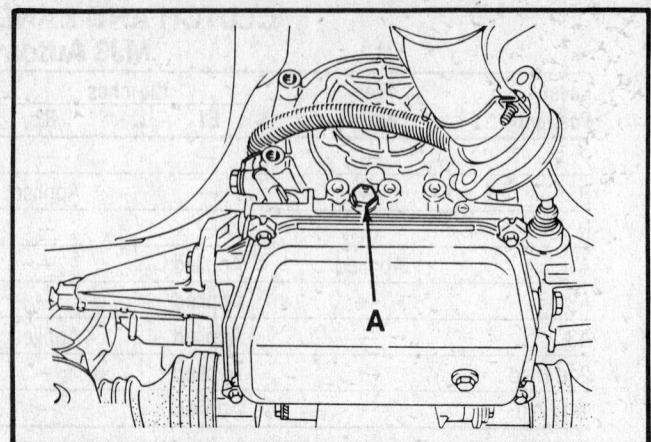

Location of the oil pressure test port plug (A)

Converter Clutch Operation and Diagnosis

The torque converter provides a smooth coupling for transmitting the engine torque to the rear case components with automatic clutch action. Increased torque is provided for moving from a standard position. The torque converter used with this transaxle is not a lockup torque converter.

The torque converter is a completely sealed unit, therefore if contaminated it must be replaced. The torque converter may vary depending on the the engine and transaxle combination being used. The converter may have an identifying decal attached to the front cover. The decal is circular in shape and states converter type and stall ratio.

TROUBLESHOOTING THE TRANSAXLE COMPUTER SYSTEM

There are 2 testers available for testing the transaxle electrical components. There is the diagnostic tester MS1700 and the diagnostic tester B.Vi.958. Both testers should be used according to the manufacturers instructions supplied with the testers.

The B.Vi.958 tester has a self checking feature. Check the tester by connecting terminal 14 to the battery and switching the tester to the test position. The test lights and the (+) red zone should light up. If they do not light, the tester is defective. It is also possible to test this system with a suitable volt/ohmmeter. Use the charts provided and a volt/ohmmeter to test the system.

Checking the 6–Way Connector

1. Unplug the connector from the computer and make the following checks:
   a. With the ignition switch in the **OFF** position, check the **B** terminal of the connector. The reading should be 4 ohms ± 3 ohms. This is used to diagnosis the backup lamps.
   b. With the ignition switch in the **ON** position, check the **A** terminal of the connector. The reading should be 12 volts ± 2 volts. This is used to diagnosis the backup lamps.
   c. With the ignition switch in the **OFF** position, check the **E** terminal of the connector. The reading should be 0 ohms. This is used to diagnosis the computer ground.
   d. With the ignition switch in the **ON** position, check the **F** terminal of the connector. The reading should be 12 volts ± 2 volts. This is used to diagnosis the current feed to the computer.
   d. With the ignition switch in the **ON** position, check the **C**

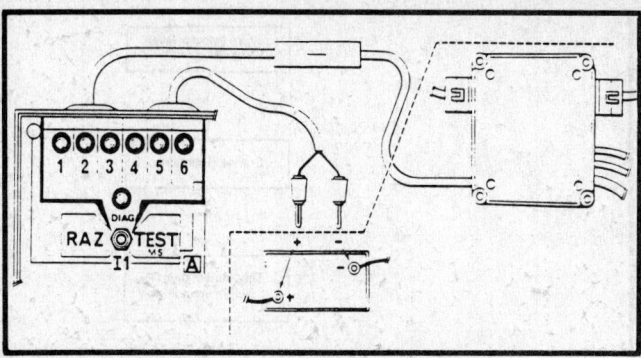

Exploded view of the self testing B.Vi.958 diagnostic tester

VEHICLE STOPPED (ENGINE RUNNING)					
Checks	Check light(s)	Good	Bad	Faulty components	Oper-ation
Solenoid Valves	1	○	⊕	Solenoid valves Harness	VII-IX-X
Road Speed Sensor	2	○	⊕	Faulty road speed sensor	
Potentio-meter	3	○	⊕	Load potentiometer harness	XI - XIV

ENGINE NOT RUNNING - IGNITION SWITCH ON				
Position of the control lever	Check light 2 is on - (do not take it into consideration)			
	Check light(s)	Good	Faulty components	Oper-ation
2nd hold	4	' ⊕ ⁵ ○	If bad, multifunction switch and harness	V - XIII
1st hold	4 and 5	' ⊕ ⁵ ⊕	If bad, check multifunction switch and harness	V - XIII
P R N D	4 and 5	' ○ ⁵ ○	If bad, check multifunction switch and harness	III - IV XII - XIII
P - N	6	⊕	If bad, check selector lever adjustment and multifunction switch operation and harness	II

⊕ Light 'ON'   ○ Light 'OFF'

Diagnostic charts to be used with diagnostic tester B.Vi.958

terminal of the connector. The reading should be 12 volts ± 2 volts. This is used to diagnosis the starter circuit.

Checking The 3–Way Connector

1. Unplug the 3–way connector from the computer and make the following checks:
    a. With the ignition switch in the **ON** position, check the **B** terminal of the connector. The reading should be 4.3 volts ± 0.5 volts.
    b. If this test proves a problem exists, check connector 7. Replace the computer if connector 7 checks out good.

Checking the Solenoid Valves and Harness

1. Unplug the 3–way connector from the computer and make the following checks:
    a. Check the continuity between terminals **A** and **C**, the reading should be 30 ohms ± 10 ohms. If there is a reading of 0, replace the wiring or solenoid valves.

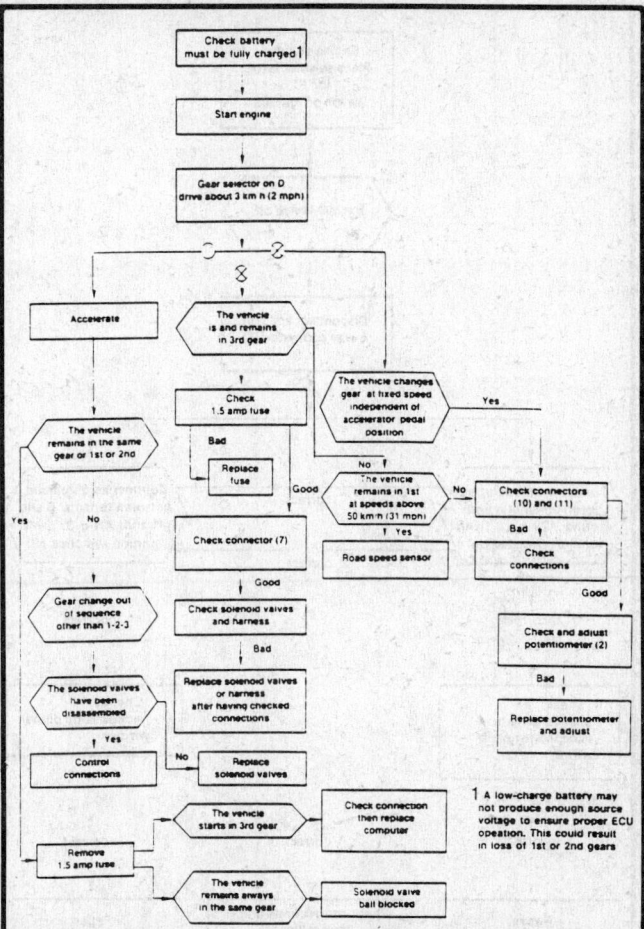

Electrical check sequence using a volt/ohmmeter

    b. Check the continuity between terminals **B** and **C**, the reading should be 30 ohms ± 10 ohms. If the reading is higher than specified, there is a poor connection.
    c. Check the continuity between terminal **C** and ground, the reading should be infinity. If the reading is not infinity, there is a short circuit between the solenoid valve windings and ground. Replace the wiring or solenoid valves.

Checking Engine Load Potentiometer

1. Unplug the connector from the potentiometer:
    a. Check the continuity between terminals **C** and **B**, the reading should be 4 kilo-ohms ± 1.
    b. Check the continuity between terminals **A** and **B**, the reading should be 2.5 kilo-ohms ± 1. Be sure to open the throttle slowly, the ohmmeter should never show infinite resistance.
    c. If the readings are different, the potentiometer is faulty or incorrectly adjusted.

Partial Check of the Multi-Function Switch

1. Unplug the 6–way connector from the computer and make the following checks at the computer socket:
    a. Check the continuity between terminals **A** and **B**, the reading should be 0 ohms with the vehicle in **R**.
    b. Check the continuity between terminals **E** and **C**, the reading should be 0 ohms with the vehicle in **P** or **N**.
    c. If there is no continuity at either of these check points, then the multi-function switch must be replaced.

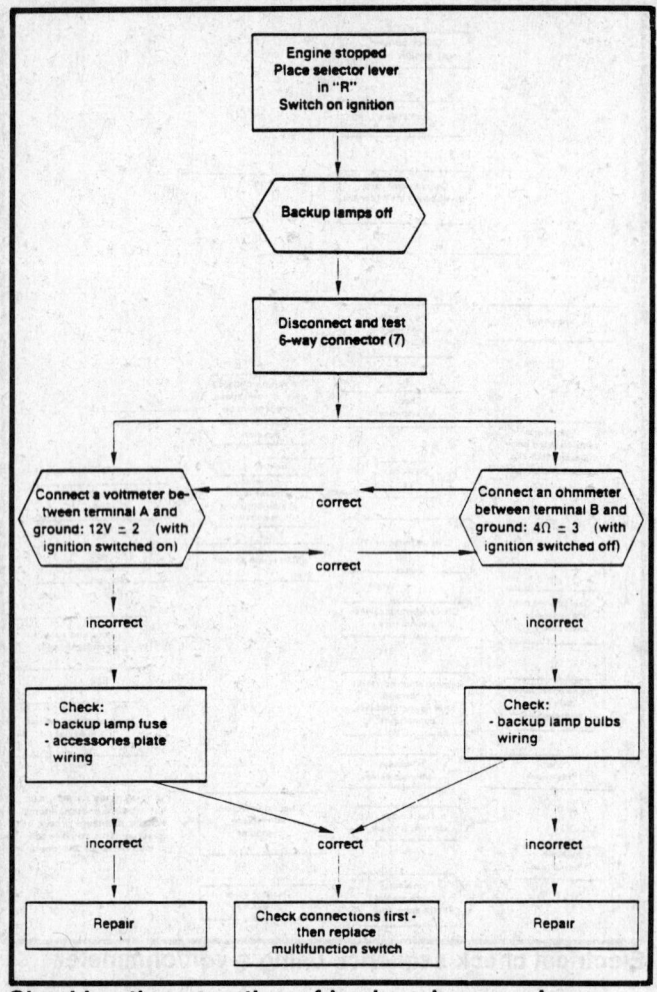

Checking the operation of back-up lamps using a volt/ohmmeter

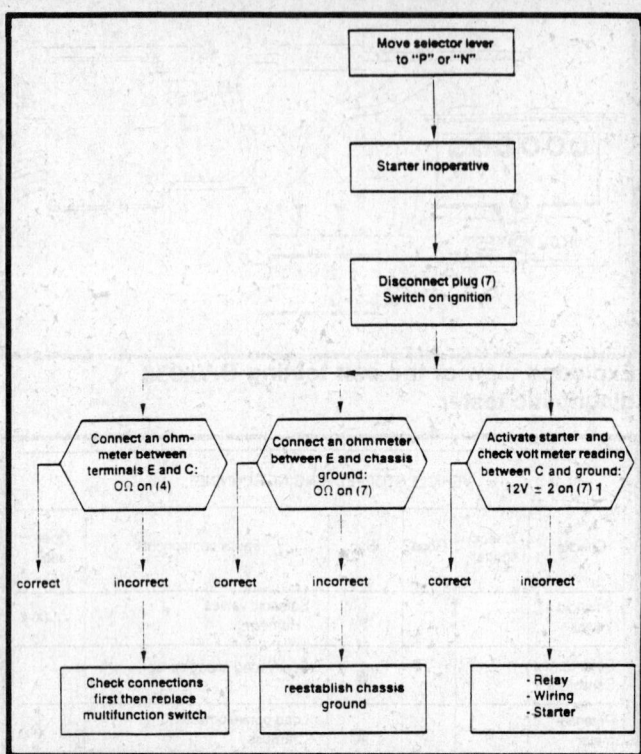

Checking the operation of starter circuit using a volt/ohmmeter

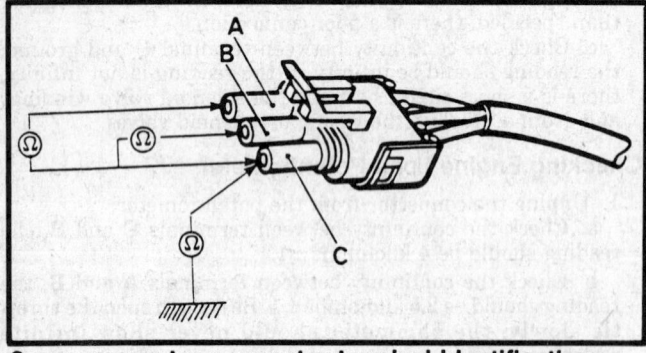

3-way computer connector terminal identifications

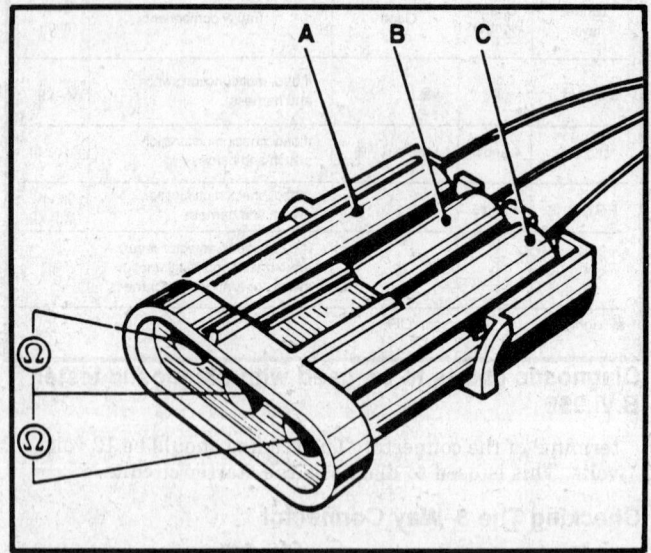

Pontentiometer connector terminal identifications

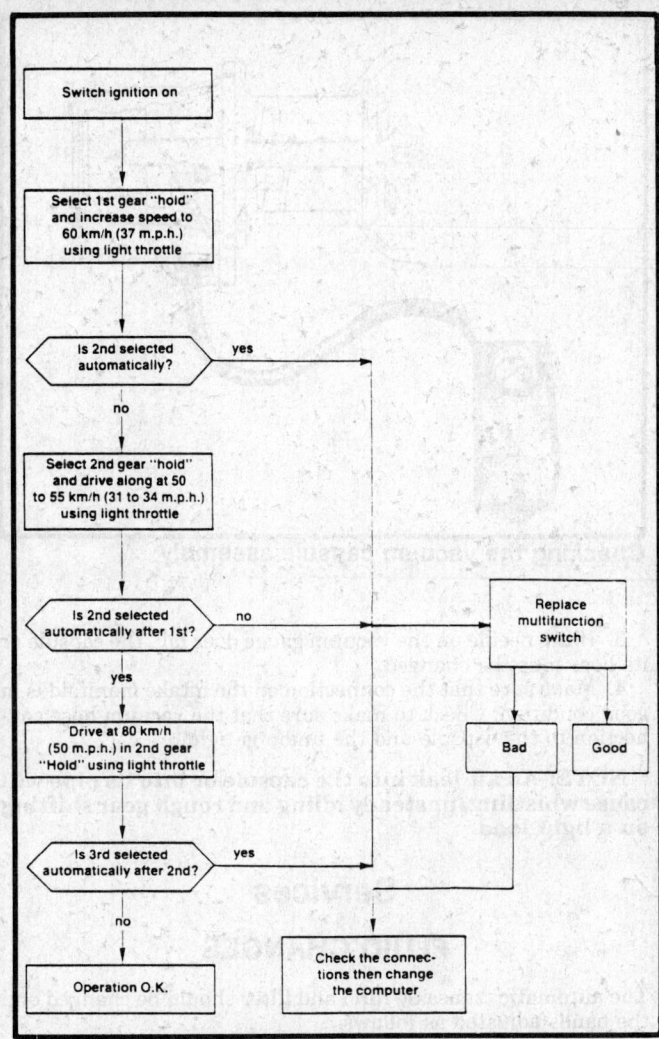

Checking the operation of the gear shifting phases using a volt/ohmmeter

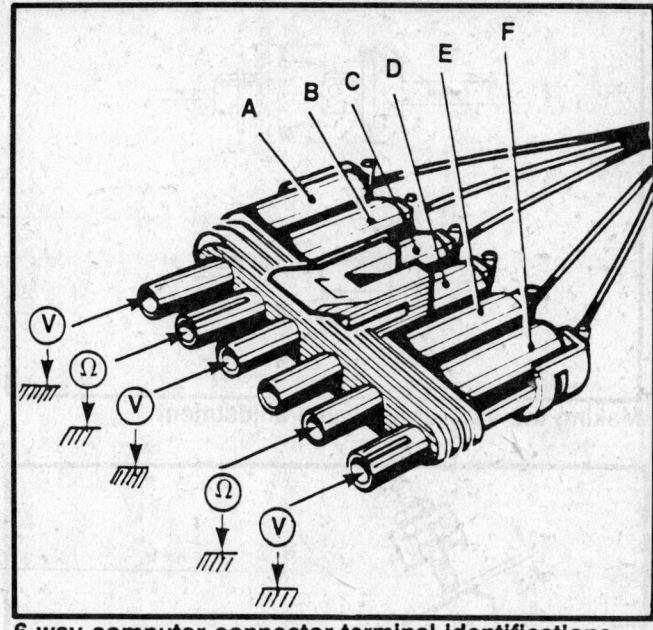

6-way computer connector terminal identifications

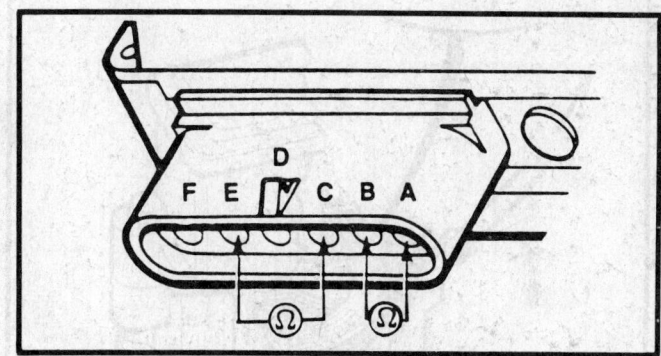

Computer socket terminal identifications

ON CAR SERVICES

Adjustments

KICKDOWN SWITCH

The kickdown switch adjustment is made with the accelerator cable.
  1. Be sure that the accelerator cable has sufficient play to allow a $\frac{1}{16}$ in. (3–4mm) movement in the stop sleeve when the accelerator pedal is completely depressed.
  2. Make sure that the cover is in position to prevent tarnishing of the contacts.

NOTE: The accelerator pedal travel, kickdown switch adjustments and governor control cable adjustments are all closely related, it is therefore wise to check and adjust them at the same time.

  3. To check the kickdown switch, connect a test lamp between the kickdown switch and the positive terminal of the battery. When the accelerator pedal is depressed the test lamp should light showing that the kickdown switch is making contact.

GOVERNOR CABLE

Before making the governor cable adjustment, be certain that the accelerator cable has been adjusted properly.
  1. Depress the accelerator pedal to the wide open throttle position (WOT).
  2. Adjust the accelerator cable to obtain 0.080 in. (2mm) compression of the spring in the cable stop. Make certain that the kickdown switch is operating properly.
  3. Adjust the governor cable adjusters on both the governor and the throttle sides to mid way position.
  4. Adjust the cable stop to obtain a clearance of 0.008–0.028

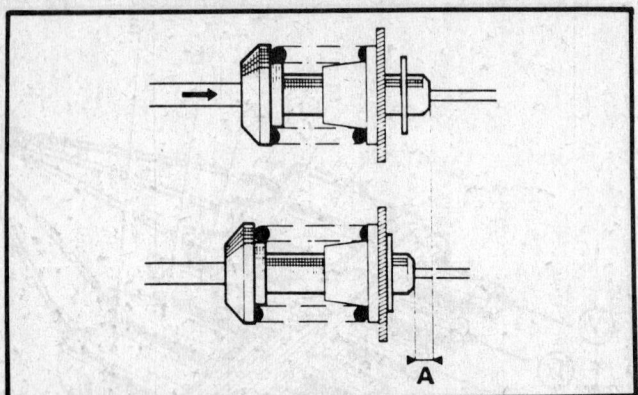

Making the accelerator cable adjustment

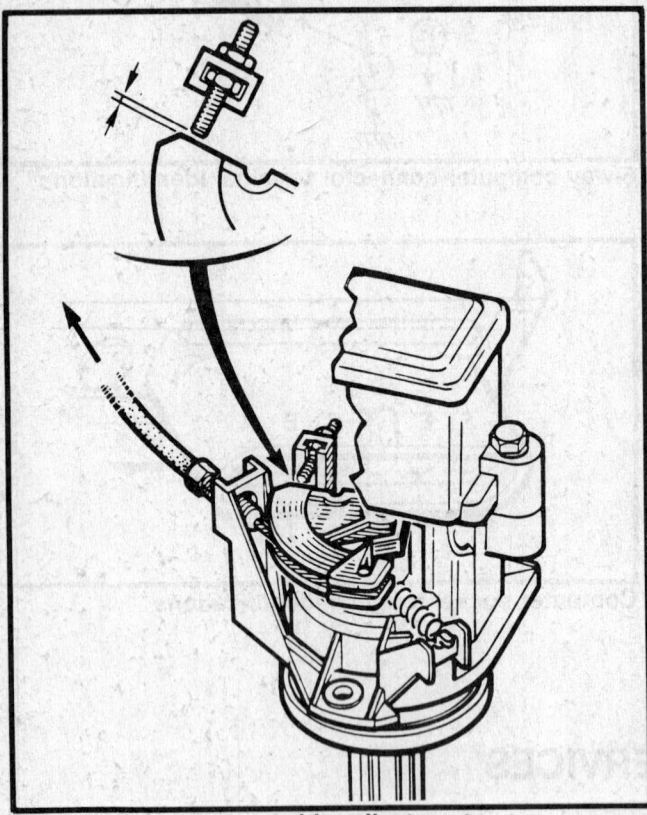

Making the governor cable adjustment

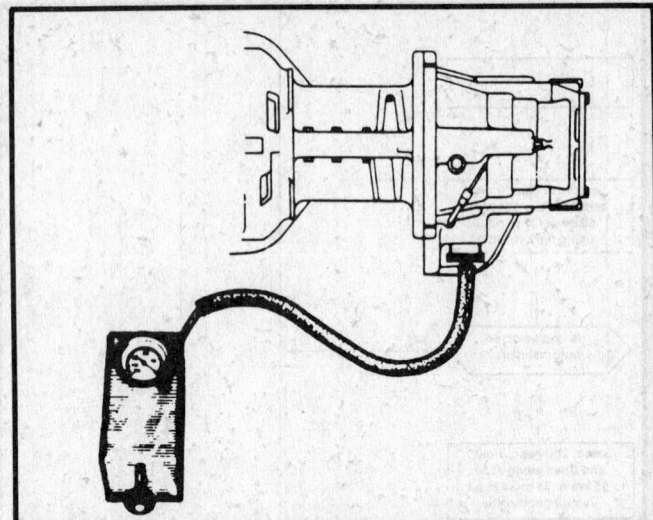

Checking the vacuum capsule assembly

3. If the needle on the vacuum gauge does fall, the capsule or its hose must be changed.

4. Make sure that the connection on the intake manifold is in good condition. Check to make sure that the vacuum hose connection to the capsule and the union is tight.

NOTE: An air leak into the capsule or into its pipe will cause whistling, unsteady idling and rough gear shifting on a light load.

Services

FLUID CHANGES

The automatic transaxle fluid and filter should be changed and the bands adjusted as follows:

    a. Normal usage – every 30,000 miles.

    b. Severe usage – every 15,000 miles.

Severe usage would be any prolonged operation with heavy loading especially in hot weather.

When refilling the transaxle, make sure only AMC/JEEP/RENAULT© ATF. The oil filter change should be made at the time of the oil change.

Drain and Refill

The fluid must be drained when hot, immediately after the engine has been turned off. This will remove all impurities suspended in the fluid.

1. Remove the transaxle dipstick. Raise and safely support vehicle. Place a container with a large opening under the transaxle oil pan.

2. Unscrew the drain plug from the transaxle oil pan.

3. Let the fluid drain for as long as possible.

4. Reinstall the drain plug into the oil pan. Torque the drain plug to 11 ft. lbs.

5. Refill the transaxle with 2⅔ quarts of the proper transaxle fluid through the dipstick tube.

6. Lower the vehicle and insert the dipstick.

7. Start the engine and allow it to idle for at least 2 minutes. Apply the parking brake and block the drive wheels. Move the selector lever momentarily to each position, ending in the **P** position.

8. Recheck the ATF fluid level, if necessary, add sufficient fluid to bring level to the the proper level.

---

in. (0.2–0.7mm) between the screw and the lever with the throttle fully open. The screw has been preset at the factory and must not be adjusted under any circumstances.

5. Verify that the length of the governor cable is approximately 0.788 in. (20mm) between the wide open throttle position and the closed position.

CHECKING THE VACUUM CAPSULE

The vacuum capsule is checked with the engine stopped.

1. Connect a suitable vacuum gauge to the vacuum hose. Apply a vacuum of approximately 15.7 in. Hg to the capsule.

2. If the needle on the vacuum gauge does not move, check the full and light throttle pressure.

9. Do not overfill. Make sure the dipstick is properly seated to seal against dirt and water entering system.

NOTE: If there is evidence of contamination or if trouble shooting indicates a problem in the converter, it must be replaced. Whenever the transmission fluid is replaced, automatic transmission fluid additive, part number 8983–100–034 or equivalent should be added. This will minimize the fluid foaming condition which occurs during normal vehicle operation. Do not add more than one bottle of automatic tranmission fluid additive per transmission oil change.

OIL PAN

Removal and Installation

1. Remove the transaxle dipstick. Raise and safely support vehicle. Place a container with a large opening under the transaxle oil pan.
2. Unscrew the drain plug from the transaxle oil pan.
3. Let the fluid drain for as long as possible.
4. Reinstall the drain plug into the oil pan. Torque the drain plug to 11 ft. lbs.
5. Loosen oil pan bolts and gently pull one corner down so any fluid left in the pan will drain. If transaxle is hot, be careful of spilling oil.
6. Remove oil pan bolts and pan.
7. Carefully inspect filter and pan bottom for a heavy accumulation of friction material or metal particles. A little accumulation can be considered normal, but a heavy concentration indicates damaged or worn parts.
8. Filter replacement is recommended when a the pan is removed. To remove the filter, remove the filter retaining bolts and and slip the filter out from under the third bolt holding it in place, do not remove the third bolt after removing the filter.
9. Be sure not damage the suction line seal. When installing the new filter be certain to install in the same position as it was removed from and torque the retaining bolts to 80 inch lbs. (9 Nm).
10. Check pan carefully for distortion, straightening the edges with a straight block of wood and a rubber mallet if necessary. Clean the pan and make sure that the magnets are positioned correctly in the pan.
11. Install a new gasket on the pan and install the pan. Torque bolts to 54 inch lbs. (6 Nm).
12. Refill the transaxle with 2⅔ quarts of the proper transaxle fluid through the dipstick tube.
13. Lower the vehicle and insert the dipstick.
14. Start the engine and allow it to idle for at least 2 minutes. Apply the parking brake and block the drive wheels. Move the selector lever momentarily to each position, ending in the **P** position.
15. Recheck the ATF fluid level, if necessary, add sufficient fluid to bring level to the the proper level.
16. Do not overfill. Make sure the dipstick is properly seated to seal against dirt and water entering system.

VALVE BODY ASSEMBLY

Removal and Installation

1. Remove the transaxle dipstick. Raise and safely support vehicle. Place a container with a large opening under the transaxle oil pan.
2. Unscrew the drain plug from the transaxle oil pan.
3. Let the fluid drain for as long as possible.
4. Reinstall the drain plug into the oil pan. Torque the drain plug to 11 ft. lbs.
5. Loosen oil pan bolts and gently pull one corner down so any fluid left in the pan will drain. If transaxle is hot, be careful of spilling oil.

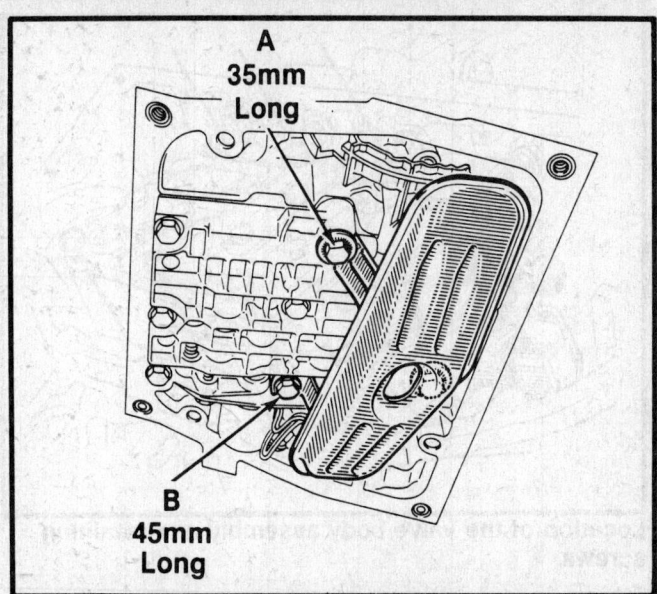

A
35mm
Long

B
45mm
Long

The correct way to install the oil filter

6. Remove oil pan bolts and pan.
7. Disconnect the solenoid valve plug from the sealed plug connector. Disconnect the solenoid ball valve wires after removing the clips. Mark the solenoid ball valves, indicating the color of the wire to which each was attached. Remove the 2 bolts holding the solenoid ball valve supporting plate and remove the valves.
8. Place large opening drain pan under transaxle, then remove the 6 bolts holding the valve body assembly to the transaxle. Hold the valve body in position while the bolts are being removed. Remove the valve body assembly from the transaxle.

──────── CAUTION ────────

Do not clamp any portion of the valve body assembly in a vise. Even the slightest distortion will result in stuck valves and leakage or fluid cross leakage. Handle the valve body with care at all times.

─────────────────────────

9. Installation is the reverse order of the removal procedure and torque the valve body bolts to 54 inch lbs. (6 Nm).
10. Install a new gasket on the pan and install the pan. Torque bolts to 54 inch lbs. (6 Nm).
11. Refill the transaxle with 2⅔ quarts of the proper transaxle fluid through the dipstick tube.
12. Lower the vehicle and insert the dipstick.
13. Start the engine and allow it to idle for at least 2 minutes. Apply the parking brake and block the drive wheels. Move the selector lever momentarily to each position, ending in the **P** position.
14. Recheck the ATF fluid level, if necessary, add sufficient fluid to bring level to the the proper level.
15. Do not overfill. Make sure the dipstick is properly seated to seal against dirt and water entering system.

SHIFT MECHANISM

Removal and Installation

1. Raise and support ther vehicle safely. Remove gear shift handle by pulling straight up on it. Remove the bezel by pressing on the left hand side and lift to disengage the prongs.
2. Remove the 4 nuts on the exhaust pipe flange. Remove the 2 bolts connecting the front and rear exhaust pipe sections.
3. Remove the exhaust pipe hanger nut. Remove the front exhaust pipe section from the vehicle.

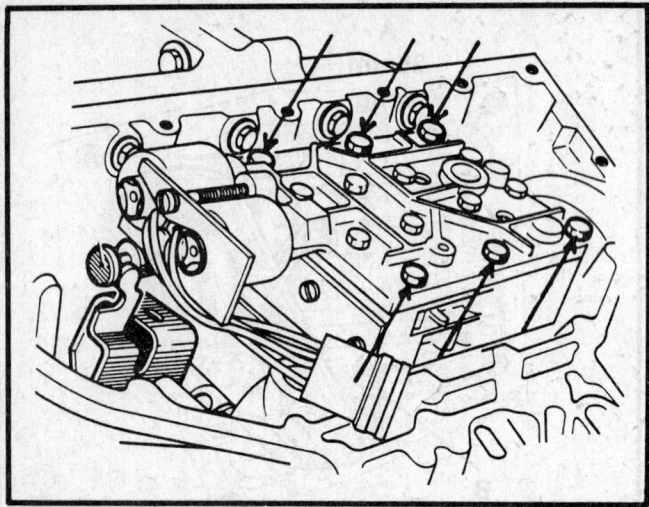

Location of the valve body assembly and retaining screws

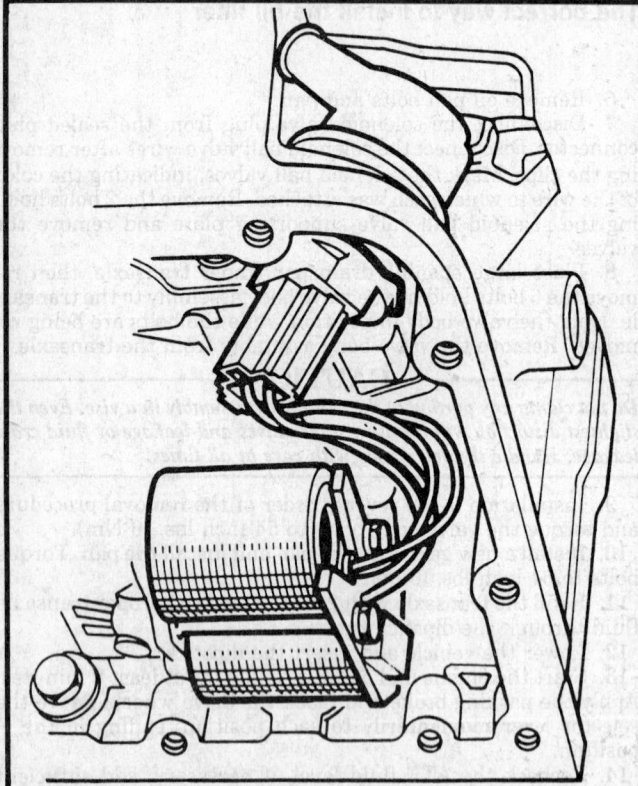

Location of the solenoid ball valves and support plate

4. Support the engine and transaxle assembly with a suitable lifting device. Snap the external control cable end off the shift lever ball stud. Lower the engine-transaxle cradle approximately ⅛ in. by loosening the rear bolts.

5. Support the transaxle assembly with a suitable transaxle jack. Remove the automatic transaxle right side support bracket.

6. Remove the shifter attaching nuts from under the vehicle.

7. Install the shift mechanism with the seal in the proper position.

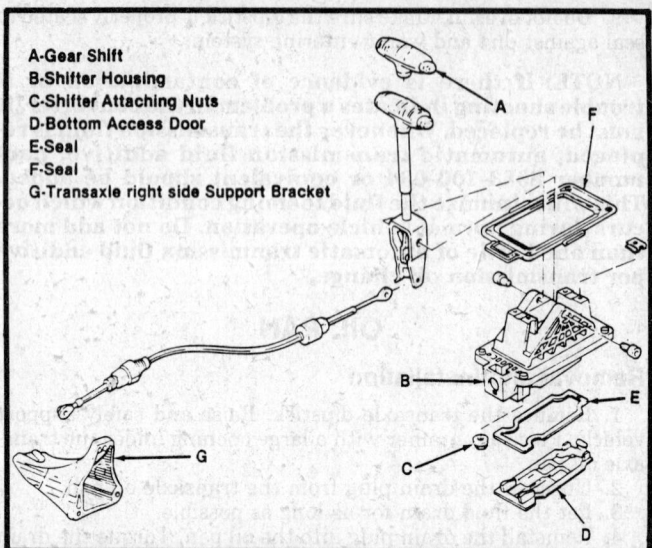

A-Gear Shift
B-Shifter Housing
C-Shifter Attaching Nuts
D-Bottom Access Door
E-Seal
F-Seal
G-Transaxle right side Support Bracket

Exploded view of the shift lever assembly

8. Position the shift mechanism into the cutout in the floor pan (board).

9. Install the retainer nuts and tighten securely.

10. Tighten the nuts on the spring loaded clamping bolts, at the catalytic converter, until the coils are completely collapsed, then back off each nut 1½ turns.

11. Tighten all fasteners securely. Snap the trim panel back into the shifter console.

12. Install the shift handle by lightly rapping it with a soft faced mallet.

SHIFT CABLE

Removal and Installation

1. Raise and support the vehicle safely. The shift mechanism must be removed to perform this procedure.

2. Unsnap the cable from the transaxle right side support bracket.

3. Using a suitable tool, open the bottom access door of the shift housing.

4. Unsnap the cable from the shifter lower end. Remove the cable lock pin.

5. Disengage the cable from the shifter housing by depressing the 2 locking tangs in the housing.

6. Snap the new cable into the shifter housing and make sure the locking tangs are in the lock position.

7. Snap the cable end onto the lower end of the shifter. Snap the access door shut with the seal in the correct position.

8. Snap the other end of the cable into the transaxle right side support bracket.

9. Adjust the shift cable as follows:

a. Install the transaxle right side support bracket and torque the bolts to 30 ft. lbs. (40 Nm).

b. Tighten the 2 rear engine to transaxle cradle bolts to 62 ft. lbs. (85 Nm).

c. Unlock the cable adjuster by popping up the lock tab.

d. Set the shift selector lever to **D** position.

e. Shift the transaxle outside lever all the way foward and back 2 detent positions (**D**).

f. Snap the cable end onto the transaxle outer lever ball stud. In this position and with the shift lever hanging under the vehicle, snap the cable adjustment lock into the lock position.

REMOVAL AND INSTALLATION

TRANSAXLE REMOVAL

The transaxle can be removed separately from the engine from underneath the vehicle, using the special transaxle jack Desvil 701 ST or equivalent with 4 studs. Install a suitable engine support tool across the front of the engine compartment. Secure the chain around the front of the exhaust port and take up the slack in the chain. This will keep the engine from tilting forward when the transaxle is removed.

1. Disconnect the negative battery cable. Raise and support the vehicle safely. Drain the transaxle fluid from the transaxle.
2. Disconnect the oxygen sensor electrical connector. Remove the hose clamp and tube from the lower end of the heat tube.
3. Remove the heat tube bracket bolt located at the rear of the engine. Remove the remaining heat tube bracket bolts and nuts, which are located under the intake manifold. Remove the heat tube.
4. Remove the bolts attaching the top dead center sensor to the converter housing and remove the sensor.
5. Remove the steering bracket. The bracket is attached to the steering rack and the steering tie rod with nuts and bolts.
6. On vehilces equipped with air conditioning, discharge the refrigerant from the A/C system. Disconnect the A/C lines at the expansion valve and retainer.
7. Remove the bolts attaching the crossmember to the side still and body.
8. Remove the front wheels. Disconnect the passenger side tie rod ball stud from the knuckle with tool T.Av. 476 or equivalent.

NOTE: Run the tie rod ball joint nut to the end of the ball stud before installing the removal tool. This protects the stud threads when loosening the stud.

9. Remove the passenger side steering tie rod.
10. Loosen the coolant expansion tank retaining strap. Pull the tank out of the strap and move the tank aside. Move the tank far enough away to permit the A/C lines foward and away from the crossmember.
11. Remove the nuts attaching the exhaust pipe to the exhaust manifold.
12. Remove the 2 bolts connecting the front and rear exhaust pipe sections. Remove the hanger nut. Remove the front exhaust pipe section from the vehicle.
13. Turn the crossmember and remove it through the wheel well opening on the passenger side of the vehicle.
14. Remove the steering knuckle upper mounting bolt. Then loosen (but do not remove) the lower bolt.

NOTE: The bolts are splined just below the head so it is necessary to remove the nut and tap the bolt out with a brass or lead mallet.

15. Remove the driveshaft roll pins with a suitable pin drift. Swing each rotor and steering knuckle outward. Then slide the driveshafts off of the transaxle output shafts.
16. Remove the mounting bracket by removing the bracket bolts.
17. Remove the wiring from the starter solenoid. Remove the rear mounting bolts. Remove the starter mounting bolts and remove the starter and locating bushing.
18. Install the drive plate tool Mot. 582 or equivalent, to hold the driveplate stationary. Remove the torque converter bolts. Remove the computer module from the bracket. Do not remove the computer module from the transaxle.
19. Disconnect the coolant lines from the heat exchanger and remove the line clamp on the side rail.
20. Disconnect the speedometer cable. Support the transaxle with a suitable transaxle jack.

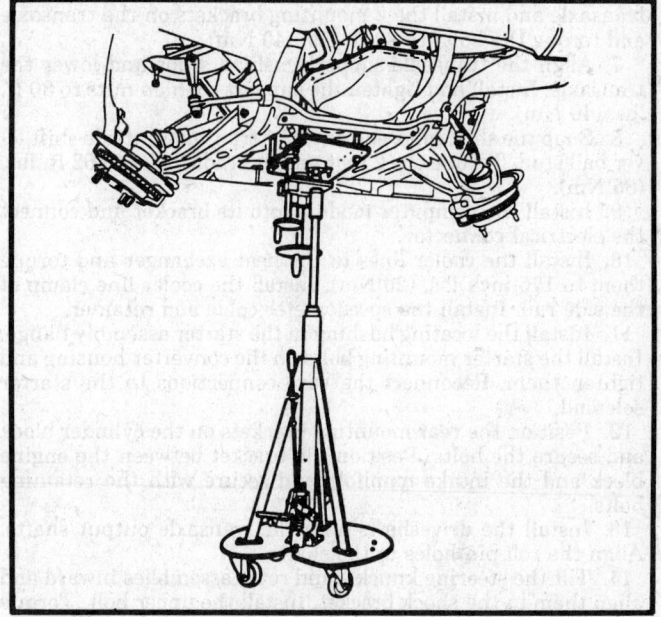

Installing the transaxle jack for removal purposes

21. Lower the the engine transaxle cradle by loosening the 2 rear bolts. Lower the cradle by 0.6 in. (15mm).
22. Remove the shift cable from the shift lever ball stud. Leave the shift cable in the right side transaxle support bracket but tie the bracket out of the way with mechanics wire.
23. Remove the ground strap from the transaxle case. Remove all transaxle to engine retaining bolts.
24. Remove the nuts that attach the transaxle support cushions to the vehicle. Remove the bolts tahat attach the 2 transaxle mounting brackets to the transaxle. Then remove the brackets.
25. Lower the transaxle carefully and guide the computer module and the cooler lines out.

NOTE: As soon as the transaxle is removed, use a suitable converter retaining plate to prevent the torque converter from separating.

TRANSAXLE INSTALLATION

If the transaxle was removed because of malfunction caused by sludge, accumulated friction material or metal particles, the oil cooler and lines must be flushed thoroughly. The transaxle and converter must be installed as an assembly; otherwise, the converter drive plate, pump bushing and oil seal will be damaged.

1. Apply a small amount of grease to the torque converter pilot area in the back of the crankshaft. Make sure that the alignment dowels are in position in the rear block face.
2. Remove the converter holding tool. Using the transaxle jack, raise the transaxle up into position while guiding the cooler lines and the computer module into position.
3. The drive plate and torque converter must be properly mated. The painted marks on the driveplate align with the marks on the torque converter.
4. Position the transaxle onto the engine dowels. Install the engine to transaxle bolts and torque them to 37 ft. lbs. (50 Nm).
5. Check the torque converter to see that it is free. Install the

torque converter bolts and torque them to 22 ft. lbs. (30 Nm). Install the drive plate tool Mot. 582 or equivalent, to hold the driveplate stationary, while tightening the bolts.

6. Install the grounding strap to the transaxle case. Raise the transaxle and install the 2 mounting brackets on the transaxle and torque the bolts to 30 ft. lbs. (40 Nm).

7. Align the transaxle support cushion studs and lower the transaxle. Install and tighten the support cushion nuts to 30 ft. lbs. (40 Nm).

8. Snap the shift cable end onto the transaxle outside shift lever ball stud. Torque the 2 rear engine cradle bolts to 62 ft. lbs. (85 Nm).

9. Install the computer module into its bracket and connect the electrical connector.

10. Install the cooler lines to the heat exchanger and torque them to 175 inch lbs. (20 Nm). Install the cooler line clamp of the side rail. Install the speedometer cable and retainer.

11. Install the locating bushing in the starter assembly flange. Install the starter mounting bolts on the converter housing and tighten them. Reconnect the wire connections to the starter solenoid.

12. Position the rear mounting brackets on the cylinder block and secure the bolts. Position the bracket between the engine block and the intake manifold and secure with the retaining bolts.

13. Install the driveshafts onto the transaxle output shafts. Align the roll pin holes in the shafts.

14. Tilt the steering knuckle and rotor assemblies inward and align them in the shock bracket. Install the upper bolt. Torque the upper and lower bolt to 148 ft. lbs. (200 Nm).

15. Line up the driveshaft using tool B.Vi. 31-01 or equivalent and install the roll pins with a suitable drift pin. Place a small amount of silicone sealant at each end of the roll pins.

16. Install the crossmember through the wheel well opening on the passenger side of the vehicle. Position the crossmember on the side sills and body and install the crossmember attaching bolts and nuts. Tighten the crossmember to body bolts first and tighten the remaining bolts.

17. On the vehicles with A/C, connect the A/C lines to the connector block on the dash panel. Secure the lines to the side sill with the retainer.

18. Connect the steering tie rods to the knuckles. Torque the tie rod nuts to 30 ft. lbs. (40 Nm).

19. Connect the steering tie rods to the steering gear bracket. Tighten the attaching bolts and nuts to 25 ft. lbs. (35 Nm). Connect the steering gear bracket to the steering gear rack. Torque the bracket bolts to 30 ft. lbs. (40 Nm). Install the locknuts and washers on the bolts and torque the nuts to 25 ft. lbs. (35 Nm).

20. Install the front wheels and torque the bolts to 66 ft. lbs. (90 Nm).

21. Install the top dead center sensor. Install the warm up tube, brackets and hoses. Connect the exhaust head pipe to the exhaust manifold.

22. Install a replacement seal on the exhaust head pipe and connect the pipe to the converter. Tighten the bolts that attach the head pipe and converter until the spring coils are touching then back off each nut 1½ turns.

23. Connect the oxygen sensor wire. Install the vacuum capsule tube. Remove the engine support tool.

24. Adjust the shift cable as necessary. Connect the negative battery cable.

25. Fill the transaxle with 3 quarts of the proper automatic transmission fluid before starting the engine. On vehicles equipped with A/C recharge the system with fresh freon. Road test the vehicle and make all and any necessary adjustments.

BENCH OVERHAUL

Before Disassembly

Cleanliness during disassembly and assembly is necessary to avoid further transaxle trouble after overhaul. Before removing any of the transaxle subassemblies, plug all the openings and clean the outside of the of the transaxle thoroughly. Steam cleaning or car wash type high pressure equipment is preferable. During disassembly, clean all parts in suitable solvent and dry each part. Do not use cloth or paper towels to dry parts. Use compressed air only. Before disassembling the transaxle, remove the torque converter, dipstick tube, wiring connections on the transaxle, the governor computer and the malfunction switch.

Converter Inspection

The torque converter is removed by simply sliding the unit out of the transaxle off the input and reaction shaft. If the converter is to be reused, set aside so it will not be damaged. Since the unit is welded and does not have a drain plugs converters subject to burnt fluid or other contamination must be replaced.

Transaxle Disassembly

OIL PAN AND FILTER

Removal

1. Make sure transaxle is held securely either in a stand or fixture.

2. Remove the pan to case bolts and gently tap pan loose. Do not insert a tool between pan and case as a prying tool or case damage may result.

3. Check pan carefully for distortion, straightening the edges of the pan with a straight block of wood and a rubber mallet if necessary. A power driven wire wheel is useful in removing glued on gaskets.

4. Carefully inspect filter and pan bottom for a heavy accumulation of friction material or metal particles. A little accumulation can be considered normal, but a heavy concentration indicates damaged or worn parts.

5. To remove the filter, remove the filter retaining bolts and remove the filter, be sure not damage the suction line seal. When installing the new filter be certain to install in the same position as it was removed from and torque the retaining bolts to 6 ft. lbs.

6. When the pan is eventually reinstalled torque the bolts evenly to 54 inch lbs. (6 Nm).

VALVE BODY

Removal

1. Place large opening drain pan under transaxle, then remove the 6 bolts holding the valve body assembly to the transaxle.

2. Hold the valve body in position while the bolts are being removed. Remove the valve body assembly from the transaxle.

REAR CASE

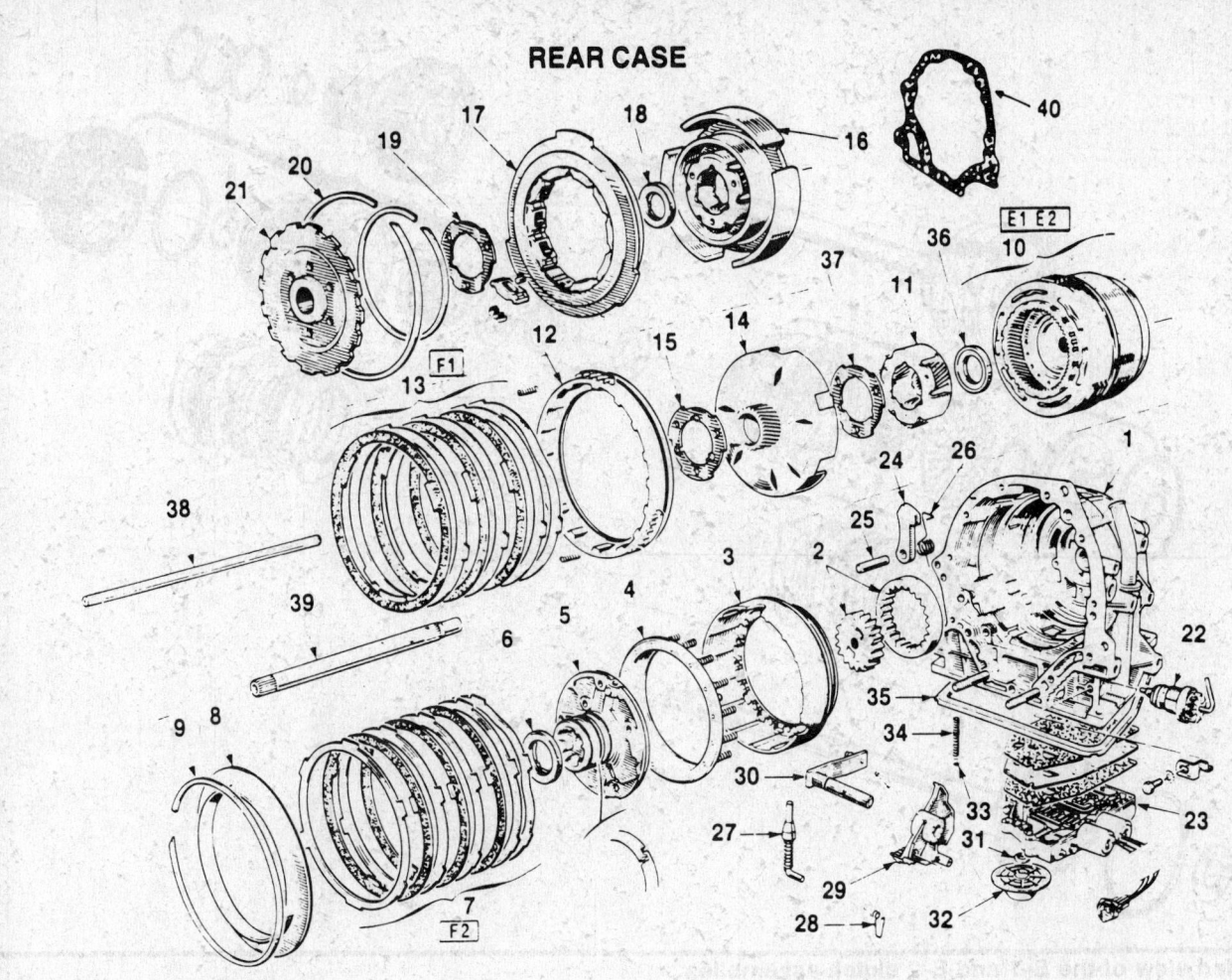

1 - Rear case	22 - Capsule
2 - Oil pump	23 - Valve Body
3 - F2 piston	24 - "Park" latch
4 - F2 cup	25 - "Park" latch shaft
5 - Feed hub	26 - "Park" latch spring
6 - Needle roller thrust bearing	27 - "Park" linkage
7 - F2 disc stack	28 - Safety clip
8 - F1 piston carrier	29 - Quadrant
9 - Snap ring	30 - Input shaft
10 - E1 - E2 clutches	31 - Suction gauze gasket
11 - Forward drive train	32 - Suction gauze
12 - F1 piston	33 - Quadrant lock ball
13 - F1 disc stack	34 - Quadrant spring
14 - E2 bellhousing	35 - Sump plate gasket
15 - Friction washer (1.5 mm thick)	36 - Needle roller bearing
16 - Reverse drive train	37 - Friction washer (1.5 mm thick)
17 - Freewheel	38 - Pump shaft
18 - Needle roller thrust bearing	39 - Turbine shaft
19 - Friction washer (thickness to be determined)	40 - Rear Case-to-Intermediary Case gasket
20 - Snap ring	
21 - "Park" wheel	

Exploded view of the rear case and its components

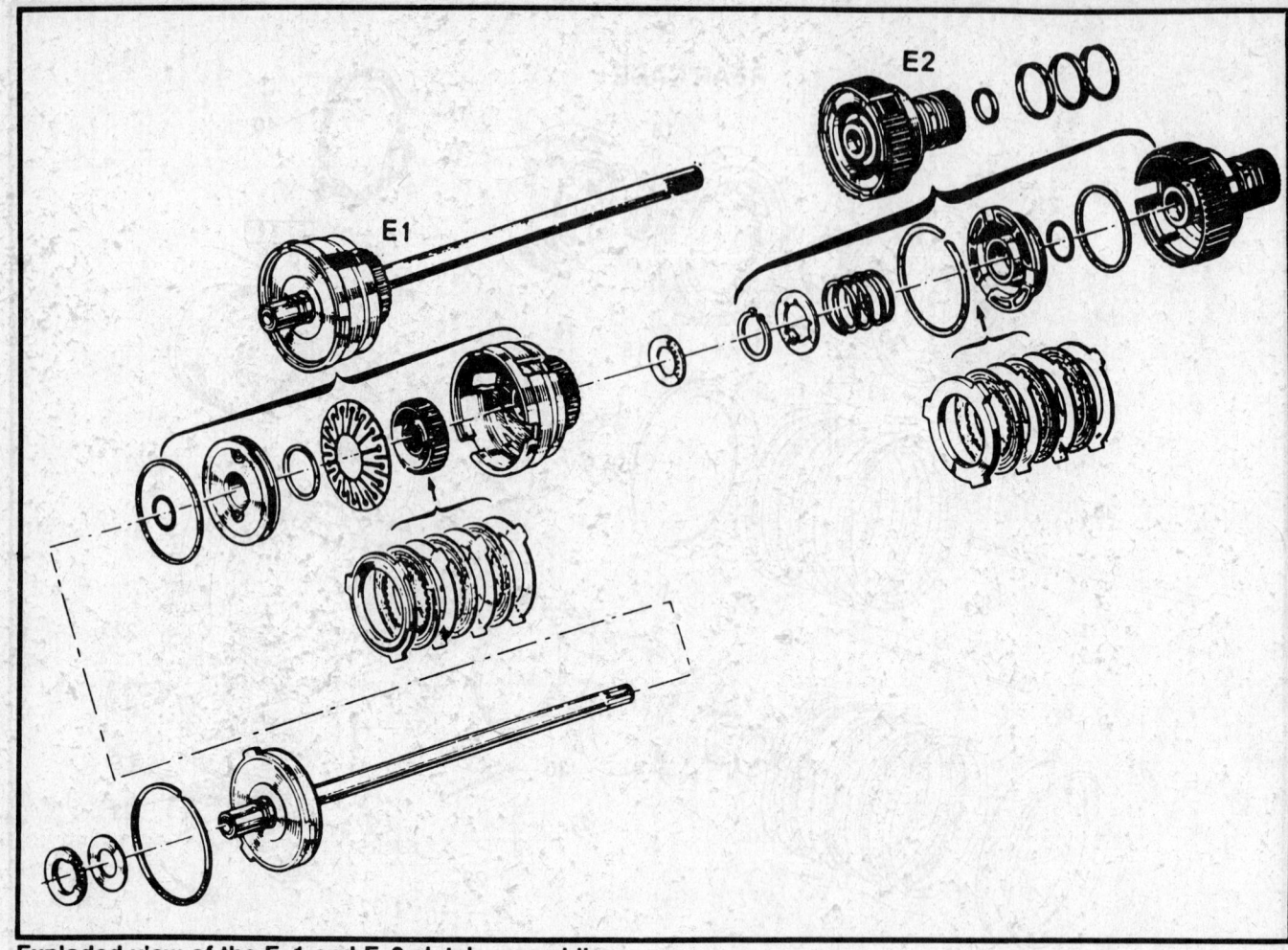

Exploded view of the E-1 and E-2 clutch assemblies

— **CAUTION** —

Do not clamp any portion of the valve body assembly in a vise. Even the slightest distortion will result in stuck valves and leakage or fluid cross leakage. Handle the valve body with care at all times.

OIL PUMP ASSEMBLY

Removal

1. Remove the oil pump housing cover.
2. Remove the oil pump shaft. Mark the direction of the oil pump ring wheel for easy reassembly.
3. Remove the oil pump gear.

TRANSAXLE COMPONENTS AND DIFFERENTIAL

Removal

1. Remove the 4 inner differential assembly bolts in the transaxle case.
2. Remove the 2 roll pins with a suitable drift pin.
3. Remove the parking latch and remove the connecting arm without separating the ball joints.
4. Remove the shaft and save the tooth quadrant. Remove the gear control linkage. The socket containing the locking ball must not be removed unless it is to be changed.

5. Set the transaxle on the end with the transaxle case resting on the oil pump housing.
6. Remove the transaxle case assembly bolts.
7. Separate the transaxle from the differential case.
8. Disassemble the parking latch by, removing the centering dowel (use a puller), the shaft, parking latch and the return spring.
9. Remove the brake mechanism fixing bolts. Remove the drive train assembly while holding the turbine shaft.
10. Keep the needle thrust bearing located inside the case.
11. Position the drive train vertically on a support and remove the various parts from the drive train as follows.
    Planetary gear train
    Sun gear assembly
    The F-1 and F-2 assembly
    The E-2 clutch
    The E-1 clutch and the turbine shaft
12. Take note of the location of the needle thrust bearings, so as to keep them in their proper location during reassembly.

Unit Disassembly and Assembly

PLANETARY GEAR TRAIN

Disassembly

1. Remove the sprag clutch.
2. Remove the adjusting shim.

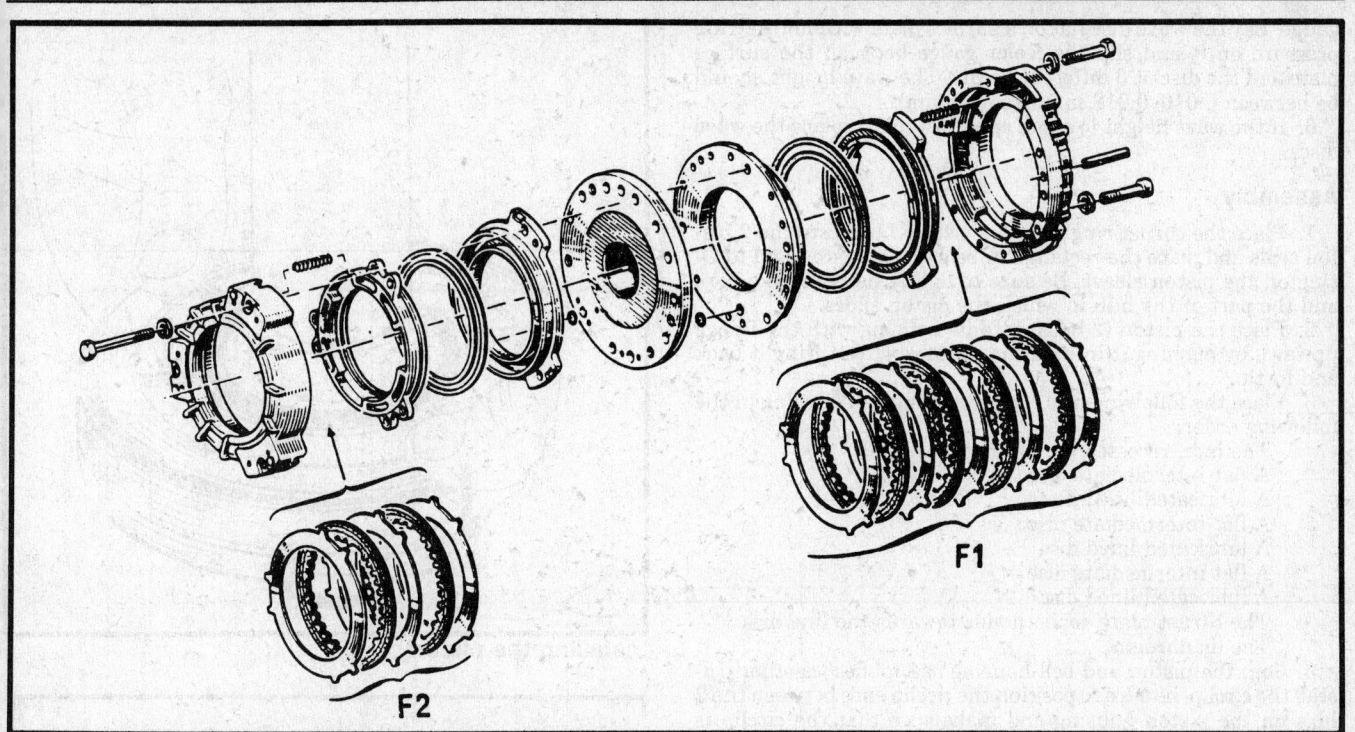

Exploded view of the F–1 and F–2 clutch assemblies

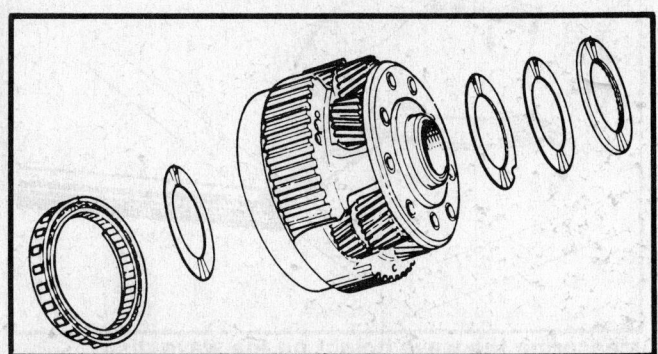

Explded view of the planetary gear train

3. Remove the needle thrust bearing plate, needle thrust bearing and the last needle thrust bearing plate.

NOTE: The thrust bearing inside the planetary gear train cannot be disassembled and the assembly must be replaced as a unit.

Inspection

1. Inspect all oil passages in the shaft and make sure they are open and clean.
2. Inspect the bearing surfaces nicks, burrs, scores or other damage. Light scratches, small nicks or burrs can be removed with crocus cloth or a fine stone.
3. Inspect all thrust plates for wear and scores, replace if damaged or worn below specifications.
4. Inspect the thrust faces of the planetary gear carriers for wear, scores or other damage, replace as required. Inspect the planetary gear carrier for cracks and pinions for broken or worn gear teeth and for broken pinion shaft welds.

Assembly

1. Install the first needle thrust bearing plate, needle thrust bearing and the last needle thrust bearing plate.
2. Install the sprag clutch on the planetary gear train. The shoulder should face towards the inside (bottom) of the carrier.
3. Check to see that the thrust bearing plate is correctly positioned.
4. Install the sun gear so that it centers and holds the inner thrust bearing.

E–1 CLUTCH

Disassembly

1. Remove the compresion ring from the needle thrust bearing before removing the needle thrust bearing.
2. The turbine shaft and the hub are one piece. Push down on the E–1 pistion housing to remove the retaining ring.
3. Remove the housing. Push the piston out by applying compressed air to the piston housing input hole.
4. Remove the diaphragm spring, thrust plate, 3 lined discs, 3 intermediate flat discs, hub and bell housing.

Inspection

1. If plates show any sign of deterioration or wear, they must be replaced. The plates and disc should be flat, they must not be warped or coned shaped.
2. Inspect the facing material on all driving discs. Replace the discs that are charred, glazed or heavily pitted. Discs should also be replaced if they show any evidence of material flaking off or if the facing material can be scrapped off easily. Inspect the driving disc splines for wear or other damage.
3. Inspect the steel plate and pressure plate surface for burning, scoring or damaged driving lugs. Replace if necessary.
4. Check to see that the discs slide easily on the hub splines and that the plates slide easily in the bell housing.
5. Check to see that the wave discs are correct with a feeler

gauge. Lay the wave disc flat on a surface plate without exerting pressure on it and slip the feeler gauge between the surface plate and the disc at 3 different points. The wave height should be between 0.010–0.018 in. (0.25–0.45mm).

6. If the wave height is out of specifications, replace the wave discs.

Assembly

1. Place the thrust ring onto the piston. Lubricate the 2 piston seals and place the rectangular seal on the piston and to O-ring on the piston sleeve. Be sure to lightly lubricate the bore and the part of the hub in which the piston slides.

2. Place the piston (2 balls) into its housing with the flange upward, by pushing it in with the thumbs while tilting it back and forth.

3. Place the following into the connecting bell housing in the following order:

    The hub, recessed part facing upward
    A flat intermediate disc
    A lubricated lined disc
    A flat intermediate disc
    A lubricated lined disc
    A flat intermediate disc
    A lubricated lined disc
    The thrust plate, smooth side towards the line disc
    The diaphragm.

4. Join the piston and bell housing assemblies together. Install the circlip, be sure to position the circlip ends between the 2 lugs on the piston housing and make sure that the circlip is properly seated in the groove all the way around.

5. Install the bearing plate for the needle thrust bearing. The seal ring after checking the ring gap play.

6. Check the operation of the E–1 clutch components by applying compressed air to the piston through the hole provided.

E–2 CLUTCH

Disassembly

1. Using a suitable tool and a arbor press, slightly compress the clutch return spring.

2. Remove the circlip, spring retainer, the spring and the 3 seal rings.

3. Remove the thrust plate circlip, the plate, 3 lined discs, 2 wave discs, the flat disc.

4. Push the piston out by applying compressed air to the piston housing input hole.

Inspection

1. If plates show any sign of deterioration or wear, they must be replaced. The plates and disc should be flat, they must not be warped or coned shaped.

2. Inspect the facing material on all driving discs. Replace the discs that are charred, glazed or heavily pitted. Discs should also be replaced if they show any evidence of material flaking off or if the facing material can be scrapped off easily. Inspect the driving disc splines for wear or other damage.

3. Inspect the steel plate and pressure plate surface for burning, scoring or damaged driving lugs. Replace if necessary.

4. Check to see that the discs slide easily on the hub splines and that the plates slide easily in the bell housing.

5. Check to see that the wave discs are correct with a feeler gauge. Lay the wave disc flat on a surface plate without exerting pressure on it and slip the feeler gauge between the surface plate and the disc at 3 different points. The wave height should be between 0.010–0.018 in. (0.25–0.45mm).

6. If the wave height is out of specifications, replace the wave discs.

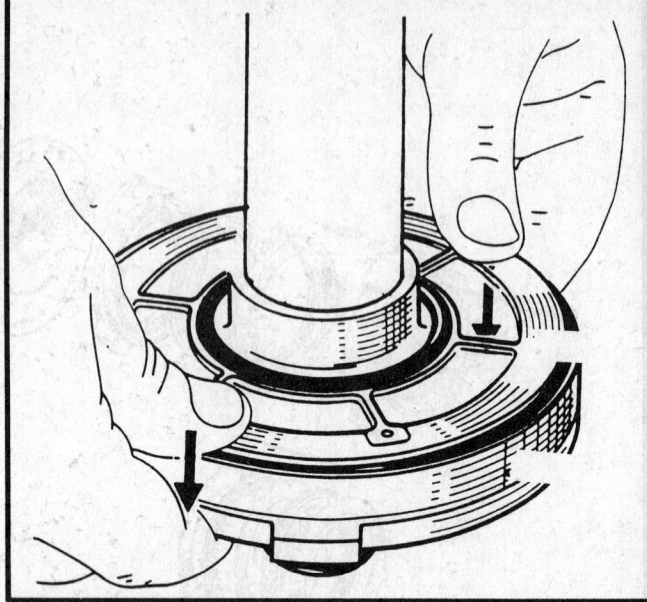

Installing the piston

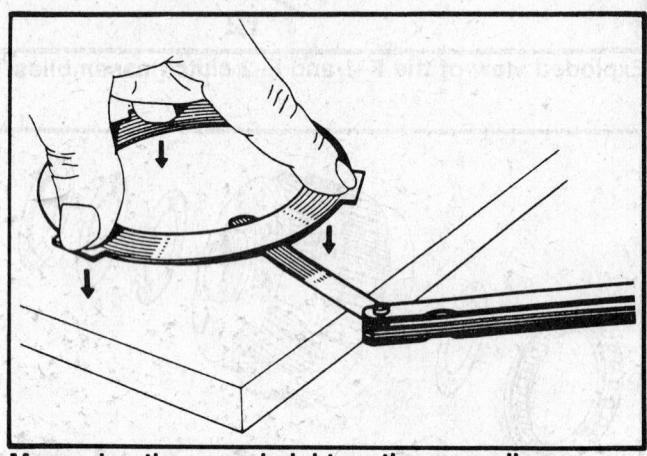

Measuring the wave height on the wave disc

Assembly

1. Install the 3 seal rings on the E–2 bell housing after checking the ring gap play, by placing the rings in the sprag clutch hub and the condition of the 3 grooves in the bell housing.

2. Lubricate the 2 piston seals and install the rectangular seal on the piston and the O-ring on the piston hub in the E–2 bell housing. Make sure that the seals fit tightly in their bores.

3. Install the piston in its place in the bell housing.

4. Using a suitable tool and a arbor press, slightly compress the clutch return spring and install the circlip, being careful to guide the spring retainer.

5. The slots in the piston and the bell housing must be lined up. Install one after the other on the piston after lubricating:

    The thrust plate
    A lubricated lined disc
    A wave disc
    A lubricated lined disc
    A wave disc
    A lubricated lined disc
    The thrust plate with the punch-marked surface towards the outside.

6. Install the circlip.

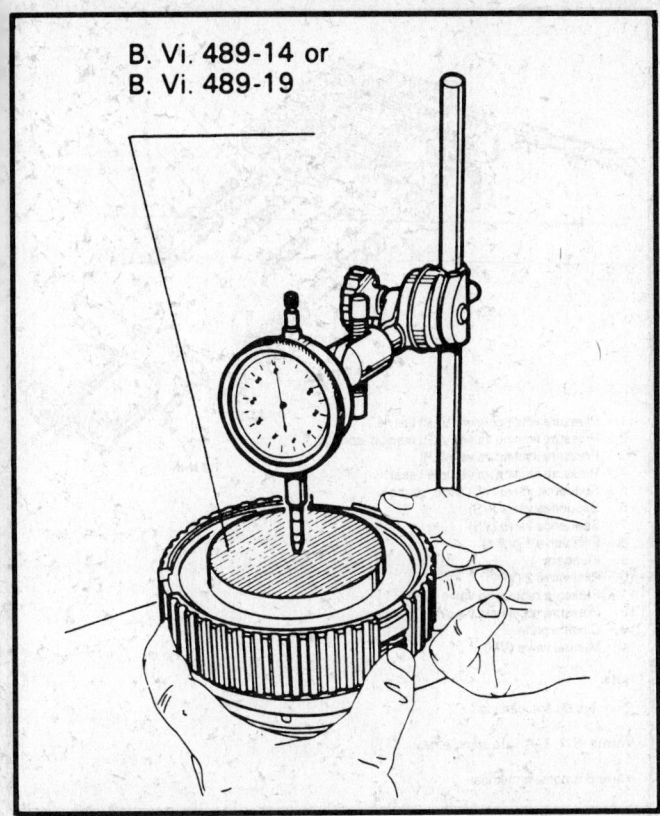

B. Vi. 489-14 or
B. Vi. 489-19

Checking the play in the E–2 clutch assembly

7. Check the operation of the E–2 clutch components by applying compressed air to the piston through the hole provided.

8. Check the endplay of the clutch as follows:

a. Place the E–2 clutch and a dial indicator gauge with bracket on a flat surface.

b. Place the B.Vi. 489–14 or B.Vi. 489–19 reference tool on the pile of the clutch discs.

c. Set the dial indicator to 0, raise the disc pile (circlip pushed up against the top groove but without compressing the waved discs) and read the off the play on the dial.

d. The play should be between 0.043–0.083 in. (1.1–2.1mm)

e. If the play is more than specified, insert a thrust plate (spacer) 0.098 in. (2.5mm) thick.

F–1 AND F–2 BRAKES

Disassembly

1. On the F–1 brake remove the following:

a. Unscrew the 3 bell housing bolts.

b. Remove the bell housing, the 6 springs and the steel discs and lined discs.

c. Save the O-ring located between the sprag clutch bearing and the piston housing.

2. On the F–2 brake remove the following

a. Unscrew the 3 bell housing bolts.

b. Remove the bell housing, the 6 springs and the steel discs and lined discs.

c. Save the O-ring located between the sprag clutch bearing and the piston housing.

d. Push the piston out by applying compressed air to the piston housing input hole.

e. Remove the piston seals.

Inspection

1. If plates show any sign of deterioration or wear, they must be replaced. The plates and disc should be flat, they must not be warped or coned shaped.

2. Inspect the facing material on all driving discs. Replace the discs that are charred, glazed or heavily pitted. Discs should also be replaced if they show any evidence of material flaking off or if the facing material can be scrapped off easily. Inspect the driving disc splines for wear or other damage.

3. Inspect the steel plate and pressure plate surface for burning, scoring or damaged driving lugs. Replace if necessary.

4. Check to see that the discs slide easily on the hub splines and that the plates slide easily in the bell housing.

5. Check to see that the wave discs are correct with a feeler gauge. Lay the wave disc flat on a surface plate without exerting pressure on it and slip the feeler gauge between the surface plate and the disc at 3 different points. The wave height should be between 0.010–0.018 in. (0.25–0.45mm).

6. If the wave height is out of specifications, replace the wave discs.

Checking and Adjusting the F–2 Brake Operating Play

This operation consists of measuring the play for the disc pile in the housing. The play is limited by, on one end the piston at the end of its travel and on the other end the bell housing.

1. Insert the piston with a seal in the F–2 piston housing.

2. Stack up a flat disc 0.059 in. (1.5mm) thick, a lined disc, the wave disc 0.079 in, (2mm) thick, which is marked with 2 notches, a lined disc and a flat disc 0.059 in. (1.5mm) thick.

3. Install the bell housing and attach the assembly to sprag the clutch hub.

4. With the dial indicator gauge point resting on a spline of the first lines disc, set the gauge to 0.

5. Raise the disc assembly so that the it makes contact with the bell housing (against the top).

6. Take measurements at several points and average the reading.

7. The play should be between 0.028–0.067 in. (0.70–1.70mm).

8. If the play is more than specified, check all parts which could affect the value, such as the piston, wave disc, line disc and bell housing. Repair or replace as necessary.

Assembly

1. Lubricate the 4 seals for the F–1 and F–2 pistons and install them in their respective housings. Check beforehand that the seals fit tightly in the brake bell housing bores.

2. Place the O-ring between the sprage clutch hub and the F–1 housing. Insert the F–1 piston in its housing, being careful not to damage the seals.

3. Stack up the flat discs and the lined discs. Place the 6 springs in their housings and cap the assembly with the F–1 bell housing.

4. Screw the 3 F–1 assembly bolts into the sprag clutch hub. Turn the assembly over and rest it on the F–1 bell housing.

5. Place the O-ring between the sprag clutch hub and the F–2 housing. Insert the F–2 piston into its housing, being careful not to damage the seals.

6. Stack up the flat discs, a lined disc and the wave disc marked with 2 notches, a lined disc and a flat disc. Place the 6 springs in their housings and cap the assembly with the F–2 bell housing.

7. Screw the 3 F–2 assembly bolts into the F–1 sprag clutch hub.

8. Check the operation of the F–1 and F–2 components by applying compressed air to the piston through the holes provided.

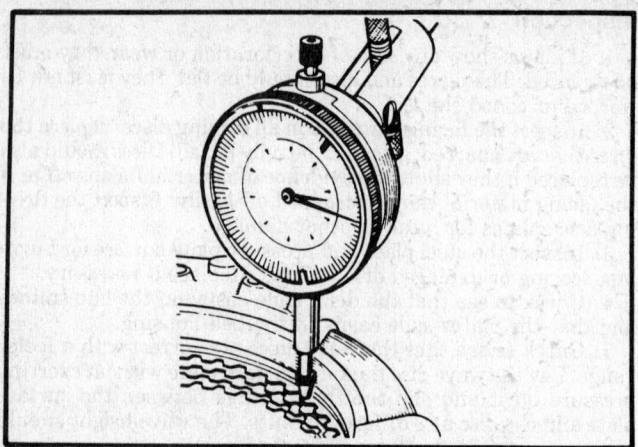

Checking the play in the F-2 brake assembly

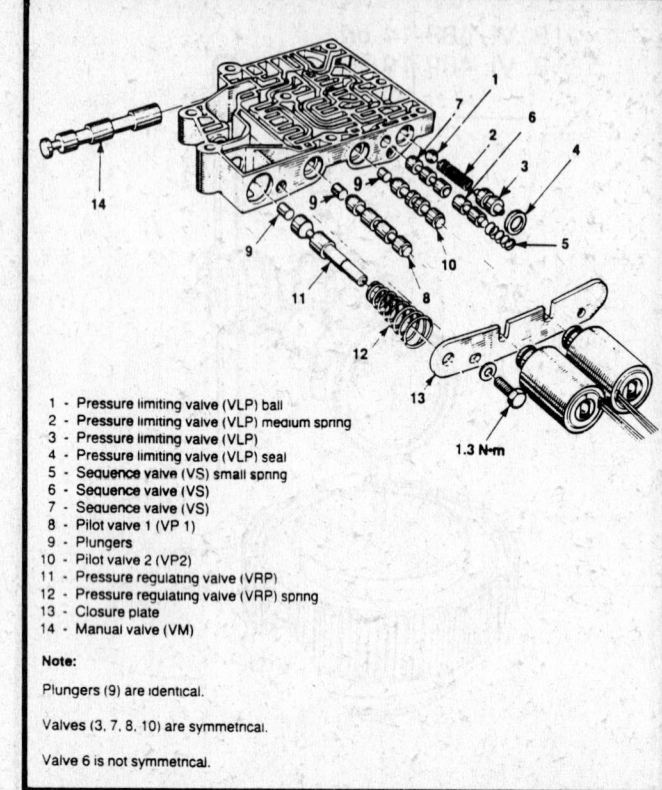

1 - Pressure limiting valve (VLP) ball
2 - Pressure limiting valve (VLP) medium spring
3 - Pressure limiting valve (VLP)
4 - Pressure limiting valve (VLP) seal
5 - Sequence valve (VS) small spring
6 - Sequence valve (VS)
7 - Sequence valve (VS)
8 - Pilot valve 1 (VP 1)
9 - Plungers
10 - Pilot valve 2 (VP2)
11 - Pressure regulating valve (VRP)
12 - Pressure regulating valve (VRP) spring
13 - Closure plate
14 - Manual valve (VM)

Note:

Plungers (9) are identical.

Valves (3, 7, 8, 10) are symmetrical.

Valve 6 is not symmetrical.

Exploded view of the disassembled valve body assembly

VALVE BODY

NOTE: The valve body and regulator assembly should not be disassembled. Only the solenoid ball valves should be changed. Whenever the transaxle is disassembled due to damaged clutches or brakes or because of poor quality gear shifting, the valve body and its regulator must be changed as an assembly.

Disassembly

Do not clamp any part of the valve body or plate in a vise, for this will cause sticking valves or excessive leakage or both. When removing and installing valves or plugs, slide them in or out very carefully. Do not use force to remove or install the valves.

When disassembling the valve body identify all valve springs with a tag for assembly reference later. Also, the oil filter screws may be longer than transfer plate screws, so do not mix them up.

1. Remove the 2 closure plate bolts, remove the manual valve and turn the unit over.
2. Remove the pressure limiting valve ball, pressure limiting valve medium spring, pressure limiting valve and pressure limiting valve seal.
3. Remove the sequence valve small spring and sequence valves.
4. Remove the pilot valve, plungers and the second pilot valve.
5. Remove the pressure regulating valve and valve spring.

Inspection

1. Thoroughly wash and blow dry all parts. Be sure all passages are clean and free from dirt or other obstructions.
2. Check the manual and throttle levers and shaft for looseness or being bent or worn excessively. If bent, replace the assembly. Check all parts for burrs or nicks. Slight imperfections can be removed with crocus cloth.
3. Using a straightedge, inspect all mating surfaces for warpage or distortion. Slight distortion can be corrected by abrading the mating surfaces on a sheet of crocus cloth on a flat piece of glass, using very light pressure. Be sure all metering holes are open in both the valve body and separator plate.
4. Use a penlight to inspect valve body bores for scratches, burrs, pits or scores. Inspect valve springs for distortion. Check valves and plugs for burrs, nicks and scores. Remove slight irregularities with crocus cloth, but do not round off the sharp edges. The sharpness of these edges is vitally important because it prevents foreign matter from lodging between the valve and the bore.

5. When valves, plugs and bores are clean and dry, they should fall freely in the bores.

Asssembly

All screws used in the valve body are tightened to the same torque, 54 inch lbs. (6 Nm).

1. Install the pressure regulating valve and valve spring.
2. Install the pilot valve, plungers and the second pilot valve.
3. Install the sequence valve small spring and sequence valves.
4. Install the pressure limiting valve ball, pressure limiting valve medium spring, pressure limiting valve and pressure limiting valve seal.
5. Install the 2 closure plate bolts, remove the manual valve and turn the unit over.

OIL PUMP

Disassembly

1. Remove the oil pump housing cover.
2. Remove the oil pump shaft. Mark the direction of the oil pump ring wheel for easy reassembly.
3. Remove the oil pump gear.

Inspection

1. Inspect the pump rotors for scoring or pitting and clean.
2. Inspect the machined surfaces on the pump body and reaction shaft support for nicks and burrs. Inspect the pump body and reaction shaft support bushings for wear or scores.
3. Inspect the pump gears for scoring and pitting. With gears cleaned and installed in the pump body, Check the oil pump shaft play.

bearing on the output shaft cannot be removed from the differential case.

9. The taper roller bearings are removed with a bearing splitter extractor. The band ring collar will have to be destroyed in order to work inside the differential housing.

10. When removing the large bearing from the differential housing, insert a steel bar into the case and place it on the flat of the bearing. Use a piece of tubing and an arbor press to remove the bearing.

11. When removing the small bearing from the differential housing, discard the snapring holding the bearing and using a 1.97 in. (50mm) diameter tube and an arbor press, press the bearing into the case.

Inspection

Inspect and clean all parts. Repair or replace the components as necessary. Be sure to dip each diffential component in automatic transaxle fluid prior to assembly.

Assembly

1. When installing the small bearing into the differential housing, position the new bearing over the opening and install using an arbor press and a piece of 2.560 in. (65mm) tube. Install a new retaining snapring.

2. When installing the large bearing into the differential housing, install it using an arbor press and a slightly shouldered steel bar 5.118 in. (130mm) long, or a 4.291–5.040 in. (125–128mm) diameter tube.

3. To install the converter and differential bearing, be sure to clean the seat area for the bearing throughly. Use emery cloth and compressed air to remove all burrs and dust.

4. Using an arbor press, install the bearing flush with the inside face of the case. Stake the bearing in place using a narrow cold chisel. The depth should be 0.051 in. (1.3mm).

NOTE: This bearing must be replaced whenever the complete transaxle or final drive is overhauled.

5. Install the taper roller bearings, using a suitable bearing installer.

6. Install the pinion bearing outer races. Install final drive pinion using a mallet and install the step-down driven gear and spacer.

7. Install a new speedometer drive oil seal.

8. Install the step-down driven gear and lock the lock plates. Install the screws and the final drive pinion nut. The final drive pinion bolts should be torqued to 118 ft. lbs.

9. Install the speedometer worm gear, step-down driving gear, thick washer and output shaft.

10. Install the ball bearings. Install the snapring, tapered washer, speedometer drive spindle, speedometer drive gear, speedometer drive seal and the snapring.

11. Install the endplay adjustment shim, spacer, closure plate bolts and the closure plate. Be sure to place a suitable sealant on the closure plate and torque the bolts to 18 ft. lbs. (25 Nm).

12. The collar must be crimped in position using an arbor press and tool B.Vi. 883 or equivalent. The tapered roller bearing must not be in position at this time. Install the ring gear using new replacement bolts. Torque the bolts to 18 ft. lbs. (25 Nm).

NOTE: The differential preload must be checked and adjusted if necessary whenever the final drive components are disassembled. The differential preload adjustment is performed without the lip seals or the pinion in place. When the differential preload shim increases in thickness, the preload increases and vice versa.

13. The differential components must be rotate under a load of 3–7 ft. lbs. (15–30 Nm) pull when new bearings are installed. These components must rotate freely and without play when bearings are reused.

Removing the oil pump shaft

4. The oil pump shaft play should be 0.014–0.031 in. (0.35–0.80 mm).

Assembly

1. Lubricate all components.

2. Install the ring wheel and be sure to use tha marks made during disassembly for wheel direction, or position the chamfer to face downward into the housing.

3. Install the gear and the pump driveshaft.

4. The pump oil seal can be replaced without removing the pump and reaction shaft support assembly from the transaxle case.

6. Using a suitable seal removal tool, remove the seal.

7. To install a new seal, lightly lubricate the new seal place the seal in the opening of the pump housing and push it into place with a suitable seal driver tool as it is tap gently.

8. Drive the new seal into the housing until the tool bottoms out.

DIFFERENTIAL COMPONENTS

Disassembly

1. Remove the endplay adjustment shim, spacer, closure plate bolts and the closure plate.

2. Remove the snapring, tapered washer, speedometer drive spindle, speedometer drive gear, speedometer drive seal and the snapring. Open the snapring and pull on the output shaft at the same time.

3. Remove the ball bearings. Push the speedometer worm gear toward the converter and pull the output shaft.

4. Remove the speedometer worm gear, step-down driving gear, thick washer and output shaft.

5. Using tool B.Vi. 953 or equivalent, block the step-down driven gear and unlock the lock plates, remove the screws and remove the final drive pinion nut.

6. Use tool B.Vi. 905 or equivalent to remove the speedometer drive oil seal it it was not removed previously.

7. Push out the final drive pinion using a mallet. Remove the step-down driven gear and spacer.

8. Remove the pinion bearing outer races. The needle roller

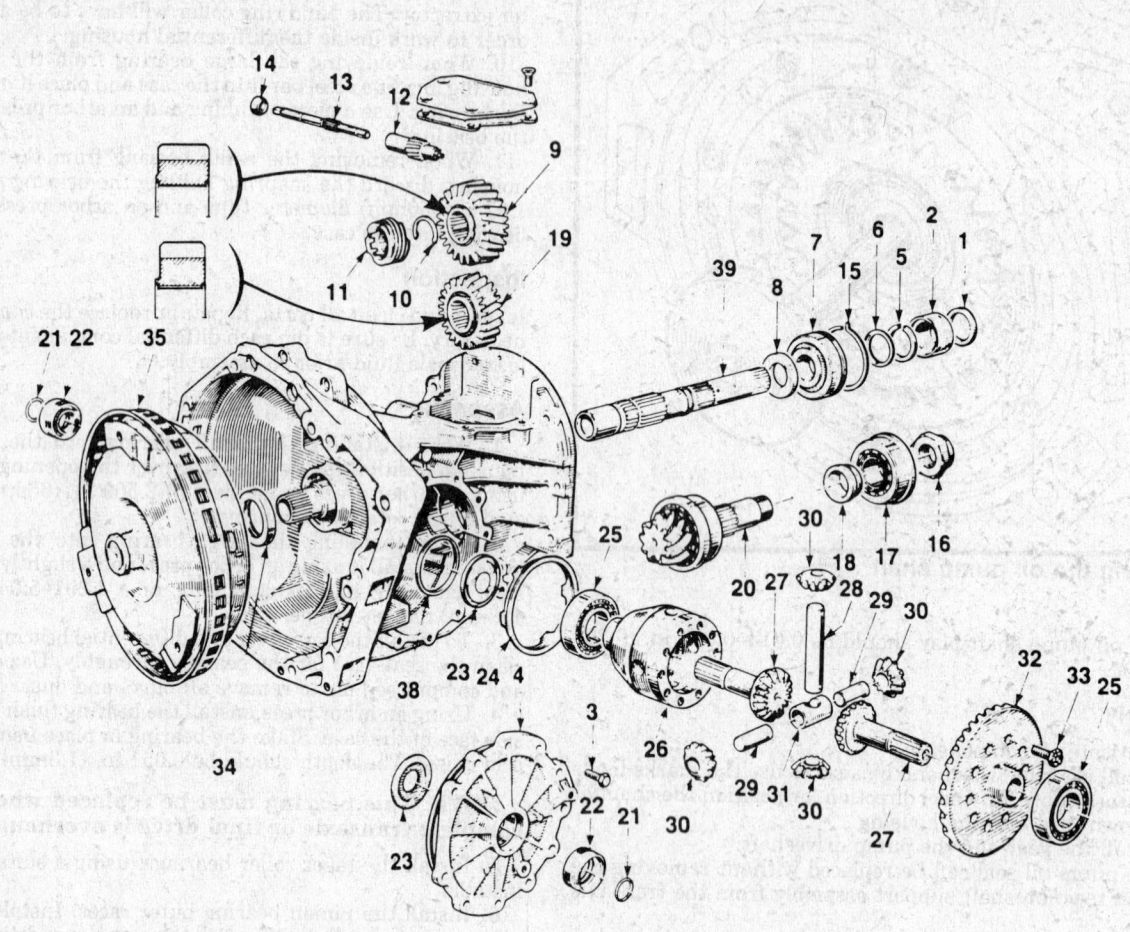

1 - End play adjusting shim	20 - Final drive pinion
2 - Spacer	21 - "O" ring
3 - Closure plate bolt	22 - Lip-type oil seal
4 - Closure plate	23 - Deflector
5 - Snap ring	24 - Collar
6 - Tapered washer	25 - Tapered roller bearing
7 - Ball bearing	26 - Differential housing
8 - Thick washer	27 - Side gears
9 - Step-down driving gear	28 - Long shaft
10 - Snap ring	29 - Short shaft
11 - Speedo. worm gear	30 - Spider gears
12 - Speedo. drive gear	31 - Core
13 - Speedo. drive spindle	32 - Ring gear
14 - Speedo. drive spindle seal	33 - Ring gear bolts
15 - Snap ring	34 - Converter oil seal
16 - Final drive pinion nut	35 - Converter
17 - Tapered roller bearing	38 - Differential preload adjusting shim
18 - Spacer	39 - Output shaft
19 - Step-down driven gear	40 - Spacers

Exploded view of the differential case and its components

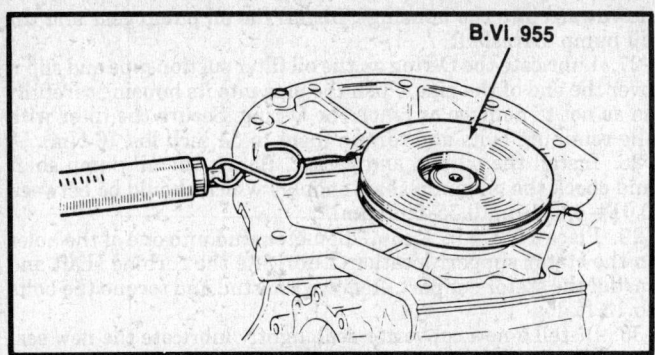

Measuring the differential pinion preload

14. The final drive pinion outer track rings should be refitted using tool B.Vi. 961 or equivalent, if new bearings are to be installed.

15. The differential pinion preload is checked without the differential installed. The thickness of the spacer determines the pinion preload.

16. Install tool B.Vi. 955 on the diifferntial pinion nut. The pinion should rotate under a load of 5–8 lbs. pull when new nearings are installed. The pinion should rotate freely and without play when the bearings are being reused. When this adjustment is complete, the differential assembly may be installed.

Transaxle Assembly

Do not use force to assemble mating parts. If parts do not assemble freely, invesitgate the cause and correct the trouble before proceeding. Always use new gaskets during assembly operations. Use only the specified automatic transaxle fluid to lubricate the transaxle parts during assembly.

With the transaxle case thoroughly cleaned and the various sub assemblies overhauled and assembled, the assembly procedure is as follows:

1. Place the E–1 assembly and the turbine shaft on a tube approximately 4 in. (100mm) in diameter. Place the needle thrust bearing into the E–1 clutch assembly with the pins facing down.

2. Roughly center the E–2 discs and slide this assembly onto the splines in the E–1 connecting bell housing. Turn gently, without forcing, to avoid damaging the discs.

3. When all the discs are properly in place, there is a play of approximately ⅛ in (4mm) between E–1 and E–2.

4. Lubricate the E–2 rings and their bearing surfaces on the sprag clutch hub.

5. Roughly center the F–2 discs and slide this assembly slowly onto the E–2 clutch assembly. Place the thrust bearing between the E–2 clutch and the sun gear assembly. Be sure the pins are facing down.

6. Center the F–1 discs and slowly lower the sun gear and planetary carrier assembly onto the F–1 brake. Make sure that all the discs are correctly positioned.

7. Install the transaxle case thrust bearing and 2 0.276 in. (7mm) diameter studs to allow the mechanism to be lowered more easily. Lubricate the seal ring housing and the location for the sprag clutch hub. Be sure that there is no burr that might interfere with the assembly.

8. Position the assembly holding it by the turbine shaft. Slowly lower the turbine shaft, making sure that the sprag clutch hub is lined up with the E–1 and E–2 clutch assemblies. Check to make sure that the sprag clutch hub fits well up against the case. The play between the E–1 and E–2 clutch should be 0.118–0.197 in. (3–5mm).

9. Remove the 2 studs and install the retaining bolts, torque them to 15 ft. lbs.

NOTE: The F–1 operating clearance should be between 0.043–0.122 in. (1.1–3.1mm).

10. Install the parking latch return spring on its shaft, the parking latch, the shaft (threaded hole upward), the centering dowel and the circlip.

11. Install the main shaft needle bearing. Install the needle thrust bearing plate onto the planetary gear carrier.

12. Install the needle thrust bearing on the output shaft in the differential case.

13. Install the endplay adjusting shim and the needle thrust bearing plate.

14. Before assembling the 2 housings, be sure that the oil seal is correctly positioned on the transaxle case.

15. Install 0.276 in. (7mm) diameter studs on the transaxle case. The 2 centering dowels the smear the sealing surface with a suitable sealant. Lubricate the turbine shaft and slowly lower the differential case onto the transaxle case.

16. Connect the 2 cases with a few bolts and torque them to 22 ft. lbs. Install the lower cover plate with a new gasket and torque the retaining bolts to 18 ft. lbs.

17. Place a dial indicator gauge bracket on the cover plate and set the pointer of the gauge on the E–1 shaft.

18. Pull on the turbine shaft, set the gauge to 0 and push the turbine shaft back again. Read off the endplay on the dial indicator gauge. The reading should be between 0.016–0.032 in. (0.4–0.8mm).

19. Once the endplay is correct, finish assembling the 2 housings, taking care to arrange the wiring clips correctly. Install the sealed junction plug equipped with a new O-ring that has been lubricated.

20. Install the assembled control shaft making sure that is has its O-ring, but do not push it all the way in because the assembled parking rod with its end in the housing and the control selector must be installed on it.

21. Install the roll pin.

22. Before installing the valve body perform the air pressure test as follows:
   a. Applying air to passage **A** will apply the F–1 brake.
   b. Applying air to passage **B** will apply the F–2 brake.
   c. Applying air to passage **C** will apply the E–2 brake.
   d. Applying air to passage **D** will apply the E–1 brake.

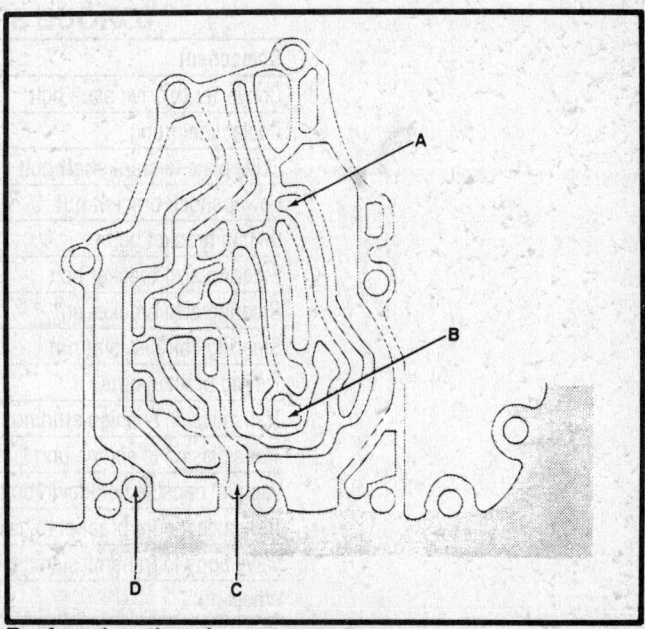

Performing the air pressure test

NOTE: Air pressure testing is used as a method of confirming proper clutch and brake operation after a repair. The tests involves substituting air pressure for fluid pressure. By applying air pressure to the appropriate case passages, movement of the piston can be felt and a soft thud may be heard as the clutch or break is applied. Check for excessive air leakage. Use dry filtered compressed air. Pressures of 30–100 psi are required to perform the tests.

23. Install the valve body assembly, as follows:

    a. The sealing surfaces on the housing and the valve body must be cleaned and free of any burrs.

    b. Be sure that the 2 centering dowels are positioned on the valve body.

    c. Be sure that the 2 toothed quadrants are properly meshed in the **P** position.

24. Install the valve body assembly onto the case housing, engaging the manual valve on the ball joint. Torque the 6 retaining bolts in progressive steps to 54 inch lbs. (6 Nm).

25. Connect the sealed junction plug and check that the marks on the valve body, solenoid ball valves and the plugs all match. Position the magnet on the solenoid ball valve retaining clamp.

26. Check that the oil pump housing is clean, lubricate and install the ring wheel (be sure to use the marks made at disassembly for the proper wheel direction or position the chamfer to face downward into the housing). Install the oil pump gear and the oil pump driveshaft.

27. Lubricate the O-ring on the oil filter suction pipe and slip it over the end of the pipe. Push the pipe into its housing carefully so as not to damage or pinch the O-ring. Secure the filter with the retaining bolts and torque them to 54 inch lbs. (6 Nm).

28. Install the oil pan and gasket. Rotate the oil pump shaft and check the oil pump shaft endplay which should be between 0.014–0.031 in. (0.35–0.80mm).

29. Place a 0.276 in. (7mm) diameter stud into one of the holes in the stator support location. Lubricate the turbine shaft and install the stator support. Remove the stud and torque the bolts to 13 ft. lbs.

30. Install a new converter seal, lightly lubricate the new seal place the seal in the opening of the pump housing and push it into place with a suitable seal driver tool as it is tap gently.

31. Drive the new seal into the housing until the tool bottoms out.

32. Install the converter after lubricating the white metal sleeve, the turbine shaft and the pump shaft splines.

33. Install the governor computer with its seal, the vacuum capsule, the wiring and the dipstick.

34. Install the transaxle assembly into the vehicle. Refill to the proper level with automatic transaxle fluid. Road test the vehicle, make all adjustments as necessary.

SPECIFICATIONS

TORQUE SPECIFICATIONS

Component	ft. lbs.	Nm
Converter to drive plate bolt	22	30
Cooler line fitting	175 ①	20
Drive plate to crankshaft bolt	51	70
Lower shock bracket nut	148	200
Oil pan bracket bolt	54 ①	6
Steering arm bracket bolt	30	40
Steering arm bracket nut	25	35
Steering link ball joint nut	30	40
Tie rod bracket nuts	25	35
Transmission cushion stud nut	30	40
Transmission to engine bolt	37	50
Vacuum capsule holddown bolt	132 ①	15
Transaxle mount bracket to transaxle case bolt	30	40
Valve body to transmission case bolt	80 ①	9
Wheel nut	66	90

① Inch lbs.

SPECIAL TOOLS

Tool Ref.	Description
B.Vi. 31-01	Set of 3 Roll Pin Drifts
B.Vi. 946	Planetary Snap Ring Installer
B.Vi. 952	Feed Hub Alignment Dowels and Front Piston Removing Tool
Mot. 50	Torque Wrench or Equivalent Beam Type Torque Wrench
Mot. 53	Drain Plug Wrench (98 mm square drive)
B. Vi. 465	Converter Oil Seal Replacement Tool and Converter Holding Lug
B. Vi. 466-04	Oil Pressure Gauge (or J-24027 with adapter 8981 320759)
B. Vi. 466-06	Oil Pressure Gauge for B. Vi. 466-04
B. Vi. 715	Tool From B. Vi. 710 Kit or use B. Vi. LM
B. Vi. 883	Differential Outside Band Installer
B. Vi. 905	Speedometer Shaft Seal Replacement Tool
B. Vi. 945	Planetary Oil Seal Installing Mandrel
B. Vi. 947	Intermediary Case Bearing Installer
B. V. 951	Differential Oil Seal Installer
B. Vi. 953	Step Down Driven Gear Holding Tool
B. Vi. 955	Differential Pinion Bearing Preload Measuring Tool
B. Vi. 958	Diagnostic Tester (or MS 1700 With Adapter)
B. Vi. 959	Output Shaft Circlip Installing Tool
B. Vi. 961	Differential Pinion Bearing Race Installing Tool
B. Vi. 962	Converter Oil Seal Installing Tool
B.Vi. 31-01	Roll Pin Punch Set
B.Vi. 465	Torque Converter Tool Set
B.Vi. 466–07	Pressure Gauge Set
B.Vi. 905-02	Speedometer Seal Tool Set
Mot. 582	Drive Plate Locking Tool
MS 1700	Electronic Diagnostic Tester
MS 1900	Engine Support Tool
T. Av. 476	Ball Joint Extractor

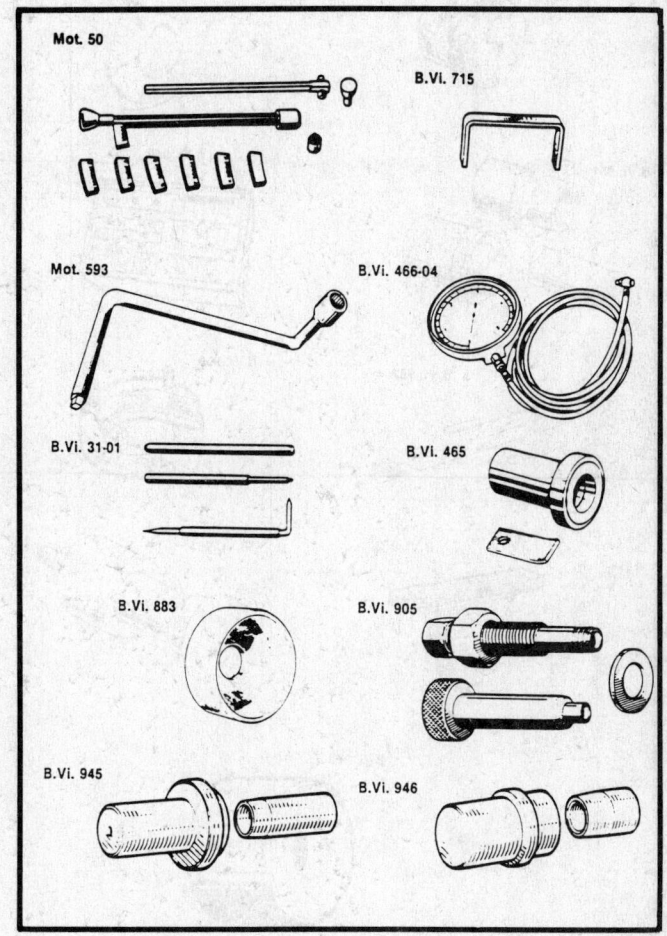

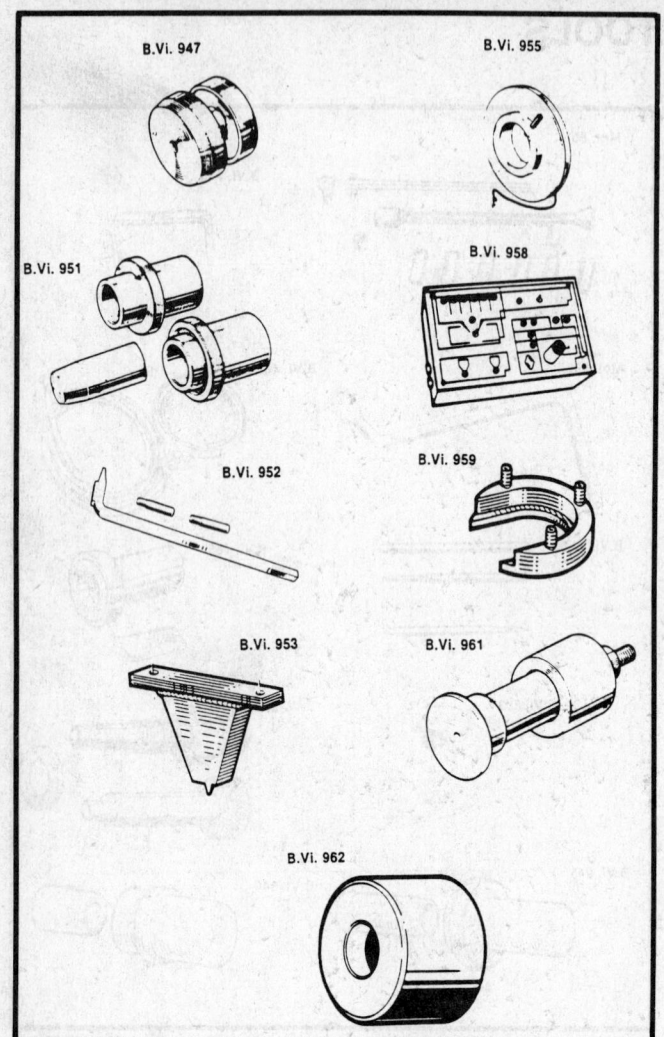

B.Vi. 947

B.Vi. 951

B.Vi. 952

B.Vi. 953

B.Vi. 955

B.Vi. 958

B.Vi. 959

B.Vi. 961

B.Vi. 962

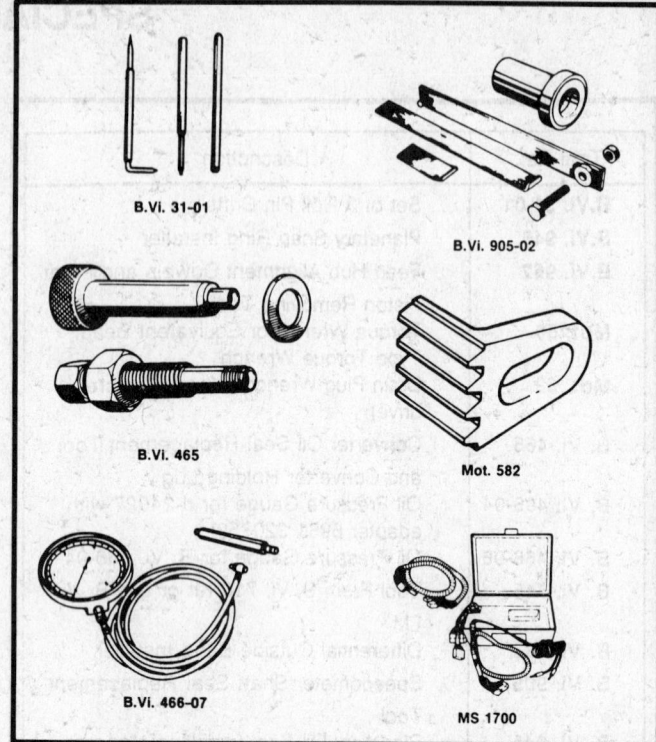

B.Vi. 31-01

B.Vi. 465

B.Vi. 466-07

B.Vi. 905-02

Mot. 582

MS 1700

Section 3

ZF-4HP-18 Transaxle
AMC/Jeep-Eagle

APPLICATION

1988–89 Premier

GENERAL DESCRIPTION

The ZF 4HP-18 is a 4 speed, automatic transaxle. Third gear ratio is 1:1. Fourth gear is an overdrive range providing an 0.74:1 gear ratio. Shifting is controlled by a governor valve, a line pressure valve, a throttle pressure regulator valve and a modulator valve. Valve operation is dependant on shift lever position, vehicle speed and throttle position.

Transaxle and Converter Identification

TRANSAXLE

The ZF 4HP-18 transaxle can be identified by a tag on the left side of the transaxle case just above the oil pan. The information on the plate consists of the builders sequence number, manufacturers part number and the transaxle type.

CONVERTER

The torque converter diameter is 10.2 in. Identification numbers or symbols, are either stamped into the cover or ink stamped on the cover surface. The torque converter used in this transaxle is not serviceable. If the converter is damaged in any way, it must be replaced.

Metric Fasteners

The ZF 4HP-18 transaxle is designed and assembled using metric fasteners. Metric measurements are used to determine clearances within the unit during servicing. Metric fasteners are required to service the unit and torque specifications must be strictly adhered to.

The metric thread is extremely close to the dimensions of the standard inch system threads and for this reason, extreme care must be taken to prevent the interchanging of inch system bolts or screws with metric bolts or screws. Mismatched or incorrect fasteners can result in damage to the transaxle unit. The fasteners should be used in the same location as they were removed from or replaced with fasteners of the same size and grade.

Capacities

NOTE: The transmission and differential sections are not integral in the ZF 4HP-18. They are separate and require different lubricants.

The ZF 4HP-18 model transaxle requires Mercon® automatic transmission fluid. This is the fluid to be used in this transaxle. Do not substitute any other type of fluid. The transaxle uses 7.4 qts. of fluid for a dry fill and 2.8 qts. for a fluid change.

The differential requires a synthetic-type SAE grade 75W–140 gear lubricant. It is the only lubricant recommended. The synthetic lubricant is designed to last the life of the differential under normal conditions. Periodic lubricant changes are not required. The capacity of the differential is 0.66 qts.

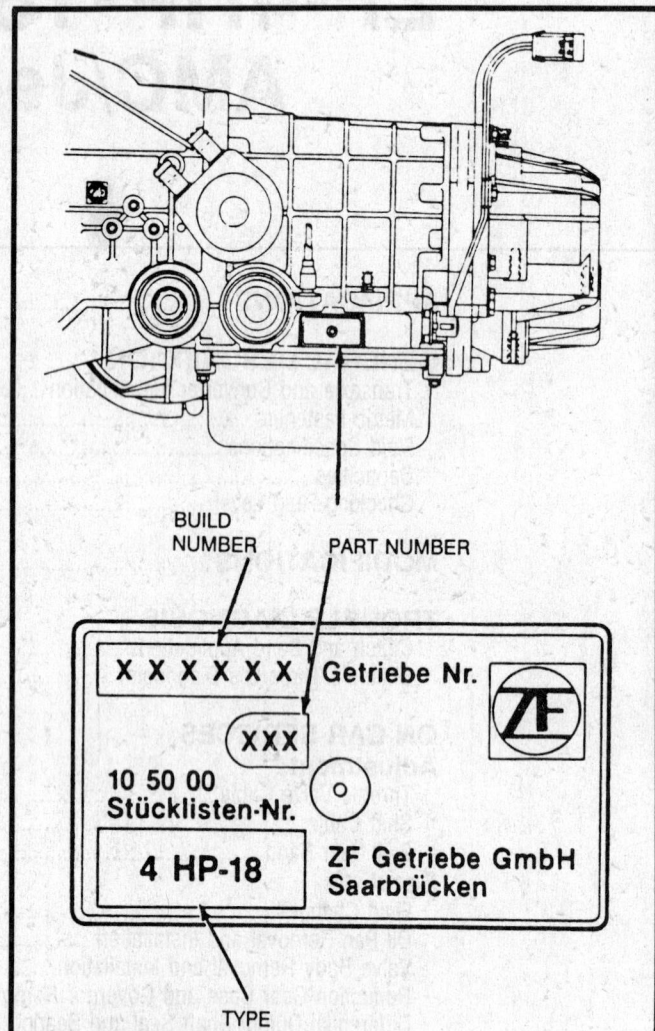

Transmission identification label and location

Checking Transaxle Fluid Levels

1. Check the level when the fluid is cold (at ambient temperature). If the fluid temperature is more than 125°F, allow it to cool before checking the level.
2. Position the vehicle on a level surface. Start and run the engine at idle.
3. Shift the transaxle through every gear range, return it to the **P** position and check the fluid level.
4. Correct level is to the cold fill mark on the dipstick.

TRANSAXLE MODIFICATIONS

No transaxle modifications have been published by the manufacturer at the time of this publication.

TROUBLE DIAGNOSIS

The ZF model 4HP-18 automatic transaxle assembly are not to be overhauled at this time. If diagnosis determines damage or malfunctions are present in the converter or transaxle, the entire assembly must be removed from the vehicle and replaced through the dealership parts exchange program.

CLUTCH AND BAND APPLICATION
ZF 4HP-18 Automatic Transaxle

	Gear Drive				
Component	First	Second	Third	Fourth	Reverse
1–3 clutch	Applied	Applied	Applied	—	—
Reverse clutch	—	—	—	—	Applied
Forward brake	—	Applied	—	—	—
2–4 band	—	Applied	—	Applied	—
First/reverse brake	Applied	—	—	—	Applied
3–4 clutch	—	—	Applied	Applied	—
Roller clutch	Applied	—	—	—	—
Sprag clutch	—	Applied	—	—	—

CHILTON'S THREE C's TRANSMISSION DIAGNOSIS CHART
ZF 4HP-18 Automatic Transaxle

Condition	Cause	Correction
Will not engage or hold in park	a) Shift cable incorrectly adjusted b) Excess clearance on detent plate c) Detent segment out of position d) Park pawl damaged	a) Adjust cable b) Adjust or replace plate c) Correct position or replace segment and rod d) Replace pawl and pin
Engine will not start	a) Neutral start switch inoperative b) Excess clearance on selector shaft	a) Replace switch b) Adjust or replace shaft
No reverse	a) Shift cable incorrectly adjusted b) Oil screen plugged c) Reverse clutch damaged d) First reverse brake damaged) Also engine will not decelerate in position one, 1st gear e) Governor sticking f) Lock-up valve 1 and reverse gear sticking	a) Adjust cable b) Replace oil screen c) Replace transmission d) Replace transmission e) Replace governor f) Replace valve body
Slips/vibrates when accelerating from stop	a) 1–2–3 clutch damaged b) First-reverse brake damaged c) Turbine shaft O-ring or pump starter malfunction d) Oil leaking into reverse clutch or seat piston ring has scored center plate	a) Replace transmission b) Replace transmission c) Replace transmission d) Replace transmission
Harsh engagement P-to-R, or N-to-R may be accompanied by improper 2–1 downshift	a) Accumulator inoperative	a) Replace valve body
Back-up lights not functioning (electrical feed/ground ok)	a) Neutral start switch malfunction	a) Replace switch
Engine will not start	a) Neutral start switch defective	a) Replace switch

SECTION 3

CHILTON'S THREE C's TRANSMISSION DIAGNOSIS CHART
ZF 4HP–18 Automatic Transaxle

Condition	Cause	Correction
Vehicle creeps in park or neutral	a) Shift cable incorrectly adjusted	a) Adjust cable
No power, poor acceleration in D range	a) Converter valve operation	a) Replace transmission
	b) Oil screen plugged	b) Replace oil screen
	c) 1–2–3 clutch defective	c) Replace transmission
	d) Roller clutch slips	d) Replace transmssion
	e) Shift cable incorrectly adjusted	e) Correct adjustment
	f) Throttle or shift valve sticking	f) Replace valve body
Harsh engagement during N-to-D shift	a) Accumulator sticking or spring broken	a) Replace valve body
	b) 1–2–3 clutch damaged	b) Replace transmission
No shift in cold or warm condition		
No 1–2 or 2–1 shift	a) Governor sticking	a) Replace governor
	b) 1–2 shift valve sticks	b) Replace valve body
No 1–2 shift	c) Forward brake or 2–4 band malfunction	c) Replace transmission
No 2–3 or 3–2 shift	d) Governor sticking	d) Replace governor
	e) 2–3 shift valve sticks	e) Replace valve body
No 2–3 shift	f) 3–4 clutch damaged	f) Replace transmission
	g) Oil supply for 3–4 clutch leaking	g) Replace transmission
No 3–4 or 4–3 shift	h) Governor sticking	h) Replace governor
	i) 3–4 shift valve sticks	i) Replace valve body
No 3–4 shift	j) Forward brake inoperative (1–2 up-shift not ok)	j) Replace transmission
	k) 2–4 band loose	k) Replace transmission
	l) 2–3–4 up-shift valve sticks	l) Replace valve body
	m) Position 3 valve sticks	m) Replace valve body
Vehicle takes off in 2nd gear (will not downshift to 1st)	a) Governor piston sticks	a) Replace governor
	b) 1–2 shift valve sticks	b) Replace valve body
	c) 2–4 band binds	c) Correct adjustment
	d) 2–4 band will not release	d) Replace transmission
Vehicle takes off in 3rd gear (will not downshift to 1st or 2nd)	e) Center ring of governor flange defective	e) Replace transmission
	f) Governor piston sticking	f) Replace governor
	g) 1–2 and 2–3 shift valve sticking	g) Replace valve body
	h) Closing cap in center plate leaking (reverse clutch always filled with oil	h) Replace transmission
Transmission shifts 1–3 (no 2nd gear)	i) 2–3 shift valve sticks	i) Replace valve body
	j) 2–3–4 shift valve sticks	j) Replace valve body
	k) 1–2–3 shift valve sticks	k) Replace valve body
Transmission shifts 1–4 (no 1–2; or 2–3 shift)	l) Engine will not accelerate	l) Replace valve body
Will not downshift to 1st at idle or no kickdown shift) Will not return to 1st gear at idle speed when stopped	a) Governor sticking	a) Replace governor
	b) Leakage in governor assembly	b) Replace transmission
	c) Shift valve binding	c) Replace valve body
No full throttle kickdown	d) Throttle valve cable incorrectly adjusted	d) Adjust cable
No kickdown shifts	e) Throttle valve cable incorrectly adjusted	e) Adjust cable
	f) Governor sticking	f) Replace governor
Harsh engagement at idle speeds	a) Accumulator malfunction	a) Replace valve body
	b) Modulator pressure too high	b) Replace valve body
	c) Clutch pack damage	c) Replace transmission
Full throttle kickdown shifts too long	d) Accumulator malfunction	d) Replace valve body
	e) Clutch pack damage	e) Replace transmission

CHILTON'S THREE C's TRANSMISSION DIAGNOSIS CHART
ZF 4HP-18 Automatic Transaxle

Condition	Cause	Correction
Full throttle and kickdown shifts too harsh Engine overspeed at 3–4 shift	f) Modulator pressure not OK g) Accumulator malfunction h) Orifice control valve sticking i) 3–4 traction valve binding j) 2–4 band slips	f) Replace valve body g) Replace valve body h) Replace valve body i) Replace valve body j) Replace transmission
Engine overspeed at 3–4 downshift	k) Time control valve and 4–3 downshift valves not coordinated l) 1–2–3 clutch damaged m) Damper function of 1–2–3 clutch and 4–3 traction valve not functioning properly	k) Replace valve body l) Replace transmission m) Replace valve body
Manual 2nd gear downshift incorrect or downshift early or late	a) Lockup valve 2 binding b) Replace governor	a) Replace valve body b) Governor piston binding
No overrun braking in D1	a) 2–4 band inoperative b) 2–4 band damaged	a) Check/replace band piston and cover O-rings if required b) Replace transmission
Manual 2–1 downshift incorrect	a) Lockup valve 1 and reverse gear binding b) Governor piston binding	a) Replace valve body b) Replace governor
No overrun braking in 1st gear	a) 1st/reverse brake damaged	a) Replace transmission
Throttle valve cable sticks	a) Cable not attached to cam b) Internal friction in cable c) Throttle pressure piston sticks	a) Connect cable to cam b) Replace cable c) Replace valve body
After long drive, noise develops and vehicle will not move in drive or reverse	a) Valve body oil screen plugged	a) Replace oil screen
Transmission noisy) Will not move in drive or reverse	a) Converter driveplate damaged b) Oil pump gears worn or damaged	a) Replace driveplate b) Replace transmission
Oil leaking from converter housing seam	a) Torque converter leaking at welded b) Pump seal leaking	a) Replace converter b) Replace pump seal
Leakage between transmission and oil pan	a) Oil pan bolts loose or pan warped b) Oil pan gasket damaged	a) Tighten bolts or replace pan b) Replace gasket
Leakage between transmission housing and differential cover	a) Cover bolts loose	a) Tighten bolts
Leakage at transmission cooler	a) Cooler attaching bolt loose b) Gasket damaged c) Cooler cracked or split	a) Tighten bolt b) Replace gasket c) Replace cooler
Leakage at 2–4 band piston cover	a) Cover O-rings worn or damaged	a) Replace O-rings
Leakage from 2–4 band retaining shaft	a) Retaining shaft O-ring damaged	a) Remove valve body and replace shaft O-ring
Leakage at output shaft	a) Bolts loose b) Seal rings damaged	a) Tighten bolts b) Replace seal rings
Oil leakage at throttle cable connection in case	a) Cable connector O-ring damaged	a) Replace O-ring; if necessary, replace cable
Leakage at differential	a) Output shaft seals or cover seal damaged	a) Replace seals
Leakage at speedometer sensor	a) Sensor or O-ring damaged	a) Replace O-ring or sensor
Leakage at breather vents in transmission or differential	a) Transmission or differential overfilled b) Incorrect fluid or lubricant	a) Correct oil level b) Replace transmission
Leakage at selector shaft	a) Seal ring damaged	a) Replace seal ring
Noise in all positions	a) Fluid level low b) Valve body leaking internally c) Oil screen plugged	a) Correct level b) Replace valve body c) Replace oil screen

CHILTON'S THREE C's TRANSMISSION DIAGNOSIS CHART
ZF 4HP-18 Automatic Transaxle

Condition	Cause	Correction
Noise at certain speeds	a) Bearing adjustment of differential	a) Replace transmission pinion gear incorrectly set
	b) Bearing adjustment of differential incorrectly set	b) Replace transmission

ON CAR SERVICES

Adjustments

THROTTLE VALVE CABLE

1. Loosen the cable locknuts and lift the threaded cable shank out of the engine bracket.
2. Place the throttle lever in idle position.
3. Pull cable wire forward and place a 1.55 in. (39.5mm) long gauge block on the wire between the cable connector and cable end.

NOTE: Vernier calipers can be substituted for the gauge block.

4. Pull cable shank rearward to the detent position (but not to the wide open throttle position).
5. The detent position will provide a definite feel, similar to a stop, when it is reached.
6. Hold the shank at the detent position and insert it in the engine bracket. Tighten the locknuts to lock it in place.
7. Remove the gauge block and verify adjustments. Detent position should be reached when travel of the cable wire is 1.55 in. (39.5mm).

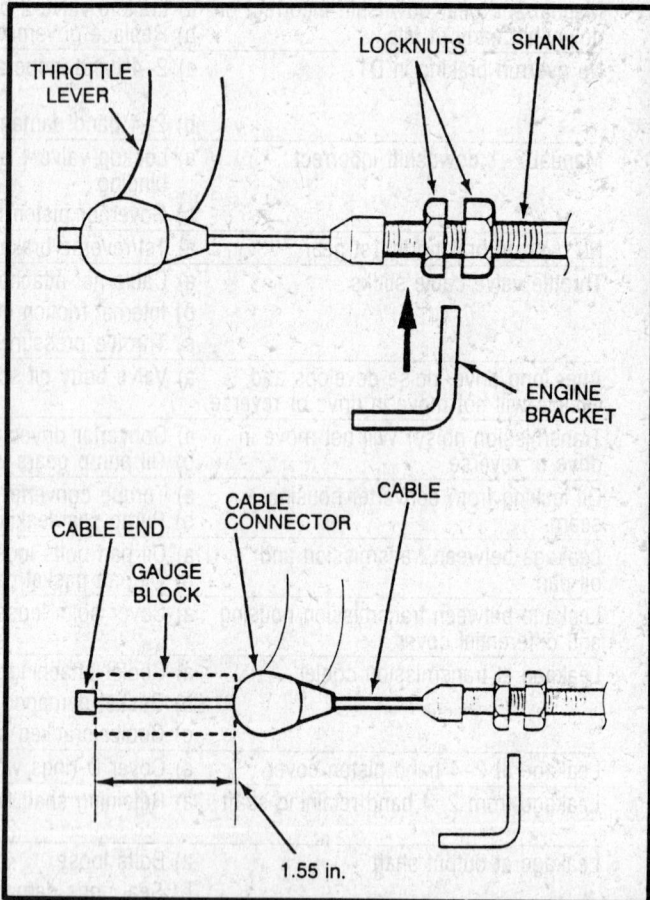

Throttle valve cable adjustment

Installing band adjusting shims

SHIFT CABLE

1. Shift the transmission into **P**.
2. Raise and safely support the vehicle.
3. Unlock the shift cable by releasing the cable adjuster clamp. Move the clamp outward to release it.
4. Move the transmission lever rearward into the park detent. Be sure the lever is centered in the detent.

NOTE: The park detent is the last rearward position.

5. Verify positive engagement of the park lock by attempting

to rotate the driveshafts. The shafts cannot be turned if the park lock is properly engaged.

6. Lock the shift cable by pressing the adjuster clamp back into position, it should lock into position. Lower the vehicle.

7. Turn the ignition key to the **LOCK** position and verify that the shift lever remains locked in **P**. It should not be possible to move the lever.

8. Turn the ignition key to the **ON** position.

9. Verify that the engine only starts when the shift lever is in the **P** or **N** positions.

NOTE: If the engine starts in any position other than park or neutral, the shift cable adjustment is incorrect or a problem exists with the multifunction switch.

10. Shift the transmission into **PARK** and verify that the key can be returned to the **LOCK** position.

2ND AND 4TH GEAR BAND

1. Raise and safely support the vehicle.

2. Remove the under-body splash shield. Loosen the nut attaching the the fill tube to the oil pan and drain the fluid.

3. Remove nuts attaching the oil pan clamps and remove the oil pan.

4. Remove the valve body bolts and remove the valve body.

5. Remove the adjusting shim from behind the nut on the band pin.

6. Using a feeler gauge, check the clearance between the band pin and the case. Correct clearance is should be between 0.049–0.059 in. (1.25–1.50mm).

7. If the clearance is not in the correct range, adjust it be adding either a thicker or thinner shim.

8. Reinstall the valve body and the oil pan.

9. Fill the transaxle with the correct grade and quantity of fluid.

Services

FLUID CHANGES

NOTE: The transmisssion and differential sections are not integral in the ZF 4HP-18. They are separate and require different lubricants.

TRANSAXLE

The manufacturer recommends that the transaxle fluid and filter be changed at 30,000 miles.

1. Raise and safely support the vehicle.

2. Remove the underbody splash shield and loosen the nut that attaches the filler tube to the oil pan. Drain the fluid.

3. When all of the fluid is drained, tighten the nut on the filler tube to 74 ft. lbs. Install the splash shield and lower the vehicle.

4. Remove the transmission dipstick and add 2.36 qts. of Mercon® transmission fluid.

5. Check and adjust the fluid as necessary.

DIFFERENTIAL

NOTE: The differential requires a synthetic-type SAE grade 75W–140 gear lubricant. It is the only lubricant recommended. The synthetic lubricant is designed to last the life of the differential under normal conditions. Periodic lubricant changes are not required. The fluid level should be checked at the regular service interval. The capacity of the differential is 0.66 qts.

1. Raise and safely support the vehicle. Remove the underbody splash shield.

2. Remove the differential drain plug and drain the fluid.

3. Install a replacement washer on the drain plug and reinstall the plug, tightening to 18 ft. lbs.

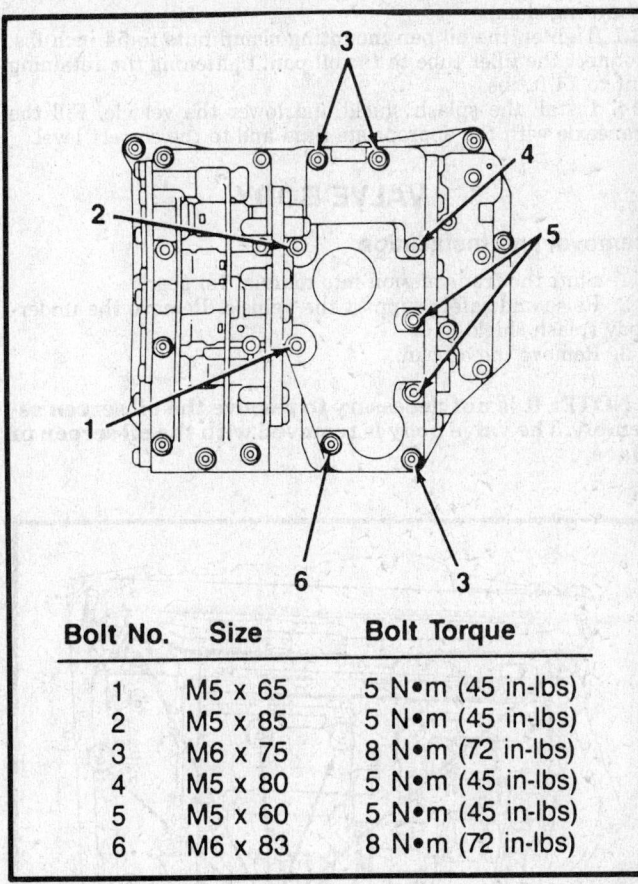

Removing the oil screen and cover

Oil screen bolt torque chart

Bolt No.	Size	Bolt Torque
1	M5 x 65	5 N•m (45 in-lbs)
2	M5 x 85	5 N•m (45 in-lbs)
3	M6 x 75	8 N•m (72 in-lbs)
4	M5 x 80	5 N•m (45 in-lbs)
5	M5 x 60	5 N•m (45 in-lbs)
6	M6 x 83	8 N•m (72 in-lbs)

4. Remove the differential fill plug and fill the differential with 75W–140 synthetic-type hypoid gear lubricant.

5. Continue adding lubricant until it starts to flow out of the fill hole. Install a new washer on the fill plug and install it. Tighten the fill plug to 37 ft. lbs.

OIL PAN

Removal and Installation

1. Raise and safely support the vehicle.
2. Remove the underbody splash shield. Drain the fluid from the transaxle.
3. Disconnect the filler tube from the transaxle after all of the fluid is drained.
4. Remove the nuts attaching the oil pan retaining clamps and the pan to the case. Remove the oil pan.
5. Remove the bolts retaining the oil screen cover. Remove the cover.
6. Remove the oil screen from the valve body. Remove the oil screen cover gasket.
7. Clean the oil pan and screen, replace the screen if necessary.
8. Install the magnet in the oil pan, it goes in the circular indentation.
9. Install a new O-ring on the screen. Coat the screen with petroleum jelly and install it in the valve body. Press the tabs on the screen into place in the valve body.
10. Install the oil screen cover and install the cover retaining bolts finger tight.
11. Tighten the oil screen cover bolts to specification.
12. Position the oil pan on the case and install the oil pan mounting clamps.
13. Tighten the oil pan mounting clamp nuts to 54 inch lbs. Connect the filler tube to the oil pan, tightening the retaining nut to 74 ft. lbs.
14. Install the splash shield and lower the vehicle. Fill the transaxle with the appropriate fluid and to the correct level.

VALVE BODY

Removal and Installation

1. Shift the transmission into manual 1st gear.
2. Raise and safely support the vehicle. Remove the underbody splash shield.
3. Remove the oil pan.

NOTE: It is not necessary to remove the oil screen assembly. The valve body is removed with the oil screen in place.

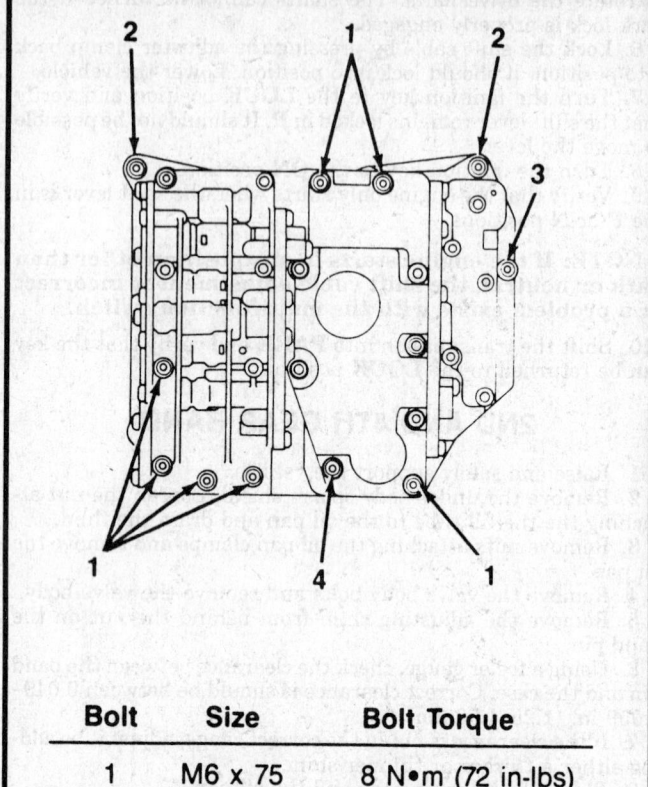

Bolt	Size	Bolt Torque
1	M6 x 75	8 N•m (72 in-lbs)
2	M6 x 30	8 N•m (72 in-lbs)
3	M6 x 27	8 N•m (72 in-lbs)
4	M6 x 83	8 N•m (72 in-lbs)

Valve body bolt torque chart

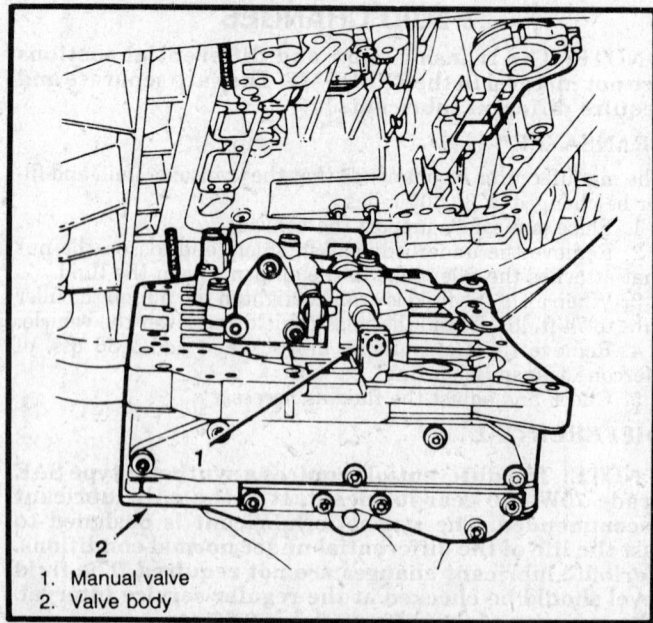

1. Manual valve
2. Valve body

Aligning the valve body for installation

4. Remove the valve body retaining bolts and remove the valve body.
5. Move the selector lever into the 1st gear detent. This is the last detent in the counterclockwise direction.

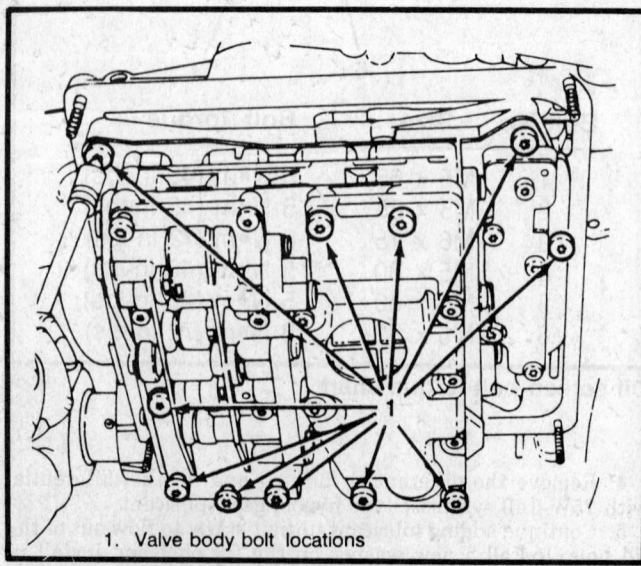

1. Valve body bolt locations

Valve body bolt locations

6. Pull the throttle cable to wide open throttle position to avoid jamming the throttle cam and piston during the valve body installation.

7. Push the manual valve all the way in to the 1st gear position.

8. Align and install the valve body on the transmission case.

9. Install and tighten the valve body bolts to 72 inch lbs. Be sure to install the correct length bolt in each position.

10. Install the oil pan. Install the underbody splash shield.

11. Fill the transmission with the correct level and grade of fluid. Adjust the throttle valve cable.

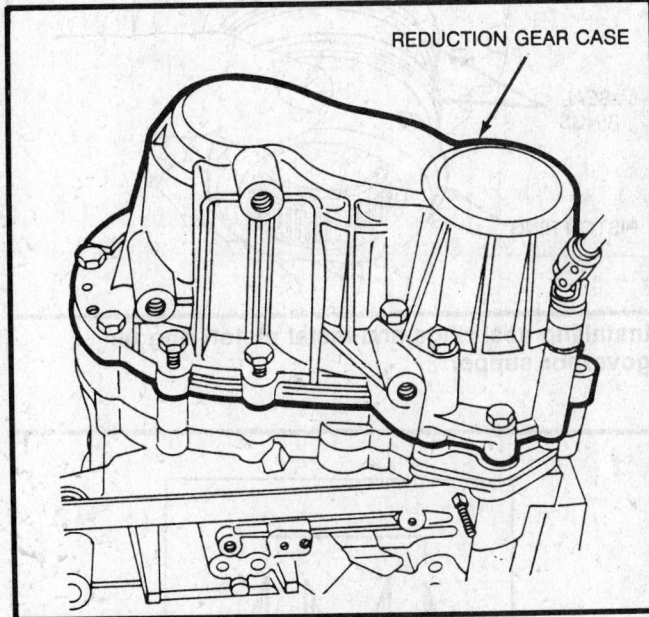

Removing the reduction gear case

REDUCTION GEAR CASE AND GOVERNOR

Removal and Installation

NOTE: The reduction gear case must be removed for access to the governor and governor support.

1. Raise and safely support the vehicle. Remove the underbody spalsh shield.

2. Disconnect the exhaust pipes. Remove the differential drain plug and drain the lubricant.

3. Remove the bolts attaching the reduction gear case to the transaxle case and remove the assembly.

4. Remove the housing flange bolts and remove the flange from the reduction gear housing.

5. Remove the spring washers from in front of the governor cover on the transaxle. Note the position of the washers for ease of reassembly.

6. Remove the governor cover and remove the governor assembly.

7. Remove the bolts attaching the valves to the governor and remove the valves.

8. Remove the 1 metal and 2 rubber seal rings from the governor body.

9. Remove the governor support retaining bolt from inside the transaxle case. Remove the governor support using an puller tool. Note the position of the 2 oil seals at the forward end of the governor support for assembly reference.

10. Remove the seals and seal rings from the support.

11. Install replacement oil seals on the governor support.

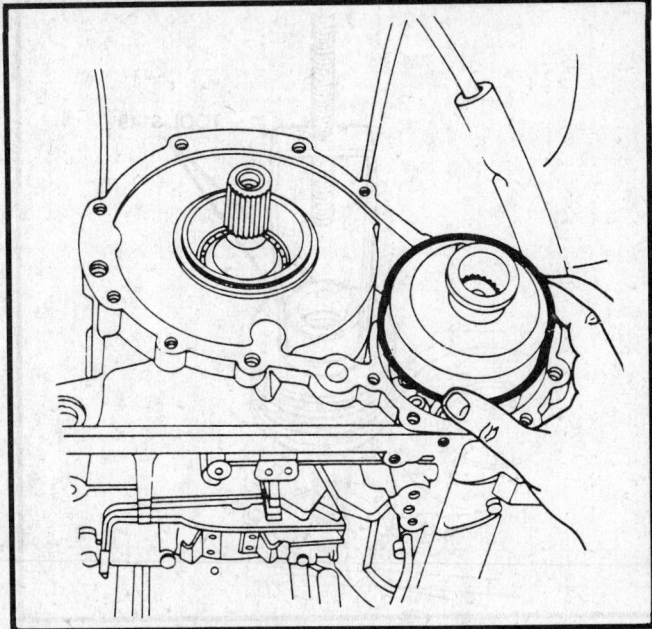

Removing the governor cover

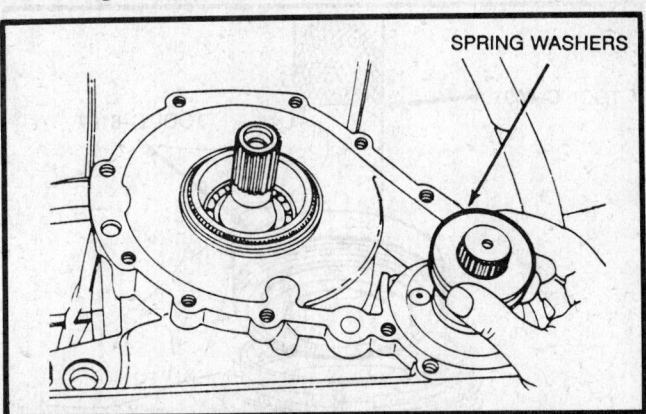

Removing the spring washers from the governor

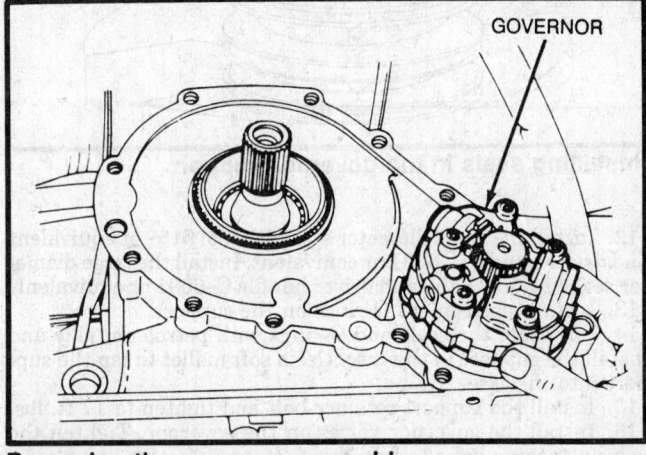

Removing the governor assembly

NOTE: Seal position is important. Install the small diameter seal with the seal lip toward the rear of the support. Install the large diameter seal with the seal lip facing out.

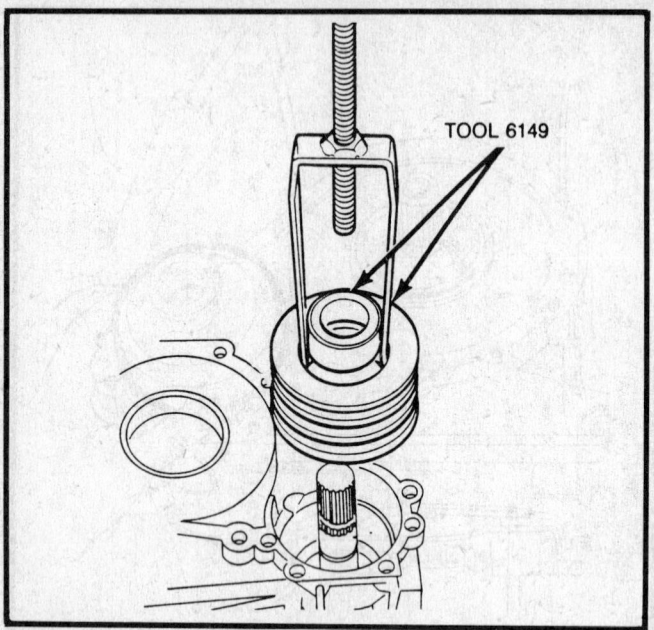

TOOL 6149

Removing the governor support

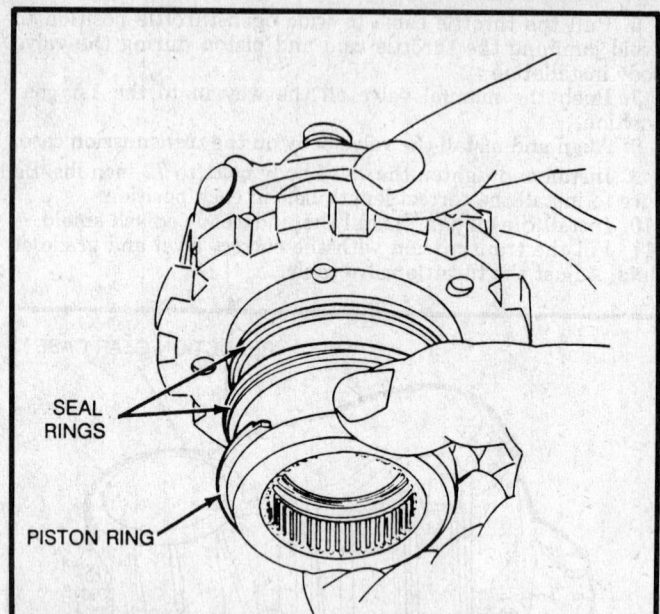

SEAL RINGS

PISTON RING

Installing seal rings and metal piston ring on governor support

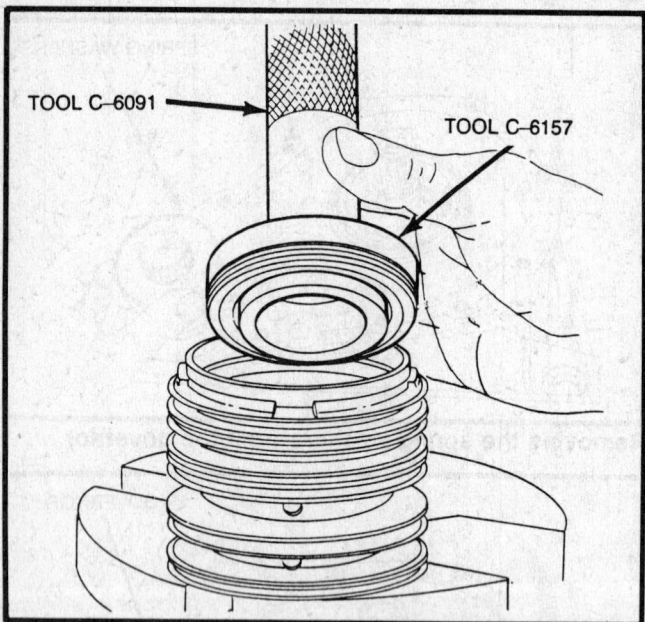

TOOL C–6091

TOOL C–6157

Installing seals in the governor support

12. Install the small diameter seal with tool 6157 or equivalent and driver handle C–6091 or equivalent. Install the large diameter seal with tool 6158 and driver handle C–6091 or equivalent.

13. Install replacement O-rings on the support.

14. Lubricate the seals and O-rings with petroleum jelly and install the support in the case. Use a soft mallet to tap the support into the case.

15. Install the support retainer bolt and tighten to 17 ft. lbs.

16. Install the governor valves on the governor. Tighten the valve attaching bolts to 8 ft. lbs.

17. Install replacement rubber seal rings and a replacement metal piston ring on the governor body.

18. Install the governor assembly in the case. Install the governor cover and assemble and install the 4 spring washers in sets.

19. Coat a replacement flange-to-case gasket with petroleum

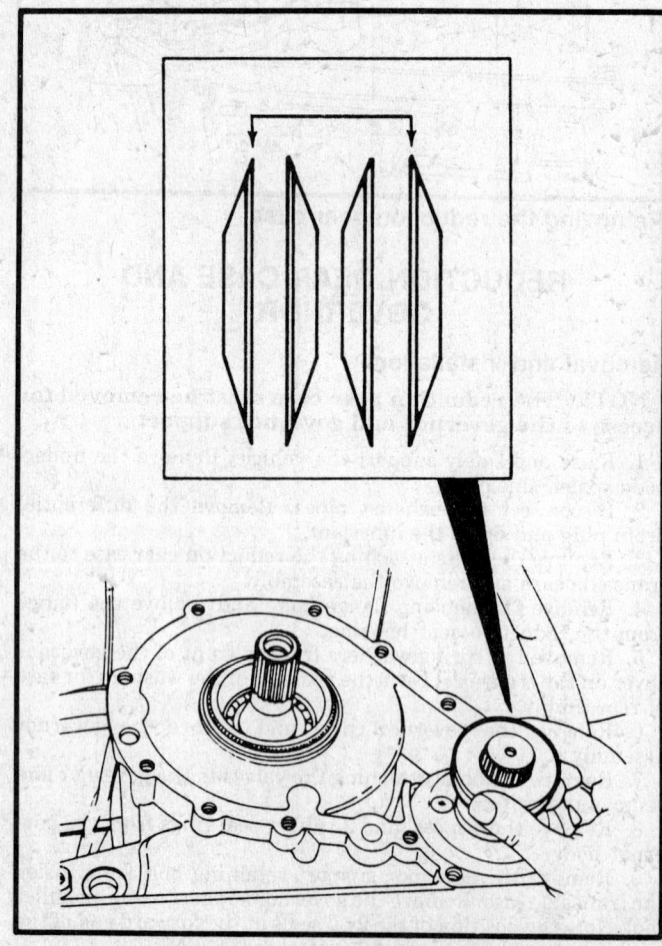

Proper installation of spring washers on the governor

jelly and position the gasket on the case. Install the flange on the case tightening the attaching bolts to 6 ft. lbs.

20. Lubricate a replacement case gasket with petroleum jelly and position it on the transmission.

21. Install the reduction gear case on the transmission. Tighten the case attaching bolts to 17 ft. lbs.

22. Install the drain plug. Remove the differential fill plug and fill the differential with the correct grade and quantity of lubricant.

23. Install the exhaust pipes and install the underbody splash shield. Lower the vehicle.

DIFFERENTIAL OUTPUT SHAFT SEAL AND BEARING

Removal and Installation

1. Raise and safely support the vehicle.
2. Remove the underbody splash shield and drain the differential lubricant.
3. Remove the roll pins attaching the driveshafts to the transaxle output shafts using a pin punch or equivalent.
4. Remove the output shaft dust cover using a small pry bar.
5. Loosen the bolt and pull the the short shaft and bearing out of the cover.
6. Pry the shaft outer seal out of the differential cover. Remove the differential fill plug from the cover.
7. Remove the differential cover bolts. Raise the transaxle as far as possible using a suitable lifting device.
8. Loosen the engine cradle nuts until there is about ½-⅞ in. space between the cradle and side sill. Do not remove the nuts completely. Lowering the cradle will allow easy cover removal.
9. Disconnect the oil filler tube and remove the cover from the case.
10. Remove the differential ring gear and case.
11. Remove the dust cover from the long output shaft. Remove the long output shaft seal using an appropriate tool.
12. Remove the long shaft retaining snapring and remove the long shaft from the case.
13. Remove the output shaft inner seals, use care not to damage the seal bores.
14. Place the long shaft in a press. Remove the snapring that retains the bearing on the shaft and press the shaft out of the bearing.
15. Press the replacement bearing onto the long shaft and install the snapring. Pack both sides of the bearing with grease. Install a replacement O-ring in the long shaft groove.

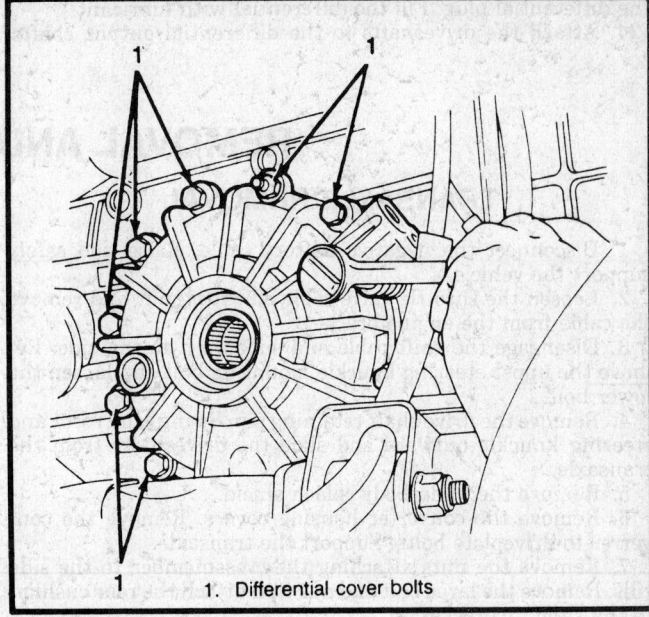

1. Differential cover bolts

Differential cover bolts

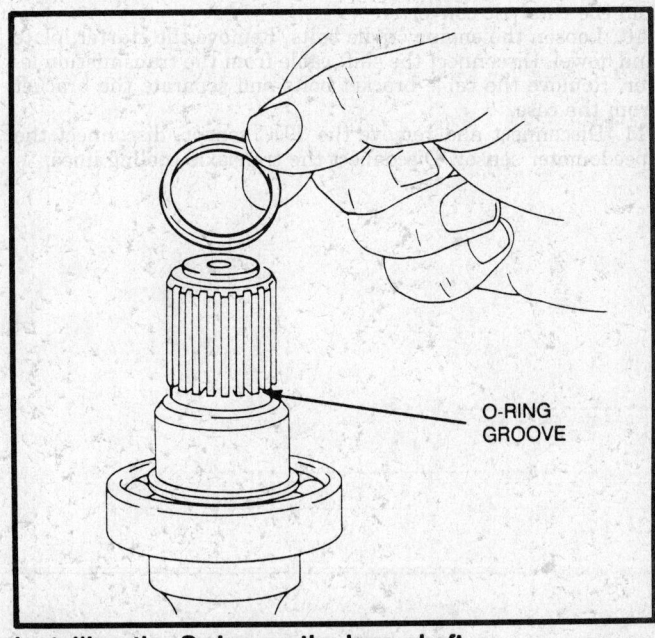

O-RING GROOVE

Installing the O-ring on the long shaft

16. Install a replacement O-ring in the short shaft groove. Install the inner shaft seals using a seal driver.
17. Install the long output shaft in the case and secure the shaft with the snapring.
18. Install the long shaft outer seal and dust cover.
19. Install the differential ring gear assembly. Install a replacement seal on the differential cover and install the differential cover on the case.
20. Install the differential cover bolts and tighten to 17 ft. lbs.
21. Tighten the engine cradle nuts and remove the jack used to support the transaxle.
22. Install the short output shaft in the case. Tighten the shaft bolt to 18 ft. lbs.
23. Install the short output outer seal and dust cover. Install

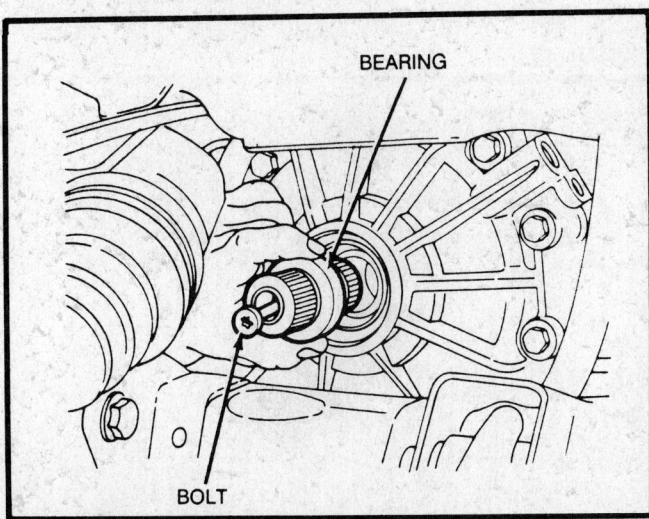

BEARING

BOLT

Removing the short shaft assembly

the differential plug. Fill the differential with lubricant.

24. Attach the driveshafts to the differential output shafts.

Use a pin punch to install the roll pins.

25. Install the underbody splash shield and lower the vehicle.

REMOVAL AND INSTALLATION

TRANSAXLE REMOVAL

1. Disconnect the negative battery cable. Raise and safely support the vehicle.

2. Loosen the throttle valve cable adjusting nut and remove the cable from the engine bracket.

3. Disengage the shift cable and support it to the side. Remove the upper steering knuckle mounting bolt and loosen the lower bolt.

4. Remove the drive shaft retaining pin. Swing each rotor and steering knuckle outward and slide the driveshafts from the transaxle.

5. Remove the underbody splash shield.

6. Remove the converter housing covers. Remove the converter-to-driveplate bolts. Support the transaxle.

7. Remove the nuts attaching the crossmember to the side sills. Remove the large bolt and nut that attach the rear cushion to the support bracket.

8. Remove the support bracket and rear cushion.

9. Disconnect the header pipes from the exhaust manifolds and the catalytic converter.

10. Loosen the engine cradle bolts. Remove the starter, plate and dowel. Disconnect the shift cable from the transmission lever. Remove the cable bracket bolts and separate the bracket from the case.

11. Disconnect and remove the TDC sensor, disconnect the speedometer sensor. Disconnect the transaxle cooling lines.

12. Remove the transaxle-to-engine bolts, pull the transaxle back and away from the engine.

TRANSAXLE INSTALLATION

1. Position the transaxle to the engine. Install the transaxle-to-engine bolts and tighten to 31 ft. lbs.

2. Connect all electrical leads, install the TDC sensor. Connect the speedometer. Install the transaxle cooler lines.

3. Attach the shift bracket to the case and tighten the bolts to 125 inch lbs. Install the shift cable into the bracket.

4. Install the starter. Connect the exhaust head pipes to the manifolds and he converter.

5. Install the rear support and cushion, install the mounting bolts and tighten to 49 ft. lbs.

6. Tighten the engine cradle bolts to 92 ft. lbs. Connect the driveshafts.

7. Install the converter-to-driveplate bolts and tighten to 24 ft. lbs. Install the converter housing covers.

8. Tilt the steering knuckles in and install the top bolts, tighten all to 148 ft. lbs.

9. Install the front wheels. Install the under body splash shield. Attach the throttle valve cable.

10. Connect the negative battery cable. Check the fluid level and check the transaxle operation.

Section 3

AR-4 Transaxle
AMC/Jeep-Eagle

APPLICATION

1987–89 Premier

GENERAL DESCRIPTION

The AR-4 automatic transaxle is 4 speed, electronically controlled fully automatic transaxle with 3 clutches and 2 brakes. The 4th gear is an overdrive range providing a 0.068:1 ratio. The transaxle and differential sections are not intergral and require different lubricants. Shifting is controlled electronically by solenoids in the valve body, speed and throttle sensors and by the transmission computer unit (TCU).

The 3 element torque converter couples the engine to the planetary gears and overdrive unit through oil and hydraulically provides additional torque multiplication when required. The converter torque multiplication feature is operational in **R**, **D1** and **D2** ranges only.

Transaxle and Converter Identification

TRANSAXLE

The AR-4 automatic transaxle can be identified by an identification tag next to the transaxle oil cooler on the passenger side of the vehicle. The information on the tag provides the transaxle type, suffix, fabrication number and plant of manufacture. The identification number "T" is used in the VIN to designate the AR-4 transaxle.

CONVERTER

The torque converter is a welded unit and cannot be disassembled for service. The torque converter diameter is 9.8 in. (250mm). Any internal malfunctions require the replacement of the converter assembly. No specific identification is available for matching the converter to the transaxle for the average repair shop.

Metric Fasteners

Metric bolt sizes and thread pitches are used for all fasteners on the AR-4 automatic transaxle. The use of metric tools is mandatory in the service of this transaxle.

Do not attempt to interchange metric fasteners for inch system fasteners. Mismatched or incorrect fasteners can result in damage to the transaxle unit through malfunctions, breakage or possible personal injury. Care should be taken to reuse the fasteners in the same location as removed, whenever possible. Due to the large number of alloy parts used, torque specifications should be strictly observed. Before installing capscrews into aluminum parts, always dip screws into oil to prevent the screws from galling the aluminum threads and to prevent seizing.

Capacities

If the pan was removed, the approximate fluid needed to fill the transaxle is 2.8 qts. (2.6L). A completely overhauled transaxle will require 5.6 qts. (5.3L) of transaxle fluid. The fluid capacities are approximate and the correct fluid level should be determined by the dipstick indicator. Only Mercon® automatic transmission fluid should be used when adding fluid or servicing the AR-4 automatic transaxle.

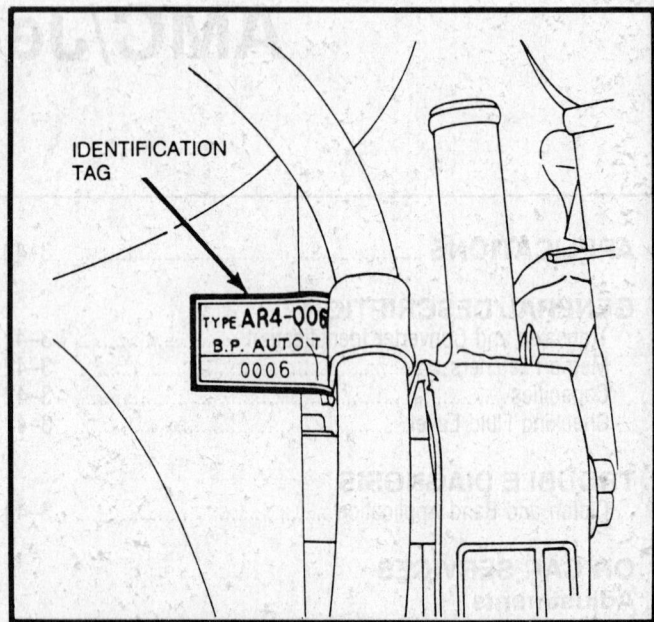

Identification location

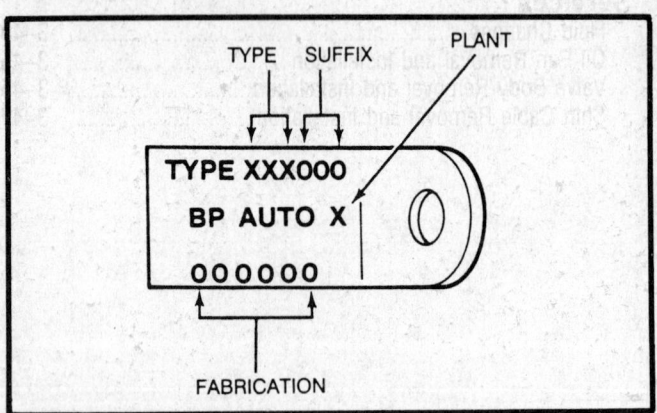

Identification tag

NOTE: The differential is a separate unit. The 4 cylinder model's differential require .89 qts (.85L) of SAE 75W-140 gear lubricant and the 6 cylinder model's differential require .73 qts (.70L) of SAE 75W-140 gear lubricant.

Checking Fluid Level

TRANSAXLE

The AR-4 transaxle is designed to operate at the hot **FULL** mark on the dipstick at normal operating temperatures, which

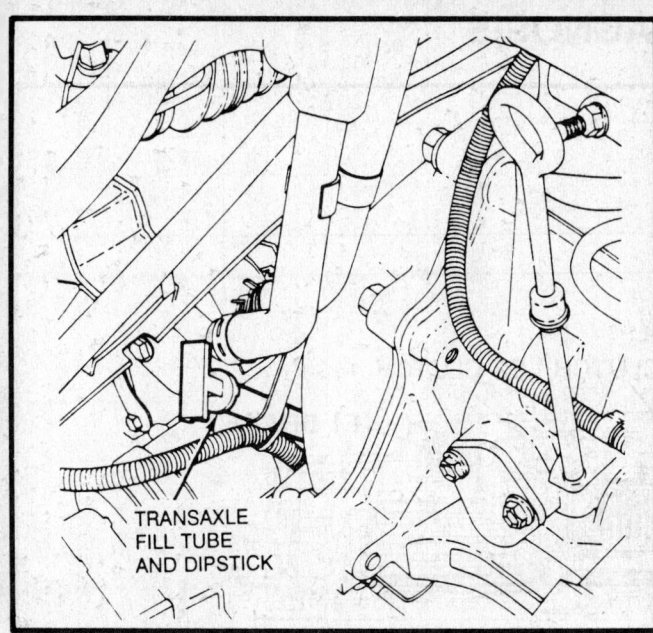

Fill tube location

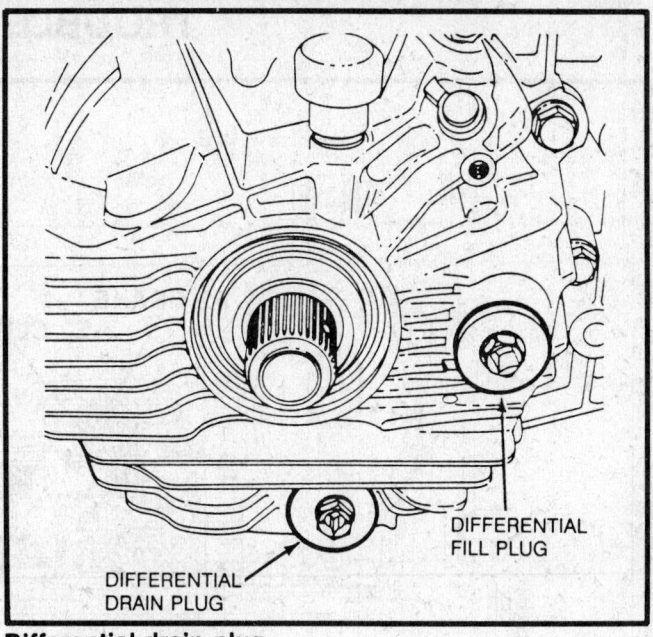

Differential drain plug

range from 190–200°F. Automatic transaxles are frequently overfilled because the fluid level is checked when cool and the dipstick level reads low. However, as the fluid warms up, the level of the fluid will rise, as much as ¾in. Note that if the transmission fluid is too hot, as it might be when operating under city traffic conditions, trailer towing or extended high speed driving, an accurate fluid level cannot be determined until the fluid has cooled somewhat, perhaps 30 minutes after shutdown. It requires 0.28 qts. (0.3L) of fluid to increase level from the **ADD** to the **FULL** mark, on the dipstick.

To determine proper fluid level under normal operating temperatures, proceed as follows:

1. Make sure vehicle is parked level.

2. Apply parking brake; move selector to **P**.
3. Start but do not race engine. Allow to idle.
4. Move selector through each range, then back to **P**, then check level. The fluid should read **FULL**.

Do not overfill the transaxle. Overfilling can cause foaming and loss of fluid from the vent. Overheating can also be a result of overfilling since heat will not transfer as readily. Notice the condition of the fluid and whether there seems to be a burnt smell or metal particles on the end of the dipstick. A milky appearance is a sign of water contamination, possibly from a damaged cooling system. All this can be a help in determining transaxle problems and their source.

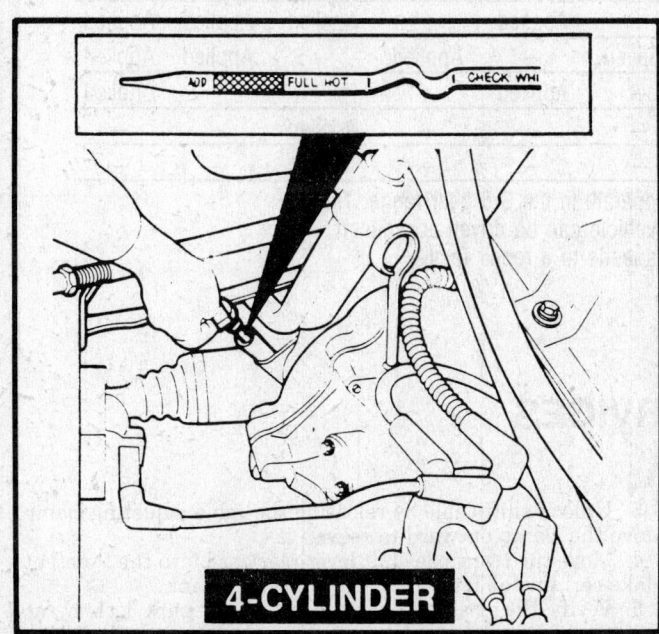

Transaxle dipstick location — 4 cylinder engine

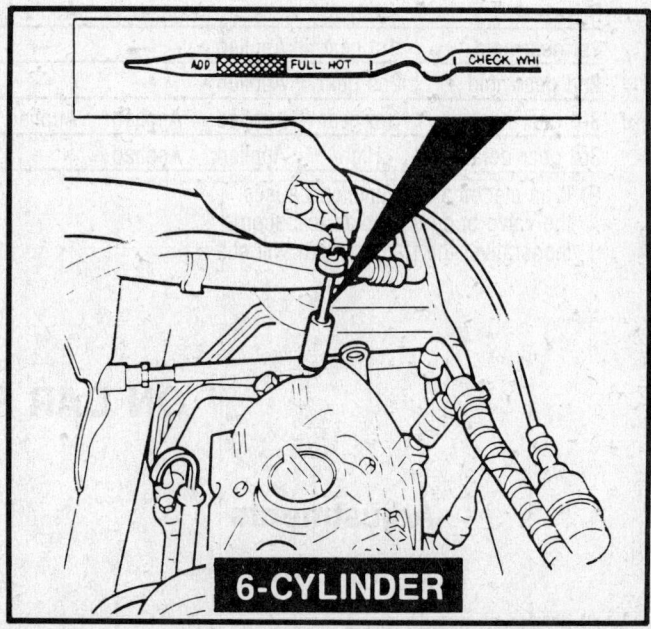

Transaxle dipstick location — 6 cylinder engine

TROUBLE DIAGNOSIS

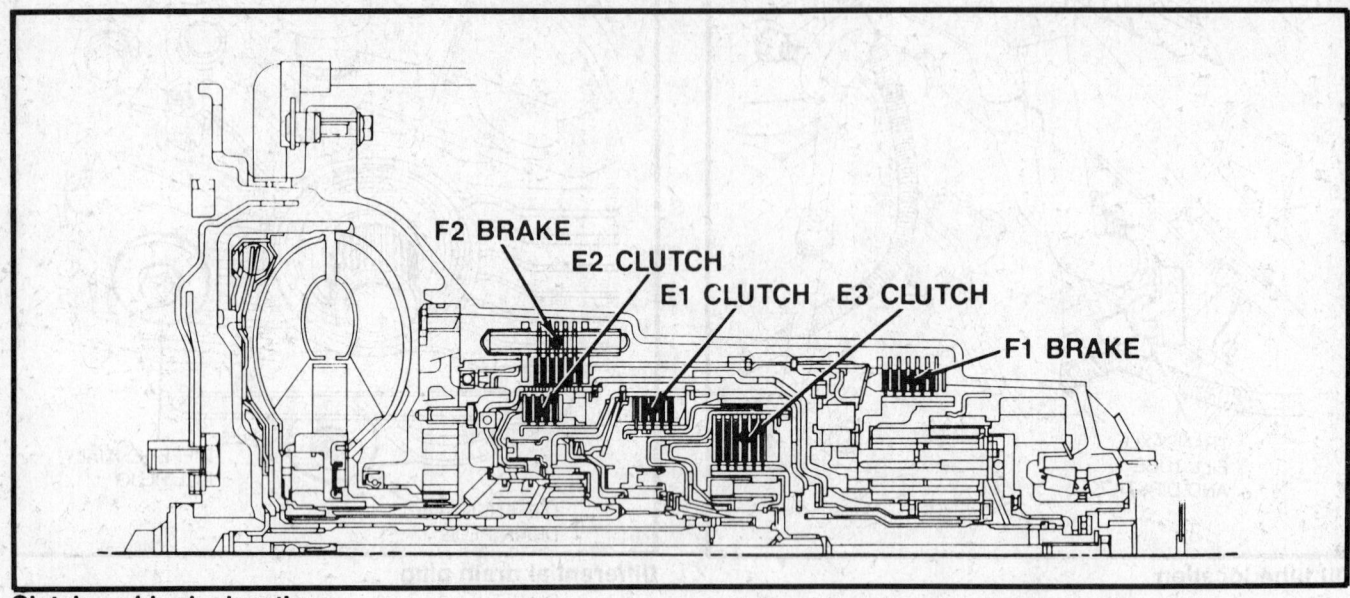

F2 BRAKE
E2 CLUTCH
E1 CLUTCH   E3 CLUTCH
F1 BRAKE

Clutch and brake locations

CLUTCH AND BAND APPLICATION

Shift Lever Position	Line Pressure Level	Clutch No. 1	Clutch No. 2	Clutch No. 3	Brake No. 1	Brake No. 2	Roller Clutch	Solenoid Valve No. 1	Solenoid Valve No. 2	Solenoid Valve No. 3
Park	Low	–	–	–	–	–	–	–	–	–
Reverse	High	–	Applied	–	Applied	–	–	–	–	–
Neutral	Low	–	–	–	–	–	–	–	–	–
Drive – 1	1st gear	Applied	–	–	–	–	Applied	–	Applied	–
Drive – 2	2nd gear	Applied	–	–	–	Applied	–	–	–	Applied
Drive – 3	3rd gear	Applied	Applied	Applied	–	–	–	Applied	–	–
Drive – 4	4th gear	–	–	Applied	Applied	–	–	Applied	Applied	Applied
1st gear hold	1st gear	Applied	–	–	Applied	–	Applied	–	Applied	Applied
2nd gear hold	2nd gear	Applied	–	–	–	Applied	–	–	–	Applied
3rd gear hold	3rd gear	Applied	Applied	Applied	–	–	–	Applied	–	–
3rd gear default①	High	Applied	Applied	–	–	–	–	–	–	–

① If an electrical malfunction causes the valve body solenoids to become inoperative, the transmission will still operate in the 3rd gear range. The vehicle can be driven at reduced speeds to a repair facility

ON CAR SERVICES

Adjustments

SHIFT CABLE

1. Shift the transaxle into **P**.
2. Raise and support vehicle safely.
3. Unlock shift cable by releasing the cable adjusting clamp. Move the clamp outward to release it.
4. Move the transaxle shift lever rearward into the **P** detent. Make certain the lever is centered in the detent.
5. Verify the positive engagement of the park lock by attempting to rotate the driveshafts. The shafts cannot be turned if the park lock is properly engaged.

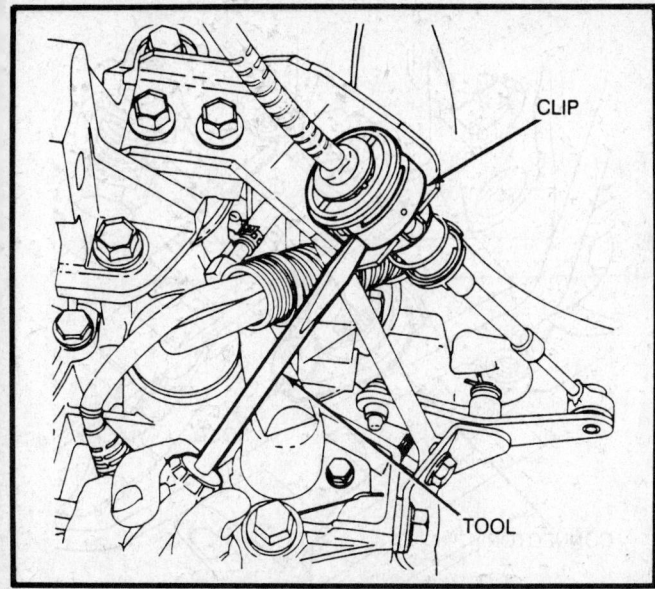

Shift cable—releasing the adjusting clamp

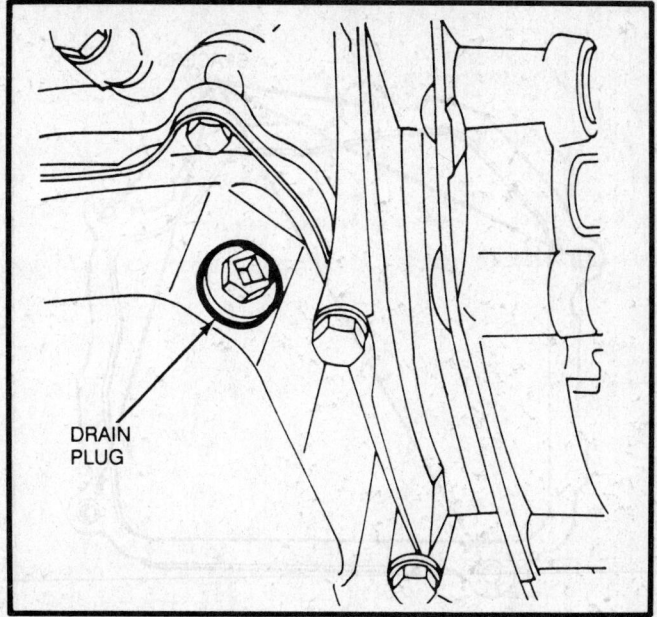

Transaxle drain plug

6. Lock the shift cable by pressing the adjuster clamp back into position. Be sure the clamp snaps into place.

7. Lower the vehicle.

8. Turn the ignition key to **LOCK** and verify that the shift lever remains locked in **P**. It should not nbe possible to move the lever out of **P**.

9. Turn the ignition key to **ON**.

10. Make certain the engine starts only when the shift lever is in **P** or **N** positions.

11. If the engine starts in any other position the cable adjustment is incorrect.

12. Shift the transaxle back into **P** and make certain the key can be returned to **LOCK** and then removed.

Services

FLUID CHANGES

The main considerations in establishing fluid change intervals are the type of driving that is done and the heat levels that are generated by such driving. Normally, the fluid and strainer would be changed at 30,000 miles. However, if the vehicle is driven under severe conditions, it is recommended that the fluid be changed and the filter screen serviced at 15,000 mile intervals. Be sure not to overfill the unit.

NOTE: The differential and transaxle sections are not integral, the differential uses SAE 75W-140 gear lubricant.

OIL PAN

Removal and Installation

1. Raise and safely support vehicle.

2. Remove the underbody splash shield bolts and remove the shield.

3. Place drain pan under transaxle oil pan and remove the drain plug.

4. Remove the oil pan bolts and remove pan.

5. Clean pan in solvent and dry with compressed air.

6. Remove the filter screen bolts and remove the filter screen from the valve body. Discard old screen and gasket.

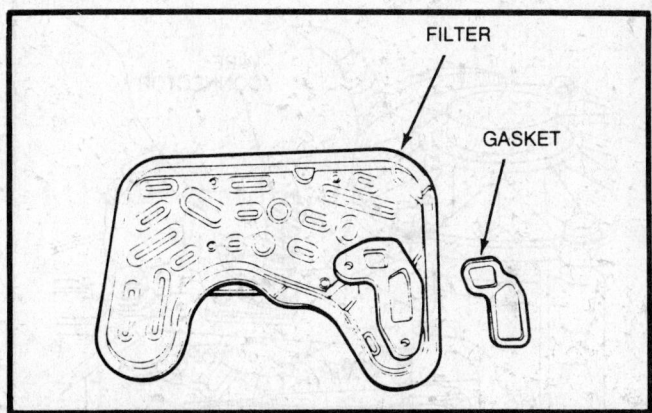

Filter and gasket

7. Install new screen and gasket, if necessary hold gasket in place on screen with petroleum jelly.

8. Torque screen bolts to 46 inch lbs. (5 Nm).

9. Install new gasket on pan dry, do not use any type of sealer, make certain to replace all gasket mounting spacers.

10. Install the pan and torque pan bolts to 90 inch lbs. (10 Nm).

11. Install drain plug with new seal ring and torque to 177 inch lbs. (20 Nm).

12. Replace the underbody splash shield.

13. Lower the vehicle.

14. Remove dipstick and fill transaxle through the fill tube with Mercon® automatic transmission fluid to the proper level.

15. With selector in **P** start engine and idle. Apply parking brake. Do not race engine.

16. Move selector through all ranges and return to **P**. Check fluid level. Add transmission fluid as necessary to bring to proper level.

VALVE BODY

Removal and Installation

1. Raise and safely support vehicle.

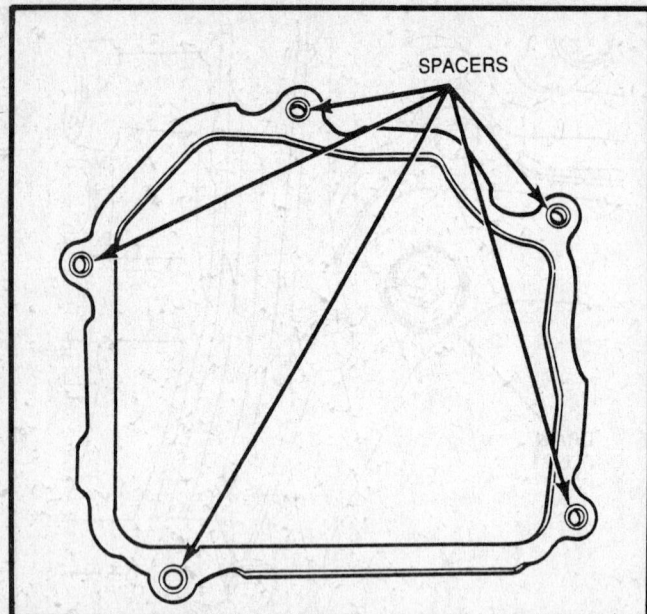

Transaxle oil pan spacers

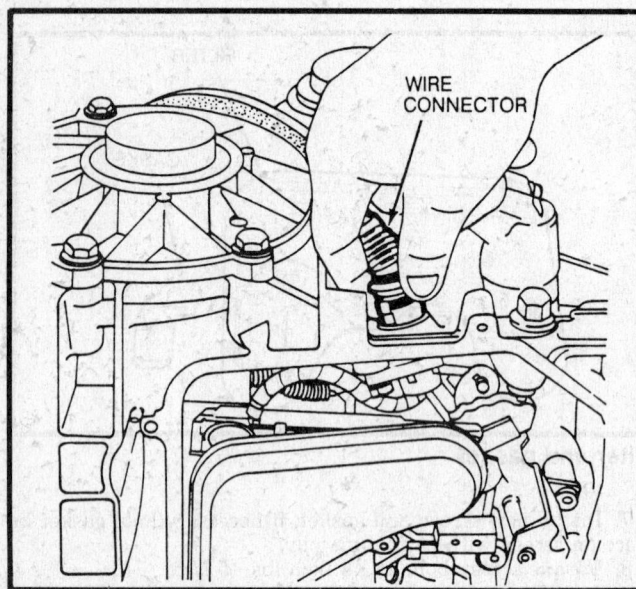

Removing wire connector

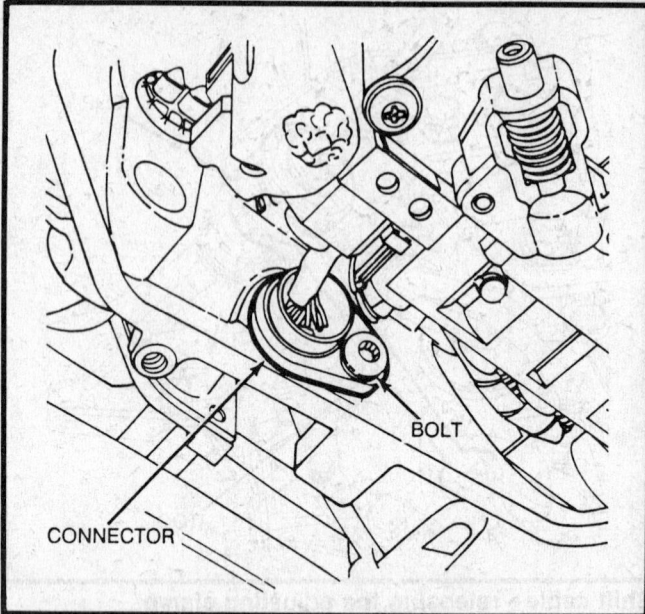

Removing solenoid harness connector

NOTE: Do not remove the 2 smaller bolts in the valve body.

12. Remove the valve body solenoid connector from the case.
13. Lower and remove the valve body.
14. Check the position of the 7 valve body baffles. If any are loose, install them in their correct locations using petroleum jelly to hold them in place.

NOTE: If any baffles fall out, make certain they are installed with the tabs facing the valve body.

15. Install a replacement O-ring on the solenoid connector and lubricate with transmission fluid.
16. Raise the valve body into position and push the solenoid connector into the transaxle case. Then align the valve body on the case and install the valve body bolts finger tight.
17. Tighten the valve body bolts to 46 inch lbs. (5 Nm) in the proper sequence.
18. Install the caliper on the manual valve, insert the metal end of the caliper first.
19. Swing the shift arm over into the channel in the caliper.
20. Install the bolt that attaches the solenoid harness connector to the case and tighten to 46 inch lbs. (5 Nm).
21. Connect the external wire harness to the solenoid connector. Squeeze the lock ring on the harness connector to install it. Listen for the connector to click into place.
22. Install new screen and gasket, if necessary hold gasket in place on screen with petroleum jelly.
23. Torque screen bolts to 46 inch lbs. (5 Nm).
24. Install new gasket on pan dry, do not use any type of sealer, make certain to replace all gasket mounting spacers.
25. Install the pan and torque bolts to 90 inch lbs. (10 Nm).
26. Install drain plug with new seal ring and torque to 177 inch lbs. (20 Nm).
27. Connect the shift cable rod to the transaxle shift lever.
28. Replace the underbody splash shield.
29. Lower the vehicle.
30. Remove dipstick and fill transaxle through the fill tube with Mercon® automatic transmission fluid to the proper level.
31. With selector in **P** start engine and idle. Apply parking brake. Do not race engine.
32. Move selector through all ranges and return to **P**. Check fluid level. Add transmission fluid as necessary to bring to proper level.

2. Remove the underbody splash shield bolts and remove the shield.
3. Place drain pan under transaxle oil pan and remove the drain plug.
4. Remove the oil pan bolts and remove pan.
5. Remove the filter from the valve body.
6. Squeeze the lock ring on the solenoid wire harness connector and remove the wire connector. Do not use pliers to squeeze the lock ring.
7. Remove the bolt attaching the valve body solenoid harness connector to the case.
8. Disconnect the shift rod from the shift lever.
9. Rotate the shift arm outward fully.
10. Disengage the caliper from the manual valve and remove the caliper and valve.
11. Remove the valve body attaching bolts.

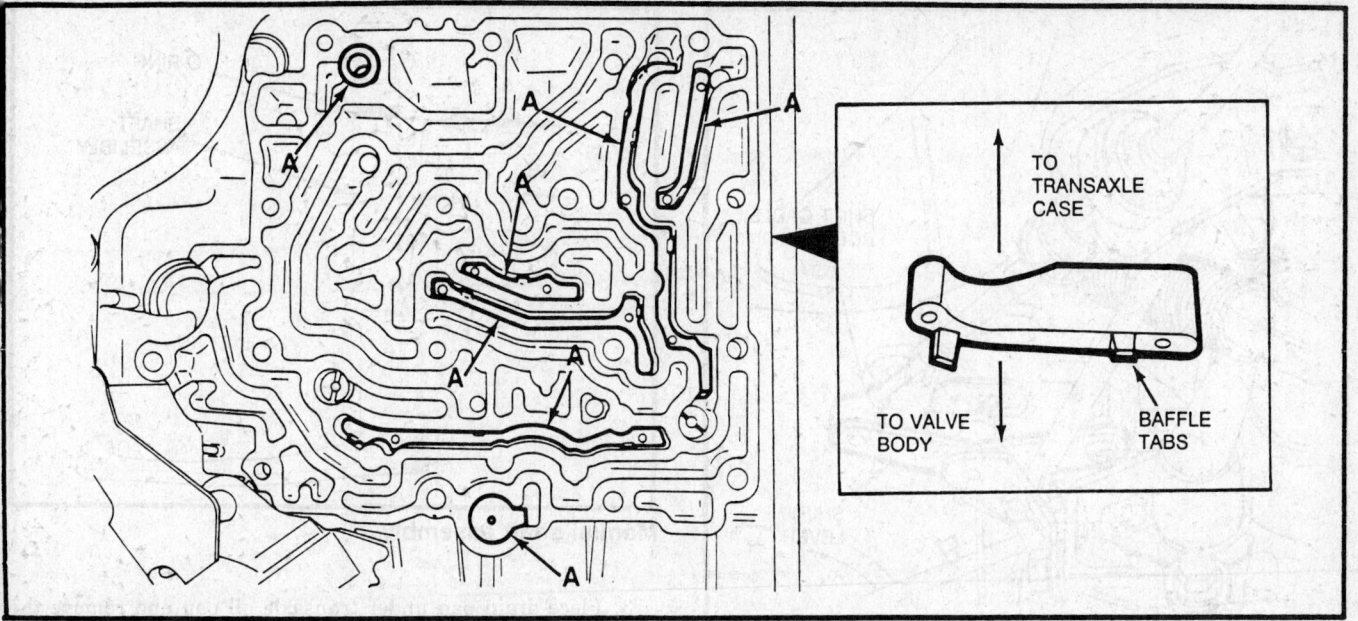

Baffle positions

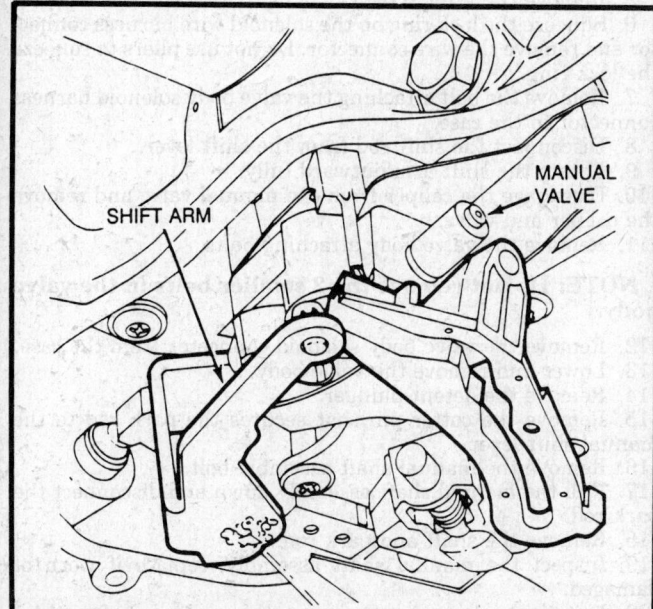

Shift rod and manual valve

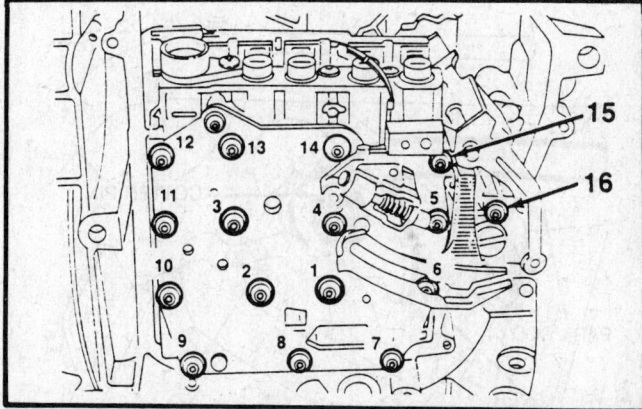

Valve body bolt locations and torque sequence

SHIFT CABLE

Removal and Installation

1. Disconnect the shift cable from the steering column shift arm, under the dash.
2. Squeeze lock tabs to release cable from the bracket.
3. Raise and support the vehicle safely.
4. Disconnect the cable from shift lever, under vehicle.
5. Squeeze lock tabs to release cable from the bracket.
6. Pull cable grommet out of the dash and remove the cable.
7. From under the vehicle, insert the cable into the drivers compartment through the cable grommet hole in the dash panel.

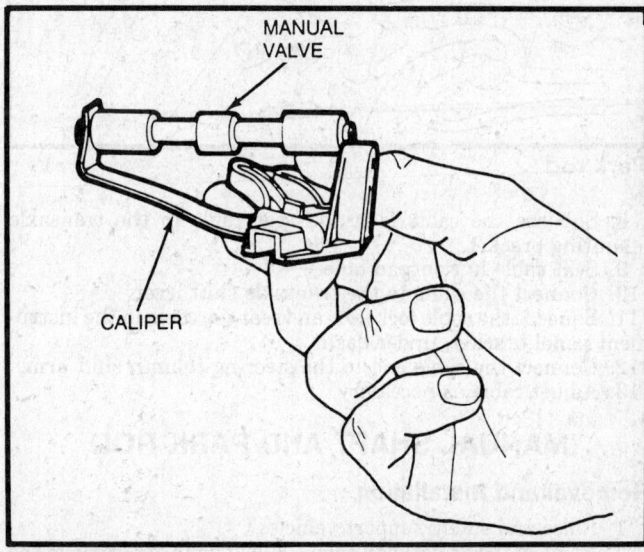

Installing the caliper onto the manual valve

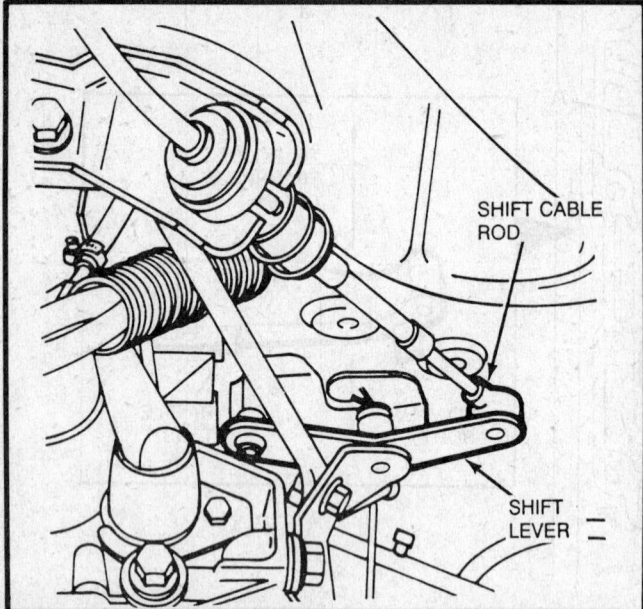

Connecting shift cable rod

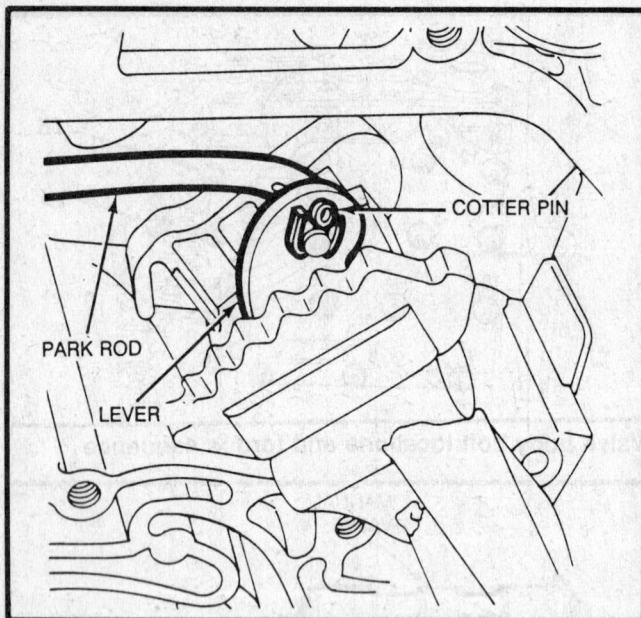

Park rod

8. Squeeze the cable lock and seat cable in the transaxle mounting bracket.
9. Seat cable in floorpan hole.
10. Connect the cable to the transaxle shift lever.
11. Squeeze the cable lock tabs and seat the cable in the instrument panel bracket, under dash.
12. Connect the cable end to the steering column shift arm.
13. Adjust cable as necessary.

MANUAL SHAFT AND PARK ROD

Removal and Installation

1. Raise and safely support vehicle.
2. Remove the underbody splash shield bolts and remove the shield.

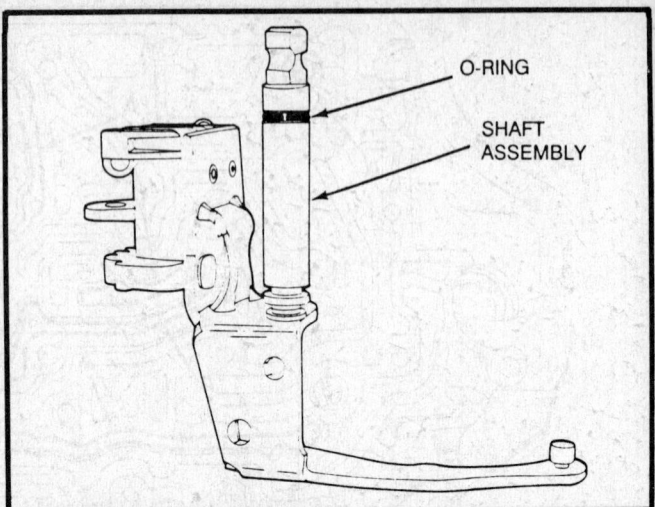

Manual shaft assembly

3. Place drain pan under transaxle oil pan and remove the drain plug.
4. Remove the oil pan bolts and remove pan.
5. Remove the filter screen.
6. Squeeze the lock ring on the solenoid wire harness connector and remove the wire connector. Do not use pliers to squeeze the lock ring.
7. Remove the bolt attaching the valve body solenoid harness connector to the case.
8. Disconnect the shift rod from the shift lever.
9. Rotate the shift arm outward fully.
10. Disengage the caliper from the manual valve and remove the caliper and valve.
11. Remove the valve body attaching bolts.

NOTE: Do not remove the 2 smaller bolts in the valve body.

12. Remove the valve body solenoid connector from the case.
13. Lower and remove the valve body.
14. Remove the detent plunger.
15. Remove the cotter pin that secures the park rod to the manual shift lever.
16. Remove the manual shaft assembly bolt.
17. Pull the manual shaft assembly down and disconnect the park rod.
18. Remove the shaft and park rod.
19. Inspect the manual shaft assembly, replace if worn of damaged.
20. Install a replacement O-ring on the manual shaft and lubricate with automatic transmission fluid.
21. Replace park rod if damaged or distorted and replace shaft bushing if damaged, cracked or worn.
22. Install the park rod in correct position.
23. Install the manual shaft assembly into the case and engage the park rod in the manual shaft lever.

NOTE: Take care not to damage the multi-function switch plunger buttons when installing the manual shaft assembly.

24. Install the retainer plate and position the plate in the manual shaft groove.
25. Install and tighten the retainer bolt to 80 inch lbs. (9 Nm).
26. Secure the park rod to the manual shaft lever with a replacement cotter pin.
27. Install a new dust seal on the manual shaft.
28. Install a new O-ring, lubricated with transmission fluid, on

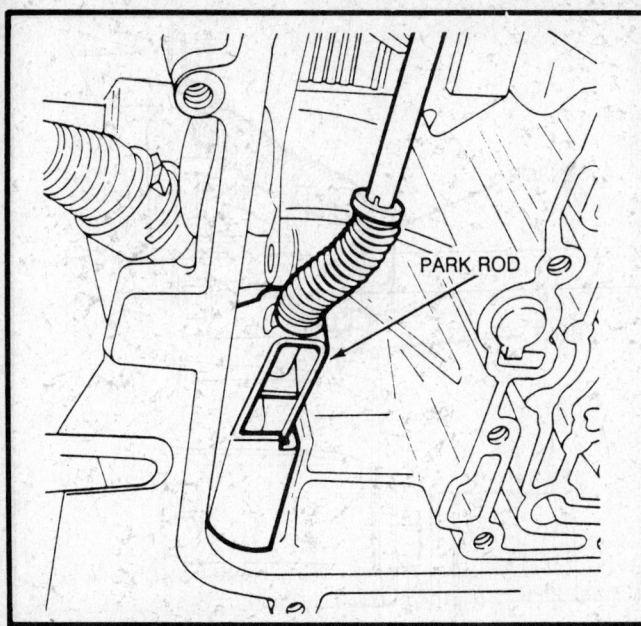

Park rod installation

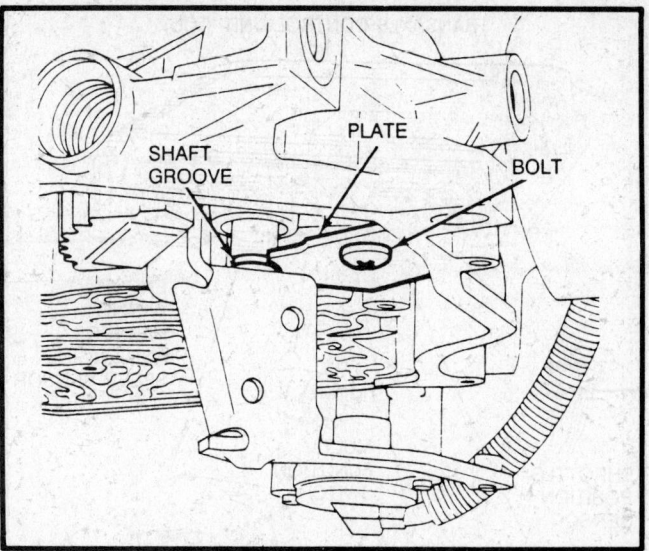

Positioning manual shaft groove

the detent plunger and install plunger. Tighten plunger to 150 inch lbs. (17 Nm).

29. Install the valve body and filter screen.

30. Check the position of the 7 valve body baffles. If any are loose, install them in their correct locations using petroleum to hold them in place.

NOTE: If any baffles fall out, make certain they are installed with the tabs facing the valve body.

31. Install a replacement O-ring on the solenoid connector and lubricate with transmission fluid.

32. Raise the valve body into position and push the solenoid connector into the transaxle case. Then align the valve body on the case and install the valve body bolts finger tight.

33. Tighten the valve body bolts to 46 inch lbs. (5 Nm) in the proper sequence.

34. Install the caliper on the manual valve, insert the metal end of the caliper first.

35. Swing the shift arm over into the channel in the caliper.

36. Install the bolt that attaches the solenoid harness connector to the case and tighten to 46 inch lbs. (5 Nm).

37. Connect the external wire harness to the solenoid connector. Squeeze the lock ring on the harness connector to install it. Listen for the connector to click into place.

38. Install new screen and gasket, if necessary hold gasket in place on screen with petroleum jelly.

39. Torque screen bolts to 46 inch lbs. (5 Nm).

40. Install new gasket on pan dry, do not use any type of sealer, make certain to replace all gasket mounting spacers.

41. Install the pan and torque bolts to 90 inch lbs. (10 Nm).

42. Install drain plug with new seal ring and torque to 177 inch lbs. (20 Nm).

43. Connect the shift cable rod to the transaxle shift lever.

44. Lower vehicle and replace the underbody splash shield.

45. Remove dipstick and fill transaxle through the fill tube with Mercon® automatic transmission fluid to the proper level.

46. With selector in **P** start engine and idle. Apply parking brake. Do not race engine.

47. Move selector through all ranges and return to **P**. Check fluid level. Add transmission fluid as necessary to bring to proper level.

MULTI-FUNCTION SWITCH

Removal and Installation

1. Disconnect the negative battery cable.
2. Raise the vehicle and support it safely.
3. Remove the switch attaching bolt and pull the multi-function switch out of the case.
4. Lower vehicle and remove windshield washer bottle.
5. Disconnect the multi-function switch harness from the transmission control unit.
6. Remove the old harness.
7. Install the new harness, making certain wiring is clear from any hot or moving parts.
8. Connect harness to transmission control unit and replace windshield washer bottle.
9. Install new O-ring on switch, lubricate with transmission fluid and install switch. Make certain the switch ground wire is on the attaching bolt.
10. Connect the negative battery cable.

SPEED SENSOR

Removal and Installation

TRANSMISSION CONTROL UNIT SENSOR

1. Disconnect the negative battery cable.
2. Disconnect the sensor electrical connector.
3. Remove the sensor bracket bolt and remove the sensor.
4. Install a new lubricated O-ring on the sensor and install the sensor.
5. Tighten the sensor mounting bracket bolt and connect the sensor electrical connector.
6. Connect the negative battery cable.

ROAD SENSOR

NOTE: The road speed sensor is the electronic pickup unit for the vehicle speedometer. It is mounted on the differential case just above the driveshaft.

1. Disconnect the negative battery cable.
2. Raise and support vehicle safely.
3. Remove the sensor bolt and pull sensor from the case.
4. Disconnect the sensor electrical connector.
5. Install a new lubricated O-ring on the sensor and reconnect the electrical connector.

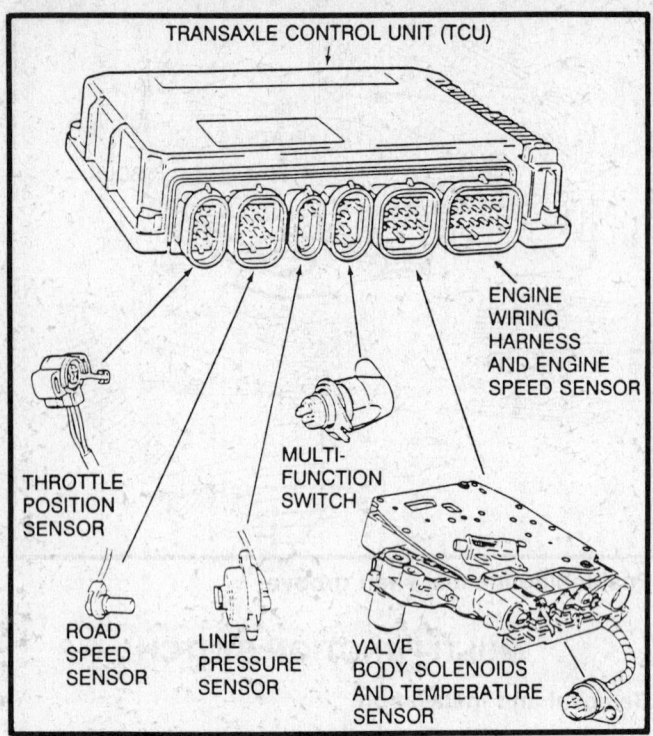

Transmission control unit (TCU)

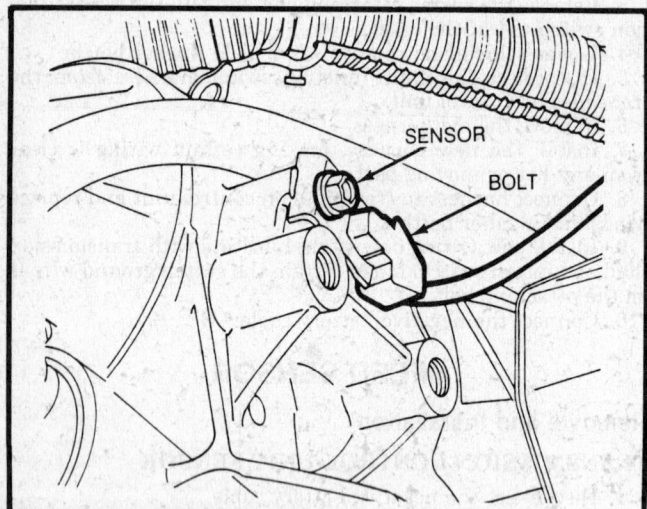

TCU speed sensor

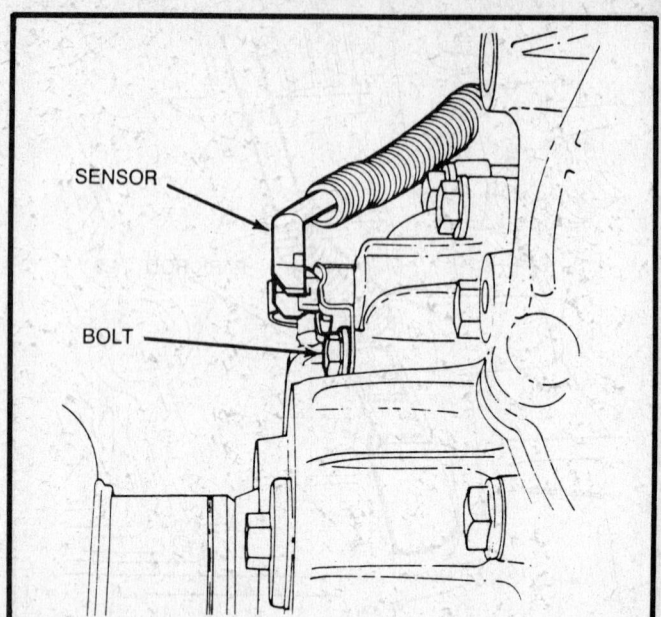

Road speed sensor

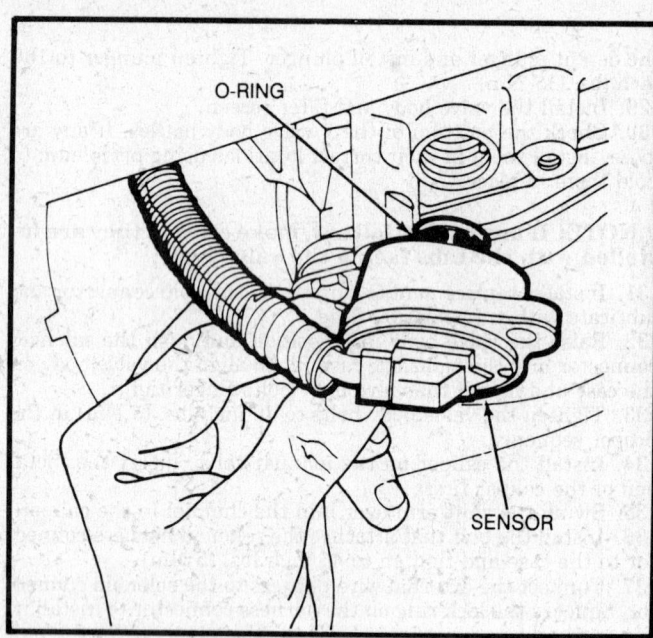

Line pressure sensor

6. Replace sensor and tighten the sensor mounting bolt.
7. Connect the negative battery cable.

LINE PRESSURE SENSOR

Removal and Installation

1. Disconnect the negative battery cable.
2. Raise and support vehicle safely.
3. Remove the underbody splash shield.
4. Remove the sensor attaching screws and pull sensor from the case.
5. Lower vehicle and remove the windshield washer bottle.
6. Disconnect the pressure line harness from the transmission control unit.

7. Remove sensor and harness from underneath vehicle.
8. Install new sensor and harness, making certain wiring is clear from any hot or moving parts.
9. Connect harness to transmission control unit and install windshield washer bottle.
10. Raise the vehicle and support safely, using a lubricated O-ring, install new sensor and tighten retaining screws.
11. Install underbody cover and lower vehicle.
12. Connect the negative battery cable.

TRANSMISSION CONTROL UNIT

Removal and Installation

1. Disconnect the negative battery cable.

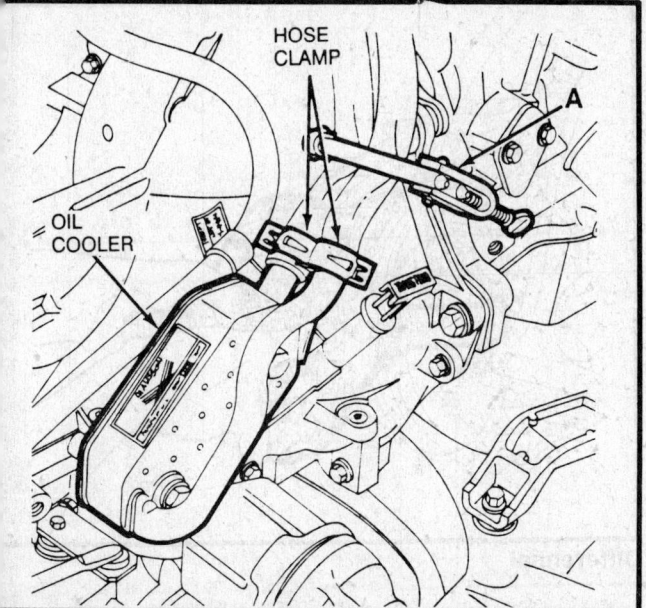

Oil cooler

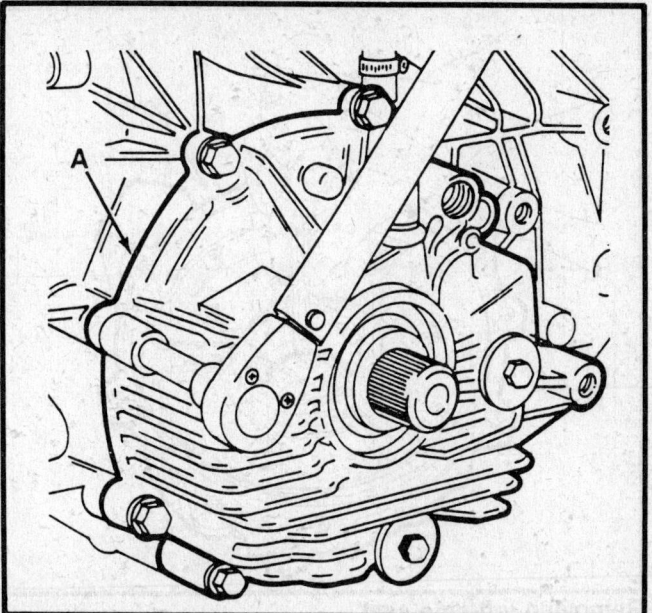

Differential cover

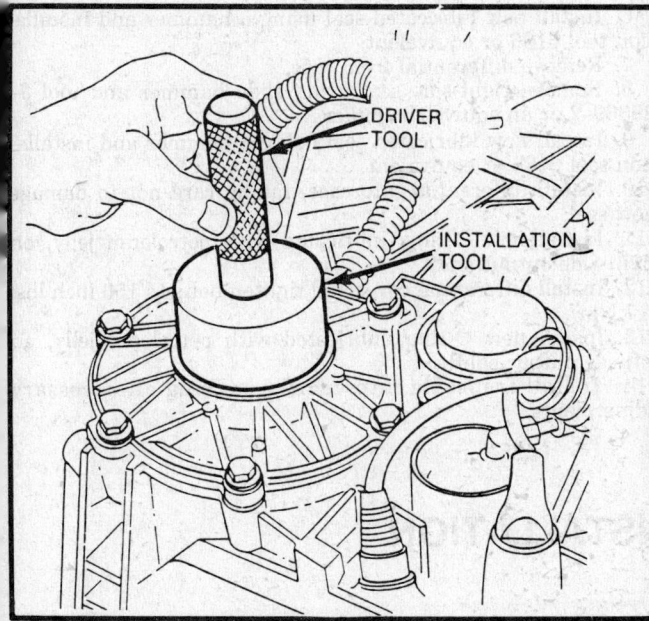

Rear plug replacement

2. Remove windshield washer bottle.
3. Unclip the strap that secures the transmission control unit to the inner fender panel.
4. Mark or tag the sensor harnesses for installation reference.
5. Disconnect the sensor harnesses from the transmission control unit.
6. Connect harnesses to new transmission control unit.
7. Replace the transmission control unit and windshield washer bottle.

OIL COOLER

Removal and Installation

1. Clamp off oil cooler hoses.

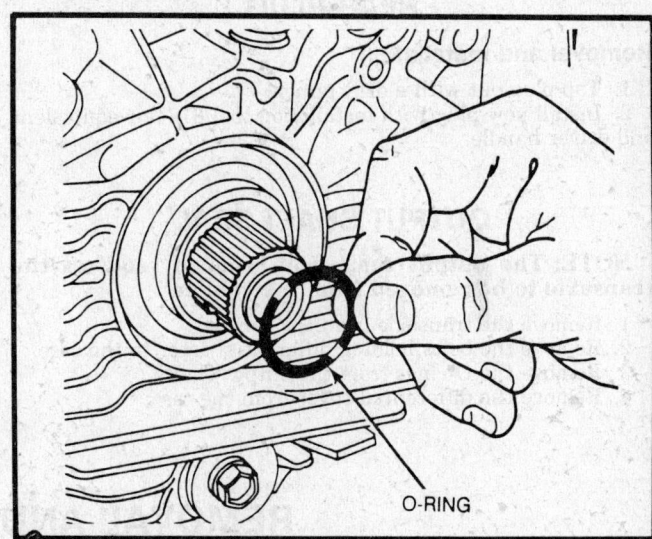

Removing output shaft O-ring

2. Remove the oil cooler bolts and remove cooler.
3. Install new O-rings on replacement cooler and new seals on cooler bolts.
4. Install cooler and torque bolts to 24 ft. lbs. (32 Nm).
5. Install oil cooler hoses and remove clamps.
6. Place hose clamps ends at a 6 o-clock position to avoid contacting the crossmember.
7. Check and add coolant as needed.

BREATHER VENT

Removal and Installation

1. Grip each vent base with pliers, twist and pull upward to remove it.
2. Unsnap cap off of new vent and start vent into case.
3. Tap vent into case with a hammer and small socket.
4. Snap cap back onto vent.

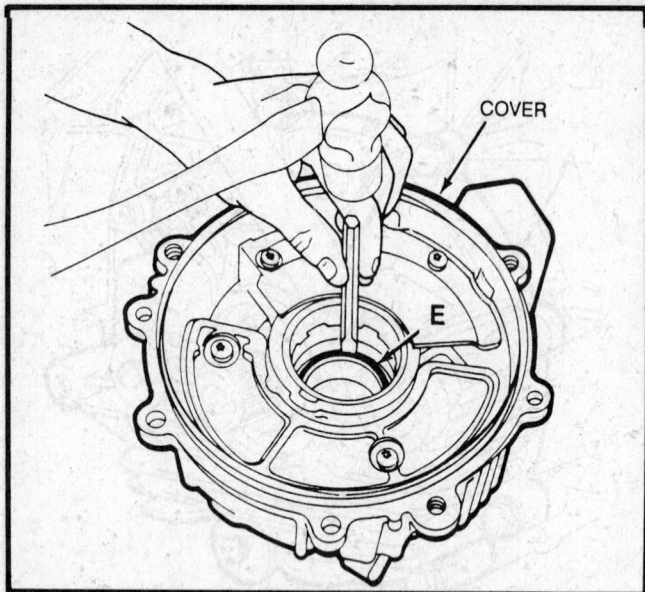

Removing left-side seal

REAR PLUG

Removal and Installation

1. Tap plug out with a drift punch.
2. Install new plug with installation tool 6184 or equivalent and driver handle.

OUTPUT SHAFT SEAL

NOTE: The output shaft seal removal requires the transaxle to be removed from the vehicle.

1. Remove the transaxle from the vehicle.
2. Remove the bolts holding differential cover to the case.
3. Remove the O-rings from the output shafts.
4. Remove the differential cover from the case.

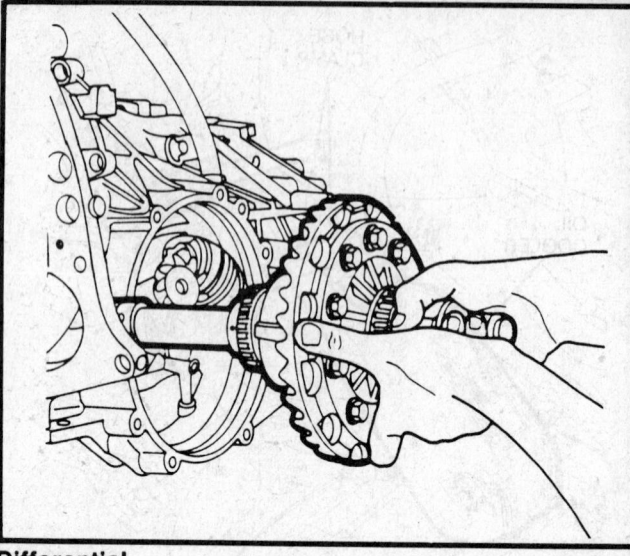

Differential

5. Remove the left-side shaft seal by tapping it out of the cover, using a hammer and drift.
6. Install new lubricated seal using a hammer and installation tool 6186 or equivalent.
7. Remove differential from case.
8. Remove right-side seal using slide hammer and tool J–29369–2 or an equivalent puller.
9. Install new lubricated seal using a hammer and installation tool 6185 or equivalent.
10. Install differential into case, taking care not to damage new seal.
11. Install new O-ring, lubricated with petroleum jelly, on right-side output shaft.
12. Install differential cover and tighten bolts to 150 inch lbs. (17 Nm).
13. Install new O-ring, lubricated with petroleum jelly, on leftside output shaft.
14. Install transaxle into vehicle, making all necessary adjustments.

REMOVAL AND INSTALLATION

TRANSAXLE REMOVAL

NOTE: Transaxle can be removed without removing the engine from the vehicle.

1. Disconnect the negative battery cable and all transaxle electrical connections.
2. Disconnect all the electrical connectors at the transmission control unit.

NOTE: Do not remove the sensors, these components will remain in place for transaxle removal.

3. Disconnect and plug transaxle cooler lines.
4. Remove the timing sensor.
5. Raise and safely support the vehicle.
6. Remove the upper strut bolt and only loosen the lower bolt. Tilt the steering knuckle outward.

NOTE: The atrut bolts are splined just under the bolt

head. Do not turn the bolt. Hold the bolt with a wrench and loosen the nuts as required.

7. Remove the underbody splash shield.
8. Remove drain plug and drain the transaxle. Replace plug when drained.
9. Remove the driveshaft retaining pin. Swing each rotor and steering knuckle outward and slide the driveshafts from the transaxle.
10. Remove the starter and heat shield.
11. Remove the converter housing covers. Remove the torque converter-to-driveplate bolts. Support the transaxle.
12. Remove the exhaust bracket.
13. Using a transmission jack, support the transaxle and remove the crossmember.
14. Disconnect the header pipes from the exhaust manifolds and the catalytic converter.
15. Disconnect the shift cable from the lever.
16. Remove the brace rod and the manual shift lever.

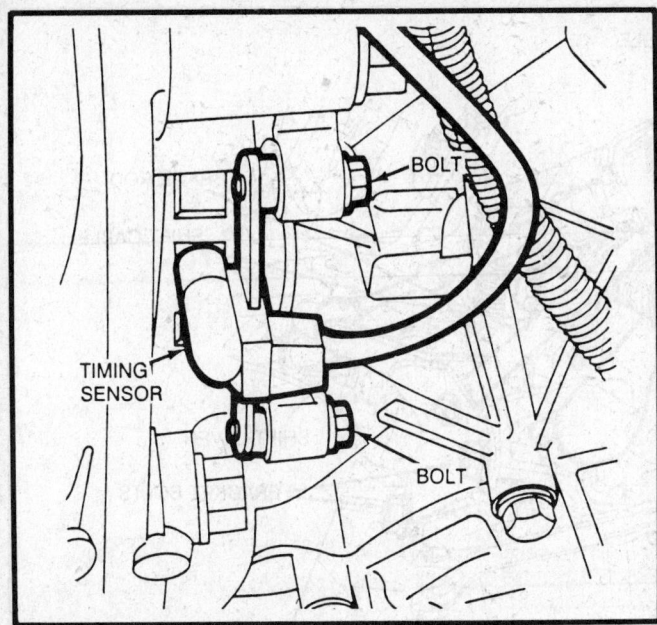

Engine timing sensor

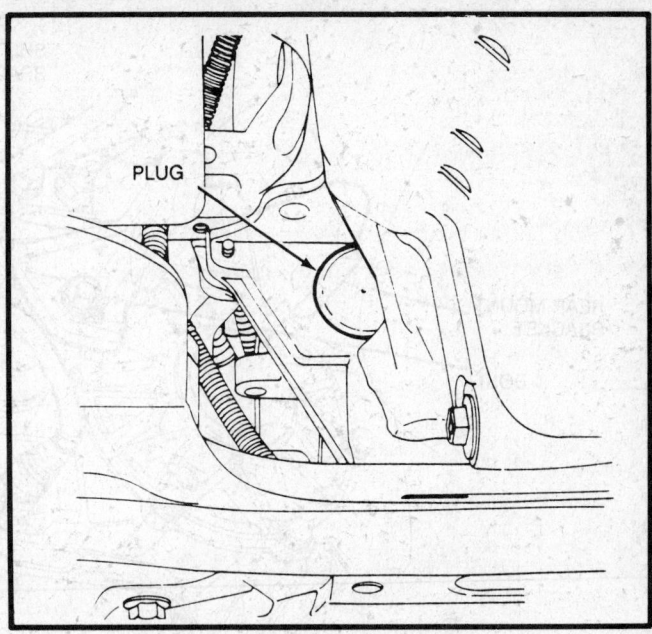

Converter housing access plug

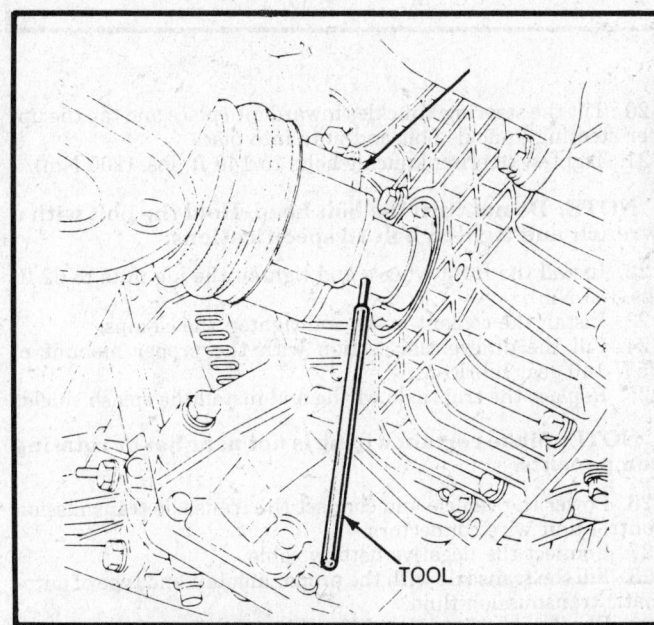

Removing driveshaft roll pin

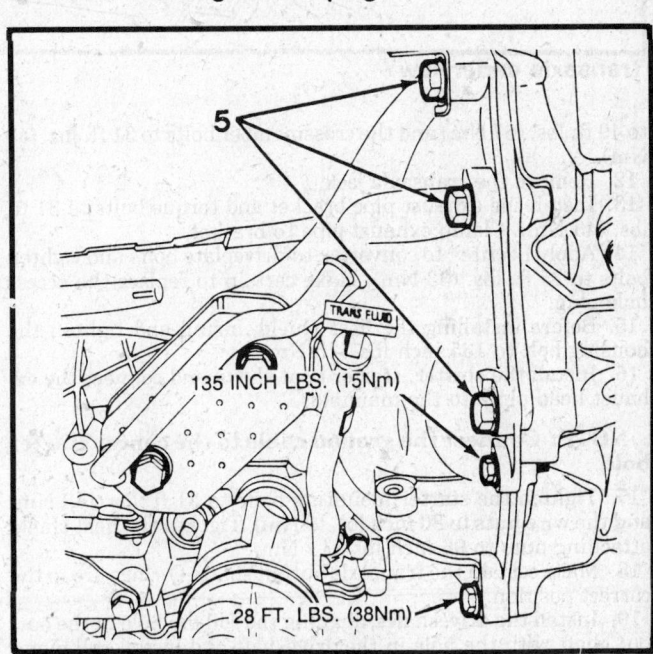

Transaxle-to-engine bolt torque

17. Remove the brace rod bracket.
18. Remove the transaxle-to-engine bolts and pull the transaxle rearward and lower from vehicle.

TRANSAXLE INSTALLATION

1. Position the transaxle to the engine. Install the transaxle-to-engine bolts and tighten top bolts to 55 ft. lbs. (75 Nm).
2. Tighten lower bolt to 28 ft. lbs. (38 Nm) and tighten small bolt to 135 inch lbs. (15 Nm).

NOTE: Make certain the dowel pins are seated in the converter housing before tightening any bolts. Also be sure the converter is aligned in the driveplate trigger wheel.

3. Check that the torque converter rotates freely.
4. Install rear mount bracket and torque to 29 ft. lbs. (40 Nm).
5. Install the shift lever bracket and torque bolts to 32 ft. lbs. (43 Nm).
6. Install the manual shift lever and torque the bolt to 110 inch lbs. (12.5 Nm).
7. Install the shift cable bracket to case. Do not tighten at this time.
8. Install the brace rod.
9. Tighten the shift cable bracket bolts to 32 ft. lbs. (43 Nm) and tighten the the brace rod bolts to 185 inch lbs. (21 Nm).
10. Snap the shift cable onto the shift lever.
11. Install the crossmember and tighten the rear mount bolt

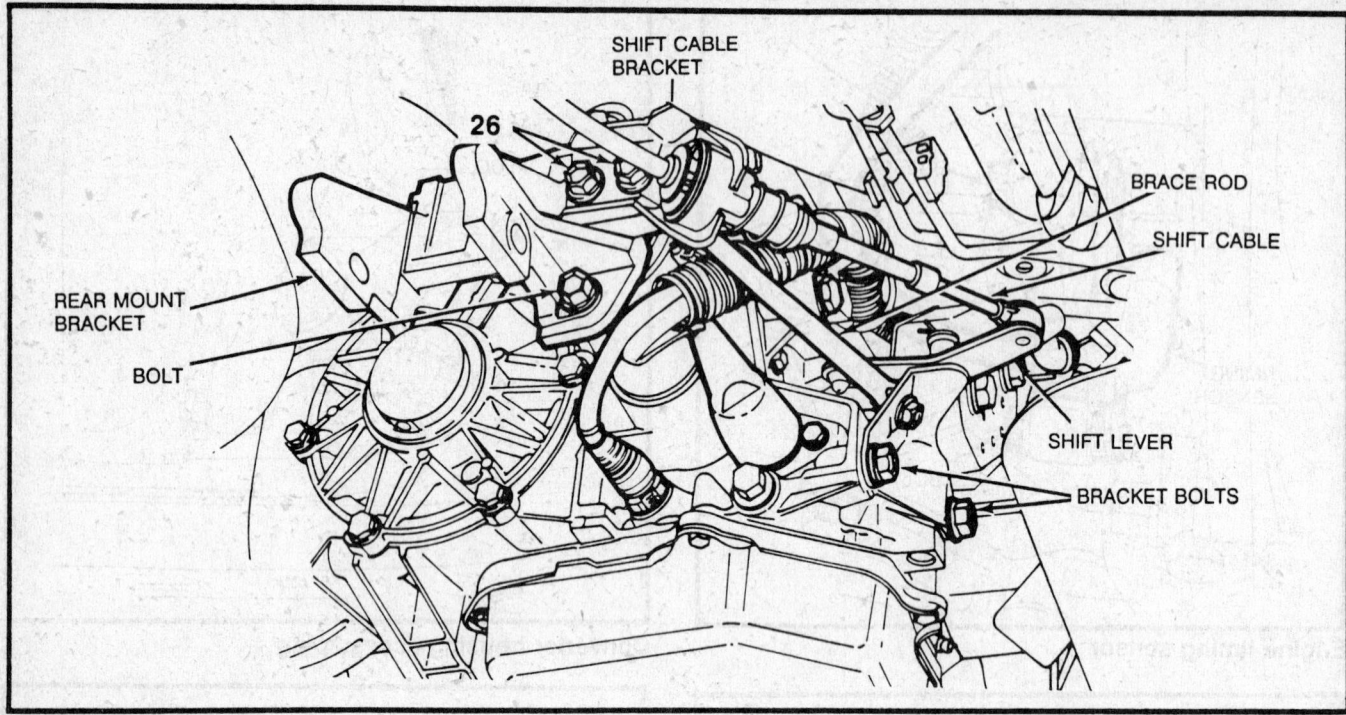

Transaxle underview

to 49 ft. lbs. (67 Nm) and the crossmember bolts to 31 ft. lbs. (43 Nm).

12. Remove the transaxle jack.

13. Install the exhaust pipe bracket and torque bolts to 31 ft. lbs. (43 Nm). Clamp exhaust pipe to bracket.

14. Apply Loctite® to converter-to-driveplate bolts and tighten bolts to 25 ft. lbs. (33 Nm). Make certain to replace the access hole plug.

15. Before installing the heat shield, install and tighten the housing bolt to 135 inch lbs. (15 Nm).

16. Install the starter, starter heat shield and connect the exhaust head pipes to the manifolds.

NOTE: Connect the ground cable to the center starter bolt.

17. Tighten the starter mounting bolts to 31 ft. lbs. (43 Nm) and the wire nuts to 80 inch lbs. (9 Nm). Tighten the heat shield attaching nuts to 96 inch lbs. (11 Nm).

18. Make certain the transaxle output shafts O-rings are in the correct position.

19. Install the driveshafts, aligning the roll pin hole in the output shaft with the hole in the driveshaft and install roll pins.

20. Tilt the steering knuckles inward into place and tap the upper steering knuckle bolt and nuts into place.

21. Tighten steering knuckle bolts to 148 ft. lbs. (200 Nm).

NOTE: Do not turn the bolt head. Hold the bolt with a wrench and tighten bolt to specifications.

22. Install the front wheels and tighten the lug nuts to 62 ft. lbs. (85 Nm).

23. Install the coolant hoses and tighten the clamps.

24. Fill the differential section with the proper amount of 75W-140 gear lubricant.

25. Replace the transaxle wiring and install the splash shield.

NOTE: Make certain wiring is not near hot or rotating components.

26. Lower the vehicle and connect the transaxle transmission control unit wire connectors.

27. Connect the negative battery cable.

28. Fill the transaxle with the proper amount and type of automatic transmission fluid.

29. Check and adjust the shift cable.

BENCH OVERHAUL

At the time of this publication transaxle overhaul information was not available from the manufacturer.

SPECIFICATIONS

E1 Clutch	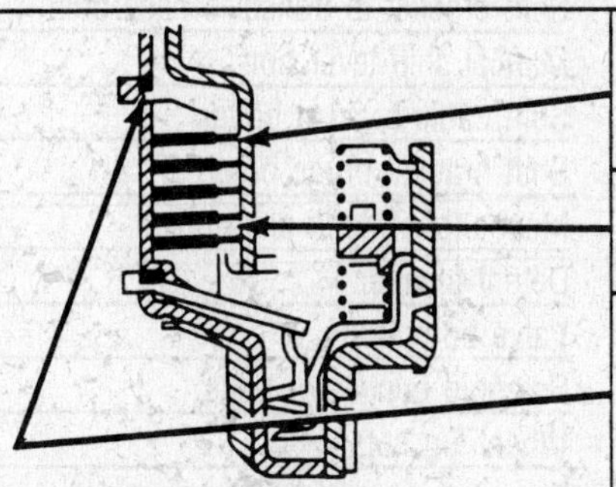	Lined Discs	4
		Intermediate flat discs	3
		End Play 1.4 - 1.6 mm (0.055 - 0.063 in) with spacer washer	
E2 Clutch	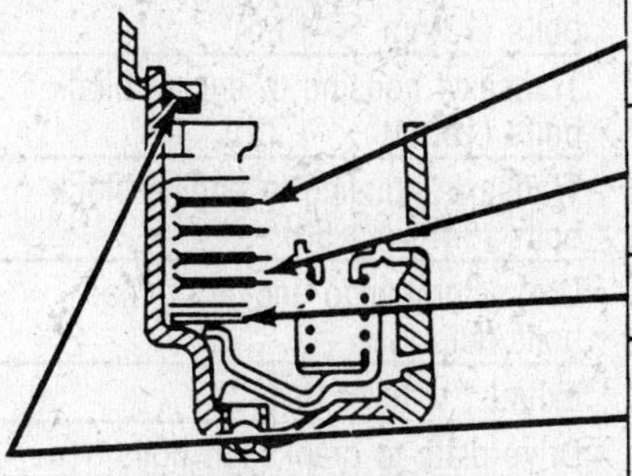	Lined discs	4
		Intermediate flat discs	5
		Spring disc	1
		End Play 1.0 - 1.4 mm (0.039 - 0.055 in) with spacer washer	
E3 Clutch	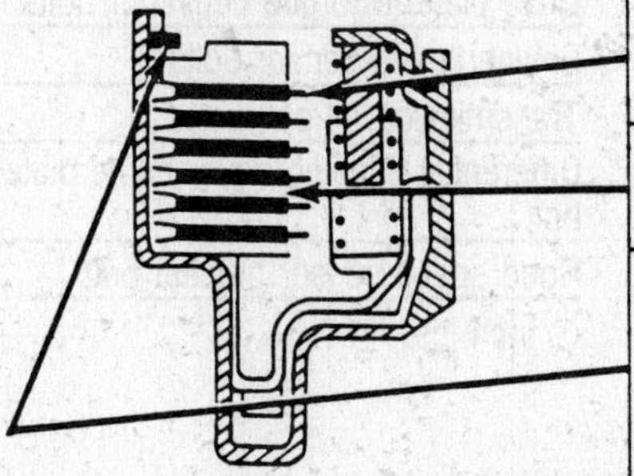	Lined discs	6
		Intermediate flat discs	6
		End Play 1.6 - 2.05 mm (0.063 - 0.081 in) with spacer washer	
F1 Brake	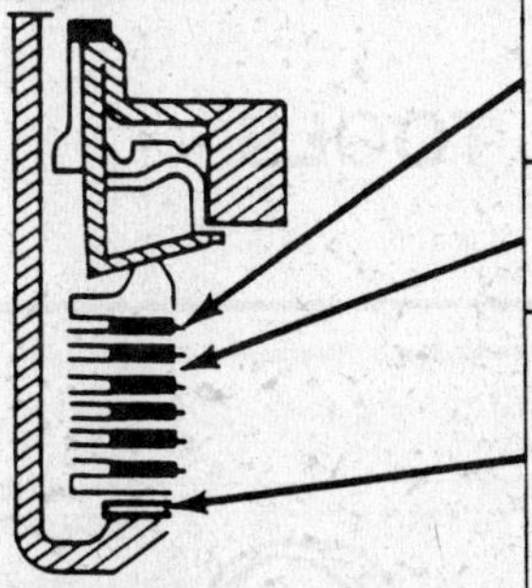	Lined discs	6
		Intermediate flat discs	6
		End Play 1.4 - 1.8 mm (0.055 - 0.070 in) with steel washer on housing side	
F2 Brake	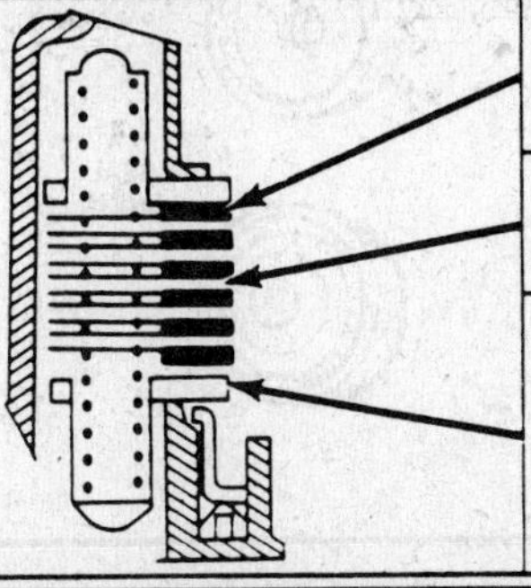	Lined discs	5
		Intermediate flat discs	4
		End Play 1.4 - 1.85 mm (0.055 - 0.073 in) with spacer plate on piston side	

TORQUE SPECIFICATIONS

Component	ft. lbs.	Nm
Differential housing drain full plugs	170–184①	19–21
Rear support bracket to transaxle case bolts	28–30	38–42
Starter shield nuts	90–102①	10–12
Rear support bracket to rear cushion bolt/nut	46–52	64–70
Exhaust pipe flange to manifold nuts	21–25	29–33
Starter wire harness nuts	75–85①	8.5–9.5
Exhaust pipe flange to catalytic cconverter nut and bolt	28–32	39–43
Starter attaching bolts	29–33	40–44
Oil cooler attaching bolts	22–26	30–34
Transmission oil pan drain plug	170–184①	19–21
Lower shock bracket nut	140–156	190–210
Rear cushion to rear crossmember nuts	22–26	30–34
Transaxle housing to engine block bolcks	52–58	71–79
Fill tube bracket to transaxle case bolt	142–158①	16–18
Starter to transaxle case bolts	29–33	41–44
Wiring harness clamp bolt	—	—
Oil screen retaining bolts	43–49①	4.5–5.5
TCU speed sensor barcket bolt	84–96①	9–11
Rear coverplate bolts	142–158①	16–18
Differential housing cover bolts	142–158①	16–18

Component	ft. lbs.	Nm
Shift bracket to transaxle case bolts	29–33	41–44
Manual shift lever bolt	96–124①	11–14
Shift cable bracket bolts	29–33	41–44
Shift bracket brace bolts	168–202①	19–22
Manual shaft lock plate bolt	84–96①	9–11
Detent plunger	170–184①	19–21
Valve body bolts	43–49①	4.5–5.5
Solenoid connector bolts	84–96①	9–11
Wheel lug nuts	59–65	81–89
Transaxle housing to engine block bolts (12mm × 1.25)	52–58	71–79
Transaxle housing to engine block bolts (10mm × 1.75)	26–30	35–41
Transaxle housing to engine block bolts (8m × 1.50)	152–168①	17–19
Crossmember to engine cradle bolts/nuts	29–33	41–44
Exhaust bracket bolts	29–33	41–44
Drive plate to crankshaft bolts	37–43 ±60°	51–57
Drive plate to torque converter bolts	23–27	31–35
Engine timing sensor bolts	68–76①	7.5–8.5
Transmission oil pan bolts	84–96①	9–11
Differential housing cover baffle plate bolt	84–96①	9–11
Road speed sensor bracket bolt	84–96①	9–11

① inch lbs.

SPECIAL TOOLS

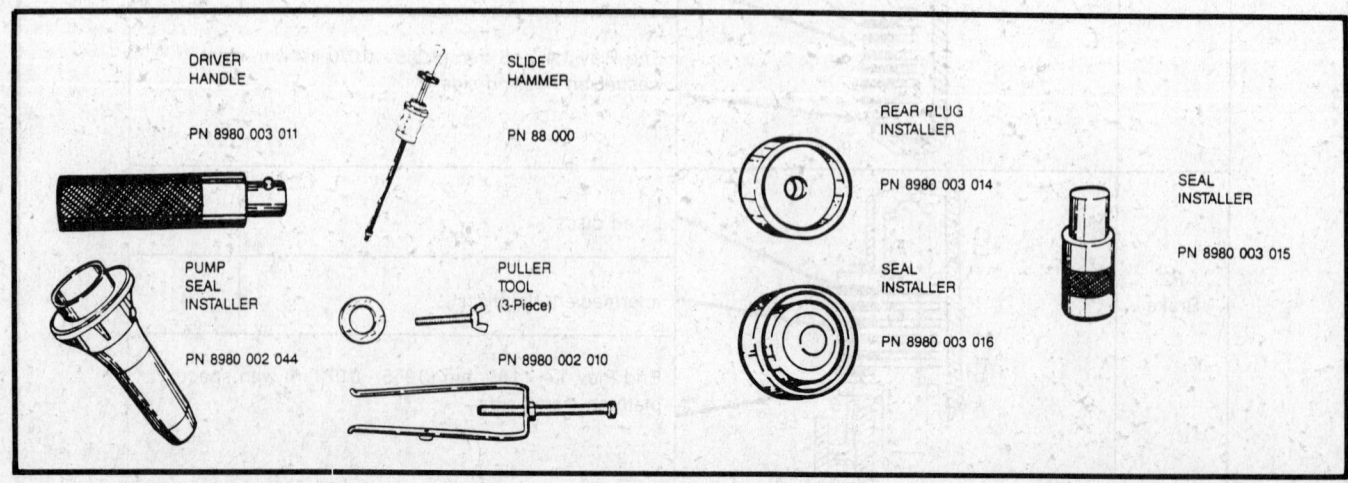

DRIVER HANDLE
PN 8980 003 011

SLIDE HAMMER
PN 88 000

REAR PLUG INSTALLER
PN 8980 003 014

SEAL INSTALLER
PN 8980 003 015

PUMP SEAL INSTALLER
PN 8980 002 044

PULLER TOOL (3-Piece)
PN 8980 002 010

SEAL INSTALLER
PN 8980 003 016

Section 3

A604 Transaxle
Chrysler Corp.

APPLICATION

1989

Acclaim, Spirit LE, Dynasty, Dynasty LE
New Yorker, New Yorker Landau,
Voyager LE, Grand Voyager SE,
Grand Voyager LE, Caravan LE,
Grand Caravan SE, Grand Caravan LE

GENERAL DESCRIPTION

Transaxle and Converter Indentification

TRANSAXLE

The A-604 Ultradrive electronic 4-speed FWD transaxle (transaxle assembly. No. 4471895) makes use of fully-adaptive controls. Adaptive controls are those which perform their functions based on real-time feedback sensor information, just as is done by electronic antilock brake controls. Although the transaxle is conventional in that it uses hydraulically-applied clutches to shift a planetary geartrain, its use of electronics to control virtually all functions is unique. The overall top gear ratio in overdrive is 2.36 and is equipped in several Chrysler models with the 3.0L V6 engine.

Operation

The transaxle provides forward ratios of 2.84, 1.57, 1.00, and 0.69 with torque converter lockup available in 2nd, direct, or overdrive gear; the Reverse ratio is 2.21. The shift lever is conventional with 6 positions: **P, R, N, OD, D,** and **L**. When in **OD** is selected, the transaxle shifts normally through all 4 speeds with lockup in overdrive; this position is recommended for most driving. The **D** position is tailored for use in hilly or mountainous driving. When **D** is selected, the transaxle uses only 1st, 2nd, and direct gears with 2-direct shift delayed to 40 mph or greater. When operating in **D** or **L** positions torque converter lockup occurs in direct gear for improved transaxle cooling when towing trailers and steep grades. If high engine coolant temperature occurs, the torque converter will also lock up in 2nd gear. The **L** position provides maximum engine braking for descending steep grades. Unlike most current transaxles, upshifts are provided to 2nd or direct at peak engine speeds if the accelerator is depressed. This provides engine over-speed protection and maximum performance.

CONVERTER

The converter is a welded unit and cannot be disassembled. The torque converter is a fluid drive coupling between the engine and transaxle. It is designed to slip at low speeds, such as when the engine is idling. As engine speed increases, the torque converter will engage the engine to the transmission. There is also a hydraulically controlled mechanical clutch inside the torque converter. This clutch is controlled by the electronic control module (ECM).

Electronic Controls

SOLENOIDS

Since the solenoid valves perform virtually all control functions, these valves must be extremely durable and tolerant of normal dirt particles. For that reason hardened-steel poppet and ball

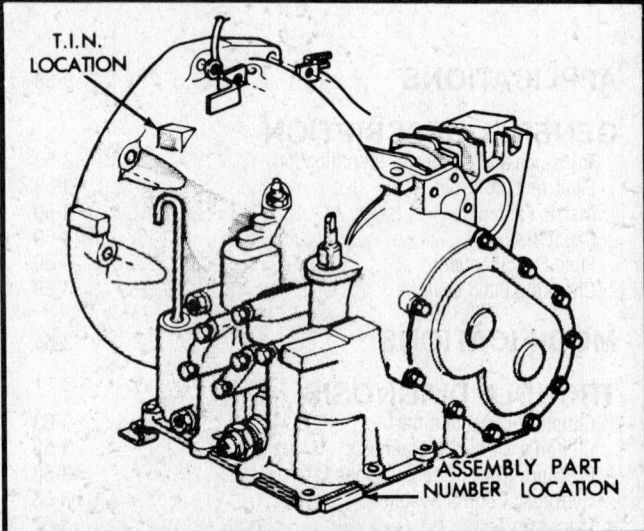

Transaxle Indentification Number (TIN) location

valves are used. These are free from any close operating clearances, and the solenoids operate the valves directly without any intermediate element. Direct operation means that these units must have very high output so that they can close against the sizeable flow areas and high line pressures. Fast response is also required to meet the control requirements.

Two of the solenoids are normally-venting and 2 are normally-applying; this was done to provide a default mode of operation. With no electrical power, the transaxle provides 2nd gear in **OD, D,** or **L** shift lever positions, neutral in **N**, reverse in **R**, and park in **P**. The choice of 2nd gear was made to provide adequate breakaway performance while still accommodating highway speeds.

SENSORS

Other electrical components include: 3 pressure switches to identify solenoid application, 2 speed sensors to read input (torque converter turbine) and output (parking sprag) speeds, and position switches to indicate the manual shift lever position. The pressure switches are incorporated in an assembly with the solenoids. Engine speed, throttle position, temperature, etc., are also observed. Some of these signals are read directly from the engine control sensors; others are read from a C^2D multiplex circuit with the engine controller.

ELECTRONICS

The control electronic unit is located underhood in a potted, diecast aluminum housing with a sealed, 60-way connector.

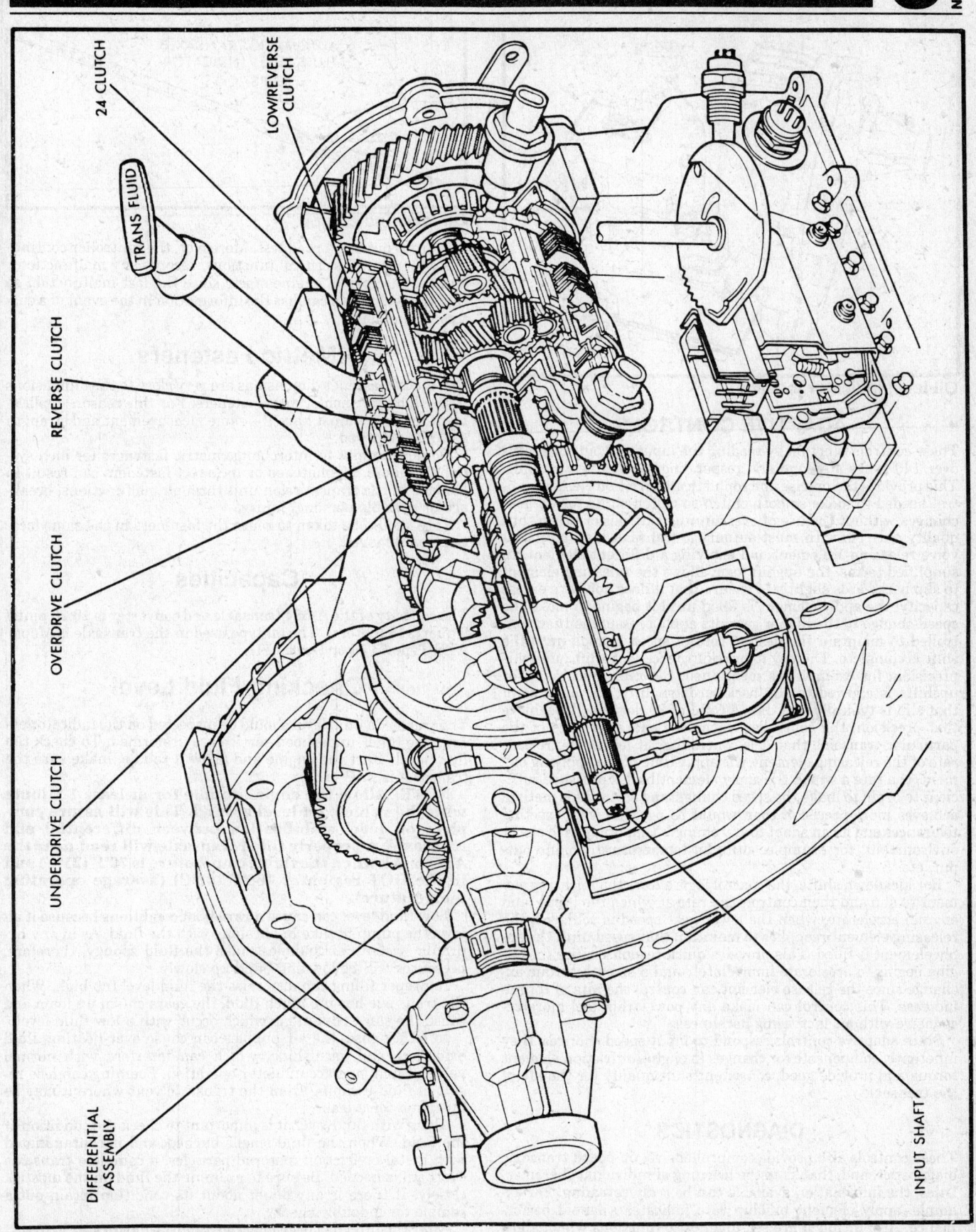

24 CLUTCH

LOW/REVERSE CLUTCH

TRANS FLUID

REVERSE CLUTCH

OVERDRIVE CLUTCH

UNDERDRIVE CLUTCH

DIFFERENTIAL ASSEMBLY

INPUT SHAFT

A604 transaxle cut-away view

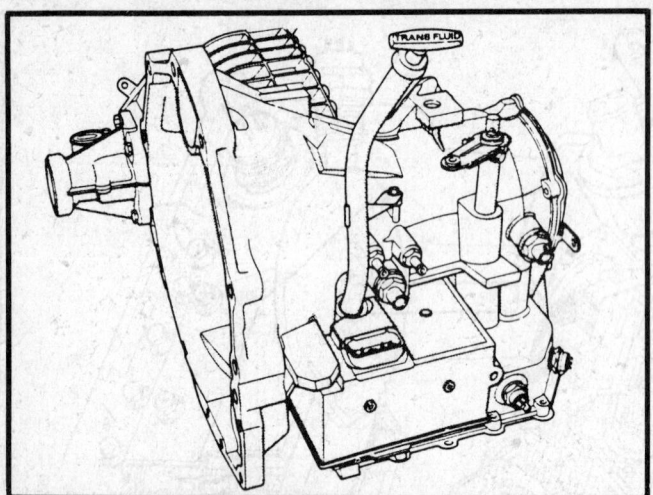

Oil level indicator location

ADAPTIVE CONTROLS

These controls function by reading the input and output speeds over 140 times a second and responding to each new reading. This provides the precise and sophisticated friction element control needed to make smooth clutch-to-clutch shifts for all gear changes without the use of overrunning clutches or other shift quality aids. As with most automatic transaxles, all shifts involve releasing 1 element and applying a different element. In simplified terms, the upshift logic allows the releasing element to slip backwards slightly to ensure that it does not have excess capacity; the apply element is filled until it begins to make the speed change to the higher gear; its apply pressure is then controlled to maintain the desired rate of speed change until the shift is complete. The key to providing excellent shift quality is precision; for example, as mentioned, the release element for upshifts is allowed to slip backwards slightly; the amount of that slip is typically less than a total of 20 degrees. To achieve that precision, the controller learns the characteristics of the particular transaxle that it is controlling; it learns the release rate of the releasing element, the apply time of the applying element, the rate a which the apply element builds pressure sufficient to begin to make the speed change, and so on. This method achieves more precision than would be possible with exacting tolerances and it can adapt to any changes that occur with age or environment, for example, altitude, temperature, engine output, etc.

For kickdown shifts, the control logic allows the releasing element to slip and then controls the rate at which the input (and engine) accelerate; when the lower gear speed is achieved, the releasing element reapplies to maintain that speed until the apply element is filled. This provides quick response since the engine begins to accelerate immediately and a smooth torque exchange since the release element can control the rate of torque increase. This control can make any powertrain feel more responsive without increasing harshness.

Since adaptive controls respond to input speed changes, they inherently compensate for changes in engine or friction element torque and provide good, consistent shift quality for the life of the transaxle.

DIAGNOSTICS

These controls also provide comprehensive, on-board transaxle diagnostics, and, thanks to the learning of individual characteristics, the information available can be truly revealing. For example, apply element buildup rate indicates solenoid performance. Also included are self-diagnostic functions which allow the technician to test the integrity of the electronic controls

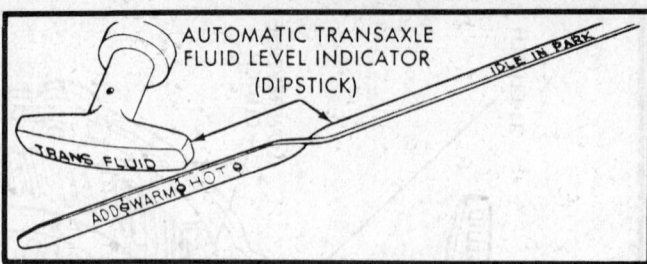

Oil level indicator

without requiring a road test. Moreover, the controller continuously monitors its critical functions, records any malfunctions, and the number of engine starts since the last malfunction so that the technician can use the information in the event of a customer complaint.

Metric Fasteners

The metric fastener dimensions are very close to the dimensions of the familiar inch system fasteners. For this reason, replacement fasteners must have the same measurement and strength as those removed.

Do not attempt to interchange metric fasteners for inch system fasteners. Mismatched or incorrect fasteners can result in damage to the transmission unit through malfunctions, breakage or possible personal injury.

Care should be taken to reuse the fasteners in the same locations as removed.

Capacities

The capacity of the A-604 transaxle and converter is 18.25 pints/9 quarts (8.6 liters). The oil type used in the transaxle is Mopar ATF Type 7176 or Dexron®II.

Checking Fluid Level

The transaxle fluid level should be inspected on the indicator every time other underhood service are preformed. To check the fluid level, start the engine and allow it to idle, make sure the transaxle is in **P** or **N**.

NOTE: Allow the engine to idle for at least 1 minute with the vehicle on level ground. This will assure complete oil level stabilization between differential and transaxle. A properly filled transaxle will read near the ADD mark when the fluid temperature is 70°F (21°C) and in the HOT region at 180°F (82°C) (average operating temperature).

Low fluid level can cause a variety of conditions because it allows the pump to take in air along with the fluid. As in any hydraulic system, air bubbles make the fluid spongy, therefore, pressures will be low and build up slowly.

Improper filling can also raise the fluid level too high. When the transaxle has too much fluid, the gears churn up foam and cause the same conditions which occur with a low fluid level.

In either case, the air bubbles can cause over-heating, fluid oxidation, and varnishing, which can interfere with normal valve, clutch, and accumulator operation. Foaming can also result in fluid escaping from the transaxle vent where it may be mistaken for a leak.

Along with fluid level, it is important to check the condition of the fluid. When the fluid smells burned, and is contaminated with metal or friction material particles, a complete transaxle overhaul is needed. Be sure to examine the fluid on the dipstick closely. If there is any doubt about its condition, drain out a sample for a double check.

After the fluid has been checked, seat the dipstick fully to seal out water and dirt.

TRANSAXLE MODIFICATIONS

Momentary Deceleration, Default to Second Gear (Limp-In) Mode or Excessive Clutch Slippage During 3–4 Upshift

On some 1989 Dynasty, New Yorker, Landau, Caravan and Voyager vehicles equipped with A604 transaxle, a default to 2nd gear (limp-in) mode or excessive clutch slippage during a 3–4 upshift are complaints that may be caused by reaction shaft support seal ring hang-up. Dirt, debris and imperfections in the area of the reaction shaft support seal rings can cause this condition. Hang-up of this seal ring may cause underdrive and/or overdrive clutch failures.

An improperly functioning seal ring can direct hydraulic pressure between the overdrive and underdrive clutches during a 3–4 upshift. Under some conditions, this may result in momentary vehicle deceleration and/or clutch drag when the clutch normally should be venting hydraulic fluid.

REPAIR PROCEDURES

CAUTION: **Do not perform this procedure unless the vehicle has 3-4 shift problems as described.**

Fault codes other than 46 and 39 must be diagnosed using regular diagnostic tests, starting with Test #1.

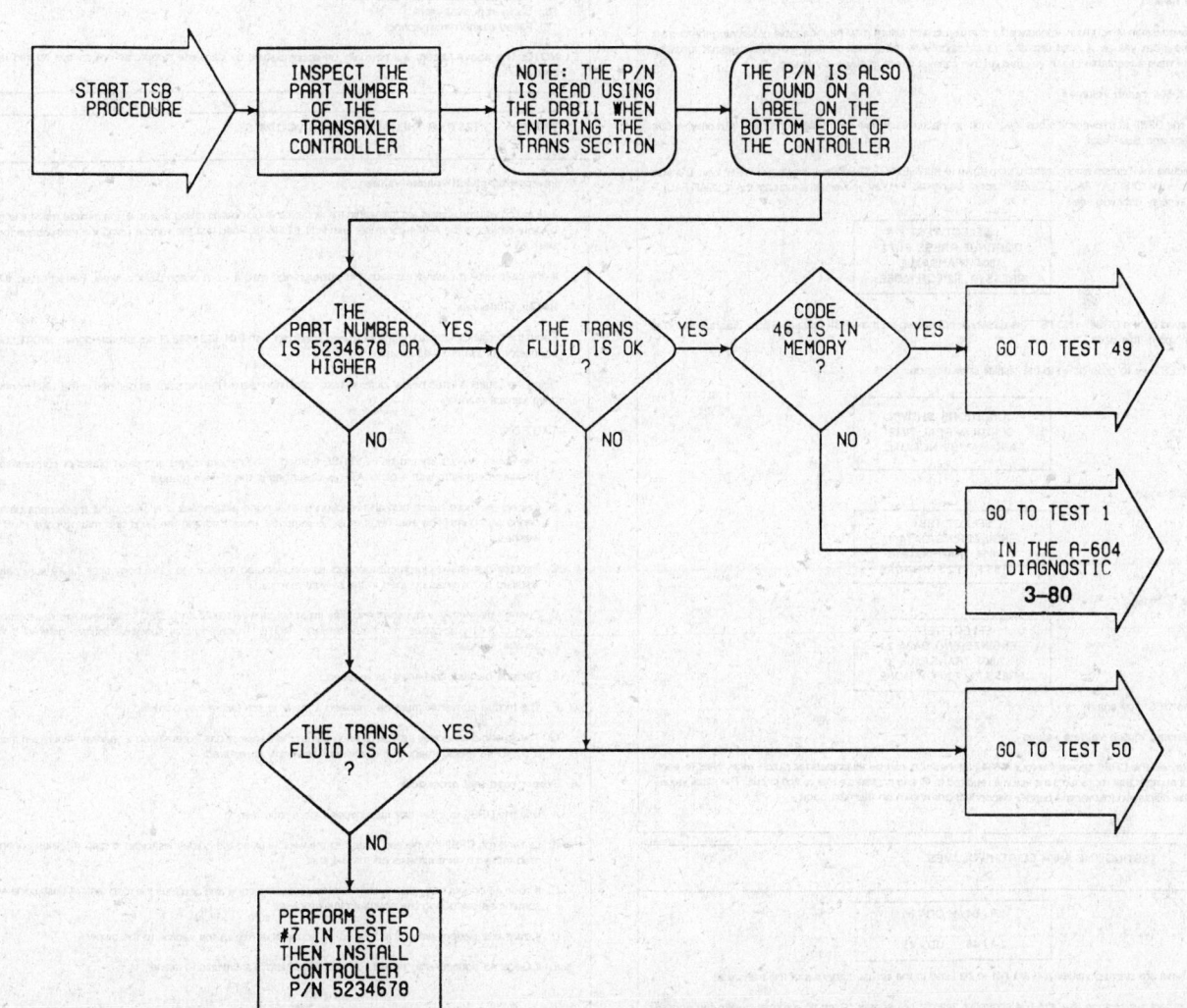

TEST 49 | CODE 46 TEST PROCEDURE

Code 46 can only be generated by an upgraded transaxle controller P/N 5234678 or later. If you find code 46 in memory, the vehicle already has the upgrade - DO NOT REPLACE THE CONTROLLER.

Code 46 is primarily set in memory after the controller has made 3 unsuccessful attempts at a proper 3-4 upshift. Controller logic then prevents the transaxle from any further upshift attempts and causes it to remain in third gear until downshifts into first or second gears have been obtained.

Code 46 will not cause a limp-in (default to second) condition.

Faulty connections at the Turbine or Output speed sensors can result in aborted 3-4 upshifts and set code 46 in memory. Carefully inspect the Turbine and Output speed sensor connectors for anything that could cause an intermittent connection to the sensor (i.e. spread, bent or misaligned terminals). If the connectors are OK, proceed with the road test below.

Road Test

Road test to confirm that code 46 can be repeated by using the following guidelines:

A. Use the DRBII to clear any fault codes before road testing.

B. Leaving the DRBII connected, road test the vehicle using the guidelines found in step #3 of Test 50, then continue to road test with an emphasis on the 3-4 shift.

C. If code 46 occurs early during the road test, erase the code and continue the road test. (A false code 46 can sometimes set during the shift learning process.)

D. If transaxle performance is judged to be acceptable, return the vehicle to the owner.

E. If code 46 continues to repeat, go to Test 50 Step 7.

TEST 50 | TESTING THE A-604 CLUTCH VOLUMES

Transaxles that have 3-4 shift problems could have normal or slightly discolored fluid but no serious clutch distress. The DRBII diagnostic tool can be used to help determine the amount of clutch wear in all A-604 clutches with the exception of reverse.

NOTE: A transmission which has experienced a sudden clutch failure may be incapable of learning the correct clutch volume index values. A road test of a transmission with this condition may exhibit an upshift runaway condition, but have acceptable clutch volumes. In this case, a clutch is obviously failing.

1. Finding A-604 clutch volumes

Connect the DRBII to the vehicle's bus diagnostic connector as shown in Transaxle Test #1. (Entering A-604 Diagnostics and Bus Tests)

After selecting the Transmission Section, drop down to the "SELECT TEST" level using the "YES" key. The first select test is the "DISPLAY FAULT CODES" display. Using the "F1" key, move to the left past the "CLEAR FAULT CODES" display until you see . . .

```
      SELECT TEST
 CONTINUE PRESS F1/F2
     A604  TRANSAXLE
  PRESS F1, F2 FOR MORE
```

. . . displayed on the DRBII. (NOTE: This display is not shown on the DRBII functional flow diagram found at the beginning of this book.)

Use the "YES" key to drop down to the display shown below.

```
  CONDITIONS SHOWN
 OCCUR IN REAL TIME
 AND MAY BE NORMAL
```

Press 'YES' again . . .

```
      SELECT TEST
  ENGINEERING DATA 1
     A604  TRANSAXLE
  PRESS F1, F2 FOR MORE
```

Press the 'F2' key . . .

```
      SELECT TEST
  ENGINEERING DATA 2
     A604  TRANSAXLE
  PRESS F1, F2 FOR MORE
```

Press the "YES" key again.

2. Understanding clutch volume values

The display on the DRBII shows the four A-604 clutches that can be examined for clutch wear. Next to each clutch is a number that represents the volume required to fill and pressurize that clutch circuit. The initial values that will be displayed following a battery disconnect are shown on the next page.

TEST 50 | TESTING THE A-604 CLUTCH VOLUMES

LR - 64	OD - 89
2-4 - 48	UD - 45

NOTE: These are start up values and are not to be used in the actual diagnosis of the transaxle.

These numbers will change as the A-604 controller "learns" or updates clutch fill volumes due to the normal usage and wear that occurs during the life of the transaxle.

New clutch discs will have maximum friction material present and tend to take less fluid to fill and apply - hence the value for these clutch circuits is smaller. As the clutch ages, the clutch clearance increases, increasing the amount of oil required to fill and apply the clutch - hence the value for these clutch circuits will be larger.

NOTE: To obtain useful clutch information on a vehicle which may have recently had its battery disconnected, the transaxle controller must be allowed to "re-learn" each clutch circuit.

3. "Teaching" clutch volume values to the A-604 controller

A. The transaxle fluid level must be properly set.
B. The transaxle must be at normal operating temperatures.
C. At least three constant throttle upshifts at approximately half throttle from a standing start through the 2-3 upshift must be made. (These learn the overdrive and 2-4 clutch)
D. At least three heavy throttle downshifts to 1st at 15 mph must be made. (These learn the low/reverse clutch)
E. At least three part throttle 4-3 downshifts between 40 and 50 mph must be made. (These learn the underdrive clutch.

4. Acceptable transaxle clutch volume value guidelines

The range of clutch volume values which have been found to be within normal wear limits are shown below:

LR - 35 TO 85	OD - 75 TO 135
2-4 - 20 TO 77	UD - 24 TO 70

5. Other factors affecting clutch volume values

1. Incorrect fluid level
2. High transaxle temperature level
3. Restricted clutch feed circuit
4. Restricted solenoid feed circuit
5. Valve body leakage
6. Leaky lip seals
7. Leaky seal rings
8. Case porosity
9. Circuit leak in pump housing
10. Circuit leak in reaction shaft support
11. Damaged accumulator seal ring
12. Clogged oil filter
13. Aerated fluid
14. Faulty oil pump
15. Insufficient clutch pack clearance
16. Sticky regulator valve
17. Failed clutch return spring

NOTE: The above factors will normally be accompanied by transaxle symptoms not always related to this procedure.

TEST 50 | TESTING THE A-604 CLUTCH VOLUMES

6. Interpreting clutch volume values

If all clutch volume values are still within the acceptable guidelines found in step 4, the vehicle may be serviced by only replacing the A-604 controller with P/N 5234678. Road test the vehicle using the instructions found in step #8.

If any clutch volume value exceeds the upper range limit, a worn clutch pack is likely. Perform step #7.

7. Repair guidelines

Begin the repair by upgrading the transaxle controller with P/N 5234678 (if not already done). (NOTE: 60-way connector torque is 35-45 in./lbs.)

Using the cautions listed below, disassemble, clean and rebuild the transaxle as outlined in the 1989 front wheel drive service manual.

CAUTION:

A. The cooler & lines should be REVERSE flushed using mineral spirits and short blasts of compressed air, followed by rinsing with 1 qt. of ATF as described in the service manual.

B. Inspect the input clutch hub and reaction shaft support assemblies. It is critical that these parts be free of debris and burrs. The seal rings must be removed, inspected and the rings and mating parts must be washed.

C. Replace distressed clutch components as required and replace the valve body filter. Make sure parts are installed properly as outlined in the service manual.

D. During reassembly, input shaft end play must fall between .005" and .025". To achieve this, a selection from a set of #4 thrust plates may be necessary. (NOTE: These end play specifications are different from the service manual.)

E. Replace gaskets and seals as required.

F. The torque converter must be changed if major clutch failure has occurred.

G. The solenoid assembly can be re-used unless the transaxle has experienced a geartrain failure. In this case a complete replacement of the solenoid assembly is required.

8. Proper road test procedure

A. Use the DRBII to clear any fault codes before road testing.

B. Leaving the DRBII connected, road test the vehicle using the guidelines found in step #3, then continue to road test with an emphasis on the 3-4 shift.

C. If code 46 occurs early during the road test, erase the code and continue the road test. (A false code 46 can sometimes set during the shift learning process)

D. If transaxle performance is judged to be acceptable, return the vehicle to the owner.

E. If Code 46 continues to repeat, contact Automatic Transmission Hotline.

TROUBLE DIAGNOSIS

CLUTCH APPLICATION CHART

Shift Lever Position	Start Safety	Park Sprag	Clutches				Low/Reverse
			Underdrive	Overdrive	Reverse	2/4	
P-Park	Applied	Applied	—	—	—	—	—
R-Reverse	—	—	—	—	Applied	—	Applied
N-Neutral	Applied	—	—	—	—	—	Applied
OD-Overdrive							
First	—	—	Applied	—	—	—	Applied
Second	—	—	Applied	—	—	Applied	—
Direct	—	—	Applied	Applied	—	—	—
Overdrive	—	—	—	Applied	—	Applied	—
D-Drive ①							
First	—	—	Applied	—	—	—	Applied
Second	—	—	Applied	—	—	Applied	—
Direct	—	—	Applied	Applied	—	—	—
L-Low ①							
First	—	—	Applied	—	—	—	Applied
Second	—	—	Applied	—	—	Applied	—
Direct	—	—	Applied	Applied	—	—	—

① Vehicle upshift and downshift speeds are increased when in these selector positions.

CHILTON THREE "C" TRANSAXLE DIAGNOSIS

Condition	Cause	Correction
Harsh engagement from N to D	a) Poor engine performance	a) Check engine tuneup
	b) Underdrive clutch worn or faulty	b) Overhaul
	c) Low/reverse clutch worn or faulty	c) Overhaul
	d) Accumulator seal rings worn or damaged	d) Replace seal rings
	e) Valve body malfunction or leakage	e) Clean or overhaul
	f) Hydraulic pressures too high	f) Adjust to specifications
	g) Engine idle speed too high	g) Adjust idle speed
Harsh engagement from N to R	a) Poor engine performance	a) Check engine tuneup
	b) Reverse clutch worn or faulty	b) Overhaul
	c) Low/reverse clutch worn or faulty	c) Overhaul
	d) Accumulator seal rings worn or damaged	d) Replace seal rings
	e) Valve body malfunction or leakage	e) Clean or overhaul

CHILTON THREE "C" TRANSAXLE DIAGNOSIS

Condition	Cause	Correction
Harsh engagement from Neutral to D	f) Hydraulic pressures too high g) Engine idle speed too high	f) Adjust to specifications g) Adjust idle speed
Delayed engagement from N to D	a) Damaged clutch seal b) Underdrive clutch worn or faulty c) Incorrect gearshift control linkage adjustment d) Accumulator seal rings worn or damaged e) Valve body malfunction or leakage f) Reaction shaft support seal rings worn or broken g) Input shaft seal rings worn or damaged h) Hydraulic pressure too low i) Oil pump faulty j) Oil filter clogged k) Fluid level low l) Fluid aerated m) Engine idle speed too low	a) Replace seal b) Overhaul c) Adjust gearshift control linkage d) Replace seal rings e) Clean or overhaul f) Replace seal ring g) Replace seal ring h) Adjust to specification i) Overhaul pump j) Replace filter k) Add as required l) Check for overfill m) Adjust idle speed
Delayed engagement from N to R	a) Damaged clutch seal b) Reverse clutch worn or faulty c) Incorrect gearshift control linkage adjustment d) Accumulator seal rings worn or damaged e) Valve body malfunction or leakage f) Reaction shaft support seal rings worn or broken g) Input shaft seal rings worn or damaged h) Hydraulic pressure too low i) Oil pump faulty j) Oil filter clogged k) Fluid level low l) Fluid aerated m) Engine idle speed too low	a) Replace seal b) Overhaul c) Adjust gearshift control linkage d) Replace seal rings e) Clean or overhaul f) Replace seal ring g) Replace seal ring h) Adjust to specification i) Overhaul pump j) Replace filter k) Add as required l) Check for overfill m) Adjust idle speed
Poor shift quality	a) Reaction shaft support seal rings worn or broken b) Hydraulic pressure too low c) Oil pump faulty d) Oil filter clogged e) Fluid level low f) Fluid aerated	a) Replace seal ring b) Adjust to specification c) Overhaul pump c) Replace filter e) Add as required f) Check for overfill
Shifts erratic	a) Poor engine performance b) Clutches worn or faulty c) Incorrect gearshift control linkage adjustment d) Valve body malfunction or leakage e) Reaction shaft support seal rings worn or broken f) Hydraulic pressure too low g) Oil pump faulty h) Oil filter clogged i) Fluid level low j) Fluid aerated	a) Check engine tuneup b) Overhaul c) Adjust gearshift control linkage d) Clean or overhaul e) Replace seal ring f) Adjust to specification g) Overhaul pump h) Replace filter i) Add as required j) Check for overfill
Drives in Neutral	a) Underdrive clutch worn or faculty b) Overdrive clutch worn or faulty c) Reverse clutch worn or faulty d) Clutches dragging e) Clutch plate clearance insufficient	a) Overhaul b) Overhaul c) Overhaul d) Check clearance e) Check clearance

CHILTON THREE "C" TRANSAXLE DIAGNOSIS

Condition	Cause	Correction
Drives in Neutral	f) Incorrect gearshift control linkage adjustment g) Valve body malfunction or leakage	f) Adjust gearshift control linkage g) Clean or overhaul
Drags or locks	a) Clutches worn or faulty b) Gear teeth chipped or damaged c) Planetary gearsets broken or seized d) Bearings worn or damaged	a) Overhaul b) Replace gear teeth c) Replace gearsets d) Replace bearings
Grating, scraping, growling noise	a) Gear teeth chipped or damaged b) Planetary gearsets broken or seized c) Bearings worn or damaged d) Driveshaft(s) bushing(s) worn or damaged	a) Replace gear teeth b) Replace gearsets c) Replace bearings d) Replace bushing(s)
Buzzing noise	a) Valve body malfunction or leakage b) Fluid level low c) Fluid aerated	a) Clean or overhaul b) Add as required c) Check for overfill
Buzzing noise during shifts only	a) Normal solenoid operation b) Solenoid sound cover loose	a) No correction b) Tighten cover
Hard to fill, oil blows out filler tube	a) High fluid level b) Oil filter clogged c) Fluid aerated	a) Remove as required b) Change filter c) Check for overfill
Transaxle overheats	a) Clutch plate clearance insufficient b) Incorrect gearshift control linkage adjustment c) Cooling system faulty d) Hydraulic pressure too low e) Oil pump faulty f) Fluid level low g) Fluid aerated h) Fluid level high i) Engine idle speed too high	a) Check clearance b) Adjust gearshift control linkage c) Service system d) Adjust to specification e) Overhaul pump f) Add as required g) Check for overfill h) Remove as required i) Adjust idle speed
Harsh upshift	a) Poor engine performance b) Overdrive clutch worn or faulty c) 2/4 clutch worn or faulty d) Hydraulic pressure too low e) Hydraulic pressure too high	a) Check engine tuneup b) Overhaul c) Overhaul d) Adjust to specification e) Adjust to specification
No upshift into overdrive	a) Overdrive clutch worn or faulty b) Engine coolant temperature too low	a) Overhaul b) Service cooling system
No lockup	a) Engine coolant temperature too low b) Valve body malfunction or leakage c) Input shaft seal rings worn or damaged d) Hydraulic pressure too low e) Oil pump faulty f) Fluid level low g) Fluid aerated	a) Service cooling system b) Clean or overhaul c) Replace seal ring d) Adjust to specification e) Overhaul pump f) Add as required g) Check for overfill
Harsh downshifts	a) Poor engine performance b) Underdrive clutch worn or faulty c) 2/4 clutch worn or faulty d) Low/reverse clutch worn or faulty e) Damaged clutch seal f) Accumulator seal ringe worn or damaged g) Valve body malfunction or leakage h) Reaction shaft support seal rings worn or broken i) Hydraulic pressure too high	a) Check engine tuneup b) Overhaul d) Overhaul d) Overhaul d) Replace seal f) Replace seal rings g) Clean or overhaul h) Replace seal ring i) Adjust to specification

CHILTON THREE "C" TRANSAXLE DIAGNOSIS

Condition	Cause	Correction
Harsh downshifts	j) Fluid level low k) Fluid aerated l) Engine idle speed too high	d) Add as required k) Check for overfill l) Adjust idle speed
High shift efforts	a) Shift linkage damaged b) Valve body malfunction or leakage	a) Check/repair linkage b) Clean or overhaul
Harsh lockup shift	a) Lockup piston sticking	a) Clean or overhaul

PRESSURE CHECK SPECIFICATIONS CHART

Shift Lever Position	Actual Gear	Under-Drive Clutch	Over-Drive Clutch	Reverse Clutch	Lockup Off	2/4 Clutch	Low/ Reverse Clutch
Park ① 0 mph	Park	0–2	0–5	0–2	60–110	0–2	115–145
Reverse ① 0 mph	Reverse	0–2	0–7	165–235	50–100	0–2	165–235
Neutral ① 0 mph	Neutral	0–2	0–5	0–2	60–110	0–2	115–145
L ② 20 mph	First	110–145	0–5	0–2	60–110	0–2	115–145
D ② 30 mph	First	110–145	0–5	0–2	60–110	115–145	0–2
D ② 45 mph	Direct	75–95	75–95	0–2	60–90	0–2	0–2
OD ② 30 mph	Overdrive	0–2	75–95	0–2	60–90	75–95	0–2
OD ② 50 mph	OD Lockup	0–2	75–95	0–2	0–5	75–95	0–2

① Engine speed at 1500 rpm
② Both front wheels must be turning at the same speed

Hydraulic Control System

NOTE: Please refer to Section 9 for all oil flow circuits.

CLUTCH AND GEAR

The A-604 transaxle consists of 3 multiple-disc input clutches, 2 multiple-disc grounded clutches, 4 hydraulic accumulators, and 2 planetary gearsets to provide 4 speeds forward and a reverse ratio. Since this transaxle is expected to operate properly with today's high-speed engines, its clutch-apply pistons were designed with centrifugally-balanced oil cavities so that quick response and good control can be achieved at any speed. A unique push/pull piston is incorporated for 2 of the 3 input clutches with out any added pressure seals; the 3rd clutch requires 1 additional seal.

HYDRAULICS

The hydraulics of the new transaxle provide the manual shift lever select function, main line pressure regulation, and torque converter and cooler flow control. Oil flow to the friction elements is controlled directly by 4 solenoid valves. The hydraulics also include a unique logic-controlled "solenoid switch valve" which locks out the 1st gear reaction element with the application of 2nd, direct, or overdrive gear elements, and redirects the 1st gear solenoid output so that it can control torque converter lockup operation. To regain access to 1st gear, a special sequence of solenoid commands must be used to uplock and move the solenoid switch valve. This precludes any application of the 1st gear reaction element with other elements applied unless specifically commanded by a properly functioning controller; it also allows 1 solenoid to control 2 friction elements.

Small, high-rate accumulators are provided in each controlled friction element circuit. These serve to absorb the pressure responses, and allow the controls to read and respond to changes that are occurring.

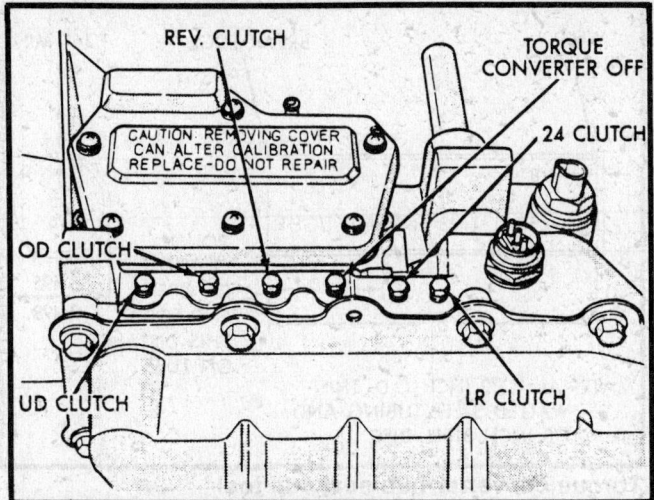

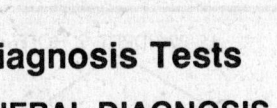

Transaxle pressure taps location

Diagnosis Tests

GENERAL DIAGNOSIS

NOTE: Before attempting any repair on the A-604 Electronic Automatic Transaxle, always check for fault codes with the DRB II.

Automatic transaxle malfunctions may be caused by 4 general conditions: poor engine malfunctions, mechanical malfunctions, and electronic malfunctions. Diagnosis of these problems should always begin by checking the easily accessible variables: fluid level and condition, gear shift cable adjustment. Then perform a road test to determine if the problem has been corrected or that more diagnosis is necessary. If the problem exists after the preliminary tests and corrections are completed, hydraulic pressure checks should be preformed.

CONTROL PRESSURE TEST

Pressure testing is a very important step in the diagnostic procedure. These tests usually reveal the cause of most transaxle problems.

Before performing pressure tests, be certain that the fluid level and the condition, and shift cable adjustments have been checked and approved. Fluid must be at operating temperature (150–200°F).

Install an engine tachometer, raise the vehicle on a hoist which allows the front wheels to turn, and position the tachometer so it can be read.

Attach 150 psi gauges to the ports as required for test being conducted. A 300 psi gauge (C–3293) is required for reverse pressure test.

Test One (Selector In L–1st Gear)

1. Attach pressure gauge to the low/reverse clutch tap.
2. Move the selector lever to the **L** position.
3. Allow the vehicle wheels to turn and increase throttle opening to achieve an indicated vehicle speed to 20 mph.
4. Low/reverse clutch pressure should read 115–145 psi.
5. This test checks the pump output, pressure regulation and condition of the low/reverse clutch hydraulic circuit and shift schedule.

Test Two (Selector In D–2nd Gear)

1. Attach a gauge to the underdrive clutch tap.

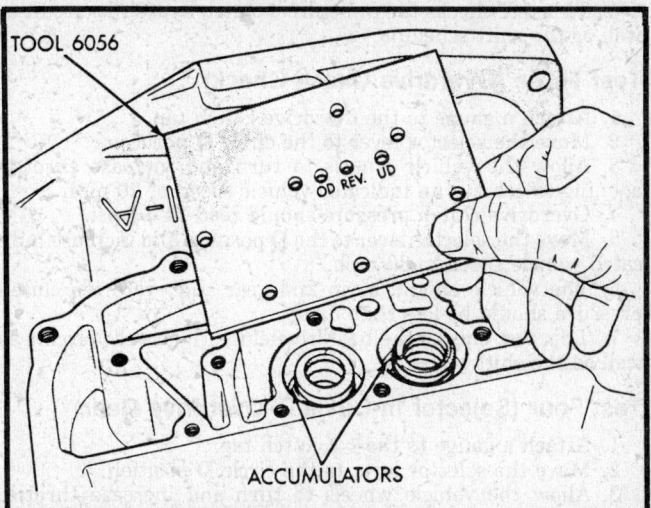

Air pressure test plate tool

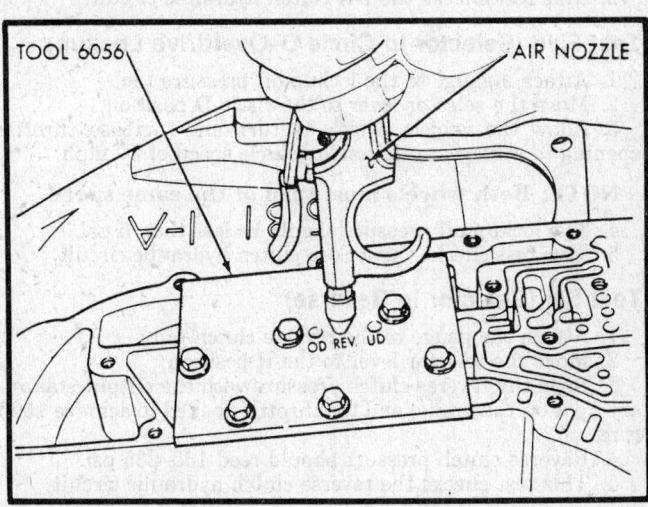

Air pressure testing the reverse clutch

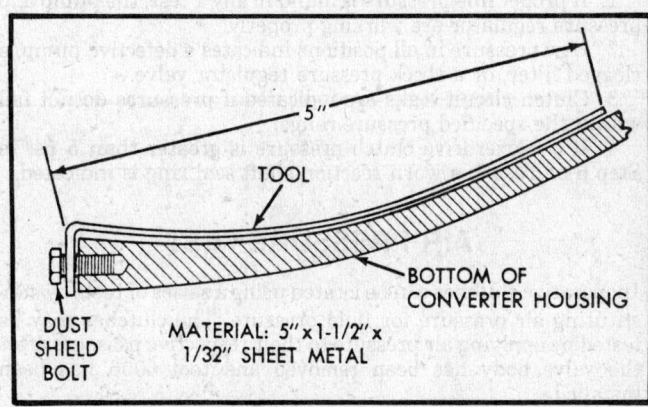

Leak locating test probe tool

2. Move the selector lever to the **D** position.
3. Allow the vehicle wheels to turn and increase throttle opening to achieve an indicated vehicle speed of 30 mph.
4. Underdrive clutch pressure should read 110–145 psi.

5. This test checks the underdrive clutch hydraulic circuit as well as the shift schedule.

Test Three (Overdrive Clutch Check)

1. Attach a gauge to the overdrive clutch tap.
2. Move the selector lever to the circle **D** position.
3. Allow the vehicle wheels to turn and increase throttle opening to achieve an indicated vehicle speed of 20 mph.
4. Overdrive clutch pressure should read 74–95 psi.
5. Move the selector lever to the **D** position and increase indicated vehicle speed to 30 mph.
6. The vehicle should be in 2nd gear and overdrive clutch pressure should be less than 5 psi.
7. This test checks the overdrive clutch hydraulic circuit as well as the shift schedule.

Test Four (Selector In Circle D–Overdrive Gear)

1. Attach a gauge to the 2–4 clutch tap.
2. Move the selector lever to the circle **D** position.
3. Allow the vehicle wheels to turn and increase throttle opening to achieve an indicated vehicle speed of 30 mph.
4. The 2–4 clutch pressure should read 74–95 psi.
5. This test checks the 2–4 clutch hydraulic circuit.

Test Five (Selector In Circle D–Overdrive Lockup)

1. Attach a gauge to the lockup off pressure tap.
2. Move the selector lever to the circle **D** position.
3. Allow the vehicle wheels to turn and increase throttle opening to achieve an indicated vehicle speed of 50 mph.

NOTE: Both wheels must turn at the same speed.

4. The lockup off pressure should be less than 5 psi.
5. This test checks the lockup clutch hydraulic circuit.

Test Six (Selector In Reverse)

1. Attach the gauge to the reverse clutch tap.
2. Move the selector lever to the **R** position.
3. Read the reverse clutch pressure with the output stationary (foot on the brake) and the throttle opened to achieve 1500 rpm.
4. Reverse clutch pressure should read 165–235 psi.
5. This test checks the reverse clutch hydraulic circuit.

Test Result Indications

1. If proper line pressure is found in any 1 test, the pump and pressure regulator are working properly.
2. Low pressure in all positions indicates a defective pump, a clogged filter, or a stuck pressure regulator valve.
3. Clutch circuit leaks are indicated if pressures do not fall within the specified pressure range.
4. If the overdrive clutch pressure is greater than 5 psi in Step 6 of Test 3, a worn reaction shaft seal ring is indicated.

AIR PRESSURE TEST

Inoperative clutches can be located using a series of tests by substituting air pressure for fluid pressure. The clutches may be tested by applying air pressure to their respective passages after the valve body has been removed and tool 6056 has been installed.

NOTE: The compressed air supply must be free of all dirt and moisture. Use a pressure of 30 psi.

Overdrive Clutch Check

Apply air pressure to the overdrive clutch apply passage and watch for the push/pull piston to move forward. The piston

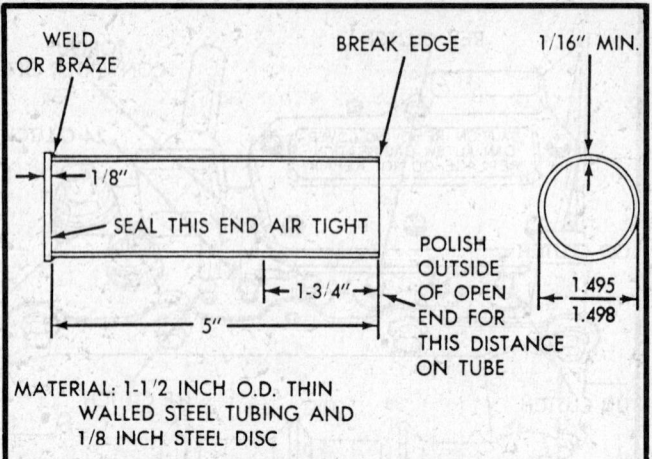

Torque converter hub seal cup tool

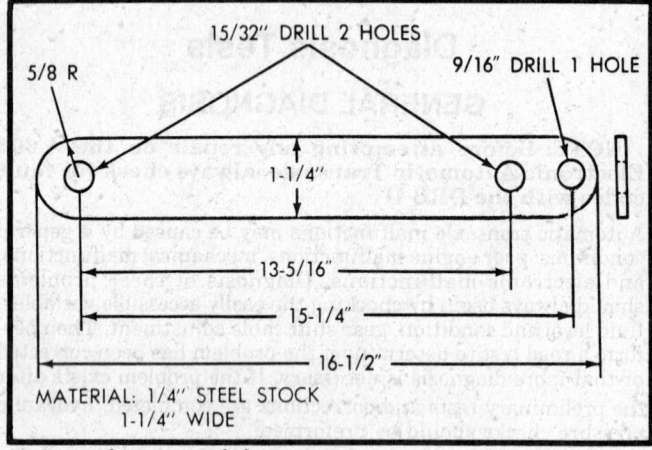

Hub seal cup retaining strap

should return to its starting position when the air pressure is removed.

Reverse Clutch Check

Apply air pressure to the reverse clutch apply passage and watch for the push/pull piston to move rearward. The piston should return to its starting position when the air pressure is removed.

2–4 Clutch Check

Apply air pressure to the feed hole located on the 2–4 clutch retainer. Look in the area where the 2–4 piston contacts the first separator plate and watch carefully for the 2–4 piston to move rearward. The piston should return to its original position after the air pressure is removed.

Low/Reverse Clutch Check

Apply air pressure to the low/reverse clutch feed hole (rear of the case, between 2 bolts holes). Then, look in the area where the low/reverse piston contacts the first separator plate and watch carefully for the piston to move forward. The piston should return to its original position after the air pressure is removed.

Underdrive Clutch Check

Because this clutch piston can not be seen, its operation is checked by function. Air pressure is applied to the low/reverse and the 2–4 clutches. This locks the output shaft. Use a piece of rubber hose wrapped around the input shaft and a pair of clamp-on pliers to turn the input shaft. Next apply air pressure to the underdrive clutch. The input shaft should not rotate with hand torque. Release the air pressure and confirm that the input shaft will rotate.

Transaxle Test

Fabricate equipment needed for the test.

The transaxle should be prepared for pressure test as follows after removal of the torque converter:

1. Install a dipstick bore plug and plug the oil cooler line fitting.

2. With rotary motion, install the converter hub seal cup over input shaft, and through the converter hub seal until the cup bottoms against the pump gear lugs. Secure with cup retainer strap using starter upper hole and opposite bracket hole.

3. Attach and clamp hose from the nozzle of tool C–4080 to the upper cooler line fitting position in the case.

--- **CAUTION** ---

Do not, under any circumstances, pressurize a transaxle to more than 10 psi.

4. Pressurize the transaxle using tool C–4080 until the pressure gauge reads 8 psi. Position the transaxle to that the pump housing and the case front may be covered with soapy solution of water. Leaks are sometimes caused by porosity in the case or the pump housing.

If a leak source is located, that part and all associated seals, O-rings, and gaskets should be replaced with new parts.

STALL SPEED TEST

--- **CAUTION** ---

Do not let anyone stand in front of the vehicle during this test.

The stall test consists of determining the engine speed obtained at full throttle in **D** position only, with the front wheels blocked. This test checks the torque converted stator clutch operation, and the holding ability of the transaxle clutch. The transaxle oil level should be checked and the engine brought to normal operating temperature before stall operation.

NOTE: Both the parking and service brakes must be fully applied and front wheels blocked while making this test.

Do not hold the throttle open any longer than is necessary to obtain a maximum engine speed reading, and never longer than 5 seconds at a time. If more than 1 stall check is required, operate the engine at approximately 1000 rpm in **N** for 20 seconds to cool the transaxle fluid between runs. If the engine speeds exceeds the maximum limits, release the accelerator immediately since transaxle clutch slippage is indicated.

Stall Speed Above Specification

If the stall speeds exceeds the maximum specified in the chart by more than 200 rpm, the transaxle clutch slippage is indicated. Follow the transaxle oil pressure and air pressure checks to determine the cause of the slippage.

Stall Speed Below Specification

Low stall speeds with a properly tuned engine indicate torque converter stator clutch problems. A road test will be necessary to identify the exact problem.

The stall speeds are 250–350 rpm below the minimum specification, and the vehicle operates properly at highway speeds, the stator overrunning clutch is slipping.

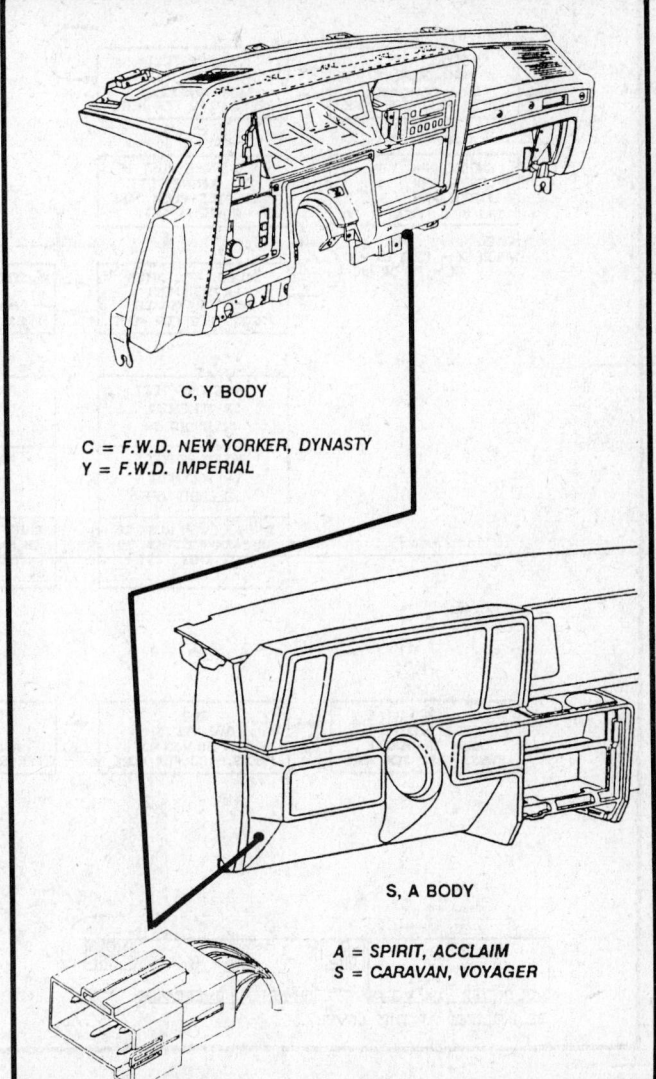

C, Y BODY

C = F.W.D. NEW YORKER, DYNASTY
Y = F.W.D. IMPERIAL

S, A BODY

A = SPIRIT, ACCLAIM
S = CARAVAN, VOYAGER

Chrysler Collision Detection (CCD) bus diagnostic connector location

If stall speed and acceleration are normal, but abnormally high throttle opening is required to maintain highway speeds, the stator clutch has seized.

Both of these stator defects require replacement of the torque converter.

Noise Diagnosis

A whining or siren-like noise due to fluid flow is normal during the stall operation with some torque converters; however, loud metallic noises from loose parts or interference within the assembly indicate a defective torque converter. To confirm that the noise originates with the torque converter, operate the vehicle at light throttle in **D** and **N** on a hoist and listen under the transaxle bell housing.

ROAD TEST

Prior to performing a road test, be certain that the fluid level and condition, and control cable adjustment have been checked and approved.

During the road test, the transaxle should be operated in each

DIAGNOSTIC READOUT BOX II (DRB II) FUNCTIONAL FLOW DIAGRAM

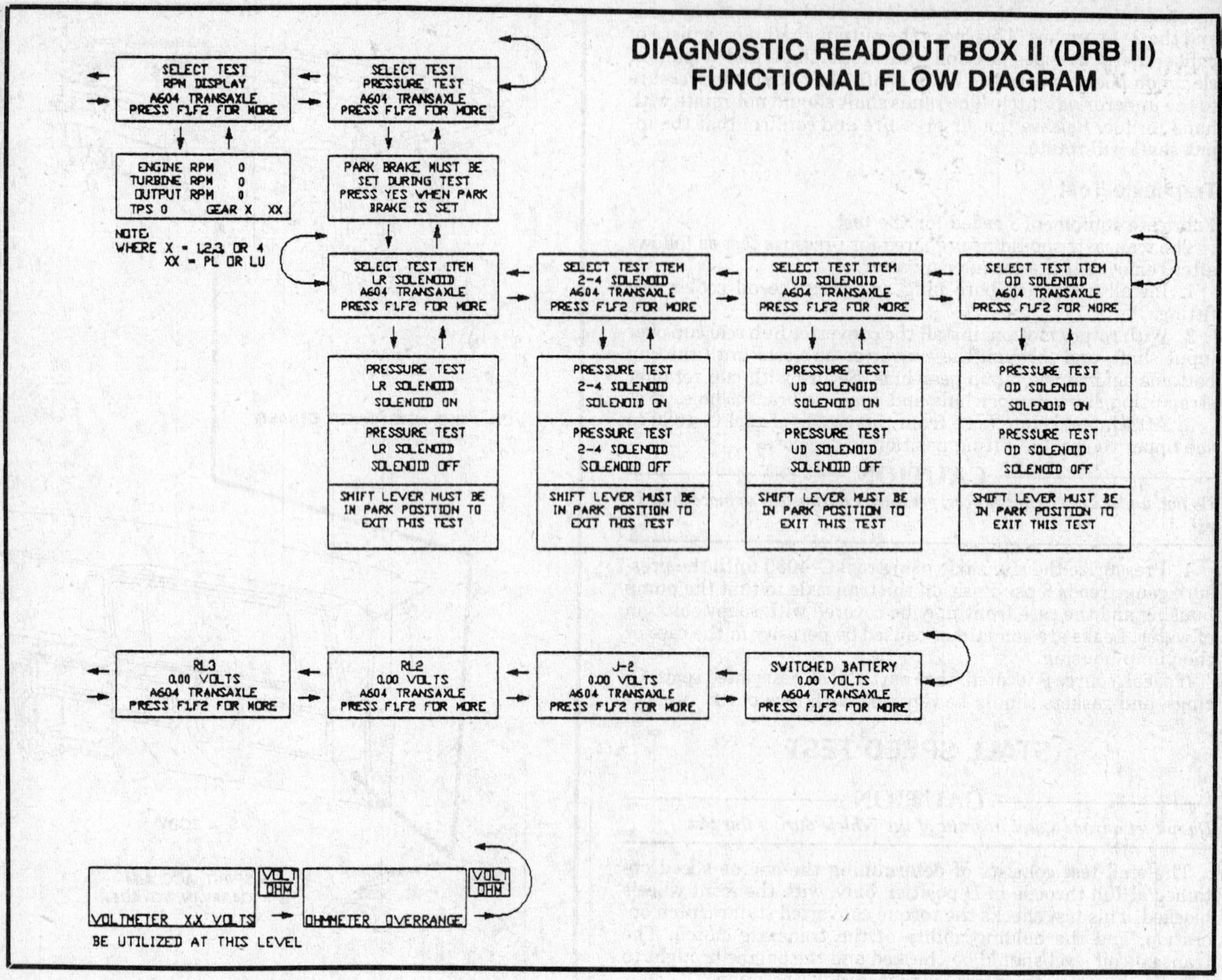

```
SELECT TEST          SELECT TEST
RPM DISPLAY          PRESSURE TEST
A604 TRANSAXLE       A604 TRANSAXLE
PRESS F1F2 FOR MORE  PRESS F1F2 FOR MORE

ENGINE RPM    0      PARK BRAKE MUST BE
TURBINE RPM   0      SET DURING TEST
OUTPUT RPM    0      PRESS YES WHEN PARK
TPS 0   GEAR X  XX   BRAKE IS SET

NOTE:
WHERE X = 1,2,3 OR 4
      XX = PL OR LU
```

```
SELECT TEST ITEM     SELECT TEST ITEM     SELECT TEST ITEM     SELECT TEST ITEM
LR SOLENOID          2-4 SOLENOID         UD SOLENOID          OD SOLENOID
A604 TRANSAXLE       A604 TRANSAXLE       A604 TRANSAXLE       A604 TRANSAXLE
PRESS F1F2 FOR MORE  PRESS F1F2 FOR MORE  PRESS F1F2 FOR MORE  PRESS F1F2 FOR MORE

PRESSURE TEST        PRESSURE TEST        PRESSURE TEST        PRESSURE TEST
LR SOLENOID          2-4 SOLENOID         UD SOLENOID          OD SOLENOID
SOLENOID ON          SOLENOID ON          SOLENOID ON          SOLENOID ON

PRESSURE TEST        PRESSURE TEST        PRESSURE TEST        PRESSURE TEST
LR SOLENOID          2-4 SOLENOID         UD SOLENOID          OD SOLENOID
SOLENOID OFF         SOLENOID OFF         SOLENOID OFF         SOLENOID OFF

SHIFT LEVER MUST BE  SHIFT LEVER MUST BE  SHIFT LEVER MUST BE  SHIFT LEVER MUST BE
IN PARK POSITION TO  IN PARK POSITION TO  IN PARK POSITION TO  IN PARK POSITION TO
EXIT THIS TEST       EXIT THIS TEST       EXIT THIS TEST       EXIT THIS TEST
```

```
RL3                  RL2                  J-2                  SWITCHED BATTERY
0.00 VOLTS           0.00 VOLTS           0.00 VOLTS           0.00 VOLTS
A604 TRANSAXLE       A604 TRANSAXLE       A604 TRANSAXLE       A604 TRANSAXLE
PRESS F1F2 FOR MORE  PRESS F1F2 FOR MORE  PRESS F1F2 FOR MORE  PRESS F1F2 FOR MORE
```

```
                              VOLT                    VOLT
                              OHM                     OHM
VOLTMETER XX VOLTS      OHMMETER OVERRANGE
BE UTILIZED AT THIS LEVEL
```

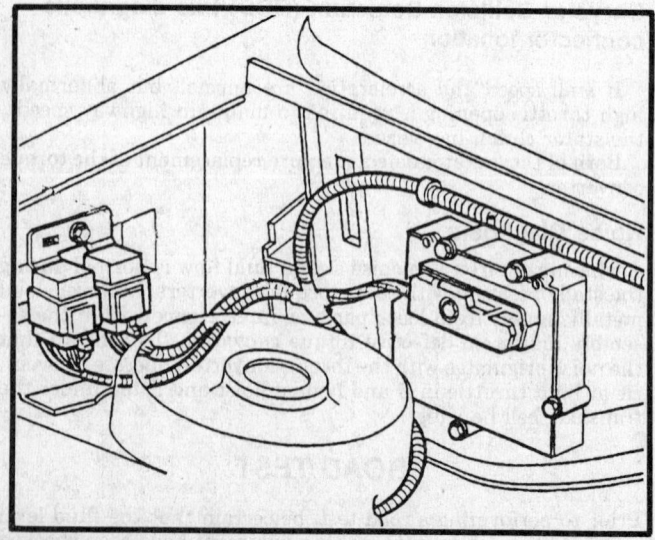

Transaxle controller, EATX relay and reverse lamp relay location—minivan

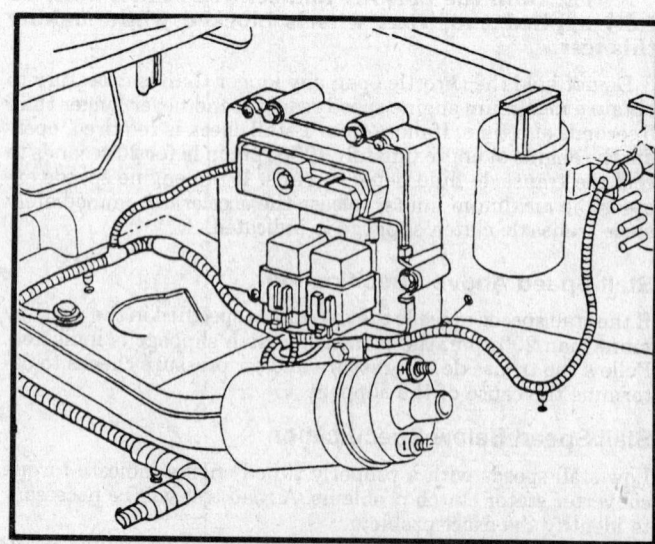

Transaxle controller, EATX relay and reverse lamp relay location—passenger car

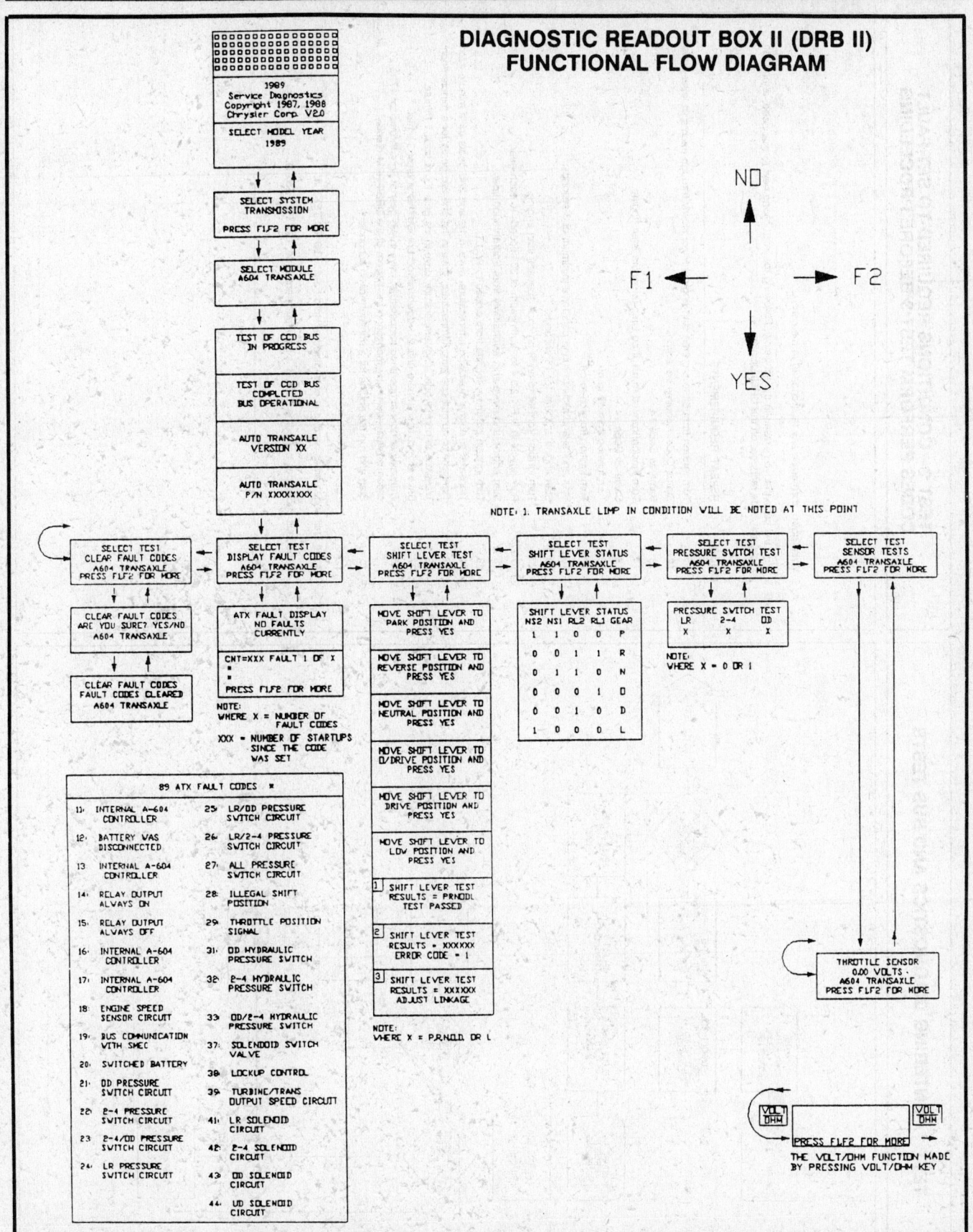

DIAGNOSTIC READOUT BOX II (DRB II)
FUNCTIONAL FLOW DIAGRAM

TEST 2 – CONDITIONS REQUIRED TO SET FAULT CODES PERFORM TEST 3 BEFORE PROCEEDING

A. Write down, then erase any fault code(s) in memory.

B. Find the code that you erased in the list below. Following the instructions next to that code, attempt to make the code reappear on the DRBII display.

CODE	REPEAT REQUIREMENTS
11	Turn ignition from off to on, then start engine. Move slowly through each shift lever position.
12	Status Code. Requires no action.
13	Same as Code 14.
14	Turn ignition from off to on. If no Limp-In occurs, start engine.
15	Same as Code 14.
16	Turn ignition from off to on.
17	Turn ignition from off to on.
18	Start engine and allow to run in park for a minimum of 3 seconds.
19	Start engine and wait for 15 seconds.
20	Turn ignition from off to on. If no code appears, start engine.
21 to 27	Run vehicle in N,R,1,2,3,4 for a minimum of 30 seconds in each gear.
28	Start engine and move shift lever slowly from Park through Low.
29	Turn ignition on, move throttle from closed to W.O.T.
31	Transaxle at normal operating temperature, drive in 1st and 2nd gears for a minute each.
32	Transaxle at normal operating temperature, drive in 1st and 3rd gears for a minute each.
33	Transaxle at normal operating temperature, drive in 1st gear for at least 1 minute.
37	Drive in 2nd, apply brake until 2-1 downshift occurs. Do this at least 3 times.
38	Transaxle at normal operating temperature, drive in 4th gear at light throttle for 17 to 20 seconds. Verify lockup by monitoring the bottom of the DRBII RPM display.
41 to 44	Start and run the engine for a minimum of 30 seconds.

C. If the fault code comes back, it is considered a "Hard Fault". GO TO TEST 4.

D. If the fault code does not come back, it is an intermittent code. GO TO TEST 9.

TEST 1 – ENTERING DIAGNOSTICS AND BUS TESTS

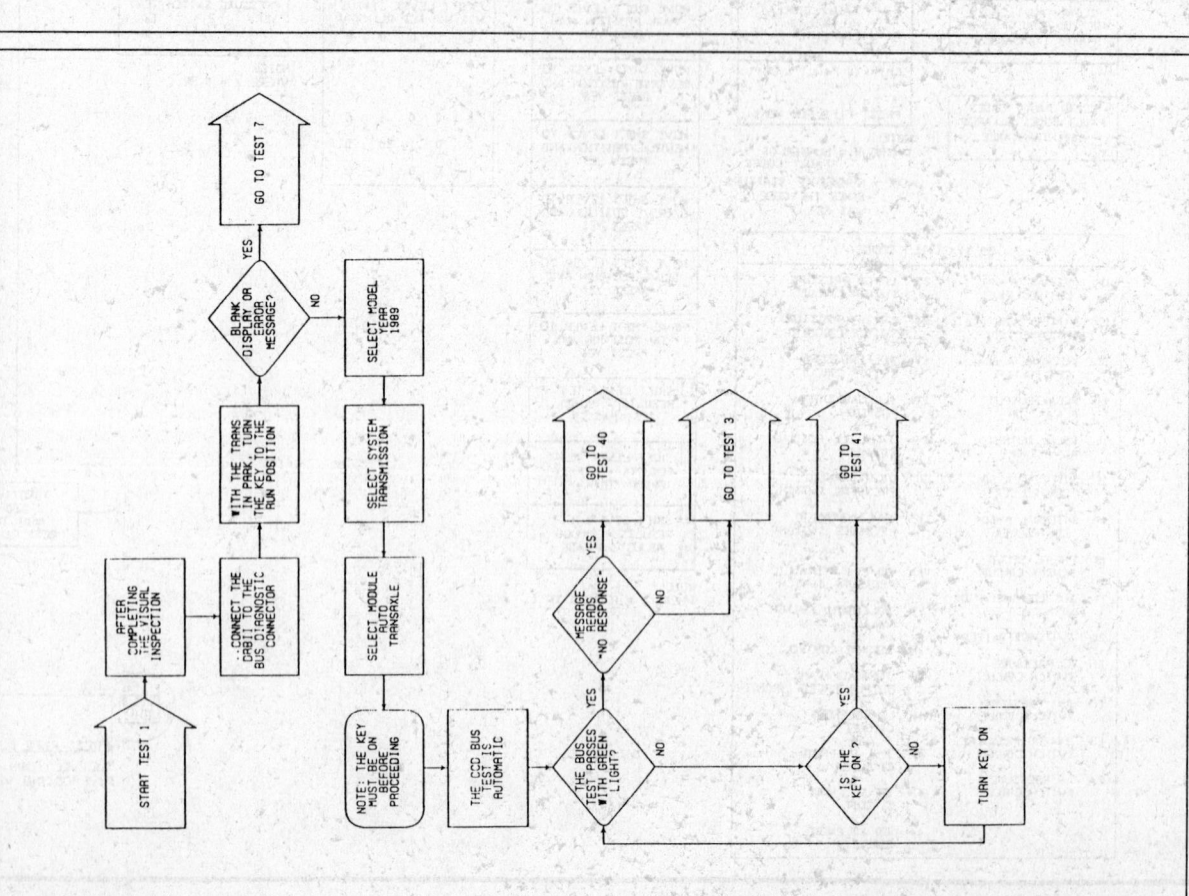

TEST 3—READING FAULT CODES PERFORM TEST 1 BEFORE PROCEEDING

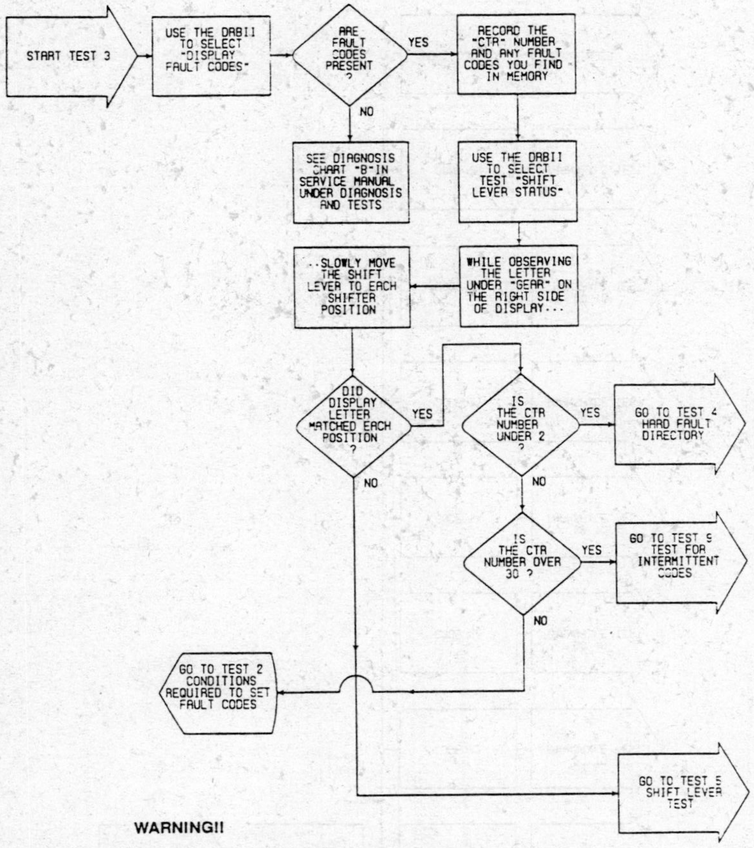
START TEST 3
USE THE DRBII TO SELECT "DISPLAY FAULT CODES"
ARE FAULT CODES PRESENT ?
YES
NO
RECORD THE "CTR" NUMBER AND ANY FAULT CODES YOU FIND IN MEMORY
SEE DIAGNOSIS CHART "B" IN SERVICE MANUAL UNDER DIAGNOSIS AND TESTS
USE THE DRBII TO SELECT TEST "SHIFT LEVER STATUS"
WHILE OBSERVING THE LETTER UNDER "GEAR" ON THE RIGHT SIDE OF DISPLAY...
..SLOWLY MOVE THE SHIFT LEVER TO EACH SHIFTER POSITION
DID DISPLAY LETTER MATCHED EACH POSITION ?
YES
NO
IS THE CTR NUMBER UNDER 2 ?
YES
NO
GO TO TEST 4 HARD FAULT DIRECTORY
IS THE CTR NUMBER OVER 30 ?
YES
NO
GO TO TEST 9 TEST FOR INTERMITTENT CODES
GO TO TEST 2 CONDITIONS REQUIRED TO SET FAULT CODES
GO TO TEST 5 SHIFT LEVER TEST

WARNING!!

DO NOT USE FAULT CODES TO DIAGNOSE TRANSMISSION PROBLEMS UNTIL AFTER YOU HAVE PERFORMED AND PASSED THE "SHIFT LEVER STATUS" TEST.

TEST 4—"HARD FAULT" CODE DIRECTORY

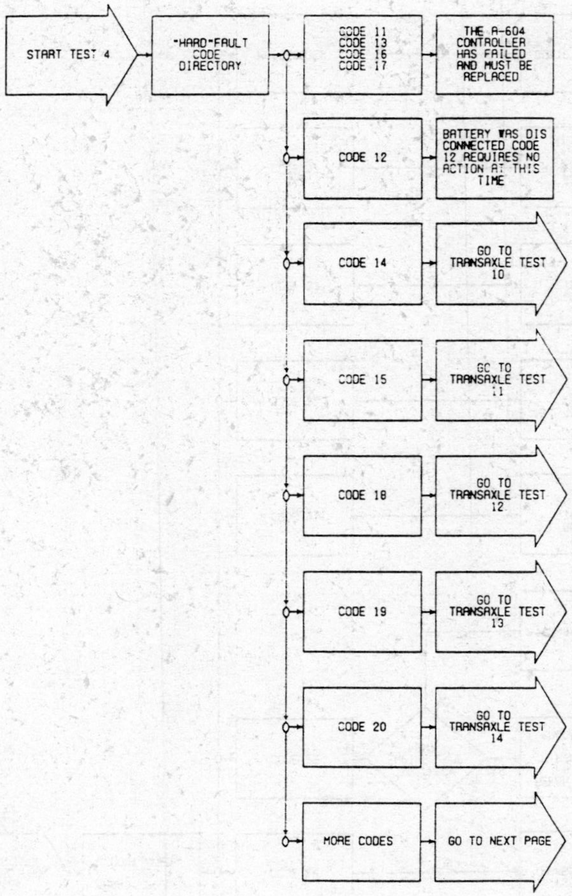
START TEST 4
"HARD" FAULT CODE DIRECTORY
CODE 11
CODE 13
CODE 16
CODE 17
THE A-604 CONTROLLER HAS FAILED AND MUST BE REPLACED
CODE 12
BATTERY WAS DISCONNECTED CODE 12 REQUIRES NO ACTION AT THIS TIME
CODE 14
GO TO TRANSAXLE TEST 10
CODE 15
GO TO TRANSAXLE TEST 11
CODE 18
GO TO TRANSAXLE TEST 12
CODE 19
GO TO TRANSAXLE TEST 13
CODE 20
GO TO TRANSAXLE TEST 14
MORE CODES
GO TO NEXT PAGE

TEST 4—"HARD FAULT" CODE DIRECTORY

TEST 4—"HARD FAULT" CODE DIRECTORY

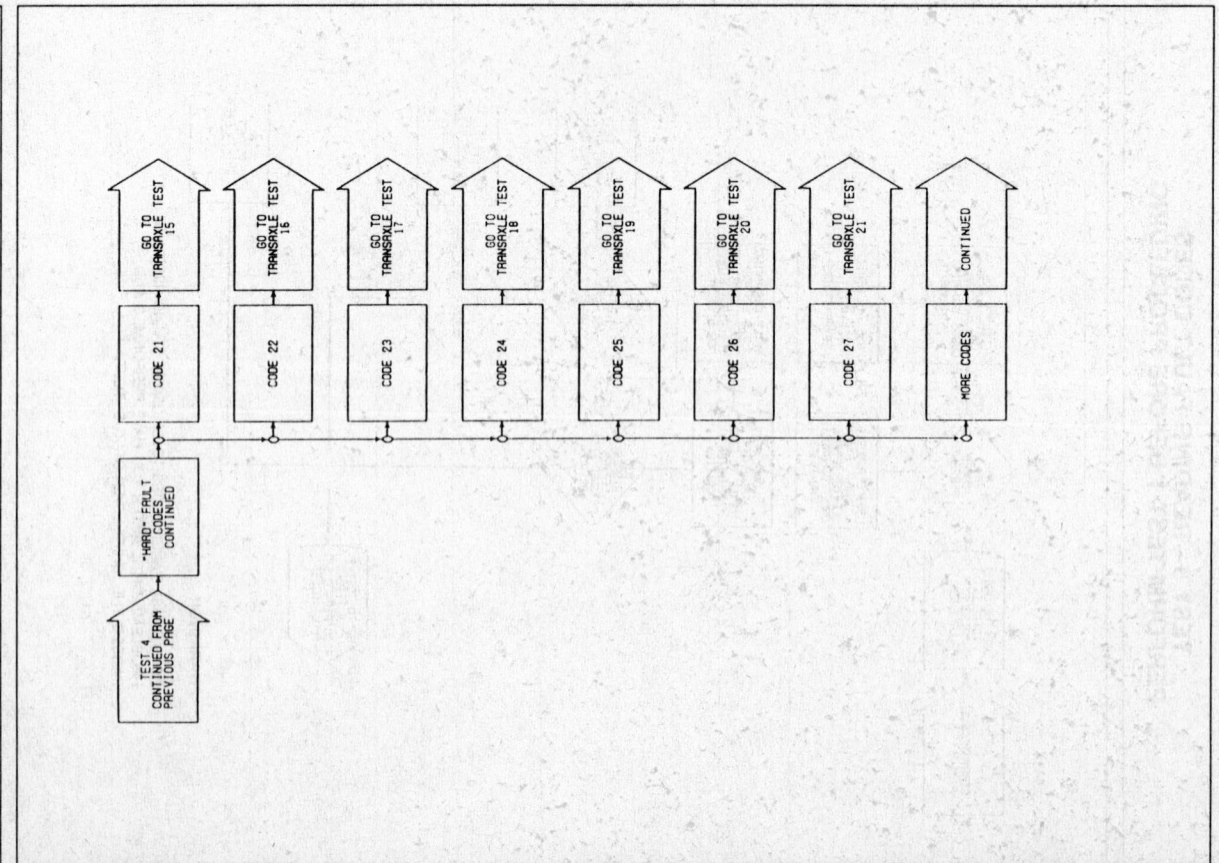

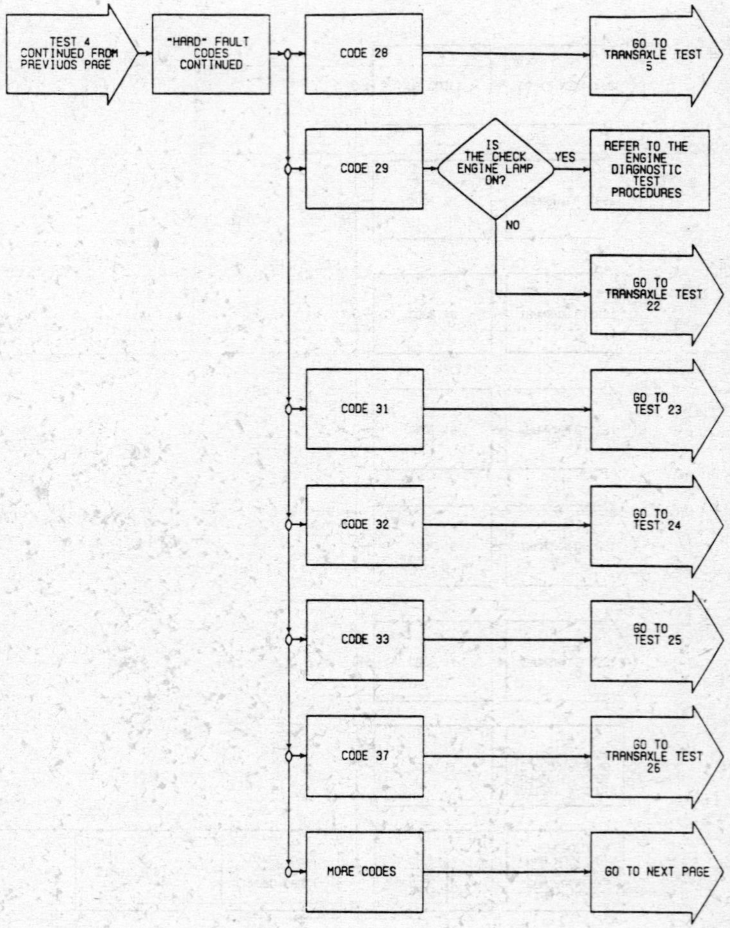

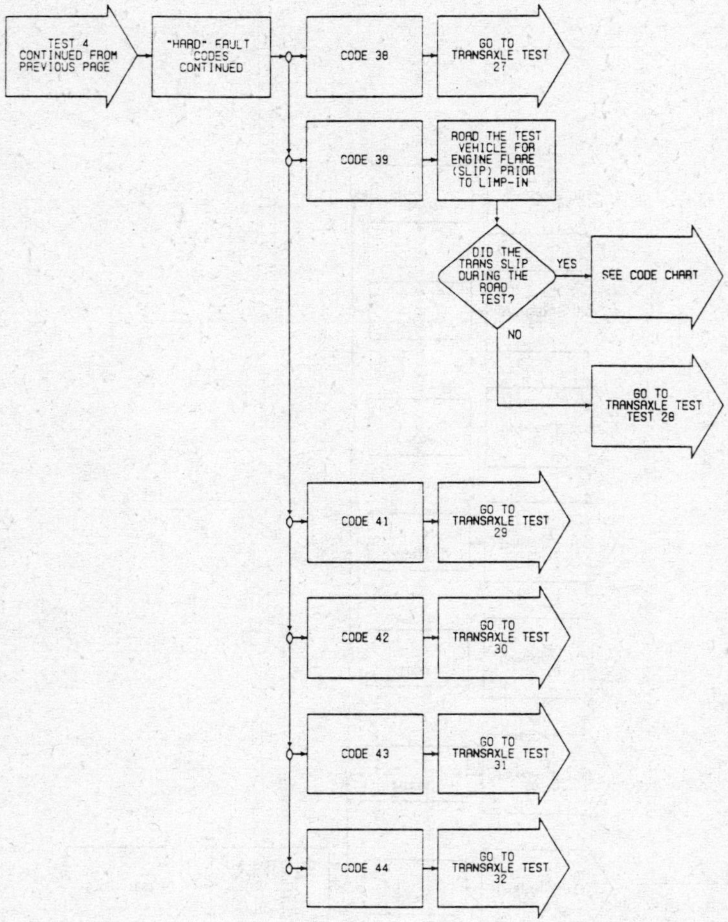

TEST 5 – SHIFT LEVER TEST
PERFORM TEST 2 BEFORE PROCEEDING

TEST 4 – "HARD FAULT" CODE DIRECTORY

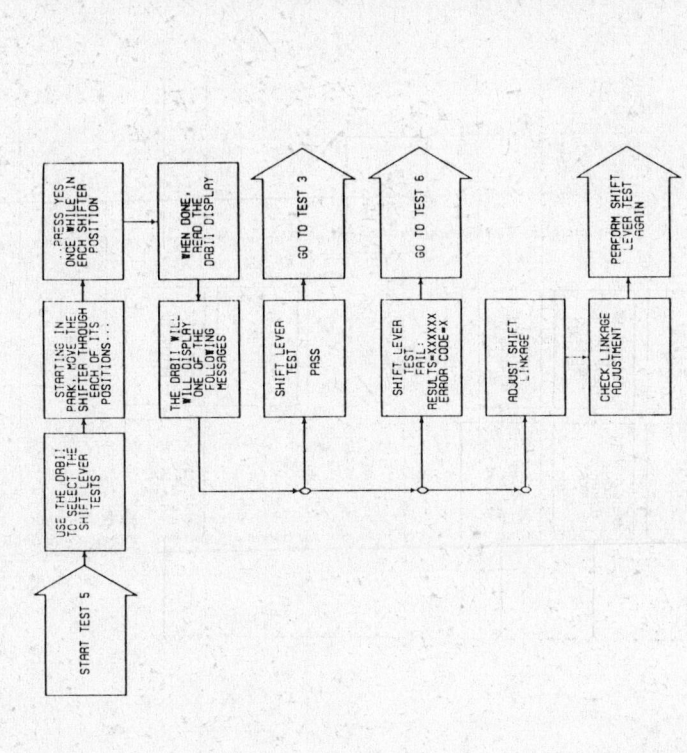

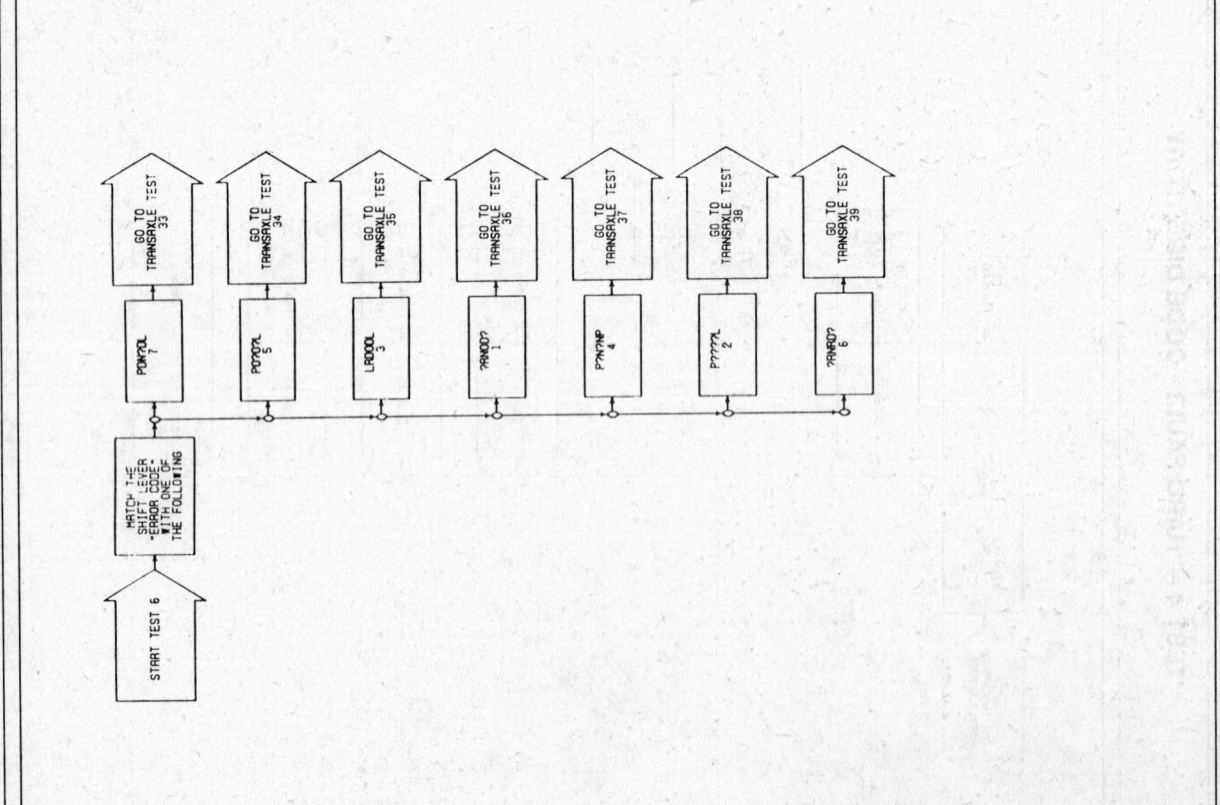

TEST 7 – DRBII ERROR MESSAGES
PERFORM TEST 1 BEFORE PROCEEDING

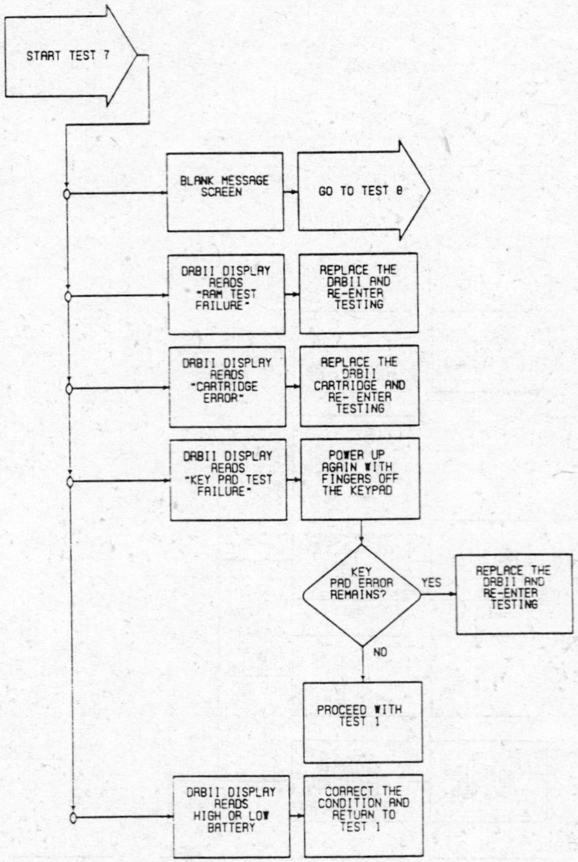

TEST 6 – FAILED SHIFT LEVER TESTS
PERFORM TEST 5 BEFORE PROCEEDING

TEST 9 – TEST FOR INTERMITTENT FAULT CODES
PERFORM TEST 2 BEFORE PROCEEDING

1. Check the following for push-outs or flaired connectors:

   A. Engine ground connection
   B. 60-way ground pins 53, 54, 57 & 58
   C. 60-way battery feed (J-11) pin 56
   D. Battery feed to EATX relay from I.O.D. connector
   E. 60-way J-2 feed pin 11

   If the above connections are OK . . . .

2. Select the intermittent code from the list below. Carefully inspect the pins and connector cavities that are listed next to the code for push-outs or terminal damage.

INTERMITTENT CODE	60-WAY PIN #	8-WAY PIN #	OTHER
11,13,16,17			Replace the A-604 controller
12			Requires no action
14	16 and 17		EATX connector/relay
15	15 and 16		EATX connector/relay
18	45		
19	4 and 43		Engine controller pin 46 and 26 (Pin 46 and 6 on Minivan)
20	16 and 17		EATX connector/relay
21	9	3 and 4	
22	47	1, 3 and 4	
23	47	1 and 4	
24	50	2 and 4	
25	50	2, 3 and 4	
26	50	2 and 4	
27	47	1 and 4	
28	1, 2, 3, 41, 42		NS connector/switch, PRNODL connector/switch
29	12 and 51		Throttle position sensor connector
31			
32			
33			
37			
38			
39	13, 14, 52		Turbine or output speed sensor connector
41	16, 20, 57, 58	4 pin 7	
42	16, 19, 57, 58	4 pin 8	
43	16.60	4 pin 6	
44	16, 59	4 pin 5	

3. If steps 1 and 2 fail to turn up a defective condition, use the DRBII to erase all fault codes and reset the start counter to zero. Road test the vehicle for proper transaxle function. If the transaxle function is acceptable, take no action at this time.

TEST 8 – TEST FOR CAUSE OF BLANK MESSAGE SCREEN
PERFORM TEST 1 BEFORE PROCEEDING

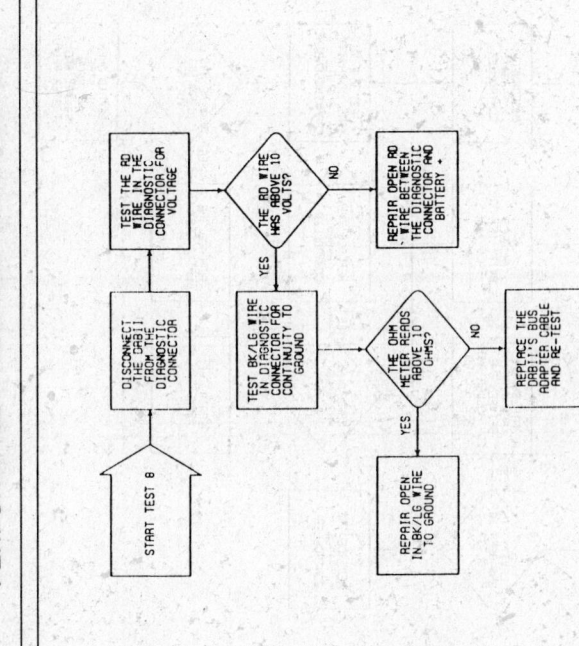

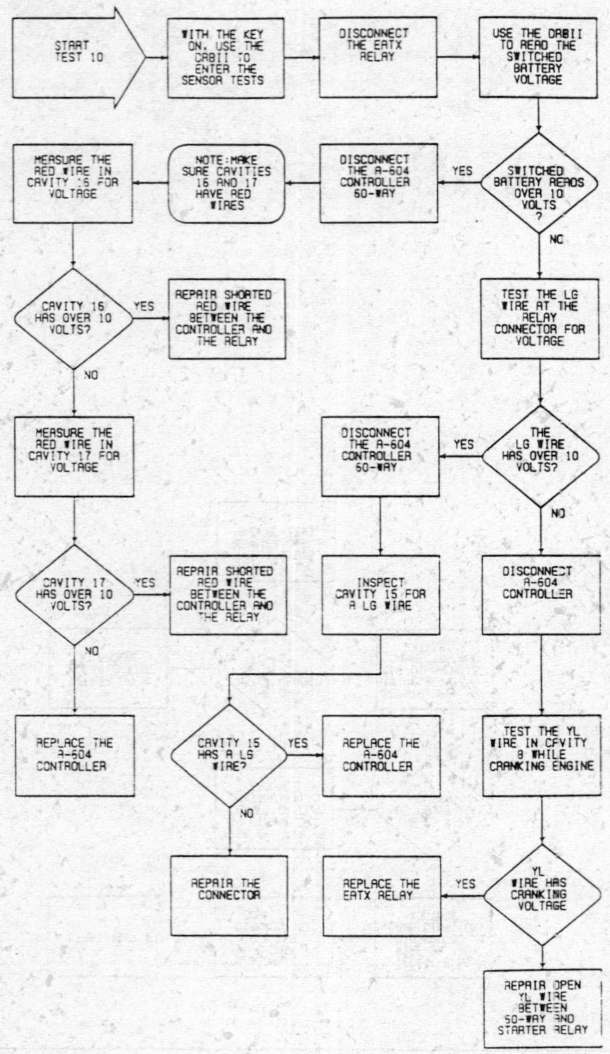

TEST 11
TEST FOR CODE 15—RELAY OUTPUT ALWAYS OFF
PERFORM TEST 3 BEFORE PROCEEDING

- START TEST 11
- DISCONNECT THE EATX RELAY
- NOTE: THE EATX RELAY HAS RD AND LG WIRES IN IT'S CONNECTOR
- TURN THE IGNITION SWITCH ON
- USE THE DRBII TO SELECT SWITCHED BATTERY UNDER SENSOR TESTS
- READ THE SWITCHED BATTERY DISPLAY ON THE DRBII
- CONNECT A JUMPER WIRE BETWEEN THE RD/WT AND THE RD WIRE
- SWITCHED BATTERY IS ABOVE 10 VOLTS?
  - YES → CONTINUE TEST 11 ON FOLLOWING PAGE
  - NO → NOTE: THE JUMPER WIRE IS STILL CONNECTED
- DISCONNECT THE A-604 60-WAY CONNECTOR
- MEASURE THE VOLTAGE AT CAVITY 16
- THE VOLTAGE IS ABOVE 10?
  - YES → REPLACE THE A-604 CONTROLLER
  - NO → REMOVE THE JUMPER WIRE FROM THE EATX RELAY CONNECTOR
- TEST THE RD/WT WIRE OF THE RELAY CONNECTOR FOR VOLTAGE
- THE VOLTAGE IS ABOVE 10?
  - YES → REPAIR THE OPEN IN THE RD/WT WIRE BETWEEN THE RELAY AND THE CONTROLLER
  - NO → REPAIR THE OPEN IN THE RD WIRE BETWEEN THE RELAY AND THE BATTERY

TEST 10
TEST FOR CODE 14—RELAY OUTPUT ALWAYS ON
PERFORM TEST 3 BEFORE PROCEEDING

- START TEST 10
- WITH THE KEY ON, USE THE DRBII TO ENTER THE SENSOR TESTS
- DISCONNECT THE EATX RELAY
- USE THE DRBII TO READ THE SWITCHED BATTERY VOLTAGE
- SWITCHED BATTERY READS OVER 10 VOLTS?
  - NO →
  - YES → DISCONNECT THE A-604 CONTROLLER 60-WAY
- NOTE: MAKE SURE CAVITIES 16 AND 17 HAVE RED WIRES
- MEASURE THE RED WIRE IN CAVITY 16 FOR VOLTAGE
- CAVITY 16 HAS OVER 10 VOLTS?
  - YES → REPAIR SHORTED RED WIRE BETWEEN THE CONTROLLER AND THE RELAY
  - NO → MEASURE THE RED WIRE IN CAVITY 17 FOR VOLTAGE
- CAVITY 17 HAS OVER 10 VOLTS?
  - YES → REPAIR SHORTED RED WIRE BETWEEN THE CONTROLLER AND THE RELAY
  - NO → REPLACE THE A-604 CONTROLLER
- TEST THE LG WIRE AT THE RELAY CONNECTOR FOR VOLTAGE
- THE LG WIRE HAS OVER 10 VOLTS?
  - YES → DISCONNECT A-604 CONTROLLER 60-WAY
    - INSPECT CAVITY 15 FOR A LG WIRE
    - CAVITY 15 HAS A LG WIRE?
      - YES → REPLACE THE A-604 CONTROLLER
      - NO → REPAIR THE CONNECTOR
  - NO → DISCONNECT A-604 CONTROLLER
- TEST THE YL WIRE IN CAVITY 8 WHILE CRANKING ENGINE
- YL WIRE HAS CRANKING VOLTAGE?
  - YES → REPLACE THE EATX RELAY
  - NO → REPAIR OPEN YL WIRE BETWEEN 60-WAY AND STARTER RELAY

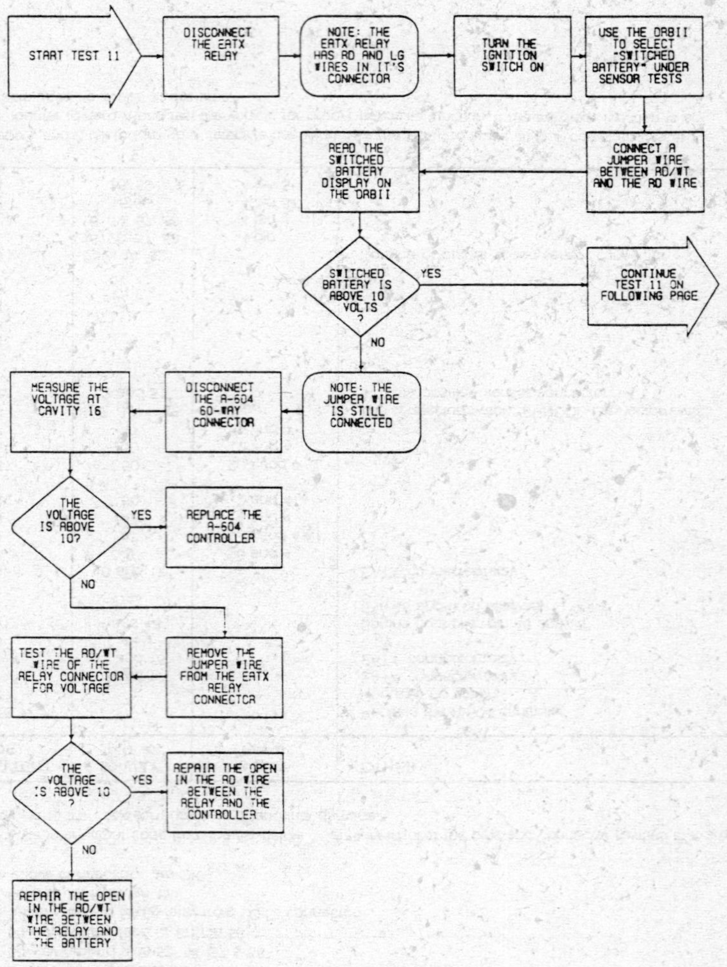

TEST 11
TEST FOR CODE 15—RELAY OUTPUT ALWAYS OFF
PERFORM TEST 3 BEFORE PROCEEDING

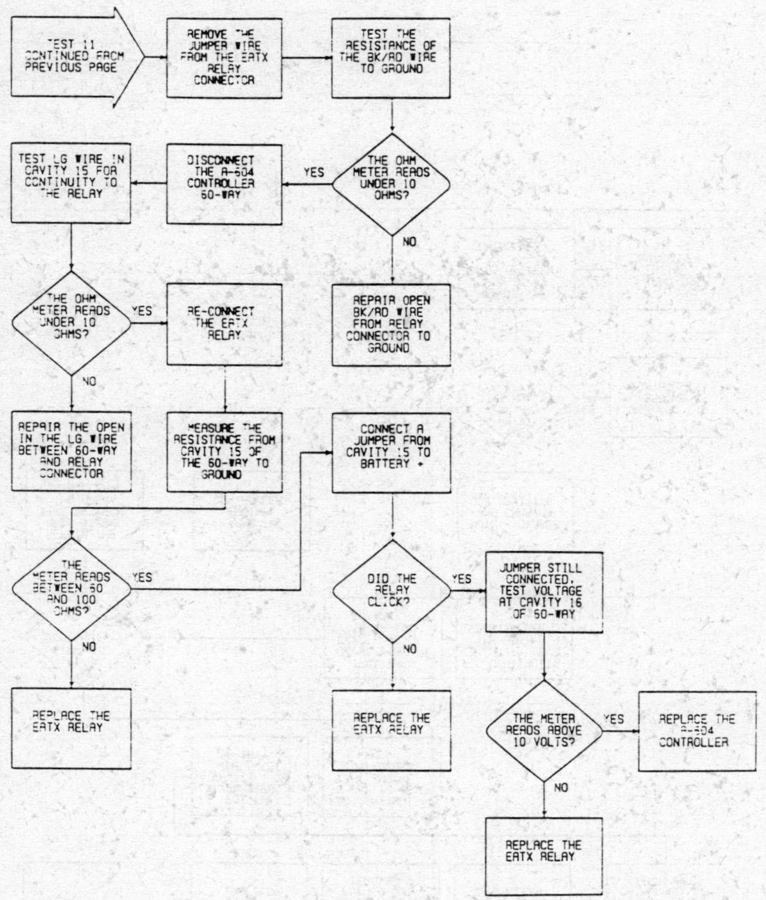
TEST 11 CONTINUED FROM PREVIOUS PAGE
REMOVE THE JUMPER WIRE FROM THE EATX RELAY CONNECTOR
TEST THE RESISTANCE OF THE BK/RD WIRE TO GROUND
THE OHM METER READS UNDER 10 OHMS?
YES
NO
REPAIR OPEN BK/RD WIRE FROM RELAY CONNECTOR TO GROUND
DISCONNECT THE A-604 CONTROLLER 60-WAY
TEST LG WIRE IN CAVITY 15 FOR CONTINUITY TO THE RELAY
THE OHM METER READS UNDER 10 OHMS?
YES
RE-CONNECT THE EATX RELAY
NO
REPAIR THE OPEN IN THE LG WIRE BETWEEN 60-WAY AND RELAY CONNECTOR
MEASURE THE RESISTANCE FROM CAVITY 15 OF THE 60-WAY TO GROUND
THE METER READS BETWEEN 60 AND 100 OHMS?
YES
NO
REPLACE THE EATX RELAY
CONNECT A JUMPER FROM CAVITY 15 TO BATTERY +
DID THE RELAY CLICK?
YES
NO
REPLACE THE EATX RELAY
JUMPER STILL CONNECTED, TEST VOLTAGE AT CAVITY 16 OF 50-WAY
THE METER READS ABOVE 10 VOLTS?
YES
REPLACE THE A-604 CONTROLLER
NO
REPLACE THE EATX RELAY

TEST 12
TEST FOR CODE 18—ENGINE SPEED SENSOR CIRCUIT
PERFORM TEST 3 BEFORE PROCEEDING

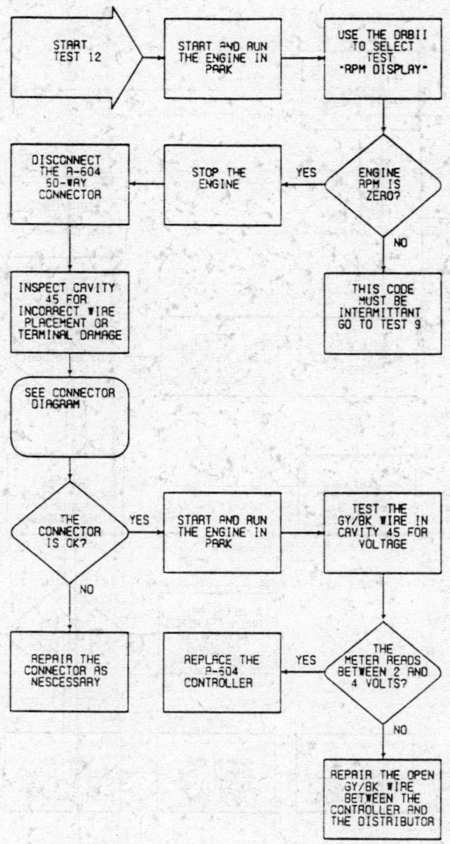
START TEST 12
START AND RUN THE ENGINE IN PARK
USE THE DRBII TO SELECT TEST "RPM DISPLAY"
ENGINE RPM IS ZERO?
YES
STOP THE ENGINE
NO
THIS CODE MUST BE INTERMITTANT GO TO TEST 9
DISCONNECT THE A-604 50-WAY CONNECTOR
INSPECT CAVITY 45 FOR INCORRECT WIRE PLACEMENT OR TERMINAL DAMAGE
SEE CONNECTOR DIAGRAM
THE CONNECTOR IS OK?
YES
NO
REPAIR THE CONNECTOR AS NESCESSARY
START AND RUN THE ENGINE IN PARK
TEST THE GY/BK WIRE IN CAVITY 45 FOR VOLTAGE
THE METER READS BETWEEN 2 AND 4 VOLTS?
YES
REPLACE THE A-604 CONTROLLER
NO
REPAIR THE OPEN GY/BK WIRE BETWEEN THE CONTROLLER AND THE DISTRIBUTOR

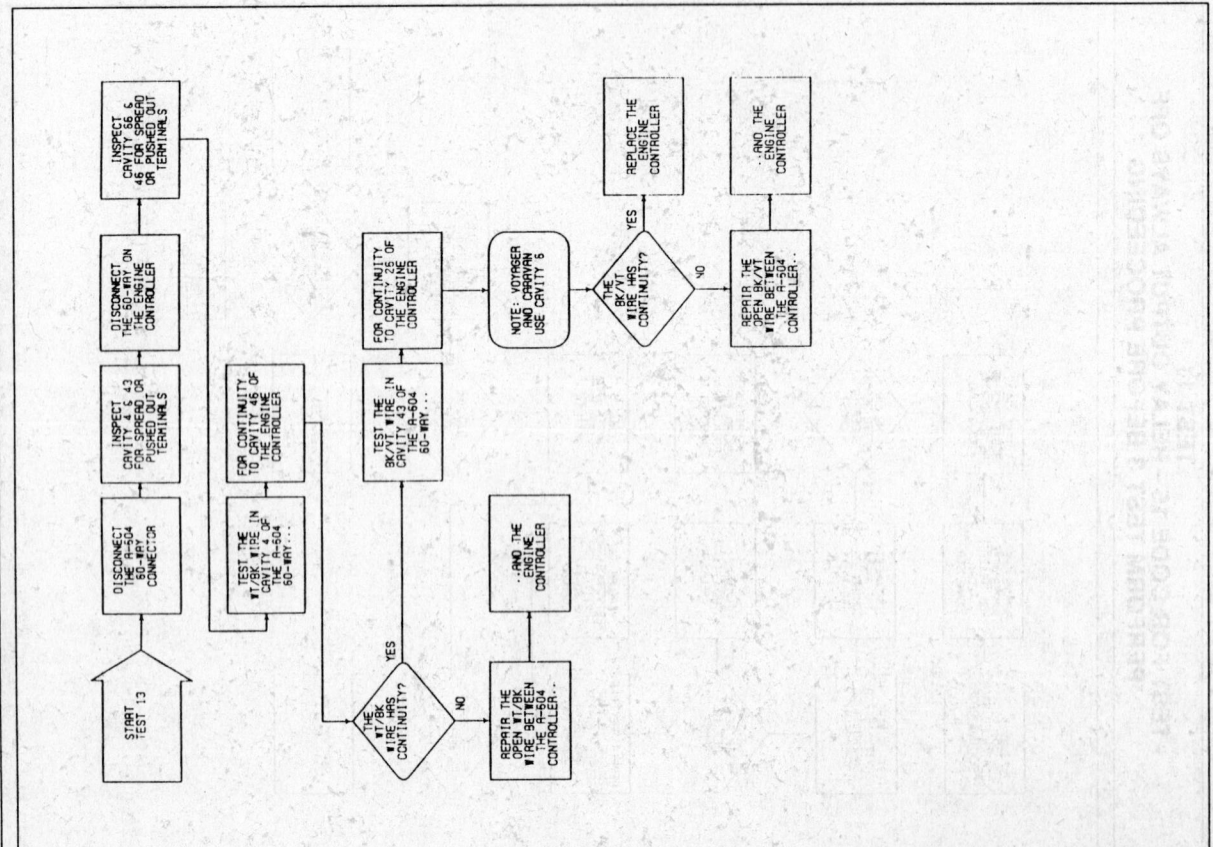

TEST 14

CODE 20 – SWITCHED BATTERY

PERFORM TEST 3 BEFORE PROCEEDING

TEST 13

CODE 19 – BUS COMMUNICATION WITH SMEC

PERFORM TEST 3 BEFORE PROCEEDING

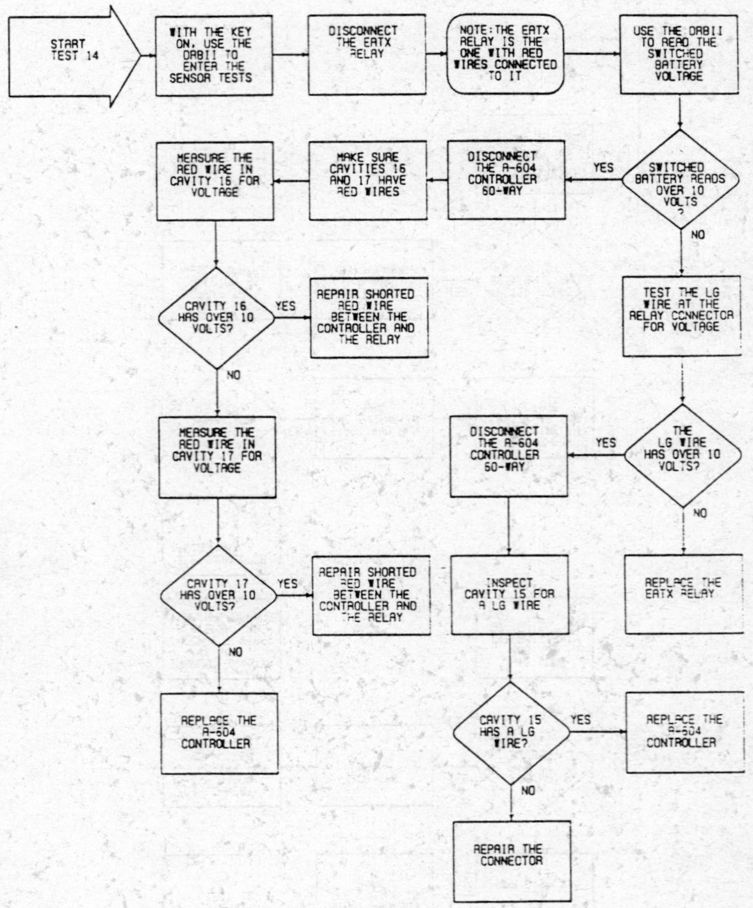

TEST 15
CODE 21 – OD PRESSURE SWITCH CIRCUIT
PERFORM TEST 3 BEFORE PROCEEDING

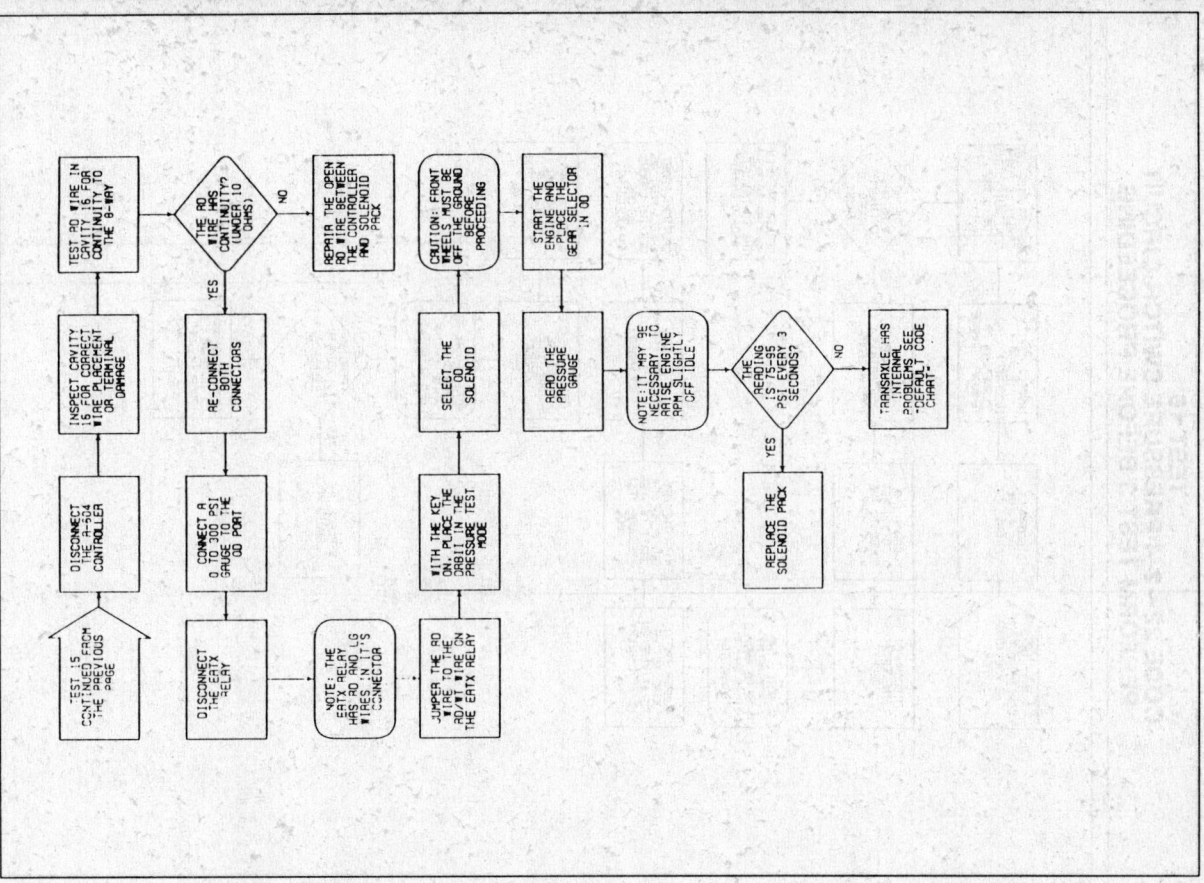

TEST 15
CODE 21 – OD PRESSURE SWITCH CIRCUIT
PERFORM TEST 3 BEFORE PROCEEDING

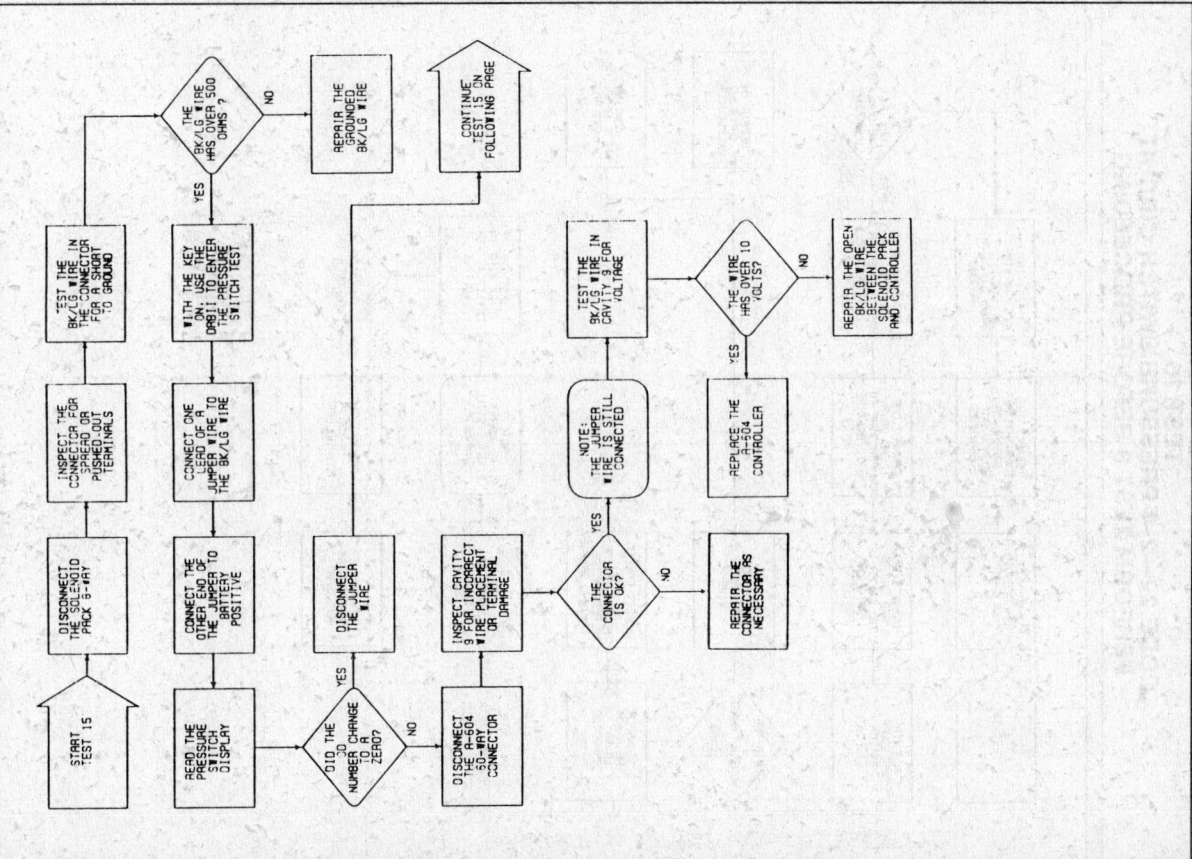

TEST 16
CODE 22 — 2-4 PRESSURE SWITCH CIRCUIT
PERFORM TEST 3 BEFORE PROCEEDING

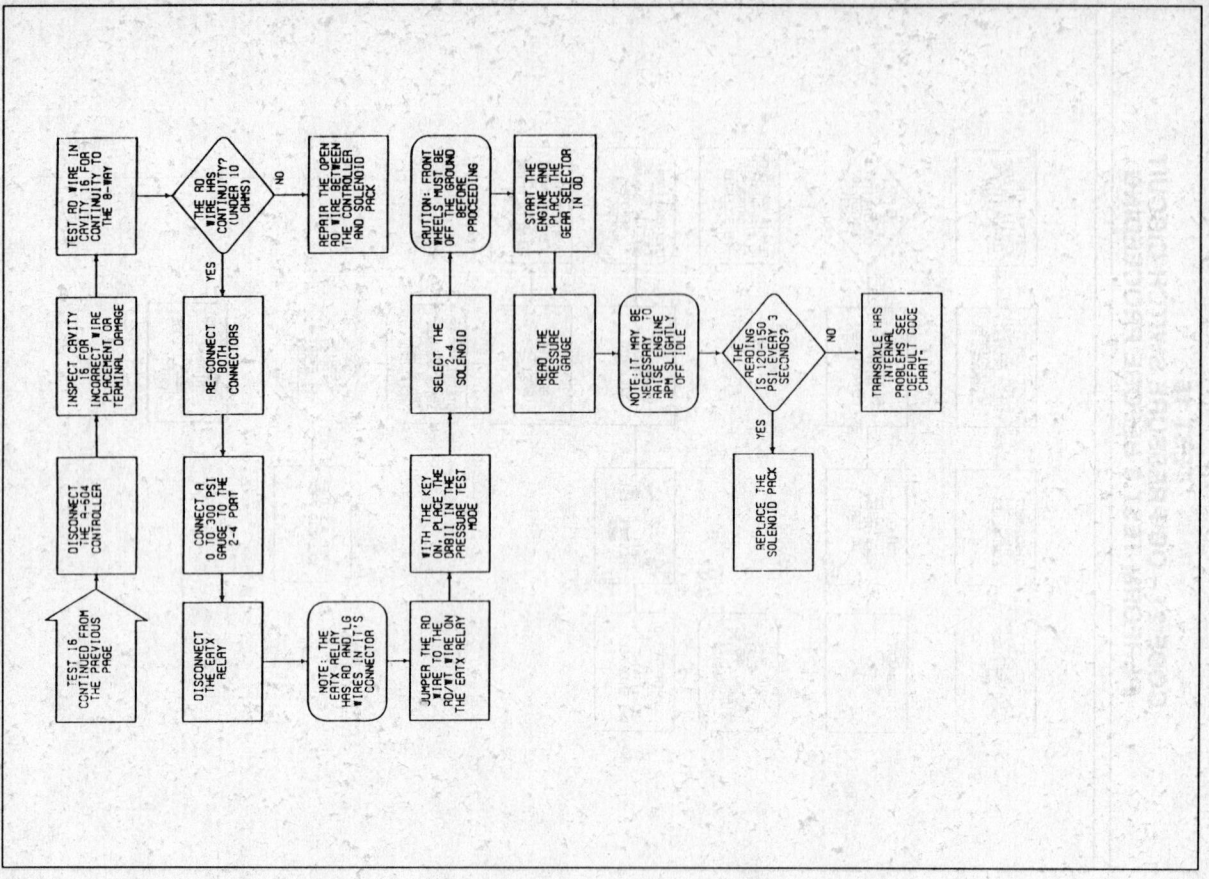

TEST 16
CODE 22 — 2-4 PRESSURE SWITCH CIRCUIT
PERFORM TEST 3 BEFORE PROCEEDING

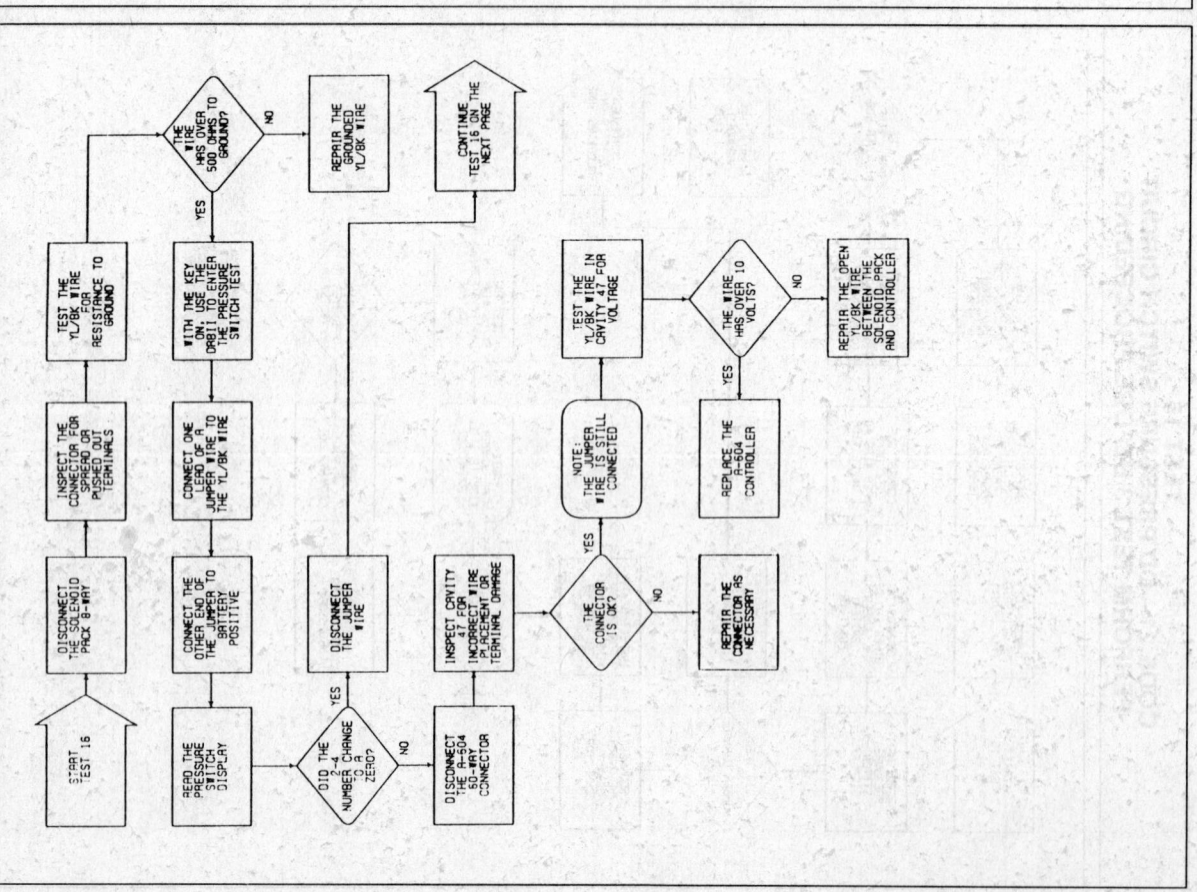

TEST 17
CODE 23 – 2-4/OD PRESSURE SWITCH CIRCUIT
PERFORM TEST 3 BEFORE PROCEEDING

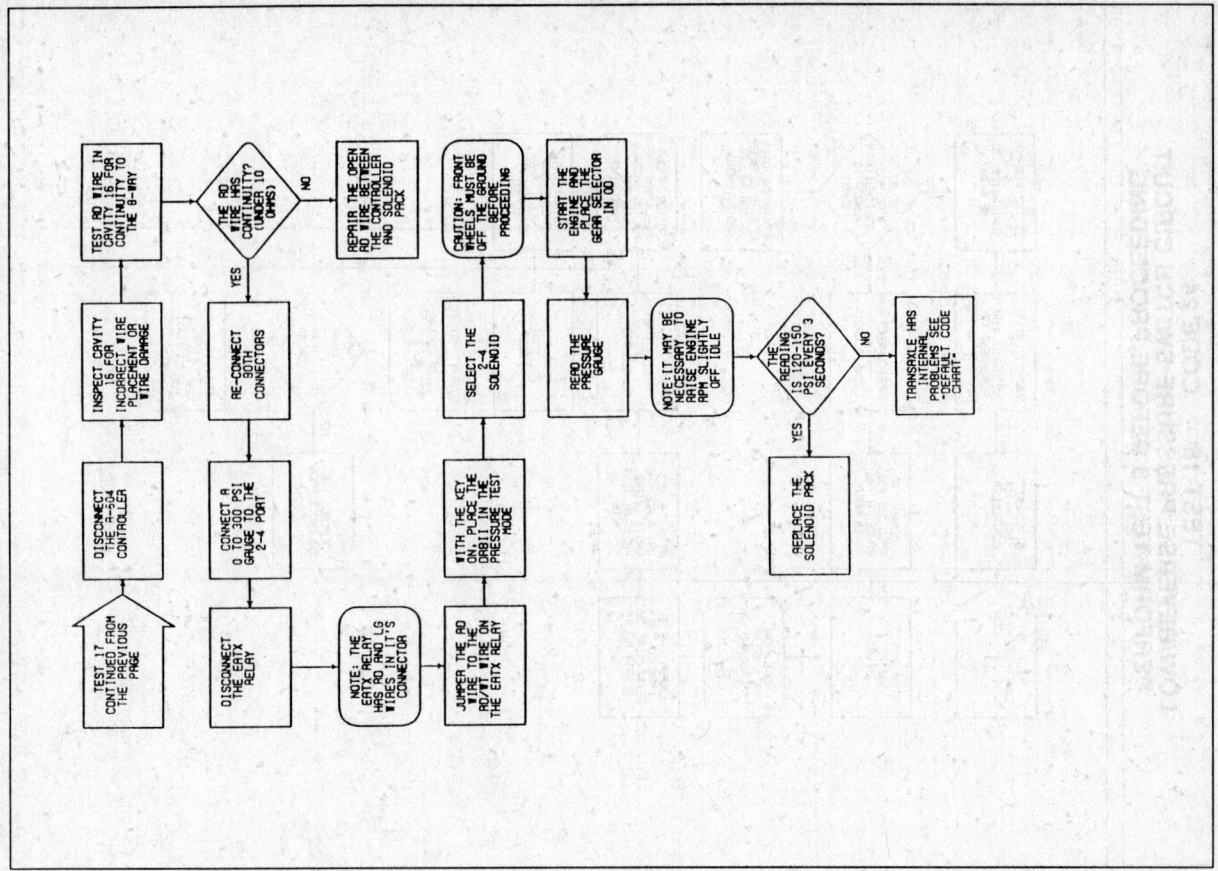

TEST 17
CODE 23 – 2-4/OD PRESSURE SWITCH CIRCUIT
PERFORM TEST 3 BEFORE PROCEEDING

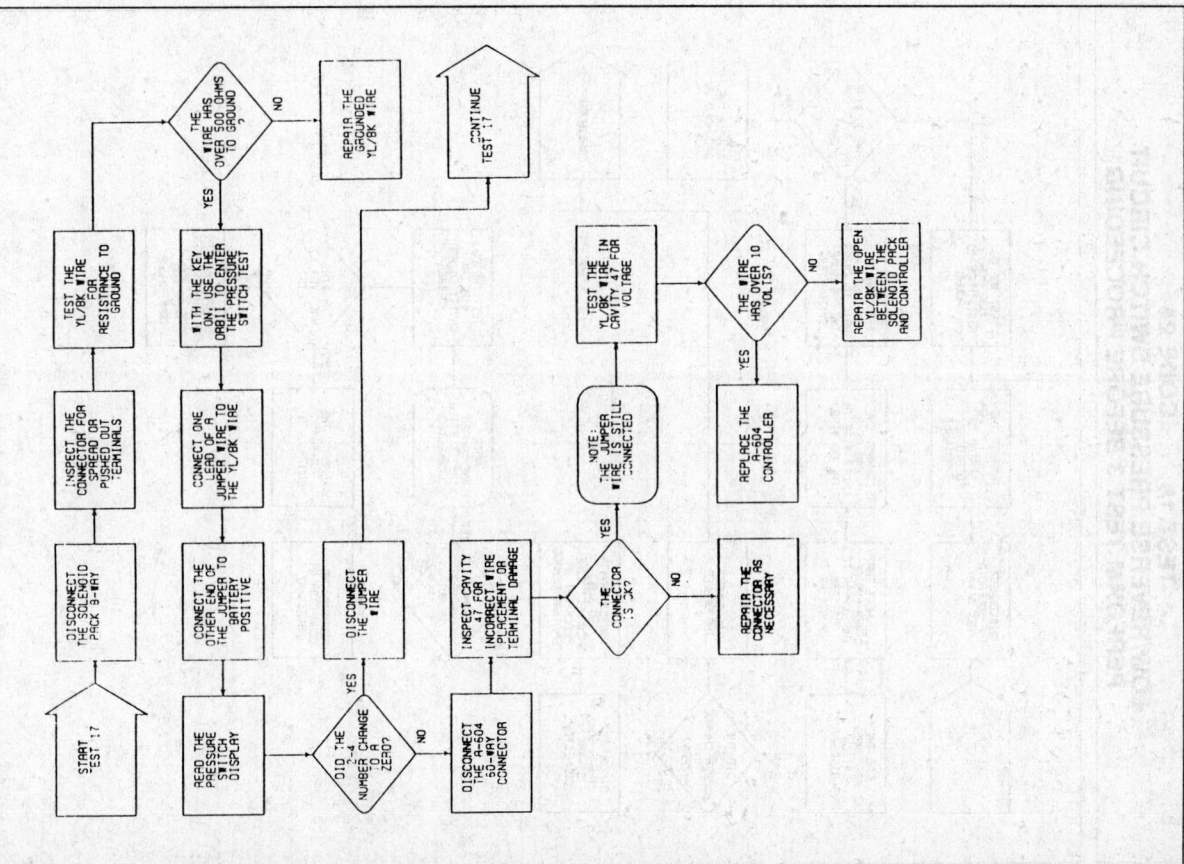

TEST 18   CODE 24
LOW/REVERSE PRESSURE SWITCH CIRCUIT
PERFORM TEST 3 BEFORE PROCEEDING

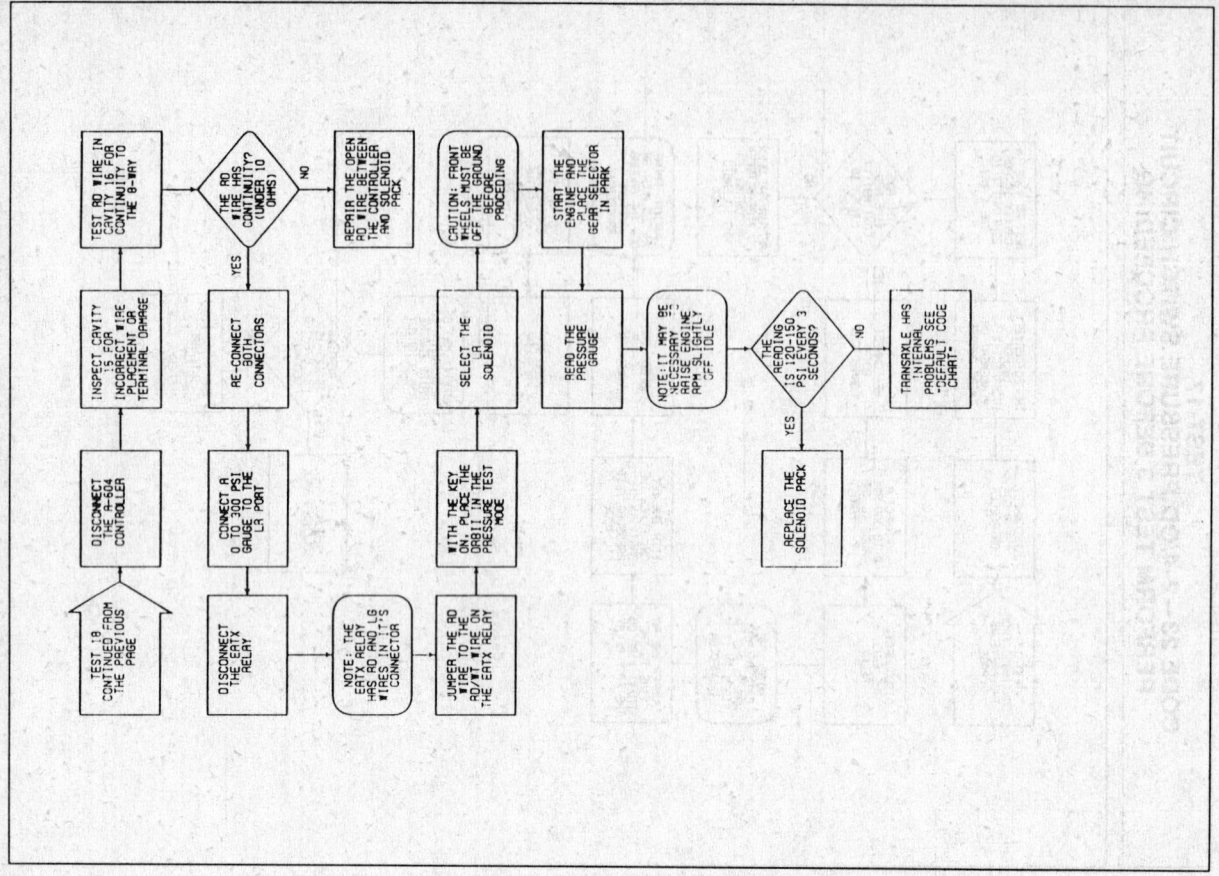

TEST 18   CODE 24
LOW/REVERSE PRESSURE SWITCH CIRCUIT
PERFORM TEST 3 BEFORE PROCEEDING

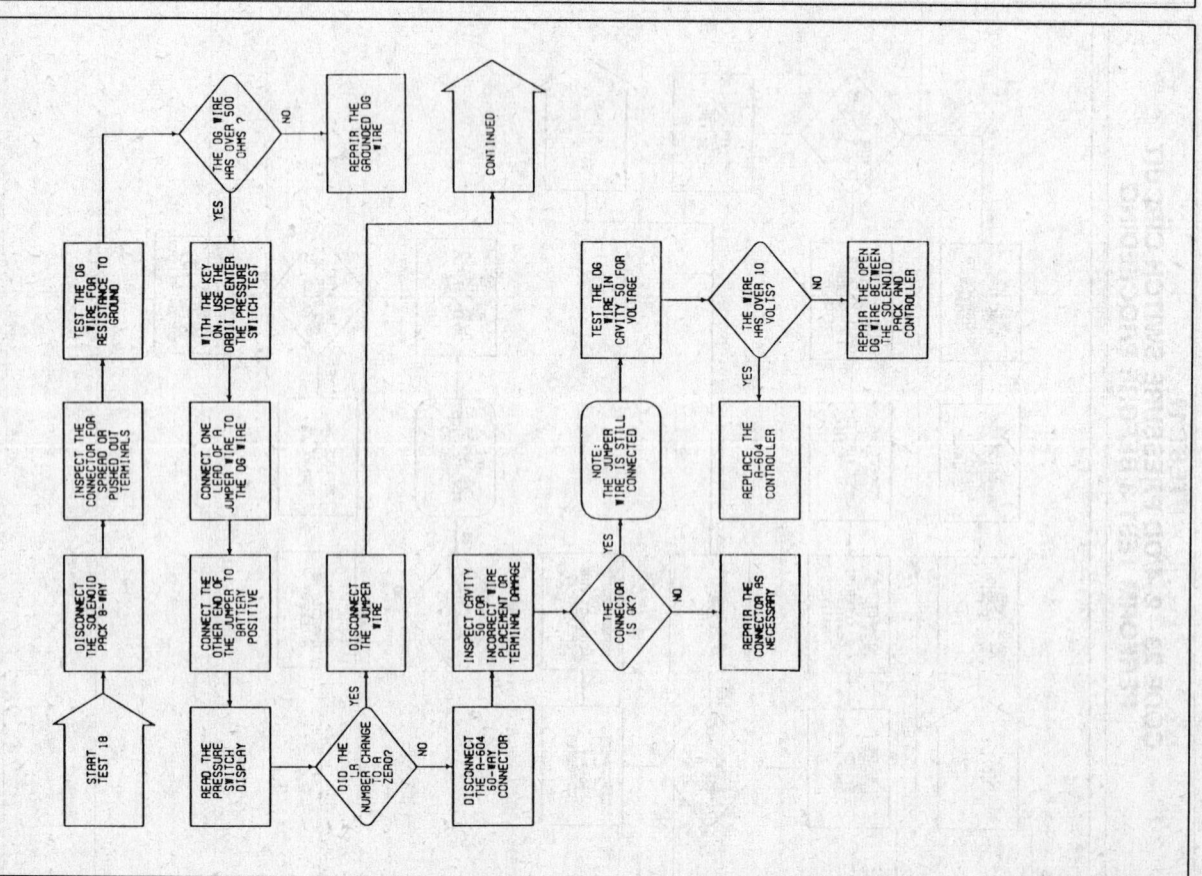

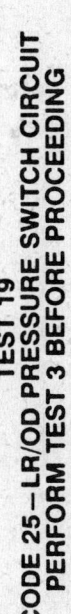

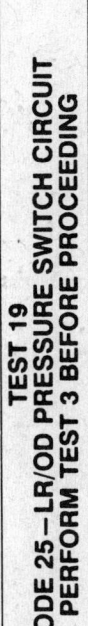

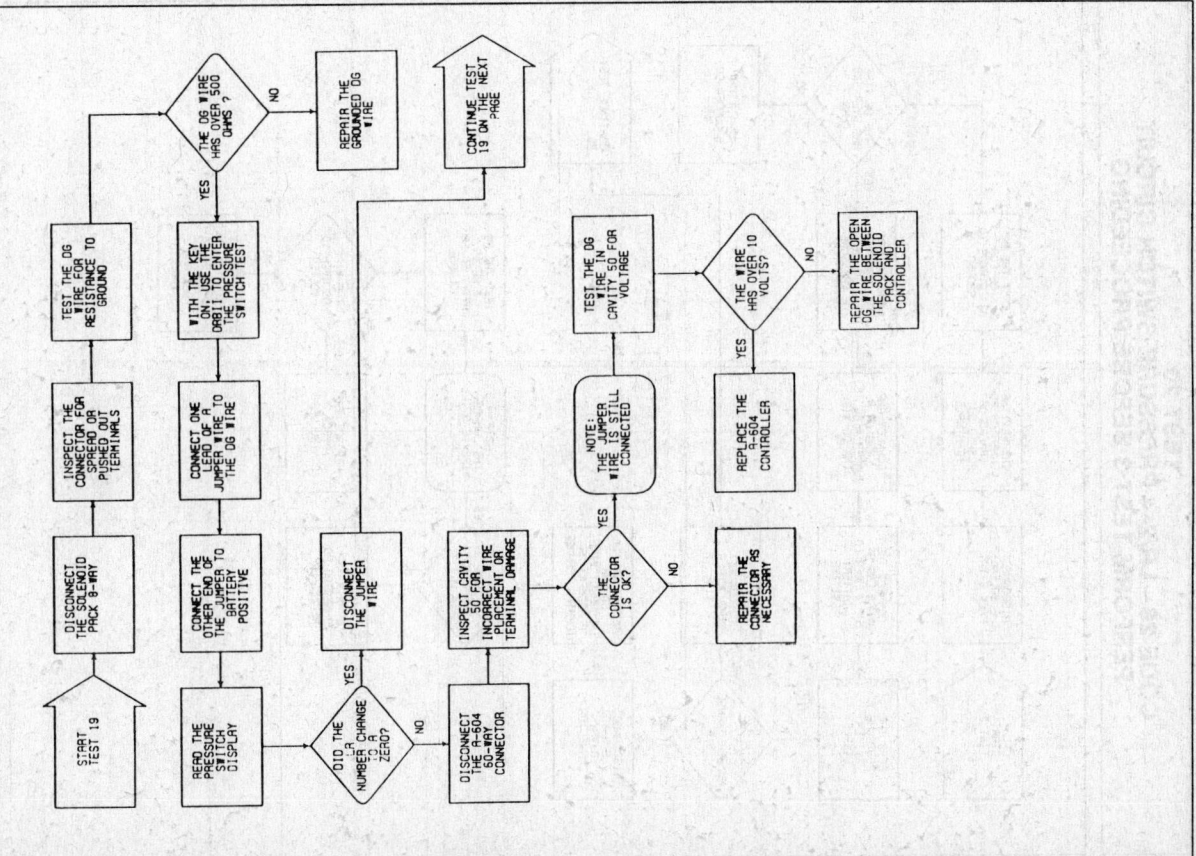

TEST 19
CODE 25—LR/OD PRESSURE SWITCH CIRCUIT
PERFORM TEST 3 BEFORE PROCEEDING

TEST 19
CODE 25—LR/OD PRESSURE SWITCH CIRCUIT
PERFORM TEST 3 BEFORE PROCEEDING

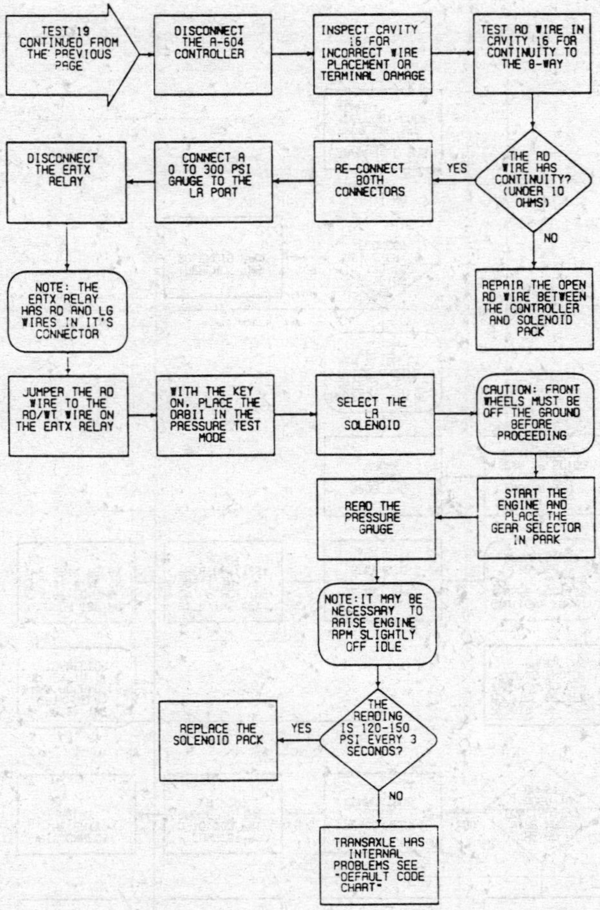

TEST 20
CODE 26 — LR/2-4 PRESSURE SWITCH CIRCUIT
PERFORM TEST 3 BEFORE PROCEEDING

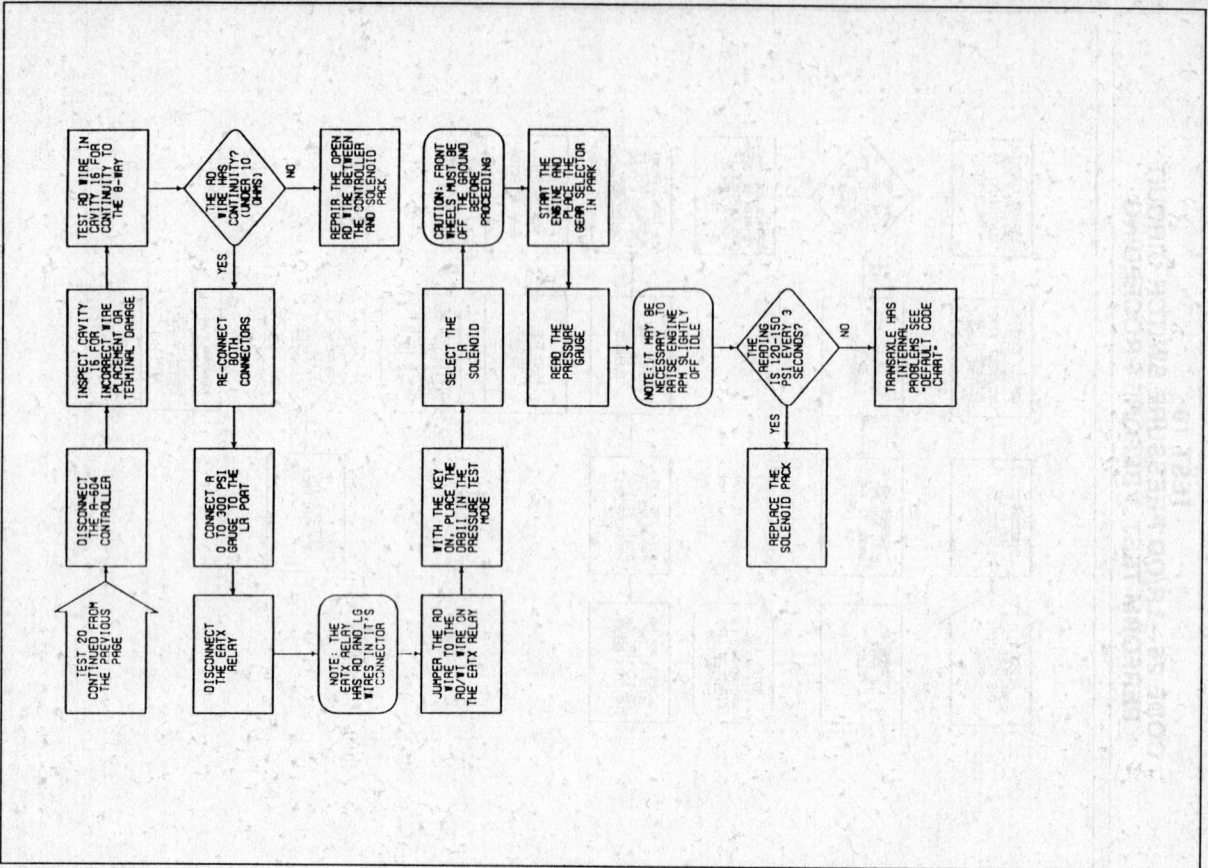

TEST 20
CODE 26 — LR/2-4 PRESSURE SWITCH CIRCUIT
PERFORM TEST 3 BEFORE PROCEEDING

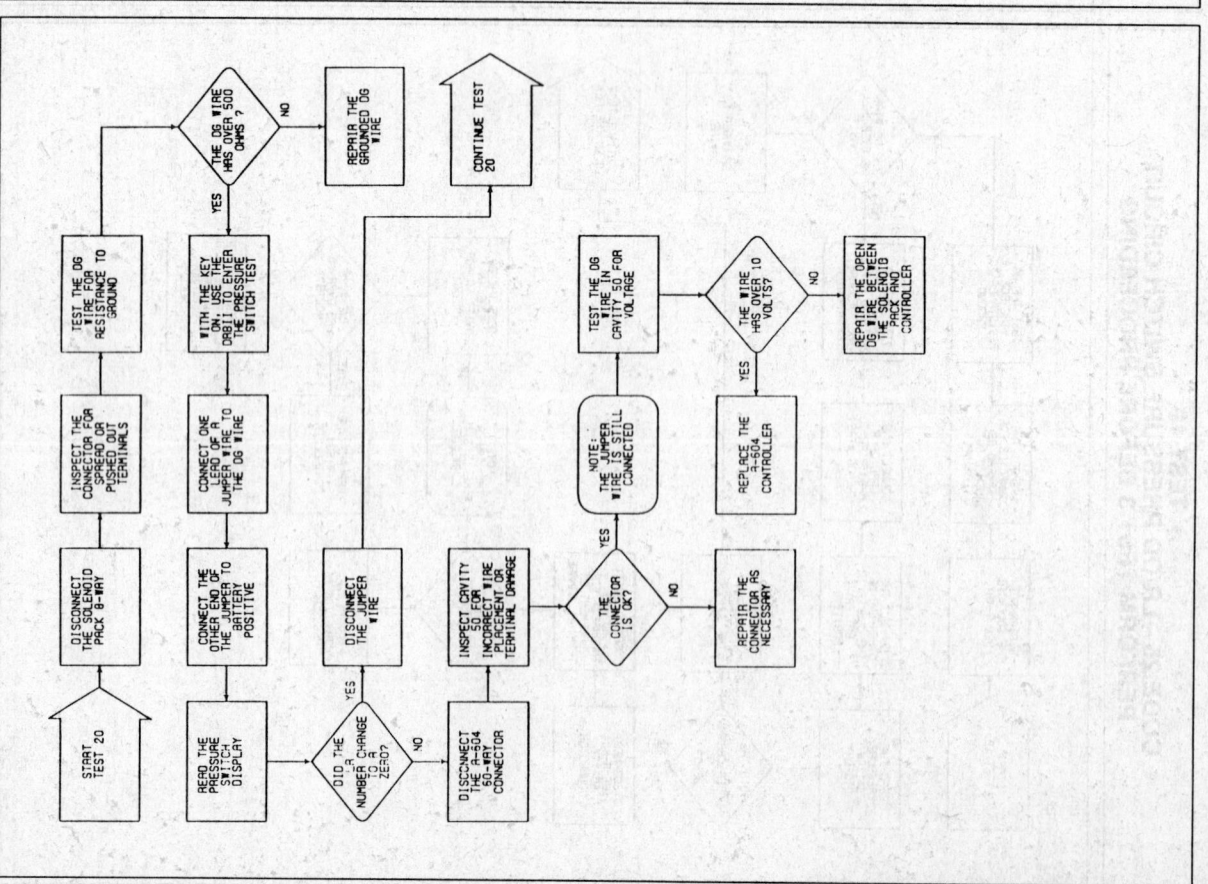

TEST 21
CODE 27 – ALL PRESSURE SWITCH CIRCUITS
PERFORM TEST 3 BEFORE PROCEEDING

TEST 21 CONTINUED FROM THE PREVIOUS PAGE

DISCONNECT THE A-604 CONTROLLER

INSPECT CAVITY 6 FOR INCORRECT WIRE PLACEMENT OR TERMINAL DAMAGE

TEST RD WIRE IN CAVITY 6 FOR CONTINUITY TO THE 8-WAY

THE RD WIRE HAS CONTINUITY? (UNDER 10 OHMS)

NO → REPAIR THE OPEN RD WIRE BETWEEN THE SOLENOID AND SOLENOID PACK

YES → RE-CONNECT BOTH CONNECTORS

CONNECT A 0 TO 300 PSI GAUGE TO THE 2-4 PORT

DISCONNECT THE EATX RELAY

NOTE: THE EATX RELAY HAS RD AND LG WIRES IN IT'S CONNECTOR

JUMPER THE RD WIRE TO THE RD/WT WIRE ON THE EATX RELAY

WITH THE KEY ON, PLACE THE DRB II IN THE PRESSURE TEST MODE

SELECT THE 2-4 SOLENOID

CAUTION: FRONT WHEELS MUST BE PLACE OFF THE GROUND BEFORE PROCEEDING

START THE ENGINE AND PLACE THE GEAR SELECTOR IN OD

READ THE PRESSURE GAUGE

NOTE: IT MAY BE NECESSARY TO RAISE ENGINE RPM SLIGHTLY OFF IDLE

THE READING IS READING 50 PSI EVERY 3 SECONDS?

NO → TRANSAXLE HAS INTERNAL PROBLEMS, SEE "DEFAULT CODE CHART"

YES → REPLACE THE SOLENOID PACK

TEST 21
CODE 27 – ALL PRESSURE SWITCH CIRCUITS
PERFORM TEST 3 BEFORE PROCEEDING

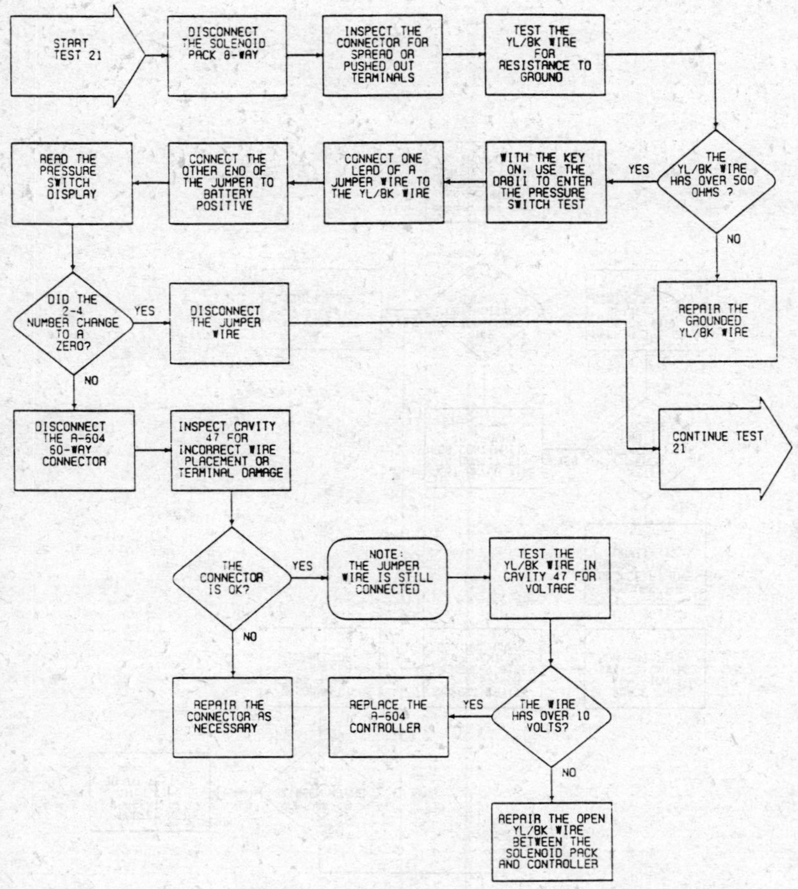

START TEST 21

DISCONNECT THE SOLENOID PACK 8-WAY

INSPECT THE CONNECTOR FOR SPREAD OR PUSHED OUT TERMINALS

TEST THE YL/BK WIRE FOR RESISTANCE TO GROUND

THE YL/BK WIRE HAS OVER 500 OHMS?

NO → REPAIR THE GROUNDED YL/BK WIRE

CONTINUE TEST 21

YES → WITH THE KEY ON, USE THE DRB II TO ENTER THE PRESSURE SWITCH TEST

CONNECT ONE LEAD OF A JUMPER WIRE TO THE YL/BK WIRE

CONNECT THE OTHER END OF THE JUMPER TO BATTERY POSITIVE

READ THE PRESSURE SWITCH DISPLAY

DID THE 2-4 NUMBER CHANGE TO A ZERO?

YES → DISCONNECT THE JUMPER WIRE

NO → DISCONNECT THE A-604 60-WAY CONNECTOR

INSPECT CAVITY 47 FOR INCORRECT WIRE PLACEMENT OR TERMINAL DAMAGE

THE CONNECTOR IS OK?

YES → NOTE: THE JUMPER WIRE IS STILL CONNECTED

TEST THE YL/BK WIRE IN CAVITY 47 FOR VOLTAGE

THE WIRE HAS OVER 10 VOLTS?

NO → REPAIR THE OPEN YL/BK WIRE BETWEEN THE SOLENOID PACK AND CONTROLLER

YES → REPLACE THE A-604 CONTROLLER

NO → REPAIR THE CONNECTOR AS NECESSARY

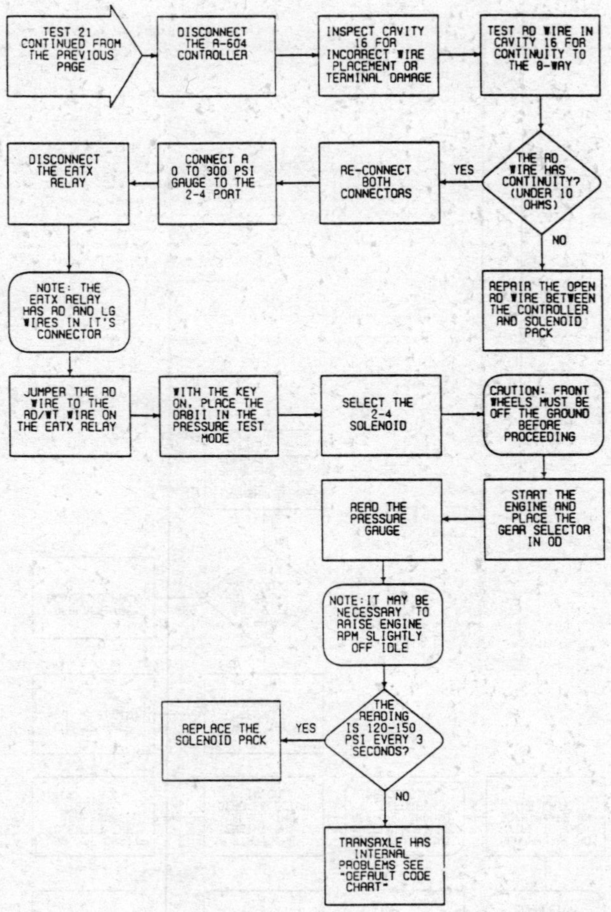

TEST 23
CODE 31 — OD HYDRAULIC PRESSURE SWITCH
PERFORM TEST 3 BEFORE PROCEEDING

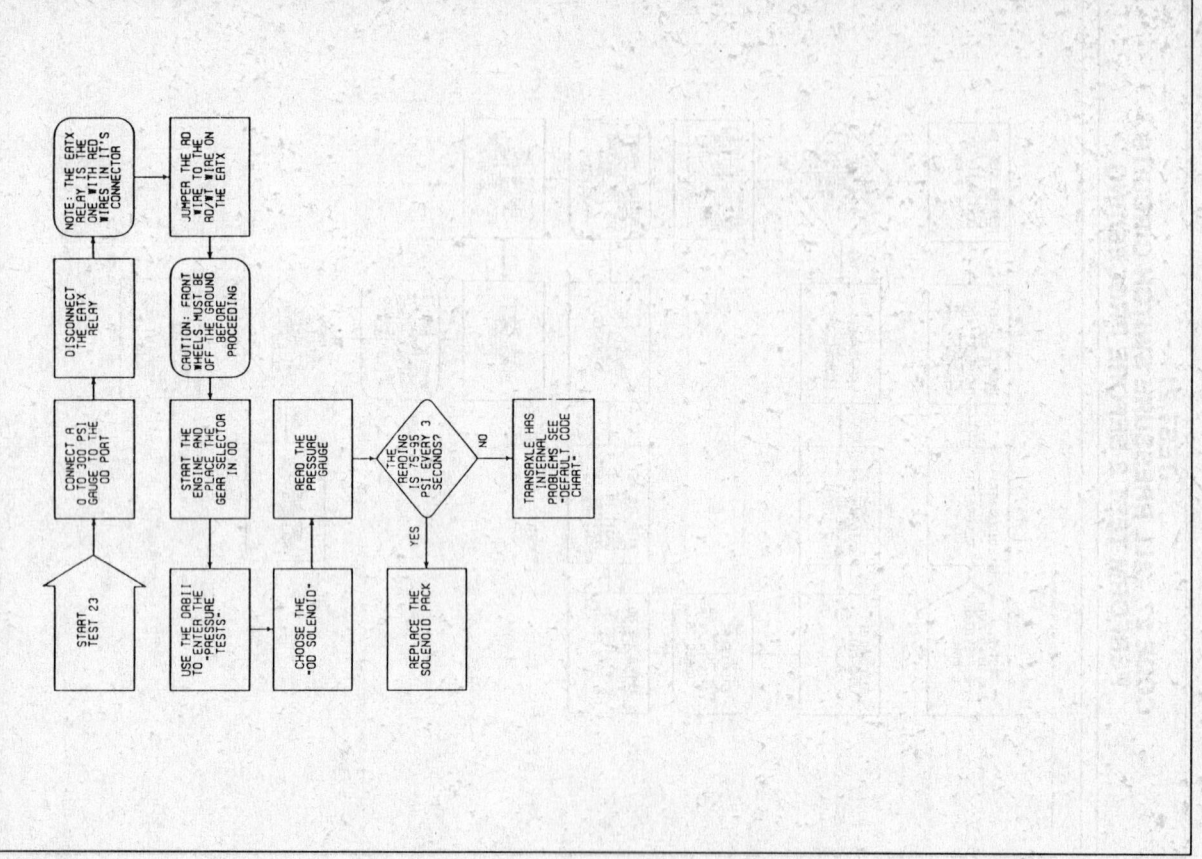

TEST 22
CODE 29 — THROTTLE POSITION SIGNAL
PERFORM TEST 3 BEFORE PROCEEDING

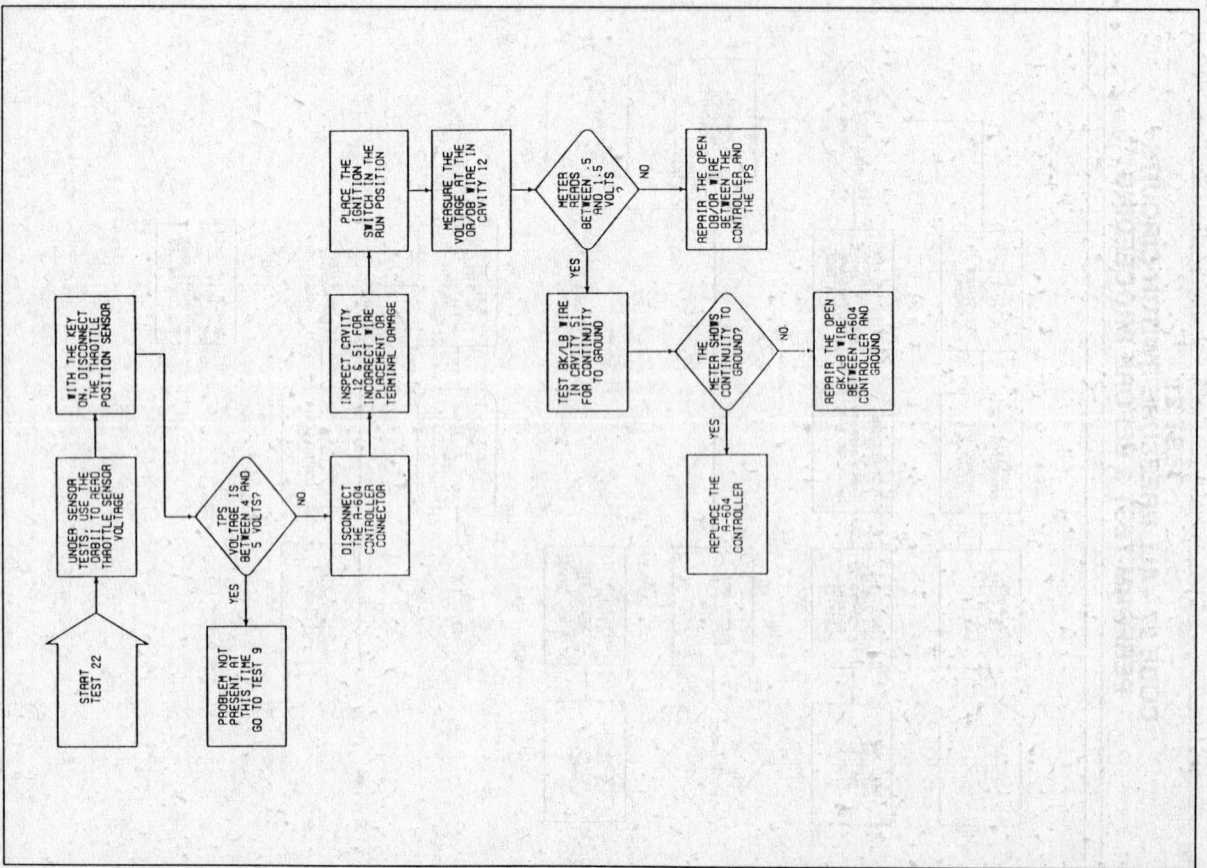

TEST 25
CODE 33 — OD/2-4 HYDRAULIC PRESSURE SWITCH
PERFORM TEST 3 BEFORE PROCEEDING

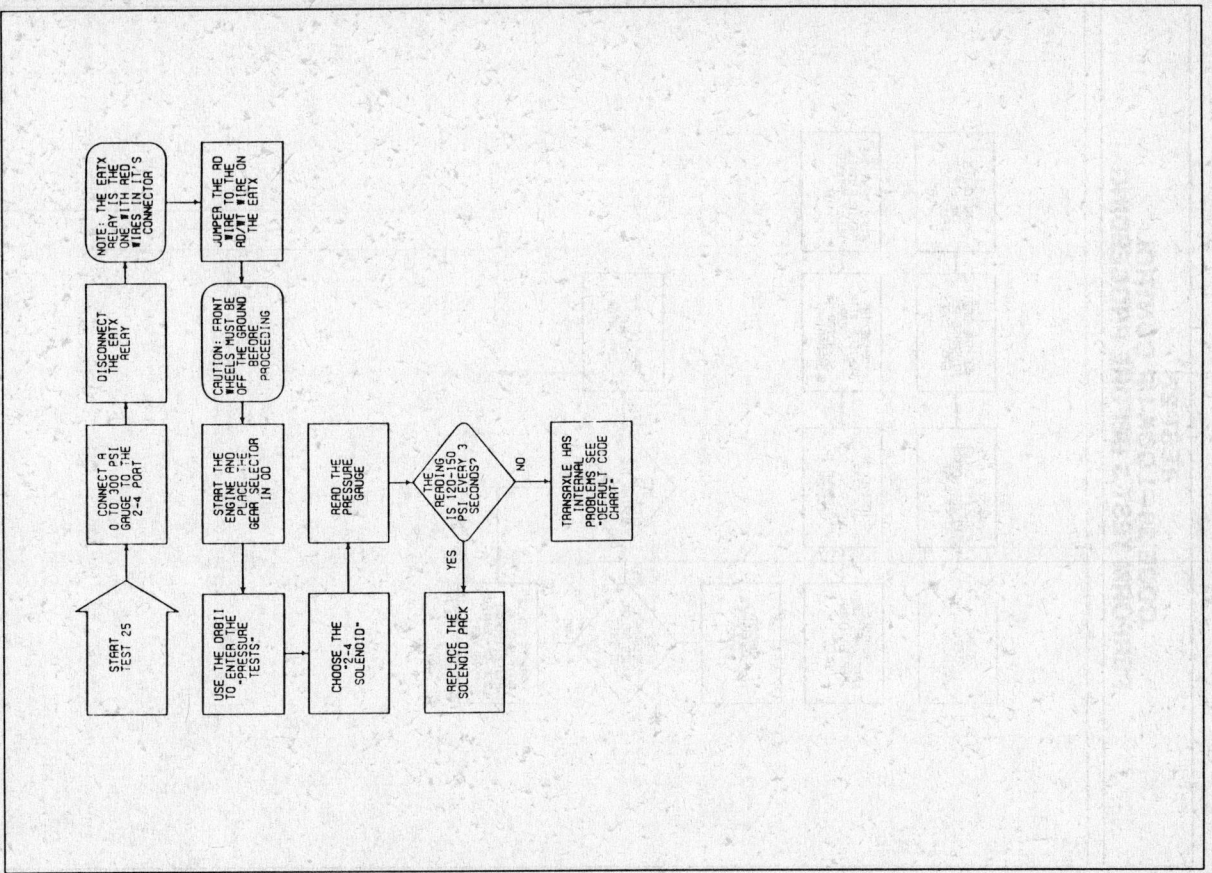

TEST 24
CODE 32 — 2-4 HYDRAULIC PRESSURE SWITCH
PERFORM TEST 3 BEFORE PROCEEDING

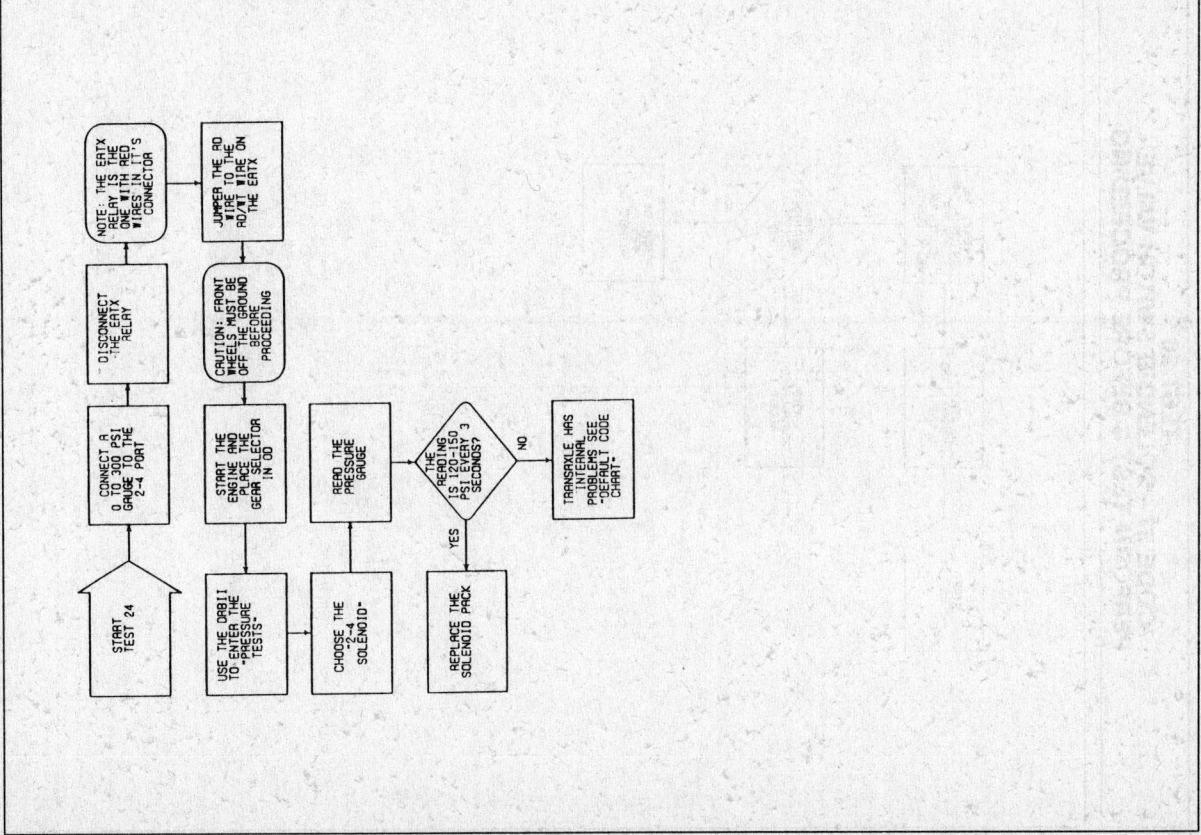

TEST 27
CODE 38 — LOCK-UP CONTROL
PERFORM TEST 3 BEFORE PROCEEDING

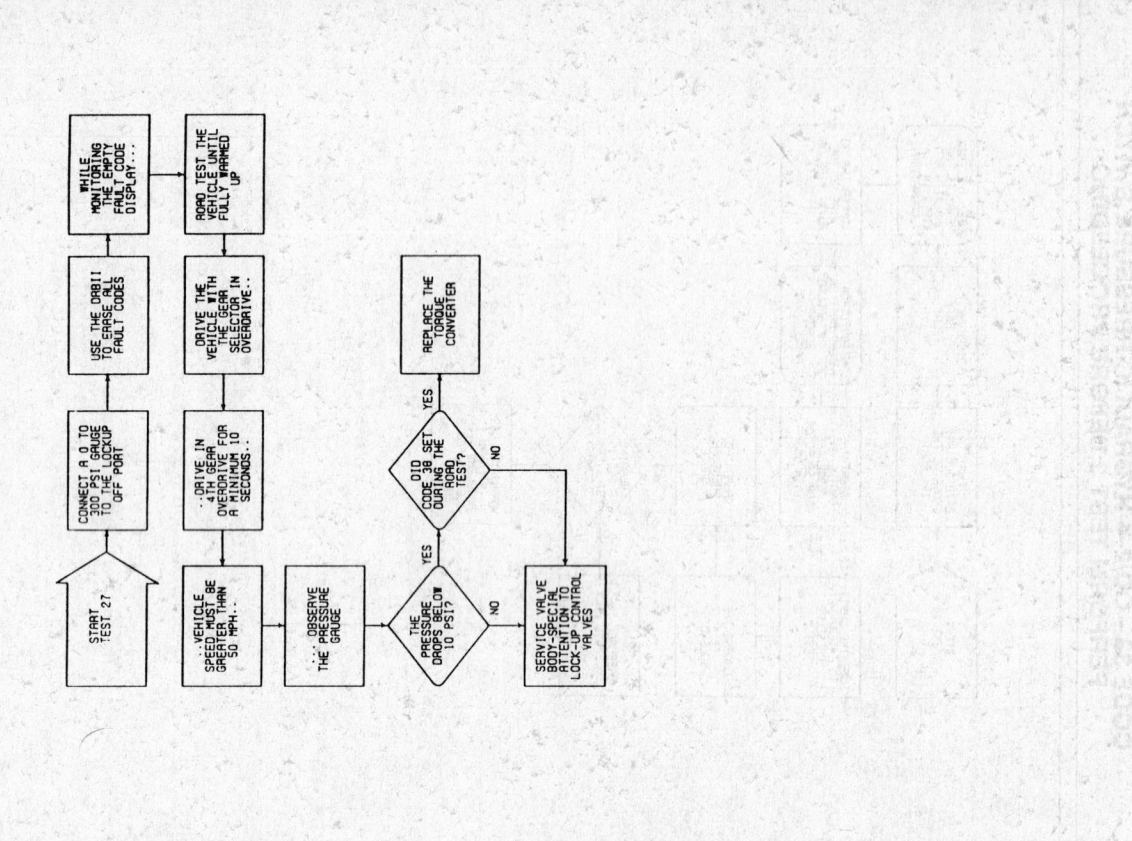

START TEST 27

CONNECT A 0 TO 300 PSI GAUGE TO THE LOCKUP OFF PORT

USE THE DRB11 TO ERASE ALL FAULT CODES

WHILE MONITORING THE EMPTY FAULT CODE DISPLAY...

ROAD TEST THE VEHICLE UNTIL FULLY WARMED UP

DRIVE THE VEHICLE WITH THE GEAR SELECTOR IN OVERDRIVE...

...DRIVE IN 4TH GEAR OVERDRIVE FOR A MINIMUM 10 SECONDS...

...VEHICLE SPEED MUST BE GREATER THAN 50 MPH...

....OBSERVE THE PRESSURE GAUGE

THE PRESSURE DROPS BELOW 10 PSI?

DID CODE 38 SET DURING THE ROAD TEST?

REPLACE THE TORQUE CONVERTER

SERVICE VALVE BODY-SPECIAL ATTENTION TO LOCK-UP CONTROL VALVES

TEST 26
CODE 37 — SOLENOID SWITCH VALVE
PERFORM TEST 3 BEFORE PROCEEDING

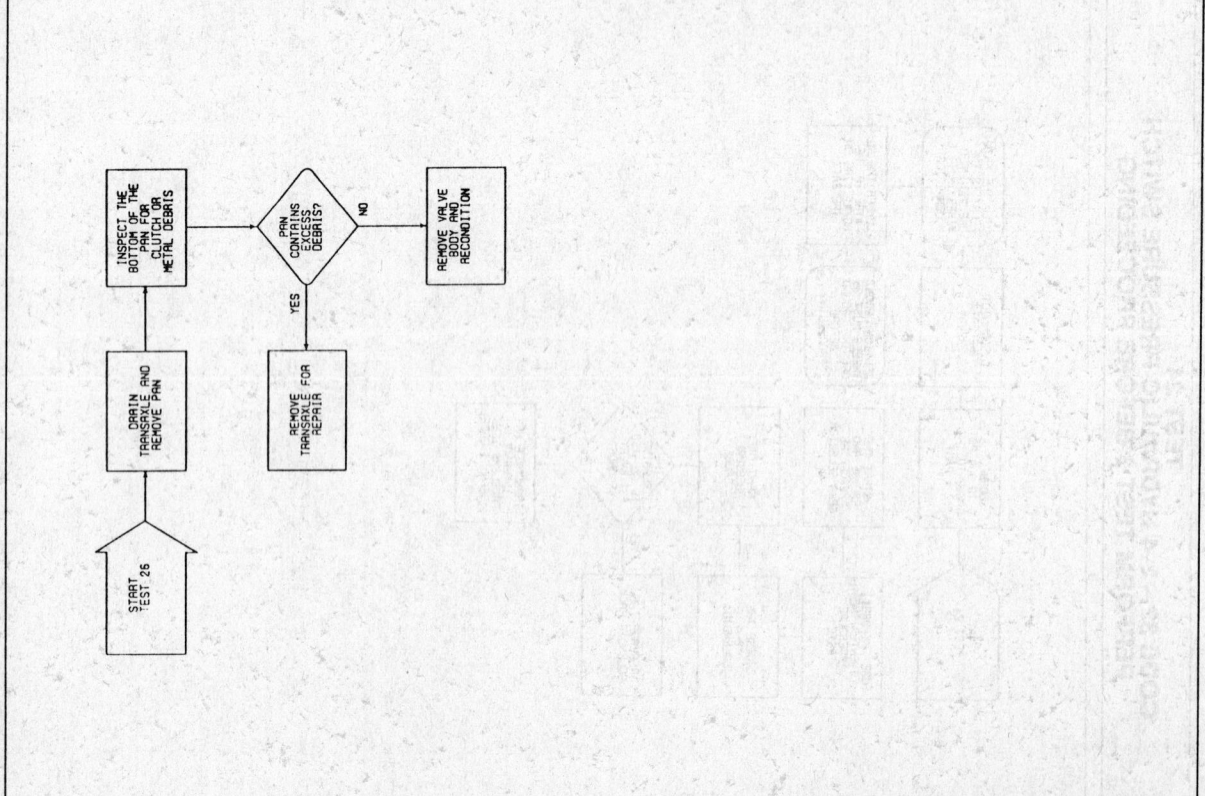

START TEST 26

DRAIN TRANSAXLE AND REMOVE PAN

INSPECT THE BOTTOM OF THE PAN FOR CLUTCH OR METAL DEBRIS

PAN CONTAINS EXCESS DEBRIS?

REMOVE FOR TRANSAXLE REPAIR

REMOVE VALVE BODY AND RECONDITION

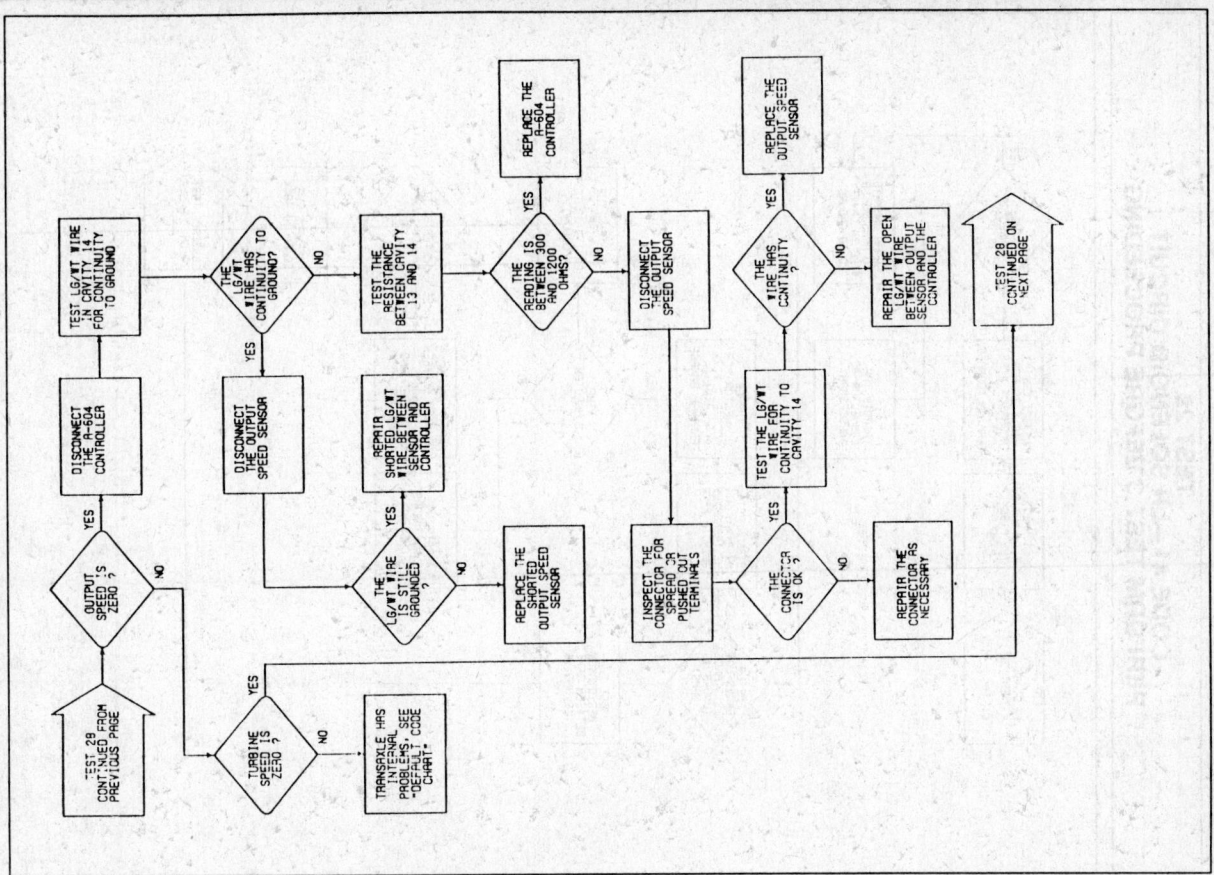

TEST 28
CODE 39 — TURBINE/TRANS OUTPUT SPEED CIRCUIT
PERFORM TEST 3 BEFORE PROCEEDING

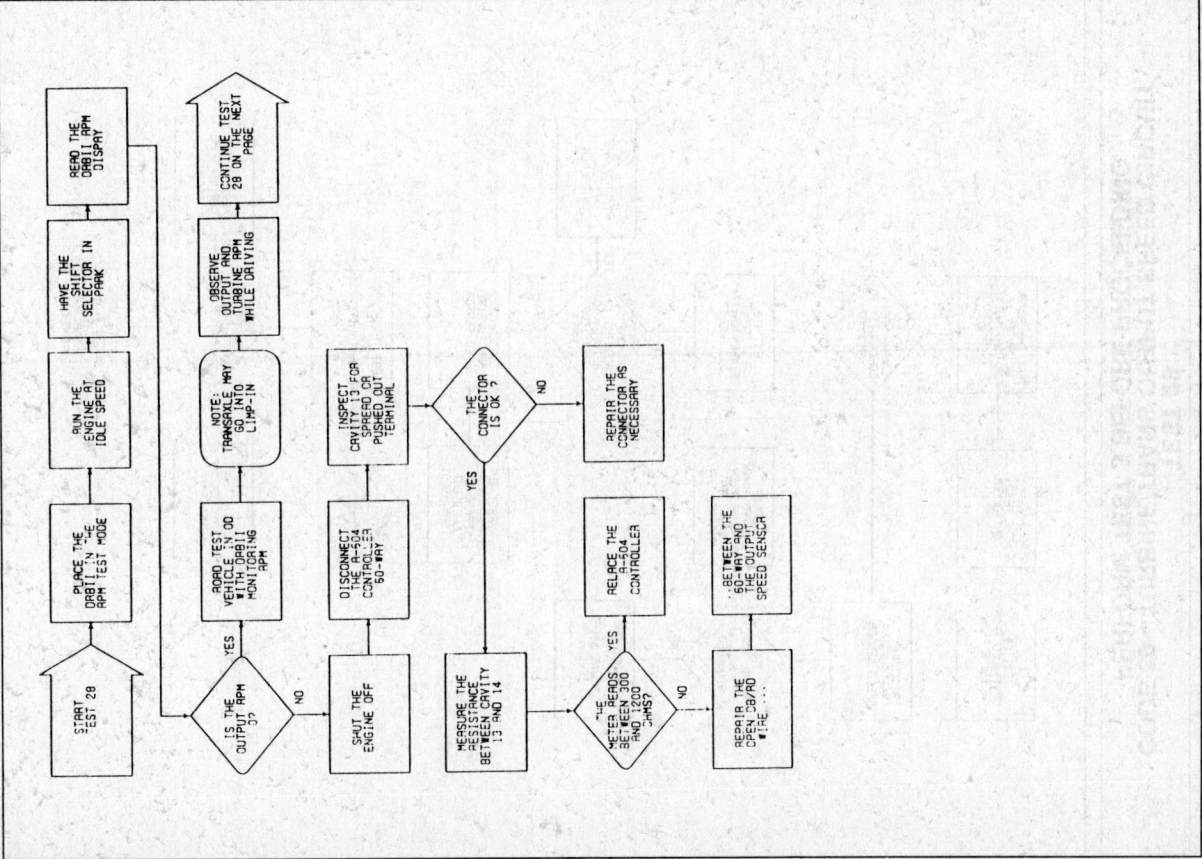

TEST 28
CODE 39 — TURBINE/TRANS OUTPUT SPEED CIRCUIT
PERFORM TEST 3 BEFORE PROCEEDING

TEST 29
CODE 41 – LR SOLENOID CIRCUIT
PERFORM TEST 3 BEFORE PROCEEDING

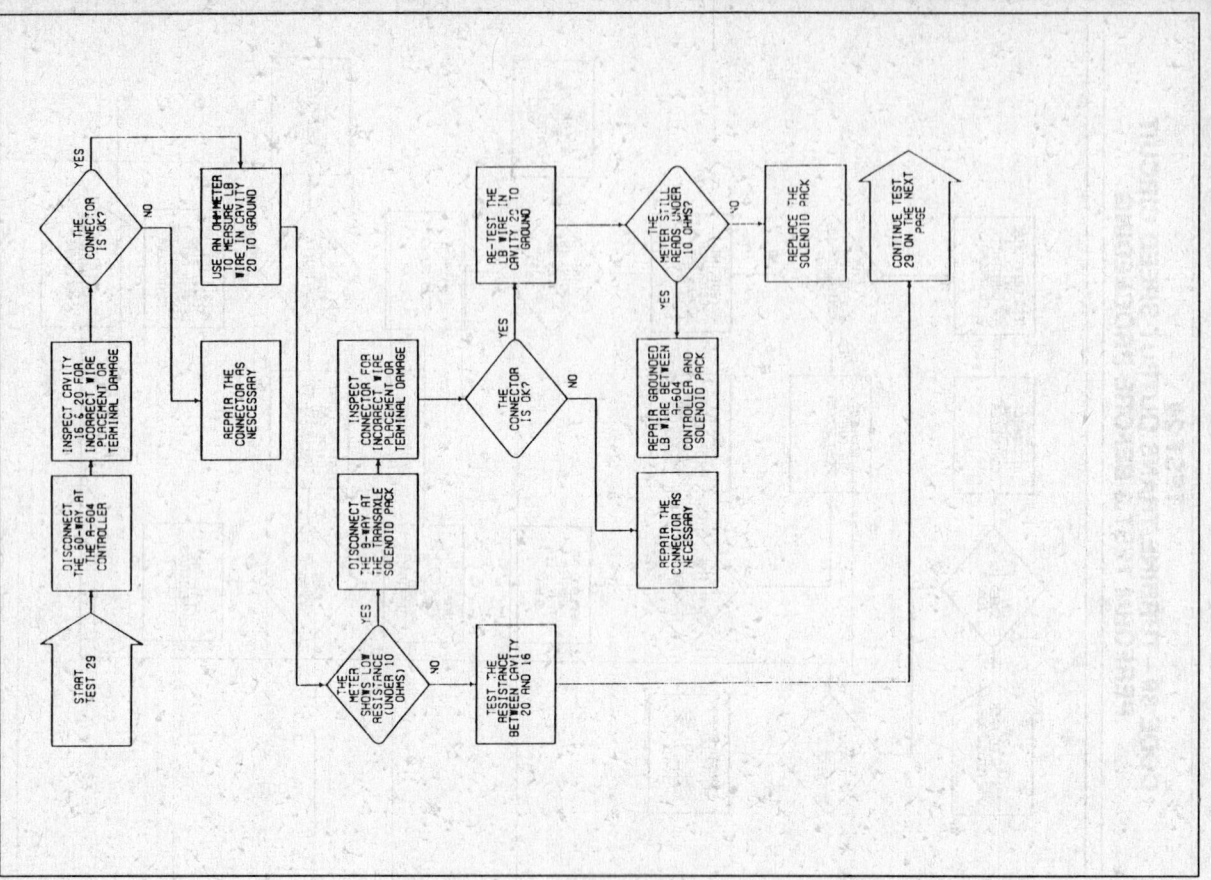

TEST 28
CODE 39 – TURBINE/TRANS OUTPUT SPEED CIRCUIT
PERFORM TEST 3 BEFORE PROCEEDING

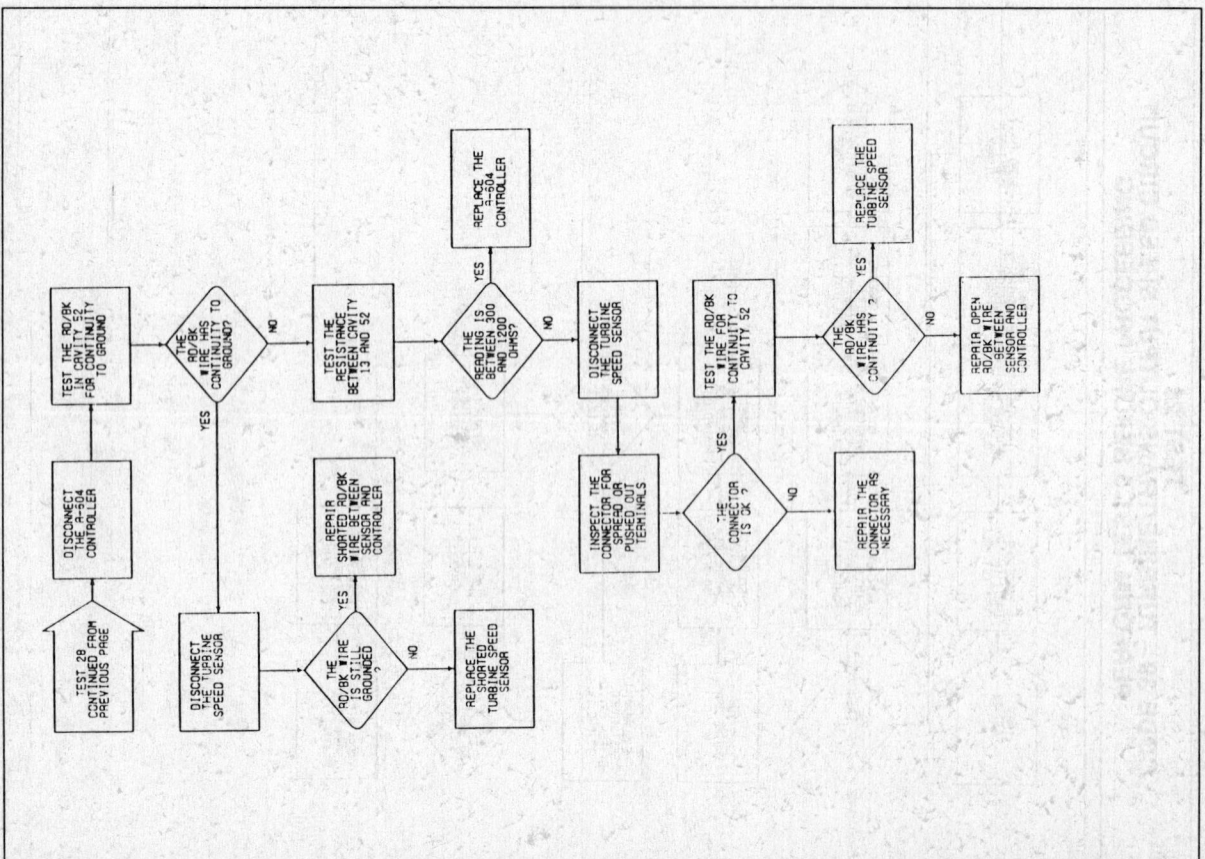

TEST 29
CODE 41 – LR SOLENOID CIRCUIT
PERFORM TEST 3 BEFORE PROCEEDING

TEST 29
CODE 41 – LR SOLENOID CIRCUIT
PERFORM TEST 3 BEFORE PROCEEDING

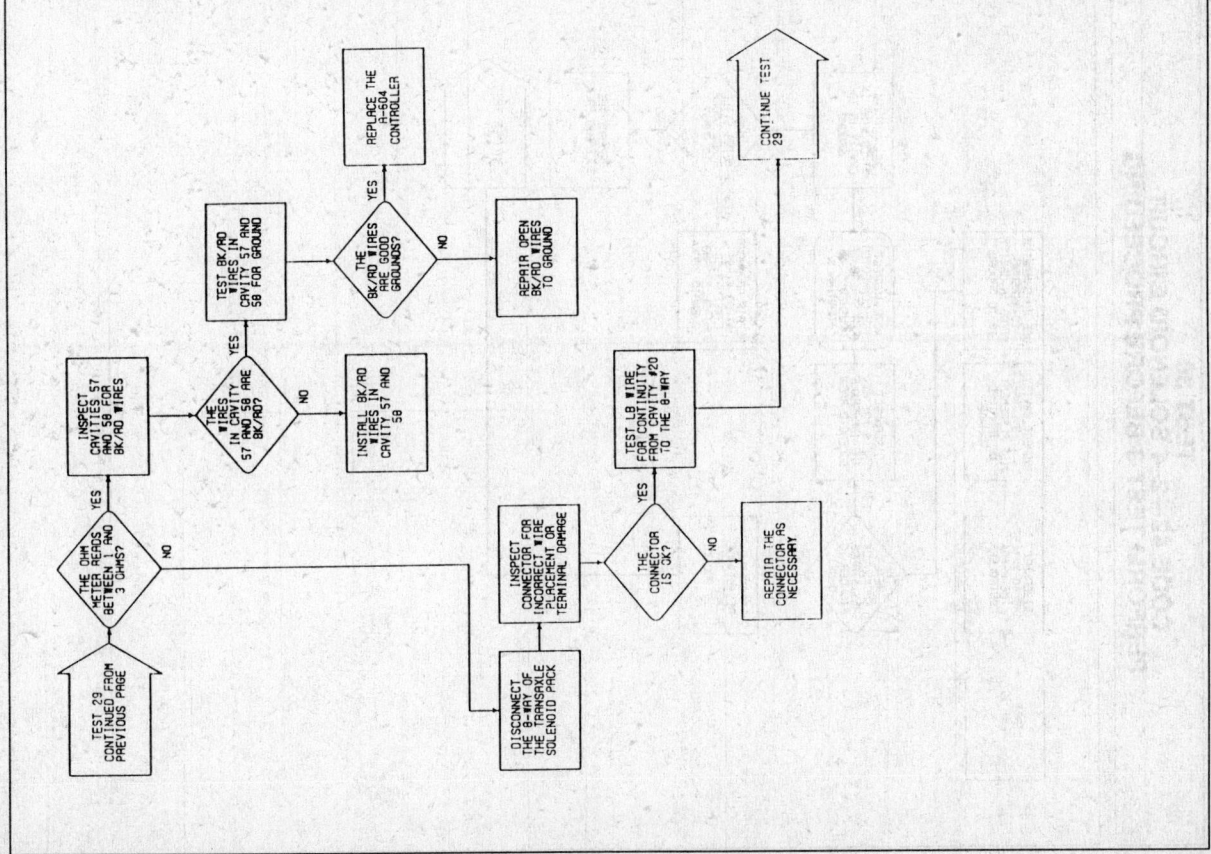

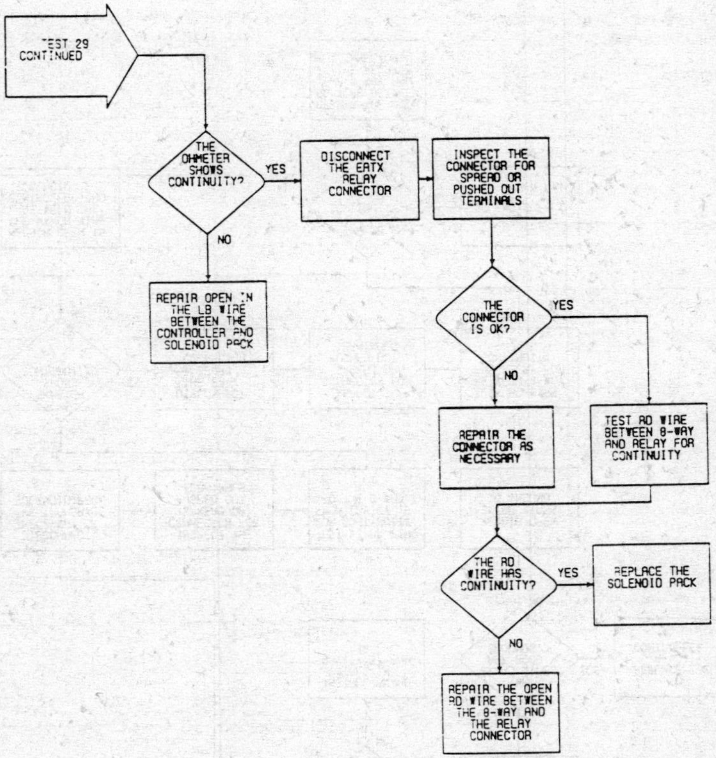

TEST 30
CODE 42—2—4 SOLENOID CIRCUIT
PERFORM TEST 3 BEFORE PROCEEDING

TEST 30
CODE 42—2—4 SOLENOID CIRCUIT
PERFORM TEST 3 BEFORE PROCEEDING

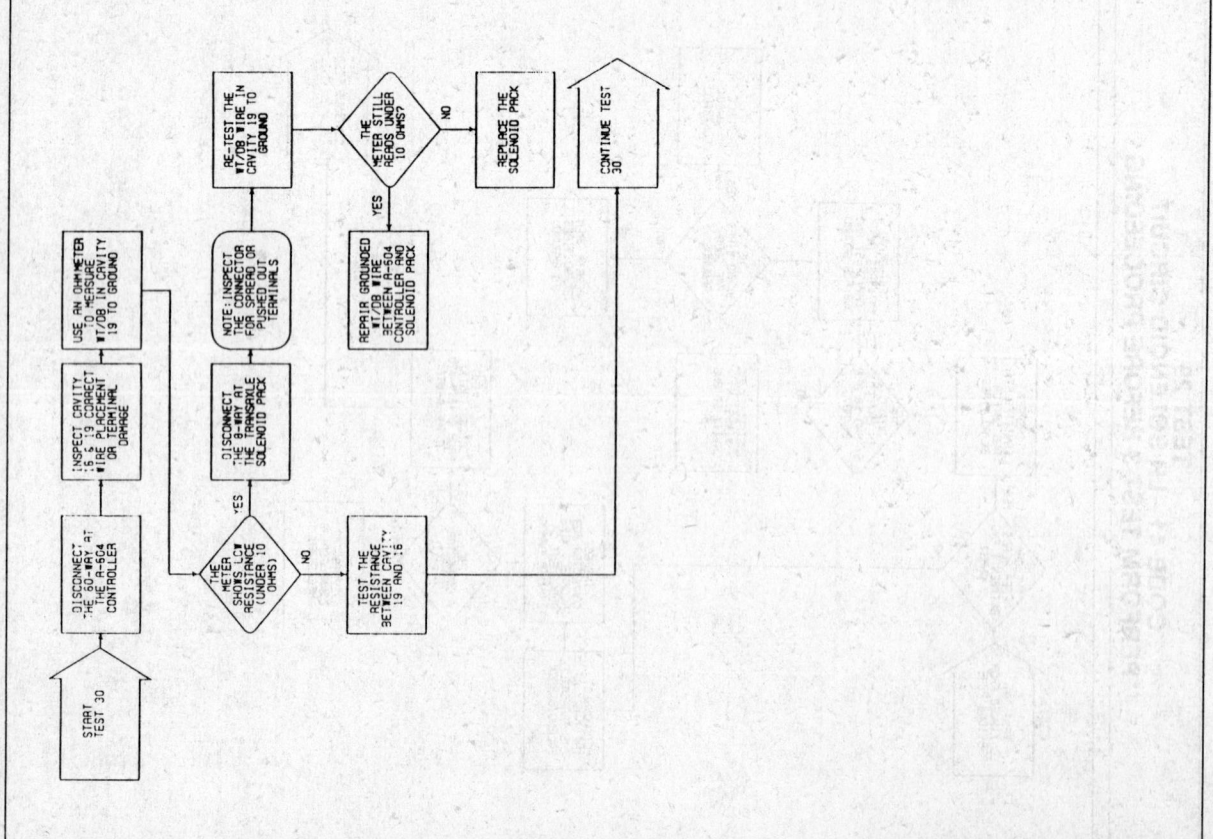

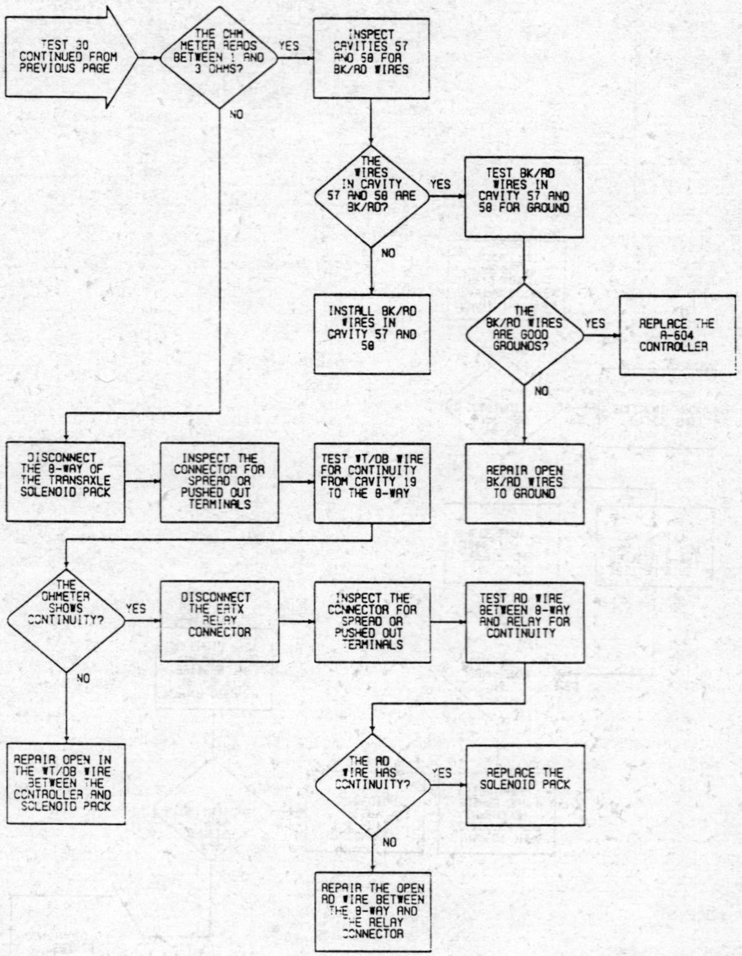

TEST 31
CODE 43 – OD SOLENOID CIRCUIT
PERFORM TEST 3 BEFORE PROCEEDING

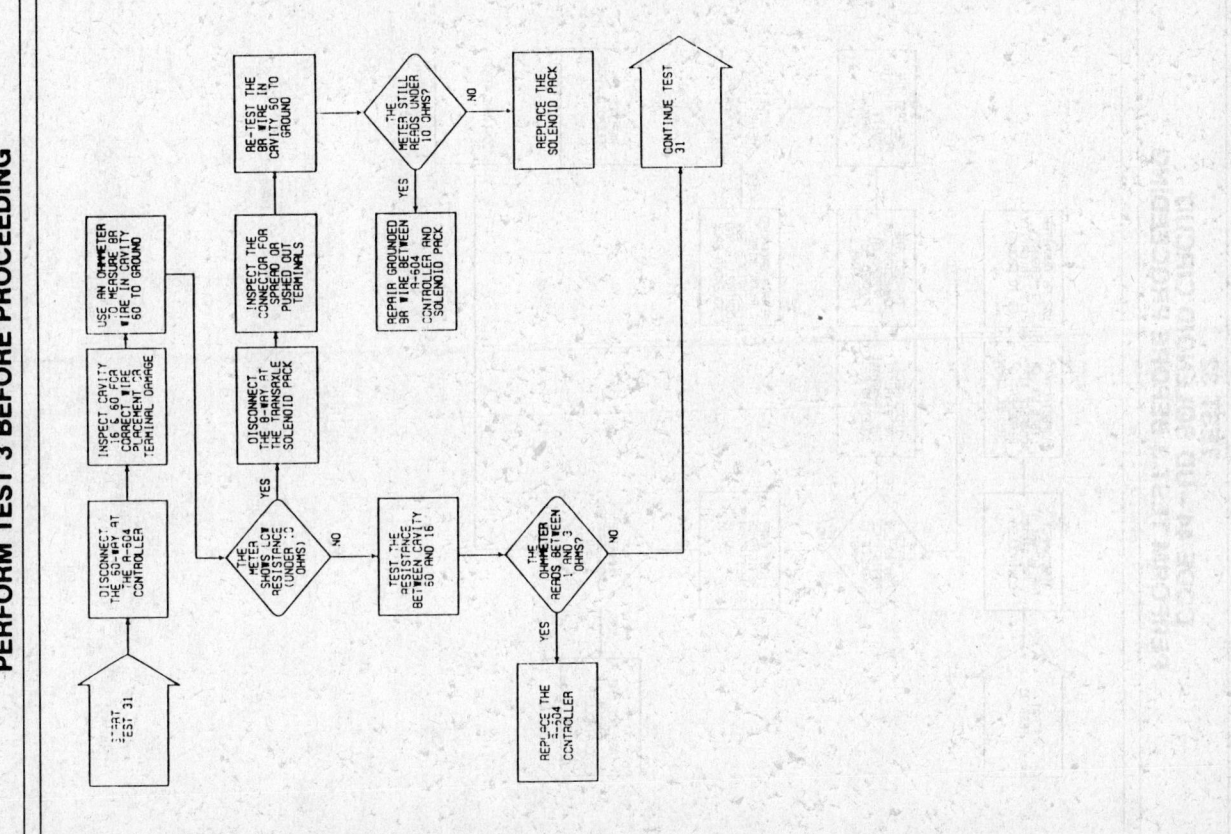

TEST 31 CONTINUED FROM PREVIOUS PAGE

DISCONNECT THE 8-WAY OF THE TRANSAXLE SOLENOID PACK

INSPECT THE CONNECTOR FOR SPREAD OR PUSHED OUT TERMINALS

TEST BR WIRE FOR CONTINUITY FROM CAVITY 50 TO THE 8-WAY

THE OHMETER SHOWS CONTINUITY?

YES → DISCONNECT THE EATX RELAY CONNECTOR

INSPECT THE CONNECTOR FOR SPREAD OR PUSHED OUT TERMINALS

TEST RD WIRE BETWEEN 8-WAY AND RELAY FOR CONTINUITY

IS THE RD WIRE CONTINUITY?

YES → REPLACE THE SOLENOID PACK

NO → REPAIR THE OPEN RD WIRE BETWEEN THE 8R AND THE RELAY CONNECTOR

NO → REPAIR OPEN IN THE BR WIRE BETWEEN THE CONTROLLER AND SOLENOID PACK

TEST 31
CODE 43 – OD SOLENOID CIRCUIT
PERFORM TEST 3 BEFORE PROCEEDING

START TEST 31

DISCONNECT THE 60-WAY AT THE A-604 CONTROLLER

INSPECT CAVITY 15 & 60 FOR CORRECT WIRE PLACEMENT OR TERMINAL DAMAGE

USE AN OHMETER TO MEASURE BR WIRE IN CAVITY 60 TO GROUND

THE METER SHOWS LOW RESISTANCE (UNDER 5 OHMS)?

YES → DISCONNECT THE 8-WAY AT THE TRANSAXLE SOLENOID PACK

INSPECT THE CONNECTOR FOR SPREAD OR PUSHED OUT TERMINALS

RE-TEST THE BR WIRE IN CAVITY 60 TO GROUND

THE METER STILL READS UNDER 10 OHMS?

YES → REPAIR GROUNDED BR WIRE BETWEEN A-604 CONTROLLER AND SOLENOID PACK

NO → REPLACE THE SOLENOID PACK

NO → TEST THE RESISTANCE BETWEEN CAVITY 50 AND 15

THE OHMETER READS BETWEEN 3 OHMS?

YES → REPLACE THE A-604 CONTROLLER

NO → CONTINUE TEST 31

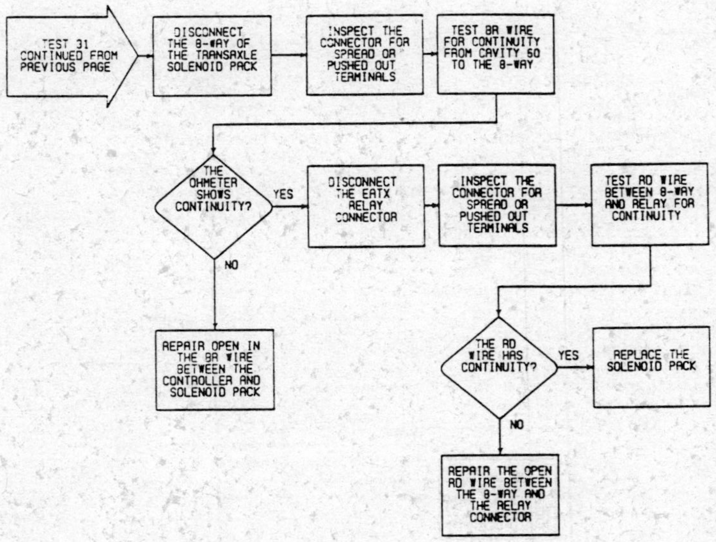

TEST 32
CODE 44 – UD SOLENOID CIRCUIT
PERFORM TEST 3 BEFORE PROCEEDING

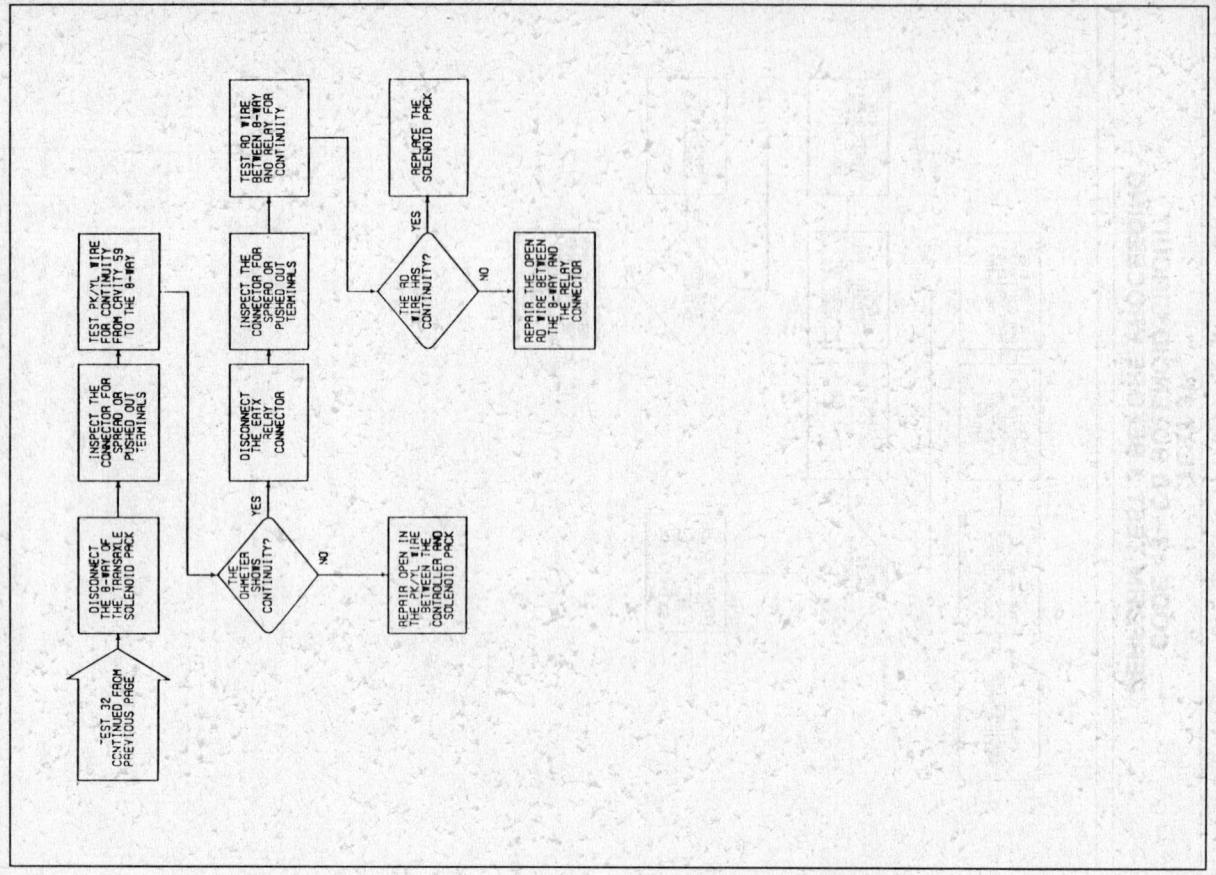

TEST 32
CODE 44 – UD SOLENOID CIRCUIT
PERFORM TEST 3 BEFORE PROCEEDING

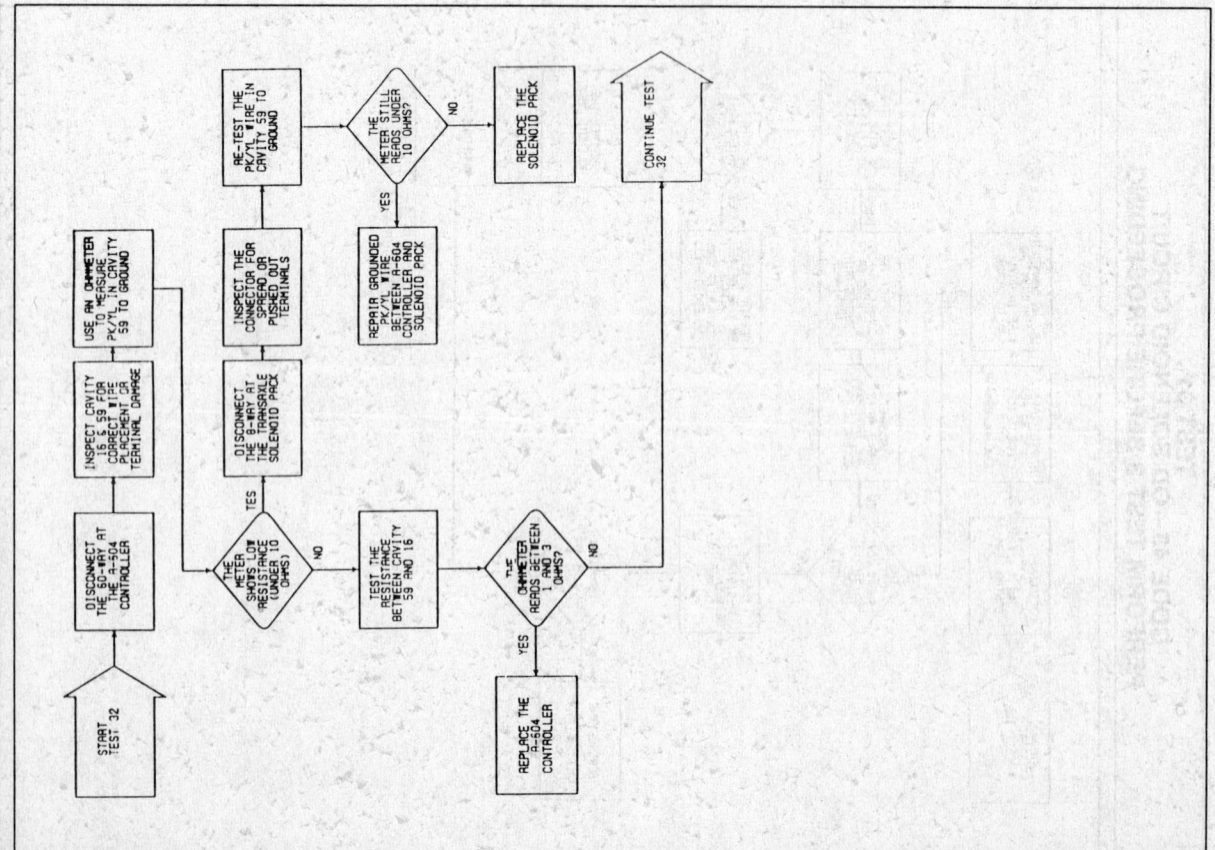

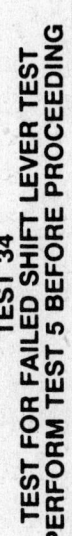

TEST 34
TEST FOR FAILED SHIFT LEVER TEST
PERFORM TEST 5 BEFORE PROCEEDING

TEST 33
TEST FOR FAILED SHIFT LEVER TEST
PERFORM TEST 5 BEFORE PROCEEDING

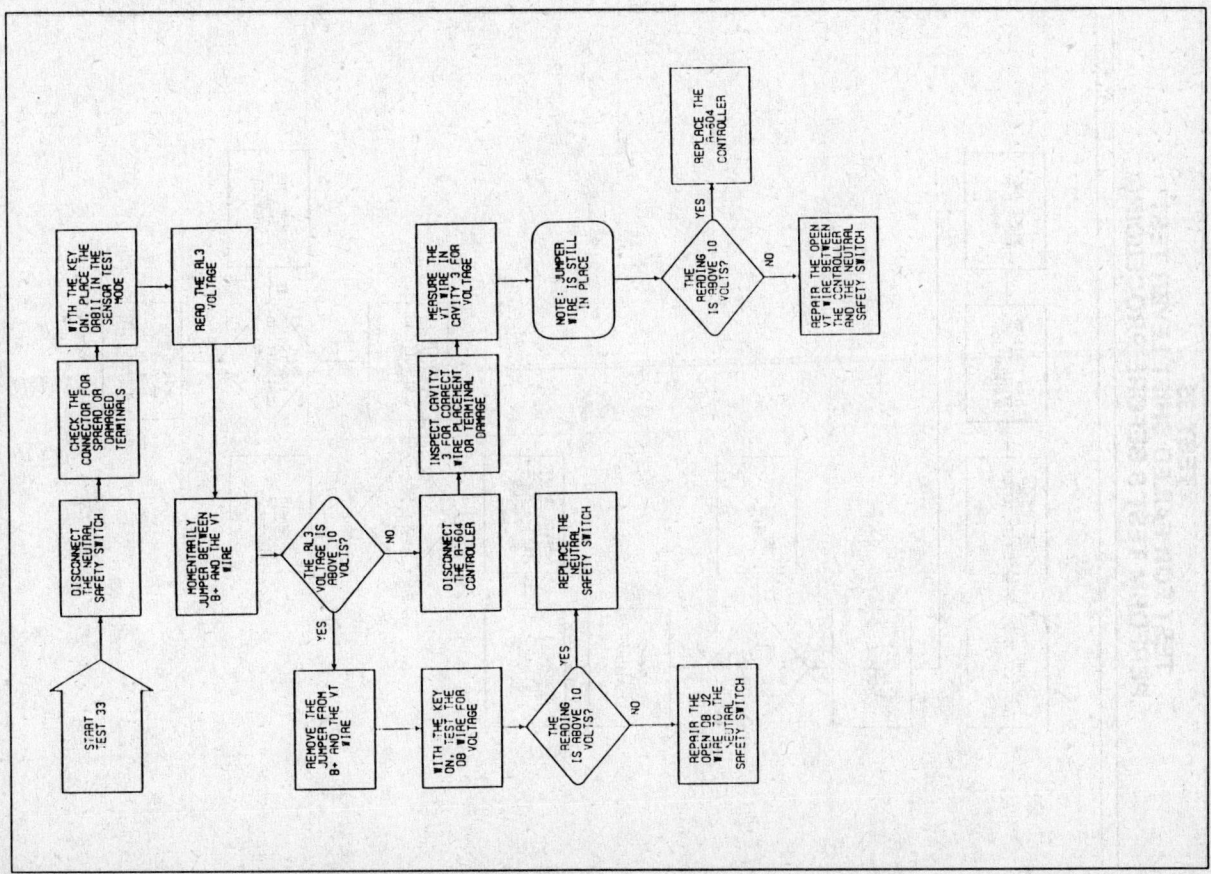

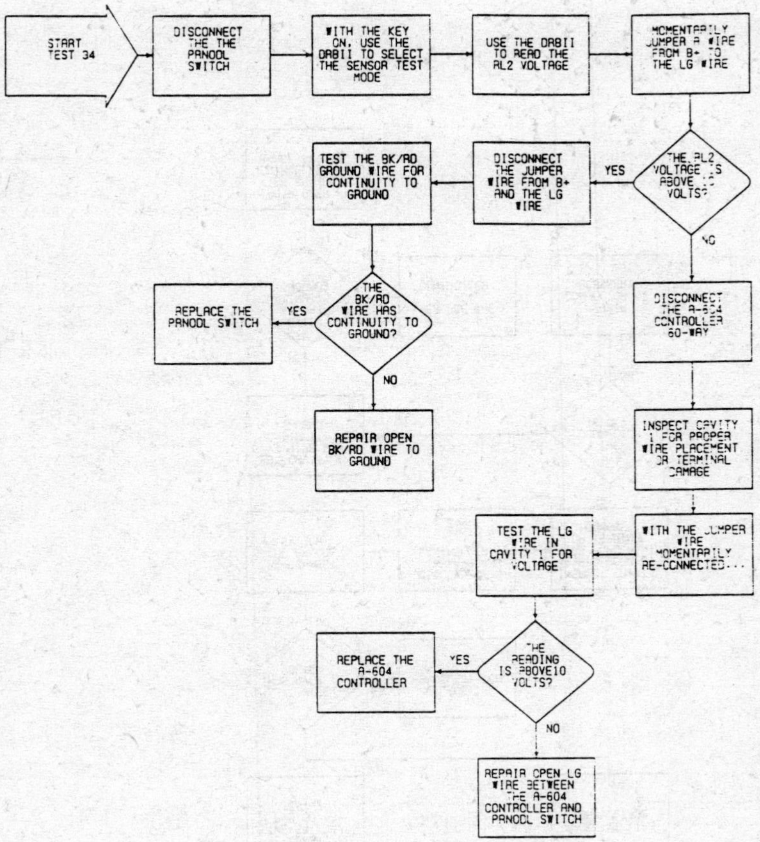

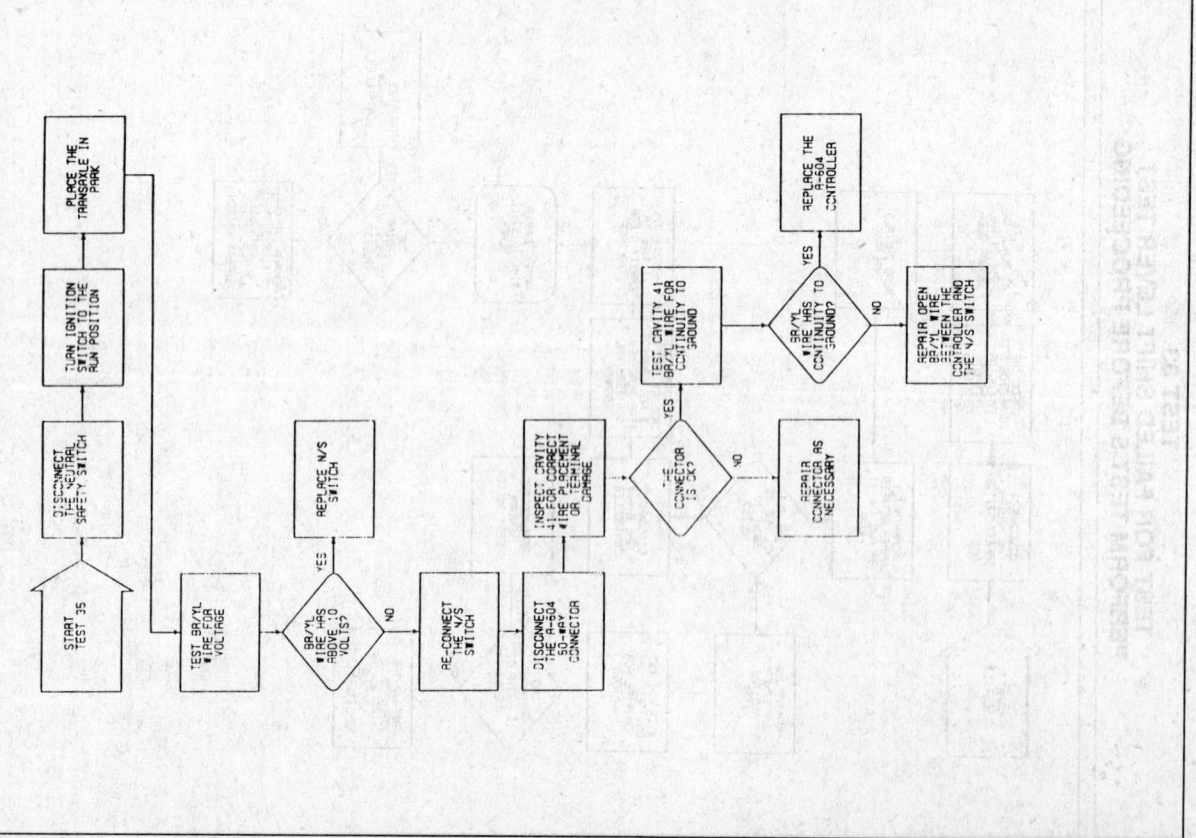

TEST 36
TEST FOR FAILED SHIFT LEVER TEST
PERFORM TEST 5 BEFORE PROCEEDING

TEST 35
TEST FOR FAILED SHIFT LEVER TEST
PERFORM TEST 5 BEFORE PROCEEDING

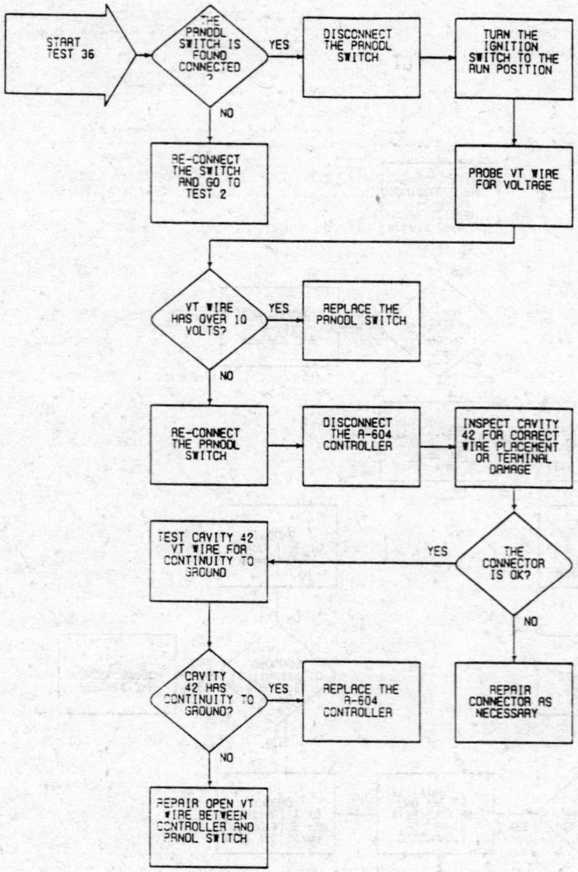

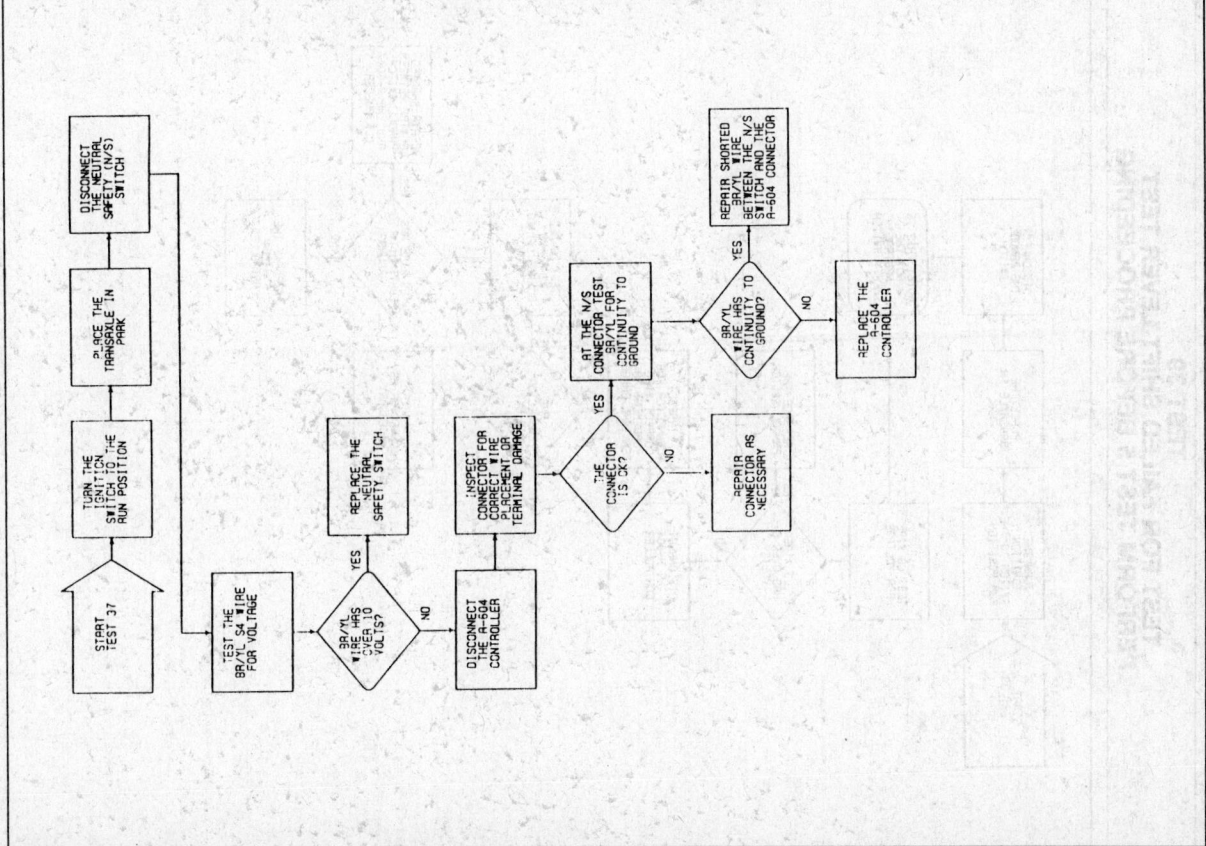

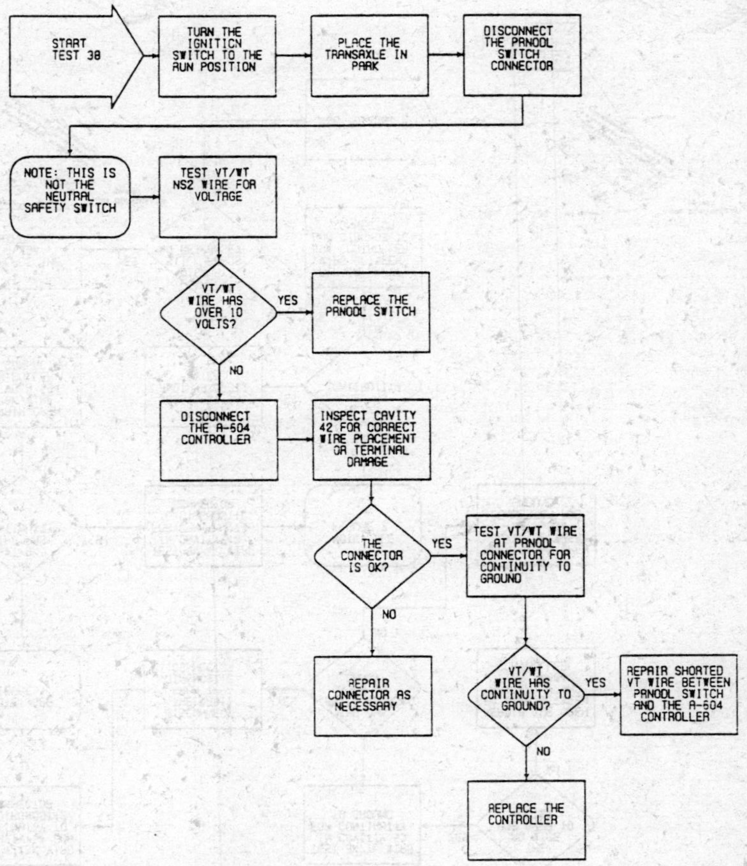

TEST 40
TEST FOR "NO RESPONSE" BUS MESSAGE
PERFORM TEST 1 BEFORE PROCEEDING

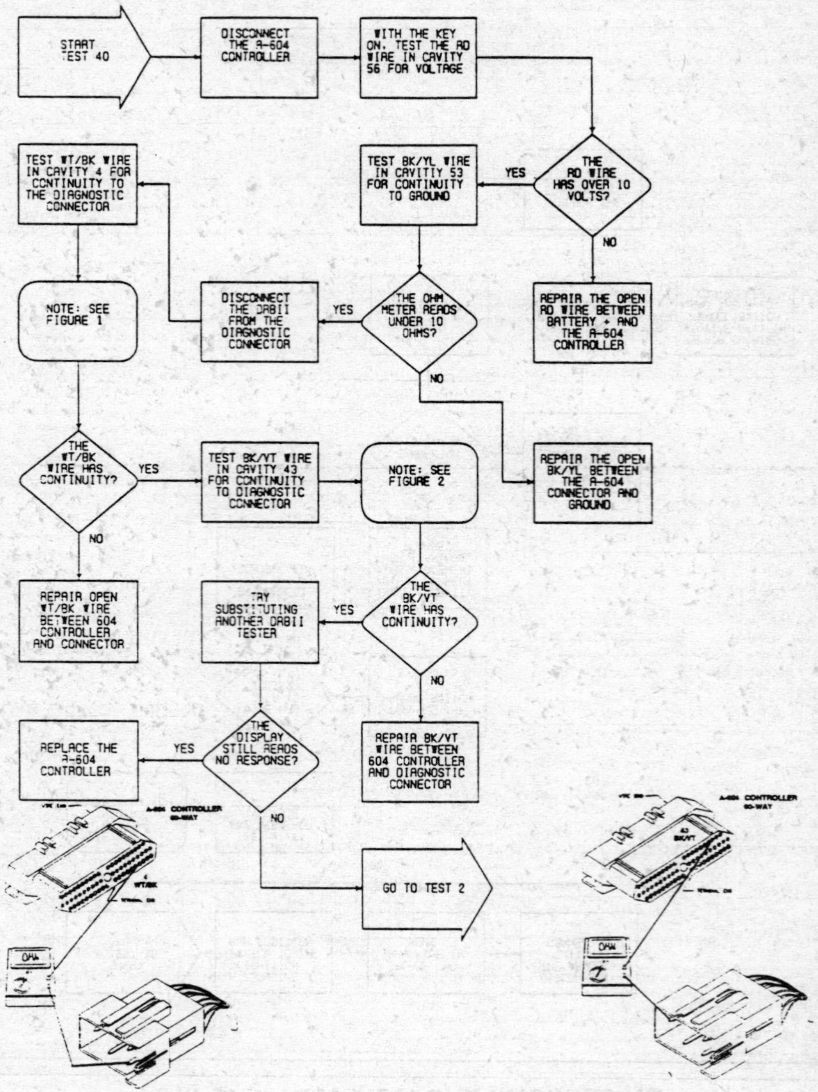

TEST 39
TEST FOR FAILED SHIFT LEVER TEST
PERFORM TEST 5 BEFORE PROCEEDING

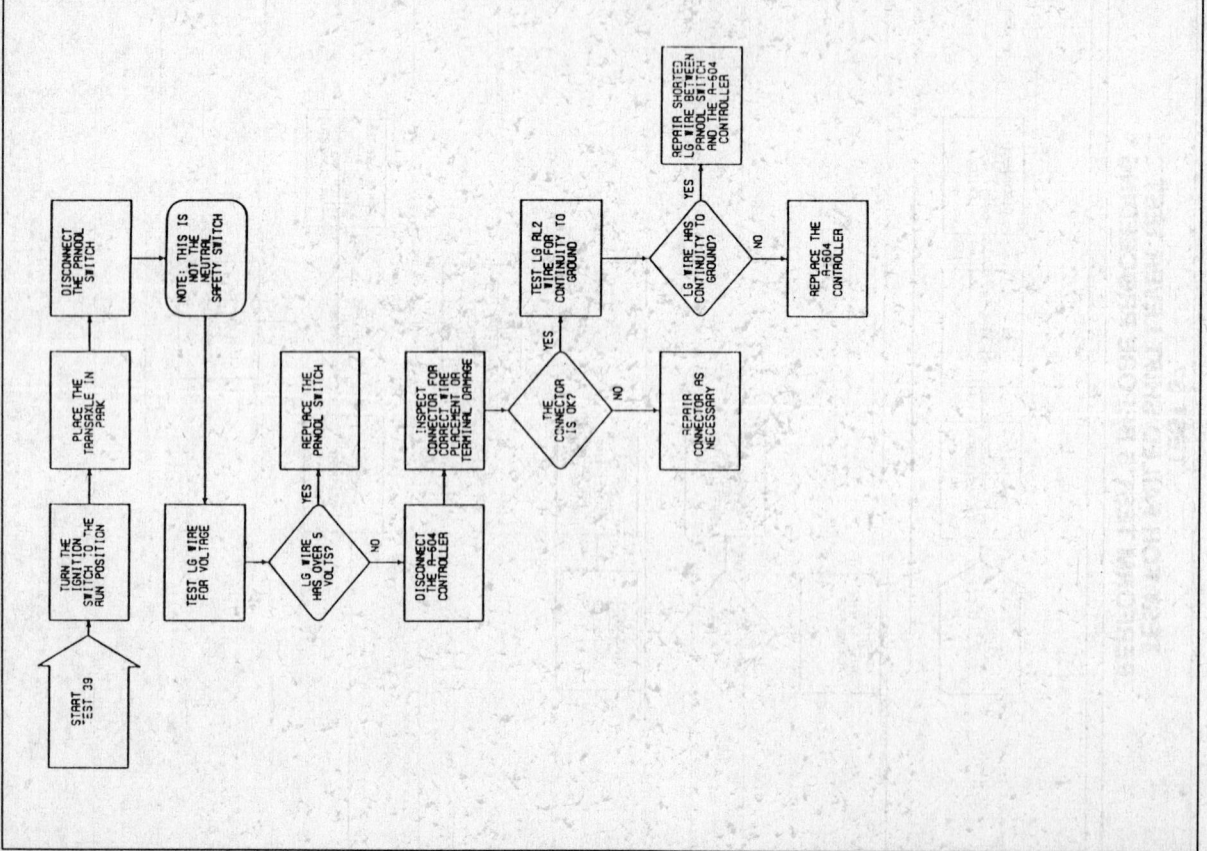

TEST 42
S-BODY FAILED BUS MESSAGE INDEX
PERFORM TEST 41 BEFORE PROCEEDING

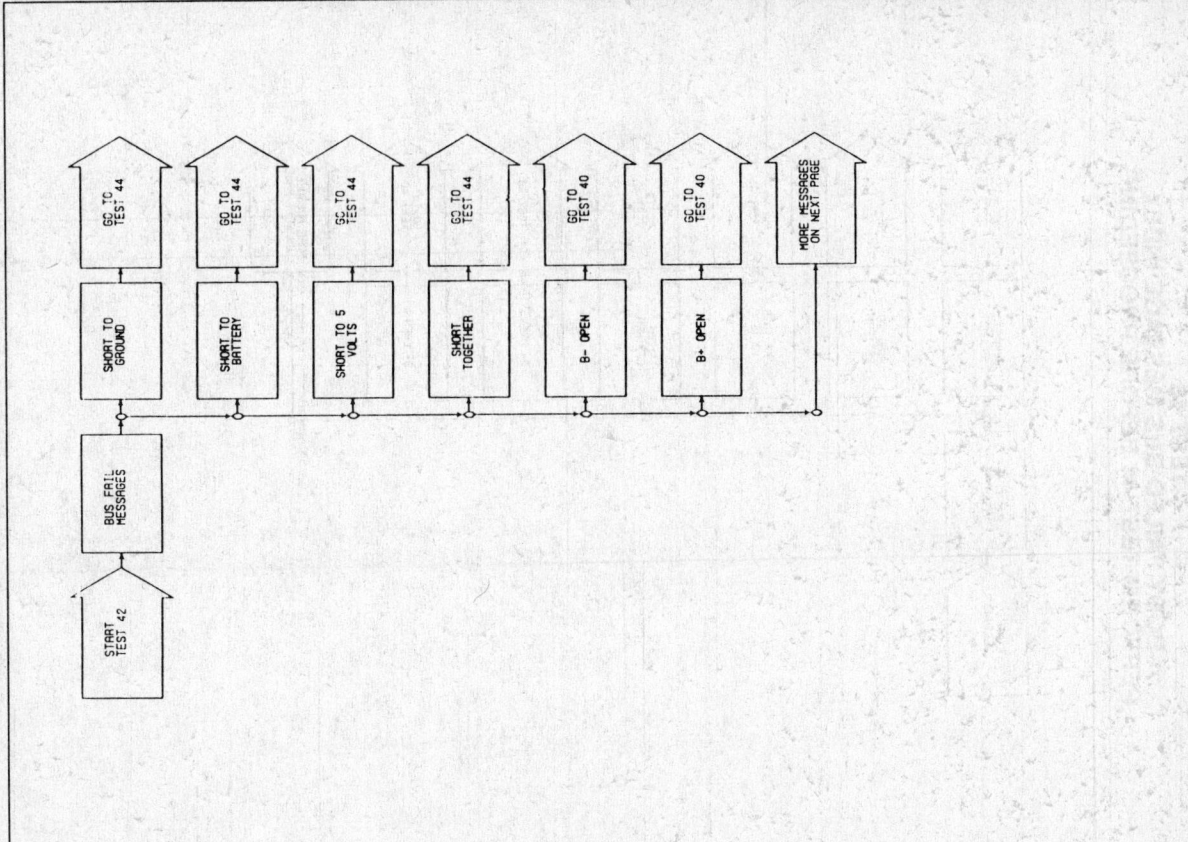

TEST 41
DETERMINING BODY CONFIGURATION
PERFORM TEST 1 BEFORE PROCEEDING

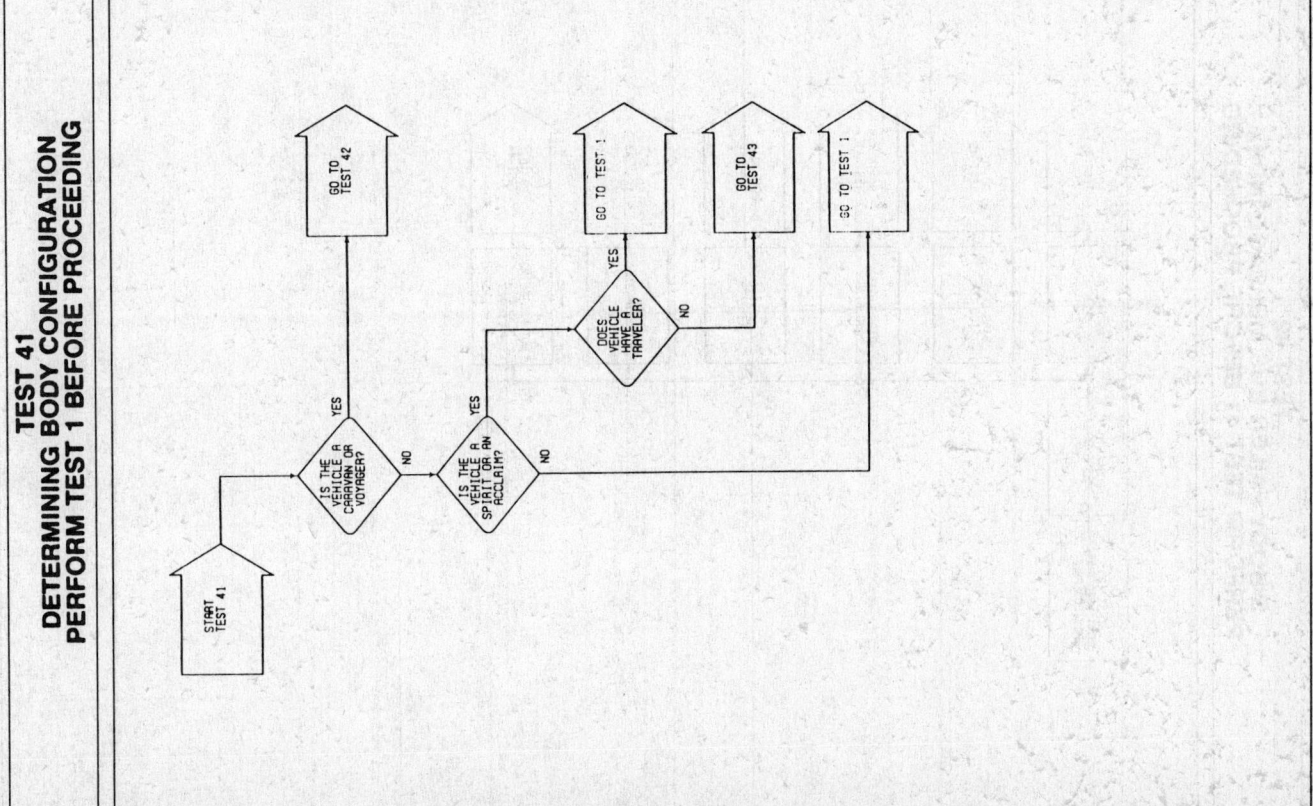

TEST 43

A-BODY FAILED BUS MESSAGE INDEX
PERFORM TEST 41 BEFORE PROCEEDING

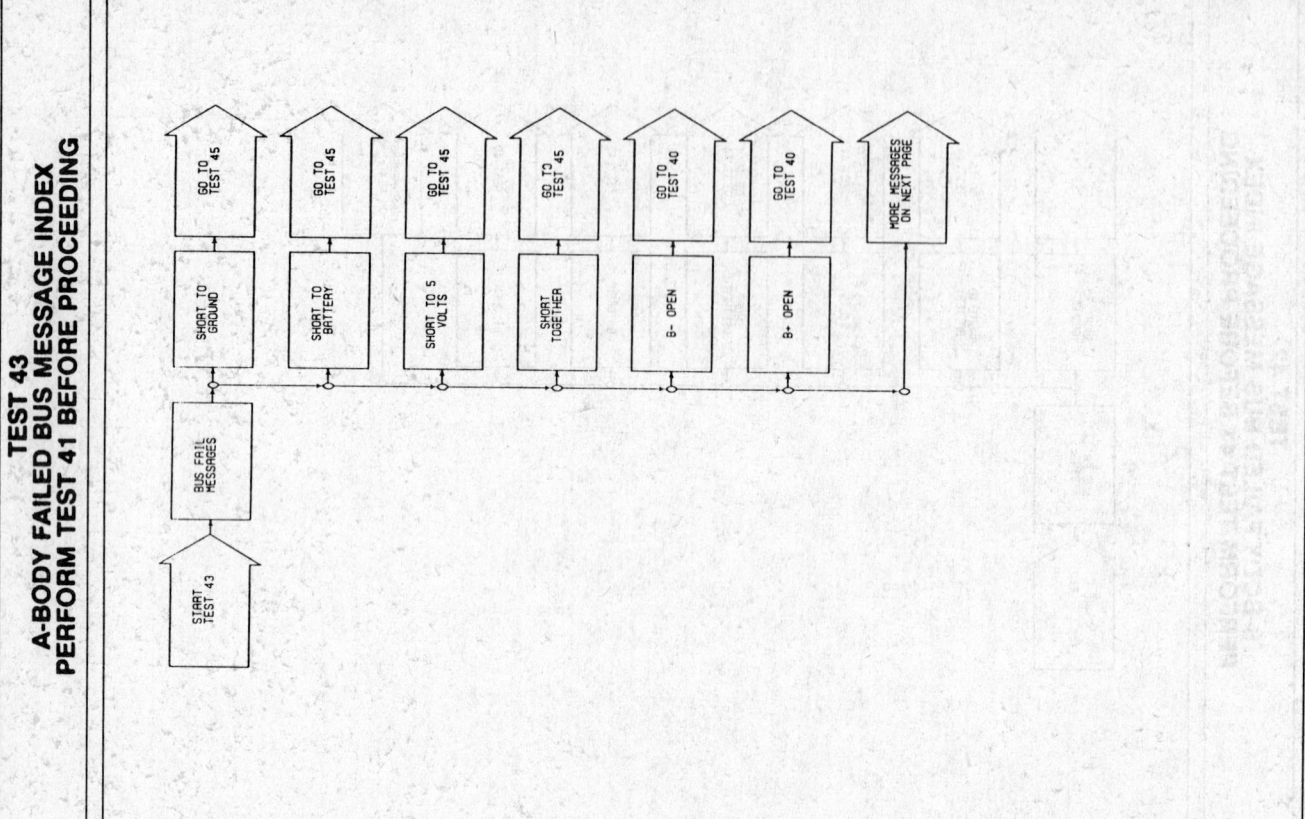

TEST 42

S-BODY FAILED BUS MESSAGE INDEX
PERFORM TEST 41 BEFORE PROCEEDING

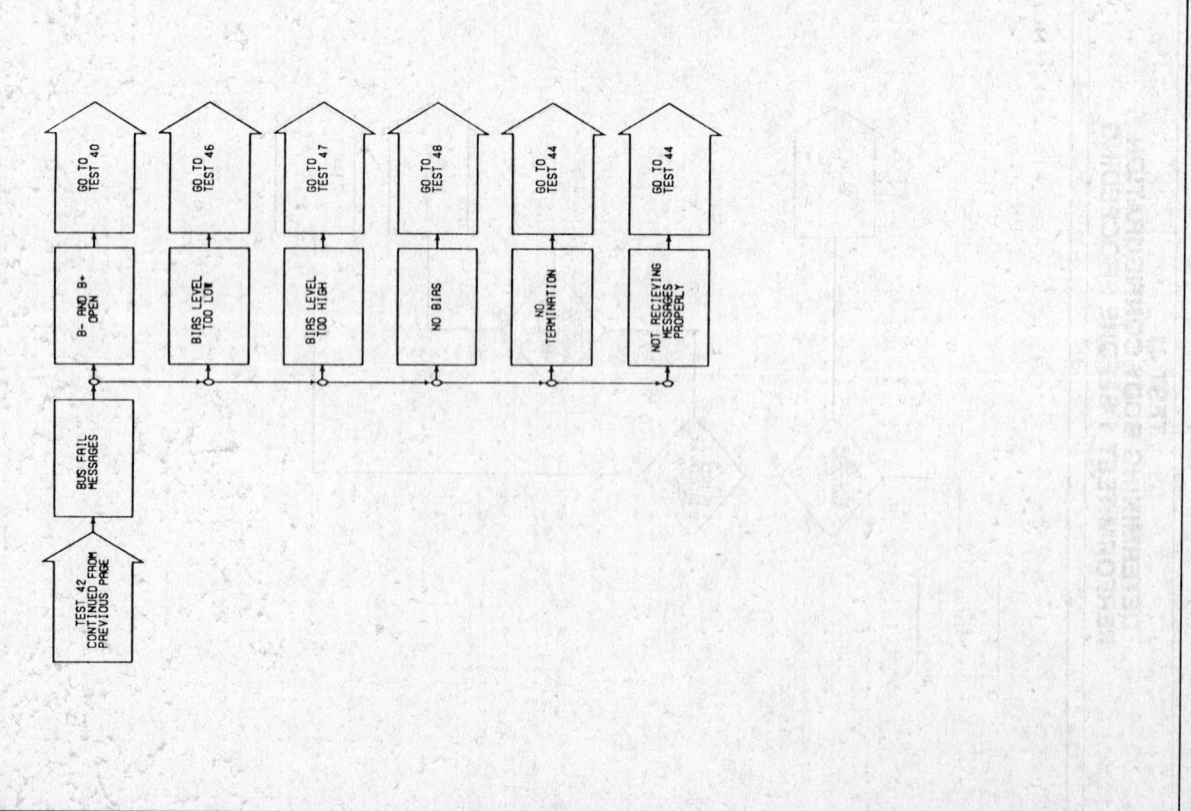

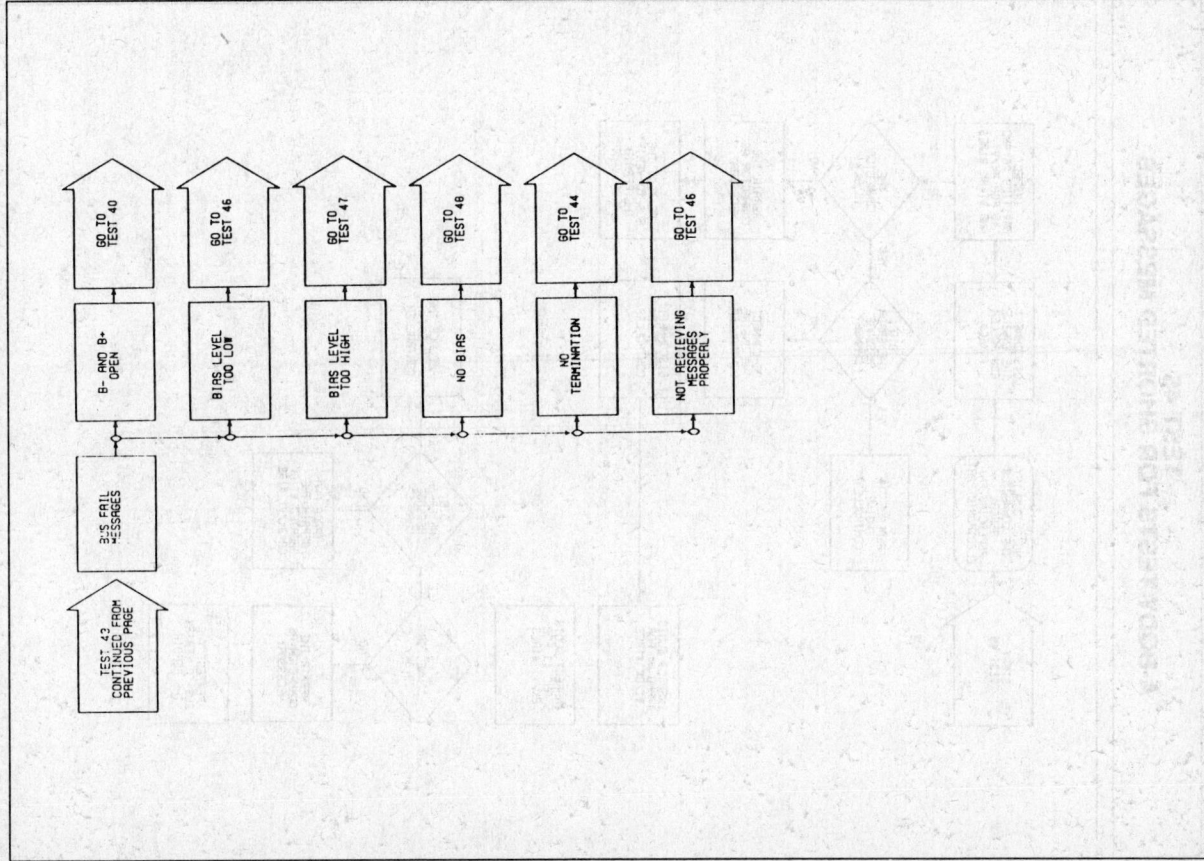

TEST 44
S-BODY TESTS FOR SHORTED MESSAGES

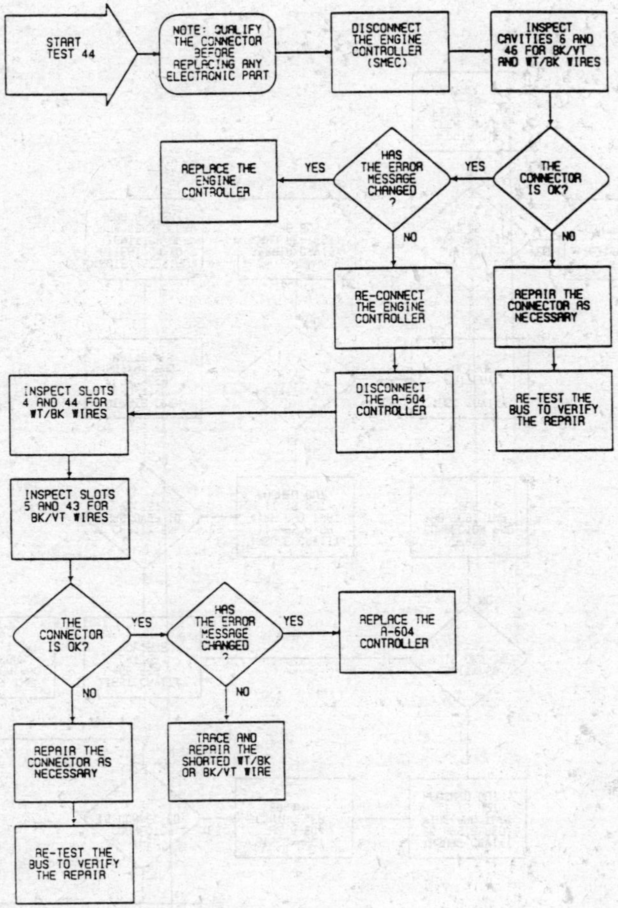

START
TEST 44

NOTE: QUALIFY THE CONNECTOR BEFORE REPLACING ANY ELECTRONIC PART

DISCONNECT THE ENGINE CONTROLLER (SMEC)

INSPECT CAVITIES 5 AND 45 FOR BK/YT AND WT/BK WIRES

THE CONNECTOR IS OK? — NO → REPAIR THE CONNECTOR AS NECESSARY → RE-TEST THE BUS TO VERIFY THE REPAIR

YES

HAS THE ERROR MESSAGE CHANGED? — NO → RE-CONNECT THE ENGINE CONTROLLER → DISCONNECT THE A-604 CONTROLLER

YES

REPLACE THE ENGINE CONTROLLER

INSPECT SLOTS 4 AND 44 FOR WT/BK WIRES

INSPECT SLOTS 5 AND 43 FOR BK/YT WIRES

THE CONNECTOR IS OK? — NO → REPAIR THE CONNECTOR AS NECESSARY → RE-TEST THE BUS TO VERIFY THE REPAIR

YES

HAS THE ERROR MESSAGE CHANGED? — NO → TRACE AND REPAIR THE SHORTED WT/BK OR BK/YT WIRE

YES

REPLACE THE A-604 CONTROLLER

TEST 43
A-BODY FAILED BUS MESSAGE INDEX
PERFORM TEST 41 BEFORE PROCEEDING

TEST 43 CONTINUED FROM PREVIOUS PAGE

BUS FAIL MESSAGES

B- AND B+ OPEN → GO TO TEST 40

BIAS LEVEL TOO LOW → GO TO TEST 46

BIAS LEVEL TOO HIGH → GO TO TEST 47

NO BIAS → GO TO TEST 48

NO TERMINATION → GO TO TEST 44

NOT RECIEVING MESSAGES PROPERLY → GO TO TEST 46

TEST 46
TESTING FOR "BUS BIAS LEVEL TOO LOW" MESSAGE

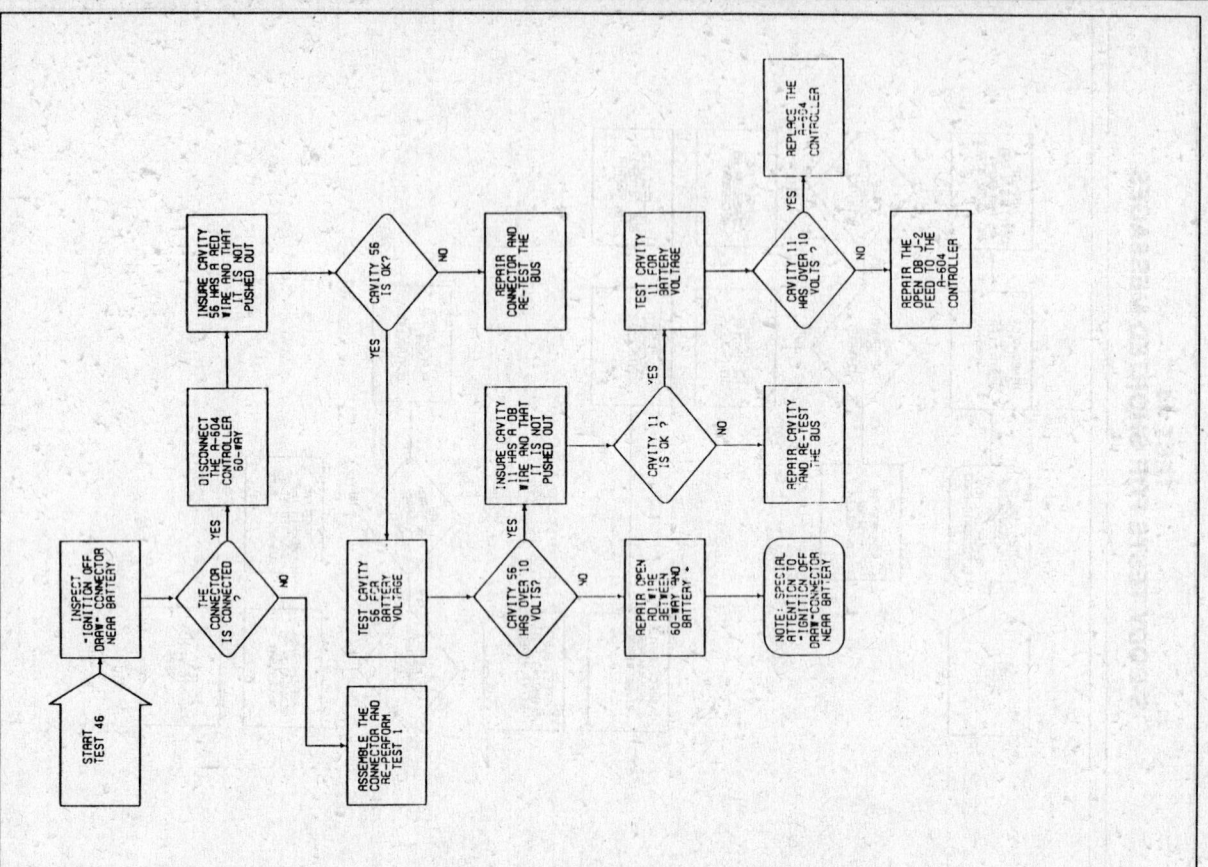

TEST 45
A-BODY TESTS FOR SHORTED MESSAGES

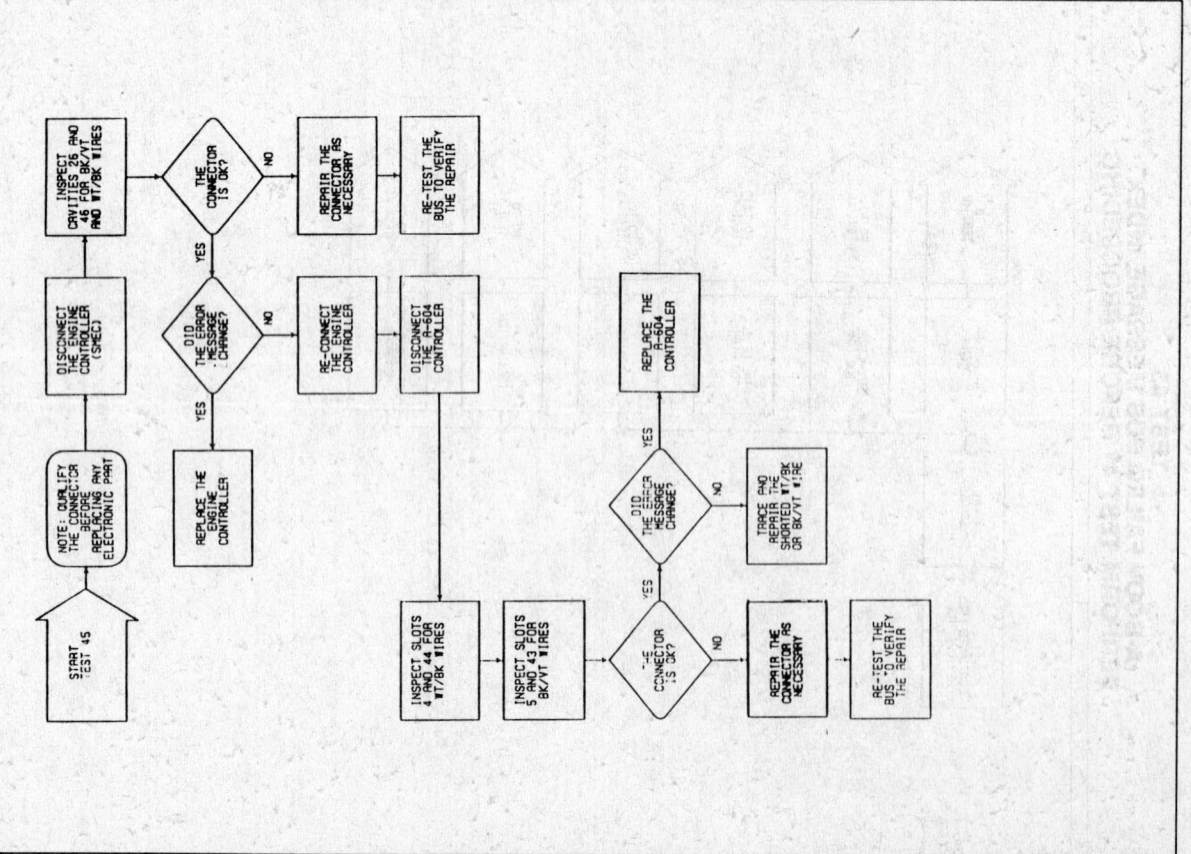

TEST 48
TESTING FOR A "NO BIAS" MESSAGE

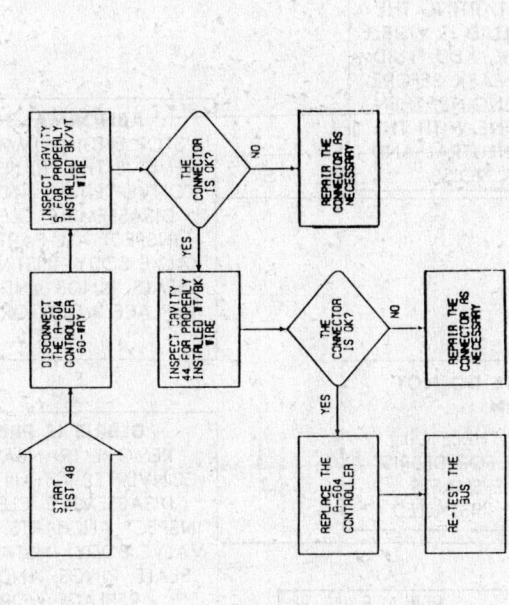

START TEST 48

↓

DISCONNECT THE A-604 CONTROLLER 60-WAY

↓

INSPECT CAVITY 5 FOR PROPERLY INSTALLED BK/VT WIRE

↓

THE CONNECTOR IS OK? — NO → REPAIR THE CONNECTOR AS NECESSARY

↓ YES

INSPECT CAVITY 44 FOR PROPERLY INSTALLED WT/BK WIRE

↓

THE CONNECTOR IS OK? — NO → REPAIR THE CONNECTOR AS NECESSARY

↓ YES

REPLACE THE A-604 CONTROLLER → RE-TEST THE BUS

TEST 47
TESTING FOR "BUS BIAS LEVEL TOO HIGH" MESSAGE

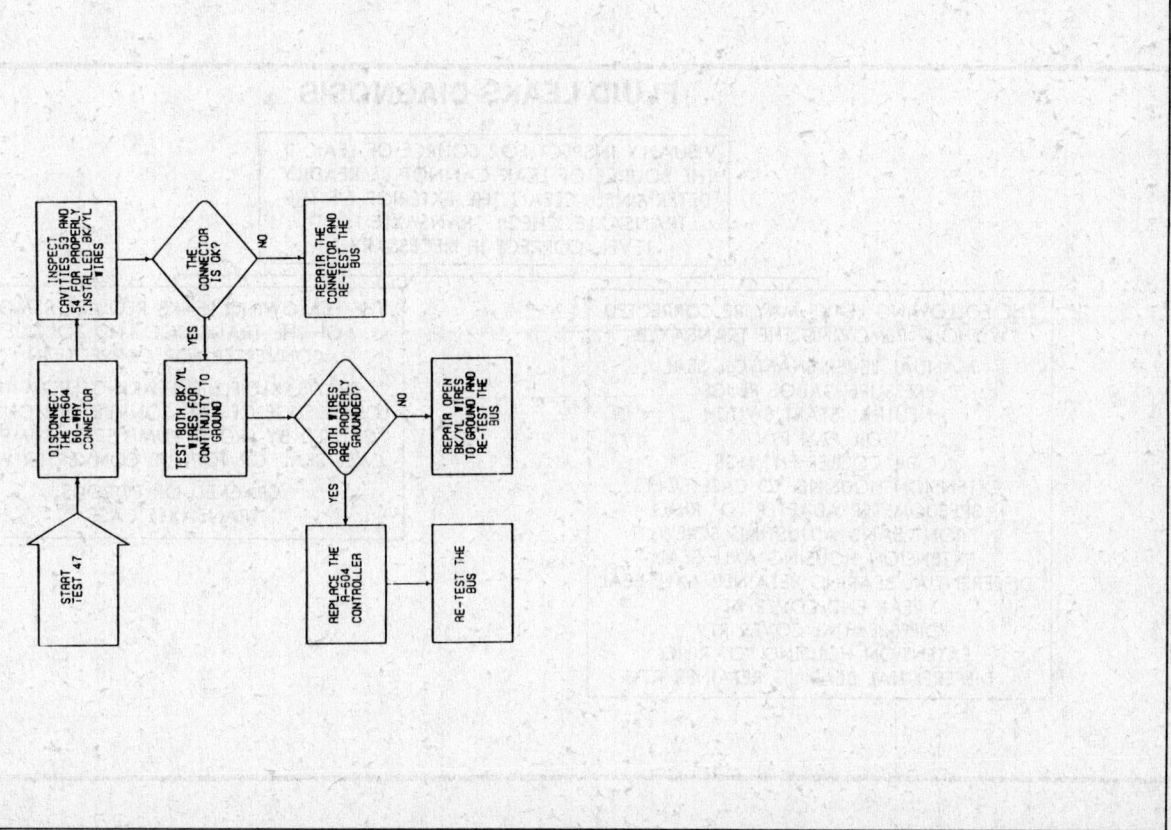

START TEST 47

↓

DISCONNECT THE A-604 60-WAY CONNECTOR

↓

INSPECT CAVITIES 53 AND 54 FOR PROPERLY INSTALLED BK/YL WIRES

↓

THE CONNECTOR IS OK? — NO → REPAIR THE CONNECTOR AND RE-TEST THE BUS

↓ YES

TEST BOTH BK/YL WIRES FOR CONTINUITY TO GROUND

↓

BOTH WIRES ARE PROPERLY GROUNDED? — NO → REPAIR OPEN BK/YL WIRES TO GROUND AND RE-TEST THE BUS

↓ YES

REPLACE THE A-604 CONTROLLER → RE-TEST THE BUS

VEHICLE WILL NOT MOVE DIAGNOSIS

CHECK THE TRANSAXLE FLUID LEVEL BEFORE STARTING THE ENGINE. IF NO FLUID IS VISIBLE ON THE DIPSTICK, ADD FLUID TO THE "ADD" MARK BEFORE STARTING THE ENGINE. THEN START THE ENGINE WITH THE TRANSAXLE IN NEUTRAL AND LISTEN FOR NOISE.

ABNORMAL NOISE, STOP ENGINE IMMEDIATELY, REMOVE THE TRANSAXLE AND CONVERTER AS AN ASSEMBLY. DISASSEMBLE, CLEAN AND INSPECT ALL PARTS. CLEAN VALVE BODY; INSTALL ALL NEW SEALS, RINGS AND GASKETS; REPLACE WORN OR DEFECTIVE PARTS.

NO ABNORMAL NOISE, MOVE THE SELECTOR TO A FORWARD DRIVE RANGE AND OBSERVE THE FRONT WHEELS FOR TURNING

DRIVE SHAFTS TURN BUT FRONT WHEELS DO NOT TURN, INSPECT FOR BROKEN DRIVE SHAFT PARTS.

DRIVE SHAFTS DO NOT TURN REMOVE ALL THREE OIL PANS. INSPECT FOR DEBRIS AND IF AXLE SHAFTS ARE PROPERLY INSTALLED.

DEBRIS IS PRESENT. REMOVE TRANSAXLE AND CONVERTER AS AN ASSEMBLY; DISASSEMBLE, CLEAN AND INSPECT ALL PARTS; CLEAN THE VALVE BODY. INSTALL ALL NEW SEALS, RINGS, AND GASKETS; REPLACE WORN OR DEFECTIVE PARTS.

NO DEBRIS. REMOVE VALVE BODY. DISASSEMBLE, CLEAN AND INSPECT ALL PARTS. REASSEMBLE, INSTALL AND CHECK PRESSURES AND OPERATION.

REPLACE TORQUE CONVERTER FLUSH COOLER AND LINES

FLUID LEAKS DIAGNOSIS

VISUALLY INSPECT FOR SOURCE OF LEAK. IF THE SOURCE OF LEAK CANNOT BE READILY DETERMINED, CLEAN THE EXTERIOR OF THE TRANSAXLE. CHECK TRANSAXLE FLUID LEVEL. CORRECT IF NECESSARY.

THE FOLLOWING LEAKS MAY BE CORRECTED WITHOUT REMOVING THE TRANSAXLE:

MANUAL LEVER SHAFT OIL SEAL
PRESSURE GAUGE PLUGS
NEUTRAL START SWITCH
OIL PAN RTV
OIL COOLER FITTINGS
EXTENSION HOUSING TO CASE BOLTS
SPEEDOMETER ADAPTER "O" RING
FRONT BAND ADJUSTING SCREW
EXTENSION HOUSING AXLE SEAL
DIFFERENTIAL BEARING RETAINER AXLE SEAL
REAR END COVER RTV
DIFFERENTIAL COVER RTV
EXTENSION HOUSING "O" RING
DIFFERENTIAL BEARING RETAINER RTV

THE FOLLOWING LEAKS REQUIRE REMOVAL OF THE TRANSAXLE AND TORQUE CONVERTER FOR CORRECTION.

TRANSAXLE FLUID LEAKING FROM THE LOWER EDGE OF THE CONVERTER HOUSING; CAUSED BY FRONT PUMP SEAL, PUMP TO CASE SEAL, CR TORQUE CONVERTER WELD.

CRACKED OR POROUS TRANSAXLE CASE.

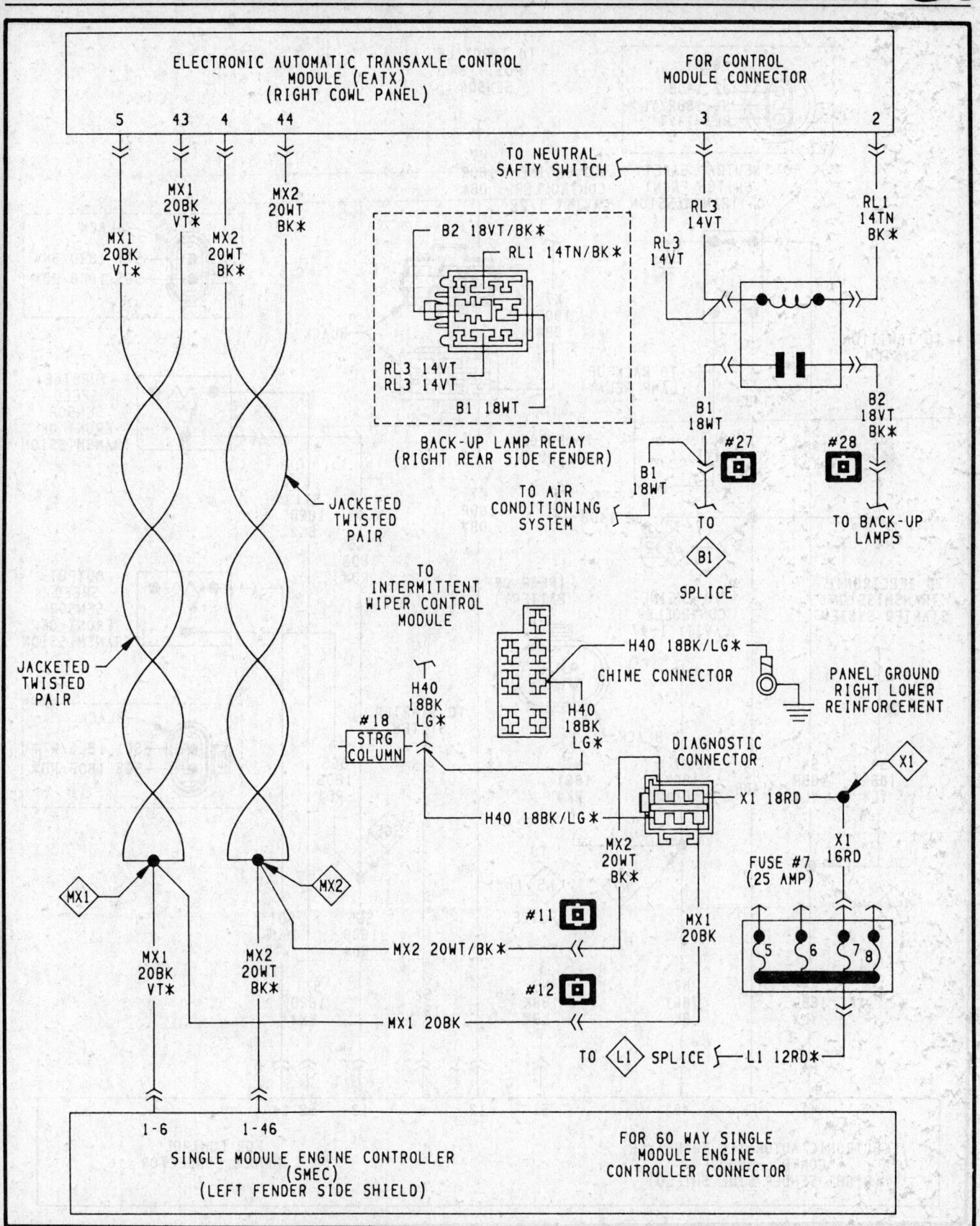

Electronic automatic transaxle wiring diagram

AUTOMATIC TRANSAXLES
A604 – CHRYSLER CORP.

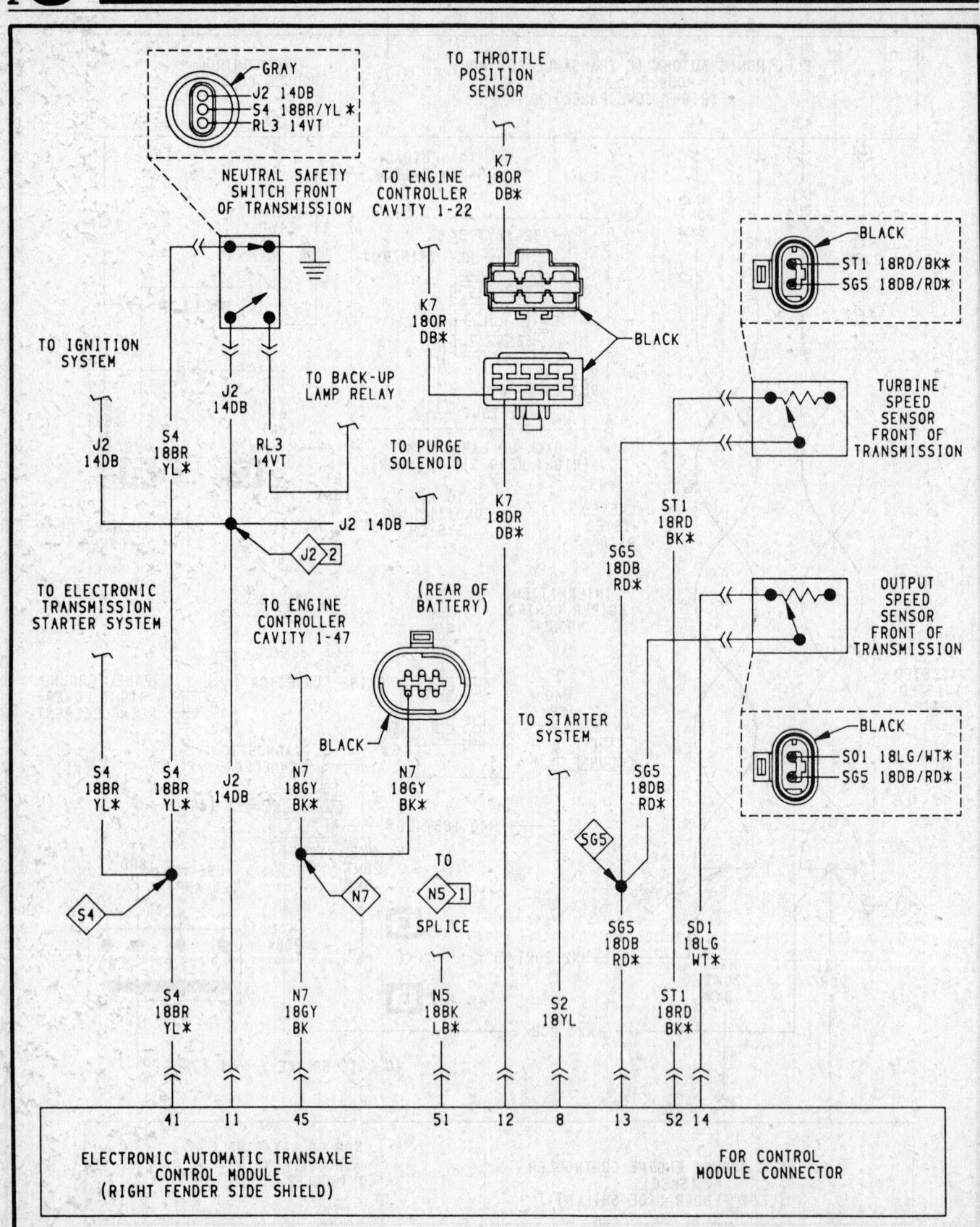

Electronic automatic transaxle wiring diagram

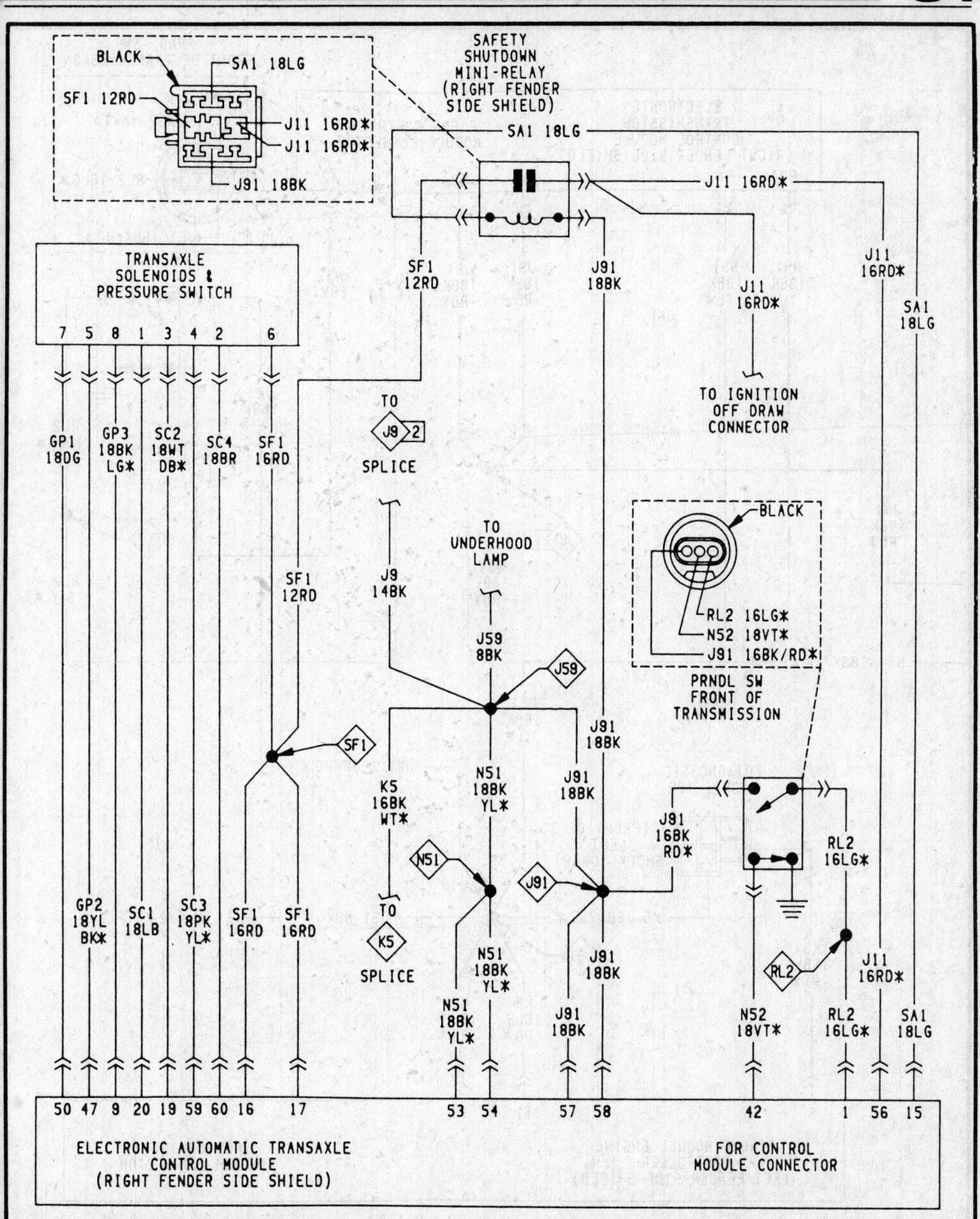

Electronic automatic transaxle wiring diagram

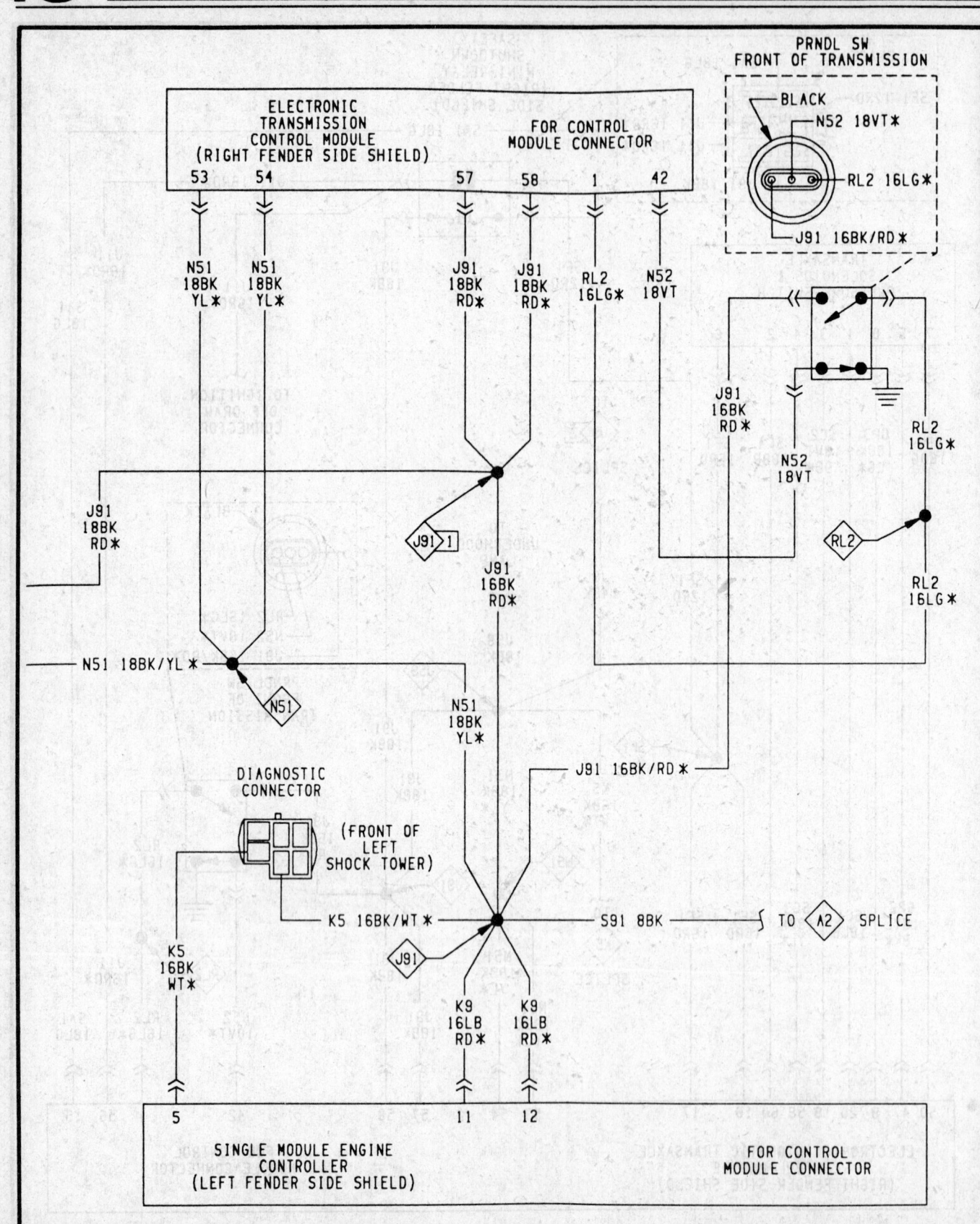

Electronic automatic transaxle wiring diagram

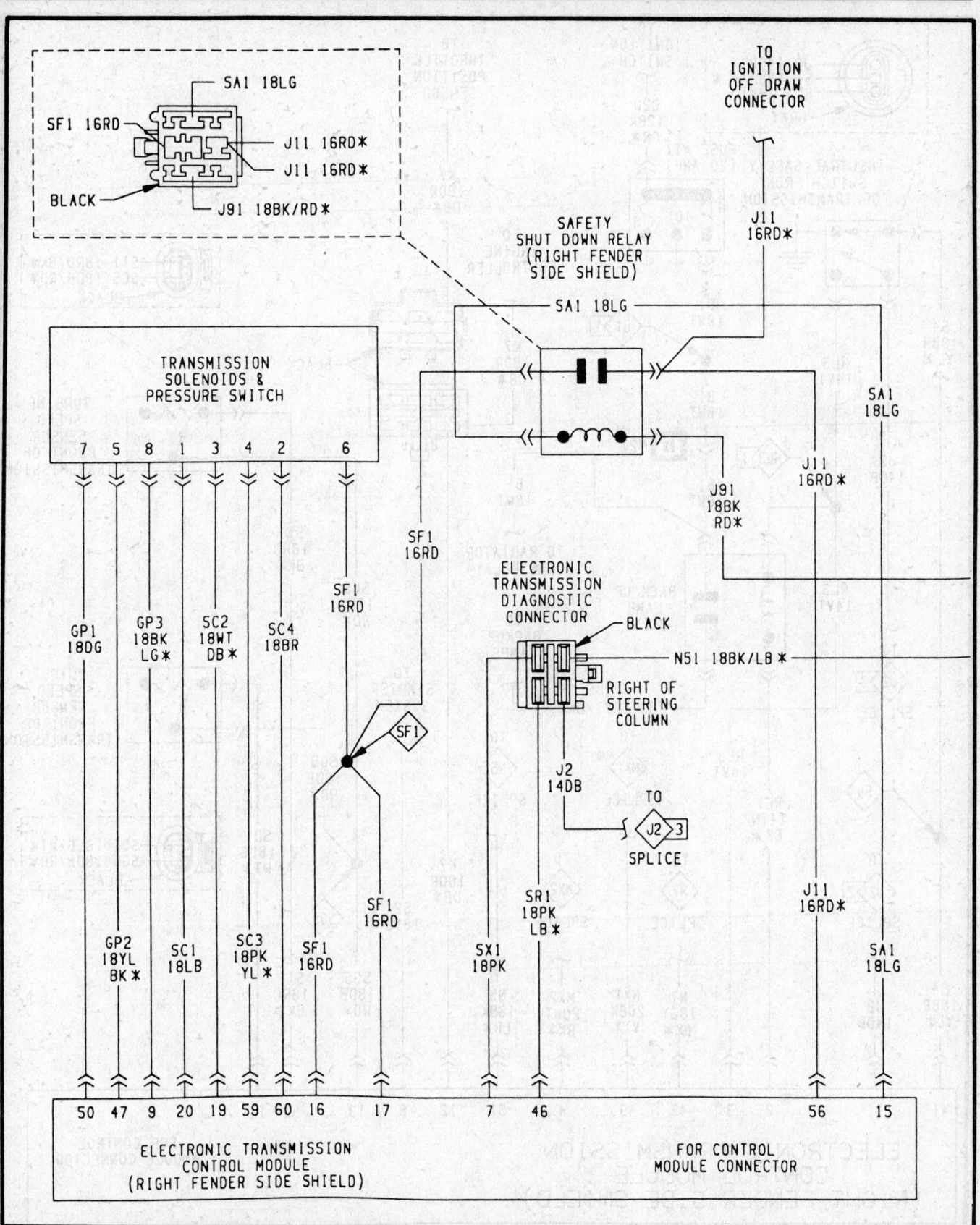

Electronic automatic transaxle wiring diagram

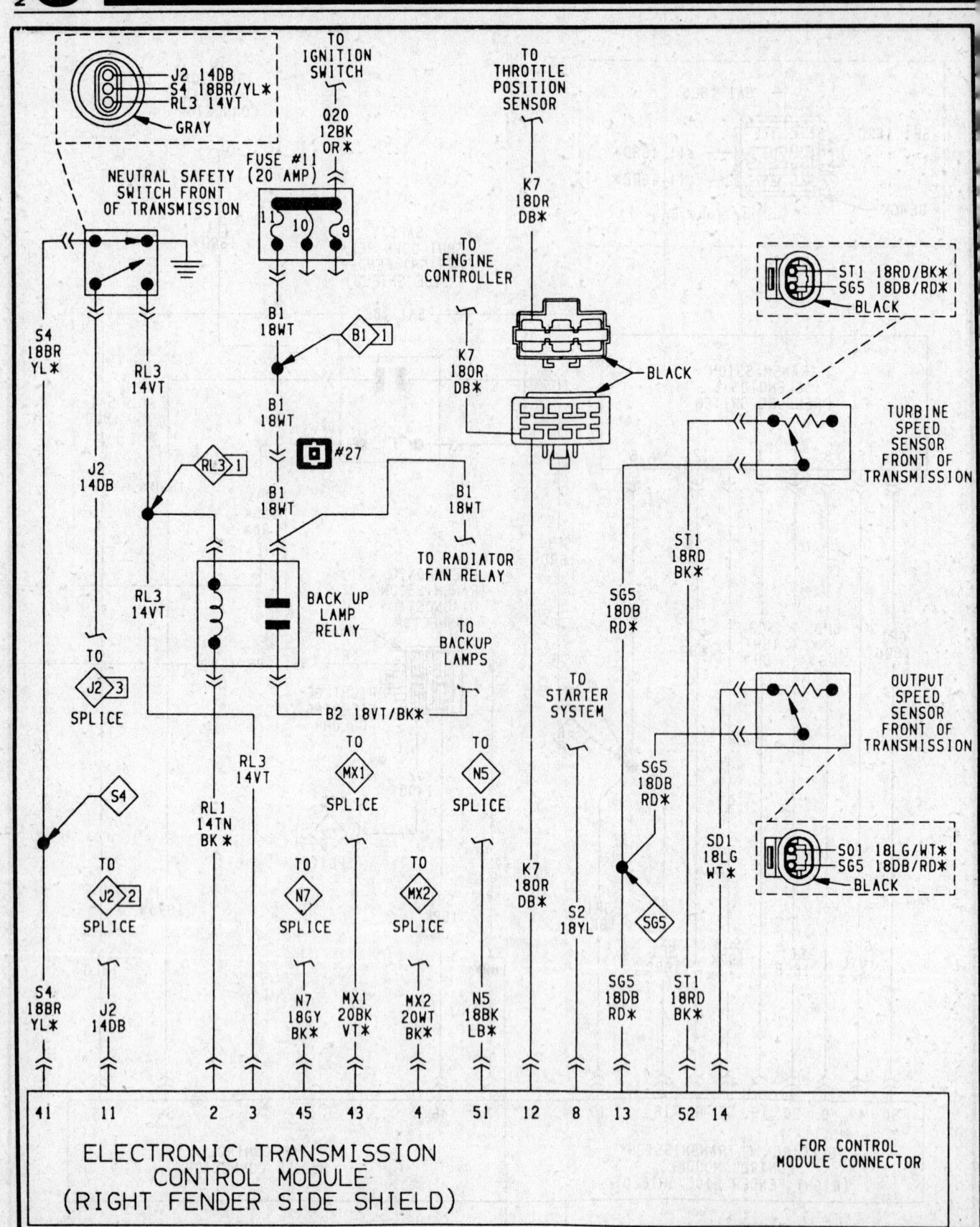

Electronic automatic transaxle wiring diagram

ABNORMAL NOISE DIAGNOSIS

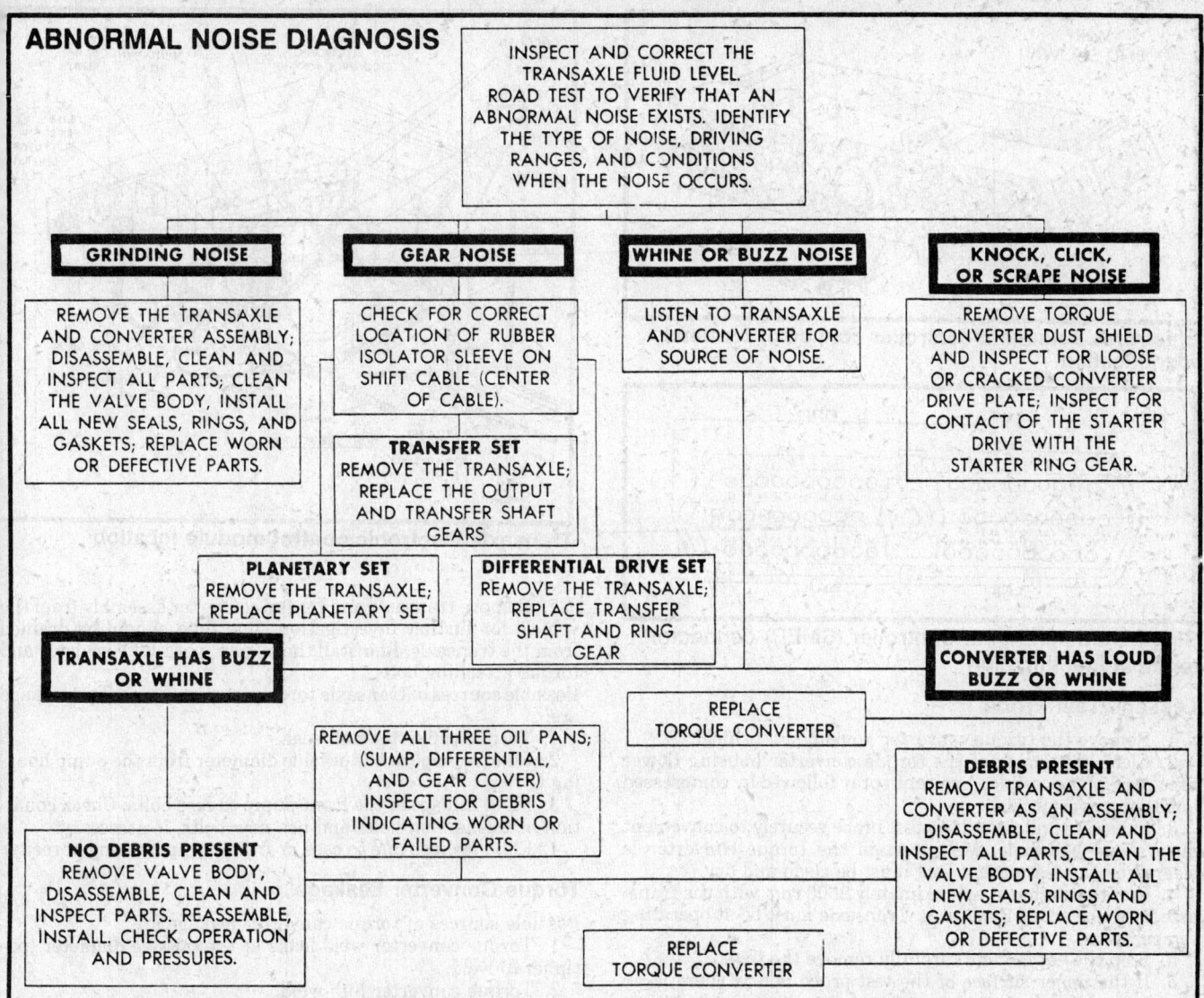

INSPECT AND CORRECT THE TRANSAXLE FLUID LEVEL. ROAD TEST TO VERIFY THAT AN ABNORMAL NOISE EXISTS. IDENTIFY THE TYPE OF NOISE, DRIVING RANGES, AND CONDITIONS WHEN THE NOISE OCCURS.

GRINDING NOISE

REMOVE THE TRANSAXLE AND CONVERTER ASSEMBLY; DISASSEMBLE, CLEAN AND INSPECT ALL PARTS; CLEAN THE VALVE BODY, INSTALL ALL NEW SEALS, RINGS, AND GASKETS; REPLACE WORN OR DEFECTIVE PARTS.

GEAR NOISE

CHECK FOR CORRECT LOCATION OF RUBBER ISOLATOR SLEEVE ON SHIFT CABLE (CENTER OF CABLE).

TRANSFER SET
REMOVE THE TRANSAXLE; REPLACE THE OUTPUT AND TRANSFER SHAFT GEARS

PLANETARY SET
REMOVE THE TRANSAXLE; REPLACE PLANETARY SET

DIFFERENTIAL DRIVE SET
REMOVE THE TRANSAXLE; REPLACE TRANSFER SHAFT AND RING GEAR

WHINE OR BUZZ NOISE

LISTEN TO TRANSAXLE AND CONVERTER FOR SOURCE OF NOISE.

KNOCK, CLICK, OR SCRAPE NOISE

REMOVE TORQUE CONVERTER DUST SHIELD AND INSPECT FOR LOOSE OR CRACKED CONVERTER DRIVE PLATE; INSPECT FOR CONTACT OF THE STARTER DRIVE WITH THE STARTER RING GEAR.

TRANSAXLE HAS BUZZ OR WHINE

CONVERTER HAS LOUD BUZZ OR WHINE

REPLACE TORQUE CONVERTER

REMOVE ALL THREE OIL PANS; (SUMP, DIFFERENTIAL, AND GEAR COVER) INSPECT FOR DEBRIS INDICATING WORN OR FAILED PARTS.

DEBRIS PRESENT
REMOVE TRANSAXLE AND CONVERTER AS AN ASSEMBLY; DISASSEMBLE, CLEAN AND INSPECT ALL PARTS, CLEAN THE VALVE BODY, INSTALL ALL NEW SEALS, RINGS AND GASKETS; REPLACE WORN OR DEFECTIVE PARTS.

NO DEBRIS PRESENT
REMOVE VALVE BODY, DISASSEMBLE, CLEAN AND INSPECT PARTS. REASSEMBLE, INSTALL. CHECK OPERATION AND PRESSURES.

REPLACE TORQUE CONVERTER

---

position to check for slipping and any variation in shifting.

In most cases, the clutch that is slipping can be determined by noting the transaxle operation in all selector positions and by comparing which internal units are applied in those positions.

The process of eliminating can be used to detect any unit which slip and to confirm proper operation of good units. However, although road test analysis can usually diagnose slipping units, the actual cause of the malfunction usually cannot be decided. Practically any condition can be caused by leaking hydraulic circuits or sticking valves.

ON-BOARD DIAGNOSTICS

The transaxle controller monitors critical input and output circuits relating to the control of the transaxle. Some of these circuits are tested continuously, and others are checked only during normal driving conditions.

If the controller senses a problem in the system, a fault code will be stored in the controller's memory. Each monitored circuit has its own designated fault code. Any stored fault code will remain in memory until erased or until displaced by more recent codes.

Converter Clutch Operation and Diagnosis

TORQUE CONVERTER CLUTCH

Fluid Leakage — Transaxle Torque Converter Housing Area

Since fluid leakage at or around the torque converter area may originate from an engine oil leak, the area should be examined closely. Factory fill fluid is dyed red and, therefore, can be distinguished from engine oil.

Prior to removing the transaxle, check the following:

1. When leakage is determined to originate from the transaxle, check fluid level prior to removal of the transaxle and torque converter.

2. High oil level can result in oil leakage out the vent in the manual shaft. If the fluid level is high, adjust to proper level.

3. After performing this operation, inspect for leakage. If a leak persists, determine if it is the torque converter or the transaxle that is leaking.

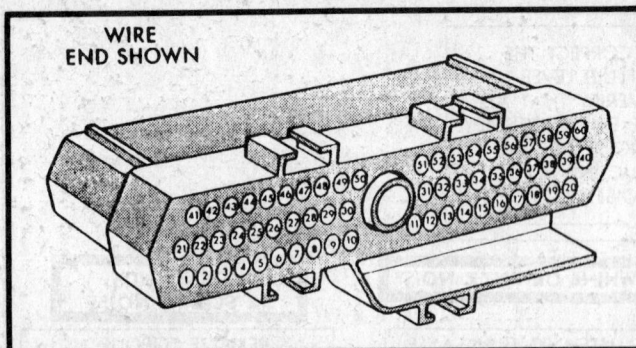

Electronic automatic controller connector terminal identification

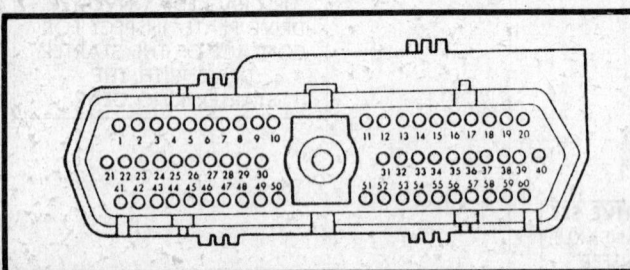

Single Module Engine Controller (SMEC) connector terminal identification

Leakage Test Probe

1. Remove the torque converter housing dust shield.
2. Clean the inside of the torque converter housing (lower area) as dry as possible. A solvent spray followed by compressed air drying is preferable.
3. Fabricate and fasten the test probe securely to convenient dust shield bolt hole. Make certain the torque converter is cleared by the test probe. Tool must be clean and dry.
4. Run the engine at approximately 2500 rpm with the transaxle in **N**, for about 2 minutes. Transaxle must be at operating temperature.
5. Stop the engine and carefully remove the tool.
6. If the upper surface of the test probe is dry, there is no torque converter leak. A path of fluid across the probe indicates a torque converter leak. Oil leaking under the probe is coming from the transaxle torque converter area.

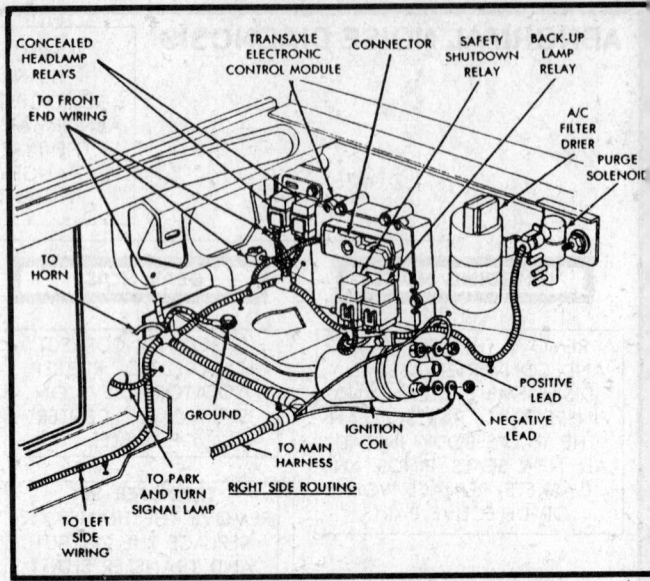

Transaxle electronic control module location

7. Remove transaxle and torque converter assembly from the vehicle for further investigation. The fluid should be drained from the transaxle. Reinstall the oil pan (with RTV sealant) and torque attaching bolts.

Possible sources of transaxle torque converter area fluid leakage are:

1. Torque converter hub seal.
2. Fluid leakage at the outside diameter from the pump housing O-ring.
3. Fluid leakage at the front pump to case bolts. Check condition of washers on bolts and use new bolts, if necessary.
4. Fluid leakage due to case or front pump housing porosity.

Torque Converter Leakage

Possible sources of torque converter leakage are:

1. Torque converter weld leaks at the outside diameter (peripheral) weld.
2. Torque converter hub weld.

NOTE: Hub weld is inside and not visible. Do not attempt to repair. Replace the torque converter.

ON CAR SERVICES

Adjustments

MANUAL LINKAGE

Gearshift Linkage

Normal operation of the PRNDL and neutral safety switch provides a quick check to confirm proper manual linkage adjustment.

Move the selector lever slowly upward until it clicks into the **P** notch in the selector gate. If the starter will operate the **P** position is correct.

After checking **P** position move the selector slowly toward **N** position until lever drops at the end of the **N** stop in the selector gate. If the starter will also operate at this point the gearshift

linkage is properly adjusted. If required, adjustment gearshift linkage as follows:

1. Set the parking brake and place the gearshift lever in **P** position.
2. Loosen the clamp bolt on the gearshift cable bracket.
3. On column shift, insure that the preload adjustment spring engages the fork on the transaxle bracket.
4. Pull the shift lever by hand all the way to the front detent position (**P**) and tighten the lock screw to 100 inch lbs. (11 Nm). Gearshift linkage should now be properly adjusted.
5. To check the adjustment, the detent position for neutral and drive should be within limits of hand lever gate stops, and the key start must occur only when the shift lever is in the park or neutral positions.

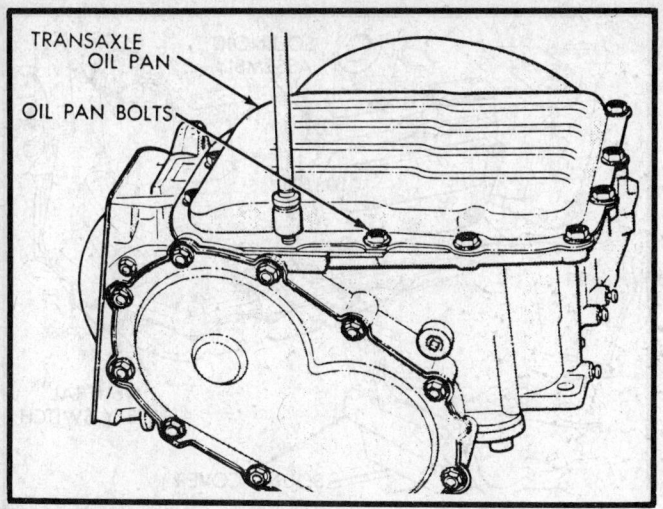

Transaxle oil pan servicing

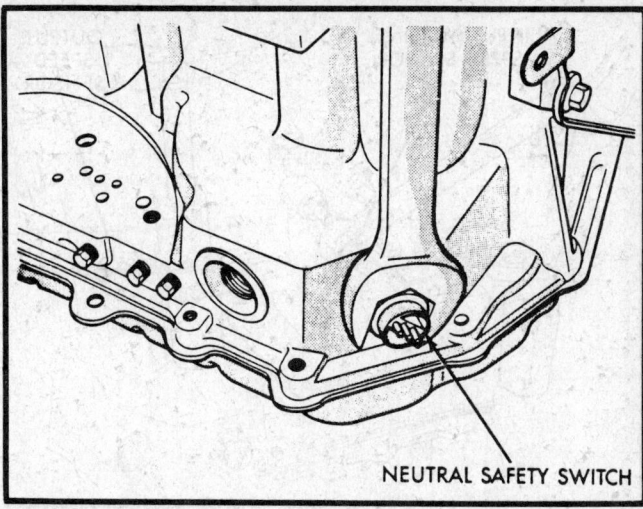

Neutral safety switch servicing

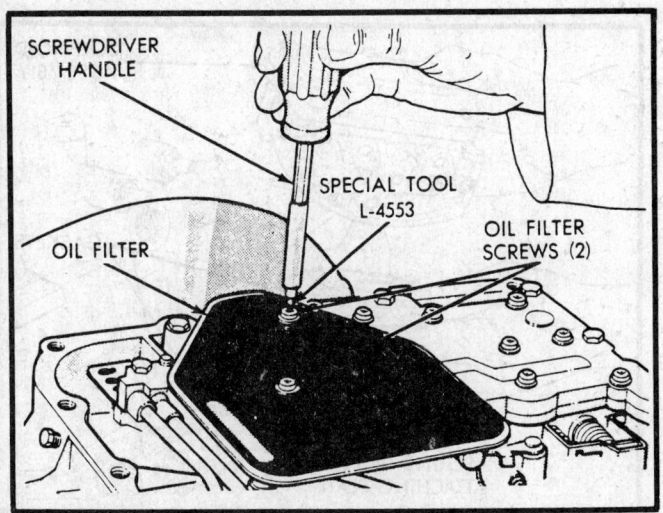

Oil filter servicing

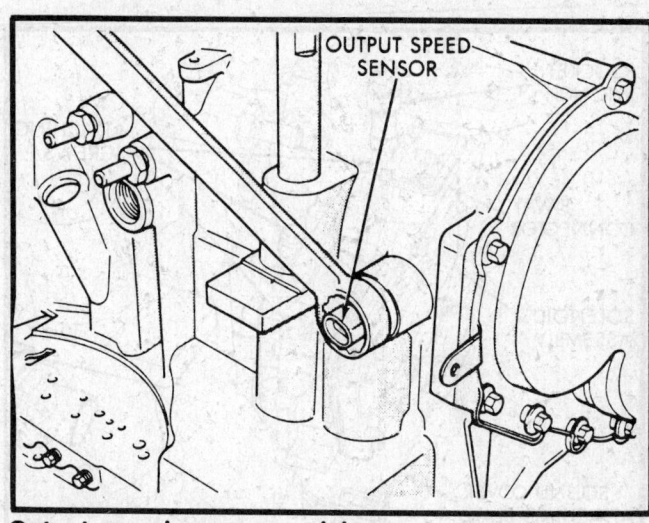

Output speed sensor servicing

SHIFT QUALITY QUICK-LEARN PROCEDURE

NOTE: This procedure will quickly optimize the shift quality after the battery has been disconnected.

The transaxle operating temperature must be warm before learning is allowed. To warm up the transaxle fluid, idle the engine for approximately 10 minutes before proceeding.

Upshift Learn Procedure

1. Maintain constant throttle opening during shifts.

NOTE: Do not move the accelerator pedal during the upshifts.

2. Accelerate the vehicle with the throttle opening angle in the range of 10–50 degrees.

3. Make approximately 15–20 upshifts—1st to 2nd, 2nd to 3rd, and 3rd to 4th upshifts.

NOTE: Accelerating from stop to approximately 45 mph each time at moderate throttle angle (20–25 degrees) is sufficient.

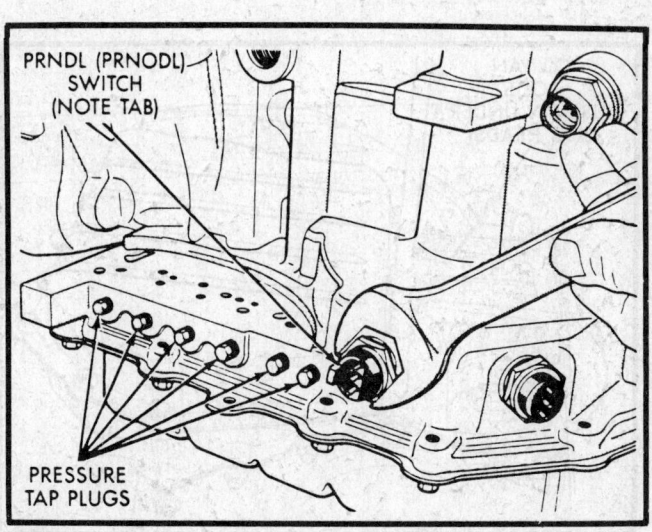

PRNDL switch servicing

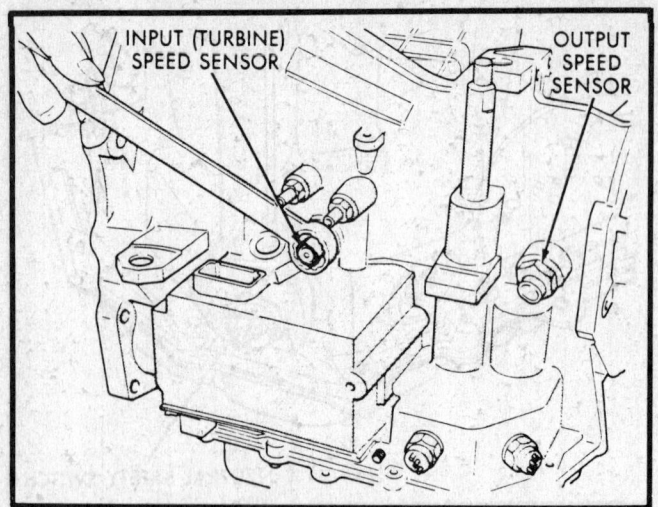

Input speed sensor servicing

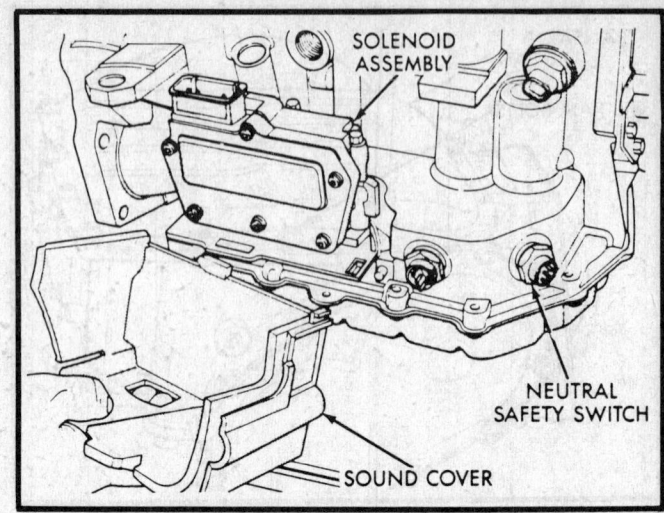

Solenoid assembly sound cover servicing

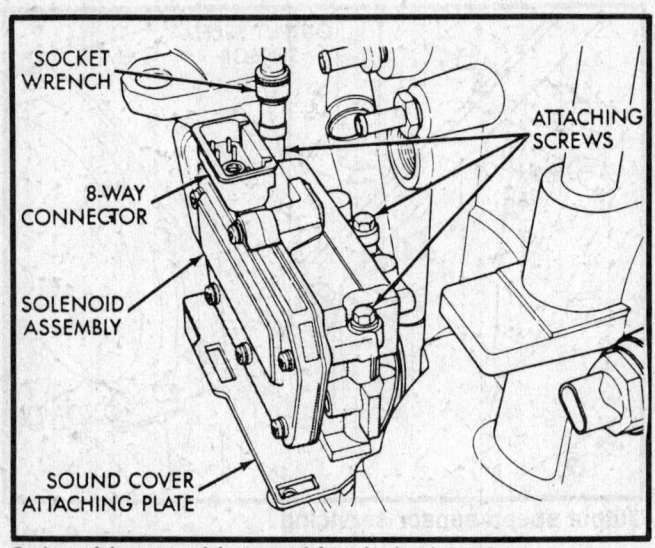

Solenoid assembly attaching bolts location

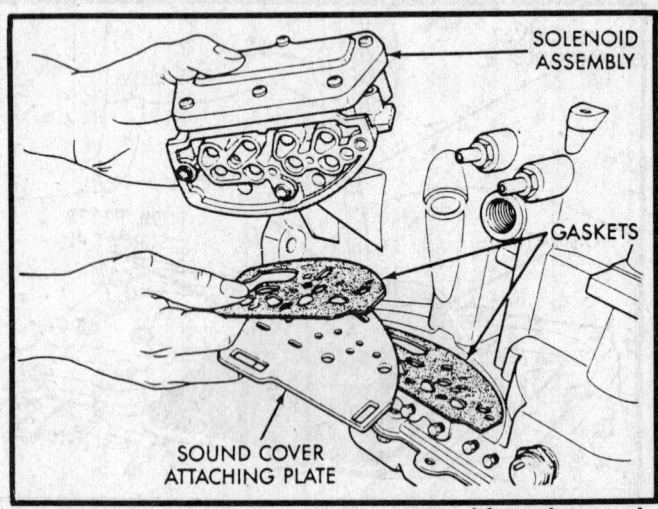

Solenoid assembly, sound cover attaching plate and gaskets

Transaxle oil pan servicing

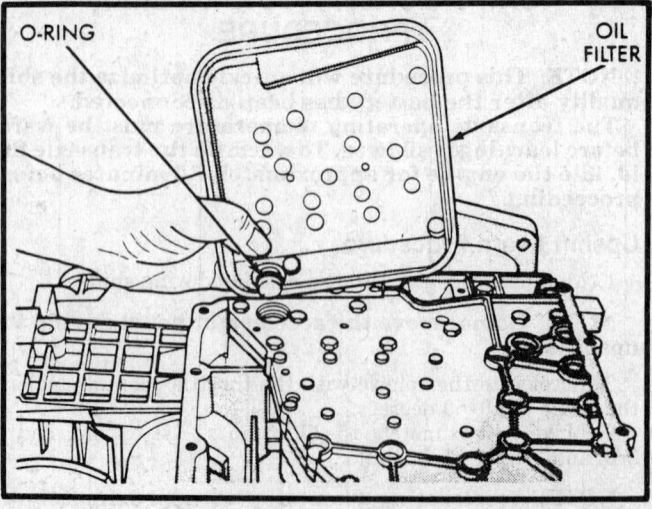

Oil filter servicing

Kickdown Learn Procedure

1. With the vehicle speed below 25 mph, make 5–8 WOT kickdowns to 1st gear from either 2nd or 3rd gear. Allow for 5 seconds or more of operation in 2nd or 3rd prior to the kickdown.
2. With the vehicle speed greater than 25 mph, make 5–8 part throttle to WOT kickdowns to either 3rd or 2nd gear from 4th gear (for example, 4–3 or 4–2 kickdowns). Allow for 5 seconds or more of operation in 4th, preferably at road-load throttle, prior to performing the kickdown.

Services

FLUID CHANGES

Fluid and filter changes are not required for average passenger vehicle usage.

Only severe usage, such as more than 50% operation in heavy city traffic during hot weather above 90°F (32°C) or police, taxi, commercial type operation and trailer towing, requires that the fluid and filter be changed, the magnet (on the inside of the oil pan) should be cleaned with a clean, dry cloth every 15,000 miles (24,000 km).

If the transaxle is disassembled for any reason, the fluid and filter should be changed.

1. Raise the vehicle and support safely. Place a drain container with a large opening under the transaxle oil pan.
2. Loosen the pan bolts and tap the pan at 1 corner to break it loose allowing fluid to drain, then remove the oil pan.
3. Install a new filter and O-ring on the bottom of the valve body.
4. Clean the oil pan and magnet. Reinstall the pan using new RTV sealant. Tighten the oil pan bolts to 165 inch lbs. (19 Nm).
5. Install 4 quarts of Mopar® ATF type 7176, or Dexron®II, through the filler tube.
6. Start the engine and allow to idle for at least 1 minute. Then, with the parking and service brakes applied, move the selector lever momentarily to each position, ending in the **P** or **N** position.
7. Add sufficient fluid to bring level to ⅛ in. below the **ADD** mark.
8. Recheck the fluid level after the transaxle is at normal operating temperature. The level should be in the **HOT** region.

NOTE: To prevent dirt from entering the transaxle, make certain that the dipstick is seated into the dipstick fill tube.

OIL PAN

Removal and Installation

1. Raise the vehicle and support safely. Place a drain container with a large opening under the transaxle oil pan.
2. Loosen the pan bolts and tap the pan at 1 corner to break it loose allowing fluid to drain, then remove the oil pan.
3. To install, reverse the removal procedure.
4. Reinstall the pan using new RTV sealant. Tighten the oil pan bolts to 165 inch lbs. (19 Nm).
5. Install 4 quarts of Mopar® ATF type 7176, or Dexron®II, through the filler tube.
6. Start the engine and allow to idle for at least 1 minute. Then, with the parking and service brakes applied, move the selector lever momentarily to each position, ending in the **P** or **N** position.
7. Add sufficient fluid to bring level to ⅛ in. below the **ADD** mark.
8. Recheck the fluid level after the transaxle is at normal operating temperature. The level should be in the **HOT** region.

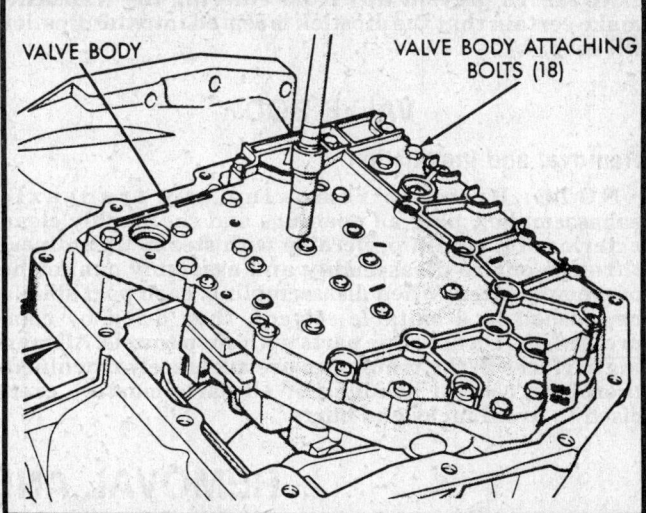

Valve body servicing

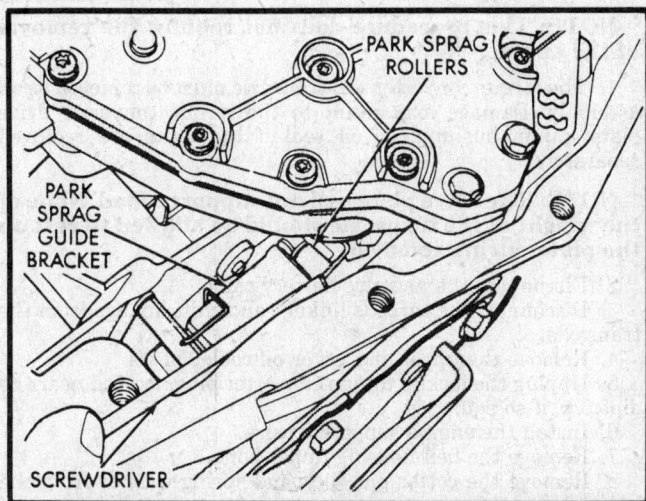

Park sprag guide bracket and park sprag rollers location

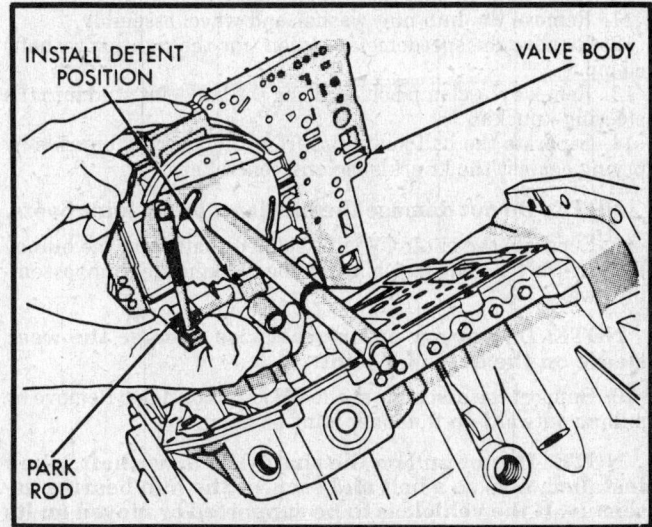

Valve body assembly servicing

NOTE: To prevent dirt from entering the transaxle, make certain that the dipstick is seated into the dipstick fill tube.

VALVE BODY

Removal and Installation

NOTE: Prior to removing any transaxle subassemblies, plug all openings and thoroughly clean exterior of the unit, preferably with steam. Cleanliness through entire disassembly and assembly cannot be overemphasized. When disassembling, each part should be washed in a suitable solvent, then dried by compressed air. Do not wipe parts with shop towels. All mating surfaces in the transaxles are accurately machined; therefore, careful handling of all parts must be exercised to avoid nicks and burrs.

1. Raise the vehicle and support safely.
2. Remove the oil pan bolts and remove the oil pan.
3. Remove the oil filter.
4. Remove the valve body attaching bolts.
5. Push the park rod rollers from the guide bracket.
6. Remove the valve body.
7. To install, reverse the removal procedure.

SOLENOID ASSEMBLY

Removal and Installation

1. Raise the vehicle and support safely.
2. Remove the input speed sensor.
3. Remove the sound cover.
4. Remove the solenoid assembly attaching bolts.
5. Remove the solenoid assembly and gaskets.
6. To install, reverse the removal procedure.

REMOVAL AND INSTALLATION

TRANSAXLE REMOVAL

NOTE: This procedure does not require the removal of the engine.

1. The torque converter and transaxle must be removed as an assembly. Damage may result to the torque converter drive plate, pump bushing, or oil seal if the units are removed separately.

NOTE: The drive plate will not support a load. None of the weight of the transaxle should be allowed to rest on the plate during removal.

2. Disconnect the negative battery cable.
3. Disconnect the throttle linkage and shift linkage from the transaxle.
4. Remove the upper and lower oil cooler hoses.
5. Unplug the lockup torque converter plug, located near the dipstick, if so equipped.
6. Install the engine support fixture.
7. Remove the bell housing upper bolts.
8. Remove the cotter pin, lock and spring washer from the hub assembly.
9. Loosen the hub nut and wheel nuts while the vehicle is on the floor and the brakes are applied.
10. Raise and support the vehicle safely.
11. Remove the hub nut, washer and wheel assembly.
12. Remove the speedometer pinion (for the right driveshaft) clamp.
13. Remove the clamp bolt securing the ball joint stud into the steering knuckle.
14. Separate the ball joint stud from the steering knuckle by prying against the knuckle leg and control arm.

NOTE: Do not damage the ball joint or CV joint boots.

15. Separate the outer CV joint splined shaft from the hub by holding the CV housing while moving the knuckle (hub) assembly away.

NOTE: Do not pry on or otherwise damage the wear sleeve on the outer CV joint.

16. Support the assembly at the CV joint housings. Remove by pulling outward on the inner joint housing.

NOTE: Do not pull on the shaft. The driveshaft, when installed, acts as a bolt and secures the hub/bearing assembly. If the vehicle is to be supported or moved on its wheels, install a bolt through the hub to insure that the hub bearing assembly cannot loosen.

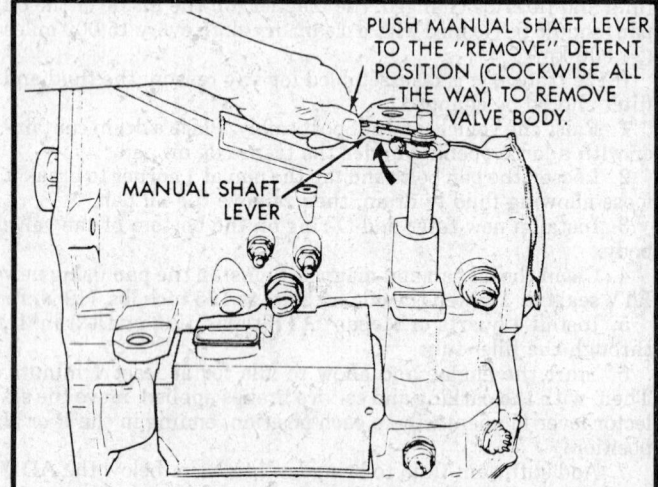

Positioning manual shaft lever for transaxle removal

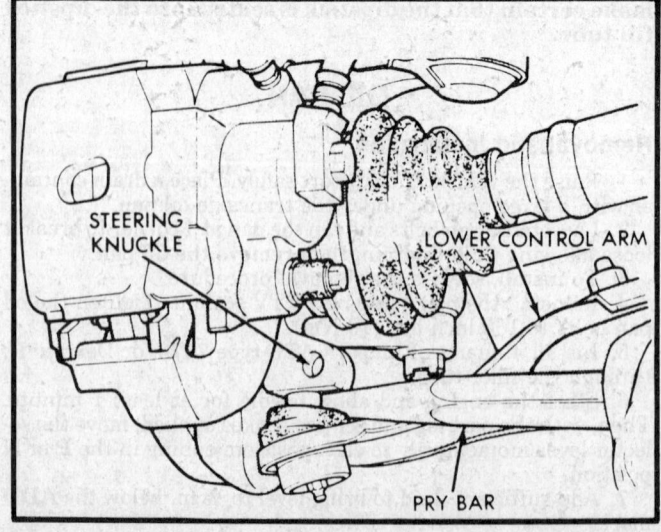

Separating lower control arm from steering knuckle

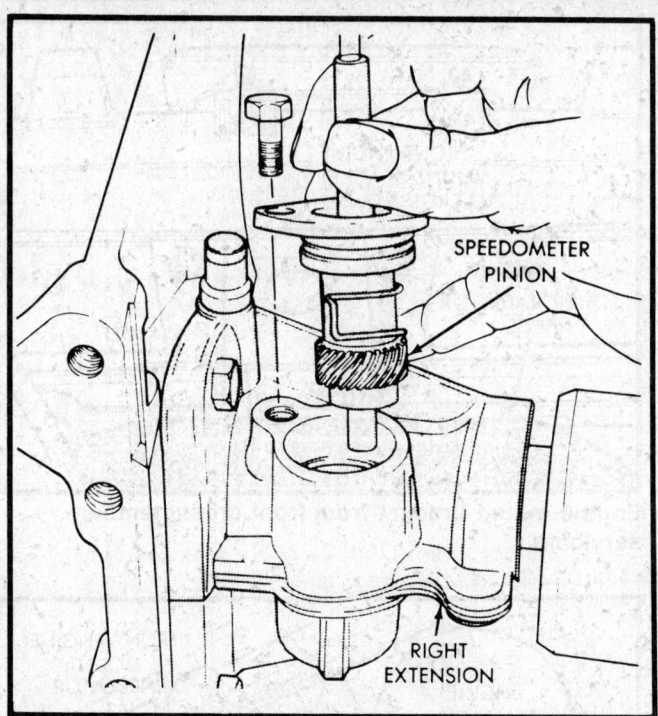

Speedometer pinion servicing

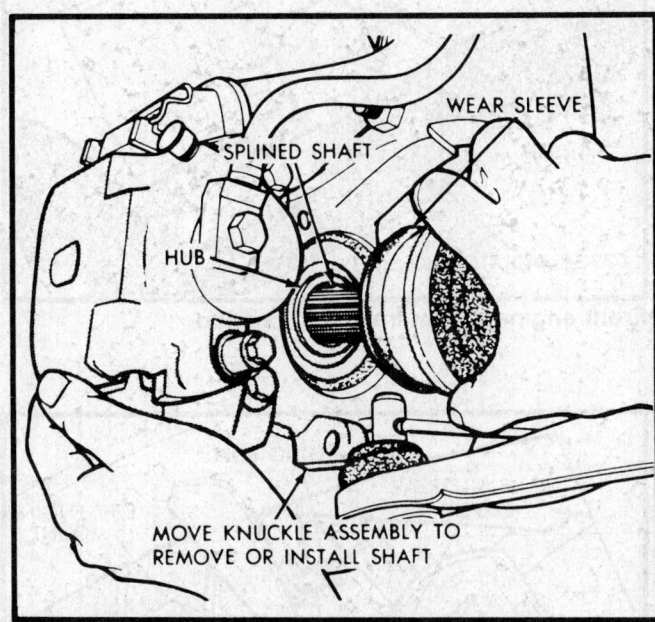

Separating drive shaft from steering knuckle

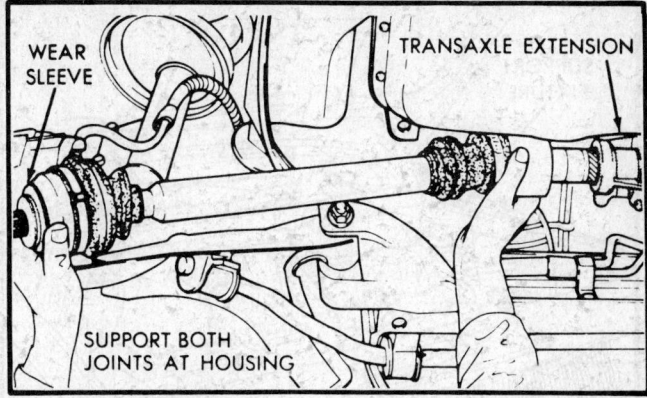

Drive shaft servicing

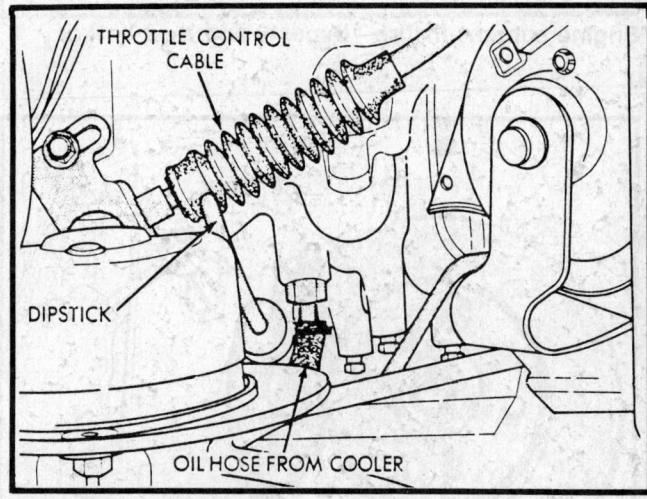

Oil cooler line location

Engine support fixture – Caravan and Voyager

17. Remove both driveshafts.
18. Remove the torque converter dust cover. Mark the torque converter and drive plate with chalk, for reassembly. Remove the torque converter mounting bolts.
19. Remove the access plug in the right splash shield to rotate the engine crankshaft.
20. Remove the wire to the neutral/park safety switch.
21. Remove the engine mount bracket from the front crossmember.
22. Remove the front mount insulator through bolt and the bell housing bolts.

23. Position the transmission jack.
24. Remove the left engine mount.
25. Remove the starter. Remove the lower bell housing bolts.
26. Pry the engine for clearance and lower the transaxle.

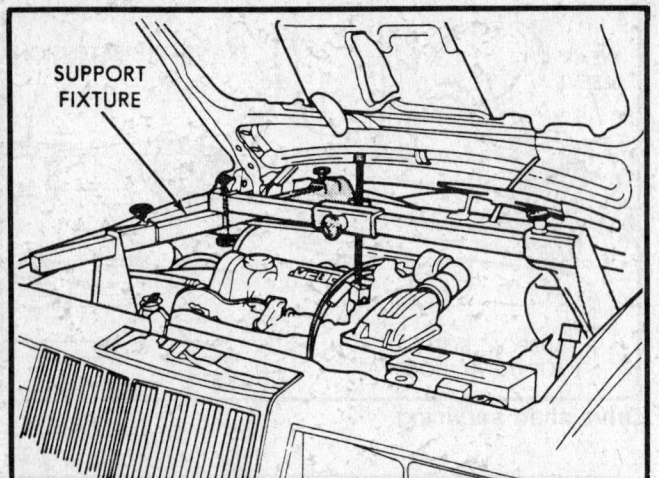

Engine support fixture—Dynasty and New Yorker

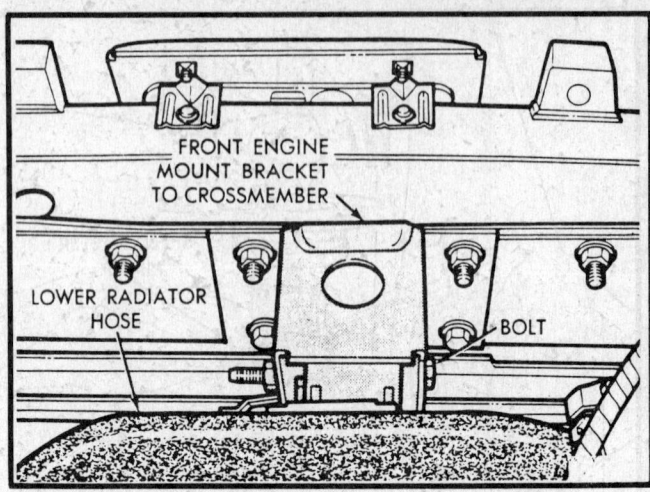

Engine mount bracket from front crossmember servicing

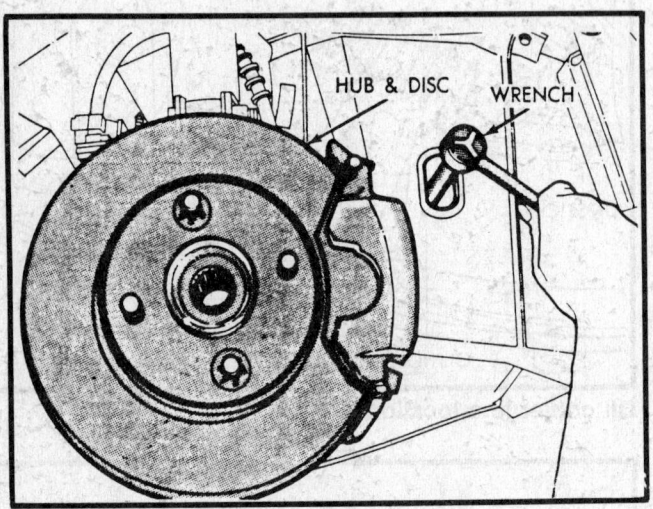

Right splash shield access plug location

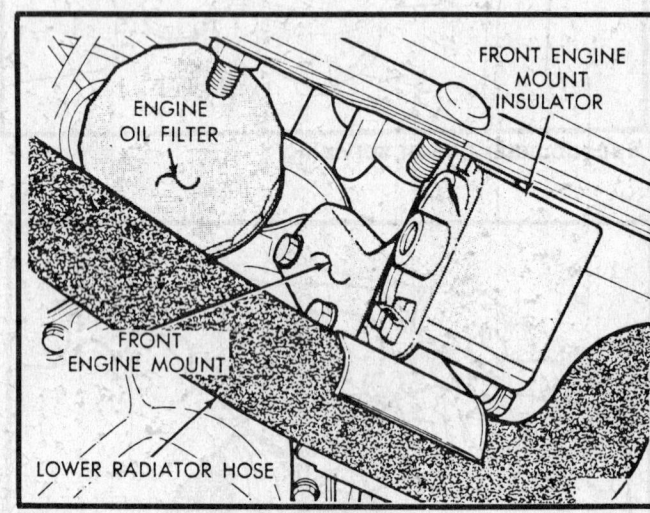

Front engine mount insulator location

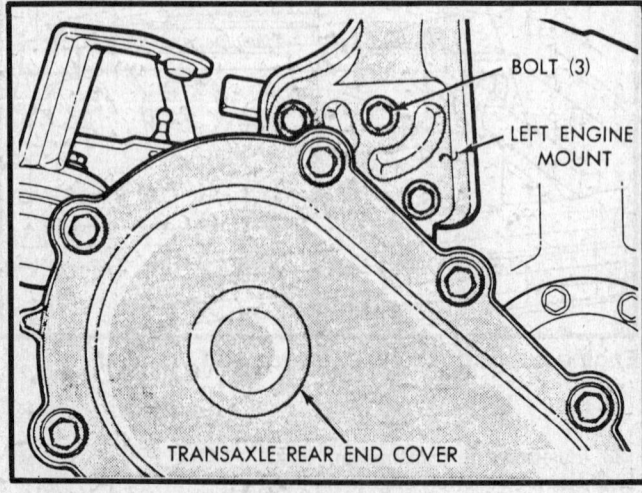

Left engine mount bolts location

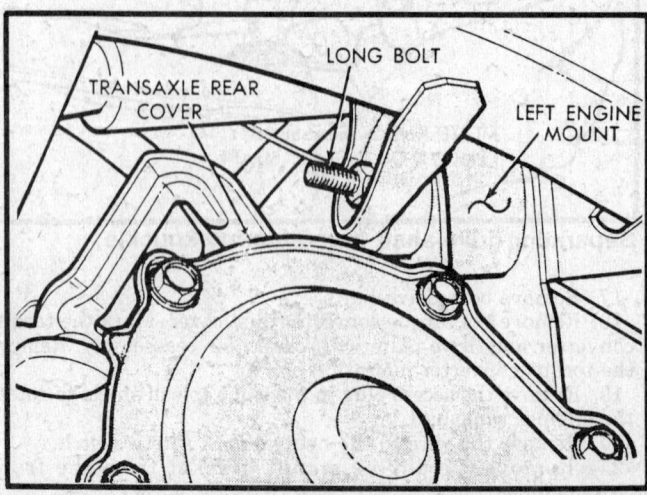

Left engine mount-from-engine bolt location

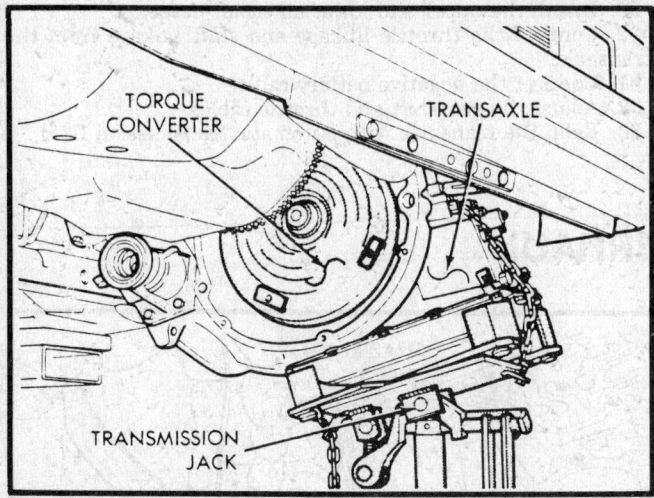

Transaxle servicing

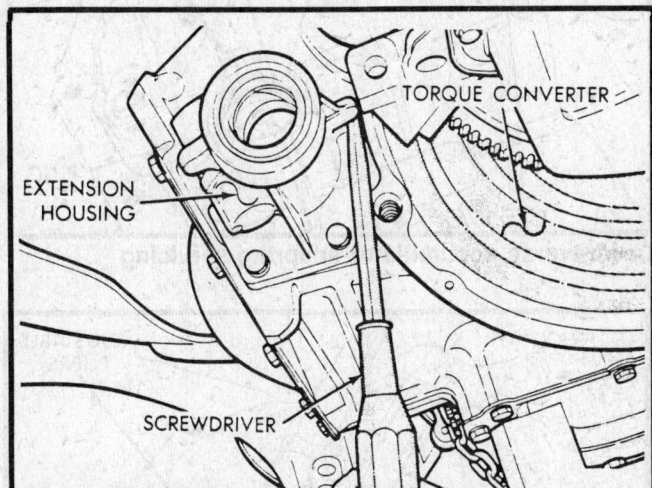

Engine clearance pry point location

TRANSAXLE INSTALLATION

1. Raise the transaxle into position.
2. Install the lower bell housing bolts. Install the starter.
3. Install the left engine mount to the engine.
4. Install the left engine mount.
5. Remove the transmission jack.
6. Install the front mount insulator through bolt and bell housing bolts.
7. Install the engine mount bracket to the front crossmember.
8. Install the wire to the neutral/park safety switch.
9. Install the access plug in the right splash shield.
10. Turn the torque converter to matchmark the driveplate made on disassembly, and install torque converter mounting bolts.
11. Install the torque converter dust cover.
12. To install the driveshafts, hold the inner joint assembly at the housing while aligning and guiding the inner joint spline into the transaxle or intermediate shaft assembly.

NOTE: When installing an A.C.I. type shaft, be sure that the tripod is engaged in the housing and the boot is not twisted.

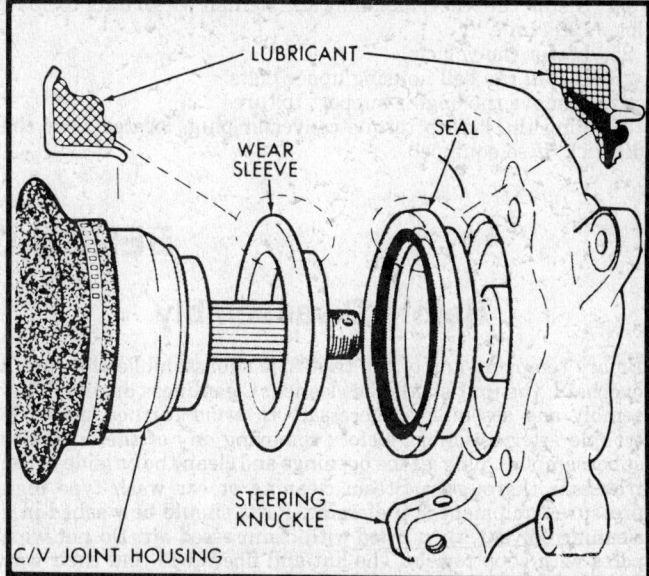

Wear sleeve and seal servicing

13. Install the inner shaft into the transaxle.

NOTE: During any service procedures where the knuckle and driveshaft are separated, thoroughly clean the seal and wear sleeve with a suitable solvent (solvent must not touch the boots) and relubricate both components prior to reinstalling driveshaft. Lubricate wear sleeve and seal with Mopar Multi-Purpose Lubricant, part number 4318063 or equivalent.

14. Apply lubricate on the full circumference of the wear sleeve and bead of lubricate that is ¼ in. (6mm) wide to seal the contact area. Fill the lip to housing cavity on the seal, complete circumference, and wet the seal lip with lubricate.
15. Push the knuckle (hub) assembly out and install the splined outer CV joint shaft in the hub.
16. Reinstall the knuckle assembly on the ball joint stud.

NOTE: The original or equivalent steering knuckle clamp bolt must be reinstalled during reassembly.

17. Install and tighten the clamp bolt to 70 ft. lbs. (95 Nm).
18. Install speedometer pinion.
19. Fill the differential with proper lubricant.
20. Install the hub nut assembly.

NOTE: If the inboard boot appears collapsed or deformed after installing the driveshaft assembly, vent the inner boot by inserting a round tipped, small diameter rod between the boot and shaft. If necessary, massage the boot to remove all puckers being careful not to allow dirt to enter or grease to leave the boot cavity. If the boot is clamped to the shaft with a rubber "garter" clamp, it need not be removed to perform this venting operation. If the boot is clamped to the shaft using a metal clamp, the clamp must be removed and discarded before the rod can be inserted. After venting, install a new service clamp, part number 5212720, or equivalent and special tool C-4653.

21. Install the washer and hub nut after cleaning foreign matter from the threads.
22. With the brakes applied, tighten the hub nut to 180 ft. lbs. (245 Nm).
23. Install the lock, washer and new cotter pin. Wrap the cotter pin prongs tightly around the nut lock.

24. Install the wheel assembly and tighten wheel nuts to 95 ft. lbs. (129 Nm).
25. Lower the vehicle.
26. Install the bell housing upper bolts.
27. Remove the engine support fixture.
28. Plug the lockup torque converter plug, located near the dipstick, if so equipped.

29. Install the upper and lower oil cooler hoses.
30. Connect the throttle linkage and shift linkage from the transaxle.
31. Connect the negative battery cable.
32. Adjust the gearshift and throttle cables.
33. Refill the transaxle with automatic transmission fluid.

BENCH OVERHAUL

Before Disassembly

Before removing any of the transaxle subassemblies for bench overhaul, the unit should be cleaned. Cleanliness during disassembly and assembly is necessary to avoid further transaxle trouble after assembly. Before removing any of the transaxle subassemblies, plug all the openings and clean the outside of the transaxle thoroughly. Steam cleaning or car wash type high pressure equipment is preferable. Parts should be washed in a cleaning solvent, then dried with compressed air. Do not wipe parts with shop towels. The lint and fibers will find their way into the valve body and other parts and cause problems later. The case assembly was accurately machined and care must be used to avoid damage. Pay attention to the torque values to avoid case distortion.

Transaxle Disassembly

CONVERTER

Removal

The torque converter is removed by sliding the unit out of the transaxle input and reaction shaft. If the converter is to be reused, set it aside so it will not be damaged. Since the units are welded and have no drain plugs, converters subject to burnt fluid or other contamination should be replaced.

OIL PAN

Removal

Loosen the pan bolts and tap the pan at a corner to break it loose allowing fluid to drain, then remove the oil pan.

VALVE BODY

Removal

1. Remove the oil filter.
2. Remove the valve body attaching bolts.
3. Push the park rod rollers from the guide bracket.
4. Remove the valve body.

ACCUMULATORS

Removal

1. Remove the underdrive clutch accumulator and return spring.
2. Remove the overdrive clutch accumulator and return spring.
3. Remove the low/reverse accumulator snapring.
4. Remove the low/reverse accumulator plug with adjustable pliers.

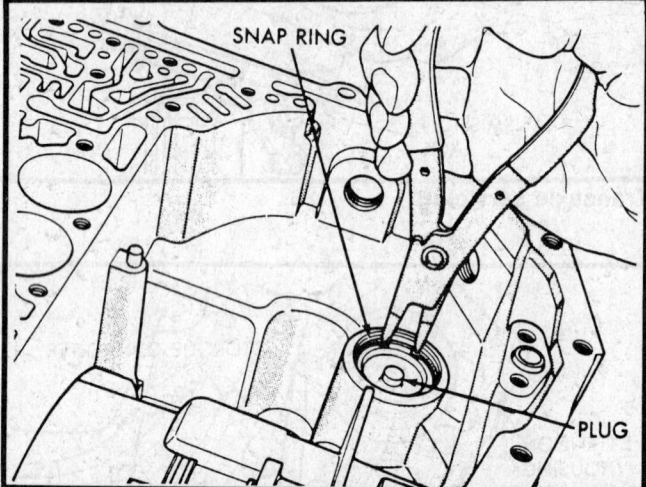

Low/reverse accumulator snapring servicing

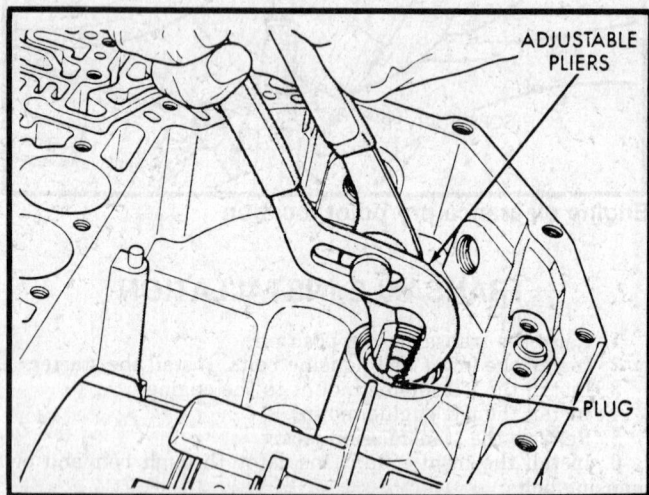

Low/reverse accumulator plug removal

5. Remove the low/reverse accumulator piston with a suitable dowel tool and petroleum jelly.
6. Remove the low/reverse accumulator piston return springs.

GOVERNOR

Removal

This transaxle utilizes electronic sensors and solenoids in place of the governor. Therefore, there is no governor assembly.

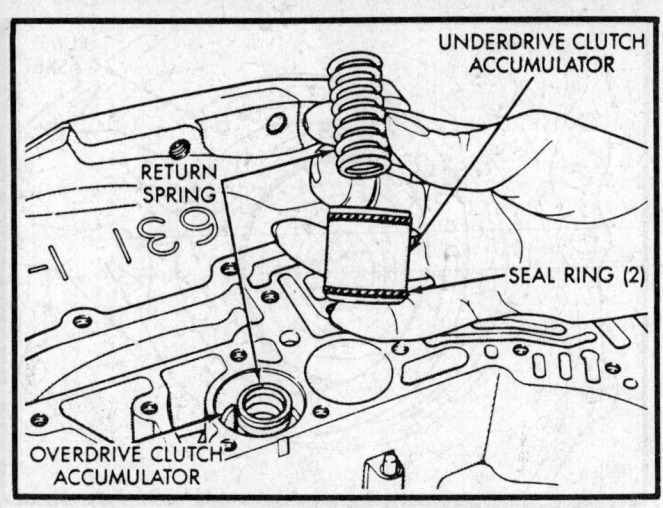

Underdrive clutch accumulator servicing

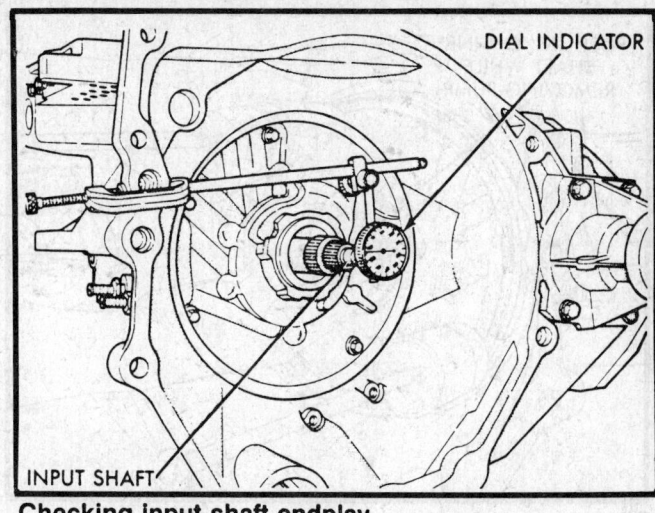

Checking input shaft endplay

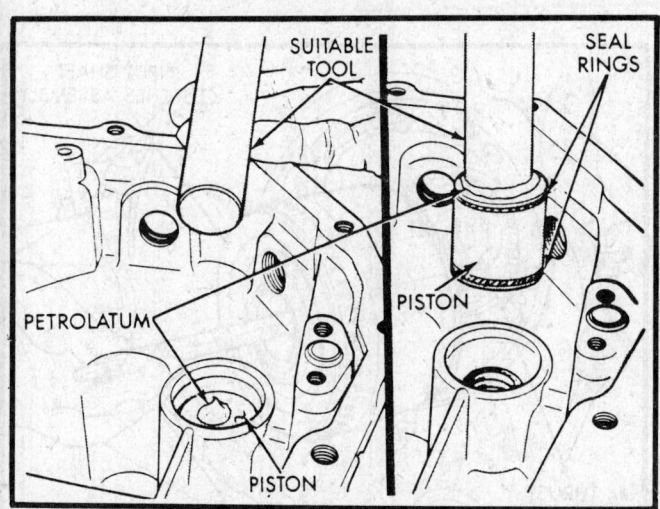

Low/reverse accumulator piston removal

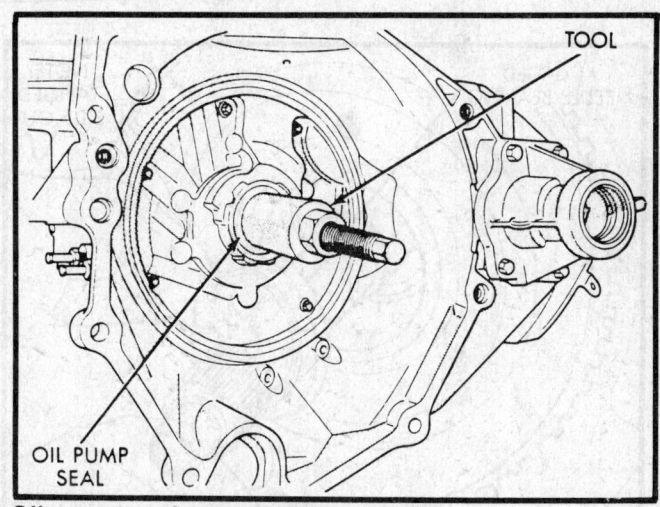

Oil pump seal removal

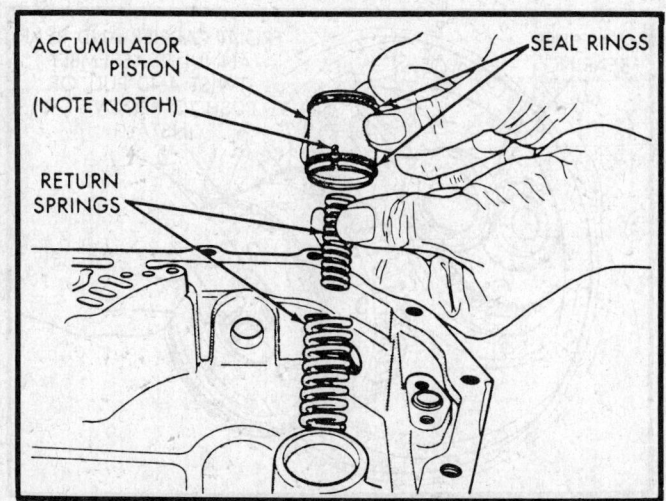

Low/reverse accumulator and return springs

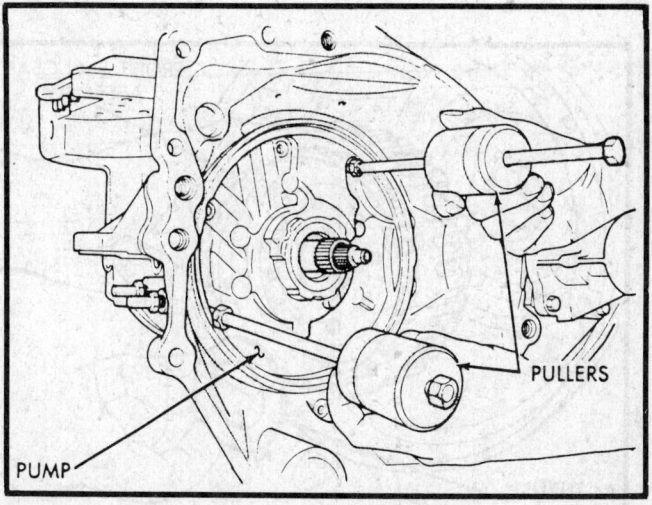

Oil pump puller tools

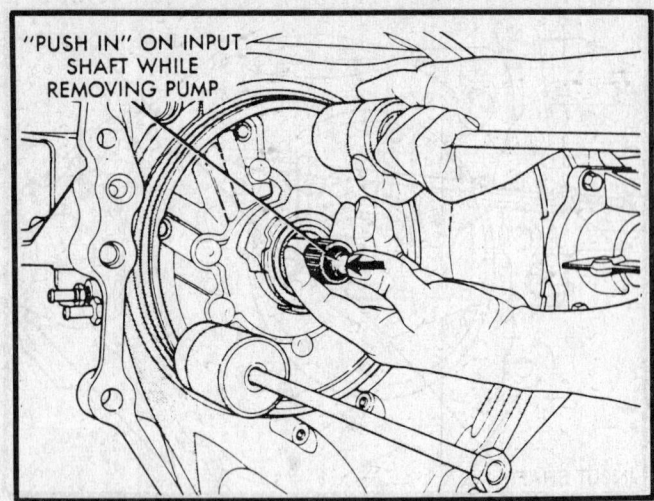

Oil pump removal

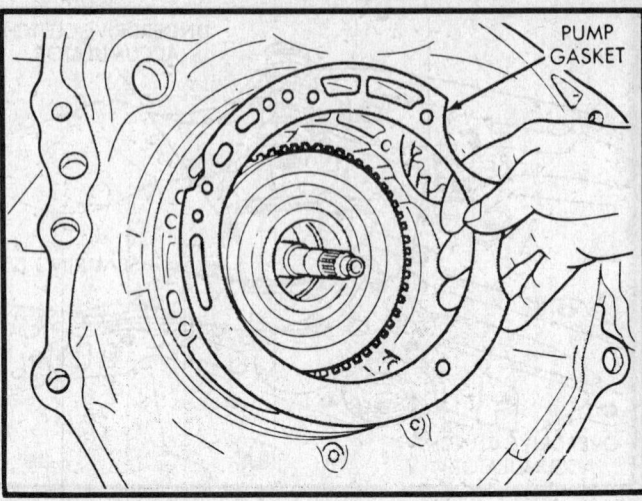

Oil pump gasket

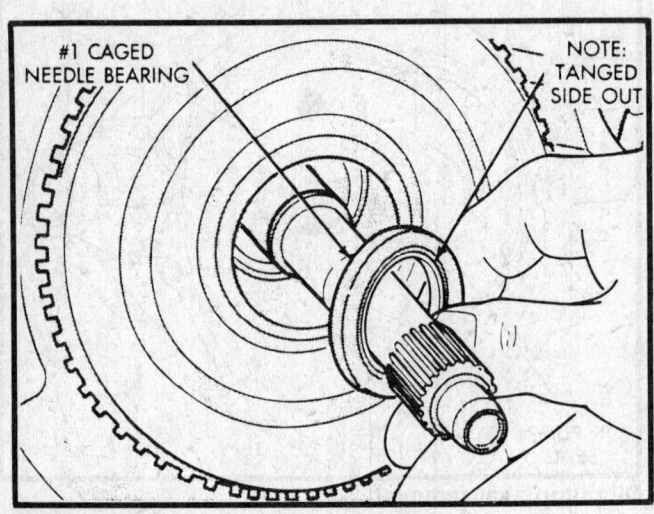

Caged needle bearing #1 assembly

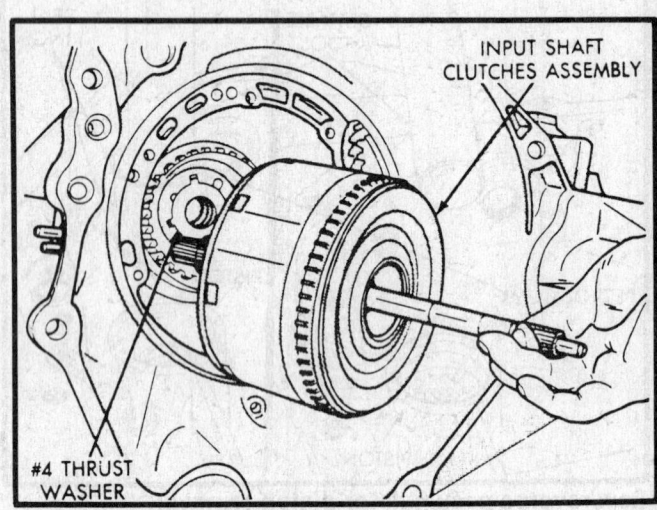

Input shaft clutches assembly

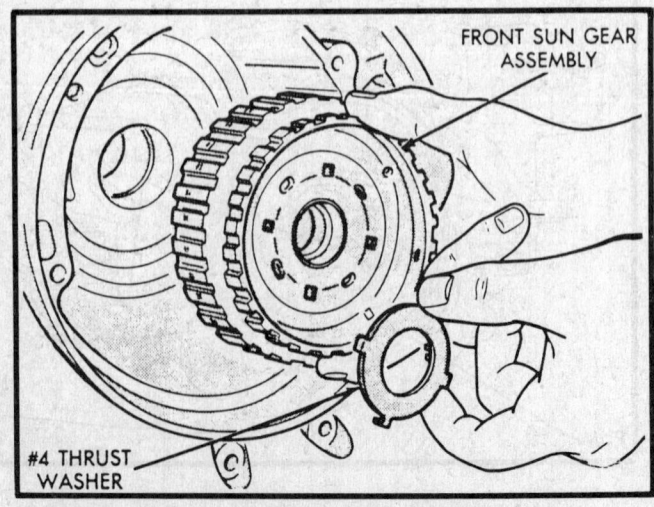

Front sun gear assembly and #4 thrust washer

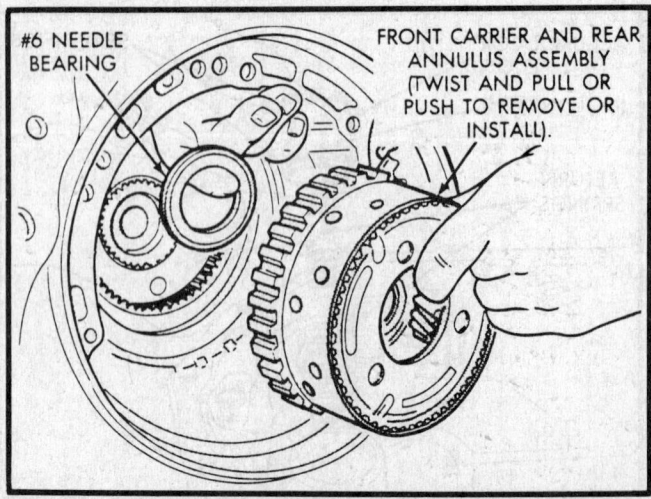

Front carrier/rear annulus assembly and #6 needle bearing

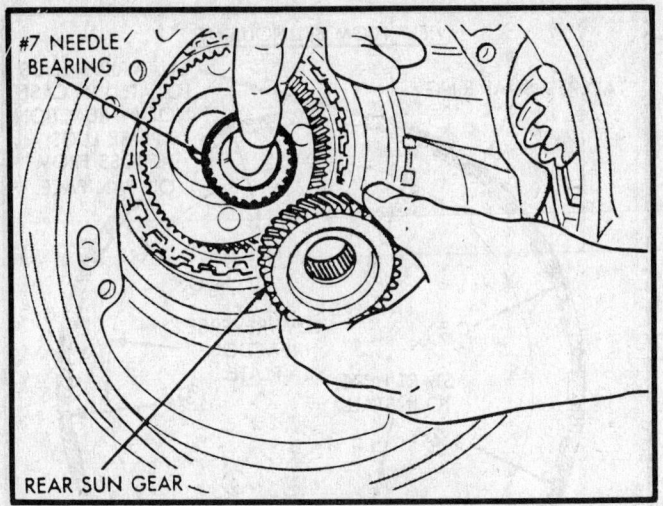

Rear sun gear and #7 needle bearing

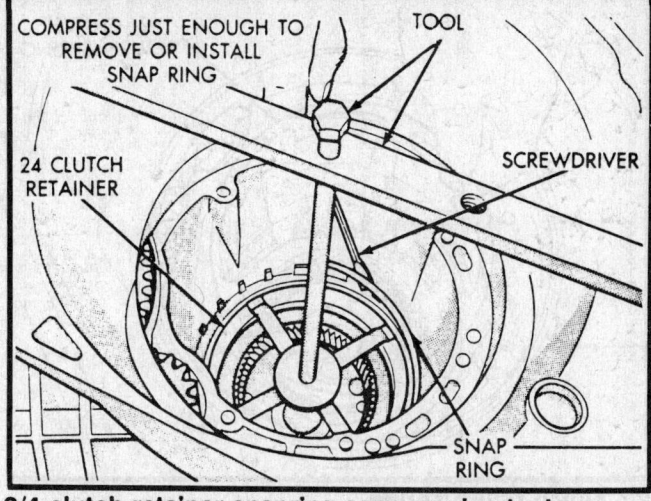

2/4 clutch retainer snapring compression tool

INPUT SHAFT ENDPLAY

Removal

Measuring input shaft endplay before disassembly will usually indicate when a No. 4 thrust plate change is required (except when major parts are replaced). The thrust washer is located behind the input shaft.

1. Attach a dial indicator to the transaxle bell housing with its plunger seated against the end of the input shaft.
2. Move the shaft in and out to obtain endplay reading. Endplay specifications are 0.012–0.030 in. (0.31–0.76mm).
3. Record the indicator reading for reference when reassembling the transaxle.

OIL PUMP

Removal

1. Remove the input speed sensor.
2. Remove the oil pump seal using tool C–3981.
3. Remove the oil pump attaching bolts.
4. Install pullers tool C–3752 to pump.
5. Push in on the input shaft while removing the pump.
6. Remove the oil pump and oil pump gasket.

INPUT SHAFT CLUTCHES ASSEMBLY

Removal

1. Remove the No. 1 caged needle bearing.
2. Remove the input shaft clutches assembly.

FRONT SUN GEAR ASSEMBLY

Removal

1. Remove the No. 4 thrust washer.
2. Remove the front sun gear assembly.

FRONT CARRIER AND REAR ANNULUS ASSEMBLY

Removal

1. Remove the front carrier and rear annulus assembly. Twist and pull to remove the assembly.
2. Remove the No. 6 needle bearing.

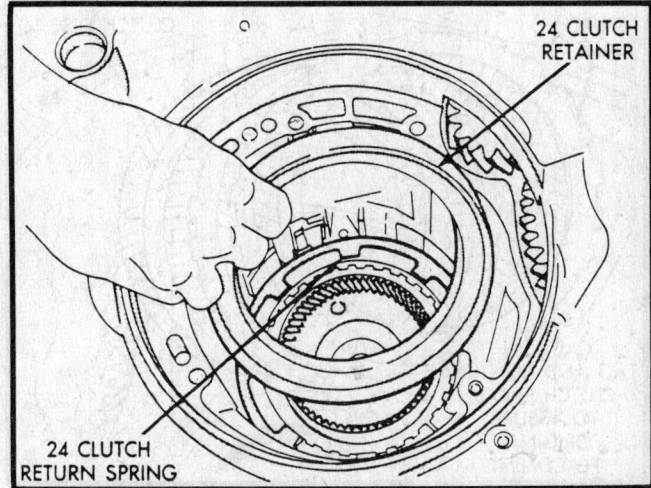

2/4 clutch retainer

REAR SUN GEAR

Removal

1. Remove the rear sun gear.
2. Remove the No. 7 needle bearing.

2–4 CLUTCH PACK

Removal

1. Install tool 5058 and compress the 2–4 clutch retainer spring just enough to remove the 2–4 clutch retainer snapring. Remove the 2–4 clutch retainer snapring.
2. Remove the 2–4 clutch retainer.
3. Remove the 2–4 clutch return spring.
4. Remove the 2–4 clutch pack. Tag and identify clutch packs to assure original replacement.

LOW/REVERSE CLUTCH PACK

Removal

1. Remove the tapered snapring. Remove in sequence.
2. Remove the low/reverse reaction plate.

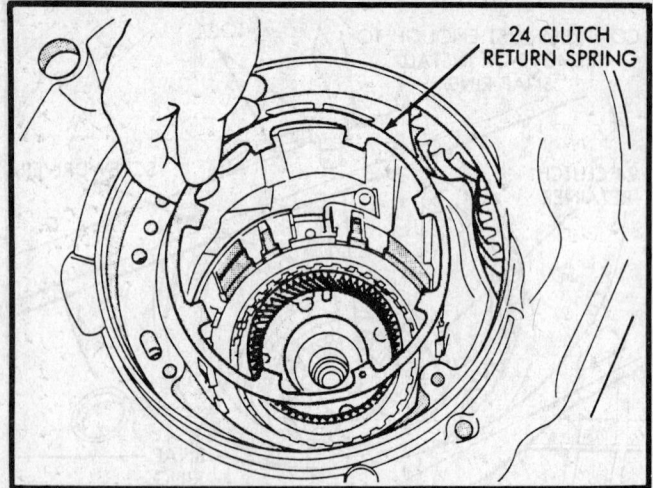

2/4 clutch return spring

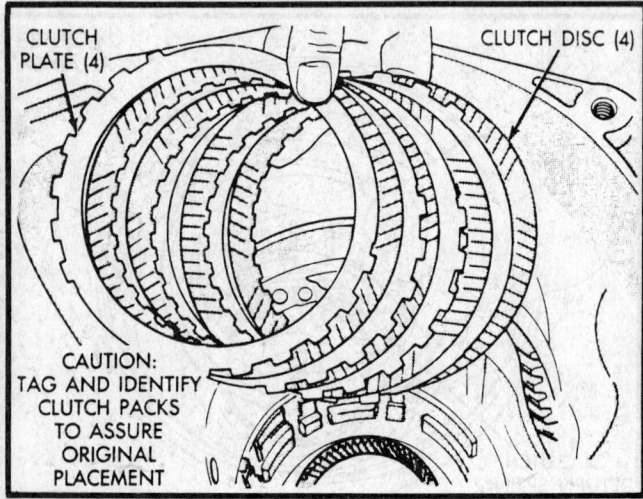

2/4 clutch pack

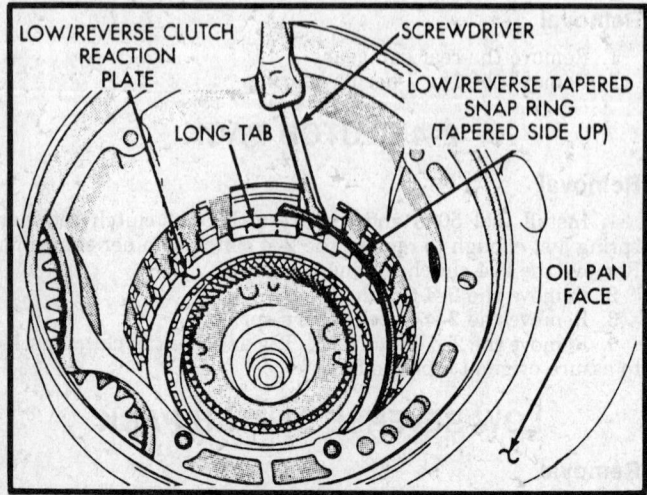

Low/reverse tapered snapring

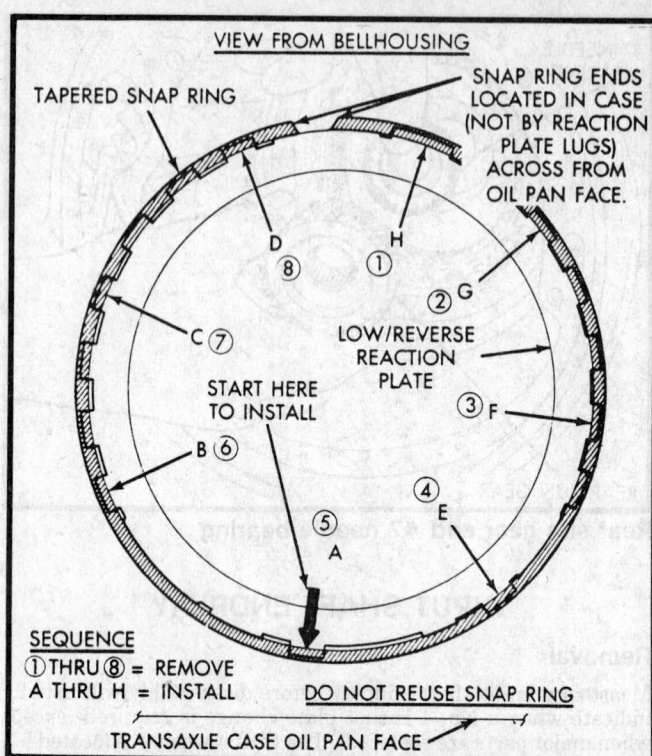

Low/reverse tapered snapring removal/installation sequence instructions

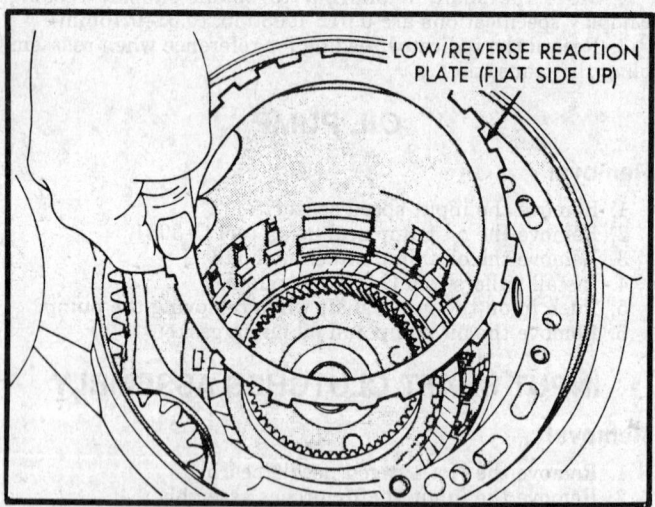

Low/reverse reaction plate

3. Remove the 1 disc from the low/reverse clutch.

4. Remove the low/reverse reaction plate snapring. Do not scratch the clutch plate.

5. Remove the low/reverse clutch pack. Tag and identify clutch packs to assure original replacement.

TRANSFER SHAFT GEAR

Removal

1. Remove the rear cover bolts.
2. Remove the rear cover.
3. Remove the transfer shaft gear nut and lockwasher using tool 6259.

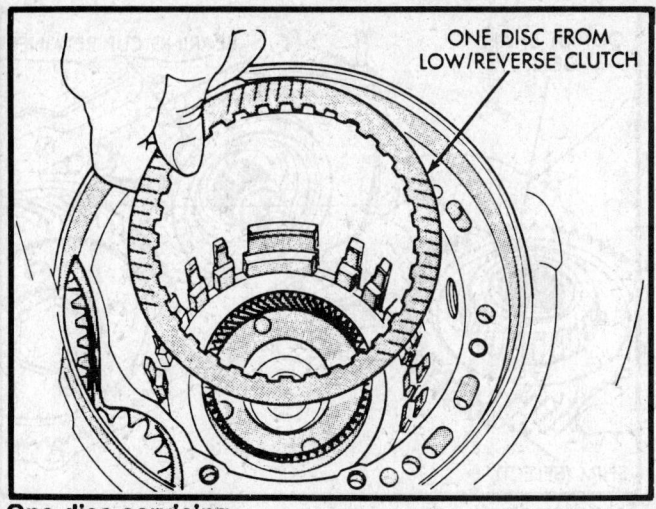

One disc servicing

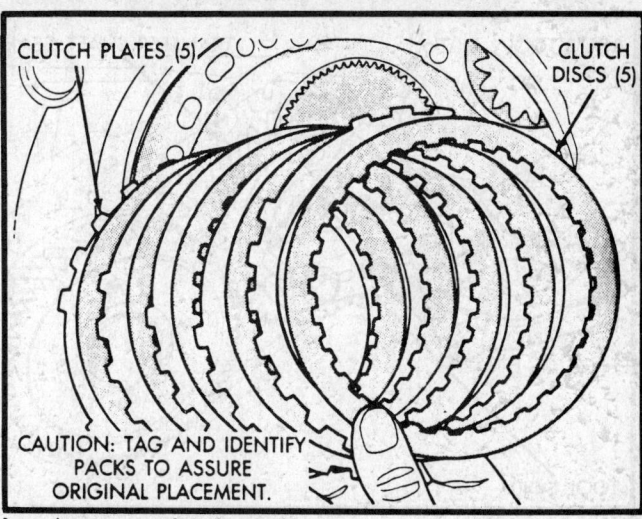

Low/reverse clutch pack

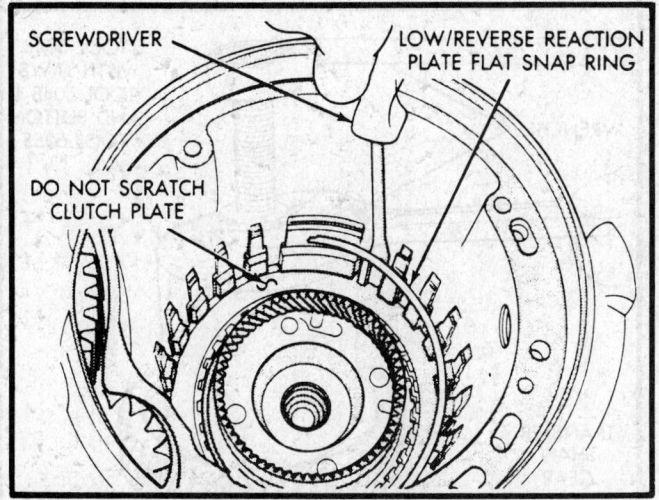

Low/reverse reaction plate snapring

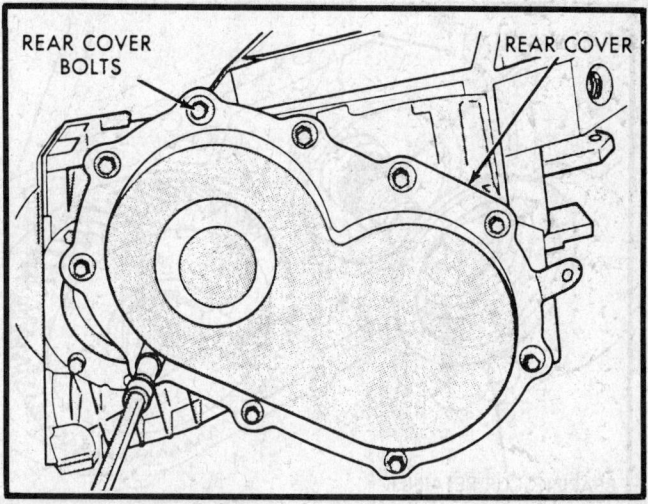

Rear cover servicing

4. Remove the transfer shaft gear and shim using puller tool L–4407 and bolts tool L–4407–6.

NOTE: If necessary, the transfer shaft bearing cone can be removed from the gear by using tool 5048 with jaws tool 5048–4 and button tool 6055.

TRANSFER SHAFT

Removal

1. Remove the transfer shaft bearing cup retainer.

NOTE: If necessary, the transfer shaft bearing cup can be removed from the transfer shaft bearing cup retainer by using tool 6062.

2. Remove the transfer shaft bearing snapring using snapring pliers tool 6051.

3. Remove the transfer shaft using tool 5049–A.

NOTE: If necessary, the transfer shaft bearing cone can be removed from the transfer shaft with the use of tool P–334 and arbor press.

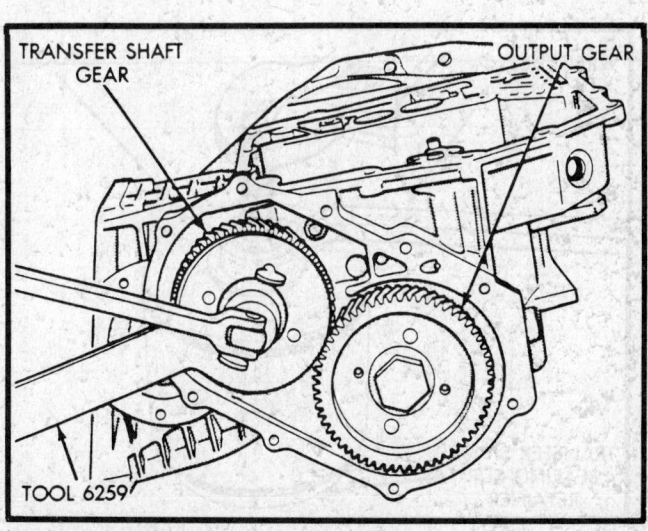

Transfer shaft gear nut removal

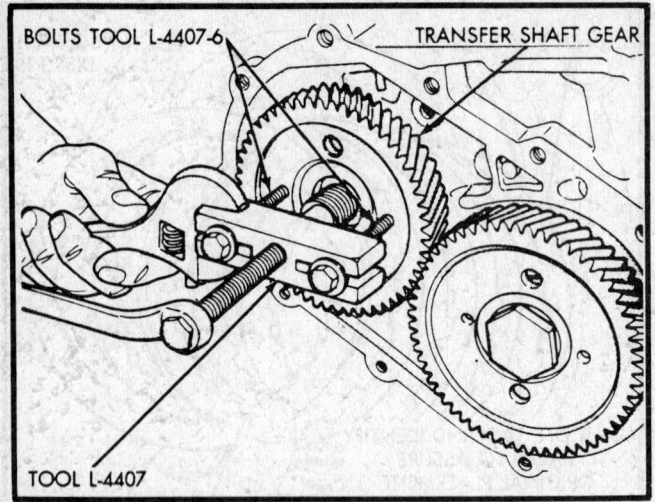

Transfer shaft gear removal tool

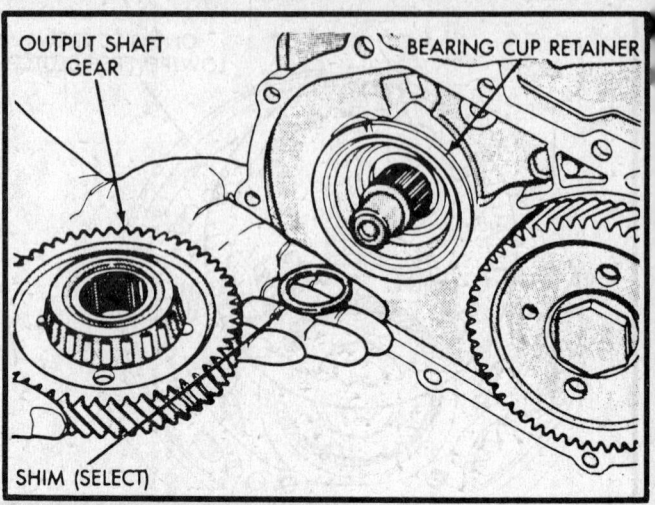

Transfer shaft gear and shim

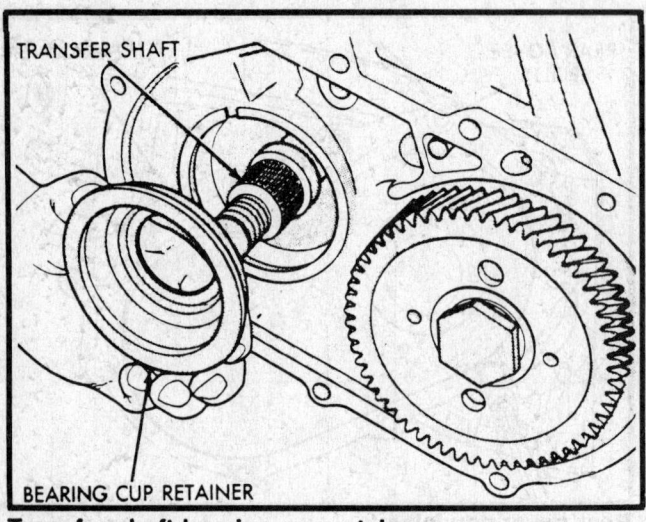

Transfer shaft bearing cup retainer

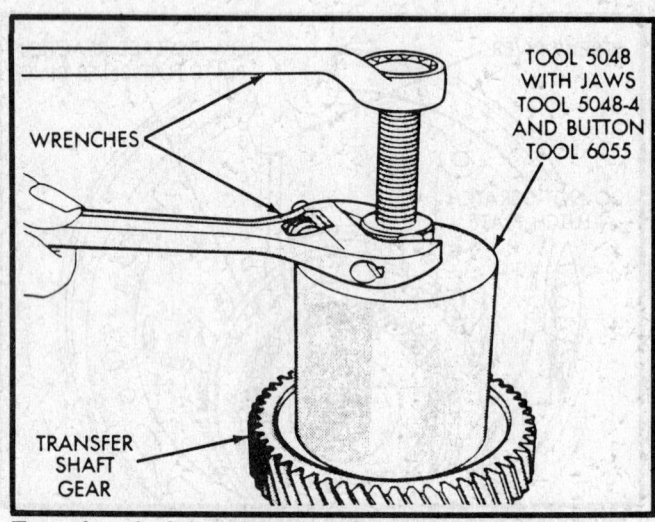

Transfer shaft bearing gear cone removal

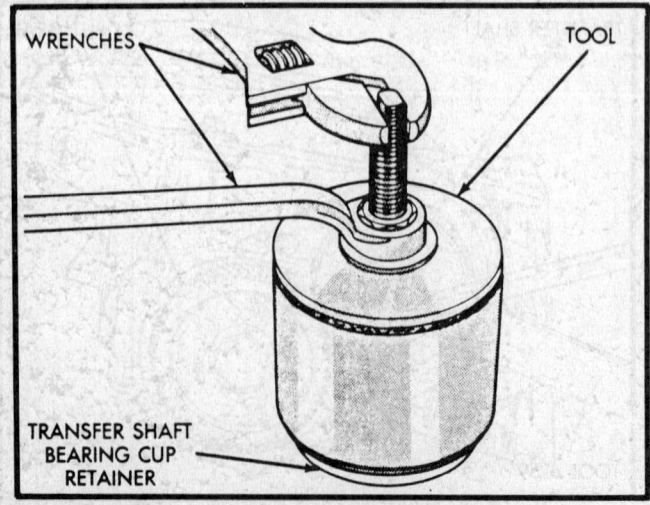

Transfer shaft bearing cup removal

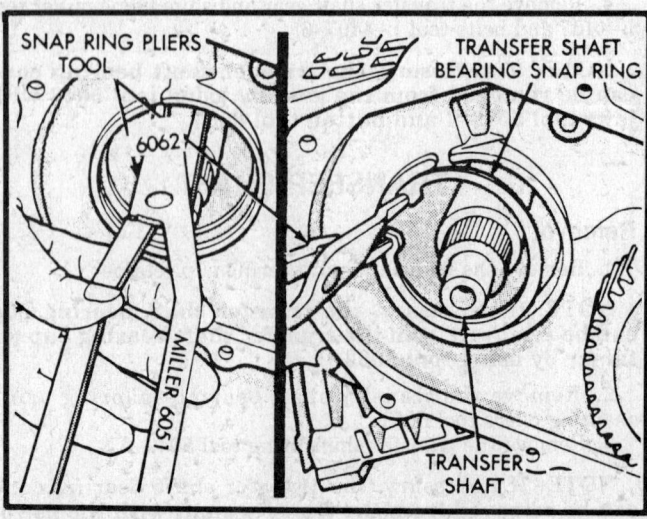

Transfer shaft bearing snapring servicing

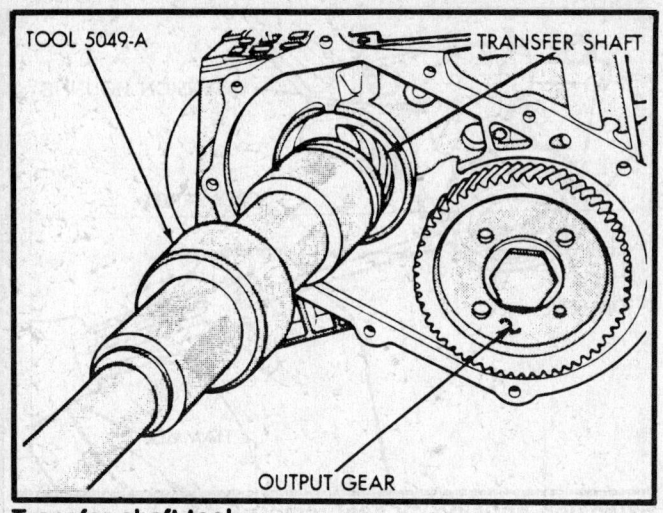

Transfer shaft tool

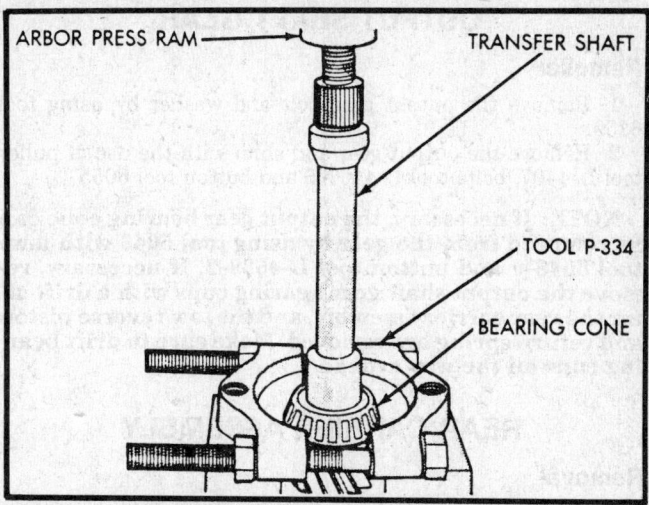

Transfer shaft bearing cone removal

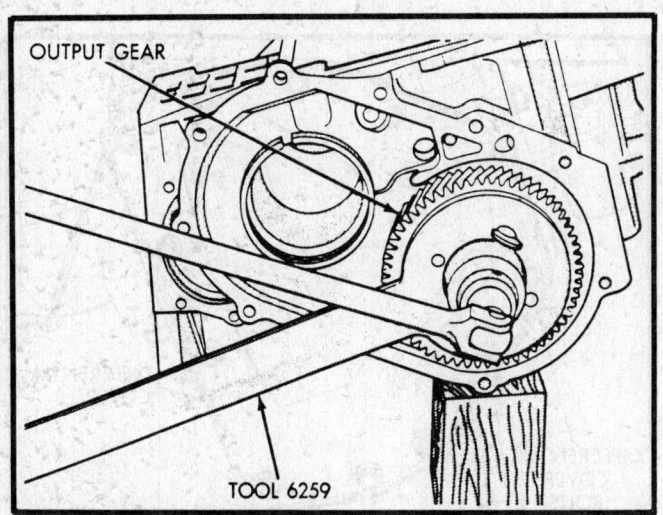

Output gear bolt removal

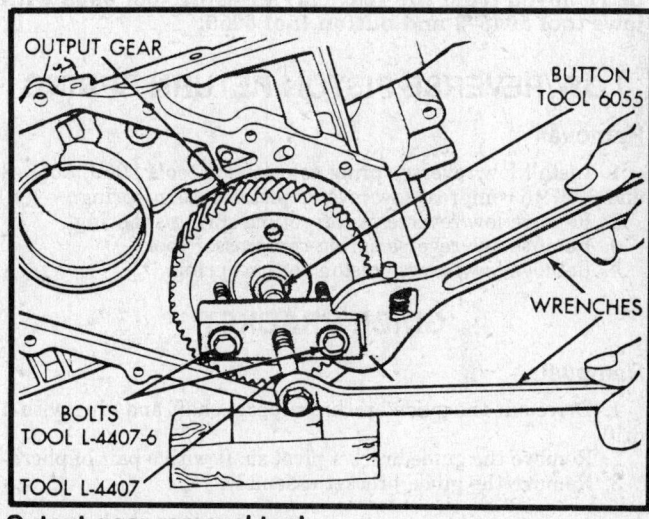

Output gear removal tool

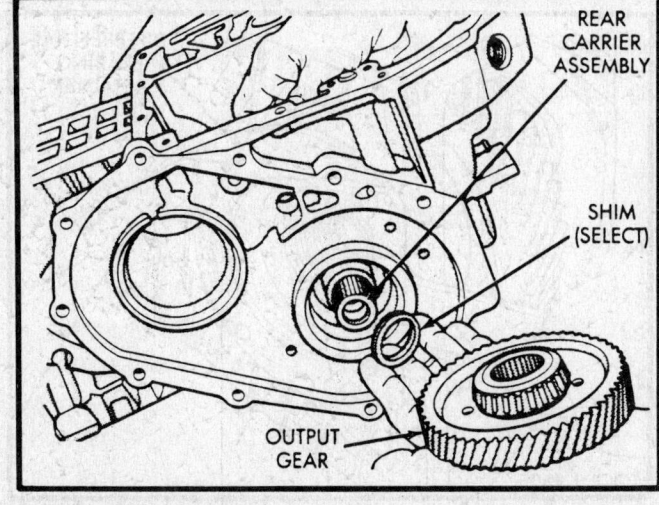

Output gear and shim

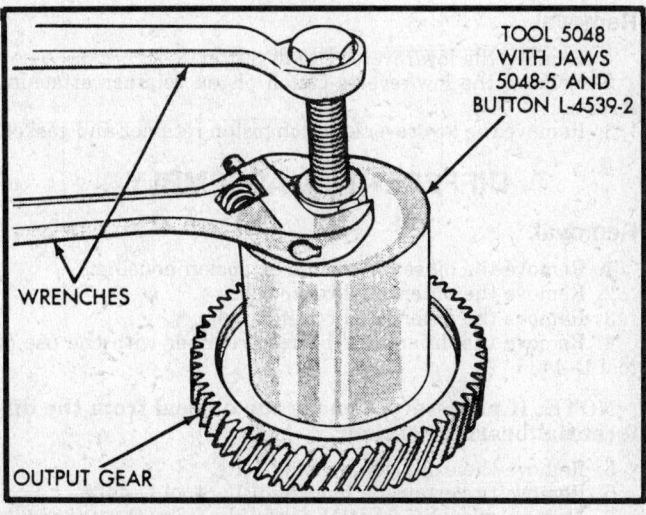

Output gear bearing cone removal

OUTPUT SHAFT GEAR

Removal

1. Remove the output gear bolt and washer by using tool 6259.
2. Remove the output gear and shim with the use of puller tool L–4407, bolts tool L–4407–6 and button tool 6055.

NOTE: If necessary, the output gear bearing cone can be removed from the gear by using tool 5048 with jaws tool 5048–5 and button tool L–4539–2. If necessary, remove the output shaft gear bearing cups with a drift after the rear carrier assembly, and the low/reverse piston and return spring are removed. Make sure to drift bearing cups all the way around.

REAR CARRIER ASSEMBLY

Removal

From the bell housing side, remove the rear carrier assembly.

NOTE: If necessary, the rear carrier bearing cone can be removed from the rear carrier using tool 5048 with jaws tool 5048–3 and button tool 6055.

LOW/REVERSE PISTON RETURN SPRING

Removal

1. Install low/reverse spring compressor tools 5059, 5058–3 and 6057 to compress low/reverse piston return spring.
2. Remove low/reverse piston return spring snapring.
3. Remove low/reverse spring compressor tool.
4. Remove low/reverse piston return spring.

GUIDE BRACKET

Removal

1. Drive out the guide bracket support shaft and plug with a drift.
2. Remove the guide bracket pivot shaft with a pair of pliers.
3. Remove the guide bracket assembly.

LOW/REVERSE CLUTCH PISTON AND RETAINER

Removal

1. Remove the low/reverse clutch piston.
2. Remove the low/reverse clutch piston retainer attaching screws.
3. Remove the low/reverse clutch piston retainer and gasket.

DIFFERENTIAL ASSEMBLY

Removal

1. Remove the oil seal from the extension housing.
2. Remove the differential cover bolts.
3. Remove the differential retainer bolts.
4. Remove the differential bearing retainer with the use of tool L–4435.

NOTE: If necessary, remove the oil seal from the differential bearing retainer.

5. Remove the extension housing bolts.
6. Remove the extension housing using tool L–4435.
7. Remove the differential assembly from the transaxle assembly.

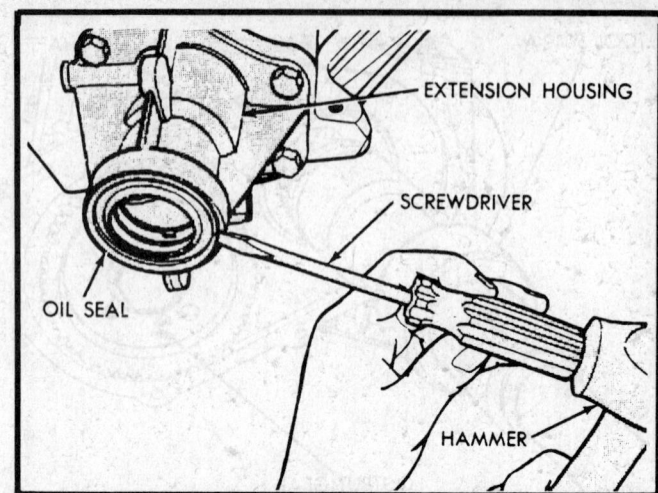

Extension housing oil seal removal

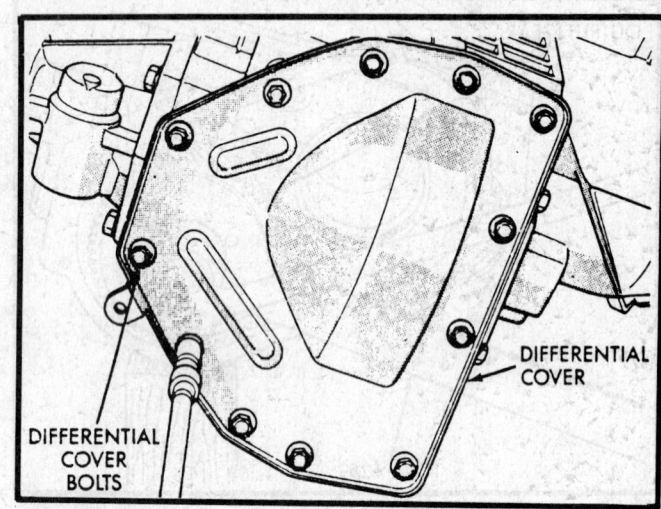

Differential cover servicing

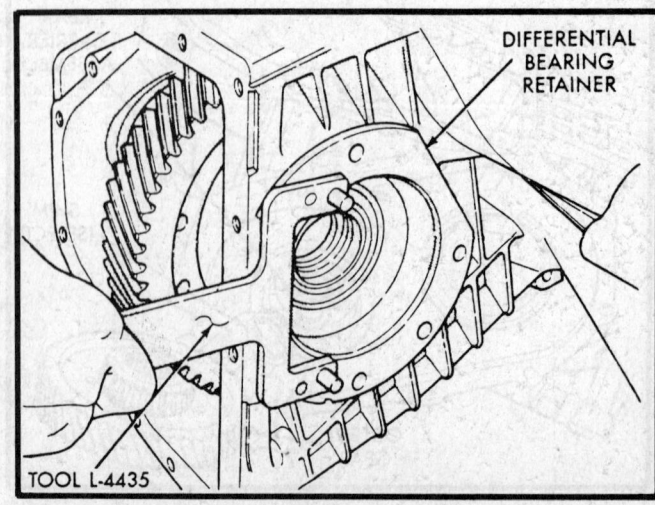

Differential bearing retainer servicing

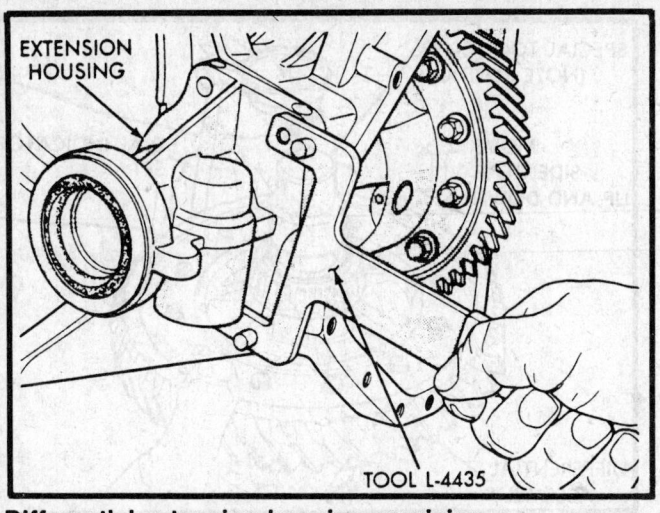

Differential extension housing servicing

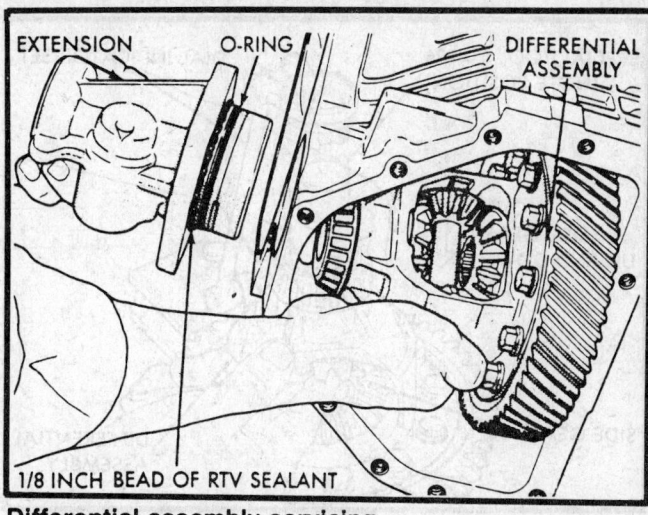

Differential assembly servicing

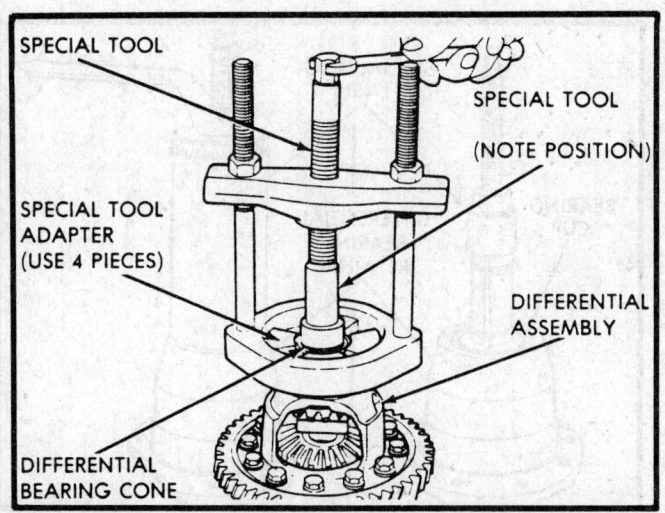

Differential assembly bearing cone (side gear side) removal

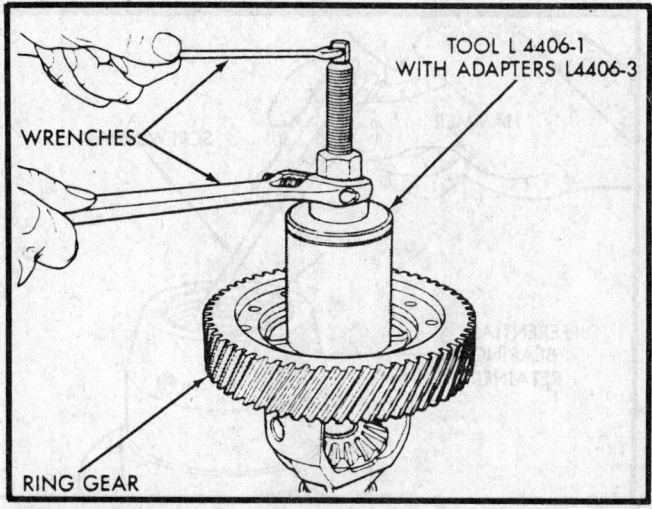

Differential assembly bearing cone (ring gear side) removal

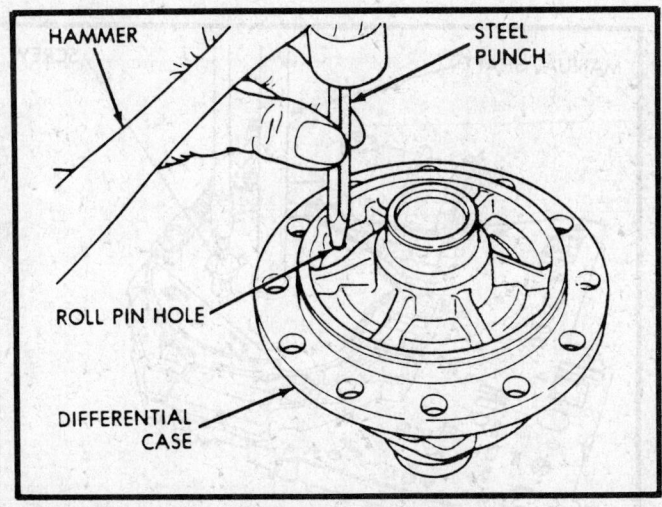

Differential pinion shaft roll pin removal

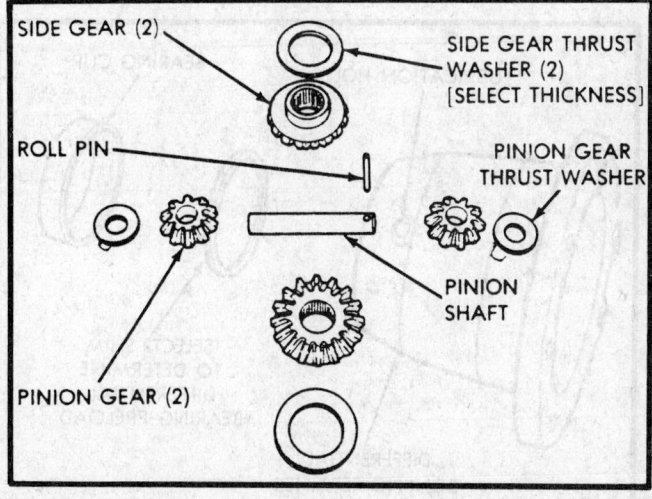

Differential gears

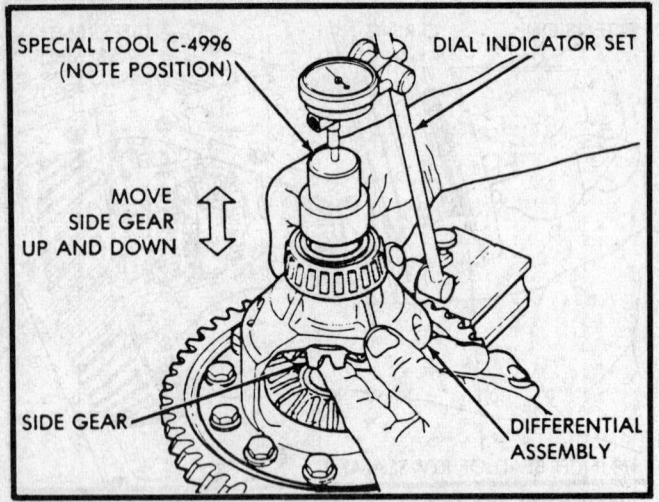

Checking differential side gear (side gear side) endplay

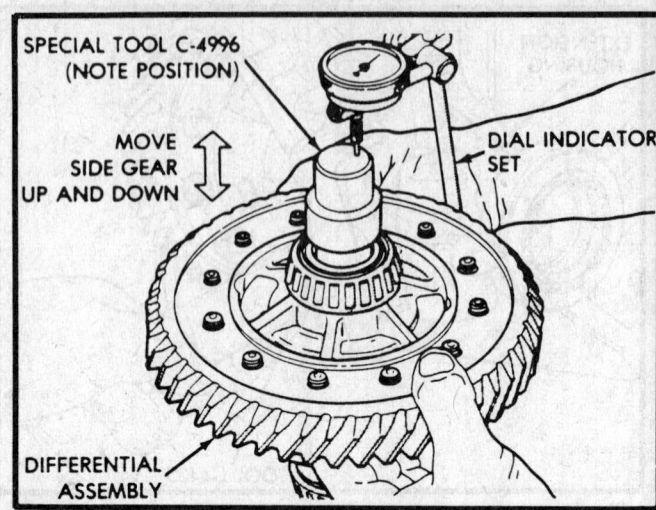

Checking differential side gear (ring gear side) endplay

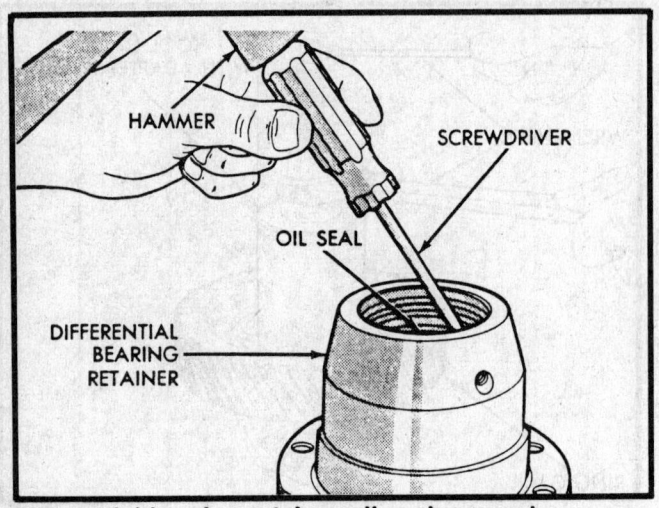

Differential bearing retainer oil seal removal

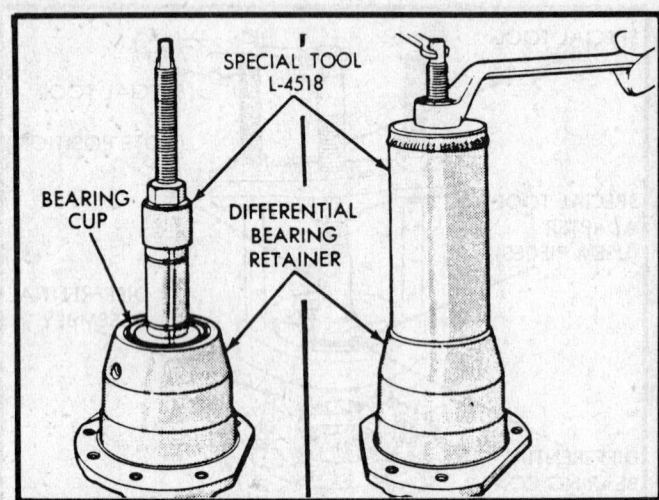

Differential bearing retainer bearing cup removal

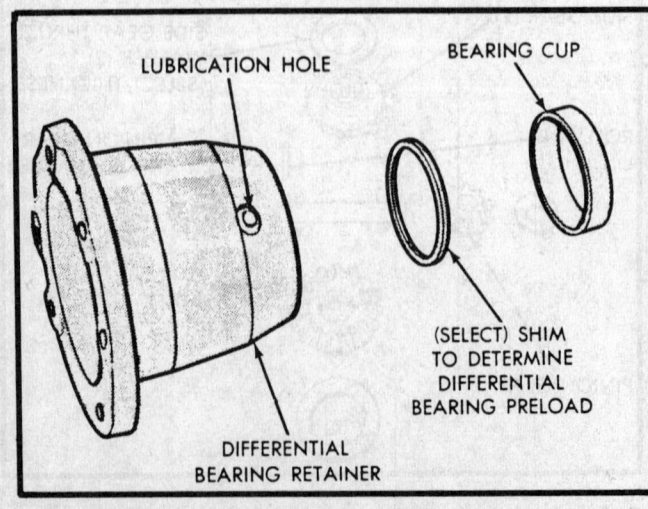

Differential bearing retainer bearing cup and shim

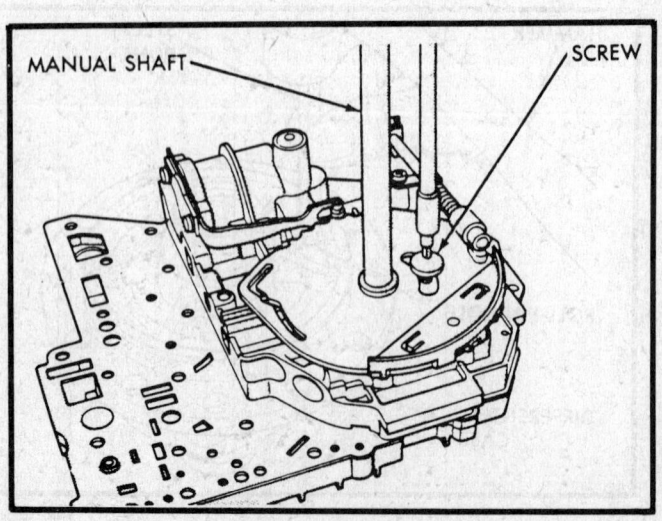

Manual shaft servicing

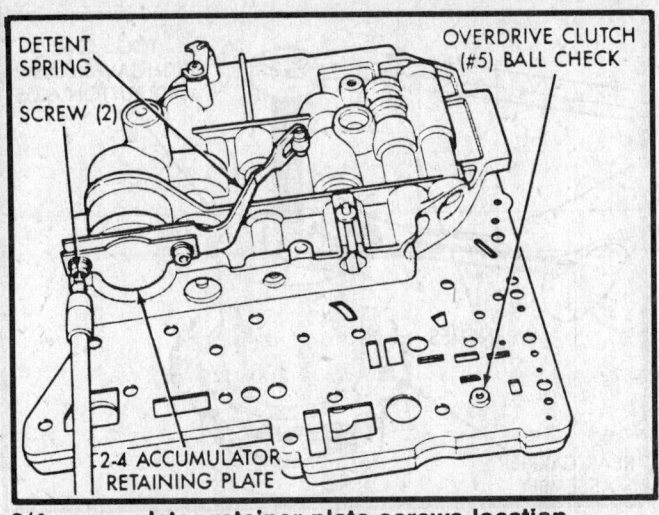

2/4 accumulator retainer plate screws location

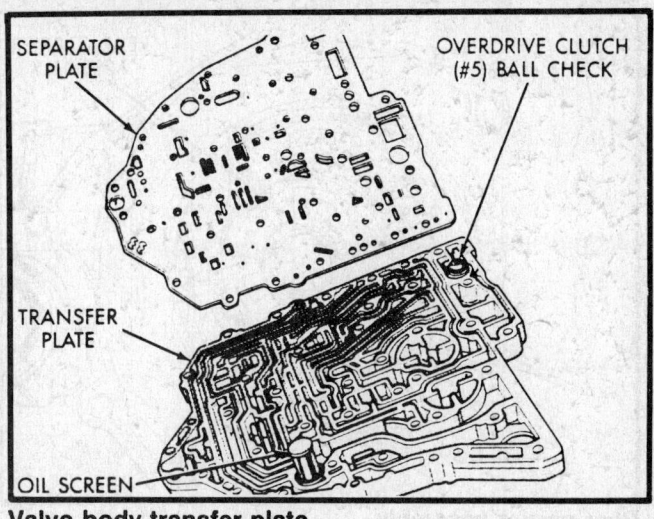

Valve body transfer plate

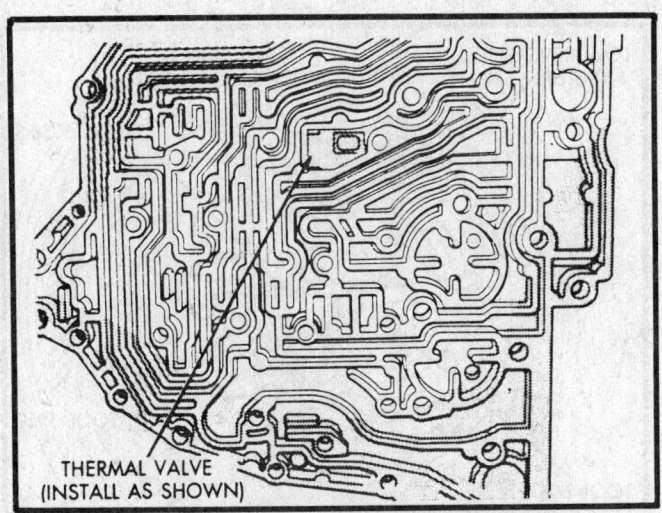

Valve body thermal valve location

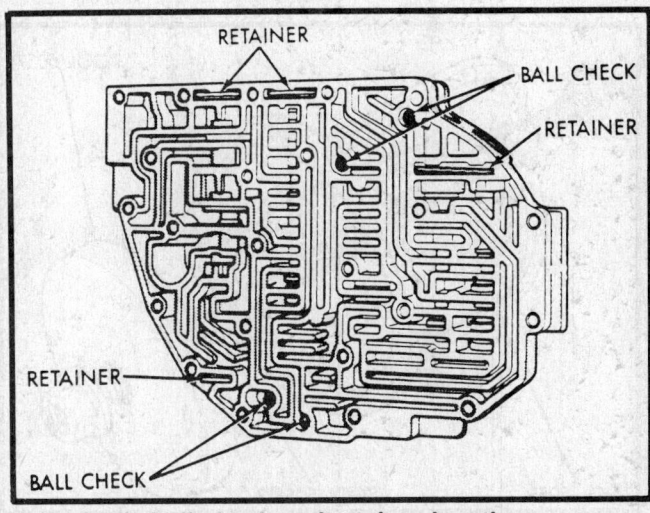

Valve body ball check and retainer locations

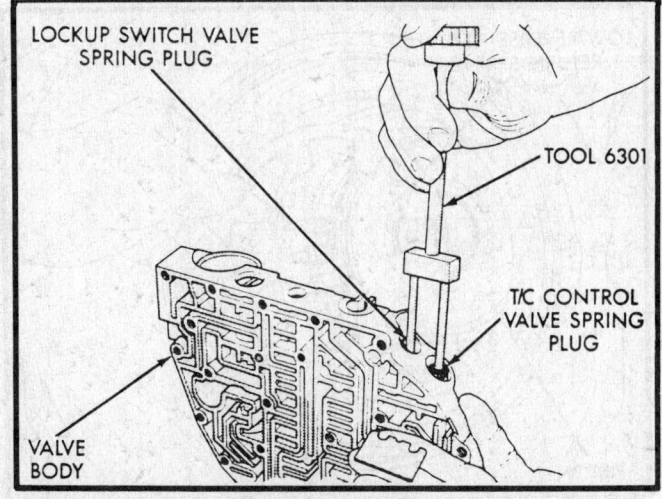

Lockup switch valve spring plug and T/C control valve spring plug servicing

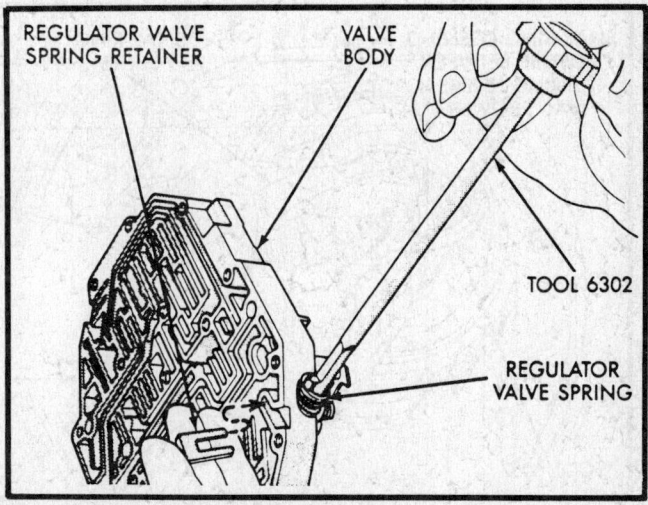

Regulator valve spring servicing

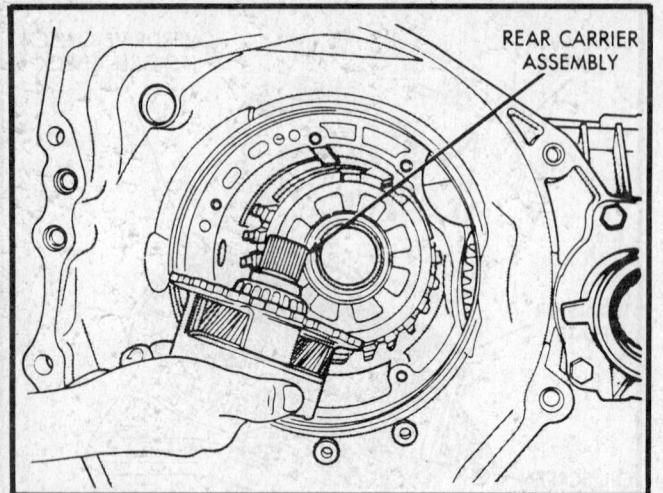

Rear carrier assembly

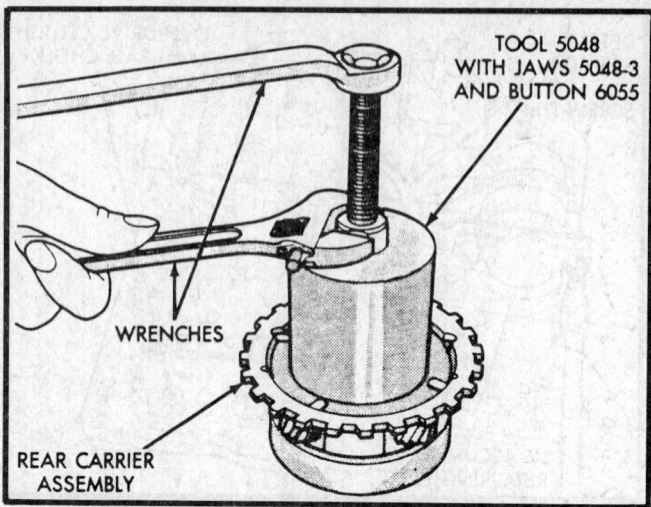

Rear carrier bearing cone removal tool

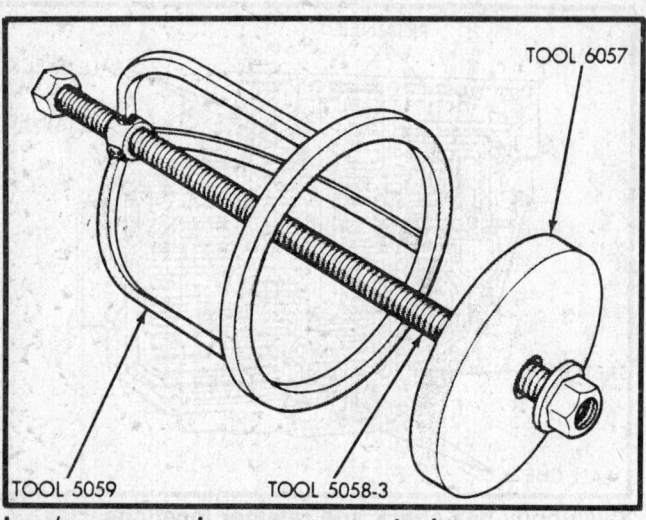

Low/reverse spring compressor tool

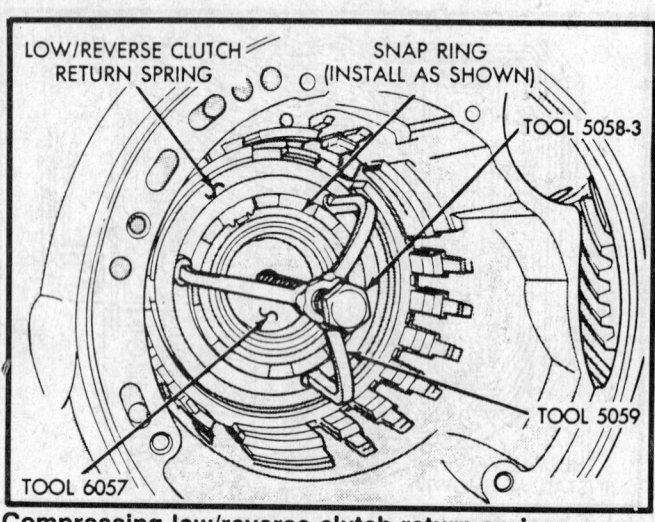

Compressing low/reverse clutch return spring

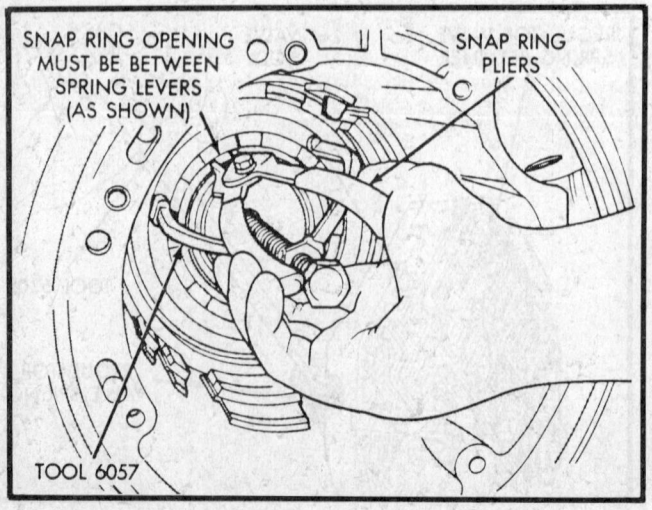

Low/reverse clutch return spring snapring servicing

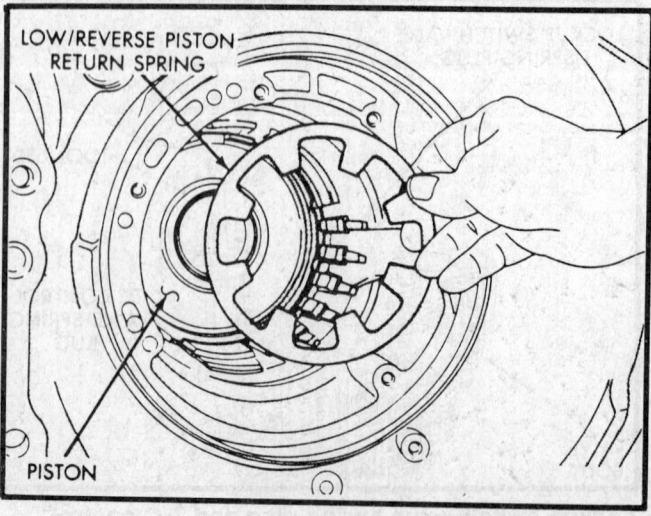

Low/reverse clutch return spring

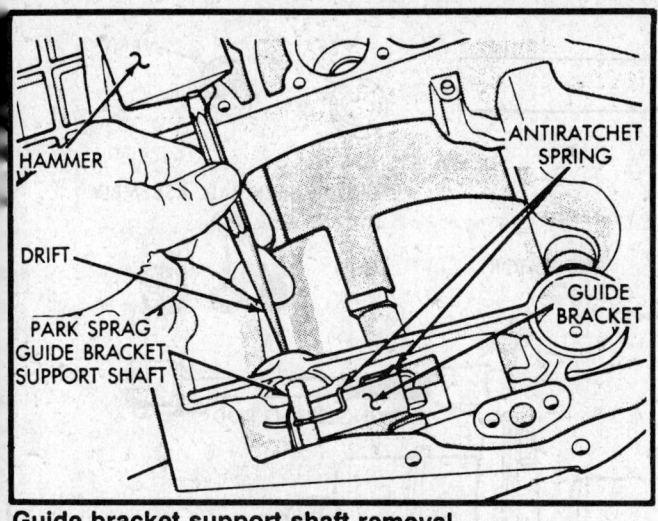

Guide bracket support shaft removal

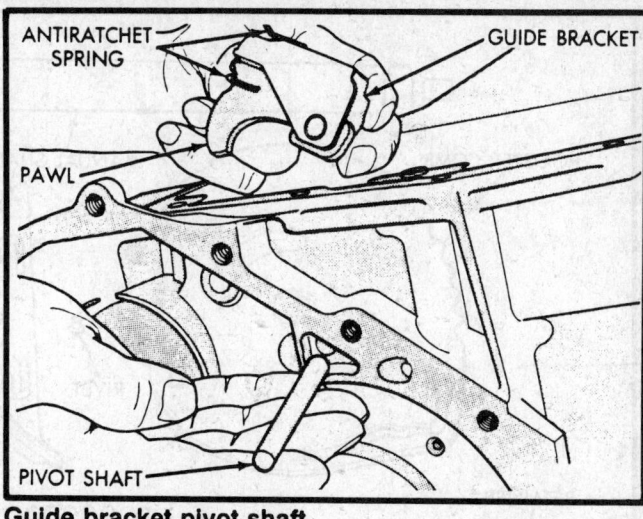

Guide bracket pivot shaft

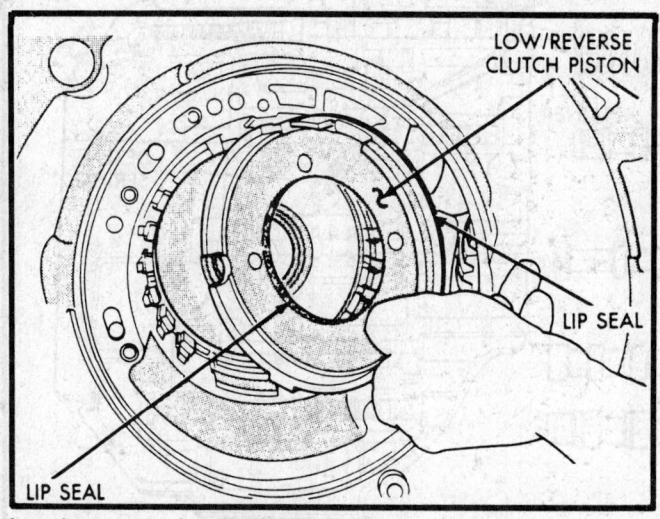

Low/reverse clutch piston

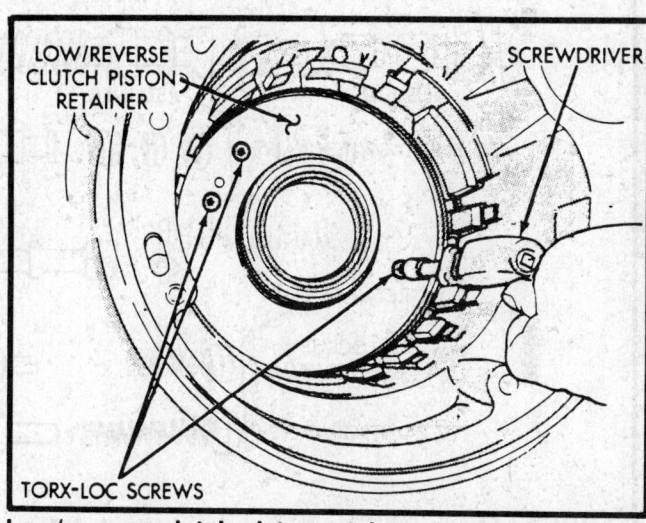

Low/reverse clutch piston retainer attaching screws

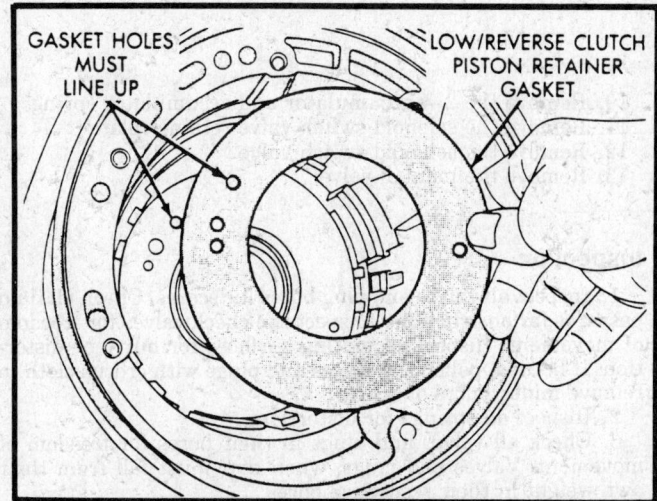

Low/reverse clutch piston retainer gasket

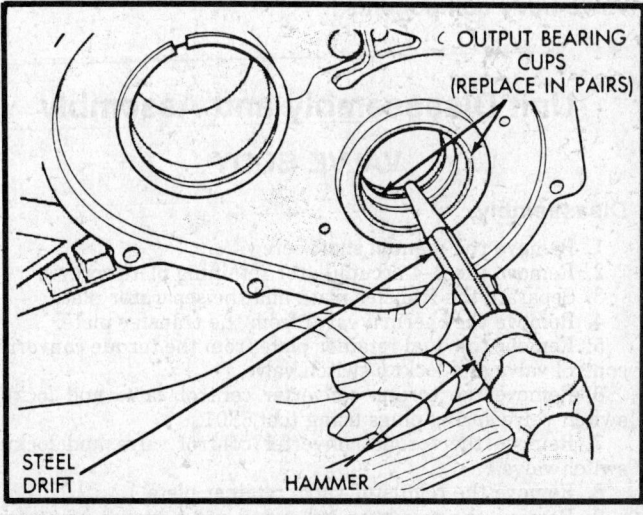

Output gear bearing cups removal

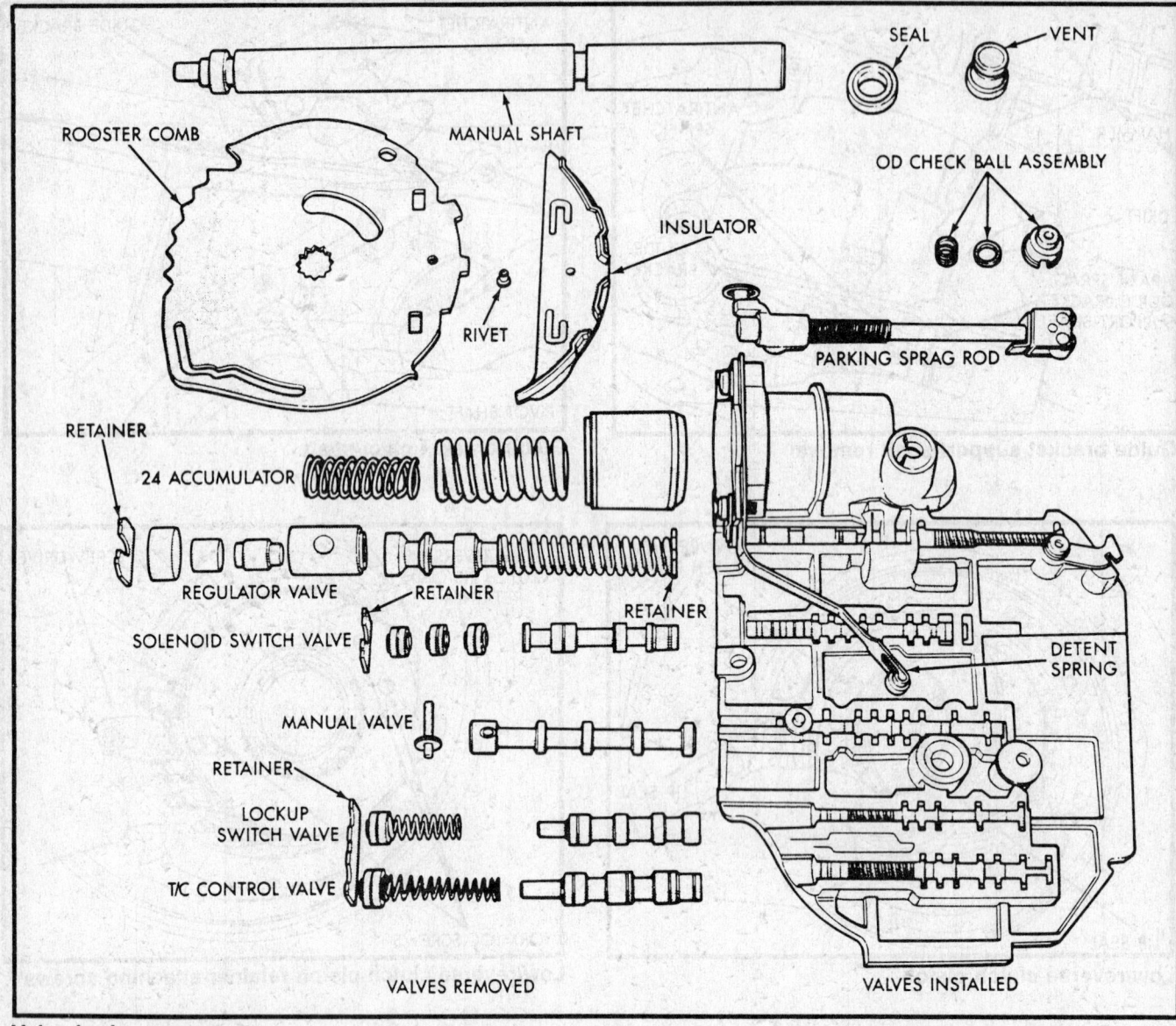

Valve body components

Unit Disassembly and Assembly

VALVE BODY

Disassembly

1. Remove the manual shaft screw.
2. Remove the 2–4 accumulator retaining plate screws.
3. Separate the transfer plate and the separator plate.
4. Remove the thermal valve from the transfer plate.
5. Remove the dual retainer plate from the torque converter control valve and lockup switch valve.
6. Remove the torque converter control valve and lockup switch valve spring plugs using tool 6301.
7. Remove the torque converter control valve and lockup switch valve.
8. Remove the regulator valve retainer plate.
9. Remove the regulator valve and valve spring using tool 6302.
10. Remove the 2–4 accumulator and accumulator springs.
11. Remove the solenoid switch valve retainer plate.
12. Remove the solenoid switch valve.
13. Remove the manual valve.

Inspection

1. Inspect all valves and plug bores for scores. Check all fluid passages for obstructions. Inspect the check valves for freedom of movement. Inspect all mating surfaces for burrs or distortion. If needed, polish the valves and plugs with crocus cloth to remove minor burrs or scores.
2. Inspect all springs for distortion.
3. Check all valves and plugs in their bores for freedom of movement. Valves and plugs, when dry, must fall from their own weight in their respective bores.
4. Roll the manual valve on a flat surface to check for a bent condition.

Assembly

1. Install the manual valve.
2. Install the solenoid switch valve.
3. Install the solenoid switch valve retainer plate.
4. Install the 2–4 accumulator and accumulator springs.
5. Install the regulator valve and valve spring using tool 6302.
6. Install the regulator valve retainer plate.
7. Install the torque converter control valve and lockup switch valve.
8. Install the torque converter control valve and lockup switch valve spring plugs using tool 6301.
9. Install the dual retainer plate from the torque converter control valve and lockup switch valve.
10. Install the thermal valve from the transfer plate.
11. Separate the transfer plate and the separator plate.
12. Install the 2–4 accumulator retaining plate screws.
13. Install the manual shaft screw.

INPUT SHAFT CLUTCHES RETAINER ASSEMBLY

Disassembly

1. With the input shaft clutches retainer assembly in a suitable holding fixture, tap down the reverse clutch reaction plate to remove the reverse clutch snapring.
2. Remove the reverse clutch snapring.
3. Pry the reverse clutch reaction plate up with a small pry tool.
4. Remove the reverse clutch reaction plate.
5. Remove the reverse clutch pack. Tag and identify the clutch packs to assure original replacement.
6. Remove the overdrive/reverse pressure plate snapring.
7. Remove the overdrive/reverse pressure plate.
8. Remove the overdrive/reverse clutch waved snapring.
9. Remove the overdrive shaft assembly and overdrive clutch pack with No. 3 thrust plate.
10. Remove the overdrive clutch pack from the overdrive shaft assembly. Tag and identify the clutch packs to assure original replacement.
11. Remove the No. 3 thrust plate and No. 4 thrust plate from the overdrive shaft assembly.
12. Remove the No. 3 thrust washer and underdrive shaft assembly.
13. Remove the No. 2 needle bearing.
14. Remove the overdrive/underdrive clutches reaction plate tapered snapring with a small pry tool. Do not scratch the reaction plate.
15. Remove the overdrive/underdrive clutch reaction plate.
16. Remove the underdrive clutch disc.
17. Remove the underdrive clutch reaction plate flat snapring.
18. Remove the underdrive clutch pack. Tag and identify clutch packs to assure original replacement.
19. Install tool 5059 with arbor press and remove underdrive retainer snapring.
20. Remove the underdrive return spring retainer and the piston return spring.
21. Remove the underdrive clutch piston.
22. Remove the input hub tapered snapring.
23. With a plastic hammer, tap on the input hub and remove the input shaft and hub assembly.
24. Remove the input clutches retainer from the overdrive/reverse piston.
25. With an arbor press ram, compress the return spring on the overdrive/reverse piston just enough to remove the snapring.
26. Remove the snapring and return spring from the overdrive/reverse piston.

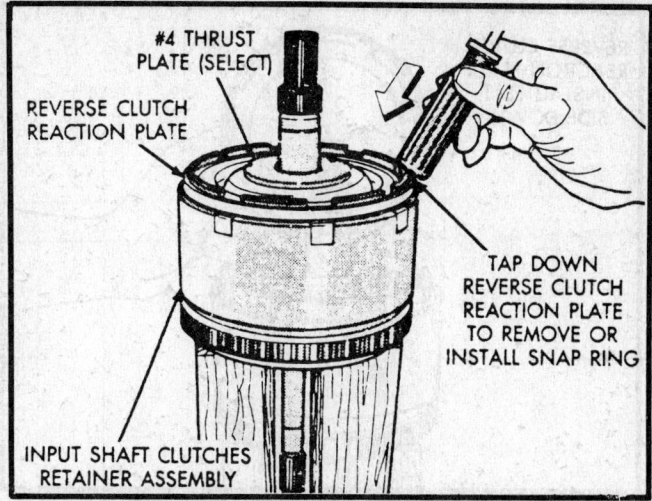

Reverse clutch reaction plate tap down

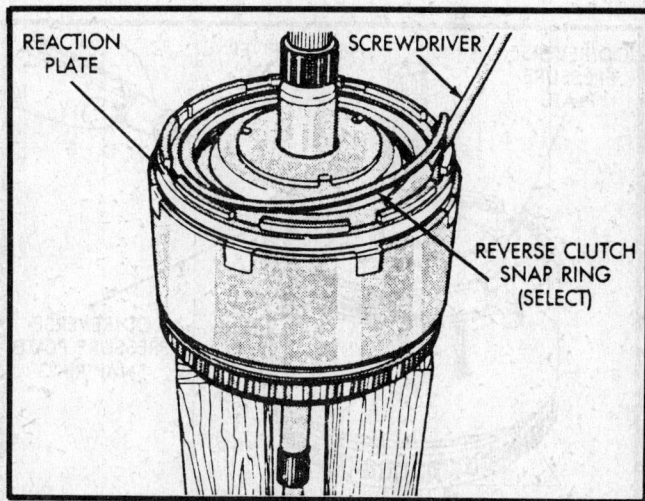

Reverse clutch snapring servicing

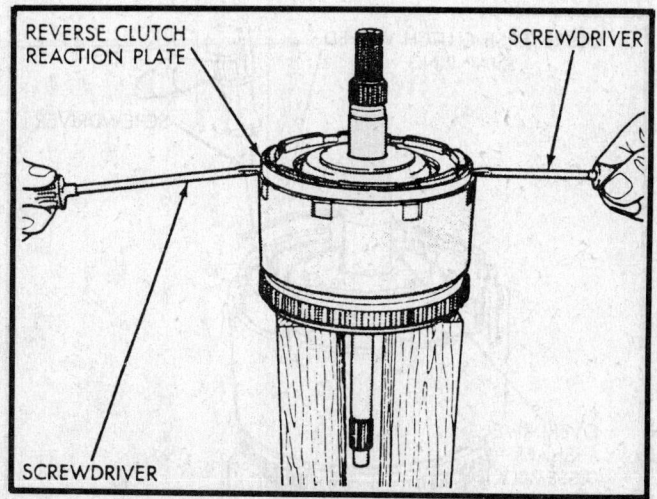

Reverse clutch reaction plate servicing

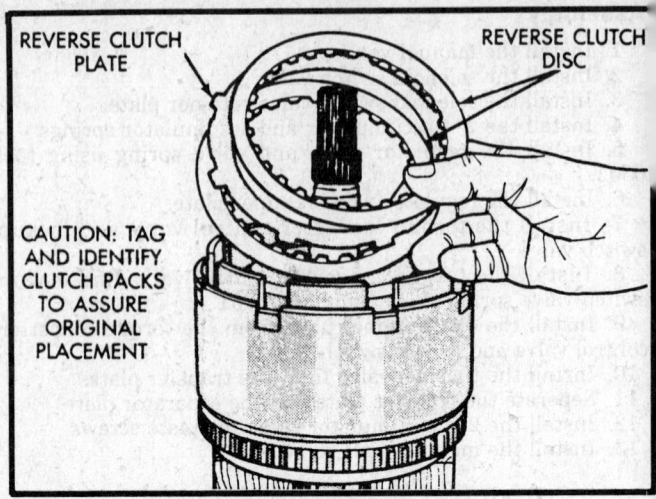

REVERSE CLUTCH REACTION PLATE (INSTALL FLAT SIDE DOWN)

Reverse clutch reaction plate

REVERSE CLUTCH PLATE

REVERSE CLUTCH DISC

CAUTION: TAG AND IDENTIFY CLUTCH PACKS TO ASSURE ORIGINAL PLACEMENT

Reverse clutch pack servicing

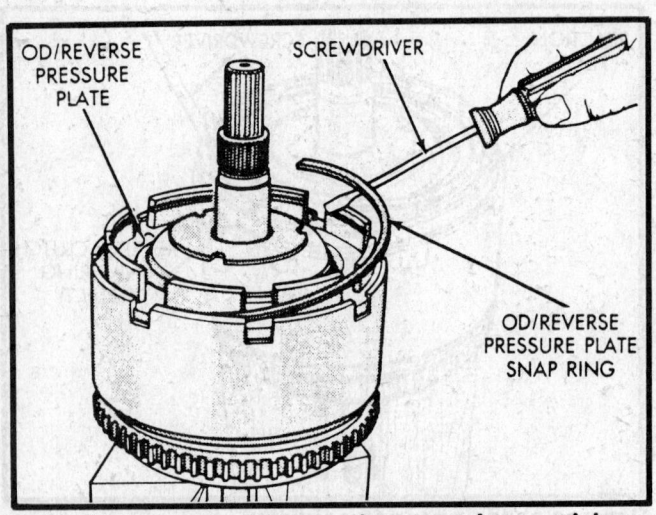

OD/REVERSE PRESSURE PLATE

SCREWDRIVER

OD/REVERSE PRESSURE PLATE SNAP RING

Overdrive/reverse pressure plate snapring servicing

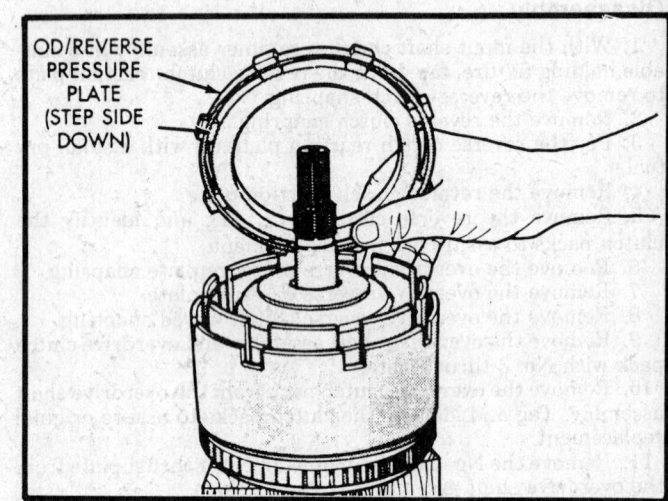

OD/REVERSE PRESSURE PLATE (STEP SIDE DOWN)

Overdrive/reverse pressure plate

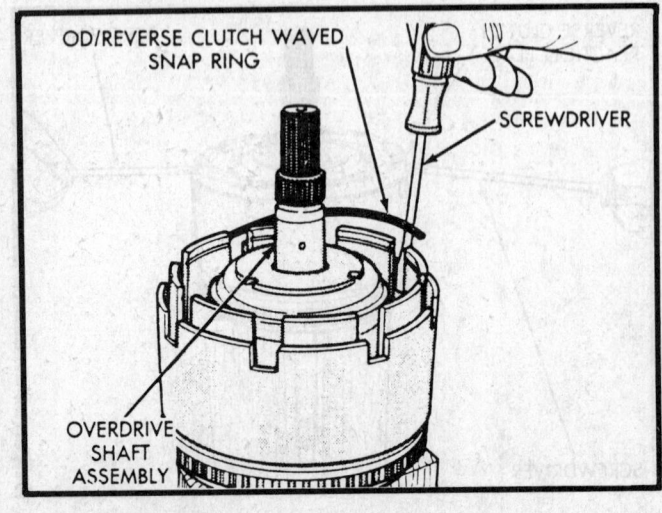

OD/REVERSE CLUTCH WAVED SNAP RING

SCREWDRIVER

OVERDRIVE SHAFT ASSEMBLY

Overdrive/reverse clutch waved snapring servicing

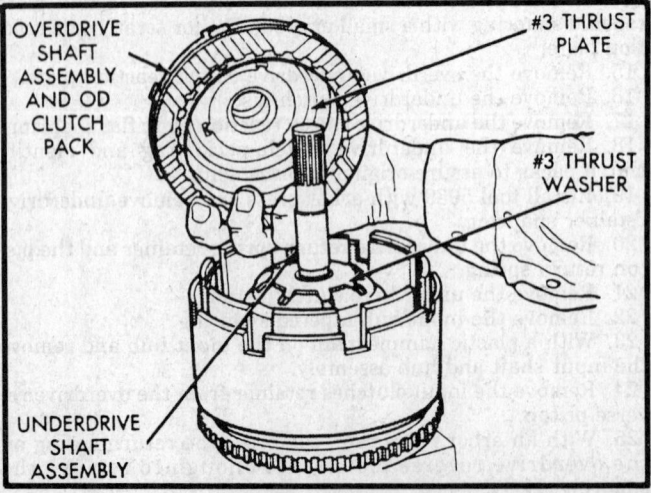

OVERDRIVE SHAFT ASSEMBLY AND OD CLUTCH PACK

#3 THRUST PLATE

#3 THRUST WASHER

UNDERDRIVE SHAFT ASSEMBLY

Overdrive shaft assembly and overdrive clutch pack servicing

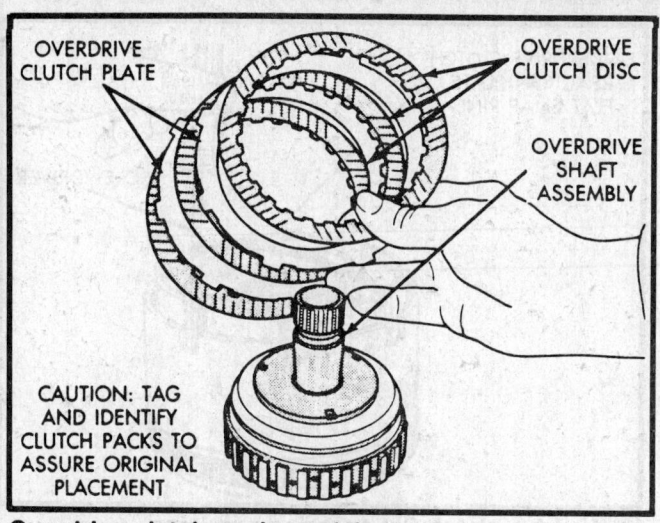

OVERDRIVE CLUTCH PLATE

OVERDRIVE CLUTCH DISC

OVERDRIVE SHAFT ASSEMBLY

CAUTION: TAG AND IDENTIFY CLUTCH PACKS TO ASSURE ORIGINAL PLACEMENT

Overdrive clutch pack servicing

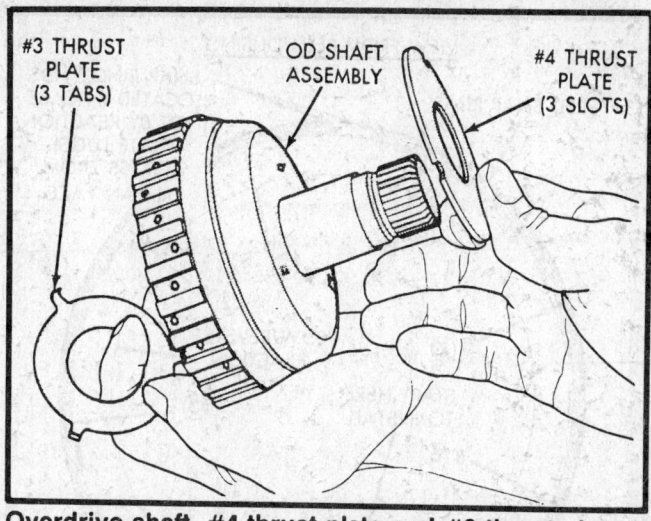

#3 THRUST PLATE (3 TABS)

OD SHAFT ASSEMBLY

#4 THRUST PLATE (3 SLOTS)

Overdrive shaft, #4 thrust plate and #3 thrust plate

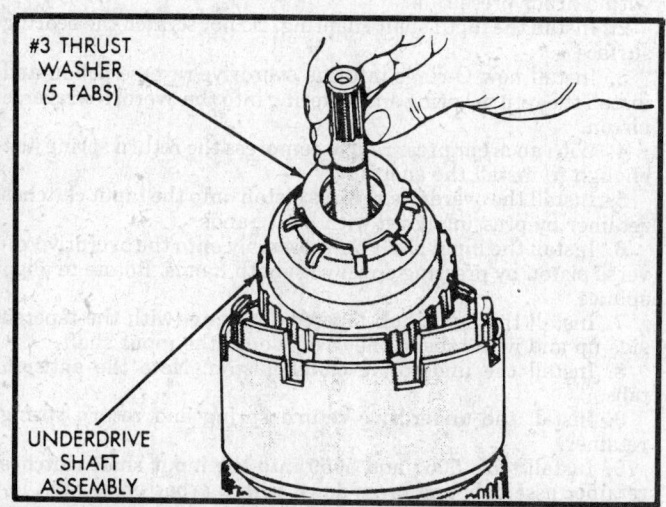

#3 THRUST WASHER (5 TABS)

UNDERDRIVE SHAFT ASSEMBLY

Underdrive shaft assembly and #3 thrust washer

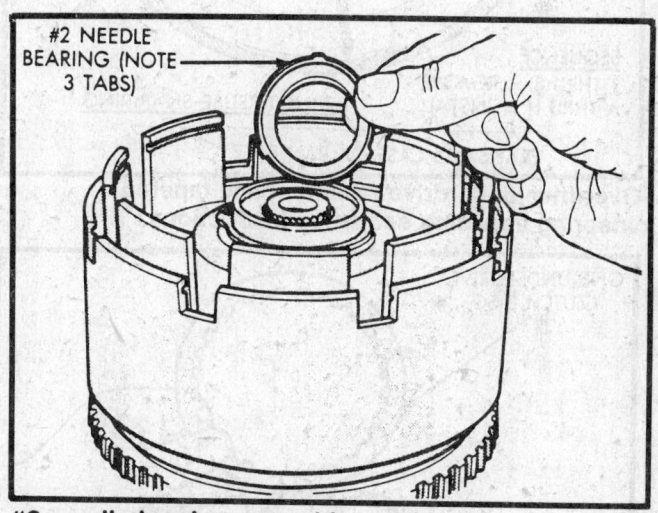

#2 NEEDLE BEARING (NOTE 3 TABS)

#2 needle bearing assembly

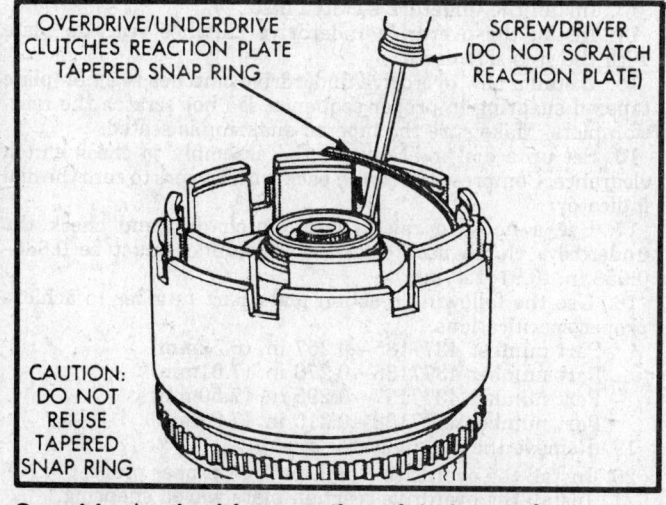

OVERDRIVE/UNDERDRIVE CLUTCHES REACTION PLATE TAPERED SNAP RING

SCREWDRIVER (DO NOT SCRATCH REACTION PLATE)

CAUTION: DO NOT REUSE TAPERED SNAP RING

Overdrive/underdrive reaction plate tapered snapring servicing

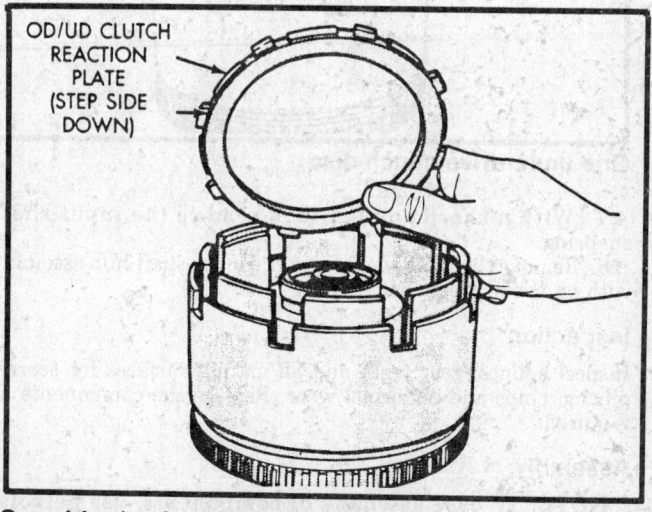

OD/UD CLUTCH REACTION PLATE (STEP SIDE DOWN)

Overdrive/underdrive reaction plate

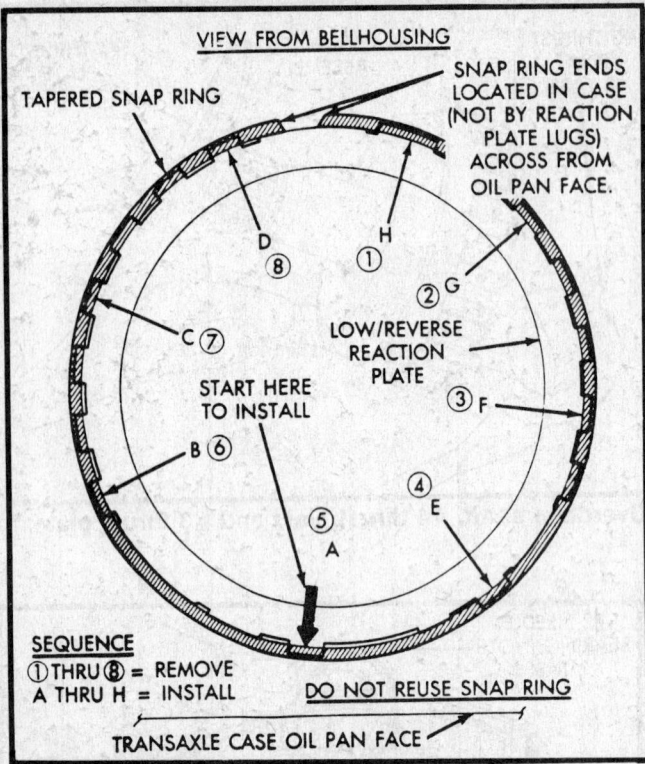

VIEW FROM BELLHOUSING

TAPERED SNAP RING

SNAP RING ENDS LOCATED IN CASE (NOT BY REACTION PLATE LUGS) ACROSS FROM OIL PAN FACE.

LOW/REVERSE REACTION PLATE

START HERE TO INSTALL

SEQUENCE
① THRU ⑧ = REMOVE
A THRU H = INSTALL

DO NOT REUSE SNAP RING

TRANSAXLE CASE OIL PAN FACE

Overdrive/underdrive reaction plate tapered snapring servicing sequence instructions

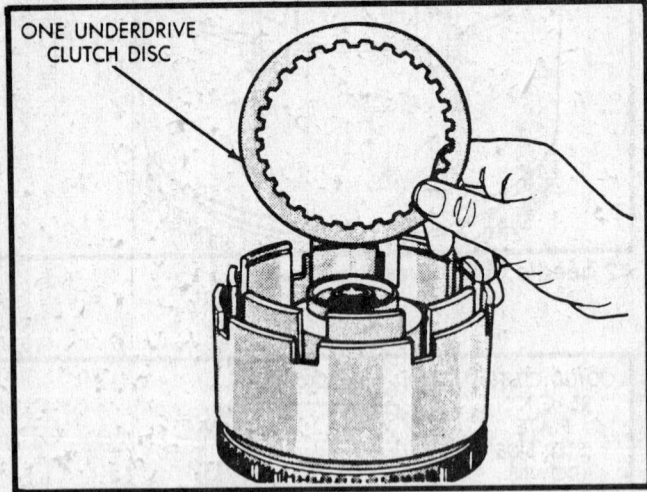

ONE UNDERDRIVE CLUTCH DISC

One underdrive clutch disc

27. With a sharp pointed tool, remove the input shaft snapring.

28. Remove the input shaft from the input shaft hub assembly with an arbor press ram.

Inspection

Inspect splines, gear teeth and all mating surfaces for scores, pitting, chips and abnormal wear. Replace the components as required.

Assembly

NOTE: To ease assembly of components, use petrolatum on all seals.

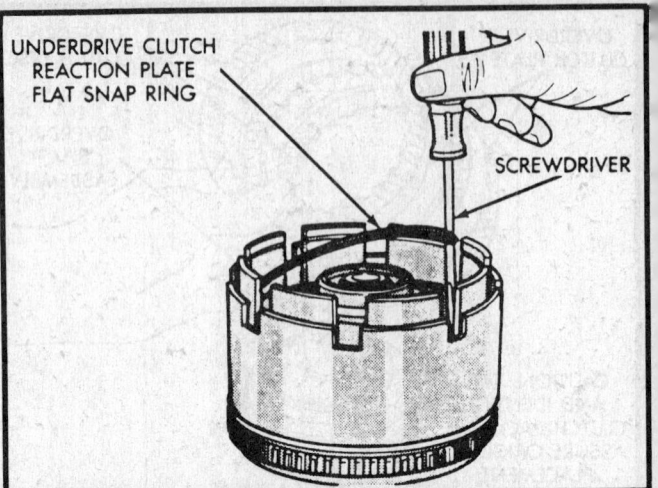

UNDERDRIVE CLUTCH REACTION PLATE FLAT SNAP RING

SCREWDRIVER

Underdrive clutch flat snapring servicing

1. Press the input shaft into the input shaft hub assembly with a arbor press ram.

2. Install the input shaft snapring. Do not scratch the bearing surface.

3. Install new O-rings into the overdrive/reverse piston and install the return spring and snapring into the overdrive/reverse piston.

4. With an arbor press ram to compress the return spring just enough to install the snapring.

5. Install the overdrive/reverse piston onto the input clutches retainer by pressing down with both hands.

6. Install the input shaft hub assembly onto the overdrive/reverse piston by pressing down with both hands. Rotate to align splines.

7. Install the input hub tapered snapring (with the tapered side up and with tabs in the cavity) onto the input shaft.

8. Install the underdrive clutch piston. Note the antispin tabs.

9. Install the underdrive return spring and return spring retainer.

10. Install tools 5067 and 5059 into the input shaft clutches retainer assembly and press down with a arbor press ram. Install the underdrive return spring retainer snapring.

11. Install the underdrive clutch pack in proper order.

12. Install the underdrive clutch reaction plate flat snapring.

13. Install the underdrive clutch disc.

14. Install the overdrive/underdrive clutches reaction plate with the step side down.

15. Install a new overdrive/underdrive clutches reaction plate tapered snapring in proper sequence. Do not scratch the reaction plate. Make sure the tapered snapring is seated.

16. Set up a dial indicator on the assembly to check clutch clearance. Compress the clutch pack with fingers to zero the dial indicator.

17. Use a hook to raise the 1 clutch disc and check the underdrive clutch pack clearance. Clearance must be 0.036–0.058 in. (0.91–1.47mm).

18. Use the following reaction plate part number to achieve proper specifications:

Part number 4377185—0.257 in. (6.52mm)
Part number 4377186—0.276 in. (7.01mm)
Part number 4377187—0.295 in. (7.50mm)
Part number 4377188—0.315 in. (7.99mm)

19. Remove the dial indicator set-up.

20. Install the overdrive clutch pack in proper order.

21. Install the overdrive reaction plate waved snapring.

22. Install the overdrive/reverse pressure plate with the step side down.

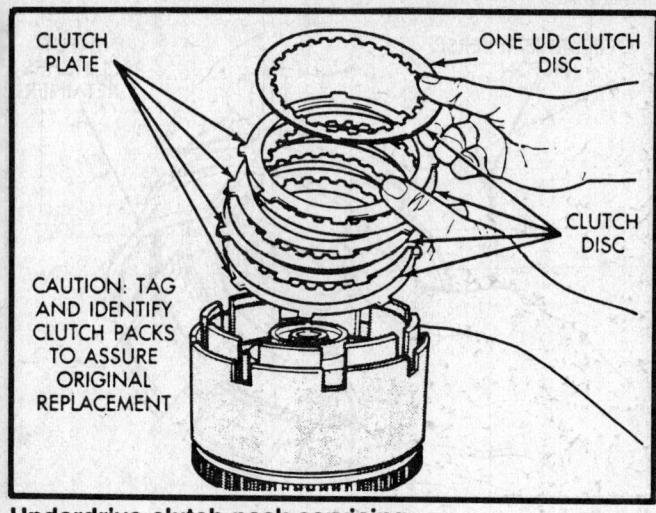

Underdrive clutch pack servicing

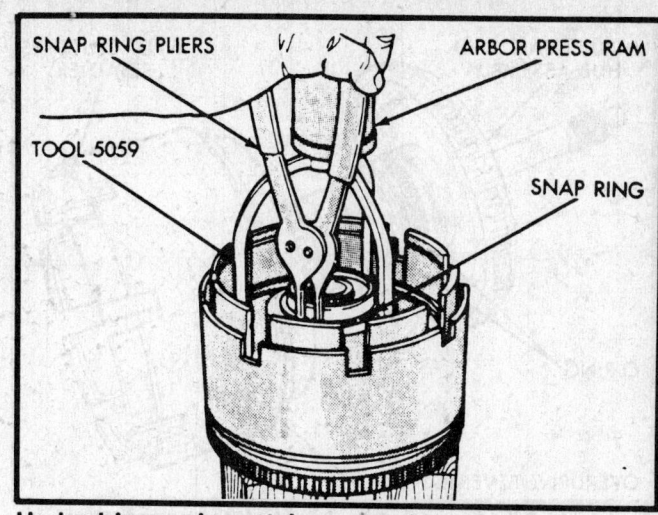

Underdrive spring retainer snapring servicing

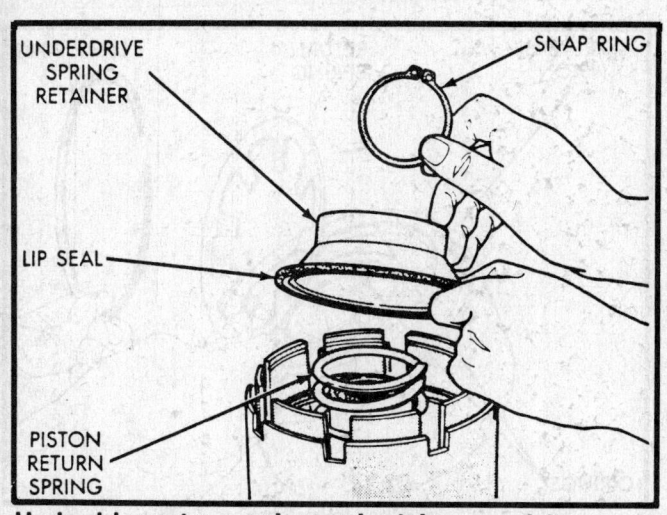

Underdrive return spring and retainer servicing

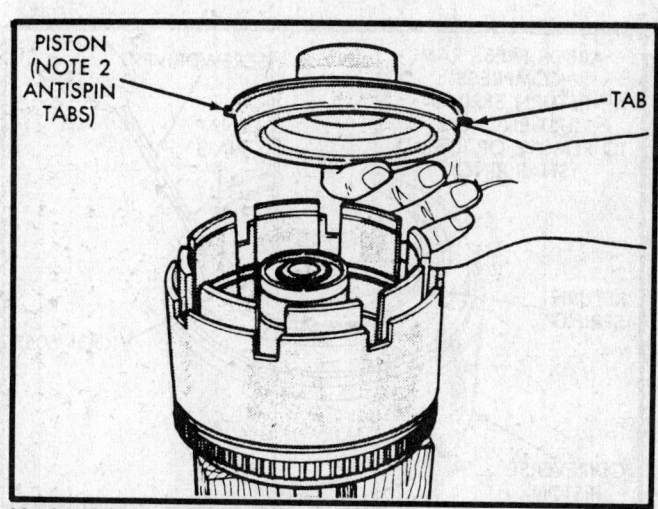

Underdrive clutch piston

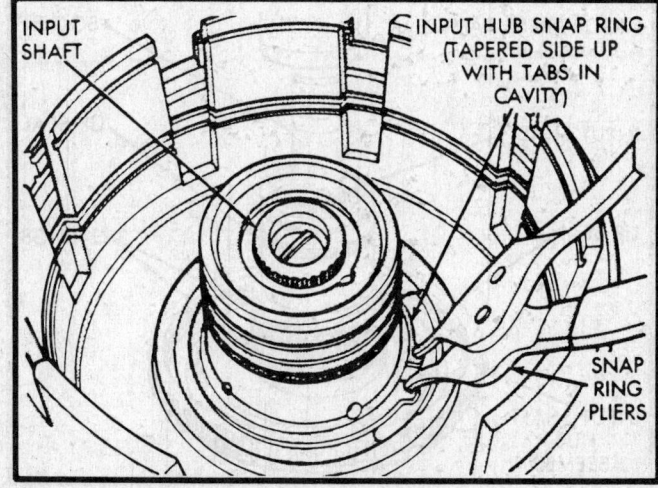

Input hub tapered snapring servicing

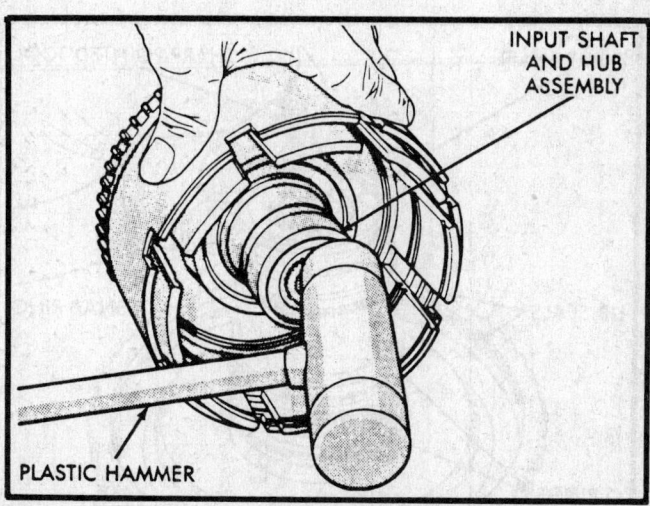

Input shaft/hub assembly servicing

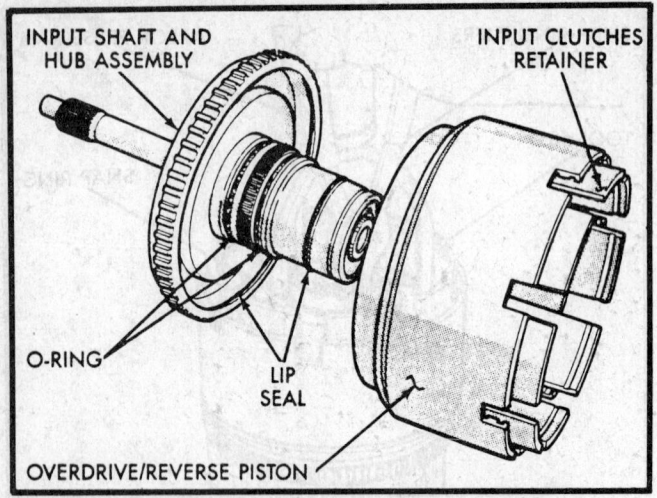

Input shaft/hub assembly, input clutches retainer and overdrive/reverse piston

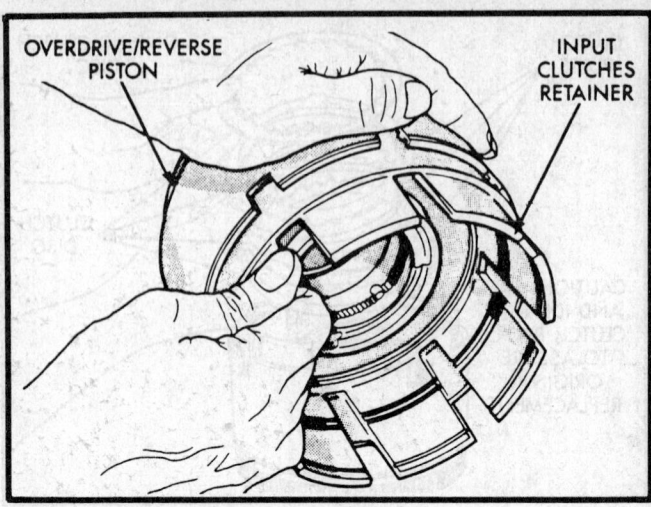

Input clutches retainer servicing

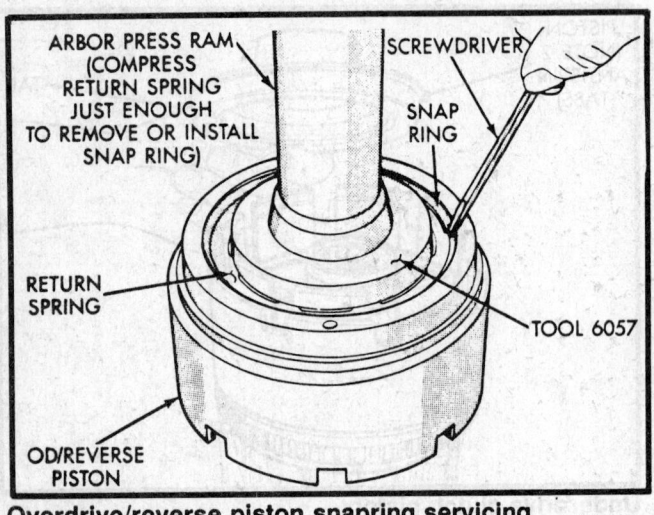

Overdrive/reverse piston snapring servicing

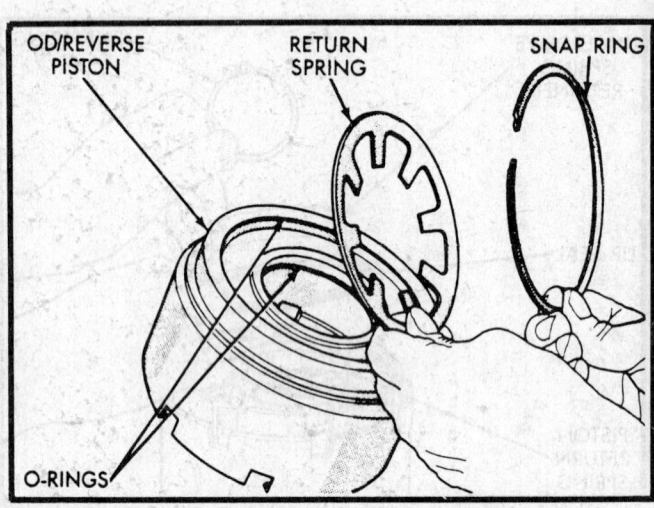

Overdrive/reverse piston return spring servicing

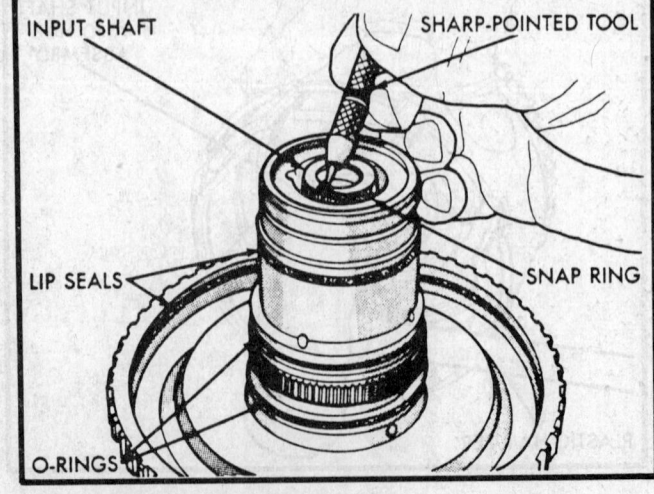

Input shaft snapring servicing

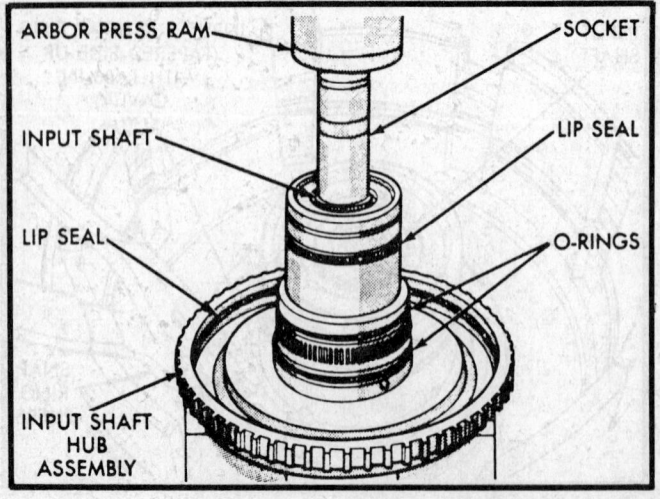

Input shaft removal

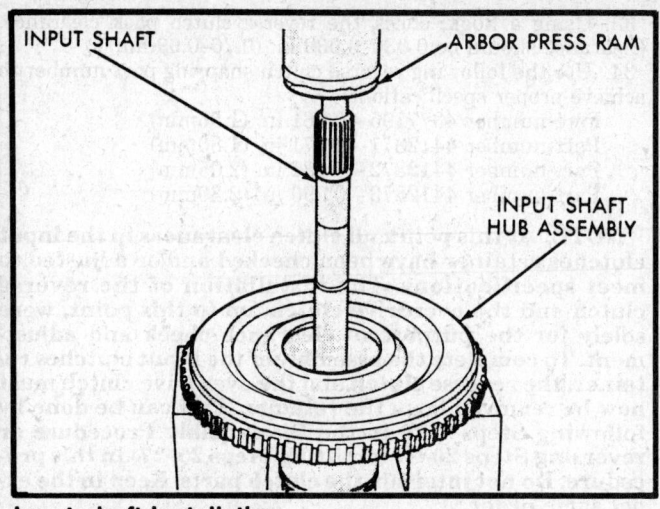

Input shaft installation

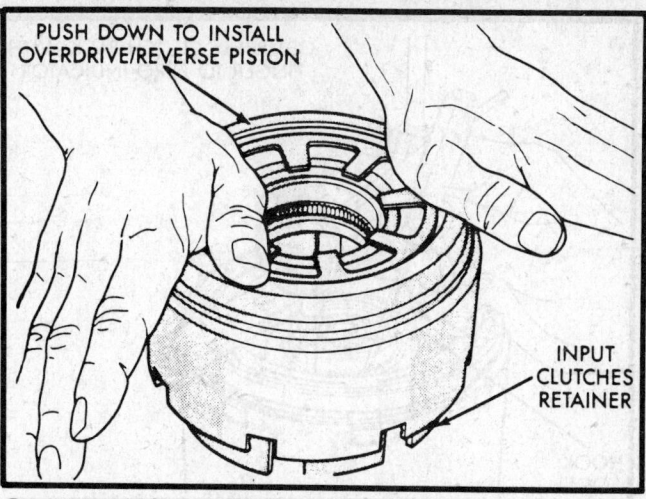

Overdrive/reverse piston installation

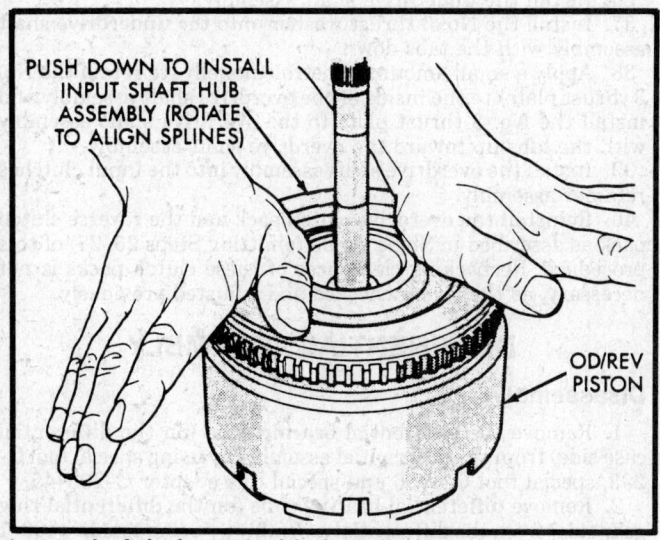

Input shaft hub assembly installation

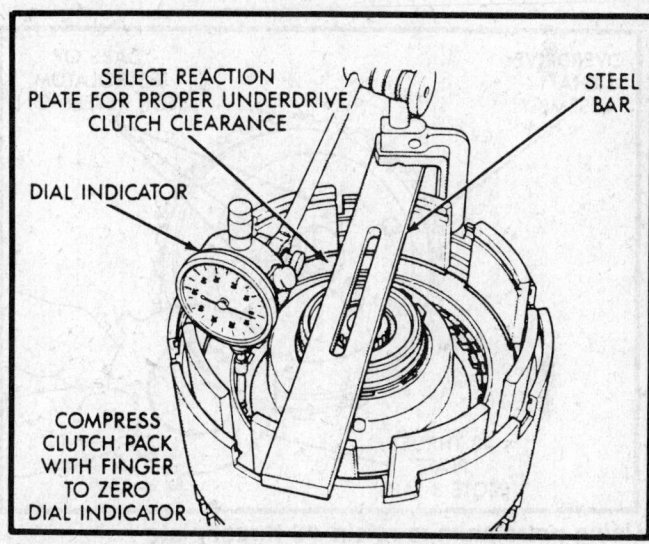

Checking underdrive clutch clearance set-up

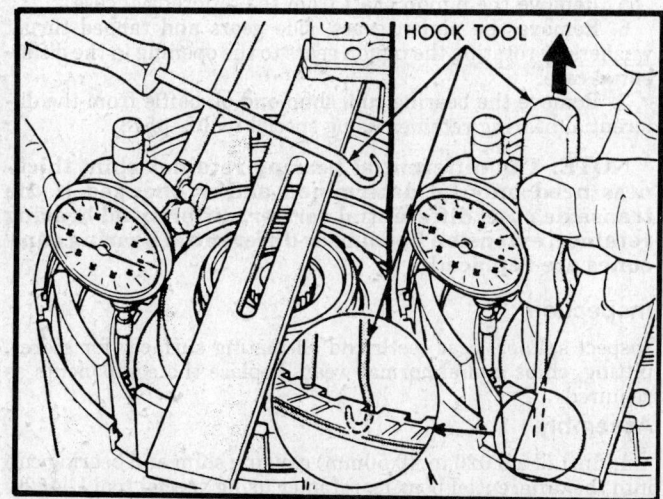

Checking underdrive clutch pack clearance

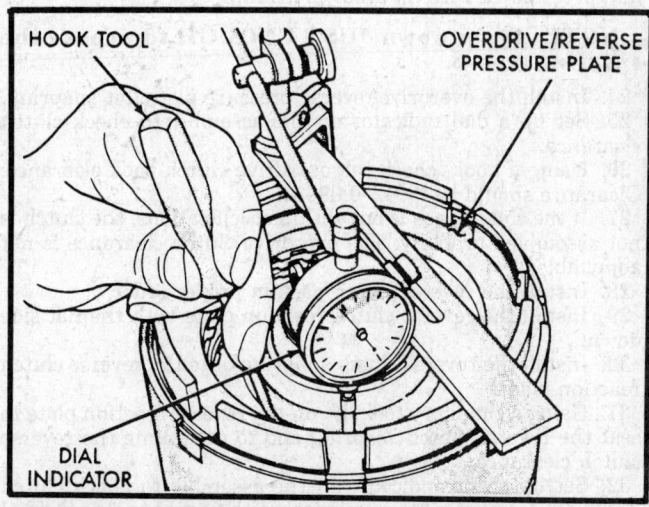

Checking overdrive clutch pack clearance

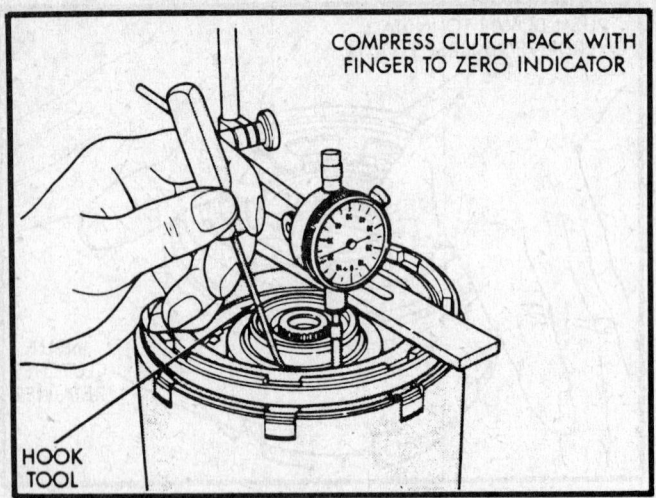

Checking reverse clutch pack clearance

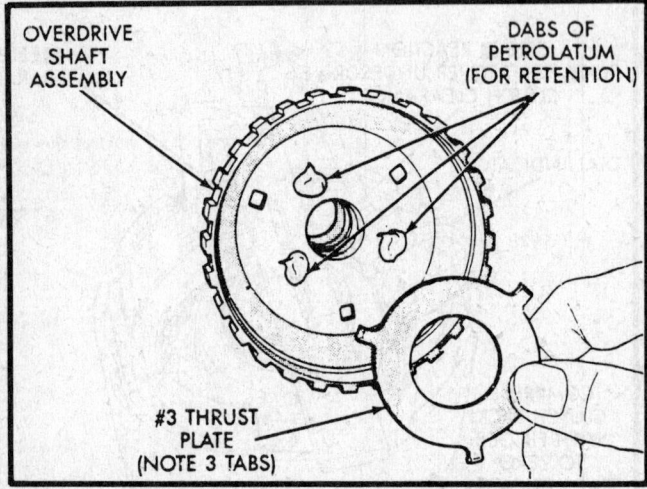

Using petrolatum to retain #3 thrust plate

23. Install tool 5059 on the overdrive/reverse pressure plate and press down with an arbor press ram.

NOTE: Press down JUST ENOUGH to expose the snapring groove.

24. Install the overdrive/reverse pressure plate flat snapring.
25. Set up a dial indicator on the assembly to check clutch clearance.
26. Using a hook, check the overdrive clutch pack clearance. Clearance should be 0.042–0.096 in.
27. If the clutch pack is not within specifications, the clutch is not assembled properly. The overdrive clutch clearance is not adjustable.
28. Install the reverse clutch pack in proper order.
29. Install the reverse clutch reaction plate with the flat side down.
30. Install the reverse clutch snapring onto the reverse clutch reaction plate.
31. Using a small pry tool, lift up the reverse reaction plate to seat the reverse clutch snapring and to determine the reverse clutch clearance.
32. Set up a dial indicator on the assembly to check clutch clearance. Compress the clutch pack with fingers to zero the dial indicator.

33. Using a hook, check the reverse clutch pack clearance. Clearance should be 0.030–0.039 in. (0.76–0.99mm).
34. Use the following reverse clutch snapring part number to achieve proper specifications:
    Part number 4377195 – 0.061 in. (1.56mm)
    Part number 4412871 – 0.071 in. (1.80mm)
    Part number 4412872 – 0.081 in. (2.05mm)
    Part number 4412873 – 0.090 in. (2.30mm)

NOTE: At this point, all clutch clearances in the input clutches retainer have been checked and/or adjusted to meet specifications. The installation of the reverse clutch and the overdrive clutch, up to this point, were solely for the purpose of clearance check and adjustment. To complete the assembly of the input clutches retainer, the reverse clutch and the overdrive clutch must now be removed from the retainer. This can be done by following Steps 1–10 in the Disassembly Procedure or reversing Steps 20–31 (omitting Steps 25–27) in this procedure. Do not intermix the clutch parts. Keep in the exact same order.

35. Install the No. 2 needle bearing with the small tabs up.
36. Install the underdrive shaft assembly.
37. Install the No. 3 thrust washer onto the underdrive shaft assembly with the tabs down.
38. Apply a small amount of petroleum jelly (to retain the No. 3 thrust plate) to the inside of the overdrive shaft assembly and install the No. 3 thrust plate to the overdrive shaft assembly with the tabs up toward the overdrive shaft assembly.
39. Install the overdrive shaft assembly into the input clutches retainer assembly.
40. Reinstall the overdrive clutch pack and the reverse clutch pack as described in Steps 20–31 (omitting Steps 25–27) of this procedure. Rechecking clearances of these clutch packs is not necessary, as they were checked and adjusted previously.

DIFFERENTIAL ASSEMBLY

Disassembly

1. Remove the differential bearing cone (on the differential case side) from the differential assembly by using special tool C–293, special tool C–4996 and special tool adapter C–293–45.
2. Remove differential bearing cone (on the differential ring gear side) from the differential assembly by using tool L–4406–1 with adapters L–4406–3.
3. Remove the ring gear bolts.
4. Remove the pinion shaft roll pin from the pinion shaft.
5. Remove the pinion shaft from the differential case.
6. Remove the pinion gears, side gears and tabbed thrust washers by rotating the pinion gears to the opening in the differential case.
7. Remove the bearing cup, shim and oil baffle from the differential bearing retainer using special tool L–4518.

NOTE: The differential bearing retainer shim thickness need only be determined and/or changed if the transaxle case, differential carrier, differential bearing retainer, extension housing or differential bearing cups/cones are replaced.

Inspection

Inspect splines, gear teeth and all mating surfaces for scores, pitting, chips and abnormal wear. Replace the components as required.

Assembly

1. Install a 0.020 in. (0.50mm) gauging shim and bearing cup into the differential bearing retainer using special tool L–4520, handle C–4171 and press. The oil baffle is not required when making shim selection.

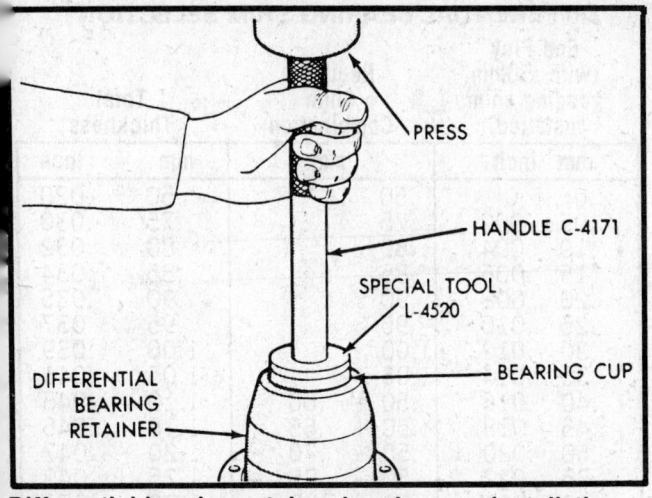

Differential bearing retainer bearing cup installation

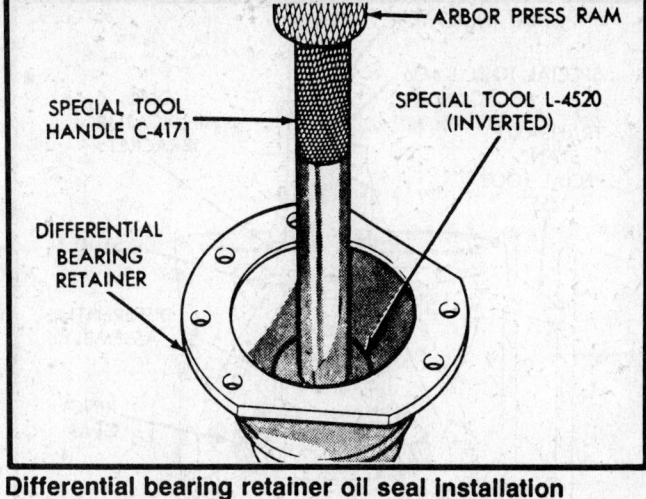

Differential bearing retainer oil seal installation

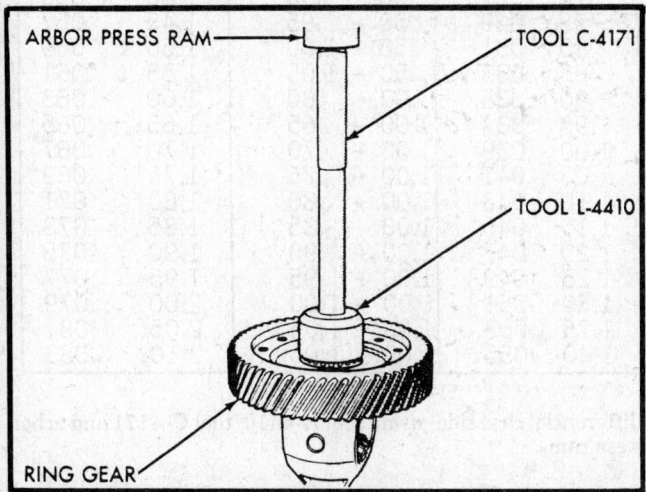

Differential bearing retainer bearing cone (ring gear side) installation

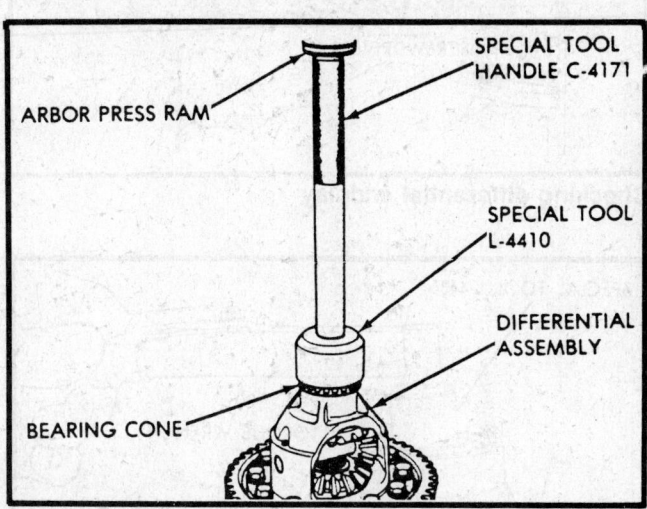

Differential bearing retainer bearing cone (side gear side) installation

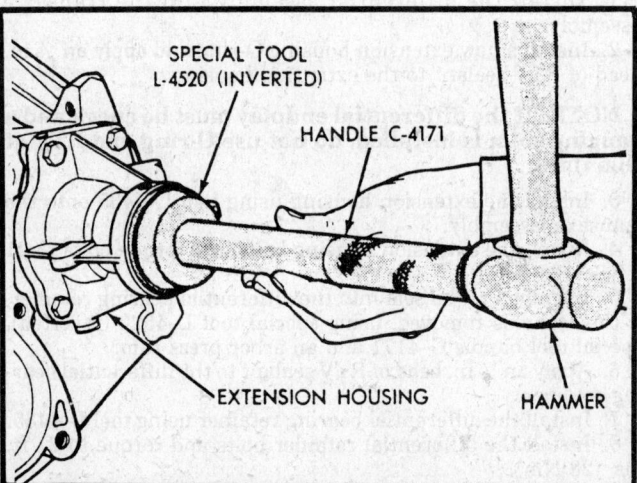

Differential extension seal installation

NOTE: The differential bearing retainer shim thickness need only be determined and/or changed if the transaxle case, differential carrier, differential bearing retainer, extension housing or differential bearing cups/cones are replaced.

2. Install pinion gear, side gears and tabbed thrust washers by rotating the pinion gears to the opening in the differential case.

3. Install the pinion shaft into the differential case. Do not install the pinion shaft roll pin at this time. If necessary, tape can be place around the differential case to hold the pinion shaft in place.

4. Install new ring gear bolts and torque to 70 ft. lbs. (95 Nm).

NOTE: Always use new ring gear bolts and torque properly.

5. Install a dial indicator and special tool C-4996 to check side gear endplay to the differential assembly (differential case side). Check the side gear endplay by moving the side gear up and down. Side gear endplay must be within 0.001–0.013 in. Thrust washers are available in 0.032, 0.037, 0.042 and 0.047 in.

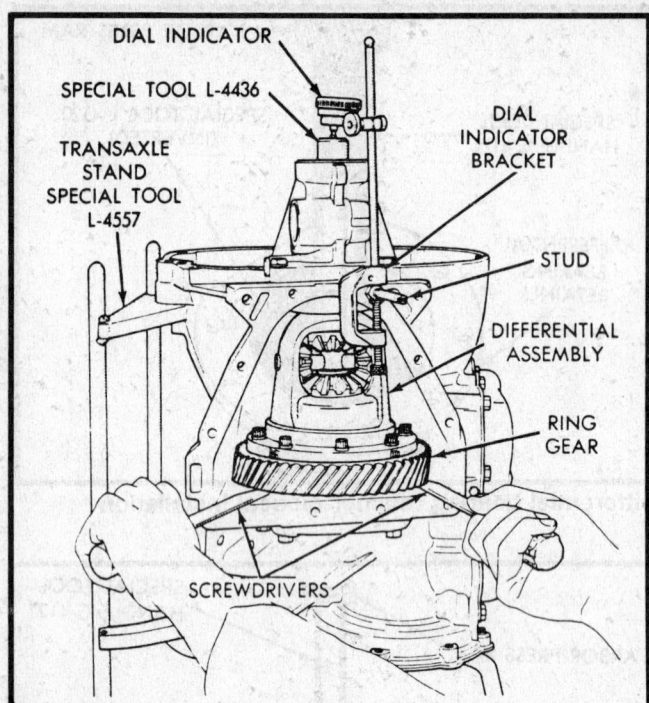

Checking differential endplay

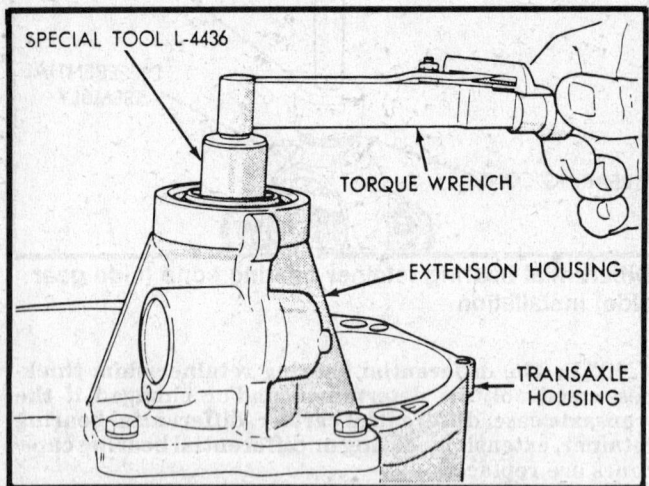

Checking differential bearings turning torque

6. Install a dial indicator and special tool C–4996 to check side gear endplay to the differential assembly (ring gear side). Check the side gear endplay by moving the side gear up and down. Side gear endplay must be within 0.001–0.013 in.. Thrust washers are available in 0.032, 0.037, 0.042 and 0.047 in..

7. When side gear endplay is within specifications, install the pinion shaft roll pin.

—————— CAUTION ——————

Make sure the pinion shaft roll pin is installed or the pinion shaft could drift and cause damage.

————————————————————————

8. Install differential bearing cone onto differential assembly (ring gear side) using tool L–4410, tool C–4171 and arbor press ram.

9. Install differential bearing cone onto differential assembly

DIFFERENTIAL BEARING SHIM SELECTION

End Play (with .50mm gauging shim Installed)		Required Shim Combination		Total Thickness	
mm	Inch	mm		mm	Inch
.0	.0	.50		.50	.020
.05	.002	.75		.75	.030
.10	.004	.80		.80	.032
.15	.006	.85		.85	.034
.20	.008	.90		.90	.035
.25	.010	.95		.95	.037
.30	.012	1.00		1.00	.039
.35	.014	1.05		1.05	.041
.40	.016	.50 +	.60	1.10	.043
.45	.018	.50 +	.65	1.15	.045
.50	.020	.50 +	.70	1.20	.047
.55	.022	.50 +	.75	1.25	.049
.60	.024	.50 +	.80	1.30	.051
.65	.026	.50 +	.85	1.35	.053
.70	.027	.50 +	.90	1.40	.055
.75	.029	.50 +	.95	1.45	.057
.80	.031	.50 +	1.00	1.50	.059
.85	.033	.50 +	1.05	1.55	.061
.90	.035	1.00 +	.60	1.60	.063
.95	.037	1.00 +	.65	1.65	.065
1.00	.039	1.00 +	.70	1.70	.067
1.05	.041	1.00 +	.75	1.75	.069
1.10	.043	1.00 +	.80	1.80	.071
1.15	.045	1.00 +	.85	1.85	.073
1.20	.047	1.00 +	.90	1.90	.075
1.25	.049	1.00 +	.95	1.95	.077
1.30	.051	1.00 +	1.00	2.00	.079
1.35	.053	1.00 +	1.05	2.05	.081
1.40	.055	1.05 +	1.05	2.10	.083

(differential case side) using tool L–4410, tool C–4171 and arbor press ram.

Transaxle Assembly

DIFFERENTIAL ASSEMBLY

Installation

1. Install the differential assembly into the transaxle assembly.

2. Install a new extension housing O-ring and apply an ⅛ in. bead of RTV sealant to the extension housing.

NOTE: If the differential endplay must be check and a gauging shim is installed, do not use O-ring and RTV at this time.

3. Install the extension housing using tool L–4435 onto the transaxle assembly.

4. Install the extension housing bolts and torque bolts to 21 ft. lbs. (28 Nm).

5. Install a new oil seal into the differential bearing retainer, if the seal was removed, using special tool L–4520 (inverted), special tool handle C–4171 and an arbor press ram.

6. Apply an ⅛ in. bead of RTV sealant to the differential bearing retainer.

7. Install the differential bearing retainer using tool L–4435.

8. Install the differential retainer bolts and torque to 21 ft. lbs. (28 Nm).

9. Apply an ⅛ in. bead of RTV sealant to the differential cover and install the differential cover.

10. Install the differential cover bolts and torque to 165 inch lbs. (19 Nm).

11. Install a new oil seal into the extension housing using special tool L–4520 (inverted) and tool handle C–4171.

Checking Differential Endplay

1. Install the transaxle assembly vertically on the support stand and install tool L–4436 into the extension.

2. Rotate the differential at least 1 full revolution to ensure the tapered roller bearings are fully seated.

3. Install a dial indicator to the case and zero the dial indicator. Place the indicator tip on the end of tool L–4436.

4. Place a small pry tool to each side of the ring gear and lift. Check the dial indicator for the amount of endplay.

NOTE: Do not damage the transaxle case and/or the differential cover sealing surface.

5. Record the endplay and refer to the Differential Bearing Shim Chart for the correct shim combination to obtain the proper bearing setting.

6. Remove the differential bearing retainer. Remove the bearing cup and the 0.020 in. (0.50mm) gauging shim.

7. Install the proper shim combination under the bearing cup. Make sure the oil baffle is installed properly in the bearing retainer, below the bearing shim and cup.

8. Install a new extension housing O-ring and apply an 1/8 in. bead of RTV sealant to the extension housing.

9. Install the extension housing and torque the extension housing bolts to 21 ft. lbs. (28 Nm).

Checking Differential Bearings Turning Torque

1. Install the transaxle assembly vertically on the support stand and install tool L–4436 into the extension.

2. Rotate the differential at least 1 full revolution to ensure the tapered roller bearings are fully seated.

3. Using an inch lbs. torque wrench installed on tool L–4436, check the turning torque of the differential. The turning torque should be between 5–18 inch lbs..

4. If the turning torque is too high, install a 0.002 in. (0.05mm) thinner shim. If the turning torque is too low, install a 0.002 in. (0.05mm) thicker shim. Repeat this procedure until 5–18 inch lbs. turning torque is obtained.

LOW/REVERSE CLUTCH PISTON AND RETAINER

Installation

1. Install the low/reverse clutch piston retainer gasket and low/reverse clutch piston retainer.

NOTE: Low/reverse clutch piston retainer gasket holes must line up.

2. Install the low/reverse clutch piston retainer attaching screws. Torque the screws to 40 inch lbs. (5 Nm).

3. Install the low/reverse clutch piston.

GUIDE BRACKET

Installation

1. Install the guide bracket assembly.
2. Install the guide bracket pivot shaft and plug.
3. Install the guide bracket support shaft and plug.

NOTE: Be sure the guide bracket and split sleeve touch the rear of the transaxle case.

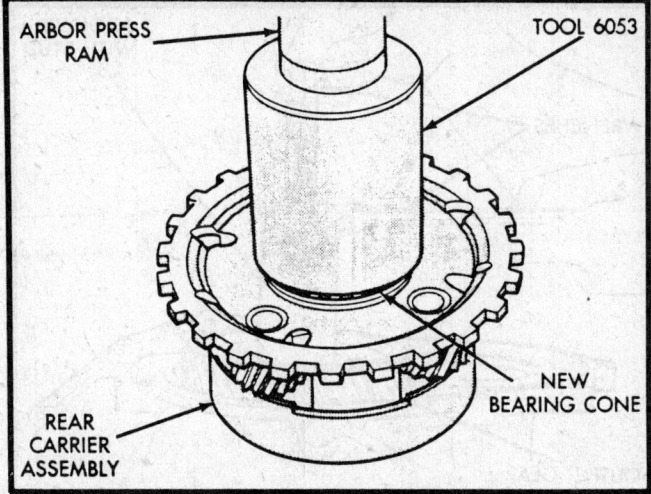

Rear carrier bearing cone installation

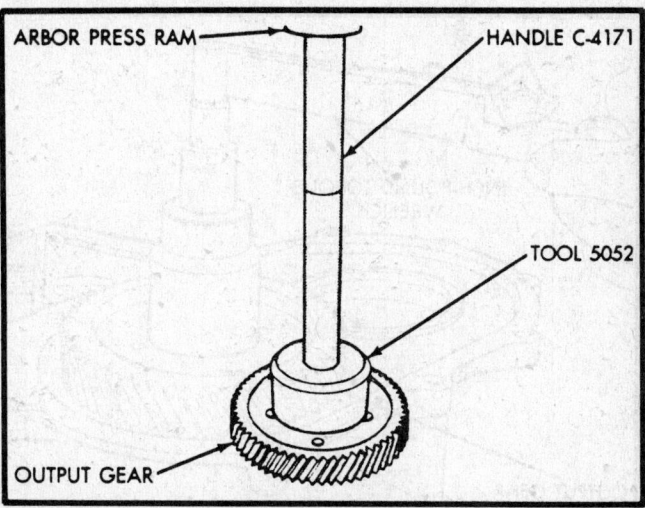

Output gear bearing cone installation

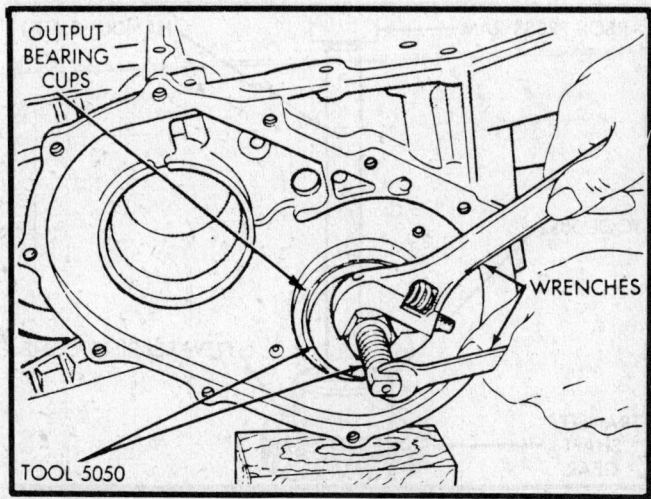

Output gear bearing cups installation

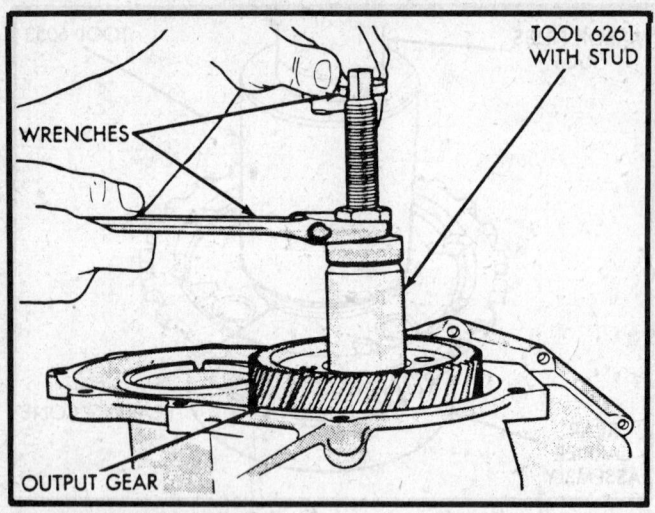

Output gear installation

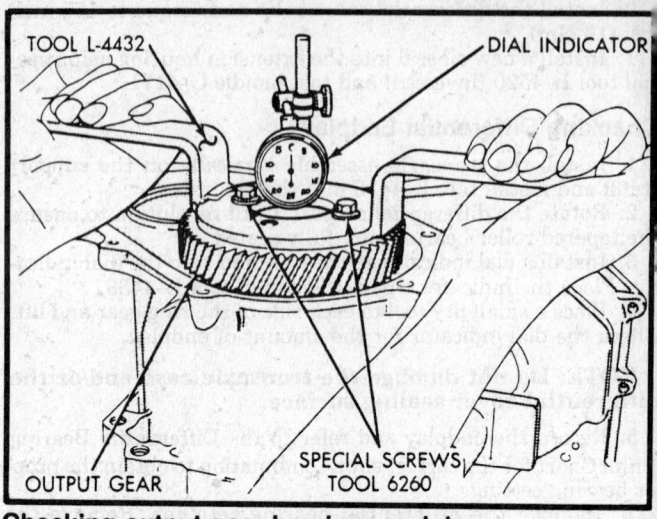

Checking output gear bearings endplay

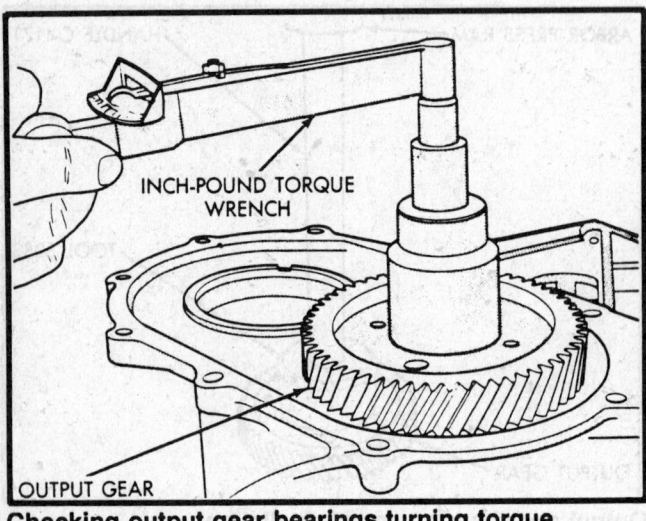

Checking output gear bearings turning torque

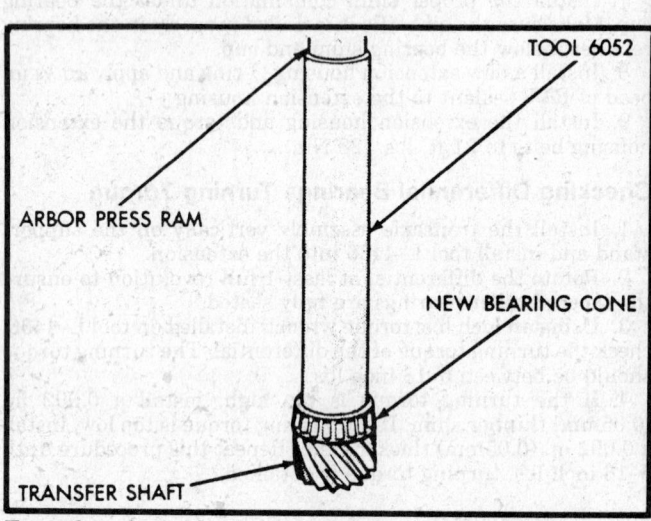

Transfer shaft bearing cone (small gear side) installation

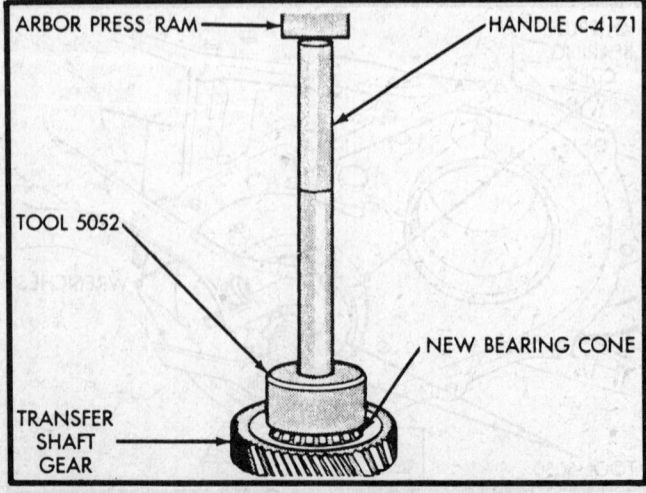

Transfer shaft bearing cone (large gear side) installation

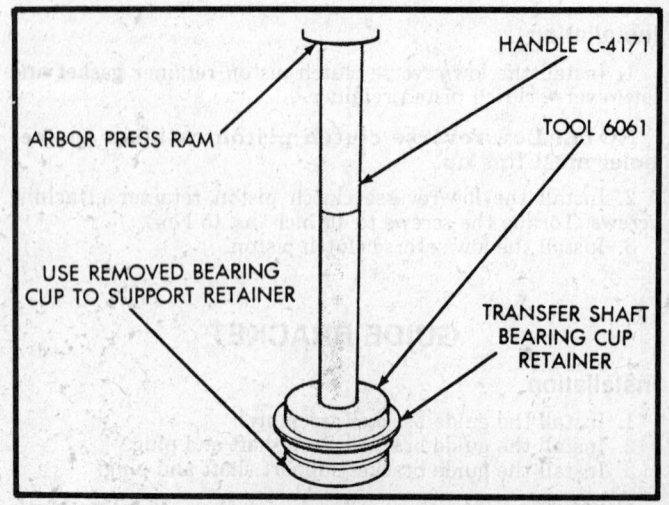

Transfer shaft bearing cup installation

LOW/REVERSE PISTON RETURN SPRING

Installation

1. Install the low/reverse piston return spring.
2. Install low/reverse spring compressor tool 5059, 5058–3 and 6057. Compress the low/reverse piston return spring.
3. Install the low/reverse piston return spring snapring.
4. Remove the low/reverse spring tools.

REAR CARRIER ASSEMBLY

Installation

1. If removed, install the rear carrier bearing cone to the rear carrier using tool 6053 and an arbor press ram.
2. Install the rear carrier assembly into the transaxle assembly (bell housing side).

OUTPUT SHAFT GEAR

Installation

1. If removed, install the output gear bearing cone using tool 5052, tool handle C–4171 and an arbor press ram.
2. If removed, install the output gear bearing cups using tool 5050.
3. Install the output gear shim and output gear.
4. Install the output gear bolt and washer using tool 6261 with stud. Use tool 6259 and torque output gear bolt to 200 ft. lbs. (271 Nm).

Checking Bearing Endplay

1. Install tool L–4432, special screws tool 6260 and a dial indicator to the output gear.
2. Move gear up and down to measure bearing endplay. Output gear endplay must have a preload of 0.0008–0.002 in. (0.02–0.05mm).
3. If the output gear endplay is not within specifications, remove the output gear following the Output Gear Removal procedure and install the proper output gear shim. Install by following the Output Gear Installation procedure and recheck the endplay.

Checking Bearing Turning Torque

1. Install proper socket onto the output gear attaching bolt. Install an inch lbs. torque wrench onto the socket.

2. Check the turning torque of the output gear. The torque should be 3–8 inch lbs..
3. If the output gear turning torque is not within specifications, remove the output gear following the Output Gear Removal procedure and install the proper output gear shim. Install by following the Output Gear Installation procedure and recheck the turning torque.

TRANSFER SHAFT

Installation

1. If removed, install the transfer shaft bearing cone using tool 6052 and an arbor press ram.
2. Install the transfer shaft using tool 5049–A.
3. Install the transfer shaft bearing snapring using snapring pliers tool 6051.
4. If removed, install the transfer shaft bearing cone onto the transfer shaft gear using tool 5052, tool handle C–4171 and an arbor press ram.
5. Install the transfer shaft bearing cup retainer.

TRANSFER SHAFT GEAR

Installation

1. If removed, install the transfer shaft bearing cone using tool 5052, tool handle C–4171 and an arbor press ram.
2. Install the transfer shaft gear and shim using tool 6261.
3. Install transfer shaft gear lockwasher and nut. Using tool 6259 to hold the transfer shaft gear, torque the transfer shaft gear nut to 200 ft. lbs. (271 Nm).
4. Check the transfer shaft endplay. The transfer shaft must have endplay of 0.002–0.004 in. (0.05–0.10mm). Install proper shim to meet specifications.
5. Apply an ⅛ in. bead of RTV sealant on the rear cover.
6. Install the rear cover.
7. Install the rear cover bolts and torque to 14 ft. lbs. (19 Nm).

LOW/REVERSE CLUTCH PACK

Installation

1. Install the low/reverse clutch pack in the proper order.
2. Install the low/reverse reaction plate snapring. Do not scratch the clutch plate.
3. Install the 1 disc onto the low/reverse clutch.
4. Install the low/reverse reaction plate (flat side up).
5. Install a new tapered snapring in sequence according to the illustration.
6. To check the low/reverse clutch clearance, install dial indicator and dial indicator tip tool 6268. Using a hook tool to raise the 1 clutch disc, check the clearance. Low/reverse clutch pack clearance is 0.042–0.065 in. (1.04–1.65mm).
7. If the low/reverse clutch pack is not within specifications, select the proper low/reverse reaction plate to achieve specifications.

    Part number 4377150 – 0.273 in. (6.92mm)
    Part number 4377149 – 0.262 in. (6.66mm)
    Part number 4377148 – 0.252 in. (6.40mm)
    Part number 4412268 – 0.242 in. (6.14mm)
    Part number 4412267 – 0.232 in. (5.88mm)
    Part number 4412266 – 0.221 in. (5.62mm)
    Part number 4412265 – 0.211 in. (5.36mm)

2–4 CLUTCH PACK

Installation

1. Install the 2–4 clutch pack in proper order.

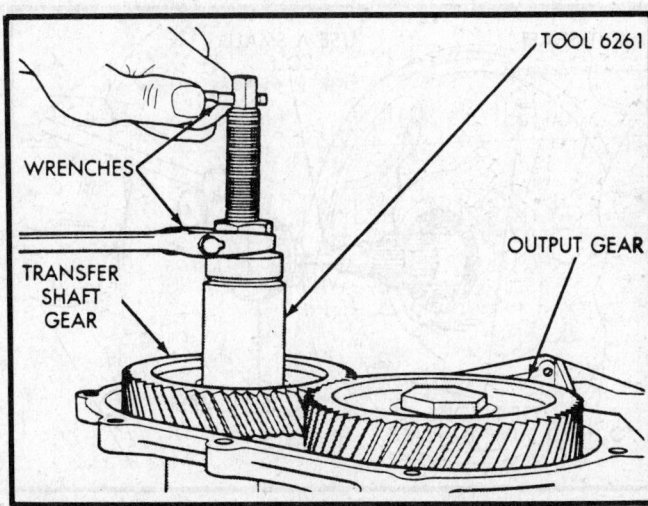

Transfer shaft gear installation

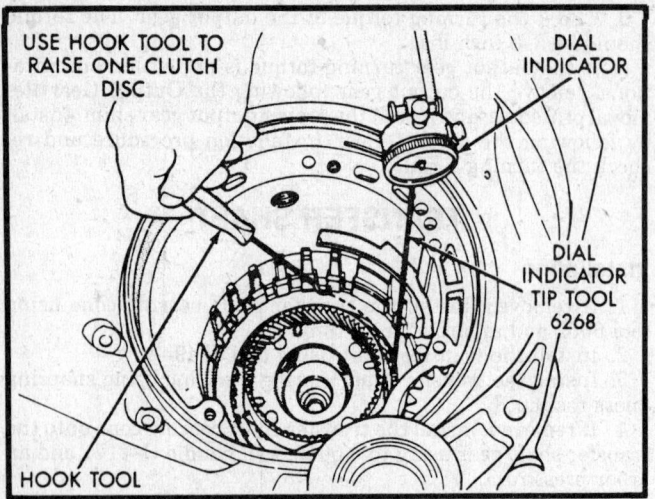

Checking low/reverse clutch clearance

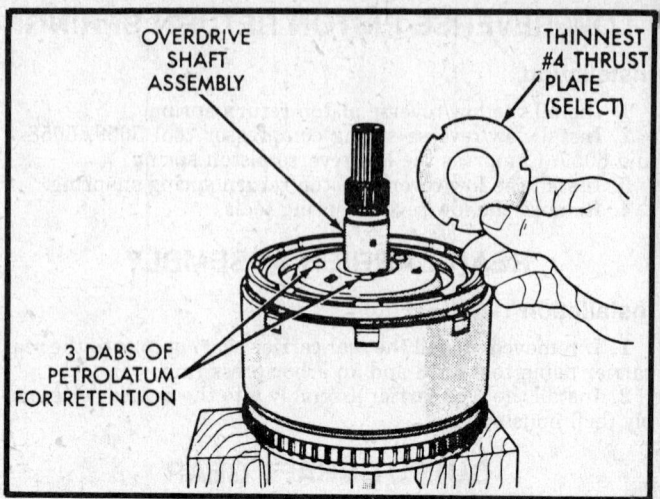

Using petrolatum to retain #4 thrust plate

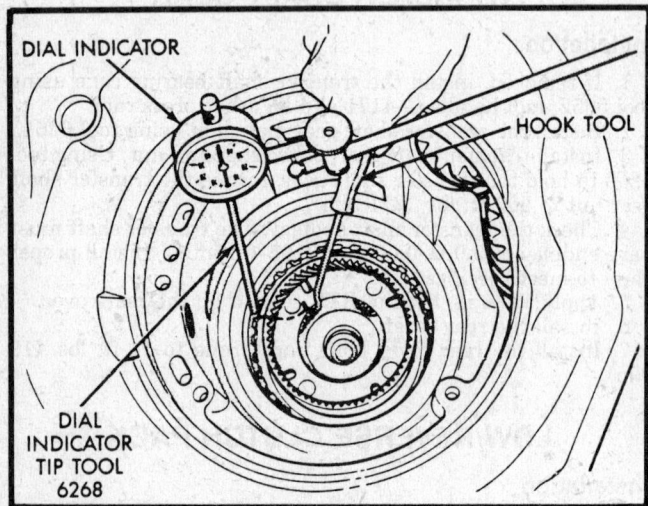

Checking 2/4 clutch clearance

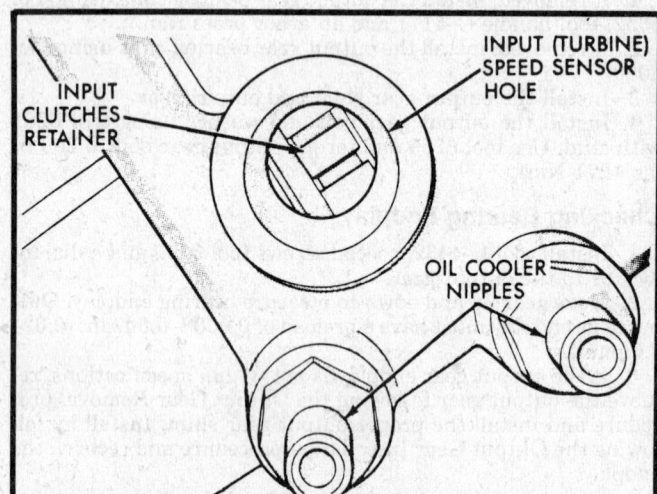

Proper input clutches retainer view through input speed sensor hole

2. Install the 2–4 clutch return spring onto the 2–4 clutch retainer. Note the position of the return spring so it is indexed properly onto the retainer.

3. Install the 2–4 clutch return spring and retainer into the transaxle assembly.

4. Install tool 5058 and compress the 2–4 clutch return spring just enough to install the 2–4 clutch retainer snapring.

5. Install the 2–4 clutch retainer snapring.

6. Install a dial indicator and dial indicator tip tool 6268 into the transaxle assembly. Press down on the clutch pack with fingers and zero the dial indicator.

7. With a hook tool, check the 2–4 clutch pack clearance. Clearance should be 0.030–0.104 in. (0.76–2.64mm). If the clutch clearance is not within specification, the 2–4 clutch pack is not assembled properly. There is no adjustment for the 2–4 clutch clearance.

REAR SUN GEAR

Installation

1. Install the No. 7 needle bearing assembly.
2. Install the rear sun gear.

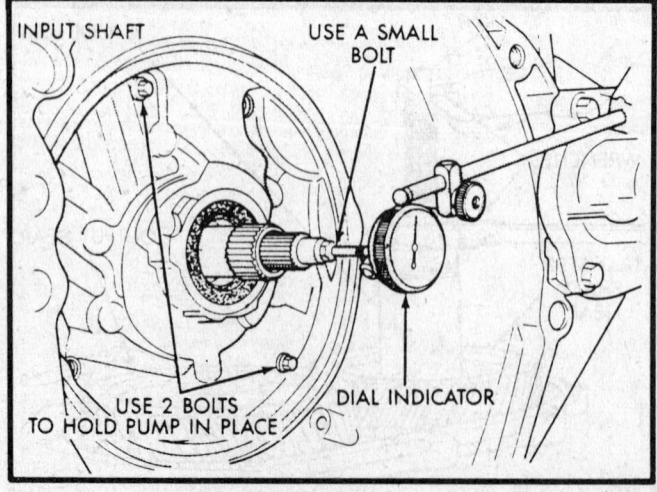

Checking input shaft endplay

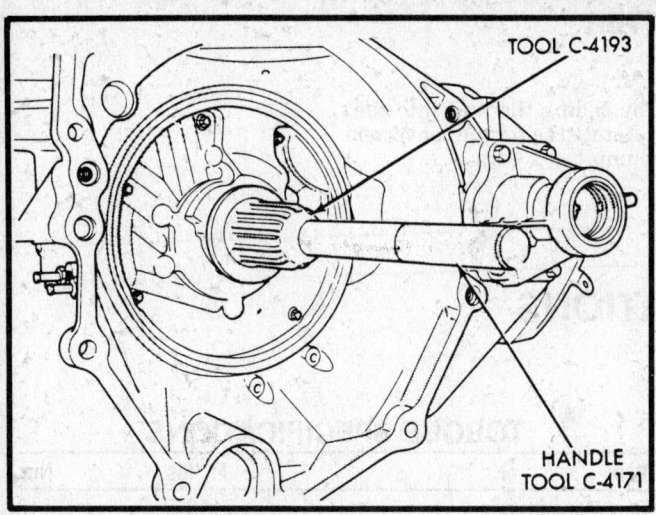

Oil pump seal installation

FRONT CARRIER AND REAR ANNULUS ASSEMBLY

Installation

1. Install the No. 6 needle bearing assembly.
2. Install the front carrier and rear annulus assembly. Twist and push to install the assembly.

FRONT SUN GEAR ASSEMBLY

Installation

1. Install the front sun gear assembly.
2. Install the No. 4 thrust washer onto the front sun gear assembly.

NOTE: If the input shaft endplay was checked before disassembly and the No. 4 thrust washer shim size is known, install the proper shim and continue assembling the transaxle unit. If not, follow the procedure to determine the No. 4 thrust plate (washer) thickness.

DETERMINING NO. 4 THRUST PLATE (WASHER) THICKNESS

1. Select the thinnest No. 4 thrust plate.
2. Apply a small amount of petroleum jelly to the input clutches retainer to hold the thrust plate in place.
3. Install the No. 4 thrust plate to the input clutches retainer.
4. Install the input clutches retainer into the transaxle unit. Make sure the input clutches retainer is completely seated.
5. To ease installation and removal, remove the oil pump O-ring.
6. Install the oil pump and install 2 bolts to hold the oil pump in place.
7. Install a dial indicator and check the input shaft endplay. Input shaft endplay must be 0.012–0.030 in. (0.31–0.76mm).
8. Once the input shaft endplay has been recorded, remove the oil pump bolts and remove the oil pump.
9. Install a oil pump O-ring onto the oil pump.
10. Remove the input shaft clutches retainer and No. 4 thrust plate.
11. Install the proper size No. 4 thrust plate and continue assembling the transaxle unit.

    Part number 4431662 — 0.037–0.039 in. (0.93–1.00mm)
    Part number 4431663 — 0.045–0.048 in. (1.15–1.22mm)

    Part number 4431664 — 0.054–0.057 in. (1.37–1.44mm)
    Part number 4431665 — 0.063–0.066 in. (1.59–1.66mm)
    Part number 4431666 — 0.071–0.074 in. (1.81–1.88mm)
    Part number 4431667 — 0.080–0.083 in. (2.03–2.10mm)
    Part number 4431668 — 0.089–0.091 in. (2.25–2.32mm)
    Part number 4431669 — 0.097–0.100 in. (2.47–2.54mm)
    Part number 4446670 — 0.106–0.109 in. (2.69–2.76mm)
    Part number 4446671 — 0.114–0.117 in. (2.91–2.98mm)
    Part number 4446672 — 0.123–0.126 in. (3.13–3.20mm)
    Part number 4446601 — 0.132–0.135 in. (3.35–3.42mm)

INPUT SHAFT CLUTCHES ASSEMBLY

Installation

1. Install the input shaft clutches assembly. Make sure the input shaft clutches assembly is completely seated.
2. Install the No. 1 caged needle bearing. Install with the tanged side out.

OIL PUMP

Installation

1. Install the oil pump gasket. Make sure the hole line up.
2. Install a new O-ring onto the oil pump and install the pump.
3. Install the oil pump attaching bolts. Torque the bolts to 23 ft. lbs. (32 Nm).
4. Install a new oil pump seal using tool C–4193 and handle tool C–4171.

GOVERNOR

Installation

This transaxle utilizes electronic sensors and solenoids in place of the governor. Therefore, there is no governor assembly.

ACCUMULATORS

Installation

1. Install the low/reverse accumulator piston return springs.
2. Install the low/reverse accumulator piston. Note the piston notch so the piston is installed correctly.
3. Install the low/reverse accumulator plug.
4. Install the low/reverse accumulator plug snapring.
5. With the seal ring installed on the overdrive clutch accumulator, install the accumulator and return spring.
6. With the seal ring installed on the underdrive clutch accumulator, install the accumulator and return spring.

VALVE BODY

Installation

1. Install the valve body by guiding the park rod rollers into the guide bracket while shifting the manual lever assembly.
2. Install the valve body attaching bolts and torque to 40 inch lbs. (5 Nm).
3. Install a new oil filter and O-ring.

OIL PAN

Installation

1. Apply an ⅛ in. bead of RTV sealant on the oil pan.
2. Install the oil pan.
3. Apply RTV sealant under the oil pan bolt heads and install the oil pan bolts. Torque the bolts to 14 ft. lbs. (19 Nm).

CONVERTER

Installation

The torque converter is installed by sliding the unit into the transaxle input and reaction shaft. Rotate the torque converter to seat the converter onto the oil pump.

SPECIFICATIONS

AUTOMATIC TRANSAXLE SPECIFICATIONS

Item	in.	mm
Pump Clearance		
Outer gear to pocket	0.0018–0.0056	0.045–0.141
Outer gear side clearance	0.0008–0.0018	0.020–0.046
Inner gear side clearance	0.0008–0.0018	0.020–0.046
Input shaft endplay	0.012–0.030	0.31–0.76
Differential side gear clearance	0.001–0.013	0.025–0.330
Clutch pack clearance		
Underdrive clutch	0.036–0.058	0.91–1.47
Overdrive clutch	0.042–0.096	1.07–2.44
Reverse clutch	0.030–0.039	0.76–0.99
Low/reverse clutch	0.042–0.065	1.07–1.65
2/4 clutch	0.030–0.104	0.76–2.64
Tapered roller bearing settings		
Output gear (preload)	0.008–0.002	0.02–0.05
Transfer shaft (endplay)	0.002–0.004	0.05–0.10
Differential (preload)	0.006–0.012	0.15–0.29

TORQUE SPECIFICATIONS

Item	Ft. lbs.	Nm
Cooler line fittings	110 ①	12
Differential cover	165 ①	19
Differential ring gear	70	95
Differential bearing retainer	21	28
Rear end cover	14	19
Extension housing	21	28
Input speed sensor	20	27
Low/Reverse clutch retainer	40 ①	5
Neutral safety switch	25	34
Oil pan to case	14	19
Output gear bolt (1.5 in. hex)	200	271
Output speed sensor	20	27
Pressure taps	45 ①	5
PRNDL switch	25	34
Pump to case	23	32
Reaction shaft to pump	23	32
Solenoid assy. to case	105 ①	12
Transfer plate to case	105 ①	12
Transfer gear nut (1.25 in. hex)	200	271
Valve body and transfer plate	40 ①	5
Vent assembly	110 ①	12
8-way solenoid connector	38 ①	4
60-way EATX connector	38 ①	4

① inch lbs.

Section 3

AXOD Transaxle
Ford Motor Co.

APPLICATION

1988–89 Continental
1986–89 Taurus and Sable

GENERAL DESCRIPTION

The AXOD transaxle is a 4-speed fully automatic overdrive transmission. The unit consists of 2 planetary gearsets, a combination planetary/differential gearset, 4 multiple plate clutches, 2 band assemblies and 2 one-way clutches. The lockup converter transmits engine power to the geartrain by means of the drive chain.

The converter clutch is controlled by the EEC-IV computer system. The fully automatic shift control responds to the road speed and engine torque demand. Operation of the EEC-IV system's electronic controls, along with the valve body hydraulic controls, operate a piston plate clutch in the torque converter to eliminate converter slippage and improve fuel economy.

Transaxle Identification

Code letters and numbers are stamped on the identification tag located on top of the converter housing. The tag denotes the serial number and the date of manufacture. The numbers are important when ordering service replacement parts.

Electronic Controls

The transaxle, being fully controlled by the EEC-IV computer system, is equipped with pressure switches and a solenoid; it responds to road speed and engine torque demand.

The internal equipment, attached to the main control assembly, consists of 3 pressure switches, an oil temperature switch (3.8L only) and a bypass clutch solenoid. A bulkhead connector/wiring assembly, attached to the middle, rear side of the chain cover assembly, provides an electrical path to the EEC-IV system.

Metric Fasteners

The transaxle is of a metric design; all bolt sizes and thread pitches are metric. Metric fastener dimensions are very close to the customary inch system fastener dimensions; replacement of the fasteners must be of the same measurement and strength as those removed.

Do not attempt to interchange metric fasteners with the customary inch system fasteners. Mismatched or incorrect fasteners can result in damage to the transaxle. Care should be taken to reuse the same fasteners in the location from which they were removed.

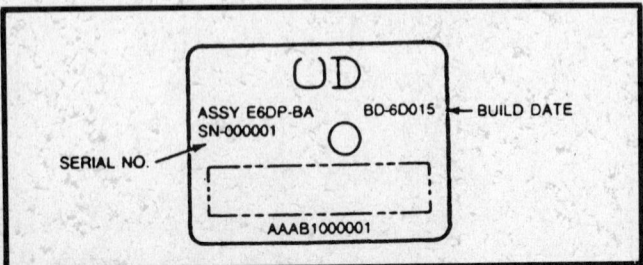

View of the transaxle identification tag

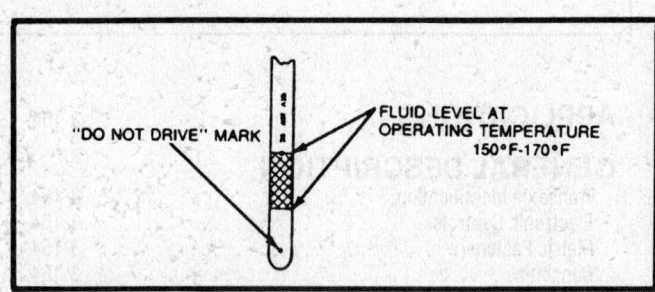

View of the dipstick

NOTE: Be sure to check the case holes for the quality of their threads. It is rather difficult to rethread bolt holes after the transaxle is installed in the vehicle.

Capacities

The fluid quantities are approximate and the correct fluid level should be determined by the dipstick indicator for the correct level. Dry fill is 13.1 qts. (12.46L).

Checking Fluid Level

NOTE: When checking the fluid level, the vehicle must be at normal operating temperatures and positioned on a flat surface. The vehicle should not be driven if the fluid level is below the dipstick's DO NOT DRIVE hole.

1. If the transaxle's oil is below 150–170°F (21–35°C), drive the vehicle until normal operating temperatures are reached.

NOTE: If the outside temperature is above 50°F (10°C), drive the vehicle 15–20 miles (24–32 km) of city driving. If the vehicle has been operated under extreme conditions in hot weather, turn the engine OFF and allow the fluid to cool for at least 30 minutes.

2. With the vehicle on a level surface, place the transaxle in **P**, idle the engine and apply the footbrake. Move the transaxle selector lever through each range; allow time in each range for the transaxle to engage.

3. Position the selector lever in **P**, fully apply the parking brake, block the drive wheels and allow the vehicle to idle.

4. Before removing the dipstick, wipe the dirt from the dipstick cap.

5. Remove the dipstick and wipe it clean. Insert it into the dipstick tube and be sure it fully seats.

6. Remove the dipstick again and observe the fluid level; it must be between the indicators.

7. If necessary to add fluid, add it through the oil filler (dipstick) tube. Add enough fluid to raise the level. Do not overfill; overfilling will cause foaming, fluid loss and transaxle malfunction.

TRANSAXLE MODIFICATIONS

Temperature Switch—3.8L Engine

A temperature switch sensor is installed on the main control assembly, near the pressure switches when this transaxle is used with the 3.8L engine.

TROUBLE DIAGNOSIS

CLUTCH AND BAND APPLICATION

Gear	Lo-Int Band	Overdrive Band	Forward Clutch	Intermediate Clutch	Direct Clutch	Reverse Clutch	Low One-Way Clutch	Direct One-Way Clutch
1st Gear Manual Low	Applied	—	Applied	—	Applied	—	Applied	Applied
1st Gear (Drive)	Applied	—	Applied	—	—	—	Applied	—
2nd Gear (Drive)	Applied	—	Applied	Applied	—	—	Holding	—
3rd Gear (Drive)	—	—	Applied	Applied	Applied	—	—	—
4th Gear (Overdrive)	—	Applied	—	Applied	Applied	—	—	Holding
Reverse (R)	—	—	Applied	—	—	Applied	Holding	—
Neutral (N)	—	—	—	—	—	—	—	—
Park (P)	—	—	—	—	—	—	—	—

CHILTON'S THREE C'S TRANSMISSION DIAGNOSIS
Ford AXOD

Condition	Cause	Correction
Oil leak	a) Damaged gasket or pan rail	a) Replace gasket, repair pan rail
	b) Distorted pan	b) Replace pan
	c) TV cable, fill tube or electrical bulkhead connector. Loose fit/damaged case. External seal damage/missing	c) Reseal TV cable, fit tube or connector. Repair or replace damaged case. Replace damaged or missing seal
	d) Manual shaft, seal damaged	d) Replace seal
	e) Governor cover and servo covers. O-ring seal damaged	e) Replace O-ring seal
	f) Cooler fittings or pressure taps Low torque, damaged threads	f) Repair damaged threads
	g) Converter or converter seal, damaged, garter spring missing. Converter hub scored or weld seam leaking	g) Inspect CV joint journal for damage. Replace seal or spring. Weld seam
	h) Halfshaft seal damaged or garter spring missing	h) Replace seal
	i) Speedometer cable or speed sensor O-ring seal damaged	i) Replace O-ring seal
Oil venting or foaming	a) Transaxle overfilled	a) Drain and fill transaxle to proper level
	b) Transmission fluid contaminated with antifreeze or engine overheating	b) Determine source of leak and repair leak
	c) Bi-metallic element stuck open	c) Replace element
	d) Oil filter plugged, damaged or missing O-rings	d) Replace filter O-rings and filter

CHILTON'S THREE C'S TRANSMISSION DIAGNOSIS
Ford AXOD

Condition	Cause	Correction
High or low oil pressure (verify with gauge)	a) Oil level too low or too high	a) Drain or fill transaxle as necessary
	b) Improper T.V. cable/linkage actuation (travel)	b) Inspect for broken or disconnected component
	c) Pressure regulator valve or spring damaged	c) Replace valve or spring
	d) Pressure relief valve damaged. Missing ball or spring	d) Replace or repair pressure relief valve
	e) Oil pump ring stuck, seals damaged, vanes damaged	e) Determine source of damage. Repair seals
	f) Oil pump driveshaft broken or damaged	f) Replace oil pump
No 1–2 shift (first gear only)	a) Governor assembly weights binding	a) Perform governor test. Replace springs
	b) Governor springs damaged, misaligned or missing	b) Replace springs
	c) Governor gears damaged	c) Replace gears
	d) Governor shaft seal damaged or missing	d) Replace seal
	e) Governor value (ball) stuck or missing	e) Replace valve ball
	f) Governor tube leaking/damaged	f) Replace governor tube
	g) Intermediate clutch plates damaged/missing	g) Replace clutch plates
	h) Intermediate clutch piston or seals damaged	h) Replace piston seals
	i) Intermediate clutch ball check stuck/damaged or missing	i) Replace damaged ball
	j) Intermediate clutch cylinder damaged	j) Replace clutch cylinder
	k) Direct/intermediate clutch hub seals damaged, missing or holes blocked	k) Replace seals or unblock holes
	l) Driven sprocket support seals damaged, missing or holes blocked	l) Replace seals or unblock holes
	m) 1–2 shift valve stuck, nicked or damaged	m) Replace valve
	n) 1–2 throttle delay valve stuck, nicked or damaged	n) Replace valve
	o) 1–2 Accumulator capacity modulator valve stuck, nicked or damaged	o) Clean or replace valve
	p) No. 9 check ball missing or damaged	p) Replace check ball
	q) Control assembly bolts too loose or too tight	q) Tighten bolts to specification
	r) Front carrier damaged	r) Inspect welds and repair
	s) Intermediate clutch tap plug loose/missing. (Located on oil pump body)	s) Tighten or replace plug
	t) T.V. cable damaged/disconnected	t) Replace cable
1–2 shift feels harsh or soft	a) High or low oil pressure	a) Perform control pressure test
	b) 1–2 Accumulator regulator valve stuck, nicked, spring missing or damaged	b) Replace valve or spring
	c) Improper T.V. cable/linkage actuation	c) Check for broken or disconnected parts
	d) 1–2 Accumulator capacity modulator valve stuck, nicked, spring missing or damaged	d) Replace valve or spring
	e) 1–2 Accumulator assembly piston stuck, seal damaged, springs damaged or missing	e) Replace piston assembly or springs
1–2 shift speed high or low	a) Governor weights binding, spring damaged, misaligned or missing	a) Perform governor test
	b) Governor gear damaged	b) Replace gear
	c) Governor shaft seal, damaged or missing	c) Replace seal
	d) Governor lube tube leaking/damaged	d) Replace tube

CHILTON'S THREE C'S TRANSMISSION DIAGNOSIS
Ford AXOD

Condition	Cause	Correction
1–2 shift speed high or low	e) Governor valve balls damaged, stuck or missing	e) Replace balls
	f) Improper T.V. cable/linkage actuation	f) Check for broken or disconnected parts
	g) T.V. control valve, T.V. plunger, T.V. line modulator valve, 1–2 throttle delay valve	g) Check and/or replace T.V. valve parts
	h) Control assembly valve(s) stuck, nicked or damaged	h) Replace valve
	i) Control assembly spring(s)—missing or damaged	i) Replace spring(s)
	j) Control assembly valve balls damaged, stuck or missing	j) Replace balls
No 2–3 shift (1–2 shift OK)	a) Low/intermediate servo apply rod (too long)	a) Install correct apply rod, if required
	b) Low/intermediate servo bore or piston damaged	b) Replace piston
	c) Low/intermediate servo piston seals damaged/missing	c) Replace seals
	d) Low/intermediate servo missing/broken return spring or retaining clip	d) Replace spring or clip
	e) Direct clutch assembly plates damaged/missing	e) Replace clutch plates
	f) Direct clutch assembly piston cylinder, or seals damaged	f) Replace piston or seals
	g) Direct clutch assembly ball check assembly stuck or missing	g) Replace check ball assembly
	h) Direct/intermediate clutch hub seals damaged or missing or holes blocked	h) Replace seals or unblock holes
	i) Driven sprocket support seals damaged or missing or holes blocked	i) Replace seals or unblock holes
	j) Direct one-way clutch assembly cage/rollers/springs damaged	j) Disassemble and inspect. Replace parts
	k) Direct one-way clutch assembly rollers missing or misassembled on inner race	k) Replace rollers
	l) Control assembly bolts too loose or too tight	l) Tighten to specification
	m) 2–3 shift valve. Valve stuck, nicked or damaged	m) Replace valve
	n) No. 4 check ball missing/damaged	n) Replace check ball
	o) Bypass solenoid not energized during wide open throttle upshift	o) Refer to Electrical System Diagnosis
	p) Case servo release passage blocked	p) Determine source of blockage
	q) Servo release tube leaking or improperly installed	q) Seal or seat tube
	r) Direct clutch pressure tap plug loose/missing on oil pump body	r) Tighten or replace
	s) TTS temperature switch on 3.8L engine	s) Refer to Electrical diagram
2–3 shift feels harsh or soft	a) Low or high oil pressure	a) Perform control pressure test
	b) Wrong low/intermediate servo apply rod length	b) Install correct apply rod, if required
	c) Low/intermediate servo piston, seal, springs or rod damaged	c) Replace piston, seal, spring or rod
	d) Backout valve stuck, nicked or spring damaged	d) Determine source of contamination or damage and replace valve or spring
2–3 shift speed high or low (1–2 shift OK)	a) Governor weights binding, springs damaged, shaft seal or valve damaged	a) Perform governor pressure test
	b) Governor tube leaking/damaged	b) Repair tube leak or replace tube

CHILTON'S THREE C'S TRANSMISSION DIAGNOSIS
Ford AXOD

Condition	Cause	Correction
2–3 shift speed high or low (1–2 shift OK)	c) Governor valve balls damaged	c) Replace valve balls
	d) Improper T.V. cable/linkage actuation	d) Service T.V. cable
	e) T.V. control valve, T.V. plunger, T.V. line modulator valve, 2–3 throttle modulator valve stuck, nicked or damaged	e) Determine source of contamination or damage and repair or replace damaged part
No 3–4 shift (1–2 and 2–3 OK)	a) Overdrive band assembly not holding	a) Perform air pressure test and replace defective part
	b) Overdrive servo apply rod (too long)	b) Install correct apply rod, if required
	c) Overdrive servo bore, piston, piston seals damaged	c) Determine source of contamination or damage. Repair damaged part
	d) Overdrive servo assembly return spring or retaining clip missing or broken	d) Replace spring or clip
	e) Forward clutch assembly return springs/ piston damaged	e) Determine source of damage. Replace springs or piston
	f) Control assembly bolts too loose or too tight	f) Tighten bolts to specification
	g) 3–4 shift valve stuck, nicked or spring damaged	g) Determine source of contamination or damage. Repair or replace valve or spring
	h) 3–4 modulator valve stuck, nicked or spring missing	h) Determine source of contamination or damage. Repair or replace valve or spring
	i) 4–3 scheduling valve stuck, nicked or spring missing	i) Determine source of contamination. Repair or replace valve or spring
3–4 shift feels harsh or soft	a) Oil pressure too high or too low	a) Perform control pressure test
	b) 3–4 Accumulator assembly piston stuck, piston seal missing or damaged	b) Determine source of damage or contamination. Replace piston or seal
	c) 3–4 Accumulator assembly springs missing or damaged	c) Replace springs
	d) No. 14 check ball missing/damaged	d) Replace ball
3–4 shift speed high or low (1–2 and 2–3 OK)	a) Governor weights binding, spring damaged or misaligned	a) Perform governor test. Replace spring or weights
	b) Governor gear, shaft seal or valve damaged	b) Replace gear, seal or valve
	c) Governor tube leaking	c) Seal or seat tube
	d) T.V. control valve, T.V. plunger, T.V. line modulator valve, 3–4 modulator valve stuck, nicked or spring(s) missing or damaged	d) Determine source of contamination or damage. Replace valve(s) or spring(s)
No converter clutch apply	a) No lock-up signal	a) Repair or replace wiring or component. Refer to Electrical System Diagnosis
	b) By-pass solenoid damaged or inoperative	b) Repair or replace wiring or component. Refer to Electrical System Diagnosis
	c) Bulkhead connector damaged	c) Repair or replace wiring or component. Refer to Electrical System Diagnosis
	d) Pinched wires	d) Repair or replace wiring or component. Refer to Electrical System Diagnosis
	e) 4–3 pressure switch, 3–2 pressure switch inoperative	e) Repair or replace wiring or component. Refer to Electrical System Diagnosis
	f) Turbine shaft, seals damaged or missing	f) Replace seals
	g) Bypass clutch control valve stuck	g) Determine source of contamination. Repair or replace valve
	h) Bypass plunger stuck	h) Repair or replace plunger
	i) Missing or damaged pump shaft seals or cup plug	i) Determine source of contamination or damage. Replace seals or plug
	j) Valve body pilot sleeve damaged/ misaligned	j) Determine source of damage. Replace pilot sleeve

CHILTON'S THREE C'S TRANSMISSION DIAGNOSIS
Ford AXOD

Condition	Cause	Correction
Converter clutch does not release	a) No unlock signal	a) Repair or replace wiring or component. Refer to Electrical System Diagnosis
	b) Bypass solenoid damaged or inoperative	b) Repair or replace wiring or component. Refer to Electrical System Diagnosis
	c) Bulkhead connector wires damaged	c) Repair or replace wiring or component. Refer to Electrical System Diagnosis
	d) Bypass clutch control valve or plunger valve stuck, nicked or damaged	d) Determine source of contamination. Repair or replace valve
	e) Solenoid filter plug (in main control)	e) Tighten or replace solenoid filter plug (in main control)
4-3 downshifts harsh	a) Incorrect overdrive servo apply rod length	a) Install correct apply rod, if required
	b) Damaged overdrive servo piston, springs or seal	b) Determine source of contamination or damage. Replace piston, seal or springs
	c) No converter clutch release	c) Refer to Electrical System Diagnosis
3-2 downshift harsh	a) Damaged or missing low/intermediate servo assembly springs	a) Determine source of contamination or damage. Replace springs
	b) Incorrect low/intermediate servo apply rod length	b) Install correct apply rod, if required
	c) 3-2 Control valve stuck, nicked or damaged	c) Determine source of contamination. Repair or replace valve
	d) No. 5 check ball missing	d) Replace check ball
	e) Intermediate clutch return spring retaining ring out of position	e) Reposition spring
3-1, 2-1 downshift harsh	a) Damaged low/intermediate servo piston, springs, or seal	a) Determine source of damage. Replace piston, seal or springs
	b) Incorrect low/intermediate servo apply rod length	b) Install correct apply rod, if required
	c) No. 9 check ball missing (3-1 only)	c) Replace check ball
No drive in drive range and no reverse in reverse range	a) Oil level low	a) Add oil
	b) Oil pressure too low	b) Perform control pressure test. Repair system
	c) Manual linkage misadjusted, disconnected, damaged, broken, bent	c) Adjust, replace or repair linkage
	d) Oil pump assembly worn or damaged	d) Determine source of damage. Replace oil pump
	e) Drive chain assembly damaged or broken	e) Determine source of damage. Replace chain
	f) Drive sprocket shaft to converter turbine spline damaged	f) Determine source of damage. Replace drive sprocket shaft
	g) Driven sprocket shaft to direct/ intermediate clutch hub damaged	g) Determine source of damage. Replace drive sprocket shaft
	h) Oil filter damaged/missing O-rings or plugged	h) Clean oil filter or replace O-rings
	i) Forward clutch assembly's clutch plates burned or missing	i) Replace clutch plates
	j) Forward clutch assembly's damaged piston seals or pistons damaged	j) Replace seals or pistons
	k) Forward clutch assembly's forward clutch ball check assembly missing or damaged	k) Replace clutch ball
	l) Forward clutch assembly's driven sprocket support seals or direct intermediate clutch hub seals damaged/ missing or holes blocked	l) Clean blocked holes or replace seals
	m) Gearset's front sun, front/rear carriers, ring gear and/or final drive assembly	m) Replace damaged component

CHILTON'S THREE C'S TRANSMISSION DIAGNOSIS
Ford AXOD

Condition	Cause	Correction
No drive in drive range and no reverse in reverse range	n) Low one-way clutch has two way rotation o) Damaged output shaft splines/ misassembled with axles p) Halfshaft splines damaged or disengaged from transaxle	n) Replace clutch o) Determine source of damage. Replace shaft or align with axles p) Service halfshaft and CV-joints
No drive. Reverse OK	a) Low/intermediate band assembly burned or broken ends b) Low/intermediate servo assembly apply rod (too short) c) Piston/seal/rod damaged d) Low/intermediate servo oil tubes or case bores damaged (leaking oil) e) 2–3 Servo regulator valve stuck	a) Determine source of damage. Replace bond assembly b) Install correct apply rod, if required c) Determine source of contamination. Replace damaged component d) Unblock tubes or case bores. Repair oil tube leaks e) Replace valve
No reverse. Drive OK	a) Reverse clutch plates burned or missing b) Reverse apply tube leaking or improperly installed	a) Determine source of damage. Replace clutch plates b) Seat or seal tube
No park range	a) Chipped or broken parking pawl or park gear b) Broken park pawl return spring c) Bent or broken actuating rod d) Manual linkage misadjusted	a) Replace pawl or gear b) Replace spring c) Replace rod d) Adjust linkage
Harsh neutral to reverse or harsh neutral to drive	a) Damaged or missing low/intermediate servo assembly springs b) Incorrect servo apply rod length c) 3–2 Control valve stuck, nicked or damaged d) No. 5 ball check. Ball missing e) Neutral-drive accumulator assembly piston stuck or seal and/or springs damaged or missing f) No. 1 check ball missing/damaged (harsh reverse) g) Main control separator plate thermal elements do not close when warm	a) Determine source of contamination or damage. Replace springs b) Install correct apply rod, if required c) Determine source of contamination. Replace valve d) Replace ball check e) Determine source of contamination. Replace piston, seal or springs f) Replace ball g) Replace thermal elements
Transaxle overheats	a) Excessive tow loads b) Improper fluid level c) Incorrect engine idle or performance d) Improper clutch or band application or oil pressure control system e) Restriction in cooler or lines f) Seized converter one-way clutch g) Dirty or sticking valve body	a) Check Owner's Manual for tow restriction b) Perform fluid level check c) Perform engine tune-up d) Perform control pressure test e) Service restriction f) Replace converter g) Clean, service or replace valve body
Transaxle fluid leaks	a) Improper fluid level b) Leakage at gaskets, seals and/or etc.	a) Perform fluid level check b) Remove all traces of lubrication on exposed surfaces of transaxle. Check the vent for free-breathing. Operate transaxle at normal temperatures and inspect for leakage

Electrical System Diagnosis

These test should only be conducted if a problem has been detected with the transaxle. If any of the following service codes appear during the Self Test, perform the AXOD Drive Cycle Test.

CODE 39: Transaxle converter bypass clutch not working properly.

CODE 59: Transaxle Hydraulic Switch (THS) 4–3 pressure switch circuit has failed open.

CODE 62: Transaxle Hydraulic Switch (THS) 4–3 and/or 3–2 pressure switch(es) has failed closed. If code appears in the "Key On, Engine Off" test, the 3–2 circuit has failed. If the code appears in the "Engine Running" test, the 4–3 circuit has failed. If the code appears in both tests, check both circuits.

CODE 69: Transaxle Hydraulic Switch (THS) 3–2 circuit has failed open.

CODE 89: Transaxle converter bypass clutch solenoid has failed open or closed.

The following codes are not transaxle related but can affect operation of the converter clutch bypass. These components should be serviced before servicing the transaxle codes.

CODE 21: Engine Coolant Temperature (ECT) sensor out of range.

CODE 22: Manifold Absolute Pressure (MAP) sensor out of range.

CODE 23: Throttle Position Sensor (TPS) out of range.

CODE 24: Air Charge Temperature (ACT) sensor out of range.

CODE 29: Vehicle Speed Sensor (VSS) nonfunctioning.

CODE 74: Brake ON/OFF (BOO) switch always open or brake not applied during Engine Running On-Demand Self Test.

CODE 75: Brake ON/OFF (BOO) switch always closed.

The following service code is transaxle related and may cause faulty engine idle speed control if not working properly.

CODE 57: Neutral Pressure Switch (NPS) failed in **N** (open). The NPS is a normally open switch that closes with hydraulic pressure; its failure will not allow the transaxle to engage in **D** or **R**. Before testing the electrical components, check for proper hydraulic operation.

NOTE: After performing the Self Test, perform the AXOD Drive Cycle Test to check for continuous codes; this test must be performed on flat terrain or a slight upgrade.

AXOD DRIVE CYCLE TEST

1. Record and zero the Self Test codes.
2. Operate the engine until normal operating temperatures are reached.
3. Place the transaxle in the **D** range, slowly accelerate to 40 mph (64 km/h) until the transaxle shifts into 3rd gear and hold the speed/throttle steady for 15 seconds or 30 seconds (above 4,000 ft.).
4. Shift the transaxle into **OD**, accelerate from 40–50 mph (64–80 km/h) until the transaxle shifts into 4th gear and hold the speed/throttle steady for 15 seconds.
5. With the transaxle in 4th gear, the speed steady and the throttle opening, lightly apply/release the brakes (to operate the brakelamps) and maintain the steady speed for the next 15 seconds.
6. Apply the brakes, come to a stop and remain stopped for the next 20 seconds with the transaxle still in **OD**.
7. Perform the Self Test and record any continuous codes.

NOTE: If any other continuous codes appear, service them first, for they could affect the transaxle's electrical operation.

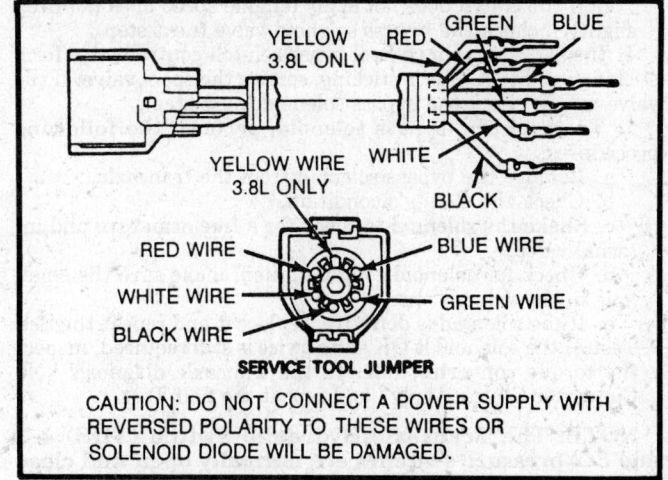

CAUTION: DO NOT CONNECT A POWER SUPPLY WITH REVERSED POLARITY TO THESE WIRES OR SOLENOID DIODE WILL BE DAMAGED.

View of the service jumper harness

DIAGNOSIS CHART INDEX

Service Code	Pinpoint Test
39	A
59	B
62	C
69	D
89	E
57	F

CODE 39

The following procedure is used to determine why the converter bypass clutch is not applying properly.

1. Make sure the vehicle harness connector is fully seated and the terminals engaged with the transaxle's bulkhead connector. If not OK, repair the connector(s) or terminal(s) and repeat the Self Test. If OK, check the solenoid resistance.

2. To check the solenoid resistance, perform the following procedures:

    a. Using a service jumper harness, connect it to the transaxle's bulkhead connector.

    b. Using an ohmmeter, connect it to the service jumper harness leads; the positive (+) lead to the red wire and the negative (−) lead to the black wire. Check the resistance, it should be 20–40 ohms. Disconnect the ohmmeter.

    c. If the reading is not OK, repeat the Self Test and service the codes as required. If the reading is OK, check the bypass clutch application.

3. To check the bypass clutch application, perform the following procedures:

    a. Using the service jumper harness, connect the Red wire to the positive (+) battery terminal.

    b. With the engine running and transaxle in 3rd gear, connect the Black wire (jumper harness) to ground; this will energize the bypass clutch solenoid.

NOTE: When connecting a power supply to the wiring, do not reverse the polarity for it will damage the solenoid diode.

    c. If the clutch applies (engine speed drops slightly), there is no electrical component failure, the bypass clutch solenoid is operating properly.

    d. Any error code produced may be caused by a slipping bypass clutch. Inspect the torque converter or refer to the transaxle diagnosis "No Converter Clutch Apply".

e. If the clutch does not apply (engine speed does not drop slightly), check the bypass solenoid valve (next step).

4. Inspect the main control bypass clutch control valve for a sticking condition. If it is sticking, service the spool valve. If the valve is OK, check the bypass solenoid (next step).

5. To check the bypass solenoid, perform the following procedures:

a. Remove the bypass solenoid from the transaxle.

b. Check the O-ring's condition.

c. Shake the solenoid to check for a free armature and internal valve.

d. Check for solenoid contamination; make sure the small hole in the valve is open.

e. If the solenoid is defective, replace it and repeat the Self Test. If the solenoid is OK and service is still required, inspect the torque converter, refer to the transaxle diagnosis "No Converter Clutch Apply" and repeat the Self Test.

NOTE: The Transaxle Hydraulic Switch (THS) 4–3 and 3–2 pressure switches are normally open and close with hydraulic pressure. With the shift selector in D and the transaxle fails to engage, a service code 59 will appear. When the transaxle fails to shift to 3rd gear, a service code 69 will appear. Before performing electrical part inspection, be sure the hydraulic system is operating correctly.

CODE 59

The following procedure is used to check the 4–3 pressure switch's failure to open.

1. Make sure the vehicle harness connector is fully seated and the terminals engaged with the transaxle's bulkhead connector. If not OK, repair the connector(s) or terminal(s) and repeat the Self Test. If OK, check the switch for continuity.

2. To check the switch for continuity, perform the following procedures:

a. Using the service jumper harness connector, attach it to the transaxle's bulkhead connector.

b. Using a ohmmeter, attach 1 lead to the Blue wire and the other to ground.

c. Start the engine and place the shift selector in **N**; the ohmmeter should show no continuity.

d. Move the shift selector to **D**; the switch should close and the ohmmeter should read less than 10 ohms.

e. When the transaxle shifts through the 1st, 2nd and 3rd gears, the switch should stay closed; when shifting to 4th gear, the switch should open.

f. If the circuit is OK, repeat the Self Test and service any codes. If the circuit is not OK, check the internal connections.

3. To check internal connections, perform the following procedures:

a. Remove the side cover from the transaxle and check that the Blue wire is firmly attached to the 4–3 pressure switch.

b. Using a ohmmeter, remove the connector from the pressure switch and check the resistance of the wire; it should be less than 2.0 ohms.

c. If the connector/wire is not OK, replace the bulkhead connector/wiring assembly and repeat the Self Test. If the connector/wire is OK, check the 4–3 pressure switch.

4. To check the 4–3 pressure switch, perform the following procedures:

a. Remove the 4–3 pressure switch and install it into a ⅛ – 27 pipe fitting. Connect the pipe fitting to low pressure air (do not use water) supply line (for testing purposes).

b. Apply 50 psi (345 kPa) to the switch and check for ruptured diaphram.

c. Submerge the switch in transaxle fluid and check for bubbles at the small vent hole near the switch terminal.

d. If bubbles appear, replace the 4–3 pressure switch and repeat the Self Test. If no bubbles appear, check the switch's resistance.

5. To check the switch's resistance, perform the following procedures:

a. Apply 50 psi (345 kPa) of air pressure to the switch.

b. Using an ohmmeter, measure the resistance between the switch's terminal and the case; it should be less than 8.0 ohms.

c. If the resistance is greater than 8.0 ohms, replace the switch, repeat the switch continuity check and repeat the Self Test; codes 39, 59, 62, 69 and 89 should no longer appear. If the resistance is less than 8.0 ohms, inspect the hydraulic circuit supplying pressure to the switch for excessive leakage and/or main control assembly operation.

CODE 62

The following procedure is used to check the 4–3 and/or 3–2 pressure switches for a failed closed condition.

NOTE: Code 62 will appear under the following Self Test situations: "Engine Running" when the 4–3 circuit has failed closed to ground, "Key On, Engine Off" when the 3–2 circuit has failed closed to ground or under both testing situations.

1. To check the wiring, perform the following procedures:

a. Remove the vehicle harness connector from the bulkhead connector.

b. Using the service jumper harness connector, attach it to the bulkhead connector.

c. Using a ohmmeter (engine Off), attach 1 lead to the White wire and the other to ground; the resistance should be infinite.

d. Using a ohmmeter (engine **OFF** and/or **RUNNING** in **N**), attach 1 lead to the Blue wire and the other to ground; the resistance should be infinite.

e. If the reading(s) are infinite, repeat the Self Test and service any code. If the reading(s) are are not infinite, check the internal wiring.

2. To check the internal wiring, perform the following procedures:

a. Remove the side cover and check for pinched, cut or grounded wiring.

b. If the wiring is pinched, cut or grounded, replace the bulkhead wiring assembly and repeat the Self Test.

c. If the wiring for the 3–2 switch is OK, inspect the 3–2 switch continuity. If the wiring for the 4–3 switch is OK, inspect the 4–3 switch's continuity.

3. To check the 3–2 and 4–3 switches continuity, perform the following procedures:

a. From each switch, remove the wiring connector.

b. Using an ohmmeter, connect 1 lead to the pressure switch terminal and the other to valve body.

c. If there is continuity, replace the defective switch and repeat the Self Test. If there is no continuity, check the internal wiring.

4. To check the internal wiring of both switches, perform the following procedures:

a. Remove the wiring connectors from both switches.

NOTE: When performing this test, make sure the wiring terminals are not contacting any metal surfaces.

b. Using an ohmmeter, connect 1 lead to the White wire and the other to ground; the resistance should be infinite.

c. Using an ohmmeter, connect 1 lead to the Blue wire and the other to ground; the resistance should be infinite.

d. If the resistance is infinite, repeat the Self Test and service any codes. If there is continuity, replace the bulkhead connector/wiring assembly and repeat the Self Test.

NOTE: The Transaxle Hydraulic Switch (THS) 4–3 and 3–2 pressure switches are normally open and close with hydraulic pressure. With the shift selector in D and the transaxle fails to engage, a service code 59 will ap-

pear. When the transaxle fails to shift to 3rd gear, a service code 69 will appear. Before performing electrical part inspection, be sure the hydraulic system is operating correctly.

CODE 69

The following procedure is used to check the 3–2 pressure switch's failure to open.

1. Make sure the vehicle harness connector is fully seated and the terminals engaged with the bulkhead connector. If not OK, repair the connector(s) or terminal(s) and repeat the Self Test. If OK, check the switch for continuity.
2. To check the switch for continuity, perform the following procedures:
 a. Using the service jumper harness connector, attach it to the bulkhead connector.
 b. Using a ohmmeter, attach 1 lead to the White wire and the other to ground.
 c. Start the engine and place the shift selector in **D, 1** or **2**; the ohmmeter should show no continuity.
 d. When the transaxle shifts to **3rd** or **4th** gears, the switch should close; resistance should be less than 10 ohms.
 e. If the circuit is OK, repeat the Self Test and service any codes. If the circuit is not OK, check the internal connections.
3. To check internal connections, perform the following procedures:
 a. Remove the side cover from the transaxle and check that the White wire is firmly attached to the 3–2 pressure switch.
 b. Using an ohmmeter, remove the connector from the pressure switch and check the resistance of the wire; it should be less than 2.0 ohms.
 c. If the connector/wire is not OK, replace the bulkhead connector/wiring assembly and repeat the Self Test. If the connector/wire is OK, check the 3–2 pressure switch.
4. To check the 3–2 pressure switch, perform the following procedures:
 a. Remove the 3–2 pressure switch and install it into a ⅛– 27 pipe fitting. Connect the pipe fitting to low pressure air (do not use water) supply line (for testing purposes).
 b. Apply 50 psi (345 kPa) to the switch and check for ruptured diaphram.
 c. Submerge the switch in transaxle fluid and check for bubbles at the small vent hole near the switch terminal.
 d. If bubbles appear, replace the 3–2 pressure switch and repeat the Self Test. If no bubbles appear, check the switch's resistance.
5. To check the switch's resistance, perform the following procedures:
 a. Apply 50 psi (345 kPa) of air pressure to the switch.
 b. Using an ohmmeter, measure the resistance between the switch's terminal and the case; it should be less than 8.0 ohms.
 c. If the resistance is greater than 8.0 ohms, replace the switch, repeat the switch continuity check and repeat the Self Test; codes 39, 59, 62, 69 and 89 should no longer appear. If the resistance is less than 8.0 ohms, inspect the hydraulic circuit supplying pressure to the switch for excessive leakage and/or main control assembly operation.

CODE 89

The following procedure is used to check the Bypass Clutch Solenoid circuit's failure.

NOTE: Code 39 may also be present; if so, refer to the diagnosis procedures.

1. Make sure the vehicle harness connector is fully seated and the terminals engaged with the bulkhead connector. If not OK, repair the connector(s) or terminal(s) and repeat the Self Test. If OK, check the solenoid's resistance.
2. To check the solenoids resistance, perform the following procedures:

 a. Using the service jumper harness attach it to the transaxle's bulkhead connector.
 b. Using an ohmmeter, connect the positive (+) lead to the Red wire and the negative (−) lead to the Black wire. Check the resistance, it should be 20–40 ohms.

NOTE: When connecting a power supply to the wiring, do not reverse the polarity for it will damage the solenoid diode.

 c. If the resistance is OK, repeat the Self Test and service any code. If the resistance is not OK, check the internal connection.
3. To check the internal connection, remove the side cover and make sure the internal connector is fully engaged with the solenoid. If the connection is not OK, fully engage the connector, check the continuity, recheck the resistance and repeat the Self Test. If the connection is OK, check the solenoid continuity.
4. To check the solenoid's continuity, perform the following procedures:
 a. Disconnect the wires from the solenoid connector.
 b. Using an ohmmeter, connect the positive (+) lead to the solenoid's positive (+) terminal and the negative (−) lead to the solenoid's negative (−) terminal; the resistance should be 20–40 ohms.
 c. If the resistance is infinite (open circuit), replace the solenoid and repeat the Self Test.
 d. If the solenoid is OK, replace the bulkhead connector/wiring assembly, reconnect the internal connectors, recheck the resistance, replace the side cover and repeat the Self Test "Key On, Engine Off On Demand"; code 89 should no longer appear.

CODE 57

The following procedure is used to check the Neutral Park Switch (NPS) for failure in **N**.

NOTE: The NPS is normally open and closes with hydraulic pressure. If the transaxle fails to engage in D or R, a service code 57 will appear. Before testing the electrical components, be sure to inspect the hydraulic system functions.

1. Make sure the vehicle harness connector is fully seated and the terminals engaged with the bulkhead connector. If not OK, repair the connector(s) or terminal(s) and repeat the Self Test. If OK, check the switch's continuity.
2. To check the switch for continuity, perform the following procedures:
 a. Using the service jumper harness connector, attach it to the bulkhead connector.
 b. Using a ohmmeter, attach 1 lead to the Green wire and the other to ground.
 c. Start the engine and place the shift selector in **N** or **P**; the resistance should be infinite.
 d. Shift the transaxle into to **R** and **D**; the switch should close and the resistance should be less than 10 ohms in both ranges.
 e. If the circuit is OK, repeat the Self Test and service any codes. If the circuit is not OK, check the internal connections.
3. To check internal connections, perform the following procedures:
 a. Remove the side cover from the transaxle and check that the Green wire is firmly attached to the neutral pressure switch.
 b. Using an ohmmeter, remove the connector from the pressure switch and check the resistance of the wire; it should be less than 2.0 ohms.
 c. If the connector/wire is not OK, replace the bulkhead connector/wiring assembly and repeat the Self Test. If the connector/wire is OK, check the neutral pressure switch.

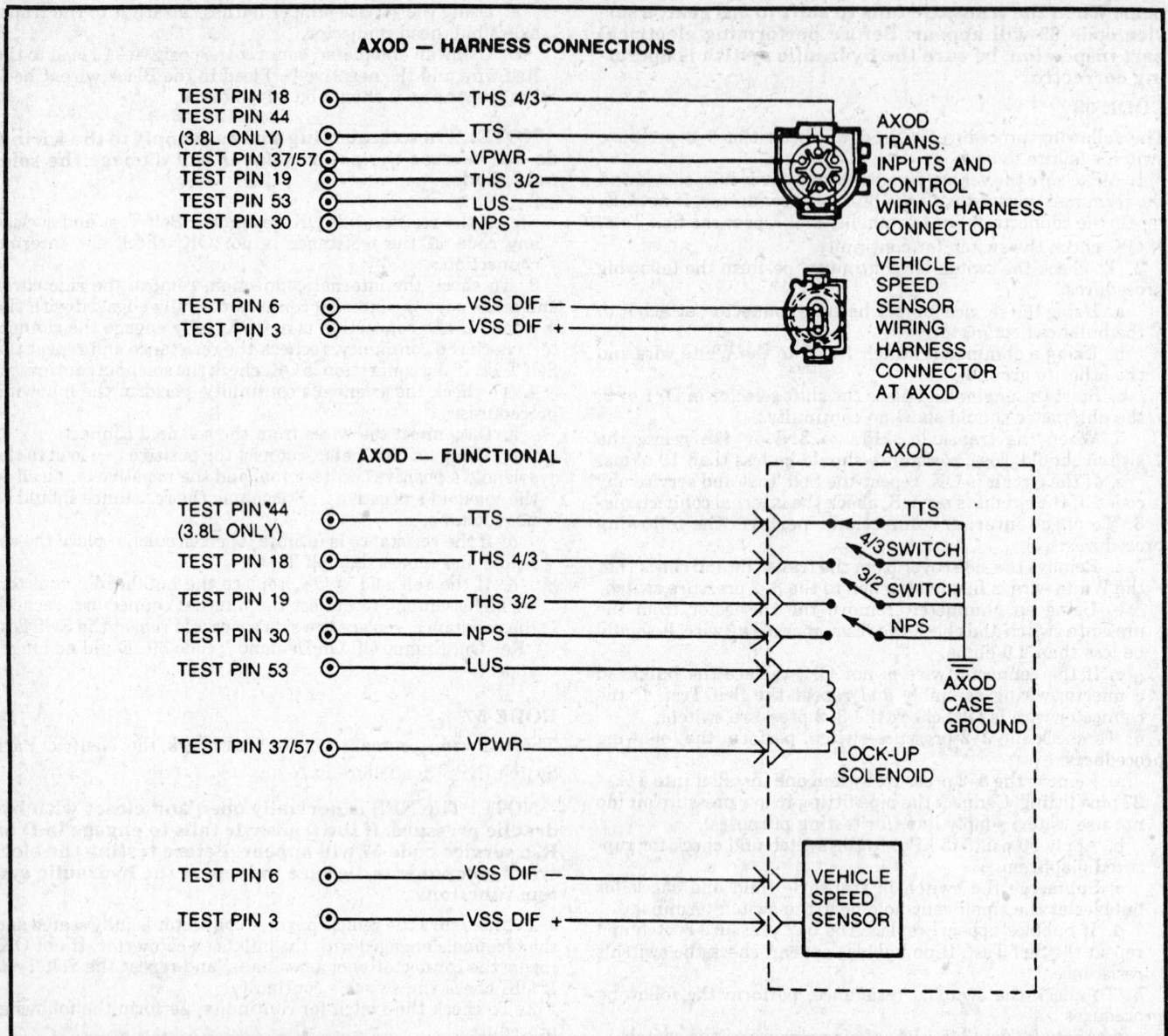

View of the pinpoint test schematic

4. To check the neutral pressure switch, perform the following procedures:

a. Remove the neutral pressure switch and install it into a ⅛—27 pipe fitting. Connect the pipe fitting to low pressure air (do not use water) supply line (for testing purposes).

b. Apply 50 psi (345 kPa) to the switch and check for ruptured diaphram.

c. Submerge the switch in transaxle fluid and check for bubbles at the small vent hole near the switch terminal.

d. If bubbles appear, replace the neutral pressure switch and repeat the Self Test. If no bubbles appear, check the switch's resistance.

5. To check the switch's resistance, perform the following procedures:

a. Apply 50 psi (345 kPa) of air pressure to the switch.

b. Using an ohmmeter, measure the resistance between the switch's terminal and the case; it should be less than 8.0 ohms.

c. If the resistance is greater than 8.0 ohms, replace the switch, repeat the switch continuity check and repeat the Self

Test; codes 39, 59, 62, 69 and 89 should no longer appear. If the resistance is less than 8.0 ohms, inspect the hydraulic circuit supplying pressure to the switch for excessive leakage and/or main control assembly operation.

Pinpoint Test

NOTE: Perform this test only when the "Key On/Engine Off Self Test" service codes 62, 67 and 89 are present; when "Engine Running Self Test" service code 62 is displayed; or when "Continuous Self Test" service codes 29, 39, 57, 59 and/or 69 are displayed. Make sure that all components are connected before performing the test.

AXOD DRIVE CYCLE TEST

1. Record and zero the Self Test codes.

2. Operate the engine until normal operating temperatures are reached.

3. Place the transaxle in the **D** range, slowly accelerate to 40

mph (64 km/h) until the transaxle shifts into 3rd gear and hold the speed/throttle steady for 15 seconds (under 4000 ft.) or 30 seconds (above 4000 ft.).

4. Shift the transaxle into **OD**, accelerate from 40 mph (64 km/h) to 50 mph (80 km/h) until the transaxle shifts into 4th gear and hold the speed/throttle steady for 15 seconds.

5. With the transaxle in 4th gear, the speed steady and the throttle opening, lightly apply/release the brakes (to operate the brake lights) and maintain the steady speed for the next 15 seconds.

6. Apply the brakes, come to a stop and remain stopped for the next 20 seconds with the transaxle still in **OD**.

7. Turn the engine **OFF**. Perform the "Run Key On/Engine Off Self Test" and record any continuous codes.

NOTE: If any other continuous codes appear, service them first, for they could affect the electrical operation.

CODE 29

This procedure is performed in an attempt to generate Code 29.

1. Perform the AXOD Drive Cycle Test. If Code 29 appears, check the Vehicle Speed Sensor (VSS) harness for continuity (next step). If codes other than 29 appear, service them first. If no codes appear, the test is complete.

2. To check the continuity of the Vehicle Speed Sensor (VSS) harness, perform the following procedures:
  a. Turn the key **OFF** and wait 10 seconds.
  b. Disconnect the VSS harness connector.
  c. From the ECA processor, disconnect the 60 pin connector. Inspect the pins for damage, corrosion, loose wires and/or etc.; repair as necessary.
  d. While leaving the processor disconnected, install the breakout box.
  e. Using a DVOM, place it on the 200 ohm scale. Measure the resistance between the VSS harness connector (Pin 3) and the breakout box. Measure the resistance between the VSS harness connector (Pin 6) and the breakout box.
  f. If the resistance is over 5 ohms, remove the breakout box, reconnect the components, service the open circuits and repeat the AXOD Drive Cycle Test for Code 29.
  g. If the resistance is under 5 ohms, inspect the VSS harness for shorts to power or ground (next step).

3. To check the VSS harness for shorts, perform the following procedures:
  a. Turn the key **OFF**. Disconnect the processor and the VSS.
  b. Using a DVOM, place it on the 200k scale. Measure the resistance between the VSS harness connector (Pin 3) and the breakout box (Pins 37, 40 and 6). Measure the resistance between the VSS harness connector (Pin 6) and the breakout box.
  c. If the resistance is under 10k ohms, remove the breakout box, reconnect the components, service the short circuits and repeat the AXOD Drive Cycle Test for Code 29.
  d. If the resistance is over 10k ohms, remove the breakout box, install a new VSS, reconnect the components and repeat the AXOD Drive Cycle Test for Code 29.
  e. If Code 29 appears, replace the processor and repeat the AXOD Drive Cycle Test. If Code 29 did not appear, replace the VSS and repeat the AXOD Drive Cycle Test for Code 29.

CODE 69

This portion of the procedure is used in an attempt to generate Code 69.

1. Perform the AXOD Drive Cycle Test. If Code 69 appears, check the 3–2 circuit for continuity (next step). If codes other than 69 appear, service them first. If no codes appear, the test is complete.

2. To check the continuity of the 3–2 circuit, perform the following procedures:
  a. Turn the key **OFF** and wait 10 seconds.
  b. Disconnect the AXOD harness connector.
  c. From the ECA processor, disconnect the 60 pin connector. Inspect the pins for damage, corrosion, loose wires and/or etc.; repair as necessary.
  d. While leaving the processor disconnected, install the breakout box.
  e. Using a DVOM, place it on the 200 ohm scale. Measure the resistance between the AXOD connector (Pin 19) and the breakout box.
  f. If the resistance is over 5 ohms, remove the breakout box, reconnect the components, service the 3–2 open circuit and repeat the AXOD Drive Cycle Test for Code 69.
  g. If the resistance is under 5 ohms, inspect the 3–2 circuit a for power short (next step).

3. To check the 3–2 circuit for a short, perform the following procedures:
  a. Turn the key **OFF**. Disconnect the processor and the AXOD harness connector.
  b. Using a DVOM, place it on the 200k scale. Measure the resistance between the 3–2 circuit connector (Pin 19) and the breakout box (Pin 37).
  c. If the resistance is under 10k ohms, remove the breakout box, reconnect the components, service the short in the 3–2 circuit and repeat the AXOD Drive Cycle Test for Code 69.
  d. If the resistance is over 10k ohms, check the processor (next step).

4. To inspect the processor, perform the following procedures:
  a. Turn the key **OFF**. Install the breakout box. Reconnect the electrical harness connector to the processor and AXOD.
  b. At the breakout box, install a jumper wire between Pin 19 and Pin 40.
  c. Perform the "Run Key On/Engine Off Test".
  d. If Code 62 or 69 does not appear, remove the breakout box and the jumper wire. Replace the processor and repeat the AXOD Drive Cycle Test for Code 69.
  e. If Code 62 or 69 appears, remove the breakout box and the jumper wire.

This portion of the test is used to check the AXOD harness and the 3–2 circuit for shorts.

1. To verify the working order of the AXOD harness, perform the following procedures:
  a. Turn the key **OFF**. Disconnect the AXOD electrical harness connector.
  b. Perform the "Run Key On/Engine Off Self Test".
  c. If Code 69 does not appear, reconnect the AXOD harness connector; test is complete.
  d. If Code 69 does appear, check the 3–2 circuit for a short to ground (next step).

2. To check the 3–2 circuit for a short to ground, perform the following procedures:
  a. Turn the key **OFF**.
  b. Disconnect the AXOD harness connector.
  c. From the ECA processor, disconnect the 60 pin connector. Inspect the pins for damage, corrosion, loose wires and/or etc.; repair as necessary.
  d. While leaving the processor disconnected, install the breakout box.
  e. Using a DVOM, place it on the 200k ohm scale. At the breakout box, measure the resistance of Pin 19 between Pin 40 and 60.
  f. If both resistances are under 10k ohms, remove the breakout box, reconnect the AXOD harness and the processor, service the short to ground and repeat the AXOD Drive Cycle Test for Code 69.
  g. If both resistances are over 10k ohms, remove the break-

out box, reconnect AXOD harness, replace the processor and repeat the AXOD Drive Cycle Test for Code 69.

CODE 59

Code Generation

This portion of the procedure is used in an attempt to generate Code 59.

1. Perform the AXOD Drive Cycle Test. If Code 59 appears, check the 4–3 circuit for continuity (next step). If codes other than 59 appear, service them first. If no codes appear, the test is complete.

2. To check the continuity of the 4–3 circuit, perform the following procedures:
   a. Turn the key **OFF** and wait 10 seconds.
   b. Disconnect the AXOD harness connector.
   c. From the ECA processor, disconnect the 60 pin connector. Inspect the pins for damage, corrosion, loose wires and/or etc.; repair as necessary.
   d. While leaving the processor disconnected, install the breakout box.
   e. Using a DVOM, place it on the 200 ohm scale. Measure the resistance between the AXOD connector (Pin 18) and the breakout box.
   f. If the resistance is over 5 ohms, remove the breakout box, reconnect the components, service the 4–3 open circuit and repeat the AXOD Drive Cycle Test for Code 59.
   g. If the resistance is under 5 ohms, inspect the 4–3 circuit a for power short (next step).

3. To check the 4–3 circuit for a short, perform the following procedures:
   a. Turn the key **OFF**. Install the breakout box.
   b. Disconnect the processor and the AXOD harness connector.
   c. Using a DVOM, place it on the 200k scale. Measure the resistance between the 4–3 circuit connector (Pin 18) and the breakout box (Pin 37).
   d. If the resistance is under 10k ohms, remove the breakout box, reconnect the components, service the short in the 4/3 circuit and repeat the AXOD Drive Cycle Test for Code 59.
   e. If the resistance is over 10k ohms, check the processor (next step).

4. To inspect the processor, perform the following procedures:
   a. Turn the key **OFF**. Install the breakout box. Reconnect the electrical harness connector to the processor and AXOD.
   b. At the breakout box, install a jumper wire between Pin 18 and Pin 40.
   c. Perform the "Run Key On/Engine Off Self Test".
   d. If Code 62 or 59 does not appear, remove the breakout box and the jumper wire. Replace the processor and repeat the AXOD Drive Cycle Test for Code 59.
   e. If Code 62 or 59 appears, remove the breakout box and the jumper wire.

Short Test

This portion of the test is used to check the AXOD harness and the 4–3 circuit for shorts.

1. To verify the working order of the AXOD harness, perform the following procedures:
   a. Turn the key **OFF**. Disconnect the AXOD electrical harness connector.
   b. Perform the "Run Key On/Engine Off Self Test".
   c. If Code 59 does not appear, reconnect the AXOD harness connector; test is complete.
   d. If Code 59 does appear, check the 4–3 circuit for a short to ground (next step).

2. To check the 4–3 circuit for a short to ground, perform the following procedures:
   a. Turn the key **OFF**.
   b. Disconnect the AXOD harness connector.

c. From the ECA processor, disconnect the 60 pin connector. Inspect the pins for damage, corrosion, loose wires and/or etc.; repair as necessary.
   d. While leaving the processor disconnected, install the breakout box.
   e. Using a DVOM, place it on the 200k ohm scale. At the breakout box, measure the resistance of Pin 18 between Pin 40 and 60.
   f. If both resistances are under 10k ohms, remove the breakout box, reconnect the AXOD harness and the processor, service the short to ground and repeat the AXOD Drive Cycle Test for Code 59.
   g. If both resistances are over 10k ohms, remove the breakout box, reconnect AXOD harness, replace the processor and repeat the AXOD Drive Cycle Test for Code 59.

CODE 39

This procedure is used in an attempt to generate Code 39.

NOTE: Should Code 59 be present, go directly to Code 59 and perform the series of checks.

Perform the AXOD Drive Cycle Test. If Code 39 appears, go to Electrical System Diagnosis and perform checks on the components. If codes other than 39 appear, service them first. If no codes appear, the test is complete.

CODE 57

This procedure is used in an attempt to generate Code 57.

1. Perform the AXOD Drive Cycle Test. If Code 57 appears, check the NPS harness circuit for continuity (next step). If codes other than 57 appear, service them first. If no codes appear, the test is complete.

2. To check the continuity of the NPS harness circuit, perform the following procedures:
   a. Turn the key **OFF** and wait 10 seconds.
   b. Disconnect the AXOD harness connector.
   c. From the ECA processor, disconnect the 60 pin connector. Inspect the pins for damage, corrosion, loose wires and/or etc.; repair as necessary.
   d. While leaving the processor disconnected, install the breakout box.
   e. Using a DVOM, place it on the 200 ohm scale. Measure the resistance between the AXOD connector (Pin 30) and the breakout box.
   f. If the resistance is over 5 ohms, remove the breakout box, reconnect the components, service the NPS open circuit and repeat the AXOD Drive Cycle Test for Code 57.
   g. If the resistance is under 5 ohms, remove the breakout box and reconnect the components.

CODE 89

This procedure is used in an attempt to generate Code 89.

1. To check the continuity of the VPWR circuit, perform the following procedures:
   a. Turn the key **OFF** and wait 10 seconds.
   b. Disconnect the AXOD harness connector.
   c. From the ECA processor, disconnect the 60 pin connector. Inspect the pins for damage, corrosion, loose wires and/or etc.; repair as necessary.
   d. While leaving the processor disconnected, install the breakout box.
   e. Using a DVOM, place it on the 200 ohm scale. Measure the resistance between the AXOD connector (Pin 37) and the breakout box.
   f. If the resistance is over 5 ohms, remove the breakout box, reconnect the components, service the LUS open circuit and repeat the this test for Code 89.
   g. If the resistance is under 5 ohms, check the LUS circuit continuity (next step).

2. To check the continuity of the LUS circuit, perform the following procedures:

a. Turn the key **OFF**. Install the breakout box.

b. Disconnect the processor and the AXOD harness connector.

c. Using a DVOM, place it on the 200 ohm scale. Measure the resistance between the AXOD harness connector (Pin 53) and the breakout box.

d. If the resistance is over 5 ohms, remove the breakout box, reconnect the components, service the open in the LUS circuit and repeat this test.

e. If the resistance is under 5 ohms, check the LUS circuit for a short to power or ground (next step).

3. To check the LUS circuit for a short to power or ground, perform the following procedures:

a. Turn the key **OFF**. Install the breakout box.

b. Disconnect the processor and the AXOD harness connector.

c. Using a DVOM, place it on the 200k scale. At the breakout box, measure the resistance Pin 53 between Pins 37 and 40.

d. If both resistances are under 10k ohms, remove the breakout box, reconnect the components, service the short in the LUS circuit. Repeat the AXOD Drive Cycle Test for Code 89; if it is still present, replace the processor and repeat the AXOD Drive Cycle Test for Code 89.

e. If both resistances are over 10k ohms, check the total circuit resistance (next step).

4. To check the total circuit resistance, perform the following procedures:

a. Turn the key **OFF**. Install the breakout box.

b. Disconnect the processor and the AXOD harness connector.

c. Using a DVOM, place it on the 200 ohm scale. At the breakout box, measure the resistance Pin 53 and Pin 57.

d. If the resistance is 20–40 ohms, remove the breakout box, replace processor and repeat the AXOD Drive Cycle Test for Code 89.

e. If the resistance is not 20–40 ohms, remove the breakout box and reconnect the processor.

CODE 62

This code is used to check the AXOD harness, the 3–2 and 4–3 circuits for shorts.

1. To verify the working order of the AXOD harness, perform the following procedures:

a. Turn the key **OFF**. Disconnect the AXOD electrical harness connector.

b. Perform the "Run Key On/Engine Off Self Test".

c. If Code 62 does not appear, reconnect the AXOD harness connector; test is complete.

d. If Code 62 does appear, check the 3–2 and 4–3 circuits for a short to ground (next step).

2. To check the 3–2 and the 4–3 circuits for a short to ground, perform the following procedures:

a. Turn the key **OFF**.

b. Disconnect the AXOD harness connector.

c. From the ECA processor, disconnect the 60 pin connector. Inspect the pins for damage, corrosion, loose wires and/or etc.; repair as necessary.

d. While leaving the processor disconnected, install the breakout box.

e. Using a DVOM, place it on the 200k ohm scale. At the breakout box, measure the resistance of Pin 18 between Pin 40 and 60.

f. At the breakout box, measure the resistance of Pin 19 between Pin 40 and 60.

g. If all resistances are under 10k ohms, remove the breakout box, reconnect all components, service the short(s) to ground and repeat the AXOD Drive Cycle Test for Code 62.

h. If all resistances are over 10k ohms, remove the breakout box, reconnect all components, replace the processor and repeat the AXOD Drive Cycle Test for Code 62.

TEMPERATURE TIMED SWITCH (TTS) – 3.8L ONLY

1. To check the TTS harness circuit continuity, perform the following procedures:

a. Turn the key **OFF** and wait 10 seconds.

b. Disconnect the AXOD harness connector.

c. From the ECA processor, disconnect the 60 pin connector. Inspect the pins for damage, corrosion, loose wires and/or etc.; repair as necessary.

d. While leaving the processor disconnected, install the breakout box.

e. Using a DVOM, place it on the 200 ohm scale. Measure the resistance between the AXOD connector (Pin 44) and the breakout box.

f. If the resistance is over 5 ohms, remove the breakout box, reconnect the components, service the TTS open circuit and drive the vehicle to verify that the drive complaint is eliminated.

g. If the resistance is under 5 ohms, check the TTS circuit for a short to the power or ground (next step).

2. To check the TTS harness circuit for a short to power or ground, perform the following procedures:

a. Turn the key **OFF**.

b. Disconnect the AXOD harness connector.

c. Disconnect the processor disconnected and install the breakout box.

d. Using a DVOM, place it on the 200k ohm scale. At the breakout box, measure the resistance between Pin 44 and Pin 37.

e. At the breakout box, measure the resistance between Pin 40 and Pin 44.

f. If all resistances are under 10k ohms, remove the breakout box, reconnect all components, service the TTS circuit's short(s) and drive the vehicle to verify that the drive complaint is eliminated.

g. If all resistances are over 10k ohms, check the processor's operation (next step).

3. To check the processor operation, perform the following procedures:

a. Turn the key **OFF** and install the breakout box.

b. Reconnect the processor and the AXOD harness.

c. Using a jumper wire at the breakout box, connect Pin 44 to Pin 40.

d. Drive the vehicle to verify the drive complaint.

e. If the drive complaint was eliminated, remove the breakout box and the jumper wire.

f. If the drive complaint was not eliminated, remove the breakout box and the jumper wire. Replace the processor.

CODE 67

1. To check the NPS input to processor voltage, perform the following procedures:

a. Turn the key **ON** and the engine **OFF**.

b. From the ECA processor, disconnect the 60 pin connector. Inspect the pins for damage, corrosion, loose wires and/or etc.; repair as necessary.

c. Reconnect the processor and install the breakout box.

d. Using a DVOM, place it on the 20 volt scale. At the breakout box, measure the voltage between Pin 30 and Pin 46.

e. If the voltage over 4 volts, check the A/C input of the neutral drive switch. Using a DVOM on the 20 volt scale, measure the breakout box Pin 10 to ground voltage; the voltage should be greater than 1.0 volt, if not replace the processor.

f. If the voltage is under 4 volts, check the NPS harness circuit for a short to ground (next step).

2. To check the NPS harness circuit for a short to ground,

perform the following procedures:

    a. Turn the key **OFF**.

    b. Disconnect the AXOD harness connector.

    c. Disconnect the processor disconnected and install the breakout box.

    d. Using a DVOM, place it on the 200k ohm scale. At the breakout box, measure the resistance of Pin 30 between Pin 40 and Pin 60.

    e. If both resistances are under 10k ohms, remove the breakout box, reconnect all components, service the NPS circuit's short and repeat the AXOD Drive Cycle Test.

    g. If both resistances are over 10k ohms, check the processor's operation (next step).

3. To check the processor's operation, perform the following procedures:

    a. Turn the key **OFF**.

    b. Install the breakout box and reconnect the processor.

    c. Disconnect the AXOD harness connector.

    d. Perform the "Run Key On/Engine Off Self Test".

    e. If Code 67 is not present, remove the breakout box, reconnect the components.

    f. If Code 67 is present, remove the breakout box, reconnect the components, replace the processor and repeat the AXOD Drive Cycle test for code 67.

Hydraulic Control System

The hydraulic shifting operation is monitored by the EEC-IV system's computer which operates a bypass clutch solenoid within the transaxle to eliminate converter slippage. Signals from the NPS Neutral, 3–2 and 4–3 pressure switches inform the computer of transaxle gear shifts so the computer may control engine operations.

The hydraulic system consists of a main control assembly (valve body), oil pump, overdrive servo, low/intermediate servo, governor and 2 reservoir areas.

Main Control Assembly (Valve Body)

The main control assembly controls the transaxle operation by directing pressurized fluid to the torque converter, band servos, clutches and governor.

Oil Pump

The oil pump, located in the control valve/pump assembly, is a variable capacity vane/rotor pump which provides pressurized fluid (proportional to demand) to operate, lubricate and cool the transaxle.

Low/Intermediate Servo

The low/intermediate servo applies the low/intermediate band in the manual low, 1st and 2nd gears.

Overdrive Servo

The overdrive servo applies the overdrive band in the 4th gear.

Governor

The governor, driven by a differential assembly gear, provides a road speed signal to the hydraulic control for shift control.

Reservoirs

Upper and lower reservoirs, dependent upon fluid temperature, are used to control the oil level. As fluid temperature rises in the lower sump, a thermostatic element closes, retaining fluid in the upper reservoir.

Diagnosis Tests

CONTROL PRESSURE TEST

1. Firmly set the parking brake and block the drive wheels.
2. Remove the pressure line tap plug from the transaxle and install the pressure gauge.
3. Start the engine, move the shift lever through the various selector positions and check the fluid pressures; refer to the control pressure chart.
4. If the fluid pressures are not within specifications, proceed to the air pressure test and/or service the main control system.

AIR PRESSURE TEST

Because of inoperative bands or clutches, a no drive condition can exist, even if the fluid pressures are correct. By substituting air pressure for fluid pressure, an erratic shift condition location can be determined.

NOTE: An inoperative forward clutch, low/intermediate one-way or low intermediate band may cause a NO DRIVE condition when the shift lever is positioned in

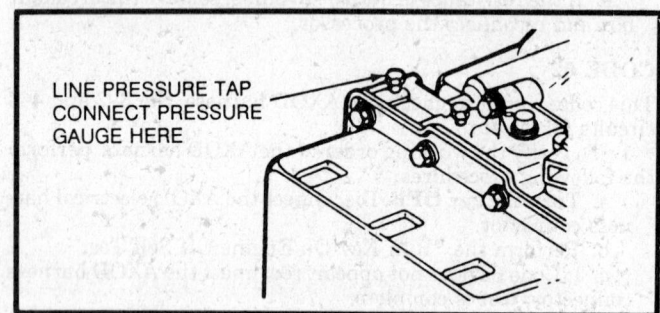

LINE PRESSURE TAP
CONNECT PRESSURE
GAUGE HERE

Location of the transaxle line pressure tap

CONTROL PRESSURE TEST

Engine	Range	Idle		Stall (WOT)	
		psi	kPa	psi	kPa
2.5L and 3.0L	P, N	81–95	558–655	—	—
	R	93–152	641–1048	242–279	1669–1924
	OD, D	81–95	558–655	158–183	1089–1262
	L	112–169	772–1165	158–183	1089–1262
3.8L	P, N	80–91	551–627	—	—
	R	93–152	641–1048	248–289	1709–1992
	OD, D	80–91	551–627	182–213	1254–1468
	L	112–169	772–1165	158–183	1089–1261

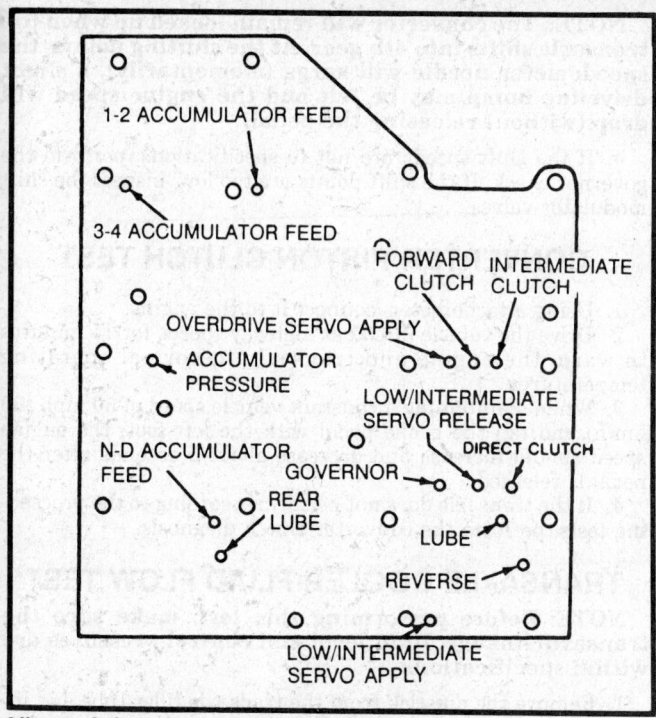

View of the air pressure test plate

OD, D or 1st gears. An inoperative direct clutch or direct one-way clutch may cause a NO COAST condition in 1st gear. A malfunctioning reverse clutch, forward clutch or low/intermediate one-way clutch may cause a NO DRIVE condition in reverse gear.

1. Raise and support the vehicle on jackstands.
2. Drain the fluid from the transaxle and remove the oil pan.
3. Remove the main control cover, the oil pump and the main control assembly.
4. Using the air pressure test plate and the chain cover gasket, install it to the main control assembly.
5. Using air pressure, introduce it to the various test plate passages as follows:

FORWARD CLUTCH

When applying air pressure to the forward clutch test port, a dull thud should be heard or movement from the piston be felt. If a hissing sound is noticed, the clutch seal(s) is leaking.

GOVERNOR

When applying air pressure to the governor test port, listen for a whistling or a sharp clicking noise; the noise indicates proper operation.

OVERDRIVE SERVO

When applying air pressure to the overdrive servo test port, the band should tighten around the overdrive drum. Due to the servo release spring's cushioning effect, band application may not be heard or felt. The servo should not leak (while holding pressure) and a dull thud (piston returning to original position) should be heard when the pressure is removed.

DIRECT CLUTCH

When applying air pressure to the direct clutch test port, a dull thud should be heard or movement of the piston should be felt. If hissing is noticed, the clutch seal(s) is leaking.

INTERMEDIATE CLUTCH

When applying air pressure to the intermediate clutch test port,

a dull thud should be heard or movement of the piston should be felt. If hissing is noticed, the clutch seal(s) is leaking.

LOW/INTERMEDIATE SERVO

When applying air pressure to the low/intermediate servo apply test port, the band should tighten around the rear planetary gearset's sun gear. Due to the servo release spring's cushioning effect, band application may not be heard or felt. The servo should not leak (while holding pressure) and a dull thud (piston returning to original position) should be heard when the pressure is removed.

While applying air pressure to the low/intermediate servo apply test port, introduce air pressure to the low/intermediate release test port; the band should loosen, a dull thud should be heard and the piston move to the release position. Remove air pressure to the apply test port, the release test port should hold air pressure without leakage. The servo requires service if leakage occurs or the piston fails to move.

LUBE AND REAR LUBE

When applying air pressure to the lube and rear lube test ports, air should move freely through the ports. If a blockage occurs, remove the test plate and check for obstructions or damage.

1-2, 3-4 AND N-D ACCUMULATORS

When applying air pressure to each accumulator feed test port, the accumulator should apply, holding air pressure. Due to the accumulator release spring's cushioning effect, accumulator application may not be heard or felt. The accumulator should not leak (while holding pressure) and a dull thud (accumulator returning to original position) should be heard when the pressure is removed.

STALL SPEED TEST

The stall test is used to test the converter's one-way clutch, forward clutch, low one-way clutch, reverse clutch, reverse clutch, low/intermediate band and engine performance.

NOTE: Be sure the engine and transaxle are at normal operating temperatures before performing this test.

1. Using a tachometer, connect it to the engine.
2. Block the drive wheels and firmly apply the parking brake. While performing the test, firmly apply the service brakes.

STALL SPEED HIGH (SLIP)

Range	Possible Source
OD, D, 1	Forward clutch Low/intermediate one-way clutch Low/intermediate band or servo
R	Forward clutch Low/intermediate one-way clutch Reverse clutch

— CAUTION —

Do not maintain wide open throttle in any gear range for more than a few seconds.

3. Start the engine and place the shift selector in a gear range (one at a time). Press the accelerator to the floor (wide open throttle) and record the engine speed reached in each range; the speeds should be within 1950–2275 rpm.

NOTE: After testing a gear range, place the shift selector in N and run the engine for 15 seconds to allow the converter to cool before testing the next range.

CAUTION

If the engine speed exceeds 2275 rpm, release the accelerator immediately; clutch or band slippage is indicated.

If the stall speeds are too low, check the engine tune-up. If the stall speeds are too high refer to the Stall Speed Diagnosis chart for possible source of the problem. If the engine is OK, remove the torque converter and check the one-way clutch for slippage.

SHIFT POINT TEST

Road Test

1. Drive the vehicle until the engine and transaxle are at normal operating temperatures.
2. Shift the transaxle to **OD** range. Apply minimum throttle pressure and note the upshift speeds and speed which the converter clutch applies.
3. Stop the vehicle and move the shift selector into **D**. Apply minimum throttle pressure and note the upshift speeds and speed which the converter clutch applies; the transaxle should make all upshifts (except 3–4 and the converter clutch apply should occur above 27 mph (46 km/h).
4. Fully depress the accelerator to wide open throttle. Depending upon vehicle speed, the transaxle should shift from 3rd-to-2nd or 3rd-to-1st and the converter clutch should release.

NOTE: If the shift lever is placed in the OD range and the accelerator is in the wide open throttle position, a 4th-to-3rd downshift can be obtained regardless of the vehicle speed.

5. When the vehicle speed is above 30 mph (48 km/h), move the shift selector from **D** to **L** and release the accelerator; the transaxle should immediately downshift to **2nd** gear. When the vehicle speed drops below 20 mph, the transaxle should downshift to **1st** gear.
6. If the transaxle does not perform according to the proceeding tests, refer to governor pressure and shift control valve diagnosis.

In-Shop Test

This test is designed to check the governor circuits, the shift delay pressures and the throttle boost.

1. Raise and support the front of the vehicle by placing supports under the suspension so the wheel are off the floor.

CAUTION

Do not exceed the speedometer reading of 60 mph (97 km/h) for the tire speed is actually twice the speedometer reading. Do not allow the suspension to hang free; damage to the velocity seals and joints may occur and heavy vibrations will be emitted.

---

2. Start the engine, place the shift lever in **OD** and apply minimum throttle pressure.
3. Note the shift speeds and the speed when the converter locks up; 1-2, 2-3, converter lockup and 3-4.

ON CAR SERVICES

Adjustments

THROTTLE VALVE CABLE

Normally, the throttle valve (T.V.) cable does not require adjustment. Only, if the main control assembly, the T.V. cable, the T.V. cable engine mounting bracket, the throttle control lever link/lever assembly, the throttle body tand/or transaxle assembly

NOTE: The converter will remain locked up when the transaxle shifts into 4th gear. At the shifting points, the speedometer needle will surge (momentarily), a slight driveline bump may be felt and the engine speed will drop (without releasing the pedal).

4. If the shift speeds are not to specifications, perform the governor check. If the shift points are too low, inspect the shift modulator valves.

CONVERTER PISTON CLUTCH TEST

1. Using a tachometer, connect it to the engine.
2. Drive the vehicle in **OD** at highway speeds for 15 minutes to warm the engine and transaxle to normal operating temperatures.
3. While maintaining a constant vehicle speed of 50 mph (80 km/h) and tap the brake pedal with the left foot; the engine speed should increase and decrease about 5 seconds after the pedal is released.
4. If the transaxle does not perform according to the proceeding tests, perform the converter clutch diagnosis.

TRANSAXLE COOLER FLUID FLOW TEST

NOTE: Before performing this test, make sure the transaxle linkage, fluid level and control pressures are within specifications.

1. Remove the dipstick from the transaxle filler tube and insert a funnel.
2. Raise and support the vehicle in a level position.
3. Remove the fluid cooler tube from the lower (return) transaxle fitting.
4. Using a hose, connect it to the fluid cooler tube and insert the other end into the funnel.
5. Firmly set the parking brake. Position the transaxle in **N**, start the engine and adjust the idle to 1000 rpm. Observe the fluid flowing into the funnel; it should be liberal and solid.
6. If the flow is not liberal, stop the engine and install the lower tube to the transaxle. Remove the upper transaxle tube, connect it to the hose and repeat the flow test.
7. If the flow is still not liberal, inspect the fluid pump for low capacity, the main circuit system for leakage and the converter drain valve or regulator valve for a sticking condition.

Converter Clutch Operation and Diagnosis

TORQUE CONVERTER CLUTCH

The torque converter clutch is a one-way clutch located within the torque converter's stator. It operates in conjunction with the piston plate clutch/damper assembly, when the EEC-IV system energizes the bypass clutch solenoid, and is designed to hold the stator stationary in the **LOCK-UP** mode. The result is improved fuel economy by eliminating converter clutch slippage.

have been replaced, should adjustment be necessary.

1. Connect the T.V. cable's eye to the transaxle throttle control lever link and the cable boot to the chain cover.
2. With the T.V. cable attached to the engine bracket, be sure the threaded shank is fully retracted. Using the index fingers, pull the spring rest upward and wiggle the threaded shank top, while pressing the shank through the spring with the thumbs.
3. Connect the T.V. cable end to the throttle body.

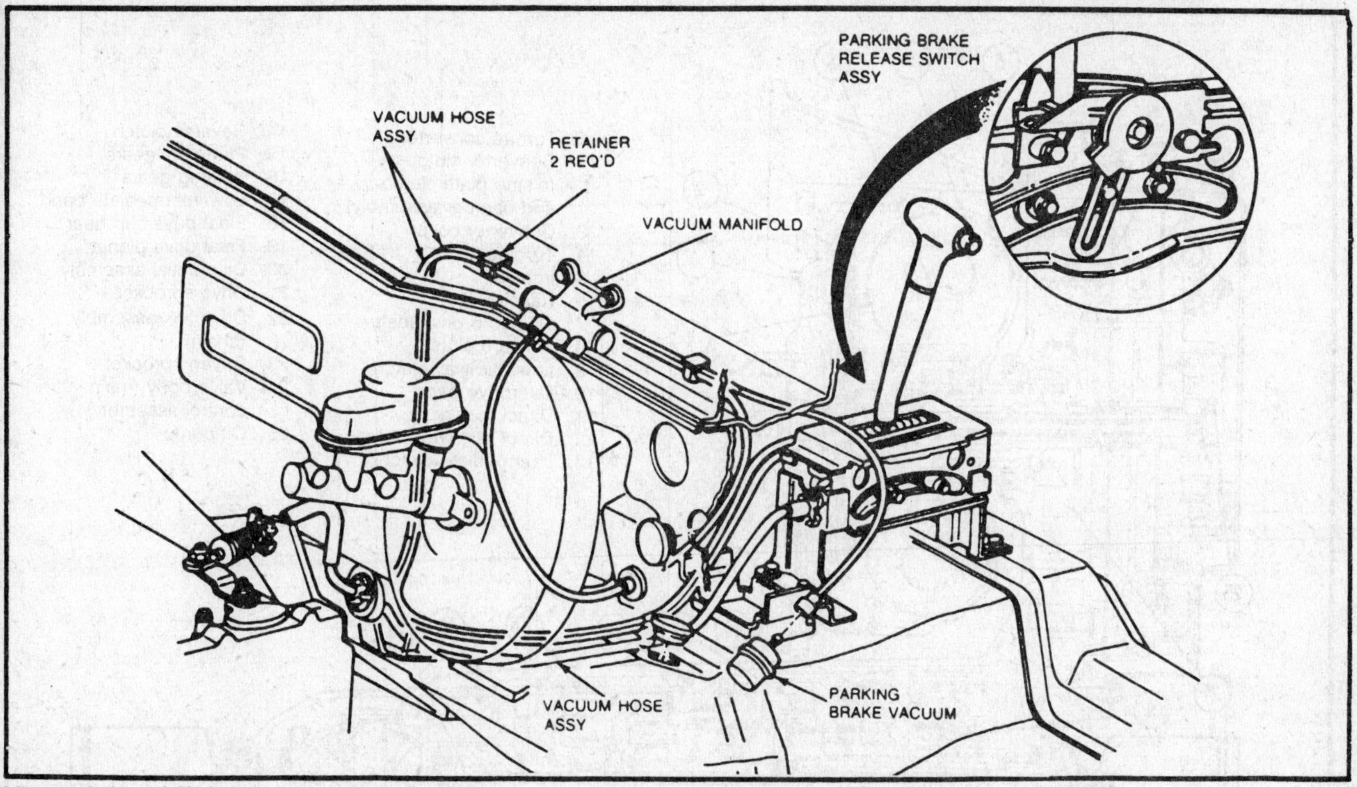

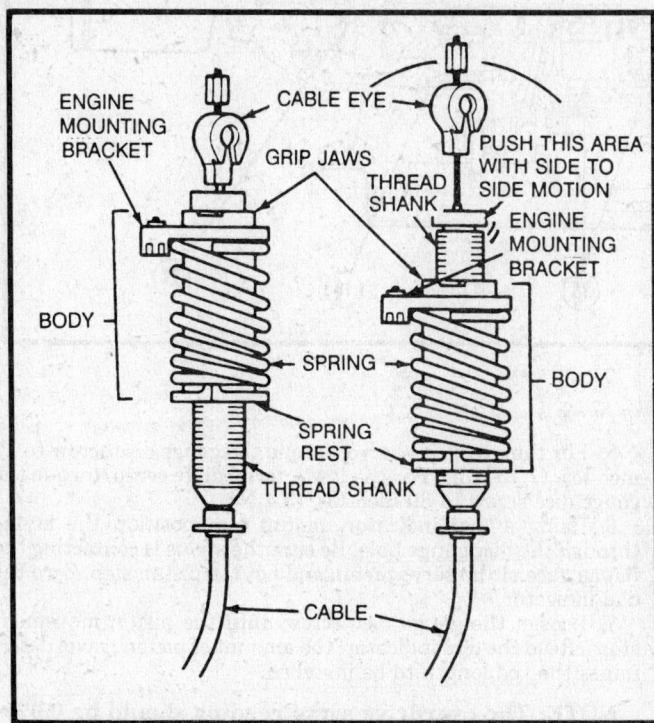

View of the shift lever control and cable

View of the throttle valve (T.V.) cable

4. Rotate the throttle lever to the wide open throttle (WOT) position and release it.

NOTE: The threaded shank must move or ratchet from the grip jaws. If movement is not noticed, inspect the system for broken or disconnected parts.

MANUAL LINKAGE

TAURUS AND SABLE

The following procedure is used for both floor and column mounted shifters.

1. Move the shift selector into the **OD** position against the rear stop.

NOTE: While the linkage is being adjusted, the shift lever must be held in the rearward position.

2. Loosen the manual lever-to-control cable retaining nut and move the lever to the **OD** position (2nd detent from the most rearward position).

3. Tighten the manual lever-to-control cable nut to 10–15 ft. lbs. (13.5–20 Nm).

4. Check the operation in each shift lever position; ensure that the park/neutral switch is functioning properly.

CONTINENTAL

This vehicle is equipped with a column shift only.

1. From the transaxle lever's pivot ball, remove the cable plastic terminal.

2. At the cable trunnion, mounted on the retaining bracket, loosen the adjusting bolt and free the cable in the trunnion.

3. From the passenger's compartment, move the shift selector into the **OD** position. Using an 8 lb. weight, suspend it from the shift lever.

4. At the transaxle, rotate the shift lever clockwise to the **L** position and counterclockwise to the **OD** position.

5. Install the shift cable plastic terminal onto the transaxle lever's pivot ball, from the flat side of the terminal.

6. Torque the trunnion's cable adjustment screw to 11–14 ft. lbs. (14–20 Nm).

7. Check the operation in each shift lever position; ensure that the park/neutral switch is functioning properly.

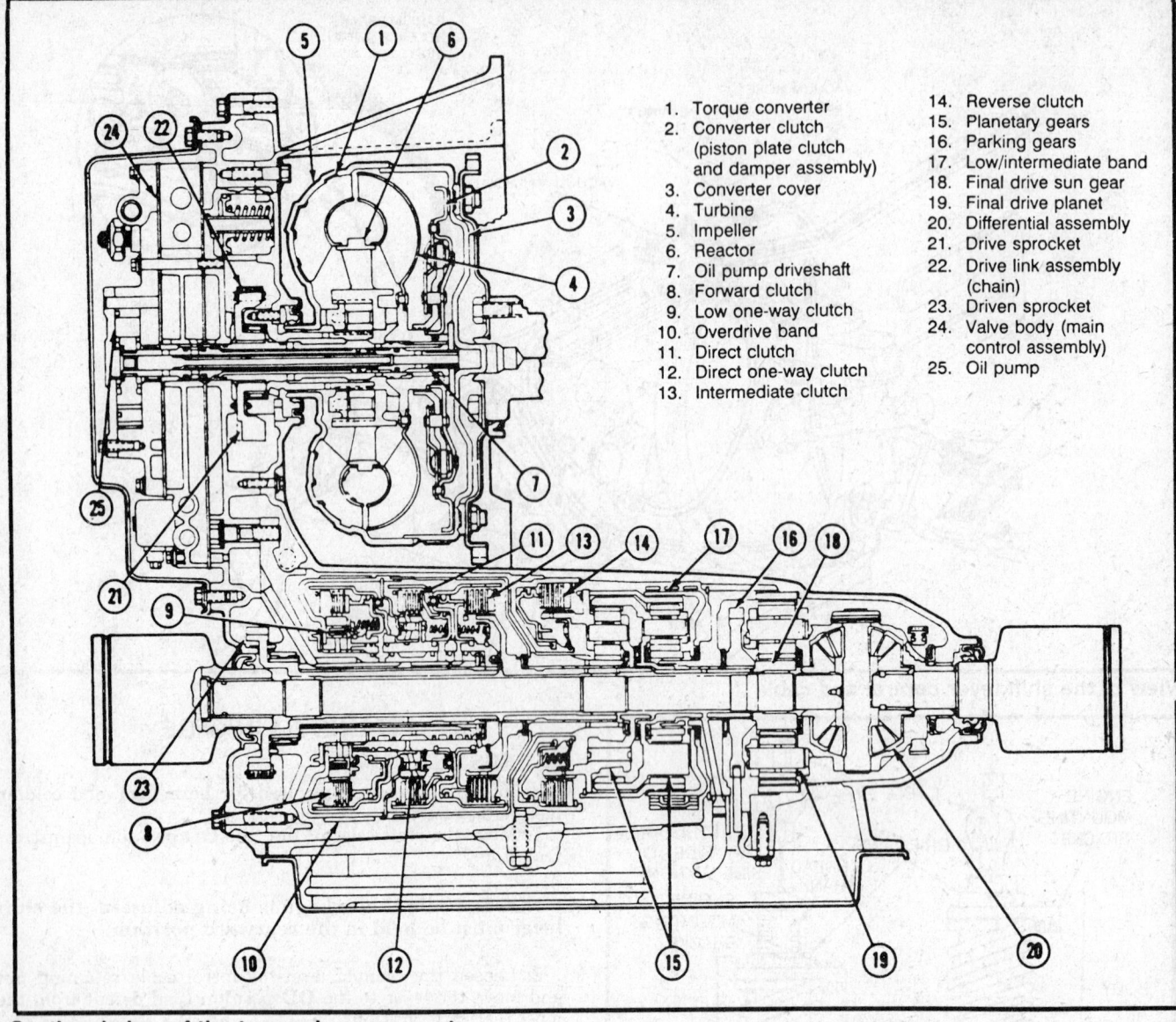

1. Torque converter
2. Converter clutch (piston plate clutch and damper assembly)
3. Converter cover
4. Turbine
5. Impeller
6. Reactor
7. Oil pump driveshaft
8. Forward clutch
9. Low one-way clutch
10. Overdrive band
11. Direct clutch
12. Direct one-way clutch
13. Intermediate clutch
14. Reverse clutch
15. Planetary gears
16. Parking gears
17. Low/intermediate band
18. Final drive sun gear
19. Final drive planet
20. Differential assembly
21. Drive sprocket
22. Drive link assembly (chain)
23. Driven sprocket
24. Valve body (main control assembly)
25. Oil pump

Sectional view of the transaxle components

LOW/INTERMEDIATE AND OVERDRIVE BANDS

The bands do not require adjustment but when the transaxle has been overhauled, the servo travel check must be performed and the servo piston rod(s) possibly be replaced.

1. If the servo covers are installed, remove the servo cover, the piston and rod.

2. Using the spring from the overdrive servo rod tool, low/intermediate servo rod tool or equivalent, install it in the case bore.

3. Install the servo piston and rod in the case bore.

NOTE: On the low/intermediate servo, the piston must be installed without the seal.

4. Using the overdrive servo rod tool, low/intermediate servo rod tool or equivalent, install it in the case bore. Using the servo cover bolts, torque the tool(s)-to-case bore to 7-9 ft. lbs. (9-12 Nm).

5. For the overdrive servo, torque the gauge disc screw to 10 inch lbs. (1.13 Nm). For the low/intermediate servo, torque the gauge disc screw to 30 inch lbs. (3.4 Nm).

6. Using a dial indicator, mount and position the stylus through the disc gauge hole. Be sure the stylus is contacting the flat surface of the servo piston and not the piston step. Zero the dial indicator.

7. Loosen the gauge disc screw until the piston movement stops. Read the dial indicator; the amount of piston travel determines the rod length to be installed.

NOTE: The overdrive servo reading should be 0.070-0.149 in. (1.8-3.8mm); the low/intermediate servo reading should be 0.216-0.255 in. (5.5-6.5mm). If a new low/intermediate band has been installed, the reading should be 0.196-0.236 in. (5-6mm).

8. Using the measurement acquired, select and install a new piston rod. Recheck the piston movement to verify the amount of piston travel.

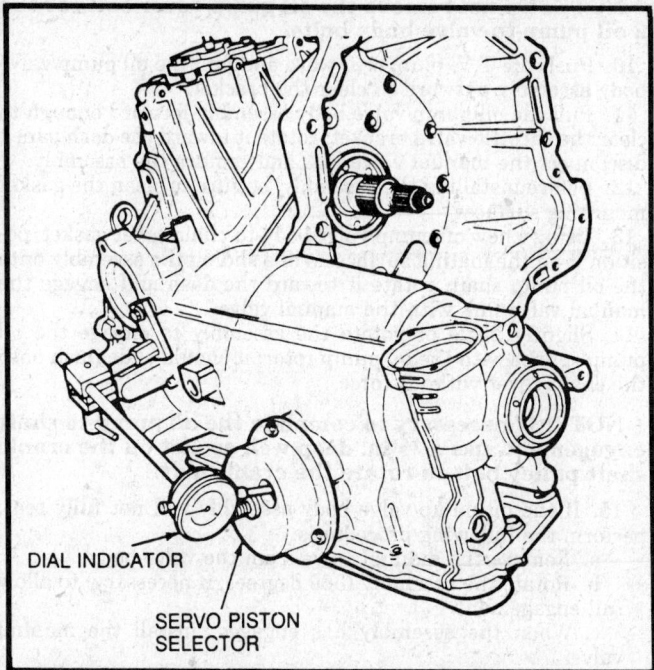

Using a dial indicator to check the servo piston movement

9. On the low/intermediate servo piston, install the seal(s).
10. Install the servo pistons and springs; be sure they are fully seated.
11. Using new gaskets, install the servo-to-case bore covers and torque the bolts to 7–9 ft. lbs. (9–12 Nm).

NOTE: When installing the low/intermediate servo cover, be sure the tab aligns with the case port. Tighten the bolts 2–3 turns at a time to prevent cocking the case cover.

Services

FLUID CHANGES

Under normal vehicle usage, the transaxle necessitates partial drain and refill procedures. Only, when operated under severe/continuous conditions or part replacement, should the transaxle be removed from service, totally drained, cleaned and refilled; at this time, the converter, cooler and cooler lines should be throughly flushed.

1. Raise and support the vehicle safely.
2. Place a drain pan under the transaxle.
3. Loosen the oil pump/valve body cover bolts and the lower pan bolts and drain the fluid into the drain pan; if necessary, use a rubber mallet to bump the cover or pan loose from the transaxle.
4. When the fluid has drained from the transaxle (except from the lower pan), remove the remaining pan bolts (working from the right side), allow the pan to drop and drain slowly. Remove the oil pump/valve body cover.
5. Clean the pan and cover, discard the gasket.
6. Using new gaskets and sealant (if necessary), install the pan and cover-to-case bolts and torque to 10–12 ft. lbs. (14–16 Nm).
7. Using the correct lubricant, refill the transaxle to the correct dipstick Level; do not overfill or foaming will occur.

8. Operate the transaxle to distribute fluid to the upper reservoir and recheck/refill to dipstick levels.

OIL PAN

Removal and Installation

1. Raise and support the vehicle safely.
2. Place a drain pan under the transaxle.
3. Loosen the lower pan bolts and drain the fluid into the drain pan; if necessary, use a rubber mallet to bump the pan loose from the transaxle.
4. When the fluid has drained from the transaxle, remove the remaining pan bolts (working from the right side), allow the pan to drop and drain slowly.
5. Clean the pan and discard the gasket.
6. Using new gaskets and sealant (if necessary), install the pan-to-case bolts and torque to 10–12 ft. lbs. (14–16 Nm).
7. Using the correct lubricant, refill the transaxle to the correct dipstick level; do not overfill, for foaming will occur.
8. Operate the transaxle to distribute fluid to the upper reservoir and recheck/refill to dipstick levels.

SIDE COVER

Removal and Installation

The side cover is located on the left-side of the transaxle and is a secondary reservoir.
1. Disconnect the battery cables, the negative cable first.
2. Remove the battery, the battery tray and the air cleaner.
3. Secure the necessary hoses, vacuum lines and wiring away from the side case.
4. If necessary, raise and support the vehicle safely.
5. Place an oil catch pan under the side cover.
6. Loosen the side cover bolts and drain the fluid. After the fluid has drained, remove the cover and gasket; if necessary, use a rubber mallet to bump the cover loose from the transaxle.
7. Remove the side cover-to-case bolts and the cover.
8. Clean the cover and discard the gasket.
9. Using new gaskets and sealant (if necessary), install the cover-to-case bolts and torque to 10–12 ft. lbs. (14–16 Nm).
10. Using the correct lubricant, refill the transaxle to the correct dipstick; do not overfill, for foaming will occur.

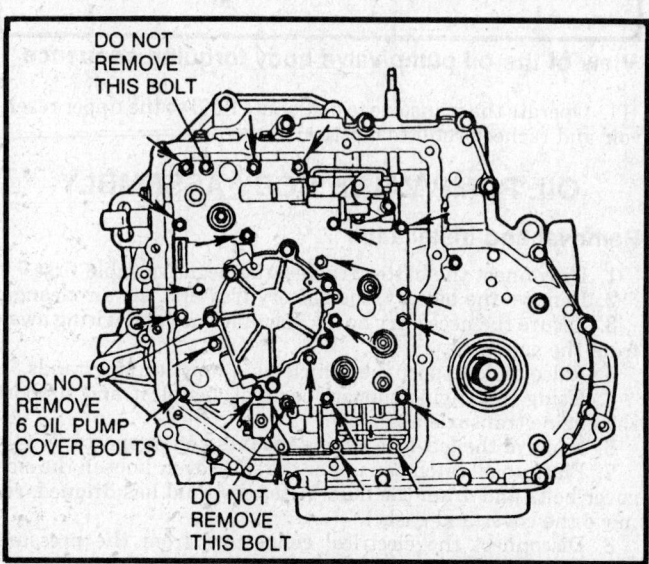

View of the oil pump/valve body assembly-to-transaxle bolts. Remove only the bolts indicated

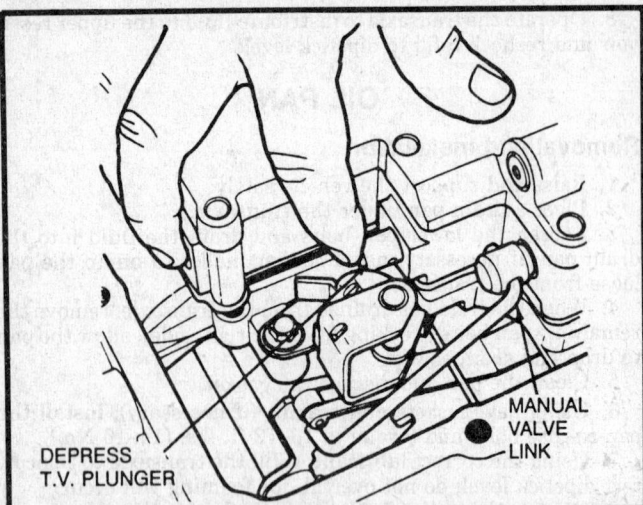

Separating the oil pump/valve body assembly from the manual valve link

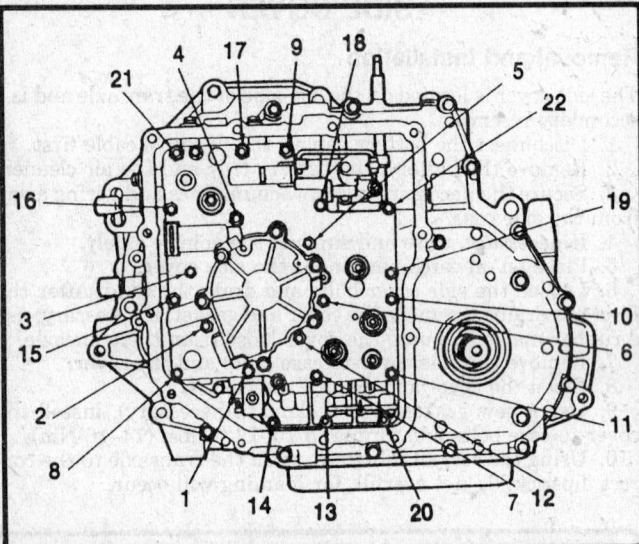

View of the oil pump/valve body torquing sequence

11. Operate the transaxle to distribute fluid to the upper reservoir and recheck/refill to dipstick levels.

OIL PUMP/VALVE BODY ASSEMBLY

Removal and Installation

1. Disconnect the battery cables, the negative cable first.
2. Remove the battery, the battery tray and the air cleaner.
3. Secure the necessary hoses, vacuum lines and wiring away from the side case.
4. Raise and support the vehicle on a hoist or jackstands.
5. Using the engine support bar tool, install it and support the engine/transaxle assembly.
6. Remove the left-side engine mounts and supports.
7. Place an oil catch pan under the side cover. Loosen the side cover bolts and drain the fluid. After the fluid has drained, remove the cover and gasket.
8. Disconnect the electrical connectors from the pressure switches and the solenoid.
9. Remove the oil pump/valve body assembly-to-transaxle bolts.

NOTE: Do not remove the oil pump cover bolts or the 2 oil pump-to-valve body bolts.

10. Push the T.V. plunger inward and pull the oil pump/valve body assembly outward to clear the bracket.
11. Pull the oil pump/valve body assembly forward enough to clear the throttle valve bracket, rotate it toward the dash panel, disconnect the manual valve link and remove the assembly.
12. Before installing the assembly, be sure to clean the gasket mounting surfaces.
13. Using a new oil pump/valve body-to-chain cover gasket, position it on the mating surface. While sliding the assembly onto the oil pump shaft, rotate it toward the dash and engage the manual valve link with the manual valve.
14. Slightly jiggle or rotate the assembly to engage the oil pump splines with the oil pump rotor; it should slide flush onto the chain cover without force.

NOTE: If necessary to complete the oil pump-to-shaft engagement, use a 7/8 in. deep well socket on the crankshaft pulley bolt to rotate the crankshaft.

15. If the oil pump/valve body assembly will not fully seat, perform the following procedures:
    a. Remove the manual valve from the valve body.
    b. Rotate the assembly (360 degrees, if necessary) to allow full engagement.
    c. When the assembly has engaged, install the manual valve.
16. If the assembly-to-chain cover bolt holes do not align, use the valve body guide pin tool or equivalent align the them; do not use the retaining bolts to perform alignment.
17. Install the oil pump/valve body assembly-to-chain cover bolts and torque them to 7–9 ft. lbs. (9–12 Nm), using the specified torquing sequence.
18. Connect the electrical connectors to the pressure switches and the solenoid.
19. Using a new side cover gasket and sealant (if necessary), install the side cover and torque the bolts to 10–12 ft. lbs. (14–16 Nm).
20. Install the left-side engine mounts and supports, remove the engine/transaxle assembly support bar and lower the vehicle to the ground.
21. Reposition the hoses, vacuum lines and wiring. Install the air cleaner, the battery tray and the battery. Reconnect the battery cables.
22. Using the correct fluid, fill the transaxle to the specified level.
23. Start the engine, move the shift selector through all ranges and check for oil leaks around the side cover.

LOW/INTERMEDIATE AND OVERDRIVE SERVO ASSEMBLIES

The servo assemblies, located on the rear side of the transaxle assembly, may be removed easily, without removing oil pans.

Removal and Installation

1. Remove the servo assembly-to-transaxle bolts and the servo assembly.
2. Check the servo body's for cracks, the piston bore for scores and the servo spring(s) for distortion.
3. Check the fluid passages for obstructions.
4. Check the band ends for cracks and the band lining for excessive wear and/or bond to the metal band. Check the band and struts for distortion.
5. Install new seals and lubricate them with petroleum jelly.
6. and the assembly into the case. Torque the servo cover screws to 7–9 ft. lbs. (9–12 Nm).

GOVERNOR

Removal and Installation

The governor is located on the top right-side of the lower case.

1. Remove the governor cover-to-transaxle bolts, the cover and seal (discard it).
2. Remove the governor, speedometer drive gear assembly and bearing (located on top of the speedometer gear) from the case.
3. Check the governor shaft seal for cracks, scoring and/or cuts.

4. Check the balance weight retaining pin for wear and the spring for distortion, damage or misalignment.
5. Check the pressure balls for scoring and free movement.
6. Check the governor drive, the driven gear and the speedometer drive gear for broken, chipped or worn teeth; replace, if necessary.
7. Using a new seal, install it onto the governor cover.
8. Position the governor assembly in the case bore, align the driven gear with the speedometer gear teeth and seat the assembly in the bore.
9. Torque the governor cover-to-case bolts to 7–9 ft. lbs. (9–12 Nm).

REMOVAL AND INSTALLATION

TRANSAXLE REMOVAL

1. Raise and support the vehicle safely. Raise the hood.
2. Using fender covers, place them on the fenders. Disconnect the negative battery cable.
3. Remove the air cleaner, the hoses and tubes. Remove the shift cable/bracket assembly-to-transaxle bolts.

NOTE: It may be necessary to place a small pry bar in the bracket slot to keep it from moving.

4. Disconnect the electrical connectors from the neutral safety switch and bulkhead connector.
5. To disconnect the throttle valve cable, perform the following procedures:
   a. Pull the cable upward and unsnap it from the throttle body lever.
   b. Remove the throttle valve cable-to-transaxle bolt, carefully lift the cable and slide it from the T.V. link.

NOTE: Be careful not to pull the cable too hard, for the internal T.V. bracket may bend.

6. From the left engine support strut, remove the nut and bolt. From the top to the transaxle, remove the torque converter housing-to-engine bolts.
7. Using an engine lifting bracket tool or equivalent and a bolt, attach it to the left-rear cylinder head; the engine lifting eye should still be connected to the front right cylinder head.
8. Using the engine support bar tool or equivalent, position it over the rocker arm covers and attach the bar chains to the lifting brackets.

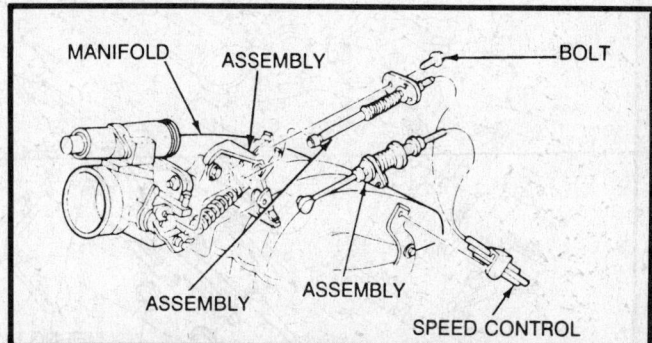
Exploded view of the accelerator cable and T.V. cable—3.8L engine

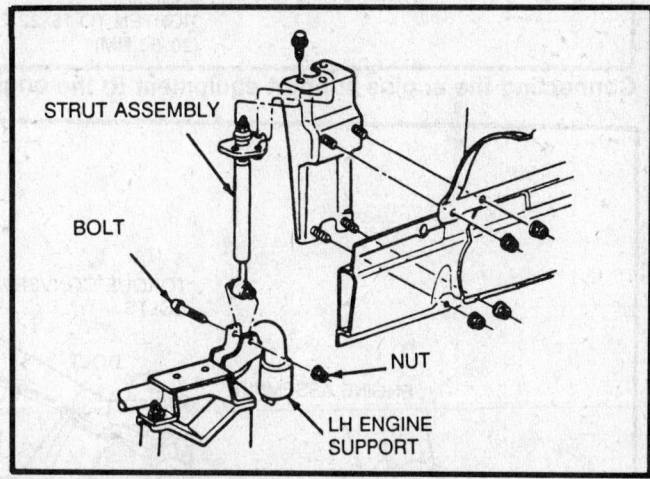
Removing the nut/bolt from the left engine support strut—3.0L engine only

NOTE: When using the 2 support points, the engine assembly will hang slightly lower at the rear (transaxle attached) or slightly lower at the front (transaxle removed). To eliminate the forward tilt, attach the left support bar chain to the No. 4 exhaust runner stud; to eliminate the rearward tilt, attach the right support bar chain between No. 2 and No. 3 exhaust manifold runners. At the front attaching point, the chain hook must face forward. Do not run the chain across the throttle cable or T.V. mechanism, for damage may occur to them.

9. Raise and support the vehicle so the wheels are off the ground. Remove both front wheels.
10. Disconnect the tie rod end from each steering knuckle. Re-

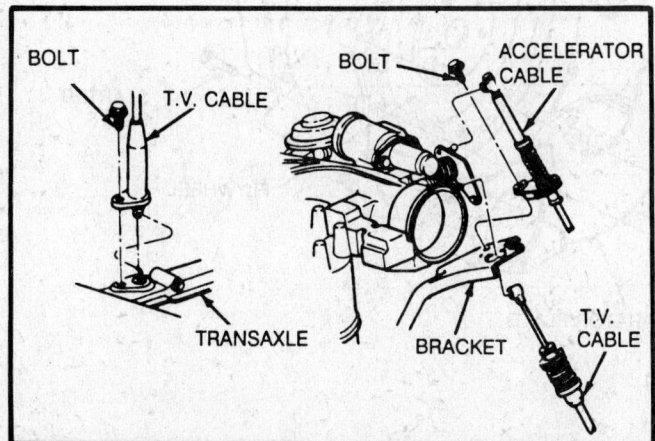
Disconnecting the throttle valve cable from the transaxle and throttle lever—3.0L engine

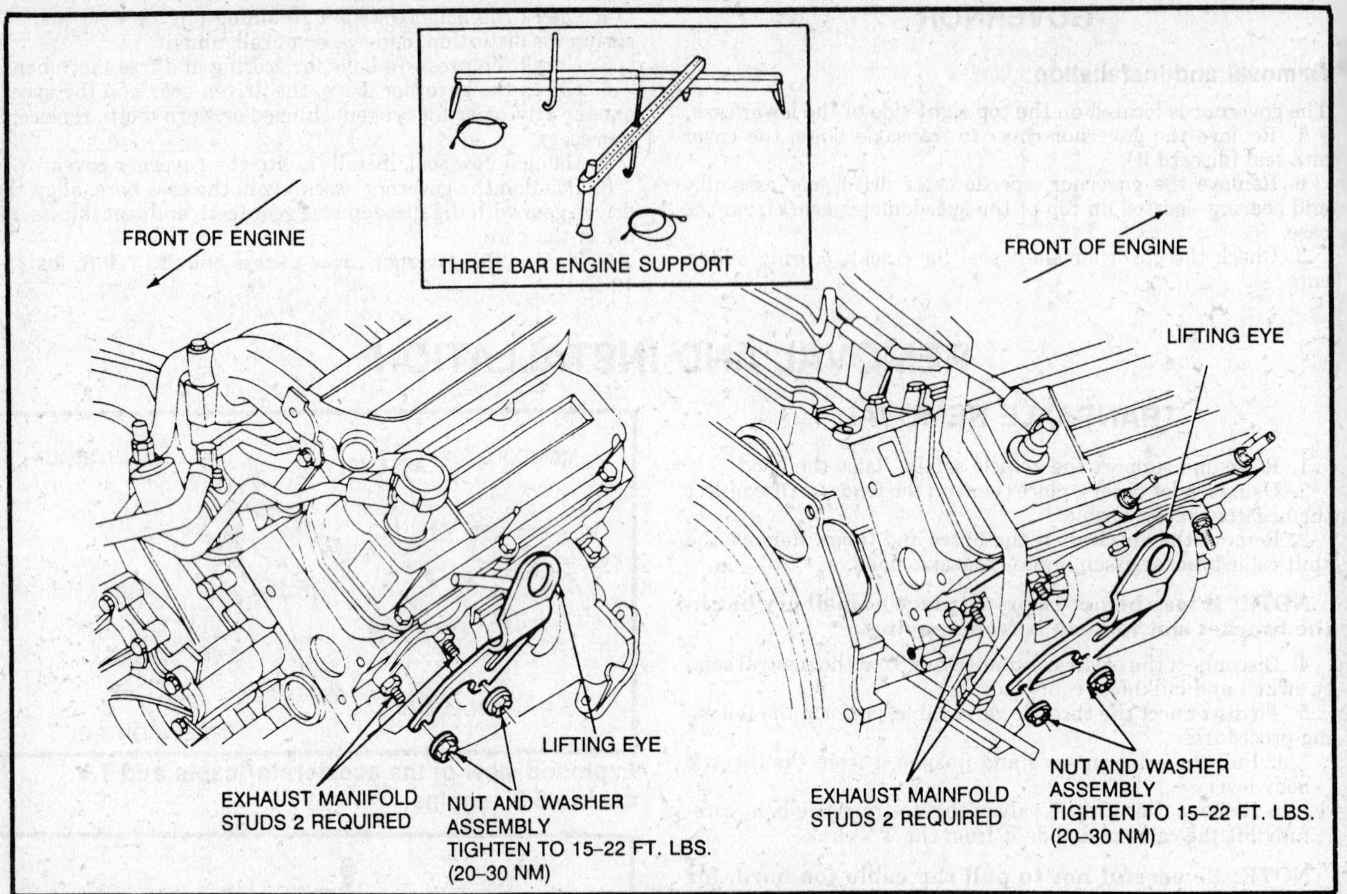

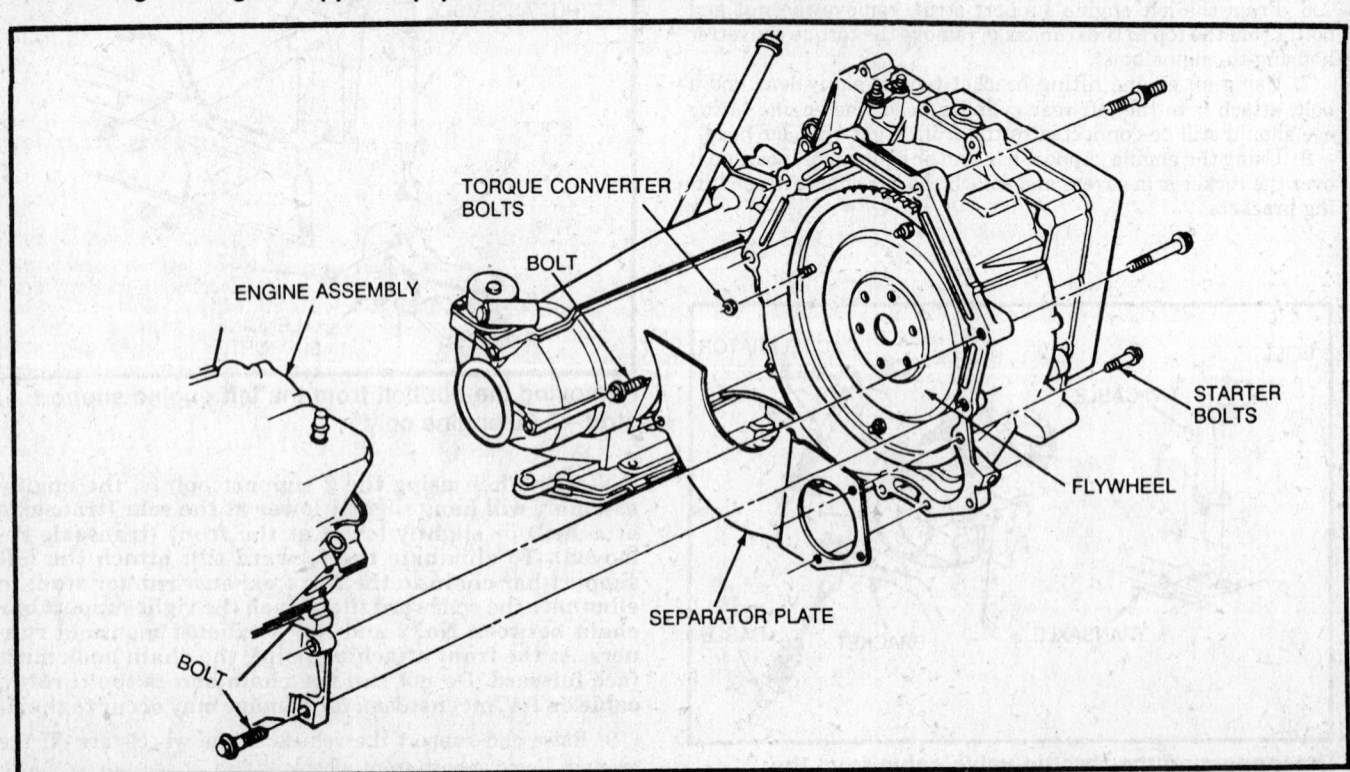

THREE BAR ENGINE SUPPORT

FRONT OF ENGINE

FRONT OF ENGINE

LIFTING EYE

LIFTING EYE

EXHAUST MANIFOLD
STUDS 2 REQUIRED

NUT AND WASHER
ASSEMBLY
TIGHTEN TO 15–22 FT. LBS.
(20–30 NM)

EXHAUST MAINFOLD
STUDS 2 REQUIRED

NUT AND WASHER
ASSEMBLY
TIGHTEN TO 15–22 FT. LBS.
(20–30 NM)

Connecting the engine support equipment to the engine—3.8L engine

TORQUE CONVERTER
BOLTS

BOLT

ENGINE ASSEMBLY

STARTER
BOLTS

FLYWHEEL

SEPARATOR PLATE

BOLT

Separating the transaxle and teparator plate from the engine

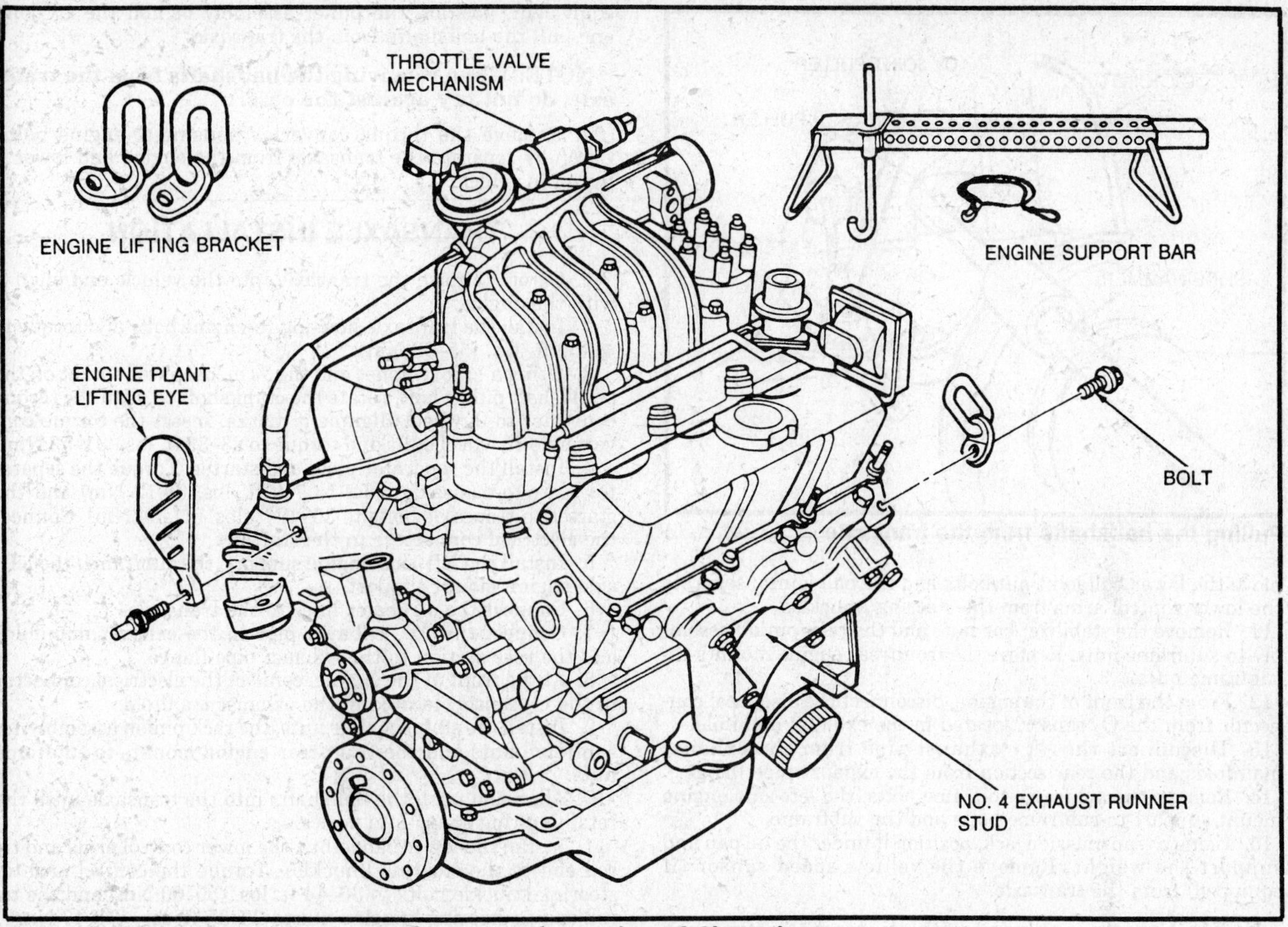

ENGINE LIFTING BRACKET

THROTTLE VALVE MECHANISM

ENGINE SUPPORT BAR

ENGINE PLANT LIFTING EYE

BOLT

NO. 4 EXHAUST RUNNER STUD

Connecting the engine support equipment to the engine—3.0L engine

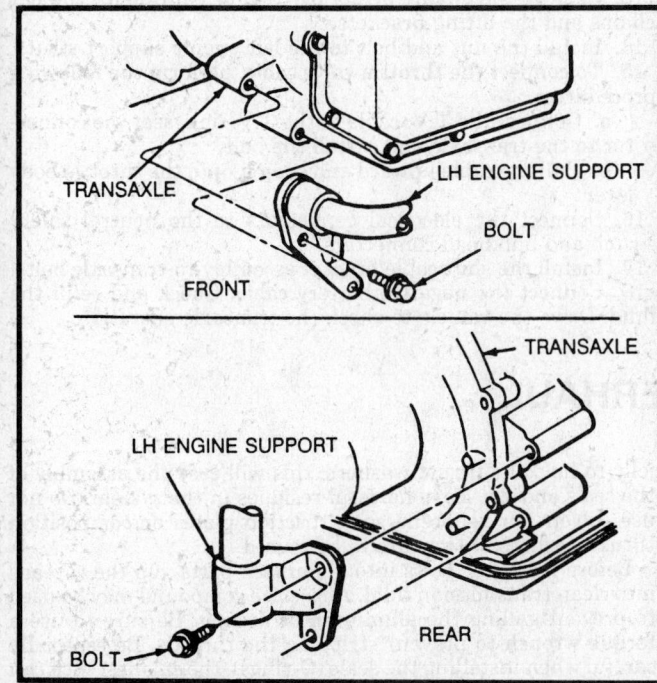

TRANSAXLE

LH ENGINE SUPPORT

BOLT

FRONT

TRANSAXLE

LH ENGINE SUPPORT

BOLT

REAR

Exploded view of the engine supports

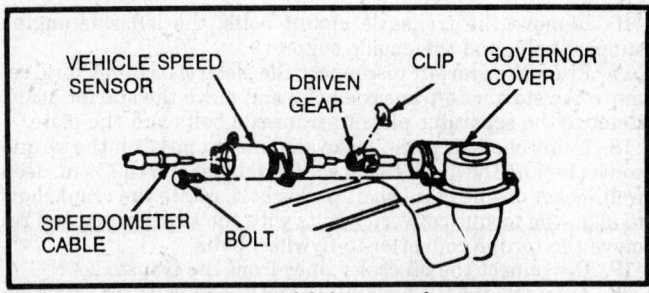

VEHICLE SPEED SENSOR

DRIVEN GEAR

CLIP

GOVERNOR COVER

SPEEDOMETER CABLE

BOLT

Exploded view of the vehicle speed sensor assembly

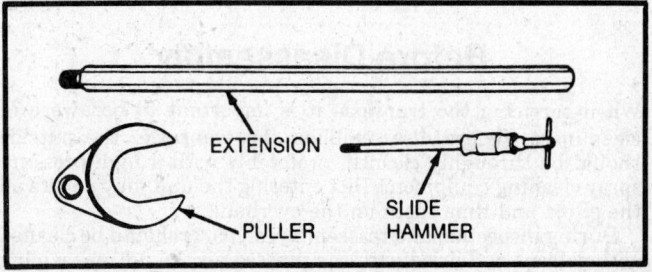

EXTENSION

SLIDE HAMMER

PULLER

View of the halfshaft removal tools

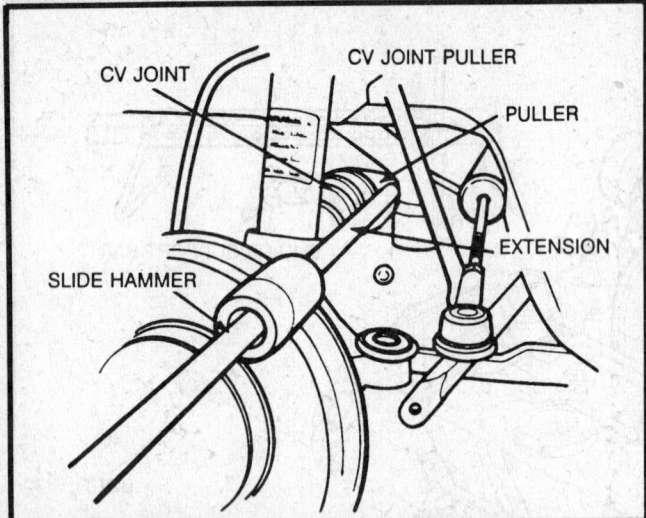

Pulling the halfshafts from the transaxle

move the lower ball joint nut/bolts and the ball joints; separate the lower control arms from the steering knuckles.

11. Remove the stabilizer bar nuts and the rack/pinion assembly-to-subframe nuts. Remove the front/rear engine mounts-to-subframe nuts.

12. From the front of the engine, disconnect the electrical connector from the O_2 sensor, located in the exhaust manifold.

13. Disconnect the "Y" exhaust pipe from the exhaust mainfolds and the rear section from the exhaust pipe flange.

14. Remove the subframe-to-frame bolts, the left-side engine mount support-to-subframe bolts and the subframe.

15. Using a transmission jack, position it under the oil pan and support the weight. Remove the vehicle speed sensor (if equipped) from the transaxle.

NOTE: Vehicles equipped with electronic instrument clusters do not use a speedometer cable.

16. Remove the transaxle mount bolts, the left-side engine support bolts and the engine support.

17. From the starter, disconnect the electrical connectors, remove the starter-to-transaxle bolts and move the starter aside. Remove the separator plate-to-transaxle bolts and the plate.

18. Using chalk or paint, make alignment marks on the torque converter and flywheel. Using a ½ in. ratchet and the ⅞ in. deep well socket on the crankshaft pulley bolt, rotate the crankshaft to align the torque converter bolts with the starter hole and remove the torque converter-to-flywheel bolts.

19. Disconnect the oil cooler lines from the transaxle.

20. Assemble the CV-joint puller tool or equivalent, a screw extension tool or equivalent, and a slide hammer puller tool or equivalent, position the puller assembly behind the CV-joint and pull the halfshafts from the transaxle.

NOTE: When removing the halfshafts from the transaxle, do not pry against the case.

21. Remove the torque converter housing-to-engine bolts. Carefully separate the transaxle from the engine and lower it from the vehicle.

TRANSAXLE INSTALLATION

1. Carefully raise the transaxle into the vehicle and align it with the engine.

2. Install the transaxle housing-to-engine bolts and torque to 41–50 ft. lbs. (55–68 Nm).

3. Using a ½ in. ratchet and the ⅞ in. deep well socket on the crankshaft pulley bolt, rotate the crankshaft to align the torque converter-to-flywheel alignment marks. Insert the torque converter-to-flywheel bolts and torque to 23–39 ft. lbs. (31–53 Nm).

4. Install the separator plate and starter. Torque the separator plate-to-transaxle bolts to 7–9 ft. lbs. (9–12 Nm) and the starter-to-transaxle bolts to 30–40 ft. lbs. (41–54 Nm). Connect the electrical connectors to the starter.

5. Install the left-side engine support, the subframe, the left-side engine mount support.

6. Connect the oil cooler lines to the transaxle.

7. Connect the "Y" exhaust pipe to the exhaust manifolds and the rear section to the exhaust pipe flange.

8. At the front of the engine, connect the electrical connector to the O_2 sensor, located in the exhaust manifold.

9. Install the stabilizer bar nuts, the rack/pinion assembly-to-subframe nuts and the front/rear engine mounts-to-subframe nuts.

10. Align and push the halfshafts into the transaxle until the retaining ring snaps into position.

11. Install the lower ball joints, the lower control arms and tie rod end to the steering knuckles. Torque the control arm-to-steering knuckle bolts to 36–44 ft. lbs. (50–60 Nm) and the tie rod end-to-steering knuckle nut to 23–35 ft. lbs. (31–47 Nm).

12. Install the wheels and lower the vehicle to the ground.

13. Remove the engine lifting bar tool or equivalent, the bar chains and the lifting brackets.

14. Install the nut and bolt to the left engine support strut.

15. To connect the throttle valve cable, perform the following procedures:

 a. Connect the T.V. cable to the T.V. link, seat the connector to the transaxle and install the bolt.

 b. Pull the cable upward and snap it onto the throttle body lever.

16. Connect the electrical connectors to the neutral safety switch and bulkhead connectors.

17. Install the shift cable/bracket assembly-to-transaxle bolts.

18. Connect the negative battery cable. Check and refill the fluid. Drive the vehicle to check the transaxle operation.

BENCH OVERHAUL

Before Disassembly

When servicing the transaxle it is important to be aware of cleanliness. Before disassembling the transaxle, the outside should be throughly cleaned, preferably with a high-pressure spray cleaning equipment. Dirt entering the unit may negate all the effort and time spent on the overhaul.

During inspection and reassembly, all parts should be cleaned with solvent and dried with compressed air; do not use wiping rags or cloths for lint may find its way into the valve body passages. Lubricate the seals with Dexron® II and use petroleum jelly to hold the thrust washers; this will ease the assembly of the seals and not leave harmful residues in the system. Do not use solvent on neoprene seals, friction plates or composition thrust washers, if they are to be reused.

Before installing bolts into aluminum parts, dip the threads into clean transmission fluid. Anti-seize compound may be used to prevent galling the aluminum or seizing. Be sure to use a torque wrench to prevent stripping the threads. Be especially careful when installing the seals (O-rings), the smallest nick can cause a leak. Aluminum parts are very susceptible to damage; great care should be used when handling them. Reusing

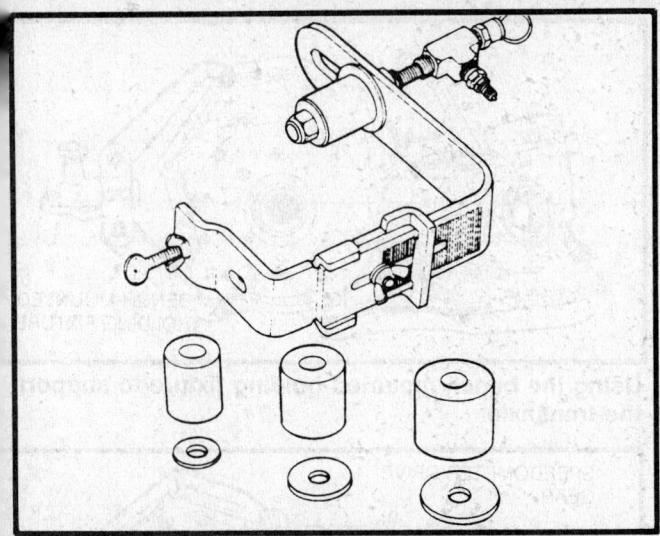

View of a Torque Converter Leak Test Kit

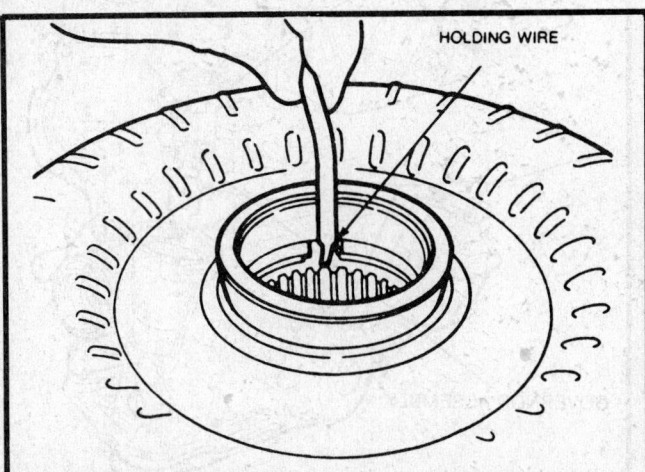

Positioning the holding wire tool in the torque converter's thrust washer slot

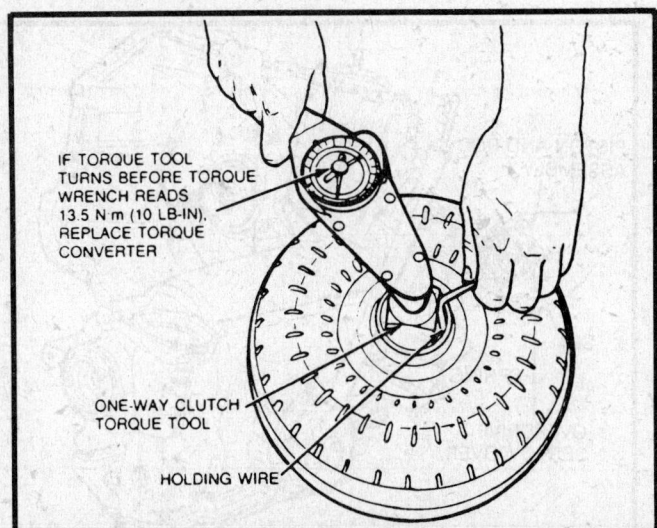

Using a torque wrench and a holding wire to check the torque converter's one-way clutch operation

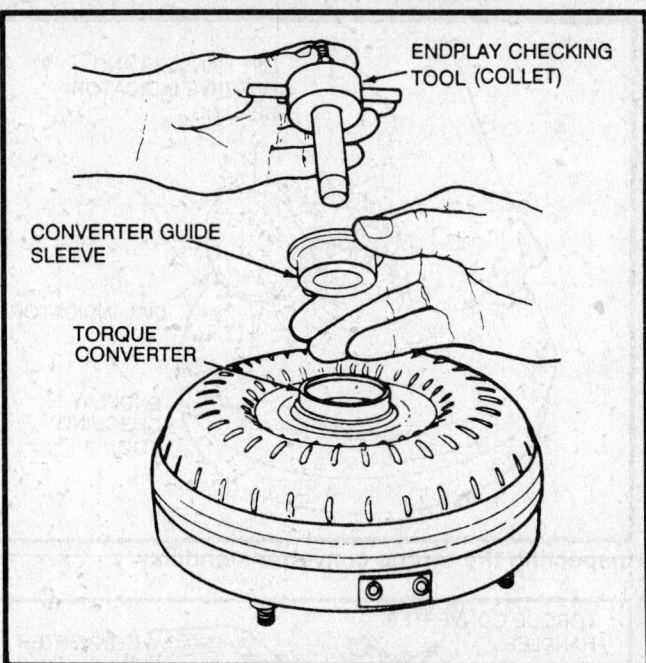

Installing the Endplay Checking and Converter Guide Sleeve tool into the torque converter

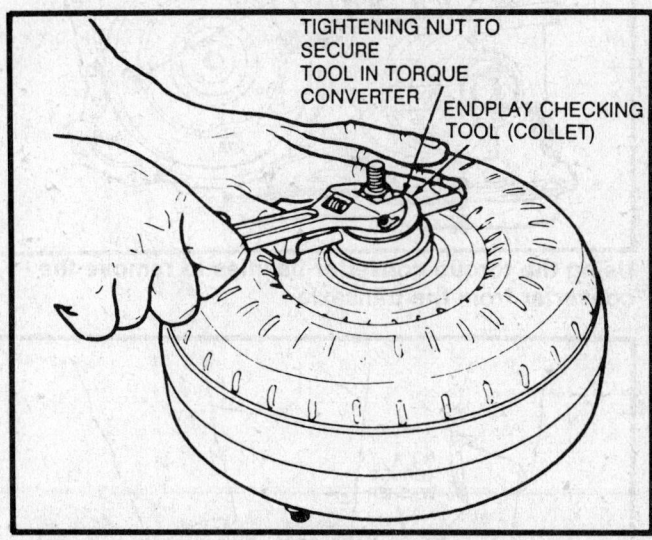

Torquing the Endplay Checking tool nut

snaprings is not recommended but should they be: compress the internal ones and compress the external ones.

Converter Inspection

The torque converter used a sealed, welded design that cannot be disassembled for service or repair; there are a few checks that can be made.

The torque converter contains approximately 2 quarts of transmission fluid. Since there is no drain plug on the unit, the fluid can only be drained through the hub. To drain the converter, invert it over a catch pan and drain the fluid. Fluid that is drained can help diagnosis the converter's condition.

1. If the fluid is discolored but does not contain metal bits or particles, the converter is usable and need not be replaced.

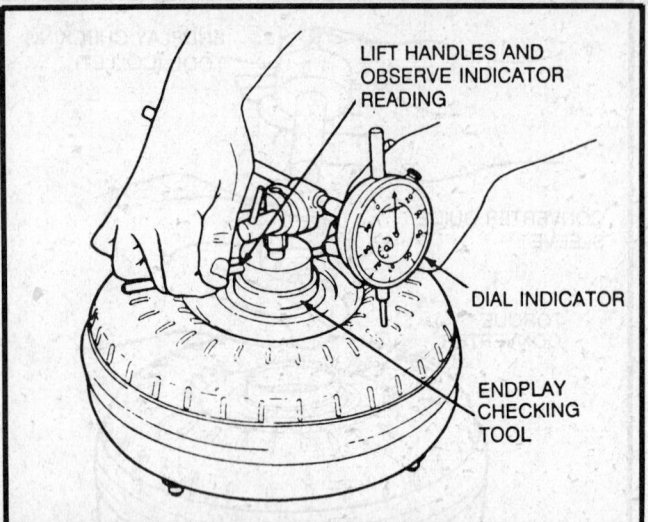

LIFT HANDLES AND OBSERVE INDICATOR READING

DIAL INDICATOR

ENDPLAY CHECKING TOOL

Inspecting the torque converter's endplay

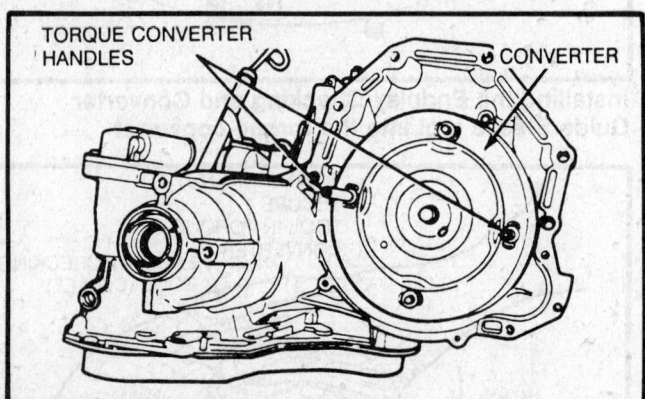

TORQUE CONVERTER HANDLES

CONVERTER

Using the torque converter handles to remove the converter from the transaxle

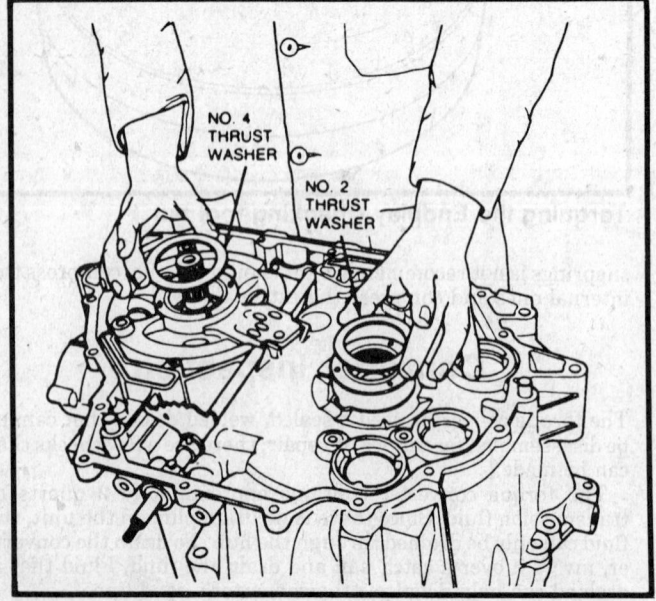

NO. 4 THRUST WASHER

NO. 2 THRUST WASHER

Removing the No. 4 and No. 2 thrust washers from the chain case

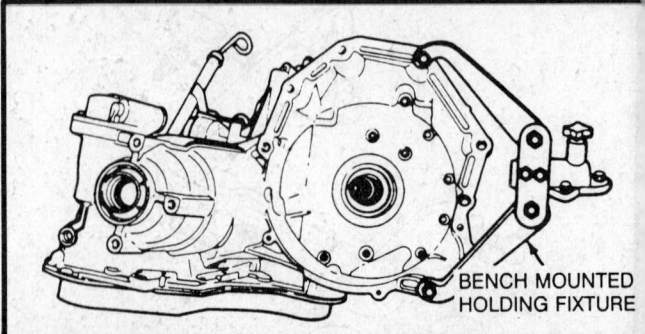

BENCH MOUNTED HOLDING FIXTURE

Using the bench mounted holding fixture to support the transaxle

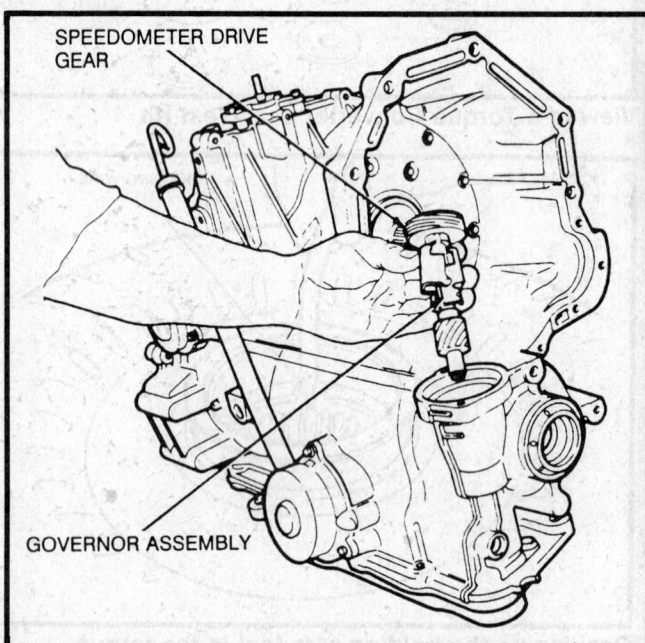

SPEEDOMETER DRIVE GEAR

GOVERNOR ASSEMBLY

Removing the governor from the transaxle

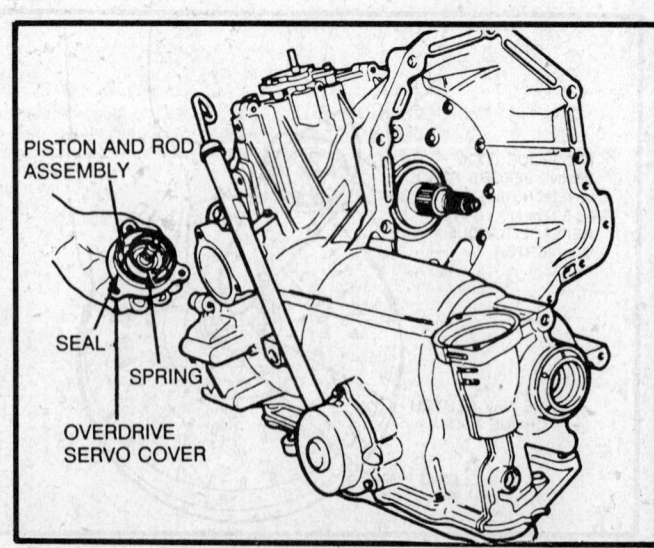

PISTON AND ROD ASSEMBLY

SEAL

SPRING

OVERDRIVE SERVO COVER

Removing the overdrive servo cover from the transaxle

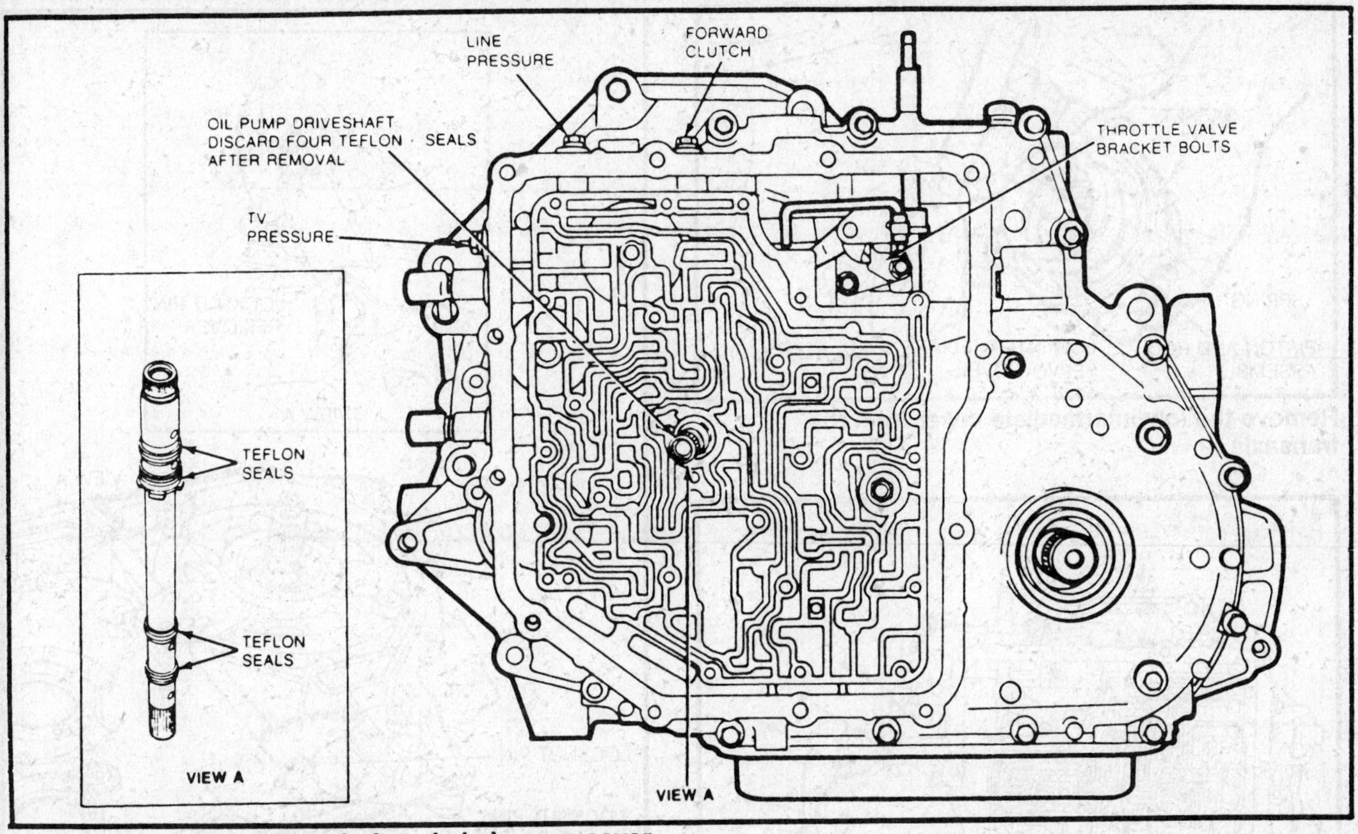

LINE PRESSURE

FORWARD CLUTCH

OIL PUMP DRIVESHAFT
DISCARD FOUR TEFLON · SEALS
AFTER REMOVAL

THROTTLE VALVE
BRACKET BOLTS

TV PRESSURE

TEFLON SEALS

TEFLON SEALS

VIEW A

VIEW A

View of the oil pump driveshaft and chain case cover

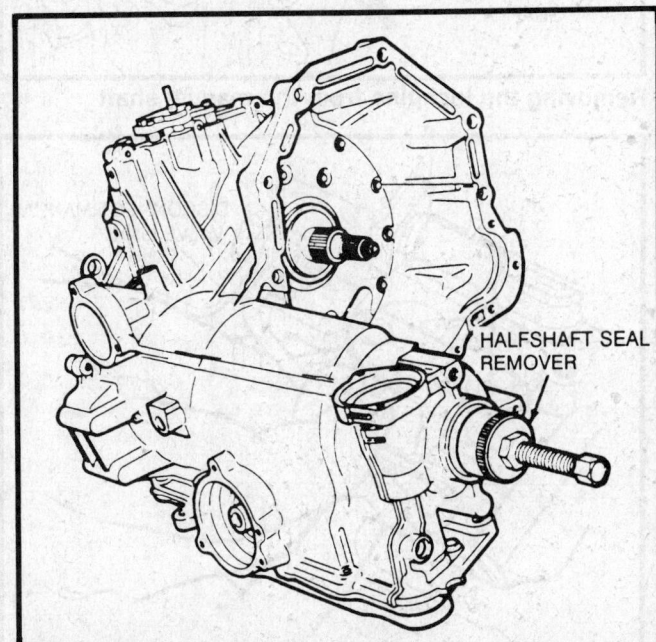

HALFSHAFT SEAL REMOVER

View of the halfshaft seal removal tool installed on the transaxle

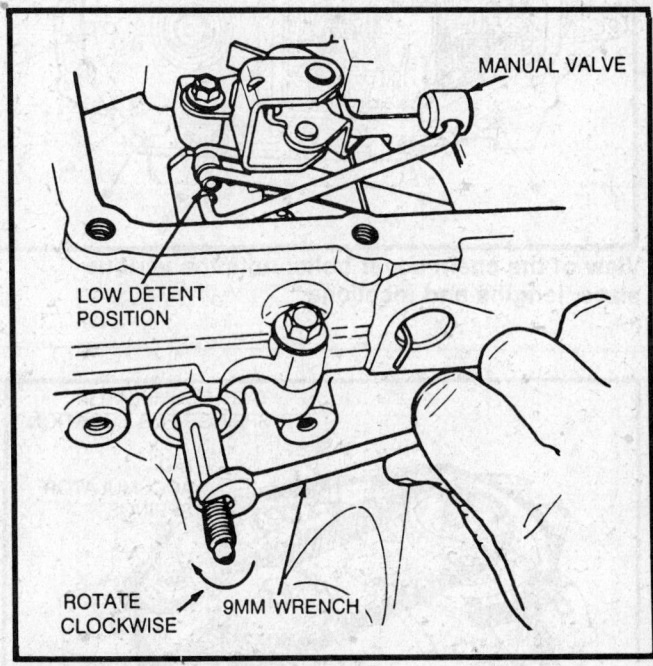

MANUAL VALVE

LOW DETENT POSITION

ROTATE CLOCKWISE   9MM WRENCH

Rotating the manual shift shaft

NOTE: Remember the fluid color is not longer a good indicator of the fluid condition. In the past, the dark color would indicate overheated transaxle fluid; with the newer fluids, this is not a positive sign of transaxle failure.

2. Metal particles in the fluid, having an aluminum paint appearance, indicating converter damage and replacement.

3. If fluid contamination is due to burned clutch plates, overheated oil or antifreeze, the converter should be cleaned or replaced.

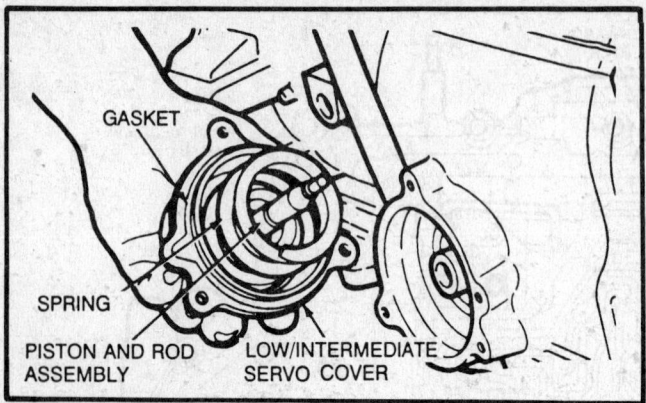

Remove the low/intermediate cover from the transaxle

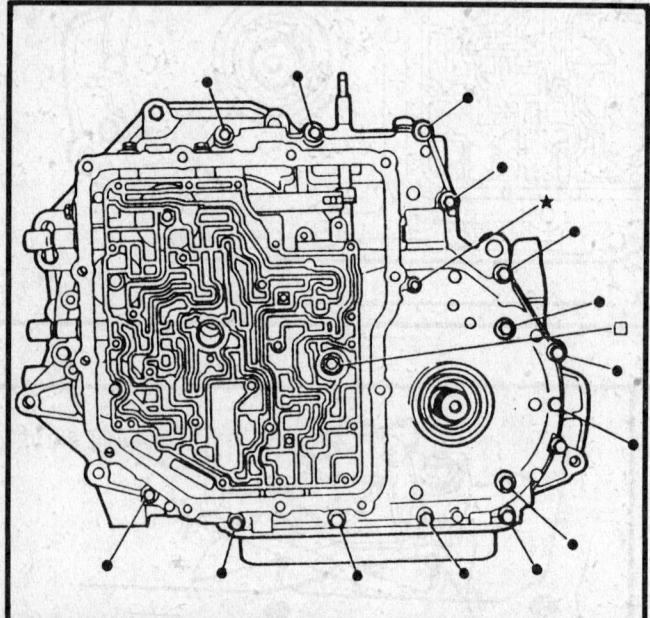

View of the chain cover bolts; note the various sizes, lengths and locations

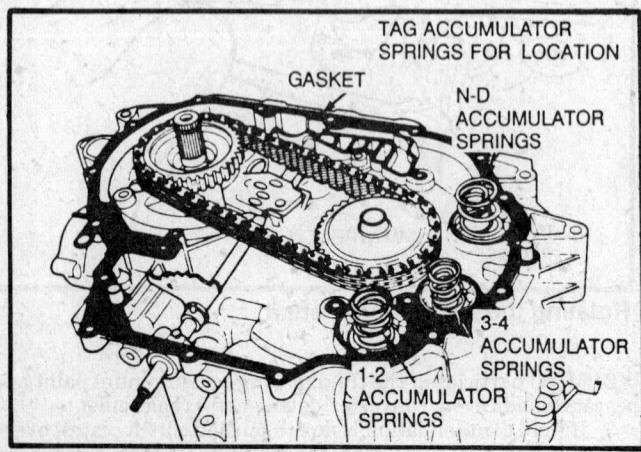

View of the accumulator springs

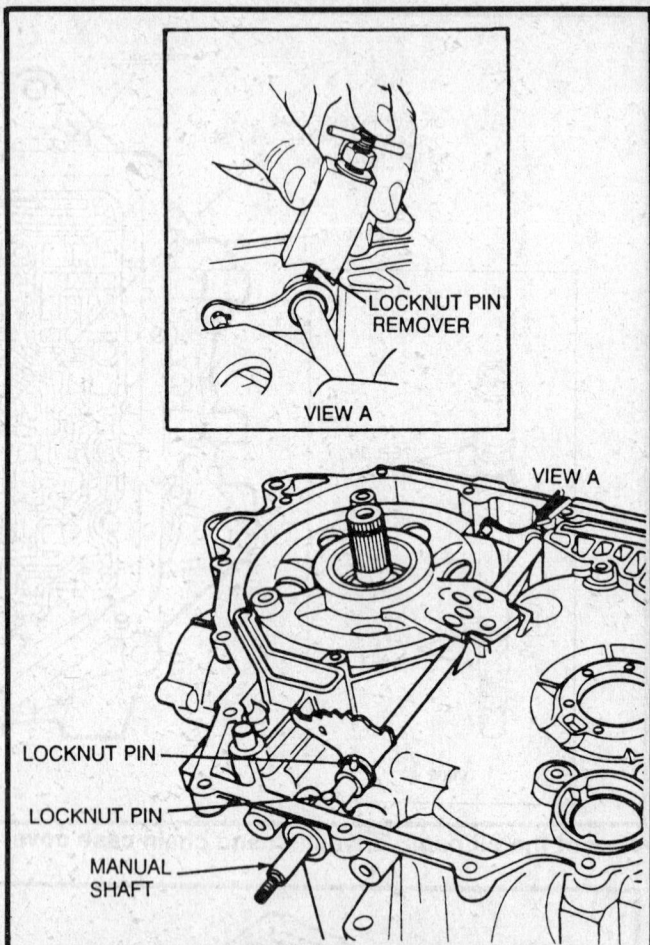

Removing the lockpins from the manual shaft

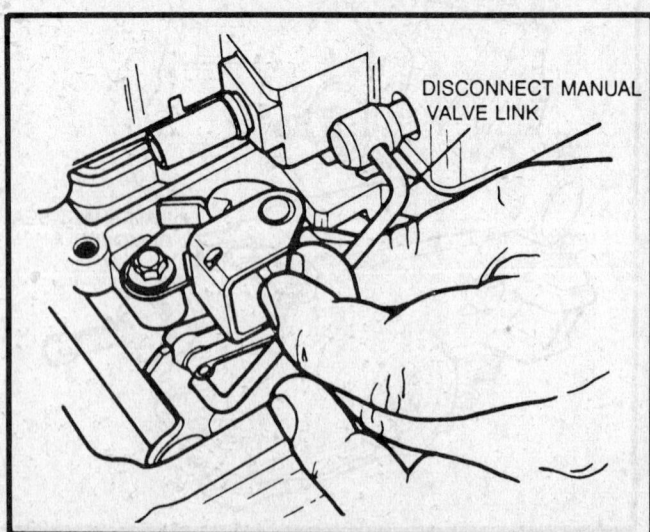

Disconnecting the manual valve link

The converter should be checked carefully for damage, especially around the seal area; remove any sharp edges or burrs from the seal surface. Do not expose the seal to any type of solvent. If the converter is to be washed with solvent, the seal must be removed.

Leakage Check

If the torque converter is suspected of leaking at the welded seams, remove it and perform the leakage check. Using a torque converter leak test Kit or equivalent, pressurize the converter and inspect the seams.

Reactor One-Way Clutch Check

To perform this test, the torque converter must be removed from the transaxle.

1. Using a holding wire, position it in the torque converter's thrust washer slot.
2. Using a torque wrench and a one-way clutch torque tool, install the assembly into the torque converter.
3. While supporting the holding wire stationary, rotate the torque wrench counterclockwise to check the torque. The torquing tool should not turn under 10 ft. lbs. (13.55 Nm); if it turns, replace the torque converter.

Endplay Check

1. Using the endplay checking tool or equivalent, and the converter guide sleeve tool or equivalent, install them into the torque converter hub.
2. Tighten the endplay checking tool nut.
3. Using a dial indicator, mount it onto the endplay checking tool. Using the indicator's stylus, contact the converter shell and zero the indicator.
4. Lift the endplay checking tool handles and note the indicator reading; if the reading changes more than 0.05 in. (1.27mm), replace the converter.

Transaxle Disassembly

TRANSAXLE UNIT

1. Using 2 torque converter handle tools or equivalent, install them onto the torque converter and pull the converter from the transaxle.
2. Using the bench mounted holding fixture tool or equivalent, mount the transaxle to it. If necessary to drain the fluid, rotate the transaxle to the vertical position (right halfshaft side down), drain the fluid into a catch pan and return it to the horizontal position.
3. Remove the governor cover-to-transaxle bolts, the cover and seal (discard it). Remove the governor, speedometer drive gear assembly and bearing (located on top of the speedometer gear) from the case.
4. Remove the overdrive servo cover-to-transaxle bolts, the cover, piston assembly and spring; discard the O-ring seal.
5. Remove the low/intermediate servo cover-to-transaxle bolts, the cover, piston assembly and spring; discard the gasket.
6. To remove the right-side output shaft seal, perform the following procedures:

NOTE: The halfshaft shaft seal is a 2-piece construction; inner rubber seal and outer metal protector.

  a. Using a shaft protector tool or equivalent, install it into the output shaft opening.
  b. Using the output shaft seal remover tool or equivalent, screw it into the metal seal protector. Tighten the tool's screw until the metal seal protector is removed and remove the protector from the tool.
  c. Reinsert the tool into the rubber seal, tighten the tool's screw and pull the seal from the transaxle.
7. From the top of the transaxle, remove the neutral safety switch-to-transaxle bolts and the switch.
8. Remove the dipstick tube-to-transaxle bolt and pull out the tube.

9. From inside the torque converter housing, remove the torque converter-to-chain cover bolts.
10. Using the seal remover tool or equivalent and a slide hammer puller, pull the oil seal from the torque converter housing shaft.
11. Remove the side cover (upper reservoir) bolts, the bolts and the gasket (discard it).
12. Disconnect the electrical connectors from the pressure switches and the solenoid.

NOTE: When disconnecting the electrical connectors, grasp the connector with one hand and push against it with the finger from the other hand.

13. At the bulkhead connector, compress the tabs (on both sides) and remove the connector from the chain cover.

NOTE: When removing the bulkhead connector, do not pull on the wiring or the connector.

14. Place a 9mm wrench on the manual shaft flats and rotate it clockwise to position the linkage in the **L** detent (valve all the way in).
15. Remove the oil pump/valve body assembly-to-chain case bolts.

NOTE: When removing the oil pump/valve body assembly, do not remove the 2 oil pump-to-valve body retaining bolts or the oil cover bolts.

16. Push the T.V. plunger inward and pull the oil pump/valve body assembly outward to clear the bracket. Rotate the assembly clockwise and remove the link from the manual valve. Disconnect the manual valve link from the detent lever and remove the oil pump/valve body assembly.
17. Remove the throttle valve bracket-to-chain cover bolts and the bracket. After pulling the oil pump driveshaft from the chain case, remove the Teflon® seals (discard them) from the shaft.
18. Rotate the transaxle to the vertical position and remove the left output shaft circlip.
19. To remove the left output shaft seal, perform the following procedures:

NOTE: The halfshaft shaft seal is a 2-piece construction; inner rubber seal and outer metal protector.

  a. Using a shaft protector tool or equivalent, install it into the output shaft opening.
  b. Using the output shaft seal remover tool or equivalent, screw it into the metal seal protector. Tighten the tool's screw until the metal seal protector is removed and remove the protector from the tool.
  c. Reinsert the tool into the rubber seal, tighten the tool's screw and pull the seal from the transaxle.
20. Remove the chain cover-to-transaxle bolts, the chain cover and the gasket (discard it).

NOTE: When removing the chain cover, be sure to note the location and length of the bolts. Be sure to tag the actuator springs so they may be installed in their correct locations during assembly.

21. From the chain cover, remove the No. 1 and No. 3 thrust washers.
22. Using both hands, grasp and lift both chain sprockets and chain assembly from the chain case. Remove the No. 2 thrust washer from the drive sprocket support and the No. 4 thrust washer from the driven sprocket support.

NOTE: The No. 4 thrust washer may stay on the driven sprocket.

23. Determine if the drive sprocket support bearing (No. 2

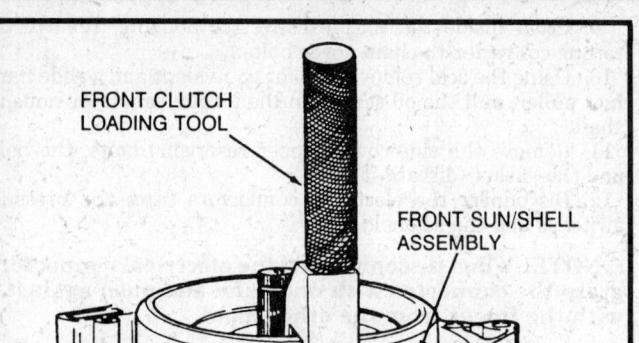

Using the Front Clutch Loading tool to remove the sun/shell assembly

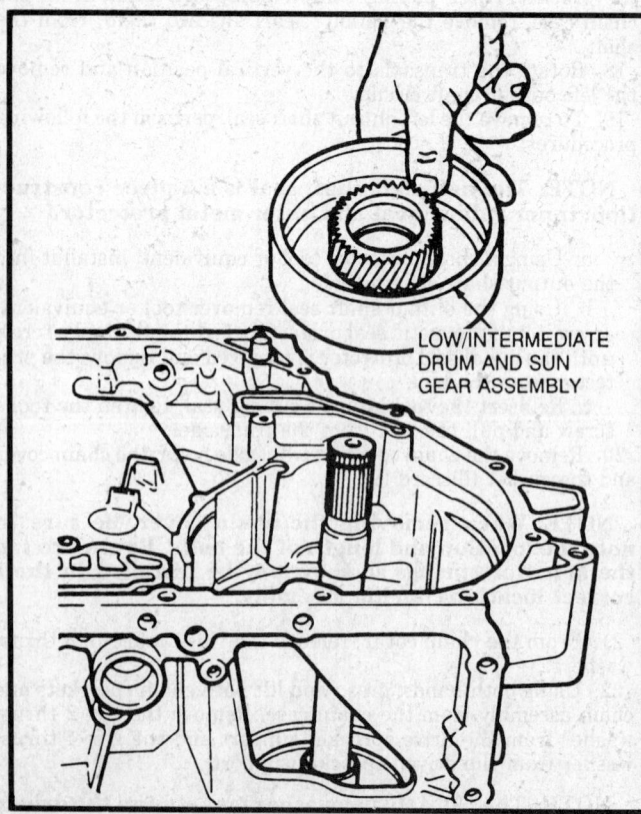

Removing the low/intermediate drum/sun gear assembly

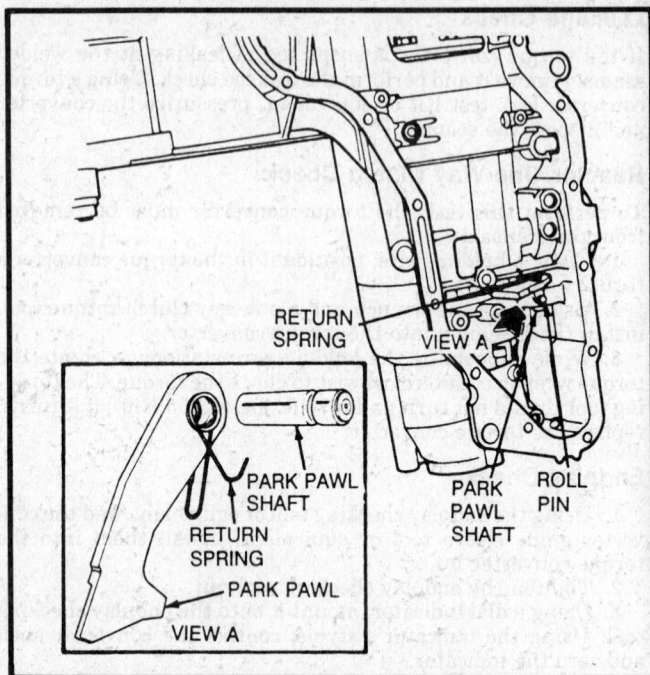

Exploded view of the park pawl assembly

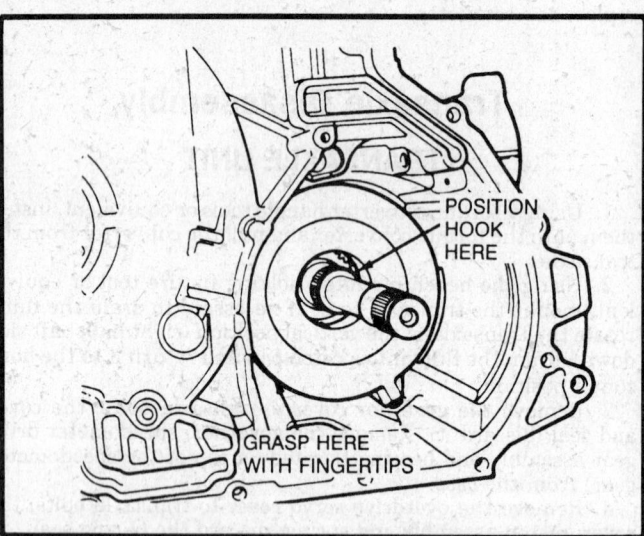

View of the reverse clutch cylinder's inner diameter

thrust washer) needs replacement; if the bearing is OK, remove the driven sprocket support-to-case housing Torx® bolts, from the torque converter housing side.

24. Using the locknut pin remover tool or equivalent, from the chain case side, remove and discard the manual shaft's lockpin and 2 roll pins; be careful not to damage the machined surfaces. Slide the manual shaft linkage from the case and pry the seal from the case.

25. Using a flat block or a straight edge, determine if the driven sprocket support's machined bolt hole surfaces are above or below the case's machined surface; this is for reassembly purposes.

26. From the chain case, remove the driven sprocket support assembly, the Teflon® seals (from the support assembly shaft) and the thrust washer (it may stay with the driven sprocket support). If the No. 8 selective thrust washer and No. 9 needle bearing were not removed with the driven sprocket support assem-

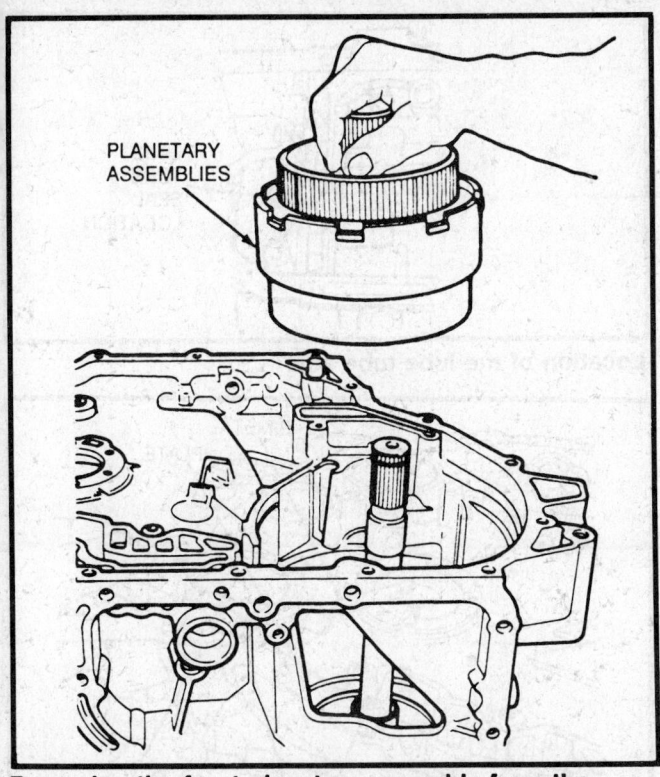

Removing the front planetary assembly from the case

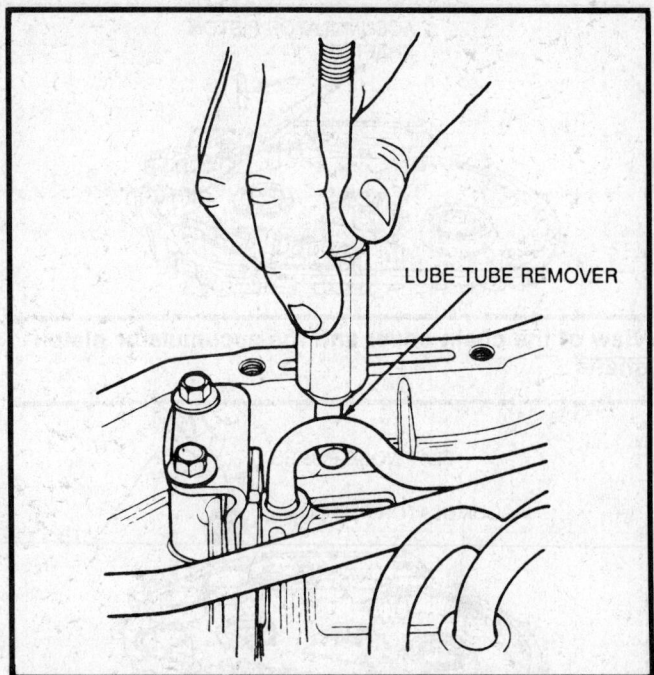

Removing the lube tubes from the transaxle

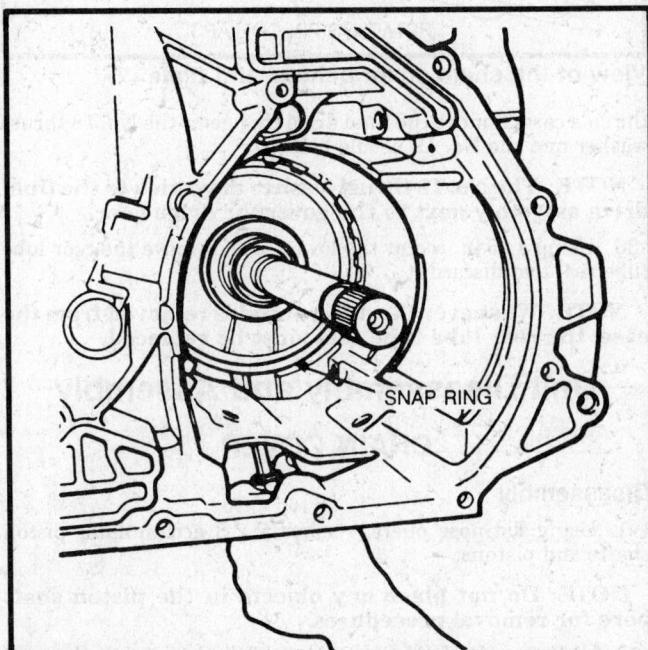

Removing the snapring from the final drive gear assembly

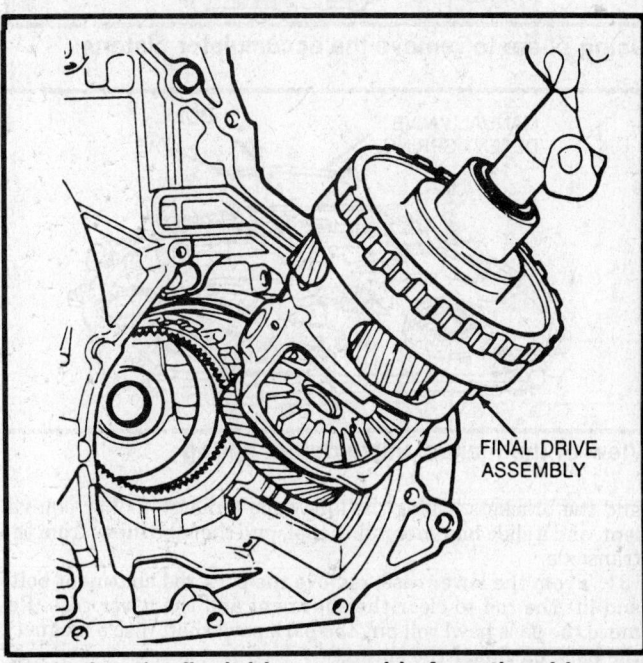

Removing the final drive assembly from the side case

bly, use a wire hook to remove them from the bottom of the chain case cylinder.

NOTE: If the driven sprocket support assembly is binding in the chain case housing, it may be necessary to back out the reverse clutch anchor bolt.

27. At the overdrive band, remove the plastic retainer and the overdrive band.

28. Install the hooked end of the front clutch loading tool or equivalent, into 1 of the sun/shell assembly's 6 holes, position the notched block over the assembly's edge, tighten the handle (do not overtighten) and lift the assembly from the case.

29. Remove the oil pan-to-transaxle cover bolts, the oil pan and gasket (discard it). Remove the reverse apply tube/oil filter bracket bolt, the bracket and the oil filter screen (discard both O-rings).

30. From the lower case, remove the lube tube bracket bolts

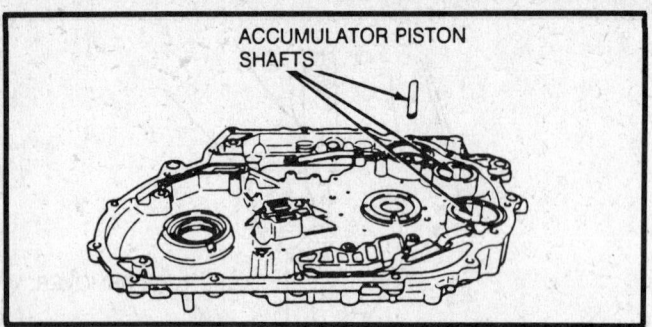

View of the chain cover and the accumulator piston shafts

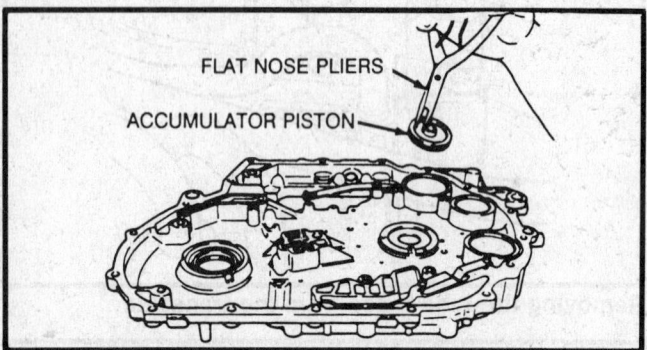

Using pliers to remove the accumulator pistons

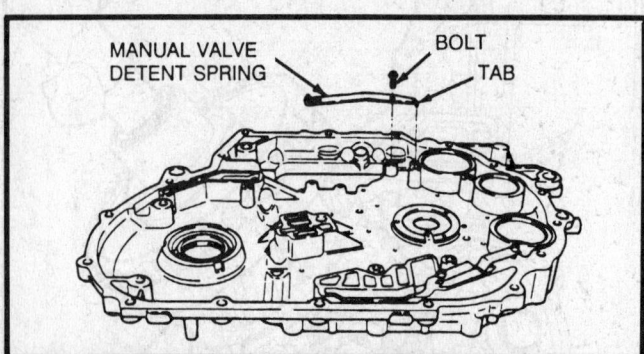

View of the manual valve detent spring

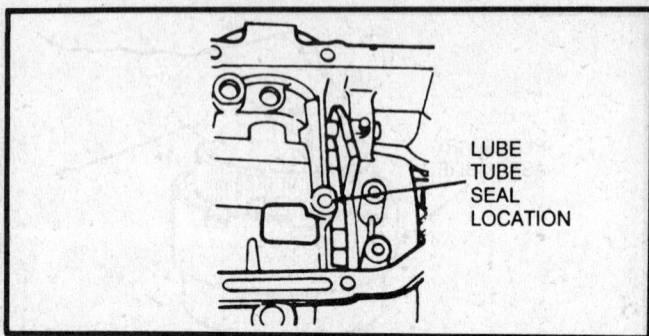

Location of the lube tube seal

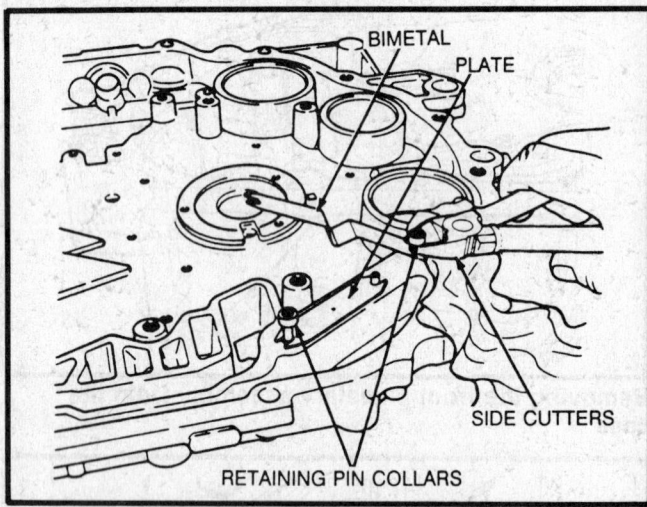

View of the chain cover bimetal and plate

the side case, remove the final drive ring gear, the No. 18 thrust washer and the No. 19 needle bearing.

NOTE: The No. 18 thrust washer may stick to the final drive assembly next to the governor drive gear.

36. Using a ⅜ in. rod at the lower case, remove the rear lube tube seal and discard it.

NOTE: Whenever the differential is removed from the case, the rear lube tube seal must be replaced.

Unit Disassembly and Assembly
CHAIN COVER

Disassembly

1. Using flat-nose pliers, remove the 3 accumulator piston shafts and pistons.

NOTE: Do not place any objects in the piston shaft bore for removal procedures.

2. Using a pair of side cutters, carefully remove the bimetal pin collars, the bimetal strip and the plate.
3. Pull the pins from the cover.
4. Remove the manual valve detent spring bolt and spring.
5. If necessary, use the stator/driven sprocket bearing remover tool or equivalent, and slide hammer puller to remove the drive sprocket support needle bearing.

Inspection

1. Using solvent, clean the chain cover.

and the brackets. Using the lube tube remover tool or equivalent, and a slide hammer puller tool, pull the lube tubes from the transaxle.

31. From the lower case, remove the park rod abutment bolts and lift the rod to clear the abutment and the lower case. Remove the park pawl roll pin, the park pawl shaft (use a magnet), the park pawl and the spring.

32. At the reverse clutch band, loosen the reverse clutch anchor pin nut and remove the Allen bolt. Rotate the transaxle to the horizontal position.

33. From the side case, locate the inner diameter of the reverse clutch cylinder, using the hooked portion of the front clutch loading tool or equivalent, grasp the cylinder's outer diameter (with fingertips) and slide the clutch assembly from the case.

34. Rotate the transaxle to the vertical position. From the side case, grasp the front planetary shaft and lift the front/rear planetary assembly from the case. Remove the low/intermediate drum/sun gear assembly and the low/intermediate band.

35. Insert a small pry bar through the lower case to remove the snapring from the final drive gear assembly. Grasp the output shaft and lift the final drive assembly from the side case. From

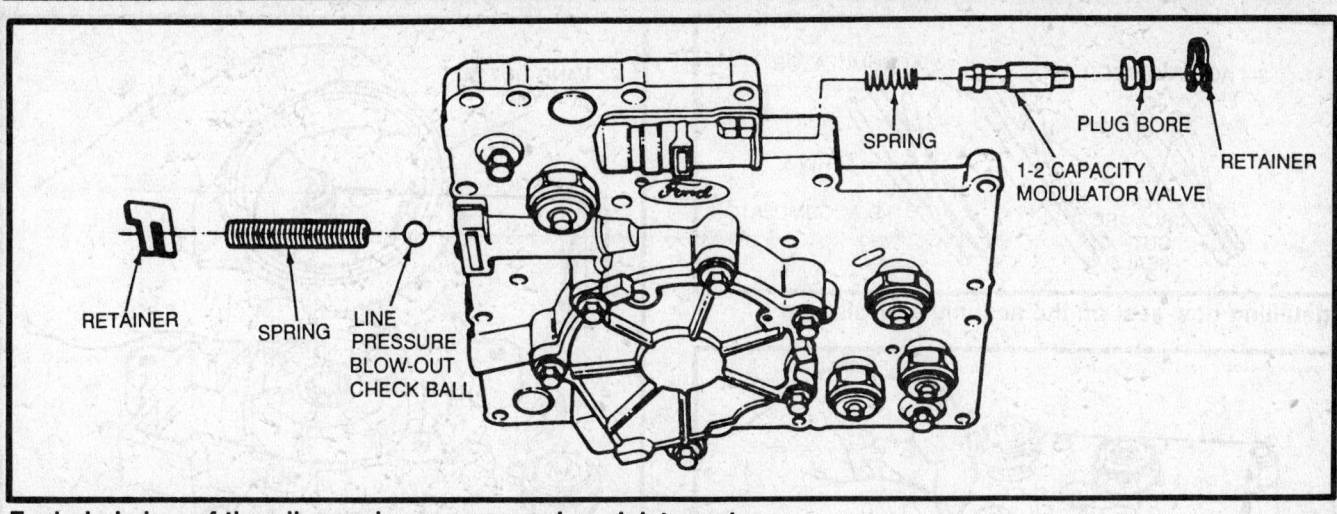

Exploded view of the oil pump's pressure and modulator valves

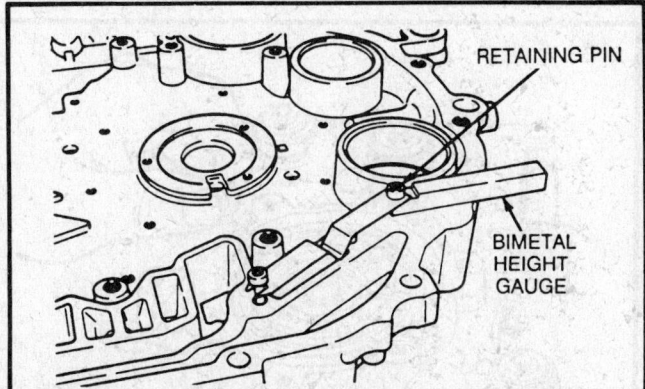

Using the Bimetal Height Gauge to adjust the retaining pin height

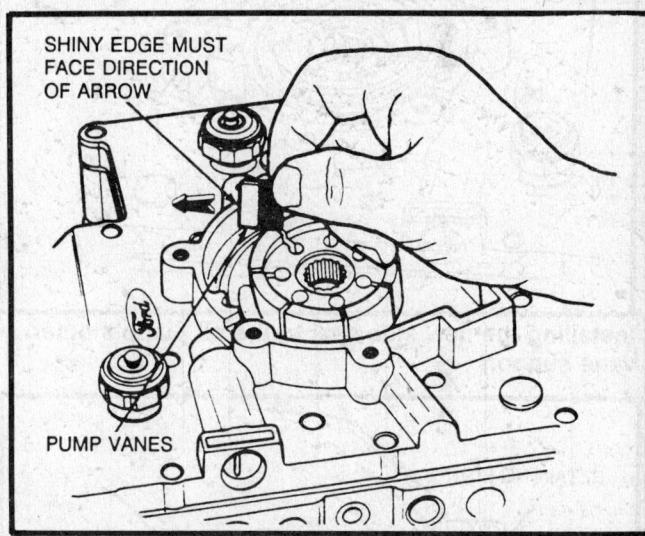

View of an oil pump's rotor vane

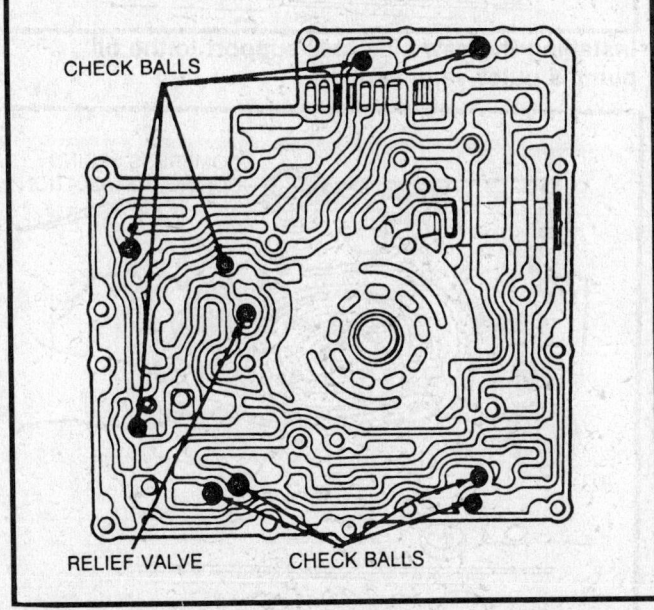

Location of the oil pump's check balls and relief valve

View of the oil pump's inner vane support

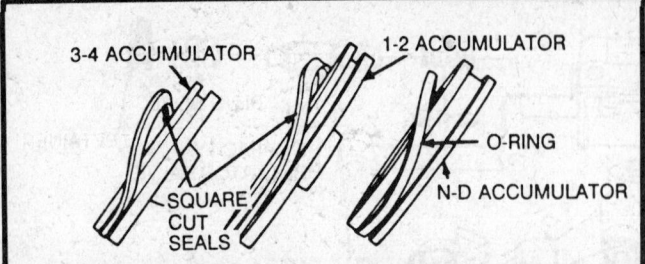

Installing new seal on the accumulator pistons

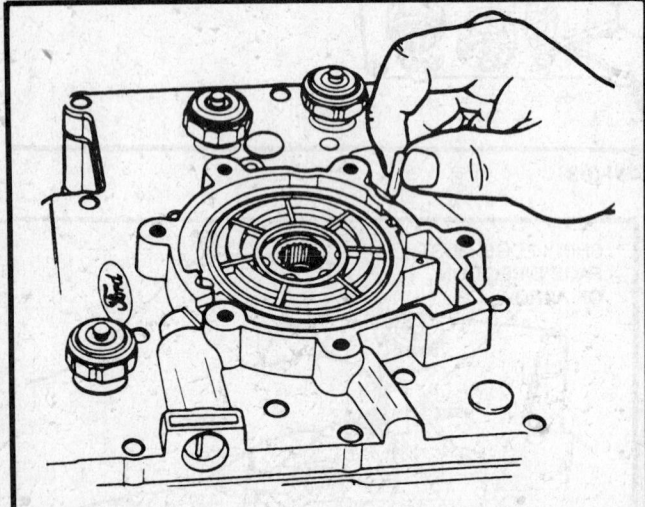

Installing the new side seal to the oil pump's outer vane support

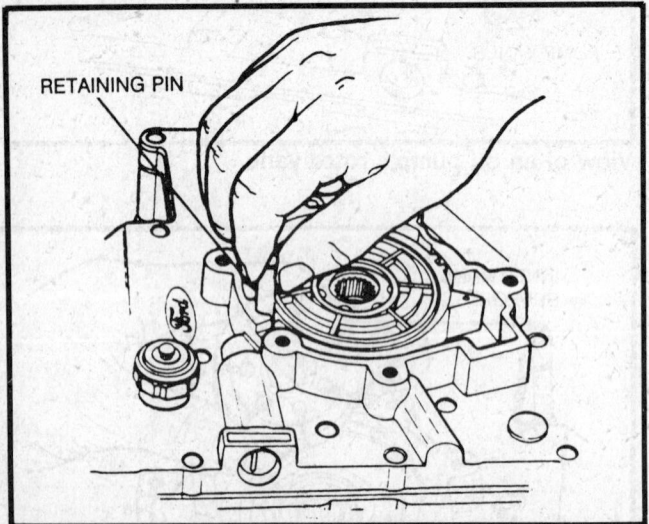

Installing the outer vane support retaining pin to the oil pump

2. Inspect the case for cracks and/or stripped threads. Inspect the gasket mounting surfaces for burrs. Check the vent for obstructions. Check the fluid passages for obstructions and leakage.

3. Check the parking linkage parts for wear and/or damage. Inspect the case bushings for scores.

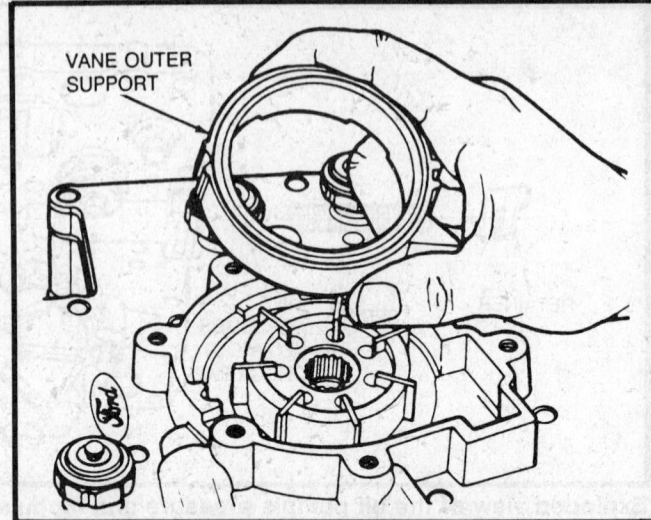

View of the oil pump's outer vane support

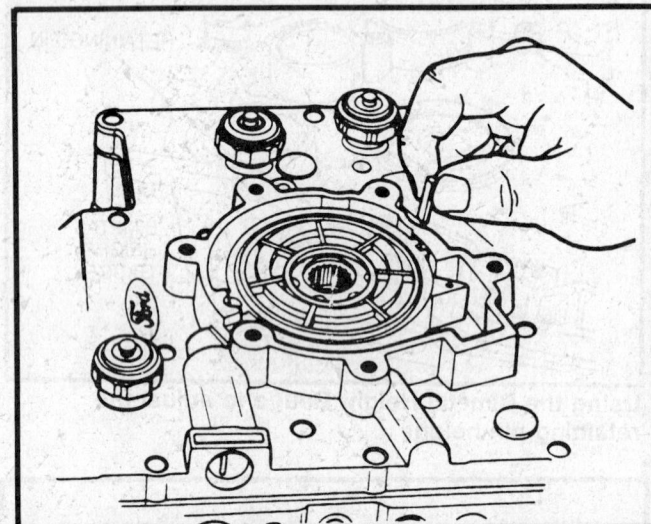

Installing the new side seal support to the oil pump's outer vane support

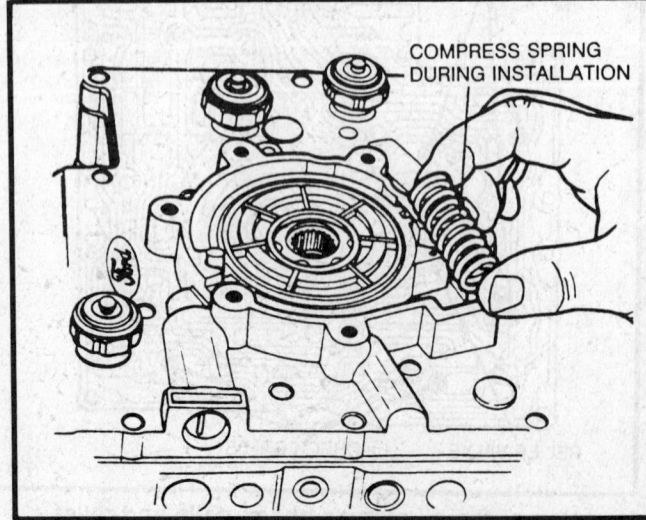

Installing the oil pump's spring

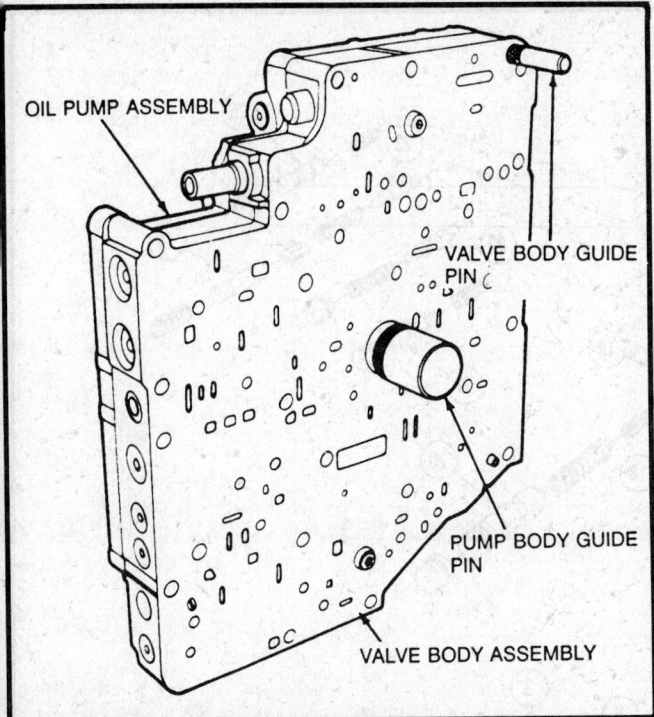

Installing the oil pump assembly to the valve body assembly

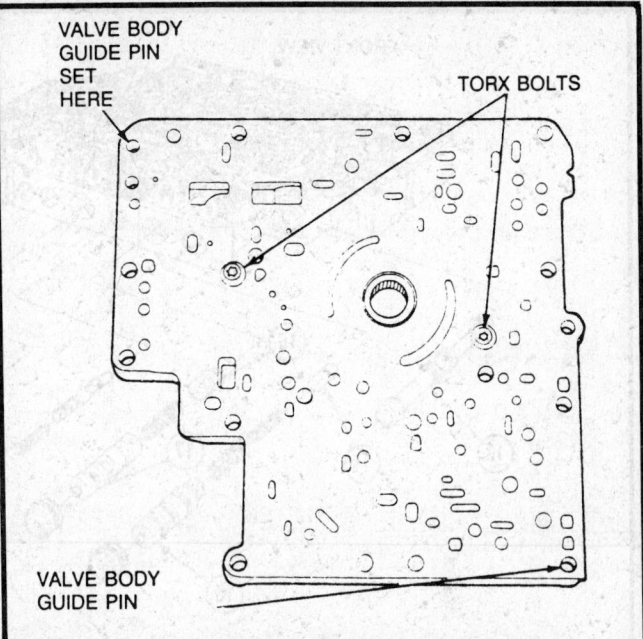

Installing the separator plate onto the oil pump housing

Assembly

1. If the drive sprocket support needle bearing was removed, use the stator/driven sprocket bearing replacer tool or equivalent, and an arbor press to the bearing into the chain cover until it seats.
2. Position the manual valve detent spring's tab in the chain cover's locator hole and install the bolts. Torque the bolt to 7–9 ft. lbs. (9–12 Nm).
3. If the bimetal retaining pins were removed, start them into the cover.
4. To install the bimetal, perform the following procedures:
   a. Position the bimetal over the retaining pins and start the retaining collars.
   b. Position the bimetal height gauge (slotted end) or equivalent, under the bimetal/retaining collar (hole side).
   c. Tap the retaining collar onto the pin until the assembly seats against the tool. Repeat the height procedure for the other bimetal retaining collar.
   d. Disconnect the bimetal's slotted end and adjust the center pin's height with the slotted end of the tool.
   e. Install the bimetal plate on the center and rear pins. Reinstall the bimetal.
5. Using new seals and O-ring, install them on the 3 accumulator pistons; use the square cut seals for the 3-4 accumulator and 1-2 accumulator pistons, while the O-ring is for the N-D accumulator.
6. Install the pistons (into the proper cylinder) and the piston shafts.

OIL PUMP

Disassembly

1. Remove the oil pump assembly-to-valve body bolts and the oil pump assembly from the valve body.
2. Remove the gasket and discard it. Place the oil pump assembly with the separator plate facing upwards.

3. Remove the separator plate-to-oil pump housing Torx® bolts and the separator plate. Remove the check ball and the relief valve; be sure to note the location of each for installation purposes.
4. Remove the oil pump cover-to-oil pump housing bolts and the cover. Using a pry bar, pry the bore spring from the oil pump housing; be careful not to damage the gasket mounting surface.

CAUTION

Be careful when removing the spring for it is under pressure and can cause personal injury.

5. From the oil pump bore's outside vane support, remove the retaining pin, the metal O-ring, the soft O-ring (discard it), the side seal (discard it), the seal support, the top vane positioning ring and the outer vane support.
6. From the oil pump rotor, remove the 7 vanes, the inner vane support and the bottom vane positioning ring.

Inspection

The only oil pump parts that are servicable are the seals. If any part is worn or damaged, replace the entire pump assembly.

Assembly

1. Using clean transmission fluid, lubricate the pump's parts.
2. Into the oil pump's bore, install the bottom vane positioning ring, the inner vane support (face the small inner diameter counterbore upward) and the vanes into the inner vane support (the shiny surface must face outwards).
3. Install the outer vane support over the inner vane support assembly, the top vane positioning ring, a new side seal support, new side seal and the outer vane support retaining pin.
4. Compress the oil pump's spring and install it between the case and outer vane tab.
5. Install the new rubber O-ring and the the metal O-ring retainer into the outer vane support groove.
6. Install the oil pump cover onto the oil pump housing and torque the bolts to 7–9 ft. lbs. (9–12 Nm). If the line pressure blow-out ball/spring and the 1-2 modulator valve/spring/plug

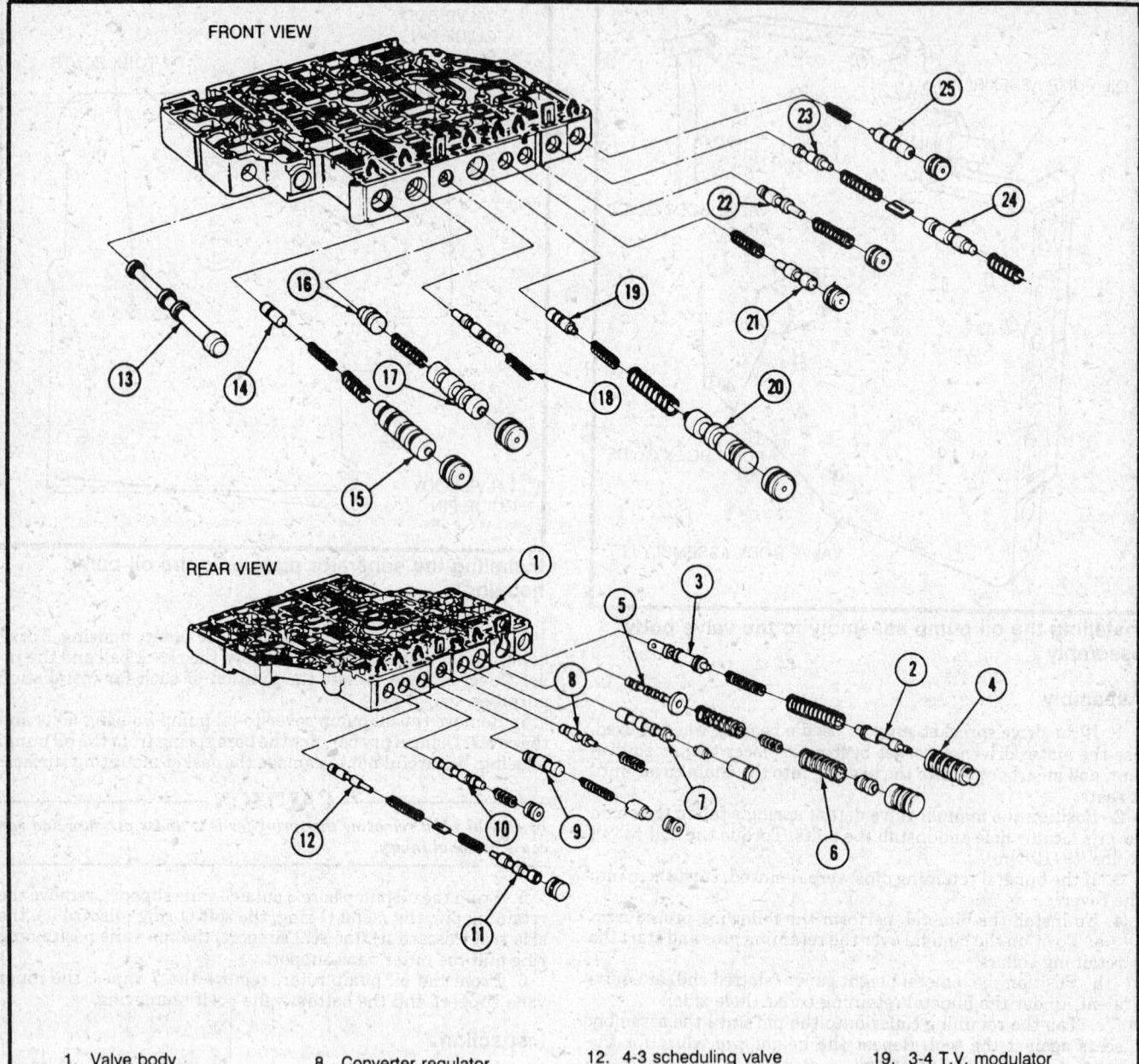

FRONT VIEW

REAR VIEW

1. Valve body
2. Throttle valve (T.V.)
3. T.V. plunger
4. T.V. valve sleeve
5. Main regulator valve
6. Main regulator boost valve
7. Converter clutch control valve
8. Converter regulator valve
9. Accumulator regulator valve
10. Backout valve
11. T.V./line modulator valve
12. 4-3 scheduling valve
13. Manual valve
14. 2-3 T.V. modulator valve
15. 2-3 shift valve
16. 1-2 throttle delay valve
17. 1-2 shift valve
18. 2-1 scheduling valve
19. 3-4 T.V. modulator valve
20. 3-4 shift valve
21. 2-4 inhibit valve
22. 3-2 control valve
23. N-D Engagement valve
24. T.V. limit valve
25. 2-3 servo regulator valve

Exploded view of the valve body components

have been removed from the housing, install them and the retaining clips.

7. Turn the oil pump housing over and install the check balls/relief valve into their proper locations.

8. Using a new gasket, position the separator plate onto the oil pump housing. Using the insert valve body guide pin set tool or equivalent, and the valve body guide pin tool or equivalent, insert them through the separator plate into the oil pump hous-

ing and torque the Torx® to 7–9 ft. lbs. (9–12 Nm); remove the pins.

9. Using a new gasket, position the oil pump assembly onto the valve body.

10. Using the pump body guide pin tool or equivalent, and the valve body guide pin tool or equivalent, install them through the valve body and into the oil pump assembly; this will align the oil pump assembly-to-valve body.

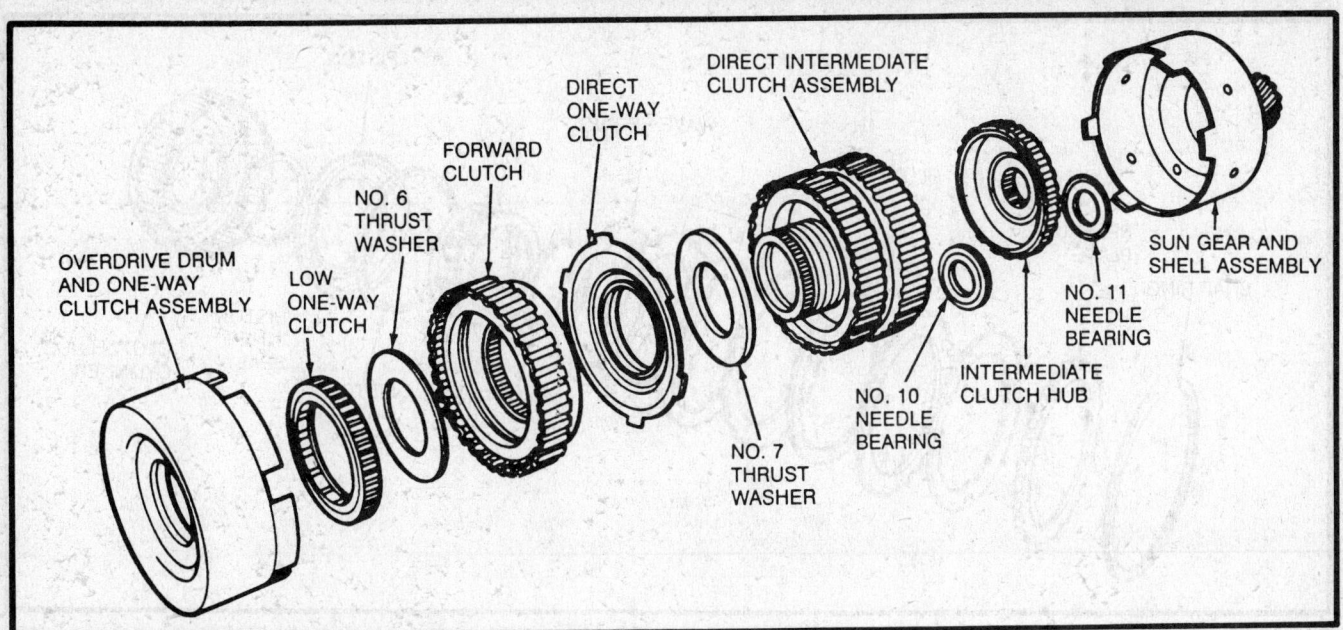

Exploded view of the shell assembly

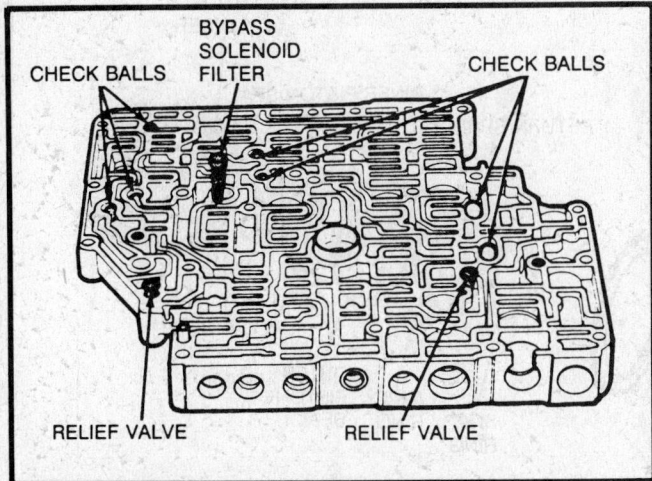

Location of the valve body's check balls, relief valves and solenoid bypass filter

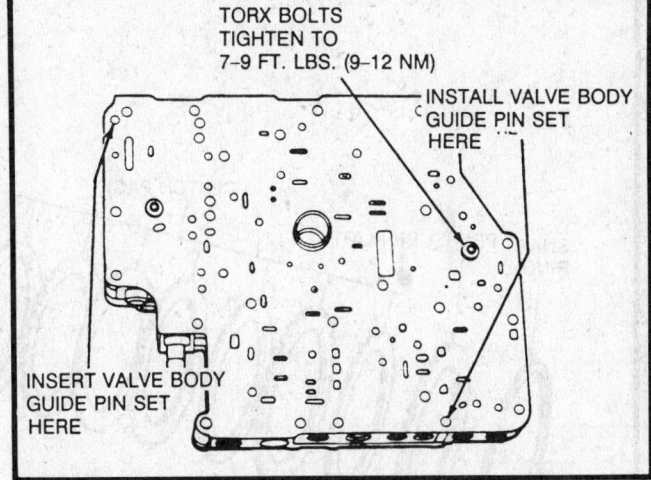

Installing the separator plate onto the valve body housing

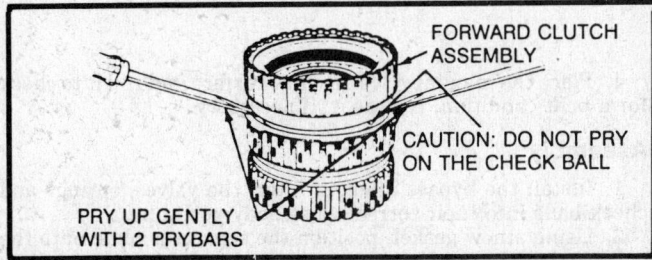

Prying the forward clutch assembly from the direct clutch hub

11. Install the oil pump assembly-to-valve body bolts and torque them to 7–9 ft. lbs. (9–12 Nm). Remove the alignment tools.

VALVE BODY

Disassembly

1. Remove the valve body-to-oil pump assembly bolts and the valve body from the oil pump assembly.

2. Remove the gasket and discard it. Place the valve assembly with the separator plate facing upwards.

3. Remove the separator plate-to-valve body Torx® bolts and the separator plate. Remove the check balls, the relief valves and bypass solenoid filter (clean it); be sure to note the location of each for installation purposes.

4. From the valve body, remove the retaining clips, the bore plugs, the valves and springs; be sure to note their locations for installation purposes.

NOTE: Since most valve are made of aluminum, they cannot be removed with a magnet. It will be necessary to remove them by tapping the valve body with the palm of

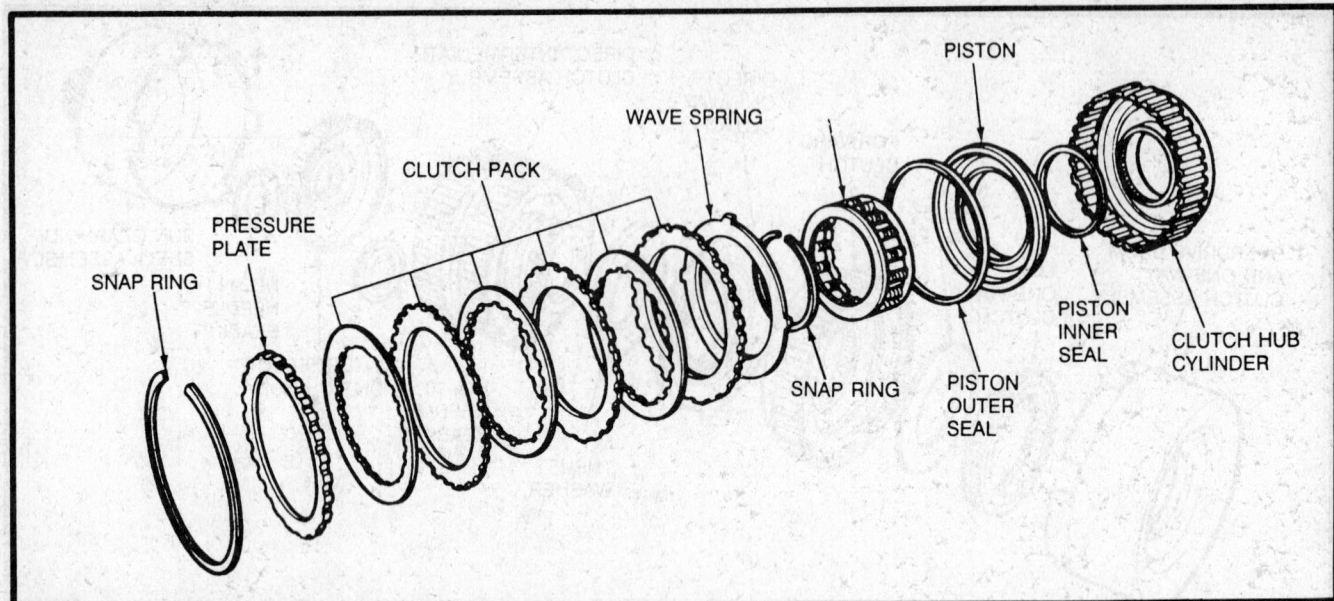

Exploded view of the forward clutch assembly

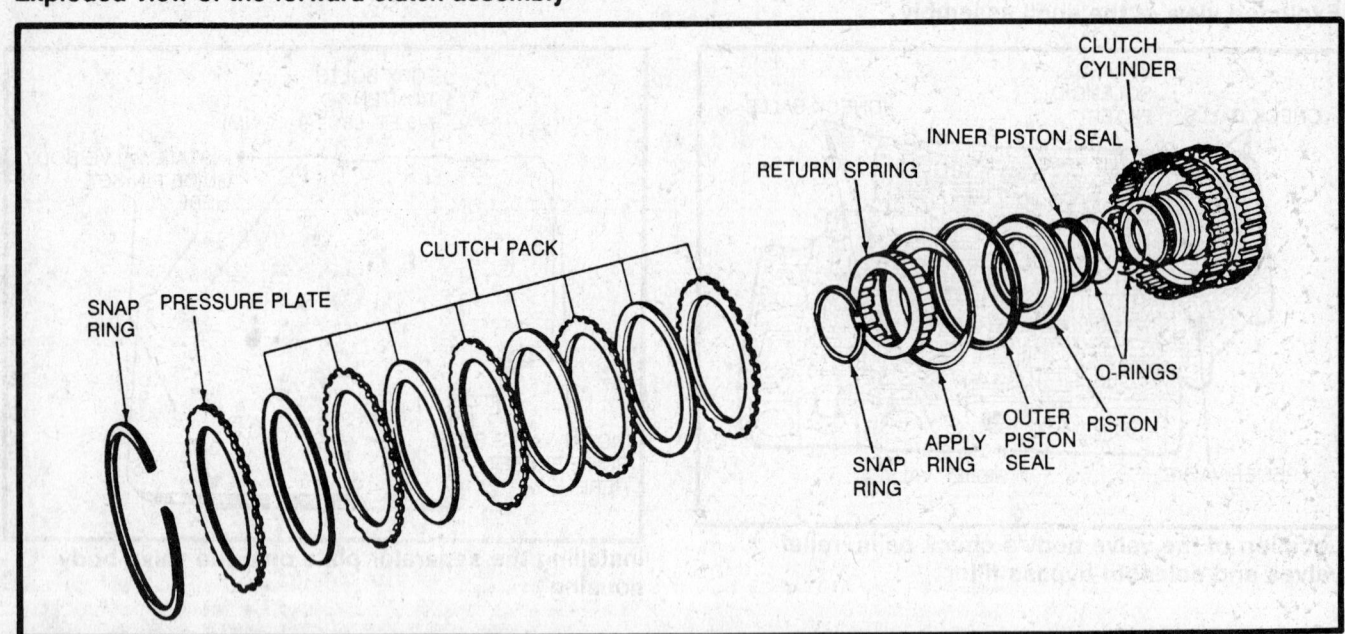

Exploded view of the direct clutch assembly

the hand or a tooth pick. If using a tooth pick, be careful not to damage the valves or the valve bore. Do not turn the throttle valve adjusting screw.

Inspection

1. Using clean solvent, wash the valves, springs and valve body; do not clean the check balls with solvent. Using moisture-free compressed air, blow dry the parts.

2. Check the valve/plug bores for scores, all passage ways for obstructions and the mounting surfaces for scores and/or burrs. If necessary, polish the valves and plugs with crocus cloth; be careful not to round their sharp edges.

3. Check the spring for distortion and the valves/plugs for free-bore movement in their bores; the valves/plugs must be free to move through their own weight.

4. Place the manual valve on a flat surface and roll it to check for a bent condition; replace it, if necessary.

Assembly

1. Install the bypass solenoid filter, the valves, springs and check balls into their correct valve body positions.

2. Using a new gasket, position the separator plate onto the valve body housing. Using the valve body guide pin set tools or equivalent, insert them through the separator plate into the valve body housing and torque the Torx® to 7–9 ft. lbs. (9–12 Nm); remove the pins.

3. Using a new gasket, position the valve body assembly onto the oil pump housing assembly.

4. Using the pump body guide pin tool or equivalent, and the valve body guide pin tool or equivalent, install them through the

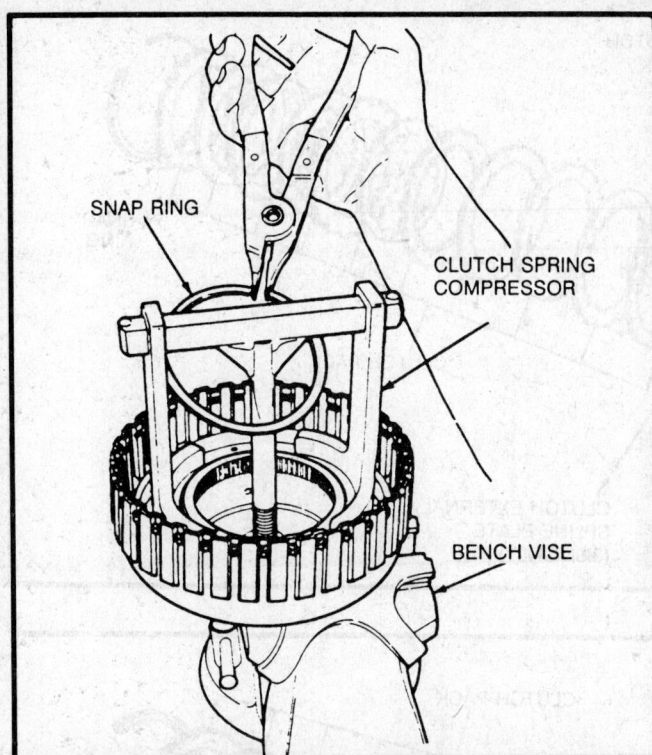

Compressing the piston assembly into the clutch hub cylinder to remove the snapring

valve body and into the oil pump assembly; this will align the oil pump assembly-to-valve body.

5. Install the oil pump assembly-to-valve body bolts and torque them to 7–9 ft. lbs. (9–12 Nm). Remove the alignment tools.

CLUTCH/SHELL ASSEMBLY

The shell assembly consists of the overdrive drum, the one-way clutch, the forward clutch, the direct clutch, the intermediate clutch and the sun gear.

Disassembly
SHELL ASSEMBLY

1. Position the shell assembly on the work bench with the sun gear facing upwards. Remove the sun gear/shell assembly from the overdrive drum.
2. Remove the No. 11 needle bearing, the intermediate clutch hub and the No. 10 needle bearing.
3. Turn the assembly over, onto the intermediate cylinder hub.
4. Remove the overdrive drum/one-way clutch assembly and the No. 6 thrust washer.
5. Using 2 pry bars, one on each side of the forward clutch assembly, pry the forward clutch upward.

NOTE: Since the forward clutch assembly is retained to the hub by O-ring seals, be sure to pry evenly. Do not position the pry bars near the check ball.

6. Remove the direct one-way clutch and the No. 7 thrust washer.

FORWARD CLUTCH ASSEMBLY

1. From the forward clutch assembly, remove the snapring, the pressure plate, the clutch pack and the wave spring.

2. Using the clutch spring compressor tool or equivalent, compress the clutch hub cylinder's piston assembly and remove the snapring.
3. Remove the compressor tool and the piston assembly.
4. From the piston, remove the outer seal. From the clutch hub cylinder, remove the inner seal.

DIRECT CLUTCH ASSEMBLY

The direct clutch assembly occupies ½ of the direct/intermediate clutch cylinder assembly.

1. From the direct clutch cylinder, remove the snapring, pressure plate and clutch pack.
2. Using the clutch spring compressor tool or equivalent, compress the clutch hub cylinder's piston assembly and remove the snapring.
3. Remove the compressor tool and the 2-piece piston assembly.
4. Separate the apply ring from the piston. From the piston, remove the outer seal. From the clutch hub cylinder, remove the inner seal.

INTERMEDIATE CLUTCH ASSEMBLY

The intermediate clutch assembly occupies ½ of the direct/intermediate clutch cylinder assembly.

1. From the intermediate clutch cylinder, remove the snapring, pressure plate and clutch pack.
2. Using the clutch spring compressor tool or equivalent, compress the clutch cylinder's piston assembly and remove the snapring.
3. Remove the compressor tool and the piston assembly.
4. From the piston, remove the outer seal. From the clutch cylinder, remove the inner seal.

REVERSE CLUTCH ASSEMBLY

1. From the reverse clutch cylinder, remove the snapring, pressure plate, clutch pack and wave spring.
2. Using the clutch spring compressor tool or equivalent, compress the clutch cylinder's piston assembly and remove the snapring.
3. Remove the compressor tool and the piston assembly.
4. From the piston, remove the outer seal. From the clutch cylinder, remove the inner seal.

Inspection
CLUTCHES

The following inspection is used to check the forward, direct, intermediate and reverse clutches.

1. Check the clutch cylinder thrust surfaces, clutch plate serrations and piston bore for burrs and/or scores. If the clutch cylinder is badly damaged or scored, replace it; otherwise, use crocus cloth to remove minor scores and/or burrs.
2. Inspect the clutch cylinder's fluid passages for obstructions; if necessary, clean them. Inspect the check balls for proper seating and freedom of movement. Check the clutch pistons for scoring; replace them, if necessary.
3. Inspect the clutch release spring for cracks and/or distortion; replace the spring, if necessary.
4. Check the steel clutch plates, composition clutch plates and pressure plate for scored or worn bearing surfaces; replace the plates, if necessary.
5. Inspect the clutch plates for fit on the clutch hub serrations and flatness; replace the plates, if they do not slide freely on the serrations.
6. Inspect the clutch hub thrust surfaces for scoring and the clutch hub splines for wear.

ONE-WAY CLUTCHES

1. Check the outer/inner races surface areas for damage and/or scoring.
2. Check the rollers, sprags and springs for wear and/or damage.

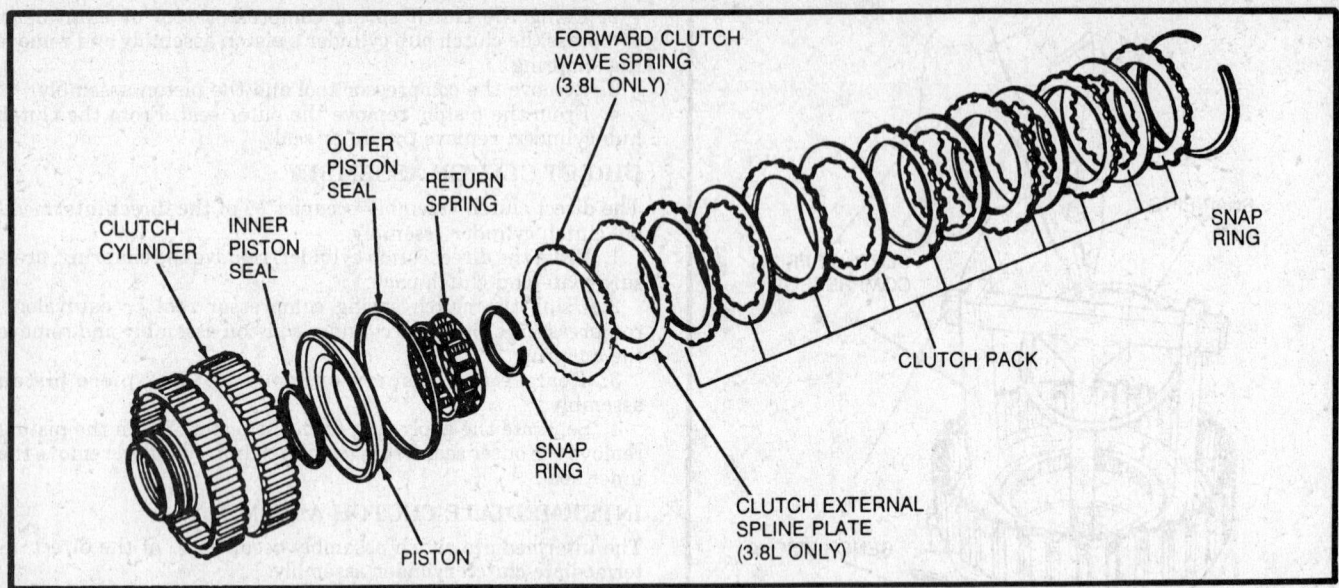

Exploded view of the intermediate clutch assembly

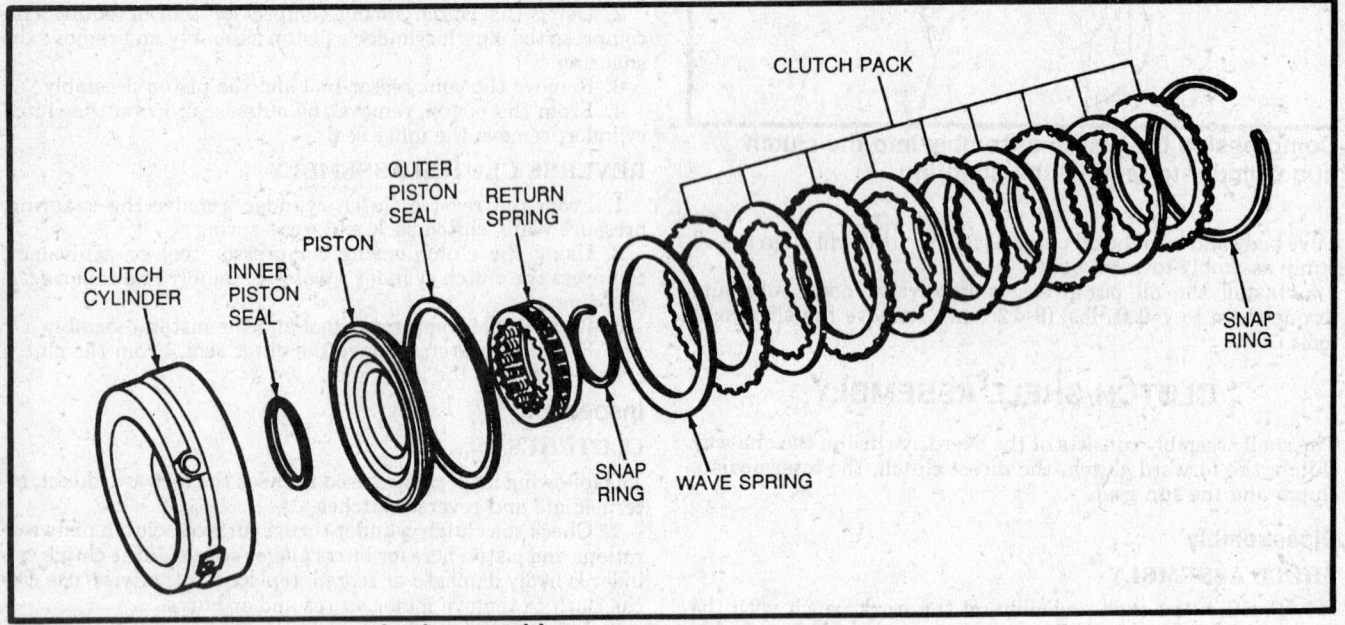

Exploded view of the reverse clutch assembly

3. Check the spring/case for damaged and/or bent spring retainers.

THRUST WASHERS

1. Using clean solvent, throughly clean the thrust bearings. Using compressed air, blow dry the bearings.
2. Check the bearings for pitting and/or roughness; replace them, if necessary.
3. Before installation, lubricate the cleaned bearings with clean transmission fluid.

Assembly

FORWARD CLUTCH ASSEMBLY

1. Using new piston seals, install them with their lips facing the bottom of the cylinder.
2. Using the forward clutch seal lip protector tool or equiva-

lent, place the piston assembly inside the tool and the tool/piston assembly into the clutch hub cylinder. Remove the installation tool.
3. Using the clutch spring compressor tool or equivalent, compress the piston assembly into the clutch hub cylinder and install the snapring. Remove the installation tool.
4. Install the wave spring, the clutch pack, the pressure plate and snapring into the clutch hub cylinder.
5. To check the clutch pack clearance, perform the following procedures:
   a. Using a dial indicator, connect it to a rigid mount.
   b. Position the forward clutch assembly on a flat surface with the clutch package facing upwards.
   c. Using at least 10 lbs. pressure, force the clutch package downward and release it.
   d. Position the dial indicator's stylus on the forward clutch's pressure plate and zero the indicator.

e. While securing the assembly on the flat surface, lift the pressure plate to the bottom of the snapring and note the indicator's reading.

f. Move the indicator to the opposite side (180 degrees) and repeat this procedure.

g. Using the 2 readings, determine the reading average; the clearance should be 0.055–0.075 in. (1.40–1.89mm).

h. If the reading is not within specifications, the snapring must be changed.

Snapring sizes:
0.049–0.053 in. (1.24–1.34mm)
0.063–0.067 in. (1.60–1.70mm)
0.077–0.081 in. (1.95–2.05mm)
0.091–0.094 in. (2.30–2.40mm)
0.104–0.108 in. (2.65–2.75mm)

i. If the snapring was replaced, recheck the clearance.

DIRECT CLUTCH ASSEMBLY

1. Using new piston seals, install them with their lips facing the bottom of the clutch cylinder.

2. Using the direct clutch seal lip protector tool or equivalent, place the piston assembly inside the tool and the tool/piston assembly into the clutch cylinder. Remove the installation tool.

3. Install the piston apply ring on top of the piston. Be sure the piston's check ball has free movement.

4. Install the return spring into the clutch cylinder by aligning the notch with the piston's check ball.

5. Using the clutch spring compressor tool or equivalent, compress the piston assembly into the clutch cylinder and install the snapring. Remove the installation tool.

6. Install the clutch pack, the pressure plate and snapring into the clutch cylinder.

7. To check the clutch pack clearance, perform the following procedures:

a. Using a dial indicator, connect it to a rigid mount.

b. Position the direct/intermediate clutch assembly on a flat surface with the direct clutch package facing upwards.

c. Using at least 10 lbs. pressure, force the clutch package downward and release it.

d. Position the dial indicator's stylus on the direct clutch's pressure plate and zero the indicator.

e. While securing the assembly on the flat surface, lift the pressure plate to the bottom of the snapring and note the indicator's reading.

f. Move the indicator to the opposite side (180 degrees) and repeat this procedure.

g. Using the 2 readings, determine the reading average; the clearance should be 0.031–0.051 in. (0.78–1.29mm).

h. If the reading is not within specifications, the snapring must be changed.

Snapring sizes:
0.047–0.051 in. (1.20–1.30mm)
0.065–0.069 in. (1.67–1.76mm)
0.084–0.088 in. (2.14–2.24mm)
0.102–0.106 in. (2.61–2.71mm)
0.119–0.123 in. (3.04–3.14mm)

i. If the snapring was replaced, recheck the clearance.

INTERMEDIATE CLUTCH ASSEMBLY

1. Using new piston seals, install them with their lips facing the bottom of the cylinder. Inspect the clutch cylinder for free check ball movement.

2. Using the forward clutch seal lip protector tool or equivalent, place the piston assembly inside the tool and the tool/piston assembly into the clutch cylinder. Remove the installation tool.

3. Using the clutch spring compressor tool or equivalent, compress the piston assembly into the clutch cylinder and install the snapring. Remove the installation tool.

4. Install the clutch pack, the pressure plate and snapring into the clutch cylinder.

5. To check the clutch pack clearance, perform the following procedures:

a. Using a dial indicator, connect it to a rigid mount.

b. Position the direct/intermediate clutch assembly on a flat surface with the intermediate clutch package facing upwards.

c. Using at least 10 lbs. pressure, force the clutch package downward and release it.

d. Position the dial indicator's stylus on the intermediate clutch's pressure plate and zero the indicator.

e. While securing the assembly on the flat surface, lift the pressure plate to the bottom of the snapring and note the indicator's reading.

f. Move the indicator to the opposite side (180 degrees) and repeat this procedure.

g. Using the 2 readings, determine the reading average; the clearance should be 0.040–0.061 in. (1.04–1.55mm).

h. If the reading is not within specifications, the snapring must be changed.

Snapring sizes:
0.049–0.053 in. (1.24–1.34mm)
0.065–0.069 in. (1.66–1.76mm)
0.081–0.085 in. (2.08–2.18mm)
0.098–1.020 in. (2.50–2.60mm)
0.114–0.118 in. (2.92–3.02mm)

i. If the snapring was replaced, recheck the clearance.

REVERSE CLUTCH ASSEMBLY

1. Using new piston seals, install them with their lips facing the bottom of the cylinder.

2. Using the reverse clutch seal lip protector tool or equivalent, place the piston assembly inside the tool and the tool/piston assembly into the clutch cylinder. Remove the installation tool. Install the return spring into the cylinder.

3. Using the clutch spring compressor tool or equivalent, compress the piston assembly into the clutch cylinder and install the snapring. Remove the installation tool.

4. Install the wave spring, the clutch pack, the pressure plate and snapring into the clutch cylinder.

5. To check the clutch pack clearance, perform the following procedures:

a. Using a dial indicator, connect it to a rigid mount.

b. Position the reverse clutch assembly on a flat surface with the clutch package facing upwards.

c. Using at least 10 lbs. pressure, force the clutch package downward and release it.

d. Position the dial indicator's stylus on the reverse clutch's pressure plate and zero the indicator.

e. While securing the assembly on the flat surface, lift the pressure plate to the bottom of the snapring and note the indicator's reading.

f. Move the indicator to the opposite side (180 degrees) and repeat this procedure.

g. Using the 2 readings, determine the reading average; the clearance should be 0.038–0.064 in. (0.97–1.63mm).

h. If the reading is not within specifications, the snapring must be changed.

Snapring sizes:
0.059–0.064 in. (1.52–1.62mm)
0.078–0.081 in. (1.98–2.08mm)
0.096–0.100 in. (2.45–2.55mm)
0.115–0.118 in. (2.92–3.02mm)

i. If the snapring was replaced, recheck the clearance.

SHELL ASSEMBLY

1. Position the intermediate clutch cylinder on the work bench with shaft end facing upwards.

2. Position the No. 7 thrust washer so its tabs (facing downward) align with the direct clutch slots.

3. Install the direct one-way clutch into the intermediate

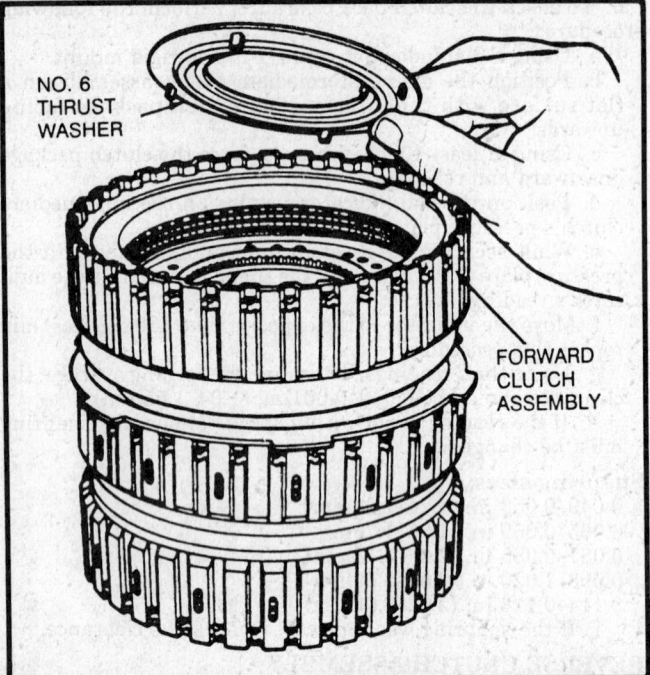

Installing the forward clutch assembly and the No. 6 thrust washer onto the intermediate clutch cylinder

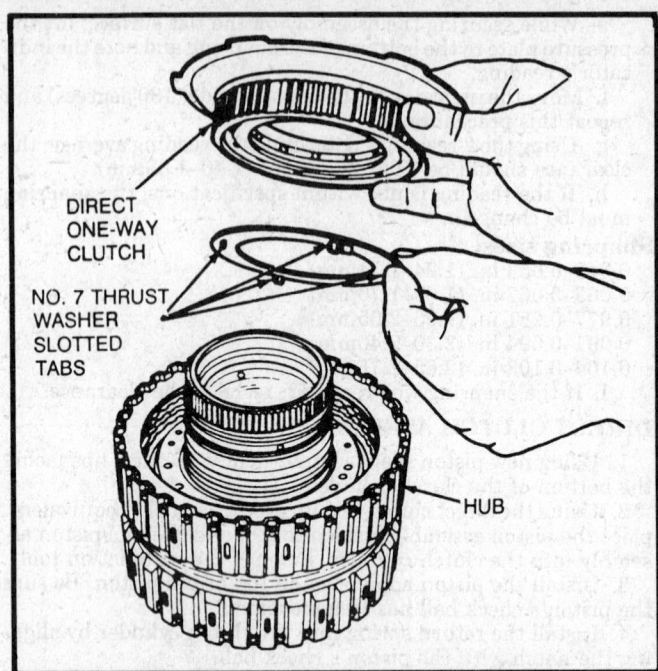

Installing the No. 7 thrust washer and the direct 1-way clutch onto the intermediate clutch cylinder

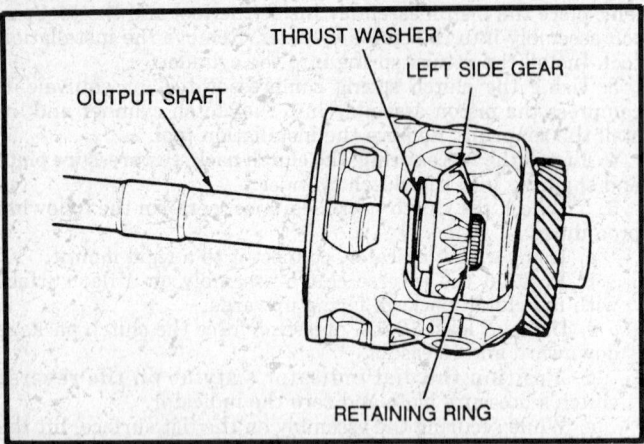

View of the differential, left side gear and output shaft assembly

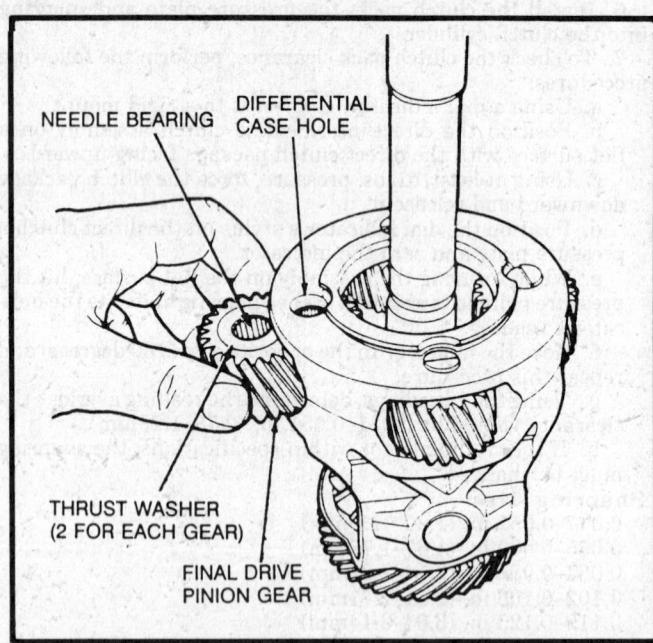

View of the pinion gears with the differential housing

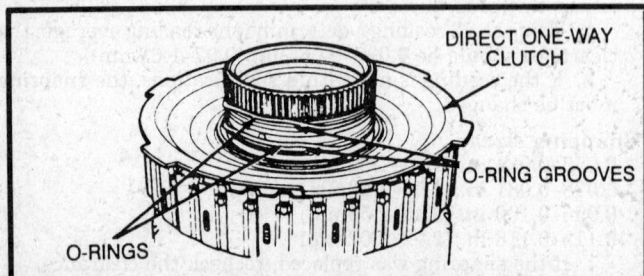

Location of the direct one-way clutch O-rings

clutch cylinder by aligning its serrations with the clutch pack splines.

4. Install new O-ring seals onto the direct one-way clutch.

5. When installing the forward clutch assembly onto the di-rect one-way clutch, be careful not to damage the O-ring seals. Install the No. 6 thrust washer (tabs facing downward) onto the forward clutch.

6. Install the overdrive drum/one-way clutch assembly over the forward clutch.

NOTE: When installing the overdrive drum/one-way clutch assembly, be sure the one-way clutch outer race groove is visible; if not, rotate the clutch counterclockwise to expose it.

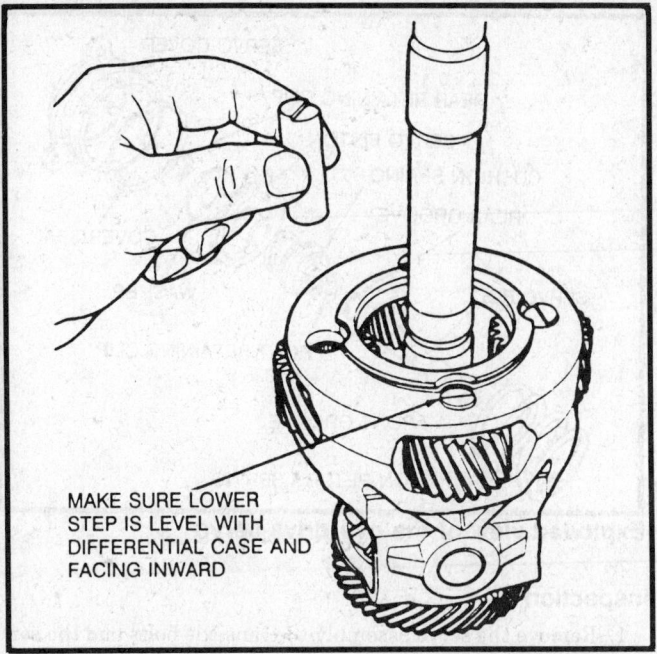

MAKE SURE LOWER STEP IS LEVEL WITH DIFFERENTIAL CASE AND FACING INWARD

Installing the pinion shafts into the differential case

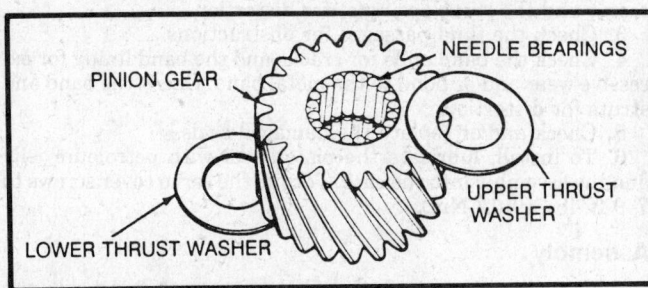

PINION GEAR — NEEDLE BEARINGS — UPPER THRUST WASHER — LOWER THRUST WASHER

View of the pinion gear assemblies

7. Turn the shell assembly over (rest it on the overdrive drum). Grease and install the No. 10 needle bearing into the intermediate clutch hub. Install the intermediate clutch hub (with No. 10 needle bearing) into the intermediate clutch cylinder; be sure the clutch plates align with the hub's serrations.

8. Install the No. 11 needle bearing (outer lip facing downward) onto the intermediate clutch hub.

9. Install the sun gear/shell assembly onto the overdrive drum assembly.

DIFFERENTIAL AND GEARSET (FINAL DRIVE)

Disassembly

1. Position the differential assembly in the vertical position (shaft facing upward).
2. Remove the snapring from the planetary pinion shaft.
3. Using a magnet, lift the planetary pinion shafts from the differential case housing. Remove the pinion gears and thrust washers from the differential case.
4. Inspect the pinion gear's needle bearings and shafts for wear and/or damage; replace them, if necessary.
5. From the top of the differential planetary assembly, remove the No. 17 needle bearing.
6. Move the differential assembly to the horizontal position. Using a drift punch, remove the roll pin from the differential

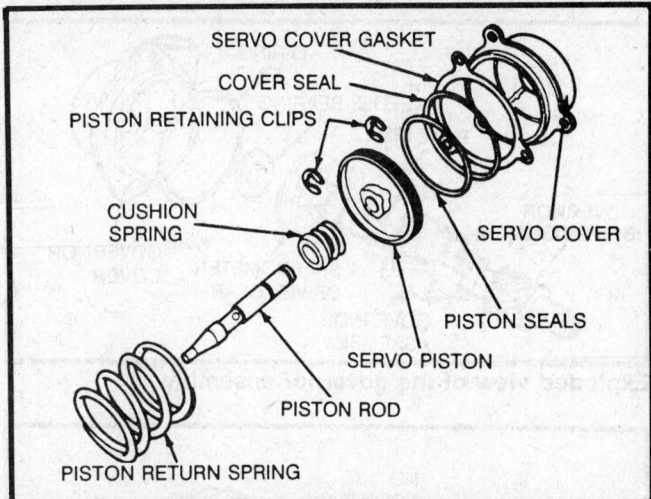

SERVO COVER GASKET — COVER SEAL — PISTON RETAINING CLIPS — CUSHION SPRING — SERVO COVER — PISTON SEALS — SERVO PISTON — PISTON ROD — PISTON RETURN SPRING

Exploded view of the low/intermediate servo

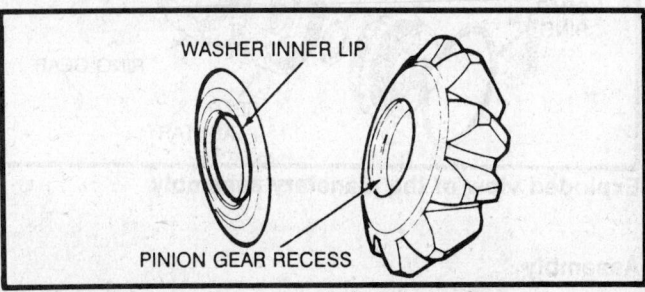

WASHER INNER LIP — PINION GEAR RECESS

View of the pinion gear and thrust washer

pinion shaft and the pinion shaft from the differential assembly.

7. Rotate the output shaft and remove the pinion gears and thrust washers.
8. Remove the right-hand side gear and thrust washer.
9. Move the output shaft toward the center of the differential housing and the left-hand side gear upward on the shaft (to gain access to the retaining ring). Remove the retaining ring and the output shaft from the differential housing. Remove the pinion gear and the thrust washer.

Inspection
OUTPUT SHAFT

1. Check the output shaft bearing surfaces for scoring and/or wear; if necessary, replace the shaft.
2. Check the output shaft splines for wear; if necessary, replace the shaft.
3. Inspect the shaft bushings for scoring and/or wear; if necessary, replace them.

PINION GEARS AND SHAFTS

1. Check the pinion gear and shafts for looseness and/or complete disengagement; be sure to check the shaft welds.
2. Check the pinion gears for freedom of rotation, damage and/or excessively worn teeth.

THRUST WASHERS

1. Using clean solvent, throughly clean the thrust bearings. Using compressed air, blow dry the bearings.
2. Check the bearings for pitting and/or roughness; replace them, if necessary.
3. Before installation, lubricate the cleaned bearings with clean transmission fluid.

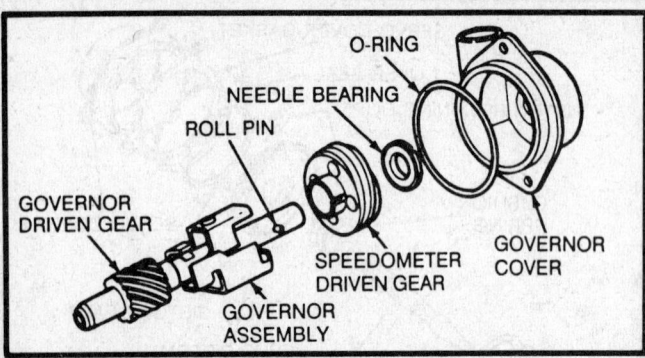

Exploded view of the governor assembly

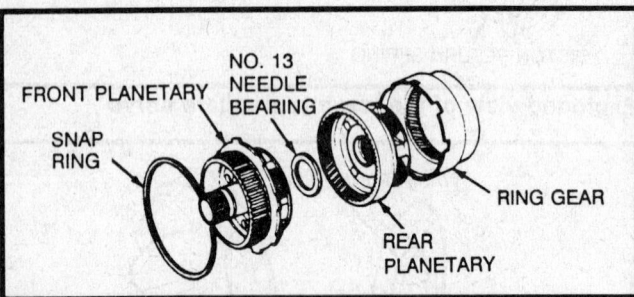

Exploded view of the planetary assembly

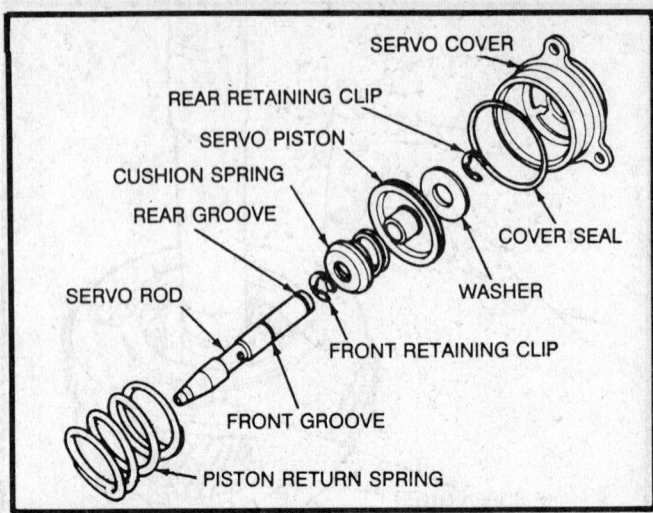

Exploded view of the overdrive servo

Assembly

1. Insert the output shaft into the differential case. Install the thrust washer, the left-hand side gear and the retaining ring onto the output shaft.
2. Install the thrust washer and the right-hand side gear into the differential case.
3. Seat the thrust washers (lips facing pinion gear) onto the pinion gears. Engage the pinion gear teeth with the side gears and rotate the output shaft to install the pinion gear assemblies into the differential housing.
4. After walking (turning the output shaft) the pinion gears into position, install the pinion shaft (tap it into position) and align the retaining pin hole with the differential housing. Using a drift punch, tap the roll pin into the differential housing/pinion shaft.
5. Install the No. 17 needle bearing (tabs facing upward) over the output shaft and seat it onto the differential housing.
6. Using a small amount of grease, install the needle bearings and the thrust washers onto the pinion gears.
7. Position the pinion gear assemblies into the differential housing and align the case holes. Install the pinion shafts through the differential case/gears until the lower shaft step is level with the differential case.
8. Install the retaining ring into the differential case grooves to hold the pinion shafts in place.

LOW/INTERMEDIATE SERVO

Disassembly

1. Remove the servo-to-transaxle cover bolts, the cover and the return spring.
2. From the cover, remove the piston and the rod.
3. From the piston assembly, remove the retaining clips, the rod and the cushion spring.
4. From the piston, remove the seal. From the cover, remove the seal and the gasket.

Inspection

1. Remove the servo assembly-to-transaxle bolts and the servo assembly.
2. Check the servo body's for cracks, the piston bore for scores and the servo spring(s) for distortion.
3. Check the fluid passages for obstructions.
4. Check the band ends for cracks and the band lining for excessive wear and/or bond to the metal band. Check the band and struts for distortion.
5. Check and/or replace the damaged seals.
6. To install, lubricate the piston seal with petroleum jelly and the assembly into the case. Torque the servo cover screws to 7–9 ft. lbs. (9–12 Nm).

Assembly

1. Onto the piston rod, install the front retaining clip, the cushion spring and the piston.
2. Compress the assembly and install the rear retaining clip.
3. Using a new piston seal, install it onto the piston. Using a new cover seal and gasket, install them onto the servo cover.
4. Using petroleum jelly, lubricate the piston seals.
5. Install the piston assembly and return spring into the servo cover.
6. Install the servo cover assembly into the transaxle case; make sure the return spring is positioned correctly.
7. Install the servo cover-to-transaxle bolts and torque them to 7–9 ft. lbs. (9–12 Nm).

OVERDRIVE SERVO

Disassembly

1. Remove the overdrive servo cover-to-transaxle bolts and the cover.
2. From the cover, remove the servo piston.
3. From the piston rod, remove the rear retaining clip, the washer, the piston, the seal (from the piston), the cushion spring and the front retaining clip.
4. Remove the seal from the cover.

Inspection

1. Remove the servo assembly-to-transaxle bolts and the servo assembly.
2. Check the servo body's for cracks, the piston bore for scores and the servo spring(s) for distortion.

3. Check the fluid passages for obstructions.
4. Check the band ends for cracks and the band lining for excessive wear and/or bond to the metal band. Check the band and struts for distortion.
5. Check and/or replace the damaged seals.
6. To install, lubricate the piston seal with petroleum jelly and the assembly into the case. Torque the servo cover screws to 7–9 ft. lbs. (9–12 Nm).

Assembly

1. Onto the piston rod, install the front retaining clip, the cushion spring, the piston and the washer.
2. Compress the assembly and install the rear retaining clip.
3. Using a new piston seal, install it onto the piston. Using a new cover seal, it onto the servo cover.
4. Using petroleum jelly, lubricate the piston seal.
5. Install the piston assembly and return spring into the transaxle; make sure the return spring is positioned correctly.
6. Install the servo cover-to-transaxle bolts and torque them to 7–9 ft. lbs. (9–12 Nm).

GOVERNOR

Disassembly

1. Remove the governor-to-transaxle bolts and the cover.
2. Remove the cover seal and discard it.
3. Remove the governor assembly from the transaxle and disassemble the speedometer drive gear bearing, the speedometer drive gear and the governor assembly.

Inspection

1. Remove the governor-to-transaxle bolts and the governor assembly from the transaxle assembly.
2. Check the governor shaft seal for cracks, scoring and/or cuts.
3. Check the balance weight retaining pin for wear and the spring for distortion, damage or misalignment.
4. Check the pressure balls for scoring and free movement.
5. Check the governor drive, the driven gear and the speedometer drive gear for broken, chipped or worn teeth; replace, if necessary.
6. To install, place the assembly into the case bore, align the driven gear with the speedometer gear teeth and seat the assembly in the bore. Torque the governor cover-to-case bolts to 7–9 ft. lbs. (9–12 Nm).

Assembly

1. Onto the governor shaft, push the speedometer drive gear and align its slots with the roll pin.
2. Onto the speedometer drive gear, install the speedometer drive gear bearing with the outer race (black side) facing upward.
3. Using a new seal, install it onto the cover.
4. Install the assembly into the transaxle and torque the cover-to-transaxle bolts to 7–9 ft. lbs. (9–12 Nm).

PLANETARY ASSEMBLY

Disassembly

1. Remove the snapring, the front planetary and the No. 13 needle bearing from the planetary assembly.
2. From the shell/ring gear assembly, remove the rear planetary.

Inspection

The individual planetary carrier parts are not serviceable, except for the differential.
1. Check the planetary assembly's pins/shafts for looseness

and/or complete disengagement; be sure to check the shaft welds. If replacement is necessary, install a new planetary assembly.
2. Check the pinion gears for freedom of rotation, damage and/or excessively worn teeth.

Assembly

1. Install the rear planetary assembly into the shell/ring gear assembly.
2. Install the No. 13 needle bearing, the front planetary and the snapring into the planetary assembly.

DRIVEN SPROCKET SUPPORT

Disassembly

Using the stator/driven sprocket bearing remover tool or equivalent, and a slide hammer, pull the needle bearing from the driven sprocket support.

Assembly

Using the Stator/Driven Sprocket Bearing Replacer tool or equivalent, press the needle bearing into the driven sprocket support.

Transaxle Assembly

UNIT ASSEMBLY

1. Place the transaxle case if the horizontal position.
2. If the drive sprocket support was removed from the torque converter housing, install it and torque the bolts to 7–9 ft. lbs. (9–12 Nm).

NOTE: Since the drive sprocket support bolts holes are offset, it can only be aligned in one direction.

3. Using the converter oil seal replacer tool or equivalent, install a new oil seal into the front of the torque converter housing; be sure the seal is equipped with a garter spring.
4. Using the output shaft seal replacer tool or equivalent, install a new oil seal into the right-side halfshaft opening; be sure the seal is equipped with a garter spring.
5. Using the AXOD endplay tool or equivalent, the step plate adapter tool or equivalent, and 2 bolts, mount the tool assembly of the right-side halfshaft opening; this assembly will be used later to perform selective thrust washer checks.
6. Turn the case so the left-side is facing upward. Install the No. 19 needle bearing (flat side facing upward and outer lip facing down) on the case boss.
7. Install the final drive ring gear (external splines facing upward) into the case; it may be necessary to use a hammer handle (tap gently) to seat the gear into the case splines.
8. Onto the final drive assembly, assemble the governor drive gear, the final drive sun gear, the paring gear, the No. 16 needle bearing, the rear planetary support, the No. 15 needle bearing and the No. 18 thrust washer.
9. Install the final drive assembly into the case and secure with the snapring; align the snapring end with the low/intermediate band anchor pin.
10. To perform the end clearance check on the No. 18 thrust washer, perform the following procedures:
   a. Using a small pry bar, place it under the differential assembly and pry upward.
   b. Using a dial indicator, attach it to the transaxle case, rest the stylus on the final drive's output shaft.
   c. Locate the AXOD tool assembly (right-side output opening) and back off the adjusting bolt until it no longer touches the shaft.
   d. Zero the dial indicator.

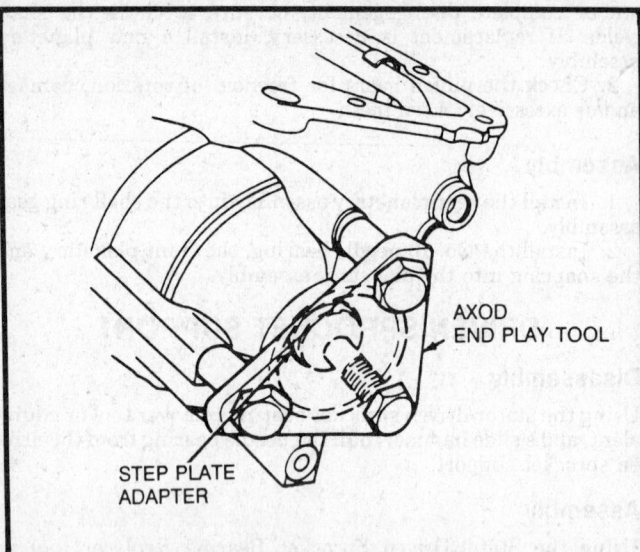

View of the adjustment tools installed in the right-side halfshaft opening

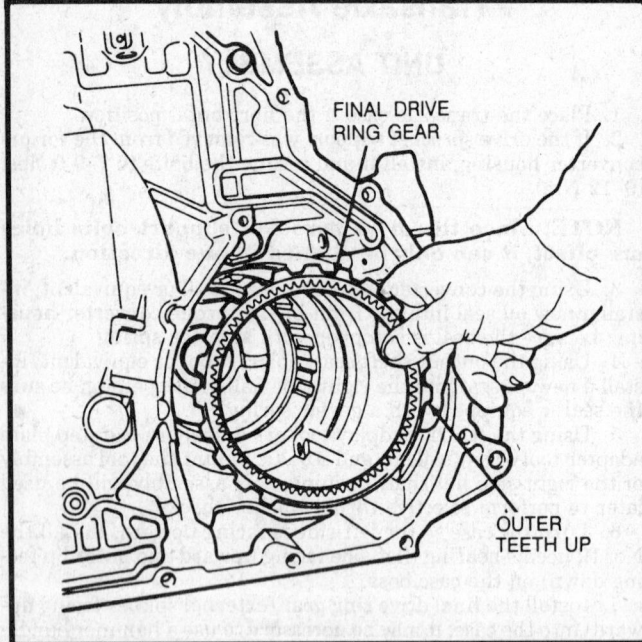

Installing the final drive ring gear into the case

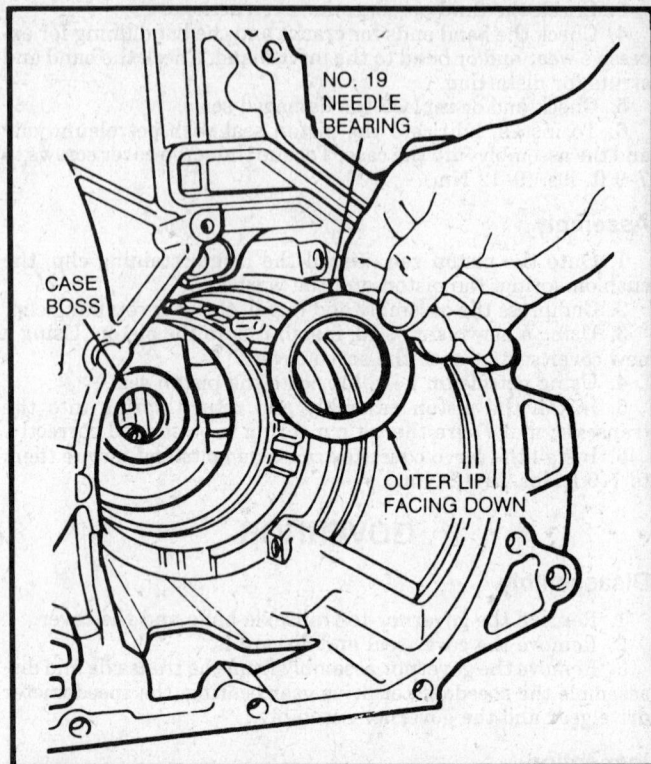

Installing the No. 19 needle bearing into the case

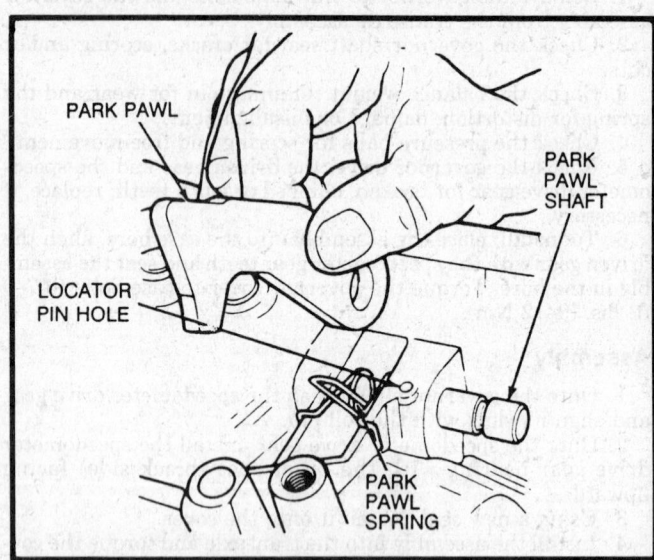

Installing the park pawl assembly

e. Torque the tool's bolt to 35–44 inch lbs. (4–5 Nm) and observe the dial indicator; the clearance should be 0.004–0.025 in. (0.1–0.65mm). If the measurement is not within specifications, the thrust washer must be replaced.

Thrust washer sizes:
Orange—0.045–0.049 in. (1.15–1.25mm)
Purple—0.055–0.059 in. (1.50–1.65mm)
Yellow—0.065–0.069 in. (1.65–1.75mm)

f. After installing another thrust washer, recheck the end clearance.

11. At the parking gear, install the park pawl, the return spring, the park pawl shaft and the locator pin; be sure the park pawl engages the park gear and returns freely.

12. Install the park rod actuating lever/park rod into the case and the park rod abutment (start the bolts). Push the park pawl

inward and locate the rod between the pawl and abutment.

13. Using a ⅜ in. drift (rod), push the lube tube seal (rubber end first) into the case (oil pan side) until it is flush.

14. At the side cover end of the case, install the low/intermediate band and align the anchor pin pocket with the anchor pin. Install the low/intermediate drum and sun gear assembly over the output shaft.

15. Assemble the planetary assembly components: the ring gear/shell assembly, the rear planetary, the No. 13 needle bearing, the front planetary and snapring; carefully slide the planetary assembly over the output shaft.

16. Install the reverse clutch into the case and engage the

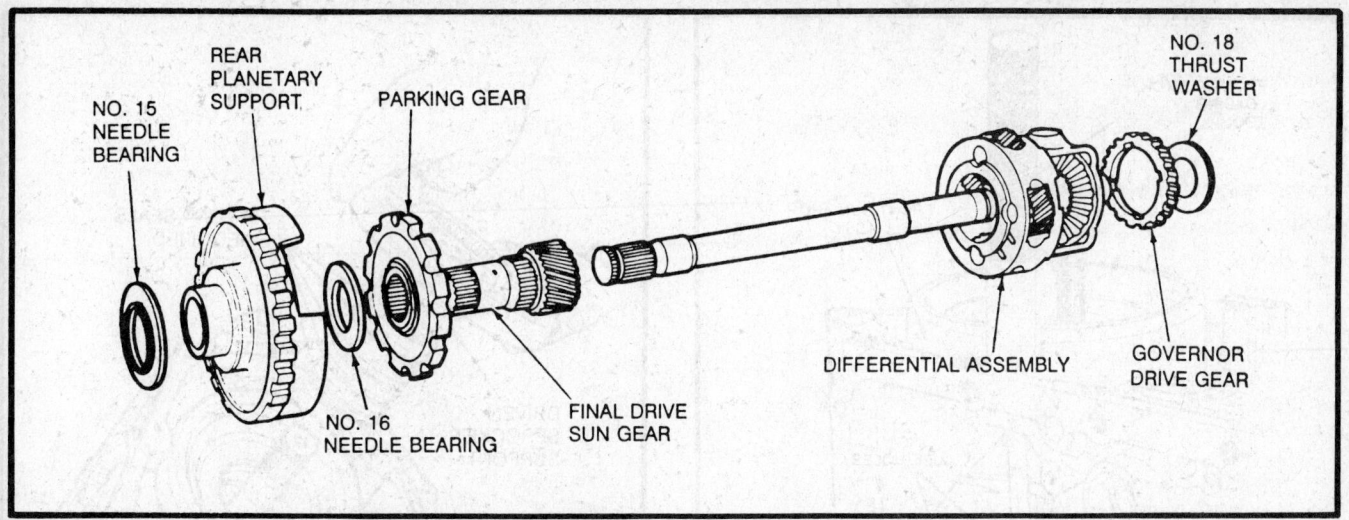

Exploded view of the final drive/planetary assembly

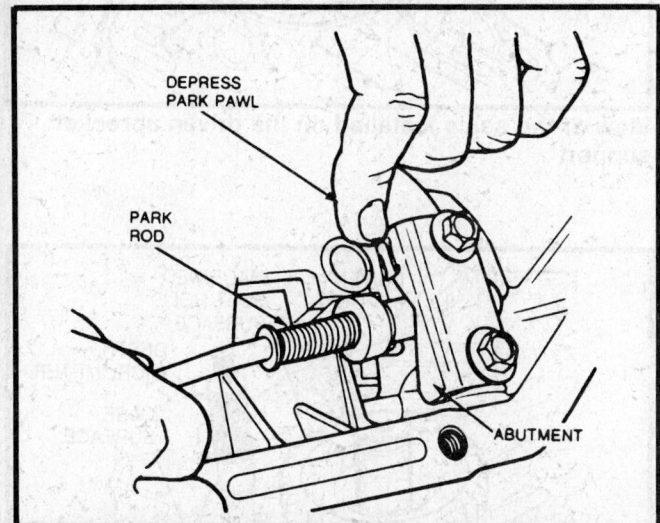

Installing the actuating rod

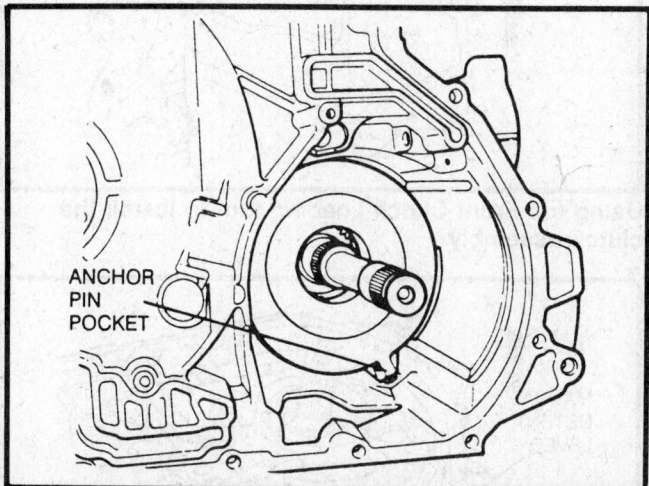

Aligning the clutch cylinder anchor pin pocket with the anchor pin case hole

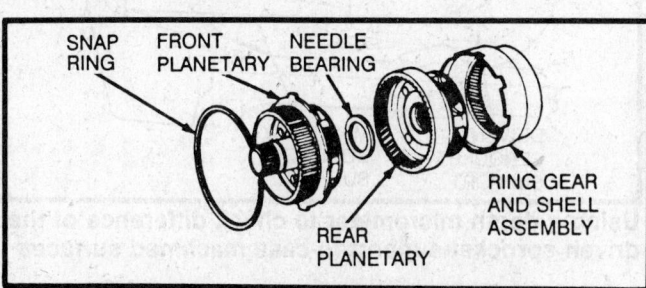

View of the planetary assembly components

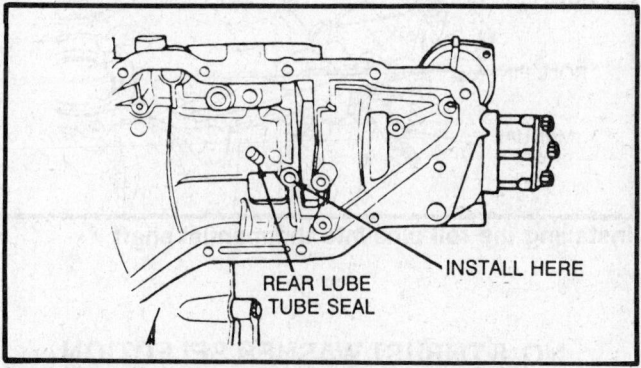

Installing the lube tube seal into the case

clutch plate by aligning the clutch cylinder anchor pin pocket with the anchor pin case hole.

17. While installing the intermediate clutch hub (when engaged with the planetary shaft splines), rotate the hub to seat the reverse clutch.

18. From the oil pan side, start the reverse anchor pin bolt but do not tighten.

19. After assembling the forward, direct and intermediate clutch assembly, attach the front clutch loading tool or equivalent, to the assembly (using a lube hole). Lower the assembly

into the case and align the shell/sun gear splines with the forward planetary; be sure the assembly is fully assembled before removing the tool.

20. Install the overdrive band and the plastic retainer (cross hairs facing upward).

21. To check the drive sprocket end clearance for the No. 5 and

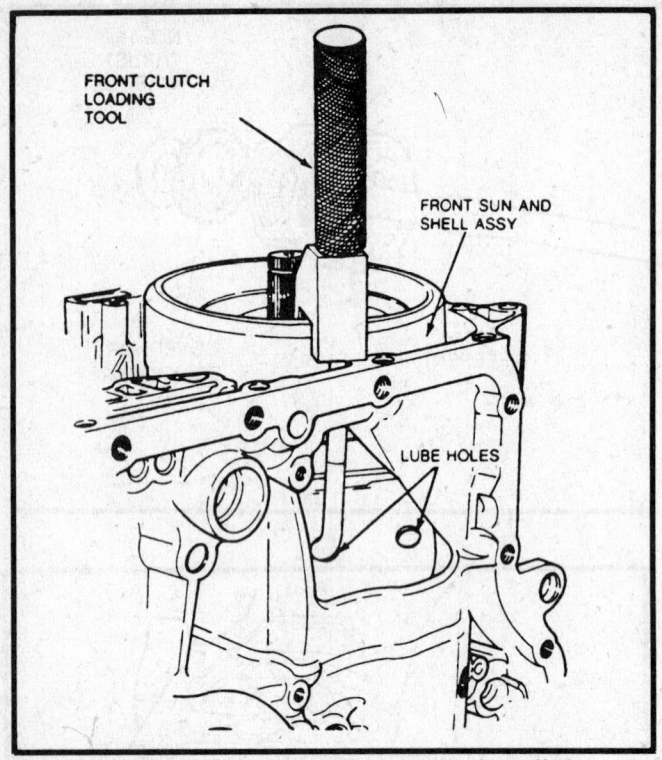

Using the Front Clutch Loading tool to install the clutch assembly

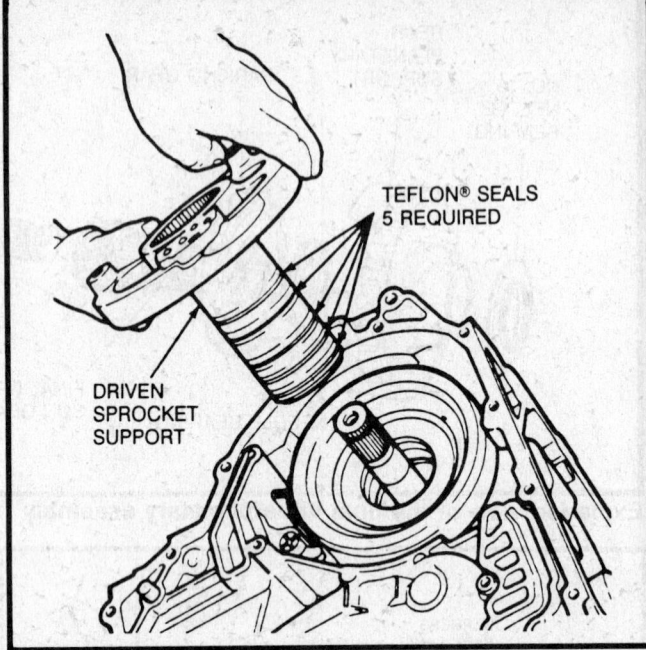

View of the seals installed on the driven sprocket support

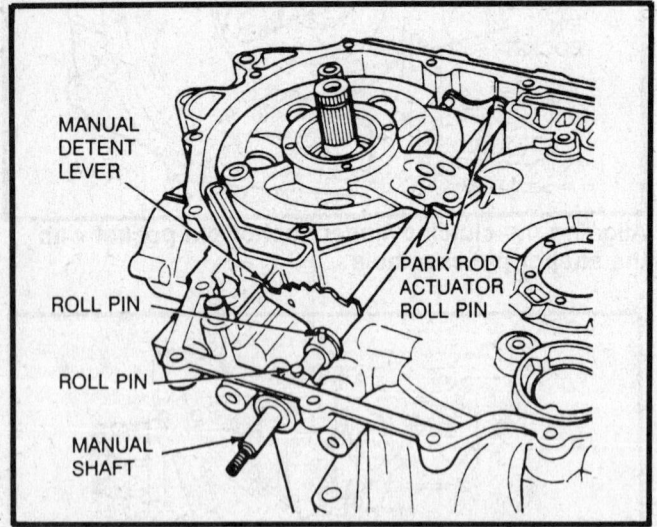

Installing the roll pins into the manual shaft

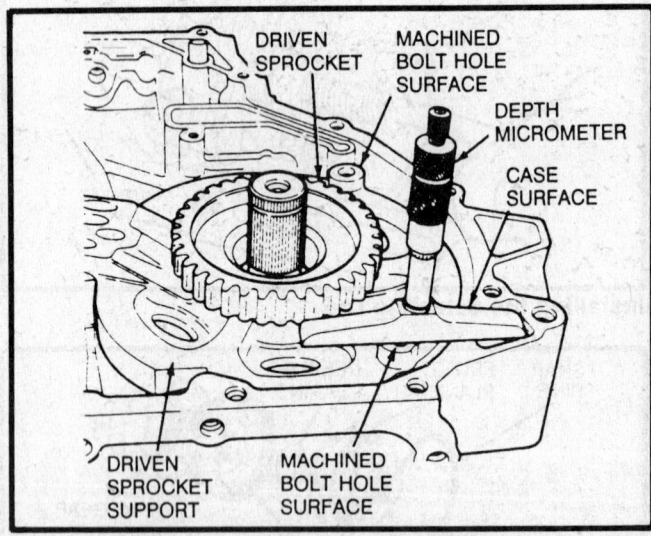

Using a depth micrometer to check difference of the driven sprocket support-to-case machined surfaces

NO. 8 THRUST WASHER SELECTION

Thrust Washer Thickness		
Inches	mm	Color
0.060–0.056	1.53–1.43	Natural
0.070–0.066	1.78–1.68	Dark green
0.079–0.075	2.02–1.92	Light blue
0.089–0.085	2.27–2.17	Red

NO. 5 THRUST WASHER SELECTION

Thrust Washer Thickness		
Inches	mm	Color
0.090–0.086	2.28–2.18	Green
0.099–0.095	2.53–2.43	Black
0.109–0.105	2.77–2.67	Natural
0.118–0.115	3.02–2.92	Red

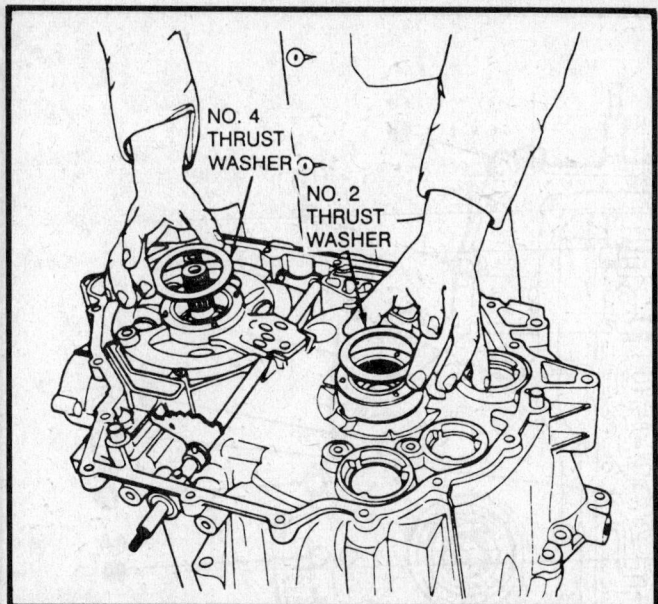

Installing the No. 2 and No. 4 thrust washers onto the case supports

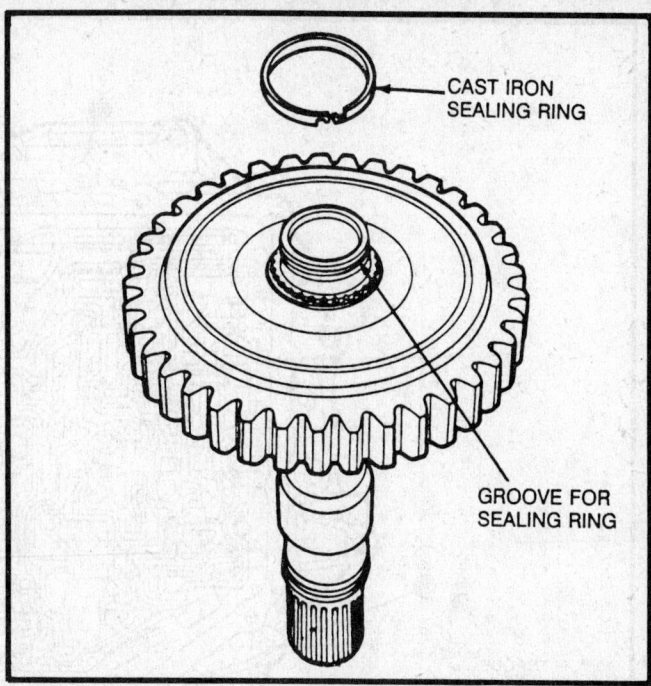

Installing the case iron sealing ring onto the input shaft

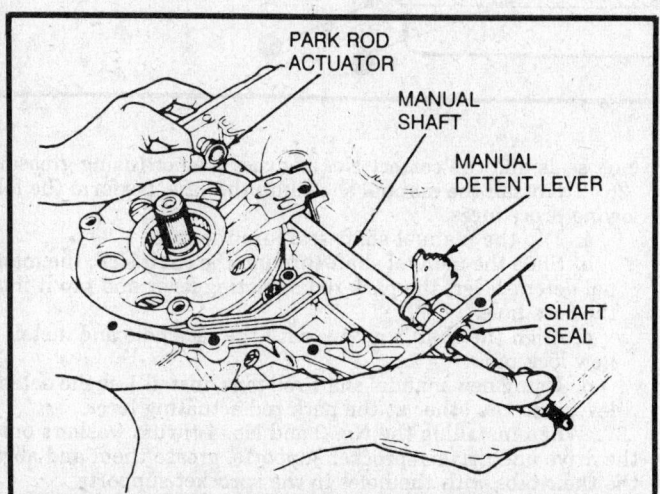

Installing the manual shaft into the transaxle case

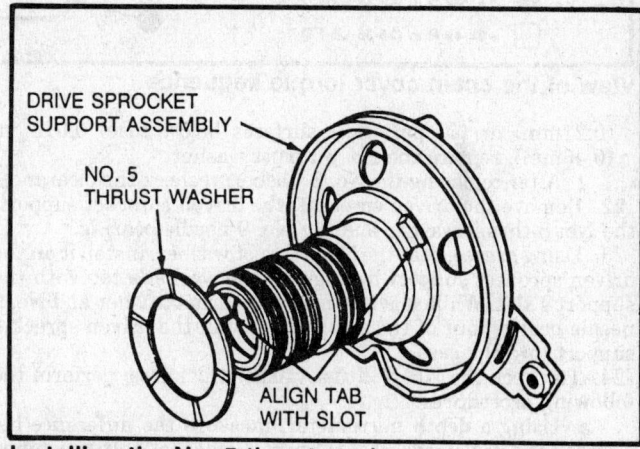

Installing the No. 5 thrust washer onto the drive sprocket support assembly

No. 8 thrust washers, perform the following procedures:

a. At the right-side output shaft, tighten the endplay check tool's screw.

b. From the driven sprocket support assembly, remove the 5 Teflon® seals (if not already removed).

c. Over the output shaft, install the No. 9 needle bearing (outer lip facing upward) and the No. 8 thrust washer.

d. If the No. 5 thrust washer is attached to the sprocket support, remove it.

e. Install the driven sprocket support and the driven sprocket to the case.

f. Determine if the machined bolt hole surfaces of the driven sprocket support are above or below the case. Using a depth micrometer, position it on the machined bolt hole surface (support hole surfaces above case) or on the case (support hole surfaces below case) and measure the averaged difference of the 2 surfaces (at both machined hole surfaces); if the average exceeds (support hole surfaces above case) 0.008 in.

Installing the No. 1 and No. 3 thrust washers onto the chain cover

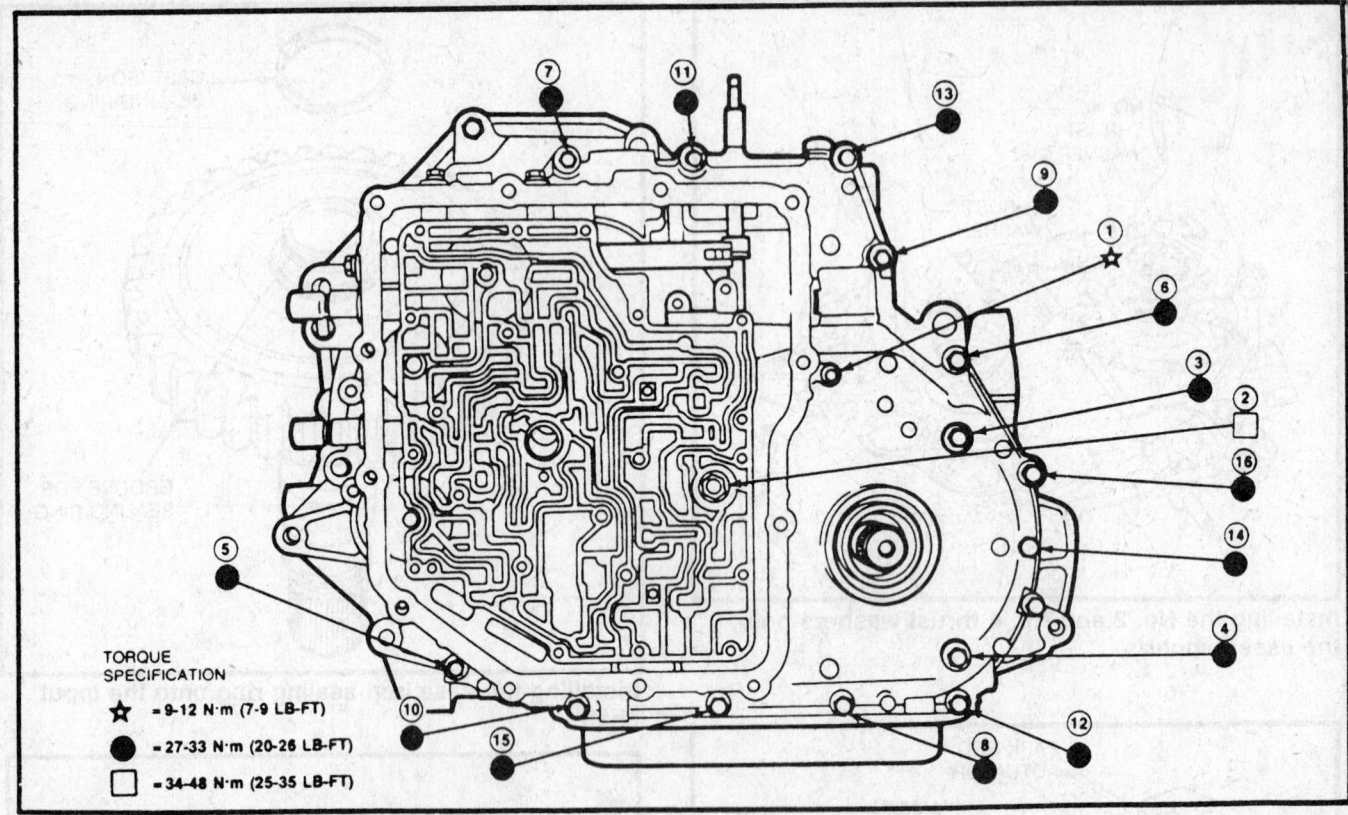

View of the chain cover torque sequence

TORQUE SPECIFICATION

☆ = 9-12 N·m (7-9 LB-FT)
● = 27-33 N·m (20-26 LB-FT)
□ = 34-48 N·m (25-35 LB-FT)

(0.21mm) or (support hole surfaces below case) 0.018 in. (0.46mm), replace the No. 8 thrust washer.

g. After replacing the No. 8 washer, recheck the clearance.

22. Remove the driven sprocket, the driven sprocket support, the No. 8 thrust washer and the No. 9 needle bearing.

23. Using grease, coat the No. 5 thrust washer, install it on the driven sprocket support by aligning the washer's tab with the support's slot. While leaving the No. 8 thrust washer and No. 9 needle bearing out of the assembly, install the driven sprocket support into the case.

24. To check the No. 5 thrust washer thickness, perform the following procedures:

a. Using a depth micrometer, measure the difference between the driven sprocket support surface (at both machined bolt holes) and the case surface; average the readings.

NOTE: The following procedure should only be used if the driven sprocket support surface is below the case surface.

b. Using the averaged reading of the No. 5 thrust washer, subtract the averaged reading of the No. 8 thrust washer; the difference should be 0–0.033 in. (0–85mm). If the difference exceeds specifications, select the correct thrust washer from the No. 5 thrust washer chart and install it.

NOTE: The following procedure should only be used if the driven sprocket support surface is above the case surface.

c. Using the averaged reading of the No. 5 thrust washer, add the averaged reading of the No. 8 thrust washer; the difference should be 0–0.033 in. (0–85mm). If the difference exceeds specifications, select the correct thrust washer from the No. 5 thrust washer chart and install it.

25. Pull the driven sprocket support from the case. Install the No. 9 needle bearing, the correct No. 8 thrust washer, the Tef-lon® seals and the correct No. 5 thrust washer (using grease).

26. To install the manual shaft into the case, perform the following procedures:

a. Tap the manual shaft seal into the case.

b. Slide the manual shaft through the shaft seal, the manual detent lever, the park rod actuating lever and tap it into the case hole.

c. Align the shaft's groove with the case hole and install a new lock pin.

d. Using new manual shaft roll pins, install 1 at the detent lever and the other at the park rod actuating lever.

27. When installing the No. 2 and No. 4 thrust washers onto the drive and driven sprocket supports, grease them and align the their tabs with the holes in the sprocket supports.

28. Lubricate and install the case iron sealing ring onto the input shaft. Assemble the chain onto the drive and driven sprockets and install the assembly into the sprocket supports; when installing, rotate the sprockets to be sure they are fully seated.

29. Onto the chain cover, align (tabs with slots) and install the No. 1 and No. 3 thrust washers.

30. Install the chain cover gasket onto the case. Install the accumulator springs into the correct case positions.

31. Carefully lower the chain cover onto the case, align the cover pins, apply gentle pressure to the cover to compress the accumulator springs and install the cover-to-case bolts. Torque (in sequence) the 8mm bolts to 7–9 ft. lbs. (9–12 Nm), the 10mm bolts to 20–26 ft. lbs. (27–33 Nm) and the 13mm bolts to 25–35 ft. lbs. (34–48 Nm).

NOTE: When installing the chain cover, be careful not to damage the input shaft's cast iron sealing ring. If the input shaft does not have some endplay after installation, remove the cover and inspect the cast iron seal for damage.

32. Torque the park rod abutment bolts to 20–22 ft. lbs. (27–

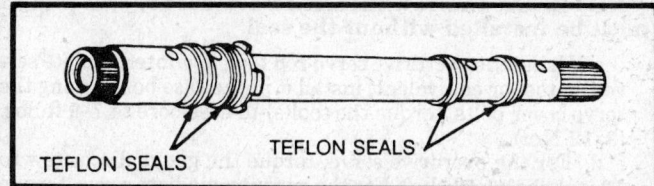

View of the Teflon® seals installed on the oil shaft

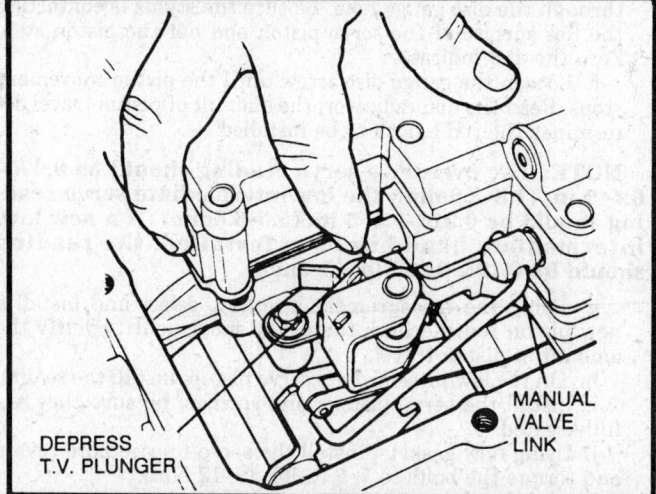

Depressing the T.V. plunger to install the valve body

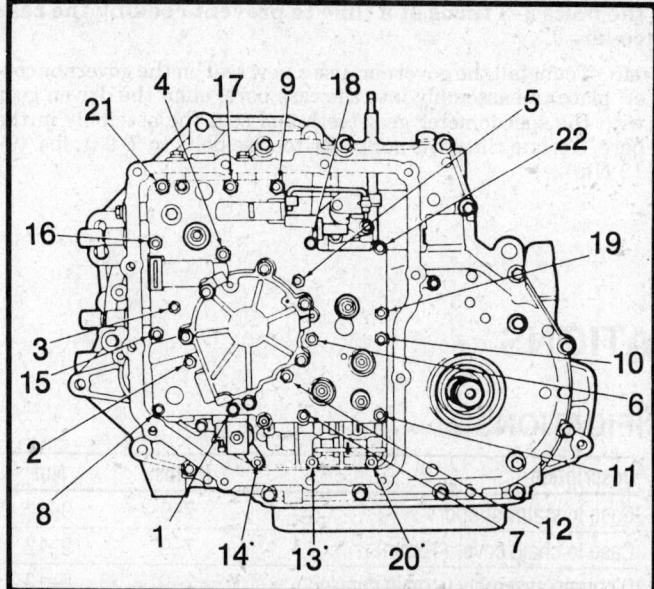

View of the valve body bolt torquing sequence

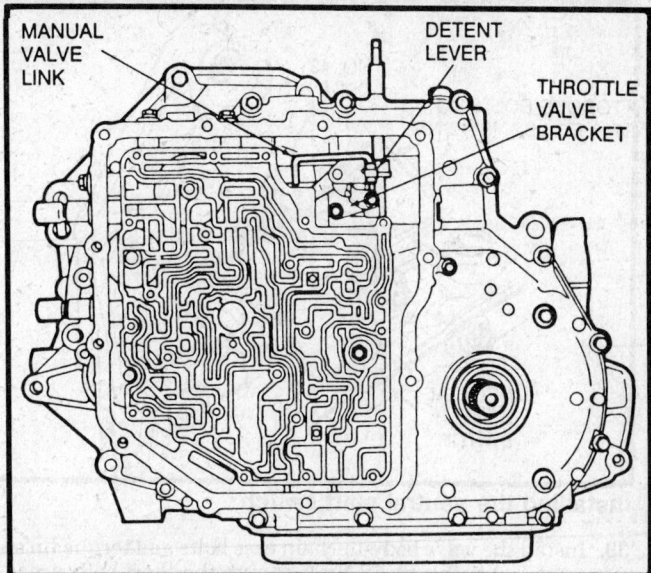

View of the throttle valve assembly

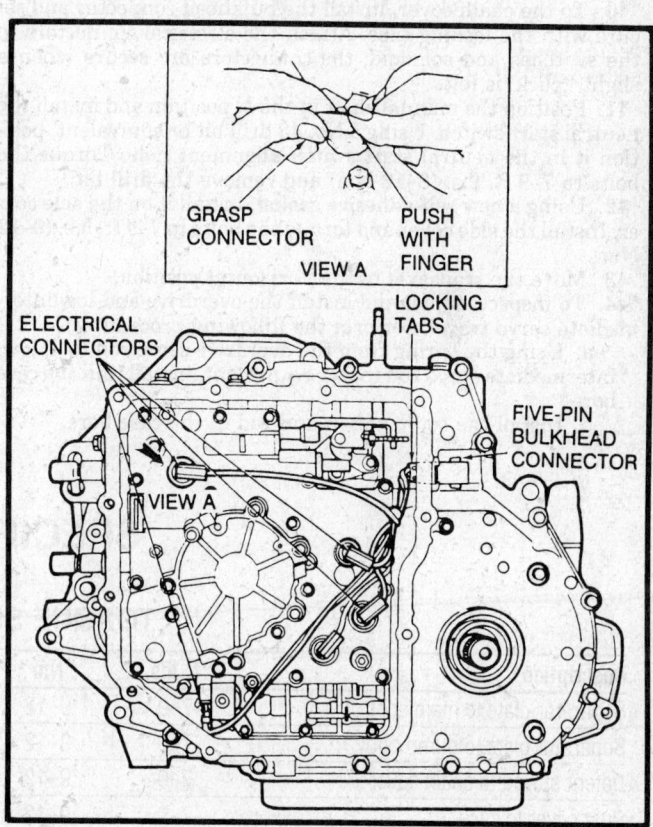

View of the valve body electrical connectors

30 Nm), the reverse drum 6mm Allen® anchor bolt to 7.5–9 ft. lbs. (10–12 Nm) and the 19mm locknut to 25–35 ft. lbs. (34–47 Nm).

33. At the oil pan side, lightly tap the lube tubes into position; using threadlock compound, coat the lube tube-to-case surfaces. Install the tube retaining brackets.

34. Install 2 new O-rings onto the oil filter and push the filter into the case. Install the reverse apply tube/oil filter bracket.

35. To install the oil pan, use a new gasket and the pan. Torque the pan-to-case bolts to 10–12 ft. lbs. (14–16 Nm).

36. Onto the oil pump shaft, install new Teflon® seals and install the shaft.

37. Through the case hole near the side cover, install the T.V. bracket with the T.V. link and torque the bolts to 7–9 ft. lbs. (9–12 Nm). Connect the manual valve link to the detent lever.

38. While installing the oil pump/valve body over the oil pump shaft, attach the manual valve link to the manual valve. Depress the T.V. plunger (to clear the T.V. bracket) and seat the oil pump/valve body.

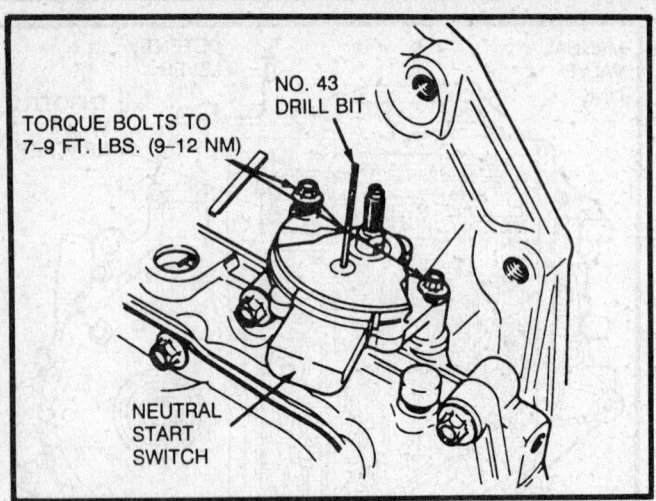

Installing the neutral start switch

39. Install the valve body-to-chain case bolts and torque (in sequence) to 7–9 ft. lbs. (9–12 Nm); be sure the short bolts are installed in their correct location.

40. To the chain cover, install the bulkhead connector and secure with the locking tabs. Attach the electrical connectors to the switches and solenoid; the connectors are secure when a slight "click" is felt.

41. Position the manual shaft in the **N** position and install the neutral start switch. Using a No. 43 drill bit or equivalent, position it in the neutral start switch alignment hole. Torque the bolts to 7–9 ft. lbs. (9–12 Nm) and remove the drill bit.

42. Using a new self-adhesive gasket, install it on the side cover. Install the side cover and torque the bolts to 7–9 ft. lbs. (9–12 Nm).

43. Move the transaxle to the horizontal position.

44. To inspect, adjust and install the overdrive and low/intermediate servo travel, perform the following procedures:

a. Using the spring from the overdrive servo rod tool, low/intermediate servo rod tool or equivalent, install it in the case bore.

b. Install the servo piston and rod in the case bore.

NOTE: On the low/intermediate servo, the piston must be installed without the seal.

c. Using the overdrive servo rod tool, low/intermediate servo rod tool or equivalent, install it in the case bore. Using the servo cover bolts, torque the tool(s)-to-case bore to 7–9 ft. lbs. (9–12 Nm).

d. For the overdrive servo, torque the gauge disc screw to 10 inch lbs. (1.13 Nm). For the low/intermediate servo, torque the gauge disc screw to 30 inch lbs. (3.4 Nm).

e. Using a dial indicator, mount and position the stylus through the disc gauge hole. Be sure the stylus is contacting the flat surface of the servo piston and not the piston step. Zero the dial indicator.

f. Loosen the gauge disc screw until the piston movement stops. Read the dial indicator; the amount of piston travel determines the rod length to be installed.

NOTE: The overdrive servo reading should be 0.070–0.149 in. (1.8–3.8mm); the low/intermediate servo reading should be 0.216–0.255 in. (5.5–6.5mm). If a new low/intermediate band has been installed, the reading should be 0.196–0.236 in. (5–6mm).

g. Using the measurement acquired, select and install a new piston rod. Recheck the piston movement to verify the amount of piston travel.

h. On the low/intermediate servo piston, install the seal(s).

i. Install the servo pistons and springs; be sure they are fully seated.

j. Using new gaskets, install the servo-to-case bore covers and torque the bolts to 7–9 ft. lbs. (9–12 Nm).

NOTE: When installing the low/intermediate servo cover, be sure the tab aligns with the case port. Tighten the bolts 2–3 turns at a time to prevent cocking the case cover.

45. To install the governor, use a new seal on the governor cover, place the assembly into the case bore, align the driven gear with the speedometer gear teeth and seat the assembly in the bore. Torque the governor cover-to-case bolts to 7–9 ft. lbs. (9–12 Nm).

SPECIFICATIONS

TORQUE SPECIFICATIONS

Description	ft. lbs.	Nm
Separator plate to main control	7–9	9–12
Separator plate to pump body	7–9	9–12
Detent spring to chain cover	7–9	9–12
Dust cover to case	7–9	9–12
T.V. control lever to chain cover	7–9	9–12
Solenoid to main control	7–9	9–12
Low-intermediate servo cover to case	7–9	9–12
Overdrive servo cover to case	7–9	9–12
Pump cover to pump body	7–9	9–12
Filler tube to case	7–9	9–12
Governor cover to case	7–9	9–12

Description	ft. lbs.	Nm
Case to stator support	7–9	9–12
Case to chain cover (10mm)	7–9	9–12
Oil pump assembly to main control	7–9	9–12
Neutral start switch to case	7–9	9–12
Valve body/solenoid to chain cover	7–9	9–12
Bracket tubes to case	7–9	9–12
T.V. cable to case	6–9	8–12
Chain cover to case (10mm)	7–9	9–12
Pump body to chain cover	7–9	9–12
Oil pan to case (lower reservoir)	10–12	14–16

TORQUE SPECIFICATIONS

Description	ft. lbs.	Nm
Main control cover to chain cover (upper reservoir)	10–12	14–16
Manual lever to manual shaft	12–16	16–22
Park abutment to case	20–22	27–30
Chain cover to case (13mm)	20–22	27–30
Case to chain cover (13mm)	24.3–26.6	33–36
Chain cover to front support (13mm)	20–22	27–30
Chain cover to front support (7mm)	25–35	34–48
Differential brace to case	25–35	34–48
Engine to case/case to engine	41–50	55–68
Case to reverse clutch screw	7–9	10–12
Case to reverse clutch nut	25–35	34–47
Pressure tap plug for chain cover and pump body	6–9	8–12
Pressure switch to pump body	6–9	8–12
Transaxle to engine	41–50	55–68
Control arm to knuckle	36–44	50–60
Stabilizer U-clamp to bracket	60–70	81–95
Stabilizer to control arm	98–125	133–169
Brake hose routing clip	8	11
Tie rod to knuckle	23–35	31–47
Manual cable bracket	10–20	14–27
Starter	30–40	41–54
Dust cover	7–9	9–12
Torque converter to flywheel	23–39	31–53
Insulator to bracket	55–70	75–90
Insulator bracket to frame	40–50	55–70
Insulator mount to transmission	25–33	34–45

SPECIAL TOOLS

Tool Number	Description
D79P-100-A	Slide hammer—universal
T59L-100-B	Impact slide hammer
T58L-101-A	Impact slide hammer
T57L-500-B	Bench Mount Holding Fixture
D80L-515-S	Puller screw
D80L-522-A	Gear and pully support bar
D80L-625-A	Shaft protector
D80L-630-3	Step plate adapter
T00L-1175-AC	Seal remover
T86P-1177-B	Output shaft seal replacer
D81P-3504-N	Locknut pin remover
T86P-3514-A1	C.V. joint puller
T86P-3514-A2	Screw extension
T00L-4201-C	Dial indicator
D79P-6000-A	Engine support bar
D81L-6001-D	Engine lifting bracket
T74P-6700-A	Output shaft seal remover
T77L-7902-A	Holding wire
T80L-7902-A	End play checking tool
T80L-7902-C	End play checking tool
T81P-7902-B	One-way clutch torque tool
T81P-7902-C	Torque converter handles
T86P-7902-A	Converter guide sleeve tool
T86P-70001-A	Lube tube remover tool

Tool Number	Description
T86P-70023-B	Overdrive servo rod tool
T86P-70023-A	Low/Intermediate servo rod tool
T86P-70043-A	Stator and driven sprocket bearing remover
T86P-70043-B	Stator and driven sprocket bearing replacer
T86P-70100-A	Valve body guide pin set
T86P-70100-B	Guide pin
T86P-70100-C	Valve body guide pin
T86P-70234-A	Direct clutch lip seal protector
T86P-70234-A	Output shaft seal replacer
T86P-70370-A	Pump body guide pin
T86P-70373-A	Direct/intermediate clutch bushing replacer
T86P-70389-A	Front clutch loading tool
T86P-70401-A	Converter oil seal replacer
T86P-70403-A	Reverse clutch outer lip seal protector
T86P-70422-A	Bimetal height gauge
T86P-70423-A	Direct clutch bearing replacer
T86P-70548-A	Forward clutch seal lip protector
T86P-77265-AH	Cooler line disconnect tool
T65L-77515-A	Clutch spring compressor
T81P-78103-A	Slide hammer adapter
ROTUNDA EQUIPMENT	
021-00047	Torque converter leak test kit
014-00737	Automatic transmission tester kit
014-00028	Torque converter and oil cooler cleaner

THRUST WASHER AND NEEDLE BEARING LOCATION

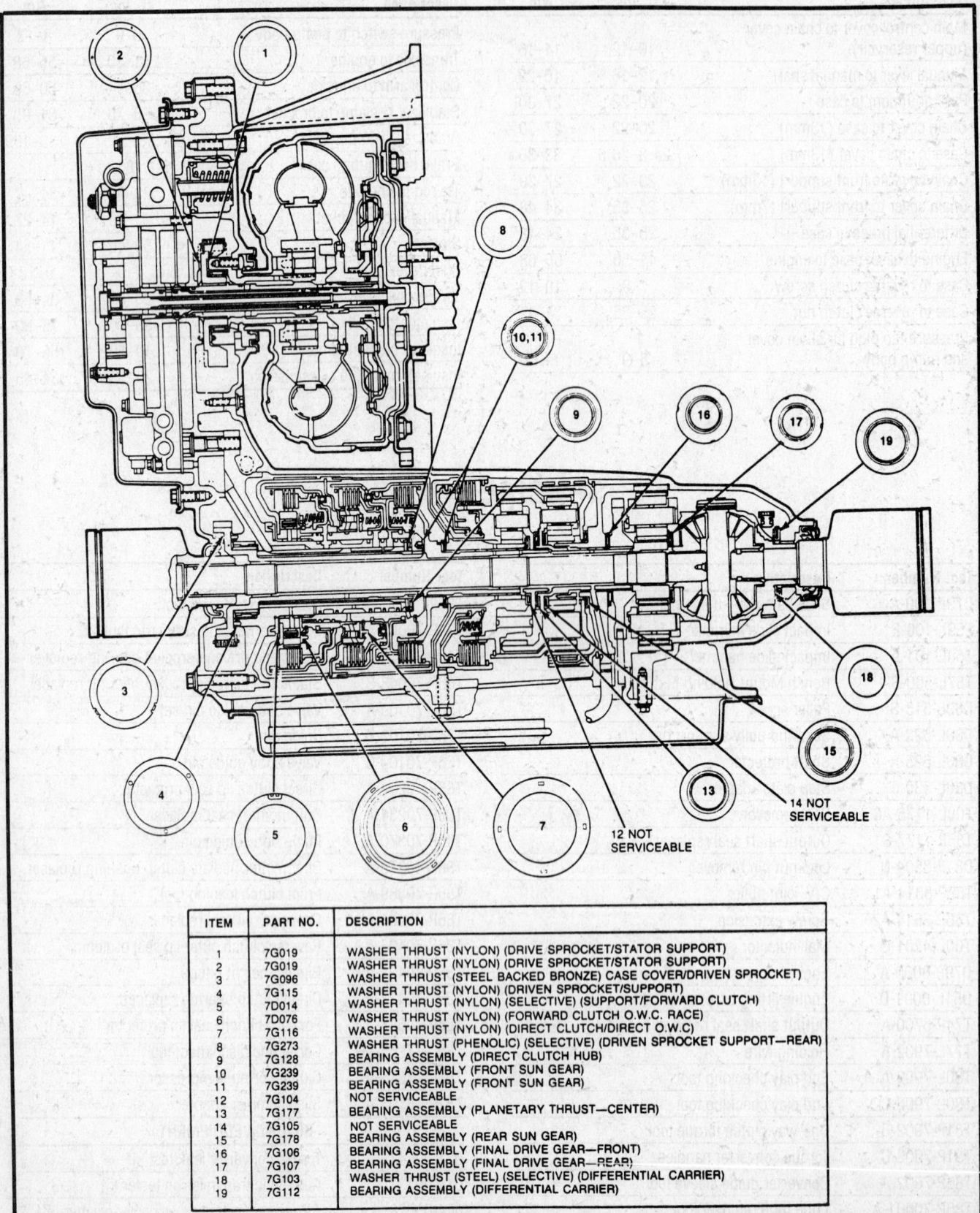

ITEM	PART NO.	DESCRIPTION
1	7G019	WASHER THRUST (NYLON) (DRIVE SPROCKET/STATOR SUPPORT)
2	7G019	WASHER THRUST (NYLON) (DRIVE SPROCKET/STATOR SUPPORT)
3	7G096	WASHER THRUST (STEEL BACKED BRONZE) CASE COVER/DRIVEN SPROCKET)
4	7G115	WASHER THRUST (NYLON) (DRIVEN SPROCKET/SUPPORT)
5	7D014	WASHER THRUST (NYLON) (SELECTIVE) (SUPPORT/FORWARD CLUTCH)
6	7D076	WASHER THRUST (NYLON) (FORWARD CLUTCH O.W.C. RACE)
7	7G116	WASHER THRUST (NYLON) (DIRECT CLUTCH/DIRECT O.W.C)
8	7G273	WASHER THRUST (PHENOLIC) (SELECTIVE) (DRIVEN SPROCKET SUPPORT—REAR)
9	7G128	BEARING ASSEMBLY (DIRECT CLUTCH HUB)
10	7G239	BEARING ASSEMBLY (FRONT SUN GEAR)
11	7G239	BEARING ASSEMBLY (FRONT SUN GEAR)
12	7G104	NOT SERVICEABLE
13	7G177	BEARING ASSEMBLY (PLANETARY THRUST—CENTER)
14	7G105	NOT SERVICEABLE
15	7G178	BEARING ASSEMBLY (REAR SUN GEAR)
16	7G106	BEARING ASSEMBLY (FINAL DRIVE GEAR—FRONT)
17	7G107	BEARING ASSEMBLY (FINAL DRIVE GEAR—REAR)
18	7G103	WASHER THRUST (STEEL) (SELECTIVE) (DIFFERENTIAL CARRIER)
19	7G112	BEARING ASSEMBLY (DIFFERENTIAL CARRIER)

Section 3

4EAT Transaxle
Ford Motor Co.

APPLICATION

1989 Ford Probe

GENERAL DESCRIPTION

The 4EAT electronically-controlled automatic transaxle is a 4 speed overdrive transaxle with a lockup torque converter. The 4EAT differs from most Ford transaxles because it is controlled by both mechanical and electronic systems. Several sensors and switches allow the 4EAT system to constantly monitor driving conditions. Signals from these sensors are sent to the 4EAT control unit, which uses the input to control shift pattern, gear position and lockup timing. The 4EAT control unit has built-in self-diagnosis, fail-safe and warning code display functions for the main input sensors and solenoid valves.

The 4 solenoid valves are located on the valve body. These valves actuate shifting and lockup by switching the oil flow through passages within the valve body. The valve body utilizes hydraulic pressure to control the application of the friction elements. The friction elements transmit power from the engine to the planetary gear unit.

A manual switch is located on the selector lever. Below it, on the selector console, is the the shift mode switch. The manual and shift mode switches provide a number of shifting and engine braking options.

The unique mechanical features of the 4EAT include a single compact combination-type planetary gear (4 speed capability) instead of the usual 2 planetary gears and a new variable capacity oil pump.

Converter Identification

CONVERTER

The torque converter is identified by either a reference or part number stamped on the converter body and is matched to a specific engine. The torque converter is a welded unit and is not repairable. If internal problems exists, the torque converter must be replaced.

Electronic Controls

The 4EAT electronic control system consists of several sensors and switches which send information to the 4EAT control unit.

The control unit utilizes the input to operate the 4EAT transaxle. The governor, used in conventional transmissions to perform shifting and lockup, is replaced in the 4EAT system by solenoid valves. These valves maintain or drain hydraulic pressure by actuating the shift and lockup control valves. The solenoid valves are controlled by the 4EAT control unit.

In the POWER mode, the transaxle shifts and the torque converter lockups occur at higher vehicle speeds to permit faster acceleration and improved performance feel. In the NORMAL mode, the shift points are selected to produce smoother engine operations and optimum fuel efficiency.

In the MANUAL SHIFT mode, the driver can use the selector lever to manually select and hold each of the lower 3 gears. A small push button on the gear selector is used to activate this mode.

Metric Fasteners

All metric fasteners are used on the 4EAT transaxle. Metric fastener dimensions are very close to the dimensions of the familiar inch system fasteners. For this reason, replacement fasteners must have the same measurement and strength as those removed.

Do not attempt to interchange metric fasteners for inch system fasteners. Mismatched or incorrect fasteners can result in damage to the transmission unit through malfunctions, breakage or possible personal injury.

NOTE: Care should be taken to reuse the fasteners in the same locations as removed.

Capacities

The 4EAT automatic transaxle use Motorcraft Mercon automatic transmission fluid. The capacity of the 4EAT automatic transaxle is 7.2 U.S. quarts or 6.8 liters.

Checking Fluid Level

1. Apply the parking brake and position wheel chocks to prevent the vehicle from rolling.

NOTE: Place the vehicle on a flat level surface. Use the low temperature scale when the fluid temperature is 148°F (68°C) or lower. Use the high temperature scale when the fluid temperature is 149°F (65°C) or higher.

4EAT SYSTEM ELECTRONIC COMPONENTS	
Components	4EAT Control Unit Input/Output
4EAT Control Unit	———
Vehicle Speed Sensor	Input
Pulse Generator	Input
Throttle Position Sensor	Input
Idle Switch	Input
Coolant Temperature Switch	Input
Fluid Temperature Switch (ATF)	Input
Brake Light Switch	Input
Neutral Safety Switch	Input
Mode Switch	Input
Manual Switch	Input
Solenoid Valve 1–2 Shift	Output
Solenoid Valve 2–3 Shift	Output
Solenoid Valve 3–4 Shift	Output
Solenoid Valve Lockup	Output

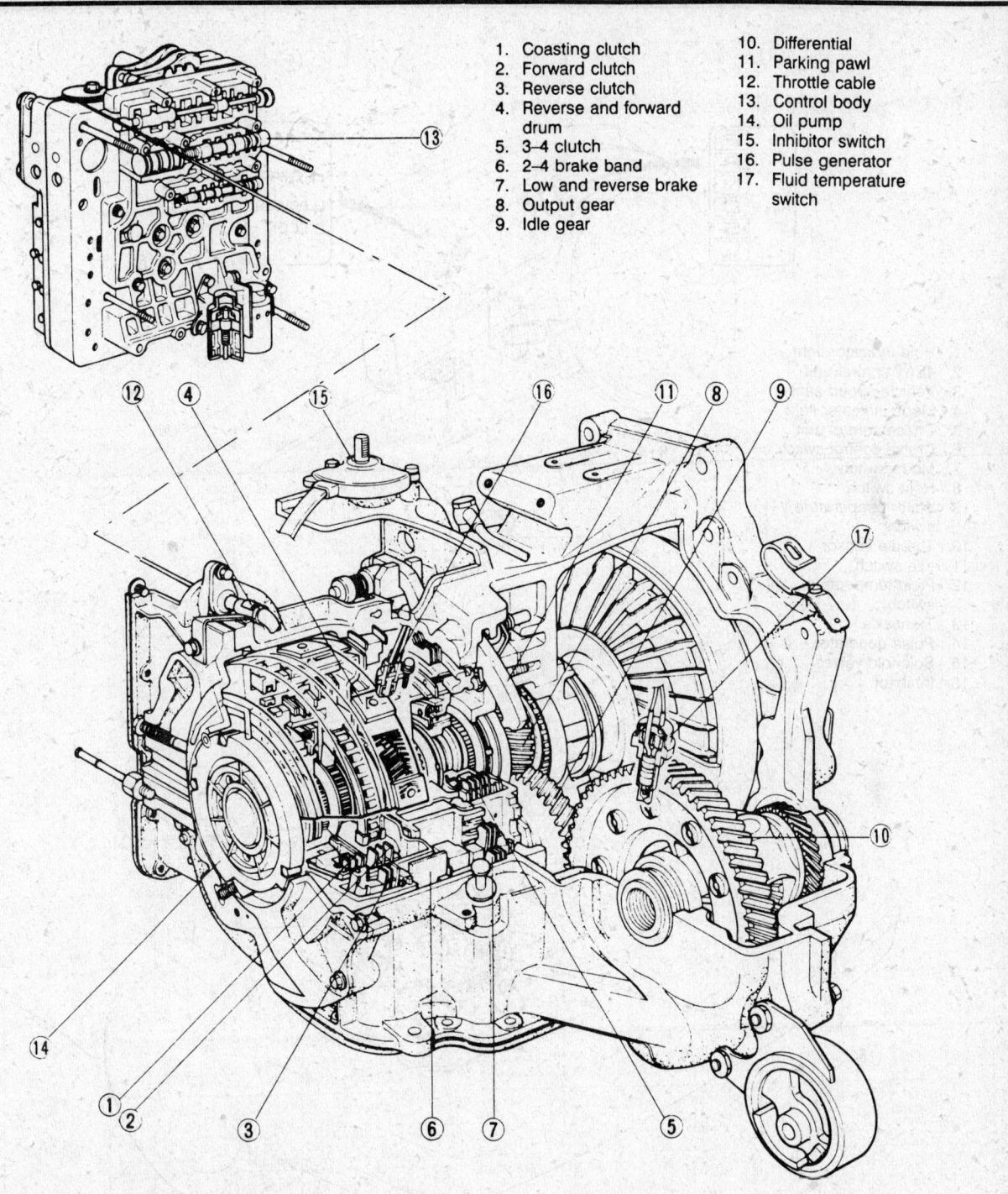

1. Coasting clutch
2. Forward clutch
3. Reverse clutch
4. Reverse and forward drum
5. 3–4 clutch
6. 2–4 brake band
7. Low and reverse brake
8. Output gear
9. Idle gear
10. Differential
11. Parking pawl
12. Throttle cable
13. Control body
14. Oil pump
15. Inhibitor switch
16. Pulse generator
17. Fluid temperature switch

Structural view of the 4EAT transaxle

2. Start the engine to allow the transmission fluid to warm up to specification.

3. With the engine idling, shift the gear selector lever from **P** to **L** and back again.

4. Let the engine idle.

5. Make sure the transmission fluid level is between the **F** and **L** marks. Add the correct fluid as required.

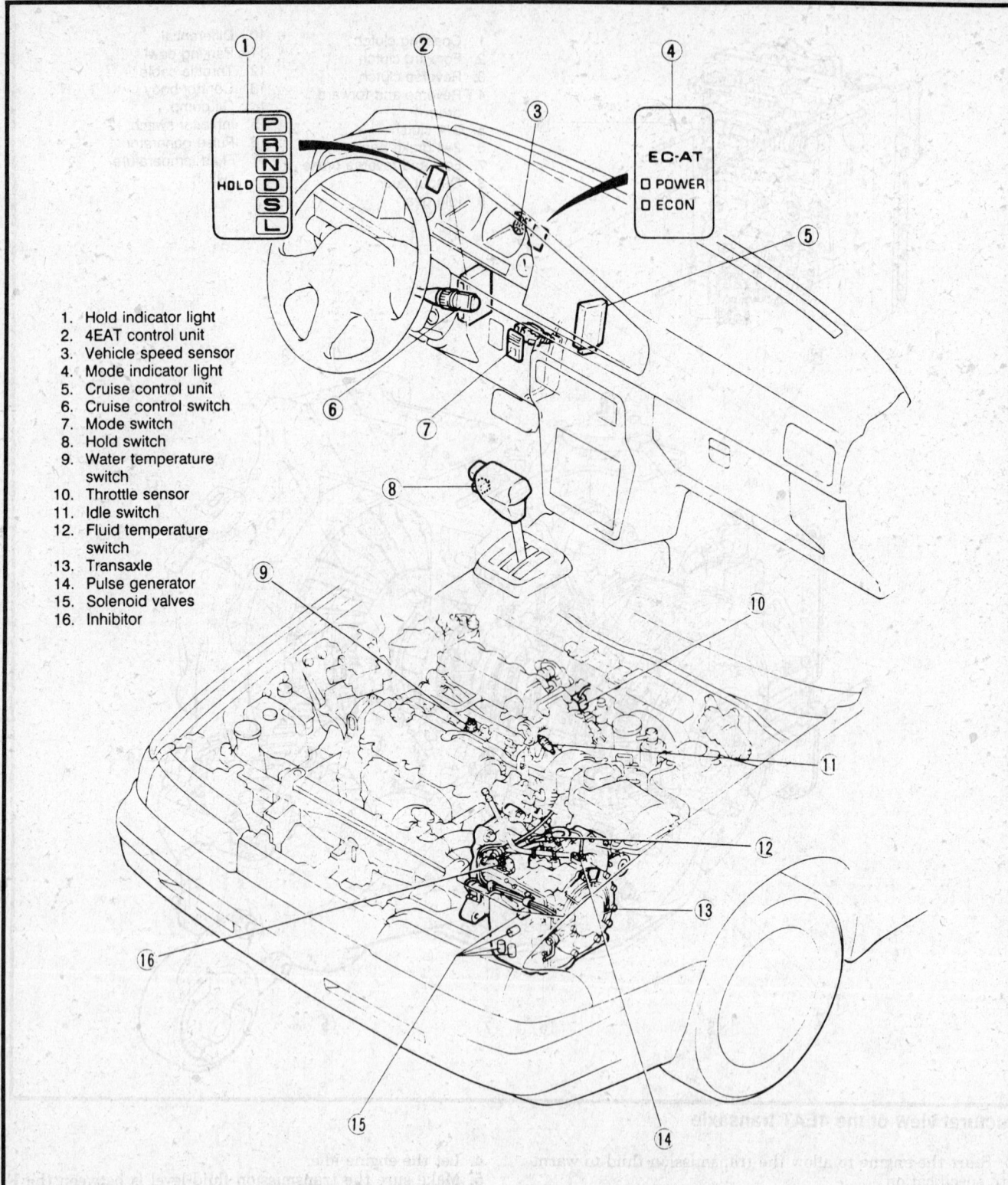

1. Hold indicator light
2. 4EAT control unit
3. Vehicle speed sensor
4. Mode indicator light
5. Cruise control unit
6. Cruise control switch
7. Mode switch
8. Hold switch
9. Water temperature switch
10. Throttle sensor
11. Idle switch
12. Fluid temperature switch
13. Transaxle
14. Pulse generator
15. Solenoid valves
16. Inhibitor

Electrical component location

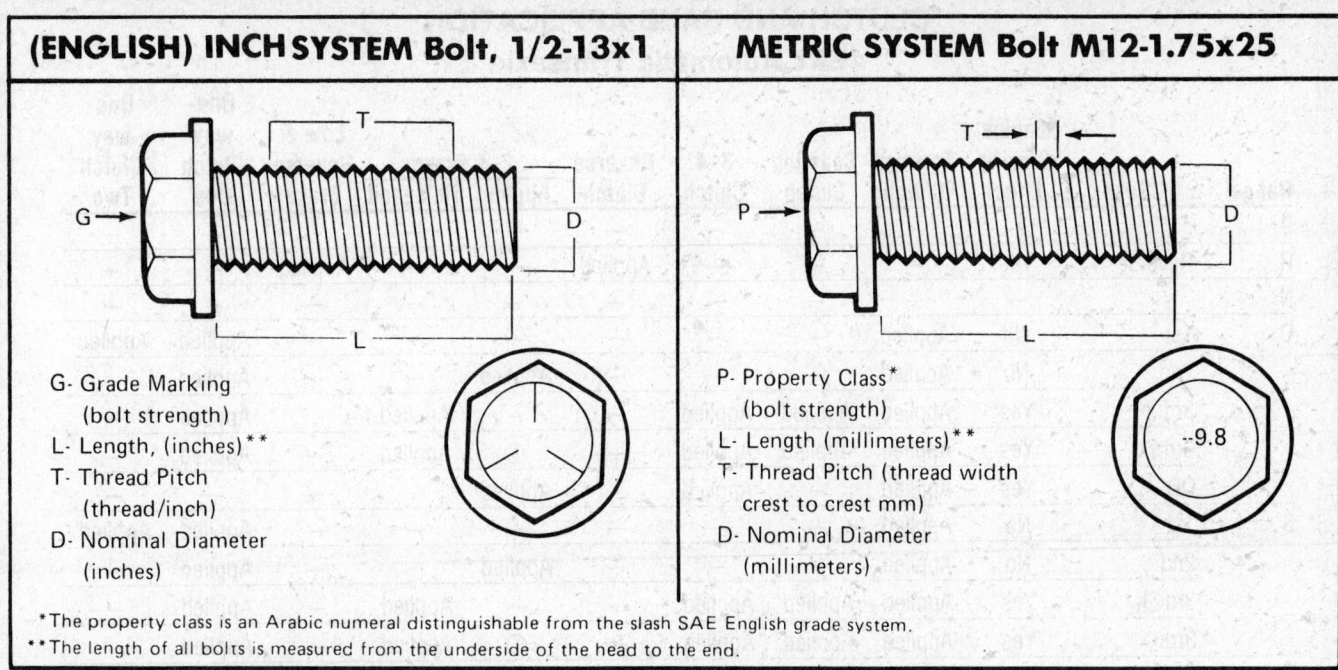

(ENGLISH) INCH SYSTEM Bolt, 1/2-13x1

G- Grade Marking
(bolt strength)
L- Length, (inches)**
T- Thread Pitch
(thread/inch)
D- Nominal Diameter
(inches)

METRIC SYSTEM Bolt M12-1.75x25

P- Property Class*
(bolt strength)
L- Length (millimeters)**
T- Thread Pitch (thread width
crest to crest mm)
D- Nominal Diameter
(millimeters)

--9.8

*The property class is an Arabic numeral distinguishable from the slash SAE English grade system.
**The length of all bolts is measured from the underside of the head to the end.

Comparison of the English Inch and Metric system bolt and thread nomenclature

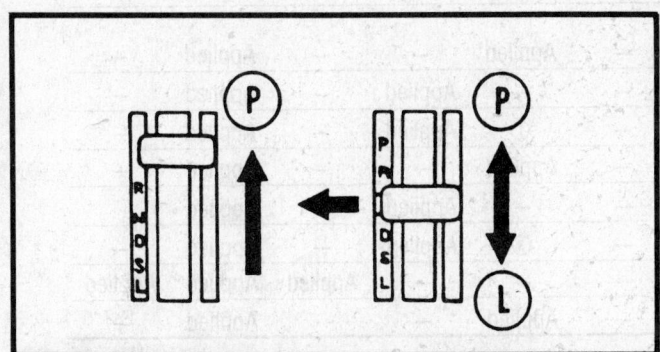

Checking transaxle fluid level — shifting gear selector

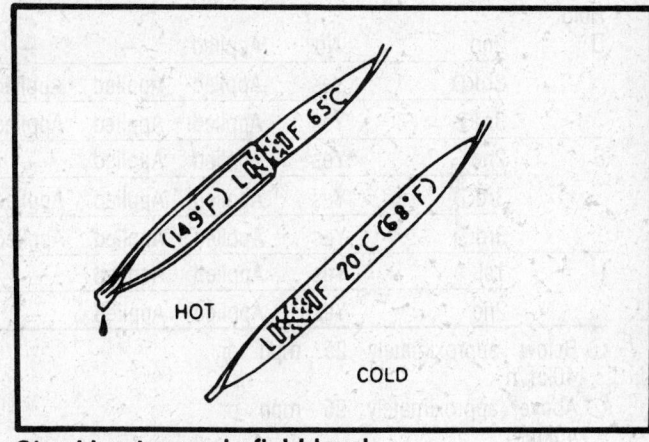

Checking transaxle fluid level

TRANSAXLE MODIFICATIONS

There have been no modifications to the 4EAT transaxle at the time of this printing.

TROUBLE DIAGNOSIS

A logical and orderly diagnosis outline and charts are provide to assist the repairman in diagnosing the problems, causes and the extent of repairs needed to bring the automatic transaxle back to its acceptable level of operation.

Preliminary checks and adjustments should be made to all electrical related components, idle speed, selector lever, kickdown cable and throttle cable. Transaxle oil level should be checked, both visually and by smell, to determine whether the fluid level is correct and to observe any foreign material in the fluid, if present. Smelling the fluid will indicate if any of the bands or clutches have been burned through excessive slippage or overheating of the transaxle.

It is most important to locate the defect, its cause and to properly repair them to avoid having the same problem re-occur.

In order to more fully understand the 4EAT automatic transaxle and to diagnose possible defects more easily, the clutch and band application chart and a general description of the hydraulic and electrical control systems are given.

CLUTCH AND BAND APPLICATION
4EAT Automatic Transaxle

Range	Gear	Engine Braking Effect	Forward Clutch	Coasting Clutch	3-4 Clutch	Reverse Clutch	2-4 Brake Applied	2-4 Brake Released	Low & Reverse Brake	One-way Clutch One	One-way Clutch Two
P		–	–	–	–	–	–	–	–	–	–
R	Reverse	Yes	–	–	–	Applied	–	–	Applied	–	–
N		–	–	–	–	–	–	–	–	–	–
D	1st	No	Applied	–	–	–	–	–	–	Applied	Applied
	2nd	No	Applied	–	–	–	Applied	–	–	Applied	–
	3rd①	Yes	Applied	Applied	Applied	–	–	Applied	–	Applied	–
	3rd②	Yes	Applied	Applied	Applied	–	③	Applied	–	Applied	–
	OD	Yes	Applied	–	Applied	–	Applied	–	–	–	–
S	1st	No	Applied	–	–	–	–	–	–	Applied	Applied
	2nd	No	Applied	–	–	–	Applied	–	–	Applied	–
	3rd①	Yes	Applied	Applied	Applied	–	–	Applied	–	Applied	–
	3rd②	Yes	Applied	Applied	Applied	–	①	Applied	–	Applied	–
L	1st	No	Applied	–	–	–	–	–	Applied	Applied	Applied
	2nd	Yes	Applied	Applied	–	–	Applied	–	–	Applied	–
Hold D	2nd	No	Applied	–	–	–	Applied	–	–	Applied	–
	3rd①	Yes	Applied	Applied	Applied	–	–	Applied	–	Applied	–
	3rd②	Yes	Applied	Applied	Applied	–	①	Applied	–	Applied	–
S	2nd	Yes	Applied	Applied	–	–	Applied	–	–	Applied	–
	3rd①	Yes	Applied	Applied	Applied	–	–	Applied	–	Applied	–
	3rd②	Yes	Applied	Applied	Applied	–	③	Applied	–	Applied	–
L	1st	Yes	Applied	Applied	–	–	–	–	Applied	Applied	Applied
	2nd	Yes	Applied	Applied	–	–	Applied	–	–	Applied	–

① Below approximately 25 mph or 40km/h
② Above approximately 25 mph or 40km/h
③ Fluid pressure to servo but band not applied due to pressure difference in servo

CHILTON'S THREE C's TRANSAXLE DIAGNOSIS
4EAT Automatic Transaxle

Condition	Cause	Correction
Engine will not crank in any shift lever position	a) Neutral start switch stuck or failed b) Neutral start switch damaged or discoonected c) 4EAT control module	a) Go to Quick Test b) Go to Quick Test c) Go to Quick Test
Engine does not crank in P	a) Selector lever and linkage out of adjustment b) Neutral start switch not correctly aligned to transmission	a) Confirm selector or linkage adjustment and operation b) Adjust neutral start switch

CHILTON'S THREE C's TRANSAXLE DIAGNOSIS
4EAT Automatic Transaxle

Condition	Cause	Correction
Engine starts in shift lever positions other than P or N	a) Shift linkage damaged, out of adjustment b) Neutral start switch short circuit c) 4EAT control module	a) Confirm selector linkage adjustment and operation b) Go to Quick Test c) Go to Quick Test
Vehicle moves in P or parking gear not disengaged when P is disengaged	a) Selector lever and linkage out of adjustment b) Parking pawl	a) Confirm selector linkage adjustment and operation b) Inspect parking pawl
Vehicle moves in N	a) Selector lever and linkage out of adjustment b) Control valve damaged	a) Confirm selector linkage adjustment and operation b) Inspect control valve. Service or replace as required
Vehicle does not move in Overdrive, D, L or R	a) Control valves b) Improper fluid level c) Oil pump dirty, broken or bad seals d) Torque converter damaged	a) Go to Quick Test b) Check and fill c) Inspect oil pump d) Inspect torque converter
Vehicle does not move in any forward shift position. Reverse OK	a) Control valves b) Forward clutch worn or damaged c) One-way clutch No. 1 worn or damaged d) Oil flow to forward clutch blocked	a) Go to Quick Test b) Inspect clutches c) Go to Operational Test d) Go to Operational Test
Vehicle does not move in reverse. Forward OK	a) Reverse clutch worn or damaged b) Low and reverse clutch slipping	a) Go to Operational Test b) Inspect clutch and clutch adjustment
Noise severe under acceleration or deceleration. Ok in P, N or steady speed	a) Speedometer cable b) Torqur converter failure c) Gear or clutch failure d) Selector cable grounding out e) Engine mounts grounding out	a) Service or replace b) Examine/service c) Examine or service d) Install and route cable as necessary e) Neutralize engine mounts
Noise in P or N. Does not stop in D at stall	a) Loose flywheel to converter bolts b) Oil pump worn c) Torque converter failure	a) Torque to specification b) Examine/servcie engine c) Examine/servcie converter or Go to Operational Test (Stall Test)
Noise in all gears. Changes power to coast	a) Final drive gearset worn b) CV joints	a) Examine/service final drive gearset b) Servcie as required
Noise in all gears—does not change power to coast	a) Defective speedometer gears gear b) Bearings worn or damaged c) Planetary gearset noisy	a) Examine/replace speed drive or driven b) Examine/replace c) Service planetary gearset
Harsh shifts (any gear)	a) Kickdown cable out of adjustment b) Valve body c) Sticking accumulators d) CV joints e) Engine mounts loose f) Throttle valve sticking g) Band adjustment h) Band servo	a) Check kickdown cable adjustment b) Inspect valve body. Go to Quick Test c) Inspect accumulators d) Service as required e) Service as required f) Inspect throttle valve g) Check band adjustment h) Inspect band servo
Soft shifts (any gears)	a) Kickdown cable b) Band adjustment c) Band servo d) Pressure regulator damaged e) ATF level f) Valve body g) Sticking accumulators h) Throttle valve sticking	a) Check kickdown cable b) Check band adjustment c) Inspect band servo d) Inspect pressure regulator e) Check and fill f) Inspect valve body. Go to Quick Test g) Inspect accumulators h) Inspect throttle valve

CHILTON'S THREE C's TRANSAXLE DIAGNOSIS
4EAT Automatic Transaxle

Condition	Cause	Correction
Erratic shifting, incorrect shift points, incorrect shift sequence	a) Kickdown cable b) Control valves c) Band adjustment d) Clutches slipping e) Fluid level and quality	a) Check kickdown cable adjustment b) Go to Quick Test c) Check band adjustment d) Inspect clutches e) Check and fill
Improper lockup	a) Control valves b) Torque converter	a) Go to Quick Test b) Inspect torque converter
Skipping gears (shift 1st to 3rd or 2nd to OD, for example)	a) Control valves b) Valve body c) 2-4 band	a) Go to Quick Test b) Inspect valve body c) Check band adjustment
Transaxle overheating	a) Impoper fluid level b) Poor engine performance c) Worn clutch, incorrect band application or poor oil pressure control d) Restriction in cooler lines e) Clogged cooler	a) Check fluid level b) Adjust according to specifications c) Go to Operational Test (Stall Test) d) Check cooler lines for kinks and damage. Clean, service or replace cooler lines e) Inspect cooler for plugging. Service as required
Drags in R like parking brake is applied	a) 2-4 band adjustment	a) Inspect band adjustment
Drags in forward gears	a) Band adjustment	a) Inspect band adjustment
Engine runaway on upshift	a) Fluid level low b) Valve body c) Oil pump d) Damaged bypass valve e) Clutches slipping	a) Check fluid level b) Inspect valve body, solenoid valve c) Inspect oil pump d) Inspect bypass valve e) Inspect clutches
Engine runaway on downshift	a) Coasting bypass valve sticking b) Clutches slipping c) Fluid level d) Oil pump	a) Go to Operational Test (Stall Test) b) Inspect clutches c) Check fluid level d) Inspect oil pump
Manual light flashing	a) Control module b) Sensors c) Circuit	a) Go to Quick Test b) Go to Quick Test c) Go to Quick Test
Mode will not switch from manual to automatic or from automatic to manual	a) Control module b) Sensors c) Circuit	a) Go to Quick Test b) Go to Quick Test c) Go to Quick Test
Excessive creep	a) Torque converter b) Kickdown cable c) Ignition timing and idle speed	a) Inspect torque converter b) Inspect kickdown cable adjustment c) Correct or adjust
No creep	a) AFT level and condition b) Kickdown cable c) Selector level d) Valve body e) Control valves f) Forward clutch g) Reverse clutch h) Oil pump	a) Check level and condition b) Inspect kickdown cable adjustment c) Confirm selector linkage adjustment and operation d) Inspect valve body e) Inspect control valves f) Inspect clutches g) Inspect clutches h) Inspect oil pump

Hydraulic Control System

NOTE: Please refer to Section 9 for all oil flow circuits.

TORQUE CONVERTER

The torque converter consists of an impeller, stator, turbine, converter clutch and converter cover. The converter clutch couples the turbine hub and the spline. During lockup, the converter clutch slides on the turbine hub and is pressed against the converter cover. Torsional damper springs are provided in the converter clutch to absorb engine torque and pulsations during lockup.

OIL PUMP

The pump consists of a cam ring, rotor vanes, guide ring, pivot roller, seal pins and oil pump flange, incorporated within the pump housing. The oil pump flange and shaft are coupled to the rotor. The other end of the shaft is coupled to the torque converter so that the rotation is the same as the engine speed. The cam ring, which rotates eccentrically with the pivot roller as a fulcrum, regulates the discharge quantity. A valve and spring are provided at the discharge port to regulate the hydraulic pressure in the variable chamber.

FLUID PASSAGES

The fluid passages are located in the oil pump, converter housing and transaxle case.

VALVE BODY

The valve body is mounted on the side of the transaxle which faces the radiator. It can be removed without removing the transaxle. The valve body consists of 4 subsections: the front, premain, main and rear control bodies.

THROTTLE VALVE

The throttle valve produces throttle pressure according to the depression of the accelerator pedal.

THROTTLE-MODULATOR VALVE

The throttle-modulator valve produces throttle-modulated pressure from throttle pressure.

PRESSURE-REGULATOR VALVE

The pressure-regulator valve adjusts the line pressure produced by the oil pump to match the current driving condition.

MANUAL VALVE

The manual valve is moved by the range selector and switches the passage for line pressure produced by the oil pump. The manual valve determines where line pressure is distributed for each selector position.

SHIFT VALVES

The 1–2 shift valve is activated by the 1–2 solenoid valve. It controls the automatic shifting between first and second gear. The 2–3 shift valve is activated by the 2–3 solenoid valve. It controls the automatic shifting between second and third gear. The 3–4 shift valve is activated by the 3–4 solenoid valve. It controls the automatic shifting between third and fourth gear.

LOW REDUCING VALVE

The low reducing valve reduces the low and reverse clutch engagement pressure, which in turn reduces low-first gear shift shock.

ACCUMULATORS

The N–OD accumulator reduces shift shock when shifting to overdrive range. The N–R accumulator reduces shift shock when shifting to reverse range. The 1–2 accumulator reduces shift shock when shifting from first to second gear. Unlike the other valves which are incorporated within the valve body, the 2–3 accumulator is located beside the bearing housing. This accumulator functions to reduce the shift shock when shifting from second to third gear.

TIMING VALVES

The 2–3 timing valve controls the 3–4 clutch engagement timing during a second to third gear shift. This timing is determined by the amount of throttle opening. The 3–2 timing valve controls the engagement timing of the 2–4 band. This timing is determined by the amount of the throttle opening during an overdrive-third to drive-second gear shift.

BYPASS VALVES

The bypass valve controls the 3–4 clutch engagement timing and shift shock during a second to third gear shift. The coasting bypass valve controls the engagement of the coasting clutch.

3–2 CAPACITY VALVE

The 3–2 capacity valve adjusts the rate at which the release pressure of the 2–4 band drains during a downshift to second gear in drive range.

LOCKUP CONTROL VALVE

The lockup control valve is activated by the lockup solenoid valve. This valve controls torque converter lockup operation.

Electronic Control System

PULSE GENERATOR

The pulse generator is a magnetic pickup sensor located on the transaxle housing. It detects the reverse-forward drum speed.

VEHICLE SPEED SENSOR

The speed sensor acts as a substitute for the pulse generator, if the pulse generator malfunctions. There are 2 types of vehicle speed sensors used on the 4EAT transaxle. One type is present on vehicles equipped with an analog cluster (sensor located within speedometer assembly) the other type is present on vehicles equipped with a digital cluster (sensor located on the transaxle housing).

THROTTLE POSITION SENSOR

The throttle position sensor is a variable resistor attached to the throttle body. The sensor detects the opening of the throttle and relays these signals to the 4EAT control unit.

IDLE SWITCH

The idle switch is attached to the throttle body, when the throttle plate is fully closed the switch sends a signal to the 4EAT control unit. The idle switch is preset at the factory and should not be adjusted.

NEUTRAL SAFETY SWITCH

The neutral safety switch is located on the transaxle case. It sends signals to the 4EAT control unit indicating the position of the manual valve (P, R, N, OD, D or L). This switch has a 0.079 in. hole which permits alignment of the switch during installation.

BRAKE LIGHT SWITCH

The brake light switch sends a signal to the 4EAT control unit when the brake pedal is depressed.

ENGINE COOLANT TEMPERATURE SWITCH

The coolant temperature switch is located on the lower portion of the intake manifold. It sends a signal to the 4EAT control unit when the engine coolant temperature is below 149°F (65°C).

FLUID TEMPERATURE SWITCH

The fluid temperature switch is located on the switch box which connects the oil cooler fluid pipe to the transaxle. It sends a signal to the 4EAT control unit when the transaxle fluid temperature is above 302°F (150°C).

SOLENOID VALVES

There are 3 solenoid valves for shifting and 1 for lockup. Located on the valve body, these valves are switched on and off by electrical signals from the control unit.

CONTROL UNIT

The control unit has internal self-diagnosis, fail-safe and warning code display functions for the the main input sensors and solenoid valves.

Diagnosis Tests

These diagnostic procedures are to be used on 4EAT equipped vehicles only. To help locate problems with the transaxle, the following sequence should be followed.

PRELIMINARY ROAD TEST

This road test, if possible, should be performed to verify the complaint. No special test equipped is used at this time.

PRELIMINARY INSPECTIONS

Visually inspect all 4EAT related components, fuses, sensors, switches etc. also inspect CV joints, engine mounts, oil cooler, halfshafts and any other external component. Inspect fluid level for burnt, discoloration or contamination of fluid. Check and adjust idle speed, if required. Check selector lever for smooth operation of the button and clicks in each position. Check transaxle for any fluid leaks from seals, lines and gaskets. Check for smooth operation of kickdown cable from idle to wide open throttle, service or replace the kickdown cable, as required. Check for proper operation of throttle cable. Adjust or replace the throttle cable as necessary. Check and inflate all tires to the proper level. After preliminary inspections review the diagnosis charts which will provide basic direction or test procedures.

QUICK TEST

This step will find fault codes that may indicate 4EAT input or output device failure. Follow Pinpoint Test step direction given in the Quick Test before continuing with the procedure. When directed to perform Quick Test, Operational Tests and Road Test for the same symptom, always perform Quick Test first.

OPERATIONAL TESTS

This step determines the causes of most basic problems that may exist. When directed to perform Operational Tests and Road Test for the same symptom always perform Operational Tests first. This action will prevent causing possible damage to the transaxle during driving.

ROAD TEST

This step isolates problems that are evident during driving. The road test is an evaluation of the 4EAT system while driving with the 4EAT tester in service. Repair or inspection of the transaxle during this test may involve major disassembly, therefore secondary road test should always be done last. The powertrain may also show problems during the test that can cause transaxle problems. If no problems are found during the road test it is likely that the problem is intermittent. Since the problem may not reoccur, the symptom should be evaluated again.

NOTE: After any repair is made, re-test the transaxle to verify if symptom is still present. If the symptom reoccurs, further testing must be performed to isolate problem. Any time fluid is drained from the transaxle, be certain the proper type and amount of fluid is replaced.

4EAT QUICK TEST

Description

The Quick test is the procedure to activate the 4EAT electronic control module self-test. The self-test is divided into 3 specialized tests: Key On- Engine Off Test, Continuous Test, Switch Monitor Test.

The processor stores the self-test program in its permanent memory. When activated, it checks the 4EAT control system by testing its memory integrity and processing capability and verifies that various sensors and actuators are connected and operating properly.

Any time a repair is made, clear memory by disconnecting the small (16-pin) connector on the control unit. Remove the 4EAT tester. Turn ignition switch **OFF**. Then repeat the test to ensure that the repair was effective.

NOTE: The Quick Test procedure should be used only when the preliminary inspection steps result in a PASS condition. If all phases of the Quick Test result in a PASS CONDITION, it is likely that the problem will be found elsewhere. Proceed to the Operational Test for further evaluation of the transaxle.

Test Steps
VEHICLE PREPARATION

NOTE: It may be necessary to disconnect or disassemble harness connector assemblies to do some of the inspections. Pin locations should be noted before disassembly.

1. Place shift lever firmly into the **P** postion and block drive wheels.
2. Start engine. Observe manual shift light.
3. Proceed to equipment hookup step.

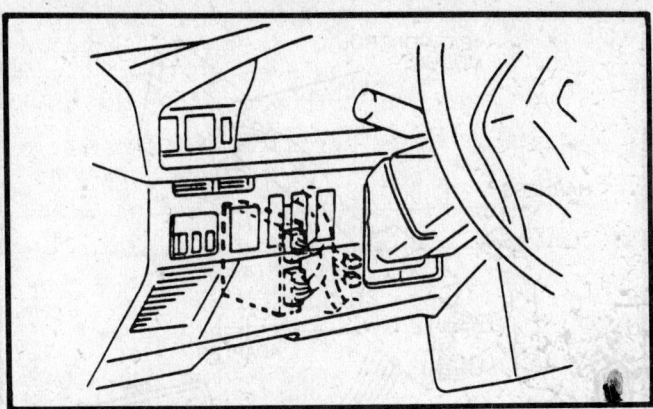

4EAT control unit location

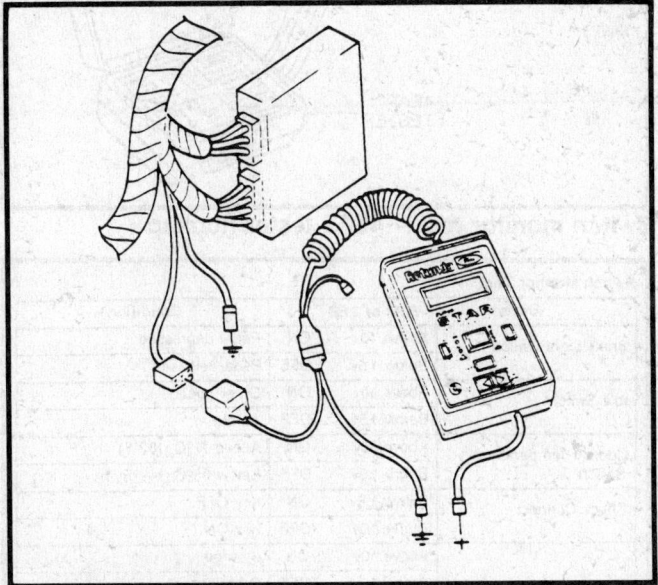

Star tester hookup

EQUIPMENT HOOKUP

1. Turn ignition key **OFF**.
2. Locate the service connector.
3. Using the Star tester
   a. Ground the Star tester.
   b. Connect the Star tester to the 6-pin 4EAT Star tester output (STO) connector.
   c. Connect the Star tester to the 1-pin 4EAT Star tester input (STI) connector.
4. Using the VOM
   a. Set the VOM on a DC voltage range to read from 0–20V.
   b. Ground the VOM lead.
   c. Connect the VOM lead to the red wire (6-pin 4EAT STO connector).
   d. Ground the single-pin 4EAT STI connector with a jumper wire.
5. Go to Key On- Engine Off Test.

KEY ON ENGINE OFF TEST

Is a system to display service codes which are present or past failures. The Star tester will display service codes and the VOM needle will pulse across the dial face representing service codes. If no codes are indicated on the Star tester or VOM and the manual shift flashed during the vehicle preperartion step, then proceed to Pinpoint Test PPQ. If the manual shift light did not flash, proceed to the Switch Monitor Test.

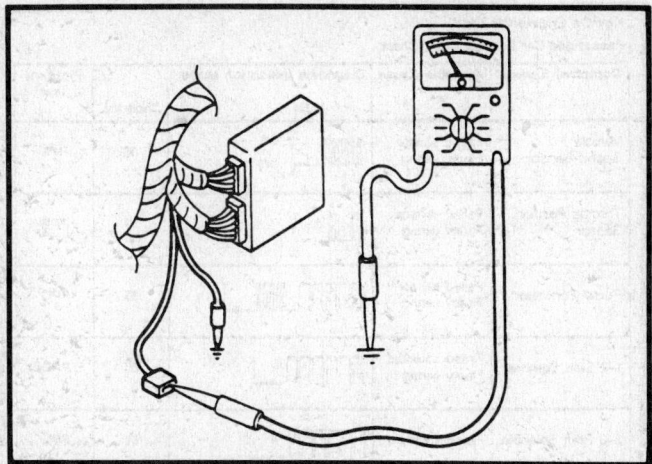

Volt/Ohm (VOM) meter hookup

1. To perform Key On- Engine Off Test verify that the vehicle has been properly prepared per vehicle preperation and equipment hookup steps.
2. Place ignition key in the **ON** position.
3. Record codes indicated by Star tester or VOM.
4. Refer to Key On- Engine Off Test passenger vehicle service code chart troubleshooting guide.

NOTE: If the manual shift light flashed during vehicle preparation step, use Key On- Engine Off passenger vehicle service code chart troubleshooting guide. If the manual shift light did not flash during vehicle preperation step, proceed to Continuous Test

CONTINUOUS TEST

Continuous memory codes are issued as a result of information stored during Continuous Test, while the vehicle was in normal operation. These codes are displayed during testing and should be used for diagnosis only when a continuous code results from previous test steps.

NOTE: Verify that the manual shift light did not flash during the vehicle preparation step before continuing with this test. It is necessary to clear the codes in memory before continuing this test. Only service those codes which are recreated by Continuous Test.

1. To clear continuous memory codes turn ignition switch **OFF**.
2. Disconnect the small (16-pin) connector on the 4EAT control unit.
3. Remove the Star tester or VOM.
4. Connect Star tester or VOM.
5. Start the engine and do not shut the engine down.
6. The system is now in the Engine Running Continuous Monitor mode.

NOTE: The Continuous Monitor mode (wiggle test) allow the technician to attempt to recreate an intermittent fault. It is necessary to drive the vehicle each time the suspect sensor and or harness is tapped, moved or wiggled. If a fault is detected, a service code will be stored in memory.

7. Refer to the Continuous Test passenger vehicle service code chart troubleshooting guide.

SWITCH MONITOR TEST

Is a check of the 4EAT control module inputs using the 4EAT tester. If a switch fails, proceed to Pinpoint test PPM. If a PASS code is received, an indication that the 4EAT control systems are OK, proceed to the Operational Test.

Key On Engine Off Test
Passenger Car Service Code Chart

Defective System	Possible Cause	Diagnosis Indication Mode VOM	Code No.	Pinpoint Test
Vehicle Speed Sensor	Failed sensor Faulty wiring	ON / OFF	06	PPA
Throttle Position Sensor	Failed sensor Faulty wiring		12	PPB
Pulse Generator	Failed sensor Faulty wiring		55	PPC
1–2 Shift Solenoid	Failed solenoid Faulty wiring		60	PPD
2–3 Shift Solenoid	Failed solenoid		61	PPE
3–4 Shift Solenoid	Failed solenoid Faulty wiring		62	PPF
Lockup Solenoid	Failed solenoid Faulty wiring		63	PPG

Diagnostic test

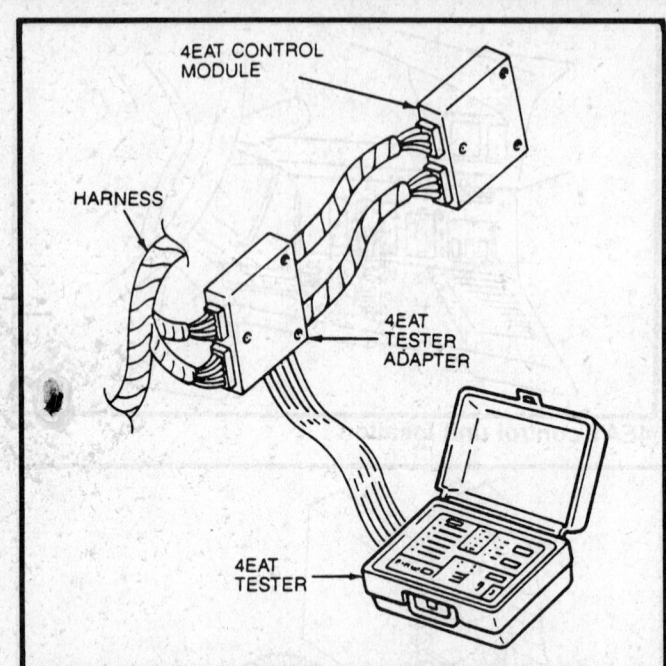

Switch monitor test— 4EAT tester hookup

Continuous Test
Passenger Car Service Code Chart

Defective System	Possible Cause	Diagnosis Indication Mode VOM	Code No.	Pinpoint Test
Vehicle Speed Sensor	Failed sensor Faulty wiring	ON / OFF	06	PPA
Throttle Position Sensor	Failed sensor Faulty wiring		12	PPB
Pulse Generator	Failed sensor Faulty wiring		55	PPC
1–2 Shift Solenoid	Failed solenoid Faulty wiring		60	PPD
2–3 Shift Solenoid	Failed solenoid		61	PPE
3–4 Shift Solenoid	Failed solenoid Faulty wiring		62	PPF
Lockup Solenoid	Failed solenoid Faulty wiring	1.2 SEC. 1.6 SEC.	63	PPG

Diagnostic test

1. To perform test disconnect vehicle harness from 4EAT control module.
2. Connect the 4EAT tester adaptor between the harness and the module.
3. Turn the 4EAT tester on.
4. Turn ignition switch **ON**.
5. Test all switches under conditions specified in the Switch Monitor Test chart.

Manual Shift Light Operation
SYSTEM OK
The manual shift light will illuminate when using manual shift mode.

Switch Monitor Test

Switch	VOM or LED		Condition
Brake Light Switch	Above 10v	ON	Pedal depressed
	Below 1.5v	OFF	Pedal released
Idle Switch	Above 10v	ON	Other speeds
	Below 1.5v	OFF	At idle
Coolant Temperature Switch	Above 10v	ON	Above 72°C (162°F)
	Below 1.5v	OFF	Below 65°C (149°F)
Check Connect	Below 1.5v	ON	Key OFF
	Above 10v	OFF	Key ON
L	Above 10v	ON	L range
	Below 1.5v	OFF	Other ranges
D	Above 10v	ON	D range
	Below 1.5v	OFF	Other ranges
Ⓓ	Above 10v	ON	Ⓓ range
	Below 1.5v	OFF	Other ranges
N or P	Below 1.5v	ON	N or P range
	Above 10v	OFF	Other ranges
Mode Switch	Above 10v	ON	Normal mode
	Below 1.5v	OFF	Power mode
Mode Indicator	Above 4.5v	OFF	Manual mode
	Below 1.5v	ON	Other mode
Manual Switch	Above 10v	ON	Switch depressed
	Below 1.5v	OFF	Switch released
Manual Indicator	Below 1.5v	ON	Manual mode
	Above 10v	OFF	Other mode
No Load Signal	Above 10v	ON	Drum speed below 80 rpm
	Below 1.5v	OFF	Drum speed above 640 rpm and N or P range
Throttle Position Sensor	Above 4.3v	ON	Throttle fully open
	Below 0.5v	OFF	Throttle closed
	Changes 0.5v		Every 1/8 position change
ATF Temperature Switch	Above 10v	OFF	ATF Temperature below 143°C (289°F)
	Below 0.5v	ON	ATF Temperature above 150°C (302°F)

Diagnostic test

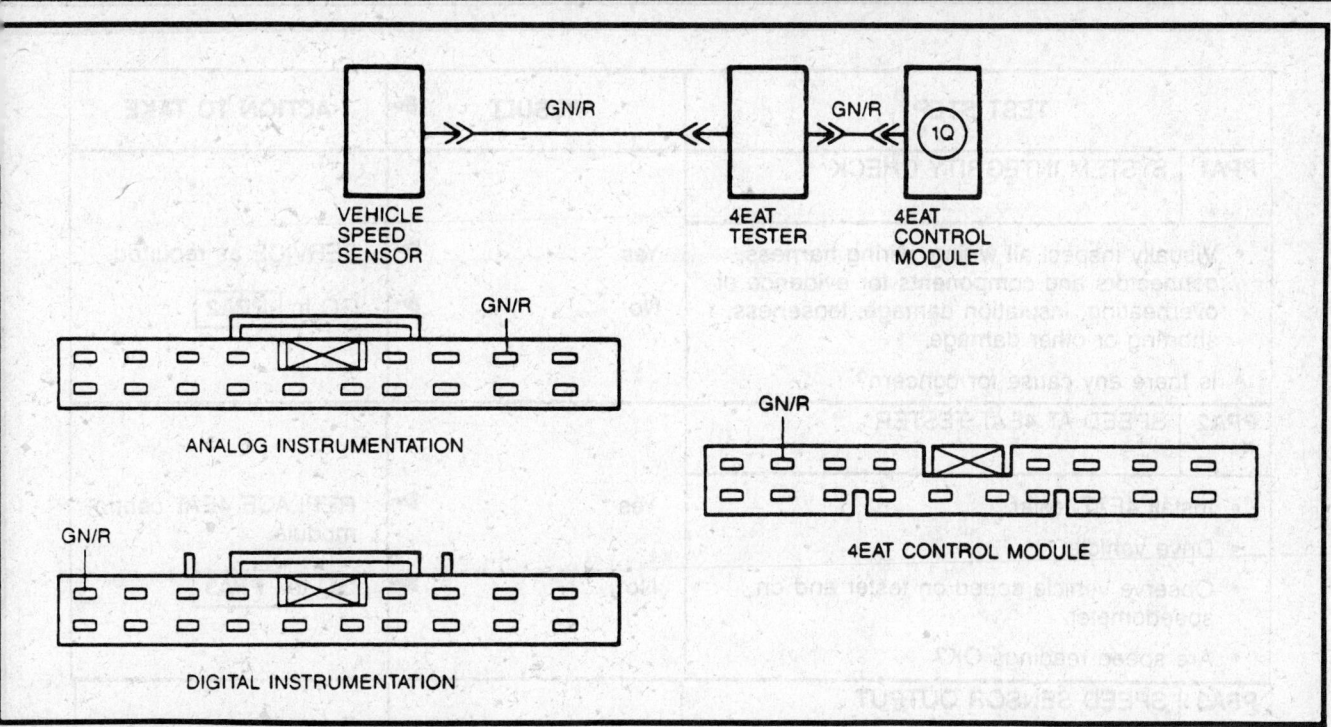

Service code 6 – pinpoint test schematic

BK Black	N Natural
BL Blue	O Orange
BR Brown	PK Pink
DB Dark Blue	P Purple
DG Dark Green	R Red
GY Gray	T Tan
GN Green	W White
LB Light Blue	Y Yellow
LG Light Green	

Standard Ford color abbreviations

SYSTEM NOT OK

If the manual shift light flashes during driving, run Key On- Engine Off Test to completion. If the manual shift light never comes on go, to Pinpoint Test PPQ.

Pinpoint Test

Each Pinpoint Test assumes that a fault has been detected in the system with direction to enter a specific repair routine. Doing any Pinpoint Test without direction may produce incorrect results and replacement of non-defective components.

In using the Pinpoint Tests, follow each step in order, starting from the first step in the appropriate test. Follow each step until the fault is found.

After completing any repairs to the 4EAT system, verify all components are properly reconnected and repeat the Quick test.

SERVICE CODE 6/PPA TEST

Enter this Pinpoint Test only when this service code is received in the Quick Test steps. This Pinpoint Test is intended to diagnose only the following: speed sensor, wiring harness, 4EAT control module.

SERVICE CODE 12/PPB TEST

Enter this Pinpoint Test only when this service code is received

in the Quick Test steps. This Pinpoint Test is intended to diagnose only the following: TP sensor, sensor harness circuit, 4EAT control module.

SERVICE CODE 55/PPC TEST

Enter this Pinpoint Test only when this service code is received in the Quick Test steps. This Pinpoint Test is intended to diagnose only the following: pulse generator, wiring harness, 4EAT control module.

SERVICE CODE 60/PPD TEST

Enter this Pinpoint Test only when this service code is received in the Quick Test steps. This Pinpoint Test is intended to diagnose only the following: 1–2 Shift Solenoid, harness circuit (BL)

SERVICE CODE 61/PPE TEST

Enter this Pinpoint Test when this service code is received in the Quick Test steps. This Pinpoint Test is intended to diagnose only the following: 2–3 Shift Solenoid, harness circuit (BL/BK)

SERVICE CODE 62/PPF TEST

Enter this Pinpoint Test when this service code is received in the Quick Test steps. This Pinpoint Test is intended to diagnose only the following: 3–4 Shift Solenoid, harness circuit (BL/O)

SERVICE CODE 63/PPG TEST

Enter this Pinpoint Test only when this service code is received in the Quick Test steps. This Pinpoint Test is intended to diagnose only the following: lockup solenoid, harness circuit (BL/W)

NO SERVICE CODE/PPM TEST

Enter this Pinpoint Test only when directed here by Quick Test steps. This Pinpoint Test is intended to diagnose only malfunctioning switches.

NO SERVICE CODE/PPQ TEST

Enter this Pinpoint Test only when directed here by Quick Test steps. This Pinpoint Test is intended to diagnose only the following: wiring harness problems such as STI and STO connectors, VPWR, KAPWR, ground and 4EAT control module.

TEST STEP	RESULT ▶	ACTION TO TAKE
PPA1 SYSTEM INTEGRITY CHECK		
• Visually inspect all wiring, wiring harness, connectors and components for evidence of overheating, insulation damage, looseness, shorting or other damage. • Is there any cause for concern?	Yes ▶ No ▶	SERVICE as required. GO to PPA2 .
PPA2 SPEED AT 4EAT TESTER		
• Install 4EAT tester. • Drive vehicle. • Observe vehicle speed on tester and on speedometer. • Are speed readings OK?	Yes ▶ No ▶	REPLACE 4EAT control module. GO to PPA3 .
PPA3 SPEED SENSOR OUTPUT		
• Key on. • VOM on 20 volt scale. • Measure voltage between speed sensor "GN/R" wire and ground. **Analog Instrumentation:** Slowly turn speedometer cable one turn. Does voltage reading 4.5 volts show four times? 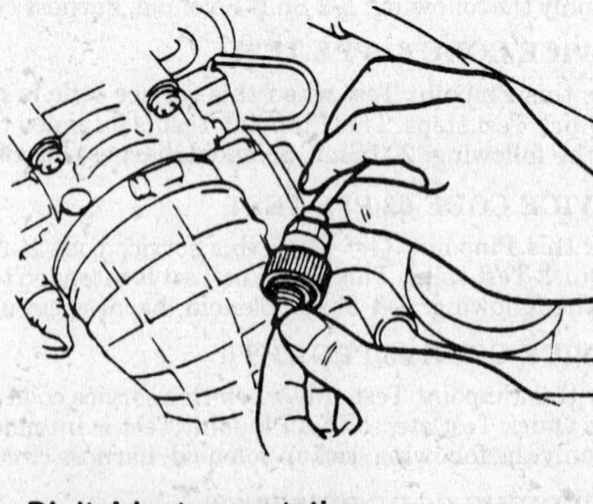 **Digital Instrumentation:** Driving . . . . Above 4.5v Vehicle stopped . . . . 4.5v or below 1.5v • Are voltage readings OK?	Yes ▶ No ▶	REPAIR "GN/R" wire from 4EAT module to speed sensor. REPLACE speed sensor. NOTE: To prevent replacement of a good speed sensor be aware that: – The rotor may be damaged – Installation of rotor or sensor may be incorrect.

Service code 6 test information

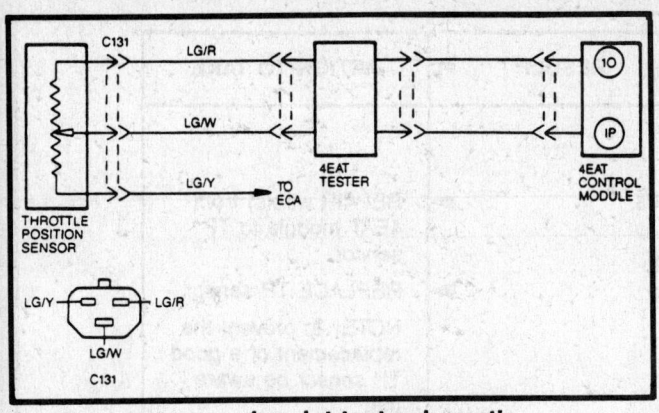

Service code 12 – pinpoint test schematic

OPERATIONAL TESTS

Description

These test are used to determine the cause of (and provide the corrective actions for) malfunctions most likely to occur. These include the torque converter, the powertrain, the friction elements (clutches and bands), the power source or hydraulic system and the associated regulating valves and controls.

OPA Test—Powertrain Function Check

This test checks for slippage of the friction components (clutches and band brakes) and the torque converter capacity.

1. To perform the test, start the engine and allow it to come to normal operating temperature or until the ATF temperature reaches 122–176°F (50–80°C). Apply both the parking and service brakes during the test.

	TEST STEP	RESULT	►	ACTION TO TAKE
PPB1	**SYSTEM INTEGRITY CHECK**			
	• Visually inspect all wiring, wiring harness, connectors and components for evidence of overheating, insulation damage, looseness, shorting or other damage. • Is there any cause for concern?	Yes No	► ►	SERVICE as required. GO to PPB2 .
PPB2	**TP SIGNAL AT 4EAT**			
	• Install 4EAT tester. • Key on. • Measure TP voltage between tester terminal 1O and ground. Key on .... 4–6v Key off .... below 1.5v Tester TP and ground terminals **Throttle** **Approximate Voltage** Closed .... 0.5v 1/8 .... 1.0v 2/8 .... 1.5v 3/8 .... 2.0v 4/8 .... 2.5v 5/8 .... 3.0v 6/8 .... 3.5v 7/8 .... 4.0v Full .... above 4.3v • Are voltage readings OK?	Yes No	► ►	REPLACE 4EAT control module. GO to PPB3 .

Service code 12 test information

TEST STEP	RESULT ►	ACTION TO TAKE
PPB3 | **TP SENSOR SIGNAL** • Leave TP sensor connected. • Key on. • Measure voltage between TP sensor "LG/R" and "LG/Y." Key on .... 4–6v Key off .... below 1.5v TP sensor "LG/W" and "LG/Y" **Throttle** **Voltage** Closed .... 0.5v 1/8 .... 1.0v 2/8 .... 1.5v 3/8 .... 2.0v 4/8 .... 2.5v 5/8 .... 3.0v 6/8 .... 3.5v 7/8 .... 4.0v Full .... above 4.3v • Are voltage readings OK?	Yes No	► REPAIR wire(s) from 4EAT module to TP sensor. ► REPLACE TP sensor. NOTE: To prevent the replacement of a good TP sensor be aware that: – Idle speeds/throttle stop adjustments may need setting. – Binding shaft/linkage.

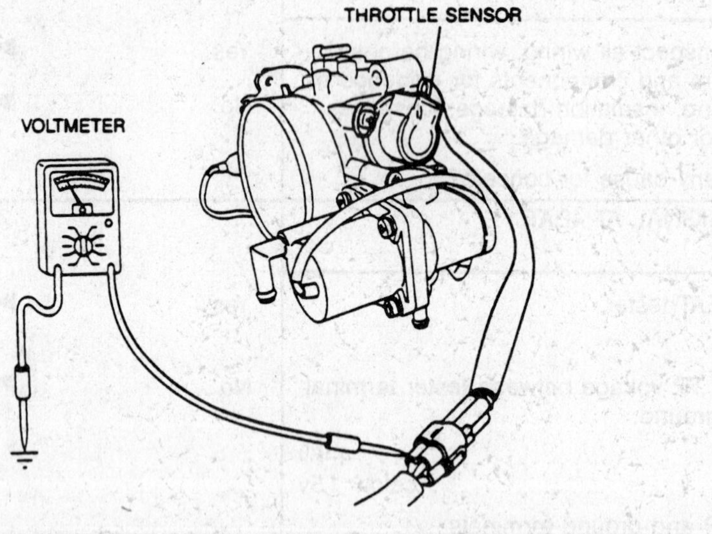

THROTTLE SENSOR

VOLTMETER

Service code 12 test information

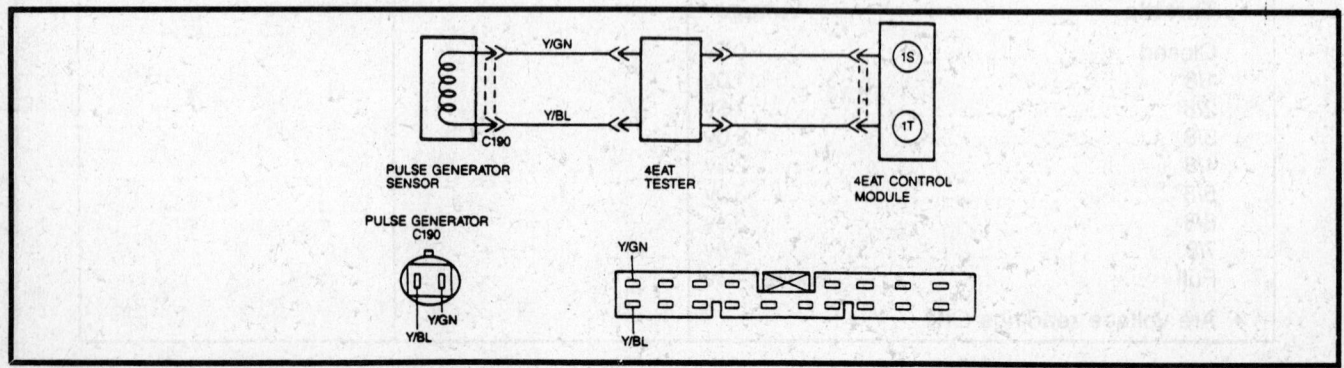

PULSE GENERATOR SENSOR   4EAT TESTER   4EAT CONTROL MODULE

Y/GN

Y/BL

C190

1S

1T

PULSE GENERATOR C190

Y/GN

Y/BL

Y/GN

Y/BL

Service code 55 – pinpoint test schematic

TEST STEP	RESULT	▶	ACTION TO TAKE
PPC1 SYSTEM INTEGRITY CHECK			
• Visually inspect all wiring, wiring harness, connectors and components for evidence of overheating, insulation damage, looseness, shorting or other damage. • Is there any cause for concern?	Yes No	▶ ▶	SERVICE as required. GO to PPC2 .
PPC2 PG SIGNAL AT 4EAT			
• Install 4EAT tester. • Drive vehicle. • Observe drum speed on tester and engine speed on tachometer. • Are speeds almost the same?	Yes No	▶ ▶	REPLACE 4EAT control module. GO to PPC3 .
PPC3 RESISTANCE AT PG SENSOR			
• Key off. • VOM on 200 ohm scale. • Measure resistance between PG sensor terminals. • Is resistance 200–400 ohms?	Yes No	▶ ▶	REPAIR wire(s) from PG sensor to 4EAT module. REPLACE PG sensor. NOTE: To prevent the replacement of a good PG sensor be aware that: – The rotor may be damaged – The rotor/sensor may not be installed properly.

Service code 55 test information

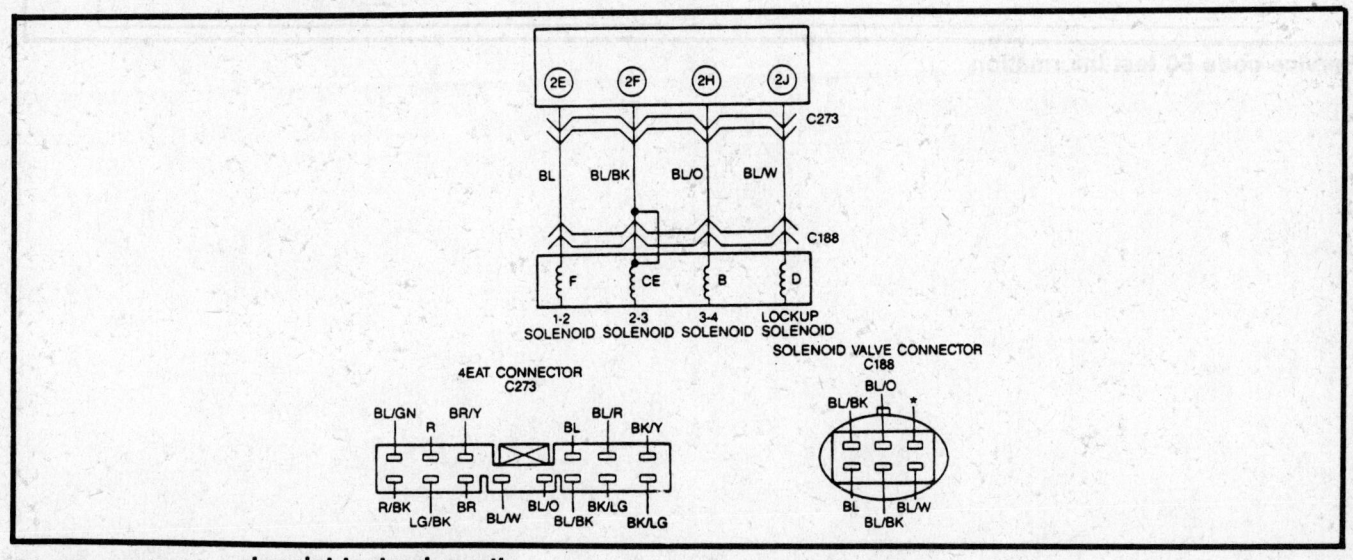

Service code 60 — pinpoint test schematic

TEST STEP		RESULT ▶	ACTION TO TAKE
PPD1	SYSTEM INTEGRITY CHECK		
	• Visually inspect all wiring, wiring harness, connectors and components for evidence of overheating, insulation damage, looseness, shorting or other damage. • Is there any cause for concern?	Yes ▶ No ▶	SERVICE as required. GO to PPD2 .

TEST STEP		RESULT ▶	ACTION TO TAKE
PPD2	SOLENOID RESISTANCE CHECK		
	• Disconnect solenoid valve (connector C188). • VOM on 200 ohm scale. • Measure resistance between connector C188 terminal F ("BL") and ground. • Is resistance between 13 to 27 ohms?	Yes ▶ No ▶	GO to PPD3 . REPLACE solenoid. NOTE: To prevent the replacement of a good solenoid be aware that: – Mechanical functions in the transaxle must operate properly.

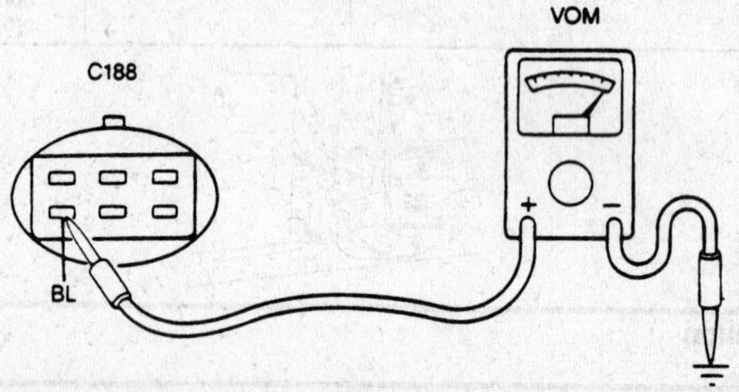

VOM

C188

BL

Service code 60 test information

TEST STEP	RESULT	▶	ACTION TO TAKE
PPD3 **CIRCUIT CONTINUITY CHECK**			
• Disconnect 4EAT control module (connector C273). • Leave solenoid valve (connector C188) disconnected. • VOM on 200 ohm scale. • Measure resistance between connector C273 terminal 2E ("BL") and connector C188 terminal F ("BL"). • Is resistance less than 5 ohms?	Yes No	▶ ▶	GO to **PPD4** . REPAIR open in "BL" wire between 4EAT control module and solenoid valve.

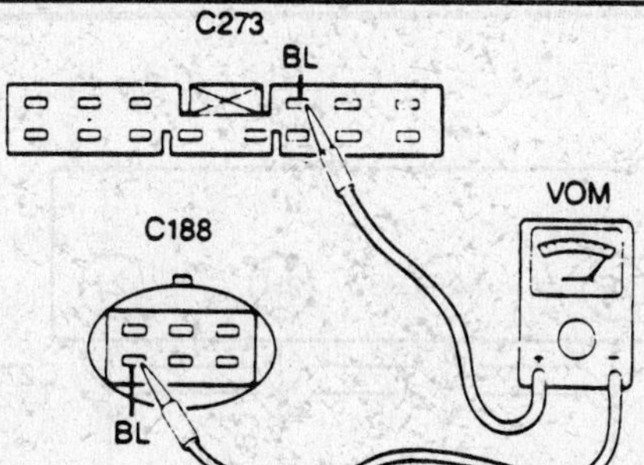

TEST STEP	RESULT	▶	ACTION TO TAKE
PPD4 **SHORT TO VPWR CHECK**			
• Leave 4EAT control module (connector C273) and solenoid valve (connector C188) disconnected. • Key on; engine off. • VOM on 20 volt scale. • Measure voltage between connector C273 terminal 2E ("BL") and ground. • Is voltage greater than 0 volts?	Yes No	▶ ▶	REPAIR "BL" wire between 4EAT control module and solenoid valve for short to VPWR. GO to **PPD5** .

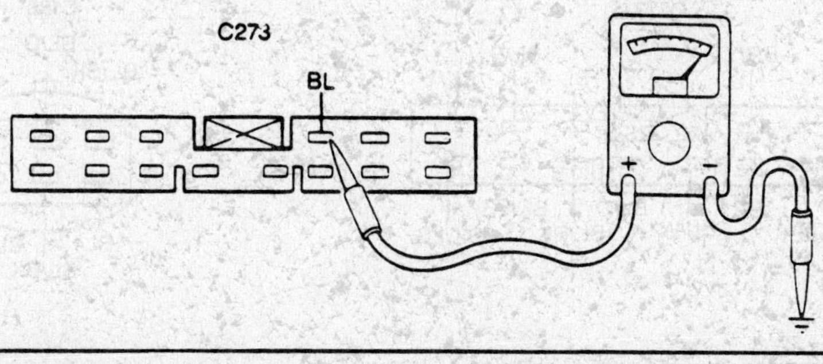

Service code 60 test information

TEST STEP		RESULT	►	ACTION TO TAKE
PPD5	**SHORT TO GROUND CHECK**			
	• Leave 4EAT control module (connector C273) and solenoid valve (connector C188) disconnected. • VOM on 200K ohm scale. • Measure resistance between connector C273 terminal 2E ("BL") and ground. • Is resistance greater than 10,000 ohms? See illustration in TEST STEP PPD4	Yes No	► ►	GO to 4EAT operational test OPS. REPAIR "BL" wire between 4EAT control module and solenoid valve for short to ground.

Service code 60 test information

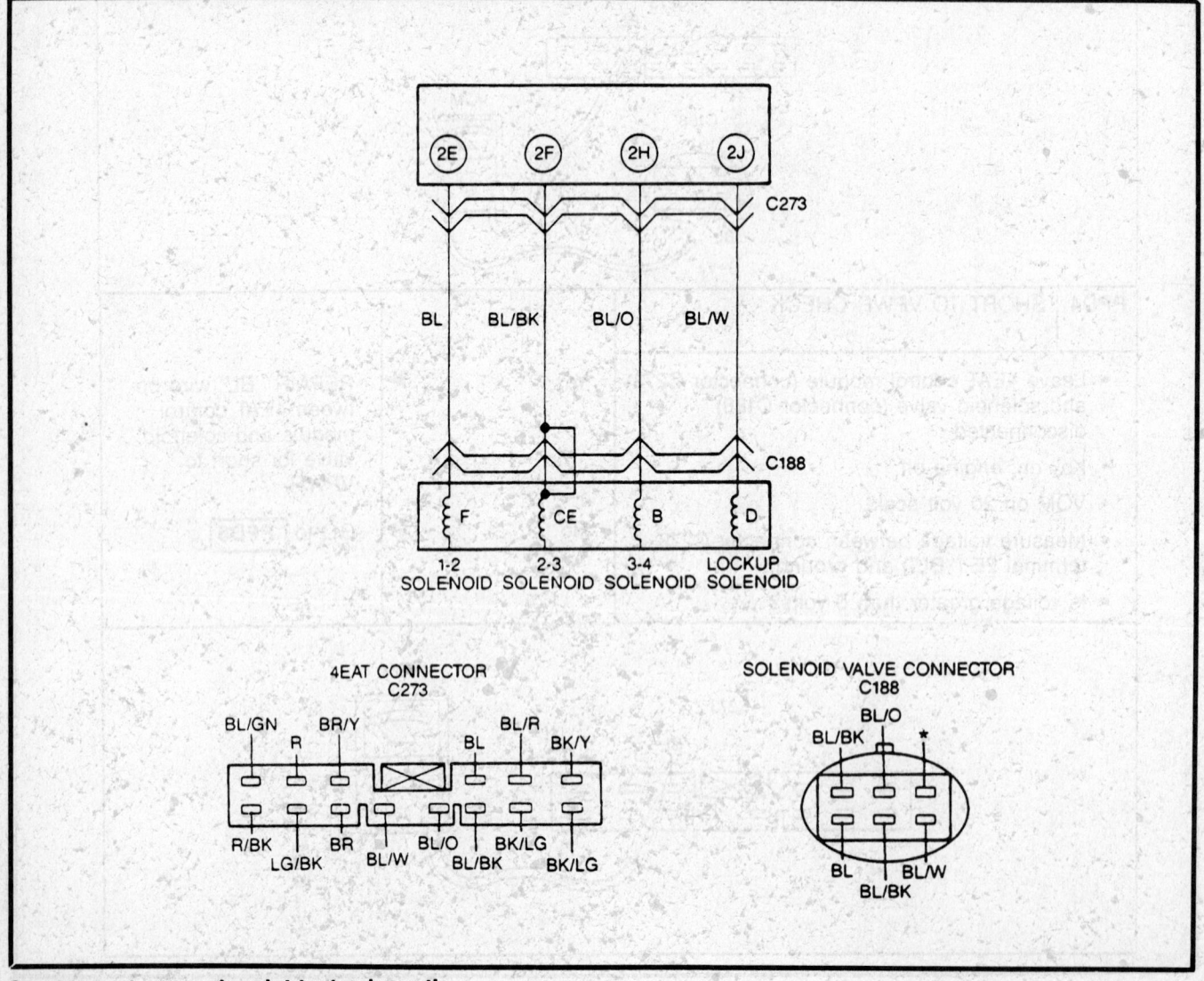

Service code 61 — pinpoint test schematic

TEST STEP	RESULT ▶	ACTION TO TAKE
PPE2 SOLENOID RESISTANCE CHECK		
• Disconnect solenoid valve (connector C188). • VOM on 200 ohm scale. • Measure resistance between connector C188 terminal C ("BL/BK") and ground, and between terminal E ("BL/BK") and ground. • Is resistance between 13 to 27 ohms?	Yes ▶ No ▶	GO to **PPE3** . REPLACE solenoid. NOTE: To prevent the replacement of a good solenoid be aware that: – Mechanical functions in the transaxle must operate properly.

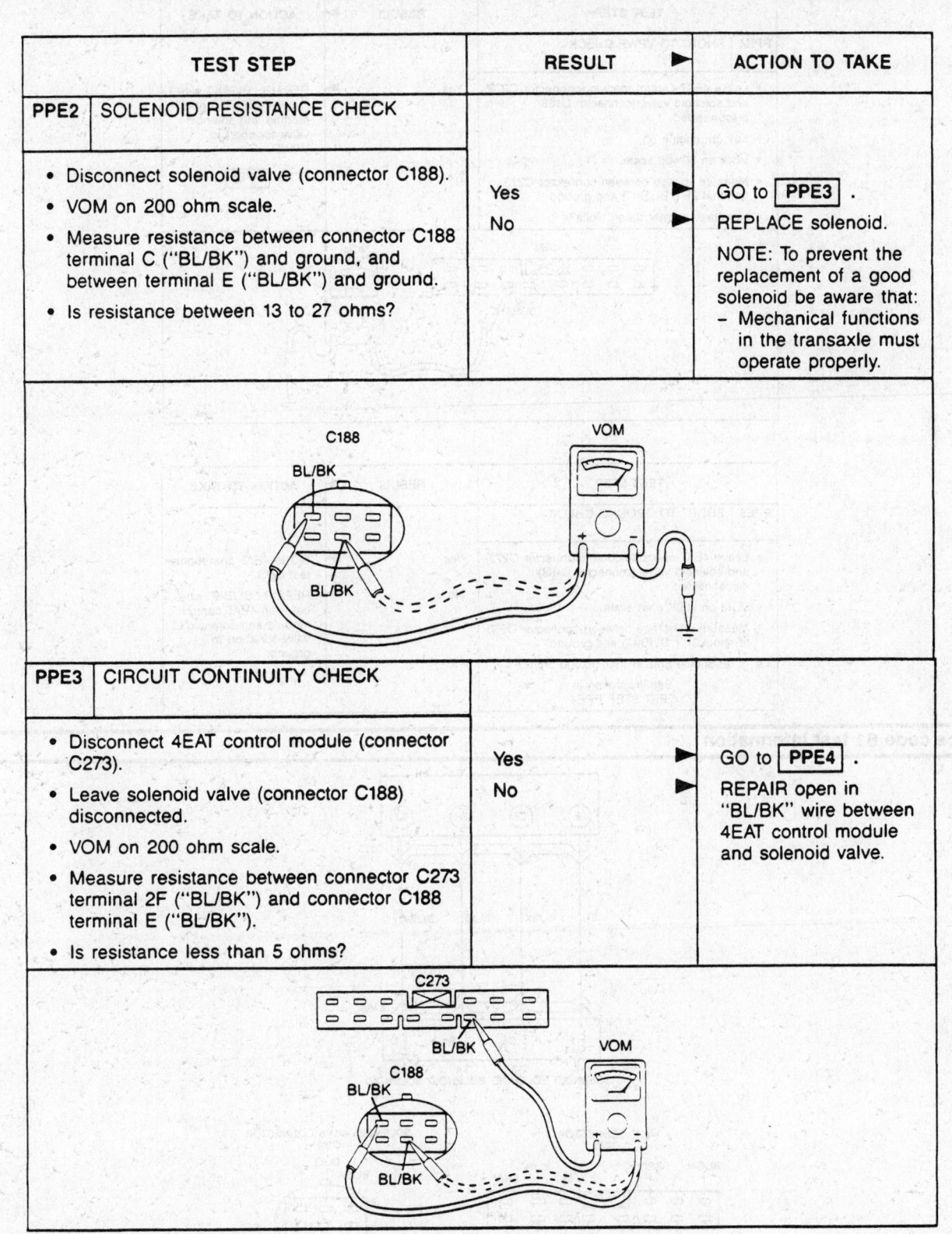

TEST STEP	RESULT ▶	ACTION TO TAKE
PPE3 CIRCUIT CONTINUITY CHECK		
• Disconnect 4EAT control module (connector C273). • Leave solenoid valve (connector C188) disconnected. • VOM on 200 ohm scale. • Measure resistance between connector C273 terminal 2F ("BL/BK") and connector C188 terminal E ("BL/BK"). • Is resistance less than 5 ohms?	Yes ▶ No ▶	GO to **PPE4** . REPAIR open in "BL/BK" wire between 4EAT control module and solenoid valve.

Service code 61 test information

TEST STEP		RESULT	▶	ACTION TO TAKE
PPE4	**SHORT TO VPWR CHECK**			
	• Leave 4EAT control module (connector C273) and solenoid valve (connector C188) disconnected.	Yes	▶	REPAIR "BL/BK" wire between 4EAT control module and solenoid valve for short to VPWR.
	• Key on; engine off.			
	• VOM on 20 volt scale.			
	• Measure voltage between connector C273 terminal 2F ("BL/BK") and ground.	No	▶	GO to PPE5 .
	• Is voltage greater than 0 volts?			

C273

BL/BK

VOM

TEST STEP		RESULT	▶	ACTION TO TAKE
PPE5	**SHORT TO GROUND CHECK**			
	• Leave 4EAT control module (connector C273) and solenoid valve (connector C188) disconnected.	Yes	▶	GO to 4EAT operational test OPS.
	• VOM on 200K ohm scale.	No	▶	REPAIR "BL/BK" wire between 4EAT control module and solenoid valve for short to ground.
	• Measure resistance between connector C273 terminal 2F ("BL/BK") and ground.			
	• Is resistance greater than 10,000 ohms?			
	See illustration in TEST STEP PPE4			

Service code 61 test information

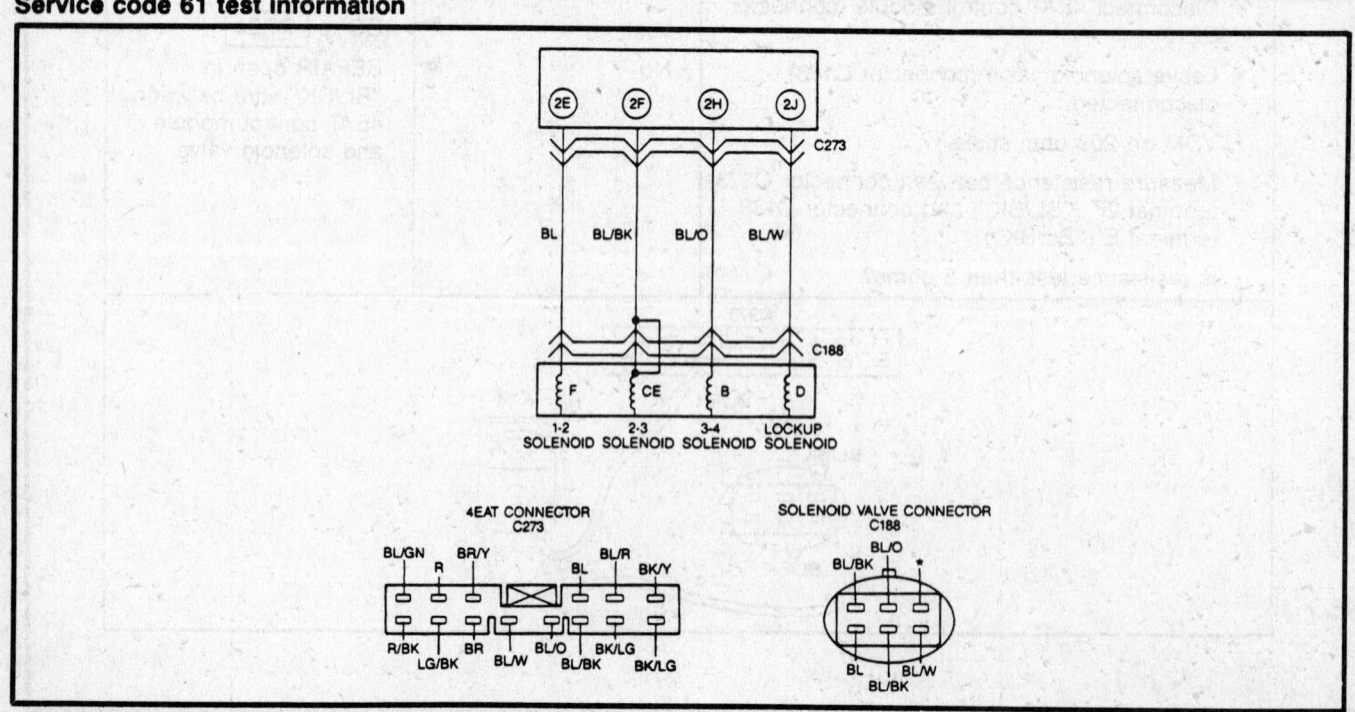

2E   2F   2H   2J

C273

BL   BL/BK   BL/O   BL/W

C188

F   CE   B   D

1-2   2-3   3-4   LOCKUP
SOLENOID   SOLENOID   SOLENOID   SOLENOID

4EAT CONNECTOR
C273

BL/GN   R   BR/Y   BL   BL/R   BK/Y

R/BK   BR   BL/O   BK/LG
LG/BK   BL/W   BL/BK   BK/LG

SOLENOID VALVE CONNECTOR
C188

BL/O
BL/BK   *

BL   BL/W
BL/BK

Service code 62 — pinpoint test schematic

TEST STEP	RESULT ▶	ACTION TO TAKE
PPF1 SYSTEM INTEGRITY CHECK		
• Visually inspect all wiring, wiring harness, connectors and components for evidence of overheating, insulation damage, looseness, shorting or other damage. • Is there any cause for concern?	Yes ▶ No ▶	SERVICE as required. GO to **PPF2**.
PPF2 SOLENOID RESISTANCE CHECK		
• Disconnect solenoid valve (connector C188). • VOM on 200 ohm scale. • Measure resistance between connector C188 terminal B ("BL/O") and ground. • Is resistance between 13 to 27 ohms?	Yes ▶ No ▶	GO to **PPF3**. REPLACE solenoid. NOTE: To prevent the replacement of a good solenoid be aware that: – Mechanical functions in the transaxle must operate properly.

PPF3 CIRCUIT CONTINUITY CHECK		
• Disconnect 4EAT control module (connector C273). • Leave solenoid valve (connector C188) disconnected. • VOM on 200 ohm scale. • Measure resistance between connector C273 terminal 2H ("BL/O") and connector C188 terminal B ("BL/O"). • Is resistance less than 5 ohms?	Yes ▶ No ▶	GO to **PPF4**. REPAIR open in "BL/O" wire between 4EAT control module and solenoid valve.

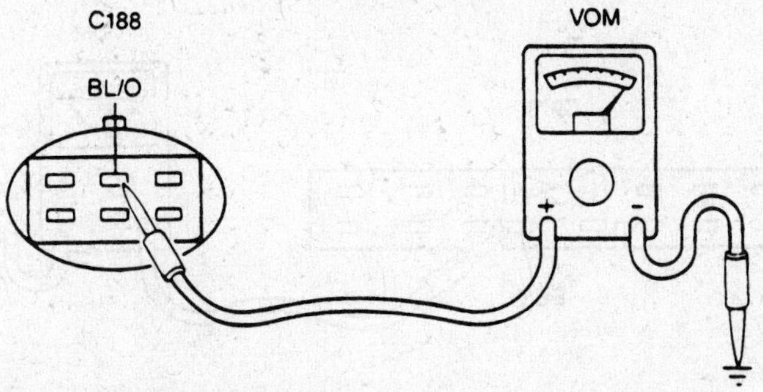

Service code 62 test information

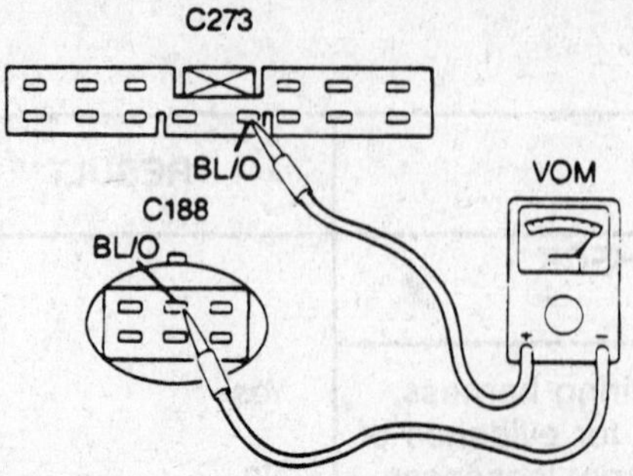

AUTOMATIC TRANSAXLES
4EAT—FORD MOTOR CO.

TEST STEP		RESULT	►	ACTION TO TAKE
PPF4	**SHORT TO VPWR CHECK**			
	• Leave 4EAT control module (connector C273) and solenoid valve (connector C188) disconnected.	Yes ►		REPAIR "BL/O" wire between 4EAT control module and solenoid for short to VPWR.
	• Key on; engine off.			
	• VOM on 20 volt scale.	No ►		GO to **PPF5** .
	• Measure voltage between connector C273 terminal 2H ("BL/O") and ground.			
	• Is voltage greater than 0 volts?			

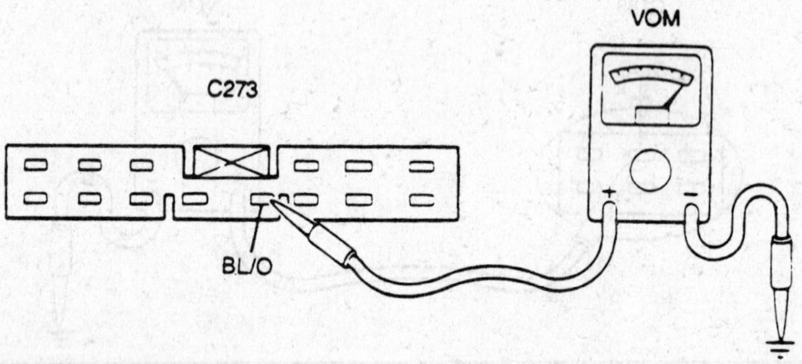

TEST STEP		RESULT	►	ACTION TO TAKE
PPF5	**SHORT TO GROUND CHECK**			
	• Leave 4EAT control module (connector C273) and solenoid valve (connector C188) disconnected.	Yes ►		GO to 4EAT operational test OPS.
	• VOM on 200K ohm scale.	No ►		REPAIR "BL/O" wire between 4EAT control module and solenoid valve for short to ground.
	• Measure resistance between connector C273 terminal 2H ("BL/O") and ground.			
	• Is resistance greater than 10,000 ohms?			
	See illustration in TEST STEP PPF4			

Service code 62 test information

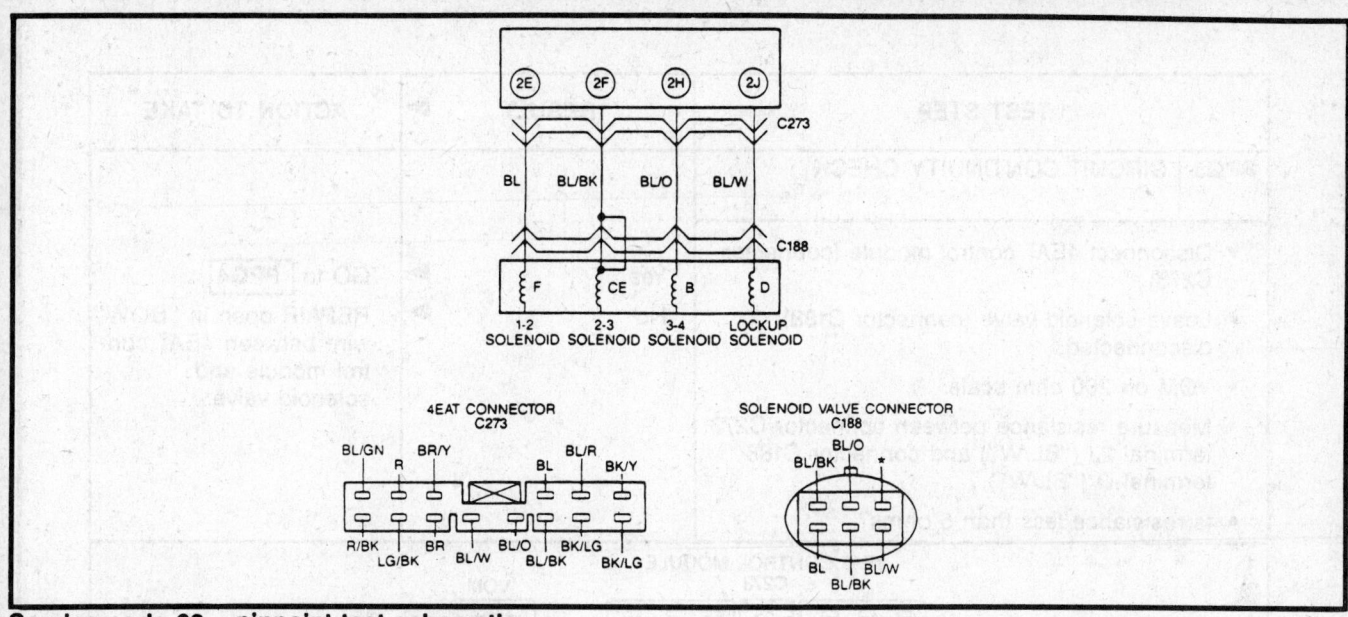

Service code 63 – pinpoint test schematic

TEST STEP		RESULT	►	ACTION TO TAKE
PPG1	**SYSTEM INTEGRITY CHECK**			
	• Visually inspect all wiring, wiring harness, connectors and components for evidence of overheating, insulation damage, looseness, shorting or other damage. • Is there any cause for concern?	Yes No	► ►	SERVICE as required. GO to PPG2 .
PPG2	**SOLENOID RESISTANCE CHECK**			
	• Disconnect solenoid valve (connector C188). • VOM on 200 ohm scale. • Measure resistance between connector C188 terminal D ("BL/W") and ground. • Is resistance between 13 to 27 ohms?	Yes No	► ►	GO to PPG3 . REPLACE solenoid. NOTE: To prevent the replacement of a good solenoid be aware that: – Mechanical functions in the transaxle must operate properly.

C188

VOM

BL/W

Service code 63 test information

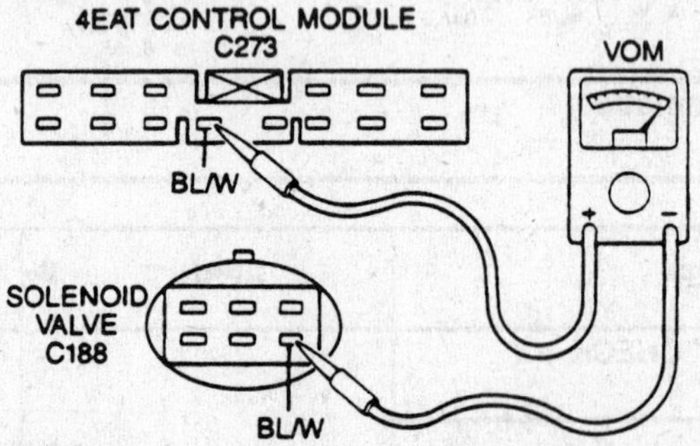

TEST STEP	RESULT ►	ACTION TO TAKE
PPG3 CIRCUIT CONTINUITY CHECK		
• Disconnect 4EAT control module (connector C273). • Leave solenoid valve (connector C188) disconnected. • VOM on 200 ohm scale. • Measure resistance between connector C273 terminal 2J ("BL/W") and connector C188 terminal D ("BL/W"). • Is resistance less than 5 ohms?	Yes ► No ►	GO to **PPG4** . REPAIR open in "BL/W" wire between 4EAT control module and solenoid valve.

4EAT CONTROL MODULE
C273
BL/W
VOM
SOLENOID VALVE
C188
BL/W

PPG4 SHORT TO VPWR CHECK		
• Leave 4EAT control module (connector C273) and solenoid valve (connector C188) disconnected. • Key on; engine off. • VOM on 20 volt scale. • Measure voltage between connector C273 terminal 2J ("BL/W") and ground. • Is voltage greater than 0 volts?	Yes ► No ►	REPAIR "BL/W" wire between 4EAT control module and solenoid valve for short to VPWR. GO to **PPG5** .

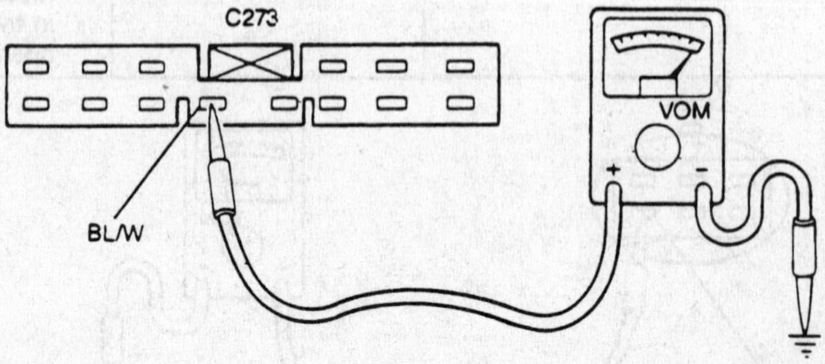

C273
BL/W
VOM

Service code 63 test information

TEST STEP		RESULT	►	ACTION TO TAKE
PPG5	SHORT TO GROUND CHECK			
	• Leave 4EAT control module (connector C273) and solenoid valve (connector C188) disconnected. • VOM on 200K ohm scale. • Measure resistance between connector C273 terminal 2J ("BL/W") and ground. • Is resistance greater than 10,000 ohms? See illustration in TEST STEP PPG4	Yes No	► ►	GO to 4EAT operational test OPS. REPAIR "BL/W" wire between 4EAT control module and solenoid valve for short to ground.

Service code 63 test information

— CAUTION —

Do not allow any one to stand either in front of or behind the vehicle during the stall test. Personal injury could result.

2. Install a tachometer to the engine. Place the selector lever in the desired detent and depress the accelerator to the wide open throttle position, noting the total rpm achieved.

NOTE: Do not hold the throttle open for more than 5 seconds at a time during the test.

3. After the test, move the selector lever to the **N** position and let the engine idle for about a minute to cool the fluid before making a second or third test.

4. Use the Stall Test Evaluation chart to verify the correlation of observed test results with possible causes for the deviations from specifications.

OPB Test—Hydraulic Control System Time Lag Check

This test checks for the time lag between selector lever shift into gear and when a shock is felt, using a stopwatch.

1. To perform the test, start the engine and allow it to come to normal operating temperature or until the ATF temperature reaches 122–176°F (50–80°C). Apply the parking during the test.

2. With the engine idling in **P** at 725–775 rpm, shift from **N** to **OVERDRIVE** and note the elapsed time until a shock is felt, using the stopwatch.

3. Idle the engine in **N** for about a minute to cool the fluid.

4. Repeat test procedure for **N** to **OVERDRIVE** manual mode and **N** to **R**.

5. Repeat procedure 3 times and average the results.

6. Use the Time Lag Evaluation chart to verify the correlation of observed test results with possible causes for the deviations from specifications.

OPC Test—Oil Pressure and Control Check

This test checks the oil pump line pressure, line pressure control, throttle control pressure and oil leakage.

1. To perform the test, start the engine and allow it to come to normal operating temperature or until the ATF temperature reaches 122–176°F (50–80°C). Apply the parking during the test.

2. Connect a tachometer to the engine.

3. Connect a pressure tester with fittings at the line pressure inspection hole (square head plug marked **L**).

4. With the engine idling in **P** at 725–775 rpm, shift the selector lever to the **D** range, then read the line pressure at idle.

5. With the foot brake firmly applied, steadily increase the engine speed to its maximum quickly read the line pressure when the engine speed remains constant, then release the accelerator.

NOTE: This test must be completed within 5 seconds, followed by cooling the ATF in the N range idling for about a minute.

6. Repeat test for each range, making certain to cool the transaxle in between tests.

7. Use the Line Pressure Test Evaluation chart to verify the correlation of observed test results with possible causes for the deviations from specifications.

OPD Test—Throttle Pressure Test

This test checks the the line pressure for checking the hydraulic components and for improper throttle cable adjustments.

1. To perform the test, start the engine and allow it to come to normal operating temperature or until the ATF temperature reaches 122–176°F (50–80°C). Apply the parking during the test.

2. Connect a tachometer to the engine.

3. Connect a pressure tester with fittings at the throttle pressure inspection hole (square head plug marked **T**).

4. With the engine idling in **P** at 725–775 rpm, shift the selector lever to the **OD** range, then read the throttle pressure at idle.

5. With the foot brake firmly applied, steadily increase the engine speed to its maximum quickly read the throttle pressure when the engine speed remains constant, then release the accelerator.

NOTE: This test must be completed within 5 seconds, followed by cooling the ATF in the neutral range idling for about a minute.

6. Use the Throttle Pressure Test Evaluation chart to verify the correlation of observed test results with possible causes for the deviations from specifications.

ROAD TEST

Description

The Road Test is an evaluation of the 4EAT performance with

TEST STEP	RESULT	ACTION TO TAKE
PPM2 BRAKE LIGHT SWITCH VOLTAGE CHECK • Disconnect 4EAT control module (connector C274). • Key on; engine off. • VOM on 20 volt scale. • Measure voltage at brake light switch connector C256 between "W/GN" wire and ground. Pedal Depressed — Above 10v Pedal Released — Below 1.5v • Are voltages OK?	Yes No	GO to PPM3 GO to PPM4

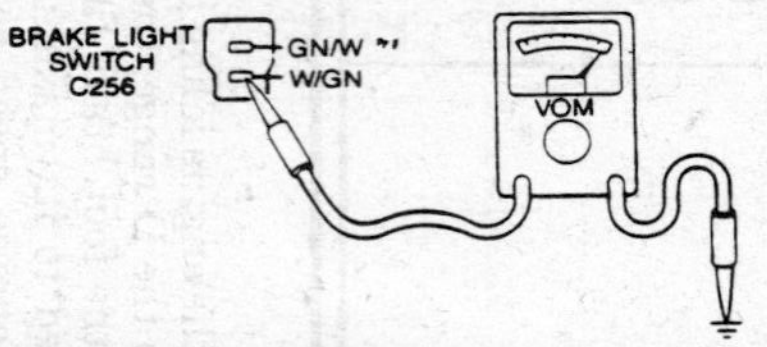

BRAKE LIGHT SWITCH C256 — GN/W, W/GN, VOM

TEST STEP	RESULT	ACTION TO TAKE
PPM3 CHECK VOLTAGE AT 4EAT CONTROL UNIT • 4EAT control module (connector C273) disconnected. • Key on; engine off. • VOM on 20 volt scale. • Measure voltage at 4EAT control module connector C274 between terminal 1N ("W/GN") and ground. Pedal Depressed — Above 10v Pedal Released — 0.0v • Are voltages OK?	Yes No	REPLACE 4EAT control module. REPAIR "W/GN" wire between 4EAT control module and brake light switch.

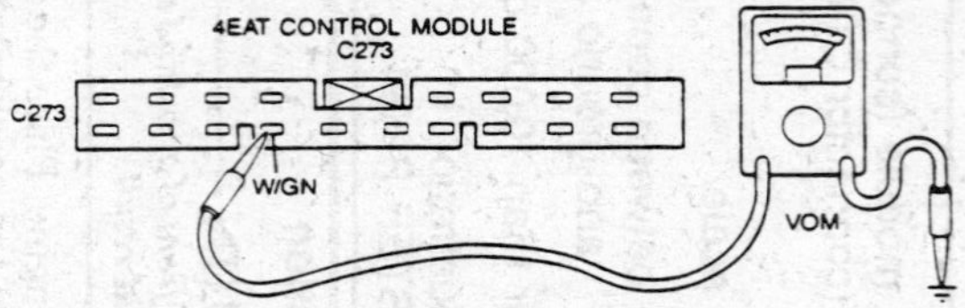

4EAT CONTROL MODULE C273 — W/GN, VOM

System integrity check

TEST STEP	RESULT	ACTION TO TAKE
PPM1 SYSTEM INTEGRITY CHECK • Visually inspect all wiring, wiring harness, connectors and components for evidence of overheating, insulation damage, looseness, shorting or other damage. • Is there any cause for concern?	Yes No	SERVICE as required. LOCATE malfunctioning switch in the table below and proceed to the appropriate Pinpoint Test Step as indicated in the "Action To Take" column.

SWITCH		ACTION TO TAKE
BRAKE LIGHT SWITCH		GO TO TEST STEP PPM2
IDLE SWITCH		GO TO TEST STEP PPM5
COOLANT TEMPERATURE SWITCH		GO TO TEST STEP PPM8
CHECK CONNECTOR		GO TO TEST STEP PPM12
NEUTRAL SAFETY SWITCH	L	GO TO TEST STEP PPM14
	D	GO TO TEST STEP PPM18
	(D)	GO TO TEST STEP PPM22
	N OR P	GO TO TEST STEP PPM26
MODE SWITCH		GO TO TEST STEP PPM28
MODE INDICATOR		GO TO TEST STEP PPM31
MANUAL SWITCH		GO TO TEST STEP PPM35
MANUAL INDICATOR		GO TO TEST STEP PPM39
NO LOAD SIGNAL		GO TO TEST STEP PPM41
THROTTLE POSITION		GO TO TEST STEP PPM44
AFT SWITCH		GO TO TEST STEP PPM45

System integrity check

System integrity check

TEST STEP	RESULT	ACTION TO TAKE
PPM6 CIRCUIT CONTINUITY CHECK • Idle switch (connector C132) disconnected. • Disconnect 4EAT control module (connector C274). • VOM on 200 ohm scale. • Measure resistance between connector C274 terminal 1L ("LG/BK") and connector C132 ("BR"). • Is resistance less than 5 ohms?	Yes No	GO to **PPM7**. REPAIR wire between 4EAT control module and idle switch for open.
PPM7 SHORT TO GROUND AND VPWR CHECK • Idle switch (connector C132) and 4EAT control module (connectors C273 and C274) disconnected. • Disconnect battery. • Key on. • VOM on 200K ohm scale. • Measure resistance between: • Connector C274 terminal 1L ("LG/BK") and ground. • Connector C274 terminal 1L ("LG/BK") and connector C273 terminal 2A ("BK/Y"). • Are resistances greater than 10,000 ohms?	Yes No	REPLACE 4EAT control module. REPAIR wire between 4EAT control module and idle switch for shorts.

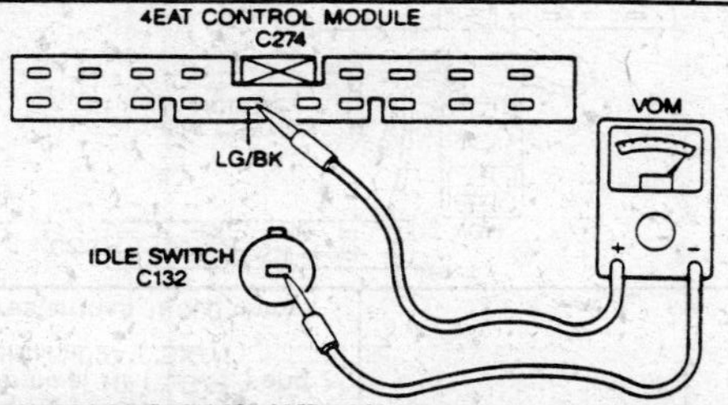

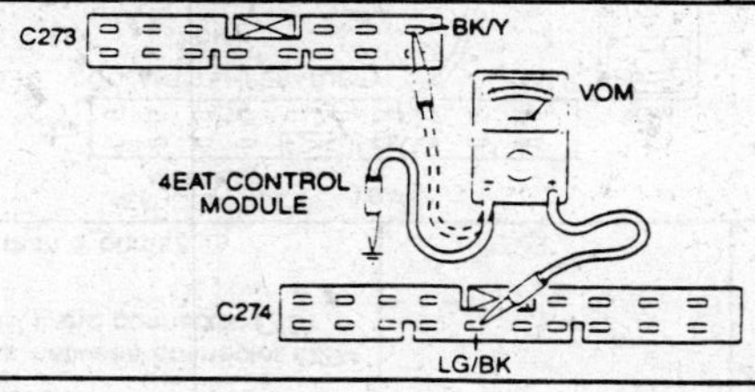

System integrity check

TEST STEP	RESULT	ACTION TO TAKE
PPM4 BRAKE LIGHT SWITCH POWER CHECK • Key on; engine off. • VOM on 20 volt scale. • Measure voltage at brake light switch (connector C256) between "GN/W" wire and ground. • Is voltage above 10 volts?	Yes No	REPAIR "W/GN" wire between brake light switch and 4EAT control module. If OK REPLACE brake light switch. REPAIR "GN/W" wire between brake light switch and fuse box.
PPM5 IDLE SWITCH FUNCTION CHECK • Disconnect idle switch (connector C132). • Measure continuity between connector C132 terminal and ground while exercising the idle switch. Throttle Position — Continuity Closed — Yes Open — No • Is the idle switch functioning OK?	Yes No	GO to **PPM6**. REPLACE idle switch.

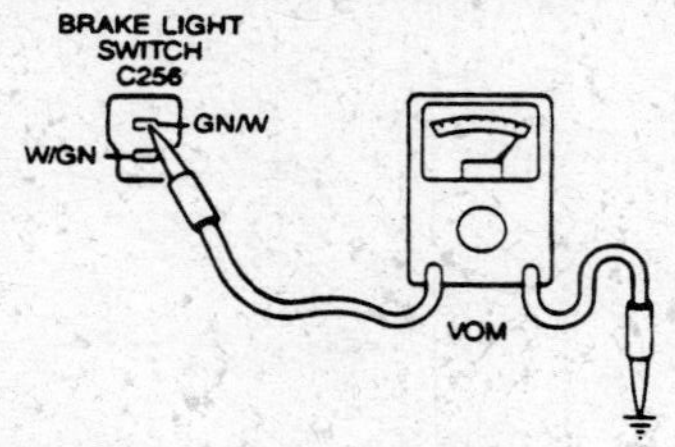

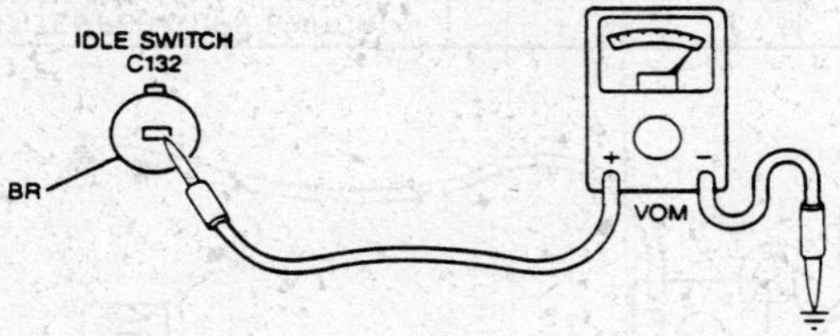

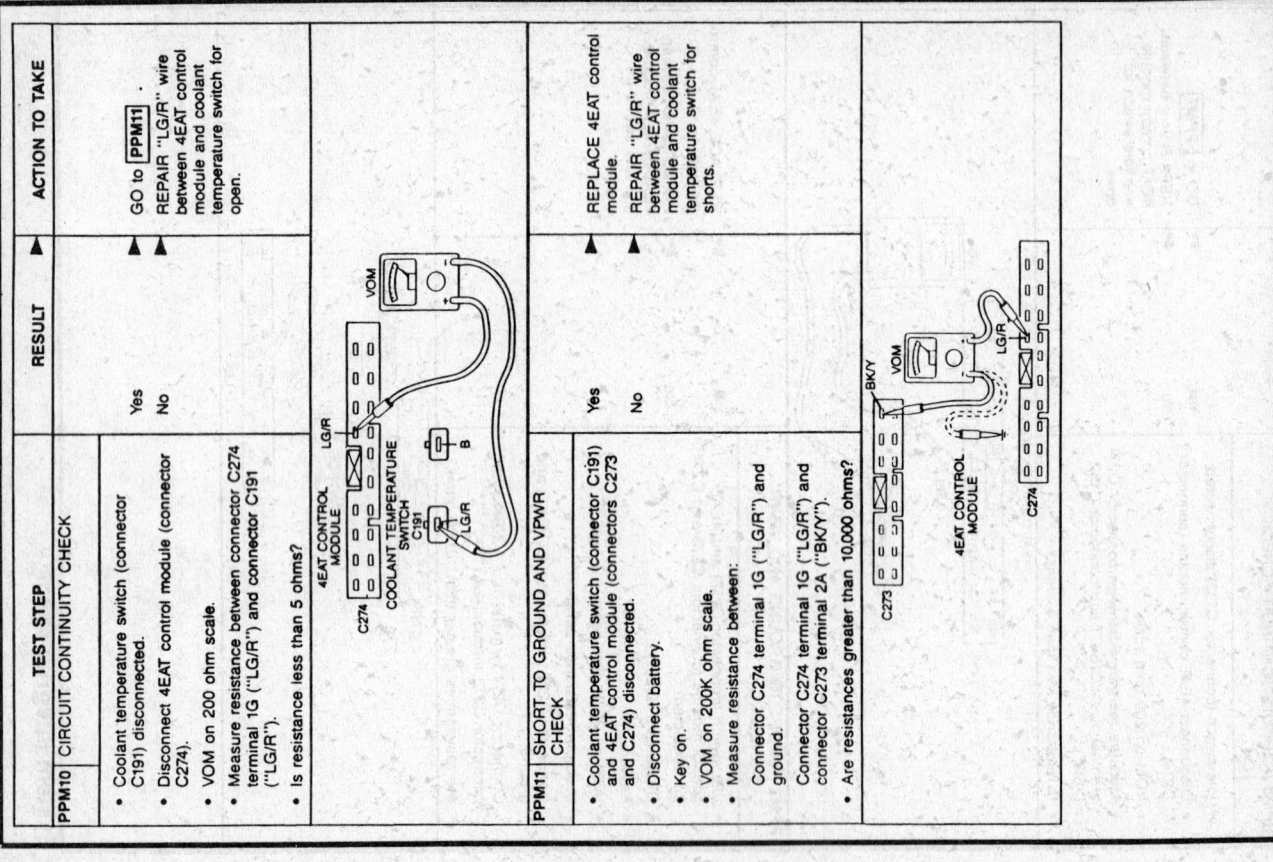

TEST STEP	RESULT	ACTION TO TAKE
PPM10 CIRCUIT CONTINUITY CHECK • Coolant temperature switch (connector C191) disconnected. • Disconnect 4EAT control module (connector C274). • VOM on 200 ohm scale. • Measure resistance between connector C274 terminal 1G ("LG/R") and connector C191 ("LG/R"). • Is resistance less than 5 ohms?	Yes No	GO to PPM11. REPAIR "LG/R" wire between 4EAT control module and coolant temperature switch for open.
PPM11 SHORT TO GROUND AND VPWR CHECK • Coolant temperature switch (connector C191) and 4EAT control module (connectors C273 and C274) disconnected. • Disconnect battery. • Key on. • VOM on 200K ohm scale. • Measure resistance between: Connector C274 terminal 1G ("LG/R") and ground. Connector C274 terminal 1G ("LG/R") and connector C273 terminal 2A ("BK/Y"). • Are resistances greater than 10,000 ohms?	Yes No	REPLACE 4EAT control module. REPAIR "LG/R" wire between 4EAT control module and coolant temperature switch for shorts.

System integrity check

TEST STEP	RESULT	ACTION TO TAKE
PPM8 COOLANT TEMPERATURE SWITCH GROUND CHECK • Disconnect coolant temperature switch (connector C906). • VOM on 200 ohm scale. • Measure resistance between connector C906 "BK" wire and ground. • Is resistance less than 5 ohms?	Yes No	GO to PPM9. REPAIR "BK" wire between coolant temperature switch and ground.
PPM9 COOLANT TEMPERATURE SWITCH FUNCTION CHECK • Coolant temperature switch (connector C906) disconnected. • Check continuity between switch terminals as follows: Coolant / Continuity Below 65°C (149°F) / Yes Above 72°C (162°F) / No • Does the coolant temperature switch function OK?	Yes No	GO to PPM10. REPLACE coolant temperature switch.

System integrity check

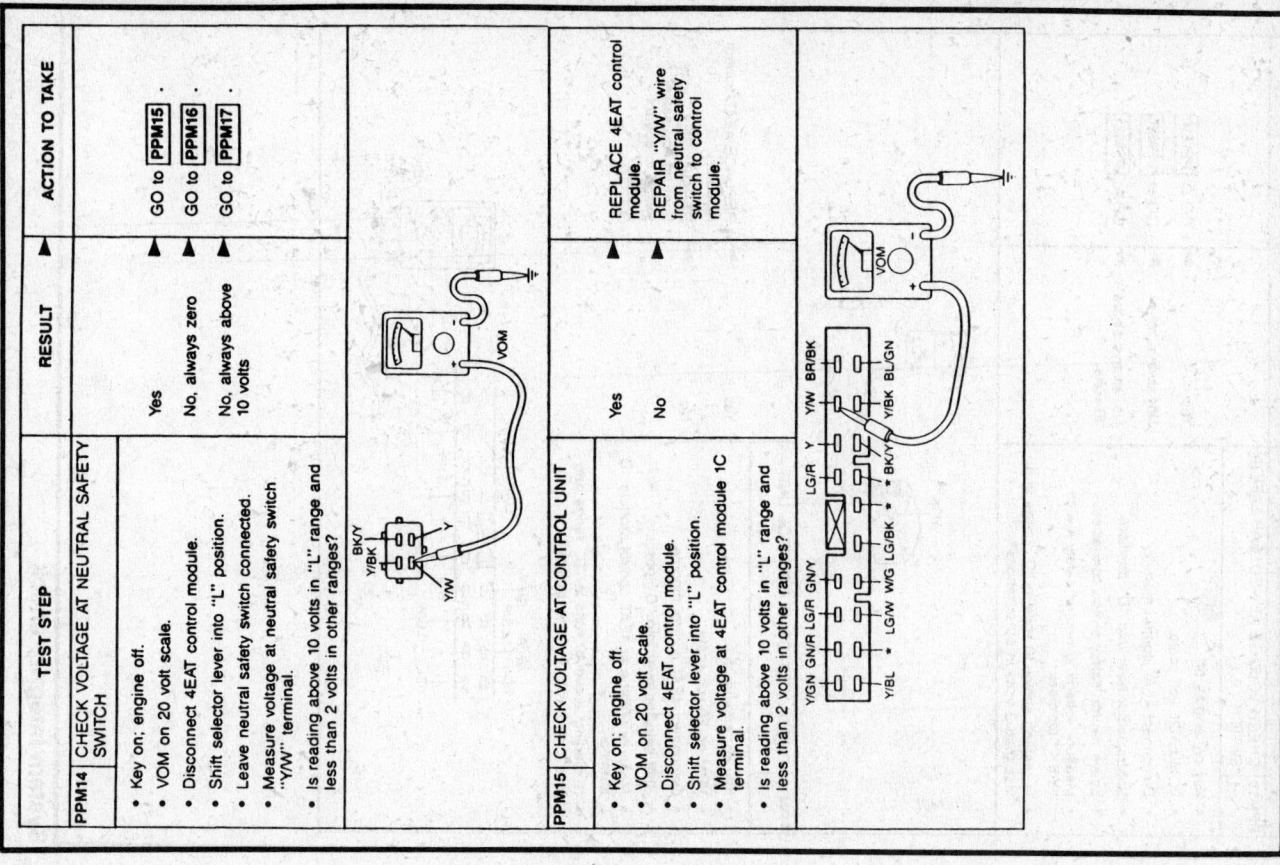

TEST STEP	RESULT	ACTION TO TAKE
PPM14 CHECK VOLTAGE AT NEUTRAL SAFETY SWITCH • Key on; engine off. • VOM on 20 volt scale. • Disconnect 4EAT control module. • Shift selector lever into "L" position. • Leave neutral safety switch connected. • Measure voltage at neutral safety switch "Y/W" terminal. • Is reading above 10 volts in "L" range and less than 2 volts in other ranges?	Yes No, always zero No, always above 10 volts	GO to **PPM15** . GO to **PPM16** . GO to **PPM17**
PPM15 CHECK VOLTAGE AT CONTROL UNIT • Key on; engine off. • VOM on 20 volt scale. • Disconnect 4EAT control module. • Shift selector lever into "L" position. • Measure voltage at 4EAT control module 1C terminal. • Is reading above 10 volts in "L" range and less than 2 volts in other ranges?	Yes No	REPLACE 4EAT control module. REPAIR "Y/W" wire from neutral safety switch to control module.

System integrity check

TEST STEP	RESULT	ACTION TO TAKE
PPM12 CIRCUIT CONTINUITY CHECK • Disconnect 4EAT control module (connector C273). • VOM on 200 ohm scale. • Measure resistance between connector C273 terminal 2P ("R/BK") and check connector terminal ("R/BK"). • Is resistance less than 5 ohms?	Yes No	GO to **PPM13** . REPAIR ("R/BK") wire between 4EAT control module and check connector for opens.

PPM13 SHORT TO GROUND AND VPWR CHECK
 	
• 4EAT control module (connector C273) disconnected.
• Disconnect battery.
• Key on.
• VOM on 200K ohm scale.
• Measure resistance between:
  Connector C273 terminal 2P ("R/BK") and ground
  Connector C273 terminal 2A ("BK/Y").
• Are resistances greater than 10,000 ohms?
	Yes
	
	No
		REPLACE 4EAT control module.
		
		REPAIR "R/BK" wire between 4EAT control module and check connector for shorts.

System integrity check

AUTOMATIC TRANSAXLES
4EAT—FORD MOTOR CO.

TEST STEP	RESULT	ACTION TO TAKE
PPM18 CHECK VOLTAGE AT NEUTRAL SAFETY SWITCH • Key on; engine off. • VOM on 20 volt scale. • Disconnect 4EAT control module. • Shift selector lever into "D" position. • Leave neutral safety switch connected. • Measure voltage at neutral safety switch "Y/BK" terminal. • Is reading above 10 volts in "D" range and less than 2 volts in other ranges?	Yes No, always zero No, always above 10 volts	GO to PPM19 GO to PPM20 GO to PPM21
PPM19 CHECK VOLTAGE AT CONTROL UNIT • Key on; engine off. • VOM on 20 volt scale. • Disconnect 4EAT control module. • Shift selector lever into "D" position. • Measure voltage at 4EAT control module 1D terminal. • Is reading above 10 volts in "D" range and less than 2 volts in other ranges?	Yes No	REPLACE 4EAT control module. REPAIR "Y/BK" wire from neutral safety switch to control module.

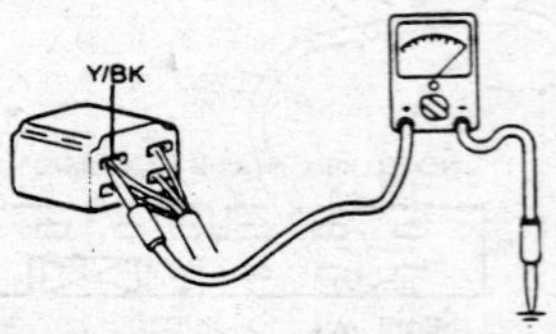

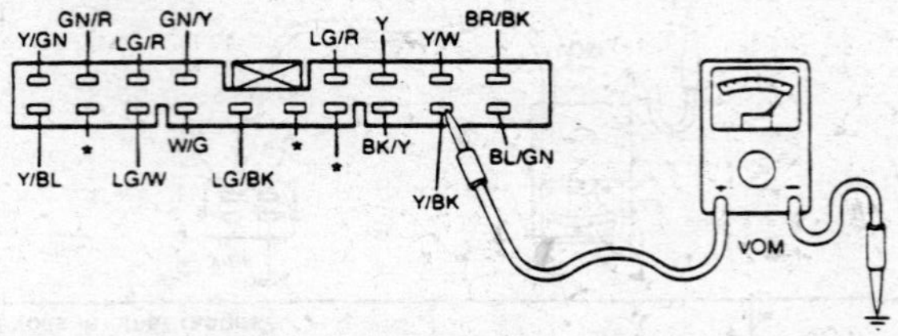

System Integrity check

TEST STEP	RESULT	ACTION TO TAKE
PPM16 CHECK VOLTAGE TO NEUTRAL SAFETY SWITCH • Key on; engine off. • VOM on 20 volt scale. • Disconnect neutral safety switch. • Measure voltage at neutral safety switch connector "BK/Y" terminal. • Is reading greater than 10 volts?	Yes No	REPLACE neutral safety switch. REPAIR "BK/Y" wire from neutral safety switch to fuse panel (15 amp meter fuse).
PPM17 CHECK FOR SHORT TO VPWR • Key on; engine off. • Disconnect 4EAT control module. • Disconnect neutral safety switch. • Measure voltage at neutral safety switch connector "Y/W" terminal. • Is reading greater than 4 volts? See illustration in TEST STEP PPM14	Yes No	REPAIR short in "Y/W" wire to VPWR or VREF. REPLACE neutral safety switch.

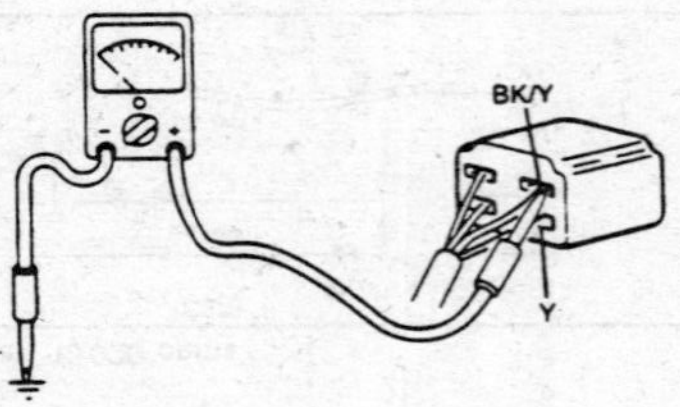

System Integrity check

System integrity check

TEST STEP	RESULT	ACTION TO TAKE
PPM23 CHECK VOLTAGE AT CONTROL UNIT • Key on; engine off. • VOM on 20 volt scale. • Disconnect 4EAT control module. • Shift selector lever into "D" position. • Measure voltage at 4EAT control module 1E terminal. • Is reading above 10 volts in "D" range and less than 2 volts in other ranges?	Yes	REPLACE 4EAT control module.
	No	REPAIR "Y" wire from neutral safety switch to control module.
PPM24 CHECK VOLTAGE TO NEUTRAL SAFETY SWITCH • Key on; engine off. • VOM on 20 volt scale. • Disconnect neutral safety switch. • Measure voltage at neutral safety switch connector "BK/Y" terminal. • Is reading greater than 10 volts? See illustration in TEST STEP PPM16	Yes	REPLACE neutral safety switch.
	No	REPAIR "BK/Y" wire from neutral safety switch to fuse panel (15 amp meter fuse).
PPM25 CHECK VOLTAGE TO NEUTRAL SAFETY SWITCH • Key on; engine off. • Disconnect 4EAT control module. • Disconnect neutral safety switch. • Measure voltage at neutral safety switch connector "Y" terminal. • Is reading greater than 4 volts? See illustration in TEST STEP PPM22	Yes	REPAIR short in "Y" wire to VPWR or VREF.
	No	REPLACE neutral safety switch.

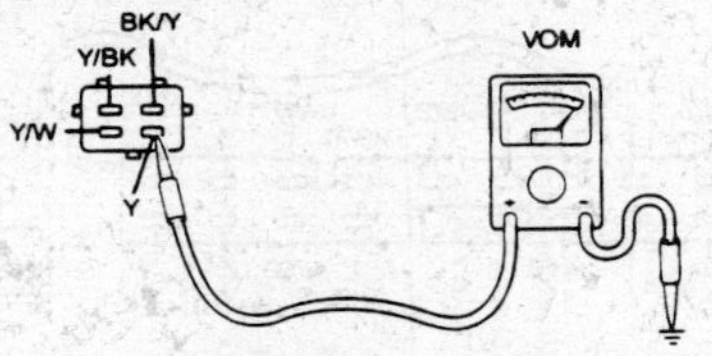

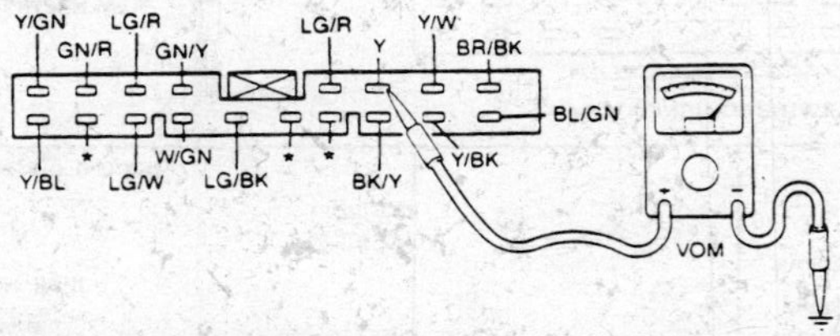

System integrity check

TEST STEP	RESULT	ACTION TO TAKE
PPM20 CHECK VOLTAGE TO NEUTRAL SAFETY SWITCH • Key on; engine off. • VOM on 20 volt scale. • Disconnect neutral safety switch. • Measure voltage at neutral safety switch connector "Y/BK" terminal. • Is reading greater than 10 volts? See illustration in TEST STEP PPM16	Yes	REPLACE neutral safety switch.
	No	REPAIR "BK/Y" wire from neutral safety switch to fuse panel (15 amp meter fuse).
PPM21 CHECK FOR SHORT TO VPWR • Key on; engine off. • Disconnect 4EAT control module. • Disconnect neutral safety switch. • Measure voltage at neutral safety switch connector "Y/BK" terminal. • Is reading greater than 4 volts? See illustration in TEST STEP PPM18	Yes	REPAIR short in "Y/BK" wire to VPWR or VREF.
	No	REPLACE neutral safety switch.
PPM22 CHECK VOLTAGE AT NEUTRAL SAFETY SWITCH • Key on; engine off. • VOM on 20 volt scale. • Disconnect 4EAT control module. • Shift selector lever in "D" position. • Leave neutral safety switch connected. • Measure voltage at neutral safety switch "Y" terminal. • Is reading above 10 volts in "D" range and less than 2 volts in other ranges?	Yes	GO to PPM23
	No, always zero	GO to PPM24
	No, always above 10 volts	GO to PPM25

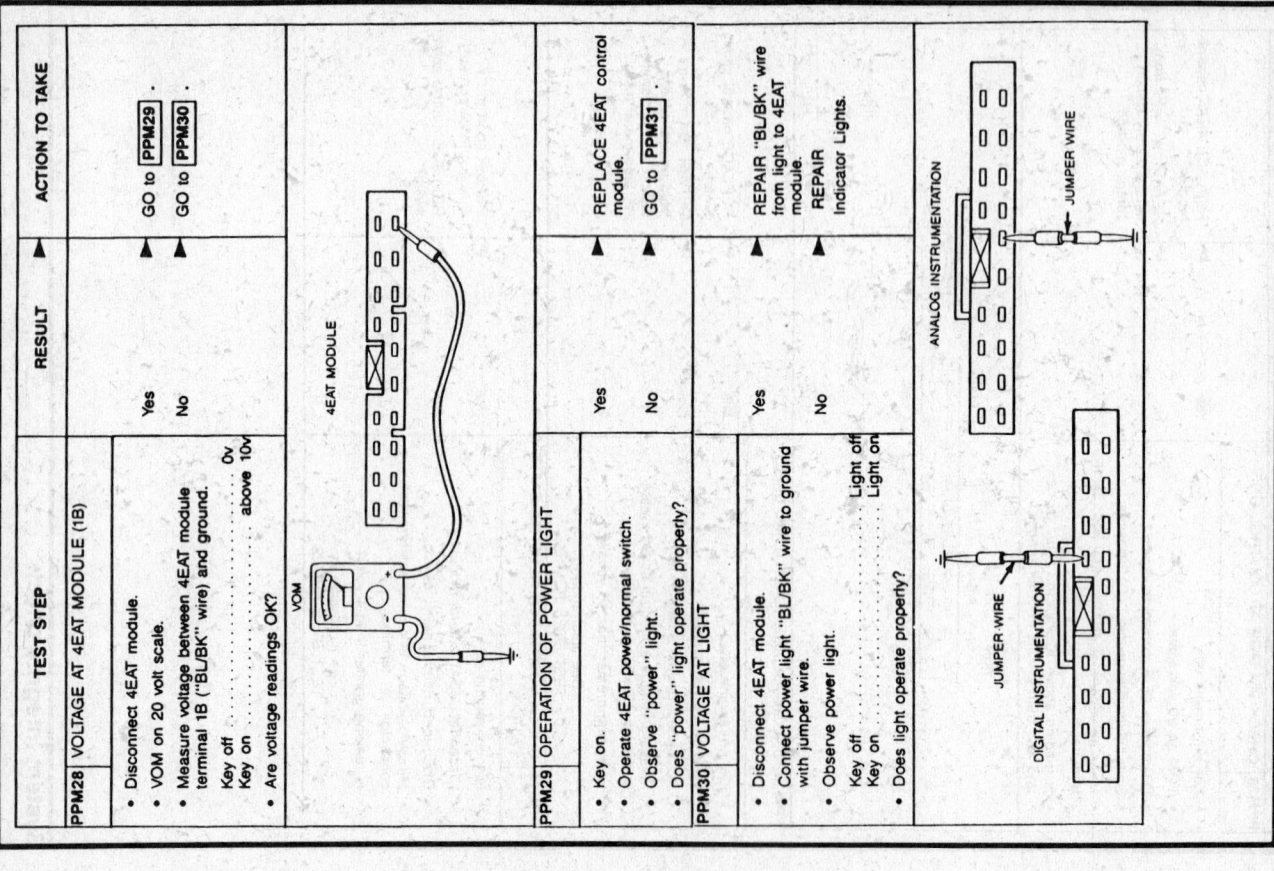

TEST STEP	RESULT	ACTION TO TAKE

PPM28 VOLTAGE AT 4EAT MODULE (1B)
• Disconnect 4EAT module.
• VOM on 20 volt scale.
• Measure voltage between 4EAT module terminal 1B ("BL/BK" wire) and ground.
  Key off 0v
  Key on .... above 10v
• Are voltage readings OK?
	Yes
	No
		GO to PPM29.
		GO to PPM30.

PPM29 OPERATION OF POWER LIGHT • Key on. • Operate 4EAT power/normal switch. • Observe "power" light. • Does "power" light operate properly?	Yes No	REPLACE 4EAT control module. GO to PPM31.

PPM30 VOLTAGE AT LIGHT
• Disconnect 4EAT module.
• Connect power light "BL/BK" wire to ground with jumper wire.
• Observe power light.
  Key off .... Light off
  Key on .... Light on
• Does light operate properly?
	Yes
	No
		REPAIR "BL/BK" wire from light to 4EAT module.
		REPAIR Indicator Lights.

4EAT MODULE

VOM

ANALOG INSTRUMENTATION

JUMPER WIRE

DIGITAL INSTRUMENTATION

JUMPER WIRE

System integrity check

TEST STEP	RESULT	ACTION TO TAKE
PPM26 CHECK VOLTAGE AT CONTROL MODULE • Key on, engine off. • VOM on 20 volt scale. • Selector lever in N or P position. • Measure voltage at 4EAT control module 1F terminal. • Is reading greater than 10 volts in N or P range and less than 2 volts in other ranges?	Yes No	GO to PPM27. REPLACE 4EAT control module.
PPM27 CHECK VOLTAGE AT NEUTRAL SAFETY SWITCH • Key on, engine off. • VOM on 20 volt scale. • Selector lever in N or P position. • Measure voltage at neutral safety switch "BK/Y" terminal. • Is reading greater than 10 volts in N or P range or less than 2 volts in other ranges?	Yes No	REPLACE neutral safety switch. REPAIR "BK/Y" wire from neutral safety switch to 4EAT control module.

BR/BK Y YW Y/BK BLGN LG/R Y BK/Y LG/R LG/BK GN/Y LG/R W/BK LG/W Y/GN GN/R Y/BL

BK/Y

System integrity check

System integrity check

TEST STEP	RESULT	ACTION TO TAKE
PPM33 4EAT SWITCH FUNCTION CHECK • Disconnect 4EAT switch (connector C320). • Check continuity between switch "BL/BK" and "BR/BK" terminals as follows: 4EAT Switch Position — Continuity Power — Yes Normal — No • Is the 4EAT switch functioning OK?	Yes No	GO to PPM34 . REPLACE 4EAT switch.
PPM34 CHECK VOLTAGE AT INSTRUMENT PANEL • Key on; engine off. • VOM on 20 volt scale. • Measure voltage at instrument panel (connector C274) as follows: Analog Instrument Panel – measure voltage between terminal 2J ("BL/BK") and ground Digital Instrument Panel – measure voltage between terminal 2G ("BL/BK") and ground. • Is voltage above 10 volts?	Yes No	REPAIR wire between instrument panel and 4EAT switch. REPAIR Warning and Indicator Lights.
PPM35 MANUAL SWITCH OPERATION • Key off. • VOM on 200 ohm scale. • Measure resistance between manual switch terminals "BR/BK" and "BK." Manual Switch — Resistance Released — above 10,000 ohms Depressed — 0 ohms • Are resistance readings OK?	Yes No	GO to PPM36 . REPLACE manual switch.

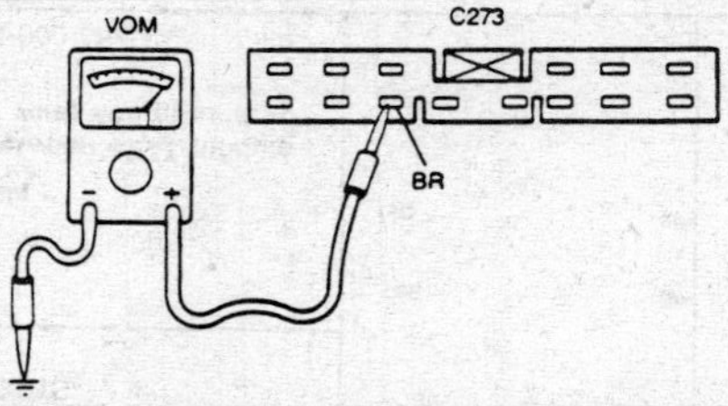

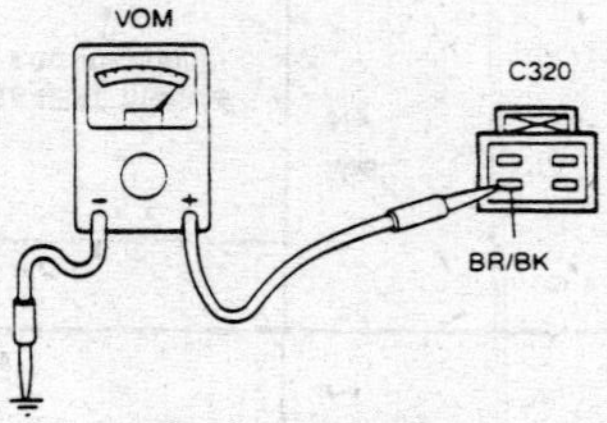

(Diagrams: ANALOG C274 / BL/BK; DIGITAL C274 / BL/BK; MANUAL SWITCH (R) C319 — BK, BR/BK; VOM)

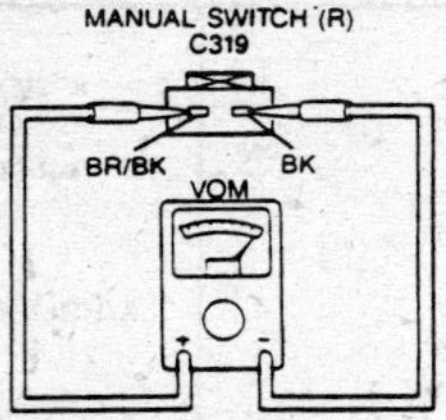

System integrity check

TEST STEP	RESULT	ACTION TO TAKE
PPM31 CHECK VOLTAGE AT 4EAT CONTROL MODULE • Disconnect 4EAT control module (connector C273). • Key on; engine off. • VOM on 20 volt scale. • Measure voltage between connector C273 terminal 2L ("BR") and ground. • Exercise the 4EAT switch between power and normal and verify the following: 4EAT Switch Position — Voltage Power — 12v Normal — 0v • Are voltages OK?	Yes No	REPLACE 4EAT control module. GO to PPM32 .
PPM32 CHECK VOLTAGE AT 4EAT SWITCH • Key on; engine off. • VOM on 20 volt scale. • Measure voltage between connector C320 ("BR/BK" wire) and ground. • Exercise the 4EAT switch between power and normal and verify the following: 4EAT Switch Position — Voltage Power — 12v Normal — 0v • Are voltages OK?	Yes No	REPAIR "BR/BK" wire between 4EAT switch and 4EAT control module. GO to PPM33 .

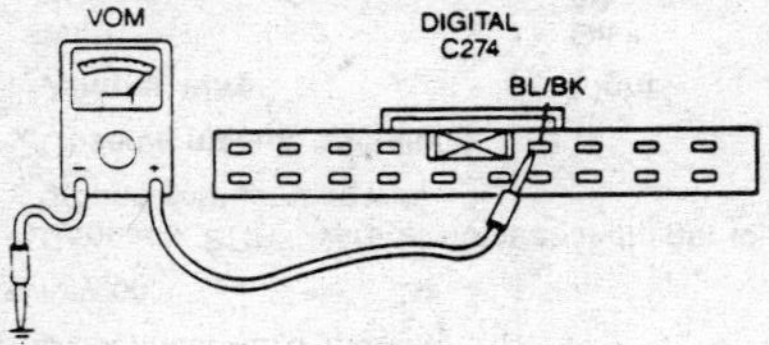

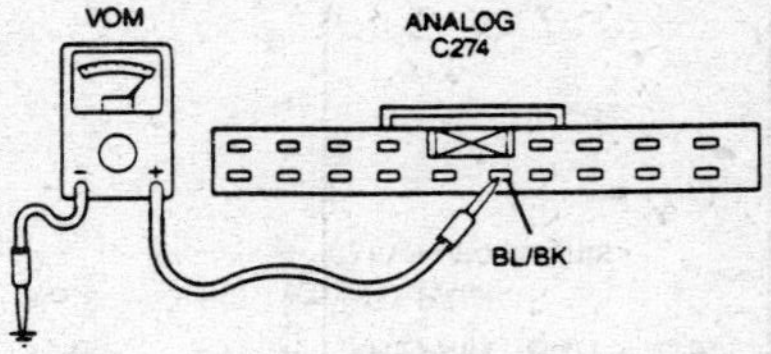

(Diagrams: C273 / BR; C320 / BR/BK; VOM)

System integrity check

TEST STEP	RESULT	ACTION TO TAKE
PPM39 OPERATION AT 4EAT MODULE • Disconnect 4EAT module. • Key on. • Connect 4EAT module terminal 2K ("BR/Y" wire) to ground with jumper wire. • Observe manual shift light: Jumper Wire — Light With — On Without — Off • Does light operate properly?	Yes No	REPLACE 4EAT module. NOTE: Be certain manual switch operated properly in Quick Test Step 5.0. GO to PPM40.
PPM40 OPERATION AT LIGHT • Disconnect 4EAT module. • Key on. • Connect "BR/Y" wire at manual shift light to ground with jumper wire. • Observe manual shift light: Jumper Wire — Light With — On Without — Off • Does light operate properly?	Yes No	REPAIR "BR/Y" wire. REPAIR Indicator Lights.

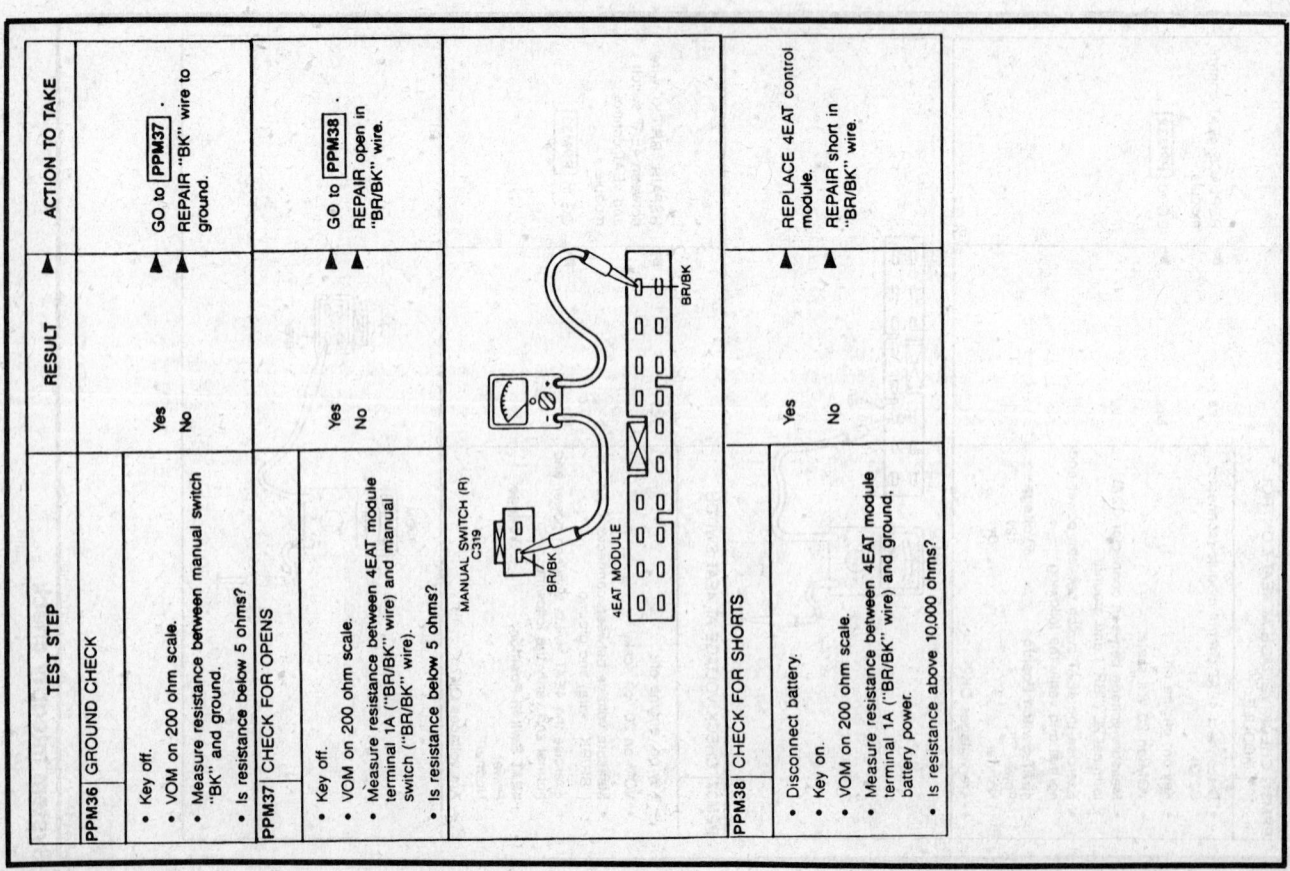

System integrity check

TEST STEP	RESULT	ACTION TO TAKE
PPM36 GROUND CHECK • Key off. • VOM on 200 ohm scale. • Measure resistance between manual switch "BK" and ground. • Is resistance below 5 ohms?	Yes No	GO to PPM37. REPAIR "BK" wire to ground.
PPM37 CHECK FOR OPENS • Key off. • VOM on 200 ohm scale. • Measure resistance between 4EAT module terminal 1A ("BR/BK" wire) and manual switch ("BR/BK" wire). • Is resistance below 5 ohms?	Yes No	GO to PPM38. REPAIR open in "BR/BK" wire.
PPM38 CHECK FOR SHORTS • Disconnect battery. • Key on. • VOM on 200 ohm scale. • Measure resistance between 4EAT module terminal 1A ("BR/BK" wire) and ground, battery power. • Is resistance above 10,000 ohms?	Yes No	REPLACE 4EAT control module. REPAIR short in "BR/BK" wire.

TEST STEP	RESULT	ACTION TO TAKE
PPM43 CHECK FOR SHORTS • Disconnect battery, 4EAT module, and ECA. • VOM on 200,000 ohm scale. • Measure resistance between 4EAT module terminal 2N "LG/BK" wire and ground, battery power. • Are resistance readings above 10,000 ohms?	Yes ▲ No ▲	▲ REFER to engine emission diagnosis ▲ REPAIR short in "LG/BK" wire to ground or battery power.
PPM44 TP SIGNAL CHECK • Key on. • VOM on 20 volts scale. • Measure voltage between TP sensor "LG/W" wire and ground. Throttle — Voltage Closed — 0.5v 1/8 — 1.0v 2/8 — 1.5v 3/8 — 2.0v 4/8 — 2.5v 5/8 — 3.0v 6/8 — 3.5v 7/8 — 4.0v Full — above 4.3v TP sensor "LG/R" wire and ground. Key off .... below 1.5v Key on .... 4–6v • Are voltage readings OK?	Yes ▲ No ▲	▲ REPAIR wire(s) in question. ▲ REPLACE throttle position sensor.
PPM45 AFT SWITCH GROUND CHECK • Disconnect AFT switch (connector C189). • VOM on 200 ohm scale. • Measure resistance between connector C189 "BK" wire and ground. • Is resistance less than 5 ohms?	Yes ▲ No ▲	▲ GO to PPM46 ▲ REPAIR "BK" wire between AFT switch and ground.

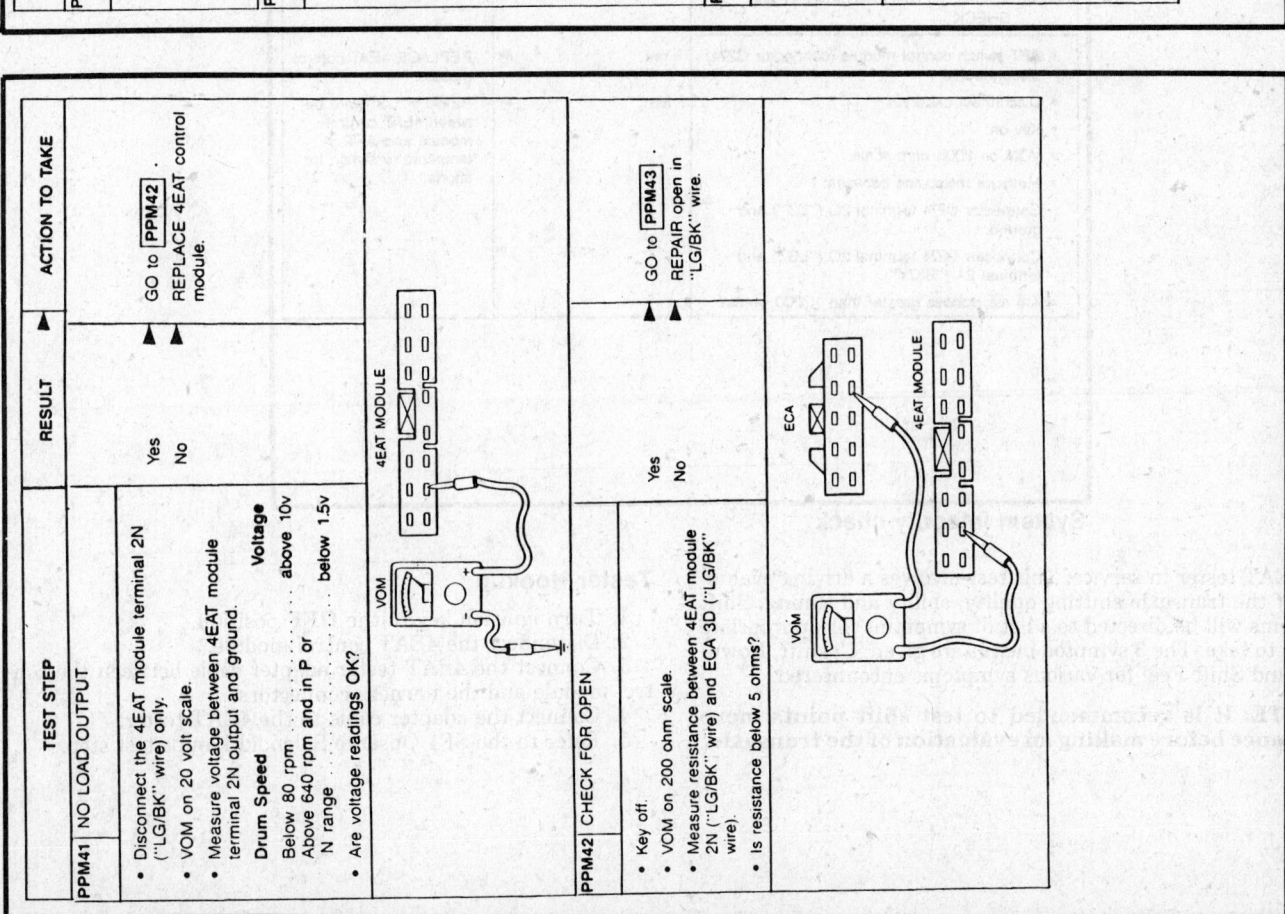

System integrity check

TEST STEP	RESULT	ACTION TO TAKE
PPM41 NO LOAD OUTPUT • Disconnect the 4EAT module terminal 2N ("LG/BK" wire) only. • VOM on 20 volt scale. • Measure voltage between 4EAT module terminal 2N output and ground. Drum Speed — Voltage Below 80 rpm .... above 10v Above 640 rpm and in P or N range .... below 1.5v • Are voltage readings OK?	Yes ▲ No ▲	▲ GO to PPM42. ▲ REPLACE 4EAT control module.
PPM42 CHECK FOR OPEN • Key off. • VOM on 200 ohm scale. • Measure resistance between 4EAT module 2N ("LG/BK" wire) and ECA 3D ("LG/BK" wire). • Is resistance below 5 ohms?	Yes ▲ No ▲	▲ GO to PPM43. ▲ REPAIR open in "LG/BK" wire.

TEST STEP	RESULT	▶	ACTION TO TAKE
PPM46 AFT SWITCH FUNCTION CHECK			
• AFT switch (connector C189) disconnected. • Check continuity between switch terminals as follows: AFT Continuity Above 150ºC (302ºF) Yes Below 143ºC (289ºF) No • Does the AFT switch function OK?	Yes No	▶ ▶	GO to PPM47 . REPLACE AFT switch.
PPM47 CIRCUIT CONTINUITY CHECK			
• AFT switch. • Disconnect 4EAT control module (connector C274). • VOM On 200 ohm scale. • Measure resistance between connector C274 terminal 2O ("LG") and connector C189 ("LG"). • Is resistance less than 5 ohms?	Yes No	▶ ▶	GO to PPM48 . REPAIR "LG" wire between 4EAT control module and AFT switch for open.

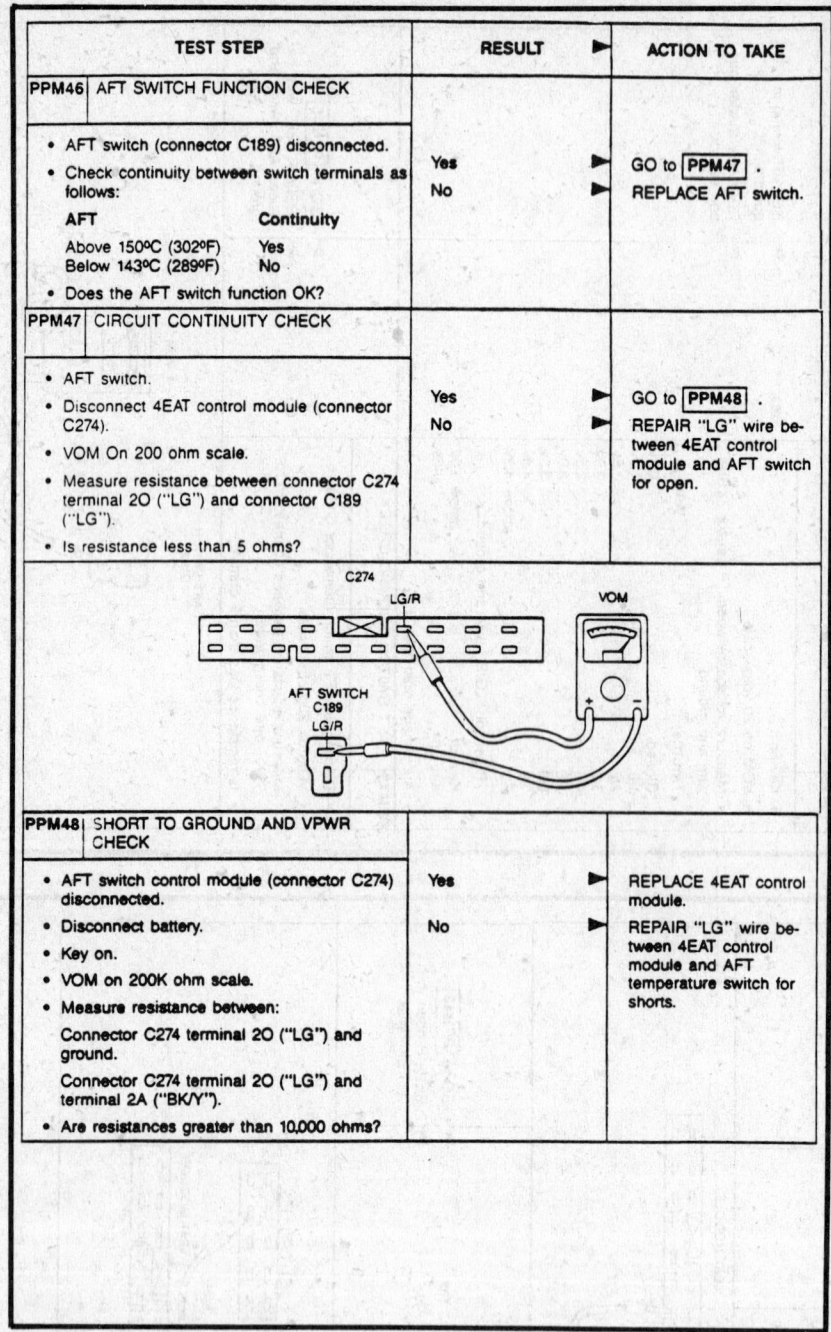

PPM48 SHORT TO GROUND AND VPWR CHECK			
• AFT switch control module (connector C274) disconnected. • Disconnect battery. • Key on. • VOM on 200K ohm scale. • Measure resistance between: Connector C274 terminal 2O ("LG") and ground. Connector C274 terminal 2O ("LG") and terminal 2A ("BK/Y"). • Are resistances greater than 10,000 ohms?	Yes No	▶ ▶	REPLACE 4EAT control module. REPAIR "LG" wire between 4EAT control module and AFT temperature switch for shorts.

System integrity check

the 4EAT tester in service. This test involves a driving evaluation of the transaxle shifting quality, ability and timing. Shift problems will be directed to a list of symptoms for appropriate action to take. The 3 sympton menus are given: Upshift, Downshift and Shift Feel for various symptoms encountered.

NOTE: It is recommended to test shift points more than once before making an evaluation of the transaxle.

Tester Hookup

1. Turn ignition key to the **OFF** position.
2. Disconnect the 4EAT control module.
3. Connect the 4EAT tester adapter cable between the control module and the harness connectors.
4. Connect the adapter cable to the 4EAT tester.
5. Refer to the SF1 Observe Solenoid Lamps test step.

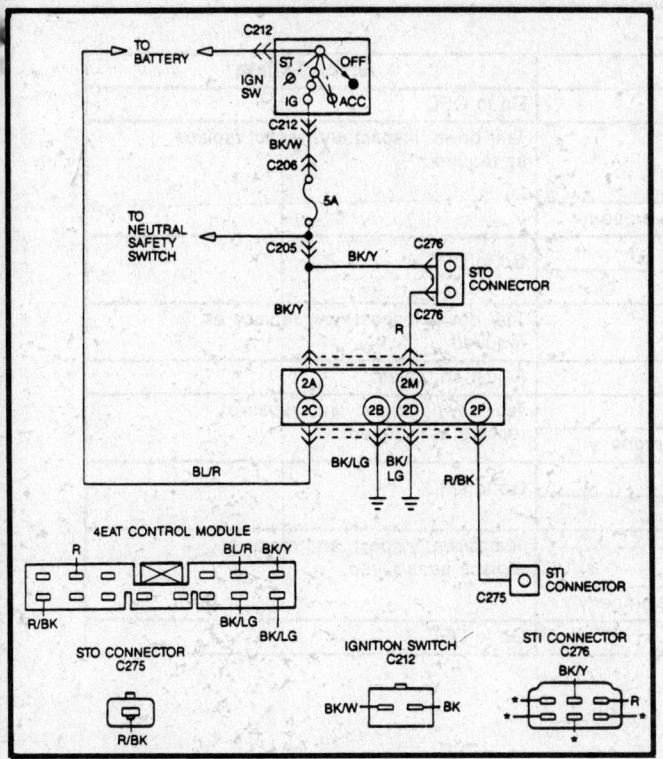

PPQ—pinpoint test schematic

TEST STEP		RESULT ▶	ACTION TO TAKE
PPQ1	**INTEGRITY**		
• Visually inspect all wiring, wiring harness, connectors and components for evidence of overheating, insulation damage, looseness, shorting or other damage. • Is there any cause for concern?		Yes ▶ No ▶	SERVICE as required. GO to PPQ2 .
PPQ2	**POWER CHECK**		
• VOM on 20 volt scale. • Measure voltage between: 4EAT control module terminal 2A ("BL/Y" wire) and ground. STO connector ("BK/Y" wire) and ground. STI connector ("R/BK" wire) and ground. Key off .... 0v Key on .... above 10v 4EAT control module terminal 2C ("BL/R" wire) and ground. Always above 10 volts. • Are voltage readings OK?		Yes ▶ No ▶	GO to PPQ3 . REPAIR wire(s) to power in question.
PPQ3	**GROUND CHECK**		
• Key off. • VOM on 200 ohm scale. • Measure resistance between 4EAT control module terminals 2B ("BK/LG" wire), 2D ("BK/LG" wire) and ground. • Is resistance below 5 ohms?		Yes ▶ No ▶	GO to PPQ4 . REPAIR "BK/LG" ground wire.
PPQ4	**STO CONTINUITY**		
• Key off. • VOM on 200 ohm scale. • Measure resistance between STO ("R" wire) connector "R" wire and 4EAT module terminal 2M. • Is resistance below 5 ohms?		Yes ▶ No ▶	REPLACE 4EAT control module. REPAIR "R" wire from STO connector to 4EAT module.

PPQ test information

Test Result	Range	Possible Cause		Action To Take
Above specification	In all ranges	Insufficient line pressure	Worn oil pump	Replace
			Oil leakage from oil pump, control valve, and/or transmission case	Tear down, inspect, and repair or replace as required.
			Stuck pressure regulator valve	
	In "D" range	One-way clutch 2 slipping		Tear down, inspect, and repair or replace as required.
	In forward ranges	Forward clutch slipping One-way clutch 1 slipping		
	In "D" (Manual) and "L" (Manual) ranges	Coasting clutch slipping		
	In "D" (Manual) and "D" (Manual) ranges	2-4 band slipping		Adjust and retest.
	In "R," "L" and "L" (Manual) ranges	Low and reverse slipping		Tear down, inspect, repair/replace as required.
	In "R" range	Low and reverse band slipping Reverse clutch slipping		Perform road test to determine whether problem is low and reverse band or reverse clutch a) Engine brake applied in 1st . . . Reverse clutch b) Engine brake not applied in 1st . . . Low and reverse band. Repair or replace as required.
Within specification*		All shift control elements within transmission are functioning normally.		Go to OPB
Below specification*		Engine out of tune		Tune engine before running Stall Test.
		One-way clutch slipping within torque converter		Tear down, inspect, repair or replace as required.

* Specification – Stall Speed:
D, D, L Ranges: 2120–2420 rpm
R Range: 2080–2380 rpm

@ Disassembly to step indicated if required after re-test.

Stall test evaluation

Shift	Result	Possible Cause	Action To Take
N – D Normal Mode	More than specification*	Insufficient line pressure	Go to OPC.
		Forward clutch slipping One-way clutch 1 slipping One-way clutch 2 slipping	Tear down, inspect and repair, replace as required.
	Less than specification*	N–D accumulator not operating properly	
		Excessive line pressure	Go to OPC.
N – D Manual Mode	More than specification*	Insufficient line pressure	
		Forward clutch slipping	Tear down, inspect, and replace as required.
		2–4 band slipping	Adjust and retest.
		One-way clutch 1 slipping	Tear down, inspect, and repair or replace as required.
	Less than specification*	1–2 accumulator not operating properly	
		Excessive line pressure	Go to OPC.
N – R	More than specification*	Insufficient line pressure	
		Low and reverse band slipping Reverse clutch slipping	Tear down, inspect, and repair or replace as required.
	Less than specification*	N–R accumulator not operating properly	
		Excessive line pressure	Go to OPC.

* Specified Time Lag
  N to D range 0.5–1.0 second
  N to R range 0.5–1.0 second

≠ Transaxle Disassembly Step required for access to component.

Time lag evaluation

LINE PRESSURE SPECIFICATIONS

	Line Pressure, kPa (psi)	
Range	D, D, L	R
Idle	353–432 (51–63)	598–942 (87–137)
Stall Speed	873–1040 (127–151)	1668–2011 (242–292)

Pressure Test Result	Range	Possible Location of Problem	Action to Take
Low	All	Worn oil pump, fluid leaking from oil pump, control valve body or transaxle case. Pressure regulator valve sticking	Tear down, inspect, repair or replace as required the complete pump or valve assembly or components
Low	D D	Fluid leaking from hydraulic circuit of forward clutch	Tear down, inspect, repair or replace components as required.
Low	R	Fluid leaking from hydraulic circuit of low and reverse band	Tear down, inspect, repair or replace components as required.
High	All	Throttle valve sticking. Throttle modulator valve sticking. Pressure regulator valve sticking.	Tear down, inspect, repair or replace components as required
Within Specified Limits	All	—	Go to OPD

Line pressure test evaluation

THROTTLE PRESSURE SPECIFICATIONS

	Throttle Pressure kPa (psi)
Idle	39–88 (6–13)
Stall Speed	471–589 (68–85)

Pressure Test Result	Position Location Of Problem	Action To Take
Not Within Specified Limits	Throttle valve sticking	Tear down, inspect, repair, clean, or replace the valve(s) as required.
	Improper adjustment of throttle cable	Remove, inspect for damage and freedom of movement, replace and adjust per shop manual as required.
Within Specified Limits	—	Go to Road Test.

Throttle pressure test evaluation

ON CAR SERVICE

Adjustments

LINE PRESSURE

1. Raise and support the vehicle safely. Remove the wheel and tire.
2. Remove the left front splash shield.
3. Remove the square head plug from the transaxle that is marked "L" and install the pressure gauge.
4. With the transaxle in **P**, start the engine. Warm up the engine to operating temperature and adjust the idle speed to 750–800 rpm for nonturbocharged vehicles or 725–775 rpm for turbocharged vehicles.
5. Adjust locknuts on the cable as follows to increase or decrease line pressure:
   a. Loosen the cable all the way so the locknuts are as far away from the throttle cam as possible.
   b. Turn the locknuts clockwise to increase or counterclockwise to decrease the line pressure to 63–66 psi.
6. Turn off the engine.
7. Remove the pressure gauge and install the square head plug in the transaxle.
8. Install the left front splash shield.
9. Install the wheel and tire.

2–4 BRAKE BAND

NOTE: The 2–4 brake band is also know as the "Busy Band" because it has a dual function in the transaxle.

1. Raise and support the vehicle safely. Remove the oil pan.

2. Loosen the locknut and tighten the piston stem to 78–95 inch lbs.
3. Loosen the piston stem 2 turns.
4. Tighten the locknut to 18–29 ft. lbs.
5. Install the oil pan. Refill the transaxle to the correct level.

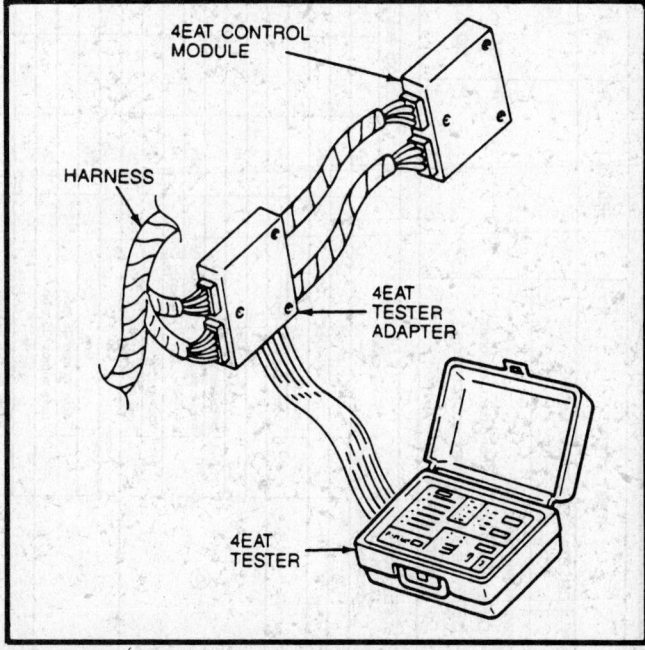

Road test—4EAT tester hookup

Road test diagnostic information

TEST STEP		RESULT	ACTION TO TAKE
SF2	**CHECK SOLENOID VOLTAGES**		TESTER lamps are not working properly. REPLACE 4EAT control module.
• Warm engine at idle. • Drive vehicle through conditions on chart. • Check voltages at solenoid terminal(s) in question. • Are voltage readings OK?		Yes No	

SELECTOR LEVER POSITION	GEAR		SOLENOID VALVE VOLTAGE			
			1-2	2-3	3-4	Lockup
P	Non					
R	Reverse		10-14v		10-14v	
N	—	1st Below approx. 11 mph		10-14v	10-14v	
		2nd Above approx. 11 mph		10-14v	10-14v	
(D)	3rd Below approx. 20 25 mph			10-14v	10-14v	
	Above approx. 25 mph	Lockup OFF	10-14v			
		Lockup ON	10-14v			10-14v
	OD	Lockup OFF			10-14v	
		Lockup ON			10-14v	10-14v
D	1st		10-14v	10-14v	10-14v	
	2nd		10-14v	10-14v	10-14v	
	3rd Below approx. 25 mph		10-14v	10-14v	10-14v	
	2nd Above approx. 25 mph		10-14v	10-14v	10-14v	
D	2nd Below approx. 68 mph		10-14v	10-14v	10-14v	
	Above approx. 68 mph		10-14v	10-14v	10-14v	
L	3rd Below approx. 25 mph		10-14v	10-14v	10-14v	
	2nd Above approx. 25 mph		10-14v	10-14v	10-14v	
Manual Switch ON	1st Below approx. 68 mph		10-14v	10-14v	10-14v	
	Above approx. 68 mph		10-14v	10-14v	10-14v	

Road test diagnostic information

TEST STEP		RESULT	ACTION TO TAKE
SF1	**OBSERVE SOLENOID LAMPS**		
• Warm engine at idle. • Drive vehicle through conditions on chart. • Observe lamps for solenoid functioning. • Do all lamps light at proper time?		Yes No	GO to OD1 GO to SF2

SELECTOR LEVER POSITION	GEAR		SOLENOID VALVE LAMPS			
			1-2	2-3	3-4	Lockup
P	Non					
R	Reverse		ON		ON	
N	—	1st Below approx. 11 mph		ON	ON	
		2nd Above approx. 11 mph		ON	ON	
(D)	3rd Below approx. 20-25 mph			ON	ON	
	Above approx. 25 mph	Lockup OFF	ON			
		Lockup ON	ON			ON
	OD	Lockup OFF			ON	
		Lockup ON			ON	ON
D	1st		ON	ON	ON	
	2nd		ON	ON	ON	
	3rd Below approx. 25 mph		ON	ON	ON	
	2nd Above approx. 25 mph		ON	ON	ON	
D	2nd Below approx. 68 mph		ON	ON	ON	
	Above approx. 68 mph		ON	ON	ON	
L	3rd Below approx. 25 mph		ON	ON	ON	
	2nd Above approx. 25 mph		ON	ON	ON	
Manual Switch ON	1st Below approx. 68 mph		ON	ON		
	Above approx. 68 mph		ON	ON		

Road test diagnostic information (OD2)

TEST STEP	RESULT	ACTION TO TAKE

OD2 SHIFT POINT CHECK
• Warm engine to operating temperature (above 162°F).
• Selector lever in D range.
• Select the economy mode.
• Manual switch off.
• Cruise control off.
• Drive vehicle:
  Accelerate at 1/2 throttle
  Accelerate at full throttle
  Operate kickdown (sudden acceleration).
• Watch 4EAT tester for shift point indication.
• Compare shift point with chart.
• Is shift point correct?
	Yes
	
	No problem on upshift
	
	No problem on downshift
		GO to OD3 .
		
		GO to Upshift symptom menu.
		
		GO to Downshift symptom menu.

Throttle Position (Throttle Position Sensor Voltage)	Shifting (Gears)	Drum Speed (rpm)	Vehicle Speed (mph)
Fully opened (4.3 volts)	1 → 2	4900 – 5450	33 – 37
	2 → 3	5100 – 5500	63 – 68
	3 → OD	5400 – 5700	102 – 109
Half throttle (1.6–2.2 volts)	1 → 2	2800 – 3350	19 – 23
	2 → 3	3000 – 3400	37 – 42
	3 → OD	2900 – 3450	55 – 66
	Lockup ON (OD)	2050 – 2500	56 – 68
	Lockup OFF (OD)	1950 – 2350	53 – 64
	OD → 3	1600 – 1950	43 – 53
	3 → 2	1200 – 1550	24 – 30
	OD → 3	3500 – 3700	95 – 101
	OD → 2	2050 – 2250	56 – 61
	OD → 1	950 – 1100	26 – 30
Kickdown	3 → 2	2950 – 3200	56 – 61
	3 → 1	1350 – 1550	26 – 30
	2 → 1	2100 – 2400	26 – 30

Road test diagnostic information (OD1)

TEST STEP	RESULT	ACTION TO TAKE

OD1 SHIFT POINT CHECK
• Warm engine to operating temperature (above 162°F).
• Selector lever in D range.
• Manual switch off.
• Select the power mode.
• Cruise control off.
• Drive vehicle:
  Accelerate at 1/2 throttle
  Accelerate at full throttle
  Operate kickdown (sudden acceleration).
• Compare shift point with chart.
• Is shift point correct?
	Yes
	
	No problem on upshift
	
	No problem on downshift
		GO to OD2 .
		
		GO to Upshift symptom menu.
		
		GO to Downshift symptom menu.

Throttle Position (Throttle Position Sensor Voltage)	Shifting (Gears)	Drum Speed (rpm)	Vehicle Speed (mph)
Fully opened (4.3 volts)	1 → 2	5000 – 5500	33 – 35
	2 → 3	5300 – 5700	65 – 70
	3 → OD	5400 – 5700	102 – 109
Half throttle (1.6–2.2 volts)	1 → 2	3500 – 4050	24 – 27
	2 → 3	3750 – 4250	47 – 53
	3 → OD	3600 – 4250	68 – 81
	Lockup ON (OD)	2500 – 3000	68 – 81
	Lockup OFF (OD)	2400 – 2850	64 – 77
	OD → 3	1950 – 2450	53 – 66
	3 → 2	1750 – 2300	33 – 43
	OD → 3	3500 – 3700	95 – 101
	OD → 2	2150 – 2350	58 – 63
	OD → 1	950 – 1100	26 – 30
Kickdown	3 → 2	3050 – 3350	40 – 63
	3 → 1	1350 – 1550	26 – 30
	2 → 1	2200 – 2400	26 – 30

Road test diagnostic Information

TEST STEP	RESULT	ACTION TO TAKE

D1 **SHIFT POINT CHECK**
• Warm engine to operating temperature (above 162°F).
• Cruise control off.
• Selector lever in D range.
• Manual switch off.
• Power or normal mode.
• Drive vehicle:
  Accelerate at 1/2 throttle
  Accelerate at full throttle.
• Compare shift point with chart.
• Is shift point correct?
NOTE: Shift points in D range, Normal or Power mode are the same.
	Yes
	
	 No problem on upshift
	
	 No problem on downshift
		GO to D2.
		
		 GO to Upshift symptom menu.
		
		 GO to Downshift symptom menu.

Throttle Position (Throttle Position Sensor Voltage)	Shifting (Gears)	Drum Speed (rpm)	Vehicle Speed (mph)
Fully opened (4.3 volts)	1 → 2	5000 – 5500	33 – 35
	2 → 3	5300 – 5700	65 – 70
	4 → 3	3750 – 4000	102 – 109
	3 → 2	3050 – 3350	40 – 63
	2 → 1	2200 – 2400	26 – 30
Half throttle (1.6-2.2 volts)	1 → 2	3500 – 4050	24 – 27
	2 → 3	3750 – 4250	47 – 53
	3 → 4	1950 – 2450	53 – 66
	3 → 2	1750 – 2300	33 – 43

TEST STEP	RESULT	ACTION TO TAKE
D2 **MANUAL RANGE CHECK** • Warm engine to operating temperature (above 162°F). • Cruise control OFF. • Selector lever in D range. • Manual switch OFF. • Power or Normal mode. • Drive vehicle until 3rd gear is obtained, then turn manual switch ON. • Decelerate vehicle. • Does 3-2 downshift occur at 66-70 mph?	Yes No	GO to D3. GO to road test symptom menu.

Road test diagnostic Information

TEST STEP	RESULT	ACTION TO TAKE
OD3 **SHIFT FEEL CHECK** • Warm engine to operating temperature (above 162°F). • Selector lever in D range. • Manual switch OFF. • Select both power and economy modes. • Cruise control OFF. • Drive vehicle from closed throttle to wide open throttle. • Does shift feel excessively harsh or slushy?	Yes No	GO to shift feel symptom menu. GO to OD4.

OD4 **MANUAL CHECK**
• Warm engine to operating temperature (above 162°F).
• Selector lever in D range.
• Select economy mode.
• Manual switch ON.
• Cruise control OFF.
• Drive vehicle (accelerate/decelerate)
• Watch 4EAT tester for shift point indication.
• Check that the following conditions are met:
  2nd-3rd upshift at 12 mph
  3rd-2nd downshift at 6 mph
  No OD gear
  No 1st gear.
• Are all conditions satisfied?
	Yes
	
	 No
		GO to OD5.
		
		 GO to road test symptom menu.

OD5 **ENGINE BRAKING CHECK** • Warm engine to operating temperature (above 162°F). • Selector lever in D range. • Select economy mode. • Manual switch OFF. • Cruise control OFF. • Drive vehicle until D gear is obtained. • Shift selecter into D range. • Is engine braking felt (in D3 only) immediately?	Yes No	GO to D1. GO to downshift symptom menu.

Road test diagnostic Information

TEST STEP	RESULT	ACTION TO TAKE
L2 MANUAL RANGE CHECK • Warm engine to operating temperature (above 162°F). • Cruise control OFF. • Selector lever in L range. • Manual switch OFF. • Power or Normal mode. • Drive vehicle until 2nd gear is obtained, then turn manual switch ON. • Decelerate vehicle. • Does 2-1 downshift occur at 27–30 mph?	Yes No	GO to L3. GO to road test symptom menu.
L3 MANUAL RANGE CHECK • Warm engine to operating temperature (above 162°F). • Cruise control. • Selector lever in L range. • Manual switch ON. • Drive vehicle. • Is 1st gear held?	Yes No	GO to L4. GO to road test symptom menu.
L4 ENGINE BRAKING CHECK • Warm engine to operating temperature (above 162°F). • Cruise control OFF. • Selector lever in L range. • Manual switch ON. • Drive vehicle in 1st gear. • Decelerate vehicle. • Is engine braking felt?	Yes No	GO to P1. GO to Downshift symptom menu.
P1 VEHICLE STOPPING TEST • Drive vehicle on level surface. • Maximum speed of 2 mph. • Shift selector lever into P range. • Does vehicle stop?	Yes No	GO to S1. PERFORM parking pawl inspection.

Road test diagnostic Info.

TEST STEP	RESULT	ACTION TO TAKE
D3 MANUAL RANGE CHECK • Warm engine to operating temperature (above 162°F). • Cruise control OFF. • Selector lever in D range. • Manual switch ON. • Drive vehicle. • Is 2nd gear held?	Yes No	GO to D4. GO to road test symptom menu.
D4 ENGINE BRAKING CHECK • Warm engine to operating temperature (above 162°F). • Cruise control OFF. • Selector lever in D range. • Manual switch OFF. • Drive vehicle until 3rd gear is obtained. • Shift selector lever into L range. • Is engine braking felt immediately?	Yes No	GO to L1. GO to downshift symptom menu.

TEST STEP	RESULT	ACTION TO TAKE

L1 SHIFT POINT CHECK
• Warm engine to operating temperature (above 162°F).
• Cruise control off.
• Selector lever in L range.
• Power or Normal mode.
• Drive vehicle:
  Accelerate at 1/2 throttle
  Accelerate at full throttle
• Compare shift point with chart.
• Is shift point correct?
	Yes
	No problem on upshift
	No problem on downshift
		GO to L2.
		GO to Upshift symptom menu.
		GO to Downshift symptom menu.

NOTE: Shift points in L range, Normal or Power mode, are the same.

Throttle Position (Throttle Position Sensor Voltage)	Shifting (Gears)	Drum Speed (rpm)	Vehicle Speed (mph)
Fully opened (4.3 volts)	1 → 2	5000 - 5500	33 - 35
	2 → 1	2200 - 2400	26 - 30
Half throttle (1.6-2.2 volts)	1 → 2	3500 - 4050	24 - 27

SHIFT FEEL SYMPTOM MENU

CONDITION	POSSIBLE CAUSE	ACTION
• Shift shock in all ranges.	– Kickdown cable out of adjustment.	– Inspect cable adjustment.
	– Throttle valve sticking or damaged.	– Clean, service or replace.
	– Control valves.	– Check for clogging blockage, service as required.
	– Coasting clutch.	– Check for wear service or replace.
	– Low and reverse band.	– Check for adjustment, wear and damage, service as required.
	– Accumulators.	– Clean, service or replace.
	– 3-4 clutch.	– Inspect, service or replace.
	– CV joints or engine mounts.	– Service or replace.
	– 2-4 band and servo.	– Check adjustment.
	– Pressure regulator valve sticking or damaged.	– Clean, service or replace.
• Harsh 1-2 shift.	– Kickdown cable broken or out of adjustment.	– Check kickdown adjustment.
• N-R shift shock.	– N-R accumulator sticking or damaged.	– Inspect and service or replace.
• 2-3 shift shock.	– 2-3 accumulator sticking or damaged.	– Inspect and service or replace.
	– 1-2 accumulator sticking or damaged.	– Inspect and service or replace.
	– Pulse generator not functioning.	– Check pickup and torque converter for damage.
• Erratic shifts.	– Kickdown cable broken or out of adjustment.	– Inspect cable adjustment.
	– Pulse generator not functioning.	– Inspect pickup and torque converter.
• Soft shift in all ranges.	– Kickdown cable broken or out of adjustment.	– Inspect cable adjustment.
	– Throttle valve sticking or damaged.	– Clean, service or replace.
	– Pressure regulator valve sticking or damaged.	– Clean, service or replace.
• 1-2 soft shift.	– Valve body.	– Inspect valve body, solenoid valves.
	– 2-4 band is too loose.	– Inspect adjustment.

Shift feel symptom diagnosis

TEST STEP		RESULT	ACTION TO TAKE
S1	CHECK SLIPPAGE		
	• Warm engine to operating temperature (above 165°F).		
	• Connect 4EAT tester.	Yes	FOLLOW direction given in chart.
	• Connect tachometer.	Yes All speeds are incorrect.	INSPECT forward clutch.
	• Drive vehicle.	No	REFER to Chilton "3C" Diagnosis Chart
	• Compare vehicle speed (and engine speed) to four indicated drum speeds.		
	• Is vehicle speed (or engine speed) above or below indicated speed.		

			DRUM SPEED				
			1000	2000	3000	4000	
Gears	Driving condition	Other condition	VEHICLE SPEED (MPH)				ACTION TO TAKE
1st	L range, Manual mode		7	11	20	27	Inspect low and reverse clutch.
1st	D range, Normal mode		7	11	20	27	Inspect one-way clutch.
2nd	D range, Manual mode		20	25	37	50	Inspect 2-4 band.
3rd	D range, Manual mode		19	38	57	76	Inspect coasting clutch.
OD	D range, Normal mode		27	55	81	109	Inspect 3-4 clutch.
OD	D mode, Lockup		1,000	2,000	3,000	4,000	Inspect Torque Converter.
			ENGINE SPEED (RPM)				

Road test diagnostic information

DOWNSHIFT SYMPTOM MENU

CONDITION	POSSIBLE CAUSE	ACTION
• Engine has momentary run-away during 3-2 downshift.	– Coasting bypass valve sticking or damaged.	– Inspect, service or replace.
	– 2-4 band and servo.	– Inspect adjustment, service or replace.
• Hesitation in 3-2 shift.	– Valve body.	– Inspect valve body, solenoid valves.
• No engine braking ⓓ to D.	– Fluid blockage to coasting clutch or failed coasting clutch.	– Check for blockage and coasting clutch condition.
	– Valve body.	– Inspect valve body, solenoid valves.
• No engine braking D to L.	– Fluid blockage to coasting clutch or failed coasting clutch.	– Inspect coasting for blockage or damage.
	– 2-4 band and servo.	– Check adjustment and inspect condition.
	– Valve body.	– Inspect valve body, solenoid valves.
	– Control valve.	– Inspect, clean or service.

Downshift symptom diagnosis

SHIFT FEEL SYMPTOM MENU

CONDITION	POSSIBLE CAUSE	ACTION
• 2-3 soft shift.	– 2-3 accumulator sticking or damaged.	– Clean, service or replace.
	– Valve body.	– Inspect valve body, solenoid valves.
• N-R soft shift.	– N-R accumulator sticking or damaged.	– Clean, service or replace.
• No lockup	– Lockup valve sticking or damaged.	– Clean, service or replace.
• Drags in reverse link parking brake is applied.	– 2-4 band is too tight.	– Check adjustment
• Slow to engage in reverse.	– Reverse clutch.	– Inspect for damage or wear; service or replace.

Shift feel symptom diagnosis

UPSHIFT SYMPTOM MENU

CONDITION	POSSIBLE CAUSE	ACTION
• No 2-3 upshift.	– 3-4 clutch spring.	– Check clutch adjustment, damage.
	– Valve body.	– Inspect valve body, solenoid valves.
• No 2nd gear (transmission shifts 1-3).	– Valve body.	– Inspect valve body, solenoid valves.
	– Loose 2-4 band.	– Adjust.
• No lock up.	– Lockup solenoid not functioning.	– Inspect solenoid and related hydraulic circuit.
	– Torque converter.	– Inspect torque converter.
• Shift points incorrect.	– Valve body.	– Inspect valve body, solenoid valves.
	– 2-4 band out of adjustment.	– Check 2-4 band adjustments.
	– Damaged or worn forward clutch.	– Inspect and service or replace.
• Engine run away when upshifting.	– Neutral safety switch.	– Check adjustment and condition.
	– Valve body.	– Clean, service or replace.
	– One way clutch no. 1.	– Inspect, service, or replace.
	– 2-4 band and servo.	– Check adjustment and condition.
	– 3-4 clutch.	– Check condition, service.
	– Bypass valve sticking or damaged.	– Clean, service, or replace.
	– Forward clutch.	– Inspect, service or replace.
• No upshift into overdrive.	– One way clutch no. 1 stuck.	– Check clutch no. 1.
	– Valve body.	– Check orifices, solenoid valves, valve body.
	– Linkage.	
• Delayed 1-2 shift.	– Valve body.	– Inspect valve body, solenoid valves.

Upshift symptom diagnosis

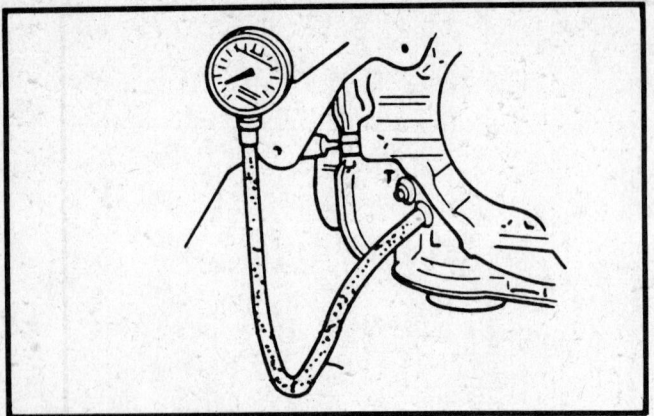

Installing pressure gauge

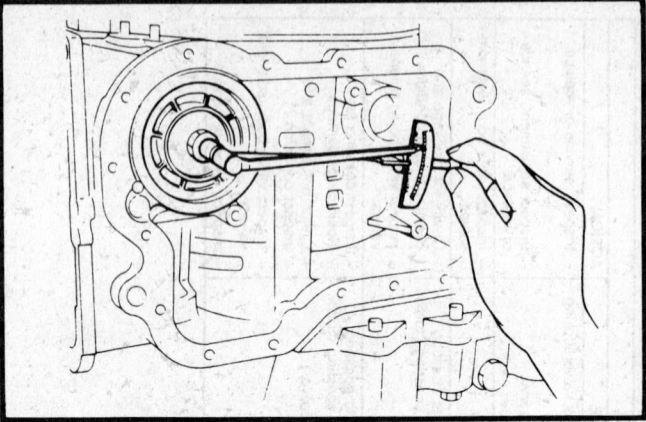

2–4 band adjustment—step 1

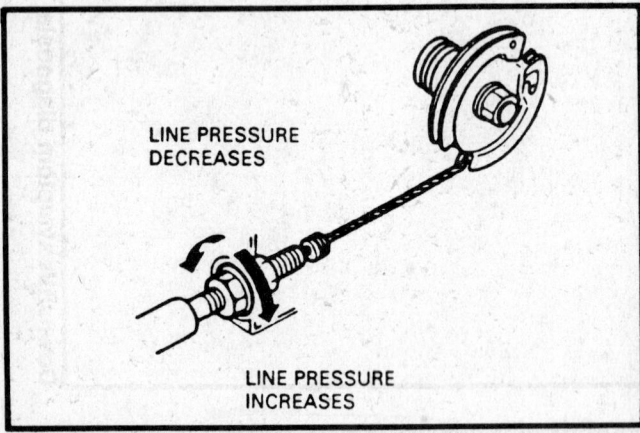
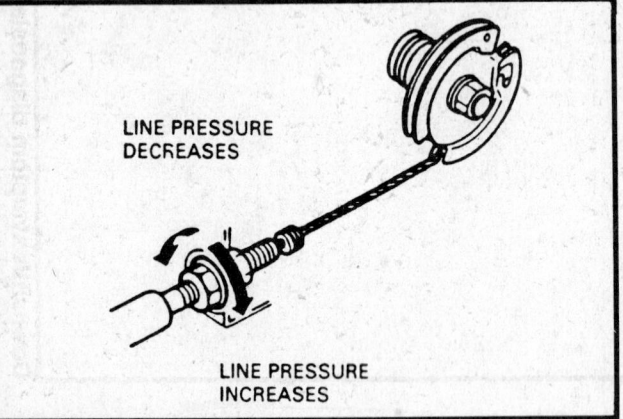

LINE PRESSURE
DECREASES

LINE PRESSURE
INCREASES

Line pressure adjustment

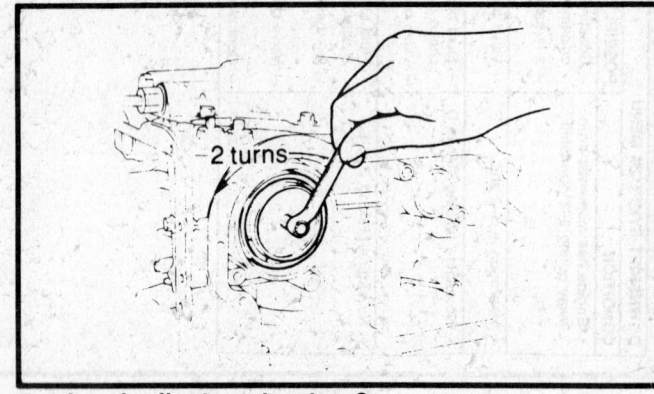

2–4 band adjustment—step 2

SHIFT CONTROL CABLE

1. Remove the selector trim panel. Disconnect the wiring harness for the programmed ride control switch.

2. Remove 4 screws securing the transaxle selector bezel assembly.

3. Lift bezel assembly to gain access to the shift cable adjuster.

4. Loosen nuts A and B. Loosen bolt C.

5. Place transaxle in **P** by moving the transaxle mounted shift lever clockwise.

6. Place the selector lever in the **P** position.

7. Torque bolt C to 67–96 inch lbs.

8. Tighten nut A until nut touches the trunnion. Torque nut B to 67–96 inch lbs. Make sure nut B seats against spacer and not the spring.

9. Install transaxle selector bezel. Verify that there is a click at each range position.

10. Make sure the linkage adjustment has not affected operation of the neutral safety switch. With the parking brake and service brakes applied, try to start the engine in each gearshift position. The engine must crank only in the **N** and **P** positions. If the engine cranks in any other gear selector lever position, check the linkage adjustment and neutral safety switch operation.

11. Connect the programmed ride control switch wiring harness. Install the selector trim panel.

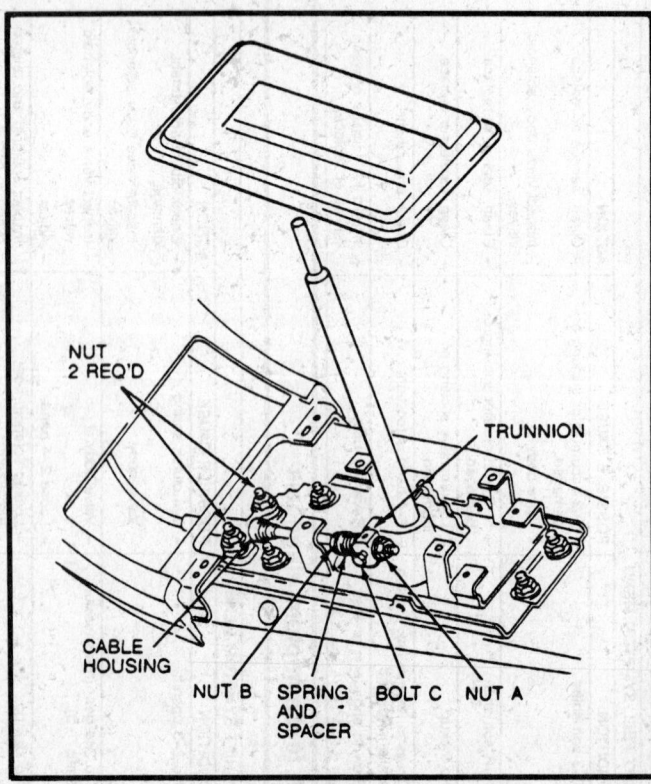

NUT
2 REQ'D

TRUNNION

CABLE
HOUSING

NUT B   SPRING   BOLT C   NUT A
         AND
         SPACER

Shift control cable adjustment

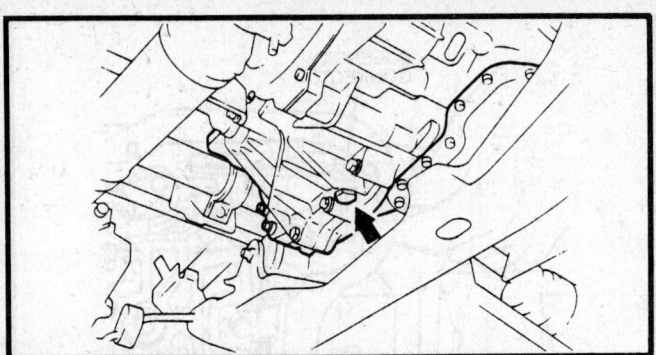

Drain plug location

Magnets in oil pan—correct location

Services

OIL PAN AND FILTER

Removal and Installation

1. Raise the vehicle and support it safely.
2. Drain the transmission fluid.
3. Remove the left side splash shield.
4. Remove the oil pan and gasket.
5. Remove the oil strainer.
6. Remove the O-ring from the oil strainer
7. To install reverse the removal procedures. Make sure to install the O-ring on the oil strainer and magnets in the correct position in the oil pan. Torque the oil strainer retaining bolts to 69–95 inch lbs. and the oil pan to case bolts to 69–95 inch lbs. Refill the transaxle.

VALVE BODY

Removal and Installation

NOTE: Before trying to service valve body make sure that a new separator plate gasket is available.

1. Remove the battery and battery carrier.
2. Disconnect the main fuse block.
3. Disconnect the 4EAT connectors and separate the 4EAT harness from the transaxle clips.
4. Raise and support the vehicle.
5. Drain the transaxle fluid.
6. Disconnect the oil cooler outlet and inlet hoses.
7. Remove the valve body cover and gasket.
8. Remove the kickdown cable from the throttle cam.
9. Disconnect the solenoid connector, pinch the tangs of the

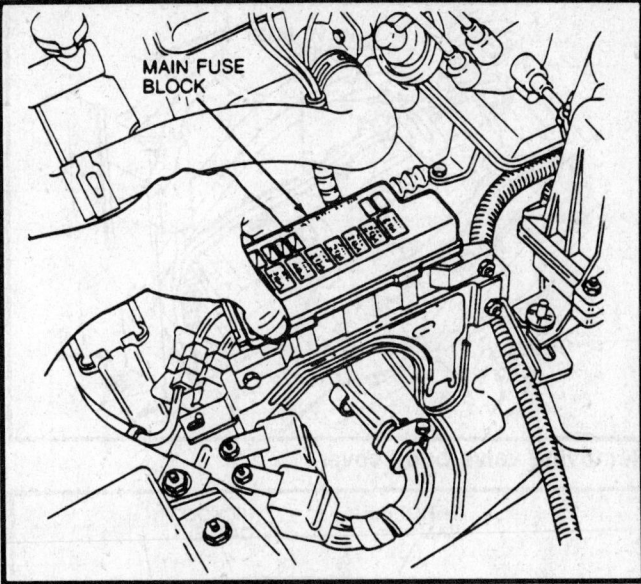

Disconnect the main fuse block

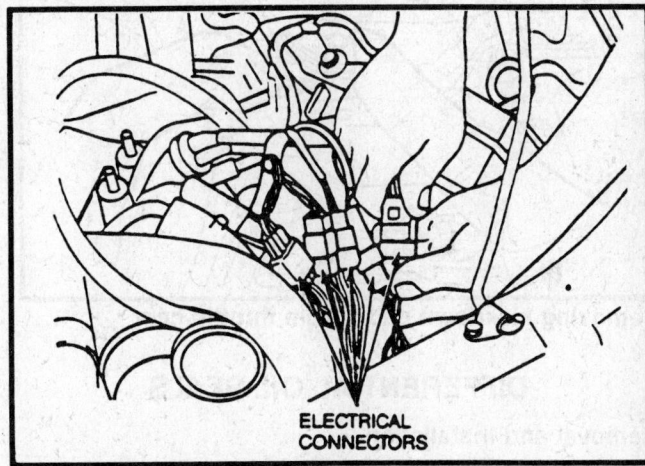

Disconnect 4EAT connectors

mating connector mounted on the transaxle case. Remove it by pushing inward.

10. Remove the attaching bolts from the valve body and carefully remove the valve body.

NOTE: Shift transaxle into reverse to place the manual plate in the correct position for installation.

11. Install the valve body, using a mirror if necessary to align the groove of the manual valve with the manual plate.
12. Tighten the valve body mounting bolts to 95–130 inch lbs.
13. Insert the solenoid connector into the transaxle case hole. Attach the mating connector.
14. Attach the kickdown cable to the throttle cam.
15. Install the valve body cover and new gasket. Tighten to 69–95 inch lbs.
16. Connect the oil cooler hoses.
17. Attach the 4EAT connectors and support the 4EAT harness on the transaxle clips.
18. Connect the main fuse block.
19. Install the battery carrier and battery.
20. Add the specified transaxle fluid and check for fluid leaks.

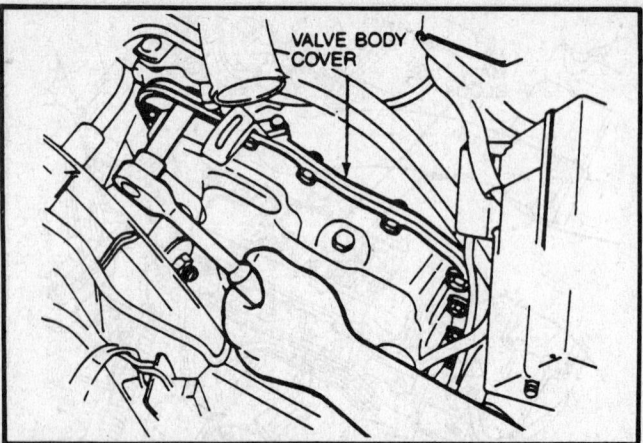

Removing valve body cover

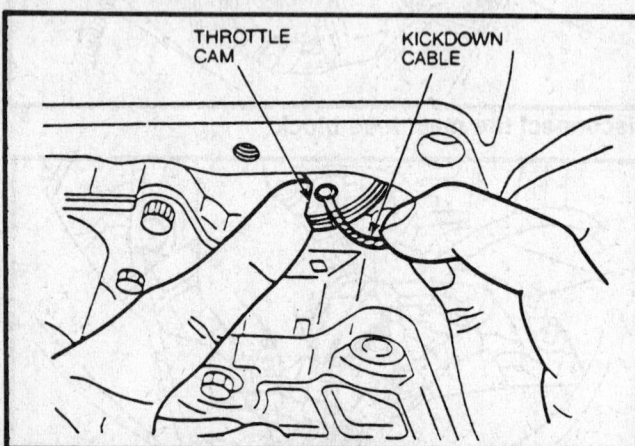

Removing kickdown cable from throttle cam

DIFFERENTIAL OIL SEALS

Removal and Installation

1. Raise and support the vehicle.
2. Remove the front wheels.
3. Remove the splash shields.
4. Drain the transaxle fluid.
5. Remove the tie rod nuts, cotter pins and disconnect the tie rod ends.
6. Remove the stabilizer link assemblies.
7. Remove the bolts and nuts from the lower arm ball joints.
8. Pull the lower arms to separate them from the knuckles.
9. Remove the right-hand joint shaft bracket.
10. Remove the halfshafts from the transaxle by prying with a bar inserted between the shaft and transaxle case. Support the halfshafts with wire.
11. Remove the differential oil seals with a flat-tip tool.
12. Tap in new differential oil seals using differential seal replacer tool T87C-77000-H or equivalent.
13. Replace the circlip located on the end of each halfshaft.
14. Install the halfshafts.
15. Attach the lower arm ball joints to the knuckles.
16. Install the tie rod ends and tighten the nuts to 22–33 ft. lbs. Install new cotter pins.
17. Install the bolts and nuts to the lower arm ball joints. Torque to 32–40 ft. lbs.
18. Install the stabilizer link assemblies. Turn the nuts on each asembly until 1.0 in. (25.4mm) of bolt thread can be measured from the upper nut. When this length is reached, secure

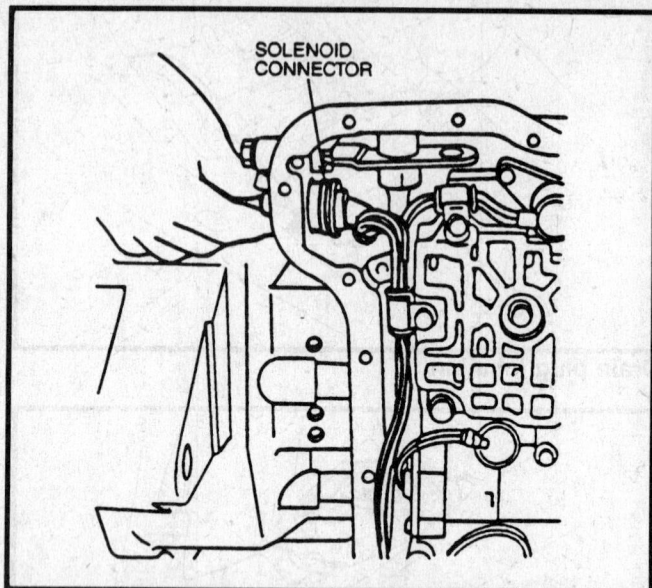

Removing solenoid connector from case.

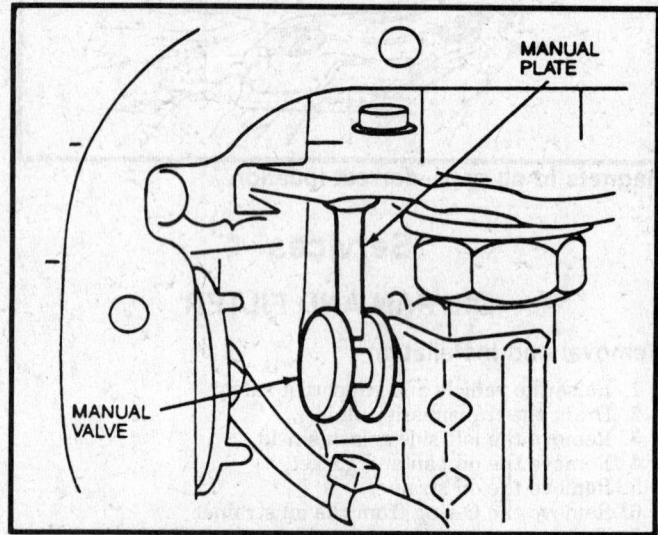

Align manual valve with manual plate

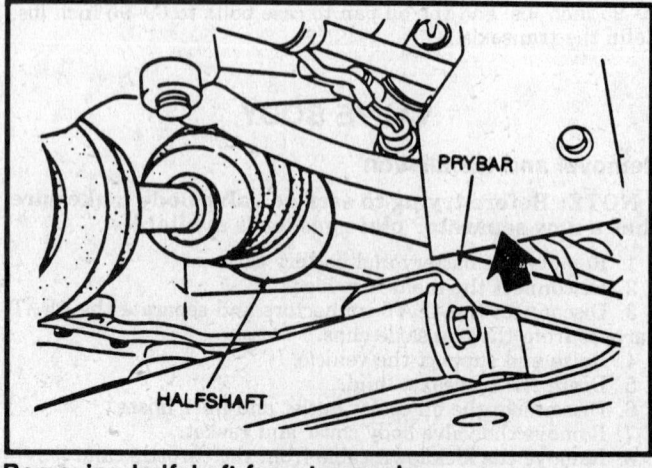

Removing halfshaft from transaxle

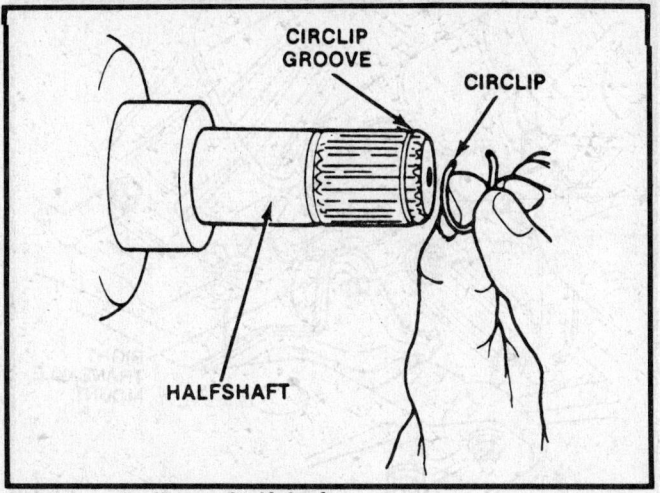

Replace circlip on halfshaft

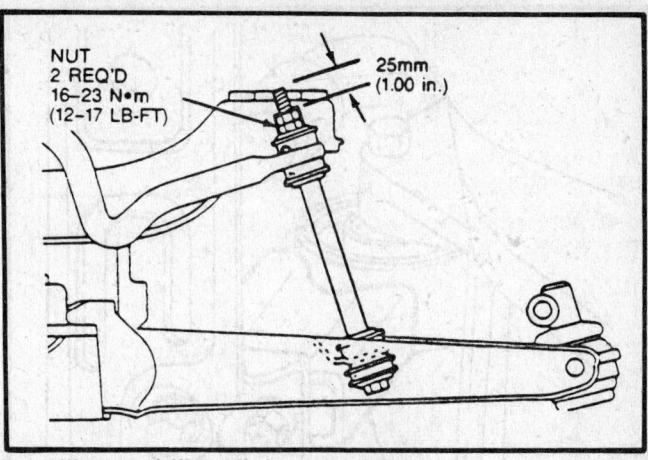

Installing stabilizer link assemblies

the upper nut and back off the lower nut until a torque of 12–17 ft. lbs. is reached.

19. Install the splash shields. Install the front wheels and tighten the lug nuts to 65–87 inch lbs.

20. Add the specified transaxle fluid and check for leaks.

OIL COOLER

Removal and Installation

1. Disconnect the oil hoses.
2. Remove the oil cooler.
3. Straighten bent fins with a flat tool or equivalent.
4. To install reverse removal procedures.

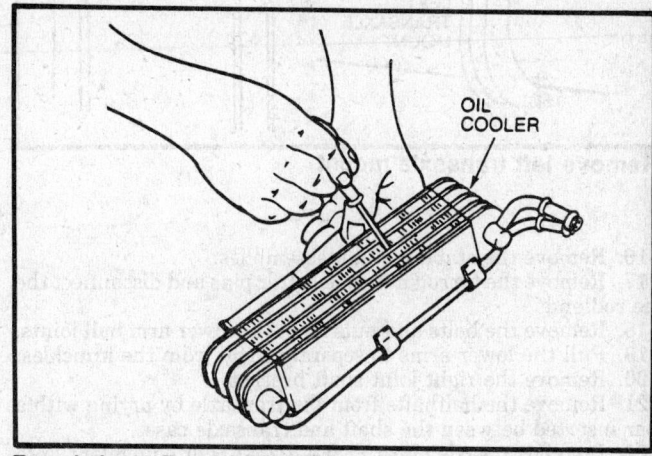

Repair bent fins in oil cooler

REMOVAL AND INSTALLATION

TRANSAXLE REMOVAL

1. Remove the battery and battery carrier.
2. Disconnect the main fuse block.
3. Disconnect the lead from the center distributor terminal.
4. Disconnect the airflow meter connector and remove the air cleaner assembly.
5. Remove the resonance chamber and bracket.
6. Disconnect the speedometer cable (electromechanical cluster) or harnes (electronic cluster).
7. Disconnect the 4EAT electrical connectors and separate the 4EAT harness from the transaxle clips.
8. Disconnect the ground wires from the transaxle case.
9. Disconnect the range selector cable from the transaxle case.
10. Disconnect the kickdown cable.
11. Raise and support the vehicle safely.
12. Remove the front wheels.
13. Remove the splash shields.
14. Drain the transaxle fluid.
15. Disconnect the oil cooler outlet and inlet hoses. Insert plugs to prevent fluid leakage.

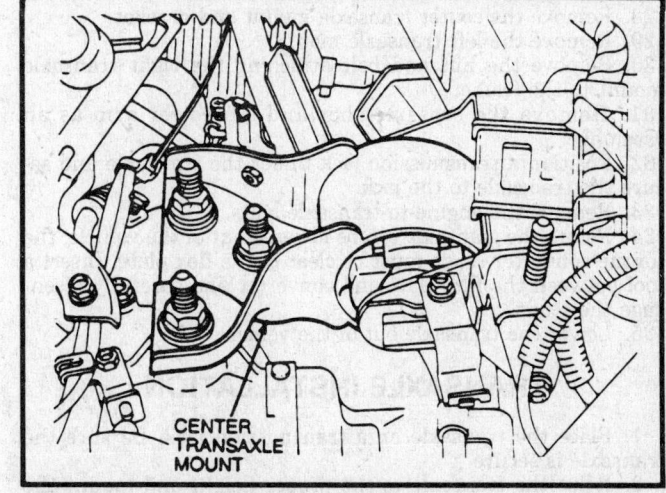

Remove center transaxle mount

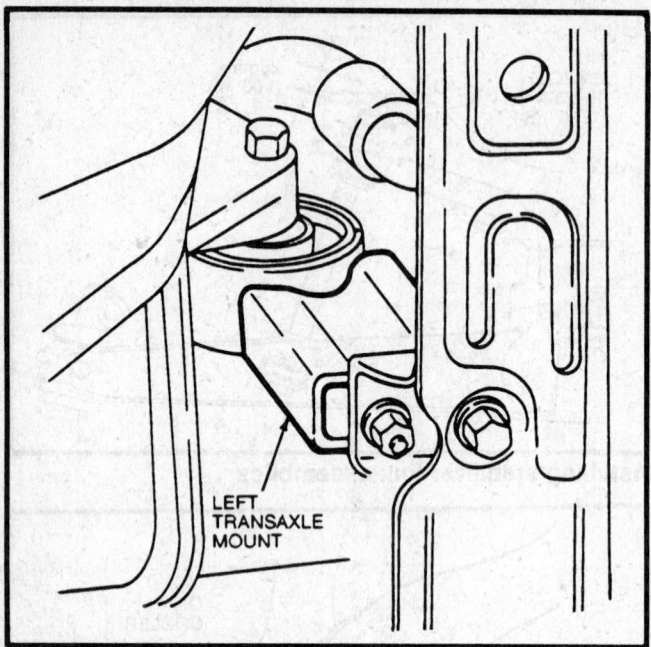

Remove left transaxle mount

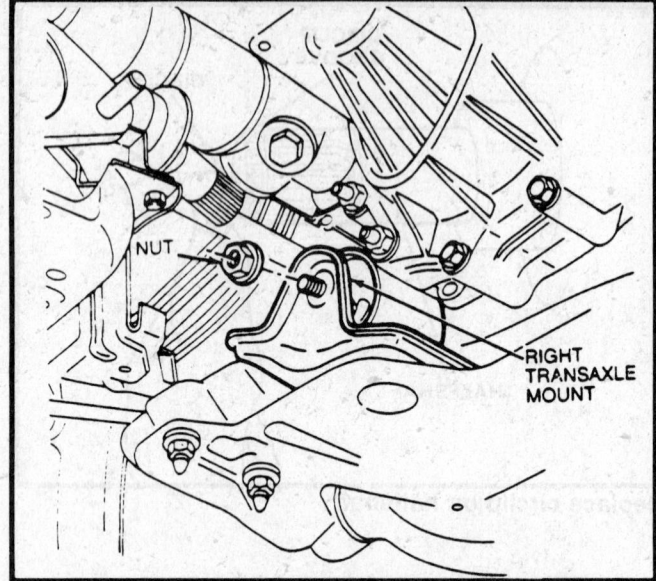

Remove nut and bolt from right transaxle mount

16. Remove the stabilizer link assemblies.
17. Remove the tie rod nuts and cotter pins and disconnect the tie rod ends.
18. Remove the bolts and nuts from the lower arm ball joints.
19. Pull the lower arms to separate them from the knuckles.
20. Remove the right joint shaft bracket.
21. Remove the halfhafts from the transaxle by prying with a bar inserted between the shaft and transaxle case.
22. Install transaxle plugs T88C–7025–AH or equivalent, into the differential side gears.

NOTE: Failure to install the transaxle plugs may allow the differential side gears to become mispositioned.

23. Remove the gusset plate-to-transaxle bolts.
24. Remove the torque converter cover.
25. Remove the torque converter nuts.
26. Remove the starter motor and access brackets.
27. Mount an engine support bar, D79P–6000–B or equivalent and attach it to the engine hanger.
28. Remove the center transaxle mount and bracket.
29. Remove the left transaxle mount.
30. Remove the nut and bolt attaching the right transaxle mount to the frame.
31. Remove the crossmember and left lower arm as an assembly.
32. Position a transmission jack under the transaxle and secure the transaxle to the jack.
33. Remove the engine-to-transaxle bolts.
34. Before the transaxle can be lowered out of the vehicle, the torque converter studs must be clear of the flex plate. Insert a tool between the flex plate and converter and carefully disengage the studs.
35. Lower the transaxle out of the vehicle.

TRANSAXLE INSTALLATION

1. Place the transaxle on a transmission jack. Be sure the transaxle is secure.
2. Raise the transaxle to the proper height and mount the transaxle to the engine.

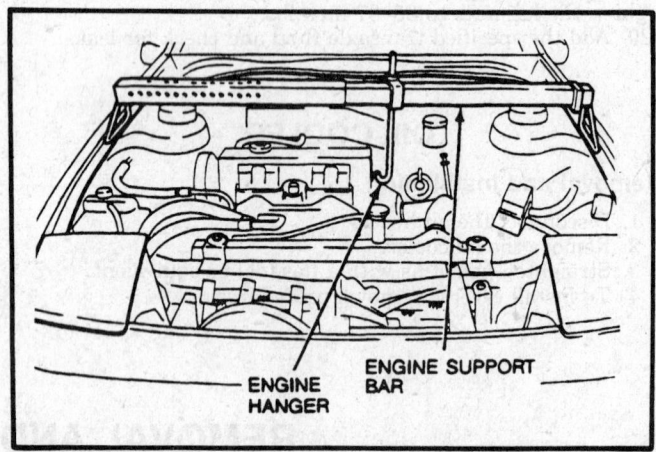

Engine support bar and engine hanger location

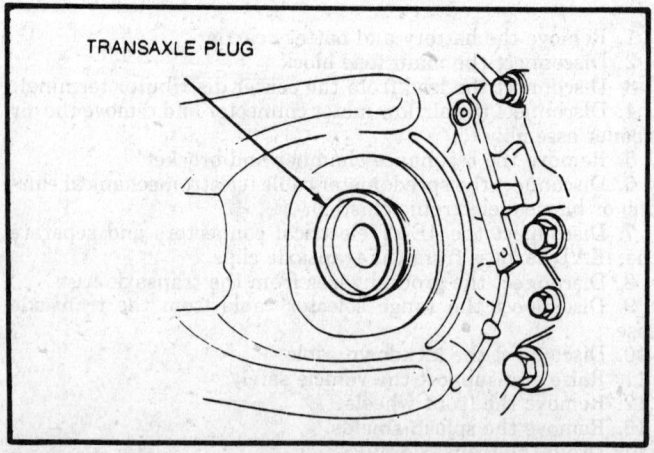

Transaxle plugs—holds differential side gears in place

NOTE: Align the torque converter studs and flex plate holes.

3. Install the engine-to-transaxle bolts and tighten to 66–86 ft. lbs.

4. Install the center transaxle mount and bracket. Tighten the bolts to 27–40 ft. lbs. and the nuts to 47–66 ft. lbs.

5. Install the left transaxle mount. Tighten the transaxle-to-mount attaching nut to 63–86 ft. lbs. Tighten the mount-to-bracket bolt and nut to 49–69 ft. lbs.

6. Install the crossmember and left lower arm as an assembly. Tighten the bolts to 27–40 ft. lbs. and the nuts to 55–69 ft. lbs.

7. Install the right transaxle mount bolt and nut. Tighten to 63–86 ft. lbs.

8. Install the starter motor and access brackets.

9. Install the torque converter nuts and tighten to 32–45 ft. lbs.

10. Install the converter cover and tighten the bolts to 69–85 inch lbs.

11. Install the gusset plate-to-transaxle bolts and tighten to 27–38 ft. lbs.

12. Replace the circlip located on the end of each halfshaft.

13. Remove the transaxle plugs and install the halfshafts.

14. Attach the lower arm ball joints to the knuckles.

15. Install the tie rod ends and tighten the nuts to 22–33 ft. lbs. Install new cotter pins.

16. Install the bolts and nuts to the lower arm ball joints. Tighten to 32–40 ft. lbs.

17. Install the stabilizer link assemblies. Turn the nuts on each assembly until 1.0 in. (25.4mm) of bolt thread can be measured from the upper nut. When then length is reached, secure the upper nut and back off the lower nut until a torque of 12–17 ft. lbs. is reached.

18. Connect the oil cooler outlet and inlet hoses.

19. Install the splash shields.

20. Install the front wheels and tighten the lug nuts to 65–87 ft. lbs.

21. Connect the kickdown cable and adjust it while performing the oil pressure test.

22. Connect the range selector cable to the transaxle case and tighten the bolt to 22–29 ft. lbs.

23. Connect the ground wires to the transaxle case and tighten to 69–95 inch lbs.

24. Connect the 4EAT electrical connectors and attach the 4EAT harness to the transaxle clips.

25. Connect the speedometer cable (electromechanical cluster) or harness (electronic cluster).

26. Install the resonance chamber and bracket and tighten to 69–95 inch lbs.

27. Install the air cleaner assembly. Tighten the bolt to 23–30 ft. lbs. and the nuts to 69–95 inch lbs.

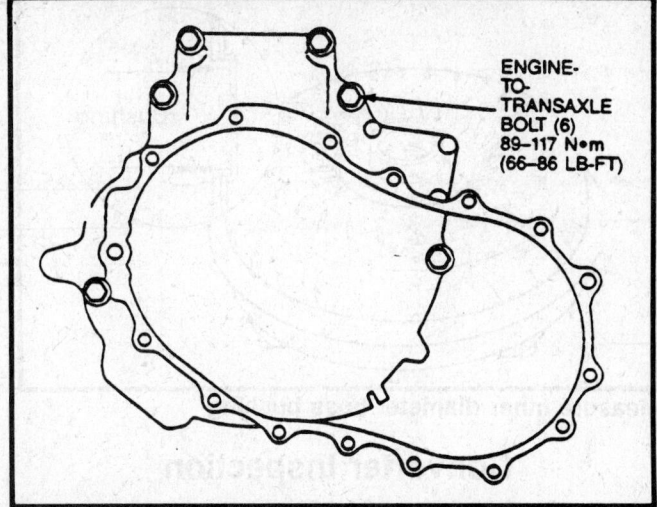

Engine to transaxle bolt location

ENGINE-TO-TRANSAXLE BOLT (6) 89–117 N•m (66–86 LB-FT)

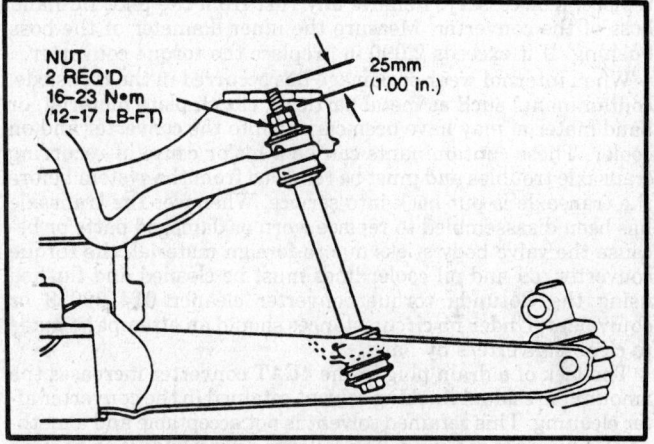

NUT 2 REQ'D 16–23 N•m (12–17 LB-FT)

25mm (1.00 in.)

Installing the stabilizer link assemblies

28. Connect the airflow meter connector.

29. Connect the center distributor terminal lead.

30. Connect the main fuse block and tighten to 69–95 inch lbs. Install the battery carrier and battery and tighten to 23–30 ft. lbs.

31. Remove the engine support bracket.

32. Add the specified transaxle fluid. Check for fluid leakage.

33. Road test vehicle for proper operation.

BENCH OVERHAUL

Before Disassembly

When servicing the unit, it is recommended that as each part is disassembled, it is cleaned in solvent and dried with compressed air. All oil passages should be blown out and checked for obstructions. Disassembly and reassembly of this unit and its parts must be done on a clean work bench. As is the case when repairing any hydraulically operated unit, cleanliness is of the utmost importance. Keep bench, tools, parts and hands clean at all times. Also, before installing bolts into aluminum parts, always dip the threads into clean transmission oil. Anti-seize com-

pound can also be used to prevent bolts from galling the aluminum and seizing. Always use a torque wrench to keep from stripping the threads. Take care with the seals when installing them, especially the smaller O-rings. The slightest damage can cause leaks. Aluminum parts are very susceptible to damage so great care should be exercised when handling them. The internal snaprings should be expanded and the external snaprings compressed if they are to be re-used. This will help insure proper seating when installed. Be sure to replace any O-ring, gasket, or seal that is removed. Lubricate all parts with ATF when assembling.

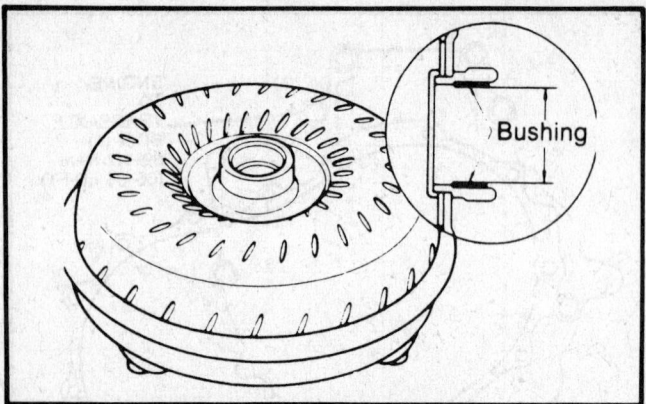

Measure inner diameter boss bushing

Converter Inspection

The torque converter is welded together and cannot be disassembled. Check the torque converter for damage or cracks and replace, if necessary. Remove any rust from the pilot hub and boss of the converter. Measure the inner diameter of the boss bushing. If it exceeds 2.090 in., replace the torque converter.

When internal wear or damage has occurred in the transaxle, contaminants such as metal particles, clutch plate material, or band material may have been carried into the converter and oil cooler. These contaminants can be a major cause of recurring transaxle troubles and must be removed from the system before the transaxle is put back into service. Whenever the transaxle has been disassembled to replace worn or damaged parts or because the valve body sticks due to foreign material, the torque converter, oil and oil cooler lines must be cleaned and flushed using the Rotunda torque converter cleaner 014–00028 or equivalent. Under no circumstances should an attempt be made to clean converters by hand.

The lack of a drain plug in the 4EAT converter increases the amount of residual flushing solvent retained in the converter after cleaning. This retained solvent is not acceptable and a method of diluting is required. The following procedure is to be used after removal of the 4EAT torque converter from the cleaning equipment. Thoroughly drain the remaining solvent through the hub. Add about a ½ quart of clean transaxle fluid into the converter. Agitate by hand. Thoroughly drain the solution through the converter hub.

Transaxle Disassembly

NOTE: Whenever the transaxle is disassemblied, the bearing preload must be adjusted. The output gear and differential bearing preload are adjusted by selecting shim(s) to insert under the bearing cups.

1. Remove the torque converter.

——————————— CAUTION ———————————
The torque converter is heavy. Be careful not to drop it.

2. Remove the oil pump shaft.
3. Mount the transaxle on a bench mounted holding fixture or equivalent.
4. Remove the dipstick tube retaining bolts and pull the tube from its slot.
5. Remove the neutral safety switch.
6. Remove the fluid temperature switch.
7. Remove the pulse generator.
8. Disconnect the solenoid connector.
9. Remove the 4EAT wiring harness and harness clip.
10. Remove the oil pipes, oil hoses and switch box as an assembly.

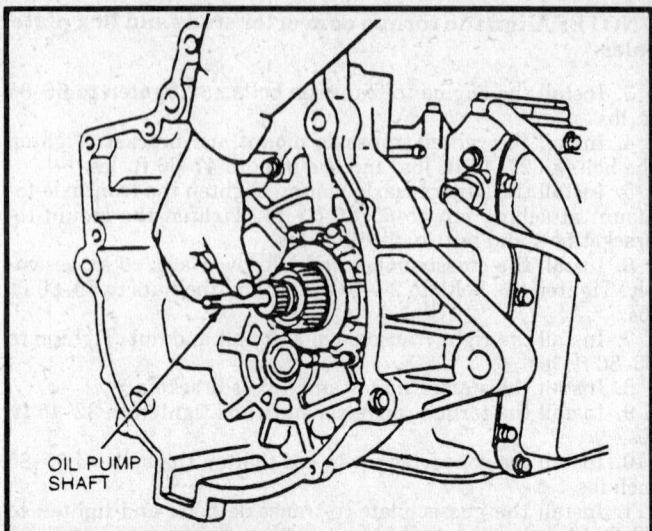

OIL PUMP SHAFT

Removing oil pump shaft

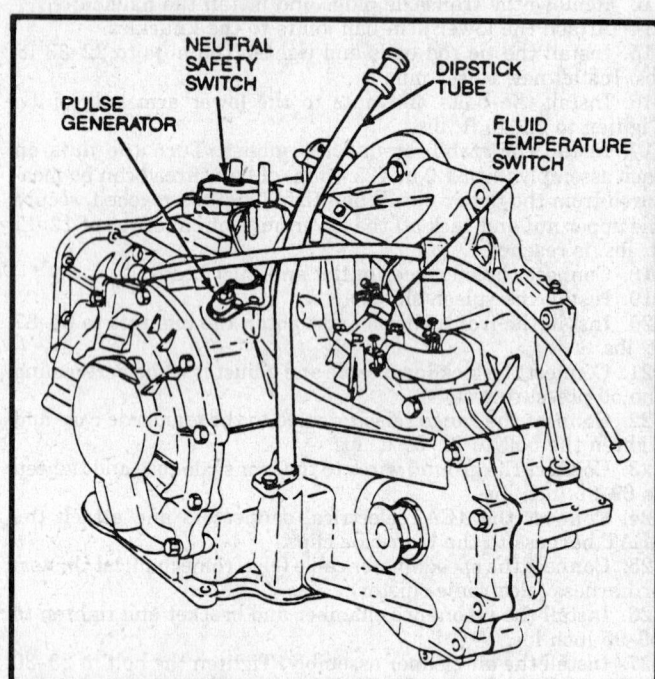

NEUTRAL SAFETY SWITCH

PULSE GENERATOR

DIPSTICK TUBE

FLUID TEMPERATURE SWITCH

Component location

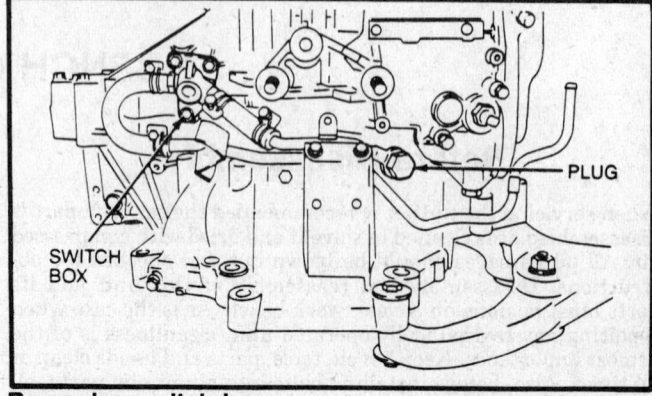

PLUG

SWITCH BOX

Removing switch box

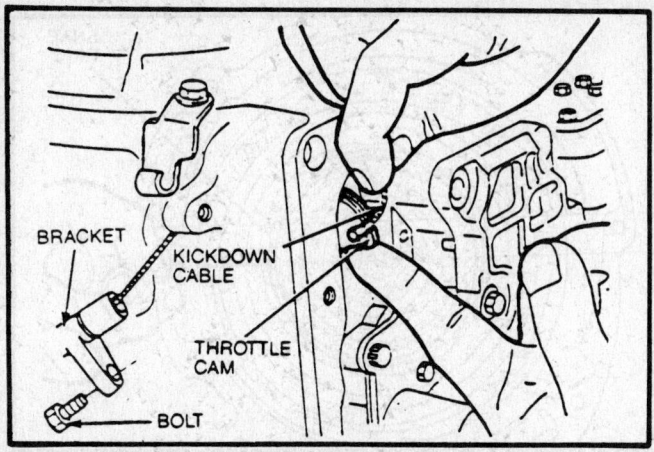

Remove kickdown cable from throttle cam

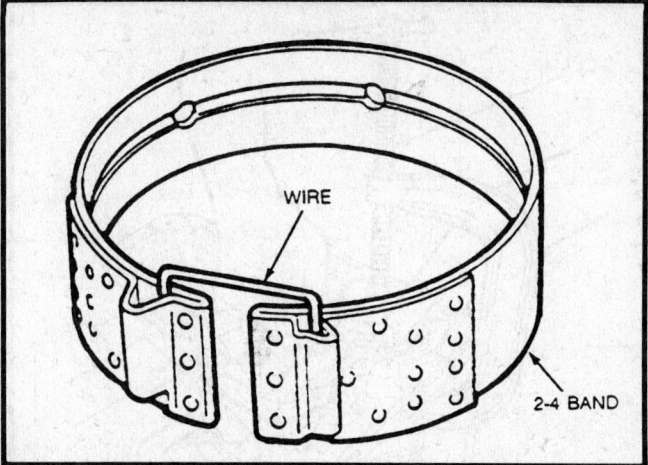

Secure the 2–4 band

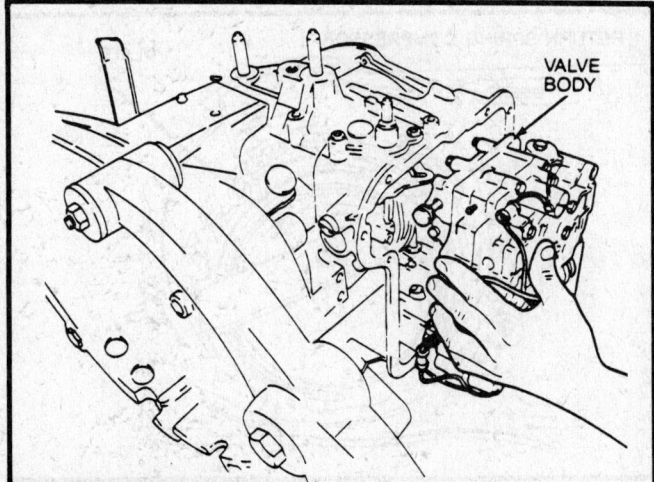

Remove valve body

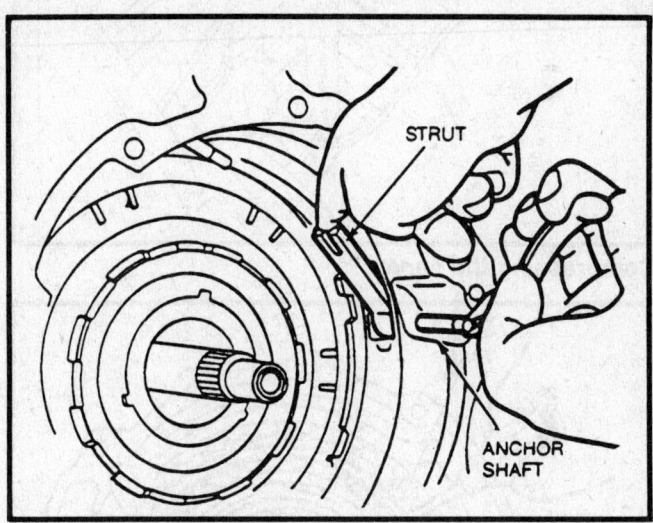

Removing anchor shaft

NOTE: Use a magnet to remove the ball and spring from the plug hole.

11. Remove the oil pan and gasket.
12. Remove the oil strainer and O-ring.
13. Remove the valve body cover and gasket.
14. Remove the kickdown cable attaching bolt and bracket.
15. Remove the kickdown cable from the throttle cam.
16. Pinch the teeth of the solenoid connector mounted on the transaxle case. Remove it by pushing inward.
17. Remove the attaching bolts from the valve body and carefully remove the valve body.
18. Remove the oil pump and gasket.
19. Remove the piston stem from the servo.
20. Remove the turbine shaft snapring.
21. Remove the clutch assembly.
22. Remove the 2–4 band.

NOTE: Secure the 2–4 band with wire to prevent warping.

23. Remove the small sun gear and one-way clutch assembly.
24. Pull the anchor shaft while holding the strut, then remove the strut.
25. Use a C-clamp and socket to compress the servo. Remove the snapring, servo and spring.
26. Remove the one-way clutch snapring.
27. Remove the one-way clutch and carrier hub assembly.
28. Remove the low and reverse clutch snapring.

29. Remove the low and reverse clutch retaining plate and drive and driven plates.
30. Remove the internal gear snapring.
31. Remove the internal gear.
32. Remove the O-ring located on the converter housing side of the turbine shaft.
33. Pull out the turbine shaft and remove the 3–4 clutch assembly.
34. Remove the transaxle case bolts and transaxle case from the converter housing. If necessary, tap lightly with a plastic hammer.
35. Remove the output shell from the output gear.
36. Compress the return spring and retainer using return spring compressor T88C–77000–AH and the plate from T87C–77000–B or equivalent.
37. Remove the retainer snapring, then the return spring and retainer.
38. Remove the return spring compressor.
39. Apply compressed air through the low and reverse clutch fluid passage to remove the low and reverse clutch piston.
40. Remove the plug, washer, spring and detent ball.
41. Remove the bracket.
42. Loosen the manual shaft nut and pull the manual shaft out.
43. Remove the nut, washer, spacer and manual plate.

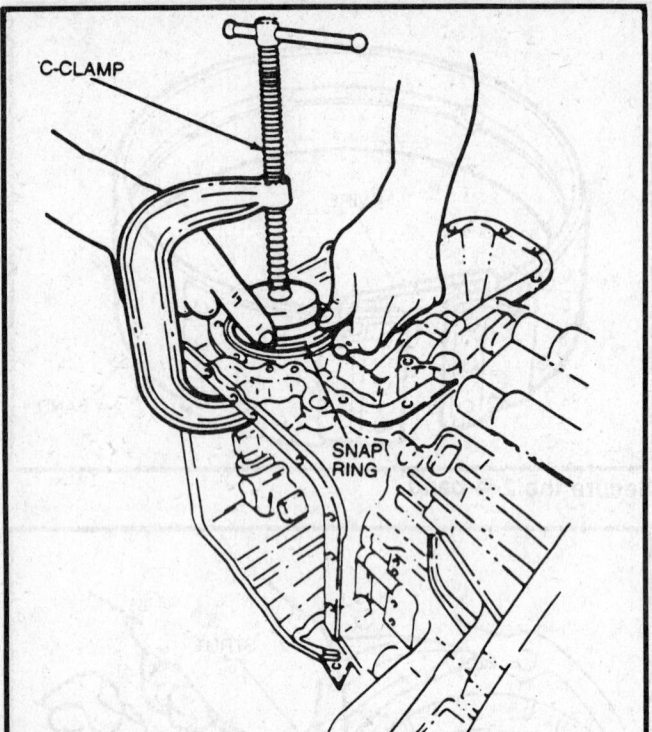

Compressing the servo

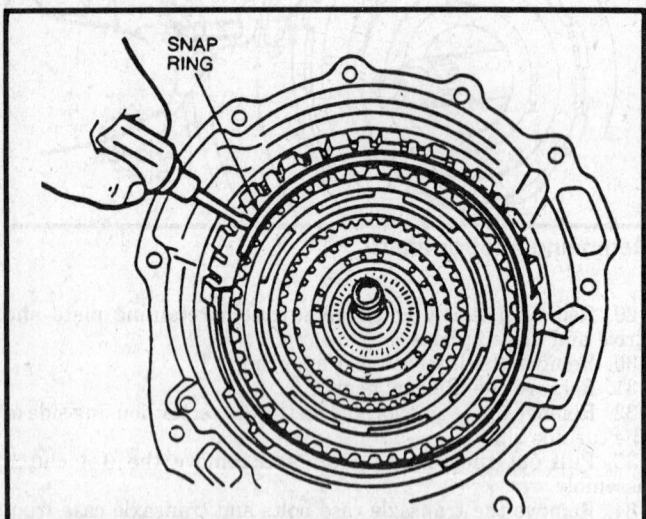

Remove low and reverse clutch snapring

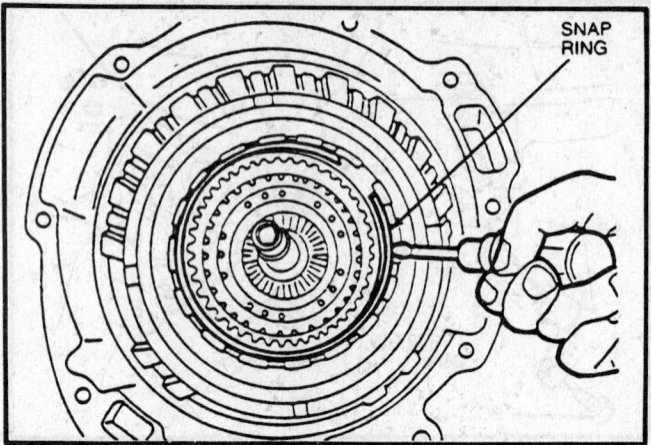

Remove internal gear snapring

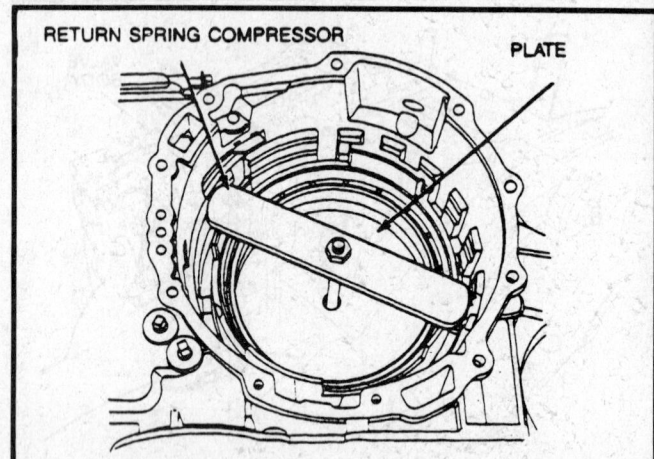

Compress return spring

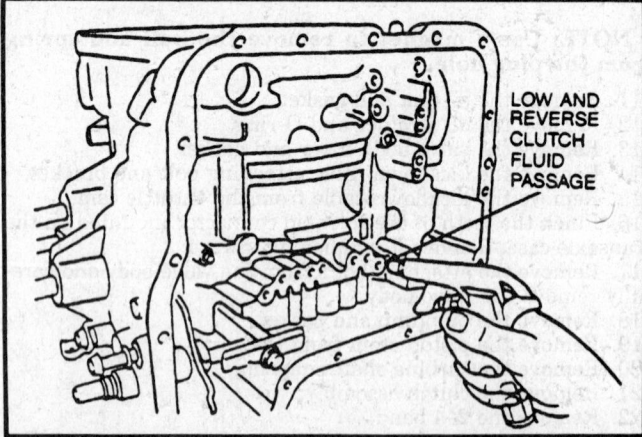

Apply compressed air to remove low and reverse clutch piston

44. Remove the actuator support.
45. Remove the parking assist lever snapring.
46. Remove the parking assist lever.
47. Remove the parking pawl snapring.
48. Pull out the parking shaft, then remove the spring and parking pawl.
49. Remove the differential.
50. Remove the 2–3 accumulator.
51. Remove the bearing housing bolt to access the roll pin.
52. Remove the roll pin using a pin punch.
53. Remove the bearing housing. If necessary, tap lightly with a plastic hammer.
54. Use a socket or equivalent to tap out the idler and output gear assemblies from the torque converter housing.

55. Remove the converter seal from the bearing/stator support using puller tool–1175–AC and slide hammer T50T–100–A or equivalent.
56. Remove the converter housing from the holding fixture.
57. Remove the bearing/stator support bolts.
58. Press the bearing/stator support out of the torque converter housing using step plate D80L–630–10 or equivalent.

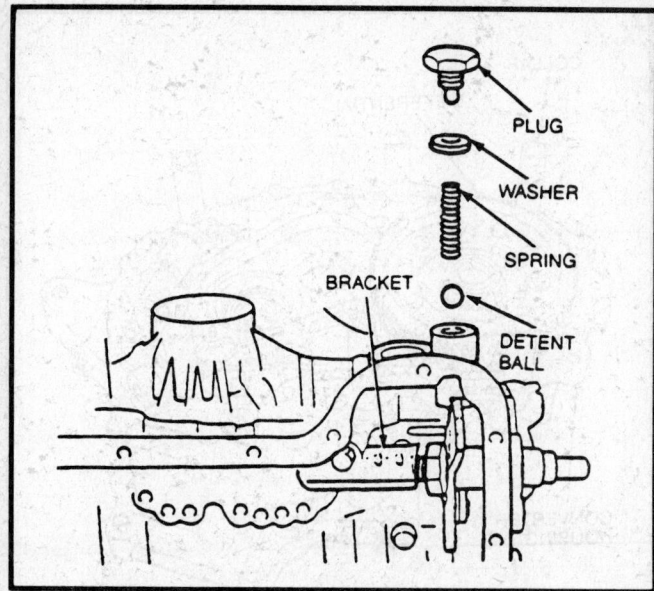

Remove plug, washer, spring and detent ball

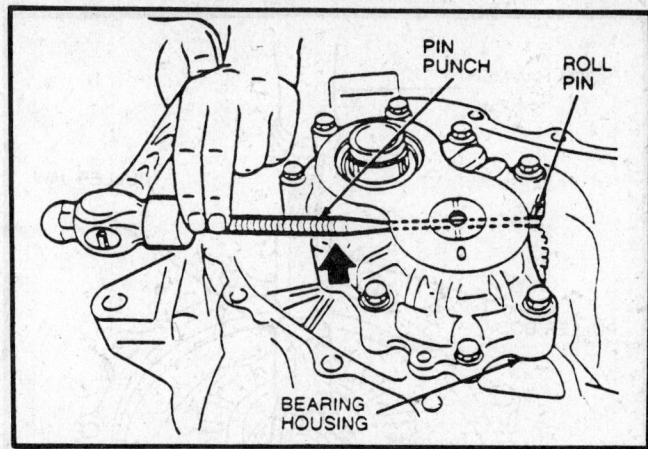

Remove roll pin from bearing housing

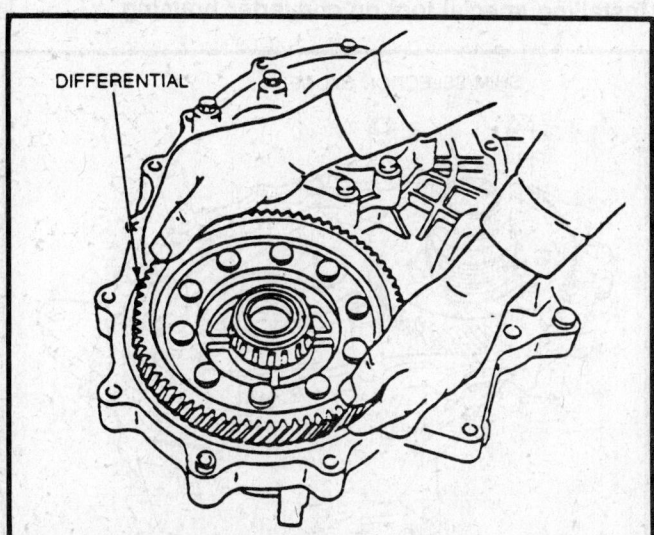

Remove the differential

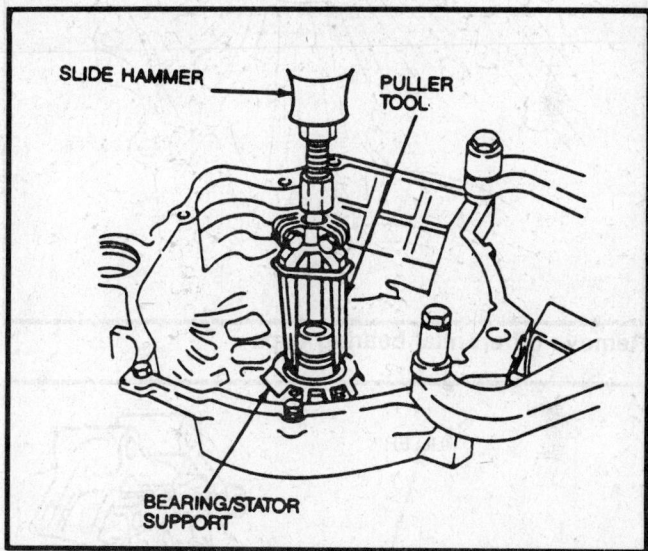

Remove converter seal from bearing stator support

59. Remove the differential bearing cups using puller jaws T86P–70043–A, puller body T73L–2196–A and slide hammer T50T–100–A or equivalent. Remove the adjustment shim(s).

60. Remove the differential oil seals using puller T77F–1102–A and slide hammer T50T–100–A or equivalent.

DIFFERENTIAL BEARING PRELOAD SHIM SELECTION

1. Remove the rear bearing cup and shims from the transaxle case using puller jaw T86P–70043–A, puller body T73L–2196–A and slide hammer T50T–100–A or equivalent.

2. Install the front bearing cup into the converter housing using driver handle T80T–4000–W and differential bearing cup replacer T88C–77000–FH or equivalent.

3. Place the differential into the converter housing.

4. Place 6 collars (part of special tool T87C–77000–J) or equivalent on the converter housing.

5. Place the rear bearing cup over the differential bearing.

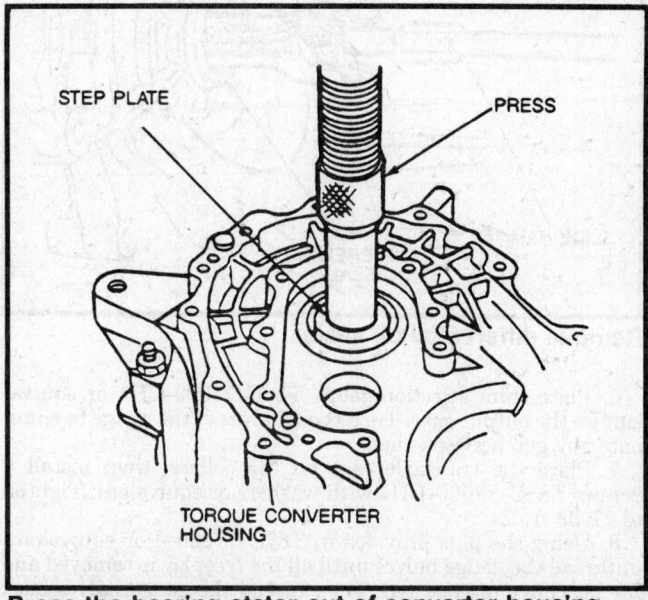

Press the bearing stator out of converter housing

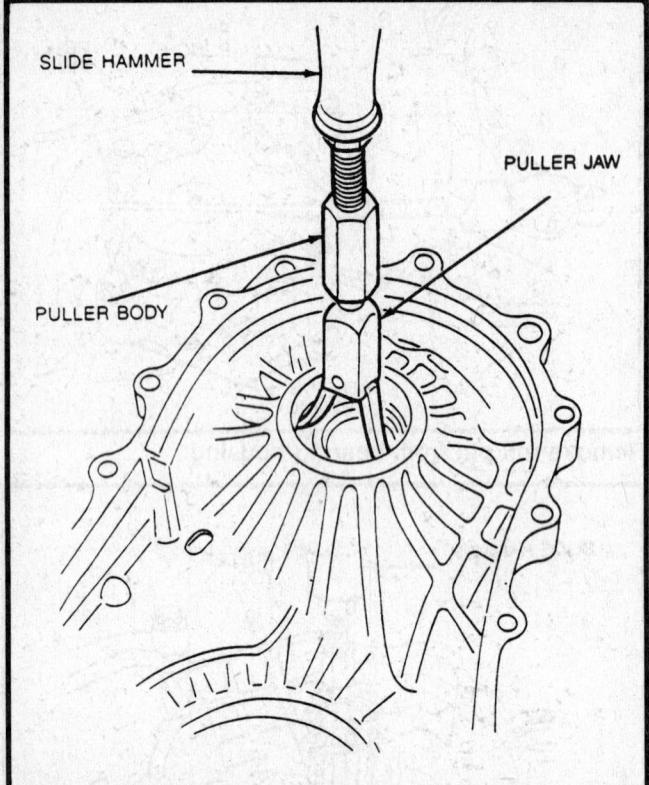

Remove differential bearing cups

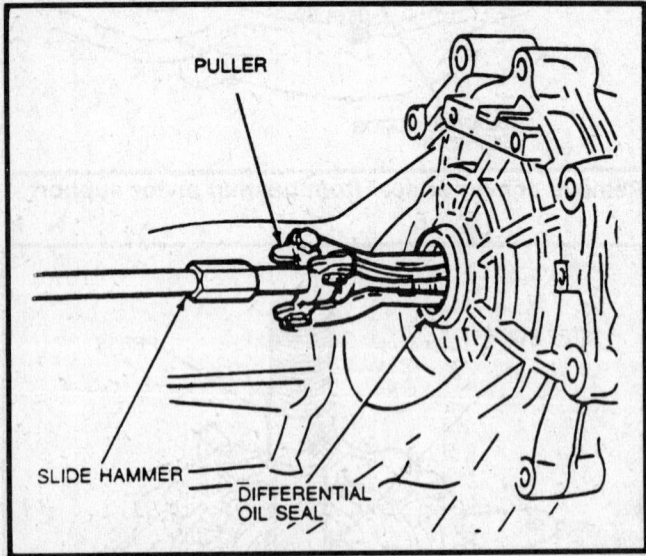

Remove differential oil seals

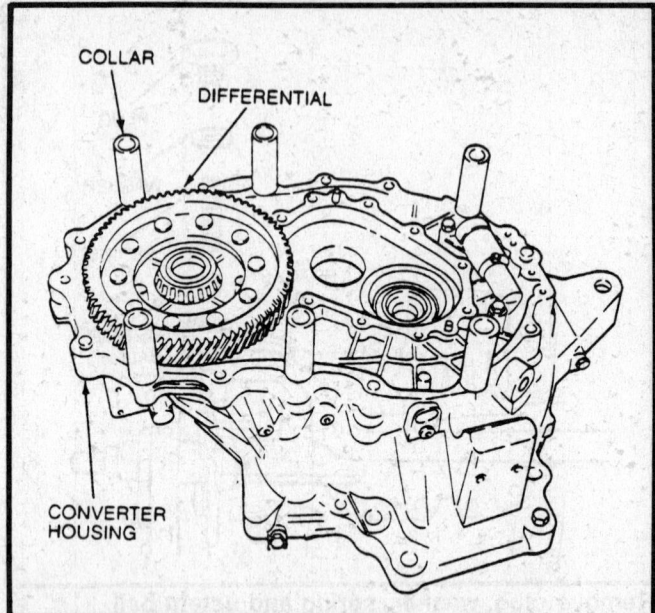

Installing special tool on converter housing

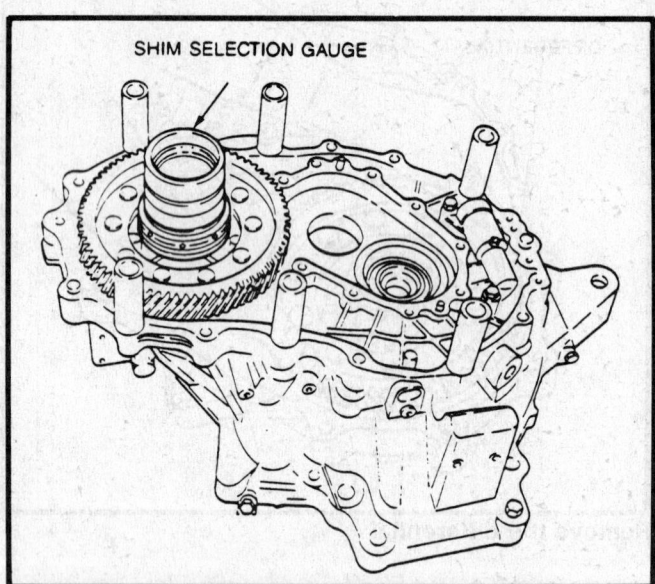

Install shim selection gauge on output gear

6. Place shim selection gauge T88C–77000–CH1 or equivalent on the output gear. Turn the 2 halves of the gauge to eliminate any gap between them.

7. Place the transaxle case on the collars, then install 6 Screws T88C–77000–CH4 with washers or equivalent. Tighten to 27–38 ft. lbs.

8. Using the pins provided in T87C–77000–J or equivalent, unthread the gauge halves until all the freeplay is removed and the bearing cup is seated. Then thread the gauge halves back together.

9. Engage torque adapter T88C–77000–L or equivalent and attach a inch lbs. torque wrench to the adapter. Measure the drag on the differential bearing.

NOTE: Read the preload when the differential starts to turn.

10. Turn the gauge using the pins (part of T87C–77000–J) or equivalent until a reading of 4.3 inch lbs. is obtained on the torque wrench.

11. Use a feeler gauge to measure the gap between the 2 halves of the gauge. Measure the gap at 4 spots, at 90 degree intervals. Use the largest measurement.

12. Add 0.0079 in. to the largest measurement. Using the differential bearing preload shim selection chart, select the shim(s) closest (or slightly larger) to this final value. Use no more than 3 shims.

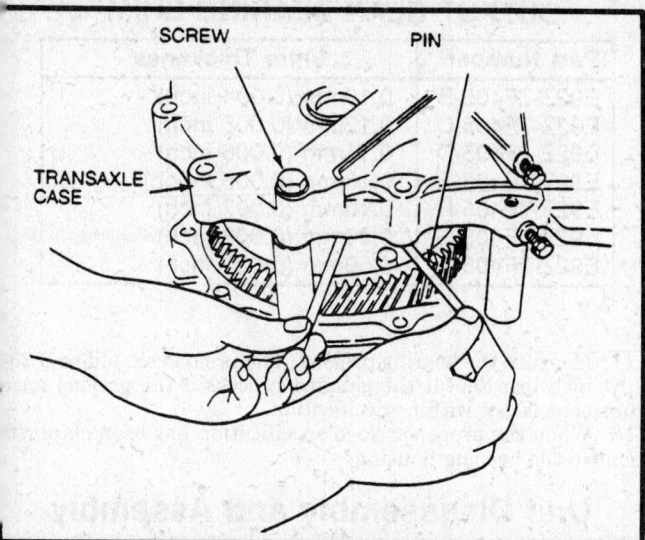

Using special tool to seat bearing cup

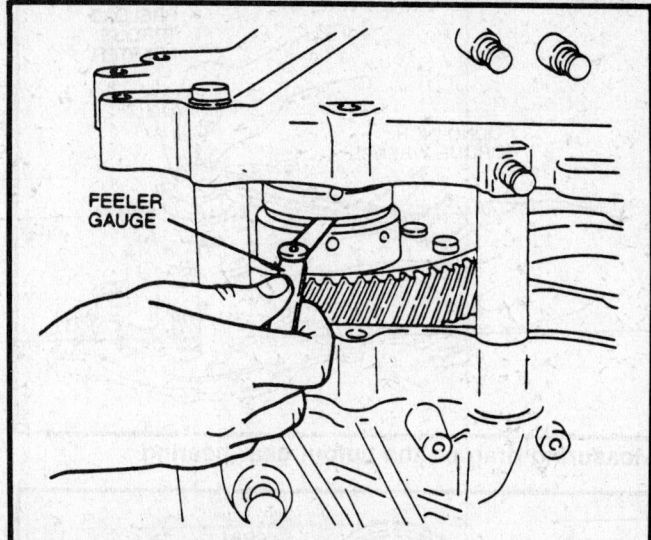

Measure gap between gauge

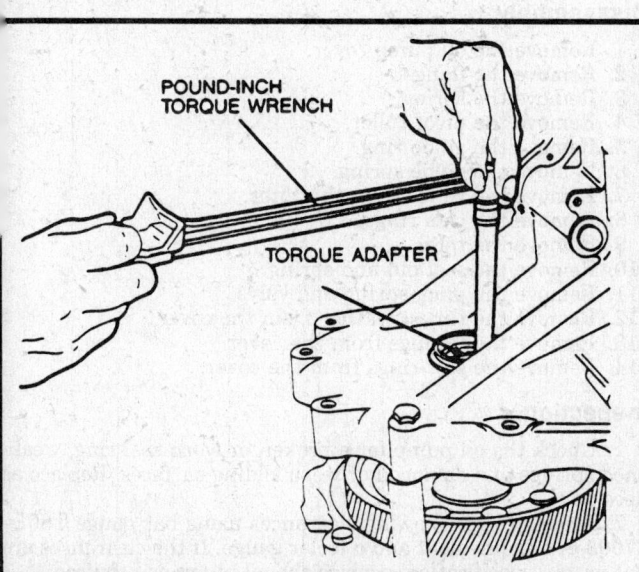

Measuring drag on the differential bearing

13. Remove the screws, washers, transaxle case, gauge and bearing cup.

14. Install the selected shim(s) and bearing cup into the transaxle case using drive handle T80T–4000–W and differential bearing cup replacer T88C–77000–FH or equivalent.

15. Install the transaxle case. Tighten the retaining bolts to 27–38 ft. lbs.

16. Measure the bearing preload. The preload should be 26–35 inch lbs. Repeat the gauging process if the preload measurement is not within specification.

17. When the proper preload specification has been obtained, remove the transaxle case.

OUTPUT GEAR BEARING PRELOAD SHIM SELECTION

1. Align the bearing stator support using guide pins T80L–77100–A or equivalent then press the support into the converter housing using step plate D80L–630–6 or equivalent.

DIFFERENTIAL BEARING SHIM

Part Number	Shim Thickness
E92Z-4067-A	0.10mm (0.004 in.)
E92Z-4067-B	0.12mm (0.005 in.)
E92Z-4067-C	0.14mm (0.006 in.)
E92Z-4067-D	0.16mm (0.0063 in.)
E92Z-4067-E	0.18mm (0.007 in.)
E92Z-4067-F	0.20mm (0.008 in.)
E92Z-4067-G	0.25mm (0.010 in.)
E92Z-4067-H	0.30mm (0.012 in.)
E92Z-4067-J	0.35mm (0.014 in.)
E92Z-4067-K	0.40mm (0.016 in.)
E92Z-4067-L	0.45mm (0.018 in.)
E92Z-4067-N	0.50mm (0.020 in.)
E92Z-4067-P	0.55mm (0.022 in.)
E92Z-4067-Q	0.60mm (0.024 in.)
E92Z-4067-R	0.65mm (0.026 in.)
E92Z-4067-S	0.70mm (0.028 in.)
E92Z-4067-T	0.75mm (0.030 in.)
E92Z-4067-U	0.80mm (0.032 in.)
E92Z-4067-V	0.85mm (0.034 in.)
E92Z-4067-W	0.90mm (0.036 in.)
E92Z-4067-X	0.95mm (0.038 in.)
E92Z-4067-Y	1.00mm (0.040 in.)
E92Z-4067-Z	1.05mm (0.042 in.)
E92Z-4067-AA	1.10mm (0.044 in.)
E92Z-4067-AB	1.15mm (0.046 in.)
E92Z-4067-AC	1.20mm (0.048 in.)

2. Remove the bearing cup and adjustment shim(s) from the bearing housing.

3. Place the output gear into the converter housing.

4. Place the bearing cup over the output gear bearing.

5. Place 4 collars (part of T87C–77000–J) or equivalent on the converter housing.

6. Place shim selection gauge T88C–77000–CH1 or equivalent on the output gear. Turn the 2 halves of the gauge to eliminate any gap between them.

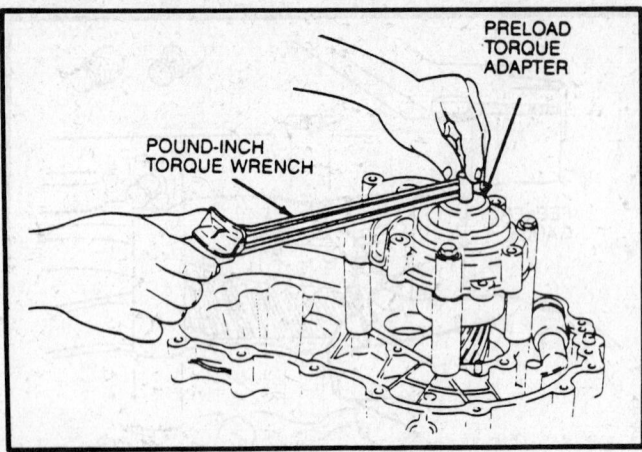

Measuring drag on the output gear bearing

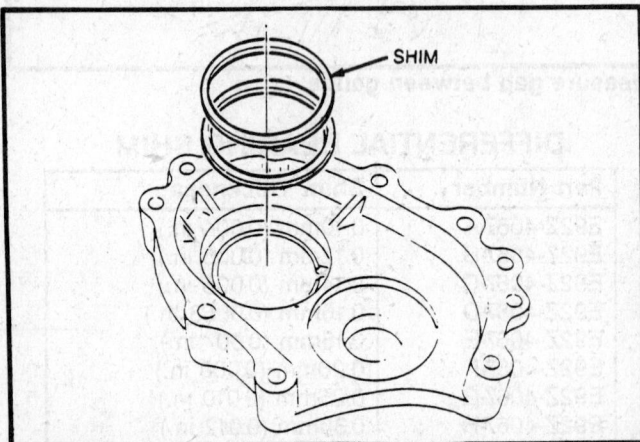

Installing shims in the bearing housing

7. Place the bearing housing on the collars, install 4 Screws T88C–77000–CH4 with washers or equivalent. Tighten to 14–19 ft. lbs.

8. Place preload torque adapter T88C–77000–DH or equivalent on the output gear.

9. Using the pins provided in T87C–77000–J or equivalent, loosen the gauge halves until all of the freeplay is removed and the bearing cup is seated. Then thread the gauge halves back together.

10. Attach a inch pound torque wrench to the torque adapter. Measure the drag on the output gear bearing.

NOTE: Read the preload when the output gear starts to turn.

11. Turn the shim selection gauge using the pins (part of T87C–77000–J) or equivalent until a reading of 4.3–7.8 inch lbs. is obtained on the torque wrench.

12. Use a feeler gauge to measure the gap between the 2 halves of the gauge. Measure the gap at 4 spots, at 90 degree intervals. Use the largest measurement.

13. Using the output gear bearing preload shim selection chart, select the shim(s) that is closest (or slightly larger) to the measured value of the gauge gap. Use no more than 7 shims.

14. Remove the screws, washers, bearing housing, gauge and bearing cup.

15. Press the selected shim(s) and bearing cup into the bearing housing using bearing installer T60K–4616–A or equivalent.

16. Install the bearing housing. Tighten the retaining bolts to 14–19 ft. lbs.

OUTPUT GEAR BEARING SHIM

Part Number	Shim Thickness
E92Z-7F405-B	0.10mm (0.004 inch)
E92Z-7F405-C	0.12mm (0.005 inch)
E92Z-7F405-D	0.14mm (0.006 inch)
E92Z-7F405-E	0.16mm (0.0063 inch)
E92Z-7F405-F	0.18mm (0.007 inch)
E92Z-7F405-G	0.20mm (0.008 inch)
E92Z-7F405-A	0.50mm (0.020 inch)

17. Measure the bearing preload. The preload should be 0.26–7.81 inch lbs. Repeat the gauging process if the preload measurement is not within specification.

18. When the proper preload specification has been obtained, remove the bearing housing.

Unit Disassembly and Assembly

OIL PUMP

Disassembly

1. Remove the oil pump cover.
2. Remove the flange.
3. Remove the spring.
4. Remove the pivot roller.
5. Remove the guide ring.
6. Remove the guide spring.
7. Remove the vanes from the rotor.
8. Remove the cam ring.
9. Remove the rotor.
10. Remove the seal pin and spring.
11. Remove the plug, spring and valve.
12. Remove the thrust washer from the cover.
13. Remove the O-rings from the cover.
14. Remove the seal rings from the cover.

Inspection

1. Check the oil pump for a broken or worn seal ring, weakened springs and damaged or worn sliding surfaces. Replace as necessary.

2. Measure the following clearances using bar gauge T80L–77003–A or equivalent and a feeler gauge. If the clearances are not within specification, replace the oil pump as required..

a. Seal pin to oil pump cover—The standard clearance should be 0.0002–0.0008 in. and the maximum allowable clearance is 0.002 in.

b. Rotor to oil pump cover—The standard clearance should be 0.0002–0.0008 in. and the maximum allowable clearance 0.002 in.

c. Cam ring to oil pump cover—The standard clearance should be 0.0002–0.0008 in. and the maximum allowable clearance 0.002 in.

d. Vane to oil pump cover—The standard clearance should be 0.0006–0.0020 in. and the maximum allowable clearance 0.003 in.

e. Vane to rotor groove—The standard clearance should be 0.0004–0.0018 in. and the maximum allowable clearance 0.0026 in.

3. Check each of the following parts for wear using the appropriate tool. If the wear limit is exceeded, replace the oil pump assembly.

a. Sleeve to oil pump body—The standard outer diameter is 1.102 in.

b. Rotor bushing—The standard inner diameter 1.102 in. and the maximum allowable inner diameter 1.104 in.

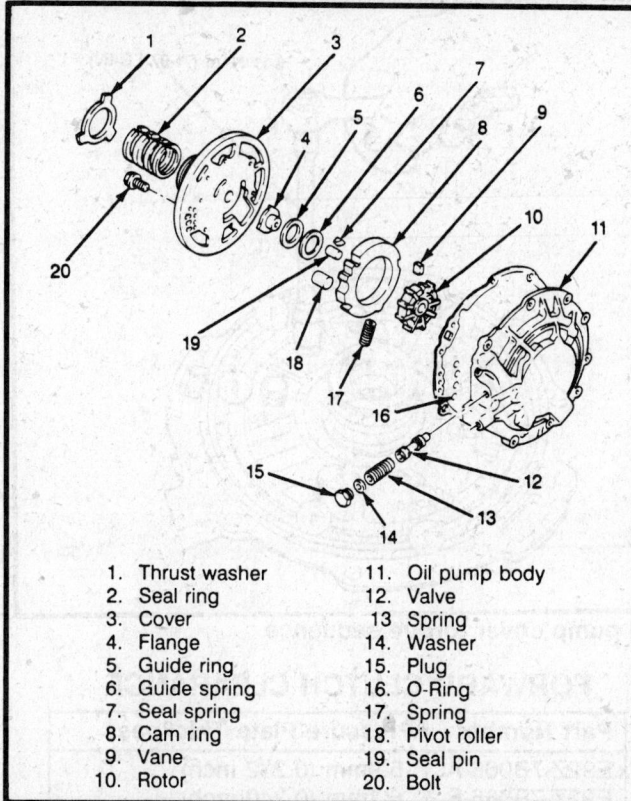

1.	Thrust washer	11.	Oil pump body
2.	Seal ring	12.	Valve
3.	Cover	13	Spring
4.	Flange	14.	Washer
5.	Guide ring	15.	Plug
6.	Guide spring	16.	O-Ring
7.	Seal spring	17.	Spring
8.	Cam ring	18.	Pivot roller
9.	Vane	19.	Seal pin
10.	Rotor	20.	Bolt

Exploded view of oil pump

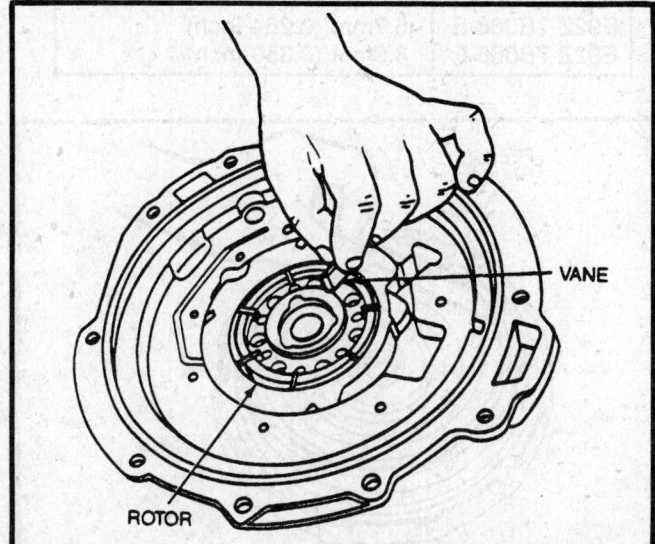

Remove vanes from rotor in oil pump

c. Guide ring—The standard outer diameter 0.278 in. and the minimum allowable outer diameter 0.272 in.

d. Valve—The standard outer diameter 0.472 in. and the minimum allowable outer diameter 0.467 in.

e. Seal pin—The standard outer diameter 0.236 in. and the minimum allowable outer diameter 0.232 in.

Assembly

1. Install the valve and spring into the oil pump body and check that the valve moves freely.

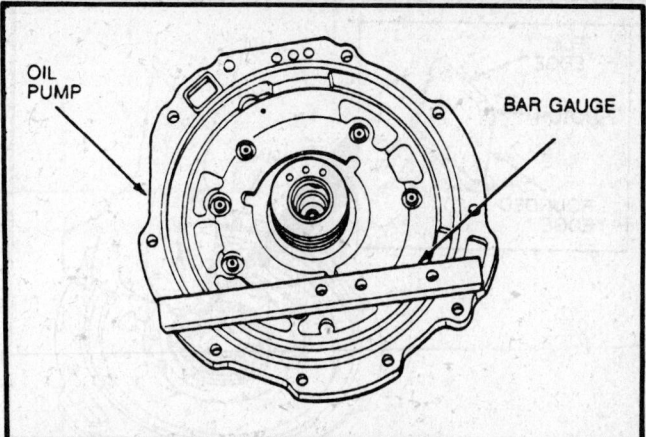

Measure clearances using bar gauge

2. Install the plug and torque to 17–26 ft. lbs.
3. Install the cam ring and pivot roller.
4. Install the rotor.
5. Install the vanes into the rotor, with the flat edges and notches facing upwards.
6. Install the guide spring.
7. Install the guide ring.
8. Install the flange with the beveled edge down.
9. Install the spring.
10. Install new O-rings.
11. Install the seal pins and springs. Install the pins with the beveled edge down and the springs facing toward the cam ring.
12. Install the oil pump cover to the oil pump body.
13. Tighten the cover bolts in sequence. Torque to 71–97 inch lbs.
14. Install the oil pump shaft and check for smooth operation.
15. Install new seal rings.
16. Apply petroleum jelly to the thrust washer and install it on the oil pump cover. The outer diameter of the thrust washer should be 3.46 in.

FORWARD CLUTCH ASSEMBLY

Disassembly

1. Remove the needle bearing.
2. Remove the snapring.
3. Remove the pressure plate.
4. Remove the forward clutch pack.
5. Remove the dished plate.

Inspection

1. Check the drive and driven plates for damage or wear. The minimum thickness should be 0.055 in.
2. Check the clutch piston, clutch drum and seal contact areas for damage or wear. Check for broken or weakened springs. The free length of each spring should be 1.173 in. Replace as necessary.

Assembly

1. Install the dished plate with the beveled side facing upward.
2. Install the forward clutch pack, pressure plate and snapring.
3. Using a feeler gauge check the forward clutch clearance. Measure between the snapring and the pressure plate.
4. If the clearance is not within 0.040–0.047 in., adjust it by selecting an appropriate pressure.
5. Set the forward and reverse drum onto the oil pump. Check each clutch operation by applying a short burst of com-

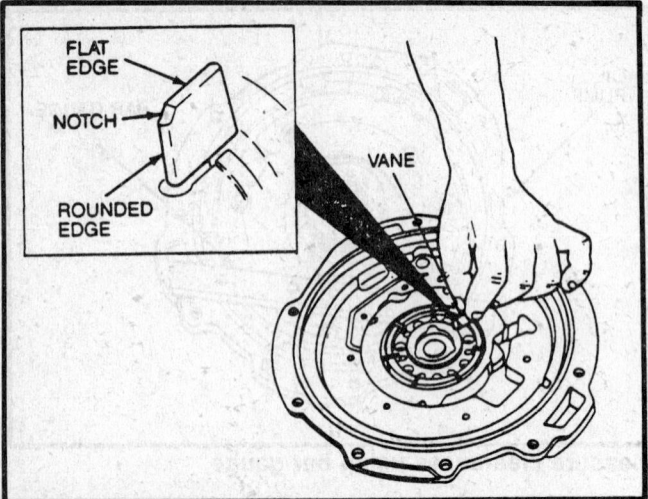

Install vanes into rotor—oil pump assembly

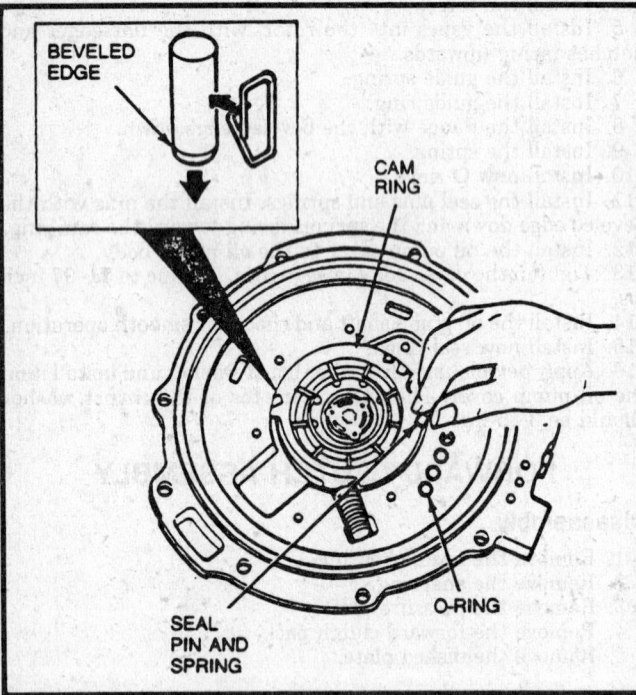

Install seal pins and springs—oil pump assembly

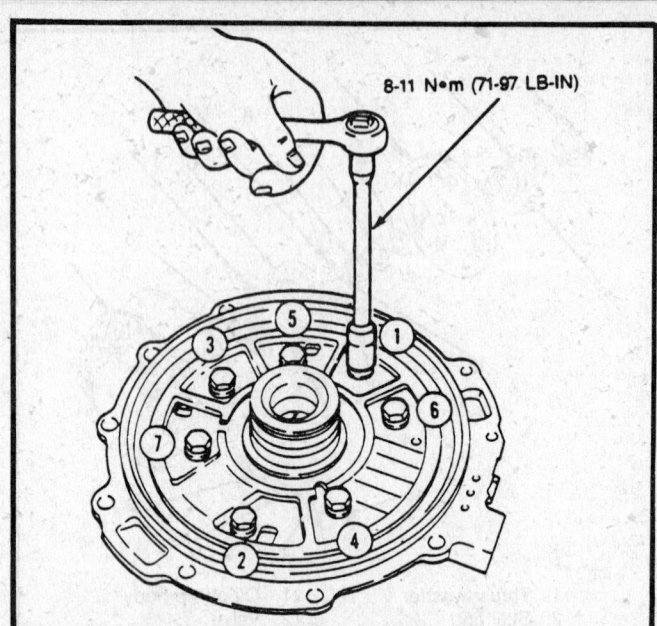

Oil pump cover torque sequence

FORWARD CLUTCH CLEARANCE

Part Number	Pressure Plate Thickness
E92Z-7B066-A	5.9mm (0.232 inch)
E92Z-7B066-B	6.1mm (0.240 inch)
E92Z-7B066-C	6.3mm (0.248 inch)
E92Z-7B066-D	6.5mm (0.256 inch)
E92Z-7B066-E	6.7mm (0.264 inch)
E92Z-7B066-F	8.9mm (0.350 inch)

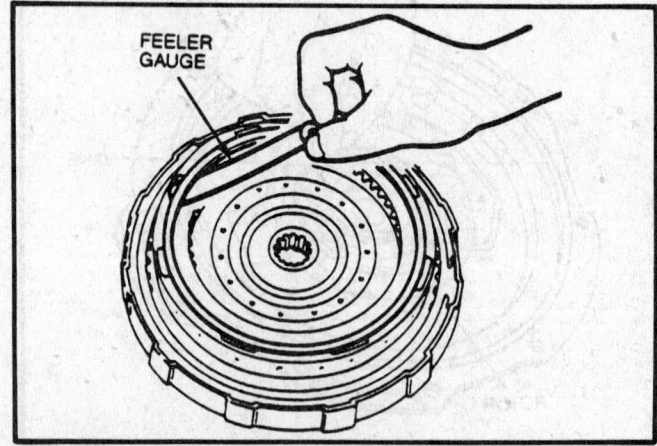

Checking forward clutch clearance

pressed air through the fluid passages. As air pressure is applies, the clutch pack should compress. The pressure should not exceed 57 psi.

6. Pour the specified amount of transaxle fluid into a pan, until the reverse piston, coasting clutch drum and coasting piston are fully submerged in the fluid. Apply a short burst of compressed air through the fluid passages. Check that no bubbles come from between the piston and drum seal. The pressure should not exceed 57 psi.

7. Apply petroleum jelly to the needle bearings and install them on both sides of the clutch assembly. The outer diameter is 3.39 in. for the oil pump side and 2.21 in. for the one-way clutch side.

COASTING CLUTCH ASSEMBLY

Disassembly

1. Remove the snapring and pressure plate.
2. Remove the coasting clutch pack.
3. Remove the dished plate.
4. Install spring compressor T65L-77505–A or equivalent and compress the return spring and retainer.
5. Remove the snapring.

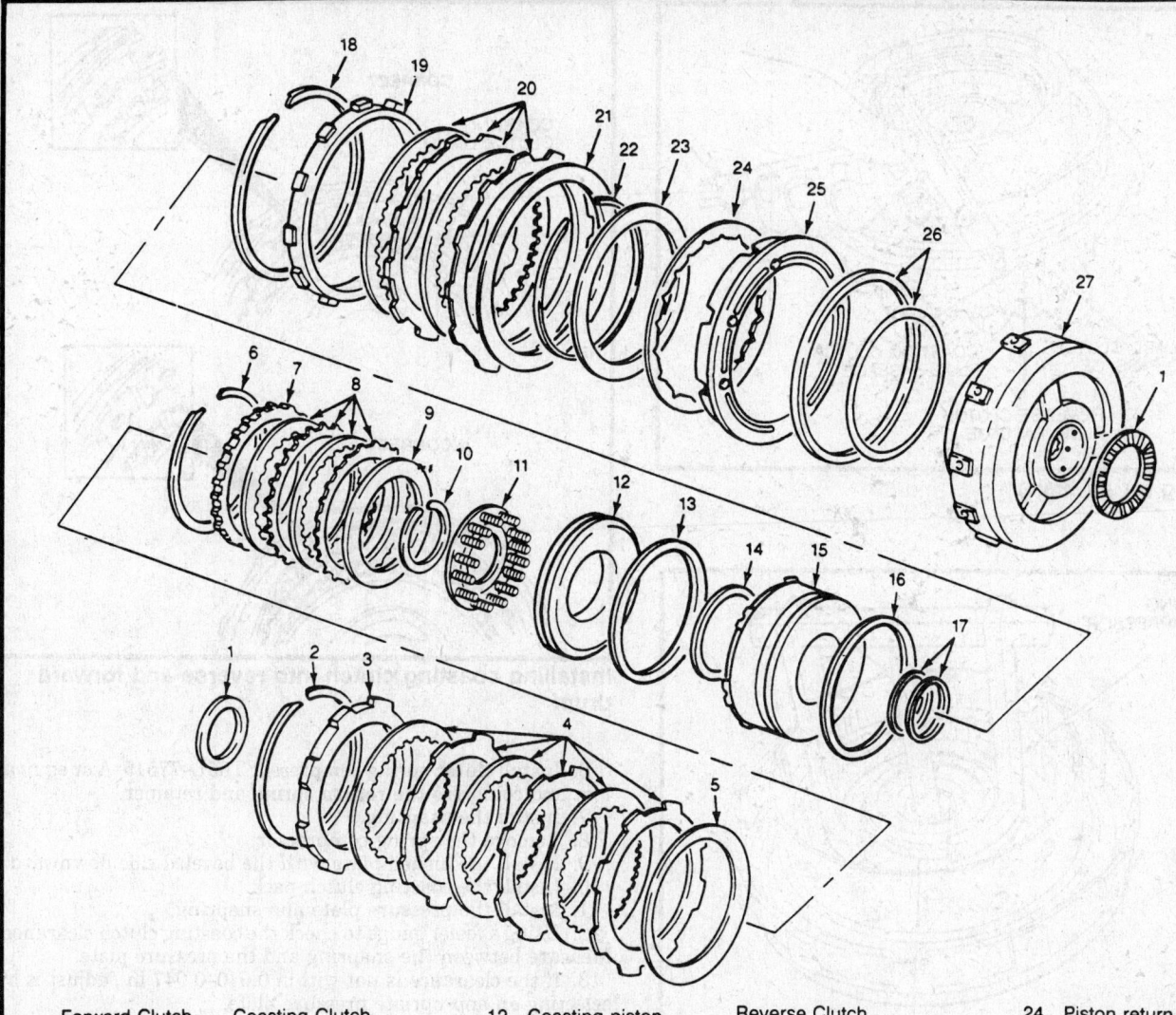

Forward Clutch	Coasting Clutch	12. Coasting piston	Reverse Clutch	24. Piston return spring
1. Needle bearing	6. Snapring	13. Outer seal	18. Snapring	25. Reverse piston
2. Snapring	7. Pressure plate	14. Inner seal	19. Pressure plate	26. Seal rings
3. Pressure plate	8. Clutch pack	15. Coasting clutch drum	20. Clutch pack	27. Reverse and forward
4. Clutch pack	9. Dished plate	16. Outer seal	21. Dished plate	drum
5. Dished plate	10. Snapring	17. Seal rings	22. Snapring	
	11. Return spring and		23. Return spring stopper	
	retainer			

Exploded view of clutch assembly

6. Remove the spring compressor.
7. Remove the return spring and retainer.
8. Remove the coasting clutch drum from the clutch assembly by applying compressed air through the fluid passage.
9. Remove the coasting piston from the coasting clutch drum by applying low pressure compressed air through the fluid passage.

Inspection

1. Check the drive and driven plates for damage or wear. The minimum thickness should be 0.055 in.
2. Check the clutch piston, clutch drum and seal contact areas for damage or wear. Check for broken or weakened springs. The free length of each spring should be 1.173 in. Replace as necessary.

Assembly

1. Apply the specified transaxle fluid to the new seals and install them on the coasting piston.
2. Attach seal protector T88C–77000–HH or equivalent to the coasting piston and install the piston into the coasting clutch drum by pushing evenly around the circumference.
3. Apply the specified transaxle fluid to a new seal and install it on the coasting clutch drum.

NOTE: Roll the outer seal lip down to ease installation.

4. Install the coasting clutch drum into the reverse and forward drum.
5. Install the return spring and retainer.

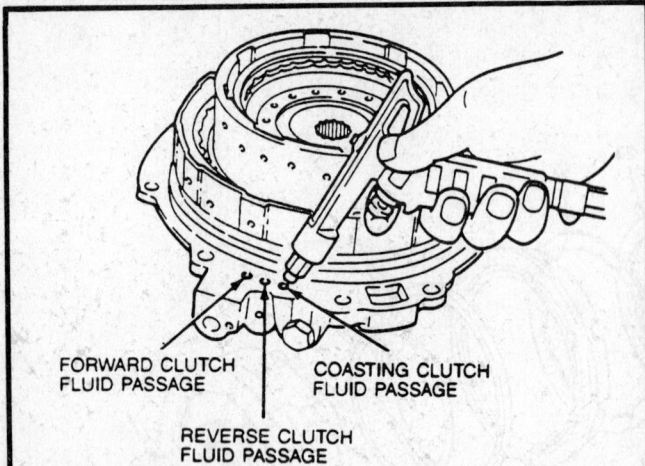

FORWARD CLUTCH FLUID PASSAGE

COASTING CLUTCH FLUID PASSAGE

REVERSE CLUTCH FLUID PASSAGE

Checking for air leaks

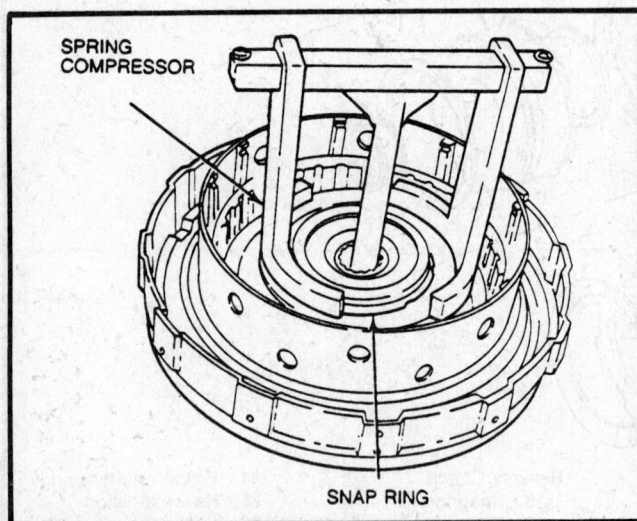

SPRING COMPRESSOR

SNAP RING

Compressing return spring and retainer to remove snapring

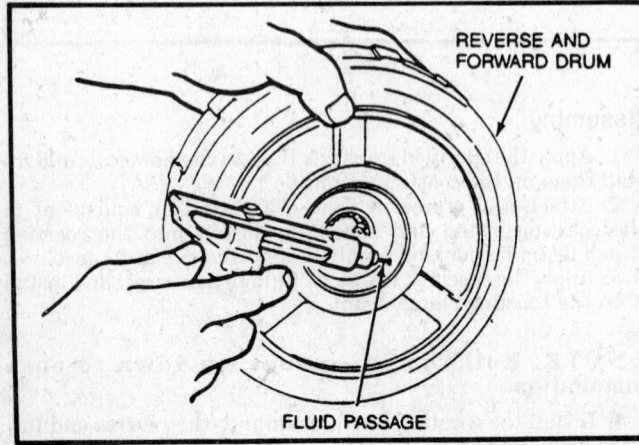

REVERSE AND FORWARD DRUM

FLUID PASSAGE

Removing coasting clutch drum by air pressure

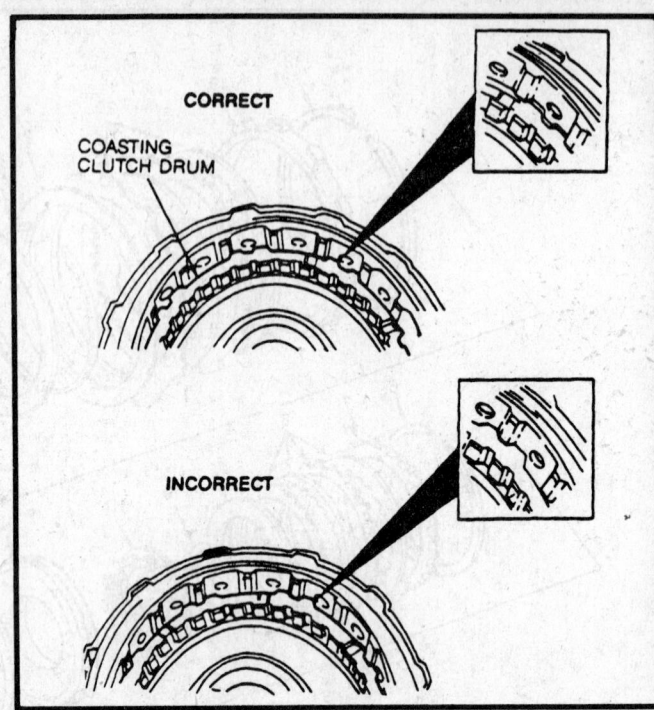

CORRECT

COASTING CLUTCH DRUM

INCORRECT

Installing coasting clutch into reverse and forward drum

6. Install clutch spring compressor T65L–77515–A or equivalent and compress the return spring and retainer.
7. Install the snapring.
8. Remove the spring compressor.
9. Install the dished plate with the beveled side downward.
10. Install the coasting clutch pack.
11. Install the pressure plate and snapring.
12. Using a feeler gauge to check the coasting clutch clearance. Measure between the snapring and the pressure plate.
13. If the clearance is not within 0.040–0.047 in., adjust it by selecting an appropriate pressure plate.

REVERSE CLUTCH

Disassembly

1. Remove the snapring.
2. Remove the pressure plate.
3. Remove the reverse clutch pack.
4. Remove the dished plate.
5. Compress the piston return spring using return spring compressor T88C–77000–AH and the plate from T87C–77000–B or equivalent.
6. Remove one end of the snapring from the groove with snapring pliers. Once started, remove the snapring with a tool.
7. Remove the spring compressor.
8. Place the clutch assembly on the oil pump.
9. Apply low pressure compressed air through the fluid passage to remove the reverse piston.

Inspection

1. Check for damaged or worn drive and driven plates. The minimum allowable drive plate thickness is 0.055 in.
2. Check for a broken or worn piston or snapring.
3. Check for a broken or weakened spring. The free length of each spring should be 0.807 in. Replace as necessary.

COASTING CLUTCH CLEARANCE

Part Number	Pressure Plate Thickness
E92Z-7B066-M	4.6mm (0.181 inch)
E92Z-7B066-G	4.8mm (0.189 inch)
E92Z-7B066-H	5.0mm (0.197 inch)
E92Z-7B066-J	5.2mm (0.205 inch)
E92Z-7B066-K	5.4mm (0.213 inch)
E92Z-7B066-L	5.6mm (0.220 inch)

REVERSE CLUTCH CLEARANCE

Part Number	Pressure Plate Thickness
E92Z-7B066-N	6.6mm (0.260 inch)
E92Z-7B066-O	6.8mm (0.268 inch)
E92Z-7B066-P	7.0mm (0.276 inch)
E92Z-7B066-Q	7.2mm (0.283 inch)
E92Z-7B066-R	7.4mm (0.291 inch)
E92Z-7B066-S	7.6mm (0.299 inch)

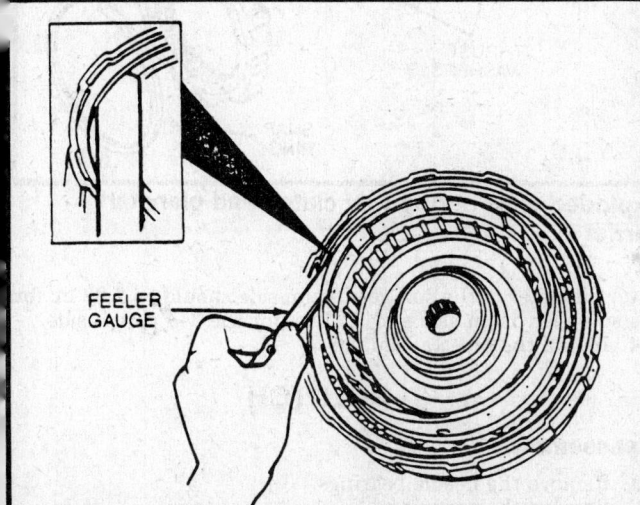

FEELER GAUGE

Checking reverse clutch clearance

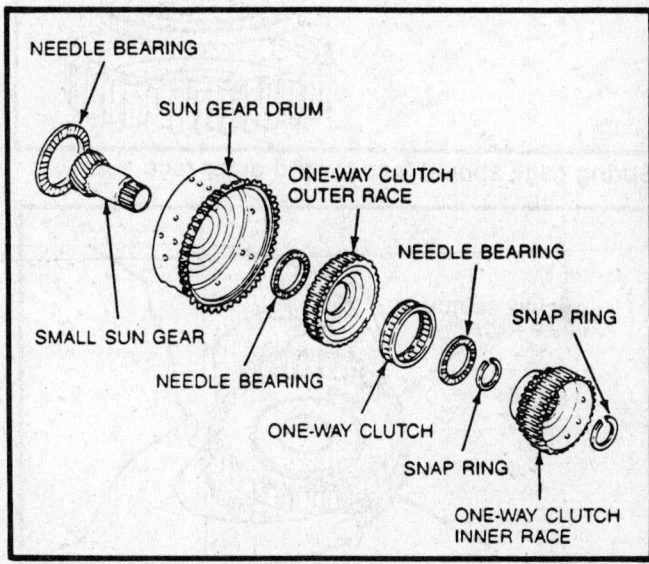

NEEDLE BEARING
SUN GEAR DRUM
ONE-WAY CLUTCH OUTER RACE
NEEDLE BEARING
SNAP RING
SMALL SUN GEAR
NEEDLE BEARING
ONE-WAY CLUTCH
SNAP RING
ONE-WAY CLUTCH INNER RACE

Exploded view small sun gear and one-way clutch

Assembly

1. Apply the specified transaxle fluid to the inner and outer faces of new seals and install them on the reverse piston.
2. Attach seal protector T88C–77000–GH or equivalent to the reverse piston. Install the reverse piston onto the reverse and forward drum by pushing evenly around the circumference. If necessary, use a tool to seat the piston. Remove the special tool seal protector.
3. Install the piston return spring with the tabs facing away from the reverse piston.
4. Install the return spring stopper with the step facing upwards.
5. Install the snapring half-way down the reverse and forward drum.
6. Compress the piston return spring using return spring compressor T88C–77000–AH and the plate from T87C–77000–B or equivalent.
7. Install the snapring with a tool.
8. Remove the spring compressor. Install the dished plate with the beveled side facing upward.
9. Install the reverse clutch pack.
10. Install the pressure plate with the step facing down.
11. Install the snapring.
12. Use a feeler gauge to check the reverse clutch clearance. Measure between the snapring and the pressure plate. if the clearance is not within 0.083–0.094 in., adjust it by selecting an appropriate pressure plate from the following chart.

SMALL SUN GEAR AND ONE-WAY CLUTCH

Disassembly

1. Remove the snapring.

2. Remove the one-way clutch inner and outer races.
3. Remove the snapring.
4. Remove the small sun gear from the sun gear drum.
5. Separate the one-way clutch inner race from the outer race.
6. Remove the one-way clutch.
7. Remove the needle bearing.

Inspection

1. Check the sun gear drum, small sun gear, bushing, clutch hub and inner and outer races for damage or wear.
2. Replace as necessary.

Assembly

1. Apply petroleum jelly to the needle bearing and install it to the one-way clutch inner race. The outer diameter is 2.44 in.
2. Install the one-way clutch into the one-way clutch outer race.

NOTE: Check that the spring cage faces toward the outer race.

3. Install the one-way clutch inner race into the one-way clutch outer race by turning the inner race counterclockwise. Make sure that the inner race turns only counterclockwise.
4. Install the small sun gear into the sun gear drum.
5. Install the snapring.
6. Install the one-way clutch inner and outer races to the sun gear drum.

NOTE: Align the splines of the one-way clutch inner race and small sun gear clutch hub.

7. Install the snapring.

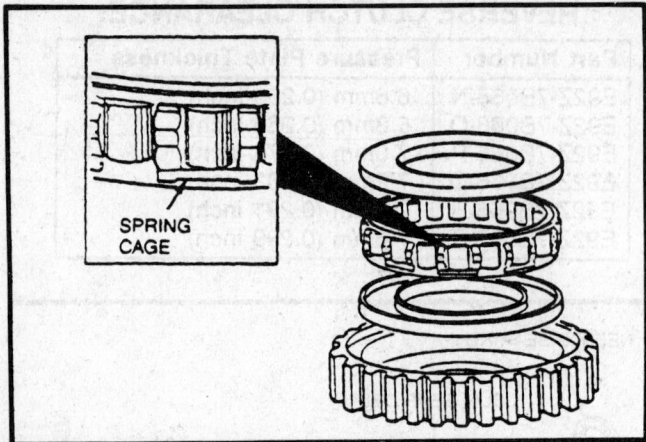

Spring cage should face toward outer race

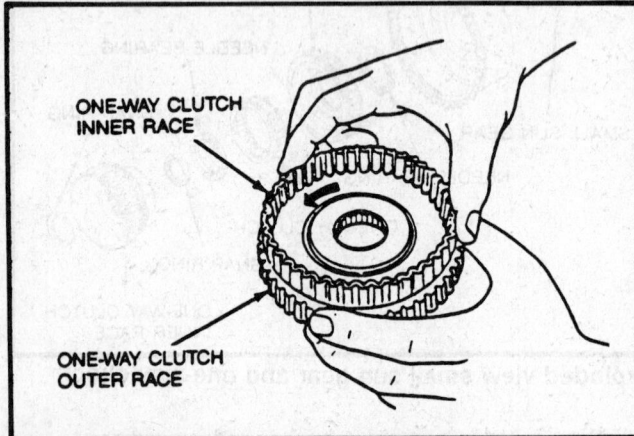

ONE-WAY CLUTCH INNER RACE

ONE-WAY CLUTCH OUTER RACE

Inner race turns only counterclockwise

8. Hold the small sun gear and make sure that the one-way clutch outer race turns smoothly and only clockwise.

9. Apply petroleum jelly to the needle bearing and install it to the sun gear drum. The outer diameter is 2.83 in.

ONE-WAY CLUTCH AND PLANETARY CARRIER ASSEMBLY

Disassembly

1. Remove the one-way clutch.
2. Remove the thrust washers.
3. Remove the snapring.
4. Remove the planetary carrier assembly from the inner race.
5. Place the one-way clutch on the inner race and make sure that the one-way clutch rotates smoothly and only clockwise.

Inspection

1. Check the inner race, thrust washers and gears for damage or wear.
2. Replace as necessary.

Assembly

1. Assemble the planetary carrier assembly to the inner race.
2. Install the snapring.
3. Apply petroleum jelly to the thrust washers and install them on the one-way clutch and planetary carrier assembly. The

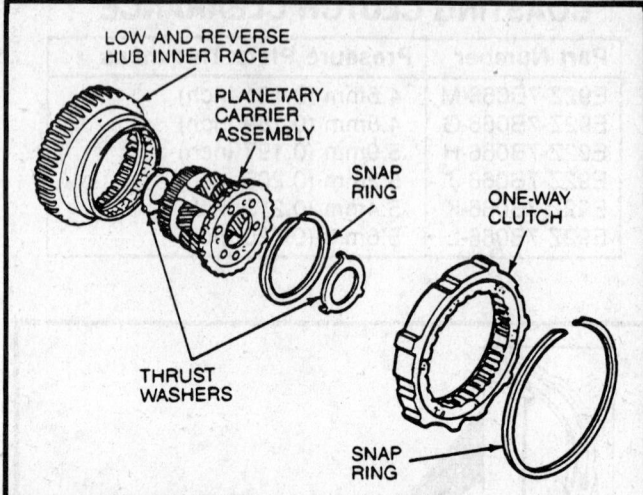

Exploded view of one-way clutch and planetary carrier

outer diameter of the sun gear drum side should be 2.83 in. for the sun gear drum side and 2.21 in. for the 3–4 clutch side.

4. Install the one-way clutch.

3–4 CLUTCH

Disassembly

1. Remove the needle bearings.
2. Remove the snapring.
3. Remove the pressure plate.
4. Remove the 3–4 clutch pack.
5. Install clutch spring compressor T65L–77515–A or equivalent and compress the return spring and retainer assembly.
6. Remove the snapring.
7. Remove the spring compressor.
8. Remove the return spring and retainer assembly.
9. Remove the 3–4 clutch piston using compressed air applied through Leak check adapter T88C–77000–JH or equivalent.
10. Remove the inner and outer seals from the 3–4 clutch piston.

Inspection

1. Check the drive and driven plates for damage or wear. The minimum thickness should be 0.055 in.
2. Check the clutch piston and clutch drum and seal contact areas for damage.
3. Check for broken or worn springs. The free length of each spring should be 1.307 in. Replace as necessary.

Assembly

1. Apply the specified transaxle fluid to the inner and outer seals and install them onto the 3–4 clutch piston.
2. Install the 3–4 clutch piston by pushing evenly around the circumference.
3. Install the return spring and retainer assembly.
4. Install clutch spring compressor T65L–77515–A or equivalent and compress the return spring and retainer assembly.
5. Install the snapring.
6. Remove the clutch spring compressor.
7. Install the 3–4 clutch pack.
8. Install the pressure plate with the step facing upward.
9. Install the snapring.
10. Use a feeler gauge to check the 3–4 clutch clearance. Measure between the snapring and the pressure plate.

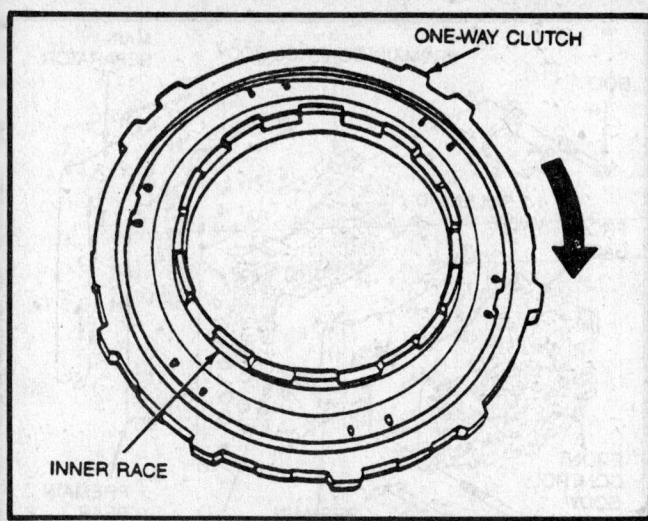

One-way clutch should rotate only clockwise

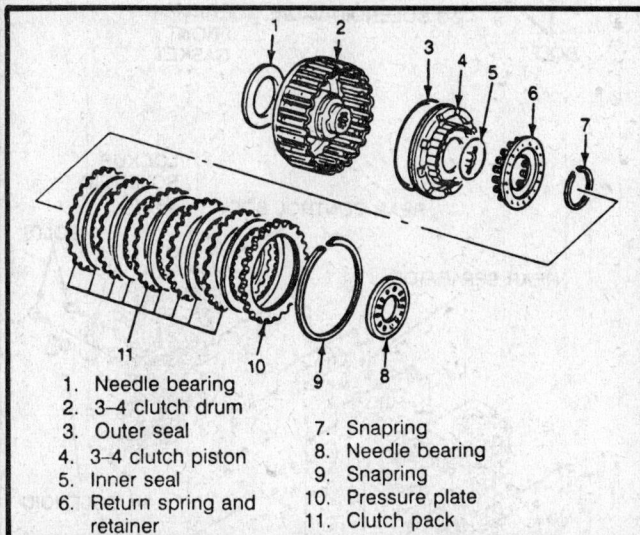

1. Needle bearing
2. 3–4 clutch drum
3. Outer seal
4. 3–4 clutch piston
5. Inner seal
6. Return spring and retainer
7. Snapring
8. Needle bearing
9. Snapring
10. Pressure plate
11. Clutch pack

Exploded view of 3–4 clutch

11. If the clearance is not within 0.051–0.059 in., adjust it by selecting a proper pressure plate.

12. Apply petroleum jelly to the needle bearings and install them on the 3–4 clutch. The outer diameter is 2.21 in. for the planetary carrier side and 2.84 in. for the output shell side.

13. Install Leak check adapter T88C–787000–JH or equivalent and apply compressed air to check operation.

NOTE: Do not apply over 57 psi of air pressure.

13. Pour the specified transaxle fluid into the clutch drum so the 3–4 clutch piston is fully submerged. Appy compressed air to check that no bubbles come from the clutch piston seal.

NOTE: Do no apply over 57 psi of air pressure. Do not apply the air pressure for more than few seconds.

2–3 ACCUMULATOR

Disassembly

1. Remove the snapring while holding in the stopper plug.
2. Remove the stopper plug.
3. Remove the spring.
4. Remove the piston.

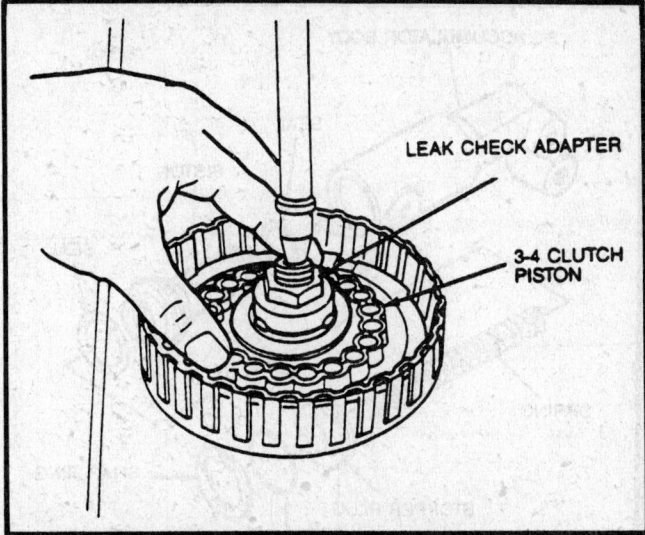

Removing 3–4 clutch piston using special tool

3–4 CLUTCH CLEARANCE

Part Number	Pressure Plate Thickness
E92Z-7B066-T	4.0mm (0.157 inch)
E92Z-7B066-U	4.2mm (0.165 inch)
E92Z-7B066-V	4.4mm (0.173 inch)
E92Z-7B066-W	4.6mm (0.181 inch)
E92Z-7B066-X	4.8mm (0.189 inch)

5. Remove the O-ring from the stopper plug.
6. Remove the seals from the piston.

Inspection

1. Check for a damaged or worn piston or stopper plug.
2. Check for a broken or worn spring. The spring free length for non-turbocharged vehicles should be 3.280 in. The spring free length for turbocharged vehicles should be 2.968 in.

Assembly

1. Apply the specified transaxle fluid to the seals and install them on the piston.
2. Apply the specified transaxle fluid to the O-ring and install it on the stopper plug.
3. Install the piston.
4. Install the spring.
5. Install the stopper plug.
6. Install the snapring while holding in the stopper plug.

VALVE BODY ASSEMBLY

Disassembly

NOTE: Each valve body bolt has a letter on the bolt head which matches the letter placed near the bolt hole. The bolts must be installed in the correct order.

1. Remove the 3–4 solenoid valve.
2. Remove the lockup solenoid valve.
3. Remove the 1–2 solenoid valve.
4. Remove the 2–3 solenoid valve.
5. Remove the brackets and wire harness.
6. Remove the fluid strainers.

NOTE: Do not turn the throttle valve adjusting screw in the main control body.

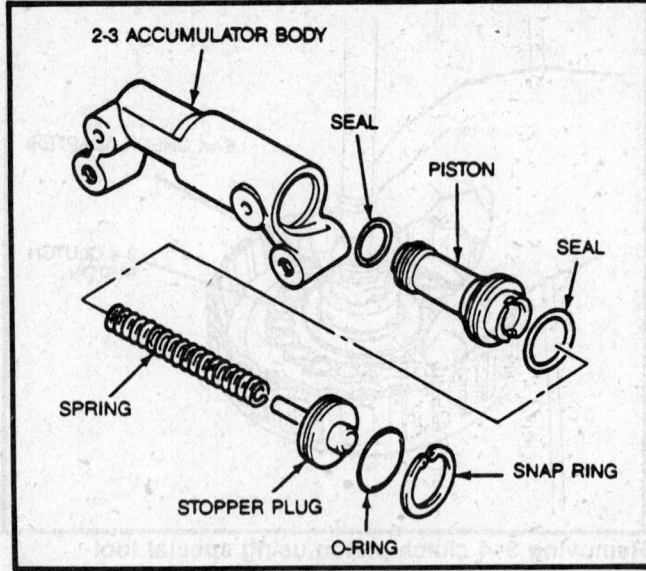

Exploded view of 2–3 accumulator

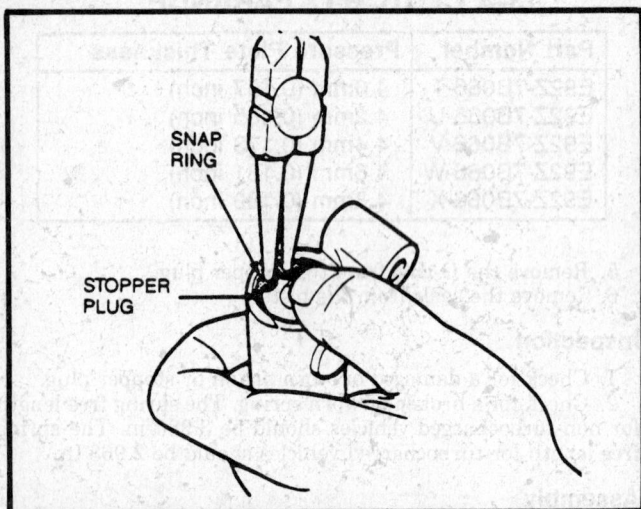

Removing snapring from accumulator

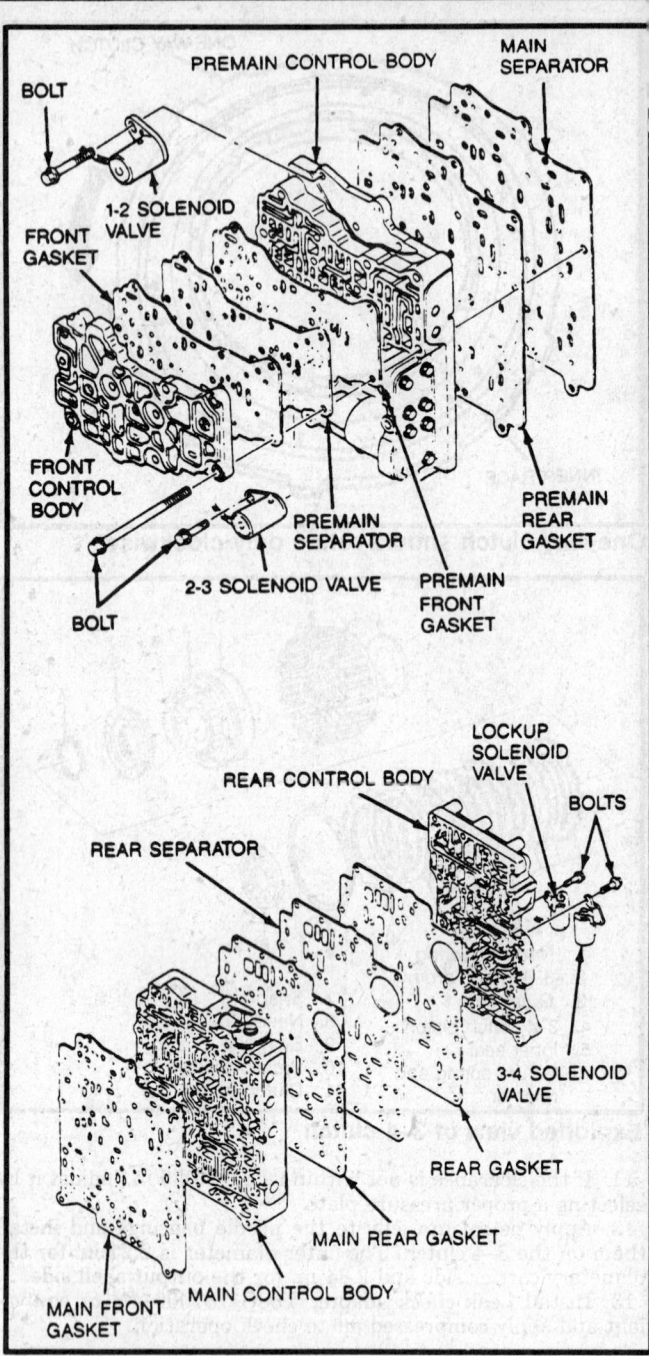

Exploded view valve body

7. Remove the O-rings.
8. Remove the front control body bolts.
9. Remove the front control body with the premain separator as a unit.
10. Remove the premain separator and front gasket from the front control body.
11. Remove the relief valve (0.031 in. orifice) and spring from the premain control body.
12. Remove the premain control body bolts, including the hexagonal head bolt.
13. Remove the premain control body and main separator as a unit.
14. Remove the premain rear gasket, main front gasket and main separator from the premain control body.
15. Remove the relief valves (0.079 in. orifice) and springs from the premain control body.
16. Remove the check ball and spring from the premain control body.
17. Remove the relief valve (0.031 in. orifice) and spring from the main control body.
18. Remove the check ball and spring from the main control body.

19. Turn the assembly over and remove rear control body bolts.
20. Remove the rear control body and rear separator as a unit.
21. Remove the main rear gasket, rear gasket and rear separator from the rear control body.
22. Remove the relief valves (0.039 in.; 0.059 in; 0.078 in. orifice) and springs from the rear control body.
23. Remove the relief valve (0.098 in. orifice) and spring from the main control body.
24. Remove the ruber ball from the main control body.

NOTE: The premain, main, rear control body individual valves and springs are removed by removing the retaining clips and bore plugs. Some valves are aluminum

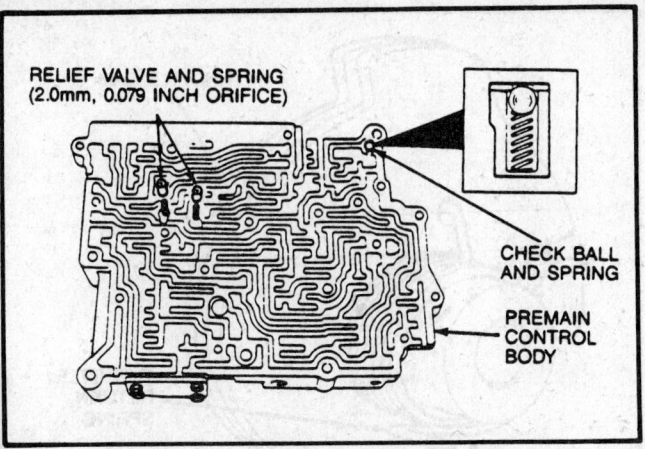

Check ball location—premain control body

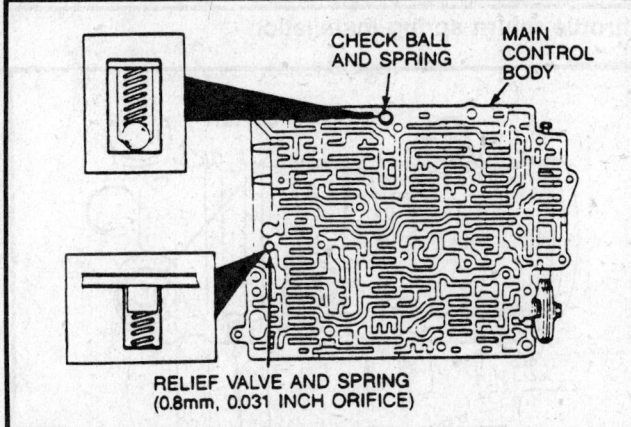

Check ball location—main control body

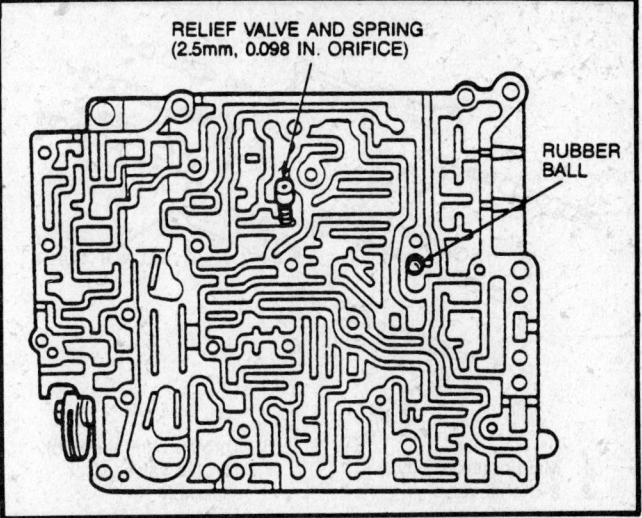

Rubber ball location—main control body

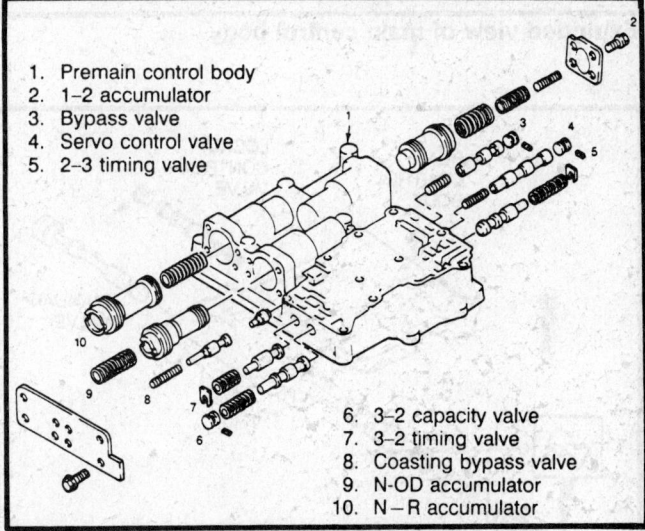

1. Premain control body
2. 1–2 accumulator
3. Bypass valve
4. Servo control valve
5. 2–3 timing valve
6. 3–2 capacity valve
7. 3–2 timing valve
8. Coasting bypass valve
9. N–OD accumulator
10. N–R accumulator

Exploded view of premain control body

and cannot be removed using a magnet. Remove these valves by tapping the valve body of the palm of the hand to slide the valve out of the bore. It may be necessary to remove the valves and springs using a pick. If so, use extreme care to prevent damaging valves or valve bores.

Inspection

1. Clean all parts thoroughly in clean solvent and blow dry with compressed air.
2. Inspect all valve and plug bores for scores. Check all fluid passages for obstructions. Inspect all mating surfaces for burrs and scores. If needed, use crocus cloth to polish valve and plugs. Avoid rounding the sharp edges of the valves and plugs with the crocus cloth.
3. Inspect all springs for distortion. Check all valves and plugs for free movement in their respective bores. Valve and plugs, when dry, must fall from their own weight into their respective bores.
4. Roll the manual valve on a flat surface to check for a bent condition. Replace any parts as necessary.

Assembly

MAIN CONTROL BODY

NOTE: When installing the throttle valve assembly, make sure that the groove is aligned with the bolt hole.

1. Install the throttle return spring on the throttle cam.
2. Tighten the throttle cam bolt to 69–95 inch lbs..

PREMAIN CONTROL BODY

1. Tighten the N–R/N–OD accumulator plate to 57–69 inch lbs.
2. Tighten the 1–2 accumulator plate to 57–69 inch lbs.
3. Do not install the bolt which holds the harness bracket.

VALVE BODY

NOTE: Do not mix up the gaskets during assembly. Match the bolt head letter with the corresponding letter on the valve body.

1. Install the relief valves (0.039 in.; 0.059 in.; 0.078 in. orifice) and springs in the rear control body.
2. Install the gaskets on both sides of the rear separator, then install it onto the rear control body.

NOTE: The rear gasket and main rear gasket are not interchangeable.

3. Install the relief valve (0.098 in. orifice) and spring in the main control body.
4. Install the rubber ball in the main control body.

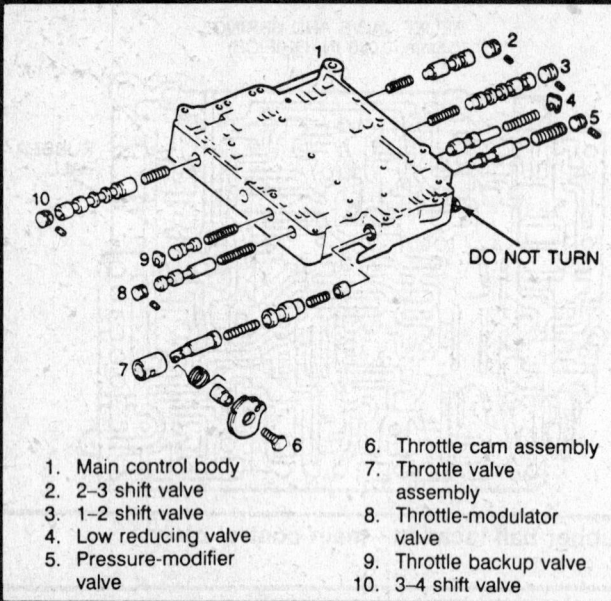

1. Main control body
2. 2–3 shift valve
3. 1–2 shift valve
4. Low reducing valve
5. Pressure-modifier valve
6. Throttle cam assembly
7. Throttle valve assembly
8. Throttle-modulator valve
9. Throttle backup valve
10. 3–4 shift valve

Exploded view of main control body

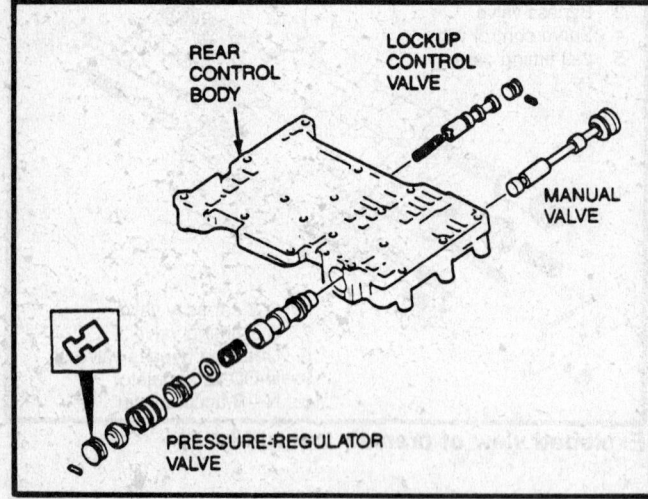

Exploded view of rear control body

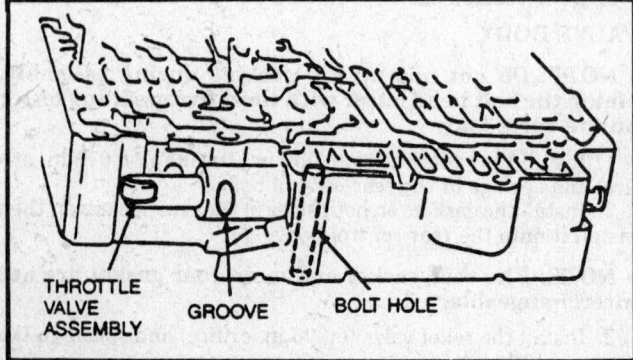

Installing throttle valve assembly

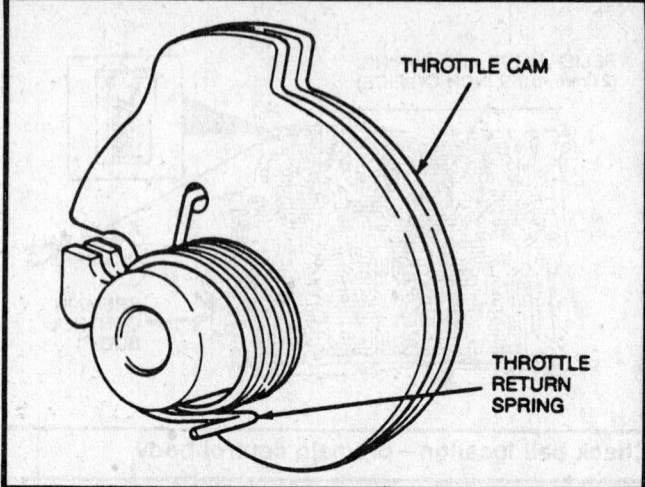

Throttle return spring installation

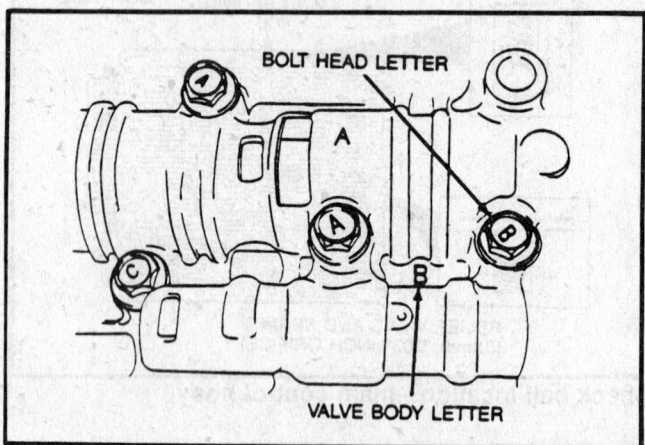

Installing bolts in valve body

5. Install the rear control body to the main control body.
6. Loosely tighten the rear control body bolts.

NOTE: Match the bolt head letter with the letter on the valve body.

7. Turn the assembly over and install the relief valve (0.031 in. orifice) and spring in the main control body.
8. Install the check ball and spring in the main control body.
9. Install the relief valves (0.079 in. orifice) and springs into the premain control body.
10. Install the check ball and spring in the premain control body.
11. Install the gaskets on both sides of the main separator, then install it onto the premain control body.

NOTE: The premain rear gasket and main front gasket are not interchangeable.

12. Set the premain control body onto the main control body.
13. Loosely tighten the premain control body bolts, including the hexagonal head bolt.
14. Install the relief valve (0.031 in. orifice and spring into the premain control body.
15. Install the gaskets on both sides of the premain separator, then install it onto the front control body.

NOTE: The front gasket and premain front gasket are not interchangeable.

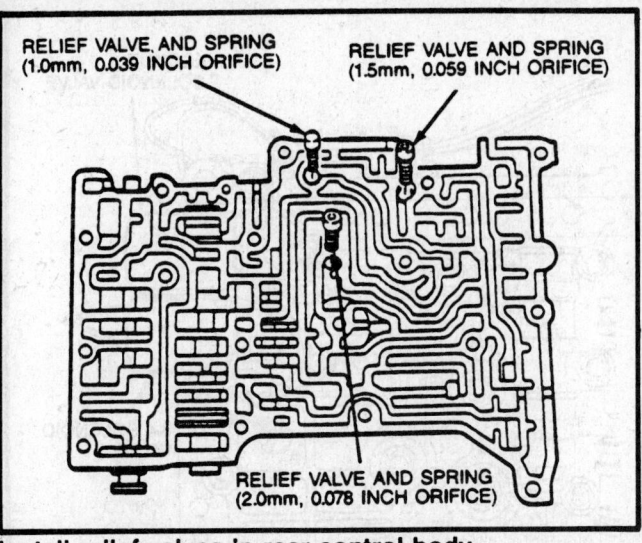

Install relief valves in rear control body

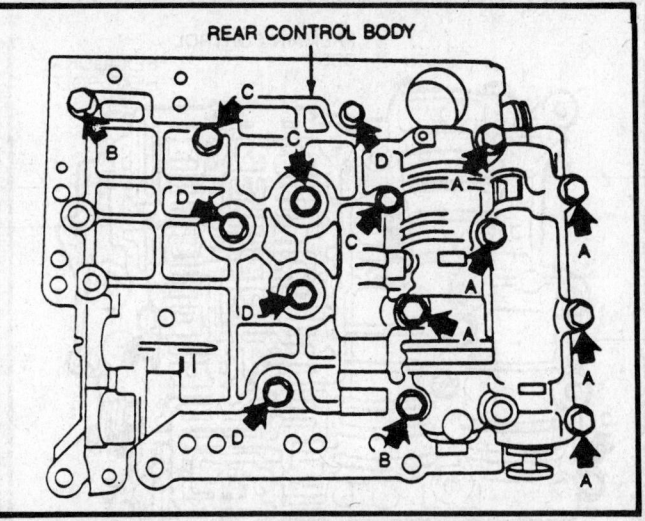

Bolt installation—rear control body

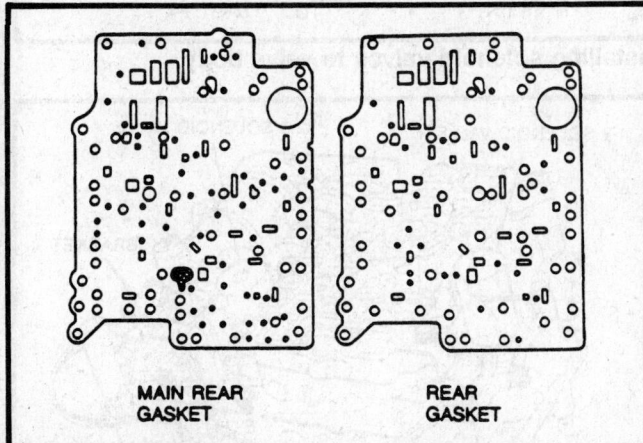

Valve body gasket

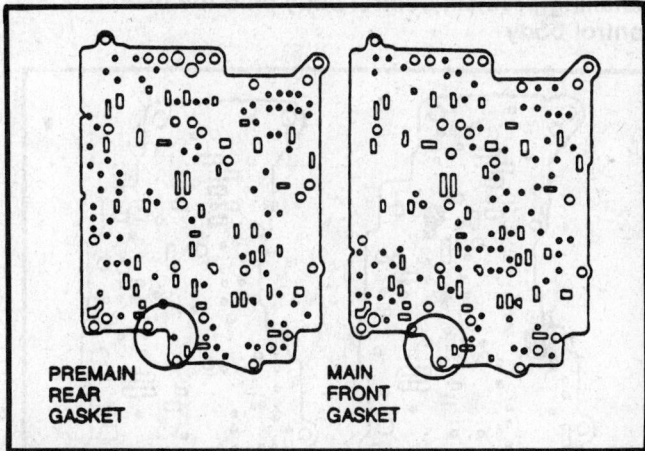

Valve body gasket

16. Install the front control body on the premain control body.
17. Loosely tighten the front control body bolts.

NOTE: Match the bolt head letter with the letter on the valve body.

18. Install 2 valve body mounting bolts for alignment.
19. Tighten the bolts on the front face of the valve body to 57–69 inch lbs.
20. Tighten the bolts on the rear face of the valve body to 57–69 inch lbs.
21. Install new fluid strainers.
22. Install new O-rings on the solenoid valves.
23. Install the 3–4 solenoid valve.
24. Install the lockup solenoid valve.
25. Tighten the solenoid valve bolts to 57–69 inch lbs.
26. Install the 1–2 solenoid valve.
27. Install the 2–3 solenoid valve.
28. Tighten the solenoid valve bolts to 57–69 inch lbs.
29. Install the brackets and wire harness.

DIFFERENTIAL

Disassembly

1. Remove the roll pin.
2. Remove the pinion shaft.

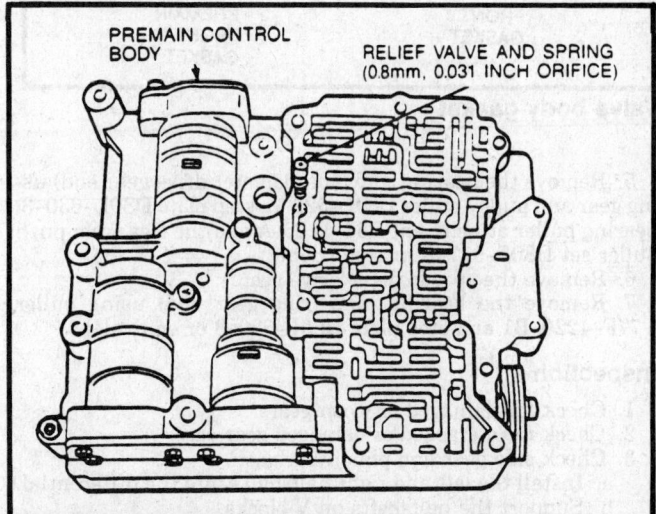

Install relief valve in premain control body

3. Remove the pinions and thrust washers by rotating them out of the gear case.
4. Remove the side gears and thrust washers.

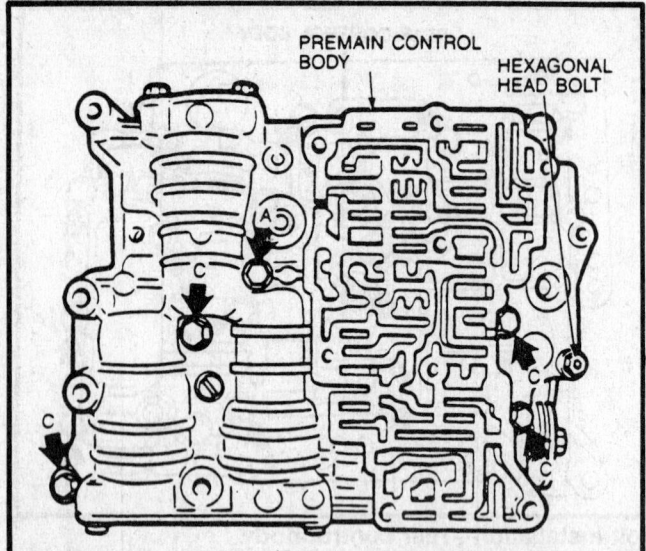

Installing premain control body onto the main control body

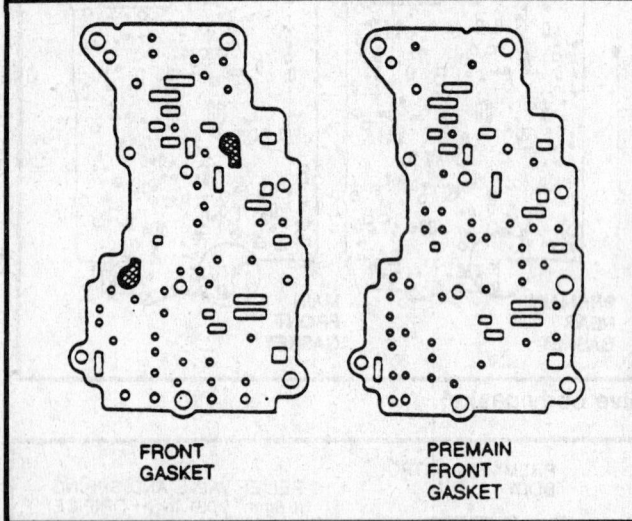

Valve body gasket

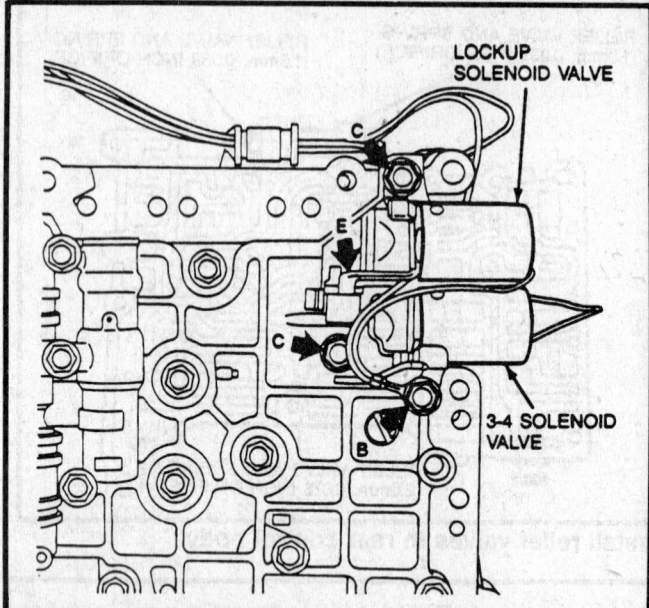

Installing solenoid valves to valve body

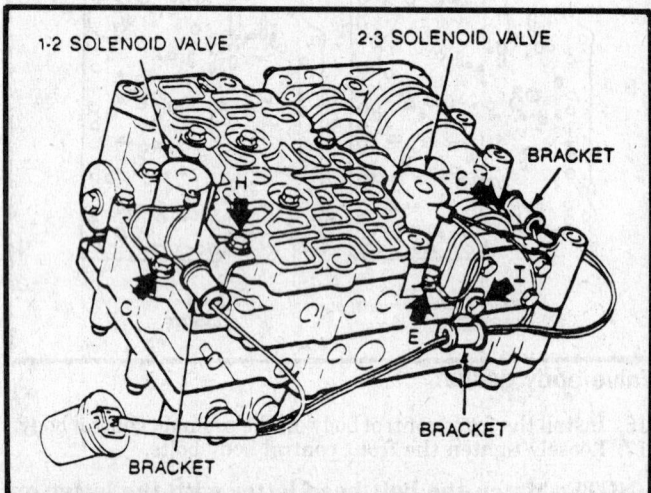

Installing solenoid valves to valve body

5. Remove the bearing core (speedometer drive gear end) using gear and pulley puller D80L–522–A, step plate D80L–630–3, bearing puller attachment D84–1123–A and the legs from push puller set D80L–927–A or equivalent.

6. Remove the speedometer drive gear.

7. Remove the bearing cone (ring gear end) using puller T77F–4220–B1 and step plate D80L–630–3 or equivalent.

Inspection

1. Check for damaged or worn gears.
2. Check for a cracked or damaged gear case.
3. Check side gear and pinion backlash.
   a. Install the left and right halfshafts into the differential.
   b. Support the halfshafts on V-blocks.
   c. Use dial indicator tool 4201–C with magnetic base/flex arm D78P–4201–C or equivalent to measure the backlash of both pinion gears. If the backlash is more then allowable, select a thrust washer with a different thickness. The backlash should be 0–0.004 in.

Assembly

NOTE: Whenever a bearing cone is removed, it must be replaced.

1. Install the speedomter drive gear and bearing cone using either driver handle T80T–4000–W or a press and differential bearing cone replacer T88C–77000–EH or equivalent.

2. Install the bearing cone (ring gear end) using either driver handle T80T–4000–W or a press and bearing cone replacer T88C–77000–EH or equivalent.

3. Install the thrust washers and pinions.

4. Install the pinion shaft.

5. Install the knock pin, then crimp it so that it cannot come out of the gear case.

6. Install the thrust washers and side gears.

OUTPUT GEAR

Disassembly

1. Remove the seal rings.

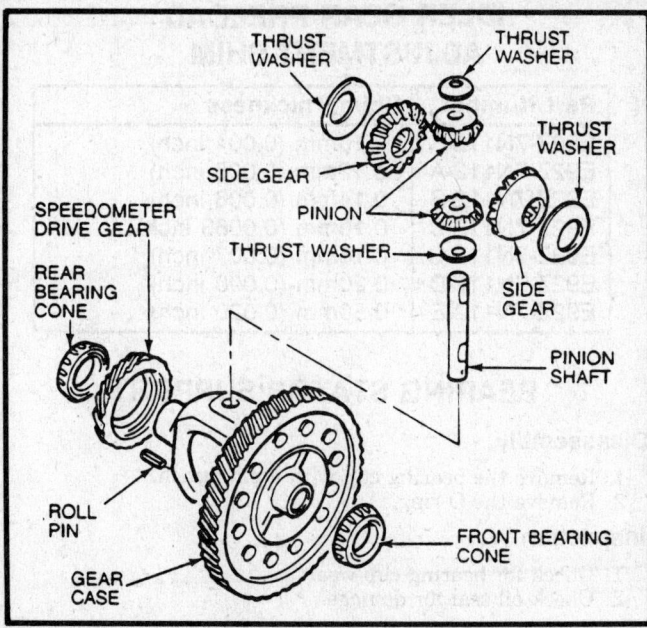

Exploded view of differential assembly

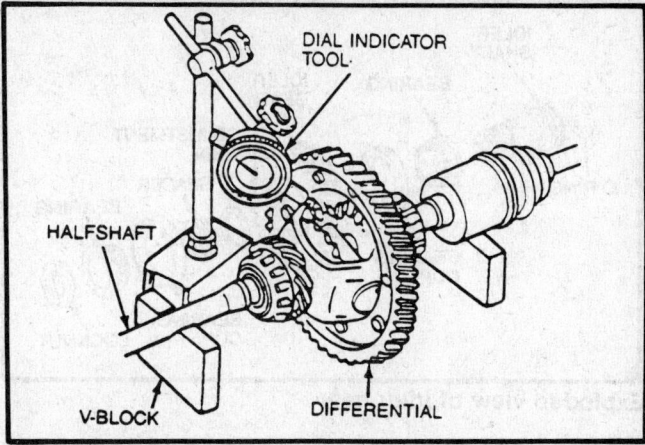

Checking side gear and pinion backlash

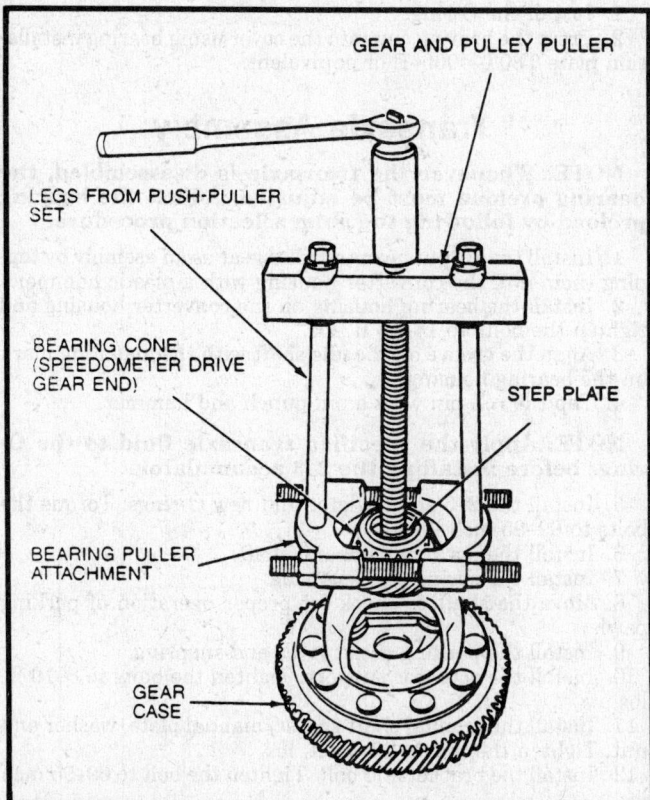

Removing the bearing cone – speedometer drive gear end

2. Press off the output gear bearings using step plate D80L–630–4 and puller D84L–1123–A or equivalent.

Inspection

1. Check for worn or damaged teeth or O-ring.
2. Check for worn or damaged seals.

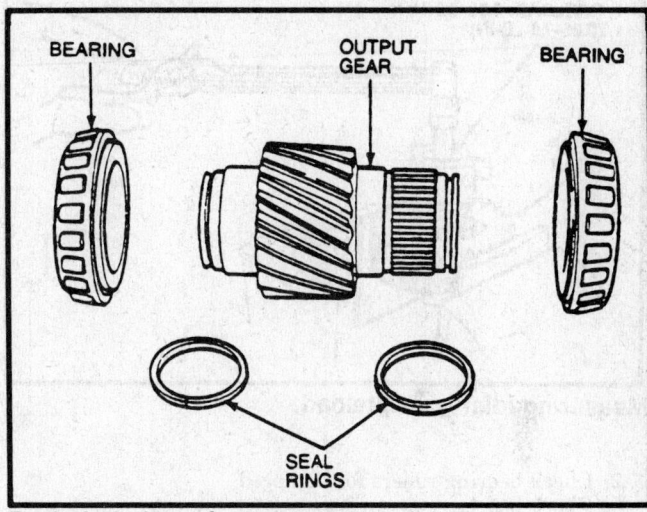

Exploded view of output gear

Assembly

1. Press on the output gear bearings using step plate D80L–630–4, bearing cone replacer T88T–7025–B and bearing installation plate T75L–1165–B or equivalent.
2. Install the seal rings.

IDLER GEAR

Disassembly

1. Secure the idler shaft in a vise using torque adapter T87C–77000–E or equivalent.
2. Remove the locknut using socket T88T–7025–A along with a 1⅝ inch socket or equivalent.
3. Remove the bearing.
4. Remove the spacer.
5. Remove the idler gear from the idler shaft.
6. Remove the adjustment shim.
7. Remove the other bearing.
8. Remove a bearing cup from the idler gear using puller D80L–943–A and slide hammer T50T–100–A or equivalent.
9. Press out the other bearing cup using step plate D80L–630–11 or equivalent.

Inspection

1. Check for worn or damaged gears.

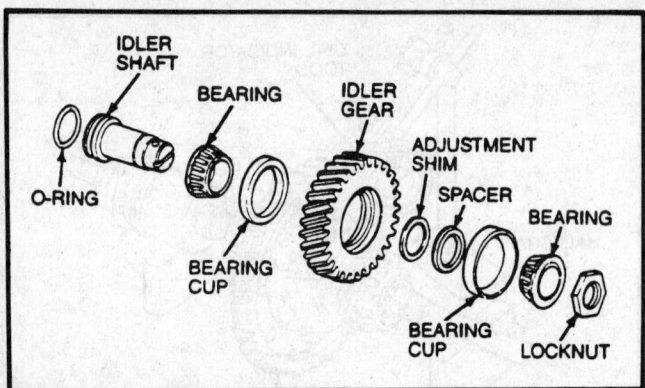

Exploded view of idler gear

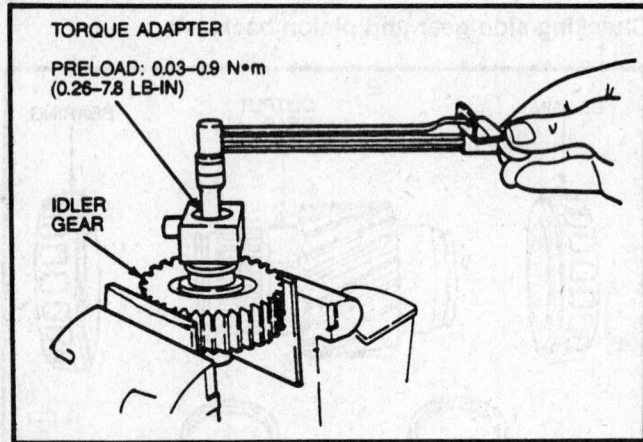

Measuring idler gear preload

2. Check bearing rollers for damaged.
3. Check bearing cups wear.

Assembly

1. Press the bearing cups into the idler gear using bearing installation plate T80T–4000–E or equivalent.
2. Install the bearing onto the idler shaft.
3. Install the adjust shim.
4. Install the spacer.
5. Install the idler gear.
6. Install the other idler gear bearing.
7. Secure the idler shaft in a vise using torque adapter T87C–77000–E or equivalent.
8. Tighten locknut to 94 ft. lbs. using socket T88T–7025–A along with a 1⅝ in. socket or equivalent.
9. Turn the idler gear and adapter over and secure the gear in a vise. Use protective plates to prevent damage to the idler gear.
10. Attach a inch lbs. torque wrench and measure the preload while tightening the locknut to 94–130 ft. lbs. The preload should be 0.26–7.8 inch lbs.

NOTE: Read the preload when the idler shaft starts to turn.

11. If the specified preload is not reached within the specified tightening torque, select an appropriate adjustment shim(s).

NOTE: The preload can be reduced by increasing the thickness of the shims, or increased by reducing the thickness of the shims. Do not use more than 7 shims.

IDLER GEAR PRELOAD ADJUSTMENT SHIM

Part Number	Shim Thickness
E92Z-7N112-F	0.10mm (0.004 inch)
E92Z-7N112-A	0.12mm (0.005 inch)
E92Z-7N112-B	0.14mm (0.006 inch)
E92Z-7N112-C	0.16mm (0.0063 inch)
E92Z-7N112-G	0.18mm (0.007 inch)
E92Z-7N112-D	0.20mm (0.008 inch)
E92Z-7N112-E	0.50mm (0.020 inch)

BEARING STATOR SUPPORT

Disassembly

1. Remove the bearing cup with a pin punch.
2. Remove the O-ring.

Inspection

1. Check for bearing cup wear.
2. Check oil seal for damage.

Assembly

1. Install the O-ring.
2. Press the bearing cup into the cover using bearing installation plate T80T–4000–E or equivalent.

Transaxle Assembly

NOTE: Whenever the transaxle is disassembled, the bearing preload must be adjusted. Adjust the bearing preload by following the shim selection procedure.

1. Install the output gear and idler gear as an asembly by tapping them into the converter housing with a plastic hammer.
2. Install the bearing housing on the converter housing and tighten the bolts to 14–19 ft. lbs.
3. Align the groove on the idle shaft with the matching mark on the bearing housing.
4. Tap the roll pin with a pin punch and hammer.

NOTE: Apply the specified transaxle fluid to the O-rings before installing the 2–3 accumulator.

5. Install the 2–3 accumulator and new O-rings. Torque the bolts to 69–95 inch lbs.
6. Install the parking pawl and shaft.
7. Install the spring and snapring.
8. Move the shaft to check for proper operation of parking pawl.
9. Install the parking assist lever and snapring.
10. Install the actuator support. Tighten the bolts to 8–10 ft. lbs.
11. Install the manual shaft spacer, manual plate, washer and nut. Tighten the nut to 30–41 ft. lbs.
12. Install the bracket and bolt. Tighten the bolt to 69–95 inch lbs.
13. Install the detent ball, spring, washer and plug. Tighten plug to 8.7–13 ft. lbs.
14. Attach seal protector T88C–77000–GH or equivalent to the low and reverse clutch piston.
15. Install the low and reverse clutch piston by pushing evenly around the circumference. Remove the protector.

NOTE: Be careful not to damage the outer seal.

16. Install the return spring and retainer.
17. Compress the return spring and retainer using return

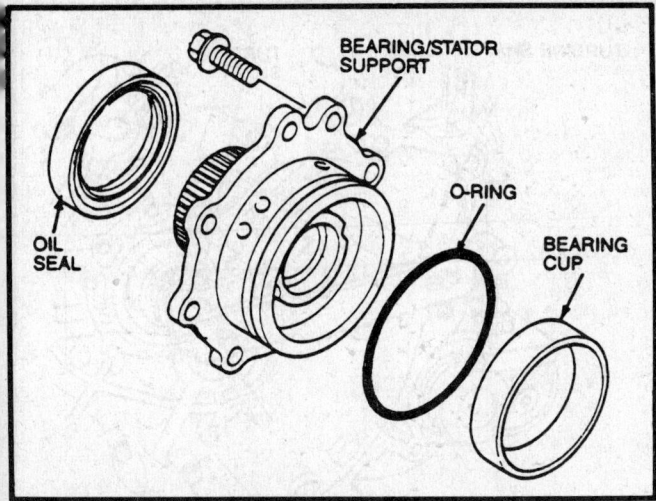

Exploded view of bearing stator support

spring compressor T88C–77000–AH and the plate from T87C–77000–B or equivalent.

18. Install the snapring.
19. Remove the return spring compressor.
20. Pour the specified transaxle fluid over the low and reverse clutch piston until it is fully submerged. Check that no bubbles appear from between the piston and seals when applying compressed air through the fluid passage.

NOTE: The compressed air must be under 57 psi and not applied for more than a few seconds.

21. Install the output shell to the output gear.
22. Install the 2.83 in. thrust washer onto the output shell.
23. Apply a thin coat of silicon sealant to the contact surfaces of the converter housing and transaxle case.
24. Install new O-rings.
25. Install the transaxle case to the converter housing. Tighten the bolts to 27–38 ft. lbs.
26. Install transaxle plugs T88C–7025–AH or equivalent to the differential side gears.

NOTE: Failure to install the transaxle plugs may allow the differential side gears to become mispositioned.

27. Place the 3–4 clutch assembly over the turbine shaft.

NOTE: Be sure that the thrust washer and needle bearing are installed in the correct position.

28. Install the turbine shaft and 3–4 clutch assembly into the transaxle case.
29. Install turbine shaft holder T88C–77000–KH or equivalent and attach it to the turbine shaft.
30. Install the internal gear.
31. Install the internal gear snapring.

NOTE: Be sure the thrust washer and needle bearing are in the correct position before installing the carrier hub assembly.

32. Install the carrier hub assembly.
33. Install the low and reverse clutch pack, retaining plate and snapring.
34. Measure the clearance between the snapring and retaining plate. The clearance should be 0.083–0.094 in. If clearance is not with specification, adjust it by selecting a retaining plate with an appropriate thickness.
35. Install the one-way clutch.

NOTE: Turning the carrier hub assembly counterclockwise eases installation of the one-way clutch.

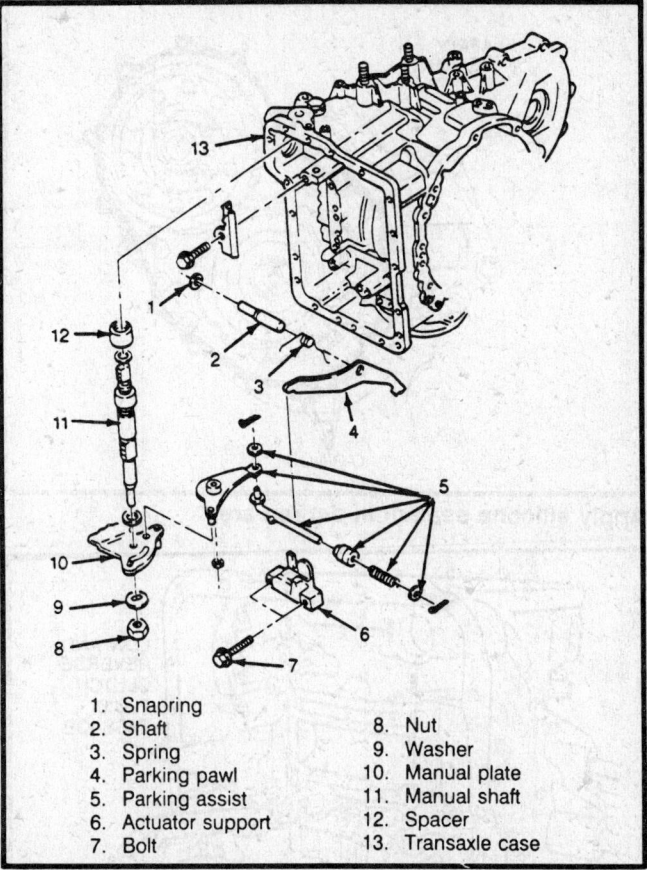

1. Snapring		
2. Shaft	8. Nut	
3. Spring	9. Washer	
4. Parking pawl	10. Manual plate	
5. Parking assist	11. Manual shaft	
6. Actuator support	12. Spacer	
7. Bolt	13. Transaxle case	

Exploded view of internal components in transaxle

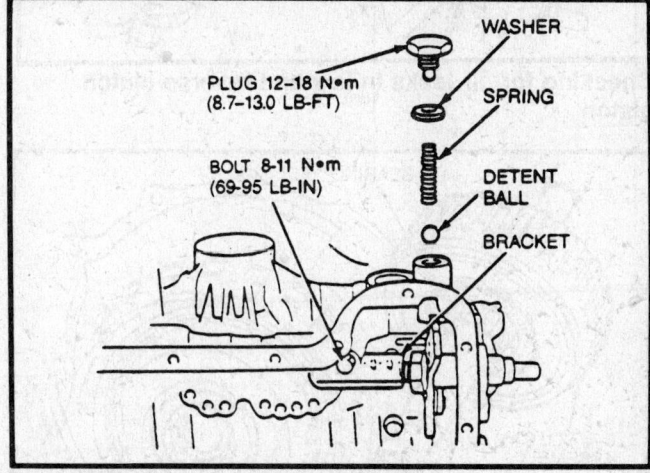

Exploded view of detent assembly

36. Install the one-way clutch snapring.
37. Install the servo spring and servo.
38. Compress the servo with a C-clamp.
39. Install the snapring, then remove the C-clamp.
40. Install the piston stem.
41. Install the anchor strut.
42. Install the 2–4 band in the transaxle case so it is fully expanded.

NOTE: Interlock the 2–4 band and anchor strut.

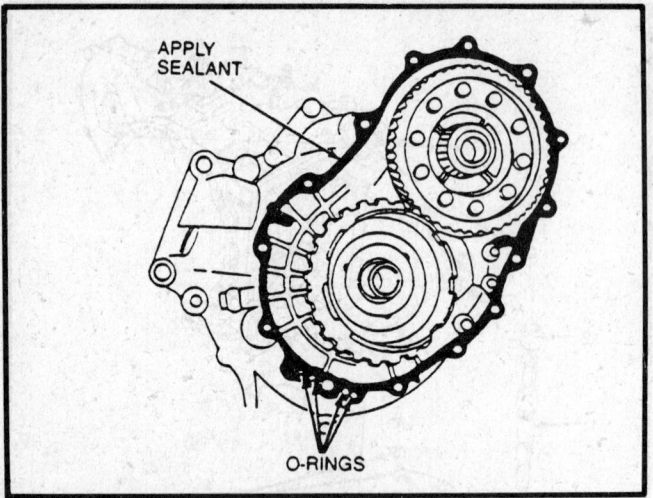

APPLY SEALANT

O-RINGS

Apply silicone sealant in darken area

LOW AND REVERSE CLUTCH FLUID PASSAGE

Checking for air leaks in low and reverse clutch piston

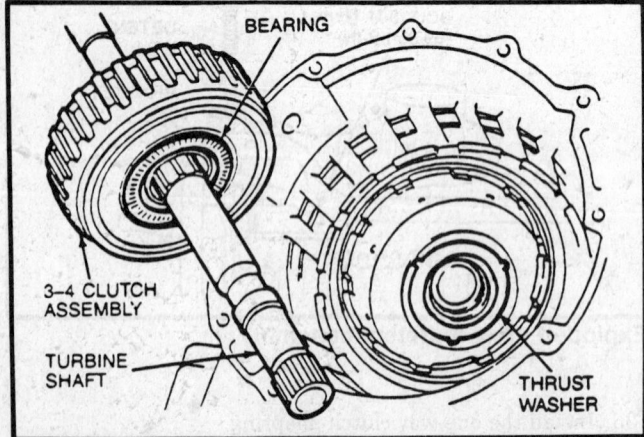

BEARING

3–4 CLUTCH ASSEMBLY

TURBINE SHAFT

THRUST WASHER

Installing the turbine shaft and 3–4 clutch assembly

43. Install the small gun gear and one-way clutch by rotating it.

NOTE: Be sure the thrust washer and needle bearing are installed in the correct position.

44. Pull the 2–4 band with a tool and install the piston stem in the correct position. Loosely tighten the piston stem by hand.

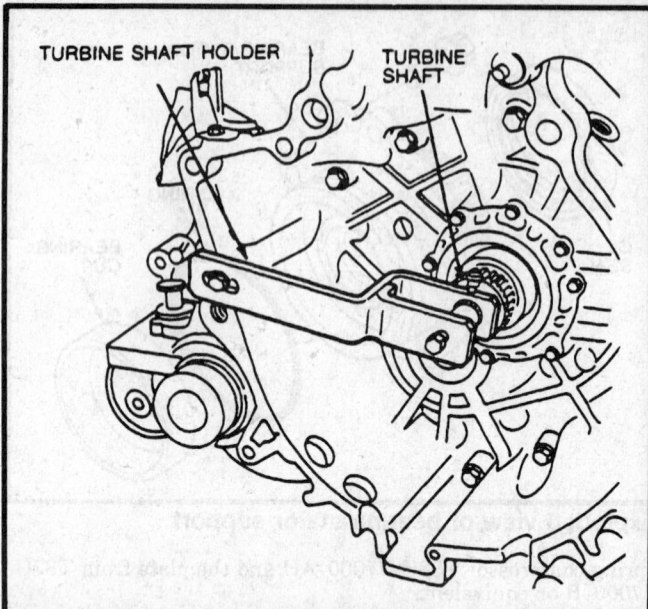

TURBINE SHAFT HOLDER

TURBINE SHAFT

Install special tool to turbine shaft

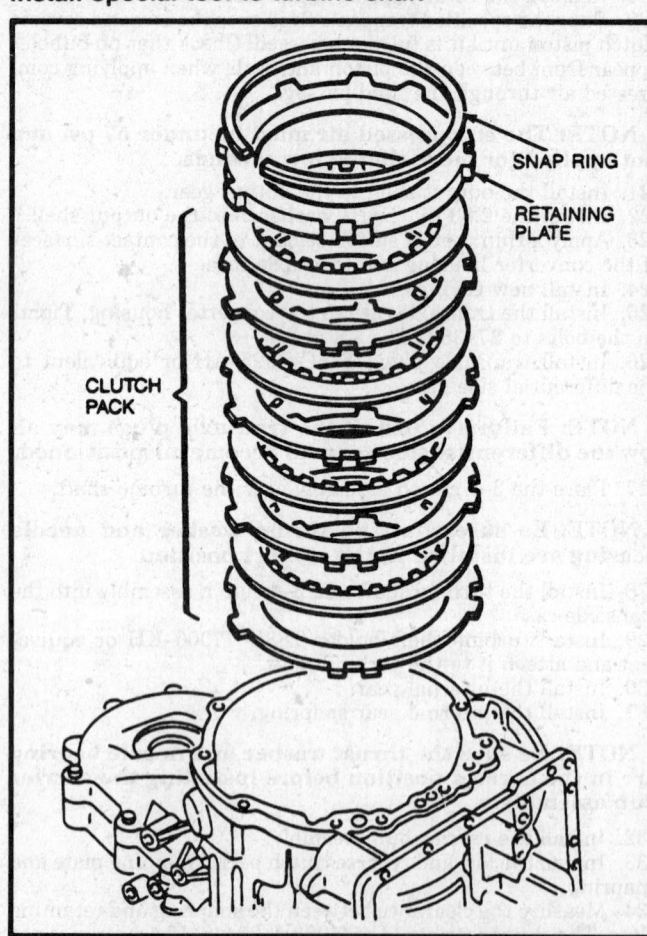

SNAP RING

RETAINING PLATE

CLUTCH PACK

Exploded view of low and reverse clutch pack

NOTE: Be sure the needle bearing is in the correct position before installing the clutch assembly.

45. Install the clutch assembly by rotating it.

LOW AND REVERSE CLUTCH PACK CLEARANCE

Part Number	Pressure Plate Thickness
E92Z-7B066-AD	6.8mm (0.268 inch)
E92Z-7B066-Y	7.0mm (0.276 inch)
E92Z-7B066-Z	7.2mm (0.283 inch)
E92Z-7B066-AA	7.4mm (0.291 inch)
E92Z-7B066-AB	7.6mm (0.299 inch)
E92Z-7B066-AC	7.8mm (0.307 inch)

46. Measure the height difference between the reverse and forward drum and transaxle case. The height difference should be 0.032 in.

47. Place the needle bearing on the clutch assembly.

48. To adjust the total endplay, remove the previous thrust washer and gasket from the oil pump. Place a 0.087 in. thrust washer on the oil pump.

49. Set the oil pump onto the clutch assembly. Measure the clearance between the transaxle case and the oil pump. Select a suitable thrust washer from the chart.

50. Remove the oil pump.

51. Place the selected thrust washer and a new gasket on the oil pump.

52. Install the oil pump onto the clutch assembly. Tighten bolts to 14–19 ft. lbs.

53. Loosen the locknut and tighten the piston stem to 78–95 inch lbs.

54. Loosen the piston stem 2 turns.

55. Tighten the locknut to 18–29 ft. lbs.

56. Install the oil strainer with a new O-ring to the transaxle. Tighten the bolts to 69–95 inch lbs.

NOTE: Be sure the magnets in the oil pan are correctly positioned.

57. Install the oil pan with a new gasket. Tighten bolts to 69–95 inch lbs.

58. Align the manual valve with the pin on the manual plate and install the valve body into the transaxle case. Tighten the bolts to 95–130 inch lbs.

59. Install the solenoid connector with a new O-ring in the transaxle case.

60. Install a new O-ring on the bracket, then feed the kickdown cable through the transaxle case and connect it to the throttle cam.

61. Install the kickdown cable attaching bolt and bracket. Tighten the attaching bolt to 69–95 inch lbs. and the bracket bolt to 14–19 ft. lbs.

62. Install the valve body cover with a new gasket. Tighten to 69–95 inch lbs.

63. Install the oil pipes, oil hoses and switch box as as assembly. Tighten the switch box bolts to 12–17 ft. lbs.

64. Install the harness clip and tighten to 69–95 inch lbs.

65. Install the ball, spring, new washers and plug. Tighten plug to 23–35 ft. lbs.

66. Install the solenoid connector.

67. Install the pulse generator and fluid temperature switch. Tighten the pulse generator bolt to 69–95 inch lbs. Tighten the fluid temperature switch to 22–29 ft. lbs.

68. Install the dipstick tube with a new O-ring. Tighten the bolts to 61–87 inch lbs.

69. Turn the manual shaft to the **N** detent position.

70. Install the neutral safety switch and loosely tighten the bolts.

71. Remove the screw and insert a 0.079 in. pin. Move the neutral safety switch until the pin engages the switch alignment hole.

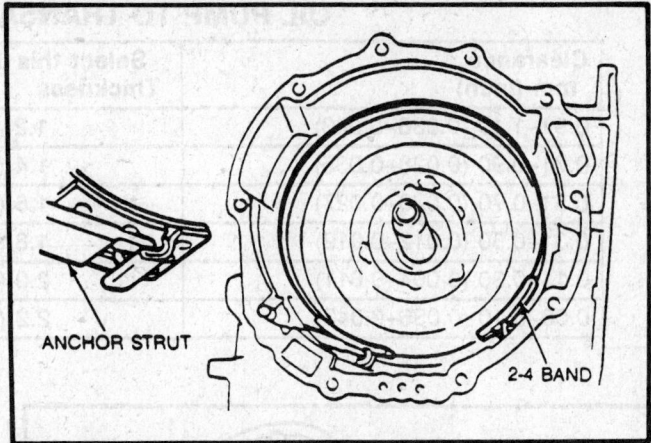

Interlock 2–4 band and anchor strut

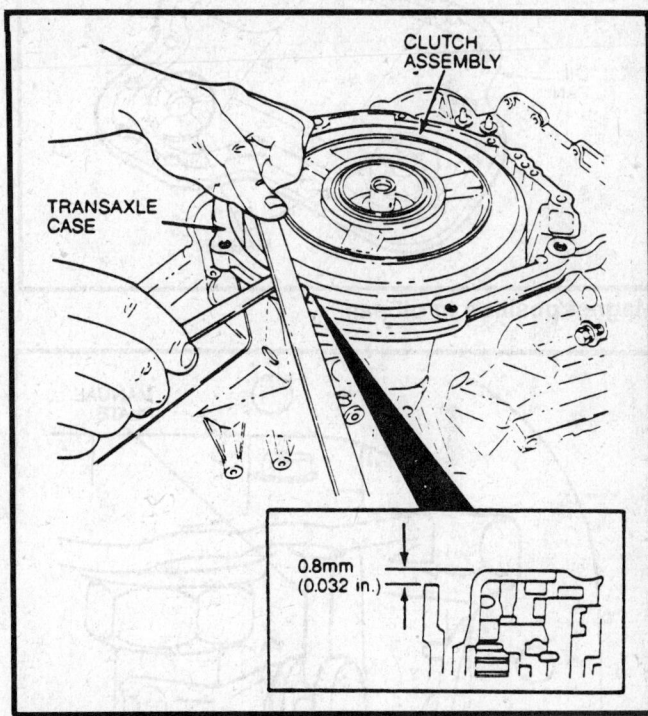

Measure the height between the reverse and forward drum and case

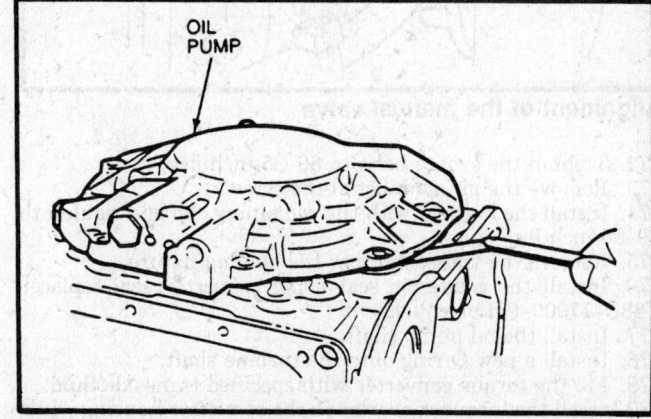

Measure clearance betwwen oil pump and case

OIL PUMP TO TRANSAXLE CASE CLEARANCE

Clearance mm (inch)	Select this Thrust Washer Thickness mm (inch)	Part Number
0.91–1.10 (0.036–0.043)	1.2 (0.047)	E92Z-7D014-E
0.71–0.90 (0.028–0.035)	1.4 (0.055)	E92Z-7D014-F
0.51–0.70 (0.020–0.027)	1.6 (0.063)	E92Z-7D014-A
0.31–0.50 (0.012–0.019)	1.8 (0.071)	E92Z-7D014-B
0.11–0.30 (0.004–0.011)	2.0 (0.078)	E92Z-7D014-C
0.00–0.10 (0.036–0.043)	2.2 (0.047)	E92Z-7D014-D

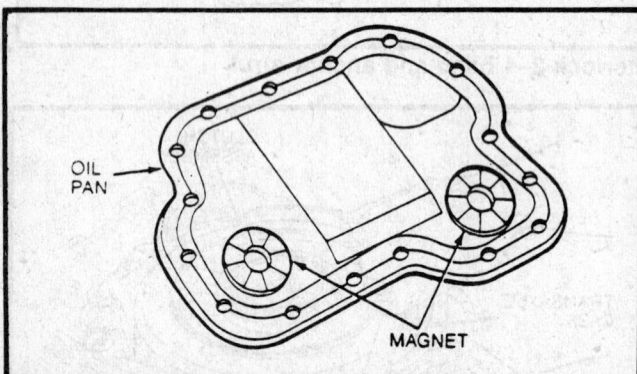

Magnet position in oil pan

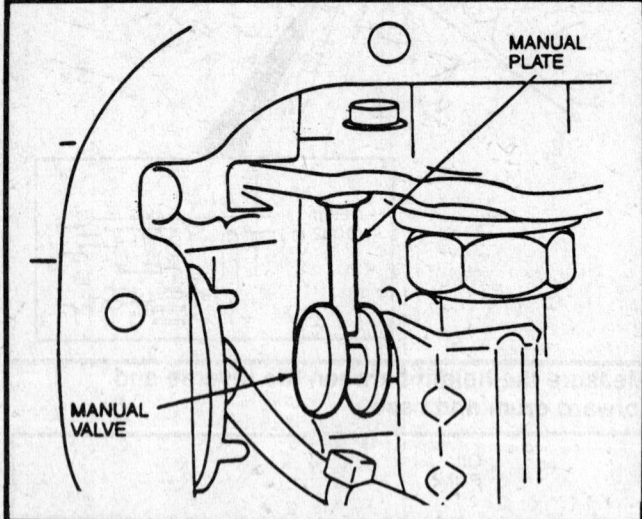

Alignment of the manual valve

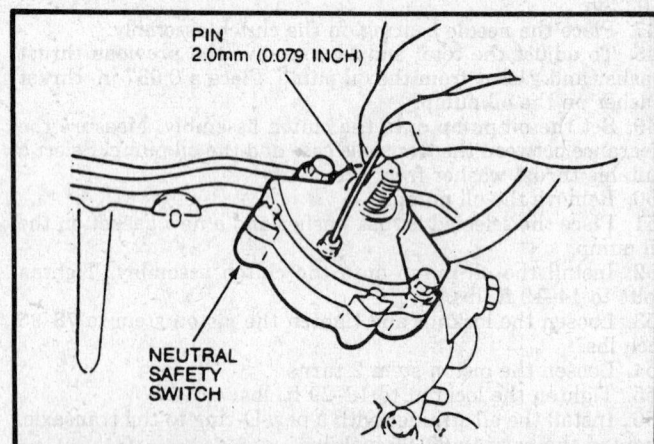

Alignment of the neutral switch

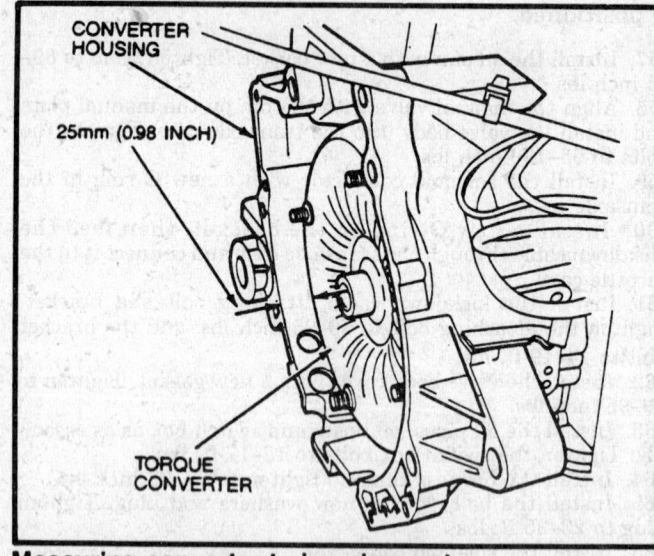

Measuring converter to housing end

72. Tighten the switch bolts to 69–95 inch lbs.
73. Remove the pin and install the screw.
74. Install the harness with the remaining clip and tighten to 69–95 inch lbs.
75. Remove the transaxle from the holding fixture.
76. Install the converter seal using converter seal replacer T88C–77000–BH or equivalent.
77. Install the oil pump shaft.
78. Install a new O-ring onto the turbine shaft.
79. Fill the torque converter with specified transaxle fluid.
80. Install the torque converter in the converter housing while rotating it to align the splines.

NOTE: Do not try to force the torque converter in, install it carefully in the transaxle.

81. Measure the distance between the torque converter and the end of the converter housing. The distance should be 0.98 in.
82. Install the right transaxle mount and tighten the bolts to 43–49 ft. lbs.
83. Install the differential oil seals using differential seal replacer T87C–77000–H or equivalent.

SPECIFICATIONS

Torque converter stall torque ratio		1.700 – 1.900:1
Gear ratio	First	2.800:1
	Second	1.540:1
	Third	1.000:1
	Fourth (OD)	0.700:1
	Reverse	2.333:1
Final gear ratio		3.700
Number of drive plates/ driven plates	Forward clutch	3/3
	Coasting clutch	2/2
	3–4 clutch	5/5
	Reverse clutch	2/2
	Low and reverse brake	4/4
Servo diameter (Piston outer dia./retainer inner dia.) mm (in.)		78mm/40mm (3.07 in./1.57 in.)
Transaxle Fluid	Type	Motorcraft MERCON or equivalent
	Capacity liters (U.S. qt., Imp. qt.)	6.8 liters (7.2 U.S. qt., 6.0 Imp. qt.)

TORQUE SPECIFICATIONS

Description	Ft. Lbs.	Inch Lbs.	Description	Ft. Lbs.	Inch Lbs.
Line pressure plug	–	43-87	2-3 accumulator	–	69-95
Bearing housing	14-19	–	Actuator support	8-10	–
Transaxle case to converter housing	27-38	–	Manual plate	30-41	–
Valve body	–	95-130	Oil pump	14-19	–
Transaxle to engine	66-86	–	Oil strainer	–	69-95
Center transaxle mount bolts	27-40	–	Oil pan	–	69-95
Center transaxle mount nuts	47-66	–	Throttle cable bracket	14-19	–
Transaxle to left mount	63-86	–	Switch box	12-17	–
Left mount to bracket	49-69	–	Oil line plug	23-35	–
Crossmember bolts	27-40	–	Pulse generator	–	69-95
Crossmember nuts	55-69	–	Fluid temperature switch	22-29	–
Right transaxle mount	63-86	–	Dipstick tube	–	61-87
Torque converter	32-45	–	Neutral safety switch	–	69-95
Converter cover	–	69-95	Throttle cam	–	69-95
Gusset plate to transaxle	27-38	–	Drain plug	29-43	–
Range sector to transaxle	22-29	–			

SPECIAL TOOLS

Tool Number	Description
T87C-77000-H	Differential seal replacer
T88C-7025-AH	Transaxle plug set
T88C-77000-AH	Return spring compressor
T88C-77000-BH	Converter seal replacer
T88C-77000-CH	Shim selection set
T88C-77000-DH	Preload torque adapter
T88C-77000-EH	Differential bearing cone replacer
T88C-77000-FH	Differential bearing cup replacer
T88C-77000-GH	Seal protector
T88C-77000-HH	Seal protector
T88C-77000-JH	Leak check adapter
T88C-77000-KH	Turbine shaft holder
T88C-77000-CH4	Screws
T88C-77000-CH5	Screws
D78P-4201-C	Magnetic base/flex arm
D80L-522-A	Puller
D80L-630-3	Step plate
D80L-630-4	Step plate
D80L-630-6	Step plate
D80L-630-10	Step plate
D80L-630-11	Step plate
D80L-927-A	Puller legs
T88C-77000-L	Torque adapter
D80L-943-A	Puller
D84L-1123-A	Puller
D87C-77000-A	Transmission test adapters
T87C-77000-J	Shim selection kit
D87L-6000-A	Engine support bar
T50T-100-A	Slide hammer

Model	Description
T57L-500-B	Bench mounting fixture
T57L-77820-A	Pressure gauge
T60K-4616-A	Bearing cup installer
T-65L-77515-A	Clutch spring compressor
T73L-2196-A	Puller body
T75L-1165-B	Bearing installation plate
T77F-1102-A	Puller
T80L-77003-A	Gauge bar
T80L-77100-A	Guide pins
T80T-4000-E	Bearing cup installation plate
T80T-4000-W	Driver handle
T86P-700043-A	Puller jaws
T87C-77000-E	Torque adapter
T88T-7025-A	Socket (55mm)
T88T-7025-B	Bearing cone replacer
TOOL-1175-AC	Puller
TOOL-4201-C	Dial indicator
T77F-4220-B1	Puller
007-00028	Super STAR II tester
059-00010	Inductive dwell-tach-volt-ohmmeter
007-00037	4EAT tester
055-00101	Tachometer
014-00737	Pressure tester
014-00456	Fittings
014-00210	Transmission jack
014-00028	Torque converter cleaner

Section 3

F3A Transaxle
Ford Motor Co.

APPLICATION

1989 Ford Festiva
1987–89 Mercury Tracer

GENERAL DESCRIPTION

The torque converter is located on the engine side and the oil pump is located on the other end of the transaxle. The front clutch, the rear clutch, front planetary and rear planetary gears are arranged in the respective order from the front, or oil pump end of the transaxle. During the section outline, the oil pump end will be referred to as the front and the converter end, or engine end, will be referred to as rear of the transaxle.

The control valve is located under the front clutch and the rear clutch assemblies. The governor is located on the outside of the case and responds to the speed of the output shaft to control operating oil pressure.

The low and reverse brake band is located on the outside of the rear planetary gears to shorten the total length of the transaxle.

The 3 shafts that are contained within the case are the oil pump driveshaft which transmit engine speed directly to the oil pump via a quill shaft inside the input shaft, the input shaft which transmits power from the torque converter turbine and drives the front clutch cover. The 3rd shaft is the output shaft which transmits power from the front planetary gear carrier and the rear planetary gear annulus, through the main drive idler gear to the differential drive gear.

Both the transaxle and the differential use a common sump with ATF fluid as the lubricant.

Transaxle and Converter Identification

TRANSAXLE

Identification tags are located on the front of the transaxle, under the oil cooler lines and identify the transaxle type and model.

CONVERTER

The torque converter is a welded unit and cannot be disassembled unless special tools are available for the purpose. A lockup torque converter is utilized, which consists of a lockup drive

plate containing centrifugally operated shoe, bracket and spring assemblies and a one-way clutch.

Metric Fasteners

Metric bolt sizes and thread pitches are used for all fasteners on the Jatco transaxle. The metric fastener dimensions are close to the dimensions of the familiar inch system fasteners and for this reason, replacement fasteners must have the same measurement and strength as those removed. Do no attempt to interchange metric fasteners for inch system fasteners. Mismatched or incorrect fasteners can result in damage to the transaxle unit through malfunctions, breakage or possible personal injury. Care should be taken to reuse the fasteners in the same locations as removed whenever possible.

Capacities

The use of Dexron®II type automatic transaxle fluid or its equivalent, is recommended for use in the F3A automatic transaxle models.

The capacity of the F3A transaxle is 6.0 U.S. quarts (5.7 L).

Checking Fluid Level

With the engine/transaxle assemblies up to normal operating temperature, move the quadrant through all the selector positions and finish in the **P** position. The correct level is between the **F** and **L** marks on the dipstick. It is important to keep the level at, or slightly below, the **F** mark on the dipstick. Do not overfill the assembly.

Transaxle oil level should be checked, both visually and by smell, to determine that the fluid level is correct and to observe any foreign material in the fluid. Smelling the fluid will indicate if any of the bands or clutches have been burned through excessive slippage or overheating of the transaxle.

It is most important to locate the defect and its cause and to properly repair them to avoid having the same problem recur.

TRANSAXLE MODIFICATIONS

Low and Reverse Clutch Hub Snapring

Transaxles which have not been previously disassembled do not have a low and reverse clutch hub snapring. This clutch hub snapring will be install on all transaxles during the rebuilding process.

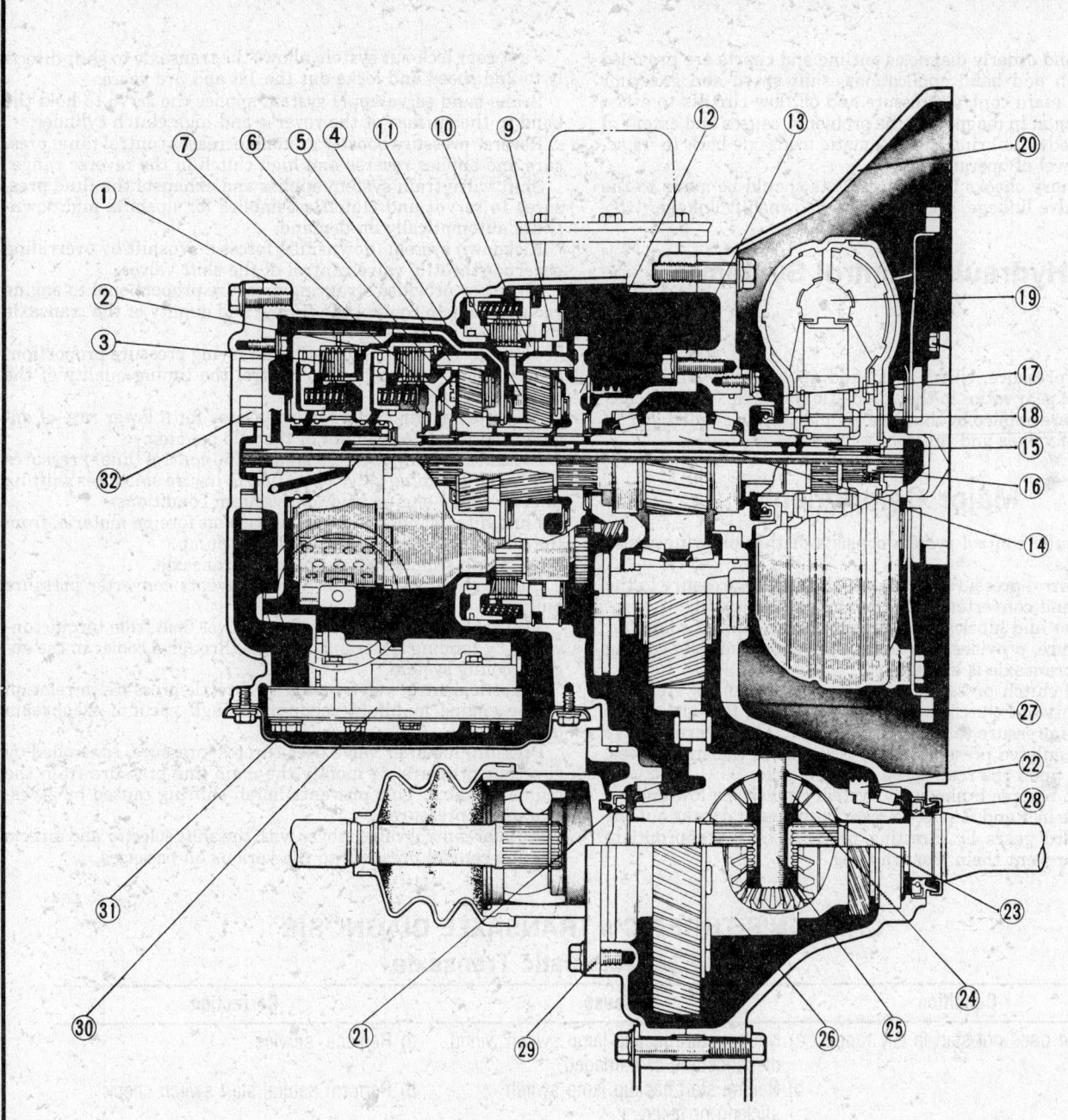

1. Transmission
2. Rear clutch
3. Front clutch
4. Connection shell
5. Rear clutch hub assembly
6. Planetary carrier
7. Sun gear
8. Low and reverse brake
9. One-way clutch
10. One-way clutch inner race
11. Planetary carrier
12. Drum hub assembly
13. Bearing housing
14. Output gear
15. Turbine shaft
16. Oil pump shaft
17. Bearing cover
18. Oil seal
19. Torque converter
20. Converter housing
21. Oil seal
22. Speedometer drive gear
23. Side gear
24. Pinion gear
25. Pinion shaft
26. Differential gear case
27. Ring gear
28. Oil seal
29. Side bearing housing
30. Control valve
31. Oil pan
32. Oil pump

Cross-section of the F3A transaxle

TROUBLE DIAGNOSIS

A logical and orderly diagnosis outline and charts are provided with clutch and band applications, shift speed and governor pressures, main control pressure and oil flow circuits to assist the repairman in diagnosing the problems, causes and extent of repairs needed to bring the automatic transaxle back to its acceptable level of operation.

Preliminary checks and adjustments should be made to the manual valve linkage, accelerator and downshift linkage.

Hydraulic Control System

Hydraulic pressure, clutch and band applications control the changing of gear ratios in the automatic transaxle. The clutches and bands are applied by the force of fluid pressure controlled by a system of valves and control mechanisms.

Major Components

The hydraulic control system consists of the following major components:

Main control pressure system which supplies pressure to the transaxle and converter when the engine is operating.

Converter and lubrication system which regulates converter fluid pressure, provides gear train lubrication and fluid cooling while the transaxle is operating.

Forward clutch pressure and governor pressure system applies the forward clutch, which is applied in all forward speeds and applies pressure to the governor valve. The governor valve supplies regulated pressure to the rear side of the shift valves, dependent upon the road speed of the vehicle.

Low and reverse brake apply system applies the low and reverse brake in 1 and R selector lever positions and locks out the 2nd and 3rd gears by directing pressure to the appropriate valves to prevent them from shifting.

First gear lock out system allows the transaxle to shift directly to 2nd speed and locks out the 1st and 3rd gears.

Brake band servo apply system applies the servo to hold the band to the surface of the reverse and high clutch cylinder.

Reverse pressure booster system increases control (line) pressure and applies reverse and high clutch in the reverse range.

Shift valve train system applies and exhausts the fluid pressures to servos and clutch assemblies for upshifts and downshifts automatically on demand.

Kickdown system (downshift) forces downshift by overriding governor/throttle valve control of the shift valves.

Governor provides a varying pressure proportional to engine vacuum to help control the timing and quality of the transaxle shifts.

Throttle T.V. system provides a varying pressure proportional to engine vacuum to help control the timing quality of the transaxle shifts.

Throttle backup system compensates for a lower rate of engine vacuum at ½ or more of throttle opening.

Pressure modifier system adjusts the control (line) pressures and 2-3 shift timing valve operation to insure smoother shifting under various engine load and vacuum conditions.

Fluid filter screens the fluid and cleans foreign material from the oil supply before entering the oil pump.

Oil pump supplies oil pressure to transaxle.

Converter pressure relief valve prevents converter pressure build up.

Transaxle fluid cooling system removes heat from torque converter by sending the transaxle fluid through a cooler in the engine cooling system.

Throttle control valve regulates throttle pressure in relation to the engine manifold vacuum through vacuum diaphragm (modulator).

Pressure modifier valve uses throttle pressure, controlled by governor pressure, to modify the main line pressure from the regulator valve. This prevents harsh shifting caused by excessive pump pressure.

Manual control valve moves with the shift selector and directs the line control pressure to the various oil passages.

CHILTON'S THREE C's TRANSAXLE DIAGNOSIS
Jatco F3A Automatic Transaxle

Condition	Cause	Correction
Engine does not start in any range	a) Neutral start/backup lamp switch wiring disconnected or damaged b) Neutral start/backup lamp switch sticking or failed	a) Replace, service b) Perform neutral start switch check
Engine does not start in P	a) Range selector and linkage	a) Service or adjust linkage
Engine starts in ranges other than P and N	a) Range selector linkage b) Neutral start/backup lamp switch loose c) Neutral start/backup lamp switch wiring short circuited	a) Perform linkage check b) Check and retighten c) Check for damage
Vehicle moves in P or parking gear not disengaged when P is disengaged	a) Range selector and linkage b) Parking linkage	a) Perform linkage check b) Check for proper operation
Vehicle moves in N	a) Range selector linkage b) Dirty or sticking valve body c) Rear clutch	a) Perform linkage check b) Clean, service or replace valve body c) Check for clutch not disengaging

CHILTON'S THREE C's TRANSAXLE DIAGNOSIS
Jatco F3A Automatic Transaxle

Condition	Cause	Correction
No drive in any gear	a) Valve body loose b) Sticky or dirty valve body c) Improper rear clutch application or damaged, worn clutch d) Low rear clutch application pressure e) Internal leakage f) Valve body loose g) Broken pump or turbine shaft	a) Tighten to specification b) Clean, service or repair valve body c) Service as required d) Perform line and pressure test e) Check pump seals f) Tighten to specification g) Perform stall test
Vehicle does not move in D (moves in 1, 2 and R)	a) Range selector linkage b) Oil pressure control system c) Dirty or sticking valve body d) One-way clutch	a) Perform linkage check b) Perform line and governor pressure tests c) Clean, service or repair valve body d) Service as required
Vehicle does not move in forward ranges, reverse OK	a) Dirty or sticking valve b) Improper rear clutch application or oil pressure control c) Damaged or worn rear clutch	a) Clean, service or repair valve body b) Check rear clutch for proper operation. Perform line pressure test c) Check and service as required
Vehicle does not move in reverse. Forward OK	a) Improper oil pressure b) Dirty or sticking valve body c) Damaged or worn low reverse clutch	a) Perform line pressure test b) Clean, service or replace valve body c) Check and service as required
Vehicle does not shift out of 1st gear in D	a) Dirty or sticking valve body b) Damaged or worn governor c) Improper oil pressure control	a) Check 1-2 shift valve operation. Clean, service or replace valve body b) Check governor valve for free movement. Service or replace governor c) Perform line pressure cut-back point and governor pressure test
Vehicle does not shift from 2 to 3 in D	a) Dirty or sticking valve body b) Governor valve c) Front clutch d) Improper oil pressure control	a) Check 2-3 shift valve operation. Clean, service or replave valve body b) Check governor valve for free movement. Service or replace governor c) Check for proper applicaton and for a worn clutch d) Perform line pressure, cut-back point and governor pressure tests
Shifts from 1 to 3 in D	a) Improper fluid level b) Dirty or sticking valve body c) Governor valve d) Band servo e) Polished or glazed band or drum	a) Perform fluid level check b) Check 1-2 shift valve for free movement. Clean, service or replace valve body c) Check governor valve for free movment. Clean, service or replace governor valve d) Check for seal leakage e) Service or replace as required
Engine overspeeds on 2-3 shift	a) Improper fluid level b) Vacuum diaphragm and piping c) Governor valve d) Improper front clutch application e) Damaged or worn front clutch f) Improper oil pressure	a) Perform fluid level check b) Service or replace c) Check governor valve for free movement. Clean, service or replace governor valve d) Check front clutch operation. Check fluid pressure line and governor e) Service as required f) Perform line pressure and cut-back point tests

CHILTON'S THREE C's TRANSAXLE DIAGNOSIS
Jatco F3A Automatic Transaxle

Condition	Cause	Correction
Practically no shift shock or slippage while 1-2 shifting	a) Improper fluid level	a) Perform fluid level check
	b) Dirty or sticking valve body	b) Clean, service or replace valve body
	c) Oil pressure control	c) Perform fluid pressure check line and governor
	d) Vacuum diaphragm and piping	d) Perform vacuum diaphragm test. Service a required
	e) Band servo	e) Check for leaking seal, service as required
	f) Polished or glazed band or drum	f) Service or replace as required
Shift points incorrect	a) Kickdown switch, kickdown solenoid and wiring	a) Check for loose connection, continuity and proper operation
	b) Vacuum diaphragm and piping	b) Check for proper operation and clogged or disconnected mline
	c) Damaged or worn governor	c) Perform governor pressure test. Check for free movement of governor valve or dirty governor
	d) Improper clutch or band application or oil pressure control	d) Perform line pressure and cut-back point test. Check clutches and bands for proper engagement
	e) Damaged vacuum diaphragm	e) Perform vacuum diaphragm check
No forced downshifts in D	a) Improper band application or oil pressure control	a) Perform line pressure test. Service or adjust as required
	b) Dirty or sticking valve body	b) Check for free movment of all valves. Clean, service or replace valve body
	c) Dirty or sticking governor valve	c) Check governor valve for free movement. Service or replace governor valve
	d) Vacuum diaphragm and piping	d) Perform vacuum diaphragm test. Check for plugged vacuum line. Service or replace as required
	e) Kickdown solenoid kickdown switch and wiring	e) Perform kickdown switch and circuit test. Service or replace as required
Does not shift from 3-2 on D to 2 shift	a) Dirty or sticking valve	a) Clean, service or replace valve body
	b) Oil pressure control system	b) Perform line and governor pressure tests
	c) Band servo	c) Check for proper operation. Service or replace as required
	d) Damaged or worn band, glazed or polished drum	d) Service or replace as required
Does not shift from 3 to 2 on D to 1 shift	a) Dirty or sticking valve body	a) Clean, service or replace as required
	b) Oil pressure control system	b) Perform line and governor pressure tests
	c) Band servo	c) Check for proper operation. Service or replace as required
	d) Damaged or worn band, glazed or polished drum	d) Service or replace as required
Kickdown operates or engine overruns when depressing pedal in 3 beyond kickdown vehicle speed limit	a) Vacuum diaphragm and piping	a) Check for sticking vacuum diaphragm and throttle valve
	b) Dirty or sticking valve body	b) Clean, service or replace as required
	c) Improper front clutch application or oil pressure control	c) Check front clutch for proper application. Perform line and governor pressure test

CHILTON'S THREE C's TRANSAXLE DIAGNOSIS
Jatco F3A Automatic Transaxle

Condition	Cause	Correction
Runaway engine on 3-2 downshift	a) Improper fluid level b) Improper band application or oil pressure system c) Band servo d) Polished or glazed band drum	a) Perform fluid level check b) Check band for proper application. Perform line pressure, cut-back point and governor pressure test c) Check for proper operation and seal leak d) Replace or service as required
No engine braking in 1	a) Improper fluid level b) Damaged or improperly adjusted manual c) Oil pressure control system d) Dirty or sticking valve body e) Low reverse brake	a) Perform fluid level check b) Perform linkage check linkage c) Perform line pressure test d) Clean, service or replace as required e) Service as required
Slow initial engagement	a) Improper fluid level b) Contaminated fluid c) Dirty or sticking valve body d) Improper clutch application or oil control pressure	a) Perform fluid level check b) Check fluid for proper condition. Check for clogged filter c) Clean, service or replace valve body d) Check rear clutch for proper application Perform line and governor pressure test
Harsh initial engagement in either forward or reverse	a) High engine idle b) Looseness in halfshafts, CV joints or engine mounts c) Vacuum diaphragm and piping d) Improper rear clutch application or oil pressure control e) Sticking or dirty valve body	a) Adjust idle to specifiaction b) Service as required c) Service as required d) Check rear clutch for proper operation. Perform line and governor pressure test e) Clean, service or replace as required
Harsh 1-2 shift	a) Weak engine performance b) Dirty or sticking body c) Vacuum diaphragm and piping d) Improper brake band application or oil pressure control	a) Tune and adjust engine to specification b) Check for free movement of 1-2 shift valve. Clean, service or replace valve body c) Perform vacuum diaphragm test. Service or replace as required d) Check band for proper operation. Perform line and governor pressure tests
Harsh 2-3 shift	a) Dirty or sticking valve body b) Improper front clutch application or oil pressure control c) Band servo d) Brake band	a) Clean, service or replace valve body b) Perform line pressure, cut-back point and governor pressure tests c) Check for proper release d) Check for proper release
Vehicle braked when shifted from 1-2	a) Dirty or sticking valve body b) Improper front clutch application or oil pressure control c) Low reverse brake d) One-way clutch	a) Clean, service or replace valve body b) Check front clutch for proper engagement. Perform line and governor pressure tests c) Check for proper disengagement or dragging clutch d) Check for seized clutch
Vehicle braked when shifted from 2-3	a) Dirty or sticking valve body b) Brake band and servo	a) Clean, service or replace valve body b) Check for proper disengagement
Noise severe under acceleration or deceleration. OK in P or N or speed	a) Speedo cable grounding out b) Shift cable grounding out c) Engine mounts bound up	a) Install and route cable as specified b) Install and route cable as specified c) Neutralize engine mounts

CHILTON'S THREE C's TRANSAXLE DIAGNOSIS
Jatco F3A Automatic Transaxle

Condition	Cause	Correction
Noise in P or N. Does not stop in Drive	a) Loose flywheel to converter bolts b) Pump c) Torque converter	a) Torque to specification b) Examine, service pump c) Examine, service converter. Perform stall test
Noise in all gears, changes power to coast	a) Final drive gearset noisy	a) Examine, service final drive gearset
Noise in all gears, does not change power to coast	a) Defective speedo gears b) Bearings worn or damaged	a) Examine, replace speed drive or driven gear b) Examine, replace
Noise in Low	a) Planetary gearset noisy	a) Service planetary gearset
Transaxle noisy in D, 2, 1 & R	a) Improper fluid level b) Improper fluid pressure control c) Rear clutch d) Oil pump e) One-way clutch f) Planetary gears	a) Perform fluid level check b) Perform line and governor pressure tests c) Check and repair as necessary d) Check, repair or replace e) Check, repair or replace as necessary f) Check or replace as necessary
Transaxle noisy, (valve noise) NOTE: Gauges may aggravate any hydraulic noises. Remove gauge and check for noise level	a) Improper fluid level b) Improper band or clutch application or oil pressure control system c) Cooler line grounding d) Dirty or sticking valve body e) Internal leakage or pump cavitation	a) Perform fluid level check b) Perform line pressure test c) Free cooler lines d) Clean, service or replace valve body e) Service or replace as required
Transaxle overheats	a) Improper fluid level b) Incorrect engine performance c) Improper clutch or band application or oil pressure control d) Restriction in cooler lines e) Dirty or sticking valve body f) Seized converter one-way clutch	a) Perform fluid level check b) Adjust according to specifications c) Perform line and pressure governor pressure tests d) Check cooler lines for kinks and damage. Clean, service or replace cooler lines e) Clean, service or replace valve body f) Replace converter

Diagnosis Tests

OIL PRESSURE CIRCUITS

In order to more fully understand the Jatco automatic transmission and to diagnose possible defects more easily, the clutch and band applications charts and a general description of the hydraulic control system is given.

To utilize the oil flow charts for diagnosing transaxle problems, the repairman must have an understanding of the oil pressure circuits and how each circuit affects the operation of the transaxle by the use of controlled oil pressure.

Control (line) pressure is a regulated main line pressure, developed by the operation of the front pump. It is directed to the main regulator valve, where predetermined spring pressure automatically moves the regulator valve to control the pressure of the oil at a predetermined rate, by opening the valve and exhausting excessive pressured oil back into the sump and holding the valve closed to build up pressure when needed.

Therefore, it is most important during the diagnosis phase to test main line control pressure to determine if high or low pressure exits. Do not attempt to adjust a pressure regulator valve spring to obtain more or less control pressure. Internal transaxle damage may result.

The main valve is the controlling agent of the transaxle which directs oil pressure to 1 of 6 separate passages used to control the valve train. By assigning each passage a number, a better understanding of the oil circuits can be gained from the diagnosis oil flow schematics.

CONTROL PRESSURE SYSTEM TEST

Control pressure tests should be performed whenever slippage, delay or harshness is felt in the shifting of the transaxle. Throttle and modulator pressure changes can cause these problems also, but are generated from the control pressures and therefore reflect any problems arising from the control pressure system.

The control pressure is initially checked in all ranges without any throttle pressure input and then checked as the throttle pressure is increased by lowering the vacuum supply to the vacuum modulator with the use of the stall test.

CLUTCH AND BAND APPLICATION CHART
Jatco F3A Automatic Transaxle

Range		Front Clutch ①	Rear Clutch ②	Low & Reverse Brake Clutch	Brake Band Operation	Servo ③ Release	One-Way Clutch	Parking Pawl
Park		—	—	On	—	—	—	On
Reverse		On	—	On	—	On	—	—
Neutral		—	—	—	—	—	—	—
Drive	Low D1	—	On	—	—	—	On	—
	Second D2	—	On	—	On	—	—	—
	Top D3	On	On	—	(On)	On	—	—
2	Second	—	On	—	On	—	—	—
1	Second 1₂	—	On	—	On	—	—	—
	Low 1₁	—	On	On	—	—	—	—

① Reverse and high clutch
② Forward clutch
③ Intermediate band

Clutch and band applications for the F3A transaxle

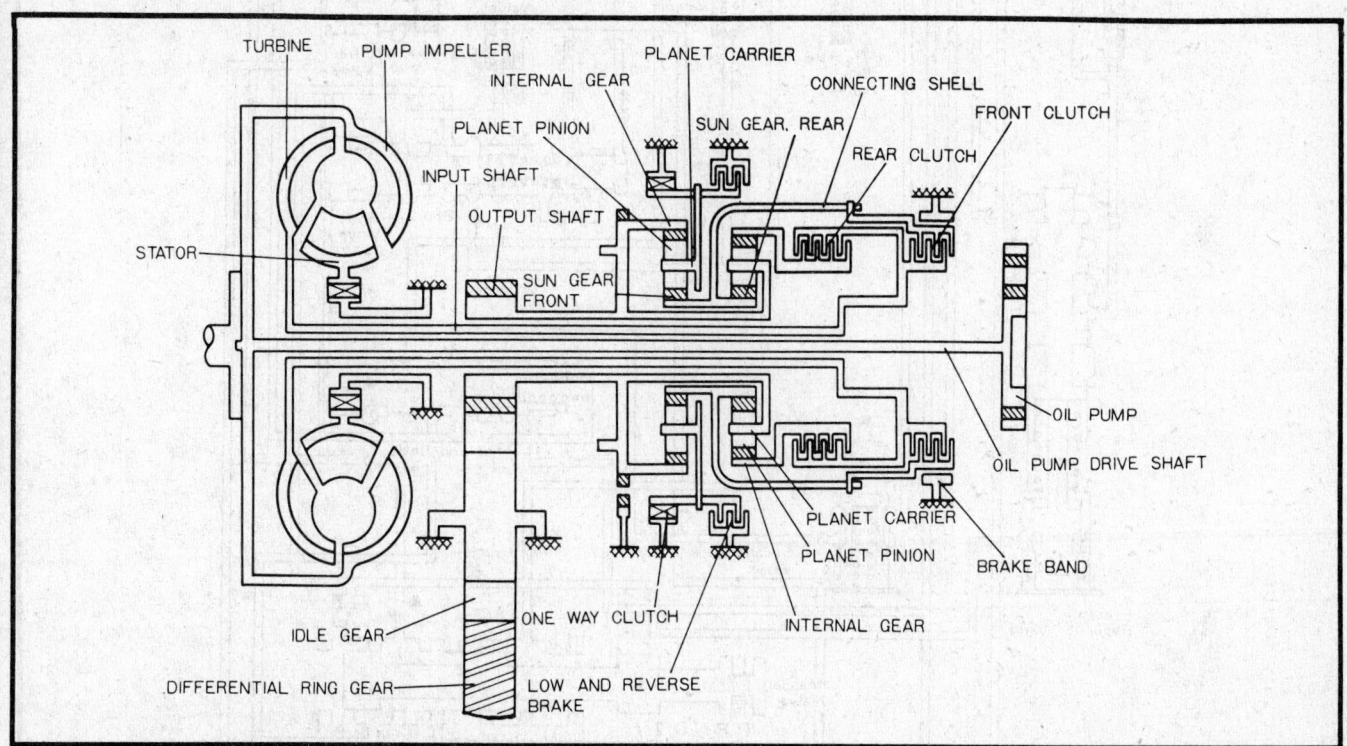

Power components of the F3A transaxle

The control pressure tests should define differences between mechanical or hydraulic failures of the transaxle.

Testing

1. Install a 0–400 psi pressure gauge to the main line control pressure tap. This may be marked ML on the side of the transaxle case.
2. Block wheels and apply both parking and service brakes.
3. Operate the engine/transaxle in the ranges on the following charts and at the manifold vacuum specified.
4. Record the actual pressure readings in each test and compare them to the given specifications.

Results

LOW PRESSURE AT IDLE IN ALL RANGES CAUSED BY:
1. EGR system, if equipped
2. Vacuum modulator
3. Manifold vacuum line
4. Throttle valve or control rod
5. Sticking regulator boost valve (pressure modifier valve)

Hydraulic control schematic

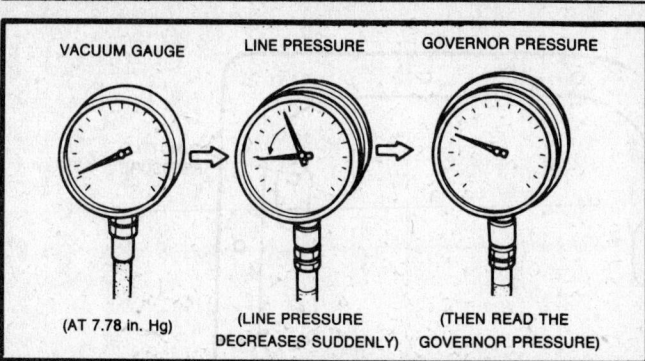

Gauges needed to test the hydraulic circuits

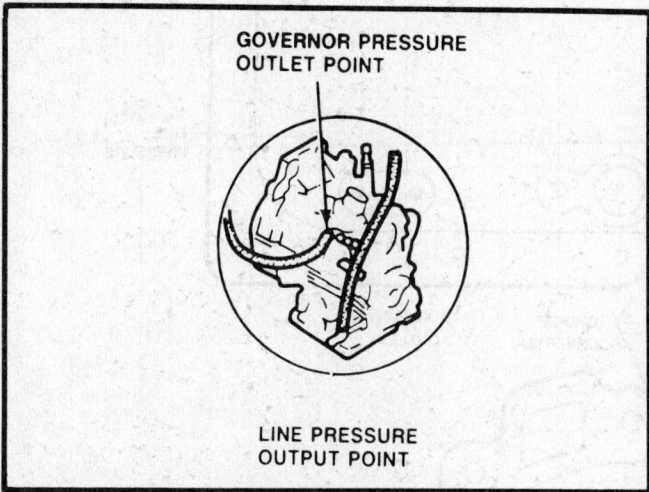

Hydraulic pressure test points

OK AT IDLE IN ALL RANGES, BUT LOW AT 10 IN. OF VACUUM IS CAUSED BY:
1. Excessive leakage
2. Low pump capacity
3. Restricted oil pan screen or filter

PRESSURE LOW IN P RANGE IS CAUSED BY:
   Valve body

PRESSURE LOW IN R IS CAUSED BY:
1. Front clutch
2. Low and reverse brake

PRESSURE LOW IN N RANGE IS CAUSED BY:
   Valve body

PRESSURE LOW IN D RANGE IS CAUSED BY:
   Rear clutch

PRESSURE LOW IN 2 RANGE IS CAUSED BY:
1. Rear clutch
2. Brake band servo

PRESSURE LOW IN 1 RANGE IS CAUSED BY:
1. Rear clutch
2. Low and reverse brake

HIGH OR LOW PRESSURE IN ALL TEST CONDITIONS IS CAUSED BY:
1. Modulator control rod broken or missing
2. Stuck throttle valve
3. Pressure modifier valve or regulator valve

POSSIBLE LOCATIONS OF PROBLEMS DUE TO LINE PRESSURE

Malfunctions

1. Low pressure when in **D**, **2**, or **R** positions could be the result of a worn oil pump, fluid leaking from the oil pump, control valve or transaxle case, or the pressure regulator valve sticking.

2. Low pressure when in **D** and **2** only could result from fluid leakage from the hydraulic circuit of the 2 ranges selected. Refer to the hydraulic fluid schematics.

3. Low fluid pressure when in the **R** position could result from a fluid leakage in the reverse fluid circuit. Refer to the hydraulic fluid schematic.

4. High pressure when idling could be the result of a broken or disconnected vacuum hose to the modulator or a defective vacuum modulator assembly.

Main Line Pressure Cut-Back Point Test

1. Connect the fluid pressure test gauge to the line pressure test port outlet of the transaxle case.

2. Connect a fluid pressure test gauge to the governor pressure test port on the transaxle case.

3. Position the gauges so that each can be seen from the driver's seat.

4. Disconnect the vacuum hose to the vacuum modulator and plug the hose.

5. Connect a vacuum pump to the vacuum modulator and position the pump so it can be operated from the driver's seat.

6. If the line pressure drops abruptly when the engine rpm is increased gradually while the selector lever is in the **D** position. Measure the governor pressure.

7. Measure the governor pressure when the vacuum is at 0 in. Hg. and at 7.9 in. Hg. The specifications are: 0.0 in. Hg – 14–23 psi (98–157 Kpa) and 7.9 in. Hg (200mm–Hg) – 6–14 psi (39–98 Kpa).

8. If the specifications are not met, check to see that the diaphragm rod has been installed or that it is more than standard. Check for a sticking valve inside the control valve assemble if the rod is correct.

Governor Pressure Test

1. Connect the fluid pressure gauge to the governor test port on the transaxle case. Position the gauge so that it is accessible to the operator.

2. Drive the vehicle with the selector lever in the **D** position.

3. Measure the governor pressure at the following speeds: The governor pressure should be 11.9–17.1 psi at 20 mph, 19.9–28.4 psi at 35 mph and 38.4–48.3 psi at 55 mph.

4. If the test results do not meet the specifications, the following should be checked:
   a. Fluid leakage from the line pressure hydraulic circuit.
   b. Fluid leakage from the governor pressure hydraulic circuit.
   c. Governor malfunctions.

AIR PRESSURE TEST

The control pressure test results and causes of abnormal pressure are to be used as a guide. Further testing or inspection could be necessary before repairs are made. If the pressures are found to be low in a clutch, servo or passageway, a verification can be accomplished by removing the valve body and performing an air pressure test. This test can be used to determine if a malfunction of a clutch or band is caused by fluid leakage in the system or is the result of a mechanical failure and also, to test the transaxle for internal fluid leakage during the rebuilding and before completing the assembly.

1. Obtain an air nozzle and adjust for 25 psi.
2. Apply air pressure (25 psi) to the passages.

Vacuum Modulator Test

The modulated throttle system, which adjusts throttle pressure for the control of the shift valves, is operated by engine manifold

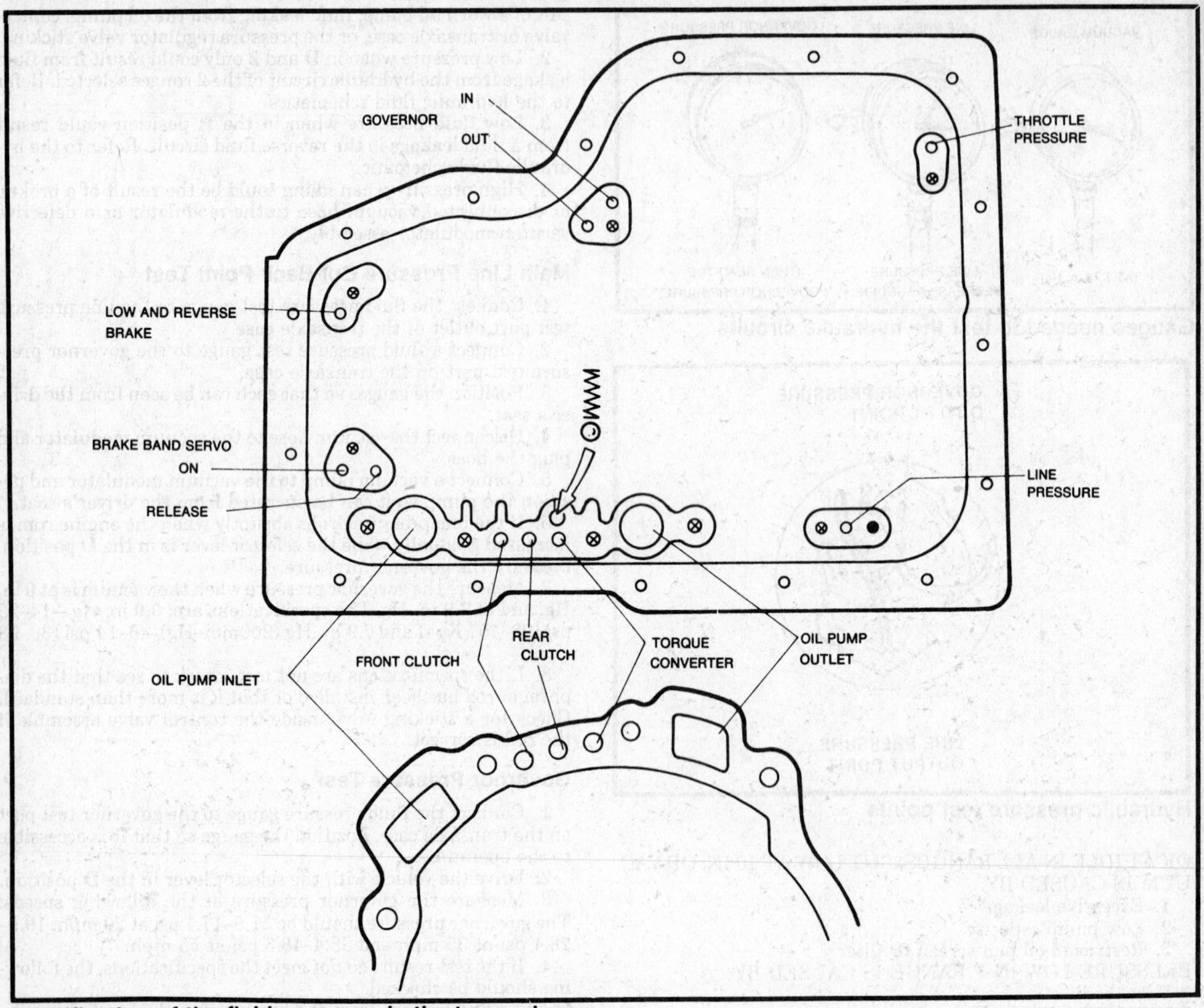

GOVERNOR

IN

OUT

THROTTLE
PRESSURE

LOW AND REVERSE
BRAKE

LINE
PRESSURE

BRAKE BAND SERVO

ON

RELEASE

OIL PUMP INLET

FRONT CLUTCH

REAR
CLUTCH

TORQUE
CONVERTER

OIL PUMP
OUTLET

Identification of the fluid passages in the transaxle case

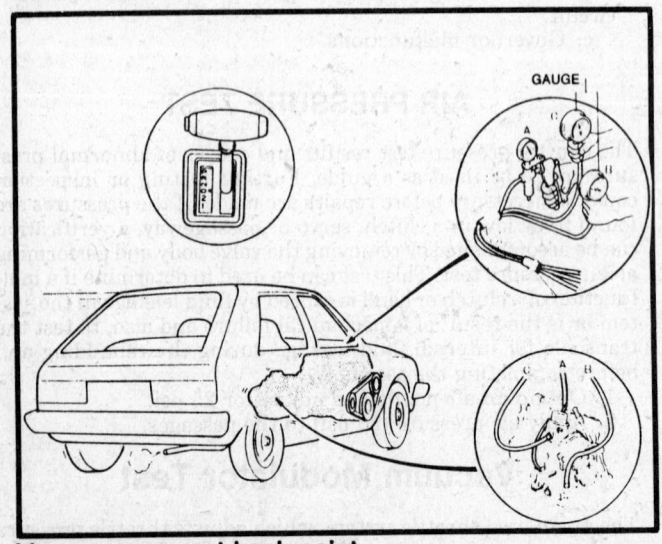

GAUGE

Line pressure cut back point

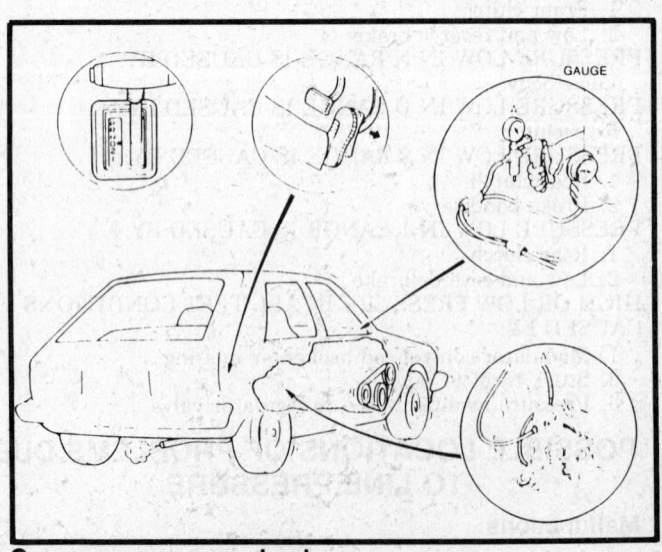

GAUGE

Governor pressure check

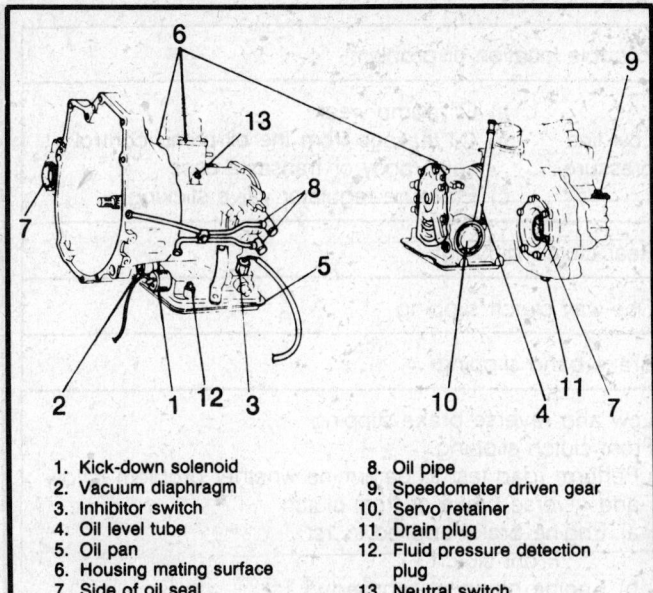

1. Kick-down solenoid
2. Vacuum diaphragm
3. Inhibitor switch
4. Oil level tube
5. Oil pan
6. Housing mating surface
7. Side of oil seal
8. Oil pipe
9. Speedometer driven gear
10. Servo retainer
11. Drain plug
12. Fluid pressure detection plug
13. Neutral switch

Possible fluid leakage locations

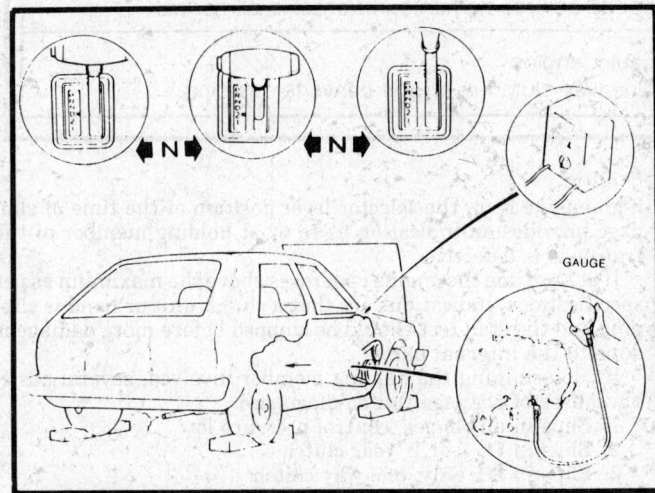

Line pressure test

vacuum through a vacuum diaphragm and must be inspected whenever a transaxle defect is apparent.

Before the vacuum modulator test is performed, check the engine vacuum supply and the condition and routing of the supply lines.

With the engine idling, remove the vacuum line at the vacuum modulator and install a vacuum gauge. There must be a steady, acceptable vacuum reading for the altitude at which the test is being performed.

If the vacuum is low, check for a vacuum leak or poor engine performance. If the vacuum is steady and acceptable, accelerate the engine sharply and observe the vacuum gauge reading. The vacuum should drop off rapidly at acceleration and return to the original reading immediately upon release of the accelerator.

If the vacuum reading does not change or changes slowly, check the vacuum supply lines for being plugged, restricted or connected to a vacuum reservoir supply. Repair the system as required.

MANIFOLD VACUUM CHECK

1. With the engine idling, remove the vacuum supply hose

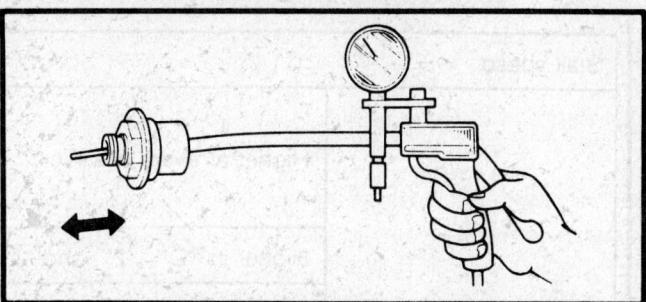

Testing the modulator with a hand vacuum pump

from the modulator nipple and check the hose end for the presence of engine vacuum with an appropriate gauge.

2. If vacuum is present, accelerate the engine and allow it to return to idle. A drop in vacuum should be noted during acceleration and a return to normal vacuum at idle.

3. If manifold vacuum is not present, check for breaks or restrictions in the vacuum lines and repair.

VACUUM MODULATOR CHECK

1. Apply at least 18 in. Hg. to the modulator vacuum nipple and observe the vacuum reading. The vacuum should hold.

2. If the vacuum does not hold, the diaphragm is leaking and the modulator assembly must be replaced.

NOTE: A leaking diaphragm causes harsh gear engagements and delayed or no up-shifts due to maximum throttle pressure developed.

On Vehicle Test

The vacuum modulator is tested on the vehicle with the aid of an outside vacuum source, which can be adjusted to maintain a certain amount of vacuum. Apply 18 inches Hg. to the vacuum modulator vacuum nipple, through a hose connected to the outside vacuum source. The vacuum should hold at the applied level without any leakdown. If the vacuum level drops off, the vacuum diaphragm is leaking and must be replaced.

Remove the vacuum hose and check transmission fluid in the hose. If the diaphragm has a leak, engine vacuum may draw transmission fluid through the hose and into the engine where it will be burned with the fuel.

Off Vehicle Test

With the vacuum modulator removed from the automatic transaxle, apply 18 in. Hg. to the modulator vacuum nipple.

The vacuum level should remain and not drop off. If the vacuum level drops, the diaphragm is leaking and the unit should be replaced.

Another test can be made with the modulator removed from the transaxle. Insert the control rod into the valve end of the diaphragm and apply vacuum to the nipple. Hold a finger over the control rod and release the vacuum supply hose. The control rod should be moved outward by the pressure of the internal return spring. If the control rod does not move outward, a broken return spring is indicated.

STALL TEST

The stall test is an application of engine torque, through the transaxle and drive train to lock up the rear wheels, which are held by the vehicle's brakes. The engine's speed is increased until the rpms are stabilized. Given ideal engine operating conditions and no slippage from transaxle clutches, bands or torque converter, the engine will stabilize at a specified test rpm.

Stall speed			Possible location of problem	
Higher than standard	Higher at every position		Low line pressure	a) Oil pump weak b) Oil leakage from the oil pump control valve body or transaxle case c) Pressure regulator valve sticking
	Higher in "D", "2", and "1"		Rear clutch slipping	
	Higher only in "D"		One-way clutch slipping	
	Higher only in "2"		Brake band slipping	
	Higher only in "R"		Low and reverse brake slipping Front clutch slipping Perform road test to determine whether problem is low and reverse brake or front clutch a) Engine brake applied in 1st .....Front clutch b) Engine brake not applied in 1st .....Low and reverse brake	
Within standard			Speed control elements in transaxle all normal	
Lower then standard			Faulty engine One-way clutch in torque converter slipping	

Stall speed trouble chart

Procedure

1. Check the engine oil level. Run the ngine until it reaches operating temperature.

2. Check the transaxle fluid level and correct as necessary. Attach a calibrated tachometer to the engine and a 0–400 psi oil pressure gauge to the transaxle control pressure tap on the right side of the case.

3. Mark the specified maximum engine rpm on the tachometer cover plate with a grease pencil to easily check if the stall speed is over or under specifications.

4. Apply the parking brake and block both front and rear wheels.

CAUTION

Do no allow anyone in front of the vehicle while performing the stall test. Secure vehicle with parking brake and blocking wheeling wheels or anchoring with chains.

5. While holding the brake pedal with the left foot, place the selector lever in **D** position and slowly depress the accelerator.

6. Read and record the engine rpm when the accelerator pedal is fully depressed and the engine rpm is stabilized. Read and record the oil pressure reading at the high engine rpm point. Stall speed – 2200-2450 rpm.

NOTE: The stall test must be made within 5 seconds.

7. Shift the selector lever into the **N** position and increase the engine speed to approximately 1000–1200 rpm. Hold this engine speed for 1–2 minutes to cool the transaxle and fluid.

8. Make similar tests in the **2**, **1** and **R** positions.

Results

HIGH ENGINE RPM

If a slipping condition occurs during the stall test, indicated by high engine rpm, the selector lever position at the time of slippage provides an indication as to what holding member of the transaxle is defective.

If at any time the engine rpm races above the maximum as per specifications, indications are that a clutch unit or band is slipping and the stall test should be stopped before more damage is done to the internal parts.

By determining the holding member involved, several possible causes of slippage can be diagnosed.

1. Slips in all ranges, control pressure low
2. Slips in D, 1 or 2, rear clutch
3. Slips in D1 only, one-way clutch
4. Slips in R only, front clutch or low and reverse brake

Perform a road test to confirm these conditions.

LOW ENGINE RPM

When low stall speed is indicated, the converter one-way clutch is not holding or the engine is in need of a major tune-up. To determine which is at fault, perform a road test and observe the operation of the transaxle and the engine. If the converter one-way clutch does not lock the stator, acceleration will be poor up to approximately 30 mph. Above mph the acceleration will be normal. With poor engine performance, acceleration will be poor at all speeds. When the one-way clutch is seized and locks the stator from turning either way, the stall test rpm will be normal. However, on a road test the vehicle will not go any faster than 50–55 mph because of the 2:1 reduction ratio in the converter.

If slippage was indicated by high engine rpm, the road test will help identify the problem area observing the transaxle operation during upshifts, both automatic and manual.

Road Test

The road test is used to confirm that malfunctions do exist within the transaxle unit, or that repairs have been accomplished

STALL TEST HOLDING MEMBER CHART

Selector Lever Position	Holding Member Applied
"D" 1st Gear	Rear clutch One-way clutch
"1" Manual	Rear clutch Low and reverse brake clutch
"2" Manual	Rear clutch Rear band
Reverse	Front clutch Low and reverse brake clutch

Line Pressure At Stall Speed	
"D" Range	128 to 156 psi
"2" Range	114 to 171 psi
"R" Range	228 to 270 psi

Line Pressure Before Stall Test—At Idle	
"D" Range	43 to 57 psi
"2" Range	114 to 171 psi
"R" Range	57 to 110 psi

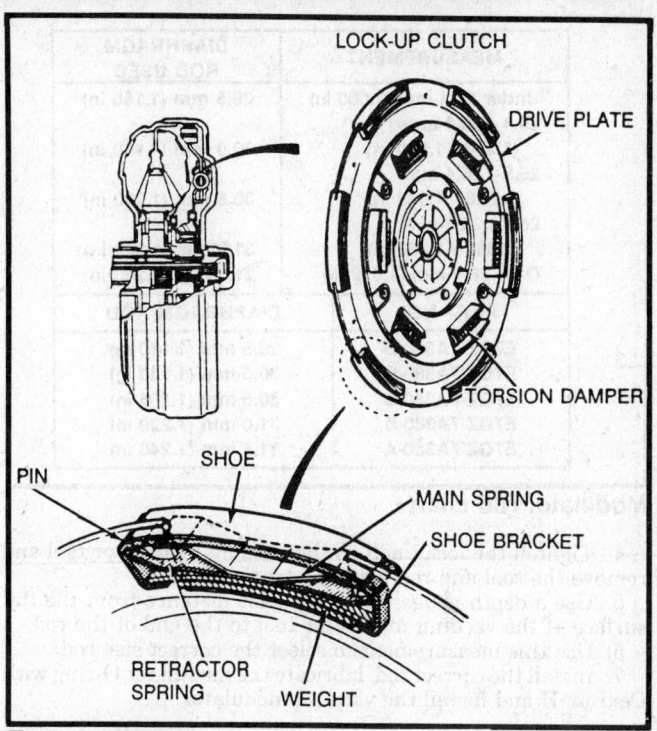

Torque converter

and the transaxle unit is either operating properly or will require additional adjustments or repairs. The road test must be performed over a pre-determined drive course that has been used before to evaluate transaxle and/or transaxle operations.

Should malfunctions occur during the road test, the selector range and road speed should be noted, along with the particular gear and shift point. By applying the point of malfunction in the operation of the transaxle, to the Clutch and Band Application Chart and the Chilton's Three "C's"; diagnosis chart, the probable causes can be pinpointed.

Some of the points to be evaluated during the road test are as follows:

1. The shift point should be smooth and have a positive engagement.
2. The shifts speed are within specifications.
3. All shifts occur during the upshifts and downshifts when in the selector lever detents, as required.
4. All downshifts occur when a forced downshift is demanded.
5. No upshift to 3rd when the selector lever is in the **2** position and the transaxle is in the 2nd speed.
6. Only 1 upshift from the 1st speed when the selector lever is in the **1** position.
7. The vehicle is firmly locked when the lever is in the **P** position.

Converter Clutch Operation and Diagnosis

TORQUE CONVERTER CLUTCH

A lockup torque converter is utilized. This eliminates the slip which is inherent in conventional torque converters. The no slip characteristics are achieved by automatically locking the converter into direct mechanical drive at high engine speed.

The lockup converter consists of a lockup drive plate containing centrifugally operated shoe, bracket and spring assemblies and a one-way clutch.

The lockup drive plate assembly is attached to the splined turbine shaft and is located inside the torque converter between the turbine and the converter cover. Torque is transmitted when the centrifugal clutch linings contact the machined inner surface of the converter housing. Torsion dampers are provided in the drive plate to absorb shock when the clutch is engaged.

NOTE: Whenever a transaxle has been disassembled, the converter and oil cooler must be cleaned.

ON CAR SERVICES

Adjustments
VACUUM MODULATOR

The vacuum modulator has no adjustments other than the replacement of the diaphragm rod. The rods are available in varied lengths as follows.

1. Raise and support the vehicle safely. Remove the vacuum modulator from its mounting.
2. Insert the vacuum diaphragm rod gauge into the mounting hole, with the beveled side out, until the tool bottoms.
3. Place the rod through the opening of the vacuum diaphragm tool until the rod bottoms out against the valve.

MEASUREMENT	DIAPHRAGM ROD USED
Under 25.4 mm (1.000 in)	29.5 mm (1.160 in)
25.4 ~ 25.9 mm (1.000 ~ 1.020 in)	30.0 mm (1.180 in)
25.9 ~ 26.4 mm (1.020 ~ 1.039 in)	30.5 mm (1.200 in)
26.4 ~ 26.9 mm (1.039 ~ 1.059 in)	31.0 mm (1.220 in)
Over 26.9 mm (1.059 in)	31.5 mm (1.240 in)
PART NO.	DIAPHRAGM ROD
E7GZ-7A380-E	29.5 mm (1.160 in)
E7GZ-7A380-C	30.0 mm (1.180 in)
E7GZ-7A380-D	30.5 mm (1.200 in)
E7GZ-7A380-B	31.0 mm (1.220 in)
E7GZ-7A380-A	31.5 mm (1.240 in)

Modulator rod chart

4. Tighten the lock knob on the vacuum modulator tool and remove the tool and rod from the transaxle case.

5. Use a depth gauge to measure the distance from the flat surface of the vacuum modulator tool to the end of the rod.

6. Use this measurement to select the correct size rod.

7. Install the correct rod, lubricate the modulator O-ring with Dexron®II and install the vacuum modulator.

NOTE: The transaxle will have to be partially drained before the vacuum modulator is removed. Add the necessary fluid and correct the level as required.

KICKDOWN SWITCH

1. Move the ignition switch to the **ON** position.

2. Loosen the kickdown switch to engage when the accelerator pedal is between $\frac{7}{8}$–$\frac{15}{16}$ in. of full travel. The downshift solenoid will click when the switch engages.

3. Tighten the attaching nut and check for proper operation.

NEUTRAL SAFETY SWITCH

No adjustment is possible on the neutral safety switch. If the engine will not start while the selector lever is in the **P** or **N** positions and the back-up lamps do not operate, check the shift control cable for proper adjustment. If shift cable adjustment is correct, the switch is defective and must be replaced.

Services

MANUAL SHIFT LINKAGE

REMOVAL AND INSTALLATION

1. Position the gear selector lever in the **N** position.

2. Remove the spring clip and pin attaching the shift cable trunnion to the transaxle shift lever.

3. Rotate the transaxle shift lever fully counterclockwise. This is the park position.

4. Rotate the transaxle shift lever clockwise 2 detents. This is the neutral position. As the lever is rotated, position it between the ends of the shift cable trunnion.

5. If the hole in the shift lever aligns with the holes in the trunnion, the cable is properly adjusted. If the holes do not align proceed to the next step.

6. Remove the shift quadrant bezel. Lift the front of the bezel to disengage it from the console.

7. Lift and rotate the quadrant to provide access.

8. Loosen the adjuster nuts on the shift cable.

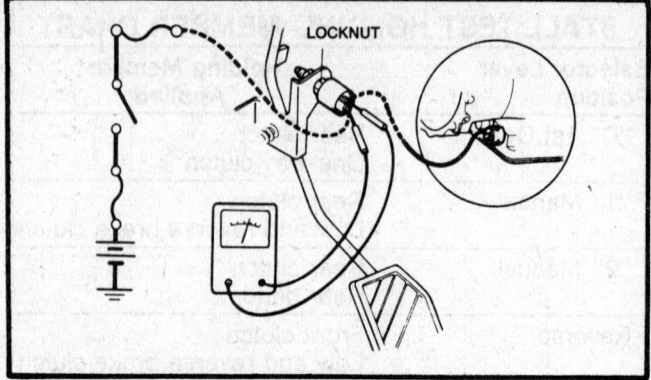

Checking the kickdown switch

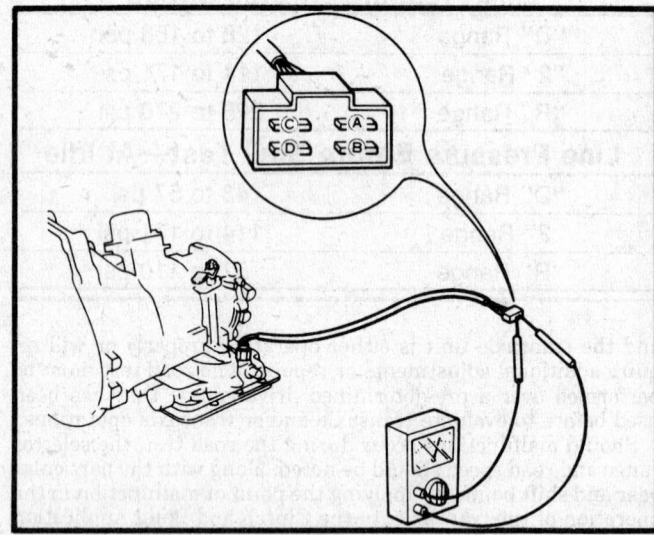

Checking the neutral safety switch

9. Position the gear selector lever in **P** position and inspect the position of the detent spring roller.

10. Loosen the attaching screws and move the detent spring forward or backward to center it in the detent.

11. Position the quadrant and install the attaching screws.

12. Position the selector lever in the **N** position.

13. Screw the adjuster nuts up or down the cable until the holes in the transaxle shift lever and the shift cable trunnion are aligned.

14. Torque the adjuster nut to 69–95 inch lbs. (8–11 Nm).

15. Check the alignment of the holes to make sure alignment was not disturbed.

16. Install the transaxle shift lever to shift cable attaching pin and retainer clip.

17. With an assistant, note the amount of freeplay when moving the shifter from **N** to **D** and compare to amount of freeplay between **N** and **R**. Adjust as necessary for equal amount of play in shifter and torque adjuster nut to 69–95 inch lbs. (8–11 Nm).

── **CAUTION** ──

Make sure the linkage adjustment has not affected operation of the neutral safety switch. With the parking brake and service brake applied, try to start the engine in each gearshift position.

18. Position the shift quadrant bezel and install the attaching screws.

FLUID CHANGES

The Jatco transaxles do not have a specific or periodic fluid

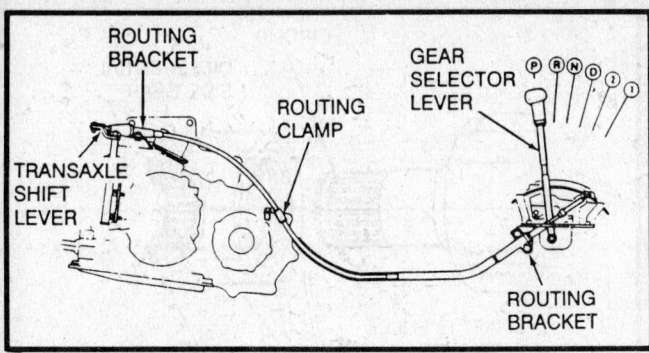

Manual shift linkage

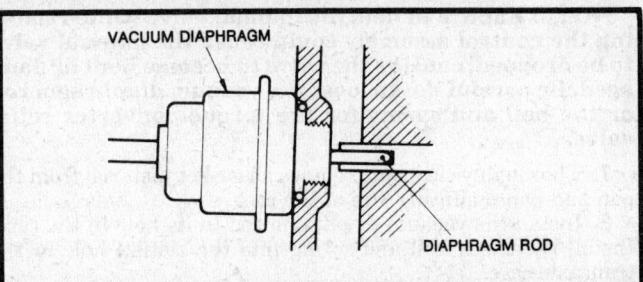

Installation of the modulator assembly

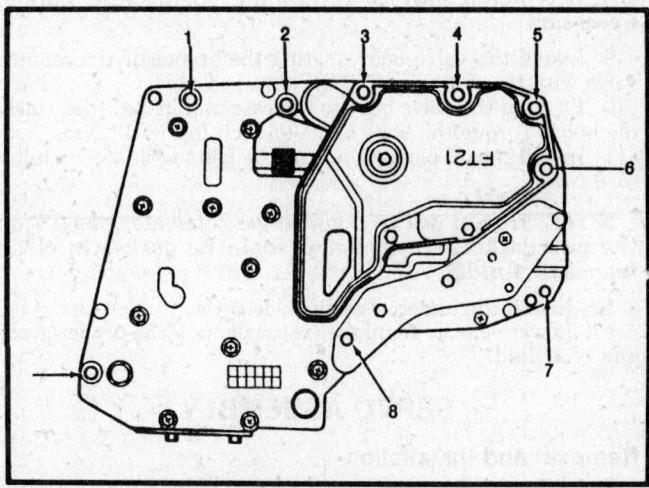

Bolt removal and torque sequence

change interval for the normal maintenance of the units. However, at the time of any major repairs or when the fluid has been contaminated, the converter, cooler and lines must be flushed to remove any debris and contaminated fluid. If the vehicle is used in continuous service or driven under severe conditions (police or taxi type operations), the transaxle should be drained, flushed and refilled at mileage intervals of 18,000–24,000 or at time intervals of 18–24 months.

NOTE: The time or mileage intervals given are average. Each vehicle operated under severe conditions should be treated individually.

1. Raise and support vehicle safely.
2. Remove the undercover and side cover to gain access to the transaxle pan and drain plug.
3. Remove the drain plug at the bottom of the transaxle case.
4. Allow the fluid to drain completely and reinstall the drain plug. Torque drain plug to 29–40 ft. lbs. (39–54 Nm).
5. Add Dexron®II type fluid to the transaxle until the desired level is reached. Approximately 3 quarts if the transaxle, not including the torque converter, was drained.

VACUUM MODULATOR

Removal and Installation

NOTE: Drain the transaxle before removing the vacuum modulator.

1. Raise the vehicle and support safely. Disconnect the vacuum hose from the modulator unit.
2. Turn the threaded modulator unit to remove it from the transaxle case.
3. Pull the actuating pin and the throttle valve from the transaxle case.
4. Remove the O-ring from the assembly.
5. Install a new O-ring on the modulator unit.
6. Install the throttle valve, the actuating pin and the vacuum modulator tubes toward the transaxle case and install the assembly into the case.
7. Tighten the vacuum modulator unit securely.

OIL PAN

Removal and Installation

1. Raise and support vehicle safely.
2. Remove the undercover and side cover to gain access to the transaxle pan and drain plug.
3. Remove the drain plug at the bottom of the transaxle case.
4. Allow the fluid to drain completely.
5. Remove the pan from the transaxle case.
6. Thoroughly clean the oil pan and filter screen.
7. Install a new washer on the drain plug and torque to 29–40 ft. lbs. (39–54 Nm).

8. Install a new pan gasket and replace pan. Torque pan bolts to 4–6 ft. lbs. (5–8 Nm).

NOTE: Do not overtighten bolts. Do not use any type of gasket sealer, RTV, etc., on the transaxle pan gasket. If necessary, soak the gasket in clean Dexron®II automatic transaxle fluid.

9. Install the undercover and side cover.
10. Remove the dipstick and add 3 quarts of Dexron®II transmission fluid.
11. Start and run engine until normal operating temperature is reached. Apply service brake and move selector through all the shift positions.

NOTE: Do no overspeed the engine during warm-up.

12. Place shift back in **P** and add fluid as necessary so reading is between the **F** and **L** marks on dipstick.

NOTE: Make certain fluid is just below the F mark. Do not overfill.

VALVE BODY

Removal and Installation

1. Disconnect the negative battery cable.
2. Raise and safely support the vehicle.
3. Remove the undercover and side cover.
4. Drain the transaxle fluid.
5. Remove the pan attaching bolts, pan and gasket.
6. Remove the valve body-to-case attaching bolts. Hold the manual valve to keep it from sliding out of the valve body and remove the valve body from the case.

NOTE: Failure to hold the manual valve while removing the control assembly could cause the manual valve to be dropped, causing the valve to become bent or damaged. Be careful not to loose the vacuum diaphragm rod or the ball and spring for the torque converter relief valve.

7. Thoroughly clean and remove all gasket material from the pan and pan mounting face of the case.
8. Install the vacuum diaphragm rod to its hole in the case. Install the check ball and spring into the slotted hole in the transaxle case.

NOTE: The ball is inserted first and then the spring. Use petroleum jelly to retain the spring and ball, if necessary.

9. Install the valve body, mating the groove of the manual valve with the driving pin of the shift rod.
10. Position the valve body to the case and install the attaching bolts. Torque the bolts to 70–95 inch lbs. (8–11 Nm).
11. Install the oil pan and torque the bolts to 43–69 inch lbs. (5–8 Nm).

NOTE: Do not use any type of gasket sealer or RTV on the pan gasket. If necessary, soak the gasket in clean transaxle fluid.

12. Install the undercover and side cover.
13. Lower vehicle. Refill the transaxle with the proper grade and type fluid.

SERVO ASSEMBLY

Removal and Installation

1. Raise and support the vehicle safely. Remove pan and valve body.
2. Remove left front wheel.
3. Remove the left lower ball joint bolt and separate the lower arm from the knuckle.
4. Separate the left drive shaft from the transaxle by prying with a bar inserted between the shaft and the case.

NOTE: A notch is provided in the side bearing housing to accommodate the bar. Do not insert the bar too far or damage to the lip of the oil seal may occur.

5. Support the halfshaft with a wire.
6. Loosen the anchor end-bolt and nut.
7. Remove the band strut.
8. Use a C-clamp and socket to compress the servo piston into the transaxle case.

—————————— CAUTION ——————————
Eye protection should be worn during servo removal.

9. Remove the servo snapring.
10. Remove the servo retainer, piston and spring by slowly loosening the C-clamp.
11. Lubricate the piston and spring with Dexron®II transmission fluid.
12. Replace the return spring. Replace the O-ring piston seal.
13. Use a C-clamp and socket to compress the assembly.
14. Install the snapring to the snapring groove.
15. Install the band strut to the band.
16. Install the anchor end-bolt to the band and torque to 8.7–10.8 ft. lbs. (12–15 Nm).
17. Back off the end-bolt 2 complete turns on carburetor equipped vehicles and 3 complete turns on EFI equipped vehicles.
18. Install the anchor end-bolt locknut and torque to 41–59 ft. lbs. (55–80 Nm).
19. Replace the clip at the end of the halfshaft with a new clip and install shaft with the clip gap at the top of the groove.

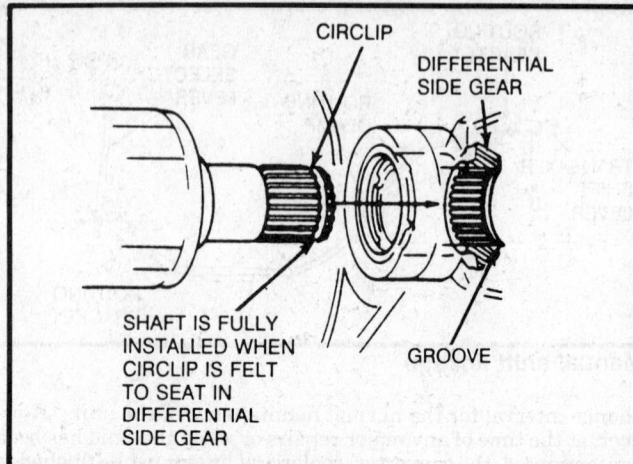

Circlip location and installation

NOTE: Do not reuse the old clip. A new clip must be installed.

20. Slide the halfshaft horizontally into the transaxle differential, supporting it at the CV joint to prevent damage to the oil seal lip. Apply even pressure to the hub until the circlips are heard to engage.

NOTE: After installation, pull both front hubs outward to confirm that the drive shafts are retained by the circlips.

21. Install the lower arm ball joint to knuckle and torque nut to 32–40 ft. lbs. (43–54 Nm).
22. Install the underside covers.
23. Install the front wheel assembly and torque lugnuts to 65–87 ft. lbs. (90–120 Nm).
24. Refill the transaxle with the proper grade and type fluid.

GOVERNOR

Removal and Installation

1. Note the position of the governor, remove the 3 retaining bolts from the governor cover assembly. Lift the governor assembly from the transaxle case.
2. Remove the 2 governor retaining screws from the governor sleeve. Remove the governor valve body.
3. Disassemble the governor valve body as required.
4. Reassemble the governor valve body.
5. Install the governor valve body to the governor sleeve.
6. Mount the governor to the transaxle case in position noted during removal.
4. Install the 3 cover/governor retaining bolts and tighten to 69–95 inch lbs. (7.8–10.8 Nm).

DIFFERENTIAL OIL SEALS

The left and right axle seals can be installed with the axles removed. Conventional seal removing and installing tools can be used. Care must be exercised to prevent damage to the seals as the axles are reinstalled into the transaxle case.

Removal and Installation

1. Support vehicle safely, remove wheel assembly and underbody covers.
2. Remove the stabilizer bar to control arm bolts, washers and bushings.
3. Remove the lower ball joint bolt and separate the lower arm from the knuckle.

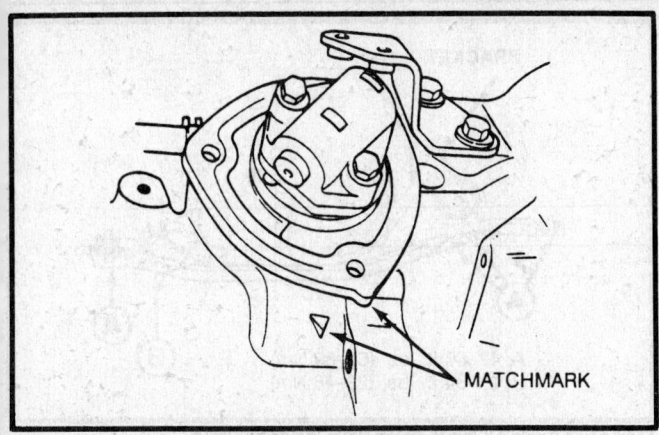

Aligning projection with mark on case

4. Partially drain the transaxle.
5. Separate the halfshaft from the transaxle by prying with a bar inserted between the shaft and the case. Tap the bar lightly to help loosen it from the differential gear.

NOTE: A notch is provided in the side bearing housing to accommodate the bar. Do not insert the bar too far or damage to the lip of the oil seal may occur.

6. Pull the halfshaft from the transaxle and support the it with a wire.
7. Pry the seal from the transaxle case using an appropriate tool.
8. Lubricate the new seal with transmission fluid and install using an appropriate tool.
9. Replace the clip at the end of the halfshaft with a new clip and install shaft with the clip gap at the top of the groove.

NOTE: Do not reuse the old clip. A new clip must be installed.

10. Slide the halfshaft horizontally into the transaxle differential, supporting it at the CV-joint to prevent damage to the oil seal lip. Apply even pressure to the hub until the circlips are heard to engage.

NOTE: After installation, pull both front hubs outward to confirm that the driveshafts are retained by the circlips.

11. Install the lower arm ball joint to knuckle and torque nut to 32–40 ft. lbs. (43–54 Nm).
12. Install the underside covers.
13. Install the front wheel assembly and torque lugnuts to 65–87 ft. lbs. (90–120 Nm).
14. Check and add Dexron®II transmission fluid as needed.

REMOVAL AND INSTALLATION

TRANSAXLE REMOVAL

The transaxle may be removed with the engine in place. The engine must be support from above, by using an engine support bar across the fenders. The procedures listed are for the Tracer. The technician should be aware that some of the procedures may vary slightly between the Tracer and Festiva, but the basic removal steps are the same.

1. Disconnect the negative cable from the battery.
2. Remove the air cleaner.
3. Loosen the front wheel lug nuts.
4. Remove the speedometer cable.
5. Disconnect the shift control cable from the transaxle by removing the clip and the bracket bolts.
6. Remove the engine ground wire from the cylinder head.
7. Remove the water pipe bracket.
8. Remove the secondary air pipe and EGR pipe bracket.
9. Remove the wire harness clip.
10. Disconnect the wiring to the inhibitor switch and kickdown solenoid.
11. Disconnect the body ground connector.
12. Remove the upper transaxle mounting bolts.
13. Disconnect the neutral switch connector at the transaxle.
14. Remove the vacuum hose from the vacuum modulator.
15. Remove and plug the cooler lines.
16. Mount the engine support bar across fenders and support the engine.
17. Raise and support the vehicle safely.
18. Remove the underbody covers.
19. Remove the tire assemblies.
20. Remove the stabilizer bar.
21. Remove the lower control arm ball joint clamp bolt and nut. Separate the ball joint from the steering knuckle.
22. Drain the transaxle.
23. Insert a pry bar between the transaxle case and halfshaft.

Supporting engine from above with support bar

Lightly tap on the end of bar until the halfshaft loosens from differential.
24. Pull the halfshaft from the transaxle and suspend under vehicle with wire.
25. Remove the crossmember to frame bolts.
26. Remove the nut attaching the positive cable to the starter and remove cable.
27. Remove the wire attach to the solenoid by grasping wire and pulling straight out.
28. Remove the starter.
29. Remove the bolts attaching the endplate to transaxle.
30. Remove the bolts attaching the torque converter to the flex plate.
31. Lean the engine toward the transaxle by loosening the engine support hook bolt.

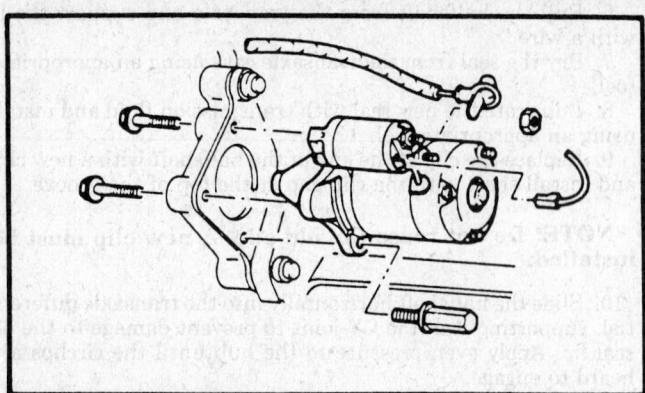

Starter bolt locations

32. Support the transaxle with a floor jack and block of wood.
33. Remove the nut and bolts that retain the engine mount bolts to the transaxle.
34. Remove the remaining transaxle mounting bolts and remove the transaxle, being careful not to allow the torque converter to separate from the transaxle.

TRANSAXLE INSTALLATION

1. Install the torque converter on the transaxle input shaft.

NOTE: Before installing the torque converter, pour a ½ qt. of Dexron*II transmission fluid into the torque converter.

2. To insure the converter is properly installed, measure the distance from converter housing to transaxle housing end. This measurement should be 0.790 in. (20mm).
3. Install the transaxle to the engine.
4. Install all but the top 2 retaining bolts and torque to 27–36 ft. lbs.(34–49Nm).

NOTE: If at all possible, it is advisable to install all of the retaining bolts, including the top bolts, before tightening. Tightening them all at the same time will avoid uneven stress on the transaxle case.

5. Raise the transaxle, using a floor jack and block of wood.
6. Align and install the torque converter to flex plate bolts and torque to 27–36 ft. lbs. (34–49Nm).
7. Install the starter and torque the bolts to 23–34 ft. lbs. (31–46 Nm).
8. Install the solenoid wire.
9. Install the positive battery cable to the solenoid.
10. Install the crossmember. Torque the motor mount nut to 21–34 ft. lbs. (28–46 Nm) and torque all other mounting bolts to 47–66 ft. lbs. (64–89 Nm).
11. Install a new clip on both halfshafts, making certain the gap in the clip is at the top of the groove when installing the shafts.

NOTE: Do not reuse the old clips. New clips must be installed.

12. Slide the halfshafts horizontally into the transaxle differential, supporting them at the CV-joint to prevent damage to the oil seal lip. Apply even pressure to the hub until the circlips are heard to engage.

NOTE: After installation, pull both front hubs outward to confirm that the driveshafts are retained by the circlips.

13. Install the lower arm ball joints to knuckle and torque nuts to 32–40 ft. lbs. (43–54 Nm).

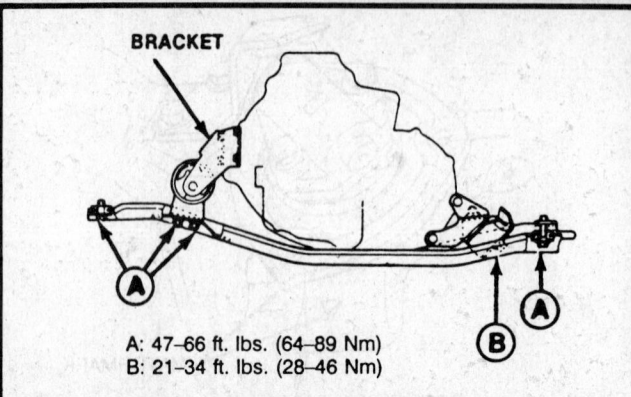

A: 47–66 ft. lbs. (64–89 Nm)
B: 21–34 ft. lbs. (28–46 Nm)

Crossmember bolt location and torque

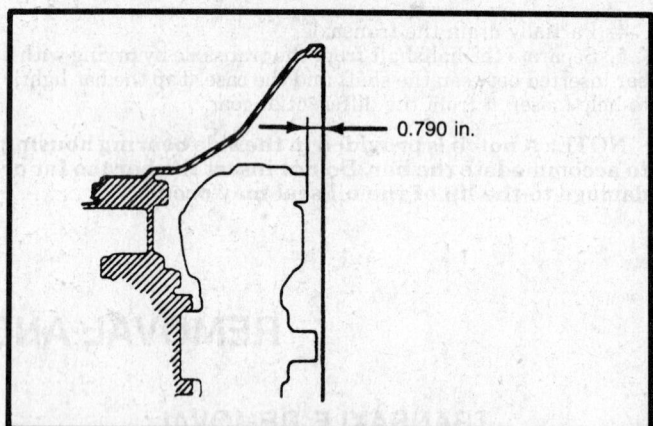

Checking converter clearance

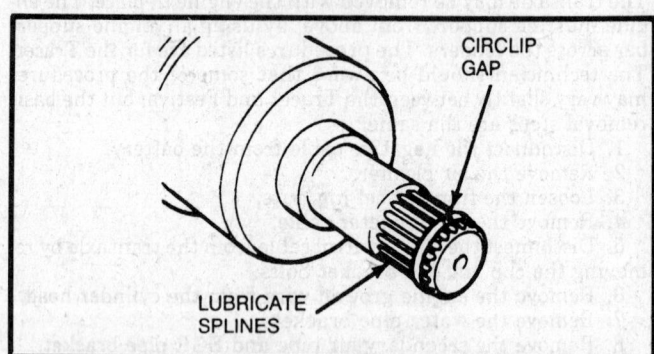

Circlip location and installation

14. Install the underside covers.
15. Install the front wheel assemblies and torque lug nuts to 65–87 ft. lbs. (90–120 Nm).
16. Lower vehicle, install upper 2 transaxle mounting bolts and torque to 47–66 ft. lbs. (64–89 Nm).
17. Remove the engine support bar.
18. Remove the plugs from the cooler lines and install cooler lines.
19. Install the vacuum line to modulator.
20. Install the neutral switch connector.
21. Install the body ground connector.
22. Connect the wiring to inhibitor switch and kickdown solenoid.
23. Install the wiring harness clips.
24. Install the secondary air pipe and EGR pipe bracket.

25. Install the engine ground wire.
26. Connect the change control cable to this transaxle. Install the mounting bracket bolts and tighten.
27. Install the speedometer cable and holddown.

28. Install the air cleaner.
29. Install all of the components that were necessary to remove the transaxle.
30. Refill the transaxle with the proper grade and type fluid.

BENCH OVERHAUL

Before Disassembly

Before removing any of the sub-assemblies, thoroughly clean the outside of the transaxle to prevent dirt from entering the mechanical parts during the repair operation.

------------------ **CAUTION** ------------------
Eye protection should be worn during procedures involving air pressure, when using spring compression tools or when removing snaprings.

During the repair of the subassemblies, certain general instructions which apply to all units of the transaxle must be followed. The instructions are given here to avoid unnecessary repetition.

Handle all transaxle parts carefully to avoid nicking or burring the bearing or mating surfaces.

Lubricate all internal parts of the transaxle before assembly with clean automatic transaxle fluid. Do not use any other lubricants except on gaskets and thrust washers which may be coated with petroleum jelly to facilitate assembly. Always install new gaskets when assembling the transaxle.

Converter Inspection

1. If the converter is to be reused, inspect the outer area of the converter for crack, inspect the bushing and seal surfaces for worn areas, scores, nicks or grooves.
2. The converter must be cleaned on the inside with cleaning solvent, dried, flushed with clean transmission fluid and drained until ready for installation.
3. Measure the converter bushing inside diameter.
4. Replace converter if bushing diameter is greater than 1.302 in. (33.075mm).

NOTE: Whenever a transaxle has been disassembled, the converter and oil cooler must be cleaned.

Transaxle Disassembly

CONVERTER AND OIL PAN

Removal

1. Remove the torque converter from transaxle by pulling it straight out of the housing.
2. If not already drained, remove the drain plug at the bottom of the transaxle case and allow the fluid to drain completely.
3. Remove the pan from the transaxle case.

VALVE BODY

Removal

1. Remove the vacuum modulator, taking care not to loosen vacuum diaphragm rod.
2. Remove the kickdown solenoid.
3. Remove the neutral safety switch.
4. Remove the valve body-to-case attaching bolts, note the position of each bolt for installation reference.

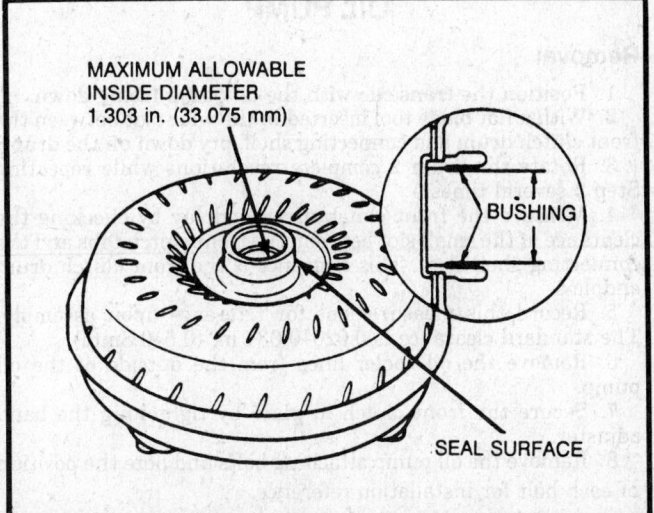

Torque converter bushing

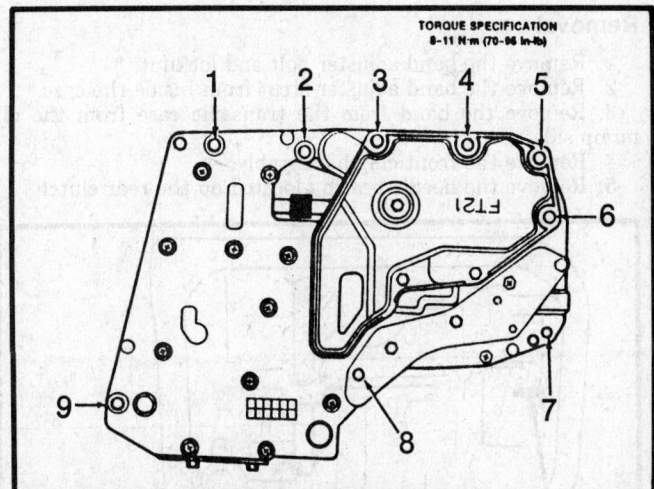

Bolt removal and torque sequence

NOTE: Be careful not to loose the ball and spring, located in the slotted hole.

5. Hold the manual valve to keep it from sliding out of the valve body and remove the valve body from the case.

NOTE: Failure to hold the manual valve while removing the control assembly could cause the manual valve to become bent or damaged. Be careful not to loose the vacuum diaphragm rod or the ball and spring for the torque converter relief valve.

6. If complete disassembly is to be done, remove the dipstick tube, speedometer driven gear, oil pump shaft and input shaft.

GOVERNOR

Removal

1. Note the position of the governor.
2. Remove the 3 retaining bolts from the governor cover assembly.
3. Lift the governor assembly from the transaxle case.
4. Remove the 2 governor retaining screws from the governor sleeve.
5. Remove the governor valve body.

OIL PUMP

Removal

1. Position the transaxle with the oil pump facing down.
2. With a flat blade tool inserted in the wide slot between the front clutch drum and connecting shell, pry down on the drum.
3. Rotate the drum 2 complete revolutions while repeating Step 2 several times.
4. Measure the front clutch drum endplay by checking the clearance of the small slot between the front clutch tabs and the connecting shell slots. This clearance is the front clutch drum endplay.
5. Record this measurement for reference upon assembly. The standard clearance is 0.020–0.031 in. (0.5–0.8mm).
6. Remove the oil cooler lines from the outside of the oil pump.
7. Secure the front clutch in place by tightening the band adjuster.
8. Remove the oil pump attaching bolts and note the position of each bolt for installation reference.

FRONT UNIT

Removal

1. Remove the band adjuster bolt and locknut.
2. Remove the band adjuster strut from inside the case.
3. Remove the band from the transaxle case from the oil pump side.
4. Remove the front clutch assembly.
5. Remove the needle bearing located on the rear clutch.

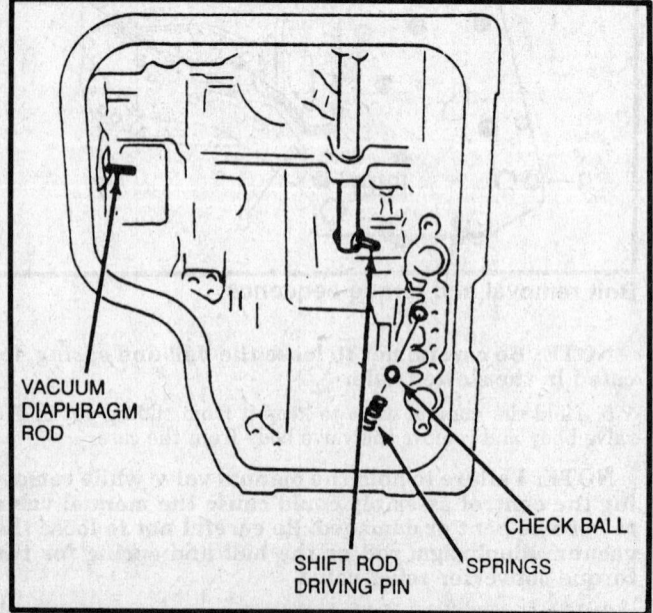

VACUUM DIAPHRAGM ROD

SHIFT ROD DRIVING PIN   SPRINGS   CHECK BALL

Transaxle and spring location

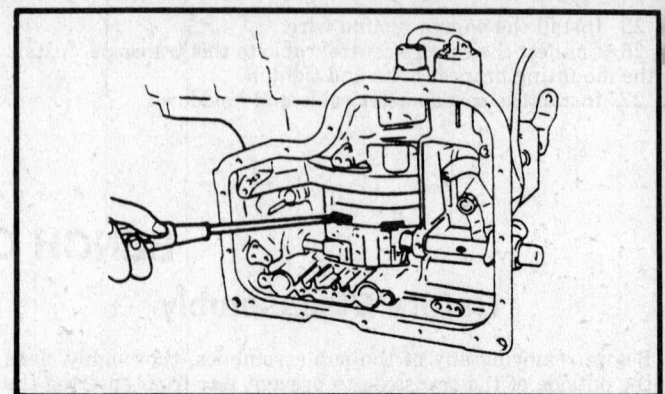

Prying clutch drum to check clearance

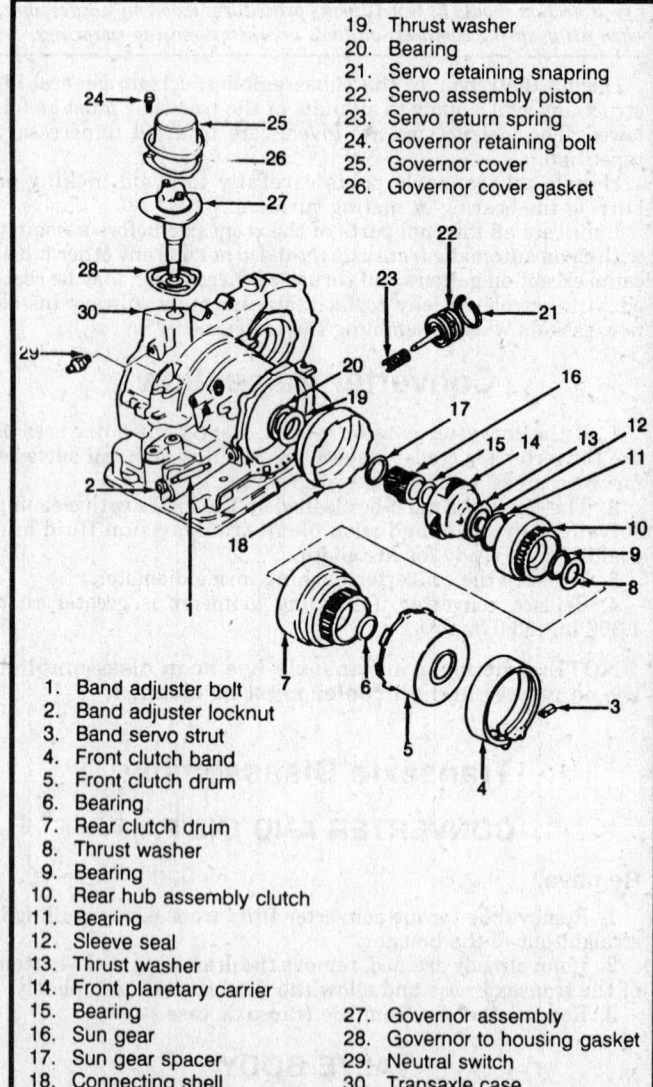

19. Thrust washer
20. Bearing
21. Servo retaining snapring
22. Servo assembly piston
23. Servo return spring
24. Governor retaining bolt
25. Governor cover
26. Governor cover gasket

1. Band adjuster bolt
2. Band adjuster locknut
3. Band servo strut
4. Front clutch band
5. Front clutch drum
6. Bearing
7. Rear clutch drum
8. Thrust washer
9. Bearing
10. Rear hub assembly clutch
11. Bearing
12. Sleeve seal
13. Thrust washer
14. Front planetary carrier
15. Bearing
16. Sun gear
17. Sun gear spacer
18. Connecting shell
27. Governor assembly
28. Governor to housing gasket
29. Neutral switch
30. Transaxle case

Transaxle exploded view—front section

6. Remove the rear clutch drum.
7. Remove the oil pump thrust washer, if washer did not stay on pump.
8. Remove the needle bearing located on the rear clutch hub assembly.

9. Remove the needle bearing and thrust washer from the planetary.
10. Remove the planetary carrier.
11. Remove the sun gear and spacer.
12. Remove the connecting shell.
13. Remove the thrust washer and needle bearing.
14. Use a C-clamp and socket to remove the servo piston into the transaxle case, if not already removed.

CAUTION

Eye protection should be worn during servo removal.

15. Remove the servo snapring.
16. Remove the servo retainer, piston and spring by slowly loosening the C-clamp.

INTERMEDIATE AND REAR UNIT

Removal

1. Remove the bolts attaching the transaxle case to the torque converter housing.
2. Carefully pry cases apart to separate the housings.
3. Pry oil lines away from case to remove.
4. Note the position of the parking pawl shaft and spring for installation reference. Remove pawl assembly by pulling the shaft straight out.
5. Remove the drum hub assembly from the case.
6. Remove the one-way clutch inner race assembly and planetary carrier from the case.
7. Remove the needle and thrust washer bearings from the planetary gear.
8. Before removing the one-way clutch, measure the clearance of the low and reverse clutch retaining plate and the one-way clutch, by using a feeler gauge. The clearance should be 0.032–0.041 in. (0.8–1.05mm).
9. Remove the snapring securing the one-way clutch and the retaining plate to the case.
10. Remove the clutch pack assembly.
11. Using a clutch compressor, place the recessed side of the large plate over the low and reverse clutch hub.
12. Place the small plate on the opposite side of the case. Insert the bolt through to clutch compressor plate and tighten the nut until the tension is relieved from the snapring.

NOTE: Transaxles which have not been previously disassembled do not have a low and reverse clutch hub snapring.

13. Remove the snapring from groove, if equipped.
14. Remove the clutch compressor tool.
15. Remove the low and reverse clutch hub.
16. Remove the springs from the low and reverse clutch piston.
17. To remove the low and reverse clutch piston, hold a wood block over the low and reverse clutch piston and apply a short burst of air to the piston application orifice in the transaxle case.

CAUTION

Wear eye protection and keep fingers out from between wood block and piston. Do not exceed 60 psi.

MANUAL LINKAGE

Removal

1. Remove the bolts attaching the parking pawl actuator guide to the case and remove the actuator guide.
2. Remove the lower nut at the end of the manual shaft assembly, hold the shaft with an open-end wrench.
3. Remove the 2 circlips from the manual shift linkage.
4. Remove the shift shaft linkage from the manual shaft.

1. Oil lines	24. Parking pawl actuator support retaining bolt
2. Parking pawl	25. Parking pawl actuator support
3. Parking pawl return spring	26. Circlip parking pawl actuator ferrule
4. Parking pawl shaft	27. Parking pawl actuator rod
5. Drum hub assembly	28. Clevis-pin
6. Needle bearing	29. Flat washer
7. Thrust washer	30. Spring
8. One-way clutch inner race	31. Ferrule
9. Planetary carrier	32. Lower manual shaft retaining nut
10. Retaining snapring	33. Manual shaft
11. Needle bearing	34. O-ring
12. Thrust washer	35. Control rod actuating lever
13. One-way clutch snapring	36. Circlip
14. One-way clutch	37. Actuating lever
15. One-way clutch retaining plate	38. Pivot pin
16. Internal spline clutch plate	39. Upper manual shaft retaining nut
17. External spline clutch plate	40. Lock washer
18. Dished plate	41. Manual shaft arm
19. Low-reverse retaining snapring	42. Control rod
20. Low-reverse clutch hub	43. Detent ball
21. Low-reverse piston	44. Detent spring
22. Outer piston seal	
23. Inner piston seal	

Transaxle exploded view—intermediate section

5. Remove the bolts from the upper shaft support and slide the manual shaft out of the transaxle case.
6. Remove the parking pawl actuator rod from the transaxle case.
7. Position the transaxle with the oil pan opening up.
8. Remove the roll pin securing the control rod to the transaxle case by lightly tapping the roll pin with a $^3/_{32}$ in. pin punch and a hammer.

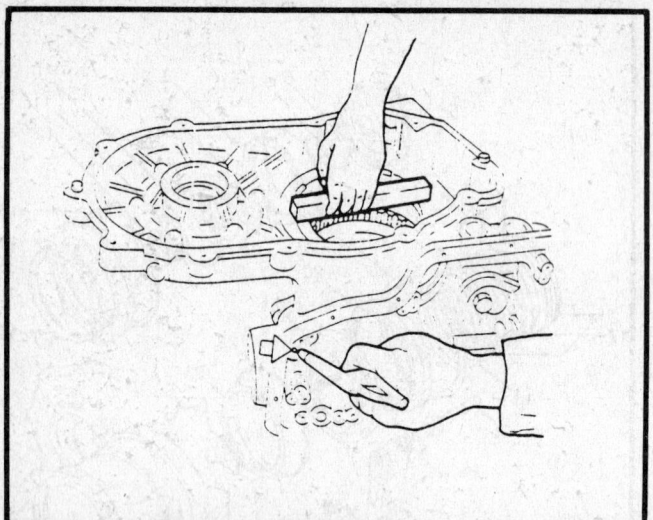

Testing low reverse clutch piston

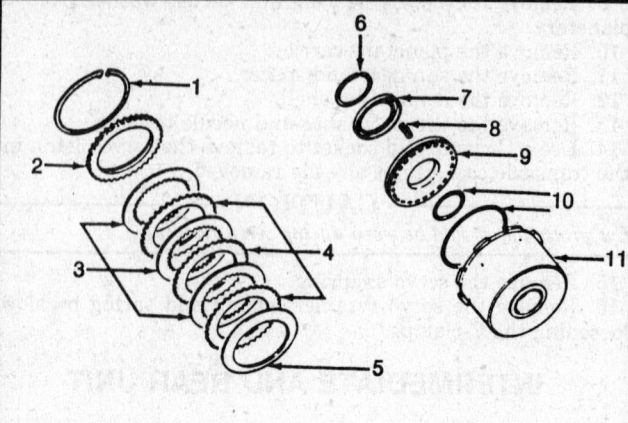

1. Snapring	7. Spring retainer
2. Retaining plate	8. Return springs
3. Internal splined disks	9. Piston
4. External splined disks	10. Seal rings
5. Dished plate	11. Rear clutch drum
6. Snapring	

Front clutch

9. Carefully slide the control rod out of the transaxle case, making sure not to lose the detent ball and spring.
10. Remove the detent ball.
11. Remove the spring.

FINAL DRIVE

Removal

1. Remove the differential assembly, by lifting it out of the case.
2. Remove the bolts attaching the output bearing and idler support to the converter housing.
3. Remove the support housing from the converter housing by lightly tapping the idler shaft with a brass drift and hammer.
4. Place the support assembly into a vise and remove the roll pin from the housing by tapping with a pin punch and hammer.
5. Carefully remove the bearing housing assembly from the vise.
6. Remove the idler gear assembly from the bearing cover.
7. Use the bearing remover to remove the bearing race from the support housing. Remove the adjustment shim from the housing. Separate or mark each shim for installation reference.
8. Using a puller and slide hammer remove the differential side bearing races from both the differential bearing housing and from the converter housing.
9. Remove the bolts and side bearing housing from the transaxle.
10. Remove the shim from the differential side bearing housing and drive out the oil seal.
11. Remove the O-ring from the differential side bearing housing.
12. Remove the oil seal from the output shaft bearing/stator support, using a puller and slide hammer.
13. Remove the output shaft bearing race from the bearing support, using a puller and slide hammer.
14. Remove the bolts and output shaft bearing/stator support by pressing it out of the case, using appropriate step plate tool.

Unit Disassembly and Assembly

NOTE: Allow all new clutch plates to soak in Dexron® II transmission fluid for a minimum of 2 hours before assembly.

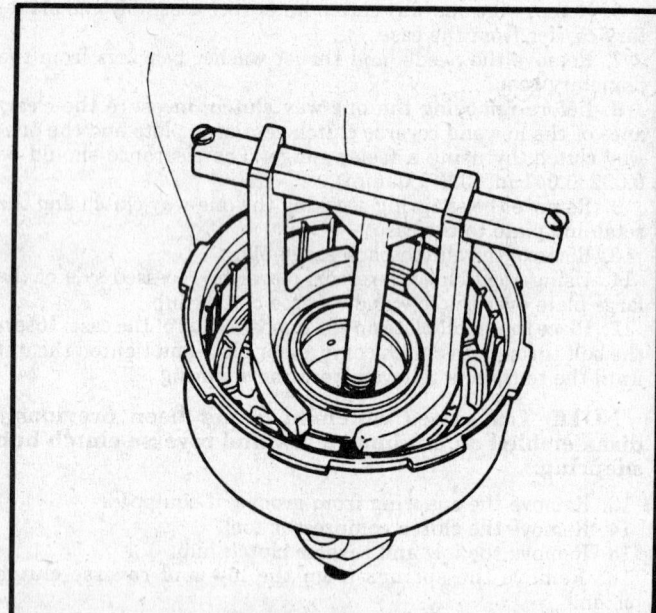

Compressing clutch plates

FRONT CLUTCH

Disassembly

1. Remove the retaining snapring from the drum.
2. Remove the retaining plate and the clutch plate assembly.
3. Remove the dished plate, noting the direction of the dish.
4. Remove the snapring from the drum hub with the use of a compressing tool.
5. Remove the piston from the drum by blowing compressed air into the apply hole in the drum. Remove the oil seals from the piston and drum hub.

Inspection

1. Inspect for damaged or worn drive plates, broken or worn

snaprings, deformed spring retainer, or weakened return springs.

NOTE: The free length of the return springs is 0.992–1.071 in. (25.2–27.2mm). If any spring is out of specification, replace all springs.

2. Inspect the drum bushing for being worn. Maximum inside diameter is 1.735 in. (44.075mm).

Assembly

1. It is good practice to install new clutch plates, both drive and driven, during the overhaul of the unit and not reuse the original plates.

2. Install the oil seals on the piston and the clutch drum hub. Lubricate the seals and grooves with vaseline or clean fluid.

3. Install the piston into the drum, being careful not to cut or damage the seals.

4. Install piston return springs to their mounting pegs on the clutch piston.

5. Place the spring retainer over the return spring.

6. Install the compressing tool and install the snapring holding the springs and spring retainer.

7. Install the dished plate with the protruding side facing the piston. Starting with a steel plate next to the dished plate, alternate with the lined plate and steel plate until 3 of each are installed.

8. Install the retaining plate and the retaining snapring.

9. Measure the front clutch clearance between the retaining plate and the snapring. The standard clearance is 0.063–0.071 in. (1.6–1.8mm). If the clearance is not correct, adjust it with the proper sized retaining plate.

10. After assembly, position the front clutch drum on the oil pump. Check clutch operation by applying air pressure to the application orifice.

REAR CLUTCH

Disassembly

1. Remove the clutch drum snapring, using an appropriate tool.

2. Remove the retaining plate, clutch plates, spacers and the dished plate from the clutch drum.

3. Place a "T" handled clutch spring compressor through the clutch drum. Install and tighten the nut of the compressor tool until the tension is relieved from the hub snapring.

4. Remove the clutch hub snapring, using an appropriate tool.

5. Remove the clutch compressor tool.

6. Place a wood block over the front of the front clutch drum. Remove the piston by applying compressed air into the fluid hole of the pump housing with the front and rear clutch assembly positioned on the oil pump extension.

CAUTION

Wear eye protection and keep fingers out from between wood block and piston. Do not exceed 60 psi.

---

7. Remove the inner and outer piston seal rings.

Inspection

Inspect for damaged or worn drive plates, broken or worn snaprings, deformed spring retainer, or weakened return springs.

NOTE: The free length of the return springs is 0.992–1.071 in. (25.2–27.2mm). If any spring is out of specification, replace all springs.

Assembly

1. Install the clutch piston into the clutch drum by pushing evenly, taking care not to damage the seals.

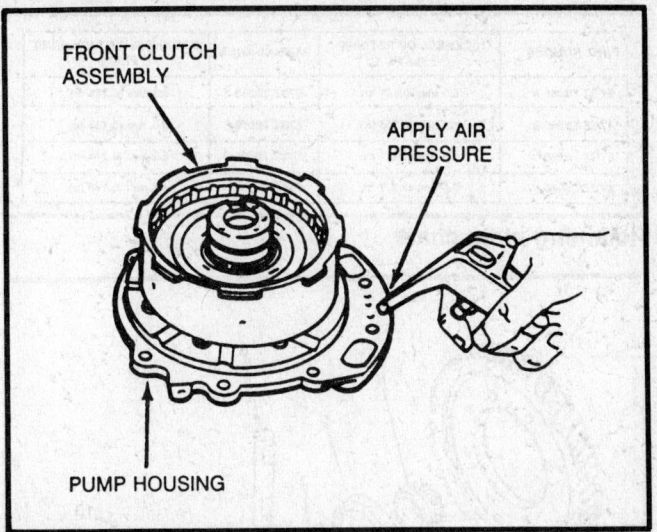

Testing front clutch assembly

PART NUMBER	THICKNESS OF RETAINING PLATE	PART NUMBER	THICKNESS OF RETAINING PLATE
E7GZ-7B066-B	5.2 mm (0.205 in)	E7GZ-7B066-E	5.8 mm (0.228 in)
E7GZ-7B066-C	5.4 mm (0.213 in)	E7GZ-7B066-F	6.0 mm (0.236 in)
E7GZ-7B066-D	5.6 mm (0.221 in)	E7GZ-7B066-G	6.2 mm (0.244 in)

Retaining plate chart

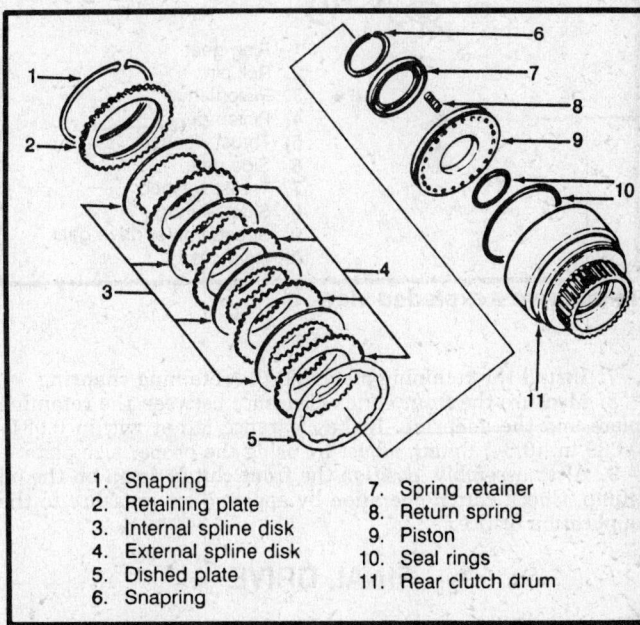

1. Snapring
2. Retaining plate
3. Internal spline disk
4. External spline disk
5. Dished plate
6. Snapring
7. Spring retainer
8. Return spring
9. Piston
10. Seal rings
11. Rear clutch drum

Rear clutch

2. Install the piston return springs to their mounting pegs on the clutch piston.

3. Place the spring retainer over the return springs.

4. Using the clutch spring compressor, press the clutch to gain access to the inner hub snapring groove.

5. Install the inner hub snapring, making certain it is fully seated in the groove. Remove compressor tool.

6. Install the dished plate with the protruding side facing the piston. Starting with a steel plate next to the dished plate, alternate with the lined plate and steel plate until 3 of each are installed.

PART NUMBER	THICKNESS OF RETAINING PLATE	PART NUMBER	THICKNESS OF RETAINING PLATE
E7GZ-7B066-A	5.0 mm (0.197 in)	E7GZ-7B066-E	5.8 mm (0.228 in)
E7GZ-7B066-B	5.2 mm (0.205 in)	E7GZ-7B066-F	6.0 mm (0.236 in)
E7GZ-7B066-C	5.4 mm (0.213 in)	E7GZ-7B066-G	6.2 mm (0.244 in)
E7GZ-7B066-D	5.6 mm (0.221 in)	E7GZ-7B066-H	4.8 mm (0.189 in)

Retaining plate chart

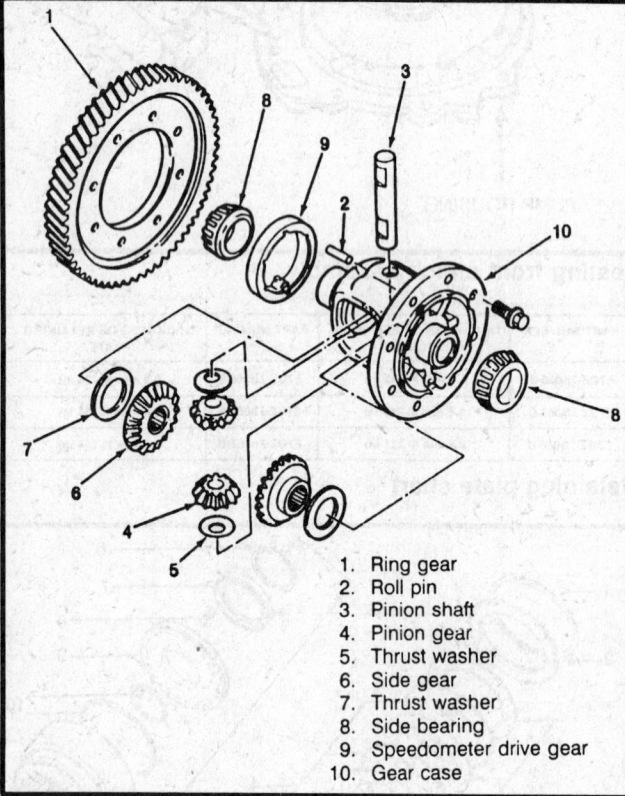

1. Ring gear
2. Roll pin
3. Pinion shaft
4. Pinion gear
5. Thrust washer
6. Side gear
7. Thrust washer
8. Side bearing
9. Speedometer drive gear
10. Gear case

Final drive — exploded view

7. Install the retaining plate and the retaining snapring.
8. Measure the front clutch clearance between the retaining plate and the snapring. If the clearance is not within 0.031–0.039 in. (0.8–1.0mm), adjust by using the proper size plate.
9. After assembly, position the front clutch drum on the oil pump. Check clutch operation by applying air pressure to the application orifice.

FINAL DRIVE

Disassembly

1. Install the halfshafts on differential and support unit in "V" blocks.
2. Measure and record the backlash of both pinion gears. Standard backlash is 0.000–0.004 in. (0.0–0.1mm).
3. Remove the ring gear.
4. Remove the pinion shaft roll pin, using a 5/32 in. diameter punch or rod at least 3 in. long.
5. Press the front bearing from the differential case, using a puller tool.

NOTE: If differential bearing is removed, it must be replaced with a new bearing and race.

6. Remove the rear bearing from the differential case, using a puller.
7. Remove the pinion shaft by sliding it out of the gear case.
8. Remove the pinion gears and thrust washers by rotating them out of the gear case.
9. Remove the side gears from the case.
10. Remove the speedometer drive gear from the case.

Inspection

1. The inspection of the components consists of checking for broken teeth, worn gears and thrust washers, or a cracked carrier housing.
2. The roller bearing must be pressed from the carrier housing and new ones pressed back on. New races must be used with new bearings.
3. The backlash of the pinion gears is 0.0–0.039 in. (0.0–0.1mm).
4. If the backlash of the pinions are not correct, replace all the thrust washers with new and recheck. If excessive clearance still exists, check the carrier for wear.

Assembly

1. Install the speedometer drive gear, align the locating tang on the gear with the groove in the gear case.
2. Install the front and rear differential bearings to the gear case with a press.
3. Locate and record the identification number on each side gear thrust washer. This information may be used when setting the backlash of the side and pinion gears. If backlash was measured when disassembled, use proper thickness thrust washer to obtain necessary backlash.
4. Coat the side gear thrust washers with Dexron®II transmission fluid and install washers and gears into the case.
5. Coat the pinion gear thrust washers with Dexron®II transmission fluid and install pinion gear and washers into the case.
6. Align pinion shaft with gears and install pinion shaft, with flat on the shaft up and the roll pin hole entering case last.
7. Install the pin through the gear case and into the pinion shaft, using an appropriate tool, until 1/16 in. below the surface of the gear case.
8. After installing the pin, stake the gear case to prevent the pin from coming out.
9. Install the ring gear to case, with the depression on the gear toward the case.
10. Align the holes in the gear with holes in case and install the bolts hand tight.
11. Tighten the bolts in a diagonal pattern in stages until torqued to 52–62 ft. lbs. (67–83 Nm).
12. Install the halfshafts on differential and support unit in "V" blocks.
13. Measure the backlash of both pinion gears. Standard backlash is 0.000–0.004 in. (0.0–0.1mm).
14. If the backlash is more than allowable, adjust by using different thickness thrust washers. Thrust washers should be the same thickness at each gear.

OUTPUT SHAFT

1. To disassemble, press off bearings.
2. Check for worn bearings or gears.
3. To reassemble, press bearing onto shaft.

IDLER GEAR

Disassembly

1. Insert hex torque adapter T87C–77000–E into the end of idler gear shaft and place the assembly into a vise.
2. Remove the locknut, using a 1½ in. socket.
3. Remove the idler gear and idler gear bearing.

Identification mark	Thickness
0	2.0 mm (0.079 in)
1	2.1 mm (0.083 in)
2	2.2 mm (0.087 in)

Pinion thrust washer identification

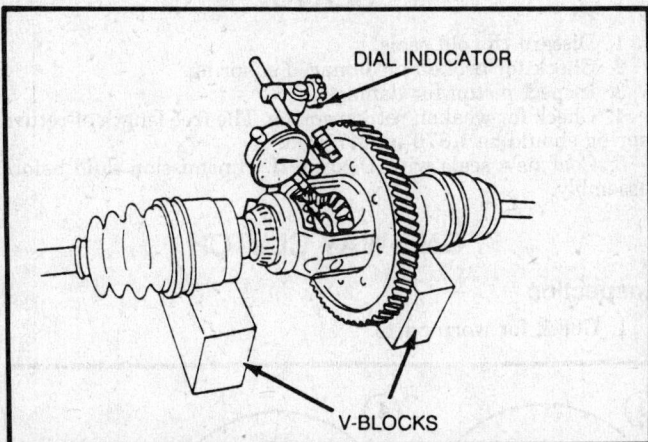

Checking backlash

4. If necessary, pull bearing race from gear, using appropriate puller.

5. Press other bearing race from gear, if necessary.

Inspection

Check for worn bearings or gears.

Assembly

1. Press the races into the idler gear, using a hydraulic press and appropriate adapters.

2. Assemble bearings, shims and locknut on the shaft and torque nut to 94 ft. lbs. (128 Nm).

3. Reposition the assembly in a vise, while protecting gear.

4. Using torque adapter tool and an inch lbs. wrench, measure the bearing preload. The correct amount of preload is 0.26–7.8 inch lbs. (0.3–9.0 Nm) while rotating tool.

5. Adjust shims as necessary to obtain proper preload.

6. When preload in correct, torque locknut to 94–130 ft. lbs. (128–177 Nm).

OIL PUMP

Disassembly

1. Remove the bolts that retain the pump cover to the pump housing.

2. Remove the pump cover, being careful not to allow the gears to fall out of the housing.

3. Mark the inner and outer gears with an indelible marker, prior to removing them.

NOTE: Do not mark the gears by pin-punching, or otherwise stressing the gear.

4. Remove the pump flange and inner and outer gears.

Inspection

1. Check the housing and cover for cracks or worn areas.

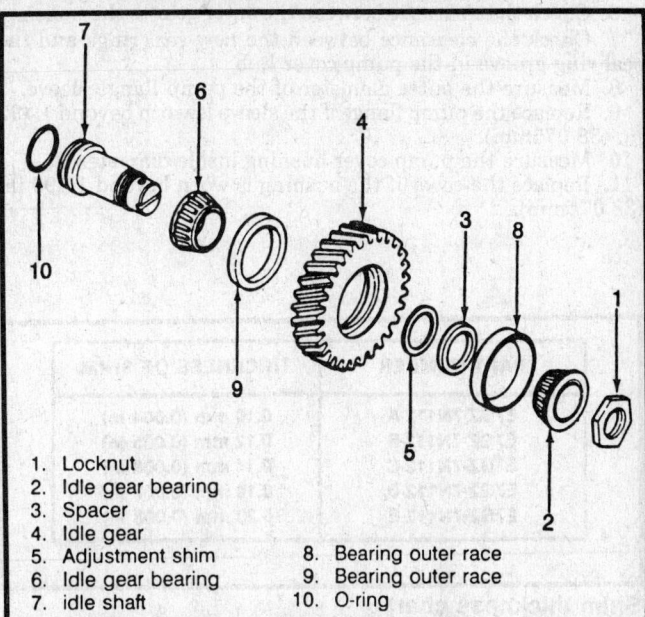

1. Locknut
2. Idle gear bearing
3. Spacer
4. Idle gear
5. Adjustment shim
6. Idle gear bearing
7. idle shaft
8. Bearing outer race
9. Bearing outer race
10. O-ring

Idler gear – exploded view

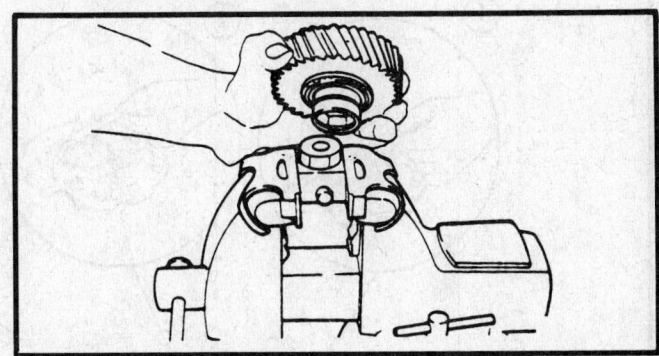

Using torque adapters

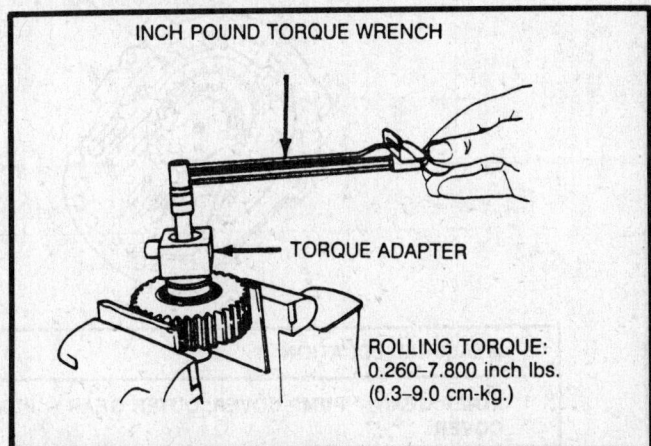

INCH POUND TORQUE WRENCH

TORQUE ADAPTER

ROLLING TORQUE:
0.260–7.800 inch lbs.
(0.3–9.0 cm-kg.)

Measuring bearing preload

2. Check the gears for wear, broken or damaged gear teeth.

3. Check the inner gear bushing of the pump housing sleeve for being worn or damaged.

4. Check the clearance of the inner gear to the pump cover and the outer gear to the pump cover.

5. Check the clearance of the outer gear teeth head to the crescent dam.

6. Check the clearance between the outer gear to the housing.

7. Check the clearance between the new seal rings and the seal ring groove in the pump cover hub.

8. Measure the outer diameter of the pump flange sleeve.

9. Replace the pump flange if the sleeve is worn beyond 1.492 in. (38.075mm).

10. Measure the pump cover bushing inside diameter.

11. Replace the cover if the bushing is worn beyond 1.499 in. (38.075mm).

PART NUMBER	THICKNESS OF SHIM
E7GZ-7N112-A	0.10 mm (0.004 in)
E7GZ-7N112-B	0.12 mm (0.005 in)
E7GZ-7N112-C	0.14 mm (0.006 in)
E7GZ-7N112-D	0.16 mm (0.007 in)
E7GZ-7N112-E	0.20 mm (0.008 in)

Shim thickness chart

Assembly

1. Assemble the gears to flange so the marks on the inner and outer gears are aligned and facing out.

2. Coat the gears with Dexron®II transmission fluid.

3. Install the pump cover to the pump housing.

4. Install the bolts and torque to 95–122 inch lbs. (11–14 Nm).

5. Install the oil pump shaft and make sure the gears turn easily.

SERVO

1. Discard the old seals.

2. Check for broken or damaged snapring.

3. Inspect piston for damage.

4. Check for weaken return spring. The free length of return spring should be 1.870 in. (47.5mm).

5. Coat new seals with Dexron®II transmission fluid before assembly.

ONE-WAY CLUTCH

Inspection

1. Check for worn parts.

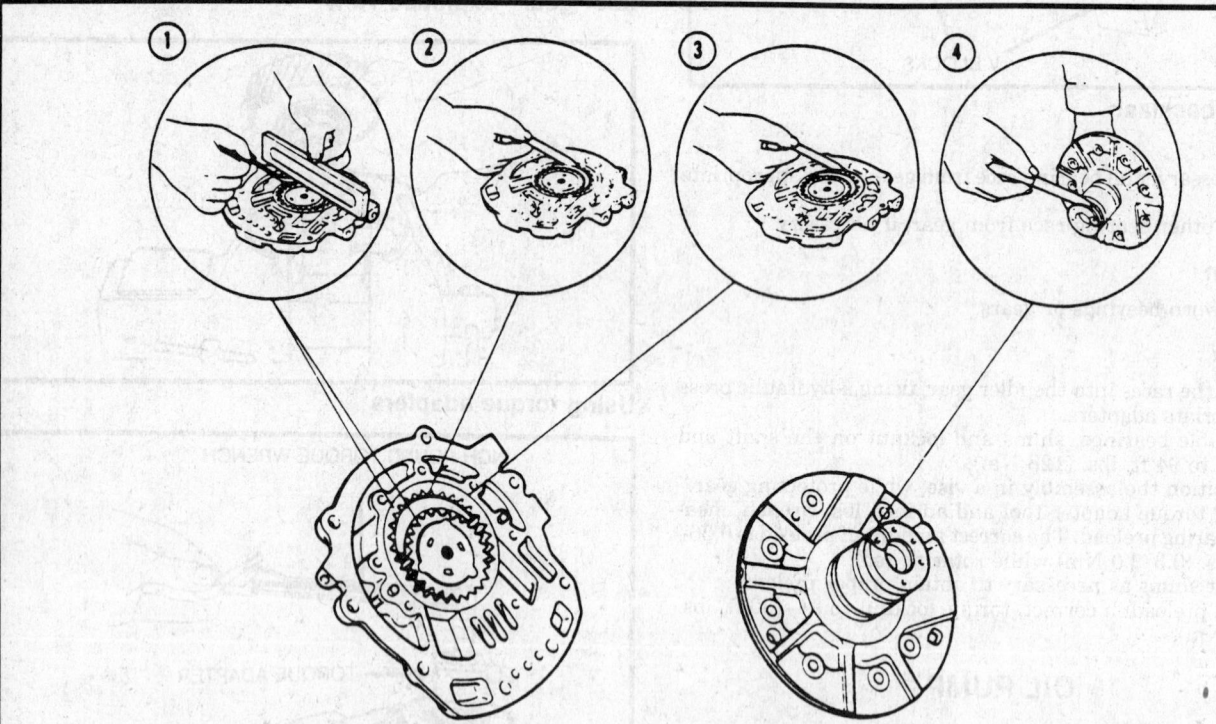

	MEASURED LOCATION	STANDARD VALUE	LIMIT
1	INNER GEAR ~ PUMP COVER: OUTER GEAR ~ PUMP COVER	0.02 ~ 0.04 mm (0.001 ~ 0.002 in)	0.08 mm (0.003 in)
2	HEAD OF OUTER GEAR TEETH ~ CRESCENT DAM	0.14 ~ 0.21 mm (0.006 ~ 0.008 in)	0.25 mm (0.010 in)
3	OUTER GEAR ~ HOUSING	0.05 ~ 0.20 mm (0.002 ~ 0.008 in)	0.25 mm (0.010 in)
4	SEAL RING ~ SEAL RING GROOVE	0.04 ~ 0.16 mm (0.002 ~ 0.006 in)	0.40 mm (0.016 in)

Checking pump and gear clearance

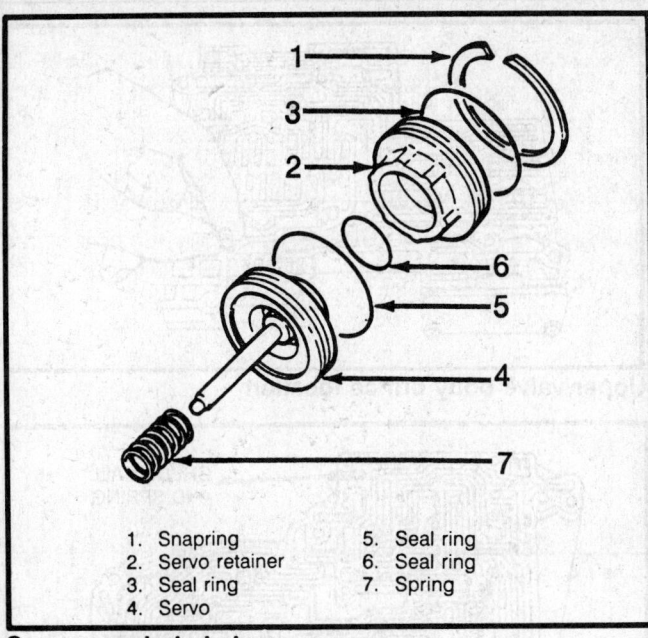

1. Snapring
2. Servo retainer
3. Seal ring
4. Servo
5. Seal ring
6. Seal ring
7. Spring

Servo – exploded view

2. Check for proper one-way operation.
3. Measure bushing, replace if greater than 5.121 in. (130.063mm).

LOW AND REVERSE CLUTCH

Inspection

1. Check for worn parts.
2. Check for weakened or damaged returned springs.
3. If any spring length is less than 1.07–1.11 in. (27.2–28.2mm), replace all springs.

DRUM HUB

Disassembly

1. Remove the parking gear spring.
2. Remove the parking gear by pushing the 2 pins which project from the drive hub.
3. Remove the snapring, the internal gear and the drive hub.

Inspection

Inspect the components for broken or worn snaprings, damaged or worn gears, or broken teeth.

Assembly

1. Assembly of the drum hub is in the reverse of its disassembly procedure.
2. Make certain the snapring and parking gear spring are in their proper positions.

PLANETARY UNITS

Disassembly

Remove snapring from one-way clutch inner race and separate planetary. The following procedures and measurements are the same for all planetary units.

Inspection

1. Inspect for worn snapring.

2. Inspect for binding, loose or rough rotation of gears.
3. Measure the clearance between the pinion washer and the planetary carrier, by using a feeler gauge. If the clearance exceeds 0.031 in. (0.8mm), replace the planetary unit.

Assembly

Clean and replace components in the reverse order of the removal procedure.

CONTROL VALVE BODY

The valve body is a high precision unit. It should be handled very carefully. Since many parts look alike, they should be kept in a well arranged order. If the clutches have been overheated or the band has been burn, make certain to disassemble, clean and inspect the valve body.

Disassembly

1. Remove the manual valve from the upper valve body.
2. Remove the bolts attaching the oil screen to the valve body and remove the oil screen.
3. Remove the 2-3 valve cover.
4. Remove the bolts attaching the upper and lower valve body, noting the position of each bolt.

NOTE: Keep the separator plate attached to the lower valve body to prevent losing the check ball, orifices and springs. If valve body is disassembled, note the locations of check ball, orifices and springs for reference during reassembly.

5. Carefully lift the lower body from the upper valve body, keeping the separator plate attached to the lower body.
6. Turn the assembly over, carefully remove the separator plate and remove the check ball and spring, 2 orifices and springs from the valve body, noting their locations.
7. Remove the orifice from the upper valve body with a magnet.
8. Note the location and position of each valve as the body is disassembled.
9. Carefully remove the side plates of the upper valve body to gain access to the valves.

NOTE: Keep the parts for each valve separated to prevent interchanging of springs that look alike.

Inspection

1. Check the valve body bores and valves for varnish or minor scoring.
2. Clean all parts, use carburetor cleaner to remove varnish.
3. If varnish or scoring is excessive, replace valve assembly.
4. Remove burrs from valves, using 600–800 grit finishing paper wet with Dexron®II transmission fluid.
5. Insert each valve separately into its bore. Do not lubricate at this time.
6. Check free movement of each valve, by tipping the valve body. Each valve should slide freely when valve body is shaken slightly.

Assembly

1. Lubricate all the components in Dexron®II transmission fluid.
2. Install the valves and springs in their correct bores.
3. Install the side plates at their correct positions and tighten the bolts to 22–30 inch lbs. (2.5–3.5 Nm).
4. Install the orifice in the upper half of the valve body.
5. Install the check ball and spring and the other 2 orifices and springs into their correct positions in the lower valve body.
6. Place the separator plate over the lower valve body. Hold-

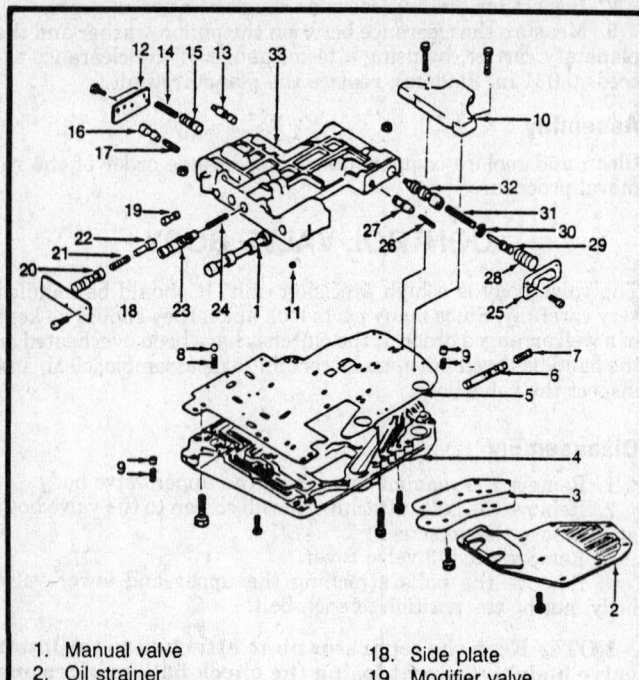

1. Manual valve
2. Oil strainer
3. 2–3 valve cover
4. Lower valve body
5. Separator plate
6. 3–2 timing valve
7. Spring
8. Check ball and spring
9. Orifice check valve and spring
10. Sub-body
11. Orifice check valve
12. Side plate
13. Vacuum throttle valve
14. Spring
15. Throttle backup valve
16. Downshift valve
17. Spring
18. Side plate
19. Modifier valve
20. 2–3 shift valve
21. Spring
22. 2–3 shift plug
23. 1–2 shift plug
24. Spring
25. Side plate
26. Spring
27. 2nd lock valve
28. Pressure regulator sleeve
29. Pressure regulator plug
30. Spring seat
31. Spring
32. Pressure regulator valve
33. Upper valve body

Valve assembly — exploded view

ing the separator plate and valve body together, turn the assembly over and place it onto the upper valve body.

7. Align the upper and lower valve body. Install attaching bolts and tighten to proper torque.

8. Install the 3-2 valve cover and torque the bolts to 26–35 inch lbs. (3–4 Nm).

9. Place valve body aside in a clean area, for installation at a later time.

GOVERNOR

Disassembly

1. Remove the governor body from the separator plate.
2. Remove the separator plate from the shaft.
3. Remove the filter from the separator plate.

NOTE: Cover the bore hole when removing the retainer plate to prevent losing the primary governor spring.

4. Remove the retainer plate for the primary governor spring by applying light pressure against the retainer plate and spring and sliding the plate out of the slot of the machined surface.

5. Remove the primary governor spring.

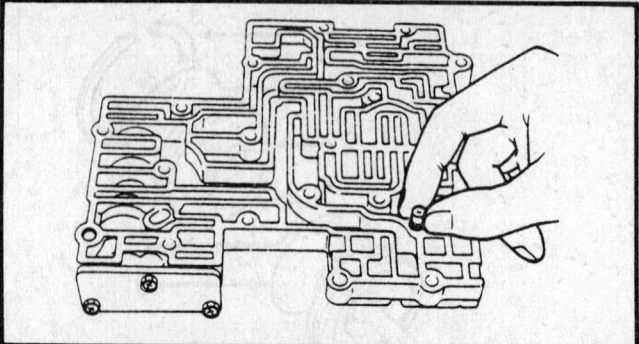

Upper valve body orifice location

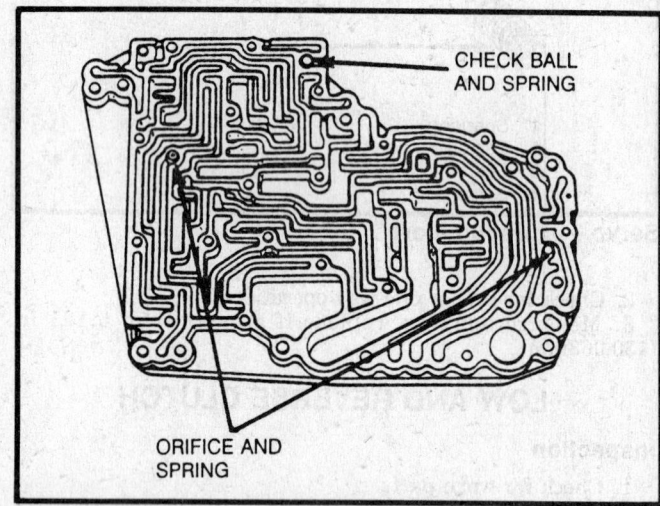

Orifice, spring and check ball location

NOTE: Cover the bore hole when removing the retainer plate to prevent losing the secondary governor spring.

6. Remove the retainer plate for the secondary governor spring by applying light pressure against the retainer plate and spring and sliding the plate out of the slot of the machined surface.

7. Remove the secondary governor spring.

8. Remove the governor driven gear roll pin, using a pin punch and hammer.

9. Remove the governor driven gear and separate the governor shaft from the sleeve.

10. Remove the seal rings from the governor shaft.

11. Remove the bearing outer race from the governor shaft.

12. Remove the needle bearing from the sleeve.

Inspection

1. Inspect the valves for scoring or sticking.

NOTE: Minor scoring or varnish may be removed with fine 600–800 grit finishing paper wet with Dexron®II transmission fluid.

2. Inspect return springs.

3. Replace the primary spring, if the diameter is not 0.34–0.87 in. (8.7–9.3mm) or free length is not 0.66–0.70 in. (16.7–17.7mm).

4. Replace the secondary spring, if the diameter is not 0.35–0.38 in. (8.95–9.55mm) or free length is not 0.50–0.54 in. (12.7–13.7mm).

5. Inspect driven gear for damaged teeth.

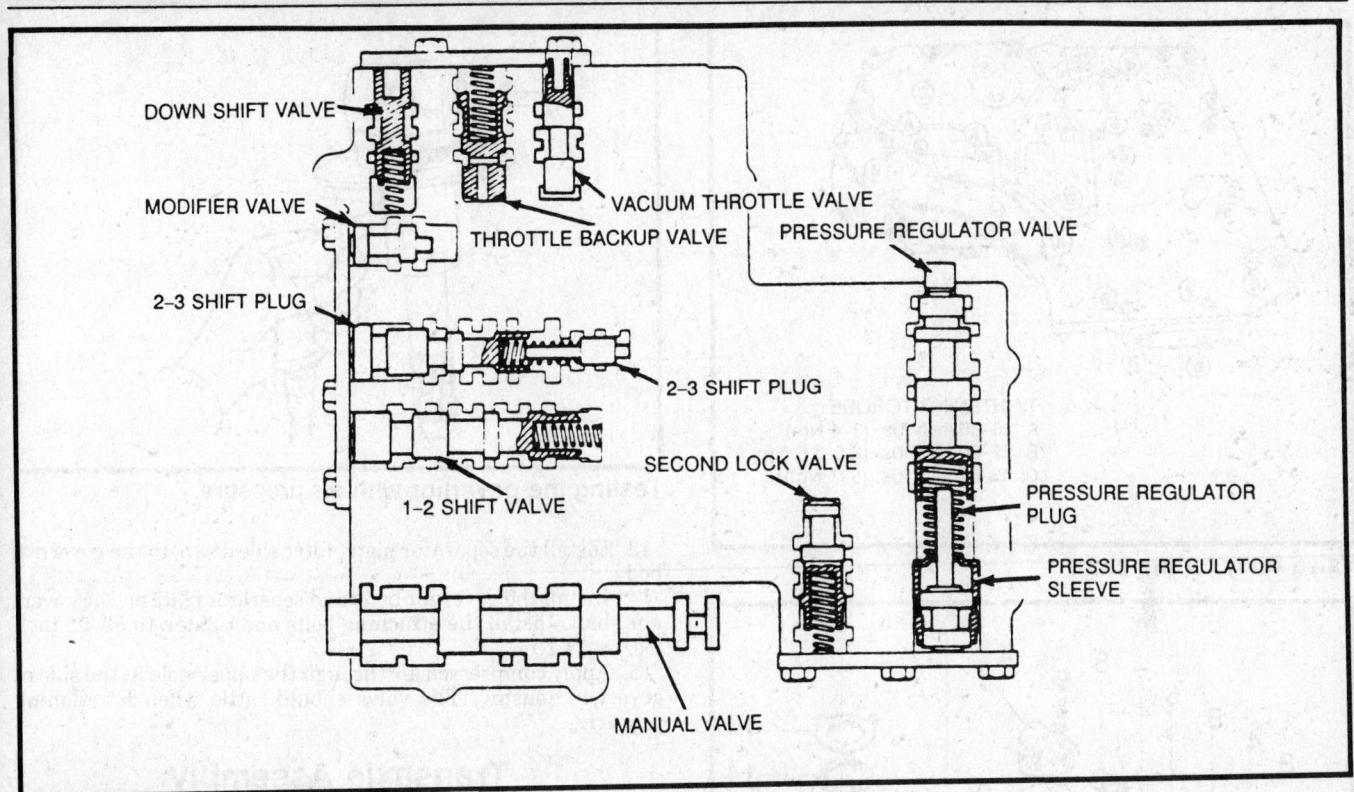

Valve location

NAME	OUTER DIA. mm (in)	FREE LENGTH mm (in)	NO. OF COILS	WIRE DIA. mm (in)
THROTTLE BACK UP	7.3 (0.287)	36.0 (1.42)	16.0	0.8 (0.031)
DOWN SHIFT	5.5 (0.217)	21.9 (0.862)	14.0	0.55 (0.022)
2-3 SHIFT	6.4 (0.252)(carb.) 6.9 (0.272)(EFI)	39.2 (1.54)(carb.) 41.0 (1.61)(EFI)	20.0	0.7 (0.028)
1-2 SHIFT	6.55 (0.258)	32.0 (1.26)	18.7 (carb.) 18.0 (EFI)	0.55 (0.022)
SECOND LOCK	5.55 (0.219)	33.5 (1.32)	18.0	0.55 (0.022)
PRESSURE REGULATOR	11.7 (0.461)	43.0 (1.69)	15.0	1.2 (0.047)
THROTTLE RELIEF	7.0 (0.276)	11.2 (0.44)	6.0	0.9 (0.035)
ORIFICE CHECK	5.0 (0.197)	15.5 (0.61)	12.0	0.23 (0.009)
3-2 TIMING	7.5 (0.295)	22.1 (0.870)	13.0	0.8 (0.031)

Valve spring size chart

6. Inspect needle bearings and thrust washer for wear.
7. Inspect for clogged or torn filter.

Assembly

1. Coat all parts with Dexron®II transmission fluid.
2. Install the seals.

3. Install the needle bearing into sleeve with the exposed bearing facing up.
4. Install the thrust washer on the governor shaft, making certain the tangs of the washer are inserted into the holes of the governor shaft.
5. Install the governor shaft into the sleeve.

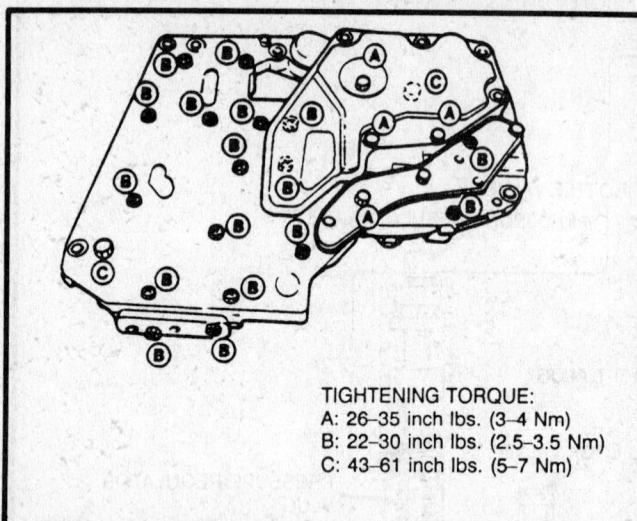

TIGHTENING TORQUE:
A: 26–35 inch lbs. (3–4 Nm)
B: 22–30 inch lbs. (2.5–3.5 Nm)
C: 43–61 inch lbs. (5–7 Nm)

Valve body torque chart

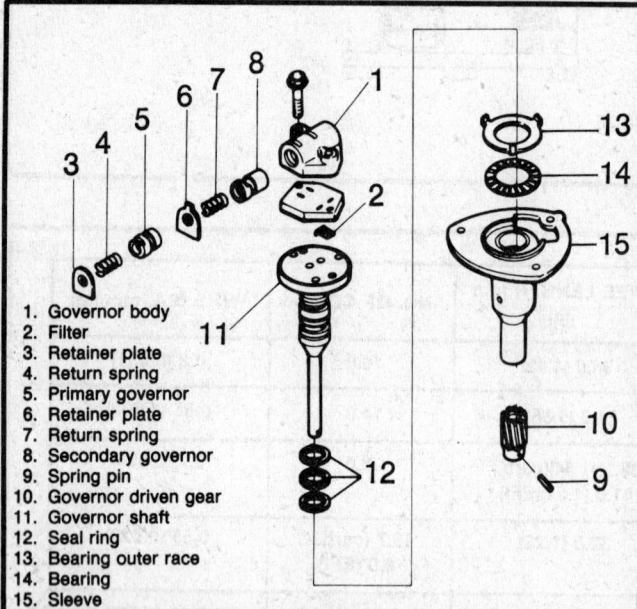

1. Governor body
2. Filter
3. Retainer plate
4. Return spring
5. Primary governor
6. Retainer plate
7. Return spring
8. Secondary governor
9. Spring pin
10. Governor driven gear
11. Governor shaft
12. Seal ring
13. Bearing outer race
14. Bearing
15. Sleeve

Governor assembly—exploded view

6. Install the governor driven gear to the governor shaft and install the roll pin, using a pin punch and hammer.

7. Install the secondary governor valve, narrow land first, into the large bore end of the governor body.

NOTE: The valve is fully seated when the narrow valve and extends out of the governor body case.

8. Install the secondary governor spring into the governor body until the spring end is seated in the recess of the secondary valve.

9. Compress the secondary spring. Install the retainer plate through the slot of the machined surface.

10. Install the primary governor valve, notched land last, into the large bore end of the governor body. The primary governor valve is fully seated when it contacts the retainer plate of the secondary valve.

11. Compress the primary spring. Install the retainer plate through the slot of the machined surface.

12. Install the filter onto the separator plate.

Testing the governor with air pressure

13. Install the separator plate, filter side down, to the governor body.

14. Install the governor body and separator plate on the governor shaft. Install the attaching bolts and tighten to 69–95 inch lbs. (8–11 Nm).

15. Apply compressed air through the upper hole in the side of governor housing. The valve should rattle when functioning properly.

Transaxle Assembly
CONVERTER HOUSING

Assembly

1. Install the differential output seal, using an appropriate tool.

2. Install the differential side bearing outer race in housing, using an appropriate tool.

3. Using guide pins, position output bearing/stator support in converter housing. Install and torque bolts to 8–10 ft. lbs. (11–14mm).

4. Using a driver and appropriate step plate press outer race for output shaft into bearing support.

5. Install the seal into stator support.

6. Using a new O-ring, install output bearing support in the transaxle case and torque bolts to 14–19 ft. lbs. (18–26 Nm).

DIFFERENTIAL BEARING PRELOAD

1. Position differential side bearing outer race in the recessed end of the gauge tool T87C–77000J. Screw the gauge tool on unit no clearance remains.

3. Place the differential in the converter housing. Place the gauge tool, with the outer race installed, over the differential side bearing.

4. Position the spacer collars in position and assemble the case halves. Torque bolts to 27–39 ft. lbs. (36–53 Nm).

5. Use the gauge wrench pins to unscrew the gauge tool and establish preload on the differential. Measure the preload using an inch lbs. torque wrench. Extend the gauge tool until the turning torque (drag) reads 4.3–6.9 inch lbs. (0.5–0.8 Nm).6. Measure the clearance at the separation of the gauge tool in order to determine the shim thickness.

7. Disassembly the gauge assembly. Install the necessary shims and bearing race in the transaxle housing and assemble the housing halves.

NOTE: Measure the clearance around the entire circumference and select shims equivalent to the maximum clearance. Do not use more than 5 shims.

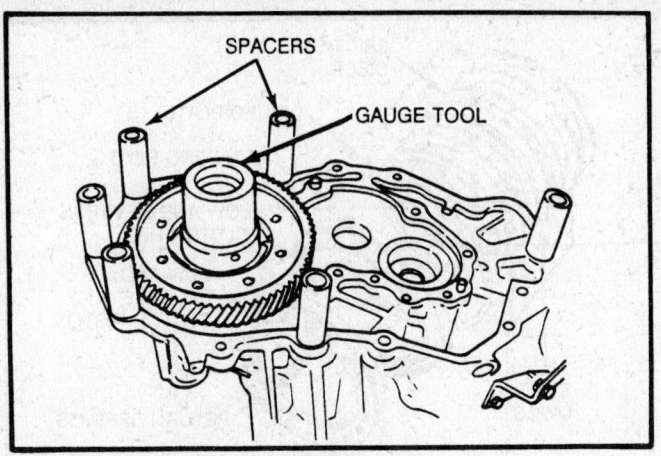

Installing bearing preload gauge

8. Test the bearing turning torque (drag) with housing assembled. If the turning torque is not 18–25 inch lbs. (2.1–2.9 Nm), repeat Steps 7 through 13.

9. Separate housing halves and install output shaft seals.

OUTPUT SHAFT BEARING PRELOAD

1.

Position the output gear and shaft into the converter housing.2.Position the 4 spacer collars.3.Insert the output shaft outer bearing race into the recessed end of the gauge tool and place the tool over the output gear shaft. Screw the halves of the gauge tool together so no clearance exists.4.Assemble the converter housing to the side bearing housing, using tool spacer bolts and torque bolts to 14–19 ft. lbs. (19–26 Nm).5.Unscrew the gauge tool, using gauge tool pins, until all the freeplay is removed and the bearing is seated.

6. Measure the drag on the output gear, by using the torque adapter tool.

7. Adjust drag to 0.36–0.65 inch lbs. (0.5–0.8 Nm), by adjusting shim thickness as necessary.

8. Disassemble the assembly tool and install selected shims and bearing race, using the appropriate tool and step plate.

9. Assembly output gear and bearing support. Torque bolts to 14–19 ft. lbs. (19–26 Nm).

10. Remeasure preload, if preload is not 0.26–7.81 inch lbs., repeat Steps 15 through 24.

11. After proper preload has been obtained, remove the bearing housing and install the idler gear assemble into the bearing housing. Replace the O-ring on the idler gear shaft.

12. Reinstall the bearing cone.

13. Torque the bearing housing bolts to 14–19 ft. lbs. (19–26 Nm).

MANUAL LINKAGE

Installation

1. Install the manual valve control rod, spring and ball detents.

2. Install the roll pin to retain the control rod.

3. Install the parking pawl actuator support and torque bolts to 8.7–11.6 ft. lbs. (12–16 Nm).

4. Install the actuating arm to the pawl rod and install circlips.

5. Install a new O-ring on the manual shaft.

6. Install the manual shaft to the transaxle case.

7. Install the manual shaft support to the transaxle case and torque the bolts to 8.7–11.6 ft. lbs. (12–16 Nm).

8. Install the shifter actuating arm to the manual shaft and align with the manual valve control rod.

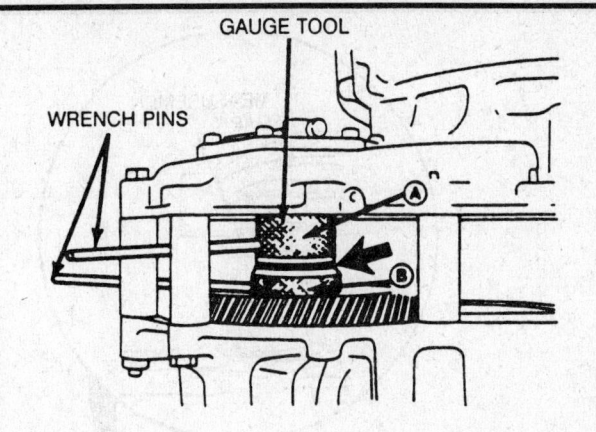

PART NUMBER	THICKNESS OF SHIM
E7GZ4067A	0.10 mm (0.004 in)
E7GZ4067A	0.12 mm (0.005 in)
E7GZ4067B	0.14 mm (0.006 in)
E7GZ4067C	0.16 mm (0.007 in)
E7GZ4067B	0.20 mm (0.008 in)
E7GZ4067C	0.30 mm (0.012 in)
E7GZ4067D	0.40 mm (0.016 in)
E7GZ4067E	0.50 mm (0.020 in)
E7GZ4067F	0.60 mm (0.024 in)
E7GZ4067G	0.70 mm (0.028 in)
E7GZ4067H	0.80 mm (0.032 in)
E7GZ4067J	0.90 mm (0.036 in)

Adjusting bearing preload

PART NUMBER	THICKNESS OF SHIM
E7GZ-7F405-A	0.10 mm (0.004 in)
E7GZ-7F405-B	0.12 mm (0.005 in)
E7GZ-7F405-C	0.14 mm (0.006 in)
E7GZ-7F405-D	0.16 mm (0.007 in)
E7GZ-7F405-E	0.20 mm (0.008 in)
E7GZ-7F405-F	0.50 mm (0.020 in)

TEST PRELOAD: 0.5 ~ 0.9 N·m (0.05 ~ 0.09 m-kg, 0.36 ~ 0.65 ft-lb)

ASSEMBLED PRELOAD: 0.03 ~ 0.9 N·m (0.3 ~ 9.0 cm-kg, 0.26 ~ 7.81 in-lb)

CAUTION
A) MEASURE THE CLEARANCE AROUND THE ENTIRE CIRCUMFERENCE, AND SELECT SHIMS EQUIVALENT TO THE MAXIMUM CLEARANCE.
B) MAXIMUM ALLOWABLE NUMBER OF SHIMS: 7

Adjusting shim chart

9. Install the nut on manual shaft and torque to 22–29 ft. lbs. (29–39 Nm).

INTERMEDIATE UNIT

Installation

1. Install new seals in the low and reverse piston and install piston in bore taking care not to damage seal.

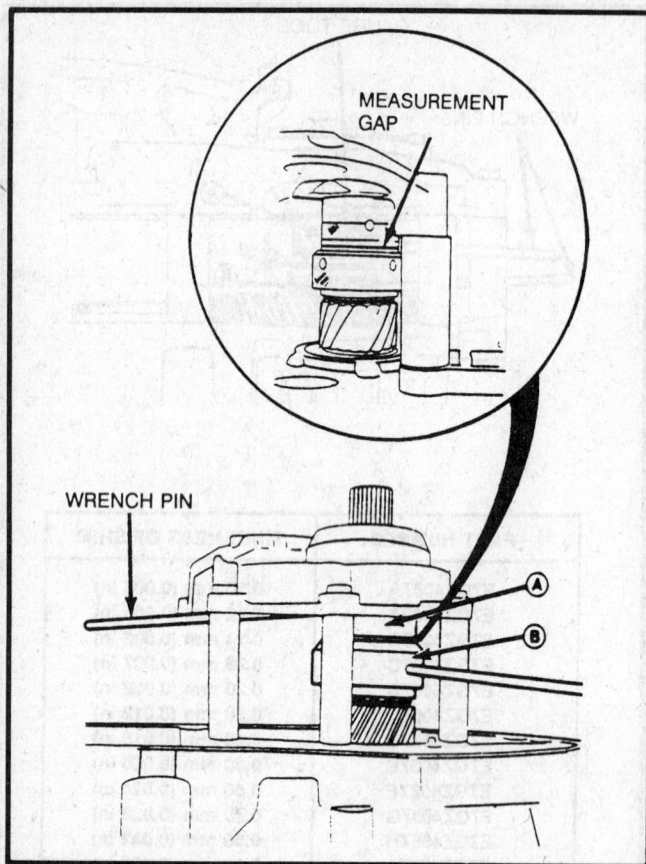

Check preload

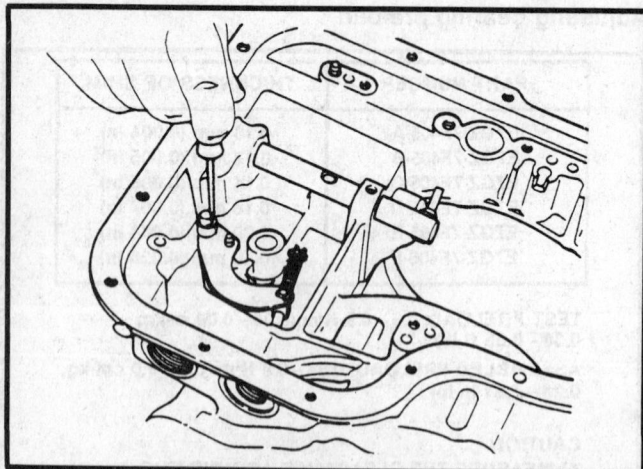

Install arm to pawl rod

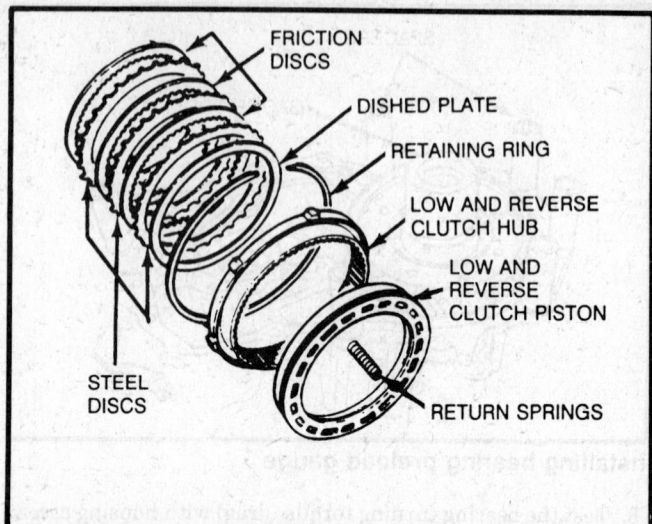

Intermediate clutch pack

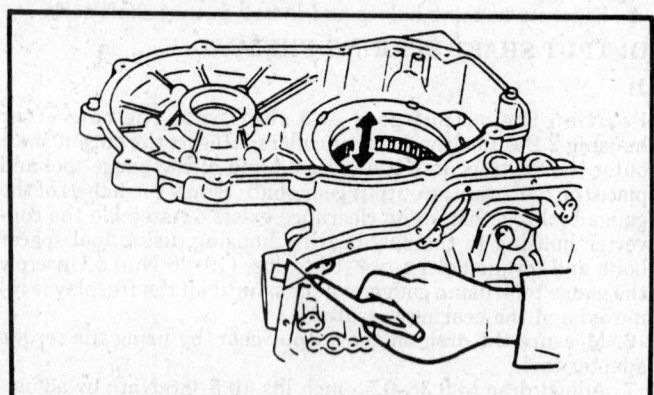

Test clutch pack

PART NUMBER	THICKNESS
E7GZ-7B066-J	7.8 mm (0.307 in)
E7GZ-7B066-K	8.0 mm (0.315 in)
E7GZ-7B066-L	8.2 mm (0.322 in)
E7GZ-7B066-M	8.4 mm (0.331 in)
E7GZ-7B066-N	8.6 mm (0.339 in)
E7GZ-7B066-P	8.8 mm (0.346 in)

Retaining plate thickness chart

2. Place the return spring and low and reverse clutch hub on top of the piston.

3. Install the clutch compressor and compress the assembly far enough to permit insertion of the retainer ring.

4. Install the dished plate to the low and reverse piston.

5. Install the clutch disc pack starting with a steel disc against the dished plate. Alternate internal and external tooth plates until all discs have been installed.

6. Install the retaining plate.

7. Install the one-way clutch with the bushing against the retaining plate. Compress the clutch assembly enough to install the retaining ring.

8. Using a feeler gauge, measure the clearance between the one-way clutch and the retaining plate.

9. If the clearance is not 0.032–0.041 in. (0.81–1.05mm), adjust shim size as necessary.

10. Apply a burst of air pressure to the application port to test clutch plate action.

— **CAUTION** —

Do not allow air pressure to exceed 60 psi. Wear eye protection.

11. Install the parking pawl, spring and anchor pin to the case.

12. Position the converter housing to receive the differential. Install the differential, meshing ring gear with idler gear.

13. Install the thrust washer over output shaft.

14. Install the bearing so that the rollers contact the thrust washer.

15. Install the assembled drum hub onto the output shaft spline.

16. Install a bearing in the recess of the drum hub. Secure the opposing thrust washer to the planetary carrier with petroleum jelly.

17. Install the planetary carrier onto the one-way clutch inner race and secure it in place with the retainer ring.

18. Install the planetary carrier/inner race assembly into the drum hub.

19. Using a plastic mallet, install the governor oil transfer lines into the transfer case.

20. Apply a $^1/_{16}$ continuous bead of gasket eliminator E1FZ–19562–A (non-silicone) onto the converter housing mating surface.

21. Assemble the transaxle halves by rotating the one-way clutch inner race as the transaxle case is lowered onto the converter housing to engage the spline teeth of the inner race with the low and reverse disks.

22. Install the bolts and torque to 22–34 ft. lbs. (29–46 Nm).

23. After the cases are together, make certain all rotating parts rotate without resistance.

FRONT UNIT

Installation

1. Install the bearing to the rear planetary carrier.

2. Install the spacer over the small end of the sun gear and insert the sun gear into the connecting shell.

3. Place the thrust bearing over the end of the sun gear protruding from the connecting shell. Hold the washer in place with petroleum jelly.

4. Install the connecting shell/sun gear assembly into the rear planetary carrier.

5. Place the thrust bearing into the front planetary carrier using petroleum jelly. Face the rollers pointing out.

6. Install the front planetary carrier into the connecting shell.

7. Install the thrust washer and matching bearing to the end of the front planetary carrier. Install the seal sleeve in the center of the front planetary carrier.

8. Install the rear clutch hub assembly over the front planetary carrier.

9. Install the thrust bearing, rollers up, in the rear clutch hub.

10. Coat the matching thrust washer with petroleum jelly. Index the tangs on the washer with the mating holes in the rear clutch and install the washer.

11. Install the rear clutch assembly to the rear clutch hub, while gently rotating the rear clutch.

12. Install the thrust bearing in the rear clutch hub, rollers up. The companion thrust washer will be installed to the end of the oil pump extension later.

13. Place the assembled front clutch over the splines of the rear clutch hub, while gently rotating the front clutch.

14. Install the intermediate band, servo, strut and adjuster bolt. Apply sealant E1FZ–19562–A (non-silicone) to threads and install bolts tight enough to hold components in place, but do not perform adjustments until pump has been installed.

GOVERNOR

Installation

1. Install the governor onto the transaxle case so that the sleeve projection is aligned with the mark on case.

2. Torque bolts to 69–95 ft. lbs. (7.8–10.8 Nm)

SERVO

Installation

1. Install the servo into the transaxle housing.

2. Use a C-clamp and deep socket to compress the servo return spring.

3. Install the retaining ring and remove C-clamp.

OIL PUMP

Installation and Measurement

TOTAL ENDPLAY

1. Remove the oil pump extension and place the housing with gears installed aside.

2. Install the oil pump extension into the front clutch housing, without the plastic adjusting washer.

3. Position a machinist straightedge over the oil pump cover in the transaxle case, be careful not to place the tool on the bolt holes.

4. Use a feeler gauge and measure the clearance between the pump and bar or transaxle and bar. The measurement should not be greater than 0.004 in. (0.10mm) with the pump below the transaxle surface, or 0.006 in. (0.15mm) with the pump cover above the case surface.

5. Replace thrust washer as necessary to obtain proper clearance.

6. Reassemble oil pump and torque the oil pump cover to housing bolts to 95–122 inch lbs. (11–14 Nm).

7. Lubricate pump with Dexron®II transmission fluid and check for free movement by inserting and turning shaft.

FRONT CLUTCH ENDPLAY

1. Use petroleum jelly to install the oil pump gasket to the oil pump.

2. Install the plastic adjusting washer to the oil pump cover using petroleum jelly.

PART NUMBER	THICKNESS OF BEARING RACE
E7GZ-7D014-A	1.2 mm (0.047 in)
E7GZ-7D014-B	1.4 mm (0.055 in)
E7GZ-7D014-C	1.6 mm (0.063 in)
E7GZ-7D014-D	1.8 mm (0.071 in)
E7GZ-7D014-E	2.0 mm (0.079 in)
E7GZ-7D014-F	2.2 mm (0.087 in)

Endplay race selection chart

3. Install the thrust washer onto the end of the pump extension using petroleum jelly.

4. Install the oil pump to the transaxle and torque bolts to 11–16 ft. lbs. (15–22 Nm).

5. Reposition the transaxle with the oil pump facing down.

6. While turning the connecting shell through 2 complete revolutions, push the front clutch down toward the oil pump, using an appropriate tool inserted into the tabs of the clutch drum.

7. Measure the clearance between the tabs of the clutch drum and the connecting shell.

8. If the endplay in not within 0.020–0.031 in (0.5–0.8mm), replace the plastic washer with an appropriate size washer.

9. Reassemble and install the oil pump.

10. Apply sealant E1FZ–19562–A (non-silicone) to threads and torque to 11–16 ft. lbs. (15–22 Nm).

VALVE BODY

Installation

1. Install the steel ball into the transaxle case.

PART NUMBER	THICKNESS OF SHIM
E7GZ-7F373-A	2.1 mm (0.083 in)
E7GZ-7F373-B	2.3 mm (0.091 in)
E7GZ-7F373-C	2.5 mm (0.098 in)
E7GZ-7F373-D	2.7 mm (0.106 in)
E7GZ-7F373-E	1.5 mm (0.059 in)
E7GZ-7F373-F	1.7 mm (0.067 in)
E7GZ-7F373-G	1.3 mm (0.051 in)

Plastic adjustment washer chart

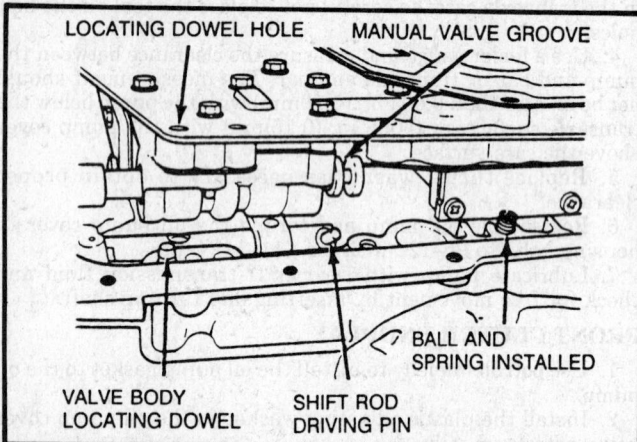

Spring and ball location

2. Install the manual valve into the valve body.
3. Align the manual valve land with the pin on the control rod. Mate the dowels in the transaxle case with the holes in the valve body.
4. Install the valve body retaining bolts and torque to 70–90 inch lbs. (8–11 Nm) in proper sequence.

INTERMEDIATE BAND ADJUSTMENT

1. Tighten adjuster bolt to 8.7–10.8 ft. lbs. (12–15 Nm).
2. Apply sealant E1FZ–19562–A (non-silicone) to adjuster screw threads and torque locknut to 41–59 ft. lbs. (55–80 Nm).

CONTROL VALVE DIAPHRAGM ROD

1. Insert the vacuum diaphragm rod gauge into the mounting hole, with the beveled side out, until the tool bottoms.
2. Place the rod through the opening of the vacuum diaphragm tool until the rod bottoms out against the valve.
3. Tighten the lock knob on the vacuum modulator tool and remove the tool and rod from the transaxle case.
4. Use a depth gauge to measure the distance from the flat surface of the vacuum modulator tool to the end of the rod.5. Use this measurement to select the correct size rod.6. Install the correct rod, lubricate the modulator O-ring with Dexron®II and install the vacuum modulator.

OIL PAN AND CONVERTER

Installation

1. Install the kickdown solenoid, coat O-ring with Dexron®II and threads with sealant E1FZ-19562 (non-silicone).

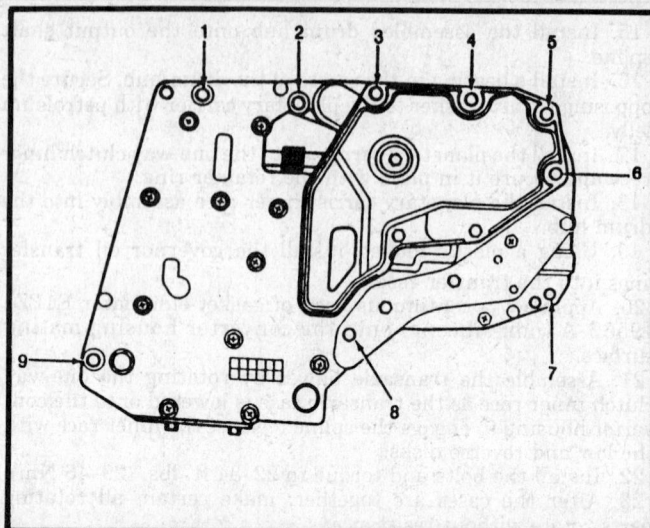

Bolt removal and torque sequence

MEASUREMENT	DIAPHRAGM ROD USED
Under 25.4 mm (1.000 in)	29.5 mm (1.160 in)
25.4 ~ 25.9 mm (1.000 ~ 1.020 in)	30.0 mm (1.180 in)
25.9 ~ 26.4 mm (1.020 ~ 1.039 in)	30.5 mm (1.200 in)
26.4 ~ 26.9 mm (1.039 ~ 1.059 in)	31.0 mm (1.220 in)
Over 26.9 mm (1.059 in)	31.5 mm (1.240 in)

PART NO.	DIAPHRAGM ROD
E7GZ-7A380-E	29.5 mm (1.160 in)
E7GZ-7A380-C	30.0 mm (1.180 in)
E7GZ-7A380-D	30.5 mm (1.200 in)
E7GZ-7A380-B	31.0 mm (1.220 in)
E7GZ-7A380-A	31.5 mm (1.240 in)

Vacuum diaphragm rod selection chart

2. Install the speedometer drive gear and torque bolts to 43–49 inch lbs. (5–8 Nm).
3. Lubricate oil filler tube end with Dexron®II and install. Torque retaining bolt to 43–69 inch lbs. (5–87 Nm).
4. Install a new pan gasket and oil pan. Torque pan bolts to 43–69 inch lbs. (5–87 Nm).

NOTE: Do not use any type of sealer or adhesive on the pan gasket. If necessary, soak the gasket in Dexron®II transmission fluid.

5. Coat the neutral safety switch threads with sealant E1FZ-19562 (non-silicone) and install.

NOTE: Switch must to torque to 14–19 ft.lbs. (19–26 Nm) for proper switch operation.

6. Install the turbine and oil pump shafts.
7. Lubricate the inside of torque converter with no more than ½ qt. of Dexron®II transmission fluid and install.
8. Measure the recess from converter to front housing mating surface. If distance is not 0.790 in. (20.0mm), converter is not seated properly.

SPECIFICATIONS

VALVE BODY

Item		EFI in. (mm)	Carburetor in. (mm)
Throttle back-up valve spring	Diameter	0.287 (7.3)	0.287 (7.3)
	Free length	1.417 (36.0)	1.420 (36.0)
Down shift valve spring	Diameter	0.219 (5.55)	0.217 (5.5)
	Free length	0.866 (22.0)	0.862 (21.9)
Throttle relief	Diameter	0.276 (7.0)	0.276 (7.0)
	Free length	0.440 (11.2)	0.440 (11.2)
2–3 shift valve spring	Diameter	0.272 (6.9)	0.252 (6.4)
	Free length	1.614 (41.0)	1.540 (39.2)
1–2 shift valve spring	Diameter	6.258 (6.55)	0.258 (6.55)
	Free length	1.260 (32.0)	1.260 (32.0)
Second lock valve spring	Diameter	0.219 (5.55)	0.219 (5.55)
	Free length	1.319 (33.5)	1.320 (33.5)
Pressure regulator valve spring	Diameter	0.461 (11.7)	0.461 (11.7)
	Free length	1.693 (43.0)	1.693 (43.0)
3-2 timing	Diameter	0.295 (7.5)	0.295 (7.5)
	Free length	0.870 (22.1)	0.870 (22.1)
Orifice check valve spring	Diameter	0.197 (5.0)	0.197 (5.0)
	Free length	–	0.610 (15.5)

SERVO

Item	Specification in. (mm)
Free length of return spring	1.87–1.93 (47.5–49.0)

GOVERNOR SPRINGS

Item		Specification in. (mm)
Primary spring	Outer diameter	0.343–0.366
	Free length	0.65–0.728 (16.5–18.5)
Secondary spring	Outer diameter	0.352–0.376 (8.95–9.55)
	Free length	0.488–0.567 (12.4–14.4)

GEAR ASSEMBLY

Item	Specification in. (mm)
Total endplay at pump	0.004–0.006 (0.1–0.15)
Endplay adjusting race	0.047 (1.2) 0.055 (1.4) 0.063 (1.6) 0.071 (1.8) 0.079 (2.0) 0.087 (2.2)
Idle gear bearing preload	0.3–7.8 (0.03–0.09)①
Preload adjusting shims	0.004 (0.10) 0.005 (0.12) 0.006 (0.14) 0.007 (0.16) 0.020 (0.50) 0.008 (0.20)
Output gear bearing preload	0.26–7.81 (0.03–0.9)①

① inch lbs. (Nm)

VACUUM DIAPHRAGM

Item	Specification in. (mm)
Available diaphragm rods	1.161 (29.5) 1.181 (30.0) 1.200 (30.5) 1.220 (31.0) 1.240 (31.5)

DRIVE AND DIFFERENTIAL

Item		Specification in. (mm)
Final gear	Type	Helical gear
	Reduction ratio	3.631
Side bearing preload		18–25 (2.1–2.9)①
Preload adjusting shims		0.004 (0.1) 0.008 (0.2) 0.012 (0.3) 0.016 (0.4) 0.020 (0.5) 0.024 (0.6) 0.028 (0.7) 0.031 (0.8) 0.035 (0.9) 0.047 (0.12) 0.055 (0.14) 0.063 (0.16)
Backlash of side gear and pinion		0–0.004 (0–0.1)
Backlash adjusting thrust washers		0.079 (2.0) 0.083 (2.1) 0.087 (2.2)

① inch lbs. (Nm)

TORQUE SPECIFICATIONS

Item	ft. lbs (Nm)
Drive plate to crankshaft	96–103 (71–76)
Drive plate to torque converter	25.3–36.2 (35–50)
Converter housing to engine	64–89 (47–66)
Converter halves	29–46 (22–34)
Converter housing to transaxle case	26.8–39.8 (37–55)
Bearing housing to converter housing	13.7–18.8 (19–26)
Side bearing housing to transaxle case	13.7–18.8 (19–26)
Bearing cover to transaxle case	8.0–10.1 (11–14)
Oil pump to transaxle case	11–16 (15–22)
Governor cover to transaxle case	7.8–10.8 (5.8–8.0)
Oil pan	3.6–5.8 (5–8)
Anchor end bolt (when adjusting band brake)	8.7–10.8 (12–15)
Anchor end bolt lock nut	41–59 (56–82)
Control valve body to transaxle case	5.8–8.0 (8–11)
Lower valve body to upper valve body	1.8–2.5 (2.5–3.5)
Side plate to control valve body	1.8–2.5 (2.5–3.5)
Reamer bolt of control valve body	3.6–5.1 (5–7)
Oil strainer of control valve	2.2–2.9 (3–4)
Governor valve body to governor shaft	5.8–8.0 (8–11)
Oil pump cover	8.0–10.1 (11–14)
Inhibitor switch	13.7–18.8 (19–26)
Manual shaft lock nut	21.7–29.0 (30–40)
Oil cooler pipe set bolt	11.6–17.4 (16–24)
Actuator for parking rod to transaxle case	8.7–11.6 (12–15)
Idle bear bearing lock nut	94–130 (130–180)

LINE PRESSURE SPECIFICATIONS

Gear	Condition	Specification psi (kPa)
R	Idling	57–100 (392–687)
	Stall	228–270 (1570–1864)
D	Idling	43–57 (294–392)
	Stall	128–156 (883–1079)
2	Idling	114–171 (785–1177)
	Stall	114–171 (785–1177)

CUT BACK POINT

Vacuum of Vacuum Pump in. Hg. (mm Hg.)	Governor Pressure psi (kPa)
0 (0)	14–23 (98–157)
7.87 (200)	6–14 (39–98)

GOVERNOR PRESSURE

mph	Governor Pressure psi (kPa)
20	13–21 (88–147)
35	27–36 (186–245)
55	58–70 (402–481)

SHIFT POINT SPEED

Throttle Condition		Shift Point mph (km/h)
CARBURETOR		
Wide open throttle	D^1–D^2	30–36 (48–58)
	D^2–D^3	60–68 (96–110)
	D^3–D^2	53–58 (85–93)
	D^2–D^1	24–26 (38–42)
Half throttle	D^1–D^2	10–19 (16–30)
	D^2–D^3	17–37 (28–60)
Fully closed throttle	D^3–D^1	6–9 (10–15)
	1_2–1_1	22–26 (35–42)
ELECTRONIC FUEL INJECTION		
Wide open throttle	D^1–D^2	30–36 (48–58)
	D^2–D^3	60–68 (96–110)
	D^3–D^2	53–58 (85–93)
	D^2–D^1	24–26 (38–42)
Half throttle	D^1–D^2	12–21 (20–34)
	D^2–D^3	37–48 (60–78)
Fully closed throttle	D^3–D^1	6–9 (10–15)
	1_2–1_1	22–26 (35–42)

TORQUE CONVERTER

Item	Specifications
Stall torque ratio	1.95–2.35
Stall torque rpm	2300–2500
Bushing diameter wear limit	1.302 in (33.075mm)

OIL PUMP

Clearance		Specification in. (mm)
Gear end float	Standard	0.0008–0.0016 (0.02–0.04)
	Limit	0.0031 (0.08)
Outer gear and crest	Standard	0.0055–0.0083 (0.14–0.21)
	Limit	0.0098 (0.25)
Outer gear and housing	Standard	0.002–0.0079 (0.05–0.20)
	Limit	0.0098 (o.25)
Oil seal ring and ring groove	Standard	0.0016–0.0063 (0.04–0.16)
	Limit	0.0157 (0.40)

LOW AND REVERSE BRAKE

Item	Specification in. (mm)
Number of friction and steel plates	3
Clearance between retaining plates and stopper	0.8–1.05 (0.032–0.041)
Clearance adjusting retaining plates	0.181 (4.6) 0.189 (4.8) 0.197 (5.0) 0.205 (5.2) 0.213 (5.4) 0.221 (5.6)
Free length of return spring	27.2–28.2 (1.07–1.11)

CLUTCH SPECIFICATIONS

Front Clutch	Specification in. (mm)
Number of driven & drive plates	3
Front clutch clearance	0.063–0.071 (1.6–1.8)
Clearance adjusting retaining plate	0.205 (5.2) 0.213 (5.4) 0.220 (5.6) 0.228 (5.8) 0.236 (6.0) 0.244 (6.2)
Return spring free length	0.992–1.071 (2.52–27.2)
Drum bushing inner diameter Standard Limit	1.7322–1.7331 (44.0–44.025) 1.7354 (44.075)
Front clutch drum end prary (clearance between drum and connecting shell)	0.020–0.032 (0.5–0.8)

CLUTCH SPECIFICATIONS

Front Clutch	Specification in. (mm)
Endplay adjusting shim	0.051 (1.3) 0.059 (1.5) 0.067 (1.7) 0.075 (1.9) 0.083 (2.1) 0.091 (2.3) 0.098 (2.5) 0.106 (2.7)

Rear Clutch	Specification in. (mm)
Number of driven and drive plates	4
Rear clutch clearance	0.031–0.059 (0.8–1.5)
Return spring free length	0.992–1.071 (25.2–27.2)

SPECIAL TOOLS

Tool	Identification
Tool–1175–AC	Seal remover
Tool–4201–C	Dial indicator
D78P–4201–C	Magnetic base for dial indicator
D79P–6000–C	Engine support bar
D80L–630–A	Step plate adapter set
D80L–943–A	Puller
D83L–7059–A	Vacuum pump
D84L–1122–A	Bearing pulling attachment
T50T–100–A	Slide hammer
T57L–500–B	Bench mounted holding fixture
T57L–77820–A	Pressure gauge
T58L–101A	Puller
T65L–77515–A	Front clutch spring compressor
T77F–1217–B	Bearing cup puller
T77F–4220–B1	Differential bearing cap puller
T80T–4000–W	Handle
T80L–77003–A	Gauge bar

Tool	Identification
T86p–70043–A	Jaws (used with T58L–101–A)
T87C–7025–C	Differential plugs
T87C–77000–A	Vacuum diaphragm rod gauge
T87C–77000–B	Clutch compressor
T87C–77000–C	Bearing cone replacer
T87C–77000–D	Bearing cone replacer
T87c–77000–E	Torque adapter
T87C–77000–G	Converter seal replacer
T87C–77000–J	Shim selection tool
014–00456	Transmission tester (Tracer ATX adapter)
014–00028	Torque converter cleaner
D80L–630–3	Plate
D80L–630–7	Plate
D80L–943–A2	Jaw puller
D79P–6000–B	Engine support bar
T86P–70043–A2	Jaw puller
T87C–77000–H	Differential seal replacer

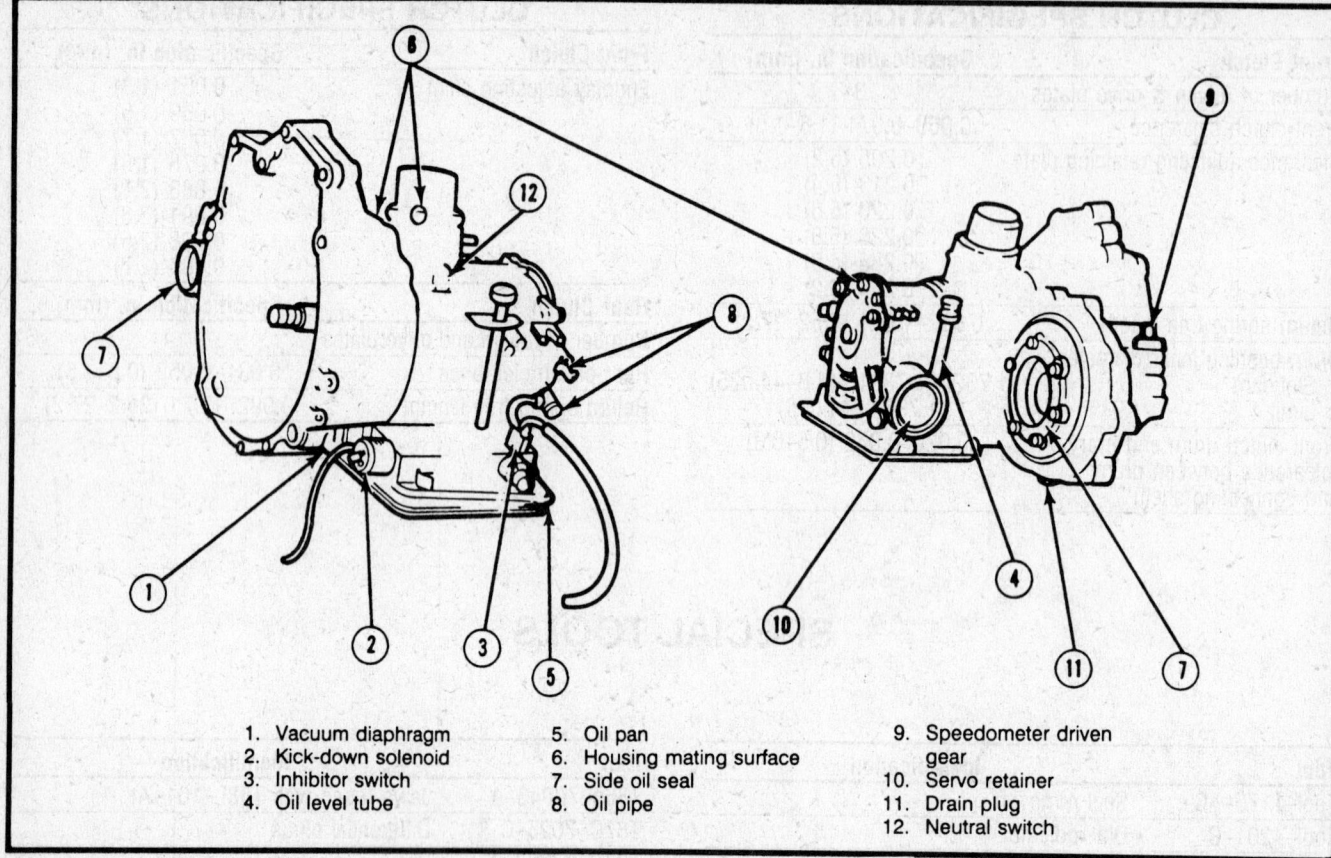

1. Vacuum diaphragm
2. Kick-down solenoid
3. Inhibitor switch
4. Oil level tube
5. Oil pan
6. Housing mating surface
7. Side oil seal
8. Oil pipe
9. Speedometer driven gear
10. Servo retainer
11. Drain plug
12. Neutral switch

Fluid leakage locations

Section 3

AW131L Transaxle
General Motors

APPLICATION

1985–89 Nova

GENERAL DESCRIPTION

The A131L transaxle is a 3 speed automatic transaxle, consisting primarily of a 4 element hydraulic torque converter, 4 multiple disc clutches, 2 one-way clutches and a band which provides the friction elements required to obtain the desired function of the compound planetary gear set. The combination of the compound planetary gear set provides 3 forward ratios and 1 reverse.

Transaxle and Converter Identification

TRANSAXLE

The transaxle identification tag is located at the top front of the transaxle case.

CONVERTER

The torque converter is equipped with a built-in lock-up clutch. It smoothly couples the engine to the planetary gears with oil and hydraulically provides additional torque multiplication when required. Changing of the gear ratios is fully automatic in relation to vehicle speed and engine torque. Vehicle speed and engine torque signals are constantly fed to the transaxle to provide the proper gear ratio for maximum efficiency and performance at all throttle openings.

Metric Fasteners

The metric fastener dimensions are very close to the dimensions of the familiar inch system fasteners and for this reason, replacement fasteners must have the same measurement and strength as those removed.

Do not attempt to interchange metric fasteners for inch system fasteners. Mismatched or incorrect fasteners can result in damage to the transaxle unit through malfunctions, breakage or possible personal injury.

Capacities

The fluid used in both the transaxle and the differential is Dexron® II automatic transmission fluid. The fluid capacity for the transaxle is 6 qts. (5.6L). The fluid capacity for the differential is 1.5 qts. (1.4L).

Checking Fluid Level

The vehicle must have been driven so that the engine and transaxle are at normal operating temperature (fluid temperature 158–176° F). If the fluid smells burnt or is black, replace it.

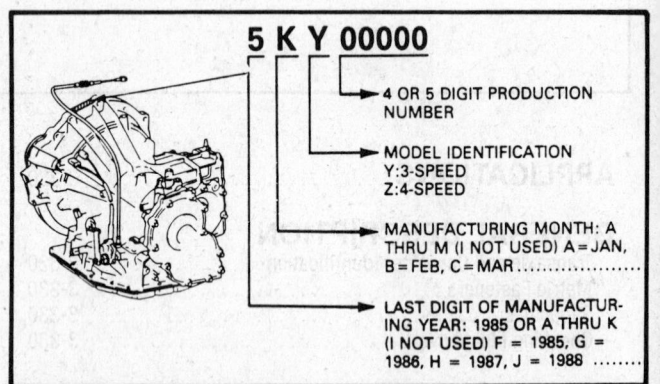

5 K Y 00000

- 4 OR 5 DIGIT PRODUCTION NUMBER
- MODEL IDENTIFICATION Y:3-SPEED Z:4-SPEED
- MANUFACTURING MONTH: A THRU M (I NOT USED) A = JAN, B = FEB, C = MAR ....
- LAST DIGIT OF MANUFACTURING YEAR: 1985 OR A THRU K (I NOT USED) F = 1985, G = 1986, H = 1987, J = 1988 ....

Transaxle identification

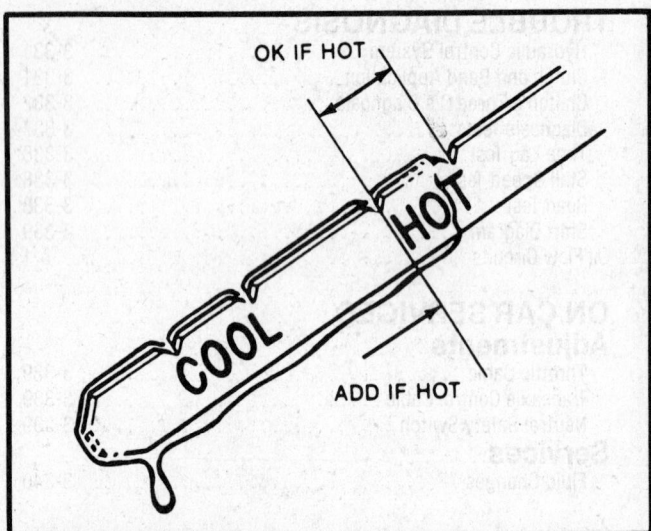

OK IF HOT

HOT

COOL

ADD IF HOT

Fluid level check

1. Park the vehicle on a level surface and set the parking brake.
2. With the engine idling, shift the selector into each gear from **P** range to **L** range and return to **P** range.
3. Pull out the transaxle dipstick and wipe it clean.
4. Push the dipstick back fully into the tube.
5. Pull out the dipstick and check that the fluid is in the **HOT** range.
6. If the level is low, add fluid. Do not overfill.

TRANSAXLE MODIFICATIONS

NOTE: There are no transaxle modifications available at the time of publication.

TROUBLE DIAGNOSIS

Hydraulic Control System

NOTE: Please refer to Section 9 for all oil flow circuits.

PUMP ASSEMBLY

The hydraulic pressure system requires a supply of transmission fluid and a pump to pressurize the fluid. The A131L transaxle uses an internal-external gear type pump with its oil intake connected to a screen assembly.

The oil pump is designed to deliver fluid to the torque converter, lubricate the planetary gear unit and supply operating pressure to the hydraulic control system. The drive gear of the oil pump and the torque converter pump are driven by the engine. The pump has a sufficient capacity of oil to supply the necessary fluid pressure throughout all forward speed ranges and reverse.

MANUAL VALVE

The manual valve is linked to the gear shift lever and directs the fluid to the gear range circuit that the lever is positioned at.

PRIMARY REGULATOR VALVE

The primary regulator valve varies the hydraulic line pressure to each component in order to conform with engine power and operate all transaxle hydraulic systems.

SECONDARY REGULATOR VALVE

This valve regulates the converter pressure and lubrication pressure. Spring tension in the valve acts in an upward direction. Converter fluid pressure and lubrication pressure are determined by the spring tension.

THROTTLE VALVE

The throttle valve acts to produce throttle pressure in response to accelerator pedal modulation or engine output. When the accelerator pedal is depressed, the downshift plug is pushed upward by the throttle cable and throttle cam. The throttle valve also moves upward by means of the spring, opening the pressure passage for creation of throttle pressure.

CUT-BACK VALVE

This valve regulates the cut-back pressure acting on the throttle valve and is activated by governor pressure and throttle pressure. By applying cut-back pressure to the throttle valve in this manner, the throttle pressure is lowered to prevent unnecessary power loss from the oil pump.

Governor pressure acts on the upper portion of the valve and as the valve is pushed downward, a passage from the throttle valve is opened and throttle pressure is applied. Because of the

CLUTCH AND BAND APPLICATION

Shift Lever Position	Gear Position	C_1	C_2	B_1	B_2	B_3	F_1	F_2
P	Parking	–	–	–	–	–	–	–
R	Reverse	–	Applied	–	–	Applied	–	–
N	Neutral	–	–	–	–	–	–	–
D	1st	Applied	–	–	–	–	–	Applied
	2nd	Applied	–	–	Applied	–	Applied	–
	3rd	Applied	Applied	–	Applied	–	–	–
2	1st	Applied	–	–	–	–	–	Applied
	2nd	Applied	–	Applied	Applied	–	Applied	–
L	1st	Applied	–	–	–	Applied	–	Applied
	2nd①	Applied	–	Applied	Applied	–	Applied	–

B_1 – No. 1 brake, 2nd coast brake
B_2 – No. 2 brake, 2nd brake
B_3 – No. 3 brake, 1st and reverse brake
C_1 – Front clutch, forward clutch
C_2 – Rear clutch, direct clutch
F_1 – No. 1 one-way clutch
F_2 – No. 2 one-way clutch
① Downshift only in L range, 2nd gear. No upshift

CHILTON'S THREE C's TRANSAXLE DIAGNOSIS

Condition	Cause	Correction
Fluid discolored or smells burnt	a) Fluid contamination b) Torque converter faulty c) Transaxle faulty	a) Replace fluid b) Replace torque converter c) Disassemble and inspect transaxle
Vehicle does not move in any forward range or reverse	a) Control cable out of adjustment b) Valve body or primary regulator valve faulty c) Transaxle faulty	a) Adjust control cable b) Inspect valve body c) Disassemble and inspect transaxle
Vehicle does not move in any range	a) Parking lock pawl faulty b) Valve body or primary regulator valve faulty c) Torque converter faulty d) Converter drive plate broken e) Oil pump intake strainer blocked f) Transaxle faulty	a) Inspect parking pawl b) Inspect valve body c) Replace torque converter d) Replace torque converter e) Clean strainer f) Disassemble and inspect transaxle
Shift lever position incorrect	a) Control cable out of adjustment b) Manual valve and lever faulty c) Transaxle faulty	a) Adjust control cable b) Inspect valve body c) Disassemble and inspect transaxle
Harsh engagement into any drive range	a) Throttle cable out of adjustment b) Valve body or primary regulator valve faulty c) Accumulator pistons faulty d) Transaxle faulty	a) Adjust throttle cable b) Inspect valve body c) Inspect accumulator pistons d) Disassemble and inspect transaxle
Delayed 1–2, 2–3 or 3–OD upshift or downshifts from OD–3 or 3–2 then shifts back to OD or 3	a) Throttle cable out of adjustment b) Governor faulty c) Valve body faulty	a) Adjust throttle cable b) Inspect governor c) Inspect valve body
Slips on 1–2, 2–3 or 3–OD upshift or slips or shudders on take-off	a) Control cable out of adjustment b) Throttle cable out of adjustment c) Valve body faulty d) Transaxle faulty	a) Adjust control cable b) Adjust throttle cable c) Inspect valve body d) Disassemble and inspect transaxle
Drag, binding or tie-up on 1–2, 2–3 or 3–OD upshift	a) Control cable out of adjustment b) Valve body faulty c) Transaxle faulty	a) Adjust control cable b) Inspect valve body c) Disassemble and inspect transaxle
Harsh downshift	a) Throttle cable out of adjustment b) Accumulator pistons faulty c) Valve body faulty d) Transaxle faulty	a) Adjust throttle cable b) Inspect accumulator pistons a) Inspect valve body d) Disassemble and inspect transaxle
No downshift when coasting	a) Governor faulty b) Valve body faulty	a) Inspect governor b) Inspect valve body
Downshift occurs too quick or too late while coasting	a) Throttle cable out of adjustment b) Governor faulty c) Valve body faulty d) Transaxle faulty	a) Adjust throttle cable b) Inspect governor c) Inspect valve body d) Disassemble and inspect transaxle
No OD–3, 3–2 or 2–1 kickdown	a) Throttle cable out of adjustment b) Governor faulty c) Valve body faulty	a) Adjust throttle cable b) Inspect governor c) Inspect valve body
No engine braking in 2 range	a) Valve body faulty b) Transaxle faulty	a) Inspect valve body b) Disassemble and inspect transaxle
Vehicle does not hold in P	a) Control cable out of adjustment b) Parking lock pawl and rod	a) Adjust control cable b) Inspect lock pawl and rod

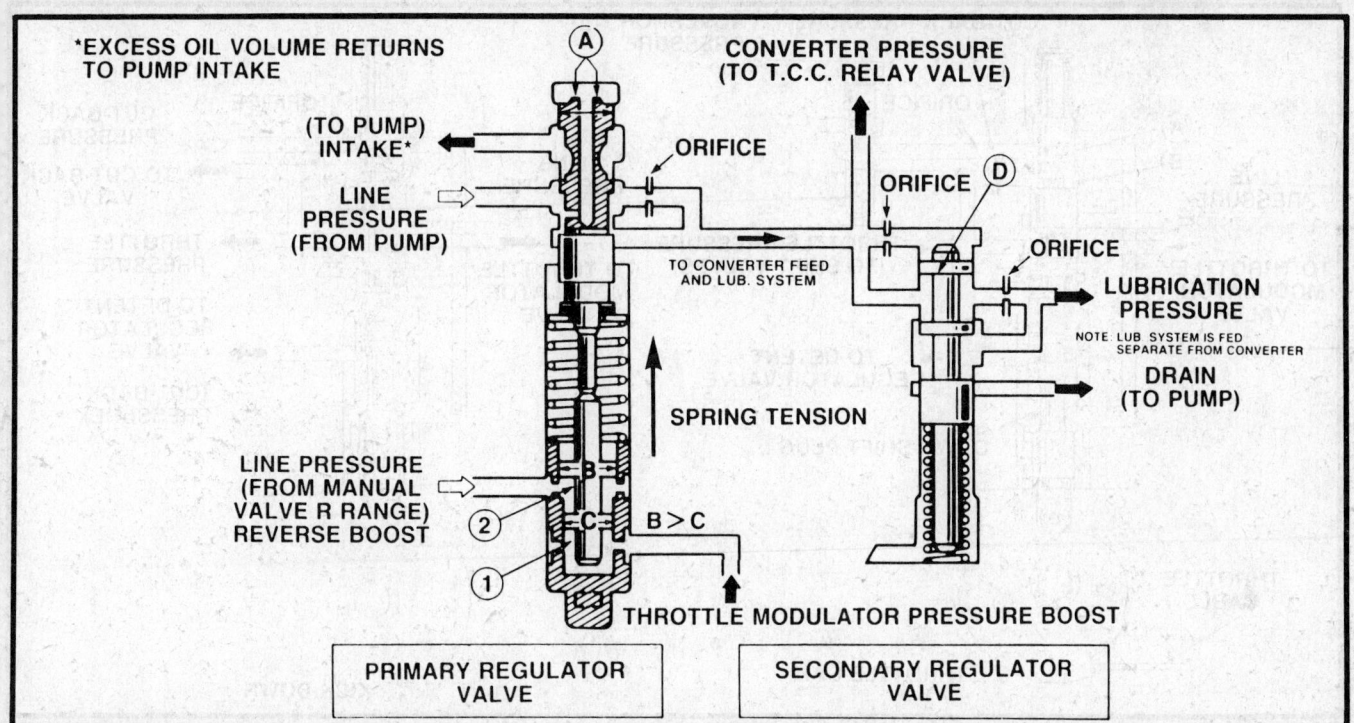

Primary and secondary regulator valves

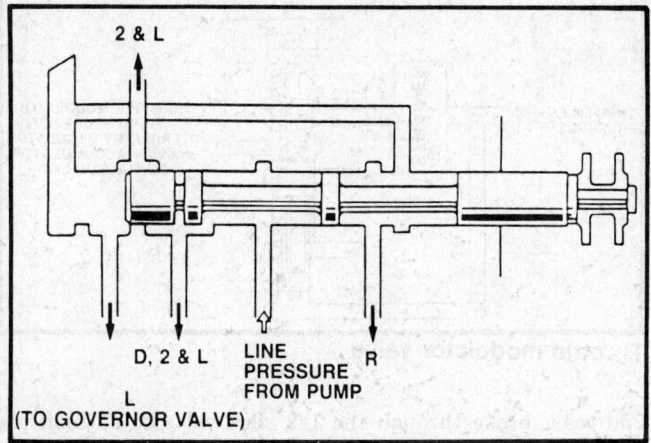

Manual valve

difference in the diameters of the valve pistons, the valve is pushed upward to balance the downward force of governor pressure and the throttle pressure becomes cut-back pressure. As the governor pressure rises, the valve is forced downward. Since the throttle pressure passage is open, the pressure becomes cutback pressure.

THROTTLE MODULATOR VALVE

This valve produces throttle modulator pressure. It reduces throttle pressure when the throttle valve opening angle is high. It causes throttle modulator pressure to act on the primary regulator valve so that line pressure performance is close to engine power performance.

DOWNSHIFT PLUG

If the accelerator pedal is depressed to nearly the fully open po-

sition, the downshift plug opens the cut-back pressure passage very wide, then causes the detent regulator valve to operate and effect kickdown.

The cut-back pressure also acts on the downshift plug when the throttle valve opening angle is less than 85%. A power assist mechanism is provided to lighten spring tension in relation to the throttle cam only to the extent of the difference in the valve piston diameters.

GOVERNOR VALVE

The governor valve is driven by the drive pinion worm gear and produces governor pressure in response to the vehicle speed. It balances the line pressure from the primary regulator valve and the centrifugal force of the governor weights to produce hydraulic pressure in proportion to vehicle speed.

DETENT REGULATOR VALVE

During kickdown, the detent regulator valve stabilizes the hydraulic pressure acting on the 1-2 and 2-3 shift valves.

LOW MODULATOR VALVE

In the L range, the low modulator valve reduces the line pressure from the manual valve. Low modulator pressure pushes down the low coast shift valve and acts on the 1st and reverse brake to cushion the apply.

Torque Converter Clutch (TCC) SIGNAL VALVE

This valve detects governor pressure and determines the TCC apply point by controlling the pressure acting on the TCC relay valve. Over a certain governor pressure, the TCC signal valve is pushed upward and line pressure from the 2–3 shift valve acts on the end of the TCC relay valve. When not in 3rd gear with the

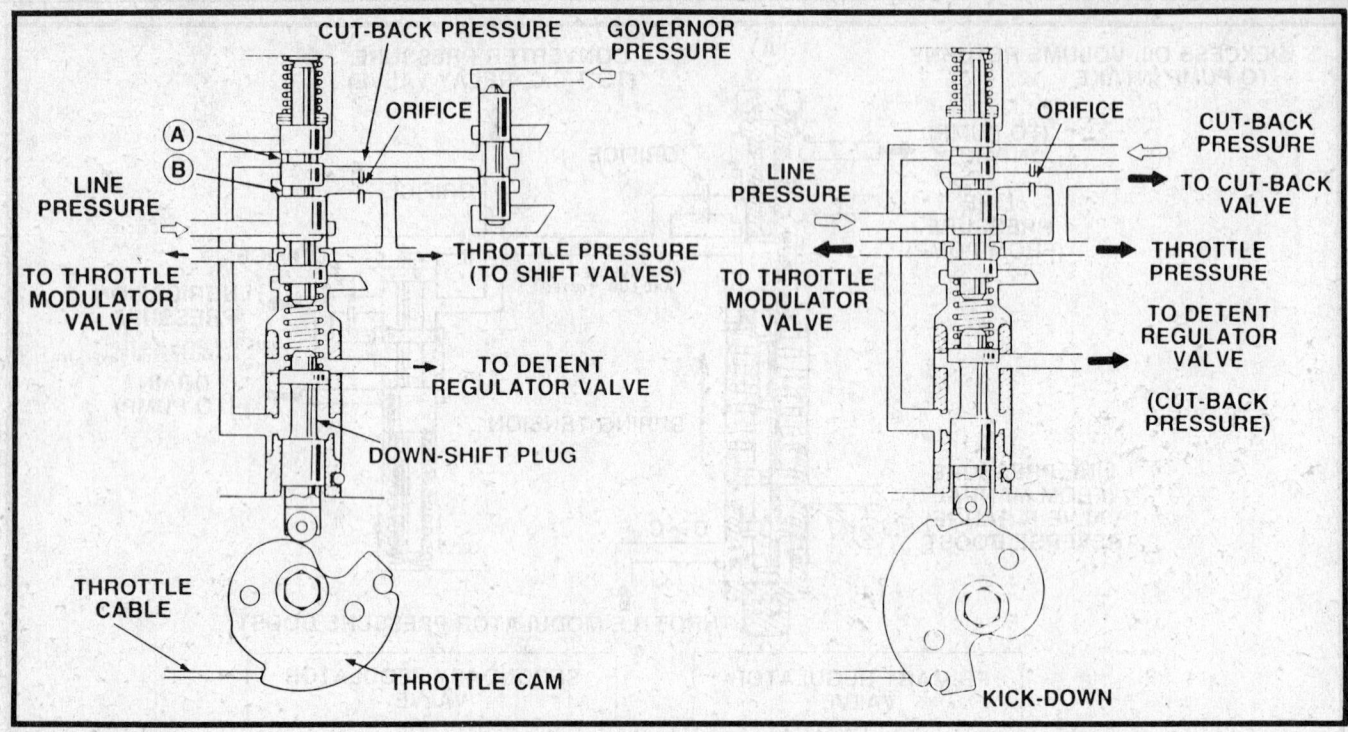

Downshift plug

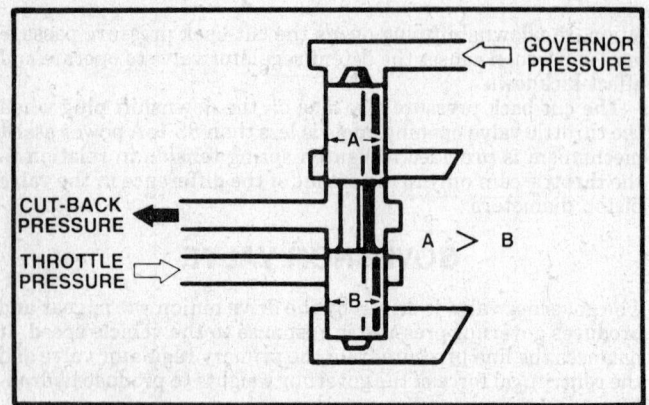

Cut-back valve

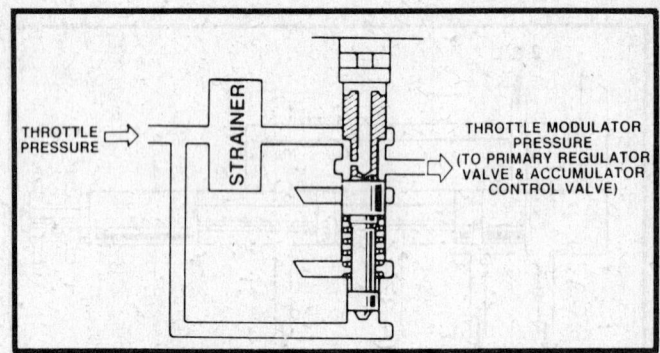

Throttle modulator valve

shift lever in **D**, line pressure from the 2–3 shift valve is not applied to the TCC signal valve, so the TCC signal valve is pushed downward by spring force.

Torque Converter Clutch (TCC) RELAY VALVE

With a fluid pressure signal (C_2 pressure) from the TCC signal valve, the TCC relay valve reverses the fluid flow through the converter. When signal pressure is applied, the TCC apply relay valve is pushed upward and the TCC is actuated. When not in 3rd gear with the shift lever in **D**, the T.C.C. relay valve is in the downward position.

2ND MODULATOR VALVE

In the manual **2** range, this valve reduces line pressure from the intermediate shift valve. 2nd modulator pressure acts on the

2nd coast brake through the 1–2 shift valve to cushion the apply.

ACCUMULATORS

The accumulators act to cushion the shifting shock. There are 3 accumulators: 1 each for the forward clutch (C_1), direct clutch (C_2) and the 2nd brake (B_2). The accumulators are located in the transaxle case. Accumulator control pressure is always acting on the back pressure side of the C_2 and B_2 pistons. This pressure along with spring tension, pushes down on the 2 pistons.

When line pressure is applied to the operating side, the pistons are pushed upward and shock is cushioned as the fluid pressure gradually rises. Operation of the C_1 piston is basically the same as that for C_2 and B_2. However the force pushing the piston downward is accomplished by spring tension only.

ACCUMULATOR CONTROL VALVE

This valve cushions shifting shock by lowering the back pressure of the direct clutch (C_2) accumulator and 2nd brake (B_2) accumulator when the throttle opening angle is small.

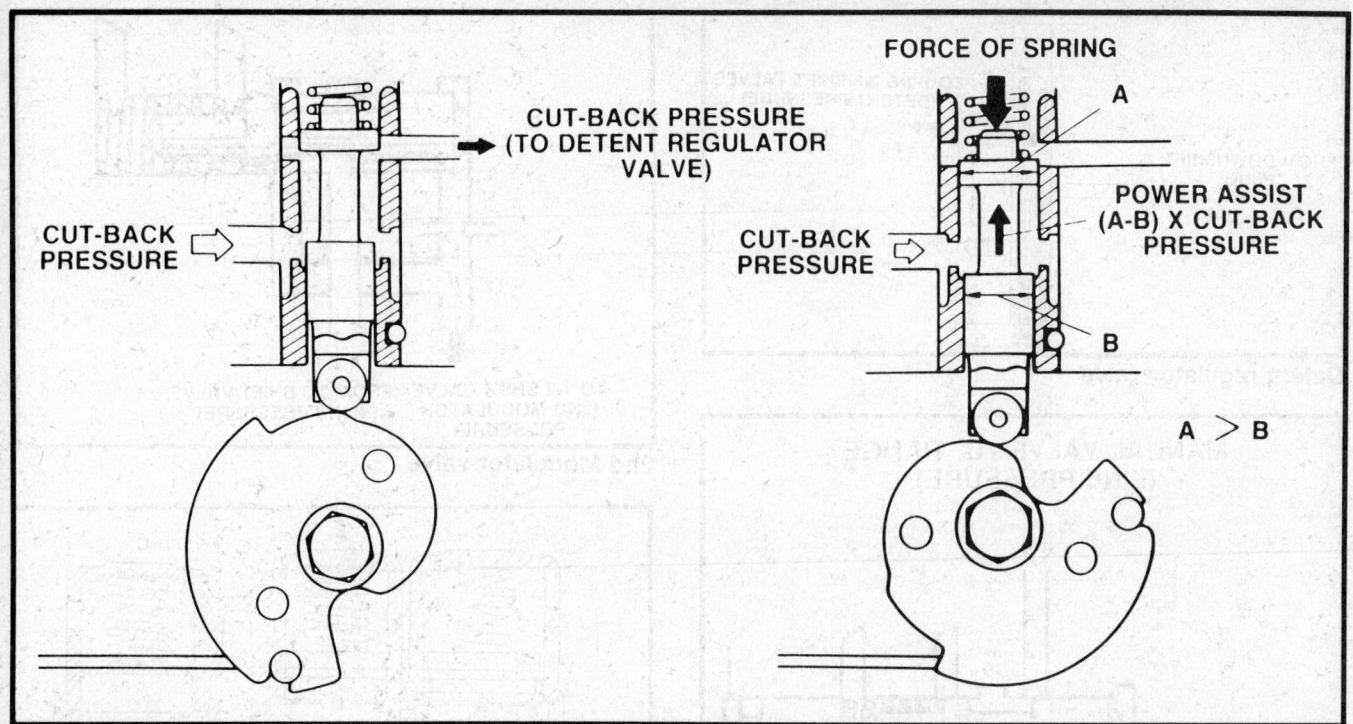

Throttle valve

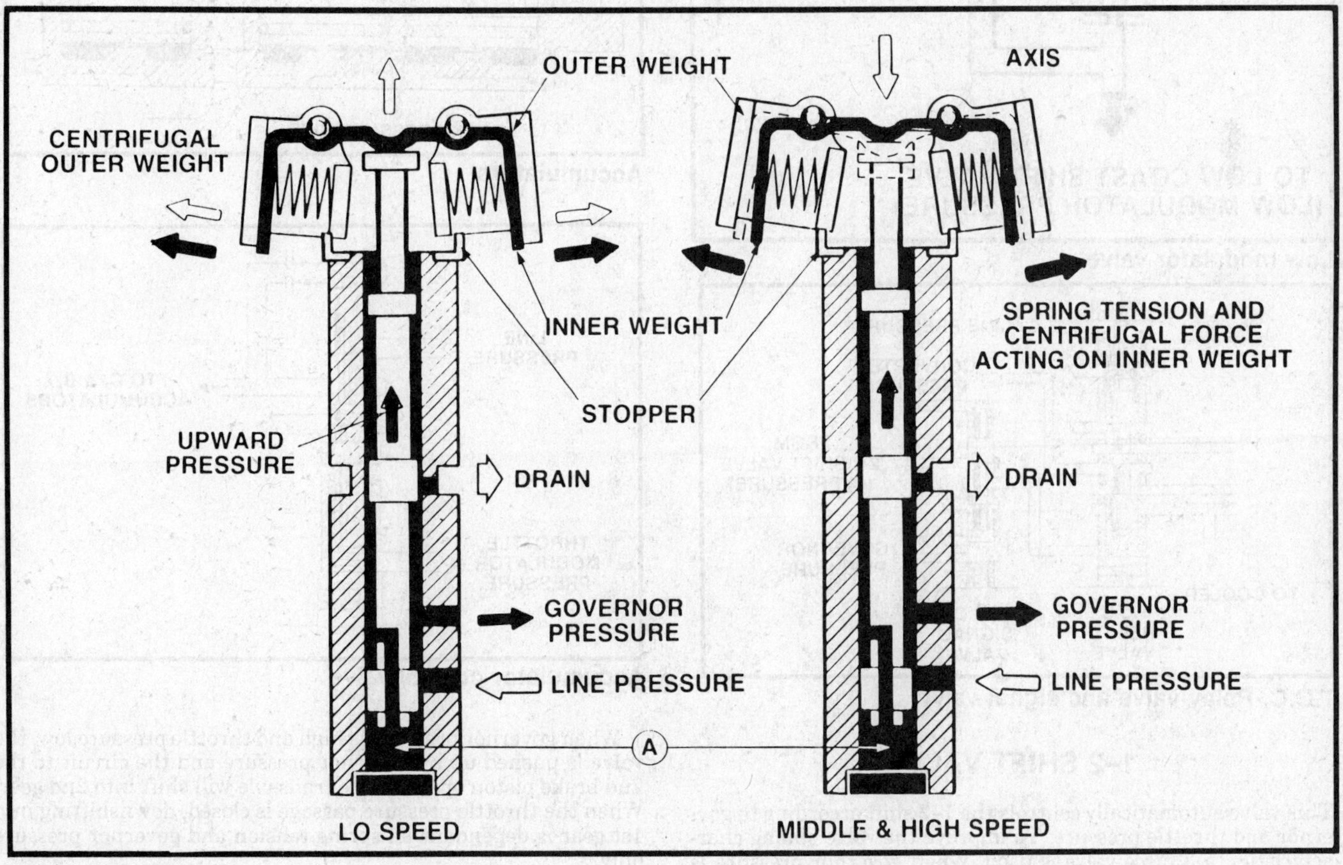

Governor valve

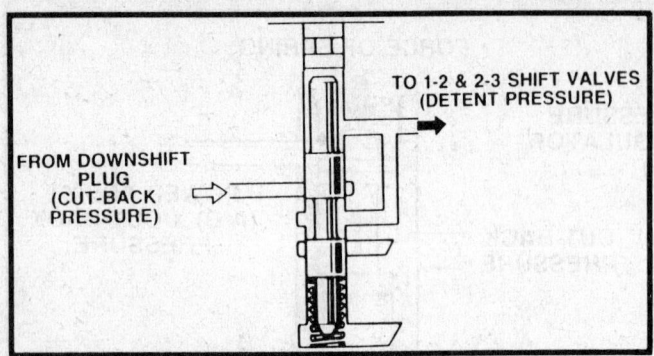

Detent regulator valve

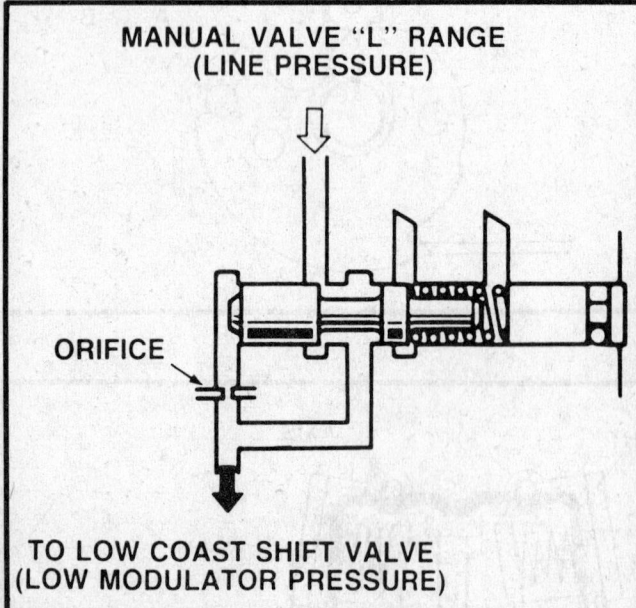

Low modulator valve

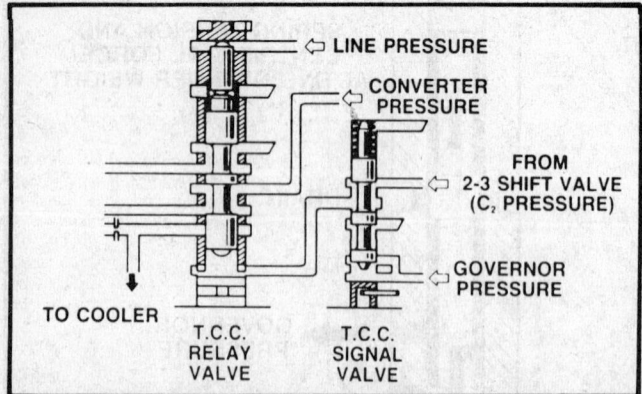

T.C.C. Relay valve and signal valve

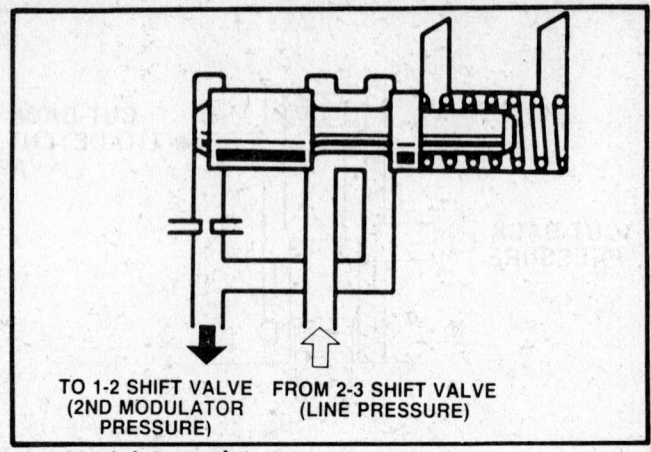

2nd Modulator valve

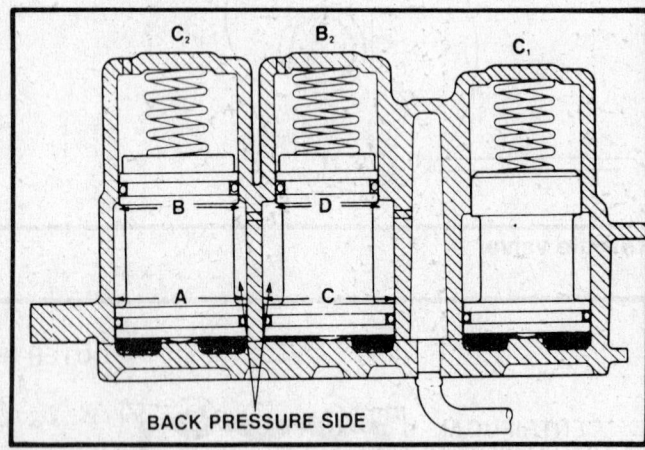

Accumulators

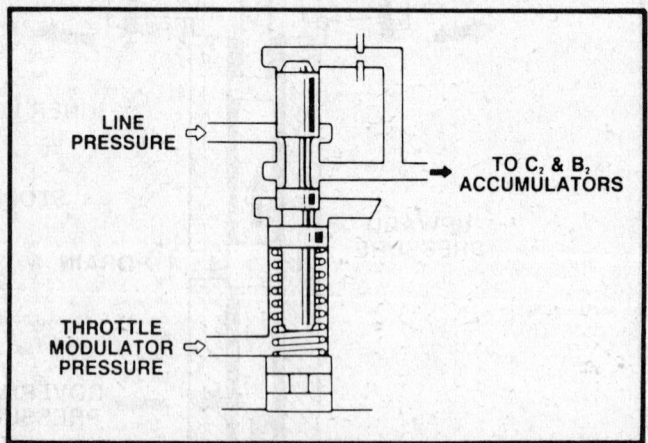

Accumulator control valve

1–2 SHIFT VALVE

This valve automatically controls the 1–2 shift according to governor and throttle pressure. To improve the valve sliding characteristics, a 3 piece valve is used. When governor pressure is low and throttle pressure is high, the valve is pushed down by throttle pressure and because the 2nd brake circuit closes, the transaxle shifts into 1st gear.

When governor pressure is high and throttle pressure low, the valve is pushed up by governor pressure and the circuit to the 2nd brake piston opens so the transaxle will shift into 2nd gear. When the throttle pressure passage is closed, downshifting into 1st gear is dependant on spring tension and governor pressure only.

Unless the downshift plug actuates and allows the detent pressure to act on the 1–2 shift valve, downshifting into 1st gear will take place at a set vehicle speed. In the **L** range, there is no

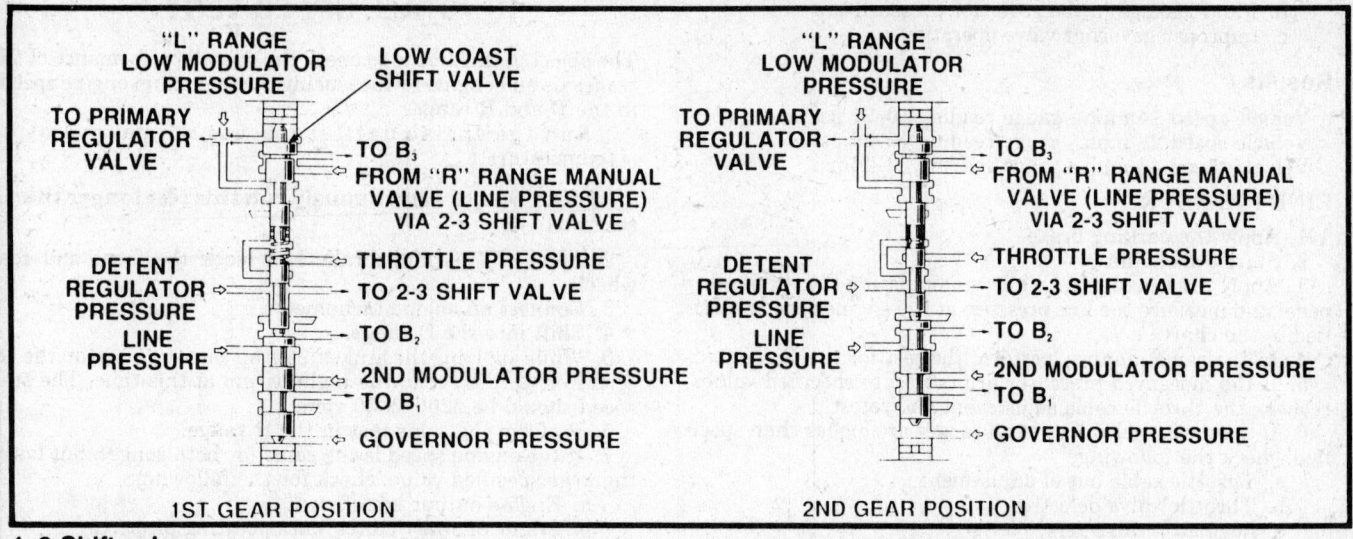

1–2 Shift valve

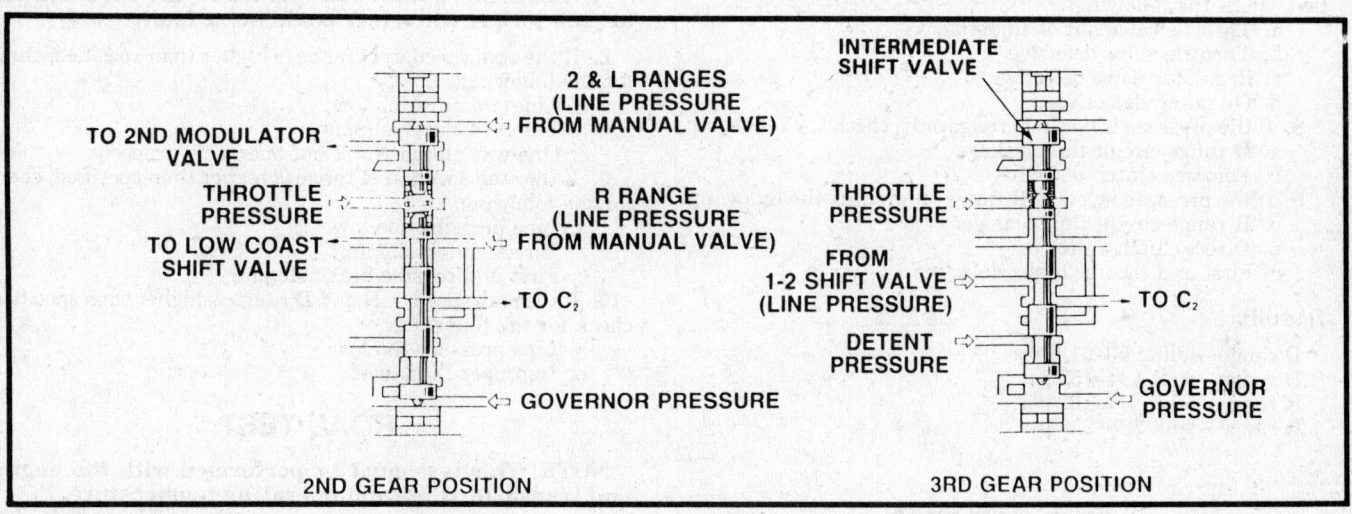

2–3 Shift valve

upshifting into 2nd gear because low modulator pressure is acting on the low coast shift valve.

2–3 SHIFT VALVE

This valve performs shifting between 2nd and 3rd gears. Control is accomplished by opposing throttle pressure and spring tension against governor pressure. When governor pressure is high, the valve is pushed up against the resistance of the throttle pressure and spring tension. This opens the passage to the direct clutch (C_2) piston to allow the shift into 3rd gear.

When governor pressure is low, the valve is pushed down by throttle pressure and spring tension to close the passage leading to the direct clutch piston, causing a downshift to 2nd gear. In the event of kickdown, the detent pressure acts on the 2–3 shift valve to permit a quicker downshift to 2nd gear. valve movement occurs due to the different size areas where pressure is applied. Since the area is larger for downshift than for upshift, downshifting takes place at a lower vehicle speed.

In the manual **2** range, line pressure from the manual valve acts on the intermediate shift valve. The valve descends and shifting into 2nd gear is accomplished but there is no upshifting

into 3rd gear. Line pressure passes through the 2nd modulator valve and 1–2 shift valve and acts on the 2nd coast brake to provide engine braking.

Diagnosis Tests

HYDRAULIC TESTS

1. Run the engine until it reaches normal operating temperature.
2. Raise the vehicle and support it safely.
3. Remove the transaxle case test plugs and mount hydraulic pressure gauges.

GOVERNOR PRESSURE

1. Apply the parking brake.
2. Start the engine.
3. Shift into **D** range and measure the governor pressure at the speeds specified in the chart.
4. If the governor pressure is not to specification, check for the following:

   a. Line pressure not to specification

b. Fluid leakage in the governor pressure cuircuit
c. Improper governor valve operation

Results

Vehicle speed 14 mph – gauge reading 10–21 psi
Vehicle speed 28 mph – gauge reading 19–29 psi
Vehicle speed 43 mph – gauge reading 33–44 psi

LINE PRESSURE

1. Apply the parking brake.
2. Start the engine.
3. Apply the brake pedal while manipulating the accelerator pedal and measure the line pressure at the engine speeds specified in the chart.
4. In the same manner, perform the test for the **R** range.
5. If the measured pressures are not up to specified values, recheck the throttle cable adjustment and retest.
6. If the measured values at all ranges are higher than specified, check the following:
   a. Throttle cable out of adjustment
   b. Throttle valve defective
   c. Regulator valve defective
7. If the measured values at all ranges are lower than specified, check the following:
   a. Throttle cable out of adjustment
   b. Throttle valve defective
   c. Regulator valve defective
   d. Oil pump defective
8. If the pressure is low in **D** range only, check the following:
   a. **D** range circuit fluid leakage
   b. Forward clutch defective
9. If the pressure is low in **R** range only, check the following:
   a. **R** range circuit fluid leakage
   b. Direct clutch defective
   c. First and reverse brake defective

Results

D range – idling 53–61 psi
D range – stall 131–152 psi
R range – idling 77–102 psi
R range – stall 205–239 psi

TIME LAG TEST

If the shift lever is shifted while the engine is idling, there will be a certain time elapse or lag before the shock can be felt. This is used for checking the condition of the forward clutch, direct clutch and 1st and reverse brake.

1. Run the engine until it reaches normal operating temperature.

NOTE: Allow 1 minute interval between tests. Make 3 measurements and take the average value.

2. Apply the parking brake.
3. Check the idle speed. With the cooling fan and A/C off and in **N** range, it should be 900 rpm with power steering and 800 rpm without power steering.
4. Move the shift lever from **N** to **D** range. Using a stop watch, measure the time it takes from shifting the lever until the shock is felt. The time lag should be less than 1.2 seconds.
5. Following Step 4, move the shift lever from **N** to **R** range. The time lag should be less than 1.5 seconds.
6. If the **N** time lag is longer than specified, check for the following:
   a. Line pressure too low
   b. Forward clutch worn
   c. Direct clutch worn
   d. First and reverse brake worn

STALL SPEED TEST

The object of this test is to check the overall performance of the transaxle and engine by measuring the maximum engine speed in the **D** and **R** ranges.
1. Run the engine until it reaches normal operating temperature.

NOTE: Do not continuously run this test longer than [ ] seconds.

2. Apply the parking brake and block the front and rear wheels.
3. Connect an engine tachometer.
4. Shift into the **D** range.
5. While applying the brakes, step all the way down on the accelerator. Quickly read the highest rpm at this time. The stall speed should be 2200–2350 rpm.
6. Perform the same test in the **R** range.
7. If the engine speed is the same for both ranges, but lower than the specified value, check for the following:
   a. Engine output insufficient
   b. Stator one-way clutch not operating properly

NOTE: If more than 600 rpm below the specified value, the torque converter could be at fault.

8. If the stall speed in **D** range is higher than specified, check for the following:
   a. Line pressure too low
   b. Forward clutch slipping
   c. One-way clutch No. 2 not operating properly
9. If the stall speed in **R** range is higher than specified, check for the following:
   a. Line pressure too low
   b. Direct clutch slipping
   c. First and reverse brake slipping
10. If the stall speed in **R** and **D** range is higher than specified, check for the following:
   a. Line pressure too low
   b. Improper fluid level

ROAD TEST

NOTE: This test must be performed with the engine and transaxle at normal operating temperature.

D RANGE TEST 1

Shift into **D** range and while driving with the accelerator pedal held constant (throttle valve opening 50% and 100%) check the following points:
1. At each of the throttle openings, check that the 1–2 and 2–3 upshifts take place and that the shift points conform to those shown in the automatic shift diagram.
2. If there is no 1–2 upshift, the governor valve may be defective or the 1–2 shift valve stuck.
3. If there is no 2–3 upshift, the 2–3 shift valve is stuck.
4. If the shift point is defective, the throttle cable is out of adjustment or the throttle valve, 1–2 shift valve and the 2-3 shift valves are defective.

D RANGE TEST 2

Check for harsh shift or soft shift slip at 1–2 and 2–3 upshifts. If the shock is severe, the line pressure is too high, the accumulator is defective or the check ball is defective.

D RANGE TEST 3

1. While driving in **D** range, 3rd gear, check for abnormal noise and vibration. This condition could also be caused by unbalance in the differential, tires or the torque converter.
2. While driving in **D** range, 2nd and 3rd gears, check the kickdown vehicle speed limits for the 2-1, 3-1 and the 3-2 kickdowns conform to the automatic shift diagram.

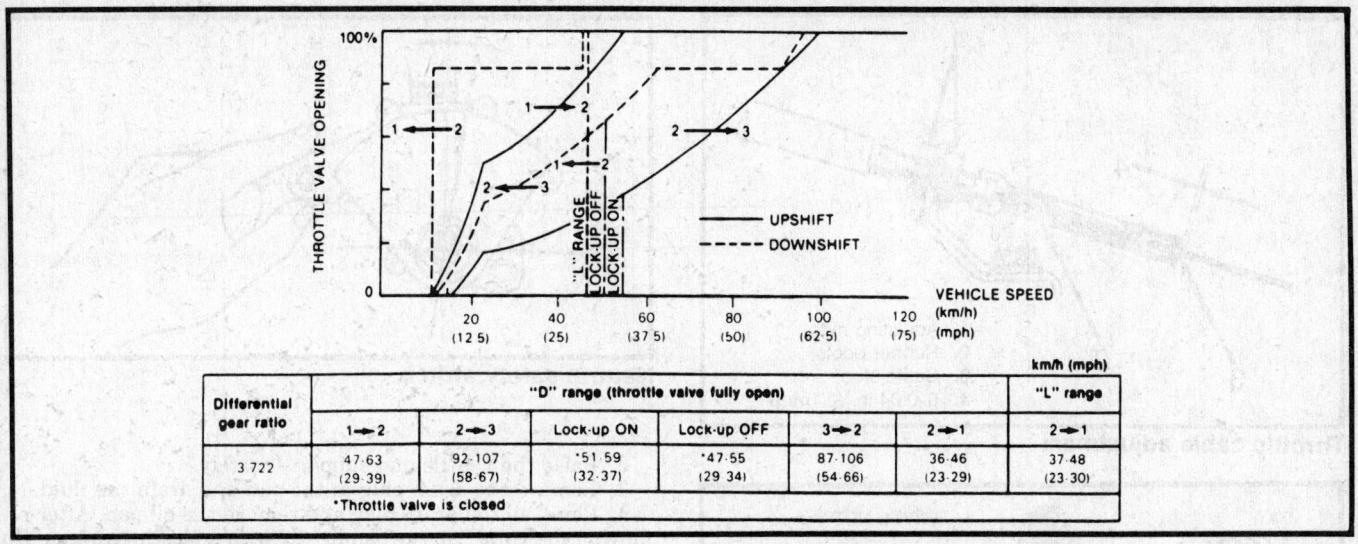

Differential gear ratio	"D" range (throttle valve fully open)						"L" range
	1→2	2→3	Lock-up ON	Lock-up OFF	3→2	2→1	2→1
3.722	47-63 (29-39)	92-107 (58-67)	*51-59 (32-37)	*47-55 (29-34)	87-106 (54-66)	36-46 (23-29)	37-48 (23-30)
*Throttle valve is closed							

Automatic shift diagram

3. While driving in **D** range, 3rd gear, shift to **2** and **L** ranges and check the engine braking effect at each of these ranges. If there is no engine braking effect at **2** range, the 2nd coast brake is defective. If there is no engine braking effect at **L** range, 1st and reverse is defective.

D RANGE TEST 4

While driving in **D** range, release the accelerator pedal and shift into **L** range. Check to see if the 3–2 and 2–1 downshift points conform to those given in the automatic shift diagram.

LOCKUP MECHANISM

While driving in **D** range at a steady speed of about 34 mph (lock-up on), lightly depress the accelerator pedal and check that the engine speed does not change abruptly.

2 RANGE TEST

1. Shift to **2** range and drive with the throttle valve opening at 50% and 100% respectively. Check the 1–2 upshift points at each of the throttle valve openings to see that it conforms to those indicated in the automatic shift diagram.
2. While driving in **2** range, 2nd gear, release the accelerator pedal and check the engine braking effect.

3. Check the kickdown from **2** range. Check the 2–1 kickdown vehicle speed limit.
4. Check for abnormal noise at acceleration and deceleration and harshness at upshift and downshift.

L RANGE TEST

1. While driving in **L** range, check that there is no upshift to 2nd gear.
2. While driving in **L** range, release the accelerator pedal and check the engine braking effect.
3. Check for abnormal noise during acceleration and deceleration.

R RANGE TEST

Shift into **R** range and while starting at full throttle, check for slipping.

P RANGE TEST

Stop the vehicle on a slight hill and after shifting into **P** range, release the parking brake. Check to see that the parking lock pawl prevents the vehicle from moving.

ON CAR SERVICES

Adjustments

THROTTLE CABLE

1. Depress the accelerator pedal all the way and check that the throttle valve opens fully. If the throttle valve does not open fully, adjust the accelerator link.
2. Fully depress the accelerator.
3. Loosen the adjustment nuts.
4. Adjust the throttle cable housing so that the distance between the end of the boot and the stopper on the cable is correct. It should be 0–0.04 in. (0–1mm).
5. Tighten the adjusting nuts and recheck the adjustment.

TRANSAXLE CONTROL CABLE

1. Loosen the swivel nut on the lever.
2. Push the manual lever fully toward the right side of the vehicle.
3. Return the lever 2 notches toward the **N** position.
4. Set the shift lever in the **N** range.
5. While holding the lever lightly toward the **R** range side, tighten the swivel nut.

NEUTRAL SAFETY SWITCH

If the engine will start with the shift selector in any range other than **N** or **P** range, adjustment is required.

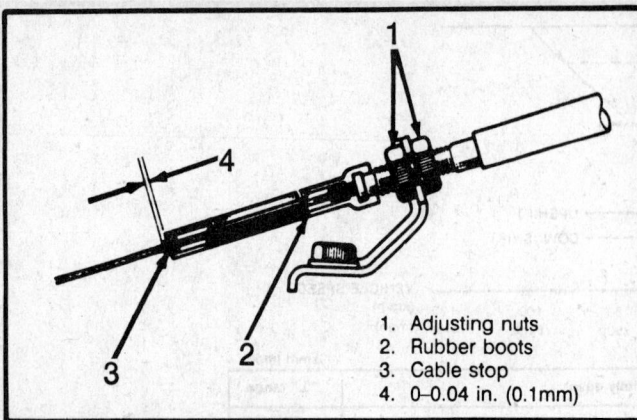

1. Adjusting nuts
2. Rubber boots
3. Cable stop
4. 0–0.04 in. (0.1mm)

Throttle cable adjustment

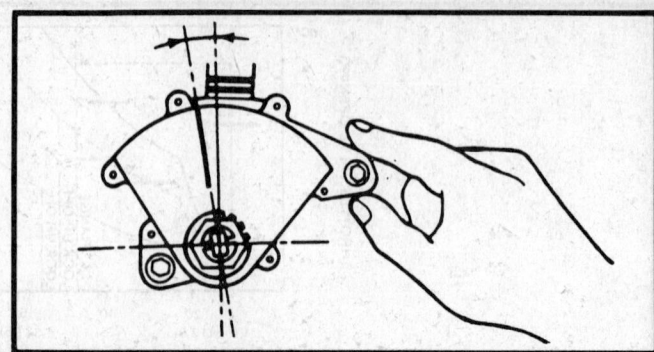

Neutral safety switch

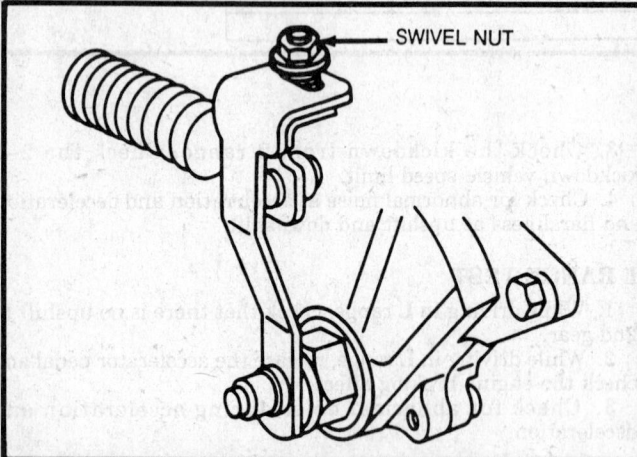

SWIVEL NUT

Control cable adjustment

1. Loosen the neutral safety switch bolts and set the shift selector in **N** range. Adjust the neutral safety switch.
2. Disconnect the neutral safety switch connector.
3. Connect an ohmmeter between the terminals.
4. Adjust the switch to the point where there is continuity between terminals.

Services

FLUID CHANGES

The conditions under which the vehicle is operated is the main consideration in determining how often the transaxle fluid should be changed. Different driving conditions result in different transaxle fluid temperatures. These temperatures effect the change intervals.

If the vehicle is driven under severe service conditions, change the fluid and filter every 15,000 miles. If the vehicle is not used under severe service conditions, change the fluid and replace the filter every 50,000 miles.

Do not overfill the transaxle. It takes 1 pint of fluid to change the level from **ADD** to **FULL** on the transaxle dipstick. Overfilling the unit can cause damage to the internal components of the automatic transaxle.

OIL PAN

Removal and Installation

1. Disconnect the negative battery cable.

2. Raise the vehicle and support it safely.
3. Remove the drain plug in the pan and drain the fluid.
4. Reinstall the drain plug and remove the oil pan. After removing the bolts, tap the pan lightly with a plastic hammer. Do not force the pan off by prying. This may cause damage to the gasket mating surface.
5. Remove the oil pan gasket material on the mating surface.
6. Remove the oil filter from the valve body.
7. Clean the inside of the oil pan before installation.
8. Clean the oil cleaner magnet and install it in the proper position.
9. Install a new filter on the valve body.
10. Install the pan with a new gasket and torque the bolts to 43 inch lbs. (4.9 Nm).
11. Fill with transmission fluid to the proper level.
12. Lower the vehicle and connect the battery cable.

VALVE BODY

Removal and Installation

1. Disconnect the negative battery cable.
2. Raise the vehicle and support it safely.
3. Remove the drain plug in the pan and drain the fluid.
4. Reinstall the drain plug and remove the oil pan. After removing the bolts, tap the pan lightly with a plastic hammer. Do not force the pan off by prying. This may cause damage to the gasket mating surface.
5. Remove the oil pan gasket material on the mating surface.
6. Remove the oil tube bracket and the oil strainer.
7. Pry out the 4 oil tubes and remove them.
8. Remove the detent spring.
9. Remove the 4 bolts and the manual valve body.
10. Loosen and remove the valve body bolts.
11. Lift the valve body assembly and disconnect the throttle cable from the cam.
12. Remove the valve body.
13. On installation, install the valve body on the case. Hold the cam down and insert the throttle cable into the slot.
14. Install the valve body with the bolts finger tight.
15. Align the manual valve with the manual lever and install the manual valve body. Torque the bolts to 84 inch lbs. (10 Nm).
16. Install the detent spring and tighten the bolts to 84 inch lbs. (10 Nm).
17. Make sure that the manual valve lever touches the center of the detent spring roller.
18. Tighten the valve body bolts to 84 inch lbs. (10 Nm).
19. Install the oil tubes, bracket and oil strainer.
20. Clean the inside of the oil pan before installation.
21. Clean the oil cleaner magnet and install it in the proper position.
22. Install the oil pan with a new gasket and torque the bolts to 43 inch lbs. (4.9 Nm).

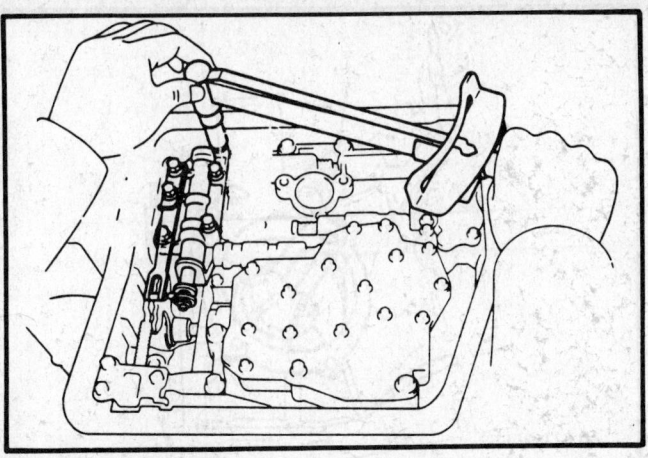

Manual valve body

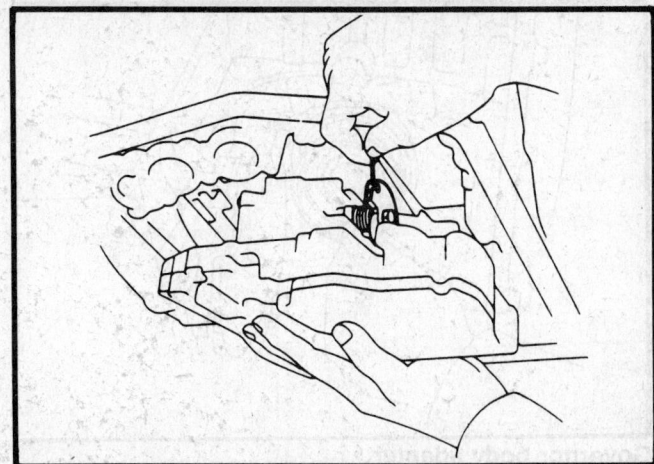

Throttle cable

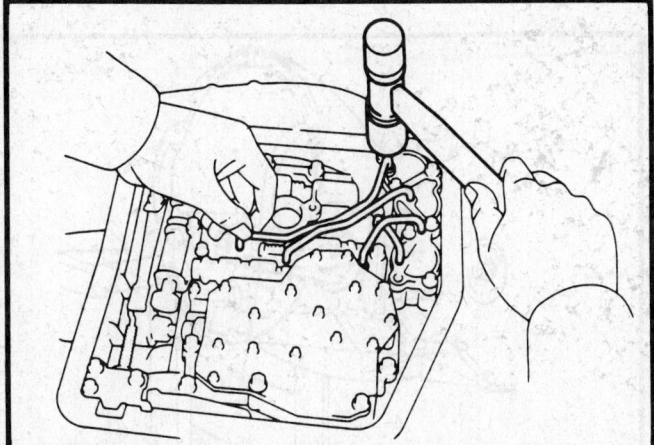

Oil tubes

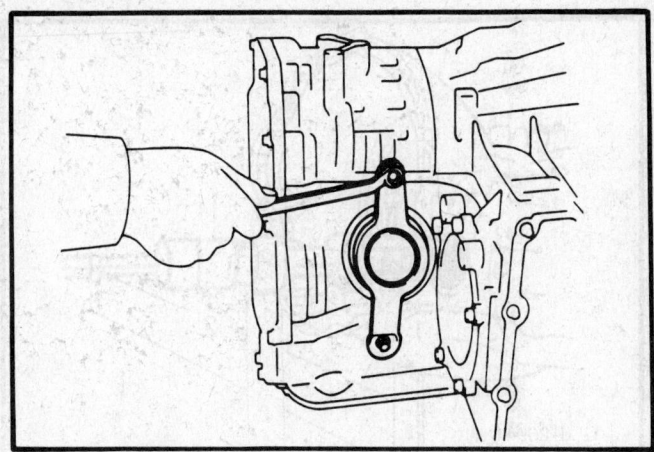

Governor cover

GOVERNOR

Removal and Installation

1. Disconnect the negative battery cable.
2. Raise the vehicle and support it safely.
3. Remove the transaxle dust cover.
4. Remnove the left hand driveshaft.
5. Remove the governor cover and O-ring.
6. Remove the governor body with the thrust washer.
7. Remove the washer.
8. Remove the governor body adapter.
9. For installation, install the governor body adapter.
10. Install the governor body with the thrust washer.
11. Install the governor cover with the O-ring.
12. Install the left hand driveshaft.
13. Install the transaxle dust cover.
14. Lower the vehicle and connect the battery cable.

DIFFERENTIAL OIL SEAL

Removal and Installation

1. Disconnect the negative battery cable.
2. Raise the vehicle and support it safely.
3. Drain the fluid from the differential.
4. Remove the driveshaft from the transaxle and the steering knuckle.

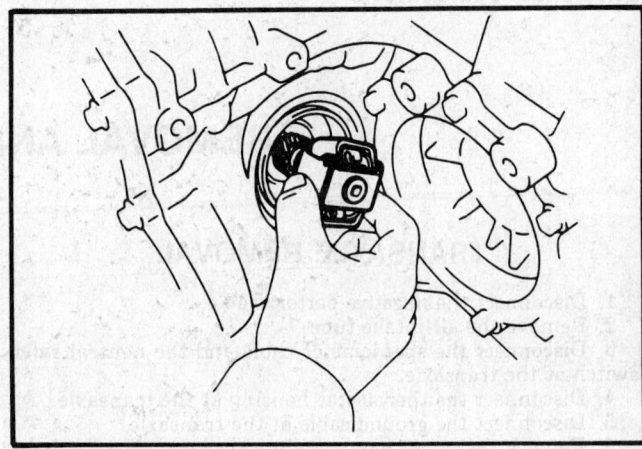

Governor valve

5. Remove the differential oil seals using tools J–26941 and J–23907.
6. Using tool J–35553, drive the oil seal into the case until its surface is flush with the surface of the case.
7. Coat the top of the oil seal with grease.
8. Install the driveshaft to the transaxle and the steering knuckle.
9. Fill with transmission fluid and check the fluid level.

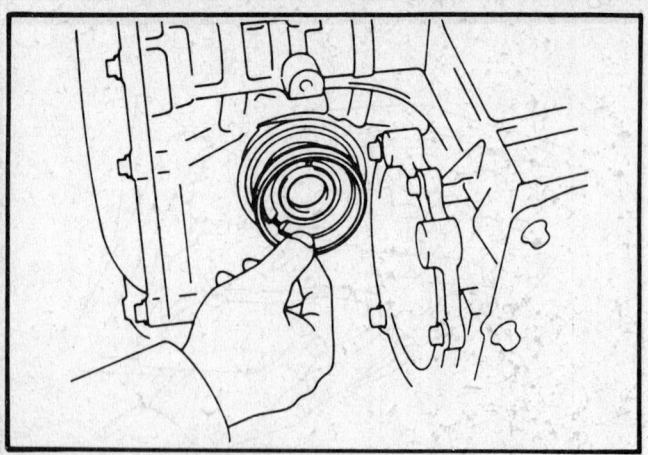

Governor body adapter

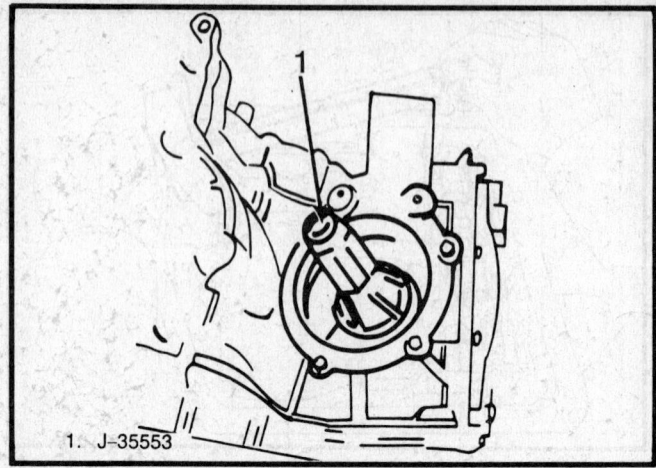

1. J–35553

Differential seal installation LH side

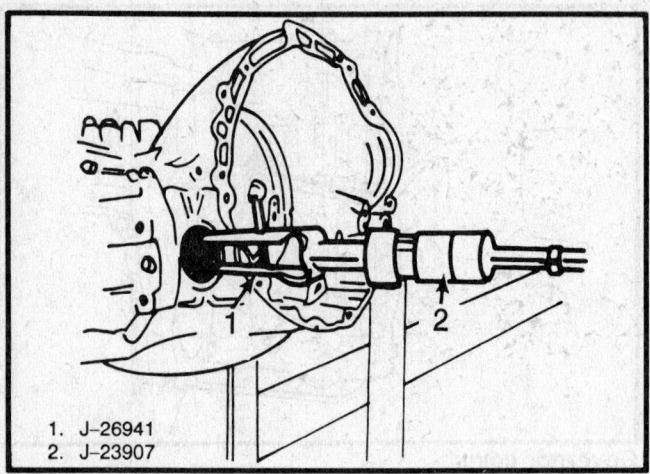

1. J–26941
2. J–23907

Differential seal removal

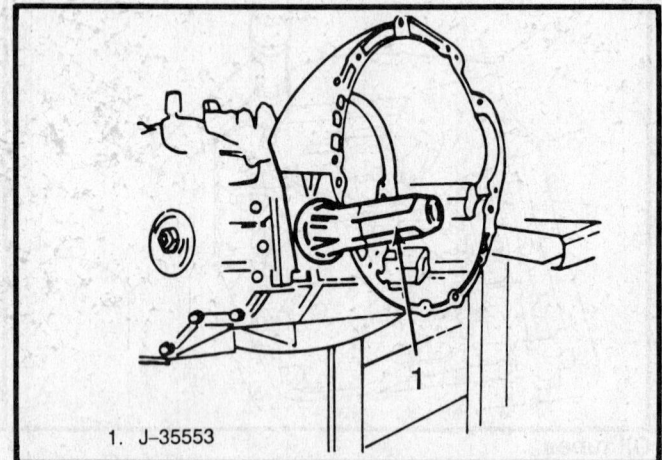

1. J–35553

Differential seal installation RH side

REMOVAL AND INSTALLATION

TRANSAXLE REMOVAL

1. Disconnect the negative battery cable.
2. Remove the air intake tube.
3. Disconnect the speedometer cable and the neutral safety switch at the transaxle.
4. Disconnect the thermostat housing at the transaxle.
5. Disconnect the ground cable at the transaxle.
6. Remove the upper mount to bracket bolt.
7. Disconnect the necessary electrical connections.
8. Disconnect the T.V. cable at the carburetor.
9. Remove the upper bell housing bolts.
10. Support the engine using an engine support tool.
11. Raise the vehicle and support it safely.
12. Remove the left wheel and tire assembly.
13. Remove the left, right and center splash shields.
14. Remove the center beam.
15. Disconnect the shift cable at the transaxle.
16. Remove the shift cable bracket.

17. Disconnect the cooler bracket.
18. Disconnect the cooler lines at the outlets.
19. Remove the inspection cover.
20. Remove the converter bolts.
21. Disconnect the left hand control arm at the ball joint.
22. Disconnect the right hand control arm at the ball joint.
23. Disconnect the right and left axle shafts at the tranxsaxle.
24. Remove the starter bolts. Remove the starter.
25. Remove the rear transaxle bolts.
26. Support the transaxle with a jack.
27. Remove the remaining mount bolts.
28. Remove the remaining bell housing bolts.
29. Remove the transaxle from the vehicle.

TRANSAXLE INSTALLATION

1. If the torque converter has been drained, refill it with 2.3 qts. (2.2L) Dexron® II automatic transmission fluid. Install the torque converter in the transaxle.

2. To be sure the torque converter is installed correctly, use a straight edge and measure from the installed surface to the front surface of the transaxle housing. The distance should be more than 0.79 in. (20mm).

3. Position the transaxle on a suitable transmission jack and align it in the vehicle.

4. Align the converter housing with the 2 dowel pins in the block and install a bolt.

5. Install the transaxle housing mounting bolts and torque the 12mm bolt to 47 ft. lbs. (64 Nm). Torque the 10mm bolts to 34 ft. lbs. (46 Nm).

6. Install the left hand engine mounting. Tighten the bolts to 38 ft. lbs. (52 Nm).

7. Install the torque converter bolts. Tighten the bolts evenly and torque to 13 ft. lbs. (18 Nm).

8. Install the engine rear end plate.

9. Install the starter.

10. Install the driveshafts.

11. Install the engine mounting center support. Tighten the bolts to 29 ft. lbs. (39 Nm).

12. Install the front and rear mounts. Tighten the bolts to 29 ft. lbs. (39 Nm).

13. Install the splash shields.

14. Install the engine under cover.

15. Lower the vehicle.

16. Install the thermostat housing.

17. Connect the oil cooler hose.

18. Connect and adjust the control cable.

19. Connect the speedometer cable.

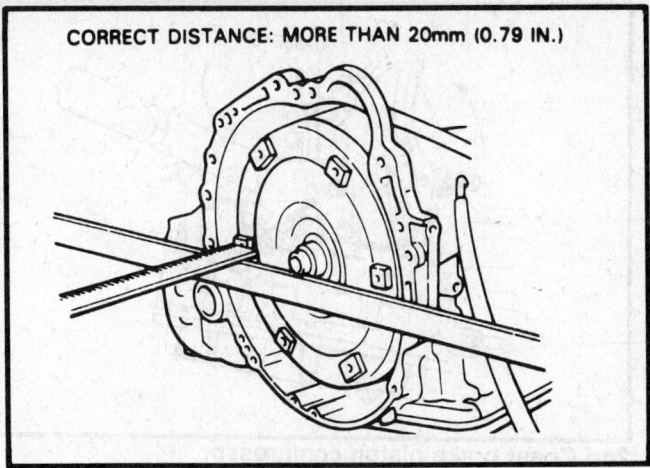

CORRECT DISTANCE: MORE THAN 20mm (0.79 IN.)

Checking the torque converter

20. Connect and adjust the throttle cable.

21. Connect the neutral safety switch connector.

22. Install the air cleaner.

23. Connect the negative battery cable.

24. Fill the transaxle with transmission fluid.

BENCH OVERHAUL

Before Disassembly

Before opening up the transaxle, the outside of the unit should be thoroughly cleaned, preferably with high pressure cleaning equipment. Dirt entering the transaxle internal parts will negate all the effort and time spent on the overhaul. During inspection and reassembly, all parts should be thoroughly cleaned with solvent and then dried with compressed air. Cloths and rags should not be used to dry the parts since lint will find its way into the valve body passages.

Lube the seals with Dexron® II automatic transmission fluid and use unmedicated petroleum jelly to hold the thrust washers and ease the assembly of the seals. Do not use solvent on neoprene seals, friction plates or thrust washers. Be wary of nylon parts if the transaxle failure was due to a cooling system problem. Nylon parts exposed to antifreeze solutions can swell and distort, so they must be replaced. Before installing bolts into aluminum parts, dip the threads in clean oil.

Converter Inspection

Make certain that the transaxle is held securey. If the torque converter is equipped with a drain plug, open the plug and drain the fluid. If there is no drain plug, the converter must be drained through the hub after pulling the converter out of the transaxle. If the oil in the converter is discolored but does not contain metal bits or particles, the converter is not damaged. Color is no longer a good indicator of fluid condition.

If the oil in the converter contains metal particles, the converter is damaged internally and must be replaced. If the cause of the oil contamination was burned clutch plates or overheated oil, the converter is contaminated and should be replaced. If the pump gears or cover show signs of damage, the converter will contain metal particles and must be replaced.

Transaxle Disassembly

1. Remove the oil cooler pipes.
2. Remove the manual shift lever.
3. Remove the neutral safety switch.
4. Remove the oil filler gauge and tube.
5. Remove the throttle cable retaining plate.
6. Remove the governor body using the following procedure:
   a. Remove the bolts and the cover bracket
   b. Remove the governor cover and O-ring
   c. Remove the thrust washer from the governor body
   d. Remove the governor body
   e. Remove the plate washer and the governor body adapter
7. Remove the pan and gasket.
8. Remove the magnet and check for chips and particles in the pan.
9. Remove the oil tube bracket and the oil strainer.
10. Remove the oil tubes.
11. Remove the manual detent spring.
12. Remove the manual valve and the manual valve body.
13. Disconnect the throttle cable from the cam and remove the valve body.
14. Remove the throttle cable from the case.
15. Remove the governor apply gasket.
16. Remove the governor oil strainer.
17. Remove the accumulator piston and springs. Loosen the bolts slowly until the spring tension is released.
18. Install the 2nd coast brake piston compressor J–35549 and remove the snapring.
19. Remove the bolts holding the oil pump to the transaxle case. Remove the pum using tools J–6125–B and J–35496 adapters.
20. Remove the direct clutch.
21. Remove the thrust washer.

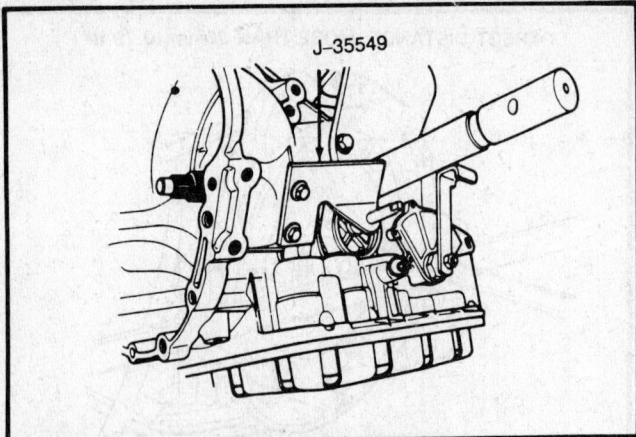

2nd Coast brake piston compressor

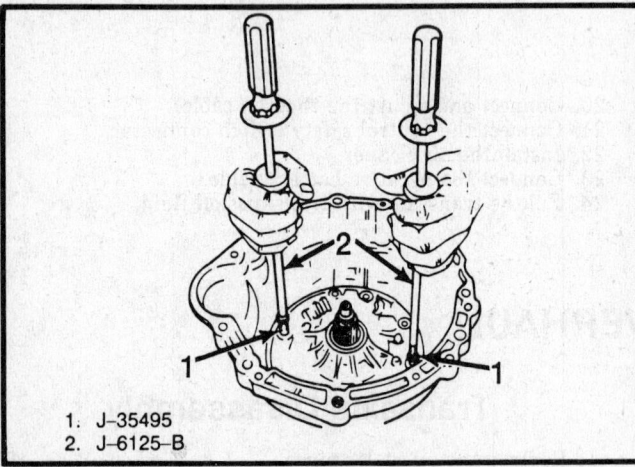

1. J-35495
2. J-6125-B

Oil pump removal

22. Remove the forward clutch drum.
23. Remove the 2nd coast brake band.
24. Remove the front planetary ring gear.
25. Remove the planetary gear.
26. Remove the sun gear, sun gear input drum, 2nd brake hub and No.1 one-way clutch.
27. Remove the 2nd coast brake band guide.
28. Remove the snapring holding the 2nd brake drum to the case.
29. Remove the 2nd brake drum and return springs.
30. Remove the 2nd brake drum gasket.
31. Remove the plates, discs and flange.
32. Blow out the piston with compressed air.
33. Remove the snapring holding the No. 2 one-way clutch outer race to the case.
34. Remove the No. 2 one-way clutch and rear planetary gear.
35. Remove the rear planetary ring gear and bearing.
36. Remove the snapring holding the flange to the case.
37. Remove the plates, discs and flanges.
38. Remove the bolts holding the rear cover to the transaxle case.
39. Remove the rear cover and intermediate shaft.
40. Remove the case gasket.
41. Remove the parking pawl bracket and parking lock rod.
42. Remove the parking lock pawl shaft, spring and parking lock pawl.

Unit Disassembly and Assembly

OIL PUMP

Disassembly

1. Remove the race from the stator shaft.
2. Remove the O-ring from the pump body.
3. Remove the oil seal rings from the back of the stator shaft.
4. Remove the thrust washer of the clutch drum from the stator shaft.
5. Remove the stator shaft. Keep the gears in assembly order.

Inspection

1. Check the body clearance of the driven gear. Push the driven gear to either side of the body. Using a feeler gauge, measure the clearance. If the clearance exceeds the limit, replace the drive gear, driven gear or pump body.
2. Check the tip clearance of both gears. Measure between the gear teeth and the crescent-shaped part of the pump body. If the clearance exceeds the limit, replace the drive gear, driven gear or pump body.
3. Check the side clearance of both gears. Using a steel straight edge and a feeler gauge, measure the side clearance of both gears. If the clearance exceeds the limit, replace the drive gear, driven gear or the pump body.
4. Inspect the front oil seal, check for wear, damage or cracks.
5. Replace the front oil seal. The seal end should be flush with the outer edge of the pump body.

Assembly

1. Install the driven gear and drive gear making sure the top of the gears are facing upward.
2. Install the stator shaft onto the pump body. Align the stator shaft with each bolt hole.
3. Tighten the bolts to 7 ft. lbs. (10 Nm).
4. Coat the thrust washer with petroleum jelly. Align the tab of the washer with the hollow of the pump body and install the thrust washer.
5. Install 2 oil seal rings on the oil pump. Do not spread the ring ends too far.
6. Check the pump drive gear rotation. Turn the drive gear and check that it rotates smoothly.
7. Install a new O-ring.
8. Install the race onto the stator shaft.

DIRECT CLUTCH

Disassembly

1. Remove the snapring from the clutch drum.
2. Remove the flange, discs and plates.
3. Compress the piston return springs and remove the snapring using tool J-23327.
4. Remove the spring retainer and springs.
5. Slide the direct clutch onto the oil pump. Apply compressed air to the oil pump to remove the piston. Remove the direct clutch from the oil pump.
6. Remove the clutch piston O-ring.

Inspection

Inspect the clutch piston. Check that the ball is free by shaking the piston. Check that the valve does not leak by applying low pressure compressed air. Inspect the discs.

Assembly

1. Coat the new O-rings with automatic transmission fluid and install them on the piston.

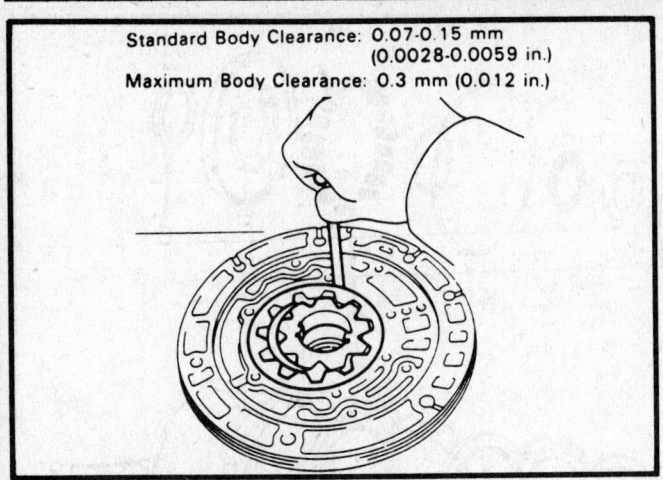

Standard Body Clearance: 0.07-0.15 mm
(0.0028-0.0059 in.)
Maximum Body Clearance: 0.3 mm (0.012 in.)

Checking body clearance

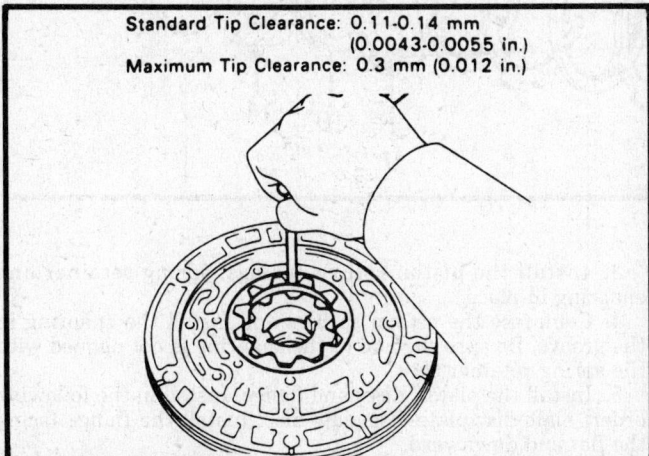

Standard Tip Clearance: 0.11-0.14 mm
(0.0043-0.0055 in.)
Maximum Tip Clearance: 0.3 mm (0.012 in.)

Checking tip clearance

2. Press the piston into the drum with the cup side up, being careful not to damage the O-ring.

3. Install the piston return springs and set the retainer and snapring in place.

4. Compress the return springs and install the snapring in the groove using tool J–23327. Install the snapring. Be sure the endgap of the snapring is not aligned with the spring retainer claw.

5. Install the plates, discs and flange. Install in order: plate-disc-plate-plate-disc. Install the flange, facing the flat end downward.

6. Install the outer snapring. Check that the endgap of the snapring is not aligned with a cutout.

7. Using compressed air, check the stroke of the direct clutch for only replacement of plate, discs and flange. If not within specification, select a proper flange. There are 2 different flange thickness.

8. Install the direct clutch onto the oil pump.

9. Apply compressed air into the passage of the oil pump body and be sure that the piston moves. If the piston does not move, disassemble and inspect.

FORWARD CLUTCH

Disassembly

1. Remove the thrust washer.

2. Remove the thrust bearings and races from both sides of the clutch.

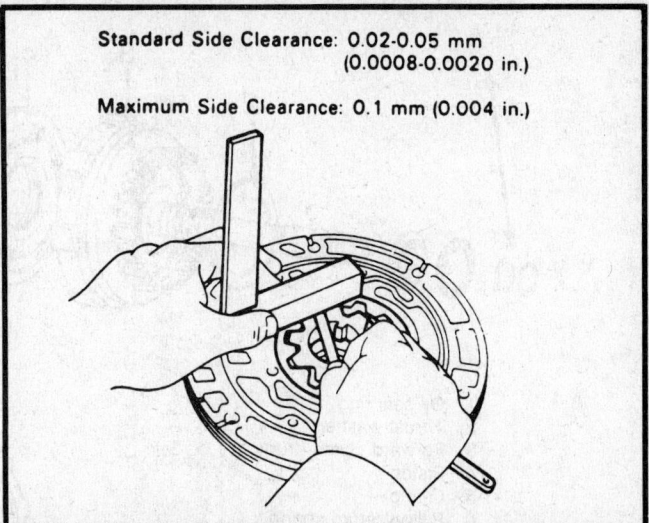

Standard Side Clearance: 0.02-0.05 mm
(0.0008-0.0020 in.)
Maximum Side Clearance: 0.1 mm (0.004 in.)

Side clearance

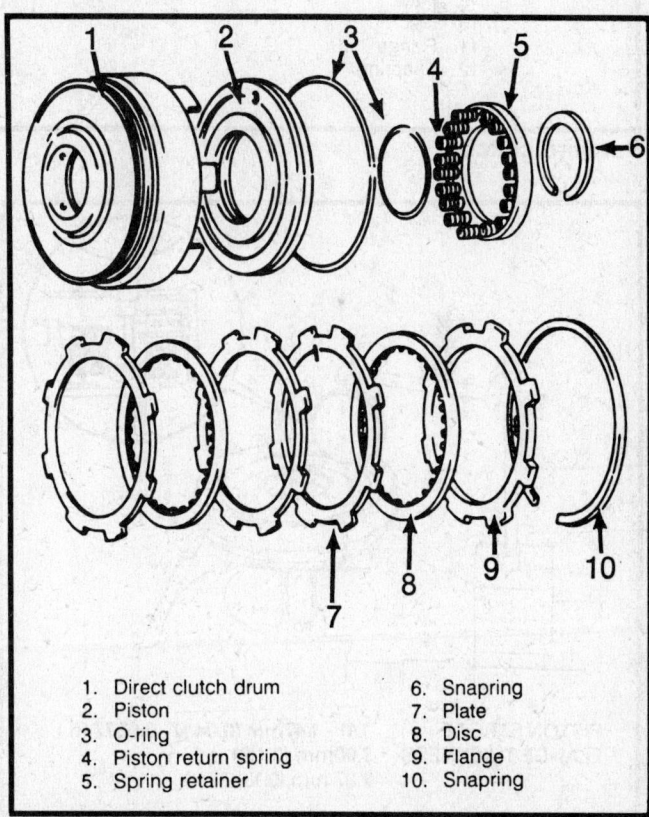

1. Direct clutch drum	6. Snapring
2. Piston	7. Plate
3. O-ring	8. Disc
4. Piston return spring	9. Flange
5. Spring retainer	10. Snapring

Direct clutch

3. Remove the snapring from the clutch drum.

4. Remove the flange, discs and plates.

5. Compress the piston return springs and remove the snapring using tools J–25018–A adapter and J–23327.

6. Remove the spring retainer and springs.

7. Apply compressed air into the oil passage to remove the piston.

Inspection

Make sure the check ball is free by shaking the piston. Check

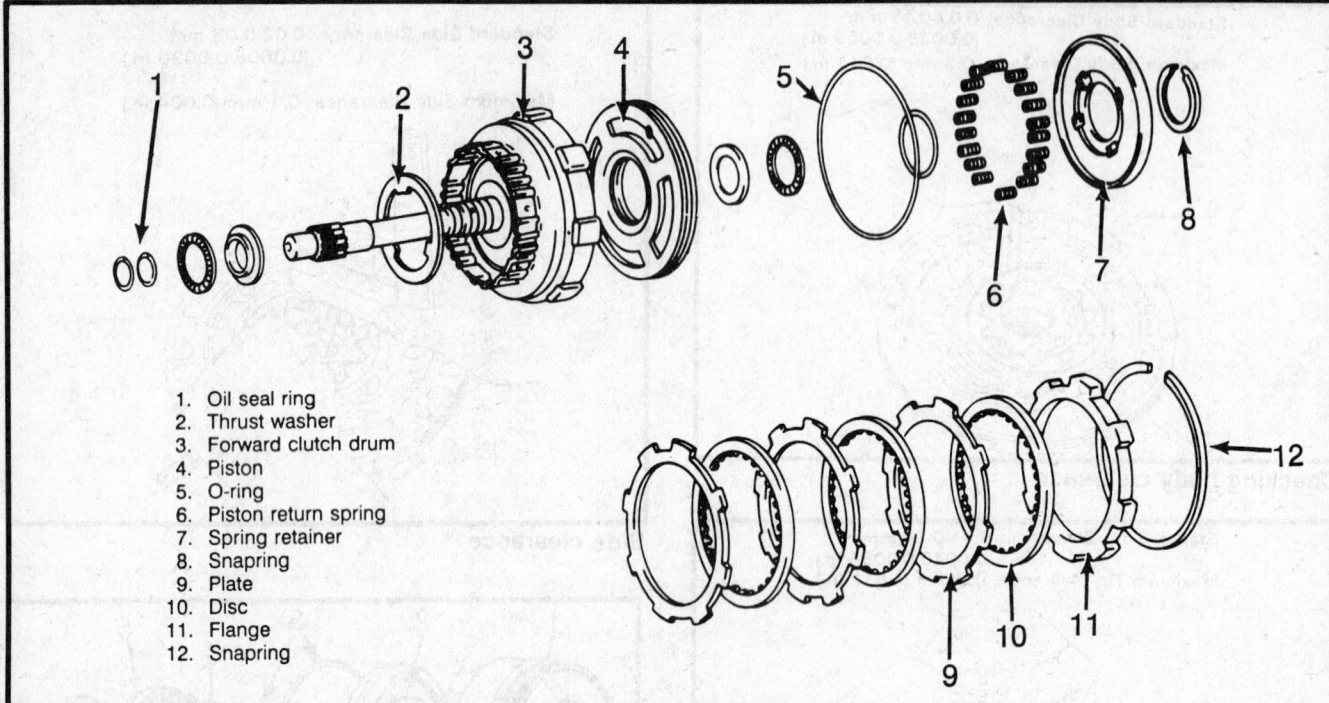

1. Oil seal ring
2. Thrust washer
3. Forward clutch drum
4. Piston
5. O-ring
6. Piston return spring
7. Spring retainer
8. Snapring
9. Plate
10. Disc
11. Flange
12. Snapring

Forward clutch

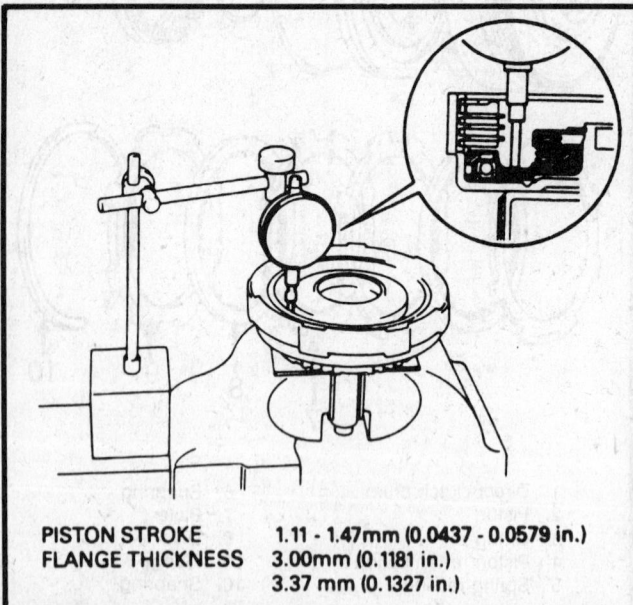

PISTON STROKE	1.11 - 1.47mm (0.0437 - 0.0579 in.)
FLANGE THICKNESS	3.00mm (0.1181 in.)
	3.37 mm (0.1327 in.)

Snapring to flange stroke

that the valve does not leak by applying low pressure compressed air. Replace the oil seal rings. Slide the rings over top of the shaft and install them into the groove. Do not spread the ring ends.

Assembly

1. Install new O-rings on the piston, coat the O-rings with automatic transmission fluid.
2. Press the piston into the forward clutch drum with the cup side up, being careful not to damage the O-ring.

3. Install the piston return springs, spring retainer and snapring in place.
4. Compress the return springs and install the snapring in the groove. Be sure the end of the snapring is not aligned with the spring retainer claw.
5. Install the plates, discs and flange. Install in the following order: plate-disc-plate-disc-plate-disc. Install the flange facing the flat end downward.
6. Install the outer snapring. Check that the endgap of the snapring is not aligned with a cutout.
7. Using compressed air, check the stroke of the direct clutch for only replacement of plate, discs and flange. If not within specification, select a proper flange. There are 2 different flange thickness.
8. Apply compressed air into the oil passage with the shaft and be sure that the piston moves. If the piston does not move, disassemble and inspect.
9. Install thrust washer, races and bearings.

ONE-WAY CLUTCH AND SUN GEAR

Disassembly

1. Check the operation of the one-way clutch by holding the sun gear and turning the hub. The hub should turn freely clockwise and should lock counterclockwise.
2. Remove the 2nd brake hub and the one-way clutch from the sun gear.
3. Remove the No. 3 planetary carrier thrust washer from sun gear input drum.
4. Remove the snapring and the sun gear input drum.

Inspection

If necessary, replace the one-way clutch.
1. Pry off the retainer.
2. Remove the one-way clutch.
3. Install the one-way clutch into the brake hub, facing the spring cage inward from the flanged side of the brake hub.

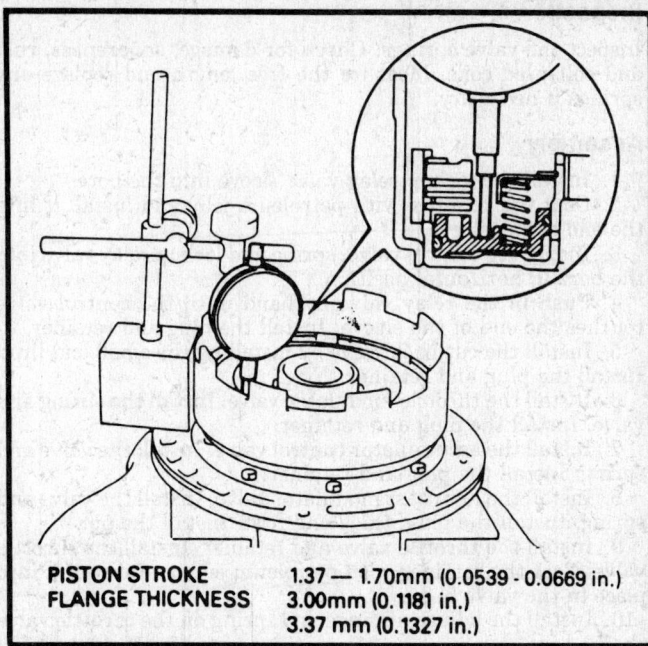

PISTON STROKE 1.37 — 1.70mm (0.0539 - 0.0669 in.)
FLANGE THICKNESS 3.00mm (0.1181 in.)
3.37 mm (0.1327 in.)

Forward clutch stroke

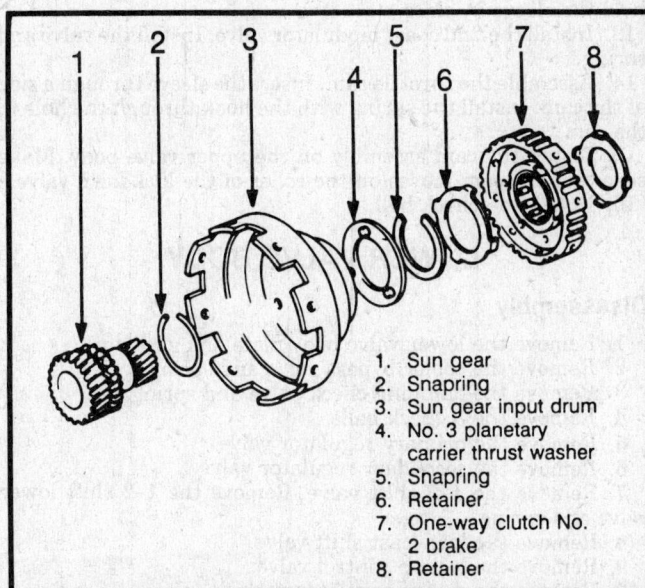

1. Sun gear
2. Snapring
3. Sun gear input drum
4. No. 3 planetary carrier thrust washer
5. Snapring
6. Retainer
7. One-way clutch No. 2 brake
8. Retainer

No. 1 one-way clutch and sun gear

4. Hold the brake hub in a vise and flatten the ears with a chisel.

5. Check the operation to make sure that the retainer is centered.

Assembly

1. Install the shaft snapring on the sun gear.

2. Install the sun gear input drum on the sun gear and install the shaft snapring.

3. Install the No. 3 planetary carrier thrust washer on the sun gear input drum.

4. Install the one-way clutch and the 2nd brake hub on the sun gear. While turning the hub clockwise, slide the one-way clutch into the inner race.

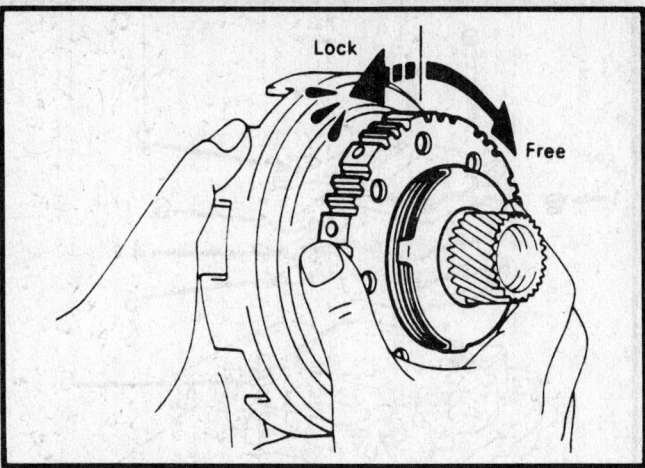

One-way clutch operation

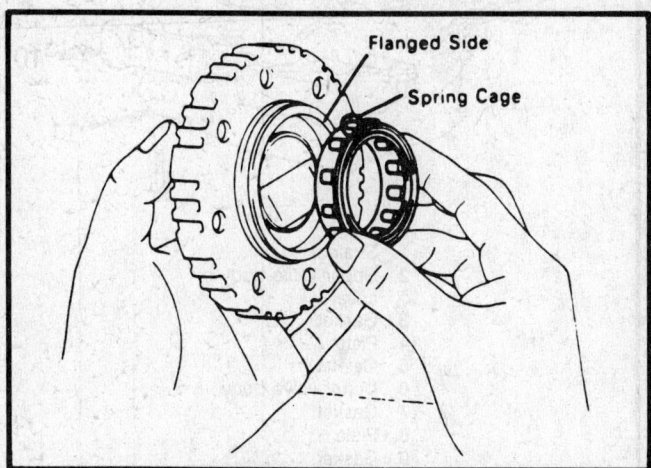

One-way clutch installation

VALVE BODY

Disassembly

1. Remove the 14 bolts and remove the remove the lower valve body cover.

2. Turn the assembly over and remove the 12 bolts from the upper valve body and upper valve body cover.

3. Remove the upper valve body cover, strainer gaskets and plate.

4. Turn the assembly over and remove the 3 bolts from the lower valve body.

5. Lift off the lower valve body and plate as a single unit. Hold the body plate to the lower valve body.

NOTE: Be careful that the check valve and ball do not fall out.

UPPER VALVE BODY

Disassembly

1. Remove the throttle valve retainer and check ball.

2. Remove the retainer for the plug with a magnetic finger and remove the plug.

3. Remove the lockup relay valve, control valve and spring.

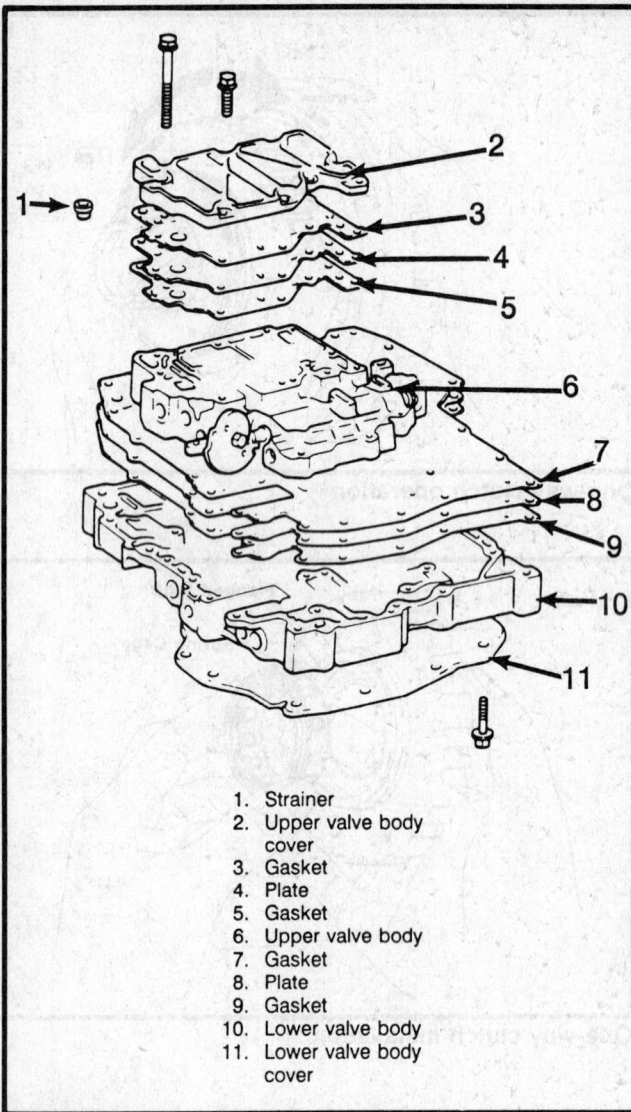

1. Strainer
2. Upper valve body cover
3. Gasket
4. Plate
5. Gasket
6. Upper valve body
7. Gasket
8. Plate
9. Gasket
10. Lower valve body
11. Lower valve body cover

Valve body

4. Remove the sleeve retainer with a magnetic finger and remove the sleeve.
5. Remove the cut-back valve by removing the retainer with a magnetic finger then remove the cut-back valve and plug.
6. Remove the throttle modulator valve by removing the retainer with a magnetic finger, then remove the plug, valve and spring.
7. Remove the accumulator control valve by removing the retainer with a magnetic finger and remove the plug, valve and spring.
8. Remove the low coast modulator valve by removing the pin with a magnetic finger then remove the plug, valve and spring.
9. Remove the 2nd coast modulator valve by removing the retainer with a magnetic finger then remove the spring and valve.
10. Remove the throttle cam. Loosen the bolt and remove the cam, spring and collar.
11. Remove the kickdown valve and spring by removing the pin with a magnetic finger, then remove the kickdown valve with the sleeve and spring.
12. Remove the throttle valve.
13. Remove the spring and adjusting rings.

Inspection

Inspect the valve springs. Check for damage, squareness, rust and collapsed coils. Measure the free length and replace any springs if necessary.

Assembly

1. Install the lockup relay valve sleeve into the bore.
2. Coat the retainer with petroleum jelly and install it into the end of the sleeve.
3. Install the control valve, spring and lockup relay valve into the bore in horizontal position.
4. Push in the relay valve by hand until the control valve touches the end of the sleeve. Install the plug and retainer.
5. Install the cut-back valve by installing the small end first. Install the plug and retainer.
6. Install the throttle modulator valve. Install the spring and valve. Install the plug and retainer.
7. Install the accumulator control valve. Install the valve and spring. Install the plug and retainer.
8. Install the low coast modulator valve. Install the valve and spring. Install the plug, thick end first. Install the pin.
9. Install the throttle valve and retainer. Install the throttle valve. Coat the retainer with petroleum jelly and install it into place in the valve body.
10. Install the adjusting rings and spring on the throttle valve shaft.
11. Install the spring into the throttle valve.
12. Install the kickdown valve and sleeve. Install the pin to hold the sleeve in place.
13. Install the 2nd coast modulator valve. Install the valve and spring.
14. Assemble the throttle cam. Insert the sleeve through a side of the cam. Install the spring with the hook through the hole in the cam.
15. Install the cam assembly on the upper valve body. Make sure that the cam moves on the roller of the kickdown valve.
16. Install the check ball.

LOWER VALVE BODY

Disassembly

1. Remove the lower valve body plate and gaskets.
2. Remove the cooler bypass valve and spring.
3. Remove the damping check valve and spring.
4. Remove the 3 check balls.
5. Remove the primary regulator valve.
6. Remove the secondary regulator valve.
7. Remove the 1–2 shift valve. Remove the 1–2 shift lower valve and spring.
8. Remove the low coast shift valve.
9. Remove the lockup control valve.
10. Remove the detent regulator valve.
11. Remove the 2–3 shift valve.
12. Remove the intermediate shift valve.
13. Remove the lockup signal valve.
14. Remove the 3–4 coast shift plug.
15. Remove the 3–4 shift plug.

Inspection

Inspect the valve springs. Check for damage, squareness, rust and collapsed coils. Measure the free length and replace any springs if necessary.

Assembly

1. Place the primary regulator valve into the bore in the horizontal position.
2. Push the valve into the bore until its tip bottoms in the bore.

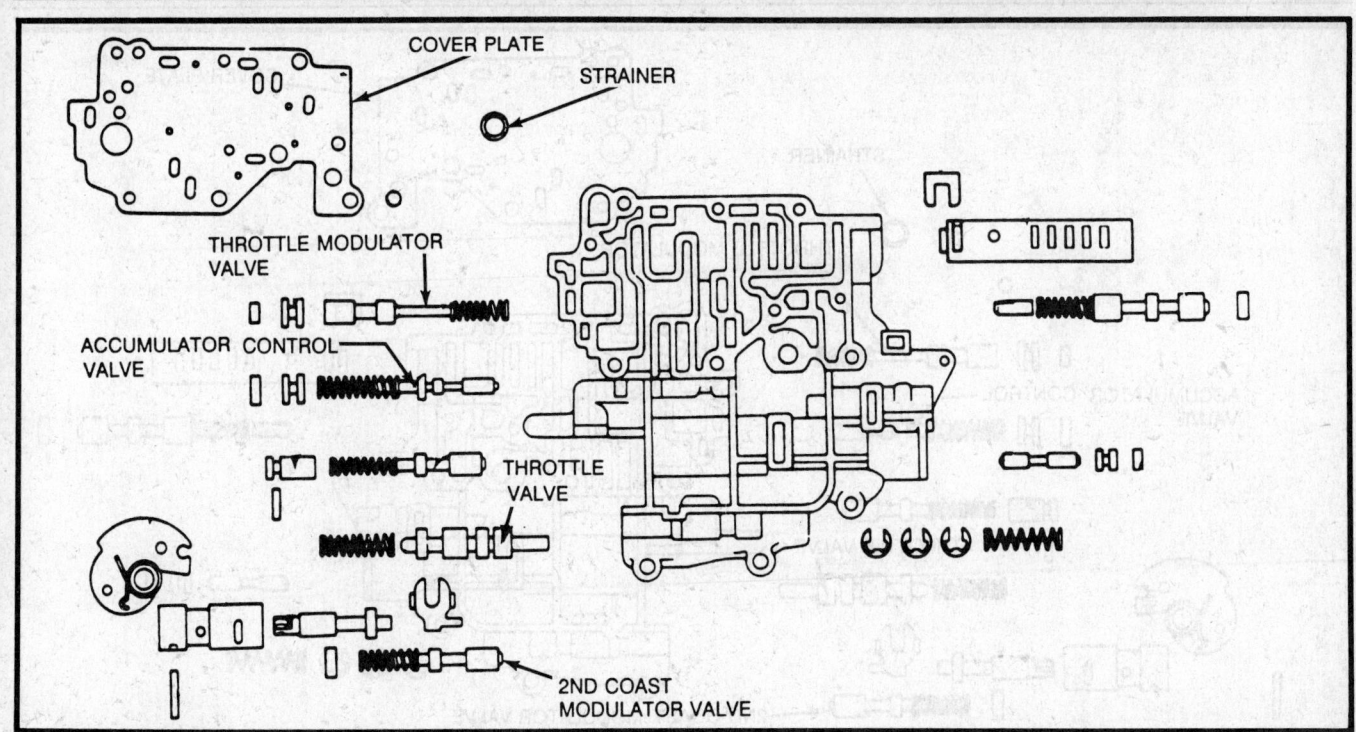

Upper valve body

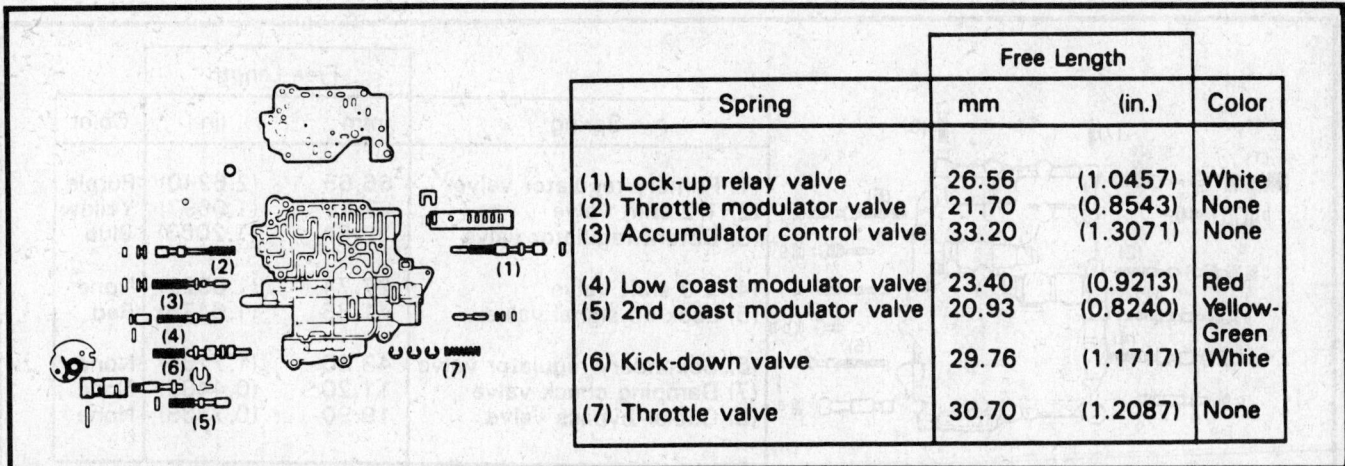

Spring	Free Length		Color
	mm	(in.)	
(1) Lock-up relay valve	26.56	(1.0457)	White
(2) Throttle modulator valve	21.70	(0.8543)	None
(3) Accumulator control valve	33.20	(1.3071)	None
(4) Low coast modulator valve	23.40	(0.9213)	Red
(5) 2nd coast modulator valve	20.93	(0.8240)	Yellow-Green
(6) Kick-down valve	29.76	(1.1717)	White
(7) Throttle valve	30.70	(1.2087)	None

Valve spring chart

3. Install the valve spring.
4. Insert the plunger with the short end first. The plunger should be recessed inside the sleeve.
5. Install the sleeve with the plunger.
6. Install the secondary regulator valve.
7. Install the 1–2 shift valve. Install the spring and upper valve.
8. Install the low coast shift valve.
9. Install the lockup control valve.
10. Install the detent regulator valve.
11. Install the intermediate shift valve.
12. Install the 2-3 shift valve.
13. Install the lock-up signal valve.
14. Install the 3-4 coast shift plug.
15. Install the 3-4 shift plug.
16. Install the spring and cooler by-pass valve.

17. Install the spring and damping check valve.
18. Install the check balls.

VALVE BODY

Assembly

Install the lower valve body on the upper valve body together with the plate.

1. Position the new gaskets and the plate on the lower valve body. Assemble the gasket having the larger cooler by-pass hole to the lower valve body.
2. Install a new gasket and plate onto the lower valve body. Install another new gasket onto the plate. Align each bolt hole in the valve body with the 2 gaskets and plate.
3. Position the lower valve body and gaskets with the plate on

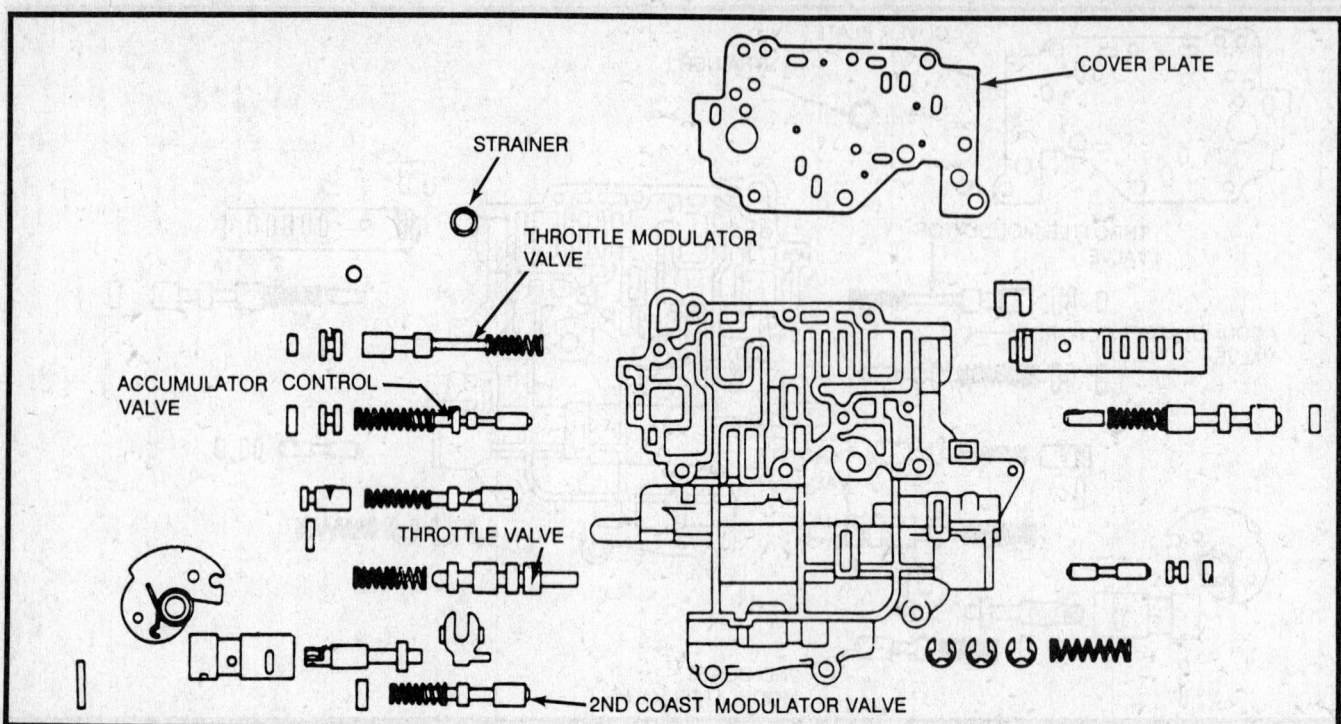

Upper valve body

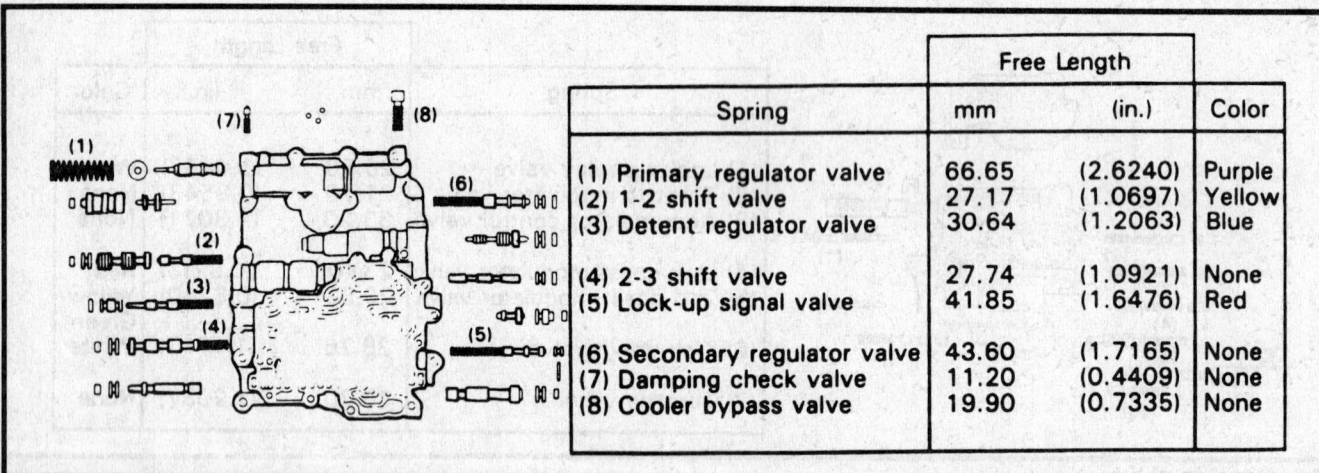

Spring	Free Length		Color
	mm	(in.)	
(1) Primary regulator valve	66.65	(2.6240)	Purple
(2) 1-2 shift valve	27.17	(1.0697)	Yellow
(3) Detent regulator valve	30.64	(1.2063)	Blue
(4) 2-3 shift valve	27.74	(1.0921)	None
(5) Lock-up signal valve	41.85	(1.6476)	Red
(6) Secondary regulator valve	43.60	(1.7165)	None
(7) Damping check valve	11.20	(0.4409)	None
(8) Cooler bypass valve	19.90	(0.7335)	None

Spring chart

top of the upper valve body. Align each bolt hole in the valve bodies with the gaskets and plate.

4. Install and finger tighten 3 bolts in the lower valve body to secure the upper valve body.

5. Turn the assembly over and finger tighten 3 bolts in the upper valve body.

6. Install the upper valve body cover new gaskets and strainer. Install the valve body cover and finger tighten the bolts.

7. Turn the assembly over and install a new gasket and the lower valve body cover.

8. Tighten the bolts of the upper and lower valve body to 48 inch lbs. (5.4 Nm).

Transaxle Assembly

Use the following guidelines before assembling the transaxle:

1. Before assembling new clutch discs, soak them in automatic transmission fluid for at least 2 hours.

2. Apply automatic transmission fluid to the sliding or rotating surfaces of parts before assembly.

3. Use petroleum jelly to keep small parts in their places.

4. Do not use adhesive cements on gaskets and similar parts.

5. When assembling the transaxle, be sure to use new gaskets and O-rings.

6. Dry all parts by blowing with compressed air. Never use the shop rags.

7. Be sure to install the thrust bearings and races in the correct direction and position.

Assembly

1. Install the parking pawl onto the case. Hook the spring ends to the case and pawl.

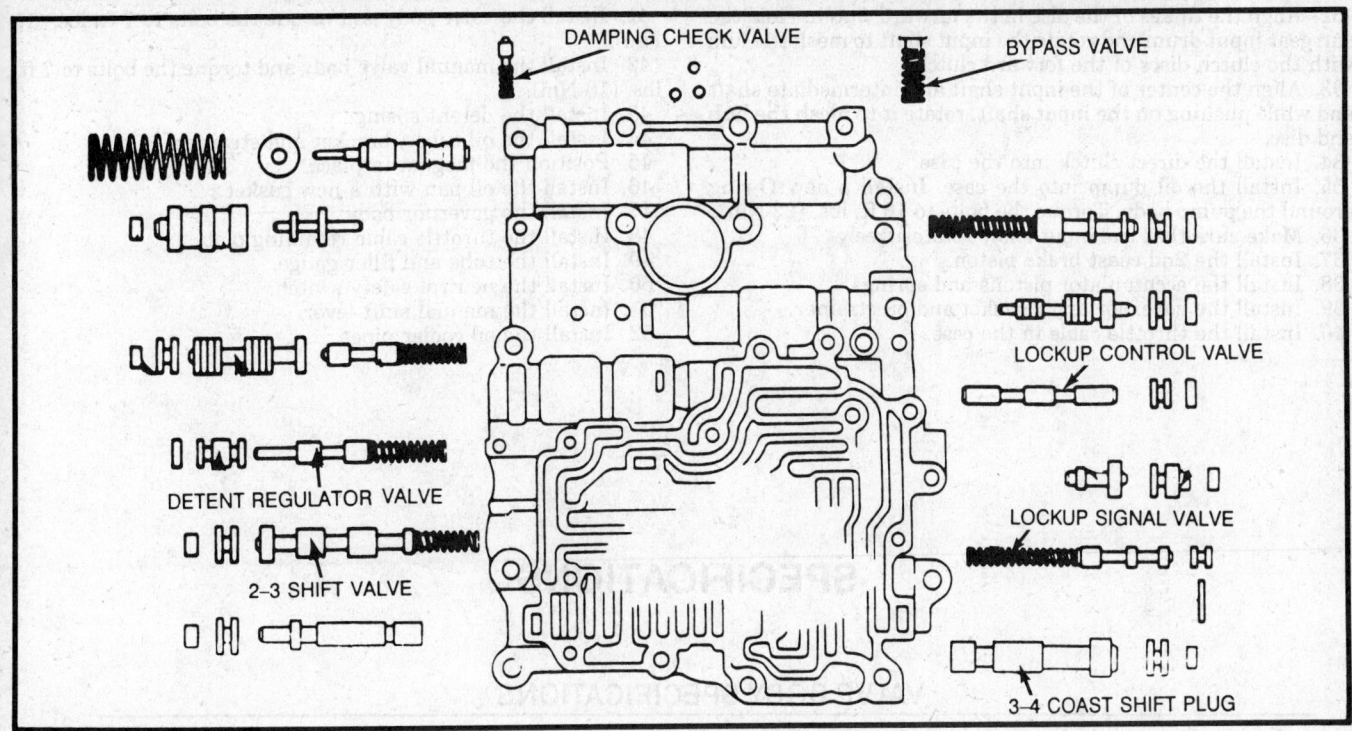

DAMPING CHECK VALVE

BYPASS VALVE

DETENT REGULATOR VALVE

2-3 SHIFT VALVE

LOCKUP CONTROL VALVE

LOCKUP SIGNAL VALVE

3-4 COAST SHIFT PLUG

Lower valve body

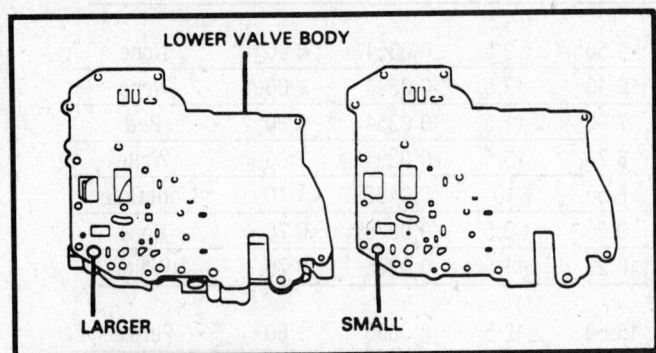

LOWER VALVE BODY

LARGER   SMALL

Valve body installation

2. Install the parking lock rod.
3. Install the parking pawl bracket.
4. Check the operation of the parking lock pawl. Make sure the counter driven gear is locked when the manual valve lever is in the **P** range.
5. Install the intermediate shaft.
6. Install the rear cover over a new gasket and torque the bolts to 18 ft. lbs. (25 Nm).
7. Check the intermediate shaft endplay. Make sure that the intermediate shaft turns smoothly.
8. Install the 1st and reverse brake in the case. Install the inner flange, facing the flat end toward the oil pump side. Install in order, 5 discs and 6 plates as follows: disc-plate-disc-plate-plate-disc-plate-plate-disc-plate-disc.
9. Install the outer flange, facing the flat end toward the piston side. Install the snapring with the endgap into the groove.
10. Check the operation of the 1st and reverse brake, apply compressed air into the oil passage in the case to check if the piston moves.
11. Install the No. 2 planetary carrier thrust washer.
12. Install the ring gear into the case.

13. Align the spline of the planetary carrier with flukes of the discs and install the planetary gear into the 1st and reverse brake discs.
14. Install the No. 2 one-way clutch into the case with the shiny side upward. Install the one-way clutch onto the inner race while turning the planetary gear clockwise.
15. Turn the planetary carrier. The carrier should turn freely clockwise and should lock counterclockwise.
16. Install the snapring endgap into the groove.
17. Install the 2nd coast brake band guide with its tip touching the case.
18. Install the 2nd brake into the case, install the flange, facing the flat end toward you.
19. Install in order: disc-plate-plate-disc-plate-plate.
20. Install the piston return spring assembly. Install each of the springs over the protrusions in the case.
21. Install the 2nd brake drum into the case. Align the groove of the drum with the bolt and place it into the case.
22. Install the snapring into the case so that the endgap is installed into the groove.
23. Check the operation of the 2nd brake. Apply compressed air into the oil passage of the case to be sure that the piston moves.
24. Install the 2nd brake drum gasket until it makes contact with the 2nd brake drum.
25. Install the No. 1 one-way clutch and 2nd brake hub. Align the flukes of the discs in the 2nd brake. Align the spine of the hub with the flukes of the discs and install the hub to the 2nd brake discs.
26. Install the sun gear and the sun gear input drum. While turning the sun gear clockwise, install it into the one-way clutch.
27. Install the front planetary gear and ring.
28. Install the planetary gear into the case.
29. Install the ring gear.
30. Install the 2nd coast brake band by installing the pin through the oil pump mounting bolt hole.
31. Install the forward clutch into the case.

32. Align the flukes of the disc in the forward clutch. Hold the sun gear input drum and rotate the input shaft to mesh the hub with the clutch discs of the forward clutch.

33. Align the center of the input shaft and intermediate shaft and while pushing on the input shaft, rotate it to mesh the hub and disc.

34. Install the direct clutch into the case.

35. Install the oil pump into the case. Install a new O-ring around the pump body. Torque the bolts to 16 ft. lbs. (22 Nm).

36. Make sure that the input shaft rotates freely.

37. Install the 2nd coast brake piston.

38. Install the accumulator pistons and springs.

39. Install the governor apply gasket and oil strainer.

40. Install the throttle cable in the case.

41. Install the valve body and torque the bolts to 7 ft. lbs. (10 Nm).

42. Install the manual valve body and torque the bolts to 7 ft. lbs. (10 Nm).

43. Install the detent spring.

44. Install the oil tubes, bracket and strainer.

45. Position the magnet in place.

46. Install the oil pan with a new gasket.

47. Install the governor body.

48. Install the throttle cable retaining plate.

49. Install the tube and filler gauge.

50. Install the neutral safety switch.

51. Install the manual shift lever.

52. Install the oil cooler pipes.

SPECIFICATIONS

VALVE BODY SPECIFICATIONS

Component	Free length in.	mm	Coil outer diameter in.	mm	No. coils	Wire diameter in.	mm	Color
Upper valve body								
Throttle modulator valve	0.8543	21.70	0.3740	9.50	9.5	0.0354	0.90	None
Accumulator control valve	1.3071	33.20	0.4094	10.40	13.5	0.0394	1.00	None
Low coast modulator valve	0.9213	23.40	0.3110	7.90	11.5	0.0354	0.90	Red
Kickdown valve	1.1717	29.76	0.3437	8.73	13.5	0.0394	1.00	White
2nd coast modulator valve	0.8240	20.93	0.3346	8.50	10	0.0433	1.10	Light Green
Throttle valve	1.2087	30.70	0.3722	9.20	9.5	0.0276	0.70	None
Lock-up relay valve	1.0457	26.56	0.4016	10.20	11.5	0.0276	0.70	White
Lower valve body (USA)								
Primary regulator valve	2.6240	66.65	0.7323	18.60	12.5	0.0630	1.60	Purple
1-2 shift valve	1.0697	27.17	0.2516	6.39	15.5	0.0217	0.55	Yellow
Detent regulator valve	1.2063	30.64	0.3110	7.90	12.5	0.0354	0.90	Blue
2-3 shift valve	1.0921	27.74	0.3268	8.30	11	0.0236	0.60	None
Lockup signal valve	1.6476	41.85	0.3189	8.10	15.5	0.0276	0.70	Red
Secondary regulator valve	1.7165	43.60	0.4291	10.90	11.5	0.0551	1.40	None
Pressure relief valve	0.4409	11.20	0.2520	6.40	7.5	0.0354	0.90	None
Cooler by-pass valve	0.7835	19.90	0.4331	11.00	8.5	0.0394	1.00	None
Lower valve body (Canada)								
Primary regulator valve	2.6240	66.65	0.7323	18.60	12.5	0.0630	1.60	None
1-2 shift valve	1.0697	27.17	0.2516	6.39	15.5	0.0217	0.55	Yellow
Detent regulator valve	1.1701	29.72	0.3110	7.90	12.5	0.0354	0.90	Gray
2-3 shift valve	1.0921	27.74	0.3268	8.30	11	0.0236	0.60	Pink
Lockup signal valve	1.5858	40.28	0.3189	8.10	15.5	0.0276	0.70	Red
Secondary regulator valve	1.7165	43.60	0.4291	10.90	11.5	0.0551	1.40	None
Pressure relief valve	0.4409	11.20	0.2520	6.40	7.5	0.0354	0.90	None
Cooler by-pass valve	0.7835	19.90	0.4331	11.00	8.5	0.0394	1.00	None

BUSHING SPECIFICATIONS

Bushing		Finished bore		Bore Limit	
		in.	mm	in.	mm
Stator support	Front	0.8465–0.8475	21.500–21.526	0.8494	21.576
	Rear	1.0630–1.0640	27.000–27.026	1.0660	27.076
Oil pump body		1.5005–1.5015	38.113–38.138	1.5035	38.188
Direct clutch drum		1.8504–1.8514	47.000–47.025	1.8533	47.075
Front planetary ring gear flange		0.7490–0.7500	19.025–19.050	0.7520	19.100
Input sun gear	Front and Rear	0.8671–0.8680	22.025–22.046	0.8699	22.096

ACCUMULATOR PISTON SPRING SPECIFICATIONS

Component	Free length		Coil outer diameter		No. coils	Wire diameter		Color
	in	mm	in	mm		in	mm	
B^2 (Center)	2.6252	66.68	0.6441	16.36	16.5	0.1024	2.60	Purple
C^1 (Transaxle rear cover side)	1.8898	48.00	0.5346	13.58	10.5	0.0906	2.30	Red
	3.1925	81.09	0.7323	18.60	17	0.0866	2.20	Yellow Green
C^2 (Torque converter side)	2.8417	72.18	0.6921	17.58	16.5	0.0906	2.30	Yellow

TORQUE SPECIFICATIONS

Part		ft. lbs.	Nm
Engine mounting		38	52
Transaxle case to Engine	12 mm	47	64
Transaxle case to Engine	10 mm	34	46
Drive plate to Crankshaft		47	64
Torque converter to Drive plate		20	27
Oil pump to Transaxle case		16	27
Oil pump body to Stator shaft		7	10
Second coast brake band guide		48 ①	5.4
Upper valve body to Lower valve body		48 ①	5.4
Valve body		7	10
Accumulator cover		7	10
Oil strainer		7	10
Oil pan		43 ①	4.9
Oil pan drain plug		36	49
Cooler pipe union nut		25	34

TORQUE SPECIFICATIONS

Part	ft. lbs.	Nm
Testing plug	65 ①	7.4
Parking lock pawl bracket	65 ①	7.4
Transaxle rear cover to Transaxle case	18	25
Neutral safety switch to Transaxle case (bolt)	48 ①	5.4
Neutral safety switch (nut)	61 ①	6.9

① Inch lbs.

OIL PUMP SPECIFICATIONS

		in.	mm
Side clearance	Std.	0.0008–0.0020	0.02–0.05
	Limit	0.004	0.1
Body clearance	Std.	0.0028–0.0059	0.07–0.15
	Limit	0.012	0.3
Tip clearance Driven gear	Std.	0.0043–0.0055	0.11–0.14
	Limit	0.012	0.3

SPECIAL TOOLS

Tool	Description
J-9617	Oil pump seal installer
J-29182	Pinion shaft bearing cup installer
J-35378	Bearing puller pilot
J-35399	Differential side bearing cup remover
J-35400	Differential side bearing housing support
J-35405	Differential preload wrench
J-35409	Differential side bearing installer
J-35455	Holding fixture
J-35467	One-way clutch tester
J-35495	Oil pump puller adapters
J-35549	Second coast brake piston compressor
J-35552	Differential side bearing cup installer
J-35553	Differential side bearing seal installer
J-35565	Intermediate shaft bearing installer
J-35661	Countergear bearing installer
J-35663	Countergear bearing cup installer
J-35664	Pinion shaft bearing installer

Tool	Description
J-35666	Pinion shaft bearing seal installer
J-35679	Band apply pin gauge
J-35683	First/reverse clutch spring compressor adapter
J-35752	Pressure gauge adapter
J-1859-03	Countergear puller
J-3289-20	Holding fixture mount
J-8001	Dial indicator set
J-8092	Driver handle
J-8614-01	Countergear holder
J-21867	Pressure gauge
J-22888	Right differential side bearing puller
J-22912-01	Bearing puller
J-23327	Clutch spring compressor
J-25018-A	Clutch spring compressor adapter
J-25025-1	Dial indicator mount
J-33411	Countergear installer
J-6125-B	Slide hammer set

Section 3

A240E Transaxle
General Motors

APPLICATION

1988–89 Nova

GENERAL DESCRIPTION

The A240E 4 speed transaxle, also called Electronic Control Transaxle (ECT), differs from the oil pressure control type transaxle in that it is controlled by a microcomputer. Trouble occurring in the ECT can stem from 1 of 3 sources: the engine, the ECT electronic control unit or the transaxle itself.

One of 2 driving modes (normal mode or power mode) can be selected in accordance with the driver's preference. If a malfunction occurrs in the electrical circuit (solenoid valve or speed sensor system), this transaxle has a self diagnosis function which causes the **OD OFF** indicator light to flash on and off only when in the **OD** mode. Should the system malfunction, the Electronic Control Module (ECM) can control the transaxle to select as gear that will allow the vehicle to operate safely.

Transaxle and Converter Identification

TRANSAXLE

The transaxle identification tag is located at the top front of the transaxle case.

CONVERTER

The torque converter is a welded unit and cannot be disassembled for repairs. Should this unit need to be replaced, both new and rebuilt units are available.

Electronic Controls

The transaxle, being fully controlled by the computer system, is equipped with solenoids; it responds to road speed and engine torque demand.

The internal equipment, attached to the main control assembly, consists of the direct clutch and 2nd brake solenoids. A bulkhead connector/wiring assembly provides an electrical path to the computer system.

If diagnostic code Nos. 42, 61, 62 or 63 occur, the overdrive indicator light will begin to blink immediately to warn the driver. An impact or shock may cause the blinking to stop, but the code will still be retained in the ECT computer memory until cancelled out. There is no warning for diagnostic code No.64.

In the event of a simultaneous malfunction of both No.1 and No.2 speed sensors, no diagnostic code will appear and the failsafe system will not function. However, when driving in the **D** range, the transaxle will not upshift from the 1st gear, regardless of the vehicle speed.

The electronic control components include the following:
ECT computer
Torque converter clutch solenoid
Neutral safety switch
Throttle position sensor
No. 2 speed sensor
No. 1 speed sensor in combination meter
No. 1 and No. 2 solenoids
Pattern selection switch
OD switch
OD OFF indicator
Stop light switch
Lockup solenoid
The lockup clutch will turn on only infrequently during nor-

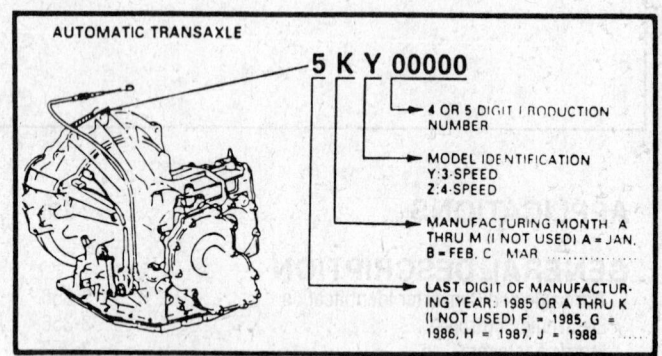

Transaxle Identification

mal 2nd and 3rd gear operation. To trigger this action, press the accelerator pedal halfway down.

Reading Diagnostic Codes

1. Turn the ignition switch and the **OD** switch to **ON**.

NOTE: Do not start the engine. The warning and diagnostic codes can be read only when the overdrive switch on the shift lever is ON. If OFF, the overdrive light will light continuously and will not blink.

2. Short the service connector terminal to the body ground, using a service wire.
3. Read the diagnostic code as indicated by the number of times the **OD OFF** light flashes.

   a. If the system is operating normally, the light will blink for 0.25 seconds every 0.50 seconds.

   b. In the event of a malfunction, the light will blink once every 0.5 second. The number of blinks will equal the 1st number and after a 1.5 second pause, the second number of the 2 digit diagnostic code. If there are 2 or more codes, there will be a 2.5 second pause between each.

   c. In the event of several trouble codes occurring simultaneously, indication will begin from the smaller value and continue to the larger.

   d. If codes 62, 63 and 64 appear, there is an electrical malfunction in the solenoid.

   e. Causes due to mechanical failure, such as a stuck switch, will not appear.

Cancelling Diagnostic Codes

After repair in the trouble area, the diagnostic code retained in memory by the ECT computer must be canceled by removing the fuse marked **STOP** for 10 seconds or more, depending on the ambient temperature (the lower the temperature, the longer the fuse must be left out), with the ignition switch off.

Cancellation can also be done by removing the negative battery terminal, but in this case other memory systems (clock, radio, etc.) will also be canceled out. The diagnostic code can also be canceled out by disconnecting the ECT computer connector.

If the diagnostic code is not canceled out, it will be retained by the ECT computer and appear along with a new code in the event of future trouble.

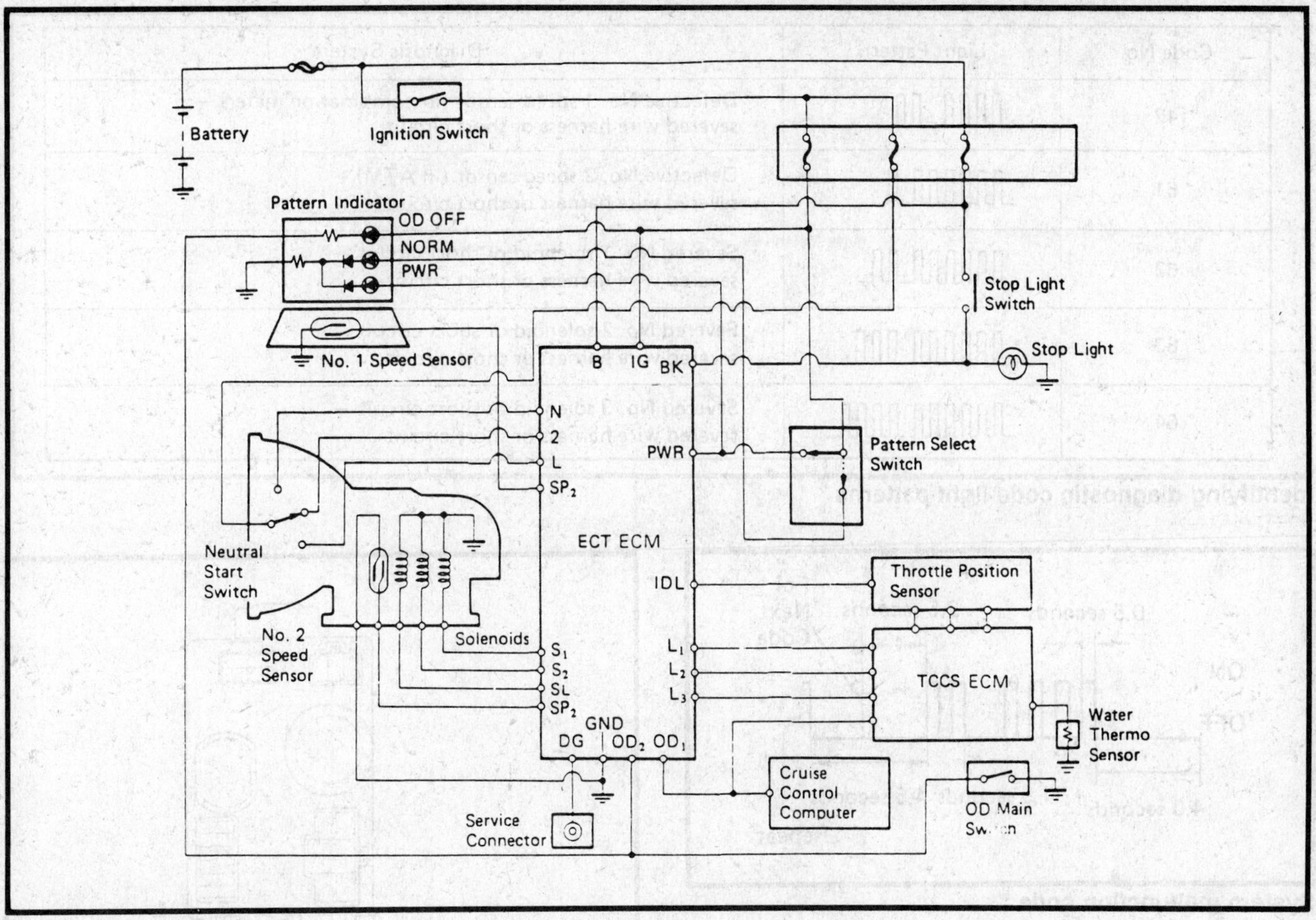

Electronic control circuit

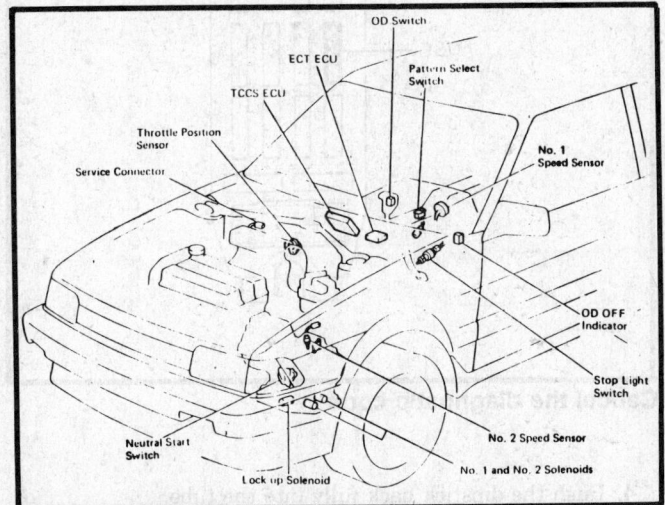

Electronic control components

Metric Fasteners

The metric fastener dimensions are very close to the dimensions of the familiar inch system fasteners and for this reason, replacement fasteners must have the same measurement and strength as those removed.

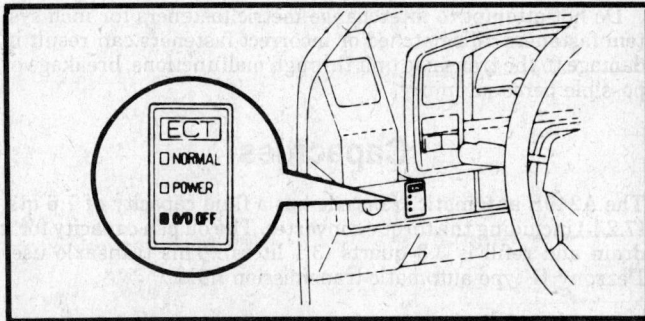

Reading diagnostic codes

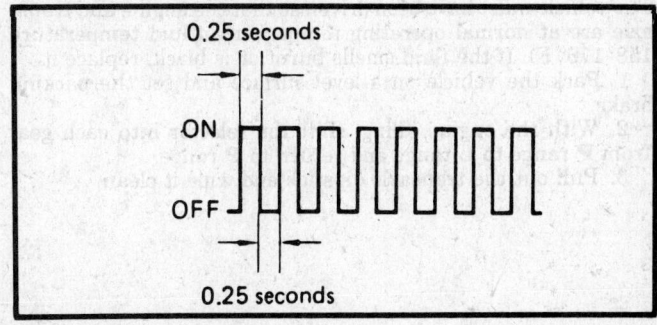

System normal code

Code No.	Light Pattern	Diagnosis System
42		Defective No. 1 speed sensor (in combination meter) – severed wire harness or short circuit
61		Defective No. 2 speed sensor (in ATM) – severed wire harness or short circuit
62		Severed No. 1 solenoid or short circuit – severed wire harness or short circuit
63		Severed No. 2 solenoid or short circuit – severed wire harness or short circuit
64		Severed No. 3 solenoid or short circuit – severed wire harness or short circuit

Identifying diagnostic code light patterns

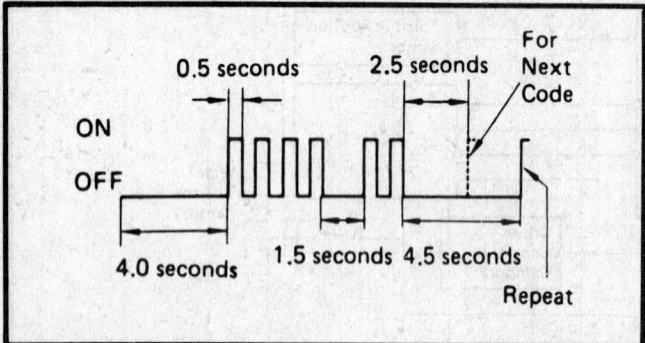

System malfunction code

Do not attempt to interchange metric fasteners for inch system fasteners. Mismatched or incorrect fasteners can result in damage to the transaxle unit through malfunctions, breakage or possible personal injury.

Capacities

The A240E automatic transaxle has a fluid capacity of 7.6 qts. (7.2 L) including the torque converter. The oil pan capacity for a drain and refill is 3.3 quarts (3.1 liters). This transaxle uses Dexron® II type automatic transmission fluid.

Checking Fluid Level

The vehicle must have been driven so that the engine and transaxle are at normal operating temperature (fluid temperature 158–176° F). If the fluid smells burnt or is black, replace it.
1. Park the vehicle on a level surface and set the parking brake.
2. With the engine idling, shift the selector into each gear from **P** range to **L** range and return to **P** range.
3. Pull out the transaxle dipstick and wipe it clean.

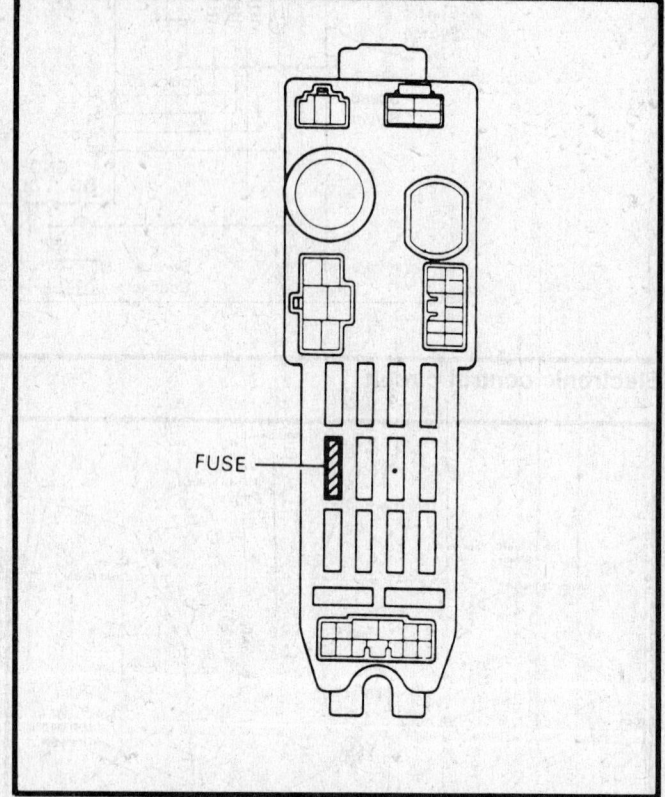

Cancel the diagnostic code

4. Push the dipstick back fully into the tube.
5. Pull out the dipstick and check that the fluid is in the **HOT** range.
6. If the level is low, add fluid. Do not overfill.

TRANSAXLE MODIFICATIONS

There are no transaxle modifications available at the time of publication.

TROUBLE DIAGNOSIS

Hydraulic Control System

The hydraulic pressure system requires a supply of transmission fluid and a pump to pressurize the fluid. The A240E transaxle uses an internal-external gear type pump with its oil intake connected to a screen assembly.

The oil pump is designed to deliver fluid to the torque converter, lubricate the planetary gear unit and supply operating pressure to the hydraulic control system. The drive gear of the oil pump and the torque converter pump are driven by the engine. The pump has a sufficient capacity of oil to supply the necessary fluid pressure throughout all forward speed ranges and reverse.

MANUAL VALVE

The manual valve is linked to the gear shift lever and directs the fluid to the gear range circuit that the lever is positioned at.

PRIMARY REGULATOR VALVE

The primary regulator valve varies the hydraulic line pressure to each component in order to conform with engine power and operate all transaxle hydraulic systems.

SECONDARY REGULATOR VALVE

This valve regulates the converter pressure and lubrication pressure. Spring tension in the valve acts in an upward direction. Converter fluid pressure and lubrication pressure are determined by the spring tension.

THROTTLE VALVE

The throttle valve acts to produce throttle pressure in response to accelerator pedal modulation or engine output. When the accelerator pedal is depressed, the downshift plug is pushed upward by the throttle cable and throttle cam. The throttle valve also moves upward by means of the spring, opening the pressure passage for creation of throttle pressure.

CUT-BACK VALVE

This valve regulates the cut-back pressure acting on the throttle valve and is activated by governor pressure and throttle pressure. By applying cut-back pressure to the throttle valve in this manner, the throttle pressure is lowered to prevent unnecessary power loss from the oil pump.

Governor pressure acts on the upper portion of the valve and as the valve is pushed downward, a passage from the throttle valve is opened and throttle pressure is applied. Because of the difference in the diameters of the valve pistons, the valve is pushed upward to balance the downward force of governor pressure and the throttle pressure becomes cut-back pressure. As the governor pressure rises, the valve is forced downward. Since the throttle pressure passage is open, the pressure becomes cut-back pressure.

THROTTLE MODULATOR VALVE

This valve produces throttle modulator pressure. It reduces throttle pressure when the throttle valve opening angle is high. It causes throttle modulator pressure to act on the primary reg-

CLUTCH AND BRAKE APPLICATION

Gear position	C_1	C_2	C_3	B_1	B_2	B_3	B_4	F_1	F_2	F_3
P-Parking	—	—	—	—	—	—	Applied	—	—	—
R-Reverse	—	Applied	—	—	—	Applied	Applied	—	—	—
N-Neutral	—	—	—	—	—	—	Applied	—	—	—
0-1st	Applied	—	—	—	—	—	Applied	—	Applied	Applied
2nd	Applied	—	—	—	Applied	—	Applied	Applied	—	Applied
3rd	Applied	Applied	—	—	Applied	—	Applied	—	—	Applied
OD	Applied	Applied	Applied	—	Applied	—	—	—	—	—
2-1st	Applied	—	—	—	—	—	Applied	—	Applied	Applied
2nd	Applied	—	—	Applied	Applied	—	Applied	Applied	—	Applied
3rd	Applied	Applied	—	—	Applied	—	Applied	—	—	Applied
1-1st	Applied	—	—	—	—	Applied	Applied	—	Applied	Applied
2nd	Applied	—	—	Applied	Applied	—	Applied	Applied	—	Applied

CHILTON'S THREE C'S TRANSAXLE DIAGNOSIS

Condition	Cause	Correction
Fluid discolored or smells burnt	a) Fluid contaminated b) Torque converter faulty c) Transaxle faulty	a) Replace fluid b) Replace torque converter c) Disassemble and inspect
Vehicle does not move in any forward range or reverse	a) Control cable out of adjustment b) Valve body or primary regulator faulty c) Parking lock pawl faulty d) Torque converter faulty e) Oil pump intake screen blocked f) Transaxle faulty	a) Adjust control cable b) Inspect valve body c) Inspect parking lock pawl d) Replace torque converter e) Clean screen f) Disassemble and inspect transaxle
Shift lever position incorrect	a) Control cable out of adjustment b) Manual valve and lever faulty c) Transaxle faulty	a) Adjust control cable b) Inspect valve body c) Disassemble and inspect
Harsh engagement into any drive range	a) Throttle cable out of adjustment b) Valve body or primary regulator faulty c) Accumulator piston faulty d) Transaxle faulty	a) Adjust throttle cable b) Inspect valve body c) Inspect accumulator piston d) Disassemble and inspect
Delayed 1-2, 2-3 or 3-OD up-shift, or down-shifts from OD-3 or 3-2 and shifts back to 4 or 3 Slips on 1-2, 2-3 or 3-OD up-shift, or slips or shudders on acceleration	a) Throttle cable out of adjustment b) Valve body faulty c) Solenoid valve faulty d) Control cable out of adjustment e) Throttle cable out of adjustment f) Valve body faulty g) Solenoid valve faulty h) Transaxle faulty	a) Adjust throttle calbe b) Inspect valve body c) Inspect valve body d) Inspect governor e) Adjust control cable f) Adjust throttle cable g) Inspect valve body h) Inspect valve body
Vehicle does not hold in P range	a) Control cable out of adjustment b) Parking lock pawl cam and spring faulty	a) Adjust control cable b) Inspect cam and spring
Drag, binding or tie-up on 1-2, 2-3 or 3-OD up-shift	a) Control cable out of adjustment b) Valve body faulty c) Transaxle faulty	a) Adjust control cable b) Inspect valve body c) Disassemble and inspect
No lockup in 2nd, 3rd or OD	a) Electronic control faulty b) Valve body faulty c) Solenoid valve faulty d) Transaxle faulty	a) Inspect electronic control b) Inspect valve body c) Inspect valve body d) Disassemble and inspect transaxle
Harsh downshift	a) Throttle cable out of adjustment b) Valve body faulty c) Transaxle faulty	a) Adjust throttle cable b) Inspect valve body c) Disassemble and inspect transaxle
No downshift when coasting	a) Governor faulty b) Valve body faulty c) Solenoid valve faulty d) Electronic control faulty	a) Inspect governor b) Inspect valve body c) Inspect solenoid valve d) Inspect electronic control
Downshift occurs too quickly or too late while coasting	a) Throttle cable out of adjustment b) Valve body faulty c) Transaxle faulty d) Solenoid valve faulty e) Electronic control	a) Adjust throttle cable b) Inspect valve body c) Disassemble and inspect transaxle d) Inspect solenoid valve e) Inspect electronic control
No OD-3, 3-2 or 2-1 kickdown	a) Throttle cable out of adjustment b) Solenoid valve faulty c) Electronic control faulty d) Valve body faulty	a) Adjust throttle cable b) Inspect solenoid valve c) Inspect electronic control d) Inspect valve body
No engine braking in 2 or L range	a) Solenoid valve faulty b) Electronic control faulty c) Valve body faulty d) Transaxle faulty	a) Inspect solenoid valve b) Inspect electronic control c) Inspect valve body d) Disassemble and inspect transaxle

ECT ELECTRONIC CONTROL DIAGNOSIS

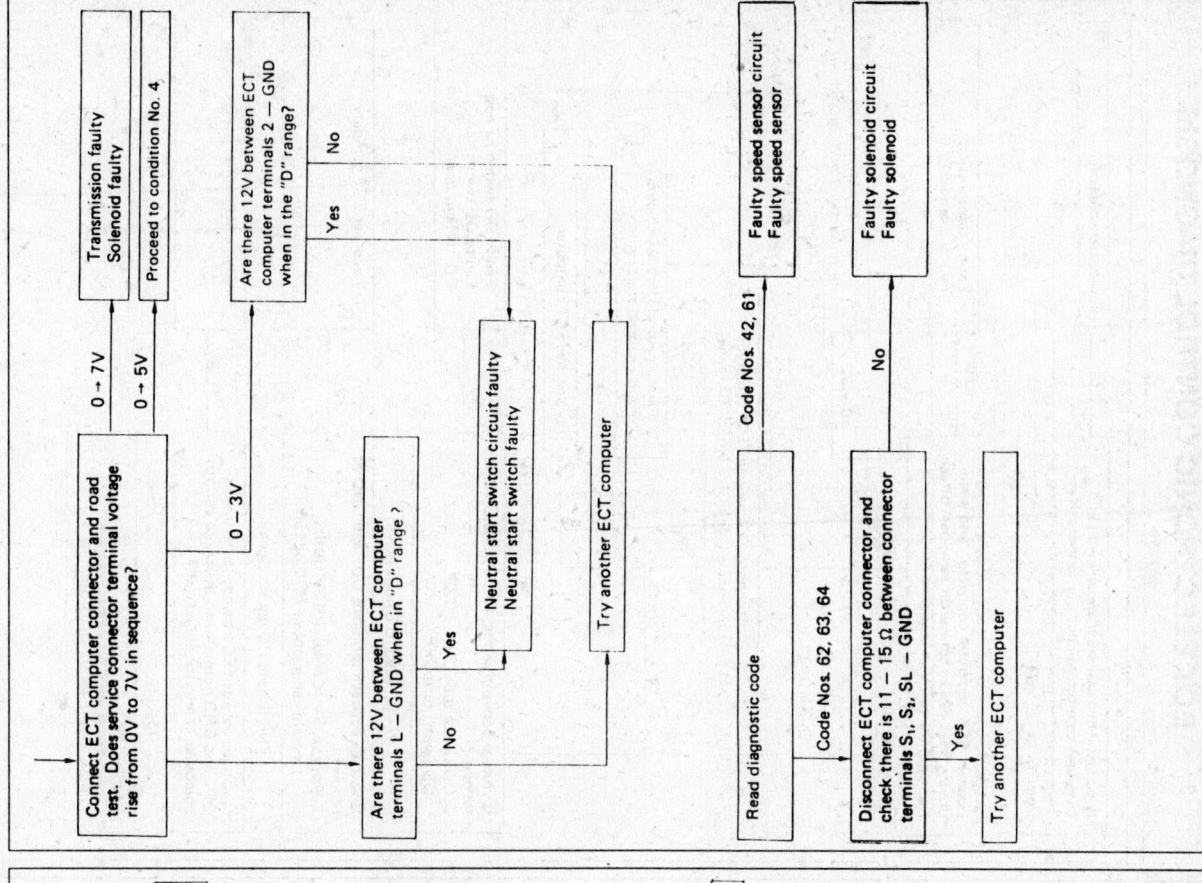

Top section flowchart (ECT ELECTRONIC CONTROL DIAGNOSIS)

Connect ECT computer connector and road test. Does service connector terminal voltage rise from 0V to 7V in sequence?

- 0 → 7V → Transmission faulty / Solenoid faulty
- 0 → 5V → Proceed to condition No. 4.
- 0 → 3V → Are there 12V between ECT computer terminals 2 — GND when in the "D" range?
  - No
  - Yes

Are there 12V between ECT computer terminals L — GND when in "D" range?
- No → Neutral start switch circuit faulty / Neutral start switch faulty
- Yes → Try another ECT computer

Read diagnostic code
- Code Nos. 42, 61 → Faulty speed sensor circuit / Faulty speed sensor
- Code Nos. 62, 63, 64 → Disconnect ECT computer connector and check there is 11 – 15 Ω between connector terminals S_1, S_2, SL – GND
  - No → Faulty solenoid circuit / Faulty solenoid
  - Yes → Try another ECT computer

Blinking while driving, overdrive indicator lights

ECT ELECTRONIC CONTROL DIAGNOSIS

Bottom section flowchart

Warm up engine
Coolant temp: 80°C (176°F)
ATF temp: 50 – 80°C (122 – 176°F)

Read diagnostic code
- Malfunction code(s) → Proceed to condition No 2
- Normal code → Connect a voltmeter to the service connector terminal and body ground. Does the terminal voltage vary with changes in throttle opening?
  - No → Is voltage between ECT computer terminals BR and GND as follows?
    - 0V: Brake pedal released
    - 12V: Brake pedal depressed
    - No → Brake signal faulty
    - Yes → Computer power source and ground faulty / Throttle position signal faulty / Terminal ECT wire open or short
  - Yes → Disconnect ECT computer connector and road test. Does the transmission operate in the respective gear when in the following ranges while driving?
    - D range ..... Overdrive
    - 2 range ..... 3rd gear
    - L range ..... 1st gear
    - No → Transmission faulty
    - Yes → Continued on next figure

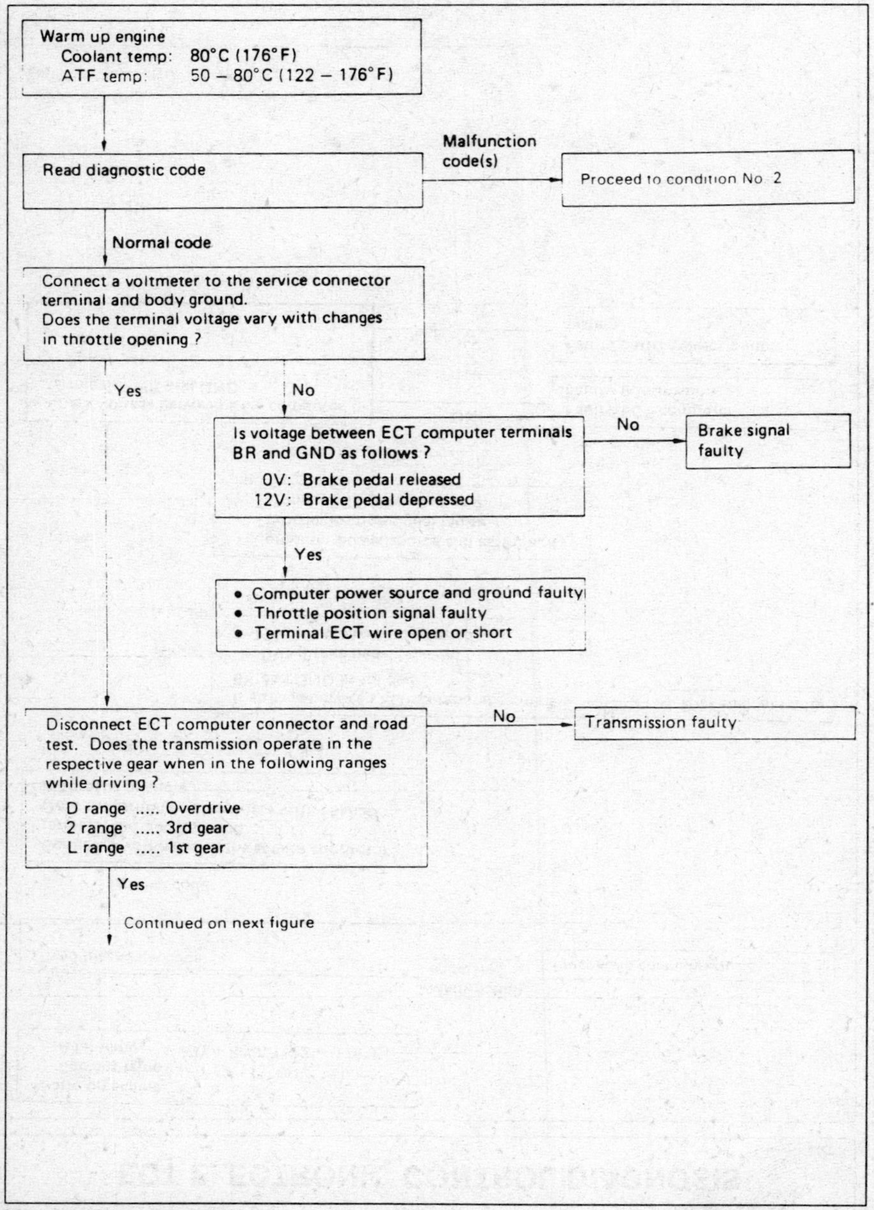

Not shifting condition

ECT ELECTRONIC CONTROL DIAGNOSIS

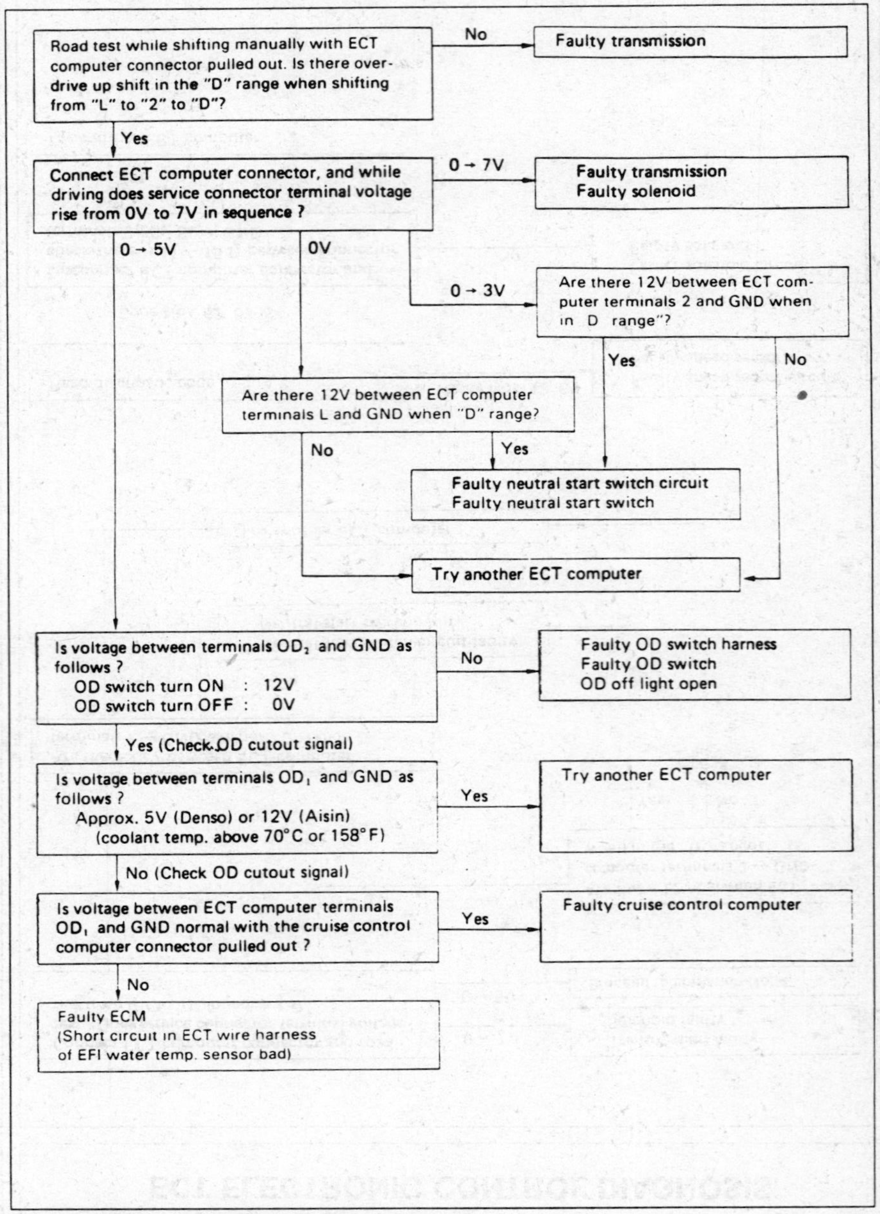

No upshift or overdrive after warm-up

Road test while shifting manually with ECT computer connector pulled out. Is there over-drive up shift in the "D" range when shifting from "L" to "2" to "D"?

No → Faulty transmission

Yes ↓

Connect ECT computer connector, and while driving does service connector terminal voltage rise from 0V to 7V in sequence ?

0 → 7V → Faulty transmission / Faulty transmission solenoid

0 → 5V / 0V

Are there 12V between ECT computer terminals L and GND when "D" range?

Yes → Faulty neutral start switch circuit / Faulty neutral start switch

No → 0 → 3V → Are there 12V between ECT computer terminals 2 and GND when in D range"?

Yes ↑ / No

Try another ECT computer

Is voltage between terminals OD₂ and GND as follows ?
OD switch turn ON : 12V
OD switch turn OFF : 0V

No → Faulty OD switch harness / Faulty OD switch / OD off light open

Yes (Check.OD cutout signal)

Is voltage between terminals OD₁ and GND as follows ?
Approx. 5V (Denso) or 12V (Aisin)
(coolant temp. above 70°C or 158°F)

Yes → Try another ECT computer

No (Check OD cutout signal)

Is voltage between ECT computer terminals OD₁ and GND normal with the cruise control computer connector pulled out ?

Yes → Faulty cruise control computer

No ↓

Faulty ECM
(Short circuit in ECT wire harness of EFI water temp. sensor bad)

ECT ELECTRONIC CONTROL DIAGNOSIS

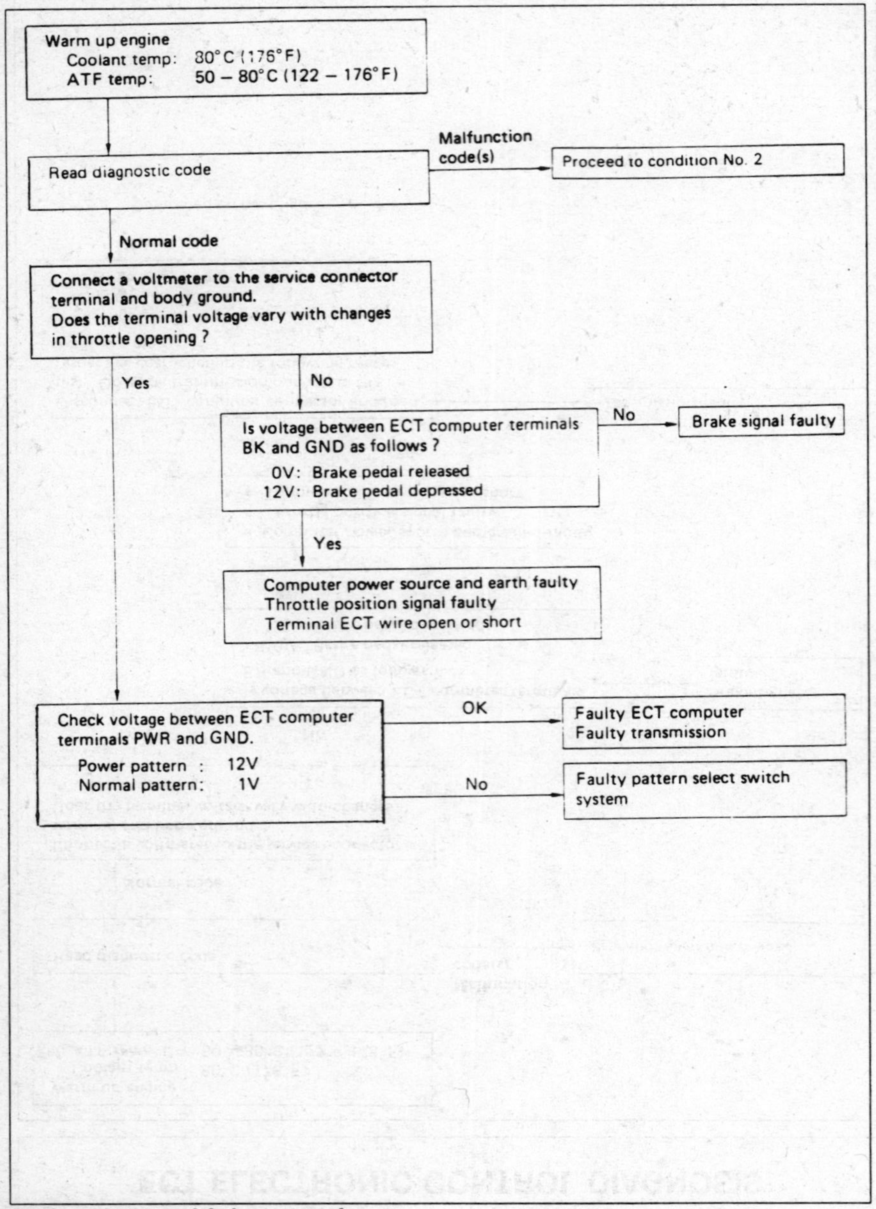

Shift point too high or too low

Warm up engine
Coolant temp: 80°C (176°F)
ATF temp: 50 – 80°C (122 – 176°F)

↓

Read diagnostic code

Malfunction code(s) → Proceed to condition No. 2

Normal code ↓

Connect a voltmeter to the service connector terminal and body ground. Does the terminal voltage vary with changes in throttle opening ?

Yes ↓ / No →

Is voltage between ECT computer terminals BK and GND as follows ?
0V: Brake pedal released
12V: Brake pedal depressed

No → Brake signal faulty

Yes ↓

Computer power source and earth faulty
Throttle position signal faulty
Terminal ECT wire open or short

Check voltage between ECT computer terminals PWR and GND.
Power pattern : 12V
Normal pattern: 1V

OK → Faulty ECT computer / Faulty transmission

No → Faulty pattern select switch system

ulator valve so that line pressure performance is close to engine power performance.

DOWNSHIFT PLUG

If the accelerator pedal is depressed to nearly the fully open position, the downshift plug opens the cut-back pressure passage very wide, then causes the detent regulator valve to operate and effect kickdown.

The cut-back pressure also acts on the downshift plug when the throttle valve opening angle is less than 85%. A power assist mechanism is provided to lighten spring tension.

GOVERNOR VALVE

The governor valve is driven by the drive pinion worm gear and produces governor pressure in response to the vehicle speed. It balances the line pressure from the primary regulator valve and the centrifugal force of the governor weights to produce hydraulic pressure in proportion to vehicle speed.

DETENT REGULATOR VALVE

During kickdown, the detent regulator valve stabilizes the hydraulic pressure acting on the 1-2 and 2-3 shift valves.

LOW MODULATOR VALVE

In the **L** range, the low modulator valve reduces the line pressure from the manual valve. Low modulator pressure pushes down the low coast shift valve and acts on the 1st and reverse brake to cushion the apply.

1–2 SHIFT VALVE

This valve automatically controls the 1–2 shift according to governor and throttle pressure. To improve the valve sliding characteristics, a 3 piece valve is used. When governor pressure is low and throttle pressure is high, the valve is pushed down by throttle pressure and because the 2nd brake circuit closes, the transaxle shifts into 1st gear.

When governor pressure is high and throttle pressure low, the valve is pushed up by governor pressure and the circuit to the 2nd brake piston opens so the transaxle will shift into 2nd gear. When the throttle pressure passage is closed, downshifting into 1st gear is dependant on spring tension and governor pressure only.

Unless the downshift plug actuates and allows the detent pressure to act on the 1–2 shift valve, downshifting into 1st gear will take place at a set vehicle speed. In the **L** range, there is no upshifting into 2nd gear because low modulator pressure is acting on the low coast shift valve.

2–3 SHIFT VALVE

This valve performs shifting between 2nd and 3rd gears. Control is accomplished by opposing throttle pressure and spring tension against governor pressure. When governor pressure is high, the valve is pushed up against the resistance of the throttle pressure and spring tension. This opens the passage to the direct clutch (C_2) piston to allow the shift into 3rd gear.

When governor pressure is low, the valve is pushed down by throttle pressure and spring tension to close the passage leading to the direct clutch piston, causing a downshift to 2nd gear. In the event of kickdown, the detent pressure acts on the 2–3 shift valve to permit a quicker downshift to 2nd gear. valve movement occurs due to the different size areas where pressure is applied.

Since the area is larger for downshift than for upshift, downshifting takes place at a lower vehicle speed. Line pressure from the manual valve acts on the intermediate shift valve. The valve descends and shifting into 2nd gear is accomplished but there is no upshifting into 3rd gear. Line pressure passes through the 2nd modulator valve and 1–2 shift valve and acts on the 2nd coast brake to provide engine braking.

Diagnosis Tests

LINE PRESSURE TEST

1. Run the engine until it reaches normal operating temperature.
2. Raise the vehicle and support it safely.
3. Remove the transaxle case test plugs and mount hydraulic pressure gauges.
4. Apply the parking brake.
5. Start the engine.
6. Apply the brake pedal while manipulating the accelerator pedal and measure the line pressure at the engine speeds specified in the chart.
7. In the same manner, perform the test for the **R** range.
8. If the measured pressure is not up to specified values, recheck the throttle cable adjustment and retest.
9. If the measured values at all ranges are higher than specified, check the following:
   a. Throttle cable out of adjustment
   b. Throttle valve defective
   c. Regulator valve defective
10. If the measured values at all ranges are lower than specified, check the following:
   a. Throttle cable out of adjustment
   b. Throttle valve defective
   c. Regulator valve defective
   d. Oil pump defective
   e. Underdrive brake defective
11. If the pressure is low in **D** range only, check the following:
   a. **D** range circuit fluid leakage
   b. Forward clutch defective
12. If the pressure is low in **R** range only, check the following:
   a. **R** range circuit fluid leakage
   b. Direct clutch defective
   c. First and reverse brake defective

The following is a list of line pressure specifications:

D range – idling 53–61 psi
D range – stall 131–152 psi
R range – idling 77–102 psi
R range – stall 205–239 psi

MANUAL SHIFTING TEST

With this test, it can be determined whether the trouble lies within the electrical circuit or is a mechanical problem in the transaxle.

1. With the engine **OFF**, remove the center cluster and disconnect the ECT computer connector.
2. If the **L**, **2** and **D** range gear positions are difficult to distinguish, do not perform the following test.
3. While driving, shift through **L**, **2** and **D** ranges and back up again. Check that the gear change corresponds to the gear position.
4. While driving, shift through **D**, **2** and **L** ranges and back down again. Check that the gear change corresponds to the gear position.
5. If any abnormality is found in the above test, do not perform the stall, time lag or road tests.

TIME LAG TEST

If the shift lever is shifted while the engine is idling, there will be a certain time elapse or lag before the shock can be felt. This is used for checking the condition of the overdrive clutch, forward clutch, direct clutch and 1st and reverse brake.

1. Run the engine until it reaches normal operating temperature.

NOTE: Allow 1 minute interval between tests. Make 3 measurements and take the average value.

2. Apply the parking brake.
3. Check the idle speed. It should be 800 rpm.
4. Move the shift lever from **N** to **D** range. Using a stop watch, measure the time it takes from shifting the lever until the shock is felt. The time lag should be less than 1.2 seconds.
5. Following Step 4, move the shift lever from **N** to **R** range. The time lag should be less than 1.5 seconds.
6. If the **N** to **D** time lag is longer than specified, check for the following:
   a. Line pressure too low
   b. Forward clutch worn
   c. No. 2 and UD one-way clutch not operating properly
7. If the **N** to **R** time lag is longer than specified, check for the following:
   a. Line pressure too low
   b. Direct clutch worn
   c. First and reverse brake worn
   d. UD brake worn

STALL SPEED

The object of this test is to check the overall performance of the transaxle and engine by measuring the maximum engine speeds in the **D** and **R** ranges.

1. Run the engine until it reaches normal operating temperature.

NOTE: Do not continuously run this test longer than 5 seconds.

2. Apply the parking brake and block the front and rear wheels.
3. Connect an engine tachometer.
4. Shift into the **D** range.
5. While applying the brakes, step all the way down on the accelerator. Quickly read the highest rpm at this time. The stall speed should be 2400–2550 rpm.
6. Perform the same test in the **R** range.
7. If the engine speed is the same for both ranges, but lower than the specified value, check for the following:
   a. Engine output insufficient
   b. Stator one-way clutch not operating properly
8. If the stall speed in **D** range is higher than specified, check for the following:
   a. Line pressure too low
   b. Forward clutch slipping
   c. One-way clutch No. 2 not operating properly
   d. UD one-way clutch not operating properly
9. If the stall speed in **R** range is higher than specified, check for the following:
   a. Line pressure too low
   b. Direct clutch slipping
   c. First and reverse brake slipping
   d. UD braking slipping
10. If the stall speed in **R** and **D** range is higher than specified, check for the following:
   a. Line pressure too low
   b. Improper fluid level
   c. UD braking slipping

ROAD TEST

NOTE: This test must be performed with the engine and transaxle at normal operating temperature.

DRIVE RANGE IN NORMAL AND POWER PATTERN RANGES

Shift into **D** range with the accelerator pedal held constant (throttle valve opening 50% and 100%). Push in one of the pattern selection buttons with the **OD** switch **ON** and check the following points:

1. 1–2, 2–3, 3–OD and lockup upshifts take place and that the shift points conform to those shown in the automatic shift diagram.
2. There is no OD upshift when the coolant temperature is below 122°F.
3. There is no lockup when vehicle speed is 6 mph less than set cruise control speed.
4. If there is no 1–2 upshift, check for the following:
   a. No. 2 solenoid stuck
   b. 1–2 shift valve stuck
5. If there is no 2–3 upshift, check for the following:
   a. No.1 solenoid stuck
   b. 2–3 shift valve stuck
6. If there is no 3–OD upshift, the 3–OD shift valve is stuck.
7. If the shift point is defective, the throttle valve, 1–2 shift valve, 2–3 shift valve and 3–OD shift valve are defective.
8. If the lockup is defective, check for the following:
   a. No. 3 solenoid stuck
   b. Lock-up relay valve stuck
9. While driving in the **D** range 2nd, 3rd gears and OD, check to see that possible kickdown vehicle speed limits for 2–1, 3–1, 3–2, OD–3 and OD–2 kickdowns conform to those in the automatic shift diagram.
10. While driving at 50 mph in **D** range OD gear, shift into **2** and **L** ranges and check the engine braking effect at each of these ranges.
11. If there is no engine braking effect at **2** range 3rd gear, the 2nd brake is defective.
12. If there is no engine braking effect at **2** range 2nd gear, the 2nd brake and 2nd coast brake are defective.
13. If there is no engine braking effect at **L** range 2nd gear, the 2nd brake and 2nd coast brake are defective.
14. If there is no engine braking effect at **L** range 1st gear, the 1st and reverse brake are defective.

LOCKUP MECHANISM

1. Connect a voltmeter to service connector terminal ECT.
2. Select normal pattern.
3. Drive at 37 mph to where 7, 5 or 3 volts appear on the voltmeter, this is the lockup range.
4. Depress the accelerator pedal and read the tachometer. If there is a big jump in the engine rpm, there is no lockup.

2 RANGE

1. Shift to **2** range and drive with the throttle valve opening at 50% and 100% respectively. Check the 1–2 upshift points at each of the throttle valve openings to see that it conforms to those indicated in the automatic shift diagram.
2. While driving in **2** range, 2nd gear, release the accelerator pedal and check the engine braking effect.
3. Check for abnormal noise at acceleration and deceleration and harshness at upshift and downshift.

L RANGE

1. While driving at 50 mph in **D** or **2** range, release the accelerator pedal and shift into **L** range and check that the 2–1 downshift points are at 32 mph.
2. While driving in **L** range, check that there is no upshift to 2nd gear.
3. While driving in **L** range, release the accelerator pedal and check the engine braking effect.
4. Check for abnormal noise during acceleration and deceleration.

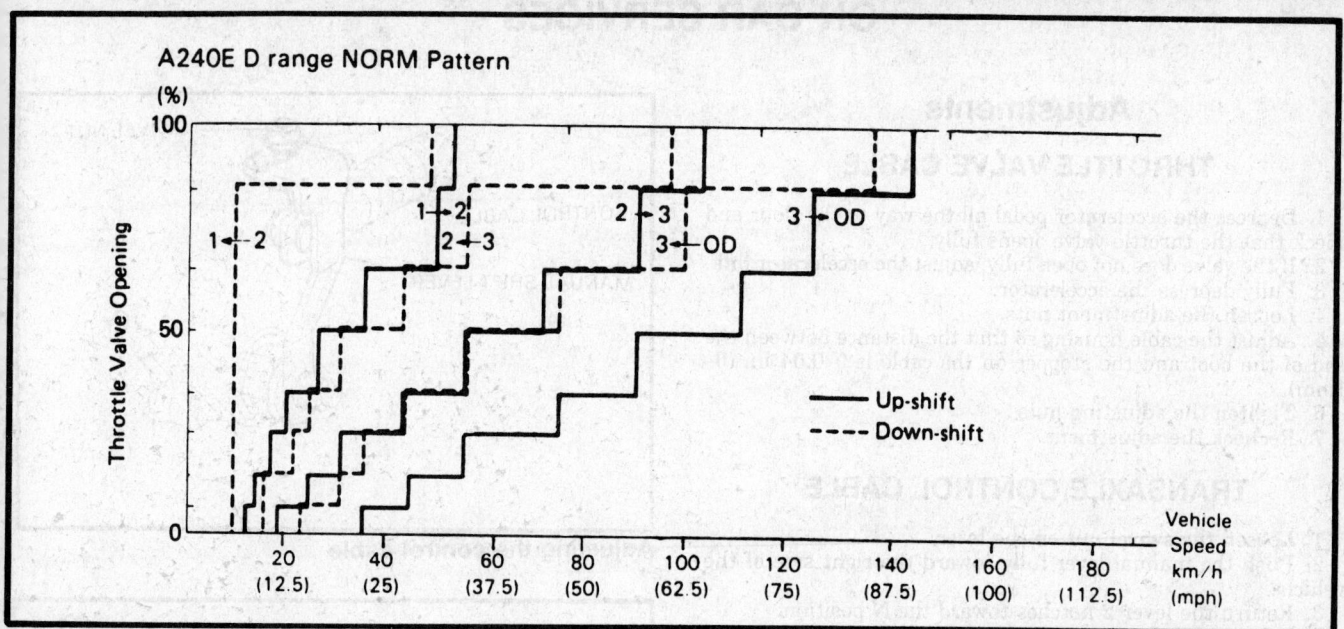

Automatic shift diagram

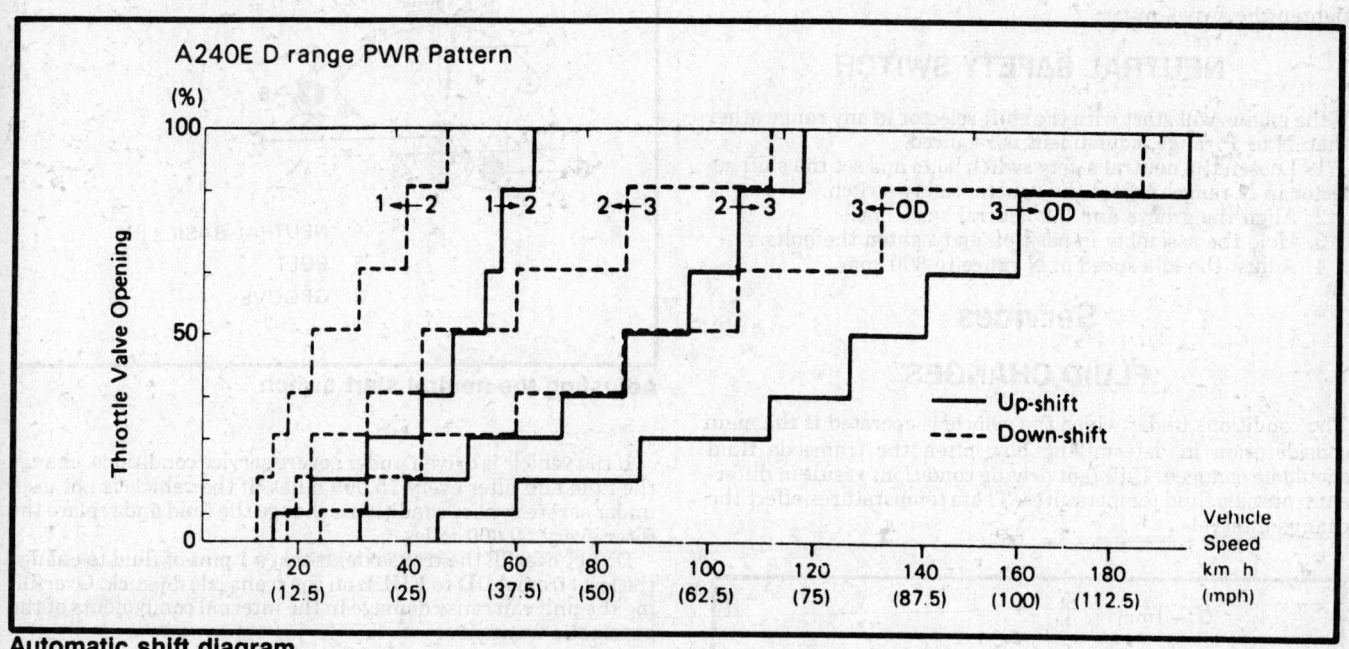

Automatic shift diagram

R RANGE

Shift into **R** range and while starting at full throttle, check for slipping.

P RANGE

Stop the vehicle on a slight hill and after shifting into **P** range, release the parking brake. Check to see that the parking lock pawl prevents the vehicle from moving.

ON CAR SERVICES

Adjustments

THROTTLE VALVE CABLE

1. Depress the accelerator pedal all the way to the floor and check that the throttle valve opens fully.
2. If the valve does not open fully, adjust the accelerator link.
3. Fully depress the accelerator.
4. Loosen the adjustment nuts.
5. Adjust the cable housing so that the distance between the end of the boot and the stopper on the cable is 0–0.04 in. (0–1mm).
6. Tighten the adjusting nuts.
7. Recheck the adjustment.

TRANSAXLE CONTROL CABLE

1. Loosen the swivel nut on the lever.
2. Push the manual lever fully toward the right side of the vehicle.
3. Return the lever 2 notches toward the N position.
4. Set the shift lever in the N range.
5. While holding the lever lightly toward the R range side, tighten the swivel nut.

NEUTRAL SAFETY SWITCH

If the engine will start with the shift selector in any range other than N or P range, adjustment is required.
1. Loosen the neutral safety switch bolts and set the shift selector in N range. Adjust the neutral safety switch.
2. Align the groove and the neutral basic line.
3. Hold the assembly in position and tighten the bolts.
4. Adjust the idle speed in N range to 800 rpm.

Services

FLUID CHANGES

The conditions under which the vehicle is operated is the main consideration in determining how often the transaxle fluid should be changed. Different driving conditions result in different transaxle fluid temperatures. These temperatures effect the change intervals.

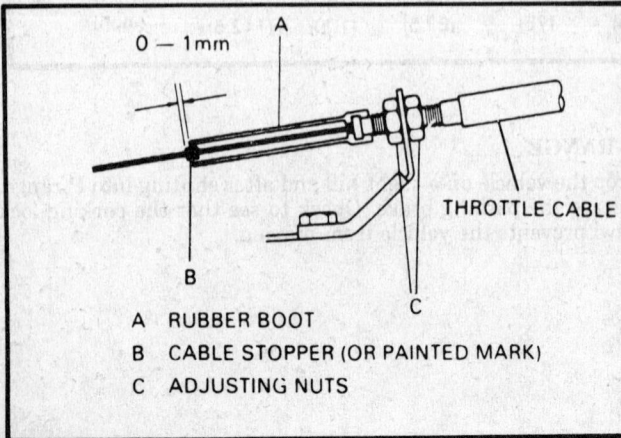

A RUBBER BOOT
B CABLE STOPPER (OR PAINTED MARK)
C ADJUSTING NUTS

Adjusting the T.V. cable

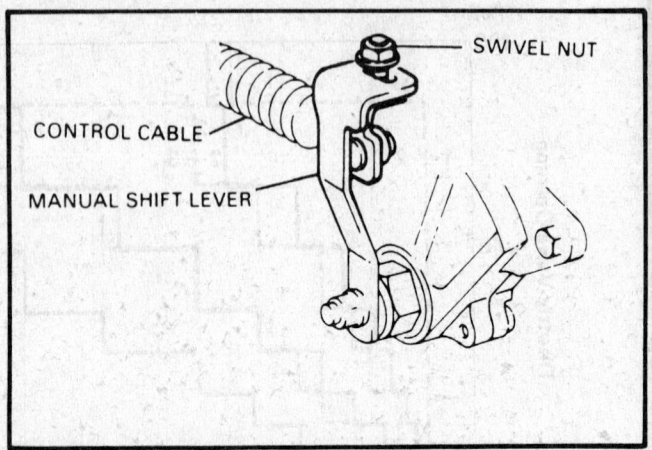

Adjusting the control cable

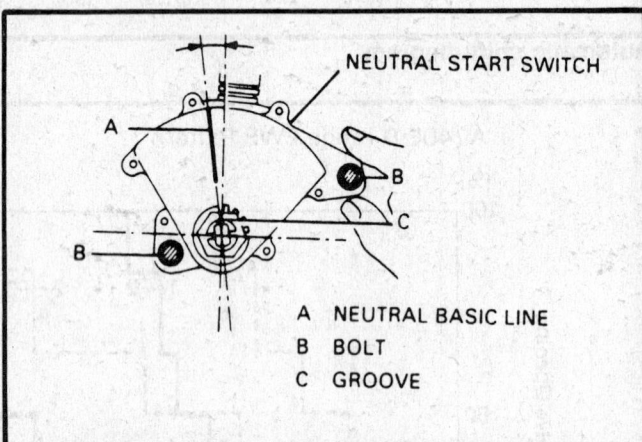

A NEUTRAL BASIC LINE
B BOLT
C GROOVE

Adjusting the neutral start switch

If the vehicle is driven under severe service conditions, change the fluid and filter every 15,000 miles. If the vehicle is not used under severe service conditions, change the fluid and replace the filter every 50,000 miles.

Do not overfill the transaxle. It takes 1 pint of fluid to change the level from ADD to FULL on the transaxle dipstick. Overfilling the unit can cause damage to the internal components of the automatic transaxle.

OIL PAN

Removal and Installation

1. Disconnect the negative battery cable.
2. Raise the vehicle and support it safely.
3. Remove the drain plug in the pan and drain the fluid.
4. Reinstall the drain plug and remove the oil pan. After removing the bolts, tap the pan lightly with a plastic hammer. Do not force the pan off by prying. This may cause damage to the gasket mating surface.
5. Remove the oil pan gasket material on the mating surface.
6. Remove the oil filter from the valve body.
7. Clean the inside of the oil pan before installation.
8. Clean the oil cleaner magnet and install it in the proper position.

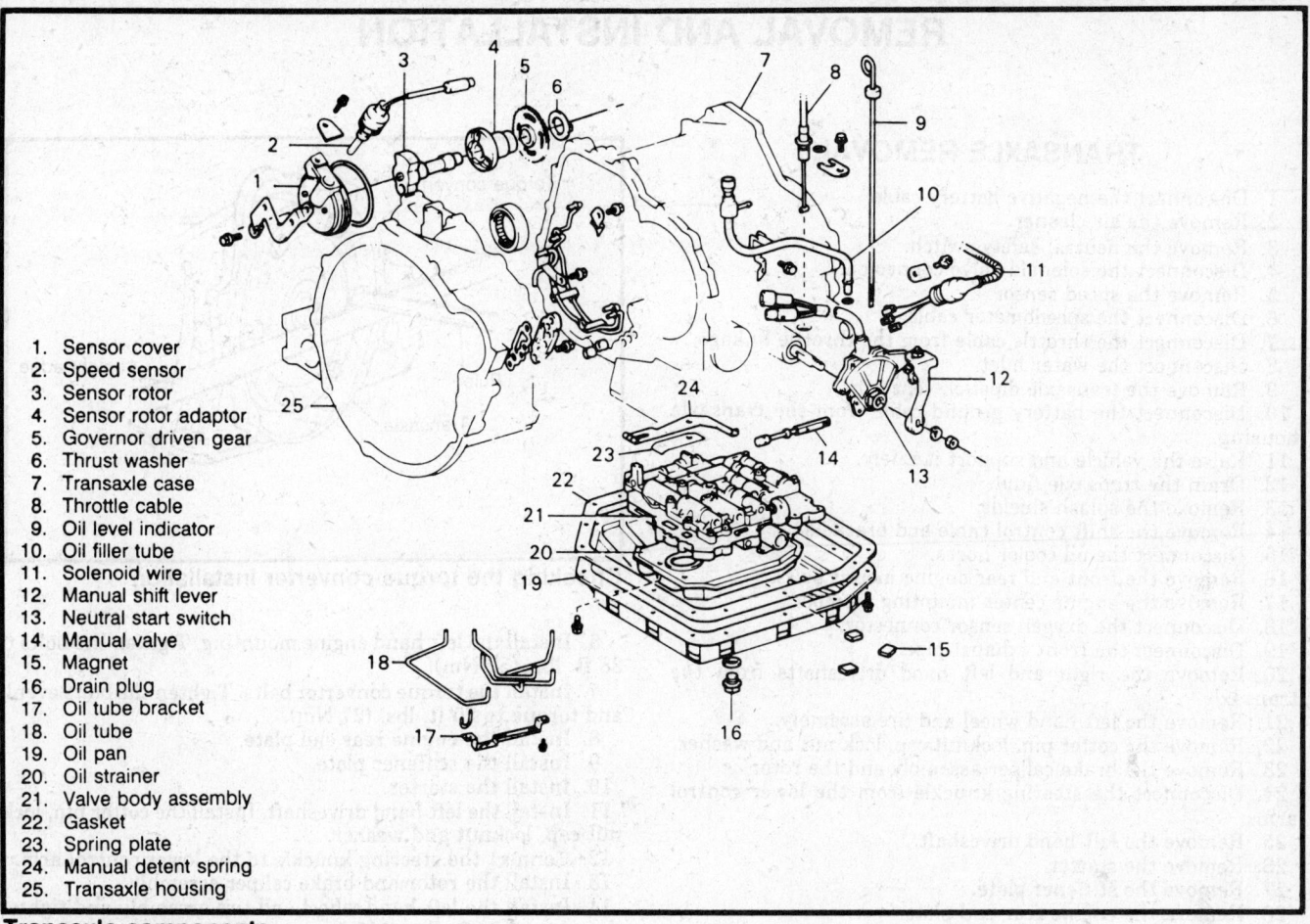

1. Sensor cover
2. Speed sensor
3. Sensor rotor
4. Sensor rotor adaptor
5. Governor driven gear
6. Thrust washer
7. Transaxle case
8. Throttle cable
9. Oil level indicator
10. Oil filler tube
11. Solenoid wire
12. Manual shift lever
13. Neutral start switch
14. Manual valve
15. Magnet
16. Drain plug
17. Oil tube bracket
18. Oil tube
19. Oil pan
20. Oil strainer
21. Valve body assembly
22. Gasket
23. Spring plate
24. Manual detent spring
25. Transaxle housing

Transaxle components

9. Install a new filter on the valve body.
10. Install the pan with a new gasket and torque the bolts to 43 inch lbs. (4.9 Nm).
11. Fill with transmission fluid to the proper level.
12. Lower the vehicle and connect the battery cable.

VALVE BODY

Removal and Installation

1. Disconnect the negative battery cable.
2. Raise the vehicle and support it safely.
3. Remove the drain plug in the pan and drain the fluid.
4. Reinstall the drain plug and remove the oil pan. After removing the bolts, tap the pan lightly with a plastic hammer. Do not force the pan off by prying. This may cause damage to the gasket mating surface.
5. Remove the oil pan gasket material on the mating surface.
6. Remove the oil tube bracket and the oil strainer.
7. Pry out the oil tubes and remove them.
8. Remove the detent spring.
9. Disconnect the 3 solenoid connectors.
10. Loosen and remove the valve body bolts.
11. Lift the valve body assembly and disconnect the throttle cable from the cam.
12. Remove the valve body.
13. Remove the 2nd brake apply gaskets.
14. On installation, install the valve body on the case. Hold the cam down and insert the throttle cable into the slot.

15. Install the valve body with the bolts finger tight.
16. Install the detent spring and tighten the bolts to 7 ft. lbs. (10 Nm).
17. Make sure that the manual valve lever touches the center of the detent spring roller.
18. Tighten the valve body bolts to 7 ft. lbs. (10 Nm).
19. Install the oil tubes, bracket and oil strainer.
20. Clean the inside of the oil pan before installation.
21. Clean the oil cleaner magnets and install it in the proper position.
22. Install the oil pan with a new gasket and torque the bolts to 43 inch lbs. (4.9 Nm).

REAR OIL SEAL

Removal and Installation

1. Disconnect the negative battery cable.
2. Raise the vehicle and support it safely.
3. Drain the fluid from the differential.
4. Remove the driveshaft from the transaxle and the steering knuckle.
5. Remove the differential oil seals using tools J–26941 or equivalent and J–23907 or equivalent.
6. Using tool J–35553 or equivalent, drive the oil seal into the case until its surface is flush with the surface of the case.
7. Coat the top of the oil seal with grease.
8. Install the driveshaft to the transaxle and the steering knuckle.
9. Fill with transmission fluid and check the fluid level.

REMOVAL AND INSTALLATION

TRANSAXLE REMOVAL

1. Disconnect the negative battery cable.
2. Remove the air cleaner.
3. Remove the neutral safety switch.
4. Disconnect the solenoid valve connector.
5. Remove the speed sensor.
6. Disconnect the speedometer cable.
7. Disconnect the throttle cable from the throttle linkage.
8. Disconnect the water inlet.
9. Remove the transaxle dipstick vent tube.
10. Disconnect the battery ground cable from the transaxle housing.
11. Raise the vehicle and support it safely.
12. Drain the transaxle fluid.
13. Remove the splash shields.
14. Remove the shift control cable and brackets.
15. Disconnect the oil cooler hoses.
16. Remove the front and rear engine mount bolts.
17. Remove the engine center mounting member.
18. Disconnect the oxygen sensor connector.
19. Disconnect the front exhaust pipe.
20. Remove the right and left hand driveshafts from the transaxle.
21. Remove the left hand wheel and tire assembly.
22. Remove the cotter pin, locknut cap, lock nut and washer.
23. Remove the brake caliper assembly and the rotor.
24. Disconnect the steering knuckle from the lower control arm.
25. Remove the left hand driveshaft.
26. Remove the starter.
27. Remove the stiffener plate.
28. Remove the engine rear end plate.
29. Remove the torque converter mounting bolts.
30. Lower the vehicle.
31. Install engine support fixture tool J–28467 or equivalent.
32. Remove the 3 bolts from the rear engine mount.
33. Raise the vehicle and support it safely.
34. Remove the transaxle from the vehicle.
35. Remove the torque converter from the transaxle.

TRANSAXLE INSTALLATION

1. Install the torque converter in the transaxle.
2. To be sure the torque converter is installed correctly, use a straight edge and measure from the installed surface to the front surface of the transaxle housing. The distance should be more than 0.79 in. (20mm).
3. Position the transaxle on a suitable transmission jack and align it in the vehicle.
4. Align the converter housing with the 2 dowel pins in the block and install a bolt.
5. Install the transaxle housing mounting bolts and torque the 12mm bolt to 47 ft. lbs. (64 Nm). Torque the 10mm bolts to 34 ft. lbs. (46 Nm).

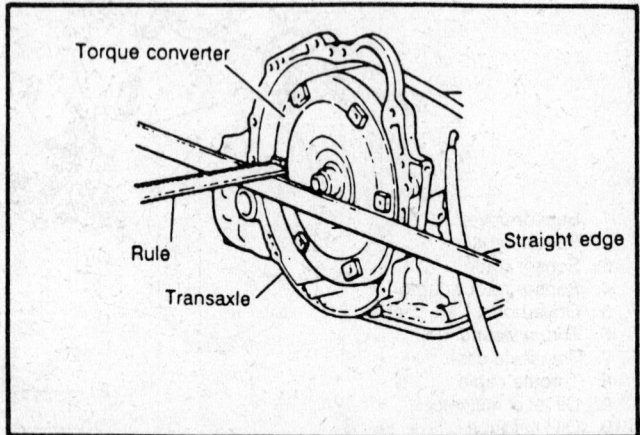

Checking the torque converter installation

6. Install the left hand engine mounting. Tighten the bolts to 38 ft. lbs. (52 Nm).
7. Install the torque converter bolts. Tighten the bolts evenly and torque to 20 ft. lbs. (27 Nm).
8. Install the engine rear end plate.
9. Install the stiffener plate.
10. Install the starter.
11. Install the left hand driveshaft. Install the cotter pin, locknut cap, locknut and washer.
12. Connect the steering knuckle to the lower control arm.
13. Install the rotor and brake caliper assembly.
14. Install the left hand wheel and tire assembly and tighten the nuts to 76 ft. lbs. (103 Nm).
15. Connect the left hand and right hand driveshafts to the transaxle.
16. Connect the front exhaust pipe.
17. Connect the oxygen sensor connector.
18. Install the engine center mounting member and tighten the bolts to 29 ft. lbs. (39 Nm).
19. Install the front and rear engine mount bolts and tighten them to 29 ft. lbs. (39 Nm).
20. Remove engine support fixture tool J–28467 or equivalent.
21. Connect the oil cooler hoses.
22. Install the shift control cable and brackets.
23. Install the splash shields.
24. Lower the vehicle.
25. Connect the battery ground cable to the transaxle housing.
26. Install the transaxle dipstick vent tube.
27. Install the water inlet.
28. Connect the throttle cable to the throttle linkage.
29. Connect the speedometer cable.
30. Install the speed sensor.
31. Connect the solenoid valve connector.
32. Install the neutral safety switch.
33. Install the air cleaner.
34. Connect the negative battery cable.

BENCH OVERHAUL

Before Disassembly

Before opening up the transaxle, the outside of the unit should be thoroughly cleaned, preferably with high pressure cleaning equipment. Dirt entering the transaxle internal parts will negate all the effort and time spent on the overhaul. During inspection and reassembly, all parts should be thoroughly cleaned with solvent and then dried with compressed air. Cloths and rags should not be used to dry the parts since lint will find its way into the valve body passages.

Lube the seals with Dexron II automatic transmission fluid and use unmedicated petroleum jelly to hold the thrust washers and ease the assembly of the seals. Do not use solvent on neoprene seals, friction plates or thrust washers. Be wary of nylon parts if the transaxle failure was due to a cooling system problem. Nylon parts exposed to antifreeze solutions can swell and distort, so they must be replaced. Before installing bolts into aluminum parts, dip the threads in clean oil.

Converter Inspection

Make certain that the transaxle is held securely. If the torque converter is equipped with a drain plug, open the plug and drain the fluid. If there is no drain plug, the converter must be drained through the hub after pulling the converter out of the transaxle. If the oil in the converter is discolored but does not contain metal bits or particles, the converter is not damaged. Color is no longer a good indicator of fluid condition.

If the oil in the converter contains metal particles, the converter is damaged internally and must be replaced. If the cause of the oil contamination was burned clutch plates or overheated oil, the converter is contaminated and should be replaced. If the pump gears or cover show signs of damage, the converter will contain metal particles and must be replaced.

Transaxle Disassembly

1. Remove the oil cooler pipes.
2. Remove the transaxle dipstick and filler tube.
3. Remove the manual shift lever.
4. Remove the neutral safety switch.
5. Remove the throttle cable retaining plate.
6. Remove the solenoid and kickdown switch wire retaining plate.
7. Remove the speed sensor, sensor rotor and adapter.
8. Remove the pan and gasket.

NOTE: Do not turn the transaxle over, before pan removal, as it will contaminate the valve body with foreign material from the bottom of the pan.

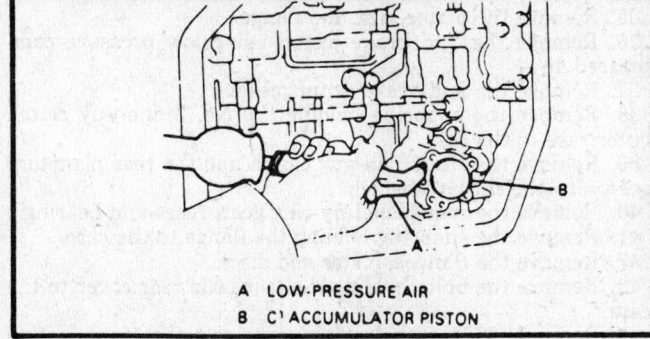

A LOW-PRESSURE AIR
B C³ ACCUMULATOR PISTON

Removing the C₃ accumulator piston

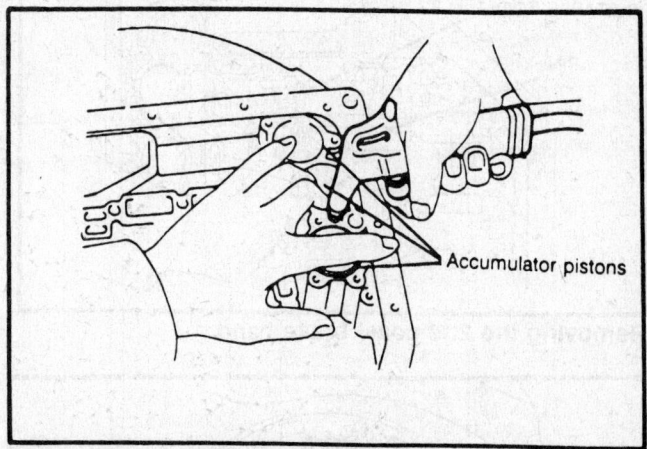

Accumulator pistons

Removing the accumulator pistons

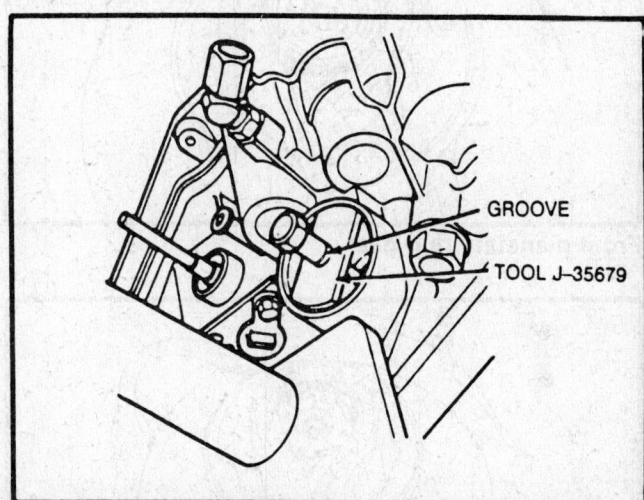

GROOVE

TOOL J–35679

Measuring the piston stroke

9. Turn the transaxle over and remove the oil tube bracket.
10. Remove the oil strainer.
11. Remove the oil tubes.
12. Remove the manual detent spring and the detent plate.
13. Disconnect the solenoid connectors.
14. Remove the valve body.
15. Remove the throttle cable from the case.
16. Disconnect the solenoid wire.
17. Remove the governor apply gasket.
18. Remove the C₃ accumulator piston and spring. Force low pressure compressed air into the hole to pop the piston out.
19. Remove the accumulator pistons and springs. Loosen the bolts 1 turn at a time until the spring tension is released. Remove the cover and gasket. It may be necessary to force low pressure compressed air into the hole to pop out pistons B₂ and C₂.
20. Measure the 2nd coast brake band piston stroke by applying a small amount of paint to the piston rod at the point where it meets the case. Using tool J–35679 or equivalent, measure the piston stroke by applying and releasing 57–114 psi (392–785 kPa) of compressed air to the hole. The piston stroke should be 0.059–0.118 in. (1.5–3.0mm).
21. If the piston stroke is more than specified, replace the pis-

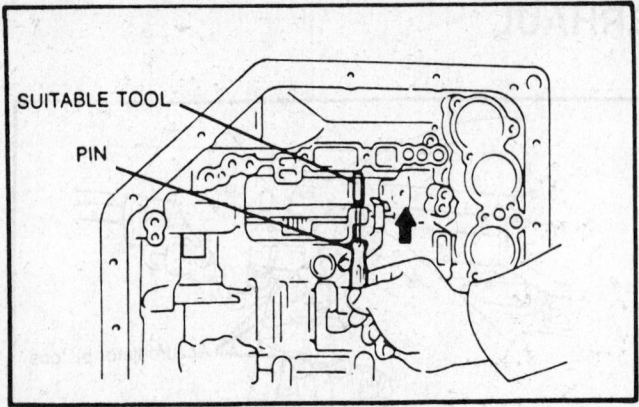

Removing the 2nd coast brake band

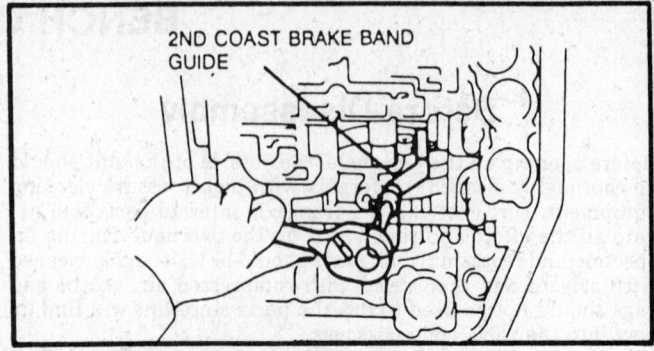

2nd coast brake band guide

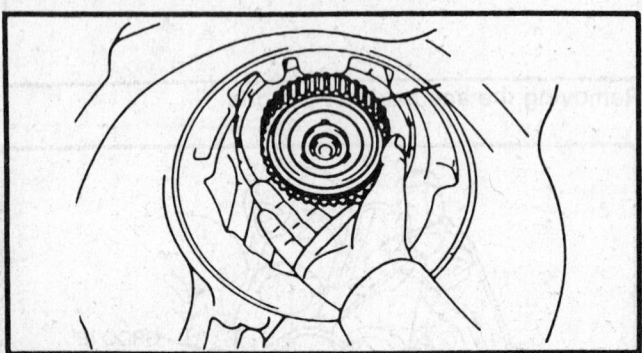

Front planetary ring gear

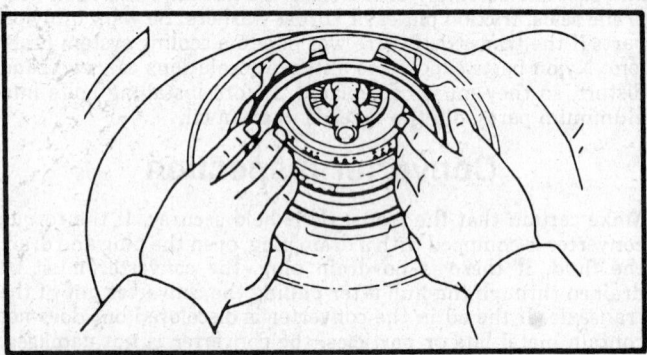

2nd brake drum

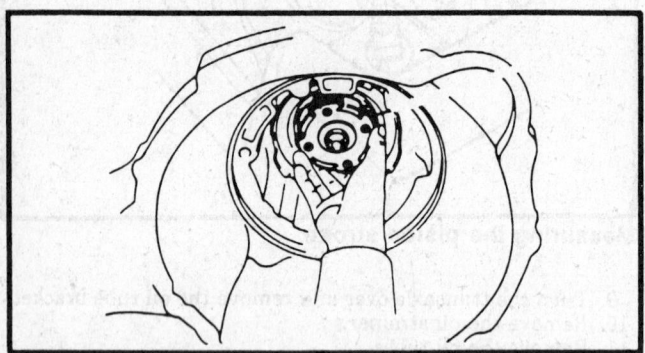

Front planetary gear

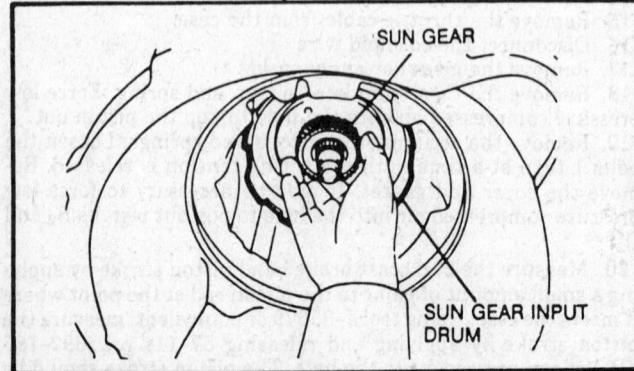

Sun gear and input drum

ton rod with a longer rod. Piston rods are available in 2.870 in. (72.9mm) or 2.811 in. (71.4mm) lengths.

22. Re-measure the piston stroke. If it is still more than specified, replace the brake band with a new band.

23. Remove the 2nd coast brake band piston snapring, cover, piston and outer return spring.

24. Remove the oil pump using tools J–6125–B slide hammer and J–35495 pulley adapter.

25. Remove the direct clutch.

26. Remove the forward clutch.

27. Remove the 2nd coast brake band by removing the pin from the oil pump mounting bolt hole.

28. Remove the front planetary ring gear with the bearing and race.

29. Remove the front planetary gear with the race.

30. Remove the sun gear, sun gear input drum and thrust washer.

31. Remove the 2nd brake hub and the No. 1 one-way clutch.

32. Remove the second coast brake band guide.

33. Remove the snapring and the 2nd brake drum.

34. Remove the 2nd brake drum piston return spring.

35. Remove the plates, disc and flange.

36. Remove the 2nd brake piston using low pressure compressed air.

37. Remove the 2nd brake drum gasket.

38. Remove the snapring holding the No. 2 one-way clutch outer race to the case.

39. Remove the No. 2 one-way clutch and the rear planetary gear with the thrust washers.

40. Remove the rear planetary ring gear, races and bearing.

41. Remove the snapring holding the flange to the case.

42. Remove the flanges, plates and discs.

43. Remove the bolts holding the transaxle rear cover to the case.

44. Remove the transaxle rear cover and the intermediate shaft.

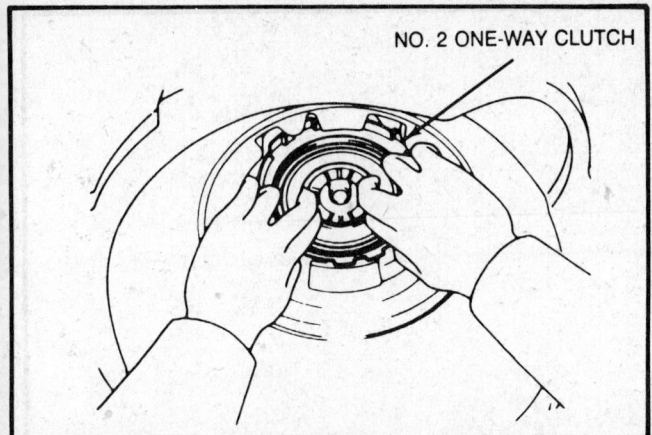

No. 2 one-way clutch and planetary gear

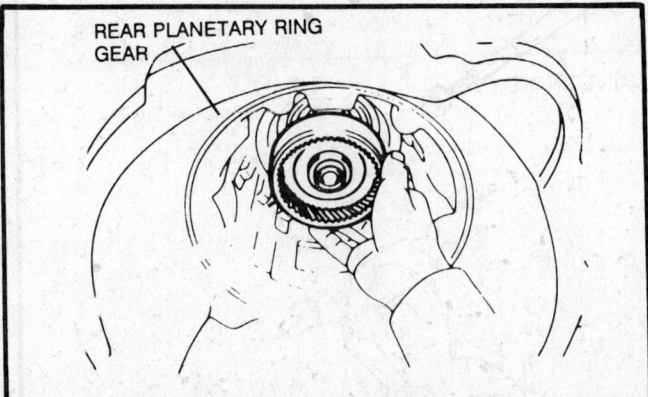

Rear planetary ring gear and bearing

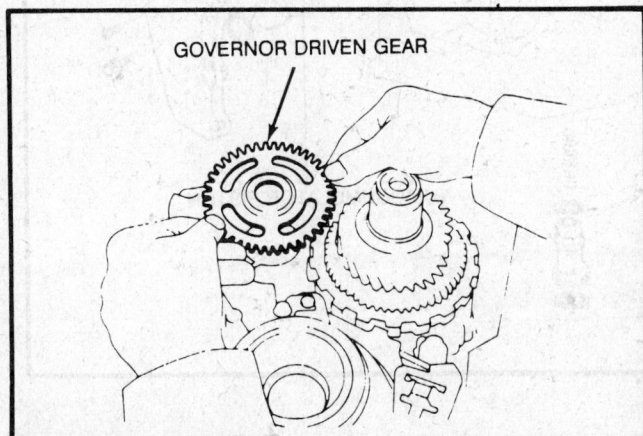

Governor driven gear

45. Remove the transaxle housing bolts and the transaxle housing.
46. Remove the differential.
47. Remove the governor driven gear and thrust washer.
48. Remove the oil seals.
49. Unstake the countershaft locknut on both sides. Attach tool J–8614–01 or equivalent to the counter driven gear and tool J–37271 or equivalent to the opposite locknut to remove the locknuts.

50. Remove the counter driven gear using tool J–1859–03 or equivalent.
51. Remove the thrust needle bearing.
52. Remove the countershaft assembly and the anti-rattle clip.
53. Remove the parking lock pawl stopper plate, torsion spring and spring guide.
54. Remove the pawl shaft clamp.
55. Remove the parking lock pawl shaft and the lock pawl.
56. Remove the parking lock sleeve.
57. Remove the cam guide bracket.
58. Remove the manual valve shaft sleeve.
59. Remove the retaining spring, manual valve shaft, manual valve lever and washer.
60. Replace the manual shaft oil seal, if necessary. Apply multipurpose grease to the oil seal lip.
61. Remove the oil seal rings.
62. Remove the oil galley cover and gasket.
63. Remove the B_4 accumulator piston and spring.
64. Remove the bearing from the case using tools J–23907 and J–26941 or equivalent.
65. Remove the 4 oil tube clamps and the oil tubes.
66. Remove the oil tube apply cover and gasket.
67. Remove the bearing from the housing using tools J–23907 and J–26941 or equivalent.

Cleaning

All disassembled parts should be washed clean, and the fluid passages and holes blown through with compressed air to make sure that they are not clogged. Dexron® II automatic transmission fluid or kerosene should be used for cleaning.

—————— **CAUTION** ——————
When using compressed air to dry parts, avoid spraying ATF or kerosene in your face.

Unit Disassembly and Assembly

OIL PUMP

Disassembly

1. Remove the race from the stator shaft.
2. Remove the O-ring from the pump body.
3. Remove the 2 oil seal rings from the back of the stator shaft.
4. Remove the thrust washer of the clutch drum from the stator shaft.
5. Remove the stator shaft.

Inspection

1. Check the body clearance of the driven gear. Push the driven gear to either side of the body. Using a feeler guage, measure the clearance. If the clearance exceeds the limit, replace the drive gear, driven gear or pump body. The standard body clearance is 0.0028–0.0059 in. (0.07–0.15mm). The maximum body clearance is 0.012 in. (0.3mm).
2. Check the tip clearance of both gears. Measure between the gear teeth and the crescent-shaped part of the pump body. If the clearance exceeds the limit, replace the drive gear, driven gear or pump body. The standard tip clearance is 0.0043–0.0055 in. (0.11–0.14mm). The maximum tip clearance is 0.012 in. (0.3mm).
3. Check the side clearance of both gears. Using a steel straight edge and a feeler gauge, measure the side clearance of both gears. If the clearance exceeds the limit, replace the drive gear, driven gear or the pump body. The standard side clearance is 0.0008–0.0020 in. (0.02–0.05mm). The maximum side clearance is 0.004 in. (0.1mm).
4. Inspect the front oil seal, check for wear, damage or cracks.

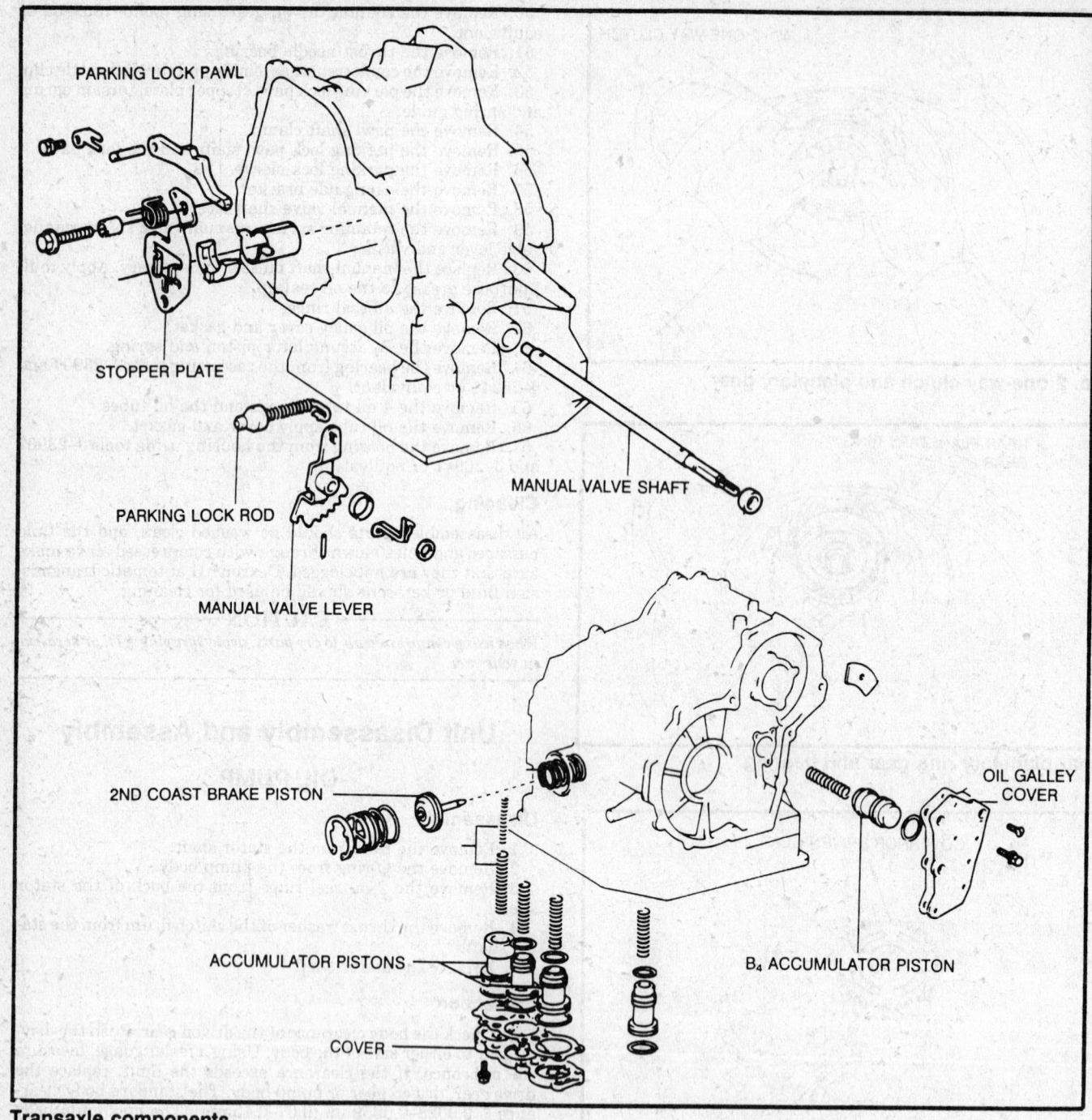

PARKING LOCK PAWL

STOPPER PLATE

PARKING LOCK ROD

MANUAL VALVE LEVER

MANUAL VALVE SHAFT

2ND COAST BRAKE PISTON

ACCUMULATOR PISTONS

COVER

OIL GALLEY COVER

B₄ ACCUMULATOR PISTON

Transaxle components

5. Replace the front oil seal. The seal end should be flush with the outer edge of the pump body.

Assembly

1. Install the driven gear and drive gear making sure the top of the gears are facing upward.
2. Install the stator shaft onto the pump body. Align the stator shaft with each bolt hole.
3. Tighten the bolts to 7 ft. lbs. (10 Nm).
4. Coat the thrust washer with petroleum jelly. Align the tab

of the washer with the hollow of the pump body and install the thrust washer.
5. Install 2 oil seal rings on the oil pump. Do not spread the ring ends too far.
6. Check the pump drive gear rotation. Turn the drive gear and check that it rotates smoothly.
7. Install a new O-ring.
8. Install the race onto the stator shaft.

DIRECT CLUTCH

Disassembly

1. Remove the snapring from the clutch drum.

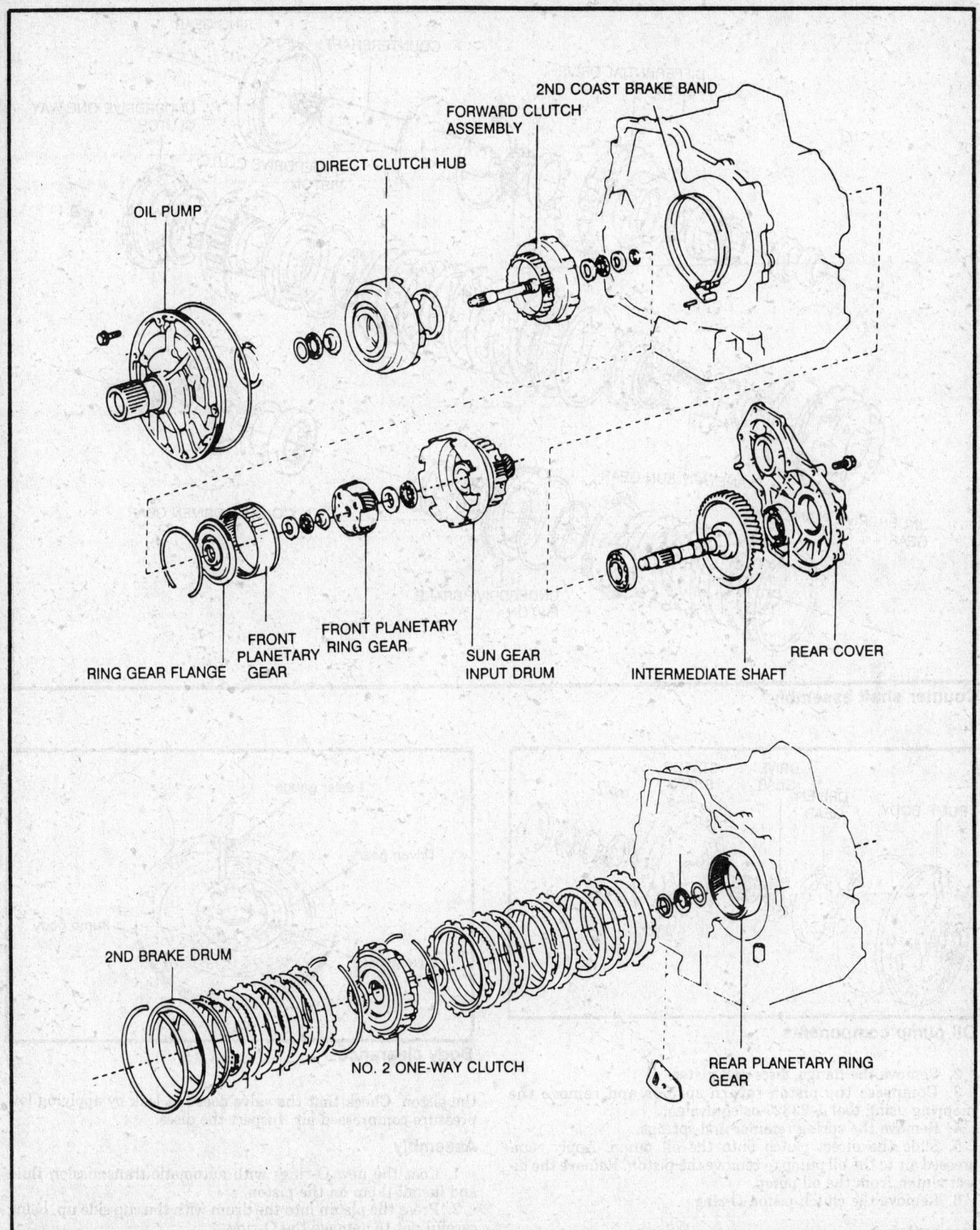

OIL PUMP

DIRECT CLUTCH HUB

FORWARD CLUTCH ASSEMBLY

2ND COAST BRAKE BAND

RING GEAR FLANGE

FRONT PLANETARY GEAR

FRONT PLANETARY RING GEAR

SUN GEAR INPUT DRUM

INTERMEDIATE SHAFT

REAR COVER

2ND BRAKE DRUM

NO. 2 ONE-WAY CLUTCH

REAR PLANETARY RING GEAR

Transaxle components

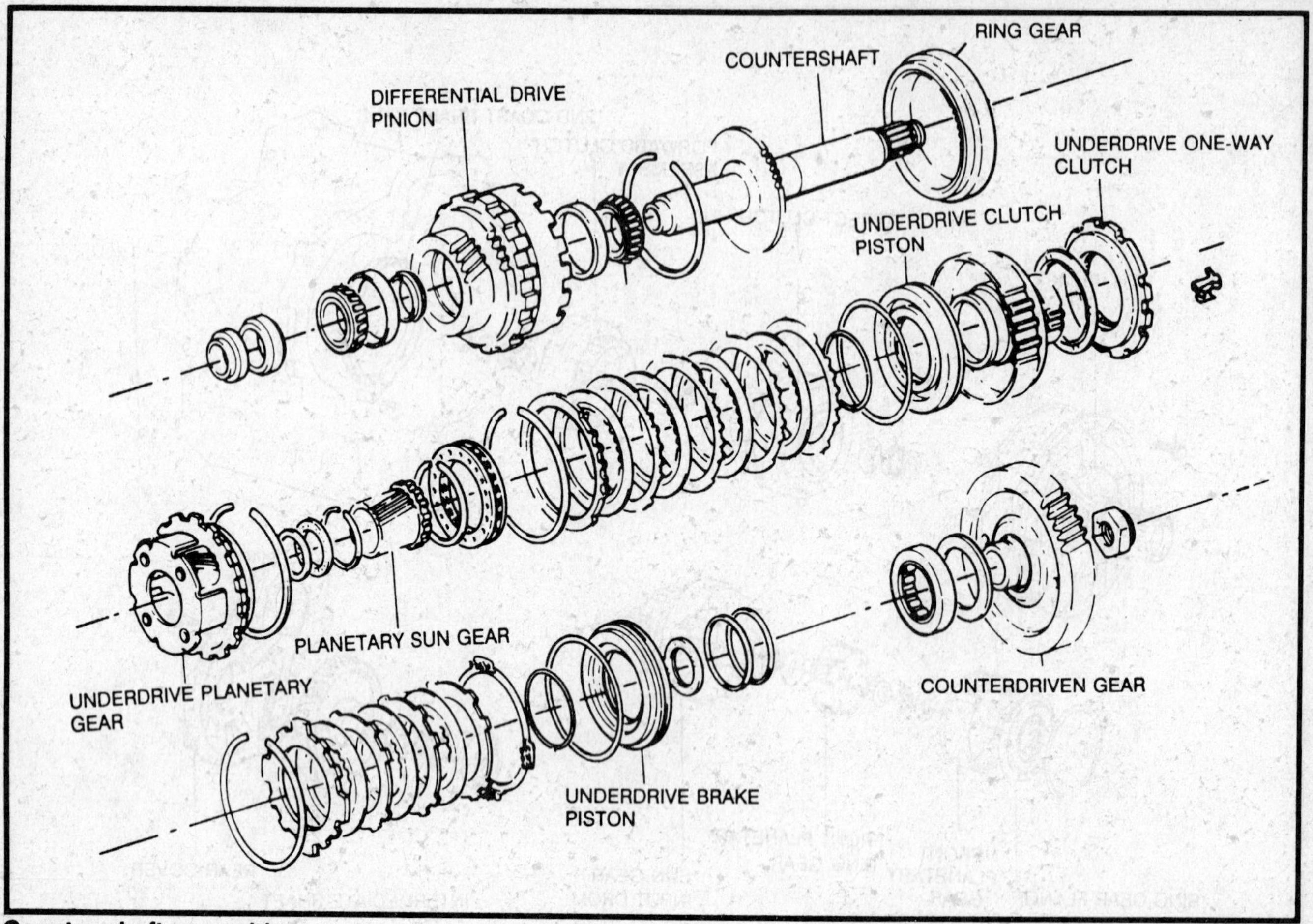

Counter shaft assembly

Oil pump components

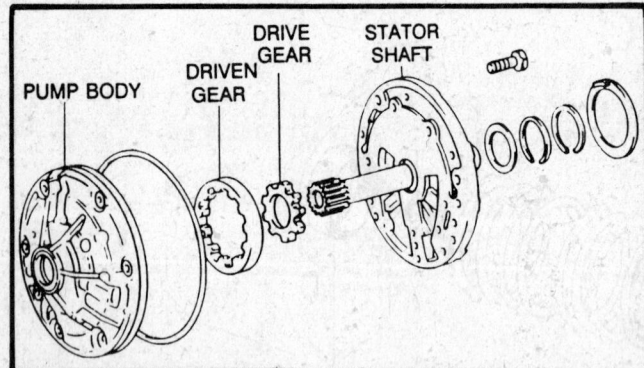

Body clearance

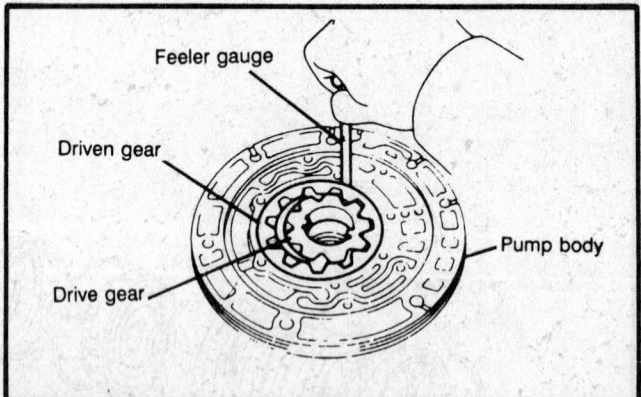

2. Remove the flange, discs and plates.

3. Compress the piston return springs and remove the snapring using tool J–23327 or equivalent.

4. Remove the spring retainer and springs.

5. Slide the direct clutch onto the oil pump. Apply compressed air to the oil pump to remove the piston. Remove the direct clutch from the oil pump.

6. Remove the clutch piston O-ring.

Inspection

Inspect the clutch piston. Check that the ball is free by shaking the piston. Check that the valve does not leak by applying low pressure compressed air. Inspect the discs.

Assembly

1. Coat the new O-rings with automatic transmission fluid and install them on the piston.

2. Press the piston into the drum with the cup side up, being careful not to damage the O-ring.

3. Install the piston return springs and set the retainer and snapring in place.

4. Compress the return springs and install the snapring in the groove using tools J–23327–1 and J–37279 or equivalent. Install the snapring. Be sure the endgap of the snapring is not aligned with the spring retainer claw.

5. Install the plates, discs and flange. Install in order: plate-disc-plate-disc-plate-disc. Install the flange, facing the flat end downward.

6. Install the outer snapring. Check that the endgap of the snapring is not aligned with a cutout.

7. Using compressed air, check the stroke of the direct clutch piston for replacement of plate, discs or flange. If not within specification, select a proper flange. There are 2 different flange thickness. The piston stroke should be 0.0445–0.0591 in. (1.13–1.50mm). The flange thicknesses are 0.1024 in. (2.6mm) and 0.1181 in. (3.0mm).

FORWARD CLUTCH

Disassembly

1. Remove the thrust washer.
2. Remove the thrust bearings and races from both sides of the clutch.
3. Remove the snapring from the clutch drum.
4. Remove the flange, discs and plates.
5. Compress the piston return springs and remove the snapring using tools J–25018–A adapter and J–23327–1 or equivalent.
6. Remove the spring retainer and springs.
7. Apply compressed air into the oil passage to remove the piston.

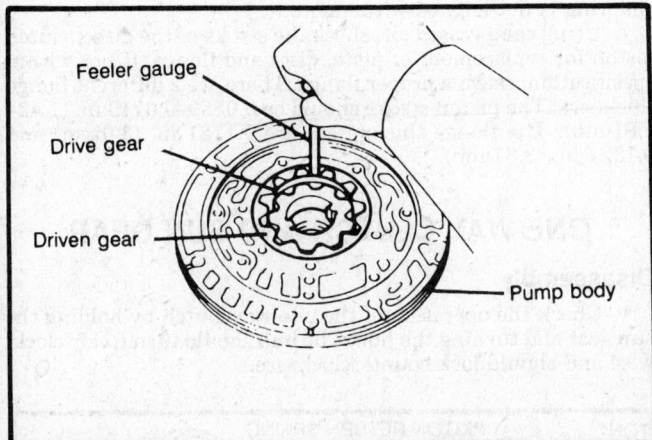

Tip clearance

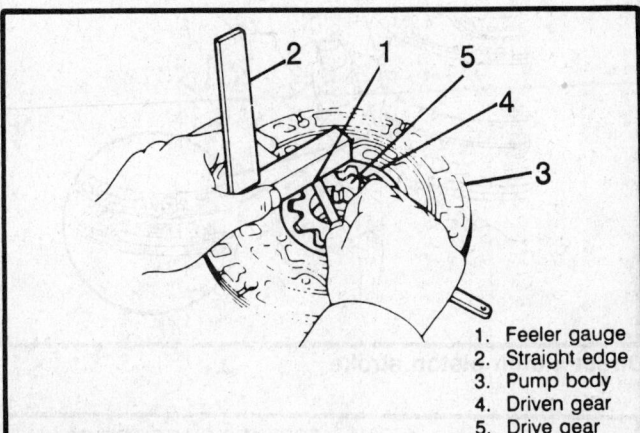

1. Feeler gauge
2. Straight edge
3. Pump body
4. Driven gear
5. Drive gear

Side clearance

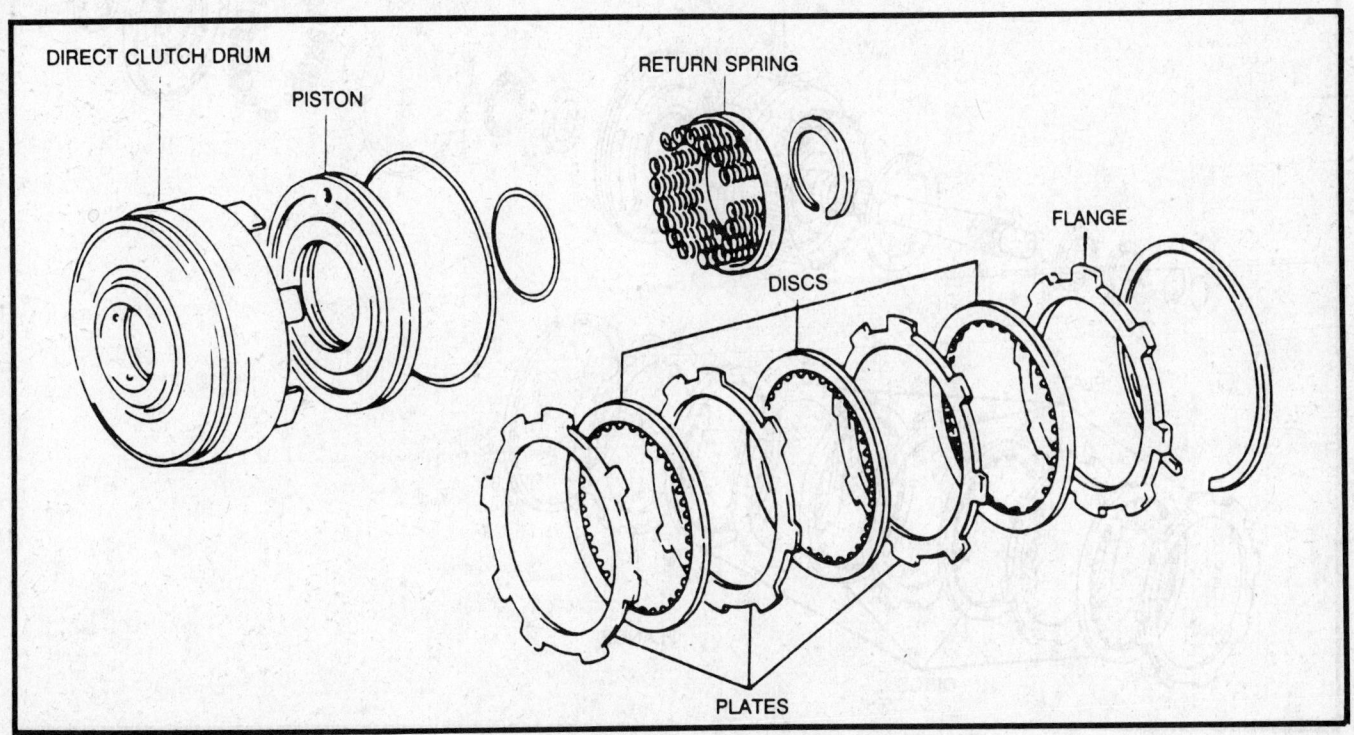

Direct clutch C₃ components

Inspection

Make sure the check ball is free by shaking the piston. Check that the valve does not leak by applying low pressure com-pressed air. Replace the oil seal rings. Slide the rings over top of the shaft and install them into the groove. Do not spread the ring ends.

Assembly

1. Install new O-rings on the piston, coat the O-rings with automatic transmission fluid.
2. Press the piston into the forward clutch drum with the cup side up, being careful not to damage the O-ring.
3. Install the piston return springs, spring retainer and snapring in place.
4. Compress the return springs and install the snapring in the groove. Be sure the end of the snapring is not aligned with the spring retainer claw.
5. Install the plates, discs and flange. Install in the following order: plate-disc-plate-disc-plate-disc. Install the flange facing the flat end downward.
6. Install the outer snapring. Check that the endgap of the snapring is not aligned with a cutout.
7. Using compressed air, check the stroke of the direct clutch piston for replacement of plate, discs and flange. If not within specification, select a proper flange. There are 2 different flange thickness. The piston stroke should be 0.0559–0.0713 in. (1.42–1.81mm). The flange thicknesses are 0.1181 in. (3.0mm) and 0.1327 in. (3.37mm).

ONE-WAY CLUTCH AND SUN GEAR

Disassembly

1. Check the operation of the one-way clutch by holding the sun gear and turning the hub. The hub should turn freely clockwise and should lock counterclockwise.

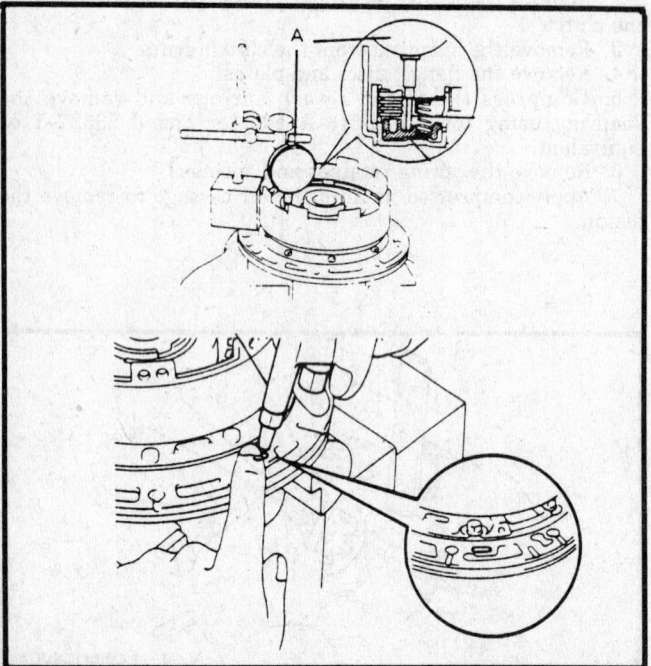

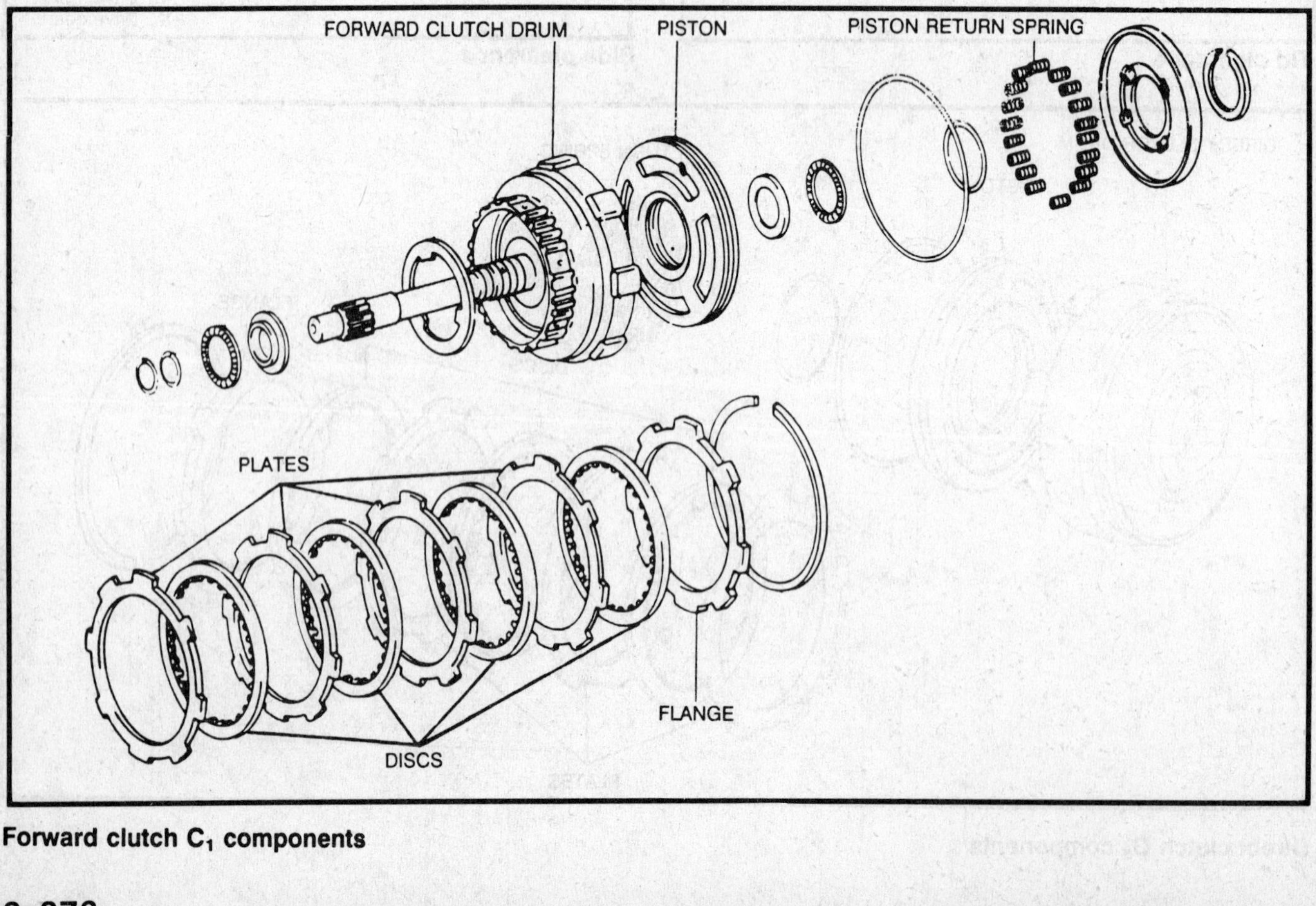

Direct clutch piston stroke

FORWARD CLUTCH DRUM PISTON PISTON RETURN SPRING

PLATES

FLANGE

DISCS

Forward clutch C$_1$ components

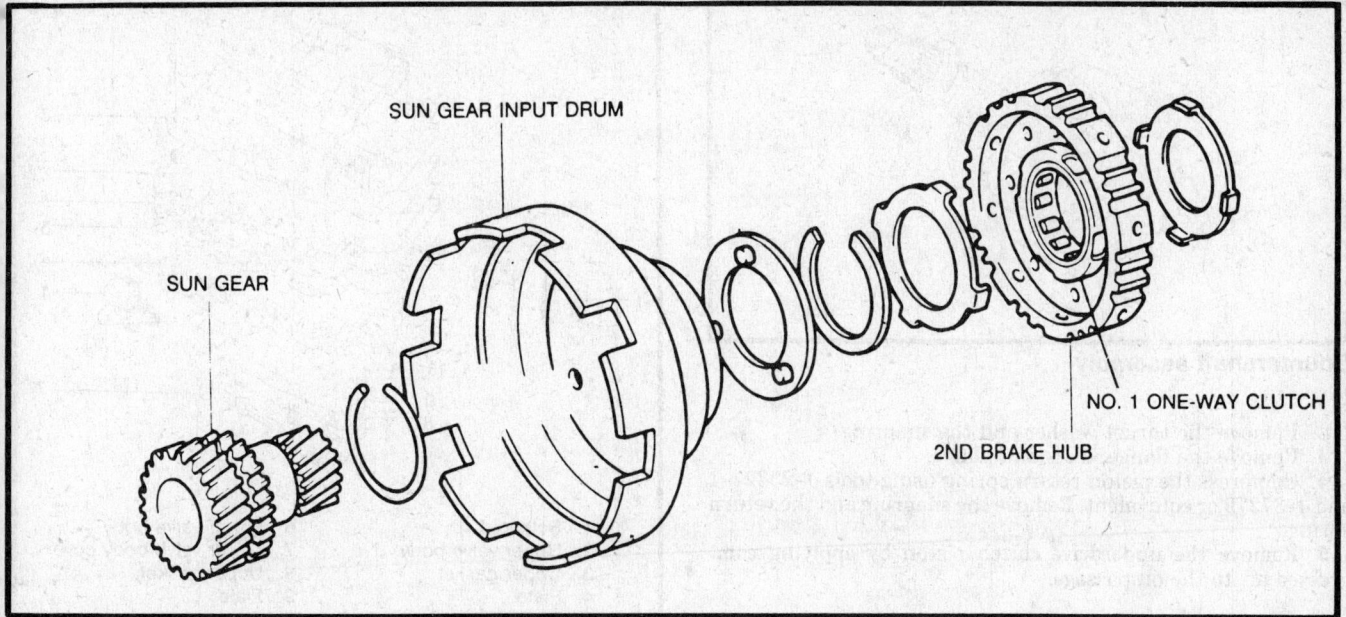

No. 1 one-way clutch and sun gear components

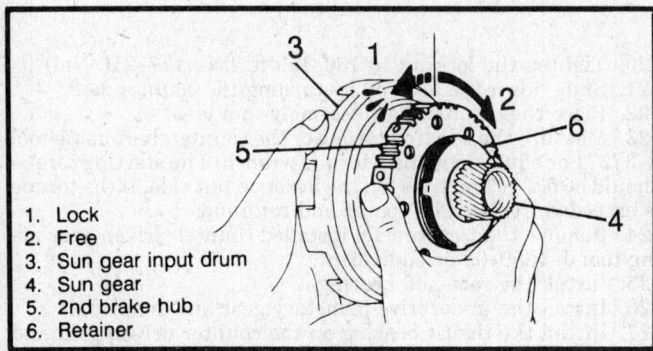

1. Lock
2. Free
3. Sun gear input drum
4. Sun gear
5. 2nd brake hub
6. Retainer

Checking No. 1 one-way clutch

2. Remove the 2nd brake hub and the one-way clutch from the sun gear.

3. Remove the No. 3 planetary carrier thrust washer from the sun gear input drum.

4. Remove the snapring and the sun gear input drum.

Inspection

If necessary, replace the one-way clutch.

1. Pry off the retainer.
2. Remove the one-way clutch.
3. Install the one-way clutch into the brake hub, facing the spring cage inward from the flanged side of the brake hub.
4. Hold the brake hub in a vise and flatten the ears with a chisel.
5. Check the operation to make sure that the retainer is centered.

Assembly

1. Install the shaft snapring on the sun gear.
2. Install the sun gear input drum on the sun gear and install the shaft snapring.
3. Install the No. 3 planetary carrier thrust washer on the sun gear input drum.
4. Install the one-way clutch and the 2nd brake hub on the

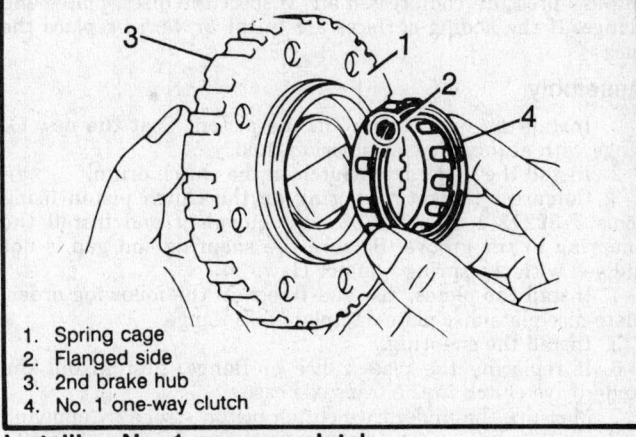

1. Spring cage
2. Flanged side
3. 2nd brake hub
4. No. 1 one-way clutch

Installing No. 1 one-way clutch

sun gear. While turning the hub clockwise, slide the one-way clutch into the inner race.

COUNTER SHAFT

Disassembly

1. Remove the bearing.
2. Remove the underdrive planetary sun gear.
3. Remove the snapring from the sun gear.
4. Remove the snapring from the countershaft assembly.
5. Remove the underdrive planetary gear.
6. Remove the thrust needle bearing and race.
7. Remove the drive pinion with the output flange, bearing, inner race and spacer. Press out the bearing using tool J–22912–01 or equivalent.
8. Remove the snapring and ring gear.
9. Remove the bearing using tools J–22912–01 and J–37273 or equivalent.
10. Remove the bearing outer race.
11. Remove the underdrive one-way clutch from the clutch drum.

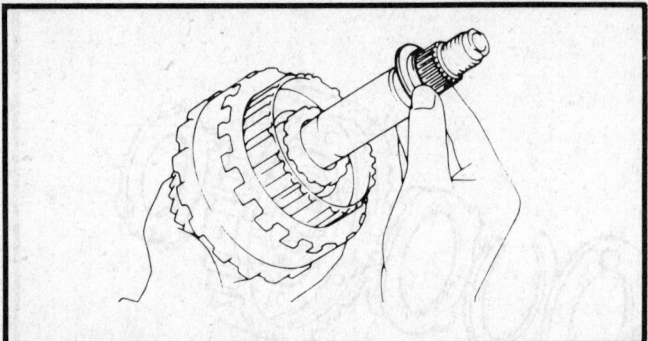

Countershaft assembly

12. Remove the thrust washer and the snapring.
13. Remove the flange, discs and plates.
14. Compress the piston return spring using tools J–23327–1 and J–37279 or equivalent. Remove the snapring and the return spring.
15. Remove the underdrive clutch piston by applying compressed air to the oil passage.

Inspection
Check that the underdrive clutch piston check ball is free by shaking the piston. Check that the valve does not leak by applying low pressure compressed air. Inspect the discs, plates and flange. If the sliding surfaces are burnt or worn, replace the part.

Assembly
1. Install the new O-rings on the piston. Coat the new O-rings with automatic transmission fluid.
2. Install the underdrive clutch in the clutch drum.
3. Compress the return spring on the clutch piston using tools J–32272–1 and J–37279 or equivalent and install the snapring in the groove. Be sure the snapring end gap is not aligned with the spring retainer claw.
4. Install the plates, disc and flange in the following order: plate-disc-plate-disc-plate-disc-plate-disc-flange.
5. Install the snapring.
6. If replacing the plates, disc or flange, first install the underdrive clutch in the transaxle case.
7. Measure the underdrive clutch piston stroke by applying and releasing low pressure compressed air and using a dial indicator. The piston stroke should be 0.0579–0.0744 in. (1.47–1.89mm).
8. If the piston stroke is less than the minimum, the parts may be misassembled.
9. If the piston stroke is not within specifications, select another flange. The flange thicknesses are 0.0803 in. (2.04mm) and 0.0945 in. (2.40mm).
10. Install the thrust washer in the clutch drum.
11. Install the underdrive one-way clutch.
12. Install the bearing outer races using tools J–8092, J–35287 and J–35663 or equivalent.
13. Install the bearing on the countershaft using tool J–37278 or equivalent.
14. Install the ring gear and snapring.
15. Install the new spacer and the drive pinion with the output flange.
16. Install the bearing inner race using a press and tool J–37278 or equivalent.
17. Install a new locknut.
18. Temporarily install the counter driven gear to the counter shaft using a press.
19. Install tool J–6814–01 or equivalent to the counter driven gear and secure the counter shaft in a vise.

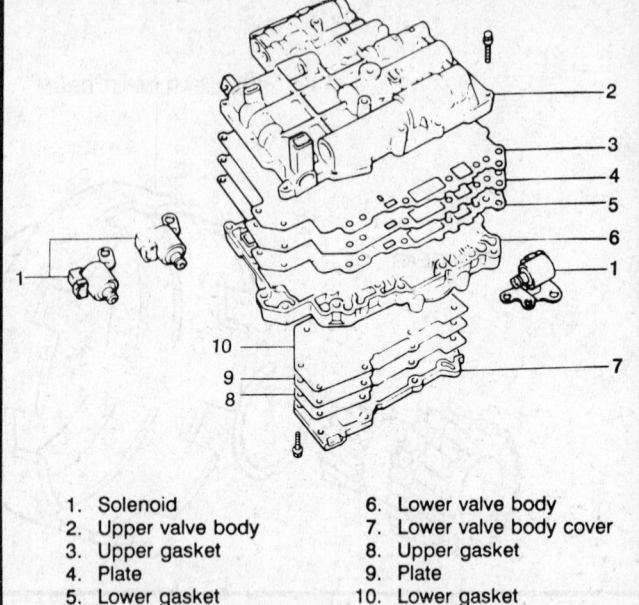

1. Solenoid	6. Lower valve body
2. Upper valve body	7. Lower valve body cover
3. Upper gasket	8. Upper gasket
4. Plate	9. Plate
5. Lower gasket	10. Lower gasket

Valve body

20. Tighten the locknut to 130–159 ft. lbs. (177–216 Nm).
21. Snug down the bearing by turning the countershaft.
22. Place the countershaft assembly in a vise.
23. Measure the starting torque of the countershaft using tool J–37271 or equivalent and a torque wrench. The starting torque should be 5.2–8.7 inch lbs. on the hexagon nut side. If the torque is exceeded, replace the spacer and retorque.
24. Remove the temporarily installed counter driven gear using tool J–1859–03 or equivalent.
25. Install the race and bearing.
26. Install the underdrive planetary gear and snapring.
27. Install the thrust bearing on the counter driven gear and stake the locknuts.

VALVE BODY

Disassembly
1. Remove the solenoid valves.
2. Remove the lower valve body cover, gaskets and plate.
3. Turn the assembly over and remove the 8 bolts from the upper valve body and upper valve body cover.
4. Turn the assembly over and remove the 9 bolts from the lower valve body.
5. Lift off the lower valve body and plate as a single unit. Hold the body plate to the lower valve body.

NOTE: Be careful of the bypass valve, pressure relief valve. Make sure the check balls, retainer, keys and pins do not fall out.

UPPER VALVE BODY

Disassembly
1. Remove the throttle valve retainer and check ball.
2. Remove the retainer for the plug with a magnetic finger and remove the plug.
3. Remove the lockup relay valve, control valve and spring.
4. Remove the sleeve retainer with a magnetic finger and remove the sleeve.

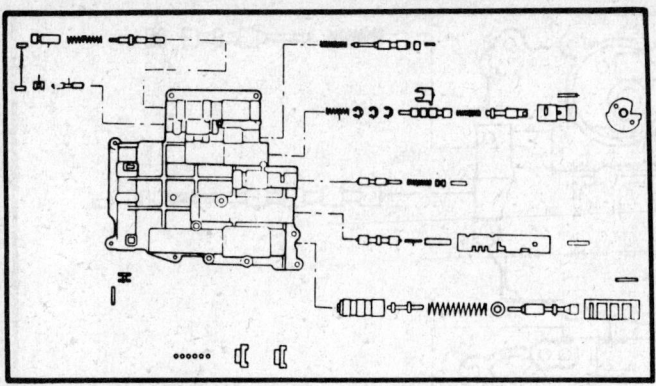

Upper valve body

UPPER VALVE BODY SPRING

Spring	Free Length		Color
	in.	(mm)	
Primary regulator valve	2.6240	66.65	Purple
Lockup relay valve	0.7402	18.80	None
Low-coast modulator valve	1.0831	27.51	Yellow
Kickdown valve	1.1717	29.76	White
Throttle valve	1.1488	29.18	Yellow green
Throttle modulator valve	1.1772	29.90	Green
Accumulator control valve	1.5039	38.20	Yellow

5. Remove the cut-back valve by removing the retainer with a magnetic finger then remove the cut-back valve and plug.

6. Remove the throttle modulator valve by removing the retainer with a magnetic finger, then remove the plug, valve and spring.

7. Remove the accumulator control valve by removing the retainer with a magnetic finger and remove the plug, valve and spring.

8. Remove the low coast modulator valve by removing the pin with a magnetic finger then remove the plug, valve and spring.

9. Remove the 2nd coast modulator valve by removing the retainer with a magnetic finger then remove the spring and valve.

10. Remove the throttle cam. Loosen the bolt and remove the cam, spring and collar.

11. Remove the kickdown valve and spring by removing the pin with a magnetic finger, then remove the kickdown valve with the sleeve and spring.

12. Remove the throttle valve.

13. Remove the spring and adjusting rings.

Inspection

Inspect the valve springs. Check for damage, squareness, rust and collapsed coils. Measure the free length and replace any springs if necessary.

Assembly

1. Install the lockup relay valve sleeve into the bore.

2. Coat the retainer with petroleum jelly and install it into the end of the sleeve.

3. Install the control valve, spring and lockup relay valve into the bore in horizontal position.

4. Push in the relay valve by hand until the control valve touches the end of the sleeve. Install the plug and retainer.

5. Install the cut-back valve by installing the small end first. Install the plug and retainer.

6. Install the throttle modulator valve. Install the spring and valve. Install the plug and retainer.

7. Install the accumulator control valve. Install the valve and spring. Install the plug and retainer.

8. Install the low coast modulator valve. Install the valve and spring. Install the plug, thick end first. Install the pin.

9. Install the throttle valve and retainer. Install the throttle valve. Coat the retainer with petroleum jelly and install it into place in the valve body.

10. Install the adjusting rings and spring on the throttle valve shaft.

11. Install the spring into the throttle valve.

12. Install the kickdown valve and sleeve. Install the pin to hold the sleeve in place.

13. Install the 2nd coast modulator valve. Install the valve and spring.

14. Assemble the throttle cam. Insert the sleeve through a side of the cam. Install the spring with the hook through the hole in the cam.

15. Install the cam assembly on the upper valve body. Make sure that the cam moves on the roller of the kickdown valve.

16. Install the check ball.

LOWER VALVE BODY

Disassembly

1. Remove the lower valve body plate and gaskets.

2. Remove the cooler bypass valve and spring.

3. Remove the damping check valve and spring.

4. Remove the 3 check balls.

5. Remove the primary regulator valve.

6. Remove the secondary regulator valve.

7. Remove the 1–2 shift valve. Remove the 1–2 shift lower valve and spring.

8. Remove the low coast shift valve.

9. Remove the lockup control valve.

10. Remove the detent regulator valve.

11. Remove the 2–3 shift valve.

12. Remove the intermediate shift valve.

13. Remove the lockup signal valve.

14. Remove the 3–4 coast shift plug.

15. Remove the 3–4 shift plug.

Inspection

Inspect the valve springs. Check for damage, squareness, rust and collapsed coils. Measure the free length and replace any springs if necessary.

Assembly

1. Place the primary regulator valve into the bore in the horizontal position.

2. Push the valve into the bore until its tip bottoms in the bore.

3. Install the valve spring.

4. Insert the plunger with the short end first. The plunger should be recessed inside the sleeve.

5. Install the sleeve with the plunger.

6. Install the secondary regulator valve.

7. Install the 1–2 shift valve. Install the spring and upper valve.

8. Install the low coast shift valve.

9. Install the lockup control valve.

10. Install the detent regulator valve.

11. Install the intermediate shift valve.

12. Install the 2–3 shift valve.

13. Install the lockup signal valve.

14. Install the 3–4 coast shift plug.

15. Install the 3–4 shift plug.

16. Install the spring and cooler bypass valve.

17. Install the spring and damping check valve.

18. Install the check balls.

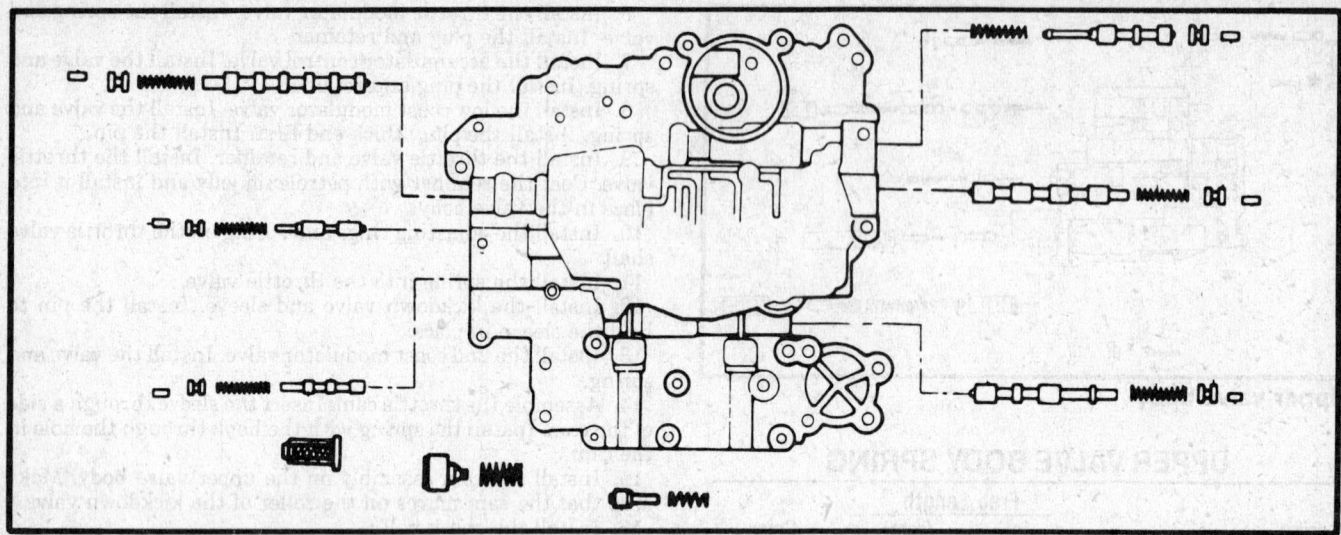

Lower valve body components

LOWER VALVE BODY SPRING

Spring	Free Length		Color
	in.	(mm)	
Secondary regulator valve	1.2937	32.86	Orange
1-2 Shift valve	1.2114	30.77	Purple
3-4 Shift valve	1.2114	30.77	Purple
2-3 Shift valve	1.2114	30.77	Purple
2nd coast modulator valve	1.1665	29.63	Red
Lockup signal valve	1.1811	30.00	Orange

VALVE BODY

Assembly

Install the lower valve body on the upper valve body together with the plate.

1. Position the new gaskets and the plate on the lower valve body. Assemble the gasket having the larger cooler bypass hole to the lower valve body.

2. Install a new gasket and plate onto the lower valve body. Install another new gasket onto the plate. Align each bolt hole in the valve body with the 2 gaskets and plate.

3. Position the lower valve body and gaskets with the plate on top of the upper valve body. Align each bolt hole in the valve bodies with the gaskets and plate.

4. Install and finger tighten 3 bolts in the lower valve body to secure the upper valve body.

5. Turn the assembly over and finger tighten 3 bolts in the upper valve body.

6. Install the upper valve body cover new gaskets and strainer. Install the valve body cover and finger tighten the bolts.

7. Turn the assembly over and install a new gasket and the lower valve body cover.

8. Tighten the bolts of the upper and lower valve body to 48 inch lbs. (5.4 Nm).

Transaxle Assembly

1. Before assembling new clutch discs, soak them in automatic transmission fluid for at least 2 hours. Apply automatic transmission fluid to the sliding or rotating surfaces of parts before assembly.

2. Use petroleum jelly to keep small parts in their places. Do not use adhesive cements on gaskets and similar parts. When assembling the transaxle, be sure to use new gaskets and O-rings.

3. Install the bearing in the transaxle housing using tools J-8092 and J-37274 and a press. Install the bearing stopper.

4. Install the oil tube apply cover. Install the oil tubes. Install the bearing in the transaxle case with the lettering facing towards the case using tools J-8092 and J-37274 or equivalent and a press.

5. Install the B4 accumulator piston and spring. Install the oil galley cover and gasket.

6. Install the oil seal rings in the transaxle case and check that they move smoothly.

7. Install the manual shaft with the washer, spacer, manual lever and retaining spring.

8. Install the pin and stake the spacer.

9. Install the cam guide bracket.

10. Install the parking lock sleeve with the protruding portion facing upward.

11. Install the parking lock pawl stopper plate, torsion spring and spring guide.

12. Install the parking lock pawl shaft, lock pawl and the pawl shaft clamp.

13. Install the underdrive brake piston and the return spring.

14. Install the plates, disc and flange in the following order: plate-disc-plate-disc-plate-disc. Install the flange facing the flat end upward.

15. Compress the return spring and install the snapring.

16. Install the underdrive one-way clutch. Install the anti-rattle clip.

17. Install the bearing and race. Install the snapring on the sun gear.

18. Install the sun gear in the transaxle case.

19. Install the countershaft assembly and the anti-rattle clip.

20. Install the thrust needle bearing.

21. Install the counter driven gear using tool J-1859-03 or equivalent.

22. Stake the countershaft locknut on both sides.

23. Install the intermediate shaft and the transaxle rear cover.

24. Install the governor driven gear and thrust washer.

25. Install the oil seals.

26. Install the 1st and reverse brake into the case.

27. Install the flange, plates and discs in the following order: flange-disc-plate-disc-plate-disc.

28. Install the snapring holding the flange to the case.
29. Install the No. 2 one-way clutch and the rear planetary gear with the thrust washers.
30. Install the rear planetary ring gear, races and bearing.
31. Install the snapring holding the No. 2 one-way clutch outer race to the case.
32. Install the second coast brake band guide.
33. Install the 2nd brake drum piston return spring.
34. Install the 2nd brake piston.
35. Install the snapring and the 2nd brake drum.
36. Install the 2nd brake drum gasket.
37. Install the No. 1 one-way clutch and the 2nd brake hub.
38. Install the sun gear, sun gear input drum and thrust washer.
39. Install the front planetary gear with the race.
40. Install the front planetary ring gear with the bearing and race.
41. Install the 2nd coast brake band.
42. Install the forward clutch.
43. Install the direct clutch.
44. Install the differential.
45. Install the transaxle housing to the case.
46. Install the oil pump.
47. Install the 2nd coast brake band piston.
48. Install the accumulator pistons and springs. Install the cover and gasket.
49. Install the 2nd brake apply gasket.
50. Install the throttle cable into the case.
51. Connect the solenoid wire.
52. Install the valve body.
53. Connect the solenoid connectors.
54. Install the manual detent spring and the detent plate.
55. Install the oil tubes.
56. Install the oil strainer.
57. Install the oil tube bracket.
58. Install the pan and gasket.
59. Install the speed sensor, sensor rotor and adapter.
60. Install the solenoid wire retaining plate.
61. Install the neutral start switch.
62. Install the manual shift lever.
63. Install the transaxle dipstick and filler tube.
64. Install the oil cooler pipes.

SPECIFICATIONS

VALVE BODY SPECIFICATIONS

Item	Free length in.	mm	Coil outer diameter in.	mm	No. coils	Wire diameter in.	mm	Color
UPPER VALVE BODY								
Primary regulator valve	2.6240	66.65	0.732	18.6	12.5	0.063	1.6	Purple
Lockup relay valve	0.7402	18.80	0.201	5.1	14.5	0.020	0.5	None
Low coast modulator valve	1.0831	27.51	0.327	8.3	12.5	0.035	0.9	Yellow
Kickdown valve	1.1717	29.76	0.3437	8.73	13.5	0.039	1.0	White
Throttle valve	1.1488	29.18	0.362	9.2	9.5	0.028	0.7	Yellow green
Throttle modulator valve	1.1772	29.90	0.354	9.0	15.5	0.035	0.9	Green
Accumulator control valve	1.5039	38.20	0.394	10.0	11.5	0.035	0.9	Yellow
LOWER VALVE BODY								
Secondary regulator valve	1.2937	32.86	0.433	11.0	11.5	0.055	1.4	Orange
1-2 shift valve	1.2114	30.77	0.382	9.7	10.5	0.035	0.9	Purple
3-4 shift valve	1.2114	30.77	0.382	9.7	10.5	0.035	0.9	Purple
2-3 shift valve	1.2114	30.77	0.382	9.7	10.5	0.035	0.9	Purple
2nd coast modulator valve	1.1665	29.63	0.327	8.3	12.5	0.039	1.0	Red
Lockup signal valve	1.1811	30.00	0.323	8.2	11.5	0.028	0.7	Orange

ACCUMULATOR PISTON SPRING SPECIFICATIONS

Item		Free length in.	mm	Coil outer diameter in.	mm	No. coils	Wire diameter in.	mm	Color
B_4 (Underdrive)		2.5756	65.42	0.7087	18.00	13.0	0.1024	2.60	None
B_2		2.6252	70.00	0.6976	17.72	15.5	0.1024	2.60	None
C_1	Inner	1.6732	42.50	0.6811	17.30	9.5	0.0906	2.30	None
	Outer	2.7992	71.10	0.9134	23.20	12.5	0.0906	2.30	White
C_2		2.4677	62.68	0.6890	17.50	18.5	0.0906	2.30	Black
C_3		2.4201	61.47	0.6193	15.73	14.5	0.0906	2.30	White

BUSHING SPECIFICATIONS

Bushing		Finished Bore		Bore Limit	
		in.	(mm)	in.	(mm)
Stator support	Front	0.8465–0.8475	21.500–21.526	0.8494	21.576
	Rear	1.0630–1.0640	27.000–27.026	1.0660	27.076
Oil pump body		1.5005–1.5015	38.138–38.138	1.5035	38.188
Direct clutch drum		1.8504–1.8514	47.000–47.025	1.8533	47.075
Front planetary ring gear flange		0.7490–0.7500	19.025–19.050	0.7520	19.100
Input sun gear (Front and Rear)		0.8671–0.8680	22.025–22.046	0.8699	22.096

OIL PUMP SPECIFICATIONS

Item		in.	mm
Side clearance	Std.	0.0008–0.0020	0.02–0.05
	Limit	0.004	0.1
Body clearance	Std.	0.0028–0.0059	0.07–0.15
	Limit	0.012	0.3
Tip clearance	Std.	0.0043–0.0055	0.11–0.14
Driven gear	Limit	0.012	0.3

CLUTCH PISTON STROKE SPECIFICATIONS

	in.	(mm)
Forward clutch (C_1)	0.0559–0.0713	1.42–1.81
Direct clutch (C_2)	0.0445–0.0591	1.13–1.50
Underdrive clutch (C_3)	0.0579–0.0744	1.47–1.89

TORQUE SPECIFICATIONS

Item	ft. lbs.	Nm
Engine mounting	38	52
Transaxle housing to Engine 12 mm	47	64
Transaxle housing to Engine 10 mm	34	46
Drive plate to Crankshaft	47	64
Torque converter to Drive plate	20	37
Oil pump to Transaxle case	18	25
Oil pump body to Stator shaft	7	10
Second coast brake band guide	48 ①	5.4
Upper valve body to Lower valve body	56 ①	6.4
Valve body	7	10
Accumulator cover	7	10
Oil strainer	7	10
Oil pan	43 ①	4.9
Oil pan drain plug	13	17
Cooler pipe union nut to Union elbow	25	34
Union elbow to Transaxle case	20	27
Testing plug	65 ①	7.4
Parking lock paw bracket	65 ①	7.4
Transaxle rear cover to Transaxle case	22	29
Neutral safety switch to Transaxle case	48 ①	5.4
Neutral safety switch	61 ①	6.9

① Inch lbs.

SPECIAL TOOLS

Tool	Description
J-9617	Oil pump seal installer
J-29182	Pinion shaft bearing cup installer
J-35378	Bearing puller pilot
J-35399	Differential side bearing cup remover
J-35400	Differential side bearing housing support
J-35405	Differential preload wrench
J-35409	Differential side bearing installer
J-35455	Holding fixture
J-35467	One-way clutch tester
J-35495	Oil pump puller adapters
J-35549	Second coast brake piston compressor
J-35552	Differential side bearing cup installer
J-35553	Differential side bearing seal installer
J-35565	Intermediate shaft bearing installer
J-35661	Countergear bearing installer
J-35663	Countergear bearing cup installer
J-35664	Pinion shaft bearing installer
J-35666	Pinion shaft bearing seal installer
J-35679	Band apply pin gauge
J-35683	First/reverse clutch spring compressor adapter
J-35752	Pressure gauge adapter
J-1859-03	Countergear puller
J-3289-20	Holding fixture mount
J-8001	Dial indicator set
J-8092	Driver handle
J-8614-01	Countergear holder
J-21867	Pressure gauge
J-22888	Right differential side bearing puller
J-22912-01	Bearing puller
J-23327	Clutch spring compressor
J-25018-A	Clutch spring compressor adapter
J-25025-1	Dial indicator mount
J-33411	Countergear installer
J-6125-B	Slide hammer set

Section 3

THM 440-4 and F7 Transaxles
General Motors

APPLICATION

THM 440-T4

Year	Body	Vehicle	Engine
1984	A	Century	2.8L 2bbl
	A	Century	3.0L 2bbl
	A	Century	3.8L MPI
	A	Celebrity	2.8L 2bbl
	A	Celebrity	4.3L Diesel
	A	Ciera	2.8L 2bbl
	A	Ciera	3.0L 2bbl
	A	Ciera	3.8L MPI
	A	6000	2.8L 2bbl
	A	6000	4.3L Diesel
1985	A	Century	2.8L 2bbl
	A	Century	3.0L 2bbl
	A	Century	3.8L MPI
	A	Century	4.3L Diesel
	C	Electra	3.0L 2bbl
	C	Electra	3.8L MPI
	C	Electra	4.3L Diesel
	C	Deville	4.1L DFI
	C	Fleetwood	4.1L DFI
	A	Celebrity	2.8L 2bbl
	A	Celebrity	2.8L MPI
	A	Celebrity	4.3L Diesel
	A	Ciera	2.8L 2bbl
	A	Ciera	3.8L MPI
	A	Ciera	4.3L Diesel
	C	Ninety-Eight	3.0L 2bbl
	C	Ninety-Eight	3.8L MPI
	C	Ninety-Eight	4.3L Diesel
	A	6000	2.8L 2bbl
	A	6000	2.8L MPI
	A	6000	4.3L Diesel
1986	A	Century	3.8L SFI
	A	Century	2.8L 2bbl
	C	Electra	3.8L SFI
	H	LeSabre	3.0L EFI
	H	LeSabre	3.8L SFI
	E	Riviera	3.8L SFI
	C	Deville	4.1L DFI
	E	Eldorado	4.1L DFI
	C	Fleetwood	4.1L DFI
	K	Seville	4.1L DFI
	A	Celebrity	2.8L 2bbl
	A	Celebrity	2.8L MPI

THM 440-T4

Year	Body	Vehicle	Engine
1986	A	Ciera	2.8L 2bbl
	A	Ciera	3.8L SFI
	C	Ninety-Eight	3.8L SFI
	H	Eighty-Eight	3.0L EFI
	H	Eighty-Eight	3.8L SFI
	E	Toronado	3.8L SFI
	A	6000	2.8L 2bbl
	A	6000	2.8L MPI
	A	6000	3.8L SFI
1987	A	Century	3.8L SFI
	A	Century	2.8L MFI
	C	Electra	3.8L SFI
	H	LeSabre	3.8L SFI
	E	Riviera	3.8L SFI
	V	Allante	4.1L DFI
	C	Deville	4.1L DFI
	E	Eldorado	4.1L DFI
	C	Fleetwood	4.1L DFI
	K	Seville	4.1L DFI
	A	Celebrity	2.8L MPI
	A	Ciera	2.8L MPI
	A	Ciera	3.8L SFI
	C	Ninety-Eight	3.8L SFI
	H	Eighty-Eight	3.8L SFI
	E	Toronado	3.8L SFI
	A	6000	2.8L MPI
	A	6000	3.8L SFI
	H	Bonneville	3.8L SFI
1988	A	Century	3.8L SFI
	A	Century	2.8L EFI
	C	Electra	3.8L SFI
	H	LeSabre	3.8L SFI
	E	Reatta	3.8L SFI
	E	Riviera	3.8L SFI
	W	Regal	2.8L MPI
	V	Allante	4.1L DFI
	C	Deville	4.5L DFI
	E	Eldorado	4.5L DFI
	C	Fleetwood	4.5L DFI
	K	Seville	4.5L DFI
	A	Celebrity	2.8L MPI
	A	Ciera	2.8L MPI
	A	Ciera	3.8L SFI

THM 440-T4

Year	Body	Vehicle	Engine
1988	C	Ninety-Eight	3.8L SFI
	H	Eighty-Eight	3.8L SFI
	E	Toronado	3.8L SFI
	W	Cutlass Supreme	2.8L MPI
	A	6000	2.8L MPI
	H	Bonneville	3.8L SFI
	W	Grand Prix	2.8L MPI
1989	A	Century	3.3L MFI
	A	Century	2.8L MFI
	C	Electra	3.8L SFI
	H	LeSabre	3.8L SFI
	E	Reatta	3.8L SFI
	E	Riviera	3.8L SFI
	W	Regal	2.8L MPI
	V	Allante	4.5L DFI
	C	Deville	4.5L DFI
	E	Eldorado	4.5L DFI
	C	Fleetwood	4.5L DFI
	K	Seville	4.5L DFI
	A	Celebrity	2.8L MPI
	A	Ciera	2.8L MPI
	A	Ciera	3.3L MFI
	C	Ninety-Eight	3.8L SFI
	H	Eighty-Eight	3.8L SFI
	E	Toronado	3.8L SFI

THM 440-T4

Year	Body	Vehicle	Engine
1989	W	Cutlass Supreme	2.8L MPI
	A	6000	2.8L MPI
	H	Bonneville	3.8L SFI
	W	Grand Prix	2.8L MPI

BBL—Barrel
DFI—Digital Fuel Injection
EFI—Electronic Fuel Injection
MFI—Multi-Port Fuel Injection
SFI—Sequential Fuel Injection

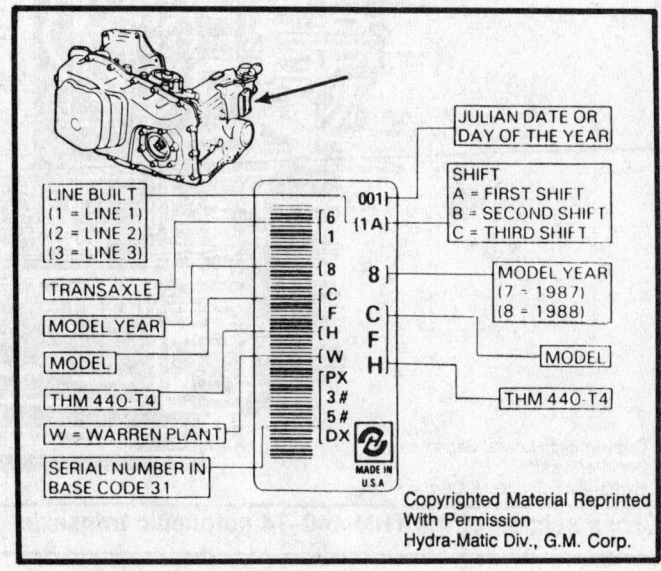

Transaxle identification data

GENERAL DESCRIPTION

Transaxle and Converter Identification

TRANSAXLE

The THM 440–T4 (ME9) and the F-7 automatic transaxles are fully automatic units. These transaxles consist of 4 multiple disc clutches, a roller clutch, a sprag and 2 bands, requiring hydraulic and mechanical applications to obtain the desired gear ratios from the compound planetary gears. The transaxle identification can be located on 1 of 3 areas of the unit. An identification plate on the side of the case, a stamped number on the governor housing or an ink stamp on the bell housing.

CONVERTER

Two types of converters are used in the varied vehicle applications. The first type is the 3 element torque converter combined with a lockup converter clutch. The second type is the 3 element torque converter combined with a viscous lockup converter clutch that has silicone fluid sealed between the cover and the body of the clutch assembly. Identification of the torque converters are either ink stamp marks or a stamped number on the shell of the converter.

Electronic Controls

The Torque Converter Clutch (TCC) system, or Cadillac's system, which uses a Viscous Converter Clutch (VCC) system, uses a solenoid operated valve in the automatic transaxle to couple the engine flywheel to the output shaft of the transaxle through the torque converter, which increases fuel economy.

For the converter clutch to apply, 2 conditions must be met:

1. Internal transaxle fluid pressure must be correct.

2. The ECM grounds a switch internally to turn **ON** a solenoid in the transaxle. This moves a check ball, which will allow the converter clutch to apply, if the hydraulic pressure is correct.

The ECM controls the TCC apply solenoid by looking at several sensors:

1. Vehicle Speed Sensor (VSS)—Speed must be above a certain value before the clutch can apply.

2. Coolant Temperature Sensor (CTS)—Engine must be warmed up before clutch can apply.

3. Throttle Position Sensor (TPS)—After the converter clutch applies, the ECM uses the information from the TPS to

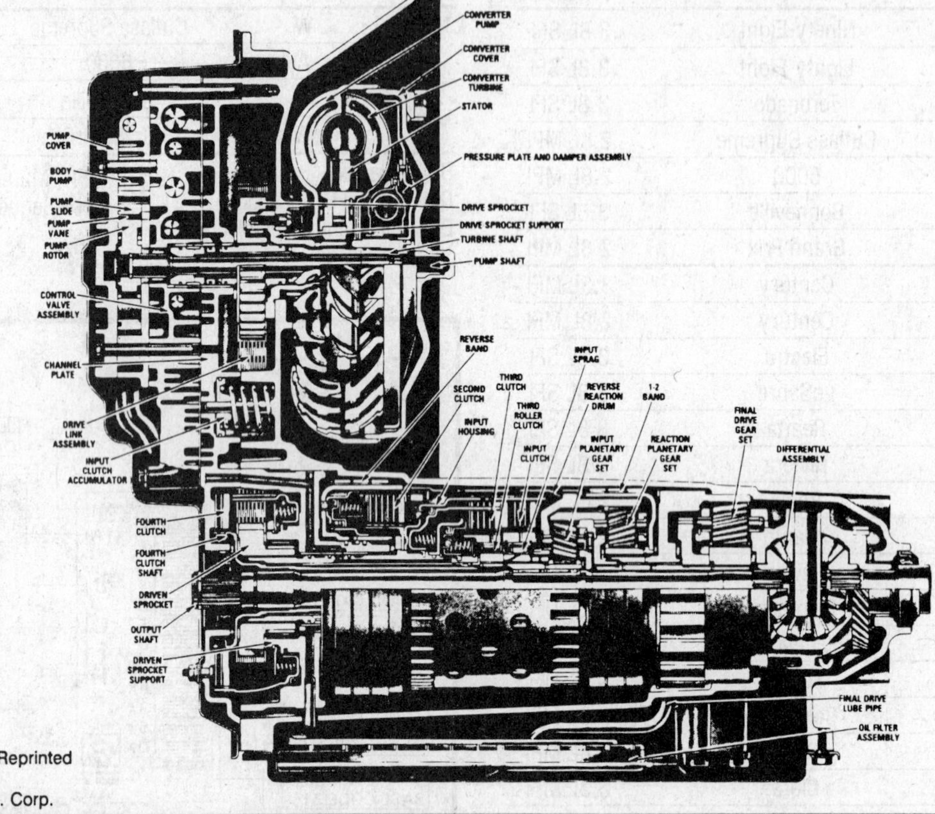

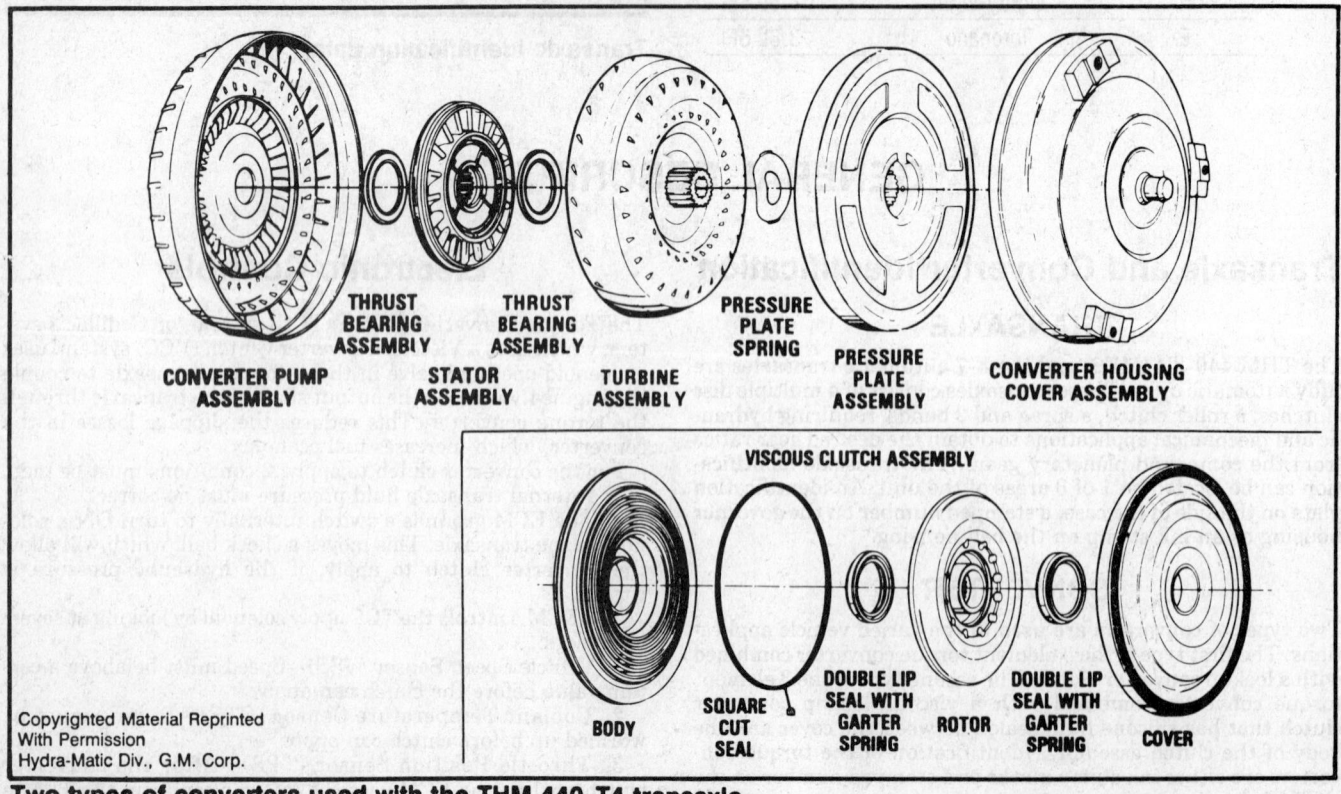

Cross section of the THM 440–T4 automatic transaxle

CONVERTER PUMP
CONVERTER COVER
CONVERTER TURBINE
STATOR
PRESSURE PLATE AND DAMPER ASSEMBLY
DRIVE SPROCKET
DRIVE SPROCKET SUPPORT
TURBINE SHAFT
PUMP SHAFT

PUMP COVER
BODY PUMP
PUMP SLIDE
PUMP VANE
PUMP ROTOR
CONTROL VALVE ASSEMBLY
CHANNEL PLATE
DRIVE LINK ASSEMBLY
INPUT CLUTCH ACCUMULATOR
FOURTH CLUTCH
FOURTH CLUTCH SHAFT
DRIVEN SPROCKET
OUTPUT SHAFT
DRIVEN SPROCKET SUPPORT

REVERSE BAND
SECOND CLUTCH
THIRD CLUTCH
INPUT HOUSING
THIRD ROLLER CLUTCH
INPUT CLUTCH
INPUT SPRAG
REVERSE REACTION DRUM
INPUT PLANETARY GEAR SET
1-2 BAND
REACTION PLANETARY GEAR SET
FINAL DRIVE GEAR SET
DIFFERENTIAL ASSEMBLY
FINAL DRIVE LUBE PIPE
OIL FILTER ASSEMBLY

THRUST BEARING ASSEMBLY
THRUST BEARING ASSEMBLY
PRESSURE PLATE SPRING
CONVERTER PUMP ASSEMBLY
STATOR ASSEMBLY
TURBINE ASSEMBLY
PRESSURE PLATE ASSEMBLY
CONVERTER HOUSING COVER ASSEMBLY

VISCOUS CLUTCH ASSEMBLY

BODY
SQUARE CUT SEAL
DOUBLE LIP SEAL WITH GARTER SPRING
ROTOR
DOUBLE LIP SEAL WITH GARTER SPRING
COVER

Two types of converters used with the THM 440–T4 transaxle

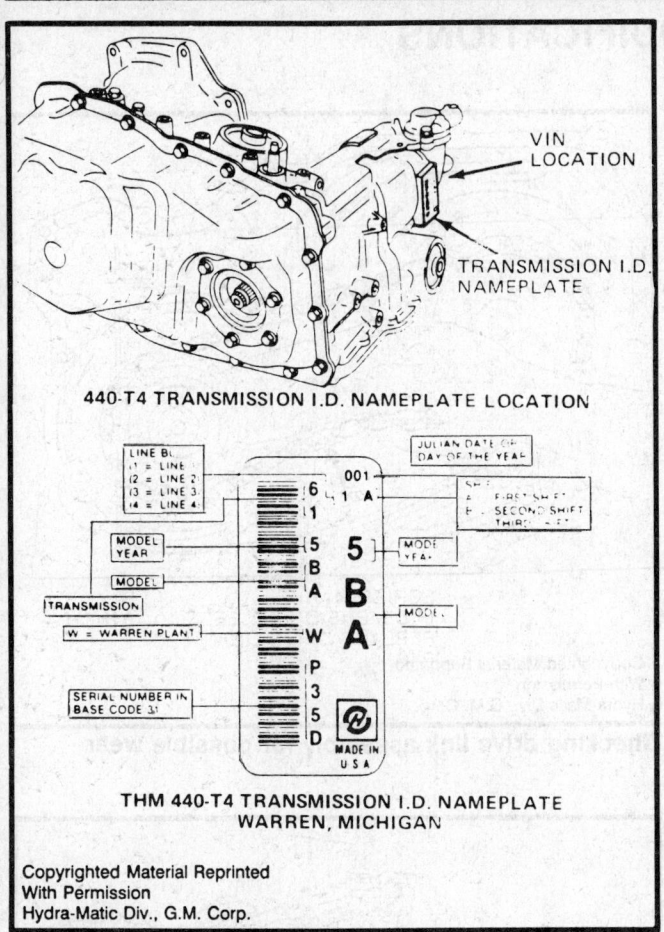

440-T4 TRANSMISSION I.D. NAMEPLATE LOCATION

THM 440-T4 TRANSMISSION I.D. NAMEPLATE WARREN, MICHIGAN

Transaxle I.D. nameplate

release the clutch when the vehicle is accelerating or decelerating at a certain rate.

4. Brake switch — Another switch switch used in the TCC circuit is a brake switch which opens the 12 volt supply to the TCC solenoid when the brake is depressed.

5. 2nd, 3rd and 4th gear switches — The 440-T4 uses 3rd and 4th gear switches which are direct inputs to the ECM. The ECM uses the switch signals for TCC engage and disengage points. The 440-T4 with torque management uses 2nd, 3rd and 4th gear switches which are direct inputs to the ECM. The ECM uses the switch signals for TCC engage and disengage points.

On Allante vehicles, the transaxle has a shift control system. The ECM controls the shift into 3rd gear by grounding the 2-3 shift solenoid circuit. To control the 4th gear shift, the ECM grounds the 3-4 solenoid circuit. The shift solenoids control the movement of the 2-3 and 3-4 shift valves by blocking or opening oil passages to move shift valves. When the shift selector is moved to the **D** position, line oil is directed to areas of the shift valve. When the solenoid is de-energized, line oil flows through the solenoid pressurizing chamber.

When the solenoid is energized by the ECM, the control chamber is allowed to exhaust through the solenoid. The solenoid simultaneously blocks line oil from entering the solenoid (so as

not to be constantly bleeding line pressure). The shift valve is moved to the upshift position by pressure. The 2-3 and 3-4 shift solenoids are controlled by the ECM for shift timing based upon other sensor input.

Metric Fasteners

The metric fastener dimensions are very close to the dimensions of the familiar inch system fasteners and for this reason, replacement fasteners must have the same measurement and strength as those removed.

Do not attempt to interchange metric fasteners for inch system fasteners. Mismatched or incorrect fasteners can result in damage to the transaxle unit through malfunctions, breakage or possible personal injury.

Care should be taken to re-use the fasteners in the same locations as removed.

Capacities

To refill the THM 440-T4 automatic transaxle after a complete overhaul, add 10 quarts of Dexron®II automatic transaxle fluid. To refill the 440-T4 automatic transaxle after the pan has been removed and replaced, add 6 quarts of Dexron®II automatic transaxle fluid. Recheck and correct the level after starting and warming the engine.

Checking Fluid Level

Transaxle Hot

1. Verify that the transaxle is at normal operating temperature. At this temperature, the end of the dipstick will be too hot to hold in the hand. Make sure that the vehicle is level.

2. With the selector in **P**, allow the engine to idle. Do not race engine. Move the selector through each range and back to **P**.

3. Immediately check the fluid level with the engine still running. Fluid level on the dipstick should be at the **FULL HOT** mark.

4. If the fluid level is low, add fluid as required, remembering that only 1 pint will bring the fluid level from **ADD** to **FULL**.

Transaxle Cold

Often it is necessary to check the fluid level when there is no time or opportunity to run the vehicle to warm the fluid to operating temperature. In this case, the fluid should be around room temperature (70°). The following Steps can be used.

1. Place the selector in **P** and start engine. Do not race engine. Move the selector through each range and back to **P**.

2. Immediately check the fluid level with the engine still running, off fast idle. Fluid level should be between the 2 dimples on the dipstick, approximately ¼ in. below the **ADD** mark on the dipstick.

3. If the fluid level is low, add fluid as required, to bring the fluid level to between the 2 dimples on the dipstick. Do not overfill. The reason for maintaining the low fluid level at room temperature is that the transaxle fluid level will rise as the unit heats up. If too much fluid is added when cold, then the fluid will rise to the point where it will be forced out of the vent and overheating can occur.

If the fluid level is correctly established at 70°F, it will appear at the **FULL** mark when the transaxle reaches operating temperature.

TRANSAXLE MODIFICATIONS

Transaxle Name Change

By September 1, 1991, Hydra-matic will have changed the name designation of the THM 440–T4 automatic transaxle. The new designation for this transaxle will be Hydra-matic 4L60. Transaxles built in 1989 and 1990 will serve as transitional years in which a dual system, made up of the old designation and the new designation will be in effect.

The name designation for the F-7 automatic transaxle will remain the same.

New Service Procedure for Checking Chain for Possible Wear

On all 1984 vehicles, when disassembling any THM 440–T4, it is important to inspect the drive link assembly (chain) for possible wear. Refer to the following service procedure:

1. Midway between the sprockets and at right angles to the chain, push the slack (bottom) strand of the chain down until finger tight and mark with crayon on opposite of teeth.
2. Push up in the same manner and put a 2nd mark, making sure that both marks are made from the same point on the chain.

NOTE: If the distance between the marks exceeds $1\frac{1}{16}$ in. (27.4mm), the chain must be replaced.

Service Information on the Input and Fourth Clutch Apply Plates

On all 1984 vehicles, when disassembling THM 440–T4 transaxles, the word **UP** may be noted on the 4th clutch apply plate and the input clutch apply plate. During reassembly of the transaxle, follow these instructions:

1. Position the side of the 4th clutch apply plate that has the word **UP** stamped on it, against the 4th clutch piston.
2. Position the side of the input clutch apply plate that has the word **UP** stamped on it (stepped side) against the 3rd clutch backing plate snapring.

Vacuum Related Shift Conditions

On all 1985 vehicles, this information is intended to assist the technician when diagnosing vacuum related shift problems. For proper operation, the THM 440–T4 requires 13–17 in. (44–57 kPa) Hg of engine vacuum at engine idle. A loss of engine vacuum can cause any of the following shift conditions:

Harsh park to reverse engagement
Harsh neutral to drive engagement
Harsh or firm light throttle upshifts
2nd speed stars
Harsh 3–2 coastdown shifts
Rough 4–3 and 2–3 manual downshifts
Slipping in drive or reverse

Low engine vacuum can be caused by a pinched, cut, plugged or disconnected vacuum line. It can also be the result of a poorly tuned engine or blocked exhaust. Also an incorrectly installed aspirator tee can give the appearance of low vacuum when the air conditioning is in operation. The aspirator tee has a "flag" with the words **MOD** and **MAN**. Make certain the modulator line is connected to the **MOD** nipple and the manifold line is connected to the **MAN** nipple as indicated by the arrows on the flag.

To check for proper vacuum, disconnect the vacuum line at

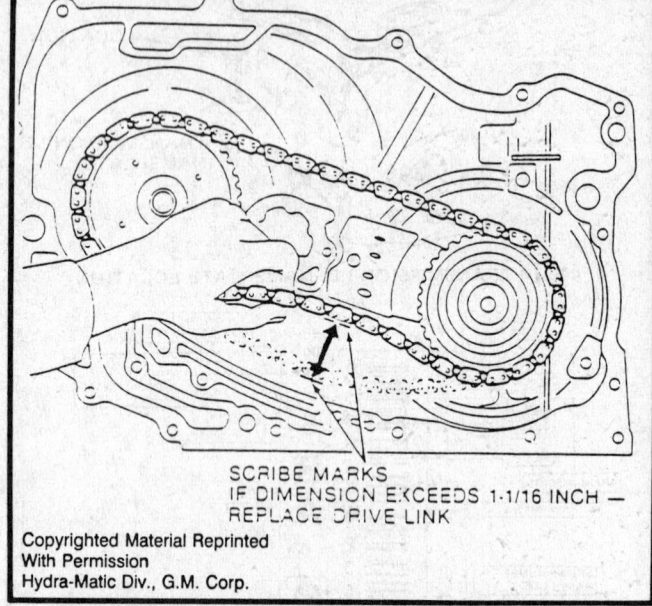

SCRIBE MARKS
IF DIMENSION EXCEEDS 1-1/16 INCH –
REPLACE DRIVE LINK

Checking drive link assembly for possible wear

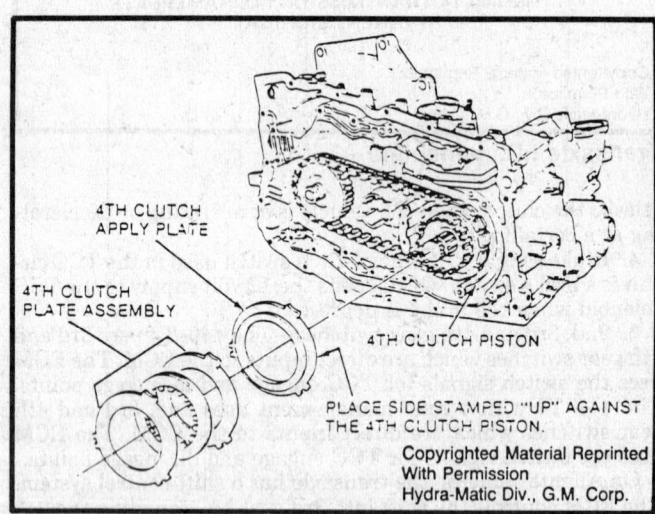

4TH CLUTCH APPLY PLATE

4TH CLUTCH PLATE ASSEMBLY

4TH CLUTCH PISTON

PLACE SIDE STAMPED "UP" AGAINST THE 4TH CLUTCH PISTON.

4th clutch assembly replacement

the modulator and install a vacuum gauge to the line. If there is insufficient vacuum locate the cause and correct as required.

If there is sufficient engine vacuum available to the modulator, remove the modulator assembly and modulator valve. Inspect the valve for nicks or scoring. Connect a hand operated vacuum device (vacuum pump) to the modulator. Pump the device until 15–20 in. (51–68 kPa) Hg of vacuum is reached; at the same time, observe the modulator plunger, it should be drawn in as the vacuum pump is operated. After reaching 15–20 in (51–68 kPa) Hg the vacuum should not bleed down for at least 30 seconds.

If the modulator is found to be functioning properly and the valve is not damaged, the shift problem is not vacuum related. At this time, attach an oil pressure gauge to the pressure tap.

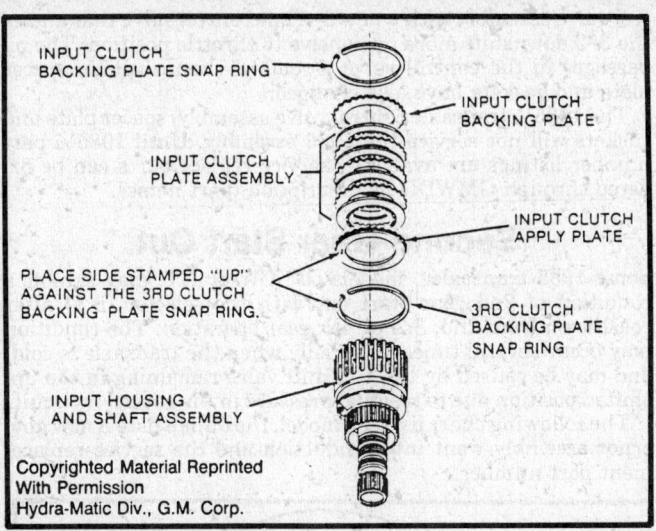

INPUT CLUTCH
BACKING PLATE SNAP RING

INPUT CLUTCH
BACKING PLATE

INPUT CLUTCH
PLATE ASSEMBLY

INPUT CLUTCH
APPLY PLATE

PLACE SIDE STAMPED "UP"
AGAINST THE 3RD CLUTCH
BACKING PLATE SNAP RING.

3RD CLUTCH
BACKING PLATE
SNAP RING

INPUT HOUSING
AND SHAFT ASSEMBLY

Copyrighted Material Reprinted
With Permission
Hydra-Matic Div., G.M. Corp.

Input clutch assembly

As a reminder, the T.V. does not control line pressure; it is used to control shift points (shift speed) only.

New Servo Spring Retainer Added

On all 1985 transaxles, models AY, BA and BS, to reduce the possibility of damage to the reverse servo seal during assembly, a servo spring retainer has been added. This retainer is identical to the one used for the 1–2 servo spring and the part number is 8656700.

Starting January 16, 1964 (Julian date, 016), all 1985 transaxles, models AY, BA and BS, were built with a new servo spring retainer.

The Julian date is on the transmission identification tag located on the side of the case by the governor.

Service Replacement Procedure for the Oil Pump Rotor, Slide and Vanes

On all 1984–85 vehicles, service parts are now available to service the oil pump rotor, slide and vanes in the pump body assembly on all THM 440–T4 transaxles. This service procedure on all THM 440–T4 transaxles must be followed to assure proper end clearance on the oil pump rotor and slide.

NOTE: Do not attempt to service the oil pump rotor, if either the pump body cover surfaces are scored. Servicing of the oil pump rotor, slides and vanes should be performed only if the selective pump rotor, slide or the vanes show wear.

1. Disassemble the oil pump.
2. Select the pump rotor, slide and vanes by the following:
   a. Use a micrometer to measure the original pump rotor, slide and vane thickness accurately. To obtain the most accurate reading, measure on flat, undamaged surfaces.
   b. Using the original part measurement, order replacement parts.
   c. Hone both sides of the replacement rotor, vanes and slide to remove any burrs and measure the replacement parts with a micrometer to assure proper selection. Incorrect rotor selection could result in a damaged oil pump assembly and/or low oil pressure. Incorrect slide could result in incorrect line pressure.

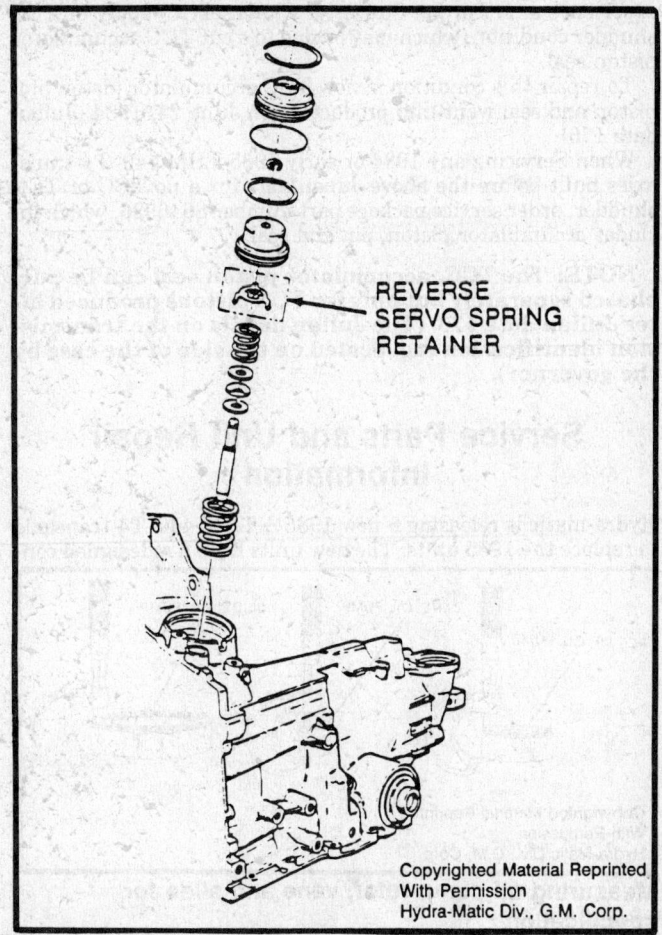

REVERSE
SERVO SPRING
RETAINER

Copyrighted Material Reprinted
With Permission
Hydra-Matic Div., G.M. Corp.

Reverse servo spring retainer

NOTE: The replacement part will provide the same clearance that the oil pump assembly was originally built with. The proper end clearance specification is 0.0025–0.0032 in. (0.0635–0.0813mm) for the rotor and vanes and 0.0013–0.0022 in. (0.0300–0.0559mm) for the slide.

Due to the factory selection of the oil seal ring, any field substitution of these parts will result in transaxle damage or could cause pump failure. These parts are serviceable only in the slide package.

The pump slide seal and the pump slide seal support can be serviced by ordering service package part number 8646916. These parts are not selective.

3. To assemble:
   a. Reassemble the oil pump assembly following.
   b. After assembling the oil pump, install the pump shaft and check for proper rotor and slide clearance by turning the pump shaft. The pump shaft should turn freely. If the pump shaft does not turn freely, recheck the pump rotor and slide selection.
   c. Install the transaxle into the vehicle.
   d. Before road testing the vehicle, install an oil pressure gauge to the transaxle and check oil pressure.

No Torque Converter Clutch (TCC) Apply or TCC Shudder

Some 1984 and some early 1985 THM 440–T4 transaxles may

experience a no Torque Converter Clutch (TCC) apply or TCC shudder condition, which may be due to a cut TCC accumulator piston seal.

To repair this condition, a new TCC accumulator piston pin, piston and seal went into production on June 24, 1984 (Julian date 176)

When Servicing any 1984 or early 1985 THM 440–T4 transaxles built before the above Julian date for a no TCC or TCC shudder, order service package part number 8646926, which includes accumulator piston, pin and seal.

NOTE: The TCC, accumulator piston seal can be purchased separately but only for TCC pistons produced after Julian date 176. (The Julian date is on the transmission identification tag located on the side of the case by the governor).

Service Parts and Unit Repair Information

Hydra-matic is releasing 8 new 1985½ THM 440–T4 transaxle to replace the 1985 units. The new units have a redesigned con-

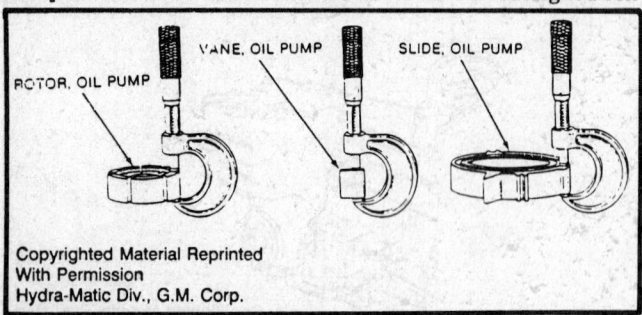

Measuring oil pump rotor, vane and slide for specification

trol valve assembly with a new 3–2 line control valve that makes the 3–2 downshift more responsive to throttle position. The oil passages in the control valve assembly, channel plate, spacer plate and gaskets have also changed.

The 1985½ transaxle control valve assembly, spacer plate and gaskets will not service the 1985 assembly. Until 1985½ part number listings are available, service replace parts can be ordered through GMWDD by description (part name).

Second Gear Start Out

Some 1985 transaxles, models CP, CW or HT, may exhibit a condition of 2nd gear start out with the selector in **D** after coastdown from 2nd, 3rd or 4th gear operation. The condition may occur several times (especially when the transaxle is cold) and may be caused by the 1–2 shift valve remaining in the upshifted position due to residual pressure in the governor circuit.

The following chart lists, by model, the Julian date a new governor assembly went into production and the service replacement part number.

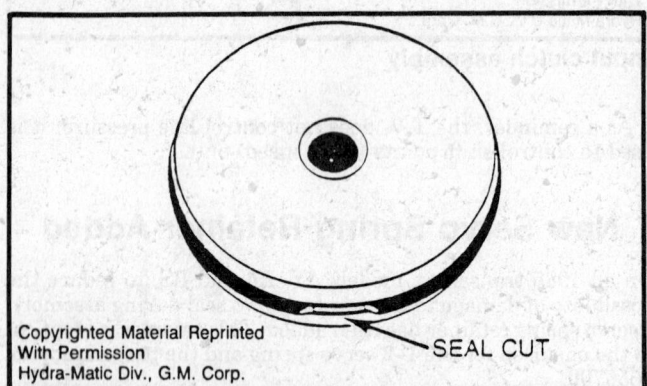

Torque converter clutch (TCC) accumulator piston and seal

PART SELECTION DATA

CHART A — Selective Pump Rotor

PART NUMBER	THICKNESS IN mm	THICKNESS IN INCHES
8656267	17.953 - 17.963	.7068 - .7072
8656268	17.963 - 17.973	.7072 - .7076
8656269	17.973 - 17.983	.7076 - .7080
8656270	17.983 - 17.993	.7080 - .7084
8656271	17.993 - 18.003	.7084 - .7088

CHART B — Selective Pump Slide, and Seals

PART NUMBER	THICKNESS IN mm	THICKNESS IN INCHES
8646911	17.983 - 17.993	.7080 - .7084
8646912	17.993 - 18.003	.7084 - .7088
8646913	18.003 - 18.013	.7088 - .7092
8646914	18.013 - 18.023	.7092 - .7096
8646915	18.023 - 18.033	.7096 - .7100

CHART C — Selective Pump Vane

PART NUMBER	THICKNESS IN mm	THICKNESS IN INCHES
8644661	17.943 - 17.961	.7064 - .7071
8644662	17.961 - 17.979	.7071 - .7078
8644663	17.979 - 17.997	.7078 - .7085

Model CP — Julian date 100 — service part number 8644961
Model CW — Julian date 81 — service part number 8644963
Model HT — Julian date 82 — service part number 8644963
To repair the 2nd gear start out on any 1985 THM 440–T4 model CP, CW, OR HT transaxle built before the listed Julian date, install the appropriate new governor assembly.

3–2 Downshift Bump

Some 1985 THM 440–T4 transaxle, models BA, BC, CM and CP may exhibit a 3–2 downshift bump. This condition may be most prevalent during a part-throttle downshift with the air conditioner operating. A slight transaxle tie-up condition which shakes or rattles the instrument panel during the downshift may also be experienced.

When servicing any 1985 transaxle, models CM and CP, for a 3–2 downshift bump, order and install service package part number 8646951.

Service package part number 8646951 contains a 3–2 control valve spring, a 1–2 servo boost valve and instruction sheet

When servicing any 1985 transaxle, models BA and BC for a 3–2 downshift bump, order and install service package part number 8646953.

Service package part number 8646593 contains a 3–2 control valve spring and instruction sheet.

Delayed Forward Engagement, Slips on Takeoff and/or 2–3 Upshift Bump or Shudder

A 1985 or 1986 THM 440–T4 transaxle may exhibit delayed forward engagement, slipping on take off from stops and/or a 2–3 upshift bump or shudder. The condition(s) may be caused by leakage in the 1–2 servo circuit, which controls apply and release of the 1–2 band.

Seals are included at both ends of the apply and release pipes and on the servo piston. A damaged seal in any position may affect operation of the servo. A leaking apply pipe circuit may cause delayed forward engagement and slipping on takeoff when in 1st or 2nd gear. A leak in the release pipe circuit may cause a 2–3 upshift bump or shudder. A 1–2 servo piston leak may cause any/all of the conditions(s).

When performing transaxle service, check transmission fluid for burned condition (burned fluid loses red color and has an acrid odor). Burned fluid may indicate major internal repair requirements.

If fluid condition is proper, inspect the servo pipe seals at both ends of each pipe and the 1–2 servo piston seals. The original pipes can be reused in field service. Replace any damaged seal when removing the seals, use care to ensure that damage to other transaxle components does not occur.

NOTE: When installing the servo pipes into the control valve assembly, it is critical that the pipes are correctly aligned with the assembly bore to ensure that seal damage does not occur.

Harsh Upshifts at High Altitudes

A 1985– A-body vehicles equipped with a 2.8L engine and a THM 440–T4 transaxle may exhibit harsh upshifts when operated at high altitudes. This condition may be caused by excessive line pressure resulting from insufficient engine vacuum.

A new vacuum modulator assembly and modulator valve have been released for service in a package, part number 8646956 for the harsh upshifts condition. The package consists of a transaxle vacuum modulator assembly, modulator valve, O-ring seal and instruction sheet

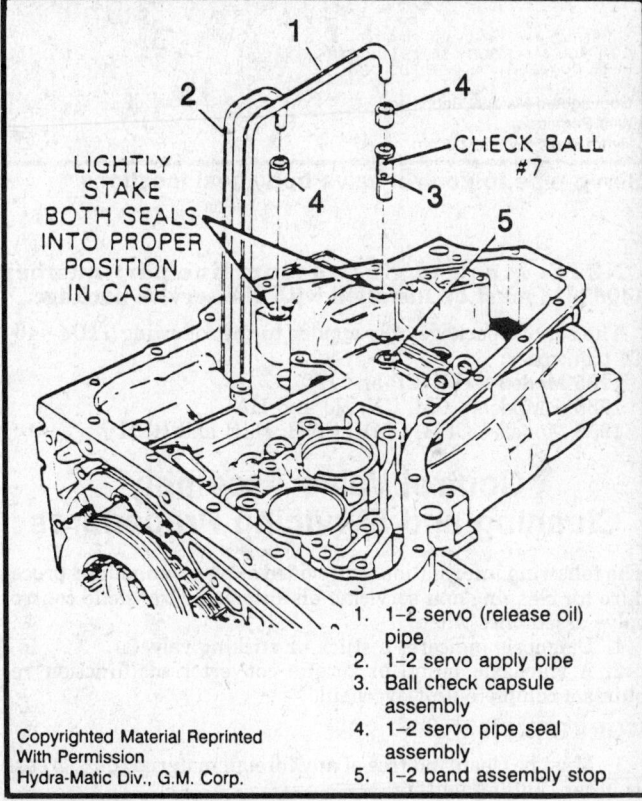

LIGHTLY STAKE BOTH SEALS INTO PROPER POSITION IN CASE.

CHECK BALL #7

1. 1–2 servo (release oil) pipe
2. 1–2 servo apply pipe
3. Ball check capsule assembly
4. 1–2 servo pipe seal assembly
5. 1–2 band assembly stop

Servo pipe to case seals

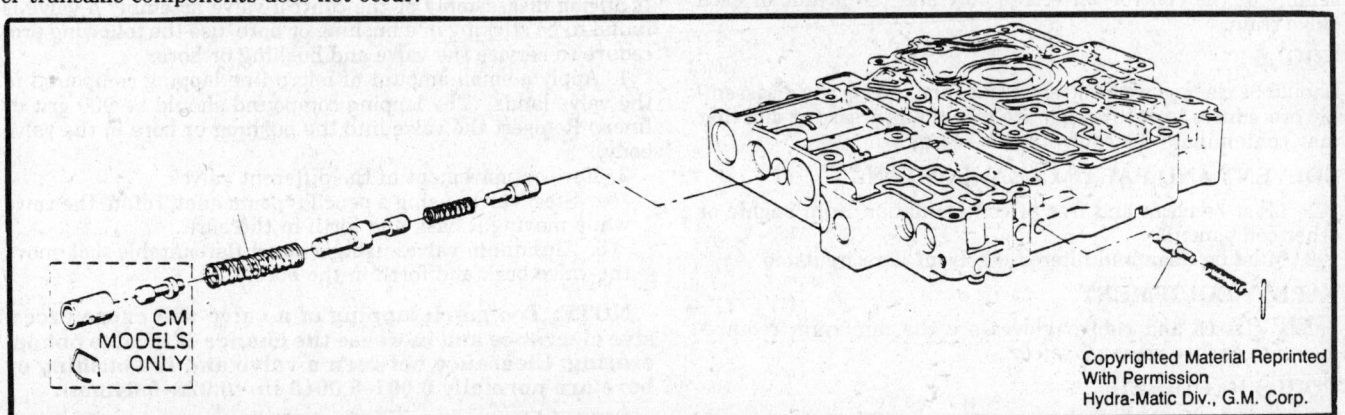

CM MODELS ONLY

3–2 control valve spring and 1–2 servo boost valve

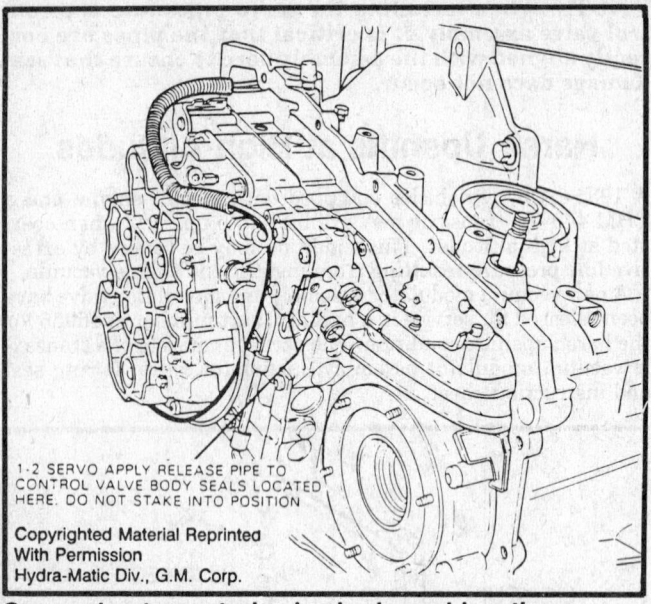

1-2 SERVO APPLY RELEASE PIPE TO CONTROL VALVE BODY SEALS LOCATED HERE. DO NOT STAKE INTO POSITION

Copyrighted Material Reprinted
With Permission
Hydra-Matic Div., G.M. Corp.

Servo pipe to control valve body seal locations

NOTE: A new engine vacuum line part number 14062624 must be installed with the service package.

The service package only applies to the following THM 440–T4 transaxles:

1985 Models – CW, CP and HT
1985½ Models – CM, CN, HJ and HA
1986 Models – CFH, CMH, CNH, HJH and HBH

Control Valve Assembly Cleaning and Servicing Procedures

The following information is provided as a recommended procedure for cleaning and servicing all automatic transaxle control valve assemblies when:

1. Diagnosis indicates a stuck or sticking valve(s).
2. A transaxle pump or torque converter malfunction requires a complete unit overhaul.

WORKBENCH

1. Must be clean and free of any foreign material (dirt, grease or other contaminants).
2. Work area should be large enough to allow for the disassembly of the control valve assembly and the layout of each valve train.

TOOLS

Should be cleaned with solvent before and during the disassembly procedures to ensure they are free of any grease or dirt that may contaminate the control valve assembly.

SOLVENT AND PARTS CLEANING TANK

1. Must be clean and free of contamination from engine or other components.
2. Must be clean and filtered if solvent is recirculated.

SAFETY EQUIPMENT

Safety glasses and rubber gloves are the minimum requirements to ensure personal safety.

TOOLS REQUIRED

a. Awl
b. Micro fine lapping compound

c. Pencil type magnet
d. Small flat blade screwdriver
e. Small non-abrasive parts cleaning brush
f. Tapered No. 49 drill bit

Cleaning and Disassembly

1. Remove the control valve assembly from the transaxle.
2. Inspect the attaching bolts and bolt holes. Remove metal chips or foreign material that may be present.
3. Place the control valve assembly in a clean tank and with clean solvent thoroughly wash the entire outer surfaces of the valve body.
4. Remove the control valve assembly from the solvent and dry it using compressed air.
5. Inspect the casting and fluid passages for foreign materials that may have accumulated in pockets. Remove the foreign material with a small suitable tool.
6. As necessary, repeat the washing and drying procedures as described in Steps 3 and 4 until all foreign materials are removed.
7. While applying a slight pressure with your finger against spring force in the valve train, remove the coiled spring pin, sleeve or clip that retains the valve train.
8. Slowly release pressure on the valve train and remove it from the valve body. A small suitable tool may be used to remove the bushing from the bore.
9. Place the valve train on a clean surface in the exact sequence as it was removed from the valve body. Follow the procedures in Steps 7, 8 and 9 to remove all valves and bushings from the valve body. (Layout of the valves, springs and bushings on a clean, lint free towel will help to keep parts organized).
10. Remove pressure switches, pipe plugs and TCC solenoid, if applicable.
11. Clean one valve train at a time by washing the valves, springs and bushings in clean solvent and drying with compressed air.
12. Clean the valve body casting with clean solvent and dry with compressed air.

Inspection of Control Valve Assembly Components

1. Inspect the valve body casting for cracks, porosity, damaged machined surfaces, nicks or burrs in valve bores and/or flatness of valve body to case mating surface (using a straight edge or by inspecting the gaskets for uniform compression).
2. Inspect valves for burrs, nicks, scratches and/or scoring.
3. Inspect valve bushings for porosity, burrs, nicks, scratches and/or scoring.
4. Inspect springs for damaged and/or distorted coils.

Stuck Valve Servicing

If during disassembly of the control valve assembly a valve is found to be sticking in a bushing or bore, use the following procedure to service the valve and bushing or bore:

1. Apply a small amount of micro fine lapping compound to the valve lands. (The lapping compound should be 900 grit or finer.) Reinsert the valve into the bushing or bore in the valve body).
2. For the movement of the different valves:
   a. Steel valves using a pencil type magnet, rotate the valve while moving it back and forth in the bore.
   b. Aluminum valves using a small flat suitable tool, move the valve back and forth in the bore.

NOTE: Too much lapping of a valve will cause excessive clearance and increase the chance of a valve not operating. Clearance between a valve and it's bushing or bore are normally 0.001–0.0015 in. (0.028–0.04mm).

3. After lapping a steel valve with a magnet, check for magnetism in the valve by holding it near some steel fillings or chips. If

the valve can pick up the fillings, de-magnetize it by using a de-magnetizing tool (different types are available at most tool stores).

4. Again check the valve for magnetism and if necessary, again, de-magnetize it. Repeat this procedure until the magnetism has been removed.

5. Thoroughly clean the valve and bushing (or bore in the valve body) with solvent and dry using compressed air.

6. Place the valve in its bushing (or bore in the valve body) and check for freeness of movement by rocking the bushing (or valve body) back and forth. The valve should travel freely in its bore. If the valve still tends to stick, repeat the lapping procedure.

NOTE: The use of a honing stone, fine sandpaper or crocus cloth is not recommended for servicing stuck valves. All valve lands have sharply machined corners that are necessary for cleaning the bore. If these corners are rounded, foreign material could wedge between the valve and bore causing the valve to stick.

Assembly

1. Make sure the valve body casting, valves and bushings are completely dry and free of cleaning solvent.

2. Lubricate all springs, valves and bushings with clean transmission fluid.

3. Reassemble the valve trains in the valve body casting and check for freedom of movement using a small suitable tool.

4. Install the control valve assembly into the transaxle.

5. Tighten the control valve assembly to case attaching bolts by starting from the center of the control valve assembly and moving outward.

NOTE: Control valve assembly to case attaching bolts must be hand torqued to the specifications. Improper torque can cause a control valve assembly to not operate properly.

Torque Converter Clutch (TCC)

A 1986 THM 440–T4 transaxle built before January 27, 1986 (Julian date 027) may exhibit a torque converter clutch apply shudder at 45–55 mph. The shudder condition may be caused by the torque converter. If the TCC apply shudder condition is exhibited, replace the torque converter with a service converter.

3rd Clutch Plates Parts Change

Third clutch plates in 1985, 2.8L Chevrolet applications of the THM 440–T4 changed to single-sided 3rd clutch plates. At the start of 1986 production, all THM 440–T4 transaxles were built with single-sided clutch plates. When servicing 3rd clutch plates on any transaxle, use the single-sided clutch plates. service package part number 8646938.

Input Shaft Seal Eliminated

All 1986 transaxles were built without an input shaft to 4th clutch shaft seal. When servicing a THM 440–T4 built prior to 1986, it is not necessary to replace the input shaft to 4th clutch shaft seal.

Converter Clutch Regulator Valve Spring Eliminated

At the start of 1986 production, the converter clutch regulator valve spring was eliminated on the following models of the THM 440–T4 transaxle: AAH, ACH, AFH, AMH, ARH, BHH, CFH, CHH, CMH, CNH, HBH and JHJ, due to recalibration and fluid

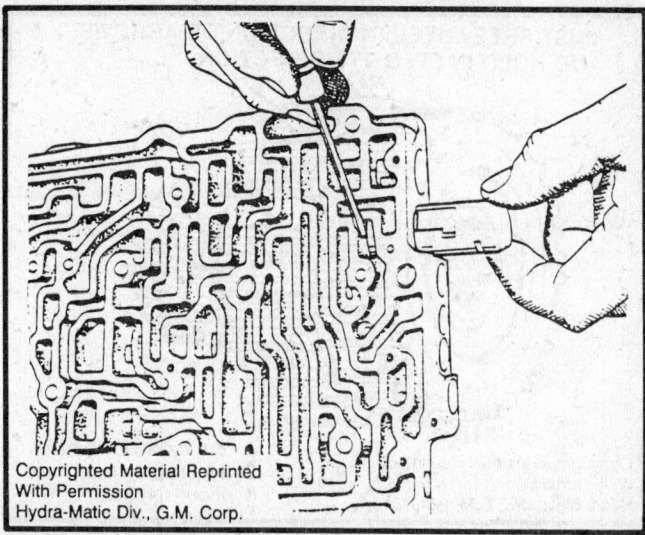

Copyrighted Material Reprinted With Permission Hydra-Matic Div., G.M. Corp.

Control valve removal

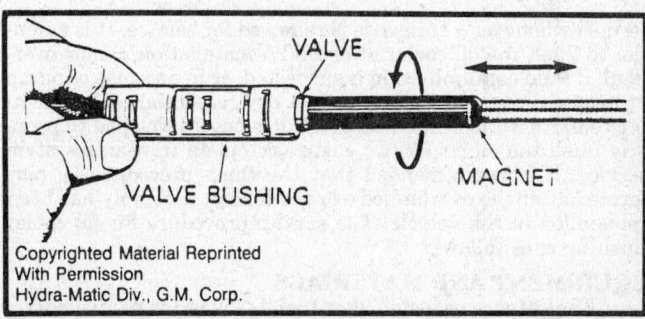

Copyrighted Material Reprinted With Permission Hydra-Matic Div., G.M. Corp.

Freeing a stuck steel type control valve with magnet

passage changes. Do not replace this spring on any listed model, as an increase of the apply feel of the transaxle converter clutch may result.

Loss of Drive and/or Reverse

Loss of drive and/or reverse on a 1984–1987 vehicles that have a THM 440–T4 transaxle with normal line pressures may be caused by the input sprag clutch assembly. This condition may be corrected by installing a new, wider input sprag clutch and related parts.

As of April 1, 1986 (Julian date 091), new input sprag clutch assembly used in later 1986 and all 1987 applications. This change is also on all Service Replacement Transmission Assemblys (SRTA) effective May 1, 1986 (Julian date 121).

Throttle Valve Lever Return Spring Eliminated

During 1985 transaxle production, the spring was removed from the throttle lever and bracket assembly to reduce throttle pedal effort. This change is also on all Service Replacement Transmission Assembly (SRTA) transaxles.

Do not install a throttle valve lever return spring on any THM 440–T4 that does not have one. When servicing a THM 440–T4, the spring can be eliminated on any 1984–85 transaxle to reduce throttle pedal effort.

Oil Cooler Flushing Procedure

On all transaxles, transmission oil cooler flushing must be per-

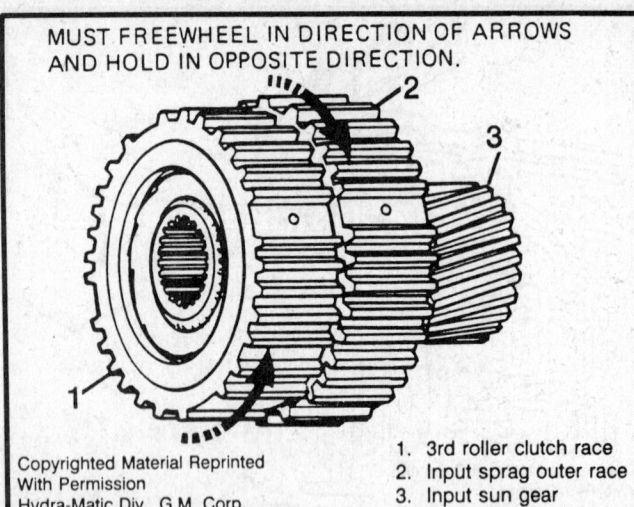

MUST FREEWHEEL IN DIRECTION OF ARROWS AND HOLD IN OPPOSITE DIRECTION.

Copyrighted Material Reprinted
With Permission
Hydra-Matic Div., G.M. Corp.

1. 3rd roller clutch race
2. Input sprag outer race
3. Input sun gear

Checking the input sprag clutch assembly for proper operation

formed whenever a transaxle is removed for service. It is essential to flush the oil cooler after SRTA installation, major overhaul, if fluid contamination is suspected, or in any case of pump or torque converter replacement. A new, essential cooler flushing tool, Kent Moore tool J–35944, has been developed to properly flush the oil cooler. To ensure complete transaxle system service, it is recommended that the flush procedure be performed after the overhauled or replacement assembly has been reinstalled in the vehicle. The service procedure for oil cooler flushing is as follows:

EQUIPMENT AND MATERIALS
a. Kent Moore cooler flusher tool J–35944 (or equivalent)
b. Biodegradable flushing solution (Available by the gallon, J–35944–20, or case, J–35944–CSE)
c. Measuring cup (supplied with tool)
d. Funnel
e. Water supply (hot water recommended in all cases if available)
f. Water hose (at least ⅝ in. diameter)
g. Air supply (with water and oil filter)
h. Air chuck (with clip if available)
i. Air pressure gauge
j. Oil drain container
k. Five gallon pail (or larger with a lid)
l. Eye protection
m. Rubber gloves

Procedure
1. After overhaul or service replacement transaxle is reinstalled in vehicle, do not reconnect oil cooler pipes.
2. Remove fill cap on tool and fill can with 0.6 liter (20–21 oz.) of Kent Moore biodegradable flushing solution. Do not overfill or tool will need to be recharged with air before backflush. Follow manufacturer's suggested procedures for proper handling of solution.

— CAUTION —

Do not substitute with any other solution. The flushing tool is designed to use only this concentrate. Use of any other solution can result in damage to the tool, cooler components, or improper flushing of the cooler.

3. Secure fill cap and pressurize the flusher can with shop air to 80–100 psi (550–700 kPa).

— CAUTION —

Shop air supply must be equipped with a water/oil filter and not exceed 120 psi (825 kPa).

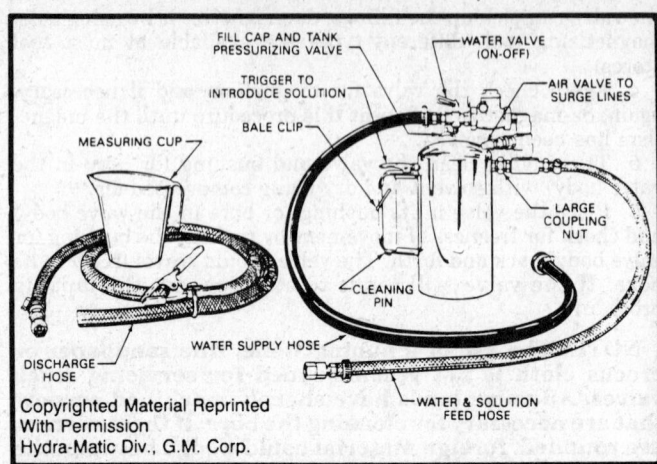

FILL CAP AND TANK PRESSURIZING VALVE
WATER VALVE (ON-OFF)
TRIGGER TO INTRODUCE SOLUTION
AIR VALVE TO SURGE LINES
MEASURING CUP
BALE CLIP
LARGE COUPLING NUT
CLEANING PIN
DISCHARGE HOSE
WATER SUPPLY HOSE
WATER & SOLUTION FEED HOSE

Copyrighted Material Reprinted
With Permission
Hydra-Matic Div., G.M. Corp.

Equipment recommended for oil cooler flushing procedure

4. Connect the discharge hose to the transaxle end of the oil pipe that goes to the top fitting at the radiator.
5. Clip discharge hose onto the oil drain container.
6. Mount the flushing tool to undercarriage of vehicle with the hook provided and connect the hose from the flushing tool to the remaining oil cooler pipe.
7. With the water valve on the tool in the **OFF** position, connect the water hose from the water supply to the tool.
8. Turn **ON** the water supply at the faucet.
9. Initial flush—switch the water valve on the tool to the **ON** position and allow the water to flow through the oil cooler for 10 seconds to remove the supply of transaxle fluid in the system.

— CAUTION —

If water does not flow through the oil cooler (system is completely plugged) do not continue flushing procedure. Turn the water off immediately and inspect the pipes and cooler for restriction. Replace the oil pipe(s) and/or cooler.

10. Switch the water valve on the tool to the **OFF** position and clip the discharge hose onto a five gallon pail with a lid or position a shop towel over the end of the discharge hose to prevent splash. Discharge will foam vigorously when solution is introduced into water stream.
11. Switch the water valve on the tool to the **ON** position and depress the trigger to mix flushing solution into the water flow. Use the bale clip provided on the handle to hold the trigger down.
12. Flush oil cooler with water and solution for 2 minutes. During this flush, attach the air supply to the air valve located on plumbing of tool for 3–5 seconds at the end of every 15–20 second interval to create a surging action.

— CAUTION —

Shop air supply must be equipped with a water/oil filter and not exceed 120 psi (825 kPa).

13. Release the trigger and switch the water valve on the tool to the **OFF** position.
14. Disconnect both hoses from the oil cooler pipes.
15. Backflush—connect hoses to the oil cooler pipes opposite from the initial flush procedures to perform a backflush.
16. Repeat Steps 11 and 12.
17. Release the trigger and allow water only to rinse the oil cooler for one minute.
18. Switch the water valve on the tool to the **OFF** position and turn the water supply **OFF** at the faucet.
19. Attach air supply to the air valve located on plumbing of tool and dry the system out with air for at least 2 minutes, or

longer if moisture is visible exiting from the oil cooler line discharge hose. Use an air chuck clip, if available, to secure the air chuck onto the air valve for ease of operation.

NOTE: Excessive residual moisture can cause corrosion in the oil cooler or cooler pipes and can damage the transaxle. If Steps 20–23 cannot be completed at this time, rinse the oil cooler and cooler pipes with transaxle fluid. Complete Steps 20–23 after reinstallation of transaxle.

20. Connect the cooler feed pipe to the transaxle.
21. If not already connected, attach the discharge hose to the cooler return pipe and place into an appropriate drain container.
22. After filling the transaxle with automatic transaxle fluid, start the engine and run for 30 seconds. This will remove any residual moisture from the oil cooler and cooler pipes, protect all components from corrosion and check flow rate through the cooler. A minimum of 2 quarts must be obtained during this 30 second run. If fluid flow is insufficient, check the fluid flow out of the transaxle by disconnecting the oil cooler feed line at the radiator and restarting the engine. Do the following according to flow rate:
   a. Insufficient feed flow – inspect the transaxle for cause.
   b. Sufficient feed flow – inspect oil cooler pipes and fittings for restrictions or leaks and repeat the oil cooler flushing procedure. Repeat the check of fluid flow out the return line and if flow is still inhibited, replace the oil cooler.
23. Remove discharge hose, reconnect cooler return pipe to transaxle and refill unit to proper fluid level. Vertical (top) connector is cooler feed, horizontal (bottom) connector is cooler return.
24. Disconnect the water supply hose from the tool.
25. Bleed air pressure from the can, remove fill cap, return any unused solution to container and rinse the can out with water. Do not store tool with solution in tank.
26. Every 3rd tool cleaning, use loosen large coupling nut and remove plumbing from tank.
27. Remove screen from plumbing and wash with water.
28. Use the cleaning pin to remove any material in the solution orifice. Orifice is located in plumbing below screen.
29. Reconnect the plumbing and fill can half full with water, secure the fill cap and pressurize the can to 80–100 psi (550–700 kPa).
30. Aim tool into the 5 gallon pail or floor drain and depress the trigger to allow water from the can to flow through the solution orifice for 30 seconds to ensure proper cleaning.
31. Bleed air pressure from can, remove the fill cap and empty the can.
32. Reconnect fill cap flushing tool.

Long and/or Delayed 2–3 Shift

A long and/or delayed 2–3 shift on a THM 440-T4 transaxle may be caused by a leaking 3rd clutch inner seal.

As of February 12, 1987 (Julian date 043), the effected parts are a new 3rd clutch piston inner seal, input housing and shaft assembly and 3rd clutch roller assembly. This change is also on all Service Replacement Transmission Assembly (SRTA) transaxles effective November 15, 1986 (Julian date 319).

Remove the transaxle, disassemble, inspect and replace with parts included in the service package part number 8646991, which include an input housing and shaft assembly, 3rd clutch piston inner seal and a complete 3rd clutch roller assembly.

Harsh Shift Conditions and On Vehicle Service Information

NOTE: Before performing any service action, make sure to diagnose the specific shift condition and altitude that affects vehicle performance. Do not assume that every condition listed applies to the vehicle.

Harsh shift conditions and the specific service information that applies to each of these conditions. However, some other items that affect transaxle operation which may also contribute to these harsh shift conditions are:
   a. Vacuum leaks (low vacuum supply to the vacuum modulator) – 13–18 in. Hg required
   b. Paint in the modulator tube restricting vacuum to the modulator causing a delayed response to throttle movement
   c. Sticking modulator valve
   d. Sticking 1–2 servo valve
   e. Missing check balls (No. 2, No. 4, or No. 12)

Very Harsh Part Throttle 3–2 Shift at 20–40 mph

On all 1985–87 transaxles, a very harsh part throttle 3–2 shift at 20–40 mph may be caused by a missing or mislocated No. 2 control 3–2 check ball. Remove the valve body to inspect for proper check ball location or damage to the spacer plate. A mislocated check ball may have bent the spacer plate. Also inspect the No. 12 check ball (1–2 servo feed check ball) to ensure it is seating properly.

Harsh 3–2 and/or 4–2 Shifts

On all 1985–87 transaxles, harsh 3–2 and 4–2 shifts at any altitude may be caused by a missing or partial hole in the spacer plate. Remove the valve body and inspect the spacer plate for a missing or partial governor passage hole (No. 25). A partial hole can be drilled out using a No. 77 drill bit to meet the hole size requirement of 0.018 in. (0.46mm). If the hole is missing, use the spacer plate gasket and control valve body as a guide to locate and drill the hole, or replace the spacer plate.

Intermittent Harsh Part Throttle 3–2 Shift

On all 1985½ transaxles except transaxles with 2.8L or 3.0L engines and all 1986 transaxles except units with 2.8L or 3.0L engines and transaxles built prior to 7/21/87 (Julian date 202), an intermittent harsh 3–2 shift may be caused by a broken 3–2 line control retainer. Remove the transaxle side cover to access the 3–2 line control valve and, if necessary, replace a broken retainer. Also ensure that the 3–2 line control valve moves freely in its bore. Use service package part number 8658678.

Harsh 3–2 Shift (High Altitude Only)

On all 1985–87 vehicles except Seville and 1986 Seville, a harsh 3–2 shift condition at high altitude may be corrected by installing the appropriate service package that contains the following items:
   a. 3–2 Control valve spring
   b. Spacer plate gaskets
   c. Instruction sheet
   Before installing a Service Replacement Transaxle Assembly (SRTA) in areas designated as "high altitude," install the new 3–2 control valve spring.
   Also ensure that the 3–2 control valve and the 1–2 servo control valve move freely in their bores.

Harsh 3–2 Shift (At Low Altitude)

On all 1986 vehicles with 2.8L, 3.0L and 3.8L engines and all 1987 vehicles with 3.8L engines, a harsh 3–2 shift at low altitude may be corrected by installing a service package that contains:
   a. 3–2 control valve spring
   b. Spacer plate gaskets
   c. Instruction sheet
   When servicing a transaxle for this condition, also ensure that the 3–2 control valve and 1–2 servo control valve move freely in their bores.

Harsh 3–2 Shift Maneuver At 17–20 mph

On all 1985½ vehicles except Seville and 1986 Seville, a 3–2

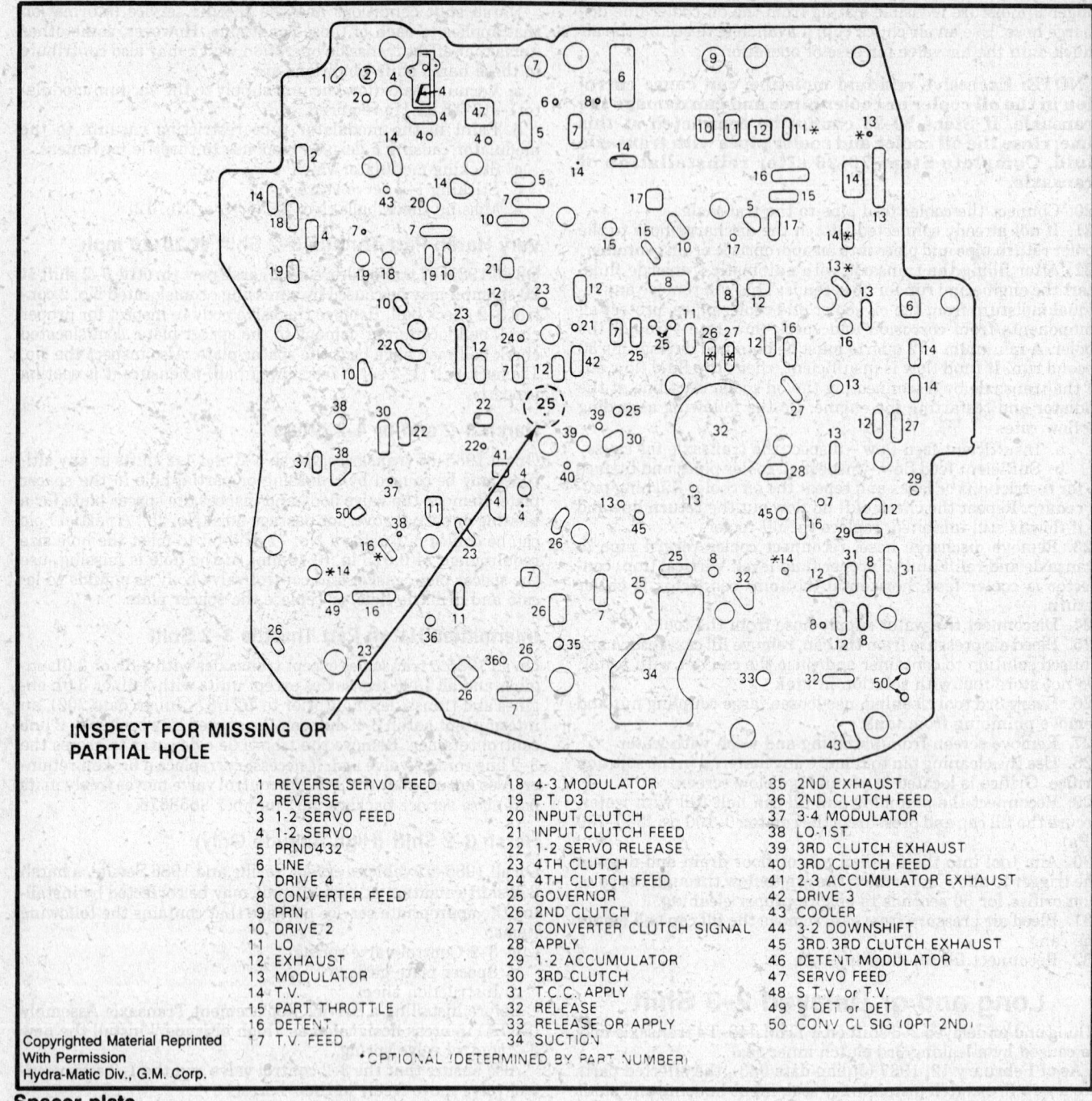

INSPECT FOR MISSING OR PARTIAL HOLE

1 REVERSE SERVO FEED	18 4-3 MODULATOR	35 2ND EXHAUST
2 REVERSE	19 P.T. D3	36 2ND CLUTCH FEED
3 1-2 SERVO FEED	20 INPUT CLUTCH	37 3-4 MODULATOR
4 1-2 SERVO	21 INPUT CLUTCH FEED	38 LO-1ST
5 PRND432	22 1-2 SERVO RELEASE	39 3RD CLUTCH EXHAUST
6 LINE	23 4TH CLUTCH	40 3RD CLUTCH FEED
7 DRIVE 4	24 4TH CLUTCH FEED	41 2-3 ACCUMULATOR EXHAUST
8 CONVERTER FEED	25 GOVERNOR	42 DRIVE 3
9 PRN	26 2ND CLUTCH	43 COOLER
10 DRIVE 2	27 CONVERTER CLUTCH SIGNAL	44 3-2 DOWNSHIFT
11 LO	28 APPLY	45 3RD 3RD CLUTCH EXHAUST
12 EXHAUST	29 1-2 ACCUMULATOR	46 DETENT MODULATOR
13 MODULATOR	30 3RD CLUTCH	47 SERVO FEED
14 T.V.	31 T.C.C. APPLY	48 S.T.V. or T.V.
15 PART THROTTLE	32 RELEASE	49 S DET or DET
16 DETENT	33 RELEASE OR APPLY	50 CONV CL SIG (OPT 2ND)
17 T.V. FEED	34 SUCTION	

* OPTIONAL (DETERMINED BY PART NUMBER)

Spacer plate

Shift maneuver is obtained by allowing the vehicle to coastdown to 17–20 mph (with closed throttle) and then stepping into the throttle to obtain a 3–2 shift.

At start of production 1987, an orifice pipe was added between the 1-2 servo release cover plate and the 3-2 coastdown valve to allow a smoother 2nd gear apply. The 4 new parts installed as a set will service certain past transaxles with a harsh 3-2 shift maneuver condition.

If the new pump body assembly has a "1 terminal" 3rd clutch switch, remove it and replace with the "2 terminal" 3rd clutch switch from the original pump body assembly.

When servicing a transaxle for the above described condition in designated high altitude areas, also install the 3-2 control valve spring package.

Also ensure that the 3-2 control valve and 1-2 servo control valve move freely in their bores.

Harsh 3–2 Coastdown Bump 3.8L at 20–40 mph

On all 1985–87 vehicles with transaxles built prior to december 18,1986 (Julian date 352) and 3.8L engines, a harsh 3–2 coastdown bump may be caused by the 1-2 servo cushion

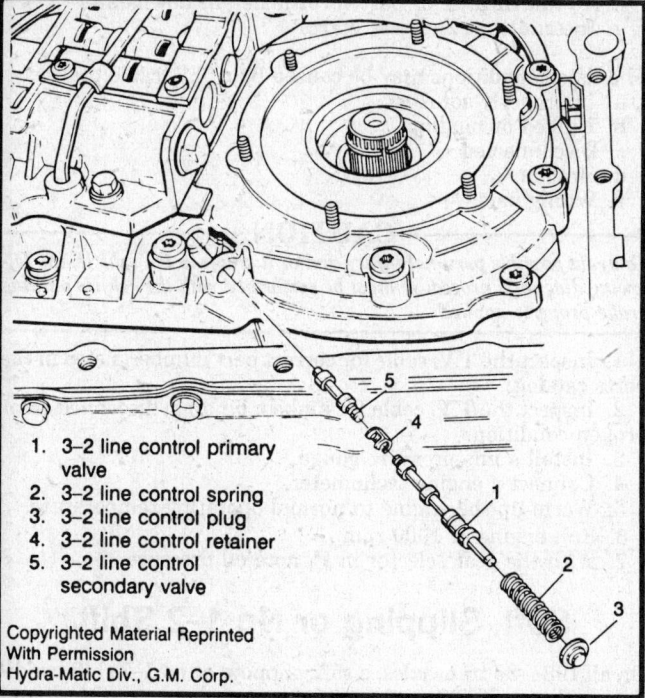

1. 3-2 line control primary valve
2. 3-2 line control spring
3. 3-2 line control plug
4. 3-2 line control retainer
5. 3-2 line control secondary valve

3-2 line control valve assembly

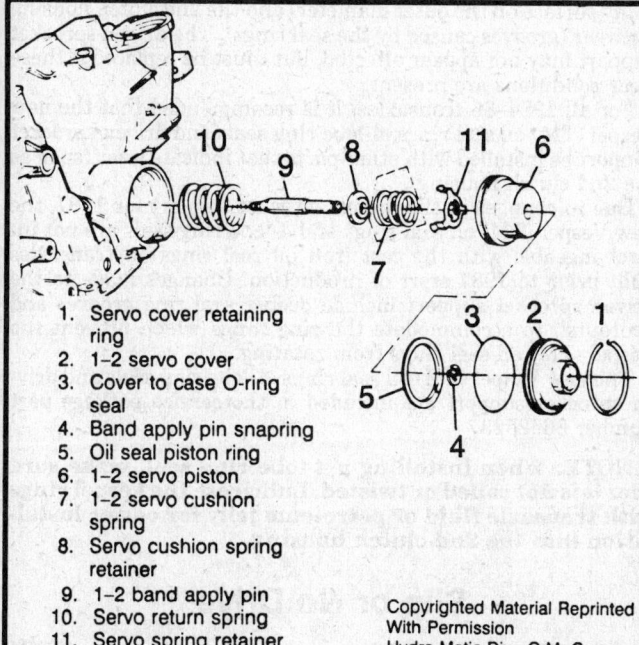

1. Servo cover retaining ring
2. 1-2 servo cover
3. Cover to case O-ring seal
4. Band apply pin snapring
5. Oil seal piston ring
6. 1-2 servo piston
7. 1-2 servo cushion spring
8. Servo cushion spring retainer
9. 1-2 band apply pin
10. Servo return spring
11. Servo spring retainer

1-2 servo assembly

spring. This condition may be corrected by replacing the 1-2 servo cushion spring. Use service package part number 8646457.

If the above condition persists, make sure the 3-2 coastdown valve (located in the oil pump body) is not stuck and moves freely in its bore.

Harsh Upshifts (High Altitude Only)

On all 1985–86 A-body vehicles equipped with 2.8L engine, 1985–87 Cadillac C and E-body vehicles with 4.1L engine and 1986 Cadillac K-body vehicles with 4.1 engine, harsh upshifts at high altitudes may be caused by high lie pressure due to low engine vacuum. This condition may be corrected on certain transaxles, by installing the appropriate aneroid modulator service package.

Transaxle model identification 6CFH, 6CMH, 6CNH, 6HBH, 6HJH – service package number 8646956

Transaxle model identification 5CM, 5CN, 5CP, 5CW, 5HA, 5HJ, 5HT – service package number 8646956

Transaxle model identification 6AAH, 6ACH, 6AFH, 6AMH – service package number 8646966

Transaxle model identification 5AF, 5AM – service package number 8646966

Transaxle model identification 6ADH, 6ARH – service package number 8646967

A new vacuum line from the engine to the vacuum modulator must also be installed when using the service packages.

A-Body Vehicles – part number 14062624
C-Body Vehicles – part number 1637147
E/K-Body Vehicles – part number 1641441

Intermittent or Complete Loss of Drive and Reverse

Intermittent or complete loss of drive and reverse on a 1984–86 vehicle equipped with a THM 440–T4 transaxle having normal line pressures may be caused by the input sprag clutch assembly. This condition may be corrected by installing a new (wider) input sprag clutch assembly and related parts.

As of April 1, 1986 (Julian date 091), all 1986 THM 440–T4 transaxles were built using a new input sprag clutch assembly. Effective May 1, 1986 (Julian date 121), all Service Replacement Transmission Assembly (SRTA) transaxles were built using the new input sprag clutch assembly.

1. Remove the transaxle from the vehicle and disassemble it to the point of removing the input sprag clutch assembly. Complete disassembly of the transaxle is not always necessary.

2. Bench check the operation of the sprag and 3rd roller clutch assembly.

3. Inspect the input sprag clutch assembly for mispositioned sprag elements and broken ribbon tabs (between the sprag elements).

4. Disassemble the input sprag clutch assembly and inspect for cracked inner or outer races and indentation marks on the inner race that would indicate sprag element "rollover".

5. Replace the input sprag clutch assembly if any of the conditions described above are present. Use the appropriate service part(s).

a. When replacing the input sprag clutch assembly on a transaxle built before April 1, 1986 (Julian date 091), use service part number 8646986.

b. When replacing the input sprag clutch assembly on a transaxle built on or after April 1, 1986 (Julian date 091), use service part number 8646985.

c. To update a transaxle built before April 1, 1986 (Julian date 0901) or a SRTA transaxle built before May 1, 1986 (Julian date 121), to use the new (wider) input sprag clutch assembly, the transaxle must contain part number 8658368 (lube dam), part number 8658407 (final drive sun shaft) and part number 8658408 (output shaft).

NOTE: These 3 correct design parts must be installed for proper lubrication of the 3rd roller clutch and new design sprag assemblies. After these parts have been assembled into the unit, the new input sprag clutch assembly and input carrier assembly, contained in the service package part number 8662906, may be used.

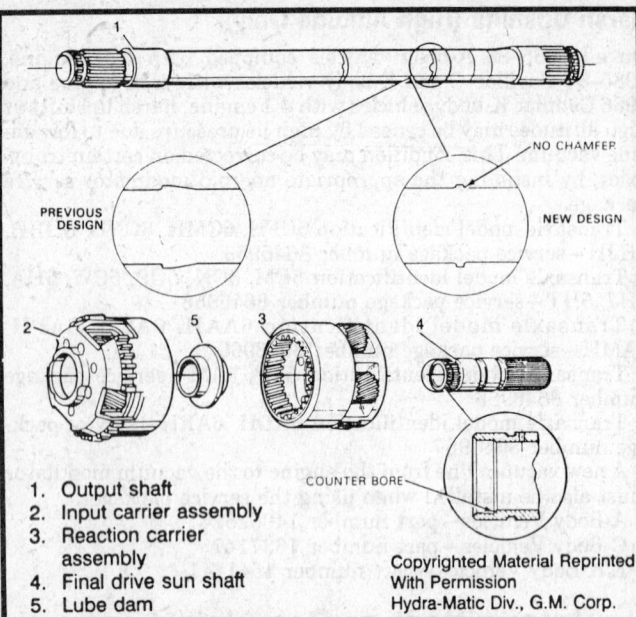

1. Output shaft
2. Input carrier assembly
3. Reaction carrier assembly
4. Final drive sun shaft
5. Lube dam

Copyrighted Material Reprinted With Permission Hydra-Matic Div., G.M. Corp.

Lube dam with associated part changes

Throttle Valve Conditions and Diagnosis

On all transaxles the throttle valve (T.V.) pressure controls the shift pattern and the amount of hydraulic line pressure used to apply clutches and bands.

NOTE: T.V. cable controls shift timing, not shift feel — line pressure is not directly affected by the T.V. cable setting.

If proper line pressure is not available, excess slippage may occur during the shift. If the T.V. cable is tailored in an effort to modify shift pattern/feel, this misadjustment can result in transaxle failure.

NOTE: Do not attempt to correct a condition by changing the T.V. cable setting from its proper adjustment. Apparent improvements from T.V. cable "tailoring" indicate a need for further diagnosis into the real cause of a condition (such as engine performance, the control valve, governor or servo assemblies, etc.).

Technicians and customers should know that certain types of heavy duty or high performance vehicles have transaxles calibrated to provide crisp, firm shifts for durability/performance. Once again, the T.V. cable must not be tailored in an effort to modify shift pattern/feel on these applications.

NOTE: Make sure engine fuel, electrical and mechanical systems are performing properly before attempting transaxle diagnosis. For example, a fouled fuel injector, cracked spark plug, damaged spark plug wire or vacuum leak can affect transaxle performance.

The T.V. system may cause one or more of the following conditions:
  a. Delayed or harsh upshifts
  b. Early and slipping upshifts
  c. No upshifts
  d. Chatters on take off
  e. 1-2 shift at full throttle only

  f. No full throttle or part throttle detent downshifts
  g. Intermittent 2nd gear starts

The listed conditions may be caused by a T.V. cable that is:
  a. Improperly adjusted
  b. Kinked or binding
  c. Disconnected
  d. Broken
  e. Wrong part

CAUTION

To avoid possible personal injury and/or damage to the vehicle, the following diagnosis procedure must be performed with the vehicle parking brake properly applied.

---

1. Inspect the T.V. cable for correct part number, listed in the parts catalog.
2. Inspect the T.V. cable for kinked, binding, disconnected or broken condition.
3. Install a line pressure gauge.
4. Connect a engine tachometer.
5. Warm up the engine to normal operating temperature.
6. Run engine at 1000 rpm.
7. With the gear selector in **P**, note oil pressure.

Soft, Slipping or No 1-2 Shift

On all 1984-86 transaxles, a soft, slipping or no 1-2 shift condition may result if the 2 cast iron seals between the driven sprocket support and 2nd clutch housing bind to the driven sprocket support and wear into the 2nd clutch housing.

Inspect the cast iron oil seal rings for wear (indicated by a shiny surface on the outer diameter) and the 2nd clutch housing for wear (grooves caused by the seal rings). The driven sprocket support may not appear affected, but must be replaced if these wear conditions are present.

For all 1984-86 transaxles, it is recommended that the new Vespel (TM) oil seal rings, 4-lobe ring seals and driven sprocket support be installed with other parts that indicate wear (such as the 2nd clutch housing).

Due to changes in the driven sprocket support for 1987, the new Vespel (TM) oil seal rings and 4-lobe ring seals are not interchangeable with the cast iron oil seal rings on transaxles built prior to 1987 start of production. Changes made to the driven sprocket support include deeper seal ring grooves and "cutouts" to accommodate the ring tangs which prevent the Vespel (TM) oil seal rings from rotating.

The new Vespel (TM) oil seal rings, 4-lobe ring seals and driven sprocket support are included in the service package part number 8662523.

NOTE: When installing a 4-lobe ring seal, make sure that it is not rolled or twisted. Lubricate the vespel rings with transaxle fluid or petroleum jelly for easier installation into the 2nd clutch housing.

Slip or No Drive

On all 1987 transaxles, a slip or no drive condition on a THM 440-T4 transaxle may be caused by low line pressure due to the pump slide binding on excessive casting flash when the slide is in the low pressure position. Modulator vacuum will not affect line pressures if this condition is present. This condition can be repaired by replacing the oil pump assembly.

THM 440-T4 transaxles built between November 26, 1986 (Julian date 330) and January 12, 1987 (Julian date 012) may exhibit this condition.

Remove the oil pump cover and pump priming springs and move the slide by hand. If excessive flash is present, the slide will bind.

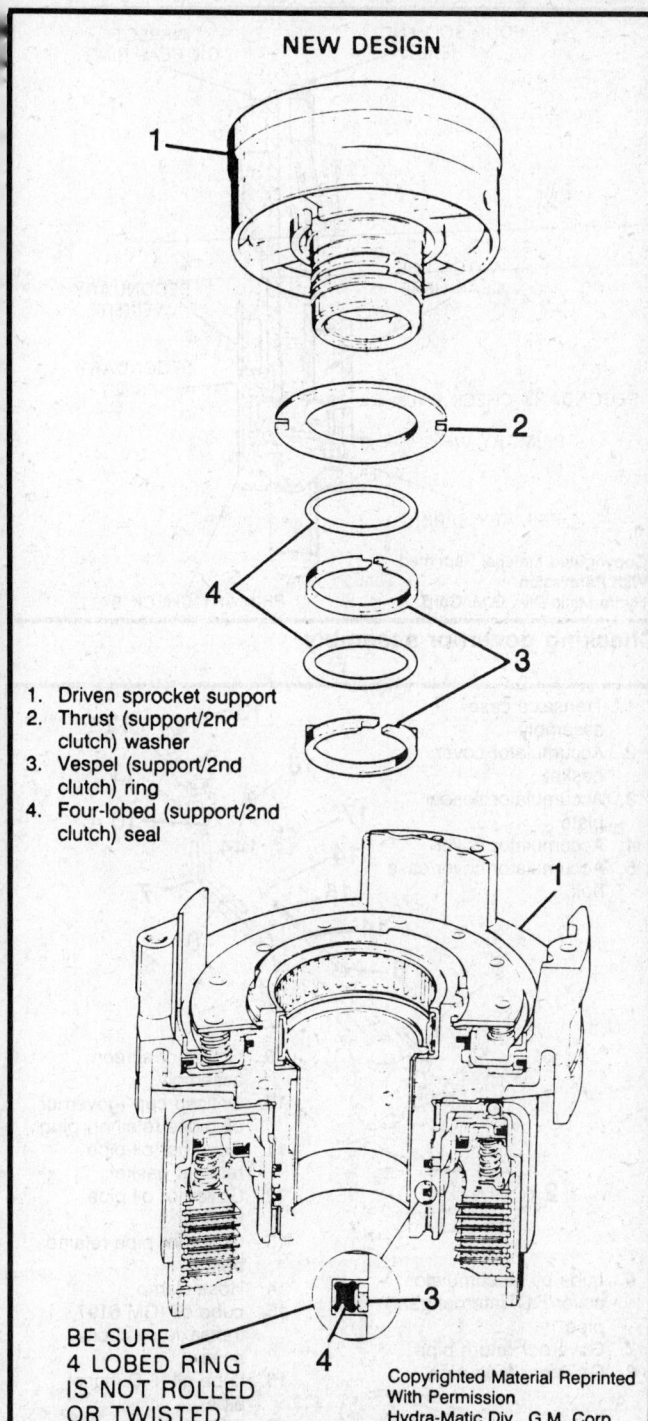

NEW DESIGN

1. Driven sprocket support
2. Thrust (support/2nd clutch) washer
3. Vespel (support/2nd clutch) ring
4. Four-lobed (support/2nd clutch) seal

BE SURE 4 LOBED RING IS NOT ROLLED OR TWISTED

Copyrighted Material Reprinted With Permission Hydra-Matic Div., G.M. Corp.

Redesigned driven sprocket support

Harsh Shifts

Harsh shifts in a 1987 2.8L fuel injected Pontiac 6000 or Pontiac 6000 LE may be caused by the installation of a 7CBH model transaxle (instead of a 7CAH model transaxle) at the vehicle assembly plant.

1987 vehicles built prior to December 1, 1986 may be equipped with a 7CBH transaxle which is calibrated for firmer shifts and used in the SE and STE models only.

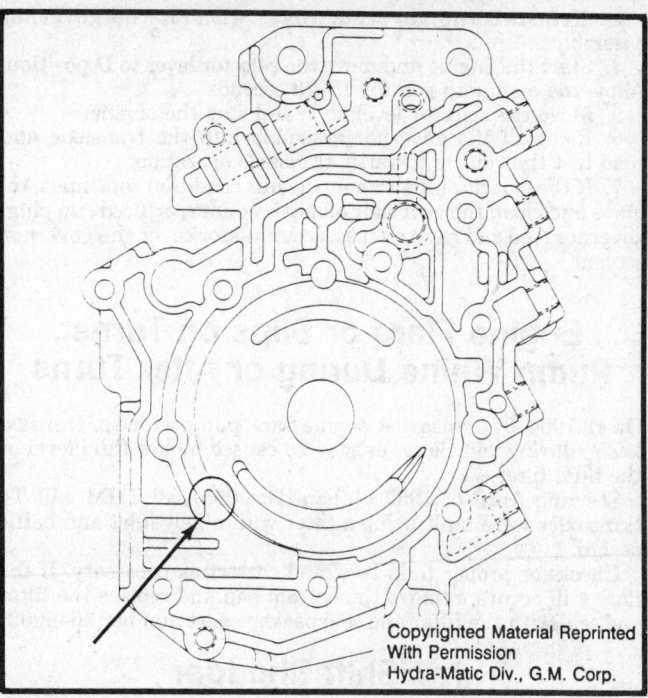

Copyrighted Material Reprinted With Permission Hydra-Matic Div., G.M. Corp.

Check for excessive casting flash

After verifying the vehicle and engine application, replace the 7CBH model transaxle with a 7CAH model transaxle.

Harsh Engagement, Double Bump or Engagement Shudder from Park or Neutral to Reverse

On all 1984–89 transaxles, a harsh engagement or engagement shudder from **P** or **N** to **R** in a THM 440–T4 transaxle may be caused by one of the items: oxidized fluid (the fluid may visually appear to be OK), or the reverse band assembly and 2nd clutch housing drum and bushing assembly.

Check engine idle speed and engine/transaxle mounts. If okay, drain and replace the transaxle fluid then road test vehicle for the above condition. If the condition still exists, replace the reverse band assembly and 2nd clutch housing drum and bushing assembly with the appropriate parts.

Reverse band assembly — 1984–89, part number 8668012

2nd clutch housing drum and bushing assembly — 1987–89, part number 8661912

2nd clutch housing drum and bushing assembly — 1984–86, part number 8662936

Erratic Shifts/No Upshifts

On all 1984–87 transaxles, erratic shifts or no upshift in a THM 440–T4 transaxle may be caused by particles of hardened Imprex® material lodging in the governor pressure channel. (Imprex® is an "impregnation plastic" used in the manufacturing of cases to help seal the case and minimize porosity.)

1. Remove the governor assembly from transaxle and clean with solvent.

2. Inspect the governor for binding weights and/or mispositioned springs. To verify operation, turn the governor upside down and pour solvent into the governor shaft. Check for leakage past the checkballs. If leakage is noted, replace the governor assembly.

3. Reinstall the governor cover without the governor assembly.

4. Start the engine and move the selector lever to **D** position. Allow the engine to run for 15–20 seconds.

5. Move the selector lever to **P** and stop the engine.

6. Reinstall the governor assembly into the transaxle and road test the vehicle to verify transaxle operation.

7. If the erratic shifts or a no upshift condition continues, remove and clean the governor oil pipe retainer, orificed cup plug, governor feed and return pipes, accumulator cover and governor screen.

Engine Flare or Slips on Turns; Pump Whine During or After Turns

On all 1984–87 transaxles, engine flare, pump whine or transaxle slip during vehicle turns may be caused by low fluid level or the fluid filter.

Starting April 6, 1987 (Julian date 095), all THM 440–T4 transaxles were built using a filter with a new inlet and baffle design.

Check for proper fluid level and correct as necessary. If the flare still occurs, remove the bottom pan and replace the filter and seal with the filter and seal package part number 8646902.

1–2 Shift Shudder

On all 1987 transaxles, a 1–2 shift shudder on a 440–T4 transaxle may be caused by out of flat 2nd clutch plates. This condition may be repaired by replacing the 2nd clutch plates with the service package part number 8662914.

Production change occurred April 15, 1987 (Julian date 105) using the new 2nd clutch plates. This change is also on all Service Replacement Transmission Assembly (SRTA) transaxles built starting April 15, 1987 (Julian date 105).

When performing a complete overhaul or servicing a transaxle for 1–2 shift shudder, remove and discard the new fiber plates from the overhaul package and the original steel plates from the 2nd clutch assembly.

NOTE: 1987 steel plates are 0.075 in. thick, 1984–86 steel plates are 0.088 in. thick. Do not interchange these plates or improper clutch travel may result. There will be a package to service 1984–86 transaxles as soon as steel plates are available.

Modulator Valve Buzz Noise

On all 1986 Cadillac vehicles and all 1987 vehicles, modulator valve buzz noise can be caused by a missing orificed cup plug in the modulator circuit of the channel plate for transaxles built prior to February 1, 1987, (Julian date 032).

Remove the transaxle from the vehicle and remove the channel plate from the transaxle. Install the orificed cup lug from the service package, part number 8646987. The cup plug is properly installed at 0.020 in. (0.0–0.5mm) below the channel plate machined surface and must be staked securely.

Intermittent No Reverse or Locks In Reverse

A 1984 through 1987 vehicle equipped with a THM 440-T4 transaxle may have an intermittent no reverse or locking in reverse condition until shifted to a forward range prior to shifting into reverse ("unloading" the parking pawl). This condition may be caused by a "dent" on the parking pawl that does not allow the pawl to release until "unloaded".

Effective May 1, 1987 (Julian date 121) all 1987 THM 440–T4

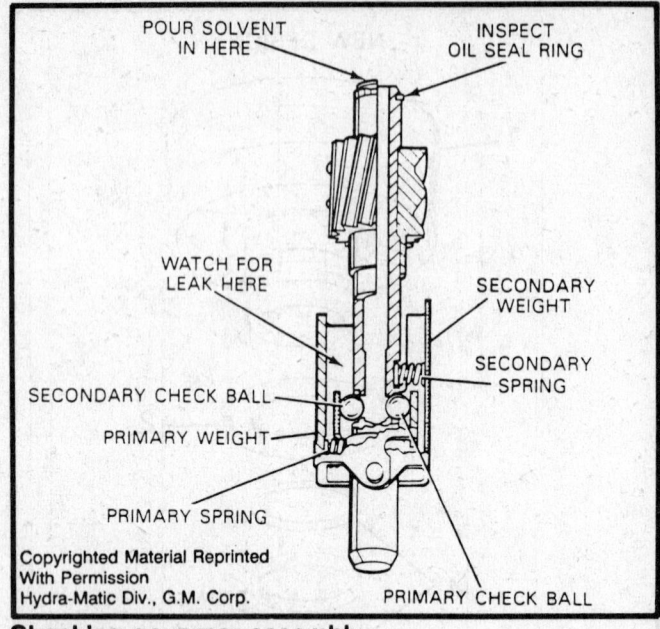

POUR SOLVENT IN HERE
INSPECT OIL SEAL RING
WATCH FOR LEAK HERE
SECONDARY WEIGHT
SECONDARY SPRING
SECONDARY CHECK BALL
PRIMARY WEIGHT
PRIMARY SPRING
PRIMARY CHECK BALL

Checking governor assembly

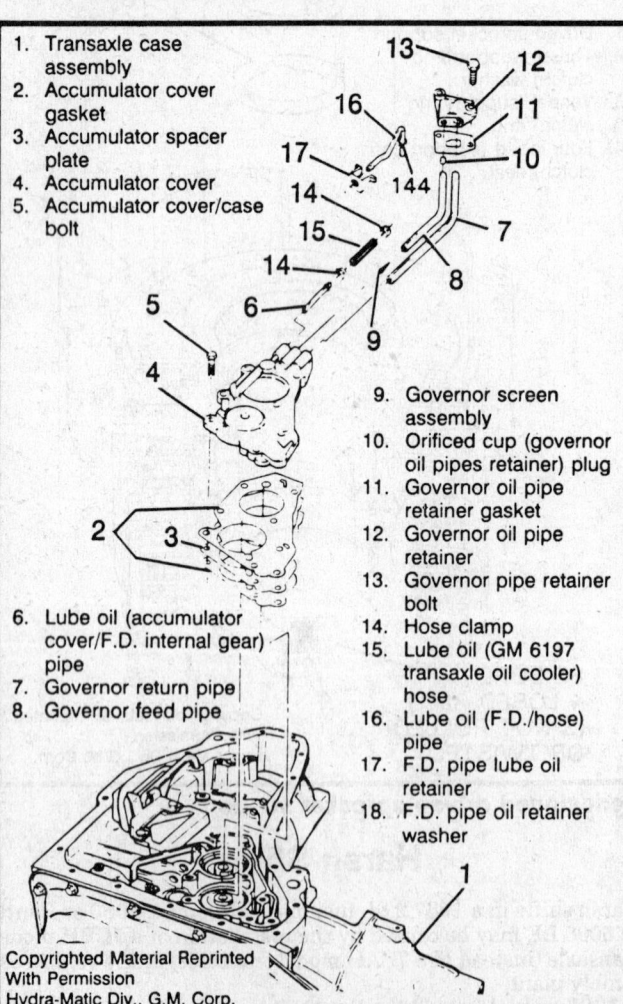

1. Transaxle case assembly
2. Accumulator cover gasket
3. Accumulator spacer plate
4. Accumulator cover
5. Accumulator cover/case bolt
6. Lube oil (accumulator cover/F.D. internal gear) pipe
7. Governor return pipe
8. Governor feed pipe
9. Governor screen assembly
10. Orificed cup (governor oil pipes retainer) plug
11. Governor oil pipe retainer gasket
12. Governor oil pipe retainer
13. Governor pipe retainer bolt
14. Hose clamp
15. Lube oil (GM 6197 transaxle oil cooler) hose
16. Lube oil (F.D./hose) pipe
17. F.D. pipe lube oil retainer
18. F.D. pipe oil retainer washer

Governor oil pipe and accumulator assembly

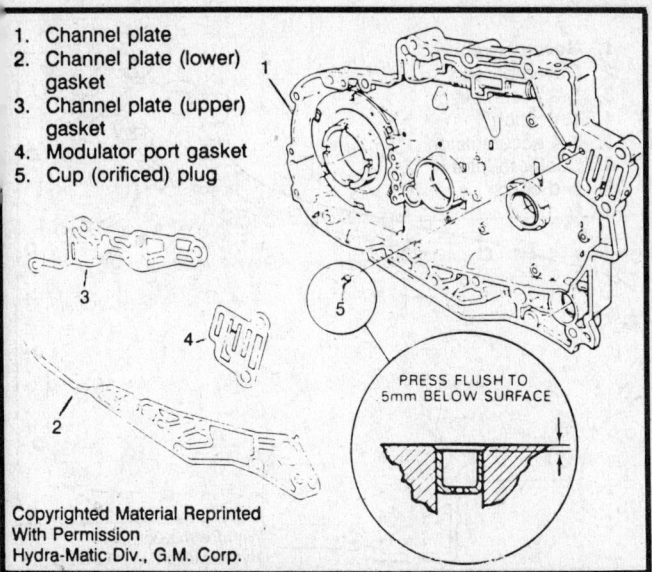

1. Channel plate
2. Channel plate (lower) gasket
3. Channel plate (upper) gasket
4. Modulator port gasket
5. Cup (orificed) plug

PRESS FLUSH TO 5mm BELOW SURFACE

Copyrighted Material Reprinted With Permission
Hydra-Matic Div., G.M. Corp.

Checking orificed cup plug

transaxles were produced with parking pawl assemblies not having a "dent".

Remove transaxle and replace the final drive internal gear/parking pawl assembly and actuator guide, plunger and spring assembly. Also inspect the parking gear for wear or damage and replace if necessary. Replacement parts are as follows:

Part number 8656372 – final drive internal gear/parking pawl assembly
Part number 8656689 – actuator guide, plunger and spring assembly
Part number 8644238 – parking gear

Before installing the replacement parts, inspect the new final drive internal gear/parking pawl assembly to make sure it does not have a "dent".

Second Gear Starts

A 1984–87 vehicle equipped with a THM 440–T4 may start out in 2nd gear instead of 1st gear. This condition could occur intermittently or all the time.

High line pressure could be a cause by holding too much governor pressure and not allowing the 1–2 shift valve to downshift. Check line pressure. Governor pressure should be below 3.0 psi at 0 mph.

If governor pressure is okay, the 1–2 shift valve, may be stuck in the upshifted position. Remove the control valve assembly and check for a sticking 1–2 shift valve, 1–2 throttle valve, or the 1–2 throttle valve spring caused by the 1–2 throttle valve bushing retainer pushed in too far. The retainer should be installed flush with the machine surface of the valve body.

Proper Fluid Level Checking Procedure

On all 1987–88 transaxles, this bulletin outlines proper hot and cold fluid level checking procedures for the transaxles.

To obtain a proper cold fluid level check for transaxles:
1. Start vehicle and cycle gear range selector through **1, 2, D, OD,** and **R** for approximately 3 seconds in each range. Complete "cold" check preparation by letting vehicle idle in **P** for 3 minutes.
2. With vehicle level, accessories turned off and engine idling in **P**, check fluid level.
3. When cold, 80°F (27°C), a full THM 440–T4 transaxle will

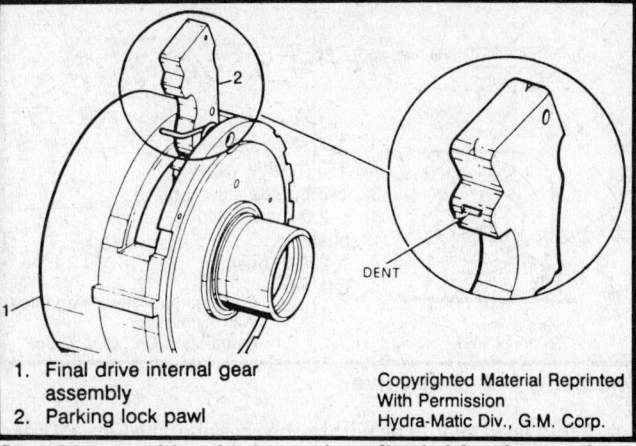

1. Final drive internal gear assembly
2. Parking lock pawl

DENT

Copyrighted Material Reprinted With Permission
Hydra-Matic Div., G.M. Corp.

Checking parking lock pawl on final drive internal gear assembly

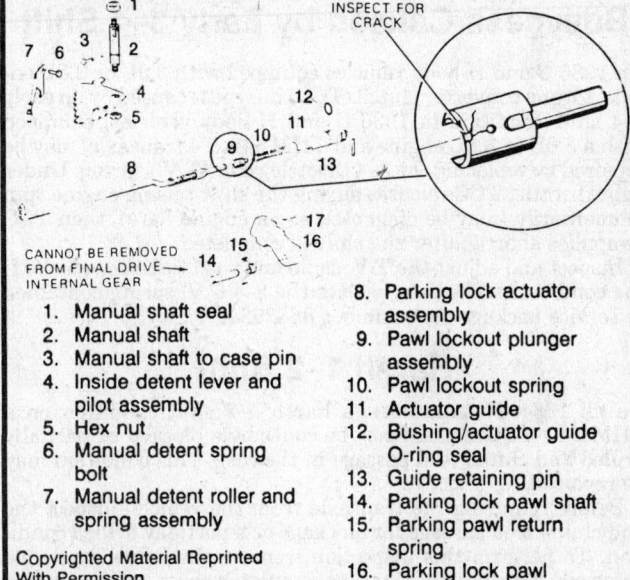

INSPECT FOR CRACK

CANNOT BE REMOVED FROM FINAL DRIVE INTERNAL GEAR

1. Manual shaft seal
2. Manual shaft
3. Manual shaft to case pin
4. Inside detent lever and pilot assembly
5. Hex nut
6. Manual detent spring bolt
7. Manual detent roller and spring assembly
8. Parking lock actuator assembly
9. Pawl lockout plunger assembly
10. Pawl lockout spring
11. Actuator guide
12. Bushing/actuator guide O-ring seal
13. Guide retaining pin
14. Parking lock pawl shaft
15. Parking pawl return spring
16. Parking lock pawl
17. Parking pawl lockout pin

Copyrighted Material Reprinted With Permission
Hydra-Matic Div., G.M. Corp.

Inspecting pawl lockout plunger assembly for cracks

show the fluid level to be above the **FULL HOT** mark on the fluid level indicator. This is a result of the fluid that is stored in the bottom pan when the transaxle is cold. As the transaxle warms to normal operating temperature, fluid is captured in the side pan lowering the fluid level to within the cross-hatched area on the fluid level indicator.

NOTE: The cold level checking procedure cannot take the place of a "hot" level check. The cold level will let the technician know that there is enough fluid in the transaxle to perform a preliminary check procedure, an accurate road test and allow normal operating temperature to be obtained prior to the necessary hot check.

To obtain a proper hot fluid level check for all THM transaxles:
1. Drive vehicle in all ranges to attain a fluid temperature of 180–200°F (80–90°C).
2. Idle at normal idle speed in **P** for 3 minutes.
3. With vehicle level, accessories turned off and engine idling in **P**, check fluid level.

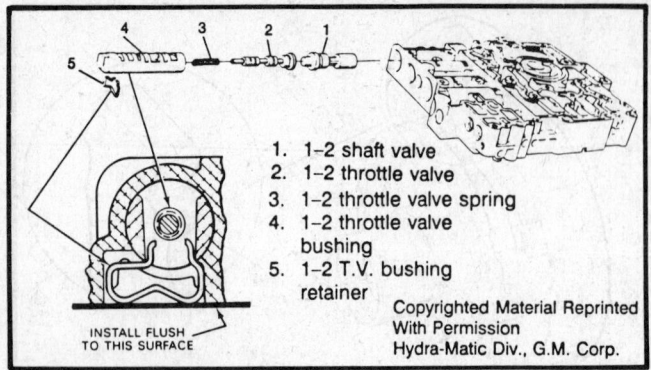

1. 1–2 shaft valve
2. 1–2 throttle valve
3. 1–2 throttle valve spring
4. 1–2 throttle valve bushing
5. 1–2 T.V. bushing retainer

INSTALL FLUSH TO THIS SURFACE

Copyrighted Material Reprinted With Permission Hydra-Matic Div., G.M. Corp.

Checking 1–2 shift valve

4. Fluid level should be within the cross-hatched area. (Read from and back of the fluid level indicator and use the lowest level.)

Torque Converter Clutch (TCC) Busyness Caused by Early 3–4 Shift

On 1986 C and H-body vehicles equipped with 3.0L or 3.8L engine, torque converter clutch (TCC) busyness caused by an early 3–4 shift condition in 1986 C and H-Body vehicles, equipped with a 3.0L or 3.8L engine and THM 440–T4 transaxle, may be repaired by replacing the 3–4 throttle valve (T.V.) spring. Under light throttle, TCC releases during the shift raising engine rpm momentarily (may be diagnosed as an engine flare), then TCC re-applies shortly after the shift is completed.

Inspect and adjust the T.V. cable and road test the vehicle. If the condition still exists, replace the 3–4 T.V. spring contained in service package part number 8662934.

Harsh 1–2 Shift

On all 1984–87 transaxles, a harsh 1–2 shift condition on a THM 440–T4 transaxle may be cause by a blocked or partially drilled 2nd clutch feed passage in the case. This condition may be repaired.

Before removing the transaxle from the vehicle, inspect the 2nd clutch feed passage for blockage or a partially drilled condition. To perform this inspection, remove the following items: transaxle bottom pan, filter, accumulator cover with governor pipes and governor pipe retainer, accumulator cover spacer plate and gaskets.

Inspect the 2nd clutch passage by measuring the hole depth which should be a minimum of 2.835 in. (72mm). If the 2nd clutch passage is properly drilled, refer to the Diagnosis Section for other possible causes of a harsh 1–2 shift condition.

If the 2nd clutch passage is not fully drilled:

1. Remove the transaxle and disassemble components up to and including the channel plate.

2. Mark an 21.64 in. (8.5mm) drill bit at 2.835 in. (72mm) from the tip using tape or other acceptable method. From the bottom pan side of the case, finish drilling the 2nd clutch passage to the proper depth as marked on the drill bit.

NOTE: Avoid drilling too deep into the 2nd clutch passage because it will damage the case.

3. Remove metal chips caused by drilling and thoroughly flush the repaired case passages with clean solvent.

4. Reassemble the transaxle.

Harsh Engagement Conditions

Harsh engagement conditions and specific service information for 1987–88 vehicles equipped with a THM 440–T4 transaxle

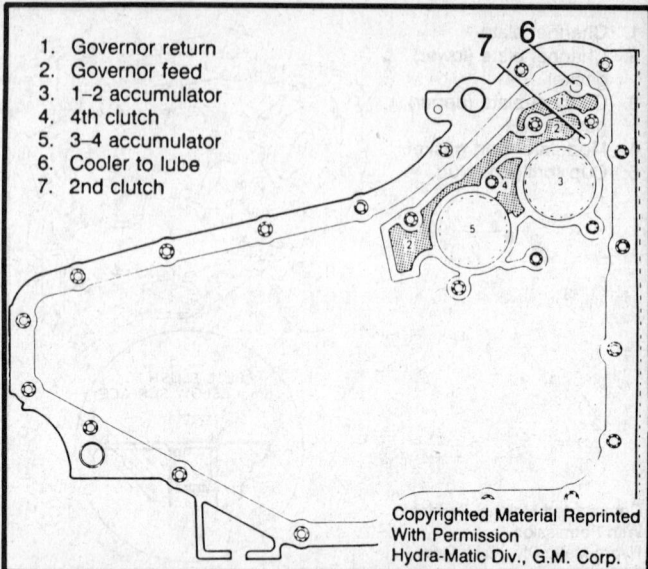

1. Governor return
2. Governor feed
3. 1–2 accumulator
4. 4th clutch
5. 3–4 accumulator
6. Cooler to lube
7. 2nd clutch

Copyrighted Material Reprinted With Permission Hydra-Matic Div., G.M. Corp.

Inspect 2nd clutch passage for drilled hole depth in case passage

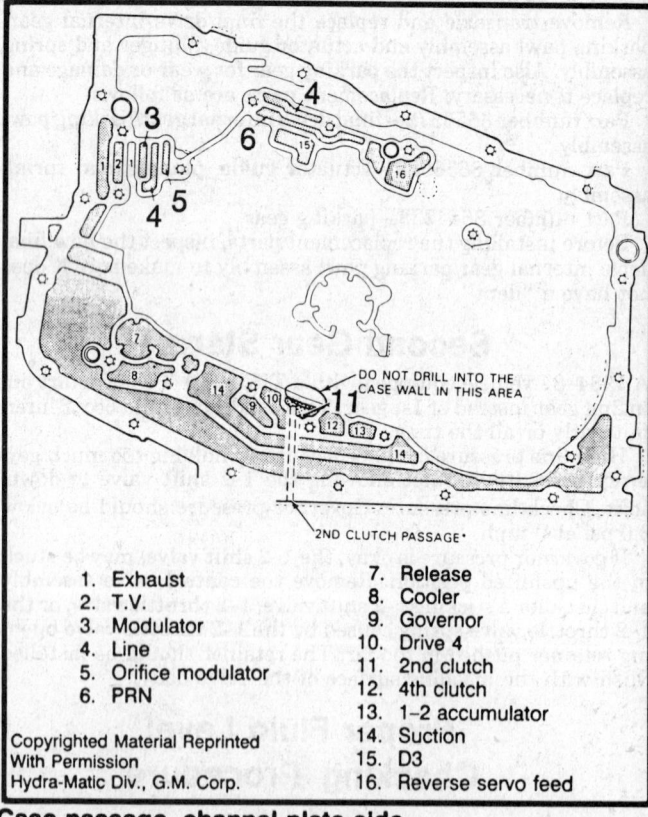

DO NOT DRILL INTO THE CASE WALL IN THIS AREA

2ND CLUTCH PASSAGE

1. Exhaust
2. T.V.
3. Modulator
4. Line
5. Orifice modulator
6. PRN
7. Release
8. Cooler
9. Governor
10. Drive 4
11. 2nd clutch
12. 4th clutch
13. 1–2 accumulator
14. Suction
15. D3
16. Reverse servo feed

Copyrighted Material Reprinted With Permission Hydra-Matic Div., G.M. Corp.

Case passage, channel plate side

follow. Other items which cause harsh engagement conditions are:

a. Vacuum leaks (low vacuum supply to the vacuum modulator) 13–18 in. Hg (33–46cm Hg) required

b. Stuck modulator valve

c. Missing No. 9 checkball

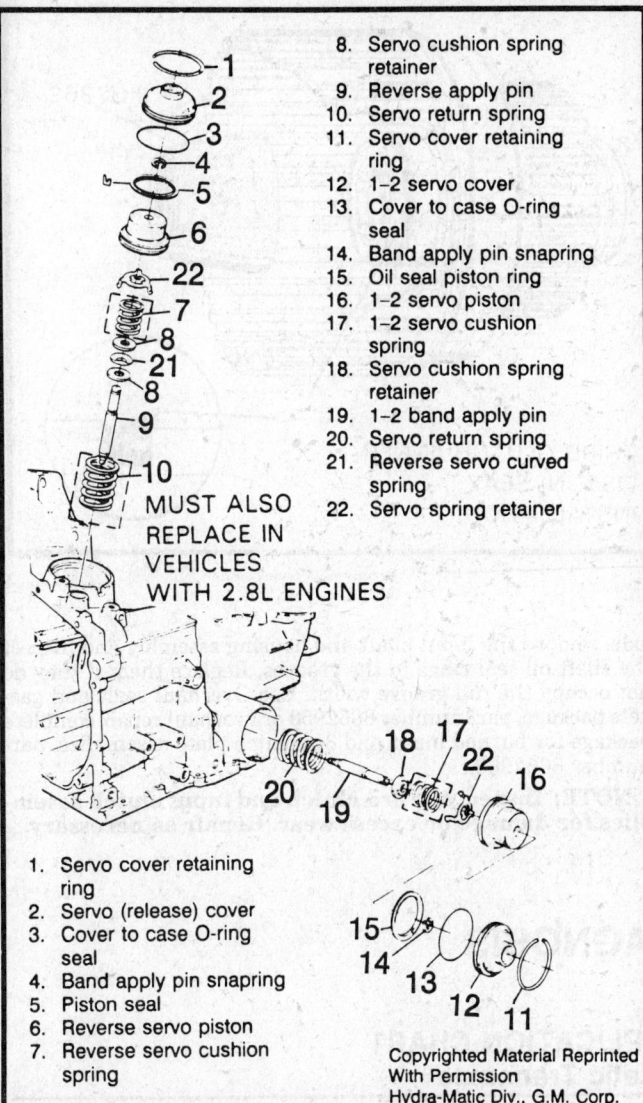

8. Servo cushion spring retainer
9. Reverse apply pin
10. Servo return spring
11. Servo cover retaining ring
12. 1–2 servo cover
13. Cover to case O-ring seal
14. Band apply pin snapring
15. Oil seal piston ring
16. 1–2 servo piston
17. 1–2 servo cushion spring
18. Servo cushion spring retainer
19. 1–2 band apply pin
20. Servo return spring
21. Reverse servo curved spring
22. Servo spring retainer

MUST ALSO REPLACE IN VEHICLES WITH 2.8L ENGINES

1. Servo cover retaining ring
2. Servo (release) cover
3. Cover to case O-ring seal
4. Band apply pin snapring
5. Piston seal
6. Reverse servo piston
7. Reverse servo cushion spring

Copyrighted Material Reprinted With Permission Hydra-Matic Div., G.M. Corp.

1–2 servo and reverse servo assemblies

Harsh Engagement From Park or Neutral To Drive or Neutral

1987–88 VEHICLES EXCEPT 2.8L ENGINE

1. Remove the 1–2 servo assembly and the reverse servo assembly from the transaxle.
2. Disassemble and replace the 1–2 servo cushion spring and the reverse servo cushion spring with part number 8668121 (reverse servo cushion spring) and part number 8668123 (1–2 servo cushion spring).
3. Install the 1–2 servo assembly and reverse servo assembly in the transaxle.

Harsh Engagement From Reverse To Drive, Park or Neutral To Drive or Reverse

1987–88 A-BODY AND 1988 W-BODY VEHICLES EQUIPPED WITH 2.8L ENGINE

1. Remove the 1–2 servo assembly and the reverse servo assembly from the transaxle.
2. Disassemble and replace the 1–2 servo cushion spring and the reverse servo cushion spring and the reverse servo return spring with part number 8668127 (reverse servo cushion spring) and part number 8668123 (1–2 servo cushion spring).

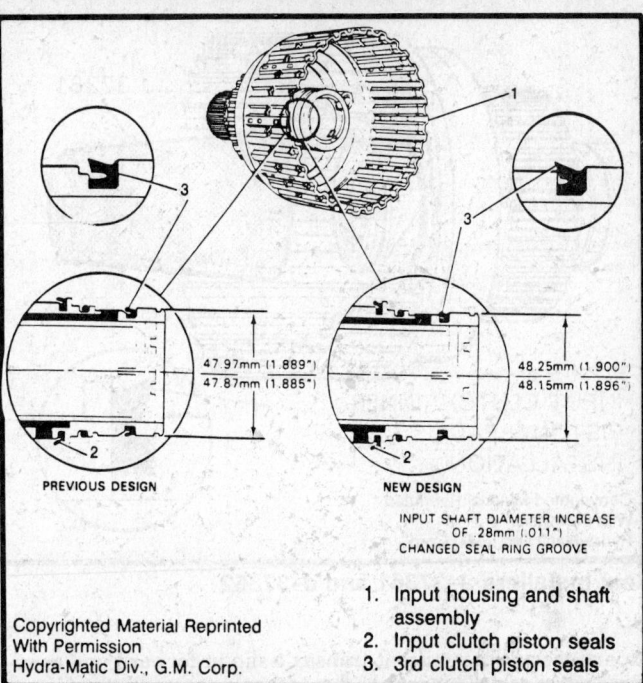

47.97mm (1.889")
47.87mm (1.885")

48.25mm (1.900")
48.15mm (1.896")

PREVIOUS DESIGN

NEW DESIGN

INPUT SHAFT DIAMETER INCREASE OF .28mm (.011") CHANGED SEAL RING GROOVE

1. Input housing and shaft assembly
2. Input clutch piston seals
3. 3rd clutch piston seals

Copyrighted Material Reprinted With Permission Hydra-Matic Div., G.M. Corp.

Input clutch housing and shaft assembly

3. Install the 1–2 servo assembly and reverse servo assembly in the transaxle.

New Input Clutch and Third Clutch Seal Installers

New seal installation tools are available for the input clutch inner piston seal and the 3rd clutch inner piston seal. These tools are to be used when servicing the input clutch assembly on all 1984–88 vehicles equipped with a THM 440–T4 transaxle.

When servicing the input clutch housing and shaft assembly on a 1984–88 THM 440–T4 transaxle use the new seal installation tools, J–37361 and J–37362. The previous design tools, J–34091 and J–34092 will work on 1984–86 transaxles only.

Governor Screen Added to Transaxle Case

On some 1989 DeVilles, Eldorados, Sevilles and Allantes a production change has been made to add a screen to the governor shaft sleeve. The screen, which is identical to the one used in the THM 125C transaxle, was added to reduce the chance of sediment entering the governor assembly.

The production change occurred on some units beginning on November 30, 1988 (Julian date 335). The change occurred on all units by December 5, 1988 (Julian date 340).

The production change included dimensional changes in the case to provide clearance for assembly of the screen.

NOTE: Do not attempt to install the screen on earlier transaxles. Critical case dimensions will not allow any further operations.

On 1989½ vehicles – Governor shaft sleeve and screen assembly – part number 8660770.

On 1984–89½ – Governor shaft sleeve – part number 8631328.

Transaxle Slips When Cold

On some 1989 DeVilles, Eldorados, Sevilles and Allantes may

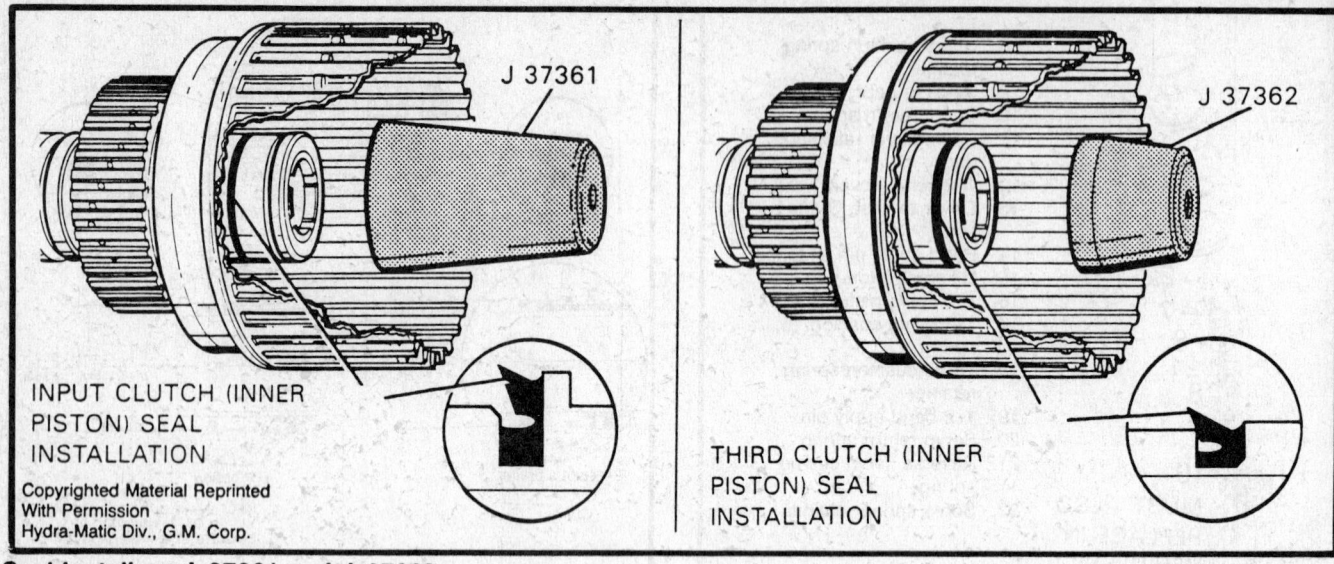

Seal Installers J–37361 and J–37362

experience an intermittent transaxle slip in forward and/or reverse when cold. This may be due to 1 or more undersized input shaft oil rings that seal the input clutch and 3rd clutch feed holes. The slipping may occur less in reverse or manual low range (due to boosted line pressure) than in the other drive ranges.

To service the THM F–7 transaxle, replace the transaxle.

To service the THM 440–T4 transaxle, disassemble the trans-axle, remove the input shaft and housing assembly and inspect the shaft oil seal rings in the grooves. Replace them if they do not occupy the full groove width. Use Overhaul seals and gaskets package, part number 8662959 or overhaul repair complete package for burned input and 3rd clutch plate assemblies, part number 8662960.

NOTE: Inspect the 3rd clutch and input clutch assemblies for damage or excess wear. Repair as necessary.

TROUBLE DIAGNOSIS

CLUTCH AND BAND APPLICATION CHART
THM 440-T4 Automatic Transaxle

Range		4th Clutch	Reverse Band	2nd Clutch	3rd Clutch	3rd Roller Clutch	Input Sprag	Input Clutch	1-2 Band
NEUTRAL PARK								①	①
DRIVE	1						HOLD	ON	ON
	2			ON			OVER-RUNNING	①	ON
	3			ON	ON	HOLD			
	4	ON		ON	①	OVER-RUNNING			
MANUAL	3			ON	ON	HOLD	HOLD	ON	
	2			ON			OVER-RUNNING	①	ON
	1			ON		HOLD	HOLD	ON	ON
REVERSE		ON					HOLD	ON	

①APPLIED BUT NOT EFFECTIVE

CHILTON'S THREE "C's" DIAGNOSIS CHART
THM 440-T4 Automatic Transaxle

Condition	Cause	Correction
Oil Leakage	a) Side cover, bottom pan and gaskets, loose bolts	a) Repair or replace cover, gasket and torque bolts
	b) Damaged seal at T.V. cable, fill tube or electrical connector	b) Replace seal as required
	c) Damaged seal assembly on manual shaft	c) Replace seal assembly as required
	d) Leakage at governor cover, servo covers, modulator, parking plunger guide, speedometer driven gear sleeve	d) Replace damaged "O" ring seals as required
	e) Converter or converter seal leaking	e) Replace converter and seal as required
	f) Axle seals leaking	f) Remove axles and replace seals as required
	g) Pressure ports or cooler line fittings leaking	g) Tighten or repair stripped threads
Fluid foaming or blowing out the vent	a) Fluid level high	a) Correct fluid level
	b) Fluid foaming due to contaminates or over-heating of fluid	b) Determine cause of contamination or overheating and repair
	c) Drive sprocket support has plugged drain back holes	c) Open drain back holes in sprocket support
	d) Thermo element not closing when hot	d) Replace thermo element
	e) Fluid filter "O" ring damaged	e) Replace fluid filter "O" ring
High or low fluid pressure, verified by pressure gauge	a) Fluid level high or low	a) Correct fluid level as required
	b) Vacuum modulator or hose leaking	b) Repair or replace hose or modulator
	c) Modulator valve, pressure regulator valve, pressure relief valve nicked, scored or damaged. Spring or ball checks missing or damaged	c) Repair or replace necessary components
	d) Oil pump or components damaged, parts missing	d) Repair or replace oil pump assembly
No drive in DRIVE range	a) Fluid level low	a) Correct fluid level
	b) Fluid pressure low	b) Refer to low fluid pressure causes
	c) Manual linkage mis-adjusted or disconnected	c) Repair or adjust manual linkage
	d) Torque converter loose on flex plate or internal converter damage	d) Verify malfunction and repair as required
	e) Oil pump or drive shaft damaged	e) Repair or replace oil pump and/or drive shaft
	f) Number 13 check ball mis-assembled or missing	f) Correct or install number 13 check ball in its proper location
	g) Damaged drive link chain, sprocket or bearings	g) Replace damaged components

CHILTON'S THREE "C's" DIAGNOSIS CHART
THM 440-T4 Automatic Transaxle

Condition	Cause	Correction
No drive in DRIVE range	h) Burned or missing clutch plates, damaged piston seals or piston, Housing check ball damaged, input shaft seals or feed passages blocked or damaged	h) Repair and/or replace damaged input clutch assembly components
	i) Input sprag and/or input sun gear assembly improperly assembled or sprag damaged	i) Correctly assemble or replace input sprag and input sun gear assembly
	j) Pinions, sun gear or internal gears damaged on input and reaction carrier assemblies	j) Repair or replace carrier assemblies as required
	k) 1-2 band or servo burned or damaged. Band apply pin incorrect in length	k) Repair or replace band and/or servo components as required
	l) 1-2 servo oil pipes leaking fluid	l) Correct oil tubes to prevent leakage
	m) Final drive assembly broken or damaged	m) Repair or replace necessary components of final drive
	n) Parking pawl spring broken	n) Replace parking pawl spring
	o) Output shaft damage, broken or misassembled	o) Repair, replace or re-assemble output shaft
First speed only, no 1-2 shift	a) Governor assembly defective	a) Repair or replace governor
	b) Number 14 check ball missing	b) Install number 14 check ball
	c) 1-2 shift valve sticking or binding	c) Repair or clean valve and bore
	d) Accumulator and/or pipes	d) Repair/renew components
	e) 2nd clutch assembly damaged	e) Repair/renew components
	f) Oil seal rings damaged on driven sprocket support	f) Replace oil seal rings
	g) Splines damaged or parts missing from reverse reaction drum	g) Repair or replace damaged components
Harsh or soft 1-2 shift	a) Fluid pressure	a) Check pressure and correct
	b) Defective accumulator assembly	b) Repair or replace accumulator assembly
	c) Accumulator valve stuck	c) Repair or clean valve and bore
	d) Missing or mislocated number 8 check ball	d) Install or re-locate number 8 check ball
High or low 1-2 shift speed	a) Disconnected or misadjusted T.V. cable	a) Connect and/or adjust T.V. cable
	b) Bent or damaged T.V. link, lever and bracket assembly	b) Repair or replace damaged components
	c) Stuck or binding T.V. valve and plunger	c) Correct binding condition or remove stuck valve and plunger
	d) Incorrect governor pressure	d) Correct governor pressure
No 2-3 upshift, 1st and 2nd speeds only	a) Defective 1-2 servo or components	a) Repair or replace 1-2 servo assembly
	b) Defective number 7 check ball and capsule assembly	b) Check, repair or replace check ball and capsule
	c) Number 11 check ball not seating	c) Check, repair or replace check ball
	d) 2-3 shift valve stuck in control valve assembly	d) Remove stuck 1-2 shift valve and repair

CHILTON'S THREE "C's" DIAGNOSIS CHART
THM 440-T4 Automatic Transaxle

Condition	Cause	Correction
No 2-3 upshift, 1st and 2nd speeds only	e) Seals damaged or blocked passages on input shaft f) Defective third clutch assembly g) Defective third roller clutch assembly h) Numbers 5, 6 and/or accumulator valve stuck	e) Replace seals and open passages f) Overhaul third clutch assembly g) Inspect, repair or replace necessary components h) Repair as required
Harsh or soft 2-3 shift	a) Fluid pressure b) Mislocated number 12 check ball	a) Test and correct fluid pressure b) Correct check ball location
High or low 2-3 shift speed	a) Disconnected or misadjusted T.V. cable b) Bent or damaged T.V. link, lever and bracket assembly c) Stuck or binding T.V. valve and plunger d) Incorrect governor pressure	a) Connect and/or adjust T.V. cable b) Repair or replace damaged components c) Correct binding condition or remove stuck valve and plunger d) Correct governor pressure
No 3-4 shift	a) Incorrect governor pressure b) 3-4 shift valve stuck in control valve assembly c) Defective 4th clutch assembly d) Spline damage to 4th clutch shaft	a) Correct governor pressure b) Free 3-4 shift valve and repair control valve assembly c) Overhaul 4th clutch assembly d) Replace 4th clutch shaft
Harsh or soft 3-4 shift	a) Fluid pressure b) Defective accumulator assembly c) Mislocated number 1 check ball	a) Test and correct fluid pressure b) Repair or replace accumulator assembly c) Correct check ball location
High or low 3-4 shift	a) Disconnected or misadjusted T.V. cable b) Bent or damaged T.V. link, lever and bracket assembly c) Stuck or binding T.V. valve and plunger d) Incorrect governor pressure	a) Connect and/or adjust T.V. cable b) Repair or replace damaged components c) Correct binding condition or remove stuck valve and plunger d) Correct governor pressure
No converter clutch apply (Vehicles equipped with E.C.M.)	a) Improper E.C.M. operation b) Electrical system of transaxle malfunctioning c) Converter clutch apply valve stuck d) Number 10 check ball missing e) Converter clutch blow-off check ball not seating or damaged f) Seals damaged on turbine shaft g) Damaged seal on oil pump drive shaft	a) Verify proper E.C.M. operation b) Test and correct electrical malfunction c) Free converter clutch apply valve and repair d) Install missing check ball e) Inspect channel plate and check ball. Repair as required f) Replace seals and inspect shaft g) Replace seal on oil pump drive shaft
No converter clutch apply (vehicles not equipped with E.C.M.)	a) Electrical system of transaxle malfunctioning	a) Test and correct electrical malfunction

CHILTON'S THREE "C's" DIAGNOSIS CHART
THM 440-T4 Automatic Transaxle

Condition	Cause	Correction
No converter clutch apply (vehicles not equipped with E.C.M.)	b) Converter clutch shift and/or apply valves stuck	b) Free converter clutch shift and/or apply valves
	c) Number 10 check ball missing	c) Install missing check ball
	d) Converter clutch blow-off check ball not seated or damaged	d) Inspect channel plate and check ball. Repair as required
	e) Seals damaged on turbine shaft	e) Replace seals and inspect shaft
	f) Damaged oil seal on seal pump drive shaft	f) Replace seal on oil pump drive shaft
Converter clutch does not release	a) Converter clutch apply valve stuck in the apply position	a) Free apply valve for converter clutch and repair as required
Rough converter clutch apply	a) Converter clutch regulator valve stuck	a) Free converter clutch regulator valve and repair as required
	b) Converter clutch accumulator piston or seal damaged	b) Replace seal or piston as required Check accumulator spring
	c) Seals damaged on turbine shaft	c) Replace seals on turbine shaft
Harsh 4-3 downshift	a) Number 1 check ball missing in control valve assembly	a) Install number 1 check ball in control valve assembly
Harsh 3-2 downshift	a) 1-2 servo control valve stuck	a) Free 1-2 servo control valve
	b) Number 12 check ball missing	b) Install number 12 check ball
	c) 3-2 control valve stuck	c) Free 3-2 control valve
	d) Number 4 check ball missing	d) Install number 4 check ball
	e) 3-2 coast valve stuck	e) Free 3-2 coast valve
	f) Input clutch accumulator piston or seal damaged	f) Replace input clutch accumulator piston and/or seal
Harsh 2-1 downshift	a) Number 8 check ball missing	a) Install number 8 check ball
No reverse	a) Fluid pressure	a) Test and correct fluid pressure
	b) Defective oil pump	b) Test and correct oil pump malfunction
	c) Broken, stripped or defective drive link assembly	c) Repair, replace as required
	d) Reverse band burned or damaged	d) Replace rear band as required
	e) Defective input clutch	e) Repair, replace defective input clutch components
	f) Defective input sprag	f) Replace defective sprag
	g) Piston or seal damaged, pin selection incorrect for rear servo assembly	g) Repair rear servo as required and install correct pin if needed
	h) Defective input and reaction carriers	h) Replace input and reaction carriers as required
No park range	a) Parking pawl, spring or parking gear damaged	a) Repair as required
	b) Manual linkage broken or out of adjustment	b) Repair linkage or adjust as required
Harsh shift from Neutral to Drive or from Neutral to Reverse	a) Number 9 check ball missing	a) Install number 9 check ball
	b) Number 12 check ball missing	b) Install number 12 check ball
	c) Thermal elements not closing when warm	c) Replace thermal elements
No viscous clutch apply (Vehicles with E.C.M.)	a) Improper E.C.M. operation	a) Verify E.C.M. operation and repair as required
	b) Damaged thermister	b) Replace thermister
	c) Damaged temperature switch	c) Replace temperature switch

Hydraulic Control System

NOTE: Please refer to Section 9 for all oil flow circuits.

OPERATION PRINCIPLES

The torque converter smoothly couples the engine to the planetary gears and the overdrive unit through fluid and hydraulically/mechanically provides additional torque multiplication when required. The combination of the compound planetary gear set provides 4 forward gear ratios and 1 reverse. The changing of the gear ratios is fully automatic is relation to the vehicle speed and engine torque. Signals of vehicle speed and engine torque are constantly being directed to the transaxle control valve assembly to provide the proper gear ratio for maximum engine efficiency and performance at all throttle openings.

TORQUE CONVERTER

The torque converter assembly serves 3 primary functions. First, it acts as a fluid coupling to smoothly connect engine power through oil to the transaxle gear train. Second, it multiplies the torque or twisting effort from the engine when additional performance is desired. Thirdly, it provides direct drive through the torque converter.

The torque converter assembly consists of a 3-element torque converter combined with a friction clutch. The 3 elements are the pump (driving member), the turbine (driven or output member) and the stator (reaction member). The converter cover is welded to the pump to seal all 3 members in an oil filled housing. The converter cover is bolted to the engine flexplate which is bolted directly to the engine crankshaft. The converter pump is therefore mechanically connected to the engine and turns at engine speed whenever the engine is operating.

The stator is located between the pump and turbine and is mounted on a one-way roller clutch which allows it to rotate clockwise but not counterclockwise.

The purpose of the stator is to redirect the oil returning from the turbine and change its direction of rotation back to that of the pump member. The energy in the oil is then used to assist the engine in turning the pump. This increases the force of the oil driving the turbine; and as a result, mulitplies the torque or twisting force of the engine.

The force of the oil flowing from the turbine to the blades of the stator tends to rotate the stator counterclockwise, but the roller clutch prevents it from turning.

With the engine operating at full throttle, transaxle in gear and the vehicle standing still, the converter is capable of multiplying engine torque by approximately 2.0:1.

As turbine speed and vehicle speed increases, the direction of the oil leaving the turbine changes. The oil flows against the rear side of the stator vanes in a clockwise direction. Since the stator is now impeding the smooth flow of oil in the clockwise direction, its roller clutch automatically releases and the stator revolves freely on its shaft.

QUADRANT POSITION

The quadrant has 7 positions indicated in the following order: **P, R, N, OD, D, 2, 1.**

P — Park position enables the transaxle output shaft to be held, thus preventing the vehicle from rolling either forward or backward. (For safety reasons, the vehicle parking brake should be used in addition to the transaxle **P** position). Because the output shaft is mechanically locked, the **P** position should not be selected until the vehicle has come to a stop. The engine may be started in the **P** position.

R — Reverse enables the vehicle to be operated in a rearward direction.

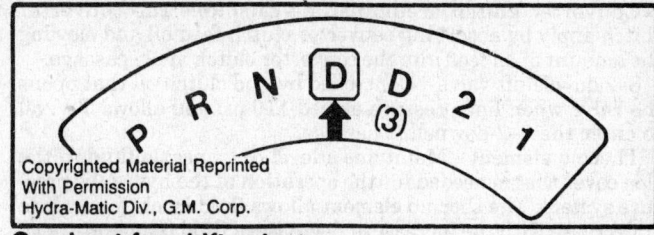

Quadrant for shift selector

N — Neutral position enables the engine to be started and operated without driving the vehicle. If necessary, this position must be selected if the engine has to be restarted while the vehicle is moving.

D — Drive is used for mostly highway driving conditions and maximum economy. Drive has 4 gear ratios, from the starting ratio, through direct drive to overdrive. Downshifts to a higher ratio are available for safe passing by depressing the accelerator.

D — Manual 3rd can be used for conditions where it is desired to use only 3 gears. This range is also useful for braking when descending slight grades. Upshifts and downshifts are the same as in **D** for 1st, 2nd and 3rd gears, but the transaxle will not shift to 4th gear.

2 — Manual 2nd adds more performance. It has the same starting ratio as Manual 3rd range, but prevents the transaxle from shifting above 2nd gear, thus retaining 2nd gear for acceleration or engine braking as desired. Manual 2nd can be selected at any vehicle speed. If the transaxle is in 3rd or 4th gear it will immediately shift to 2nd Gear.

1 — Manual low can be selected at any vehicle speed. The transaxle will shift to 2nd gear if it is in 3rd or 4th gear, until it slows below approximately 40 mph (64km/h), at which time it will downshift to 1st gear. This is particularly beneficial for maintaining maximum engine braking when descending steep grades.

DESCRIPTION OF HYDRAULIC COMPONENTS

Manual valve — Mechanically connected to the shift selector. It is fed by line pressure from the pump and directs pressure according to which range the driver has selected.

1–2 servo — A hydraulic piston and pin that mechanically applies the 1–2 band in 1st and 2nd gear. Also absorbs 3rd clutch oil to act as an accumulator for the 2–3 shift.

Reverse servo — A hydraulic piston and pin that mechanically applies the reverse band when **R** range is selected by the driver.

Modulator valve — Is controlled by the vacuum modulator assembly and regulates line pressure, into a modulator pressure that is proportional to engine vacuum (engine torque).

Modulator assembly — By sensing engine vacuum, it causes the modulator valve to regulate modulator pressure that is proportional to engine torque (inversely proportional to engine vacuum).

1–2 accumulator piston — Absorbs 2nd clutch oil to provide a cushion for the 2nd clutch apply. The firmness of the cushion is controlled by the 1–2 accumulator valve.

3–4 accumulator piston — Absorbs 4th clutch oil to provide a cushion for the 4th clutch apply. The firmness of the cushion is controlled by the 1–2 accumulator valve.

1–2 servo thermo elements — When cold, it opens another orifice to the servo, to provide less of a restriction for a quick servo apply. When warm, it blocks 1 of the 2 orifices to the servo apply. When warm, it blocks 1 of the 2 orifices to the servo and slow the flow of oil and provide a good neutral/drive shift feel.

Input clutch accumulator — Absorbs input clutch apply oil to cushion the input clutch apply.

Converter clutch accumulator — Cushions the converter clutch apply by absorbing converter clutch feed oil and slowing the amount of oil feed into the converter clutch apply passage.

3-2 downshift valve — Controlled by 2nd clutch oil that opens the valve when line pressure exceed 110 psi and allows T.V. oil to enter the 3-2 downshift passage.

Thermo element — Maintains a level of transaxle fluid in the side cover that is needed for the operation of the hydraulic pressure system. The thermo element allows fluid levels to increase or decrease with the increase or decrease of fluid temperature.

1-2 shift valve train — Shifts the transaxle from 1st to 2nd gear or 2nd to 1st gear, depending on governor, T.V., detent, or low oil pressures.

3-4 M.T.V. valve — Modulates T.V. pressure going to the 3-4 throttle valve to a lower pressure so that a light throttle 3-4 upshift will not be delayed.

2-3 accumulator valve — Receives line pressure from the manual valve and controlled by modulator pressure. The 2-3 accumulator valve, in 3rd gear and overdrive, varies 1-2 servo. Apply (2-3 accumulator) oil pressure in proportion to changes in modulator pressure (engine torque).

3-2 control valve — Controlled by governor oil, it controls the 3-2 downshift timing by regulating the rate at which the 3rd clutch releases and the 1-2 band applies.

2-3 shift valve train — Shifts the transaxle from 2nd to 3rd gear or 3rd to 1st gear, depending on governor T.V., detent or drive 2 oil pressures.

3-4 shift valve train — Shifts the transaxle from 3rd to 4th gear or 4th to 3rd gear, depending on governor, 3-4 M.T.V., 4-3 M.T.V., part throttle, or drive 3 oil pressures.

4-3 M.T.V. valve — Modulates T.V. pressure going to the 3-4 throttle valve to a lower pressure to prevent an early downshift at light to medium throttle.

Reverse servo boost valve — Under hard acceleration the higher line pressure will open the valve to provide a quick feed to the reverse servo and prevent the reverse band from slipping during application.

1-2 servo control valve — Closed by 2nd oil during a **D** range 3-2 downshift, it slows down the 1-2 servo apply.

1-2 servo boost valve — Under hard acceleration the higher line pressure will open the valve to provide a quick feed to the 1-2 servo and prevent the 1-2 band from slipping during application.

Converter clutch apply valve — Controlled by the converter clutch solenoid, it directs oil to either the release or the apply side of the converter clutch.

Converter clutch regulator valve — Controlled by T.V. pressure and fed by converter clutch feed pressure it regulates converter clutch apply pressure.

1-2 accumulator valve — Receives line pressure from the manual valve and controlled by modulator pressure. It varies 1-2 and 3-4 accumulator pressure in proportion to changes in modulator pressure (engine torque).

Pressure relief check ball — Prevents line pressure from exceeding 245-360 psi.

Converter clutch shift valve plug — Allows 2nd oil to feed into the converter clutch signal passage. The plug is used on models with vehicles equipped with computer command control.

Converter clutch shift valve train (non-C3 systems) — Sends signal oil to the converter clutch apply valve and together with the converter clutch solenoid determines whether the clutch should be released or applied. It is controlled by governor, T.V. and detent oil.

T.V. limit valve — Limits the line pressure fed to the throttle valve to 90 psi.

Throttle valve — A regulating valve that increases T.V. pressure as the accelerator pedal is depressed and is controlled by T.V. plunger movement.

T.V. plunger — Controlled by the throttle lever and bracket assembly and linked to the accelerator pedal. When accelerating, this valve compresses the throttle tralve spring causing the throttle valve to increase T.V. pressure. It also controls the opening of the part throttle and detent ports.

Pressure regulator valve — Controls line pressure by regulating pump output and is controlled by the pressure regulator spring, the reverse boost valve and the line boost valve.

Pressure regulator valve with isolator — Same function as pressure regulator valve except isolator system assists in stabilizing the pressure regulator system.

Reverse boost valve — Boosts line pressure by pushing the pressure regulator valve up when acted on by Park, Reverse, Neutral (PRN) oil or low oil pressure.

Line boost valve — Boosts line pressure by pushing the pressure regulator valve up when acted on by modulator oil pressure.

Second clutch signal pipe — Directs 2nd clutch oil to apply or release the 1-2 control valve.

CLUTCH EXHAUST CHECK BALLS

To complete the exhaust of apply oil when the input, 2nd, or 3rd clutch is released, an exhaust check ball assembly is installed near the outer diameter of the clutch housings. Centrifugal force, resulting from the spinning clutch housings, working on the residual oil in the clutch piston cavity would give a partial apply of the clutch plates if it were not exhausted. The exhaust check ball assembly is designed to close the exhaust port by clutch apply pressure seating the check ball when the clutch is being applied.

When the clutch is released and clutch apply oil is being exhausted, centrifugal force on the check ball unseats it and opens the port to exhaust the residual oil from the clutch piston cavity.

CHECK BALLS

1. Fourth clutch check ball: Forces 4th clutch oil to feed through 1 orifice and exhaust through a different orifice.

2. 3-2 control check ball: Forces exhausting 1-2 servo release oil to either flow through an orifice or the regulating 3-2 control valve.

3. Part throttle and drive 3 check ball: Separates part throttle and drive 3 oil passages to the 3-4 shift valve.

4. Third clutch check ball: Forces 3rd clutch oil to feed through 1 orifice and exhaust through a different orifice.

5. 2-3 accumulator feed check ball: In 3rd gear and 4th gear forces D4 oil to be orificed into the 1-2 servo (2-3 accumulator).

6. 2-3 accumulator exhaust check ball: In 1st gear, allows the 2-3 accumulator exhaust passage to feed and apply the 1-2 servo unrestricted. In 3rd gear, forces exhausting 1-2 servo oil to either flow through an orifice or the regulating 2-3 accumulator valve.

7. Third clutch accumulator ball and spring: In 3rd gear, it closes the 1-2 servo release passage exhaust. On a 3-2 downshift after 1-2 servo release oil has dropped to a low pressure, the spring will unseat the check ball and allow the oil to exhaust completely.

8. Second clutch check ball: Forces 2nd clutch oil to feed through 1 orifice and exhaust through a different orifice.

9. Reverse servo feed check ball: Forces oil feeding the reverse servo to orifice, but allows the oil to exhaust freely.

10. Converter clutch release/apply check ball: Separates converter clutch release and converter clutch apply passages to the clutch blow-off ball.

11. Third/Lo-1st check ball: Separates the 3rd clutch and lo-1st passages to the 3rd clutch.

12. 1-2 servo feed check ball: Forces oil feeding the apply side of the 1-2 servo to orifice but allows the oil to exhaust unrestricted.

13. Input clutch/reverse check ball: Minimizes neutral—drive and neutral—reverse apply time by allowing the park, reverse, neutral (PRN) circuit to feed and apply the input clutch quicker.

14. Detent/modulator check ball: Allows detent oil to apply

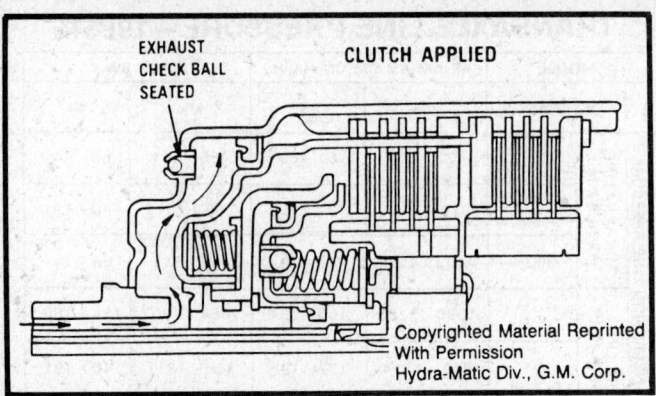

Clutch exhaust check ball applied

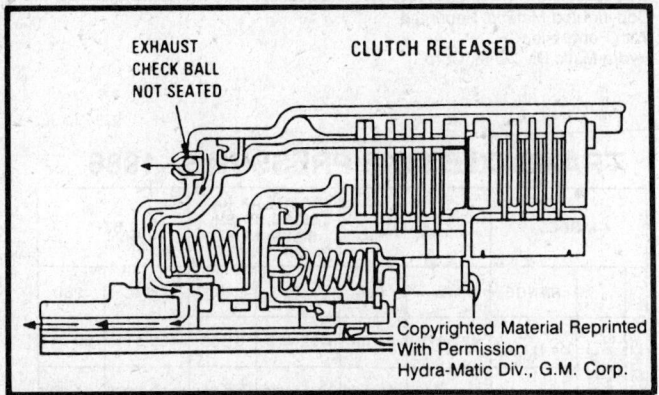

Clutch exhaust check ball released

1. 4th clutch check ball
2. 3rd clutch check ball
3. 2–3 accumulator feed check ball
4. Reverse servo feed check ball

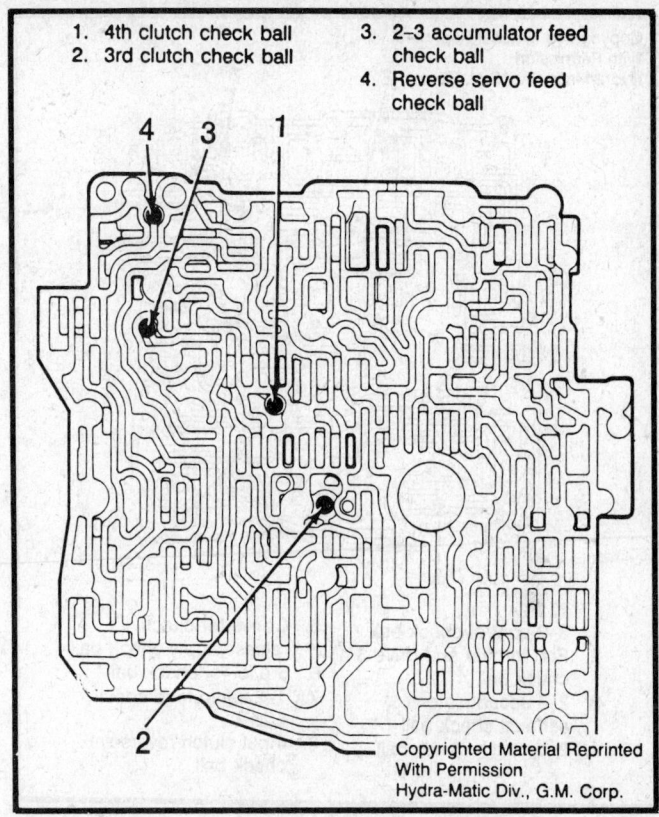

Control valve check ball locations – 1984–85

1. 4th clutch check ball
2. 3rd clutch check ball
3. 2–3 accumulator feed check ball
4. Reverse servo feed check ball
5. 3rd clutch exhaust screen

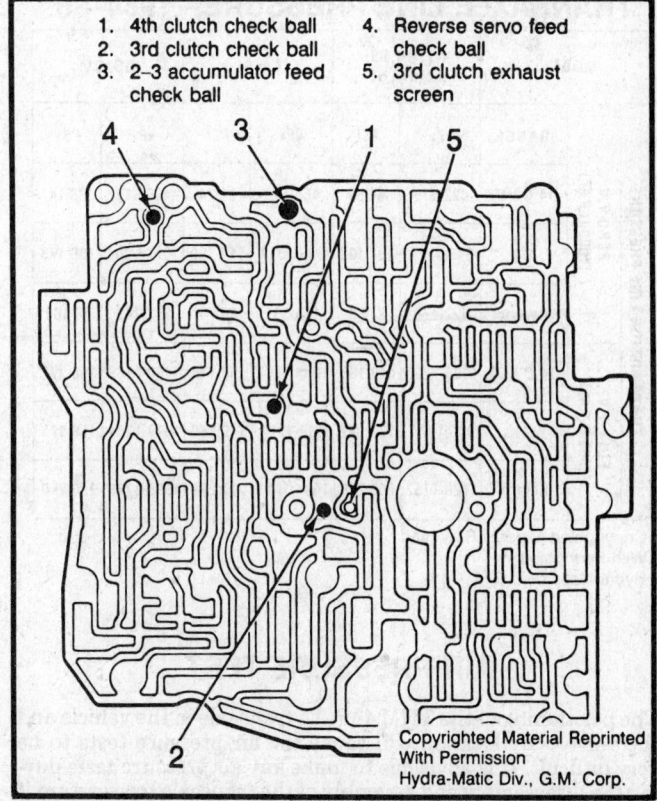

Control valve check ball locations – 1985½–89

force to the pressure regulator system during part or full throttle detent and when driving at high altitude.

15. Converter clutch blow off check ball: Prevents converter clutch release or apply pressure from exceeding 100 psi.

16. Low blow off check ball: Prevents low-1st pressure to the 3rd clutch from exceeding 70 psi in manual low.

17. Cooler check ball: When the engine is shut off the spring seats the ball to prevent converter drainback.

Diagnosis Tests

CONTROL PRESSURE TEST

Before proceeding, check the transaxle fluid to make sure that it is at the proper level. Note the fluid color. Burned fluid loses its red color and has an acrid odor.

NOTE: If the oil is burned and/or clutch plate material is found in the oil pan, overhaul may be required.

1. Check the following:
   a. T.V. cable adjustment
   b. Outside manual linkage and correct
   c. Engine tune
2. Connect an oil pressure gauge to the transaxle.
3. Connect a tachometer to the engine.
4. Apply the parking braking and chock the drive wheels.
5. Check the oil pressures with the brakes applied at all times. Take the line pressure readings in the ranges and at the engine rpm indicated in the chart.

NOTE: Total running time is not to exceed 2 minutes.

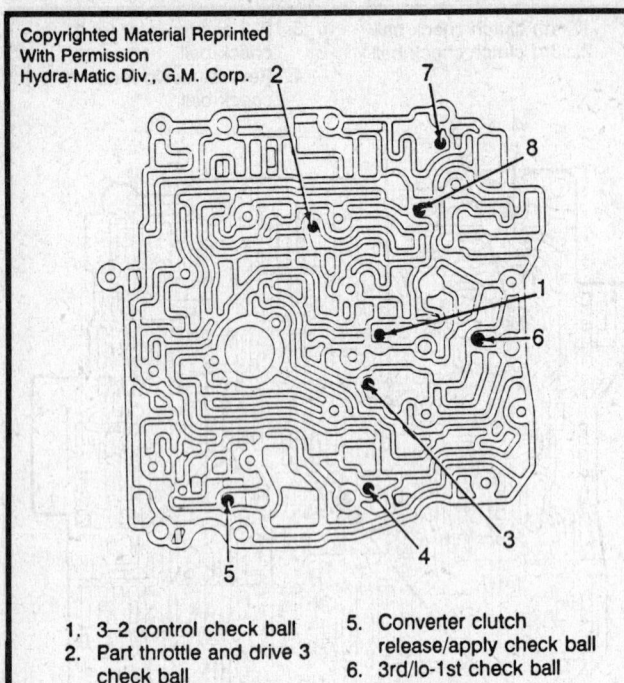

1. 3–2 control check ball
2. Part throttle and drive 3 check ball
3. 2–3 accumulator exhaust check ball
4. 2nd clutch check ball
5. Converter clutch release/apply check ball
6. 3rd/lo-1st check ball
7. 1–2 servo feed check ball
8. Input clutch/reverse check ball

Channel plate check ball locations

TRANSAXLE LINE PRESSURE – 1984–85

	MODEL		AY, BN, BS, BU, CW, HT		BA, BC		OB, OV	
		RANGE	kPa	PSI	kPa	PSI	kPa	PSI
TRANSMISSION LINE PRESSURE	ZERO T.V. (1000 R.P.M.)	D4,D3,D2	422-475	61-69	455-511	66-74	455-511	66-74
		D1	946-1324	137-192	968-1317	140-190	1074-1204	156-175
		Reverse	422-475	61-69	455-511	66-74	663-743	96-108
	FULL T.V. (1000 R.P.M.)	D4,D3,D2	1024-1260	149-183	1058-1297	153-188	1090-1189	158-172
		D1	946-1324	137-192	968-1317	140-190	1074-1204	156-175
		Reverse	1428-1757	207-255	1494-1831	217-266	1585-1729	230-250

AIR PRESSURE TEST

The positioning of the THM 440–T4 transaxle in the vehicle and the valve body location will cause the air pressure tests to be very difficult. It is advisable to make any air pressure tests during the disassembly and assembly of the transaxle to ascertain if a unit is operating.

TRANSAXLE LINE PRESSURE – 1985½

	MODEL		AF, AM, BV, CM, CN, HA, HJ		BR, BW	
		RANGE	kPa	PSI	kPa	PSI
TRANSMISSION LINE PRESSURE	MINIMUM LINE (1250 R.P.M.)	P,N, D4,D3,D2	422 - 475	61 - 69	455 - 511	66 - 74
		D1	946 - 1324	137 - 192	968 - 1317	140 - 191
		REV.	422 - 475	61 - 69	455 - 511	66 - 74
	FULL LINE (1250 R.P.M.)	N, D4, D3, D2	1030 - 1266	150 - 184	1064 - 1302	154 - 189
		D1	946 - 1324	137 - 192	968 - 1317	140 - 191
		REV.	1436 - 1764	209 - 257	1502 - 1838	218 - 267

TRANSAXLE LINE PRESSURE – 1986

	MODEL		AA, AU		AF, AM, AR, BA, BB, BC, BD, BH, BL, BM, BP, BT, CM, CN, HJ		BZ	
		RANGE	kPa	PSI	kPa	PSI	kPa	PSI
TRANSMISSION LINE PRESSURE	MINIMUM LINE (1250 R.P.M.)	P,N, D4,D3,D2	422-475	61-69	422-475	61-69	455-511	66-74
		D1	946-1324	137-192	998-1276	145-185	1112-1399	161-203
		REV.	422-475	61-69	422-475	61-69	455-511	66-74
	FULL LINE (1250 R.P.M.)	N, D4, D3, D2	1030-1266	150-184	1152-1393	167-202	1186-1429	172-207
		D1	946-1324	137-192	998-1276	145-185	1112-1399	161-203
		REV.	1436-1764	209-257	1573-1901	228-276	1619-1951	235-283

TRANSAXLE LINE PRESSURE – 1987

	MODEL		7ADH, 7AFH, 7AHH, 7ALH, 7ARH, 7CAH, 7CBH		7ACH, 7BBH, 7BCH, 7BJH, 7BKH, 7BNH, 7BRH, 7BSH, 7BTH, 7BUH, 7BZH, 7FBH, 7FCH, 7FJH, 7FKH, 7FLH, 7FNH, 7FRH, 7FSH, 7FTH, 7FUH, 7FZH, 7HAH, 7HCH	
		RANGE	kPa	PSI	kPa	PSI
TRANSMISSION LINE PRESSURE	MINIMUM LINE (1250 R.P.M.)	D4,D3,D2	422 - 475	61 - 69	422 - 475	61 - 69
		D1	946 - 1324	137 - 192	998 - 1276	145 - 185
		P,R,N	422 - 475	61 - 69	422 - 475	61 - 69
	FULL LINE (1250 R.P.M.)	D4,D3,D2	1030 - 1266	150 - 184	1152 - 1393	167 - 202
		D1	946 - 1324	137 - 192	998 - 1276	145 - 185
		P,R,N	1436 - 1764	209 - 257	1573 - 1901	228 - 276

TRANSAXLE LINE PRESSURE — 1988–89 EXCEPT THM F7

		8BJH, 8BKH, 8BRH, 8BTH, 8BYH, 8FBH, 8FCH, 8FJH, 8FSH		8AAH, 8ABH, 8AFH, 8ANH, 8ATH, 8AWH		8CFH, 8CMH, 8CRH, 8CTH, 8CXH, 8CWH	
	RANGE	kPa	PSI	kPa	PSI	kPa	PSI
MINIMUM LINE @ 1250 R.P.M. (18 In. Hg. Vacuum At Modulator)	D4,D3,D2	422 - 475	61 - 69	544 - 1034	79 - 150	422 - 475	61 - 69
	D1	998 - 1276	145 - 185	998 - 1276	145 - 185	946 - 1324	137 - 192
	P,R,N	422 - 475	61 - 69	640 - 1216	93 - 176	422 - 475	61 - 69
FULL LINE @ 1250 R.P.M. (0 In. Hg. Vacuum At Modulator)	D4,D3,D2	1152 - 1393	167 - 202	1022 - 1536	148 - 223	1030 - 1266	149 - 184
	D1	998 - 1276	145 - 185	998 - 1276	145 - 185	946 - 1324	137 - 192
	P,R,N	1573 - 1901	228 - 275	1202 - 1807	174 - 262	1436 - 1764	208 - 256

Copyrighted Material Reprinted
With Permission
Hydra-Matic Div., G.M. Corp.

TRANSXALE LINE PRESSURE 1988–89 THM F7

		8APZ	
	RANGE	kPa	PSI
MINIMUM LINE @ 1250 R.P.M. (18 In. Hg. Vacuum At Modulator)	D4,D3,D2	455 - 511	66 - 74
	D1	1112 - 1399	161 - 203
	P,R,N	455 - 511	66 - 74
FULL LINE @ 1250 R.P.M. (0 In. Hg. Vacuum At Modulator)	D4,D3,D2	1186 - 1429	172 - 207
	D1	1112 - 1399	161 - 203
	P,R,N	1619 - 1951	235 - 283

Copyrighted Material Reprinted
With Permission
Hydra-Matic Div., G.M. Corp.

STALL SPEED TEST

General Motors does not recommend performing a stall test because of the excessive heat that is generated within the transaxle by the converter during the test.

Recommendations are to perform the control pressure test and road test to determine and localize any transaxle malfunctions.

ROAD TEST

Shift Check

1. Start the engine.
2. Depress the brake pedal.
3. Move the gear selector from **P** to **R** to **N** to **D**. The gear selections should be immediate and not harsh.

Upshifts and Torque Converter Clutch Apply

1. Position the gear selector in **OVERDRIVE D** range.
2. Accelerate using a steady increasing throttle pressure.
3. Note the shift speed point gear engagements for 2nd gear, 3rd gear and Overdrive.
4. Note the speed shift point for the torque converter clutch apply. This should occur while in 3rd or Overdrive. If the apply is not noticed, check the torque converter clutch.

NOTE: The torque converter clutch will not engage if the engine coolant has not reached a minimum operating temperature of 130°F (54°C).

Part Throttle Detent Downshift

At vehicle speeds of 40–55 mph (64–88 kph), quickly depress the accelerator to a half open position. The torque converter clutch should release and the transaxle should downshift to 3rd gear immediately.

Full Throttle Detent Downshift

At vehicle speeds of 40–55 mph (64–88 kph), quickly depress the accelerator to a wide open position. The torque converter clutch should release and the transaxle should downshift to 2nd gear immediately.

Manual Downshift

At vehicle speeds of 40–55 mph (64–88 kph), release the accelerator pedal while moving the gear selector lever to 3rd gear. The torque converter clutch should release and the transaxle should downshift to 3rd gear immediately. The engine should slow the vehicle down.

Move the gear selector to **OVERDRIVE D** and accelerate to 40–45 mph (64–72 kph). Release the accelerator pedal while moving the gear selector to 2nd gear. The torque converter clutch should be released and the transaxle should downshift to 2nd gear immediately. The engine should slow the vehicle down.

Move the gear selector to **OVERDRIVE D** and accelerate to 25 mph (40 kph). Release the accelerator pedal while moving the gear selector to 1st gear. The torque converter clutch should be released and the transaxle should downshift to 1st gear immediately. The engine should slow the vehicle down.

Coastdown Downshift

With the gear selector in **OVERDRIVE D**, accelerate the vehicle to 4th gear with the torque converter clutch applied. Release the accelerator pedal and lightly apply the brakes. The torque converter clutch should release and the transaxle should downshift.

Manual Gear Range Selection

MANUAL 3RD

With the vehicle stopped, position the gear selector in 3rd and accelerate. Note the 1st to 2nd gear shift point and the 2nd to 3rd gear shift point.

MANUAL 2ND

With the vehicle stopped, position the gear selector in 2nd and accelerate. Note the 1st to 2nd gear shift point. Accelerate to 25 mph (40 kph). A 2nd to 3rd gear shift should not occur and the torque converter clutch should not engage.

MANUAL 1ST

With the vehicle stopped, position the gear selector in 1st and accelerate to 15 mph (24 kph). No upshift should occur and the torque converter clutch should not engage.

REVERSE

With the vehicle stopped, position the gear selector in **R** and slowly accelerate and note the reverse gear operation.

CONVERTER STATOR OPERATION TEST

The torque converter stator assembly and its related roller clutch can possible have one of 2 different type malfunctions.
1. The stator assembly freewheels in both directions.
2. The stator assembly remains locked up at all times.

Malfunction Type One

If the stator roller clutch becomes ineffective, the stator assembly freewheels at all times in both directions. With this condition, the vehicle will tend to have poor acceleration from a standstill. At speeds above 30–35 mph (50–55 kph), the vehicle may act normal. If poor acceleration problems are noted, it should first be determined that the exhaust system is not blocked, the engine is in good tune and the transmission is in 1st gear when starting out.

If the engine will freely accelerate to high rpm in **N**, it can be assumed that the engine and exhaust system are normal. Driving the vehicle in **R** and checking for poor performance will help determine if the stator is freewheeling at all time.

Malfunction Type Two

If the stator assembly remains locked up at all times, the engine rpm and vehicle speed will tend to be limited or restricted at high speeds. The vehicle performance when accelerating from a standstill will be normal. Engine over-heating may be noted. Visual examination of the converter may reveal a blue color from the over-heating that will result.

Converter Clutch Operation and Diagnosis

TORQUE CONVERTER CLUTCH

The converter clutch mechanically connects the engine to the drive train and eliminates the hydraulic slip between the pump and turbine. When accelerating, the stator gives the converter the capability to multiply engine torque (maximum torque multiplication is 2.1:1) and improve vehicle acceleration. At this time the converter clutch is released. When the vehicle reaches cruising speed, the stator becomes inactive and there is no multiplication of engine torque (torque multiplication is 1.0:1). At this time the converter is a fluid coupling with the turbine at almost the same speed as the converter pump. The converter clutch can now be applied to eliminate the hydraulic slip between the pump and turbine and improve fuel economy.

The converter clutch cannot apply in **P**, **R**, **N** and **D** Range – 1st gear.

On vehicles equipped with computer command control, converter clutch operation is controlled by the solenoid. The solenoid is controlled by the brake switch, 3rd clutch pressure switch and the computer command control system.

Converter Clutch Applied

The converter clutch is applied when oil pressure is exhausted between the converter pressure plate and the converter cover and pressure is applied to push the pressure plate against the converter cover.

When the solenoid is energized converter signal oil, from the converter clutch plug, pushes the converter clutch apply valve to the left. Converter clutch release oil then exhausts and converter clutch apply oil from the converter clutch regulator valve pushes the converter pressure plate against the converter to apply the converter clutch.

Converter Clutch Released

The converter clutch is released when oil pressure is applied between the converter cover and the converter pressure plate.

Converter feed pressure from the pressure regulator valve passes through the converter clutch apply valve into the release passage. The release oil feeds between the pump shaft and the turbine shaft to push the pressure plate away from the converter cover to release the converter clutch.

Converter Clutch Apply Feel

Converter clutch apply feel is controlled by the converter clutch regulator valve and the converter clutch accumulator.

The converter clutch regulator valve is controlled by T.V. and controls the pressure that applies the converter clutch. The converter clutch accumulator absorbs converter feed oil as converter release oil is exhausting. Less oil is then fed to the converter clutch regulator valve and the apply side of the converter clutch. This gives a cushion to the converter clutch apply.

VISCOUS CONVERTER CLUTCH

Viscous Converter Clutch Applied

The viscous converter clutch is capable of applying at approximately 25 mph providing that the transaxle is in 2nd gear and the transaxle oil temperature is below 200°F (93.3°C). (This temperature is monitored by the ECM through the thermistor.) When transaxle oil temperatures are above 200°F (93.3°C) but below 315°F (157°C) the viscous clutch will not apply until approximately 38 mph. If transaxle oil temperature exceeds 315°F (157°C) a temperature switch located in the channel plate will open and release the viscous clutch to protect the transaxle from overheating.

TROUBLESHOOTING THE TORQUE CONVERTER CLUTCH

Before diagnosing the torque converter clutch system as being at fault in the case of rough shifting or other malfunctions,

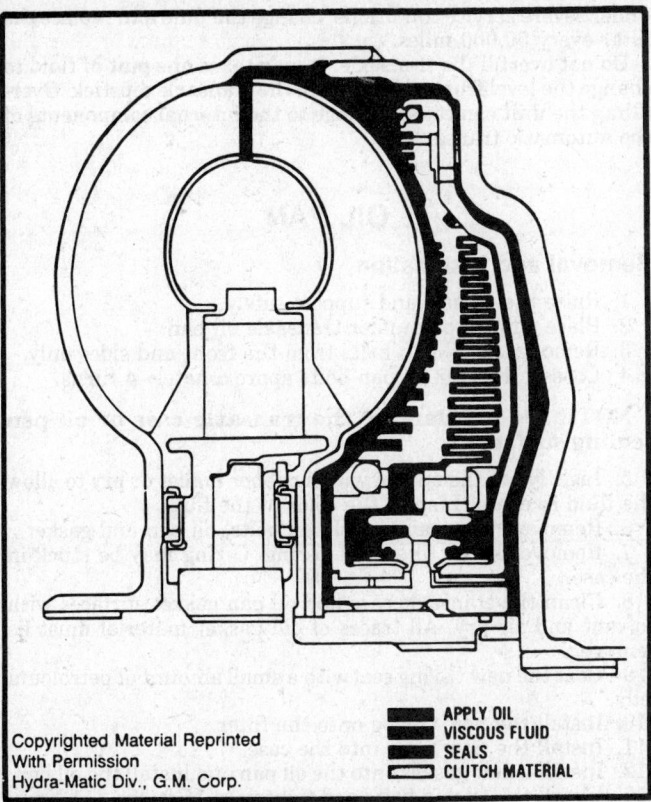

APPLY OIL
VISCOUS FLUID
SEALS
CLUTCH MATERIAL

Copyrighted Material Reprinted
With Permission
Hydra-Matic Div., G.M. Corp.

Viscous converter clutch applied

make sure that the engine is in at least a reasonable state of tune. Also the following points should be checked:

1. Check the transmission fluid level and correct as necessary.

2. Check the manual linkage adjustment and correct as necessary.

3. Road test the vehicle to verify the complaint. Make sure that the vehicle is at normal operating temperature.

CAUTION

When inspecting the stator and turbine of the torque converter clutch unit, a slight drag is normal when turned in the direction of freewheel rotation because of the pressure exerted by the waved spring washer, located between the turbine and the pressure plate.

Torque Converter Clutch—Electrical Controls

Two types of electrical control systems are used to control the **APPLY** function of the torque converter clutch assembly. Both systems use the third clutch pressure switch and a solenoid. The difference in the 2 systems is that the vehicle speed sensing controls are not the same.

Computer Command Control System

Vehicles equipped with the computer command control system utilize the following components to accomplish the **APPLY** function of the torque converter clutch assembly.

1. Vacuum sensor—which sends engine vacuum information to the electronic control module.

2. Throttle position sensor—which sends throttle position information to the electronic control module.

3. Vehicle speed sensor—which sends vehicle speed information to the electronic control module.

4. Electronic control module—which energizes and grounds the transaxle electrical system.

5. Brake release switch—which avoids stalling the engine when braking. An time that the brakes are applied the torque converter clutch is released.

6. Third gear switch—which prevents operation until third gear speed is obtained.

ON CAR SERVICES

Adjustments

THROTTLE VALVE (T.V.) CABLE

2.5L AND 2.8L ENGINES

1. Check to see that the cable is in the full non-adjustment position.

2. Without twisting or kinking cable, insert cable slug into idler pulley (cam) slot.

3. Accelerator cable must be installed before adjustment.

4. Rotate the idler pulley (cam) in a counterclockwise direction to 65 inch lbs. (7.3 Nm).

3.8L ENGINE

1. With the engine stopped, depress and hold down the readjust tab at the T.V. cable adjuster.

2. Move the cable conduit until it stops against the fitting.

3. Release the readjustment tab.

4. Rotate the throttle lever by hand to its full travel position.

5. The slider must move (ratchet) toward the lever when the lever is rotated to its full travel position.

SHIFT CONTROL CABLE

COLUMN SHIFT CONTROL WITH CABLE ADJUSTER

1. Place the shift lever in **N**. Neutral can be found by rotating the selector shaft clockwise from **P** through **R** to **N**.

2. Place the shift control assembly in **N**.

3. Push the tab on the cable adjuster to adjust the cable in the cable mounting bracket.

COLUMN SHIFT CONTROL WITHOUT CABLE ADJUSTER

1. Position the selector lever in **N**.

2. Position the transaxle lever in **N**. Obtain **N** position by turning the transaxle lever clockwise from **P** through **R** into **N**.

3. Loosely assemble the pin part of the shift cable through the transaxle lever slotted hole.

4. Tighten the nut to 20 ft. lbs. (27 Nm). The lever must be held out of **P** when tightening the nut.

CONSOLE SHIFT CONTROL

1. Disconnect the negative battery cable at the battery.

2. Place the transaxle into **1st** gear position.

3. Loosen the shift cable attaching nuts at the transaxle lever.

4. Remove the console trim plate and slide shifter boot up shifter handle. Remove the console.

5. With the shift lever in **1st** gear position (pulled to the left and held against the stop) insert a yoke clip to hold the lever hard against the reverse lockout stop. Install af $^5/_{32}$ in. or No. 22 drill bit into the alignment hole at the side of the shifter assembly.

6. Remove the lash from the transaxle by rotating the lever in the direction away from the cable (do not force the cable) while tightening the nut.

7. Tighten the nut at the lever.

8. Remove the drill bit and yoke at the shifter assembly.

9. Install the console, shifter boot and the trim plate.

10. Connect the negative battery cable at the battery.

11. Road test the vehicle to check for a good neutral gate feel during shifting. It may be necessary to fine tune the adjustment after road testing.

PARK/NEUTRAL START AND BACKUP LIGHT SWITCH

1. Place the transaxle control shifter assembly in the **N** notch in the detent plate.

2. Loosen the switch attaching screws.

3. Rotate the switch on the sifter assembly to align the service adjustment hole with carrier tang hole. Insert a $^3/_{32}$ in. (2.34mm) maximum diameter gauge pin to a depth of $^5/_8$ in. (15mm).

4. Tighten the attaching screws.

5. Remove the gauge pin.

PARK LOCK CONTROL CABLE

1. Position the selector lever in **P**. Lock the steering column.

2. Position the transaxle lever into the **P** position.

3. Install the cable-to-shifter mounting bracket with the spring yoke.

4. Install the cable-to-park lock pin on the shifter. Install the lock pin. Push the lock button on the cable housing in to set the cable length.

5. Check the cable operation in the following manner:

   a. Turn the ignition key to the **LOCK** position.

   b. Press the detent release button in the shifter handle.

   c. Pull the shifter lever rearward.

   d. The shifter lock-hook must engage into the shifter base slot, within 2 degrees maximum movement of the shifter lever.

   e. Turn the ignition key to the **OFF** position.

   f. Repeat Steps b–c. The selector lever must be able to move rearward to the **L** (1 on some vehicles) position.

   g. Repeat Steps a–d to assure that the adjustment nut has not slipped during check.

   h. Return the key to the **LOCK** position and check key removal.

Services

FLUID CHANGES

The conditions under which the vehicle is operated is the main consideration in determining how often the transaxle fluid should be changed. Different driving conditions result in different transaxle fluid temperatures. These temperatures affect change intervals.

If the vehicle is driven under severe service conditions, change the fluid and filter every 15,000 miles. If the vehicle is not used under severe service conditions, change the fluid and replace the filter every 50,000 miles.

Do not overfill the transaxle. It only takes one pint of fluid to change the level from add to full on the transaxle dipstick. Overfilling the unit can cause damage to the internal components of the automatic transaxle.

OIL PAN

Removal and Installation

1. Raise the vehicle and support safely.

2. Place a drain pan under transaxle oil pan.

3. Remove the oil pan bolts from the front and sides only.

4. Loosen the rear oil pan bolts approximately 4 turns.

NOTE: Do not damage the transaxle case or oil pan sealing surfaces.

5. Lightly tap the oil pan with a rubber mallet or pry to allow the fluid to drain. Inspect the color of the fluid.

6. Remove the remaining oil pan bolts, oil pan and gasket.

7. Remove the oil filter and O-ring. O-ring may be stuck in the case.

8. Clean the transaxle case and oil pan gasket surfaces with solvent and air dry. All traces of old gasket material must be removed.

9. Coat the new O-ring seal with a small amount of petroleum jelly.

10. Install the new O-ring onto the filter.

11. Install the new filter into the case.

12. Install a new gasket onto the oil pan and install the oil pan.

13. Install the oil pan bolts and tighten to 15 ft. lbs. (11 Nm).

14. Lower the vehicle.

15. Fill the transaxle to the proper level with Dexron®II fluid or equivalent.

16. Check the cold fluid level reading for initial fill. Do not overfill.

17. Check the oil pan gasket for leaks.

VALVE BODY

Removal and Installation

1. Disconnect the negative cable from the battery.

2. Raise and support the vehicle safely.

3. Remove the case side cover pan.

4. Remove the pump assembly.

5. Remove the 1–2 servo pipe clip from the valve body.

6. Remove the valve body-to-channel plate bolts.

7. Remove the valve body keeping the spacer plate with the transaxle.

8. Remove the spacer plate and gasket.

9. Retain the check balls in their proper locations with petroleum jelly.

10. Install the spacer plate and gasket.

11. Install the valve body and gasket.

12. Install the valve body-to-channel plate bolts. Torque to 10 ft. lbs. (14 Nm).

NOTE: Do not use an impact type tool on the valve body or pump assembly.

13. Install the 1–2 servo pipe clip to the valve body.

14. Install the pump assembly.

15. Install the case side cover pan.

16. Lower the vehicle.

17. Connect the negative battery cable to the battery.

18. Refill the transaxle to the proper level.

19. Adjust the T.V. cable. Check for leaks.

REVERSE SERVO ASSEMBLY

Removal and Installation

1. Raise and support the vehicle safely.
2. Disconnect the exhaust crossover pipe.
3. Depress the servo cover.
4. Remove the snapring, servo cover, servo piston, sealing ring, apply pin and servo spring.
5. Install the servo spring, apply pin, sealing ring, servo piston, servo cover and snapring.
6. Connect the exhaust crossover pipe.
7. Lower the vehicle.

1–2 SERVO ASSEMBLY

Removal and Installation

1. Raise and support the vehicle safely.
2. Disconnect the exhaust crossover pipe.
3. Depress the servo cover.
4. Remove the snapring, servo cover, servo piston, sealing ring, apply pin and servo spring.
5. Install the servo spring, apply pin, sealing ring, servo piston, servo cover and snapring.
6. Connect the exhaust crossover pipe.

GOVERNOR

Removal and Installation

1. Raise the vehicle and support safely.
2. Disconnect the speedometer cable.
3. Remove the governor cover attaching bolts.
4. Remove the governor cover and seal.
5. Remove the governor assembly (including the sleeve and the speedometer drive gear).
6. Install the governor assembly.
7. Install the governor cover and new seal.
8. Install the governor cover attaching bolts and torque to 97 inch lbs. (11 Nm).
9. Connect the speedometer cable.
10. Lower the vehicle.

REMOVAL AND INSTALLATION

TRANSAXLE REMOVAL

A-BODY VEHICLES

1. Disconnect the negative battery cable.
2. Remove the air cleaner and disconnect the T.V. cable at the throttle body.
3. Disconnect the shift linkage at the transaxle.
4. Install the engine support fixture. Tool J–28467 is recommended.
5. Disconnect all electrical connectors.
6. Remove the 3 bolts from the transaxle to the engine.
7. Disconnect the vacuum line at the modulator.
8. Raise the vehicle and suitably support it.
9. Remove the left front wheel and tire assembly.
10. Remove the left hand ball joint from the steering knuckle.
11. Disconnect the brake line bracket at the strut.

NOTE: A drive axle seal protector tool J–34754 should be modified and installed on any drive axle prior to service procedures on or near the drive axle. Failure to do so could result in seal damage or joint failure.

12. Remove the drive axles from the transaxle.
13. Disconnect the pinch bolt at the intermediate steering shaft. Failure to do so could cause damage to the steering gear.
14. Remove the frame to stabilizer bolts.
15. Remove the stabilizer bolts at the control arm.
16. Remove the left front frame assembly.
17. Disconnect the speedometer cable or wire connector from the transaxle.
18. Remove the extension housing to engine block support bracket.
19. Disconnect the cooler pipes.
20. Remove the right and left insulator attaching bolts.
21. Remove the flywheel splash shield.
22. Remove the converter cover and converter-to-flywheel bolts.
23. Remove all of the remaining transaxle to engine bolts except one.
24. Position a jack under the transaxle.
25. Remove the remaining transaxle to engine bolt and remove the transaxle.

BUICK AND OLDSMOBILE C-BODY VEHICLES

1. Disconnect the negative terminal from the battery. Disconnect the wire connector at the mass air flow sensor.
2. Remove the air intake duct and the mass air flow sensor as an assembly.
3. Disconnect the cruise control assembly and the the shift control linkage.
4. Label and disconnect the following:
   a. Park/Neutral switch
   b. Torque converter clutch
   c. Vehicle speed sensor
   d. Vacuum modulator hose at the modulator
5. Remove the 3 top transaxle-to-engine block bolts and install an engine support fixture.
6. Remove both front wheels and turn the steering wheel to the full left position.
7. Remove the right front ball joint nut and separate the control arm from the steering knuckle.
8. Remove the right halfshaft.

NOTE: Be careful not to allow the drive axle splines to contact any portion of the lip seal.

9. Using a medium pry bar, remove the left halfshaft; be careful not to damage the pan. Install drive axle boot seal protectors.
10. Remove 3 bolts at the transaxle and 3 nuts at the cradle member. Remove the left front transaxle mount.
11. Remove the right front mount-to-cradle nuts. Remove the left rear transaxle mount-to-transaxle bolts.
12. Remove the right rear transaxle mount. Remove the engine support bracket-to-transaxle case bolts.
13. Remove the flywheel cover, matchmark the flywheel-to-torque converter and remove the flywheel-to-converter bolts.

NOTE: Be sure to matchmark the flywheel-to-converter relationship for proper alignment upon reassembly.

14. Remove the rear cradle member-to-front cradle dog leg.
15. Remove the front left cradle-to-body bolt and the front cradle dog leg-to-right cradle member bolts.
16. Install a transaxle support fixture into position.

17. Remove the cradle assembly by swinging it aside and supporting it with jackstand.
18. Disconnect and plug the oil cooler lines at the transaxle.

NOTE: A bolt is located between the transaxle and the engine block; it is installed in the opposite direction.

19. Remove the remaining lower transaxle-to-engine bolts and lower the transaxle from the vehicle.

CADILLAC C-BODY VEHICLES

1. Disconnect the negative terminal from the battery. Remove the air cleaner and the T.V. cable.
2. Disconnect the shift linkage from the transaxle. Using an engine support fixture tool, connect it to and support the engine.
3. Label and disconnect the electrical connectors from the following items:
   a. Converter clutch
   b. Vehicle speed sensor
   c. Vacuum line at the modulator
4. Remove the upper bell housing-to-engine bolts and studs.
5. Raise and support the front of the vehicle. Remove both front wheels.
6. From the left side of the vehicle, disconnect the lower ball joint from steering knuckle. Remove both drive axles from the transaxle.
7. Remove the stabilizer bar-to-left control arm bolt.
8. Remove the left front cradle assembly.
9. Remove the extension housing-to-engine support bracket.
10. Disconnect and plug the oil cooler lines at the transaxle case.
11. Remove the right and left transaxle mount attachments.
12. Remove the flywheel splash shield. Matchmark the torque converter-to-flywheel and remove the converter-to-flywheel bolts.
13. Remove the lower bellhousing bolts except the lower rear on (No. 6).
14. Using a floor jack, position it under the transaxle and remove the last bell housing bolt.

NOTE: To reach the last bell housing bolt, use a 3 in. socket wrench extension through the right wheel arch opening.

15. Remove the transaxle assembly.

H-BODY VEHICLES

1. Disconnect the negative battery cable. Disconnect the wire connector at the mass air flow sensor.
2. Remove the air intake duct and the mass air flow sensor as an assembly.
3. Disconnect the cruise control assembly. Disconnect the shift control linkage.
4. Tag and disconnect the torque converter clutch, park/neutral switch, vehicle speed sensor and vacuum modulator hose at the modulator.
5. Remove the top transaxle to engine block bolts. Install an engine support fixture.
6. Remove both front wheels and turn the steering wheel to the full left position.
7. Remove the right front ball joint nut and separate the control arm from the steering knuckle.
8. Remove the right drive axle. Be careful not to allow the drive axle splines to contact any portion of the lip seal.
9. Remove the left drive axle using a suitable pry bar. Be careful not to damage the pan. Install drive axle boot seal protectors.
10. Remove bolts at the transaxle and nuts at the cradle member. Remove the left front transaxle mount.
11. Remove the right front mount to cradle nuts. Remove the left rear transaxle mount to transaxle bolts.
12. Remove the right rear transaxle mount as in Step 10. Remove the engine support bracket to transaxle case bolts.

13. Remove the flywheel cover. Remove the flywheel to converter bolts. Be sure to matchmark the flywheel to converter relationship for proper alignment upon reassembly.
14. Remove the bolts attaching the rear cradle member to the front cradle dog leg.
15. Remove the front left cradle to body bolt. Remove the front cradle dog leg to right cradle member bolts.
16. Install a transaxle support fixture into position.
17. Remove the cradle assembly by swinging it aside and supporting it with a suitable stand.
18. Disconnect and cap the oil cooler lines at the transaxle.

NOTE: A bolt is located between the transaxle and the engine block and is installed in the opposite direction.

19. Remove the remaining lower transaxle to engine bolts. Lower the transaxle assembly away from the vehicle.

1986–87 RIVIERA AND TORONADO

NOTE: To perform this procedure, secure an engine support tool J–28467 or equivalent and a drive axle remover tool J–33008 or equivalent.

1. Disconnect the negative battery cable. Install the engine support fixture.
2. Disconnect the vacuum line from the modulator; electrical connections involved with the transaxle; transaxle valve cable at the throttle body and at the transaxle; the cruise control servo.
3. Disconnect the shift selector bracket and cable from the transaxle. Disconnect the neutral safety switch.
4. Remove the top 3 transaxle mounting bolts.
5. Remove the bolts that fasten the wiring harness to the transaxle. Remove the driveline dampener bracket.
6. Raise and support the front of the vehicle.
7. Disconnect and drain the transaxle oil cooler lines at the transaxle.
8. Remove the torque converter cover. Scribe the relationship between the flexplate and the converter so the same relationship may be established on reinstallation for balance. Remove the converter-to-flexplate bolts, turning the crankshaft (as necessary).
9. Remove the left side transaxle mounting bolts. Remove the engine mounting nuts.
10. Disconnect the sway bar links. Disconnect the left side ball joint from the knuckle.
11. Disconnect the left side driveshaft from the transaxle using a special tool J–33008 or equivalent.
12. Disconnect the left side of the frame by removing the bolts.
13. Position a floor jack under the transaxle and support it securely.
14. Remove the 2 remaining engine-to-transaxle bolts.

NOTE: One of the bolts is located between the transaxle case and the block, it is installed in the direction opposite to the others.

15. Remove the engine-to-transaxle bracket.
16. Remove the right drive axle from the transaxle and hang it securely.
17. Remove the transaxle.

1986–89 ELDORADO, SEVILLE AND 1987–89 ALLANTE

1. Disconnect the negative battery cable. Remove the air cleaner assembly. Disconnect the transaxle throttle valve cable.
2. Remove the cruise control servo and bracket assembly. Disconnect the electrical connectors going to the distributor, oil pressure sending unit and transaxle.
3. Remove the bracket for the engine oil cooler lines.
4. Remove the shift linkage bracket from the transaxle and the manual shift lever from the manual shift shaft; leave the cable attached to the lever and bracket.

5. Remove the fuel line bracket and disconnect the neutral safety switch connector.

6. Remove the vacuum modulator.

7. Remove the throttle valve cable support bracket and engine oil cooler line bracket. Remove the bell housing bolts except the left and right side bolts; note the bolt lengths and positions.

8. Remove the air injection reactor crossover pipe fitting and reposition the pipe. Remove the radiator hose bracket and transaxle mount-to-bracket nuts.

9. Install an engine support fixture, noting the positions of the hooks.

10. Raise and support the front of the vehicle.

11. Remove both front wheels, the right and left stabilizer link bolts. Remove the ball joint cotter pins and nuts and press the ball joints from the steering knuckles.

12. Remove the air conditioner splash shield and the mount cover for the forwardmost cradle insulator.

13. Remove the hose connections from the ends of the air injection reactor pipes. Remove the vacuum hoses and the wire loom from the clips at the front of the cradle.

14. Remove the engine mount and dampener-to-cradle attachments. Remove the transaxle mount-to-cradle attachments. Remove the wire loom clip from the transaxle mount bracket and lower the vehicle.

15. Using the 2 left side support hooks on the engine support fixture to raise the transaxle 2 inches from its normal position. Raise and support the front of the vehicle.

16. Remove the right front and left rear transaxle-to-cradle bolts and the left stabilizer mount bolts. Remove the foremost cradle mount insulator bolt and the left cradle member, separate the right front corner first.

17. Remove the air injection reactor management valve/bracket assembly from the transaxle mount bracket and reposition the bracket to the transaxle stud bolts.

18. Lower the front of the vehicle. Lower the transaxle to its normal position to gain access to the transaxle mounting bracket. Remove the mounting bracket.

19. Raise and support the front of the vehicle. Remove the right rear transaxle mount-to-transaxle bracket. Remove the engine-to-transaxle brace bolts that pass into the transaxle VSS connector.

20. Mark the relationship between torque converter and flexplate for reassembly in the same position. Remove the flywheel covers, then, remove the torque converter bolts, rotating the crankshaft with a socket wrench as necessary to gain access. Position a jack under the transaxle to support it.

21. Remove the left and right bell housing bolts; note the bolt lengths and positions.

NOTE: Access may be gained through the right wheelhouse opening to remove the bolt on the right side; use a 3 foot long socket extension to reach it.

22. Disconnect the oil cooler lines at the transaxle, drain them and plug the openings. Then, install drive axle boot seal protectors and disconnect the driveshafts at the transaxle. Suspend the drive axles out of the way and remove the transaxle.

1988–89 REATTA, RIVIERA AND TORONADO

1. Disconnect the negative battery cable. Remove the air intake duct.

2. Disconnect the throttle valve cable from the transaxle and the throttle body. Disconnect the cruise control servo and cable.

3. Remove the exhaust pipe crossover.

4. Disconnect the shift control linkage lever from the manual shaft and the mounting bracket from the transaxle.

5. Disconnect the electrical harness connectors from the neutral start/backup light switch, the torque converter clutch (TCC) and the vehicle speed sensor (VSS).

6. From the vacuum modulator, disconnect the hose.

7. Remove the upper transaxle-to-engine bolts.

8. Using the engine support fixture tool J–28467 or equiva-

lent, attach it to the engine, turn the wing nuts to relieve the tension on the engine cradle and mounts.

9. Turn the steering wheel to the full left position.

10. Raise and support the front of the vehicle. Remove both front wheel assemblies.

11. Using the drive axle seal protector tool J–34754 or equivalent, install one on each halfshaft. Remove both front ball joint-to-steering knuckle nuts and separate the control arms from the steering knuckles.

12. Using a medium pry bar, pry the halfshaft from the transaxle and support it on a wire; Do not remove the halfshaft from the steering knuckle.

NOTE: When removing the halfshaft, be careful not to damage the seal lips.

13. Remove the right rear transaxle-to-frame nuts, the left rear transaxle mount-to-transaxle bolts and the right rear transaxle mount.

14. From the left control arm, remove the stabilizer shaft.

15. Remove the flywheel cover bolts and the cover.

16. Matchmark the torque converter-to-flywheel bolts for reinstallation purposes. Remove the torque converter-to-flywheel bolts and push the torque converter back into the transaxle.

17. Remove the partial frame-to-main frame bolts, the partial frame-to-body bolts and the partial frame.

18. Disconnect and plug the oil cooler tubes from the transaxle.

19. Remove the lower transaxle-to-engine bolts.

NOTE: One bolt is located between the engine and the transaxle case and is positioned in the opposite direction.

20. Lower the transaxle from the vehicle; be careful not to damage the hoses, lines and wiring.

W-BODY VEHICLES

1. Disconnect the negative terminal from the battery. Remove the air cleaner, bracket, mass air flow (MAF) sensor and air tube as an assembly.

2. Disconnect the exhaust crossover from the right-side manifold and remove the left-side exhaust manifold, then, raise and support the manifold/crossover assembly.

3. Disconnect the T.V. cable from the throttle lever and the transaxle.

4. Remove the vent hose and the shift cable from the transaxle.

5. Remove the fluid level indicator and the filler tube.

6. Using the engine support fixture tool J–28467 or equivalent and the adapter tool J–35953 or equivalent, install them on the engine.

7. Remove the wiring harness-to-transaxle nut.

8. Label and disconnect the wires for the speed sensor, TCC connector and the neutral safety/backup light switch.

9. Remove the upper transaxle-to-engine bolts.

10. Remove the transaxle-to-mount through bolt, the transaxle mount bracket and the mount.

11. Raise and safely support the vehicle.

12. Remove the front wheel assemblies.

13. Disconnect the shift cable bracket from the transaxle.

14. Remove the left-side splash shield.

15. Using a modified drive axle seal protector tool J–34754 or equivalent, install one on each drive axle to protect the seal from damage and the joint from possible failure.

16. Using care not to damage the halfshaft boots, disconnect the halfshafts from the transaxle.

17. Remove the torsional and lateral strut from the transaxle. Remove the left-side stabilizer link pin bolt.

18. Remove the left frame support bolts and move it out of the way.

19. Disconnect the speedometer wire from the transaxle.

20. Remove the transaxle converter cover and matchmark the converter to the flywheel for assembly.
21. Disconnect and plug the transaxle cooler pipes.
22. Remove the transaxle-to-engine support.
23. Using a transmission jack, position and secure it to the transaxle and remove the remaining transaxle-to-engine bolts.
24. Make sure that the torque converter does not fall out and remove the transaxle from the vehicle.

NOTE: The transaxle cooler and lines should be flushed any time the transaxle is removed for overhaul, or to replace the pump, case or converter.

TRANSAXLE INSTALLATION

A-BODY VEHICLES
1. Install the transaxle into place.
2. Install the transaxle-to-engine bolts and torque to 55 ft. lbs. (75 Nm).
3. Install the converter-to-flywheel bolts and torque to 46 ft. lbs. (62 Nm). Retorque the first bolt after all 3 bolts have been tightened.
4. Install the flywheel splash shield.
5. Install the right and left insulator attaching bolts and torque to 40 ft. lbs. (55 Nm).
6. Connect the cooler pipes and torque tube nuts to 20 ft. lbs. (27 Nm).
7. Install the extension housing support bracket.
8. Connect the speedometer cable.
9. Install the frame assembly.
10. Install the stabilizer shaft.
11. Install the driveshafts.
12. Install the brake line bracket at the strut.
13. Install the pinch bolt and nut at the steering knuckle.
14. Install the wheel assemblies.
15. Lower the vehicle.
16. Connect the vacuum line at the modulator.
17. Tighten the remaining transaxle-to-engine bolts to 55 ft. lbs. (75 Nm).
18. Connect all electrical connectors.
19. Connect the shift linkage at the transaxle.
20. Connect the T.V. cable.
21. Install the air cleaner and the negative battery cable.
22. Fill the transaxle with transaxle fluid and check adjustments.

BUICK AND OLDSMOBILE C-BODY VEHICLES
1. Install the transaxle into the vehicle.
2. Install the lower transaxle-to-engine bolts and torque to 55 ft. lbs. (75 Nm).
3. Connect the cooler pipes at the transaxle and torque to 16 ft. lbs. (22 Nm).
4. Install the right and left drive axle splines into the case past the lip seal.
5. Attach the ball joint to the lower steering knuckle and torque to 48 ft. lbs. (65 Nm).
6. Remove the transaxle support fixture.
7. Install the cradle assembly.
8. Install the left frame-to-body attaching bolts.
9. Install the front frame strut to the right frame member bolts.
10. Install the front frame strut to the rear frame member bolts.
11. Install the flywheel-to-converter bolts and torque to 46 ft. lbs. (62 Nm). Retorque the first bolt after all 3 bolts have been tightened.
12. Install the flywheel cover and attaching bolts.
13. Connect the stabilizer link to the control arm bolt.
14. Install the engine support bracket-to-transaxle case bolts.
15. Install the right rear transaxle mount. Torque the 3 nuts to frame member to 30 ft. lbs. (41 Nm). Torque the 2 bolts to the transaxle case to 40 ft. lbs. (55 Nm).

16. Install the left rear transaxle mount to the transaxle bolts and torque to 30 ft. lbs. (41 Nm).
17. Install the right front transaxle mount to frame nuts.
18. Install the left front transaxle mount. Torque the 3 bolts at the transaxle to 40 ft. lbs. (55 Nm). Install the 3 nuts at the frame member.
19. Install the driveshafts.
20. Install the ball stud to the steering knuckle.
21. Install the wheel assemblies.
22. Lower the vehicle.
23. Remove the engine support fixture.
24. Install the remaining top transaxle to engine bolts and torque to 55 ft. lbs. (75 Nm).
25. Connect the vacuum modulator hose at the modulator.
26. Connect all electrical connectors.
27. Connect the shift control linkage.
28. Connect the cruise control accessories.
29. Connect the T.V. cable at the throttle body and at the transaxle.
30. Install the air intake duct and mass air flow sensor.
31. Connect the battery negative cable.
32. Check the fluid level and all adjustments.

CADILLAC C-BODY VEHICLES
1. Install the transaxle assembly.

NOTE: To reach the last bell housing bolt, use a 3 in. socket wrench extension through the right wheel arch opening.

2. Install the lower bellhousing bolts and torque to 55 ft. lbs. (75 Nm).
3. Install the flywheel splash shield.
4. Install the right and left transaxle mount attachments.
5. Connect the oil cooler lines at the transaxle case.
6. Install the extension housing-to-engine support bracket.
7. Install the left front cradle assembly.
8. Install the stabilizer bar-to-left control arm bolt.
9. Install both drive axles to the transaxle. From the left side of the vehicle, connect the lower ball joint to steering knuckle.
10. Install both front wheels.
11. Install the upper bell housing-to-engine bolts and studs.
12. Connect the electrical connectors to the following items:
    a. Converter clutch
    b. Vehicle speed sensor
    c. Vacuum line at the modulator
13. Connect the shift linkage to the transaxle. Remove engine support fixture tool.
14. Install the air cleaner and the TV cable. Connect the negative terminal to the battery.
15. Check the fluid level and all adjustments.

H-BODY VEHICLES
1. To install, position the transaxle into the vehicle.
2. Install the lower transaxle-to-engine bolts and torque to 55 ft. lbs. (75 Nm).
3. Connect the cooler pipes at the transaxle and torque to 16 ft. lbs. (22 Nm).
4. Install the right and left drive axle splines into the case past the lip seal.
5. Attach the ball joint to the lower steering knuckle and torque to 48 ft. lbs. (65 Nm).
6. Remove the transaxle support fixture.
7. Install the cradle assembly.
8. Install the left frame-to-body attaching bolts.
9. Install the front frame strut to the right frame member bolts.
10. Install the front frame strut to the rear frame member bolts.
11. Install the flywheel-to-converter bolts and torque to 46 ft. lbs. (62 Nm). Retorque the first bolt after all 3 bolts have been tightened.

12. Install the flywheel cover and attaching bolts.

13. Connect the stabilizer link to the control arm bolt.

14. Install the engine support bracket-to-transaxle case bolts.

15. Install the right rear transaxle mount. Torque the 3 nuts to frame member to 30 ft. lbs. (41 Nm). Torque the 2 bolts to the transaxle case to 40 ft. lbs. (55 Nm).

16. Install the left rear transaxle mount to the transaxle bolts and torque to 17 ft. lbs. (41 Nm).

17. Install the right front transaxle mount to frame nuts.

18. Install the left front transaxle mount. Torque the 3 bolts at the transaxle to 40 ft. lbs. (55 Nm). Install the 3 nuts at the frame member.

19. Install the driveshafts.

20. Install the ball stud to the steering knuckle.

21. Install the wheel assemblies.

22. Lower the vehicle.

23. Remove the engine support fixture.

24. Install the remaining top transaxle to engine bolts and torque to 55 ft. lbs. (75 Nm).

25. Connect the vacuum modulator hose at the modulator.

26. Connect all electrical connectors.

27. Connect the shift control linkage.

28. Connect the cruise control accessories.

29. Connect the T.V. cable at the throttle body and at the transaxle.

30. Install the air intake duct and mass air flow sensor.

31. Connect the battery negative cable.

32. Check the fluid level and all adjustments.

1986–87 RIVIERA AND TORONADO

1. Slide the transaxle into position and then install the 2 lower engine-to-transaxle bolts, torquing to 55 ft. lbs. (75 Nm).

2. Install the engine-to-transaxle bracket. Install the left side frame assembly bolts.

3. Install the engine mounting nuts. Install the left side transaxle mounting bolts.

4. Install the right driveshaft to the transaxle.

5. Install the engine-to-transaxle bracket.

6. Install the 2 remaining engine-to-transaxle bolts.

7. Connect the left side of the frame by removing the bolts.

8. Connect the left side driveshaft to the transaxle.

9. Connect the left side ball joint to the knuckle. Connect the sway bar links.

10. Install the engine mounting nuts. Install the left side transaxle mounting bolts.

11. Install the converter-to-flexplate bolts, turning the crankshaft (as necessary). Install the torque converter cover.

12. Connect the transaxle oil cooler lines at the transaxle.

13. Lower the front of the vehicle.

14. Install the driveline dampener bracket. Install the bolts that fasten the wiring harness to the transaxle.

15. Install the top 3 transaxle mounting bolts.

16. Connect the neutral safety switch. Connect the shift selector bracket and cable to the transaxle.

17. Connect the vacuum line to the modulator; electrical connections involved with the transaxle; transaxle valve cable at the throttle body and at the transaxle; the cruise control servo.

18. Remove the engine support fixture.

19. Connect the battery negative cable.

20. Check the fluid level and all adjustments.

1986–89 ELDORADO, SEVILLE AND 1987–89 ALLANTE

1. Install the transaxle into place.

2. Install the lower bell housing bolts and torque to 55 ft. lbs. (75 Nm).

3. Install the converter-to-flexplate bolts and torque to 46 ft. lbs. (63 Nm).

4. Install the flexplate splash shield.

5. Install the cooler lines to the case.

6. Install the driveshafts and remove the drive axle boot seal protectors.

7. Install the engine-to-transaxle brace bolts that pass into the transaxle VSS connector. Install the right rear transaxle mount-to-transaxle bracket. Lower the front of the vehicle.

8. Install the mounting bracket. Raise and safely support the vehicle.

9. Install the air injection reactor management valve/bracket assembly to the transaxle mount bracket.

10. Install the foremost cradle mount insulator bolt and the left cradle member. Install the right front and left rear transaxle-to-cradle bolts and the left stabilizer mount bolts.

11. Lower the front of the vehicle. Remove the engine support fixture.

12. Raise and support the vehicle. Install the wire loom clip to the transaxle mount bracket. Install the transaxle mount-to-cradle attachments. Install the engine mount and dampener-to-cradle attachments.

13. Install the vacuum hoses and the wire loom to the clips at the front of the cradle. Install the hose connections to the ends of the air injection reactor pipes.

14. Install the air conditioner splash shield and the mount cover for the forwardmost cradle insulator.

15. Install the ball joint cotter pins and nuts. Press the ball joints to the steering knuckles. Install the right and left stabilizer link bolts and both front wheels.

16. Lower the front of the vehicle.

17. Install the radiator hose bracket and transaxle mount-to-bracket nuts. Install the air injection reactor crossover pipe fitting.

18. Install the bell housing bolts. Install the throttle valve cable support bracket and engine oil cooler line bracket.

19. Install the vacuum modulator.

20. Install the fuel line bracket and connect the neutral safety switch connector.

21. Install the shift linkage bracket to the transaxle and the manual shift lever to the manual shift shaft.

22. Install the bracket for the engine oil cooler lines.

23. Install the cruise control servo and bracket assembly. Connect the electrical connectors going to the distributor, oil pressure sending unit and transaxle.

24. Connect the transaxle throttle valve cable. Install the air cleaner assembly. Connect the negative battery cable.

25. Adjust the transaxle valve cable and the shift linkage. Refill the transaxle to the proper level. Operate the engine until normal operating temperatures are reached. Adjust the level until it is correct.

1988–89 REATTA, RIVIERA AND TORONADO

1. Raise the transaxle to the vehicle; be careful not to damage the hoses, lines and wiring.

2. Install the lower transaxle-to-engine bolts.

3. Connect the oil cooler tubes to the transaxle.

4. Install the partial frame, the partial frame-to-main frame bolts and the partial frame-to-body bolts.

5. Install the torque converter-to-flywheel bolts.

6. Install the flywheel cover and bolts.

7. To the left control arm, install the stabilizer shaft.

8. Install the right rear transaxle mount, the left rear transaxle mount-to-transaxle bolts and the right rear transaxle-to-frame nuts.

9. Install the halfshaft to the transaxle.

NOTE: When installing the halfshaft, be careful not to damage the seal lips.

10. Connect the control arms to the steering knuckles. Install both front ball joint-to-steering knuckle nuts. Remove the drive axle seal protector tool.

11. Install both front wheel assemblies. Lower the front of the vehicle.

12. Install the upper transaxle-to-engine bolts.

13. Remove the engine support fixture tool.

14. Connect the hose to the vacuum modulator.

15. Connect the electrical harness connectors to the neutral start/backup light switch, the torque converter clutch (TCC) and the vehicle speed sensor (VSS).

16. Install the shift control linkage lever mounting bracket to the transaxle and connect the shift control linkage lever to the manual shaft.

17. Install the exhaust pipe crossover.

18. Connect the cruise control servo and cable. Connect the throttle valve (T.V.) cable to the transaxle and the throttle body.

19. Install the air intake duct. Connect the negative battery cable.

20. Check and/or adjust the T.V. and shift control cables. Check and/or refill the transaxle fluid. Road test the vehicle and check for leaks.

W-BODY VEHICLES

1. Put a small amount of grease on the pilot hub of the converter and make sure that the converter is properly engaged with the pump.

2. Raise the transaxle to the engine while guiding the right-side halfshaft into the transaxle.

3. Install the lower transaxle mounting bolts, tighten to 55 ft. lbs. and remove the jack.

4. Align the converter with the marks made previously on the flywheel and install the bolts hand tight.

5. Torque the converter bolts to 46 ft. lbs.; retorque the first bolt after the others.

6. Install the starter assembly. Install the left side halfshaft.

7. Install the converter cover, oil cooler lines and cover. Install the sub-frame assembly. Install the lower engine mount retaining bolts and the transaxle mount nuts.

8. Install the right and left ball joints. Install the power steering rack, heat shield and cooler lines to the frame.

9. Install the right and left inner fender splash shields. Install the tire assemblies.

10. Lower the vehicle. Connect all electrical leads. Install the upper transaxle mount bolts, tighten to 55 ft. lbs.

11. Attach the crossover pipe to the exhaust manifold. Connect the EGR tube to the crossover.

12. Connect the T.V. cable and the shift cable. Install the air cleaner and inlet tube.

13. Remove the engine support tool. Connect the negative battery cable.

14. Adjust the transaxle valve cable and the shift linkage. Refill the transaxle to the proper level. Operate the engine until normal operating temperatures are reached. Adjust the level until it is correct.

BENCH OVERHAUL

Before Disassembly

NOTE: Cleanliness is an important factor in the overhaul of the transaxle.

Before opening up the transaxle, the outside of the unit should be thoroughly cleaned, preferably with high-pressure cleaning equipment such as a car wash spray unit. Dirt entering the transaxle internal parts will negate all the effort and time spent on the overhaul. During inspection and reassembly, all parts should be thoroughly cleaned with solvent, then dried with compressed air. Wiping cloths and rags should not be used to dry parts since lint will find its way into valve body passages. Wheel bearing grease, long used to secure thrust washers and to lube parts should not be used. Lube seals with Dexron®II and use ordinary unmedicated petroleum jelly to hold thrust washers to ease assembly of seals, since it will not leave a harmful residue as grease often will. Do not use solvent on neoprene seals, friction plates or thrust washers. Be wary of nylon parts if the transaxle failure was due to a failure of the cooling system. Nylon parts exposed to antifreeze solutions can swell and distort and so must be replaced (Speedo gears, some thrust washers, etc.). Before installing bolts into aluminum parts, always dip the threads into clean oil. Anti-seize compound is also a good way to prevent the bolts from galling the aluminum and seizing. Always use a torque wrench to keep from stripping the threads. Take care of the seals when installing them, especially the smaller O-rings. The internal snaprings should be expanded and the external snaprings should be compressed, if they are to be reused. This will help insure proper seating when installed.

Converter Inspection

1. Inspect the converter for leaks as followed:

a. Install pressurizing adapter tool J–21369–B or equivalent. Tighten the hex nut.

b. Fill the converter with approximately 80 psi.

c. Submerge in water and check for leaks.

CAUTION

After leak testing, bleed pressurized air from the converter before removing the tool.

d. Remove the tool.

2. Inspect the converter hub surfaces for signs of scoring or wear.

3. Inspect the converter bushing for damage, cracks or scoring.

4. Inspect converter internal end clearance.

a. Screw the upper and lower knurled knobs of tool J–35138 or equivalent, together. Be sure collet end is not expanded.

b. Insert tool in the torque converter hub.

c. Slide the tapered plug portion of the tool into the torque converter hub to ensure proper tool alignment.

d. Hold the upper knurled knob and turn the wing nut clockwise until hand tight to expand the collet into the converter turbine hub. Then loosen the wing nut (counterclockwise) until the tool is just loose enough to allow up and down movement while not removable from the converter (generally 2½ turns or more).

e. Hold the upper knurled knob and wing nut and turn the lower knurled knob clockwise until hand tight to clamp the tool in the converter turbine hub.

f. Attach the magnetic base (tool J–26900–13 or equivalent) to the torque converter and set up the dial indicator (tool J–8001 or equivalent) so that the indicator tip is in the center of the tool wing nut.

g. To make the end play check, push the upper knurled knob down, zero out dial indicator and pull the lower knurled knob up. Be sure the tapered plug stays seated in the converter hub. The end play is the difference between up and down position. Do not allow the wing nut to turn when measuring. Allowable clearance is 0–0.019 in. (0–0.50mm). Torque converter must be replaced if the clearance exceeds maximum limit.

h. Remove the tool by holding the upper knurled counterclockwise until the collet can be removed from the torque converter turbine hub.

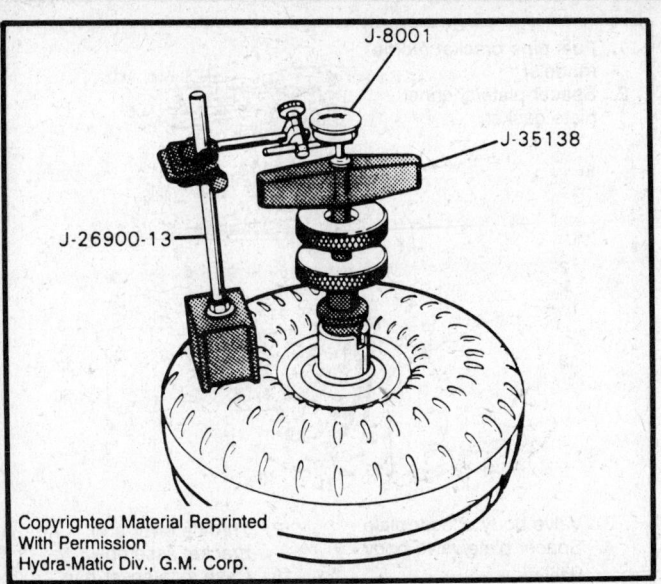

J-8001

J-35138

J-26900-13

Copyrighted Material Reprinted
With Permission
Hydra-Matic Div., G.M. Corp.

Checking torque converter endplay

Transaxle Disassembly
TORQUE CONVERTER

Removal

1. Make certain that the transaxle is held securely.
2. Pull the converter straight out of the transaxle. Be careful since the converter contains a large amount of oil. There is no drain plug on the converter so the converter should be drained through the hub.

NOTE: The transaxle fluid that is drained from the converter can help diagnose transaxle problems.

3. If the oil in the converter is discolored but does not contain metal bits or particles, the converter is not damaged and need not be replaced. Remember that color is no longer a good indicator of transaxle fluid condition. In the past, dark color was associated with overheated transaxle fluid. It is not a positive sign of transaxle failure with the newer fluids like Dexron®II.
4. If the oil in the converter contains metal particles, the converter is damaged internally and must be replaced. The oil may have an aluminum pain appearance.
5. If the cause of oil contamination was due to burned clutch plates or overheated oil, the converter is contaminated and should be replaced.

OIL PAN

Removal

1. Remove the oil pan attaching bolts. Carefully bump the pan with a rubber mallet to free the pan. If the pan is pried loose instead, be very careful not to damage the gasket surfaces. Discard the pan gasket.
2. Inspect the bottom of the pan for debris that can give an indication of the nature of the transaxle failure.
3. Check the pan for distorted gasket flanges, especially around the bolt holes, since these are often dished-in due to overtorque. They can be straightened with a block of wood and a rubber mallet if necessary.

OIL FILTER

Removal

1. The oil filter is retained by a clip as well as the interface fit

of the oil intake tube and O-ring. Move the clip out of the way and pull the filter from the case.
2. Discard the O-ring from the intake pipe. Often the O-ring will stick to its bore in the case.
3. The oil pressure regulator is in the bore next to the oil filter intake pipe opening. If it is to be removed, use snapring pliers to remove the retaining ring and then pull the pressure regulator bushing assembly from the case.

GOVERNOR

Removal

1. Since the speedometer drive gear is attached to the governor assembly, first remove the speedometer driven gear attaching bolt and the retaining clip.
2. Remove the speedometer driven gear from the governor cover. Remove the governor cover and discard the O-ring.
3. Remove the governor assembly along with the speedometer drive gear thrust bearing.
4. Remove the modulator retainer and lift out the modulator. Discard the O-ring. Lift out the modulator valve using a magnet.

REVERSE AND/OR 1–2 SERVO

Removal

1. To remove the reverse and/or 1–2 servo assembly, the cover will have to be depressed to relieve the spring pressure on the snapring that retains the cover. The factory type tool for this is similar to a clamp that hooks to the case and applies with a screw operated arm. The object is to release the spring holding pressure the cover has on the snapring.
2. Pliers can be used to grasp the servo cover to remove it. Discard the seals. Make sure that the cover seal ring is not stuck in the case groove where it might be overlooked.
3. Remove the servo assembly and the servo return springs. Remove the apply pin from the servo assembly.

NOTE: The servo assemblies are not interchangeable due to the reverse servo pin being longer than the 1–2 pin. Keep the servo assemblies separate.

OIL PUMP

Removal

1. Disconnect the side cover attaching nuts and bolts and remove the side cover. Discard the gaskets.
2. Detach the solenoid wiring harness from the case connector and pressure switch. Remove the throttle valve assembly from the valve body.
3. Remove the oil pump bolts and lift the oil pump assembly from the valve body.

VALVE BODY

Removal

1. Remove the valve body retaining bolts. Remove the valve body from the channel plate.
2. Remove the check balls from the spacer plate. Detach the spacer plate and discard the gaskets.
3. Remove the check balls from the channel plate.

OIL PUMP SHAFT AND CHANNEL PLATE

Removal

1. Remove the oil pump shaft by sliding it out of the channel

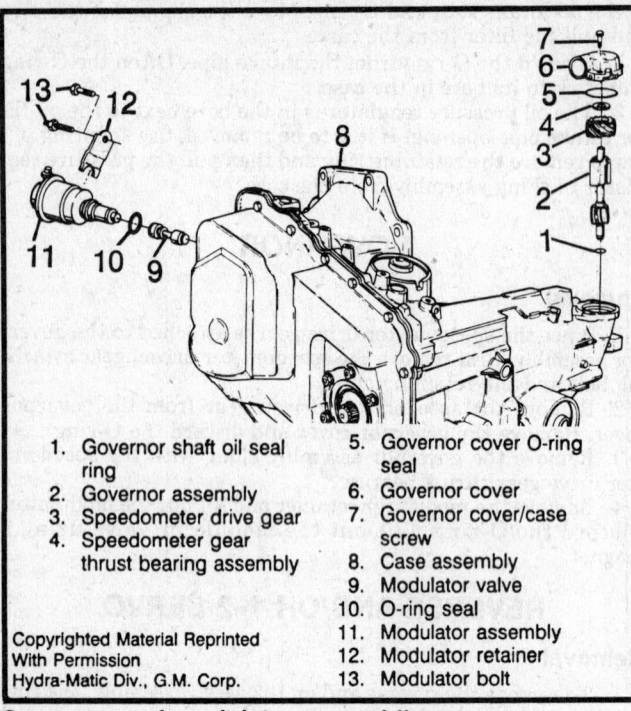

1. Governor shaft oil seal ring
2. Governor assembly
3. Speedometer drive gear
4. Speedometer gear thrust bearing assembly
5. Governor cover O-ring seal
6. Governor cover
7. Governor cover/case screw
8. Case assembly
9. Modulator valve
10. O-ring seal
11. Modulator assembly
12. Modulator retainer
13. Modulator bolt

Governor and modulator assemblies

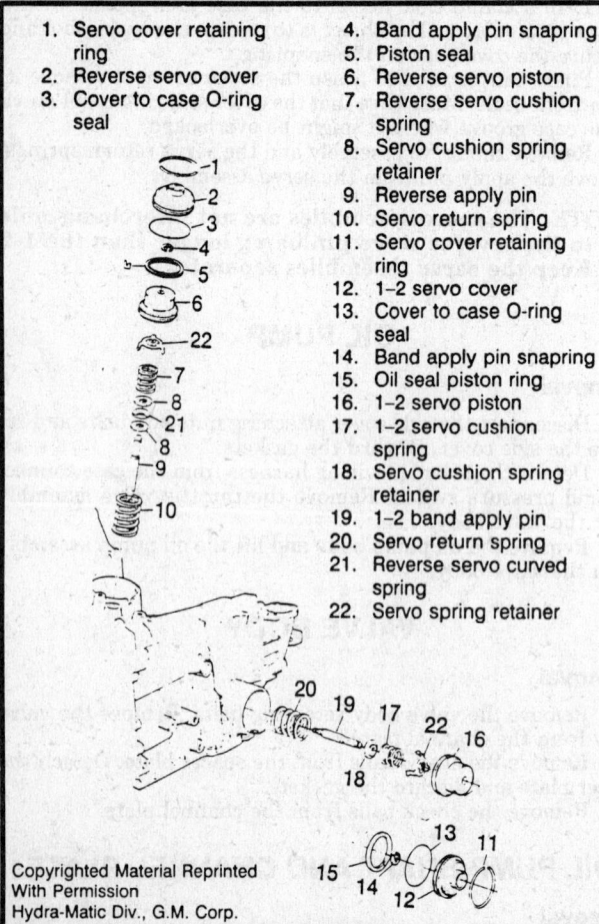

1. Servo cover retaining ring
2. Reverse servo cover
3. Cover to case O-ring seal
4. Band apply pin snapring
5. Piston seal
6. Reverse servo piston
7. Reverse servo cushion spring
8. Servo cushion spring retainer
9. Reverse apply pin
10. Servo return spring
11. Servo cover retaining ring
12. 1–2 servo cover
13. Cover to case O-ring seal
14. Band apply pin snapring
15. Oil seal piston ring
16. 1–2 servo piston
17. 1–2 servo cushion spring
18. Servo cushion spring retainer
19. 1–2 band apply pin
20. Servo return spring
21. Reverse servo curved spring
22. Servo spring retainer

1–2 and reverse servo assemblies

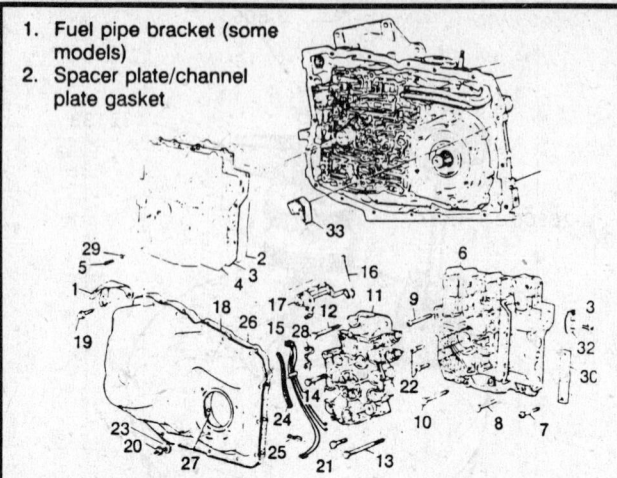

1. Fuel pipe bracket (some models)
2. Spacer plate/channel plate gasket

3. Valve body spacer plate
4. Spacer plate/valve body gasket
5. Converter clutch solenoid screen assembly
6. Control valve assembly
7. Valve body to channel plate bolt
8. Valve body to channel plate hex bolt
9. Valve body to driven support bolt
10. Valve body to case bolt
11. Pump assembly
12. Pump body to case bolt
13. Pump cover to channel plate bolt
14. Pump cover to valve body bolt
15. Wiring harness
16. Throttle lever to cable link
17. Throttle lever and bracket assembly
18. Case side cover pan
19. Special screws
20. Flanged hex nut
21. Pump body/channel plate bolt
22. Valve body/channel plate bolt
23. Conical washer
24. Conduit wire
25. Two wire clip
26. Side cover to case gasket
27. Side cover to channel plate gasket
28. Wire conduit clip
29. Converter clutch solenoid screen O-ring (not used on early models)
30. Clamping plate
31. Servo pipe retainer bolt
32. Servo pipe retainer bracket
33. Oil wier

Side cover, pump, valve body and parts

plate assembly. Place the detent lever in the **P** position and remove the manual valve clip.

2. Remove the channel plate attaching bolts and lift the channel plate from the transaxle case.

3. Remove the accumulator piston and the converter clutch accumulator piston and spring. Discard all gaskets.

FOURTH CLUTCH, SHAFT AND OUTPUT SHAFT
Removal

1. Remove the 3 clutch plates along with the apply plate. Remove the thrust bearing.

NOTE: The thrust bearing may still be on the case cover from earlier disassembly.

2. Remove the 4th clutch and shaft assembly. This will expose the output shaft.

3. Rotate the output shaft until the output shaft C-ring is visible. Remove the C-ring.

4. Pull the output shaft from the transaxle being careful not to damage it.

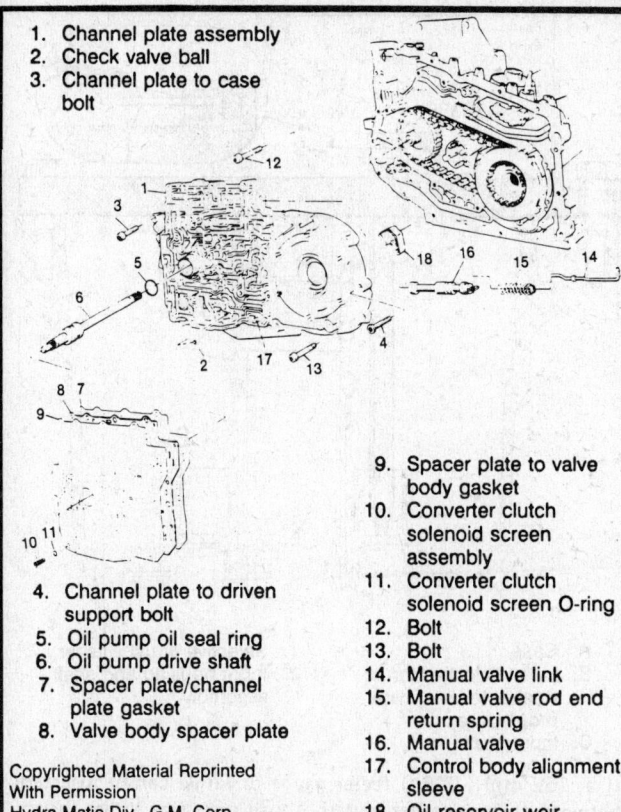

1. Channel plate assembly
2. Check valve ball
3. Channel plate to case bolt

4. Channel plate to driven support bolt
5. Oil pump oil seal ring
6. Oil pump drive shaft
7. Spacer plate/channel plate gasket
8. Valve body spacer plate

9. Spacer plate to valve body gasket
10. Converter clutch solenoid screen assembly
11. Converter clutch solenoid screen O-ring
12. Bolt
13. Bolt
14. Manual valve link
15. Manual valve rod end return spring
16. Manual valve
17. Control body alignment sleeve
18. Oil reservoir weir

Oil pump driveshaft and channel plate

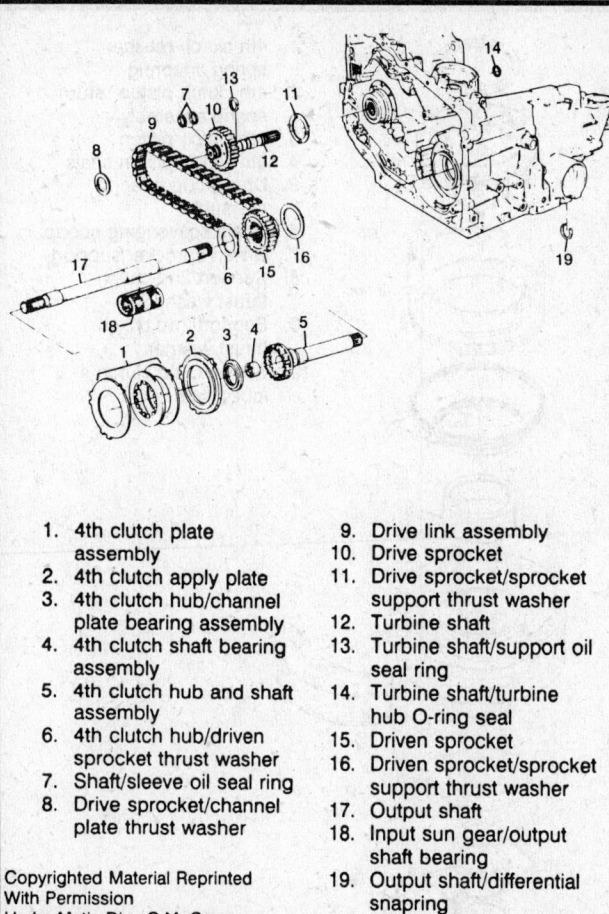

1. 4th clutch plate assembly
2. 4th clutch apply plate
3. 4th clutch hub/channel plate bearing assembly
4. 4th clutch shaft bearing assembly
5. 4th clutch hub and shaft assembly
6. 4th clutch hub/driven sprocket thrust washer
7. Shaft/sleeve oil seal ring
8. Drive sprocket/channel plate thrust washer

9. Drive link assembly
10. Drive sprocket
11. Drive sprocket/sprocket support thrust washer
12. Turbine shaft
13. Turbine shaft/support oil seal ring
14. Turbine shaft/turbine hub O-ring seal
15. Driven sprocket
16. Driven sprocket/sprocket support thrust washer
17. Output shaft
18. Input sun gear/output shaft bearing
19. Output shaft/differential snapring

Drive link assembly, output shaft, 4th clutch shaft and clutch assembly

DRIVE LINK ASSEMBLY

Removal

1. Remove the turbine shaft O-ring located at the front of the unit.

2. Reach through the access holes in the sprockets and slip the snaprings from their grooves.

3. Remove the sprockets and the chain as an assembly. It will required alternately pulling on the sprockets until the bearings come out of their support housings.

NOTE: If the sprockets are difficult to remove, use 2 small pieces of masonite or similar material to act both as wedges and as pads for a pry bar. Do not pry on the chain or the case.

4. After removing the drivelink assembly, take note as to the position of the colored link on the chain. It should be facing out. Remove the thrust washers.

5. Lift out the drive sprocket support and remove the thrust washer located on the casing.

CHECK INPUT UNIT ENDPLAY

The factory tools for checking the endplay on this unit are somewhat elaborate and it is unlikely that every shop will be equipped in the same manner. However, the object is to pre-load the output shaft to remove the clearance. The factory tool mounts on the output end of the transaxle and a knob and screw arrangement can be tightened, forcing the output shaft upwards. A dial indicator is mounted on the end of the input shaft. By raising the input shaft with a suitable bar (again, the factory

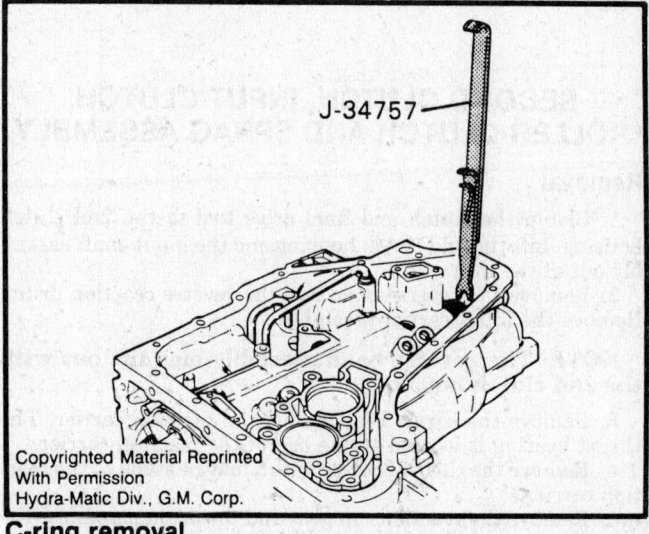

J-34757

C-ring removal

tool is special and grips the input shaft splines) the input unit endplay can be measured. Input shaft endplay should be 0.020–0.042 in.

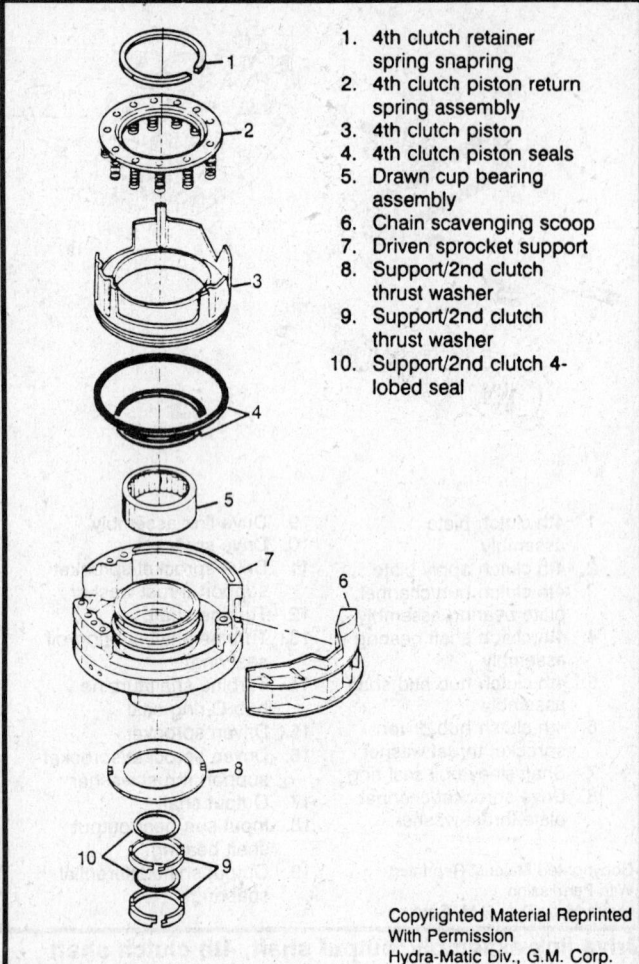

1. 4th clutch retainer spring snapring
2. 4th clutch piston return spring assembly
3. 4th clutch piston
4. 4th clutch piston seals
5. Drawn cup bearing assembly
6. Chain scavenging scoop
7. Driven sprocket support
8. Support/2nd clutch thrust washer
9. Support/2nd clutch thrust washer
10. Support/2nd clutch 4-lobed seal

Driven sprocket support

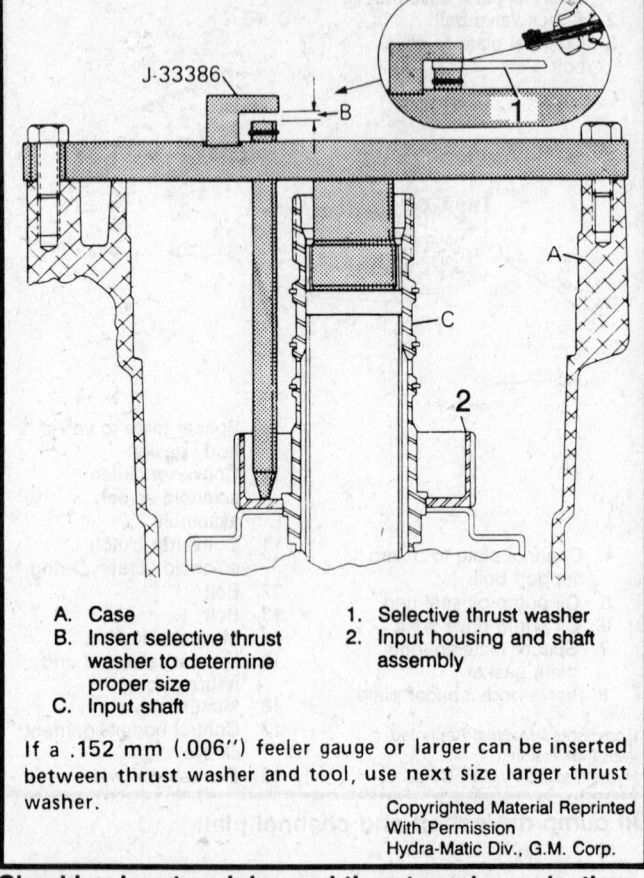

A. Case
B. Insert selective thrust washer to determine proper size
C. Input shaft

1. Selective thrust washer
2. Input housing and shaft assembly

If a .152 mm (.006") feeler gauge or larger can be inserted between thrust washer and tool, use next size larger thrust washer.

Checking input endplay and thrust washer selection chart

SECOND CLUTCH, INPUT CLUTCH, ROLLER CLUTCH AND SPRAG ASSEMBLY

Removal

1. Clamp the clutch and final drive tool to the 2nd clutch housing. Lift the 2nd clutch housing and the input shaft assembly out of the unit.
2. Remove the reverse band and the reverse reaction drum. Remove the input carrier assembly.

NOTE: The reverse band assembly may lift out with the 2nd clutch housing.

3. Remove the thrust bearing and the reaction carrier. The thrust bearing is located at one end of the reaction carrier.
4. Remove the thrust bearing which may be stuck to the reaction carrier.
5. Remove the reaction sun gear and the drum assembly. Remove the 1–2 band.

NOTE: The 1–2 band assembly should not be cleaned in cleaning solvent.

6. Remove the bearing ring and the sun gear shaft. A final drive internal bushing will be found on the sun gear shaft.

FINAL DRIVE ASSEMBLY

Removal

1. With a suitable tool, remove the snapring at the head of the internal final drive gear.
2. Clamp the clutch and final drive tool to the final drive internal gear and lift it out.
3. The final drive carrier will be removed with the final drive internal gear.

MANUAL SHAFT/DETENT LEVER AND ACTUATOR ROD

Removal

1. It is not necessary to disassembly the manual shaft, detent lever or the actuator rod unless replacement is needed.
2. Remove the manual shaft and detent lever retaining bolts and remove the shaft lever.
3. Remove the actuator rod assembly and check for wear or damage.
4. Remove the actuator guide assembly and check for damage.

MANUAL LINKAGE/ACTUATOR REPLACEMENT

Removal

1. Remove the manual shaft locknut and pin and lift out the manual shaft with the detent lever.

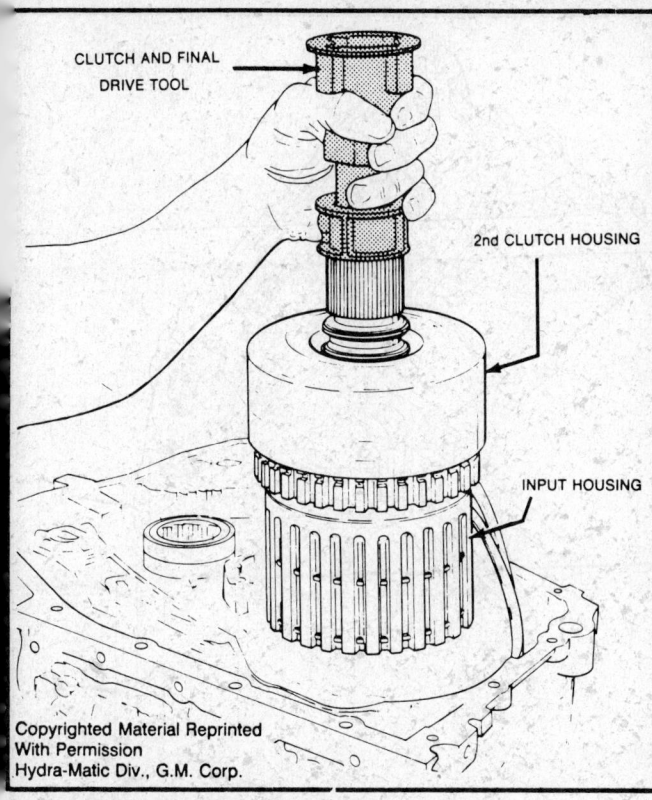

CLUTCH AND FINAL DRIVE TOOL

2nd CLUTCH HOUSING

INPUT HOUSING

Input housing and shaft removal

2. Remove the retaining pin from the case and detach the actuator guide assembly.

3. Remove the O-ring from the actuator guide and discard the O-ring.

4. The parking lock pawl assembly cannot be removed from the final drive internal gear.

NOTE: If the manual shaft seal is needed to be replaced, remove the axle oil seal along with the converter seal and then remove the manual shaft seal from its mounting in the transaxle case.

Unit Disassembly and Assembly
TRANSAXLE CASE

1. Clean the case and inspect carefully for cracks. Make certain that all passages are clean and that all bores and snapring grooves are clean and free from damage. Check for striped bolt holes. Check the case bushings for damage.

2. A new manual shaft seal can be installed at this time, along with a new axle oil seal and converter seal. Tap the seals into place with a suitable tool. The seal lips must face into the case.

3. Check the drive sprocket support assembly for damage. If it requires replacement, a slide hammer type puller can be used to pull the bearing from the sprocket support. Once the bearing is out, inspect the bore for wear or damage. The new bearing should be driven in straight and with care so as not to damage it.

4. If the parking pawl and related parts are to be removed, begin by turning the transaxle to the oil pan side up. Use a punch to remove the cup plug. Remove the parking pawl shaft retainer, then the shaft, pawl and return spring. Check the pawl for cracks.

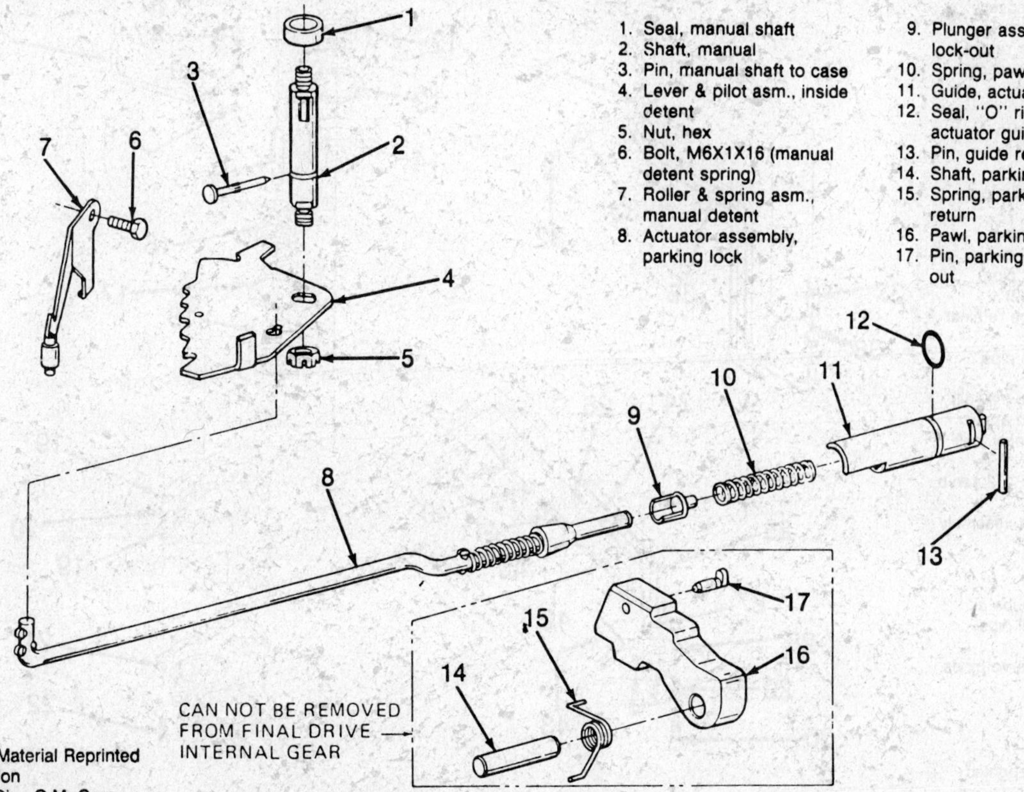

1. Seal, manual shaft
2. Shaft, manual
3. Pin, manual shaft to case
4. Lever & pilot asm., inside detent
5. Nut, hex
6. Bolt, M6X1X16 (manual detent spring)
7. Roller & spring asm., manual detent
8. Actuator assembly, parking lock
9. Plunger assembly, pawl lock-out
10. Spring, pawl lock-out
11. Guide, actuator
12. Seal, "O" ring (bushing/actuator guide)
13. Pin, guide retaining
14. Shaft, parking lock pawl
15. Spring, parking pawl return
16. Pawl, parking lock
17. Pin, parking pawl lock-out

CAN NOT BE REMOVED FROM FINAL DRIVE INTERNAL GEAR

Exploded view of manual linkage assembly

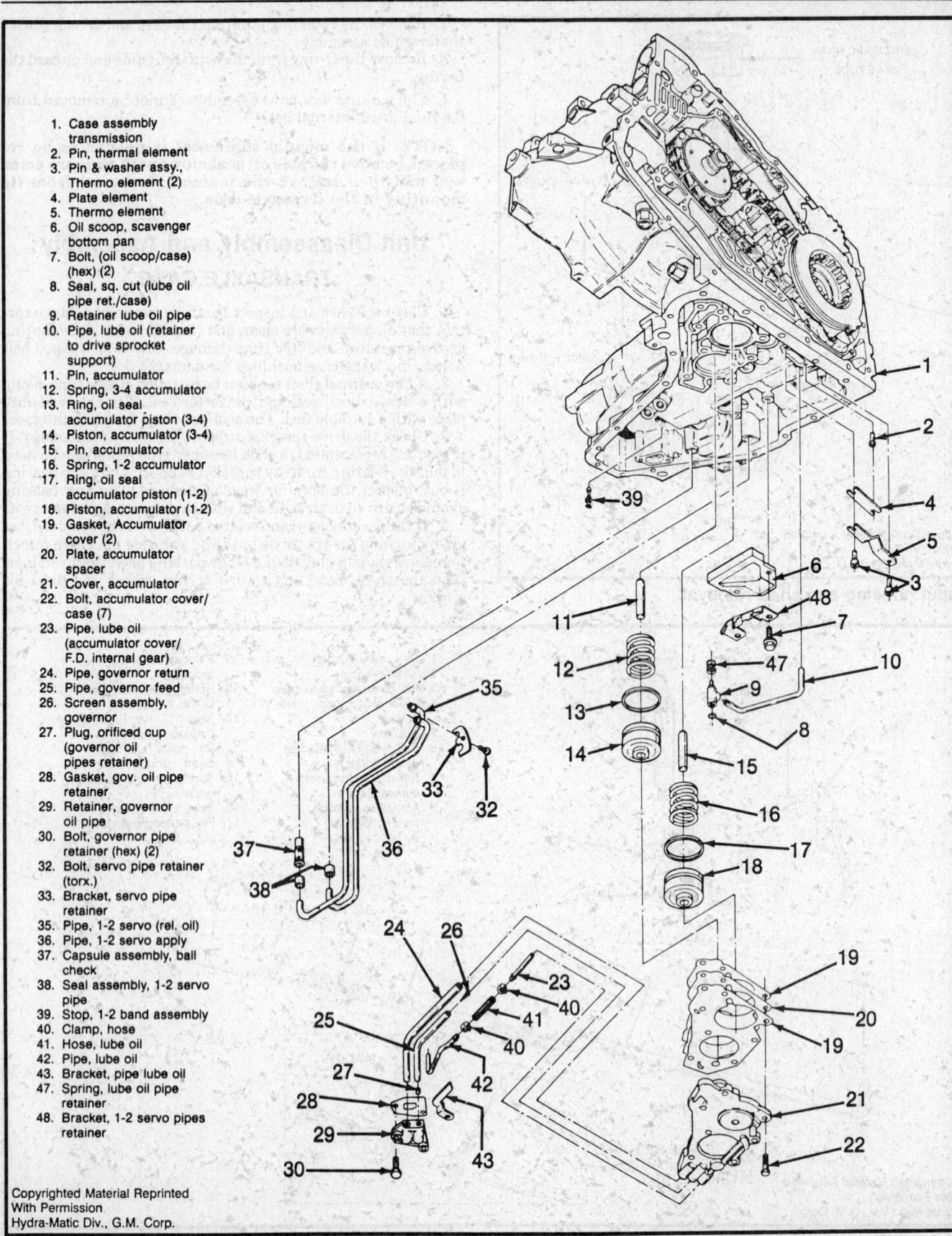

1. Case assembly transmission
2. Pin, thermal element
3. Pin & washer assy., Thermo element (2)
4. Plate element
5. Thermo element
6. Oil scoop, scavenger bottom pan
7. Bolt, (oil scoop/case) (hex) (2)
8. Seal, sq. cut (lube oil pipe ret./case)
9. Retainer lube oil pipe
10. Pipe, lube oil (retainer to drive sprocket support)
11. Pin, accumulator
12. Spring, 3-4 accumulator
13. Ring, oil seal accumulator piston (3-4)
14. Piston, accumulator (3-4)
15. Pin, accumulator
16. Spring, 1-2 accumulator
17. Ring, oil seal accumulator piston (1-2)
18. Piston, accumulator (1-2)
19. Gasket, Accumulator cover (2)
20. Plate, accumulator spacer
21. Cover, accumulator
22. Bolt, accumulator cover/ case (7)
23. Pipe, lube oil (accumulator cover/ F.D. internal gear)
24. Pipe, governor return
25. Pipe, governor feed
26. Screen assembly, governor
27. Plug, orificed cup (governor oil pipes retainer)
28. Gasket, gov. oil pipe retainer
29. Retainer, governor oil pipe
30. Bolt, governor pipe retainer (hex) (2)
32. Bolt, servo pipe retainer (torx.)
33. Bracket, servo pipe retainer
35. Pipe, 1-2 servo (rel. oil)
36. Pipe, 1-2 servo apply
37. Capsule assembly, ball check
38. Seal assembly, 1-2 servo pipe
39. Stop, 1-2 band assembly
40. Clamp, hose
41. Hose, lube oil
42. Pipe, lube oil
43. Bracket, pipe lube oil
47. Spring, lube oil pipe retainer
48. Bracket, 1-2 servo pipes retainer

Exploded view of the governor control body, accumulator cover, pistons and component parts

1. Plate assembly, 4th clutch
2. Plate, 4th clutch apply
3. Bearing assembly, 4th clutch hub/channel plate
4. Bearing assembly, 4th clutch shaft
5. Hub & shaft assembly, 4th clutch
6. Washer, thrust (4th clutch hub/driven sprocket)
7. Ring, oil seal (shaft/sleeve) (2)
8. Washer, thrust (drive sprocket/channel plate)
9. Ring, snap (turbine shaft/drive sprocket)
10. Link assembly, drive
11. Sprocket, drive
12. Washer, thrust (drive sprocket/sprocket support)
13. Shaft, turbine
14. Ring, oil seal (turbine shaft/support)
15. Seal, "O" ring (turbine shaft/turbine hub)
16. Bearing assembly, drawn cup
17. Support, drive sprocket
18. Bushing, drive sprocket support
19. Sprocket, driven
20. Washer, thrust (driven sprocket/sprocket support)
21. Ring, snap (4th clutch ret. spring)
22. Spring asm., 4th clutch piston return
23. Piston, 4th clutch
24. Seals, 4th clutch piston
25. Case, transmission
26. Connector, cooler (1)
27. Pin, dowel
28. Vent assembly
29. Plug, pipe (line pressure)

32. Pin, anchor (1-2 band) (2)
33. Pin, anchor (reverse band) (2)
34. Plug, case servo (orifice)
35. Plug, cup (park lock-out)
36. Screw, nameplate
37. Nameplate
38. Plug, pipe (governor pressure)
39. Bushing, case
40. Seal assembly, axle oil
41. Helix seal assembly, (converter oil)
42. Screw, button head (4) case/drum sprocket)
43. Ring, servo cover retaining
44. Cover, servo (reverse)
45. Seal, "O" ring (cover to case)
46. Ring, snap (band apply pin)
47. Ring, oil seal piston
48. Piston, reverse servo
49. Spring, reverse servo cushion
50. Retainer, servo cushion spring
51. Pin, reverse apply

52. Spring, servo return
53. Ring, servo cover retaining
54. Cover, servo (1-2)
55. Seal, "O" ring (cover to case)
56. Ring, snap (band apply pin)
57. Ring, oil seal piston
58. Piston, 1-2 servo
59. Spring, 1-2 servo cushion

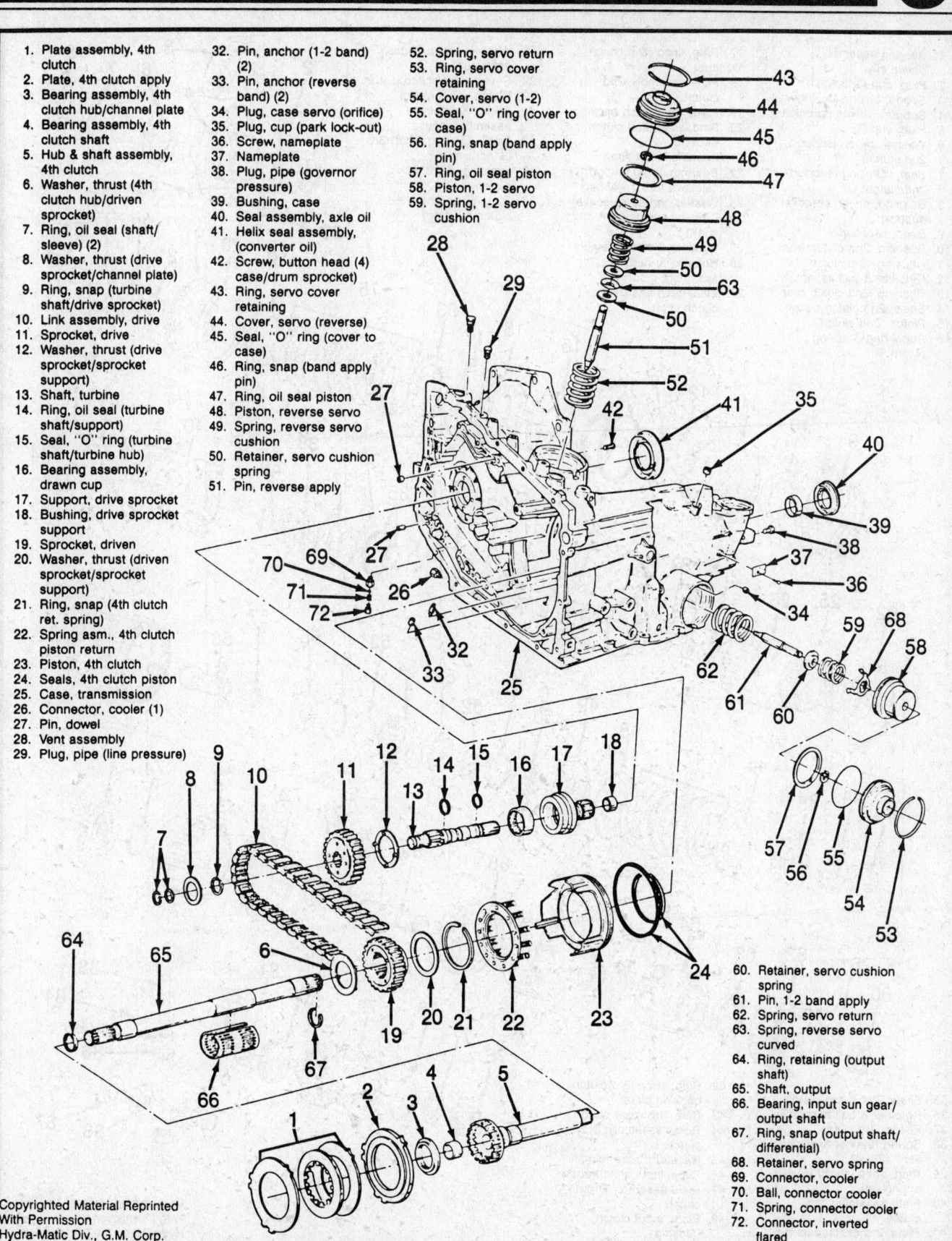

60. Retainer, servo cushion spring
61. Pin, 1-2 band apply
62. Spring, servo return
63. Spring, reverse servo curved
64. Ring, retaining (output shaft)
65. Shaft, output
66. Bearing, input sun gear/output shaft
67. Ring, snap (output shaft/differential)
68. Retainer, servo spring
69. Connector, cooler
70. Ball, connector cooler
71. Spring, connector cooler
72. Connector, inverted flared

Exploded view of case assembly drive link and sprocket

1. Bearing assembly, drawn cup
2. Plug, cup (orificed)
3. Scoop, chain scavenging
4. Support, driven sprocket
5. Plug, cup (4)
6. Washer, thrust (support/2nd clutch)
7. Seal, "O" ring (support/2nd clutch)
8. Bushing, driven sprocket support
9. Band, reverse
10. Bushing, 2nd clutch front
11. Housing, 2nd clutch
12. Retainer & ball assembly
13. Bushing, 2nd clutch rear
14. Seals, 2nd clutch piston
15. Piston, 2nd clutch
16. Apply ring & spring return

17. Ring, snap (2nd clutch hub)
18. Plate assembly, 2nd clutch
19. Plate, 2nd clutch backing
20. Ring, snap (2nd clutch backing)
21. Bushing, input shaft
22. Bearing, thrust (support/selective thrust washer)
23. Washer, thrust (selective)
24. Ring, oil seal (input shaft)
25. Retainer & ball assembly
26. Housing & shaft assembly, input
27. Seal, input shaft/4th clutch shaft

28. Washer, thrust (input shaft/sun)
29. Seals, input clutch piston
30. Piston, input clutch
31. Spring & retainer assembly, input
32. Seal, "O" ring (shaft/3rd cl. housing)
33. Housing, 3rd clutch piston
34. Ring, snap (shaft/3rd clutch housing)

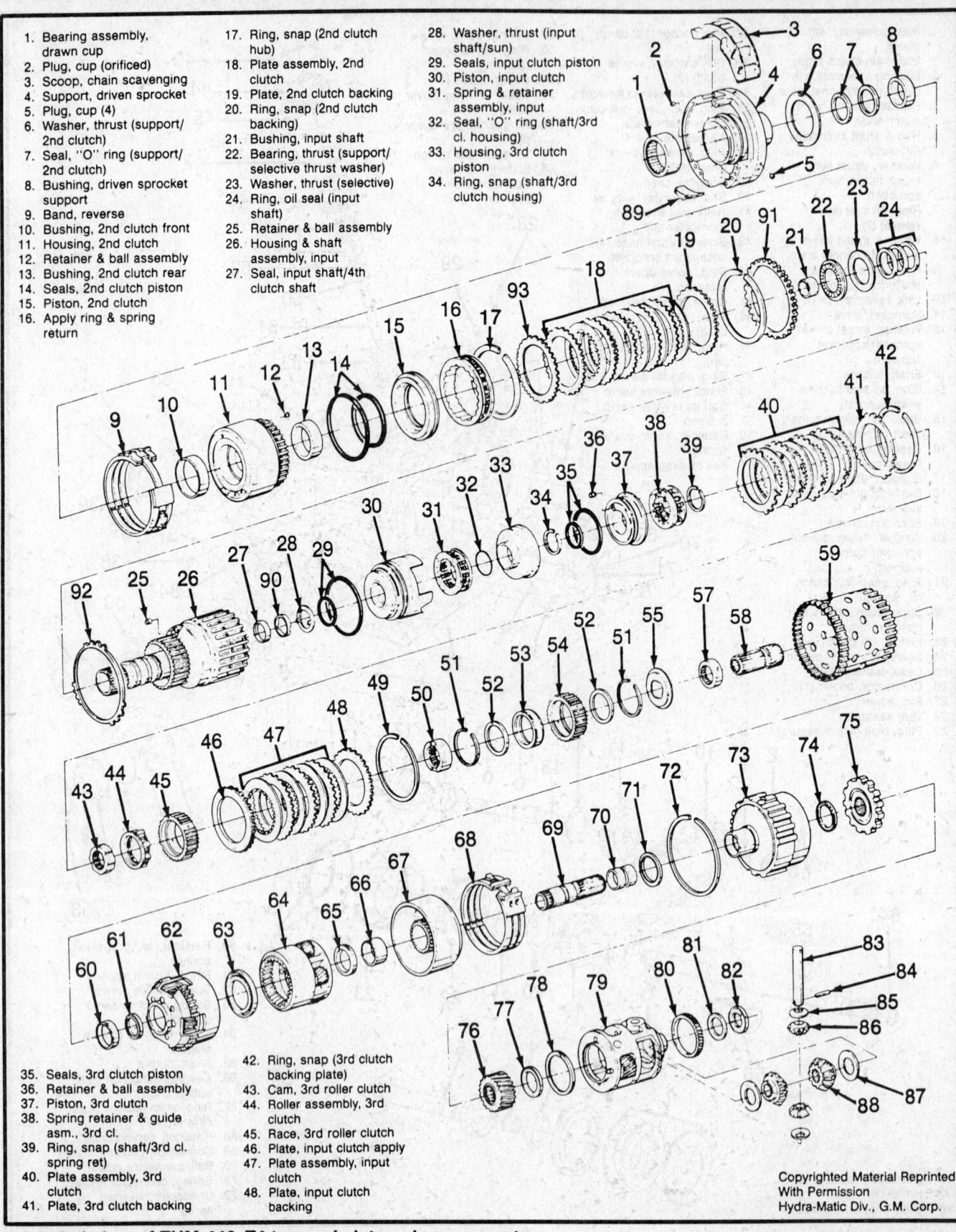

35. Seals, 3rd clutch piston
36. Retainer & ball assembly
37. Piston, 3rd clutch
38. Spring retainer & guide asm., 3rd cl.
39. Ring, snap (shaft/3rd cl. spring ret)
40. Plate assembly, 3rd clutch
41. Plate, 3rd clutch backing

42. Ring, snap (3rd clutch backing plate)
43. Cam, 3rd roller clutch
44. Roller assembly, 3rd clutch
45. Race, 3rd roller clutch
46. Plate, input clutch apply
47. Plate assembly, input clutch
48. Plate, input clutch backing

Exploded view of THM 440–T4 transaxle internal components

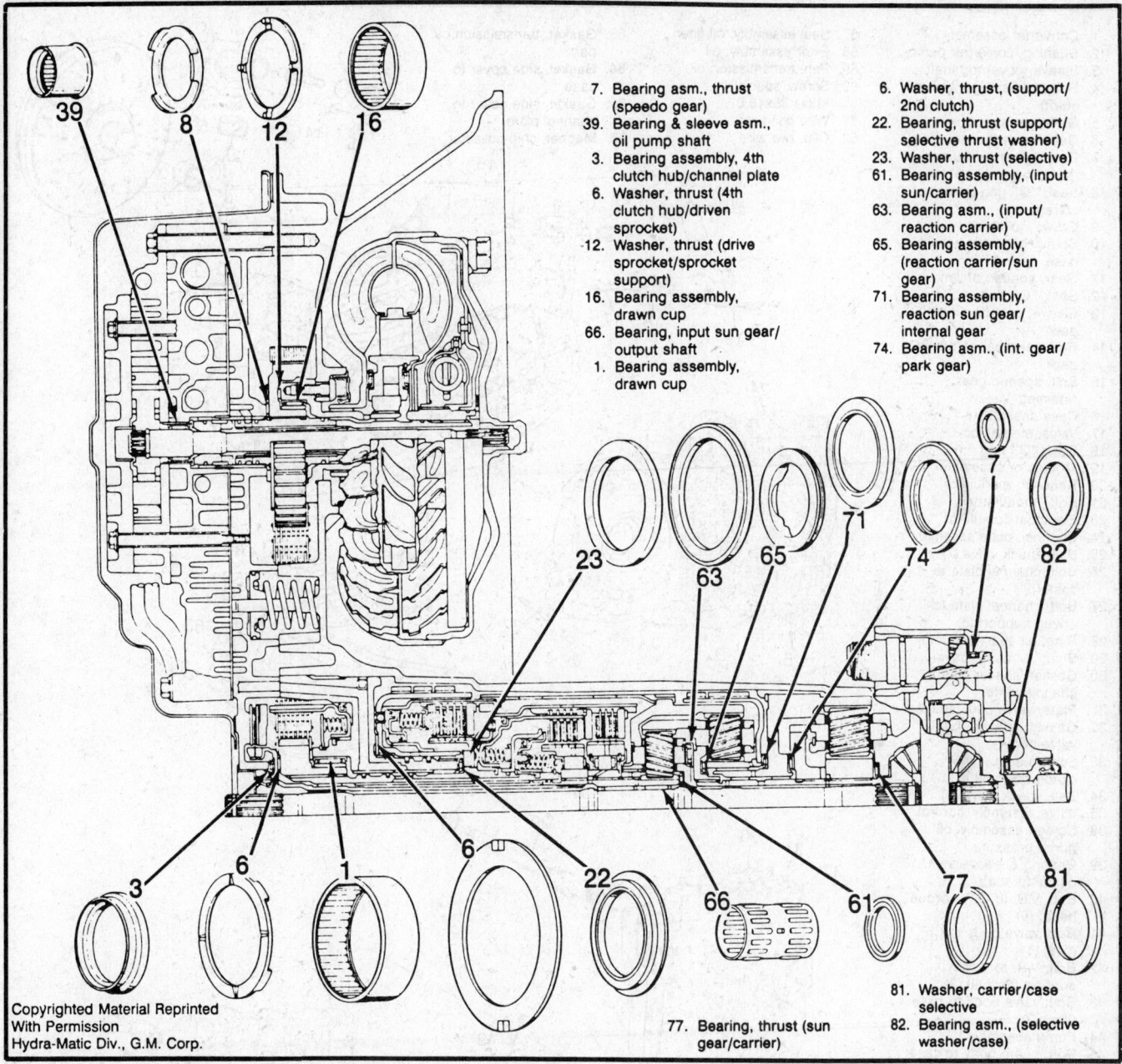

7. Bearing asm., thrust (speedo gear)
39. Bearing & sleeve asm., oil pump shaft
3. Bearing assembly, 4th clutch hub/channel plate
6. Washer, thrust (4th clutch hub/driven sprocket)
12. Washer, thrust (drive sprocket/sprocket support)
16. Bearing assembly, drawn cup
66. Bearing, input sun gear/output shaft
1. Bearing assembly, drawn cup

6. Washer, thrust, (support/2nd clutch)
22. Bearing, thrust (support/selective thrust washer)
23. Washer, thrust (selective)
61. Bearing assembly, (input sun/carrier)
63. Bearing asm., (input/reaction carrier)
65. Bearing assembly, (reaction carrier/sun gear)
71. Bearing assembly, reaction sun gear/internal gear
74. Bearing asm., (int. gear/park gear)

81. Washer, carrier/case selective
82. Bearing asm., (selective washer/case)
77. Bearing, thrust (sun gear/carrier)

Location of thrust bearings and washers in the drive train

FINAL DRIVE UNIT

Disassembly

1. Remove the final drive gear snapring and lift out the final drive gear unit. Lift out the bearing assembly and the parking gear.

2. Remove the final drive sun gear along with the final drive carrier and the governor drive gear.

3. Remove the carrier washer and the bearing assembly.

4. Place the final drive carrier on its side and remove the differential pinion shaft by tapping out the pinion shaft retaining pin.

5. Remove the pinion thrust washer and the differential pinion. Remove the 2 side gear thrust washers and the 2 differential side gears.

Inspection

1. Clean all parts well and check for damage or excessive wear. Check the gears for burrs and cracks.

2. Inspect the washers and replace any that appear damaged or warped.

3. Check the bearing assemblies for any mutilation and replace as needed.

Assembly

1. Install the differential side gears and washers into the final drive carrier.

2. Install the pinion thrust washers onto the differential pinions. A small amount of petroleum jelly can be used to hold the washers in place.

3. Place the pinions and washers into the final drive carrier.

1. Converter assembly
2. Bushing, converter pump
3. Sleeve, governor shaft
4. Ring, oil seal (governor shaft)
5. Governor assembly
6. Gear, speedometer drive
7. Bearing asm., thrust (speedo gear)
8. Seal, "O" ring (governor cover)
9. Cover, governor
10. Screw, governor cover/ case
11. Gear, speedo driven
12. Seal, "O" ring
13. Sleeve, speedo driven gear
14. Retainer, speedo driven gear
15. Bolt, speedo gear retaining
16. Case assembly
17. Valve, modulator
18. Seal, "O" ring
19. Modulator assembly
20. Retainer, modulator
21. Bolt, (modulator)
23. Electrical connector
24. Channel, plate assembly
25. Ball, check valve (7)
26. Bolt, channel plate to case (5)
27. Bolt, channel plate to driven support (6)
28. Ring, oil seal (oil pump)
29. Shaft, oil pump drive
30. Gasket, spacer plate/ channel plate
31. Plate, valve body spacer
32. Gasket, spacer plate/ valve body
33. Screen asm., conv. clutch solenoid
34. Ball, check valve (5)
35. Valve assembly, control
38. Screen assembly, oil pump pressure
39. Bearing & sleeve asm., oil pump shaft
40. Bolt, V.B. to C.P. (torque head) (6)
41. Bolt, valve body to C.P. (hex) (1)
42. Bolt, V.B. to driven support (torque) (2)
43. Bolt, valve body to case (hex) (3)
44. Pump assembly
45. Bolt, pump body to case (hex) (2)
46. Bolt, pump cover to C.P. (hex) (10)
47. Bolt, pump cover to valve body (hex) (1)
48. Harness, wiring
49. Link throttle lever to cable
50. Lever & bracket assembly, throttle
51. Pan, case side cover
52. Screw, special M8x1.25x16.0
53. Nut, flanged hex (M6x1.0)
54. Bolt, M6x1.0x35 LG. P.B./C.P. hex (1)
55. Bolt, M6x1.0x45 LG. V.B./C.P. (2)
56. Washer, conical

57. Seal assembly, oil filter
58. Filter assembly, oil
59. Pan, transmission oil
60. Screw, special M8x1.25x16.0
61. Wire conduit
62. Clip, two wire

63. Gasket, transmission oil pan
64. Gasket, side cover to case
65. Gasket, side cover to channel plate
66. Magnet, chip collector

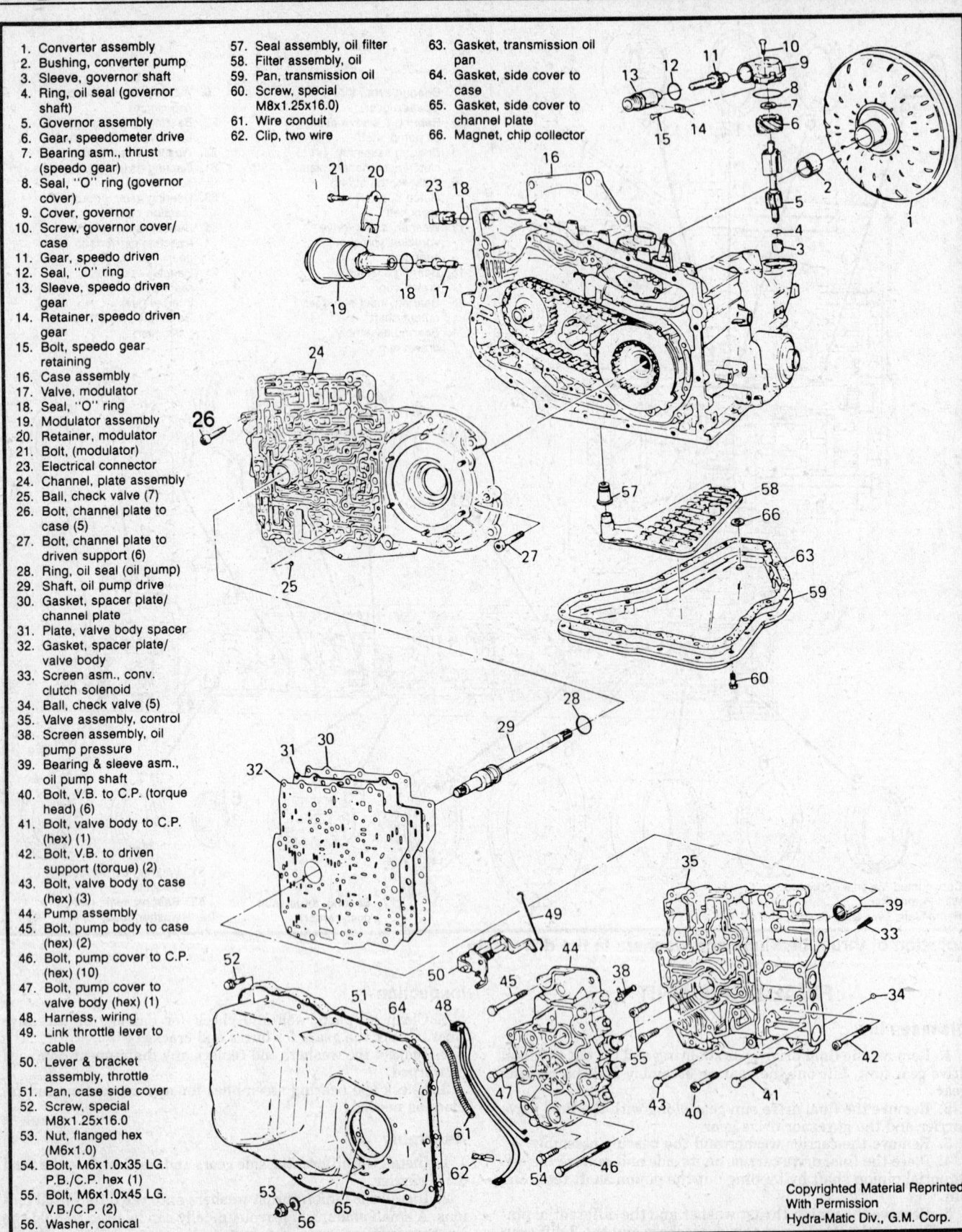

Exploded view of the THM 440–T4 automatic transaxle

4. Insert the differential pinion shaft into the final drive carrier to check alignment of the pinions, then remove.

5. If the pinions are out of alignment, correct and reinstall the differential pinion shaft. Tap the pinion shaft retaining pin into position.

6. Assemble the sun gear into the final drive carrier with the stopped side facing out. Install the parking gear onto the sun gear.

7. Install the thrust bearing assembly into the final drive internal gear and place the unit onto the final drive carrier.

8. Install the thrust washer and the thrust bearing onto the carrier hub. Install the snapring making sure it seats properly in its groove.

FINAL DRIVE SUN GEAR SHAFT

Disassembly

1. Lift off the reverse reaction drum and the input carrier assembly.

2. Remove the reaction carrier bearing, which may be stuck to the input carrier assembly.

3. Remove the internal gear bearing and the final drive sun gear.

4. Lift out the 1–2 band from the reaction sun gear and drum assembly.

5. Remove the bearing assembly from the reaction sun gear and drum assembly.

Inspection

1. Inspect the final drive sun gear shaft for damaged splines. Replace if necessary.

2. Inspect the 1–2 band assembly for damage from heat or excessive wear. Check the band assembly for lining separation or lining cracks.

NOTE: The 1–2 band assembly is presoaked in a friction solution and should not be washed in a cleaning solvent.

3. Inspect the sun gear/drum assembly for any scoring or damaged teeth.

4. Inspect the thrust bearings for damage. Replace as required.

5. Check the reaction carrier assembly for pinion endplay. Pinion endplay should be 0.23–0.61mm.

6. Check for pinion damage or internal gear damage. Replace as needed.

Assembly

1. Position the inside race of the thrust bearing against the final drive internal gear.

2. Install the reaction sun gear and drum assembly into the case.

3. Position the thrust bearing inside the reaction carrier and retain with petroleum jelly.

4. Install the reaction carrier and rotate until all the pinions engage with the sun gear.

5. Install the reverse reaction drum making sure that all the spline teeth engage with the input carrier.

THIRD ROLLER CLUTCH AND INPUT SUN GEAR AND SPRAG

Disassembly

1. Remove the input sprag and 3rd roller clutch from the input sun gear.

2. Remove the input sun gear spacer and retainer from the sun gear.

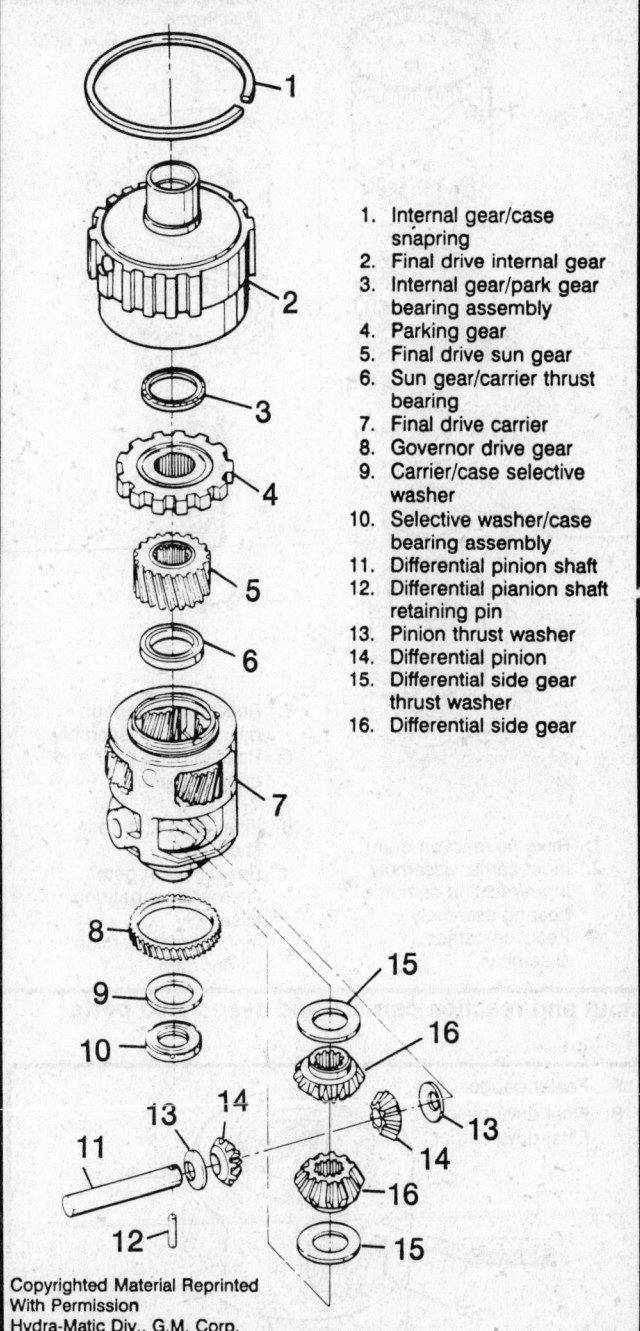

1. Internal gear/case snapring
2. Final drive internal gear
3. Internal gear/park gear bearing assembly
4. Parking gear
5. Final drive sun gear
6. Sun gear/carrier thrust bearing
7. Final drive carrier
8. Governor drive gear
9. Carrier/case selective washer
10. Selective washer/case bearing assembly
11. Differential pinion shaft
12. Differential pianion shaft retaining pin
13. Pinion thrust washer
14. Differential pinion
15. Differential side gear thrust washer
16. Differential side gear

Final drive assembly

3. Remove the snapring and lift off the input sprag wear plate and the 3rd roller clutch race and cam from the roller assembly.

4. Disassemble the input sprag assembly by removing the inner race from the sprag assembly.

5. Remove the snapring that holds the wear plate and lift out the wear plate and sprag assembly.

Inspection

1. Clean all parts in cleaning solvent and blow dry using compressed air.

2. Inspect the outer race and roller cam for any cracks or scoring. Replace as required.

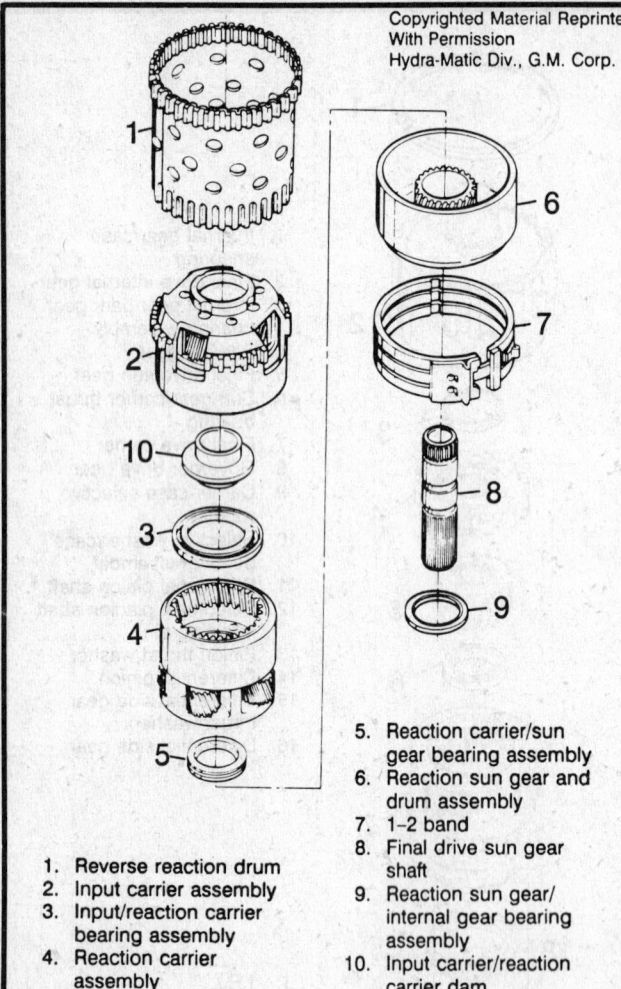

Copyrighted Material Reprinted With Permission Hydra-Matic Div., G.M. Corp.

5. Reaction carrier/sun gear bearing assembly
6. Reaction sun gear and drum assembly
7. 1-2 band
8. Final drive sun gear shaft
9. Reaction sun gear/internal gear bearing assembly
10. Input carrier/reaction carrier dam

1. Reverse reaction drum
2. Input carrier assembly
3. Input/reaction carrier bearing assembly
4. Reaction carrier assembly

Input and reaction carriers and associated parts

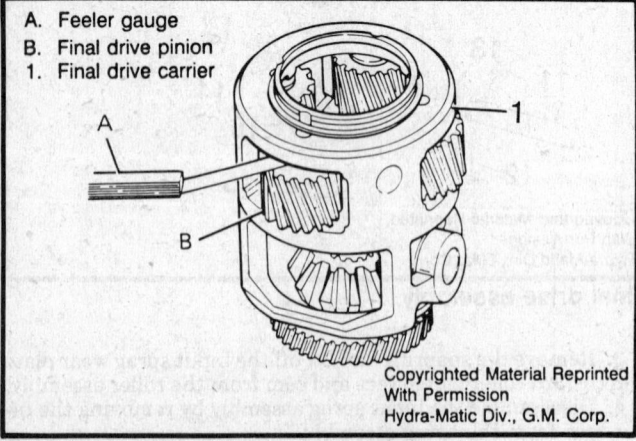

A. Feeler gauge
B. Final drive pinion
1. Final drive carrier

Copyrighted Material Reprinted With Permission Hydra-Matic Div., G.M. Corp.

Checking final drive pinion endplay

3. Inspect the roller assembly for damaged rollers and springs. Replace any loose rollers by depressing the spring and inserting the roller.
4. Inspect the sprag assembly for damaged sprags or cages and replace as required.

5. Inspect the inner race and wear plates for any scoring or damage. Replace as required.

Assembly

1. Position 1 wear plate against the snapring and hold in position with petroleum jelly.
2. Insert the wear plate with the snapring against the sprag assembly.
3. Install the spacer on the input sun gear and place the sprag retainer over the spacer.
4. Install the sprag snapring. Make sure the snapring seats properly.
5. Install the sprag assembly and the roller clutch onto the sun gear.

INPUT CLUTCH ASSEMBLY

Disassembly

1. Remove the input clutch snapring and remove the input clutch backing plate.
2. Remove the steel and composition clutch plates, along with the input clutch apply plate.
3. Remove the 3rd clutch snapring and remove the 3rd clutch backing plate.
4. Remove the steel and composition clutch plates, along with the 3rd clutch waved plate.
5. Remove the snapring from the spring retainer and lift out the 3rd clutch piston from its housing.
6. Remove the 3rd clutch piston inner seal from the shaft.
7. Compress the 3rd clutch piston housing and remove the snapring. Remove the 3rd clutch piston housing.
8. Remove the O-ring seal and take out the spring retainer. Remove the input clutch piston and inner seal.

Inspection

1. Wash all parts in cleaning solvent and blow dry using compressed air.
2. Inspect all parts for scoring, wear or damage.
3. Inspect the input clutch housing for damaged or worn bushings.
4. Check the 4th clutch shaft seal and replace if damaged or cut.
5. Repair or replace any parts found to be defective.

Assembly

1. Lubricate all parts with automatic transmission fluid prior to assembling.
2. Install the input clutch piston seal with the piston seal protector. Position the input piston in the housing.
3. Install the O-ring on the input shaft making sure it seats properly. Install the spring retainer in the piston.
4. Install the 3rd clutch piston housing into the input housing. Compress the 3rd clutch housing with a clutch spring compressor and install the snapring.
5. Install the 3rd clutch inner seal on the 3rd clutch piston and install the 3rd clutch piston.
6. Install the 3rd clutch spring retainer and compress the spring retainer using the clutch spring compressor and install the snapring.
7. Install the 3rd clutch plates and the 3rd clutch backing plate. install the snapring.

NOTE: When installing the 3rd clutch plates, start with a steel plate and alternate between composition and steel plates. When installing the 3rd clutch backing plate, make sure that the stepped side is facing up.

8. Install the input clutch apply plate with the notched side facing the snapring. Install the input clutch plates.

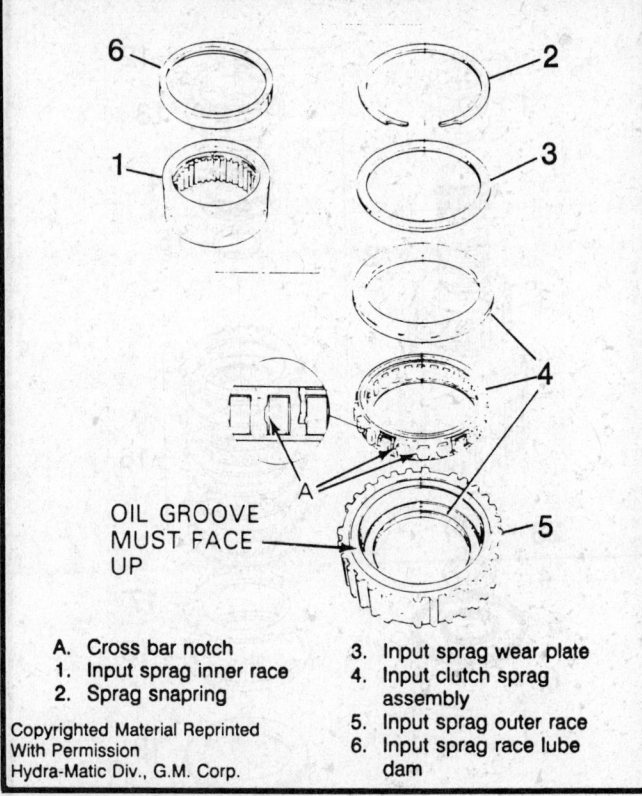

A. Cross bar notch
1. Input sprag inner race
2. Sprag snapring
3. Input sprag wear plate
4. Input clutch sprag assembly
5. Input sprag outer race
6. Input sprag race lube dam

Proper installation of input sprag

NOTE: When installing the input clutch plates, start with a composition plate and alternate between steel and composition plates.

9. Install the input clutch backing plate and secure with a snapring.

RETAINER AND BALL ASSEMBLY

Replacement (Optional)

1. Remove the retainer and ball assembly from the housing with a $\frac{3}{8}$ in. (9.5mm) drift.
2. Tap in a new retainer using a $\frac{3}{8}$ in. (9.5mm) drift.

PISTON SEAL

Replacement (Optional)

1. Remove the input clutch piston seal and the 3rd clutch piston seal.
2. Inspect the clutch piston for any remaining seals and remove.
3. Install a new input clutch piston seal and a new 3rd clutch piston seal. Lubricate with transmission fluid.

FOURTH CLUTCH SHAFT SEAL

Replacement (Optional)

1. Remove the lock up sleeve using a suitable tool and remove the oil seal.
2. Install the new oil seal into the input shaft making sure that the seal tab aligns with the slot in the shaft.
3. Install the lock up sleeve in the shaft using a bench press.

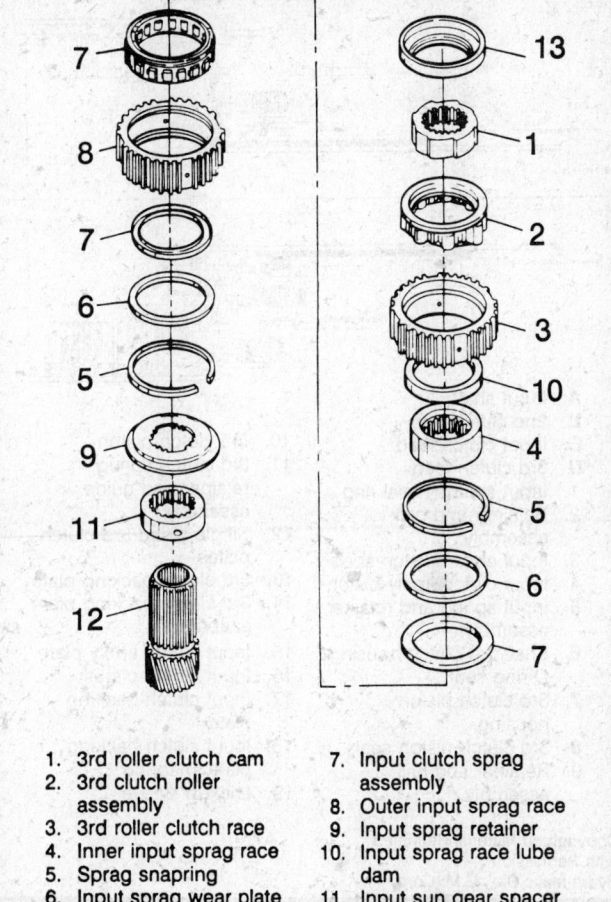

1. 3rd roller clutch cam
2. 3rd clutch roller assembly
3. 3rd roller clutch race
4. Inner input sprag race
5. Sprag snapring
6. Input sprag wear plate
7. Input clutch sprag assembly
8. Outer input sprag race
9. Input sprag retainer
10. Input sprag race lube dam
11. Input sun gear spacer
12. Input sun gear
13. 3rd roller clutch dam

Sprag and roller clutch assembly

INPUT SHAFT SEAL

Replacement (Optional)

1. Remove the seal rings from the input shaft with a suitable tool.
2. Adjust the seal protector so that the bottom matches the seal ring groove.
3. Lubricate the oil seal ring and place it on the seal protector.
4. Slide the seal into position with the seal pusher over the seal protector.
5. Size the seal with a seal sizer and gently work the tool over the seal with a twisted motion.

SECOND CLUTCH HOUSING

Disassembly

1. Remove the 2nd clutch hub snapring and lift out the 2nd clutch wave plate.

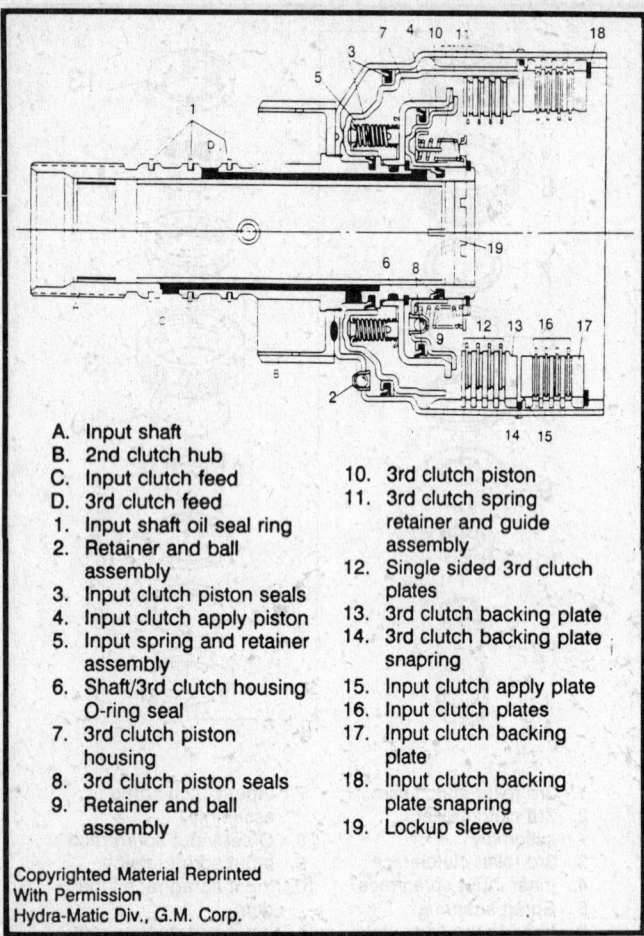

A. Input shaft
B. 2nd clutch hub
C. Input clutch feed
D. 3rd clutch feed
1. Input shaft oil seal ring
2. Retainer and ball assembly
3. Input clutch piston seals
4. Input clutch apply piston
5. Input spring and retainer assembly
6. Shaft/3rd clutch housing O-ring seal
7. 3rd clutch piston housing
8. 3rd clutch piston seals
9. Retainer and ball assembly
10. 3rd clutch piston
11. 3rd clutch spring retainer and guide assembly
12. Single sided 3rd clutch plates
13. 3rd clutch backing plate
14. 3rd clutch backing plate snapring
15. Input clutch apply plate
16. Input clutch plates
17. Input clutch backing plate
18. Input clutch backing plate snapring
19. Lockup sleeve

Input clutch cross view

2. Remove the 2nd clutch plate assembly and the 2nd clutch backing plate.

3. Remove the next snapring and remove the 2nd clutch housing support.

4. Remove the thrust bearing and thrust washer. Remove the reverse band.

5. Remove the 2nd clutch housing. Remove the 2nd clutch piston seals which may be stuck on the 2nd clutch housing.

6. Remove the 2nd clutch piston and the spring return apply ring.

Inspection

1. Wash all parts in cleaning solvent and blow dry using compressed air.

2. Inspect all parts for scoring, wear or damage.

3. Inspect the 2nd clutch piston and seal for damage or warping.

4. Repair or replace damaged parts as required.

Assembly

1. Lubricate a new piston seal with automatic transmission fluid and install in the 2nd clutch piston.

2. Install a new retainer and ball assembly into the 2nd clutch housing using a ⅜ in. (9.5mm) drift.

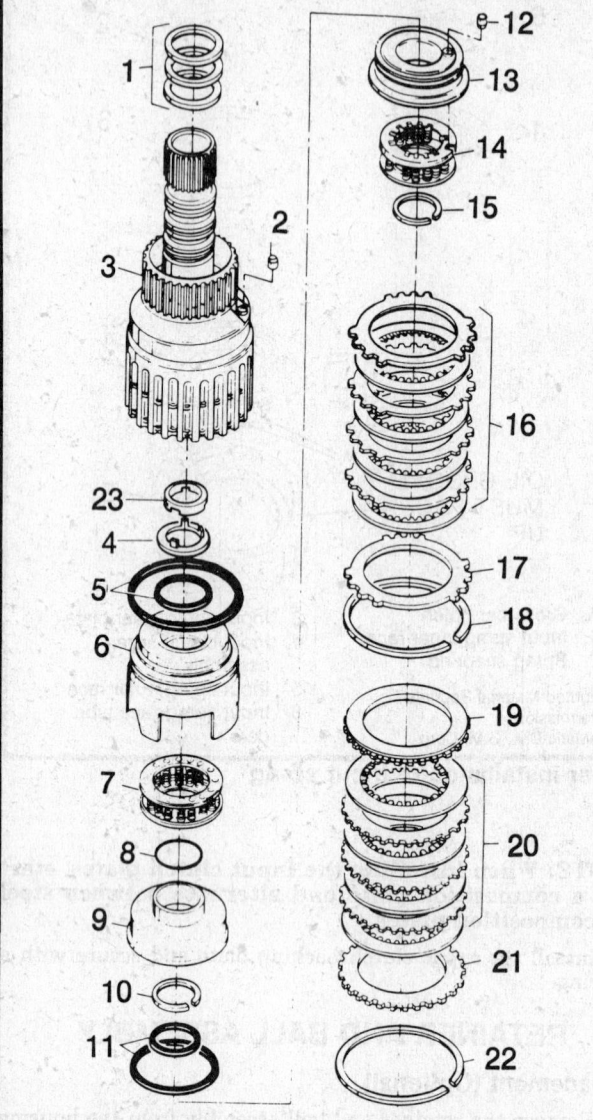

1. Input shaft oil seal ring
2. Retainer and ball assembly
3. Input housing and shaft assembly
4. Input shaft/sun thrust washer
5. Input clutch piston seals
6. Input clutch piston
7. Input spring and retainer assembly
8. Shaft/3rd clutch housing O-ring seal
9. 3rd clutch piston housing
10. Shaft/3rd clutch housing O-ring seal
11. 3rd clutch piston seals
12. Retainer and ball assembly
13. 3rd clutch piston
14. 3rd clutch spring retainer and guide assembly
15. Shaft/3rd clutch spring retainer snapring
16. 3rd clutch plate assembly
17. 3rd clutch backing plate
18. 3rd clutch backing plate snapring
19. Input clutch apply plate
20. Input clutch plate assembly
21. Input clutch backing plate
22. Input clutch backing plate snapring
23. Lockup sleeve

Input clutch assembly

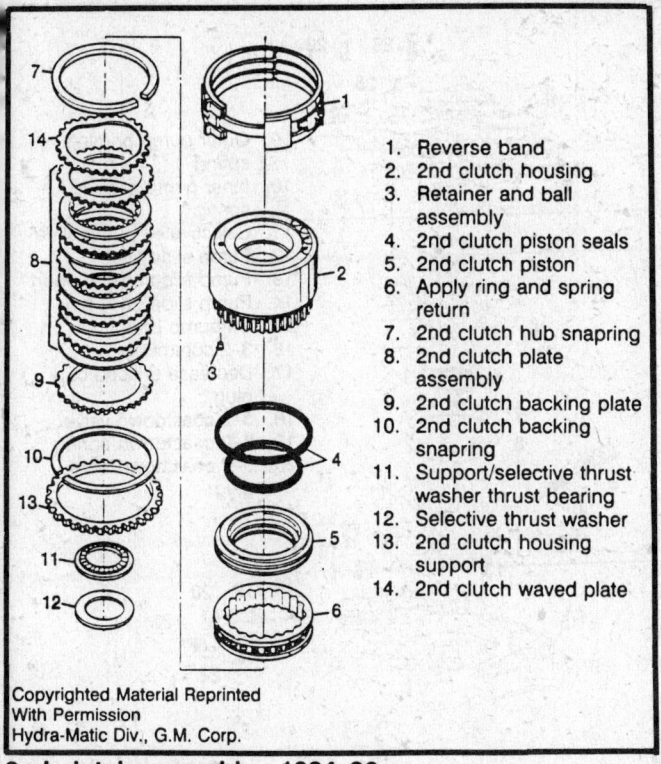

1. Reverse band
2. 2nd clutch housing
3. Retainer and ball assembly
4. 2nd clutch piston seals
5. 2nd clutch piston
6. Apply ring and spring return
7. 2nd clutch hub snapring
8. 2nd clutch plate assembly
9. 2nd clutch backing plate
10. 2nd clutch backing snapring
11. Support/selective thrust washer thrust bearing
12. Selective thrust washer
13. 2nd clutch housing support
14. 2nd clutch waved plate

2nd clutch assembly — 1984–86

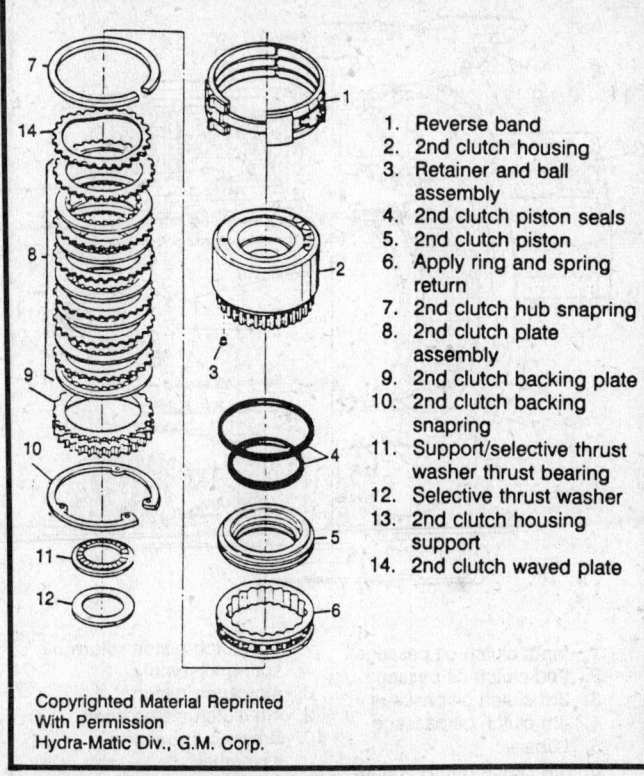

1. Reverse band
2. 2nd clutch housing
3. Retainer and ball assembly
4. 2nd clutch piston seals
5. 2nd clutch piston
6. Apply ring and spring return
7. 2nd clutch hub snapring
8. 2nd clutch plate assembly
9. 2nd clutch backing plate
10. 2nd clutch backing snapring
11. Support/selective thrust washer thrust bearing
12. Selective thrust washer
13. 2nd clutch housing support
14. 2nd clutch waved plate

2nd clutch assembly — 1987–89

3. Install the 2nd clutch piston into the 2nd clutch housing. Make sure the seals are not damaged.

4. Install the spring return apply ring into the 2nd clutch housing. Using a spring compressor, compress the spring return apply ring and insert the snapring.

5. Install the 2nd clutch plates starting with steel and alternating with composition plates.

NOTE: The 2nd clutch composition plates are pre-soaked and do not require soaking in solvent.

6. Install the reverse band and the thrust bearing and thrust washers.

7. Install the clutch housing support and secure with a snapring.

8. Install the backing plate and the 2nd clutch plates. Install the waved plate and the snapring.

DRIVEN SPROCKET SUPPORT

Disassembly

1. Using a suitable tool, compress the 4th clutch spring assembly and remove the snapring.

2. Remove the 4th clutch piston and the piston seals. Discard the piston seals.

3. Remove the bearing assembly from the driven sprocket support.

4. Remove the chain scavenging scoop and the oil reservoir wire.

5. Remove the thrust washer and the O-ring seals.

Inspection

1. Clean all parts thoroughly in solvent and blow dry using compressed air.

2. Inspect the driven sprocket support for cracks or damage.

3. Inspect the seals and pistons for damage. Replace as necessary.

4. Check the spring retainer for distorted or damaged springs.

5. Inspect the oil reservoir weir and the chain scavenging scoop for cracks or damage.

6. Repair or replace any damaged parts as required.

Assembly

1. Lubricate new O-rings and install them behind the thrust washer on the driven sprocket support.

2. Install the oil reservoir weir and the chain scavenging scoop on the driven sprocket support.

3. Install the bearing assembly on the driven sprocket support, between the oil reservoir weir and the chain scavenging scoop.

4. Install new seals on the 4th clutch piston and install the 4th clutch piston.

5. Install the 4th clutch spring assembly and using a suitable tool, compress the springs and insert the snapring.

OIL PUMP

Disassembly

1. Remove the pump bolts from the cover. Lift off the pump cover. Remove the pump cover sleeve and the vane ring.

2. Remove the pump rotor and the bottom vane ring. Remove the oil seal ring and the O-ring from the oil pump slide.

3. Remove the oil pump slide. Enclosed in the oil pump slide are the pump slide seal and support along with the inner and outer pump priming springs.

NOTE: The pump rotor, vane rings and oil pump slide are factory matched units. Therefore, if any parts need replacing, all parts must be replaced.

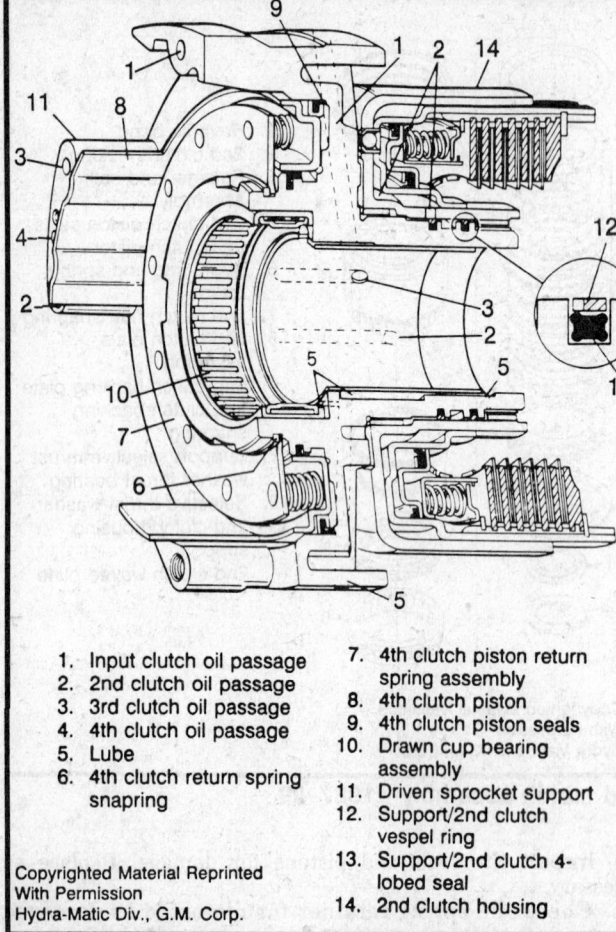

1. Input clutch oil passage
2. 2nd clutch oil passage
3. 3rd clutch oil passage
4. 4th clutch oil passage
5. Lube
6. 4th clutch return spring snapring
7. 4th clutch piston return spring assembly
8. 4th clutch piston
9. 4th clutch piston seals
10. Drawn cup bearing assembly
11. Driven sprocket support
12. Support/2nd clutch vespel ring
13. Support/2nd clutch 4-lobed seal
14. 2nd clutch housing

Driven sprocket support and 2nd clutch cross view

4. Remove the pivot pin and the roll pin from the oil pump body.

5. Remove the 3–2 coast down valve, spring and bore plug from the oil pump body. Remove the oil pressure switches.

Inspection

1. Clean all parts thoroughly in solvent and blow dry using compressed air.

2. Check the pump body for warping or cracks. Make sure that the oil passages are free of debris.

3. Check the oil pump slide and springs for excessive wear.

4. Check the rotor and vanes for any damage. Inspect the pump slide seal and support for any cracks.

5. Repair or replace damaged parts as needed.

Assembly

1. Install the 3–2 coast down valve along with the spring and bore plug into the oil pump body.

2. Install the lower vane ring into the pump pocket. Install the pump slide into the pump pocket being careful not to dislodge the lower vane ring.

3. Install the pump slide seal and support into the oil pump.

4. Insert the inner priming spring into the outer priming spring. Press the springs into the pump body.

5. Install the O-ring seal onto the oil pump slide. Install the oil seal ring onto the oil pump slide.

6. Install the oil pump rotor onto the oil pump body. Insert the pump vanes into the oil pump rotor. Install the upper vane ring onto the oil pump rotor.

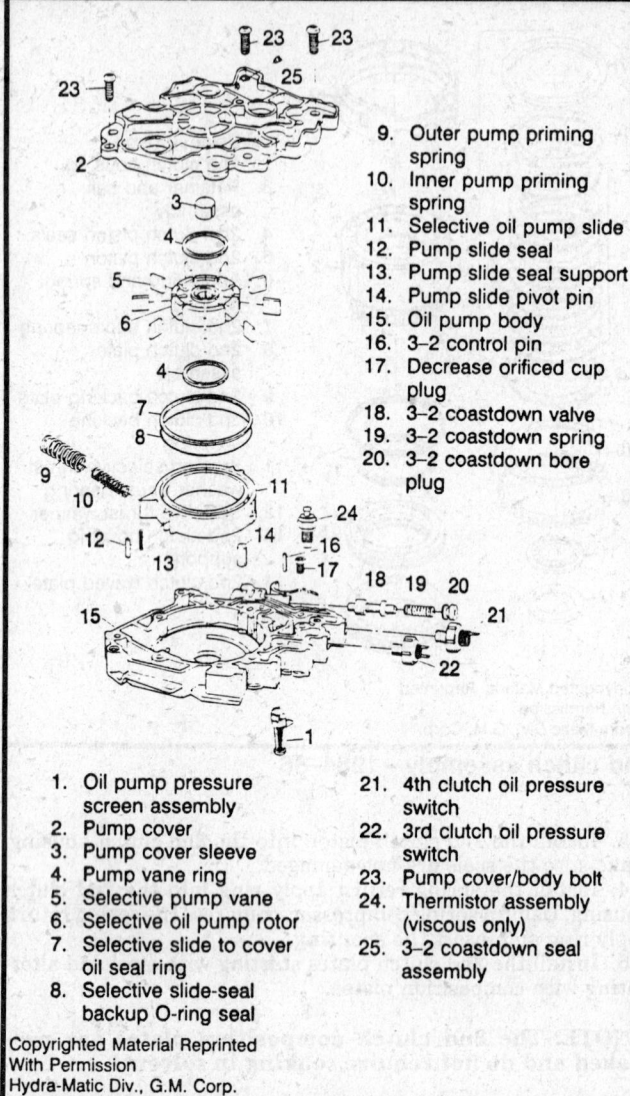

9. Outer pump priming spring
10. Inner pump priming spring
11. Selective oil pump slide
12. Pump slide seal
13. Pump slide seal support
14. Pump slide pivot pin
15. Oil pump body
16. 3–2 control pin
17. Decrease orificed cup plug
18. 3–2 coastdown valve
19. 3–2 coastdown spring
20. 3–2 coastdown bore plug

1. Oil pump pressure screen assembly
2. Pump cover
3. Pump cover sleeve
4. Pump vane ring
5. Selective pump vane
6. Selective oil pump rotor
7. Selective slide to cover oil seal ring
8. Selective slide-seal backup O-ring seal
21. 4th clutch oil pressure switch
22. 3rd clutch oil pressure switch
23. Pump cover/body bolt
24. Thermistor assembly (viscous only)
25. 3–2 coastdown seal assembly

Oil pump assembly

NOTE: The pump vanes must be installed flush with the top of the oil pump rotor.

7. Install the pump cover onto the oil pump body. Install the cover bolts.

8. Install the oil pressure switches into the oil pump body.

CONTROL VALVE

Disassembly

NOTE: As each part of the valve train is removed, place the pieces in order and in a position that is relative to the position on the valve body to lessen the chances for error in assembly. None of the valves, springs or bushings are interchangeable.

1. Lay the valve body on a clean work bench with the machined side up and the line boost valve at the top. The line boost valve should be checked for proper operation before its removal. If it is necessary to remove the boost valve, grind the end of a No. 49 drill to a taper (a small Allen wrench an sometimes be

substituted) and lightly tap the drill into the roll pin. Push the line boost valve out of the top of the valve body.

2. The throttle valve should be checked for proper operation before removing it, by pushing the valve against the spring. If it is necessary to remove the throttle valve, first remove the roll pin holding the T.V. plunger bushing and pull out the plunger and bushing. Remove the throttle valve spring. Remove the blind hole roll pin using the drill method.

3. On the same side of the valve body, move to the next bore down. Remove the straight pin and remove the reverse boost valve and bushing, as well as revere boost spring and the pressure regulator assembly.

NOTE: Transaxle on vehicles equipped with a diesel engine will not have a reverse boost spring or a pressure regulator modulator spring.

4. Move to the other side of the valve body and from the top bore remove the 1–2 throttle valve bushing retainer and lift out the throttle valve bushing and the 1–2 shift valve assembly.

5. Move to the next bore and remove the spring pin and lift out the 2–3 accumulator bushing assembly.

6. At the next bore down, remove the 3–2 control sleeve and the 3–2 control valve assembly.

7. Move to the next bore and remove the spring pin. Remove the 2–3 throttle valve bushing and its components. On Allante, remove the 2–3 shift solenoid assembly.

8. Move to the next bore and remove the coiled spring pin. Remove the 3–4 throttle valve assembly. On Allante, remove the 3–4 shift solenoid assembly.

9. The 2 remaining bores contain the 1–2 servo pipe lip seals, which are removed.

10. At the side of the valve body, are the servo assemblies. Remove the coiled spring pins and detach the servo valves and springs.

Inspection

1. Wash all bushings, springs and valves in solvent. Blow dry using compressed air.

2. Inspect all valves and bushings for any scoring or scratches.

3. Check the springs for collapsed coils and bore plugs for damage.

4. Repair or replace any defective parts as needed.

Assembly

1. Install the reverse servo boost valve and spring into its proper location in the valve body. Install the 1–2 servo control valve and the 1–2 servo boost valve into the valve body. Install the correct springs behind each valve and insert the coiled spring pins.

2. Install new servo pipe lip seals. Move to the bore next to the servo pipe lip seals and install the 3–4 throttle assembly. Install the coiled spring pin. On Allante, install the 3–4 shift solenoid assembly.

3. Move to the next bore and install the 2–3 throttle valve bushing and its components. Install the spring pin. On Allante, install the 2–3 shift solenoid assembly.

4. Move to the next bore and in the following order install 3–2 isolater valve and spring, 3–2 control valve and spring and the 3–2 control sleeve.

5. Move to the next bore and install the 2–3 accumulator bushing assembly. Install the spring pin.

6. Move to the last bore of the side and install in the following order the 1–2 shift valve and throttle valve, the throttle valve spring and the 1–2 throttle valve bushing. Insert the 1–2 throttle valve bushing retainer into the 1–2 throttle valve bushing.

7. Move to the other side of the valve body and install the pressure regulator valve assembly. Install the reverse boost valve and bushing. Install the straight pin.

NOTE: The reverse boost spring and a pressure regulator modulator spring will only be found on transaxles equipped with a gas engine.

8. Install in the next bore the throttle valve assembly. Secure the assembly with the spring pin.

9. Install the line boost valve assembly. Insert the retainer clip.

10. Move to the next bore and install throttle valve feed valve assembly. Make sure the valve stop plate is in its proper position.

11. Move to the next bore and install the converter clutch shift valve assembly securing it with the bushing and a coiled spring pin.

12. The next bore is the pump pressure valve and bushing locations. Secure these units with a spring pin.

13. Moving to the next bore, install the 1–2 accumulator assembly. Make sure that the valve bore plug is in place over the 1–2 accumulator valve.

14. Assemble the converter clutch valves into the next 2 bore holes.

15. Install the 2nd clutch pipes in the top of the valve body. Install the release cover plate gasket and cover.

CHANNEL PLATE

Disassembly

1. Remove the modulator port gasket and the upper channel plate gasket. Remove the lower channel plate gasket and discard all gaskets.

2. Remove the input clutch accumulator piston and spring. Discard the input clutch ring seal.

3. Remove the converter clutch accumulator piston and the converter clutch spring. Discard the converter clutch seal. Remove the axle oil seal.

4. Remove the manual valve assembly. Detach the manual valve clip. Remove the channel plate stud from the case side of the channel plate.

Inspection

1. Wash all parts in solvent and blow dry using compressed air.

2. Check all parts for excessive wear or damage. Check the channel plate for cracks or warping.

3. Repair or replace any defective parts as required.

Assembly

1. Install the channel plate stud to the channel plate. Attach the manual valve clip to the manual valve assembly. Install the manual valve assembly into the channel plate.

2. Press in a new axle oil seal using a suitable tool. Install a new converter clutch seal. Place the converter clutch piston on its shaft with a new seal. Install the converter clutch spring.

3. Install the input clutch piston with a new input clutch seal. Install the input clutch spring.

Transaxle Assembly

Before the assembly of the transaxle begins, make certain that the case and all other parts are clean that all parts are serviceable or have been overhauled. Inspect the case carefully for cracks or any signs of porosity. Inspect the vents to make sure that they are open. Check the case lugs, the intermediate servo bore and snapring grooves for damage. Check the bearings that are in the case and replaced if they appear to be worn.

NOTE: If the bearings are replaced, they must be installed with the bearing identification facing up.

The converter seal should be replaced. After all these prelimi-

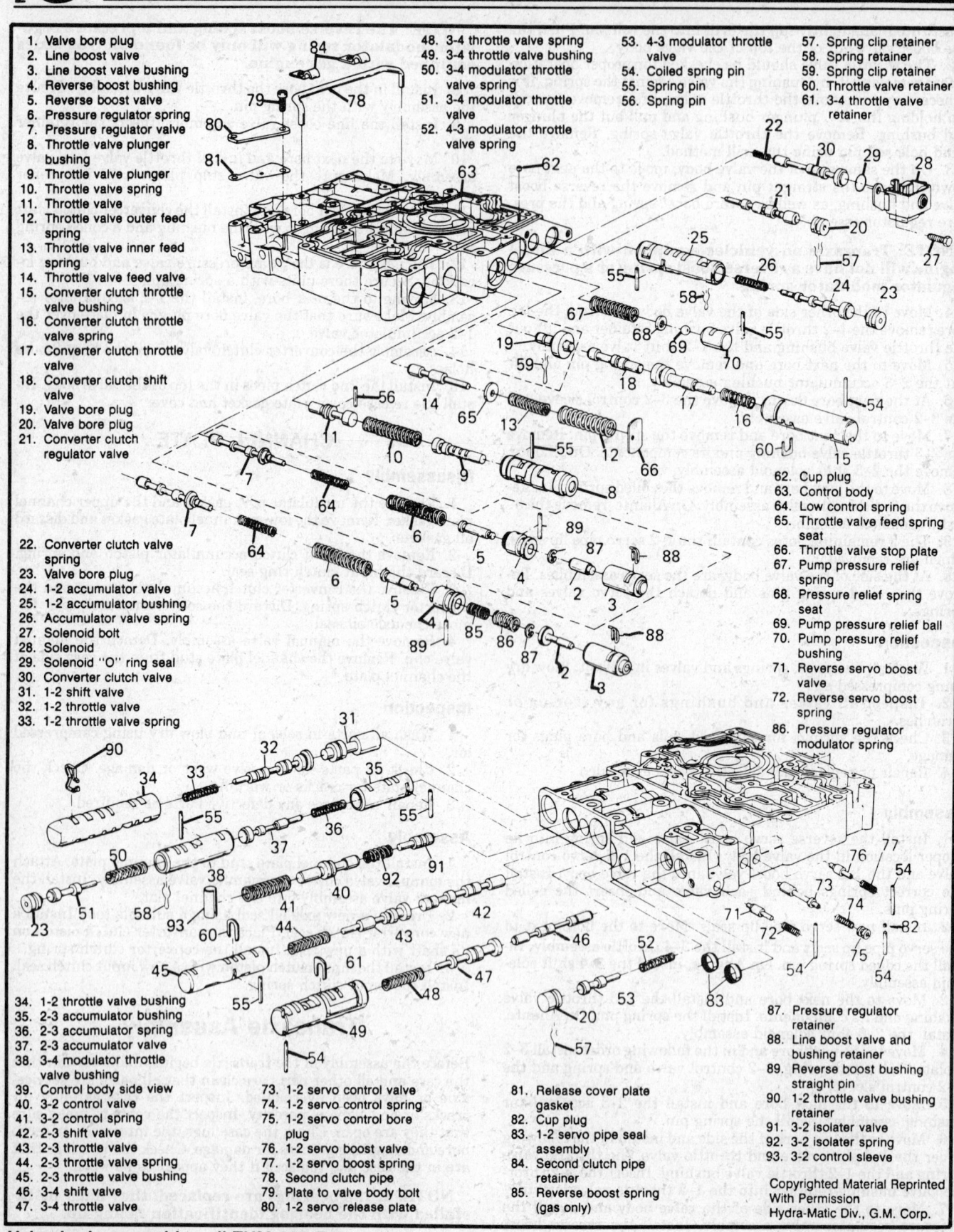

1. Valve bore plug
2. Line boost valve
3. Line boost valve bushing
4. Reverse boost bushing
5. Reverse boost valve
6. Pressure regulator spring
7. Pressure regulator valve
8. Throttle valve plunger bushing
9. Throttle valve plunger
10. Throttle valve spring
11. Throttle valve
12. Throttle valve outer feed spring
13. Throttle valve inner feed spring
14. Throttle valve feed valve
15. Converter clutch throttle valve bushing
16. Converter clutch throttle valve spring
17. Converter clutch throttle valve
18. Converter clutch shift valve
19. Valve bore plug
20. Valve bore plug
21. Converter clutch regulator valve
22. Converter clutch valve spring
23. Valve bore plug
24. 1-2 accumulator valve
25. 1-2 accumulator bushing
26. Accumulator valve spring
27. Solenoid bolt
28. Solenoid
29. Solenoid "O" ring seal
30. Converter clutch valve
31. 1-2 shift valve
32. 1-2 throttle valve
33. 1-2 throttle valve spring
34. 1-2 throttle valve bushing
35. 2-3 accumulator bushing
36. 2-3 accumulator spring
37. 2-3 accumulator valve
38. 3-4 modulator throttle valve bushing
39. Control body side view
40. 3-2 control valve
41. 3-2 control spring
42. 2-3 shift valve
43. 2-3 throttle valve
44. 2-3 throttle valve spring
45. 2-3 throttle valve bushing
46. 3-4 shift valve
47. 3-4 throttle valve

48. 3-4 throttle valve spring
49. 3-4 throttle valve bushing
50. 3-4 modulator throttle valve spring
51. 3-4 modulator throttle valve
52. 4-3 modulator throttle valve spring
53. 4-3 modulator throttle valve
54. Coiled spring pin
55. Spring pin
56. Spring pin
57. Spring clip retainer
58. Spring retainer
59. Spring clip retainer
60. Throttle valve retainer
61. 3-4 throttle valve retainer
62. Cup plug
63. Control body
64. Low control spring
65. Throttle valve feed spring seat
66. Throttle valve stop plate
67. Pump pressure relief spring
68. Pressure relief spring seat
69. Pump pressure relief ball
70. Pump pressure relief bushing
71. Reverse servo boost valve
72. Reverse servo boost spring
86. Pressure regulator modulator spring

73. 1-2 servo control valve
74. 1-2 servo control spring
75. 1-2 servo control bore plug
76. 1-2 servo boost valve
77. 1-2 servo boost spring
78. Second clutch pipe
79. Plate to valve body bolt
80. 1-2 servo release plate
81. Release cover plate gasket
82. Cup plug
83. 1-2 servo pipe seal assembly
84. Second clutch pipe retainer
85. Reverse boost spring (gas only)
87. Pressure regulator retainer
88. Line boost valve and bushing retainer
89. Reverse boost bushing straight pin
90. 1-2 throttle valve bushing retainer
91. 3-2 isolater valve
92. 3-2 isolater spring
93. 3-2 control sleeve

Valve body assembly – all THM 440-T4

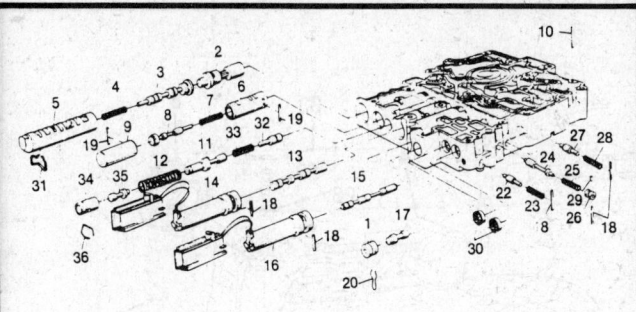

1. Valve bore plug
2. 1–2 shift valve
3. 1–2 throttle valve
4. 1–2 throttle valve spring
5. 1–2 throttle valve bushing
6. 2–3 accumulator bushing
7. 2–3 accumulator spring
8. 2–3 accumulator valve
9. 3–4 modulator plug
10. Spring pin
11. 3–2 control valve
12. 3–2 control spring
13. 2–3 shift valve
14. 2–3 shift solenoid assembly
15. 3–4 shift valve
16. 3–4 shift solenoid assembly
17. 4–3 manual throttle valve
18. Coiled spring pin
19. Spring pin
20. Spring clip retainer
21. Control body
22. Reverse servo boost valve
23. Reverse servo boost spring
24. 1–2 servo control valve
25. 1–2 servo control spring
26. 1–2 servo control bore plug
27. 1–2 servo boost valve
28. 1–2 servo boost spring
29. Cup plug
30. 1–2 servo pipe seal assembly
31. 1–2 throttle valve bushing retainer
32. 3–2 accumulator valve
33. 3–2 accumulator spring
34. 3–2 throttle valve bias bushing
35. 3–2 throttle valve bias valve
36. 3–2 throttle valve bias retainer

Valve body assembly—all THM F7

nary checks have been made, begin the reassembly of the transaxle. Make certain that the transaxle is held securely in the proper support fixture.

MANUAL LINKAGE/ACTUATOR REPLACEMENT

Installation

1. Install the O-ring to the actuator guide and install the actuator guide assembly.
2. Install the actuator guide retaining pin to the case.
3. Install the manual shaft with the detent lever. Install the locknut and torque to 25 ft. lbs. (34 Nm). Insert the retaining pin into the case.

MANUAL SHAFT/DETENT LEVER AND ACTUATOR ROD

Installation

1. Install the actuator guide assembly.
2. Install the actuator rod assembly.
3. Install the shaft lever and install the manual shaft and detent lever retaining bolts.

1. 3–2 coastdown seal assembly
2. Line boost valve
3. Line boost valve bushing
4. Reverse boost bushing
5. Reverse boost valve
6. Pressure regulator spring
7. Pressure regulator valve
8. Throttle valve plunger bushing
9. Throttle valve plunger
10. Throttle valve spring
11. Throttle valve
12. Throttle valve feed outer spring
13. Throttle valve feed inner spring
14. Throttle valve feed valve
15. Valve bore plug
16. Converter clutch regulator valve
17. Converter clutch valve spring
18. Valve bore plug
19. 1–2 accumulator valve
20. 1–2 accumulator bushing
21. Accumulator valve spring
22. Solenoid bolt
23. Solenoid
24. Converter clutch solenoid O-ring
25. Converter clutch valve
26. Spring pin
27. Spring pin
28. Spring clip retainer
29. Spring retainer
30. Control body
31. Pressure regulator isolator spring
32. Throttle valve feed spring seat
33. Throttle valve valve stop plate
34. Pump pressure relief spring
35. Pressure relief spring seat
36. Pump pressure relief ball
37. Pump pressure relief bushing
38. Plug and release cover assembly pipe
39. 2nd clutch-to-1–2 servo control valve pipe
40. Plate/valve body bolt
41. Release cover plate gasket
42. 2nd clutch pipe retainer
43. Reverse boost spring
44. Pressure regulator module boost spring
45. Pressure regulator retainer
46. Line boost valve and bushing retainer
47. Reverse boost bushing straight pin
48. Converter clutch regulator valve spring— some models
49. Throttle valve assist spring

Valve body assembly—all THM F7

FINAL DRIVE ASSEMBLY

Installation

1. The final drive carrier will be installed with the final drive internal gear.
2. Clamp the clutch and final drive tool to the final drive internal gear and install it.

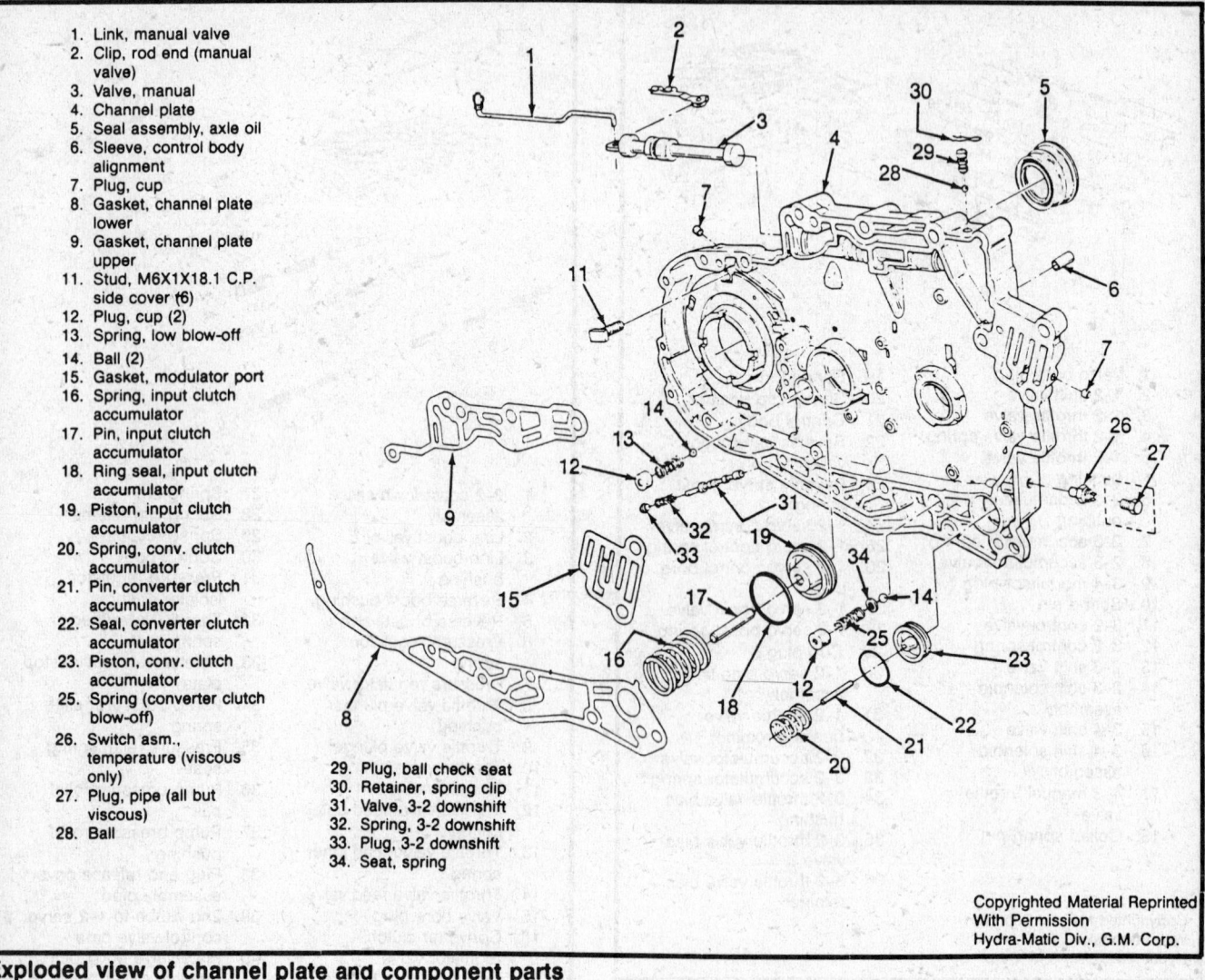

1. Link, manual valve
2. Clip, rod end (manual valve)
3. Valve, manual
4. Channel plate
5. Seal assembly, axle oil
6. Sleeve, control body alignment
7. Plug, cup
8. Gasket, channel plate lower
9. Gasket, channel plate upper
11. Stud, M6X1X18.1 C.P. side cover (6)
12. Plug, cup (2)
13. Spring, low blow-off
14. Ball (2)
15. Gasket, modulator port
16. Spring, input clutch accumulator
17. Pin, input clutch accumulator
18. Ring seal, input clutch accumulator
19. Piston, input clutch accumulator
20. Spring, conv. clutch accumulator
21. Pin, converter clutch accumulator
22. Seal, converter clutch accumulator
23. Piston, conv. clutch accumulator
25. Spring (converter clutch blow-off)
26. Switch asm., temperature (viscous only)
27. Plug, pipe (all but viscous)
28. Ball

29. Plug, ball check seat
30. Retainer, spring clip
31. Valve, 3-2 downshift
32. Spring, 3-2 downshift
33. Plug, 3-2 downshift
34. Seat, spring

Exploded view of channel plate and component parts

3. With a suitable tool, install the snapring at the head of the internal final drive gear.

SECOND CLUTCH, INPUT CLUTCH, ROLLER CLUTCH AND SPRAG ASSEMBLY

Installation

1. Install the sun gear shaft and the bearing ring.
2. Install the 1–2 band. Install the reaction sun gear and the drum assembly.
3. Install the thrust bearing into the reaction carrier.
4. Install the reaction carrier.
5. Install the input carrier assembly. Install the reverse band and the reverse reaction drum.
6. Install the 2nd clutch housing and the input shaft assembly into the unit.

DRIVE LINK ASSEMBLY

Installation

1. Install the thrust washer. Install the drive sprocket support.

2. Position the drivelink assembly, onto the drive and driven sprockets. The drive link must be installed the same way as it was removed. It should be facing out.
3. Install the sprockets and the chain as an assembly. It will required alternately pushing on the sprockets until the bearings go onto of their support housings.
4. Reach through the access holes in the sprockets and slip the snaprings onto their grooves.
5. Install the turbine shaft O-ring located at the front of the unit.

FOURTH CLUTCH, SHAFT AND OUTPUT SHAFT

Installation

1. Install the output shaft into the transaxle being careful not to damage it.
2. Place the C-ring in the installation part of tool J-28583 and install the C-ring.
3. Install the 4th clutch shaft assembly.
4. Install the clutch apply plate with the stamped **DN** facing down. Install the steel clutch plate, then the composition plate, then the last steel clutch plate.

OIL PUMP SHAFT AND CHANNEL PLATE

Installation

1. Install the accumulator pistons and pins into the channel plate assembly. Install the 3 channel plate gaskets onto the channel plate and retain with petrolatum. Install the input clutch accumulator spring and the converter clutch spring into the case.
2. Install the channel plate into the transaxle case. Install the channel plate attaching bolts.
3. Align the manual detent roller and spring assembly to the detent lever and tighten the screws.

VALVE BODY

Installation

1. Install the 8 check balls into the channel plate.
2. Install the fluid reservoir weir.
3. Install the spacer plate/channel plate gasket. Install the spacer plate. Torque the bolts to 10 ft. lbs. (14 Nm). Install the spacer plate/valve body gasket.
4. Slide the fluid pump driveshaft through the drive sprocket hole.
5. Install the converter clutch solenoid screen.
6. Install the remaining check balls into the control valve assembly and retain with petrolatum.
7. Install the valve body onto the channel plate. Put the 1–2 servo pipes into the holes in the side of the valve body. Install the valve body retaining bolts. Torque the bolts to 10 ft. lbs. (14 Nm).

OIL PUMP

Installation

1. Position the oil pump assembly onto the valve body. Install the oil pump bolts. Torque to 10 ft. lbs. (14 Nm).
2. Install the solenoid wiring harness into the case connector and pressure switch.
3. Install the release pipe cover gasket and cover. Install the attaching screws.
4. Install the throttle valve assembly onto the valve body.
5. Install the side cover gasket on the case and position the side cover onto the case. Install the attaching screws, washer and nuts.

REVERSE AND/OR 1–2 SERVO

Installation

1. Install the accumulator springs and pistons. Install the accumulator pin through the piston hole.
2. To install the reverse and/or 1–2 servo assembly, install the piston and spring into the servo bore. Then install the cover. Depress the cover and install the snapring.

GOVERNOR

Installation

1. Install the speedometer drive gear onto the governor assembly.
2. Install the thrust bearing on the speedometer drive gear. The inside race goes against the gear or black side up.
3. Install the governor cover O-ring. Install the governor cover onto the case. Install the governor control body bolts and torque to 20 ft. lbs. (27 Nm).

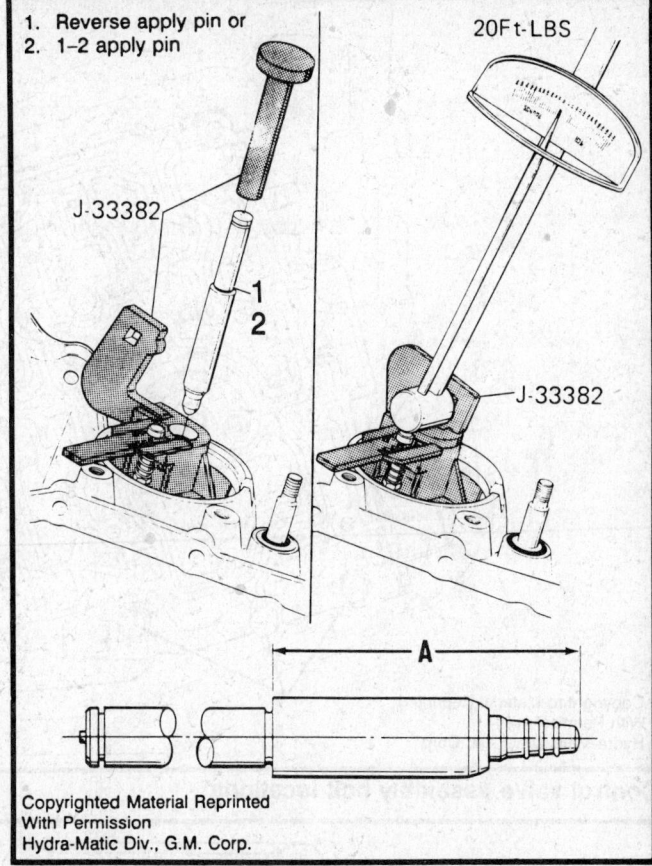

1. Reverse apply pin or
2. 1–2 apply pin

20 Ft-LBS

J-33382

1
2

J-33382

A

Checking 1–2 apply pin or reverse apply pin

4. Install the modulator valve into the case. Install the modulator O-ring onto the modulator and install in the case. Install the retainer and bolt. Torque to 20 ft. lbs. (27 Nm).

OIL FILTER

Installation

1. If the oil pressure regulator bushing assembly was removed, install it. Install the oil pressure regulator bushing assembly snapring.
2. Install the oil filter with a new O-ring. Attach the clips.

OIL PAN

Installation

1. Install the new oil pan gasket onto the oil pan.
2. Install the oil pan onto the case.
3. Install the oil pan attaching bolts. Torque to 10 ft. lbs. (13 Nm).

TORQUE CONVERTER

Installation

1. Install the converter assembly, making sure it is installed fully toward the rear of the transaxle.
2. The converter will be properly installed when the distance between the case mounting face and the front face of the converter lugs is a minimum of ½ in. (13mm).

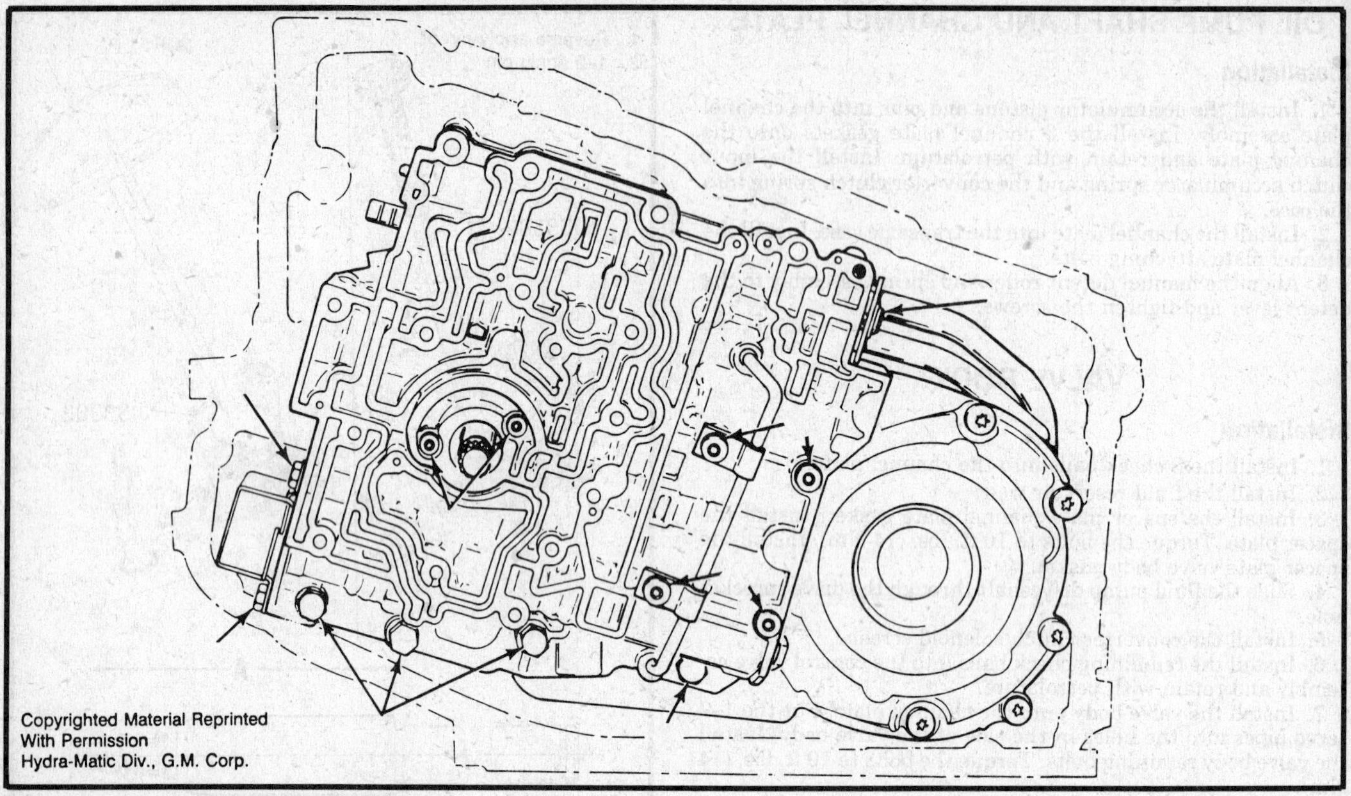

Control valve assembly bolt locations

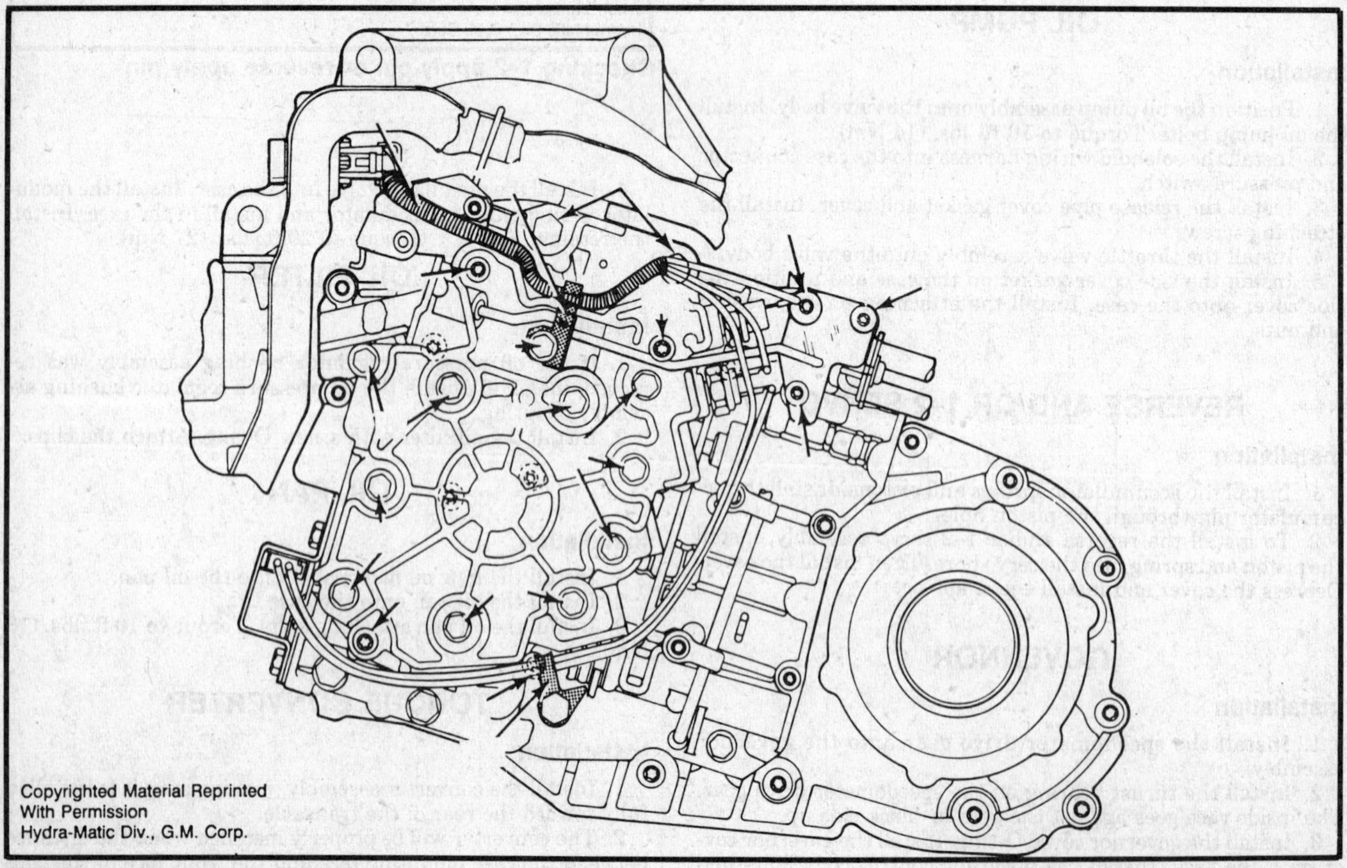

Oil pump assembly bolt location

SPECIFICATIONS

TORQUE SPECIFICATIONS

Item	Foot Pounds	N•m
Cooler Fitting Connector	30	41
Modulator to Case	20	27
Pump Cover to Channel Plate	10	14
Pump Cover to Pump Body	20	27
Pump Cover to Pump Body (Torx Head)	20	27
Pipe Plug	10	14
Case to Drive Sprocket Support	20	27
Manifold to Valve Body	10	14
Governor to Case	20	27
Pressure Switch	10	14
Solenoid to Valve Body	10	14
Detent Spring to Valve Body	10	14
Case Side Cover to Channel Plate	10	14
Pump Cover to Valve Body	10	14
Pump Cover to Channel Plate	10	14
Valve Body to Case (Torx Head)	20	27
Valve Body to Case	20	27
Pump Body to Case	20	27
Valve Body to Channel Plate	10	14
Valve Body to Channel Plate (Torx Head)	10	14
Channel Plate to Case (Torx Head)	20	27
Channel Plate to Driven Sprocket Support (Torx Head)	20	27
Side Cover to Case	10	14
Accumulator Cover to Case	20	27
Oil Scoop to Case	10	14
Governor Control Body Retainer	20	27
Transmission Oil Pan to Case	10	14
Manual Shaft to Inside Detent Lever (Nut)	25	34

THRUST WASHER GUIDE

I.D. Number	Dimension (in.)	Color
1	2.90-3.00	Orange/Green
2	3.05-3.15	Orange/Black
3	3.20-3.30	Orange
4	3.35-3.45	White
5	3.50-3.60	Blue
6	3.65-3.75	Pink
7	3.80-3.90	Brown

THRUST WASHER GUIDE

I.D. Number	Dimension (in.)	Color
8	3.95-4.05	Green
9	4.10-4.20	Black
10	4.25-4.35	Purple
11	4.40-4.50	Purple/White
12	4.55-4.65	Purple/Blue
13	4.70-4.80	Purple/Pink
14	4.85-4.95	Purple/Brown
15	5.00-5.10	Purple/Green

FINAL DRIVE ENDPLAY

I.D. Number	Thickness
1	0.059-0.062 inches (1.50-1.60mm)
2	0.062-0.066 inches (1.60-1.70mm)
3	0.066-0.070 inches (1.70-1.80mm)
4	0.070-0.074 inches (1.80-1.90mm)
5	0.074-0.078 inches (1.90-2.00mm)
6	0.078-0.082 inches (2.00-2.10mm)

REVERSE BAND APPLY PIN

IDENTIFICATION	DIMENSION A
2 WIDE BANDS	70.86 - 71.01
3 GROOVES & WIDE BAND	71.91 - 72.06
2 GROOVES & WIDE BAND	72.96 - 73.11
1 GROOVE & WIDE BAND	74.01 - 74.16
NO GROOVE	75.03 - 75.18
1 GROOVE	76.08 - 76.23
2 GROOVE	77.13 - 77.28
3 GROOVE	78.18 - 78.33
4 GROOVE	79.20 - 79.35

1–2 BAND APPLY PIN

IDENTIFICATION	DIMENSION A
1 RING & WIDE BAND	56.24 - 56.39
1 RING	57.23 - 57.38
2 RINGS	58.27 - 58.42
3 RINGS	59.31 - 59.46
WIDE BAND	60.34 - 60.49
2 RINGS & WIDE BAND	61.34 - 61.49

SPECIAL TOOLS

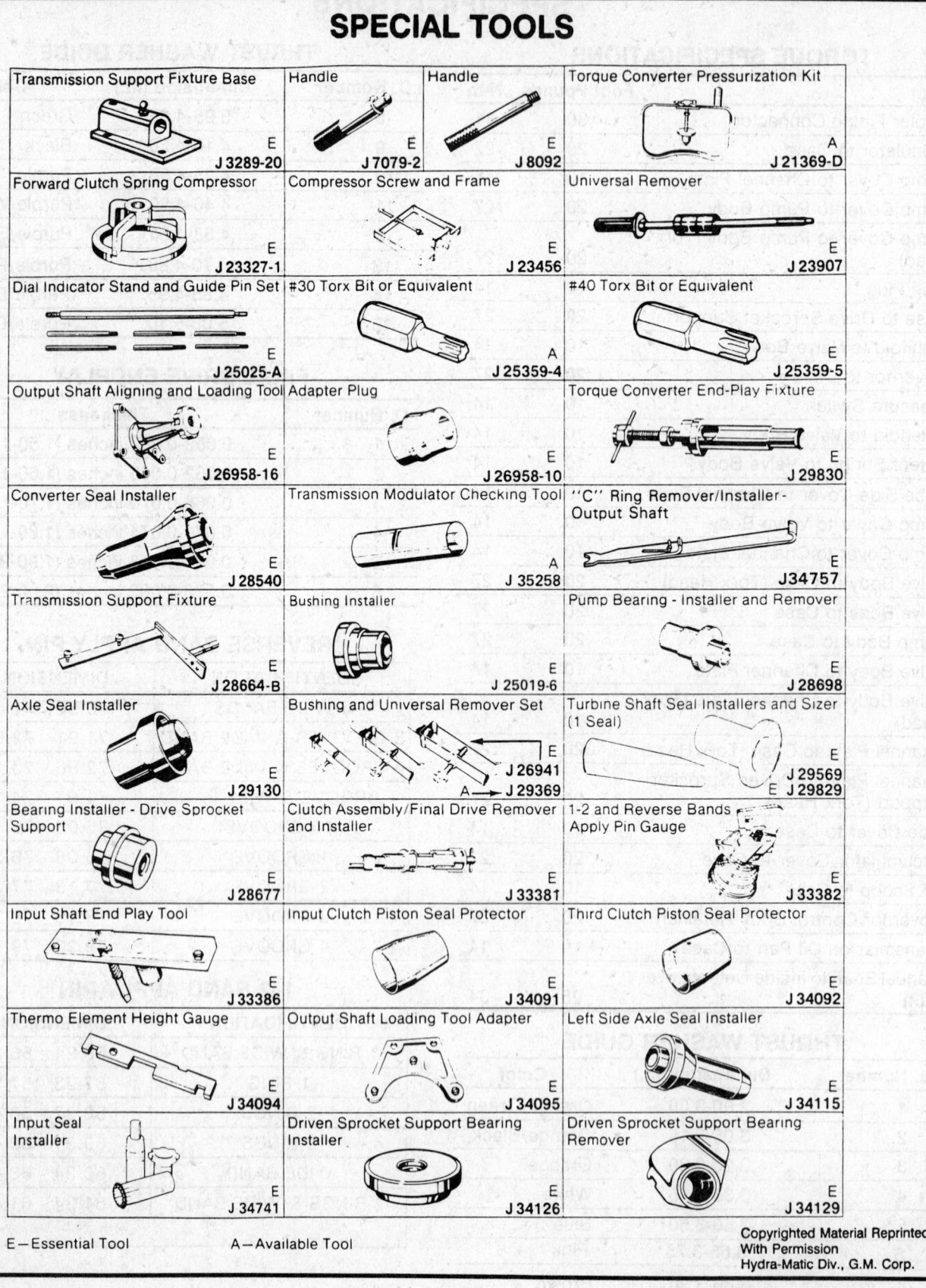

Transmission Support Fixture Base E **J 3289-20**	Handle E **J 7079-2**	Handle E **J 8092**	Torque Converter Pressurization Kit A **J 21369-D**
Forward Clutch Spring Compressor E **J 23327-1**	Compressor Screw and Frame E **J 23456**		Universal Remover E **J 23907**
Dial Indicator Stand and Guide Pin Set E **J 25025-A**	#30 Torx Bit or Equivalent A **J 25359-4**		#40 Torx Bit or Equivalent E **J 25359-5**
Output Shaft Aligning and Loading Tool E **J 26958-16**	Adapter Plug E **J 26958-10**		Torque Converter End-Play Fixture E **J 29830**
Converter Seal Installer E **J 28540**	Transmission Modulator Checking Tool A **J 35258**		"C" Ring Remover/Installer- Output Shaft E **J 34757**
Transmission Support Fixture E **J 28664-B**	Bushing Installer E **J 25019-6**		Pump Bearing - Installer and Remover E **J 28698**
Axle Seal Installer E **J 29130**	Bushing and Universal Remover Set E **J 26941** A **J 29369**		Turbine Shaft Seal Installers and Sizer (1 Seal) E **J 29569** E **J 29829**
Bearing Installer - Drive Sprocket Support E **J 28677**	Clutch Assembly/Final Drive Remover and Installer E **J 33381**		1-2 and Reverse Bands Apply Pin Gauge E **J 33382**
Input Shaft End Play Tool E **J 33386**	Input Clutch Piston Seal Protector E **J 34091**		Third Clutch Piston Seal Protector E **J 34092**
Thermo Element Height Gauge E **J 34094**	Output Shaft Loading Tool Adapter E **J 34095**		Left Side Axle Seal Installer E **J 34115**
Input Seal Installer E **J 34741**	Driven Sprocket Support Bearing Installer E **J 34126**		Driven Sprocket Support Bearing Remover E **J 34129**

E — Essential Tool   A — Available Tool

Section 3

Sprint and Metro Transaxle
General Motors

APPLICATION

1986–88 Sprint, 1989 Geo Metro

GENERAL DESCRIPTION

The transaxle is a 3 speed fully automatic overdrive transmission. The unit consists of 2 planetary gears, 2 disc clutches, a band brake, a disc brake and a one-way clutch. The fully automatic shift control which responds to the road speed and engine torque demand.

Transaxle and Converter Identification

TRANSAXLE

Code letters and numbers are stamped on the identification tag located on the left side (front) of the transaxle housing. The tag denotes the serial number and the date of manufacture. These numbers are important when ordering service replacement parts.

CONVERTER

The 3 element torque converter consists of a pump, turbine and stator; disassembly is not possible. The pump is mounted to the crankshaft, the turbine to the input shaft and stator to the transaxle case by way of a one-way clutch. Its torque increases when starting, accelerating and driving up hill; while driving at constant speed, it functions as a fluid clutch.

Electronic Controls

The transaxle, being fully controlled by the computer system, is equipped with 2 solenoids; it responds to road speed and engine torque demand.

The internal equipment, attached to the main control assembly, consists of the direct clutch and 2nd brake solenoids. A bulkhead connector/wiring assembly, attached to the middle, rear side of the chain cover assembly, provides an electrical path to the computer system.

Metric Fasteners

The transaxle is of a metric design; all bolt sizes and thread pitches are metric. Metric fastener dimensions are very close to the customary inch system fastener dimensions; replacement of the fasteners must be of the same measurement and strength as those removed.

Do not attempt to interchange metric fasteners with the customary inch system fasteners. Mismatched or incorrect fasteners can result in damage to the transaxle. Care should be taken to reuse the same fasteners in the location from which they were removed.

NOTE: Be sure to check the case holes for the quality of their threads. It is rather difficult to rethread bolt holes after the transaxle is installed in the vehicle.

Capacities

The fluid quantities are approximate and the correct fluid level should be determined by the dipstick indicator for the correct level. Dry fill is 4.7 qts. (4.5L)

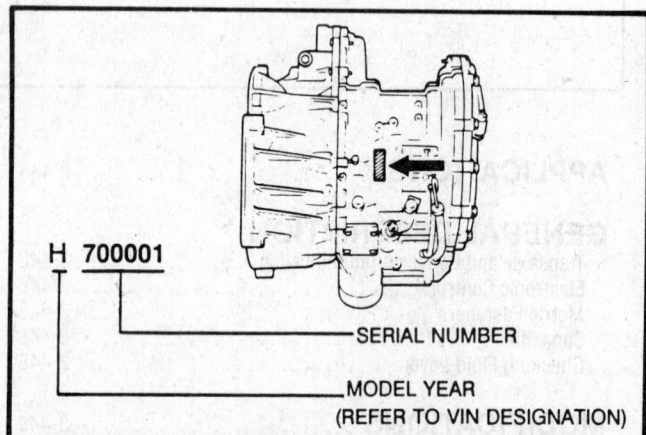

Location and description of the transaxle's identification number

Checking Fluid Level

Transaxle at Normal Operating Temperature

DIPSTICK COOL TO THE TOUCH

NOTE: The following procedure is used to check the fluid level after the transaxle has been overhauled, the fluid drained or the valve body serviced. This check is only temporary, be sure to perform the HOT check procedures before driving the vehicle.

1. With the vehicle on a level surface, place the transaxle in **P**, idle (do not race) the engine for 5 min. and apply the parking brake. Move the selector lever through each range; allow time in each range for the transaxle to engage.
2. Position the selector lever in **P**, fully apply the parking brake, block the drive wheels and allow the vehicle to idle.
3. Before removing the dipstick, wipe the dirt from the dipstick cap.
4. Remove the dipstick and wipe it clean. Insert it into the dipstick tube and be sure it fully seats.
5. Remove the dipstick again and observe the fluid level; it must be between the **FULL COLD** and **LOW COLD** indicators.
6. If necessary to add fluid, add it through the oil filler (dipstick) tube. Add enough fluid to raise the level. Do not overfill; overfilling will cause foaming, fluid loss and transaxle malfunction.

DIPSTICK HOT TO THE TOUCH

NOTE: When checking the fluid level, the vehicle must be at normal operating temperatures and positioned on a flat surface. The vehicle should not be driven if the fluid level is below the dipstick's DO NOT DRIVE hole.

1. If the oil is below 158–176°F (70–80°C), drive the vehicle until normal operating temperatures are reached.

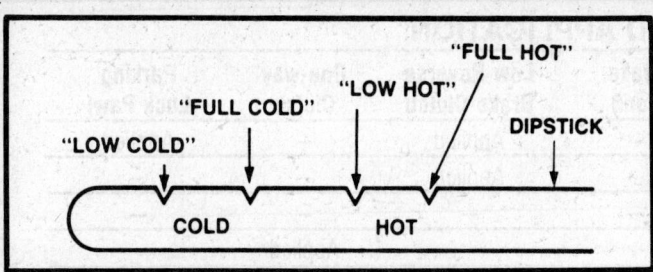

View of the dipstick fluid level indicators

NOTE: If the outside temperature is above 50°F (10°C), drive the vehicle 15–20 miles (24–32 km) of city driving. If the vehicle has been operated under extreme conditions in hot weather, turn the engine OFF and allow the fluid to cool for at least 30 minutes.

2. With the vehicle on a level surface, place the transaxle in **P**, idle (do not race) the engine and apply the parking brake. Move the selector lever through each range; allow time in each range for the transaxle to engage.

3. Position the selector lever in **P**, fully apply the parking brake, block the drive wheels and allow the vehicle to idle.

4. Before removing the dipstick, wipe the dirt from the dipstick cap.

5. Remove the dipstick and wipe it clean. Insert it into the dipstick tube and be sure it fully seats.

6. Remove the dipstick again and observe the fluid level; it must be between the **FULL HOT** and **LOW HOT** indicators.

7. If necessary to add fluid, add it through the oil filler (dipstick) tube. Add enough fluid to raise the level. Do not overfill; overfilling will cause foaming, fluid loss and transaxle malfunction.

TRANSAXLE MODIFICATIONS

Differential Side and Pinion Gear Wear

Some 1986–87 vehicles may experience operational problems due to wear of the differential side and pinion gears. The following serial numbers refer to the last 8 VIN digits and include all previous vehicles, HK740463 (2 Door) and HK740416 (4 Door).

Refer to the differential case assembly replacement procedures and replace the assembly with part number 96057455.

Direct Clutch Drum Bushing Wear

Some 1986–87 vehicles may experience operational problems due to wear of the differential side and pinion gears. The following serial numbers refer to the last 8 VIN digits and include all previous vehicles, HK740463 (2 Door) and HK740416 (4 Door).

Several sets of replacement parts are available from GM. Order the correct set according to the extent of repair or replacement that is required.

PART NUMBER INFORMATION

Previous Part No.	Qty.	New Part No.	Qty.	Part Name
35677–12010	3	35677–20020①	2	Disc, clutch (for 2nd brake)
35648–32010	3	Same①	4	Plate, clutch (for 2nd brake)
90501–25011	1	90501–26014①	1	Spring (B2 Accumulator piston)

① Parts are interchangable as a set only

TROUBLE DIAGNOSIS

NOTE: Before performing the wiring troubleshooting procedures, make sure the wiring is undamaged, the electrical connectors are firmly connected and the vacuum switch hoses are securely connected.

NOTE: Before performing the electrical checking procedures, make sure the ignition switch is turned OFF and the controller's electrical connector is disconnected.

NOTE: Before performing the electrical checking procedures on the accelerator and vacuum switches, firmly apply the parking brake, block the drive wheels, place the shift selector into P and the engine must be running.
Any checks with an asterisk mark (*) should be carried out within 5 seconds or damage may result. Release the accelerator after each continuity test, for long engine

operation at a high speed can cause overheating of the transaxle fluid.

Hydraulic Control System

The main components of the hydraulic control system are: the valve body, oil pump, manual valve, throttle valve, primary regulator valve, secondary regulator valve, B2 control valve, cooler bypass valve, 1–2 shift valve, 2–3 shift valve, accumulator and direct clutch/2nd brake solenoids.

VALVE BODY

The valve body is located inside the oil pan. It contains the various valves which control oil pressure to the clutches and bands.

CLUTCH AND BAND APPLICATION

Range	Gear	Forward Clutch	Direct Clutch	Brake Band	Low-Reverse Brake Clutch	One-way Clutch	Parking Lock Pawl
P	Parking	–	–	–	Applied	–	Applied
R	Reverse	–	Applied	–	Applied	–	–
N	Neutral	–	–	–	–	–	–
D	1st	Applied	–	–	–	Applied	–
	2nd	Applied	–	Applied	–	–	–
	3rd	Applied	Applied	–	–	–	–
2	1st	Applied	–	–	–	Applied	–
	2nd	Applied	–	Applied	–	–	–
L	1st	Applied	–	–	Applied	Applied	–
	2nd①	Applied	–	Applied	–	–	–

① To prevent over-resolution of engine, this 2nd gear is operated only when selector lever is shifted to L range at the speed of more than 34 mph (55 km/h)

CHILTON'S THREE C's TRANSAXLE DIAGNOSIS
Sprint

Condition	Cause	Correction
No 1–2 upshift	a) Sticking 1–2 shift valve b) 2nd gear solenoid stuck open c) Defective controller or poor electrical connection	a) Free or replace 1–2 shift valve b) Free or replace 2nd gear solenoid c) Replace controller or fix electrical connection
Harsh engagement during 1–2 upshift	a) Defective 2nd gear accumulator b) Worn brake band c) Sticking 2nd gear check ball	a) Replace 2nd gear accumulator b) Replace brake band c) Replace 2nd gear check ball
No 2–3 upshift	a) Sticking 2–3 shift valve b) Direct clutch solenoid stuck open c) Defectice controller or poor electrical connection	a) Free or replace 2–3 shift valve b) Free or replace direct clutch solenoid c) Replace controller or fix electrical connection
Harsh engagement during 2–3 upshift	a) Worn direct clutch b) Sticking direct clutch check ball	a) Replace direct clutch b) Replace direct clutch check ball
No upshift	a) Defective back drive solenoid b) Defective shift selector	a) Inspect wiring or replace back drive solenoid b) Adjust or replace shift selector
Harsh engagement during gear selection or gear change due to poor line pressure	a) Defective regulator valve b) Defective throttle valve c) Unadjusted accelerator cable	a) Replace regulator valve b) Replace throttle valve c) Adjust accelerator cable
Harsh engagement shifting from N to R	a) Worn low/reverse clutch b) Sticking low reverse clutch check ball	a) Replace low/reverse clutch b) Replace low/reverse check ball
Harsh engagement when shifting from N to D	a) Defective forward clutch accumulator b) Worn forward clutch c) Sticking forward clutch check ball	a) Replace forward clutch accumulator b) Replace forward clutch c) Replace forward clutch check ball
Slippage in any drive range with engine speed at 2000–2400 rpm	a) Transaxle failure a) Fluid below normal	a) Rebuild or replace transaxle b) Check and/or fill transaxle

CHILTON'S THREE C's TRANSAXLE DIAGNOSIS
Sprint

Condition	Cause	Correction
Slippage in any drive range with engine speed below 2000–2400 rpm	a) Defective torque converter b) Poor engine power	a) Replace torque converter b) Tune or adjust engine
Slippage in any drive range with engine speed above 2000–2400 rpm and proper fluid pressure	a) Transaxle failure	a) Rebuild or replace transaxle
Slippage in any drive range with engine speed above 2000–2400 rpm and poor fluid pressure	a) Defective oil pump b) Defective regulator valve c) Defective throttle valve d) Misadjusted acceleartor cable	a) Replace oil pump b) Replace regulator valve c) Adjust or replace throttle valev d) Adjust accelerator cable
Slippage with shift selector in the D range only and engine speed is above 2000–2400 rpm	a) If the engine speed drops to the transaxle solenoid wire is disconnected a defective one-way clutch is indicated b) If the engine speed does not drop to 2000–2400 rpm when the transaxle solenoid wire is disconnected and the fluid pressure is OK a worn forward clutch is indicated c) If the engine speed does not drop to 2000–2400 rpm when the transaxle solenoid wire is disconnected and the fluid pressure is not OK an oil leak in the forward clutch or D range oil circuit is present	a) Replace one-way clutch b) Replace forward clutch c) Repair the forward clutch or D range circuit oil leak
Slippage with shift selector in the R range only and the engine speed is above the 2000–2400 range	a) If the engine speed drops to when the transaxle solenoid wire is disconnected a worn low reverse clutch is indicated b) If the engine speed does not drop to 2000–2400 rpm when the transaxle solenoid wire is disconnected and the fluid pressure is OK a worn direct clutch is indicated c) If the engine speed does not drop to 2000–2400 rpm when the transaxle solenoid wire is disconnected and the fluid pressure is not OK a worn direct clutch or R range oil circuit leak is present	a) Replace the low reverse clutch b) Replace the direct clutch c) Replace the direct clutch or R range circuits oil leak
No 3–2 or 2–1 downshift	a) Defective accelerator switch b) Defective controller or poor electrical connector	a) Replace accelerator switch b) Replace controller or fix electrical connector
No engine braking when shifted into 2nd range	a) Defective brake band	a) Replace brake band
No engine braking when shifted into low range	a) Defective low reverse clutch	a) Replace low reverse clutch

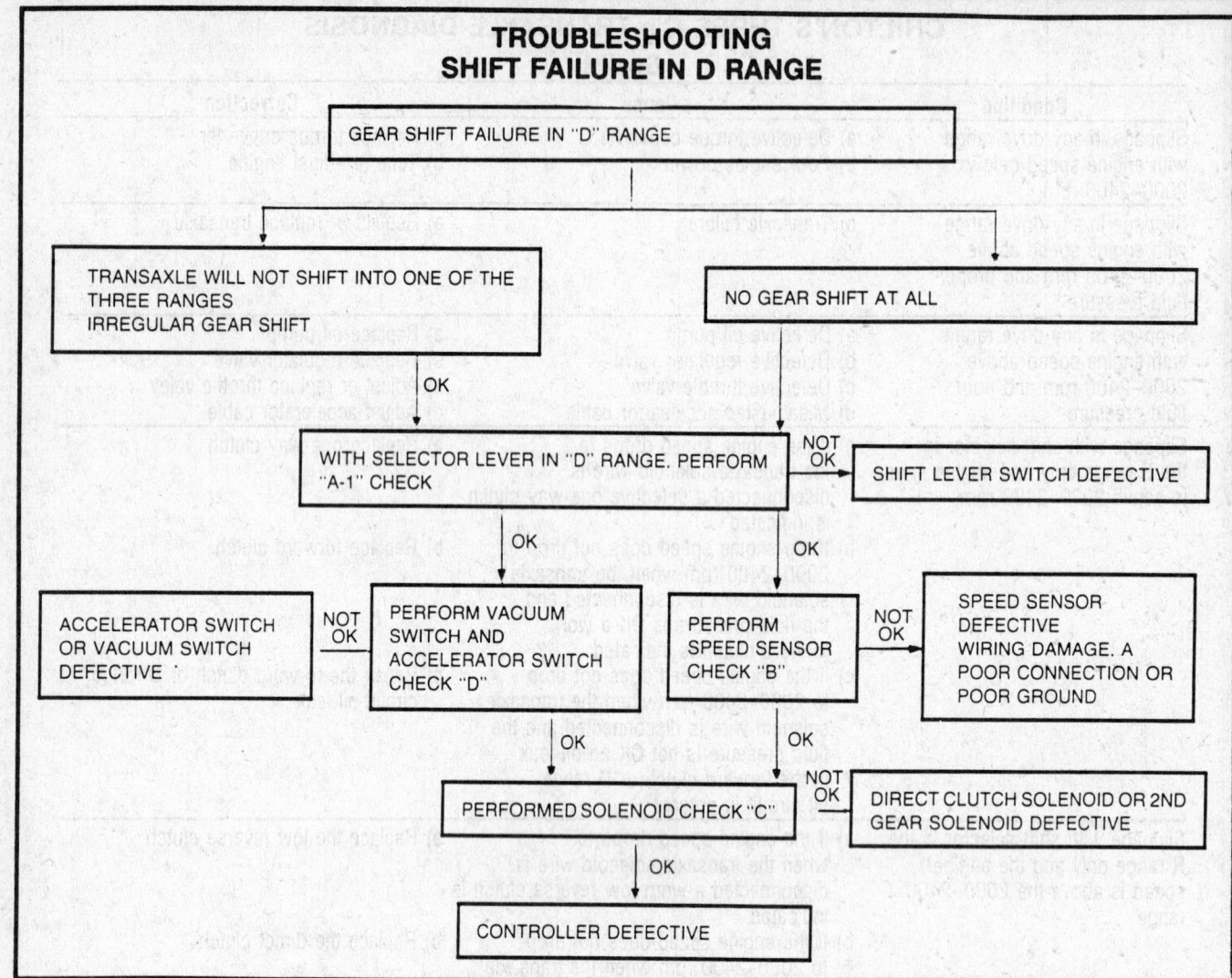

TROUBLESHOOTING
SHIFT FAILURE IN D RANGE

GEAR SHIFT FAILURE IN "D" RANGE

TRANSAXLE WILL NOT SHIFT INTO ONE OF THE THREE RANGES IRREGULAR GEAR SHIFT

NO GEAR SHIFT AT ALL

WITH SELECTOR LEVER IN "D" RANGE. PERFORM "A-1" CHECK

NOT OK — SHIFT LEVER SWITCH DEFECTIVE

ACCELERATOR SWITCH OR VACUUM SWITCH DEFECTIVE

NOT OK — PERFORM VACUUM SWITCH AND ACCELERATOR SWITCH CHECK "D"

PERFORM SPEED SENSOR CHECK "B"

NOT OK — SPEED SENSOR DEFECTIVE WIRING DAMAGE. A POOR CONNECTION OR POOR GROUND

PERFORMED SOLENOID CHECK "C"

NOT OK — DIRECT CLUTCH SOLENOID OR 2ND GEAR SOLENOID DEFECTIVE

CONTROLLER DEFECTIVE

OIL PUMP

The internal gear type oil pump, located directly behind the torque converter, is operated by a splined shaft to the torque converter hub. Its purpose is to feed oil to the torque converter, lubricate parts and deliver oil pressure to each clutch and brake solenoid.

MANUAL VALVE

The manual valve, located on the upper valve body, is directly connected the shift selector lever by a cable. It's purpose is to mechanically open and close the oil passage to the respective oil pressure circuit (range) according to the selector lever movement.

THROTTLE VALVE

The throttle valve, located in the upper valve body, is connected to the accelerator pedal by a cable and produces throttle pressure corresponding to the accelerator pedal movement.

Depressing the accelerator pedal, causes the throttle cam to push the shift plug, compressing 2 springs, to move the throttle

valve; the line pressure passage opens and procedures throttle pressure. Throttle pressure is also applied to the rear of the throttle valve to push it backward. Throttle pressure is determined by the springs pressure and position of the shift plug, applied to the primary/secondary regulator valves to regulate the line pressure.

PRIMARY REGULATOR VALVE

The primary regulator valve, located in the upper valve body, regulates the oil pressure (produced by the oil pump) to correspond to each condition of use. It's operation is controlled throttle pressure, springs and line pressure (in reverse).

SECONDARY REGULATOR VALVE

The secondary regulator valve, located on the lower valve body, regulates the oil pressure to the torque converter and supplies lubrication to each part by means of the throttle pressure and spring.

B2 CONTROL VALVE

The B2 control valve, located in the lower valve body, operates

TROUBLESHOOTING
SHIFT FAILURE IN 2 RANGE

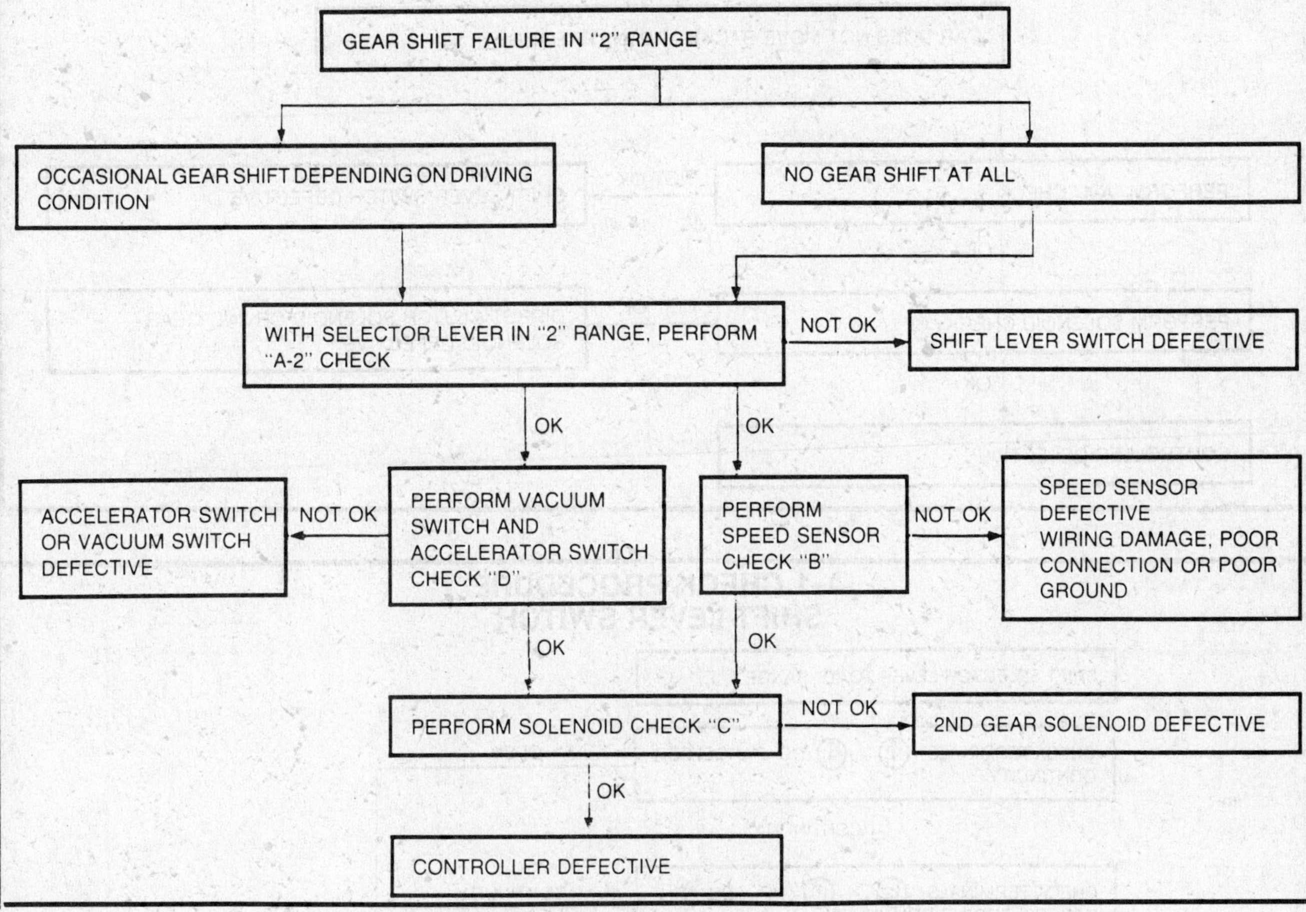

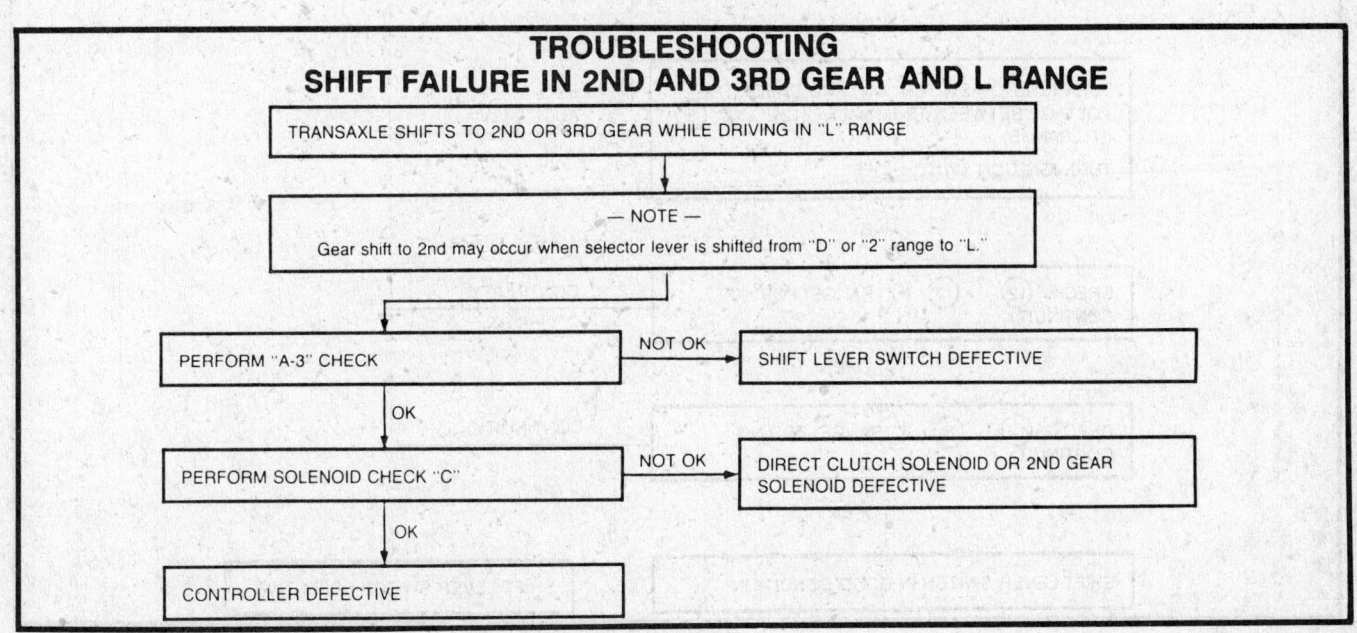

TROUBLESHOOTING
SHIFT FAILURE IN 2ND AND 3RD GEAR AND L RANGE

TRANSAXLE SHIFTS TO 2ND OR 3RD GEAR WHILE DRIVING IN "L" RANGE

— NOTE —
Gear shift to 2nd may occur when selector lever is shifted from "D" or "2" range to "L."

PERFORM "A-3" CHECK → NOT OK → SHIFT LEVER SWITCH DEFECTIVE

OK

PERFORM SOLENOID CHECK "C" → NOT OK → DIRECT CLUTCH SOLENOID OR 2ND GEAR SOLENOID DEFECTIVE

OK

CONTROLLER DEFECTIVE

TROUBLESHOOTING
NO REVERSE

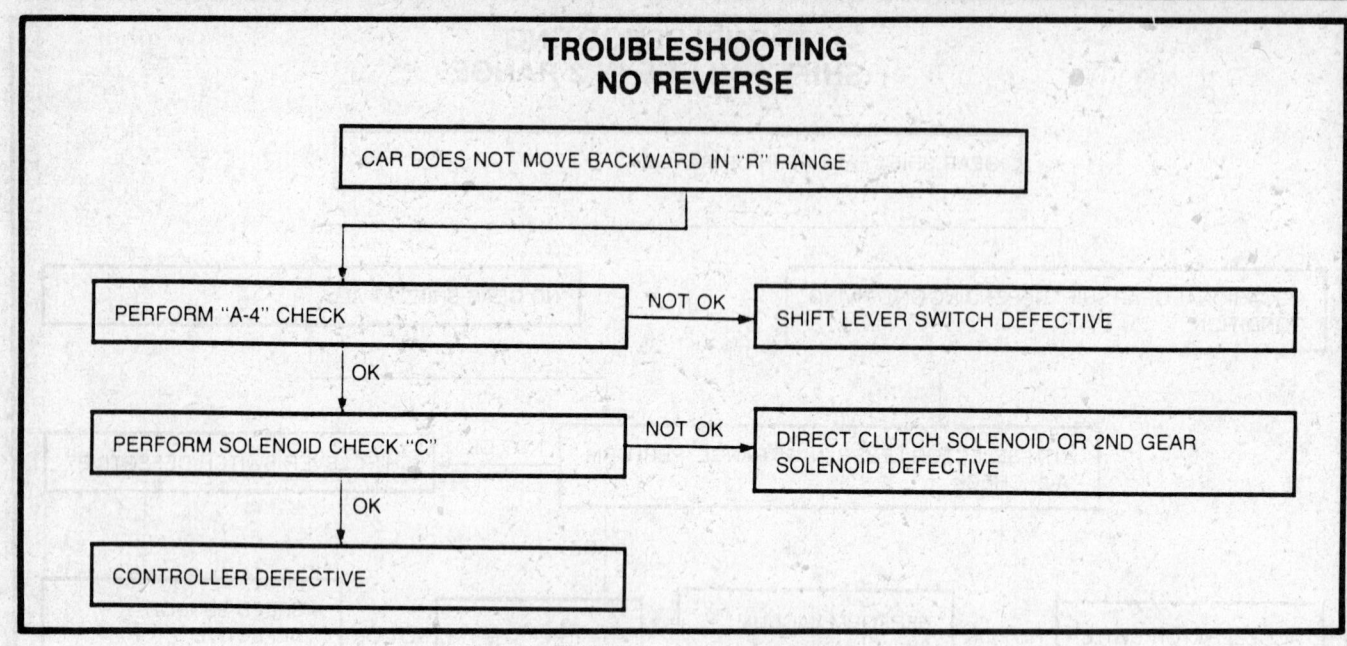

CAR DOES NOT MOVE BACKWARD IN "R" RANGE

↓

PERFORM "A-4" CHECK — NOT OK → SHIFT LEVER SWITCH DEFECTIVE

↓ OK

PERFORM SOLENOID CHECK "C" — NOT OK → DIRECT CLUTCH SOLENOID OR 2ND GEAR SOLENOID DEFECTIVE

↓ OK

CONTROLLER DEFECTIVE

A–1 CHECK PROCEDURE
SHIFT LEVER SWITCH

SHIFT SELECTOR LEVER TO "D" RANGE

↓

CHECK TERMINALS (12) - (4) ("D" RANGE) FOR CONTINUITY — OPEN → SHIFT LEVER SWITCH DEFECTIVE

↓ CONTINUITY

CHECK TERMINALS (12) - (16) ("P" AND "N" RANGES) FOR NO CONTINUITY — CONTINUITY → SHIFT LEVER SWITCH DEFECTIVE

↓ OPEN

TURN IGNITION SWITCH "ON" AND CHECK THE VOLTAGE BETWEEN TERMINALS (12) AND (5) ("R" RANGE)
TURN IGNITION SWITCH "OFF" — ABOUT 12V → SHIFT LEVER SWITCH DEFECTIVE

↓ OV

CHECK (12) - (17) ("2" RANGE) FOR NO CONTINUITY — CONTINUITY → SHIFT LEVER SWITCH DEFECTIVE

↓ OPEN

CHECK (12) - (8) ("L" RANGE) FOR NO CONTINUITY — CONTINUITY → SHIFT LEVER SWITCH DEFECTIVE

↓ OPEN

SHIFT LEVER SWITCH IN GOOD CONDITION

SHIFT LEVER SWITCH DEFECTIVE

in the **L** range to reduce the line pressure shock acting on the 1st/reverse brake.

COOLER BYPASS VALVE

The cooler bypass valve, located in the lower valve body, is designed to keep the oil pressure in the torque converter constant.

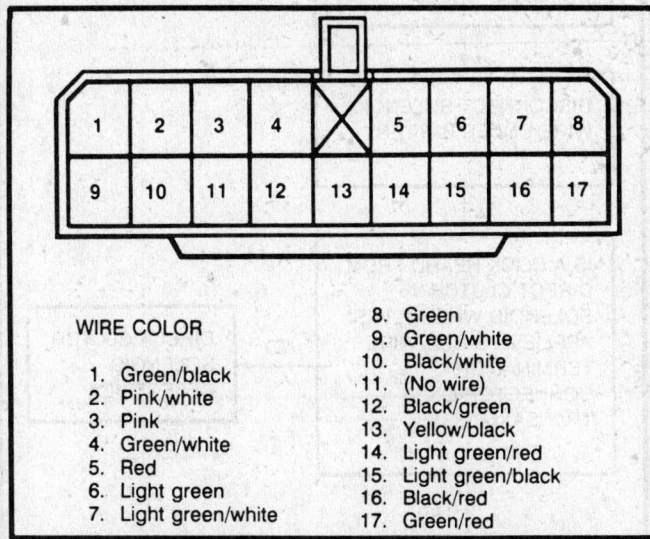

WIRE COLOR

1. Green/black
2. Pink/white
3. Pink
4. Green/white
5. Red
6. Light green
7. Light green/white
8. Green
9. Green/white
10. Black/white
11. (No wire)
12. Black/green
13. Yellow/black
14. Light green/red
15. Light green/black
16. Black/red
17. Green/red

View of the controller's wiring harness connector

1–2 SHIFT VALVE

The 1–2 shift valve, located in the lower valve body, provides the gear shift between the 1st and 2nd gears.

When the controller operates the 2nd brake solenoid, line pressure is applied to the shift valve, the valve moves providing line pressure to the 2nd brake, thus, shifting from 1st-to-2nd gear. When the 2nd brake solenoid is de-energized, a spring forces the shift valve to return, thus, shifting from 2nd-to-1st gear.

NOTE: When the shift selector is placed in L or R range, the 2nd brake solenoid operates applying fluid pressure to the 1st/reverse brake.

2–3 SHIFT VALVE

The 2–3 shift valve, located in the lower valve body, provides the gear shift between the 2nd and 3rd gears.

When the controller operates the direct clutch solenoid, line pressure is applied to the shift valve, the valve moves providing line pressure to the direct clutch, thus, shifting from 2nd-to-3rd gear. When the direct clutch solenoid is de-energized, a spring forces the shift valve to return, thus, shifting from 3rd-to-2nd gear.

A–2 CHECK PROCEDURE
SHIFT LEVER SWITCH

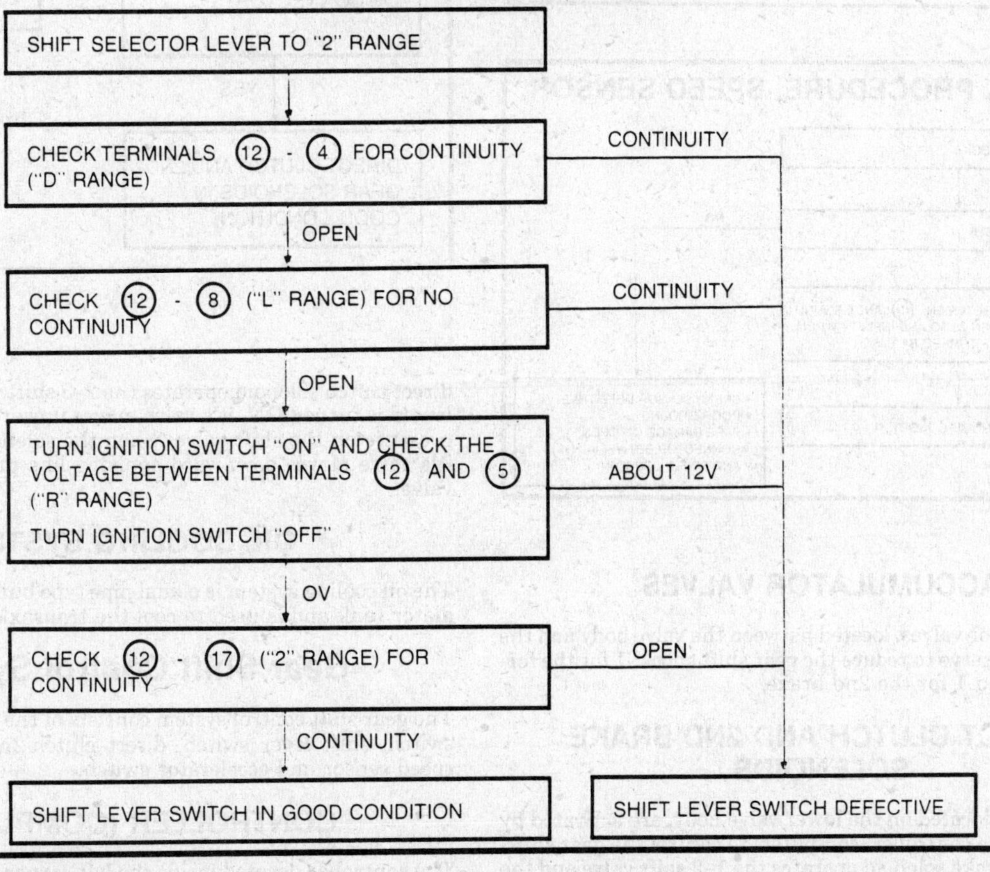

SHIFT SELECTOR LEVER TO "2" RANGE

↓

CHECK TERMINALS ⑫ - ④ FOR CONTINUITY ("D" RANGE) ———→ CONTINUITY

↓ OPEN

CHECK ⑫ - ⑧ ("L" RANGE) FOR NO CONTINUITY ———→ CONTINUITY

↓ OPEN

TURN IGNITION SWITCH "ON" AND CHECK THE VOLTAGE BETWEEN TERMINALS ⑫ AND ⑤ ("R" RANGE)
TURN IGNITION SWITCH "OFF" ———→ ABOUT 12V

↓ OV

CHECK ⑫ - ⑰ ("2" RANGE) FOR CONTINUITY ———→ OPEN

↓ CONTINUITY

SHIFT LEVER SWITCH IN GOOD CONDITION   SHIFT LEVER SWITCH DEFECTIVE

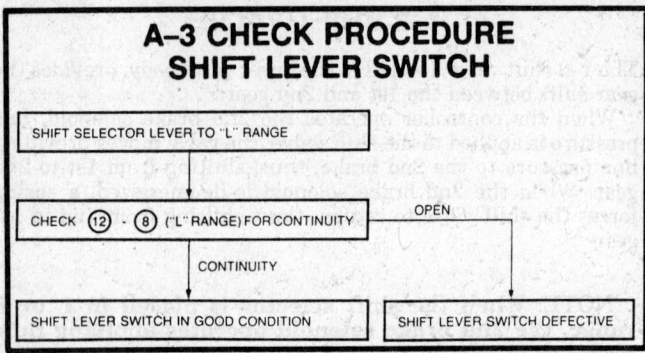

A-3 CHECK PROCEDURE
SHIFT LEVER SWITCH

SHIFT SELECTOR LEVER TO "L" RANGE

↓

CHECK ⑫ - ⑧ ("L" RANGE) FOR CONTINUITY — OPEN →

↓ CONTINUITY

SHIFT LEVER SWITCH IN GOOD CONDITION   SHIFT LEVER SWITCH DEFECTIVE

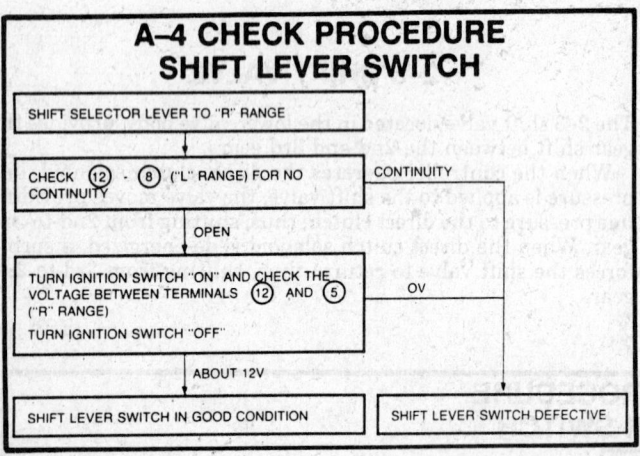

A-4 CHECK PROCEDURE
SHIFT LEVER SWITCH

SHIFT SELECTOR LEVER TO "R" RANGE

↓

CHECK ⑫ - ⑧ ("L" RANGE) FOR NO CONTINUITY — CONTINUITY →

↓ OPEN

TURN IGNITION SWITCH "ON" AND CHECK THE VOLTAGE BETWEEN TERMINALS ⑫ AND ⑤ ("R" RANGE) TURN IGNITION SWITCH "OFF" — OV →

↓ ABOUT 12V

SHIFT LEVER SWITCH IN GOOD CONDITION   SHIFT LEVER SWITCH DEFECTIVE

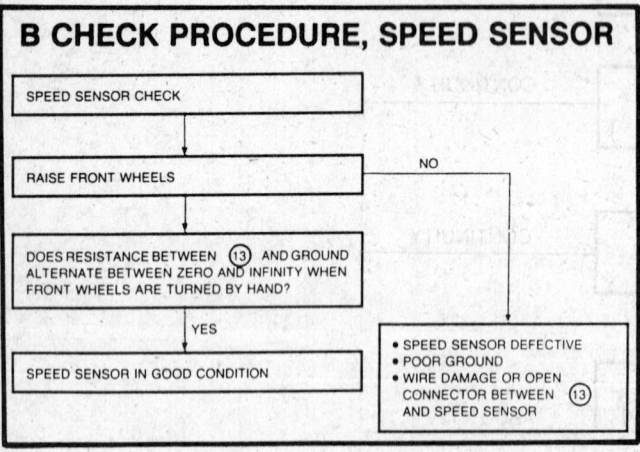

B CHECK PROCEDURE, SPEED SENSOR

SPEED SENSOR CHECK

↓

RAISE FRONT WHEELS — NO →

↓

DOES RESISTANCE BETWEEN ⑬ AND GROUND ALTERNATE BETWEEN ZERO AND INFINITY WHEN FRONT WHEELS ARE TURNED BY HAND?

↓ YES

SPEED SENSOR IN GOOD CONDITION

- SPEED SENSOR DEFECTIVE
- POOR GROUND
- WIRE DAMAGE OR OPEN CONNECTOR BETWEEN ⑬ AND SPEED SENSOR

ACCUMULATOR VALVES

The accumulator valves, located between the valve body and the main housing, serve to reduce the gear shift shock; 1 for the forward clutch and 1 for the 2nd brake.

DIRECT CLUTCH AND 2ND BRAKE SOLENOIDS

The solenoids, located on the lower valve body, are activated by signals from the controller (computer) to control the gear shifting. The 2nd brake solenoid operates the 1-2 shift valve and the

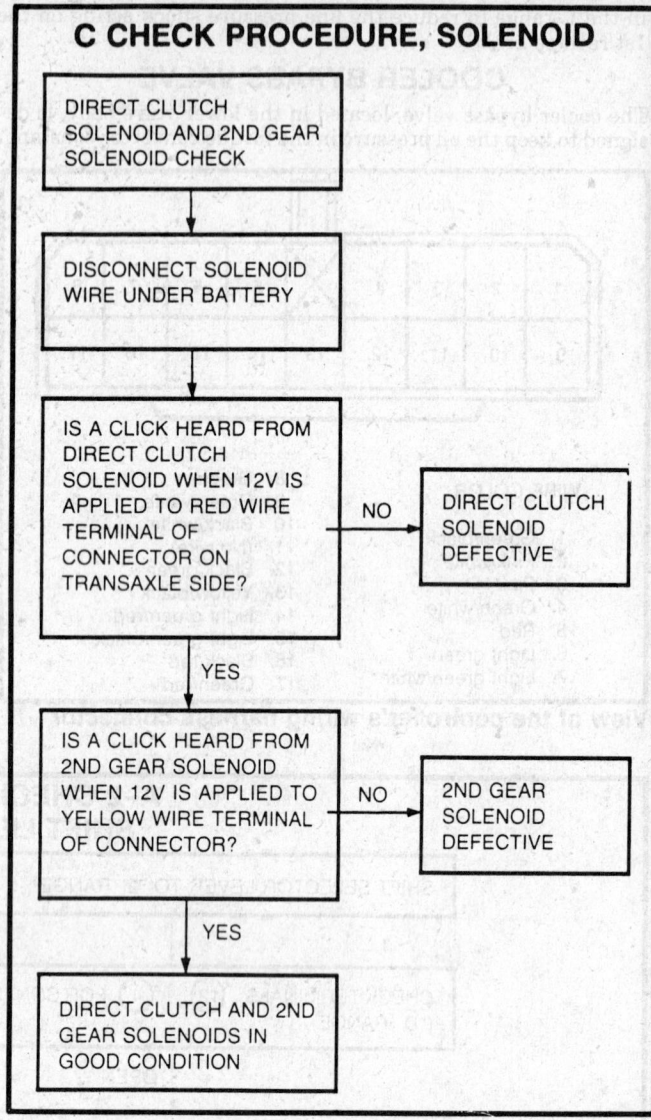

C CHECK PROCEDURE, SOLENOID

DIRECT CLUTCH SOLENOID AND 2ND GEAR SOLENOID CHECK

↓

DISCONNECT SOLENOID WIRE UNDER BATTERY

↓

IS A CLICK HEARD FROM DIRECT CLUTCH SOLENOID WHEN 12V IS APPLIED TO RED WIRE TERMINAL OF CONNECTOR ON TRANSAXLE SIDE? — NO → DIRECT CLUTCH SOLENOID DEFECTIVE

↓ YES

IS A CLICK HEARD FROM 2ND GEAR SOLENOID WHEN 12V IS APPLIED TO YELLOW WIRE TERMINAL OF CONNECTOR? — NO → 2ND GEAR SOLENOID DEFECTIVE

↓ YES

DIRECT CLUTCH AND 2ND GEAR SOLENOIDS IN GOOD CONDITION

direct clutch solenoid operates the 2-3 shift valve. When the solenoid is turned **ON**, it's valve moves upward to relieve the line pressure on the shift valve; when the solenoid is turned **OFF**, it's valve moves downward applying line pressure to the shift valve.

OIL COOLING SYSTEM

The oil cooling system is a dual pipe type built into the lower radiator tank and is used to cool the transaxle fluid.

Gear Shift Control System

The gear shift control system consists of the controller, vacuum switch, shift lever switch, direct clutch/2nd brake solenoids, speed sensor and accelerator switch.

CONTROLLER (COMPUTER)

The controller, located inside the left corner of the main instru-

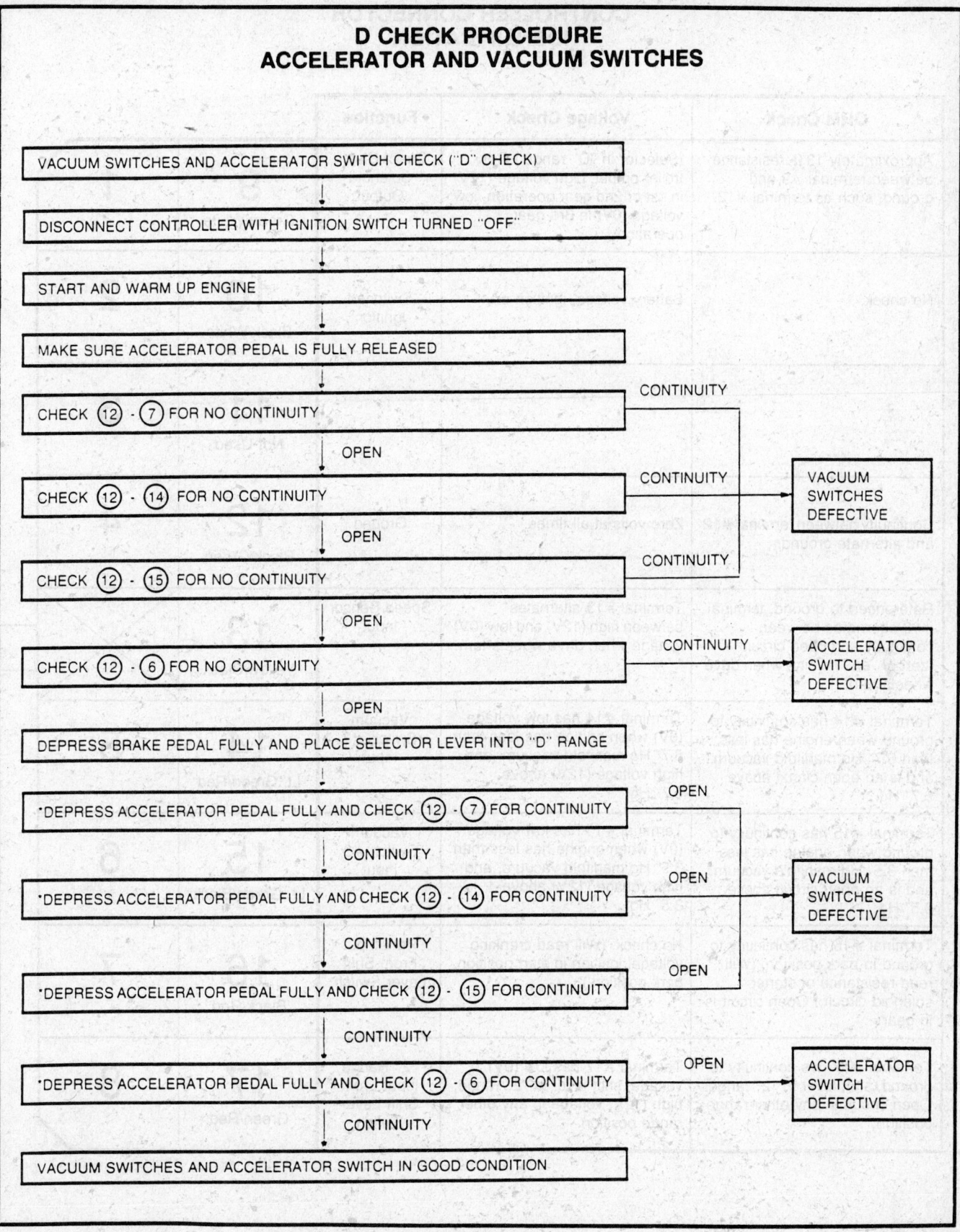

D CHECK PROCEDURE
ACCELERATOR AND VACUUM SWITCHES

VACUUM SWITCHES AND ACCELERATOR SWITCH CHECK ("D" CHECK)

DISCONNECT CONTROLLER WITH IGNITION SWITCH TURNED "OFF"

START AND WARM UP ENGINE

MAKE SURE ACCELERATOR PEDAL IS FULLY RELEASED

CHECK ⑫ - ⑦ FOR NO CONTINUITY — CONTINUITY

  OPEN

CHECK ⑫ - ⑭ FOR NO CONTINUITY — CONTINUITY → VACUUM SWITCHES DEFECTIVE

  OPEN

CHECK ⑫ - ⑮ FOR NO CONTINUITY — CONTINUITY

  OPEN

CHECK ⑫ - ⑥ FOR NO CONTINUITY — CONTINUITY → ACCELERATOR SWITCH DEFECTIVE

  OPEN

DEPRESS BRAKE PEDAL FULLY AND PLACE SELECTOR LEVER INTO "D" RANGE

*DEPRESS ACCELERATOR PEDAL FULLY AND CHECK ⑫ - ⑦ FOR CONTINUITY — OPEN

  CONTINUITY

*DEPRESS ACCELERATOR PEDAL FULLY AND CHECK ⑫ - ⑭ FOR CONTINUITY — OPEN → VACUUM SWITCHES DEFECTIVE

  CONTINUITY

*DEPRESS ACCELERATOR PEDAL FULLY AND CHECK ⑫ - ⑮ FOR CONTINUITY — OPEN

  CONTINUITY

*DEPRESS ACCELERATOR PEDAL FULLY AND CHECK ⑫ - ⑥ FOR CONTINUITY — OPEN → ACCELERATOR SWITCH DEFECTIVE

  CONTINUITY

VACUUM SWITCHES AND ACCELERATOR SWITCH IN GOOD CONDITION

CONTROLLER CONNECTOR
IDENTIFICATION

OHM Check	Voltage Check	Function		
Approximately 13 Ω resistance between terminal #9 and ground, such as terminal #12.	(Selector in "D" range.) Controller output: high voltage (12V) in 1st or 2nd gear operation, low voltage (0V) in 3rd gear operation.	Direct Clutch Solenoid Output	**9** Green/White	**1**
No check.	Battery voltage, ignition on.	Switched Ignition	**10** Black/White	**2**
			11 Not Used	**3**
Continuity between terminal #12 and alternate ground.	Zero volts at all times.	Ground	**12** Black/Green	**4**
Referenced to ground, terminal #13 alternates between continuity and open circuit (zero Ω and infinity) when drive wheels turn.	Terminal #13 alternates between high (12V) and low (0V) voltage when drive wheels turn.	Speed Sensor Input	**13** Yellow/Black	✕
Terminal #14 has continuity to ground when engine has less than 6.7" Hg manifold vacuum, and is an open circuit above 6.7" Hg.	Terminal #14 has low voltage (0V) when engine has less than 6.7" Hg manifold vacuum, and high voltage (12V) above 6.7" Hg.	Vacuum Switch #2 Input	**14** Lt. Green/Red	**5**
Terminal #15 has continuity to ground when engine has less than 3.5" Hg manifold vacuum, and is an open circuit above 3.5" Hg.	Terminal #15 has low voltage (0V) when engine has less than 3.5" Hg manifold vacuum, and high voltage (12V) above 3.5" Hg.	Vacuum Switch #3 Input	**15** Lt. Green/Black	**6**
Terminal #16 has continuity to ground in park position. (Will read resistance of starter solenoid circuit.) Open circuit is in gear.	No check. (Will read cranking voltage, ignition in start position, park position.)	Park Input From Shift Lever Switch	**16** Black/Red	**7**
Terminal #17 has continuity to ground, shift lever in "2" range. Open circuit in any other range position.	Terminal #17 has low (0V) voltage, shift lever in "2" range, high (12V) voltage in any other range position.	"2" Range Input From Shift Lever Switch	**17** Green/Red	**8**

CONTROLLER CONNECTOR
IDENTIFICATION

		Function	Voltage Check	OHM Check
9	1 Green/Black	2nd Gear Solenoid Output	(Selector in "D" Range.) Controller output: high voltage (12V) in first gear operation, low voltage (0V) in 2nd or 3rd gear operation.	Approximately 13 Ω resistance between terminal #1 and ground such as terminal #12.
10	2 Pink/White	Output to ECM Speed Signal	Same as terminal #13.	Same as terminal #13.
11	3 Pink	Output to ECM Park Signal	Same as terminal #16.	Same as terminal #16.
12	4 Green/White	"D" Range Input From Shift Lever Switch	Terminal #4 has low voltage (0V), shift lever in "D" range, high voltage (12V) in any other range position.	Terminal #4 has continuity to ground, shift lever in "D" range, open circuit in any other range position.
13				
14	5 Red	Reverse Input From Shift Lever Switch	Terminal #5 has high voltage (12V), shift lever in "R" range, low voltage (0V) in any other range position.	No check. (Will read resistance of backup lamp circuit in any range position.)
15	6 Lt. Green	Wide-Open Throttle Input From Accelerator Switch	Terminal #6 has low voltage (0V) at more than 90% accelerator pedal travel, high voltage (12V) at less than 90% accelerator pedal travel.	Terminal #6 has continuity to ground at more than 90% accelerator pedal travel. Open circuit at less than 90% accelerator pedal travel.
16	7 Lt. Green/White	Vacuum Switch #1 Input	Terminal #7 has low voltage (0V) when engine has less than 11.8" Hg manifold vacuum, and high voltage (12V) above 11.8" Hg.	Terminal #7 has continuity when engine has less than 11.8" Hg manifold vacuum, and is an open circuit above 11.8" Hg.
17	8 Green	"L" Range Input From Shift Lever Switch	Terminal #8 has low voltage (0V), shift lever in "L" range, high voltage (12V) in any other range position.	Terminal #8 has continuity to ground, shift lever in "L" range, open circuit in any other range position.

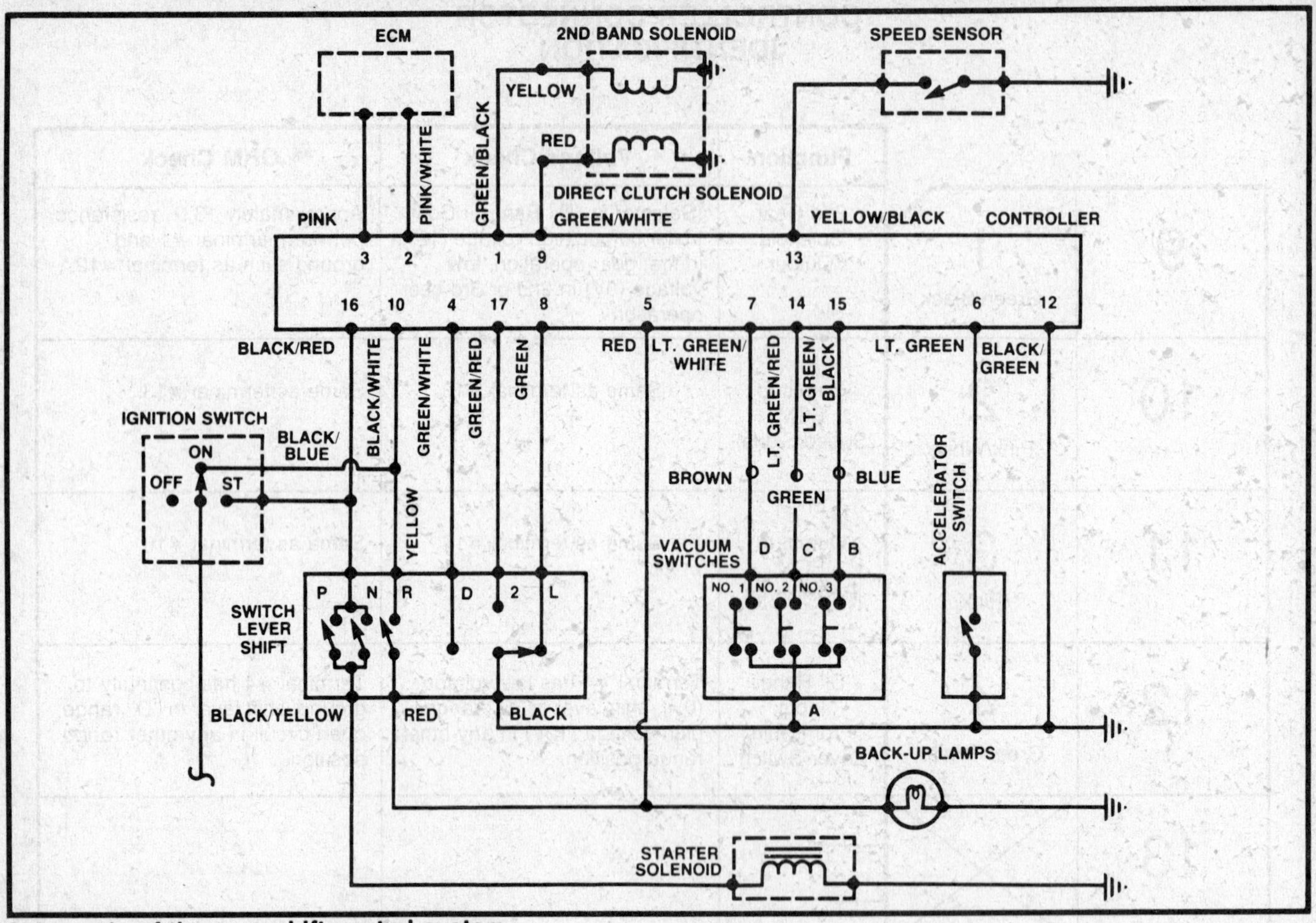

Schematic of the gear shift control system

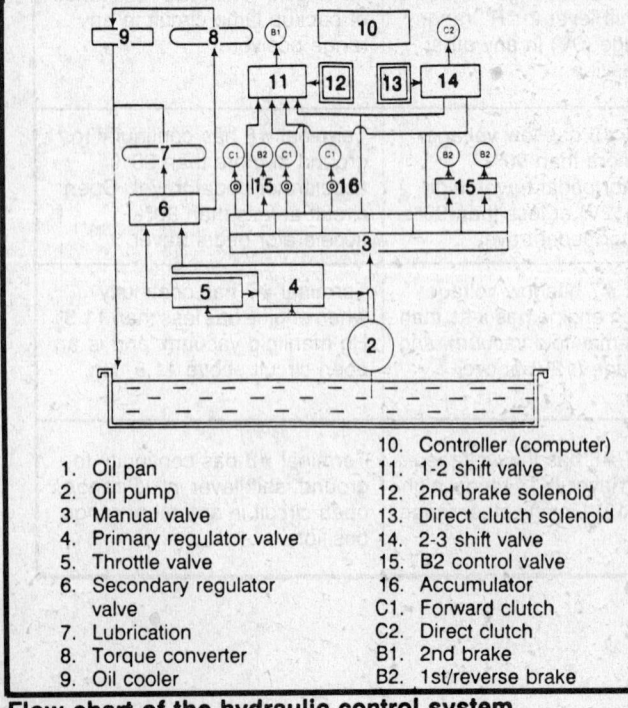

Flow chart of the hydraulic control system

1. Oil pan
2. Oil pump
3. Manual valve
4. Primary regulator valve
5. Throttle valve
6. Secondary regulator valve
7. Lubrication
8. Torque converter
9. Oil cooler
10. Controller (computer)
11. 1-2 shift valve
12. 2nd brake solenoid
13. Direct clutch solenoid
14. 2-3 shift valve
15. B2 control valve
16. Accumulator
C1. Forward clutch
C2. Direct clutch
B1. 2nd brake
B2. 1st/reverse brake

ment panel, collects information from the accelerator switch, 3 vacuum switches, shift lever switch and speed sensor. After monitoring the information, it sends out signals to open/close the direct clutch and 2nd brake solenoids to control the transaxle's shifting.

VACUUM SWITCHES

Three vacuum switches, each having its own range of operation, monitor the throttle valve opening (engine load) and send the information to the controller.

SHIFT LEVER SWITCH

The shift lever switch, located on the gear shift selector, changes the shift lever positions into electrical signals and sends them to the controller. The switch's contact points (**P** and **N**) are connected to the starter motor circuit; the starter cannot be activated unless the shift selector is in the proper position.

DIRECT CLUTCH AND 2ND BRAKE SOLENOIDS

The solenoids, located on the lower valve body, are activated by signals from the controller (computer) to control the gear shifting. The 2nd brake solenoid operates the 1–2 shift valve and the direct clutch solenoid operates the 2–3 shift valve.

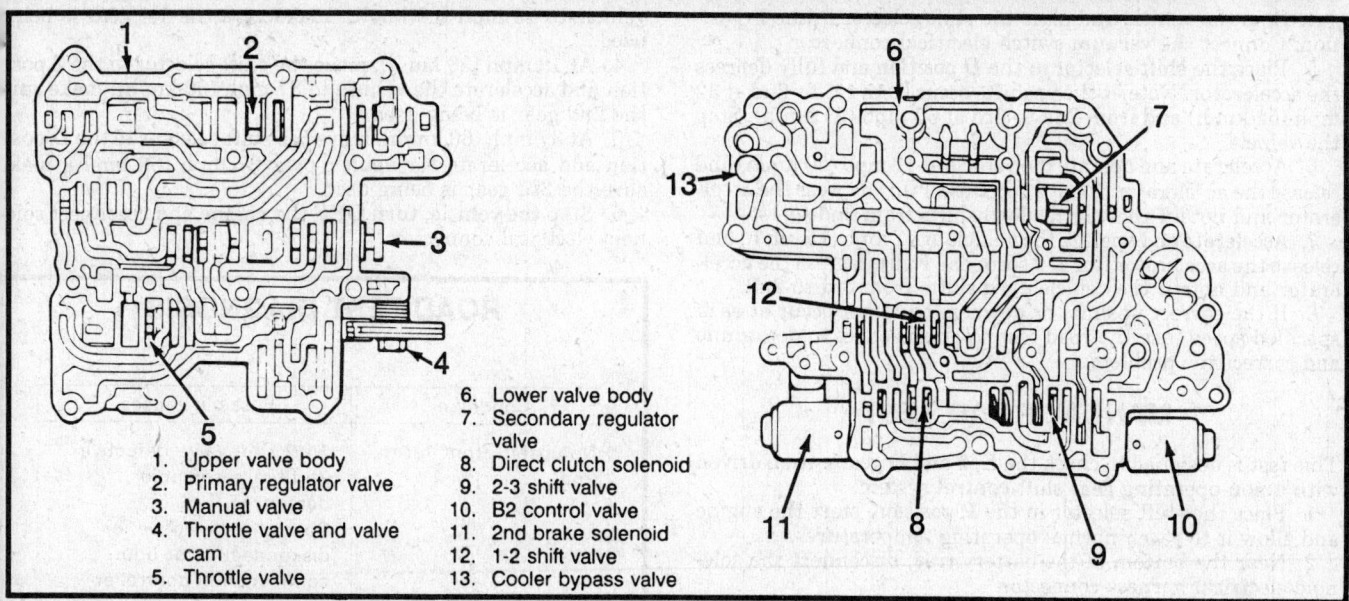

1. Upper valve body
2. Primary regulator valve
3. Manual valve
4. Throttle valve and valve cam
5. Throttle valve
6. Lower valve body
7. Secondary regulator valve
8. Direct clutch solenoid
9. 2-3 shift valve
10. B2 control valve
11. 2nd brake solenoid
12. 1-2 shift valve
13. Cooler bypass valve

Location of the valve body components

SPEED SENSOR

The speed sensor, built into the speedometer, consists of a lead switch and a magnet. As the magnet (attached to the speedometer cable) rotates, it's magnetic field causes the lead switch to turn **ON** and **OFF**. While the switching frequency increases or decreases in proportion with the vehicle speed, it is sent to the controller as pulse signals.

ACCELERATOR SWITCH

The accelerator switch, mounted on the accelerator pedal bracket, turns **ON** when the accelerator pedal is depressed 2.0–2.2 in. (50–56mm) and signals the controller of the throttle valve opening.

Diagnosis Tests

CONTROL PRESSURE TEST

This test is designed to check the oil pressure system by measuring the operating oil pressure.
1. Operate the vehicle until the transaxle's fluid is at normal operating temperatures. Make sure the oil level is between **FULL HOT** and **LOW HOT** and the transaxle shows no signs of oil leaks.
2. With the engine turned **OFF**, remove the oil plug (upper rear side of the oil pan) and install an oil pressure gauge in the threaded hole.
3. Install a tachometer onto the engine.
4. Firmly apply the parking brake and block the drive wheels.
5. Place the shift selector in the **P** position and start the engine.
6. Fully depress the brake pedal and place the shift selector in the **D**. Check the oil pressure at 700–800 rpm and at 2000–2400 rpm; the oil pressure should be 29–57 psi (200–400 kPa) and 57–85 psi (400–600 kPa) respectively.

NOTE: Do not operate the engine at high speed for more than 5 seconds for the oil temperature may rise excessively high.

7. Fully depress the brake pedal and place the shift selector in

the **R** position. Check the oil pressure at 700–800 rpm and at 2000–2400 rpm; the oil pressure should be 29–57 psi (200–400 kPa) and 57–85 psi (400–600 kPa) respectively.

STALL SPEED TEST

This test is designed to check the overall performance.

NOTE: Do not operate the engine at high speed for more than 5 seconds for the oil temperature may rise excessively high.

1. Operate the vehicle until the transaxle's fluid is at normal operating temperatures. Make sure the oil level is between **FULL HOT** and **LOW HOT**.
2. Install a tachometer onto the engine.
3. Firmly apply the parking brake and block the drive wheels.
4. Place the shift selector in the **P** position and start the engine.
5. Fully depress the brake pedal. Place the shift selector in the **D** and fully depress the accelerator. While watching the tachometer, note when the engine speed becomes constant (stall speed). When the stall speed has been reached, immediately release the accelerator.
6. Fully depress the brake pedal and place the shift selector in the **R** position. While watching the tachometer, note when the engine speed becomes constant (stall speed). When the stall speed has been reached, immediately release the accelerator.
7. The stall speed should be within 2000–2400 rpm; if not, use the stall speed diagnosis chart to determine and correct the problem.

ROAD TEST

This test is designed to check the upshifts and downshifts at specific speeds.
1. Operate the engine until normal operating temperatures are reached.
2. Disconnect the vacuum switch(s) electrical harness connector.
3. Place the shift selector in the **D** position, depress the accelerator ½ stroke and accelerate the vehicle. Note, if the upshifts occur from 1st-to-2nd at 15 mph (25 km/h) and from 2nd-to-3rd at 38 mph (62 km/h).

4. Stop the vehicle and place the shift selector in the **P** position. Connect the vacuum switch electrical connector.

5. Place the shift selector in the **D** position and fully depress the accelerator. Note, it the upshifts occur from 1st-to-2nd at 32 mph (52 km/h) and from 2nd-to-3rd at 60 mph (97 km/h). Stop the vehicle.

6. Accelerate and operate the vehicle at 18 mph (30 km/h) and release the accelerator (for 1–2 seconds). Fully depress the accelerator and note if the vehicle downshifts from 2nd-to-1st.

7. Accelerate and operate the vehicle at 47 mph (75 km/h) and release the accelerator (for 1–2 seconds). Fully depress the accelerator and note if the vehicle downshifts from 3rd-to-2nd.

8. If the correct upshifts or downshifts do not occur at each specified speed, use the road test diagnosis chart to determine and correct the problem.

MANUAL ROAD TEST

This test is designed to check the **L**, **2** and **D** gears when driven with a non-operating gear shift control system.

1. Place the shift selector in the **P** position, start the engine and allow it to reach normal operating temperatures.

2. Near the bottom of the battery tray, disconnect the solenoid electrical harness connector.

3. Place the shift selector in the **L** position and accelerate the

vehicle to 18 mph (30 km/h); make sure the 1st gear is being used.

4. At 18 mph (30 km/h), move the shift selector to the **2** position and accelerate the vehicle to 37 mph (60 km/h); make sure the 2nd gear is being used.

5. At 37 mph (60 km/h), move the shift selector to the **D** position and accelerate the vehicle over 37 mph (60 km/h); make sure the 3rd gear is being used.

6. Stop the vehicle, turn **OFF** the engine and reconnect solenoid electrical connector.

ROAD TEST DIAGNOSIS

Condition	Possible causes
No upshift from 1st to 2nd	1 – 2 shift valve defective 2nd brake solenoid defective Controller defective, or disconnection or poor connection in controller electric circuit
No upshift from 2nd to 3rd	2 – 3 shift valve defective Direct clutch solenoid defective Controller defective, or disconnection or poor connection in controller electric circuit
No downshift from 2nd to 1st or 3rd to 2nd	Accelerator switch defective Controller defective, or disconnection or poor connection in controller electric circuit

Engine rpm	Line pressure	
	"D" range	"R" range (changed)
700 - 800 rpm	2 - 4 kg/cm² 28.5 - 56.8 psi 200 - 400 kPa	5.5 - 8 kg/cm² 78.3 - 113.7 psi 550 - 800 kPa
2,000 - 2,400 rpm (Stall speed)	4 - 6 kg/cm² 56.9 - 85.3 psi 400 - 600 kPa	8.5 - 12 kg/cm² 120.9 - 170.6 psi 850 - 1,200 kPa

Control pressure test chart

CONTROL PRESSURE DIAGNOSIS

Line pressure measured	Possible cause
Higher than specification in "D" & "R" ranges	Regulator valve defective Throttle valve defective Accelerator cable and oil pressure control cable maladjusted
Lower than specification in "D" & "R" ranges	Oil pump defective Regulator valve defective Throttle valve defective Accelerator cable and oil pressure control cable maladjusted
Lower than specification only in "D" range	Forward clutch oil pressure system oil leakage "D" range oil pressure system oil leakage
Lower than specification only in "R" range	Direct clutch oil pressure system oil leakage 1st – reverse brake oil pressure system oil leakage "R" range oil pressure system oil leakage

STALL SPEED DIAGNOSIS

Stall speed measured	Possible causes
Lower than specification	Engine output insufficient
	Torque converter defective
Higher than specification in "D" range	Forward clutch slippage
	One-way clutch defective
Higher than specification in "R" range	Direct clutch slippage
	1st – reverse brake slippage

ENGINE BRAKE TEST

1. While driving the vehicle in the **D** position and in 3rd gear, move the shift selector to the **2** position and note if the engine brake operates. If the engine fails to brake, the 2nd brake is defective.
2. While driving the vehicle in the **D** position and in 3rd gear, move the shift selector to the **L** position and note if the engine brake operates. If the engine fails to brake, the 1st/reverse brake is defective.

PARK TEST

1. Stop the vehicle on a slope, move the shift selector to the **P** position and firmly apply the parking brake.
2. Turn the engine **OFF**, release the parking brake and note if the vehicle remains stationary.

ON CAR SERVICES

Adjustments

OIL PRESSURE CONTROL CABLE

The oil pressure control cable operates the throttle valve cam.
1. Inspect and/or adjust the accelerator cable play by performing the following procedures:
   a. At the carburetor, check the amount of play in the accelerator cable; it should be 0.40–0.59 in. (10–15mm) cold or 0.12–0.19 in. (3–5mm) warm.
   b. If necessary to adjust, loosen the locknut and turn the adjustment nut until the correct specifications are met.
   c. After adjustment, tighten the locknut.
2. Operate the engine until normal operating temperatures are reached and allow the engine to idle; make sure the carburetor is not on the fast idle step.
3. From near transaxle's dipstick tube, remove the oil pressure control cable cover. Using a feeler gauge, check that the boot-to-inner cable stopper clearance is 0–0.02 in. (0–0.5mm).
4. If the clearance is not within specifications, perform the following procedures:
   a. Loosen the **A** adjusting nuts (engine side of bracket) and turn them to adjust the clearance.
   b. If the adjustment (engine side) fails to establish the clearance, tighten the nuts and move the other side (dipstick side) of the bracket.
   c. Loosen the **B** adjusting nuts (dipstick side of bracket) and turn them to adjust the clearance.
   d. After adjustment is complete, tighten the adjusting nuts, recheck adjustment and install the cover.

BACK DRIVE SOLENOID

1. Remove the console cover and loosen the solenoid mounting screws.
2. Move the shift selector into the **P** position.
3. Using grease, lubricate the upper/lower edges of the lock plate.
4. Adjust the solenoid so the following situations exist:
   a. When the ignition switch is turned **OFF**, the solenoid is inoperative; when the ignition switch is turned **ON**, the solenoid is operative.
   b. There is to be no clearance between the lock plate and the guide plate.

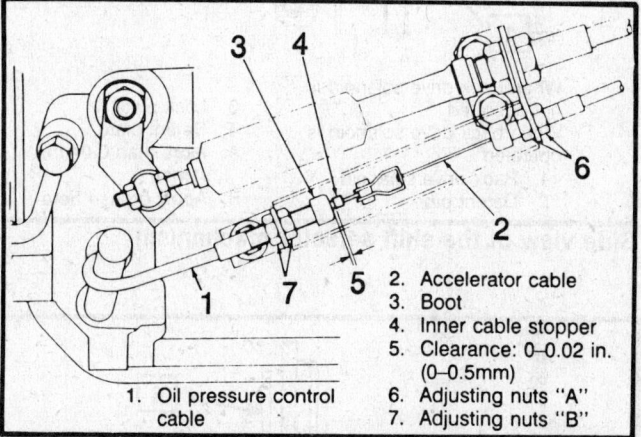

2. Accelerator cable
3. Boot
4. Inner cable stopper
5. Clearance: 0–0.02 in. (0–0.5mm)
6. Adjusting nuts "A"
7. Adjusting nuts "B"
1. Oil pressure control cable

Checking and adjusting the oil pressure control cable

5. After adjusting the solenoid, tighten the solenoid's mounting screws.
6. After tightening the solenoid screws, the following situations must exist:
   a. When the ignition switch is turned **OFF**, the shift selector should be locked in the **P** position and cannot be moved to any other position.
   b. When the ignition switch is turned **ON**, the shift selector can be moved from **P** to any other position.
   c. If the manual release knob is pulled and the ignition switch is turned **OFF**, the shift selector can be shifted from **P** to any other position.
7. Install the console cover.

BACK DRIVE CABLE

1. Place the shift selector into the **P** position.
2. Loosen both (**A** and **B**) back drive cable nuts.
3. Pull the outer wire forward so there is no deflection on the inner wire and tighten both nuts (hand tight); tighten **A** first and **B** second. Tighten both nuts securely.
4. After tightening the nuts, check the following situations:
   a. With the shift selector in the **P** position, the ignition key can be turned from **ACC** to **LOCK** position and removed from the ignition switch.

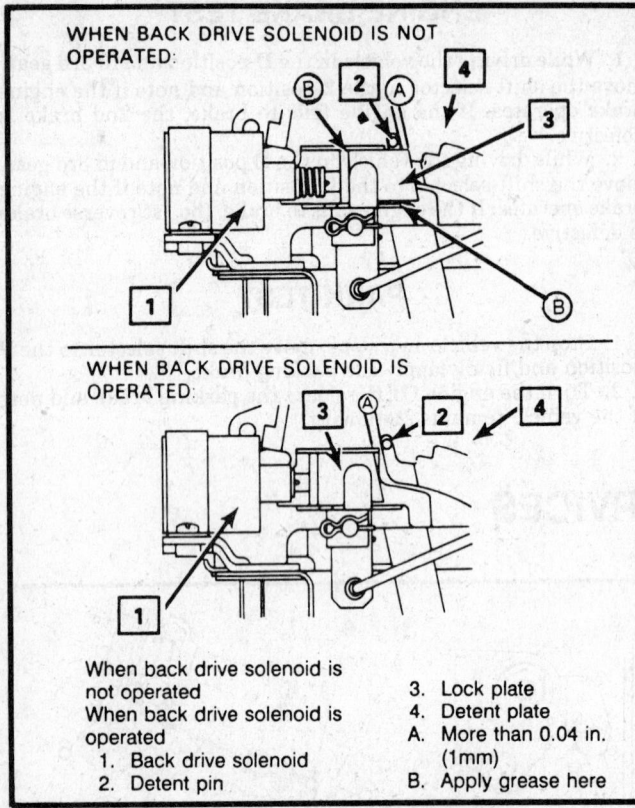

WHEN BACK DRIVE SOLENOID IS NOT OPERATED:

WHEN BACK DRIVE SOLENOID IS OPERATED:

When back drive solenoid is not operated
When back drive solenoid is operated
1. Back drive solenoid
2. Detent pin
3. Lock plate
4. Detent plate
A. More than 0.04 in. (1mm)
B. Apply grease here

Side view of the shift selector mechanism

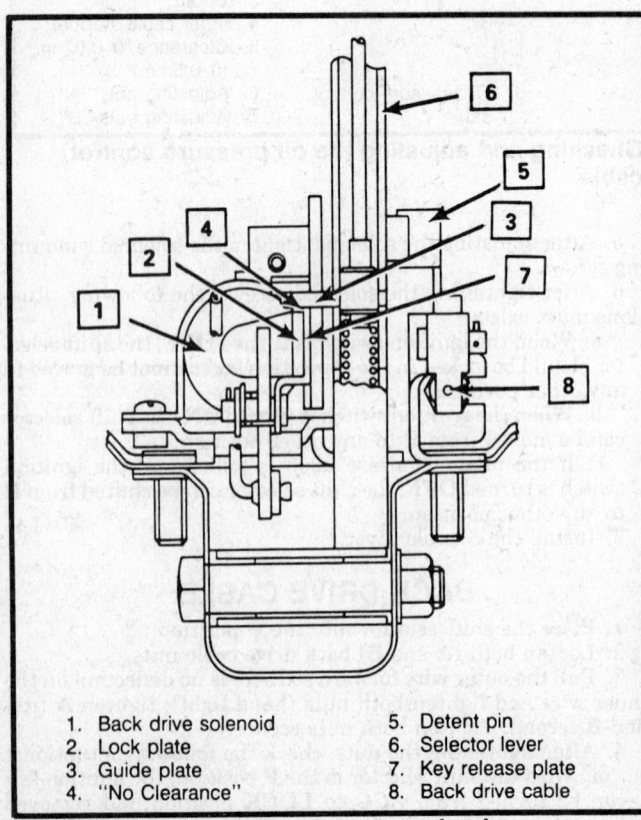

1. Back drive solenoid
2. Lock plate
3. Guide plate
4. "No Clearance"
5. Detent pin
6. Selector lever
7. Key release plate
8. Back drive cable

Front view of the shift selector mechanism

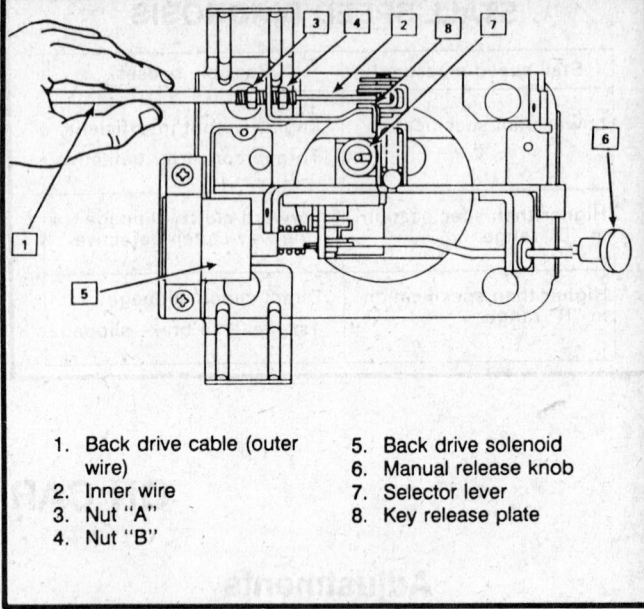

1. Back drive cable (outer wire)
2. Inner wire
3. Nut "A"
4. Nut "B"
5. Back drive solenoid
6. Manual release knob
7. Selector lever
8. Key release plate

Adjusting the back drive cable

b. With the shift selector in any position, other than **P**, the ignition key cannot be turned from **ACC** to **LOCK** position.

SHIFT SELECTOR CABLE

1. At the shift lever on the transaxle, loosen the shift selector cable adjusting nuts.

NOTE: It may be necessary to remove the shift lever switch.

2. Move the shift lever into the **N** position. From inside the vehicle, move the shift selector lever into the **N** position.

3. At the shift selector cable, turn adjusting nut **A** (hand tight) until it contacts the manual shift cable joint. Using a wrench, tighten adjusting nut **B**.

4. After the cable is adjusted, check for the following situations:

    a. Move the shift selector lever into the **P** position and start the engine; the vehicle should not move.

    b. Move the shift selector lever into the **N** position; the vehicle should not move under power.

    c. Move the shift selector lever into the **D, 2** and **L** positions; the vehicle should move under power.

    d. Move the shift selector lever into the **R** position; the vehicle should move rearward under power.

SHIFT LEVER SWITCH

1. Remove the shift lever switch from the transaxle.

2. Using a flat blade prybar, turn the shift lever switch joint to align it with the shift lever shaft; stop at the position where a click is heard from the joint.

3. Install the switch and torque the bolt to 10–16 ft. lbs. (13–23 Nm). Install the couplers and the clamp.

4. After the switch is installed, check for the following situations:

    a. Firmly apply the parking brake and block the drive wheels.

    b. Move the shift selector lever to the **P** position. Turn the ignition switch **ON** and verify that the starter motor operates.

change the level from add to full on the dipstick. Overfilling can cause damage to the internal components of the automatic transaxle.

Procedure

1. Raise and support the vehicle safely. If the transaxle is hot, allow it to cool.
2. Remove the drain plug and drain the fluid into a drain pan.
3. After draining, install the drain plug and gasket into the pan; torque the plug to 13–16 ft. lbs. (18–23 Nm).
4. Remove the dipstick and install a funnel in it's place. Using 3.16 qts. (1.5L) of Dexron®II automatic transmission fluid, install it through the dipstick tube.

NOTE: If refilling the transaxle after an overhaul (torque converter reused), use 3.7 qts. (3.5L) of fluid. If refilling the transaxle after an overhaul (torque converter dry), use 4.7 qts. (4.5L) of fluid.

5. Check the fluid level at both room temperature and operating temperature.

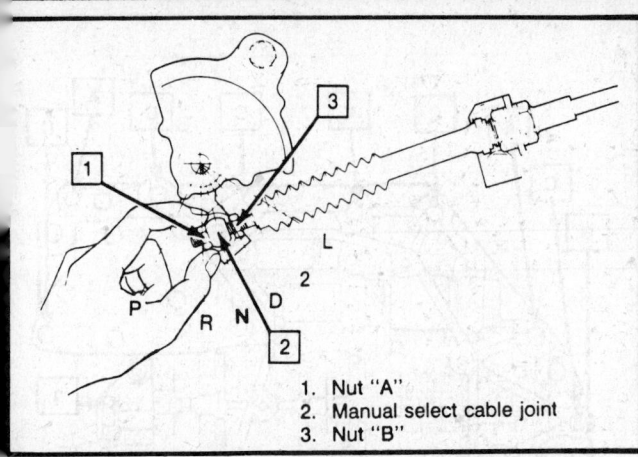

1. Nut "A"
2. Manual select cable joint
3. Nut "B"

Adjusting the shift lever cable

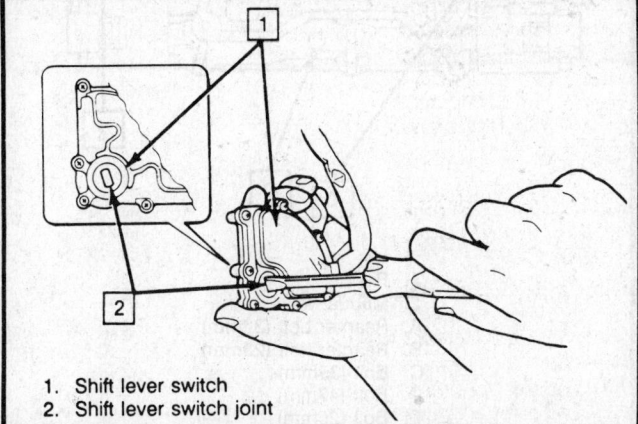

1. Shift lever switch
2. Shift lever switch joint

Adjusting the shift lever switch

c. Move the shift selector lever to the **N** position. Turn the ignition switch **ON** and verify that the starter motor operates.
d. Move the shift selector lever to the **L** position and back to the **N** position. Turn the ignition switch **ON** and verify that the starter motor operates.
e. Move the shift selector lever to the **P** position. Turn the ignition switch **ON** and verify that the starter motor operates.
f. Move the shift selector lever to any position, except the **P** or **N** positions. Turn the ignition switch **ON** and verify that the starter motor operates.
g. Turn the ignition switch **ON**, do not start the engine, move the shift selector lever into the **R** position and check that the backup lights turn **ON**.
h. If any of these situations do not exist, remove the shift lever switch and reperform the adjustment procedures.

Services

FLUID CHANGES

Under normal driving conditions, the fluid should be changed every 100,000 miles (160,000 km). Under severe driving conditions, the fluid should be changed every 15,000 miles (25,000 km). The following conditions are considered severe:
  a. Heavy city traffic where the outside temperature reaches 90°F (32°C)
  b. Very hilly or mountainous areas
  c. Commercial use, such as, taxi, police or delivery service
Do not overfill the transaxle. It only takes 1 pint of fluid to

OIL PAN

Removal and Installation

1. Raise and support the vehicle safely. Drain the transaxle; if it is hot, allow it to cool.
2. Remove the stabilizer bar-to-chassis bolts and the bar.
3. Using a floor jack and a block of wood, support the transaxle by not blocking the oil pan.
4. Remove the transaxle mounting member bolts and the member.
5. Remove the oil pan bolts. Using a plastic hammer, tap around the oil pan to remove it; do not use a prybar.
6. Using a gasket scraper or a putty knife, clean the gasket from the oil pan and transaxle.
7. Using solvent, clean the oil pan; be sure to place the magnet directly below the oil strainer.
8. Using a new gasket, sealant (if necessary), install the oil pan. Using sealant on the cross grooved (on head) bolts, torque the bolts to 3–4 ft. lbs. (4–6 Nm).
9. Install the transaxle mounting member. Torque the member-to-transaxle nuts to 29–36 ft. lbs. (40–50 Nm) and the member-to-chassis bolts to 36–43 ft. lbs. (50–60 Nm).
10. Install the stabilizer bar. Torque the stabilizer bar-to-chassis bolts to 22–40 ft. lbs. (30–55 Nm).
11. Refill the transaxle with Dexron®II transmission fluid.

DIRECT CLUTCH AND 2ND BRAKE SOLENOIDS

Removal and Installation

1. Raise and support the vehicle safely.
2. Drain the transaxle and remove the oil pan.
3. Disconnect the electrical connectors from the direct clutch and 2nd brake solenoids.
4. Remove the solenoids.

NOTE: If removing the wiring harness, remove it with the grommet from the upper side of the transaxle.

5. When installing the wiring harness, use a new grommet (O-ring) seal if the old one is damaged.
6. Install the solenoids into the case; if the O-ring seals are damaged, replace them.
7. Install the electrical connectors to the solenoids.
8. Install the oil pan and refill with clean fluid.

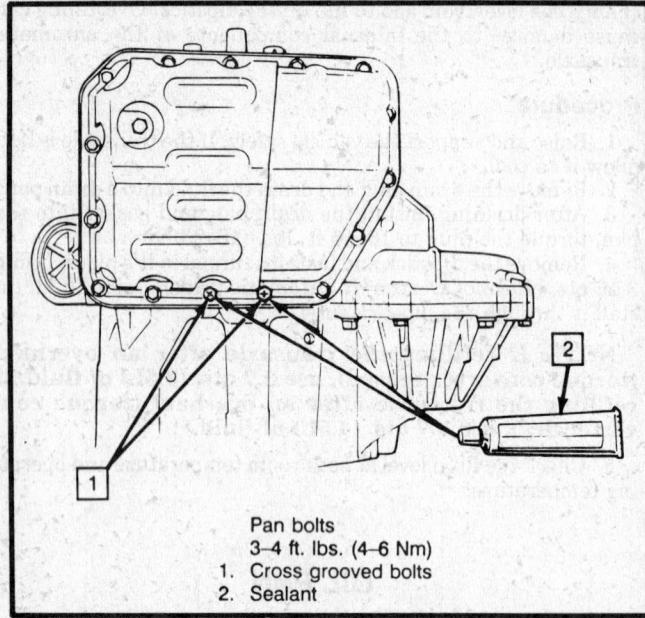

Pan bolts
3–4 ft. lbs. (4–6 Nm)
1. Cross grooved bolts
2. Sealant

Installing sealant on the cross grooved oil pan bolts

VALVE BODY

Removal and Installation

1. Raise and support the vehicle safely.
2. Drain the fluid and remove the oil pan.
3. Remove the direct clutch and 2nd brake solenoids.
4. Using a small prybar, pry both oil tubes from the lower valve body.
5. Disconnect the oil pressure control cable from the throttle valve cam and remove the cable.
6. Remove the oil strainer-to-valve body bolts and the strainer.
7. Remove the valve body-to-transaxle bolts and the valve body.
8. To install the valve body, position it into the case by aligning the manual valve with the manual shift lever pin; make sure that the accumulator spring is seated. First, torque both reamer (A and B) bolts to 6–8.5 ft. lbs. (8–12 Nm), secondly, torque all remaining bolts (in diagonal order) to 6–8.5 ft. lbs. (8–12 Nm).
9. Connect the oil pressure cable to the throttle valve cam, by holding the cam down and sliding the cable end into the slot.
10. Using a soft hammer, carefully tap the oil tubes into the valve body; make sure to insert them into the flange position securely.

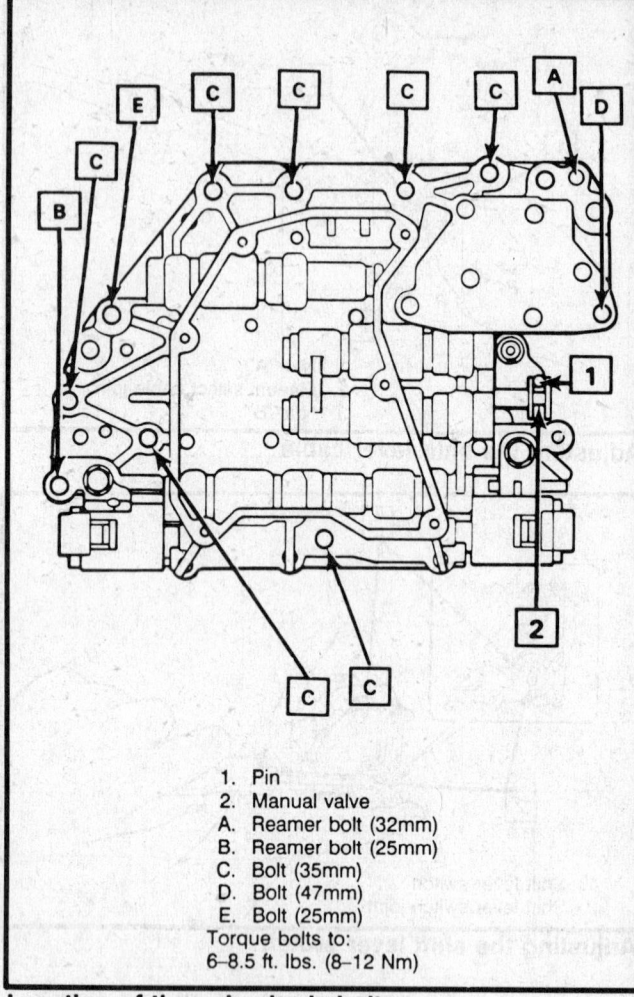

1. Pin
2. Manual valve
A. Reamer bolt (32mm)
B. Reamer bolt (25mm)
C. Bolt (35mm)
D. Bolt (47mm)
E. Bolt (25mm)
Torque bolts to:
6–8.5 ft. lbs. (8–12 Nm)

Location of the valve body bolts

11. Install the solenoids and connect the electrical connectors to them.
12. Install the oil strainer-to-valve body and torque the bolts to 3–4 ft. lbs. (4–6 Nm); be sure to install the solenoid wire clamp.
13. Using solvent, clean the oil pan; be sure to place the magnet directly below the oil strainer.
14. Using a new gasket, sealant (if necessary), install the oil pan. Using sealant on the cross grooved (on head) bolts, torque the bolts to 3–4 ft. lbs. (4–6 Nm).

REMOVAL AND INSTALLATION

TRANSAXLE REMOVAL

1. From the air cleaner, remove the air suction guide.
2. Disconnect both cables from the battery and the negative (−) cable from the transaxle. Remove the battery and the battery tray.
3. From the transaxle, disconnect the solenoid coupler, the shift lever switch coupler and the wiring harness.
4. Separate the oil pressure control cable from the accelerator cable. From the transaxle, disconnect the accelerator cable and the shift selector cable.
5. Remove the starter motor. Place a catch pan under the transaxle and drain the fluid.
6. Disconnect and plug the oil cooler tubes at the transaxle.
7. Raise and support the vehicle safely. Remove the exhaust pipe and the lower clutch housing plate.

NOTE: Before removing the torque converter-to-drive plate bolts, make alignment marks on the torque converter and drive plate for assembly purposes.

8. Using a prybar, insert it through the notch (underside of transaxle) to lock the drive plate gear. Remove the torque converter-to-drive plate bolts.

9. To remove the left halfshaft, perform the following procedures:

    a. From the wheel hub, remove the center cap, the split pin and the driveshaft nut.

    b. Remove the lug nuts and the front wheels.

    c. Using a prybar, position it between the differential case and the halfshaft's inboard joint, pry the joint until the snapring disconnects from the side gear.

    d. Remove both stabilizer bar-to-chassis brackets and the ball stud-to-steering knuckle bolt. Pull the stabilizer bar downward to disconnect the ball joint from the steering knuckle.

    e. Carefully remove the halfshaft from the differential case and the steering knuckle to prevent tearing the boots.

10. Using a prybar, disconnect the right halfshaft from the differential case.

11. Remove the transaxle mounting member bolts and the member. Using a floor jack and a piece of wood, support the transaxle.

12. Remove the left transaxle mount.

13. Remove the transaxle-to-engine bolts. Slide the transaxle from the engine (to prevent damaging the crankshaft, drive plate or torque converter) and lower it from the vehicle.

TRANSAXLE INSTALLATION

1. Using grease, lubricate the cup around the center of the torque converter.

2. Measure the distance **A** between the torque converter and the transaxle housing; it should be at least 0.85 in. (21.4mm). If the distance is less than specified, the torque converter is improperly installed; remove and reinstall it.

3. When installing the transaxle, guide the right halfshaft into the differential case; make sure the snapring seats in the differential gear.

4. To install the left halfshaft, perform the following procedures:

    a. Clean and lubricate the halfshaft splines with grease.

    b. Carefully install the halfshaft into the steering knuckle and the differential case to prevent tearing the boots; make sure the snapring seats in the differential gear.

    c. Install the ball joint stud into the steering knuckle and torque the bolt to 36–50 ft. lbs. (50–70 Nm).

    d. Install the stabilizer bar-to-chassis brackets and torque the bolts to 22–39 ft. lbs. (30–55 Nm).

    e. Torque the halfshaft hub nut to 108–195 ft. lbs. (150–270 Nm) and install the split pin (to the shaft) and the center cap.

    f. Torque the lug nuts to 29–50 ft. lbs. (40–70 Nm).

5. Torque the transaxle housing-to-engine bolts to 12–16.5 ft. lbs. (16–23 Nm), the mounting member-to-chassis bolts to 40 ft. lbs. (55 Nm), the mounting member-to-transaxle nuts to 33 ft. lbs. (45 Nm) and the transaxle-to-mount bolts to 40 ft. lbs. (55 Nm).

6. Using a prybar, insert it through the notch (underside of transaxle) to lock the drive plate gear and torque the torque converter-to-drive plate bolts to 13–14 ft. lbs. (18–19 Nm).

7. Install the oil cooler lines and the starter.

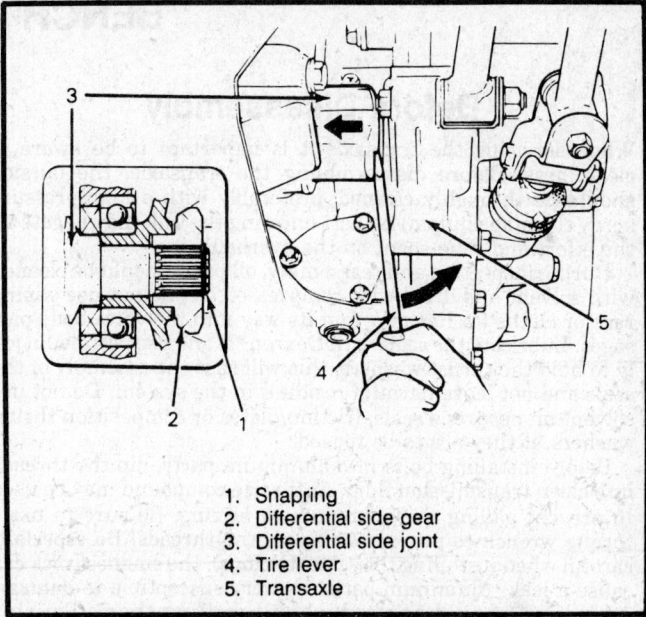

1. Snapring
2. Differential side gear
3. Differential side joint
4. Tire lever
5. Transaxle

Prying the halfshaft from the differential case

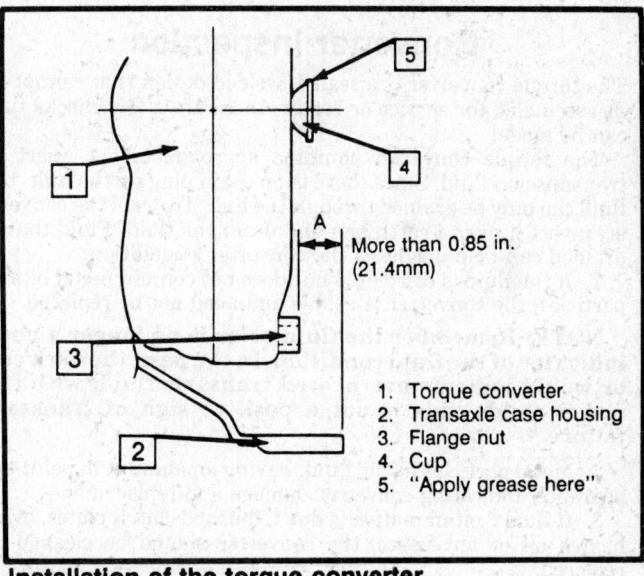

More than 0.85 in. (21.4mm)

1. Torque converter
2. Transaxle case housing
3. Flange nut
4. Cup
5. "Apply grease here"

Installation of the torque converter

8. After connecting the oil pressure control cable to the accelerator cable, check and/or adjust the cable play.

9. Connect the wiring harness, the shift lever switch coupler and the solenoid coupler to the transaxle.

10. Install and adjust the select cable and shift switch.

11. Install the battery tray and the battery. Connect the battery cables to the battery and the negative (−) battery cable to the transaxle.

12. Install the air suction guide to the air cleaner.

13. Refill and check the fluid level.

BENCH OVERHAUL

Before Disassembly

When servicing the transaxle it is important to be aware of cleanliness. Before disassembling the transaxle, the outside should be throughly cleaned, preferably with a high-pressure spray cleaning equipment. Dirt entering the unit may negate all the effort and time spent on the overhaul.

During inspection and reassembly, all parts should be cleaned with solvent and dried with compressed air; do not use wiping rags or cloths for lint may find its way into the valve body passages. Lubricate the seals with Dexron®II and use petroleum jelly to hold the thrust washers; this will ease the assembly of the seals and not leave harmful residues in the system. Do not use solvent on neoprene seals, friction plates or composition thrust washers, if they are to be reused.

Before installing bolts into aluminum parts, dip the threads into clean transmission fluid. Anti-seize compound may be used to prevent galling the aluminum or seizing. Be sure to use a torque wrench to prevent stripping the threads. Be especially careful when installing the seals (O-rings), the smallest nick can cause a leak. Aluminum parts are very susceptible to damage; great care should be used when handling them. Reusing snaprings is not recommended but should they be: compress the internal ones and compress the external ones.

Converter Inspection

The torque converter is a sealed, welded design that cannot be disassembled for service or repair; there are a few checks that can be made.

The torque converter contains approximately 1 quart of transmission fluid. Since there is no drain plug on the unit, the fluid can only be drained through the hub. To drain the converter, invert it over a catch pan and drain the fluid. Fluid that is drained can help diagnosis the converter's condition.

1. If the fluid is discolored but does not contain metal bits or particles, the converter is usable and need not be replaced.

NOTE: Remember the fluid color is no longer a good indicator of the fluid condition. In the past, the dark color would indicate overheated transaxle fluid; with the newer fluids, this is not a positive sign of transaxle failure.

2. Metal particles in the fluid, having an aluminum paint appearance, indicating converter damage and replacement.

3. If fluid contamination is due to burned clutch plates, overheated oil or antifreeze, the converter should be cleaned or replaced.

The converter should be checked carefully for damage, especially around the seal area; remove any sharp edges or burrs from the seal surface. Do not expose the seal to any type of solvent. If the converter is to be washed with solvent, the seal must be removed.

Transaxle Disassembly

1. Pull the torque converter from the front of the transaxle.
2. Remove the bolts from the rear cover and the solenoid wire harness clamps. Using a holding fixture tool, mount the transaxle to it.
3. Remove the dipstick, the dipstick tube and the fluid cooling lines.
4. Place an oil catch pan under the transaxle and drain the fluid.

NOTE: Before draining the fluid from the transaxle, do not turn it over for the foreign matter in the pan will contaminate the valve body.

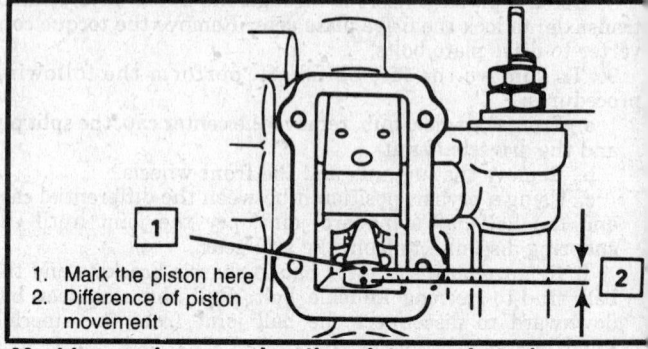

1. Mark the piston here
2. Difference of piston movement

Marking and measuring the piston rod stroke

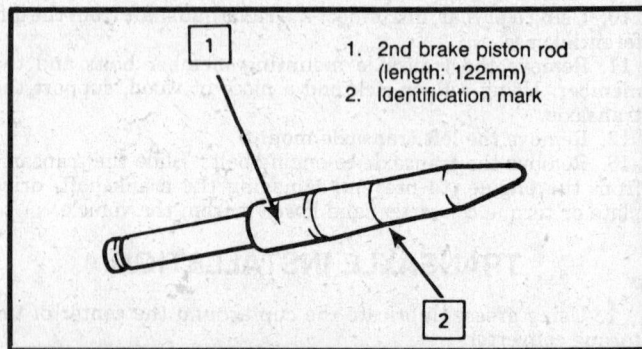

1. 2nd brake piston rod (length: 122mm)
2. Identification mark

View of the 2nd brake band piston

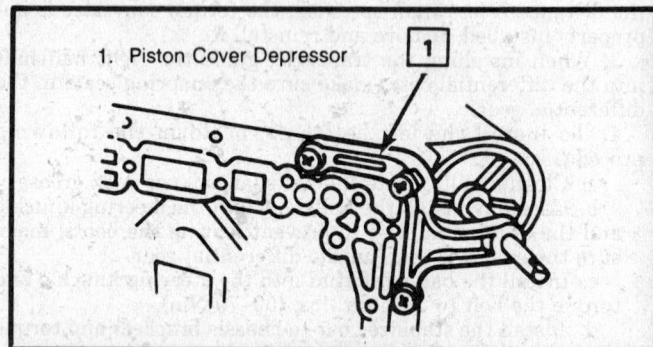

1. Piston Cover Depressor

Using the piston cover depressing tool to compress the 2nd brake piston

5. Remove the oil pan bolts. Using a soft mallet, tap the oil pan from the transaxle and remove the gasket.
6. From the bottom of the transaxle, disconnect the electrical connectors from the direct clutch and 2nd brake solenoids.
7. Using a prybar, pry the oil tubes from the valve body.
8. Using a pair of pliers, disconnect the oil control cable from the throttle valve cam and remove the cable from the transaxle.
9. Remove the oil strainer-to-valve body bolts, the strainer, the valve body-to-transaxle case bolts and the valve body.
10. Using a rag and 15 psi (100 kPa) of compressed air, place the rag over the accumulator pistons, force the compressed air into the piston holes, pop them out and catch the them with the rag.
11. Remove the 2nd brake band cover and gasket. To check the 2nd brake piston stroke, perform the following procedures:
   a. Scribe a mark on the piston rod.

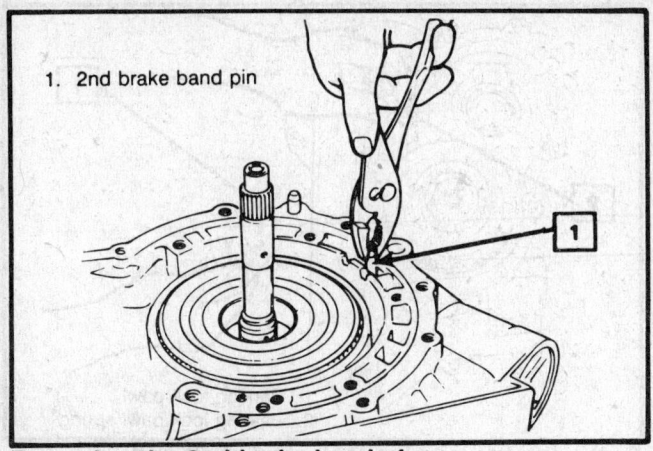

1. 2nd brake band pin

Removing the 2nd brake band pin

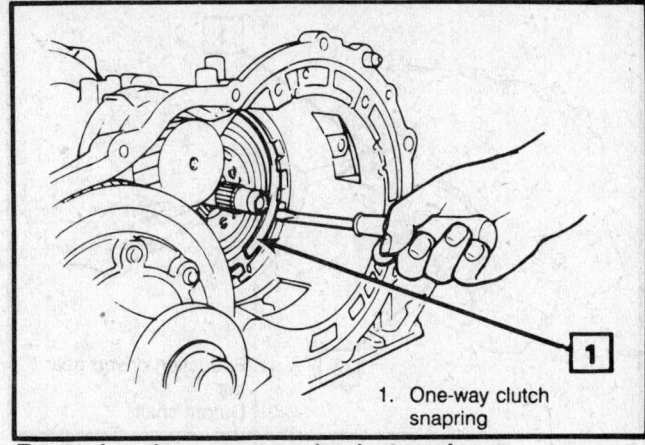

1. One-way clutch snapring

Removing the one-way clutch snapring

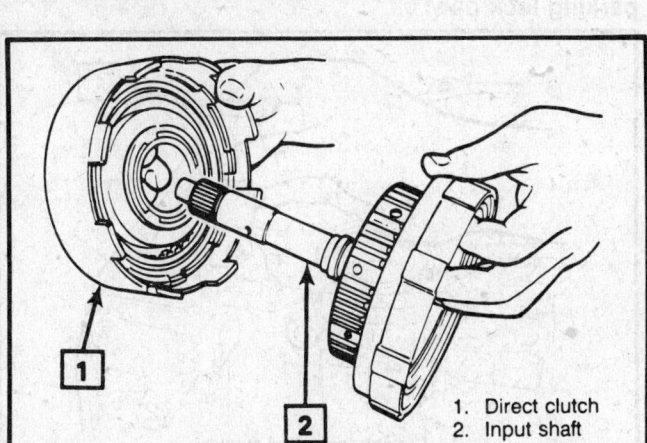

1. Direct clutch
2. Input shaft

Removing the direct clutch from the input shaft

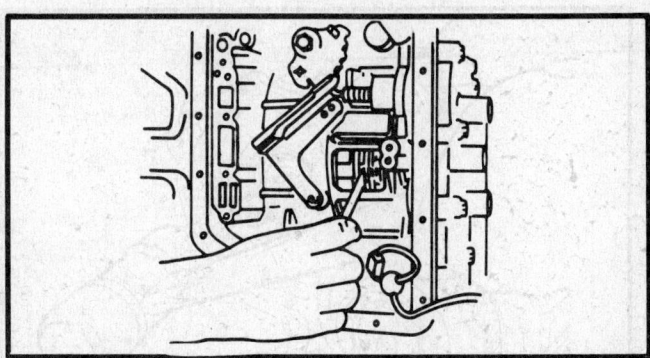

Using a feeler gauge to check the 1st/reverse brake clearance

planetary ring gear, the ring gear bearing, the planetary sun gear and the front planetary gear bearing.

19. Using a small prybar, remove the one-way clutch snapring from the housing. Remove the one-way clutch, the rear planetary gear, the rear planetary ring gear, the ring gear bearing and the washers.

20. Using a feeler gauge, place it between the snapring and the 1st/reverse brake; the clearance should be 0.023–0.075 in. (0.58–1.92mm). If the measurement is out of specifications, replace the 1st/reverse brake plate or disc with a new one.

21. Using a small prybar, remove both 1st/reverse snaprings. Remove the 1st/reverse brake flange, discs, plates, damper plate and the differential gear assembly.

22. From the rear of the transaxle, remove the rear cover bolts/nuts and the cover; it may be necessary to use a plastic hammer to lightly tap the rear cover from the transaxle.

23. To remove the reduction driven gear, perform the following procedures:

   a. Using a hammer and a chisel, remove the stake mark from the retaining nut.

   b. Move the shift selector lever to the **P** position; make sure the output shaft cannot turn.

   c. Using a wrench, carefully loosen and remove the retaining nut; do not use a hammer, for the parking lock pawl and output shaft may be damaged.

   d. Remove the reduction driven gear.

24. Using a plastic hammer, drive the counter shaft from the transaxle.

25. Using the output shaft remover tool or equivalent, position it (the tool's legs in the case notches) on the outer race of the internal output shaft bearing (inside the transaxle) and drive the output shaft from the transaxle.

   b. Apply low pressurized air into the oil hole and measure the 2nd brake piston rod stroke; it should be 0.06–0.11 in. (1.5–3.0mm).

   c. If out of specifications, replace the 2nd brake band or the piston rod (with a different length); the piston rod is available in 2 lengths.

12. To remove the 2nd brake piston, install a piston cover depressor tool or equivalent, onto the transaxle case and tighten the bolt to compress the piston spring. Using a small prybar, remove the snapring. Remove the depressor tool and the 2nd brake piston.

13. At the solenoid wire harness, remove the wire holding the plate retaining nut and pull out the solenoid wire.

14. To remove the oil pump, perform the following procedures:

   a. Remove the oil pump bolts.

   b. Using a pair of slide hammers, equipped with adapters, pull the oil pump from the transaxle.

15. Remove the bell housing-to-transaxle case bolts, tap around with housing (with a plastic hammer) and remove the bell housing.

16. Using a pair of pliers, pull the 2nd brake band pin from the transaxle housing.

17. Grasp the input shaft and remove the direct/forward clutch assembly; be careful, for the ring gear bearing race and bearing, which may be sticking to the clutch assembly, may drop out.

18. From the housing, remove the 2nd brake band, the front

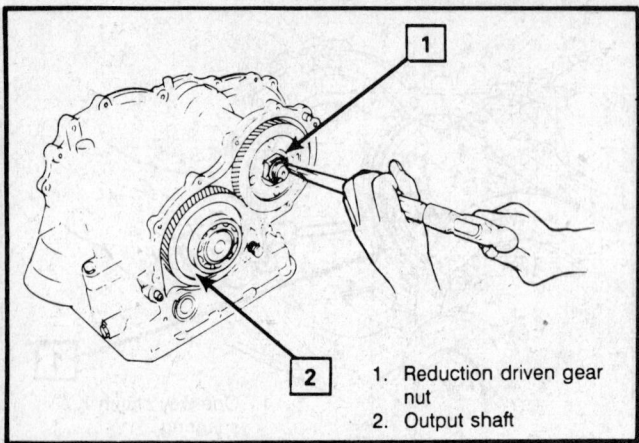

1. Reduction driven gear nut
2. Output shaft

Removing the reduction driven gear nut

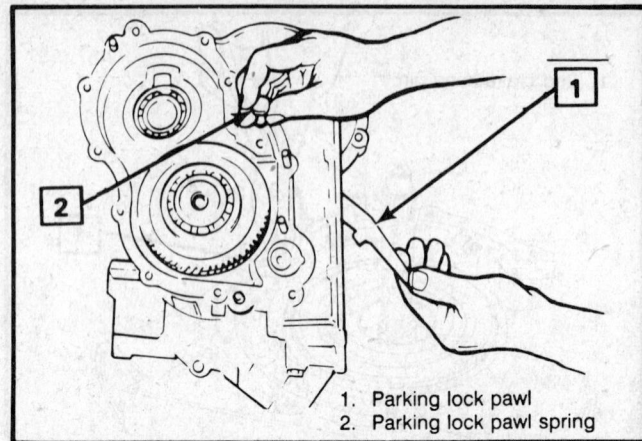

1. Parking lock pawl
2. Parking lock pawl spring

Removing the parking lock pawl shaft and parking lock pawl

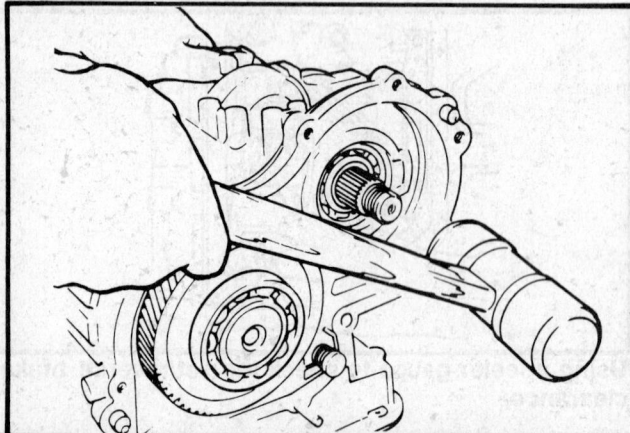

Driving the countershaft from the transaxle

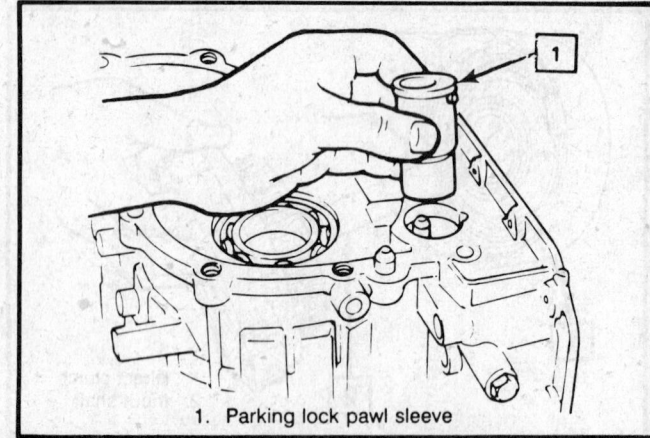

1. Parking lock pawl sleeve

Removing the parking lock pawl sleeve

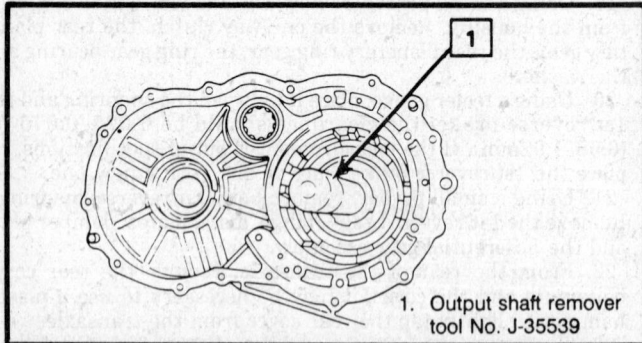

1. Output shaft remover tool No. J-35539

Using the output shaft remover tool to drive the output shaft from the transaxle

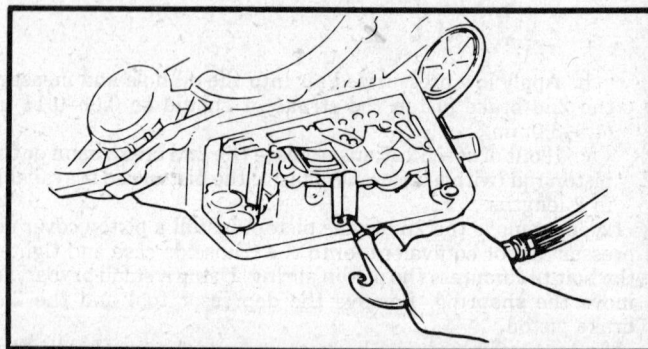

Using air pressure to remove the 1sr/reverse brake piston from the case

26. To remove the parking lock pawl, perform the following procedures:
    a. Pull out the parking lock pawl shaft and the spring.
    b. Remove the parking lock pawl.
    c. Pull out the parking lock pawl sleeve.
    d. Remove the manual detent spring assembly and the manual shift shaft.
27. To remove the 1st/reverse brake piston, perform the following procedures:
    a. Using a small prybar, push the return spring assembly downward and pry the snapring from the flange.
    b. Lift the return spring assembly from the case.

    c. Using low pressurized air, apply it to the oil hole and force the 1st/reverse piston from the case.

Unit Disassembly and Assembly
DIRECT CLUTCH

Disassembly

1. Using a Vernier® scale, measure the height between the snapring and the clutch flange; the height should be 0.098–0.120 in. (2.49–3.06mm). If the height is within specifications,

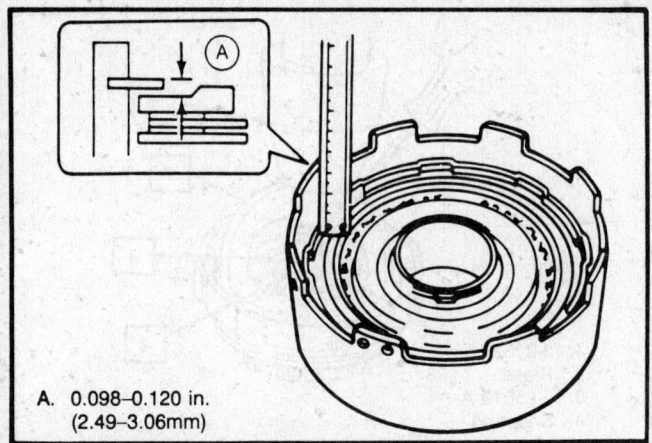

A. 0.098–0.120 in.
(2.49–3.06mm)

Measuring the direct clutch height

the clutch is OK; if the height is not within specifications, replace the clutch discs or plates.

2. Using a prybar, remove the large clutch plate snapring.

3. Remove the clutch flange, discs and plates.

4. Using a clutch spring compressor tool or equivalent, and a shop press, compress the piston return springs and remove the small snapring with a small prybar.

5. Remove the spring seat and the return spring assembly.

6. To remove the direct clutch piston, apply low pressurized air through oil hole in the drum; the piston should pop out. If the piston does not come out, use a pair of needle-nose pliers and lift it out.

7. Remove the inner seal from the drum and the outer seal from the piston.

Inspection

1. Check the piston for free movement of the check valve (steel ball).

2. Using low pressurized air, check for leakage of the check valve; if faulty, replace the piston.

Assembly

1. Using Dexron®II transmission fluid, lubricate the new O-rings seals; fit the inner seal into the drum and the outer seal onto the piston.

2. When installing the piston into the drum, be careful the O-ring does not get twisted or caught.

3. Install the clutch return spring assembly and the spring seat.

4. Using a clutch spring compressor tool or equivalent, and a shop press, compress the piston return springs and install the small snapring with a small prybar.

NOTE: Make sure the snapring is fully seated in the 4 spring seat projections. Do not compress the return spring more than necessary.

5. Install the discs, plates and flange in the following order: plate, disc, plate, plate, disc and flange.

NOTE: If installing new clutch discs, soak them in Dexron®II fluid for at least 2 hours before assembly.

6. Install the large snapring. After assembly, measure the height between the clutch flange and the snapring; it should be 0.098–0.120 in. (2.49–3.06mm). If the height is not within specifications, with new clutch plates and discs installed, install the different clutch flange. Clutch flanges are available in 2 thicknesses: 0.118 in. (3.00mm) and 0.132 in. (3.37mm).

7. Apply low pressurized air to the oil hole in the drum to check the piston movement.

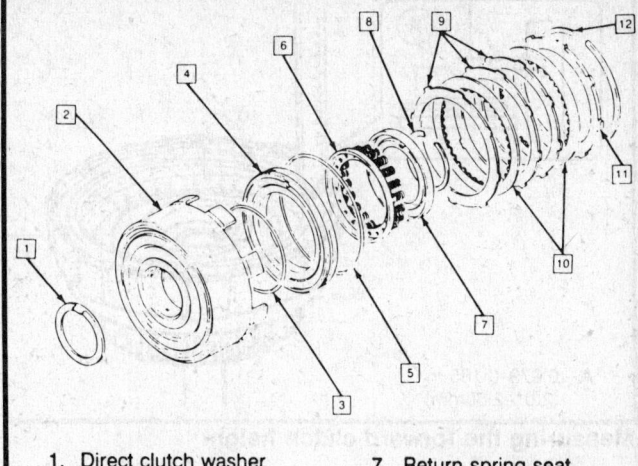

1. Direct clutch washer
2. Direct clutch drum
3. Inner seal
4. Direct clutch piston
5. Outer seal
6. Return spring assembly
7. Return spring seat
8. Clutch plate snapring
9. Clutch plate
10. Clutch disc
11. Clutch flange
12. Clutch plate snapring

Exploded view of the direct clutch assembly

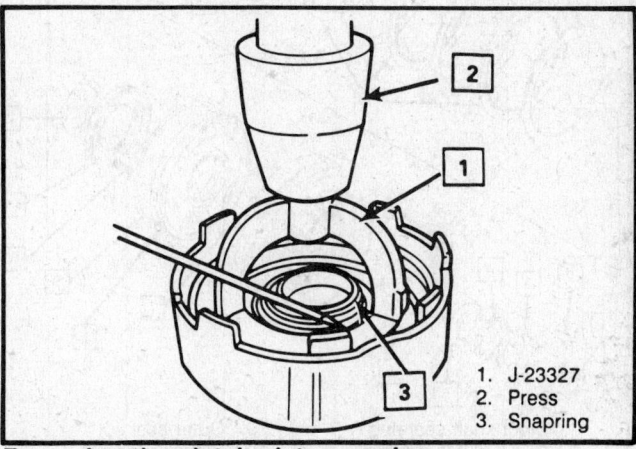

1. J-23327
2. Press
3. Snapring

Removing the clutch plate snapring

FORWARD CLUTCH

Disassembly

1. Using a Vernier® scale, measure the height between the snapring and the clutch flange; the height should be 0.079–0.105 in. (2.01–2.68mm). If the height is within specifications, the clutch is OK; if the height is not within specifications, replace the clutch discs or plates.

2. Using a prybar, remove the large clutch plate snapring.

3. Remove the clutch flange, discs and plates.

4. Using a clutch spring compressor tool or equivalent, an adapter tool and a shop press, compress the return springs and remove the small snapring with a small prybar.

NOTE: When compressing the return spring, be careful not to compress them more than necessary.

5. Remove the spring seat and the return springs.

6. To remove the forward clutch piston, apply low pressurized air through oil hole in the input shaft; the piston should pop out. If the piston does not come out, use a pair of needle-nose pliers and lift it out.

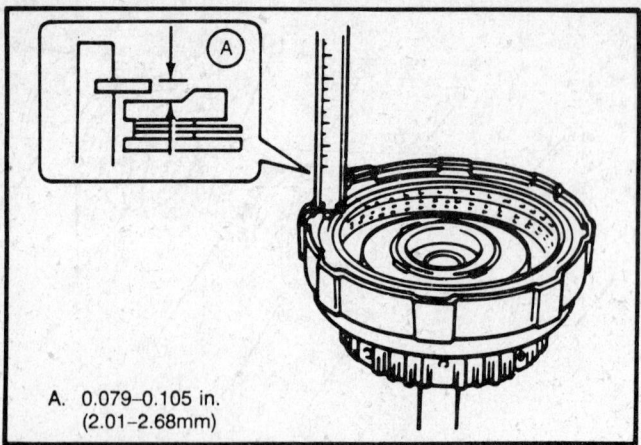

A. 0.079–0.105 in.
(2.01–2.68mm)

Measuring the forward clutch height

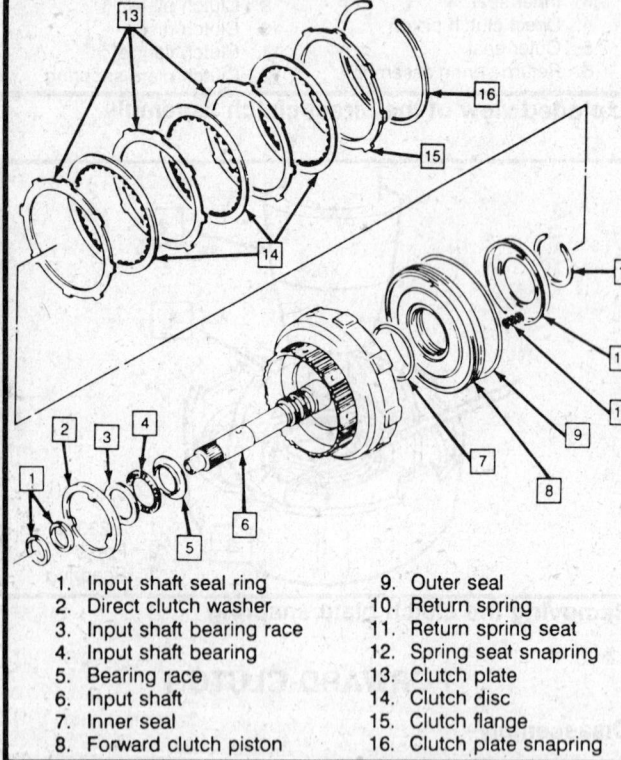

1. Input shaft seal ring
2. Direct clutch washer
3. Input shaft bearing race
4. Input shaft bearing
5. Bearing race
6. Input shaft
7. Inner seal
8. Forward clutch piston
9. Outer seal
10. Return spring
11. Return spring seat
12. Spring seat snapring
13. Clutch plate
14. Clutch disc
15. Clutch flange
16. Clutch plate snapring

Exploded view of the forward clutch assembly

7. Remove the inner and outer seals (O-rings) from the piston.

Inspection

1. Check the clutch piston for free movement of the check valve (ball).
2. Using low pressurized air, check for leakage of the check valve; if faulty, replace the clutch piston.

Assembly

1. Using Dexron®II transmission fluid, lubricate the new O-rings seals; fit them onto the piston.
2. When installing the piston into the input shaft drum, be careful the O-ring seals do not get twisted or caught.

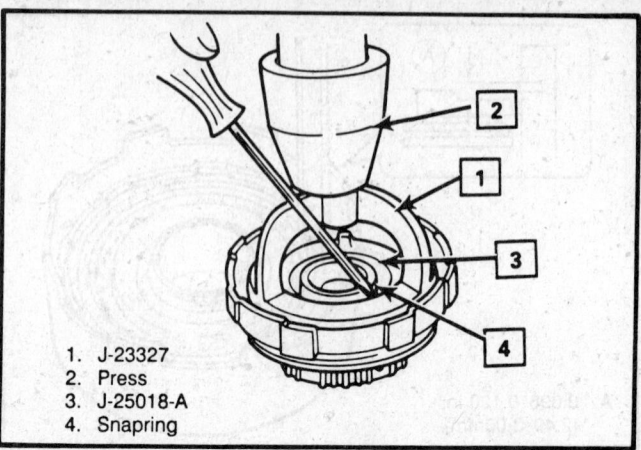

1. J-23327
2. Press
3. J-25018-A
4. Snapring

Removing the snapring from the forward clutch assembly

3. Install the piston return springs and the spring seat.
4. Using a clutch spring compressor tool or equivalent, an adapter tool and a shop press, compress the return springs and install the small snapring.

NOTE: **Make sure the snapring is fully seated in the 4 spring seat projections. Do not compress the return spring more than necessary.**

5. Install the discs, plates and flange in the following order: plate, disc, plate, disc, plate, disc and flange.

NOTE: **If installing new clutch discs, soak them in Dexron®II fluid for at least 2 hours before assembly.**

6. Install the large snapring. After assembly, measure the height between the clutch flange and the snapring; it should be 0.079–0.105 in. (2.01–2.68mm). If the height is not within specifications, with new clutch plates and discs installed, install the different clutch flange. Clutch flanges are available in 2 thicknesses: 0.118 in. (3.00mm) and 0.132 in. (3.37mm).
7. Apply low pressurized air to the oil hole in the input shaft to check the clutch piston movement.

DIFFERENTIAL CASE

Disassembly

1. Using a wheel puller tool and a plug tool, pull the side bearings and the speedometer driven gear from the differential case.
2. Using a hammer and a pin punch, drive the pinion shaft roll pin from the differential case.
3. Remove the pinion shaft, pinion gears and side gears from the differential case.
4. Remove the ring gear-to-differential case bolts and the ring gear.

Inspection

1. Using Dexron®II fluid or kerosene, wash the parts throughly.
2. Inspect the gear teeth for excessive signs of wear; minor nicks or scratches may be removed with an oil stone. If necessary, replace the damaged or worn parts.
3. Inspect the thrust washers for signs of excessive wear, distortion or damage; if necessary, replace them.

Assembly

1. Using Dexron®II fluid, lubricate the parts before installation.
2. Install the side washers and the side gears.
3. Install the pinion washers, the pinion gears and the pinion shaft.

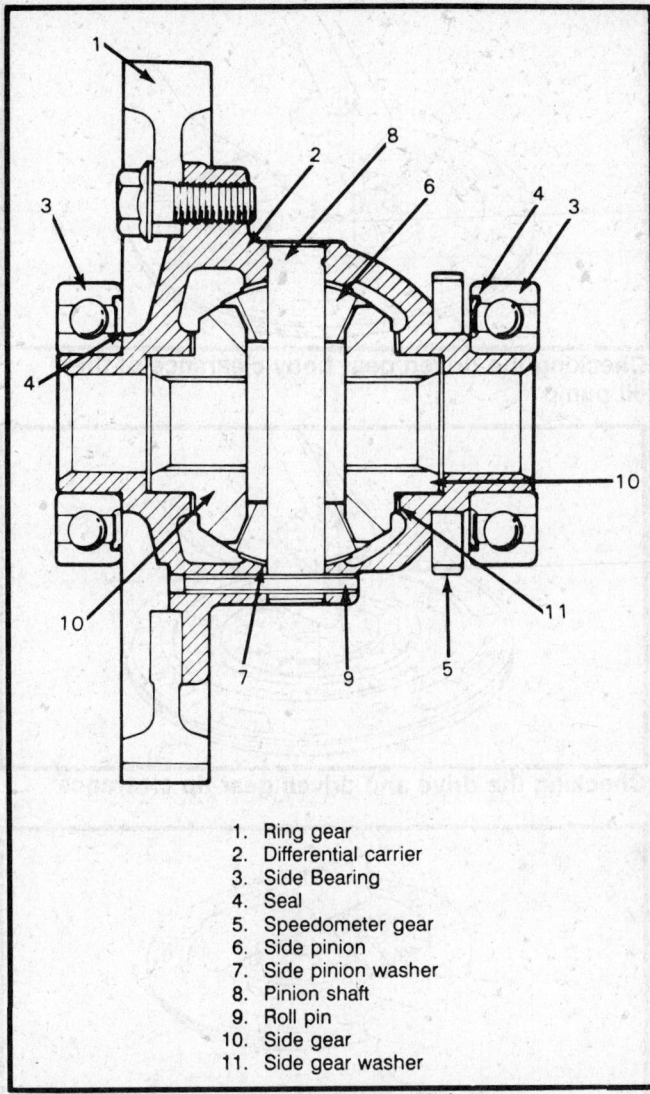

1. Ring gear
2. Differential carrier
3. Side Bearing
4. Seal
5. Speedometer gear
6. Side pinion
7. Side pinion washer
8. Pinion shaft
9. Roll pin
10. Side gear
11. Side gear washer

Crossectional view of the differential case

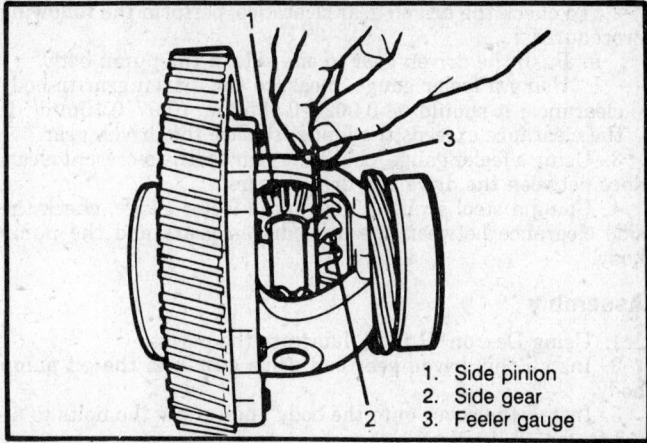

1. Side pinion
2. Side gear
3. Feeler gauge

Measuring the backlash of the pinion and side gears

	mm	IN.
Available side gear	0.90	0.035
	0.95	0.037
Washer sizes	1.00	0.039
	1.05	0.041
	1.10	0.043
	1.15	0.045
	1.20	0.047

List of the side gear washer sizes

4. Using a feeler gauge, measure the backlash of the side pinions and side gears; it should be 0–0.009 in. (0.01–0.25mm). If the backlash is not within specifications, adjust it by changing the thickness of the side washers.

5. Align the pinion shaft hole with the differential case hole and install the roll pin.

6. Install the ring gear and torque the bolts to 58–72 ft. lbs. (80–100 Nm).

7. Using a shop press, press the speedometer gear onto the differential case.

8. Using a bearing installation tool or equivalent, and a hammer, drive both side bearings (seal side facing case) onto the differential case.

OIL PUMP

Disassembly

1. Remove both cover seal rings and the O-ring.
2. Remove the cover-to-body bolts and the front cover.

Inspection

1. Check the oil pump seal for wear, cracks or damage; if necessary, replace the seal.

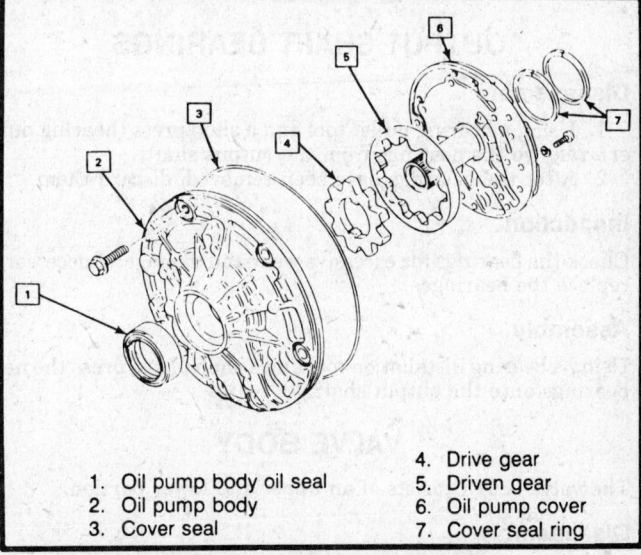

1. Oil pump body oil seal
2. Oil pump body
3. Cover seal
4. Drive gear
5. Driven gear
6. Oil pump cover
7. Cover seal ring

Exploded view of the oil pump assembly

2. To check the driven gear clearance, perform the following procedures:

a. Push the driven gear to one side of the pump body.

b. Using a feeler gauge, measure the driven gear-to-body clearance; it should be 0.0028–0.0059 in. (0.07–0.15mm). If the clearance exceeds the limits, replace the driven gear.

3. Using a feeler gauge, check the gear tooth-to-cresent clearance between the drive and driven gears.

4. Using a steel straight edge and a feeler gauge, check the side clearance between the drive/driven gears and the pump body.

Assembly

1. Using Dexron®II fluid, lubricate the parts.

2. Install the driven gear and drive gear into the oil pump body.

3. Install the cover onto the body and torque the bolts to 6–8.5 ft. lbs. (8–12 Nm).

4. Lubricate both oil pump seal rings and install them onto the pump.

5. Install the O-ring onto the cover; make sure it is not twisted and fully seated into the groove.

6. Rotate the drive gear and check it for smooth rotation.

COUNTERSHAFT BEARINGS

Disassembly

1. Using a prybar inside the case, remove the countershaft bearing snaprings.

2. Remove the rear cover (backing plate).

3. Using a bearing remover tool and a slide hammer, remove both countershaft bearings.

Inspection

Check the bearings for excessive wear and damage; if necessary, replace the bearings.

Assembly

1. Insert the countershaft spacer and roller bearing into the case. Using the bearing installation tool and a hammer, drive the bearing into the case until it is seated. Install the snapring.

2. Install the ball bearing into the case. Using the bearing installation tool and a hammer, drive the bearing into the case until it is seated.

3. Install the bearing backing plate and the snapring.

OUTPUT SHAFT BEARINGS

Disassembly

1. Using a bearing puller tool and a shop press (bearing puller), remove the bearings from the output shaft.

2. After the bearings have been removed, discard them.

Inspection

Check the bearings for excessive wear and damage; if necessary, replace the bearings.

Assembly

Using a bearing installation tool and a shop press, press the new bearings onto the output shaft.

VALVE BODY

The valve body consists of an upper and lower portion.

Disassembly

1. Remove the upper valve body-to-lower valve body bolts;

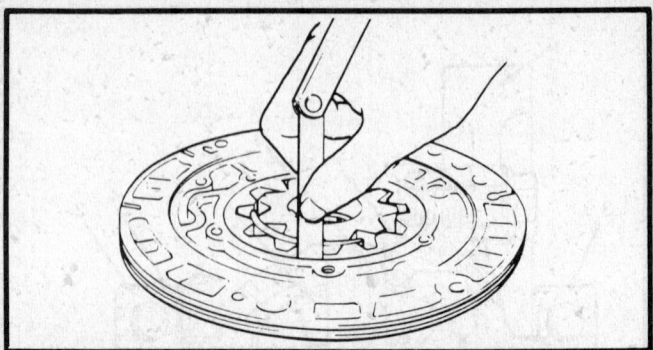
Checking the driven gear body clearance of the oil pump

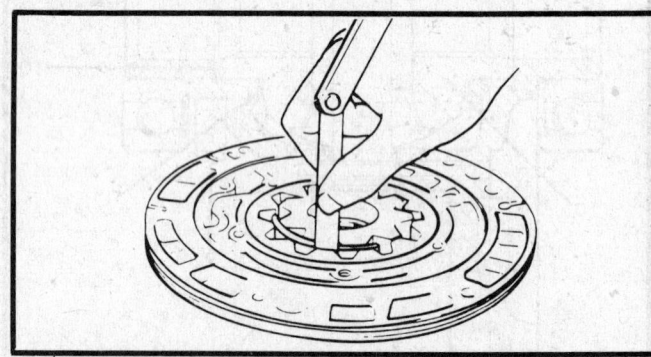
Checking the drive and driven gear tip clearance

Checking the drive and driven gear side clearance

when separating the valve bodies, be careful not drop the check balls.

2. From the upper valve body, remove the throttle valve cam bolt, cam and spring.

3. From the lower valve body, remove the 2nd brake solenoid, the direct clutch solenoid, the lower valve body cover bolts, cover and gasket (discard it).

4. Using a needle-nose pliers, remove the valve plug keys.

NOTE: Even though the valve components appear to be similar, they are different; be sure to keep them separated.

5. When removing the valves (from each body) and keep the corresponding spring together with each valve.

6. Using Dexron®II fluid, throughly wash each part. Using compressed air, blow out the fluid passages and holes.

Inspection

1. Inspect the check balls for damage or a sticking condition.

2. Check the valves for free movement, damage or scoring.

3. Check the springs for binding.

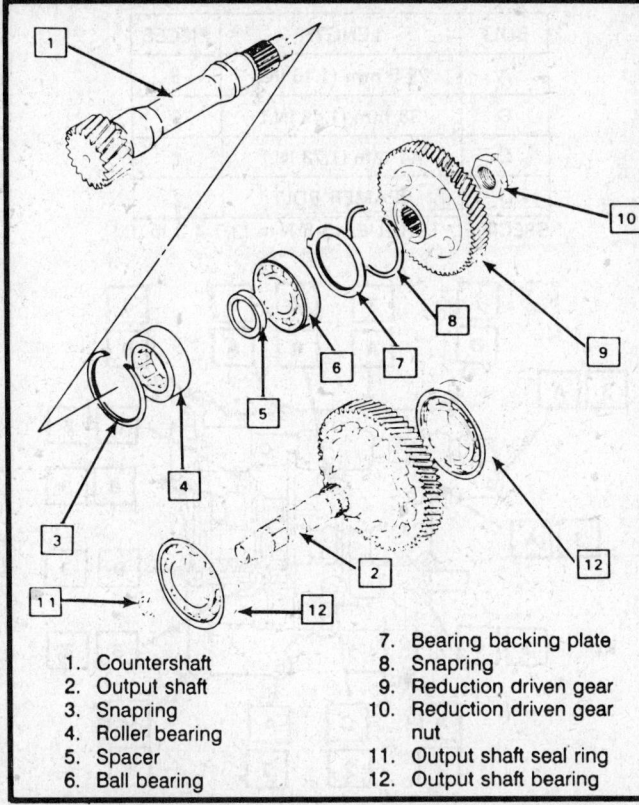

1. Countershaft
2. Output shaft
3. Snapring
4. Roller bearing
5. Spacer
6. Ball bearing
7. Bearing backing plate
8. Snapring
9. Reduction driven gear
10. Reduction driven gear nut
11. Output shaft seal ring
12. Output shaft bearing

Exploded view of the countershaft and output shaft assemblies

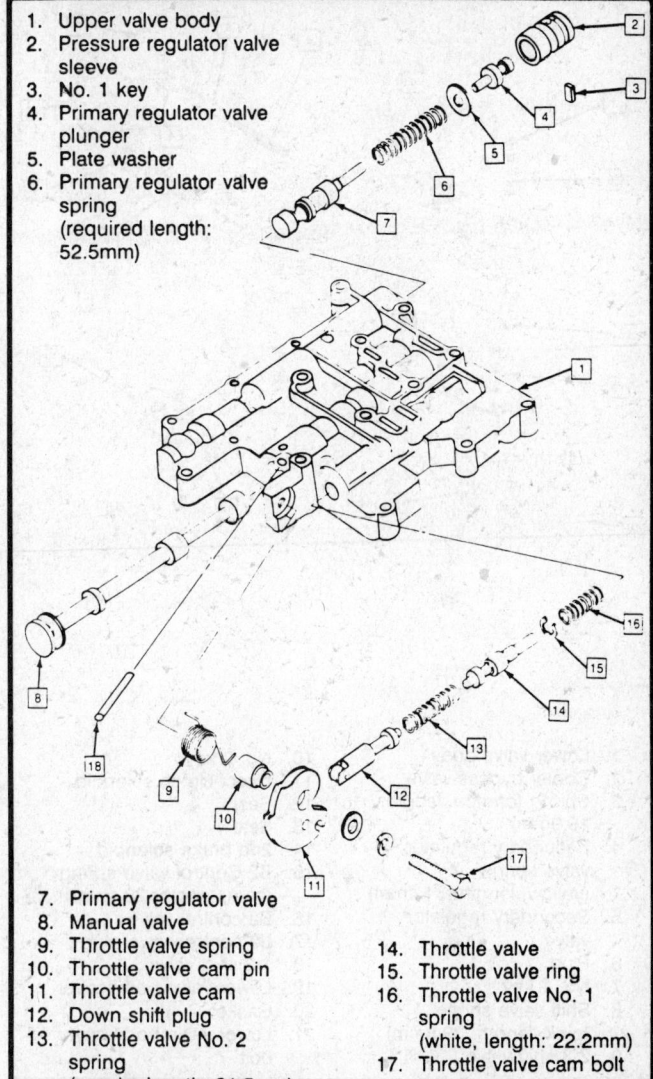

1. Upper valve body
2. Pressure regulator valve sleeve
3. No. 1 key
4. Primary regulator valve plunger
5. Plate washer
6. Primary regulator valve spring
   (required length: 52.5mm)
7. Primary regulator valve
8. Manual valve
9. Throttle valve spring
10. Throttle valve cam pin
11. Throttle valve cam
12. Down shift plug
13. Throttle valve No. 2 spring
   (purple, length: 31.5mm)
14. Throttle valve
15. Throttle valve ring
16. Throttle valve No. 1 spring
   (white, length: 22.2mm)
17. Throttle valve cam bolt
18. Nozzle neutral drain

Exploded view of the upper valve body components

4. Check the seals for nicks, cracks or deterioration; replace them, if necessary.

Assembly

1. When assembling the lower valve body, use a new gasket, install the lower valve body cover and torque the bolts to 3–4 ft. lbs. (4–6 Nm).
2. Assemble the throttle valve cam to the upper valve body and torque the bolt to 4.5–6.5 ft. lbs. (6–9 Nm).
3. Position the check balls in the correct positions in the lower valve body.
4. When assembling the valve bodies, use a new gasket, install the bolts and perform the following procedure:
   a. Install all of the bolts, in their correct locations, finger tight.
   b. Torque the No. 2 bolts to 3.7–4.3 ft. lbs. (5–6 Nm).
   c. Torque the No. 3 bolts to 3.7–4.3 ft. lbs. (5–6 Nm).
   d. Torque the No. 4 bolts to 3.7–4.3 ft. lbs. (5–6 Nm).
   e. Torque the No. 1 bolts to 3.7–4.3 ft. lbs. (5–6 Nm).

Transaxle Assembly

1. To install the manual shift shaft and parking lock pawl into the transaxle case, perform the following procedures:
   a. Install the lower washer and parking lock rod to the manual shift shaft.

NOTE: When installing the manual shift shaft, be careful not to damage the oil seal lip.

   b. Install the manual shift shaft into the case, followed by the manual detent spring. Torque the manual detent spring nut/bolt to 6.0–8.5 ft. lbs. (8–12 Nm).
   c. Install the upper washer and manual shift lever to the manual shift shaft. Torque the upper/lower nuts to 20–23.5 ft. lbs. (27–33 Nm).
   d. After torquing the nuts, check the manual shift shaft for rotation smoothness.
   e. Assemble the restrictor pin and snapring to the parking lock pawl sleeve and install the assembly into the case.
   f. Shift the manual shift lever into **P**, install the parking lock pawl, the lock pawl shaft and the lock pawl spring. Move the manual shift lever to make sure the parking lock pawl moves smoothly.
2. To install the 1st/reverse brake piston, perform the following procedures:
   a. Using Dexron®II fluid, lubricate the piston's inner/outer seals and fit them to the piston.
   b. Install the piston into the case so the spring holes are facing upward; be sure the seals are not twisted or caught.
   c. Position the return spring assembly on the piston; make sure the springs (of the assembly) are fitted securely in the piston holes.
   d. Using prybars, press the return spring assembly downward and install the snapring.
3. Using a driver handle tool or equivalent, a countershaft in-

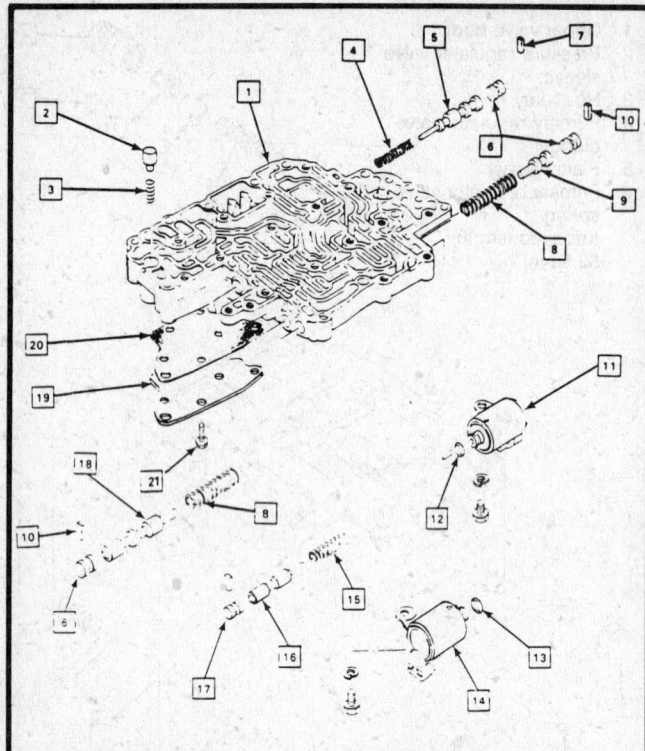

1. Lower valve body
2. Cooler bypass valve
3. Spring (orange, length: 19.9mm)
4. Secondary regulator valve spring (yellow, length: 31.4mm)
5. Secondary regulator valve
6. Plug
7. No. 1 key
8. Shift valve spring (pink, length: 39.6mm)
9. 2-3 shift valve
10. No. 2 key
11. Direct clutch solenoid
12. Seal
13. Seal
14. 2nd brake solenoid
15. B2 Control valve spring (blue, length: 28.1mm)
16. B2 control valve
17. B2 control valve plug
18. 1-2 shift valve
19. Lower valve body cover
20. Gasket
21. Lower valve body cover bolt

Exploded view of the lower valve body components

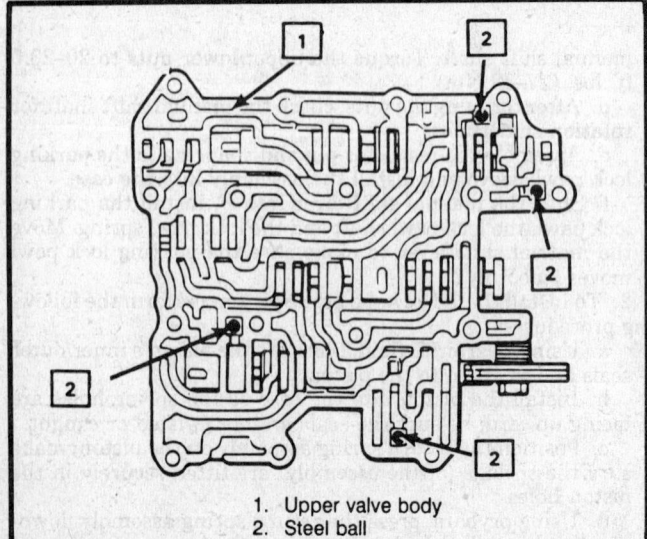

1. Upper valve body
2. Steel ball

Location of the check balls in the upper valve body

BOLT	LENGTH	PIECES
A	29.5 mm (1.16 IN.)	6
B	38 mm (1.49 IN.)	6
C	44 mm (1.73 IN.)	2
D	REAMER BOLT	2

SPECIFIED TORQUE: 5-6 N·m (3.7-4.3 lb. ft.)

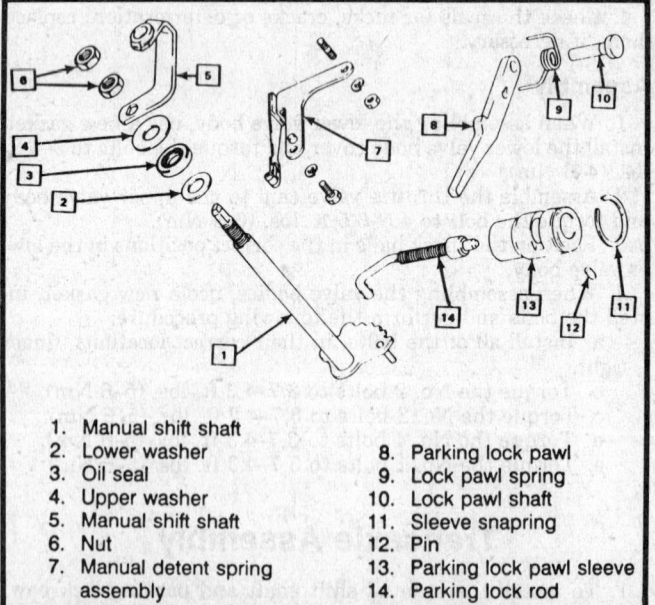

Description and location of the valve body bolts

1. Manual shift shaft
2. Lower washer
3. Oil seal
4. Upper washer
5. Manual shift shaft
6. Nut
7. Manual detent spring assembly
8. Parking lock pawl
9. Lock pawl spring
10. Lock pawl shaft
11. Sleeve snapring
12. Pin
13. Parking lock pawl sleeve
14. Parking lock rod

Exploded view of the manual shift shaft, parking lock pawl and related parts

stallation tool or equivalent, and a hammer, drive the counter-shaft into the case until it is seated in the bearings.

NOTE: When driving the countershaft, make sure the spacer is in position and do not drive the shaft excessively hard, for the snapring may become damaged.

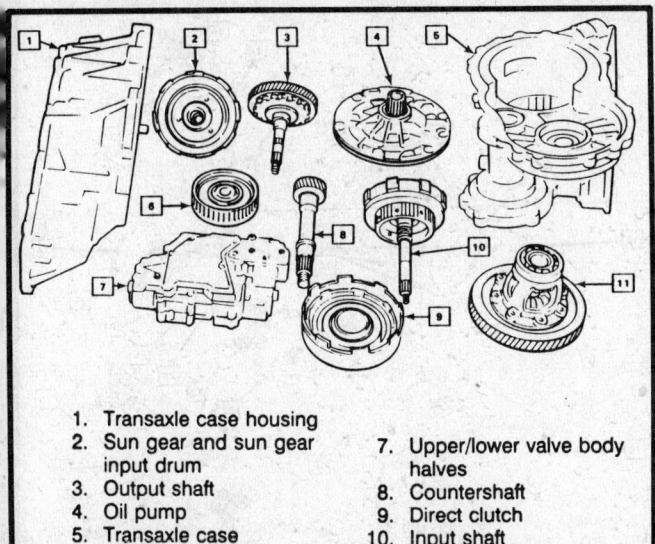

1. Transaxle case housing
2. Sun gear and sun gear input drum
3. Output shaft
4. Oil pump
5. Transaxle case
6. Front planetary
7. Upper/lower valve body halves
8. Countershaft
9. Direct clutch
10. Input shaft
11. Differential

View of the transaxle components

4. To install the output shaft, perform the following procedures:

a. Move the manual shift lever into a position other than **P**.

b. Using a bearing installation tool or equivalent, and a hammer, drive the output shaft into the case until it seats.

5. To install the reduction driven gear, perform the following procedures:

a. Position the reduction driven gear on the countershaft, engaging the gear teeth with the output shaft gear.

b. Move the manual shift lever into the **P** position; make sure the output shaft is locked and cannot move.

c. Install the driven gear nut and torque it to 86–108 ft. lbs. (110–150 Nm).

d. Using a chisel and a hammer, stake the gear nut in 2 places.

6. To install the rear transaxle cover, perform the following procedures:

a. Using a new gasket, install the rear cover. Make sure the output shaft bearing enters the rear cover bearing hole smoothly. Rotate the output shaft and check for abnormal gear sounds.

b. Install the rear cover bolts/nuts and torque the bolts to 12–16 ft. lbs. (16–23 Nm) and the nuts to 8–10 ft. lbs. (11–15 Nm).

NOTE: If the holding fixture tool is being used, only ½ the rear cover bolts can be installed; install the remaining bolts after the tool is removed.

7. To seat the output shaft, perform the following procedures:

a. Using the output shaft remover/installer tool or equivalent, align 4 of the tool's projections in 4 case notches.

b. Using a hammer, lightly tap the tool to seat the bearing and output shaft against the rear cover; do not hammer on the shaft directly.

8. Install the differential gear assembly by engaging the final gear teeth with the countershaft teeth; be careful not to damage the gear teeth surfaces.

9. To install the 1st/reverse brake parts, perform the following procedures:

a. Install the damper plate (convex side facing upward) onto the return spring assembly; do not reverse the direction of the plate.

b. Install the discs, plates and flange in the following order: plate, disc, plate, disc, plate, disc, plate, disc and flange (flat side facing downward).

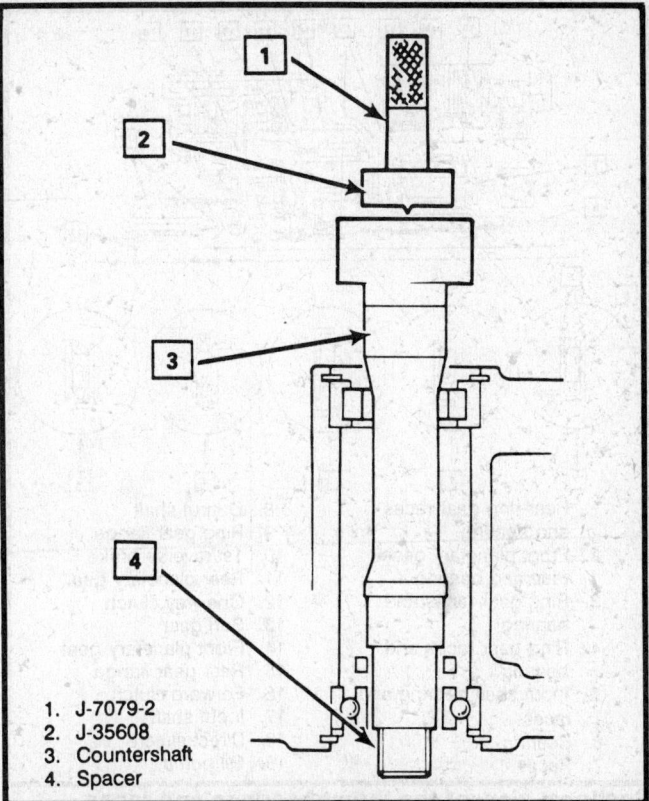

1. J-7079-2
2. J-35608
3. Countershaft
4. Spacer

Installing the countershaft into the case

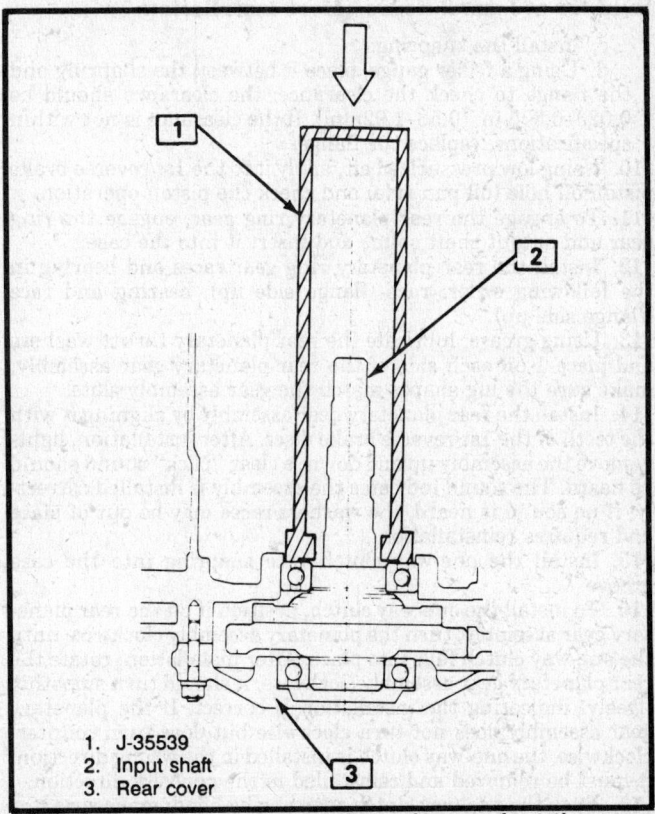

1. J-35539
2. Input shaft
3. Rear cover

Seating the output shaft and bearing against the rear cover

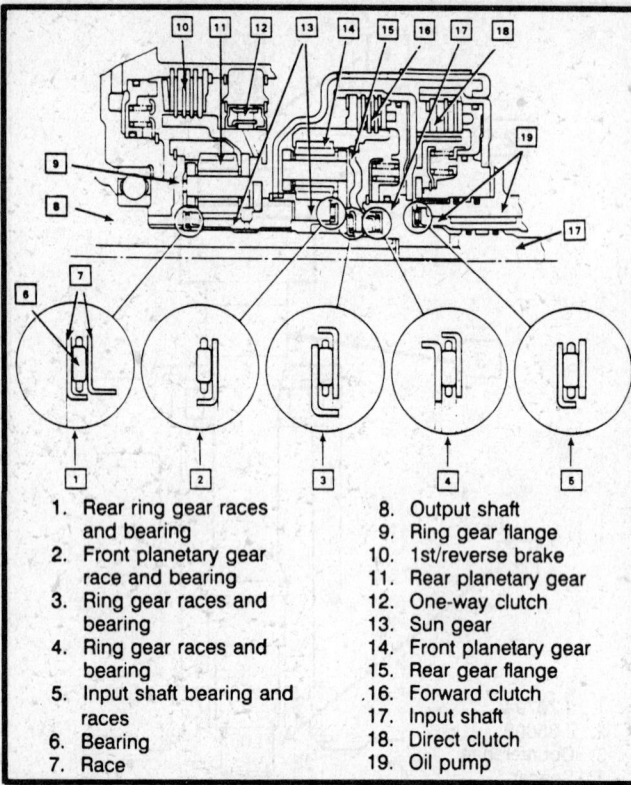

1. Rear ring gear races and bearing
2. Front planetary gear race and bearing
3. Ring gear races and bearing
4. Ring gear races and bearing
5. Input shaft bearing and races
6. Bearing
7. Race
8. Output shaft
9. Ring gear flange
10. 1st/reverse brake
11. Rear planetary gear
12. One-way clutch
13. Sun gear
14. Front planetary gear
15. Rear gear flange
16. Forward clutch
17. Input shaft
18. Direct clutch
19. Oil pump

Sectional view of the thrust bearings and races

NOTE: If installing new discs, soak them in Dexron® II fluid for at least 2 hours before installation.

c. Install the snapring.

d. Using a feeler gauge, place it between the snapring and the flange to check the clearance; the clearance should be 0.023–0.075 in. (0.58–1.92mm). If the clearance is not within specifications, replace the flange.

10. Using low pressurized air, apply it to the 1st/reverse brake piston oil hole (oil pan side) and check the piston operation.

11. To engage the rear planetary ring gear, engage the ring gear and output shaft spline and insert it into the case.

12. Install the rear planetary ring gear races and bearing in the following order: race (flange side up), bearing and race (flange side up).

13. Using grease, lubricate the rear planetary thrust washers and place 1 on each side of the rear planetary gear assembly; make sure the lug shapes match the gear assembly slots.

14. Install the rear planetary gear assembly by aligning it with the teeth of the 1st/reverse brake discs. After installation, lightly move the assembly up and down; a clear "click" sound should be heard. The sound indicates the assembly is installed correctly; if no sound is heard, the washers/races may be out of place and requires reinstallation.

15. Install the one-way clutch race snapring into the case groove.

16. To install the one-way clutch, position it on the rear planetary gear assembly, turn the planetary assembly clockwise until the one-way clutch falls into place. After installation, rotate the rear planetary gear assembly clockwise, it should turn smoothly (freely) indicating the installation is correct. If the planetary gear assembly does not turn clockwise but does turn counterclockwise, the one-way clutch is installed in the wrong direction; it must be removed and reinstalled in the opposite direction.

17. Push the one-way clutch snapring by hand; make sure it is fully seated and the snapring ring ends are between the lugs.

18. Using grease, apply it to the sun gear thrust washer. In-

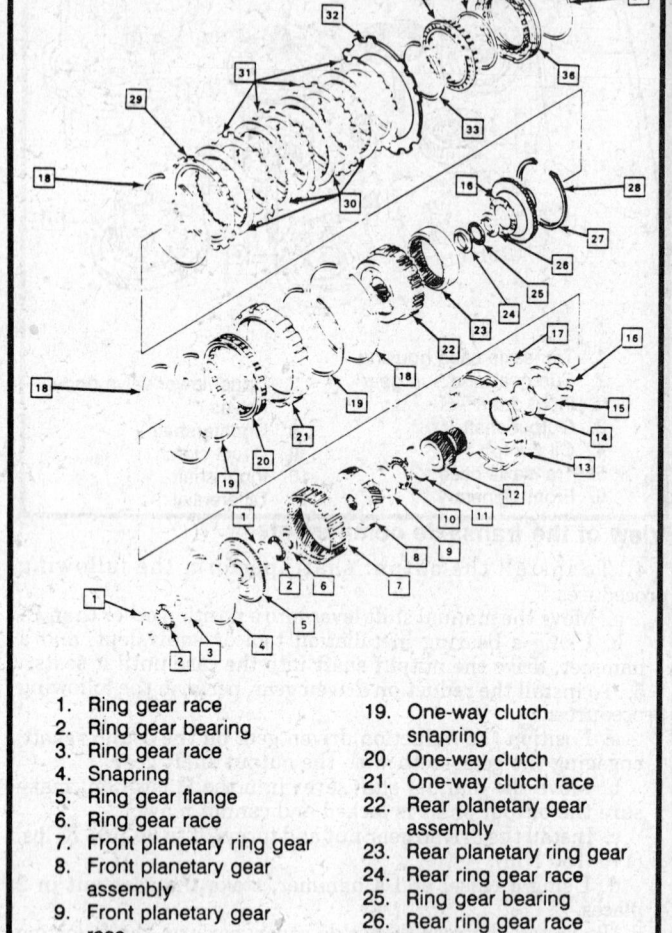

1. Ring gear race
2. Ring gear bearing
3. Ring gear race
4. Snapring
5. Ring gear flange
6. Ring gear race
7. Front planetary ring gear
8. Front planetary gear assembly
9. Front planetary gear race
10. Front planetary gear bearing
11. Input drum snapring
12. Sun gear
13. Sun gear input drum
14. Snapring
15. Planetary thrust washer
16. Rear planetary thrust washer
17. Sun gear pin
18. One-way clutch race snapring
19. One-way clutch snapring
20. One-way clutch
21. One-way clutch race
22. Rear planetary gear assembly
23. Rear planetary ring gear
24. Rear ring gear race
25. Ring gear bearing
26. Rear ring gear race
27. Ring gear flange
28. Ring gear snapring
29. 1st/reverse brake flange
30. 1st/reverse brake disc
31. 1st/reverse brake plate
32. 1st/reverse brake damper plate
33. Return spring snapring
34. 1st/reverse brake return spring
35. Piston inner seal
36. 1st/reverse brake piston
37. Piston outer seal

Exploded view of the planetary gears and related parts

stall the thrust washer and pin to the sun gear. Make sure the pin is fitted in the thrust washer notch.

19. Install the sun gear assembly by engaging it with the rear planetary gear; be careful not to damage the bushing (inside the sun gear). After installation, lightly move the sun gear up and down; it should make a clear "click" sound. If no sound is heard, the washers may be out of place; remove and reinstall the sun gear.

20. Install the front planetary gear bearing and race (flange side down) on the sun gear.

21. To install the front planetary gear assembly, turn it in either direction until it engages with the sun gear. After installation, lightly move the assembly up and down; it should make a clear "click" sound, indicating it is properly installed. If no sound is heard, the bearing and race may be out of position; remove, check and reinstall the assembly.

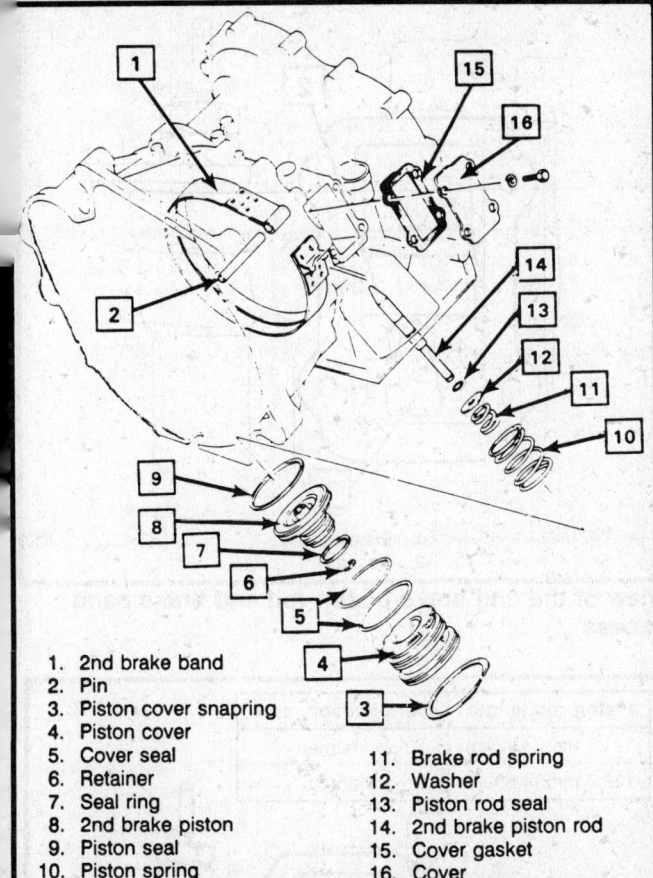

1. 2nd brake band
2. Pin
3. Piston cover snapring
4. Piston cover
5. Cover seal
6. Retainer
7. Seal ring
8. 2nd brake piston
9. Piston seal
10. Piston spring
11. Brake rod spring
12. Washer
13. Piston rod seal
14. 2nd brake piston rod
15. Cover gasket
16. Cover

Exploded view of the 2nd brake components

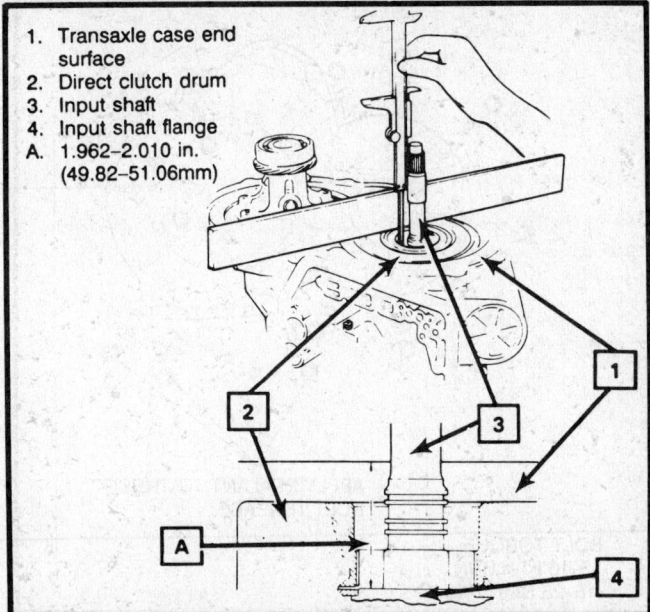

1. Transaxle case end surface
2. Direct clutch drum
3. Input shaft
4. Input shaft flange
A. 1.962–2.010 in. (49.82–51.06mm)

Measuring the distance between the case end surface and input shaft flange.

22. On the front planetary gear assembly, install these items in the following order: the ring gear race (flange side up), the ring gear bearing and ring rear race (flange side down).

23. Install the front planetary ring gear assembly. After installation, lightly move the assembly up and down; it should make a clear "click" sound, indicating it is properly installed. If no sound is heard, the bearing and races may be out of position; remove, check and reinstall the assembly.

24. Install the 2nd brake band in the correct direction in the case; do not bend it too much, for it can become damaged.

25. To install the 2nd brake band pin, dip it in Dexron®II fluid and insert it in the case hole aligned with the 2nd brake band hole.

26. To install the 2nd brake piston, perform the following procedures:
    a. Using Dexron®II fluid, lubricate the piston rod, seal and seal ring. Install the piston spring and piston assembly into the case.
    b. Using Dexron®II fluid, lubricate both cover seals and install the piston cover on the case.
    c. Using the piston cover depressor tool or equivalent, compress the piston cover and install the snapring.

27. Inspect the output shaft seal ring for wear or damage; replace it, if necessary. Install the seal on the output shaft; be careful not to expand it too much.

28. Using grease, lubricate the input shaft and install the input shaft seal rings on the shaft; be careful not to expand it too much.

29. Using grease, apply it to the direct clutch washer and position it (grooved face outward) on the direct clutch; the grease will hold the washer in place.

30. To install the direct clutch, align the discs teeth and place it on the input shaft. After installation, lightly move the assembly up and down; it should make a clear "click" sound, indicating it is properly installed. If no sound is heard, the assembly is not installed correctly; remove and reinstall it.

31. Using grease, apply it to the ring gear races and bearing. Install these items in the following order: the 1.41 in. (35.8mm) ring gear race (flange side down), the bearing and the 1.49 in. (37.9mm) ring gear race on the ring gear.

32. To install the input shaft and forward/direct clutch assembly, support the input shaft (direct clutch installed), align the forward clutch discs and lower it into the case by turning it back and forth; be careful the bearing and race do not fall off. After installation, lightly move the assembly up and down; it should make a clear "click" sound, indicating it is properly installed. If no sound is heard, the assembly is not installed correctly; remove and reinstall it.

33. To check the components for correct installation, perform the following procedures:
    a. Using a steel straight-edge, position it across the transaxle case.
    b. Using a depth micrometer or vernier scale, measure the distance from the input shaft flange to the upper straight-edge surface (A). Subtract the straight-edge's width from measurement (A); the final calculation is the input shaft flange-to-case distance, it should be 1.962–2.010 in. (49.82–51.06mm).
    c. If the measurement is not within specifications, disassemble the component parts and reinstall them properly.

34. To install the transaxle case housing, perform the following procedures:
    a. Using a new gasket, install the transaxle case housing; be sure the gasket does not protrude inside the housing.
    b. When installing the case bolts, notice that 3 have star-shaped grooves in their heads, these bolts require sealant on their threads; do not apply sealant on the other bolts. Torque the bolts to 12–16.5 ft. lbs. (16–23 Nm).

35. Using grease, apply it to the input shaft bearing race and install it (flange side outward), with the bearing, on the forward clutch; make sure the bearing does not get positioned on the race flange. Using grease, apply it to the other input shaft bearing race and install it onto the oil pump.

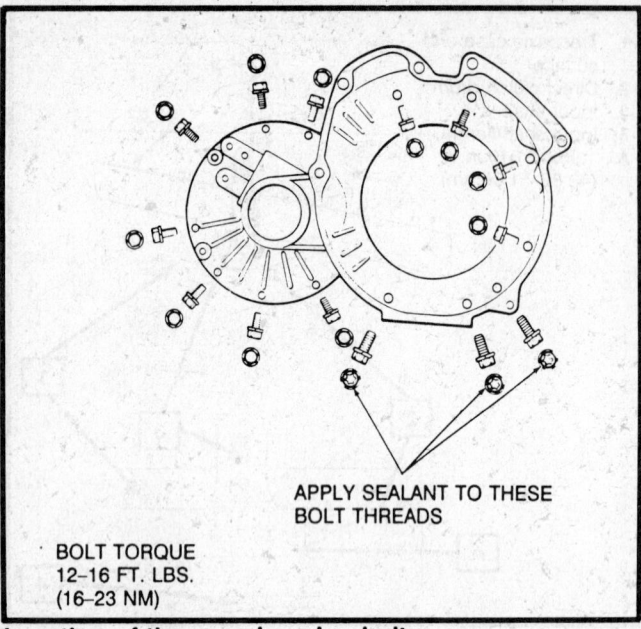

APPLY SEALANT TO THESE
BOLT THREADS

BOLT TORQUE
12–16 FT. LBS.
(16–23 NM)

Location of the case housing bolts

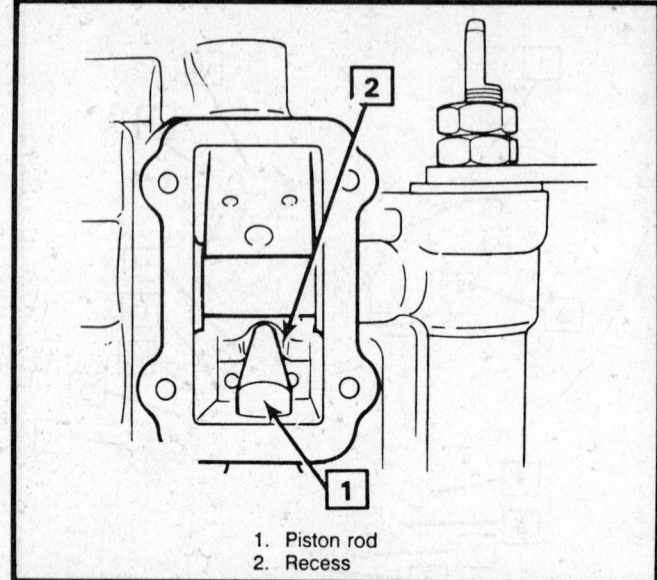

1. Piston rod
2. Recess

View of the 2nd brake piston rod and brake band recess

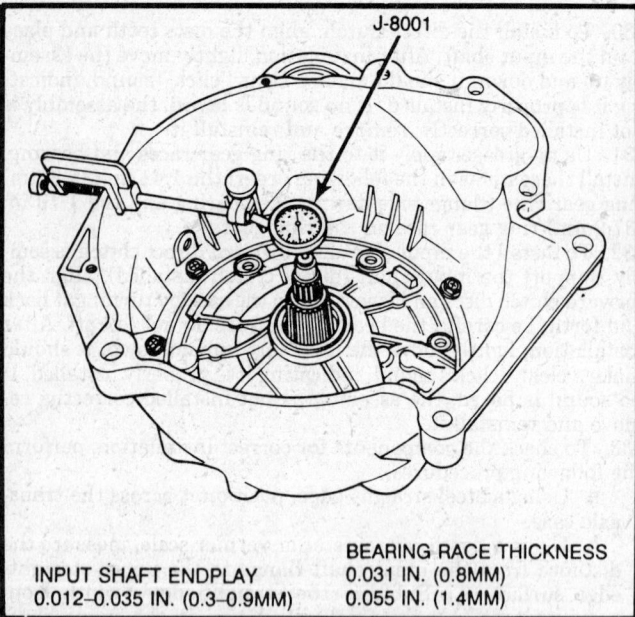

J-8001

INPUT SHAFT ENDPLAY
0.012–0.035 IN. (0.3–0.9MM)

BEARING RACE THICKNESS
0.031 IN. (0.8MM)
0.055 IN. (1.4MM)

Measuring the endplay of the input shaft

Piston rod length	Identification mark
121.3 mm (4.77 in)	Unmarked
122.7 mm (4.83 in)	Marked

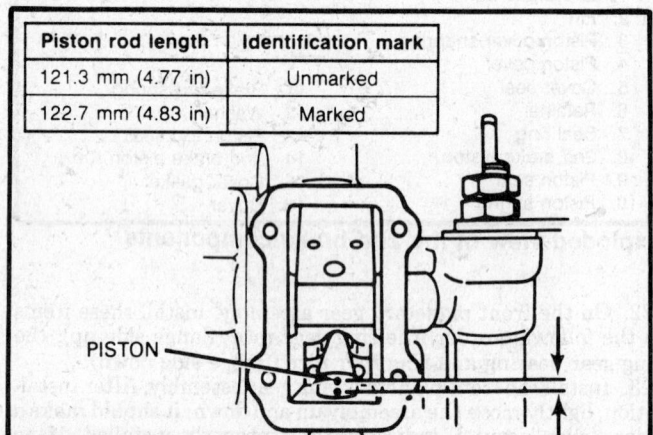

PISTON

Measuring the piston rod stroke

36. Using grease, apply it to the direct clutch washer and install it on the oil pump; fit the washer's flange into notch of the oil pump body.

37. Using grease, lubricate a new oil pump cover seal (O-ring) and install it the outer groove of the oil pump; make sure the seal is not twisted or extruded.

38. To install the oil pump, position the pump in the case, align the bolt holes and install the bolts. Make sure the direct clutch washer does not fall off and the input shaft seal rings or pump cover seal rings do not come off or get damaged. Torque the bolts to 13.5–19.5 ft. lbs. (18–27 Nm).

39. To check the input shaft endplay, perform the following procedures:

a. Using a dial indicator, position it on the tip of the input shaft and zero it.

b. Lift the input shaft and measure the amount of movement; it should be 0.012–0.035 in. (0.3–0.9mm). If the endplay is not within specifications, remove the oil pump and replace the input shaft bearing race (oil pump side).

40. To install the solenoid wiring harness, perform the following procedures:

a. Insert the solenoid wire holding plate in the groove of the solenoid wire grommet and the solenoid wire to the stud bolt.

b. Using a lock washer and a nut, secure the holding plate.

c. To the rear cover, install both solenoid wire clamps and secure them with the rear cover bolts.

41. To check the 2nd brake band for correct installation, look through the 2nd brake band cover hole to make sure the 2nd brake piston rod end is aligned with the center of the brake band recess. If the rod end contacts outside the brake band recess, insert a thin wire in the brake band fitting and pull the 2nd brake band up so it's recess aligns properly with the rod end.

42. To check the 2nd brake piston stroke, perform the following procedures:

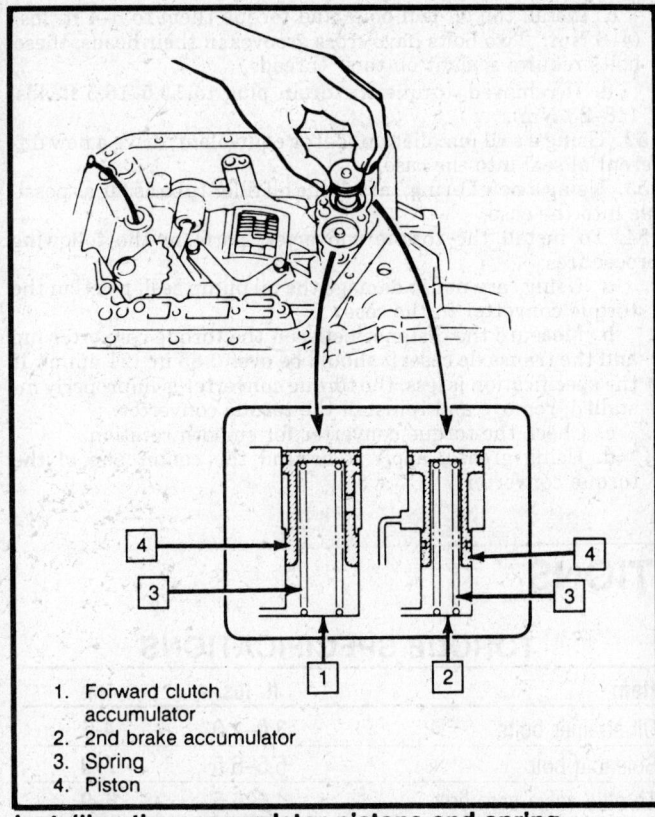

1. Forward clutch accumulator
2. 2nd brake accumulator
3. Spring
4. Piston

Installing the accumulator pistons and spring

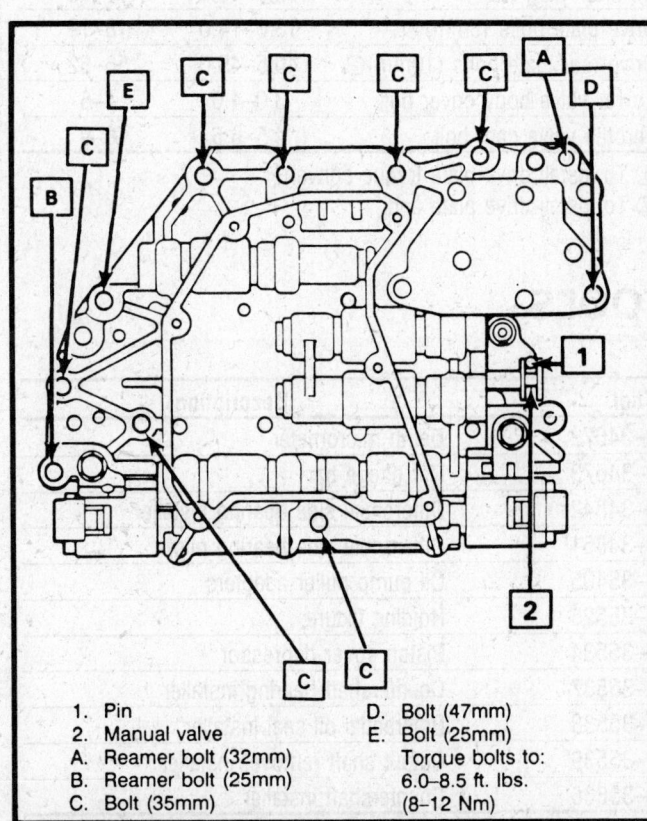

1. Pin
2. Manual valve
A. Reamer bolt (32mm)
B. Reamer bolt (25mm)
C. Bolt (35mm)
D. Bolt (47mm)
E. Bolt (25mm)
Torque bolts to:
6.0–8.5 ft. lbs.
(8–12 Nm)

Installing the lower valve body

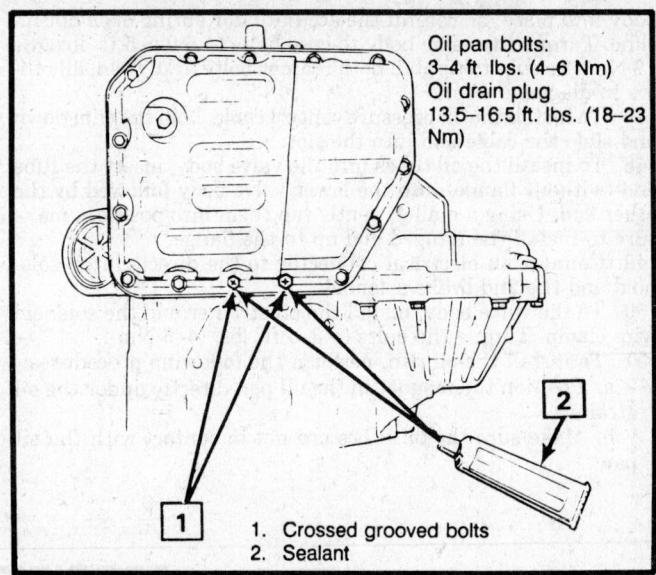

Oil pan bolts:
3–4 ft. lbs. (4–6 Nm)
Oil drain plug
13.5–16.5 ft. lbs. (18–23 Nm)

1. Crossed grooved bolts
2. Sealant

Installing the oil pan bolts

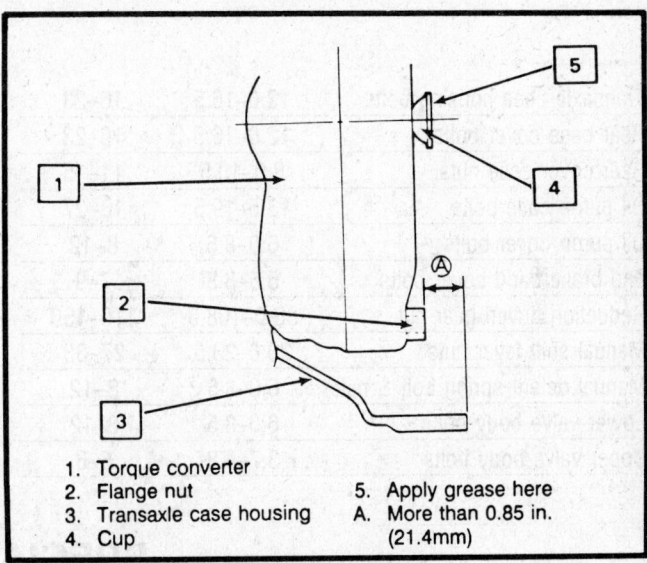

1. Torque converter
2. Flange nut
3. Transaxle case housing
4. Cup
5. Apply grease here
A. More than 0.85 in. (21.4mm)

Installation of the torque converter

   a. Scribe a mark on the piston rod.
   b. Apply low pressurized air into the oil hole and measure the 2nd brake piston rod stroke; it should be 0.06–0.11 in. (1.5–3.0mm).
   c. If out of specifications, replace the 2nd brake band or the piston rod (with a different length); the piston rod is available in 2 lengths.
43. Using a new gasket, install the 2nd brake band cover and torque the bolts to 5.5–6.5 ft. lbs. (7–9 Nm).
44. Install the oil pressure control cable into the case.
45. To install the accumulator pistons, perform the following procedures:
   a. Using Dexron®II fluid, dip the new seal rings and install them onto the pistons.
   b. Install the pistons in the case; be careful the seal rings do not fall off.
   c. Insert the spring into the 2nd brake accumulator piston.
46. To install the lower valve body into the case, align the manual valve with the manual shift lever pin and lower the valve

body into place; be careful the accumulator spring does not incline. Torque the valve body-to-case bolts to 6.0–8.5 ft. lbs. (8–12 Nm); be sure to tighten both reamer bolts first, then, all others in diagonal order.

47. To install the oil pressure control cable, hold the cam down and slide the cable end into the slot.

48. To install the oil tubes into the valve body, insert the tube end (without flange) into the lower valve body followed by the other end. Using a mallet, gently tap them into position; make sure to install the flanged end up to the flange.

49. Connect an electrical connector to the direct clutch solenoid and the 2nd brake solenoid.

50. To the valve body, install the oil strainer and the solenoid wire clamp. Torque the bolts to 3–4 ft. lbs. (4–6 Nm).

51. To install the oil pan, perform the following procedures:

   a. Position the magnet in the oil pan directly under the oil strainer.

   b. Make sure the oil tubes are not in contact with the oil pan.

   c. Install the oil pan bolts and torque them to 3–4 ft. lbs. (4–6 Nm). Two bolts have cross grooves in their heads; these bolts require sealant on their threads.

   d. If removed, torque the drain plug to 13.5–16.5 ft. lbs. (18–23 Nm).

52. Using a seal installation tool or equivalent, drive a new differential seal into the case.

53. Using a new O-ring, install the oil filler tube as far as possible into the case.

54. To install the torque converter, perform the following procedures:

   a. Using care not to damage the oil pump seal, position the torque converter in the case.

   b. Measure the distance between the torque converter lug and the transaxle case; it should be over 0.85 in. (21.4mm). If the specification is less, the torque converter is improperly installed; remove and reinstall the torque converter.

   c. Check the torque converter for smooth rotation.

   d. Using grease, apply it around the center cup of the torque converter.

SPECIFICATIONS

Transaxle case housing bolts	12.0–16.5	16–23
Rear case cover bolts	12.0–16.5	16–23
Rear cover case nuts	8.0–10.5	11–15
Oil pump case bolts	13.5–19.5	18–27
Oil pump cover bolts	6.0–8.5	8–12
2nd brake band cover bolts	5.5–6.5	7–9
Reduction driven gear nut	80.0–108.0	110–150
Manual shift lever nuts	20.0–23.5	27–33
Manual detent spring bolt & nut	6.0–8.5	8–12
Lower valve body bolts	6.0–8.5	8–12
Upper valve body bolts	3.7–4.3	5–6

TORQUE SPECIFICATIONS

Item	ft. lbs.	Nm
Oil strainer bolts	3.0–4.0	4–6
Solenoid bolt	5.5–6.5	7–9
Throttle valve cam bolt	4.5–6.5	6–9
Oil pan bolts	4–6	—
Oil drain plug	13.5–16.5	18–23
Drive plate bolts (8mm)①	13.0–14.0	18–19
Drive rear plate bolts (10mm)②	40.5–45.0	56–62
Lower valve body cover bolt	3.0–4.0	4–6
Throttle valve cam bolt	4.5–6.5	6–9

① To install drive plate torque converter
② To install drive plate and

SPECIAL TOOLS

Tool	Description
J–6125–B	Oil pump puller slide hammers
J–7079–2	Driver handle
J–8001	Dial indicator set
J–8092	Driver handle
J–9617	Oil pump seal installer
J–22888	Output shaft bearing installer
J–23327	Clutch spring compressor
J–23907	Slide hammer
J–25018–A	Clutch spring compressor adapter
J–29369	Differential bearing puller
J–29369–1	Countershaft ball bearing remover
J–29369–2	Countershaft roller bearing remover

Tool	Description
J–34672	Depth micrometer
J–34673	Flat gauge bar
J–34842	Differential side bearing installer
J–34851	Differential side bearing pilot
J–35495	Oil pump puller adapters
J–35525	Holding fixture
J–35534	Piston cover depressor
J–35537	Countershaft bearing installer
J–35538	Differential oil seal installer
J–35539	Output shaft remover/installer
J–35608	Countershaft installer

Section 4
AW4 Transmission
AMC/Jeep-Eagle

APPLICATION

1986–89 Cherokee, Wagoneer and Comanche

GENERAL DESCRIPTION

The AW-4 automatic transmission is a 4-speed, electronically controlled transmission. This transmission consists of a lockup torque converter, oil pump, 3 planetary gear sets, clutch and brake units, hydraulic accumulators, a valve body which is controlled by electronic solenoids and a transmission computer unit.

The valve body solenoids are activated by electrical signals generated from the transmission computer unit. Signal sequence is determined by throttle position and vehicle speed.

Transmission and Converter Identification

TRANSMISSION

The AW-4 automatic transmission identification plate is attached to the right rear side of the automatic transmission case. This data plate provides the transmission part number, build date, model code and transmission serial number. Also included on this identification tag are the year and month that the transmission was built.

CONVERTER

The AW-4 automatic transmission uses a lockup torque converter. The lockup mechanism consists of a sliding clutch piston, coil springs and clutch friction material. All of the lockup clutch components are incorporated inside of the torque converter assembly. The clutch friction material is attached to the torque converter front cover. The clutch piston and torsion springs are attached to the turbine hub. The function of the torsion springs is to dampen engine firing impulses and loads that occur during the initial phase of the torque converter lockup function.

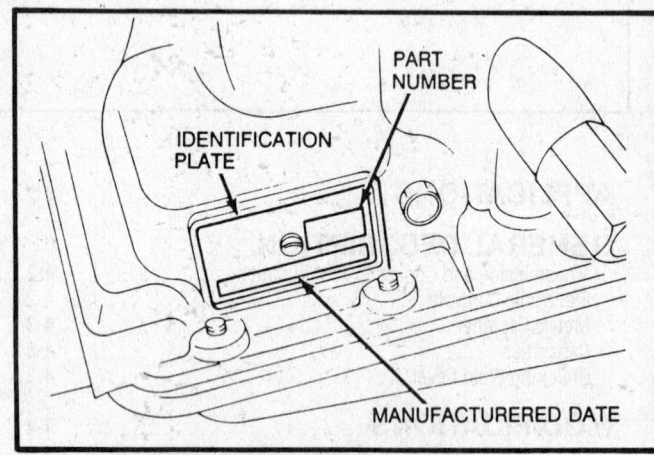

AW-4 transmission identification plate

Torque converter lockup is controlled by valve body solenoid number 3 and by the lockup relay valve. When lockup speed is reached, the solenoid routes line pressure to the lockup clutch through the relay valve. Lockup operation is provided in 2nd, 3rd, and 4th gear ranges only.

Electronic Controls

The AW-4 automatic transmission is electronically controlled in the forward gear ranges. The controls consist of the transmission computer unit, valve body solenoids, and sensors. These sensors monitor vehicle speed, throttle opening, shift lever position and brake pedal application.

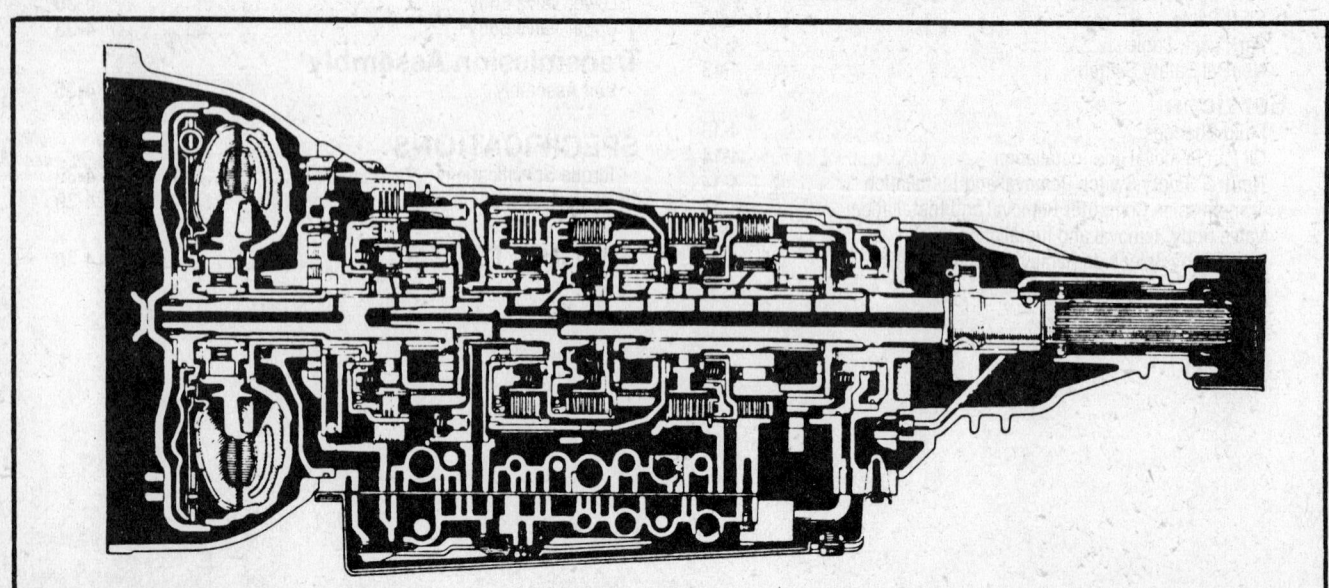

AW-4 automatic transmission

TRANSMISSION COMPUTER UNIT

The transmission computer unit determines shift and torque converter lockup timing based on signals received from the sensors. The transmission computer unit also activates and deactivates the valve body solenoids.

Two separate shift modes are programmed into the transmission computer unit. The first (comfort) mode, provides normal shift speeds and points. The second (power) mode, provides higher engine speeds and shift points when extra acceleration and torque are needed. Both of these shift modes are activated by a switch, which is located on the instrument panel.

The transmission computer unit incorporates a built in diagnostic program. Problems in the transmission circuitry or components can be diagnosed with the use of the MS1700 tester or the DRB II tester. Once the problem is noted it is stored in the transmission computer unit memory. The problem is stored until it is fixed and the computer is cleared by the technican. To erase the stored problem, disconnect and reconnect the **TRANS** fuse in the transmission computer unit wiring harness.

The transmission computer unit is located under the instrument panel on the passenger side of the vehicle.

VALVE BODY SOLENOIDS

The solenoids are mounted on the valve body and operated by the transmission control unit. These solenoids control operation of the torque converter lockup and shift valves in response to input signals from the transmission computer unit.

SENSORS

The sensors include the throttle position sensor, the speed sensor, the neutral safety switch and the brake pedal application switch.

The throttle position sensor is located on the throttle body. It electronically determines throttle position and relays this data to the transmission computer unit in order to control shift points and torque converter lockup.

The speed sensor consists of a rotor and a magnet. It is located on the transmission output shaft. A switch is mounted on the transmission extension housing or adapter. The sensor switch is activated each time the rotor and the magnet complete a revolution. The speed sensor signals are transmitted to the transmission computer unit through a wiring harness.

The neutral safety switch is located on the valve body manual shaft. The switch sends a signal from the shift linkage and manual valve position to the transmission computer unit, through an interconnecting wiring harness. The switch also prevents the engine from starting in any selectlor lever detent position other than **P** or **N**.

The brake application switch releases the lockup clutch in the torque converter whenever the vehicle brakes are applied. The switch is located on the brake pedal bracket and signals the transmission computer unit when the brake pedal is depressed or released.

Metric Fasteners

Metric tools will be required to service this transmission. Due to the large number of alloy parts used in this transmission, torque specifications should be strictly observed. Before installing capscrews into aluminum parts, dip the bolts into clean transmission fluid as this will prevent the screws from galling the aluminum threads, thus causing damage.

Metric fastener dimensions are very close to the dimensions of the familiar inch system fasteners. For this reason replacement fasteners must have the same measurement and strength as the original fastener.

Do not attempt to interchange meteric fasteners for inch system fasteners. Mismatched or incorrect fasteners can cause damage to the automatic transmission unit and possible personal injury. Care should be taken to reuse fasteners in their original locations.

Capacities

The fluid capacities are approximate and the correct fluid level should be determined by the dipstick indicator. After complete transmission overhaul the AW-4 transmission should hold approximately 8½ quarts of automatic transmission fluid. After pan and filter service, the AW-4 transmission should hold approximately 5 quarts of automatic transmission fluid. Transmissions used in 1986–88 vehicles should use Jeep automatic transmission fluid or Dexron® II. Transmissions used in 1989 vehicles should use Mercon® automatic transmission fluid.

Checking Fluid Level

The correct transmission fluid level is to the **FULL** mark on the dipstick indicator stick. Before checking the transmission fluid level be sure that the transmission is at normal operating temperature. Before checking the fluid level shift the transmission selector lever from the **P** detent to the **1–2** detent and then back into the **P** detent. Check the fluid level with the transmission selector lever in the **P** detent and the engine at curb idle speed.

The transmission fluid should be clear and free of foreign material or particles. If the transmission fluid is dark brown or black in color and smells burnt, it has been overheated and should be changed.

The transmission operation chould be checked if the unit contains large quanities of metal particles or clutch disc friction material. A small quanity of friction material or metal particles in the fluid pan is normal. These particles are usually generated during the brake in-period and indicate normal seating of the various transmission components.

The automatic transmission fluid should be changed every 30,000 miles or 30 months under normal driving conditions.

1. Run the engine until normal operating temperature is reached.

2. Position the vehicle on a flat surface. Depress the parking brake.

3. Check the idle speed and adjust, as required.

4. Move the transmission selector lever through all the shift detents and then position the selector lever in the **P** detent.

5. Remove the dipstick indicator level and wipe it clean. Insert the dipstick indicator level until it seats.

6. Remove the dipstick indicator level and check the fluid reading. It should be between the **ADD** and **FULL** marks on the dipstick. Correct the fluid level, as required.

7. Do not overfill the transmission, it takes about a pint of transmission fluid to raise the level from the **ADD** to the **FULL** mark on the dipstick indicator.

TRANSMISSION MODIFICATIONS

Information regarding any modifications to the AW-4 automatic transmission is not available at the time of publication.

TROUBLE DIAGNOSIS

CLUTCH AND BAND APPLICATION
AW–4 Automatic Transmission

Shift Lever Position	Gear	Valve Body Solenoid No.1	Valve Body Solenoid No.2	Over-Drive Clutch	Forward Clutch	Direct Clutch	Over-Drive Brake	Second Coast Brake	Second Brake	First/Reverse Brake	Over-Drive One-way Clutch	No. 1 One-way Clutch	No. 2 One-way Clutch
P	Park	On	Off	Applied	—	—	—	—	—	—	—	—	—
R	Reverse	On	Off	Applied	—	Applied	—	—	—	Applied	Applied	—	—
N	Neutral	On	Off	Applied	—	—	—	—	—	—	—	—	—
D	First	On	Off	Applied	Applied	—	—	—	—	—	Applied	—	Applied
	Second	On	On	Applied	Applied	—	—	—	Applied	—	—	Applied	Applied
	Third	Off	On	Applied	Applied	Applied	—	—	Applied	—	Applied	—	—
	OD	Off	Off	—	Applied	Applied	Applied	—	Applied	—	—	—	—
3	First	On	Off	Applied	Applied	—	—	—	—	—	Applied	—	Applied
	Second	On	On	Applied	Applied	—	—	Applied	Applied	—	Applied	Applied	—
	Third	Off	On	Applied	Applied	Applied	—	—	Applied	—	Applied	—	—
1–2	First	On	Off	Applied	Applied	—	—	—	—	Applied	Applied	—	Applied
	Second	On	On	Applied	Applied	—	—	Applied	Applied	—	Applied	Applied	—

CHILTON'S THREE C's TRANSMISSION DIAGNOSIS
AW–4 Transmission

Condition	Cause	Correction
Fluid discolored or smells burnt	a) Fluid contaminated b) Torque converter faulty c) Transmission faulty	a) Replace fluid b) Replace torque converter c) Disassemble and repair transmission
Vehicle does not move in any forward range or reverse	a) Shift linkage out of adjustment b) Valve body or primary regulator faulty c) Park lock pawl faulty d) Torque converter faulty e) Converter drive plate broken f) Oil pump intake screen blocked g) Transmission faulty	a) Adjust linkage b) Inspect/repair valve body c) Repair park pawl d) Replace torque converter e) Replace drive plate f) Clean screen g) Disassemble and repair transmission
Shift lever position incorrect	a) Shift linkage out of adjustment b) Manual valve and lever faulty	a) Adjust linkage b) Repair valve body
Harsh engagement (all ranges)	a) Throttle cable out of adjustment b) Valve body or primary regulator faulty c) Accumulator pistons faulty d) Transmission faulty	a) Adjust throttle cable b) Repair valve body c) Repair pistons d) Disassemble and repair

CHILTON'S THREE C's TRANSMISSION DIAGNOSIS
AW–4 Automatic Transmission

Condition	Cause	Correction
Delayed 1–2, 2–3 or 3–OD upshift or downshifts from 4–3 or 3–2 and shifts back to 4 or 3	a) Electronic control problem b) Valve body faulty c) Solenoid faulty	a) Find faulty part with MS 1700 tester or DRB II tester b) Repair valve body c) Repair solenoid
Slips on 1–2, 2–3 or 3–OD upshift or slips or shudders on take-off	a) Shift linkage out of adjustment b) LP cable out of adjustment c) Valve body faulty d) Solenoid faulty e) Transmission faulty	a) Adjust linkage b) Adjust cable c) Repair valve body d) Replace solenoid e) Disassemble and repair transmission
Drag or bind in 1–2, 2–3 or 3–OD upshift	a) Shift linkage out of adjustment b) Valve body faulty c) Transmission faulty	a) Adjust shift linkage b) Repair valve body c) Disassemble and repair transmission
No lockup in 2nd, 3rd or OD	a) Electronic control problem b) Valve body faulty c) Solenoid faulty d) Transmission faulty	a) Repair MS 1700 tester or DRB II tester b) Repair valve body c) Replace solenoid d) Disassemble and repair transmission
Harsh downshift	a) Throttle cable out of adjustment b) Throttle cable and cam faulty c) Accumulator pistons faulty d) Valve body faulty e) Transmission faulty	a) Adjust cable b) Replace cable and cam c) Repair pistons d) Repair valve body e) Transmission faulty
No downshift when coasting	a) Valve body faulty b) Solenoid faulty c) Electronic control problem	a) Repair valve body b) Replace solenoid c) Locate problem with MS 1700 tester or DRB II tester
Downshift late or early during coast	a) Throttle cable faulty b) Valve body faulty c) Transmission faulty d) Solenoid faulty e) Electronic control problem	a) Replace cable b) Repair valve body c) Disassemble and repair transmission d) Replace solenoid e) Locate problem with MS 1700 tester or DRB II tester
No OD–3, 3–2 or 2–1 kickdown	a) Solenoid faulty b) Electronic control problem c) Valve body faulty	a) Replace solenoid b) Locate problem with MS 1700 tester or DRB II tester c) Repair valve body
No engine braking in 1–2 position	a) Solenoid faulty b) Electronic control problem c) Valve body faulty d) Transmission faulty	a) Replace solenoid b) Loacte problem with MS 1700 tester or DRB II tester c) Repair valve body d) Disassemble and repair transmission
Vehicle does not hold in Park	a) Shift linkage out of adjustment b) Parking lock pawl cam and spring faulty	a) Adjust shift linkage b) Replace cam and spring

Hydraulic Control System

The hydraulic system consists of the transmission oil pump, the valve body and solenoids and 4 hydraulic accumulators.

The transmission fluid pump provides the required system lubrication and operating pressure.

The valve body controls the application of the clutches, brakes, second coast band and torque converter lockup clutch. The valve body solenoids control the sequencing of the 1–2, 2–3 and 3–4 shift valves within the valve body. The solenoids are activated by signals from the transmission computer unit.

The accumulators are used in the clutch and brake feed circuits to control initial apply pressure. Spring loaded accumulator pistons modulate the initial surge of apply pressure for smooth engagement.

TRANSMISSION OIL PUMP COMPONENTS

A rotor type oil pump is used in this transmission. The pump gears are mounted in the oil pump body. The drive gear is operated by the torque converter hub. Drive tangs on the hub engage in the drive slots of the drive gear.

VALVE BODY COMPONENTS

Automatic transmission working pressure is supplied to the clutch and brake apply circuits through the valve body assembly. The valve body consists of an upper body assembly, lower body assembly, separator plate and upper and lower gaskets. Various spool valves, sleeves, plugs and springs are also located within both valve body assembly sections. The manual valve, 1–2 shift valve, primary regulator valve, accumulator control valve, check balls, solenoids and oil strainers are located in the lower valve body assembly. The remaining control and shift valves plus check balls and an additional oil strainer are located in the upper valve body assembly.

The manual valve is operated by the gearshift linkage. The valve diverts fluid to the apply circuits according to shift lever position

The primary regulator valve modulates line pressure to the clutches and brakes according to engine load. The valve is actuated by throttle valve pressure. During high load operation, the valve increases line pressure to maintain positive clutch and

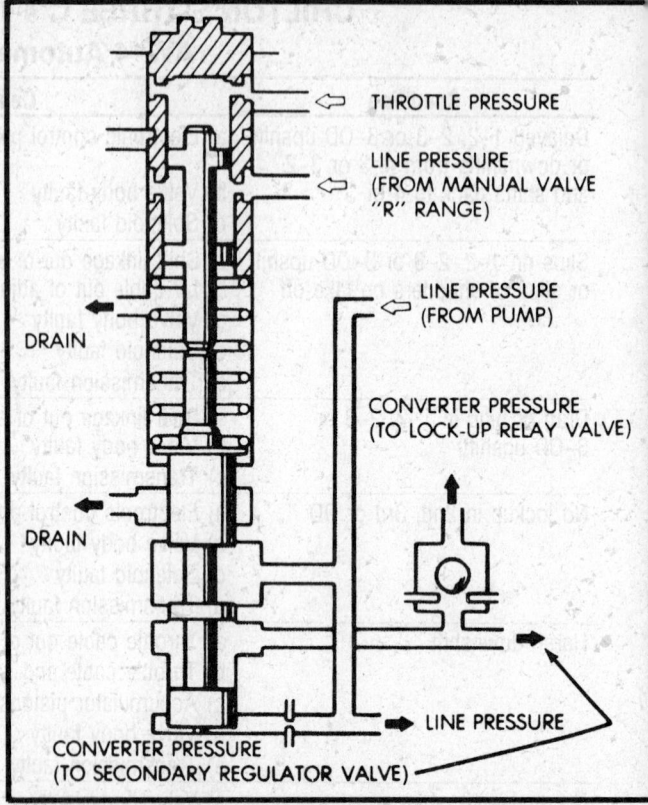

AW-4 transmission—primary regulator valve circuitry

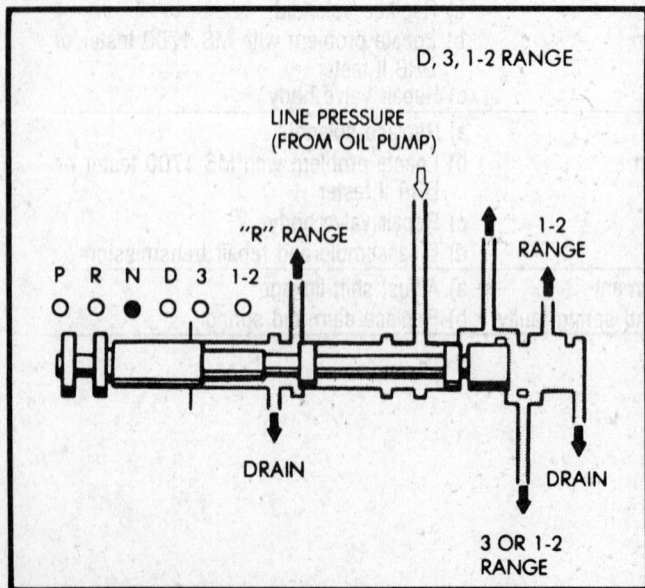

AW-4 transmission—manual valve circuitry

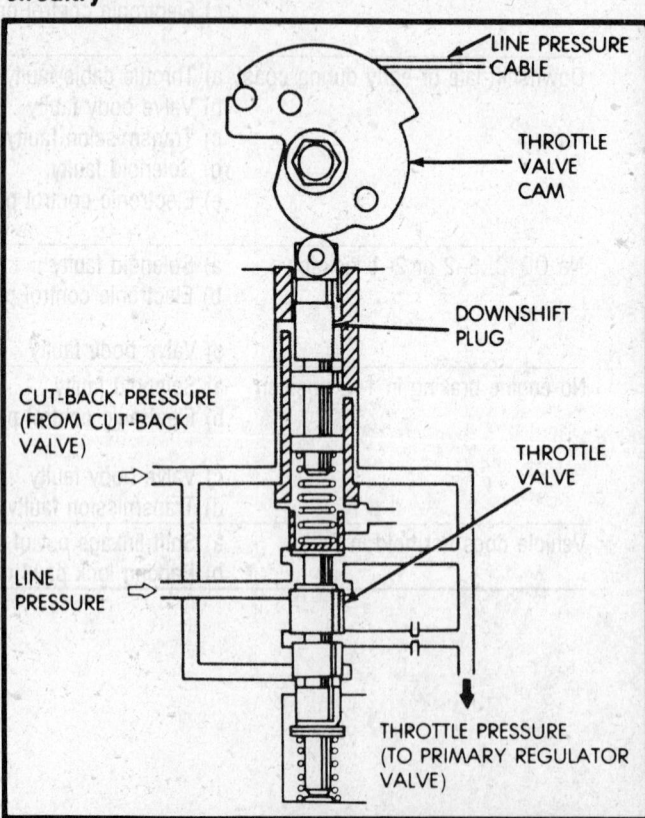

AW-4 transmission—throttle valve and downshift plug circuitry

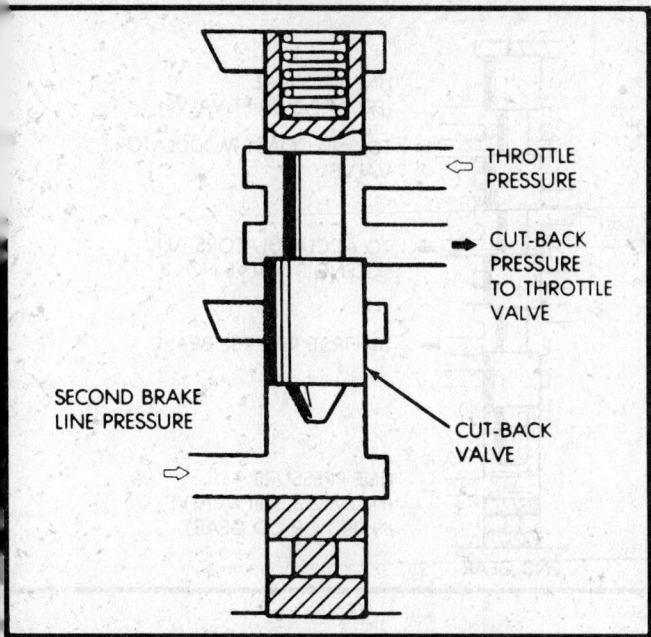

AW-4 transmission — cut back valve circuitry

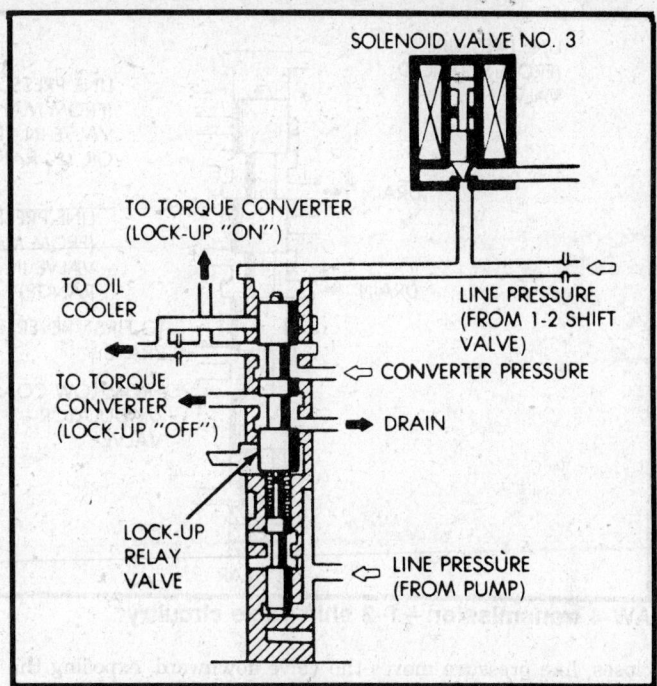

AW-4 transmission — lockup relay valve circuitry

brake engagement. At light load, the valve decreases line pressure just enough to maintain somooth engagemant.

The throttle valve and downshift plug control throttle pressure to the primary regulator valve. These valves are operated by the throttle valve cam line pressure cable in response to engine throttle position. Throttle valve pressure is also modulated by the cut back valve in 2nd, 3rd and 4th gear ranges.

The cut back valve helps prevent excessive pump pressure buildup in 2nd, 3rd and 4th gear. This valve is actuated by throttle pressure and by line pressure from the second brake. This valve also aids in regulating line pressure by controlling the amount of cut back pressure to the throttle valve.

The secondary regulator valve regulates converter lockup clutch and transmission lubrication pressure. When primary regulator valve pressure exceeds the specification for converter lockup clutch engagement or transmission lubrication, the secondary regulator valve is moved upward, exposing the drain port. Excess pressure than bleeds off, as required. As pressure drops, spring tension moves the valve downward closing the drain port.

The lockup relay valve controls the fluid flow to the torque converter lockup clutch. The valve is operated by line pressure from the 1–2 shift valve and is controlled by the third solenoid valve.

The 1–2 shift valve controls 1–2 upshifts and downshifts. The valve is operated by the second valve body solenoid and line pressure from the manual valve, second coast modulator valve and the 2–3 shift valve. When the transmission computer unit deactivates the solenoid, line pressure at the top of the valve moves the valve down, thus closing the second brake accumulator feed port. As the solenoid is activated and the drain port opens, spring force moves the valve upward and exposes the second brake feed port for the shift into 2nd gear.

The 2–3 shift valve controls 2–3 upshifts and downshifts. The valve is acutated by the first valve body solenoid and by line pressure from the manual valve and primary regulator valve. When the transmission computer unit activates the first valve body solenoid, line pressure at the top of the 2–3 valve is released through the solenoid drain port. Spring tension than moves the valve upward to hold the valve in the 2nd gear position. As the solenoid is deactivated, line pressure than moves

the valve down exposing the direct clutch feed port for the shift to 3rd gear.

The 3–4 shift valve is operated by the second valve body solenoid and by line pressure from the manual valve, the 2–3 valve and the primary regulator valve. As the transmission computer unit activates the second valve body solenoid, line pressure at the top of the 3–4 valve is released through the solenoid valve drain port. Spring tension than moves the valve upward, exposing the overdrive clutch accumulator feed port in order to apply the clutch. When the solenoid is deactivated and the drain port

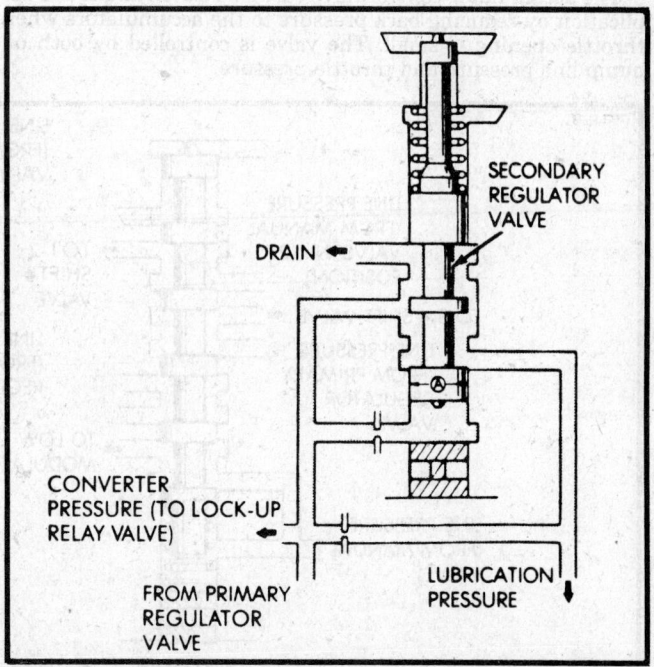

AW-4 transmission — secondary regulator valve circuitry

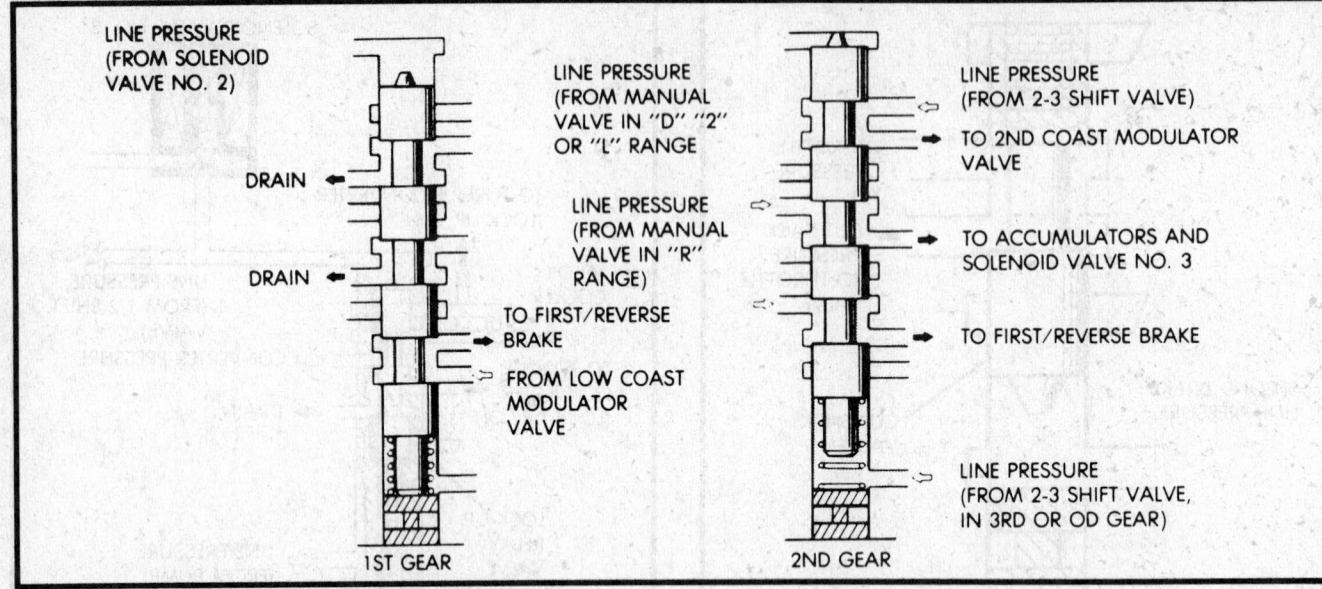

AW-4 transmission — 1-2 shift valve circuitry

closes, line pressure moves the valve downward, exposing the overdrive brake accumulator feed port for the shift into 4th gear. In the **1-2** or **3** gearshift lever detents, line pressure from the 2-3 shift valve is applied to the lower end of the 3-4 valve. This holds the valve upward thus closing off the overdrive brake feed port to prevent a shift into 4th gear.

The second coast modulator valve momentarily reduces line pressure from the 1-2 shift valve in order to cushion application of the second coast brake. The valve is operative only when the shift lever and manual valve are in the 3rd gear detent.

The low coast modulator valve momentarily reduces line pressure from the 2-3 shift valve to cushion the application of the first/reverse brake. The valve is operative only when the shift lever and the manual valve are in the 1-2 gear detent.

The accumulator control valve cushions clutch and brake application by reducing back pressure to the accumulators when throttle opening is small. The valve is controlled by both oil pump line pressure and throttle pressure.

This transmission uses 3 valve body solenoids. The first and second valve body solenoids control shift valve operation by applying or releasing line pressure as indicated by the transmission computer unit signal. The third valve body solenoid controls operation of the torque converter lockup clutch in response to signals from the transmission computer unit. When the first and second valve body solenoids are activated, the solenoid plunger is moved off of its seat thus opening the drain port to release line pressure. When either solenoid is deactivated, the plunger closes the drain port. The third valve body solenoid operates in reverse. When the solenoid is deactivated, the solenoid plunger is moved from its seat thus opening the drain port in order to release line pressure. When the solenoid is activated, the plunger closes the drain port.

ACCUMULATORS

Four accumulators are used to cushion the application of the clutches and brakes. The accumulators consist of spring loaded

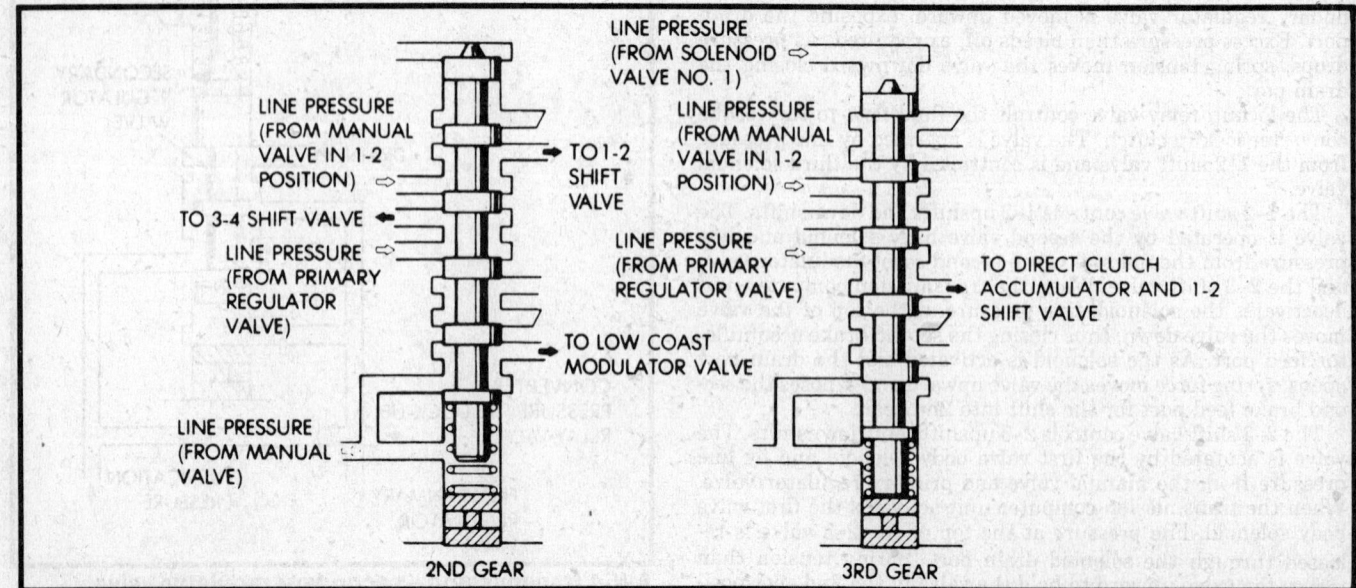

AW-4 transmission — 2-3 shift valve circuitry

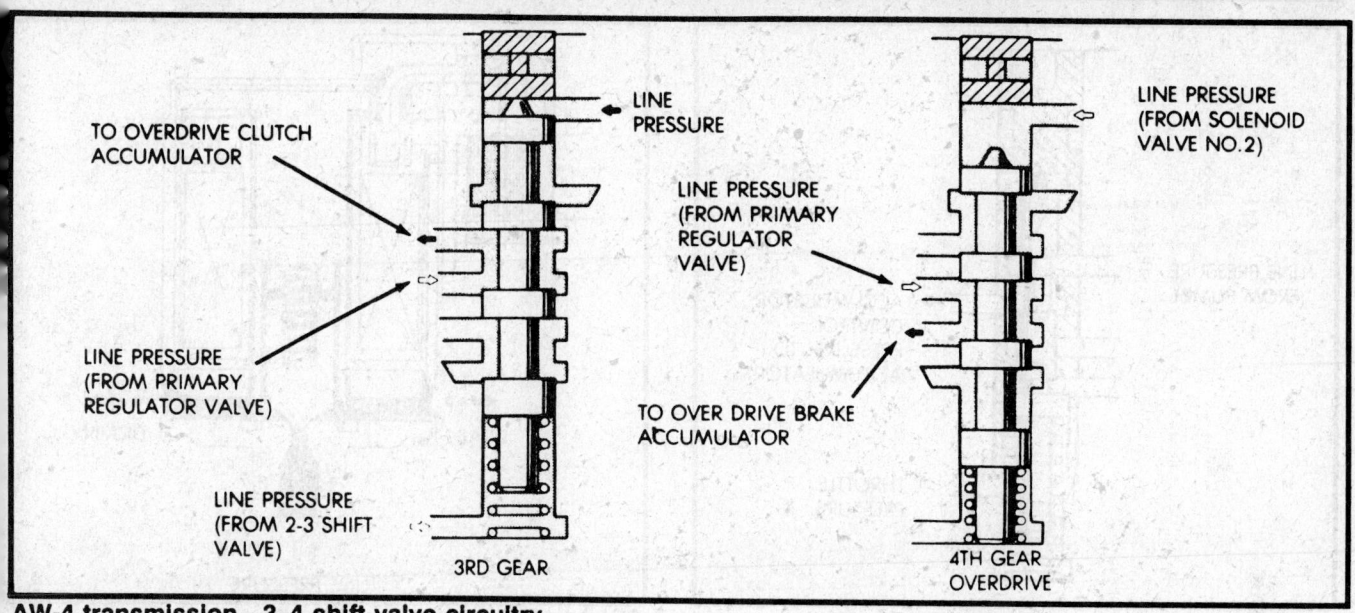

AW-4 transmission – 3–4 shift valve circuitry

pistons which dampen the initial surge of apply pressure in order to provide smooth engagement during transmission gear shifts. Control pressure from the accumulator control valve is continously applied to the back pressure side of the accumulator pistons. This pressure, plus spring tension holds the pistons down. As line pressure from the shift valves enters the opposite end of the piston bore, control pressure and spring tension momentarily delay application of full line pressure in order to cushion engagement. All of the accumulators are located inside the transmission case assembly.

Diagnosis Tests

The AW-4 automatic transmission is an electronically controlled transmission. Shift points and sequence in the forward gear ranges are controlled by the transmission computer unit.

Before attempting transmission repair, it will be necessary to determine if the transmission is at fault and than whether the fault is mechanical or electrical.

The transmission computer unit that is used with the AW-4 transmission has a self diagnostic program. The program is compatible with the MS1700 tester or the DRB II tester. The tester will identify faults in the electrical control system. The road test, control pressure test, stall speed test and time lag test will identify faults in the mechanical functions of the transmission.

PRE TEST DATA

1. Check and adjust the shift linkage.
2. Check line pressure cable operation. Correct, as required.
3. Check engine throttle operation. Correct, as required.

AW-4 transmission – second coast modulator valve circuitry

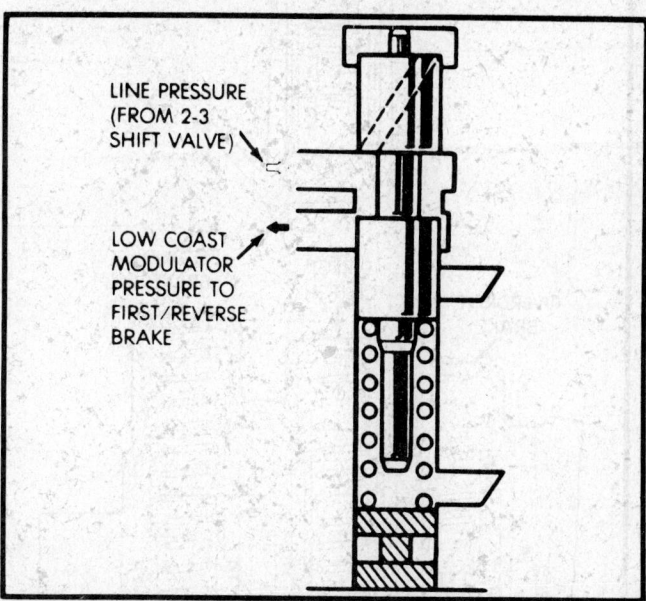

AW-4 transmission – low coast modulator valve circuitry

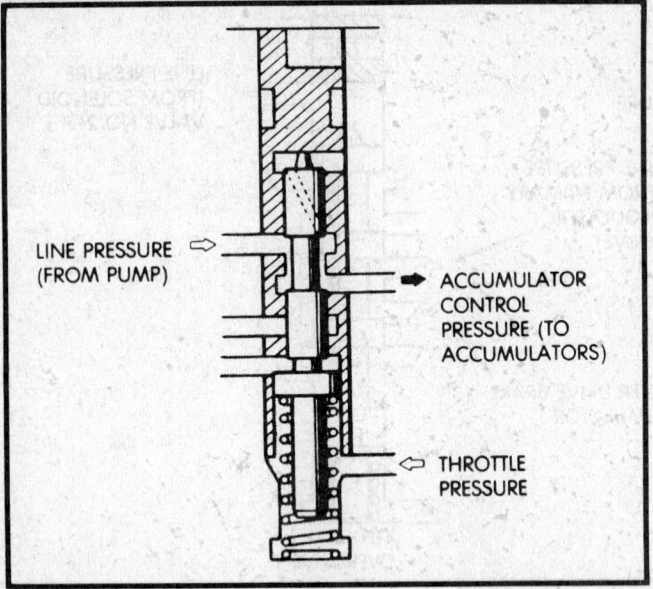

AW-4 transmission – accumulator control valve circuitry

4. Check transmission fluid level. Correct, as required.
5. Check the neutral safety switch. Adjust, as required.
6. Check TPS adjustment and operation. Adjust or replace the sensor, as required.

MANUAL SHIFTING TEST

1. Stop the engine. Disconnect the transmission computer unit or the transmission computer unit fuse.

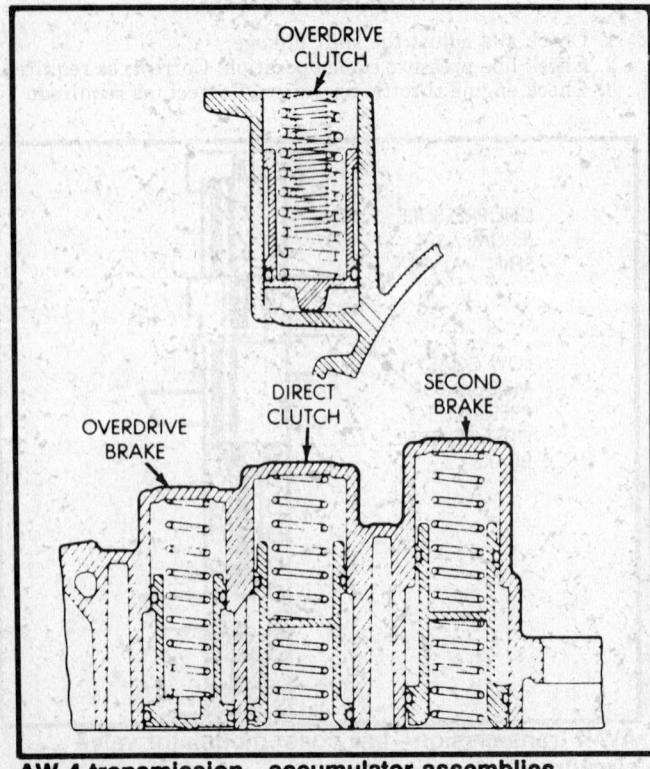

AW-4 transmission – accumulator assemblies

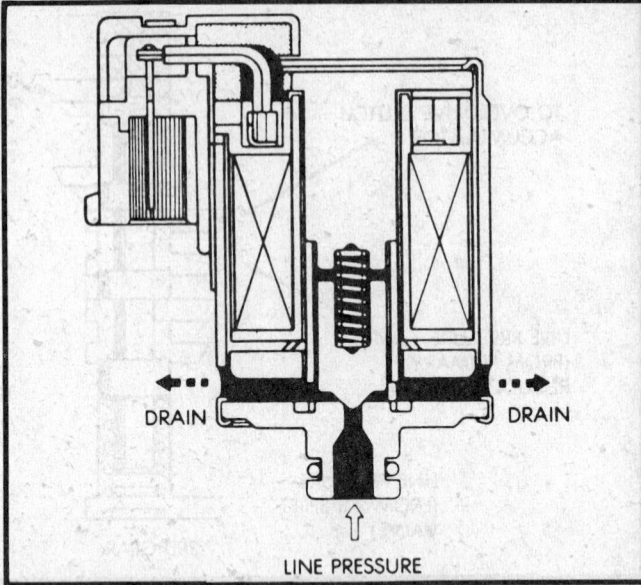

AW-4 transmission – valve body solenoids

2. Road test the vehicle. Shift the transmission selector lever into each gear range.
3. The transmission should lock in the **P** detent. The transmission should back up in the **R** detent. The transmsision should not move in the **N** detent.
4. The transmission should have 1st gear only when the selector lever is positioned in the **1-2** detent. The transmission should have 3rd gear only when the selector lever is positioned in the **3** detent. The transmission should have overdrive (4th) gear only when the selector lever is positioned in the **D** detent.
5. If the transmission does not operate as indicated, refer to the diagnosis charts. Do not perform the stall speed test or the timelag test.
6. If the transmission does perform as indicated, and all forward gear ranges were not difficult to distinguish, continue the road test.
7. Manually downshift the transmission from the **D** detent to the **3** detent and than from the **3** detent to the **1–2** detent. Manually upshift the transmission through all forward ranges.

NOTE: Do not overspeed the engine during this test. Ease off the throttle and allow the vehicle to slow down before downshifting.

8. If the transmission operation is acceptable, perform the stall speed test, time lag test and the control pressure test.
9. If a transmission shifting problem is encountered, refer to the diagnosis charts.

CONTROL PRESSURE TEST

1. Run the engine until the transmission reaches normal operating temperature.
2. Connect the control pressure gauge to the test port, which is located on the passenger side of the transmission.
3. Depress the parking brake. Block the drive wheels. Check and adjust the engine idle speed. Apply the service brakes.

NOTE: Do not allow anyone to stand in front of or behind the vehicle while the following steps are being performed.

4. Shift the transmission into the **D** detent. Record the line pressure with the engine at idle speed. The control pressure specification should be 53–61 psi.

5. With the selector lever in the **D** detent, depress the accelerator to the wide open throttle position. Record the line pressure. The control pressure specification should be 161–196 psi. Do not maintain wide open throttle for more than a few seconds at a time.

6. Shift the transmission into the **R** detent. Record the line pressure with the engine at idle speed. The control pressure specification should be 73–87 psi.

7. With the selector lever in the **R** detent, depress the accelerator to the wide open throttle position. Record the line pressure. The control pressure specification should be 223–273 psi. Do not maintain wide open throttle for more than a few seconds at a time.

8. If the control line pressure is not within specification, adjust the line pressure cable and repeat the control pressure test.

9. If the line pressures are higher than specification, check for a defective line pressure cable, or a worn, sticking or damaged throttle valve, downshift plug, throttle cam or primary regulator valve.

10. If the line pressures are lower than specification, check for a defective line pressure cable, or a worn, sticking or damaged throttle valve, downshift plug, throttle cam or primary regulator valve. Also check for defective oil pump gears and housing and a worn overdrive clutch assembly.

11. If the line pressure is low in the **D** detent, check the forward clutch assembly for wear and damage. Also check for fluid leakage in the drive circuit.

12. If the line pressure is low in the **R** detent, check the shift linkage and the manual valve for proper adjustment. Check the direct clutch assembly and the first/reverse brake for wear and damage. Also check for fluid leakage in the reverse circuit.

AIR PRESSURE TEST

The air pressure test can be used to determine if cross passages are present within the transmission case or valve body assembly. This test is also used to determine if the clutch passages are open.

STALL SPEED TEST

1. Run the engine until the transmission reaches normal operating temperature.

2. Connect a tachometer to the engine, position it so that it can be viewed from the drivers seat.

3. Depress the parking brake. Block the drive wheels. Check and adjust the engine idle speed. Apply the service brakes.

4. If equipped with 4WD, shift the transfer case into 2WD **HIGH** position. Start the engine.

NOTE: Do not allow anyone to stand in front of or behind the vehicle while the following steps are being performed.

5. Shift the transmission selector lever into the **D** detent. Depress the accelerator to the wide open throttle position and record the maximum rpm reading. Stall speed should be 2100–2400 rpm. Do not maintain wide open throttle for more than a few seconds at a time.

6. Release the throttle and shift the transmission into the **N** detent. Allow the transmission fluid to cool for about 15–20 seconds.

7. Shift the transmission selector lever into the **R** detent. Depress the accelerator to the wide open throttle position and record the maximum rpm reading. Stall speed should be 2100–2400 rpm. Do not maintain wide open throttle for more than a few seconds at a time.

8. If the engine rpm specification is lower than specification, check engine performance. Check the stator clutch in the torque converter, as it may not be holding if the engine rpm speed was less than 1500 rpm.

9. If the engine rpm specification is higher than specification, check for low fluid level, low line pressure or the overdrive one-way clutch not holding.

10. If the engine rpm specification is higher than specified in the **D** range, check for low line pressure, forward clutch slippage, the number 2 one-way clutch not holding or the overdrive one-way clutch not holding.

11. If the engine rpm specification is higher than specified in the **R** range, check for low line pressure, direct clutch slippage, first/reverse brake slippage or the overdrive one-way clutch not holding.

ROAD TEST

When road testing the vehicle, be sure that the transmission is at normal operating temperature. Operate the transmission in each shift detent to check for slipping or any variation in the shifting patern. Note whether the shifts are harsh or spongy. By utilizing the clutch and band application chart with any malfunctions noted, the defective unit or circuit can be found.

TIME LAG TEST

The time lag test checks the general condition of the overdrive clutch, forward clutch, rear clutch and first/reverse brake. Condition is indicated by the amount of time required for clutch/brake engagement with the engine at normal idle speed. Engagement time is measured for the **D** and **R** detents.

1. Check and adjust the transmission fluid level. Run the engine until the transmission reaches normal operating temperature.

2. Depress the parking brake. Turn the air conditioning off. If equipped with 4WD, shift the transfer case into the 2WD **HIGH** position.

3. Start the engine and check the idle speed, correct as required.

4. Position the transmission selector lever in the **N** detent. Set the stop watch.

5. During the following tests, start the stop watch as soon as the selector lever reaches the **D** and **R** detents.

6. Shift the transmission selector lever into the **D** detent and record the time it takes for engagement. Engagement time should be 1.2 seconds maximum. Repeat the test at least twice.

7. Reset the stop watch. Shift the transmission selector lever into the **N** detent.

8. Shift the transmission selector lever into the **r** detent and record the time it takes for engagement. Engagement time should be 1.5 seconds maximum. Repeat the test at least twice.

9. If engagement is longer than specification with the selector lever in the **D** detent, check for misadjusted shift linkage, low line pressure, worn forward clutch assembly or a worn and damaged overdrive clutch.

10. If engagement is longer than specification with the selector lever in the **R** detent, check for misadjusted shift linkage, low line pressure, worn direct clutch assembly, worn first/reverse brake or a worn and damaged overdrive clutch.

ON CAR SERVICES

Adjustments

THROTTLE CABLE

1. Turn the ignition switch to the **OFF** position.
2. Fully retract the cable plunger. Press the cable button all the way down. Push the cable button inward.

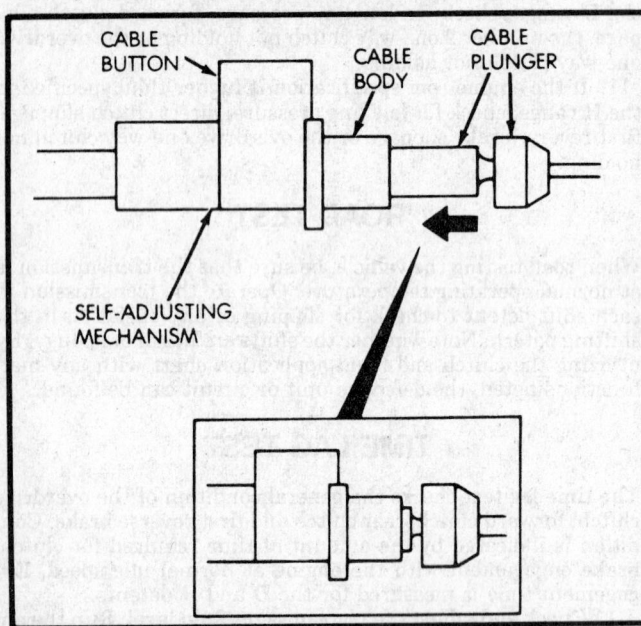

AW-4 transmission—throttle cable adjustment

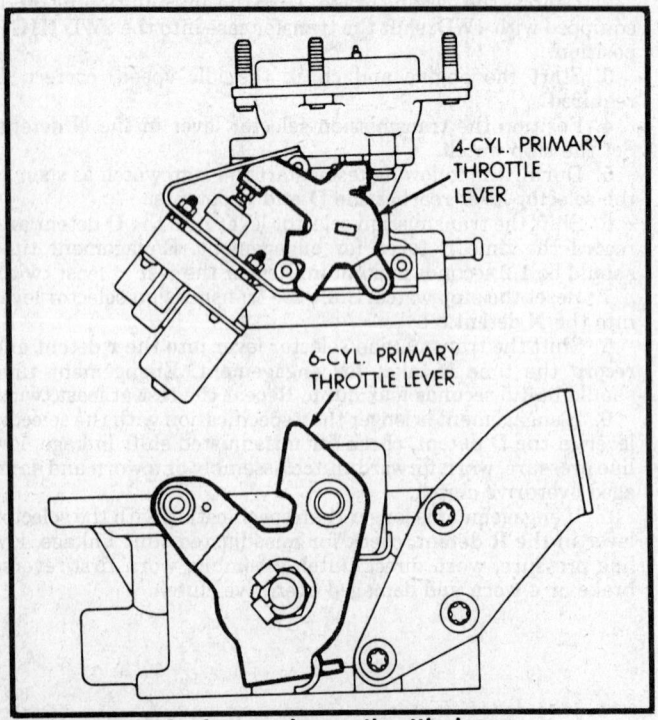

AW-4 transmission—primary throttle lever positioning

3. Rotate the primary throttle lever to the wide open throttle lever position and let the cable plunger extend.
4. Release the lever when the plunger is fully extended. The cable is now adjusted.

THROTTLE POSITION SENSOR

1. Loosen the TPS adjusting screws. Partially retighten a retaining screw in order to secure the sensor for adjustment.
2. If a voltmeter is used for adjustment, connect the positive lead to terminal **B** and the negative lead to terminal **D**.
3. If the MS1700 tester or the DRB II tester is being used, connect it according to the manufacturers instructions.
4. Observe the equipment reading and rotate the TPS until output voltage is 82% of input voltage, or about 4.2 volts.
5. Tighten the TPS retaining screws. Recheck the adjustment.
6. If required output voltage cannot be obtained or input voltage is considerably less than 5.0 volts, replace the TPS assembly.

SHIFT CABLE ADJUSTMENT

1. Be sure that the transmission selector lever is in the **P** detent.
2. Raise and support the vehicle safely.
3. Release the cable adjuster clamp in order to unlock the cable. Unsnap the cable from the bracket.
4. Move the transmission selector lever all the way rear ward into the **P** detent. The lever is located on the manual valve shaft at the left side of the transmission case.

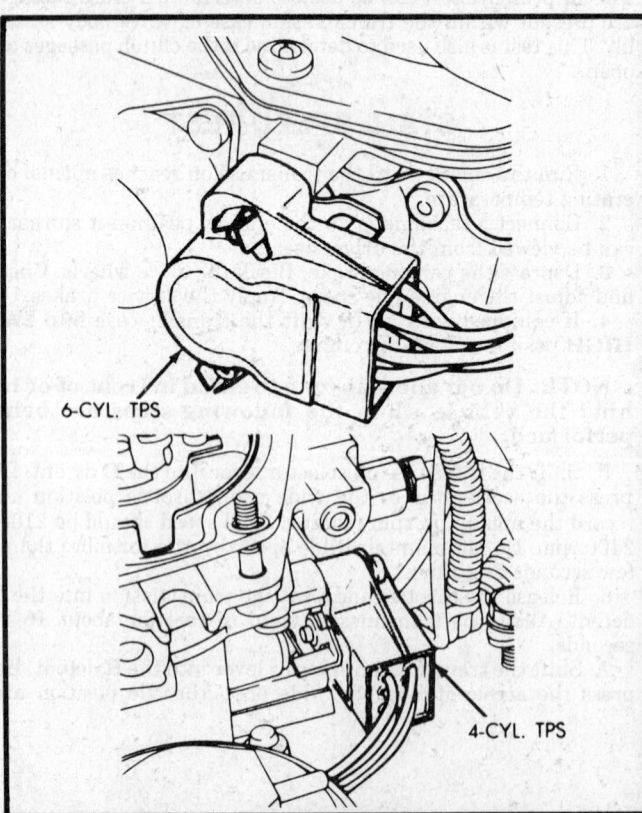

AW-4 transmission—throttle position sensor identification

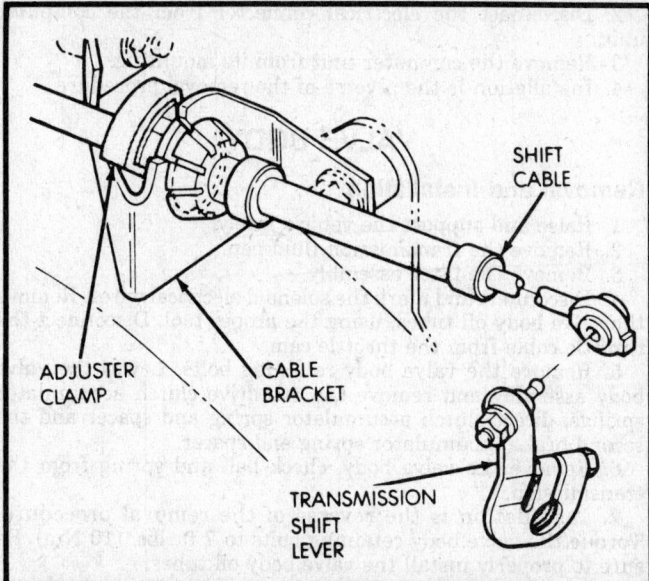

AW-4 transmission—shift cable adjustment

5. Verify that the transmission is in the **P** position by attempting to rotate the driveshaft, it should not turn.
6. Snap the cable into the cable bracket. Lock the cable by pressing the cable adjuster clamp down until it snaps into place.
7. The engine should only start in the **P** or **N** detent.

PARK LOCK CABLE ADJUSTMENT

1. Be sure that the transmission selector lever is in the **P** detent.
2. Be sure that the ignition switch is in the **LOCK** position.
3. Remove the shift lever bezel and console screws. Raise the bezel and the console to gain access to the cable.
4. Pull the cable lock button upward in order to release the cable.
5. Pull the cable forward. Release the cable and press the cable lock button down until it snaps into place.
6. Check the movement of the release shift handle button on vehicles equipped with a floor shifter, it should not press inward.
7. Check the movement of the release lever on vehicles equipped with a column shifter, the selector lever should not move.
8. Turn the ignition switch to the **ON** position.
9. If equipped with a floor shifter, press the shifter release button. If equipped with a column shifter, move the selector lever.
10. Shift the selector lever into the **N** detent. If the cable adjustment is correct, the ignition switch cannot be turned to the **LOCK** position.
11. Shift the selector lever into the **D** detent. If the cable adjustment is correct, the ignition switch cannot be turned to the **LOCK** position.
12. Position the selector lever into the **P** detent. Check the ignition switch operation. It is correct if the ignition switch can be turned to the **LOCK** position and the release button, on floor shifter equipped vehicles or the selector lever, on column shifter equipped vehicles does not move.

NEUTRAL SAFETY SWITCH

1. Position the transmission selector lever in the **N** detent.
2. Raise and support the vehicle safely.

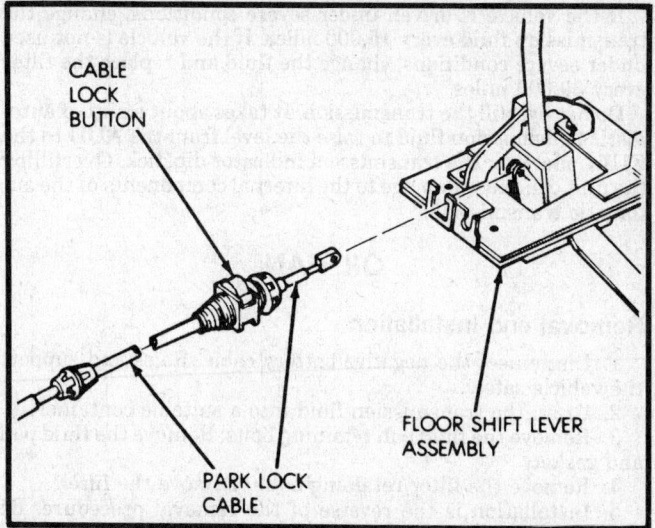

AW-4 transmission—park lock cable adjustment

3. Loosen the switch retaining bolt. Rotate the switch in order to align the neutral standard line with the vertical groove on the manual valve shaft.
4. Align the switch standard line with the groove or flat on the manual valve shaft.
5. Torque the switch adjusting bolt to 9 ft. lbs. (13 Nm). Bend the washer lock tabs over the switch retaining nut in order to secure it in place.
6. Lower the vehicle and check the switch operation.

Services
FLUID CHANGES

The conditions under which the vehicle is operated is the main consideration in determining how often the transmission fluid should be changed. Different driving conditions result in different transmission fluid temperatures. These temperatures affect change intervals.

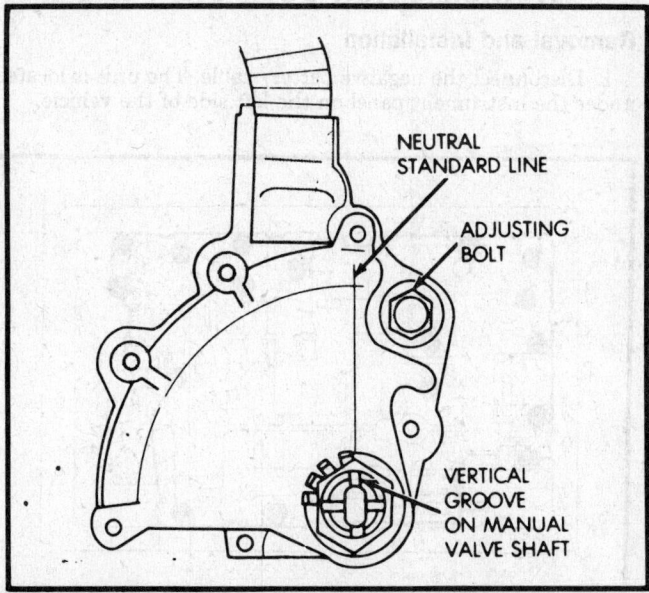

AW-4 transmission—neutral safety switch adjustment

If the vehicle is driven under severe conditions, change the transmission fluid every 15,000 miles. If the vehicle is not used under severe conditions, change the fluid and replace the filter every 30,000 miles.

Do not overfill the transmission. It takes about a pint of automatic transmission fluid to raise the level from the **ADD** to the **FULL** mark on the transmission indicator dipstick. Overfilling the unit can cause damage to the internal components of the automatic transmission.

OIL PAN

Removal and Installation

1. Disconnect the negative battery cable. Raise and support the vehicle safely.
2. Drain the transmission fluid into a suitable container.
3. Remove the fluid pan retaining bolts. Remove the fluid pan and gasket.
4. Remove the filter retaining bolts. Remove the filter.
5. Installation is the reverse of the removal procedure. Be sure to use a new gasket or RTV sealant, as required.
6. Fill the transmission to specification with the proper grade and type automatic transmission fluid.
7. Run the engine until the transmission reaches normal operating temperature. Recheck the fluid level and correct, as required.

NEUTRAL SAFETY SWITCH

Removal and Installation

1. Disconnect the negative battery cable. Raise and support the vehicle safely.
2. Disconnect the electrical connector from the switch assembly.
3. Pry the washer lock tabs upward. Remove the switch retaining nut and the tabbed washer.
4. Remove the switch adjusting bolt. Slide the neutral safety switch off of the manual valve shaft.
5. Installation is the reverse of the removal procedure. Adjust the neutral safety switch, as required.

TRANSMISSION COMPUTER UNIT

Removal and Installation

1. Disconnect the negative battery cable. The unit is located under the instrument panel on the left side of the vehicle.

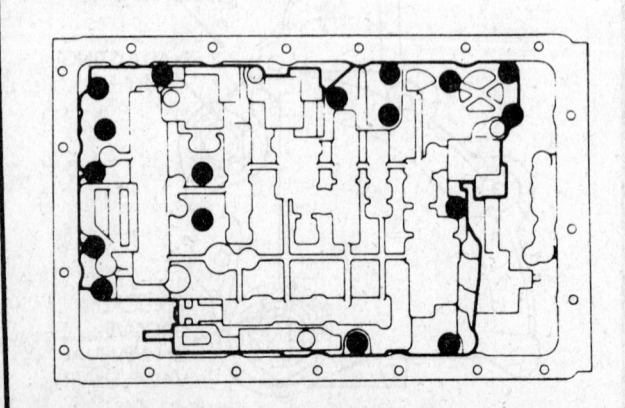

AW-4 transmission—valve body retaining bolt location

2. Disconnect the electrical connector from the computer unit.
3. Remove the computer unit from its mounting.
4. Installation is the reverse of the removal procedure.

VALVE BODY

Removal and Installation

1. Raise and support the vehicle safely.
2. Remove the transmission fluid pan.
3. Remove the filter assembly.
4. Disconnect and mark the solenoid electrical wires. Remove the valve body oil tubes, using the proper tool. Disconnect the throttle cable from the throttle cam.
5. Remove the valve body retaining bolts. Lower the valve body assembly and remove the overdrive clutch accumulator springs, direct clutch accumulator spring and spacer and the second brake accumulator spring and spacer.
6. Remove the valve body, check ball and spring from the transmission.
7. Installation is the reverse of the removal procedure. Torque the valve body retaining bolts to 7 ft. lbs. (10 Nm). Be sure to properly install the valve body oil tubes.

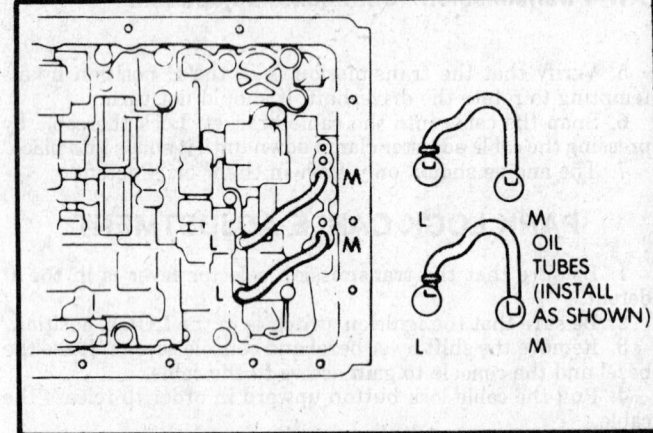

AW-4 transmission—valve body oil tube installation

8. Be sure to use a new gasket or RTV sealant, as required. Fill the transmission to specification with the proper grade and type automatic transmission fluid.
9. Run the engine until the transmission reaches normal operating temperature. Recheck the fluid level and correct, as required.

VALVE BODY SOLENOIDS

Removal and Installation

1. Raise and support the vehicle safely.
2. Remove the transmission fluid pan. Remove the filter assembly.
3. Disconnect and mark the solenoid electrical wires. Remove the solenoid retaining bolt. Remove the solenoid from the valve body.

NOTE: Be sure that no other components fall out of the valve body when the solenoids are removed from the valve body.

4. To test the solenoid connect the test leads of an ohmmeter to the solenoid mounting bracket and to the solenoid wire terminal. Resistance should be 11–15 ohms. Replace the solenoid, as required.
5. Installation is the reverse of the removal procedure.

Torque the solenoid retaining bolts to 7 ft. lbs. (10 Nm).

6. Be sure to use a new gasket or RTV sealant, as required. Fill the transmission to specification with the proper grade and type automatic transmission fluid.

7. Run the engine until the transmission reaches normal operating temperature. Recheck the fluid level and correct, as required.

MANUAL VALVE SHAFT SEAL

Removal and Installation

1. Disconnect the negative battery cable. Raise and support the vehicle safely.
2. Remove the neutral safety switch. Remove the transmission fluid pan. Remove the valve body assembly.
3. Remove the bolts that retain the park rod bracket to the transmission case. Remove the park rod from the shift sector.
4. Cut the spacer sleeve, using a chisel. Remove it from the manual valve shaft.
5. Remove the pin from the shaft and sector, using a punch. Remove the shaft and the sector from the transmission case.
6. Pry the shaft seals out of the transmission case.
7. Inspect the components for wear and damage. Repair or replace defective components as required.
8. Installation is the reverse of the removal procedure. Be sure to coat the new seals with petroleum jelly prior to installation.
9. Be sure to use a new gasket or RTV sealant, as required. Fill the transmission to specification with the proper grade and type automatic transmission fluid.
10. Run the engine until the transmission reaches normal operating temperature. Recheck the fluid level and correct, as required.

THROTTLE CABLE

Removal and Installation

1. Disconnect the negative battery cable.
2. Disconnect the throttle cable from the throttle linkage. Compress the cable mounting ears and remove the cable from the linkage bracket.
3. Raise and support the vehicle safely. Remove the transmission fluid pan.
4. Disengage the cable from the throttle valve cam. Remove the cable bracket bolt. Remove the cable and the bracket from the transmission.
5. Remove and discard the cable seal.
6. Installation is the reverse of the removal procedure. Be sure to lubricate the new seal with clean transmission fluid prior to installation.
7. Be sure to use a new gasket or RTV sealant, as required. Fill the transmission to specification with the proper grade and type automatic transmission fluid.
8. Run the engine until the transmission reaches normal operating temperature. Recheck the fluid level and correct, as required.

ACCUMULATOR PISTONS AND SPRINGS

Removal and Installation

1. Disconnect the negative battery cable. Raise and support the vehicle safely.
2. Drain the transmission fluid. Remove the transmission fluid pan and filter assembly. Remove the valve body assembly.
3. Using compressed air, remove the accumulator pistons. To accomplish this, apply air through the small feed hole next to each accumulator piston bore. Catch the accumulator piston assembly as it exits the bore.

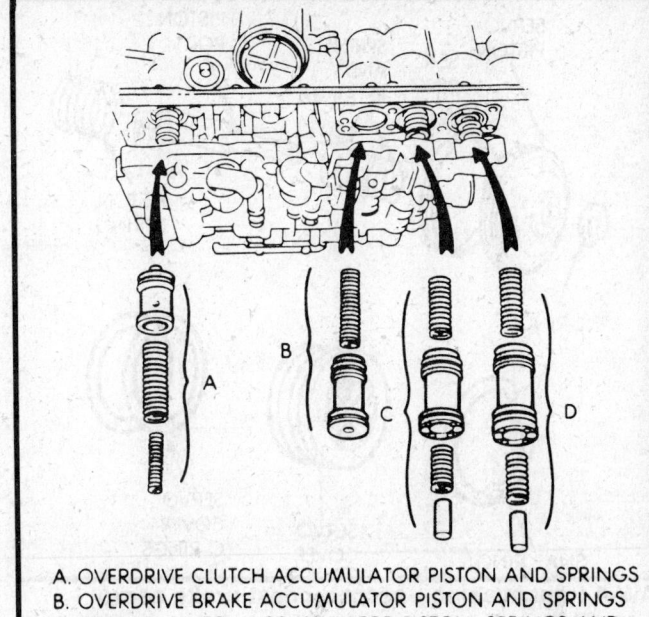

A. OVERDRIVE CLUTCH ACCUMULATOR PISTON AND SPRINGS
B. OVERDRIVE BRAKE ACCUMULATOR PISTON AND SPRINGS
C. SECOND CLUTCH ACCUMULATOR PISTON, SPRINGS AND SPACER
D. SECOND CLUTCH ACCUMULATOR PISTON, SPRINGS AND SPACER

AW-4 transmission—accumulator piston assembly

NOTE: Use only enough air pressure to ease each accumulator piston out of the bore. Mark each accumulator piston assembly for reinstallation. Do not intermix the accumulator piston assemblies.

4. Remove and discard the accumulator piston O-ring seals. Check the accumulator piston springs, replace as required. Check the accumulator piston assemblies, repair or replace defective components as required.
5. Installation is the reverse of the removal procedure. Be sure to lubricate the O-rings with clean transmission fluid prior to installation.
6. Be sure to use a new gasket or RTV sealant, as required. Fill the transmission to specification with the proper grade and type automatic transmission fluid.
7. Run the engine until the transmission reaches normal operating temperature. Recheck the fluid level and correct, as required.

SECOND COAST BRAKE SERVO

Removal and Installation

1. Disconnect the negative battery cable. Raise and support the vehicle safely.
2. Drain the transmission fluid. Remove the transmission fluid pan and filter assembly. Remove the valve body assembly.
3. Using compressed air, remove the servo piston and cover. To accomplish this, apply air through the oil hole in the servo boss to ease the piston out of the bore.
4. Remove and discard the seal and O-rings from the cover and piston. Repair or replace defective components, as required.
5. Installation is the reverse of the removal procedure. Be sure to lubricate the O-rings with clean transmission fluid prior to installation.
6. Be sure that the servo piston rod is properly engaged in the second coast brake band.
7. Be sure to use a new gasket or RTV sealant, as required.

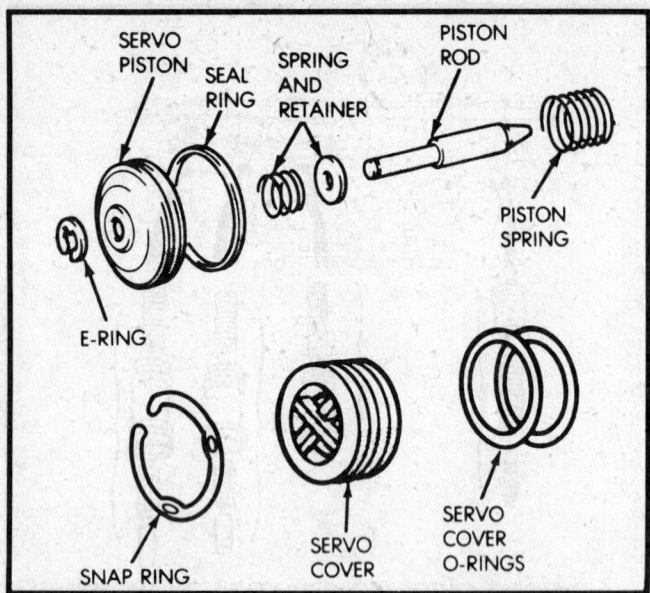

AW-4 transmission—second coast brake servo assembly

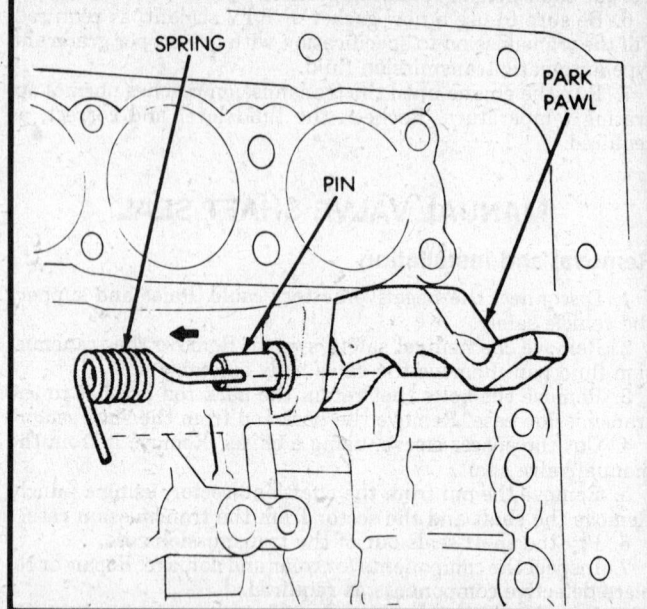

AW-4 transmission—parking pawl spring installation

Fill the transmission to specification with the proper grade and type automatic transmission fluid.

8. Run the engine until the transmission reaches normal operating temperature. Recheck the fluid level and correct, as required.

PARK ROD AND PAWL

Removal and Installation

1. Disconnect the negative battery cable. Raise and support the vehicle safely.
2. Drain the transmission fluid. Remove the transmission fluid pan and filter assembly. Remove the valve body assembly.
3. Remove the bolts that retain the park lock bracket to the transmission case. Remove the park lock rod from the manual valve shaft sector. Remove the park rod.
4. Remove the park pawl, pin and spring. Repair or replace defective components as required.
5. Installation is the reverse of the removal procedure. Be sure that the spring is properly positioned.
6. Be sure to use a new gasket or RTV sealant, as required. Fill the transmission to specification with the proper grade and type automatic transmission fluid.

7. Run the engine until the transmission reaches normal operating temperature. Recheck the fluid level and correct, as required.

REAR OIL SEAL

Removal and Installation

1. Disconnect the negative battery cable. Raise and support the vehicle safely.
2. As necessary, disconnect or remove the driveshaft, crossmember, shift linkage, electrical connectors, hoses, transfer case and exhaust system in order to gain access to the rear oil seal.
3. On 4WD vehicles, remove the seal from the adaptor housing, using the proper tool.
4. On 2WD vehicles, remove the dust shield and remove the seal from the extension housing, using the proper tool.
5. Installation is the reverse of the removal procedure. Fill the transmission to specification with the proper grade and type automatic transmission fluid.
6. Run the engine until the transmission reaches normal operating temperature. Recheck the fluid level and correct, as required.

REMOVAL AND INSTALLATION

TRANSMISSION REMOVAL

1. Disconnect the negative battery cable. Remove the transmission dipstick indicator.
2. Raise and support the vehicle safely. Drain the transmission fluid.
3. Remove the upper half of the transmission dipstick tube. Disconnect and plug the fluid cooler lines.
4. Properly support the engine and the transmission assembly, using the proper equipment.
5. Disconnect the transmission linkage. Disconnect the transfer case linkage, if equipped with 4WD.

6. Disconnect all the required electrical and vacuum connections. Disconnect the speedometer cable.
7. Remove the required exhaust system components. Remove the driveshaft. If equipped wth 4WD, remove the front driveshaft.
8. Remove the rear crossmember. Disconnect the transmission throttle cable.
9. Remove the starter. Remove the torque converter to flex plate retaining bolts.
10. Remove the torque converter housing to engine retaining bolts.
11. Properly secure the transmission and the transfer case, if equipped to a transmission jack.

12. Remove the assembly from the vehicle. Remove the torque converter from the transmission. Separate the transmission from the transfer case, if equipped.

TRANSMISSION INSTALLATION

1. Position and secure the transmission on the transmission jack. Install the torque converter. If equipped, install the transfer case.

2. Install the assembly. Install the torque converter housing to engine retaining bolts. Install the torque converter to flex plate retaining bolts.

3. Install the starter. Connect the transfer case linkage, vacuum lines and electrical connections, if equipped.

4. Install the required exhaust components. Install the rear crossmember.

5. Install the driveshaft. Install the front driveshaft, if equipped.

6. Connect the speedometer cable. Connect the transmission electrical harness. Connect the fluid lines.

7. Connect the throttle valve cable. Install the upper dipstick tube into the lower dipstick tube, using a new O-ring.

8. Lower the vehicle. Fill the transmission to specification with the proper grade and type automatic transmission fluid.

9. Run the engine until the transmission reaches normal operating temperature. Recheck the fluid level and correct, as required.

BENCH OVERHAUL

Before Disassembly

Cleanliness is an important factor in the overhaul of the AW-4 automatic transmission. Before opening up this unit, the entire outside of the transmission assembly should be cleaned, preferable with a high pressure washer such as a car wash spray unit. Dirt entering the transmission internal parts will negate all the time and effort spent on the overhaul. During inspection and reassembly all parts should be thoroughly cleaned with solvent then dried with compressed air. Wiping cloths and rags should not be used to dry parts since lint will find its way into the valve body passages.

Wheel bearing grease, long used to hold thrust washers and lube parts, should not be used. Lube seals with clean transmission fluid and use ordinary unmedicated petroleum jelly to hold the thrust washers and to ease the assembly of seals, since it will not leave a harmful residue as grease often will. Do not use solvent on neoprene seals, friction plates if they are to be reused, or thrust washers. Be wary of nylon parts if the transmission failure was due to failure of the cooling system. Nylon parts exposed to water or antifreeze solutions can swell and distort and must be replaced.

Before installing bolts into aluminum parts, always dip the threads into clean transmission fluid. Antiseize compound can also be used to prevent bolts from galling the aluminum and seizing. Always use a torque wrench to keep from stripping the threads. Take care when installing new O-rings, especially the smaller O-rings. The internal snaprings should be expanded and the external rings should be compressed, if they are to be reused. This will help insure proper seating when installed.

Converter Inspection

After the torque converter is removed from the transmission, the stator roller clutch can be checked by inserting a finger into the splined inner race of the roller clutch and trying to turn the race in both directions. The inner race should turn freely in the clockwise direction, but not turn in the counterclockwise direction. The inner race may tend to turn in the counterclockwise direction, but with great difficulty, this is to be considered normal. Do not use such items as the driven sprocket support or the shafts to turn the race, as the results may be misleading. Inspect the outer hub lip and the inner bushing for burrs or jagged edges to avoid injury to your fingers when testing the torque converter.

Transmission Disassembly

1. Position the transmission assembly in a suitable holding fixture.

2. The converter pulls out of the transmission. Be careful since the converter contains a large amount of fluid.

3. Remove both halves of the dipstick indicator tube. Remove the clamp that attaches the wire harness and throttle pressure cable to the transmission.

4. Remove the shift lever from the manual valve shaft at the left side of the transmission.

5. Remove the neutral safety switch. If equipped, remove the speedometer driven gear. Remove the speed sensor.

6. Remove the torque converter housing retaining bolts. Separate the torque converter housing from the transmission assembly.

7. On 2WD vehicles, remove the extension housing retaining bolts. Remove the extension housing from the transmission case.

8. On 4WD vehicles, remove the adaptor housing retaining bolts. Remove the adaptor housing from the transmission case.

9. On 2WD vehicles, use an inside micrometer and measure the inside diameter of the extension housing bushing. The diameter should be 1.4996 in. (38.09mm) or less. If not within specification, replace the extension housing.

10. Remove the speedometer drive gear snapring. Remove the gear and the gear spacer, if equipped.

11. Remove the speed sensor rotor and key. Position a block of wood between the rotor and the transmission in order to remove the rotor.

12. Remove the transmission fluid pan. Remove the filter.

13. Remove the valve body oil feed tubes. Disconnect the solenoid electrical wires.

14. Remove the harness bracket bolt. Remove the harness and the bracket.

15. Remove the valve body retaining bolts. Disconnect the throttle cable from the throttle cam. Remove the valve body from the transmission.

16. Remove the accumulator springs, spacers and check ball and spring.

17. Using compressed air, remove the second brake and clutch accumulator pistons. Apply air pressure through the feed port and ease the pistons out of the bore.

18. Using compressed air, remove the overdrive brake accumulator piston and the overdrive clutch accumulator piston. Remove the throttle cable.

19. Remove the oil pump retaining bolts. Using a suitable puller remove the oil pump assembly from the transmission. Remove the race from the oil pump.

20. Pull out the 4th gear overdrive planetary gear and overdrive direct clutch assembly. Remove the race from the 4th gear overdrive planetary.

21. Remove the thrust bearing, race and overdrive planetary ring gear.

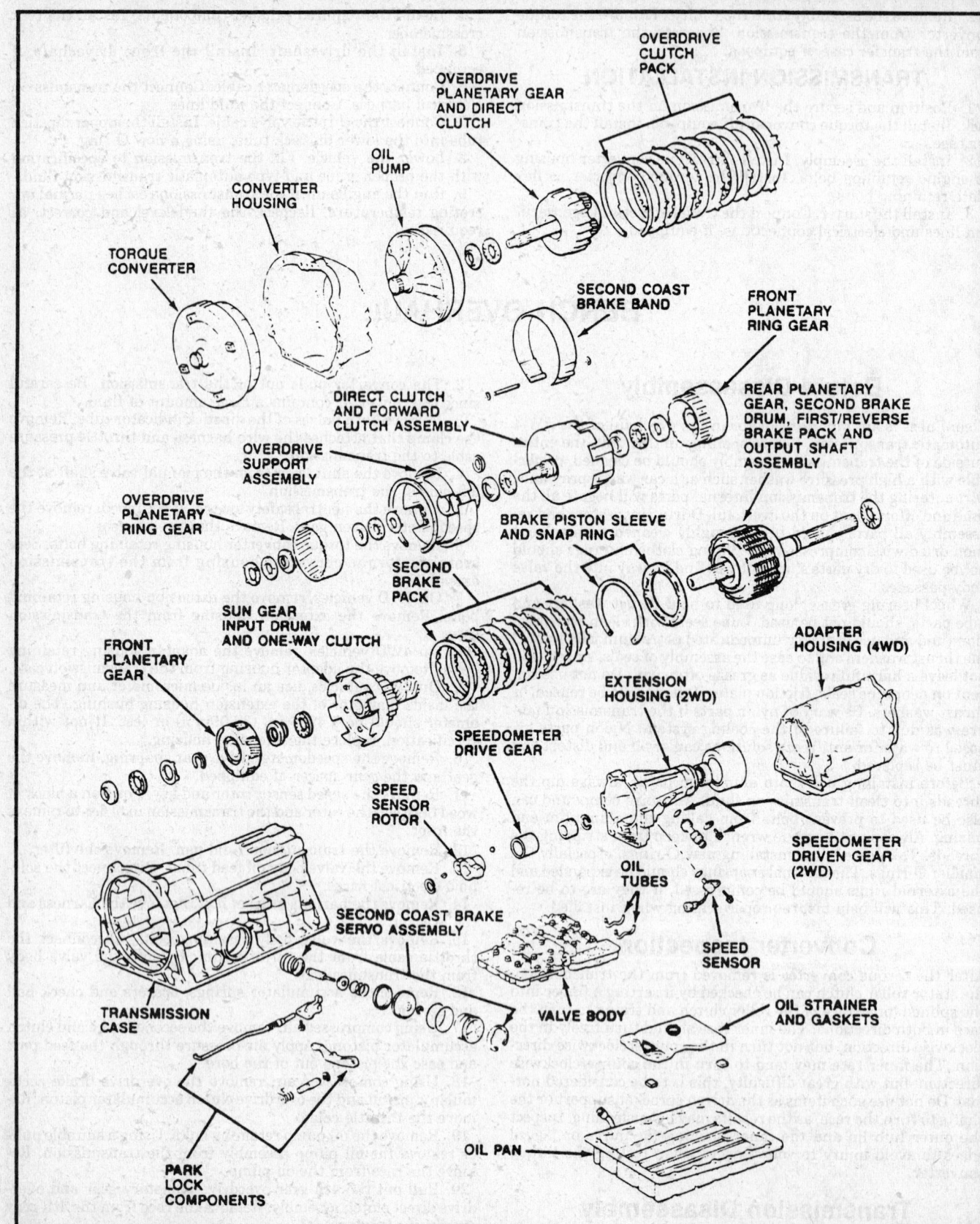

AW-4 transmission—exploded view of major assemblies

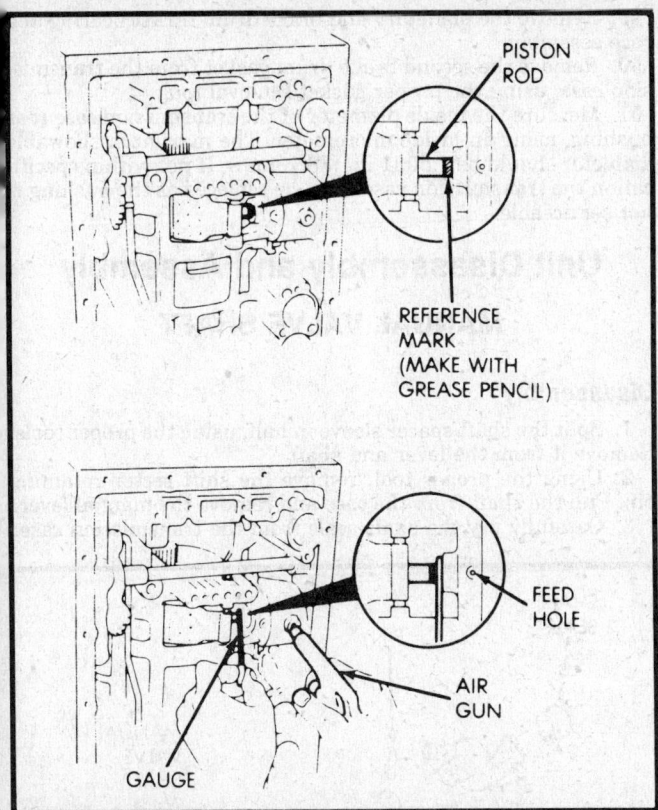

AW-4 transmission – second coast piston rod stroke measurement

22. To measure the stroke length of the overdrive brake piston, install a dial indicator gauge on the transmission case.

23. Mount the gauge tool so that it contacts the piston. Apply 57–114 psi air pressure through the piston apply port.

24. Note the piston stroke reading on the dial indicator gauge, it should be 0.055–0.669 in. (1.40–1.70mm) for vehicles equipped with a 6 cylinder engine and 0.052–0.0638 in. (1.32–1.62mm) for vehicles equipped with a 4 cylinder engine. If not within specification, replace the brake pack retainer.

OVERDRIVE BRAKE RETAINER SELECTION

Retainer	Thickness	
No.	in.	mm
26	0.130	3.3
25	0.138	3.5
12	0.124	3.6
24	0.146	3.7
11	0.150	3.8
23	0.154	3.9
Not Marked	0.157	4.0

25. Remove the overdrive brake snapring. Remove the overdrive support lower race. Remove the upper bearing and race assembly.

26. Remove the overdrive support bolts. Remove the overdrive support snapring, using the proper tool.

27. Using a bridge type puller, remove the overdrive support from the transmission case.

28. Remove the race from the hub of the overdrive support. Remove the overdrive brake discs and plates.

29. Measure the disc thickness using a micrometer. Minimum disc thickness specification should be 0.0724 in. (1.84mm). Replace the discs if not within specification.

30. To measure the stroke length of the second coast brake piston, make a reference mark on the piston rod.

31. Apply 57–114 psi of air pressure through the piston feed hole and check the stroke length using gauge tool BVIFM-40/41 or equivalent.

32. The stroke length specification should be 0.059–0.118 in (1.5–3.0mm). If not within specification, install a new piston rod and recheck the stroke length.

NOTE: Replacement piston rods are available in 2.811 in (71.4mm) length or 2.870 in. (72.9mm) length.

33. If the stroke length is still not correct, replace the second coast brake band.

34. Using tool BVIFM-29 or equivalent, remove the second coast brake piston snapring. Remove the piston cover and piston assembly by applying compressed air through the piston feed hole.

35. Disassemble the second coast brake piston, as required.

36. Remove the direct and the forward clutch assembly. Remove the thrust bearing and the race from the clutch hub.

37. Remove the second coast brake band E-clip from the band pin. Remove the brake band.

38. Remove the front planetary ring gear front bearing race. Remove the front planetary ring gear.

39. Remove the thrust bearing and the rear race from the ring gear. Remove the planetary thrust race.

40. To relieve the load on the planetary snapring, loosen the transmission holding fixture. Turn the transmission over and allow the output shaft to support the transmission weight. Position wood blocks under the shaft in order to protect the splines.

41. Remove the planetary snapring. Remove the planetary gear assembly.

42. Remove the sun gear, input drum and one-way clutch as an assembly.

43. Measure the second brake clutch pack clearance. It should be 0.0244–0.0780 in (0.62–1.98mm) for vehicles equipped with a 6 cylinder engine and 0.0350–0.0846 in. (0.89–2.15mm) for vehicles equipped with a 4 cylinder engine. Replace the discs, if not within specification.

44. Remove the second brake clutch pack snapring. Remove the second brake clutch pack. Measure the disc thickness, using a micrometer. Minimum disc thickness should be 0.0724 in. (1.84mm). Replace the discs, if not within specification.

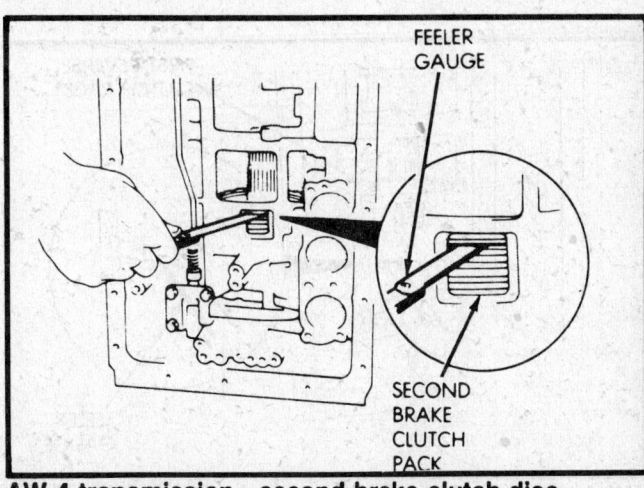

AW-4 transmission – second brake clutch disc thickness check

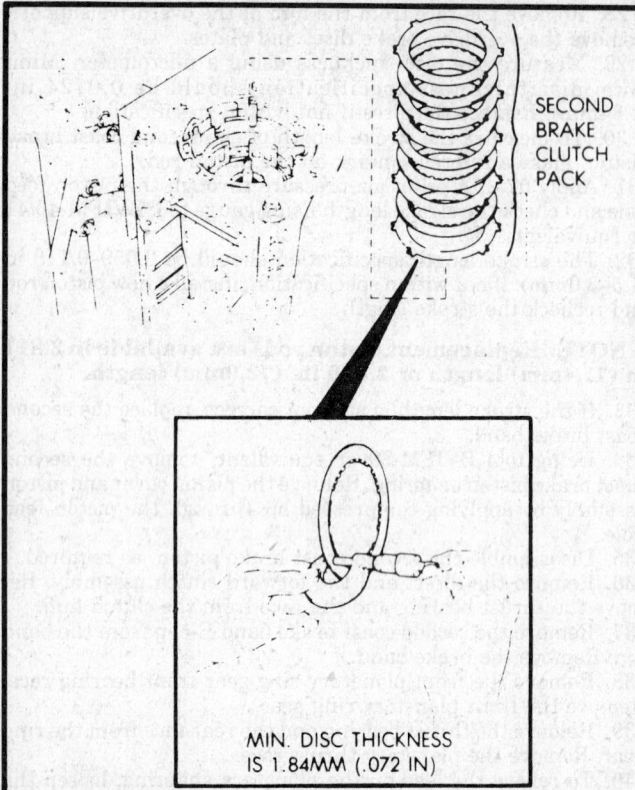

SECOND
BRAKE
CLUTCH
PACK

MIN. DISC THICKNESS
IS 1.84MM (.072 IN)

AW-4 transmission—second brake clutch disc thickness check

45. Remove the park rod bracket retaining bolts. Disconnect the park rod from the manual shaft lever. Remove the park rod and bracket. Remove the park pawl spring, pin and pawl.

46. Measure the clearance of the 1st/reverse brake clutch pack. Clearance should be 0.0276–0.787 in (0.70–2.00mm) for vehicles equipped with a 6 cylinder engine and 0.0236–0.0685 in. (0.60–1.74mm) for vehicles equipped with a 4 cylinder engine. Replace the discs, if not within specification.

47. Remove the second brake piston sleeve. To avoid damaging the transmission case, cover the removal tool with tape.

48. Remove the rear planetary gear, second brake drum and output shaft as a complete assembly.

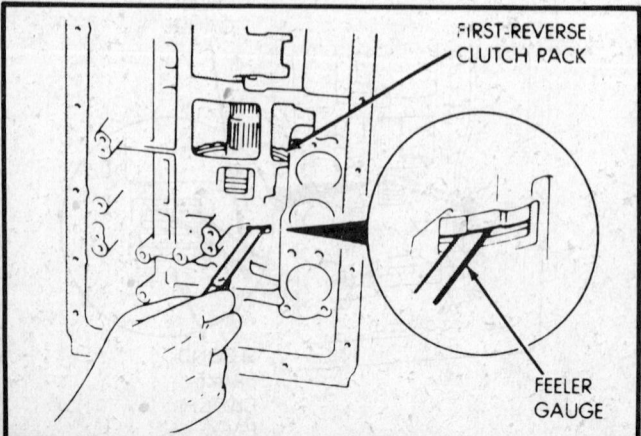

FIRST-REVERSE
CLUTCH PACK

FEELER
GAUGE

AW-4 transmission—first/reverse brake clutch pack clearance check

49. Remove the planetary and brake drum thrust bearing and race assembly.

50. Remove the second brake drum gasket from the transmission case, using the proper gasket removal tool.

51. Measure the inside diameter of the transmission case rear bushing, using an inside micrometer. The maximum allowable diameter should be 1.5031 in. (38.18mm). If not within specification the transmission case must be replaced as the bushing is not serviceable.

Unit Disassembly and Assembly
MANUAL VALVE SHAFT

Disassembly

1. Split the shaft spacer sleeve in half, using the proper tools. Remove it from the lever and shaft.

2. Using the proper tool, remove the shift sector retaining pin. Pull the shaft from the case and remove the manual lever.

3. Carefully pry the shaft seals from the transmission case.

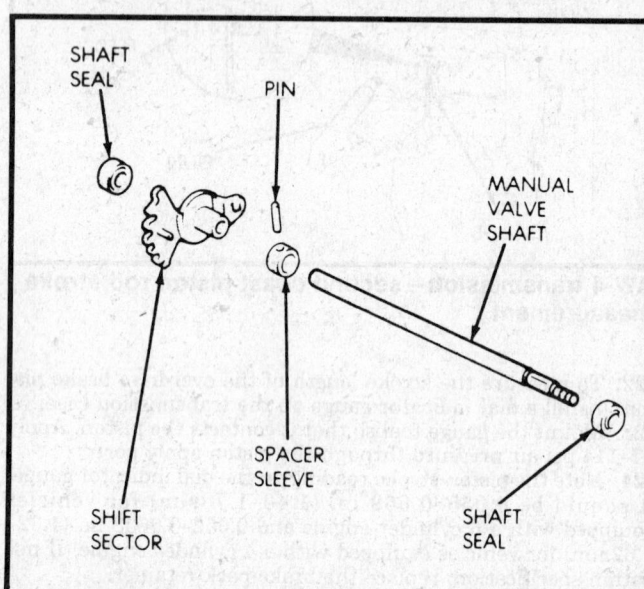

SHAFT
SEAL

PIN

MANUAL
VALVE
SHAFT

SPACER
SLEEVE

SHIFT
SECTOR

SHAFT
SEAL

AW-4 transmission—manual valve shaft components

Inspection

1. Inspect all components. Repair or replace defective components as required.

2. Replace all seals, prior to installation coat them with petroleum jelly.

Assembly

1. Install a new spacer sleeve on the shift sector. Install the sector and sleeve on the shaft. Install the shaft into the transmission case.

2. Align the sector and sleeve. Install a new retaining pin.

3. Align the notch in the sleeve with the depression in the sector. Stake the sleeve in 2 positions.

4. Check that the lever and the shaft rotate freely.

OIL PUMP

Disassembly

1. Remove the pump body O-ring. Remove the pump seal rings.

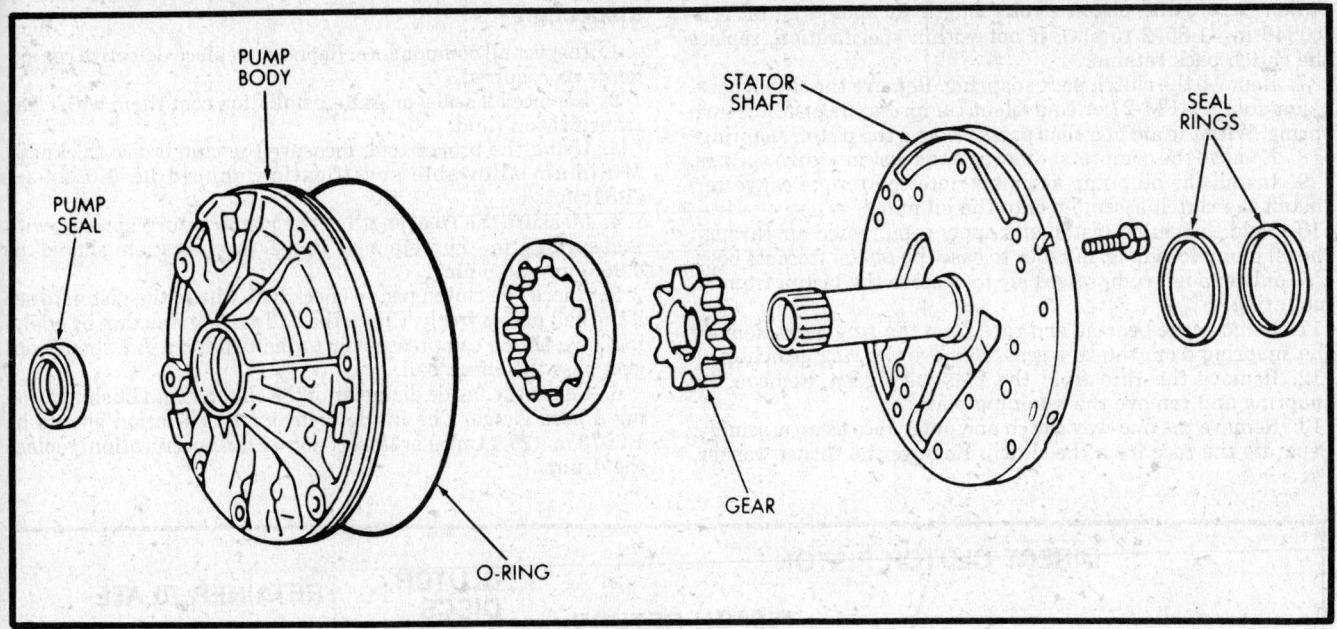

AW-4 transmission—oil pump and related components

2. Remove the bolts that retain the stator shaft to the pump body. Separate the components.

3. Remove the drive gear and driven gear and driven gear from the pump body.

4. Measure the inside diameter of the pump body, using a bore gauge. The specification should be 1.5035 in. (38.19mm) or less. If not within specification, replace the pump body.

5. Measure the inside diameter of the stator shaft bushing. Take these measurements at the front and rear of the bushing. The front diameter specification should be 0.08496 in. (21.58mm) or less. The rear diameter specification should be 1.0661 in. (27.08mm) or less. If not within specification, replace the stator shaft.

6. Measure the oil pump clearances. Clearance between the oil pump driven gear and the oil pump body should be 0.012 in. (0.3mm) or less. Clearance between the tips of the oil pump gear teeth should be 0.012 in. (0.3mm) or less. Clearance between the rear surface of the oil pump housing and the oil pump gears should be 0.004 in. (0.1mm) or less. Replace the oil pump body and gears if not within specification.

7. Remove the oil pump seal, using the proper removal tool.

Inspection

1. Inspect all components. Repair or replace defective components as required.

2. Replace all seals, prior to installation coat them with clean transmission fluid.

3. Lubricate the oil pump gears with clean transmission fluid, prior to installation.

Assembly

1. Using tool BVIFM-38 or equivalent lubricate and install a new oil pump seal. Lubricate and install the pump gears into the pump body.

2. Assemble the stator shaft and pump body. Torque the retaining bolts to 7 ft. lbs. (10 Nm).

3. Install a new O-ring on the pump body and new seal rings on the stator shaft.

4. Install the oil pump into the torque converter to check pump gear rotation. The gears must rotate smoothly when turned clockwise and counterclockwise.

OVERDRIVE PLANETARY GEAR AND CLUTCH

Disassembly

1. To check the operation of the one-way clutch in the clutch drum, hold the drum and turn the planetary shaft clockwise and counterclockwise.

2. The planetary shaft should turn counterclockwise freely, but lock when turned counterclockwise. Replace the assembly if it does not function properly.

3. Remove the overdrive clutch from the planetary gear. Remove the thrust bearing and race assembly from the clutch drum.

4. To measure the stroke length of the clutch piston, mount the oil pump on the torque converter, than mount the the clutch on the oil pump.

5. Install a dial indicator gauge on the clutch and position the indicator stylus on the clutch piston.

6. Apply compressed air through the feed hole in the oil

CLUTCH/BRAKE PACK SELECTION

Component	Engine	Discs Required	Plates Required	Retainer Required
Overdrive brake	6 cyl.	4	3	2
	4 cyl.	3	2	2
Second brake	6 cyl.	5	4	1
	4 cyl.	4	3	1
Overdrive direct clutch	6 cyl.	2	2	1
	4 cyl.	2	2	1
Direct clutch	6 cyl.	4	4	1
	4 cyl.	3	3	1
Forward clutch	6 cyl.	6	6	1
	4 cyl.	5	5	1
1st/reverse brake	6 cyl.	7	7	1
	4 cyl.	6	6	1

pump. Record the piston stroke length. It should be 0.0728–0.0846 in. (1.85–2.15mm). If not within specification, replace the clutch pack retainer.

7. Remove the clutch pack snapring. Remove the clutch pack. Using tool BVIFM-27 or equivalent compress the piston return spring. With the aid of a shop press remove the piston snapring.

8. Remove the compressor tool and the piston return springs.

9. Install the oil pump assembly onto the torque converter. Install the clutch assembly onto the oil pump.

10. Hold the clutch piston and apply compressed air through the oil pump feed hole, in order to ease the piston from its bore. Use only enough compressed air to remove the piston from its mounting.

11. Remove the bearing and race from the ring gear. Remove the snapring from the ring gear. Remove the ring gear hub.

12. Remove the race from the planetary gear. Remove the snapring and remove the retaining plate.

13. Remove the one-way clutch and outer race as an assembly. Separate the race from the clutch. Remove the thrust washer.

Inspection

1. Inspect all components. Repair or replace defective components as required.

2. Replace all seals, prior to installation coat them with clean transmission fluid.

3. Using the proper tool, measure the clutch disc thickness. Minimum allowable specification should be 0.0724 in. (1.84mm).

4. Measure the free length of the piston return springs, with the springs in the retainer. Proper specification should be 0.0661 in. (16.8mm).

5. Check the clutch piston check ball. Shake the piston to see if the ball moves freely. Check the ball sealing function by applying low volume compressed air to the ball inlet. Air should not leak past the check ball.

6. Check the inside diameter of the clutch drum bushings, using a bore gauge. The inside diameter specification should be 1.0673 in. (27.11mm) or less. If not within specification, replace the drum.

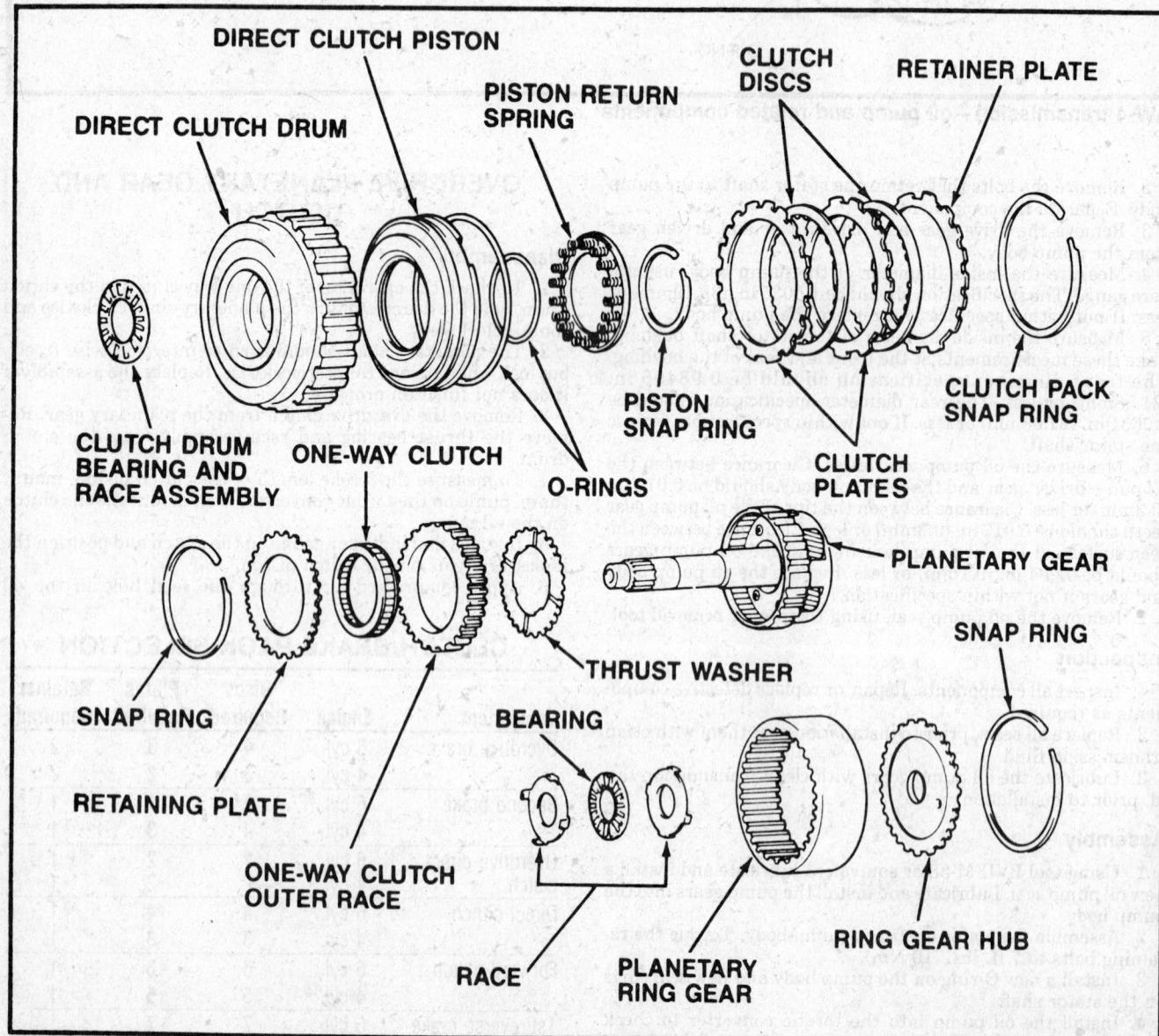

AW-4 transmission — overdrive planetary gear and clutch assembly

7. Check the inside diameter of the planetary gear bushing. The inside diameter specification should be 0.04437 in. (11.27mm) or less. If not within specification, replace the planetary gear.

Assembly

1. Install the thrust washer in the planetary gear. Note that the grooved side of the washer faces up and toward the front.

2. Install the one-way clutch in the race. The flanged side of the clutch must face upward.

3. Install the assembled one-way clutch and outer race in the planetary gear. Be sure that the flanged side of the clutch is facing upward.

4. Install the clutch pack retaining plate and snapring in the planetary gear.

5. Coat the planetary race with petroleum jelly and install it on the planetary gear. Check the outside diameter of the race, it should be 1.646 in. (41.8mm). Check the inside diameter of the race, it should be 1.067 in. (27.1mm).

6. Install the hub in the planetary ring gear. Install the snapring. Coat the race and the bearing with petroleum jelly. Install the planetary ring gear.

7. Check the race size. The outside diameter of the race should be 1.882 in. (47.8mm). The inside diameter of the race should be 0.953 in. (24.2mm).

8. Check the bearing size. The outside diameter of the bearing should be 1.843 in. (46.8mm). The inside diameter of the race should be 1.024 in. (26mm).

9. Lubricate and install new O-rings on the clutch piston. Install the piston in the clutch drum.

10. Install the piston return springs in the clutch piston. Install the piston snapring. Compress the piston return springs using the spring compressor tool and the shop press.

11. Install the clutch pack in the drum. Install the steel plate first, then a disc. Continue this sequence until all plates and discs are installed.

12. Install the clutch pack retainer with the flat side side facing downward. Install the retainer snapring. Compress the springs, using tool BVIFM-27 or equivalent.

13. Recheck the clutch piston stroke length. If not within specification, install new clutch discs or a select fit retainer.

14. Install the clutch drum bearing and race assembly. Be sure that the bearing rollers face upward. The outside diameter of the assembled bearing and race should be 1.976 in. (50.2mm). The inside dioameter of the component should be 1.138 in. (28.9mm).

PISTON STROKE LENGTH SELECTION

Location	Engine	Specification in.	mm
Direct clutch	All	0.0539–0.0640	1.37–1.60
Overdrive brake	6 cyl.	0.0551–0.0669	1.40–1.70
	4 cyl.	0.0200–0.0638	1.32–1.62
Second coast brake	All	0.0590–0.1180	1.50–3.00
Forward clutch	6 cyl.	0.1469–0.1807	3.73–4.59
	4 cyl.	0.1346–0.1655	3.42–4.23
Overdrive direct clutch	All	0.0278–0.0846	1.82–2.15

15. Install the clutch on the planetary gear.

16. To check the one-way clutch operation, hold the drum and turn the planetary shaft clockwise and counterclockwise. The shaft clockwise, it should turn freely. Turn the shaft counterclockwise, it should lock.

OVERDRIVE SUPPORT

Disassembly

1. To check the brake piston operation, mount the overdrive support on the clutch assembly.

2. Apply compressed air through the support feed hole and observe the brake piston movement.

3. The piston should move smoothly and not bind or stick. If the piston does not perform properly, replace the piston and the support.

4. Remove the thrust bearing front race, thrust bearing and rear race.

5. Turn the overdrive support over and remove the bearing race and the clutch drum thrust washer.

6. Using tool BVIFM-26 or equivalent, compress the piston return spring and remove the piston snapring.

7. Mount the overdrive support in the direct clutch and remove the piston, using compressed air. Use the same feed hole as used when checking piston operation.

8. Remove and discard the overdrive support O-rings. Remove the overdrive support seal rings.

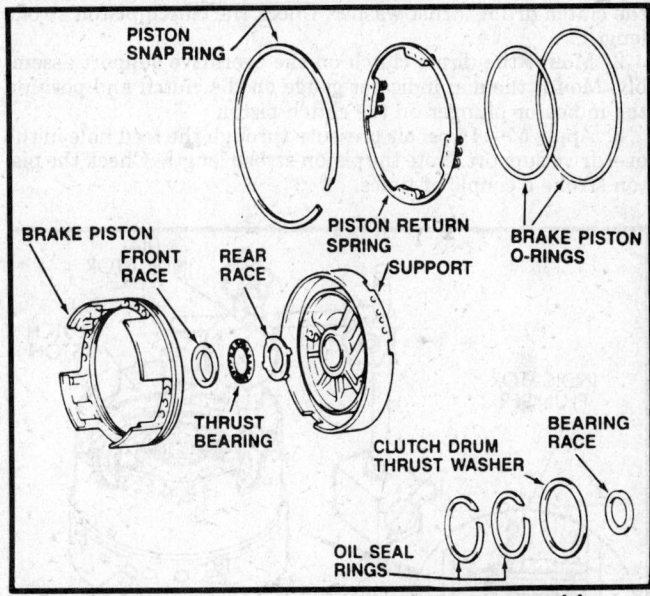

AW-4 transmission – overdrive support assembly

Inspection

1. Measure the free length of the piston return springs with the springs mounted in the retainer. Spring length should be 0.733 in. (18.61mm).

2. Clean the overdrive support components and dry them using compressed air.

3. Inspect all components. Repair or replace defective components as required.

4. Replace all seals, prior to installation coat them with clean transmission fluid.

5. Inspect the overdrive support and brake piston. Replace the overdrive support and piston if either part is worn or damaged.

Assembly

1. Lubricate the overdrive support seal rings. Compress the rings and install them on the overdrive support.

2. Lubricate and install new O-rings on the brake piston. Carefully seat the piston in the overdrive support.

3. Install the return springs on the brake piston. Using the proper tool, compress the return springs and install the snapring.

4. Install the support bearing race and clutch drum thrust washer.

5. Install the thrust bearing and the front and rear bearing races. The thrust bearing rollers should face upward.

6. Check the thrust race sizes.
The front race outer diameter should be 1.882 in. (47.8mm).
The front race inside diameter should be 1.209 in. (30.7mm).
The rear race outer diameter should be 1.882 in. (47.8mm).
The rear race inside diameter should be 1.350 in. (47.7mm).

7. Check the thrust bearing sizes. The outer bearing diameter should be 1.878 in. (47.7mm). The inside bearing diameter should be 1.287 in. (32.7mm).

8. Check the brake piston operation. The piston should move smoothly and not bind or stick.

DIRECT CLUTCH

Disassembly

1. Remove the direct clutch from the forward clutch. Remove the clutch drum thrust washer. Check the clutch piston stroke length.

2. Mount the direct clutch on the overdrive support assembly. Mount the dial indicator gauge on the clutch and position the indicator plunger on the clutch piston.

3. Apply 57–114 psi air pressure through the feed hole in the overdrive support. Note the piston stroke length. Check the piston stroke a couple of times.

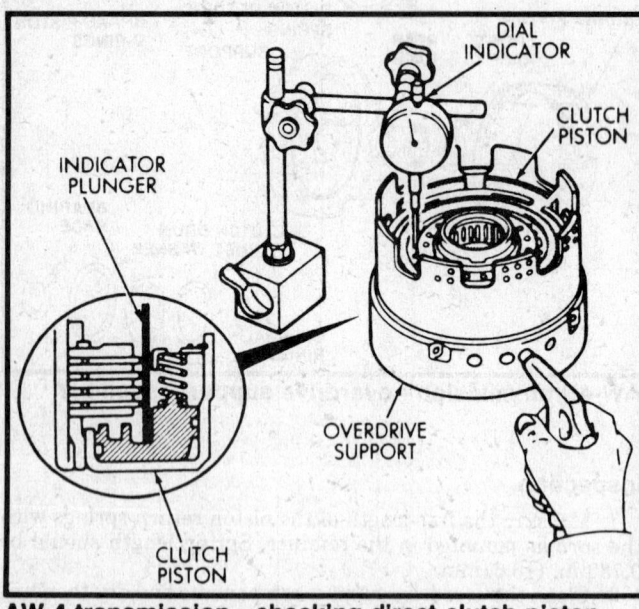

AW-4 transmission—checking direct clutch piston stroke length

4. Piston stroke length should be 0.0539–0.0642 in. (1.37–1.60mm). If the specification is not within the limits either the clutch pack retainer or the clutch discs must be replaced.

5. Using tool BVIFM-27 or equivalent, remove the clutch pack snapring. Remove the retainer and the clutch pack from the drum.

6. Compress the clutch piston return springs using tool BVIFM-27. Remove the clutch piston snapring.

7. Remove the compressor tool and the return spring. Remove the clutch piston.

8. Remount the clutch on the overdrive support. Apply com-

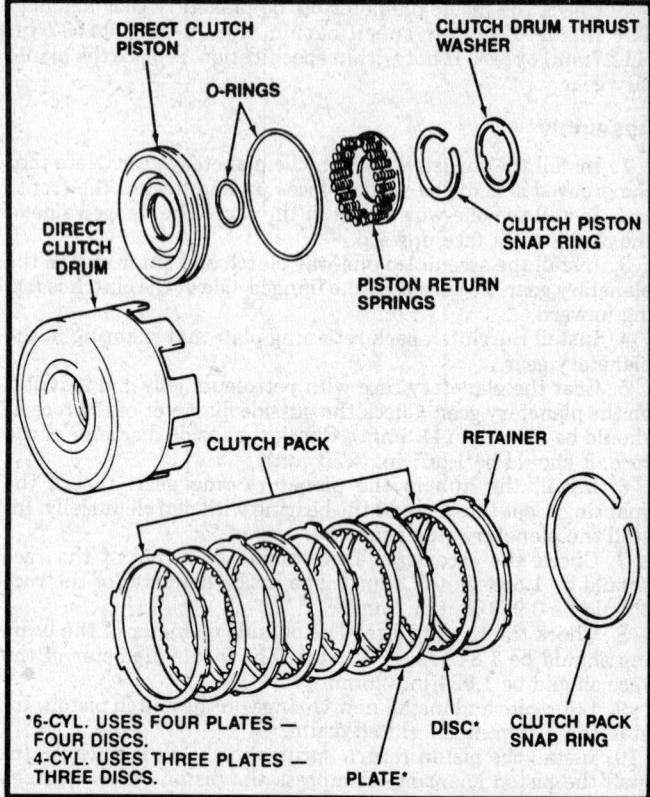

AW-4 transmission—direct clutch assembly

pressed air through the piston feed hole in the overdrive support in order to remove the piston. Use only enough compressed air to remove the piston.

9. Remove and discard the clutch piston O-rings.

Inspection

1. Inspect all components. Repair or replace defective components as required.

2. Replace all seals, prior to installation coat them with clean transmission fluid.

3. Measure the clutch disc thickness. The minimum allowable thickness is 0.0724 in. (1.84mm). If not within specification, replace the clutch discs.

4. Measure the free length of the piston return springs with the springs in the retainer. The free length specification should

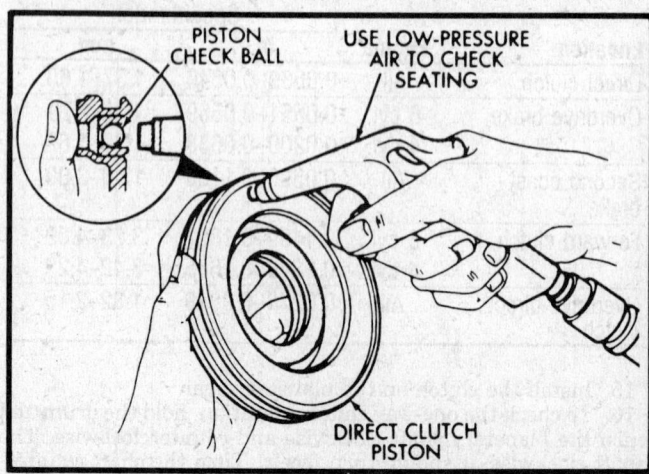

AW-4 transmission—piston check ball seating

be 0.0839 in. (2.32mm). If not within specification, replace the return springs.

5. Check the clutch piston check ball. Shake the piston to see if the ball moves freely. Check the ball seat by applying low volume compressed air to the ball inlet.

6. Measure the inside diameter of the clutch drum bushing. The inside diameter should be less than 2.1248 in. (53.97mm). If not within specification, replace the drum.

Assembly

1. Lubricate and install the replacement O-rings on the clutch piston. Install the clutch piston in the drum. Install the return springs on the piston.

2. Compress the piston return springs and install the snapring. Be sure that the snapring end gap is not aligned with the spring retainer tab.

3. Install the clutch discs and plates. Install the plate and then the disc, until all the plates and discs are installed.

4. Install the clutch pack retainer in the drum. Install the clutch pack snapring.

5. Check the snapring position. As required, shift the snapring until the end gap is not aligned with any notches in the clutch drum.

6. Recheck the clutch piston stroke length. If correct continue.

7. If the clutch piston stroke length is incorrect, replace the clutch discs or use a different thickness clutch pack retainer.

8. Lubricate the clutch drum thrust washer with pertroleum jelly and install it in the drum.

9. Mount the direct clutch assembly on the forward clutch assembly. Check the assembled height it should be 2.767–2.815 in. (70.3–71.5mm).

10. If the assembled height is incorrect, the clutches are not seated properly.

11. If the assembled height is correct, remove the direct clutch from the forward clutch.

FORWARD CLUTCH

Disassembly

1. To check the forward clutch piston stroke, position the overdrive support assembly on wood blocks. Mount the forward clutch drum on the support.

2. Remove the bearing and the race form the forward clutch drum.

3. Install a dial indicator gauge on the clutch drum. Position the dial indicator plunger against the clutch piston.

4. Apply compressed air through the right side feed hole in the support. Note the piston stroke length on the dial indicator.

5. Stroke length should be 0.1469–0.1807 in. (3.73–4.59mm) for transmissions used in vehicles equipped with a 6 cylinder engine. Stroke length should be 0.1346–0.1665 in. (3.42–4.23mm) for transmissions used in vehicles equipped with a 4 cylinder engine.

6. Replace the clutch discs if the stroke length is not within specification.

7. Remove the clutch pack snapring. Remove the retainer and the clutch pack. Remove the clutch pack cushion plate.

8. Using tool BVIFM-27, compress the clutch springs and remove the piston snapring. Remove the tool and the piston return springs.

9. Remount the forward clutch drum on the overdrive support. Apply compressed air through the feed hole in the support in order to remove the piston.

10. Use only enough compressed air to ease the piston out of the drum. Remove and discard the clutch piston O-rings.

11. Remove the clutch drum O-ring from the rear hub of the drum. Remove the seal rings from the clutch drum shaft. Remove the thrust bearing and the race assembly from the clutch drum.

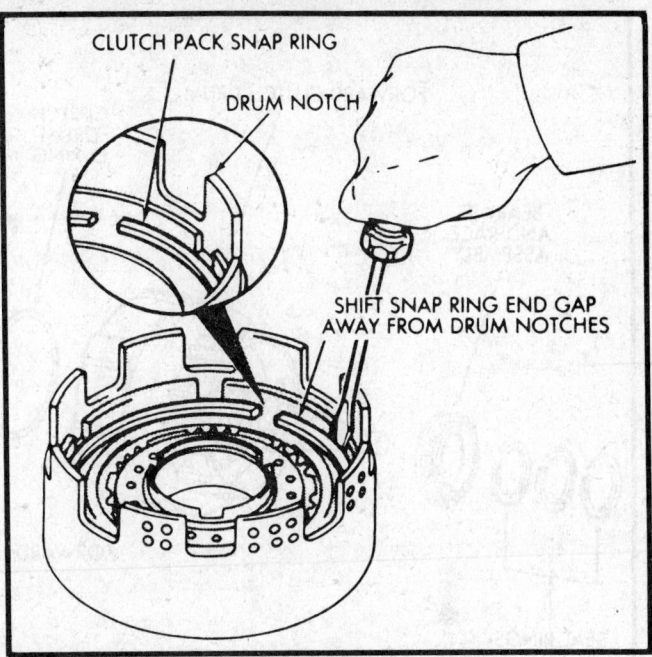

AW-4 transmission–clutch pack snapring positioning

Inspection

1. Inspect all components. Repair or replace defective components as required.

2. Replace all seals, prior to installation coat them with clean transmission fluid.

3. Measure the clutch disc thickness, using a micrometer. The minimum allowable thickness should be 0.0595 in. (1.51mm) for transmissions used in vehicles equipped with a 6 cylinder engine and 0.0724 in. (1.84mm) for transmissions used in vehicles equipped with a 4 cylinder engine.

4. Measure the free length of the piston return springs with the springs in the retainer. The free length specification should be 0.767 in. (19.47mm). If not within specification, replace the return springs and the retainer.

5. Check the clutch piston check ball. The ball should move freely. Check the ball seat by applying low volume compressed air to the ball inlet. The ball should seat firmly and not leak air.

6. Measure the inside diameter of the clutch drum hub. The inside diameter should be less than 0.9480 in. (24.08mm). If not within specification, replace the clutch drum.

Assembly

1. Lubricate the bearing and the race assembly with petroleum jelly and install it in the clutch drum. Be sure that the race side of the assembly faces downward and toward the drum and that the bearing rollers face up.

2. Coat the new clutch drum shaft seal rings with petroleum jelly. Before installing the drum shaft seal rings, squeeze each ring so that the ring ends overlap. This tightens the ring and makes clutch installation easier.

3. Install the seal rings on the shaft. Keep the rings closed as tightly as possible during installation. Avoid overspreading them.

4. Mount the clutch drum on the overdrive support. Lubricate and install a new O-ring on the clutch drum hub.

5. Lubricate and install new O-rings on the clutch piston. Install the piston in the drum. Install the piston return springs.

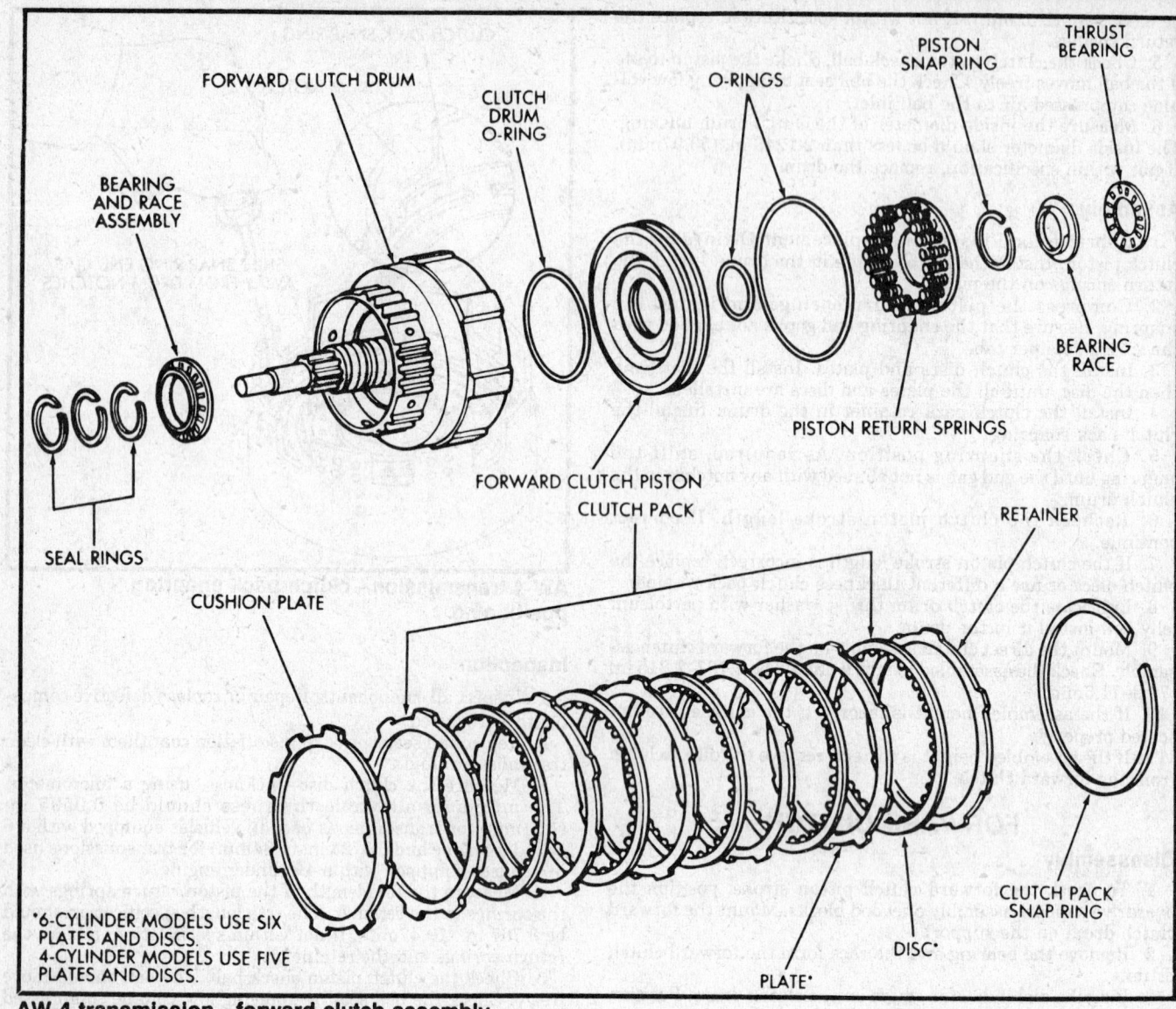

AW-4 transmission—forward clutch assembly

6. Using tool BVIFM-27 and a shop press, install the piston snapring. Be sure that the snapring end gap is not aligned with any notches in the drum.

7. Install the cushion plate in the drum. Be sure that the concave side of the plate faces down.

8. Install the clutch discs, plates and retainer. Install the tabbed plate followed by a disc, until all the plates and discs are installed. Install the clutch pack snapring.

9. Recheck the clutch piston stroke length. If not within specification, replace the clutch discs.

10. Lubricate the race and bearing with petroleum jelly. Install them in the clutch drum. Be sure that the bearing rollers face upward and the race lip is seated in the drum.

11. Check the bearing and the race size. The outer diameter of the bearing should be 1.839 in. (46.7mm). The outer diameter of the race should be 1.925 in. (48.9mm). The inner diameter of the bearing and the race should be 1.024 in. (26.0mm).

12. Mount the forward clutch on the direct clutch. Check the assembled height. It should be 2.767–2.815 in. (70.3–71.5mm).

FRONT PLANETARY GEAR

Disassembly

1. Remove the ring gear from the planetary gear. Remove the front bearing and both races from the ring gear.

2. Remove the tabbed thrust race from the planetary gear. Remove the snapring that retains the planetary gear to the shaft. Remove the gear.

3. Remove the rear bearing and the race from the planetary gear.

4. Measure the inside diameter of the ring gear bushing. The maximum allowable diameter is 0.9489 in. (24.08mm). Replace the ring gear if the bushing inside diameter is greater than specification.

Inspection

1. Inspect all components. Repair or replace defective components as required.

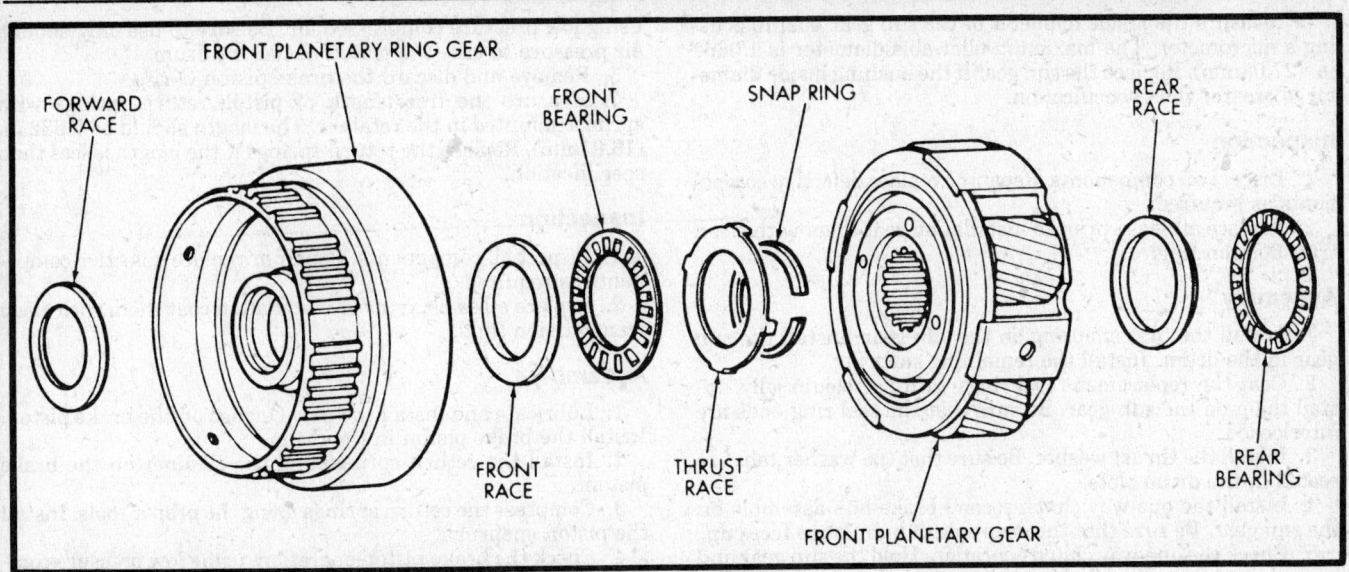

AW-4 transmission — front planetary gear components

2. Replace all seals, prior to installation coat them with clean transmission fluid.

Assembly

1. Lubricate the planetary and ring gear bearings and their races with petroleum jelly.
2. Identify the planetary bearings and races before installation.
  The outer diameter of rear bearing is 1.878 in. (47.7mm).
  The inner diameter of the rear bearing is 1.398 in. (35.5mm).
  The outer diameter of the rear race 1.874 in. (47.6mm).
  The inner diameter of the rear race is 1.327 in. (33.7mm).
  The outer diameter of the front race is 2.110 in. (53.6mm).
  The inner diameter of the front race is 1.201 in. (30.5mm).
  The outer diameter of the front bearings is 1.878 in. (47.7mm).
  The inner diameter of the front bearings is 1.283 in. (32.6).
  The outer diameter of the forward race is 1.850 in. (47.0mm).
  The inner diameter of the forward race is 1.043 in. (26.5mm).

3. Install the rear race and bearing in the gear. Turn the planetary assembly over and install the thrust race.
4. Install the front race and bearing and the forward race in the ring gear.

SUN GEAR AND NO. 1 ONE-WAY CLUTCH

Disassembly

1. Hold the sun gear and turn the second brake hub clockwise and than counterclockwise. The hub should rotate freely clockwise, but lock when turned counterclockwise. Replace the one-way clutch and hub if it does not operate properly.
2. Remove the one-way clutch/second brake hub assembly from the drum. Remove the thrust washer from the drum. Remove both seal rings from the sun gear.
3. Support the sun gear on a wood block. Remove the first sun gear snapring and separate the drum from the gear.
4. Remove the remaining snapring from the sun gear.

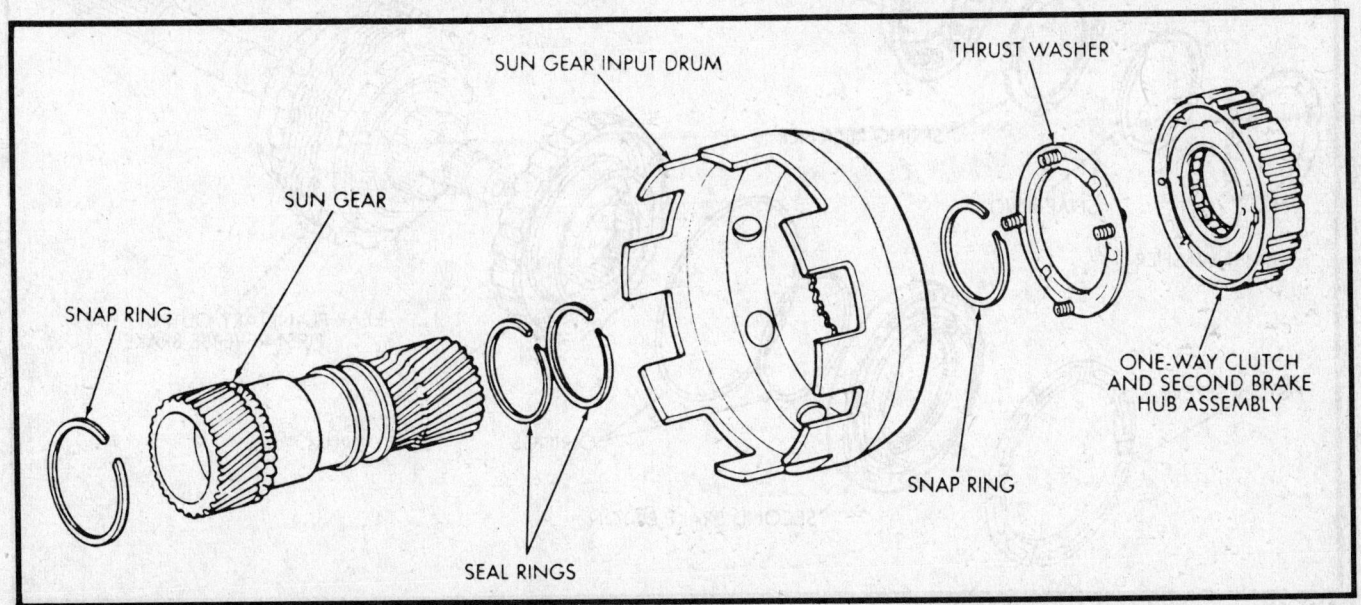

AW-4 transmission — sun gear and one-way clutch assembly

5. Measure the inside diameter of the sun gear bushings using a micrometer. The maximum allowable diameter is 1.0661 in. (27.08mm). Replace the sun gear if the bushing inside diameter is greater than specification.

Inspection

1. Inspect all components. Repair or replace defective components as required.
2. Replace all seals, prior to installation coat them with clean transmission fluid.

Assembly

1. Install the first snapring on the sun gear. Install the sun gear in the drum. Install the remaining snapring.
2. Coat the replacement seal rings with petroleum jelly. Install them on the sun gear. Be sure that the seal ring ends are interlocked.
3. Install the thrust washer. Be sure that the washer tabs are seated in the drum slots.
4. Install the one-way clutch/second brake hub assembly on the sun gear. Be sure that the deep side of hub flange faces up.
5. Check the one-way clutch operation. Hold the sun gear and turn the second brake hub clockwise and than counterclockwise. The hub should turn clockwise freely, but lock when turned counterclockwise.

SECOND BRAKE

Disassembly

1. Remove the second brake drum from the output shaft. Set the output shaft assembly aside.
2. Remove the thrust washer from the second brake drum.
3. Using tool BVIFM-27 or equivalent and a shop press, compress the piston return springs.
4. Remove the compressor tool. Remove the spring retainer and the return springs.
5. Remove the second brake piston and sleeve from the drum,

using low pressure compressed air. Be sure to use only enough air pressure to ease the piston out of the drum.
6. Remove and discard the brake piston O-rings.
7. Measure the free length of piston return springs with springs mounted in the retainer. The length should be 0.632 in. (16.05mm). Replace the return springs if the length is less than specifiication.

Inspection

1. Inspect all components. Repair or replace defective components as required.
2. Replace all seals, prior to installation coat them with clean transmission fluid.

Assembly

1. Lubricate and install the new O-rings on the brake piston. Install the brake piston in the drum.
2. Install the return springs and the retainer on the brake piston.
3. Compress the return springs using the proper tools. Install the piston snapring.
4. Check the brake piston operation, using low pressure compressed air. Apply air pressure through the feed hole in the drum. The piston should move smoothly when applying and releasing air pressure.
5. Coat the thrust washer with petroleum jelly and install it in the drum. Be sure that the washer notches are aligned with the tabs on the spring retainer.

REAR PLANETARY, NO. 2 ONE-WAY CLUTCH AND OUTPUT SHAFT

Disassembly

1. Remove the output shaft from the gear assembly. Remove and discard the shaft seal ring. Remove the brake pack from the planetary gear.
2. Measure the thickness of each brake pack disc. The mini-

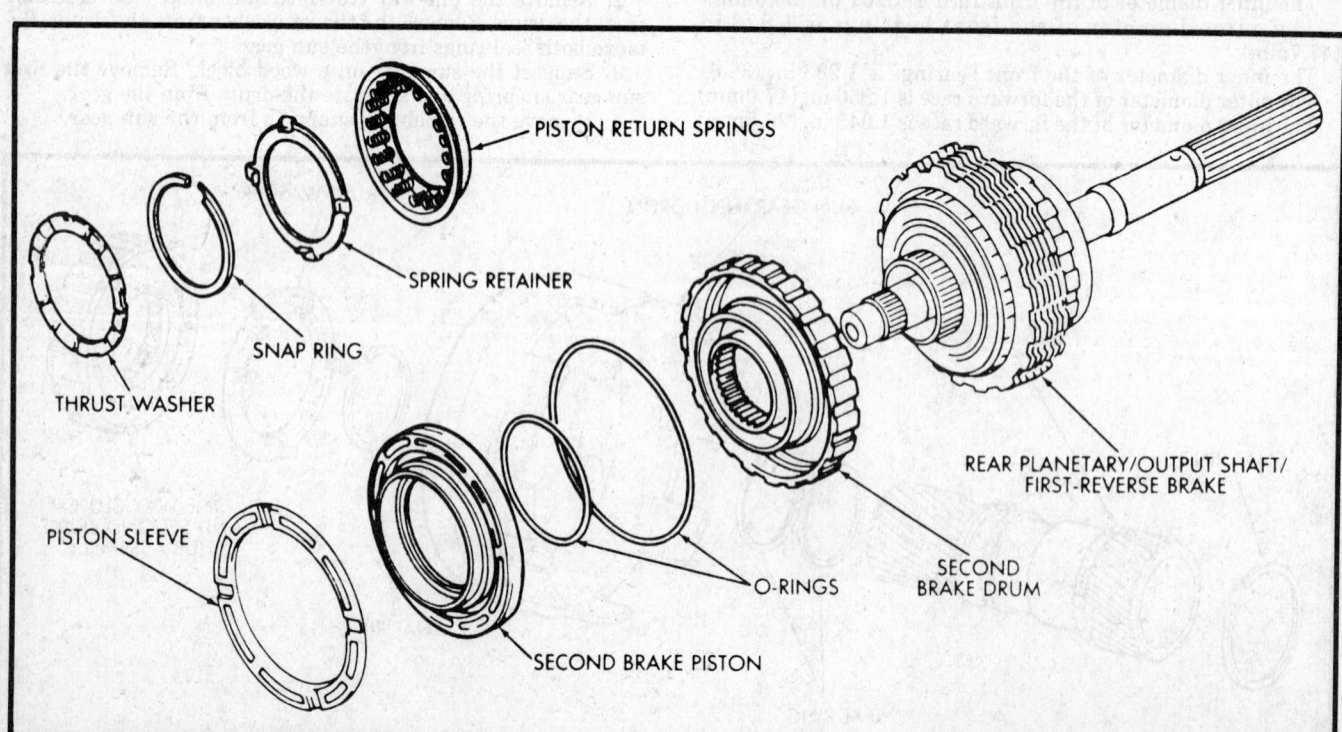

PISTON RETURN SPRINGS

SPRING RETAINER

SNAP RING

THRUST WASHER

PISTON SLEEVE

SECOND BRAKE PISTON

O-RINGS

SECOND BRAKE DRUM

REAR PLANETARY/OUTPUT SHAFT/ FIRST-REVERSE BRAKE

AW-4 transmission—second brake assembly

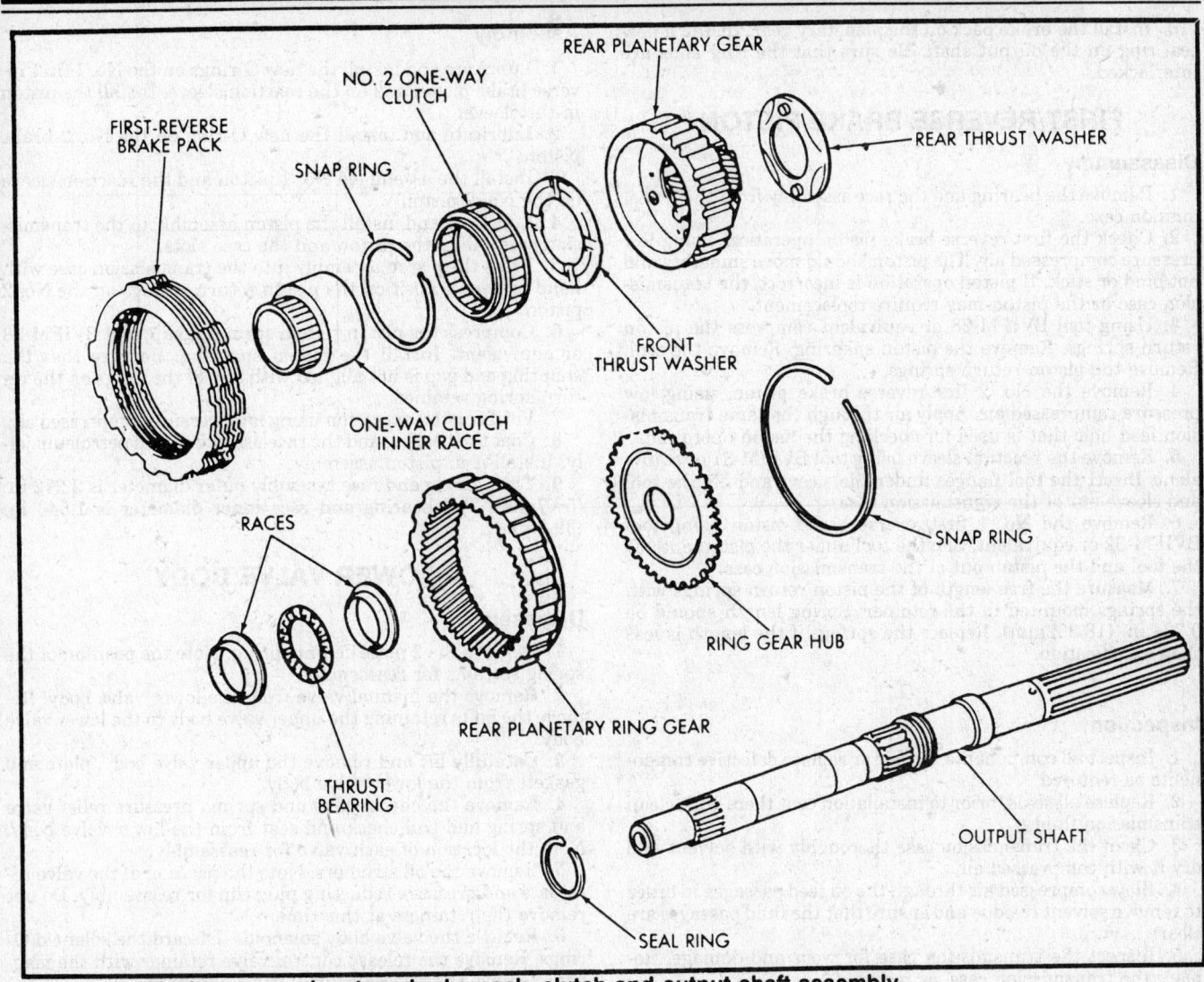

AW-4 transmission—rear planetary, brake pack, clutch and output shaft assembly

mum thickness is 0.0594 in. (1.51mm). Replace all of the discs if any disc is thinner than specification. Remove the planetary gear from the ring gear.

3. Check the No. 2 one-way clutch. Hold the planetary gear and turn the clutch inner race in both directions. The race should turn freely counterclockwise, but lock when turned clockwise. Replace the one-way clutch if it does not perform properly.

4. Remove the clutch inner race from the planetary gear. Remove the clutch snapring. Remove the No. 2 one-way clutch from the planetary gear assembly.

5. Remove the front and rear thrust washers from the planetary gear assembly. Remove the thrust bearing and washers from the ring gear.

6. Remove the ring gear snapring. Remove the ring gear hub.

Inspection

1. Inspect all components. Repair or replace defective components as required.

2. Replace all seals, prior to installation coat them with clean transmission fluid.

Assembly

1. Install the hub and the snapring in the ring gear.

2. Identify the ring gear thrust bearing and races.
The outer diameter of the bottom race is 1.764 in. (44.8mm).
The inner diameter of the bottom race is 1.087 in. (27.6mm).
The outer diameter of the bearing is 1.760 in. (44.7mm).
The inner diameter of the bearing is 1.185 in. (30.1mm).
The outer diameter of the upper race is 1.764 in. (44.8mm).
The inner diameter of the upper race is 1.134 in. (28.8mm).

3. Lubricate the ring gear thrust bearing and races with petroleum jelly. install them in ring gear.

4. Coat the planetary thrust washers with petroleum jelly. Install them in gear.

5. Install the No. 2 one-way clutch in the planetary gear. Be sure that the flanged side of clutch faces up.

6. Install the clutch retaining snapring. Install the clutch inner race. Turn the race counterclockwise to ease installation.

7. Verify that the one-way clutch is operating properly. Hold the gear and turn the inner race in both directions. The race should turn freely counterclockwise, but lock when turned clockwise.

8. Install the planetary gear in the ring gear.

9. Assemble the clutch discs and the clutch plates. The installation sequence is disc first, then a plate. Use 7 discs and plates in a transmission that is used in a vehicle equipped with a 6 cylinder engine. Use 6 discs and plates in a transmission that is used in a vehicle equipped with a 4 cylinder engine.

10. Install the brake pack on the planetary gear. Install a new seal ring on the output shaft. Be sure that the ring ends are interlocked.

FIRST/REVERSE BRAKE PISTON

Disassembly

1. Remove the bearing and the race assembly from the transmission case.

2. Check the first/reverse brake piston operation, using low pressure compressed air. The piston should move smoothly and not bind or stick. If piston operation is incorrect, the transmission case or the piston may require replacement.

3. Using tool BVIFM-28 or equivalent compress the piston return springs. Remove the piston snapring. Remove the tool. Remove the piston return springs.

4. Remove the No. 2 first/reverse brake piston, using low pressure compressed air. Apply air through the same transmission feed hole that is used for checking the piston operation.

5. Remove the reaction sleeve using tool BVIFM-31 or equivalent. Insert the tool flanges under the sleeve and lift the tool and sleeve out of the transmission case.

6. Remove the No. 1 first/reverse brake piston using tool BVIFM-32 or equivalent. Slip the tool under the piston and lift the tool and the piston out of the transmission case.

7. Measure the free length of the piston return springs with the springs mounted in the retainer. Spring length should be 0.724 in. (18.382mm). Replace the springs if the length is less than specification.

Inspection

1. Inspect all components. Repair or replace defective components as required.

2. Replace all seals, prior to installation coat them with clean transmission fluid.

3. Clean the transmission case thoroughly with solvent and dry it with compressed air.

4. Blow compressed air through the oil feed passages in order to remove solvent residue and ensure that the fluid passages are clear.

5. Inspect the transmission case for wear and damage. Replace the transmission case, as required.

Assembly

1. Lubricate and install the new O-rings on the No. 1 first/reverse brake piston and on the reaction sleeve. Install the piston in the sleeve.

2. Lubricate and install the new O-ring on the No. 2 brake piston.

3. Install the assembled No. 1 piston and the reaction sleeve on the No. 2 piston.

4. Lubricate and install the piston assembly in the transmission case. Align the piston and the case slots.

5. Press the piston assembly into the transmission case with hand pressure. Position the piston return springs on the No. 2 piston.

6. Compress the piston return springs, using tool BVIFM-28 or equivalent. Install the piston snapring. Be sure that the snapring end gap is not aligned with any of the tangs on the return spring retainer.

7. Verify piston operation using low pressure compressed air.

8. Coat the bearing and the race assembly with petroleum jelly. Install it in piston assembly.

9. The bearing and race assembly outer diameter is 2.272 in. (57.7mm). The bearing and race inner diameter is 1.543 in. (39.2mm).

LOWER VALVE BODY

Disassembly

1. Remove the 2 piece detent spring. Note the position of the spring sections for reassembly.

2. Remove the manual valve from the lower valve body. Remove the bolts retaining the upper valve body to the lower valve body.

3. Carefully lift and remove the upper valve body, plate and gaskets from the lower valve body.

4. Remove the check valve and spring, pressure relief valve and spring and ball check and seat from the lower valve body. Note the location of each valve for reassembly.

5. Remove the oil strainers. Note the position of the valve retainers and pressure reducing plug clip for reassembly. Do not remove the retainers at this time.

6. Remove the valve body solenoids. Discard the solenoid O-rings. Remove the release control valve retainer with the magnet. Remove the release control valve and plug.

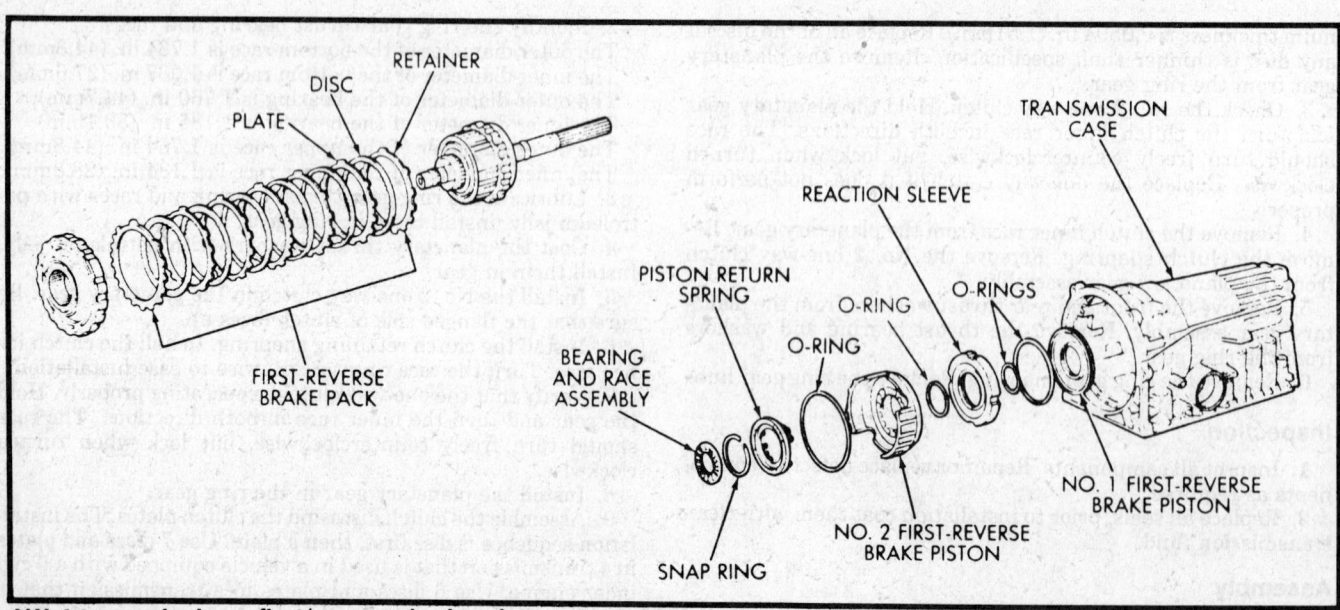

AW-4 transmission—first/reverse brake piston assembly

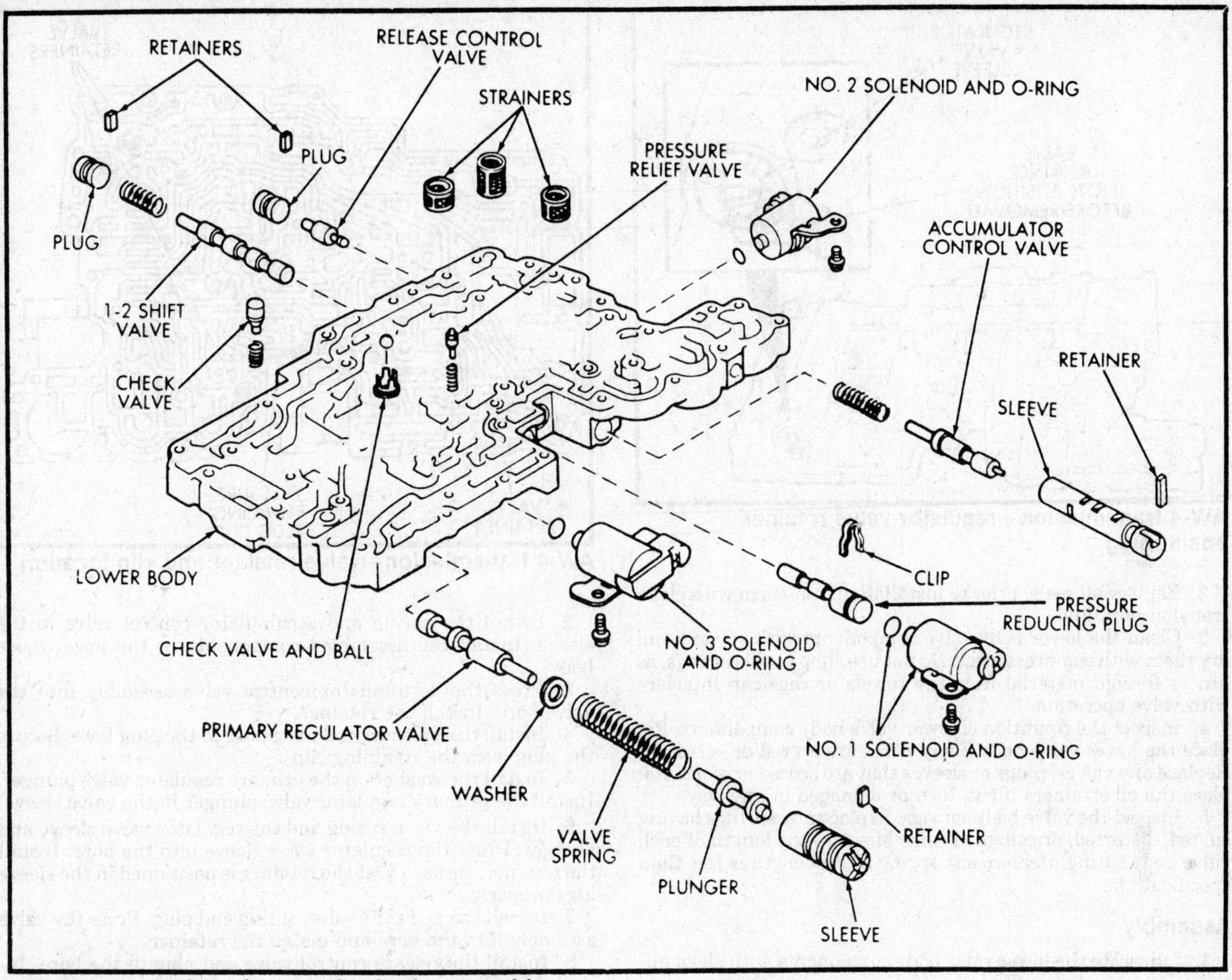

RETAINERS
RELEASE CONTROL VALVE
PLUG
STRAINERS
PRESSURE RELIEF VALVE
NO. 2 SOLENOID AND O-RING
ACCUMULATOR CONTROL VALVE
PLUG
1-2 SHIFT VALVE
CHECK VALVE
RETAINER
SLEEVE
LOWER BODY
CLIP
PRESSURE REDUCING PLUG
CHECK VALVE AND BALL
NO. 3 SOLENOID AND O-RING
PRIMARY REGULATOR VALVE
WASHER
NO. 1 SOLENOID AND O-RING
RETAINER
VALVE SPRING
PLUNGER
SLEEVE

AW-4 transmission – lower valve body assembly

7. Remove the 1-2 shift valve retainer. Remove the valve plug, valve spring and valve.

NOTE: The primary regulator valve sleeve and plunger are under tension from the valve spring. Be sure to exert counterpressure on the spring while removing the valve retainer in order to prevent components from flying out.

8. To remove the primary regulator valve, note the position of the valve retainer for reassembly. Press the valve sleeve inward and remove the retainer, using a magnet.

9. Slowly release the pressure on the sleeve and remove the sleeve, spring and washer and the valve. Use of a magnet to remove the valve is necessary.

10. Remove the regulator valve and plunger from the sleeve. Remove the retaining clip. Using the proper tool, remove the pressure reducing plug.

11. Remove the accumulator control valve retainer. Remove the control valve assembly. Remove the spring and the control valve from the valve sleeve.

Inspection

1. Inspect all components. Repair or replace defective components as required.

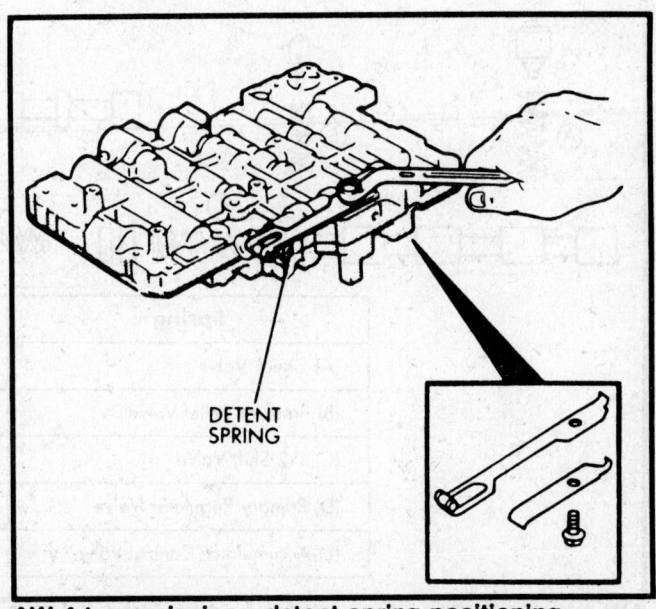

DETENT SPRING

AW-4 transmission – detent spring positioning

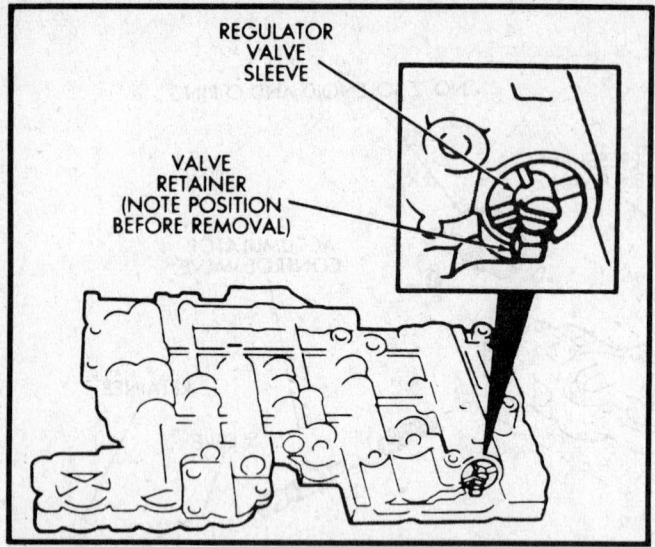

AW-4 transmission—regulator valve retainer positioning

2. Replace all seals, prior to installation coat them with clean transmission fluid.

3. Clean the lower body valve components with solvent and dry them with compressed air. Do not use shop towels or rags, as lint or foreign material from the towels or rags can interfere with valve operation.

4. Inspect the condition of lower valve body components. Replace the lower valve body if any bores are scored or corroded. Replace any valves, plugs or sleeves that are scored or worn. Replace the oil strainers if cut, torn or damaged in any way.

5. Inspect the valve body springs. Replace any springs having rusted, distorted, or collapsed coils. Measure the length of each valve body spring. Replace any spring if free length is less than specification.

Assembly

1. Lubricate the lower valve body components with clean automatic transmission fluid.

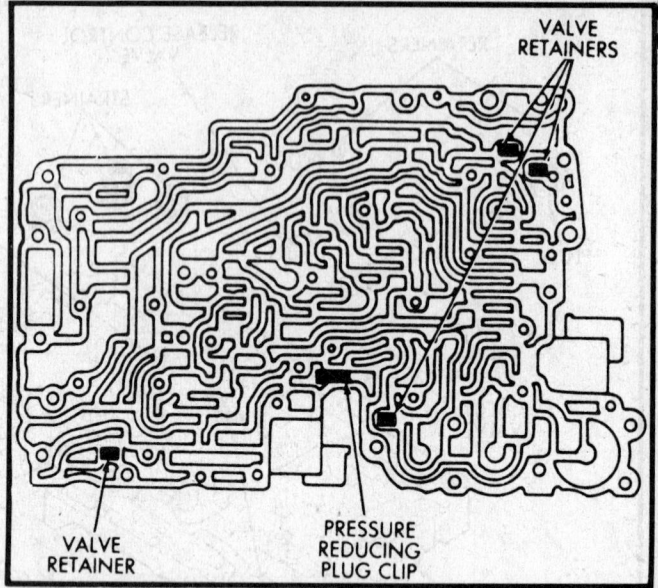

AW-4 transmission—valve retainer and clip location

2. Install the spring and accumulator control valve in the sleeve. Install the assembled components in the lower valve body.

3. Press the accumulator control valve assembly into the valve bore. Install the retainer.

4. Install the pressure reducing plug in the plug bore. Secure the plug with the retaining clip.

5. Install the washer on the primary regulator valve plunger. Install the primary regulator valve plunger in the valve sleeve.

6. Install the valve spring and the regulator valve sleeve and plunger. Press the regulator valve sleeve into the bore. Install the retainer. Be sure that the retainer is positioned in the sleeve lugs properly.

7. Install the 1–2 shift valve, spring and plug. Press the valve assembly into the bore and install the retainer.

8. Install the release control valve and plug in the bore. Install the valve retainer.

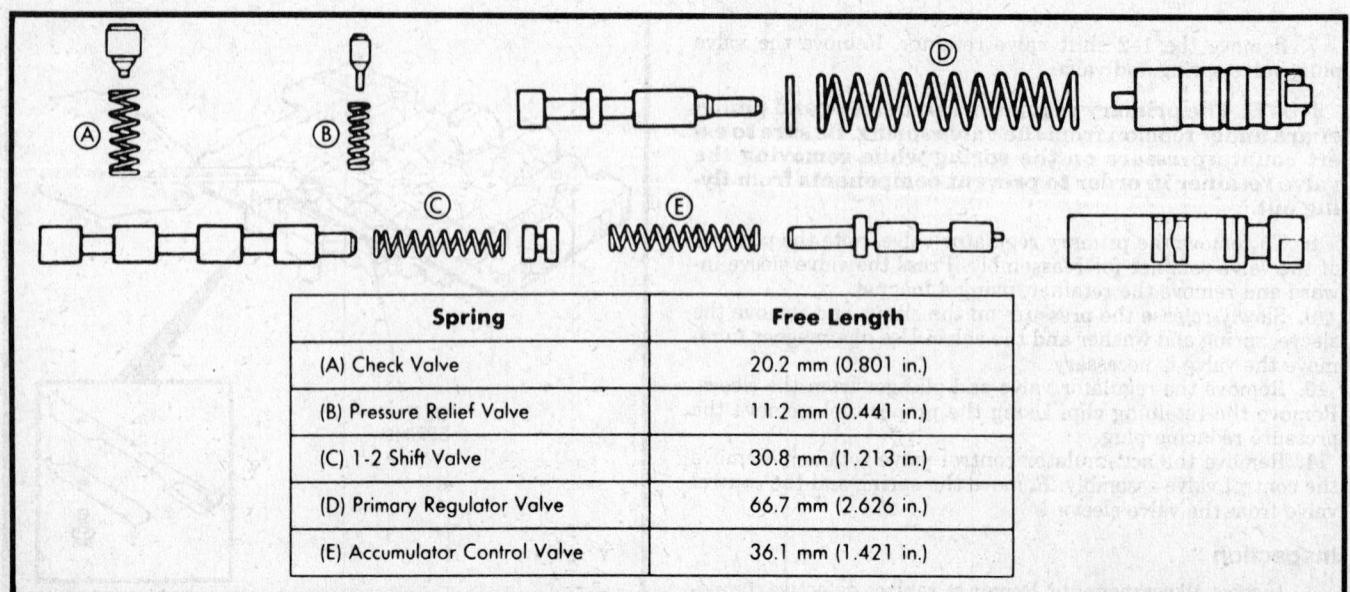

Spring	Free Length
(A) Check Valve	20.2 mm (0.801 in.)
(B) Pressure Relief Valve	11.2 mm (0.441 in.)
(C) 1-2 Shift Valve	30.8 mm (1.213 in.)
(D) Primary Regulator Valve	66.7 mm (2.626 in.)
(E) Accumulator Control Valve	36.1 mm (1.421 in.)

AW-4 transmission—lower valve body spring dimension data

9. Install the replacement O-rings on the solenoids. Install the solenoids on the valve body. Torque the solenoid retaining bolts to 7 ft. lbs. (10 Nm).

10. Install the oil strainers. Be sure to identify the strainers prior to installation. The strainers are all the same diameter but are different lengths. Two strainers are 0.443 in. (11.0mm) long and the other strainer is 0.76 in. (19.5mm) long.

11. Install the check valves and springs seats.

UPPER VALVE BODY

1. Remove the 2 piece detent spring. Note the position of the spring sections for reassembly.

2. Remove the manual valve from the lower valve body. Remove the bolts retaining the upper valve body to the lower valve body.

3. Carefully lift and remove the upper valve body, plate and gaskets from the lower valve body.

4. Remove the upper valve body plate and gaskets. Discard the gaskets.

5. Remove the strainer and the 9 check balls. Note the check ball and strainer position for reassembly.

6. Remove the valve stop and the throttle cam. Remove the throttle valve pin using a magnet. Remove the downshift plug, valve spring and throttle valve.

7. Turn the upper valve body over and remove the throttle valve adjusting rings and spring. Note the number of adjusting rings, if the valve is equipped with them.

8. Remove the 3–4 shift valve retainer, using a magnet. Remove the valve plug, spring and the 3–4 shift valve.

9. Remove the second coast modulator valve retainer. Remove the valve plug, spring and valve.

10. Remove the lock-up relay valve retainer. Remove the relay valve and sleeve assembly. Remove the lock-up relay valve and the spring and plunger from the valve sleeve.

11. Remove the secondary pressure regulator valve retainer. Remove the plug, regulator valve and spring.

12. Remove the cut-back valve retainer. Remove the plug, cut-back valve and spring.

13. Remove the 2–3 shift valve retainer. Remove the plug, spring and the 2–3 shift valve.

14. Remove the low coast modulator valve retainer. Remove the valve plug, spring and the low coast modulator valve.

Inspection

1. Inspect all components. Repair or replace defective components as required.

2. Replace all seals, prior to installation coat them with clean transmission fluid.

3. Clean the upper body components with solvent and dry them with compressed air. Do not use shop towels or rags as lint or foreign material from the towels or rags can interfere with valve operation.

4. Inspect the condition of the upper valve body components. Replace the upper valve body if any of the bores are scored or corroded. Replace any valves, plugs or sleeves if scored or worn. Replace the oil strainer if cut, torn or damaged in any way.

5. Inspect the valve body springs. Replace any spring having rusted, distorted, or collapsed coils. Measure the length of each spring. Replace any spring if the free length is less than specification.

Assembly

1. Lubricate the valves, springs, plugs, sleeves and the valve bores in the upper valve body with clean automatic transmission fluid. Note position of the valve retainers and stop for reassembly reference.

2. Install the low coast modulator valve, spring and plug in the valve bore. Press valve plug inward and install the retainer.

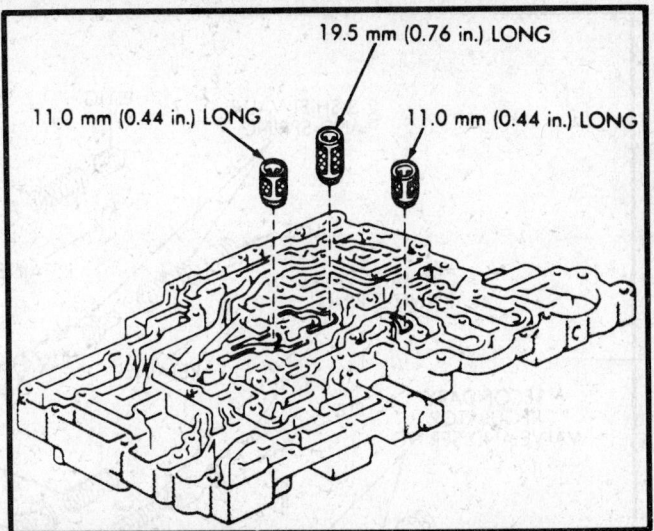

AW-4 transmission—oil strainer identification and location

3. Install the 2–3 shift valve, spring and plug in the valve bore. Press the plug inward and install retainer.

4. Install the cut-back valve spring, valve and plug. Press the plug inward and install retainer.

5. Install the secondary regulator valve spring, valve and plug in the valve bore. Press the plug inward and install the retainer.

6. Assemble the lock-up relay valve. Install the spring and plunger in the valve sleeve. Install the assembled valve in the sleeve.

7. Install the assembled lock-up relay valve in the valve bore. Install the retainer.

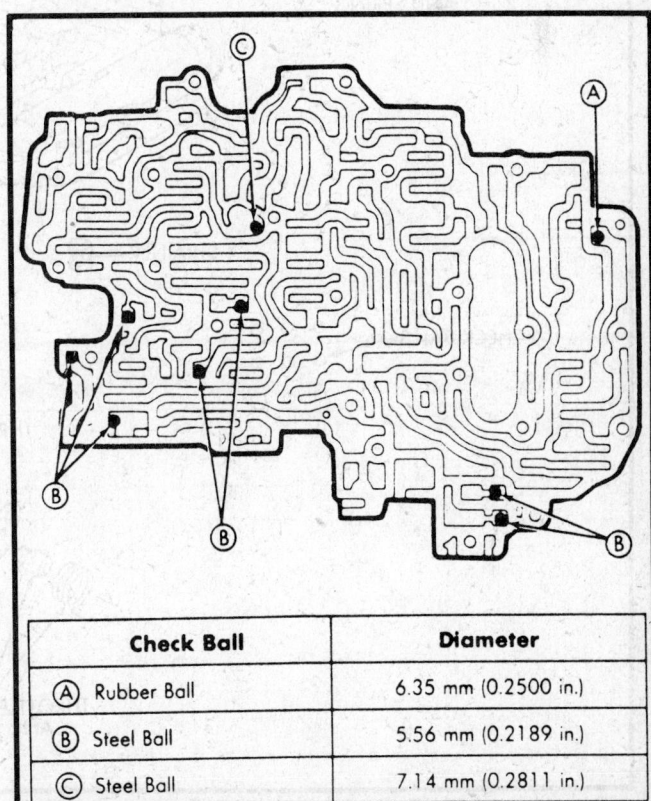

Check Ball	Diameter
Ⓐ Rubber Ball	6.35 mm (0.2500 in.)
Ⓑ Steel Ball	5.56 mm (0.2189 in.)
Ⓒ Steel Ball	7.14 mm (0.2811 in.)

AW-4 transmission—check ball and strainer location

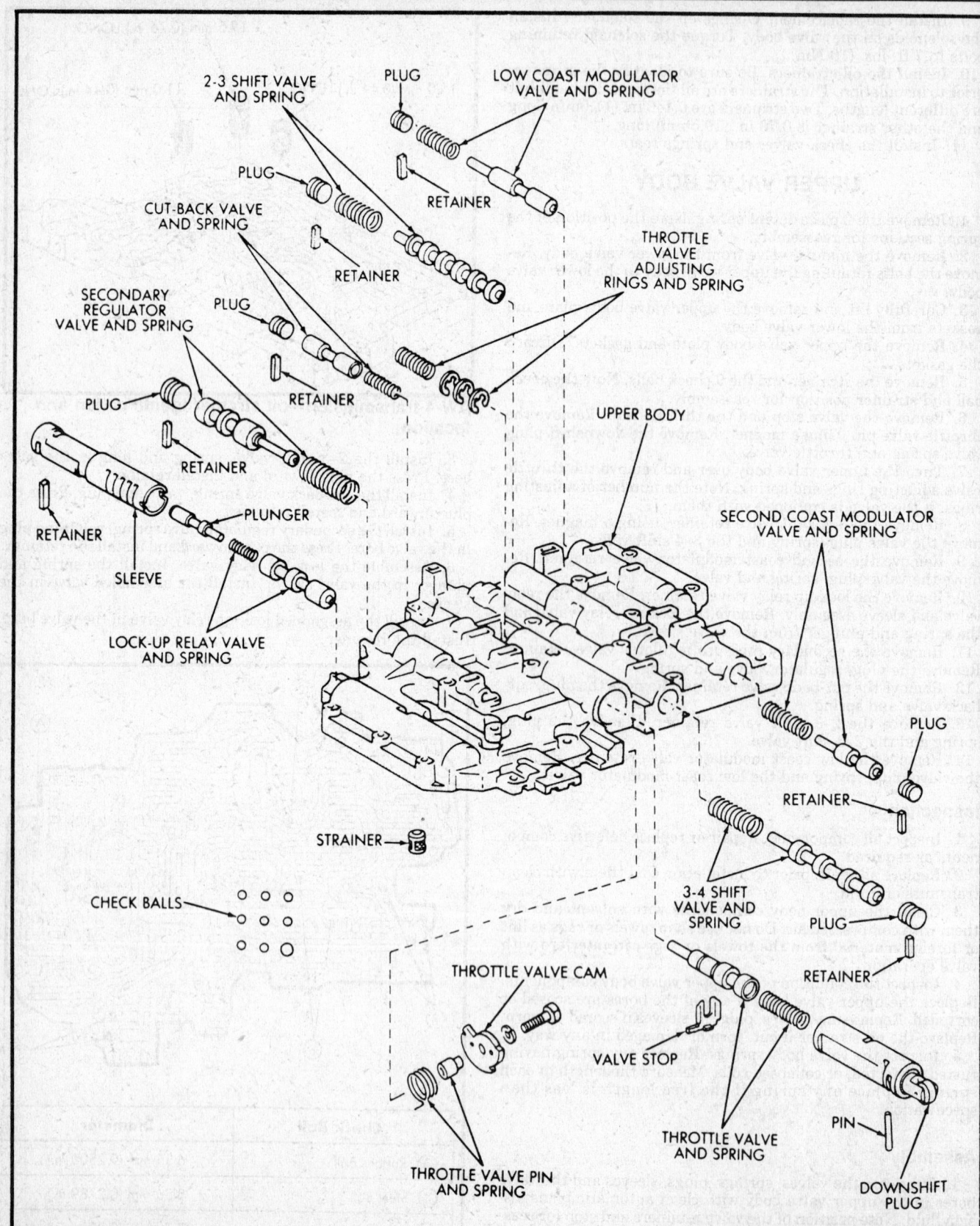

2-3 SHIFT VALVE AND SPRING

PLUG

LOW COAST MODULATOR VALVE AND SPRING

PLUG

CUT-BACK VALVE AND SPRING

RETAINER

THROTTLE VALVE ADJUSTING RINGS AND SPRING

SECONDARY REGULATOR VALVE AND SPRING

PLUG

RETAINER

PLUG

RETAINER

UPPER BODY

PLUG

RETAINER

RETAINER

PLUNGER

SECOND COAST MODULATOR VALVE AND SPRING

RETAINER

SLEEVE

LOCK-UP RELAY VALVE AND SPRING

PLUG

RETAINER

STRAINER

3-4 SHIFT VALVE AND SPRING

PLUG

CHECK BALLS

RETAINER

THROTTLE VALVE CAM

VALVE STOP

THROTTLE VALVE AND SPRING

PIN

THROTTLE VALVE PIN AND SPRING

DOWNSHIFT PLUG

AW-4 transmission—upper valve body assembly

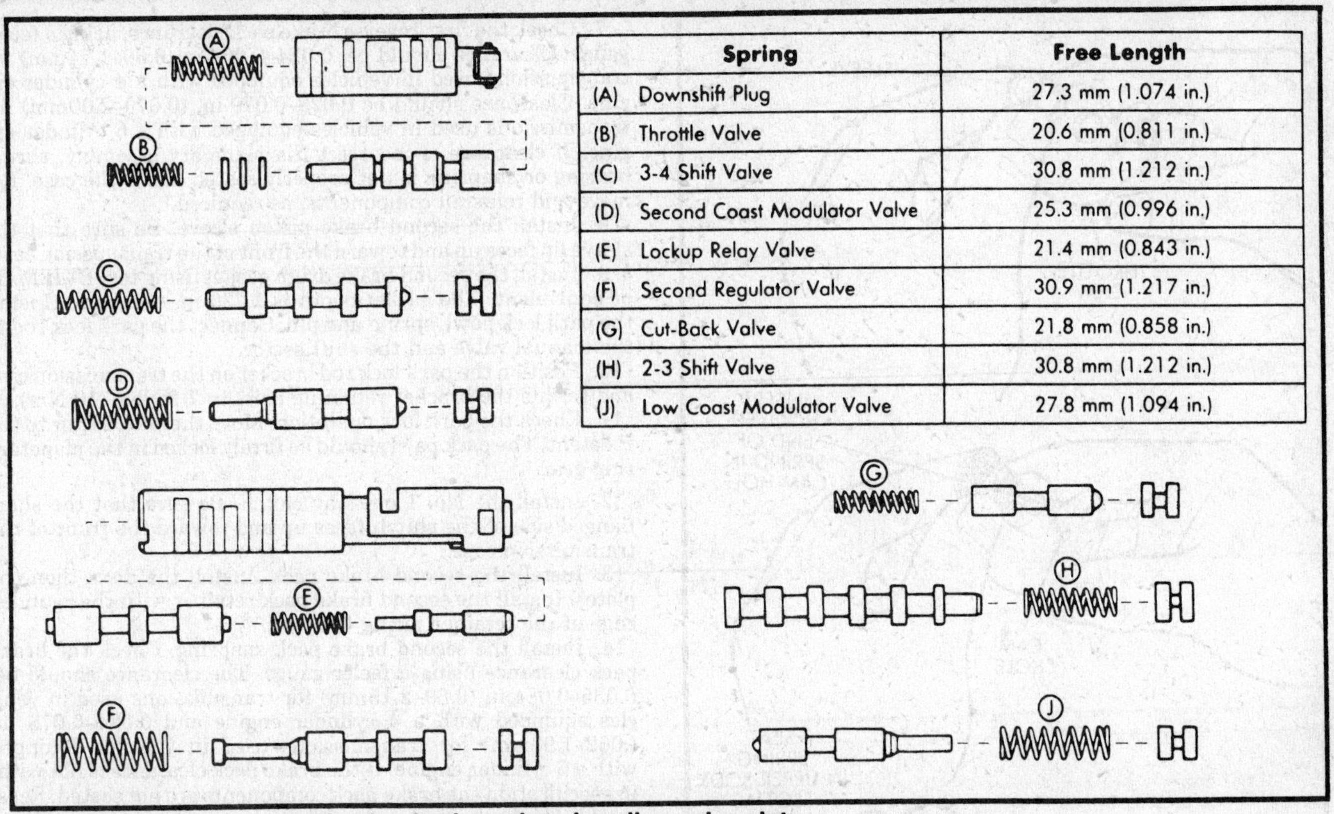

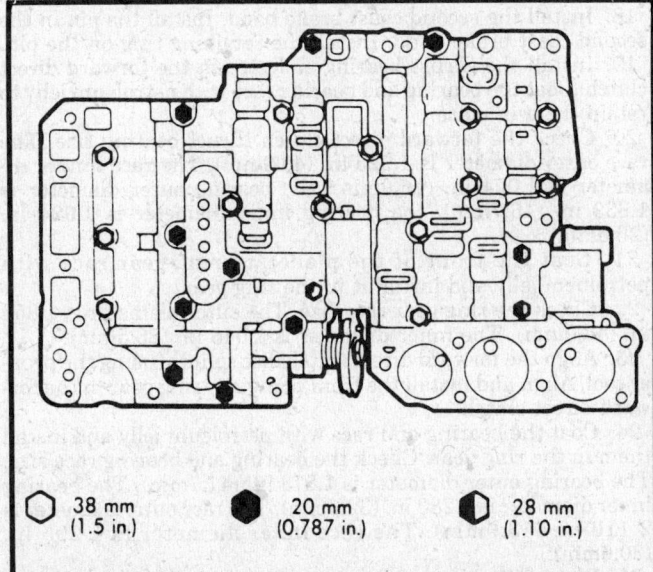

	Spring	Free Length
(A)	Downshift Plug	27.3 mm (1.074 in.)
(B)	Throttle Valve	20.6 mm (0.811 in.)
(C)	3-4 Shift Valve	30.8 mm (1.212 in.)
(D)	Second Coast Modulator Valve	25.3 mm (0.996 in.)
(E)	Lockup Relay Valve	21.4 mm (0.843 in.)
(F)	Second Regulator Valve	30.9 mm (1.217 in.)
(G)	Cut-Back Valve	21.8 mm (0.858 in.)
(H)	2-3 Shift Valve	30.8 mm (1.212 in.)
(J)	Low Coast Modulator Valve	27.8 mm (1.094 in.)

AW-4 transmission—upper valve body and spring dimension data

8. Install the second coast modulator valve, spring and plug in the valve bore. Press the plug inward and install the retainer.

9. Install the 3–4 shift valve, spring and plug in the bore. Press the plug inward and install the retainer.

10. Install the throttle valve in the valve bore. Push the valve into place and install the valve stop.

11. On transmissions that use adjusting rings, turn the upper valve body over and install the adjusting rings. Be sure to install the same number of rings as removed.

AW-4 transmission—valve body bolt location and identification

◯ 38 mm (1.5 in.)   ⬢ 20 mm (0.787 in.)   ⬡ 28 mm (1.10 in.)

12. Install the throttle valve adjusting spring in the bore and onto the end of the throttle valve.

13. Install the downshift spring and plug in the throttle valve bore. Press the plug inward against the throttle valve and spring. Install the retainer pin.

14. Install the sleeve in the throttle cam. Install the spring on the cam. Hook the curved end of the spring through the hole in the cam.

15. Mount the cam on the upper body. Install the cam retaining bolt and spacer. Torque the bolt to 7 ft. lbs. (10 Nm).

16. Be sure that the straight end of the spring is seated in the upper valve body slot.

17. Install the check balls in the upper valve body. Refer to illustration for check ball identification and location. Install the oil strainer.

18. To install the upper valve body to the lower valve body, position a new No. 1 gasket on the upper valve body.

19. Positon the valve body plate on the No. 1 gasket. Positon a new No. 2 gasket on the valve body plate and align the gaskets and plate, usie the bolt holes as guides.

20. Install the valve body bolts. Different length bolts are used. Torque the valve body bolts to 56 inch lbs. (6.4 Nm).

21. Install manual valve. Install the detent spring. Torque the spring retaining bolt to 7 ft. lbs. (10 Nm).

Transmission Assembly

NOTE: During the assembly of the transmission, be sure to lubricate components with clean transmission fluid or petroleum jelly, as required.

1. If any of the tranmission components are still assembled after the overhaul checking procedures have been done, disassemble these components as necessary in preparation for transmission reassembly.

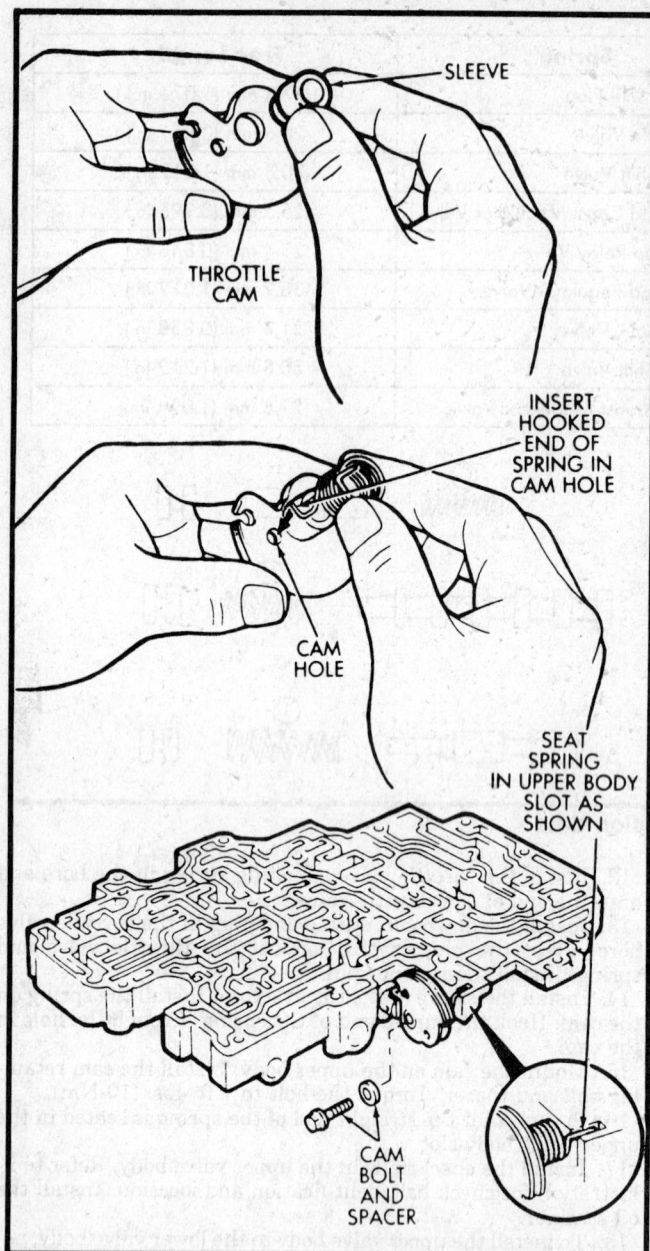

AW-4 transmission—throttle cam positioning

7. Check the first/reverse brake pack clearance, using a feeler gauge. Clearance should be, 0.024–0.069 in (0.60–1.74mm) for transmissions used in vehicles equipped with a 4 cylinder engine. Clearance should be 0.028–0.079 in. (0.070–2.00mm) for transmissions used in vehicles equipped with a 6 cylinder engine. If clearance is incorrect the planetary assembly, thrust bearing or snapring is not properly seated inside the case. Remove and reinstall components, as required.

8. Install the second brake piston sleeve. Be sure that the sleeve lip faces up and toward the front of the transmission case.

9. Install the second brake drum gasket using tool BVIFM-33 or equivalent. The gasket depth is 1.720 in. (43.7mm). Install the park lock pawl, spring and pin. Connect the park lock rod to the manual valve and the shift sector.

10. Position the park lock rod bracket on the transmission case and torque the bracket retaining bolts to 7 ft. lbs. (10 Nm).

11. Check the park lock operation. Move the shift sector to the **P** detent. The park pawl should be firmly locked in the planetary ring gear.

12. Install the No. 1 one-way clutch. Be sure that the short flanged side of the clutch faces up and toward the front of the transmission case.

13. Install the second brake pack. Install the discs then the plates. Install the second brake pack retainer with the rounded edge of the retainer facing the disc.

14. Install the second brake pack snapring. Check the brake pack clearance using a feeler gauge. The clearance should be, 0.035–0.084 in (0.89–2.15mm) for transmissions used in vehicles equipped with a 4 cylinder engine and 0.024–0.078 in. (.062–1.98mm) for transmissions used in vehicles equipped with a 6 cylinder engine. If the brake pack clearance is not within specification the brake pack components are not seated. Reassemble the brake pack, as required.

15. Install the planetary sun gear and the input drum. Be sure that the drum thrust washer tabs are seated in the drum. Use petroleum jelly to hold the thrust washer in position, as necessary.

16. Install the front planetary gear on the sun gear. Support the output shaft with wood blocks. Install the planetary snapring on the sun gear, using tool BVIFM-30 or equivalent.

17. Install the tabbed thrust race on the front planetary gear. The washer tabs face down and toward the gear. The race outer diameter is 1.882 in. (47.8mm). the race inner diameter is 1.350 in. (34.3mm).

18. Install the second coast brake band. Install the pin in the second coast brake band. Install the retaining ring on the pin.

19. Install the thrust bearing and race in the forward direct clutch. Coat the bearing and bearing race with petroleum jelly to retain them in place.

20. Check the forward direct clutch thrust bearing size. The race outer diameter is 1.925 in. (48.9mm). The race innner diameter is 1.024 in. (26.0mm). the bearing outer diameter is 1.839 in. (46.7mm). the bearing inner diameter is 1.024 in. (26.0mm).

21. Coat the front of the planetary ring gear race with petroleum jelly and install it in the ring gear.

22. Check the ring gear race size. The outer diameter is 1.850 in. (47.0mm). The inner diameter is 1.045 in. (26.5mm).

23. Align the forward direct clutch disc splines, using the proper tool. Align and install the front planetary ring gear in the forward direct clutch.

24. Coat the bearing and race with petroleum jelly and install them in the ring gear. Check the bearing and bearing race size. The bearing outer diameter is 1.878 in. (47.7mm). The bearing inner diameter is 1.283 in. (32.6mm). The race outer diameter is 2.110 in. (53.6mm). The race inner diameter is 1.205 in. (30.6mm).

25. Rotate the front of the transmission case downward and install the assembled planetary gear forward direct clutch assembly.

2. Verify correct thrust bearing and race installation during reassembly.

3. To install the rear planetary gear, second brake drum and output shaft, verify the No. 10 thrust bearing and race specification. The bearing and race outer diameter is 2.272 in. (57.7mm). The bearing and race inside diameter is 1.543 in. (39.2mm).

4. Coat the thrust bearing and race assembly with petroleum jelly and install it in the transmission case. Be sure that the race faces down and the bearing rollers face up.

5. Align the teeth of the second brake drum and the clutch pack. Align the rear planetary output shaft assembly teeth with the tranmission case slots and install assembly in the tranmsission case.

6. Install the rear planetary snapring using tool BVIFM-29, or equivalent. The chamfered side of the snapring must face up and toward the front of the transmission case.

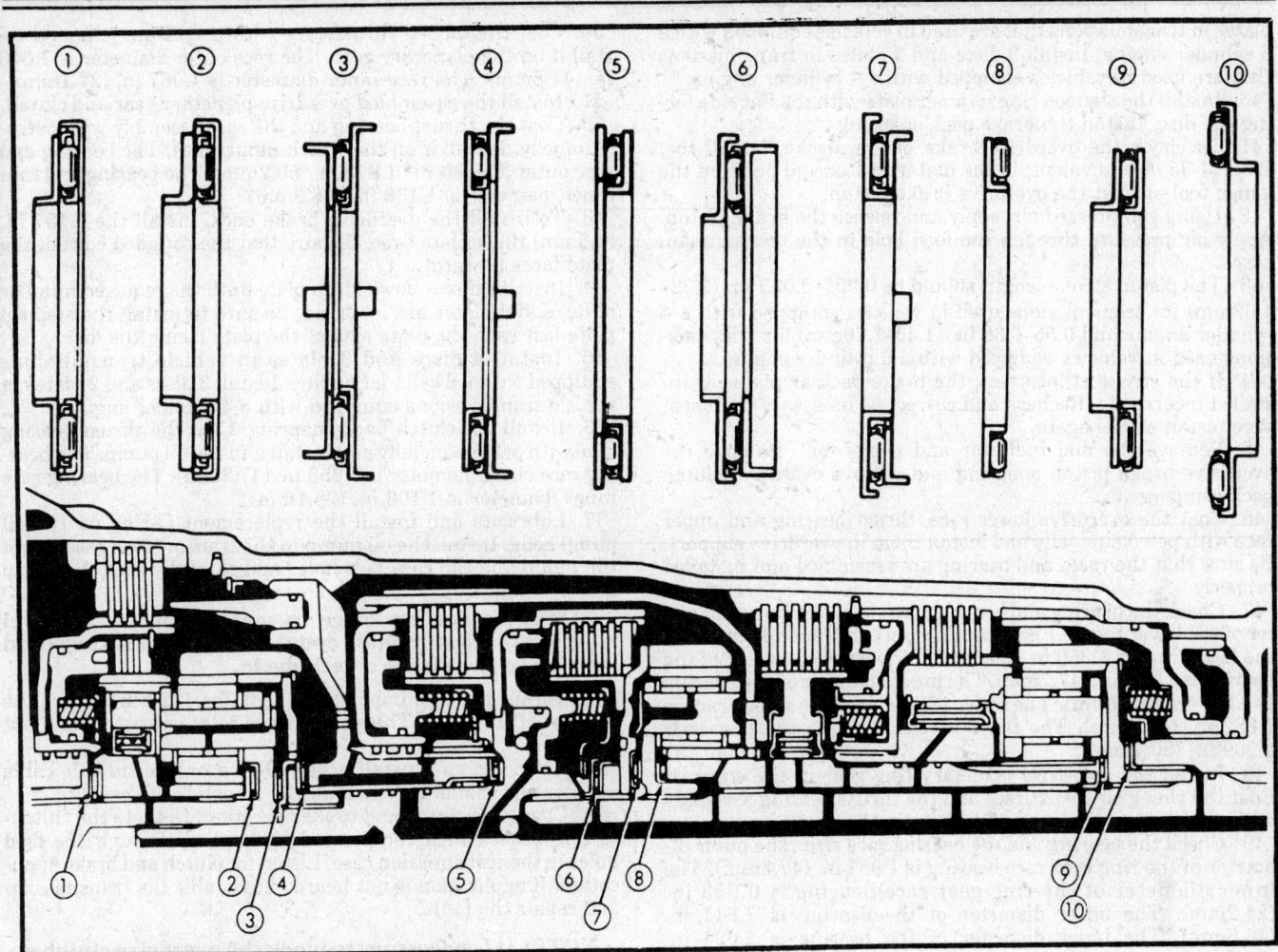

AW-4 transmission – thrust bearing data

26. Check the clearance between the sun gear input drum and the direct clutch drum. The clearance should be 0.3860–0.4654 in. (9.8–11.8mm). If the clearance is incorrect the planetary gear forward direct clutch assembly is not seated or it is improperly assembled. Remove the assembly and correct, as required.

27. Coat the thrust bearing and the race assembly with petroleum jelly and install it on the clutch shaft. Be sure that the bearing faces up and toward the front of the transmission case. Check the bearing and bearing race size. The bearing and race outer diameter is 1.882 in. (47.8mm). The bearing and race inner diameter is 1.301 in. (33.6mm).

28. Assemble the second coast brake piston components. Install the assembled second coast brake piston in the transmission case.

29. Install the replacement seals on the second coast brake piston cover. Install the cover in the transmission case.

30. Install the second coast brake piston snapring, using tool BVIFM-29 or equivalent.

31. To check the second coast brake piston stroke, make a reference mark on the brake piston rod. Apply 57–114 psi of compressed air through the feed hole. Alternately apply and release the air pressure in order to operate the piston.

32. Check the stroke, using the proper gauge tool. Use gauge tool BVIFM40 or equivalent for transmissions used in vehicles wquipped with a 4 cylinder engine and use gauge tool BVIFM-41 or equivalent for transmissions used in vehicles equipped with a 6 cylinder engine.

33. If the stroke length is incorrect, the piston, cover or snapring is not seated properly. Reassemble these components and recheck the stroke, as required.

34. Coat the thrust race and tabbed washer with petroleum jelly and install them on overdrive support. Check the race size. the race outer diameter is 2.004 in. (50.9mm). The race inner diameter is 1.426 in. (36.2mm).

35. Install the overdrive support in the transmission case. Use both of the long bolts to help align and guide the support into position.

36. Install the overdrive support snapring using tool BVIFM-29 or equivalent. Be sure that the chamfered side of the snapring faces up and toward the front of the transmission case. The snapring ends must be aligned with the case opening and with the ring ends approximately 0.94 in. from the centerline of the case opening.

37. Install and torque the overdrive support bolts to 19 ft. lbs. (25 Nm). Using a dial indicator gauge check the output shaft endplay. The endplay should be 0.0106–0.0339 in. (0.27–0.86mm).

38. If the output shaft endplay is incorrect, one or more of the installed components is not seated properly. Reassemble the components, as required and recheck the endplay.

39. Install the overdrive clutch pack. Be sure to install the thickest clutch plate first and check that the rounded edge of the plate faces up. Install the first disc followed by a plate until the correct number of discs trand plates are used. Install 4 discs and 3

plates in transmissions that are used in vehicles equipped with a 6 cylinder engine. Install 3 discs and 2 plates in transmissions that are used in vehicles equipped with a 4 cylinder engine.

40. Install the stepped ring retainer plate with the flat side facing the disc. Install the brake pack snapring.

41. To check the overdrive brake piston stroke, install tool BVIFM-35 or equivalent, in the dial indicator and position the gauge tool against the overdrive brake piston.

42. Using compressed air, apply and release the brake piston. Apply air pressure through the feed hole in the transmission case.

43. The piston stroke length should be 0.052–0.063 in. (1.32–1.62mm) for transmissions used in vehicles equipped with a 4 cylinder engine and 0.55–0.66 in. (1.40–1.70mm) for transmissions used in vehicles equipped with a 6 cylinder engine.

44. If the stroke is incorrect, the brake pack or piston is installed incorrectly. Recheck and correct as necessary and measure piston stroke again.

45. Remove the dial indicator and gauge tool. Remove the overdrive brake piston snapring and remove overdrive clutch pack components.

46. Coat the overdrive lower race, thrust bearing and upper race with petroleum jelly and install them in overdrive support. Be sure that the races and bearing are assembled and installed properly.

47. Check the bearing and bearing race sizes. The outer diameter of the lower race is 1.882 in. (47.8mm). the inner diameter of the lower race is 1.350 in. (34.3mm). The outer diameter of the bearing is 1.878 in. (47.7mm). The inner diameter of the bearing is 1.287 in. (32.7mm). The outer diameter of the upper race is 1.882 in. (47.8mm). The inner diameter of the upper race is 1.209 in. (30.7mm).

48. Install the overdrive planetary ring gear in the support. Coat the ring gear thrust race and the thrust bearing assembly with petorleum jelly and install them in the gear.

49. Check the bearing and the bearing race size. The outer diameter of the ring gear race bearing is 1.882 in. (47.8mm). The inner diameter of the ring gear race bearing is 0.953 in. (24.2mm). The outer diameter of the bearing is 1.844 in. (46.8mm). The inner diameter of the bearing is 1.024 in. (26.0mm).

50. Coat the tabbed thrust race with petroleum jelly and install it on the planetary gear. The race outer diameter is 1.646 in. (41.8mm). The race inner diameter is 1.067 in. (27.1mm).

51. Install the assembled overdrive planetary gear and clutch.

52. Coat the thrust bearing and the race assembly with petroleum jelly. Install it on the clutch input shaft. The bearing and race outer diameter is 1.976 in. (50.2mm). The bearing and race inner diameter is 1.138 in. (28.9mm).

53. To install the overdrive brake pack, install the 0.157 in. (4.0mm) thick plate first. Be sure that the rounded edge of the plate faces upward.

54. Install a disc followed by a plate until the required number of discs and plates are installed. Be sure to install the stepped plate last with the plate side of the plate facing the disc.

55. Install 4 discs and 3 plates in vehicle transmissions equipped with a 6 cylinder engine. Install 3 discs and 2 plates in vehicle transmissions equipped with a 4 cylinder engine.

56. Install the clutch pack snapring. Coat the thrust bearing race with petroleum jelly and install it in the oil pump. The bearing race outer diameter is 1.858 in. (47.2mm). The bearing race inner diameter is 1.106 in. (28.1mm).

57. Lubricate and install the replacement O-ring on the oil pump body. Install the oil pump in the transmission case. Align the pump and the case bolt holes and carefully ease the pump into position.

NOTE: Do not use force to seat the pump. The seal rings on the stator shaft could be damaged if they bind or stick to the direct clucth drum.

58. Torque the oil pump bolts to 16 ft. lbs. (22 Nm). Check the input shaft rotation. The shaft should rotate smoothly and not bind.

59. Lubricate and install a new O-ring on the throttle cable adapter and install the cable in the transmission case.

60. Check the clutch and brake operation. Operate the clutches and brakes with compressed air applied through the feed holes in the transmission case. Listen for clutch and brake application. If application is not heard, diassemble the transmission and repair the fault.

NOTE: It is necessary to block the overdrive clutch accumulator feed hole No. 8 in order to check the direct clutch operation.

61. Lubricate and install new O-rings on the accumulator pistons. Assemble and install the accumulator piston components.

62. Install a new check ball body and spring. Position the valve body assembly on the transmission case. Install the detent spring.

63. Align the manual valve, detent spring and shift sector.

ACCUMULATOR COMPONENT SELECTION

Item	Component	Diameter in. (mm)	Length in. (mm)
Second brake accumulator	Pin A	0.472 (12.0)	1.386 (35.2)
	Spring B, 4 cyl.	0.748 (19.0)	1.653 (42.0)
	Spring B, 6 cyl.	0.764 (19.4)	1.496 (38.0)
	Piston C	1.453 (36.9)	2.697 (68.5)
	Spring D, 4 cyl.	0.772 (19.6)	2.106 (53.5)
	Spring D, 6 cyl.	0.775 (19.7)	2.106 (53.5)
Direct clutch accumulator	Pin E	0.539 (13.7)	1.307 (33.2)
	Spring F, 4 cyl.	0.819 (20.8)	1.535 (39.0)
	Spring F, 6 cyl.	0.831 (21.1)	1.433 (36.4)
	Piston G	1.453 (36.9)	2.465 (62.6)
	Spring H	0.799 (20.3)	1.893 (48.1)
Overdrive brake accumulator	Piston I	1.256 (31.9)	2.047 (52.0)
	Spring J	0.626 (15.9)	2.598 (66.0)
Overdrive clutch accumulator	Spring K	0.551 (14.0)	1.811 (46.0)
	Spring L	0.799 (20.3)	2.937 (74.6)
	Piston M	1.177 (29.9)	1.929 (49.0)

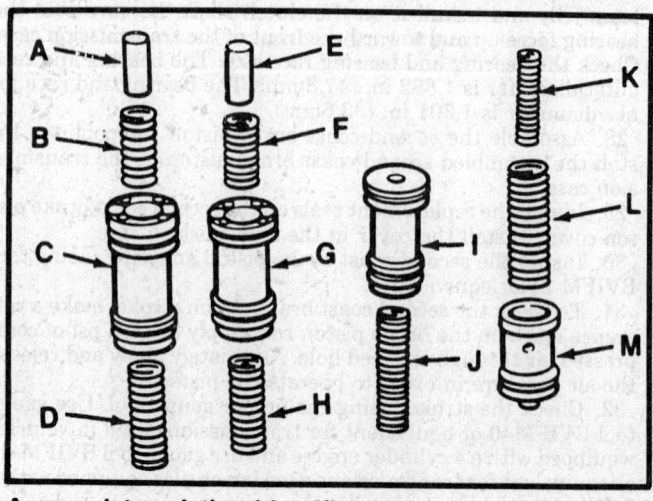

Accumulator pistion identification

Connect the throttle cable to the throttle valve cam. Install and torque the valve body to transmission case bolts to 7 ft. lbs. (10 Nm).

64. Connect the valve body solenoid wires to the solenoids. Install a new O-ring on the solenoid harness adapter and secure the adapter to the transmission case.

65. Install the valve body oil tubes. Tap the tubes into place using a plastic mallet. Be sure that the flanged tube ends and straight tubes ends are installed correctly..

66. Install new gaskets on the oil screen and install the screen on the valve body. Torque the screen bolts to 7 ft. lbs. (10 Nm).

67. Install a magnet in the oil pan. Be sure that the magnet does not interfere with valve body oil tubes.

68. Apply RTV sealer, to the gasket surface of the oil pan. The sealer bead should be 0.04 in. (1mm) wide. Install a new gasket on the oil pan. Install the oil pan. Torque the pan bolts to 65 inch lbs. (7.4 Nm).

69. Install the speed sensor rotor and key on the output shaft. Install the spacer and speedometer drive gear on the output shaft. Install the retaining snapring.

70. Install the spacer and the speedometer drive gear on the output shaft. Install the retaining snapring.

71. Apply a bead of sealer to the sealing surface at rear of the transmission case. Install the extension housing (2WD vehicles) or adapter housing (4WD vehicles). Torque the retaining bolts to 25 ft. lbs. (34 Nm).

72. Install the speed sensor. Torque the sensor bolt to 65 inch lbs. (7.4 Nm) Connect the sensor wire harness connector.

73. Install the speedometer driven gear. Torque the gear retaining bolt to 175 inch lbs. (19 Nm).

74. Install the torque converter housing. Torque the 12mm diameter housing bolts to 42 ft. lbs. (57 Nm). Torque the 10mm diameter housing bolts to 25 ft. lbs. (34 Nm).

75. Install the transmission shift control lever on the manual valve shaft. Do not install the lever retaining nut at this time.

76. Move the shift control lever all the way to the rear. Then move it 2 detent positions forward.

77. Install the neutral saftey switch on the manual valve shaft and tighten switch adjusting bolt just enough to keep the switch from moving.

78. Install the neutral safety switch tabbed washer and retaining nut. Torque the nut to 61 inch lbs. (6.9 Nm), but do not bend any of the washer tabs against the nut.

79. Align the neutral safety switch standard line with the groove or flat on the manual shaft. Torque the neutral safety switch adjusting bolt to 9 ft. lbs. (13 Nm).

80. Install the shift control lever on the manual valve shaft. Torque the lever retaining nut to 12 ft. lbs. (16 Nm).

81. Install the retaining clamp for the wire harness and the throttle cable. Install the torque converter.

82. Check that the converter is seated by measuring the distance between the torque converter housing flange and one of the torque converter mounting pads.

83. Use a straightedge and vernier calipers to measure this distance. On vehicles equipped with a 4 cylinder engine, the distance should be 0.689 in. (17.5 mm). On vehicles equipped with a 6 cylinder engine, the distance should be 0.650 in. (16.5mm).

84. Install the lower half of the transmission fill tube. Install the upper half of the transmission fill tube after the transmission is installed in the vehicle.

SPECIFICATIONS

TORQUE SPECIFICATIONS

Component	Service Set-to-torque ft. lbs.	Nm	Service Recheck Torque ft. lbs.	Nm
Converter housing bolt				
10mm	25	34	23–27	32–36
12mm	42	57	40–43	55–59
Extension housing bolt	25	34	23–27	32–36
Speed sensor bolt	65①	7.4	57–75①	6.4–8.4
Speedometer housing bolt	175①	19	160–185①	18–20
Shift lever nut	12	16	11–13	15–17
Neutral safety switch bolt	9	13	8–10	12–14
Neutral safety switch nut	61①	6.9	53–70	5.9–7.9
Solenoid harness bolt	65①	7.4	57–75	6.4–8.4
Oil pan bolts	65①	7.4	57–75	6.4–8.4
Oil pan drain plugs	15	20	14–16	19–21
Oil screen bolt	88①	10	80–96①	9–11
Valve body bolt (to case)	88①	10	80–96	9–11
Valve body bolt (to valve body)	56①	6.4	54–58①	6–6.8
Detent spring bolt	88①	10	80–96①	9–11
Oil pump bolt (to case)	17	22	16–18	21–23

TORQUE SPECIFICATIONS

Component	Service Set-to-torque ft. lbs.	Nm	Service Recheck Torque ft. lbs.	Nm
Oil pump bolt (to stator shaft)	88①	10	80–96①	9–11
OD support bolt (to case)	19	25	18–20	23–27
Park pawl bracket	88①	10	80–96①	9–11

① Measurement in inch lbs.

BUSHING SPECIFICATIONS

Bushing Location	Maximum Allowance Inside Diameter in.	mm
Extension housing	1.4996	38.09
Direct clutch drum	2.1248	53.97
Overdrive planetary gear	0.4437	11.27
Overdrive direct clutch drum	1.0673	21.11
Front startor shaft	0.8496	21.58
Rear startor shaft	1.0661	27.08
Oil pump body	1.5035	38.19
Transmission case	1.5031	38.18

ENDPLAY AND CLEARANCE SPECIFICATIONS

Component	Engine	Specification in.	mm
Output shaft endplay		0.0106–0.0339	0.27–0.86
1st/Reverse brake pack clearance	6 cyl.	0.0280–0.0790	0.70–2.00
	4 cyl.	0.0240–0.0690	0.60–1.74
Second brake pack clearance	6 cyl.	0.0350–0.0840	0.89–2.15
	4 cyl.	0.0240–0.0780	0.62–1.98
Clutch discs All except 1st/reverse and forward		0.00724	1.84

Component	Engine	Specification in.	mm
Forward clutch disc	6 cyl.	0.0594	1.51
	4 cyl.	0.0724	1.84
6 cyl. direct clutch plates	Thin (1)	0.905	2.3
	Thick (3)	0.118	3.0
4 cyl. Direct clutch plates	Thin (1)	0.118	3.0
	Thick (2)	0.1574	4.0
Forward clutch plate	6 cyl.	0.070	1.8
	4 cyl.	0.078	2.0
1st/reverse brake disc		0.0594	1.51

SPECIAL TOOLS

TOOL REF. NUMBER	DESCRIPTION
B.Vi. FM 25	PUMP PULLER
B.Vi. FM 26	OVERDRIVE SPRING COMPRESSOR
B.Vi. FM 27	PISTON SPRING COMPRESSOR
B.Vi. FM 28	PISTON SPRING COMPRESSOR
B.Vi. FM 29	SNAP RING PLIERS
B.Vi. FM 30	SNAP RING PLIERS
B.Vi. FM 31	BRAKE SLEEVE PULLER
B.Vi. FM 32	PISTON PULLER
B.Vi. FM 33	SEAL INSTALLER
B.Vi. FM 34	SEAL INSTALLER
B.Vi. FM 35	GAUGE
B.Vi. FM 36	CLUTCH TEST TOOL (CONVERTER)
B.Vi. FM 37	CLUTCH TEST TOOL (CONVERTER)
B.Vi. FM 38	SEAL INSTALLER
B.Vi. FM 39	SEAL REMOVER
B.Vi. FM 40	1.5 mm WIRE GAUGE
B.Vi. FM 41	3.0 mm WIRE GAUGE
B.Vi. KM 01	SEAL INSTALLER 2WD
J-29184	SEAL INSTALLER 4WD

B.Vi. FM 35

B.Vi. FM 36

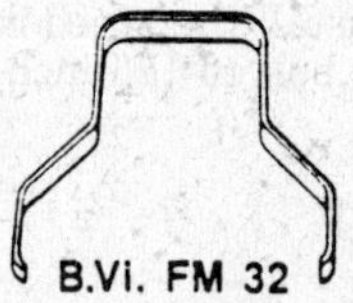

B.Vi. FM 32

B.Vi. FM 37

B.Vi. FM 40

B.Vi. FM 41

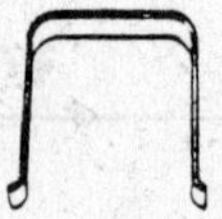

B.Vi. FM 31

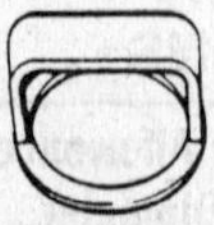

B.Vi. FM 27

B.Vi. FM 38

B.Vi. KM.01 OR J-29184

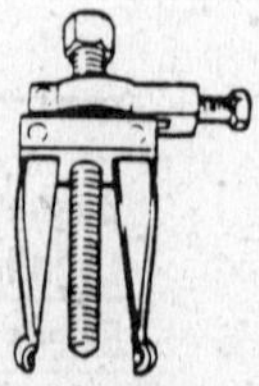

B.Vi. FM 39

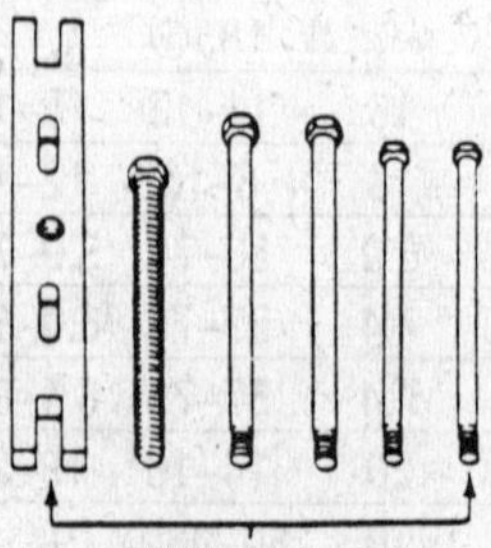

B.Vi. FM 25

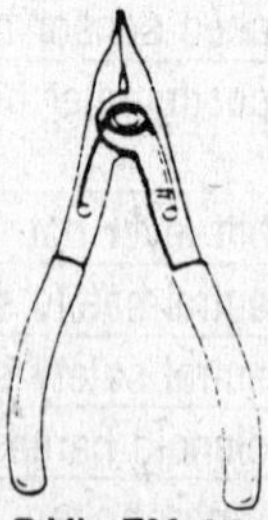

B.Vi. FM 30

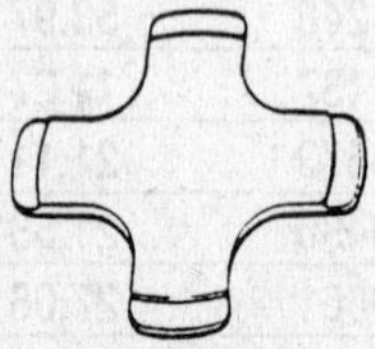

B.Vi. FM 26

B.Vi. FM 33

B.Vi. FM 34

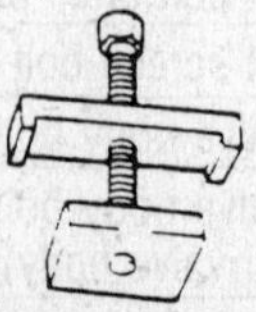

B.Vi. FM 29

B.Vi. FM 28

Section 4

A500 Transmission
Chrysler Corp.

APPLICATION

1988–89 Dodge Dakota

GENERAL DESCRIPTION

The front portion of the A-500 4 speed overdrive automatic transmission is a modified version of the A-998 3 speed Loadflite automatic transmission. The rear unit, or overdrive unit, replaces the extension housing and provides a overdrive gear with a gear ratio of 0.69–1.

The first 3 gear ratios of the A-500 have the same gear ratios and torque capacity that was offered in the 3 speed Loadflite transmission. The addition of the 4th gear overdrive to the Loadflite gives the added features of increased fuel economy , prolonged engine life and less engine noise at cruising speed.

The overdrive unit is designed to withstand up to 400 lbs. of torque. Because of the high loads and long periods of time that can be spent in overdrive, all the thrust bearings are needle bearings. The overdrive has added approximately 50 lbs. of weight and 6½ in. of length to the A-998 transmission.

The 4th gear (overdrive) is electronically controlled and hydraulically activated. A variety of sensor inputs are fed to the Single Module Engine Controller (SMEC) which controls a solenoid mounted on the valve body. The solenoid will energize and close a vent, allowing a 3–4 upshift. The SMEC also controls the operation of the lockup torque converter using many of the same sensor inputs.

A lockup torque converter, which is electronically controlled and hydraulically activated, will also be used with this transmission. 4th gear (overdrive) and lockup will only occur during certain conditions determined by the SMEC.

When the vehicle is traveling in 3rd gear over 25 mph, the SMEC uses the following information to allow the transmission to shift. The SMEC checks the coolant sensor signal for a 60° fahrenheit minimum temperature. It also checks the engine sensor speed, the vehicle speed sensor, the throttle position sensor and the MAP sensor.

The steering column shift selector remains at 6 positions. Overdrive will be engaged automatically in **D**. A separate overdrive **OFF** switch will be located on the instrument panel. This switch will override the SMEC and shift out of overdrive and prevent further shifts into overdrive. If the overdrive **OFF** switch is activated again the automatic operation is restored. The switch has an indicator light when the overdrive is turned off. The switch also resets on key-off so that the automatic overdrive feature is restored.

The use of fault codes aid in diagnosing the electronic components used to operate the overdrive and lockup torque converter. Other features in conjunction with this unit include.

1. The output shaft of the 3 speed section is now an intermediate shaft.

2. The 3 speed section rear drum is retained on the support with a snapring.

3. The governor and speedometer drive have been relocated to the rear of the output shaft.

4. The overdrive case now contains 2 output shaft bearings.

5. There are no rotating seal rings or pressurized oil for the overdrive and direct clutches in the overdrive housing. The governor is the only component receiving pressurized oil through the slip fit tubes. Pressurized oil for the overdrive lubrication circuit is supplied through the intermediate shaft.

6. Governor pressure and overdrive pressure taps are provided in the rear of the transmission case for in-vehicle transmission pressure testing.

7. The valve body is modified by adding several new valves. There is an overdrive solenoid, a 3–4 shift valve, a 3–4 timing valve, a 3–4 accumulator and a 3–4 shuttle valve. Once in 4th (overdrive) gear, the lockup solenoid, lockup valve and lockup timing valve accomplish the hydraulics to lock the converter turbine to the torque converter housing.

8. The direct drive and overdrive gear ratios are supplied by a 3rd planetary gear set, a direct clutch, an overdrive clutch and an overrunning clutch. A very strong spring, rated at up to 800 lbs. (5516 kPa), holds the sun gear to the annulus for direct drive. For coasting or reverse gear, power flows only through the direct clutch.

9. The lockup timing valve releases the torque converter to normal operation prior to the 4–3 downshift.

10. All closed throttle 3–4 upshifts will occur at 25–28 mph., regardless of the axle ratio.

11. All closed throttle 4–3 downshifts will occur at 25 mph., regardless of the axle ratio.

12. No 3–4 upshifts can be achieved, regardless of the vehicle speed, if the throttle opening is greater than 70% approximately.

Transmission and Converter Identification

TRANSMISSION

The 7 digit transmission part number is usually stamped on the left side of the transmission case just above the oil pan mating surface. This number is followed by a 4 digit code number which indicates the date of manufacture. The final 4 digit number group stamped on the transmission case represents the transmission serial number.

CONVERTER

Because the lockup converter is completely enclosed within the converter and cannot be seen, look for lockup converters to have an identifying decal attached to the front cover. The decal is circular in shape and states converter type and stall ratio such as **LOCKUP** and **LS** (Low Stall) or **HS** (High Stall).

NOTE: The torque converters no longer come equipped with drain plugs and therefore cannot be flushed if contaminated, only replaced.

Electronic Controls

The 4th gear (overdrive) is electronically controlled and hydraulically activated. A variety of sensor inputs are fed to the Single Module Engine Controller (SMEC) which controls a solenoid mounted on the valve body. The solenoid will energize and close a vent, allowing a 3–4 upshift. The SMEC also controls the operation of the lockup torque converter using many of the same sensor inputs.

A lockup torque converter, which is electronically controlled and hydraulically activated, will also be used with this transmission. 4th gear (overdrive) and lockup will only occur during certain conditions determined by the SMEC.

When the vehicle is traveling in 3rd gear over 25 mph, the SMEC uses the following information to allow the transmission to shift. The SMEC checks the coolant sensor signal for a 65°F minimum temperature. It also checks the engine sensor speed, the vehicle speed sensor, the throttle position sensor and the MAP sensor.

Th 25 mph speed limit is actually the lowest speed the transmission will stay in overdrive, during a coast down. The upshift into overdrive will be somewhat higher than 25 mph.

The engine speed is compared to the vehicle speed so that the SMEC can determine if the transmission is in 3rd gear . The SMEC must know this before it will allow the 3–4 shift to occur. This also prevents the possibility of a 2–4 downshift occuring. This signal comes from the ignition distributor.

The throttle position signal is compared to the engine speed signal to determine when to engage or disengage the overdrive unit. This signal comes from the throttle position sensor.

The SMEC must see all of the criteria stated above before it will energize the overdrive solenoid and go into overdrive.

The steering column shift selector remains at 6 positions. Overdrive will be engaged automatically in **D**. A separate overdrive **OFF** switch will be located on the instrument panel. This switch will override the SMEC and shift out of overdrive and prevent further shifts into overdrive. If the overdrive **OFF** switch is activated again the automatic operation is restored. The switch has an indicator light when the overdrive is turned off. The switch also resets on key-off so that the automatic overdrive feature is restored.

The use of fault codes help to diagnose the electronic components used to operate the overdrive and lockup torque converter.

Metric Fasteners

The metric fastener dimensions are very close to the dimensions of the familiar inch system fasteners and for this reason, replacement fasteners must have the same measurement and strength as those removed.

Do not attempt to interchange metric fasteners for inch system fasteners. Mismatched or incorrect fasteners can result in damage to the transmission unit through malfunctions, breakage or possible personal injury.

Care should be taken to reuse the fasteners in the same locations as removed.

Common metric fastener strength property classes are 9.8 and 12.9 with class identification embossed on the head of each bolt. The inch strength classes range from grade 2–8 with the line identification embossed on each bolt head. Markings on the bolt head correspond to 2 lines less than actual grade (for example grade 8 bolt will exhibit 6 embossed lines on the bolt head). Some metric nuts will be marked with a single digit strength identification numbers on the nut face.

Capacities

Chrysler products using lockup torque converters and models equipped with extra transmission coolers will all vary slightly in their capacity. Therefore, check fluid level carefully. The complete refill oil capacity of the A-998 transmission is 8.5 quarts (8.1 liters) and 10.5 quarts (9.6 liters) for the A-500 transmission.

Checking Automatic Transmission Fluid Level

The Chrysler type automatic transmission are designed to operate with fluid level at the **FULL** mark on the dipstick indicator. The fluid level can be checked with the transmission at normal operating temperature or with the transmission at room temperature. Do not overfill the transmission.

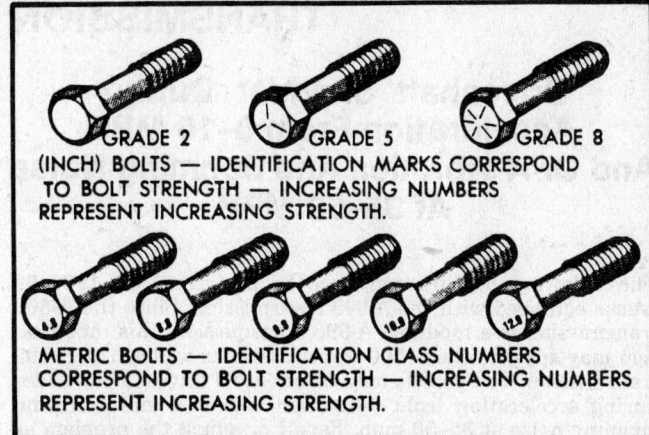

GRADE 2 (INCH) BOLTS — IDENTIFICATION MARKS CORRESPOND TO BOLT STRENGTH — INCREASING NUMBERS REPRESENT INCREASING STRENGTH.

METRIC BOLTS — IDENTIFICATION CLASS NUMBERS CORRESPOND TO BOLT STRENGTH — INCREASING NUMBERS REPRESENT INCREASING STRENGTH.

Inch and Metric thread notation and bolt identification

NOTE: When the automatic transmission fluid is replaced or topped off, MOPAR® ATF should be used. DEXRON® II type fluid should be used, only if the recommended fluid is not available.

TRANSMISSION AT NORMAL OPERATING TEMPERATURE

Approximately 180°F — Dipstick Hot To The Touch

1. With the vehicle on a level surface, engine idling, wheels blocked and the parking brake applied, move the selector lever through all the gear positions and return to the **N** position. Allow the engine to idle.
2. Clean the dipstick area of dirt and remove the dipstick from the filler tube. Wipe the dipstick indicator clean and reinsert the dipstick back into the filler tube and seat firmly.
3. Remove the dipstick from the filler tube again and check the fluid level as indicated on the dipstick indicator. The fluid level should be at the **FULL** mark.
4. If necessary, add fluid through the filler tube to bring the fluid level to its proper height.
5. When the fluid level is correct, fully seat the dipstick in the filler tube to avoid entrance of dirt or other foreign matter.

TRANSMISSION AT ROOM TEMPERATURE

Approximately 70°F — Dipstick Cool To The Touch

1. With the vehicle on a level surface, engine idling, wheels blocked and the parking brake applied, move the selector lever through all the gear positions and return to the **N** position. Allow the engine to idle.
2. Clean the dipstick area of dirt and remove the dipstick from the filler tube. Wipe the dipstick indicator clean and reinsert it back into the filler tube and seat firmly.
3. Remove the dipstick from the filler tube again and check the fluid level as indicated on the dipstick indicator. The fluid level should be at the **ADD ONE PINT** mark on the dipstick.
4. If necessary, add fluid through the filler tube to bring the fluid level to its proper height.
5. Reset the dipstick into the filler tube to avoid the entrance of dirt or foreign materials.
6. Upon bringing the transmission to its normal operating temperature, the fluid level should be at the **FULL** mark on the dipstick, due to the expansion of the fluid through heat.

TRANSMISSION MODIFICATIONS

Driveshaft Shudder During Acceleration From 0–10 MPH And Or A Vibration And Booming Noise At 35–50 MPH

The following modification is to be performed on 1987–89 trucks equipped with the A-998 transmission. Since the A-500 transmission is a modified A-998 transmission, this modification may apply to the A-500 transmission as well as the A-998 transmission. The vehicle may experience a driveshaft shudder during acceleration from 0–10 mph and or a vibration and booming noise at 35–50 mph. Repair or adjust the problem as follows:

1. Attach a suitable tachometer to the engine. Road test the vehicle to verify the condition.
2. The diagnosis procedure for acceleration shudder is performed from a standing start. Accelerate with medium to heavy acceleration from 0–15 mph while watching for the shudder. If the shudder is evident, note the engine rpm.
3. In the case of vibration and/or booming noise, road test the vehicle in the 35–55 mph range. If a vibration and/or booming noise is evident, note the engine rpm where the problem is most perceptible.
4. With the vehicle stopped and transmission in the N position, run the engine up through the same rpm ranges and note if the same condition is present.
5. If neither of these problems are present while running up the engine and either or both of the above conditions are have been verified, it will be necessary to remove the 2 piece driveshaft and install a single piece driveshaft as follows:

    a. Remove the front and rear driveshaft assembly.

    b. Unbolt and remove the driveshaft center bearing support cross member.

    c. Install a new 1 piece driveshaft and torque the U-joint strap bolts to 14 ft. lbs. (68 Nm).

    d. Road test the vehicle to verify repairs. The driveshaft required are as follows.

    e. A wheel base of 124 in. with a 7¼ rear axle requires driveshaft part number 4384625.

    f. A wheel base of 124 in. with a 8¼ rear axle requires driveshaft part number 4384605.

TROUBLE DIAGNOSIS

CLUTCH AND BAND APPLICATION
A-500 Overdrive Transmission

Lever Position	A500 Over- Drive	Start Safety	Parking Sprag	Transmission Clutches Front	Rear	Running	Lockup	Bands KD Front	Reverse/Rear	Overdrive OD	Clutches Running	Direct
P-Park	—	Applied	Applied	—	—	—	—	—	—	—	—	—
R-Reverse	2.21	—	—	Applied	—	—	—	—	Applied	—	—	Applied
O-Drive												
First	2.74	—	—	—	Applied	Applied	—	—	—	—	Applied	Applied
Second	1.54	—	—	—	Applied	—	—	Applied	—	—	Applied	Applied
Third	1.00	—	—	Applied	Applied	—	—	—	—	—	Applied	Applied
2-Second												
First	2.74	—	—	—	Applied	Applied	—	—	—	—	Applied	Applied
Second	1.54	—	—	—	Applied	—	—	Applied	—	—	Applied	Applied
1-Low	2.74	—	—	—	Applied	Applied	—	—	Applied	—	Applied	Applied

CHILTON'S THREE C'S TRANSMISSION DIAGNOSIS PROCEDURE
A-500 Overdrive Transmission

Condition	Cause	Correction
Harsh engagement from N to D or R	a) Engine idle speed too high b) Valve body malfunction c) Hydraulic pressure too high d) Worn or faulty rear clutch	a) Adjust to specification b) Clean or overhaul c) Adjust to specification d) Overhaul rear clutch

CHILTON'S THREE C'S TRANSMISSION DIAGNOSIS PROCEDURE
A-500 Overdrive Transmission

Condition	Cause	Correction
Delayed engagement from N to D or R	a) Hydraulic pressure too low	a) Adjust to specification
	b) Valve body malfunction	b) Clean or overhaul
	c) Malfunction in low/reverse servo, band or linkage	c) Overhaul
	d) Low fluid level	d) Add as required
	e) Manual linkage adjustment	e) Adjust as required
	f) Oil filter clogged	f) Change filter and fluid
	g) Faulty oil pump	g) Overhaul pump
	h) Bad input shaft seals	h) Replace seal rings
	i) Idle speed too low	i) Adjust to specifications
	j) Bad reaction shaft support seals	j) Replace seal rings
	k) Bad front clutch	k) Overhaul
	l) Bad rear clutch	l) Overhaul
Runaway upshift	a) Hydraulic pressure too low	a) Adjust to specifications
	b) Valve body malfunction	b) Clean or overhaul
	c) Low fluid level	c) Add as required
	d) Oil filter clogged	d) Change filter and fluid
	e) Aerated fluid	e) Check for overfilling
	f) Manual linkage ajustment	f) Adjust as required
	g) Bad reaction shaft support seals	g) Replace seal rings
	h) Malfunction in kickdown servo, band or linkage	h) Overhaul
	i) Bad front clutch	i) Repair as needed
No upshift	a) Hydraulic pressure too low	a) Adjust to specifications
	b) Valve body malfunction	b) Clean or overhaul
	c) Low fluid level	c) Add as required
	d) Manual linkage adjustment	d) Adjust as required
	e) Incorrect throttle linkage adjustment	e) Adjust as required
	f) Bad seals on governor support	f) Replace seals
	g) Bad reaction shaft support seals	g) Replace seal rings
	h) Governor malfunction	h) Service or replace unit
	i) Malfunction in kickdown servo, band or linkage	i) Overhaul
	j) Bad front clutch	j) Overhaul
3-2 Kickdown runaway	a) Hydraulic pressure too low	a) Adjust to specifications
	b) Valve body malfunction	b) Clean or overhaul
	c) Low fluid level	c) Add as required
	d) Aerated fluid	d) Check for overfilling
	e) Incorrect throttle linkage adjustment	e) Adjust as reqiured
	f) Kickdown band out of adjustment	f) Adjust to specifications
	g) Bad reaction shaft support seals	g) Replace seal rings
	h) Malfunction in kickdown servo, band or linkage	h) Overhaul
	i) Bad front clutch	i) Overhaul
No kickdown or normal downshift	a) Valve body malfunction	a) Clean or overhaul
	b) Incorrect throttle linkage adjustment	b) Adjust as required
	c) Governor malfunction	c) Service or replace unit
	d) Malfunction in kickdown servo, band or linkage	d) Overhaul

CHILTON'S THREE C'S TRANSMISSION DIAGNOSIS PROCEDURE
A-500 Overdrive Transmission

Condition	Cause	Correction
Shifts erratic	a) Hydraulic pressure too low	a) Adjust to specifications
	b) Valve body malfunction	b) Clean or overhaul
	c) Low fluid level	c) Add as required
	d) Manual linkage adjustment	d) Adjust as required
	e) Oil filter clogged	e) Change filter and fluid
	f) Faulty oil pump	f) Overhaul oil pump
	g) Aerated fluid	g) Check for overfilling
	h) Incorrect throttle linkage adjustment	h) Adjust as required
	i) Bad seals on governor support	i) Replace seals
	j) Bad reaction shaft support seals	j) Replace seal rings
	k) Governor malfunction	k) Service or replace unit
	l) Malfunction in kickdown servo, band or linkage	l) Overhaul
	m) Bad front clutch	m) Overhaul
Slips in forward drive positions	a) Hydraulic pressure too low	a) Adjust to specifications
	b) Valve body malfunction	b) Clean or overhaul
	c) Low fluid level	c) Add as required
	d) Manual linkage adjustment	d) Adjust as required
	e) Oil filter clogged	e) Change filter and fluid
	f) Faulty oil pump	f) Overhaul pump
	g) Bad input shaft seals	g) Replace seal rings
	h) Aerated fluid	h) Check for overfilling
	i) Incorrect throttle linkage adjustment	i) Adjust as required
	j) Overrunning clutch not holding	j) Overhaul or replace
	k) Bad rear clutch	k) Overhaul
Slips in R only	a) Hydraulic pressure too low	a) Adjust as required
	b) Low/reverse band out of adjustment	b) Adjust to specifications
	c) Valve body malfunction	c) Clean or overhaul
	d) Malfunction in low/reverse servo, band or linkage	d) Overhaul
	e) Low fluid level	e) Add as required
	f) Manual linkage adjustment	f) Adjust as required
	g) Faulty oil pump	g) Overhaul pump
	h) Aerated fluid	h) Check for overfilling
	i) Bad reaction shaft support seals	i) Replace seal rings
	j) Bad front clutch	j) Overhaul
Slips in all positions	a) Hydraulic pressure too low	a) Adjust as required
	b) Valve body malfunction	b) Clean or overhaul
	c) Low fluid level	c) Add as required
	d) Oil filter clogged	d) Change fluid and filter
	e) Faulty oil pump	e) Overhaul pump
	f) Bad input shaft seals	f) Replace seal rings
	g) Aerated fluid	g) Check for overfilling
No drive in any position	a) Hydraulic pressure too low	a) Adjust to specifications
	b) Valve body malfunction	b) Clean or overhaul
	c) Low fluid level	c) Add as required
	d) Oil filter clogged	d) Change filter and fluid
	e) Faulty oil pump	e) Overhaul pump
	f) Planetary gear sets broken or seized	f) Replace affected parts
No drive in forward drive positions	a) Hydraulic pressure too low	a) Adjust to specifications
	b) Valve body malfunction	b) Clean or overhaul
	c) Low fluid level	c) Add as required
	d) Bad input shaft seals	d) Replace seal rings
	e) Overrunning clutch not holding	e) Overhaul or replace
	f) Bad rear clutch	f) Overhaul
	g) Planetary gear sets broken or seized	g) Replace affected parts

CHILTON'S THREE C'S TRANSMISSION DIAGNOSIS PROCEDURE
A-500 Overdrive Transmission

Condition	Cause	Correction
No drive in R	a) Hydraulic pressure too low	a) Adjust to specifications
	b) Low/reverse band out of adjustment	b) Adjust to specifications
	c) Valve body malfunction	c) Clean or overhaul
	d) Malfunction in low/reverse servo, band or linkage	d) Overhaul
	e) Manual linkage adjustment	e) Adjust as required
	f) Bad input shaft seals	f) Replace seal rings
	g) Bad front clutch	g) Overhaul
	h) Bad rear clutch	h) Overhaul
	i) Planetary gear sets broken or seized	i) Replace affected parts
Drives in N	a) Valve body malfunction	a) Clean or overhaul
	b) Manual linkage adjustment	b) Adjust as required
	c) Insufficient clutch plate clearance	c) Overhaul clutch pack
	d) Bad rear clutch	d) Overhaul
	e) Rear clutch dragging	e) Overhaul
Drags or locks	a) Stuck lock-up valve	a) Clean or overhaul
	b) Low/reverse band out of adjustment	b) Adjust to specifications
	c) Kickdown band adjustment too tight	c) Adjust to specifications
	d) Planetary gear sets broken or seized	d) Replace affected parts
	e) Overrunning clutch broken or seized	e) Overhaul or replace
Grating, scraping or growling noise	a) Low/reverse band out of adjustment	a) Adjust to specifications
	b) Kickdown band out of adjustment	b) Adjust to specifications
	c) Output shaft bearing or bushing bad	c) Replace
	d) Planetary gear sets broken or seized	d) Replace affected parts
	e) Overrunning clutch broken or seized	e) Overhaul or replace
Buzzing noise	a) Valve body malfunction	a) Clean or overhaul
	b) Low fluid level	b) Add as required
	c) Aerated fluid	c) Check for overfilling
	d) Overrunning clutch inner race damaged	d) Overhaul or replace
Hard to fill, oil blows out filler tube	a) Oil filter clogged	a) Change filter and fluid
	b) Aerated fluid	b) Check for overfilling
	c) High fluid level	c) Bad converter check valve
	d) Breather clogged	d) Clean, change fluid
Transmission overheats	a) Engine idle speed too high	a) Adjust to specifications
	b) Hydraulic pressure too low	b) Adjust to specifications
	c) Low fluid level	c) Add as required
	d) Manual linkage adjustment	d) Adjust as required
	e) Faulty oil pump	e) Overhaul pump
	f) Kickdown band adjustment too tight	f) Adjust to specifications
	g) Faulty cooling system	g) Service vehicle's cooling system
	h) Insufficient clutch plate clearance	h) Overhaul clutch pack
Harch upshift	a) Hydraulic pressure too low	a) Adjust to specifications
	b) Incorrect throttle linkage adjustment	b) Adjust as required
	c) Kickdown band out of adjustment	c) Adjust to specifications
	d) Hydraulic pressure too high	d) Adjust to specifications
Delayed upshift	a) Incorrect throttle linkage adjustment	a) Adjust as required
	b) Kickdown band out of adjustment	b) Adjust as required
	c) Bad seals on governor, support	c) Replace seals
	d) Bad reaction shaft support seals	d) Replace seal rings
	e) Governor malfunction	e) Service or replace unit
	f) Malfunction in kickdown servo, band or linkage	f) Overhaul
	g) Bad front clutch	g) Overhaul

CHILTON THREE C's TRANSMISSION DIAGNOSIS
A-500 Overdrive Transmission

Condition	Cause	Correction
No reverse or slips in reverse	a) Failed direct clutch b) Overdrive spring lost c) Wrong overdrive piston selected proper spacer	a) Replace the clutch b) Replace the spring load c) Replace with the bearing spacer
No overdrive shift	a) Blown fuse b) Faulty overdrive c) Faulty wiring or connectors d) Faulty overdrive switch e) Faulty SMEC f) Failed overdrive clutch g) Wrong overdrive piston bearing spacer selected h) Valve body malfunction	a) Replace the fuse b) Replace the solenoid solenoid c) Repair or replace as necessary d) Repair or replace as necessary e) Replace SMEC f) Replace the clutch g) Replace with the proper spacer h) Repair or replace the internal components as necessary
Runaway overdrive shift	a) Failed overdrive overrunning clutch	a) Replace the overrunning clutch
Overdrive shift occurs immediately after the 2-3 shift	a) Faulty overdrive solenoid (not venting) b) Lower valve body malfunction c) Faulty wiring or connectors d) Faulty SMEC	a) Replace overdrive solenoid b) Repair or replace the valve body or its internal components as necessary c) Repair or replace as necessary d) Replace SMEC
Excessively delayed overdrive shift	a) Wrong overdrive piston bearing b) Faulty sensor	a) Replace with the proper spacer b) Replace the sensor
No 4-3 downshift	a) Faulty lockup solenoid b) Lower valve body malfunction c) Faulty wiring or connectors d) Faulty SMEC	a) Replace lockup solenoid b) Repair or replace the valve body or its internal components as necessary c) Repair or replace as necessary d) Replace SMEC
No 4-3 downshift with overdrive off switch	a) Faulty overdrive b) Faulty lockup solenoid c) Faulty wiring or connectors d) Faulty SMEC	a) Replace overdrive switch a) Replace lockup solenoid c) Repair or replace as necessary d) Replace SMEC
Torque converter locks up in 2nd and 3rd gears	a) Faulty lockup solenoid (not venting)	a) Replace or repair solenoid valve
Harsh shift 1–2, 2–3 & 3–2	a) Faulty lockup solenoid (not venting)	a) Replace lockup solenoid
Low governor pressure	a) Leaking governor tubes. Bent, loose fit or governor seal rings broken or worn	a) Repair or replace as necessary
Noisy	a) Failed overdrive piston bearing b) Failed gear train needle thrust bearing c) Failed overdrive planetary d) Failed overdrive overrunning clutch	a) Replace bearing b) Replace thrust bearing c) Replace planetary assembly d) Replace the clutch

CHILTON THREE C's LOCKUP TORQUE CONVERTER DIAGNOSIS
A–500 Overdrive Transmission

Condition	Cause	Correction
No lockup	a) Faulty oil pump	a) Replace the oil pump
	b) Sticking governor valve	b) Repair or replace as necessary
	c) Valve body malfunction. Stuck switch valve, lock valve or fail-safe valve	c) Repair or replace valve body or its internal components
	d) Faulty torque converter	d) Replace torque converter
	e) Failed locking clutch	e) Replace torque converter
	f) Leaking turbine hub seal	f) Replace torque converter
	g) Faulty input shaft or seal ring	g) Repair or replace as necessary
Will not unlock	a) Sticking governor valve	a) Repair or replace as necessary
	b) Valve body malfunction. Stuck switch valve, lockup valve or fail-safe valve	b) Repair or replace the valve body or its internal components as necessary
Stays locked up at too a speed in Direct	a) Sticking governor valve	a) Repair or replace as necessary
	b) Valve body malfunction. Stuck switch valve, lockup valve or fail-safe valve	b) Repair or replace the valve body or its internal components as necessary
Locks up or drags in low or second	a) Faulty oil pump	a) Replace the oil pump
	b) Valve body malfunction. Stuck switch valve, lockup valve or fail-safe valve	b) Repair or replace the valve body or its internal components as necessary
Sluggish or stalls in reverse	a) Faulty oil pump	a) Replace oil pump
	b) Plugged oil cooler, cooler lines	b) Flush or replace cooler and flush line and fittings
	c) Valve body malfunction. Stuck switch valve, lockup valve or fail-safe valve	c) Repair or replace the valve body or its internal components as necessary
Loud chatter during lockup engagement (cold)	a) Faulty torque converter	a) Replace torque converter
	b) Failed locking clutch	b) Replace torque converter
	c) Leaking turbine hub seal	c) Replace torque converter
Vibration or shudder during lockup Engagement	a) Faulty oil pump	a) Replace oil pump
	b) Valve body malfunction	b) Repair or replace the valve body or its internal components as necessary
	c) Faulty torque converter	c) Replace torque converter
	d) Engine needs tune-up	d) Tune-up engine
Vibration after lockup engagement	a) Faulty torque converter	a) Replace torque converter
	b) Exhaust system strikes the underbody	b) Align the exhaust system
	c) Engine needs tune-up	c) Tune-up engine
	d) Throttle linkage misadjusted	d) Adjust throttle linkage
Vibration when revved in neutral	a) Torque converter out of balance	a) Replace torque converter
Overheating. Oil blows out of the dipstick tube or pump seal	a) Plugged cooler, cooler lines or or fittings	a) Flush or replace cooler and flush lines
	b) Stuck switch valve	b) Repair switch valve in the valve body or replace valve body
Shudder after lockup engagement	a) Plugged cooler, cooler lines fittings	a) Flush or replace cooler and flush lines
	b) Faulty oil pump	b) Replace oil pump
	c) Valve body malfunction	c) Repair or replace the valve body or its internal components as necessary
	d) Faulty torque converter	d) Replace torque converter
	e) Engine needs tune-up	e) Tune-up engine
	f) Exhaust system strikes the underbody	f) Align the exhaust system
	g) Failed locking clutch	g) Replace torque converter
Torque converter locks up in 2nd and 3rd gears	a) Faulty lockup solenoid not venting	a) Replace or repair

Hydraulic Control System

NOTE: Please refer to Section 9 for all oil flow circuits.

The hydraulic control system has 4 important functions to perform in order to make the transmission fully automatic. These functions are, the pressure supply system, the pressure regulating system, the flow control valve system and the clutches, band servos and accumulator systems.

An explanation of each system follows to assist the technician in understanding the oil flow circuitry within the torqueflite automatic transmissions.

THE PRESSURE SUPPLY SYSTEM

The pressure supply system consists of the oil pump driven by the engine through the torque converter. The oil pump furnishes the fluid pressure for all the hydraulic and lubrication requirements.

THE PRESSURE REGULATING SYSTEM

The pressure regulating system consists of the pressure regulator valve which controls line pressure at the value dependent upon throttle opening. The governor valve transmits regulated pressure to the valve body to control upshifts and downshifts, in conjunction with the vehicle speed.

The throttle valve transmits regulated pressure to the transmission to control the upshifts, downshifts and lockup speeds when the transmission is equipped with a lockup converter assembly. The throttle pressure operates in conjunction with the throttle opening.

THE FLOW CONTROL VALVE SYSTEM

1. The manual valve provides the different transmission drive ranges as selected by the vehicle operator.

2. The 1–2 shift valve automatically shifts the transmission from 1st speed to 2nd or from 2nd speed to 1st speed, depending upon the vehicle road speed.

3. The 2–3 shift valve automatically shifts the transmission from 2nd to 3rd speed or from 3rd speed to 2nd speed, depending upon the vehicle speed.

4. The kickdown valve makes possible a forced downshift from 3rd to 2nd, 2nd to 1st, or 3rd to 1st speeds, depending upon the vehicle speed, by depressing the accelerator past the detent feel near the wide open throttle (WOT).

5. The throttle pressure plug, at the end of the 2–3 shift valve, provides a 3–2 downshift with varying throttle openings, again depending upon the vehicle speed.

6. The 1–2 shift control valve transmits 1–2 shift control pressure to the transmission accumulator piston to control the kickdown band capacity on the 1–2 upshift and 3–2 downshifts. The limit valve is used to determine the maximum speed at which a 3–2 throttle downshift can be made.

7. The shuttle valve has 2 functions and they are accomplished independently of each other. The first function is to provide a fast release of the kickdown band and to provide a smooth front clutch engagement when the vehicle operator makes a closed throttle upshift from 2nd to 3rd speed. The second function of the shuttle valve is to regulate the application of the kickdown servo and band when making 3rd to 2nd kickdown.

8. On automatic transmissions equipped with the lockup converter assembly, the lockup valve automatically applies the torque converter lockup clutch if the vehicle is above a predetermined speed when in the 3rd (direct) gear ratio.

9. The failsafe valve restricts feed to the lockup clutch if the front clutch apply pressure drops. This valve permits lockup only in the 3rd (direct) gear and provides a fast lockup release during a kickdown.

10. The switch valve directs fluid to apply the lockup clutch in 1 position and release it in the other and also directs fluid to the cooling and lubrication systems.

11. Transmissions not equipped with the lockup converter use a control valve to limit the pressure to the lubrication and cooling system and to direct main line pressure to the converter.

THE CLUTCHES, BAND SERVOS AND ACCUMULATOR SYSTEM

The front and rear clutch pistons and both servo pistons are moved hydraulically to engage the clutches and apply the bands. The pistons are released by spring tension when the hydraulic pressure is released. On the 2–3 upshift, the kickdown servo piston is released by spring tension and hydraulic pressure.

The accumulator controls the hydraulic pressure on the apply side of the kickdown servo during the 1–2 shift, thereby cushioning the kickdown band application at any throttle opening.

Diagnostic Tests

HYDRAULIC PRESSURE TEST

Before starting the pressure test, make sure the fluid level is correct and linkage is adjusted properly. A good pressure test is an important part of diagnosing transmission problems. Oil flow charts are supplied for hydraulic circuitry details.

1. Check fluid level and linkage adjustments. Remember that fluid must be at operating temperature (150–200°F) during tests.

2. Install engine tachometer and route wires so that it can be read under the car.

3. Raise vehicle on hoist so that rear wheels can turn. It may be helpful to disconnect throttle valve and shift rod from transmission levers so that they can be shifted from under the vehicle.

4. Two size gauges are needed: one 100 psi and the other a 300 or 400 psi. The higher pressure gauge is required for the "reverse" test.

Test 1 (Selector in 1)

The purpose of this test is to check pump output, the pressure regulation and also to check on the condition of the rear clutch and rear servo hydraulic circuits.

1. Hook up gauges to line and rear servo ports.

2. Adjust engine speed to 1000 rpm.

3. Shift into **1** position. (Selector lever on transmission all the way forward.)

4. Read pressures on both gauges as the throttle lever on transmission is moved from the full forward position to full rearward position.

5. Line pressure should read from 54–60 psi with the throttle lever forward and it should gradually increase as the lever is moved rearward, to 90–96 psi.

6. The rear servo pressure should read about the same as the line pressure, to within 3 psi.

Test 2 (Selector in 2)

The purpose of this test is to check pump output, the pressure regulation and also to check on the condition of the rear clutch and lubrication hydraulic circuits.

1. Attach gauge to the line pressure port on the right hand side of the unit and install a T-fitting into the rear cooler line so that lubrication pressure can be recorded.

2. Adjust engine speed to 1000 rpm.

3. Shift into **2** position (this is 1 detent rearward from the full forward position of the selector lever).

4. Read pressures on both gauges as the throttle lever on transmission is moved from the full forward position to full rearward position.

5. Line pressure should read from 54–60 psi with the throttle lever forward and it should gradually increase as the lever is moved rearward, to 90–96 psi.

6. Lubrication pressure should be between 5–15 psi with the throttle lever forward and between 10–30 psi with lever rearward.

Test 3 (Selector in D)

The purpose of this test is to check pump output, the pressure regulation and also to check on the condition of the rear clutch and front clutch and hydraulic circuits.

1. Attach gauges to the line pressure port and also to the front servo release port, on the right hand side of the unit.

2. Adjust engine speed to 1600 rpm.

3. Shift into **D** position. (This is 2 detents rearward from the full forward position of the selector lever).

4. Read pressures as the throttle lever on the transmission is moved from the full forward position to full rearward position.

5. Line pressure should read from 54–60 psi with the throttle lever forward and it should gradually increase as the lever is moved rearward.

6. The front servo release is pressurized only in direct drive and should be the same as the line pressure reading within 3 psi, up to the downshift point.

TEST 4 (Selector in Reverse)

The purpose of this test is to check pump output, pressure regulation and also to check on the condition of the front clutch and rear servo hydraulic circuits. Also, at this time, a check can be made for leakage into the rear servo, due to case porosity, cracks, valve body or case warpage which can cause reverse band burn out.

1. Attach the 300 psi (or higher) gauge to the rear servo apply port at the right hand rear of the unit.

2. Adjust engine speed to 1600 rpm.

3. Shift into **R** position. (This is 4 detents rearward from the full forward position of the selector lever.)

4. Read pressure on gauge. It should be between 230–260 psi.

5. By moving the selector lever back to the **D** position, the pressure at the rear servo should drop to zero. This checks for leakage into the rear servo, which would result in the reverse band burning out.

Analyzing the Pressure Test

1. If the proper line pressure from the minimum to maximum is found in any one test, the pump and pressure regulator are working properly.

2. If there is low pressure in **D**, **1** and **2**, but there is a correct pressure reading in **R**, then there is leakage in the rear clutch circuit.

3. if there is low pressure in **D** and **R**, but there is correct pressure in **1**, then there is leakage in the front clutch circuit.

4. If there is low pressure in **R** and **1**, but there is correct pressure in **2**, then there is leakage in the rear servo circuit.

5. If there is low line pressure in all positions then there could be a defective pump, a clogged filter, or a stuck pressure regulator valve.

GOVERNOR PRESSURE

The governor pressure only needs to be tested if the transmission shifts at the wrong vehicle speeds, when the throttle rod is correctly adjusted.

1. Connect a 100 psi gauge to the governor pressure opening. This is on the left hand side, near the bottom, near the extension housing mounting flange.

2. Pressures are recorded by operating in 3rd gear.

3. If the pressures are wrong at a given speed, the governor valve or the weights are sticking. The pressure should respond

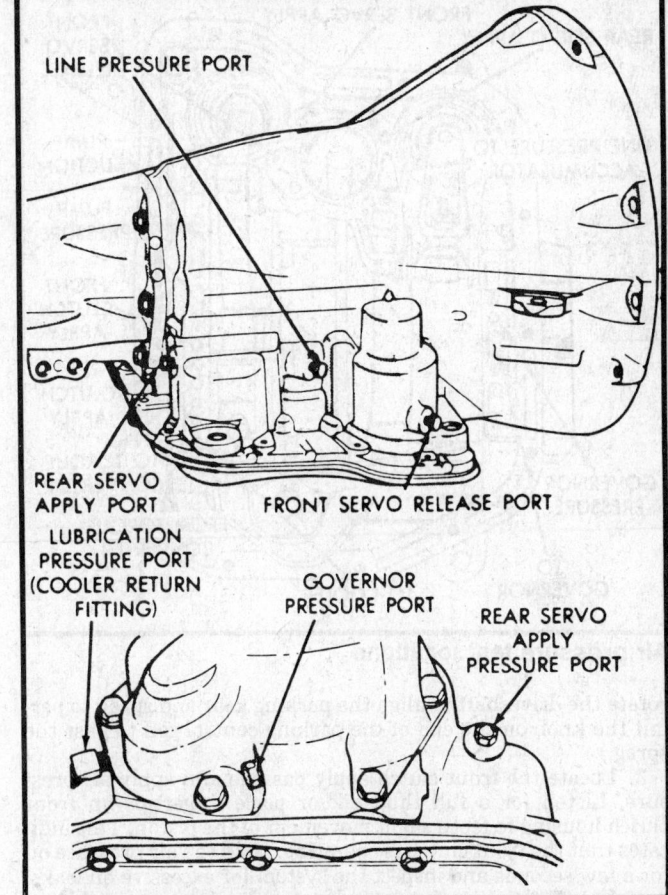

Pressure test locations

smoothly to any changes in rpm and should drop to 0–1½ psi when the vehicle is stopped. If there is high pressure at stand still (more than 2 psi) then the transmission will be prevented from downshifting.

THROTTLE PRESSURE

This transmission has no provision for testing throttle pressure with a gauge. The only time incorrect throttle pressure should be suspected is if the part throttle up-shift speeds are either too slow in coming or occur too early in relation to vehicle speeds. Engine runaway on either up shifts or down shifts can also be an indicator of incorrect (low) throttle pressure setting. The throttle pressure really should not be adjusted until the throttle linkage is checked and adjustment has been verified to be right.

CLUTCH AND SERVO AIR PRESSURE TESTS

Even though all fluid pressures are correct and the hydraulic pressure test checks, out, it is still possible to have a no drive condition, due to inoperative clutches or bands. The inoperative units can be located by using tests, with air pressure instead of hydraulic pressure. To make an air pressure test the following points should be observed.

1. Compressed air should be set to about 30 psi and must be free of dirt and moisture.

2. After the vehicle is safely supported or on a hoist, remove pan and carefully remove the valve body assembly. (If necessary,

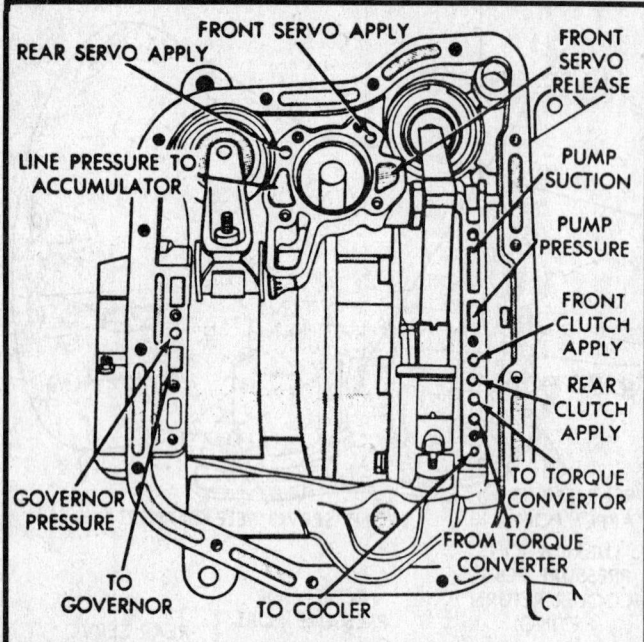

Air pressure test locations

rotate the driveshaft to align the parking gear and sprag to permit the knob on the end of the parking control rod to pass the sprag.)

3. Locate the front clutch apply passage and apply air pressure. Listen for a full thud and/or place fingertips on front clutch housing to feel a slight movement of the piston. This indicates that the front clutch is operating. Hold the air pressure on for a few seconds and inspect the system for excessive oil leaks.

4. Locate the rear clutch apply passage air pressure. Listen for a dull thud and/or place fingertips on rear clutch housing to feel a slight movement of the piston. This indicates that the rear clutch is operating. Hold the air pressure on for a few seconds and inspect the system for excessive oil leaks.

5. Locate the front servo apply passage and apply air pressure. This tests the kickdown servo and operation of the servo is indicated by the front band tightening. The spring tension on the servo piston should release the band.

6. Locate the rear servo apply passage and apply air pressure. This tests the Low and Reverse servo and operation of the servo is indicated by the rear band tightening. The spring tension on the servo piston should release the band.

7. If, after the air pressure tests, correct operation of the clutches and servos are confirmed and the complaint was no upshift or erratic shifts, then the problem is in the valve body.

STALL SPEED TEST

Stall speed testing involves determining the maximum engine rpm obtainable at full throttle with the rear wheels locked and the transmission in **D** position.

─── CAUTION ───

Never allow anyone to stand in front of the car when performing a stall test. In addition, always block the front wheels and have both the parking and service brakes fully applied during the test.

─── CAUTION ───

Do not hold the throttle open any longer than necessary and never longer than 5 seconds at a time. If more than 1 stall test is required, operate the engine at 1,000 RPM in neutral for at least 20 seconds to cool the transmission fluid between runs.

1. Connect tachometer to engine.
2. Check and adjust transmission fluid level as necessary.
3. Operate engine until transmission fluid reaches operating temperature (approx. 175° F).
4. Block front wheels.
5. Fully apply parking brakes.
6. Fully apply service brakes.
7. Open throttle completely and record maximum engine rpm registered on tachometer, in **D**.
8. If engine speed exceeds maximum stall speed, release the accelerator immediately. The indicates that transmission slippage is occurring.
    a. Torque converter diameter — 10 ¾ in.
    b. Engine stall speed rpm — 1900–2100.
9. Shift transmission into **N**, operate engine for 20 seconds, stop engine, shift into **P** and release brakes.
10. If the values read on the tachometer do not agree with the information in the stall speed specifications chart, refer to the problem diagnosis below.

Stall Speed Too High

If the stall speed exceeds the maximum specified in the chart by more than 200 rpm, transmission clutch slippage is indicated. Refer to the hydraulic pressure test and air pressure test procedures to find the cause of slippage.

Stall Speed Too Low

Low stall speeds with a properly tuned engine indicate a torque converter stator clutch problem. The condition should be confirmed by road testing prior to converter replacement. If stall speeds are 250–350 rpm below the minimum specified in the cart and the car operates properly at highway speeds but has poor low speed acceleration, the stator overrunning clutch is slipping and the torque converter should be replaced.

Stall Speed Normal

If stall speeds are normal but road testing shows that abnormally high throttle opening is required to maintain highway speeds even though low speed acceleration is normal, the stator overrunning clutch is seized and the torque converter must be replaced.

Converter Clutch Operation and Diagnosis
TORQUE CONVERTER CLUTCH

The 4th gear (overdrive) is electronically controlled and hydraulically activated. A variety of sensor inputs are fed to the Single Module Engine Controller (SMEC) which controls a solenoid mounted on the valve body. The solenoid will energize and close a vent, allowing a 3–4 upshift. The SMEC also controls the operation of the lockup torque converter using many of the same sensor inputs.

A lockup torque converter, which is electronically controlled and hydraulically activated, will also be used with this transmission. 4th gear (overdrive) and lockup will only occur during certain conditions determined by the SMEC.

The transmission locked or unlocked is controlled by a solenoid. First the coolant temperature is sensed. If the actual temperature is below 150°F, the solenoid will remain de-energized (unlocked). Once this reference temperature is reached, mph, vacuum and the throttle position sensor determine the locked or unlocked of the transmission.

If the throttle position sensor is closed, the transmission will always be unlocked. The transmission will remain unlocked for a programmed period after the throttle is opened. If the actual mph is above the low reference value entry into the lockup region occurs. If the actual mph is below the low reference value, entry into the lockup region will not occur (solenoid de-energized).

The state of the transmission locked or unlocked, is determined by a set of vacuum verus mph curves. Two hysteresis bands are present. Once in a lockup region the vacuum must fall below or rise above the unlock vacuum reference points in order to enter the unlock (lockup) region. Lockup (solenoid energized) of the transmission is delayed a programmable period of time after entry into the lockup region occurs. There will be a drop in rpm when lockup takes place.

TROUBLESHOOTING THE LOCKUP TORQUE CONVERTER

The Single Module Engine Controller (SMEC) has been programmed to monitor several different circuits of the fuel injection system. This monitoring is called On Board Diagnosis. If a problem is sensed with a monitored circuit, often enough to indicate an actual problem, its fault code is stored in the SMEC module for eventual display to the service technician. If the problem is repaired or ceases to exist, the SMEC cancels the fault code after 50–100 ignition key on/off cycles.

Fault Codes

Fault codes are 2 digit numbers that identify which circuit is bad. In most cases, they do not identify which component is bad in a circuit. When a fault code appears (either by flashes of the power loss/limited (check engine) lamp or by watching the diagnostic read out tool (DRB-II), or equivalent, it indicates that the SMEC has recognized an abnormal signal in the system. Fault codes indicate the results of a failure but do not always identify the failed component directly.

Accessing Trouble Code Memory

There are 2 methods used in accessing trouble codes. The first method is the use of a diagnostic readout box tool (DRB-II) or equivalent, the second method is observing the power loss/limited (check engine) lamp.

The diagnostic readout box (DRB-II) is used to put the system into a Diagnostic Test Mode, Circuit Actuation Test Mode, Switch Test Mode, Engine Running Test Mode and Sensor Test Mode. Four of these modes of testing are called for at certain points of the driveability test procedure. A fifth test mode is available with the engine running. The following is a description of each test mode:

1. Diagnostic Test Mode—This mode is used to see if there are any fault codes stored in the on-board diagnostic system memory.

2. Circuit Actuation Test Mode (CTM Test)—This mode is used to turn a specific circuit on and off in order to check it. CTM test codes are used in this mode.

3. Switch Test Mode—This mode is used to determine if specific switch inputs are being received by the logic module.

4. Sensor Test Mode—This mode is used to see the output signals of certain sensors as received by the logic module.

5. Engine Running Test Mode—This mode is used to determine if the oxygen feedback system is switching from rich to lean and lean to rich.

DIAGNOSIS USING READOUT BOX

The diagnostic readout box (DRB-II) is used to put the on-board diagnostic system in 4 different modes of testing as called for in the driveability test procedure.

1. Connect tool diagnostic read out box (DRB-II) or equivalent, to the mating connector located in the wiring harness in the engine compartment near the SMEC.

2. Start the engine if possible, cycle the transmission selector and the A/C switch if applicable. Shut off the engine.

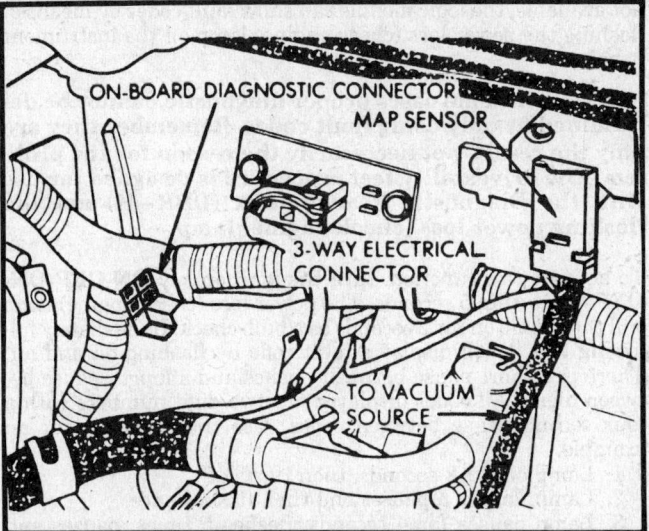

Location of the diagnostic connector

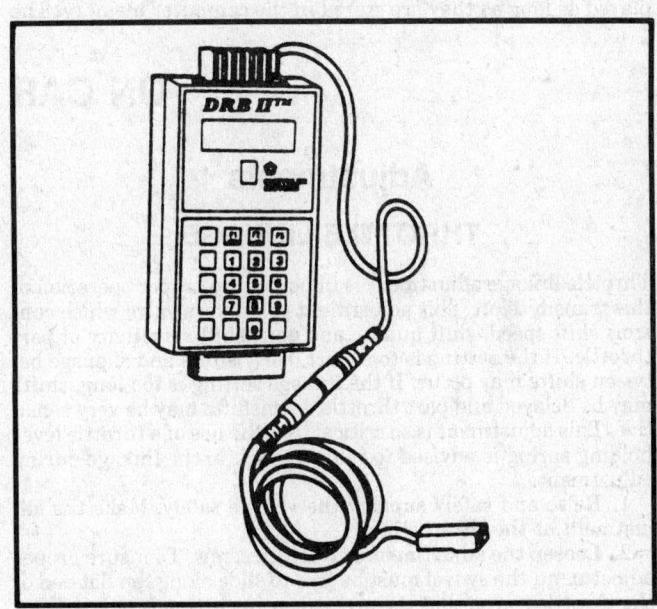

Typical diagnostic readout box

3. Place the read/hold switch on the readout box (DRB-II) in the read position. Turn the ignition key **ON-OFF-ON-OFF-ON** within 5 seconds. Record all the fault codes shown on the diagnostic readout box (DRB-II). Observe the check engine lamp on the instrument panel the lamp should light for 3 seconds then go out (bulb check).

NOTE: The display of codes can be stopped by moving the read/hold switch to the hold position. Returning to the read position will continue the displaying of codes. To erase the fault codes, access the erase fault code data on the diagnostic readout box (DRB-II).

DIAGNOSIS USING POWER LOSS/LIMIT (CHECK ENGINE) LAMP

The power loss/limit (check engine) lamp has 2 modes of operation. If for some reason the diagnostic readout box (DRB-II) is not available, the logic module can show fault codes by means of flashing the power loss (check engine) lamp on the instrument panel

NOTE: In some cases proper diagnostic cannot be determined by only using fault codes. Remember they are only the result, not necessarily the reason for the problem. The driveability test procedure is designed for use with the Diagnostic Readout Box (DBR–II) not the flashing power loss (check engine) lamp.

To activate this function, turn the ignition key **ON-OFF-ON-OFF-ON** within 5 seconds. The power loss (check engine) lamp will then come on for 2 seconds as a bulb check. Immediately following this it will display a fault code by flashing on and off. There is a short pause between flashes and a longer pause between digits. All codes displayed are two digit numbers with a four second pause between codes. Use the following for an example.

1. Lamp on for 2 seconds, then turns off.
2. Lamp flashes 5 pauses and then flashes once.
3. Lamp pauses for 4 seconds, flashes 5 times, pauses and then flashes 5 times.

The two codes are 51 and 55 . Any number of codes can be displayed as long as they are stored in the computer memory. The lamp will flash until all of them are displayed.

NOTE: In some cases proper diagnosis cannot be determined by only using fault codes. Remember they are only the results, not necessarily the reason for the problem.

4. Unlike the diagnostic readout box (DRB–II), the power loss lamp (check engine) cannot do the following.
   a. Once the lamp begins to display fault codes, it can not be stopped. If the code count is forgotten or lost, it is necessary to start over.
   b. The lamp can not perform the actuation test, sensor read test, switch test mode and engine running test modes.

Fault Code Description

The only fault codes that actually pertains to the transmission itself, are fault codes 37 and 45. Code 37 is used one both the Dakota trucks equipped with single point and dual point injection systems. This code is the PTU Solenoid Circuit. Code 37 is stating that an open or shorted condition is detected in the torque converter part throttle unlock solenoid circuit. Code 45 is used on the Dakota trucks equipped with only the dual point injection system. This code is for the Overdrive Circuit. Code 45 is stating an open or shorted condition detected in the overdrive solenoid circuit.

ON CAR SERVICES

Adjustments

THROTTLE LINKAGE

Throttle linkage adjustment is important to proper operation of this transmission. This adjustment positions a valve which controls shift speed, shift quality and downshift sensitivity at part throttle. If the setting is too short, early shifts and slippage between shifts may occur. If the linkage setting is too long, shifts may be delayed and part throttle downshifts may be very sensitive. This adjustment is so critical that the use of a throttle lever holding spring is advised to remove slack in the linkage during adjustment.

1. Raise and safely support the vehicle safely. Make the adjustment at the throttle lever.
2. Loosen the adjustment swivel lock screw. To insure proper adjustment, the swivel must be free to slide along the flat end of the throttle rod so that the preload spring action is not restricted. Disassemble and clean or repair the parts to assure free action, if necessary.
3. Hold the transmission lever firmly forward against its internal stop and tighten the swivel lock screw to 100 inch lbs.
4. The adjustment is finished and linkage backlash was automatically removed by the preload spring.
5. Lower the vehicle. Test the linkage freedom of operation by moving the throttle rod rearward, slowly releasing it to confirm it will return fully forward.

GEAR SHIFT LINKAGE

The gear shift linkage adjustment is important because the linkage positions the manual valve in the valve body. Incorrect adjustment will result in the vehicle creeping in **N**, premature clutch wear, delayed engagement in any gear or a no-start in the **P** or **N** condition.
Proper operation of the neutral start switch will provide a quick check of linkage adjustment as follows:
1. Turn key to **ON** to unlock column and shift lever.

Exploded view of the gearshift linkage

2. Move shift lever slowly until it clicks into the **P** detent. Try to start engine. If starter does operate, **P** position is correct.
3. Stop the engine. Repeat, only this time moving lever to **N**. Try to start engine. If starter does operate, the **N** position is correct and linkage is properly adjusted.
4. Adjust the linkage as follows:
   a. Use a suitable tool to force the rod from the grommet in the lever (pry only where the grommet and rod attach, not the rod itself) then cut away the old grommet. Use suitable pliers to snap the new grommet into the lever and rod into the grommet.
   b. To insure the proper adjustment, make sure the adjustable swivel block is free to turn on the shift rod. Disassemble and clean or repair parts to assure free action , if necessary.

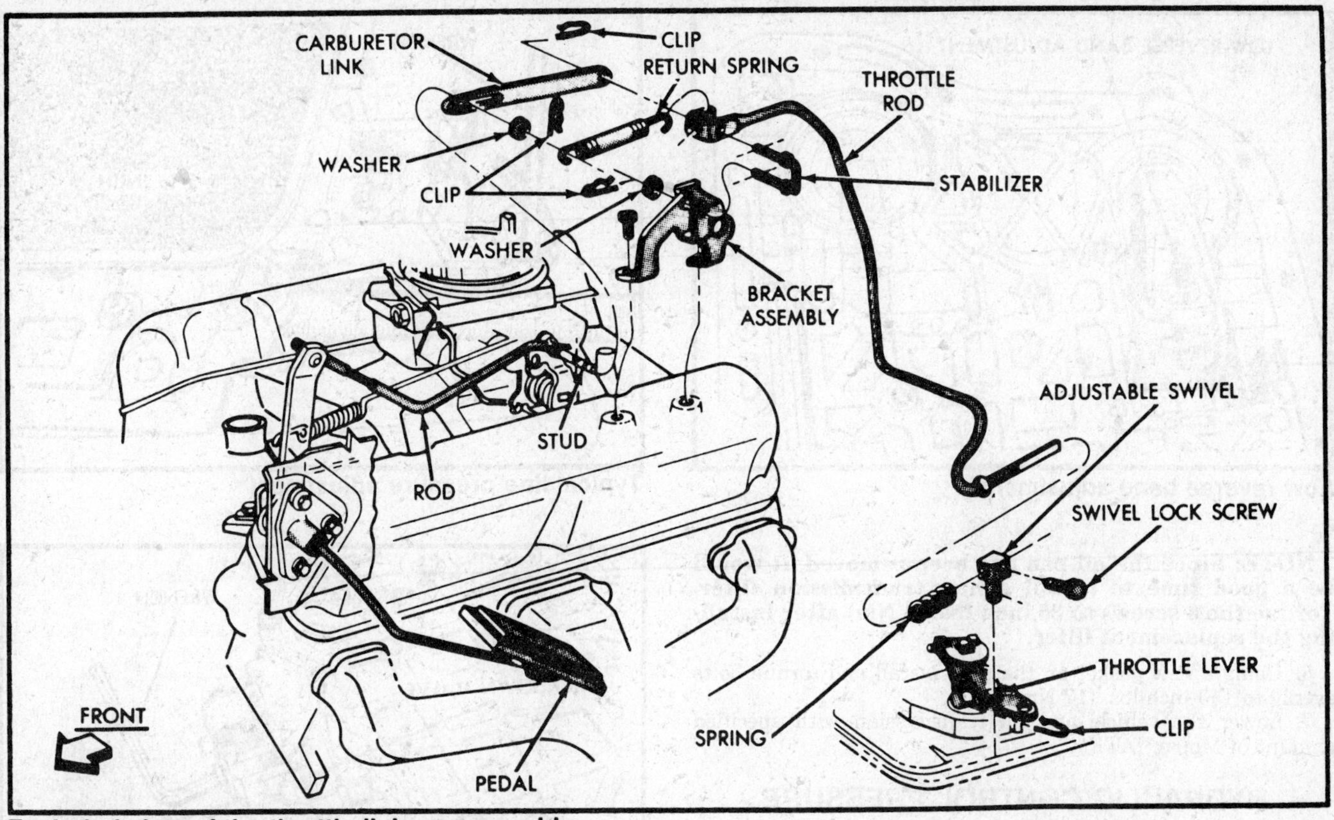

Exploded view of the throttle linkage assembly

c. Place the gearshift in the **P** position. With all the linkage assembled and the adjustable swivel lockbolt loose, move the shift lever on the transmission all the way to the rear detent (park) position.

d. Tighten the adjustment swivel lockbolt to 90 inch lbs. (10 Nm).

e. Check the detent position for **N** and **D**. They should be within limits of hand lever gate stops. The key start must occur only when the shift lever is in the **P** or **N** positions.

KICKDOWN (FRONT) BAND ADJUSTMENTS

The kickdown (front) band adjustment is done from the outside of the transmission. While somewhat difficult to reach, it can

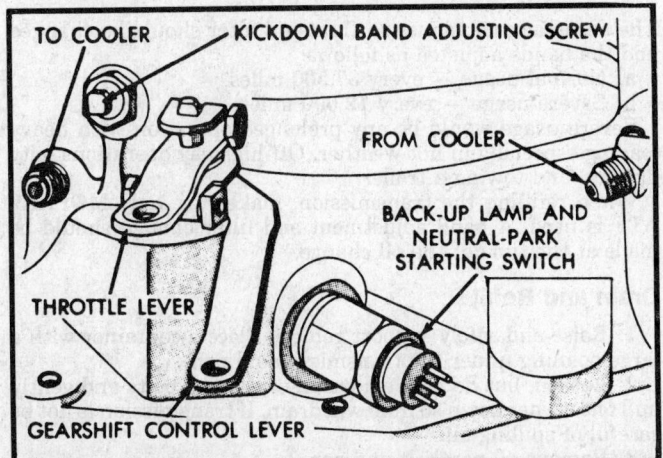

Kickdown band adjusting screw location along with other external controls

nevertheless be adjusted while still in the vehicle. The front band adjusting screw is located on the left side of the transmission case just above the manual lever and throttle lever.

1. Raise and support the vehicle safely.
2. Loosen adjusting screw locknut and back off locknut 5 turns.
3. Check that adjusting screw turns freely. Using special tool wrench C-3380-A with adapter C-3705 or equivalent. Tighten the band adjusting screw to 47–50 inch lbs. (5 Nm). If the adapter is not being used, tighten adjusting screw to 72 inch lbs. (8 Nm) torque, using a small torque wrench and a $^5/_{16}$ square socket.
4. Back off adjusting screw 2 turns.
5. Hold the adjusting screw in this position and tighten the screw locknut to 30 ft. lbs. (41 Nm) making sure that adjuster screw setting does not change.

REAR BAND ADJUSTMENT

The rear band adjustment is an inside adjustment so the pan must be removed.

1. Raise and support the vehicle safely.
2. Remove oil pan and drain fluid.
3. Look carefully at fluid, filter and pan bottom for a heavy accumulation of friction material or metal particles. A little accumulation can be considered normal, but a heavy concentration indicates damaged or worn parts.
4. Adjust the band by loosening locknut approximately 5 turns, then tightening the band adjusting screw to 72 inch lbs. (8 Nm) using a small torque wrench and a ¼ hex head socket or tool C-3380-A.
5. Back off adjusting screw approximately 4 turns. Hold the adjusting screw in this position and tighten the locknut to 25 ft. lbs.

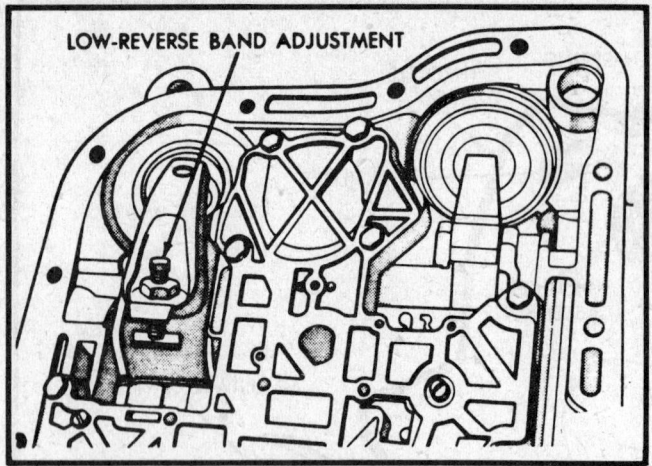

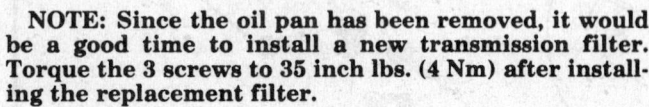

Low reverse band adjustment

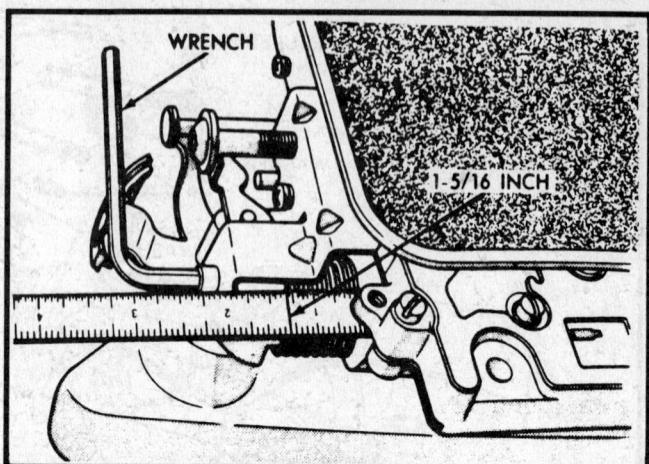

Typical line pressure adjustment

NOTE: Since the oil pan has been removed, it would be a good time to install a new transmission filter. Torque the 3 screws to 35 inch lbs. (4 Nm) after installing the replacement filter.

6. Using a new gasket on the pan, install and torque bolts evenly to 150 inch lbs. (17 Nm).

7. Lower the vehicle and fill transmission with specified amount of Mopar® ATF.

HYDRAULIC CONTROL PRESSURE ADJUSTMENT

There are 2 pressure adjustments that can be performed on the valve body. They are line pressure and throttle pressure both the line pressure and throttle pressure are independent of each other since each affects the shift quality and timing. Both adjustments must be performed properly and in the correct sequence. The line pressure adjustment must be performed first. To adjust the line pressure, remove the valve body, then follow this procedure:

1. Measure the distance from the valve body to the inner edge of the adjusting screw, using an accurate steel scale. The distance should be $1\frac{5}{16}$ in. (3.3cm).

2. If adjustment is needed, turn the screw in or out to obtain the $1\frac{5}{16}$ in. (3.3cm) setting.

NOTE: Because of manufacturing tolerances, the above dimension is an approximate setting and it may be necessary to vary this setting to get the proper pressure. The adjusting screw may be turned with an allen wrench. One complete turn of the adjusting screw changes the line pressure about $1\frac{2}{3}$ psi. To increase the pressure, turn the adjusting screw counterclockwise, while clockwise decreases the pressure.

3. Adjust the throttle pressure as follows:

   a. Since a special tool C-3763 is recommended by the factory, it will require that a tool be made to insert between the throttle lever cam and kickdown valve.

   b. Push the gauge tool (¼ in. block, 7 in.long x 0.629 in. wide) inward to compress the kickdown valve against its spring and to bottom the throttle valve in the valve body.

   c. Maintain the pressure against the kickdown valve spring and turn the throttle lever stop screw until the screw head touches the throttle lever tang and throttle lever cam touches the gauge tool along the 0.629 in. width. Be sure the adjustment is made with the spring fully compressed and the valve bottomed in the valve body.

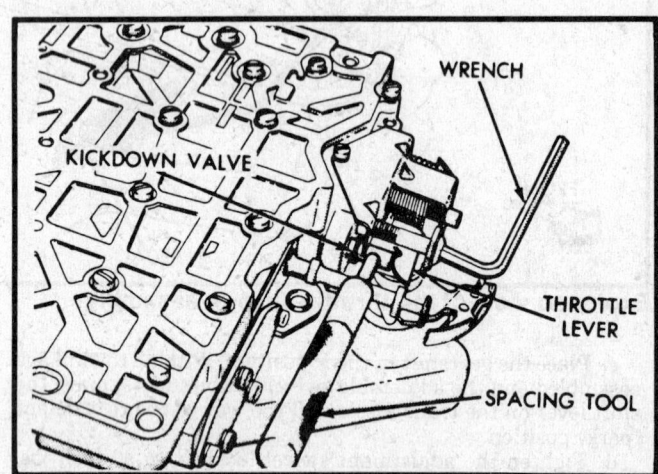

Making the throttle pressure adjustment

Services

FLUID CHANGES

The automatic transmission fluid and filter should be changed and the bands adjusted as follows:

   a. Normal usage — every 37,500 miles.

   b. Severe usage — every 12,000 miles.

Severe usage would be any prolonged operation with heavy loading especially in hot weather. Off-highway operations (city driving) and towing a trailer.

When refilling the transmission, make sure only MOPAR© ATF is used. A band adjustment and filter change should be made at the time of the oil change.

Drain and Refill

1. Raise and safely support vehicle. Place a container with a large opening under the transmission oil pan.

2. Loosen, but do not remove all of the pan bolts and gently pull one corner down so fluid will drain. If transmission is hot be careful of spilling oil.

3. Remove oil pan bolt and pan.

4. Perform any necessary band adjustments and/or filter change.

5. Check pan carefully for distortion, straightening the edges with a straight block of wood and a rubber mallet if necessary. Clean pan well.

NOTE: If there is evidence of contamination or if trouble shooting indicates a problem in the converter, it must be replaced.

6. Install new gasket on pan and torque the bolts to 150 inch lbs. (17 Nm).

7. Lower the vehicle, pour 4 quarts of MOPAR© ATF through the filler tube.

8. Start the engine and allow it to idle for at least 2 minutes. Apply the parking brake and block the drive wheels. Move the selector lever momentarily to each position, ending in the **N** position.

9. Recheck the ATF fluid level, if necessary, add sufficient fluid to bring level to the **ADD ONE PINT** mark.

10. Recheck fluid level after transmission is at normal operating temperature. The normal level should be between the **FULL** mark and **ADD ONE PINT** mark.

11. Do not overfill. Make sure the dipstick is properly seated to seal against dirt and water entering system.

OIL PAN

Removal and Installation

1. Raise and safely support the vehicle.

2. Loosen oil pan bolts and gently pull one corner down so fluid will drain. If transmission is hot, be careful of spilling oil.

3. Remove oil pan bolts and pan.

4. Carefully inspect filter and pan bottom for a heavy accumulation of friction material or metal particles. A little accumulation can be considered normal, but a heavy concentration indicates damaged or worn parts.

NOTE: Filter replacement is recommended when a pan is removed. Also, rear band can be adjusted if necessary.

5. Check pan carefully for distortion, straightening the edges with a straight block of wood and a rubber mallet if necessary. Clean pan well.

6. Install new gasket on pan and install. Torque bolts to 150 inch lbs. (17 Nm).

7. Lower the vehicle, pour 4 quarts of MOPAR© ATF through the filler tube.

8. Start the engine and allow it to idle for at least 2 minutes. Apply the parking brake and block the drive wheels. Move the selector lever momentarily to each position, ending in the **N** position.

9. Recheck the ATF fluid level, if necessary, add sufficient fluid to bring level to the **ADD ONE PINT** mark.

10. Recheck fluid level after transmission is at normal operating temperature. The normal level should be between the **FULL** mark and **ADD ONE PINT** mark.

11. Do not overfill. Make sure the dipstick is properly seated to seal against dirt and water entering system.

VALVE BODY AND ACCUMULATOR PISTON

Removal and Installation

1. Raise and safely support vehicle.

2. Remove pan and drain fluid.

3. Disconnect throttle and shift levers from transmission.

4. Unplug neutral switch harness and unscrew switch. Disconnect the electronic lockup solenoid wire from inside of the wiring connector at the rear of the transmission case.

5. Place large opening drain pan under transmission, then remove the 10 bolts holding the valve body to the transmission.

Hold the valve body in position while the bolts are being removed.

6. Gently lower valve body out of the transmission and pull it forward, out of the case. It may be necessary to rotate the driveshaft so that the parking gear and sprag align to permit the knob on the end of the parking control rod to pass the sprag.

7. Remove accumulator piston and spring from transmission case and inspect for wear, nicks or cracks. Check spring for cracks or distortion. Clean for inspection or replacement of parts as necessary.

NOTE: If seal for valve body manual shaft is leaking, it is not necessary to remove valve body to replace seal. Simply drive the seal out of the case with a small punch and drive in a new seal using a $^{15}/_{16}$ in. socket as a driver. Be careful not to scratch the manual lever shaft or the manual lever shaft seal.

--- CAUTION ---

Do not clamp any portion of the valve body or transfer plate in a vise. Even the slightest distortion will result in stuck valves and leakage or fluid cross leakage. Handle the valve body with care at all times.

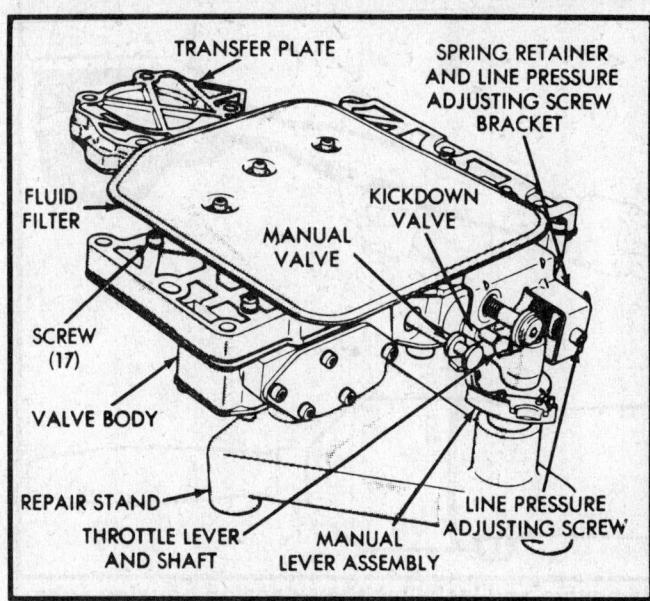

Typical valve body assembly

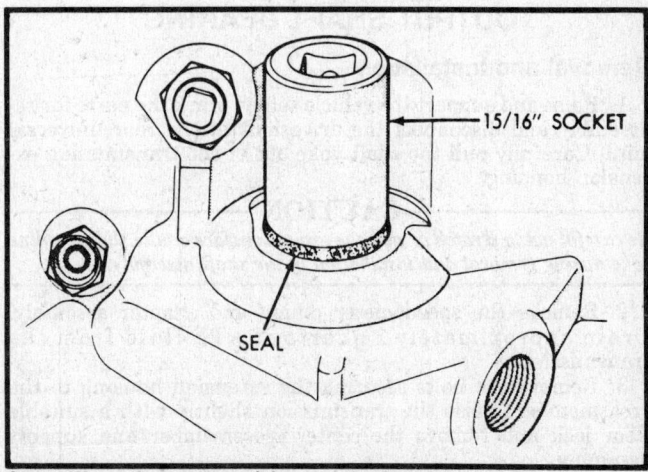

Installing the manual lever shaft seal

EXTENSION HOUSING YOKE SEAL

Removal and Installation

1. Raise and support the vehicle safely. Mark the parts for re-assembly and disconnect the driveshaft at the rear universal joint, Carefully pull the shaft yoke out of the transmission extension housing.

CAUTION

Be careful not to scratch or nick the ground surface on the sliding spline yoke during removal and installation of the shaft assembly.

---

2. Using seal removal tool C-3985 or equivalent, remove the old seal.

3. To install a new seal, position the seal in the opening of the extension housing and drive it into the housing with a suitable seal driver.

4. Carefully guide the front universal joint yoke into the extension housing and on the mainshaft splines. Align the marks made at removal and connect the driveshaft to the rear axle pinion shaft yoke.

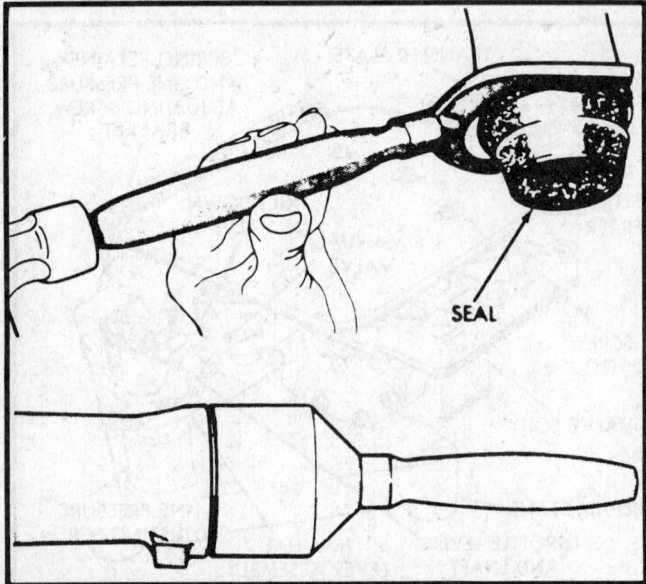

Removing and installing the extension housing yoke seal

EXTENSION HOUSING BUSHING AND OUTPUT SHAFT BEARING

Removal and Installation

1. Raise and support the vehicle safely. Mark the parts for re-assembly and disconnect the driveshaft at the rear universal joint, Carefully pull the shaft yoke out of the transmission extension housing.

CAUTION

Be careful not to scratch or nick the ground surface on the sliding spline yoke during removal and installation of the shaft assembly.

---

2. Remove the speedometer pinion and adapter assembly. Drain approximately 2 quarts of ATF fluid from the transmission.

3. Remove the bolts securing the extension housing to the crossmember. Raise the transmission slightly with a suitable floor jack and remove the center crossmember and support assembly.

4. Remove the extension housing to transmission bolts.

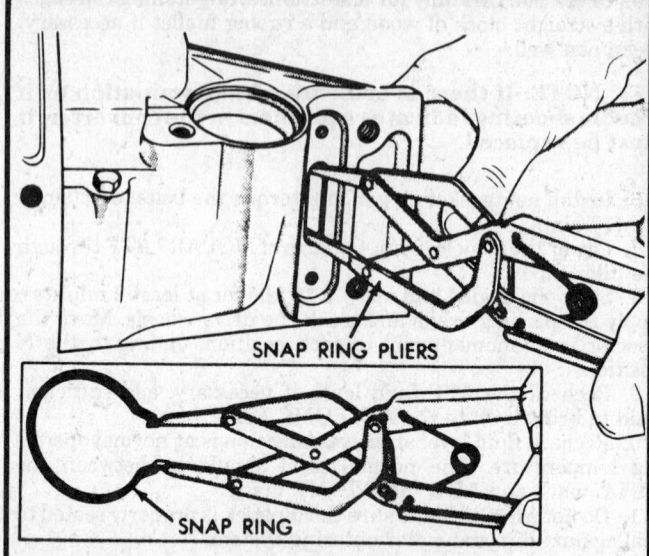

Removing or installing the output shaft bearing snapring

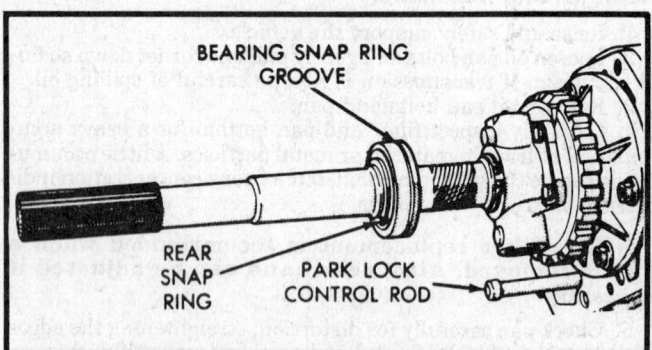

Installing a new oil seal into the housing

NOTE: When removing or installing the extension housing, the gearshift lever must be in the 1 (low) position. This positions the parking lock control rod rearward so it can be disengaged or engaged with the parking lock sprag.

5. Remove the screws, plate and gasket from the bottom of the extension housing mounting pad. Spread the snapring from the output shaft bearing

6. With the snapring spread as far as possible, carefully tap the extension housing rearward to allow the parking lock control knob to clear the parking sprag and remove the housing.

7. Using a heavy duty pair of snapring pliers, remove the output shaft bearing snapring and remove the bearing from the shaft.

8. Install a new bearing onto the shaft with the outer race ring groove toward the front and install the heavy duty snapring.

9. Remove the oil seal with a seal removal tool C-3985 or equivalent. Press or drive out the bushing with tool C-3396 or equivalent.

10. Slide a new bushing on the installing end of bushing tool C-3396 or equivalent. Align the oil hole in the bushing with the oil slot in the housing, press or drive the bushing into place.

11. Drive a new seal into the housing with tool C-3995 or equivalent.

12. Install the extension housing with a new gasket and torque

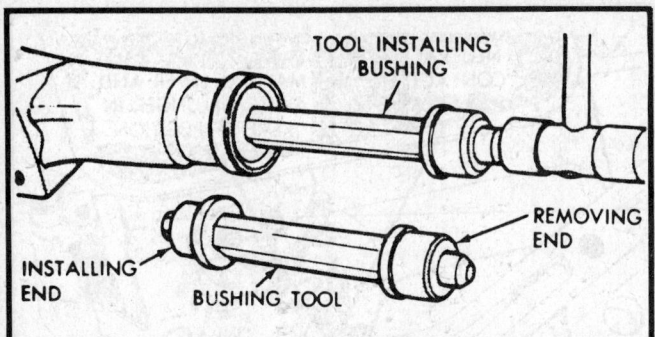

Replacing the extension housing bushing

the retaining bolts to 32 ft. lbs. (43 Nm). Torque the housing to support bolt to 50 ft. lbs. (68 Nm). Add the proper ATF fluid to the transmission to bring it up to the proper level.

GOVERNOR AND PARKING GEAR

Removal and Installation

1. Raise and support the vehicle safely. Remove the extension housing and output shaft bearing.
2. Carefully remove the snapring from the weight end of the governor valve shaft. Slide the valve and shaft assembly out of the governor body.
3. Remove the large snapring from the weight end of the governor body, lift out the governor weight assembly.
4. Remove the snapring from inside the governor weight, remove the inner weight and spring from the outer weight.
5. Remove the snapring from behind the governor body. Slide the governor and support assembly off the output shaft.
6. Remove the bolts and separate the governor body and screen from the parking gear.
7. Inspect all parts for burrs and wear. Inspect all moving parts for free movement, replace or repair as necessary.
8. Install by assembling the governor body and screen to support and tighten bolts finger tight. Be sure that the oil passage of the governor body aligns with the passage in the support.
9. Position the support and governor assembly on the output shaft. Align the assembly so the valve shaft hole in the governor body aligns with the hole in output shaft, slide the assembly into place. Install the snapring behind the governor body. Use new valve body support bolts and tighten the valve body to support bolts to 95 inch lbs. (11 Nm). The support bolts have a self locking nylon patch and cannot be reused.
10. Assemble the governor weights and spring and secure with a snapring inside of the larger governor weight. Place the weight assembly in the governor body and install the snapring.
4. Place the governor valve onto the valve shaft, insert the assembly into the body through governor weights. Install the valve shaft retaining snapring. Inspect the valve and weight assembly for free movement after installation.
5. Install the output shaft bearing and extension housing.

PARK LOCK

Removal and Installation

1. Raise and support the vehicle safely. Remove the extension housing.
2. Slide the shaft out of the extension housing to remove the parking sprag and spring.
3. Remove the snapring and slide the curved reaction plug and pin assembly out of the housing.
4. To remove the parking lock control rod, it is necessary to remove the valve body.
5. Installation is the reverse order of the removal procedure.

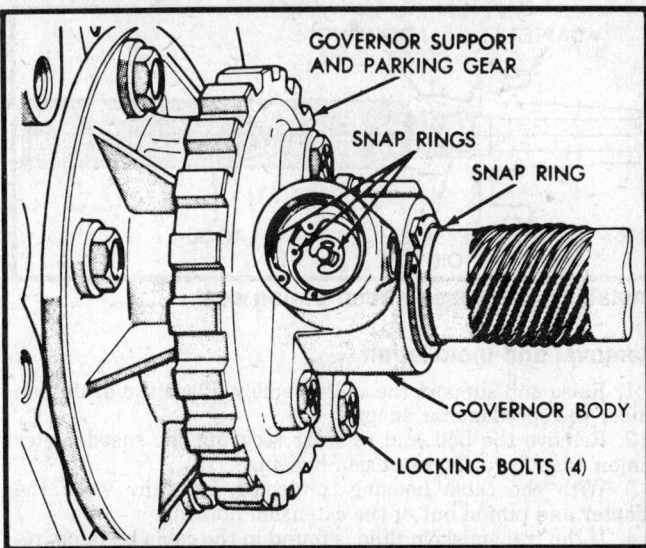

Removing the governor snapring

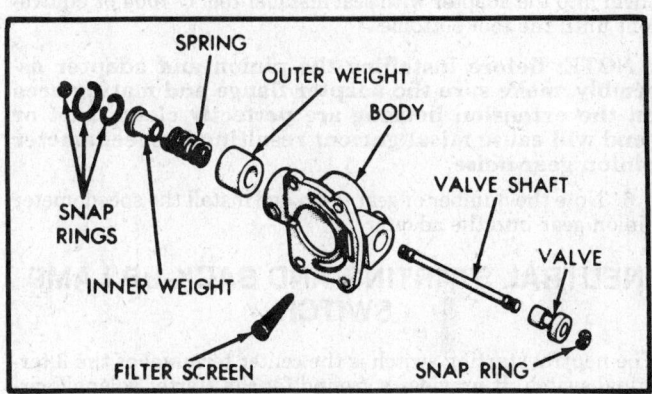

Typical governor assembly

SPEEDOMETER PINION GEAR

Any time the speedometer pinion adapter is removed, a new O-ring (black in color) must be installed on the outside diameter of the adapter.

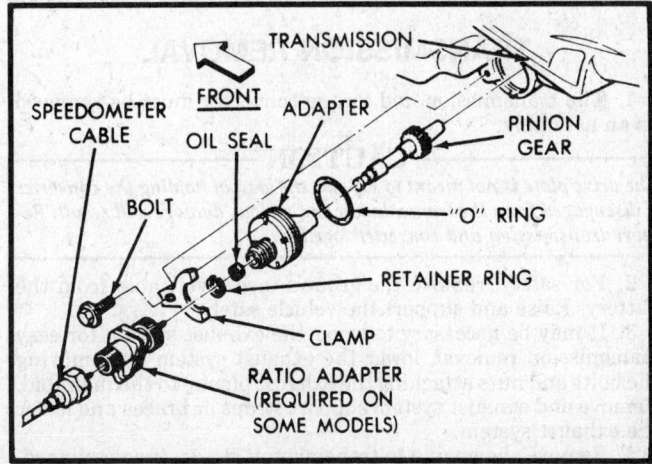

Exploded view of the speedometer drive assembly

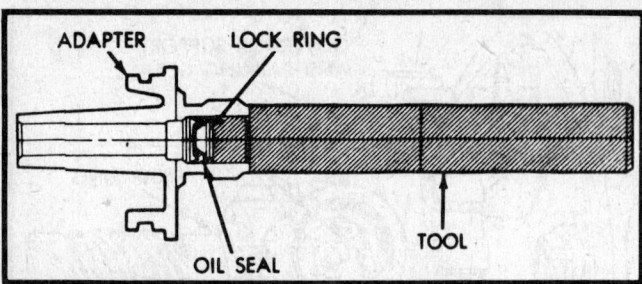

Installing the speedometer pinion seal

Removal and Installation

1. Raise and support the vehicle safely. Place the drain pan under the speedometer adapter.

2. Remove the bolt and retainer securing the speedometer pinion adapter in the extension housing.

3. With the cable housing connected, carefully work the adapter and pinion out of the extension housing.

4. If the transmission fluid is found in the cable housing, replace the seal in the adapter.

5. Start the seal and retainer ring in the adapter and push them into the adapter with seal installer tool C-4004 or equivalent until the tool bottoms.

NOTE: Before installing the pinion and adapter assembly, make sure the adapter flange and mating area on the extension housing are perfectly clean. Dirt or sand will cause misalignment resulting in speedometer pinion gear noise.

6. Note the number of gear teeth and install the speedometer pinion gear into the adapter.

NEUTRAL STARTING AND BACK-UP LAMP SWITCH

The neutral starting switch is the center terminal of the 3 terminal switch. It provides a ground for the starter solenoid circuit through the selector lever in only the **P** and **N** positions. Proper operation of the neutral start switch can be checked as follows:

1. Turn key to **ON** to unlock column and shift lever.

2. Move shift lever slowly until it clicks into the **P** detent. Try to start engine. If starter does operate, **P** position is correct.

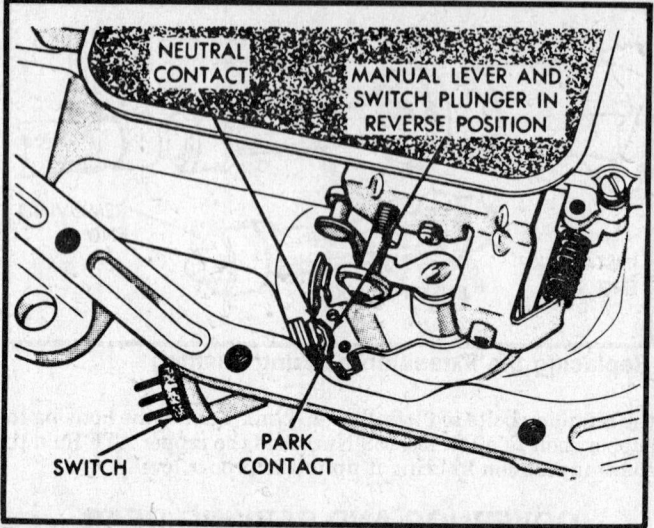

Removing or installing the neutral/back-up lamp switch

3. Stop the engine. Repeat, only this time moving lever to the **N** position. Try to start engine. If starter does operate, **N** position is correct and linkage is properly adjusted.

4. Remove the switch as follows:

a. Unscrew the switch from the transmission case allowing the fluid to drain into a suitable container.

b. Move the selector lever to **P** and then to **N** positions and inspect to see that the switch operating lever fingers are centered in the switch opening in the case.

c. Screw the switch and new seal into the transmission case and torque the switch to 25 ft. lbs. (34 Nm). Retest the switch with a suitable test lamp.

d. Add the proper ATF fluid to the transmission to bring it up to the proper level.

e. The back-up lamp switch circuit is through the 2 outside terminal of the 3 terminal switch.

f. To test the switch, remove the wiring connector from the switch and test for continuity between the 2 outside pins.

g. Continuity should exist only with the transmission in the **R** position.

h. No continuity should exist from either pin to the transmission case.

REMOVAL AND INSTALLATION

TRANSMISSION REMOVAL

1. The transmission and torque converter must be removed as an assembly.

――――――――― CAUTION ―――――――――
The drive plate is not meant to support the load of holding the converter if disengaged from the transmission and serious damage will result. Remove transmission and converter together.
――――――――――――――――――――――――

2. For safety, remove the ground (negative) cable from the battery. Raise and support the vehicle safely.

3. It may be necessary to lower the exhaust system for easy transmission removal, lower the exhaust system by removing the bolts and nuts attaching the exhaust pipe(s) to the manifold. Remove and exhaust system support straps or braces and lower the exhaust system.

4. Remove the engine to transmission struts, if so equipped. Remove and plug the cooler lines at the transmission.

5. Remove the starter motor and cooler line bracket.

6. Remove the torque converter access cover. Loosen the oil pan bolts, tap the pan to break it loose and let the fluid drain into a suitable drain pan.

7. Reinstall the pan temporarily with a few of the pan bolts. Mark the torque converter and drive plate to aid in reassembly. The crankshaft flange bolt circle, inner and outer circle of the holes in the drive plate and the 4 tapped holes in the front face of the torque converter all have 1 hole offset so these parts will be installed in the original position. This maintains the balance of the engine and torque converter.

8. Rotate the engine clockwise with the socket wrench on the crankshaft bolt to position the bolts attaching the torque converter to the drive plate and remove the bolts.

9. Mark the parts for reassemble then disconnect the driveshaft at the rear universal joint Carefully pull the shaft assembly out of the extension housing.

10. Disconnect the wire connector from the back-up lamp and neutral starting switch and lockup solenoid wiring connector.

Disconnect the spedometer cable and remove the oil fill tube.

11. Disconnect the gear shift rod and torque shaft assembly from the transmission.

NOTE: When it is necessary to disassemble the linkage rods from levers that use a plastic grommet as retainers, the grommets should be replaced with new ones.

12. Use a suitable tool to force the rod from the grommet in the lever and cut away the old grommet. Use pliers to snap the new grommet into the lever and rod into the grommet.

13. Disconnect the throttle rod from the lever at the left side of the transmission. Remove the linkage bell crank from the transmission, if so equipped.

14. Install the engine support fixture tool C-3487-A or equivalent with frame hooks, so as to support the rear of the engine.

15. Raise the transmission slightly with a suitable transmission jack to relieve the load on the supports.

16. Remove the bolts supporting the transmission mount to the crossmember and crossmember to frame and remove the crossmember.

17. Remove all bell housing bolts. Carefully work the transmission and torque converter assembly rearward off the engine block dowels and disengage the torque converter hub from the end of the crankshaft.

NOTE: Attach a small C-clamp to the edge of the bell housing to hold the torque converter in place during transmission removal.

18. Lower the transmission and remove the assembly from under the vehicle. To remove the torque converter assembly, remove the C-clamp from the edge of the bell housing and carefully slide the assembly out the transmission.

19. Remove the overdrive unit retaining bolts. Very carefully pull the overdrive unit off of the intermediate shaft. A bearing and select spacer may be either on the overdrive piston on the rear of the transmission case, sliding hub or intermediate shaft.

NOTE: Once the overdrive unit is pulled back approximately 1 in., it is free to fall, if unsupported.

TRANSMISSION INSTALLATION

If the transmission was removed because of malfunction caused by sludge, accumulated friction material or metal particles, the oil cooler and lines must be flushed thoroughly. Also, once the transmission is out, the engine block can be inspected for leaking core hole plugs or oil gallery plugs that would otherwise be inaccessable. The transmission and converter must be installed as an assembly; otherwise, the converter drive plate, pump bushing and oil seal will be damaged.

1. Reinstall the overdrive unit, if it had been removed and torque the retaining bolts to 25 ft. lbs.

2. The pump rotors must be aligned so that the converter will fully seat. Slide converter over the input and reaction shaft. Make sure the converter hub slots are engaging the pump inner rotor lugs as the converter is slid inward. Test for full engagement by placing a straightedge on the face of the case. Measure from the straightedge to the lug (square piece with tapped hole for drive plate) on the front cover. The dimension should be at least ½ in. when the converter is pushed all the way into the transmission. This is very important.

3. Attach a small C-clamp to the edge of the converter housing to hold the converter in place during installation. Check the converter drive plate for cracks or distortion and if necessary, replace it. Drive plate to crankshaft bolts should be torqued to 55 ft. lbs. and the torque should be checked even if bolts were not removed.

4. Coat the hole in the crankshaft that will receive the converter hub with Multi-Purpose grease. With transmission and

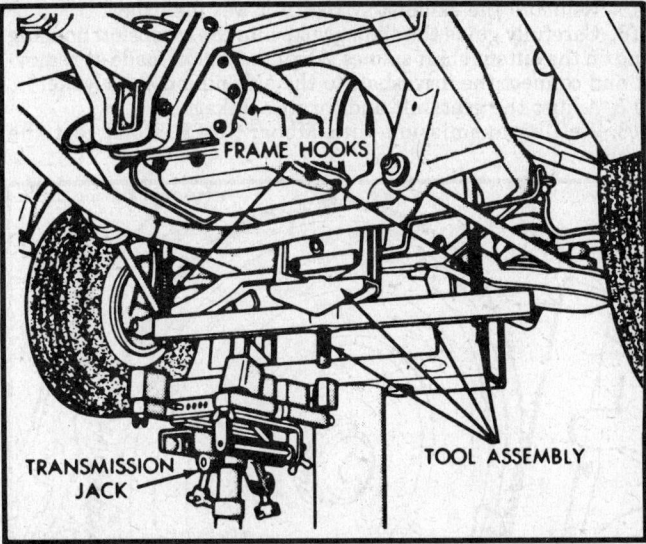

Typical engine support fixture

converter assembly held securely on the jack, align as necessary with the engine.

5. Rotate the converter so that the mark that was made on the converter during removal will align with the mark on the drive plate. The offset holes in the plate are located next to the ⅛ in. hole in the inner circle of the plate. Carefully work transmission forward onto the block dowels with converter hub entering the crankshaft opening. Remove the C-clamp before pushing the assembly fully home.

NOTE: If the converter or drive plate has been replaced, or the marks made at removal are lost, examine crankshaft flange to see how the plate and converter must line up because of the offset holes. Then mark the plate and converter (paint, chalk) for assembly.

6. When the transmission is in position, install the converter housing bolts and torque then to 30 ft. lbs. (41 Nm) install the vibration dampener removed from the driveline tunnel, if so equipped.

7. Install the crossmember to the frame and lower the transmission to install the mount on the extension to the crossmember, tighten all bolts. Remove engine support fixture.

8. Using alignment marks made at disassembly, align speedometer adapter and install. Install oil fill tube.

9. Connect the throttle rod to the transmission lever. Connect the gearshift rod and torque the shaft assembly to the transmission lever and frame.

10. When it is necessary to disassemble the linkage rods from levers that use a plastic grommet as retainers, the grommets should be replaced with new ones. Use a suitable tool to force the rod from the grommet in the lever and cut away the old grommet. Use pliers to snap the new grommet into the lever and rod into the grommet.

11. Place the wire connector on the combination back-up and neutral/park starting switch. Connect the wiring to the lockup solenoid wiring connector at the rear of the transmission case.

12. Using a socket on the engine vibration damper, rotate engine clockwise as needed to install converter to drive plate bolts, making sure the marks made previously match up. Torque these bolts to 22 ft. lbs.

13. Install converter access cover, starter and hook up cooler lines.

14. Install the engine to transmission struts, if so equipped. Tighten the bolts holding the strut to transmission before the strut to engine bolts.

15. Reinstall the exhaust system if it was disturbed.
16. Carefully guide the sliding yoke into the extension housing and on the outout shaft splines. Align the marks made at removal and connect the driveshaft to the axle pinion shaft yoke.
17. Adjust the gearshift and throttle linkage.
18. Refill transmission with Mopar® ATF. Road test the vehicle.

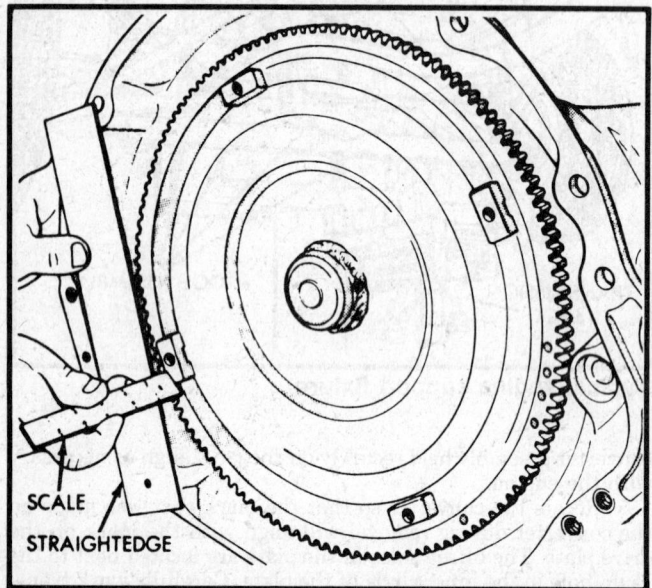

Measuring the torque converter for full engagement into transmision

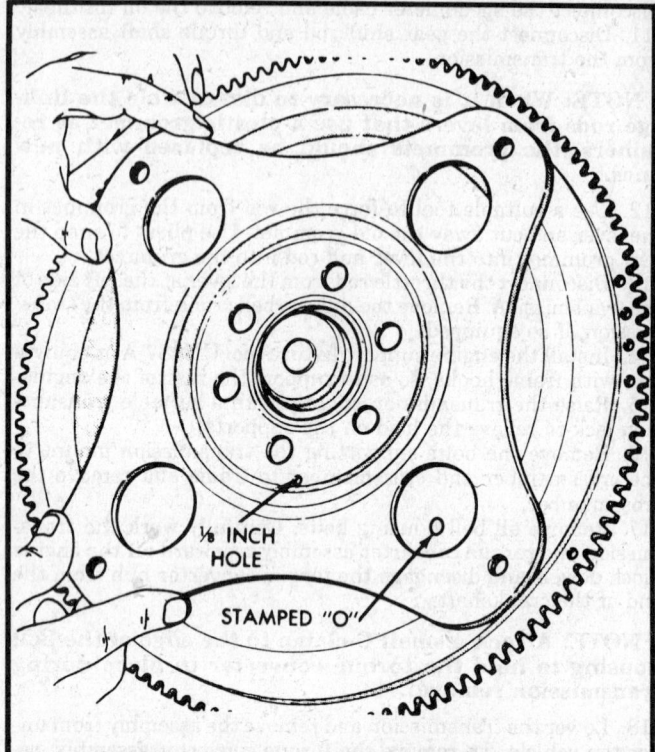

Torque converter and drive plate marking

BENCH OVERHAUL

Before Disassembly

Cleanliness during disassembly and assembly is necessary to avoid further transmission trouble after assembly. Before removing any of the transmission subassemblies, plug all the openings and clean the outside of the of the transmission thoroughly. Steam cleaning or car wash type high pressure equipment is preferable. During disassembly, clean all parts in a suitable solvent and dry each part. Do not use cloth or paper towels to dry parts. Use compressed air only.

ENDPLAY MEASUREMENT

Measuring the endplay before disassembling the unit will indicate whether a thrust washer change is required and will save a considerable amount of time at assembly
1. Mount transmission in a holding fixture or otherwise secure and rig up a dial indicator so that the stylus is against the forward end of the input shaft.
2. Move input shaft to the back as far as it will go and zero the indicator.
3. Pull the input shaft forward to obtain the endplay reading.
4. Mark this figure down for future reference and remove indicator.

Converter Inspection

The torque converter is removed by simply sliding the unit out of the transmission off the input and reaction shaft. If the converter is to be reused, set aside so it will not be damaged. Since the units are welded and have no drain plugs, converters subjected to burnt fluid or other contamination must be replaced.

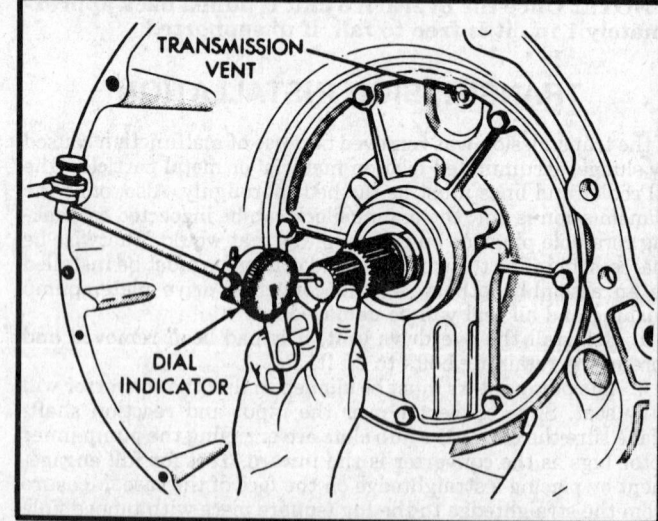

Measuring the input shaft end play

Transmission Disassembly

OIL PAN AND FILTER

Removal

1. Make sure transmission is held securely either in a stand or fixture.

2. Remove the pan to case bolts and gently tap pan loose. Do not insert a tool between pan and case as a prying tool or case damage may result.

3. Check pan carefully for distortion, straightening the edges of the pan with a straight block of wood and a rubber mallet if necessary. A power driven wire wheel is useful in removing glued on gaskets.

4. There are only 3 screws used to hold the filter to the valve body. A new filter must be installed whenever the pan is removed for transmission service. Remove screws, discard filter. The filter retaining screws may be a special Torx® drive screw head which requires the proper Torx® drive bit to remove the screws.

5. When the pan is eventually reinstalled torque the bolts evenly to 150 inch lbs.

VALVE BODY

Removal

1. Loosen the clamp bolts and remove the gearshift and throttle levers from the transmission.

2. Unscrew the neutral/back-up light switch. Disconnect the lockup solenoid wire from the wiring connector at the rear of the transmission case.

3. Remove the 10 bolts holding the valve body to the transmission. Remove the **E** clip that holds the parking lock rod to the valve body manual lever.

4. Lift valve body, freeing the lock rod from the manual lever. Remove the valve body assembly from its mating surface and place it on a shop bench.

5. At this time, remove the accumulator piston spring and piston, keeping them separate from the servo pistons and springs remove next.

EXTENSION HOUSING

Removal

1. Remove the speedometer pinion and adapter assembly.
2. Remove the extension housing to transmission bolts.

NOTE: When removing or installing the extension housing, the gearshift lever must be in the 1 (low) position. This positions the parking lock control rod rear-ward so it can be disengaged or engaged with the parking lock sprag.

3. Remove the screws, plate and gasket from the bottom of the extension housing mounting pad. Spread the snapring from the output shaft bearing

4. With the snapring spread as far as possible, carefully tap the extension housing rearward to allow the parking lock control knob to clear the parking sprag and remove the housing.

5. Using a heavy duty pair of snapring pliers, remove the output shaft bearing snapring and remove the bearing from the shaft.

GOVERNOR AND SUPPORT

Removal

1. Carefully remove the snapring from the weight end of the governor valve shaft (smaller side of governor) slide valve and shaft assembly out of the governor body.

2. Carefully remove the snapring from behind the governor body and slide the governor body and support assembly off of the output shaft.

OIL PUMP AND REACTION SHAFT SUPPORT

Removal

1. Tighten the front band adjusting screw until the band is tight on the front clutch retainer. This prevents the front clutch retainer from coming out with the pump which might cause unnecessary damage to the clutches.

2. Remove the the oil pump housing retaining bolts.
3. Using 2 slide hammers, bump the unit outward evenly.

FRONT BAND AND FRONT CLUTCH

Removal

1. Loosen the front band adjuster screws and remove the band strut. Slide the band out of the case.
2. Slide front clutch assembly out of the case.

INPUT SHAFT AND REAR CLUTCH

Removal

1. Grasp input shaft and slide input shaft and rear clutch assembly out of the case.

2. Be careful not to lose the thrust washer located between the rear end of the input shaft and the forward end of the output shaft.

PLANETARY GEAR ASSEMBLIES, SUN GEAR AND DRIVING SHELL

Removal

1. While supporting the output shaft and driving shell, carefully slide the assembly forward and out of the case, being very careful of the output shaft's surface.

NOTE: While it is possible to remove the planetaries and driving shell at one time, it may be easier to remove the front planetary/annulus first.

REAR BAND AND LOW-REVERSE DRUM

Removal

1. Loosen the band adjusting screw and remove the band strut and link.

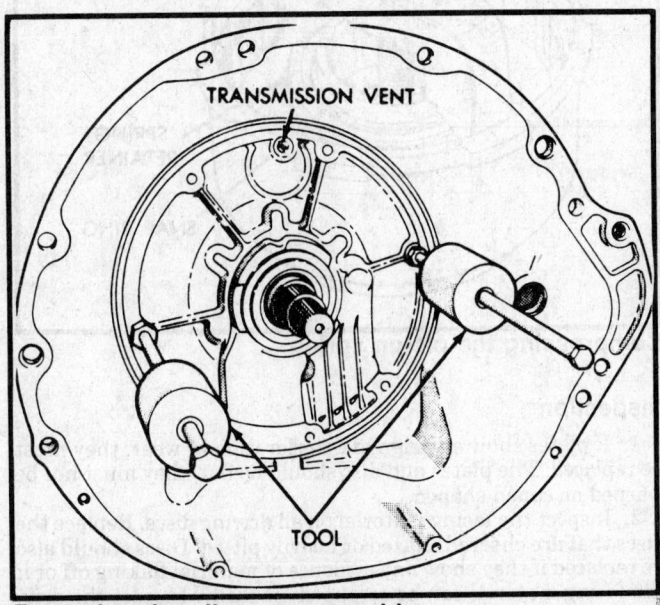

TRANSMISSION VENT

TOOL

Removing the oil pump assembly

2. Remove the low reverse drum from the case.

OVERRUNNING CLUTCH

Removal

Due to the possibility of the overrunning clutch breaking loose from the case on high mileage vehicles, the clutch should be carefully inspected and the springs replaced. The rollers tend to apply unevenly due to decreasing spring pressure. This forces the inner race, or hub to one side moving the rest of the gear train with it. With long-nose pliers, pull out 1 roller and spring and inspect for wear. If badly worn, unit replacement is recommended.

1. Note the position of the overrunning clutch rollers and springs before disassembly, to assist in reassembly.
2. Carefully slide out the clutch hub and remove the rollers and springs.

KICKDOWN (FRONT) SERVO

Removal

1. Compress the kickdown servo piston rod guide until it bottoms in case bore. This can be done by pushing with a suitable tool or by compressing with a C-clamp on a suitable adapter, like a socket, or by using an engine valve spring compressor type tool. (In this case it is not necessary to remove port plug).
2. If not using a C-clamp or compressor, then insert a suitable tool through the port to hold the servo rod guide down far enough to remove the snapring.
3. After snapring removal, press guide back down to release the tool and slowly release rod guide.
4. Remove rod guide, springs and piston rod from the case.

— CAUTION —

Do not attempt to remove the rod using pliers. If the rod sticks in the case, work it gently to release it. Keep spring and parts separate. Do not allow front and rear servo parts to get mixed.

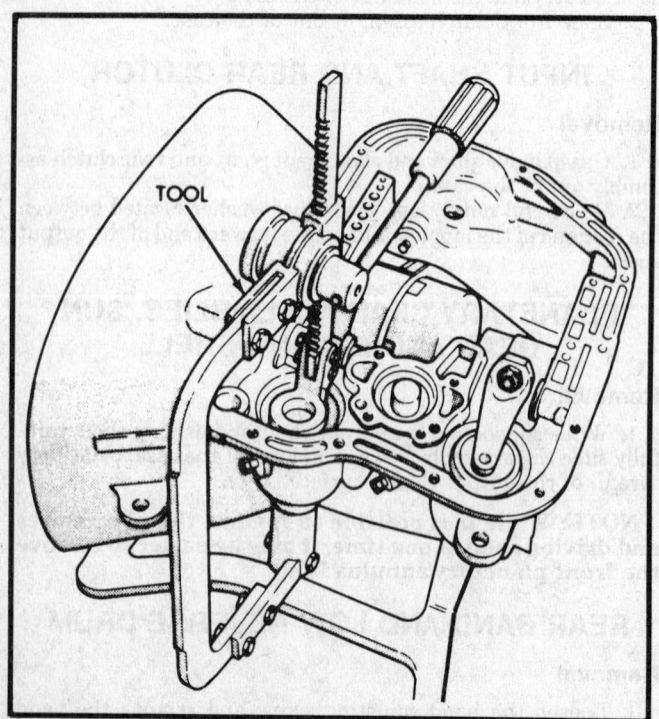

Compressing the kickdown servo spring

LOW-REVERSE (REAR) SERVO

Removal

1. Compress the low and reverse servo piston spring by using a engine valve spring compressor tool and remove the snapring.
2. Remove the spring retainer, spring and servo piston and plug assembly from the case.

OVERDRIVE UNIT

Removal

1. Remove the overdrive unit retaining bolts.
2. Very carefully pull the overdrive unit off of the intermediate shaft.
3. A bearing and select spacer may be either on the overdrive piston on the rear of the transmission case, sliding hub or intermediate shaft.

NOTE: Once the overdrive unit is pulled back approximately 1 in., it is free to fall, if it is unsupported.

Unit Disassembly and Assembly

FRONT CLUTCH

Disassembly

1. Remove large snapring and lift off pressure plate and clutch plates.
2. With a spring compressor, squeeze piston spring retainer down far enough to remove snapring. Remove spring and retainer.
3. Turn clutch retainer assembly over and tap on a block of wood to remove piston. Remove and discard seals from hub and piston.

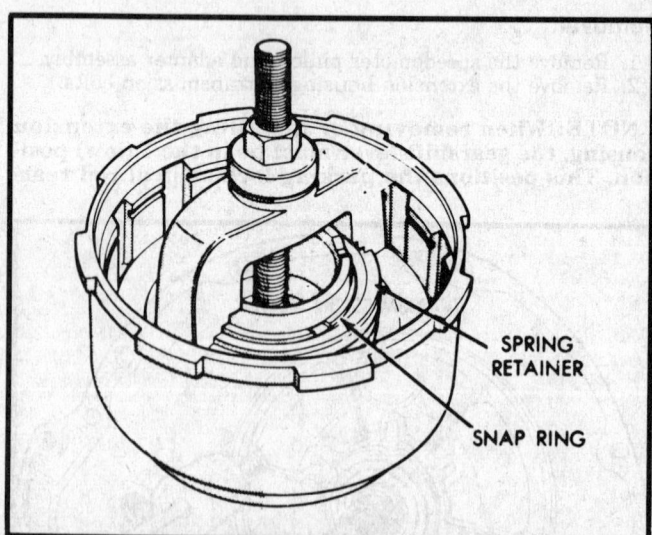

Compressing the piston spring

Inspection

1. If plates show any sign of deterioration or wear, they must be replaced. The plates and disc should be flat, they must not be warped or coned shaped.
2. Inspect the facing material on all driving discs. Replace the discs that are charred, glazed or heavily pitted. Discs should also be replaced if they show any evidence of material flaking off or if the facing material can be scrapped off easily. Inspect the driving disc splines for wear or other damage.

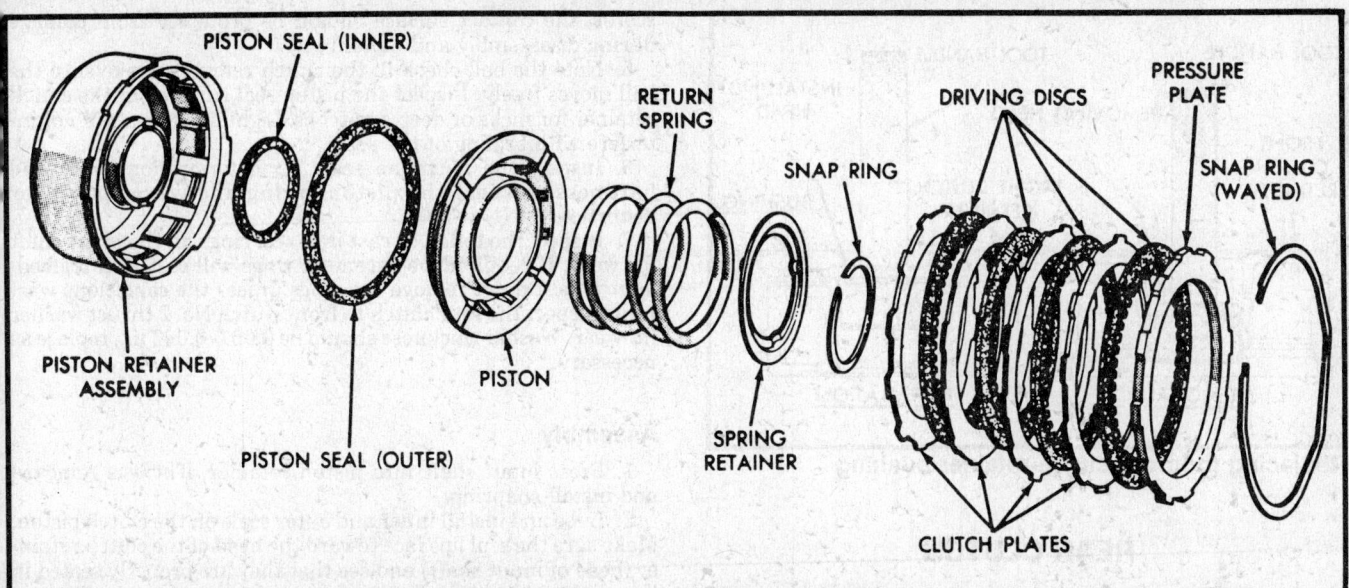

PISTON SEAL (INNER)

RETURN SPRING

DRIVING DISCS

PRESSURE PLATE

SNAP RING

SNAP RING (WAVED)

PISTON RETAINER ASSEMBLY

PISTON

PISTON SEAL (OUTER)

SPRING RETAINER

CLUTCH PLATES

Exploded view of the front clutch assembly

3. Inspect the steel plate and pressure plate surface for burning, scoring or damaged driving lugs. Replace if necessary.

4. Inspect the steel plate grooves in the clutch retainer for smooth surfaces, plates must travel freely in the grooves. Inspect the band contacting surface on the clutch retainer for scores, the contact surface should be protected from damage during disassembly and handling.

5. Note the ball check in the clutch retainer, make sure the ball moves freely. Inspect the piston seal surfaces in the clutch retainer for nicks or deep scratches. Light scratches will not interfere with sealing of the seals.

6. Inspect retainer assembly bushing for wear or scores. If bushing is to be replaced, use the following procedure:

   a. Turn the clutch retainer over (open end down) on a clean smooth surface and place removing head tool SP-3627 or equivalent in the bushing. Install the handle tool C-4171 or equivalent in removing head.

   b. Drive the bushing straight down and out of the clutch retainer bore. Be careful not to cock the tool in the bore.

   c. Turn the clutch retainer over (open end up) on a clean smooth surface. Slide a new bushing on the head tool SP-3626 or equivalent and start them in the clutch retainer bore.

   d. Drive the new bushing into the clutch retainer until it bottoms out. Thoroughly clean the clutch retainer before assembly and installation.

7. Inspect the inside bore of the piston for score marks, if light, remove with a suitable crocus cloth. Inspect the seals for deterioration, wear and hardness. Inspect the piston spring, retainer and snapring for distortion.

8. Clean all parts well, then install seal on retainer hub.

Assembly

1. Lubricate and install the inner seal on the hub of the clutch retainer. Make sure the lip of the seal faces down and properly seated in the groove.

2. Install the outer seal on the clutch piston, with the lip of the seal toward the bottom of the clutch retainer. Apply a coat of ATF fluid to the outer edge of the seals and press the seal to the bottom of its groove around the piston diameter for easier installation of the piston assembly.

3. Place the piston assembly into the retainer and carefully seat the piston in the bottom of the retainer.

4. Install spring, retainer and with spring compressor, install snapring into the hub groove. Remove the spring compressor.

5. Soak all plates in suitable automatic transmission fluid and install 1 steel plate followed by a lined plate (disc) making sure the correct number of plates are used, since it may vary from unit to unit and application to application.

6. Install pressure plate and snapring, be sure that snapring is properly seated.

7. Insert a feeler gauge between the pressure plate and the snapring, under the raised waved part to measure the maximum clearance. The clutch plate clearance should be with 5 discs — 0.075–0.152 in.

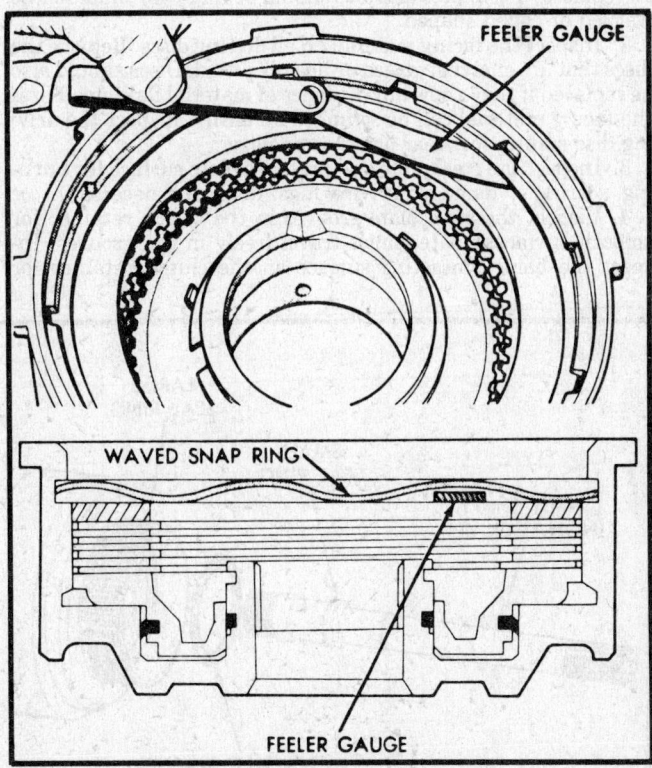

FEELER GAUGE

WAVED SNAP RING

FEELER GAUGE

Measure the front clutch plate clearance

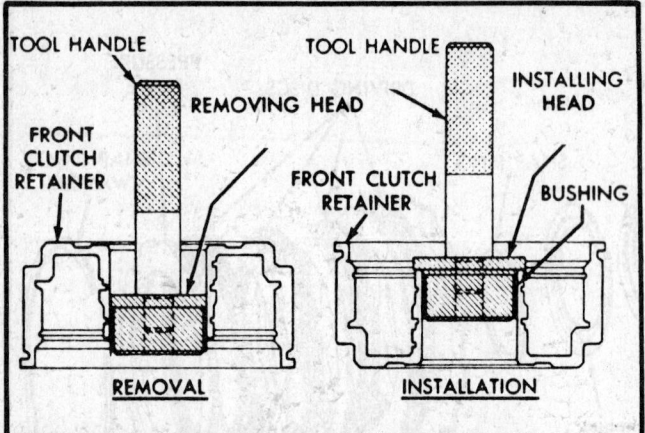

Replacing the front clutch retainer bushing

REAR CLUTCH

Disassembly

1. Remove the large snapring retaining the pressure plate. This is a selective fit snapring; handle it carefully. Take out pressure plate, clutches and inner pressure plate.

2. Pry one end of the wave spring out of its groove in the clutch retainer and remove along with clutch piston spring.

3. Turn retainer assembly over and tap on a block of wood to remove piston. Remove and discard seals from piston.

4. Remove snapring and press out input shaft if required.

Inspection

1. If plates show any sign of deterioration or wear, they must be replaced. The plates and disc should be flat, they must not be warped or coned shaped.

2. Inspect the facing material on all driving discs. Replace the discs that are charred, glazed or heavily pitted. Discs should also be replaced if they show any evidence of material flaking off or if the facing material can be scrapped off easily. Inspect the driving disc splines for wear or other damage.

3. Inspect the steel plate and pressure plate surface for burning, scoring or damaged driving lugs. Replace if necessary.

4. Inspect the steel plate grooves in the clutch retainer for smooth surfaces, plates must travel freely in the grooves. Inspect the band contacting surface on the clutch retainer for

scores, the contact surface should be protected from damage during disassembly and handling.

5. Note the ball check in the clutch retainer, make sure the ball moves freely. Inspect the piston seal surfaces in the clutch retainer for nicks or deep scratches. Light scratches will not interfere with sealing of the seals.

6. Inspect the neoprene seals for deterioration, wear and hardness. Inspect the piston spring and wave spring for distortion.

7. Inspect the teflon or cast iron seal rings on the input shaft for wear. If required, replacement rings will cast iron hooked-joint type. Do not remove the rings unless the conditions warrant. Inspect the rear clutch to front clutch No. 2 thrust washer for wear. Washer thickness should be 0.061–0.063 in., replace as necessary.

Assembly

1. Press input shaft into piston retainer, if it was removed and install snapring.

2. Lube and install inner and outer seals on the clutch piston. Make sure the seal lips face toward the head of the clutch retainer (head of input shaft) and see that they are properly seated in the piston in bottom of retainer.

3. Install the piston assembly into the retainer and with a twisting motion, seat the piston in the bottom of the retainer. Place the clutch piston spring on top of the piston in the retainer. Start one end of the wave spring in its retainer groove, tapping it progressively in place until it is fully seated in the groove.

4. Install inner pressure plate, with the raised portion of the plate resting on the spring.

5. Soak all plates in automatic transmission fluid and install making sure correct No. of plates is used, since it may vary from unit to unit and application to application. Make sure a lined plate is installed first, then a steel, until all are installed. Install the outer pressure plate and selective snapring.

6. Measure rear clutch plate clearance by pressing down firmly on the outer plate (it may require an assistant) then using a feeler gauge between the plate and snapring. The clutch plate clearance should be with 4 discs — 0.032–0.055 in.

NOTE: Rear clutch pack clearance is very important in obtaining proper clutch engagement and shaft quality. Clearance can be adjusted by the use of various thickness outer snaprings. Snaprings are available in 0.060, 0.076 and 0.098 in. thickness.

7. Grease the cupped side of the No. 3 thrust plate and install the cupped side over the input shaft.

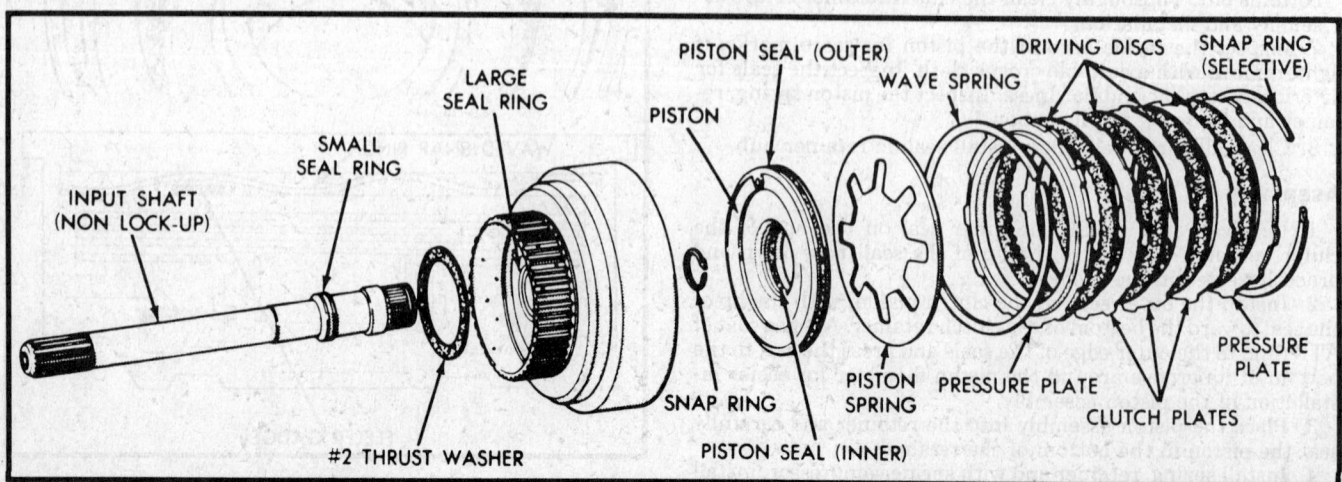

Exploded view of the rear clutch

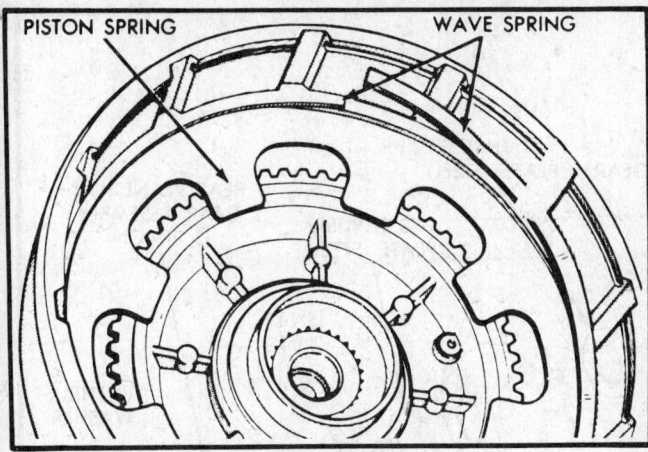

Installing the rear clutch spring

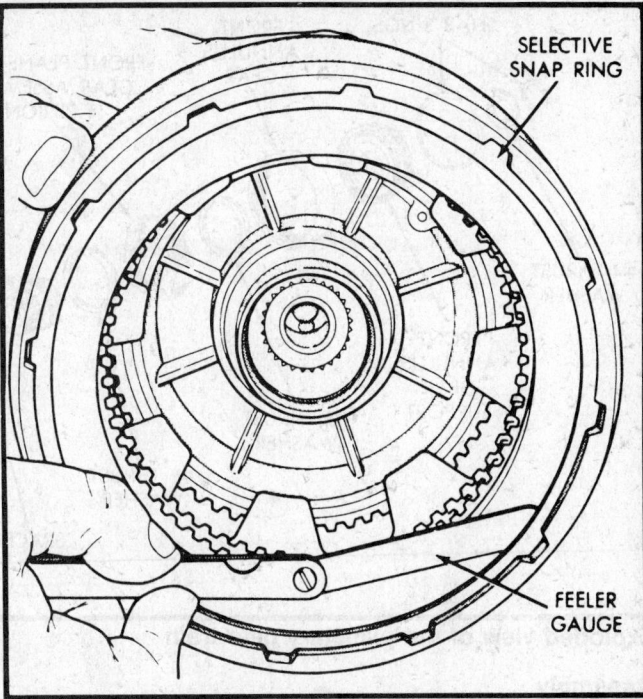

Measuring the rear clutch plate clearance

PLANETARY GEAR TRAIN

Endplay

Before disassembly, endplay of the planetary gear assemblies, sun gear and driving shell should be measured. Stand the gear train upright with the forward end of the output shaft on a block of wood. This causes all the parts to slide forward against the selective snapring on the front of the shaft. Insert feeler gauges between the rear annulus gear support hub and the shoulder on the output shaft. The clearance should be between 0.005–0.048 in. If clearance is not within these sizes, replace thrust washers, any worn parts and selective thickness snaprings at assembly.

Disassembly

1. Remove the selective No. 3 thrust washer from the tip of the output shaft.
2. Remove the selective snapring and slide the front planetary assembly from the shaft.
3. Remove the snapring and No. 4 thrust washer from the hub of the planetary; slide front annulus gear and support off the planetary gear set. Remove the No. 5 thrust washer from

the front side of the planetary gear assembly. Remove the No. 6 thrust washer from the rear side of the planetary gear assembly. If necessary, remove the snapring from the front of the annulus gear to separate the support from the annulus gear.

4. Slide the sun gear, driving shell and the rear planetary off of the output shaft.
5. Lift the sun gear and the driving shell off of the rear planetary assembly. Remove the snapring and the No. 8 thrust plate (steel) from the sun gear. Slide the sun gear out of the driving shell and remove the snapring and the No. 7 thrust plate from the opposite end of the sun gear, if necessary.
6. Remove the No. 9 thrust washer from the forward side of the rear planetary and separate the planetary from the rear annulus.
7. Remove the No. 10 thrust washer from the rear side of the planetary assembly and if necessary, remove the snapring from the rear annulus gear to separate the support from the annulus gear.

Inspection

1. Inspect all oil passages in the shaft and make sure they are open and clean.
2. Inspect the bearing surfaces on the output shaft for nicks, burrs, scores or other damage. Light scratches , small nicks or burrs can be removed with crocus cloth or a fine stone.
3. Inspect the speedometer drive gear for any nicks or burrs and remove with a sharp edged stone.
4. Inspect the bushing in the sun gear for wear or scores, replace the sun gear assembly if the bushings are damaged.
5. Inspect all thrust washers for wear and scores, replace if damaged or worn below specifications.
6. Inspect the thrust faces of the planetary gear carriers for wear, scores or other damage, replace as required. Inspect the planetary gear carrier for cracks and pinions for broken or worn gear teeth and for broken pinion shaft welds.
7. Inspect the annulus gear and driving gear teeth for damage. Replace distorted lock rings. Clean all parts well, blow dry.

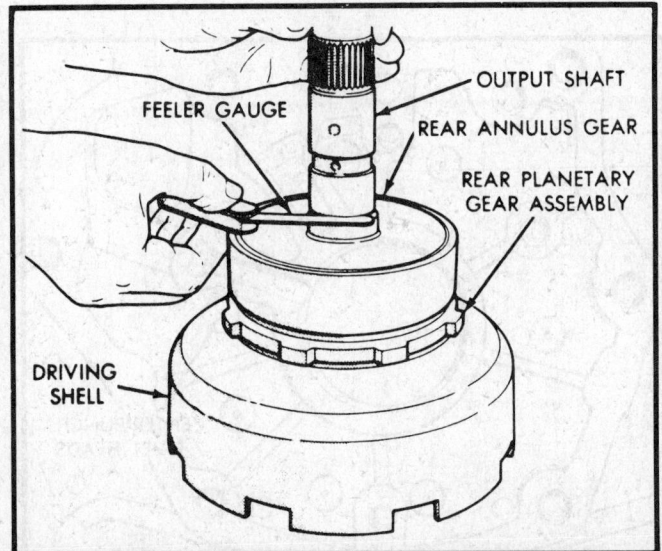

Measuring the end play of the planetary gear train

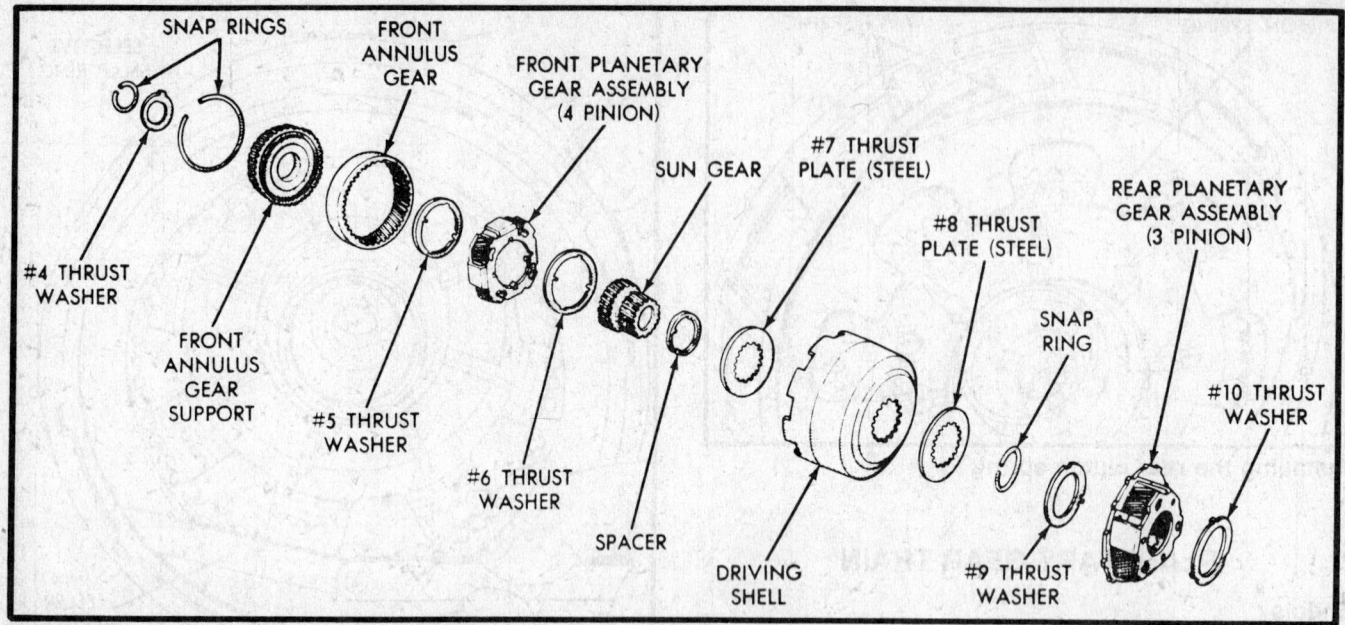

Exploded view of the planetary gear train

Assembly

1. To assemble, place rear annulus gear support in annulus gear and install snapring.
2. Put the No. 10 thrust washer on the back of the rear planetary, insert into the rear annulus and follow with the No. 9 thrust washer on the front side of the planetary.
3. From the back of the rear annulus gear, insert the output shaft, slowly working it through the planetary until splines on the shaft are meshed with the splines of annulus gear support.
4. Install the No. 7 thrust plate and snapring on one end of the sun gear. Insert the sun gear through the front side of the driving shell, install No. 8 thrust plate and snapring.
5. Carefully slide the driving shell and sun gear assembly onto the output shaft, meshing the sun gear teeth with the rear planetary pinion teeth.
6. Place the front annulus gear support in the annulus gear and install the snapring.
7. Put the No. 5 thrust washer on the front side of the front planetary gear assembly. Put the front planetary in front of the front annulus gear, install the No. 4 thrust washer over the planetary hub and install the snapring. Put the No. 6 thrust washer on the rear side of the planetary gear assembly.

8. Carefully work the front planetary and annulus gear assembly onto the shaft meshing the planetary pinions with the sun gear.
9. With all components in place, install the selective snapring on the front of the output shaft. Remeasure the endplay. The clearance can be adjusted by the use of various thickness snaprings. Snaprings are available in 0.042, 0.064 and 0.084 in. thickness.

OVERRUNNING CLUTCH

Inspection

Check rollers for signs of wear or out-of-round. They must be free from flat spots and chipped edges. Check the cam for wear and the springs for distortion. If the overrunning clutch cam or spring retainer is worn, or damaged, the service replacement contains a cam with tapped holes and retaining bolts.

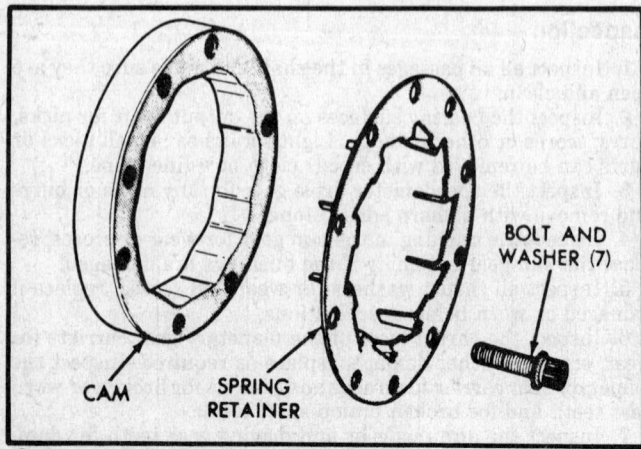

Overrunning clutch replacement

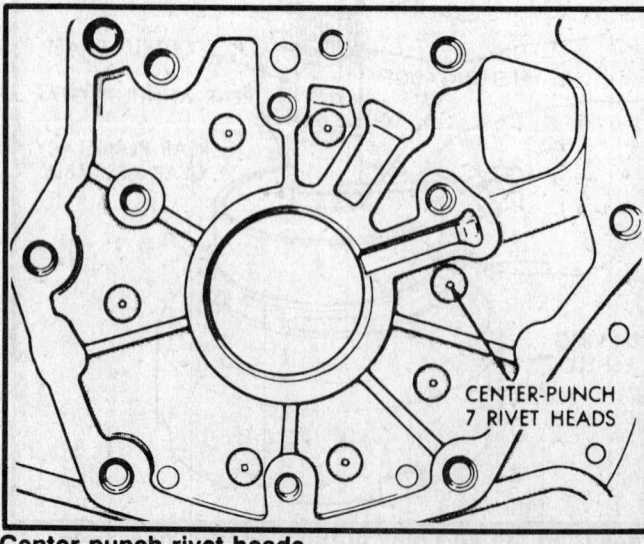

Center punch rivet heads

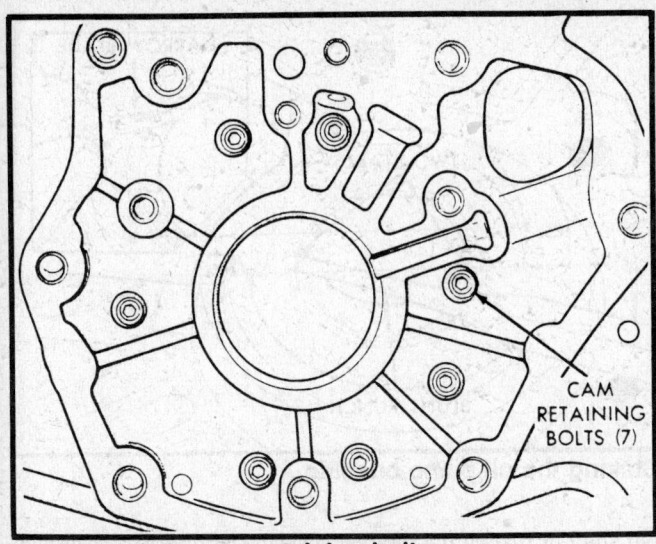

Location of the cam retaining bolts

Overrunning Clutch Cam Replacement

The service parts are retained in the case with bolts instead of rivets. To install proceed as follows:

1. Remove the 4 bolts holding the output shaft support to the transmission case and remove, tapping with a soft hammer if required.
2. Center punch the rivets exactly in the center of each rivet head.
3. Using a ⅜ in. drill bit, drill through each rivet head being careful not to drill into the transmission case. Remove remainder of rivet head and drive out rivets with a punch.
4. Enlarge carefully the holes with a $^{17}/_{64}$ in. drill bit. Clean case so that no clips remain and check for burrs around drilled holes.
5. Drive cam from case.
6. Position new cam and spring retainer in case, align bolt holes and install, but do not tighten bolts. Note that the cone shaped washers on the bolts must be installed to that the inner diameter is coned toward the bolt head.
7. If necessary, tap the cam into the case and tighten bolt evenly to 100 inch lbs.
8. Install output shaft support. It may require using 2 bolts with heads cut off, as pilot studs to help align the support. Tap firmly into case with soft hammer.

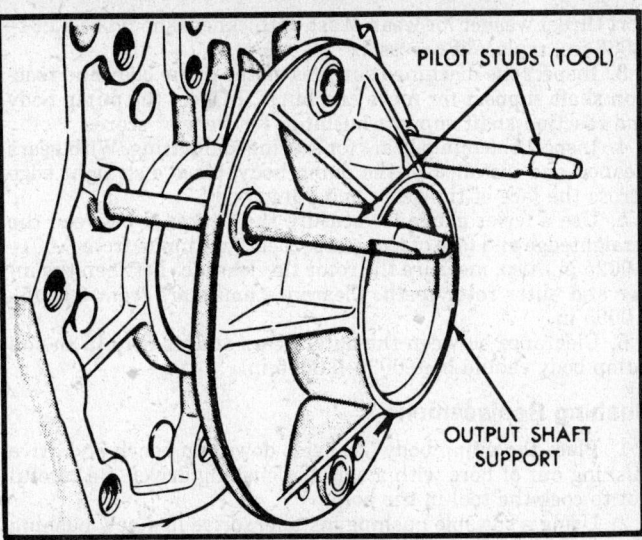

Installing the output shaft support

9. Tighten bolts to 150 inch lbs. (17 Nm).

OIL PUMP

Disassembly

Because this unit is equipped with a lockup torque converter, it is important that the oil pump be within the specified clearance limits. In any overhaul, the oil pump bushing should be replaced.

1. Remove the 6 bolts attaching the pump to the reaction shaft support and remove the support. Remove and discard O-ring and oil seal, which may need to be driven out with a blunt punch.
2. Apply a small amount of machinist's bluing on one spot on the inner and outer rotors and scribe a mark across the rotors for correct tooth alignment at reassembly.

Inspection

1. Inspect reaction shaft support for cracks or burrs on the sealing ring grooves; seal rings will have to be removed to allow clearance for the No. 1 thrust washer to be removed. Inspect pump rotors for scoring or pitting and clean well.
2. Inspect front clutch piston retainer to reaction shaft sup-

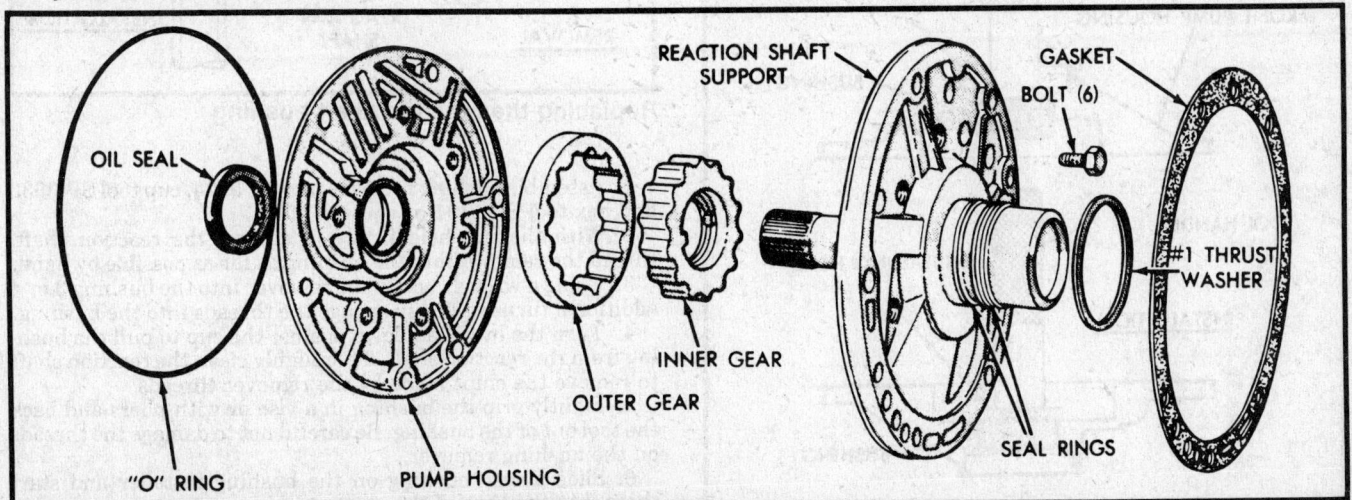

Exploded view of the oil pump and reaction shaft support

port thrust washer for wear. Washer thickness should be 0.061–0.063 in., replace if necessary.

3. Inspect the machined surfaces on the pump body and reaction shaft support for nicks and burrs. Inspect the pump body and reaction shaft support bushings for wear or scores.

4. Inspect the pump gears for scoring and pitting. With gears cleaned and installed in the pump body, place a straight edge across the face of the gears and pump body.

5. Use a feeler gauge to measure the clearance between the straightedge and face of the gears. Clearance limits from 0.001–0.0025 in. Also, measure the rotor tip clearance between the inner and outer rotor teeth. Clearance limits are from 0.0045–0.0095 in.

6. Clearance between the outer gears and its bore in the oil pump body should be 0.0035–0.0075 in.

Bushing Replacement

1. Place the pump body (seal side down) on bench and drive bushing out of bore with a suitable bushing driver. Be careful not to cock the tool in the bore.

2. Using a suitable bushing installer, drive in a new bushing until it bottoms in the oil pump cavity. Be careful not to cock the tool during installation. When the bushing is in place, stake it in several places with a blunt punch. A gentle tap will do.

3. Using a suitable tool, clean off the burrs and high spots caused by the stake. Don't use a file or any tool that would remove too much metal. Rinse pump body in solvent.

4. Install the pump rotors in the pump body. Place a straightedge across the rotor faces and pump body. Using a feeler gauge measure the clearance between the straightedge and feeler gauge. Clearance limits are 0.001–0.003 in. (0.254–0.762mm).

5. Turn the rotors so that the center of a tooth on each rotor is aligned. Measure the clearance between the tips of the teeth. Measure 4 times, turning the inner rotor ¼ turn between measurements. Rotor tip clearance should be 0.005–0.010 in. (0.1270–0.2540mm). Measure the clearance between the outer surface of the outer rotor and the pump bore. The clearance should be 0.004 to 0.008 in. (0.1016 to 0.2043mm).

6. Inspect reaction shaft support bushing. If the bushing has failed or is badly worn, then inspect support assembly. If the in-

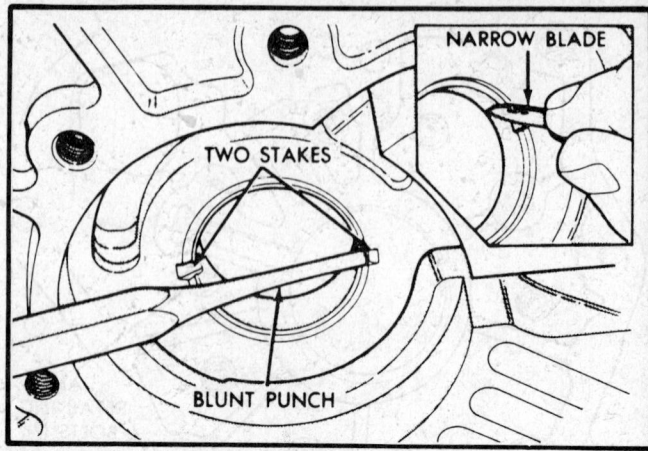
Staking the oil pump bushing

put shaft or rear clutch retainer seal ring lands are worn or badly grooved, the entire support assembly should be replaced. If just the bushing is to be replaced, use the following procedure.

Reaction Shaft Bushing Replacement

Do not clamp any part of the reaction shaft or support in a vise. Special type removal tools grab the bushing from the inside which is then bumped out with the tool slide hammer. Do not damage support assembly.

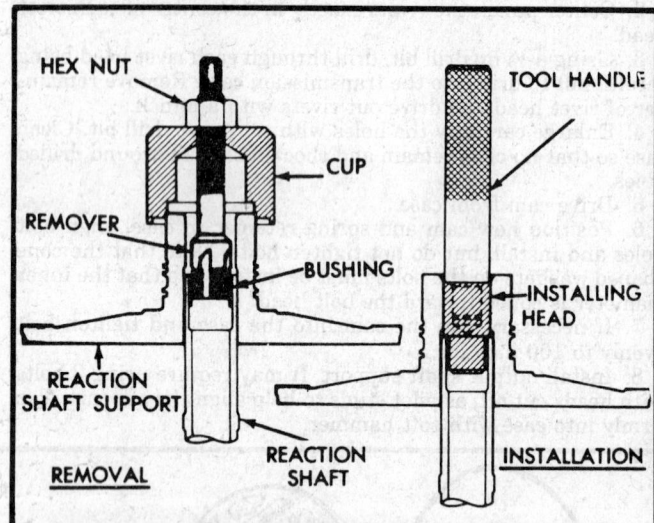
Replacing the reaction shaft bushing

1. Assemble bushing remover tool SP-5324, cup tool SP-3633 and hex tool SP-1191 or equivalents.

2. With the cup held firmly in against the reaction shaft, thread the remover into the bushing as far as possible by hand.

3. Using a wrench, screw the remover into the bushing 3 or 4 additional turns to firmly engage the threads into the bushing.

4. Turn the hex head down against the cup to pull the bushing from the reaction shaft. Thoroughly clean the reaction shaft to remove the chips made by the remover threads.

5. Lightly grip the bushing in a vise or with pliers and back the tool out of the bushing. Be careful not to damage the threads on the bushing remover.

6. Slide a new bushing on the bushing installer and start them into the bore of the reaction shaft.

7. Support the reaction shaft upright on a clean smooth sur-

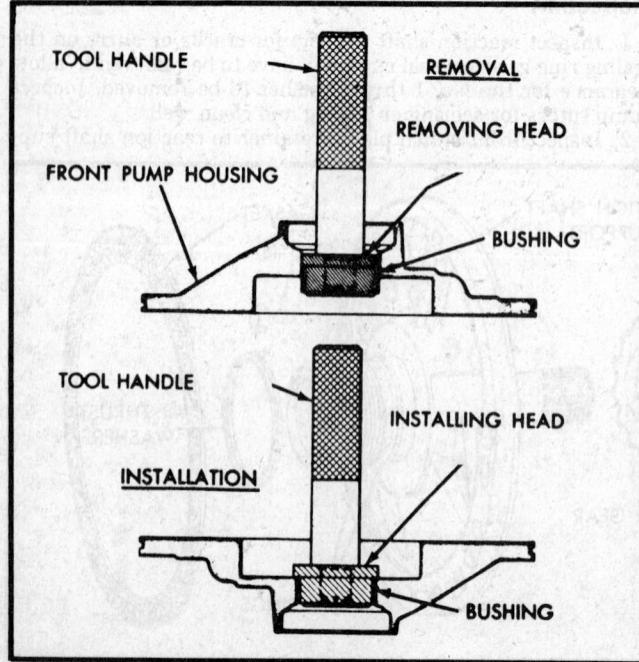
Replacing the oil pump bushing

face and drive the bushing into the shaft until the tool bottoms out.

8. Thoroughly clean the reaction shaft support assembly before installation.

Assembly

1. Place the reaction shaft support in assembling tool C-3759, with the hub of the support tool resting on a smooth flat surface bench. Screw 2 pilot studs into the threaded holes of the reaction shaft support flange.

2. Assemble and place the pump gears in the center of the support.

3. Lower the pump body over the pilot studs, insert tool C-3756 or equivalent through the pump body and engage the pump inner gear.

4. Rotate the pump gears with the tool to center the gears in the pump body, then with the pump body firm against the reaction shaft support, tighten the clamping tool securely.

5. Invert the pump and reaction shaft support assembly with clamping tool intact. Install the support to pump body bolts and tighten to 175 inch lbs. (20 Nm). Remove the clamping tool, pilot studs and gear alignment tool.

NOTE: If difficulty was encountered removing the pump at first, it may be well to expand the case with a heat lamp before attempting to install pump.

6. Place a new oil seal in the opening of the pump housing (lip of the seal facing inward), drive a seal into the housing until the tool bottoms out.

OIL PUMP SEAL

Removal and Installation

The pump oil seal can be replaced without removing the pump and reaction shaft support assembly from the transmission case.

1. Screw the seal remover tool C-3981 or equivalent into the seal, tighten the screw portion of the tool to remove the seal.

2. To install a new seal, place the seal in the opening of the pump housing (lid side facing inward).

3. Using tool C-4193 and handle tool C-4171 or equivalent, drive the new seal into the housing until the tool bottoms out.

KICKDOWN SERVO AND BAND

Disassembly

1. Remove the small snapring from the servo piston.
2. Remove the washer, spring and piston rod assembly from the servo piston.

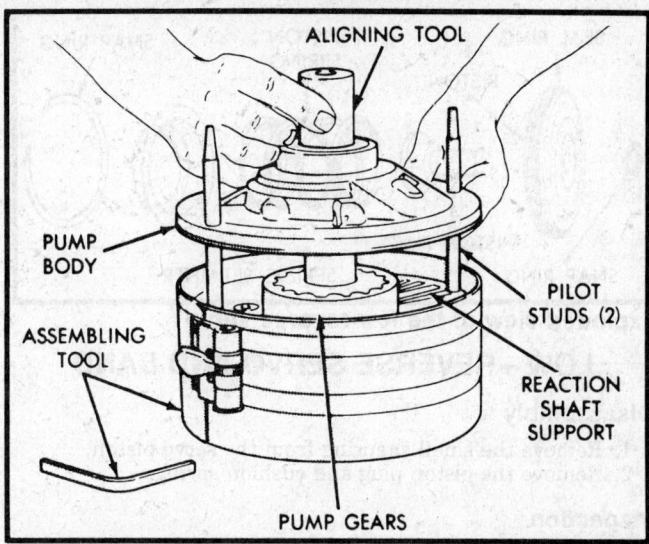

Assembling the oil pump and reaction shaft support

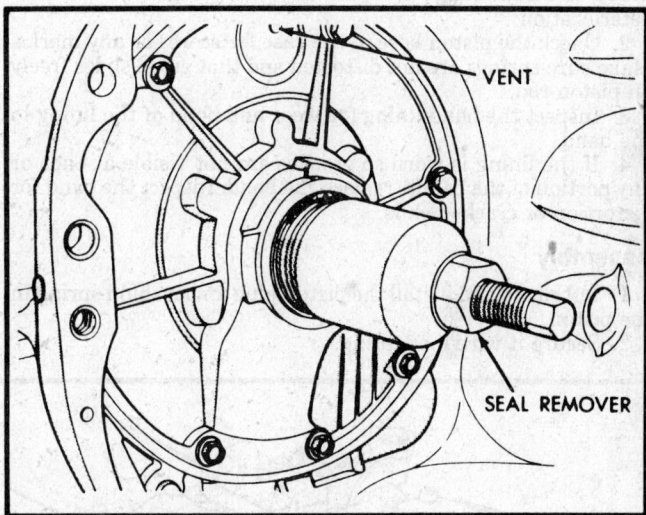

Removing the oil pump seal

Inspection

1. Inspect carefully the piston and guide seal rings for wear and make sure they turn freely. It usually is not necessary to remove the seal rings unless they show signs of wear or deterioration.

2. Check the piston bore in the case for scores or any marks. Make sure springs are not distorted and that guide slides freely on piston rod.

3. Inspect the band lining for wear and bond of the lining to the band. Inspect the lining for black burn marks, glazing, non-uniform wear pattern and flaking.

4. If the lining is worn so grooves are not visible at ends or any portion of the bands, replace the band. Inspect the band for distortion or cracked ends.

Assembly

1. Grease the O-ring and install the piston rod.
2. Install the piston rod into the servo piston.
3. Install the spring, flat washer and snapring to complete the assembly.

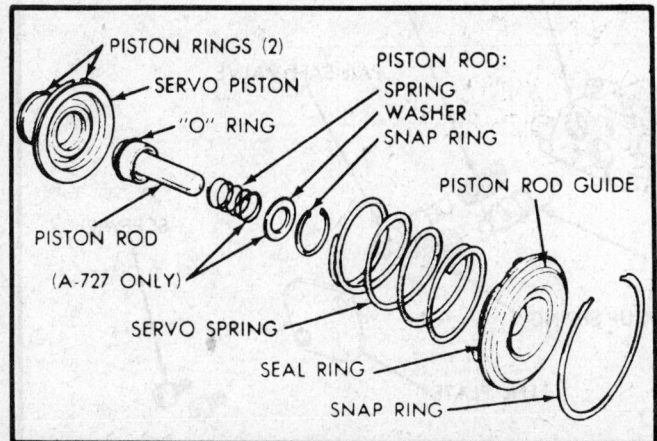

Exploded view of the kickdown (front) servo

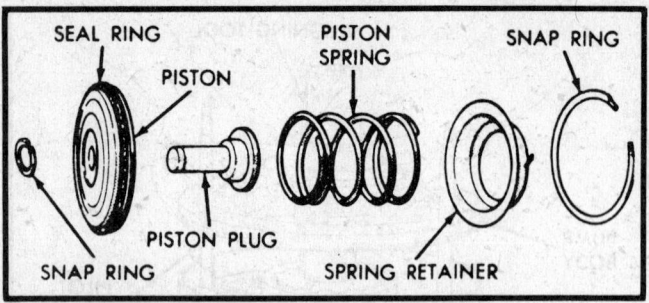

Exploded view of the low-reverse servo

LOW—REVERSE SERVO AND BAND

Disassembly

1. Remove the small snapring from the servo piston.
2. Remove the piston plug and cushion spring.

Inspection

1. Inspect carefully the piston and guide seal rings for wear and make sure they turn freely. It usually is not necessary to remove the seal rings unless they show signs of wear or deterioration.
2. Check the piston bore in the case for scores or any marks. Make sure springs are not distorted and that guide slides freely on piston rod.
3. Inspect the band lining for wear and bond of the lining to the band.
4. If the lining is worn so grooves are not visible at ends or any portion of the bands, replace the band. Inspect the band for distortion or cracked ends.

Assembly

1. Lubricate and install the piston plug and cushion spring in the piston.
2. Secure it with a snapring.

VALVE BODY

Disassembly

CAUTION

Do not clamp any part of the valve body or plate in a vise, for this will cause sticking valves or excessive leakage or both. When removing and installing valves or plugs, slide them in or out very carefully. Do not use force to remove or install the valves.

NOTE: When disassembling the valve body identify all valve springs with a tag for assembly reference later. Also, oil filter screws are longer than transfer plate screws. Do not mix them.

1. Remove the E-clip and park control rod from the manual lever.
2. Place the valve body on a suitable clean work bench. Remove the screws from the oil filter and remove the filter.
3. Remove the top and bottom screws from the spring retainer and adjustment screw bracket.
4. Hold the spring retainer firmly against the spring force while removing the last retaining screw from the side of the valve body. Do not alter the settings of the throttle pressure adjusting screws, while removing the line pressure adjusting screw assembly and switch valve regulator springs and valves from their bores.
5. Slide the switch valve and regulator valve out of their bores.
6. Remove the screws from the lockup module and carefully remove the tube (note the long end of the tube for assembly) and lockup module. Disassemble lockup module, tagging the springs.
7. Remove the transfer plate retaining screws and lift off the transfer plate and separator plate assembly.
8. Remove the lockup solenoid retaining screw and pull the solenoid from its bore in the transfer plate. Remove the screws from the separator plate and separate parts for cleaning.
9. Remove the rear clutch check ball, reverse servo ball check

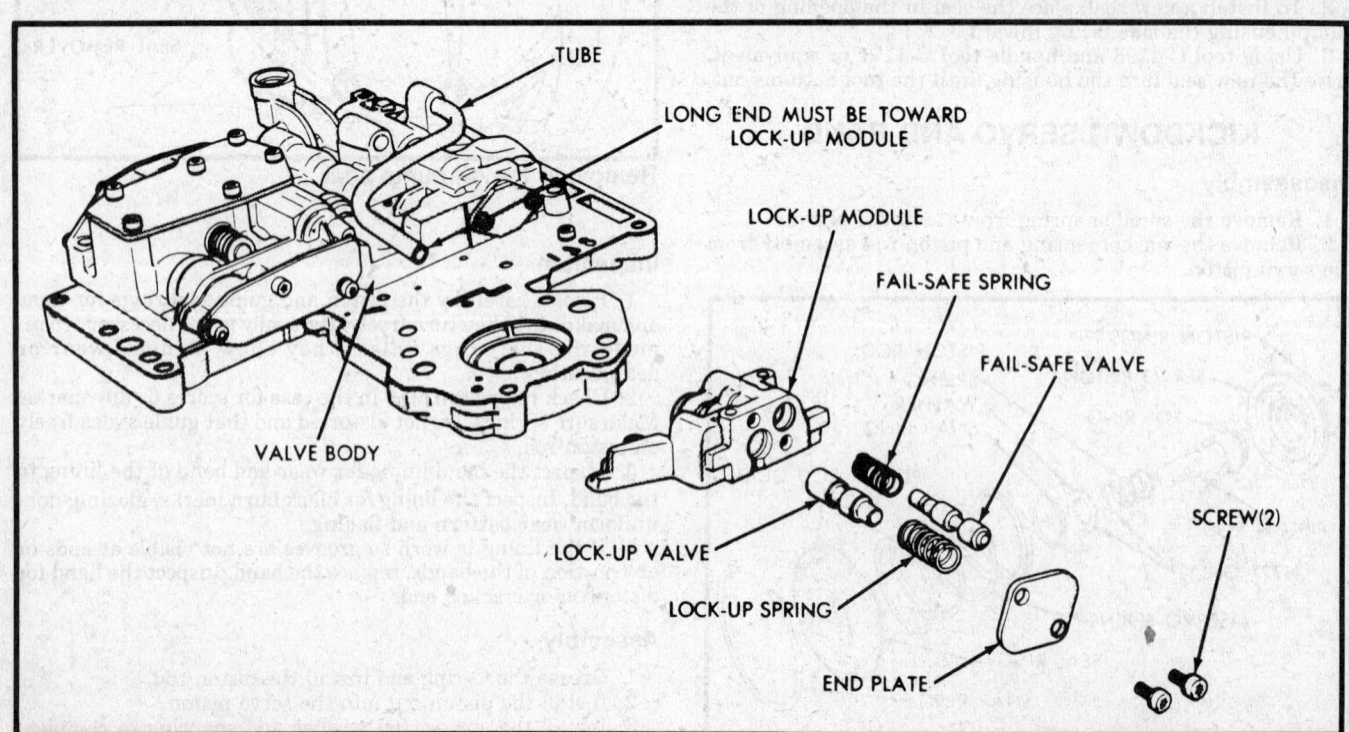

Exploded view of the lockup module

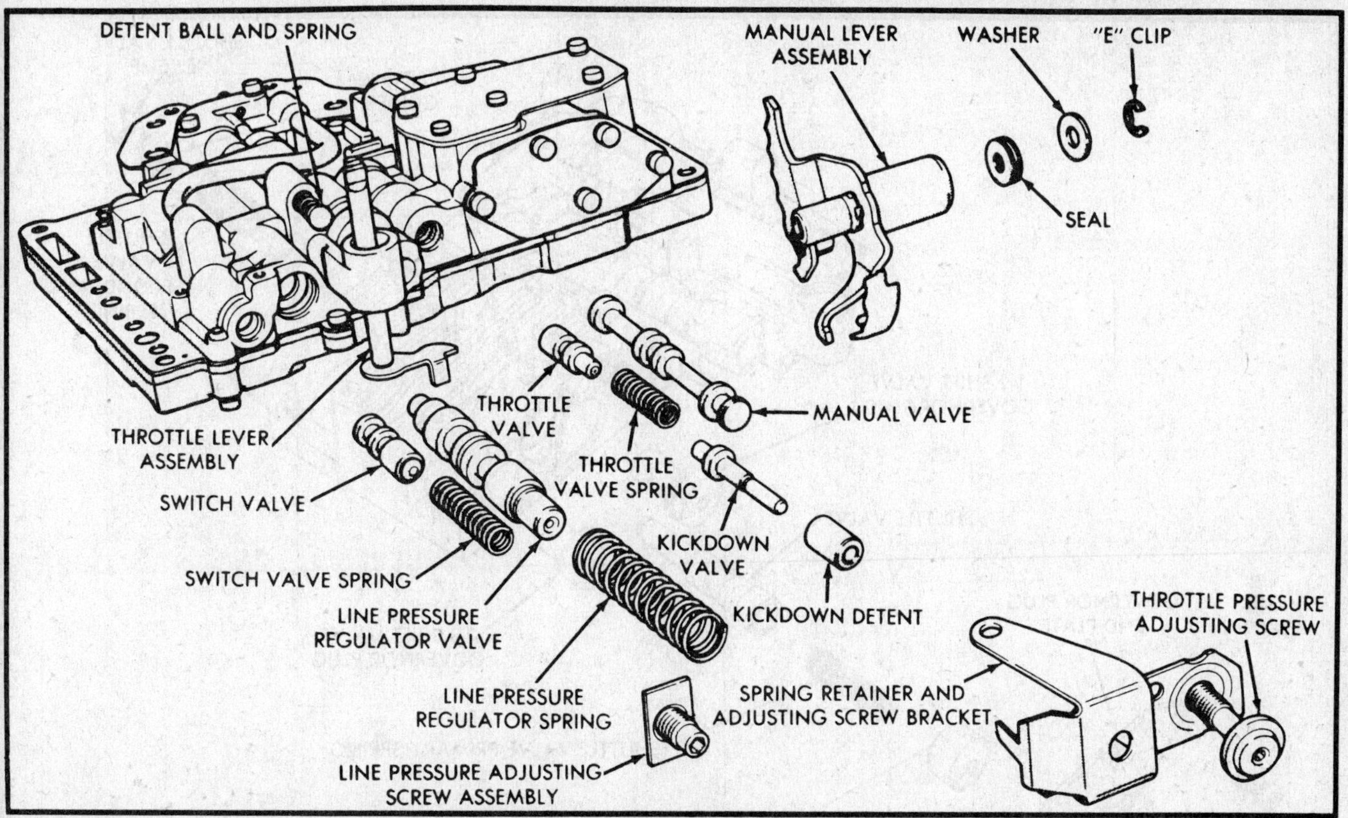

DETENT BALL AND SPRING

MANUAL LEVER ASSEMBLY

WASHER

"E" CLIP

SEAL

THROTTLE LEVER ASSEMBLY

SWITCH VALVE

SWITCH VALVE SPRING

LINE PRESSURE REGULATOR VALVE

THROTTLE VALVE

THROTTLE VALVE SPRING

MANUAL VALVE

KICKDOWN VALVE

KICKDOWN DETENT

THROTTLE PRESSURE ADJUSTING SCREW

LINE PRESSURE REGULATOR SPRING

LINE PRESSURE ADJUSTING SCREW ASSEMBLY

SPRING RETAINER AND ADJUSTING SCREW BRACKET

Exploded view of the pressure regulators and manual controls

and line pressure regulator valve screen from the separator plate, clean all parts.

10. Remove the 7 balls from the valve body.

11. Disassemble the lockup module as follows:

    a. Remove the end cover.

    b. Remove the lockup spring and valve.

    c. Remove the fail-safe valve and spring.

    d. Be sure to tag these springs as they are removed, for reassembly identification.

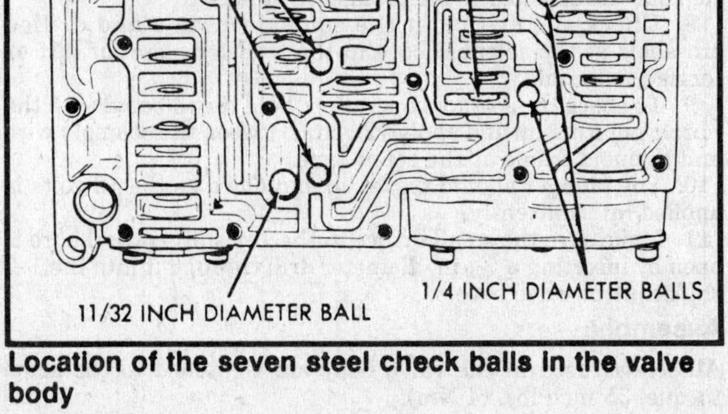

12. Turn the valve body over and remove the shuttle valve cover plate. Remove the governor plug end plate and slide out the shuttle valve throttle plug and spring, the 1–2 shift valve governor plug and the 2–3 shift valve governor plug.

13. To remove the shuttle valve, remove the E-clip and slide the shuttle valve out of its bore. Also remove the secondary spring and guides which were held in by the E-clip.

14. To remove the manual lever and throttle lever, first remove the E-clip and washer. The manual lever detent ball is

1/4 INCH DIAMETER BALLS

SMALL ORIFICE INTO 1-2 SHIFT CONTROL BORE

1/4 INCH DIAMETER BALLS

11/32 INCH DIAMETER BALL

Location of the seven steel check balls in the valve body

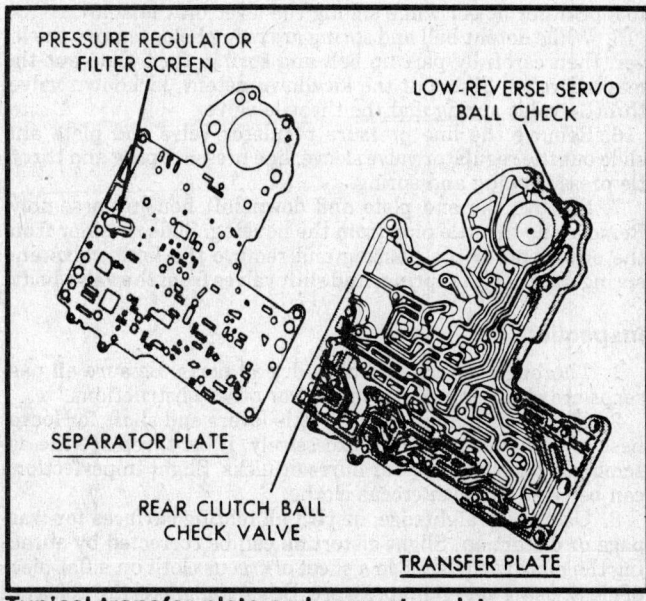

PRESSURE REGULATOR FILTER SCREEN

LOW-REVERSE SERVO BALL CHECK

SEPARATOR PLATE

REAR CLUTCH BALL CHECK VALVE

TRANSFER PLATE

Typical transfer plate and separator plate

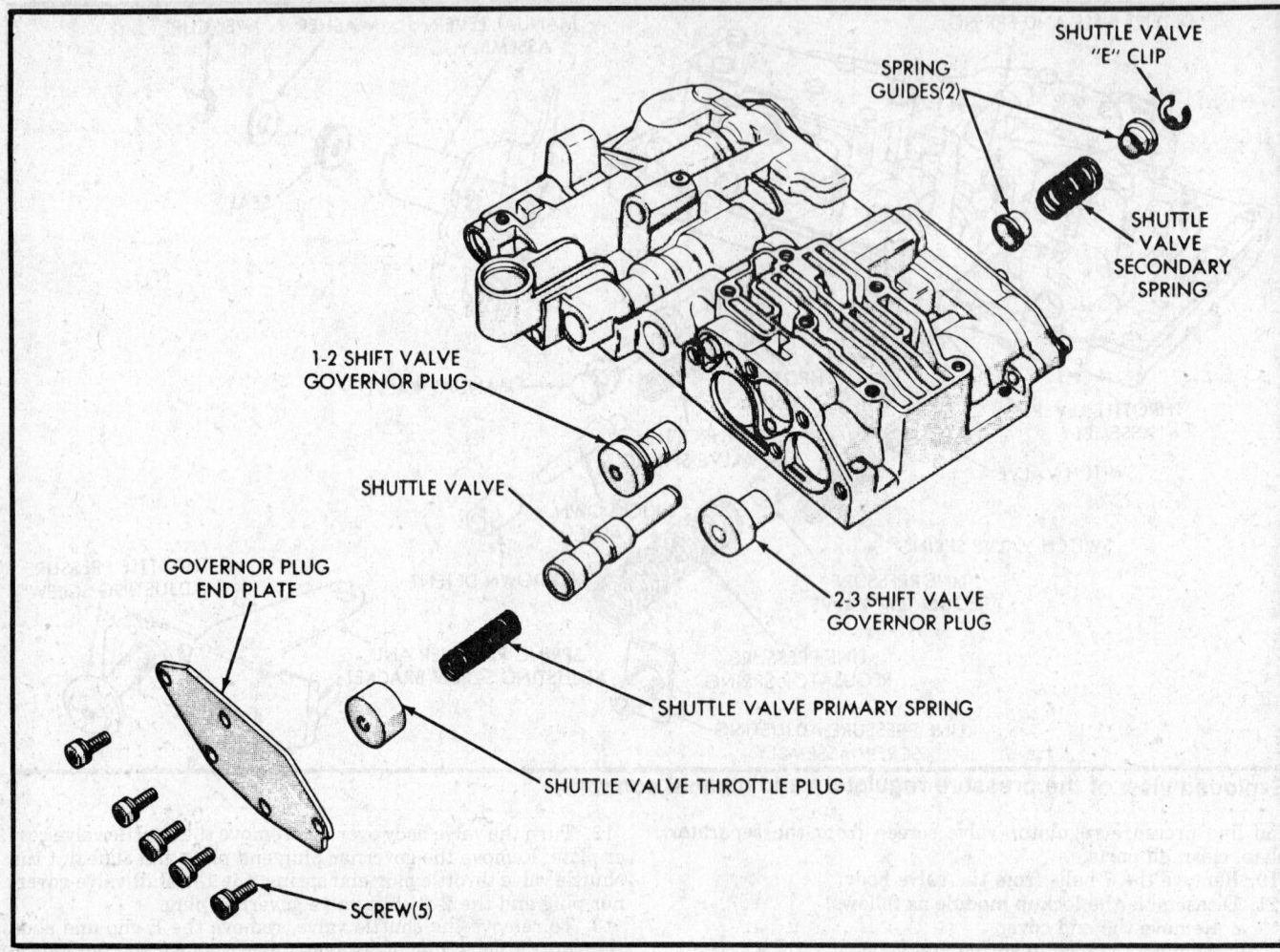

Exploded view of the shuttle valve and governor plugs

spring loaded and if the lever is removed the ball will jump out and may cause injury or be lost. Hold detent ball with a suitable tool or other object while sliding the lever off the shaft.

15. While detent ball and spring are being held, remove the lever, then carefully pick up ball and spring, then slide out the manual valve. Slide out the kickdown detent, kickdown valve, throttle valve spring and the throttle valve.

16. Remove the line pressure regulator valve end plate and slide out the regulator valve sleeve, line pressure plug and throttle pressure plug and spring.

17. Remove the end plate and downshift housing assembly. Remove the throttle plug from the housing. Slide retainer from the other end of the housing and remove the limit valve and spring. Remove the springs and shift valves from the valve body.

Inspection

1. Thoroughly wash and blow dry all parts. Be sure all passages are clean and free from dirt or other obstructions.

2. Check the manual and throttle levers and shaft for looseness or being bent or worn excessively. If bent, replace the assembly. Check all parts for burrs or nicks. Slight imperfections can be removed with crocus cloth.

3. Using a straightedge, inspect all mating surfaces for warpage or distortion. Slight distortion can be corrected by abrading the mating surfaces on a sheet of crocus cloth on a flat piece of glass, using very light pressure. Be sure all metering holes are open in both the valve body and separator plate.

4. Use a penlight to inspect valve body bores for scratches, burrs, pits or scores. Inspect valve springs for distortion. Check valves and plugs for burrs, nicks and scores. Remove slight irregularities with crocus cloth, but do not round off the sharp edges. The sharpness of these edges is vitally important because it prevents foreign matter from lodging between the valve and the bore.

5. When valves, plugs and bores are clean and dry, they should fall freely in the bores.

6. Inspect the lockup solenoid assembly for a cut and or broken wire, melted or disorted coil, cut or nicked O-rings, etc.

7. Shake the solenoid to verify that plunger is free to travel. Replace the solenoid if the plunger is stuck.

8. Check the orifice in the solenoid nozzle and drilled crosshole at the solenoid bore in the transfer plate for dirt or forgien material.

9. To check the solenoid operation, hold the solenoid with the nozzle pointing up and apply 12 volts between the solenoid wire and solenoid frame at the screw hole.

10. The plunger should travel up and down as the 12 volts is applied intermittently.

11. Make sure the small orifice in the 1–2 shift control bore is open by inserting a $\frac{1}{32}$ in. diameter drill through it into the 1–2 shift control valve bore.

Assembly

All screws used in the valve body are tightened to the same torque, 35 inch lbs. (4 Nm).

1. After all cleaning and checking, slide shift valves and springs into their proper valve body bores.

2. Assemble the 3–2 limit valve housing by inserting the limit valve and spring into the downshift assembly housing and slide the retainer into its groove. Install the throttle plug in the housing then position the assembly against the shift valve springs in the valve body.

3. Install end plate and tighten screws.

4. Install regulator valve throttle pressure plug spring, plug, sleeve and line pressure plug then fasten end plate to the valve body.

5. To assembly the shuttle valve and governor plugs, plate the 1–2 and 2–3 shift valve governor plugs in their respective bores. Install the shuttle valve and hold it in the bore while putting on the secondary spring and guides and the E-clip. Install the primary shuttle valve primary spring and shuttle valve throttle plug. Install the governor plug end plate and tighten the retaining screws. Install the shuttle valve cover plate and tighten the retaining screws.

6. Install the throttle valve, throttle valve spring, kickdown valve and kickdown detent.

7. Slide the manual valve into its bore, then install the throttle lever and shaft on the valve body. Insert the detent spring and ball in its bore in the valve body. Depress ball with a piece of tubing cut on an angle and slide manual valve over the throttle shaft so that it engages the manual valve and detent ball. Install seal, retaining washer and E-clip.

8. Install the 7 balls in the transfer plate. Install rear clutch ball and low-reverse servo ball check into the transfer plate and regulator valve screen into the separator plate.

9. Install the screws and place the transfer plate on the valve body, being careful to align the filter screen. Install the 17 screws finger tight, (the 3 longer screws are for the oil filter) starting at the center and working outward, tighten the screws to 35 inch lbs. (4 Nm).

NOTE: To help insure against cross-leakage due to a warped case, some rebuilders do not tighten the valve body assembly screws until they have torqued the valve body itself to the case.

10. Slide the switch valve and line pressure valves and their spring into their respective bores.

11. Install the pressure adjusting screw and bracket assembly on the springs and fasten the screw that goes into the side of the valve body. Start the top and bottom screws, then torque the side screw to 35 inch lbs. (4 Nm), then, the top and bottom screws. Install the oil filter and torque the screws to 35 inch lbs. (4 Nm).

12. Install the lockup valve and spring. Install the fail-safe spring and valve into the lockup module. Install the lockup module to the transfer and separator plate assembly with the retaining screws.

13. Insert the lockup solenoid nozzle (with O-ring) into the bore in the transfer plate and install the retaining screw. Route the lockup solenoid wire between the solenoid and limit valve housing cover and underneath the edge of the oil filter.

NOTE: The correct wire routing is very important. The wire must be routed away from the low-reverse band lever.

14. After the valve body has been serviced and completely assembled, measure the throttle and line pressure. If the diagnostic test, done before the transmission was disassembled, were satisfactory, use the original settings.

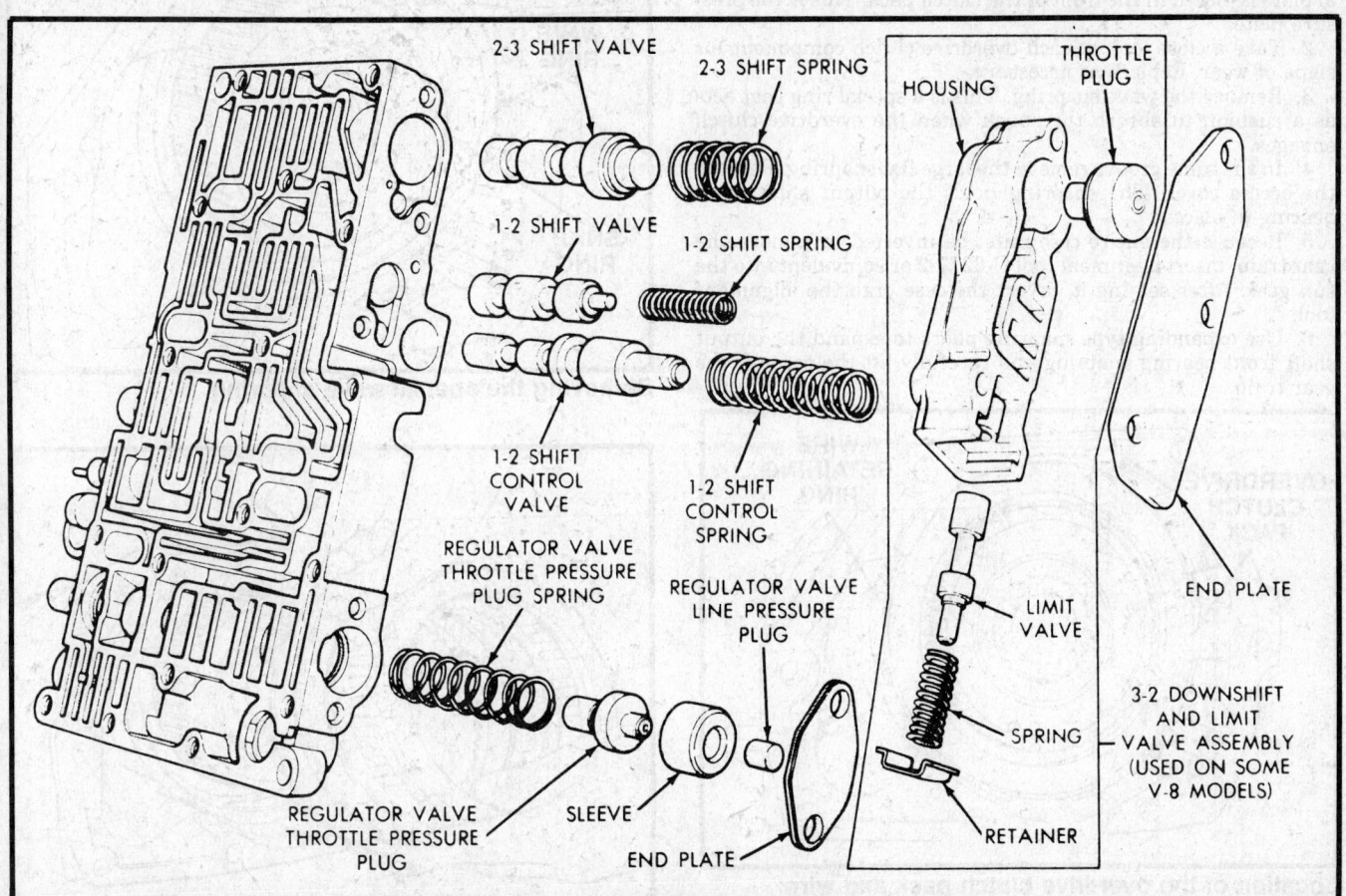

2-3 SHIFT VALVE
2-3 SHIFT SPRING
HOUSING
THROTTLE PLUG
1-2 SHIFT VALVE
1-2 SHIFT SPRING
1-2 SHIFT CONTROL VALVE
1-2 SHIFT CONTROL SPRING
REGULATOR VALVE THROTTLE PRESSURE PLUG SPRING
REGULATOR VALVE LINE PRESSURE PLUG
LIMIT VALVE
END PLATE
REGULATOR VALVE THROTTLE PRESSURE PLUG
SLEEVE
END PLATE
SPRING
RETAINER
3-2 DOWNSHIFT AND LIMIT VALVE ASSEMBLY (USED ON SOME V-8 MODELS)

Exploded view of the shift valves and pressure regulator valve plugs

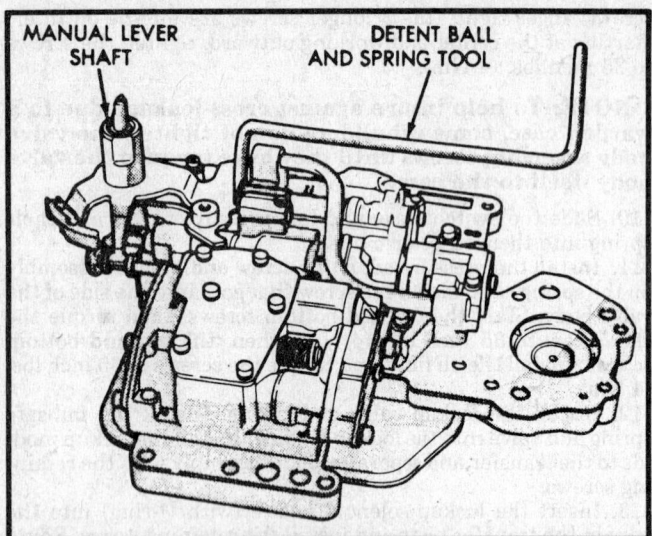

Installing the detent spring and ball

15. Install the parking lock rod and E-clip retainer to the manual lever.

OVERDRIVE UNIT

Disassembly

1. Remove the overdrive clutch wire retaining rings and pull out the alternating plates and discs. Note that the heaviest metal plate is placed in the front of the clutch pack. This is the pressure plate.

2. Take a close look at each overdrive clutch component for signs of wear. Replace as necessary.

3. Remove the wave snapring. This is a special ring that acts as a cushion to absorb the shock when the overdrive clutch engages.

4. In the same groove remove the large flat snapring. Remove the access cover. The snapring holds the output shaft front bearing in place.

5. Because the entire case must be inverted to remove the gear train, insert alignment tool C-6277-2 or equivalent into the sun gear. After seating it, invert the case onto the alignment tool.

6. Use expanding type snapring pliers to expand the output shaft front bearing snapring and carefully lift the case off the gear train.

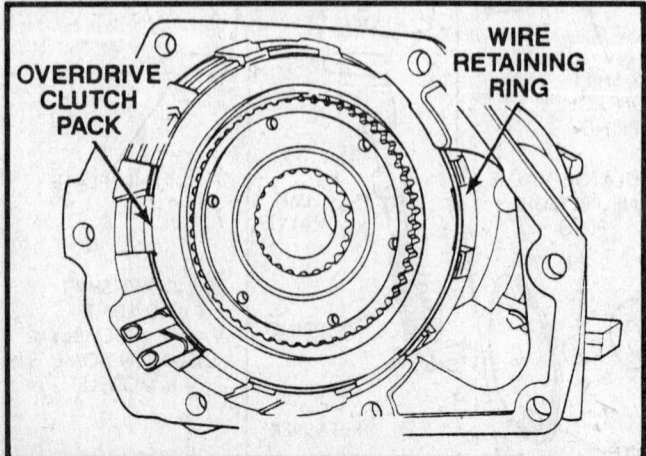

Location of the overdrive clutch pack and wire retaining ring

7. Remove the governor retaining snapring. Remove the governor and shaft key. This will prevent damaging the governor when the direct clutch spring is compressed in an arbor press. Set the gear train aside and continue disassembly of the case components.

8. Remove the output shaft front bearing snapring and remove the governor support snapring. Take the governor support with the slip-fit (pressure) tubes out of the case.

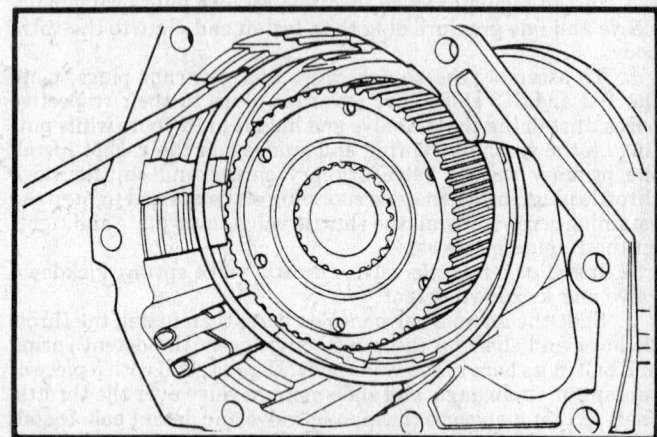

Removing the large flat snap ring

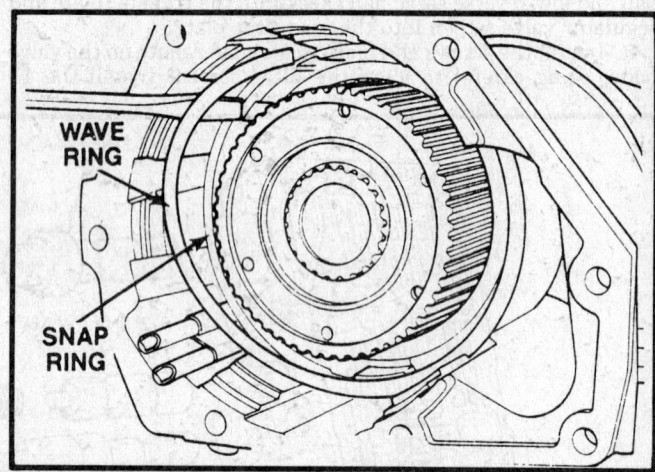

Removing the special wave snapring

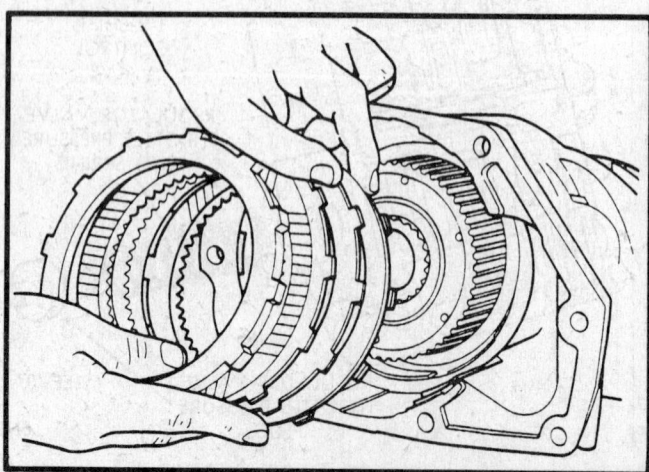

Inspecting the clutch components

9. Using locking snapring pliers, remove the output shaft rear bearing snapring. Tap the overdrive case downward on the bench to remove the rear bearing.

10. To remove the parking mechanism, first remove the reaction plug snapring. Compress the snapring just enough to allow its removal.

11. Unscrew the bolt securing the dowel and parking pawl, another light tap to the case on the bench will cause the dowel and the parking pawl components to drop out on the bench.

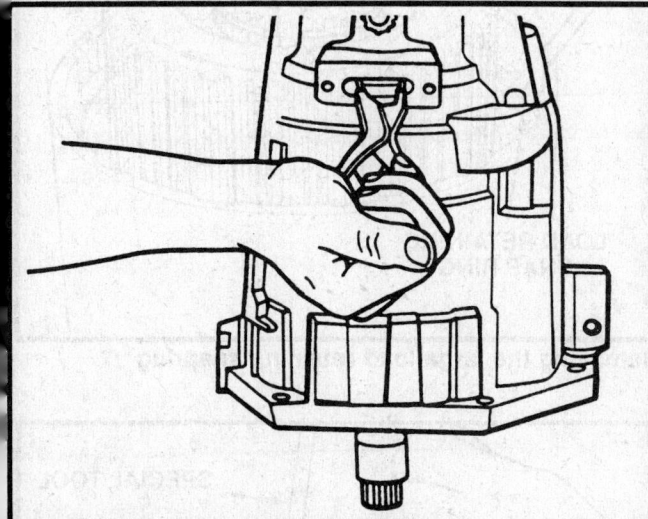

Removing the front bearing snapring

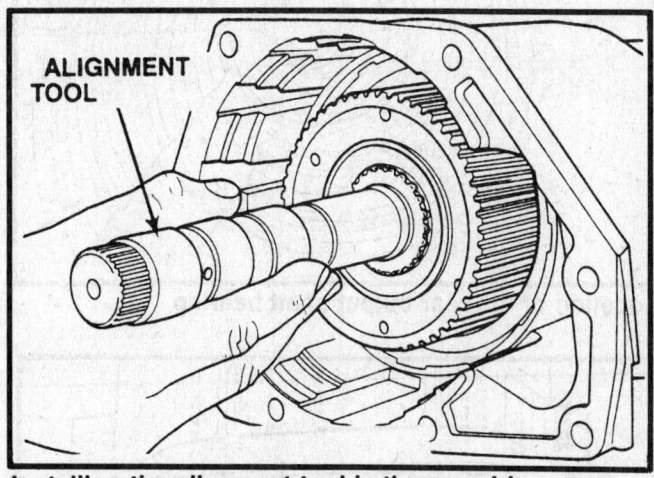

Installing the alignment tool in the overdrive case

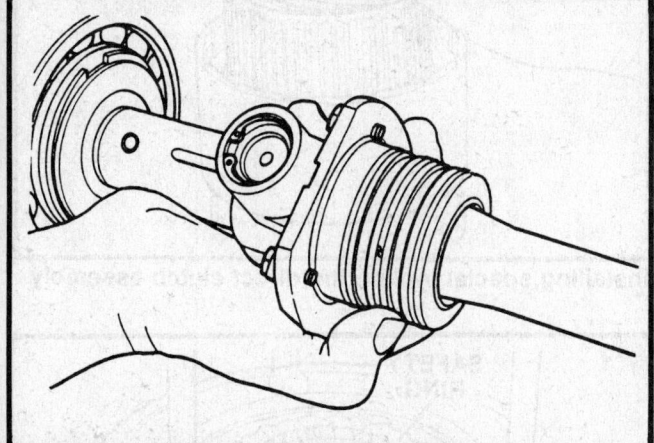

Removing the governor and shaft key

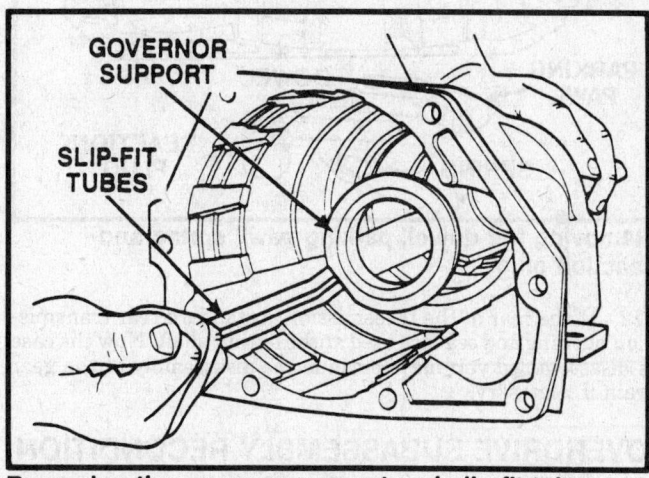

Removing the governor support and slip-fit tubes

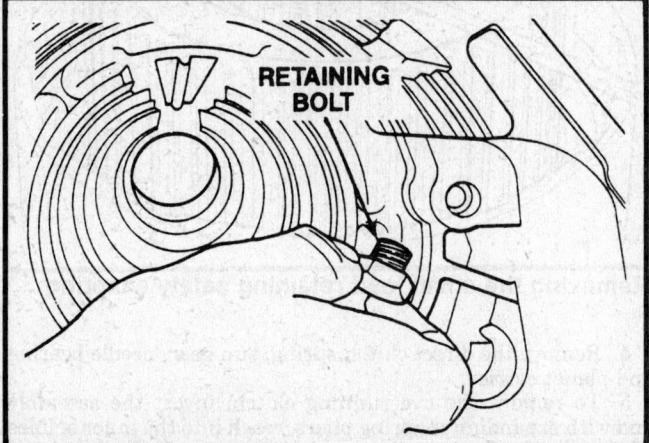

Removing the dowel and parking pawl retaining bolt

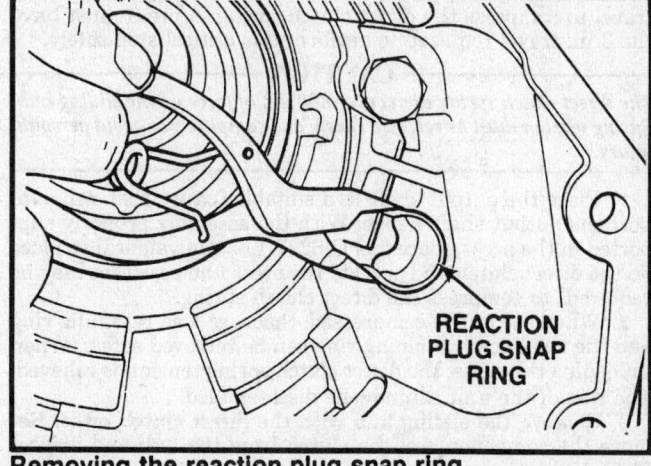

Removing the reaction plug snap ring

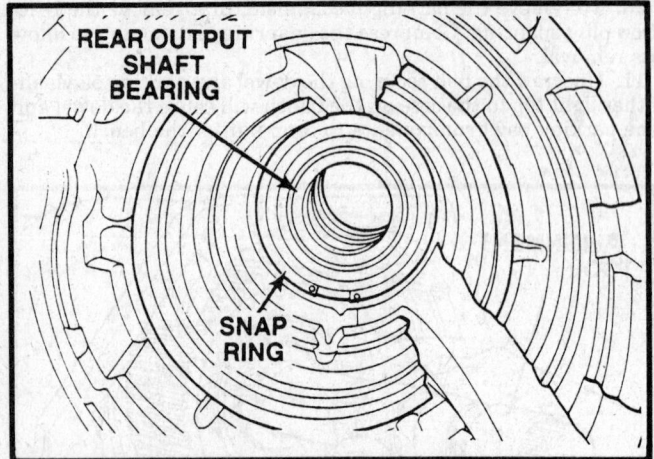

Location of the rear output shaft bearing

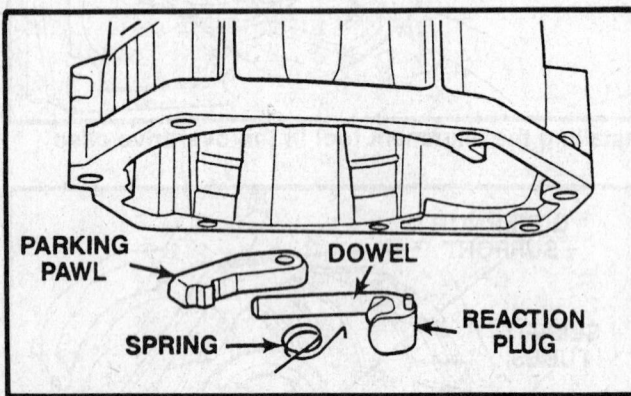

Removing the dowel, parking pawl, spring and reaction plug

12. At the rear of the transmission, a standard rear transmission bushing and seal are used at the output shaft. Now the case is disassembled you may continue the disassembly of the gear train if necessary.

OVERDRIVE SUBASSEMBLY RECONDITION

Disassembly

It is of the upmost importance to use of a press capable of 3 in. of travel to compress the direct clutch spring. A press must have the 3 in. travel required to perform this critical step safely.

CAUTION

The direct clutch spring exerts over 800 lbs. of force on the sliding hub. Spring tension must be released slowly and completely to avoid personal injury.

---

1. Place the output shaft in a suitable fixture that will support the output shaft flange. With the assembly properly supported in the press, place tool C-6227-1 or equivalent into place on the direct clutch and operate the press (an assistant may be required) to compress the direct clutch spring.

2. When the hub is compressed, the large load retaining ring and the small load retaining ring can be removed safely. When unloading the press, the direct clutch spring tension is relieved. The rest of the unit can now be disassembled.

3. Remove the sliding hub with the direct clutch on it. Remove the components of the clutch from the hub and inspect them 1 at a time.

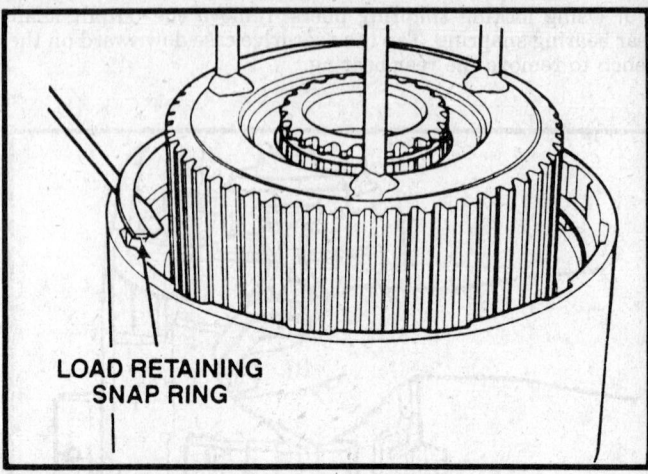

Removing the large load retaining snapring

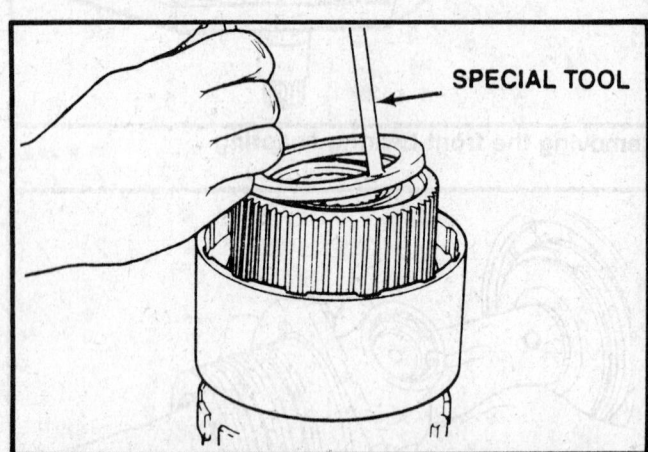

Installing special tool on the direct clutch assembly

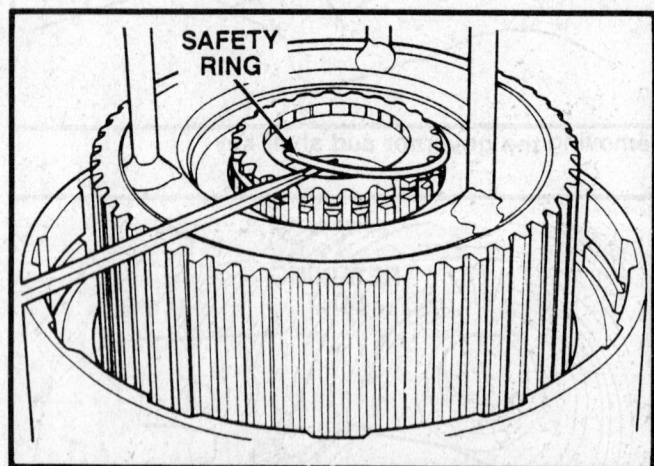

Removing the small load retaining safety snapring

4. Remove the direct clutch spring, sun gear, needle bearing and planet carrier.

5. To remove the overrunning clutch, invert the assembly and with expanding snapring pliers, reach into the inner splines of the clutch. Remove the overrunning clutch intact with a quick counterclockwise twist. Also, remove the needle bearing.

6. Mark the direct clutch drum and annulus for reassembly. Two wire retaining rings secure the direct clutch drum to the annulus. Remove the inner one first, then the one behind the gear of the drum. Slide the drum from the annulus.

7. Mark the annulus and output shaft for exact reassembly. To remove the annulus gear (a snapring secures it to the output shaft), a light tap with a soft mallet will pop it off the shaft. Also remove the output shaft front bearing.

Assembly

Before assembling, clean all parts and dry them with compressed air. Do not clean or dry parts with shop towels as lint deposits could plug the oil filter.

1. To assemble the overdrive unit, align the mating marks and insert the shaft through the back of the annulus and secure it with a snapring.

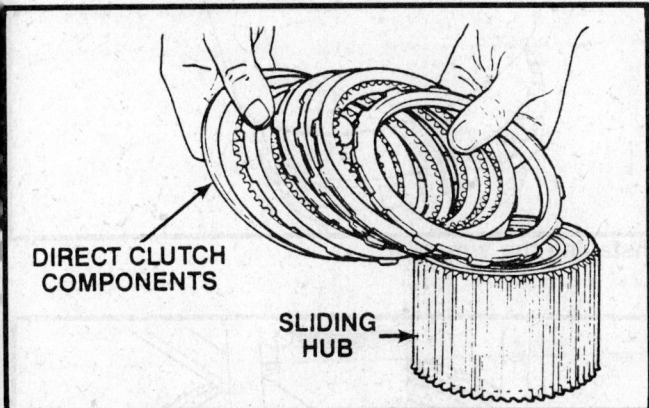

Inspecting the direct clutch components

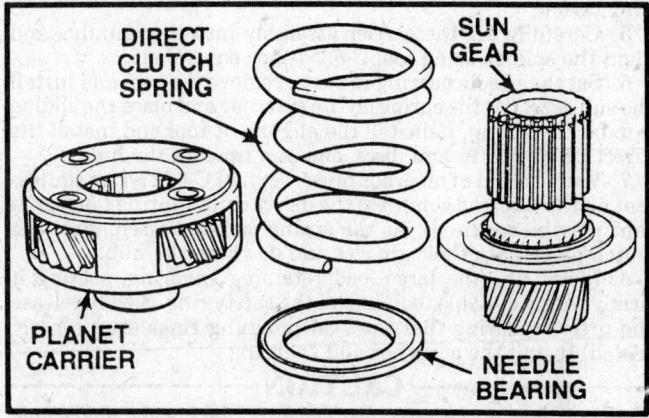

Exploded view of the direct clutchspring, planet carrier, sun gear and needle bearing

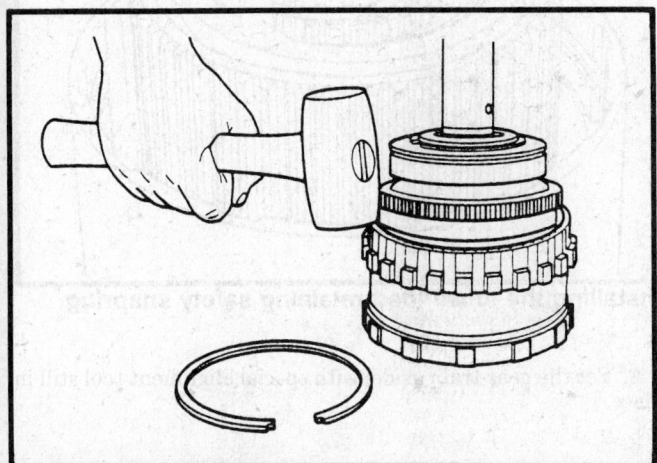

Removing the annulus

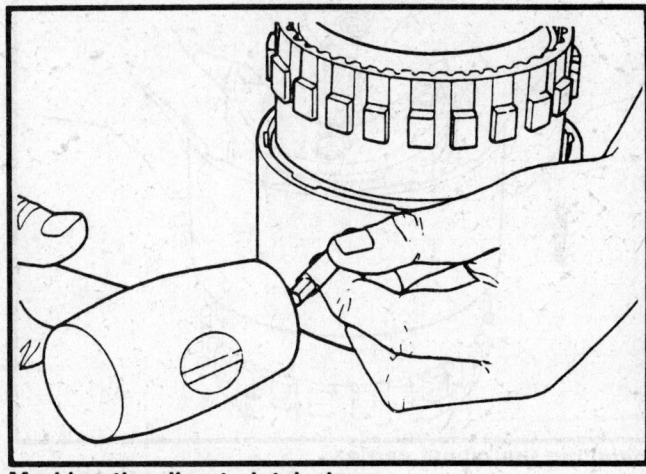

Marking the direct clutch drum

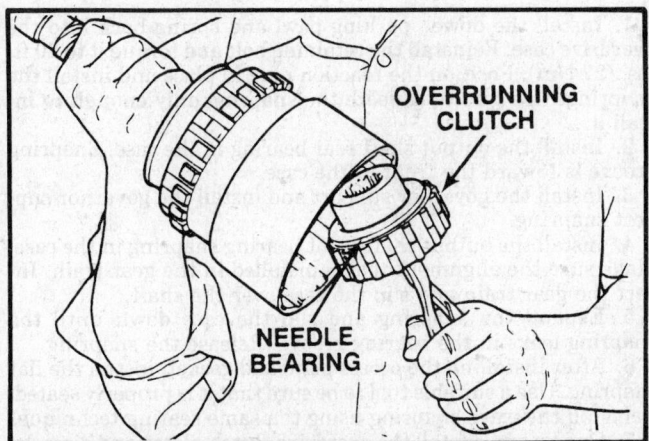

Removing the overrunning clutch

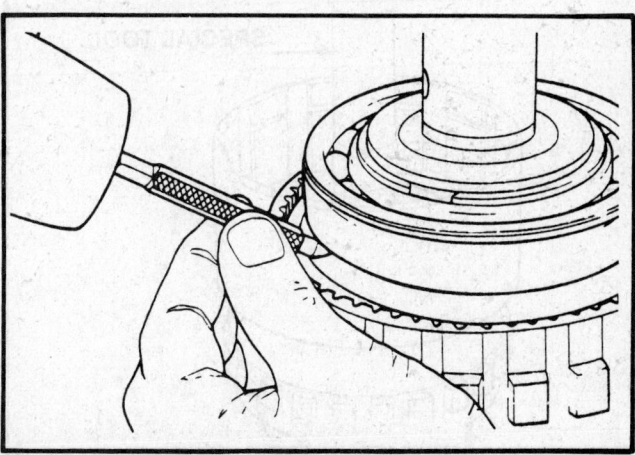

Marking the annulus 1and output shaft

2. Set the direct clutch drum face down and align the mating marks. Insert the annulus lugs into the slots inside the drum.

3. Install the rear retaining ring first. Invert the assembly. Slide the drum forward to expose the retaining ring groove. Install the front wire retaining ring to secure the drum.

4. Hold the overrunning clutch upside down with expanding snaping pliers. place the needle bearing against the back face of the clutch. Hold the shaft assembly upside down and with an upward, counterclockwise twisting motion, install the overrunning clutch.

5. Carefully set the carrier assembly into the annulus and align the splines using tool C-6227-2 or equivalent.

6. Set the needle bearing in place, remove the tool and install the sun gear. Set the spring on the sun gear and place the sliding hub on the spring. Reinstall the alignment tool and install the direct clutch plates and discs, one at a time on the hub.

7. With the aid of an arbor press, set tool C-6227-1 or equivalent on the hub and compress the direct clutch spring (an assistant may be required). As the spring is compressed, slide the clutch plates into their grooves and down on the hub.

8. Install the the large load retaining snapring, seating it firmly with a suitable tool. Install the safety ring. Slowly release the press, ensuring that the load-retaining rings are properly seated. Install the governor and snapring.

CAUTION

The direct clutch spring exerts over 800 lbs. of force on the sliding hub. Spring tension must be released slowly to avoid personnal injury.

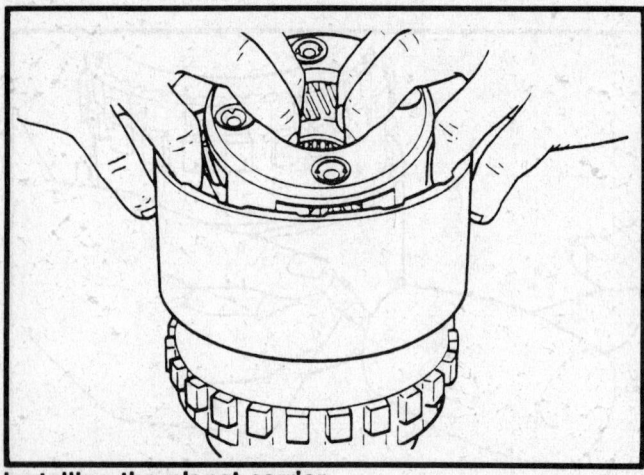

Installing the planet carrier

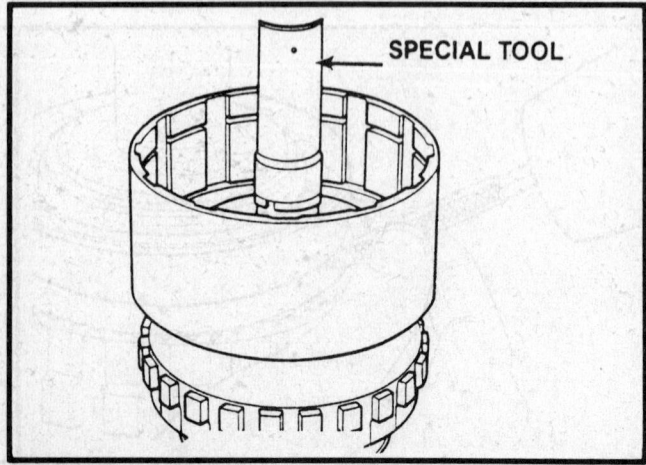

Aligning the splines

SPECIAL TOOL

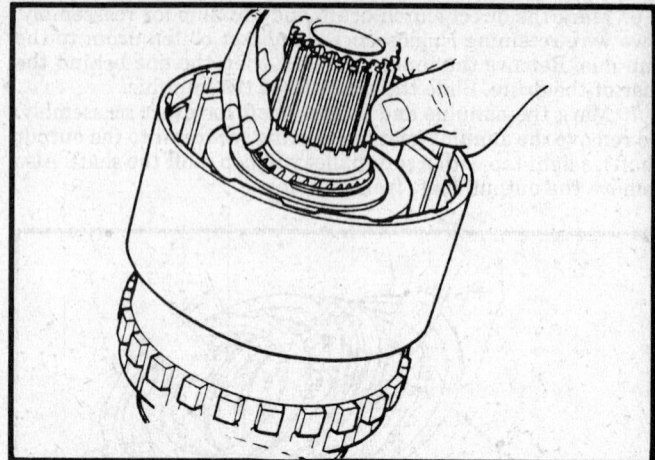

Installing the sun gear

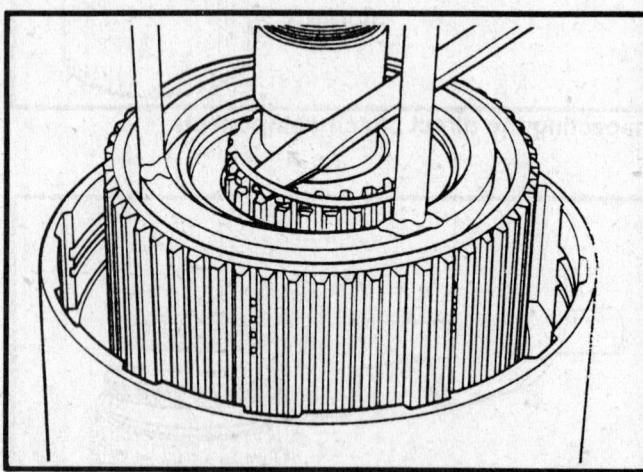

Installing the small load retaining safety snapring

9. Set the gear train aside, with special alignment tool still in place.

OVERDRIVE UNIT

Assembly

1. Install the dowel, parking pawl and spring back into the overdrive case. Reinstall the retaining bolt and torque it to 20 ft. lbs. (27 Nm). Position the reaction plug in place and install the snapring. Use care to squeeze the snapring only enough to install it.

2. Install the output shaft rear bearing in the case. Snapring groove is toward the front of the case.

3. Install the governor support and install the governor support snapring.

4. Install the output shaft front bearing snapring in the case. Make sure the alignment tool is installed in the gear train. Invert the gear train and slip the case over the shaft.

5. Expand the snapring and slip the case down until the snapring locks in the bearing groove. Release the snapring.

6. After installing the access plate and gasket, install the flat snapring. Use a suitable tool to be sure that it is properly seated. Reinstall the wave snapring using tha same seating technique.

7. One by one, install the overdrive clutch plates and discs, be certain to put the thichest plate in last.

8. Position the overdrive unit vertically in a large vise. To determine the proper intermediate shaft spacer thickness, insert tool C-6312 (depth gauge) or equivalent through the sun gear. Be sure that the tool bottoms out against the carrier spline shoulder. Position tool C-6311 across the overdrive case face. Using a dial caliper tool C-6311 Measure the distance to the top of the tool C-6312.

9. Use the measurements that follow as a guide to select the proper thickness spacer.

  a. A measurement of 0.7336–0.7505 in. will require a spacer thickness of 0.159–0.158 in., the spacer part number will be 4431916.

  b. A measurement of 0.7506–0.7675 in. will require a spacer thickness of 0.176–0.175 in., the spacer part number will be 4431917.

  c. A measurement of 0.7676–0.7855 in. will require a spacer thickness of 0.194–0.193 in., the spacer part number will be 4431918.

  d. A measurement of 0.7856–0.8011 in. will require a spacer thickness of 0.212–0.211 in., the spacer part number will be 4431919.

10. To determine the proper shim thickness for the overdrive piston, position tool C-6311 or equivalent across the overdrive case face. Using a suitable dial caliper tool C-4962 position it over tool C-6311 (straight edge) or equivalent, measure the distance to the sliding hub bearing seat.

11. This measurement should be taken at 4 locations 90° apart. Add all measurements together and divide by 4. Use the measurements that follow as a guide to select the proper thickness spacer.

  a. A measurement of 1.7500–1.7649 in. will require a spacer thickness of 0.108–0.110 in., the spacer part number will be 4431730.

  b. A measurement of 1.7650–1.7799 in. will require a spacer thickness of 0.123–0.125 in., the spacer part number will be 4431585.

  c. A measurement of 1.7800–1.7949 in. will require a spacer thickness of 0.138–0.140 in., the spacer part number will be 4431731.

  d. A measurement of 1.7950–1.8099 in. will require a spacer thickness of 0.153–0.155 in., the spacer part number will be 4431586.

  e. A measurement of 1.8100–1.8249 in. will require a spacer thickness of 0.168–0.170 in., the spacer part number will be 4431732.

  f. A measurement of 1.8250–1.8399 in. will require a spacer thickness of 0.183–0.185 in., the spacer part number will be 4431587.

  g. A measurement of 1.8400–1.8549 in. will require a spacer thickness of 0.198–0.200 in., the spacer part number will be 4431733.

  h. A measurement of 1.8550–1.8699 in. will require a spacer thickness of 0.213–0.215 in., the spacer part number will be 4431588.

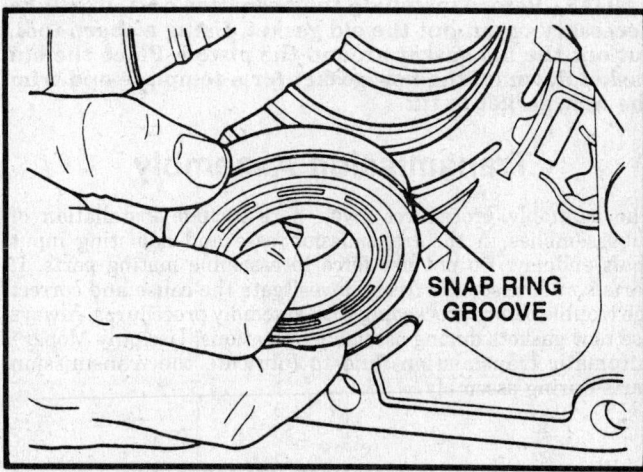

Installing the rear output shaft bearing

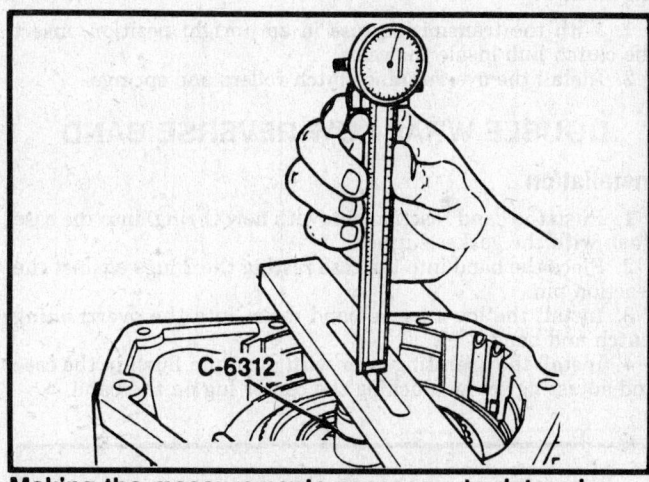

Making the measurements necessary to determine the proper intermediate shaft spacer thickness

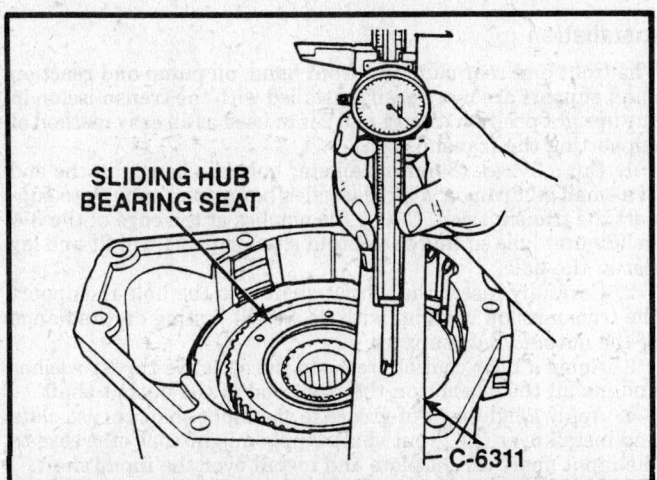

Making the measurements necessary to determine the proper overdrive piston shim thickness

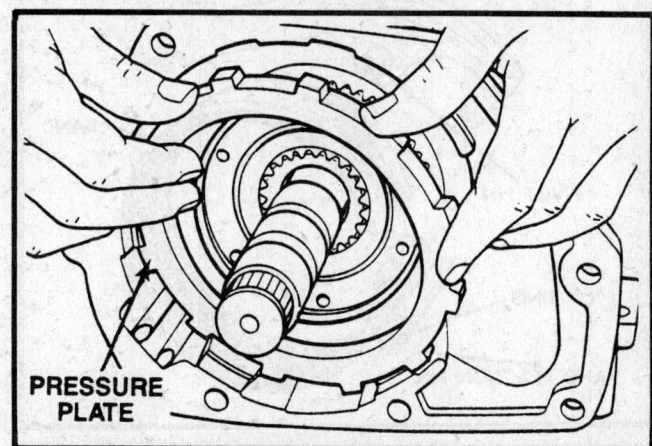

Installing the overdrive clutch plates

i. A measurement of 1.8700–1.8849 in. will require a spacer thickness of 0.228–0.230 in., the spacer part number will be 4431734.

j. A measurement of 1.8850–1.8999 in. will require a spacer thickness of 0.243–0.245 in., the spacer part number will be 4431590.

NOTE: Before installing the overdrive unit, it will be necessary to cut out the old gasket. Using a sharp tool, cut out the old gasket around the piston. Place the old gasket down on the new gasket for a template and trim the new gasket to fit.

Transmission Assembly

The assembly procedures given here include installation of subassemblies in the transmission case and adjusting input shaft endplay. Do not use force to assemble mating parts. If parts so not assemble freely, invesitgate the cause and correct the trouble before proceeding with assembly procedures. Always use new gaskets during assembly operations. Use only Mopar® automatic transmission fluid to lubricate the transmission parts during assembly.

OVERRUNNING CLUTCH

Installation

1. With the transmision case in an upright position, insert the clutch hub inside the cam.
2. Install the overrunning clutch rollers and springs.

DOUBLE WRAP LOW-REVERSE BAND

Installation

1. Push the band reaction pin (with new O-ring) into the case flush with the gasket surface.
2. Place the band into the case resting the 2 lugs against the reaction pin.
3. Install the low-reverse band drum into the overrunning clutch and band.
4. Install the operating lever with pivot pin flush in the case and adjusting screw touching the center lug on the band.

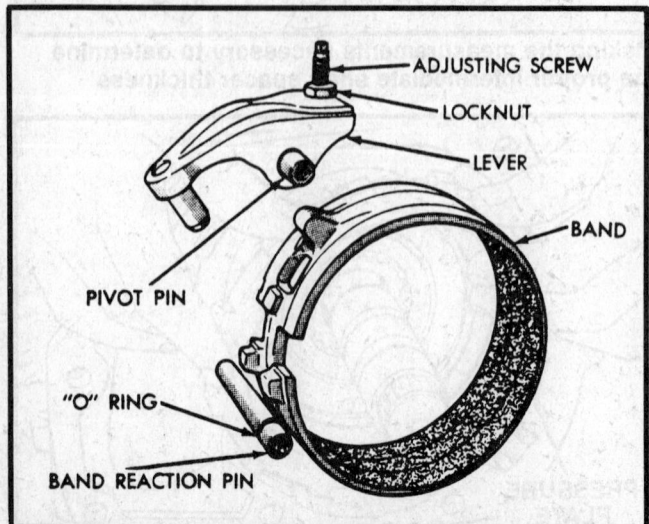

Exploded view of the double wrap band assembly

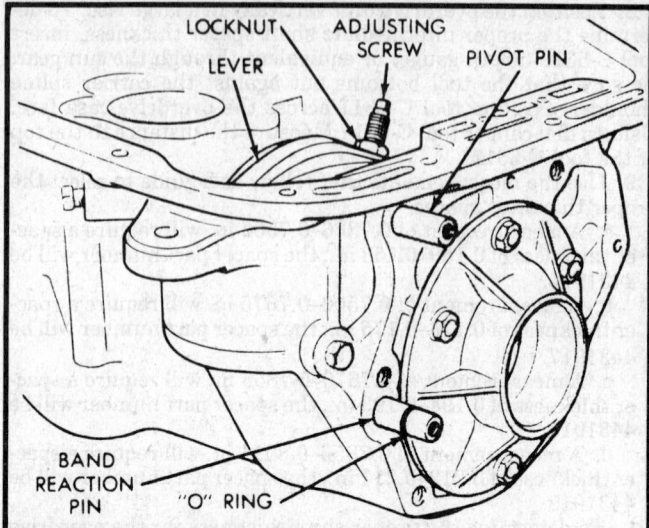

Typical double wrap band linkage

KICKDOWN SERVO

Installation

1. Carefully push the servo piston assembly into the case bore. Install the spring, guide and snapring.
2. Compress the kickdown servo spring by using the engine valve spring compressor tool C-3422-A or equivalent and install the snapring.

PLANETARY GEAR ASSEMBLIES, SUN GEAR AND DRIVING SHELL

Installation

1. While supporting the assembly in the case, insert the output shaft through the rear support.
2. Carefully work the assembly rearward engaging the rear planetary carrier lugs into the low-reverse drum slots.
3. Be careful not to damage the ground surfaces on the output shaft during installation.

FRONT AND REAR CLUTCH ASSEMBLIES

Installation

The front and rear clutches, front band, oil pump and reaction shaft support are more easily installed with the transmission in the upright position. Step 1 and 2 is to used as an easy method of supporting the transmission.

1. Cut a 3½ in. (89mm) diameter hole in a bench, in the end of a small oil drum or a large wooden box strong enough to support the transmission. Cut or file notches at the edge of the 3½ in. (89mm) hole so that the output shaft support will fit and lay flat in the hole.
2. Carefully insert the output shaft into the hole to support the transmission upright, with its weight resting on the flange of the output shaft support.
3. Apply a light coat of grease to the selective thrust washer and install the washer on the front end of the output shaft.
4. Apply a light coat of grease to the input shaft thrust plate and install over the input shaft. Apply a light coat of grease to the input shaft thrust plate and install over the input shaft.
5. If the input shaft endplay is not within specifications, (0.022–0.091 in.), when tested before disassembly, replace the thrust washer with one of proper thickness.

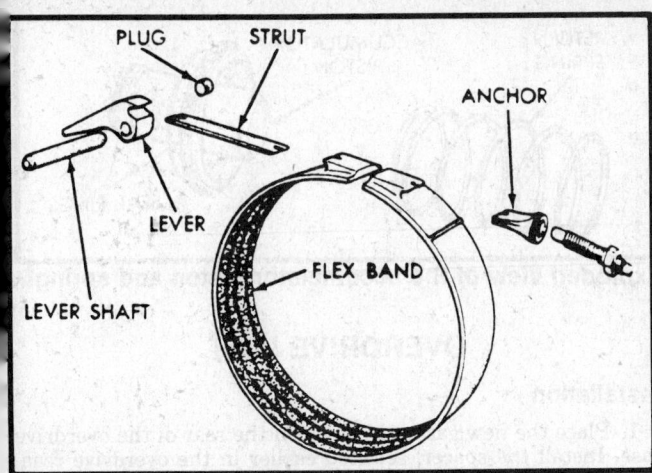

Exploded view of the kickdown band assembly

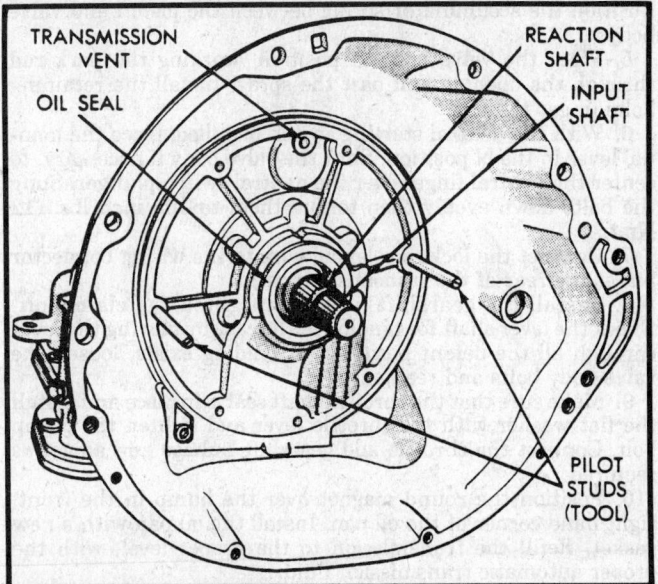

Installing the oil pump

6. Align the front clutch plate inner splines and place the assembly in position on the rear clutch. Be sure the front clutch plate splines are fully engaged on the rear clutch splines.

7. Align the rear clutch plate inner splines, grasp the input shaft and lower the clutch assemblies into the transmission case.

8. Carefully work the clutch assemblies in a circular motion to engage the rear clutch splines over the splines of the front annulus gear. Be sure the front clutch drive lugs are fully engaged in the slots in the driving shell.

KICKDOWN BAND

Installation

1. Slide the kickdown band over the front clutch assembly.

2. Install the kickdown band strut, screw in the adjuster just enough to hold the strut and anchor in place.

OIL PUMP AND REACTION SHAFT SUPPORT

Installation

If difficulty was encountered removing the pump, it may be well to expand the case with a heat lamp before attempting to install pump.

1. Install the No. 1 thrust washer on the reaction shaft support hub.

2. Screw the pilot studs tool C-3288-B or equivalent into the opening of the pump case. Install a new gasket over the pilot studs.

3. Place a new rubber seal ring in the groove on the outer flange of the pump housing. Make sure the seal ring is not twisted. Coat the seal ring with grease for easy installation.

4. Install the pump assembly into the case, tap it lightly with a soft mallet, if necesary. Remove the pilot studs and install the bolts and snug down evenly. Rotate the input and output shafts to see if any binding exists and torque the bolts to 175 inch lbs. (20 Nm). Check the shafts again for free rotation.

5. Adjust both bands.

GOVERNOR AND SUPPORT

Installation

1. Position the support and governor body assembly on the output shaft. Align the assembly so that the governor valve shaft hole in the governor body aligns with the hole in the output shaft and slide the assembly into place.

2. Install the snapring behind the governor body. Torque the body to support self-locking bolts to 95 inch lbs. (11 Nm).

3. Place the governor valve on the valve shaft, insert the assembly into the body and through the governor weights. Install the valve shaft retaining snapring.

OUTPUT SHAFT BEARING AND EXTENSION (OR ADAPTER ON 4WD VEHICLES)

Installation

1. Install the bearing on the shaft with its outer race ring groove toward the front. Press or tap the bearing tight against the shoulder and install the rear snapring.

2. On 4WD vehicles, use ATF lubricant on the output shaft bearing O-ring. Drive the bearing into the adapter using tool C-4203 or equivalent inverter with handle C-4171 or equivalent.

3. Place a new extension housing gasket on the transmission case. Position the output shaft bearing retaining snapring as far as possible then carefully tap the extension housing (or adapter) into place. Make sure that the snapring is fully seated in the bearing groove.

4. Install and tighten the extension housing (or adapter) bolts to 32 ft. lbs.

5. Install the gasket, plate and screws on the bottom of the extension housing mounting pad.

6. Be sure to re-measure the input shaft endplay and adjust as necessary.

VALVE BODY AND ACCUMULATOR PISTON INSTALLATION

Installation

1. Make sure that the combination back-up lamp/neutral start switch is not installed in the transmission case.

2. Place the valve body manual lever in the **MANUAL LOW** position to move the parking rod to the rear position.

3. Using a suitable tool to push the park sprag into the engagement with the parking gear, turning the output shaft to verify engagement. This will allow the knob of the end of the parking rod to move past the sprag as the valve body is installed.

4. Install the accumulator piston in the transmission case.

Position the accumulator spring between the piston and valve body.

5. Place the valve body in position, working the park rod through the opening and past the sprag. Install the retaining bolts finger tight.

6. With the neutral starting switch installed, place the manual lever in the **N** position. Shift the valve body if necessary, to center the neutral finger over the neutral switch plunger. Snug the bolts down evenly then torque them to 105 inch lbs. (12 Nm).

7. Connect the lockup solenoid wire to the wiring connector pin at the rear of the transmission case.

8. Install the gearshift lever and tighten the clampbolt. Check the lever shaft for binding in the case by moving the lever through all the detent positions. If binding exists, loosen the valve body bolts and realign.

9. Make sure that the throttle shaft seal is in place and install the flat washer with the throttle lever and tighten the clamp bolt. Connect the throttle and gearshift linkage and adjust as required.

10. Position the round magnet over the bump in the front, right hand corner of the oil pan. Install the oil pan with a new gasket. Refill the transmission to the proper level, with the proper automatic transmission fluid.

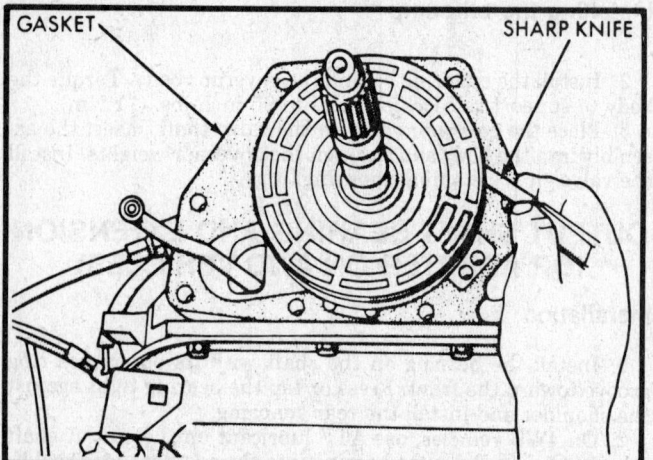

Removing the old gasket from the overdrive unit

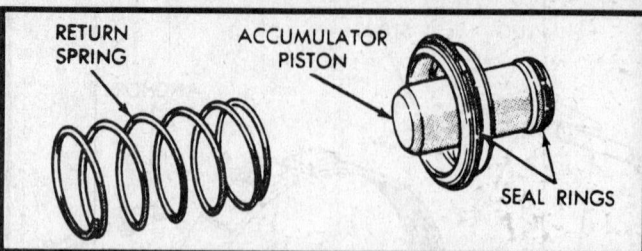

Exploded view of the accumulator piston and spring

OVERDRIVE UNIT

Installation

1. Place the new gasket in place on the rear of the overdrive case. Install the spacer, selected earlier in the overdrive reassembly, on the intermediate shaft.

2. Place the spacer, selected earlier in the overdrive reassembly, in position over the piston on the main portion of the transmission. Install the sliding hub bearing over the intermediate shaft against the sliding hub.

— **CAUTION** —
The shoulder on the inside diameter of the bearing must face forward. A small amount of petroleum jelly or equivalent should be used to hold the shim and bearing into position.

3. Carefully lift the overdrive unit and slide it onto the intermediate shaft. Insert the parking rod into the reaction plug.

— **CAUTION** —
Extreme caution must be used not to tilt the unit as this could cause the carrier and overrunning clutch splines to rotate out of alignment. If this happens, it will be necessary to remove the overdrive unit and align them with tool C-6227-2 or equivalent.

4. Align the slip-fit governor tubes and push the unit forward until it touches the transmission case. Install the attaching bolts and torque them in a crisscross pattern to 25 ft. lbs. (34 Nm).

5. Install the crossmember, speedometer cable and driveshaft using the marks made at disassembly. Refill to the proper level with Mopar® ATF.

SPECIFICATIONS

TORQUE SPECIFICATIONS

A500 Automatic (LoadFlite)	Ft. Lbs.	N·m		Ft. Lbs.	N·m
Cooler Line Fitting	155*	18	Neutral Starter Switch	25	34
Converter Drive Plate to			Oil Pan Bolt	150*	17
Crankshaft Bolt	55	75	Oil Pump Housing to		
Converter Drive Plate to Torque			Transmission Case Bolt	175	20
Converter Bolt	270*	31	Output Shaft Support Bolt	150*	17
Extension Housing to			Pressure Test Take-Off Plug	120*	14
Transmission Case Bolt	32	43	Reaction Shaft Support to Oil		
Extension Housing to Insulator			Pump Bolt	175*	20
Mounting Bolt	50	68	Reverse Band Adjusting		
Governor Body to Support Bolt	95	11	Screw Locknut	25	34
Kickdown Band Adjusting			Speedometer Drive Clamp Screw	100*	11
Screw Locknut	30	41	Transmission to Engine Bolt	30	41
Kickdown Lever Shaft Plug	150*	17	Valve Body Screw	35*	4
Lock-up Solenoid Wiring			Valve Body to Transmission		
Connector	150*	17	Case Bolt	105*	12
*Inch Pounds				*Inch Pounds	

GENERAL TRANSMISSION DATA

Transmission Model:	A-998		A-500	
TYPE	Automatic 3-Speed		Automatic 4-Speed Overdrive	
TORQUE CONVERTER DIAMETER (Standard)	10-3/4 inches		10-3/4 inches	
	U.S.A. Measure	Metric Measure	U.S.A. Measure	Metric Measure
OIL CAPACITY—TRANSMISSION AND TORQUE CONVERTER	17.1 pts.	8.1 Liter	20.4 pts.	9.6 Liter

Use "MOPAR ATF PLUS" (Automatic Transmission Fluid) Type 7176

COOLING METHOD .... Water-Heat Exchanger

LUBRICATION .... Pump (Gear Type)

GEAR RATIOS:

	First	Second	Third	Reverse	Overdrive
	2.74	1.54	1 to 1	2.21	0.69 to 1

PUMP CLEARANCES:
- Outer Gear to Case Bore .... .0035 to .0075 inch
- End Clearance—Gears .... .0004 to .0025 inch

GEAR TRAIN END PLAY .... .005 to .048 inch

INPUT SHAFT END PLAY .... .022 to .091 inch

SNAP RINGS:
- Rear Clutch Snap Ring (Selective) ....
  - .060 to .062 inch
  - .068 to .070 inch
  - .076 to .078 inch
  - .098 to .100 inch
- Output Shaft (Forward End) ....
  - .040 to .044 inch
  - .062 to .066 inch
  - .082 to .086 inch

CLUTCH PLATE CLEARANCE:
- Front Clutch .... 5 Disc .075 to .152 inch
- Rear Clutch .... 4 Disc .032 to .055 inch

CLUTCHES:

	A-998	A-500
Number of Front Clutch Discs	5	5
Number of Rear Clutch Discs	4	4
Number of Direct Clutch Discs	—	5
Number of Overdrive Clutch Discs	—	3

BAND ADJUSTMENTS:

	A-998	A-500
Kickdown (Front) Turns*	2-1/2	2-1/2
Low-Reverse (Internal) Turns*	4	4

*Backed off from 72 inch-pounds (8 N·m).

THRUST WASHERS: A-998/A-500

- Reaction Shaft Support Thrust Washer .... #1 .061 to .063 inch
- Rear Clutch Retainer Thrust Washer .... #2 .061 to .063 inch
- Input Shaft Thrust Plate .... .024 to .026 inch
- Output Shaft Thrust Washer .... #3 Selective
  - .052 to .054 inch (Tin)
  - .068 to .070 inch (Red)
  - .083 to .086 inch (Green)
- Front Annulus Thrust Washer .... #4 .121 to .125 inch
- Front Carrier (To Annulus) Thrust Washer .... #5 .048 to .050 inch
- Front Carrier (To Drive Shell) Thrust Washer .... #6 .048 to .050 inch
- Sun Gear Drive Shell Thrust Plate .... #7 .050 to .052 inch / #8 .050 to .052 inch
- Rear Carrier (To Drive Shell) Thrust Washer .... #9 .048 to .050 inch
- Rear Carrier (To Annulus) Thrust Washer .... #10 .048 to .050 inch

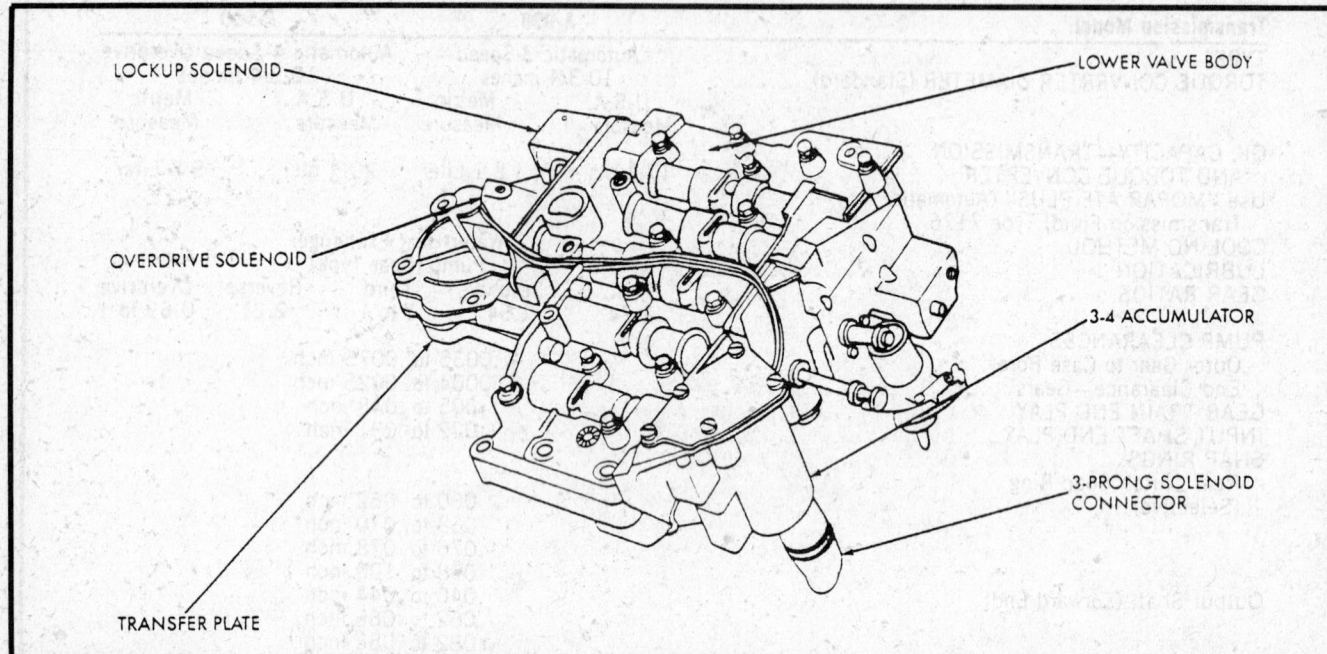

LOCKUP SOLENOID

OVERDRIVE SOLENOID

TRANSFER PLATE

LOWER VALVE BODY

3-4 ACCUMULATOR

3-PRONG SOLENOID CONNECTOR

A–500 valve body

3-4 TIMING VALVE

LOWER VALVE BODY HOUSING

3-4 ACCUMULATOR PISTON

3-4 SHIFT VALVE

3-4 ACCUMULATOR HOUSING

END COVER PLATE

PLUG

3-4 SHUTTLE VALVE

OVERDRIVE SOLENOID (BLACK WIRE)

SPRING RETAINER

LOCKUP VALVE

LOCKUP TIMING VALVE

LOCKUP SOLENOID (WHITE WIRE)

STEEL SEPARATOR PLATE

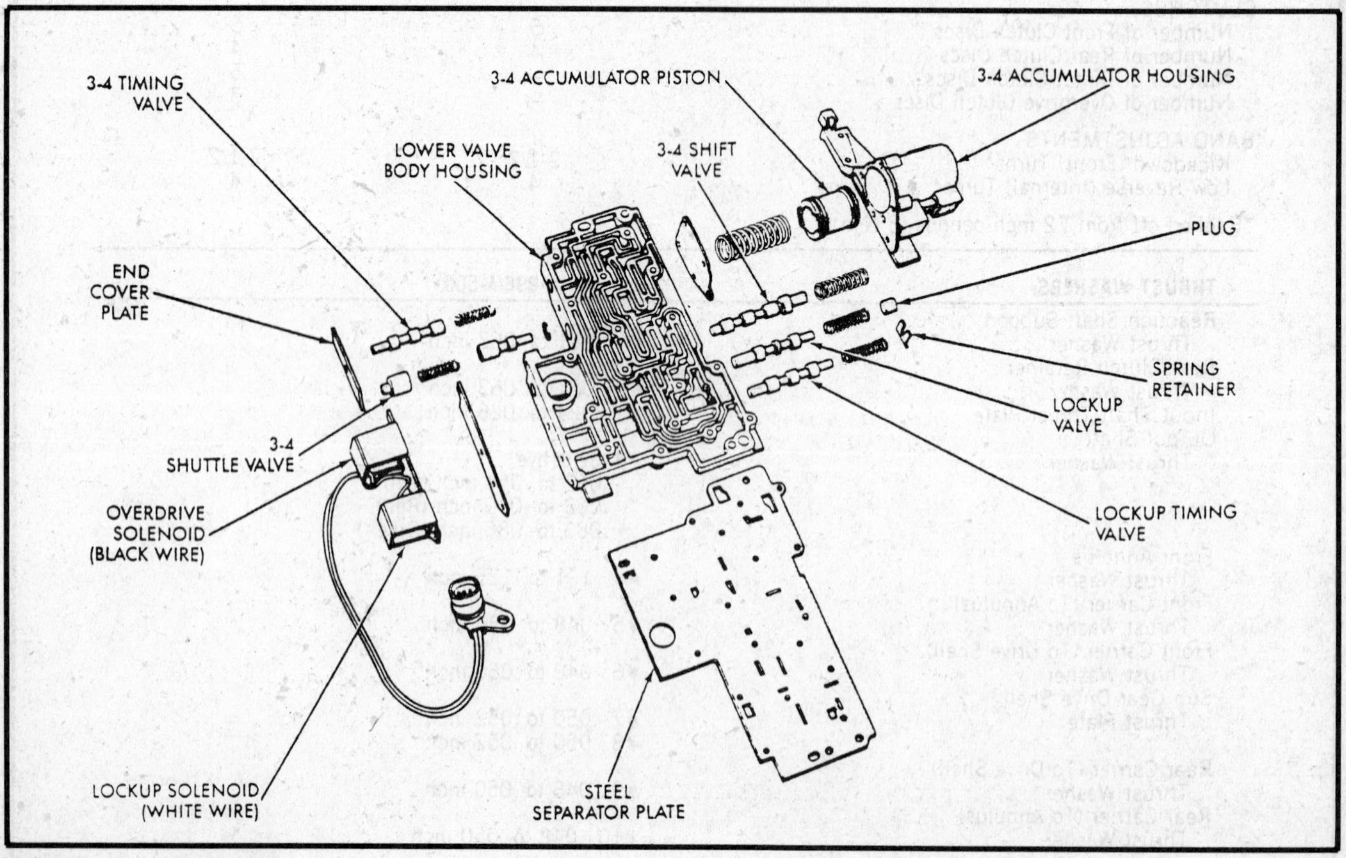

Valve body components

Section 4

KM148, AW372 and AW372L Transmissions
Chrysler Corp.

APPLICATION

KM148			AW372 AND AW372L		
Year	Vehicle	Engine	Year	Vehicle	Engine
1987–89	Dodge Ram 50	2.6L	1987–89	Dodge Ram	2.0L
	Dodge Raider	2.6L			

GENERAL DESCRIPTION

The automatic transmissions used are the AW372, AW372L and KM148. The AW372 transmission is designed for use in vehicles equipped with 2WD and the 2.0L or 2.6L engines. The AW372L transmission is designed for use in vehicles equipped with 2WD and the 2.4L engine. The KM148 transmission is designed for use in vehicles equipped with 4WD and the 2.6L engine.

Basically these transmissions are the same with a few slight differences: The AW372 and KM148 are identical, except the AW372 does not incorporate a transfer case, the AW372L, like the AW372 does not use a transfer case but utilizes a hydraulically controlled lockup type torque converter clutch. The AW372 and KM148 use a one-way clutch (sprag type) torque converter.

All of these transmissions consists of 3 multiple disc clutches, 3 one-way clutches, 4 multiple disc brakes and 2 planetary gear sets to provide 4 forward ratios and a reverse ratio.

The transfer case on the KM148 has a high/low and a 2WD/4WD position. By operating the transfer control lever, running at 2WD high (2H), 4WD high (4H) of 4WD low (4L) can be selected freely.

Transmission and Converter Identification

The transmission can be identified by the third line on the Vehicle information code plate, which is located on the top section of the cowl outer panel, in the engine compartment. The plate shows model code, engine model, transmission model and body color code. Additional information such as, the serial number, fixed number, classification, manufacturing year and month can all be found on the left side of the transmission directly above the pan.

The KM148 and AW372 automatic transmissions utilizes a torque converter that consists of an impeller turbine stator, a one-way clutch and front and rear covers. It is a non serviceable, sealed constructed unit, in which the surfaces of the outer and inner covers are welded together.

The AW372L automatic transmission utilizes a torque converter that has a built in hydraulically controlled lockup clutch, which prevents torque converter loss or slippage in medium and high speed ranges, as well as economizing fuel consumption.

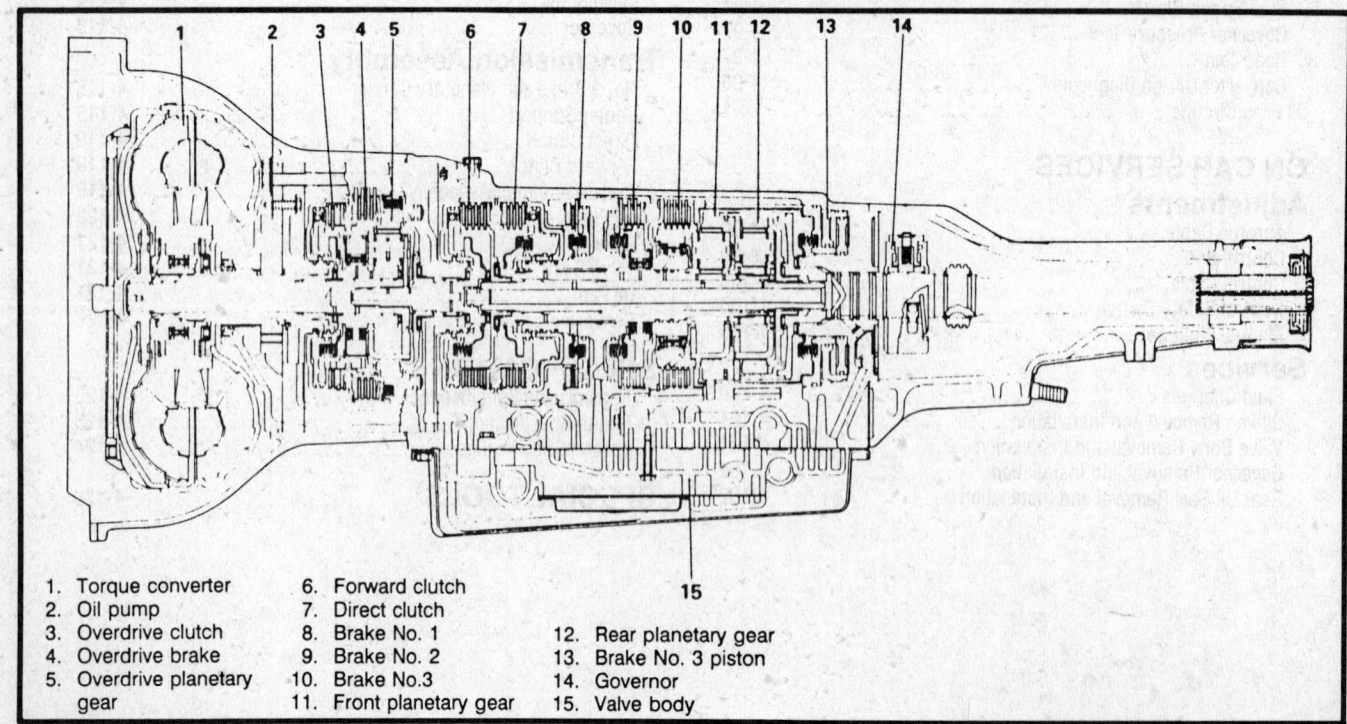

1. Torque converter
2. Oil pump
3. Overdrive clutch
4. Overdrive brake
5. Overdrive planetary gear
6. Forward clutch
7. Direct clutch
8. Brake No. 1
9. Brake No. 2
10. Brake No. 3
11. Front planetary gear
12. Rear planetary gear
13. Brake No. 3 piston
14. Governor
15. Valve body

Cross-sectional view of the AW372 automatic transmission

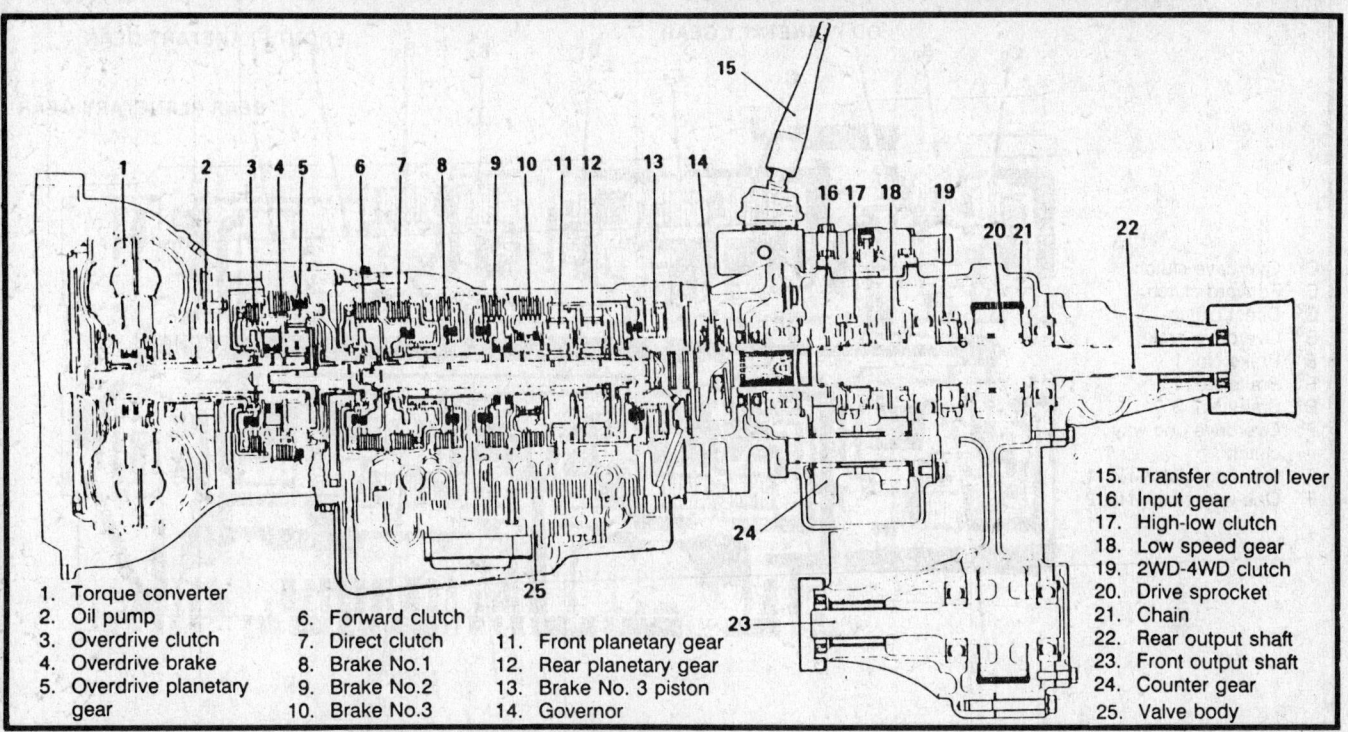

1. Torque converter	15. Transfer control lever
2. Oil pump	16. Input gear
3. Overdrive clutch	17. High-low clutch
4. Overdrive brake	18. Low speed gear
5. Overdrive planetary	19. 2WD-4WD clutch
gear	20. Drive sprocket
6. Forward clutch	21. Chain
7. Direct clutch	22. Rear output shaft
8. Brake No.1	23. Front output shaft
9. Brake No.2	24. Counter gear
10. Brake No.3	25. Valve body
11. Front planetary gear	
12. Rear planetary gear	
13. Brake No. 3 piston	
14. Governor	

Cross-sectional view of the KM148 automatic transmission

Engaging and disengaging the lockup clutch is controlled by the change in direction of hydraulic fluid flow in the torque converter. This unit is also non serviceable.

Torque converters are coded by the manufacturer and sold through varied parts networks. Specific part numbers are used to identify the converters and to allow proper match up to the transmission. When replacing a converter, verify the replacement unit is the same as the unit originally used with the engine/transmission combination.

Metric Fasteners

Metric bolts and fasteners are used in attaching the transmission to the engine and also in attaching the transmission to the chassis crossmember mount.

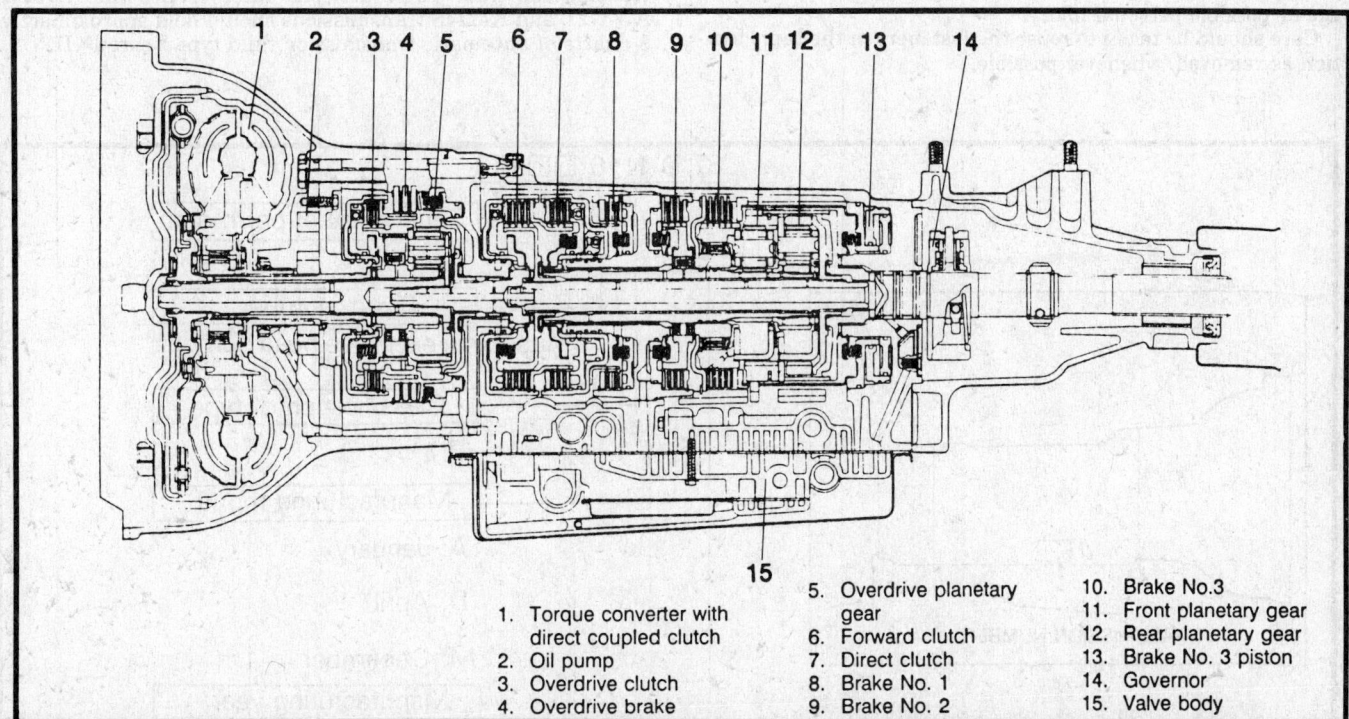

1. Torque converter with	5. Overdrive planetary	10. Brake No.3
direct coupled clutch	gear	11. Front planetary gear
2. Oil pump	6. Forward clutch	12. Rear planetary gear
3. Overdrive clutch	7. Direct clutch	13. Brake No. 3 piston
4. Overdrive brake	8. Brake No. 1	14. Governor
	9. Brake No. 2	15. Valve body

Cross-sectional view of the AW372L automatic transmission with direct coupled clutch torque converter

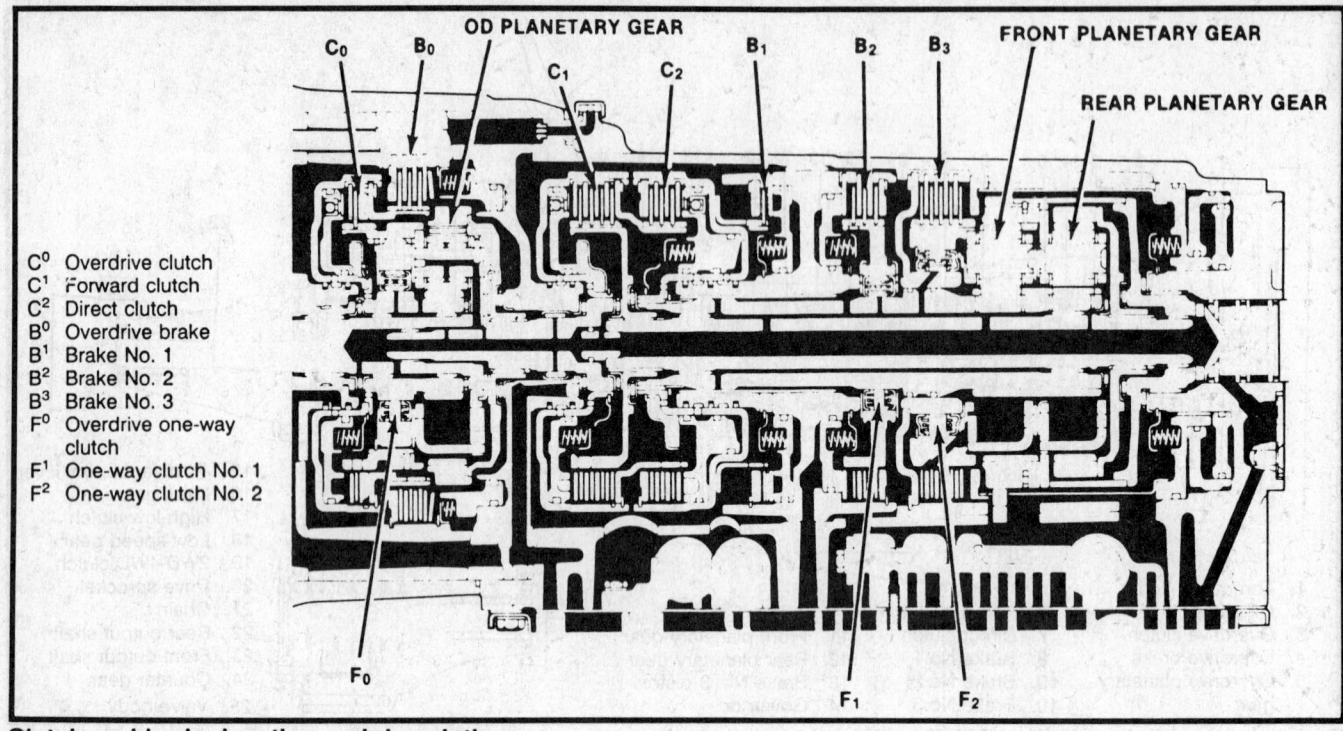

C⁰ Overdrive clutch
C¹ Forward clutch
C² Direct clutch
B⁰ Overdrive brake
B¹ Brake No. 1
B² Brake No. 2
B³ Brake No. 3
F⁰ Overdrive one-way
    clutch
F¹ One-way clutch No. 1
F² One-way clutch No. 2

Clutch and brake location and description

The metric fastener dimensions are very close to the dimensions of the familiar inch system fasteners and for this reason replacement fasteners must have the same measurement and strength as those removed.

Do not attempt to interchange metric fasteners for inch system fasteners. Mismatched or incorrect fasteners can result in damage to the transmission unit through malfunctions, breakage or possible personal injury.

Care should be taken to reuse the fasteners in the same location as removed, whenever possible.

Capacities

The fluid capacities are approximate and the correct fluid level should be determined by the dipstick indicator. After complete transmission overhaul the AW372, AW372L and KM148 transmissions should hold approximately 7.6 quarts of automatic transmission fluid. After pan and filter service the AW372, AW372L and KM148 transmissions should hold approximately 3 quarts of automatic transmission fluid type Dexron® II.

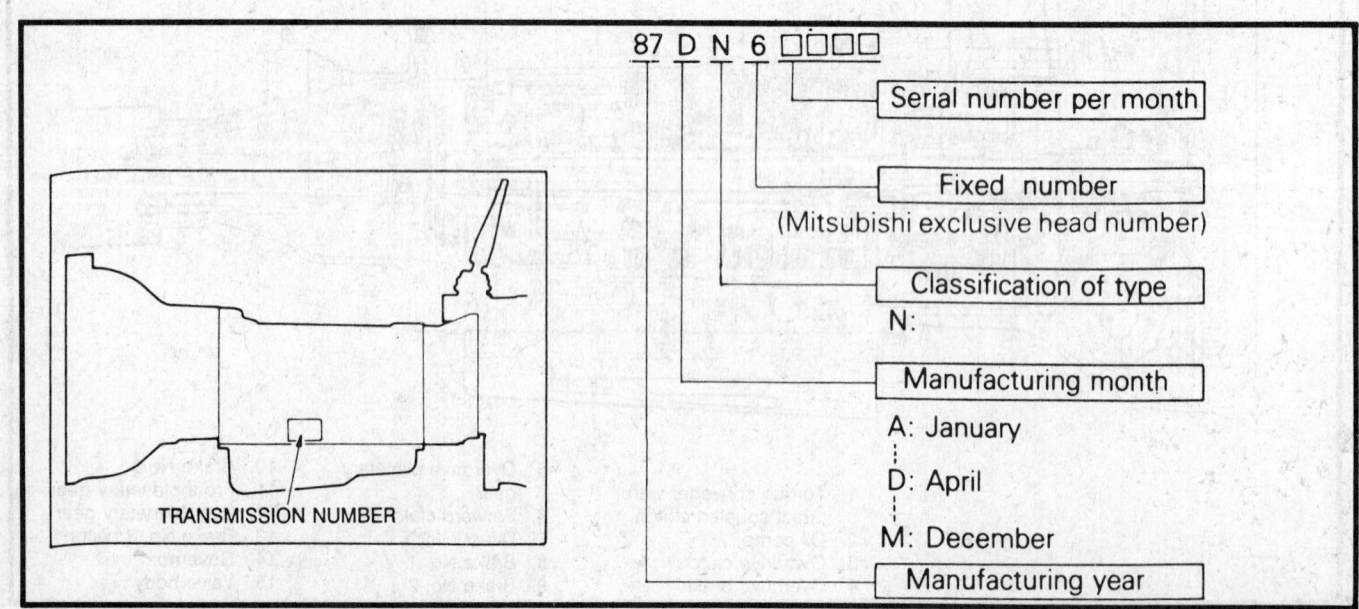

Transmission identification information plate

FLUID CAPACITY
All capacities given in quarts

Year	Vehicle	Transmission	Fluid Type	Pan Capacity①	Overhaul Capacity
1987–89	Dodge Raider	KM148	Dexron®II	3.2	7.6
	Dodge Ram 50	AW372	Dexron®II	2.9	7.2
	Dodge Ram 50	KM148	Dexron®II	3.2	7.6

① Approximate specification

Checking Fluid Level

1. Start the engine and allow to idle for at least a couple of minutes. With the parking brake applied, move the selector lever through all of its positions. Finally, place the selector lever in the **N** position.

2. After the transmission has warmed up to the normal operating temperature, recheck the fluid level. The level must be between the cold upper limit and hot lower limit marks on the dipstick. Insert the dipstick fully to prevent dirt from entering the transmission.

NOTE: A fully cooled transmission will show an oil level below the bottom the of the dipstick mark, even when correctly filed with oil.

3. If the oil level is too low, the oil pump will suck up air which can be clearly heard. The oil will foam and provide incorrect dipstick level results during an oil level checkup. Wait a few minutes until the oil foam has resided, add oil and recheck the oil level.

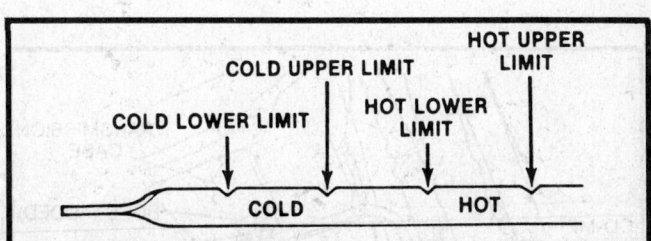

Transmission dipstick levels

4. Excessive transmission fluid must be drained, otherwise the transmission gears would be splashing in oil. The temperature will increase unnecessarily, resulting in foaming oil being ejected through the breather. Continuous operation under such circumstances can lead to transmission damage.

TRANSMISSION MODIFICATIONS

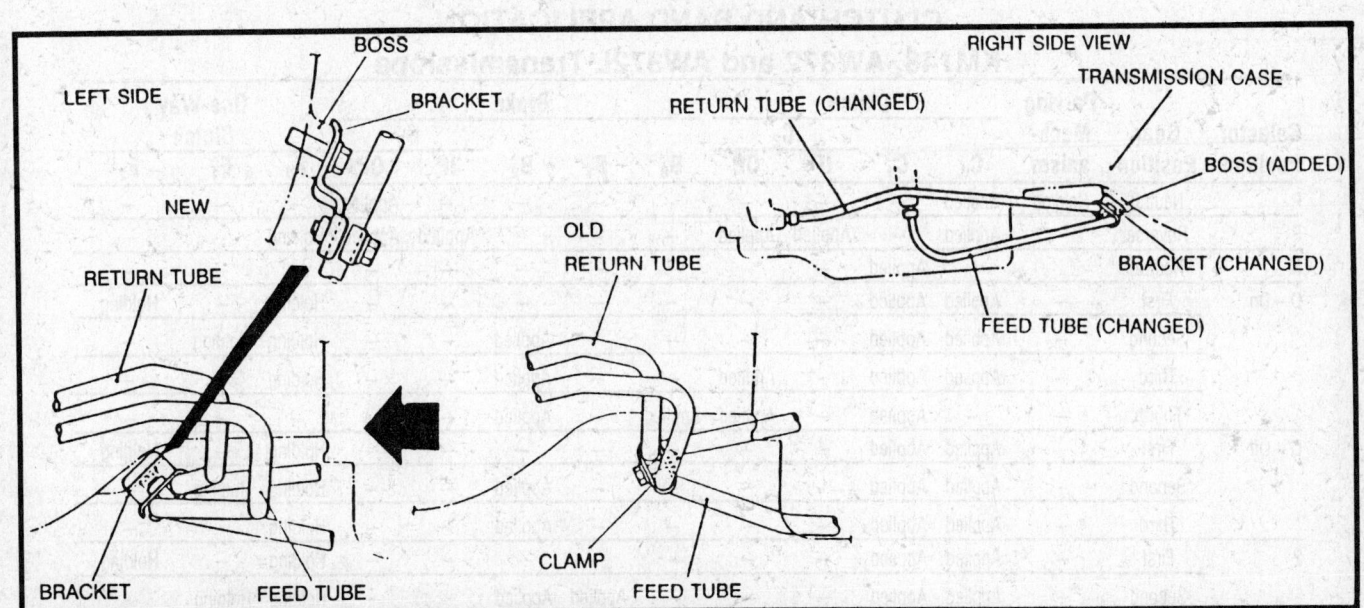

Transmission cooler line modification – KM148 automatic transmission

Check Ball Positioning and Cooler Line Changes

Corrections to the positioning of the valve body check balls and transmission cooler lines on the KM148 require that changes be made on the 1987 Mitsubishi Montero, Chrysler Ram 50 and Ram Raider.

RAM 50

On the 2WD vehicles, the shape of the transmission lines have been changed.

On both the 2WD and 4WD vehicles, the cooler line clamp has been changed to a bracket.

On both 2WD and 4WD vehicles, a threaded boss has been added to the transmission case to accommodate the new bracket mounting bolt.

RAM RAIDER AND MONTERO

The cooler line clamp has been eliminated and a threaded boss has been added to the transmission case to accommodate the new bracket mounting bolt.

RAM 50, RAM RAIDER AND MONTERO

Install the steel check ball in its designated position. The other 3 rubber check balls are identical and may be installed in any other position.

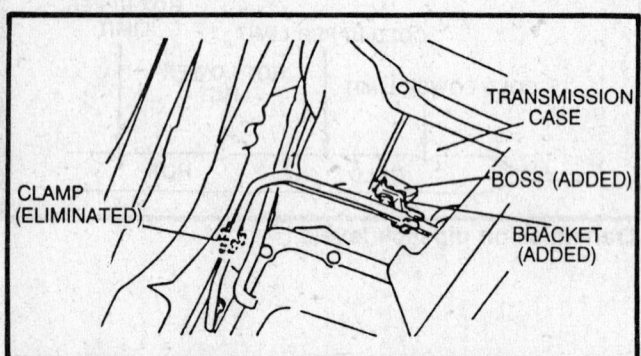

Transmission cooler line clamp and threaded boss modification—KM148 automatic transmission

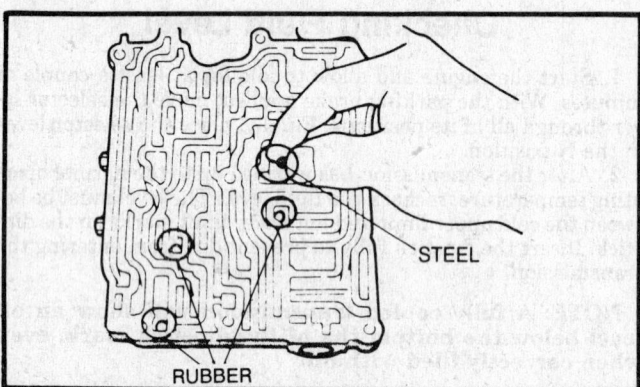

Valve body check ball positions

TROUBLE DIAGNOSIS

CLUTCH AND BAND APPLICATION
KM148, AW372 and AW372L Transmissions

Selector Position	Gear Position	Parking Mechanism	C₀	C₁	C₂ IP	C₂ OP	B₀	B₁	B₂	B₃ IP	B₃ OP	F₀	F₁	F₂
P	Neutral	Holding	Applied	–	–	–	–	–	–	–	Applied	–	–	–
R	Reverse	–	Applied	–	Applied	Applied	–	–	–	Applied	Applied	Holding	–	–
N	Neutral	–	–	Applied	–	–	–	–	–	–	–	–	–	–
D – On	First	–	Applied	Applied	–	–	–	–	–	–	–	Holding	–	Holding
	Second	–	Applied	Applied	–	–	–	–	Applied	–	–	Holding	Holding	–
	Third	–	Applied	Applied	–	Applied	–	–	Applied	–	–	Holding	–	–
	Fourth	–	–	Applied	–	Applied	Applied	–	Applied	–	–	–	–	–
D – Off	First	–	Applied	Applied	–	–	–	–	–	–	–	Holding	–	Holding
	Second	–	Applied	Applied	–	–	–	–	Applied	–	–	Holding	Holding	–
	Third	–	Applied	Applied	–	–	–	–	Applied	–	–	Holding	–	–
2	First	–	Applied	Applied	–	–	–	–	–	–	–	Holding	–	Holding
	Second	–	Applied	Applied	–	–	Applied	Applied	–	–	–	Holding	Holding	–
L	First	–	Applied	Applied	–	–	–	–	–	Applied	Applied	Holding	–	Holding

CHILTON'S THREE C's TRANSMISSION DIAGNOSIS
KM148, AW372 and AW372L Transmissions

Condition	Cause	Correction
No starter action in P or N) Starter motor action in all other selector positions) Back-up lights inoperative	a) Neutral safety switch out of adjustment	a) Replace or adjust switch as needed
Excessive thump into D, 1st or R	a) Engine idle too high b) Throttle cable out of adjustment c) Valves sticking in control valve body	a) Adjust idle speed b) Adjust or replace throttle cable c) Clean control valve body or replace as necessary
Vehicle moves with selector lever in N	a) Manual linkage out of adjustment b) Fault in front clutch support housing c) Fault in stator supportshaft bearing d) Fault in forward sun gear shaft seals	a) Adjust manual likage b) Replace front clutch support housing c) Replace stator support shaft bearing d) Replace forward sun gear shaft seals
Stall speed in D and R range is equal to each other but lower than nominal value	a) Engine output is low b) Stator one-way clutch is faulty c) Faulty torque converter is suspected if it is lower than nominal by more than 600 rpm	a) Check engine performance and repair condition b) Replace stator one-way clutch c) Replace torque converter
Stall speed in D range is higher than nominal	a) OD clutch slipping b) OD one-way clutch faulty c) Forward clutch slipping d) One-way clutch No. 2 faulty e) Low line pressure	a) Replace OD clutch b) Replace one-way clutch c) Replace forward clutch d) Replace No. 2 one-way clutch e) See line pressure diagnosis
Stall speed in R range is higher than nominal	a) OD clutch slipping b) OD one-way clutch faulty c) Direct clutch slipping d) Brake No. 3 slipping e) Low line pressure	a) Replace OD clutch b) Replace one-way clutch c) Replace direct clutch d) Replace brake No. 3 e) See line pressure diagnosis
Hydraulic pressure higher than nominal in all ranges	a) Regulator valve faulty b) Throttle valve faulty c) Throttle control cable incorrectly adjusted	a) Replace regulator valve b) Replace throttle valve c) Adjust throttle valve cable
Hydraulic pressure lower than nominal in D range	a) Large fluid leaks in D range hydraulic circuit b) Forward clutch faulty c) OD clutch faulty	a) Eliminate leakage b) Replace forward clutch c) Replace OD clutch
Hydraulic pressure lower than nominal in R range	a) Large fluid leaks in R range hydraulic circuit b) Brake No. 3 faulty c) Direct clutch faulty d) OD clutch faulty	a) Eliminate leakage b) Replace brake No. 3 c) Replace direct clutch d) Replace OD clutch

CONVETER CLUTCH DIAGNOSIS
KM148, AW372 and AW372L Transmissions

Condition	Cause	Correction
No drive at any position due to clutch torque converter engaged	a) Abnormal signal slippage in damper clutch torque converter system b) Malfunctioning sealing in solenoid valve torque converter	a) Replace b) Replace

CONVETER CLUTCH DIAGNOSIS
KM148, AW372 and AW372L Transmissions

Condition	Cause	Correction
Excessive vibration	a) Decreased signal slippage from CPU (Computer Processing Unit)	a) Replace
Inoperative damper clutch torque	a) No signal lock-up from CPU b) Lock-up line pressure low c) Opened or shorted circuit of solenoid valve	a) Replace b) Replace c) Replace
Increased fuel consumption	a) Damper clutch torque converter does not engage because of a stuck valve	a) Clean up
Lock-up torque converter does not release	a) Decreased driving effort in facing of clutch plate b) Burn out clutch disc c) Damper clutch torque converter system solenoid valve stuck open	a) Replace b) Replace c) Replace
Increased vibration due to no control of slipping ratio	a) Sticking shaft in throttle opening sensor	a) Replace
No drive at any position	a) Seized or stuck thrust bearing in torque converter b) Deformed crankshaft bushing in torque converter c) Broken or cracked drive plate d) Low oil level	a) Replace b) Replace c) Replace d) Refill with fluid
Increased noise due to inoperative	a) Deformed or worn locking-ring in torque converter	a) Replace
Excessive slips when starting	a) Low oil level b) Worn over running clutch in torque converter	a) Refill with fluid b) Replace
Selector lever operation is stiff	a) Incorrect adjustment of pushbutton b) Incorrect adjustment of control cable c) Excessive wear of detent plate d) Excessive wear of pin at end of selector e) Worn contact surfaces of bushbutton and sleeve	a) Adjust b) Adjust c) Replace d) Replace e) Replace
Starter motor does not operate with the selector lever in the N or P position	a) Malfunction in inhibitor switch b) Incorrect adjustment of control cable	a) Replace b) Adjust
Vehicle does not move	a) Low automatic transmission fluid level b) Broken planetary gear carrier	a) Correct b) Replace

Hydraulic Control System

NOTE: Please refer to Section 9 for all oil flow circuits.

The hydraulic control system mainly consists of the oil pump to generate hydraulic pressure, the governor to detect vehicle speed and the valve body assembly to control the clutches and brakes.

The oil pump is of the gear type. It generates hydraulic pressure suppling fluid to the torque converter, to activate the hydraulic control system and provides lubrication to all frictional parts.

The valve body contains valves to distribute the hydraulic pressure from the oil pump to each component and to control the hydraulic pressure. The throttle valve opening and vehicle speed determine hydraulic pressure. The primary regulator valve automatically controls hydraulic pressure, preventing excessive pressure build up by the pump.

The secondary regulator valve controls the converter pressure, the lubrication oil pressure and the cooler pressure. The pressure relief valve regulates maximum hydraulic pressure generated by the oil pump to maintain the safety of the hydraulic pressure circuit.

The torque converter fluid, which has been heated up during operation is channeled into the cooler on the engine side, here the fluid is cooled down. The check valve (for cooler bypass), reduces the fluid pressure for the cooler in order to ensure safe cooler operation.

The governor is installed on the output shaft and changes line pressure from the primary regulator valve to governor pressure. Governor pressure increases as the vehicle speed increases.

The manual valve is is mechanically connected by the manual shift rod or cable, which in turn is linked to the selector lever in the passenger compartment. This valve changes the fluid passages for each gear selector position (P, R, N, D, 2 and L).

Downshift is achieved by movement of the kickdown valve. At ¾ throttle position, the kickdown valve moves until the detent regulator valve port is opened. This allows detent pressure to flow to the 1–2, 2–3 and 3–4 shift valves to downshift. The detent regulator valve regulates the hydraulic detent pressure applied to the 1–2, 2–3 and 3–4 shift valves through the kickdown valve to limit the speed during a downshift.

The intermediate modulator valve regulates line pressure and supplies it to brake No. 1 to reduce the shock when the engine brake is applied in the 2nd speed in **D2** range. The low coast modulator, reduces line pressure to low coast modulator pressure when the selector lever is in the **L** range operation.

The 1–2 shift valve automatically controls the shift from 1st gear to 2nd gear or vice versa depending on governor pressure and throttle pressure. The 2–3 shift valve automatically controls a 2–3 or 3–4 shift in accordance with the governor pressure and throttle pressure.

The 3–4 shift valve automatically controls a 3–4 or 4–3 shift in accordance with the governor pressure and throttle pressure. The 3–4 shift valve receives upward force from throttle pressure at the top end, line pressure at the middle portion and spring force. It also receives upward force from the governor pressure at its lower piston.

The cutback valve, operated by governor pressure and throttle pressure, controls cutback pressure which is applied to the throttle valve. Applying cutback pressure to the throttle valve lowers the throttle pressure. Consequently, line pressure is lowered by applying the lowered throttle pressure to the primary regulator valve, thus preventing unnecessary loss of power by the oil pump.

The reverse clutch sequence valve reduces shock when a shift is made into **R** range. It is controlled by line pressure acting on the inner piston of the direct clutch C2.

When the shift lever is changed from **D** position to **D2** position while in 4th gear (OD), the transmission shifts to 3nd gear and to 2nd gear. Thus the D–2 down timing valve allows a smooth transition from 4th gear to 2nd gear.

Accumulators are provided for C1, C2 and B2, respectively to dampen shocks when each is actuated. The area of the pressure receiving side of the accumulator piston is made greater than that of the back pressure side. The line pressure is always applied to the back pressure side, keeping the piston in the up position. When the circuit to the pressure receiving side opens causing the line pressure to be applied to the piston, the piston is slowly pushed downward, thus dampening shocks when each device is operated.

The 4th (OD) control system utilizes a solenoid valve to electrically select the hydraulic circuit to shift into 4th speed. When the OD-off switch on the select lever is turned ON, the OD solenoid is energized to select a circuit to set the 4th speed. When the OD-off switch is turned off, the OD-off indicator light, on the meter panel comes on.

The OD-off switch is located on the select lever on the driver's side seat. The OD solenoid valve is installed to the left of the transmission case.

THROTTLE VALVE SYSTEM

The throttle valve controls the throttle pressure with the power demand of the driver.

When the accelerator pedal is depressed, the throttle cable, which is linked to the pedal, is pulled to turn the throttle cam. This in turn pushes the kickdown valve to the right. Consequently, the throttle valve is moved to the right by a spring, thus opening a line pressure passage. On the other hand, throttle pressure is applied to the back of throttle valve land No. 2, pushing the valve to the left. Cut back pressure acts on land No. 3 to the position where all forces balance. In this condition, the throttle valve closes the line pressure port.

The throttle pressure is applied to the 1–2, 2–3 and 3–4 shift valve and works against governor pressure. This pressure is applied to the primary and secondary regulator valves, thus controlling line pressure by balancing throttle valve pressure against governor pressure.

Diagnosis Tests
GENERAL DIAGNOSTIC SEQUENCE

Before starting any test procedures, a selected sequence should be followed in the diagnosis of any automatic transmission malfunction. A suggested sequence is as follows:

1. Inspect the fluid level and correct as required.
2. Check the freedom of movement of the downshift linkage and adjust as required.
3. Check the manual linkage synchronization and adjust as required.
4. Install a 400 psi oil pressure gauge to the main line pressure port on the transmission case. Should this arrangement be used on a road test, route and secure the hose so as not to drag or be caught during the test.
5. Perform the road test over a predetermined route to verify shift speeds and engine performance. Refer to the pressure gauge during all shifts for irregularities in the pressure readings. With the aid of a helper, record all readings for reference.
6. During the road test, governor operation can be noted and the shift speeds recorded as the throttle valves are moved through various positions. Should further testing of the governor system be needed, this can be accomplished when the vehicle is returned to the service center, by a shift test.
7. Should a verification of engine performance or initial gear engagement be needed, a stall test can be used to aid in pinpointing a malfunction.
8. Perform a case air pressure test, should the malfunction indicated internal transmission pressure leakage.

CONTROL PRESSURE TEST

Control pressure tests should be performed whenever slippage, delay or harshness is felt in the shifting of the transmission. Throttle pressure changes can cause these problems also, but are generated from the control pressures and therefore reflect any problems arising from the control pressure system.

The control pressure is first checked in all ranges without any throttle pressure. The control pressure tests should define differences between mechanical or hydraulic failures of the transmission.

CONTROL PRESSURE DIAGNOSIS

Condition	Cause	Correction
Hydraulic pressure higher than nominal in all ranges	a) Regulator valve faulty b) Throttle valve faulty c) Throttle control cable incorrectly adjusted	a) Replace regulator valve b) Replace throttle valve c) Adjust throttle valve

CONTROL PRESSURE DIAGNOSIS

Condition	Cause	Correction
Hydraulic pressure lower than nominal in D range	a) Large fluid leaks in D range hydraulic circuit b) Forward clutch faulty c) OD clutch faulty	a) Eliminate leakage c) Replace forward clutch c) Replace OD clutch
Hydraulic pressure lower than nominal in R range	a) Large fluid leaks in R range hydraulic circuit b) Brake No. 3 faulty c) Direct clutch faulty d) OD clutch faulty	a) Eliminate leakage b) Replace brake No. 3 c) Replace direct clutch d) Replace OD clutch
Hydraulic pressure lower than nominal in all ranges	a) Oil pump faulty b) Regulator valve faulty c) Throttle valve faulty d) Throttle control cable incorrectly adjusted e) OD clutch faulty	a) Replace oil pump b) Replace regulator valve c) Replace throttle valve d) Check and adjust throttle cable e) Replace OD clutch

AIR PRESSURE

Air pressure testing is helpful in locating leak points during diassembly and in verifying that the fluid circuits are not leaking during build-up. If the road test discloses which clutch or servo is not holding, that is the circuit to be air tested. Use air pressure regulated to about 25 psi and check for air escaping to detect leakage. If the pressures are found to be low in a clutch, servo or passage-way, a verification can be accomplished by removing the valve body and performing an air pressure test.

1. To determine if a malfunction of a clutch or brake is caused by fluid leakage in the system or is the result of a mechanical failure.
2. To test the transmission for internal fluid leakage during the rebuilding and before completing the assembly.

Procedure

1. Raise and support the vehicle safely. Remove the oil pan.
2. Remove the valve body and place it in and clean area.
3. Obtain an air nozzle and adjust for 25 psi.
4. Apply low compressed air pressure (25 psi.) to the each passage and test the operation of the clutches and brakes.

NOTE: When appling low pressure compressed air to each passage, a dull thud will normally be heard, if a hissing or no thud is heard the transmission must be removed, disassembled and checked further.

STALL TEST

The stall test is used to check the maximum engine rpm (no more increase in engine rpm at wide open throttle) with the selector lever in the D, 2, 1, R positions and to determine if any slippage is occurring from the clutches, bands or torque converter. The engine operation is noted and a determination can be made as to its performance.

Before performing pressure test, perform basic checks and adjustment including fluid level and condition check and throttle cable adjustment. Prior to pressure test, the engine and transmission must have been warmed up enough, the engine coolant temperature to 180–195° F (80–90°C) and the transfer must be in 2WD high.

1. Check the engine oil level, start the engine and bring to normal operating temperature.

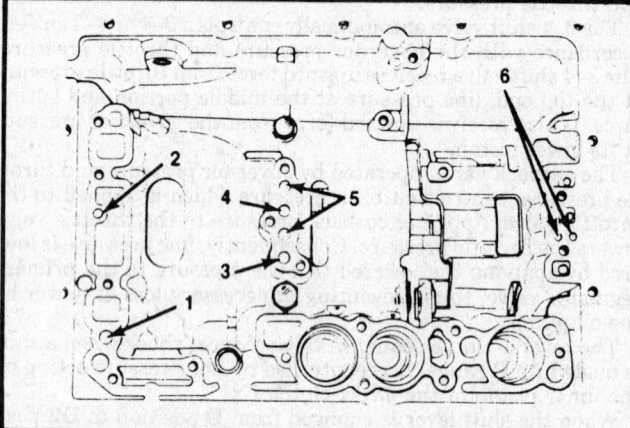

Air pressure test ports

2. Check the transmission fluid level and correct as necessary. Attach a calibrated tachometer to the engine and a 0–400 psi oil pressure gauge to the transmission control pressure tap on the left side of the case.
3. Mark the specified maximum engine rpm on the tachometer cover plate with a grease pencil to immediately check if the stall speed is over or under specifications.
4. Apply the parking brake and block both front and rear wheels.

— CAUTION —
Do not allow anyone in front or rear of the vehicle while performing the stall test.

5. While holding the brake pedal with the left foot, place the selector lever in the D position and slowly depress the accelerator.
6. Read and record the engine rpm when the accelerator pedal is fully depressed and the engine rpm is stabilized. Read and record the oil pressure reading at the high engine rpm point.

— CAUTION —
The stall test must be made within 8 seconds.

STALL SPEED SPECIFICATIONS

Vehicle Application	Engine (liters)	Transmission	Stall Speed rpm	
			Minimum	Maximum
Mitsubishi Montero	2.6	KM148	2100	2400
Mitsubishi Truck	2.0	AW372	1800	2100
Mitsubishi Truck	2.6	KM148	2100	2400
Dodge Raider	2.6	KM148	2100	2400
Dodge Ram 50	2.0	AW372	1800	2100
Dodge Ram 50	2.6	KM148	2100	2400

7. Shift the selector lever into the **N** position and increase the engine rpm to approximately 1000–1200. Hold the engine speed for 1–2 minutes to cool the converter, transmission and fluid.

8. Make similar tests in the **R** position.

— **CAUTION** —

If at any time the engine rpm exceeds the maximum as per the specifications, indications are that a clutch unit or brake is slipping and the stall test should be stopped before more damage is done to the internal parts.

GOVERNOR PRESSURE TEST

Procedure

1. Raise and support the vehicle safely. Remove the plug from the governor pressure gauge using a suitable adapter tool.
2. Position the gauge inside the vehicle for easy access.
3. Appy the parking brake and start the engine.
4. Release the parking brake.
5. Place the selector lever in the **D** range and measure the governor pressure.

NOTE: If the governor pressure is not within specification, incorrect line pressure, oil leakes from the governor pressure circuit or faulty governor is suspected.

GOVERNOR PRESSURE TEST

Output Shaft Speed rpm	Governor Pressure		
	2.0L psi (kPa)	2.4L psi (kPa)	2.6L psi (kPa)
1000	19–22 (128)–150)	18–23 (130–160)	20–24 (138–166)
2000	33–38 (226)–264)	33–38 (230–270)	36–41 (246–284)
3200	54–62 (373)–431)	54–63 (380–440)	59–66 (402–460)

LINE PRESSURE TEST

	Line Pressure	
	D Range psi (kPa)	R Range psi (kPa)
At idle	66–76 (452–529)	100–116 (687–804)
At stall	144–169 (991–1166)	214–270 (1471–1863)

STALL SPEED TEST RESULTS

Condition	Cause
Stall speed in D and R range is equal to each other but lower than nominal value	a) Engine output is low b) Stator one-way clutch is faulty. Faulty torque converter is suspected if it is lower than nominal by more than 600 rpm
Stall speed in D range is higher than nominal	a) OD clutch slipping b) OD one-way clutch faulty c) Forward clutch slipping d) One-way clutch No. 2 faulty e) Low line pressure
Stall speed in R range is higher than nominal	a) OD clutch slipping b) OD one-way clutch faulty c) Direct clutch slipping d) Brake No. 3 slipping e) Low line pressure

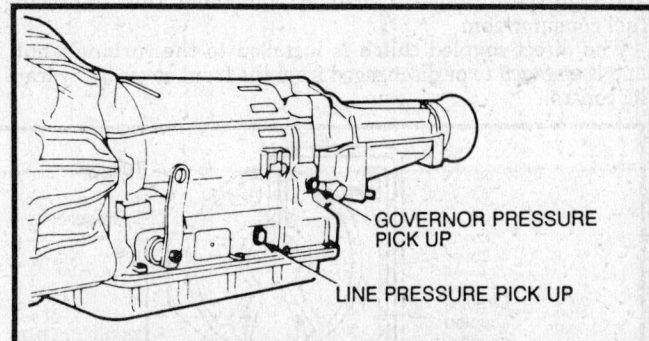

Governor and line pressure test points

ROAD TEST

Prior to performing the road test, be sure to make basic checks including check and adjustment of fluid level and condition and adjustment of the throttle cable. For road testing, the transfer case must be placed in the 2H (2WD-high) position.

In the road test, various changes during transmission operation must be observed, slippage conditions are checked at each shift position.

D Range 3rd Speed Test

1. Place the selector in **D** position range 3rd speed and listen for abnormal noise and vibration.

2. Check carefully as abnormal noise and vibration are sometimes caused by unbalanced driveshaft, differential, tires, torque converter, engine, etc.

2 Range Test

1. Shift to **2** position and start with the throttle valve at 50% full open. Check to see if the 1st and 2nd speed upshift point at these throttle openings, meet the shift pattern.

2. Kickdown at 2nd speed in **2** range, to check that 2nd to 1st kickdown speed limits meet the shift pattern.

3. Check for abnormal noise during acceleration and deceleration, check for shock during upshift and downshift.

L Range Test

1. Shift the selector into the **L** range and check that upshift to 2nd speed does not take place.

2. Check for abnormal noise during acceleration and deceleration.

R Range Test

1. Shift to the **R** range and start forward with full throttle to check for slippage.

2. While the vehicle is running, lightly depress the accelerator pedal to check for slippage.

P Range Test

With the vehicle parked on a slope (about 5 degrees or steeper), shift to the **P** range and release the parking brake to check to see that the parking brake system functions to keep the vehicle stationary.

Converter Clutch Operation and Diagnosis

A direct-coupled clutch is incorporated in the torque converter; it corresponds to a manual transmission clutch.

As a result, torque converter loss or slippage in the medium and high speed ranges is virtually eliminated, thus improving fuel consumption.

The direct-coupled clutch is installed to the turbine's hub, and is engaged to or disengaged from the front cover by hydraulic control.

ENGAGEMENT

When the vehicle is driven in overdrive 4th gear, the line pressure circuit acting on the 2 part of the signal valve is obstructed by the 3–4 shift valve, with the result that the line pressure from the 3–4 shift valve is then applied to the 1 part of the signal valve.

When the speed of the vehicle equals a certain specified speed (approximately 34 mph (55 km/h) or higher, the spring force pressing the signal valve is overcome by the governor pressure, with the result that the signal valve is pressed upward, and line pressure is applied to the lower part of the relay valve. Line pressure is applied to the upper part of the relay valve at all times, and this plus the spring force press the relay valve downward, but, because the (B) diameter is greater than the diameter of the (A) part, the (B-A) X line pressure) force overcomes the force of the spring, thus pressing the relay valve upward. As a result, the converter pressure acts upon the right side of the direct-coupled clutch, thus causing it to engage with the front cover.

DISENGAGEMENT

When the vehicle is driven in a gear other than overdrive (4th gear), the line pressure from the 3–4 shift valve does not act upon the (1) part of the signal valve. The line pressure from the 3–4 shift valve, however, does act upon the (2) part of the signal valve, and this plus the force of the spring cause the signal valve to be forced upward.

When the vehicle speed becomes the certain designated speed or less, the governor pressure decreases, and the signal valve is pressed upward by the spring force. As a result, because the line pressure does not act upon the lower part of the relay valve, the relay valve remains in the pushed down condition due to the spring force and the line pressure acting on the upper part of the relay valve. Consequently, the converter pressure acts upon the left side of the direct-coupled clutch, and the clutch is disengaged from the front cover.

Testing the Converter Clutch

1. Perform a converter stall speed test to determine if trouble is in the converter clutch or transmission.

2. If the stall speed in **D** and **R** range is equal to each other but lower than the nominal valve:

    a. The engine output is low.

    b. The stator one-way clutch is faulty.

NOTE: A faulty torque converter is suspected if the stall speed is lower than nominal by more than 600 rpm.

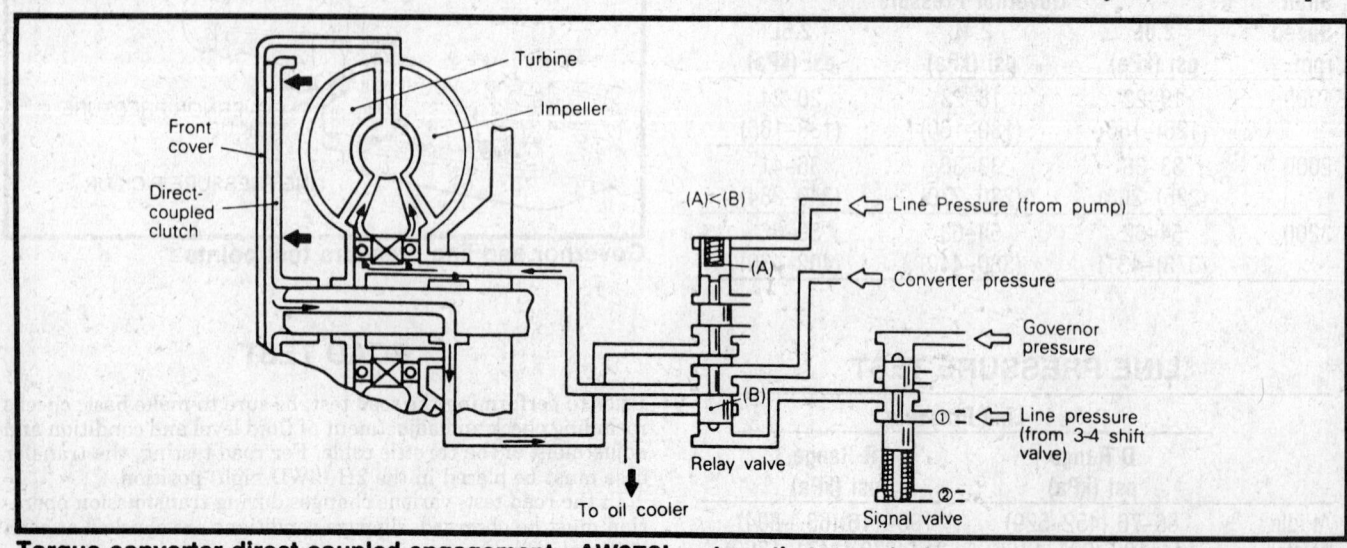

Torque converter direct-coupled engagement—AW372L automatic transmission

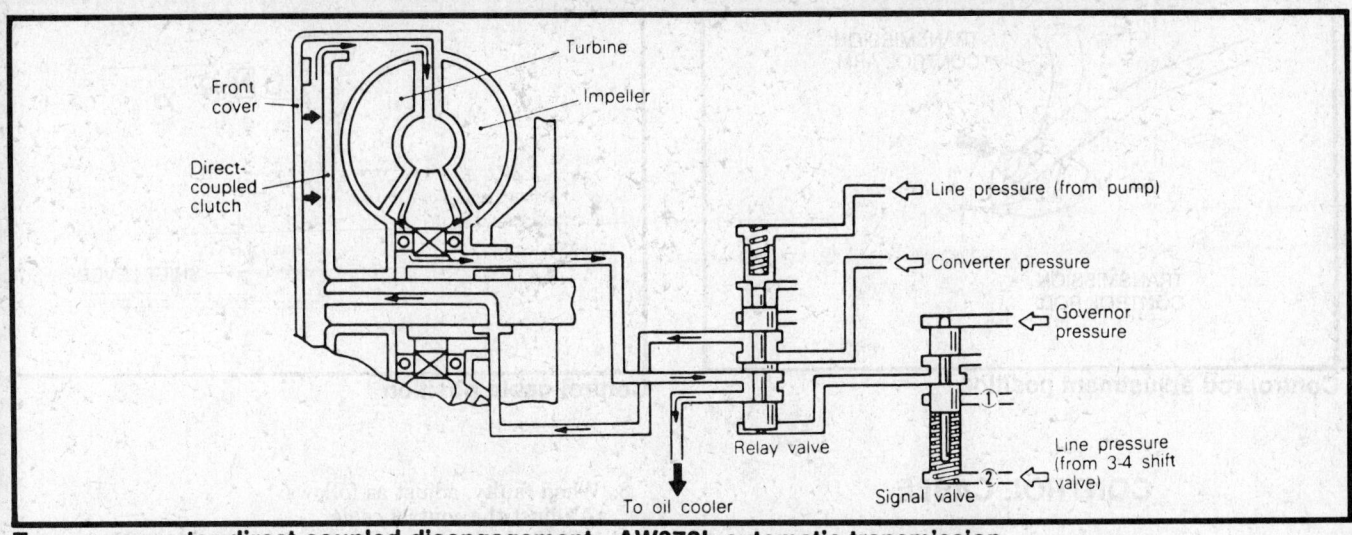

Torque converter direct-coupled disengagement—AW372L automatic transmission

ON CAR SERVICES

Adjustments

THROTTLE CABLE

1. Check the engine idle adjustment. If necessary, readjust.

CAUTION

When engine idle adjustment has been performed, always adjust the throttle control cable.

2. Make sure that no bending or deformation exists on the carburetor throttle lever and throttle cable bracket.

3. Measure the length between the inner cable stopper and the cover end with the carburetor throttle valve full open. If it is not within the standard value, adjust the inner cable bracket moving upward or downward. Standard value: 2.047–2.086 in. (52–53mm).

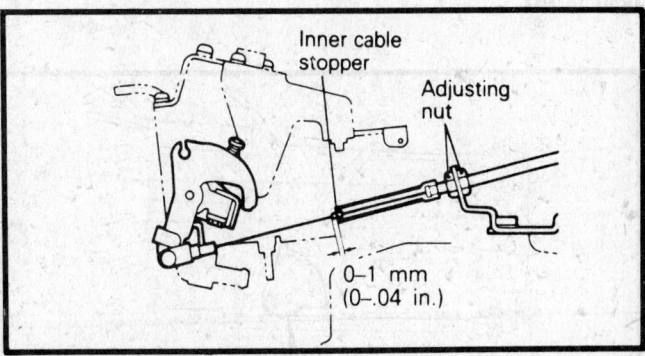

Throttle cable adjustment

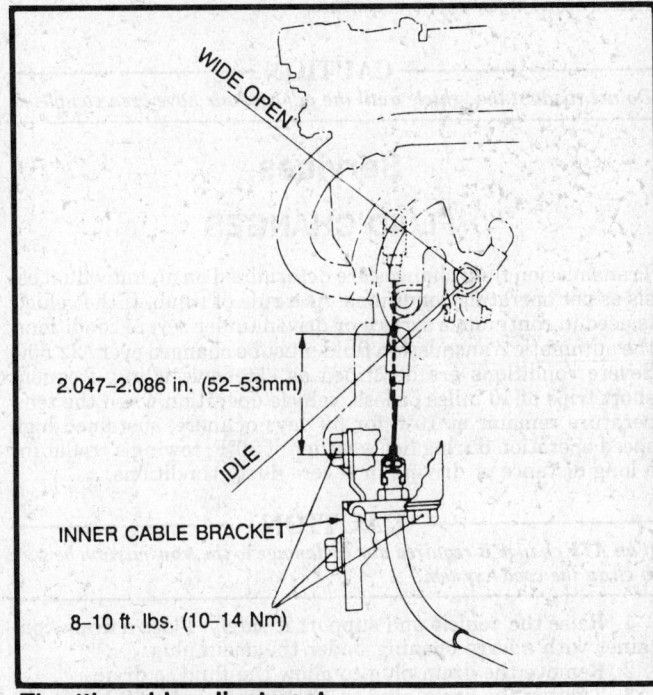

Throttle cable adjustment

CONTROL ROD

1. Move the transmission and shift lever to the **N** position and install the transmission control arm, rod and nut about center. Tighten the nut.

2. Check while driving, to be sure that the transmission is set to each range when the selector lever is shifted to each position.

3. Check while driving, to be sure that the overdrive is activated and canceled correctly when the overdrive switch is used.

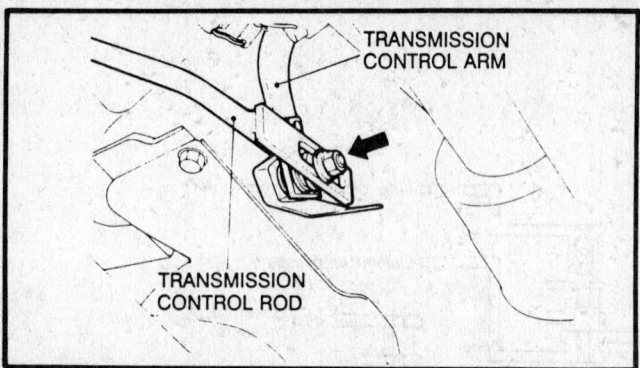

Control rod adjustment position

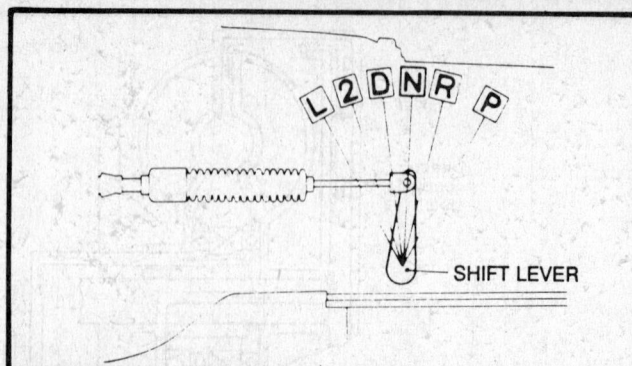

Control cable position

CONTROL CABLE

No adjustment is necessary to the control cable. Visually inspect the cable for wear and smooth operation.

NOTE: When handling the control cable be careful not to bend or kink it.

NEUTRAL SAFETY SWITCH

ALL VEHICLES

1. Be sure that the engine only starts with selector lever in **N** or **P** and not in any other range.
2. Be sure that the backup lamp lights up only with selector lever in **R** and not in any other range. Be sure that all indicators light in **P-L**.

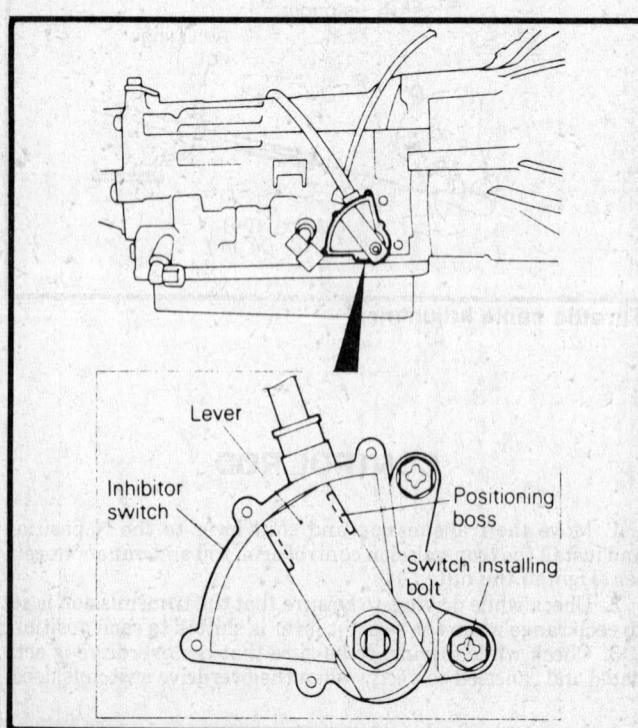

Lever

Inhibitor switch

Positioning boss

Switch installing bolt

Inhibitor switch adjustment

3. When faulty, adjust as follows:
  a. Adjust the control cable.
  c. Shift the lever on the transmission side to **N** range.
  b. Loosen the switch installing bolt.
  c. Adjust the switch by aligning the shift lever with the positioning boss located on the switch.
  d. Tighten the switch mounting bolt to 3–5 ft. lbs. (4–7 Nm).
  e. Recheck for correct inhibitor switch operation.

MANUAL LINKAGE

Before starting the engine, move the shift lever through each gear range, feeling the detents in the transmission. The detents and the shift selector should be synchronized. The neutral safety switch is installed on the selector lever. After checking normal operation of this switch, place the selector lever in the the **N** position. If the notch of the selector lever on the transmission side faces directly down, the linkage has been adjusted correctly. If not an adjustment is required.

――――――――――― **CAUTION** ―――――――――――
Do not roadtest the vehicle until the adjustments have been completed.

Services

FLUID CHANGES

Transmission fluid changes are determined on an individual basis as per operating conditions. As a rule of tumb, If the vehicle is used in continuous service or driven under severe conditions, the automatic transmission fluid must be changed every 22,500. Severe conditions are described as extensive idling, frequent short trips of 10 miles or less, vehicle operation when the temperature remains at 10°F for 60 days or more, sustained high speed operation during hot weather of 90°F, towing a trailer for a long distance or driving in severe dusty conditions.

――――――――――― **CAUTION** ―――――――――――
If an ATF change is required due to damage to the transmission be sure to clean the cooler system.

1. Raise the vehicle and support it safely. Place a drain container with a large opening under the drain plug.
2. Remove the drain plug to allow the fluid to drain.
3. Tighten the drain plug to 13–17 ft. lbs. (18–23 Nm).
4. Pour clean ATF through the oil level gauge hole until its level reaches the cold lower limit of the level gauge.
5. Start the engine and allow it to idle for at least 2 minutes.

With the parking brake and service brake applied, move the selector lever through all positions and finally place it in the **N** or **P** position.

6. Add fluid to bring the level to the **Cold** mark on the dipstick. With the transmission at normal operating temperature, recheck the fluid level. The fluid level must be between the **Hot** marks.

7. Insert the oil level gauge securely to avoid water and dust from entering.

NOTE: By smelling the fluid, a burnt odor indicates a major transmission failure with overhaul required. Should burned flakes, solid residue or varnish in the fluid or on the dipstick be evident, overhaul of the unit is indicated.

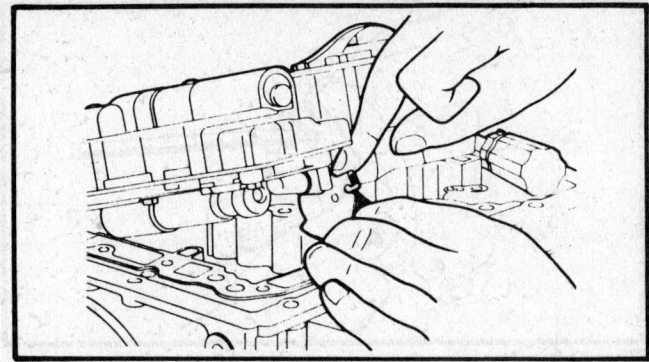
Removing the throttle cable from the valve body

OIL PAN

Removal and Installation

1. Raise and support the vehicle safely, remove the pan drain plug and allow the transmission fluid to drain.
2. Remove the transmission pan retaining bolts.
3. Remove the transmission oil pan and gasket.
4. Examine metallic particles in the oil pan. Remove the magnet and use it to collect any steel chips. Look carefully at the chips and particles in the oil pan and on the magnet to determine where the wear occurs in the transmission.
5. Clean the pan throughly, examine for distortion and repair or replace as needed.

NOTE: Steel metalic particles indicate: bearing wear or gear and clutch plate wear. Brass non-magnetic particles indicate bushing wear.

6. Remove all gasket material on the mating surfaces of the pan and transmission case.
7. Install the magnet in the oil pan and install the oil pan with a new gasket. Torque the retaining bolts to 3.3 ft. lbs. (4.5 Nm).

— CAUTION —
Make sure that the magnet does not interfere with the oil pipes.

8. Install the drain plug with a new gasket. Torque to 5.4 ft. lbs. (7.5 Nm).

VALVE BODY

Removal and Installation

1. Raise and support the vehicle safely. Remove the pan drain plug and allow the transmission fluid to drain out.
2. Remove the transmission pan retaining bolts.
3. Remove the transmission oil pan and gasket.
4. Remove the tubes by prying up both ends of each tube with a with a suitable tool.
5. Remove the strainer.
6. Remove the valve body retaining bolts.
7. Lift the valve body and disconnect the throttle cable from the cam. Remove the valve body.
8. Prior to installing the valve body, make sure the accumulator pistons are pressed fully into the bore.
9. Align the manual valve with the pin on the manual valve lever and position the valve body into place.
10. Prior to installing the retaining bolts, attach the throttle cable and make sure that the lower spring is installed on the B2 or C2 piston.
11. Install the retaining bolts in the valve body and tighten the bolts uniformly to 7.2 ft. lbs. (10 Nm).
12. Install the detent spring.
13. Install the oil strainer and tighten the bolts to 3.3 ft. lbs. (4.5 Nm).

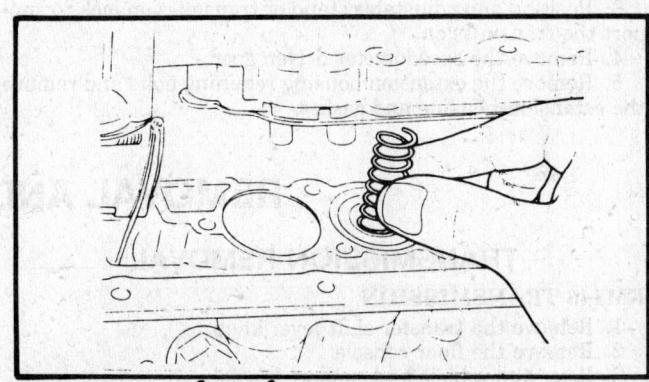
Installing the B² or C² piston lower spring

14. Using a plastic hammer, install the oil pipes into the position.

— CAUTION —
Be careful not to bend or damage the pipes.

15. Install the magnet in the oil pan and install the oil pan with a new gasket.

— CAUTION —
Make sure that the magnet does not interfere with the oil pipes.

16. Install the drain plug with a new gasket. Torque to 5.4 ft. lbs. (7.5 Nm).

GOVERNOR

Removal and Installation

4WD VEHICLES

1. Raise the vehicle and support it safely.
2. Drain the transmission and transfer case fluids.
3. Remove both front and rear driveshafts from the vehicle.
4. Position an adjustable stand or transmission jack to support the transmission.
5. Remove the transfer case assembly.
6. Remove the governor body lock bolt.
7. While lifting the retaining clip with a suitable tool, slide the governor off the output shaft.
8. Installation is the reverse order of the removal procedure.

2WD VEHICLES

1. Raise the vehicle and support it safely.
2. Matchmark the driveshaft and remove from the vehicle.

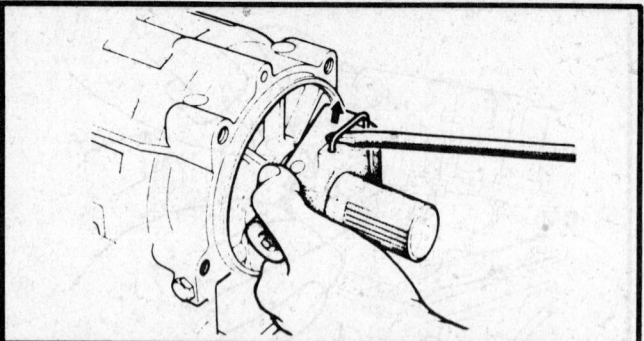

Removing the governor from the output shaft

6. Remove the speedometer drive gear.
7. Loosen the staked part of the governor lock plate.
8. Remove the governor body lock bolt.
9. While lifting the retaining clip with a suitable tool, slide the governor off the output shaft.
10. Remove the governor strainer lock plate screws, plate and remove the strainer.
11. Installation is the reverse order of the removal procedure. Torque the extension housing retaining bolts to 25 ft. lbs. (34.5 Nm) and the driveshaft retaining bolts to 36–43 ft. lbs. (50 Nm).

REAR OIL SEAL

Removal and Installation

ALL VEHICLES

1. Raise and support the vehicle safely.
2. Remove the driveshaft. Use a special puller tool to remove the dust shield and oil seal from the extension housing.
3. When installing the oil seal, apply grease to the lip.
4. When installing the dust seal, soak it with fluid.
5. Install the oil seal and dust shield using a special installer tool.

3. Position and adjustable stand or transmission jack to support the transmission.
4. Remove the speedometer driven gear.
5. Remove the extension housing retaining bolts and remove the extension housing and gasket.

REMOVAL AND INSTALLATION

TRANSMISSION REMOVAL

KM148 TRANSMISSION

1. Remove the transfer shift lever knob.
2. Remove the floor console.
3. Raise the vehicle and support it safely.
4. Remove the skid plate and undercover.
5. Drain the transmission and transfer case fluids.
6. Remove the throttle cable snap pin and clevis pin, position the throttle cable to the side.
7. Remove the transfer case protector.
8. Remove the shift control cable snap pin and disconnect the cable from the shaft.
9. Disconnect the speedometer cable.
10. Disconnect the neutral safety switch connection from the inhibitor switch.
11. Remove the rear driveshaft.
12. Remove the front driveshaft.
13. Remove the starter motor mounting bolts and remove the starter motor.
14. Remove exhaust pipe bracket retaining bolts.
15. Remove the torque converter housing inspection cover retaining bolts.
16. Remove the torque converter to flywheel retaining bolts.

—————— CAUTION ——————

The torque converter to flywheel retaining bolts are special bolts and should not be mixed in or exchanged with bolts not specifically designed for the converter.

17. Disconnect the oil cooler return lines.
18. Remove the oil fill tube.
19. Position a transmission jack to support the transmission.
20. Disconnect the engine support insulator and crossmember.
21. Disconnect the transfer case mounting bracket.
22. Lower the crossmember from the vehicle.
23. Disconnect the transmission and transfer case assembly from the engine by pulling it slowly toward the rear of the vehicle.
24. When lowering the transmission and transfer case assembly, tilt the front of the transmission downward and slowly lower the assembly forward until it is clear.

25. Place the transmission in a suitable holding fixture.

AW372 TRANSMISSION

1. Raise the vehicle and support it safely.
2. Remove the under cover.
3. Drain the transmission fluid.

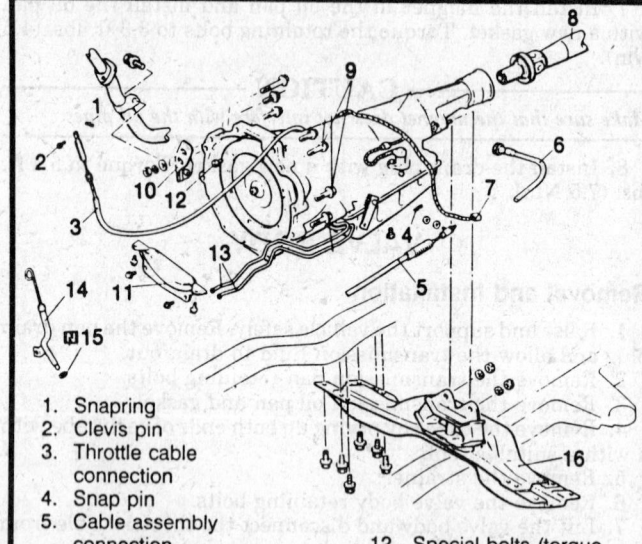

1. Snapring
2. Clevis pin
3. Throttle cable connection
4. Snap pin
5. Cable assembly connection
6. Speedometer cable connection
7. Inhibitor switch connection
8. Driveshaft
9. Starter motor retaining bolts
10. Exhaust pipe mounting bracket
11. Bell housing cover
12. Special bolts (torque converter)
13. Oil feed tube and oil return tube connection
14. Filler tube
15. O-ring
16. Rear engine support insulator and crossmember

Exploded view of the AW372 automatic transmission and related components

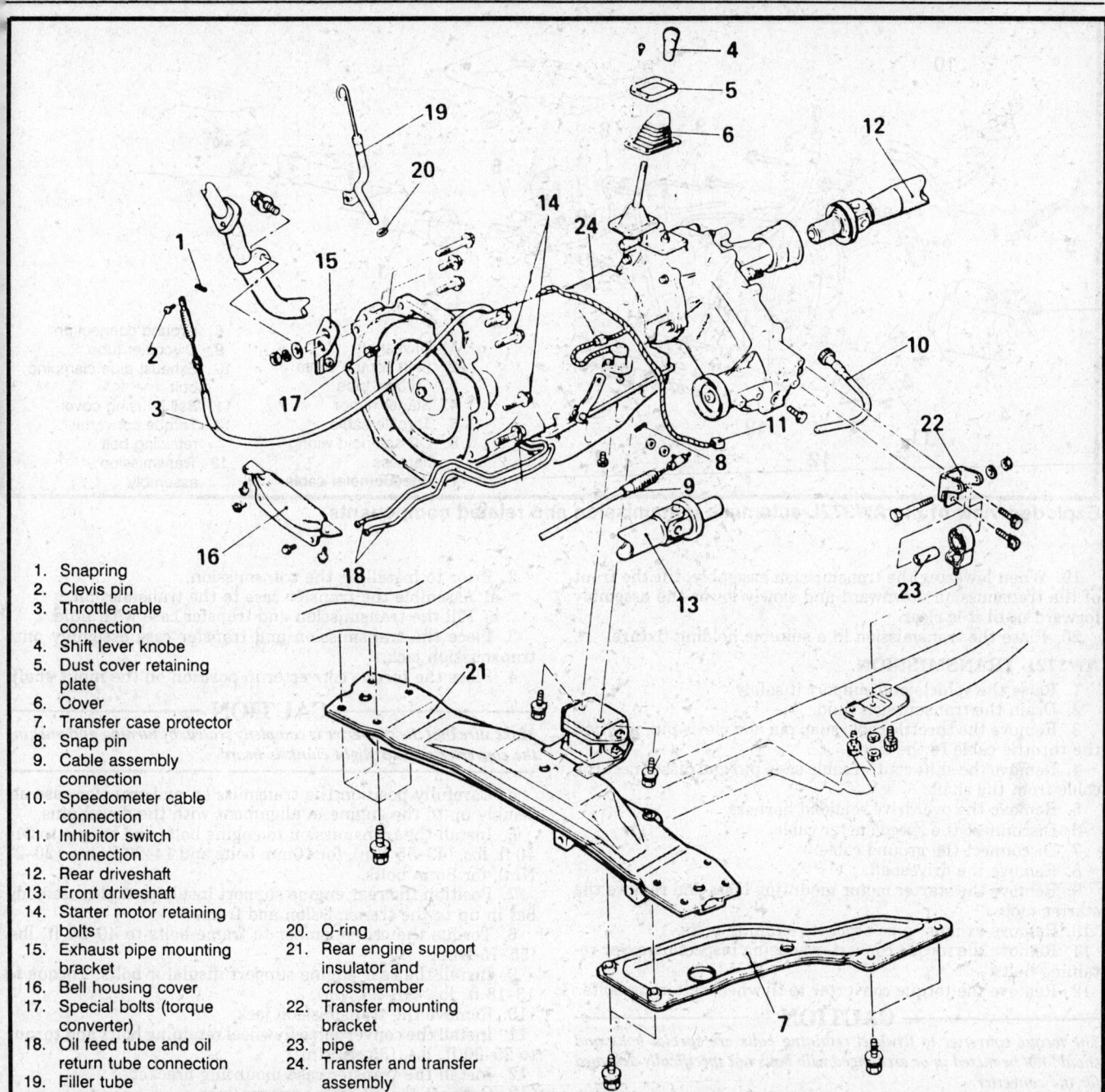

1. Snapring
2. Clevis pin
3. Throttle cable connection
4. Shift lever knobe
5. Dust cover retaining plate
6. Cover
7. Transfer case protector
8. Snap pin
9. Cable assembly connection
10. Speedometer cable connection
11. Inhibitor switch connection
12. Rear driveshaft
13. Front driveshaft
14. Starter motor retaining bolts
15. Exhaust pipe mounting bracket
16. Bell housing cover
17. Special bolts (torque converter)
18. Oil feed tube and oil return tube connection
19. Filler tube
20. O-ring
21. Rear engine support insulator and crossmember
22. Transfer mounting bracket
23. pipe
24. Transfer and transfer assembly

Exploded view of the KM148 automatic transmission and related components

4. Remove the throttle cable snap pin and clevis pin, position the throttle cable to the side.
5. Remove the shift control cable snap pin and disconnect the cable from the shaft.
6. Disconnect the speedometer cable.
7. Disconnect the neutral safety switch connection from the inhibitor switch.
8. Remove the driveshaft.
9. Remove the starter motor mounting bolts and remove the starter motor.
10. Remove exhaust pipe bracket retaining bolts.
11. Remove the torque converter housing inspection cover retaining bolts.
12. Remove the torque converter to flywheel retaining bolts.

─────────── **CAUTION** ───────────
The torque converter to flywheel retaining bolts are special bolts and should not be mixed in or exchanged with bolts not specifically designed for the converter.
──────────────────────────────────

13. Disconnect the oil cooler return lines.
14. Remove the oil fill tube.
15. Position a transmission jack to support the transmission.
16. Disconnect the rear engine support insulator and crossmember.
17. Lower the crossmember from the vehicle.
18. Disconnect the transmission assembly from the engine by pulling it slowly toward the rear of the vehicle.

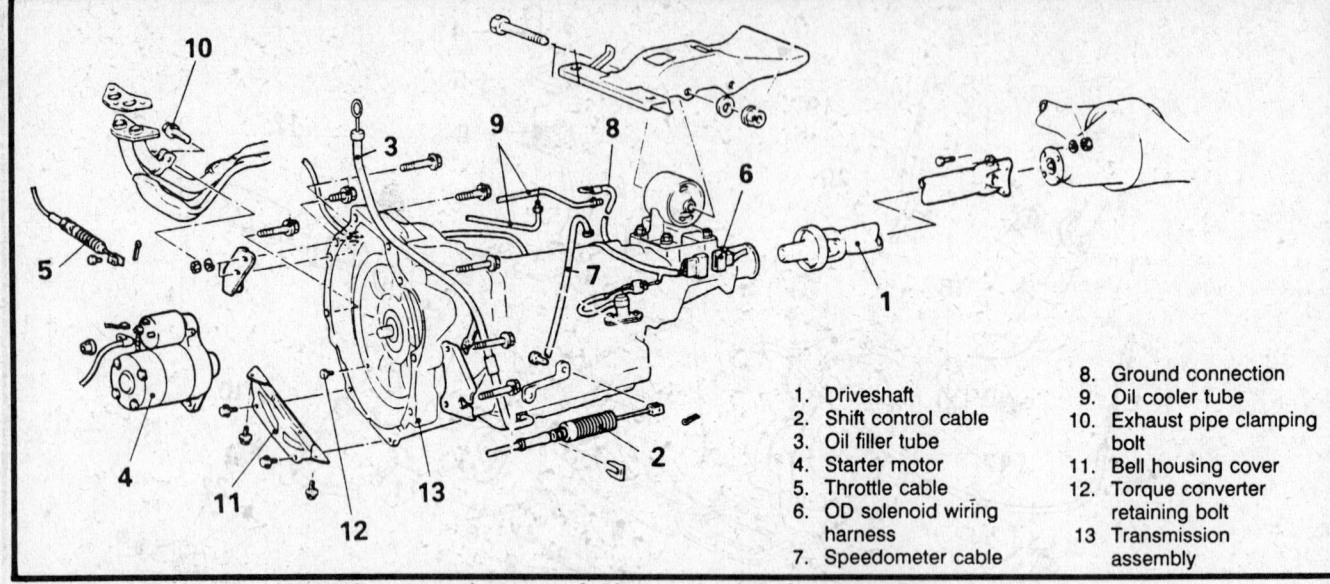

1. Driveshaft
2. Shift control cable
3. Oil filler tube
4. Starter motor
5. Throttle cable
6. OD solenoid wiring harness
7. Speedometer cable
8. Ground connection
9. Oil cooler tube
10. Exhaust pipe clamping bolt
11. Bell housing cover
12. Torque converter retaining bolt
13. Transmission assembly

Exploded view of the AW372L automatic transmission and related components

19. When lowering the transmission assembly, tilt the front of the transmission downward and slowly lower the assembly forward until it is clear.
20. Place the transmission in a suitable holding fixture.

AW372L TRANSMISSION

1. Raise the vehicle and support it safely.
2. Drain the transmission fluid.
3. Remove the throttle cable snap pin and clevis pin, position the throttle cable to the side.
4. Remove the shift control cable snap pin and disconnect the cable from the shaft.
5. Remove the overdrive solenoid harness.
6. Disconnect the speedometer cable.
7. Disconnect the ground cable.
8. Remove the driveshaft.
9. Remove the starter motor mounting bolts and remove the starter motor.
10. Remove exhaust pipe bracket retaining bolts.
11. Remove the torque converter housing inspection cover retaining bolts.
12. Remove the torque converter to flywheel retaining bolts.

— CAUTION —

The torque converter to flywheel retaining bolts are special bolts and should not be mixed in or exchanged with bolts not specifically designed for the converter.

13. Disconnect the oil cooler return lines.
14. Remove the oil fill tube.
15. Position a transmission jack to support the transmission.
16. Disconnect the rear engine support insulator and crossmember.
17. Disconnect the transmission assembly from the engine by pulling it slowly toward the rear of the vehicle.
18. When lowering the transmission assembly, tilt the front of the transmission downward and slowly lower the assembly forward until it is clear.
19. Place the transmission in a suitable holding fixture.

TRANSMISSION INSTALLATION

KM148 TRANSMISSION

1. Raise the vehicle and support it safely.

2. Prior to installing the transmission:
   a. Assemble the transfer case to the transmission.
   b. Fill the transmission and transfer case with fluid.
3. Place the transmission and transfer case assembly on a transmission jack.
4. Place the torque converter in position on the input shaft.

— CAUTION —

Make sure that the converter is completly seated, by turning and pushing the converter until a slight clunk is heard.

5. Carefully position the transmission and transfer case assembly up to the engine in alignment with the dowel pins.
6. Install the transmission to engine bolts and torgue to 31–40 ft. lbs. (43–55 Nm), for 10mm bolts and 14–20 ft. lbs. (20–27 Nm), for 8mm bolts.
7. Position the rear engine support insulator and crossmember in up to the transmission and frame.
8. Torque the crossmember to frame bolts to 40–54 ft. lbs. (55–75 Nm).
9. Install the rear engine support insulator bolts. Torque to 13–18 ft. lbs. (18–25 Nm).
10. Remove the transmission jack.
11. Install the converter to flywheel retaining bolts and torque to 25–30 ft. lbs. (35–42 Nm).
12. Install the transfer case mounting bracket.
13. Connect the oil cooler return lines.
14. Install the special torque converter to flywheel retaining bolts.

— CAUTION —

The torque converter to flywheel retaining bolts are special bolts and should not be mixed in or exchanged with bolts not specifically designed for the converter.

15. Install the torque converter housing inspection cover retaining bolts.
16. Install the exhaust pipe bracket retaining bolts.
17. Install the starter motor mounting bolts and install the starter motor.
18. Install the front driveshaft.
19. Install the rear driveshaft.
20. Connect the neutral safety switch connection to the neutral safety switch.

21. Fill the transmission and transfer case with fluid.

22. Start the engine and test transmission operation in all ranges.

AW372 TRANSMISSION

1. Raise the vehicle and support it safely.
2. Place the transmission on a transmission jack.
3. Place the torque converter in position on the input shaft.

--- **CAUTION** ---

Make sure that the converter is completely seated, by turning and pushing the converter until a slight clunk is heard.

---

4. Carefully position the transmission assembly up the the engine in alignment with the dowel pins.
5. Install the transmission to engine bolts and torque to 31–40 ft. lbs. (43–55 Nm), for 10mm bolts and 14–20 ft. lbs. (20–27 Nm), for 8mm bolts.
6. Position the rear engine support insulator and crossmember in up to the transmission and frame.
7. Torque the crossmember to frame bolts to 29–36 ft. lbs. (40–50 Nm).
8. Install the rear engine support insulator nuts. Torque to 14–17 ft. lbs. (20–24 Nm).
9. Remove the transmission jack.
10. Install the converter to flywheel retaining bolts and torque to 25–30 ft. lbs. (35–42 Nm).
11. Connect the oil cooler return lines.
12. Install the torque converter to flywheel retaining bolts.

--- **CAUTION** ---

The torque converter to flywheel retaining bolts are special bolts and should not be mixed in or exchanged with bolts not specifically designed for the converter.

---

13. Install the torque converter housing inspection cover retaining bolts.
14. Install the exhaust pipe bracket retaining bolts and bracket.
15. Install the starter motor mounting bolts and install the starter motor.
16. Install the driveshaft.
17. Connect the neutral safety switch connection to the neutral safety switch.
18. Connect the speedometer cable.
19. Install the shift control cable snap pin and connect the cable to the shaft.

20. Install the throttle cable snap pin and clevis pin and connect the throttle cable.
21. Fill the transmission with fluid.
22. Lower the vehicle to the ground and test the transmission operation in all ranges.

AW372L TRANSMISSION

1. Raise the vehicle and support it safely.
2. Place the transmission on a transmission jack.
3. Place the torque converter in position on the input shaft.

--- **CAUTION** ---

Make sure that the converter is completely seated, by turning and pushing the converter until a slight clunk is heard.

---

4. Carefully position the transmission assembly up to the engine in alignment with the dowel pins.
5. Install the transmission to engine bolts and torgue to 31–40 ft. lbs. (43–55 Nm), for 10mm bolts and 14–20 ft. lbs. (20–27 Nm), for 8mm bolts.
6. Install the rear engine support mount bolt and nut. Torque to 50–65 ft. lbs. (70–90 Nm).
7. Remove the transmission jack.
8. Install the converter to flywheel retaining bolts and torque to 25–30 ft. lbs. (35–42 Nm).
9. Install the oil fill tube.
10. Connect the oil cooler return lines.
11. Install the torque converter to flywheel retaining bolts.

--- **CAUTION** ---

The torque converter to flywheel retaining bolts are special bolts and should not be mixed in or exchanged with bolts not specifically designed for the converter.

---

12. Install the torque converter housing inspection cover and retaining bolts.
13. Install the exhaust pipe bracket and retaining bolts.
14. Install the starter motor mounting bolts and install the starter motor.
15. Install the driveshaft.
16. Connect the ground cable.
17. Connect the speedometer cable.
18. Install the overdrive solenoid harness.
19. Install the shift control cable snap pin and disconnect the cable from the shaft.
20. Install the throttle cable snap pin and clevis pin and install the throttle cable.
21. Lower the vehicle to the floor. Fill the transmission with fluid and test the transmission operation in all ranges.

BENCH OVERHAUL

Before Disassembly

All disassembled parts should be washed clean and the fluid passages and holes blown through with compressed air to make sure that they are not clogged.

--- **CAUTION** ---

When using compressed air to dry parts, avoid spraying ATF or cleaning solvents, as personal injury may occur.

After cleaning, all parts should be arranged in proper order to allow a thorough inspection.

When disassembling the valve body, be sure to keep each valve together with its own spring.

New brake and clutch discs that are to be used for replace-

ment must be soaked in ATF for at least 2 hours before assembly.

Converter Inspection

1. Remove the torque from the transmission, if not already done.
2. Insert a special wrench tool into the inner race of the one-way clutch of the torque converter.
3. Insert a special stopper tool so that it installs in the notch of the converter hub and the other race of the one-way clutch.
4. Test the one-way clutch: The clutch should lock when turned counterclockwise and should rotate freely and smoothly clockwise. Less than 22 inch lbs. (2.5 Nm) of torque should be required to rotate the clutch clockwise. If necessary, clean the converter and retest the clutch. Replace the converter if the clutch still fails the test.

Transmission Disassembly

TORQUE CONVERTER

Removal

With the transmission secured on a work bench or a suitable transmission holding fixture, grasp the torque converter firmly and pull the assembly straight out of the transmission.

NOTE: The torque converter is a heavy unit and care must be exercised to handle the weight.

The torque converter is a sealed unit and is non-serviceable. If failure occurs, it must be replaced.

OIL PAN

Removal

1. Removal the pan retaining bolts and remove the pan and gasket.
2. Examine metallic particles in the oil pan. Remove the magnet and use it to collect any steel chips. Look carefully at the chips and particles in the oil pan and on the magnet to determine where the wear occurs in the transmission.

VALVE BODY

Removal

1. With the transmission mounted in a suitable holding fixture remove the oil pan.
2. Remove the tubes by prying up both ends of each tube with a with a suitable tool.
3. Remove the strainer.
4. Remove the valve body retaining bolts.
5. Lift slightly the valve body and disconnect the throttle cable from the cam, and remove the valve body.

GOVERNOR

Removal

1. On the AW372 and AW372L, remove the extension housing.
2. Remove the speedometer drive gear.
3. Remove the governor body lock bolt.
4. While lifting the retaining clip with a suitable tool, slide the governor off the output shaft.

OIL PUMP

Removal

1. Remove the oil pump retaining bolts.

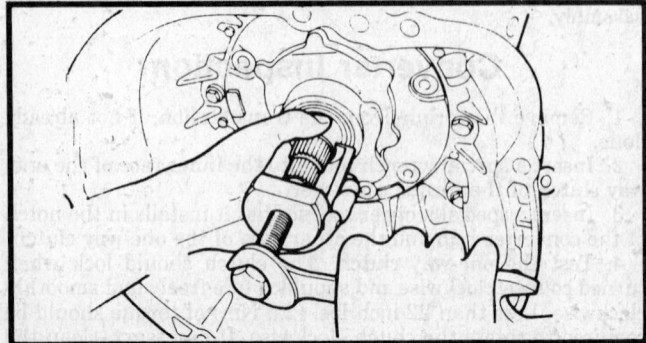

Removing the oil pump

Appling low pressure air to force pistons out the case

2. Position a suitable pulling tool on the shaft in back of the spline.
3. Turn bolt of the pulling tool to free the pump.

─── **CAUTION** ───
Be careful not to damage the shaft bushing surface.

4. Grasp the front pump stator shaft and pull the pump from the case.
5. Remove the bearing and race behind the oil pump.

OVERDRIVE CLUTCH ASSEMBLY

Removal

1. Remove the converter housing.
2. Using a 10mm socket, push the plastic throttle cable retainer out of the transmission case to remove the cable with the retainer.
3. Position a rag to catch each piston. Blow low pressure compressed air of about 14.5 psi into each of the holes. Remove the pistons and springs.

─── **CAUTION** ───
Wear protective eye wear and keep face away to avoid injury. Do not use high pressure air.

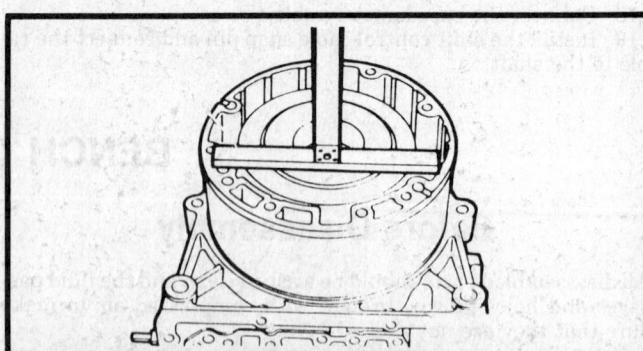

Measure the distance between the top of the overdrive case and clutch cylinder

4. Remove the parking lock linkage.
5. Remove the cam plate.
6. Remove the parking lock rod.
7. Remove the spring, pivot pin and parking lock pawl.
8. Remove the manual lever and shaft.
9. Using a hammer and punch, drive out the pin retaining the manual lever shaft.

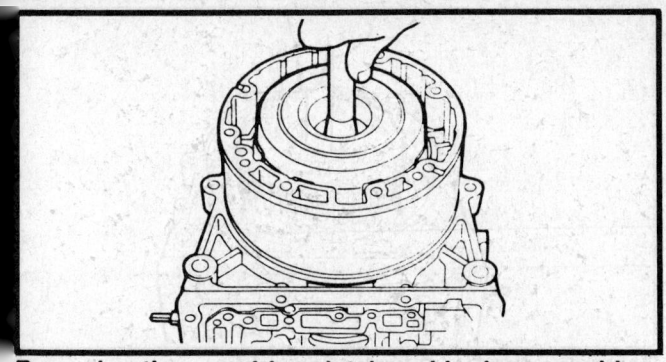

Removing the overdrive clutch and brake assembly

10. Slide the shaft out of the case and remove the detent plate.
11. Place the transmission on a suitable holding stand for more efficient work.
12. Position a suitable measuring tool on the overdrive case and measure the distance between the top of overdrive case and clutch cylinder. Make a note of the distance for reassembly.
13. Grasp the shaft and pull out the overdrive clutch assembly. Watch for bearings and races on both sides of the assembly.
14. Remove the overdrive case and brake as follows: Hold both sides of the overdrive case and pull it out from the transmission case. Watch for bearings and races on both sides of the assembly.
15. Position a suitable measuring tool in the case. Measure the distance between the top of case flange and the clutch drum. Make a note of the finding for reassembly.

FORWARD CLUTCH

Removal

1. After the overdrive unit has been removed, the forward clutch may be removed.
2. Grasp the shaft and pull out the forward clutch assembly. Remove the bearings and races on both sides of the assembly.

DIRECT CLUTCH

Removal

1. After the forward clutch has been removed the direct clutch may be removed.
2. Remove the direct clutch by grasping the clutch hub and pulling it out from the case.

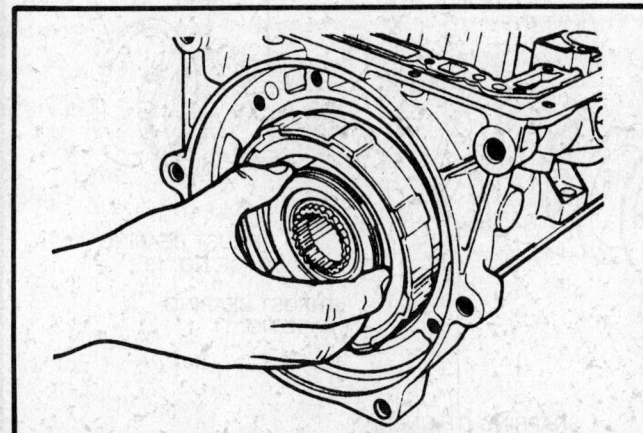

Removing the direct clutch

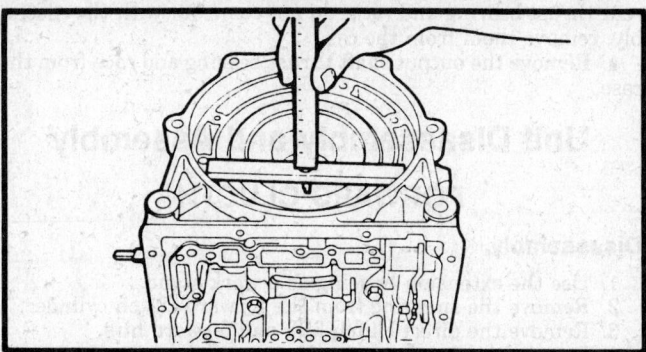

Measure the distance between the top of the case and the clutch drum

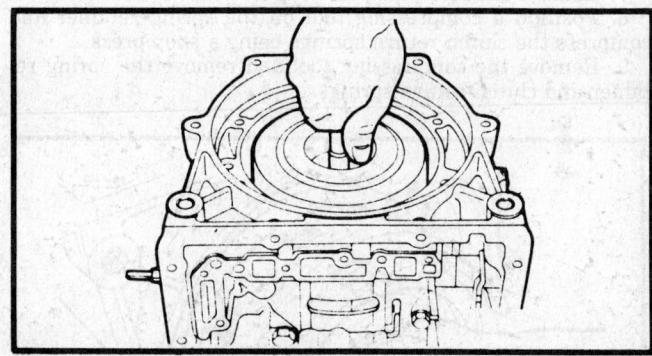

Removing the forward clutch

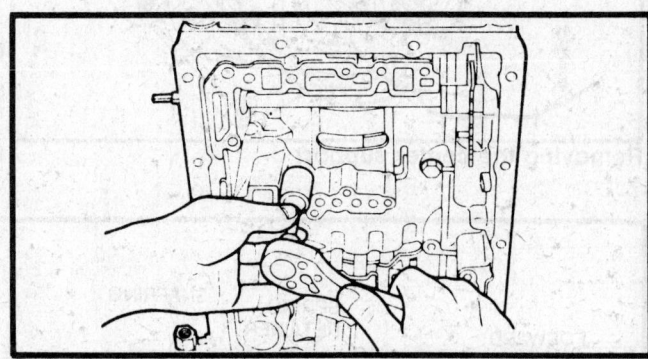

Removing the center support retaining bolts

CENTER SUPPORT

Removal

1. Remove the center support retaining bolts.
2. Grasp the center support assembly and pull out the center support with sun gear from the case.

NO. 3 BRAKE AND PLANETARY CARRIER

Removal

1. Remove the snapring in front of the planetary carrier.
2. Remove the reaction plate retaining ring using a suitable tool.
3. Remove the No. 3 brake and planetary carrier assembly by pulling out the intermediate shaft. If the brake apply tube and

rear thrust bearing and races do not come out with the assembly, remove them from the case.

4. Remove the output shaft thrust bearing and race from the case.

Unit Disassembly and Assembly

FORWARD CLUCTH

Disassembly

1. Use the extension housing as a work stand.
2. Remove the snapring from the forward clutch cylinder.
3. Remove the direct clutch hub and forward hub.
4. Remove the thrust bearing No. 12 and the races No. 11 and No. 13.
5. Remove the clutch disc.
6. Remove the snapring.
7. Remove the remaining clutch plates and discs.
8. Position a compressing tool on the spring retainer and compress the clutch return springs using a shop press.
9. Remove the compressing tool and remove the spring retainer and clutch return springs.

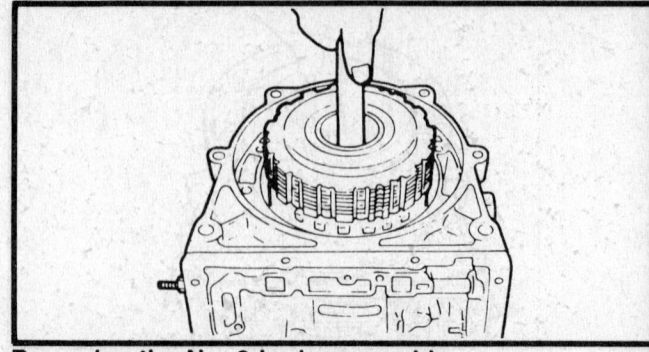
Removing the No. 3 brake assembly

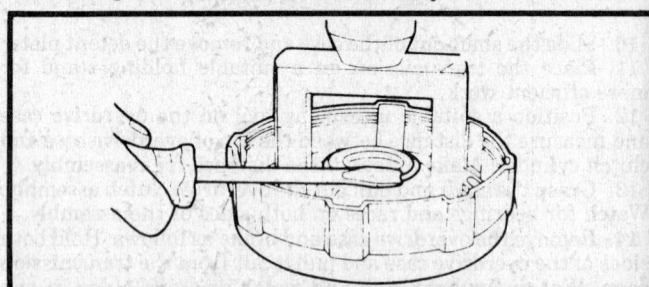
Compressing the clutch return springs

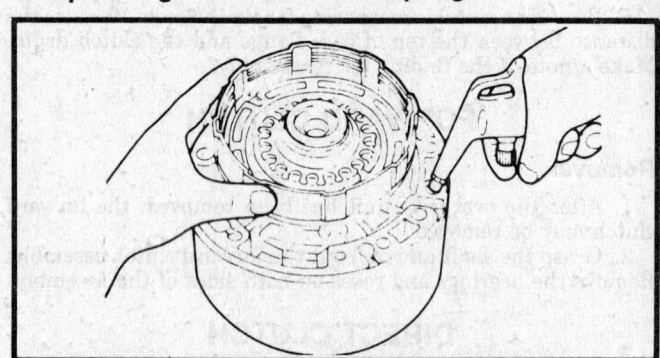
Removing the clutch piston with compressed air

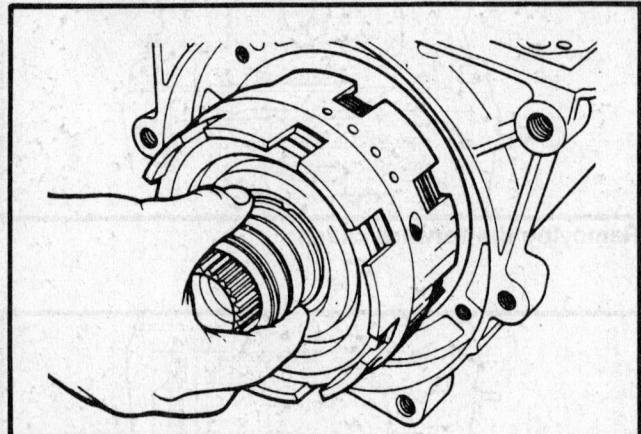
Removing the center support

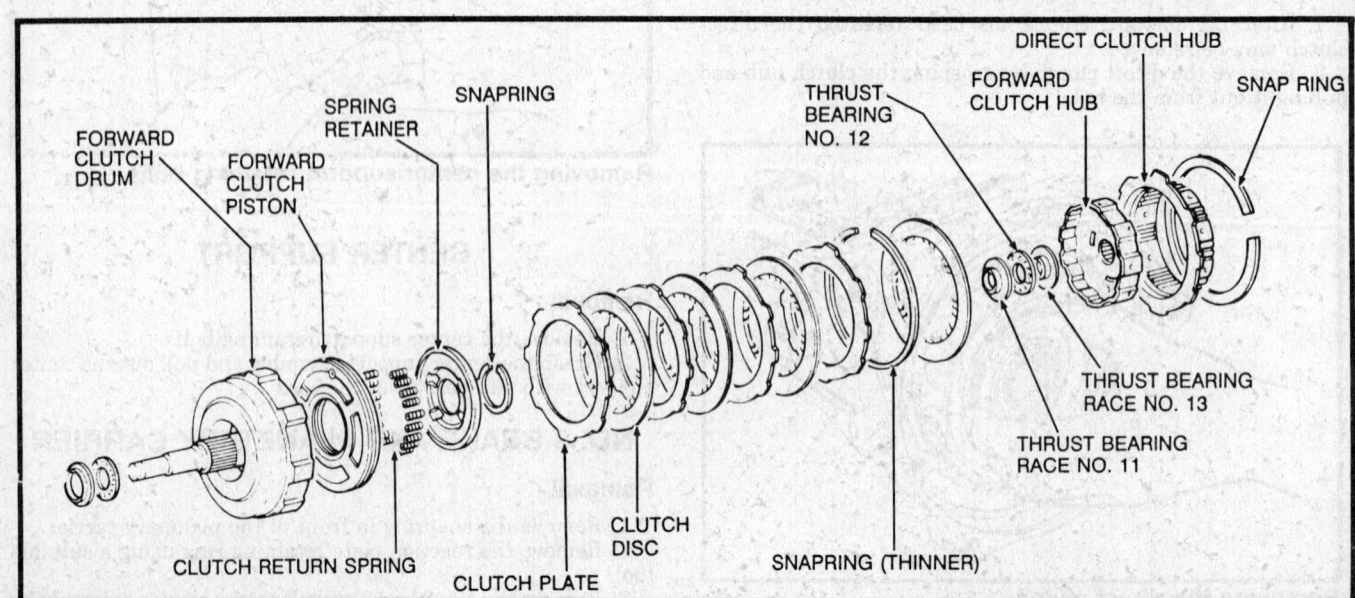

FORWARD CLUTCH DRUM

FORWARD CLUTCH PISTON

SPRING RETAINER

SNAPRING

THRUST BEARING NO. 12

FORWARD CLUTCH HUB

DIRECT CLUTCH HUB

SNAP RING

THRUST BEARING RACE NO. 13

THRUST BEARING RACE NO. 11

CLUTCH RETURN SPRING

CLUTCH PLATE

CLUTCH DISC

SNAPRING (THINNER)

Exploded view of the forward clutch assembly

10. Assemble the forward clutch cylinder and piston on the overdrive case and force out the piston by compressed air.

    a. Slide the forward clutch cylinder and piston onto the overdrive case.

    b. Apply compressed air to the overdrive case to remove the piston.

    c. Remove the forward clutch cylinder from the overdrive case.

11. Remove the O-rings from the forward clutch cylinder and piston.

Inspection

Wash the removed parts and dry with compressed air. Check the the following and replace faulty parts.

1. Check the input shaft and clutch cylinder for excessive wear and binding of thrust bearing contact surfaces. Check for damage of splines and for wear of the OD case seal ring contact surface.

2. Check the forward clutch cylinder for wear and damage of clutch drum teeth and for wear or binding of the piston sliding surface. Also, check for damage and binding of the thrust bearing seating surface.

3. Check the front clutch for abnormal wear and damage of teeth, splines and hub thrust surface.

4. Check the clutch disc and clutch plate for wear and binding of friction surfaces and from wear and damage from engagement with the cylinder and hub.

5. Check the clutch return spring for damage and cracks. Check for spring outside wear and deterioration.

6. Check the clutch piston for wear and damage of the surface in contact with the cylinders. Shake the piston to check if the check ball is binding or free. Also apply low pressure compressed air to the piston for air leaks.

7. Check the direct clutch for abnormal wear or damage.

NOTE: Prepare the new discs by soaking them at least 2 hours in clean ATF.

Assembly

1. Install new O-rings on the forward clutch piston and coat with clean ATF.

2. Press the forward clutch piston into forward clutch cylinder with the cup side up (check ball down). Be careful not to damage the O-rings.

3. Install the clutch return springs, spring retainer and snapring in place.

4. Compress the clutch return springs and install the spapring in the groove.

    a. Position the compressing tool on the spring retainer and compress the springs using a shop press.

    b. Install the snapring in place. Be sure the end gap of the snapring is not aligned with the spring retainer claw.

5. Install the clutch discs and plates without assembling the snapring.

NOTE: New clutch discs should be soaked in automatic transmission fluid for at least 2 hours before installation.

6. Using low pressure compressed air, blow all excess fluid from the discs.

——————— **CAUTION** ———————

High pressure air will damage discs.

7. Install the clutch plates and discs alternately. Do not install the snapring (thinner) at this time.

8. Check the piston stroke of the forward clutch.

    a. Install the direct clutch hub and snapring.

    b. Install the forward clutch cylinder assembly onto the

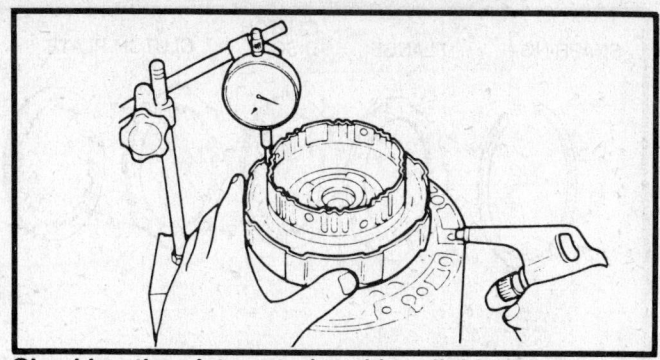

Checking the piston stroke with a dial indicator

overdrive case. Using a dial indicator, measure the stroke by applying and releasing the compressed air of 58–116 psi. (400–800 kPa). Standard stroke is 0.563–0.1154 in. (1.43–2.93mm). If the stroke exceeds the limit, the clutch discs and plates are probably worn. If the stroke is less than the limit, parts may be misassembled or there may be excess automatic transmission fluid on the discs.

    c. After the check, remove the snapring and direct clutch hub.

9. Compress and lower the snapring into the groove by hand. Check that the ends of the snapring are not aligned with any of the cutouts.

10. Install the clutch disc.

11. Install the thrust bearing No. 12 and the races No. 11 and No. 13, coat with petroleum jelly.

12. Install the forward clutch hub while aligning the disc lugs with the hub teeth. Make sure the hub meshes with all the discs and is fully inserted.

13. Install the direct clutch hub and snapring. Check that the snapring ends are not aligned with any of the cutouts.

DIRECT CLUTCH

Disassembly

1. Remove the snapring from the direct clutch cylinder.

2. Remove the flange, clutch discs and plates.

NOTE: Do not allow the clutch discs to dry out.

3. Position a compressing tool on the spring retainer and compress the piston return springs with a shop press. Remove the snapring.

4. Remove the spring retainer and piston return springs.

5. Assemble the direct clutch cylinder and piston set, on the center support and force out the piston by compressed air.

6. Side the direct clutch cylinder and piston set onto the center support.

7. Appy compressed air to the center support to remove the piston.

8. Remove the direct clutch from the center support.

9. Remove the O-rings from the direct clutch piston.

Inspection

Wash the removed parts and dry with compressed air. Check the the following and replace faulty parts.

1. Check the clutch cylinder for wear and damage to the grooves and piston sliding surfaces, thrust bearing surface and the seal ring sliding surface.

2. For inspection of the clutch disc, plate, piston and spring.

3. Check the clutch disc and clutch plate for wear and binding of friction surfaces and from wear and damage from engagement with the cylinder and hub.

4. Check the clutch return spring for damage and cracks. Also check for spring outside wear and deterioration.

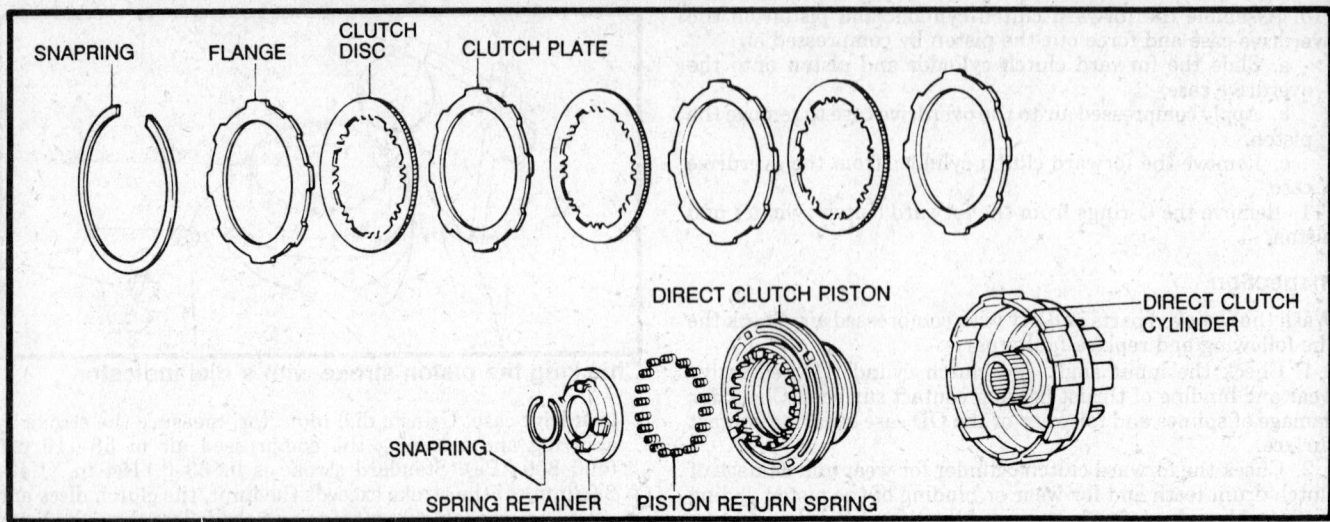

Exploded view of the direct clutch

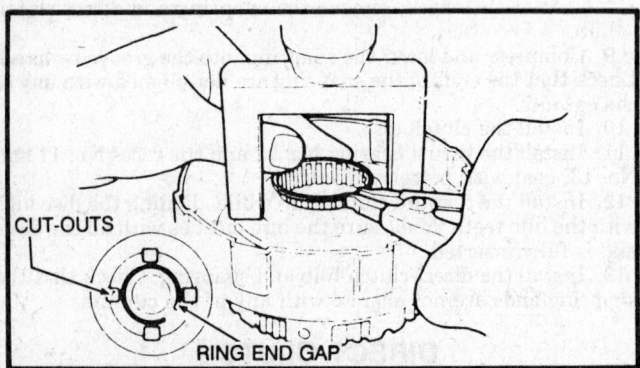

Compressing the direct clutch piston

5. Check the clutch piston for wear and damage of the surface in contact with the cylinders. Shake the piston to check if the check ball is binding or free. Also apply low pressure compressed air to the piston for air leaks.

6. Check the direct clutch for abnormal wear or damage.

Assembly

1. Install new O-rings on the direct clutch piston. Coat the O-rings with automatic transmission fluid.

2. Install the direct clutch piston in the direct clutch cylinder. Press the direct clutch piston into the cylinder with the cup side facing up, being careful not to damage the O-rings.

3. Install the piston return springs and set the retainer with the snapring in place.

4. Compress the piston return springs and install the snapring.

5. Position the compressing tool on the spring retainer and compress the springs using a shop press. Install the snapring. Be sure the end gap of the snapring is not aligned with the spring retainer claw.

6. Install the clutch discs, plates and flange.

NOTE: New clutch discs should be soaked in automatic transmission fluid for at least 2 hours before installation.

7. Using low pressure compressed air, blow all excess fluid from the clutch discs.

————— **CAUTION** —————

High pressure air will damage the discs.

8. Install the parts in the following order: clutch plate, clutch disc, clutch plate, clutch disc, flange (flat end facing down).

9. Install the snapring. Check that the snapring ends are not aligned with any of the cutouts.

10. Check the piston stroke of the direct clutch. Install the direct clutch onto the center support. Using a dial indicator, measure the stroke by applying and releasing the compressed air of 58–116 psi. (400–800 kPa). Standard stroke is 0.0358–0.0783 in. (0.91–1.99mm). If the stroke exceeds the limit, the clutch discs and/or plates are probably worn. If the stroke is less than the limit, parts may be misassembled or there may be excess automatic transmission fluid on the discs.

CENTER SUPPORT

Disassembly

1. Remove the snapring from the end of the planetary sun gear shaft.

2. Pull the center support assembly from the planetary sun gear.

3. Remove the snapring from the front of the center support assembly (No. 1 brake).

4. Remove the flange, clutch disc and plate No. 1 brake.

5. Position a compressing tool on the spring retainer and compress the springs with a shop press. Remove the snapring.

6. Remove the spring retainer and the brake return springs.

7. Blow compressed air through the center support oil hole to remove the No. 1 brake piston.

8. Remove the No. 1 brake piston O-rings.

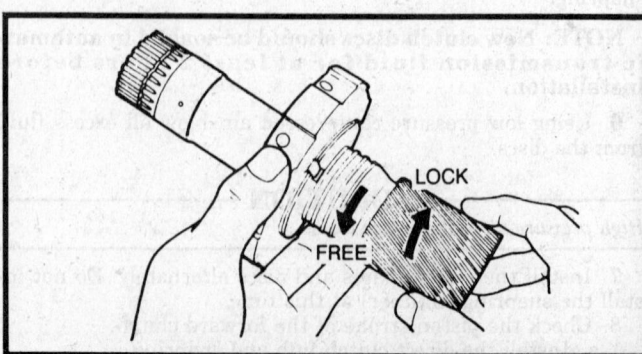

Checking the one-way clutch operation

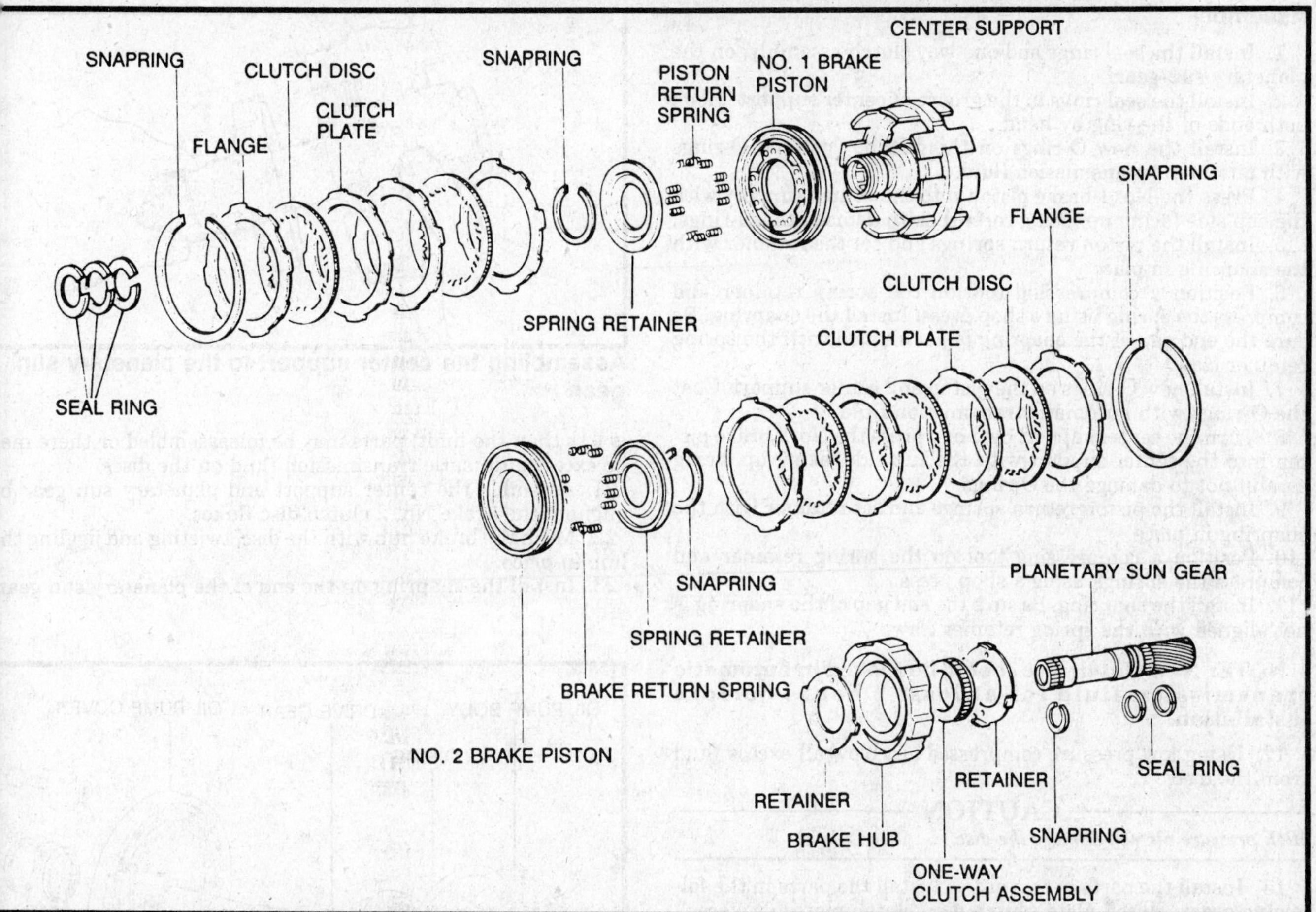

Exploded view of the center support

9. Turn the center support assembly over and remove the rear snapring (No. 2 brake).

10. Position the compressing tool on the spring retainer and compress the springs with a shop press. Remove the snapring.

11. Remove the spring retainer and the brake return springs.

12. Blow compressed through the center support oil hole to remove the No. 2 brake piston.

13. Remove the No. 2 brake piston O-rings.

14. Remove the oil seal rings from the center support.

15. Remove the one-way clutch assembly and oil seal rings from the planetary sun gear.

16. Inspect the one-way clutch assembly by holding the No. 2 brake hub and turn the planetary sun gear. The sun gear should turn freely counterclockwise and should lock clockwise. If the one-way clutch does not operate properly, replace it.

17. If it is necessary to replace the one-way, bend the tabs back with a tapered punch.

18. Pry off the retainer with a suitable tool. Leave the other retainer on the hub.

19. Remove the one-way clutch.

20. Install the one-way clutch into the brake hub facing the spring cage toward the front.

21. Hold the brake hub in a soft jawed vice and bend the tabs with a suitable tool.

22. Check to make sure that the retainer is centered.

Inspection

Wash the removed parts and dry with compressed air. Check the the following and replace faulty parts.

1. Check the center support for damage and deterioration of the seal rings, for abnormal wear and binding of bushin and ofr wear of clutch plate slots.

2. Check the brake piston for damage of its outside surface in contact with the center support cylinder.

3. Check the clutch disc and clutch plate for wear and binding of friction surfaces and from wear and damage from engagement with the cylinder and hub.

4. Check the clutch return spring for damage and crackes. Also check for spring outside wear and deterioration.

5. Check the clutch piston for wear and damage of the surface in contact with the cylinders. Shake the piston to check if the check ball is binding or free. Also apply low pressure compressed air to the piston for air leaks.

6. Check the direct clutch for abnormal wear or damage.

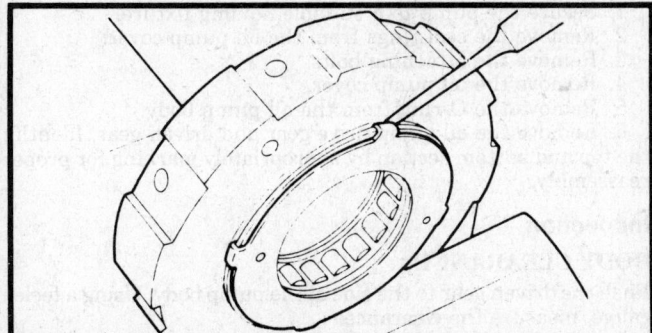

Removing the one-way clutch

Assembly

1. Install the seal rings and one-way clutch assembly, on the planetary sun gear.
2. Install the seal rings in the groove of center support. Hook both ends of the ring by hand.
3. Install the new O-rings on the piston. Coat the O-rings with automatic transmission fluid.
4. Press the No. 1 brake piston into the center support with the cup side facing up, being careful no to damage the O-rings.
5. Install the piston return springs and set the retainer with the snapring in place.
6. Position a compressing tool on the spring retainer and compress the spring using a shop press. Install the snapring. Be sure the end gap of the snapring is not aligned with the spring retainer claw.
7. Install new O-rings on the piston and center support. Coat the O-rings with automatic transmission fluid.
8. Turn the center support over and press the No. 2 brake piston into the center support with the cup side facing up, being careful not to damage the O-rings.
9. Install the piston return springs and set retainer with the snapring in place.
10. Position a compressing tool on the spring retainer and compress the springs using a shop press.
11. Install the snapring. Be sure the end gap of the snapring is not aligned with the spring retainer claw.

NOTE: New clutch disc should be soaked in automatic transmission fluid for at least 2 hours berfore installation.

12. Using low pressure compressed air, blow all excess fluid from the disc.

----- **CAUTION** -----
High pressure air will damage the disc.

13. Install the parts in this order: Install the parts in the following order: clutch plate, clutch disc, clutch plates (2 pieces), clutch disc, flange (rounded end facing down).
14. Install the snapring in the center support. Check that the snapring ends are not aligned with any of the cutouts.
15. Check the piston stroke of the No. 1 brake. Using a dial indicator, measure the stroke by applying and releasing the compressed air of 58–116 psi. (400–800 kPa). Standard stroke is 0.0315–0.0681 in. (0.80–1.73mm). If the stroke exceeds the limit, the clutch discs and/or plates are probably worn. If the stroke is less than the limit, parts may be misassembled or there may be excess automatic transmission fluid on the discs.
16. Turn the center support over and install the No. 2 brake, clutch plates, discs and flange.

NOTE: New clutch discs should be soaked in automatic transmission fluid for at least 2 hours before installation.

17. Using low pressure compressed air blow the excess fluid from the discs.

----- **CAUTION** -----
High presure air will damage the the disc.

18. Install the parts in the following order: Install the parts in the following order: clutch plate, clutch disc, clutch plate, clutch disc, clutch plate, clutch disc, flange.
19. Install the snapring in the center support. Check that the snapring ends are not aligned with any of the cutouts.
20. Check the piston stroke of the No. 2 brake. Using a dial indicator, measure the stroke by applying and releasing the compressed air of 58–116 psi. (400–800 kPa). Standard stroke is 0.0398–0.0896 in. (1.01–2.25mm). If the stroke exceeds the limit, the clutch discs and/or plates are probably worn. If the stroke

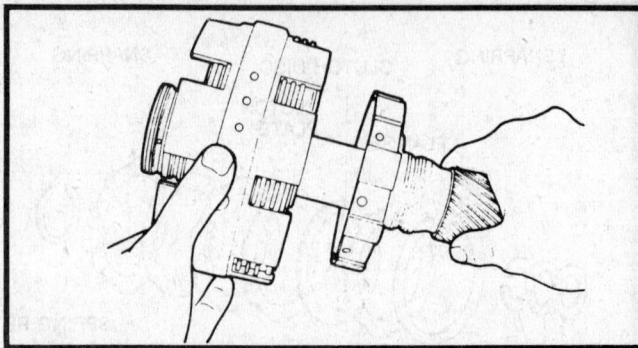

Assembling the center support to the planetary sun gear

is less than the limit, parts may be misassembled or there may be excess automatic transmission fluid on the discs.

21. Assemble the center support and planetary sun gear by aligning the brake No. 2 clutch disc flukes.
22. Mesh the brake hub with the disc, twisting and jiggling the hub in place.
23. Install the snapring on the end of the planetary sun gear.

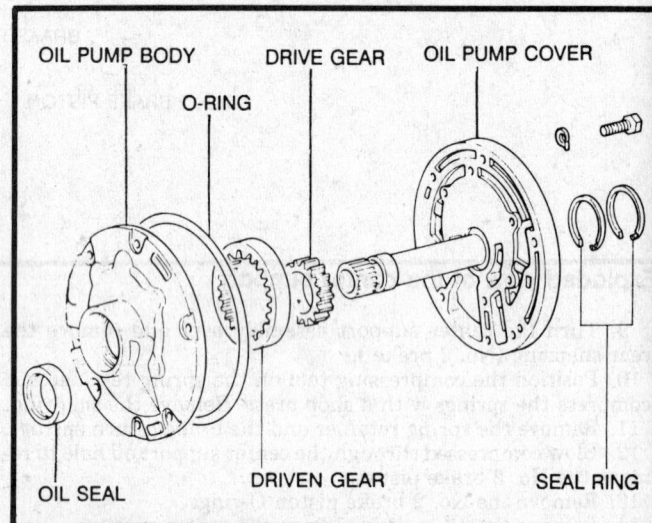

OIL PUMP BODY   DRIVE GEAR   OIL PUMP COVER
O-RING
OIL SEAL   DRIVEN GEAR   SEAL RING

Exploded view of the oil pump

OIL PUMP

Disassembly

1. Secure the pump in a suitable holding fixture.
2. Remove the seal rings from the oil pump cover.
3. Remove the attaching bolts.
4. Remove the oil pump cover.
5. Remove the O-ring from the oil pump body.
6. Remove the oil pump drive gear and driven gear. Identify the top and bottom section by appropriately marking for proper reassembly.

Inspection

BODY CLEARANCE

Push the driven gear to the side of the pump body. Using a feeler gauge, measure the clearance.
     Standard value: 0.003–0.006 in. (0.07–0.15mm).
     Limit: 0.012 in. (0.3mm).

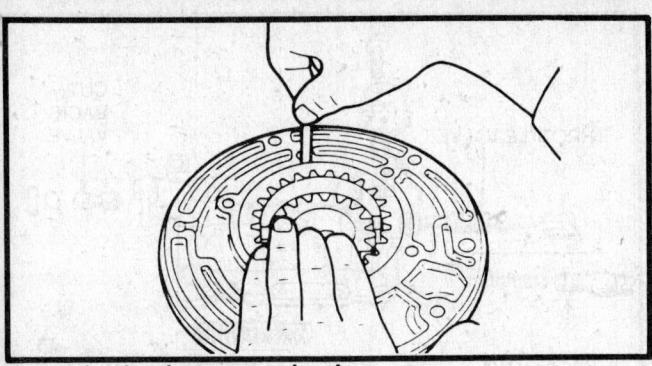

Pump body clearance check

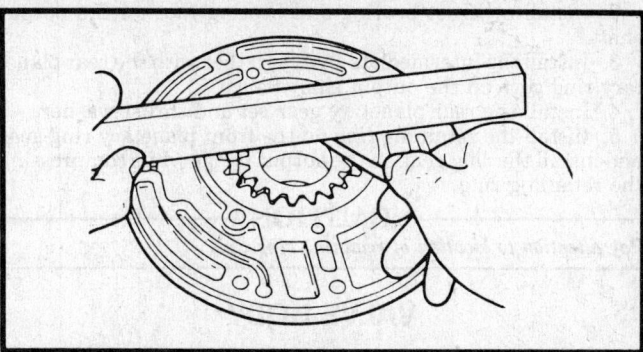

Pump side clearance check

TIP CLEARANCE

Measure the gap between the drive and driven gear teeth and the cresent-shaped part of pump body.

Standard value: 0.0043–0.0055 in. (0.11–0.14mm).

Limit: 0.012 in. (0.3mm).

SIDE CLEARANCE

Using a steel straightedge and a feeler gauge, measure the side clearance of drive and driven gears.

Standard value: 0.0008–0.0020 in. (0.02–0.05mm).

Limit: 0.004 in. (0.2 mm).

FRONT OIL SEAL

Check for wear, damage or cracks. If necessary, replace the oil seal by the following steps.

a. Pry the oil seal off using a suitable tool.

b. Install a new oil seal.

NOTE: The seal end should be flush with outer edge of pump body.

Assembly

1. Secure the pump in a suitable holding fixture.

2. Install the driven and drive gears on the oil pump body in correct directions according to the marks put during disassembly.

3. Install the oil pump cover on the body.

4. Align the bolt holes in cover with those in body. Install the attaching bolts with wave washers finger tight.

5. Install a pointed tool to align the body and cover.

6. Tighten the pump cover bolts to 4.5–6.5 ft. lbs. (6–8.5 Nm).

7. Remove the tool.

8. Install the seal rings on the pump cover by spreading apart and sliding them into the groove. Hook both ends by hand.

9. Install a new O-ring on the pump. Make sure the O-ring is not twisted and is fully seated in the groove.

REAR PLANAETARY UNIT

Disassembly

1. Loosen the retaining ring and remove the intermediate shaft (front planetary ring gear and rear planetary gear) from the output shaft assembly.

2. Remove the front planetary ring gear, thrust washer and rear planetary gear from the intermediate shaft.

3. Remove retaining ring from the rear of the intermediate shaft and remove rear planetary ring gear and thrust bearing.

Inspection

Wash the removed parts and dry with air. Check the following and replace faulty parts.

1. Check the front planetary ring gear for wear and damage of internal gear teeth and parking pawl teeth.

2. Check the intermediate shaft for wear and damage of the splines and bushing seating surfaces and for clogging of oil holes in the shaft.

3. Check the rear planetary gear for wear of the carrier thrust surface and for play in the thrust direction of the pinion.

4. Check the rear planetary ring gear for wear and damage of the internal gear teeth and internal splines.

5. Check the output shaft for wear and damage of flange thrust bearing surface and shaft bushing seating surface and for clogging of shaft oil hole and governor oil way.

6. Check the thrust washer and thrust race for wear and binding of the bearing surface.

7. Check the seal ring for wear and damage. Also check the groove.

Reassembly

1. Install a thrust bearing on the intermediate shaft and install the rear planetary ring gear and hold it in place with the retaining ring.

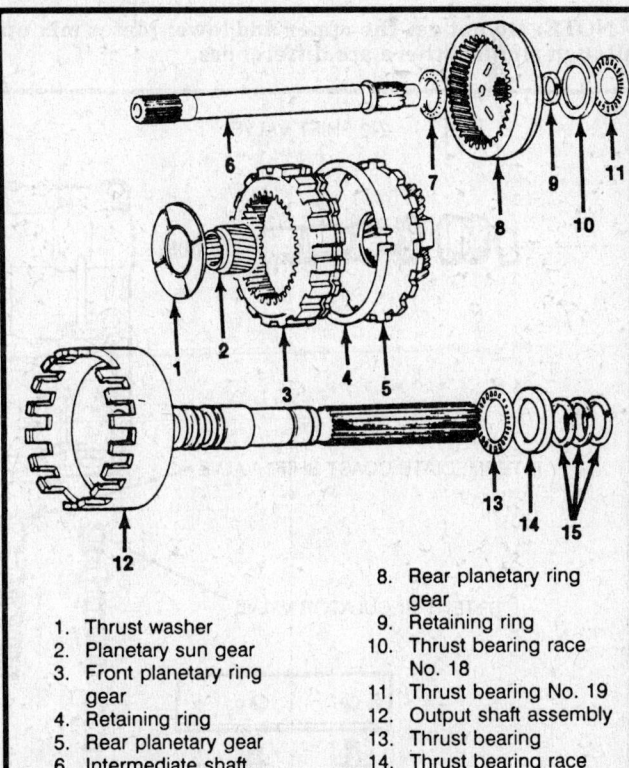

1. Thrust washer
2. Planetary sun gear
3. Front planetary ring gear
4. Retaining ring
5. Rear planetary gear
6. Intermediate shaft
7. Thrust bearing No. 17
8. Rear planetary ring gear
9. Retaining ring
10. Thrust bearing race No. 18
11. Thrust bearing No. 19
12. Output shaft assembly
13. Thrust bearing
14. Thrust bearing race
15. Seal ring

Exploded view of the planetary gear set

2. Install a thrust bearing and bearing race on the output shaft.

3. Install the intermediate shaft together with the rear planetary ring gear on the output shaft flange.

4. Install the rear planetary gear set and thrust washer.

5. Install the retaining ring on the front planetary ring gear and install the ring gear on the output flange while compressing the retaining ring.

CAUTION

Pay attention to location of retaining ring ends.

VALVE BODY

Disassembly

NOTE: Keep the disassembled parts orderly for efficient reassembly operation. Attach tags to springs for identification. When disassembling the valve, do not attempt to remove the valve with undue force. The valve and valve bore could be damaged or burred, leading to faulty valve operation. When removing the front upper and rear valve bodies from the lower valve body, use care not to lose check balls and springs.

1. Place the valve body assembly on a clean work bench.
2. Remove the manual valve.
3. Remove the lower valve body retaining bolts.
4. Turn the valve body upside down and remove the upper valve body retaining bolts.
5. Separate the lower valve body from the upper front valve body.
6. Remove the detent plate.
7. Remove the lower valve body from the rear upper valve body.
8. Remove the separator attaching bolts and remove the separator plate.

NOTE: Do not get the upper and lower plates mix up, altough similar, there are differences.

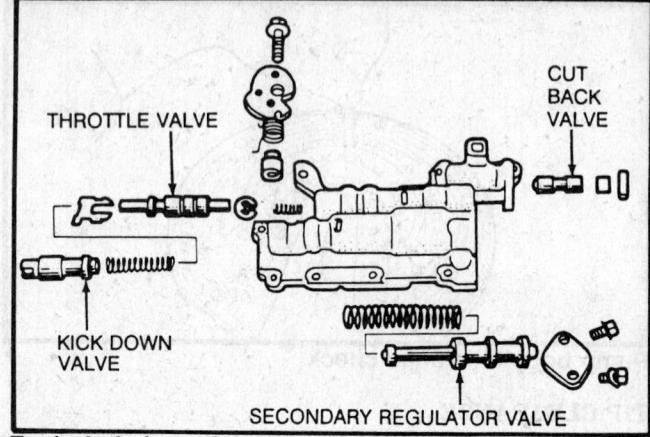

Exploded view of the upper front valve body and related components

9. Remove the lower valve body gasket from the lower valve body.

10. Remove the rubber check ball at this time and take note to its location.

11. Remove the cutback valve plug and remove the cutback valve and retainer.

12. Remove the throttle cam spring and cam from the upper front valve body. Take note to the spring location prior to removal.

13. Remove the kickdown valve, throttle valve primary spring, remove the key plate and E-rings, throttle secondary spring and the throttle valve. Note order of removal for correct installation later.

14. Remove front valve end cover and remove the secondary regulator valve spring and secondary valve from the front upper valve body.

15. Remove the lower valve body cover and gasket.

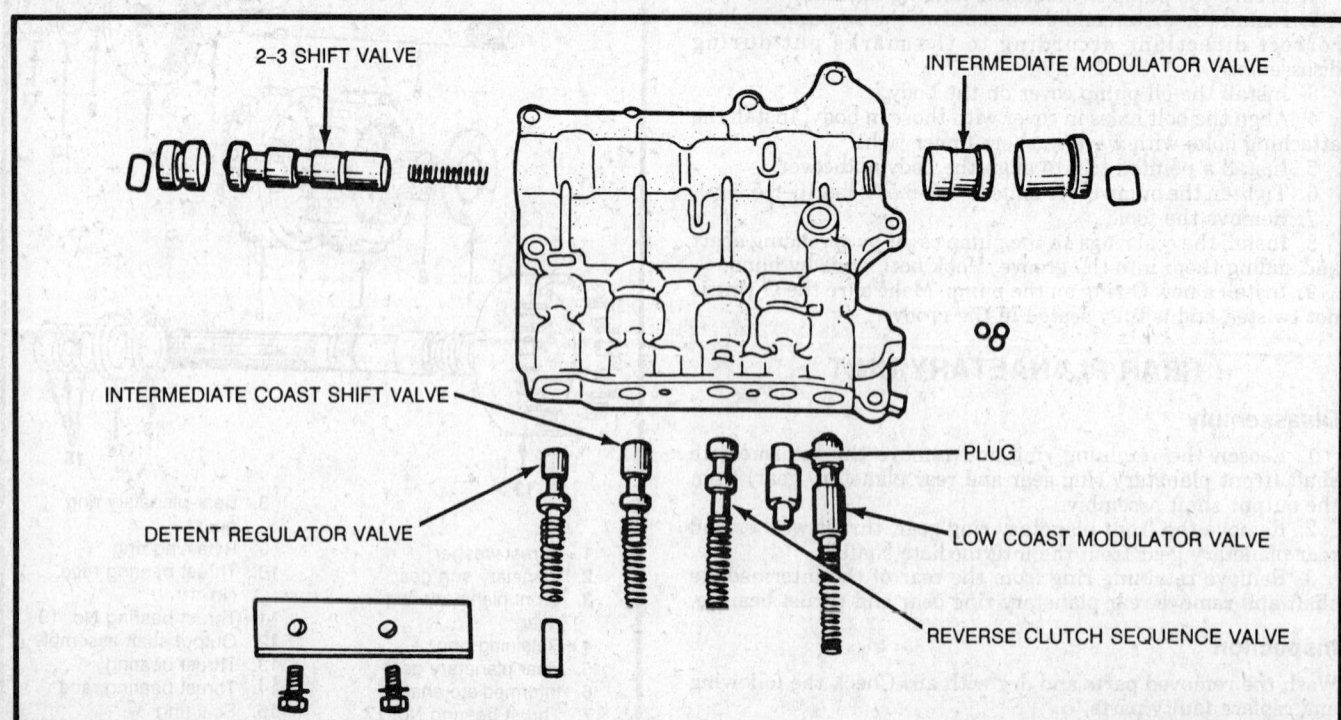

Exploded view of the upper rear valve body and related components

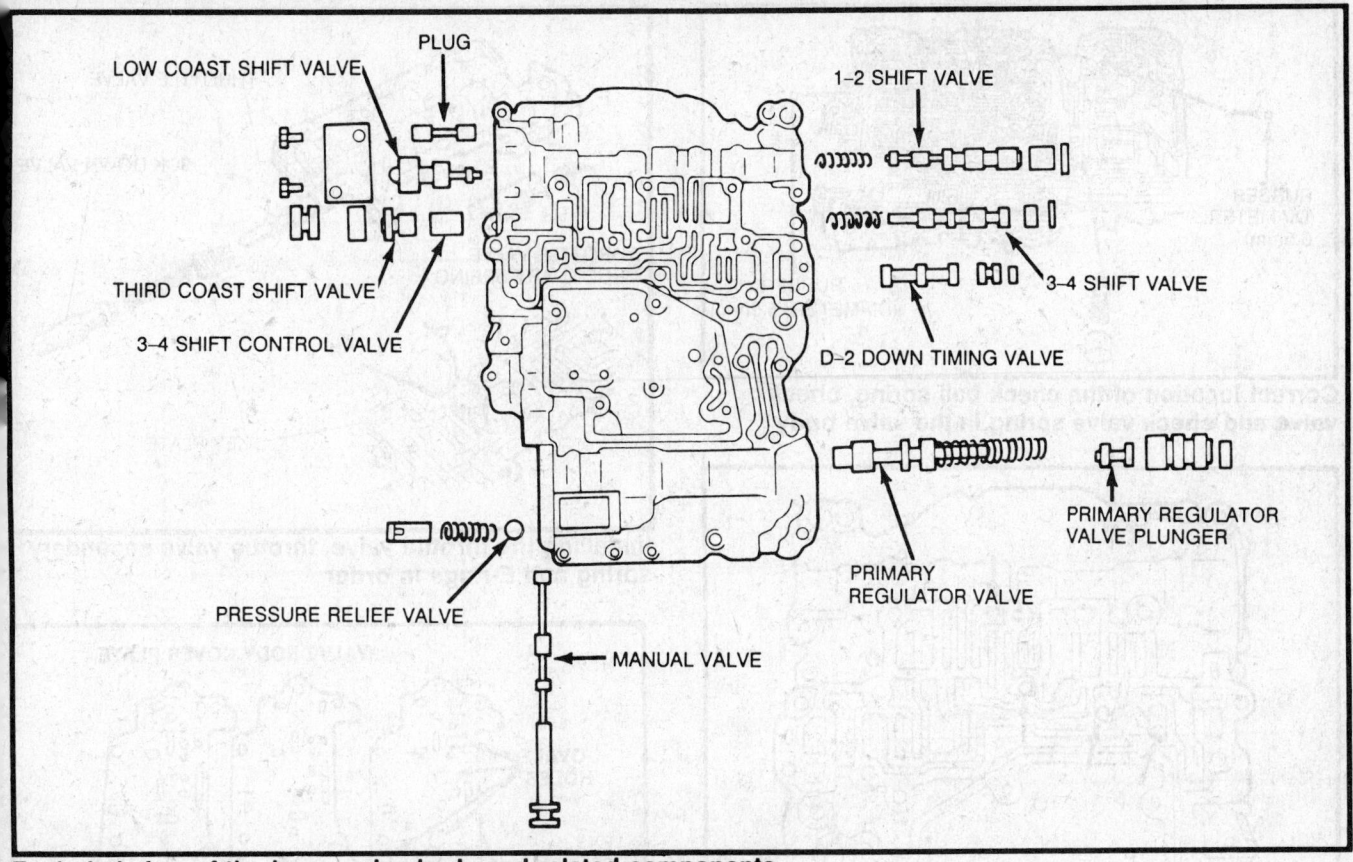

Exploded view of the lower valve body and related components

NOTE: Take particular notice in comparing the upper and lower gaskets at this time, the lower gasket has oval holes to accommodate the check balls. Do not get the upper and lower gaskets mix up.

16. Remove the rubber check balls at this time paying particular attention to the location of each ball.
17. Remove the rear valve cover and remove the valve springs, intermediate coast modulator valve, reverse brake sequence valve, plug and low coast modulator.
18. Remove the detent regulator valve, spring and retainer.
19. Remove the intermediate coast shift valve, plug and retainer.
20. Remove the 2–3 shift valve, spring, 2–3 shift valve plug and retainer from the upper rear valve body.
21. Remove the D–2 down timing valve, plug and seat.
22. Remove the 3–4 shift valve, spring, plug and locating pin.
23. Remove the check valve and check valve spring. Note location.
24. Remove the pressure relief valve, spring and retainer.
25. Remove the 1–2 shift valve spring, low coast shift valve, plug and low coast shift valve cover.
26. Remove the 1–2 shft valve, valve plug and insert retainer.
27. Remove the primary regulator valve retainer, primary regulator valve, spring, pluger and sleeve from the lower valve body.

INSPECTION

Wash the removed parts and dry with air. Then make the following checks.

—— **CAUTION** ——

When making checks, use care not to damage the valve land outside and valve body bores.

1. Check the valves for damage and wear.
2. Insert the valves in the valve body and check for smooth rotation and sliding.
3. Check for damage and wear of valve bores and for clogging of oil passages.
4. Check for damage or wear of the valve body plate and check balls.
5. Check for clogging of the oil strainer.
6. Check the springs and replace if broken or excessively deteriorated.

ASSEMBLY

—— **CAUTION** ——

Before reassembly, wash the parts in a clean detergent and dry with air. Do not wipe dry with rags. Entry of dust could cause faulty valve operation.

1. Install primary regulator valve, spring, plunger and sleeve in the lower valve body in order. Insert retainer to hold the valve in the valve body.
2. Install 1–2 shift valve, valve plug and insert retainer.
3. Install 1–2 shift valve spring, low coast shift valve, plug, and low coast shift valve cover.
4. Install pressure relief valve, spring and retainer.
5. Install spring, check valve and check valve spring at illustrated locations.
6. Install the spring, 3–4 shift valve, plug, and locating pin.
7. Install the D–2 down timing valve, plug, and seat.
8. Install 2–3 shift valve spring, 2–3 shift valve, 2–3 shift valve plug, and retainer in the upper rear valve body.
9. Install intermediate coast shift valve, plug and retainer.

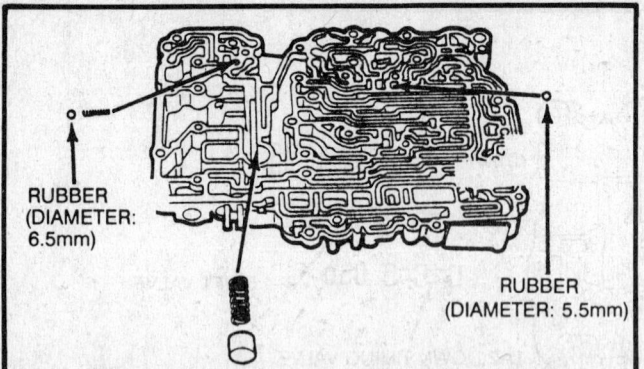

Correct location of the check ball spring, check valve and check valve spring in the valve body

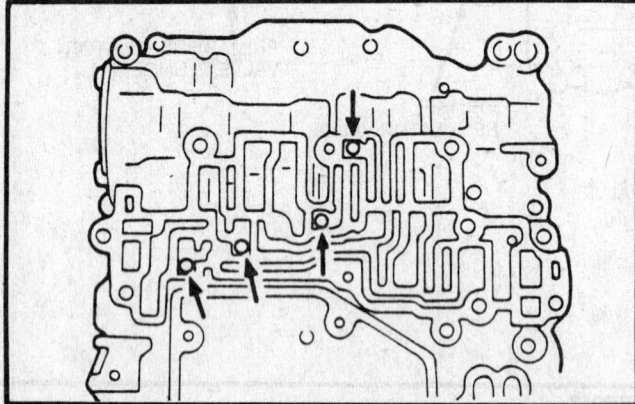

Correct location of the rubber check balls in the lower valve boby

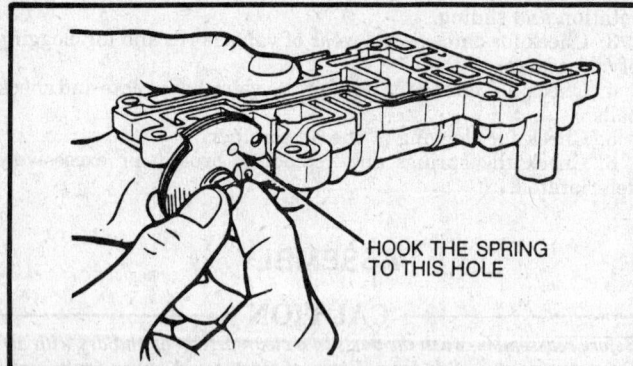

Installing the throttle and cam spring

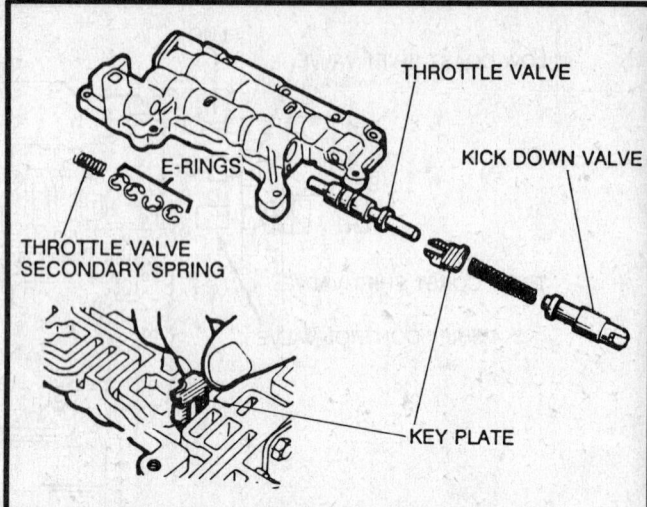

Installing the throttle valve, throttle valve secondary spring and E-rings in order

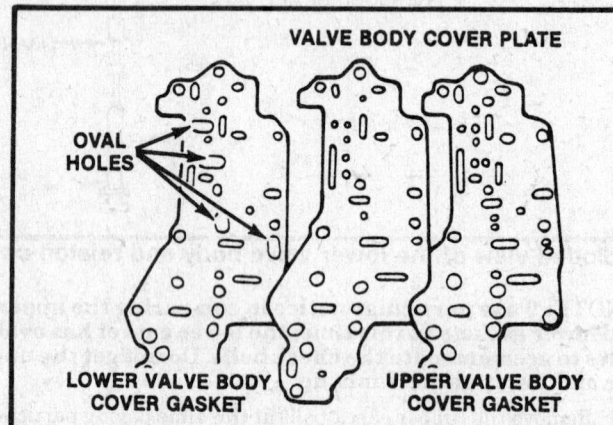

Oval hole location for check balls—lower valve body

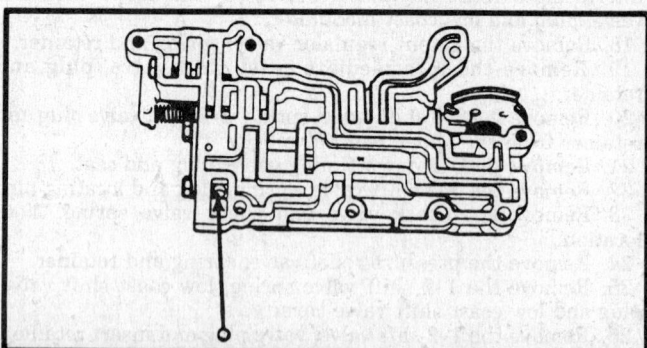

Install the rubber check ball in this location—lower front valve body

10. Install detent regulator valve, spring and retainer in that order.

11. Install low coast modulator valve, plug, reverse brake sequence valve and intermediate coast modulator valve.

12. Install valve springs.

13. Install rear valve cover.

14. Place the rubber check balls in the lower valve body at proper locations.

15. When installing the lower valve body cover, use the correct gasket. The lower valve body gasket is equipped with oval holes for the check balls.

16. Insert secondary regulator valve spring and the secondary regulator valve in the front upper valve body. Install front valve end cover.

17. Insert throttle valve, throttle valve secondary spring, E-rings, and key plate in the proper location. Install the throttle valve primary and kickdown valve.

—————— **CAUTION** ——————

Install the same number of E-rings as before disassembly for the correct throttle valve adjustment. Insertion of the throttle valve key plate at the incorrect location could cause faulty valve operation.

18. Install the throttle cam and spring on the upper front valve body and tighten the bolts temporarily. When installing, note the location of the spring end of the body side. Hook the other end of the spring to the cam and bolt the cam to the valve body. After installation, check that the throttle cam turns through a full stroke smoothly.

CAUTION

Hook the spring to the correct hole.

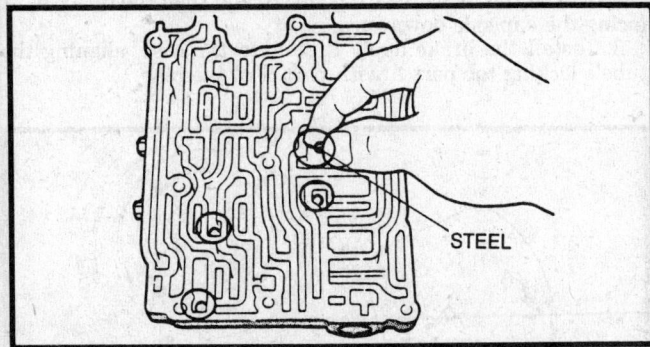

Steel check ball must be place in this location

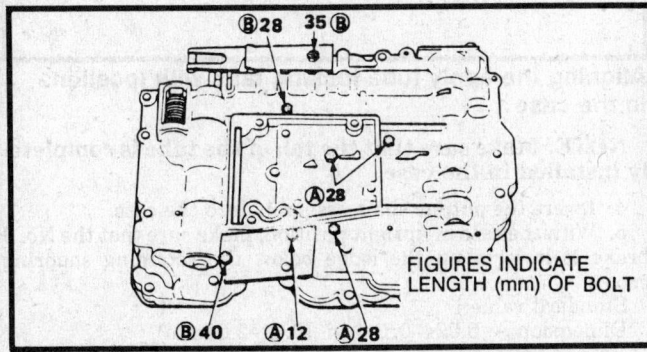

Tighting bolts indicated by A or B — lower valve body side

19. Install cutback valve, valve plug and retainer. Install the cutback plug with the larger land end facing out.
20. Install the rubber check ball in its location.
21. Place a new lower valve body gasket on the lower valve body.

CAUTION

Do not mix the upper and lower gaskets up, although similar, there are differences.

22. Install the separator plate and temporarily tighten the bolts.
23. Place a gasket for upper valve body, aligning with separator plate.
24. Install the steel check ball in its designated location. The 3 rubber check balls are identical and may be installed in any other location.
25. Install the lower valve body onto the rear upper valve body and temporarily tighten the bolts indicated by A. Be careful not to disturb the check valve position on the rear upper valve body.
26. Remove the 2 bolts previously tighten.
27. Install the lower valve body onto the rear upper valve body and temporarily tighten the bolts indicated by B.
28. Install the detent plate.
29. Install the lower valve body onto the upper front valve body and temporarily tighten the bolts indicated at the left of the lower valve body side.

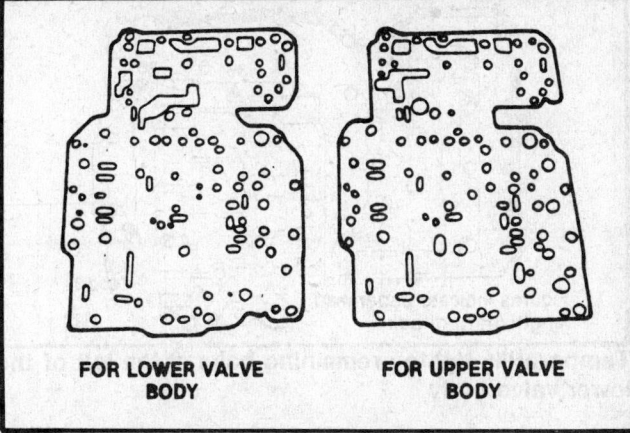

Upper and lower valve body gaskets

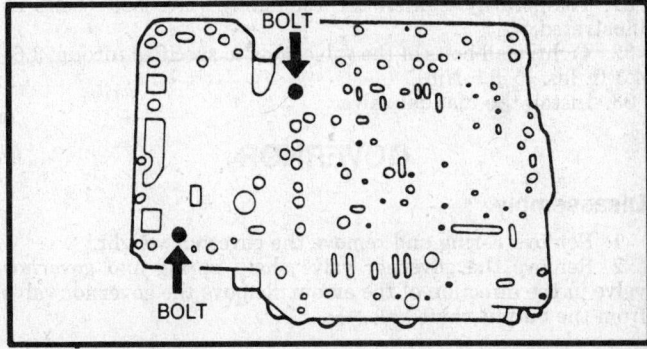

Separator plate

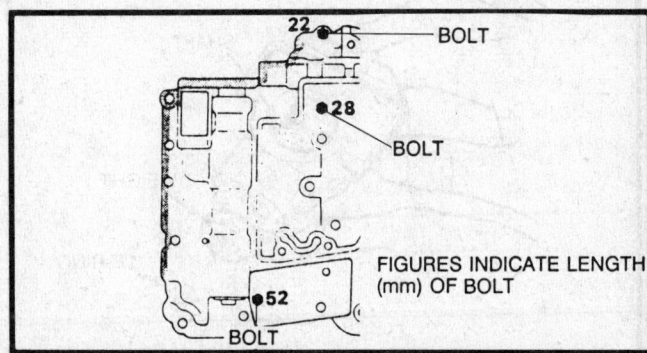

Tighten bolts indicated — upper valve body side

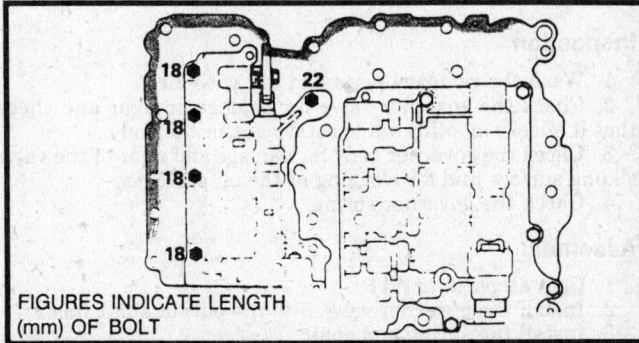

Tighten bolts indicated — upper valve body side

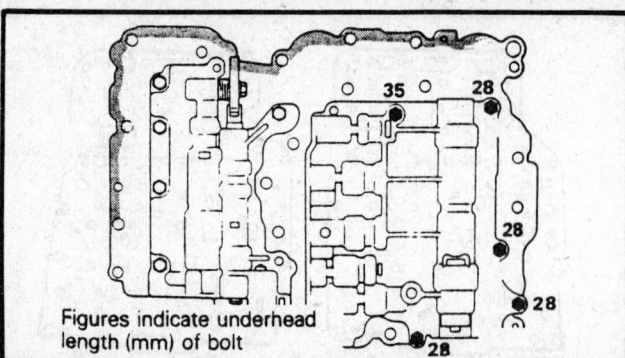

Temporarilly tighten remaining bolts at the left of the lower valve body

30. Turn the valve body upside down and temporarily tighten the indicated bolts from the upper valve body side.
31. Temporarily tighten the remaining valve body bolts as illustrated.
32. Tighten all bolts of the valve body to specified torque. 3.6–4.3 ft. lbs. (5–5.5 Nm).
33. Install the manual valve.

GOVERNOR

Disassembly

1. Remove E-ring and remove the governor weight.
2. Remove the governor valve shaft, spring and governor valve in the direction of the arrow. Remove the governor valve from the output shaft hole.

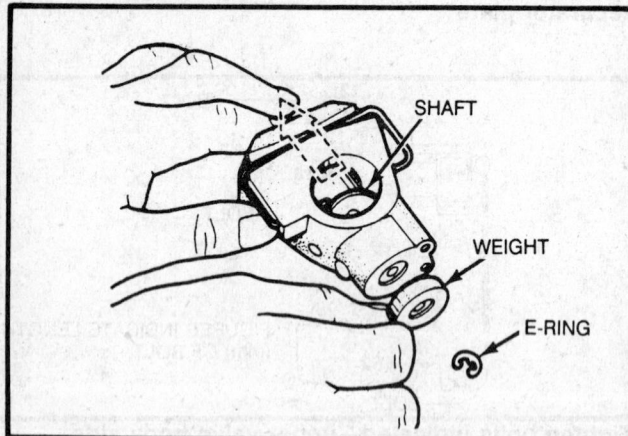

Governor

Inspection

1. Wash the removed parts and dry with air.
2. Check the governor valve for damage or wear and check that it slides smoothly while rotating it in the body.
3. Check the governor body for damage and wear of the valve sliding surface and for clogging of the oil passages.
4. Check the governor spring.

Assembly

1. Coat all parts in ATF.
2. Install the governor valve into the output shaft hole.
3. Install the spring and shaft.
4. Install the weight and E-ring.

Transmission Assembly

ASSEMBLY

NOTE: **Before assembly, make sure that all component assemblies are assembled correctly.**

1. Place the transmission in a suitable holding fixture for more efficient work. Place shock absorbing material between the case and holding fixture to prevent damage to the case.
2. Install the thrust bearing No. 20 and then the race No. 21 facing the cup side downward.
3. Install the brake apply tube onto the case, aligning the tube's locking tab part A with part B of the case.

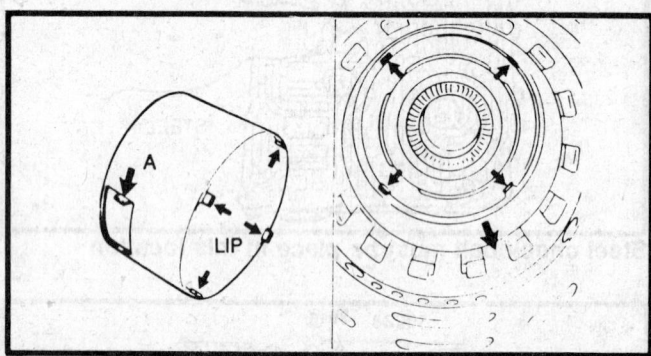

Aligning the apply tube locking tabs with locations in the case

NOTE: **Make sure that the tab of the tube is completely installed in the case.**

4. Insert the output shaft assembly into the case.
5. With the case in upright position, make sure that the No. 3 brake is lower than the ledge below the retaining snapring groove.
Standard value:
Dimension A: 0.024–0.104 in. (0.61–2.64mm).

NOTE: **If the the No. 3 brake is not lower than the ledge, components may be misassembled or there may be excess ATF between the disc and plate.**

6. Install the reaction plate positioning the notched tooth of the reaction plate toward the valve body side of the case. Push it into place.

NOTE: **The reaction plate is correctly installed if the retaining snapring groove is fully visible.**

7. Using a suitable tool, install the retaining snapring. Compress the snapring and push into place by hand. Work around

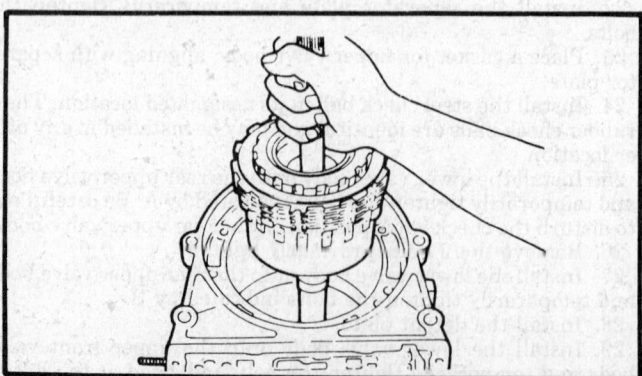

Installing the output shaft and assembly

the case. Visually check to make sure that the ring is fully seated. Make sure that the ends of the snapring are between the lugs.

8. Push the center support assembly into the case while aligning the oil hole and bolt hole of the center support with those of the body side.

9. Install the center support bolts with wave washers. Finger tighten the bolts.

10. Install the direct clutch in the case while turning the clutch to mesh its hub with the center support.

11. Check for correct installation of the direct clutch. If the direct clutch is fully meshed with the center support, the splined center of the clutch will be flush with the end of the planetary sun gear shaft.

12. After being coated with petroleum jelly, install the thrust bearing race No. 16 over the splined end of the direct clutch in case with its lip toward the direct clutch.

13. After being coated with petroleum jelly, install the thrust bearing No. 15 and race No. 14 on the forward clutch, with the race's lip outward.

14. Install the forward clutch assembly in the case by aligning the flukes of the direct clutch discs and mesh them with the forward clutch hub. Push the forward clutch assembly into the case.

--- CAUTION ---
Be careful not to allow the thrust bearing to drop out.

15. Check for proper installation of the forward clutch as follows:

  a. Position a suitable measuring tool on the transmission case.

  b. Measure the distance between the top surface of the tool and forward clutch assembly. If the distance corresponds to that during disassembly, the forward clutch is installed correctly.

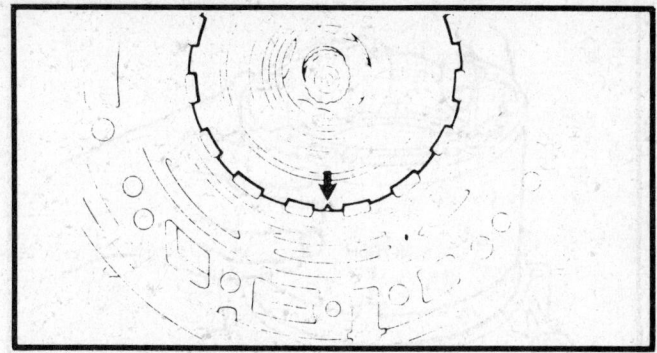

Reaction plate position

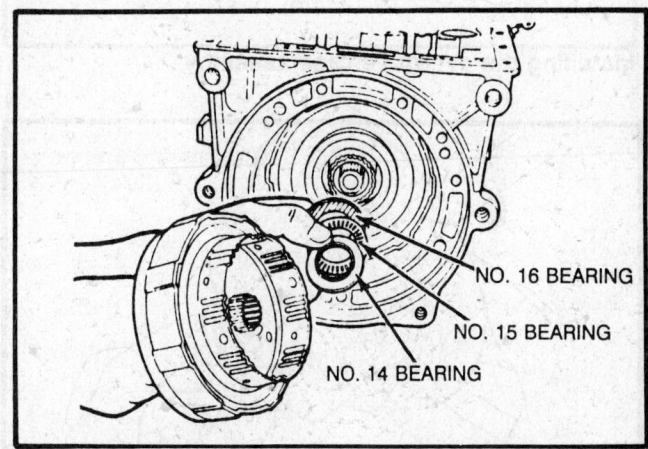

NO. 16 BEARING

NO. 15 BEARING

NO. 14 BEARING

Installing the No. 14, 15 and 16 thrust bearing

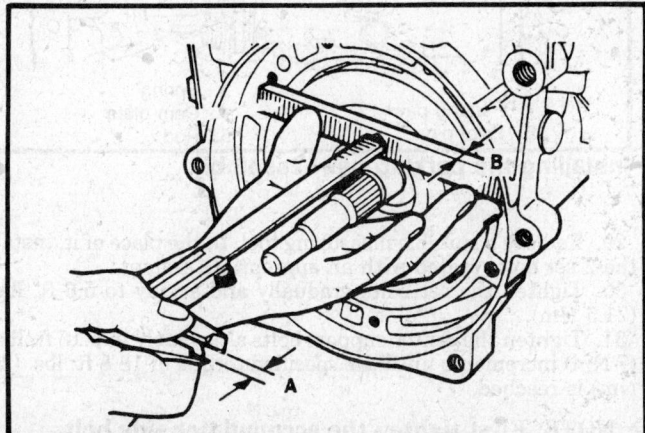

Checking the forward clutch installation height

16. Remove the measuring tool from the case.

17. After being coated with petroleum jelly, install the thrust bearing No. 10 on the forward clutch.

18. After being coated with petroleum jelly, install the thrust race No. 9 on the overdrive case end with its lip toward the overdrive case.

19. Insert the overdrive case gently into the transmission case through the guide pins with the part indicated by arrow facing in the direction shown.

20. Coat the thrust washers with petroleum jelly. Install the washers on the overdrive planetary gear.

NOTE: The washer lugs should be inserted in the holes.

21. Install the overdrive clutch in the case by aligning the disc flukes in the overdrive case. Align the flukes with the slots of the overdrive clutch and press the overdrive clutch into the overdrive case.

--- CAUTION ---
Be careful not to let the thrust washer drop.

22. Check for correct installation of the overdrive clutch as follows:

  a. Position a suitable measuring tool on the overdrive case.

  b. Measure the distance between the top surface of the tool and the overdrive clutch. If the distance corresponds to that during disassembly, the overdrive clutch is installed correctly.

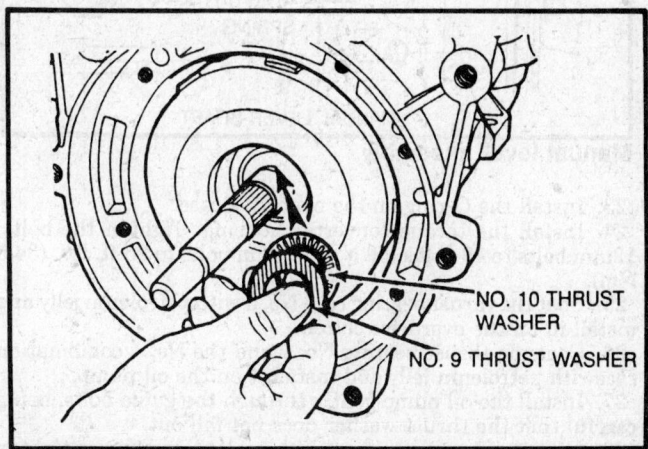

NO. 10 THRUST WASHER

NO. 9 THRUST WASHER

Installing thrust washers No. 9 and 10

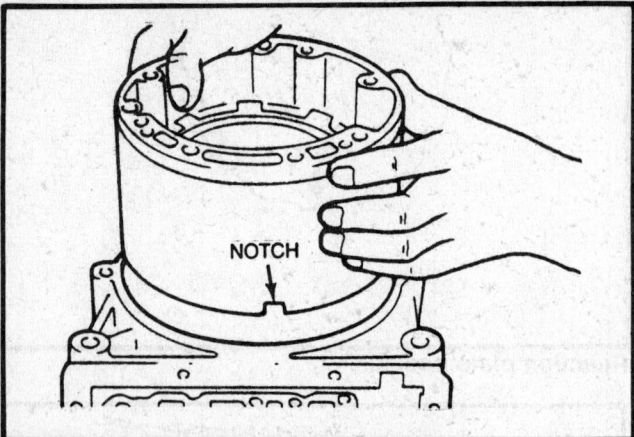

Installing the overdrive case assemby

Installing the thrush washer on the overdrive planetary gear

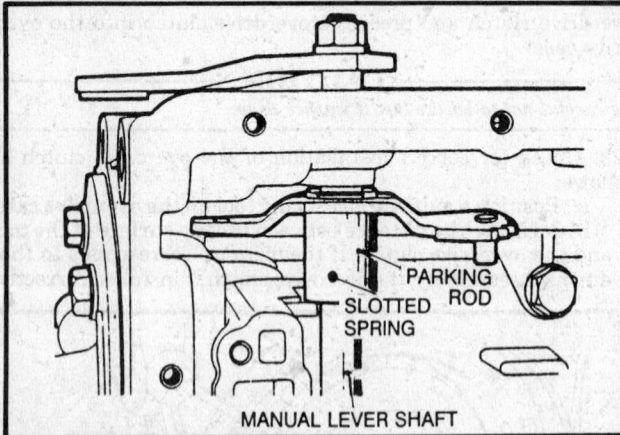

Manual lever assembly

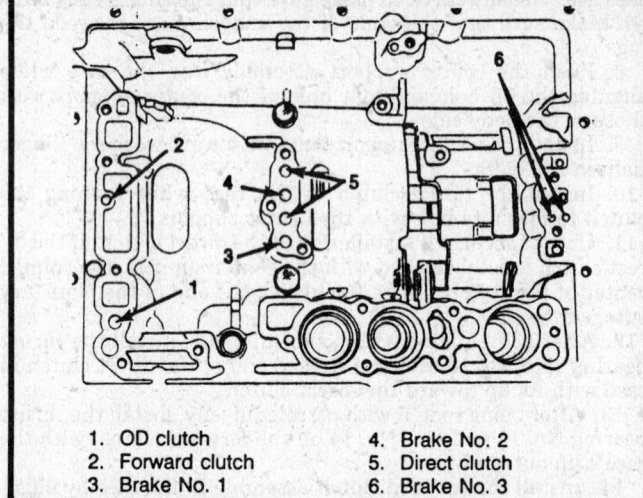

1. OD clutch	4. Brake No. 2
2. Forward clutch	5. Direct clutch
3. Brake No. 1	6. Brake No. 3

Appy low pressure air pressure to test clutch and brake operation

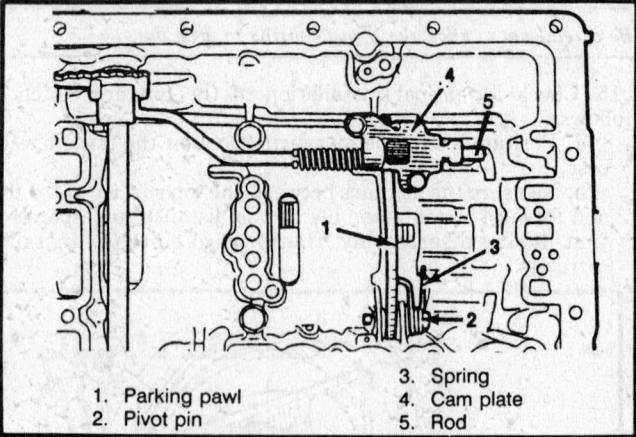

1. Parking pawl	3. Spring
2. Pivot pin	4. Cam plate
	5. Rod

Installing the parking pawl assembly

23. Install the O-ring on the overdrive case.
24. Install the torque converter housing. Tighten the bolts: 12mm bolts to 42 ft.lbs (58 Nm), 10mm bolts to 25 ft. lbs. (34.5 Nm).
25. Coat the thrust bearing race No. 3 with petroleum jelly and install in on the overdrive clutch.
26. Coat the thrust bearing No. 2 and the No. 1 combination racewith petroleum jelly and install it on the oil pump.
27. Install the oil pump gently through the guide bolts, being careful that the thrust washer does not fall out.
28. Coat the pump retaining with sealant and finger tighten them.

29. Remove a suitable measuring tool. In the place of it, install the 2 set bolts coated with an appropriate sealant.
30. Tighten the set bolts gradually and evenly to 5.6 ft. lbs. (21.5 Nm).
31. Tighten the center support bolts alternately in 5.16 ft. lbs. (7 Nm) increments until the specified torque of 18.8 ft. lbs. (26 Nm) is reached.

NOTE: First tighten the accumulator side bolt.

32. Check the operation of the pistons by appling low pressure compressed air into the passages indicated in the figure and listen for noise from piston movement.
   a. Overdrive clutch
   b. Overdrive brake
   c. Forward clutch
   d. Direct clutch
   e. Brake No. 1
   f. Brake No. 2
   g. Brake No. 3
If the pistons do not move, disassemble and inspect them.
33. Check the input shaft and output shaft:
   a. Make sure that the input shaft has play in axial direction and that it turns.
   b. Make sure that the output shaft has an appropriate endplay of: 0.012–0.035 in. (0.3–0.9mm).

34. Install the parking rod assembly on the manual valve lever and insert the manual shaft in transmission case.

35. Drive in a new slotted spring pin with the slot at a right angle to the shaft.

36. Install the parking pawl, pivot pin and spring in the case.

37. Install the cam plate on the case with the attaching bolts. Make sure that the parking rod protrudes from the cam plate. Tighten the bolts to 4.5–6.5 ft. lbs. (6–8.5 Nm). Make sure the pawl moves freely.

CAUTION

Be careful, as it is possible for the cam plate to be installed too far forward, where it will bind the pawl.

38. Check the operation of the parking lock pawl. The planetary gear output shaft must be locked when the manual valve lever is in the **P** range.

39. Install a new O-ring on the throttle cable.

40. Install the throttle cable in the case by pushing the cable through the case, being careful not to damage the O-ring. Check for full seating.

41. Install the accumulator piston and springs.

42. Place the valve body on the transmission as follows: Make sure the accumulator pistons are pressed fully into the bore. Align the manual valve with the pin on the manual valve lever, and lower valve body into place.

43. Lift a side of the valve body and attach the throttle cable.

44. Make sure that the lower spring is installed on the B^2 or C^2 piston.

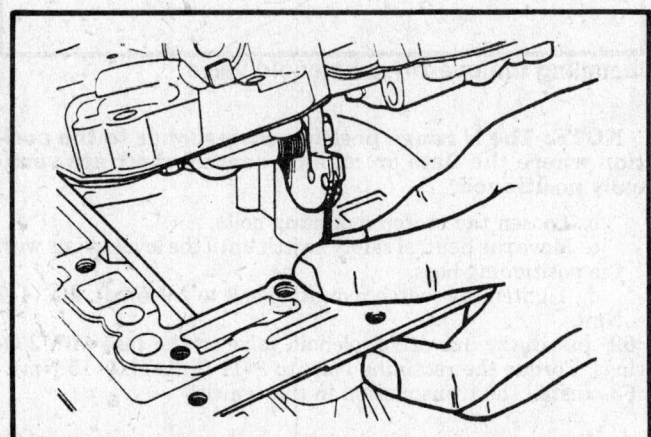

Connecting the throttle cable to the valve body

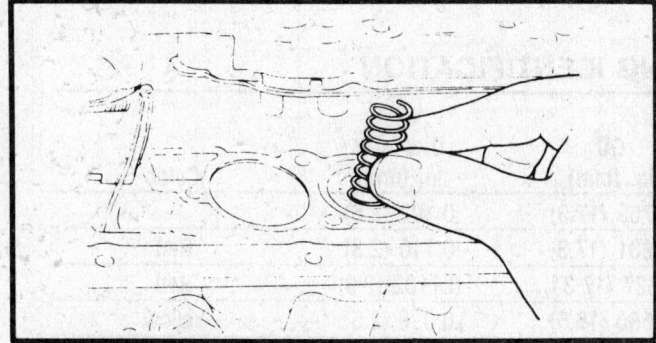

Installing the lower spring

45. Install the bolts in the valve body and tighten the bolts to 6–85 ft. lbs. (8–11 Nm).

46. Install the detent spring.

47. Install the oil strainer and tighten the bolts to 3.6–4.3 ft. lbs. (5–5.5 Nm).

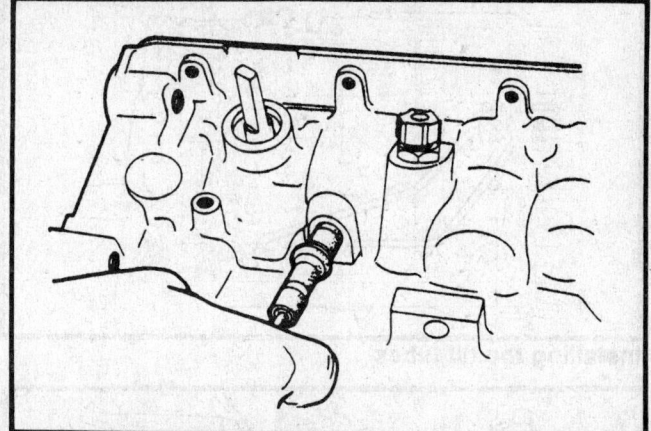

Installing the throttle cable

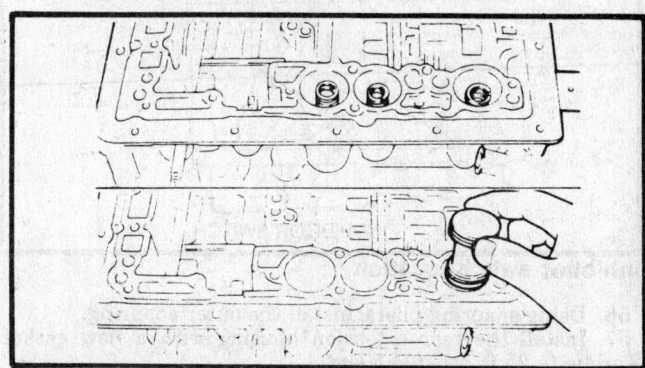

Installing the accumulator and springs

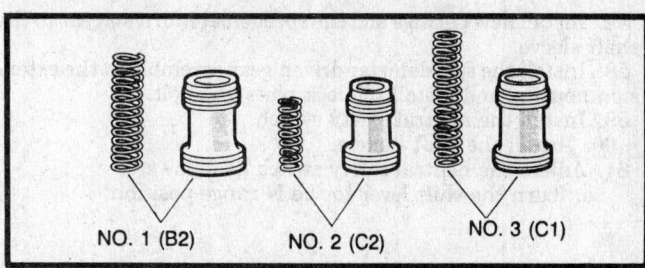

NO. 1 (B2)   NO. 2 (C2)   NO. 3 (C1)

Accumlator piston and spring identification

48. Using a plastic hammer, install the oil pipes into position.

CAUTION

Be careful not to bend or damage the pipes.

49. Install the magnet in the oil pan and install the oil pan with a new gasket. Torque pan retaining bolts to 3–3.5 ft. lbs. (4–4.5 Nm).

CAUTION

Make sure that the magnet does not interfere with the oil pipes.

50. Install the drain plug with a new gasket. Torque to 13–16 ft. lbs. (18–22 Nm).

51. Install the governor line strainer on the transmission case and then install the plate.

52. Install the governor and speedometer drive gear on the output shaft.

53. Install the lock plate and bolt and stake the lock plate.

54. Install the snapring and lock ball.

55. Slide the speedometer gear onto the shaft.

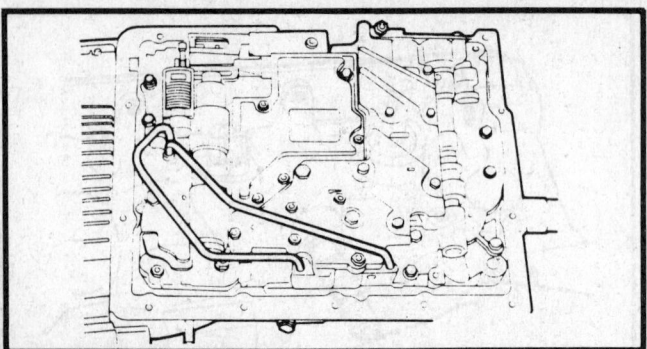

Installing the oil tubes

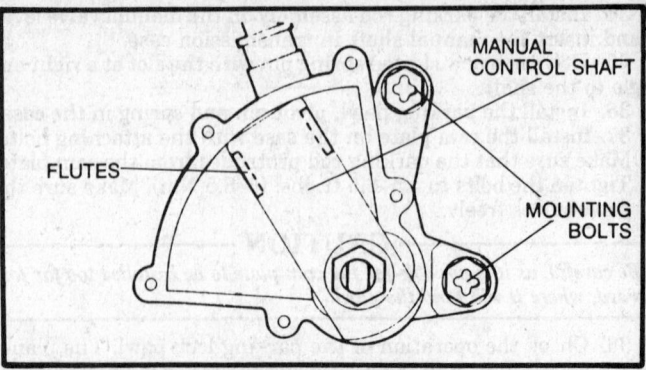

Inhibitor switch adjustment position

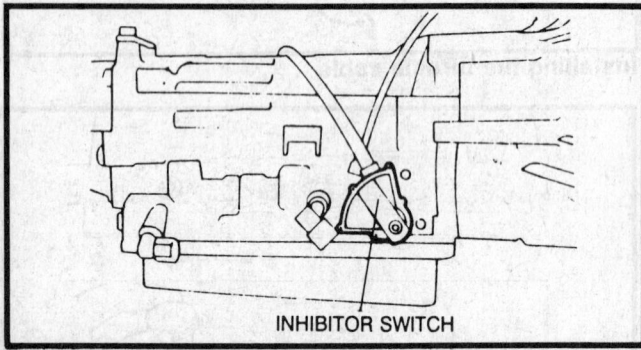

Inhibitor switch location

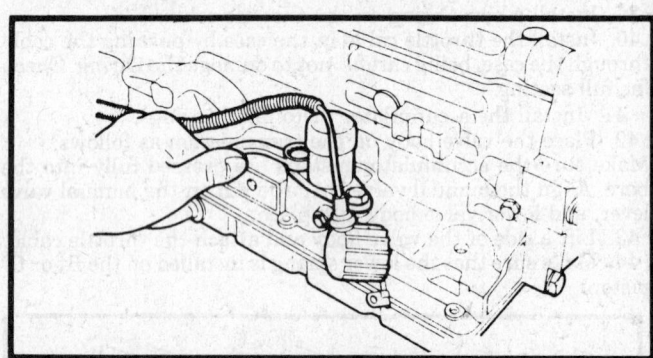

Installing the overdrive solenoid valve

56. Using snapring pliers, install the outer snapring.
57. Install the rear extension housing with a new gasket. Torque to 25 ft. lbs. (34.5 Nm).

NOTE: Do not use sealant on gasket.

54. Install new O-rings and the speedometer driven gear to the shaft sleeve.
58. Install the speedometer driven gear assembly in the extension housing and install the lock plate and bolt.
59. Install the neutral safety switch.
60. Install the shift handle.
61. Adjust the neutral safety switch as follows:
   a. Turn the shift lever to the **N** range position.

NOTE: The N range position corresponds to the position where the flats on manual control shaft are vertically positioned.

   b. Loosen the switch mounting bolts.
   c. Move the neutral safety switch until the lever aligns with the positioning boss.
   d. Tighten the switch mounting bolt to 2.9–5.1 ft. lbs. (4–7 Nm).
62. Install the overdrive solenoid valve on the case with 2 O-rings. Torque the retaining bolts to 8–11 ft. lbs. (10–15 Nm).
63. Install the transmission in the vehicle.

SPECIFICATIONS

ACCUMULATOR SPRING IDENTIFICATION

Spring	Engine (liters)	Free Length in. (mm)	OD in. (mm)	Wire Diameter in. (mm)	Color
B_2, No. 1	2.0	2.626 (66.7)	0.705 (17.9)	0.102 (2.6)	—
B_2, No. 1	2.6	2.626 (66.7)	0.681 (17.3)	0.110 (2.8)	Red
B_2	2.4	2.6252 (66.68)	0.627 (17.34)	0.1102 (2.8)	Red
C_2, No. 2	2.0	2.409 (61.2)	0.650 (16.5)	0.098 (2.5)	Yellow
C_2, No. 2	2.6	2.173 (55.2)	0.646 (16.4)	0.09 (2.3)	—
C_2, No. 1	2.4	1.2886 (32.73)	0.5827 (14.80)	0.512 (1.3)	Green
C_2, No. 2	2.4	1.7016 (43.22)	0.5449 (13.84)	0.0787 (2.0)	Red
C_1, No. 3	2.0, 2.6	2.547 (64.7)	0.689 (17.5)	0.079 (2.0)	—
C_1	2.4	2.5465 (64.88)	0.6890 (17.50)	0.787 (2.0)	—

ACCUMULATOR PISTON
IDENTIFICATION

Piston	OD in. (mm)	Length in. (mm)
B_2, No. 1	1370 (34.8)	1909 (48.5)
C_2, No. 2	1252 (31.8)	1772 (45)
C_1, No. 3	1252 (31.8)	1949 (49.5)

TORQUE SPECIFICATIONS
AW372L Transmission

Items	ft. lbs.	Nm
12mm torque converter housing	42.0	58
10mm torque converter housing	25.0	34.5
Extension housing	25.0	34.5
Oil pump	15.6	21.5
Center pump	18.8	26
Upper valve body to lower valve body	4.0	5.5
Valve body	7.2	10
Oil strainer	4.0	5.5
Oil pan	3.3	4.5
Oil drain plug	13–17	18–23
Oil pump cover bolt	5.4	7.5
Cooler pipe union nut	18.1	25
Testing plug	5.4	7.5
Parking lock pawl bracket	5.4	7.5
Inhibitor switch bolt	2.9–5.1	4–7
Selector handle installing screw	1.4 or more	2 or more
Shift lever shaft	13–17	18–24
Oil cooler tube flare nut	29–36	40–50
Oil cooler tube clamp	2–4	3–5
Oil cooler tube bracket	7–10	9–14
Propeller shaft installing bolt	36–43	50–60
Rear engine mount installing bolt	50–65	70–95
Exhaust pipe clamp bolt	14–22	20–30
Starter motor installing bolt	20–25	27–34
Torque converter installing bolt	25–30	35–42
Engine and transmission tightening bolt		
Bolts with 0.39 (10mm) outside dia.	31–40	43–55
Bolts with 0.31 (8mm) outside dia.	14–20	20–27

TORQUE SPECIFICATIONS
KM148 and AW372 Transmissions

Items	ft. lbs.	Nm
Converter housing attaching bolt		
10mm diameter bolt	20–30	27–41
12mm diameter bolt	35–49	47–66
Oil pump assembly attaching bolt	13–18	18–24
Oil pump body and cover tightening bolt	4.5–6.5	6–8.5
Center support attaching bolt	18–20	24–27
Adapter attaching bolt	20–30	27–41
Cover plate attaching screw	4.5–6.5	6–8.5
All bolts for valve body	3.6–4.3	5–5.5
Throttle cam attaching bolts	4.5–6.5	6–8.5
Valve body assembly attaching bolt	6–8.5	8–11
Oil screen attaching bolt	3.6–4.3	5–5.5
Parking cam plate attaching bolt	4.5–6.5	6–8.5
Oil pan attaching bolt	3–3.5	4–4.5
Union	15–21	20–29
Elbow connector	15–21	20–29
Plug for hydraulic test	4.5–6.5	6–8.5
Oil pan drain plug	13–16	18–22
OD solenoid valve attaching bolt	8–11	10–15
Plug	8–11	10–15
Manual lever attaching nut	11–13	14–17
Transmission mounting bolt	31–40	43–55
Exhaust pipe mounting bracket mounting bolt	15–20	20–27
Special bolt	25–30	35–42
Rear engine support insulator to transmission		
2WD	14–17	20–24
4WD	13–18	18–25
Bell housing cover mounting bolt	6–7	8–10
Exhaust clamp mounting bolt	14–21	20–30
Starter motor mounting bolt	16–23	22–32
No. 2 crossmenber mounting bolt		
2WD	29–36	40–50
4WD	40–54	55–75
Steering wheel lock nut	25–33	35–45

GENERAL SPECIFICATIONS

Items	AW372	KM148	AW372L
Torque converter type	3 elements, 1 stage, 2 phase	3 elements, 1 stage, 2 phase	3 element, 1 stage, 2 phase with a lock-up clutch
Stall torque ratio	1.96	1.96	2.26
One-way clutch	Sprag type	Sprag type	Sprag type
Transmission Type	Forward 4 stages Reverse 1 stage Single row planetary gear and Simpson planetary gear type	Forward 4 stages Reverse 1 stage Single row planetary gear and Simpson planetary gear type	Forward 4 stages Reverse 1 stage Single row planetary gear and Simpson planetary gear type

GENERAL SPECIFICATIONS

Items	AW372	KM148	AW372L
Control element			
Clutch	Multi disc type, 3 sets	Multi disc type, 3 sets	Mutli disc type, 3 sets
Brake	Multi disc type, 4 sets	Multi disc type, 4 sets	Multi disc type, 4 sets
One-way clutch	Sprag type, 3 sets	Sprag type, 3 sets	Sprag type, 3 sets
Gearbox ratio			
1st	2.826	2.826	2.828
2nd	1.493	1.493	1.493
3rd	1.000	1.000	1.000
4th	0.688	0.688	0.688
Reverse	2.703	2.703	2.703
Shift control method	Column shift type	Column shift type	Floor shift type
Select pattern	PRND2L and overdrive switch	PRND2L and overdrive switch	PRND2L and overdrive switch
Oil pump type	Gear type	Gear type	Gear type
Driving method	Directly connected to engine via torque converter	Directly connected to engine via torque converter	Directly connected to engine via torque converter
Hydraulic control method	Detection of throttle opening and vehicle speed	Detection of throttle opening and vehicle speed	Detection of throttle opening and vehicle speed
Oil cooling method	Water cooling type	Air and water cooling type (dual system)	Water cooling type
Transfer type	—	Constant mesh type	—
Shift control method	—	Single lever, floor shift type	—
Speed change ratio			
low	—	1.944	—
high	—	1.000	—
Speed meter gear ratio	—	22/8	—

COMPONENT SPECIFICATIONS

Items		Standard		Limit	
		in.	mm	in.	mm
Transmission control	Sleeve and selector lever end dimension	0.559–0.587	14.2–14.9	—	—
Oil pump	Side clearance	0.0008–0.0020	0.02–0.50	0.004	0.1
	Body clearance	0.0028–0.0058	0.07–0.15	0.012	0.3
	Tip clearance (driven gear)	0.0043–0.0055	0.11–0.14	0.012	0.3
Clutch and brake piston stroke	Overdrive clutch (C^0)	0.0614–0.0996	1.56–2.53	—	—
	Forward clutch (C^1)	0.0563–0.1154	1.43–2.93	—	—
	Direct clutch (C^2)	0.0358–0.783	0.91–1.99	—	—
	No. 1 brake (B^1)	0.0135–0.0681	0.80–1.73	—	—
	No. 2 brake (B^2)	0.0398–0.0886	1.01–2.25	—	—
Brake clearance	Overdrive brake (B^0)	0.0256–0.0870	0.65–2.21	—	—
	No. 3 brake (B^3)	0.0240–0.1309	0.61–2.64	—	—
Bushing bore	Stator support—front	0.8465–0.8475	21.501–21.527	0.8495	21.577
	Stator support—rear	0.9065–0.9075	23.025–23.501	0.9095	23.138
	Oil pump body	1.5005–1.5015	38.113–38.138	1.5035	38.188

COMPONENT SPECIFICATIONS

Items		Standard in.	Standard mm	Limit in.	Limit mm
Bushing bore	Overdrive sun gear (front and rear)	0.9080–0.9090	23.062–23.088	0.9109	23.138
	Overdrive input shaft	0.4409–0.4418	11.200–11.221	0.4437	11.271
	Sun gear (front and rear)	0.8465–0.8475	21.501–21.527	0.8495	21.577
	Center support	1.4325–1.4335	36.386–36.411	1.4355	36.461
	Transmission case	1.5005–1.5015	38.113–38.138	1.5035	38.188
	Output shaft	0.7087–0.7097	18.001–18.026	0.7117	18.076
	Extension housing	1.5605–1.5615	39.636–39.661	1.5634	39.711
Thermo switch	Continuity temperature	122°F	50°C	—	—
	Input shaft endplay	0.012–0.035	0.3–0.9	—	—
	Overdrive brake clearance	0.014–0.062	0.35–1.6	—	—
Overdrive clutch return spring	Free length	0.587	14.9	—	—
Overdrive brake return spring	Free length	0.634	16.1	—	—

VALVE BODY VALVE SPRING IDENTIFICATION

Valve Body	Springs	Outer Diameter in. (mm)	Free Length in. (mm)	Number of Turns	Wire Diameter in. (mm)	Identification color
Upper front	Spring for throttle valve	0.338 (8.58)	0.757 (19.24)	8	0.028 (0.71)	—
	Spring for kickdown valve	0.428 (10.87)	1.710 (43.44)	15.5	0.047 (1.20)	Orange
	Spring for secondary regulator valve	0.686 (17.43)	2.806 (71.21)	15	0.076 (1.93)	Green
Upper rear	Spring for intermediate modulator valve	0.356 (9.04)	1.073 (27.26)	9.5	0.043 (1.10)	Green
	Spring for sequence valve	0.367 (9.32)	1.327 (33.72)	13	0.052 (1.32)	Yellow
	Spring for low coast modulator valve	0.364 (9.24)	1.667 (42.35)	15	0.033 (0.84)	—
	Spring for 2–3 shift valve	0.353 (0.96)	1.382 (35.10)	12.5	0.030 (0.76)	White
	Spring for detent regulator valve	0.350 (8.90)	1.198 (30.43)	13	0.035 (0.90)	Green
Lower	Spring for 1–2 shift valve	0.298 (7.56)	1.363 (34.62)	13	0.022 (0.56)	—
	Spring for 3–4 shift valve	0.417 (10.60)	1.385 (35.18)	14.5	0.043 (1.10)	Green
	Spring for pressure relief valve	0.517 (13.14)	1.265 (32.14)	9	0.080 (2.03)	—
	Spring for check valve	0.544 (13.82)	1.312 (33.32)	7	0.052 (1.32)	Yellow
	Spring for primary regulator valve	0.677 (17.20)	2.409 (61.20)	13	0.071 (1.80)	White
	Spring for primary regulator valve damping	0.196 (4.97)	0.787 (20.00)	16	0.016 (0.40)	—

SPECIAL TOOLS

Tool (Number and name)	Use	Tool (Number and name)	Use
MD998218 Wrench 	Inspection of torque converter	MD998212 Oil pump puller 	Removal of oil pump
MD998219 Stopper 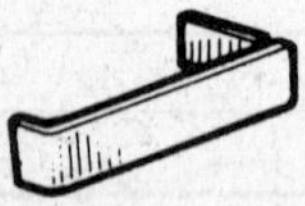	Inspection of torque converter	MD998412 Guide 	Installation of oil pump
MD999563 (includes MD998331) Oil pressure gage (1000 kPa) (142 psi) 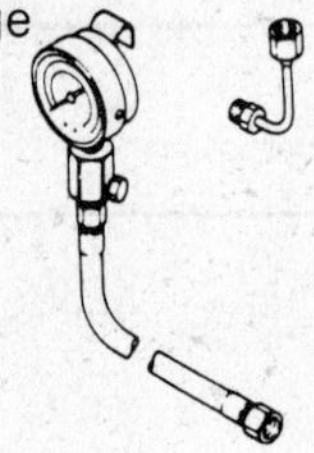	Measurement of oil pressure	MD998330 (includes MD998331) Oil pressure gage (3000 kPa) (427 psi) 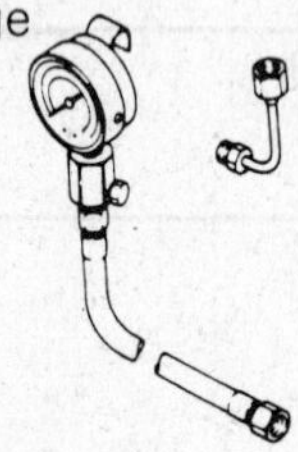	Measurement of oil pressure
MD998206 Adapter 	Connection of oil pressure gage	MD998903 Spring compressor 	Disassembly and assembly of clutch and brake
MD998335 Oil pump band 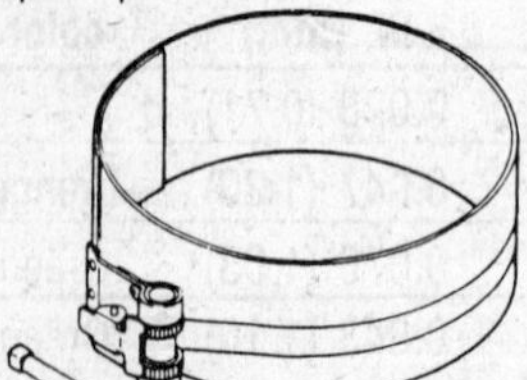	Assembly of oil pump	MD998353 Torque driver set 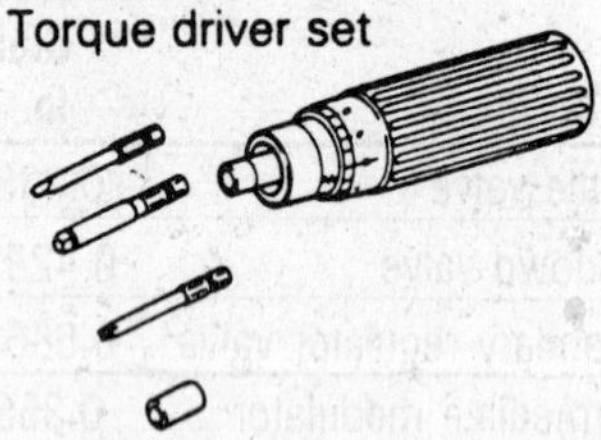	Tightening of valve body screw
MD998210 Bolt 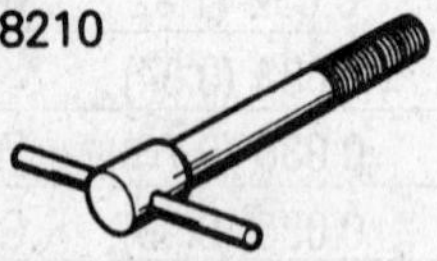	Disassembly and assembly of No.3 brake spring	MD998217 Gage 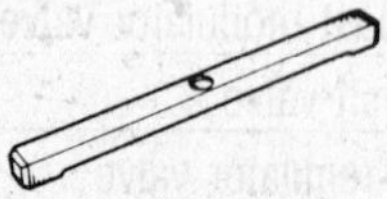	Check of quality of assembly condition
MD998211 Retainer 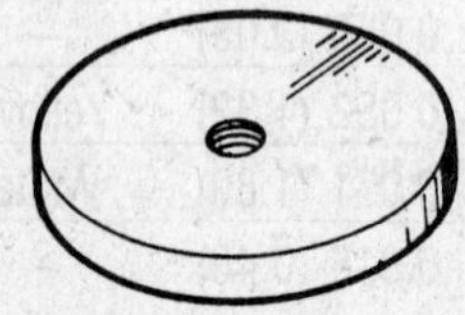	Disassembly and assembly of No.3 brake spring	DT-1001-A Steering wheel puller 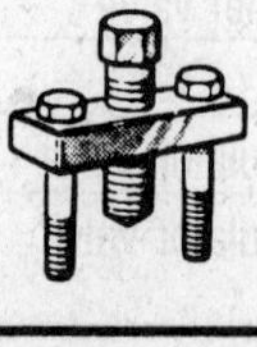	Removal of the steering wheel

Section 4

AOD Transmission
Ford Motor Co.

APPLICATION

AOD

Year	Engine	Vehicle
1984	5.0L (CFI)	Mustang/Capri
	3.8L (CFI)/5.0L (CFI)	LTD/Marquis
	3.8L (CFI)/5.0L (CFI)	Thunderbird/Cougar
	5.0L (CFI)	Mark VII/Continental
	5.0L (CFI)/5.8L (Carb.)	Crown Victoria/Grand Marquis
	5.0L (CFI)	Town Car
	5.0L (Carb.)	E-150/250
	5.0L (Carb.)	F-150/250 Pickup
1985–86	5.0L (CFI)/5/0L (EFI)	Mustang/Capri
	3.8L (CFI)/5.0L (CFI)	LTD/Marquis
	3.8L (CFI)/5.0L (EFI)	Thunderbird/Cougar
	5.0L (EFI)	Mark VII/Continental
	5.0L (EFI)/5.8L (Carb.)	Crown Victoria/Grand Marquis

Year	Engine	Vehicle
1985–86	5.0L (CFI)/5.0L (EFI)	Town Car
	5.0L (Carb.)	E-150/250
	5.0L (Carb.)	F-150/250 Pickup
1987	5.0L HO (EFI)	Mustang
	3.8L (CFI)/5.0L (EFI)	Thunderbird/Cougar
	5.0L (EFI)	Mark VII/Continental
	5.0L (EFI)/5.8L (Carb.)	Crown Victoria/Grand Marquis
	5.0L (EFI)	Town Car
1988–89	5.0L HO (EFI) -	Mustang
	3.8L (EFI)/5.0L (EFI)	Thunderbird/Cougar
	5.0L (EFI)	Mark VII
	5.0L (EFI)/5.8L (Carb.)	Crown Victoria/Grand Marquis
	5.0L (EFI)	Town Car

GENERAL DESCRIPTION

The automatic overdrive transmission (AOD) differs from conventional 3 speed transmissions in that the planetary gear set operates in 4th gear. The AOD provides fully automatic operation in either **D** or **OD** positions.

OD—this is the normal driving position for the AOD transmission. In this position the transmission starts in 1st gear and as the vehicle accelerates, it automatically upshifts to 2nd, 3rd and 4th gear. The transmission will automatically downshift as vehicle speed decreases.

NOTE: The transmission will not shift into or remain in overdrive when the accelerator is pushed to the floor.

D—in this position the transmission operates as in **OD** except that there will be no shift into the overdrive gear. This position may be used when driving up or down mountainous roads to provide better perfomance and engine breaking than the **OD** position. The transmission may be shifted from **D** to **OD** or **OD** to **D** at any time and at any speed, while in motion.

1 (LOW)—this position can be used when maximum engine braking is desired. To help brake the vehicle on hilly roads where **D** does not provide enough braking, shift the selector to **1** (LOW). At speeds above 25 mph, the transmission will shift to 2nd gear and remain in 2nd gear. When the vehicle speed drops below 25 mph, the transmission will shift to 1st gear and remain in 1st gear.

Forced downshifts—at vehicle speeds from 55–25 mph in **OD** or **D**, the transmission will downshift to 2nd gear when the accelerator is pushed to the floor. At vehicle speeds below 25 mph, the transmission will downshift to 1st gear when the accelerator is pushed to the floor. At most vehicle speeds in **OD**, the transmission will downshift from 4th to 3rd gear when the accelerator is pushed for moderate to heavy acceleration.

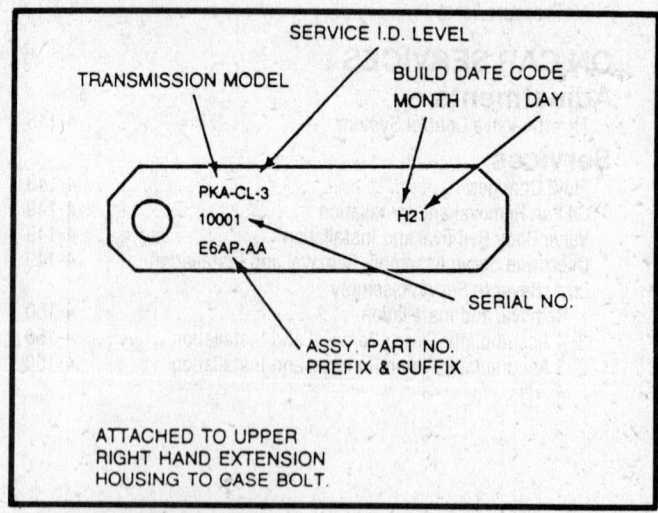

AOD identification tag

Transmission and Converter Identification

TRANSMISSION

The AOD automatic transmission is identified by the letter **T** stamped on the vehicle certification label, mounted on the left

TORQUE CONVERTER APPLICATION

Vehicle Application	Engine Disp.	Trans. Type	Converter Size	Stall Speed (RPM) Min.	Stall Speed (RPM) Max.
Thunderbird/Cougar	3.8L CFI 2V	AOD	12"	2082	2409
Mustang	5.0L (HO) SEFI	AOD	12"	2066	2457
Ford Crown Victoria/ Mercury Grand Marquis	5.0L SEFI	AOD	12"	2062	2400
Lincoln Town Car	5.0L SEFI	AOD	12"	2061	2399
Continental/Mark	5.0L SEFI	AOD	12"	2032	2446
Thunderbird/Cougar/ Mark VII LSC	5.0L SEFI	AOD	12"	2032	2346
Ford Crown Victoria/ Mercury Grand Marquis	5.8L (HO)	AOD	12"	1543	1857

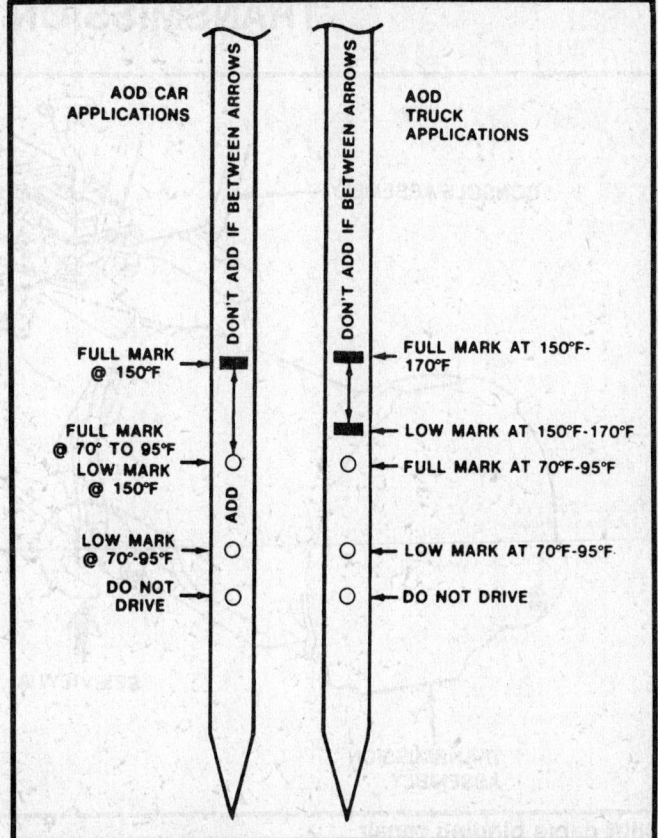

Fluid level dipstick

driver's door body pillar post. The identification tag is located on one of the extension housing bolts. The identification tag indicates the model code, the part number prefix, build code and transmission serial number.

CONVERTER

The AOD torque converter is identified by either a reference or part number stamped on the converter body and is matched to a specific engine. The torque converter is a welded unit and is not repairable. If internal problems exists, the torque converter must be replaced.

Metric Fasteners

Metric bolts and nuts are used in the construction of the transmission, along with the familiar inch system fasteners. The dimensions of both systems are very close and for this reason, replacement fastener must have the same measurement and strength as those removed. Do not attempt to interchange metric fasteners for inch system fasteners. Mismatched or incorrect fasteners can result in damage to the transmission unit through malfunctions, breakage or personal injury. Care should be exercised to replace the fasteners in the same locations as removed.

Capacities

Only Motorcraft Dexron®II or equivalent fluid, meeting Ford Motor Co.'s specifications ESP-M2C1-166HP, should be used in the AOD transmission. Failure to use the proper fluid could result in internal transmission damage. The pan capacity is approximately 4 quarts. The total overhaul capacity is 12 quarts.

Checking Fluid Level

The AOD transmission is designed to operate with the fluid level between the **ADD** and **FULL** mark of the dipstick, with the transmission at normal operating temperature of 155–170°F. If the fluid level is at or near the bottom indicator on the dipstick, either cold or hot, do not drive the vehicle until fluid has been added.

Transmission at Room Temperature

70–95°F, DIPSTICK COOL TO THE TOUCH

1. With the vehicle on a level surface, engine idling, wheels blocked and foot brake applied, move the selector lever through the gear positions to engage each gear and to fill the oil passages with fluid.
2. Place the selector lever in the **P** position and apply the parking brakes, allowing the engine to idle.

3. Clean the dipstick area of dirt and remove the dipstick from the filler tube. Wipe the dipstick clean and re-insert it back into the filler tube and seat it firmly.
4. Remove the dipstick from the filler tube again and check the fluid level as indicated on the dipstick. The level should be between the cold low mark and the cold full mark on the dipstick indicator.
5. If necessary, add enough fluid to bring the level to its cold full mark. Re-install the dipstick and seat it firmly in the filler tube.
6. When the transmission reaches normal operating temperature of 155–170°F, re-check the fluid level and correct as required to bring the fluid to its hot level mark.

Transmission at Normal Operating Temperature

155–170°F, DIPSTICK HOT TO THE TOUCH

1. With the vehicle on a level surface, engine idling, wheels blocked and foot brake applied, move the selector lever through the gear positions to engage each gear and to fill the passageways with fluid.
2. Place the selector lever in the **P** position and apply the parking brake, allowing the engine to idle.
3. Clean the dipstick area of dirt and remove the dipstick from the filler tube. Wipe the dipstick clean, re-insert the dipstick into the filler tube and seat firmly.
4. Again remove the dipstick from the filler tube and check the fluid level as indicated on the dipstick. The level should be between the **ADD** and **FULL** marks. If necessary, add enough fluid to bring the fluid level to the **FULL** mark.
5. When the fluid level is correct, fully seat the dipstick in the filler tube.

TRANSMISSION MODIFICATIONS

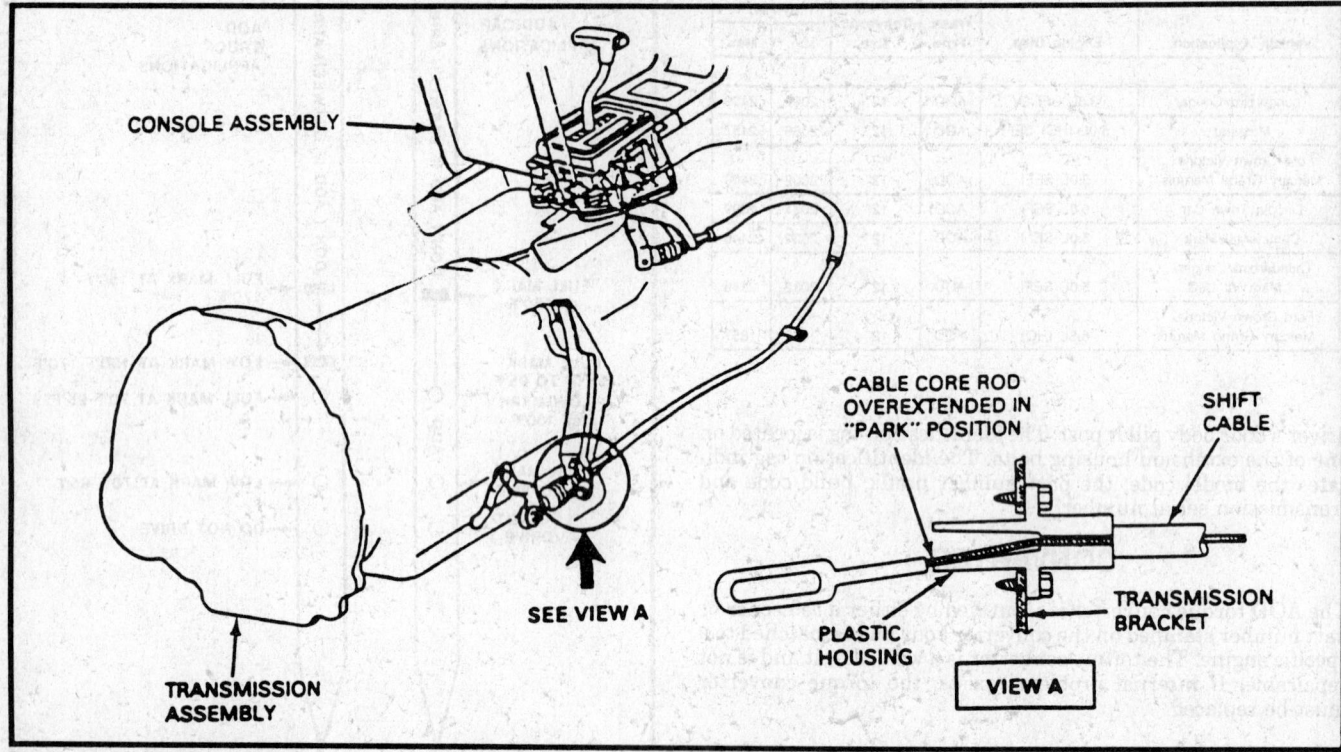

Shift cable binding repair

Transmission Fluid Leak at Cooler Line Connections

1985–87 FORD AND LINCOLN/MERCURY

In the event that service is required for a disconnected transmission cooler line, the quick-connect fitting should not be reused because it may not reseal properly and can result in repeat repair.

To correct the problem, the cooler lines must be modified using the following procedure:

1. Remove and discard the quick-connect fitting connector from the radiator or transmission case.

NOTE: Rework the connectors in sets, do not rework only one connector at a time.

2. Cut off the tubing as close as possible to the formed bead, using a tubing cutter.
3. Slide a $5/16 \times 1/2–20$ thread tube nut on the tube.
4. Make a double flare tube end.
5. Install the proper size and type connectors into the transmission case or radiator. Use thread sealer on the male threads of the connector.
6. Install thread tube nuts onto connectors. Torque to 12–18 ft. lbs.

Shift cable Lockup in Park

Transmissions that lockup in the **P** mode on some 1987 Thunderbird/Cougar vehicles with floor shift gear selectors may be caused by a shift cable bracket that is not positioned correctly on the gear selector. This allows the shift cable to catch on the plastic cable housing when the gear selector is positioned in **P**.

To correct this, install a new design gear selector and shift cable bracket using the following service procedure:

1. Remove the boot that seals the shift cable onto the transmission.
2. Check if shift cable core rod extends past the plastic cable housing when gear selector is positioned in **P**.
3. If the cable core rod extends past the housing, replace the gear selector with part number E8SZ–7210 and shift cable bracket with part number E7SZ–7B229–B.

TROUBLE DIAGNOSIS

CHILTON THREE C's TRANSMISSION DIAGNOSIS
Ford AOD

Condition	Cause	Correction
No / delayed forward engagement. Reverse OK	a) Improper fluid level	a) Check fluid level
	b) Manual linkage misadjusted or damaged	b) Check and adjust or repair as required
	c) Low line pressure	c) Control pressure test, note results
	d) Valve body bolts too loose or tight	d) Torque to specification 80–100 inch lbs. (9–11 Nm)
	e) Valve body dirty or sticking valves	e) Determine source of contamination. Repair as required
	f) Misassembled or leaking oil filter	f) Visually check oil filter for leaks at crimps. Verify proper assembly of oil filter to valve body gasket. Inspect rubber sealing grommet for nicks or cuts. Torque attaching bolts to specification
	g) 2–3 accumulator piston seal (small) cut/worn-piston bore in case damaged; piston damaged	g) Determine cause of failure and repair as required
	h) Forward clutch assembly burnt or damaged. Piston seals worn or cut. Cylinder ball check not seating. Stator support seal rings or ring grooves damaged or worn	h) Determine cause of failure and repair as required
No forward engagement. OD and 3	a) Planetary (low) one-way clutch	a) Repair as required
No / delayed reverse engagement. Forward OK	a) Improper fluid level	a) Check fluid level
	b) Low line pressure in reverse	b) Control pressure test, note results
	c) Manual linkage misadjusted or damaged	c) Check and adjust or repair as required. Manual linkage check
	d) Valve body bolts too loose or tight	d) Torque to specification 80–100 inch lbs. (9–11 Nm)
	e) Misassembled or leaking oil filter	e) Visually check oil filter for leaks at crimps. Verify proper assembly of oil filter to valve body gasket. Inspect rubber sealing grommet for nicks or cuts. Torque attaching bolts to specification
	f) Valve body dirty or sticking valves	f) Determine source of contamination then repair as required
	g) Reverse clutch assembly burnt or worn. Piston seals worn or cut. Piston ball check not seating. Stator support seal rings or ring grooves worn or damaged. Abuse	g) Determine cause of failure then repair as required
No / delayed engagement forward and reverse	a) Pump gear damaged (no engagement)	a) Replace and repair as required
	b) Output shaft broken (no engagement only)	b) Repair as required
	c) Turbine shaft broken (no engagement only)	c) Repair as required
No / delayed reverse engagement and no engine breaking in manual low (1)	a) Low reverse band or servo piston burnt or worn. Servo seal worn or cut. Servo bore damaged. Servo piston sticking in bore. Low line pressure	a) Determine cause of failure, then repair as required
Harsh engagements or initial engagement clunk (warm engine)	a) Improper fluid level	a) Check fluid level
	b) Throttle linkage misadjusted (long), disconnected, sticking, damaged or return spring disconnected	b) Adjust throttle linkage
	c) Engine curb idle too high	c) Check engine curb idle

Condition	Cause	Correction
Harsh engagements or initial engagement clunk (warm engine)—Continued	d) Valve body bolts—loose/too tight	d) Torque to specification 80–100 inch lbs. (9–11 Nm)
	e) Misassembled/leaking oil filter	e) Visually check oil filter for leaks at crimps. Verify proper assembly of oil filter to valve body gasket. Inspect rubber sealing grommet for nicks or cuts. Torque attaching bolts to specification
	f) Valve body dirty or sticking valves. Throttle valve (forward and reverse). 2–3 backout valve (forward only)	f) Determine source of contamination. Repair as required
	g) Engine rpm above specification	g) Adjust engine rpm to specification
	h) Throttle valve linkage misadjusted	h) Adjust throttle linkage
	i) Worn, damaged or loose U-joint (front/rear), slip yoke, rear axle, rear suspension	i) Repair as necessary
	j) Excessive transmission endplay	j) Check transmission endplay. Replace selective thrust washer if necessary
Forward engagement slips, shudders or chatters	a) Improper fluid level	a) Check fluid level
	b) Low throttle pressure or throttle valve rod misadjusted (short)	b) Adjust throttle valve rod
	c) Manual linkage misadjusted or damaged	c) Check and adjust or repair as required. Manual linkage check
	d) Low line pressure	d) Control pressure test
	e) Valve body bolts too loose or tight	e) Torque to specification 80–100 inch lbs. (9–11 Nm)
	f) Misassembled or leaking oil filter	f) Visually check oil filter for leaks at crimps. Verify proper assembly of oil filter to valve body gasket. Inspect rubber sealing grommet for nicks or cuts. Torque attaching bolts to specification
	g) Valve body dirty or sticking valves	g) Determine source of contamination. Repair as required
	h) Forward clutch piston ball check not seating	h) Replace forward clutch cylinder. Repair transmission as required
	i) Forward clutch piston seal cut or worn	i) Replace seal and repair clutch as required
	j) Contamination blocking forward clutch feed hold	j) Determine source of contamination, then repair as required
	k) Low one-way clutch (planetary) damaged	k) Repair as required. Determine cause of failure
Reverse shudder / chatters / slips	a) Improper fluid level	a) Check fluid level
	b) Low line pressure in reverse	b) Control pressure test
	c) Reverse servo or servo bore damaged	c) Determine cause of failure. Repair as required
	d) Misassembled or leaking oil filter	d) Visually check oil filter for leaks at crimps. Verify proper assembly of oil filter to valve body gasket. Inspect rubber sealing grommet for nicks or cuts. Torque attaching bolts to specification
	e) Reverse clutch drum bushing damaged	e) Determine cause of failure. Repair as required
	f) Reverse clutch—short one friction plate	f) Rebuild with proper number of plates
	g) Reverse clutch stator support seal rings/ring grooves worn/damaged	g) Determine cause of failure. Repair as required
	h) Reverse clutch piston seal cut or worn	h) Determine cause of failure then repair as required

Condition	Cause	Correction
Poor vehicle acceleration at higher speed 1st and 2nd gears. All engine speeds in 3rd and 4th. (Stall test will check OK)	a) Torque converter one-way clutch locked up	a) Replace torque converter
All upshifts harsh or delayed or no upshifts	a) Improper fluid level	a) Check fluid level
	b) Throttle linkage misadjusted (long), disconnected, sticking, or damaged or return spring disconnected	b) Adjust throttle linkage. Repair as required
	c) Manual linkage misadjusted or damaged	c) Check and adjust or repair as required. Manual linkage check
	d) Governor sticking	d) Perform governor test. Repair as required
	e) Line pressure too high or low	e) Control pressure test. Repair as required
	f) Valve body bolts too loose or tight	f) Torque to specification 80–100 inch lbs. (9–11 Nm)
	g) Misassembled or leaking oil filter	g) Visually check oil filter for leaks at crimps. Verify proper assembly of oil filter to valve body gasket. Inspect rubber sealing grommet for nicks or cuts. Torque attaching bolts to specification
	h) Valve body dirty or sticking valves. Throttle valve or throttle pressure limit valve	h) Determine source of contamination. Repair as required
Mushy, early or pile up—all upshifts	a) Improper fluid level	a) Check fluid level
	b) Throttle linkage misadjusted (short), sticking or damaged	b) Adjust throttle linkage. Repair as required
	c) Low line pressure	c) Control pressure test
	d) Valve body bolts too loose or tight	d) Torque to specification 80–100 inch lbs. (9–11 Nm)
	e) Misassembled or leaking oil filter	e) Visually check oil filter for leaks at crimps. Verify proper assembly of oil filter to valve body gasket. Inspect rubber sealing grommet for nicks or cuts. Torque attaching bolts to specification
	f) Valve body valve sticking. Throttle valve or throttle pressure limit valve	f) Determine source of contamination. Repair as required
	g) Governor valve sticking	g) Perform governor test. Repair as required
No 1–2 upshifts	a) Improper fluid level	a) Check fluid level
	b) Throttle linkage misadjusted (long), disconnected or sticking	b) Adjust throttle linkage
	c) Manual linkage misadjusted or damaged	c) Check and adjust or repair as required. Manual linkage check
	d) Low line pressure to intermediate friction clutch	d) Control pressure test. Note results
	e) Governor valve sticking	e) Perform governor test. Repair as required
	f) Valve body bolts too loose or tight	f) Torque to specification 80–100 inch lbs. (9–11 Nm)
	g) Misassembled or leaking oil filter	g) Visually check oil filter for leaks at crimps. Verify proper assembly of oil filter to valve body gasket. Inspect rubber sealing grommet for nicks or cuts. Torque attaching bolts to specification
	h) Valve body dirty or sticking valves. 1–2 shift valve or throttle valve	h) Determine source of contamination. Repair as required
Upshifts 1–3	a) Intermediate clutch assembly burnt. Piston seals worn or cut. Piston not positioned properly. Improper stack up, low line pressure.	a) Determine cause of failure then repair as required
	b) Intermediate one-way clutch damaged	b) Repair as required

Condition	Cause	Correction
Rough or harsh delayed 1–2 upshift	a) Improper fluid level	a) Check fluid level
	b) Poor engine performance	b) Tune-up engine
	c) Throttle linkage misadjusted (long), damaged or disconnected	c) Adjust throttle linkage. Repair as required
	d) Line pressure too high or low	d) Control pressure test. Note results
	e) Valve body bolts too loose or tight	e) Torque to specification 80–100 inch lbs. (9–11 Nm)
	f) Misassembled or leaking oil filter	f) Visually check oil filter for leaks at crimps. Verify proper assembly of oil filter to valve body gasket. Inspect rubber sealing grommet for nicks or cuts. Torque attaching bolts to specification.
	g) Valve body dirty or sticking valves. Rough shift—1–2 capacity modulator, 1–2 accumulator, 1–2 accumulator exhaust port blocked. Delayed shift—2–3 throttle modulator	g) Determine source of contamination, then repair as required
	h) Governor valve sticking	h) Perform governor test. Repair as required
Mushy, early, soft or slipping 1–2 upshift	a) Improper fluid level	a) Check fluid level
	b) Throttle linkage misadjusted (short) or damaged	b) Adjust throttle linkage. Repair as required
	c) Low line pressure	c) Control pressure test. Note results
	d) Valve body bolts loose/too tight	d) Torque to specification 80–100 inch lbs. (9–11 Nm)
	e) Misassembled/leaking oil filter	e) Visually check oil filter for leaks at crimps. Verify proper assembly of oil filter to valve body gasket. Inspect rubber sealing grommet for nicks or cuts. Torque attaching bolts to specification
	f) Valve body dirty or sticking valves. Throttle valve, throttle pressure limit valve, 2–3 throttle pressure limit (early) or 1–2 capacity modulator	f) Determine source of contamination. Repair as required
	g) Intermediate friction clutch burnt or worn. Clutch piston seals cut or worn. Clutch piston not aligned with pump body. Excessive clutch pack clearance	g) Determine cause of failure then repair as required
	h) Clutch piston upside down	h) Install properly. Bleedhole to be at 12 o'clock
	i) Governor valve sticking	i) Perform governor test. Repair as required
No 2–3 upshift	a) Improper fluid level	a) Check fluid level
	b) Throttle linkage misadjusted (long), sticking or damaged	b) Adjust throttle linkage. Repair as required
	c) Low line pressure to direct clutch	c) Control pressure test. Note results
	d) Valve body bolts too loose or tight	d) Torque to specification 80–100 inch lbs. (9–11 Nm)
	e) Misassembled or leaking oil filter	e) Visually check oil filter for leaks at crimps. Verify proper assembly of oil filter to valve body gasket. Inspect rubber sealing grommet for nicks or cuts. Torque attaching bolts to specification
	f) Valve body dirty/sticking valves. 2–3 shift valve	f) Determine source of contamination, then repair as required
	g) Direct clutch assembly burnt or worn. Piston seals cut/worn. Piston ball check stuck (not seating). Output shaft seal rings (small, Teflon) worn/cut. Collector body seal rings (large cast iron) worn	g) Perform stall test. Determine cause of failure then repair as required

Condition	Cause	Correction
No 2–3 upshift—Continued	h) Converter damper hub weld broken	h) Perform Converter Damper Hub Weld Check. Replace torque converter if required
Harsh / delayed 2–3 upshift	a) Improper fluid level	a) Check fluid level
	b) Poor engine performance	b) Tune-up engine
	c) Throttle linkage misadjusted (long), sticking or damaged	c) Adjust throttle linkage. Repair as required
	d) Valve body bolts too loose or tight	d) Torque to specification 80–100 inch lbs. (9–11 Nm)
	e) Misassembled or leaking oil filter	e) Visually check oil filter for leaks at crimps. Verify proper assembly of oil filter to valve body gasket. Inspect rubber sealing grommet for nicks or cuts. Torque attaching bolts to specification
	f) Valve body dirty/sticking valves. Throttle valve, throttle pressure limit valve, 2–3 backout valve (harsh backout shift), 2–3 capacity modulator (rough), or 2–3 throttle pressure modulator (delayed)	f) Determine source of failure. Repair as required
	g) 2–3 accumulator piston drain hole plugged/omitted	g) Remove 2–3 accumulator piston and visually inspect for plugging condition or omission
	h) 2–3 accumulator piston seals cut/worn	h) Replace seals, determine cause of failure, repair as required
Soft, early or mushy 2–3 upshift	a) Improper fluid level	a) Check fluid level
	b) Throttle linkage misadjusted (short) or bent	b) Adjust throttle linkage. Repair as required
	c) Valve body bolts too loose or tight	c) Torque to specification 80–100 inch lbs. (9–11 Nm)
	d) Misassembled or leaking oil filter	d) Visually check oil filter for leaks at crimps. Verify proper assembly of oil filter to valve body gasket. Inspect rubber sealing grommet for nicks or cuts. Torque attaching bolts to specification
	e) Valve body dirty or sticking valves. Throttle valve, throttle pressure limit valve, 2–3 throttle pressure limit valve (early), 2–3 capacity modulator valve, or 2–3 backout valve (mushy)	e) Determine source of contamination then repair as required
	f) Direct clutch assembly burnt/worn. Clutch piston seals cut/worn. Clutch piston ball check stuck/not seating. Output shaft seal rings (small Teflon) worn. Collector body seal rings (large cast) worn on output shaft	f) Perform stall test. Determine cause of failure. Repair as required
No 3–4 upshift	a) Improper fluid level	a) Check fluid level
	b) Throttle linkage—misadjusted (long)/ bent/sticking	b) Adjust throttle linkage. Repair as required
	c) Low pressure to overdrive band servo	c) Control pressure test. Note results
	d) Valve body bolts too loose or tight	d) Torque to specification 80–100 inch lbs. (9–11 Nm)
	e) Misassembled or leaking oil filter	e) Visually check oil filter for leaks at crimps. Verify proper assembly of oil filter to valve body gasket. Inspect rubber sealing grommet for nicks or cuts. Torque attaching bolts to specification
	f) Valve body dirty/sticking valves. 3–4 shift valve. Throttle valve. 3–4 shuttle valve	f) Determine source of contamination, then repair as required

Condition	Cause	Correction
No 3–4 upshift—Continued	g) Overdrive band assembly burnt or worn. OD band not seated to case. OD servo not seated to band end seat. OD servo apply blocked. OD servo seals worn/cut. OD servo bore damaged	g) Determine cause of failure, repair as required
	h) 3–4 accumulator piston seals worn or cut. 3–4 accumulator piston drain passage blocked	h) Determine cause of failure. Repair as required
Harsh/delayed 3–4 upshift	a) Improper fluid level	a) Check fluid level
	b) Throttle linkage misadjusted (long) or bent	b) Adjust throttle linkage. Repair as required
	c) Valve body bolts too loose or tight	c) Torque to specification 80–100 inch lbs. (9–11 Nm)
	d) Misassembled or leaking oil filter	d) Visually check oil filter for leaks at crimps. Verify proper assembly of oil filter to valve body gasket. Inspect rubber sealing grommet for nicks or cuts. Torque attaching bolts to specification
	e) Valve body dirty or sticking valves. 3–4 shift valve, throttle valve, throttle pressure limit valve, 3–4 shuttle valve (rough), 3–4 backout valve (rough backout shifts) or 3–4 throttle pressure modulator valve	e) Determine source of contamination then repair as required
Slips, shudder soft or early 3–4 upshift	a) Improper fluid level	a) Check fluid level
	b) Throttle linkage misadjusted (short), bent or sticking	b) Adjust throttle linkage. Repair as required
	c) Low pressure to overdrive band servo	c) Control pressure test. Note results
	d) Valve body bolts too loose or tight	d) Torque to specification 80–100 inch lbs. (9–11 Nm)
	e) Misassembled or leaking oil filter	e) Visually check oil filter for leaks at crimps. Verify proper assembly of oil filter to valve body gasket. Inspect rubber sealing grommet for nicks or cuts. Torque attaching bolts to specification
	f) Valve body dirty or sticking valves. 3–4 backout valve (soft), throttle valve, 3–4 shuttle valve (soft), or 3–4 throttle pressure modulator valve (early)	f) Determine source of contamination, then repair as required
	g) Overdrive band assembly burnt/worn. Overdrive band not seated to case. Overdrive servo not seated to band end seat. Overdrive servo apply blocked. Overdrive servo seals worn/cut. Overdrive servo bore damaged. 3–4 accumulator piston seals worn or cut. 3–4 accumulator piston drain passage blocked	g) Determine cause of failure. Repair as required
Erratic shifts	a) Improper fluid level	a) Check fluid level
	b) Throttle linkage binding or sticking	b) Inspect throttle linkage. Repair as required
	c) Valve body bolts—loose/too tight	c) Torque to specification 80–100 inch lbs. (9–11 Nm)
	d) Misassembled/leaking oil filter	d) Visually check oil filter for leaks at crimps. Verify proper assembly of oil filter to valve body gasket. Inspect rubber sealing grommet for nicks or cuts. Torque attaching bolts to specification

Condition	Cause	Correction
	e) Valve body dirty or sticking valves	e) Perform line pressure test, note results and source of contamination, then repair as required
	f) Governor valve sticking	f) Perform governor test. Repair as required
	g) Output shaft collector body seal rings (large cast iron) worn/cut	g) Repair as required
Shift hunting 3–4, 4–3	a) Poor engine performance. EGR solenoid defective	a) Tune-up engine. Replace solenoid
	b) Throttle linkage misadjusted	b) Inspect and adjust throttle linkage as required
	c) Manual linkage misadjusted	c) Check and adjust or repair as required. Manual linkage check adjustment
No engine breaking—manual low "pull-in"	a) Low reverse band is not holding	a) Refer to condition "No reverse engagement. Forward OK"
Shift efforts high	a) Manual shift linkage damaged/misadjusted	a) Check and adjust or repair as required. Manual linkage check adjustment
	b) Inner manual lever nut loose	b) Torque nut to specification
	c) Manual lever retainer pin damaged	c) Adjust manual linkage and install new pin
No kickdown or hard to get kickdown	a) Misadjusted throttle linkage (short). Carburetor throttle lever sticking. Carburetor misadjusted	a) Inspect and adjust throttle linkage. Repair as required. Adjust to specification
Transmission leaks	a) Torque converter Seam weld leaks. Drain plug loose/cross threaded. Impeller hub pitted/worn	a) Replace or repair as required
	b) Oil pump Impeller hub seal cut or worn. Overdrive seal cut/pinched. Gasket misaligned. Bolts loose	b) Replace or repair as required
	c) Lever seals in case Manual lever seal cut/worn. Throttle lever seal cut/worn	c) Replace or repair as required
	d) Case fittings Cooler line fittings loose or cross threaded. Pressure plugs loose or cross threaded	d) Replace or repair as required
	e) Case Porosity or cracked	e) Replace or repair as required
	f) Oil pan Gasket misaligned or damaged. Bolts loose or cross threaded. Pan damaged	f) Replace or repair as required
	g) Extension housing Gasket misaligned or damaged. Bolts loose. Seal cut/worn. Bushing worn or damaged. Speedometer cable connection	g) Replace or repair as required
	h) Filler tube Out top of tube, at bottom of tube. Cut or worn seal. Case porosity. Damaged tube	h) Check converter drainback valve. Replace seal. Replace case. Replace tube
	i) Case breather vent	i) Repair as required
	j) Engine-power steering leak	j) Correctly identify fluid; isolate leakage area; repair leak
Harsh coasting downshift clunk	a) Anti-clunk spring not seated properly	a) Reposition anti-clunk spring properly
	b) Throttle linkage misadjusted (long)	b) Adjust throttle linkage, repair as required

Condition	Cause	Correction
Improper shift timing—4-3 Backout shift 4-3 Shift on full back out (foot off accelerator Pedal) accompanied by 3–4 shift when accelerator depressed	a) Loose governor—output shaft snap ring not seated b) Worn or broken output shaft seal rings-large diameter c) Worn seal ring grooves d) Worn collector bore e) Output shaft holes blocked	a) Repair as required b) Repair as required c) Repair as required d) Repair as required e) Repair as required
No start in P	a) Manual linkage misadjusted b) Plug connector for the neutral start switch does not fit properly	a) Adjust manual linkage b) Check plug connection
No start in P and N	a) Plug connector for the neutral start switch does not fit properly	a) Check plug connection

CLUTCH AND BAND APPLICATION

	Interm. Friction Clutch	Interm. One-Way Clutch	Overdrive Band	Reverse Clutch	Forward Clutch	Planetary One-Way Clutch	Low-Reverse Band	Direct Clutch
1st Gear Manual Low					Applied	Holding	Applied	
2nd Gear Manual Low	Applied	Holding	Applied		Applied			
1st Gear — Ⓓ(OVERDRIVE) or D(3)					Applied	Holding		
2nd Gear — Ⓓ(OVERDRIVE) or D(3)	Applied	Holding			Applied			
3rd Gear — Ⓓ(OVERDRIVE) or D(3)	Applied				Applied			Applied
4th Gear — Ⓓ(OVERDRIVE)	Applied		Applied					Applied
Reverse (R)				Applied			Applied	

Hydraulic Control System

Before the transmission can transfer the input power from the engine to the drive wheels, hydraulic pressures must be developed and routed to the varied components to cause them to operate, through numerous internal systems and passages. A basic understanding of the components, fluid routings and systems, will aid in the trouble diagnosis of the transmission.

OIL PUMP

The oil pump is a positive displacement pump, meaning that as long as the pump is turning and fluid is supplied to the inlet, the pump will deliver fluid in a volume proportionate to the input drive speed. The pump is in operation whenever the engine is operating, delivering more fluid than the transmission needs, with the excess being bled off by the pressure regulator valve and routed to the sump. It should be remembered, the oil pump is driven by a shaft which is splined into the converter cover and through a drive gear insert. The gears, in turn, are installed in a body, which is bolted to the pump support at the rear of the transmission case.

Should the oil pump fail, fluid would not be supplied to the transmission to keep the converter filled, to lubricate the internal working parts and to operate the hydraulic controls.

PRESSURE REGULATOR SYSTEM

The pressure regulator system controls the main line pressure at pre-determined levels during the vehicle operation. The main oil pressure regulator valve and spring determines the psi of the main line control pressure. The main line control pressure is regulated by balancing pressure at the end of the inner valve land, against the valve spring. When the pump begins fluid delivery and fills the passages and transmission components, the spring holds the valve closed and there is no regulation. As the pressure rises, the pressure regulator valve is moved against the spring tension, opening a passage to the torque converter. Fluid then flows into the converter, the cooler system and back to the lubrication system. As the pressure continues its rise, the pressure regulator valve is moved further against the spring tension and at a predetermined psi level and spring tension rate, the valve is moved further to open a passage, allowing excess pressurized fluid to return to the sump. The valve then opens and closes in a vibrating type action, dependent upon the fluid requirements of the transmission. A main line oil pressure booster valve is used to increase the line pressure to meet the needs of higher pressure, required when the transmission torque load increases, to operate the clutches and band servo.

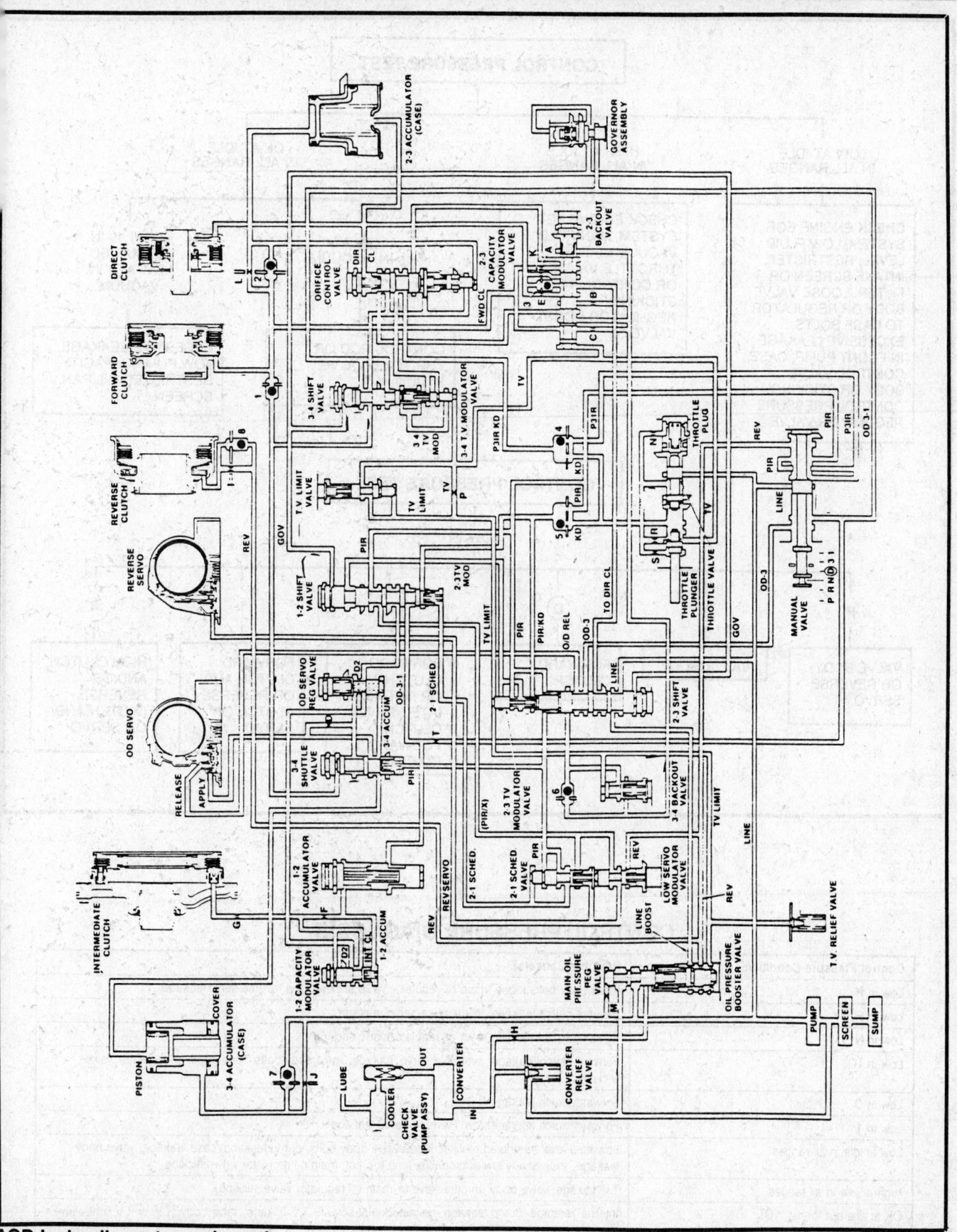

AOD hydraulic system schematic

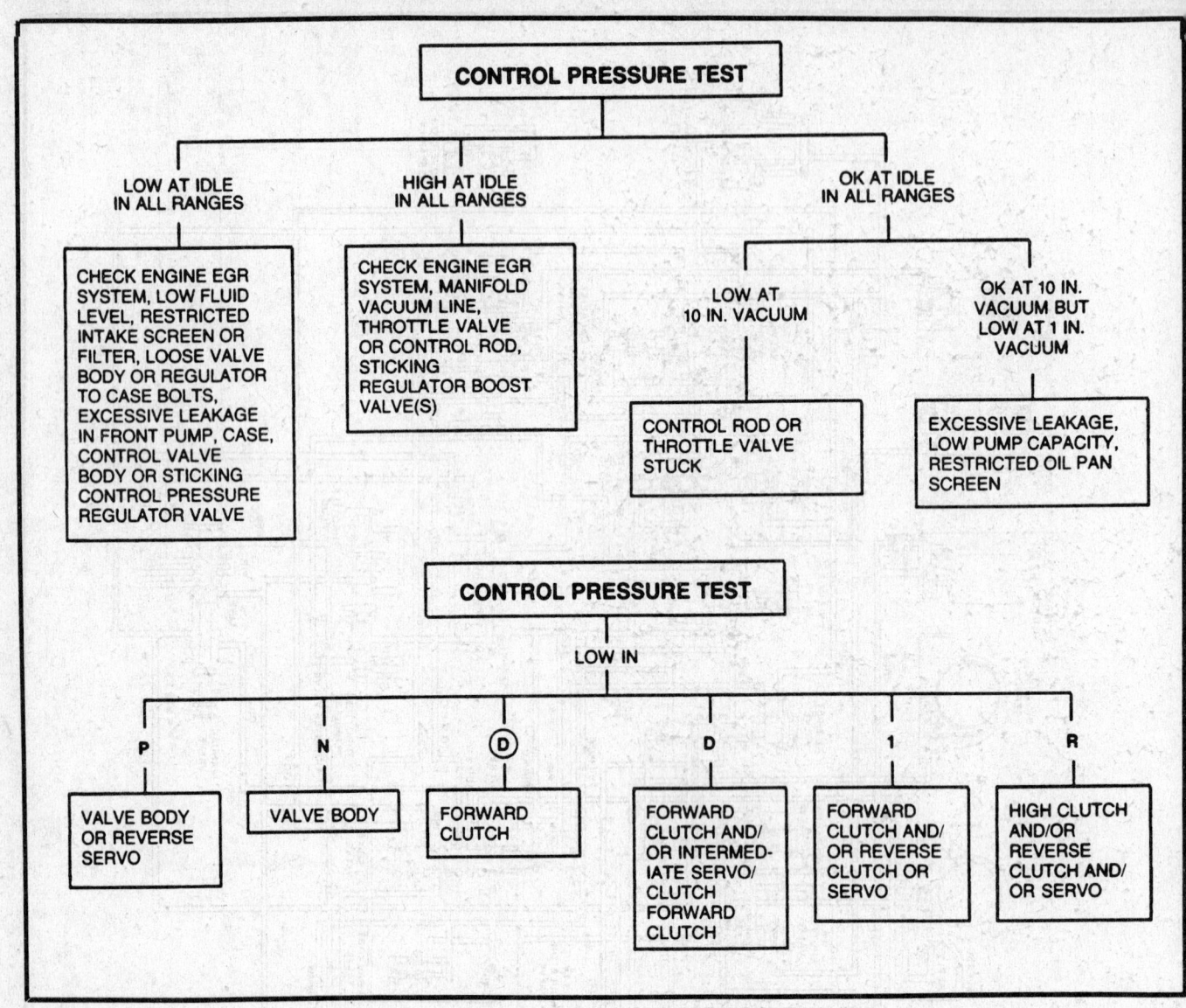

CONTROL PRESSURE DIAGNOSIS

Control Pressure Condition	Possible Cause(s)
Low in P	Valve body bolts loose, main oil regulator valve sticking, low reverse servo leakage.
Low in R	Reverse clutch leakage, low reverse servo leakage.
Low in N	Valve body bolts loose, main oil regulator valve sticking.
Low in (D)	Forward clutch leakage, overdrive servo leakage, valve body bolts loose, main oil regulator valve sticking.
Low in D	Forward clutch leakage.
Low in 1	Forward clutch leakage, low. Reverse servo leakage.
Low at idle in all ranges	Low fluid level, restricted oil filter, loose valve body bolts, pump leakage, case leakage, valve body leakage, excessively low engine idle, fluid too hot, main oil regulator valve sticking.
High at idle in all ranges	T.V. linkage, valve body (throttle valve or main oil regulator valve sticking).
OK at idle but low at WOT	Internal leakage, pump leakage, restricted inlet screen, T.V. linkage, valve body (T.V. or T.V. limit valve sticking, main oil regulator valve sticking).

LINE PRESSURE SPECIFICATIONS

Engine	Operation Range	Idle		W.O.T. Stall	
		Throttle Pressure	Line Pressure	Throttle Pressure	Line Pressure
5.0L SEFI, 5.0L HO SEFI, 5.8L	P,N, Ⓓ, D,1	0	55-65	79-91	180-215
	R	0	75-90	79-91	250-290
3.8L	P,N, Ⓓ, D,1	0	55-65	74-86	176-204
	R	0	75-90	74-86	241-279

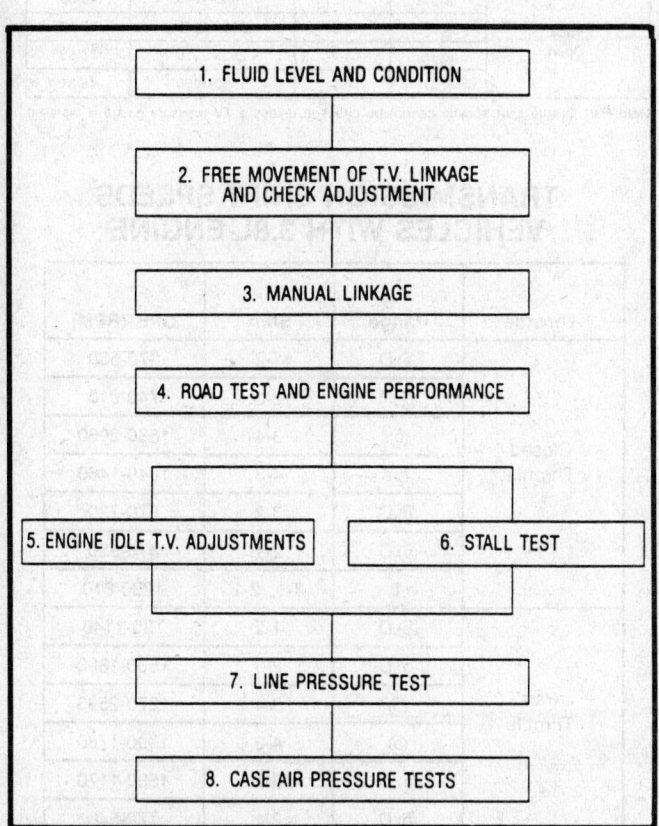

1. FLUID LEVEL AND CONDITION

2. FREE MOVEMENT OF T.V. LINKAGE AND CHECK ADJUSTMENT

3. MANUAL LINKAGE

4. ROAD TEST AND ENGINE PERFORMANCE

5. ENGINE IDLE T.V. ADJUSTMENTS

6. STALL TEST

7. LINE PRESSURE TEST

8. CASE AIR PRESSURE TESTS

General diagnostic sequence

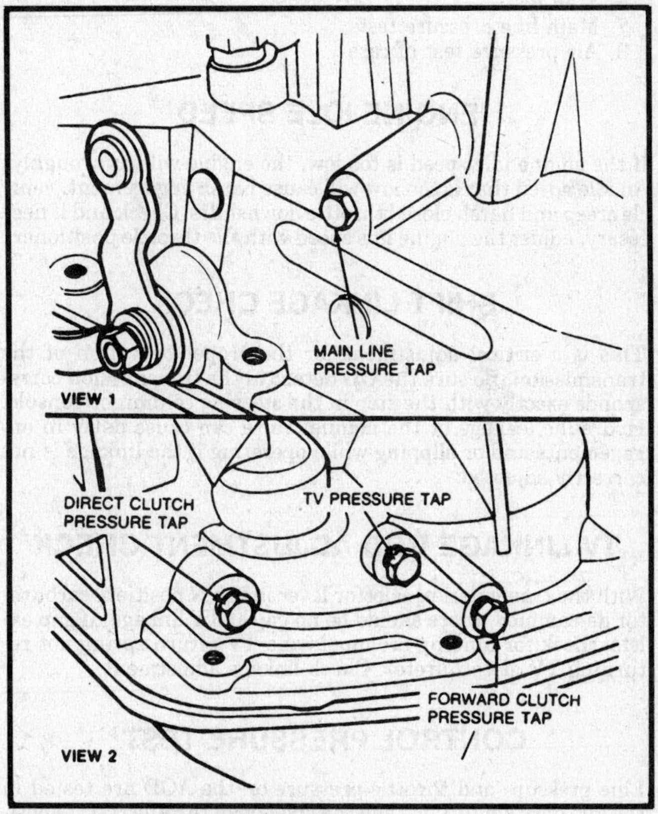

MAIN LINE PRESSURE TAP

VIEW 1

DIRECT CLUTCH PRESSURE TAP

TV PRESSURE TAP

FORWARD CLUTCH PRESSURE TAP

VIEW 2

Control pressure tap locations

MANUAL CONTROL VALVE

Main line control pressure is always present at the manual control valve. Other than required passages, such as to the converter fill, the lubricating system and certain valve assemblies, the manual valve must be moved to allow the pressurized fluid to flow to the desired components or to charge certain passages in order to engage the transmission components in their applicable gear ratios.

GOVERNOR ASSEMBLY

The governor assembly reacts to vehicle road speed and provides a pressure signal to the control valves. This pressure signal causes automatic upshifts to occur as the road speed increases and permits downshifts as the road speed decreases. The governor has 3 hydraulic passages, an exhaust governor pressure out and line pressure in, controlled by springs and weights, with the weight position determined by centrifugal force as the governor assembly rotates.

Throttle Valve (T.V.) Control Systems

The AOD transmission uses three T.V. control systems. On all vehicles equipped with 3.8L CFI engines and 5.8L carbureted engines, a T.V. control rod linkage is used. On vehicles equipped with 3.8L EFI engines, a manual locking T.V. cable control system is used. All vehicles equipped with 5.0L SEFI and 5.8L HO SEFI engines, use a self locking T.V. cable system.

Diagnostic Tests

A general diagnosis sequence should be followed to determine in what area of the transmission a malfunction exists. The following sequence is suggested by the manufacturer to diagnose and test the operation of the AOD transmission.

1. Inspect fluid level and condition.
2. Freedom of movement of the T.V. linkage and verify adjustment.
3. Correct positioning of the manual linkage.
4. Road test and engine performance.
5. Engine idle and T.V. adjustment.
6. Stall test.
7. Main line pressure test.
8. Air pressure test of case.

ENGINE IDLE SPEED

If the engine idle speed is too low, the engine will run roughly. An idle speed that is too low will cause harsh engagement, vehicle creep and harsh closed throttle downshifts. Check and if necessary, adjust the engine idle speed with the throttle positioner.

SHIFT LINKAGE CHECK

This is a critical adjustment for the proper operation of the transmission. Be sure the **OD** detent in the transmission corresponds exactly with the stop in the steering column or console. Hydraulic leakage at the manual valve can cause delay in engagements and/or slipping while operating if the linkage is not correctly adjusted.

TV LINKAGE ROD ADJUSTMENT CHECK

With the transmission selector lever in the **N** position, carburetor de-cammed, there should be no gap at TV linkage. If gap exists, check for binding grommets and TV return spring not returning TV at carburetor. Check linkage adjustment.

CONTROL PRESSURE TEST

Line pressure and throttle pressure on the AOD are tested in the idle position (0 T.V.) and the wide-open throttle (WOT) position. In each of the modes the reverse reading will be higher than the others.

1. Check the T.V. linkage for correct aadjustment.
2. Connect a 0–300 psi. gauge to the line pressure port of the transmission case. The gauge should have enough hose to be read while running the engine.
3. Connect a 0–100 psi. pressure gauge to the T.V. port on the right side of the transmission case.

NOTE: WOT readings should be taken at full stall. Run the engine at fast idle in NEUTRAL between tests for cooling.

4. Run the engine until it reaches normal operating temperature.

TRANSMISSION SHIFT SPEEDS VEHICLES WITH 5.8L ENGINE

Throttle	Range	Shift	OPS (RPM)	Column Number 1
Closed Throttle (See Note)	⒟,D	1-2	370-530	11-15
	⒟,D	2-3	720-890	21-26
	⒟,	3-4	1460-1850	42-53
	⒟,	4-3	1580-1200	46-35
	⒟,	3-2	870-700	25-20
	⒟,D	2-1	470-320	14-9
	1	3-1, 2-1	730-810	36-23
Part Throttle (See Note)	⒟,D	1-2	670-1050	19-30
	⒟,D	2-3	1350-1780	39-51
	⒟,	3-4	1790-2420	52-70
	⒟,	4-3	1760-1340	51-39
	⒟,D	3-2	1390-830	40-24
	⒟,D	2-1	750-500	22-14
Wide Open	⒟,D	1-2	1400-1940	40-56
	⒟,D	2-3	2650-3020	77-87
	⒟,D	3-2	2530-2170	73-63
	⒟,D	2-1	1560-1060	45-31

Note: Part throttle shift speeds cannot be checked unless a TV pressure gauge is installed.

TRANSMISSION SHIFT SPEEDS VEHICLES WITH 3.8L ENGINE

Throttle	Range	Shift	OPS (RPM)
Closed Throttle	⒟,D	1-2	370-530
	⒟,D	2-3	740-910
	⒟	3-4	1680-2060
	⒟	4-3	1840-1460
	⒟,D	3-2	870-720
	⒟,D	2-1	470-320
	1	3-1, 2-1	1230-810
Part Throttle	⒟,D	1-2	730-1140
	⒟,D	2-3	1500-1890
	⒟	3-4	1970-2590
	⒟	4-3	1990-1780
	⒟,D	3-2	1580-1170
	⒟,D	2-1	770-540
Wide Open	⒟,D	1-2	1430-1900
	⒟,D	2-3	2630-3000
	⒟,D	3-2	2570-2220
	⒟,D	2-1	1520-1060

5. Apply the parking and service brakes. Shift the transmission through all of the ranges and record the line pressure and throttle pressure for each position. Compare the readings with the specifications.

STALL SPEED DIAGNOSIS

Selector Position	Stall Speeds High	Stall Speeds Low
Overdrive & D	Planetary One-Way Clutch	
Overdrive, D & 1	Forward Clutch	
Overdrive, D, 1 & R	General Problems Pressure Test. Check TV Cable Adjustment if Not Done Prior to Test.	Converter Stator One-Way Clutch or Engine Performance
R	High and/or Reverse Clutch or Low Reverse Band or Servo	

TRANSMISSION SHIFT SPEEDS VEHICLES WITH 5.0L ENGINE

Throttle	Range	Shift	OPS (RPM)
Closed Throttle (See Note)	Ⓓ,D	1-2	310-460
	Ⓓ,D	2-3	680-830
	Ⓓ	3-4	1300-1680
	Ⓓ	4-3	1440-1060
	Ⓓ,D	3-2	800-660
	Ⓓ,D	2-1	410-240
	1	3-1, 2-1	1100-730
Part Throttle (See Note)	Ⓓ,D	1-2	670-1020
	Ⓓ,D	2-3	1330-1710
	Ⓓ	3-4	1600-2210
	Ⓓ	4-3	1600-1200
	Ⓓ,D	3-2	1440-1020
	Ⓓ,D	2-1	690-480
Wide Open	Ⓓ,D	1-2	1370-1800
	Ⓓ,D	2-3	2470-2810
	Ⓓ,D	3-2	2420-2080
	Ⓓ,D	2-1	1450-1020

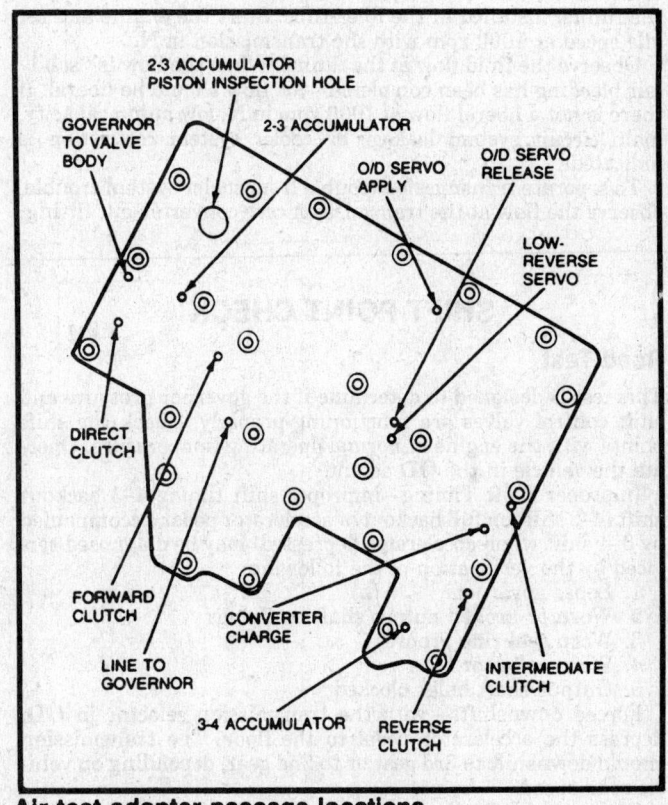

Air test adapter passage locations

NOTE: Clutch and servo leakage may or may not show up on the control pressure test. This is because the pump has a high output volume and the leak may not be severe enough to cause a pressure drop. Pressure loss caused by a major leak is more likely to show up at idle than WOT, where the pump is delivering full volume.

DIRECT CLUTCH PRESSURE TEST

The direct clutch pressure test is designed to to diagnose a low-pressure condition or leakage in the direct clutch circuit. A difference of 15 psi. or more between direct clutch pressure and line pressure (read at the forward clutch pressure tap) will prevent a normal 3–4 shift.

1. Attach 0–300 psi. pressure gauges to the forward clutch pressure tap and to the direct clutch pressure tap.

NOTE: Gauges must be accurate enough to distinguish a 15 psi. difference and have enough hose to be read while operating the vehicle.

2. Drive the vehicle. When pressure is applied to the direct clutch , note the difference between the line pressure and direct clutch pressure.

3. If the difference in the gauge readings is more than 15 psi. there could be a leak in the direct clutch pressure circuit.

STALL TEST

The stall test checks converter clutch operation and installation, the holding ability of the forward clutch, reverse clutch, the low/reverse bands, the planetary one-way clutch and engine performance.

1. Run the engine until it reaches normal operating temperature. Check the T.V. for proper adjustment.

2. Connect a tachometer to the engine. Apply the parking and service brakes.

3. In each of the gearshift positions, press the accelerator to the floor and hold it long enough to let the engine get to full rpm. While making the test, do not hold the throttle open for more than 5 seconds at a time.

4. Note the results of the test in each gear range. After checking each range, run the engine at 1000 rpm for 15 seconds to cool the converter before the next test.

TRANSMISSION FLUID FLOW CHECK

The linkage, fluid and control pressure must be within specifications before performing this flow check.

Remove the transmission dipstick from the filler tube. Place a funnel in the transmission filler tube. Raise the vehicle, remove the cooler return line from its fitting in the case. Attach a hose to the cooler return line and fasten the free end of the hose in the funnel installed in the filler tube. Start the engine and set idle speed at 1000 rpm with the transmission in **N**.

Observe the fluid flow at the funnel. When the flow is "solid" (air bleeding has been completed), the flow should be liberal. If there is not a liberal flow at 1000 rpm in **N**, low pump capacity, main circuit system leakage or cooler system restriction is indicated.

To separate transmission trouble from cooler system trouble, observe the flow at the transmission case converter-out fitting.

SHIFT POINT CHECK

Road Test

This test is designed to determine if the governor pressure and shift control valves are functioning properly. Check the shift points with the engine at normal operating temperature. Operate the vehicle in the **OD** detent.

Improper Shift Timing—improper shift timing 4–3 backout shift (4–3 shift on full backout of accelerator pedal, accompanied by 3–4 shift when accelerator depressed) may be diagnosed/serviced by the verification of the following:

1. Loose governor
2. Worn or broken output shaft seal rings
3. Worn seal ring grooves
4. Worn collector bore
5. Output shaft holes blocked

Forced downshifts—with the transmission selector in **OD**, depress the accelerator pedal to the floor. The transmission should downshift to 3rd gear or to 2nd gear, depending on vehicle road speed.

Closed throttle downshifts—closed throttle downshifts should be extremely difficult to detect. It may be necessary to attach 0–100 psi. pressure gauges to the forward and direct clutch taps in order to detect 4–3 and 2–3 coast down shifts. A 4–3 coast (closed throttle) downshift is signified by the application of the forward clutch (the pressure reading from the forward clutch pressure apply will indicate an increase in pressure from 0–60 psi). A 3–2 coast downshift is signified by the release of the direct clutch. A 2–1 downshift should be imperceptible (the pressure reading from the gauge on the direct clutch pressure tap will indicate a decrease in pressure from 60–0 psi.

In Shop Check

A shift test can be performed in the shop to check for 1–2, 2–3 and 3–4 upshifts.

1. Raise and safely support the vehicle so that the rear wheels are off the ground.

----------------- **CAUTION** -----------------
Never exceed 60 mph speedometer speed with the vehicle raised.

2. Place the transmission lever in **OD** and make a minimum throttle 1–2, 2–3 and 3–4 upshift.
3. When the shifts occur, the speedometer needle will make a

momentary surge and the driveline will bump.

4. Check the shift points against the specifications. If the shift points are within specification, the 1–2, 2–3 and 3–4 shift valves and governor are ok.

5. If the shift points are not within specification, perform a governor check to isolate the problem.

AIR PRESSURE TEST

A no drive condition can exist, even with the correct transmission fluid pressure, because of inoperative clutches or band. Erratic shifts could be caused by a stuck governor valve. The inoperative units can be located through a series of checks by substituting air pressure for the fluid pressure to determine the location of the malfunction.

A no drive condition in **D** and **2** may be caused by an inoperative band or one-way clutch. When there is no drive in **1**, the difficulty could be caused by improper functioning of the direct clutch or band and the one-way clutch. Failure to drive in **R** range could be caused by a malfunction of the reverse clutch or one-way clutch.

When a slip problem is evident, whether it is in the valve body or in the hydraulic system beyond the valve body, the air pressure tests can be very valuable.

To properly air test the transmission, a main control to case gasket and the following special service tools or equivalent will be required.

  a. Adapter plate tool T82L–7006–A
  b. Adapter plate attaching screws tool T82P–7006–C
  c. Air nozzle tool 7000–DE
  d. Air nozzle rubber tip tool 7000–DD

With the main control body removed, position the adapter plate and gasket on the transmission. Install the adapter plate attaching screws and tighten the screws to 80–100 inch lbs. (9–11 Nm) torque. Note that each passage is identified on the plate. Using the air nozzle equipped with the rubber tip, apply air pressure to each passage in the following order:

Overdrive Servo

Apply air pressure to the OD servo appy passage in the service plate tool. Operation of the band is indicated by the tightening of the band around the reverse clutch drum. The OD servo will return to the release position as a result of spring force from the release spring. Also, when the servo returns to the release position, a thud can be felt on the OD servo cover. The band will then relax.

Direct Clutch

Apply air pressure to the forward clutch apply passage in the service tool plate. A dull thud can be heard or movement of the piston can be felt on the case as the clutch piston is applied. If the clutch seal(s) are leaking a hissing sound will be heard.

Intermediate Clutch

Apply air pressure to the intermediate clutch apply passage in the service tool plate. A dull thud can be heard or movement of the piston can be felt on the case as the clutch piston is applied. If the clutch seal(s) are leaking a hissing sound will be heard.

Reverse Clutch

Apply air pressure to the reverse clutch apply passage in the service tool plate. A dull thud can be heard or movement of the piston can be felt on the case as the clutch piston is applied. If the clutch seal(s) are leaking a hissing sound will be heard.

Forward Clutch

Apply air pressure to the forward clutch apply passage in the service plate. A dull thud can be heard or movement of the piston can be felt on the case as the clutch piston is applied.

3–4 Accumulator

Apply air pressure to the 3–4 accumulator apply passage, the accumulator should unseat.

Low/Reverse Servo

Apply air pressure to the low/reverse servo apply passage in the service plate. A dull thud can be heard when the low/everse servo band tightens around the planetary assembly drum surface. Also, movement of the ring gear can be detected.

2–3 Accumulator

Apply air pressure to the 2–3 accumulator apply passage in the

service plate. The accumulator piston should unseat. This can be detected by inserting a metal rod into the 2–3 piston inspection hole. When the piston unseats, the rod will move. Also a dull thud can be heard when the piston is applied.

Governor

In order to air pressure test the line to governor passage and the governor to valve body passage, the driveshaft, crossmember and extension housing must be removed.

Apply air pressure to the line to governor passage in the service plate while checking the governor valve. If air is escaping from the governor valve then the passage is unobstructed.

To air pressure check the governor to valve body passage, remove the governor. Apply air pressure to the passage while checking the holes in the output shaft. If air escapes any of the holes, the passage is unobstructed.

ON CAR SERVICES

Adjustments

THROTTLE VALVE CONTROL SYSTEM

5.8L Carbureted Engine

The T.V. control linkage is set to its proper length during initial assembly using the sliding trunnion block at the transmission end of the T.V. control rod. Under normal circumstances, it should not be necessary to to alter this adjustment. Any required adjustment of the T.V. control linkage can normally be accomplished using the adjustment screw on the linkage lever at the carburetor.

Major linkage adjustment (sliding trunnion on rod) may only be required after maintenance involving the removal and/or replacement of the carburetor, T.V. control rod assembly or the transmission. Minor linkage adjustment (adjustment screw on the linkage lever) may be required after installing a new main control assembly, or after idle speed adjustments greater than 50 rpm and to correct poor transmission shift quality.

MINIMUM IDLE STOP

When the linkage is correctly adjusted, the T.V. control lever on the transmission will be at its internal idle stop position (lever up as far as it will travel) when the carburetor throttle lever is at its minimum idle stop. There will be a light contact force between the the throttle lever and end of the linkage lever adjustment screw. Due to flexibility in the linkage system, the linkage lever adjustment screw would have to be backed out approximately 3 turns before a gap between the screw and throttle lever could be detected.

At WOT, the T.V. control lever on the transmission may or may not be at its wide open stop. The WOT throttle position must not be used as the reference point in adjusting the linkage.

LINKAGE ADJUSTMENT AT CARBURETOR

1. Set carburetor at minimum idle stop. Place shift lever in **N** and set parking brake.
2. Back out linkage lever adjusting screw all the way (screw end is flush with lever face).
3. Turn in adjusting screw until a clearance of 0.005 in. is reached (check with feeler gauge).

NOTE: To eliminate the effect of friction, push the linkage lever forward and release before checking clearance between end of screw and throttle.

4. Turn in screw 3 turns (3 turns are preferred. If travel is limited, 1 turn is sufficient).

5. If it is not possible to turn in adjusting screw at least 1 turn, if there was insufficient screw adjusting capacity to obtain an initial gap, adjustment at the transmission is necessary.

LINKAGE ADJUSTMENT AT TRANSMISSION

The linkage lever adjustment screw has limited adjustment capability. If it is not possible to adjust the T.V. linkage using this screw, the length of the T.V. control rod assembly must be readjusted using the following procedure. This procedure must also be followed whenever a new control rod assembly is installed.

1. Set carburetor at its minimum idle stop. Place the shift lever in **N** and set the parking brake.
2. Set the linkage adjustment screw at approximately midrange.
3. If a new T.V. control rod assembly is being installed, connect the rod to the linkage lever at the carburetor.
4. Raise and safley support the vehicle.
5. Loosen the bolt on the sliding trunnion block on the T.V. control rod assembly. Remove any corrosion from the control rod and free the trunnion block so that it slides freely on the control rod.
6. Push up on the lower end of the control rod to ensure that the linkage lever at carburetor is firmly against the throttle lever. Release the tension on the rod, rod must stay up.
7. Push the T.V. control lever on the transmission up against its internal stop firmly. Tighten the bolt on the trunnion block, do not release the force on the block until the bolt is tightened.
8. Lower the vehicle and verify that the throttle lever is still against the minimum idle stop or throttle solenoid positioner stop. If not, repeat the adjustment procedure.

3.8L EFI and 5.0L HO/SEFI Engines

The T.V. control system is set and locked to its proper length during initial assembly by pushing down on the locking lever at the throttle body end of the cable assembly. When the lever is unlocked, the cable is released for adjustment. The take up spring at this end of the cable automatically tensions the cable when released. With the slack taken up and the locking lever pushed, the take up spring plays no part in the operation of the system.

Under normal circumstances, it should not be necessary to alter or readjust, the initial setting of the T.V. control cable. Situations requiring the readjustment of the T.V. control cable include maintenance involving the removal and/or replacement of the throttle body, transmission, T.V. cable assembly or main control assembly.

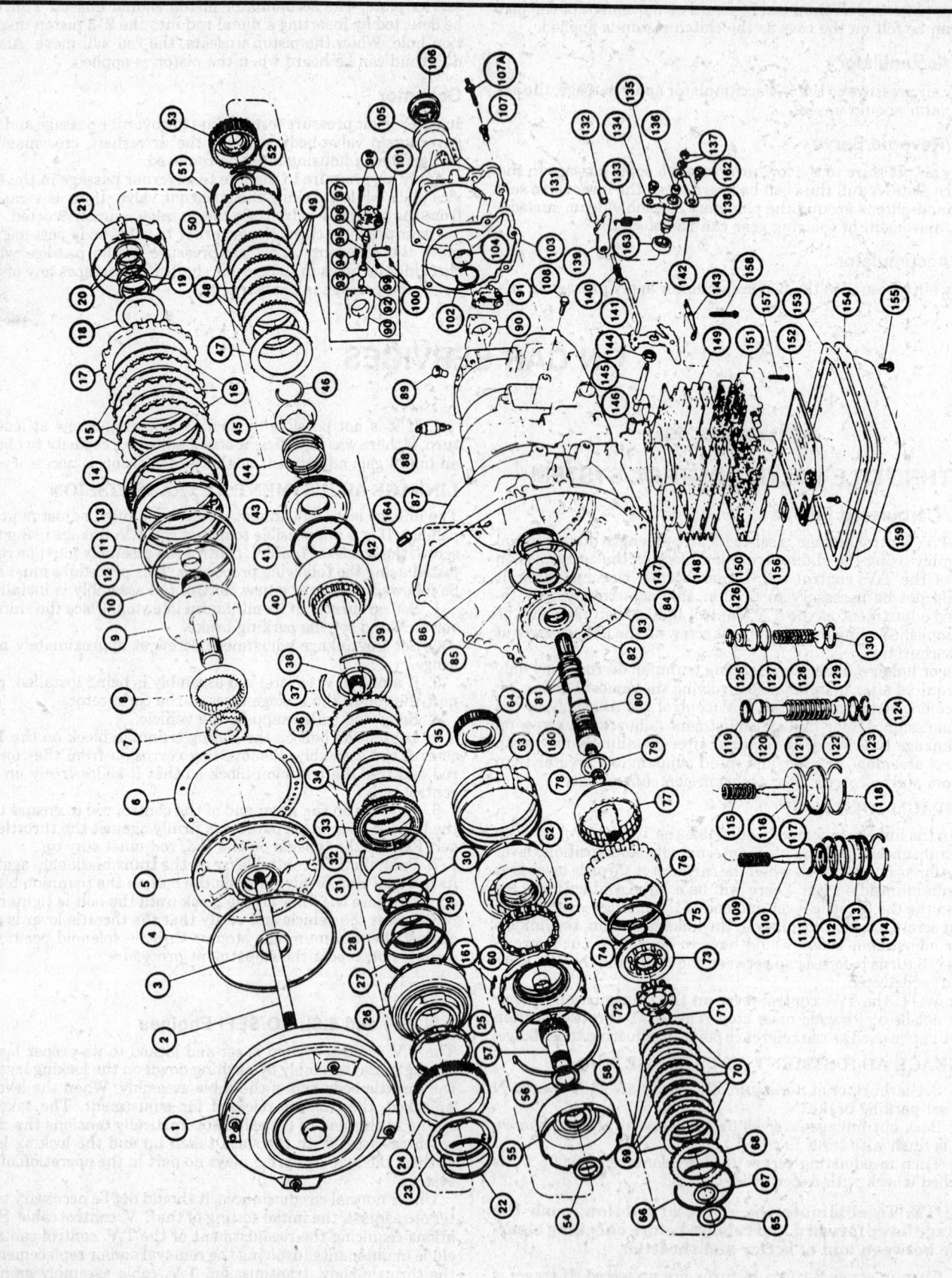

Exploded view of the AOD transmission

1. Torque converter
2. Direct drive shaft
3. Front pump seal
4. Front pump O-ring
5. Front pump body
6. Front pump gasket
7. Front pump drive gear
8. Front pump driven gear
9. Front pump stator support
10. Intermediate piston inner lip seal
11. Intermediate piston outer lip seal
12. Front pump bushing
13. Intermediate clutch piston
14. Intermediate clutch piston return spring
15. Intermediate clutch external spline steel plates
16. Intermediate clutch internal spline friction plates
17. Intermediate clutch pressure plates
18. Front pump No. 1 thrust washer
19. Stator support seal rings—reverse clutch
20. Stator support seal rings—forward clutch
21. Overdrive band
22. Intermediate one-way clutch retaining snapring
23. Intermediate one-way clutch retaining plate
24. Intermediate one-way clutch outer race
25. Intermediate one-way clutch assembly
26. Reverse clutch drum
27. Reverse clutch piston seal
28. Reverse clutch piston
29. Reverse clutch inner piston seal
30. Thrust ring
31. Reverse clutch piston return spring
32. Retaining snapring
33. Reverse clutch front pressure plate
34. Forward and reverse clutch internal spline friction plate
35. Reverse clutch external spline steel plate

36. Forward and reverse clutch rear pressure plate
37. Reverse clutch retaining ring
38. No. 2 thrust washer
39. Turbine shaft
40. Forward clutch cylinder and turbine shaft
41. Forward clutch outer piston seal
42. Forward clutch inner piston seal
43. Forward clutch piston
44. Forward clutch piston return spring
45. Return spring retainer
46. Retaining snapring
47. Waved plate
48. Forward clutch external spline steel plate
49. Forward and reverse clutch internal spline friction plate
50. Forward and reverse clutch pressure plate
51. Retaining snapring
52. No. 3 needle bearing—forward clutch
53. Forward clutch hub
54. No.4 needle bearing
55. Reverse sun gear and drive shell
56. No. 5 needle bearing
57. Forward sun gear
58. Center support retaining ring
59. Center support
60. Center support planetary
61. Planetary one-way clutch and cage spring and roller
62. Planetary assembly
63. Reverse band
64. Direct clutch hub
65. No. 7 needle bearing
66. Retaining snapring
67. Thrust spacer
68. Direct clutch pressure plate
69. Direct clutch internal splined plate
70. Direct clutch external splined plate
71. Retaining snapring
72. Return spring and retainer
73. Direct clutch piston

74. Direct clutch piston inner seal
75. Direct clutch piston outer seal
76. Ring gear and park gear
77. Direct cylinder
78. Output shaft steel seal rings
79. No. 8 needle bearing
80. Output shaft
81. Large output shaft seal
82. Output shaft seal
83. Retaining snapring
84. Retaining snapring
85. Rear case bushing
86. No. 9 needle bearing
87. Case assembly
88. Neutral start switch
89. Vent cap
90. Governor counterweight
91. Governor body assembly
92. Governor plug
93. Governor sleeve
94. Governor oil screen assembly
95. Governor valve spring
96. Governor valve
97. Governor body
98. Bolt
99. Clip
100. Bolt
101. Governor valve cover
102. Snapring
103. Extension housing bracket
104. Extension housing bushing
105. Extension housing
106. Extension housing seal
107. Extension housing bolt
107A. Extension housing stud
108. Pipe plug
109. Overdrive servo piston return spring
110. Overdrive servo piston
111. Overdrive servo piston seal
112. Overdrive servo cover seals
113. Overdrve servo cover
114. Retaining snapring
115. Reverse servo piston return spring
116. Reverse servo piston

117. Reverse servo cover
118. Snapring
119. 3–4 accumulator valve seal
120. 3–4 accumulator valve
121. 3–4 accumulator valve return spring
122. 3–4 accumulator cover
123. 3–4 accumulator cover seal
124. Snapring
125. 2–3 accumulator valve small seal
126. 2–3 accumulator valve
127. 2–3 accumulator valve large seal
128. 2–3 accumulator valve return spring
129. 2–3 accumulator cover
130. Snapring
131. Park pawl shaft
132. Guide cup
133. Park pawl return spring
134. Manual lever
135. Grommet
136. Throttle lever oil seal
137. Attaching nut and lock washer
138. Throttle lever
139. Park pawl
140. Park pawl actuating rod
141. Inner manual lever
142. Roll pin
143. Detent spring
144. Attaching nut
145. Inner throttle lever
146. Throttle torsion spring
147. Valve body reinforcement plate
148. Separator plate gasket
149. Separator plate
150. Separator plate gasket
151. Valve body
152. Oil filter and grommet
153. Oil pan gasket
154. Oil pan
155. Bolt
156. Oil filter gasket
157. Bolt
158. Bolt
159. Bolt
160. Governor drive ball
161. Anti clunk spring
162. Grommet
163. Oil seal assembly
164. Connector assembly
165. Bolt

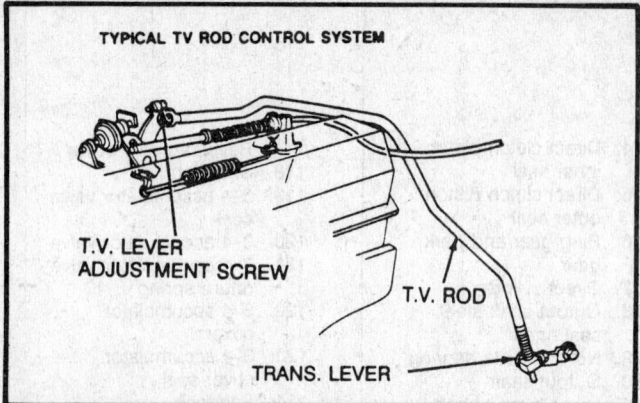

T.V rod system components

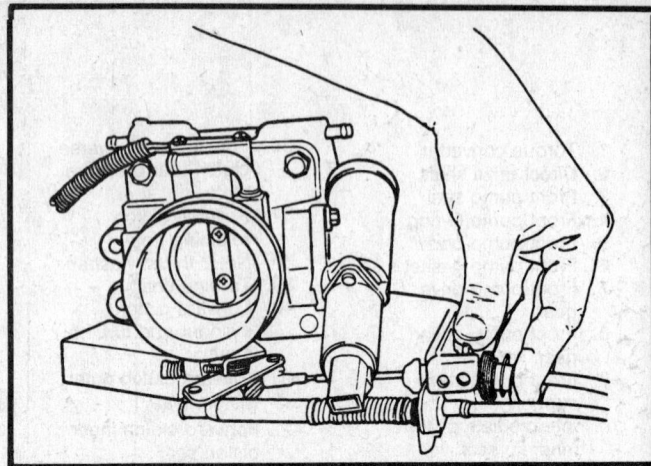

Adjusting the T.V. pressure at the cable

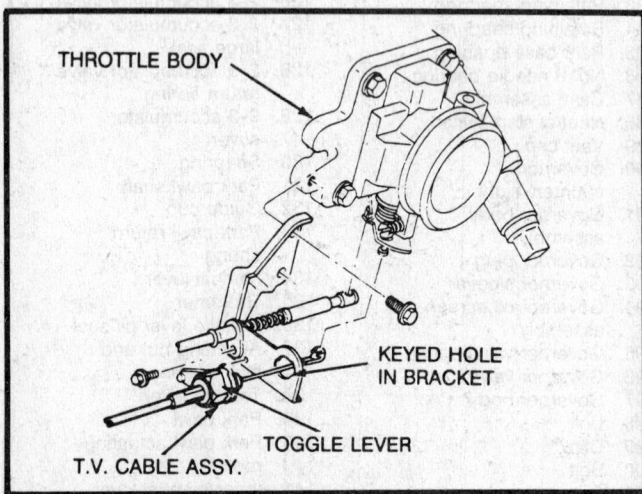

T.V. cable system attachment

NOTE: The EFI engine uses an air bypass valve (ISC, that does not affect throttle position. Therefore, idle automatic setting does not affect T.V. cable adjustment.

LINKAGE ADJUSTMENT USING T.V. CONTROL PRESSURE

To correctly perform this procedure, the use of a T.V. pressure gauge with hose (0–60 psi) T86L–70002–A or equivalent is required. Also, T.V. cable gauge tool T86L–70332–A or equivalent is needed for correct adjustment.

1. Attach the T.V. pressure gauge to the T.V. port on the transmission.

2. Insert the tapered end of the cable gauge tool between the crimped slug end of the cable and plastic cable fitting that attaches to the throttle lever. Push gauge as far in as it will go.

3. Run the engine until it reaches normal operating temperature. The transmission fluid temperature should be approximatelt 100–150°F.

4. Set the parking brake and place the shift lever in **N**, the T.V. pressure should be between 30–40 psi. For best transmission operaton, set T.V. pressure as close as possible to 33 psi.

NOTE: T.V. pressure must be set with the transmission in N.

5. Using a small pry bar, pry up the white toggle lever on the cable adjuster located behind the throttle body cable mounting bracket. The adjuster pre-load spring should cause the the ad-

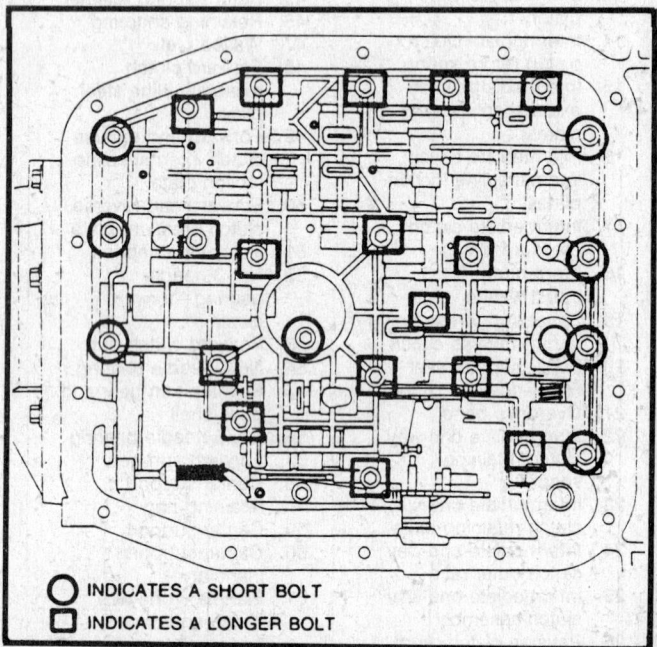

○ INDICATES A SHORT BOLT
□ INDICATES A LONGER BOLT

Valve body bolt locations

justing slider to move away from the throttle body and T.V. pressure should increase.

6. Push on the slider form behind bracket until T.V. pressure is 33 psi. While still holding slider, push down on toggle lever as far as it will go, locking the slider in position. Toggle lever must be completely down for proper locking on cable.

7. Remove gauge tool, allowing cable spring to return to its normal idling position. With the engine still idling, T.V. pressure must be at or near 0 psi (less than 5 psi.). If the T.V. pressure is not in this range, repeat the adjustment procedure but lower the setting to 30 psi. Recheck the pressure.

8. Remove the T.V. gauge and check transmission shift operation.

Services
FLUID CHANGES

Normal maintenance and lubrication requirements do not necessitate periodic transmission fluid changes. When used under

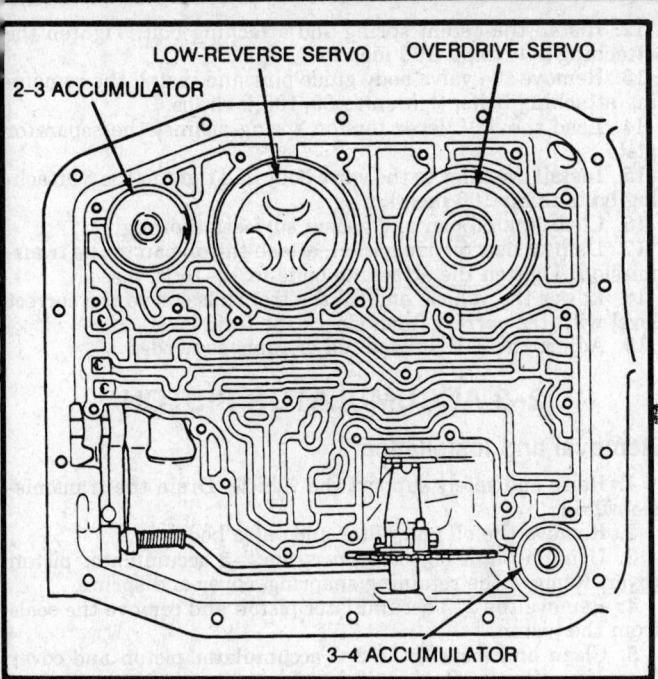

Servo locations

continuous or severe conditions the fluid should be changed more frequently than when used in normal circumstances.

The specified fluid to use in the AOD transmission is Mercon® fluid or an equivalent fluid that meets Ford specification ESP–M2C–185–C. Use of fluid that does not meet this specification could result in transmission failure.

The fluid capacity of the AOD for an complete service, including converter drain and fill, is 12.3 qts. The drain and refill service capacity is approximately 3 qts.

OIL PAN

Removal and Installation

1. Raise the vehicle and support safely. Place a drain pan under the oil pan and loosen the pan attaching bolts.

2. Allow the fluid to drain from the oil pan, to the level of the pan flange. Remove the pan attaching bolts in such a manner as to allow the oil pan to drop slowly, draining more of the fluid from the oil pan.

3. Remove the oil pan and drain the remaining fluid into the container. Discard the old gasket and clean the oil pan.

NOTE: The torque converter on the AOD transmission can be drained also. This can be accomplished by removing the dust cover and then removing the drain plug from the converter. The drain plug is accessible by turning the converter.

4. Clean or replace the oil filter screen. Install a new gasket on the oil pan and install the pan on the transmission. Tighten the oil pan attaching bolt to 6–10 ft. lbs.

5. Lower the vehicle and fill the transmission to the correct level with the specified fluid. Re-check the level as required, using the room temperature checking procedure.

VALVE BODY

Removal and Installation

1. Raise and safely support the vehicle.
2. Starting at the rear and working toward the front, loosen

the oil pan attaching bolts and drain the fluid from the transmission.

3. Remove the transmission pan attaching bolts, the pan and gasket.

4. Remove the filter-to-valve body attaching bolts and remove the filter, grommet and gasket.

5. Remove the detent spring attaching bolt and spring.

6. Remove the 24 valve body attaching bolts and remove the valve body. Discard the gasket.

7. Clean and inspect the valve body.

8. Using the valve body guide pins, T80L–77100–A or equivalent, position the valve body to the case. Make sure the inner manual lever and inner T.V. levers are engaged.

9. Install the 24 valve body-to-case bolts and tighten to 80–100 inch lbs.

10. Install the detent spring and attaching bolt. Tighten the attaching bolt to 80–100 inch lbs.

11. Remove the valve body guide pins and install the remaining attaching bolts, tighten to 80–100 inch lbs.

12. Load the T.V. lever torsion spring against the separator plate.

13. Install the filter to the valve body and tighten the 3 attaching bolts to 80–100 inch lbs.

14. Clean the oil pan and gasket surfaces thoroughly.

15. Using a new oil pan gasket, attach the oil pan to the transmission. Tighten the attaching bolts to 12–16 ft. lbs.

16. Lower the vehicle and fill the transmission to the correct level with the correct fluid. Check the fluid level.

17. Adjust the linkage rod or cable as needed.

OVERDRIVE SERVO ASSEMBLY

Removal and Installation

1. Raise and safely support the vehicle. Drain the transmission fluid from the vehicle.

2. Remove the oil pan, filter and valve body.

3. Depress the overdrve servo piston cover with a blunt object and remove the snapring retaining the piston.

4. Using servo piston remover, T80L–77030–B or equivalent, apply low air pressure to the servo piston release passage in order to remove the overdrive servo piston cover and spring.

5. Remove the piston from the cover. Remove the rubber seals from the piston and cover.

6. Clean and inspect the servo piston for nicks or burrs. Clean and inspect the servo piston pocket in the case for burrs.

7. Install new seals on the servo piston and cover. Lubricate the seals with clean transmission fluid. Install the servo piston into the cover and lubricate with clean transmission fluid.

8. Assemble the return spring to the servo piston. Install the overdrive piston cover and spring into the overdrive servo pocket and case. Make sure the servo rod contacts the overdrive band apply pocket.

9. Using a blunt object, depress the overdrive servo and install the retaining snapring.

7. Using the valve body guide pins, T80L–77100–A or equivalent, position the valve body to the case. Make sure the inner manual lever and inner T.V. levers are engaged.

8. Install the 24 valve body-to-case bolts and tighten to 80–100 inch lbs.

9. Install the detent spring and attaching bolt. Tighten the attaching bolt to 80–100 inch lbs.

10. Remove the valve body guide pins and install the remaining attaching bolts, tighten to 80–100 inch lbs.

11. Load the T.V. lever torsion spring against the separator plate.

12. Install the filter to the valve body and tighten the 3 attaching bolts to 80–100 inch lbs.

13. Clean the oil pan and gasket surfaces thoroughly.

14. Using a new oil pan gasket, attach the oil pan to the trans-

mission. Tighten the attaching bolts to 12–16 ft. lbs.

15. Lower the vehicle and fill the transmission to the correct level with the correct fluid. Check the fluid level.

16. Adjust the linkage rod or cable as needed.

LOW/REVERSE SERVO ASSEMBLY

Removal and Installation

1. Raise and safely support the vehicle. Drain the transmission fluid.

2. Remove the oil pan, filter and valve body.

3. Depress the reverse servo piston cover with a blunt object and remove the retaining snapring.

4. To remove the reverse servo piston and spring, apply low air pressure to the servo piston release passage using tool T80L–77030–B or equivalent.

5. Cover the servo piston pocket to prevent the piston from falling out of the case when the air pressure is applied.

6. Clean and inspect the reverse servo piston, cover and spring.

7. Assemble the return spring to the servo piston. Install the servo piston and spring into the cover and into the case.

8. Using a blunt object, depress the reverse servo piston and install the retaining snapring.

9. Using the valve body guide pins, T80L–77100–A or equivalent, position the valve body to the case. Make sure the inner manual lever and inner T.V. levers are engaged.

10. Install the 24 valve body-to-case bolts and tighten to 80–100 inch lbs.

11. Install the detent spring and attaching bolt. Tighten the attaching bolt to 80–100 inch lbs.

12. Remove the valve body guide pins and install the remaining attaching bolts, tighten to 80–100 inch lbs.

13. Load the T.V. lever torsion spring against the separator plate.

14. Install the filter to the valve body and tighten the 3 attaching bolts to 80–100 inch lbs.

15. Clean the oil pan and gasket surfaces thoroughly.

16. Using a new oil pan gasket, attach the oil pan to the transmission. Tighten the attaching bolts to 12–16 ft. lbs.

17. Lower the vehicle and fill the transmission to the correct level with the correct fluid. Check the fluid level.

18. Adjust the linkage rod or cable as needed.

3–4 ACCUMULATOR PISTON

Removal

1. Raise and safely support the vehicle. Drain the transmission fluid.

2. Remove the oil pan, filter and valve body.

3. Depress the 3–4 accumulator piston cover with a blunt object and remove the retaining snapring.

4. Slowly release the tension on the 3–4 accumulator cover and remove the piston cover and piston. On some models a spring is also used.

5. Remove the seals from the accumulator piston and cover.

6. Clean and inspect the accumulator piston and cover.

7. Install new seals on the piston and cover.

8. Lubricate the seals with clean transmission fluid. Install the 3–4 accumulator piston and spring into the case. Install the cover.

9. Depress the cover into the piston pocket and install the retaining snapring.

10. Using the valve body guide pins, T80L–77100–A or equivalent, position the valve body to the case. Make sure the inner manual lever and inner T.V. levers are engaged.

11. Install the 24 valve body-to-case bolts and tighten to 80–100 inch lbs.

12. Install the detent spring and attaching bolt. Tighten the attaching bolt to 80–100 inch lbs.

13. Remove the valve body guide pins and install the remaining attaching bolts, tighten to 80–100 inch lbs.

14. Load the T.V. lever torsion spring against the separator plate.

15. Install the filter to the valve body and tighten the 3 attaching bolts to 80–100 inch lbs.

16. Clean the oil pan and gasket surfaces thoroughly.

17. Using a new oil pan gasket, attach the oil pan to the transmission. Tighten the attaching bolts to 12–16 ft. lbs.

18. Lower the vehicle and fill the transmission to the correct level with the correct fluid. Check the fluid level.

19. Adjust the T.V linkage rod or cable as needed.

2–3 ACCUMULATOR PISTON

Removal and Installation

1. Raise and safely support the vehicle. Drain the transmission fluid.

2. Remove the oil pan, filter and valve body.

3. Using a blunt object depress the 2–3 accumulator piston cover. Remove the retaining snapring, cover and spring.

4. Remove the 2–3 accumulator piston and remove the seals from the piston.

5. Clean and inspect the 2–3 accumulator piston and cover for nicks or burrs. Replace if damaged.

6. Install new seals on the 2–3 accumulator piston and install the piston into the case.

7. Install the return spring and cover. Depress the 2–3 accumulator cover and install the retaining snapring.

8. Using the valve body guide pins, T80L–77100–A or equivalent, position the valve body to the case. Make sure the inner manual lever and inner T.V. levers are engaged.

9. Install the 24 valve body-to-case bolts and tighten to 80–100 inch lbs.

10. Install the detent spring and attaching bolt. Tighten the attaching bolt to 80–100 inch lbs.

11. Remove the valve body guide pins and install the remaining attaching bolts, tighten to 80–100 inch lbs.

12. Load the T.V. lever torsion spring against the separator plate.

13. Install the filter to the valve body and tighten the 3 attaching bolts to 80–100 inch lbs.

14. Clean the oil pan and gasket surfaces thoroughly.

15. Using a new oil pan gasket, attach the oil pan to the transmission. Tighten the attaching bolts to 12–16 ft. lbs.

16. Lower the vehicle and fill the transmission to the correct level with the correct fluid. Check the fluid level.

17. Adjust the T.V linkage rod or cable as needed.

EXTENSION HOUSING BUSHING AND REAR SEAL

Removal and Installation

1. Raise and safely support the vehicle.

2. Disconnect the driveshaft at the transmission. To keep the driveline balance, mark the driveshaft yoke and axle flange so that the driveshaft can be installed in its original position.

3. Remove the rear seal from the transmission using a seal remover, T74P–77248–A or equivalent.

4. After removing the seal, the bushing can be removed using a bushing remover, T77L–7697–A or equivalent.

5. Inspect the seal bore for nicks or burrs, any burrs can be removed with crocus cloth.

6. Install new bushing using a bushing installer, T80L–77034–A or equivalent.

7. Install a new seal into the extension housing using a seal installer, T61L–7657–A or equivalent. The seal should be firmly

seated in the bore. Coat the inside diameter of the seal with a long life multi-purpose lubricant.

8. Install the driveshaft aligning the marks made during removal.

EXTENSION HOUSING

Removal and Installation

1. Raise and safely support the vehicle.
2. Disconnect the parking brake cable from the equalizer.
3. Disconnect the driveshaft at the transmission. To keep the driveline balance, mark the driveshaft yoke and axle flange so that the driveshaft can be installed in its original position.
4. Disconnect the speedometer cable from the extension housing.
5. Remove the engine rear suport-to-extension housing bolts. Place a suitable lifting device under the transmission and raise it enough to remove the weight from the engine support.
6. Remove the bolt that secures the rear engine support to the crossmember and remove the support.
7. Place a drain pan under the rear of the transmission case. Lower the transmission and remove the extension housing attaching bolts. Slide the extension housing off the output shaft and allow the fluid to drain.
8. Remove and discard the extension housing gasket.
9. Clean the extension housing and transmission mounting surfaces. Remove any sealant from bolts and bolt holes. Position a new gasket on the transmission.
10. Coat all of the attaching bolts with thread sealer. Position the extension housing and install the attaching bolts, tightening to 16–20 ft. lbs.
11. Using a suitable lifting device, raise the transmission high enough to position the rear engine support on the crossmember.
12. Install the support-to-crossmember bolt and tighten to 25–35 ft. lbs.
13. Lower the transmission and install the support-to-extension housing bolts, tighten to 50–70 ft. lbs.
14. Connect the speedometer cable to the extension housing. Connect the parking brake cable to the equalizer.
15. Install the driveshaft in the transmission, aligning the matchmarks made during removal.
16. Lower the vehicle and fill the transmission to the correct level with the appropriate fluid. Run the engine and recheck the fluid level.

GOVERNOR

Removal and Installation

1. Raise and safely support the vehicle.
2. Remove the extension housing. Remove the governor-to-output shaft retaining snapring.
3. Using a soft faced hammer, tap the governor assembly off the output shaft. Remove the governor drive ball.

4. Remove the governor-to-counterweight attaching screws and lift the governor from the counterweight.
5. Lubricate the governor valve parts with clean transmission fluid. Make certain that the valve moves freely in the valve body bore.
6. Position the governor valve body on the counterweight with the cover facing towards the front of the vehicle. Install the attaching screw and tighten to 50–60 inch lbs.
7. Position the governor drive ball into the pocket of the output shaft.
8. Align the keyway in the counterweight to the governor drive ball. Slide the governor assembly onto the output shaft. If necessary, gently tap the governor into position with a soft faced hammer.
9. Reinstall the governor-to-output shaft retaining snapring. Clean the mounting surface on the transmission and on the extension housing. Position a new gasket on the transmission.
10. Install the extension housing.

NEUTRAL SAFETY SWITCH

Removal and Installation

TOWN CAR, 1984–87 CONTINENAL, CROWN VICTORIA/GRAND MARQUIS

1. Set the parking brake and palce the transmission shift lever in the **1** position.
2. Open the hood and remove the air cleaner assembly. Disconnect the negative battery cable.
3. Disconnect the neutral safety switch connector by lifting the harness off the switch without using a side to side motion.
4. Remove the neutral safety switch and O-ring seal. The switch can be removed by using a 24 in. long extension and universal adapter, the access path is along the left side of the firewall.
5. Install the neutral safety switch and O-ring into the transmission, tightening to 8–11 ft. lbs.
6. Connect the neutral safety switch electrical lead.
7. Connect the negative battery cable. Check the operation of the switch in each gear position.
8. Install the air cleaner assembly.

MARK VII, THUNDERBIRD/COUGAR, MUSTANG/CAPRI

1. Place the transmission shift lever in the **1** position. Disconnect the negative battery cable.
2. Raise and safely support the vehicle.
3. Disconnect the neutral safety switch electrical connector.
4. Remove the neutral safety switch and seal O-ring.
5. Install the neutral safety switch and O-ring into the transmission, tightening to 8–11 ft. lbs.
6. Connect the neutral safety switch electrical lead.
7. Lower the vehicle.
8. Connect the negative battery cable. Check the operation of the switch in each gear position.

REMOVAL AND INSTALLATION

TRANSMISSION REMOVAL

1. Disconnect the negative battery cable. Raise and safely support the vehicle.
2. Place a drain pan under the transmission and drain the fluid. Once the fluid is drained, install 2 bolts in the oil pan to keep it in place.
3. Remove the converter drain plug access cover. Remove the converter to flywheel attaching nuts.
4. Place a drain pan under the converter. Turn the converter

to gain access to the converter drain plug and remove the plug. When the fluid is drained, reinstall the drain plug.
5. Disconnect the dirveshaft from the rear axle and slide the shaft back to remove it form the transmission. To maintain driveline balance matchmark the driveshaft flange and the rear axle yoke.
6. Disconnect the cable from the terminal on the starter. Remove the attaching bolts and remove the starter.
7. Disconnect the neutral safety switch wire from the neutral safety switch.

8. Remove the rear mount-to-crossmember attaching bolts and the crossmember-to-frame attaching bolts. Remove the engine rear support-to-extension housing attaching bolts.

9. Disconnect the T.V. linkage from the T.V. lever ball stud. On Thunderbird/Cougar, disconnect the T.V. linkage from the bellcrank lever stud and remove the bracket bolt.

10. Disconnect the manual rod from the transmission manual lever. Remove the bolts securing the bellcrank bracket to the case.

11. Using a suitable lifting device, raise the transmission enough to allow removal of the rear mount. Remove the rear mount from the crossmember and remove the crossmember from the side supports.

12. Disconnct the oil cooler lines from the fittings on the transmission. Disconnect the speedometer cable from the extension housing.

13. Remove the bolts securing the transmission filler tube to the cylinder block. Remove the filler tube from the transmission.

14. Secure the transmission to the lifting device and remove the engine-to-transmission bolts.

15. Carefully move the transmission and converter assembly away from the engine and lower the assembly from under the vehicle.

TRANSMISSION INSTALLATION

1. Position the converter on the transmission, make sure the converter is fully seated on the pump gear by rotating the converter.

2. With the converter properly installed, place the transmission on a lifting device. Lift the transmission into position under the vehicle.

3. Align the converter with the flywheel. Move the transmission assembly forward into position, use care not to damage the flywheel and converter pilot.

4. Install the transmission-to-engine bolts and tighten to 40–50 ft. lbs.

5. Install a new O-ring on the transmission filler tube and insert the filler tube in the transmission case. Install the attaching bolt.

6. Connect the speedometer cable to the extension housing. Connect the cooler lines and tighten to 18–23 ft. lbs.

7. Position the crossmember on the side rails and install the rear nount on the crossmember. Install the attaching bolt and nut.

8. Secure the engine support to the extension housing. Secure the crosmember to the side supports tightening the bolts to 70–100 ft. lbs.

9. Install the bellcrank assembly onto the converter housing and tighten the bolts to 20–30 ft. lbs.

10. Connect the T.V. linkage rod to the to the T.V. lever ball stud. Connect the manual linkage rod to the manual lever.

11. Install the converter to flywheel attaching nuts, tighten to 20–34 ft. lbs.

12. Install the converter housing access cover, tighten the bolts to 12–16 ft. lbs.

13. Install the starter motor and connect the cable to the terminal. Connect the neutral safety switch wires.

14. Install the driveshaft, aligning the matchmarks made during disassembly.

15. Lower the vehicle and attach the negative battery cable. Fill the transmission to the correct level with the specified fluid.

16. Adjust the T.V. linkage, idle and manual linkage as necessary.

BENCH OVERHAUL

Before Disassembly

When servicing this unit, it is recommended that as each part is disassembled, it is cleaned in solvent and dried with compressed air. All oil passages should be blown out and checked for obstructions. Disassembly and reassembly of this unit and its parts must be done on a clean work bench. As is the case when repairing any hydraulically operated unit, cleanliness is of the utmost importance. Keep work area, tools, parts and hands clean at all times. Also, before installing bolts into aluminum parts, always dip the threads into clean transmission oil. Antiseize compound can also be used to prevent bolts from galling the aluminum and seizing. Always use a torque wrench to keep from stripping the threads. Take care with the seals when installing them, especially the smaller O-rings. The slightest damage can cause leaks. Aluminum parts are very susceptible to damage so great care should be exercised when handling them. The internal snaprings should be expanded and the external snaprings compressed if they are to be re-used. This will help insure proper seating when installed. Be sure to replace any O-ring, gasket, or seal that is removed, although often the Teflon seal rings, when used, will not need to be removed unless damaged. Lubricate all parts with Dexron® II when assembling.

Inspection

CONVERTER ENDPLAY CHECK

1. Insert endplay checking tool, T80L–7902–A or equivalent, into the converter pump drive hub until it bottoms.

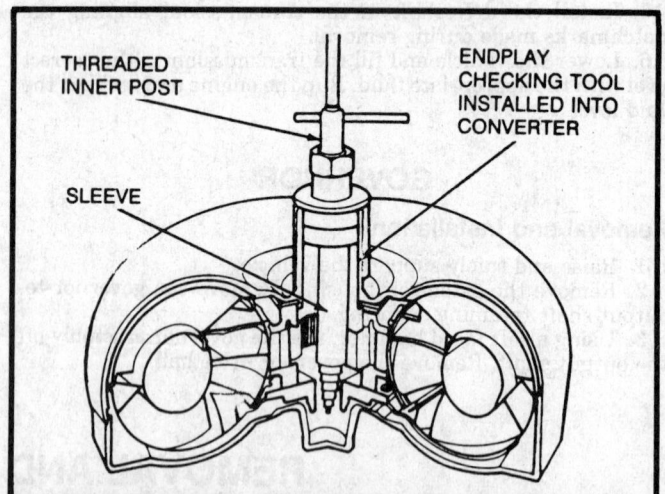

Checking converter endplay

2. Expand the sleeve in the turbine spline by tightening the threaded inner post until the tool is securely locked into the spline.

3. Attach dial indicator tool, 4201–C or equivalent, to the tool. Position the indicator button on the converter pump drive hub and set the dial face at 0.

4. Lift the tool upward as far as it will go and note the indicator reading. The indicator is the total endplay which the turbine

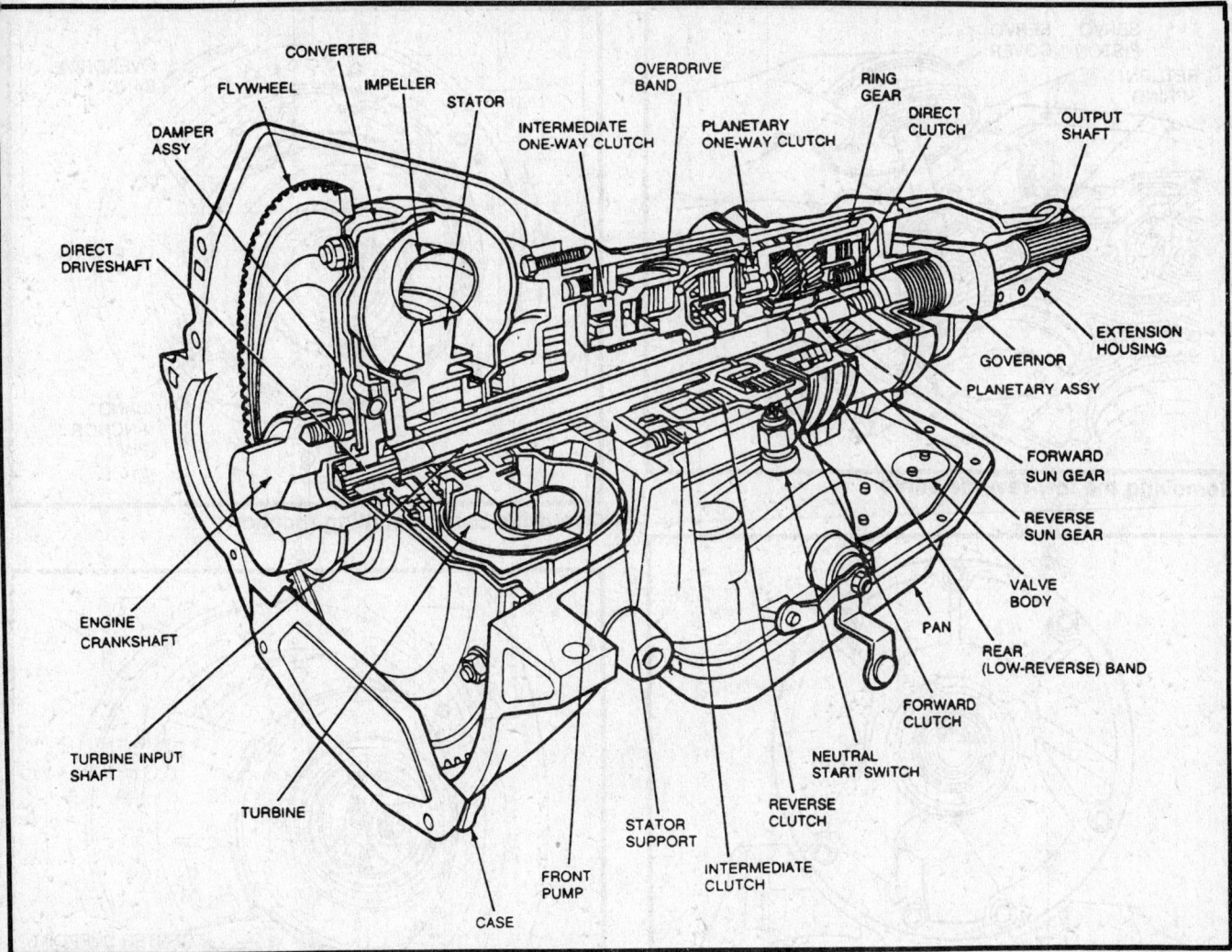

AOD component locations

and stator share. Replace the converter unit if the total endplay exceeds 0.50 in.

5. Remove the tools from the converter.

CONVERTER DAMPER/HUB ASSEMBLY WELD CHECK

1. Position a suitable converter holding fixture, T83L–7902–A3 or equivalent, in a vise.

2. Place the converter on top of the holding fixture, aligning the pilot hub and 1 stud in the appropriate holes.

3. Insert a rod torque adapter tool, T83L–7902–A1 or equivalent, into the converter making sure the splines engage the damper assembly.

4. Install the pilot guide T83L–7902–A2 or equivalent, over the rod torque adapter turning tool and onto impeller hub.

5. Hold the converter snug to the holding fixture while tightening.

6. Turn the shaft clockwise and counterclockwise applying approximately 50 ft. lbs. of pressure with a ¾ in. drive socket and torque wrench.

7. The shaft should not turn more than 2 degrees.

8. If there is a grinding noise and/or if the shaft turns more than 2 degrees, the converter damper assembly, welds, rivets or reaction hub are broken. Replace the torque converter.

REACTOR ONE-WAY CLUTCH CHECK

1. Align the slot in the thrust washer with the slot in the holding lug.

NOTE: To align the slots, use tool, T81P–7902–B or its equivalent to turn the reactor.

2. Position the holding wire, T77L–7902–A or its equivalent, in the holding lug.

3. While holding the wire in position in the lug, install the one-way clutch torquing tool, T76L–7902–C or equivalent, in the reactor spline.

4. Continue holding the wire and turn the torquing tool counterclockwise with a torque wrench. The converter one-way clutch should lock-up and hold at 10 ft. lbs. of torque. The converter one-way clutch should rotate freely in clockwise direction.

5. If the clutch fails to lock-up and hold at 10 ft. lbs, replace the converter.

Transmission Disassembly

1. Remove the transmission from the vehicle and mount it in a suitable holding fixture.

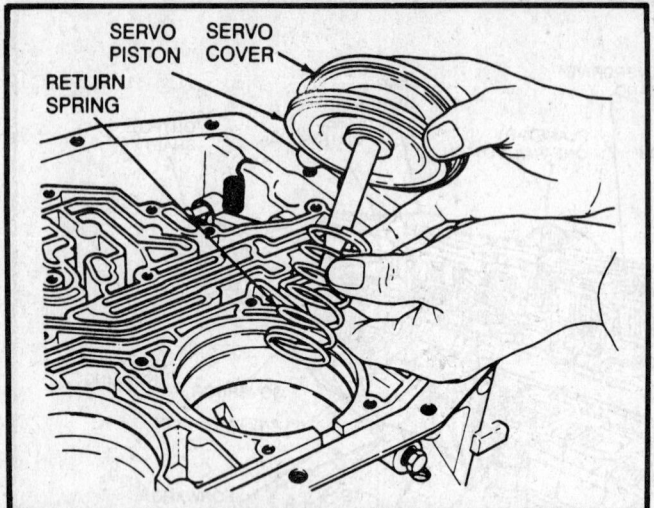

Removing the low-reverse servo

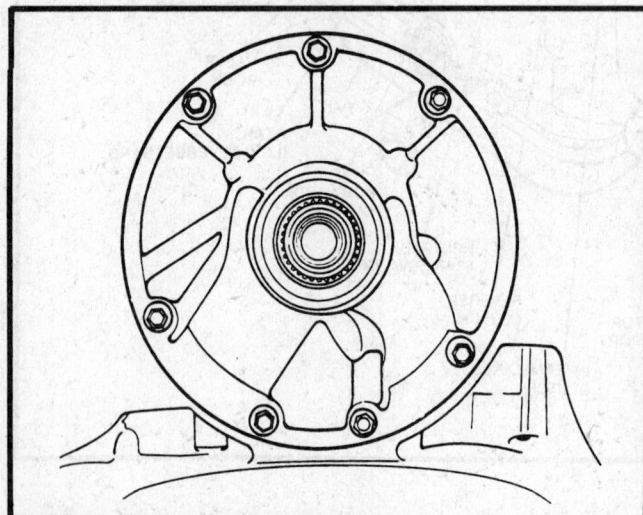

Pump attaching bolt locations

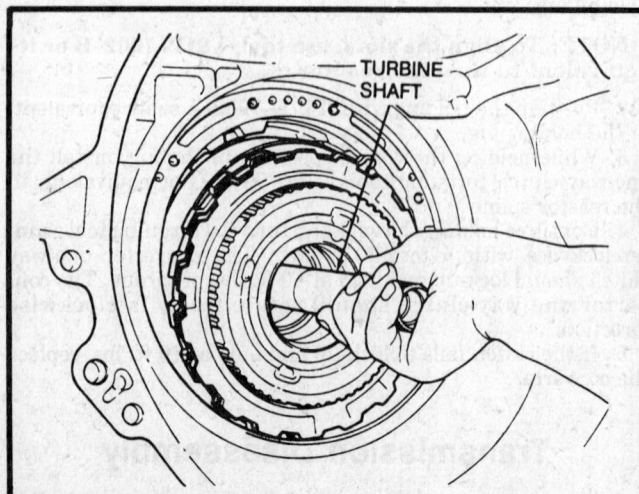

Removing the turbine shaft and clutch packs

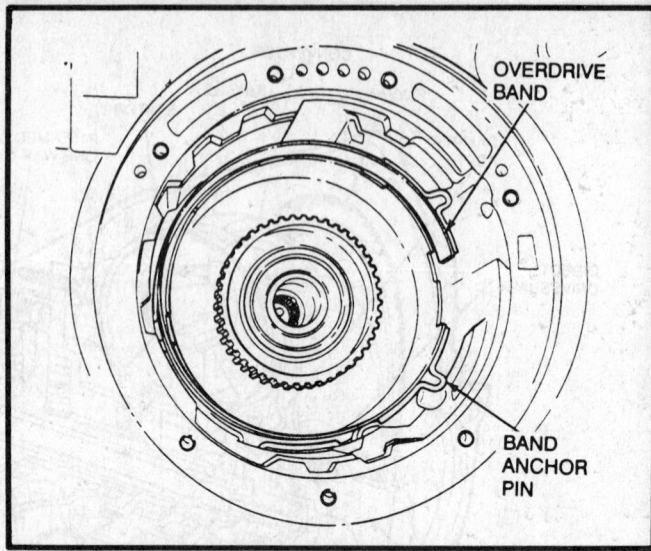

Overdrive band mounting location

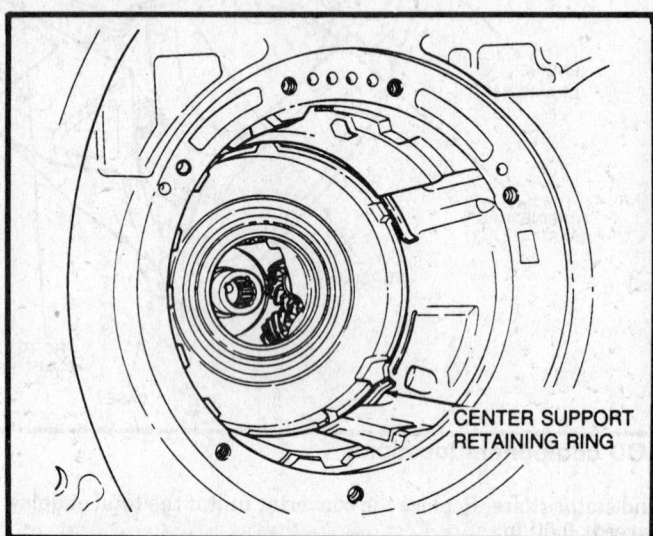

Location of center support retaining ring

2. Remove the torque converter from the inside the bell housing by pulling it straight out.

3. Remove the bolts attaching the oil pan and remove the oil pan. Discard the gasket. Remove the bolts retaining the oil filter and remove the filter, grommet and gasket.

4. Remove the manual lever detent spring and roller assembly. Remove the remaining valve body retaining bolts and remove the valve body.

5. Remove the 3–4 accumulator cover and piston, the overdrive servo cover and piston, the low reverse servo cover and piston and the 2–3 accumulator.

6. Place the transmission in a vertical position. Remove the pump body attaching bolts and remove the pump assembly from the case, using slide hammer tool T59L–100–B or equivalent.

7. Place the transmission in a horizontal position. Grasp the turbine shaft and pull it from the case.

NOTE: When the turbine shaft is removed, the intermediate clutch pack, reverse and forward clutch packs and the intermediate one-way clutch will also come out. Care should be taken not to damage the overdrive band friction material when removing these components.

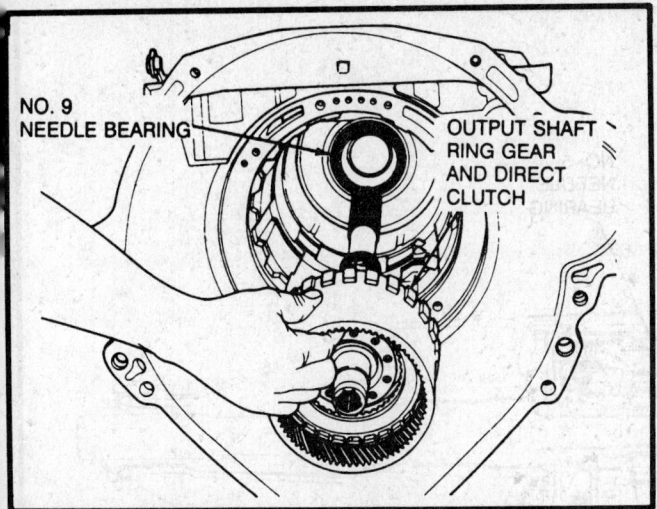

Removing the output shaft and direct clutch assembly

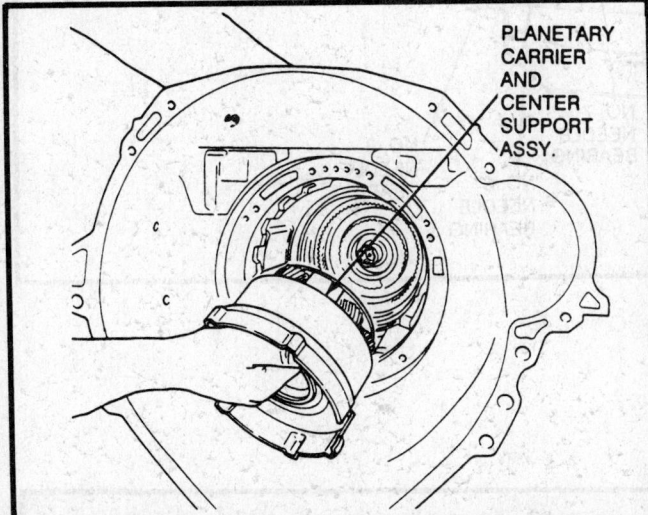

Removing the planetary carrier and center support

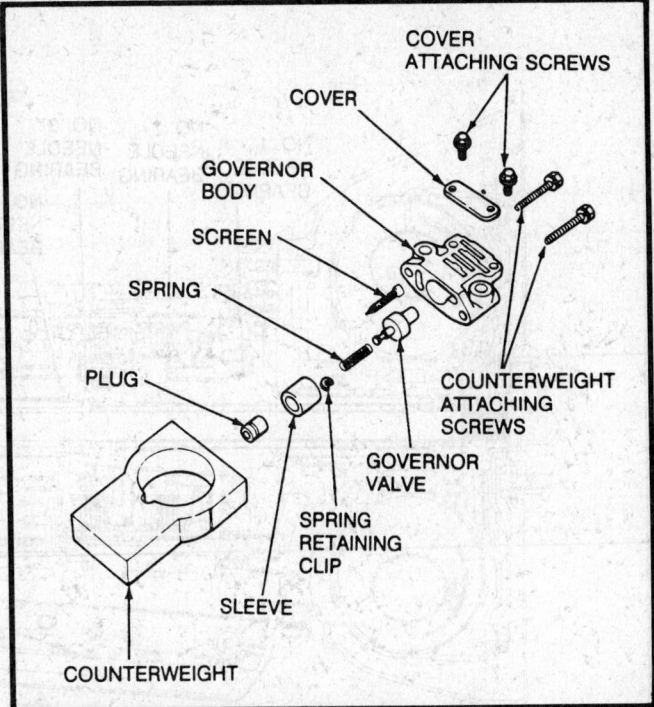

Exploded view of the governor assembly

move the output shaft, the ring gear and the direct clutch through the front of the case, as an assembly.

18. Remove the output shaft No. 9 needle bearing from the rear of the case.

19. Remove the intermediate clutch pack from the intermediate one-way clutch. Remove the reverse clutch assembly from the forward clutch assembly.

Unit Disassembly and Assembly

GOVERNOR

Disassembly

1. Remove the screws attaching the counterweight to the governor body and remove the governor cover screws.

2. Remove the governor cover. Remove the plug, sleeve and governor valve from the governor body.

3. Remove the screen from the governor body.

Inspection

1. Inspect the governor valves and bores for scores. Minor scores may be removed from the valves with crocus cloth. Replace the governor if the valves or body are deeply scored.

2. Inspect the governor screen for obstructions. The screen must be free of foreign material. If contaminated, clean thoroughly in a suitable solvent and blow dry.

3. Check for free movement of the valves in their bores. The valves should slide freely in the bores when dry. Inspect the fluid passages in the governor body and counterweight for obstructions.

4. Check the mating surfaces of the governor valve and the counterweight for burrs or scratches.

Assembly

1. Install the clip and sleeve on the governor valve. Install the governor valve in the governor body.

8. Disengage the overdrive band from the anchor pins and remove it from the case.

9. Remove the forward clutch hub and the No. 3 needle bearing from the case as an assembly.

10. Remove the forward sun gear, No. 5 needle bearing, reverse sun gear, drive shell and the No. 4 needle bearing as an assembly.

11. Remove the center support retaining ring, note the position of the tabs for reassembly.

12. Using a small pry bar, pry the anti-clunk spring from between the center support and the case. Note the location of the spring for reassembly.

13. Remove the center support and planetary carrier as an assembly. Remove the reverse band.

14. If the direct clutch hub did not come out with the planetary, lift it out of the direct clutch.

15. Rotate the transmission so that the extension housing is in an upright position. Remove the extension housing mounting bolts and remove the extension housing.

16. Rotate the transmission into a horizontal position. Remove the governor retaining ring and the governor from the output shaft.

17. Remove the governor drive ball from the output shaft. Re-

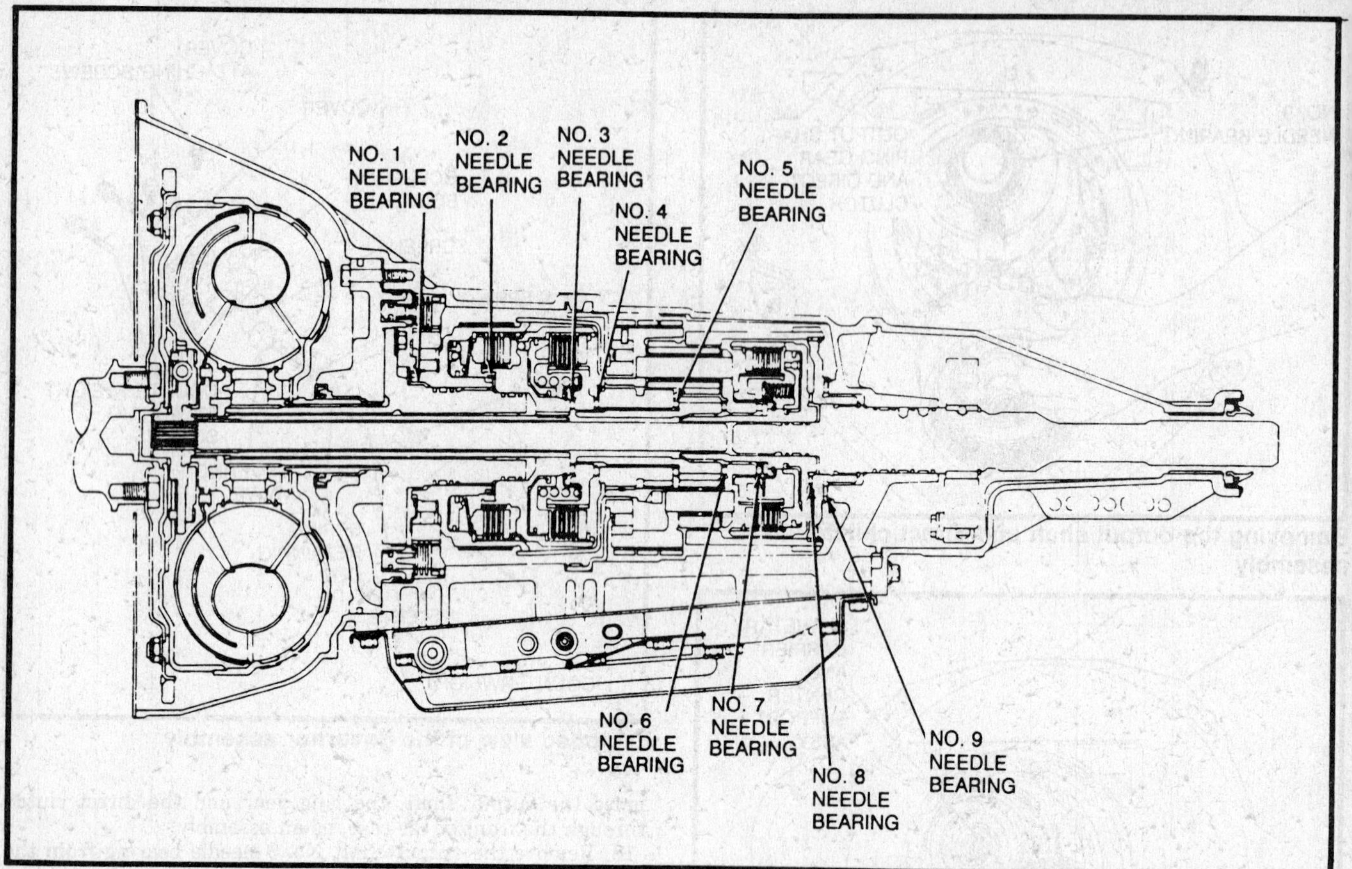

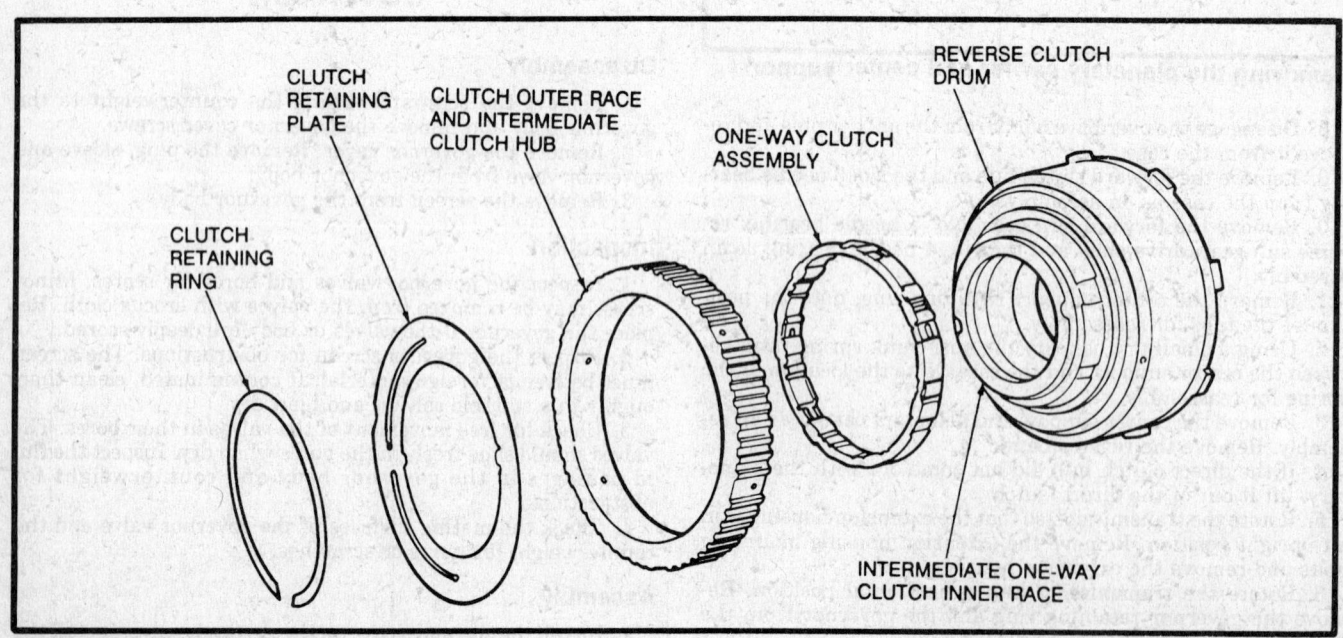

NO. 1 NEEDLE BEARING
NO. 2 NEEDLE BEARING
NO. 3 NEEDLE BEARING
NO. 4 NEEDLE BEARING
NO. 5 NEEDLE BEARING
NO. 6 NEEDLE BEARING
NO. 7 NEEDLE BEARING
NO. 8 NEEDLE BEARING
NO. 9 NEEDLE BEARING

Thrust bearing locations

CLUTCH RETAINING RING
CLUTCH RETAINING PLATE
CLUTCH OUTER RACE AND INTERMEDIATE CLUTCH HUB
ONE-WAY CLUTCH ASSEMBLY
REVERSE CLUTCH DRUM
INTERMEDIATE ONE-WAY CLUTCH INNER RACE

Intermediate one-way clutch assembly

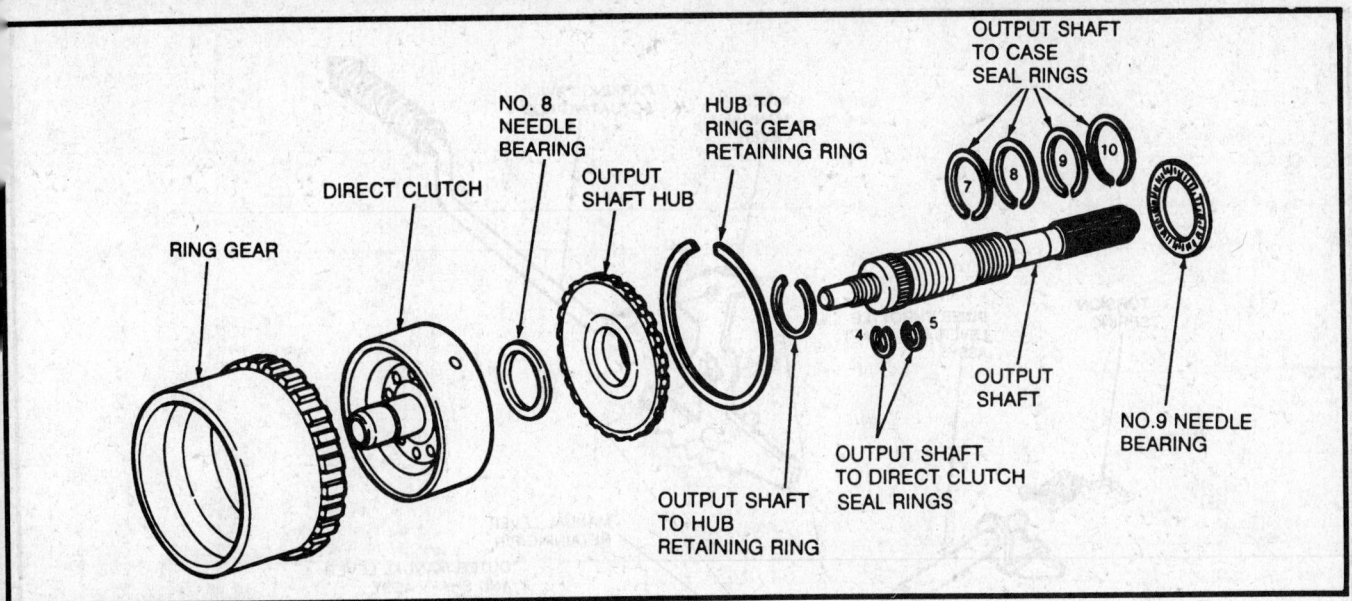

Output shaft assembly

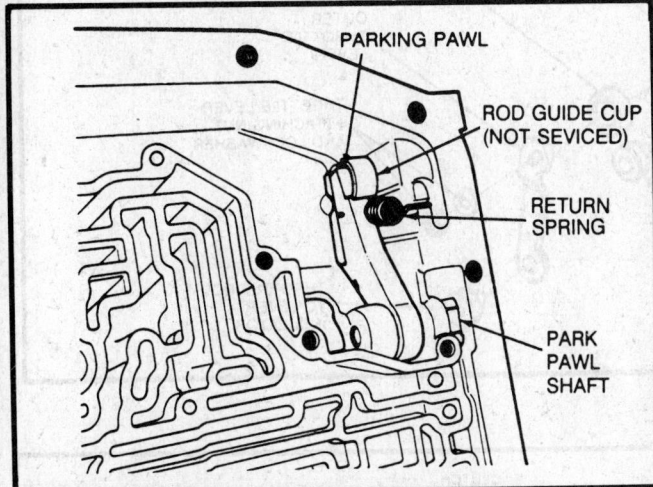

Parking pawl component locations

2. Install the sleeve in the governor body with the points outward. Install the plug in the sleeve with the knurled face inward.

3. Position the cover and install the attaching screws, tightening to 20–30 inch lbs.

4. Install the screen in the body with the steel band facing inward and the top of the screen facing out.

5. Position the governor body on the counterweight and install the retaining screws. Tighten the retaining screws to 50–60 inch lbs.

PARKING PAWL

Disassembly

1. Slide the park pawl shaft out of the rear of the case and remove the parking pawl.

2. Remove the return spring.

Assembly

1. Hook the squared end of the spring into the notch on the park pawl.

2. Hold the pawl and spring in place and hook the curved end of the spring into the recess in the case.

3. Install the park pawl shaft by sliding it into the case.

INTERMEDIATE/ONE-WAY CLUTCH

Disassembly

1. Using expanding type snapring pliers, remove the snapring that retains the clutch.

2. Remove the clutch retaining plate. Remove the clutch outer race by lifting on the race while turning counterclockwise.

3. Carefully lift the one-way clutch from the inner race.

Inspection

1. Inspect the clutch outer race for burrs or spline damage.

2. Inspect the clutch inner race for burrs.

3. Check the clutch hub splines for wear. The clutch hub is attached to the reverse clutch drum.

Assembly

1. Install the one-way clutch over the inner race.

2. Install the clutch outer race by placing it over the one-way clutch and turning it counterclockwise.

3. Install the clutch retaining plate and install the retaining snapring.

OUTPUT SHAFT

Disassembly

1. Remove the ring retaining the output shaft hub to the ring gear.

2. Separate the output shaft and hub assembly from the ring gear.

3. Remove the direct clutch from the ring gear and the No. 8 needle bearing from the back of the direct clutch.

4. Remove the 4 output shaft seal rings and the hub-to-output shaft retaining ring. Separate the hub from the output shaft.

5. Remove the 2 direct clutch seal rings from the output shaft.

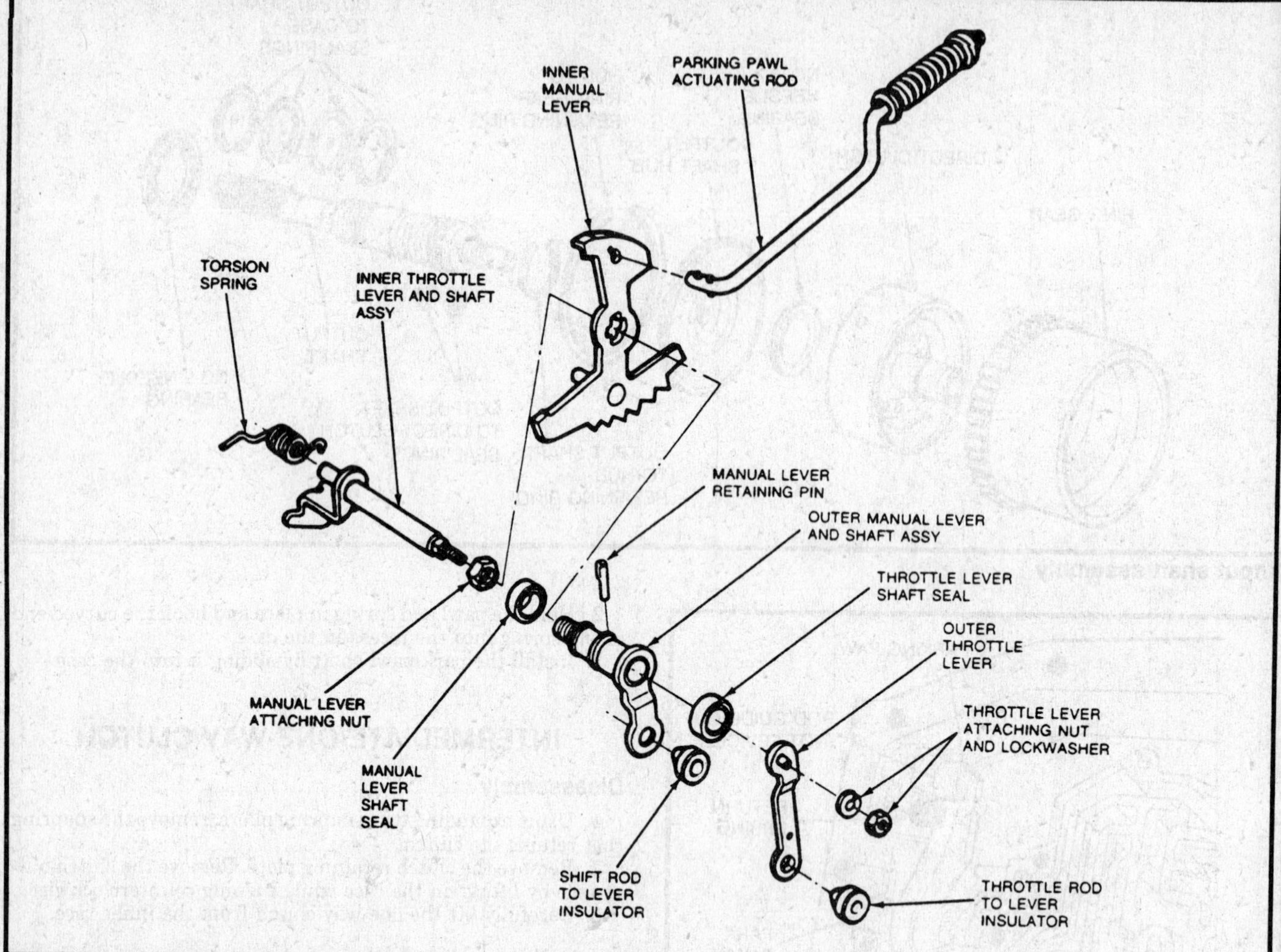

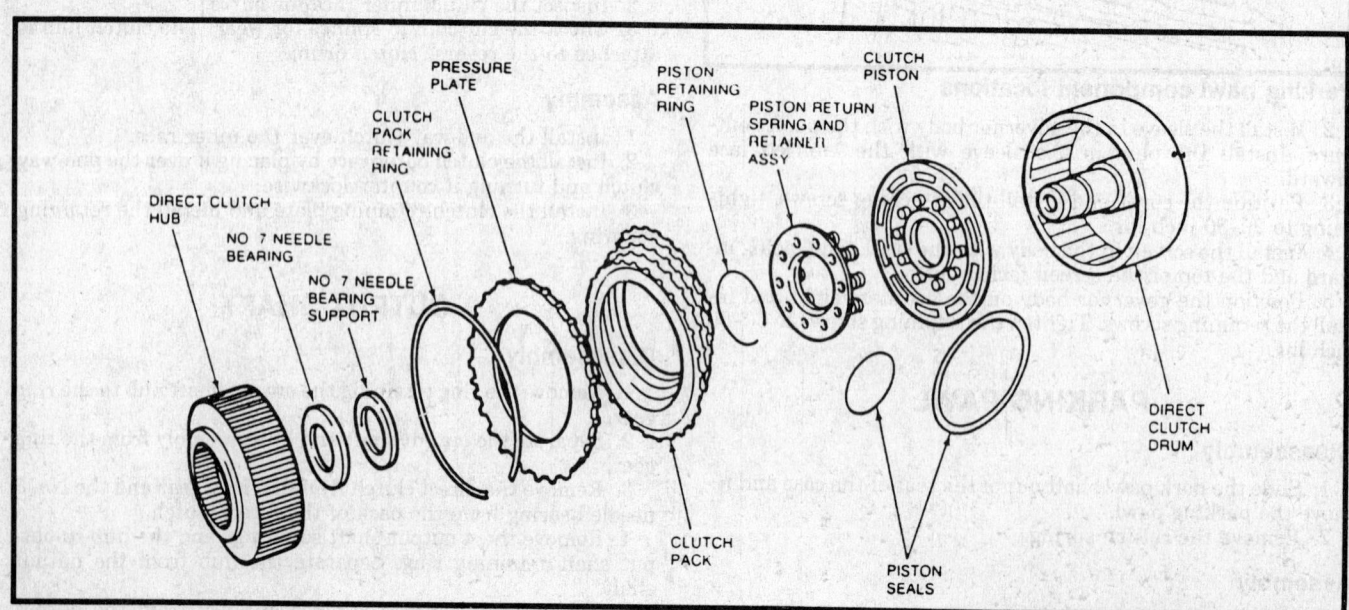

Manual and throttle linkage assembly

(Labels in upper diagram:) INNER MANUAL LEVER · PARKING PAWL ACTUATING ROD · TORSION SPRING · INNER THROTTLE LEVER AND SHAFT ASSY · MANUAL LEVER RETAINING PIN · OUTER MANUAL LEVER AND SHAFT ASSY · THROTTLE LEVER SHAFT SEAL · OUTER THROTTLE LEVER · MANUAL LEVER ATTACHING NUT · THROTTLE LEVER ATTACHING NUT AND LOCKWASHER · MANUAL LEVER SHAFT SEAL · SHIFT ROD TO LEVER INSULATOR · THROTTLE ROD TO LEVER INSULATOR

(Labels in lower diagram:) PRESSURE PLATE · CLUTCH PACK RETAINING RING · PISTON RETAINING RING · CLUTCH PISTON · PISTON RETURN SPRING AND RETAINER ASSY · DIRECT CLUTCH HUB · NO 7 NEEDLE BEARING · NO 7 NEEDLE BEARING SUPPORT · DIRECT CLUTCH DRUM · CLUTCH PACK · PISTON SEALS

Direct clutch assembly

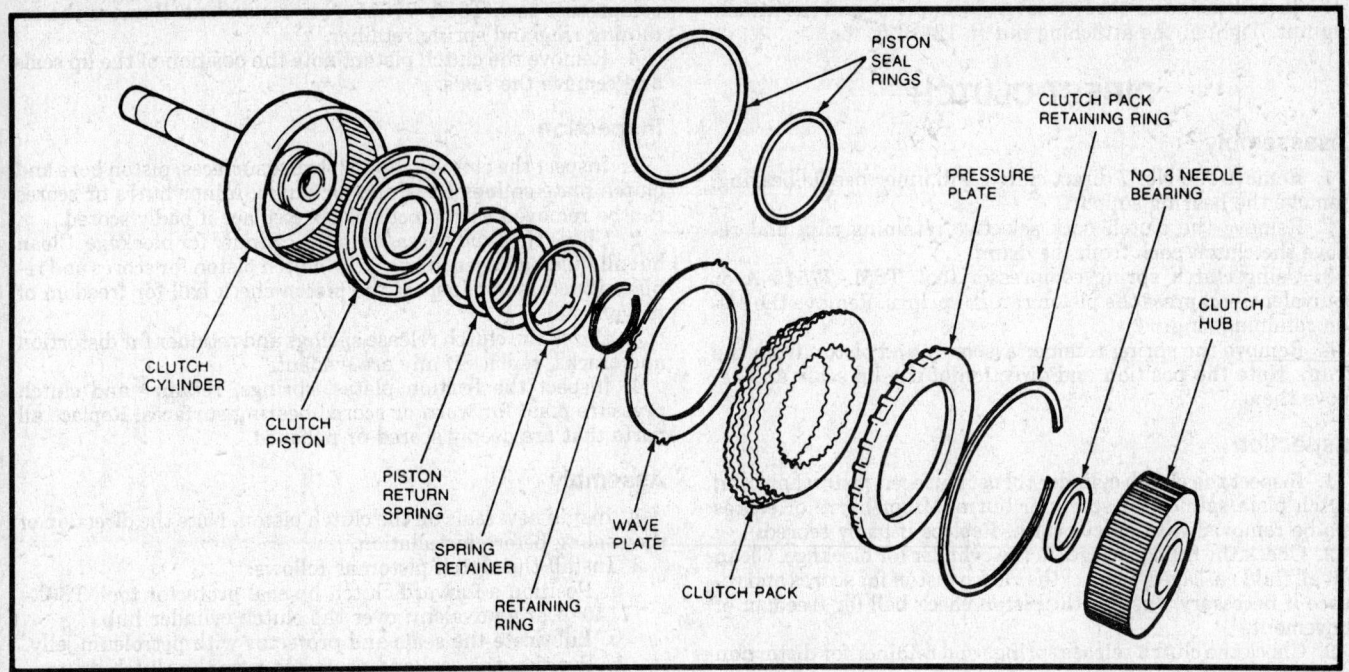

Forward clutch assembly

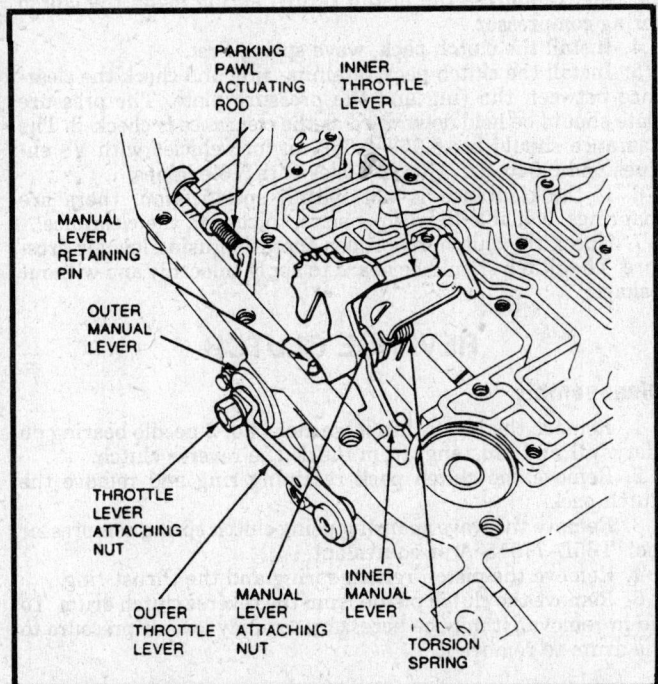

Manual and throttle linkage component locations

Inspection

1. Check the output shaft splines for damage or wear. Replace the shaft if the splines are excessively worn.
2. Inspect the ring gear for damaged or chipped teeth.
3. Check the needle bearing for freedom of movement and damaged bearings.
4. Replace any damaged or worn components. Replace all seal rings.

Assembly

1. Install new direct clutch O-rings on the output shaft.
2. Install 4 outshaft seal rings and the hub. Install the hub-to-output shaft retaining ring.
3. Install the direct clutch assembly and the needle bearing onto the direct clutch.
4. Install the output shaft and hub assembly onto the ring gear.
5. Install the output shaft retaining ring.

MANUAL AND THROTTLE LINKAGE

Disassembly

1. Loosen the attaching nut on the throttle lever. Hold the lever firmly while loosening to prevent damage to the valve body and remove the throttle lever.
2. Using an awl, remove the lever shaft seal from the case.
3. Using a small prybar, remove the manual shaft retaining pin from the case.
4. Using a 21mm wrench, remove the manual lever attaching nut while securely holding the inner manual lever. Thread the nut off the shaft and remove the lever.
5. Remove the inner throttle lever and T.V. lever torsion spring.
6. Remove the inner manual lever and parking pawl actuating rod as an assembly.
7. Remove the manual lever shaft seal from the case using an slide hammer type, seal removal tool.

Assembly

1. Install a new manual lever seal into the case.
2. Install the inner manual lever and park pawl actuating rod as an assembly.
3. Install the inner throttle lever and T.V. torsion spring. Install the outer manual lever into the case and install the inner manual lever retaining nut. Tighten to 19–27 ft. lbs.
4. Install the manual lever shaft retaining pin. Install a new outer manual lever seal.

5. Install the outer throttle lever, lockwasher and the attaching nut. Tighten the attaching nut to 12–16 ft. lbs.

DIRECT CLUTCH

Disassembly

1. Remove the No. 7 direct clutch hub inner needle bearing. Remove the bearing support.
2. Remove the clutch pack selective retaining ring and remove the clutch pack from the drum.
3. Using clutch spring compressor tool, T65L–77515–A or equivalent, compress the piston return springs. Remove the piston retaining ring.
4. Remove the spring retainer assembly and piston from the drum. Note the position and direction of the lip seals and remove them.

Inspection

1. Inspect the clutch cylinder thrust surfaces, piston bore and clutch plate splines for scores or burrs. Minor burrs or scores can be removed with crocus cloth. Replace if badly scored.
2. Check the fluid passages in the cylinder for blockage. Clean out all fluid passages. Inspect the clutch piston for scores and replace if necessary. Inspect the piston check ball for freedom of movement.
3. Check the clutch release springs and retainer for distortion and cracks, replace if any are evident.
4. Inspect the friction plates, springs, retainer and clutch pressure plate for worn or scored bearing surfaces. Replace all parts that are deeply scored or polished.

Assembly

1. Install the inner piston seal on the clutch drum as follows:
   a. Position a direct clutch lip seal protector tool, T80L–77234–A or equivalent, over the clutch drum hub.
   b. Lubricate the seal and protector with petroleum jelly.
   c. Position the seal over the installer tool with the sealing lip facing down.
   d. Push the seal down until it snaps off the end of the protector onto the clutch hub.
   e. Remove the seal protector from the hub.
   f. Slide the seal up until it seats on the seal groove.
2. Install the outer clutch piston seal. Note the direction of the sealing lip, the lip points away from the spring posts.
3. Install the clutch apply piston, coat the piston, seals and the clutch drum sealing area with petroleum jelly.
4. Install the piston spring, retainer and retaining ring using clutch spring compressor tool, T65L–77515–A.
5. Install the clutch pack. Install the clutch pack selective retaining ring and check the clearance between the ring and the pressure plate using a feeler gauge. The clearance should be; 0.050–0.067 in. for V8 engines and 0.040–0.057 in. for V6 engines.
6. If the clearance is not within specification, there are snaprings available in various sizes, to correct the clearance.
7. Check the clutch for proper operation using low air pressure. The clutch should be heard to apply smoothly and without leakage.
8. Install the No. 7 needle bearing support. Install the No. 7 needle bearing.

FORWARD CLUTCH

Disassembly

1. Remove the clutch hub and the No. 3 needle bearing.
2. Remove the clutch pack selective retaining ring and remove the clutch pack.
3. Compress the piston return spring using clutch spring

compressor tool, T65L–77515–A or equivalent. Remove the retaining ring and spring retainer.
4. Remove the clutch piston, note the position of the lip seals and remove the seals.

Inspection

1. Inspect the clutch cylinder thrust surfaces, piston bore and clutch plate splines for scores or burrs. Minor burrs or scores can be removed with crocus cloth. Replace if badly scored.
2. Check the fluid passages in the cylinder for blockage. Clean out all fluid passages. Inspect the clutch piston for scores and replace if necessary. Inspect the piston check ball for freedom of movement.
3. Check the clutch release springs and retainer for distortion and cracks, replace if any are evident.
4. Inspect the friction plates, springs, retainer and clutch pressure plate for worn or scored bearing surfaces. Replace all parts that are deeply scored or polished.

Assembly

1. Install new seals on the clutch piston. Note the direction of the sealing before installation.
2. Install the clutch piston as follows:
   a. Position a forward clutch lip seal protector tool, T80L–77140–A or equivalent, over the clutch cylinder hub.
   b. Lubricate the seals and protector with petroleum jelly.
   c. Position the seal and protector over the clutch drum.
   d. Push the piston to the bottom of the drum.
3. Install the piston return spring, spring retainer and retaining ring. Compress the piston return spring using the clutch spring compressor.
4. Install the clutch pack, wave spring first.
5. Install the clutch pack retaining ring and check the clearance between the ring and the pressure plate. The pressure plate should be held downward as the clearance is checked. The clearance should be; 0.050–0.089 in. for vehicles with V8 engines and 0.040–0.071 for vehicles with V6 engines.
6. If the clearance is not within specification, there are snaprings available in various sizes, to correct the clearance.
7. Check the clutch for proper operation using low air pressure. The clutch should be heard to apply smoothly and without leakage.

REVERSE CLUTCH

Disassembly

1. Remove the No. 2 thrust washer (No. 2 needle bearing on Mark VII and Mustang) from inside the reverse clutch.
2. Remove the clutch pack retaining ring and remove the clutch pack.
3. Remove the wave snapring using clutch spring compressor tool, T65L–77515–A or equivalent.
4. Remove the piston return spring and the thrust ring.
5. Remove the clutch piston from the reverse clutch drum. To aid in removal, it may be necessary to apply low air pressure to the drum to remove it.

Inspection

1. Inspect the drum band surface, the bushing and thrust surfaces for scoring. Minor scoring can be removed with crocus cloth.
2. Inspect the clutch piston bore and the piston inner and outer bearing surfaces for scoring. Check the air bleed ball valve in the clutch piston for free movement. Check the orifice to make sure it is not plugged.
3. Check the fluid passages for obstructions. All fluid passages must be clean and free of obstruction.
4. Inspect the clutch plates for wear, scoring and fit on the clutch splines. Replace all plates that are badly heat distressed,

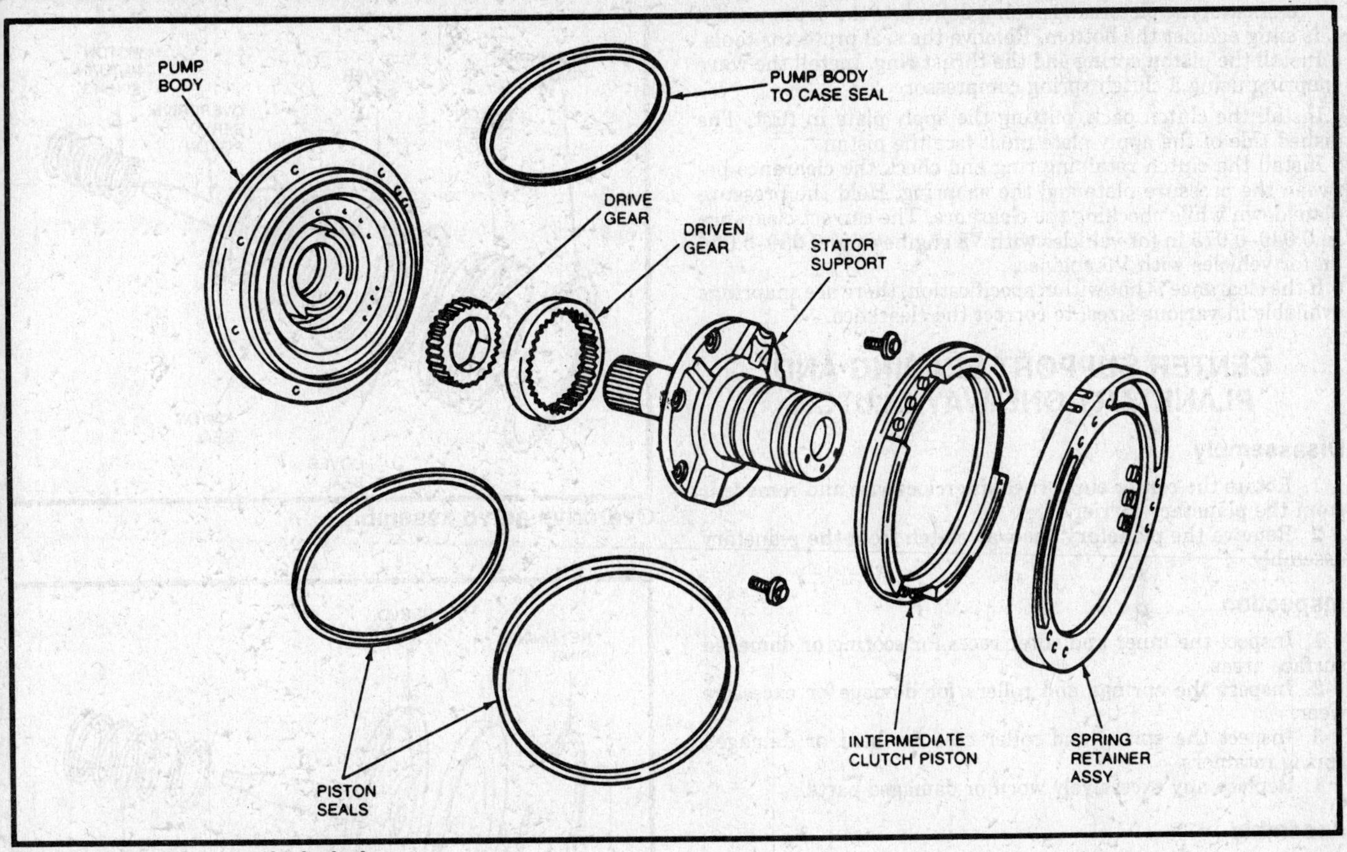

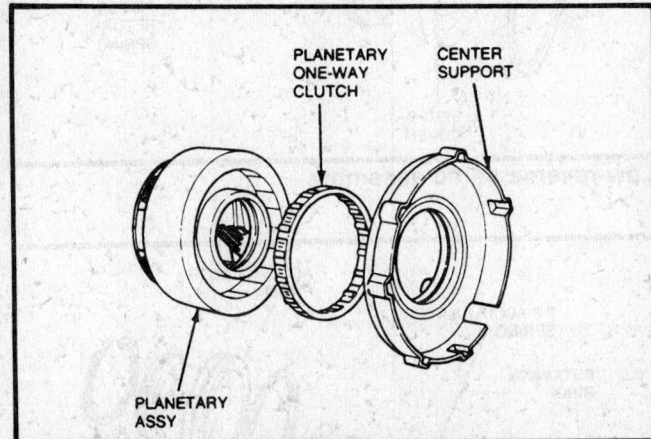

Pump assembly—exploded view

PUMP BODY

PUMP BODY TO CASE SEAL

DRIVE GEAR

DRIVEN GEAR

STATOR SUPPORT

PISTON SEALS

INTERMEDIATE CLUTCH PISTON

SPRING RETAINER ASSY

PLANETARY ONE-WAY CLUTCH

CENTER SUPPORT

PLANETARY ASSY

Center support and planetary one-way clutch assembly

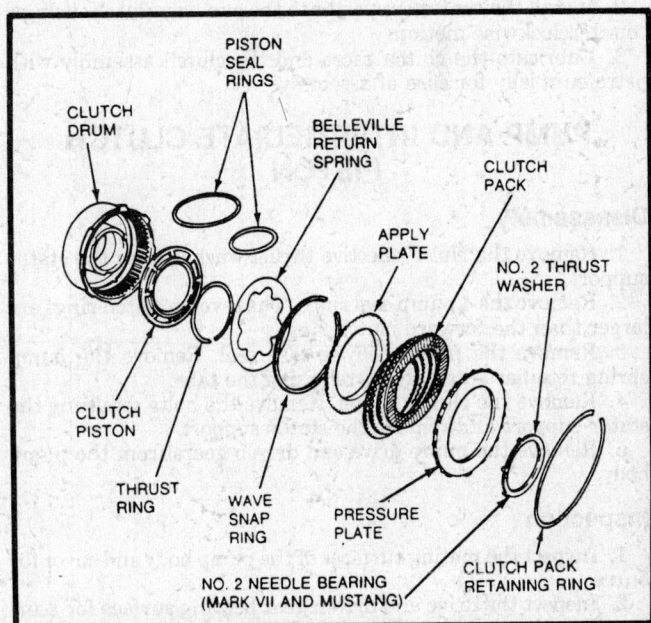

CLUTCH DRUM

PISTON SEAL RINGS

BELLEVILLE RETURN SPRING

APPLY PLATE

CLUTCH PACK

NO. 2 THRUST WASHER

CLUTCH PISTON

THRUST RING

WAVE SNAP RING

PRESSURE PLATE

CLUTCH PACK RETAINING RING

NO. 2 NEEDLE BEARING (MARK VII AND MUSTANG)

Reverse clutch assembly

worn or do not move freely in the hub.

5. Inspect the clutch pressure plate for scores on the clutch plate bearing surface. Check the clutch release springs for distortion.

Assembly

1. Install new seals on the clutch piston.

NOTE: Because the seals used on the reverse clutch piston are cut square, the direction of the seal during installation is not important.

2. Install the clutch piston into the reverse clutch drum in

the following sequence:

a. Coat the piston seals and the inside of the clutch drum with petroleum jelly.

b. Install inner seal protector, T80L-7403-B or equivalent and outer seal protector, T80L-77403-A or equivalent, into the clutch drum.

c. Install the piston and push it down into the drum until it is snug against the bottom. Remove the seal protector tools.

3. Install the piston spring and the thrust ring. Install the wave snapring using a clutch spring compressor.

4. Install the clutch pack, putting the apply plate in first. The dished side of the apply plate must face the piston.

5. Install the clutch retaining ring and check the clearance between the pressure plate and the snapring. Hold the pressure plate down while checking the clearance. The correct clearance is; 0.040–0.075 in for vehicles with V8 engines and 0.030–0.056 in. for vehicles with V6 engines.

6. If the clearance is not within specification, there are snaprings available in various sizes, to correct the clearance.

CENTER SUPPORT BEARING AND PLANETARY ONE-WAY CLUTCH

Disassembly

1. Rotate the center support counterclockwise and remove it from the planetary carrier.

2. Remove the planetary one-way clutch from the planetary assembly.

Inspection

1. Inspect the inner and outer races for scoring or damaged surface areas.

2. Inspect the springs and rollers for damage or excessive wear.

3. Inspect the spring and roller case for bent or damaged spring retainers.

4. Replace any excessively worn or damaged parts.

Assembly

1. Install the one-way clutch into the planetary carrier.

2. Install the center support into the one-way clutch, using a counterclockwise motion.

3. Lubricate the clutch races and the clutch assembly with petroleum jelly for ease of assembly.

PUMP AND INTERMEDIATE CLUTCH PISTON

Disassembly

1. Remove the No. 1 selective thrust washer from the stator support.

2. Remove the 4 pump seal rings. The reverse clutch rings are larger than the forward clutch rings.

3. Remove the pump body-to-case seal. Remove the pump spring retainer assembly by releasing the tabs.

4. Remove the clutch piston. Remove the bolts retaining the stator support and remove the stator support.

5. Remove the pump drive and driven gears from the pump body.

Inspection

1. Inspect the mating surfaces of the pump body and cover for burrs.

2. Inspect the drive and driven gear bearing surface for scoring. Check the gear teeth for burrs.

3. Check fluid passages for obstructions.

4. If any parts are excessively worn or damaged, replace the pump as a unit.

5. Check the large seal ring groove on the pump body for damage.

Assembly

1. Install the pump gears into the pump body. The chamfers

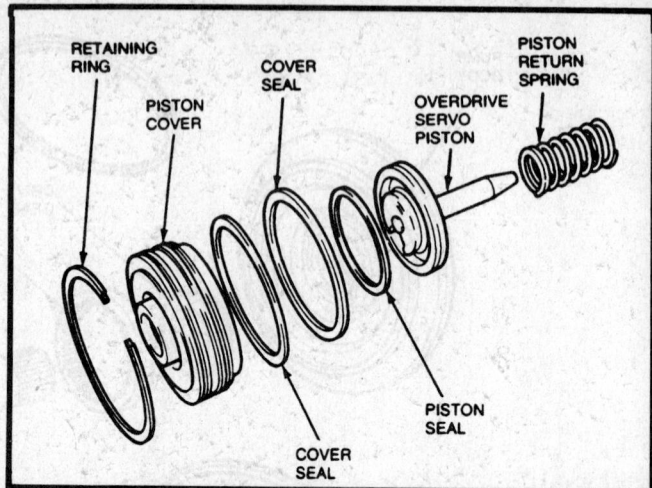

Overdrive servo assembly

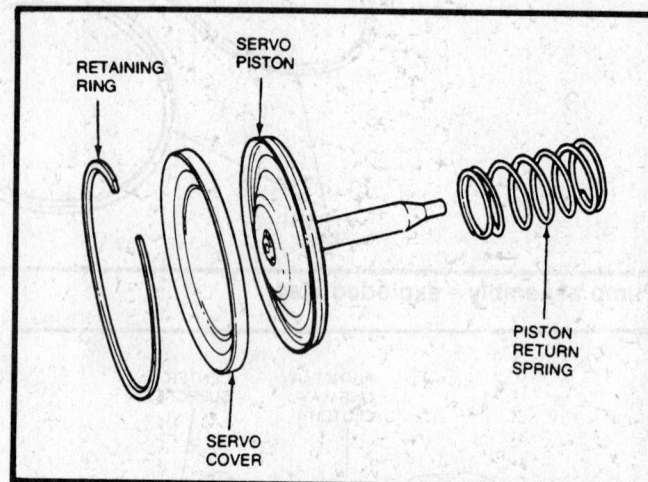

Low-reverse servo assembly

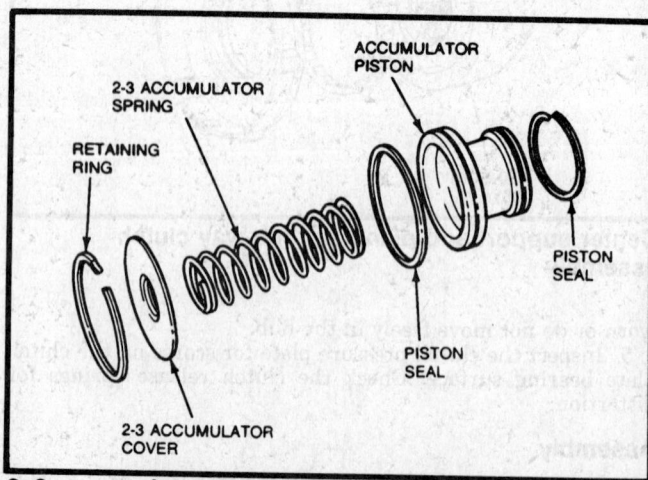

2–3 accumulator assembly

on the gears must face towards the pump.

2. Install the stator support to the pump body, tightening the attaching bolts to 12–16 ft. lbs.

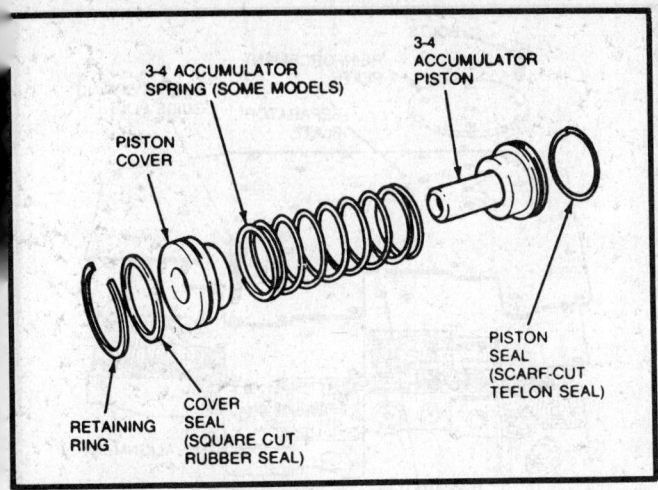

3–4 accumulator assembly

3. Install a new pump to case seal. Install new seal on the piston.

4. Install the clutch piston by first coating the seals with petroleum jelly and then installing the piston into the pump body. Push it all the way into the bore.

NOTE: The piston bleed hole must be located at the 12 o'clock position.

5. Snap the spring retainer assembly into position on the pump.

6. Install new pump seal rings. Stator support seal rings are are the largest seal rings and are for the reverse clutch. These rings are closest to the pump. Stator support seal rings are for the forward clutch and are the furthest from the pump.

ACCUMULATORS AND SERVOS

Disassembly and Assembly
3–4 AND 2–3 ACCUMULATORS

Install new seals on the accumulator piston and cover, be sure the diagonal cuts on the piston seal are aligned properly. On some transmission applications, the 3–4 accumulator may be built with a spring.

LOW/REVERSE SERVO

Inspect the sealing edge on both the servo cover and the apply piston. Replace the cover or piston if any damage is evident. The length of the rod that is attached to the piston may vary from transmission to transmission. There are 3 possible lengths; a single groove on the piston indicates the shortest possible length and 2 or 3 grooves on the rod indicate longer lengths. Do not interchange rods when assembling the transmission, use only the length rod that was removed.

OVERDRIVE SERVO

Pull the overdrive servo from the piston cover and inspect it. Install new seals on the piston and cover before reassembly. To aid in assembly, the piston seal should be lubricated with petroleum jelly.

VALVE BODY

Disassembly

1. Remove and discard the valve body gasket. Remove the bolts from the reinforcement plates and detent spring guide bolt from the separator plate.

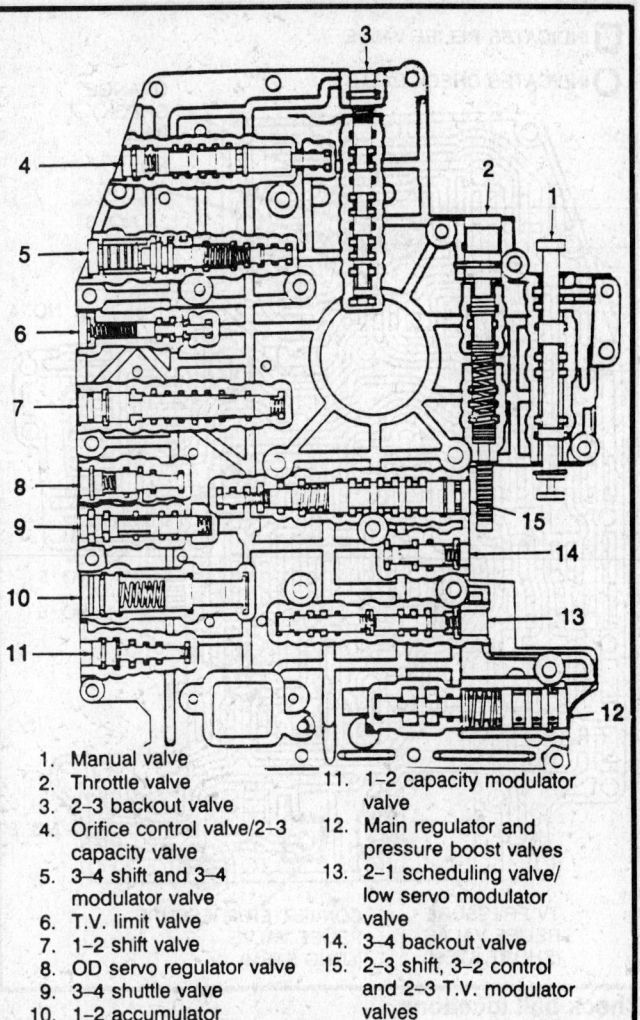

1. Manual valve
2. Throttle valve
3. 2–3 backout valve
4. Orifice control valve/2–3 capacity valve
5. 3–4 shift and 3–4 modulator valve
6. T.V. limit valve
7. 1–2 shift valve
8. OD servo regulator valve
9. 3–4 shuttle valve
10. 1–2 accumulator
11. 1–2 capacity modulator valve
12. Main regulator and pressure boost valves
13. 2–1 scheduling valve/ low servo modulator valve
14. 3–4 backout valve
15. 2–3 shift, 3–2 control and 2–3 T.V. modulator valves

Valve body – valve locations

2. Remove the separator plate, reinforcement plates and separator plate gasket.

3. Remove the 2 relief valves and the 7 check balls from the valve body. Note the location of the orange check ball, it is not interchangeable with the black check balls.

NOTE: The check balls are numbered 1 through 8, check ball number 7 was eliminated.

4. Slide the manual valve out of its bore.

5. To remove the throttle control valve, remove the retaining clip and slide the throttle sleeve out of the bore. Remove the pre-load spring, throttle plug, throttle control valve and throttle plunger.

6. To remove the 2–3 back out valve, remove the retaining clip and slide the valve and spring from the bore.

7. To remove the 2–3 capacity modulator valve, remove the spring retainer plate and slide the valve bore plug out of the bore. Remove the orifice control valve and spring, the second spring retainer plate and the 2–3 capacity modulator valve and sring.

8. To remove the 3–4 modulator/shift valves, remove the clip retaining the valves and slide the sleeve and plug from the bore. Remove the 3–4 shift valve and spring, 3–4 T.V. modulator valve and spring from the bore.

9. To remove the T.V. limit valve, remove the spring retainer plate and slide the limit valve and spring from the bore.

10. To remove the 1–2 shift valve, remove the clip retaining

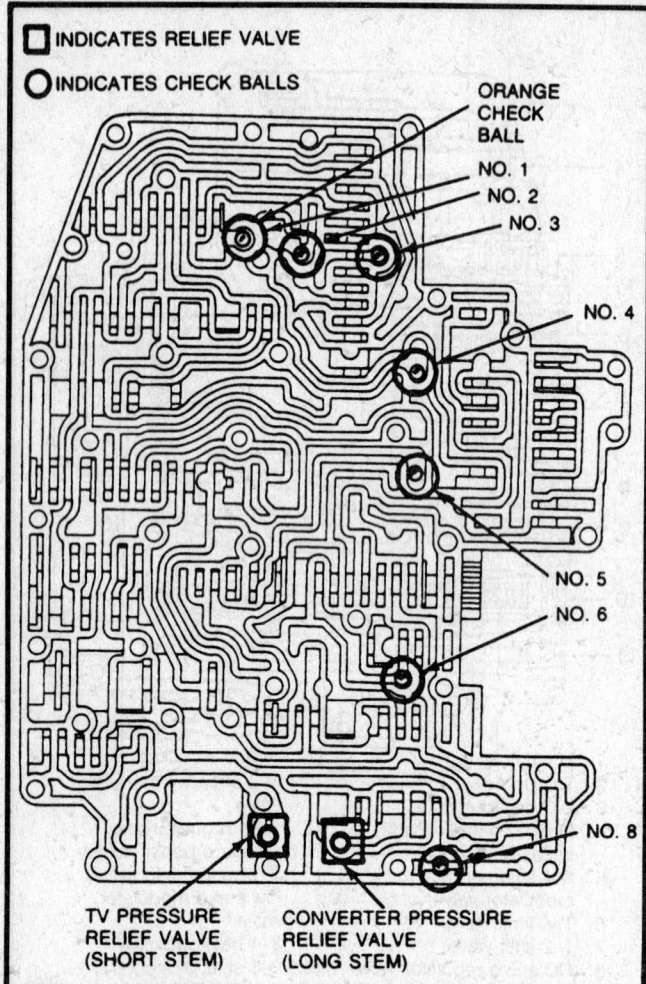

☐ INDICATES RELIEF VALVE

◯ INDICATES CHECK BALLS

ORANGE CHECK BALL

NO. 1
NO. 2
NO. 3
NO. 4
NO. 5
NO. 6
NO. 8

TV PRESSURE RELIEF VALVE (SHORT STEM)

CONVERTER PRESSURE RELIEF VALVE (LONG STEM)

Check ball locations

the bore plug and slide the bore plug, valve and spring from the bore.

11. To remove the OD servo regulator valve, remove the spring retainer plate and slide the bore plug, valve and spring from the valve body.

12. To remove the 3–4 shuttle valve, remove the spring retainer plate and slide the bore plug, valve and spring from the valve body.

13. To remove the 1–2 accumulator valve, remove the clip retaining the bore plug and remove it. Remove the O-ring seal and slide the 1–2 accumulator valve and spring from the bore.

14. To remove the 1–2 capacity modulator valve, remove the clip retaining the bore plug and remove it. Remove the the 1–2 accumulator valve and spring from the bore. Remove the 1–2 capacity modulator valve and spring.

15. To remove the main pressure regulator valve, remove the clip retaining the boost sleeve. Remove the boost valve and spring, main regulator valve spring and seat. Slide the main pressure regulator valve from the bore.

16. To remove the low servo/2–1 scheduling valves, remove the spring retaining plate, slide the low servo modulator valve and spring. Remove the second spring retainer and slide the 2–1 scheduling valve from the bore.

17. To remove the 3–4 back out valve, remove the spring retainer plate and slide the valve from the bore.

18. To remove the 2–3 shift/2–3 moulator valves—remove the clip retaining the bore plug and remove the bore plug. Slide the

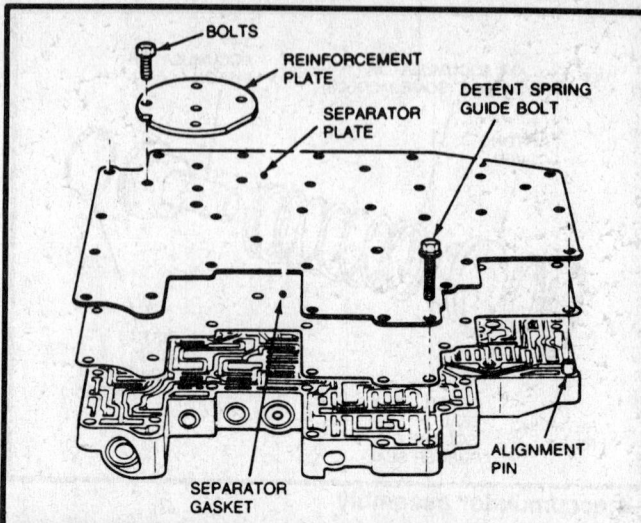

BOLTS
REINFORCEMENT PLATE
DETENT SPRING GUIDE BOLT
SEPARATOR PLATE
ALIGNMENT PIN
SEPARATOR GASKET

Installing separator plate on valve body

2–3 shift valve and spring, 3–2 control valve and 2–3 modulator valve and spring from the bore.

Inspection

1. Clean all parts thoroughly in solvent and blow dry with free compressed air.

2. Inspect all valve and plug bores for scoring. Check all fluid passages for obstructions. Inspect the check valves for freedom of movement and all mating surfaces for burrs or distortion.

3. Inspect all springs for distortion. Check all valves and plugs for freedom of movement in their bores. Valves and plugs should fall freely from their bores when dry.

4. Roll the manual valve on a flat surface to make sure it is not bent.

5. All burrs or scoring can be removed with crocus cloth. Do not round out the flat edges of valves with the cloth.

Assembly

1. Assemble each of the valves in their respective bores making sure that they move freely.

2. Lay the valve body on a flat surface and install the 7 check balls in their correct location. Make sure the orange ball is in the correct location, it is not interchangeable with the black check balls.

3. Install the 2 pressure relief valves in the valve body.

4. Install 2 alignment pins, T80L–77100–A or equivalent, into the valve body. Using a new separator plate gasket, install the separator plate over the alignment pins. Position the 3 reinforcement plates and loosely install the valve body bolts. Loosely install the detent spring guide bolt.

5. Starting at the center reinforcement plate and working outward, tighten the 11 attaching bolts to 80–100 inch lbs. Tighten the detent spring guide bolt to 80–100 inch lbs. Remove the alignment pins.

Transmission Assembly

1. Install the No. 9 needle bearing in the transmission case. Install the No. 7 bearing support and direct clutch hub in the direct clutch.

2. Install the output shaft, direct clutch and ring gear as an assembly. Install the governor drive ball and the governor assembly. Install the governor retaining ring, the face of the governor should be almost flush with the counterweight.

3. Install the low/reverse band into the front of the case. Make sure the band is seated on the anchor pin.

NOTE: When the band is properly installed, the center of the band actuating rod seat can be seen through the servo piston bore.

4. Install the center support and planetary assembly into the case. Align the planet carrier splines with the direct clutch hub splines.

NOTE: The planet carrier and center support assembly cannot be installed unless the notch in the center support is aligned with the overdrive band anchor pin.

5. Install the center support anti-clunk spring, the tabs on the spring must face outward. Install the center support retaining ring.

6. Before installing the low/reverse servo piston, the piston rod length must be determined. Use the following procedure to determine the length of piston rod needed:

    a. Lubricate the low/reverse piston seal to ease assembly.

    b. Install the low/reverse servo piston and return spring. Do not install the cover or retaining ring.

    c. Install servo piston selection tool, T80L–77030–A or equivalent. Tighten the band apply bolt on the servo piston select tool to 50 inch lbs.

    d. Attach dial indicator tool, TOOL–4201–C or equivalent and position the indicator stem on the flat portion of the piston. Zero the dial indicator.

    e. Back the bolt out of the selector tool until the piston stops against the bottom of the tool.

    f. Read the amount of piston travel on the dial indicator. If the travel is within 0.112–0.237 in., the travel is within specification. If the travel is not within specification, there are 3 piston lengths available; 2.936 in. (1 groove), 2.989 in. (2 grooves) and 3.043 in. (3 grooves). Select the proper rod to bring the travel within specification. Remove the service tools.

    g. Lubricate the low/reverse servo piston cover seal and install the cover and retaining ring.

7. Install the reverse clutch on the forward clutch assembly. Be sure the No. 2 thrust washer is in position.

8. Install the No. 3 needle bearing and forward clutch hub in the forward clutch. Position the No. 4 needle bearing on the forward clutch hub and install the drive shell.

9. Install the No. 5 needle bearing and forward sun gear on the drive shell. Install the drive shell, forward clutch and reverse clutch as an assembly. Rotate the output shaft as necessary, to aid in engaging the sun gear with the planetary gears.

10. Install the overdrive band, make sure the band anchor is properly positioned on the anchor pin.

11. Lubricate the overdrive servo cover seals to ease assembly and install the servo in the case. With the overdrive servo installed, inspect the apply pin and band for proper position and engagement.

12. Install the intermediate clutch pack components, by first installing the pressure plate then the clutch pack and finally the selective steel plate.

13. Measure the intermediate clutch clearance using a depth micrometer D80P–4201–A or equivalent and endplay gauge bar T80L–77003–A or equivalent. Set the endplay tool across the pump case mounting. Locate the micrometer end play gauge bar and read the depth. The depth at the intermediate clutch separator plate should be; 1.634–1.636 in. for vehicles with V8 engines and 1.629–1.640 in. for vehicles with V6 engines.

NOTE: Maintain downward pressure on the clutch pack while measuring depth.

14. If the depth is not within tolerance, there are 4 different sized separator plates available to correct the depth; 0.071–0.067 in., 0.081–0.077 in., 0.091–0.087 in. and 0.101–0.097 in. Install the corrective plate, if necessary and recheck the clearance.

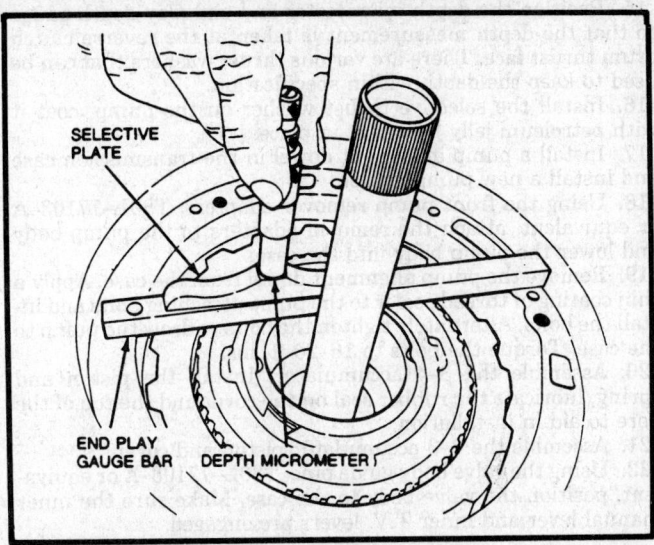

Checking intermediate clutch clearance

SELECTIVE THRUST WASHER ENDPLAY

Depth	Washer No.	Washer Size	Washer Color
37.668-38.113mm (1.483-1.500 inch)	1	0.050-0.054 inch	Green
38.114-38.540mm (1.501-1.517 inch)	2	0.068-0.072 inch	Yellow
38.541-38.970mm (1.518-1.534 inch)	3	0.085-0.089 inch	Natural
38.971-39.408mm (1.535-1.551 inch)	4	0.102-0.106 inch	Red
39.409-39.827mm (1.552-1.568 inch)	5	0.119-0.123 inch	Blue

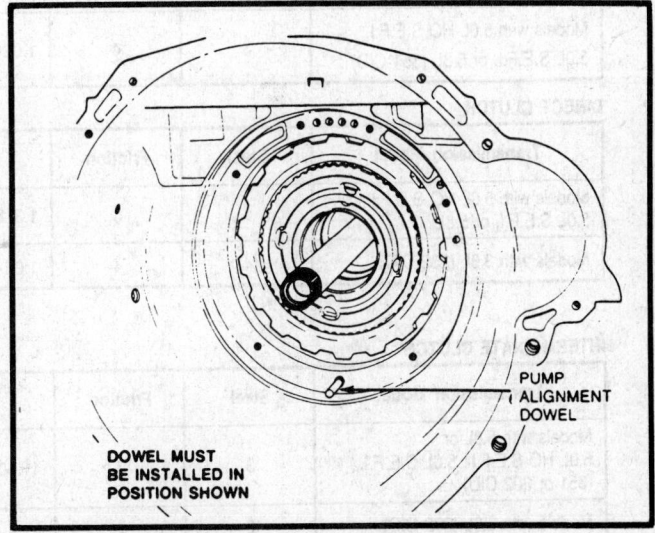

Installing the pump alignment dowel

15. Position the depth micrometer and end play depth gauge so that the depth measurement is taken at the reverse clutch drum thrust face. There are various thrust washers that can be used to keep the depth within specification.

16. Install the selective thrust washer on the pump, coat it with petroleum jelly to hold it in place.

17. Install a pump alignment dowel in the transmission case and install a new pump gasket.

18. Using the front pump remover adapters, T80L–77103–A or equivalent, attach the removal adapters to the pump body and lower the pump body into the case.

19. Remove the pump alignment dowel from the case. Apply a thin coating of thread sealer to the pump attaching bolts and install the bolts. Alternately tighten the bolts to draw the pump to the case. Torque the bolts to 16–20 ft. lbs.

20. Assemble the 3–4 accumulator. Install the piston and spring, lubricate the rubber seal on the cover and the top of the bore to aid in installation.

21. Assemble the 2–3 accumulator piston and cover.

22. Using the valve body guide pins, T80L–77100–A or equivalent, position the valve body to the case. Make sure the inner manual lever and inner T.V. levers are engaged.

23. Install the 24 valve body-to-case bolts and tighten to 80–100 inch lbs.

24. Install the detent spring and attaching bolt. Tighten the attaching bolt to 80–100 inch lbs.

25. Remove the valve body guide pins and install the remaining attaching bolts, tighten to 80–100 inch lbs.

26. Load the T.V. lever torsion spring against the separator plate.

27. Install the filter to the valve body and tighten the 3 attaching bolts to 80–100 inch lbs.

28. Clean the oil pan and gasket surfaces thoroughly.

29. Using a new oil pan gasket, attach the oil pan to the transmission. Tighten the attaching bolts to 12–16 ft. lbs.

30. Clean the mounting surface on the transmission and on the extension housing. Remove any sealant from the bolts and the case bolt holes. Install a new gasket on the transmission, coat the extension housing mounting bolts with thread sealant and install them. Tighten the mounting bolts to 16–20 ft. lbs.

31. Install the direct driveshaft by sliding it into the pump. Install the torque converter, be sure the converter is fully seated in the pump.

SPECIFICATIONS

CLUTCH SPECIFICATIONS

FORWARD CLUTCH

Transmission Model	Steel	Friction	Clearance	Selective Snap Rings-Thickness
Models with 3.8L (232 CID)	4*	4	1.02-1.80mm (0.040-0.071 inch)	0.060-0.064 0.074-0.078 0.088-0.092 0.102-0.106
Models with 5.0L HO S.E.F.I., 5.0L S.E.F.I. or 5.8L (302 or 351 CID)	5*	5	1.27-2.26mm (0.050-0.089 inch)	

*Plus a waved plate (installed next to piston).

REVERSE CLUTCH

Transmission Model	Steel	Friction	Clearance	Selective Snap Rings-Thickness
Models with 3.8L (232 CID)	2	3	0.76-1.42mm (0.030-0.056 inch)	0.060-0.064 0.074-0.078 0.088-0.092 0.102-0.106
Models with 5.0L HO S.E.F.I., 5.0L S.E.F.I. or 5.8L (351 CID)	3	4	1.02-1.91mm (0.040-0.075 inch)	

DIRECT CLUTCH

Transmission Model	Steel	Friction	Clearance	Selective Snap Rings-Thickness
Models with 5.0L HO S.E.F.I., 5.0L S.E.F.I. or 5.8L	5	5	1.3-1.77mm (0.050-0.067 inch)	0.050-0.054 0.064-0.068 0.078-0.082 0.092-0.096
Models with 3.8L (232 CID)	4	4	1.02-1.44mm (0.040-0.057 inch)	

INTERMEDIATE CLUTCH

Transmission Model	Steel	Friction	Gauge Dim.	Selective Steel Plates-Thickness
Models with 5.8L or 5.0L HO S.E.F.I., 5.0L S.E.F.I., (351 or 302 CID)	3	3	41.504-41.808mm (1.634-1.646 inch)	0.067-0.071 0.077-0.081 0.087-0.091 0.097-0.101
Models with 3.8L (232 CID)	2	2	41.4-41.7mm (1.628-1.640 inch)	

TORQUE CONVERTER ENDPLAY DATA

Transmission	New or Rebuilt	Used
All	.023" Max.	.050" Max.

SELECTIVE SERVO PISTON

Rod Length*	I.D.	Rod Length*	I.D.	Rod Length*	I.D.
2.936	1 Groove	2.989	2 Groove	3.043	3 Groove

*Measured from the piston surface to the end of the rod.

SELECTIVE THRUST WASHER DATA

Depth	Thickness	Color Code	Depth	Thickness	Color Code
37.668-38.113mm (1.483-1.500 inch)	0.050-0.054	Green	38.971-39.408mm (1.535-1.551 inch)	.102-.106	Red
38.114-38.540mm (1.501-1.517 inch)	0.068-0.072	Yellow	39.409-39.827mm (1.552-1.568 inch)	.119-.123	Blue
38.541-38.970mm (1.518-1.534 inch)	0.085-0.089	Natural			

*The thrust washer is located on the stator support which is attached to the back of the pump housing.

TORQUE SPECIFICATIONS

Description	N·m	Lb-Ft	Description	N·m	Lb-Ft
Stator Support to Pump Body	16-22	12-16	Radiator Connectors Push Connector to Tank	16-24	12-18
Front Pump to Case	22-27	16-20	Threaded Connector to Tank	24-31	18-23
Reinforcing Plate to Valve Body	9-14	80-120 lb-in	Tube Nut to Threaded Connector	16-24	12-18
Separator Plate to Valve Body	9-11	80-100 lb-in	Converter to Flywheel	27-46	20-34
Valve Body to Case	9-11	80-100 lb-in	Converter Housing Access Cover to Converter Housing	16-22	12-16
Filter to Valve Body	9-14	80-120 lb-in			
Oil Pan to Case	8-13.5	6-10	Detent Spring Attaching Bolt	9-14	80-120 lb-in
Extension to Case	22-27	16-20	Inner Manual Lever to Shaft	26-37	19-27
Governor Body to Counterweight	6-7	50-60	Outer Throttle Lever to Shaft	16-22	12-16
Governor Body Cover to Governor Body	2.3-3.4	20-30	Push Connect Fitting to Case	24-31	18-23
			Converter Plug to Converter	11-38	8-28
Transmission Connectors Push Connector to Case	24-31	18-23	Neutral Start Switch to Case	11-15	8-11
Tube Nut to Connector	16-24	12-18	Pressure Plug to Case	8-16	6-12
			Transmission to Engine	55-68	40-50

SPECIAL TOOLS

Tool Number	Description	Tool Number	Description
T50T-100-A	Slide Hammer	T83L-7902-A	Converter Checking Tool
T59L-100-B	Impact Slide Hammer	T83L-7902-A1	Rod Torque Adapter
T58L-101-A	Shift Shaft Seal Remover	T83L-7902-A2	Pilot Guide
TOOL-1175-AC	Front Pump Seal and Rear Case Bushing Remover	T83L-7902-A3	Holding Fixture
T71P-19703-C	O-Ring Pick	T82L-9500-AH	Cooler Line Disconnect Tool
D80P-4201-A	Depth Micrometer (Also Commercially Available)	T80L-77030-B	Servo Piston Remover (Also used for air pressure checks)
TOOL-4201-C	Dial Indicator	T80L-77034-A	Extension Housing Bushing Replacer
T57L-500-B	Bench Mounted Holding Fixture	T80L-77100-A	Valve Body Guide Pins
T73L-6600-A	Pressure Gauge	T80L-77103-A	Front Pump Remover Adapter
TOOL-7000-DE	Air Nozzle	T80L-77110-A	Rear Case Bushing Replacer
T82L-7006-A	Air Test Adapter Plate	T80L-77140-A	Forward Clutch Lip Seal Protector (Inner)
T82P-7006-C	Air Test Adapter Plate Screws	T80L-77234-A	Direct Clutch Lip Seal Protector (Inner)
T84P-7341-A	Shift Linkage Grommet Removal Tool	T74P-77247-A	Neutral Start Switch Socket
T61L-7657-A	Extension Housing Seal Replacer	T74P-77248-A	Extension Housing Seal Remover
T77L-7697-A	Extension Housing Bushing Remover	T80L-77254-A	Lip Seal Protector
D84P-70332-A	Rod TV Control Pressure Gauge Block	T80L-77268-A	Front Pump Bushing Replacer
T86L-70332-A	Cable TV Control Pressure Gauge Tool	T80L-77268-B	Front Pump Bushing Remover
T86L-70002-A	TV Pressure Gauge with Hose	T80L-77403-A	Reverse Clutch Seal Protector (Outer)
D80L-77001-A	Adapter Fitting	T80L-77403-B	Reverse Clutch Seal Protector (Inner)
T80L-77003-A	End Play Gauge Bar	T80L-77405-A	Reverse Clutch Spring Compressor Plate
T80L-77005-A	Intermediate Clutch Lip Seal Protector (Inner and Outer)	T74P-77498-A	Shift Shaft Seal Replacer
T80L-77030-A	Servo Piston Selection Tool	T65L-77515-A	Clutch Spring Compressor
TOOL-7000-DD	Rubber Tip for Air Nozzle	T80L-77515-A	Forward Clutch Spring Compressor Adapter
T80L-7902-A	End Play Checking Tool	T63L-77837-A	Front Pump Seal Replacer
T76L-7902-C	Converter Clutch Torquing Tool	T68P-7D158-A	Forward Clutch Lip Seal Protector (Outer)
T77L-7902-A	Converter Clutch Holding Tool	T86P-77265-AH	Cooler Line Disconnect Tool (Push Connect Fittings)

Section 4

A4LD Transmission
Ford Motor Co.

APPLICATION

A4LD

Year	Vehicle	Engine
1985	Bronco II	All
	Ranger	All
1986	Aerostar	All
	Bronco II	All
	Ranger	All
1987	Mustang	2.3L, 5.0L
	Thunderbird	2.3L
	Aerostar	All
	Bronco II	All
	Ranger	All
1988–89	Mustang	2.3L, 5.0L
	Scorpio	2.9L
	Thunderbird	2.3L
	Aerostar	All
	Bronco II	All
	Ranger	All

GENERAL DESCRIPTION

Transmission and Converter Identification

TRANSMISSION

The A4LD is a 4 speed overdrive automatic transmission with a lockup torque converter. It is similar to the C-3 (3 speed) automatic transmission. It is the first Ford Motor Company production automatic transmission to use electronic controls integrated in the on-board computer system. The hydraulic lockup and unlock function of the torque converter is electronically controlled by the on-board computer EEC-IV system.

All vehicles are equipped with a safety standard certification Label on the driver's side door lock post. Refer to the stamped code in the space marked **Trans.** for proper transmission identification. The transmission is also identified by a tag on the transmission body, attached to the lower left hand extension attaching bolt.

CONVERTER

The converter is a welded unit and is not to be repaired. If a transmission malfunction is traced to the torque converter, replacement of the converter is recommended.

Electronic Controls

The torque converter incorporates electrical and hydraulic lockup components. The EEC-IV system controls a converter clutch solenoid in the main control which hydraulically operates the piston/plate clutch in the converter to provide a solid drive transmission function.

Metric Fasteners

Metric bolts may be used in attaching the transmission to the engine and also in attaching the transmission to the crossmember mount. The metric fastener dimensions are very close to the dimensions of the familiar inch system fasteners and for this

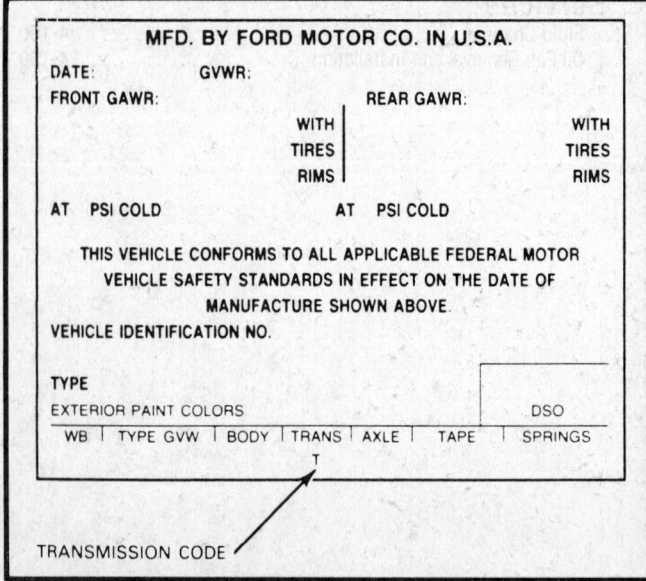

Transmission Identification

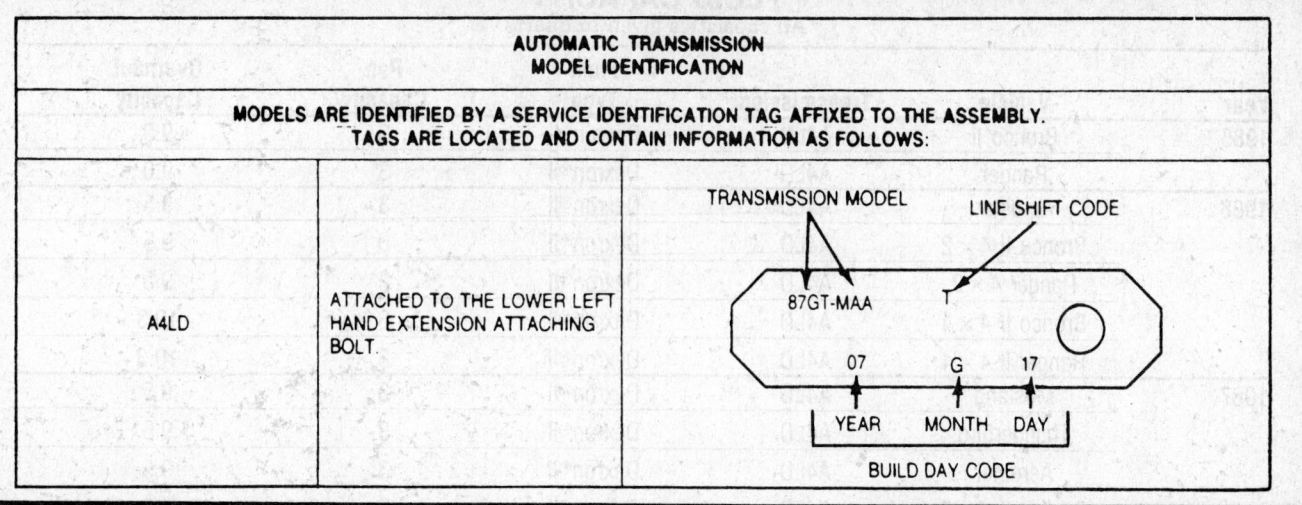

Transmission tag

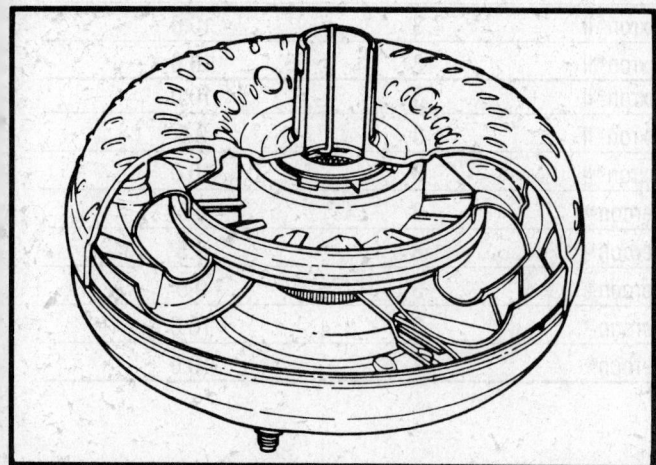

Torque converter assembly

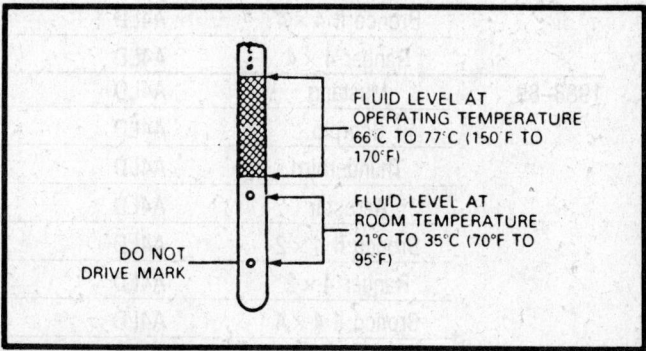

Dipstick reading

reason, replacement fasteners must have the same measurement and strength as those removed.

— CAUTION —

Do not attempt to interchange metric fasteners for inch system fasteners. Mismatched or incorrect fasteners can result in damage to the transmission unit through malfunctions or breakage and cause personal injury.

Capacities

The A4LD automatic transmission has a fluid capacity of approximately 8–10 quarts including the torque converter if it has been overhauled or flushed. If the torque converter has not been drained, the fluid capacity is 4 quarts. Use Dexron® II or Motorcraft Mercon® automatic transmission fluid. Bring the transmission to normal operating temperature and recheck the fluid level. Do not overfill the unit.

Checking Fluid Level

OPERATING TEMPERATURE

The automatic transmission should be checked at an operating temperature of 150–170° F (66–77° C). The dipstick should be

hot to the touch. The dipstick reading should be within the cross-hatched area.

ROOM TEMPERATURE

If the transmission is not at operating temperature and it becomes necessary to check the fluid level, it may be checked at a room temperature of 70–95° F (21–35° C). The dipstick should be cool to the touch. The dipstick reading should be between the holes.

1. With the transmission in **P**, engine at idle rpm, foot brakes applied and vehicle on level surface, move the selector lever through each range allowing time to engage the transmission.

2. Return the selector lever to **P**, applying the parking brake fully and block the wheels. Do not turn off the engine during the fluid level check.

3. Pull the dipstick out of the filler tube, wipe it clean and push it all the way back into the tube. Make sure that it is fully seated.

4. Pull the dipstick out of the filler tube again and check the fluid level. Before adding fluid, check for the correct type to use. It is usually stamped on the dipstick.

5. If necessary, add enough fluid through the filler tube to raise the level to the correct position. Over filling the transmission will result in foaming, loss of fluid through the vent and possible transmission malfunction.

6. Install the dipstick checking that it is fully seated in the tube.

FLUID CAPACITY
All capacities given in quarts

Year	Vehicle	Transmission	Fluid Type	Pan Capacity	Overhaul Capacity
1985	Bronco II	A4LD	Dexron®II	3	9.0
	Ranger	A4LD	Dexron®II	3	9.0
1986	Aerostar	A4LD	Dexron®II	3	9.5
	Bronco II 4×2	A4LD	Dexron®II	3	9.5
	Ranger 4×2	A4LD	Dexron®II	3	9.5
	Bronco II 4×4	A4LD	Dexron®II	3	10.3
	Ranger II 4×4	A4LD	Dexron®II	3	10.3
1987	Mustang	A4LD	Dexron®II	3	9.5
	Thunderbird	A4LD	Dexron®II	3	9.5
	Aerostar	A4LD	Dexron®II	3	9.5
	Bronco II 4×2	A4LD	Dexron®II	3	9.5
	Ranger 4×2	A4LD	Dexron®II	3	9.5
	Bronco II 4×4	A4LD	Dexron®II	3	10.0
	Ranger 4×4	A4LD	Dexron®II	3	10.0
1988–89	Mustang	A4LD	Dexron®II	3	10.0
	Scorpio	A4LD	Dexron®II	3	9.5
	Thunderbird	A4LD	Dexron®II	3	10.0
	Aerostar	A4LD	Mercon®	3	9.5
	Bronco II 4×2	A4LD	Mercon®	3	9.5
	Ranger 4×2	A4LD	Mercon®	3	9.5
	Bronco II 4×4	A4LD	Mercon®	3	10.0
	Ranger 4×4	A4LD	Mercon®	3	10.0

TRANSMISSION MODIFICATIONS

Front Pump Installation

A new pump bolt (part number E800512-S72) silver color, has been released with increased torque specifications, 9.6–11 ft. lbs. (13–15 Nm). Whenever overhauling the A4LD transmission, replace all old design pump bolts (black colored) with the new bolts and increase the torque. Do not increase the torque specification with the old design bolts.

When installing the housing and pump to case, always install new aluminum washers (part number E830124-S) under the bolt. Use front pump alignment tools (kit no. T74P-77103-X) for installation.

Front Pump Seal Blow Out

Whenever this condition is found in 1985–87 vehicles, a new housing/seal assembly has been released and must be used for service to prevent repeat repairs. If new tools are not available to remove, replace and restake the seal, then seal repairs on housings with staked seals will require replacement of the housing assembly.

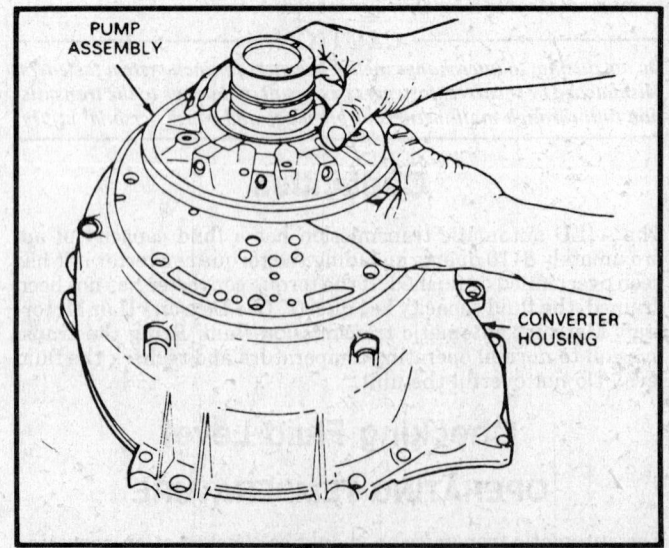

Front oil pump installation

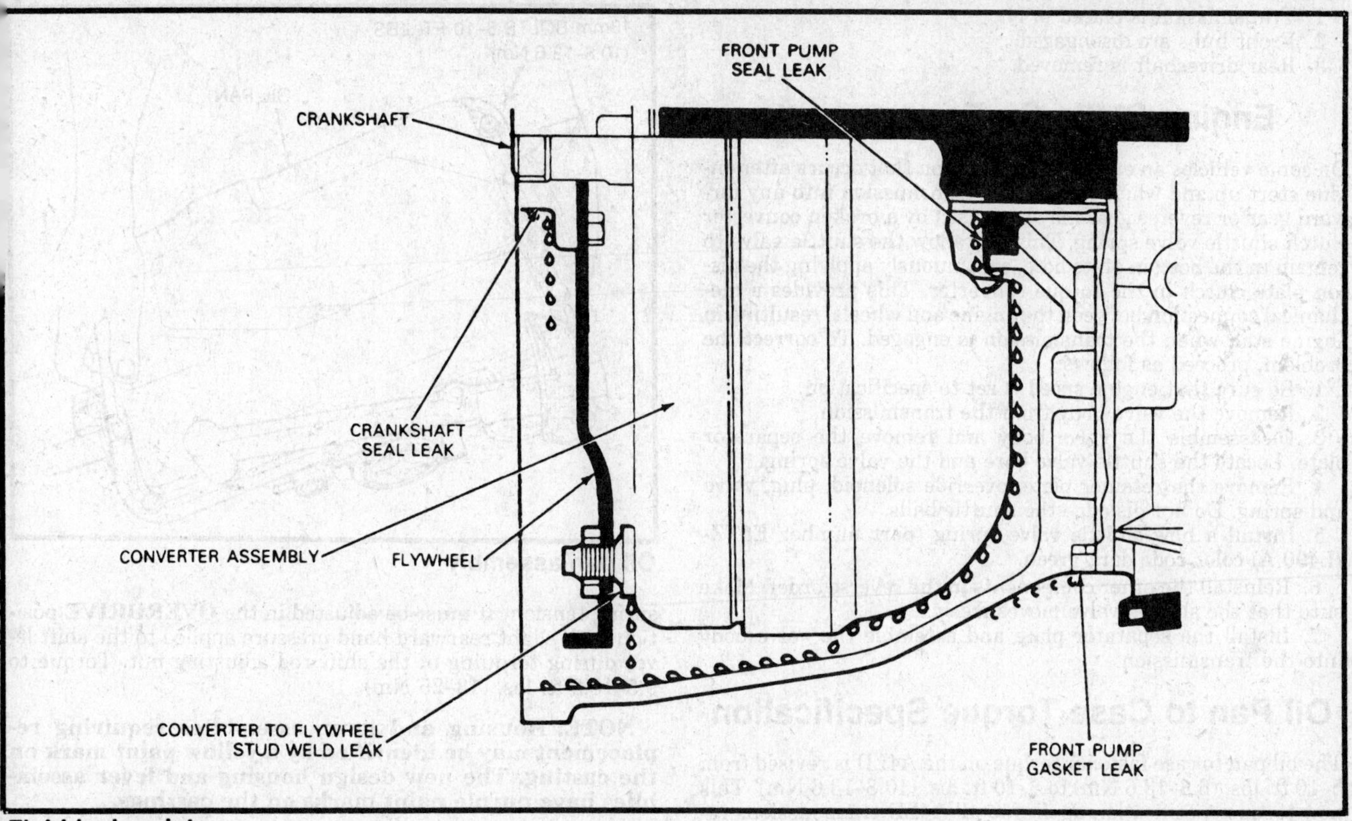

FRONT PUMP
SEAL LEAK

CRANKSHAFT

CRANKSHAFT
SEAL LEAK

CONVERTER ASSEMBLY   FLYWHEEL

CONVERTER TO FLYWHEEL
STUD WELD LEAK

FRONT PUMP
GASKET LEAK

Fluid leak points

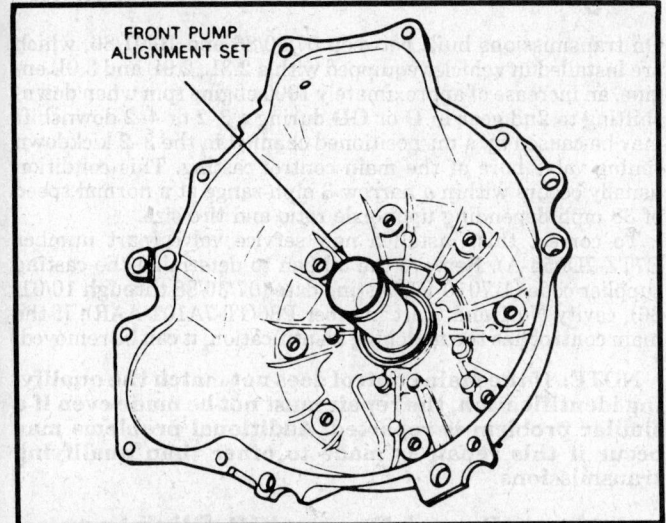

FRONT PUMP
ALIGNMENT SET

Front oil pump alignment

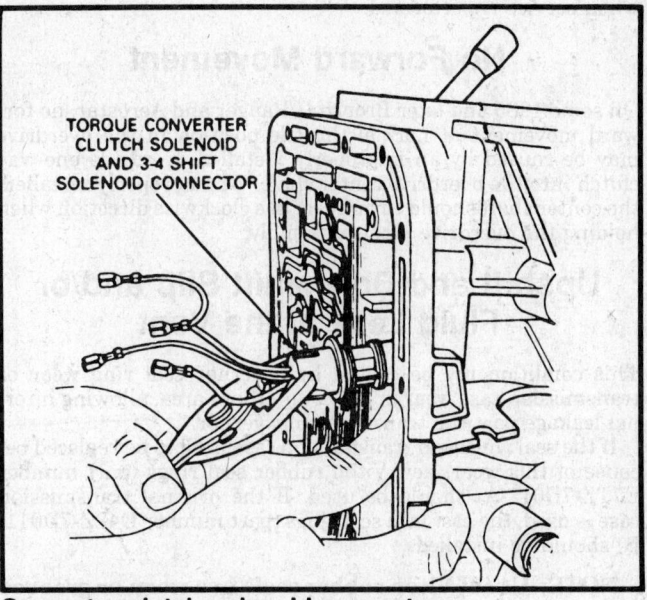

TORQUE CONVERTER
CLUTCH SOLENOID
AND 3-4 SHIFT
SOLENOID CONNECTOR

Converter clutch solenoid connector

Converter Override Clutch Connector Leak

There may be a leak at the converter clutch override connector and transmission case. This condition may be caused by sump fluid migrating up the override connector wires and depositing at the terminals at the top of the connector. This condition may be corrected by replacing the switch (part number E5TZ-7E449-A).

Burnt Fluid After Towing

Some Bronco II/Ranger vehicles, equipped with 4WD and an electronic transfer case, may sustain transmission damage while being towed by another vehicle. The electronic transfer case does not have a neutral position, so it cannot be shifted into **N** as can be done with the manually operated transfer case. If towing is necessary, make sure of the following:

1. Transmission is placed in **N**.
2. Front hubs are disengaged.
3. Rear driveshaft is removed.

Engine Stalls On Engagement

On some vehicles an engine stall condition that occurs after engine start up and when shifting the transmission into any forward gear or reverse gear may be caused by a broken converter clutch shuttle valve spring. This will allow the shuttle valve to remain in the bottom of its bore, continuously applying the piston plate clutch in the torque converter. This provides a mechanical connection between the engine and wheels, resulting in engine stall when the transmission is engaged. To correct the problem, proceed as follows:
1. Be sure that engine speed is set to specification.
2. Remove the valve body from the transmission.
3. Disassemble the valve body and remove the separator plate. Locate the shuttle valve bore and the valve spring.
4. Remove the retainer plate, override solenoid, plug, valve and spring. Do not dislodge the shuttle balls.
5. Install a new shuttle valve spring (part number E5TZ-7L490-A) color code dark green.
6. Reinstall the other components in the reverse order. Make sure that the shuttle valve moves freely.
7. Install the separator plate and assemble the valve body into the transmission.

Oil Pan to Case Torque Specification

The oil pan to case fastener torque on the A4LD is revised from 5–10 ft. lbs. (6.8–13.6 Nm) to 8–10 ft. lbs. (10.8–13.6 Nm). This new torque specification applies to all A4LD transmissions regardless of case type and will ensure a proper oil pan to case seal when service is performed.

No Forward Movement

On some 1985 and later Bronco II/Ranger and Aerostar, no forward movement at normal throttle position in the overdrive may be caused by an improperly installed overdrive one-way clutch into the overdrive center shaft. When properly installed, the center shaft should turn freely in a clockwise direction when holding the overdrive planet assembly.

Upshift and Downshift Slip and/or Fluid Leak at the Vent

This condition my be caused by governor seal ring wear or transmission case wear in the counterbore area, allowing internal leakage past the transmission governor.

If the seal rings and transmission case need to be replaced because of this wear, new Viton rubber seal rings (part number E7TZ-7D011-A) should be used. If the original transmission case is used, the cast iron seal rings (part number D4ZZ-7D011-B) should be installed.

NOTE: Use of Viton rubber seals in a worn or grooved transmission case will result in a recurrence of leakage past the governor.

Selector Lever Vibration

On some 1987 Mustangs, a rattling noise from the transmission shifter housing and lever assembly while traveling on rough roads may be caused by the spring tension of the transmission shifter assembly being too weak.

To correct this, install a new design transmission housing and lever assembly (part number E7ZZ-7210-C) which has higher

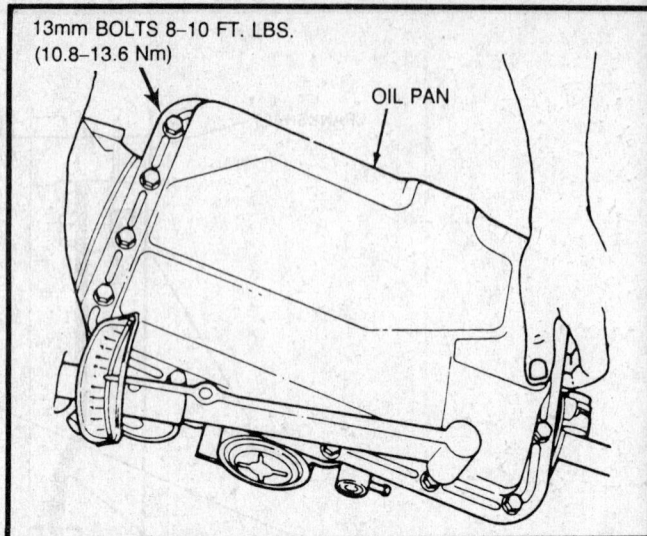

13mm BOLTS 8–10 FT. LBS. (10.8–13.6 Nm)

OIL PAN

Oil pan assembly

spring tension. It must be adjusted in the **OVERDRIVE** position with slight rearward hand pressure applied to the shift lever during torquing of the shift rod adjusting nut. Torque to 9.5–18.5 ft. lbs. (13–25 Nm).

NOTE: Housing and lever assemblies requiring replacement may be identified by a yellow paint mark on the casting. The new design housing and lever assemblies have purple paint marks on the castings.

Engine RPM Increases on Downshift

On transmissions built between 07/30/86 and 10/01/86, which are installed in vehicles equipped with a 2.3L, 2.9L and 3.0L engine, an increase of approximately 1000 engine rpm when downshifting to 2nd gear in **D** or **OD** during a 3–2 or 4–2 downshift may be caused by a mispositioned channel in the 3–2 kickdown timing valve bore of the main control casting. This condition usually occurs within a narrow 3 mph range at a normal speed of 38 mph depending upon axle ratio and tire size.

To correct this, install a new service valve (part number E7TZ-7D054-A). Remove the oil pan to determine the casting supplier code (1-7010-D), casting date (07/30/86 through 10/01/86), cavity No.1 and (part number P86GT-7A101-AAR). If the main control has the matching identification, it can be removed.

NOTE: If the main control does not match the qualifying identification, the repair must not be made even if a similar problem is reported. Additional problems may occur if this repair is made to other than qualifying transmissions.

Upshift and Downshift Slipping

Some 1986–87 Aerostars may be equipped with a transmission that slips during upshifts and downshifts. This problem may be caused by the manual linkage not properly adjusted to specification. To correct this, adjust the manual linkage using the following service procedure:
1. From inside the vehicle, place the shift lever in the **OD** position.
2. From below the vehicle, loosen the adjustment screw on the shift cable and remove the end fitting from the manual lever ball stud.
3. Position the manual lever in the **OD** position by moving the lever all the way rearward, and then moving it 3 detents forward. Hold the shift lever against the **OD** rear stop.

4. Connect the cable end fitting to the manual lever. Tighten the adjustment screw to 45–60 inch lbs. (5–7 Nm).

5. After adjustment, check for **P** engagement. The control lever must move to the right when engaged in the **P** detent. Check the transmission control lever in all detent positions with the engine running to make sure of correct detent action.

Erratic or No 3–4 Upshift or 4–3 Downshift

Some 1987–88 vehicles may experience and erattic or no 3–4 upshift or 4–3 downshift condition. This condition may be caused by normal levels of contamination in the transmission fluid. This causes the 3–4 shift solenoid to stick in the open or closed position. The 3–4 shift solenoid is external of the transmission filter which makes it sensitive to normal levels of contamination.

To correct this, install a new 3–4 shift solenoid and sleeve/screen assembly. The sleeve/screen assembly will protect the new 3–4 shift solenoid from contamination. Both components are contained in service kit (part number E8TZ-7M107-A).

Front Oil Pump to Converter Housing Bolt

On the 1987–88 Mustang and Thunderbird, 1986–88 Aerostar and 1985–88 Bronco II/Ranger, the front oil pump to converter housing bolts for the 1988 transmission cannot be used on prior model year transmissions. Two types of front oil pump to converter housing bolts are currently available for service. The M–6 bolts are used to service 1987 and prior transmission. The M–8 bolts are used to service the 1988 transmission only. The M–8 bolt size is M–8 × 1 with fine threads and has a torque range of 17–20 ft. lbs. (23–27 Nm).

NOTE: The 1987 and prior model year M–6 bolts, front oil pump support, oil pump adapter plate and converter housing assemblies are not to be used to service 1988 A4LD transmissions.

Snapring and Output Shaft

Aerostar extended vans require the use of a 2.0mm snapring and matching output shaft. During the 1989 model year some A4LD transmissions used in other vehicle and light truck applications, are built with either the 1.2mm snapring and matching output shaft or the 2.0mm snapring and matching output shaft. The snaprings and output shafts are not interchangeable because of the difference in size.

If service is required on the snapring or output shaft, it will be necessary to determine which size snapring is needed. The 1.2mm and 2.0mm snaprings are packaged together for service.

NOTE: The 2.0mm snapring and matching output shaft can be used to service prior model year A4LD transmissions.

Transmission Fluid Leak

On some 1988 Scoropios, transmission fluid leakage at the converter housing to transmission case may be caused by the existing converter housing to transmission case attaching bolts. The bolts may not provide adequate sealing qualities.

To correct this, install new design converter housing to transmission case attaching bolts (part number E804594-S72) that have an integral O-ring. Torque the new bolts to 28–38 ft. lbs. (38–52 Nm).

NOTE: If the transmission requires disassembly, always install the new design converter housing to transmission case attaching bolts at the time of reassembly.

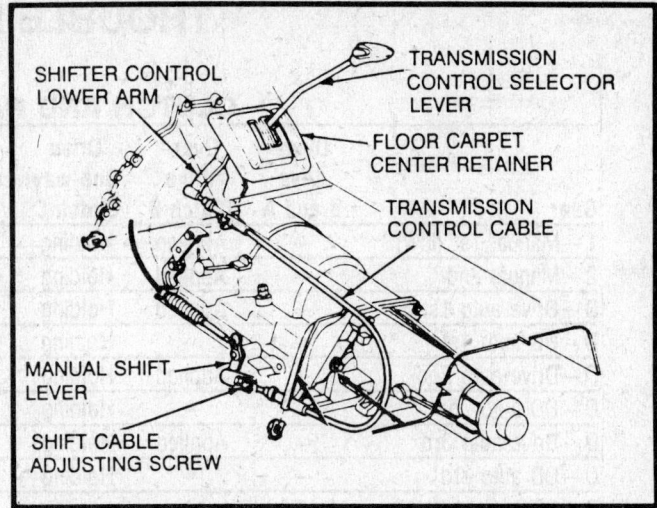
Shift control linkage

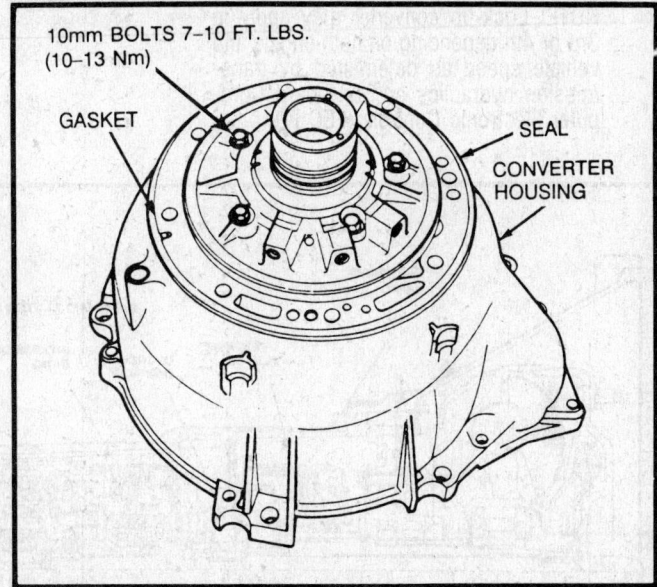
Front oil pump to housing bolts

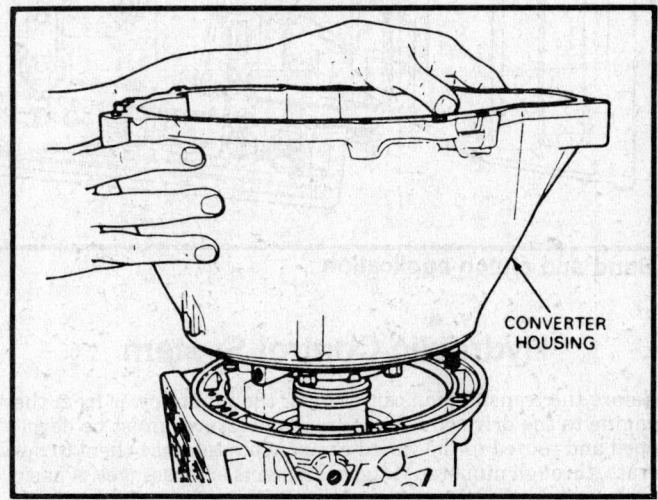
Converter housing to transmission case

TROUBLE DIAGNOSIS

CLUTCH AND BAND APPLICATION

Gear	Over-drive B and A	Over-drive Clutch B	Drive One-way Clutch C	Inter-mediate Band D	Reverse and High Clutch E	Forward Clutch F	Low and Reverse Band G	One-way Clutch H	Gear Ratio
1—Manual 1st (low)	–	Applied	Holding	–	–	Applied	Applied	Holding	2.47:1
2—Manual 2nd	–	Applied	Holding	Applied	–	Applied	–	–	1.47:1
D—Drive auto 1st	–	Applied	Holding	–	–	Applied	–	Holding	2.47:1
D—OD auto 1st	–	–	Holding	–	–	Applied	–	Holding	2.47:1
D—Drive auto 2nd	–	Applied	Holding	Applied	–	Applied	–	–	1.47:1
D—OD auto 2nd	–	–	Holding	Applied	–	Applied	–	–	1.47:1
D—Drive auto 3rd	–	Applied	Holding	–	Applied	Applied	–	–	1.00:1
D—OD auto 3rd	–	–	Holding	–	Applied	Applied	–	–	1.00:1
D—OD automatic 4th	Applied	–	–	–	Applied	Applied	–	–	0.75:1
Reverse	–	Applied	Holding	–	Applied	–	Applied	–	2.10:1

NOTE: Lock-up converter may apply in 3rd or 4th depending on both engine and vehicle speed as determined by transmission hydraulics and on-board Computer Electronic Controls (EEC IV)

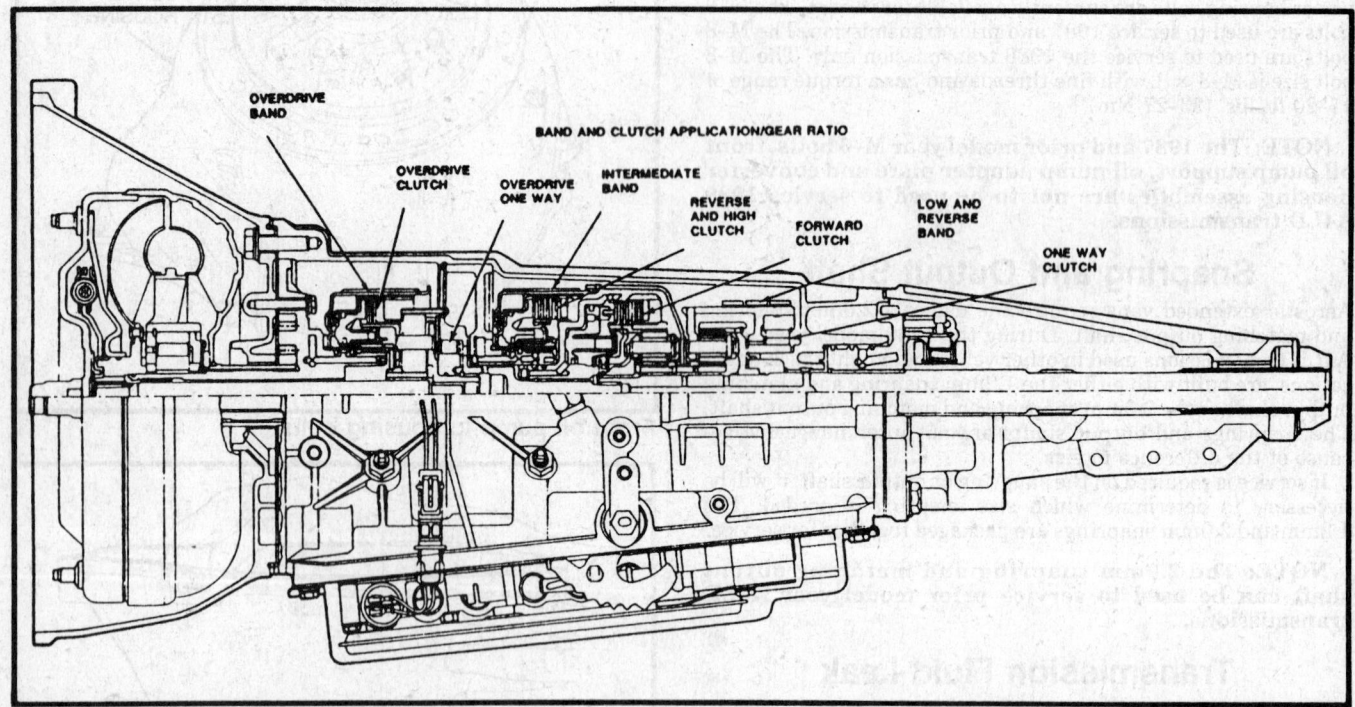

Band and clutch application

Hydraulic Control System

Before the transmission can transfer the input power from the engine to the drive wheels, hydraulic pressures must be developed and routed to the varied components to cause them to operate, through numerous internal systems and passages. A basic understanding of the components, fluid routings and systems, will aid in the trouble diagnosis of the transmission.

OIL PUMP

The oil pump is a positive displacement pump, meaning that as long as the pump is turning and fluid is supplied to the inlet, the pump will deliver fluid in a volume proportionate to the input drive speed. The pump is in operation whenever the engine is operating, delivering more fluid than the transmission needs, with the excess being bled off by the pressure regulator valve

CHILTON'S THREE C's TRANSMISSION DIAGNOSIS
A4LD Automatic Transmission

Condition	Cause	Correction
Converter clutch does not engage	a) Converter clutch solenoid is not being energized electrically. Wires to solenoid shorted or an open circuit. Transmission case connector not sealed. Open or short circuit inside of solenoid. Malfunctioning engine coolant temperature sensor, throttle position sensor or manifold absolute pressure sensor. Vacuum line disconnected from the MAP sensor	a) Perform EEC-IV diagnostic check key on, engine off
	b) Brake switch malfunction	b) Perform EEC-IV diagnostic check, engine running
	c) Malfunctioning EEC-IV processor	c) Run diagnostic check on processor
	d) Converter clutch solenoid is being energized electronically but foreign material on solenoid valve is preventing valve closure	d) Remove transmission oil pan. Remove valve body. Remove solenoid and check operation of solenoid. Clean if necessary
	e) Converter clutch shuttle valve stuck in unlock position (against plug) or too high a load spring	e) Remove valve body. Check operation of converter clutch shuttle valve. Remove any contamination. Spring load should be approximateley 2 lbs @ 0.512 in.
	f) Converter clutch shift valve stuck in downshift position	f) Remove valve body. Check operation of converter clutch shift valve. Remove any contamination. Be sure valve moves freely
	g) Torque converter internal malfunction preventing lock-up piston application	g) Remove transmission. Replace converter
Converter clutch always engaged even at zero road speed. (Symptom: vehicle will move only when the engine is accelerated to a high rpm and transmission selector level is into D	a) Converter clutch shift valve stuck in lock position	a) Remove transmission valve body. Check to see that converter clutch shift valve moves freely
	b) Converter clutch shuttle valve stuck in locked position	b) Remove valve body. Check converter clutch shuttle valve for ease of movement
	c) Lock-up piston in torque converter	c) Remove transmission. Replace converter
Converter clutch will not disengage on coastdown	a) malfunctioning throttle position sensor (should unlock at closed throttle)	a) Perform EEC-IV diagnpostic check, key on, engine off
	b) Converter clutch solenoid sticking	b) Remove valve body. Check operation of of solenoid. Replace if required
Slow initial engagement	a) Improper fluid level	a) Perform fluid level check
	b) Damaged or improperly adjusted manual linkage	b) Service or adjust manual linkage
	c) Contaminated fluid	c) Perform fluid condition check
	d) Improper clutch and band application or low main control pressure	d) Perform control pressure test
Rough initial engagement in either forward or reverse	a) Imprpoer fluid level	a) Perform fluid level check
	b) High engine idel	b) Adjust to specification
	c) Automatic choke on (warm temperature)	c) Service as required
	d) Looseness in the driveshaft U-joints or engine mounts	d) Service as required

CHILTON'S THREE C's TRANSMISSION DIAGNOSIS
A4LD Automatic Transmission

Condition	Cause	Correction
Rough initial engagement in either forward or reverse	e) Improper clutch band application or oil control pressure	e) Perform control pressure test
	f) Sticking or dirty valve body	f) Clean, service or replace valve body
	g) Converter clutch not disengaging	g) Check converter clutch engagement/ disengagement
Harsh engagements (warm engine)	a) Improper fluid level	a) Perform fluid level check
	b) Engine curb idle speed too high	b) Check engine curb idle speed
	c) Valve body bolts too loose or tight	c) Tighten to specification
	d) Valve body dirty, sticking valves	d) Determine source of contamination. Service as required
No or delayed forward engagement. Reverse OK	a) Improper fluid level	a) Perform fluid level check
	b) Manual linkage misadjusted or damaged	b) Check and adjust or service as required
	c) Low main control pressure (leakage). Forward clutch center support seal rings leaking	c) Control pressure test. Note results
	d) Forward clutch assembly burnt, damaged, leaking. Check ball in cylinder, leaking piston seal rings	d) Perform air pressure test
	e) Valve body bolts too loose ot tight	e) Tighten to specification
	f) Valve body dirty, sticking valves	f) Determine source of contamination. Service as required
	g) Transmission filter plugged	g) Replace filter
	h) Pump damaged or leaking	h) Visually inspect pump gear. Replace pump if necessary
No or delayed reverse engagement	a) Improper fluid level	a) Perform fluid level check
	b) Manual linkage misadjusted or damaged	b) Check and adjust or service as required
	c) Low main control pressure in reverse	c) Control pressure test
	d) Reverse clutch assembly burnt, worn or leaking; check ball in piston, leaking piston seal rings	d) Perform air pressure test
	e) Valve body bolts too loose or tight	e) Tighten to specification
	f) Valve body dirty, sticking valves	f) Determine source of contamination. Service as required
	g) Transmission filter plugged	g) Replace filter
	h) Pump damaged	h) Visually inspect pump gears. Replace pump if necessary
	i) Low/reverse servo piston seal cut or leaking	i) Perform air pressure test. Check and replace piston seal. Check and replace low/reverse band
No engagement in drive or forward (any position) or reverse	a) Improrper fluid level	a) Perform fluid level check
	b) Low main control pressure	b) Perform control pressure test
	c) Mechanical damage	c) Check splines on turbine, input shaft, and OD carrier, OD one-way clutch, center shaft, forward clutch, forward carrier and output shaft. Replace if necessary
No engagement or drive in D (2 & 1 OK)	a) Manual linkage misadjusted	a) Adjust manual linkage
	b) Rear one-way clutch damaged	b) Replace rear one-way clutch
	c) Dirty or contaminaited transmission fluid	c) Clean transmission and valve body
	d) Overdrive one-way clutch damaged	d) Repair or replace
Vehicle creeping in neutral	a) Forward clutch failing to disengage	a) Clean transmission

CHILTON'S THREE C's TRANSMISSION DIAGNOSIS
A4LD Automatic Transmission

Condition	Cause	Correction
No or delayed reverse engagement and/or no engine braking in manual low (1)	a) Improper fluid level b) Linkage out of adjustment c) Low reverse servo piston seal leaking d) Low reverse band burnt or worn e) Overdrive clutch, overdrive one-way clutch damaged f) Polished, glazed low/reverse band or drum g) Rear one-way clutch damaged	a) Perform fluid level check b) Service or adjust linkage c) Check and replace piston seal d) Perform air pressure test e) Replace as required f) Service or replace as require4d g) Replace
No engine braking in manual 2nd gear	a) Intermediate band out of adjustment b) Improper band or clutch application or oil pressure control system c) Intermediate servo leaking d) Overdrive clutch, OD one-way clutch damaged e) Glazed band	a) Adjust intermediate band b) Perform control pressure test c) Perform air pressure test of intermediate servo for leakage. Service as required d) Replace as required e) Service or replace as required
Forward engagement slips, shudders, chatters	a) Improper fluid level b) Manual linkage misadjusted, damaged c) Low main control pressure d) Valve body bolts too loose or tight e) Valve body dirty, sticking valves f) Forward clutch piston ball check not sealing, leaking g) Forward clutch piston seals cut or worn h) OD one-way clutch damaged i) Rear one-way clutch damaged	a) Perform fluid level check b) Check and adjust or service as required c) Perform control pressure test d) Tighten to specification e) Determine source of contamination. Service as required f) Replace forward clutch piston. Service transmission as required g) Replace seal and service clutch as required h) Replace as required i) Determine cause of condition. Service as required
Reverse shudders, chatters, slips	a) Improper fluid level b) Low main control pressure in reverse c) Low/reverse servo leaking d) OD and/or rear one-way clutch damaged e) OD and/or rear revers/high clutch drum bushing damaged f) OD and/or rear/high clutch center support seal rings, ring grooves worn or damaged g) OD and/or rear reverse/high clutch piston seals cut or worn h) Low/reverse servo piston damaged or worn i) Low/reverse band out of adjustment or damaged j) Looseness in the driveshaft, U-joints or engine mounts k) Low/reverse servo piston, or bores damaged	a) Perform fluid level check b) Perform control pressure test c) Air pressure test. Visually inspect seal rings and piston bore d) Determine cause of condition. Service as required e) Determine cause of condition. Service as required f) Detetermine condition. Service as mt,f) required g) Determine cause of condition. Service mt,g) as required h) Service as required i) Adjust and inspect low/reverse band j) Service as required k) Perform air pressure check

CHILTON'S THREE C's TRANSMISSION DIAGNOSIS
A4LD Automatic Transmission

Condition	Cause	Correction
No drive, slips or chatters in 1st gear in D. All other gears normal	a) Damaged or worn rear one-way clutch	a) Service or replace rear one-way clutch
No drive, slips or chatters in 2nd gear	a) Intermediate band out of adjustment b) Improper band or clutch application or control pressure c) Damaged or worn intermediate servo d) Dirty or sticking valve body e) Polished, glazed intermediate band	a) Adjustment intermediate band b) Perform control pressure test c) Perform air pressure test d) Clean, service or replace valve body e) Replace or service as required
Starts up in 2nd or 3rd	a) Improper band and/or clutch application or oil pressure control system b) Damaged, worn or sticking governor c) Valve body loose d) Dirty or sticking valve body e) Cross leaks between valve body and case mating surfce	a) Perform control pressure test b) Perform governor check. Replace or service governor, clean screen c) Tighten to specification d) Clean, service or replace valve body e) Service or replace valve body and or case as required
Shift points incorrect	a) Improper fluid level b) Vacuum line damaged, clogged or leaks c) Improper operation of EGR system d) Improper speedometer gear installed e) Improper clutch or band application or oil pressure control system f) Damaged or worn governor g) Vacuum diaphragm bent, sticks or leaks h) Dirty or sticking valve body	a) Perform fluid level check b) Perform vacuum supply test c) Service or replace as required d) Replace gear e) Perform shift test and control f) Service or replace governor, clean screen g) Service or replace as required h) Clean, service or replace valve body
All upshifts harsh, delayed or no upshifts	a) Improper fluid level b) Manual linkage misadjusted or damaged c) Governor sticking d) Main control pressure too high e) Valve body bolts too loose or tight f) Valve body dirty or sticking valves g) Vacuum leak to diaphragm unit h) Vacuum diaphragm bent, sticking, leaks	a) Perform fluid level check b) Check and adjust or service as required c) Perform governor test. Service as required d) Perform control test. Service as required e) Tighten to specification f) Determine source of contamination. Service as required g) Perform vacuum supply and diaphragm test. Check vacuum lines to diaphragm unit. Service as required h) Check diaphragm unit. Service as required
All upshifts mushy or early	a) Low main control pressure b) Valve body bolts too loose or tight c) Valve body or throttle control valve sticking d) Governor valve sticking e) Kickdown linkage misadjusted, sticking or damaged	a) Perform control pressure. Note results b) Tighten to specification c) Determine source of contamination. Service as required d) Perform governor test. Repair as required e) Adjust linkage, service as required

CHILTON'S THREE C's TRANSMISSION DIAGNOSIS
A4LD Automatic Transmission

Condition	Cause	Correction
No 1–2 upshift	a) Improper fluid level	a) Perform fluid level check
	b) Kickdown system damaged	b) Replace damaged parts
	c) Manual linkage misadjusted or damaged	c) Check and adjust or service as required
	d) Governor valve sticking	d) Perform governor test. Service as required
	e) Intermediate band out of adjustment	e) Adjust intermediate band
	f) Vacuum leak to diaphragm unit	f) Check vacuum lines to diaphragm. Service as required
	g) Vacuum diaphragm bent, sticking, leaks	g) Check diapraghm unit. Service as required
	h) Valve body bolts too loose or tight	h) Valve body dirty or sticking valves
	i) Intermediate band and/or servo assembly burnt	i) Perform air pressure test
Rough, harsh or delayed 1–2 upshift	a) Improper fluid level	a) Perform fluid level check
	b) Poor engine performance	b) Tune engine
	c) Kickdown linkage misadjusted	c) Adjust linkage
	d) Intermediate band out of adjustment	d) Adjust intermediate band
	e) Main control pressure too high	e) Perform control pressure test
	f) Governor valve sticking	f) Perform governor test. Service as required
	g) Damaged intermediate servo	g) Perform air pressure test on intermediate servo
	h) Engine vacuum leak	h) Check engine vacuum lines. Check vacuum diaphragm unit. Perform vacuum supply and diaphragm test. Service as required
	i) Valve body too loose or tight	i) Tighten to specifications
	j) Valve body dirty or sticking valves	j) Determine source of contaminiation. Service as required
	k) Vacuum leak to diaphragm unit	k) Check vacuum lines to diaphragm unit. service as required
	l) Vacuum diaphragm bent, sticking or leaks	l) Check diaphragm unit. Service as required
Mushy, early, soft or slipping	a) Improper fluid level	a) Perform fluid level check
	b) Main regulator or throttle valve sticking	b) Service as required
	c) Incorrect engine performance	c) Tune engine as required
	d) Intermediate band out of adjustment	d) Adjust intermeidate band
	e) Low main control pressure	e) Perform control pressure test
	f) Valve body bolts too loose or tight	f) Tighten to specification
	g) Valve body dirty or sticking valves	g) Determine source of contamination. Service as required
	h) Governor valve sticking	h) Perform governor test. Service as required
	i) Damaged intermediate servo or band	i) Perform air pressure test. Service as required
	j) Polished or glazed intermediate band or drum	j) Service or replace as required
No 2–3 upshift	a) Low fluid level	a) Perform fluid level check
	b) Kickdown system damaged	b) Replace damaged parts
	c) Low main control pressure to reverse high clutch	c) Perform control pressure test. Note results
	d) Valve body bolts too loose or tight	d) Tighten to specification

CHILTON'S THREE C's TRANSMISSION DIAGNOSIS
A4LD Automatic Transmission

Condition	Cause	Correction
No 2–3 upshift	e) Valve body dirty or sticking valves	e) Determine source of contamination. Service as required
	f) Reverse/high clutch assembly burnt or worn	f) Determine cause of condition. Service as required
Harsh or delayed 2–3 upshift	a) Incorrect engine performance	a) Check engine tune-up
	b) Engine vacuum leak	b) Check engine vacuum lines. Check vacuum diaphragm unit. Perform vacuum supply and diaphragm test. Service as required
	c) Kickdown system damaged	c) Replace damaged parts
	d) Damaged or worn intermediate servo release and reverse/high clutch piston check ball	d) Air pressure test the intermediate servo. Apply and release the reverse/high clutch piston check ball
	e) Valve body bolts too loose or tight	e) Tighten to specification
	f) Valve body dirty or sticking valves	f) Determine source of condition. Service as required
	g) Vacuum diaphragm bent, sticking or leaks	g) Check diaphragm. Replace as required
	h) Throttle valve stuck	h) Service as required
Soft, early or mushy 2–3 upshift	a) Kickdown system damaged	a) Replace damaged parts
	b) Valve body bolts too loose or tight	b) Tighten to specification
	c) Valve body dirty or sticking valves	c) Determine source of contamination. Service as required
	d) Vacuum diaphragm or T.V. control rod bent, sticking, leaks	d) Check diaphragm and rod. Replace as required
	e) Throttle valve stuck	e) Service as required
Erratic shifts	a) Poor engine performance	a) Check engine tune-up
	b) Vacuum line damaged	b) Service as required
	c) Valve body bolts too loose or tight	c) Tighten to specification
	d) Valve body dirty or sticking valves	d) Perform air pressure test. Note results Determine source of contamination. Service as required
	e) Governor valve stuck	e) Perform governor test. Service as required
	f) Output shaft collector body seal rings damaged	f) Service as required
Shifts 1–3 in OD or D	a) Intermediate band out of adjustment	a) Adjust band
	b) Damaged intermediate servo and/or internal leaks	b) Perform air pressure test. Service front servo and/or internal leaks
	c) Improper band or clutch application or oil pressure control system	c) Perform control pressure test
	d) Polished or glazed band or drum	d) Service or replace band or drum
	e) Dirty or sticking valve body or governor	e) Clean, service or replace valve body or governor
	f) Governor valve stuck	f) Perform governor test. Service as required
	g) Kickdown system out of adjustment	g) Adjust kickdown system
Engine overspeeds on 2–3 shift	a) Kickdown system damaged	a) Replace damaged parts
	b) Improper band or clutch application or oil pressure control system	b) Perform control pressure test
	c) Damaged or worn reverse/high clutch and/or intermediate servo piston	c) Perform air pressure test. Service as required

CHILTON'S THREE C's TRANSMISSION DIAGNOSIS
A4LD Automatic Transmission

Condition	Cause	Correction
Engine overspeeds on 2–3 shift	d) Intermediate servo piston seals cut or leaks	d) Replace seals. Check for leaks
	e) Dirty or sticking valve body	e) Clean, service or replace valve body
	f) Throttle valev stuck	f) Service as required
	g) Damaged vacuum diaphragm	g) Replace vacuum diaphragm
Rough or shudder 3–2 shift at closed throttle in D	a) Incorrect engine idle or performance	a) Tune and adjust engine idle
	b) Improper kickdown linkage adjustment	b) Service or adjust kickdown linkage
	c) Improper clutch or band application or oil pressure control system	c) Perform control pressure test
	d) Improper governor operation	d) Perform governor test. Service as required
	e) Dirty or sticking valve body	e) Clean, service or replace valve body
No 3–4 upshift	a) Kickdown system damaged	a) Replace damaged parts
	b) Vacuum line damaged	b) Repair or replace as required
	c) Vacuum diaphragm damaged	c) Repair or replace as required
	d) Throttle valve sticking	d) Repair or replace as required
	e) OD servo damaged or leaking	e) Check and replace OD piston seal if required
	f) Polished or glazed OD band or drum	f) Service or replace OD band or drum
	g) Dirty or sticking valve body	g) Clean, service or replace valve body. Check 3–4 shift valve for freedom of movement
	h) Dirty or sticking 3–4 solenoid	h) Clean, service or replace 3–4 solenoid and filter sleeve assembly
Slipping 4th gear	a) OD servo damaged or leaking	a) Check and replace OD piston seal
	b) Polished or glazed OD band or drum	b) Service or replace OD band on drum
Engine stall speed exceeded in OD, D or R	a) Vacuum system	a) Check and service vacuum system
	b) Low main control pressure	b) Control pressure test. Check and clean valve body. Replace valve body gasket. Check or service pump
Engine stall speed exceeded in R	a) Low/reverse servo or band damaged	a) Check engine braking in 1. If not OK check, service or replace if required the low/reverse servo and band
	b) Reverse and high clutch damaged	b) If low/reverse servo OK, check and repair reverse and high clutch
Engine stall speed exceeded in OD or D. OK in R	a) OD one-way clutch or rear one-way clutch damaged	a) Check engine stall speeds in 2 and 1 If OK, repair OD or rear one-way clutches. Clean transmission
1–2 upshift is above 40 mph (64 km/h)	a) Vacuum system	a) Check and service hoses and vacuum diaphragm if required
	b) Main control pressure	b) Perform control pressure test
	c) Governor damaged or worn	c) Perform governor check. Replace or service governor
	d) Dirty or sticking valve body	d) Clean, service or replace valve body
Kickdown shift speeds too early	a) Kickdown system damaged	a) Replace damaged parts
	b) Main control pressure	b) Perform control pressure test
	c) Governor damaged or worn	c) Perform governor check. Replace or service governor

CHILTON'S THREE C's TRANSMISSION DIAGNOSIS
A4LD Automatic Transmission

Condition	Cause	Correction
No kickdown into 2nd gear between 40–60 mph (64–100 km/h) on OD or D	a) Kickdown system damaged b) Main control pressure c) Dirty or sticking valve body d) Kickdown cable overadjusted	a) Replace damaged parts b) Perform control pressure test c) Ckeck kickdown valve. Clean or replace valve body d) Adjust kickdown cable
No shift into 2nd gear with accelerator 3–4 depressed at 25 mph (40 km/h) in OD or D	a) Main control pressure b) Governor damaged or worn c) Dirty or sticking valve body	a) Perform control pressure test b) Check governor c) Clean or replace valve body
When moving selector from OD or D to manual 1 at 55 mph (86 km/h) with accelerator released, no braking felt from downshift to 2nd gear	a) Main control pressure b) Intermediate band out of adjustment c) Overdrive clutch damaged	a) Perform control pressure test b) Adjust band. Check intermediate servo c) Repair or replace overdrive clutch
When moving selector from OD or D to manual 1 at 55 mph (86 km/h) with accelerator released, shift into 1st gear occurs over 45 mph (72 km/h)	a) Main control pressure b) Dirty or sticking valve body c) Governor damaged or worn d) Kickdown linkage misadjusted or stuck	a) Perform main control pressure test b) Clean or replace valve body c) Perform governor check. Replace or service governor d) Adjust or repair kickdown linkage
When moving selector from OD or D to manual 1 at 55 mph (86 km/h) with accelerator released, 1st gear shift occurs under 15 mph (24 km/h)	a) Main control pressure b) Dirty or sticking valve body c) Low/reverse servo damaged d) Governor damaged or worn service governor e) Overdrive clutch damaged	a) Perform main control pressure test b) Clean or replace valve body c) Check and service as required d) Perform governor check. e) Repair or replace as required
No forced downshifts	a) Kickdown cable damaged b) Kickdown cable overadjusted c) Damaged internal kickdown linkage d) Improper clutch or band application or oil pressure control system e) Dirty or sticking governor f) Dirty or sticking valve governor	a) Replace damaged parts b) Adjust kickdown cable c) Service internal kickdown linkage d) Perform control pressure test e) Service or replace governor, clean screen f) Clean, service or replace valve body
Engine overspeeds on 3–2 downshift	a) Linkage out of adjustment b) Intermediate band out of adjustment c) Improper band or clutch application and one-way clutch or oil pressure control system d) Damaged or worn intermediate servo e) Polished or glazed band or drum f) Dirty or sticking valve body	a) Service or adjust linkage b) Adjust intermediate band c) Perform control pressure test. Service clutch d) Perform air pressure test. Check the intermediate servo. Service servo and/or seals e) Service or replace as required f) Clean, service or replace valve body
Shift efforts high	a) Manual shaft linkage damaged or misadjusted b) Inner manual lever nut loose misadjusted c) Manual lever retainer pin damaged	a) Check and adjust or service as required b) Tighten nut to specification c) Adjust linkage and install pin
Transmission overheats	a) Improper fluid level b) Incorrect engine idle or performance c) Improper clutch or band application or oil pressure control system	a) Perform fluid level check b) Tune or adjust engine idle c) Perform control pressure test

CHILTON'S THREE C's TRANSMISSION DIAGNOSIS
A4LD Automatic Transmission

Condition	Cause	Correction
Transmission overheats	d) Restriction in cooler lines	d) Service rectriction
	e) Seized converter one-way clutch	e) Replace one-way clutch
	f) Dirty or sticking valve body	f) Clean, service or replace valve body
Transmission leaks	a) Case breather vent	a) Check the vent for free breathing. Repair as required
	b) Leakage at gasket, seal, etc.	b) Remove all traces of lube on exposed surfaces of transmission. Check the vent for free breathing. Operate transmission at normal temperatures and perform fluid leakage check. Service as required
Poor vehicle acceleration	a) Poor engine performance	a) Check engine tune-up
	b) Torque converter one-way clutch slipping	b) Replace torque converter
Transmission noisy. Valve resonance b) Service or adjust linkage NOTE: Gauges may aggravate any hydraulic resonance. Remove gauge and check for resonance level	a) Improper fluid level	a) Perform fluid level check b) Linkage out of adjustment
	c) Improper band or clutch application or oil pressure control system	c) Perform control pressure test
	d) Cooler lines grounding	d) Free up cooler lines
	e) Dirty or sticking valve body	e) Clean, service or replace valve body
	f) Internal leakage or pump cavitation	f) Service as required
Engine stalls when shifting into forward or reverse	a) Low engine idle	a) Verify that engine idle speeds are set
	b) Broken converter clutch shuttle valve spring	b) Replace converter clutch shuttle valve spring

and routed to the sump. It should be remembered, the oil pump is driven by a shaft which is splined into the converter cover and through a drive gear insert. The gears, in turn, are installed in a body, which is bolted to the pump support at the rear of the transmission case.

Should the oil pump fail, fluid would not be supplied to the transmission to keep the converter filled, to lubricate the internal working parts and to operate the hydraulic controls.

PRESSURE REGULATOR SYSTEM

The pressure regulator system controls the main line pressure at pre-determined levels during vehicle operation. The main oil pressure regulator valve and spring determines the psi of the main line control pressure. The main line control pressure is regulated by balancing pressure at the end of the inner valve land, against the valve spring. When the pump begins fluid delivery and fills the passages and transmission components, the spring holds the valve closed and there is no regulation. As the pressure rises, the pressure regulator valve is moved against the spring tension, opening a passage to the torque converter. Fluid then flows into the converter, the cooler system and back to the lubrication system. As the pressure continues its rise, the pressure regulator valve is moved further against the spring tension and at a predetermined psi level and spring tension rate, the valve is moved further to open a passage, allowing excess pressurized fluid to return to the sump. The valve then opens and closes in a vibrating type action, dependent upon the fluid requirements of the transmission. A main line oil pressure booster valve is used to increase the line pressure to meet the needs of higher pressure, required when the transmission torque load increases, to operate the clutches and band servo.

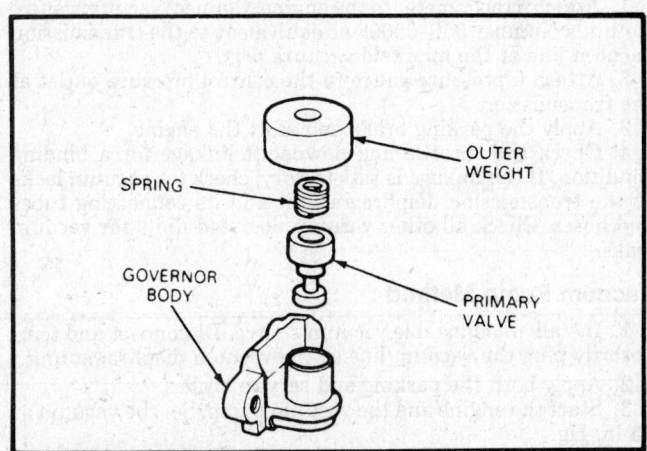

Governor assembly

MANUAL CONTROL VALVE

Main line control pressure is always present at the manual control valve. Other than required passages, such as to the converter fill, the lubricating system and to certain valve assemblies, the manual valve must be moved to allow the pressurized fluid to flow to the desired components or to charge certain passages in order to engage the transmission components in their applicable gear ratios.

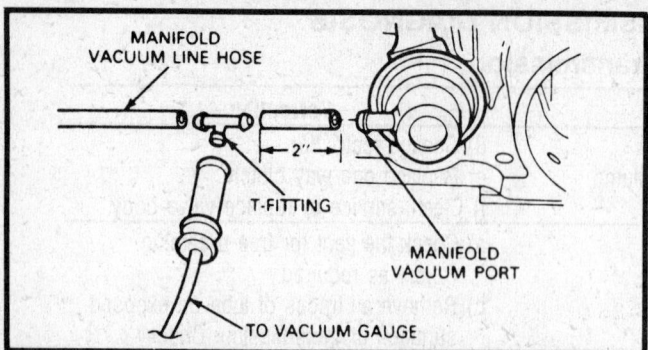

Control pressure test—engine vacuum procedure

GOVERNOR ASSEMBLY

The governor assembly reacts to vehicle road speed and provides a pressure signal to the control valves. This pressure signal causes automatic upshifts to occur as the road speed increases and permits downshifts as the road speed decreases. The governor has 3 hydraulic passages, an exhaust governor pressure out and line pressure in, controlled by springs and weights, with the weight position determined by centrifugal force as the governor assembly rotates.

Diagnosis Tests

CONTROL PRESSURE TEST

There are 2 methods of performing the control pressure test. The first is to perform the test using the engine vacuum. The other is to use a remote vacuum source, such as a hand operated vacuum pump.

Engine Vacuum Method

1. Attach a tachometer to the engine. Connect vacuum gauge, Rotunda Number 059–00008 or equivalent to the transmission vacuum line at the manifold vacuum port.
2. Attach a pressure gauge to the control pressure outlet at the transmission.
3. Apply the parking brake and start the engine.
4. Check the throttle and downshift linkage for a binding condition. If the linkage is satisfactory, check for vacuum leaks at the transmission diaphragm unit and its connecting tubes and hoses. Check all other vacuum operated units for vacuum leaks.

Vacuum Pump Method

1. Install an adjustable vacuum source. Disconnect and temporarily plug the vacuum line at the vacuum diaphragm unit.
2. Apply both the parking and service brakes.
3. Start the engine and the vacuum pump. Set the vacuum at 15 in. Hg.
4. Read and record the control pressure in all selector positions.
5. Run the engine up to 1000 rpm and reduce the vacuum to 10 in. Hg.
6. Read and record the pressure in all of the forward drive ranges.
7. Keep the engine at 1000 and reduce the vacuum to 1 in. Hg.
8. Read and record the pressure in all forward drive ranges and reverse.

AIR PRESSURE TEST

A no drive condition can exist, even with the correct transmis-

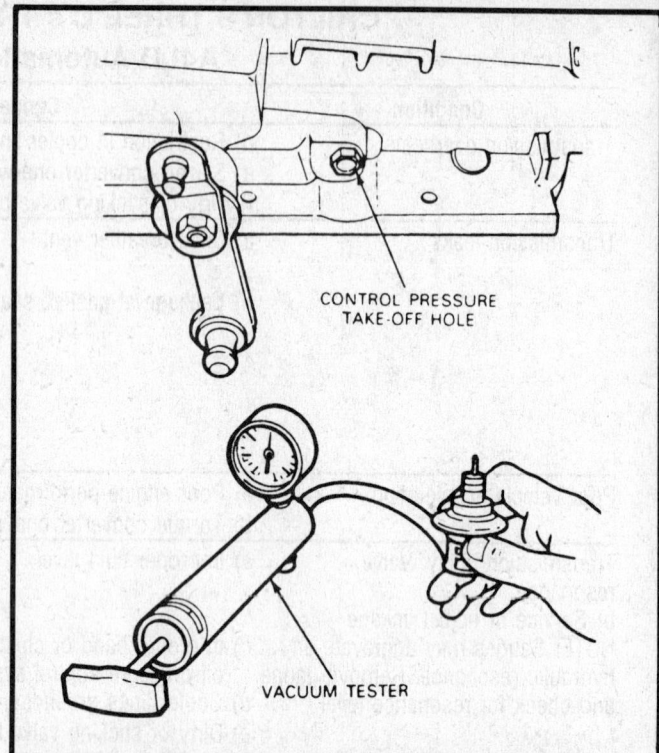

Control pressure test—vacuum pump method

sion fluid pressure, because of inoperative clutches or bands. The inoperative units can be located through a series of checks by substituting air pressure for fluid pressure to determine the locations of the malfunction.

To make the air pressure checks, loosen the oil pan bolts and lower the edge to drain the transmission fluid. Remove the oil pan and the control valve body assembly. The inoperative clutches or bands can be located by introducing low pressure compressed air into the various transmission case passages. If the servos do not operate, disassemble, clean and inspect them to locate the source of the trouble. If air pressure applied to either of the clutch passages fails to operate a clutch or operates both clutches at once, remove and with air pressure check the fluid passages in the case and front pump to detect obstructions.

FORWARD CLUTCH

Apply low pressure compressed air to the transmission case forward clutch passages. A dull thud can be heard when the clutch piston is applied. If no noise is heard, place the finger tips on the input shell and again apply air pressure to the forward clutch passage. Movement of the piston can be felt as the clutch is applied.

GOVERNOR

Apply low pressure compressed air pressure to the forward clutch feed to governor passage and listen for a sharp clicking or whistling noise. The noise indicates governor valve movement.

OVERDRIVE SERVO

Hold the air nozzle in the overdrive servo apply passage. Operation of the servo is indicated by a tightening of the overdrive band around the overdrive drum. Continue to apply low pressure compressed air to the servo apply passage and introduce air pressure into the overdrive servo release passage. The overdrive servo should stroke off releasing the overdrive band.

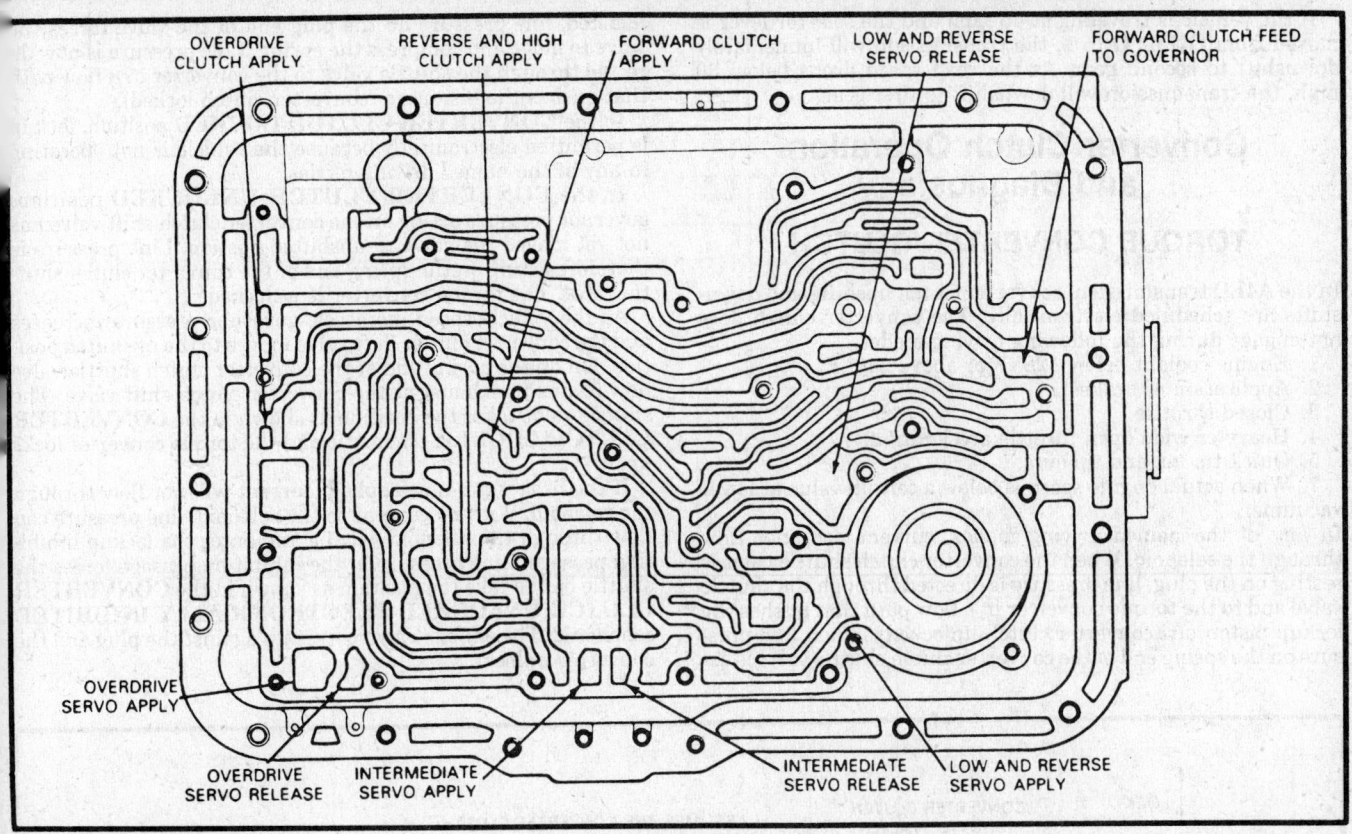

OVERDRIVE CLUTCH APPLY — REVERSE AND HIGH CLUTCH APPLY — FORWARD CLUTCH APPLY — LOW AND REVERSE SERVO RELEASE — FORWARD CLUTCH FEED TO GOVERNOR — OVERDRIVE SERVO APPLY — OVERDRIVE SERVO RELEASE — INTERMEDIATE SERVO APPLY — INTERMEDIATE SERVO RELEASE — LOW AND REVERSE SERVO APPLY

Air pressure checks

OVERDRIVE CLUTCH

Applied in **D, 2, 1** and **R** ranges. Apply low pressure compressed air to the overdrive clutch feed passage. A dull thud indicates that the overdrive clutch piston has moved to the applied position.

REVERSE/HIGH CLUTCH

Apply low pressure compressed air to the reverse/high clutch. A dull thud indicates that the piston has moves to the applied position. If no noise is heard, place the finger tips on the clutch drum and again apply air pressure to detect movement of the piston.

INTERMEDIATE SERVO

Hold the air nozzle in the intermediate servo apply passages. Operation of the servo is indicated by a tightening of the intermediate band around the drum. Continue to apply low pressure compressed air to the servo apply passage and introduce air pressure into the intermediate servo release passage. The intermediate servo should release the band against the apply pressure.

LOW-REVERSE SERVO

Apply low pressure compressed air to the low-reverse servo. The low-reverse band should tighten around the drum if the servo is operating properly.

STALL SPEED TEST

The stall test checks converter one-way clutch operation and installation, the holding ability of the forward clutch, reverse clutch, the low-reverse bands, the planetary one-way clutch and engine performance.

The test should be done only with the engine coolant and transmission fluid at the proper levels and at operating temper-ature. Apply the service and the parking brakes for each stall test.

1. Mark the specified stall rpm for the vehicle on the tachometer.
2. Connect the tachometer to the engine.
3. In each of the drive and reverse range, press the accelerator to the floor and hold it just long enough to let the engine get to full rpm. Do not hold the throttle wide open for more than a few seconds at a time.
4. After each range, move the selector lever to **N** and run the engine at 1000 rpm for 15 seconds to cool the converter before making the next test.

NOTE: If the engine speed recorded by the tachometer exceeds the maximum limit, releases the accelerator immediately, because clutch or band slippage is indicated.

ROAD TEST

This test will determine if the electronics, governor and shift control valves are functioning properly. Check the throttle upshifts with the selector in the **OD** range.

The transmission should start in 1st gear and shift through 2nd, 3rd and 4th **OD** gears and then lock the converter clutch. A wide open throttle lockup and 3–4 shift is not possible. A 4–3 wide open throttle kickdown can always be obtained regardless of road speed.

When the selector lever is in the **D** position, the transmission will make all automatic upshifts except the 3–4. When the selector lever is at **2**, the transmission can operate only in second gear.

With the transmission in 3rd gear and the road speed over 45 mph, the transmission should shift to second gear when the selector lever is moved from **D** to **2** to **1**.

If the vehicle is traveling at 45 mph and the selector lever is moved from **OD** or **D** to **1**, the transmission will immediately downshift to second gear. As the road speed drops below 30 mph, the transmission will downshift to first gear.

Converter Clutch Operation and Diagnosis

TORQUE CONVERTER CLUTCH

In the A4LD transmission, converter clutch upshifts and downshifts are scheduled electronically. The converter clutch does not engage during the following driving modes.

1. Engine coolant below 128° F or above 240° F.
2. Application of brakes.
3. Closed throttle.
4. Heavy or wide open throttle acceleration.
5. Quick tip ins and tip outs.
7. When actual engine speed is below a certain value at lower vacuums.

In any of the named driving modes, current does not flow through the solenoid. When the converter clutch shuttle valve is resting on the plug, line pressure is directed through the shuttle valve and to the torque converter in a flow path that pushes the lockup piston off (converter clutch unlocked). When line pressure on the spring end of the converter clutch shuttle valve is ex-hausted, line pressure on the plug end of the valve forces the valve to move and compress the spring. Line pressure is now directed through the shuttle valve to the converter in a flow path that pushes the piston on (converter clutch locked).

In the **CONVERTER CLUTCH LOCKED** position, lockup is permitted electronically because the vehicle is not operating in any of the named driving modes.

In the **CONVERTER CLUTCH UNLOCKED** position, governor pressure acting on the converter clutch shift valve has not yet moved the valve to upshifted postion. Line pressure is therefore acting on the spring end of the converter clutch shuttle valve. The torque converter is unlocked.

As the vehicle speed increases, governor pressure increases and the converter clutch shift valve moves to the upshifted position. Oil on the spring end of the converter clutch shuttle valve now drains to exhaust at the converter clutch shift valve. The shuttle valve takes the position as shown in the **CONVERTER CLUTCH LOCKED** schematic and the torque converter locks up.

If the brakes are now applied, current will not flow through the solenoid. With no current to the solenoid, line pressure can flow through the solenoid valving and enter the lockup inhibition passage. Line pressure in the inhibition passage forces the shuttle ball to take the position as shown in the **CONVERTER CLUTCH UNLOCKED ELECTRONICALLY INHIBITED** schematic. The shuttle valve moves up against the plug and the converter unlocks.

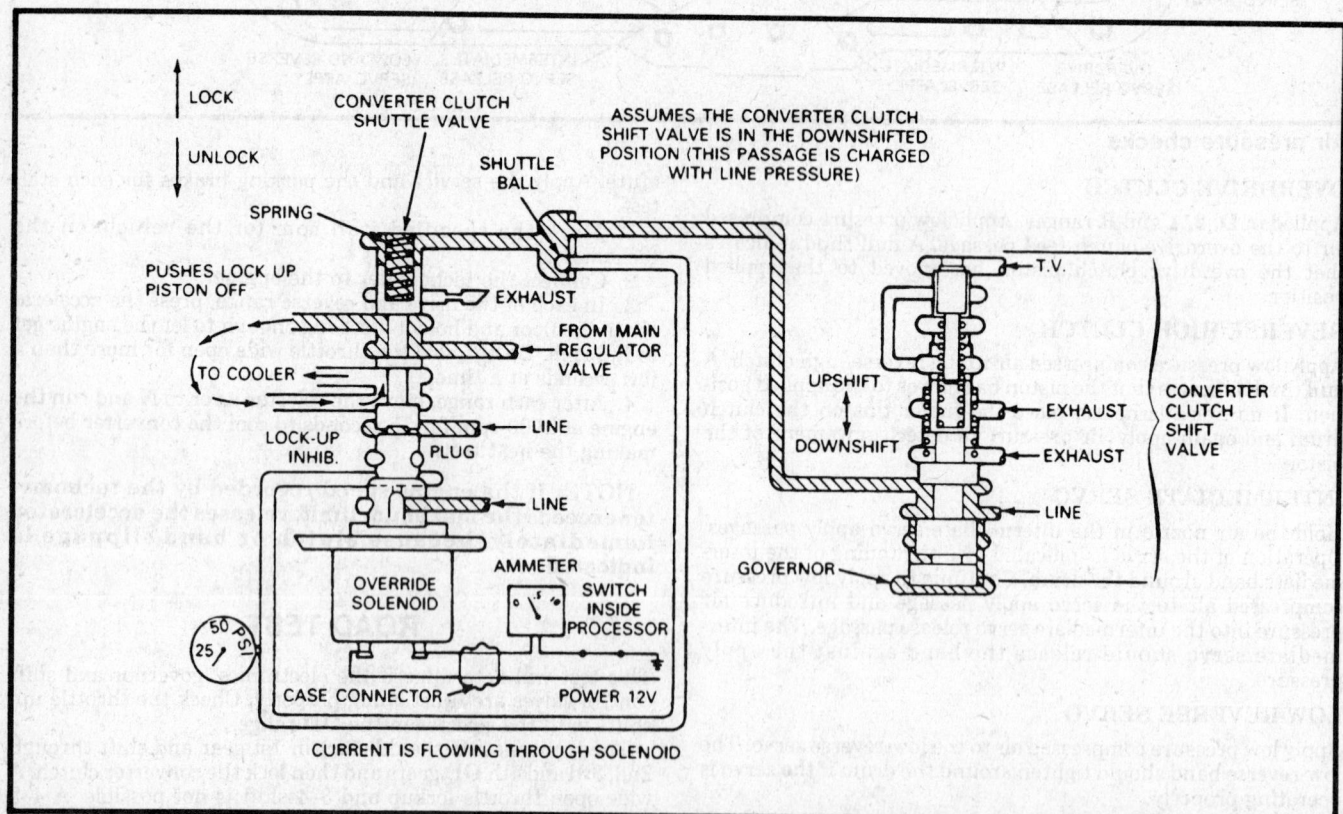

Converter clutch system

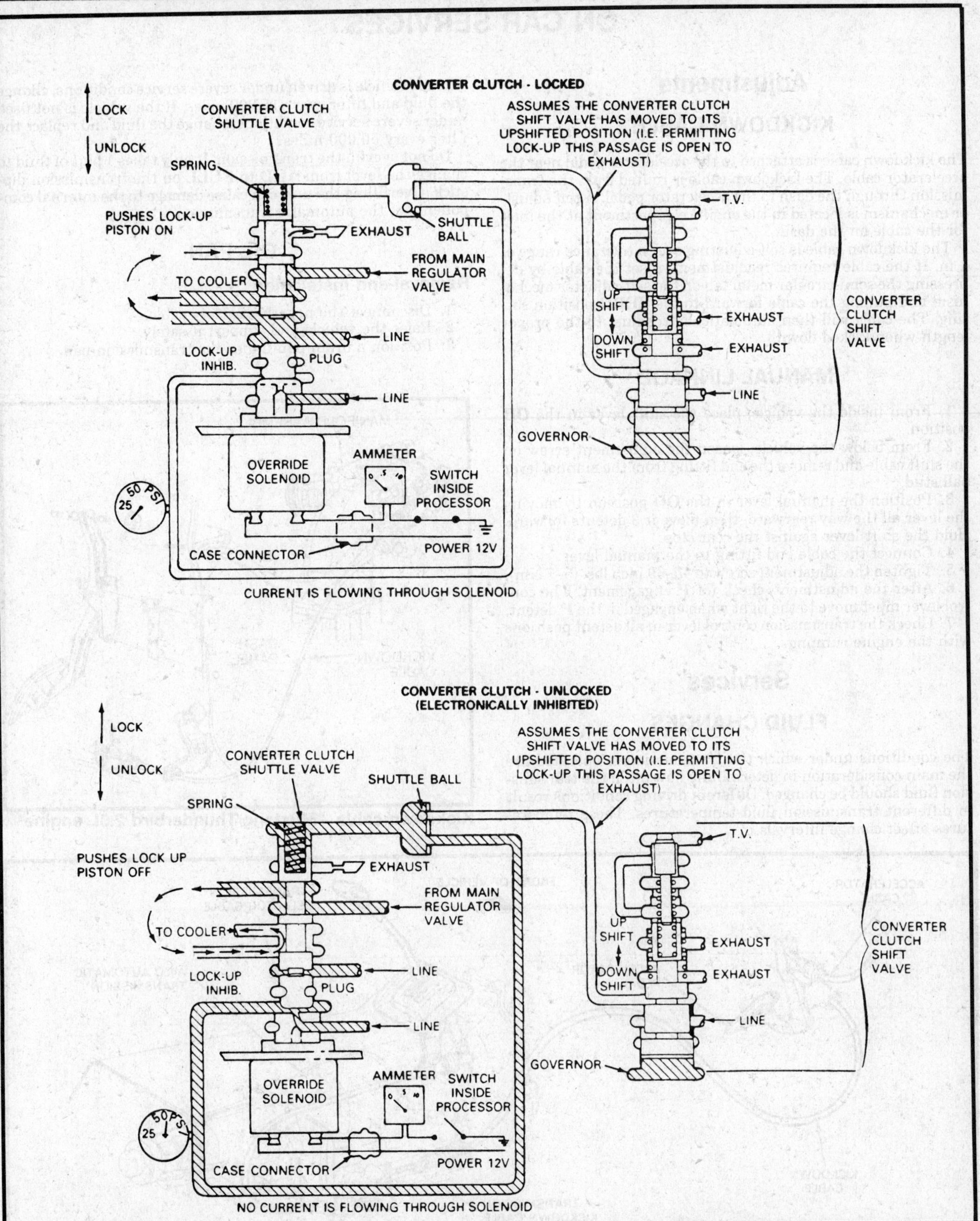

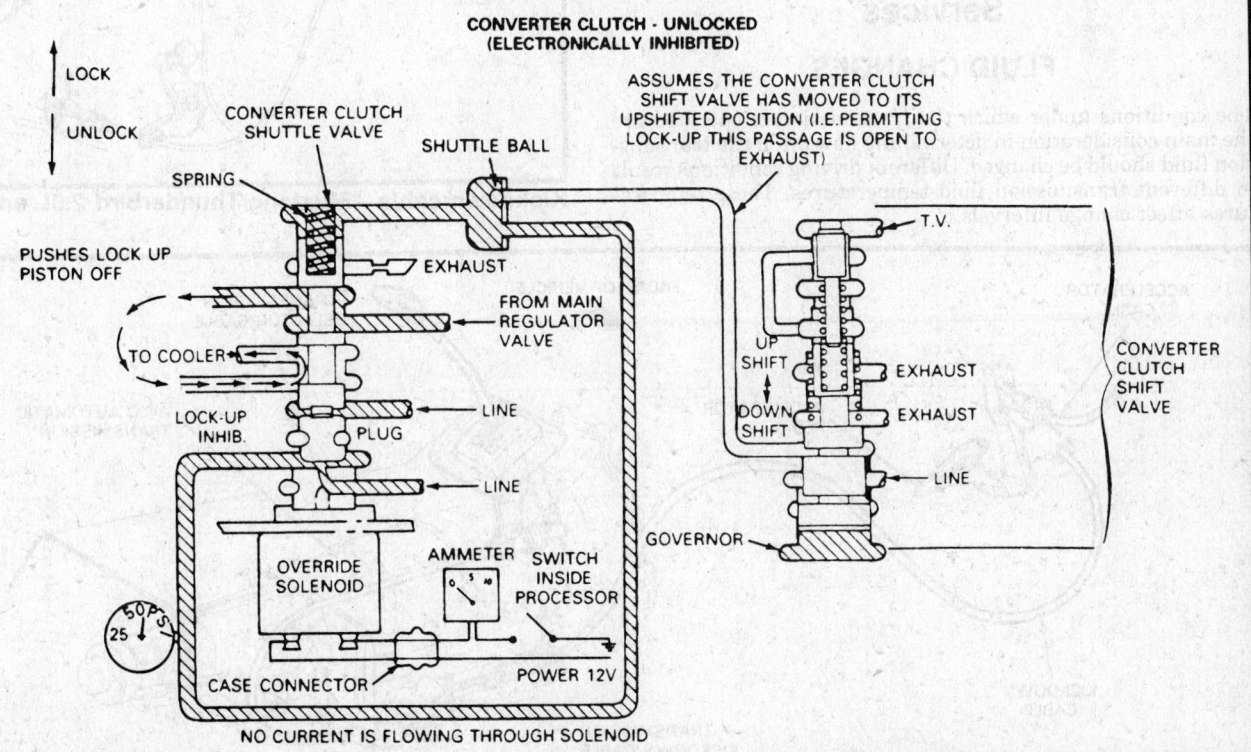

Converter clutch system

ON CAR SERVICES

Adjustments

KICKDOWN CABLE

The kickdown cable is attached to the accelerator pedal near the accelerator cable. The kickdown cable is routed from the transmission through the dash to the accelerator pedal. A self adjuster mechanism is located in the engine compartment at the inlet for the cable on the dash.

The kickdown cable is self-adjusting over a tolerance range of 1 in. If the cable requires readjustment, reset the cable by depressing the semi-circular metal tab on the self-adjuster mechanism and pulling the cable forward to the **ZERO** position setting. The cable will then automatically readjust to the proper length when kicked down.

MANUAL LINKAGE

1. From inside the vehicle, place the shift lever in the **OD** position.
2. From below the vehicle, loosen the adjustment screw on the shift cable and remove the end fitting from the manual lever ball stud.
3. Position the manual lever in the **OD** position by moving the lever all the way rearward, then move it 3 detents forward. Hold the shift lever against the rear stop.
4. Connect the cable end fitting to the manual lever.
5. Tighten the adjustment screw to 45–60 inch lbs. (5–7 Nm).
6. After the adjustment, check for **P** engagement. The control lever must move to the right when engaged in the **P** detent.
7. Check the transmission control lever in all detent positions with the engine running.

Services

FLUID CHANGES

The conditions under which the transmission is operated are the main consideration in determining how often the transmission fluid should be changed. Different driving conditions result in different transmission fluid temperatures. These temperatures affect change intervals.

If the vehicle is driven under severe service conditions, change the fluid and filter every 15,000 miles. If the vehicle is not used under severe service conditions, change the fluid and replace the filter every 50,000 miles.

Do not overfill the transmission. It only takes 1 pint of fluid to change the level from **ADD** to **FULL** on the transmission dipstick. Overfilling the unit can cause damage to the internal components of the automatic transmission.

OIL PAN

Removal and Installation

1. Disconnect the negative battery cable.
2. Raise the vehicle and support it safely.
3. Position a drain pan under the transmission pan.

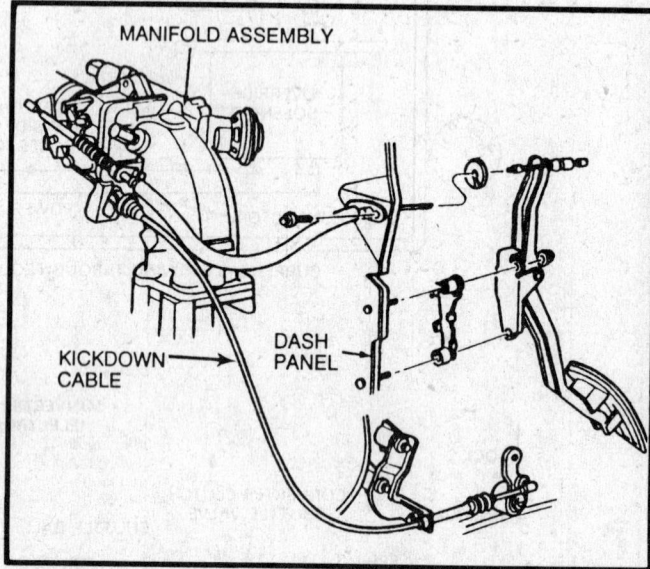

Kickdown cable—Mustang/Thunderbird 2.3L engine

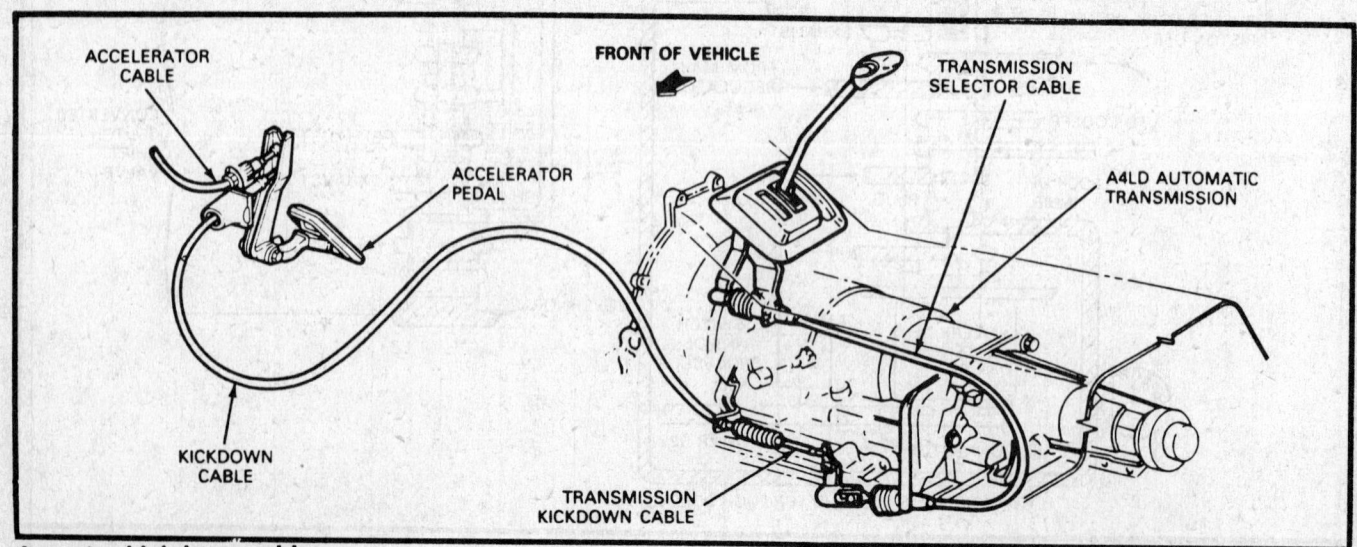

Aerostar kickdown cable

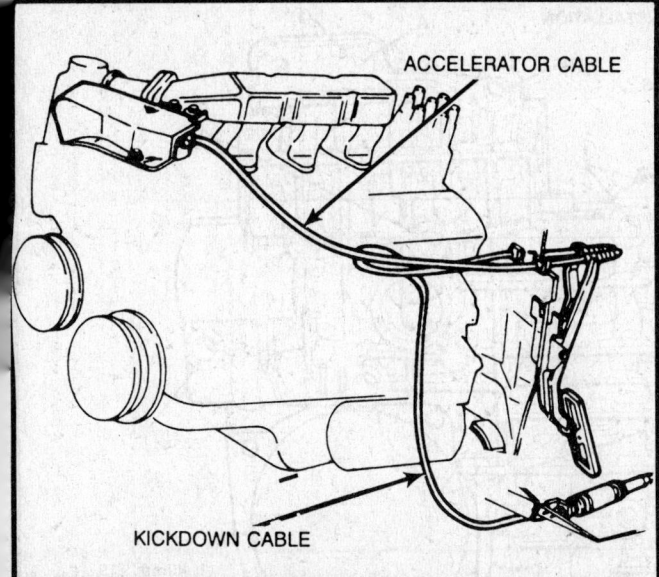

Kickdown cable – Ranger/Bronco II

4. Starting at the rear, loosen, but do not remove the pan bolts.

5. Loosen the pan from the transmission and allow the fluid to drain gradually.

6. Remove all of the pan bolts except 2 at the front or rear and allow the fluid to continue draining.

7. Remove the pan. Clean the old gasket from the pan and the transmission case.

8. Install a new gasket on the pan. Install the pan on the transmission case.

9. Install the pan bolts and torque them to 8–10 ft. lbs. (11–13 Nm).

10. Install 3 quarts of Dexron® II or Mercon® type transmission fluid into the filler tube (converter not drained). When refilling a dry transmission and converter, install 5 quarts of fluid into the filler tube.

11. Start the engine and run it until it reaches normal operating temperature.

12. Check the fluid level after moving the gear selector through all ranges. Correct the fluid level as necessary.

VALVE BODY

Removal and Installation

1. Disconnect the negative battery cable.
2. Raise the vehicle and support it safely.
3. Remove the oil pan.
4. Remove the filter screen and gasket.
5. Remove the low/reverse servo cover, piston, spring and gasket.
6. Disconnect the 2 wires at the converter clutch solenoid and the 2 wires at the 3–4 shift solenoid.
7. Remove the bolts and while easing the valve body out of the transmission, unlock and detach the selector lever connecting link. Remove the valve body and the gasket.
8. Attach and lock the selector lever connecting rod to the manual valve and ease the valve body into the case.
9. Tighten all bolts except the filter screen bolt in the correct sequence to 71–97 inch lbs. (8.0–11.0 Nm).
10. Install the low-reverse servo cover, piston, spring and gasket.
11. Install the converter clutch solenoid wires.
12. Install the filter screen and gasket.

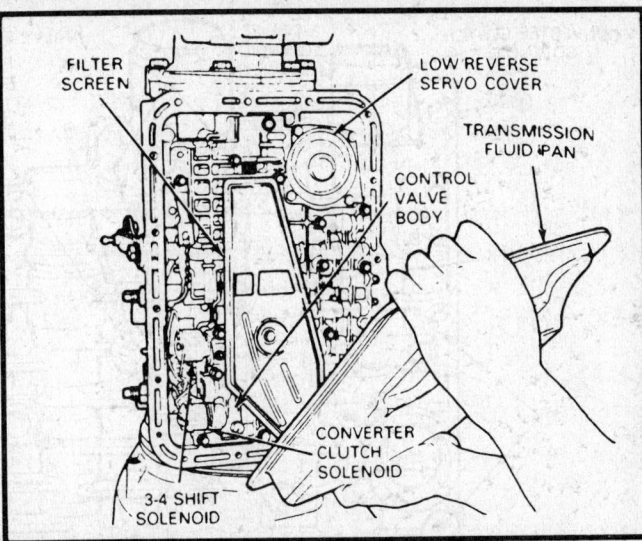

Oil pan and valve body – removal and installation

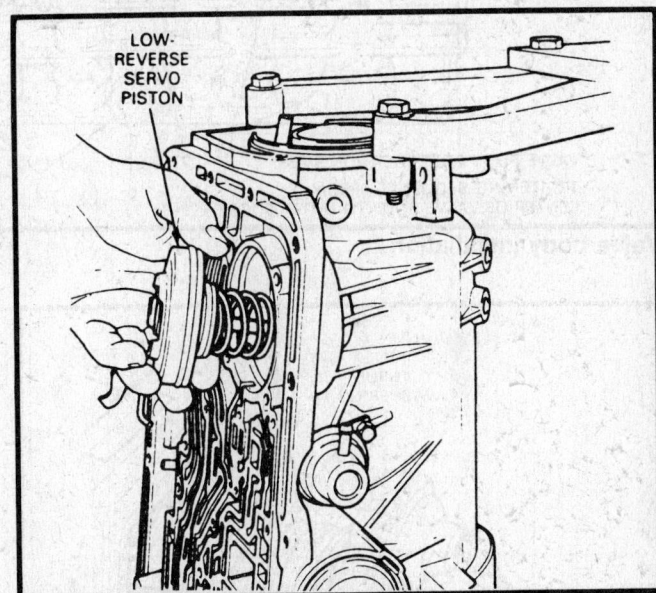

Low/Reverse servo assembly

13. Install the oil pan and fill with specified transmission fluid to the correct level.

LOW/REVERSE SERVO ASSEMBLY

Removal and Installation

1. Disconnect the negative battery cable.
2. Raise the vehicle and support it safely.
3. Remove the oil pan.
4. Remove the filter screen and gasket.
5. Remove the low/reverse servo cover, piston, spring and gasket.
6. Installation is the reverse of the removal procedure. Refill the transmission.

GOVERNOR

Removal and Installation

1. Disconnect the negative battery cable.

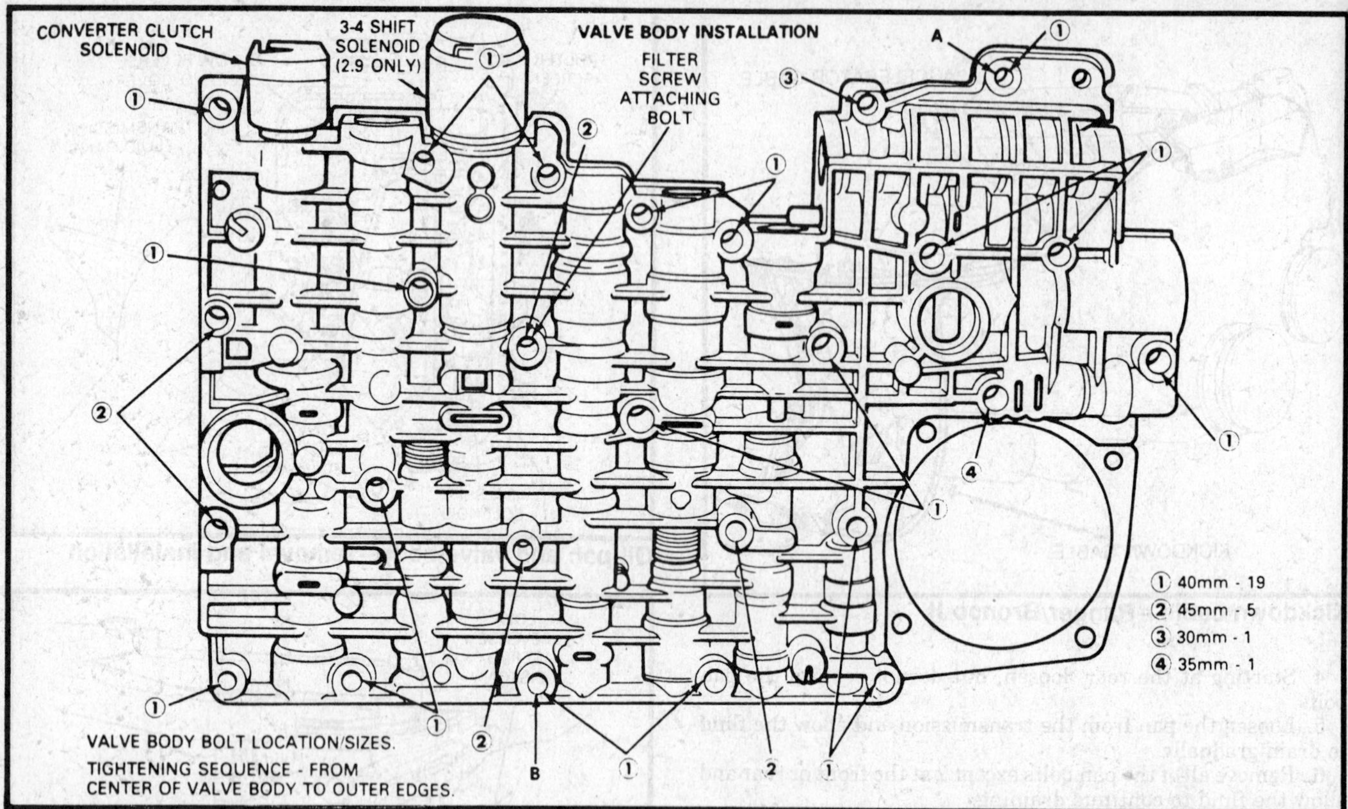

CONVERTER CLUTCH
SOLENOID

3-4 SHIFT
SOLENOID
(2.9 ONLY)

VALVE BODY INSTALLATION

FILTER
SCREW
ATTACHING
BOLT

A

① 40mm - 19
② 45mm - 5
③ 30mm - 1
④ 35mm - 1

VALVE BODY BOLT LOCATION/SIZES.
TIGHTENING SEQUENCE - FROM
CENTER OF VALVE BODY TO OUTER EDGES.

B

Valve body installation

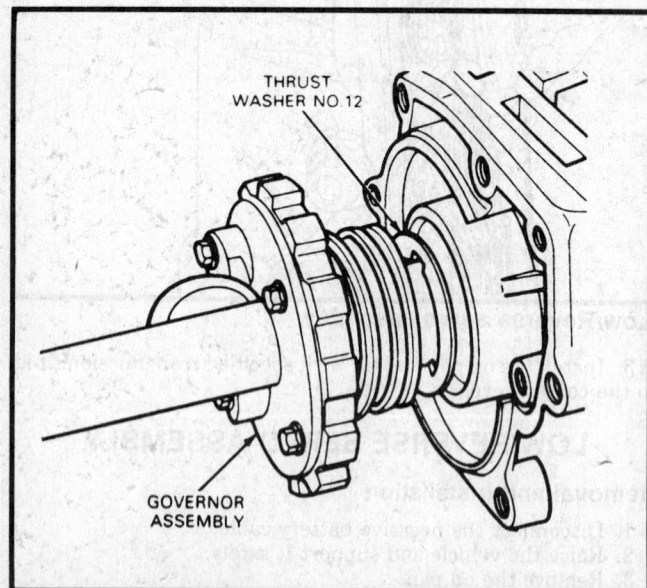

THRUST
WASHER NO.12

GOVERNOR
ASSEMBLY

Governor assembly

2. Raise the vehicle and support it safely.
3. Remove the extension housing.
4. Remove the governor body to oil collector body attaching bolts.

5. Remove the governor body, valve, spring and weight from the collector body.

NOTE: The components are not retained once the governor body to oil collector body attaching bolts have been removed. It is necessary to hold the governor body and components while removing or installing.

6. Assemble the governor body and components.
7. Position the governor body over the oil feed holes of the oil collector body.
8. Install the governor body to oil collector body attaching bolts and tighten to 84–120 inch lbs. (9.5–13.6 Nm).

REAR OIL SEAL

Removal and Installation

1. Raise the vehicle and support it safely.
2. Remove the driveshaft. Make scribe marks on the driveshaft end yoke and rear axle companion flange to assure proper positioning of the driveshaft during assembly.
3. Remove the extension housing seal using tool T71P-7657-A or equivalent.
4. Before installing a new seal, inspect the sealing surface of the universal joint yoke for scores. Inspect the counterbore of the housing for burrs. Remove any burrs using crocus cloth.
5. Install the new seal using tool T74P-77052-A or equivalent. Coat the inside diameter at the end of the rubber boot portion of the seal and the front universal joint spline with Multi-Purpose Long-Life Lubricant.

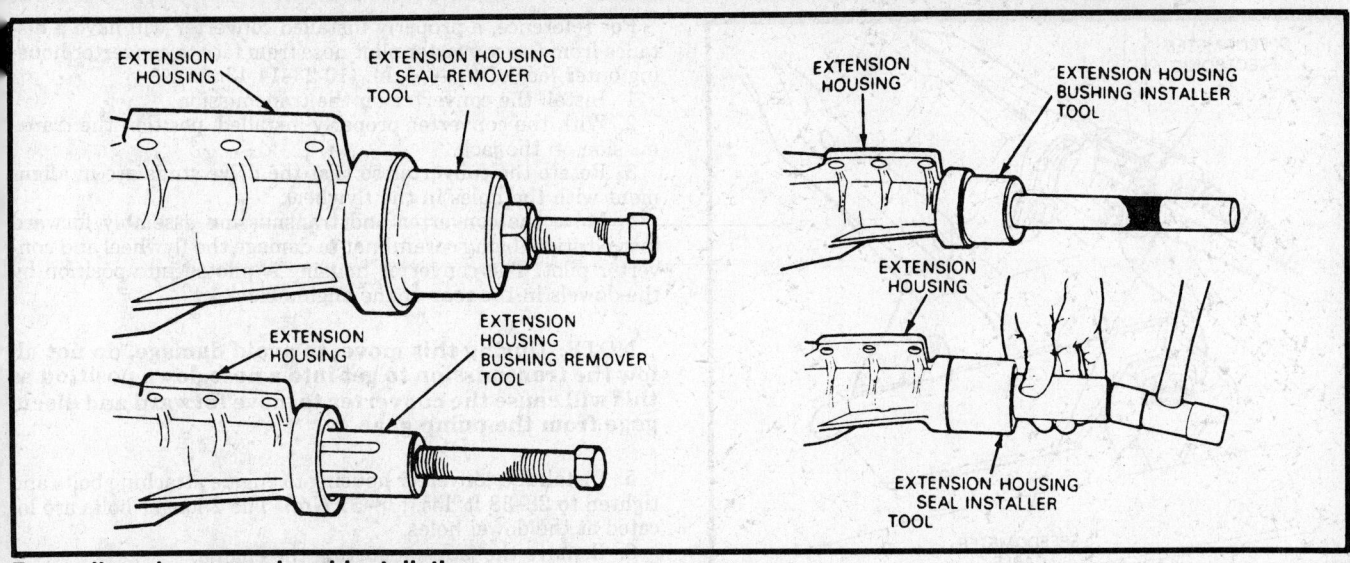

Rear oil seal – removal and installation

REMOVAL AND INSTALLATION

TRANSMISSION REMOVAL

1. Disconnect the negative battery cable.
2. Raise the vehicle and support it safely.
3. Position a drain pan under the transmission pan.
4. Starting at the rear, loosen, but do not remove the pan bolts.
5. Loosen the pan from the transmission and allow the fluid to drain gradually.
6. Remove all of the pan bolts except 2 at the front or rear and allow the fluid to continue draining.
7. Remove the converter access cover from the lower right side of the converter housing on the 3.0L engine. Remove the cover from the bottom of the engine oil pan on the 2.3L engine. Remove a bolt on the access cover of the 2.9L engine and swing the cover open. Remove the access cover and adapter plate bolts from the lower left side of the converter housing on all other applications.
8. Remove the flywheel to converter attaching nuts. Use a socket and breaker bar on the crankshaft pulley attaching bolt. Rotate the pulley clockwise as viewed from the front to gain access to each of the nuts.

NOTE: On belt driven overhead cam engines, never rotate the pulley in a counterclockwise direction as viewed from the front.

9. Scribe a mark indexing the driveshaft to the rear axle flange. Remove the driveshaft.
10. Remove the speedometer cable from the extension housing.
11. Disconnect the shift rod or cable at the transmission manual lever and retainer bracket.
12. Disconnect the downshift cable from the downshft lever. Depress the tab on the retainer and remove the kickdown cable from the bracket.
13. Disconnect the neutral start switch wires, converter clutch solenoid and the 3–4 shift soleniod connector.
14. Remove the starter mounting bolts and the ground cable. Remove the starter.

15. Remove the vacuum line from the transmission vacuum modulator.
16. Remove the filler tube from the transmission.
17. Position a transmission jack under the transmission and raise it slightly.
18. Remove the engine rear support to crossmember bolts.

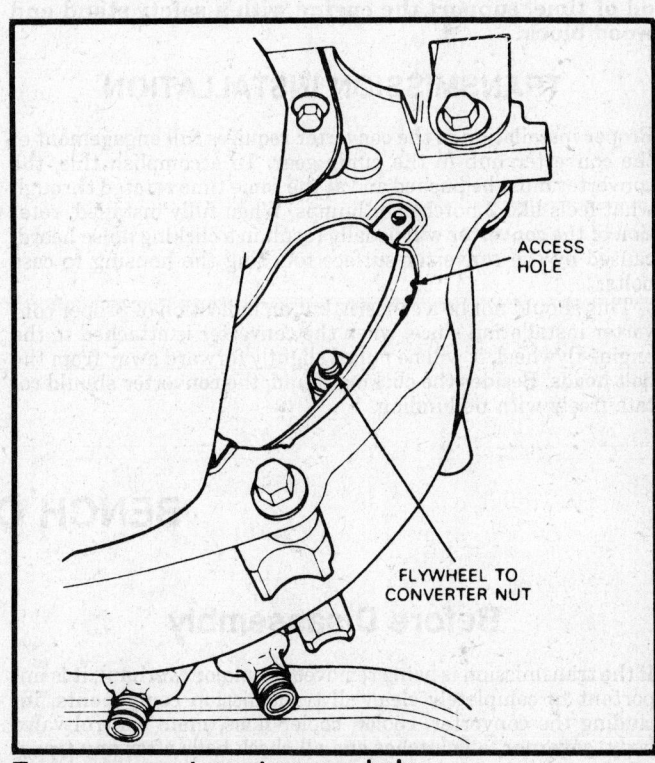

Torque converter nut access hole

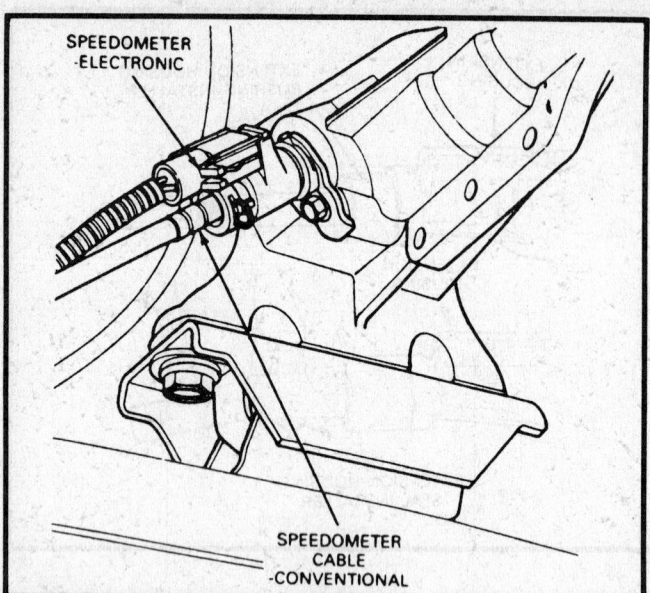

SPEEDOMETER
-ELECTRONIC

SPEEDOMETER
CABLE
-CONVENTIONAL

Speedometer cable connection

19. Remove the crossmember to frame side support attaching nuts and bolts. Remove the crossmember.
20. Remove the converter housing to engine bolts.
21. Slightly lower the jack to gain access to the oil cooler lines. Disconnect the oil cooler lines at the transmission. Plug all openings to keep dirt and contamination out.
22. Move the transmission to the rear so it disengages from the dowel pins and the converter is disengaged from the flywheel. Lower the transmission from the vehicle.
23. Remove the torque converter from the transmission.

NOTE: If the transmission is to be removed for a period of time, support the engine with a safety stand and wood block.

TRANSMISSION INSTALLATION

Proper installation of the converter requires full engagement of the converter hub in the pump gear. To accomplish this, the converter must be pushed and at the same time rotated through what feels like 2 notches or bumps. When fully installed, rotation of the converter will usually result in a clicking noise heard, caused by the converter surface touching the housing to case bolts.

This should not be a concern, but an indication of proper converter installation since, when the converter is attached to the engine flywheel, it will be pulled slightly forward away from the bolt heads. Besides the clicking sound, the converter should rotate freely with no binding.

For reference, a properly installed converter will have a distance from the converter pilot nose from face to converter housing outer face of $7/16$–$9/16$ in. (10.23–14.43mm).

1. Install the converter on the transmission.
2. With the converter properly installed, position the transmission on the jack.
3. Rotate the converter so that the drive studs are in alignment with the holes in the flywheel.
4. Move the converter and transmission assembly forward into position, being careful not to damage the flywheel and converter pilot. The converter housing is piloted into position by the dowels in the rear of the engine block.

NOTE: During this move, to avoid damage, do not allow the transmission to get into a nose down position as this will cause the converter to move forward and disengage from the pump gear.

5. Install the converter housing to engine attaching bolts and tighten to 28–38 ft. lbs. (38–51 Nm). The 2 longer bolts are located at the dowel holes.
6. Remove the jack supporting the engine.
7. Raise the transmission. Position the crossmember to the frame side supports. Install the attaching bolts and tighten to 20–30 ft. lbs. (27–41 Nm).
8. Lower the transmission and install the rear engine to crossmember nut and tighten to 60–80 ft. lbs. (82–108 Nm). Remove the transmission jack.
9. Install the filler tube in the transmission.
10. Install the oil cooler lines in the retaining clip at the cylinder block. Connect the lines to the transmission case.
11. Install the vacuum hose on the transmission vacuum unit. Install the vacuum line into the retaining clip.
12. Connect the neutral start switch plug to the neutral start switch. Connect the converter clutch solenoid wires and the 3–4 shift solenoid wires.
13. Install the starter and tighten the bolts to 15–20 ft. lbs. (20–27 Nm).
14. Install the flywheel to converter attaching nuts and tighten to 20–34 ft. lbs. (27–46 Nm).
15. Connect the muffler inlet pipe to the exhaust manifold.
16. Connect the transmission shift rod or cable to the manual lever.
17. Connect the downshift cable to the downshift lever.
18. Install the speedometer cable or sensor.
19. Install the driveshaft making sure to line up the scribe marks made during removal on the driveshaft and axle flange. Tighten the companion flange U-bolt attaching nuts to 70–95 ft. lbs. (95–130 Nm).
20. Adjust the manual and downshift linkages.
21. Lower the vehicle. Connect the negative battery cable.
22. Fill the transmission to the proper level with the specified fluid.
23. Check the transmission, converter and oil cooler lines for leaks.

BENCH OVERHAUL

Before Disassembly

If the transmission is being removed for major overhaul, it is important to completely clean all transmission components, including the converter, cooler, cooler lines, main control valve body, governor, all clutches and all check balls after any transmission servicing that generates contamination. These contaminants are a major cause for recurring transmission troubles and must be removed from the system before the transmission is put back into service.

Thorough cleaning of the transmission exterior will reduce the possibility that damaging contaminants might enter the sub-assemblies during disassembly and assembly.

When building up sub-assemblies, each component part should be lubricated with clean transmission fluid. Also lubri-

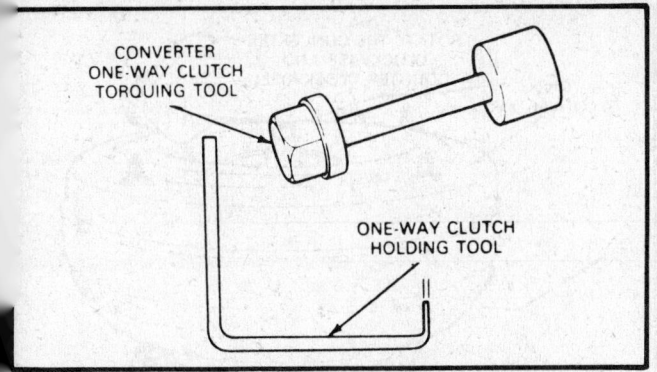

Endplay and one-way clutch checking tools

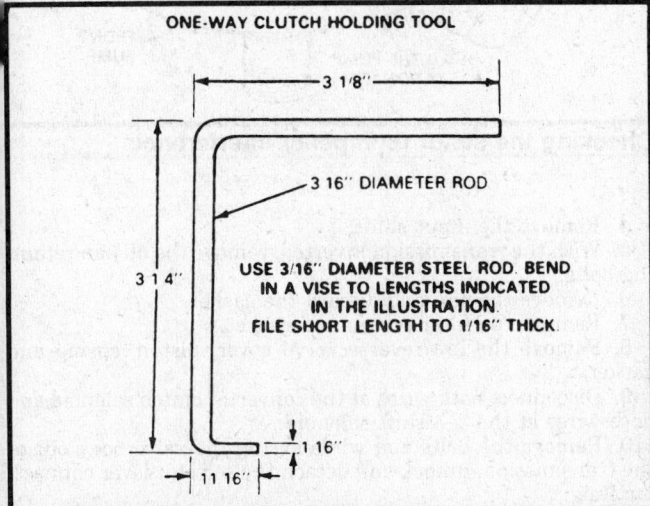

One-way clutch holding tool

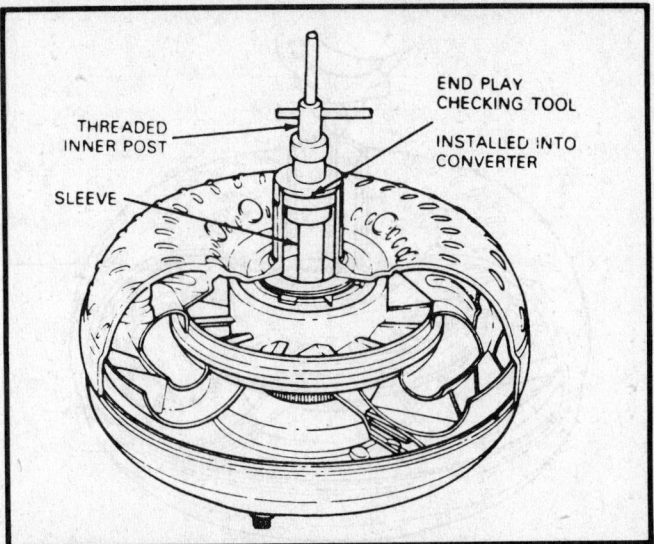

Endplay tool installed into the converter

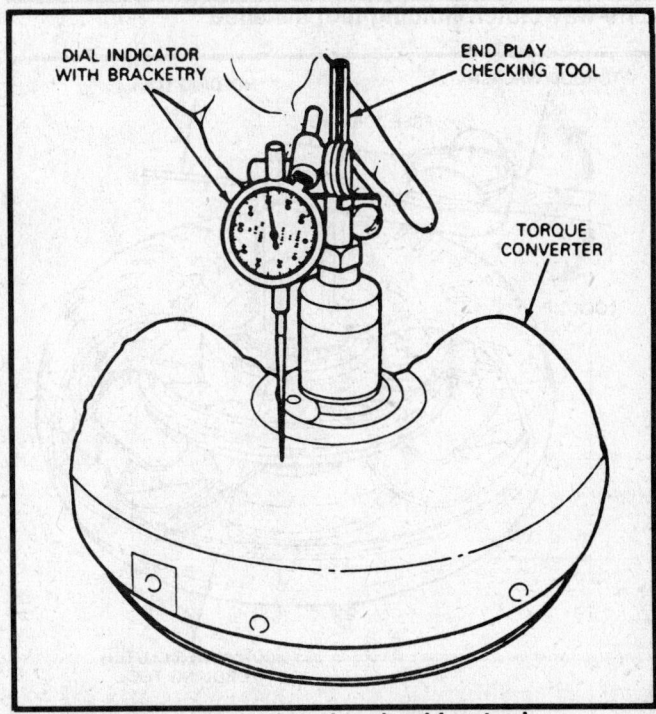

Dial indicator attached to the checking tool

cate the sub-assemblies as they are installed in the case. Needle bearings, thrust washers and seals should be lightly coated with petroleum jelly during transmission assembly.

Converter Inspection

Checking Converter Endplay

1. Insert endplay checking tool T80L-7902-A or equivalent into the converter impeller hub until it bottoms.
2. Expand the sleeve in the turbine spline by tightening the threaded inner post until the tool is securely locked in the spline.
3. Attach a dial indicator tool 4201-C or equivalent to the endplay checking tool. Position the indicator button on the converter impeller housing and set the dial face at 0.
4. Lift the tool upward as far as it will go and note the indicator reading. The indicator reading is the total endplay which the turbine and stator share. Replace the converter unit if the total endplay exceeds the limits.
5. Loosen the threaded inner post to free the tool and then remove the tool from the converter.

Checking Converter One-Way Clutch

1. Use one-way clutch holding tool D84L-7902-A or equivalent. Insert the tool in 1 of the grooves in the stator thrust washer.
2. Insert the converter one-way clutch torquing tool T77L-7902-B or equivalent in the converter impeller hub so as to engage the one-way clutch inner race.

3. Attach a torque wrench to the one-way clutch torquing tool. With the one-way clutch holding tool held stationary, turn the torque wrench counterclockwise. The clutch should lock up and hold a 10 ft. lbs. (14 Nm) torque. The clutch should rotate freely in a clockwise direction.
4. If the clutch fails to lock up and hold at 10 ft. lbs. (14 Nm) torque, replace the torque converter.

Checking Stator to Impeller Interference

1. Position the front pump assembly on a bench with the spline end of the stator support pointing up.
2. Mount a converter on the pump with the splines of the one-way clutch inner race engaging the mating splines of the stator support. The impeller hub will then engage the pump drive gear.
3. Hold the pump stationary and try to rotate the torque con-

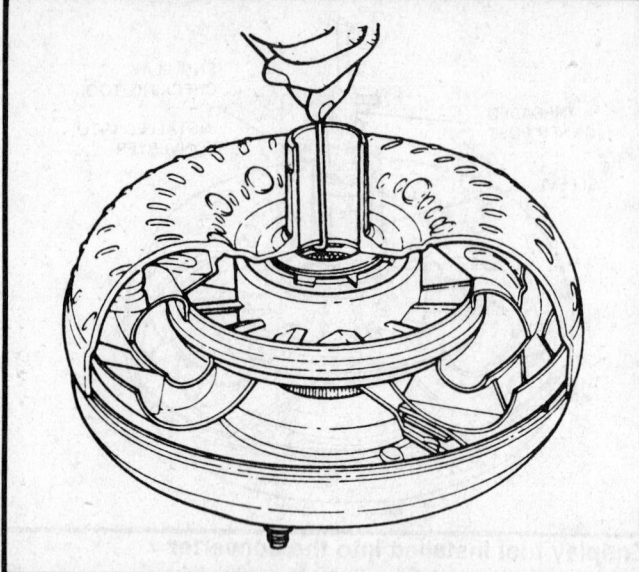

One-way clutch holding tool installed

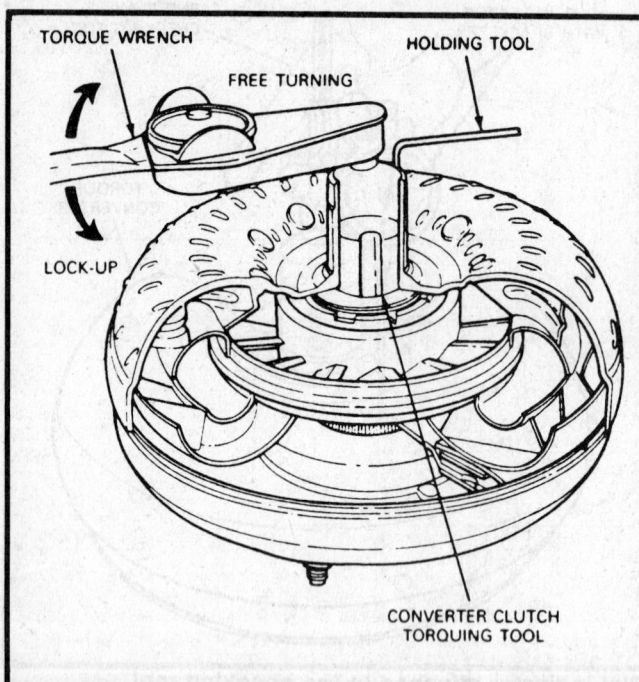

One-way clutch torquing tool

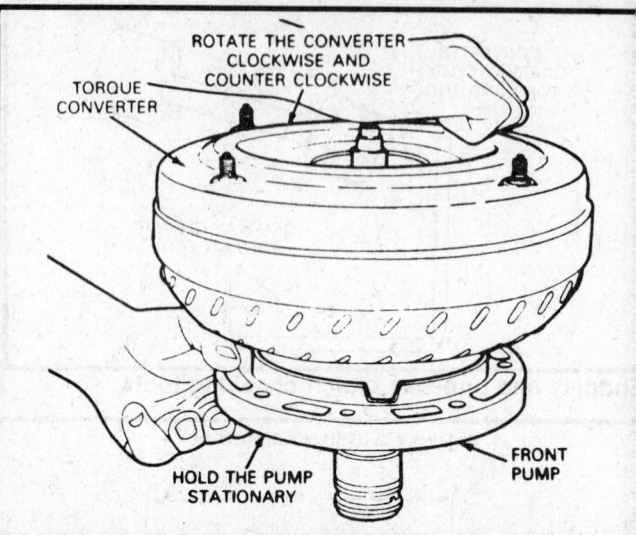

Checking the stator to impeller interference

verter both clockwise and counterclockwise. The converter should rotate freely without any signs of interference or scraping within the converter assembly.

4. If there is an indication of scraping, the trailing edges of the stator blades may be interfering with the leading edges of the impeller blades. In such cases, replace the converter.

Transmission Disassembly

1. If the converter is equipped with a drain plug, remove the plug and drain the fluid from the converter.
2. Pull the converter off of the mainshaft and if necessary, drain the fluid out of the hub opening.
3. Mount the transmission in a suitable holding fixture.

4. Remove the input shaft.
5. With the transmission inverted, remove the oil pan retaining bolts.
6. Remove the pan and discard the gasket.
7. Remove the filter screen and gasket.
8. Remove the low/reverse servo cover, piston, spring and gasket.
9. Disconnect both wires at the converter clutch solenoid and both wires at the 3–4 shift solenoid.
10. Remove the bolts and while easing the valve body out of the transmission, unlock and detach the selector lever connecting link.
11. Remove the valve body and the gasket.
12. Remove the retaining bolt that holds the center support.
13. Remove the extension housing.
14. Remove the parking pawl and the return spring.
15. Remove the governor body to oil collector body attaching bolts.
16. Remove the governor body, valve, spring and weight from the collector body.

NOTE: The components are not retained once the governor body to oil collector body attaching bolts have been removed. It is necessary to hold the governor body and components while removing or installing.

17. Remove the converter housing and the oil pump as an assembly. Rotate and lift so that the clutches stay in place.
18. Loosen the overdrive band locknut and back off the adjusting screw.
19. Remove the anchor and apply struts.
20. Lift out the overdrive clutch assembly and band.
21. Remove the hydraulic pump oil seal.
22. Remove the hydraulic pump from the converter housing and remove the steel plate with the O-ring.
23. Lift out the overdrive one-way clutch and planetary assembly.
24. Remove the center support retaining snapring.
25. Remove the overdrive apply lever and shaft.
26. Remove the overdrive control bracket from the valve body side of the case.

NOTE: The overdrive apply lever does not have a boss on the shaft hole as compared to the intermediate apply lever. The overdrive apply lever shaft is longer as compared to the intermediate apply lever shaft.

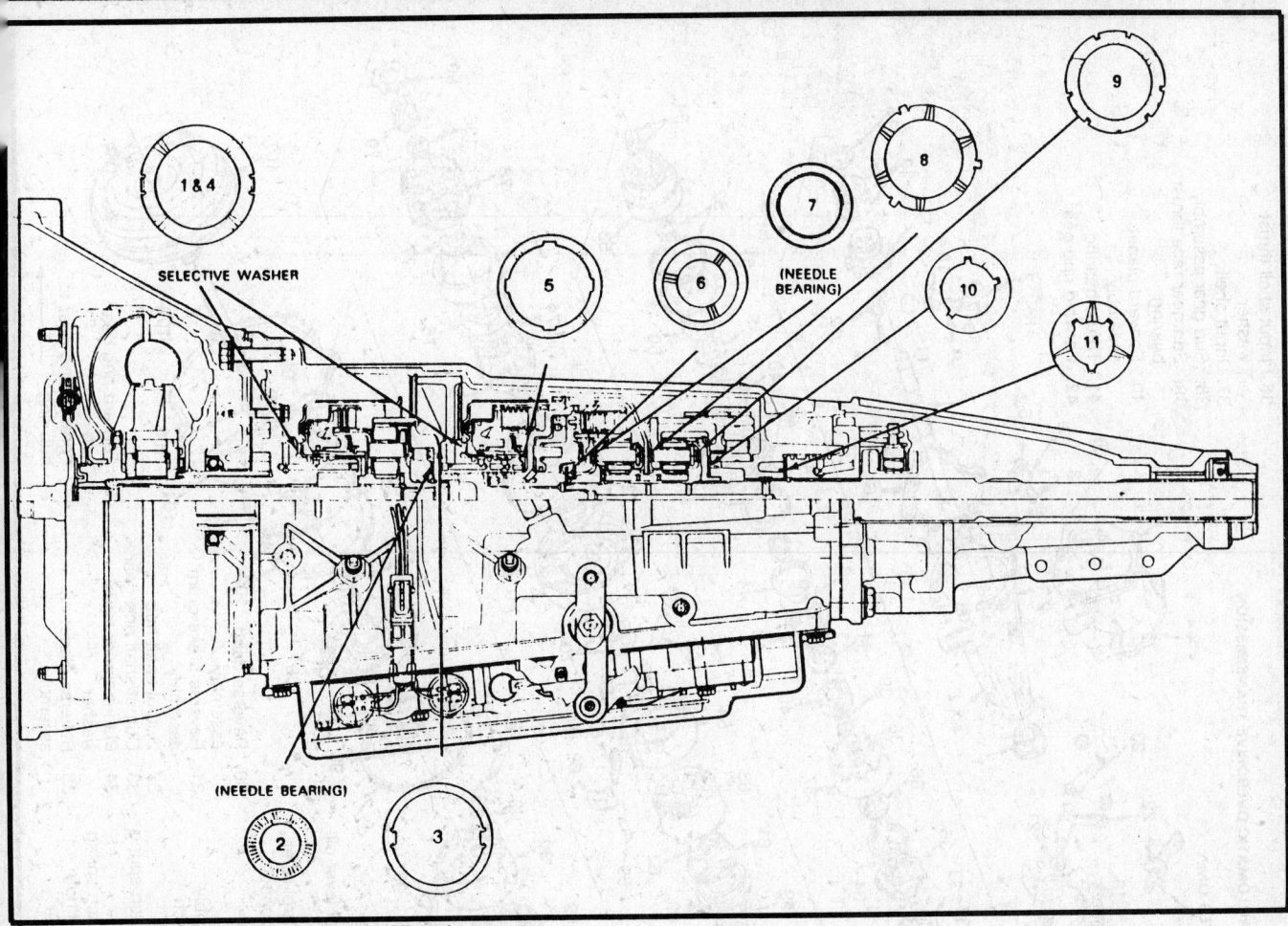

Thrust washer location and identification

27. Remove the thrust washer on top of the center support. Identify the thrust washer for reassembly.
28. Remove the center support being careful to pry upward evenly.
29. Remove the thrust washer below the center support. Identify the thrust washer for reassembly.
30. Loosen the intermediate band locknut and back off the adjusting screw.
31. Remove the anchor and apply struts.
32. Remove the reverse/high and forward clutch assembly.
33. Remove the intermediate band. Identify as intermediate and identify which end is the apply side or the anchor side for reinstallation.
34. Remove the forward planet assembly.
35. Remove the sun gear shell.
36. Remove the reverse planet assembly. Note and identify the thrust washers on both sides. They are identical.
37. Remove the snapring and the output shaft ring gear.
38. Remove the low/reverse drum and one-way clutch assembly.
39. Remove the low/reverse servo from the valve body side of the case. Remove the low/reverse band.
40. Remove the intermediate apply lever and shaft. This apply lever has a boss on the shaft hole and the shaft is shorter than the overdrive shaft.
41. Remove the output shaft.
42. Remove the park gear/collector body assembly from the rear of the case.
43. Remove the vacuum diaphragm and the throttle valve actuator rod.

44. Remove the throttle valve from the bore after verifying that it moves freely in the bore.
45. Remove the intermediate servo cover snapring. The transmission case is notched out to permit easy snapring removal.
46. Remove the intermediate servo cover, piston and spring and tag them for identification.
47. Remove the overdrive servo cover, piston and spring and tag the parts for identification.

— **CAUTION** —
Covers can pop off due to spring pressure behind the piston.

48. Remove the neutral start switch.
49. Remove the kickdown lever nut and O-ring seal.
50. Remove the linkage centering pin taking precautions not to damage the case flange.
51. Remove the manual lever, internal kickdown lever and park pawl rod and detent plate assembly.
52. Remove the lever shaft oil seal.
53. Remove the torque converter clutch solenoid connector. A tab on the outside of the case on the backside of the connector must be depressed while pulling with pliers.

Unit Disassembly and Assembly
VALVE BODY

Disassembly

1. Remove the screws that retain the separator plate and gasket to the valve body.

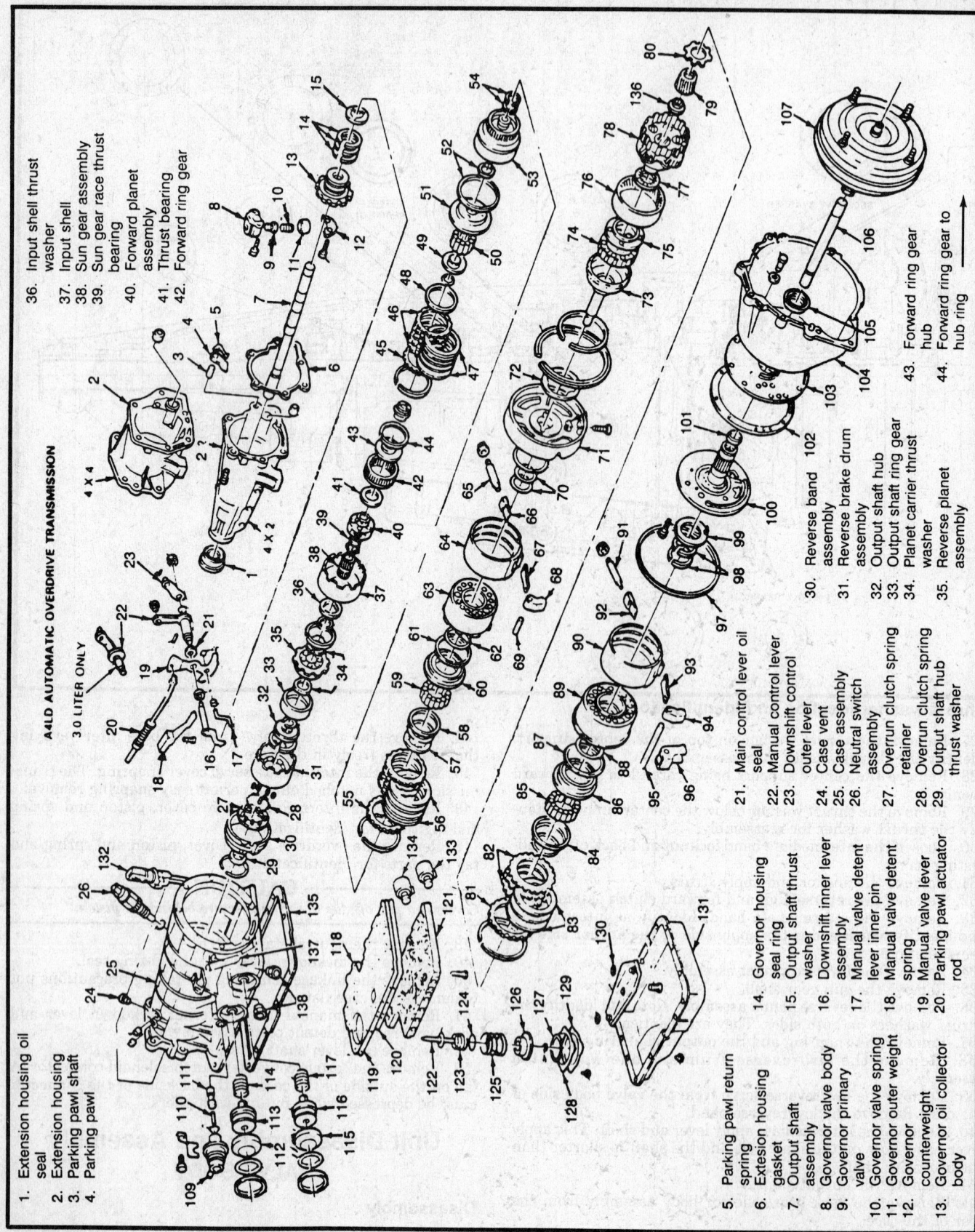

A4LD AUTOMATIC OVERDRIVE TRANSMISSION

3.0 LITER ONLY

4 X 4

4 X 2

1. Extension housing oil seal
2. Extension housing
3. Parking pawl shaft
4. Parking pawl
5. Parking pawl return spring
6. Extesion housing gasket
7. Output shaft assembly
8. Governor valve body
9. Governor primary valve
10. Governor valve spring
11. Governor outer weight
12. Governor counterweight
13. Governor oil collector body
14. Governor housing seal ring
15. Output shaft thrust washer
16. Downshift inner lever
17. Manual control inner lever
18. Manual valve detent lever inner pin
19. Manual valve lever
20. Parking pawl actuator rod
21. Main control lever oil seal
22. Manual control lever
23. Downshift control outer lever
24. Case vent
25. Case assembly
26. Neutral switch assembly
27. Overrun clutch spring
28. Overrun clutch spring retainer
29. Output shaft hub thrust washer
30. Reverse band assembly
31. Reverse brake drum assembly
32. Output shaft hub
33. Output shaft ring gear
34. Planet carrier thrust washer
35. Reverse planet assembly
36. Input shell thrust washer
37. Input shell
38. Sun gear assembly
39. Sun gear race thrust bearing
40. Forward planet assembly
41. Thrust bearing
42. Forward ring gear
43. Forward ring gear hub
44. Forward ring gear to hub ring

Exploded view of the transmission assembly

4–198

45. Forward clutch pressure plate
46. Forward clutch plate
47. Forward clutch plate
48. Forward clutch cushion spring
49. Forward clutch cushion spring retainer
50. Forward clutch piston spring
51. Forward clutch piston
52. Clutch piston oil seal
53. Forward clutch cylinder
54. Forward clutch cylinder seal
55. Clutch pressure reverse plate
56. Clutch high plate
57. Brake drum thrust washer
58. Reverse clutch piston spring retainer
59. Reverse clutch piston spring
60. Reverse clutch piston
61. Clutch piston oil seal
62. High clutch piston inner seal
63. Intermediate brake drum
64. Intermediate servo band
65. Reverse band adjusting screw
66. Intermediate brake band anchor strut
67. Intermediate brake band apply strut

68. Intermediate band servo lever
69. Intermediate band actuator lever shaft
70. High clutch seal ring
71. Center overdrive support
72. Center suport thrust washer
73. Center overdrive shaft
74. Overdrive overrun clutch
75. Overdrive clutch washer
76. Overdrive ring gear
77. Overdrive inner race bearing
78. Overdrive planet gear carrier
79. Overdrive sun gear
80. Overdrive clutch adapter
81. Overdrive clutch pressure plate
82. Overdrive clutch plate
83. Overdrive clutch spline plate
84. Spring retainer
85. Overdrive clutch piston spring
86. Overdrive clutch piston
87. Overdrive clutch piston outer seal
88. Overdrive clutch piston inner seal
89. Overdrive drum assembly
90. Overdrive band assembly

91. Overdrive band adjusting screw
92. Overdrive brake drum anchor strut
93. Overdrive brake drum apply strut
94. Overdrive band servo lever
95. Overdrive band adjusting lever shaft
96. Overdrive bracket
97. Front oil pump seal
98. Intermediate brake drum seal
99. Input thrust weasher
100. Front pump support and gear assembly
101. Front pump support seal
102. Oil pump gasket
103. Oil pump adapter plate
104. Converter housing
105. Front oil pump seal
106. Input shaft
107. Converter assembly
108. TV Control diaphragm clamp
109. TV Control diaphragm assembly
110. TV Control rod
111. Throttle control valve
112. Intermediate band servo cover and seal
113. Intermediate piston and rod assembly
114. Intermediate band servo piston spring
115. Overdrive band servo cover and seal

116. Overdrive piston and rod assembly
117. Overdrive band servo piston spring
118. Valve body separater gasket
119. Valve body separating plate
120. Valve body separating gasket
121. Main control assembly
122. Reverse band servo piston rod
123. Reverse servo spring
124. Reverse band servo piston oil seal
125. Reverse servo piston spring
126. Reverse servo piston and rod assembly
127. Reverse band servo retainer oil seal
128. Reverse servo separator plate cover gasket
129. Reverse band servo piston cover
130. Oil pan screen assembly
131. Oil pan
132. Converter clutch override connecter
133. Overdrive shift solenoid connector
134. 3-4 Shift solenoid connector
135. Oil pan gasket
136. Sun gear thrust bearing race
137. Lube oil inlet tube
138. Integral thrust washer

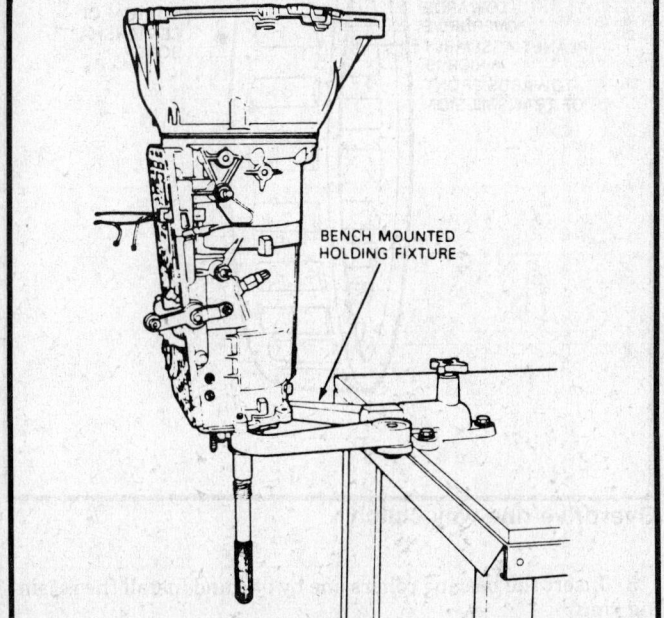

BENCH MOUNTED HOLDING FIXTURE

Bench mounted holding fixture

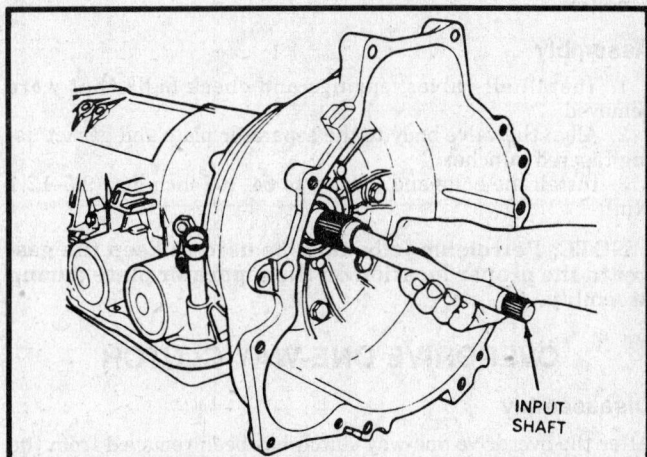

INPUT SHAFT

Removing the input shaft

2. With the separator plate and gasket removed, the following can be removed from the valve body:
    a. Converter pressure relief valve and spring
    b. T.V. pressure relief valve and spring
    c. Shuttle balls
    d. Accumulator check valve

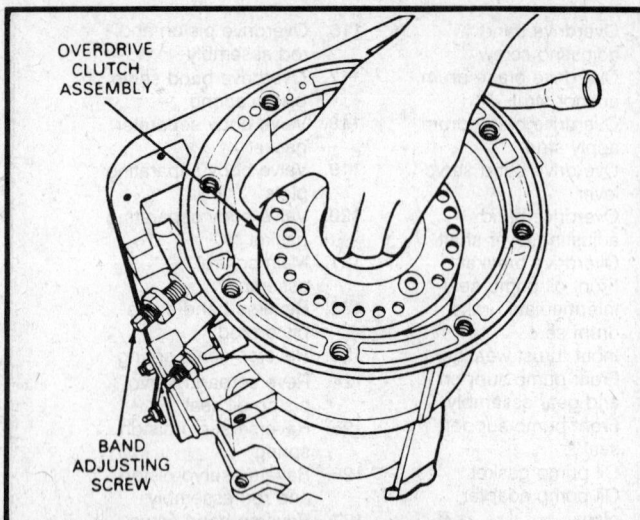

Removing the overdrive clutch and band

e. Filter that is retained by the separator plate at the converter clutch solenoid location

Inspection

1. Clean all parts thoroughly in clean solvent and blow dry with moisture free compressed air.
2. Inspect all valve and plug bores for scores.
3. Check all fluid passages for obstructions.
4. Inspect the check valve for free movement.
5. Inspect all mating surfaces for burrs or distortion.
6. Inspect all plugs and valves for burrs or scores.
7. Use crocus cloth to polish valves and plugs. Avoid rounding the sharp edges of the valves and plugs with the cloth.
8. Inspect all springs for distortion.
9. Check all valves and plugs for free movement in their respective bores. Valves and plugs, when dry, must fall from their own weight in their respective bores.
10. Roll the manual valve on a flat surface to check for bent condition.

Assembly

1. Install all valves, springs and check balls that were removed.
2. Align the valve body to the separator plate and gasket using tapered punches.
3. Install the bolts and tighten to 84–107 inch lbs. (9.5–12.1 Nm).

NOTE: Petroleum jelly must be used to keep the gasket in the proper location on the separator plate during assembly.

OVERDRIVE ONE-WAY CLUTCH

Disassembly

After the overdrive one-way clutch has been removed from the transmission case, it is very easily disassembled by removing the retaining ring.
1. Remove the retaining ring.
2. Lift out the cage with the springs and bearing rollers as a unit.

Assembly

1. Clean all parts and check for wear.
2. Install the cage with the springs.

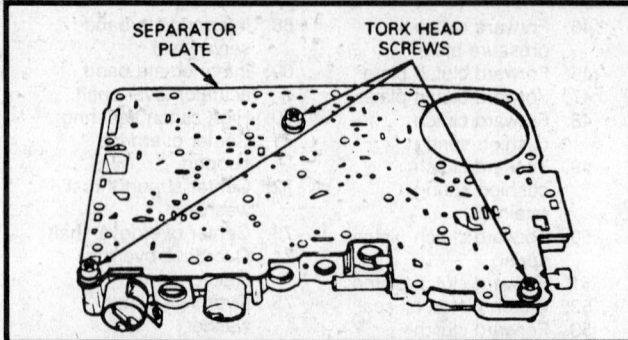

Separator plate and gasket attached to the valve body

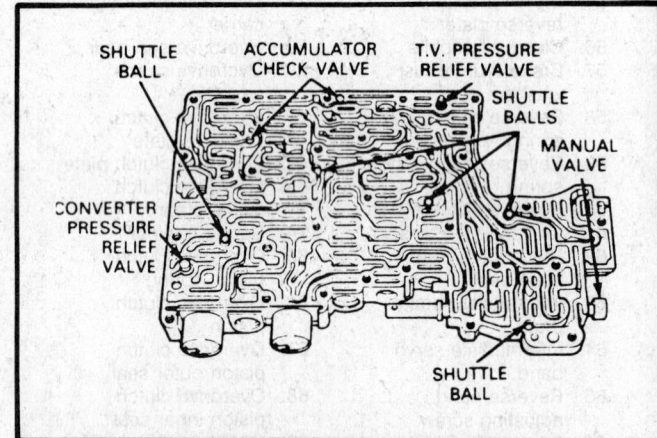

Separator plate and gasket removed

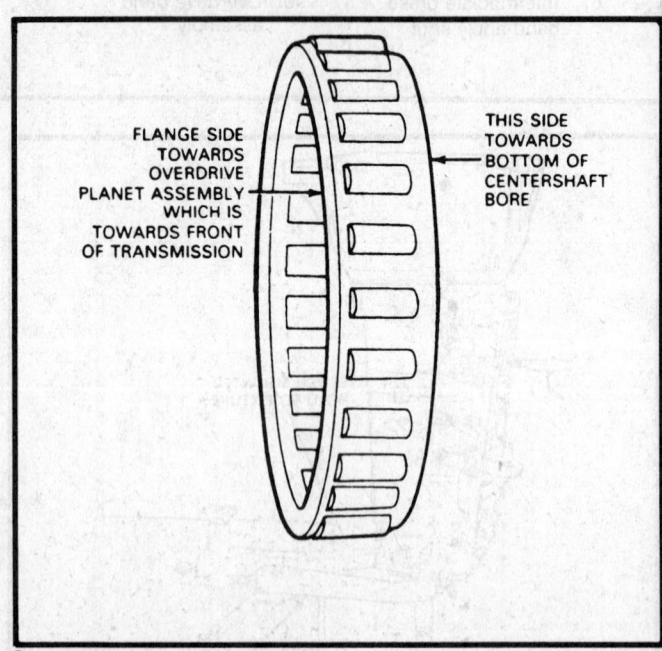

Overdrive one-way clutch

3. Insert the bearing rollers one by one and install the retaining ring.
4. Install the one-way clutch assembly into the center shaft so that the flanges of the inner and outer cages are toward the

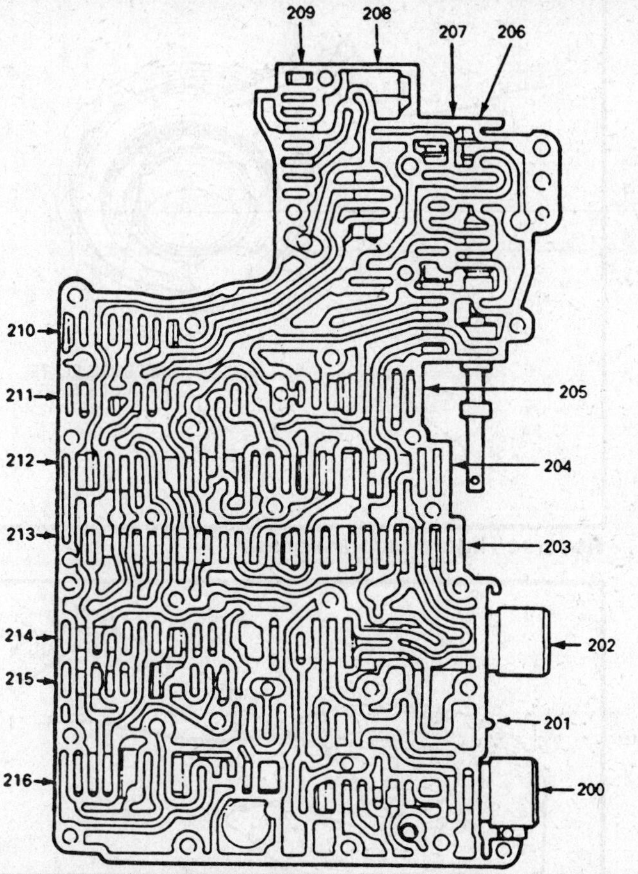

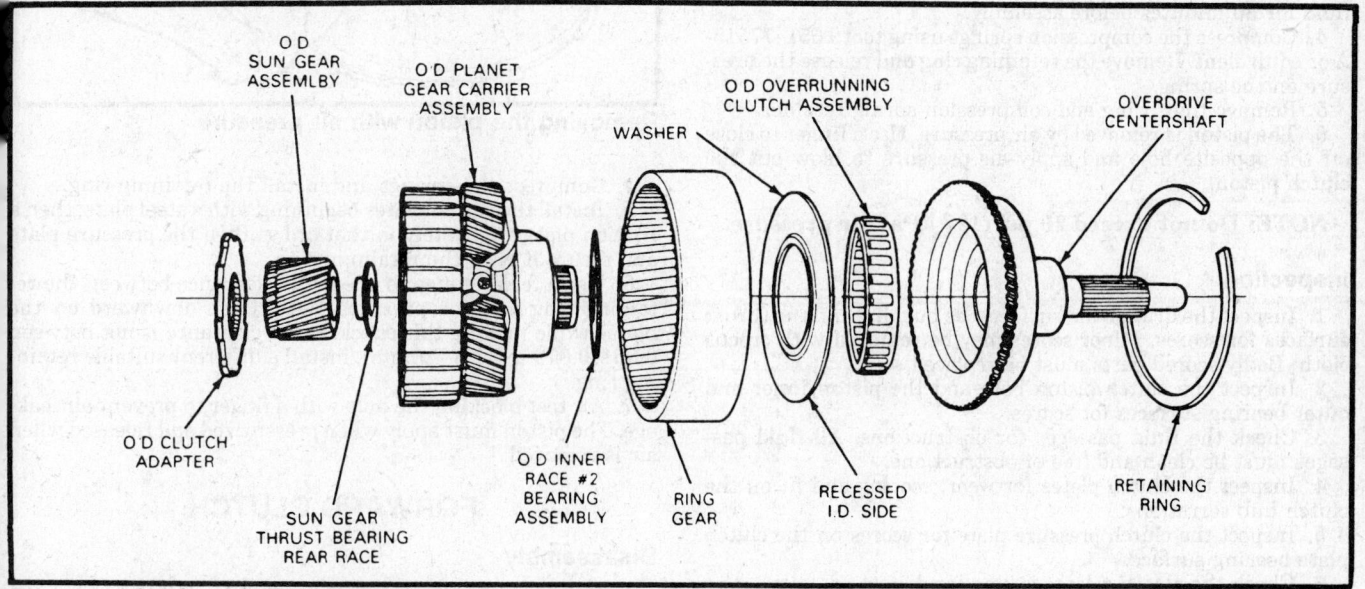

200. CONVERTER CLUTCH OVERRIDE SOLENOID, CONVERTER CLUTCH CONTROL VALVE
201. 3-4 SHIFT VALVE, 3-4 T.V. MODULATOR VALVE
202. 3-4 SHIFT SOLENOID, 3-4 SHIFT VALVE, OIL INLET SCREEN, CONVERTER CLUTCH SHIFT VALVE
203. 2-3 SHIFT VALVE, 2-3 T.V. MODULATOR VALVE
204. 1-2 SHIFT VALVE, D2 SHIFT VALVE
205. GOVERNOR COAST BOOST VALVE, LINE PRESURE COAST BOOST VALVE (2 AND LOW)
206. MANUAL VALVE
207. THROTTLE DOWNSHIFT VALVE (KICKDOWN)
208. MAIN OIL PRESSURE BOOSTER VALVE, MAIN OIL PRESSURE REGULATOR VALVE
209. CUTBACK VALVE
210. TORQUE DEMAND CONTROL VALVE
211. 1-2 TRANSITION VALVE, 2-3 BACKOUT VALVE, ENGAGEMENT CONTROL VALVE
212. T.V. PRESSURE BOOST VALVE
213. 3-2 COAST CONTROL VALVE
214. 3-2 KICKDOWN TIMING
215. CLUTCH RELEASE VALVE, 3-2 INTERMEDIATE SERVO RELEASE CONTROL VALVE
216. INTERMEDIATE SERVO ACCUMULATOR VALVE, OVERDRIVE SERVO ACCUMULATOR VALVE, 3-4 BACKOUT VALVE

Valve body valve identification

One-way clutch and planetary assembly

overdrive planet assembly which is toward the front of the transmission.

5. Position the overdrive clutch washer between the overdrive planet carrier and centershaft. It must be installed so that the recessed I.D. faces toward not against the sprag clutch.

6. After assembly, perform a build-up check. The center shaft should turn clockwise when holding the overdrive planet assembly.

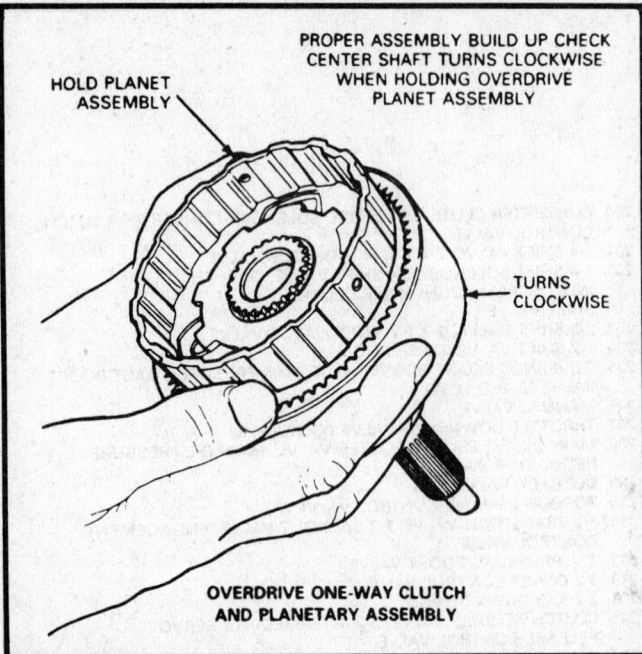

Build-up check

REVERSE/HIGH CLUTCH

Disassembly

1. Remove the pressure plate retainer ring and remove the plate neck.
2. Inspect the steel clutch plates and clutch lining plates for wear, damage or effects of overheating. Replace the entire set if necessary.
3. If new plates are to be used, immerse them in transmission fluid for 30 minutes before assembly.
4. Compress the compression springs using tool T65L-77515-A or equivalent. Remove the retaining ring and release the pressure on the spring.
5. Remove the spring and compression spring retainer.
6. The piston is removed by air pressure. Use a finger to close off the opposite hole and apply air pressure to blow out the clutch piston.

NOTE: Do not exceed 20 psi (137 kPa) air pressure.

Inspection

1. Inspect the drum band surface, the bushing and the thrust surfaces for scores. Minor scores may be removed with crocus cloth. Badly scored parts must be replaced.
2. Inspect the clutch piston bore and the piston inner and outer bearing surfaces for scores.
3. Check the fluid passages for obstructions. All fluid passages must be clean and free of obstructions.
4. Inspect the clutch plates for wear, scoring and fit on the clutch hub serrations.
5. Inspect the clutch pressure plate for scores on the clutch plate bearing surface.
6. Check the clutch release spring for distortion.
7. The clutch cylinders have check balls. Inspect the check balls for freedom of movement and proper seating.

Assembly

1. Install new seal rings on the clutch piston.
2. Install the clutch piston into the clutch body.
3. Install the compression spring tand the spring retainer.

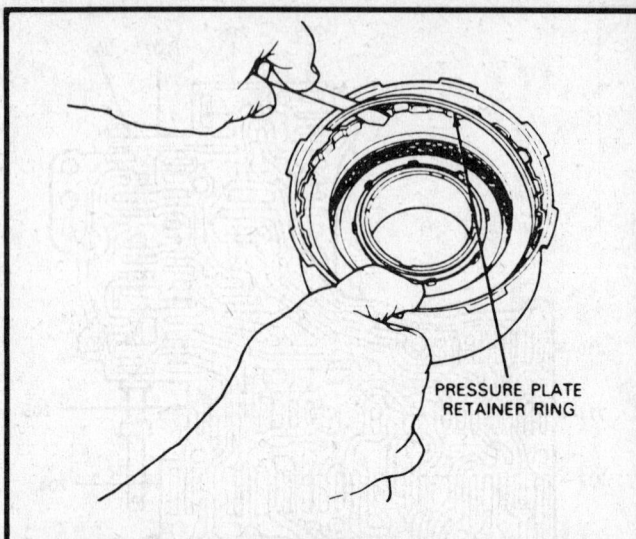

Reverse/High clutch assembly

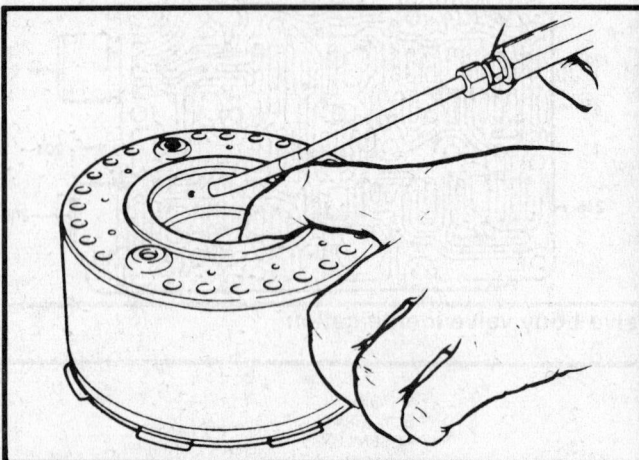

Removing the piston with air pressure

4. Compress the springs and install the retaining ring.
5. Install the clutch plates beginning with a steel plate, then a friction plate alternately in that order, then the pressure plate and secure it with the retaining ring.
6. Use a feeler gauge to check the clearance between the retaining ring and the pressure plate. Push downward on the plates while making this check. If the clearance is not between 0.051–0.079 in. (1.3–2.0mm), install a different suitable retaining ring.
7. Air test blocking the hole with a finger to prevent air leakage. The piston must apply when pressurized and released when air is removed.

FORWARD CLUTCH

Disassembly

1. Remove the pressure plate retainer ring and remove the plate neck.
2. Inspect the steel clutch plates and clutch lining plates for wear, damage or effects of overheating. Replace the entire set if necessary.
3. If new plates are to be used, immerse them in transmission fluid for 30 minutes before assembly.
4. Compress the compression springs using tool T65L-77515-

A or equivalent. Remove the retaining ring and release the pressure on the spring.

5. Remove the spring and compression spring retainer.

6. The piston is removed by air pressure. Use a finger to close off the opposite hole and apply air pressure to blow out the clutch piston.

NOTE: Do not exceed 20 psi (137 kPa) air pressure.

Inspection

1. Inspect the clutch cylinder thrust surfaces, piston bore, and clutch plate serrations for scores or burrs. Minor scores or burrs may be removed with crocus cloth. Replace the clutch cylinder if it is badly scored or damaged.

2. Check the fluid pressure in the clutch cylinder for obstructions. Clean out all fluid passages.

3. Inspect the clutch piston for scores and replace if necessary. Inspect the piston check ball for freedom of movement and proper seating.

4. Check the clutch release springs for distortion and cracks.

5. Inspect the composition clutch plates, steel clutch plates and clutch pressure plate for worn or scored bearing surface.

6. Check the clutch plates for flatness and fit on the clutch hub serrations.

7. Check the clutch hub thrust surfaces for scores and the clutch hub splines for wear.

8. Check the input shaft for damaged or worn splines.

9. Inspect the bushing in the stator support for scores.

Assembly

1. Install new seal rings on the clutch piston.

2. Install the clutch piston into the clutch body.

3. Install the compression spring and the spring retainer.

4. Compress the springs and install the retaining ring.

5. Install the clutch plates beginning with a steel plate, then a friction plate alternately in that order, then the pressure plate and secure it with the retaining ring.

6. Use a feeler gauge to check the clearance between the retaining ring and the pressure plate. Push downward on the plates while making this check. If the clearance is not between 0.055–0.083 in. (1.4–2.1mm), install a different suitable retaining ring.

7. Air test blocking the hole with a finger to prevent air leakage. The piston must apply when pressurized and released when air is removed.

OVERDRIVE CLUTCH

Disassembly

1. Remove the pressure plate retainer ring and remove the plate neck.

2. Inspect the steel clutch plates and clutch lining plates for wear, damage or effects of overheating. Replace the entire set if necessary.

3. If new plates are to be used, immerse them in transmission fluid for 30 minutes before assembly.

4. Compress the compression springs using tool T65L-77515-A or equivalent. Remove the retaining ring and release the pressure on the spring.

5. Remove the spring and compression spring retainer.

6. The piston is removed by air pressure. Use a finger to close off the opposite hole and apply air pressure to blow out the clutch piston.

NOTE: Do not exceed 20 psi (137 kPa) air pressure.

Inspection

1. Inspect the outer and inner races for scores or damaged surface areas where rollers contact the races.

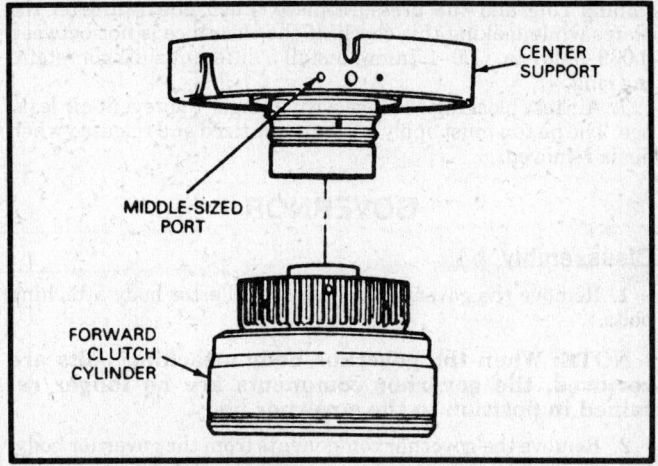

Forward clutch assembly

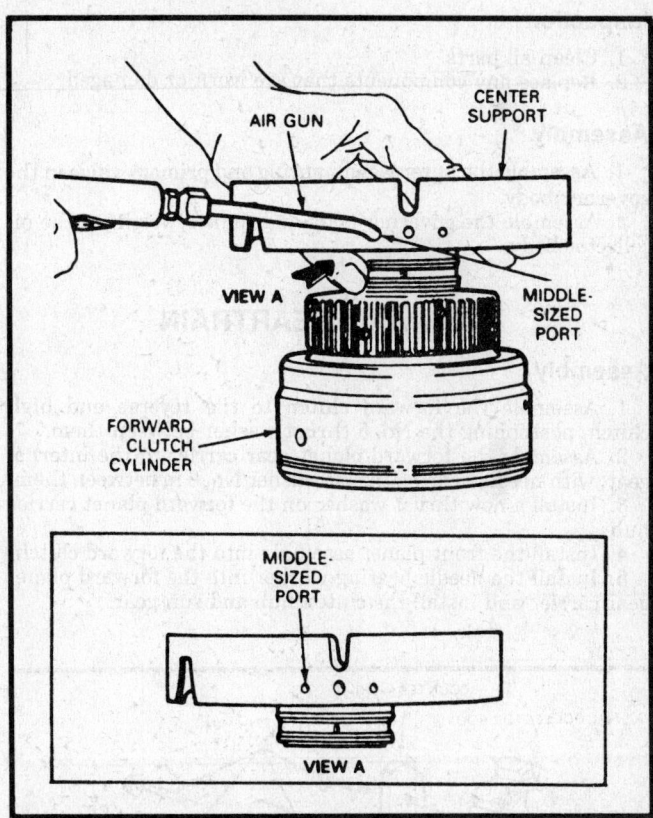

Applying the piston with air pressure

2. Inspect the rollers and springs for excessive wear or damage.

3. Inspect the spring and roller cage for bent or damaged spring retainers.

Assembly

1. Install new seal rings on the clutch piston.

2. Install the clutch piston into the clutch body.

3. Install the compression spring and the spring retainer.

4. Compress the springs and install the retaining ring.

5. Install the clutch plates beginning with a steel plate, then a friction plate alternately in that order, then the pressure plate and secure it with the retaining ring.

6. Use a feeler gauge to check the clearance between the re-

taining ring and the pressure plate. Push downward on the plates while making this check. If the clearance is not between 0.039–0.067 in. (1.0–1.7mm), install a different suitable retaining ring.

7. Air test blocking the hole with a finger to prevent air leakage. The piston must apply when pressurized and released when air is removed.

GOVERNOR

Disassembly

1. Remove the governor body to oil collector body attaching bolts.

NOTE: When the governor body attaching bolts are removed, the governor comonents are no longer retained in position to the governor body.

2. Remove the governor components from the governor body.
3. Remove the counterwieght.

Inspection

1. Clean all parts.
2. Replace any components that are worn or damaged.

Assembly

1. Assemble the outer weight spring and primary valve in the governor body.
2. Assemble the governor body and counterweight to the oil collector body.

FORWARD GEARTRAIN

Assembly

1. Assemble the forward clutch to the reverse and high clutch, positioning the No. 5 thrust washer between them.
2. Assemble the forward planet gear carrier to the internal gear, with needle bearing thrust washer No. 8 in between them.
3. Install a new thrust washer on the forward planet carrier hub.
4. Install the front planet assembly into the forward clutch.
5. Install the needle bearing washer into the forward planet gear carrier and install the clutch hub and sun gear.

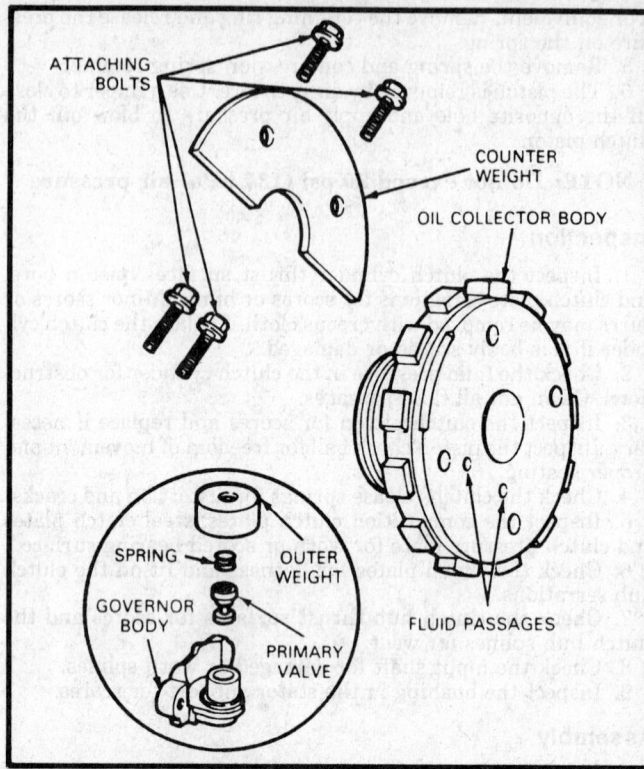

Governor components

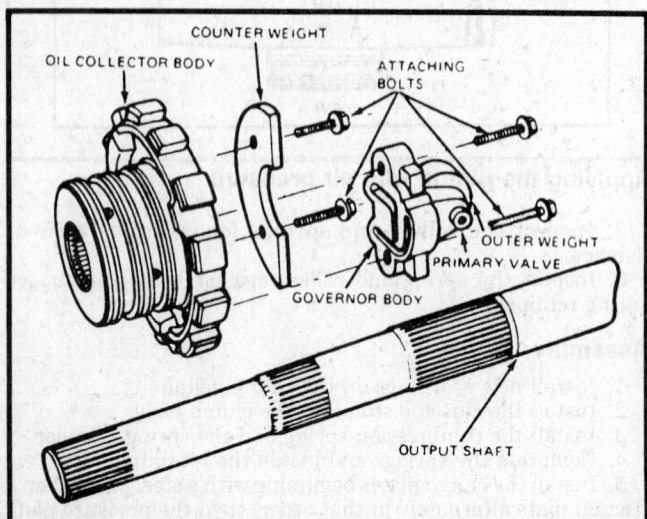

Governor assembly

Transmission Assembly

Before beginning assembly of the transmission, the following high clutch seal sizing must be performed:

1. Install the new high clutch seals on the support hub.
2. Apply a liberal amount of petroleum jelly to the center support hub and seals.
3. Use the overdrive brake drum as a sizing tool. Rotate the center support while inserting it into the brake drum.
4. Observe the seals as they enter the cavity to see that they do not roll over or get cut.
5. Seat the center support fully into the overdrive drum and allow to stand for several minutes so that the seals seat in the grooves.

NOTE: If this is not done, the seals can be cut or rolled over when entering the intermediate brake drum cavity.

After the seal sizing procedure is completed, set the assembly aside until it is required for reassembly.

1. Install thrust washer No. 12 into the back of the transmission case.
2. Install the collector body in the rear of the case.
3. Install the output shaft.
4. Install the governor on the collector body and tighten to 84–120 inch lbs. (9–14 Nm).
5. Install thrust washer No. 11 into the case from the front.
6. Install the low/reverse drum using the overrunning clutch replacement guide tool T74P-77193-A or equivalent.
7. Install the output shaft ring gear and snapring onto the output shaft.
8. Install thrust washer No. 10, reverse planet assembly and thrust washer No. 9.
9. Use petroleum jelly to hold the thrust washers in position on the planet assembly.
10. Install the snapring in the drum to hold the planet assembly in place.

REVERSE HIGH CLUTCH • THRUST WASHER NO. 5 • INTEGRAL THRUST WASHER-7A045 • NEEDLE BEARING NO. 8 • NEEDLE BEARING WASHER • CLUTCH HUB WITH SUN GEAR

FORWARD CLUTCH STAMPED STEEL • INTERNAL GEAR • FORWARD PLANET GEAR CARRIER

Forward geartrain assembly

11. Install the low/reverse band.
12. Replace the servo piston or O-ring, if necessary.
13. Install the low/reverse servo piston to hold the band in position.
14. Replace the piston or O-ring, if necessary.
15. Install the intermediate servo spring, piston, cover and snapring.
16. Replace the piston or O-ring, if necessary.
17. Install the overdrive servo spring, piston, cover and snapring.
18. Locate and identify the intermediate servo apply lever and shaft. The intermediate servo apply lever is the lever that has the boss on the shaft hole and the shaft is shorter than the overdrive shaft.
19. Install the intermediate apply lever and shaft into the case.
20. Install the complete forward clutch and reverse and high clutch assemblies.
21. Install the intermediate band and apply strut.
22. Install the intermediate band anchor strut and proceed to the transmission rear endplay check.

The transmission rear endplay check determines the amount of space existing between the thrust washer surfaces of the overdrive center support and the intermediate brake drum. It also determines the thickness of the No. 4 thrust washer that is required to obtain an endplay of 0.012–0.022 in. (0.30–0.54mm).

To perform the endplay check, fabricate a depth gauge fixture from an overdrive center support. An ⅛ in. hole must be drilled through the thrust washer surface of the center support. This allows depth micrometer D80P-4201-A or equivalent access to the area between the thrust surfaces of the support and the intermediate brake drum. Remove the rubber seals from the center support to allow easy insertion into the intermediate brake drum.

23. Place the depth micrometer over the drilled hole in the fabricated depth gauge fixture. Extend the micrometer probe until it is flush with the thrust washer surface of the fixture. Record the micrometer reading. This is reading **A**.
24. Install the depth gauge and input shaft fixture into the intermediate brake drum and make sure it is fully seated in the transmission case. Allow the center support fixture to slide into the intermediate brake drum using its own weight. The fixture axially locates the drum in its proper position.
25. Position the depth micrometer over the drilled hole in the fixture.
26. Continue extending the micrometer probe until it contacts the thrust washer surface of the intermediate brake drum. This is reading **B**.
27. Subtract reading **A** from reading **B**. The difference between these readings is dimension **A**. This is the space between the thrust surfaces.
28. Remove and rotate the fixture 180° and repeat Steps 23 through 27.

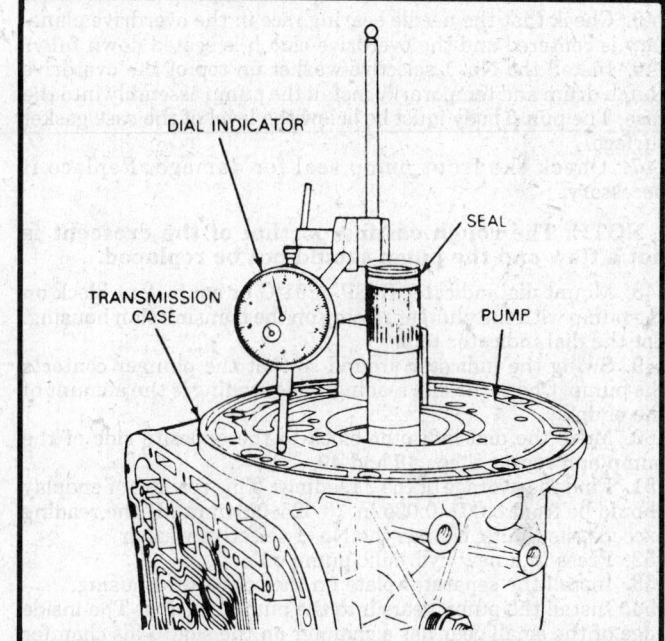

DIAL INDICATOR • SEAL • TRANSMISSION CASE • PUMP

Checking endplay

29. Average the 2 dimension A readings to obtain a final dimension A reading.
30. Select the proper thrust washer required to obtain the specified endplay of 0.012–0.022 in. (0.30–0.54mm). If dimension **A** is outside the specified limits, this indicates improper assembly, missing parts or parts out of specification.
31. Remove the depth gauge and overdrive fixture from the overdrive drum.
32. Position the correct No. 4 selective washer on the rear of the center support using petroleum jelly.
33. Insert the input shaft through the center support and into the splines in the forward clutch cylinder.
34. Install the center support into the case checking to make sure that it is square with the case and the 5mm allen bolt retainer nut is oriented with the bolt hole in the case.
35. Do not apply any pressure to the center support. Allow the center support to slide into the intermediate brake drum using its own weight. When the support is fully seated, remove the input shaft.
36. Position the No. 3 thrust washer on top of the center support.
37. Install the large snapring to retain the center support in

position with the taper of the snapring towards the front of the transmission.

NOTE: The 2 ends of the snapring should be positioned in the wide shallow cavity located in the 5 o'clock position.

38. Install the 5mm allen head bolt that retains the center support to the case.

39. Install the sun gear and overdrive clutch adapter into the overdrive planet assembly and one-way clutch.

40. Center the needle bearing race inside of the planetary. Be sure it stays centered and positioned with the extruded lip toward the sun gear.

41. Install the overdrive planet assembly and one-way clutch into the case.

42. Install the overdrive drum assembly.

43. Install the overdrive bracket, apply lever and shaft.

44. Install the overdrive band and apply strut. Install the anchor strut.

45. Check that the needle bearing race in the overdrive planetary is centered and the overdrive clutch is seated down fully.

46. Install the No. 1 selective washer on top of the overdrive clutch drum and temporarily install the pump assembly into the case. The pump body must be below the level of the case gasket surface.

47. Check the front pump seal for damage. Replace if necessary.

NOTE: The rough casting portion of the crescent is not a flaw and the pump should not be replaced.

48. Mount dial indicator D78P-4201-G or equivalent block on the pump with the plunger resting on the transmission housing. Set the dial indicator to 0.

49. Swing the indicator around so that the plunger contacts the pump. Check the dial reading. This reading is the amount of the endplay.

50. Move the dial indicator block to the opposite side of the pump and repeat Steps 48 and 49.

51. Find the average of the 2 readings. This reading of endplay should be from 0.001–0.025 in. (0.025–0.64mm). If the reading exceeds the limits, change the No. 1 selective washer.

52. Press in a new hydraulic pump oil seal.

53. Install the separator plate on the converter housing.

54. Install the pump gears into the pump housing. The inside edge of the small gear has a chamfer on the side. This chamfer must be positioned toward the front of the transmission. The larger gear has a dimple on the side which must be positioned toward the front of the transmission.

55. Install the pump assembly into the separator plate and converter housing and install the bolts finger tight.

56. Align the pump in the converter housing using tool T74P-77103-X or equivalent. This tool must be used in order to prevent seal leakage, pump breakage or bushing failure.

57. Before removing the alignment tool, tighten the bolts to 7–10 ft. lbs. (10–13 Nm).

58. Install the input shaft into the pump and install the converter into the pump gears. Rotate the converter to check for free movement, then remove the converter and the input shaft.

59. Coat the converter housing gasket with petroleum jelly and position it on the housing. Install the seal on the converter housing.

60. Install the No. 1 selective washer on the rear of the pump using petroleum jelly.

61. Align the converter housing and the pump to the transmission. Install the bolts with new aluminum washers and tighten to 27–38 ft. lbs. (37–52 Nm).

62. Adjust the overdrive band using tool T71P-77370-A or equivalent.

63. Install a new locknut on the adjusting screw and tighten to 10 ft. lbs. (14 Nm). Back off the adjusting screw 2 turns. Hold the adjusting screw from turning and tighten the locknut to 35–45 ft. lbs. (48–61 Nm).

64. Adjust the intermediate band using the same procedure. Back off the adjusting screw 2½ turns before tightening the locknut.

65. Install the shift lever oil seal using tool T74P-77498-A or equivalent.

66. Install the internal shift linkage including the external manual control lever and centering pin. Tighten to 30–40 ft. lbs. (41–54 Nm).

67. Install the O-ring, kickdown lever and 13mm nut. Tighten to 7–10 ft. lbs. (10–14 Nm).

68. Install the neutral start switch and tighten to 84–120 inch lbs. (9.5–13.6 Nm).

69. Install the converter clutch solenoid connector.

70. Install the throttle valve, vacuum diaphragm, retaining clamp and bolt.

71. Align the valve body to separator plate and gasket using tapered punches. Install the bolts and tighten to 84–107 inch lbs. (9.5–12.1 Nm).

72. Attach and lock the selector lever connecting rod to the manual valve and ease the control body into the case.

73. Tighten all bolts except the filter screen bolt in the correct sequence to 71–97 inch lbs. (8.0–11.0 Nm).

74. Install the low-reverse servo cover, piston, spring and gasket.

75. Install the converter clutch solenoid wires.

76. Install a new servo cover gasket and tool T74P-77190-A or equivalent and tighten with the attaching bolts. Tighten the servo tool attaching screw to 35 inch lbs. (4 Nm).

77. Install a dial indicator on the transmission case and position the indicator on the piston pad. Set the dial indicator to 0.

78. Back out the servo tool adjusting screw until the piston bottoms out on the tool. Record the distance the servo piston travelled. If the piston travel is between 0.120–0.220 in. (3–5.6mm), it is within specification. If the piston travel is greater than 0.220 in. (5.6mm), use the next longer piston and rod.

79. Remove the servo adjusting tool and reverse servo piston checking spring.

80. Install the servo piston assembly, accumulator spring, gasket and cover. Tighten the bolts to 7–10 ft. lbs. (10–13 Nm).

81. Install new O-rings on the screen and lubricate with petroleum jelly. Install the filter screen and tighten the bolt to 71–97 inch lbs. (8–11 Nm).

82. Install the oil pan and gasket to the case. Tighten the bolts to 5–10 ft. lbs. (7–14 Nm).

83. Install the parking pawl and its return spring in the extension housing and preload.

84. Using a new gasket, install the extension housing. correctly seat the operating parking rod in the extension guide cup. Tighten the bolts and studs to 27–38 ft. lbs. (37–52 Nm).

85. Replace the extension housing seal and bushing.

SPECIFICATIONS

TORQUE SPECIFICATIONS

Description	ft. lbs.	Nm
Transmission to engine	28–38	38–51.5
Converter housing lower cover to converter housing	12–16	16.3–21.7
Converter housing and pump to case	27–39	36.6–52.9
Oil pump to converter housing	9.6–11	13–15
Center support (OD) to case	80–115①	9.0–13.0
Extension housing to case	27–39	36.6–52.9
Oil pan to case	8–10	11–13.5
Main control to case	71–97①	8–11
Separator plate to valve body	54–72①	6.1–8.1
Detent spring to valve body	80–107①	9–12.1
Neutral start switch to case	84–120①	9.5–13.6
Reverse servo to case	80–115①	9–13
Vacuum diaphragm retainer clip to case	80–106①	9–12
Governor assembly to oil collector body	84–120①	9.5–13.6
Outer downshift lever to inner lever shaft nut	7–11	9.5–15
Manual lever nut	30–40	40.7–54.2
Overdrive band adjusting screw locknut to case	35–45	47.5–61
Intermediate band adjusting screw locknut to case	35–45	47.5–61
Converter to flywheel attaching nut	20–34	27.1–46.1
Cooler line to case connector	18–23	24.4–31.2
Push connect cooler to line fitting case	18–23	24.4–31.2
Pressure plug to case	7–11	9.5–14.9

① inch lbs.

TORQUE CONVERTER ENDPLAY

New or rebuilt converter	Used converter
0.023 in. (Max.)	0.050 in.
0.58mm (Max.)	1.27mm (Max.)

SELECTIVE SNAPRINGS

Part Number	Thickness		Diameter	
	in.	mm	in.	mm
OVERDRIVE AND REVERSE/HIGH CLUTCH				
E 860126–S	0.0539	1.37	5.122	130.1
E 860127–S	0.0681	1.73	5.122	130.1
E 860128–S	0.0819	2.08	5.122	130.1
E 860129–S	0.0961	2.44	5.122	130.1
FORWARD CLUTCH				
E 860115–S	0.0539	1.37	4.925	125.1
E 860116–S	0.0681	1.73	4.925	125.1
E 860117–S	0.0819	2.08	4.925	125.1
E 860118–S	0.0961	2.44	4.925	125.1

CLUTCH PLATES

Engine (liter)	Steel	Friction	Clearance in.
FORWARD CLUTCH			
2.3 EFI	5	5	0.055–0.083
2.3 turbo	5	5	0.055–0.083
3.0 EFI	5	5	0.055–0.083
OVERDRIVE CLUTCH			
2.3 EFI	3	3	0.039–0.067
2.3 EFI turbo	3	3	0.039–0.067
3.0 EFI	3	3	0.039–0.067
REVERSE/HIGH CLUTCH			
2.3 EFI	4	4	0.051–0.079
2.3 turbo	5	5	0.051–0.079
3.0 EFI	5	5	0.051–0.079

CHECKS AND ADJUSTMENTS

Operation	Specification
Transmission endplay (front)	0.001–0.025 in. 0.025–0.685mm Less gasket
Transmission endplay (rear)	0.012–0.022 in. 0.30–0.54mm
Overdrive and intermediate band	Remove and discard locknut. Install new lockout. Tighten adjusting screw 10 turns. Back off 2 turns for overdrive or 2½ turns for intermediate band. Hold screw and tighten locknut

SELECTIVE THRUST WASHERS

Location	Transmission Endplay	Part Number	Thickness in.	(mm)	Number Stamped on Washer
No. 1 thrust washer front pump support	Front 0.001–0.0025 in. 0.0025–0.625mm without gasket	84DT–7D014–AA	0.053–0.055	1.35–1.40	1
		84DT–7D014–BA	0.060–0.062	1.55-1.60	2
		84DT–7D014–CA	0.068–0.070	1.75–1.80	3
		84DT–7D014–DA	0.076–0.078	1.95–2.00	4
		84DT–7D014–EA	0.084–0.086	2.15–2.20	5
		84DT–7D014–FA	0.092–0.094	2.35–2.40	6
No. 4 thrust washer OD center support	Rear 0.012–0.022 in. 0.30–0.54mm	84DT–7D014–FA	0.092–0.094	2.35–2.40	6

SPECIAL TOOLS

Tool Number	Description
T50T–100–A	Impact slide hammer
T57L–500–B	Bench mounted holding fixture
TOOL–4201–C	Dial indicator with bracket
D78P–4201–G	Dial indicator
TOOL–7000–DD	Rubber tip for air nozzle
TOOL–7000–DE	Air nozzle assembly
T67P–7341–A	Shift linkage tool
T84P–7341–A	Shift linkage tool
T84P–7341–B	Shift linkage tool
T71P–7657–A	Extension housing seal remover
T77L–7697–E	Extension housing bushing remover
T77L–7697–F	Extension housing bushing replacer
T80L–7902–A	Torque converter endplay checking tool
T74P–77000–A	C–3 service set
T74P–77001–A	Transmission mounting adapter
T74P–77028–A	Front servo cover compressor
D80P–4201–A	Depth micrometer
T74P–77052–A	Extension housing seal replacer
T74P–77103–X	Front pump alignment set
T74P–77190–A	Servo rod selecting guide

Tool Number	Description
T74P–77193–A	Overrunning clutch replacing guide
T74P–77247–A	Neutral start switch socket
T74P–77248–A	Seal remover
T74P–77248–B	Front pump seal replacer
T71P–77370–A	Band adjustment torque wrench set
T74P–77404–A	Lip seal protector
T74P–77498–A	Seal replacer
T65L–77515–A	Clutch spring compressor
T74P–77548–B	Lip seal protector
T57L–77820–A	Pressure gauge 0–700 psi
T77L–7902–B	Converter one-way clutch torquing tool
D84L–7902–A	One-way clutch holding tool
T82L–9500–AH	Cooler line disconnect tool
T87L–77248–AH	Front pump seal replacer
T87L–77248–BH	Seal staking tool
ROTUNDA EQUIPMENT	
014–00737	Automatic transmission tester
014–00028	Torque converter cleaner
021–00047	Torque converter leak tester

Section 4

E40D Transmission
Ford Motor Co.

APPLICATION

1989 E–250, E–350 over 8500 lbs. GVW except 4.9L engine
1989 F–250, F–350 over 8500 lbs. GVW except 4.9L engine
1989 F-Super Duty series vehicles

GENERAL DESCRIPTION

The E40D transmission is a fully automatic electronically controlled, 4 speed unit with a 3 element locking torque converter. The main operating components of the E40D transmission include a converter clutch, 6 multiple disc friction clutches, a band, 2 sprag one-way clutches and a roller one-way clutch which provide for the desired function of 3 planetary gear sets.

In the **OVERDRIVE** range, automatic operation of all 4 gears is possible. The overdrive cancel switch, located on the vehicle's dashboard, disables overdrive operation and enables automatic operation through the first 3 gears.

Manual gear selection is available in the **1** and **2** range. The 2nd gear is commanded when the gear selector is in the **2** range and when downshifted into the **1** range at speeds above approximately 35 mph for gasoline engines and 30 mph for diesel engines. The 1st gear is commanded in the **1** range at startups and when downshifted into **1** range below approximately 35 mph for gasoline engines and 30 mph for diesel engines.

Transmission and Converter Identification

TRANSMISSION

The transmission identification tag is located on the left hand side of the transmission case to the rear of the manual level position sensor.

CONVERTER

The torque converter is identified by either a reference or part number stamped on the converter body and is matched to a specific engine. The torque converter is a welded unit and is not repairable. If internal problems exists, the torque converter must be replaced.

Electronic Controls

On gasoline engine equipped vehicles, with gear selection in the

OVERDRIVE range, the converter clutch operation is controlled by the EEC–IV control system. Operating conditions are relayed to EEC–IV by various sensors throughout the vehicle. The EEC–IV compares these conditions with electronically stored parameters and logically determines the state that the transmission should operate at.

For diesel engine applications, the E40D transmission utilizes a computerized electronic transmission control module which will process various engine, transmission and vehicle inputs but without the engine control function.

Metric Fasteners

Metric bolts and fasteners may be used in attaching the transmission to the engine and also in attaching the transmission to the chassis crossmember mount. The metric fastener dimensions are very close to the dimensions of the familiar inch system fasteners, and for this reason, replacement fasteners must have the same measurement and strength as those removed.

--- **CAUTION** ---
Do not attempt to interchange metric fasteners for inch system fasteners. Mismatched or incorrect fasteners can result in damage to the transmission unit through malfunctions or breakage and possible personal injury.

Capacities

The E40D automatic transmission use Motorcraft Mercon® automatic transmission fluid. The capacity of the E40D automatic transmission is 16.4 qts. or 15.5L for 2WD drive transmission types and 16.9 qts. or 16L for 4WD drive transmission.

Checking Fluid Level

The automatic transmission is designed to operate with the fluid level between the **ADD** and **FULL** mark on the dipstick at an operating temperature of 150°F–170°F (65°C–77°C). Fluid level

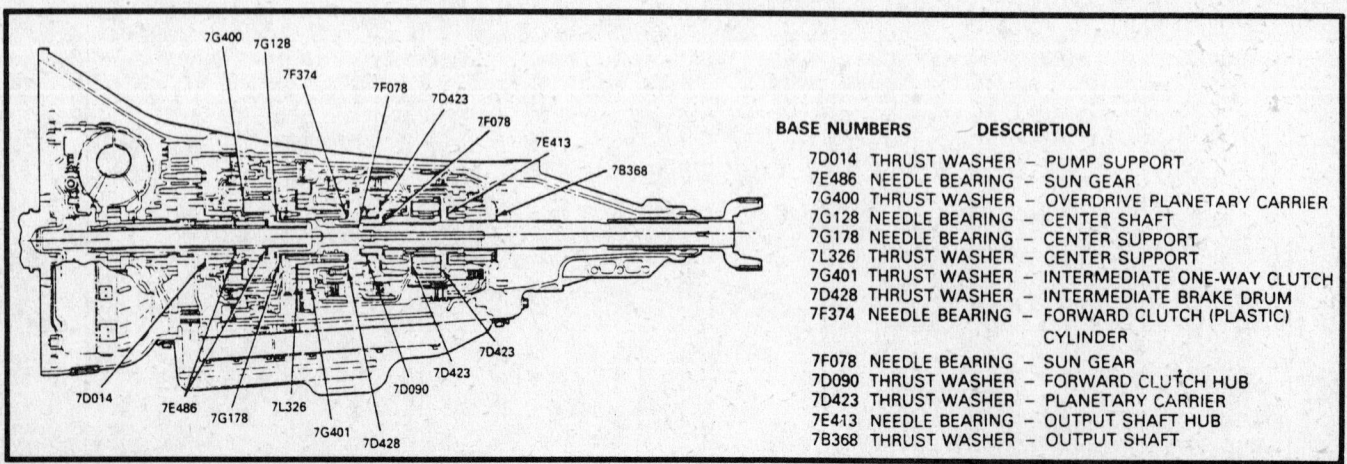

BASE NUMBERS	DESCRIPTION
7D014	THRUST WASHER – PUMP SUPPORT
7E486	NEEDLE BEARING – SUN GEAR
7G400	THRUST WASHER – OVERDRIVE PLANETARY CARRIER
7G128	NEEDLE BEARING – CENTER SHAFT
7G178	NEEDLE BEARING – CENTER SUPPORT
7L326	THRUST WASHER – CENTER SUPPORT
7G401	THRUST WASHER – INTERMEDIATE ONE-WAY CLUTCH
7D428	THRUST WASHER – INTERMEDIATE BRAKE DRUM
7F374	NEEDLE BEARING – FORWARD CLUTCH (PLASTIC) CYLINDER
7F078	NEEDLE BEARING – SUN GEAR
7D090	THRUST WASHER – FORWARD CLUTCH HUB
7D423	THRUST WASHER – PLANETARY CARRIER
7E413	NEEDLE BEARING – OUTPUT SHAFT HUB
7B368	THRUST WASHER – OUTPUT SHAFT

Thrust washer and neddle bearing location

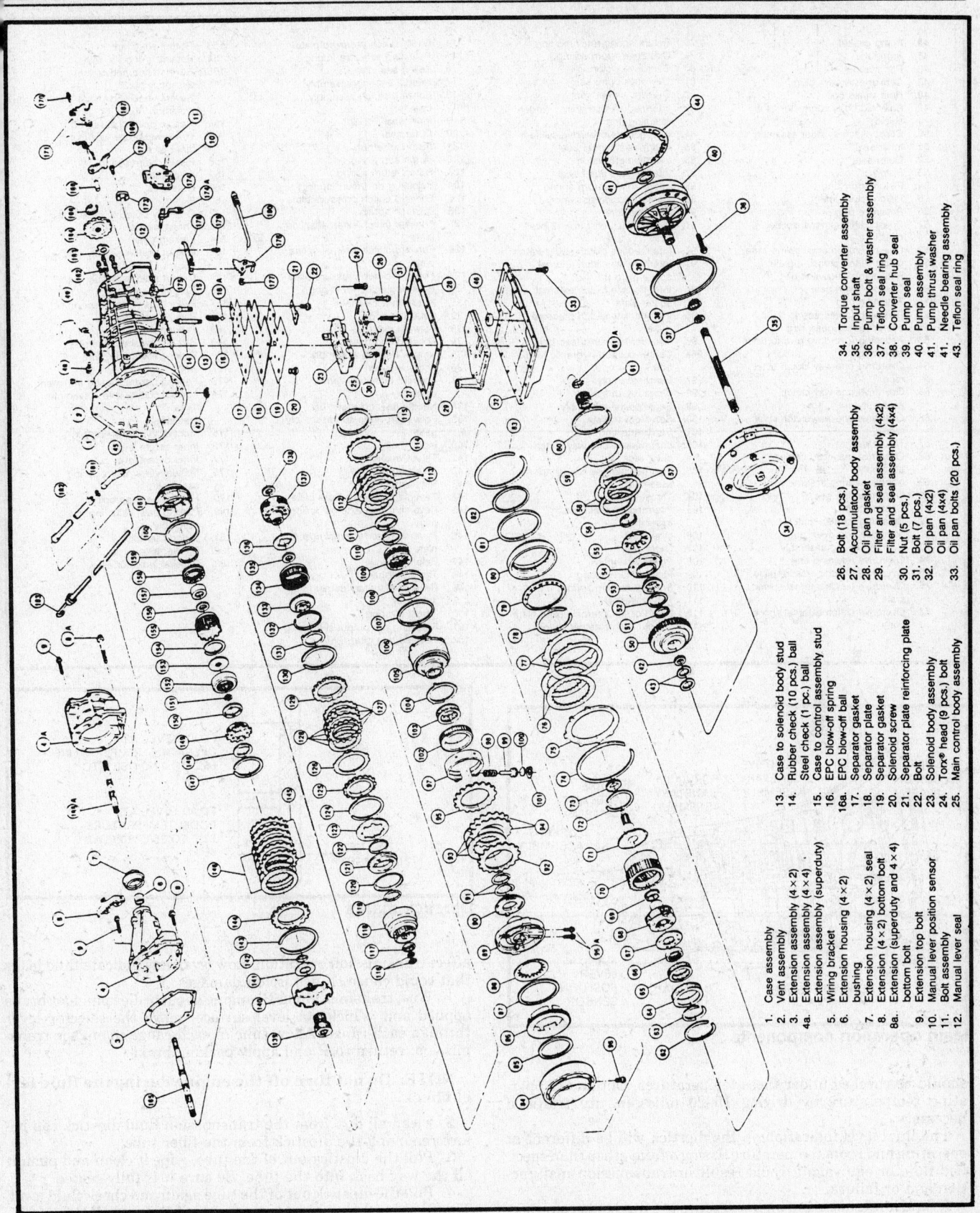

1. Case assembly
2. Vent assembly
3. Extension assembly (4×2)
4. Extension assembly (4×4)
4a. Extension assembly (superduty)
5. Wiring bracket
6. Extension housing (4×2) bushing
7. Extension housing (4×2) seal
8. Extension (4×2) bottom bolt
8a. Extension (superduty and 4×4) bottom bolt
9. Extension top bolt
10. Manual lever position sensor
11. Bolt assembly
12. Manual lever seal

13. Case to solenoid body stud
14. Rubber check (10 pcs.) ball
15. Steel check (1 pc.) ball
15. Case to control assembly stud
16. EPC blow-off spring
16a. EPC blow-off ball
17. Separator gasket
18. Separator plate
19. Separator gasket
20. Solenoid screw
21. Separator plate reinforcing plate
22. Bolt
23. Solenoid body assembly
24. Torx® head (9 pcs.) bolt
25. Main control body assembly

26. Bolt (18 pcs.)
27. Accumulatoor body assembly
28. Oil pan gasket
29. Filter and seal assembly (4x2)
29. Filter and seal assembly (4x4)
30. Nut (5 pcs.)
31. Bolt (7 pcs.)
32. Oil pan (4x2)
32. Oil pan (4x4)
33. Oil pan bolts (20 pcs.)

34. Torque converter assembly
35. Input shaft
36. Pump bolt & washer assembly
37. Teflon seal ring
38. Converter hub seal
39. Pump seal
40. Pump assembly
41. Pump thrust washer
41. Needle bearing assembly
43. Teflon seal ring

Exploded view E40D transmission

44. Pump gasket	78. Return spring retaining ring	114. Direct clutch pressure plate	153. Output shaft hub
45. Stub tube	79. Overdrive return spring	115. Retaining selective fit ring	154. Retaining ring
46. Pan magnet	80. Overdrive piston	116. Teflon seal ring	155. Reverse hub and clutch assembly (4x2)
47. Converter access plug	81. Overdrive outer seal	117. Needle bearing assembly	Reverse hub and clutch assembly (4x4)
48. Heat shield bolt	82. Overdrive inner seal	118. Forward clutch assembly cylinder	156. Needle bearing assembly
49. Solenoid body connector heat shield	83. Intermediate/overdrive cylinder retaining ring	119. Inner seal	157. Low/reverse one way clutch inner race
50. Coast clutch cylinder assembly	84. Intermediate/overdrive cylinder	120. Outer seal	158. Piston return spring
51. Inner seal	85. Intermediate inner seal	121. Piston assembly	159. Inner seal
52. Outer seal	86. Intermediate piston	122. Piston apply ring	160. Outer seal
53. Piston	87. Intermediate outer seal	123. Piston return spring	161. Piston
54. Piston apply ring	88. Intermediate return spring	124. Retaining (for return spring) ring	162. One way clutch to case bolts
55. Piston return spring	89. Center support assembly	125. Forward clutch pressure plate	163. Thrust washer
56. Retaining ring	90. Thrust washer	126. Cushion spring	164. Parking gear
57. Coast clutch external spline plate	91. Direct clutch cast iron (2 pcs.) seal	127. Forward clutch external spline plate	165. Output shaft assembly (4x2) 165a.
58. Coast clutch internal spline plate	92. Intermediate clutch apply plate	128. Forward clutch internal spline plate	Output shaft assembly (4x4)
59. Coast clutch pressure plate	93. Intermediate clutch internal spline plate	129. Forward clutch pressure plate	166. Retaining ring
60. Retaining selective fit ring	94. Intermediate clutch external spline plate	130. Retaining selective fit ring	167. Parking pawl return spring
61. Overdrive sun gear	95. Intermediate clutch pressure plate	131. Plastic thrust washer	168. Parking pawl pin
61a. Retaining ring	96. Cylinder hydraulic feed bolt	132. Retaining ring	169. Parking pawl
62. Retaining (outer race to overdrive owc) ring	96a. Center support hydraulic feed bolt	133. Forward hub	170. Bolt and washer assembly
63. Retaining (overdrive owc to outer race) ring	97. Band assembly	134. Forward ring gear	171. Parking rod guide plate
64. Overdrive one-way clutch outer race	98. Servo return spring	135. Needle bearing assembly	172. Bolt
65. Overdrive one-way clutch assembly	99. Servo piston assembly	136. Thrust washer	173. Parking pawl actuating abutment
66. Overdrive one-way clutch inner race	100. Servo cover plate	137. Forward planetary carrier assembly	174. Manual control lever assembly 174a
67. Thrust washer	101. Servo retaining ring	138. Needle bearing assembly	Insulator
68. Overdrive planetary carrier assembly	102. Intermediate one way clutch outer race	139. Forward/reverse sun assembly gear	175. Manual lever retaining pin
69. Needle bearing assembly	103. Intermediate one way clutch assembly	140. Input shell	176. Inner detent lever
70. Overdrive ring gear	104. Thrust washer	141. Thrust washer	177. Inner detent lever nut
71. Center shaft	105. Intermediate brake drum assembly	142. Retaining ring	178. Manual valve detent spring assembly
72. Retaining (center shaft to overdrive ring gear) ring	106. Inner seal	143. Retaining ring	179. Hex flange head bolt
73. Needle bearing assembly	107. Outer seal	144. Reverse clutch pressure plate	180. Parking pawl actuating rod assembly
74. Overdrive retaining ring	108. Piston assembly	145. Reverse clutch external spline plate	181. O-ring filler tube
75. Overdrive clutch pressure plate	109. Piston return spring	146. Reverse clutch internal spline plate	182. Oil filler tube assy.
76. Overdrive clutch internal spline plate	110. Spring retaining spring	147. Retaining ring	183. Oil level indicator assy.
77. Overdrive clutch external spline plate	111. Thrust washer	148. Thrust washer	
	112. Direct clutch internal spline plate	149. Reverse planetary carrier assembly	
	113. Direct clutch external spline plate	150. Thrust washer	
		151. Retaining (for output shaft) ring	
		152. Reverse ring gear	

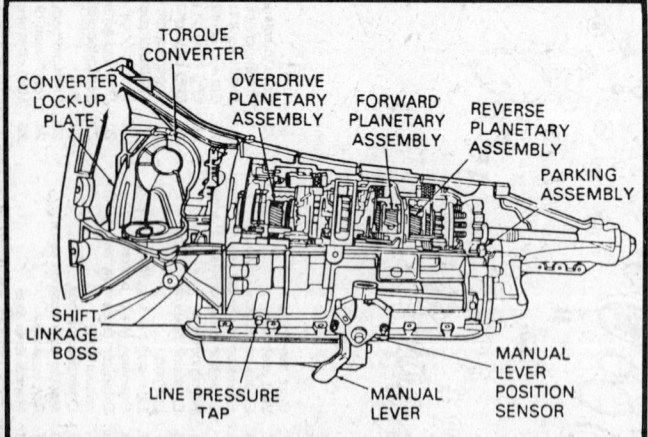

Main operation components

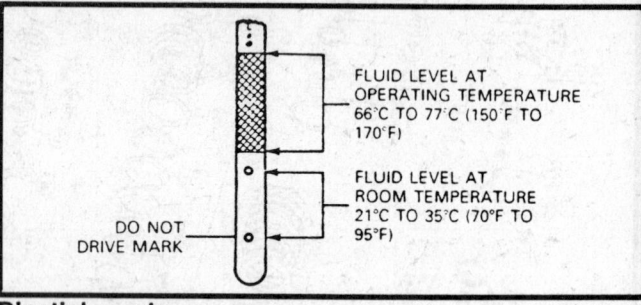

Dipstick marks

should be checked under these temperatures. Obtain the operating temperature by driving 15–20 miles in city traffic if necessary.

The fluid level indication on the dipstick will be different at operating and room temperature. Using a fluid other than specified fluid or equivalent, could result in transmission malfunction and or failure.

A fluid level that is too high will cause the fluid to become aerated. Aerated fluid will cause low control pressure and the aerated fluid may be forced out the vent. A fluid that is too low will

affect transmission operation. Low level may indicate fluid leaks that could cause transmission damage.

1. With transmission in **P**, engine at curb idle rpm, foot brake applied and vehicle on level surface, move the selector lever through each range. Allow time in each range to engage transmission, return to **P** and apply parking brake.

NOTE: Do not turn off the engine during the fluid level check.

2. Clean all dirt from the transmission fluid dipstick cap before removing the dipstick from the filler tube.

3. Pull the dipstick out of the tube, wipe it clean and push it all the way back into the tube. Be sure it is fully seated.

4. Pull the dipstick out of the tube again and check fluid level. The fluid level should be between the **ADD** and **FULL** mark.

5. Correct the fluid level, as required. Install the dipstick, making sure it is fully seated in the tube.

TRANSMISSION MODIFICATIONS

There have been no modifications to the E40D transmission at the time of this printing.

TROUBLE DIAGNOSIS

A logical and orderly diagnosis outline and charts are provide to assist the repairman in diagnosing the problems, causes and the extent of repairs needed to bring the automatic transmission back to its acceptable level of operation.

Preliminary checks and adjustments should be made to all related components. Transmission oil level should be checked, both visually and by smell, to determine whether the fluid level is correct and to observe any foreign material in the fluid, if present. Smelling the fluid will indicate if any of the bands or clutches have been burned through excessive slippage or overheating of the transaxle.

It is most important to locate the defect and its cause and to properly repair them to avoid having the same problem reoccur.

In order to more fully understand the E40D automatic transmission and to diagnose possible defects more easily, the clutch and band application chart and a general description of the hydraulic and electrical control systems are given.

Hydraulic Control System

TORQUE CONVERTER

The torque converter consists of: converter clutch (piston plate clutch and damper assembly), converter cover, turbine, impeller, reactor (sometimes called a stator) and a impeller hub. The torque converter couples the engine to the input shaft. Provides torque multiplication and absorbs engine shock caused by gear shifting.

OIL PUMP

The E40D uses a positive displacement gerotor type pump. The pump provides transmission fluid to the torque converter, lube circuit and the remaining hydraulic circuits. The pump assembly is primarily made up of 3 parts, the pump body, the control body and the reactor support. The pump body contains the pocket for the gerotor gearset. The control body contains the active ports for the pump and the bores for 3 of the hydraulic control valves: the main regulator valve, converter clutch regulator valve and coverter clutch control valve. The reactor support is pressed into the control body and supports the coast clutch cylinder, torque coverter and input shaft.

The gerotor pump consists of 2 elements. These include the inner rotor which is driven at engine speed and the outer rotor that is driven by the inner rotor. Because the inner and outer rotors have 1 tooth difference, the outer rotor runs offset from the inner and at a slower speed. This action causes the rotors to separate, causing a void in the pump cavity. This void is filled by fluid caused by atmospheric pressure on the sump fluid.

As the pump rotates, a separate chamber is created which moves

CLUTCH AND BAND APPLICATION

			Friction Elements						One-way Clutches Drive		
Gear	Coast	Inter-mediate	Direct	Forward	Reverse	Over-drive	Band		O/D OWC	Inter-mediate OWC	Low Reverse OWC
OD-1st	①	—	—	Applied	—	—	—		Holding	—	Holding
D1	Coast	Coast	Coast	Coast	Coast	Coast	Coast		OR ①	—	OR
OD-2nd	①	Applied	—	Applied	—	—	—		Holding	Holding	OR
D2	Coast	Coast	Coast	Coast	Coast	Coast	Coast		OR ①	OR	OR
OD-3rd	①	Applied	Applied	Applied	—	—	—		Holding	OR	OR
D3	Coast	Coast	Coast	Coast	Coast	Coast	Coast		OR ①	OR	OR
OD-4th	—	Applied	Applied	Applied	—	Applied	—		OR	OR	OR
D4	Coast	Coast	Coast	Coast	Coast	Coast	Coast		OR	OR	OR
1	Applied	—	—	Applied	Applied	—	—		Ineff	—	Ineff
2	Applied	Applied	—	Applied	—	—	Applied		—	Ineff	OR
R	Applied	—	Applied	—	Applied	—	—		Ineff	—	Ineff

OD—Overdrive
OWC—One-way clutch
OR—Overrunning
① In D Range with overdrive cancel switch pressed, the coast clutch is applied and the OD one-way is by-passed

Ineff—Indicates that a related component renders the one-way inoperative (without load) unless the component slips

CHILTON'S THREE C'S DIAGNOSIS

Condition	Cause	Correction
Fluid venting or foaming	a) Check fluid level	a) Drain transmission to proper level
	b) Inspect transmission fluid for contamination with anti-freeze or engine overheating	b) Determine source of leak. Service as required
	c) Inspect transmission fluid filter for damaged seal or misassembly to pump	c) Replace filter seals or reassemble fluid filter
Stalls when stopping	a) Poor engine performance	a) Check engine and service as required
	b) Check fluid level	b) Drain or fill transmission to proper level
	c) Check electronic engine control operation	c) Perform Quick Test
	d) Test converter clutch. Converter clutch does not release	d) Refer to service procedure
Shift efforts high	a) Inspect manual shift linkage for damage or misadjustment	a) Service as required
	b) Inspect manual lever retainer pin for damage	b) Adjust linkage and install new pin
	c) Check detent spring	c) Replace detent spring
	d) Inspect inner manual lever nut	d) Tighten nut to specifications
Poor vehicle performance	a) Poor engine performance	a) Perform Quick Test
	b) Test converter clutch. Converter clutch does not release	b) Refer to service procedure
	c) Inspect torque converter one-way clutch. One-way clutch locked up	c) Replace converter
Vehicle will not start	a) Inspect ignition switch. Misadjusted or defective	a) Adjust or replace as required
	b) Check electronic engine control operation	b) Perform Quick Test
Transmission overheats	a) Excessive tow loads	a) Check owner's manual for tow restriction
	b) Check fluid level	b) Drain or fill transmission to proper level
	c) Check electronic engine control operation	c) Perform Quick Test
	d) Inspect transmission cooler and cooler lines for restriction	d) Service as required
	e) Test converter clutch. Converter clutch does not apply	e) Refer to service procedure
	f) Inspect valve body. Dirty or sticky valves	f) Clean, service or replace valve body
	g) Inspect torque converter one-way clutch. One-way clutch locked up	g) Replace converter
No 1st gear, starts in higher gear	a) Check line pressure. Low line pressure	a) Perform line pressure test
	b) Check solenoid operation	b) Refer to electrical diagnosis. Service as required
	c) Inspect D2 valve, 2-3 shift valve and 3-4 shift valve for missing springs or sticky valves	c) Service as required
No 1-2 upshift	a) Check fluid level	a) Drain or fill transmission to the proper level
	b) Check manual linkage	b) Service as required
	c) Test line pressure. Low to intermediate friction clutch	c) Perform line pressure test
	d) Check solenoid operation (S2 solenoid suspected)	d) Service as required
	e) Inspect valve body bolts for correct torque	e) Tighten bolts to specification
	f) Inspect valve body. Dirty/sticky valves	f) Service as required
	g) Inspect 1-2 shift valve for damage	g) Service as required
	h) Inspect D2 valve for missing spring or sticky valve	h) Service as required
	i) Inspect intermediate clutch accumulator regulator valve for damage	i) Service as required

CHILTON'S THREE C'S DIAGNOSIS

Condition	Cause	Correction
No 1-2 upshift	j) Inspect intermediate clutch accumulator. Plunger stuck or damaged. Springs missing or damaged	j) Service as required
	k) Inspect intermediate clutch assembly. Clutch plates damaged/missing. Piston or seals damaged. Ball check stuck/missing. Feedbolt loose/missing/sealant leak. Clutch hub damaged	k) Service as required
	l) Inspect intermediate one-way clutch assembly for damaged cage/sprags or misassembled on inner race	l) Disassemble and inspect. Service as required
1-2 Shift harsh or soft	a) Check for high or low line pressure	a) Perform line pressure test
	b) Service line modulator pressure high or low	b) Refer to service procedure
	c) Inspect valve body bolts for correct torque	c) Tighten bolts to specification
	d) Inspect intermediate clutch accumulator regulator valve. Valve stuck, nicked or damaged. Spring missing or tangled	d) Service as required
	e) Inspect valve body. Dirty or sticky valves	e) Service as required
	f) Inspect intermediate clutch accumulator. Plunger stuck or damaged. Springs missing or tangled	f) Service as required
2-3 Shift harsh or soft	a) Check for high or low line pressure	a) Perform line pressure test
	b) Sevice line modulator pressure high or low	b) Refer to service procedure
	c) Inspect valve body bolts for correct torque	c) Tighten bolts to specification
	d) Inspect intermediate clutch accumulator regulator valve. Valve stuck, nicked or damaged. Spring missing or tangled	d) Service as required
	e) Inspect intermediate clutch accumulator. Plunger stuck or damaged. Springs missing or tangled	e) Service as required
	f) Inspect valve body. Dirty or sticky valves	f) Service as required
	g) Inspect pump air bleed check valve for leak or damage	g) Service as required
	h) Inspect intermediate clutch assembly. Clutch plates damaged/missing. Piston or seals damaged. Ball check stuck or missing. Feedbolt loose/missing sealant leak. Clutch hub damaged	h) Service as required
No 2-3 upshift	a) Check fluid level. Fluid level high or low	a) Drain or fill transmission to the proper level
	b) Check line pressure. Low to direct clutch	b) Perform line pressure test
	c) Check solenoid operation (S1 solenoid)	c) Refer to electrical diagnosis
	d) Inspect valve body bolts for correct torque	d) Tighten bolts to specification
	e) Inspect valve body. Dirty or sticky valves	e) Service as required
	f) Inspect 2-3 shift valve for being stuck, nicked or damaged	f) Service as required
	g) BS5 check ball missing. Plate seat damaged	g) Replace BS5 check ball and plate
	h) Inspect direct clutch assembly. Clutch plates damaged/missing. Piston or seals damaged. Ball check assembly stuck or missing	h) Service as required
	i) Inspect direct clutch cylinder. Seals damaged or missing or holes blocked	i) Service as required

CHILTON'S THREE C'S DIAGNOSIS

Condition	Cause	Correction
No 2-3 upshift	j) Inspect center support. Damaged, feedbolts loose or missing. Center support O.D. or case bore damaged/leaking. Teflon seal damaged	j) Service as required
2-3 Shift harsh or soft	a) Check line pressure. High or low line pressure	a) Perform line pressure test
	b) Service line modulator pressure high or low	b) Refer to service procedure
	c) Inspect valve body bolts for correct torque	c) Tighten bolts to specification
	d) Inspect valve body. Dirty or sticky valves	d) Service as required
	e) Inspect direct clutch accumulator regulator valve. Valve stuck, nicked or damaged. Spring missing or tangled	e) Service as required
	f) Inspect direct clutch accumulator. Springs missing or tangled. Plunger nicked or damaged	f) Service as required
	g) Inspect direct clutch assembly. Clutch plates damaged/missing. Piston or seals damaged. Ball check assembly stuck or missing	g) Service as required
	h) Inspect direct clutch cylinder. Seals damaged, missing or holes blocked	h) Service as required
	i) Inspect center support. Damaged, feedbolts loose or missing. Center support O.D. or case bore damaged/leaking. Teflon seal damaged	i) Service as required
No 3-4 upshift	a) Check fluid level. Fluid level high or low	a) Drain or fill transmission to the proper level
	b) Check for high or low line pressure	b) Perform line pressure test
	c) Check S2 solenoid operation	c) Refer to electrical diagnosis procedure. Service as required
	d) Inspect valve body bolts for correct torque	d) Tighten bolts to specification
	e) Inspect valve body. Dirty or sticky valves	e) Service as required
	f) Inspect 3-4 shift valve. Valve stuck, nicked or damaged. Springs missing or tangled	f) Service as required
	g) Inspect overdrive accumulator regulator valve. Valve stuck, nicked or damaged. Spring missing or tangled	g) Service as required
	h) Inspect overdrive clutch assembly. Clutch plates burnt or worn. Overdrive clutch cylinder damaged/feedbolt loose or missing/sealant leaking. Cylinder ball check assembly stuck or missing	h) Service as required
3-4 Shift harsh or soft	a) Check for line pressure high or low	a) Perform line pressure test
	b) Service line modulator pressure high or low	b) Refer to service procedure
	c) Inspect valve body bolts for correct torque	c) Tighten bolts to specification
	d) Inspect valve body. Dirty or sticky valves	d) Service as required
	e) Inspect overdrive accumulator regulator valve. Valve stuck, nicked/damaged. Spring missing or tangled	e) Service as required
	f) Inspect overdrive accumulator. Accumulator plunger stuck or damaged. Springs missing or tangled	f) Service as required

CHILTON'S THREE C'S DIAGNOSIS

Condition	Cause	Correction
3-4 Shift harsh or soft	g) Inspect overdrive clutch assembly. Clutch plates burnt or worn. Overdrive clutch cylinder damaged or feedbolt loose or missing. Cylinder ball check assembly stuck or missing	g) Service as required
Shifts 1-3	a) Check for fluid level high or low	a) Drain or fill transmission to the proper level
	b) Check S1 solenoid operation	b) Refer to electrical service procedure. Service as required
	c) Inspect D2 shift valve. Dirty or sticky. Spring missing or damaged	c) Service as required
	d) Inspect intermediate clutch accumulator regulator valve. Valve sticky or dirty	d) Service as required
	e) Inspect intermediate friction clutch. May be burnt or worn	e) Replace intermediate friction clutch
	f) Inspect intermediate one-way clutch assembly. Damaged cage/sprags. Misassembled on inner race	f) Disassemble and inspect. Service as required
Shift speed high or low	a) Check for fluid level high or low	a) Drain or fill transmission to the proper level
	b) Check electronic engine control operation	b) Perform Quick Test
	c) Inspect vehicle speed sensor. Wrong gear/damaged gear	c) Repair or replace as necessary
4-3 Downshift harsh	a) CB7 check ball missing. Plate seat damaged	a) Replace CB7 check ball and plate
3-2 Downshift harsh	a) CB6 check ball missing. Plate seat damaged	a) Replace CB6 check ball and plate
2-1 Downshift harsh	a) CB14 check ball missing. Plate seat damaged	a) Replace CB14 check ball and plate
No drive in drive range	a) Check for low fluid level	a) Fill transmission to the proper level
	b) Check for low line pressure	b) Perform line pressure test
	c) Inspect manual linkage (internal and external). Misadjusted, disconnected, damaged, broken or bent	c) Service as required
	d) Check transmission filter inside oil pan	d) Replace filter if plugged
	e) Inspect valve body and pump control body bolts for correct torque	e) Tighten bolts to specification
	f) Inspect pump control body and valve body. Dirty or sticky valves	f) Service as required
	g) Inspect overdrive one-way clutch. Improperly assembled/damaged. Damaged sprags or races	g) Service as required
	h) Inspect forward clutch assembly. Burnt or missing clutch plates. Damaged piston or seals. Forward clutch ball check assembly missing or damaged. Center support seals damaged or missing/holes blocked/feedbolt loose or missing. Forward clutch hub damaged	h) Service as required
	i) Inspect reverse one-way clutch. Improper installation or damaged rollers	i) Service as required
	j) Inspect front sun gear/shell for damage	j) Replace front gear/shell
	k) Inspect front and rear carrier. Damaged pinions/lugs to rear ring gear	k) Determine source of damage. Service as required
	l) Inspect reverse ring gear for damaged gears/lugs to forward carrier	l) Service as required
	m) Inspect output shaft for damage splines	m) Replace output shaft

CHILTON'S THREE C'S DIAGNOSIS

Condition	Cause	Correction
No reverse	a) Check for low fluid level	a) Fill transmission to the proper level
	b) Inspect manual linkage. Misadjusted, disconnected, damaged, broken or bent	b) Service as required
	c) Check for low line pressure	c) Perform line pressure test
	d) Check transmission filter inside oil pan	d) Replace filter if plugged
	e) Inspect valve body and pump control body bolts for correct torque	e) Tighten bolts to specification
	f) Inspect pump control body and valve body. Dirty or sticky valves	f) Service as required
	g) Inspect direct clutch accumulator regulator valve. Valve stuck, nicked or damaged. Spring missing or tangled	g) Service as required
	h) BS5 check ball missing. Plate seat damaged	h) Replace BS5 check ball and plate
	i) Inspect direct clutch assembly (if 3rd gear inoperative). Damaged piston or seals. Burnt or missing clutch plates. Direct clutch ball check assembly missing or damaged. Center support seals damaged or missing or holes blocked. Direct clutch hub damaged	i) Service as required
	j) Inspect coast clutch assembly for leakage	j) Service as required
	k) Inspect reverse clutch. Burnt or missing clutch plates. Damaged piston or seals	k) Service as required
	l) Inspect front and rear carrier. Damaged pinions/lugs to rear ring gear	l) Determine source of damage. Service as required
No park range	a) Inspect manual shift linkage for damage or misadjustment	a) Service as required
	b) Damaged park mechanism. Chipped or broken parking pawl or parking gear. Broken park pawl return spring. Bent or broken actuating rod	b) Determine source of damage. Service as required
Harsh neutral to drive or neutral to reverse engagements	a) Check for low fluid level	a) Fill transmission to the proper level
	b) Check electronic engine control operation	b) Perform Quick Test
	c) Worn/damaged/loose U-joint, slip yoke, rear axle or rear suspension	c) Service as required
	d) Inspect valve body bolts for correct torque	d) Tighten bolts to specification
	e) Engagement control valve. Valve stuck, nicked or damaged	e) Service as required
	f) CB13 check ball missing. Plate seat damaged	f) Replace CB13 check ball and plate
	g) Inspect direct clutch accumulator regulator valves. Valve sticking or dirty. Spring missing or tangled	g) Service as required
	h) Inspect direct clutch accumulator. Accumulator plunger stuck. Accumulator seal damaged or missing. Springs missing or tangled	h) Service as required
	i) Inspect forward clutch assembly. Burnt or missing clutch plates. Damaged piston or seals. Forward clutch ball check assembly missing or damaged. Center support seals damaged or missing/holes blocked/feedbolt loose or missing. Forward clutch hub damaged	i) Service as required
	j) Inspect reverse clutch for leakage	j) Identify source of leakage. Service as required
	k) Excessive transmission end play	k) Check transmission end play. Replace selective thrust washer

CHILTON'S THREE C'S DIAGNOSIS

Condition	Cause	Correction
No forced downshifts	a) Check for fluid level high or low	a) Drain or fill transmission to the proper level
	b) Check electronic engine control operation	b) Perform Quick Test
	c) Inspect valve body bolts for correct torque	c) Tighten bolts to specification
	d) Inspect valve body. Dirty or sticky valves	d) Service as required
No engine braking in manual one	a) Check for low fluid level	a) Fill transmission to the proper level
	b) Check for low line pressure	b) Perform line pressure test
	c) Check S1 solenoid operation	c) Refer to electrical diagnosis procedure
	d) Inspect for dirty or sticky valves. Reverse clutch modulator, D2 4-3-2 timing or 2-3 or coast clutch shift valves	d) Service as required
	e) Check ball missing. BS1, BS3 or CB1. Plate seat damaged	e) Replace check balls and plate
	f) Inspect coast clutch. Worn or burnt. Piston or seals damaged. Stator support damaged or holes blocked. Coast clutch hub damaged or holes blocked	f) Service as required
	g) Inspect reverse clutch. Worn or burnt. Piston or seals damaged	g) Service as required
No engine braking in manual second	a) Check for low fluid level	a) Fill transmission to the proper level
	b) Check for low line pressure	b) Perform line pressure test
	c) Inspect for dirty or sticky valves. 4-3-2 timing, D2, 2-3 or coast clutch shift valve	c) Service as required
	d) Check ball missing, BS1, BS3 or CB1. Plate seat damaged	d) Replace check balls and plate
	e) Check intermediate servo	e) Perform air pressure test of servo for leakage. Service as required
	f) Inspect intermediate band or drum, may be worn or burnt	f) Service as required
	g) Inspect coast clutch, may be worn or burnt. Piston or seals damaged. Stator support damaged or holes blocked. Coast clutch hub damaged or holes blocked	g) Service as required
Erratic shifts	a) Check for high or low fluid level	a) Drain or fill transmission to the proper level
	b) Check electronic engine control operation	b) Perform Quick Test
	c) Inspect vehicle speed sensor. Damaged or defective	c) Service as required
	d) Inspect valve body bolts for correct torque	d) Tighten bolts to specification
	e) Inspect valve body. Dirty or sticky valves	e) Service as required
Shift hunting	a) Check for high or low fluid level	a) Drain or fill transmission to the proper level
	b) Check electronic engine control operation	b) Perform Quick Test
High or low line pressure	a) Check for high or low fluid level	a) Drain or fill transmission to the proper level
	b) Electronic pressure control solenoid malfunction	b) Refer to electrical diagnosis procedure. Service as required
	c) Main regulator valve or spring. Dirty or sticky valve. Damaged spring	c) Determine source of damage or contamination. Service as required
	d) Pump assembly. Gears damaged, broken or worn	d) Determine source of damage. Service as required
No convertor clutch apply	a) Check for high or low fluid level	a) Drain or fill transmission to the proper level

CHILTON'S THREE C'S DIAGNOSIS

Condition	Cause	Correction
No convertor clutch apply	b) Electrical system or electronic engine control. No lock-up signal. S3 solenoid malfunction. Bulkhead connector damaged. Pinched wires	b) Refer to electrical diagnosis procedure. Service as required
	c) Inspect stator shaft Teflon seal for damage	c) Replace stator shaft seal
	d) Converter clutch control valve dirty or sticky	d) Service as required
Converter clutch does not release	a) Check for high or low fluid level	a) Drain or fill transmission to the proper level
	b) Electrical system or electronic engine control. No unlock signal. S3 solenoid malfunction. Bulkhead connector damaged. Pinched wires	b) Refer to electrical diagnosis procedure. Service as required
	c) Converter clutch control valve dirty or stuck valve	c) Service as required
Line modulator pressure high or low	a) Check for high or low line pressure	a) Perform line pressure test
	b) Inspect line pressure modulator valve. Valve stuck or damaged. Plunger or sleeve stuck or damaged	b) Service as required

fluid from the void to the compression area. The rotors squeeze the fluid out to the hydraulic system which creates the flow necessary for control line pressure from the pressure regulator.

CONTROL VALVES

MAIN REGULATOR BOOSTER VALVE

This valve reacts to pressure from the manual 1 circuit and the electronic pressure control solenoid to force, directly or through a spring force, the main regulator valve back toward its rest position resulting in increased line pressure.

MAIN REGULATOR VALVE

This valve regulates line pressure by allowing excess pump output to force the valve from its rest position. As the valve moves, the excess flow is exhausted into the converter charge passage or the sump, thereby relieving excess pressure. The regulated line pressure is variable and dependent on the spring force on the valve and the magnitude of the manual 1 circuit and electronic pressure control force against the main regulator booster valve.

NOTE: This valve boosts control line pressure during reverse or manual gear operation.

CONVERTER CLUTCH REGULATOR VALVE

This valve regulates line pressure to the converter. The maximum pressure to the torque converter is 113 psi.

CONVERTER CLUTCH CONTROL VALVE

The valve position is solenoid controlled and directs flow to the converter, which either applies or releases the converter clutch.

LINE MODULATOR VALVE

The line modulator valve provides a controlled pressure to an accumulator valve train which controls the pressure applied to the friction clutches. Line modulator pressure acts on an accumulator plunger which sets the output of the accumulator regulator valve during a shift.

MANUAL VALVE

The manual valve motion is controlled by the position of the transmission manual lever. This is connected mechanically to the transmission shift selector. The manual valve directs line

pressure input from the main regulator valve to 1 of 4 circuits. The circuits are the overdrive–2–1 circuit, 2 circuit, 1 circuit and the reverse circuit.

SOLENOID REGULATOR VALVE

This valve regulates pressure to 50 psi for use by the 4 shift solenoids. The output is also used for 4–3–2 shift timing.

SHIFT VALVES

LOW/REVERSE MODULATOR VALVE

This valve regulates pressure into the low and reverse clutch assembly.

3–4 SHIFT VALVE

This valve directs flow into the overdrive clutch when in rest position (during 4th gear) and directs flow into coast clutch shift valve when shifted.

2–3 SHIFT VALVE

This valve supplies fluid to the direct clutch in 3rd and 4th gears. It directs the flow in 1st and 2nd gear drive range to shift 3–4 shift valve. It also supplies fluid to the 1–2 shift valve in manual 1 and manual 2.

D2 VALVE

This valve shifts 1–2 shift valve during reverse operation.

1–2 SHIFT VALVE

This valve directs fluid to the intermediate clutch in 2nd, 3rd and 4th gears. It stops the flow in 1st gear. In manual gears it also sends flow to the band in 2 and to the reverse clutch in 1.

SHIFT TIMER PLUNGER

In manual pull in, it delays the shifting of the 4–3–2 shift timer valve thereby delaying the application of the band or the reverse clutch.

4–3–2 SHIFT TIMER VALVE

During manual pull in, it directs the flow into the 2–3 shift valve.

ENGAGEMENT CONTROL VALVE

During higher electronic pressure control this valve increases pressure to the forward clutch during forward engagement and direct clutch during reverse engagement.

1-2 MANUAL TRANSITION VALVE

This valve prevents the band from coming on during manual 1 and 2 upshift until the low/reverse clutch is off.

COAST CLUTCH SHIFT VALVE

This valve when shifting during manual pull in or when overdrive range is cancelled, directs fluid to the coast clutch, otherwise it stops oil flow.

OVERDRIVE CLUTCH ACCUMLATOR PLUNGER AND VALVE

This valve regulates line pressure supplied to the overdrive friction clutch by using the valve to constrict the flow. Valve regulated pressure is determined by the force of line modulator pressure and the inner and outer springs acting against the accumulator plunger.

DIRECT CLUTCH ACCUMULATOR PLUNGER AND VALVE

This valve regulates line pressure supplied to the direct friction clutch by using the valve to constrict the flow. Valve regulated pressure is determined by the force of line modulator pressure and the inner and outer springs acting against the accumulator plunger.

INTERMEDIATE CLUTCH ACCUMULATOR

This valve regulates line pressure supplied to the intermediate friction clutch by using the valve to constrict the flow. Valve regulated pressure is determined by the force of line modulator pressure and the inner and outer springs acting against the accumulator plunger.

LINE PRESSURE MODULATOR PLUNGER AND VALVE

This valve provides a modulated pressure dependent upon the electronic pressure control, which acts in the accumulator body to resist accumulator valve movement and thereby increase clutch application pressure.

Electronic Controls

GASOLINE ENGINE

On vehicles equipped with gasoline engines, the operation of E40D automatic transmission is controlled by the EEC–IV system.

THROTTLE POSITION SENSOR (TPS)

The throttle position sensor is a potentiometer mounted on the throttle body. It consists of a lever positioned between the throttle valve and a variable resistor. The throttle position sensor detects the opening of the throttle plate and sends this information to the ECA as a varying voltage signal.

MANIFOLD ABSOLUTE PRESSURE SENSOR (MAP)

The manifold absolute pressure sensor uses pressure to produce an electrical voltage signal. The frequency of this voltage signal varies with intake manifold pressure. This sensor sends the signal to the ECA, which determines altitude from manifold pressure. The ECA can then adjust the transmission shift schedule for different altitudes.

PROFILE IGNITION PICKUP SIGNAL (PIP)

The profile ignition pickup signal is produced by a Hall Effect device in the distributor. It tells the ECA the engine rpm and the crankshaft position.

BRAKE ON/OFF SWITCH (BOO)

The brake on/off switch tells the ECA whether the brakes are applied or not. The switch is closed when the brakes are applied and open when they are not.

MANUAL LEVER POSITION SENSOR (MLPS)

This sensor tells the ECA which position the shift lever is in. It is located on the outside of the transmission, at the manual lever.

VEHICLE SPEED SENSOR (VSS)

The vehicle speed sensor is a magnetic pickup that sends an signal to the ECA. This signal is proportional to the transmission output shaft rpm and tells the ECA what the vehicle speed is.

TRANSMISSION OIL TEMPERATURE SENSOR (TOT)

The transmission oil temperature sensor is a temperature sensitive device called a thermistor. It sends a voltage signal that varies with the transmission oil temperature to the ECA. The ECA uses this signal to determine whether a cold start shift schedule is necessary. The cold start shift schedule lowers shift speeds to allow for increased viscosity of the cold transmission fluid. This sensor is located on the solenoid body in the transmission sump.

OVERDRIVE CANCEL SWITCH AND INDICATOR LIGHT

When the overdrive cancel switch is pressed, the indicator light comes on and a signal is sent to the ECA. The ECA then energizes solenoid 4, applying the coast clutch cancelling 4th gear operation.

NOTE: The overdrive cancel switch indicator light will come on if the variable force solenoid (VFS) fails.

SOLENOIDS

The ECA controls the E40D transmission operation through 4 on/off solenoids and 1 variable force solenoid. These solenoids are housed in the transmission valve body assembly. Solenoids 1 and 2 provide gear selection of the 1st through 4th gears by controlling the pressure to the 3 shift valves. Solenoid 3 provides converter clutch control by shifting the converter clutch control valve. Solenoid 4 provides coast clutch control for overdrive lockout by shifting the coast clutch shift valve. This solenoid can be activated either by pressing the overdrive cancel switch or by selecting the **R**, **1** or **2** range with the transmission selector lever.

The variable force solenoid (VFS) is an electrohydraulic actuator combining a solenoid and a regulating valve. It produces electronic pressure control which regulates transmission line pressure by producing resisting forces to the main regulator valve and the line modulator valve. These 2 modified pressures control the clutch application pressures.

DIESEL ENGINE

On vehicles equipped with diesel engines, the operation of the E40D transmission is controlled by the transmission control system (Transmission electronic control assembly).

FUEL INJECTION PUMP LEVER SENSOR (FIPL)

The fuel injection pump lever sensor is a potentiometer similar to the TP sensor used on gasoline engines. This sensor is attached to the fuel injection pump and is operated by the throttle lever. It sends a varying voltage signal to the transmission electronic control assembly module, telling the module how much fuel is being delivered to the engine.

If a malfunction occurs in the sensor circuit, the transmission control system will recognize that the sensor signal is out of specification. The transmission electronic control assembly module will then operate the transmission in a high capacity mode to prevent transmission damage. This high capacity mode causes harsh upshifts and engagements, a sign that transmission diagnosis is required.

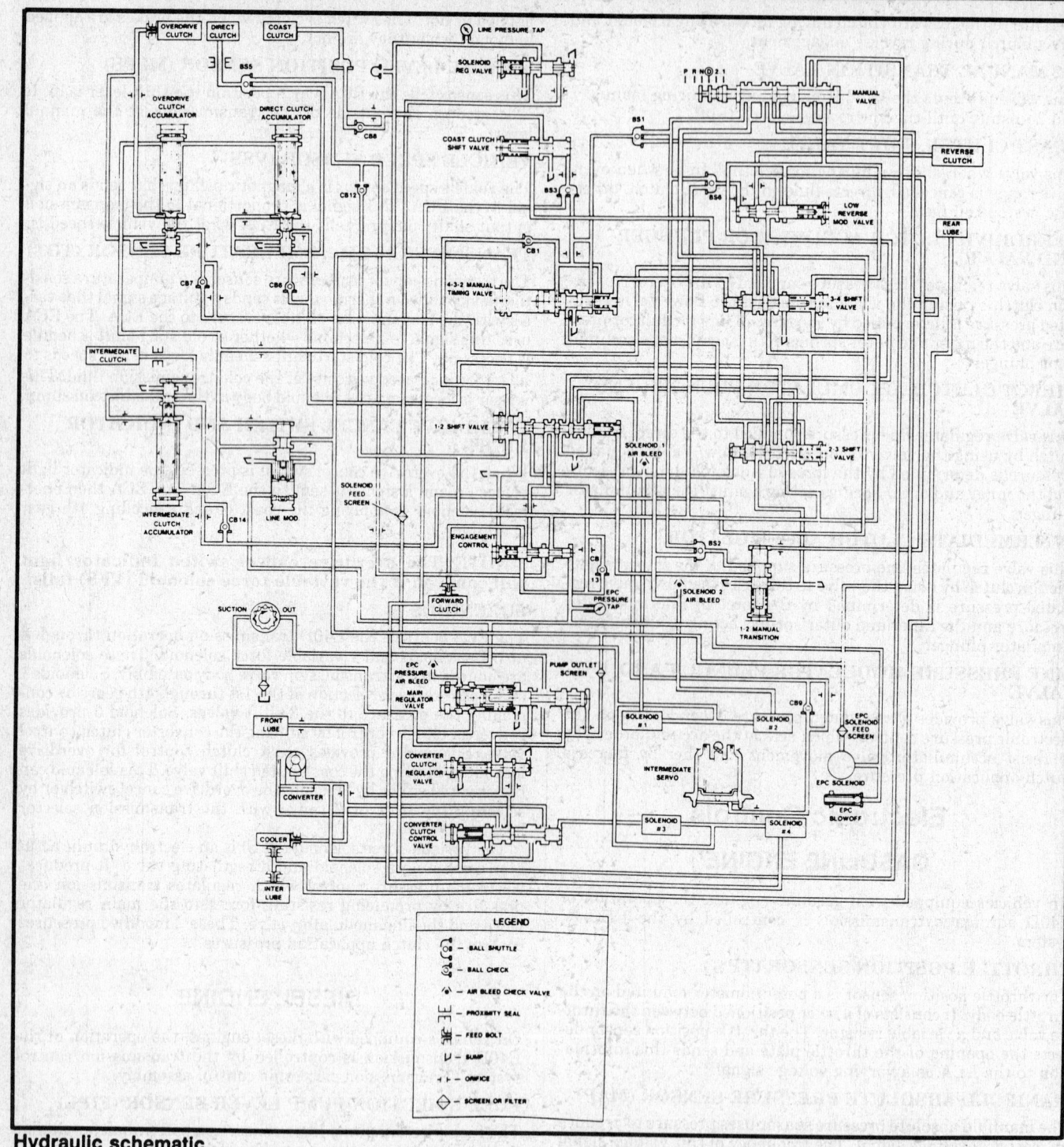

Hydraulic schematic

BAROMETRIC PRESSURE SENSOR (BP)

The barometric pressure sensor operates in the same as the MAP sensor, except that its measures barometric pressure instead of intake manifold pressure. The transmission electronic control assembly module uses the signal from the BP sensor to determine the altitude at which the vehicle operates then adjust the shift schedule for that altitude.

ENGINE RPM SENSOR

The engine RPM sensor indicates the engine speed with information from the fuel injection pump gear.

BRAKE ON/OFF SWITCH (BOO)

The brake on/off Switch tells the transmission electronic control

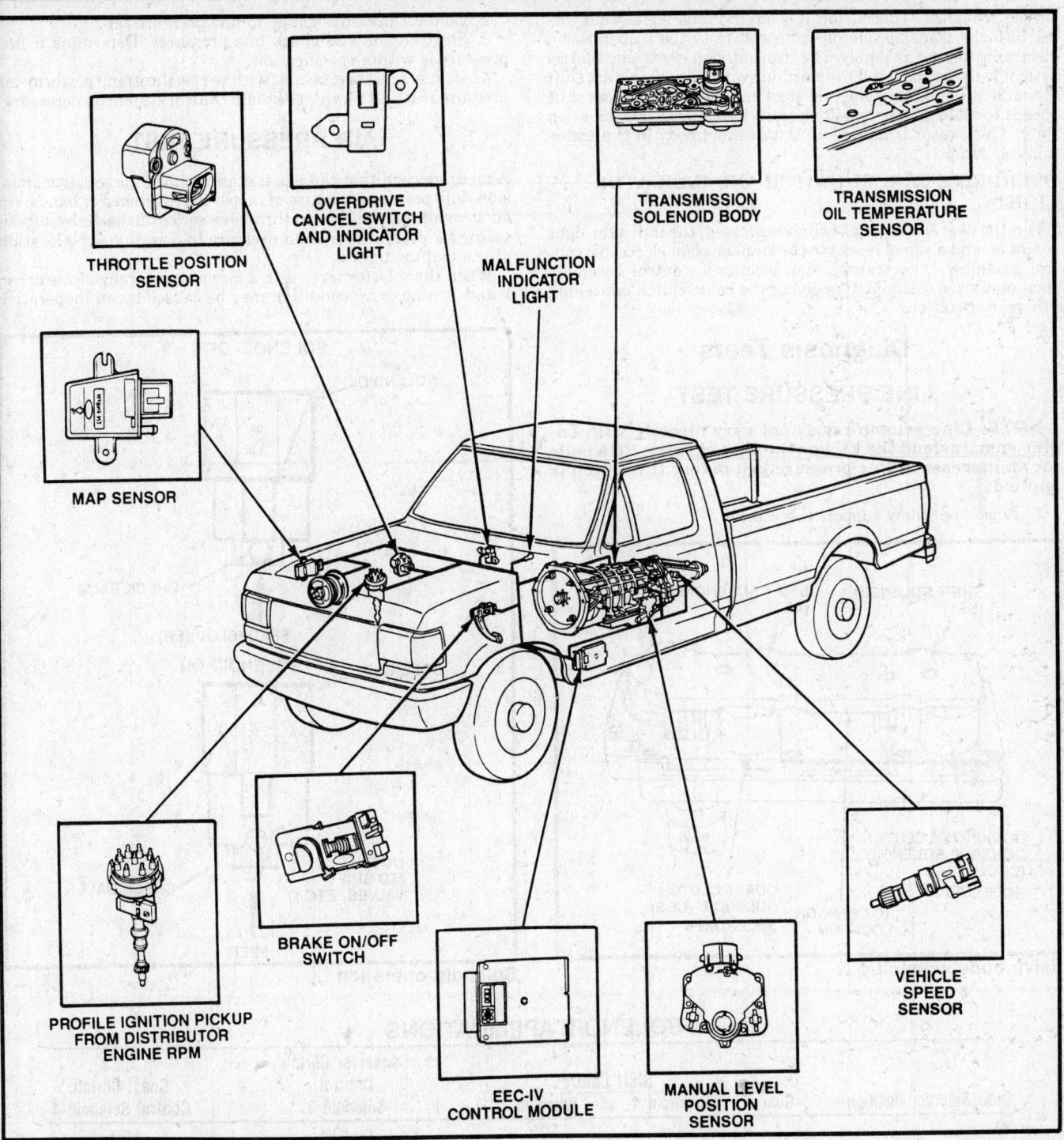

THROTTLE POSITION SENSOR

OVERDRIVE CANCEL SWITCH AND INDICATOR LIGHT

MALFUNCTION INDICATOR LIGHT

TRANSMISSION SOLENOID BODY

TRANSMISSION OIL TEMPERATURE SENSOR

MAP SENSOR

PROFILE IGNITION PICKUP FROM DISTRIBUTOR ENGINE RPM

BRAKE ON/OFF SWITCH

EEC-IV CONTROL MODULE

MANUAL LEVEL POSITION SENSOR

VEHICLE SPEED SENSOR

Transmission and engine sensor locations

assembly whether the brakes are applied or not. The switch is closed when the brakes are applied and open when they are not.

MANUAL LEVER POSITION SENSOR (MLPS)

This sensor tells the transmission electronic control assembly which position the shift lever is in. It is located on the outside of the transmission, at the manual lever.

VEHICLE SPEED SENSOR (VSS)

The vehicle speed sensor is a magnetic pickup that sends an signal to the transmission electronic control assembly. This signal is proportional to the transmission output shaft rpm and tells to the transmission electronic control assembly vehicle speed.

TRANSMISSION OIL TEMPERATURE SENSOR (TOT)

The transmission oil temperature sensor is a temperature sensitive device called a thermistor. It sends a voltage signal that varies with the transmission oil temperature to the transmission electronic control assembly. The transmission electronic control assembly uses this signal to determine whether a cold start shift schedule is necessary. The cold start shift schedule lowers shift speeds to allow for increased viscosity of the cold transmission fluid. This sensor is located on the solenoid body in the transmission sump.

OVERDRIVE CANCEL SWITCH AND INDICATOR LIGHT

When the overdrive cancel switch is pressed, the indicator light comes on and a signal is sent to the transmission electronic control assembly. The transmission electronic control assembly then energizes solenoid 4, applying the coast clutch cancelling 4th gear operation.

Diagnosis Tests

LINE PRESSURE TEST

NOTE: Line pressure does not vary directly with engine rpm. Instead the ECA or the transmission ECA calls for an increase in line pressure just before the clutch is applied.

1. Raise and safely support the vehicle.

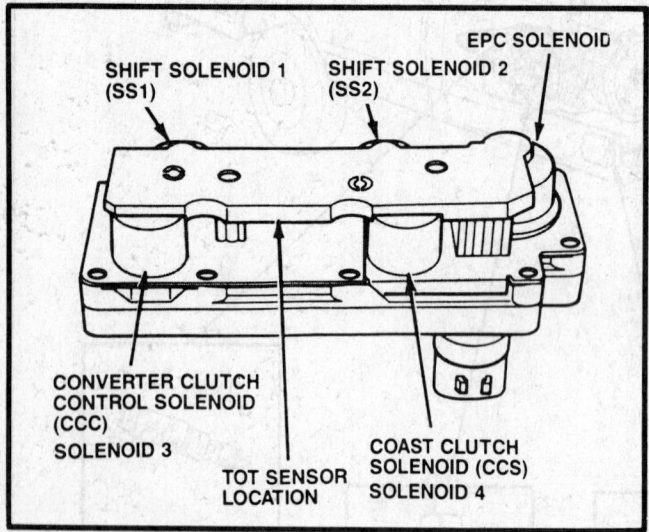

Valve body solenoids

2. Connect pressure gauge to line pressure tap.
3. Start engine and check line pressures. Determine if line pressure is within specification.
4. If line pressure is not within specification, perform air pressure test and service the main control system as necessary.

AIR PRESSURE TEST

A no drive condition can exist, even with the correct transmission fluid pressure, because of inoperative clutches or bands. An erratic shift can be located through a series of checks by substituting air pressure for fluid pressure to determine the location of the malfunction.

When the selector lever is in a forward gear range (overdrive, 2 and 1) a no drive condition may be caused by an inoperative

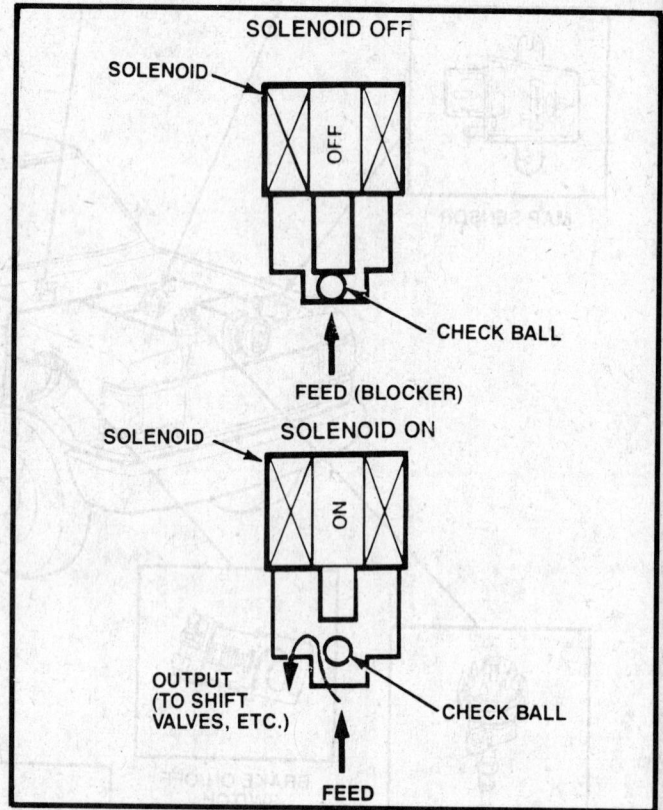

Solenoid operation

SOLENOID APPLICATIONS

Gear Selector Position	Gear	Shift Control Solenoid 1	Shift Control Solenoid 2	Converter Clutch Control Solenoid 3	Coast Clutch Control Solenoid 4
OD	4	Off	Off	On/Off	Off
	3	Off	On	On/Off	Off
	2	On	On	On/Off	Off
	1	On	Off	On/Off	Off
OD	3	Off	On	Based on EEC-IV Strategy	On
Overdrive Cancel	2	On	On	Based on EEC-IV Strategy	On
Switch Pressed	1	On	Off	Based on EEC-IV Strategy	On
2	2	Off	Off	Based on EEC-IV Strategy	Off
1	1	On	Off	Off	Off

LINE PRESSURE SPECIFICATIONS CHART

Engine	Range	Idle		Stall	
		psi	kPa	psi	kPa
5.8L	P, N	55–65	379–448	—	—
	R	85–110	586–758	240–265	1655–1827
	OD, 2	55–65	379–448	156–174	1076–1200
	1	74–99	510–682	157–182	1082–1255
7.3L Diesel	P, N	55–65	379–448	—	—
	R	105–130	723–896	240–265	1655–1827
	OD, 2	55–65	379–448	156–174	1076–1200
	1	74–99	510–682	161–186	1110–1282
7.5L	P, N	55–65	379–448	—	—
	R	90–115	621–792	240–265	1655–1827
	OD, 2	55–65	379–448	156–174	1076–1200
	1	74–99	510–682	157–182	1082–1255

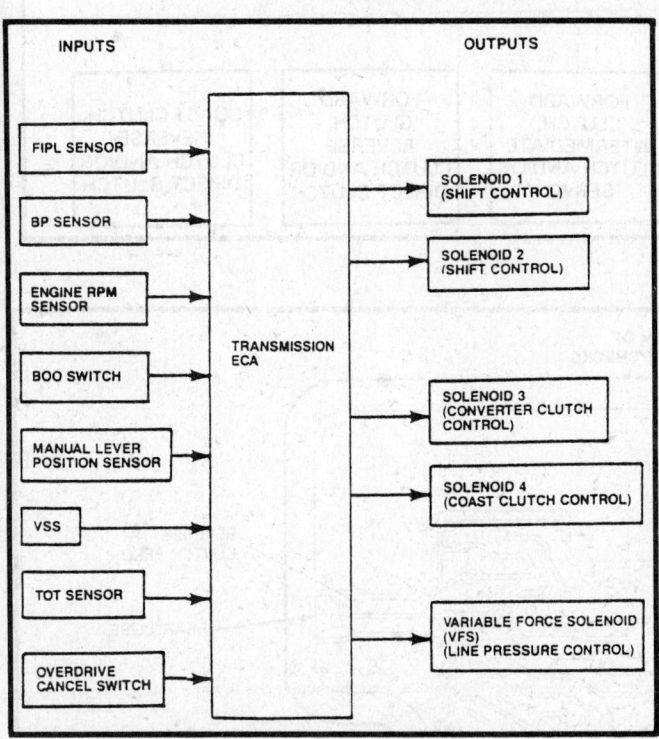

Transmission ECA inputs and outputs

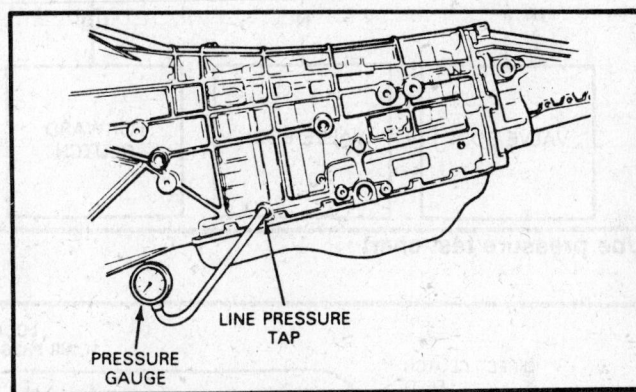

Line pressure tap location

STALL TEST

The stall test checks the operation of the following items: converter one-way clutch, forward clutch, low/reverse one-way clutch, reverse clutch, overdrive one-way clutch, direct clutch, coast clutch and the engine performance.

— **CAUTION** —

Do not allow any one to stand either in front of or behind the vehicle during the stall test. Personal injury could result.

1. Apply the brakes. Brock the drive wheels. Run engine to normal operating temperature then connect the tachometer to the engine.
2. Press the accelerator pedal to floor (WOT) in each transmission range. Record the rpm reached in each range. The stall speeds should be in the appropriate range. On the 5.8L engine the stall speed should be between 2100–2460 rpm. On the 7.3L Diesel engine the stall speed should be between 1650–1910 rpm and on the 7.5L engine it should be betwwen 1840–2155 rpm.
3. After testing each of the following ranges overdrive, 2, 1 and reverse, move selector lever to **N** and run engine for about 15 seconds to allow converter to cool before testing next range.

NOTE: Do not maintain wide open throttle (WOT) in any gear range for more than 5 seconds.

4. If engine rpm recorded by the tachometer exceeds maxi-

forward clutch, overdrive one-way clutch or low/reverse one-way clutch. No manual low (1) coast could be caused by an inoperative coast clutch or the reverse clutch. Failure to move in reverse gear could be caused by a problem in the reverse clutch, overdrive one-way clutch or the direct clutch.

1. Raise the vehicle and safely support.
2. Drain the transmission fluid and remove the oil pan.
3. Remove the filter and the seal asembly, solenoid body and the main control assemblies.
4. The inoperative clutches can be located by introducing air pressure into the various test passages.

NOTE: A dull thud can be heard, or movement of the piston felt when clutch piston is applied. If clutch seal(s) are leaking, a hissing sound will be heard.

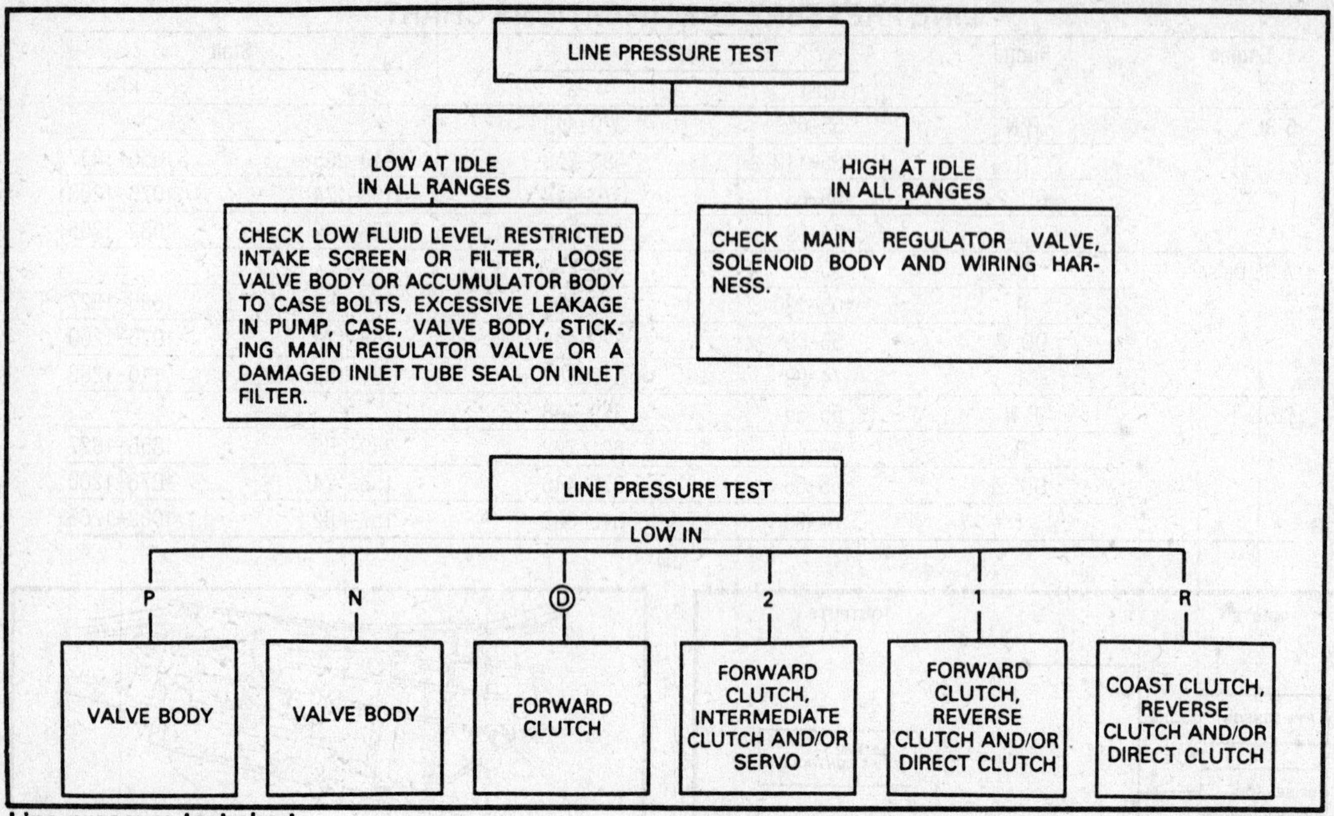

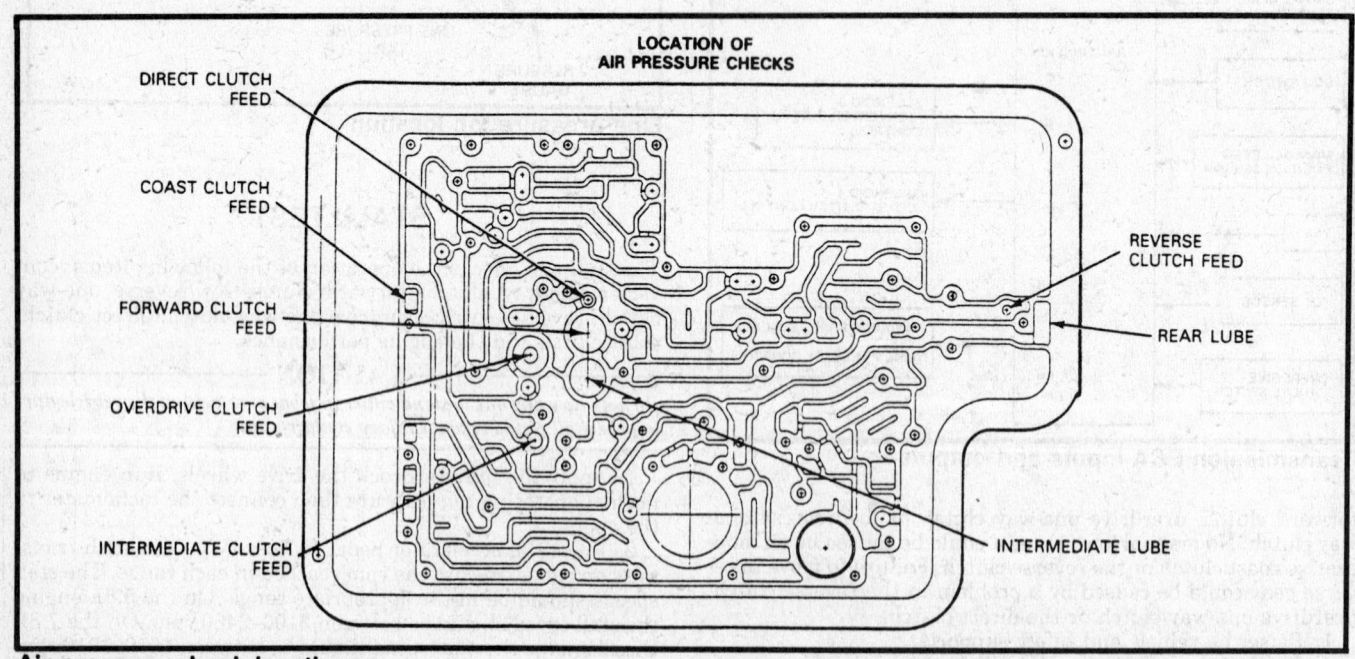

Line pressure test chart

Air pressure check locations

mum specified rpm, then release the accelerator pedal immediately. Clutch or band slippage is indicated by this test result.

5. If the stall speeds were too high, refer to the stall speed diagnosis chart. If the stall speeds were too low, check engine performance. If engine performance is correct, remove the torque converter and check the torque converter reactor one-way clutch for slippage.

Range	Possible Source
D	Forward Clutch Overdrive One-Way Clutch Low/Reverse One-Way Clutch
R	Direct Clutch Overdrive One-Way Clutch Reverse Clutch
2	Forward Clutch Overdrive One-Way Clutch Intermediate Clutch Intermediate One-Way Clutch
1	Forward Clutch Reverse Clutch and Low/Reverse One-Way Clutch Coast Clutch and Overdrive One-Way Clutch

Stall speed diagnosis chart

TRANSMISSION FLUID COOLER FLOW TEST

The transmission linkage adjustment, fluid level and line pressure must be within specifications before performing this test.
1. Remove the dipstick from filler tube and place a funnel in the filler tube.
2. Raise the vehicle and support safely.
3. Remove the cooler return line (rear fitting) from fitting on transmission case and connect a hose to the cooler return line. Insert other end of hose into the funnel in the dipstick tube.
4. Start the engine and run at idle with transmission in **N** range.
5. Observe the fluid flow at the funnel. When fluid flow is solid, the flow should be liberal and the test is completed.
6. If the flow is not liberal, stop the engine. Disconnect the hose from the cooler return line and connect it to the converter out line fitting (front fitting) on the transmission case.
7. Start engine and observe the fluid flow. If fluid flow is not liberal, check the transmission oil cooler for blockage and or the transmission oil pump assembly.

SHIFT POINT TEST

This test verifies that the shift control system is operating properly.

Road Test
1. Bring engine transmission up to normal operating temperature.
2. Operate the vehicle in the overdrive range.
3. Apply minimum throttle pressure and observe the upshift speeds and speeds at which the converter and clutch apply.
4. With vehicle in overdrive (4th gear), depress overdrive cancel switch. The transmission should downshift into 3rd gear.
5. Depress the accelerator pedal to the floor (WOT). The transmission should shift from 3rd to 2nd, or 3rd to 1st depending on vehicle speed and the converter clutch should release and then reapply.
6. With vehicle in the overdrive range above 50 mph and less than half throttle, move transmission selector from overdrive range to the 2nd range and release accelerator pedal. The transmission should immediately downshift into 2nd gear. With vehicle remaining in 2nd gear range, move transmission selector into 1st gear range, and release accelerator pedal. Transmission should downshift into 1st gear at speeds below 30–35 mph.
7. If transmission fails to upshift or downshift, adjustment and or repair is necessary.

In-Shop Test
1. Raise and support the vehicle safely. Run the engine to the normal operating temperature is reached.

NOTE: Do not exceed 60 mph indicated speedometer speed. Do not exceed recommended tire speed rating.

2. To check shift valves, place the transmission in the overdrive range. Apply throttle pressure and observe the upshift speeds.
3. At the shift points, the speedometer needle will make a momentary surge, a slight drive line bump may be felt and the engine speed will drop without releasing the accelerator pedal.
4. If transmission fails to upshift or downshift adjustment and or repair is necessary.

ELECTRICAL TESTS FOR GASOLINE ENGINES

When performing trouble diagnosis to E40D transmission, perform the Electronic Engine Control (EEC–IV) Quick Test. This will determine if any service codes for the transmission exist. These service codes may appear during the EEC–IV Quick Test. Service these codes first and repeat the EEC–IV Quick Test before continuing with the transmission diagnosis.

EEC–IV Quick Test Service Codes

CODE 26
TOT SENSOR OUT OF SELF-TEST RANGE

The transmission oil temperature (TOT) sensor registers a temperature not in the allowable range of testing. The test should be repeated with the transmission heated to the correct testing temperature.

CODE 47
4WD SWITCH CLOSED

The transmission transfer case is activated into 4WD drive. Release the 4WD drive and repeat the test.

CODE 65
OVERDRIVE CANCEL SWITCH NOT CHANGING STATE

The operation of the overdrive cancel switch was not recorded during the Engine On Quick Test. Service the switch and or wiring connections

CODE 67
MANUAL LEVER POSITION SENSOR OUT OF RANGE/ AC ON

If the AC clutch is on during the test, this code will appear. Shut off the AC or defrost and repeat the test. If the AC unit was off during the test, go to Transmission Quick Test Service Code 67.

Transmission Quick Test Service Codes

NOTE: If any of the following service codes appear during the EEC–IV Quick Test, perform the Drive Cycle Test for continuous codes.

CODE 49
1–2 SHIFT ERROR

The engine speed drop during the 1 to 2 shift. It does not fall within tolerance limits.

CODE 56
TRANSMISSION OIL TEMPERATURE SENSOR INDICATED -40°F SENSOR CIRCUIT OPEN

The voltage drop across the transmission oil temperature sensor exceeds the scale set for the temperature of -40°F.

CODE 59
2–3 SHIFT ERROR

The engine speed drop during the 2 to 3 shift. It does not fall within tolerance limits.

CODE 62
CONVERTER CLUTCH FAILURE

The EEC–IV module picks up excessive amount of converter slip while converter is scheduled to be locked up.

CODE 66
TRANSMISSION OIL TERMPERATURE OIL SENSOR INDICATED 315°F SENSOR CIRCUIT GROUNDED

The voltage drop across the transmission oil temperature sensor does not reach the scale set for the temperature of 315°F.

CODE 67
MANUAL LEVER POSITION SENSOR OUT OF RANGE/AC ON

The indicated voltage drop across the MLPS (manual lever position sensor) exceeds the limits established for each position. With AC or defrost on the fault results from the AC clutch being on during Quick Test.

CODE 69
3–4 SHIFT ERROR

The engine speed drop during the 3 to 4 shift. It does not fall within tolerance limit.

CODE 91
SHIFT SOLENOID 1 CIRCUIT FAILURE

The solenoid 1 circuit fails to provide voltage drop across the solenoid. The circuit is open or shorted, or an EEC driver failure exist.

CODE 92
SHIFT SOLENOID 2 CIRCUIT FAILURE

The solenoid 2 circuit fails to provide voltage drop across the solenoid. The circuit is open or shorted, or an EEC driver failure exist.

CODE 93
CCS SOLENOID CIRCUIT FAILURE

Solenoid 4 (coast clutch solenoid) fails to provide voltage drop across the solenoid. The circuit is open or shorted, or an EEC driver failure exist.

CODE 94
CCS SOLENOID CIRCUIT FAILURE

Solenoid 3 (converter clutch solenoid) fails to provide voltage

Error Codes	Pinpoint Test
49	AA
56	BB
59	AA
62	CC
66	BB
67	EE
69	AA
91	GG
92	GG
93	GG
94	GG
98	HH
99	HH

Electrical diagnosis chart index

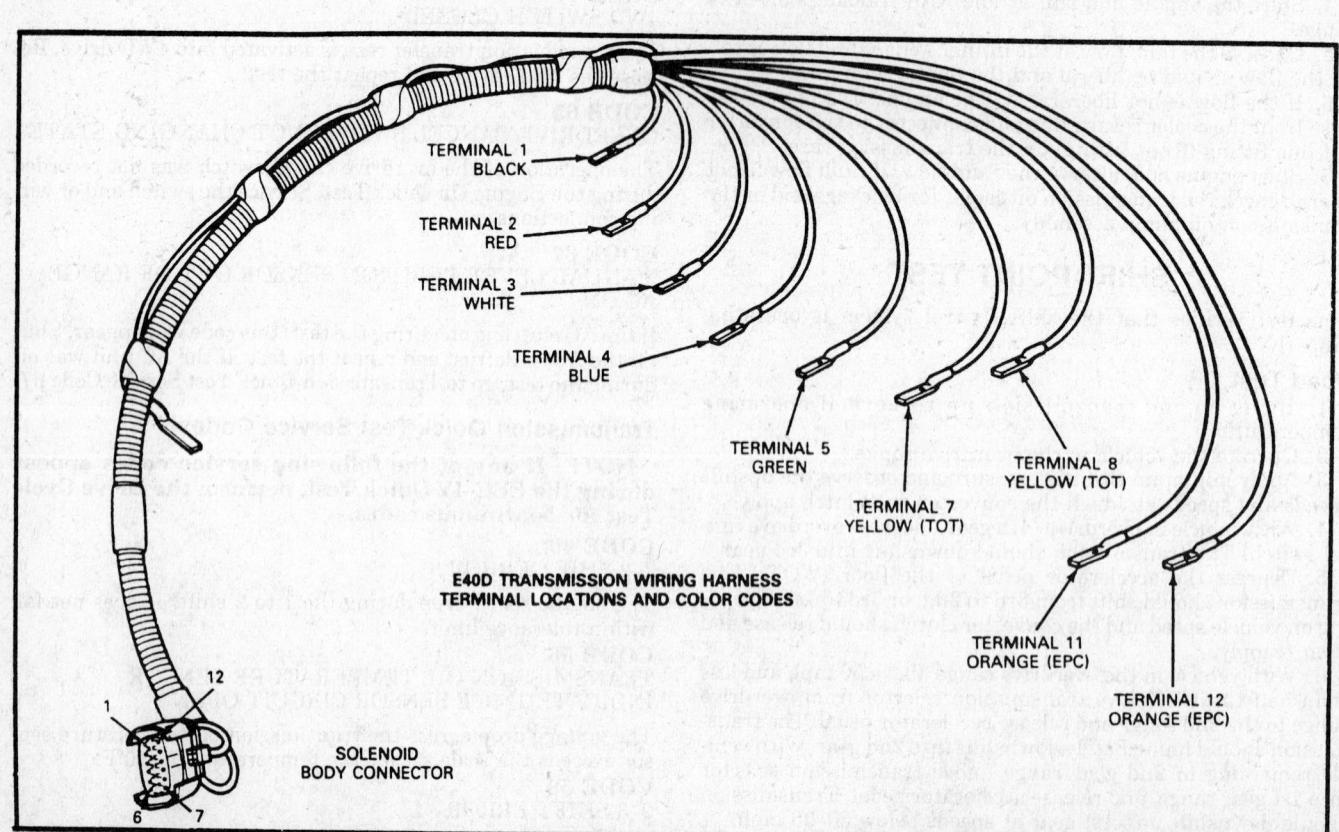

TERMINAL 1
BLACK

TERMINAL 2
RED

TERMINAL 3
WHITE

TERMINAL 4
BLUE

TERMINAL 5
GREEN

TERMINAL 7
YELLOW (TOT)

TERMINAL 8
YELLOW (TOT)

TERMINAL 11
ORANGE (EPC)

TERMINAL 12
ORANGE (EPC)

**E40D TRANSMISSION WIRING HARNESS
TERMINAL LOCATIONS AND COLOR CODES**

SOLENOID
BODY CONNECTOR

E40D transmission test harness

rop across the solenoid. The Circuit open or shorted, or EEC driver failure exist.

CODE 98
FAILURE MODE AND EFFECTS MAGAGEMENT FAILURE/FAILED EPC OUTPUT DRIVER

During the Quick Test, the voltage through the EPC (electronic pressure control) solenoid is checked and compared to a voltage through the solenoid after a time delay. An error will be noted if the change tolerance is exceeded.

CODE 99
EPC SOLENOID CIRCUIT FAILURE/SHORT

The voltage measured across the electronic pressure control (EPC) solenoid is less than a calculated minimum voltage.

Drive Cycle Test

After performing the EEC–IV Quick Test, the following drive cycle test for checking the E40D transmission continuous codes should be performed. Faults have to appear 4 times consecutively for continuous codes 49, 59 and 69 to be set in memory and 5 times consecutively for continuous code 62 to be set in memory.

1. Record the EEC–IV Quick Test codes.
2. Verify that the transmission fluid level is correct and engine is at operating temperature.

3. With transmission in **OVERDRIVE** range, press the overdrive cancel switch (light should illuminate) and moderately accelerate from stop to 40 mph. This will allow the transmission to shift into 3rd gear. Hold speed and throttle opening steady for a minimum of 15 seconds (30 seconds above 4000 feet altitude).

4. Depress the overdrive cancel switch (light should turn off) and accelerate from 40 mph to 50 mph). This will allow the transmission to shift into 4th gear. Hold speed and the throttle position steady for a minimum of 15 seconds.

5. With transmission in 4th gear, maintaining steady speed and throttle opening, lightly apply and release the brake (to operate brake lights). Then hold speed and throttle steady for an additional 15 seconds minimum.

6. Bring vehicle to a stop and remain stopped for a minimum of 20 seconds with the transmission in **OVERDRIVE** range.

7. Perform test at least 5 times then perform EEC–IV Quick Test and record continuous codes. If the codes appear, refer to the Electrical Diagnosis Chart Index for appropriate Pinpoint Test.

NOTE: If any other service codes appear, service those codes first as they could affect the electrical operation of the transmission. After the servicing of any error codes perform the Quick Test again to recheck for the fault.

SERVICE CODES: 49, 59 AND 69 — PINPOINT TESTS AA

TEST STEPS		RESULTS ▶	ACTION TO TAKE
AA1	CHECK HARNESS CONNECTIONS		
	Check that the vehicle harness connector is fully engaged on the transmission bulkhead connector.	(OK) ▶	GO to **AA2**.
	Check that the vehicle harness connector terminals are fully engaged in the connector.	(OK) ▶	SERVICE or REPLACE as required. REPEAT QUICK TEST
AA2	CHECK RESISTANCE OF SOLENOID		
	NOTE: Refer to the E4OD Transmission Wiring Harness Terminal Locations and Color Codes preceding these Pinpoint Tests.	20-30 ohms ▶	GO to **AA3**.
	Install service jumper harness to the transmission bulkhead connector. (Do not pry vehicle harness connector off with a screwdriver.)*	High resistance ▶	REPLACE solenoid body and REPEAT QUICK TEST
	Connect ohmmeter negative lead to the black wire on the service harness and the positive lead to the white wire on the service harness. This is to test solenoid 1.		
	Record the resistance.		
	Resistance should be between 20-30 ohms.		
	Connect ohmmeter negative lead to the black wire on the service harness and the positive lead to the red wire on the service harness. This is to test solenoid 2.		
	Record the resistance.		
	Resistance should be between 20-30 ohms.		

SERVICE CODES: 49, 59 AND 69 — PINPOINT TESTS AA (Continued)

TEST STEPS		RESULTS	▶	ACTION TO TAKE
AA3	CHECK SOLENOID FOR SHORT TO GROUND			
	Install service jumper harness to transmission bulkhead connector. (Do not pry vehicle harness connector off with a screwdriver.)*	Continuity	▶	REPLACE Solenoid Body. REPEAT QUICK TEST.
	Check for continuity between an engine ground and appropriate wire with an ohmmeter or other low current tester (less than 200 milliamps).	No continuity	▶	GO to **AA4**.

Solenoid	Wire
1	White
2	Red

	Connection should show no continuity (infinite resistance).			
AA4	CHECK SOLENOID REGULATOR VALVE			
	Tear down to solenoid regulator valve.	(OK)	▶	CLEAR errors and REPEAT QUICK TEST
	Inspect solenoid regulator valve for damage or contamination.			
	Check for stuck or missing spring.			
		(OK̸)	▶	Service as required.

*Remove solenoid body connector by pushing on the center tab and pulling on the wiring harness.
Do not attempt to pry tab with a screwdriver. Remove heat shield from transmission before removing connector.

SERVICE CODES: 56 AND 66 — PINPOINT TESTS BB

TEST STEPS		RESULTS	▶	ACTION TO TAKE
BB1	CHECK HARNESS CONNECTIONS			
	Check that the vehicle harness connector is fully engaged on the transmission bulkhead connector.	(OK)	▶	GO to **BB2**.
	Check that the vehicle harness connector terminals are fully engaged in the connector.	(OK̸)	▶	SERVICE or REPLACE as required. REPEAT QUICK TEST
BB2	CHECK TOT SENSOR RESISTANCE			
	NOTE: Refer to the E4OD Transmission Wiring Harness Terminal locations and Color Codes preceding these Pinpoint Tests.	Resistance in range	▶	GO to **BB3**.
	Install service jumper harness to the transmission bulkhead connector. (Do not pry vehicle harness connector off with a screwdriver.)*	Resistance greater than 100K	▶	REPLACE solenoid body and REPEAT QUICK TEST

SERVICE CODES: 56 AND 66 — PINPOINT TESTS BB

TEST STEPS	RESULTS	▶	ACTION TO TAKE
BB2 CHECK TOT SENSOR RESISTANCE			
Carefully touch the transmission oil pan on the driver's side, away from the exhaust system, to approximate the temperature. After running the Quick Test, the transmission oil pan should be warm to the touch. (As a guide, warm to the touch is about 41-70 degrees C [105-158 degrees F]).	Resistance out of range	▶	PERFORM SECOND TEST listed in this step. REPEAT QUICK TEST
Connect ohmmeter negative lead and the positive lead to the yellow wires on the service harness.			
Record the resistance.			
Resistance should be approximately in the following ranges.			

TRANSMISSION FLUID TEMPERATURE

Degrees C	(Degrees F)	Resistance (Ohms)
0- 20	(32- 58)	37K- 100K
21- 40	(59-104)	16K- 37K
41- 70	(105-158)	5K- 16K
71- 90	(159-194)	2.7K- 5K
91-110	(195-230)	1.5K- 2.7K
111-130	(231-266)	0.8K- 1.5K

TEST STEPS	RESULTS	▶	ACTION TO TAKE
If the resistance was not the appropriate temperature range but was between 0.8K and 100K ohms, perform the following test. If the transmission is cold, run the transmission to heat it up. If the transmission is warm, allow the transmission to cool. Check TOT sensor resistance again. Compare the resistance with the initial resistance. Resistance should decrease if transmission was heated and should increase if transmission was allowed to cool. If the correct change in resistance occurs, REPEAT QUICK TEST.			
BB3 CHECK TOT SENSOR FOR SHORT TO GROUND			
Install service jumper harness to transmission bulkhead connector. (Do not pry vehicle harness connector off with a screwdriver.)*	Continuity	▶	REPLACE solenoid body and REPEAT QUICK TEST.
Check for continuity between engine ground and one yellow wire with an ohmmeter or other low current tester (less than 200 milliamps).			
Repeat the continuity check with the other yellow wire.	No continuity	▶	If code was a continuous code, inspect transmission fluid to determine if fluid is burnt. If burnt, teardown transmission and inspect for damage. SERVICE as required and REPEAT QUICK TEST
Connection should show no continuity (infinite resistance).			

*Remove solenoid body connector by pushing on the center tab and pulling on the wiring harness. Do not attempt to pry tab with a screwdriver. Remove heat shield from transmission before removing connector.

SERVICE CODE: 62 — PINPOINT TEST CC

TEST STEPS	RESULTS ▶	ACTION TO TAKE
CC1 CHECK HARNESS CONNECTIONS • Check that the vehicle harness connector is fully engaged on the transmission bulkhead connector. • Check that the vehicle harness connector terminals are fully engaged in the connector.	(OK) ▶ (OK̸) ▶	GO to **CC2**. SERVICE or REPLACE as required. REPEAT QUICK TEST
CC2 CHECK RESISTANCE OF SOLENOID **NOTE: Refer to the E4OD Transmission Wiring Harness Terminal locations and Color Codes preceding these Pinpoint Tests.** • Install service jumper harness to the transmission bulkhead connector. (Do not pry vehicle harness connector off with a screwdriver.)* • Connect ohmmeter negative lead to the black wire on the service harness and the positive lead to the green wire on the service harness. This is to test converter clutch solenoid. • Record the resistance. • Resistance should be between 20-30 ohms.	20-30 ohms ▶ High resistance ▶	GO to **CC3**. REPLACE solenoid body and REPEAT QUICK TEST
CC3 CHECK SOLENOID FOR SHORT TO GROUND • Install service jumper harness to transmission bulkhead connector. (Do not pry vehicle harness connector off with a screwdriver.)* • Check for continuity between engine ground and green wire with an ohmmeter or other low current tester (less than 200 milliamps).	No continuity ▶ Continuity ▶	GO to **CC4**. Replace Solenoid Body and REPEAT QUICK TEST
CC4 CHECK CONVERTER CLUTCH REGULATOR VALVE AND CONVERTER CLUTCH CONTROL VALVE • Tear down to converter clutch regulator valve and converter clutch control valve. • Inspect valves for damage or contamination. • Check for struck or missing spring.	(OK) ▶ (OK̸) ▶	CLEAR errors and REPEAT continuous drive tests. SERVICE as required.

*Remove solenoid body connector by pushing on the center tab and pulling on the wiring harness.
   Do not attempt to pry tab with a screwdriver. Remove heat shield from transmission before
removing connector.

SERVICE CODE: 67 — PINPOINT TEST EE

TEST STEPS	RESULTS ▶	ACTION TO TAKE
EE1 ADJUST MANUAL LEVER POSITION SENSOR Apply the parking brake. Place transmission in Neutral position.	(OK) ▶ (ØK) ▶	GO to **EE2**. ADJUST sensor according to adjustment procedures
EE2 CHECK OPERATION OF MANUAL LEVER POSITION SENSOR Insert Manual Lever Position Sensor test harness into the Manual Lever Position Sensor connector. Plug test box into power supply With transmission in Park, press the buttons on the box. The ____ light should light only when the P button is pushed. Repeat the test for R, N, ⒟, 2 and 1.	(OK) ▶ (ØK) ▶	REPEAT QUICK TEST REPLACE Manual Lever Position Sensor and REPEAT QUICK TEST

SERVICE CODES: 91, 92, 93 AND 94 — PINPOINT TEST GG

TEST STEPS	RESULTS ▶	ACTION TO TAKE
GG1 CHECK HARNESS CONNECTIONS Check that the vehicle harness connector is fully engaged on the transmission bulkhead connector. Check that the vehicle harness connector terminals are fully engaged in the connector.	(OK) ▶ (ØK) ▶	GO to **GG2**. SERVICE or REPLACE as required. REPEAT QUICK TEST
GG2 CHECK RESISTANCE OF SOLENOID NOTE: Refer to the E4OD Transmission Wiring Harness Terminal locations and Color Codes preceding these Pinpoint Tests Install service jumper harness to the transmission bulkhead connector. (Do not pry vehicle harness connector off with a screwdriver.)* Connect ohmmeter negative lead to the black wire on the service harness and the positive lead to the appropriate wire on the service harness.	20-30 ohms ▶ High resistance ▶	GO to **GG3**. REPLACE solenoid body and REPEAT QUICK TEST

Error Code	Wire
91	White
92	Red
93	Green
94	Blue

Record the resistance.

Resistance should be between 20-30 ohms.

SERVICE CODES: 91, 92, 93 AND 94 — PINPOINT TEST GG

TEST STEPS	RESULTS ▶	ACTION TO TAKE
GG3 CHECK SOLENOID FOR SHORT TO GROUND		
Install service jumper harness to transmission bulkhead connector. (Do not pry vehicle harness connector off with a screwdriver.)*	Continuity ▶	REPLACE solenoid body and REPEAT QUICK TEST
Check for continuity between engine ground and appropriate wire with an ohmmeter or other low current tester (less than 200 milliamps).	No continuity ▶	REPEAT QUICK TEST
Error Code / Wire 91 White, 92 Red, 93 Green, 94 Blue		Problem should not reoccur if the solenoid body passed previous tests.
Connection should show no continuity (infinite resistance).		

*Remove solenoid body connector by pushing on the center tab and pulling on the wiring harness. Do not attempt to pry tab with a screwdriver. Remove heat shield from transmission before removing connector.

SERVICE CODES: 98 AND 99 — PINPOINT TEST HH

TEST STEPS	RESULTS ▶	ACTION TO TAKE
HH1 CHECK HARNESS CONNECTIONS		
Check that the vehicle harness connector is fully engaged on the transmission bulkhead connector.	(OK) ▶	GO to **HH2**.
Check that the vehicle harness connector terminals are fully engaged in the connector.	(not OK) ▶	SERVICE or REPLACE as required. REPEAT QUICK TEST
HH2 CHECK RESISTANCE OF SOLENOID		
NOTE: Refer to the E4OD Transmission Wiring Harness Terminal locations and Color Codes preceding these Pinpoint Tests.	4.0-6.5 ohms ▶	GO to **HH3**.
Install service jumper harness to the transmission bulkhead connector. (Do not pry vehicle harness connector off with a screwdriver.)*	High resistance ▶	REPLACE solenoid body and REPEAT QUICK TEST
Connect ohmmeter negative lead and positive lead to the orange wires on the service harness.		
Record the resistance. Resistance should be between 4.0-6.5 ohms.		
HH3 CHECK SOLENOID FOR SHORT TO GROUND		
Install service jumper harness to transmission bulkhead connector. (Do not pry vehicle harness connector off with a screwdriver.)*	Continuity ▶	REPLACE solenoid body and REPEAT QUICK TEST
Check for continuity between engine ground and one of the orange wires with an ohmmeter or other low current tester (less than 200 milliamps).		
Repeat the continuity check with the other orange wire.	No continuity ▶	REPEAT QUICK TEST Problem should not reoccur if the solenoid body passed previous tests.
Connection should show no continuity (infinite resistance).		

*Remove solenoid body connector by pushing on the center tab and pulling on the wiring harness. Do not attempt to pry tab with a screwdriver. Remove heat shield from transmission before removing connector.

ON CAR SERVICES

Services

FLUID CHANGE

The conditions under which the vehicle is operated is the main consideration in determining how often the transmission fluid should be changed. Different driving conditions result in different transmission fluid temperatures. These temperatures affect change intervals.

If the vehicle is driven under severe service conditions, change the fluid and filter every 40,000 miles. If the vehicle is not used under severe service conditions, change the fluid and replace the filter every 100,000 miles.

OIL PAN

Removal and Installation

1. Raise the vehicle and support safely.
2. Place a drain pan under the transmission.
3. Loosen the oil pan attaching bolts and drain the fluid from the transmission.
4. When fluid has drained to level of pan flange, remove the rest of the pan bolts working from the right hand side and allow it to drop and drain slowly.
5. When all fluid has drained from the transmission, remove and thoroughly clean the pan. Discard the gasket.
6. Place a new gasket on the pan and install the pan on the transmission.
7. Lower the vehicle refill the transmission. Start the engine and check the fluid level.

EXTENSION HOUSING GASKET

Removal and Installation

1. Raise and support the vehicle safely.
2. Remove the front driveshaft, if equipped. Remove the rear driveshaft.
3. Remove transmission mounting pad nuts and bolts.
4. On 4WD models only, remove shift linkage from transfer case shift lever.
5. On 4WD models only, remove 4WD drive switch connector from transfer case, use care not to overextend tabs.
6. Disconnect wire harness locators from extension housing wire bracket.
7. On 4WD models only, remove wire harness locators from left hand side of the crossmember.
8. Remove the speedometer cable.
9. On 4WD models only, remove transfer case vent hose from the detent place.
10. On 4WD models only, place transmission stand fixture on universal high lift transmission jack or equivalent and position under transfer case.
11. Remove the 9 extension housing bolts using a 13mm box wrench or equivalent.
12. Slide the transfer case rearward and downward to remove, and discard extension housing gasket from housing and transfer case mating surfaces.
13. Position the extension housing gasket on the extension housing.
14. Raise the extension housing into position and install the 9 extension housing bolts. Tighten to 20–29 ft. lbs.

NOTE: On 4WD models only, attach transfer case vent hose to detent plate and install the 4WD drive connector.

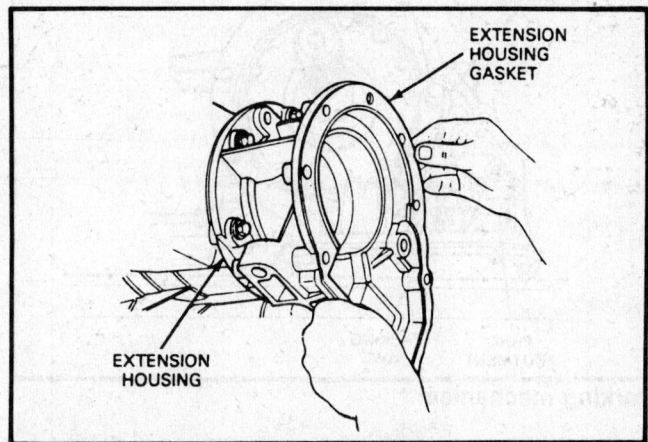

Installing extension housing gasket

15. Install the wire harness locator into extension housing wire bracket.
16. Install the transmission mounting pad bolts and nuts and torque to 60–80 ft. lbs. for all F Series or 50–70 ft. lbs. for all E Series.
17. Remove the universal high lift transmission jack or equivalent. Install the speedometer cable.
18. Install the front driveshaft, if equipped. Install the rear driveshaft.
19. Start the engine and check the fluid level. Fill the transmission to the proper level with the specified fluid.

PARKING MECHANISM

Removal and Installation

1. Raise and support the vehicle safely. Remove the extension housing from the transmission.
2. Remove the 2 bolts using a 13mm socket or equivalent from the park rod guide plate.
3. Remove the parking pawl return spring, pin and parking pawl from the transmission case.
4. Remove the Torx® head bolt (40A bit) and the parking pawl abutment.
5. Install the parking pawl, pin and the return spring. The spring end rests on the inside surface of case.
6. Install the parking pawl abutment with Torx® head bolt (40A bit). Torque to 16–20 ft. lbs.
7. Using a 13mm socket or equivalent, attach the park rod guide plate with 2 bolts and washers. Tighten to 16–20 ft. lbs. Check that the plate dimple is facing inward.
8. Install the extension housing and refill the transmission. Start engine and check the fluid level.

VALVE BODY AND INTERMEDIATE BAND SERVO

Removal and Installation

1. Raise and support the vehicle safely. Remove the solenoid body connector heat shield, loosen both bolts using an 8mm socket or equivalent.
2. Remove the slotted heat shield and the solenoid body connector by pushing on the center tab and pulling on the wire harness.

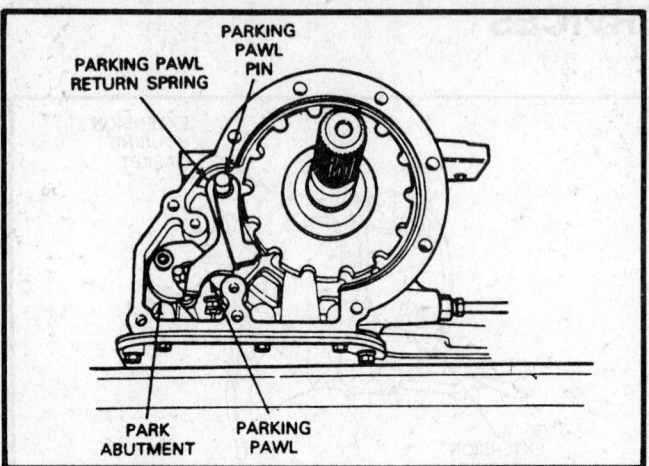

Parking mechanism

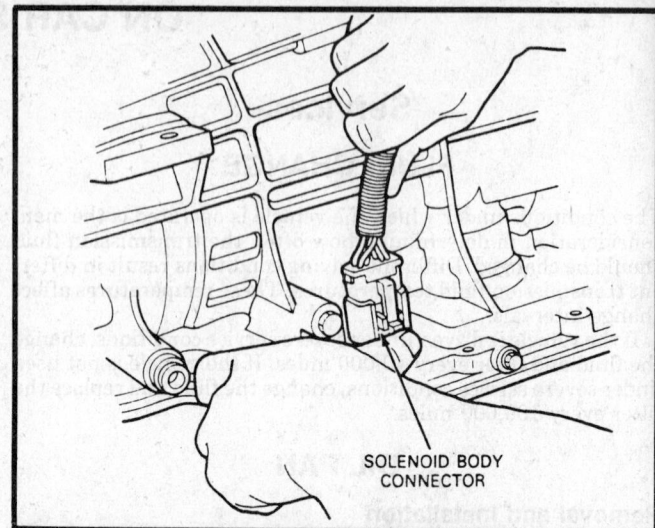

Removing solenoid electrical connector

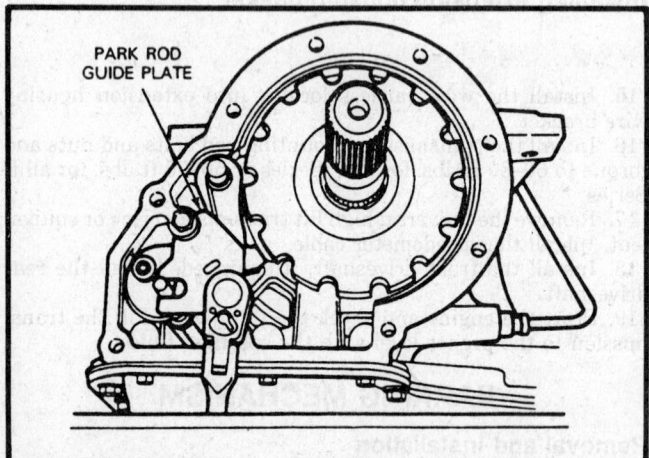

Removing park rod guide plate

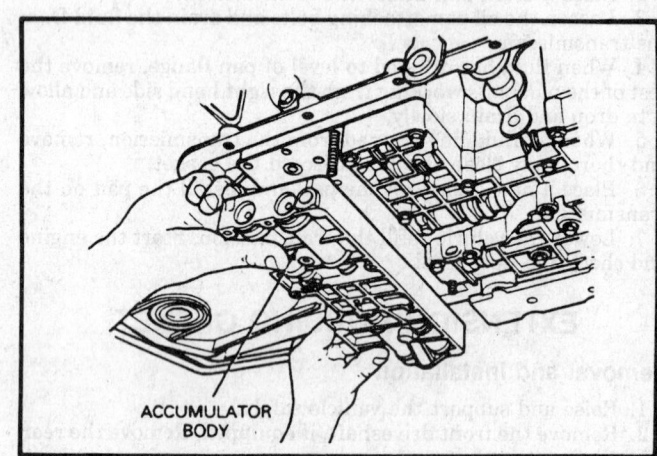

Removing accumulator body

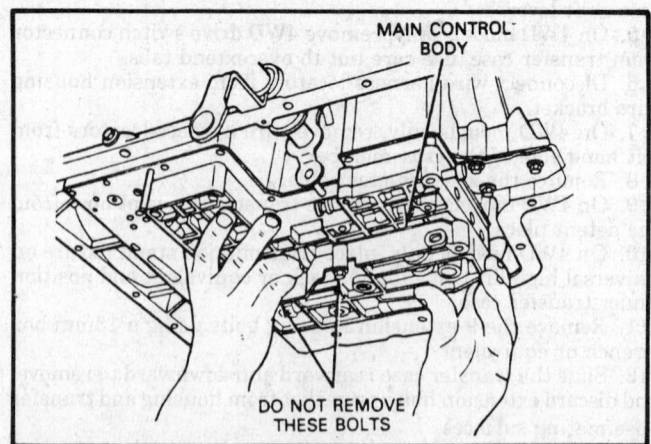

Removing main control body

NOTE: Do not attempt to pry tab with pry bar. Remove the heat shield from the transmission before attempting to remove the connector.

3. Check the electrical connectors for terminal conditions, corrosion and contamination. Service as required.

4. Remove the 15 back and side pan bolts using a 10mm socket or equivalent.

5. Place a drain pan or equivalent under the transmission pan. Loosen transmission pan bolts and remove the transmission pan.

6. Remove the filter and seal assembly by carefully pulling and rotating the filter as necessary. If seal remains in bore, carefully remove using O-ring tool T71P–19703–C or equivalent. Discard the filter and seal.

7. Remove the 11 accumulator body bolts using an 8mm socket or equivalent and 2 nuts using a 10mm socket or equivalent. Remove the accumulator body.

8. Remove the 14 main control body bolts using an 8mm socket or equivalent and 2 nuts using a 10mm socket or rquivalent. Remove the main control body.

NOTE: Do not remove the 2 center bolts on the main control body.

9. Remove the 9 solenoid body bolts using a Torx® (30A bit)

and 1 nut using a 10mm socket or equivalent. Push down on the solenoid body receptacle to remove solenoid body.

10. Remove the solenoid screen by turning counterclockwise and pulling out. Remove the 3 reinforcing plate bolts using an 8mm socket or equivalent. Remove the plate.

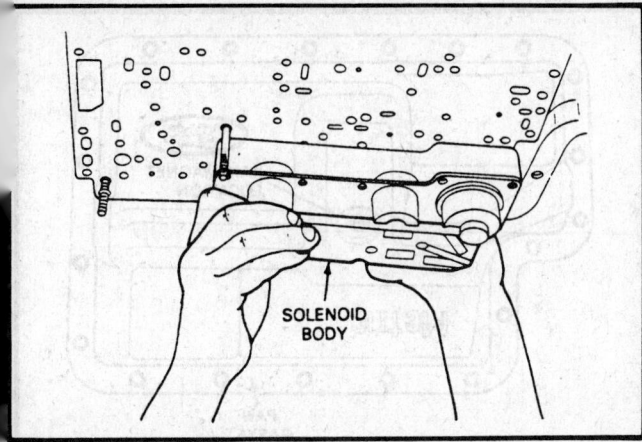

Removing solenoid body

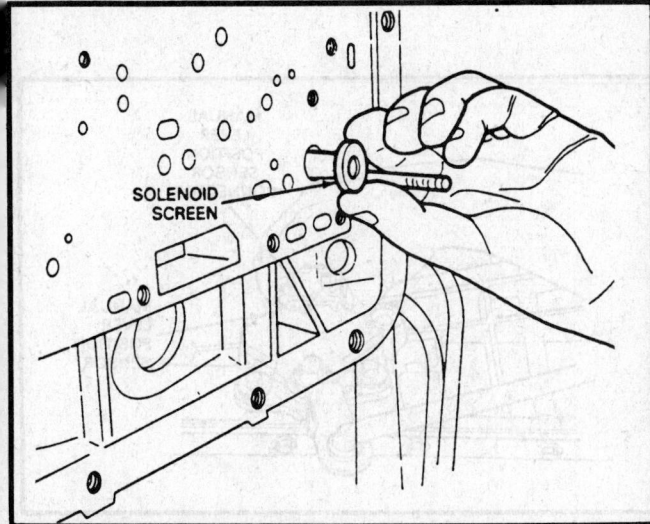

Removing solenoid screen

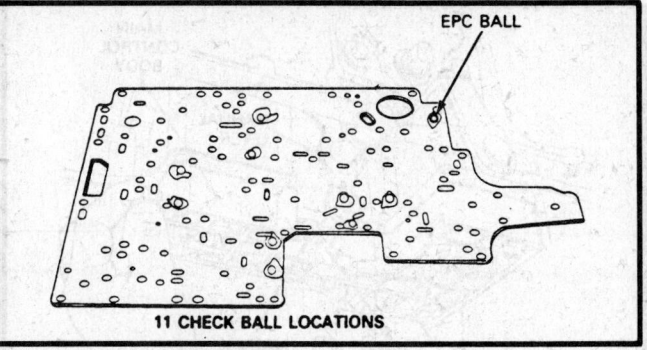

Check ball locations

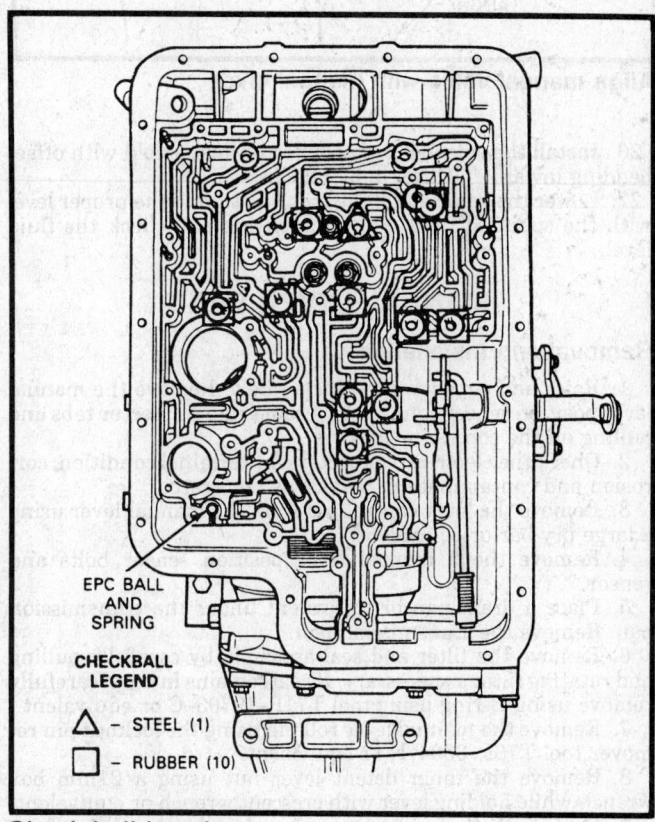

Check ball locations

11. Carefully lower the separator plate and gasket so that check balls, EPC ball and spring are retained.

12. Remove the servo snapring and retaining plate, piston and rod assembly and servo spring.

13. Install the servo spring, servo piston and rod assembly.

14. Install the servo retaining plate and snapring. Grease the separator plate with petroleum jelly to hold new separator to control gasket.

15. Position the new separator to case gasket on separator plate.

16. Lubricate the separator case gasket with petroleum jelly.

17. Grease the valve body pockets with petroleum jelly. Put 11 check balls (10 rubber and 1 steel), EPC spring and greased (petroleum jelly) EPC ball into position.

18. Install the separator plate and gaskets. Install the 3 reinforcing plate bolts using an 8mm socket or equivalent. Tighten to 80–100 inch lbs.

NOTE: Check the location of check balls and EPC ball at this point of the installation. The stamped marking UP on the reinforcing plate must be visible.

19. Install the solenoid screen and lock in place by turning clockwise. Install the main control body over the studs. Align the manual valve with the manual lever.

20. Attach the valve body with 2 nuts and 14 bolts. Torque to 80–100 inch lbs.

21. Install the accumulator body over the studs and attach with 2 nuts and 11 bolts. Torque to 80–100 inch lbs.

22. Install the solenoid body over the stud and attach with 9 Torx® (30A bit) bolts and 1 nut. Torque to 80–100 inch lbs.

NOTE: Prior to installing the solenoid body assembly, coat the case connector bore with M1C172–A grease or equivalent.

23. Install a new filter and a seal assembly by lubricating the seal with transmission fluid and pressing the filter into place. Position the gasket onto pan and check the condition and placement of pan magnet.

24. Install the 20 pan bolts. Tighten to 10–12 ft. lbs.

25. Completely seat the solenoid body connector into the solenoid valve body receptacle. An audible click sound indicates proper installation of this connector.

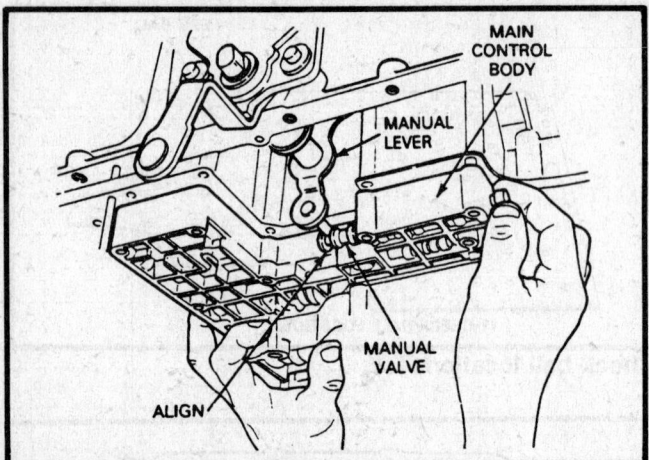

Align manual valve with manual lever

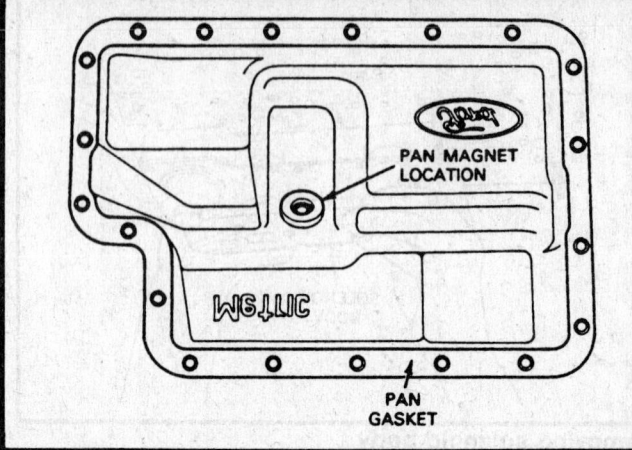

Pan magnet location

26. Install the solenoid body connector heat shield with offset bending inward. Tighten to 6–9 ft. lbs.

27. Lower the vehicle. Fill the transmission to the proper level with the specified fluid. Start the engine and check the fluid level.

MANUAL LEVER SEAL

Removal and Installation

1. Raise and support the vehicle safely. Remove the manual lever position sensor connector by squeezing connector tabs and pulling on the connector harness.

2. Check the electrical connectors for terminal condition, corrosion and contamination. Service as requirerd.

3. Remove the lever control rod from the manual lever using a large pry bar or equivalent.

4. Remove the 2 manual lever position sensor bolts and sensor.

5. Place a drain pan or rquivalent under the transmission pan. Remove the transmission pan.

6. Remove the filter and seal assembly by carefully pulling and rotating filter as necessary. If seal remains in bore, carefully remove using O-ring using tool T71P–19703–C or equivalent.

7. Remove the manual lever roll pin using the locknut pin remover tool T78P–3504–N or equivalent.

8. Remove the inner detent lever nut using a 21mm box wrench while holding lever with crescent wrench or equivalent.

9. Remove the inner detent lever and park actuating rod assembly from manual lever. Remove manual the lever.

10. Remove the manual lever seal using a pry tool, being careful not to score the transmission bore.

11. Clean bore opening with cleaner and install a new seal using shift lever seal replacer tool T74P–77498–A or equivalent.

12. Install the manual lever, inner detent lever, park actuating rod assembly and nut. The inner detent lever must be sealed on flats of the shaft and rod assembly must be through guide plate. The inner lever pin must be aligned with manual lever.

13. Torque the inner detent lever nut using a 21mm crows foot tool while holding lever with a crescent wrench or equivalent. Torque to 30–40 ft. lbs.

14. Install the manual lever roll pin and manual lever position sensor with 2 bolts and washers. Do not tighten bolts at this time. Align manual lever position sensor for **N** gear position using gear position sensor adjuster tool T89T–70010–J or equivalent. Tighten bolts to 55–75 inch lbs.

15. Install the manual lever position sensor connector. An audible click sound indicates proper installation.

16. Install the shift linkage.

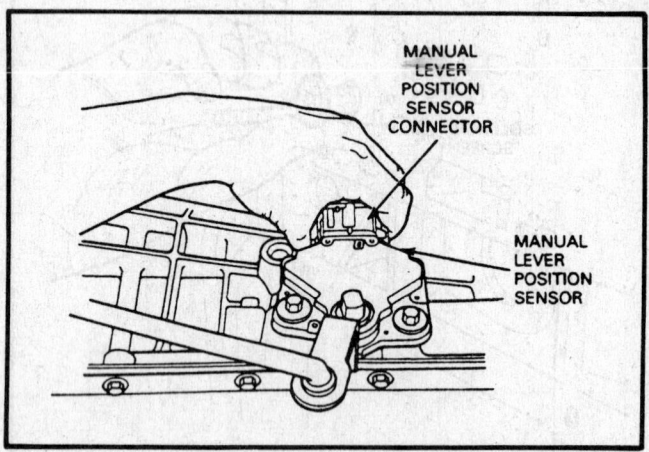

Removing manual lever position sensor connector

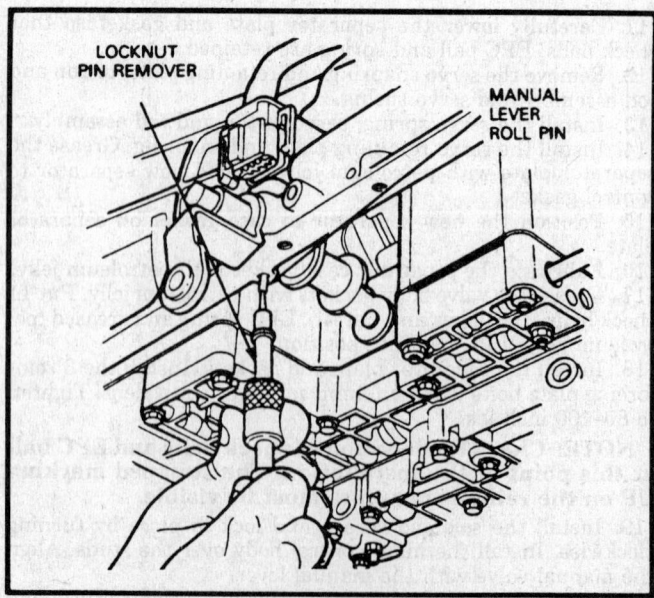

Removing manual lever roll pin

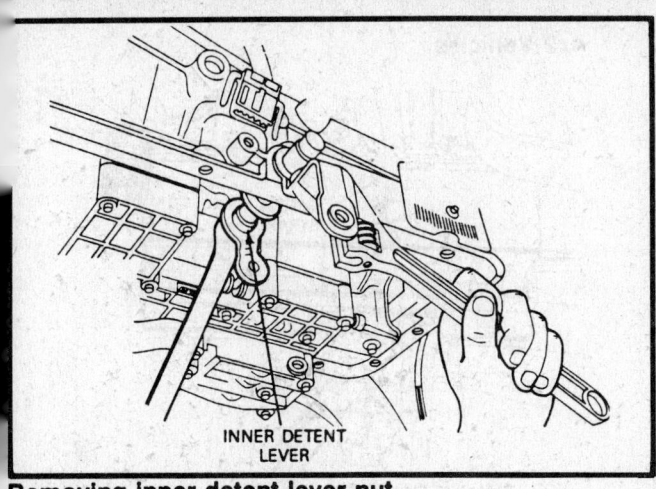

Removing inner detent lever nut

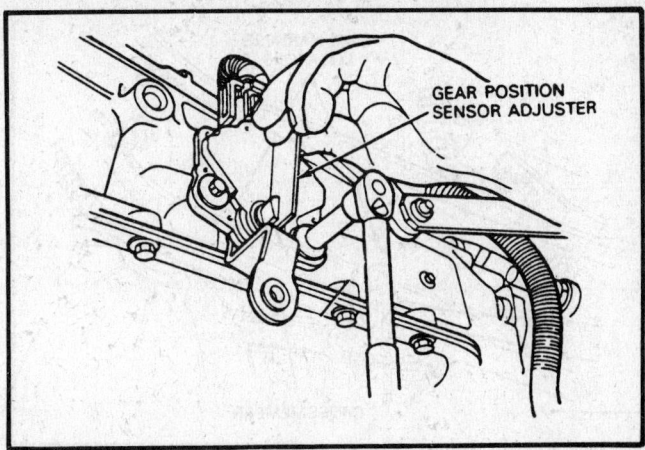

GEAR POSITION SENSOR ADJUSTER

Align manual lever position sensor with special tool

17. Install a new filter and seal assembly by lubricating the seal with transmission fluid and pressing the filter into place. Using petroleum jelly to hold new pan gasket, position gasket onto pan. Check condition and placement of pan magnet.

18. Install the transmission pan. Torque to 10–12 ft. lbs.
19. Lower the vehicle and refill the transmission. Start the engine and check the fluid level.

REMOVAL AND INSTALLATION

TRANSMISSION REMOVAL

1. Disconnect negative battery cable at the battery. Remove the transmission dipstick.
2. Place transmission selector in **N** position. Raise and safely support the vehicle.
3. On 4WD models only, remove the front driveshaft. Remove the rear driveshaft. On F-Super Duty vehicles, remove the transmission mounted parking brake.
4. Disconnect the shift linkage. On 4WD models only, remove the shift linkage from transfer case shift lever.
5. Remove the manual lever position sensor connector by squeezing connector tabs and pulling on connector.

NOTE: Do not attempt to pry tab with pry bar. Remove the heat shield from the transmission before attempting to remove the connector.

6. Remove the solenoid body connector heat shield.
7. Remove the solenoid body connector by pushing on the center tab and pulling on the wire harness.
8. On 4WD models only, remove the 4WD drive switch connector from the transfer case. Use care not to overextend tabs.
9. Remove the wire harness locator from the extension housing wire bracket. On 4WD models only, remove the wire harness locators from left hand side of the crossmember.
10. Remove the speedometer cable and the lower converter bolts.
11. Remove the rear engine cover plate bolts. Remove the starter.
12. Using a $^{15}/_{16}$ socket or equivalent, rotate the crankshaft bolt to gain access to converter nuts. Remove the 4 converter mounting nuts and discard the nuts.
13. Place a transmission stand fixture tool 014–00763 or equivalent on a universal transmission jack and position under the transmission.

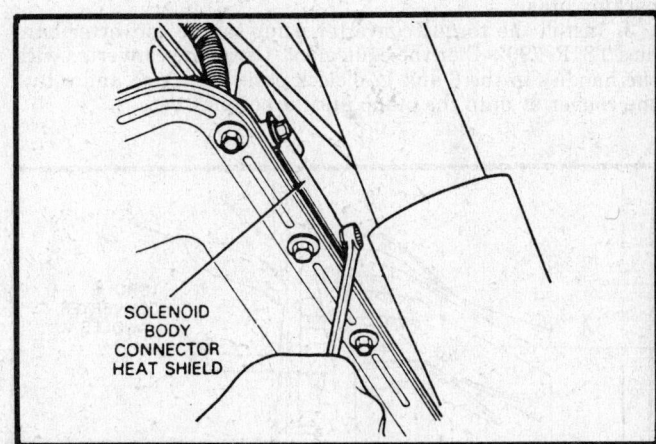

SOLENOID BODY CONNECTOR HEAT SHIELD

Removing heat shield

— **CAUTION** —

Use a safety strap to secure the transmission to the transmission stand fixture.

14. Loosen the 2 rear transmission mounting pad nuts. Remove the retaining bolts and remove the crossmember from the transmission.
15. Remove the transmission cooling lines from the case. Cap cooling lines and plug fittings at transmission.
16. Remove the 6 bell housing bolts. Back out the converter pilot from the flywheel and gently lower the transmission while observing for obstructions.
17. Install torque converter handles, T81P–8902–C or equivalent on the converter with handles in the 6 and 12 o'clock positions.

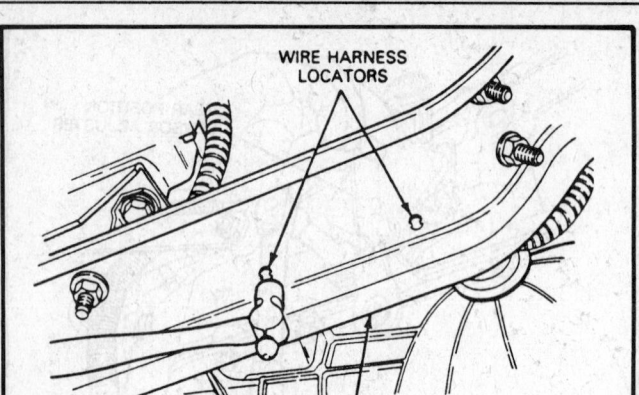

Wire harness—4x4 models

18. Remove the transmission filler tube. On 4WD models only, remove the transfer case vent hose form detent bracket and the transfer case from the transmission. On F-Super Duty models, remove the transmission mounted parking brake.

TRANSMISSION INSTALLATION

1. Place the transmission onto a transmission stand fixture tool 014–4–763 or equivalent.
2. On 4WD models only, install the transfer case to transmission. On F-Super Duty models, install transmission mounted parking brake.
3. Install the torque converter using torque converter handles T81P–7902–C or the equivalent. Carry the converter with the handles in the 6 and 12 o'clock positions. Push and rotate the converter onto the pump until it bottoms out.

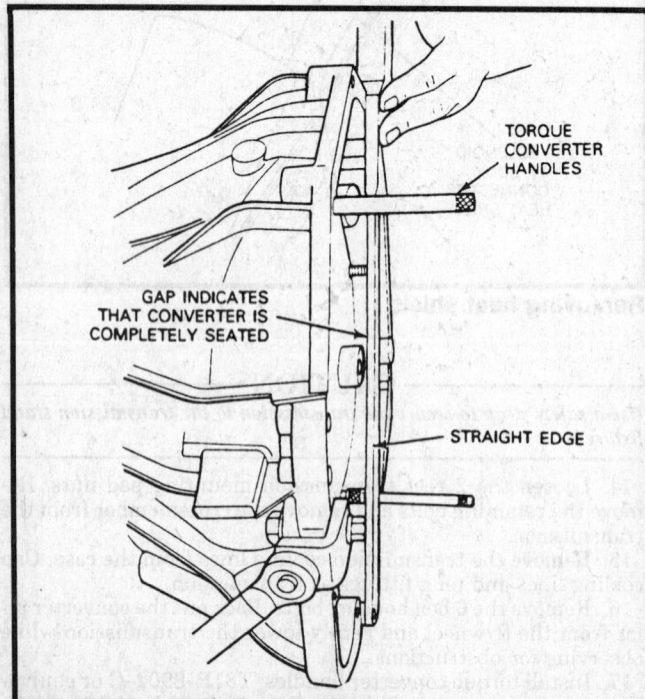

Checking converter installation

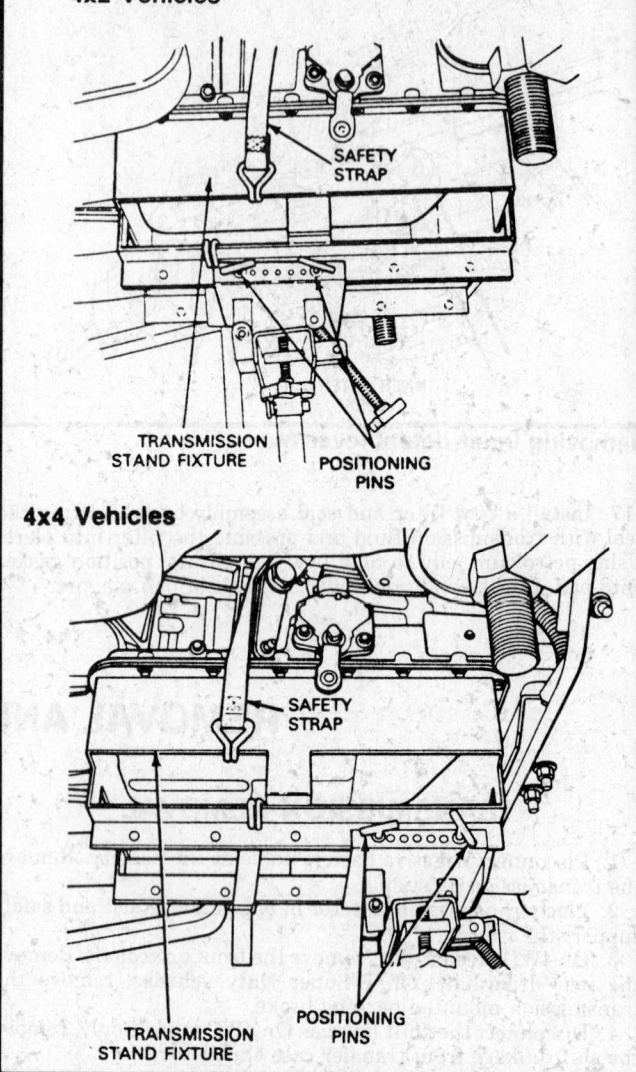

Placement of positioning pins

NOTE: Check the seating of the converter by placing a straightedge across the bell housing. There must be a gap between the converter pilot face and the straightedge.

4. Remove the converter handles. Check the condition of filler tube O-ring, if damaged or worn replace the O-ring. Install the filler tube.
5. Rotate the converter studs to align with flywheel mounting holes. Raise transmission into position while observing for any obstructions. Do not allow converter drive flats to disengage from pump gear. Use rubber converter drain plug cover or equivalent to aid in the alignment of the converter studs.

NOTE: Use care not to damage the flywheel and convert pilot. The converter must rest squarely against the flywheel. This indicates that the converter pilot is not binding in the engine crankshaft.

6. Alternately snug up the bell housing bolts and final torque to 40–50 ft. lbs.
7. Install the rubber converter drain plug cover and transmission cooling lines. Tighten lines to 18–23 ft. lbs.

8. Install the crossmember and the transmission retaining bolts. Remove the safety strap and the universal high lift transmission jack.

9. Rotate the crankshaft to gain access to converter studs. Install new stud nuts and torque to 20–30 ft. lbs.

10. Install the starter motor, rear engine plate cover and lower dust cover. Tighten to 12–16 ft. lbs.

11. Install the speedometer cable.

12. Completely seat the solenoid body connector into solenoid valve body recepticle. An audible click sound indicates proper installation.

13. Install the solenoid body connector heat shield with offset bending inward. Tighten to 6–9 ft. lbs.

14. On 4WD models only, install wire harness locators into crossmember.

15. Install the wire harness locator into extension housing wire bracket.

16. On 4WD models only, install the 4WD drive switch connector and connect the transfer case shift linkage.

17. Install the manual lever position sensor connector. An audible click sound indicates proper installation.

18. Install the shift linkage. On 4WD models only, install the shift rod to transfer case shift lever.

19. Install the rear driveshaft and install the front driveshaft on 4WD models.

20. Lower the vehicle, connect the negative battery cable and refill the transmission. Start the engine and check the fluid level.

21. Road test vehicle for proper operation and correct shift patterns.

BENCH OVERHAUL

Before Disassembly

When servicing the unit, it is recommended that as each part is disassembled, it is cleaned in solvent and dried with compressed air. All oil passages should be blown out and checked for obstructions. Disassembly and reassembly of this unit and its parts must be done on a clean work bench. As is the case when repairing any hydraulically operated unit, cleanliness is of the utmost importance. Keep bench, tools, parts and hands clean at all times. Also, before installing bolts into aluminum parts, always dip the threads into clean transmission oil. Anti-seize compound can also be used to prevent bolts from galling the aluminum and seizing. Always use a torque wrench to keep from stripping the threads. Take care with the seals when installing them, especially the smaller O-rings. The slightest damage can cause leaks. Aluminum parts are very susceptible to damage so great care should be exercised when handling them. The internal snaprings should be expanded and the external snaprings compressed if they are to be reused. This will help insure proper seating when installed. Be sure to replace any O-ring, gasket, or seal that is removed. Lubricate all parts with the specified transmission fluid when assembling.

Converter Inspection

The torque converter is welded together and cannot be disassembled. Check the torque converter for damage or cracks and replace, if necessary. Remove any rust from the pilot hub and boss of the converter.

When internal wear or damage has occurred in the transmission, metal particles, clutch plate material, or band material may have been carried into the converter. These contaminants are a major cause of recurring transmission troubles and must be removed from the system before the transmission is put back into service. The converter must be cleaned by using the torque converter cleaner tool 014–00028 or equivalent. Under no circumstances should an attempt be made to clean converter by hand agitation with solvent.

CONVERTER ENDPLAY CHECK

1. Insert tool T80L–7902–A or equivalent into the converter pump drive hub until it bottoms out.

2. Expand the sleeve in the turbine spline by tightening the threaded inner post until the tool is securely locked into the spline.

3. Attach a dial indicator with bracketry tool–4201–C or

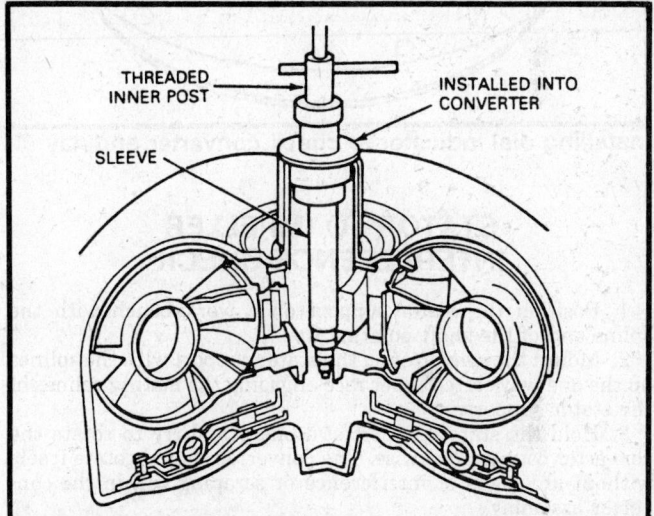

THREADED INNER POST
INSTALLED INTO CONVERTER
SLEEVE

Checking converter endplay

equivalent to the tool. Position the indicator button on the converter pump drive hub and set the dial face at zero.

4. Lift the tool upward as far as it will go and note the indicator reading. The indicator reading is the total endplay which the turbine and stator share. Replace the converter unit if the total endplay exceeds the limits. The torque converter endplay on a new or rebuilt converter should be 0.021 in. (0.533mm) maximum. The torque converter endplay on a used converter should be 0.50 in. (1.25mm) maximum.

5. Loosen the threaded inner post to free the tool, and then remove the tool from the converter.

TORQUE CONVERTER ONE-WAY CLUTCH INSPECTION

In order to test the converter one-way clutch, insert fingers into the torque converter. Reaching the first splined segment, attempt to spin it. The segment should rotate freely clockwise and should not turn counterclockwise without the converter turning with it. If the segment rotates freely counterclockwise or does not rotate freely clockwise, the one-way clutch has failed and the torque converter should be replaced.

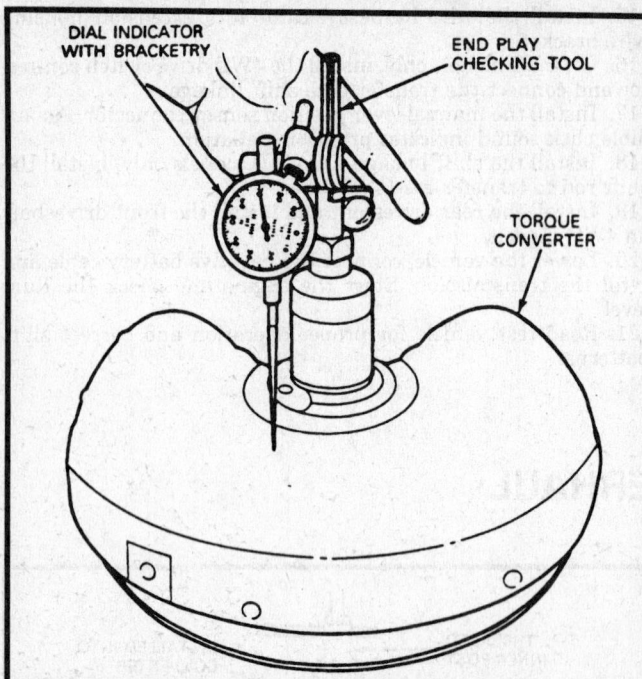

Installing dial indicator to check converter endplay

STATOR TO IMPELLER INTERFERENCE CHECK

1. Position the stator support on a work bench with the spline end of the shaft pointing up.
2. Mount the converter on the stator support with the splines on the one-way clutch inner race engaging the mating splines of the stator support.
3. Hold the stator support stationary and try to rotate the converter counterclockwise. The converter should rotate freely without any signs of interference or scraping within the converter assembly.
4. If there is an indication of scraping, the trailing edges of the stator blades may be interfering with the leading edges of the impeller blades. In such cases, replace the converter. The stator support may remain in pump assembly during this test.

STATOR TO TURBINE INTERFERENCE CHECK

1. Position the converter on the work bench front side down.
2. Install a stator support to engage the mating splines of the stator support shaft.
3. Install the input shaft, engaging the splines with the turbine hub.
4. Hold the stator shaft stationary and attempt to rotate the turbine with the input shaft. The turbine should rotate freely in both directions without any signs of interference or scraping noise.
5. If interference exists, the stator front thrust washer may be worn, allowing the stator to hit the turbine. In such cases, the converter must be replaced.
6. Check the converter crankshaft pilot for nicks or damaged surfaces that could cause interference when installing the converter into the crankshaft.
7. Check the converter impeller hub for nicks or sharp edges that would damage the pump seal. The stator support may remain in pump assembly during this test.

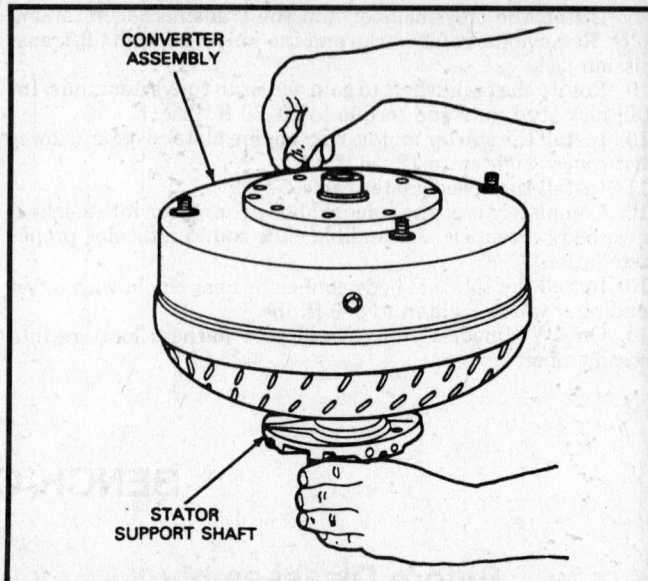

Checking stator to impeller interference

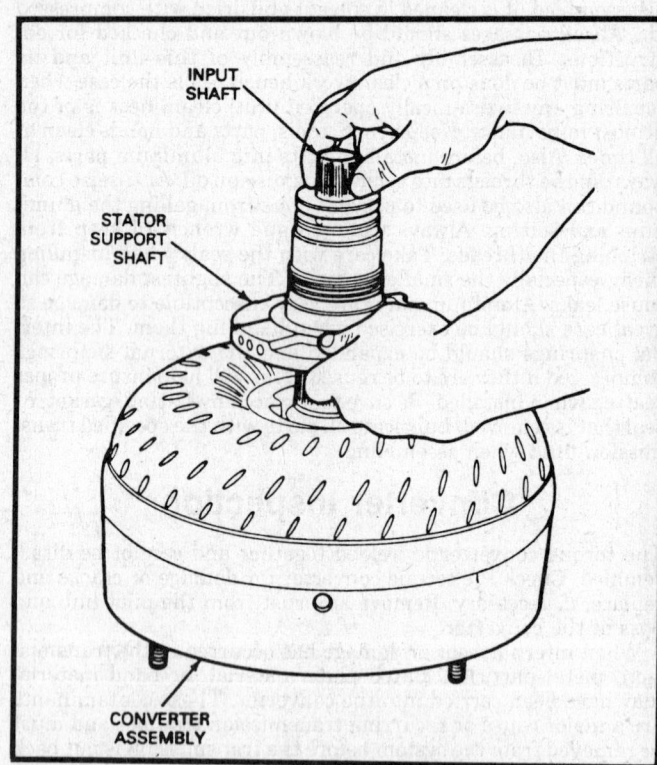

Checking stator to turbine interference

Transmission Disassembly

1. Remove the input shaft from transmission and mount the transmission in a suitable holding fixture.
2. Thoroughly clean the solenoid body connector area to avoid contamination. Rotate the transmission so that pan is facing up. Remove the pan and gasket, discard the gasket.
3. Remove the filter and seal assembly by carefully pulling and rotating the filter as necessary. If seal remains in bore, carefully remove using O-ring tool T71P–19703–C or equivalent.

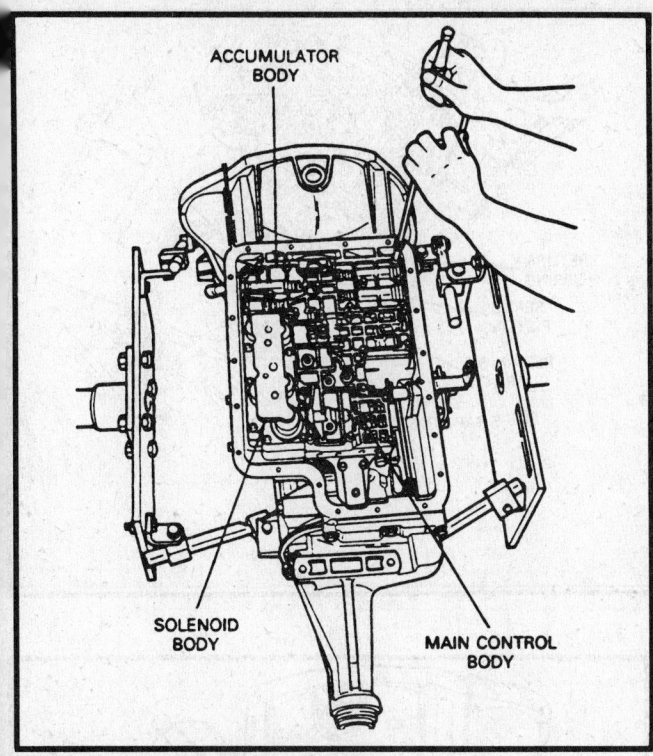

Internal component locations

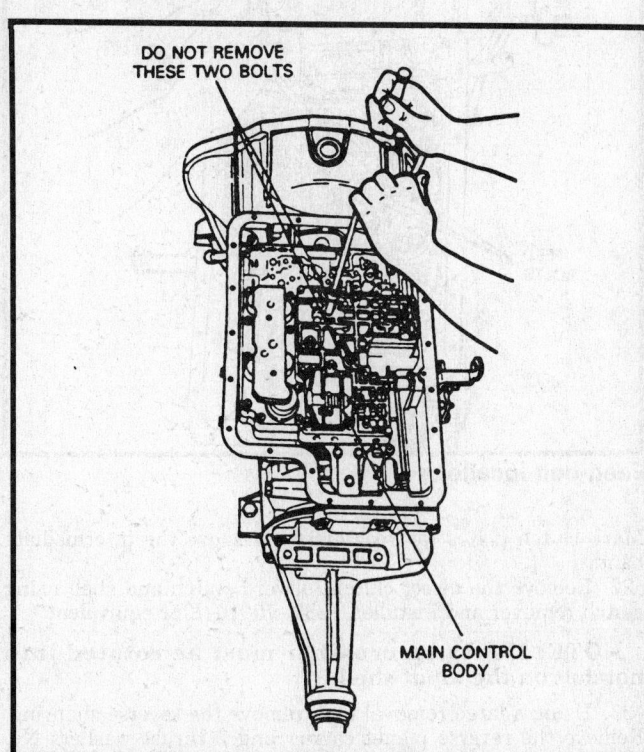

Main control body locations

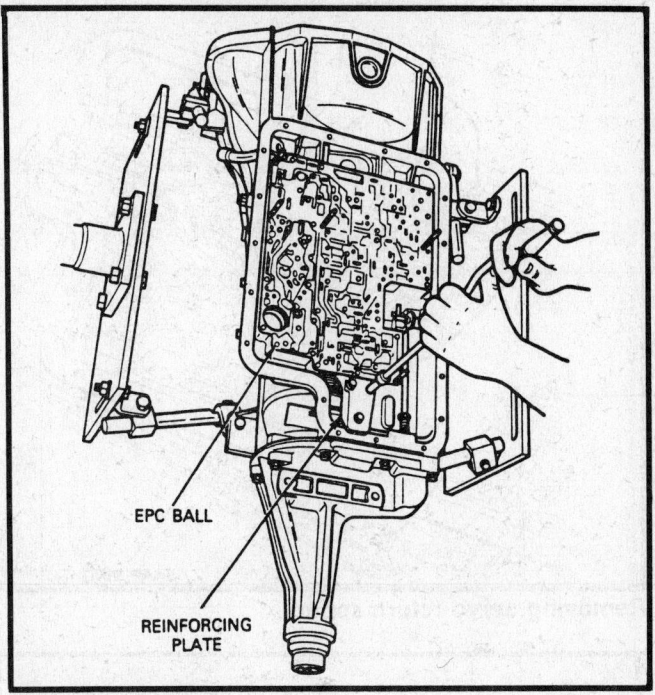

EPC ball location

6. Push up on the solenoid body connector while removing solenoid body. Remove the solenoid screen, by turning counterclockwise and pull out.

7. Remove the 3 reinforcing plate bolts and remove the plate.

NOTE: The EPC ball is spring loaded under the separator plate.

8. Remove the separator plate, 2 gaskets, EPC ball and blowoff spring, discard gaskets. Remove 1 steel and 10 rubber check balls from transmission, using a small tool. Do not damage the rubber check balls.

9. Remove the servo snapring, retaining plate, piston/rod assembly and servo spring. Apply slight downward pressure to plate while remove snapring.

10. Remove the 3 feed bolts. Discard the feed bolts.

11. Rotate the transmission so that bell housing is facing up. Remove 9 pump bolts. Discard the pump bolt washers.

12. Use 2 threaded holes in pump and install pump puller adapter T89T–70010–A or equivalent. Install a slide hammer T59L–100–B or equivalent into adapter and remove the pump.

13. Remove the pump gasket and No. 7D014 thrust washer. Discard the gasket.

14. Lift out the coast clutch assembly. Remove the needle bearing assembly No. 7E486 between the front pump and the sun gear.

15. Remove the large snapring using a large removal tool.

16. Remove the overdrive pressure plate and clutch pack and mark for reassembly. Remove the overdrive ring gear and center shaft assembly and needle bearing assembly No. 7G178.

17. Install the clutch spring compressor T89T–70010–F or equivalent into the case. Tighten center bolt to 65 inch lbs.

18. Remove the large snapring with a large removal tool. Loosen the spring compressor center bolt and remove the compressor tool.

19. Remove the intermediate/overdrive cylinder assembly. Remove the intermediate return spring.

20. Remove the center support and thrust washer No. 7L326.

21. Remove the intermediate pressure plate and clutch plates.

4. Remove the accumulator body and the main control body

NOTE: Do not remove the 2 center bolts.

5. Remove the 9 solenoid body bolts using a Torx® (30A bit) and 1 nut.

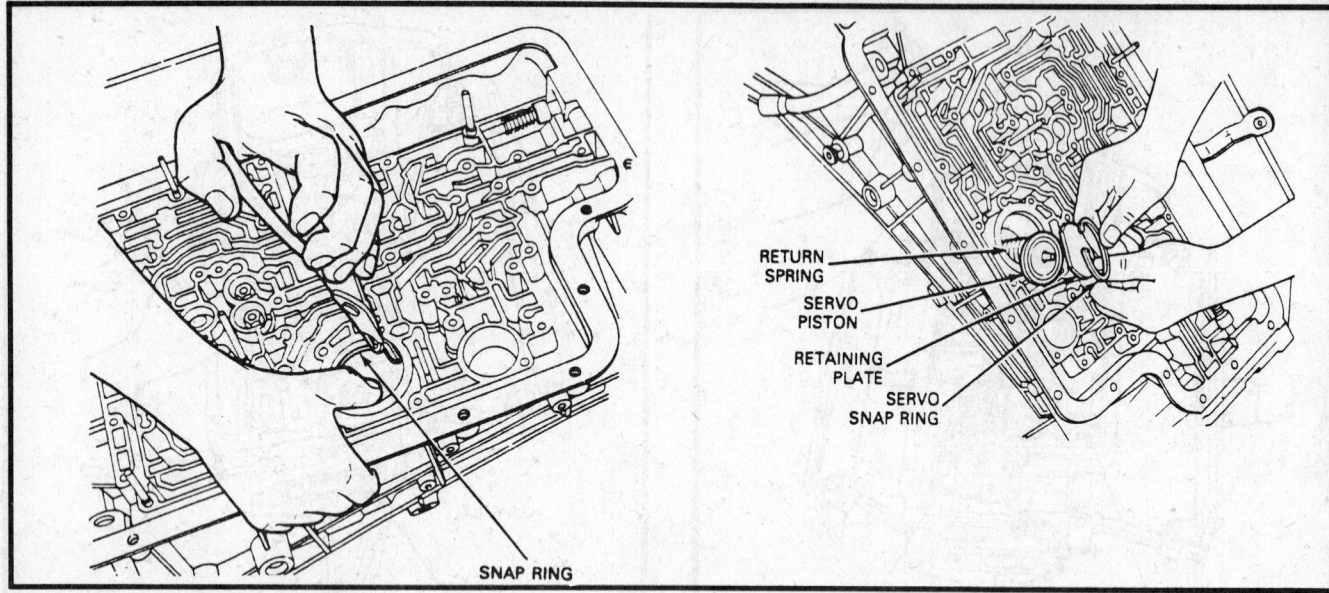

RETURN SPRING
SERVO PISTON
RETAINING PLATE
SERVO SNAP RING

SNAP RING

Removing servo return spring

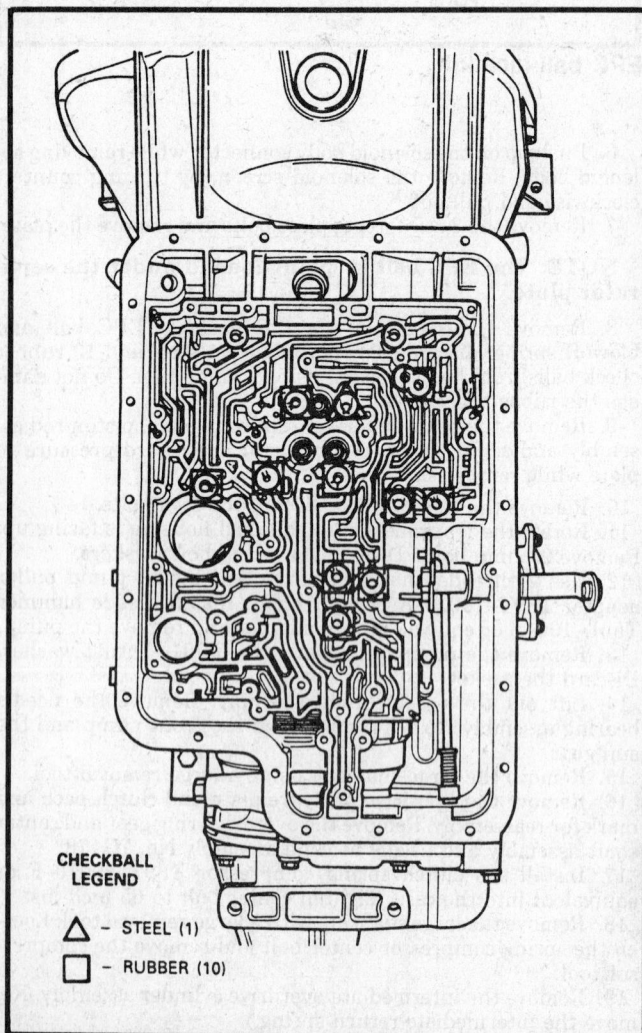

CHECKBALL LEGEND

△ - STEEL (1)

□ - RUBBER (10)

Checkball location

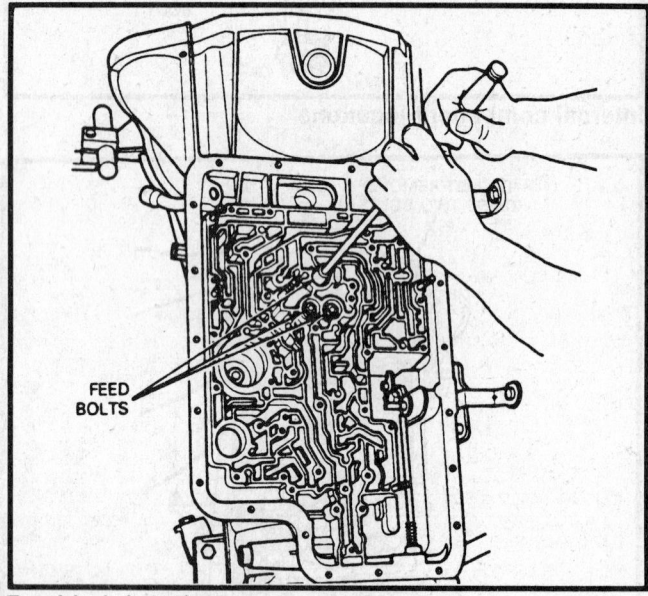

FEED BOLTS

Feed bolt locations

Mark clutch plates for reassembly. Remove the intermediate band.

22. Remove the direct clutch forward clutch and shell using clutch remover and installer T89T–70010–E or equivalent.

NOTE: Hooks on crossbar must be rotated into notches on the input shell.

23. Using a large removal tool, remove the reverse snapring. Remove the reverse planet carrier and 2 thrust washers No. 7D423.

24. Remove the output shaft snapring. Discard the snapring.

25. Remove the ring gear and hub assembly, and needle bearing assembly No. 7E413.

26. Remove the reverse hub and the one-way clutch assembly.

27. Using the proper tool remove the reverse clutch snapring. Remove the reverse pressure plate and clutch pack. Mark for reassembly.

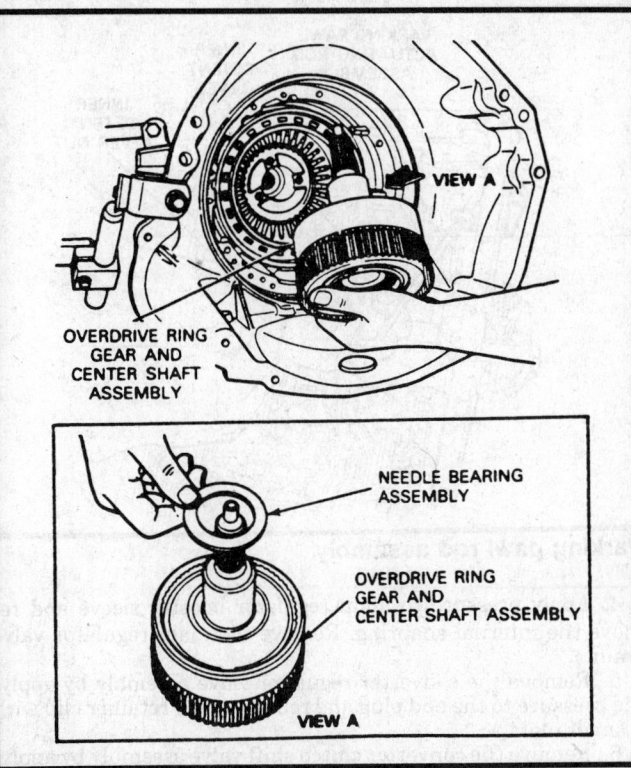

Removing overdrive ring gear and centershaft assembly

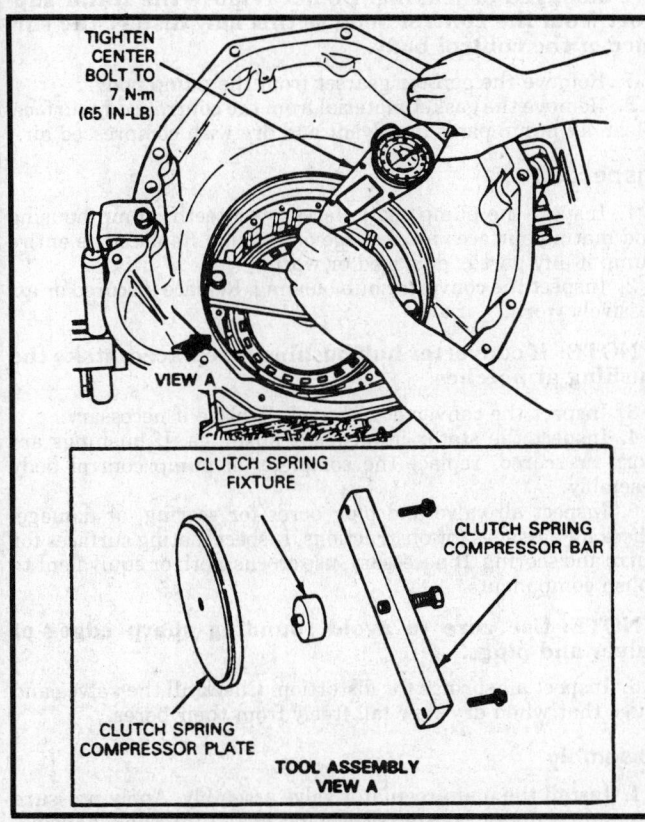

Install clutch spring compressor into case

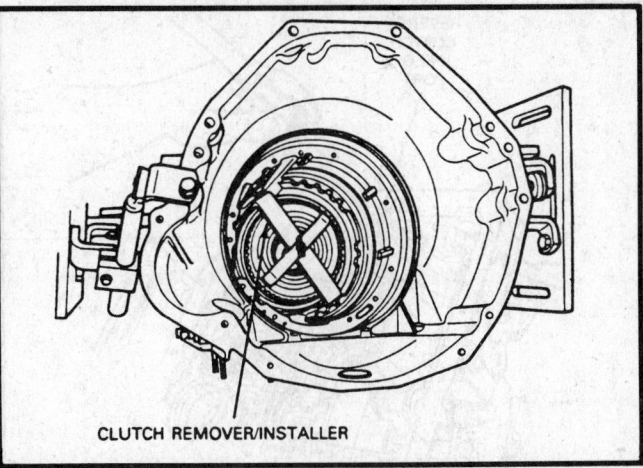

Removing direct clutch/forward clutch and shell from case

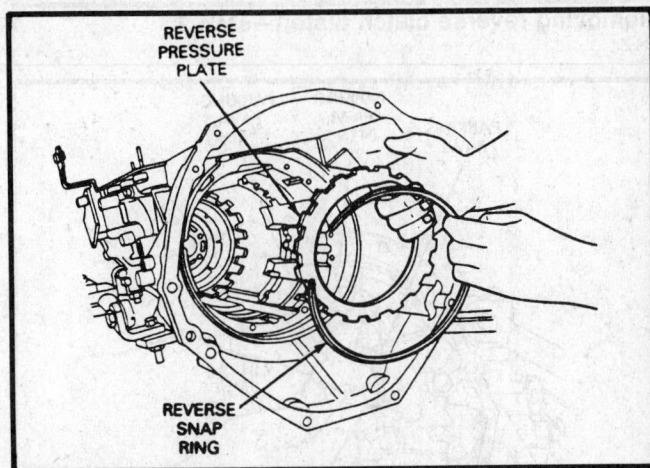

Removing reverse clutch piston—step 1

28. Rotate the transmission so that pan surface is facing up. Remove the 9 extension housing bolts. Remove the wiring bracket, extension housing and gasket, discard gasket.

29. Remove the output shaft, park gear and thrust washer No. 7B368.

30. Remove the 5 bolts from the low/reverse one-way clutch inner race. Remove the reverse clutch, return spring and inner race. Install the reverse clutch pressure plate and snapring, to hold reverse clutch piston during removal.

31. Blow compressed air into the reverse clutch feed port. This will blow out the reverse clutch piston against the pressure plate.

32. Remove the snapring, reverse clutch pressure plate and piston from case.

33. Rotate the transmission so that pan surface is facing down. Remove the park pawl return spring, pin and parkwing pawl from the case.

34. Remove the 2 bolts from the parking rod guide plate.

35. Remove the Torx® head bolt (40A bit) and parking pawl abutment.

36. Using side cutters or locknut pin remover T78P–3504–N or equivalent remove manual lever roll pin from the case.

37. Remove the inner detent lever nut, while holding the lever with crescent wrench or equivalent.

38. Remove the inner detent lever and parking pawl actuating rod assembly from the manual lever.

39. Remove the 2 bolts and the manual lever position sensor.

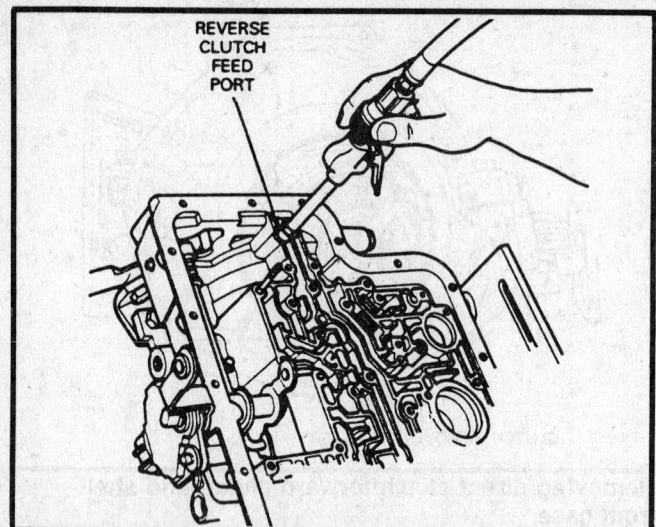

Removing reverse clutch piston – step 2

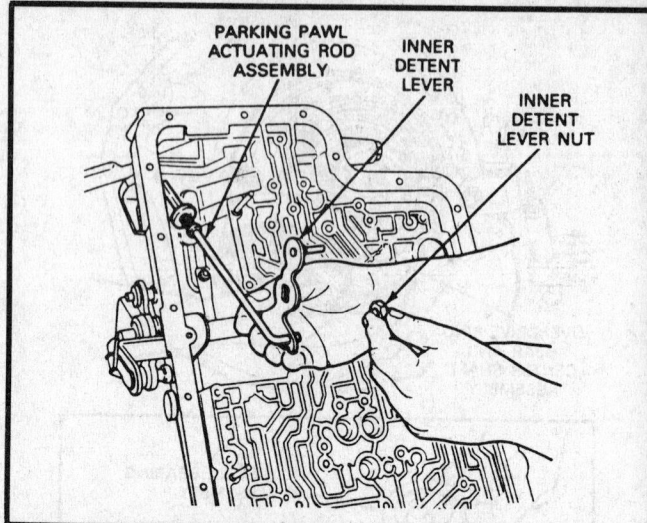

Parking pawl rod assembly

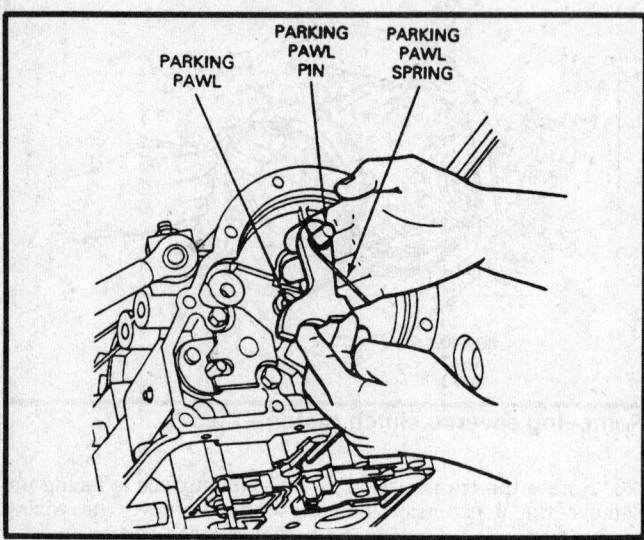

Parking pawl assembly

40. Remove the manual lever and the manual lever seal using seal remover T74P–77248–A and slide hammer T50T–100–A or equivalents.

41. If necessary, remove the stub tube using channel lock pliers or equivalent.

Unit Disassembly and Assembly

OIL PUMP

Disassembly

1. Remove the 2 Teflon® coast clutch seals from the stator support. Remove the converter clutch seal from the front of the stator support. Remove the pump outer diameter square cut seal.

2. Obtain a banding tool prior to removing pump body bolts. This tool is needed to align the pump with the control body assembly during reassembly.

3. Remove the 11 bolts and separate the pump control body from the pump body.

4. Apply pressure to main regulator booster sleeve and remove the internal snapring. Remove the main regulator valve train.

5. Remove the converter regulator valve assembly by applying pressure to the end plug and removing the retainer clip with a small tool.

6. Remove the converter clutch shift valve assembly by applying pressure to the end plug and removing retainer clip with a small tool.

NOTE: Do not remove any of the cup plugs unless they are damaged or leaking. Do not remove the stator support from the control body as this may distort the surface of the control body.

7. Remove the gerotor gearset from the pump body.

8. Remove the gasket material from the control body surface. Clean all pump parts in solvent and dry with compressed air.

Inspection

1. Inspect the pump gears, faces, gear teeth, pump housing and mating surfaces for damage or scoring. Replace the entire pump if any part is damaged or worn.

2. Inspect the converter hub bushing. Replace if scored or excessively worn.

NOTE: If converter hub bushing is replaced, stake the bushing at notches.

3. Inspect the converter hub seal. Replace if necessary.

4. Inspect the stator input shaft bushings. If bushings are worn or scored, replace the complete oil pump control body assembly.

5. Inspect all valve and plug bores for scoring, or damage. Check all passages for obstructions. Inspect mating surfaces for burrs and scoring. If necessary, use crocus cloth or equivalent to polish components.

NOTE: Use care to avoid rounding sharp edges of valves and plugs.

6. Inspect all springs for distortion. Check all the valves and plugs that when dry they fall freely from their bores.

Assembly

1. Install the main regulator valve assembly. Apply pressure to main regulator booster sleeve and install internal snapring. Make sure that the snapring is properly seated.

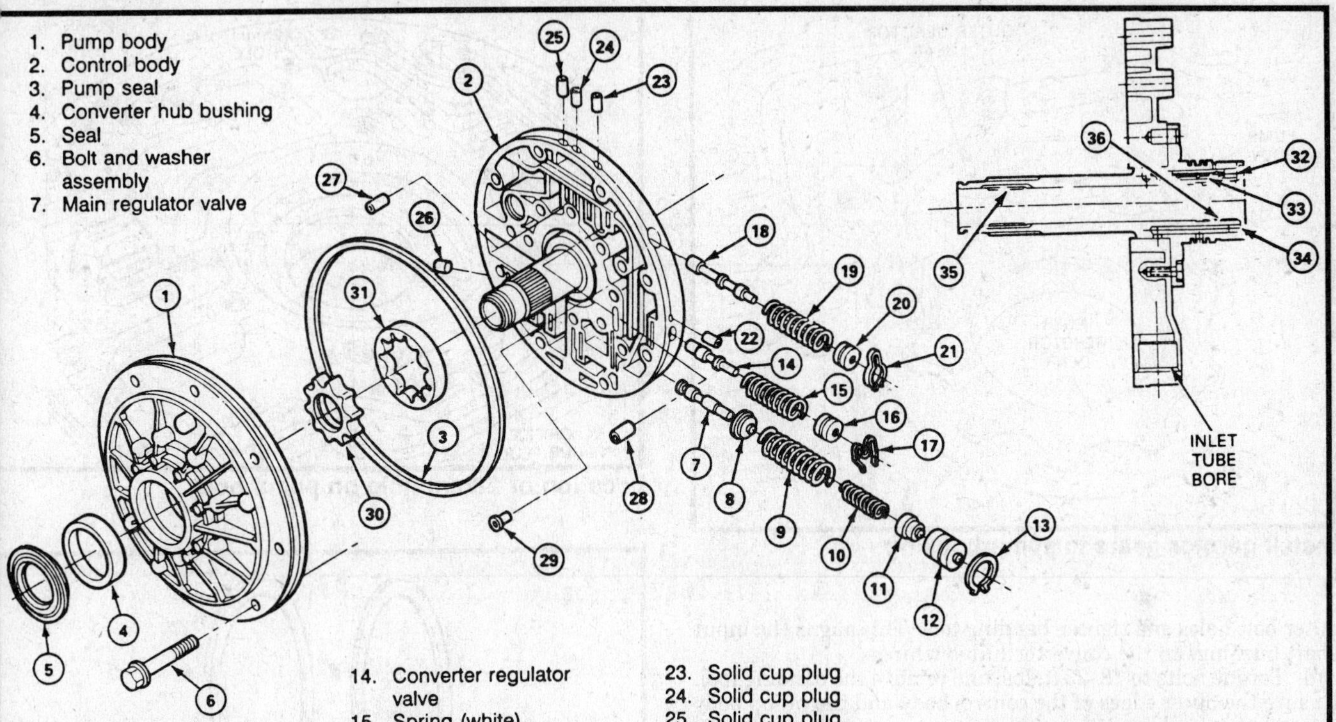

1. Pump body
2. Control body
3. Pump seal
4. Converter hub bushing
5. Seal
6. Bolt and washer assembly
7. Main regulator valve

8. Spring retainer
9. Outer spring (green)
10. Inner spring (green)
11. Main regulator booster valve
12. Main regulator booster sleeve
13. Retainer

14. Converter regulator valve
15. Spring (white)
16. Plug
17. Clip
18. Converter clutch control valve
19. Spring (yellow)
20. Plug
21. Clip
22. Solid cup plug

23. Solid cup plug
24. Solid cup plug
25. Solid cup plug
26. Solid cup plug
27. Orificed cup plug (0.077–0.083)
28. Orificed cup plug (0.049–0.055)
29. Air bleed check valve assembly
30. Inner gerotor gear

31. Outer gerotor gear
32. Orificed cup plug (0.057–0.062)
33. Valve assembly
34. Solid cup plug
35. Front input shaft bushing
36. Rear input shaft bushing

INLET TUBE BORE

Exploded view of oil pump

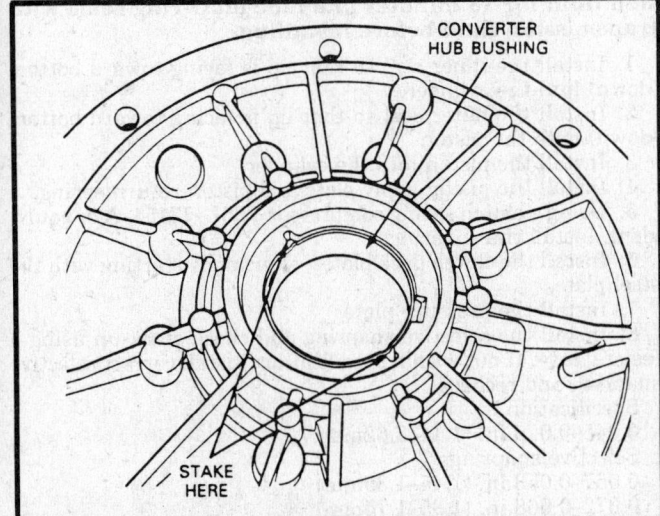

CONVERTER HUB BUSHING

STAKE HERE

Hub bushing replacement

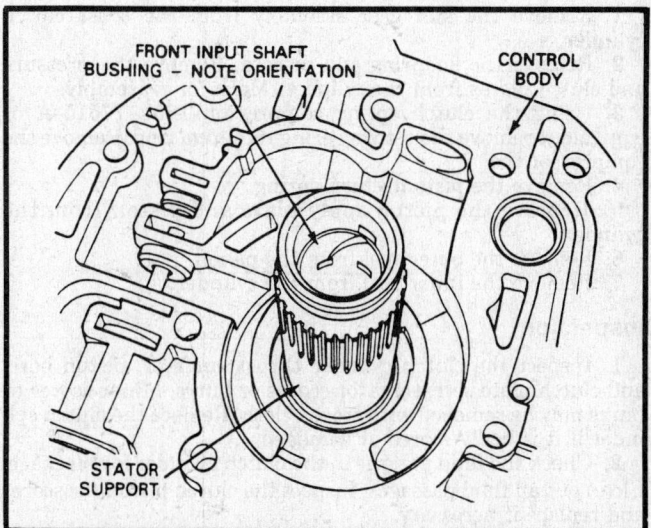

FRONT INPUT SHAFT BUSHING – NOTE ORIENTATION

CONTROL BODY

STATOR SUPPORT

Stator input shaft bushing

2. Install the converter shuttle valve assembly.
3. Lightly coat the gerotor gears with petroleum jelly and install in the pump housing.

NOTE: The dot on the inner gerotor gear must face the control body assembly.

4. Lower the control body and stator assembly onto the pump body, aligning the 28mm round hole in the control body with the 28mm hole in the pump body.
5. Loosely install bolts into the pump body. Install banding tool D89L–77000 or equivalent with clamp by filter inlet. Align

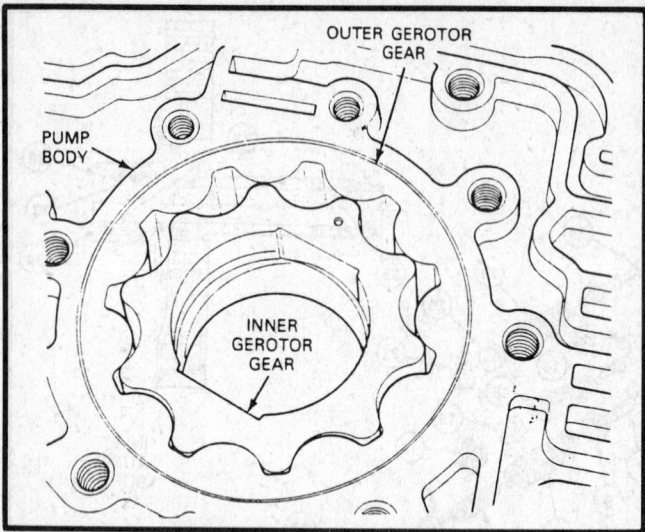

Install gerotor gears in pump housing

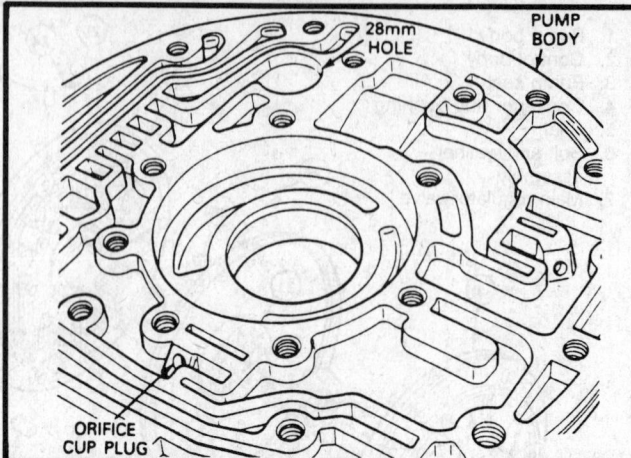

Location of 28mm hole on pump body

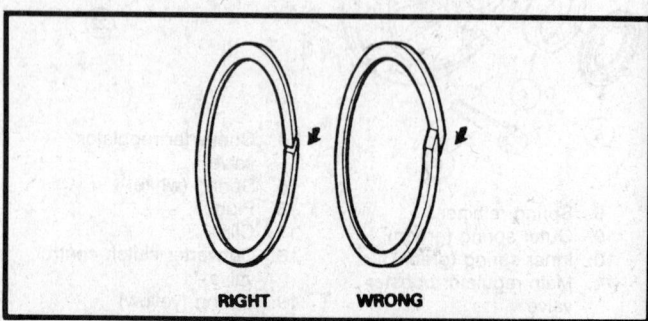

Correct installation of seals in pump assembly

outer bolt holes and tighten banding tool. This aligns the input shaft bushings to the converter hub bushings.

6. Torque bolts to 18–23 ft. lbs. and remove the banding tool. Ensure the outer edges of the control body and the pump body are completely aligned.

7. Install the coast clutch Teflon® seals. Install converter lockup seal on front of stator support.

8. Install the pump outer diameter seal. Be sure groove is clean and free of burrs. Lubricate outer diameter seal with transmission fluid before installing pump into transmissin case.

COAST CLUTCH CYLINDER ASSEMBLY

Disassembly

1. Remove the sun gear assembly from the coast clutch cylinder.

2. Remove the snapring and discard. Remove the pressure and clutch plates from the cylinder. Mark for reasembly.

3. Using the clutch spring compressor T65L–77515–A or equivalent remove the return spring retaining ring. Remove the compressor tool.

4. Remove the piston return spring.

5. Remove the piston apply plate and piston from the cylinder.

6. Remove the outer seal from the piston.

7. Remove the inner seal from the cylinder.

Inspection

1. Inspect the clutch cylinder thrust surfaces, piston bore, and clutch plate serrations for scores or burrs. Minor scores or burrs may be removed with crocus cloth. Replace the clutch cylinder if it is badly scored or damaged.

2. Check the fluid passage in the clutch cylinder for blockage. Clean out all fluid passages. Inspect the clutch piston for scores and replace if necessary.

3. Check the clutch release spring for distortion and cracks.

4. Inspect the composition clutch plates, steel clutch plates, and clutch pressure plate for worn or scored bearing surfaces. Replace all parts that are deeply scored or burred.

5. Check the clutch plates for flatness and fit on the clutch hub serrations. Discard any plate that does not slide freely on the serrations or that is not flat.

6. Check the clutch hub thrust surfaces for scores and the clutch hub splines for wear.

Assembly

NOTE: Soak all the friction plates in clean transmission fluid for 15 minutes and lube all O-ring seals with transmission fluid before installing.

1. Install the inner seal so that lip is facing toward bottom (down) into the cylinder.

2. Install the outer seal so that lip is facing toward bottom (down) onto the piston.

3. Install the piston into the cylinder.

4. Install the piston apply plate and piston return spring.

5. Using a clutch spring compressor T65L–77151–A or equivalent, install the snapring.

6. Install the clutch pack plates, alternately starting with the steel plate.

7. Install the pressure plate.

8. Install the selective snapring and check stack-up using a feeler gauge. If not within specification, install correct selective snapring and recheck.

Specification
0.045–0.025 in. (1.14–0.62mm)
Selective snaprings
0.057–0.053 in. (1.45–1.35mm)
0.072–0.068 in. (1.85–1.75mm)
0.088–0.084 in. (2.25–2.15mm)

9. Install the overdrive sun gear with the short end of gear down into the coast clutch cylinder.

OVERDRIVE RING GEAR AND CENTER SHAFT ASSEMBLY

Disassembly

1. Remove the inner race.

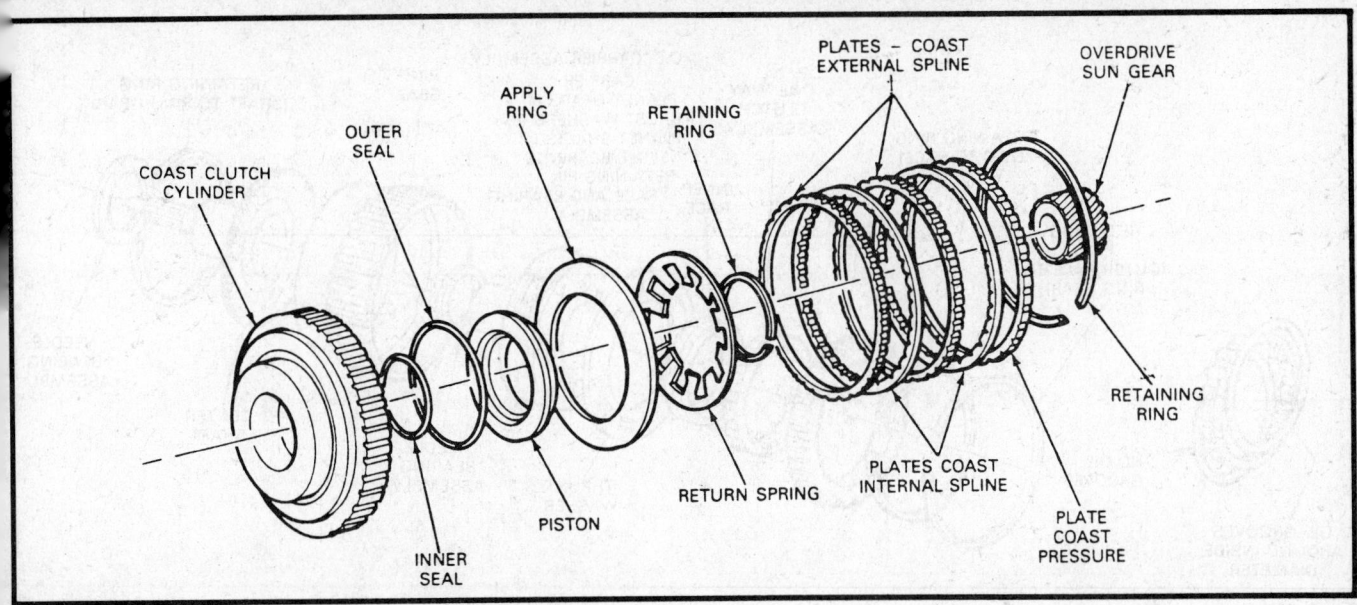

PLATES – COAST EXTERNAL SPLINE

OVERDRIVE SUN GEAR

APPLY RING

OUTER SEAL

RETAINING RING

COAST CLUTCH CYLINDER

RETAINING RING

INNER SEAL

PISTON

RETURN SPRING

PLATES COAST INTERNAL SPLINE

PLATE COAST PRESSURE

Exploded view of coast clutch cylinder assembly

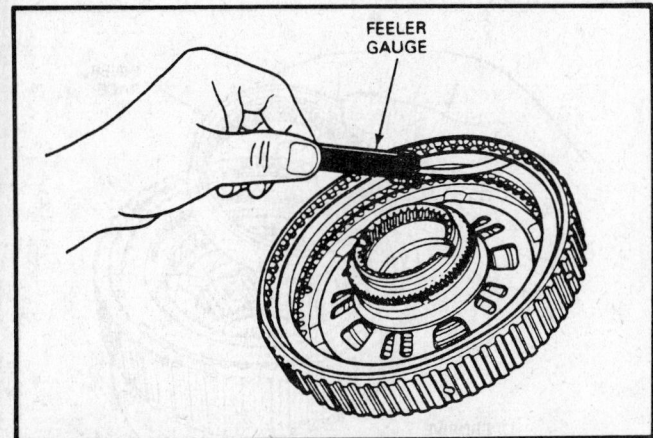

FEELER GAUGE

Checking stack-up in clutch asembly

2. Remove the small (inner) snapring and one-way clutch assembly.

3. Remove the large snapring and the outer race assembly from ring gear.

4. Remove the thrust washer No. 7G400 from front of carrier.

5. Remove the overdrive carrier from ring gear assembly.

6. Remove the needle bearing assembly No. 7G128 from rear face of carrier using the appropriate tool.

7. Remove the center shaft to ring gear wave type snapring. Remove the center shaft from ring gear.

Inspection

1. Inspect the outer and inner races for scores or damaged surface areas.

2. Inspect the rollers for excessive wear or damage.

NOTE: Individual parts of the planet carrier are not serviceable.

3. The pins and shafts in the planet assembly should be checked for loose fit and or complete disengagement.

4. Inspect the pinion gears for damaged or excessively worn teeth.

5. Check for free rotation of the pinon gears.

Assembly

1. Install the center shaft into the overdrive ring gear with retaining ring.

2. Install the needle bearing assembly No. 7G128 on rear face of carrier.

3. Install the overdrive carrier into center shaft and ring gear assembly.

4. Install the thrust washer No. 7G400 on front of the carrier.

5. Install the outer race assembly into the ring gear with snapring groove facing up and attach ring gear with snapring.

NOTE: The overdrive one-way clutch end caps must be installed correctly. The end cap with the scallops on the inner diameter must be toward the front of the transmission for proper lubrication.

6. Place the top (thick) end cap onto the one-way clutch. Place the thin end cap onto the bottom of the one-way clutch.

7. Install the one-way clutch assembly. The date code on the outside of thick end cap must be visible. Secure in place with snapring.

8. Install the inner race and make sure the inner race rotates counterclockwise.

INTERMEDIATE/OVERDRIVE CYLINDER ASSEMBLY

Disassembly

1. Using a suitable tool compress the overdrive return spring.

2. Remove the snapring and compressor tool assembly.

3. Remove the return spring and the overdrive piston.

4. Remove the outer and inner seals, using O-ring tool T71P–19703–C or equivalent.

5. Remove the intermediate piston.

6. Remove the intermediate/overdrive inner seal from cylinder bore, using O-ring tool T71P–19703–C or equivalent.

7. Remove the outer seal from the intermediate piston.

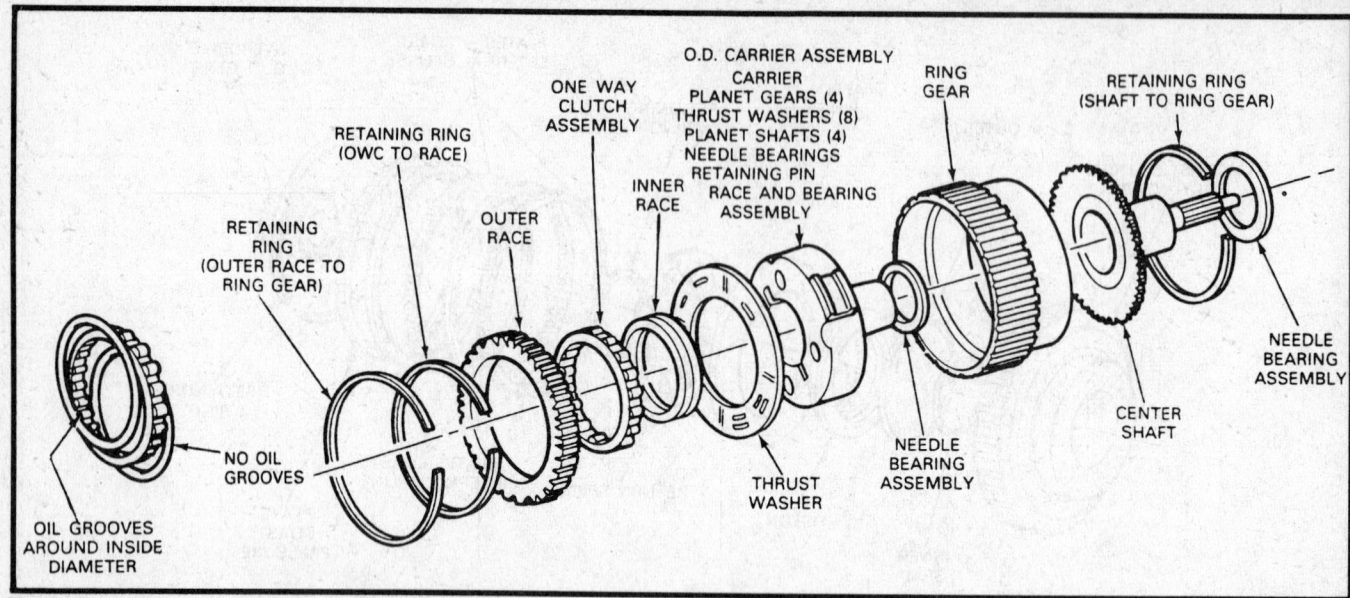

Exploded view of overdrive ring gear and center shaft assembly

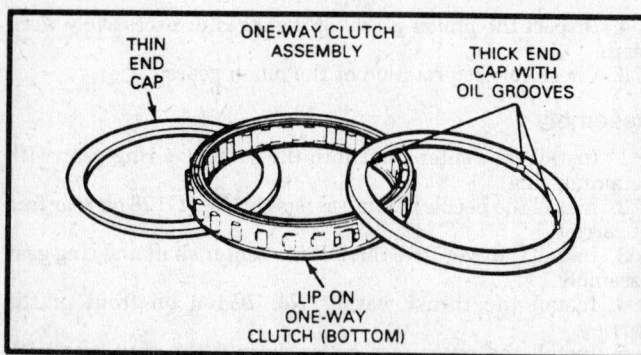

Correct installation of one-way clutch end caps

Inspection

1. Inspect the clutch cylinder thrust surfaces, piston bore, and clutch plate serrations for scores or burrs. Minor scores or burrs may be removed with crocus cloth. Replace the clutch cylinder if it is badly scored or damaged.
2. Check the fluid passage in the clutch cylinder for blockage. Clean out all fluid passages. Inspect the clutch piston for scores and replace if necessary.
3. Check the clutch release spring for distortion and cracks.
4. Inspect the composition clutch plates, steel clutch plates, and clutch pressure plate for worn or scored bearing surfaces. Replace all parts that are deeply scored or burred.
5. Check the clutch plates for flatness and fit on the clutch hub serrations.

NOTE: **Replace any plate that does not slide freely on the serrations or that is not flat.**

6. Check the clutch hub thrust surfaces for scores and the clutch hub splines for wear.

Assembly

1. Install the outer seal onto intermediate piston with lip seal facing down towards cylinder.
2. Install the intermediate/overdrive inner seal onto cylinder bore with lip seal facing down towards cylinder.

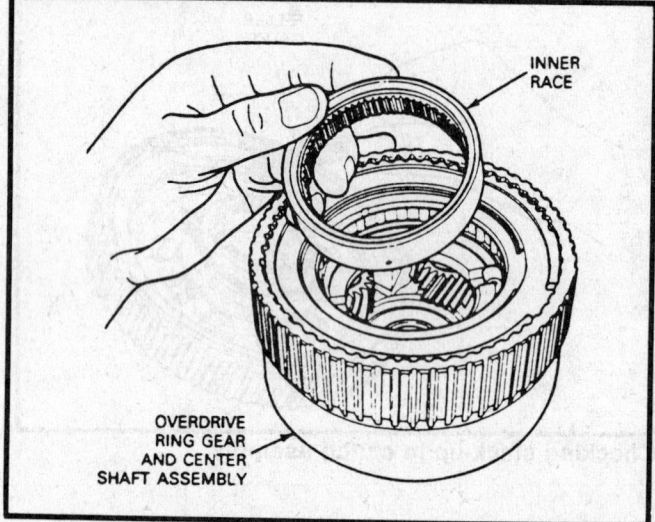

Installation of inner race

3. Install the intermediate piston.
4. Install the overdrive outer and inner seals with lip seal facing down towards the cylinder.
5. Install the overdrive piston and return spring. Make note that the spring fingers are facing up.
6. Using a suitable tool compress the return spring and install the snapring. Remove the tool assembly.

CENTER SUPPORT

Disassembly

Remove the 2 cast iron outer seal rings using a suitable tool.

Assembly

Install the 2 cast iron seal rings on the center support.

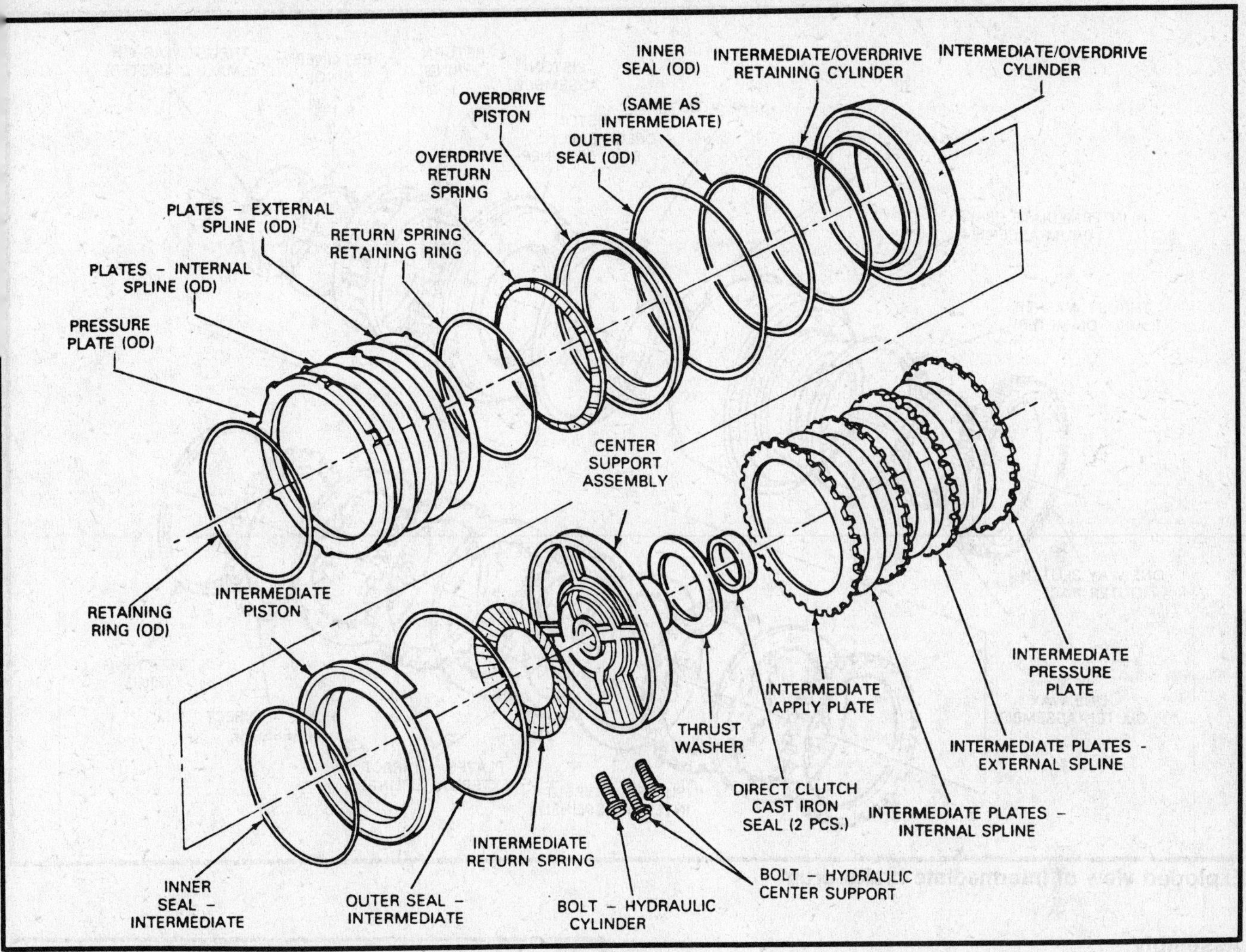

INNER SEAL (OD)

INTERMEDIATE/OVERDRIVE RETAINING CYLINDER

INTERMEDIATE/OVERDRIVE CYLINDER

OVERDRIVE PISTON

(SAME AS INTERMEDIATE)

OUTER SEAL (OD)

OVERDRIVE RETURN SPRING

RETURN SPRING RETAINING RING

PLATES – EXTERNAL SPLINE (OD)

PLATES – INTERNAL SPLINE (OD)

PRESSURE PLATE (OD)

CENTER SUPPORT ASSEMBLY

RETAINING RING (OD)

INTERMEDIATE PISTON

INTERMEDIATE PRESSURE PLATE

THRUST WASHER

INTERMEDIATE APPLY PLATE

INTERMEDIATE PLATES – EXTERNAL SPLINE

DIRECT CLUTCH CAST IRON SEAL (2 PCS.)

INTERMEDIATE PLATES – INTERNAL SPLINE

INTERMEDIATE RETURN SPRING

BOLT – HYDRAULIC CENTER SUPPORT

INNER SEAL – INTERMEDIATE

OUTER SEAL – INTERMEDIATE

BOLT – HYDRAULIC CYLINDER

Exploded view of intermediate/overdrive cylinder assembly

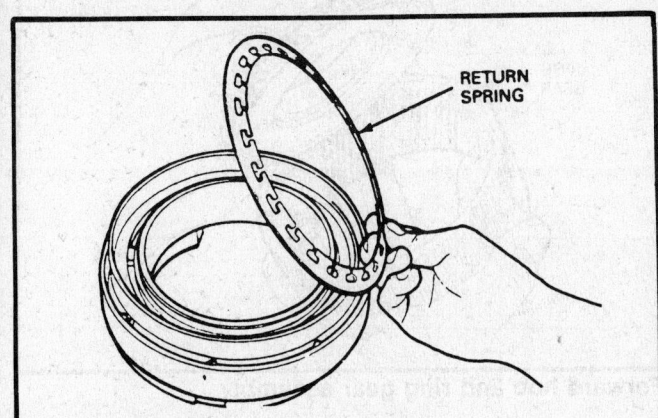

RETURN SPRING

Correct installation of return spring

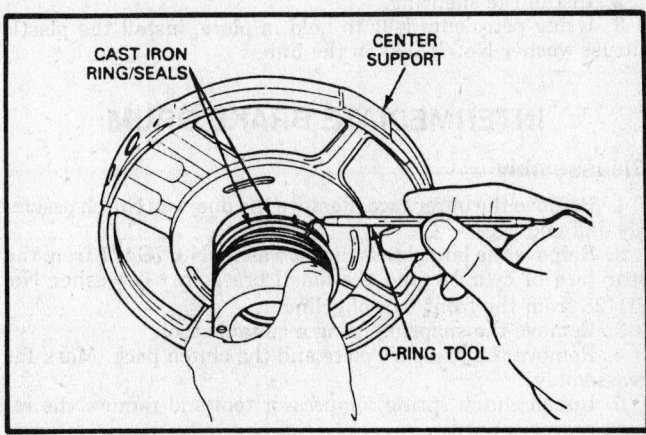

CAST IRON RING/SEALS

CENTER SUPPORT

O-RING TOOL

Center support assembly

FORWARD HUB AND RING GEAR

Disassembly

1. Remove the plastic thrust washer No. 7D090 from the front face of hub.

2. Remove the snapring using suitable tool.
3. Remove the forward hub from the ring gear.

Inspection

Check the clutch hub thrust surfaces for scores and the clutch hub splines for wear or damage.

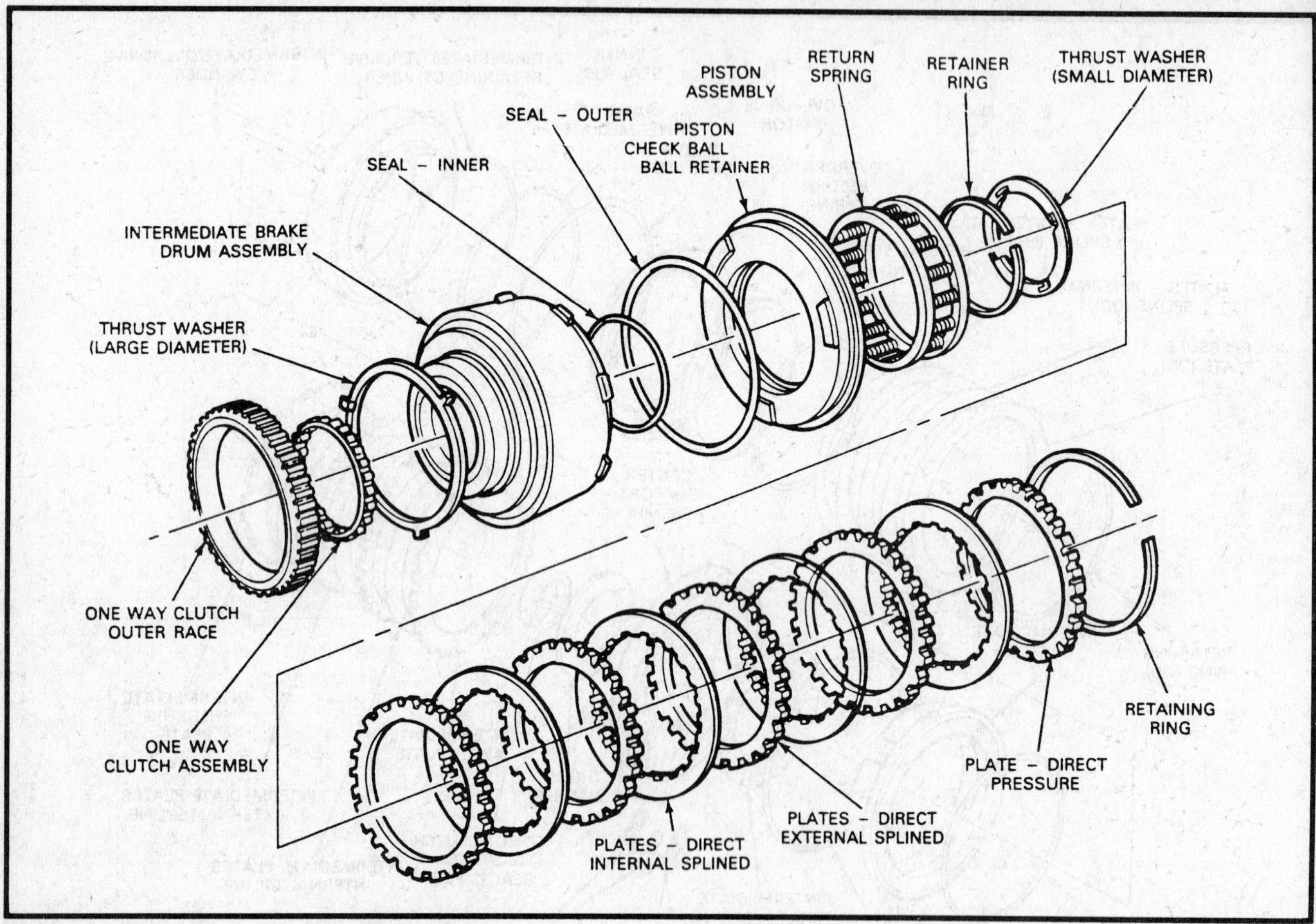

SEAL – INNER

SEAL – OUTER

PISTON ASSEMBLY

PISTON CHECK BALL
BALL RETAINER

RETURN SPRING

RETAINER RING

THRUST WASHER (SMALL DIAMETER)

INTERMEDIATE BRAKE DRUM ASSEMBLY

THRUST WASHER (LARGE DIAMETER)

ONE WAY CLUTCH OUTER RACE

ONE WAY CLUTCH ASSEMBLY

PLATES – DIRECT INTERNAL SPLINED

PLATES – DIRECT EXTERNAL SPLINED

PLATE – DIRECT PRESSURE

RETAINING RING

Exploded view of intermediate brake drum

Assembly

1. Install the forward hub into the gear.
2. Install the snapring.
3. Using petroleum jelly to hold in place, install the plastic thrust washer No. 7D090 on the hub.

INTERMEDIATE BRAKE DRUM

Disassembly

1. Remove the outer race. Remove the one-way clutch assembly and end caps.
2. Remove the large brass thrust washer No. 7G401 from the rear face of cylinder and the small brass thrust washer No. 7D428 from the front face of cylinder.
3. Remove the snapring using a suitable tool.
4. Remove the pressure plate and the clutch pack. Mark for reassembly.
5. Install clutch spring compressor tool and remove the return spring snapring.
6. Remove the return spring assembly.
7. Remove the piston from the intermediate brake drum.
8. Remove inner and outer seals from the drum using O-ring tool T71P–19703–C or equivalent.

Inspection

1. Inspect the clutch cylinder thrust surfaces, piston bore, and clutch plate serrations for scores or burrs. Minor scores or

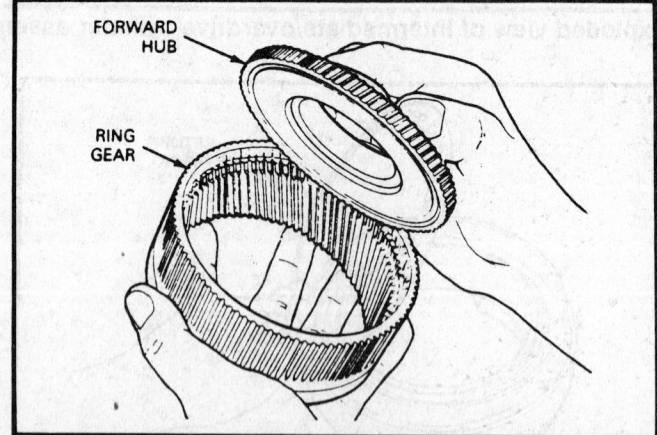

FORWARD HUB

RING GEAR

Forward hub and ring gear assembly

burrs may be removed with crocus cloth. Replace the clutch cylinder if it is badly scored or damaged.

2. Check the fluid passage in the clutch cylinder for blockage. Clean out all fluid passages. Inspect the clutch piston for scores and replace if necessary. Inspect the check balls for freedom of movement and proper seating.
3. Check the clutch release spring for distortion and cracks.
4. Inspect the composition clutch plates, steel clutch plates, and clutch pressure plate for worn or scored bearing surfaces.

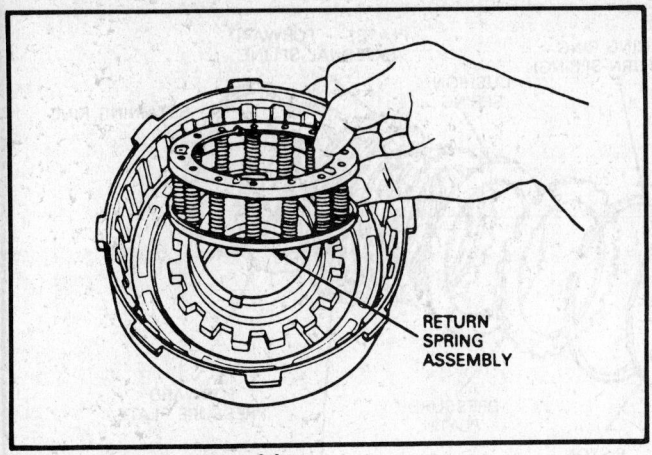

Return spring assembly

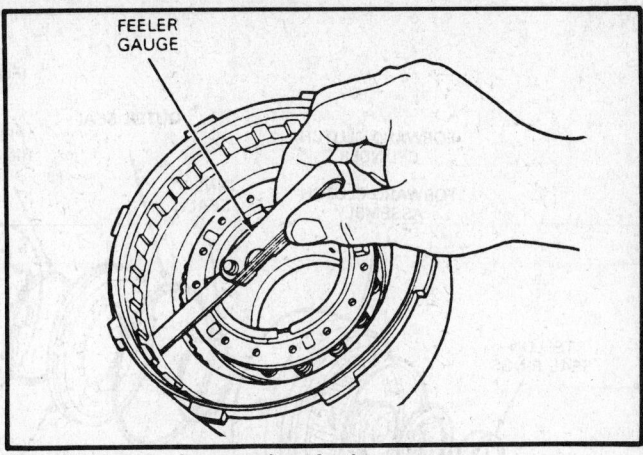

Checking stack-up using feeler gauge

5. Check the clutch plates for flatness and fit on the clutch hub serrations. Discard any plate that does not slide freely on the serrations or that is not flat.

6. Check the clutch hub thrust surfaces for scores and the clutch hub splines for wear.

Assembly

1. Install the inner seal into the cylinder with seal groove facing down.

2. Install the outer seal into the intermediate brake drum with seal groove facing down.

3. Inspect the piston check ball for freedom of movement.

4. Install piston into drum and return spring assembly. Using clutch spring compressor tool T65l–77515–A or equivalent, install the snapring. Ensure that the protrusions on the spring retainer are properly engaged with the lugs on the clutch piston.

5. Install the 4 plate clutch pack, starting with the steel plate. Install the pressure plate.

NOTE: Soak the clutch plates with clean transmission for 15 minutes before installing.

6. Install the selective snapring. Check the stack-up using a feeler gauge. If not with specification, install correct snapring and recheck.
Specification:
0.060–0.045 in. (1.52–1.15mm)
Selective snaprings:
0.065–0.069 in. (1.65–1.75mm)
0.074–0.078 in. (1.88–1.98mm)
0.083–0.087 in. (2.10–2.20mm)

7. Install the small brass thrust washer No. 7D428 on face of the cylinder.

8. Install the large brass thrust washer No. 7G401 on face of cylinder.

9. Install the intermediate one-way clutch end cap, one-way clutch assembly, outer race, and outer end cap over inner race.

NOTE: The lip is up on one-way clutch.

10. Install outer race so that the race turns counterclockwise.

FORWARD CLUTCH ASSEMBLY

Disassembly

1. Remove the needle bearing assembly from inner face of the cylinder.

2. Remove the needle bearing assembly No. 7F374.

3. Remove both Teflon® seal rings from the grooves.

4. Remove the snapring and rear pressure plate.

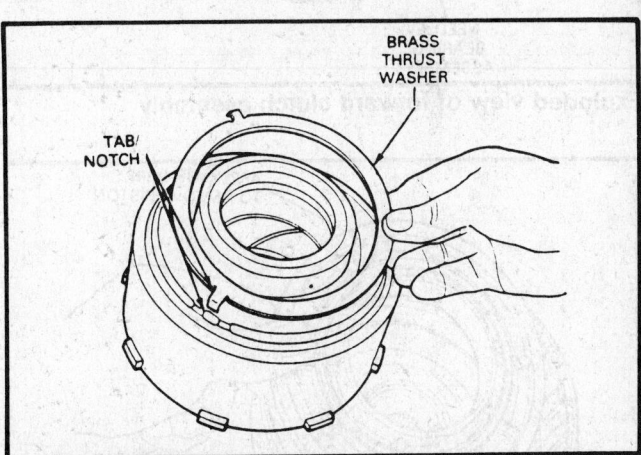

Correct installation of large brass washer on assembly

5. Remove the 4 plate clutch pack, cushion spring and front pressure plate. Mark for reassembly.

6. Remove the return spring snapring and return spring.

7. Remove the steel ring from the piston groove.

8. Remove the piston from the cylinder by applying compressed air to the piston.

9. Remove the outer seal from piston.

10. Remove the inner seal from the cylinder.

Inspection

1. Inspect the clutch cylinder thrust surfaces, piston bore, and clutch plate serrations for scores or burrs. Minor scores or burrs may be removed with crocus cloth. Replace the clutch cylinder if it is badly scored or damaged.

2. Check the fluid passage in the clutch cylinder for blockage. Clean out all fluid passages. Inspect the clutch piston for scores and replace if necessary. Inspect the check balls for freedom of movement and proper seating.

3. Check the clutch release spring for distortion and cracks.

4. Inspect the composition clutch plates, steel clutch plates, and clutch pressure plate for worn or scored bearing surfaces.

5. Check the clutch plates for flatness and fit on the clutch hub serrations. Discard any plate that does not slide freely on the serrations or that is not flat.

6. Check the clutch hub thrust surfaces for scores and the clutch hub splines for wear.

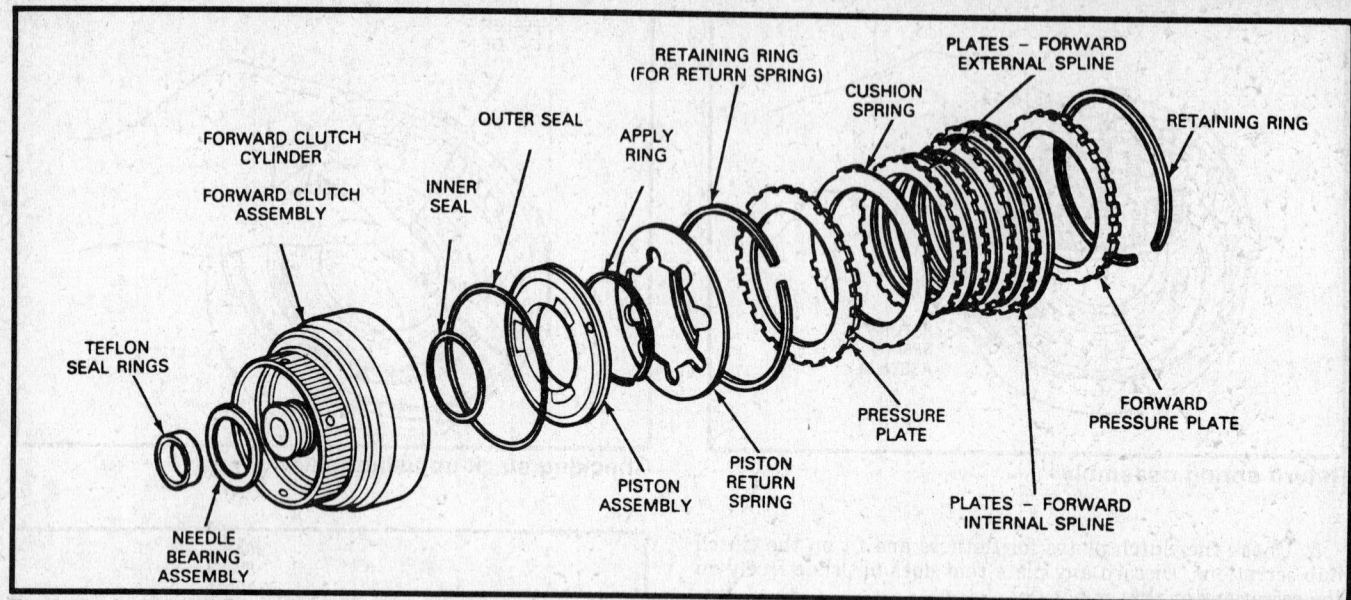

Exploded view of forward clutch assembly

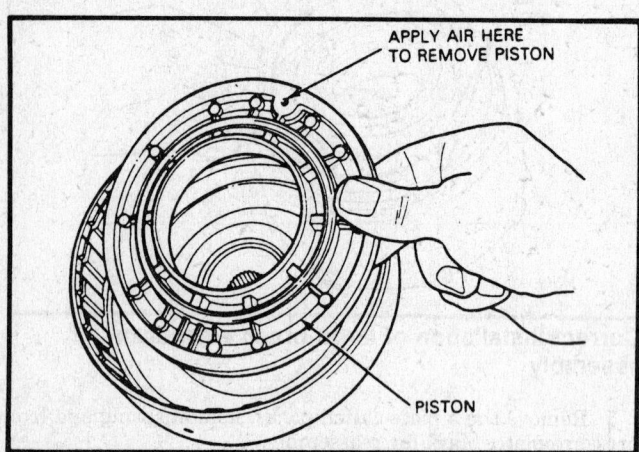

Removing piston from cylinder with air pressure

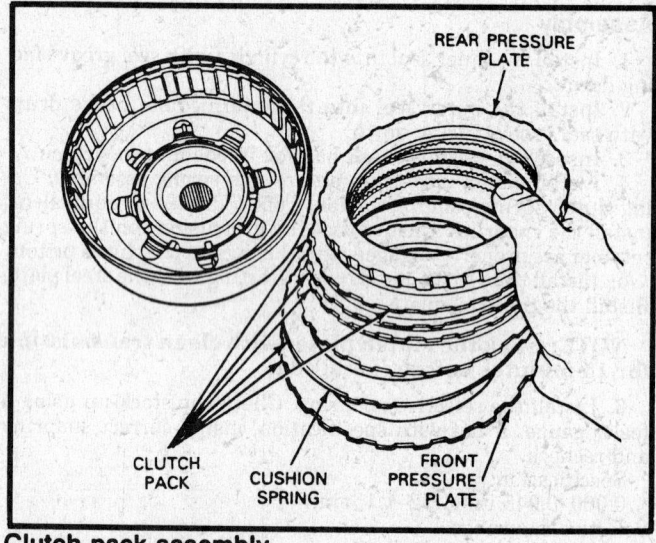

Clutch pack assembly

Assembly

1. Install the inner seal in the cylinder.
2. Install the outer seal on the piston.
3. Inspect the piston check ball for freedom of movement.
4. Install piston into cylinder using lip seal protector T77L–77548–A or equivalent.
5. Install the steel ring into the groove on the piston.
6. Install the retrun spring with the return spring fingers against the piston steel ring.
7. Install the snapring and the front pressure plate.
8. Install cushion spring.
9. Install the 4 steel plates and 4 friction plates alternately, starting with a steel plate.

NOTE: Soak the clutch plates with clean transmission fluid for 15 minutes before installing.

10. Install the rear pressure plate and the selective snapring.
11. Check the stack-up clearance, using a feeler gauge. If not with specification install correct snapring and recheck.
Specification:
0.055–0.030 in. (1.40–0.76mm)

Selective snaprings:
0.056–0.060 in. (1.42–1.52mm)
0.074–0.078 in. (1.88–1.98mm)
0.092–0.096 in. (2.34–2.44mm)
0.110–0.114 in. (2.79–2.90mm)
0.128–0.132 in. (3.25–3.35mm)
12. Install the Teflon® seal rings in the grooves.
13. Install the needle bearing assembly No. 75374 over Teflon® seal snout.
14. Install the needle bearing assembly on inner face of cylinder, with notched inner race facing outward.

FORWARD CARRIER

Disassembly

1. Remove the needle bearing assembly No. 7F078 from the carrier.
2. Remove the thrust washer No. 7D423 from the front side of the carrier.

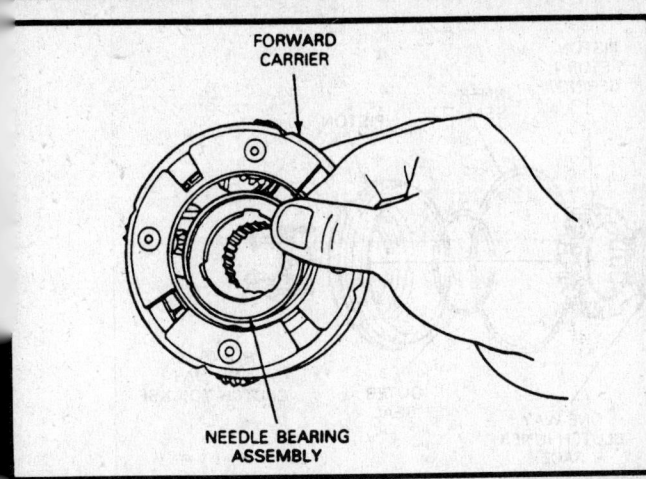

Forward carrier assembly

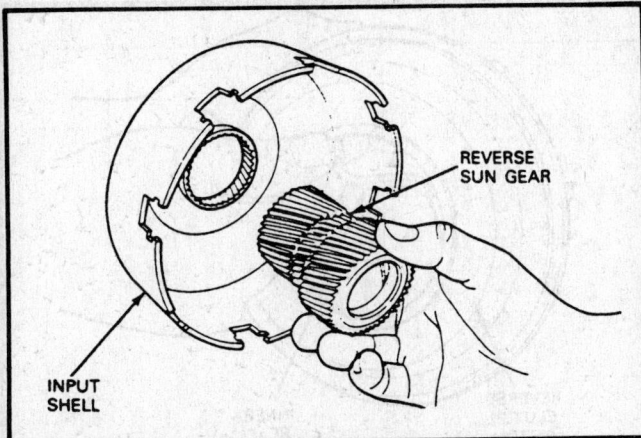

Installing reverse sun gear into input shell

Inspection

1. The pins and shafts in the planet assembly should be checked for loose fit and or complete disengagement.

NOTE: Individual parts of the planet carrier are not serviceable.

2. Inspect the pinion gears for damaged or excessively worn teeth.
3. Check for free rotation of the pinon gears.

Assembly

1. Place thrust washer No. 7D423 on front side of carrier, using petroleum jelly to hold in place. The thrust washer tabs go into the carrier.
2. Install the needle bearing assembly on the inner face of the carrier. The notched inner race should face outward.

INPUT SHELL

Disassembly

1. Remove the snapring from the reverse sun gear using snapring pliers.
2. Remove the thrust washer No. 7D066 from the input shell.
3. Remove the reverse sun gear from input shell.

Inspection

1. Check the input shell for cracks or damage.
2. Check the reverse sun gear for wear.

Assembly

1. Install the reverse sun gear into the input shell so that lube hole in the sun gear is between the stand off pads on the shell.
2. Install the input shell thrust washer No. 7D066 onto the reverse sun gear.
3. Install the snapring onto the reverse sun gear using snapring pliers.

REVERSE PLANET CARRIER

Disassembly

1. Remove the rear thrust washer No. 7D423.
2. Remove the front thrust washer No. 7D423.

Inspection

1. The pins and shafts in the planet assembly should be checked for loose fit and or complete disengagement.

NOTE: Individual parts of the planet carrier are not serviceable.

2. Inspect the pinion gears for damaged or excessively worn teeth.
3. Check for free rotation of the pinon gears.

Assembly

1. Install the front thrust washer No. 7D423. Hold the thrust washer in place by using petroleum jelly.
2. Install rear thrust washer No. 7D423. Hold the thrust washer in place by using petroleum jelly.

REVERSE ONE-WAY CLUTCH

Disassembly

1. Remove the reverse hub and needle bearing assembly No. 7E413 from the reverse one-way clutch hub.
2. Remove the snapring from the reverse one-way clutch hub.
3. Remove the brass thrust washer and rollers from the reverse clutch hub.

Inspection

1. Inspect the outer and inner races for scores or damaged surface areas where the rollers or sprags contact the races.
2. Inspect the rollers, sprags and springs for excessive wear or damage.
3. Inspect the spring and cage for bent or damaged spring retainers.

Assembly

1. Install the one-way clutch rollers and the brass thrust washer No. 7E194.
2. Install the snapring onto the one-way clutch hub.
3. Install the needle bearing assembly No. 7E413 with the smooth race surface facing up. Lightly grease the thrust washer with petroleum jelly to hold in place upon installation.

REVERSE CLUTCH PISTON

Disassembly

1. Remove the outer piston seal.
2. Remove the inner piston seal.

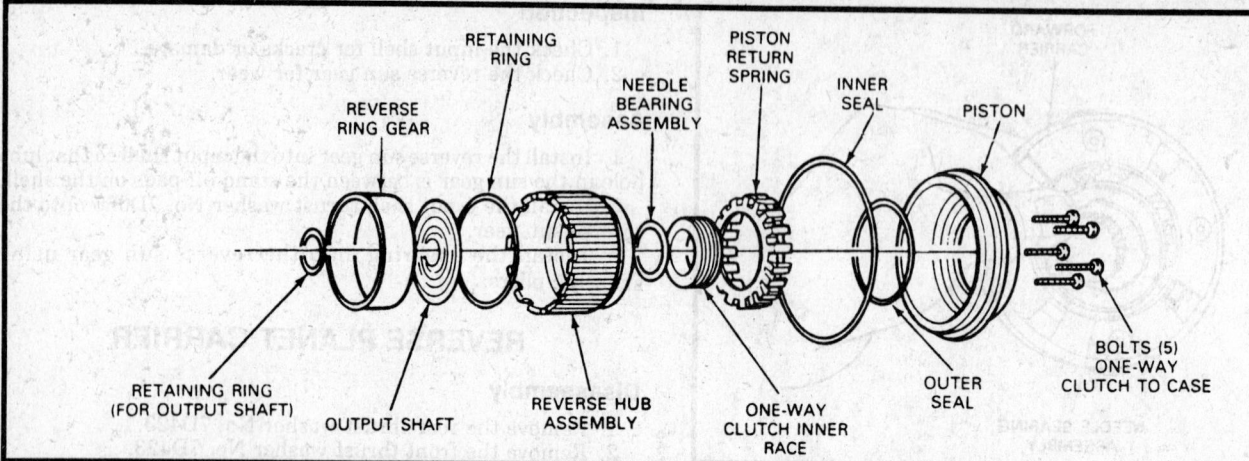

Exploded view of reverse one-way clutch

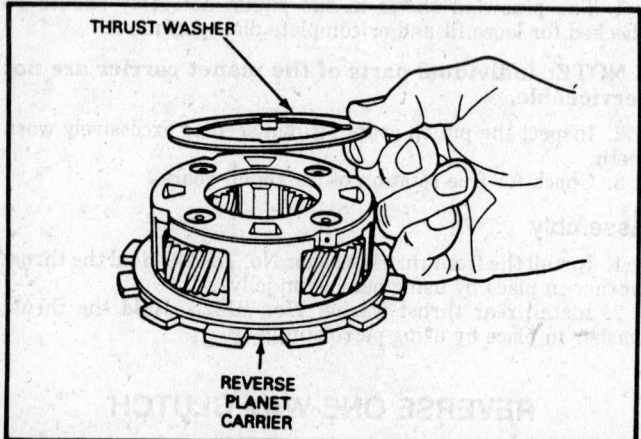

Reverse planet carrier

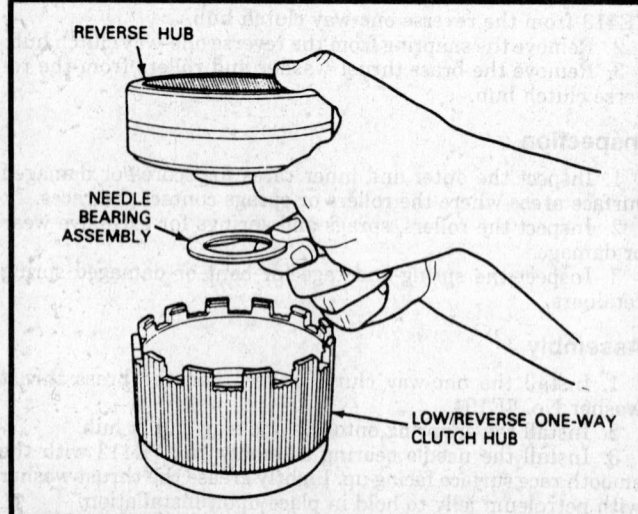

Removing neddle bearing assembly from hub

Inspection

Check piston surface for cracks or damage. Always check piston groves for distortion so that the piston seal will seat properly upon installation.

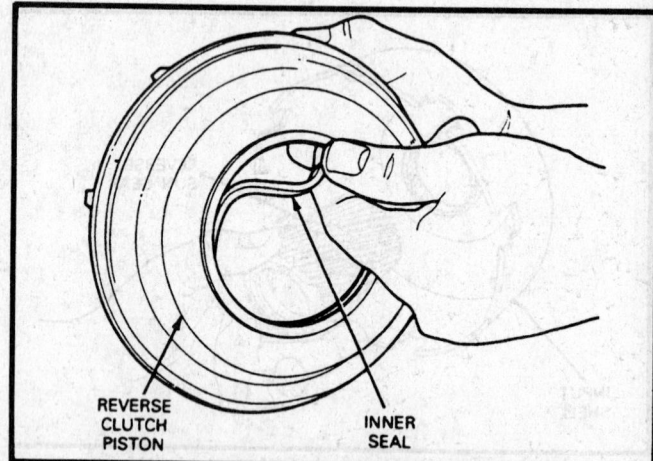

Removing inner seal from reverse clutch piston

Assembly

1. Install the inner piston seal.
2. Install the outer piston seal.

EXTENSION HOUSING

Disassembly

1. Using a suitable tool remove the extension housing seal.
2. On 2WD models, check the extension housing bushing for wear or damage. If wear is visible replace the bushing as the new extension housing seal will fail under these conditions.

Assembly

1. Install extension housing seal, using a suitable tool.
2. Install the extension housing bushing in the tailshaft by carefully driving the bushing in place using a suitable tool.

ASSEMBLY OF SUBASSEMBLIES

Assembly

1. Place the thrust washer No. 7D428 onto the intermediate brake drum. Lightly grease thrust washer with petroleum jelly to hold in correct location.
2. Install the forward clutch onto the intermediate brake drum.

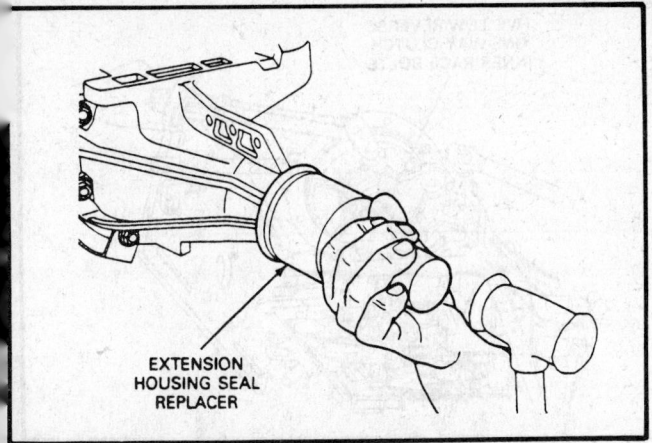

Installing rear seal in extension housing

3. Install the needle bearing assembly No. 7F078 onto the intermediate brake drum and forward clutch assembly.

NOTE: Lightly grease with petroleum jelly the needle bearing assembly. Notched inner race must be facing outward (up).

4. Grease with petroleum jelly the plastic thrust washer No. 7D090 and place onto the forward clutch hub. Place forward clutch hub into the intermediate brake drum and forward clutch assemblies.

5. Grease with petroleum jelly the thrust washer No. 7D423 and place onto the forward planet carrier. Place carrier into assembly.

6. Install the needle bearing assembly No. 7F078 into forward carrier assembly.

NOTE: Lightly grease with petroleum jelly the needle bearing to hold in place. The notched inner race surface should face up.

7. Align the input shell notches with intermediate brake drum.

8. Install the input shell onto the assembly.

9. Install the needle bearing assembly No. 7F374 into the front end of forward clutch assembly.

10. Install the intermediate brake drum, forward clutch and input shell remover/install T89T–70010–E or equivalent.

Transmission Assembly

NOTE.: Soak all the friction clutch plates in clean transmission for 15 minutes. Lightly lubricate all the O-ring seals before installing using transmission fluid and grease all thrust washers with petroleum jelly, to hole in place during assembly.

1. Mount transmission in suitable holding fixture. Rotate the transmission so that bell housing is facing up.

2. Install the inner and outer seals on the reverse clutch piston.

3. Install the reverse clutch piston using a suitable tool. Remove tool after installing piston.

4. Install the reverse piston return spring assembly and one-way clutch inner race.

5. Attach to case with 5 (11mm) bolts and torque to 18–25 ft. lbs.

6. Install a 6 internal spline plate reverse clutch pack starting with an external spline plate. Alternate external spline plates with internal spline plates. Install snapring.

NOTE: No stack-up clearance measurement is required.

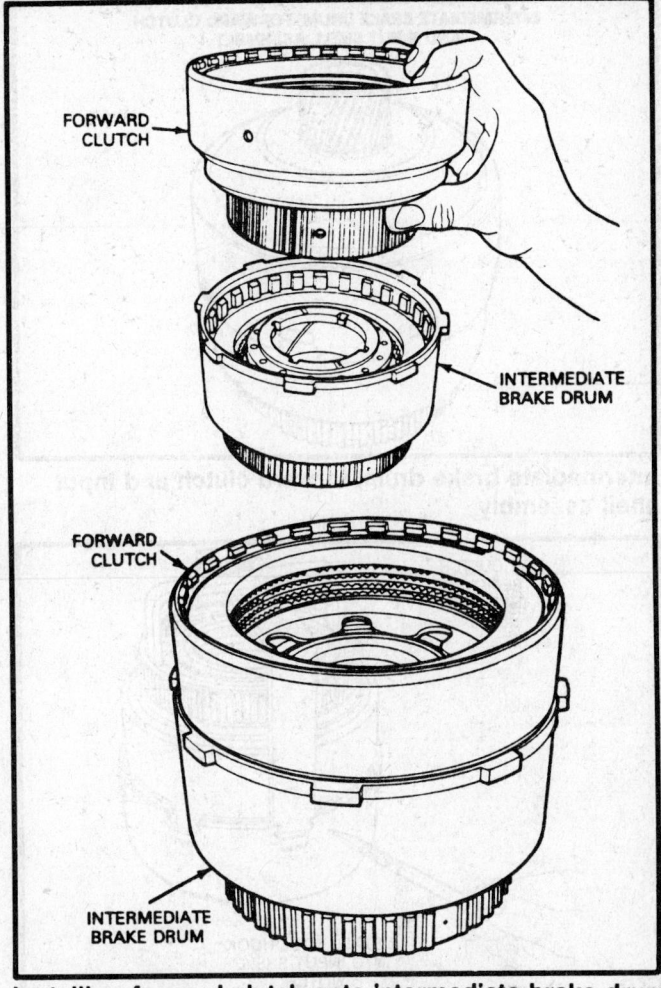

Installing forward clutch onto intermediate brake drum

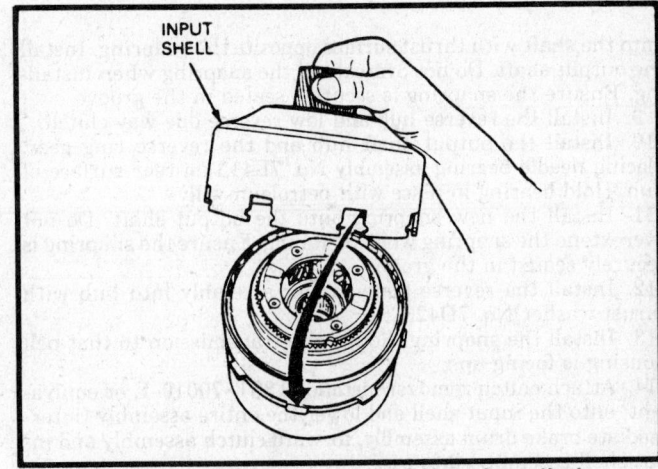

Input shell to intermediate brake drum installation

7. Rotate transmission to horizontal position. Grease with petroleum jelly the steel side of the thrust washer No. 7B368 and place on the rear of case so that bronze side is facing outward.

8. Install the snapring onto the output shaft. Slide park gear

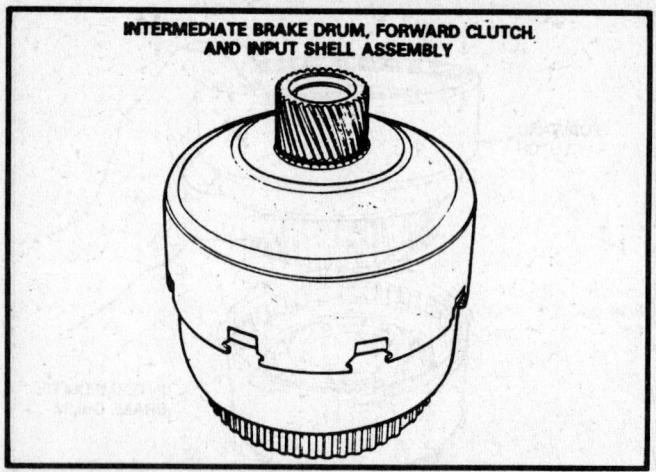

Intermediate brake drum, forward clutch and input shell assembly

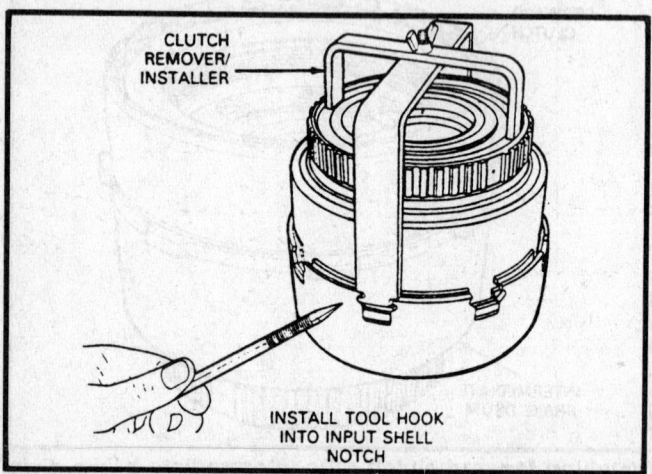

Input shell assembly with special tool installed

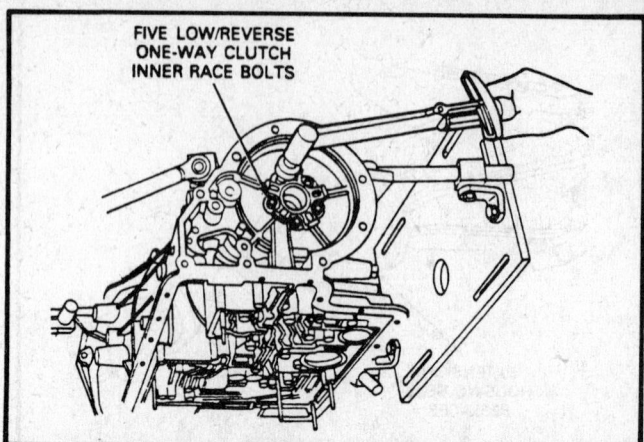

Installing inner race bolts

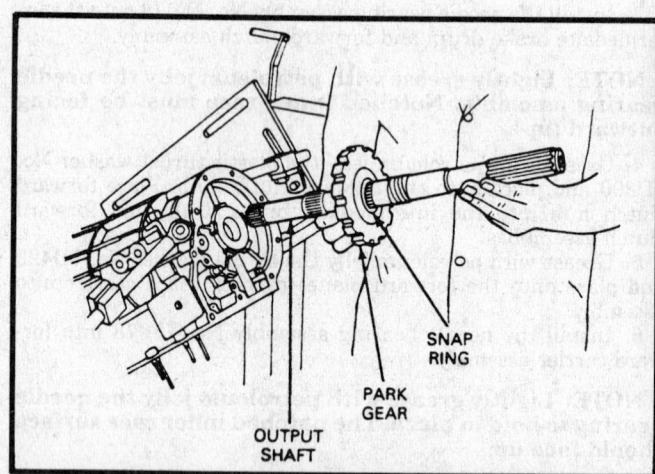

Install snapring—do not overextended snapring

onto the shaft with thrust surface opposite the snapring. Install the output shaft. Do not overextend the snapring when installing. Ensure the snapring is securely seated in the groove.

9. Install the reverse hub and low reverse one-way clutch.

10. Install the output shaft hub and the reverse ring gear, placing needle bearing assembly No. 7E413 on rear surface of hub. Hold bearing in place with petroleum jelly.

11. Install the new snapring onto the output shaft. Do not overextend the snapring when installing. Ensure the snapring is securely seated in the groove.

12. Install the reverse plate carrier assembly into hub with thrust washer No. 7D423.

13. Install the snapring. Rotate the transmission to that bell housing is facing up.

14. Attach clutch remover/installer T89T–70010–E or equivalent, onto the input shell and lower the entire assembly (intermediate brake drum assembly, forward clutch assembly and input shell assembly) into case.

NOTE: It may be necessary to rotate output shaft to seat reverse sun gear.

15. Install the intermediate band so that 1 ear is resting on the reaction pin.

16. Install the servo snapring, retaining plate, piston and rod assembly and servo spring. Apply slight downward pressure to plate while removing the snapring.

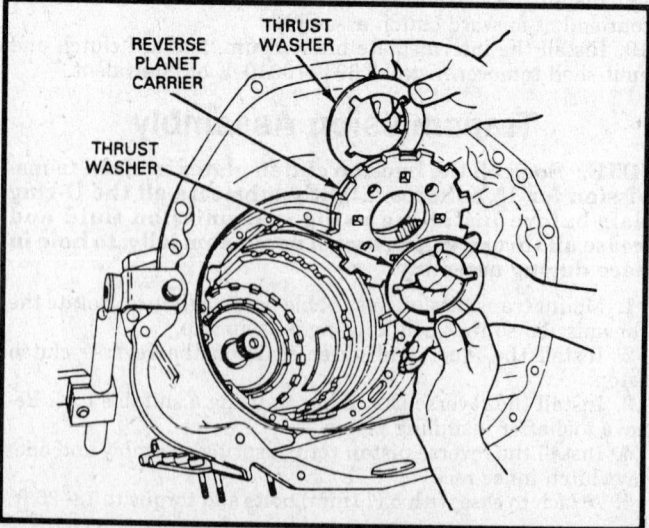

Installing reverse plate carrier assembly

17. Install the intermediate pressure plate. Install the cluch pack starting with internal spline plate. Install the apply plate.

18. Determine the endplay. The transmission rear endplay check determines the amount of space existing between the

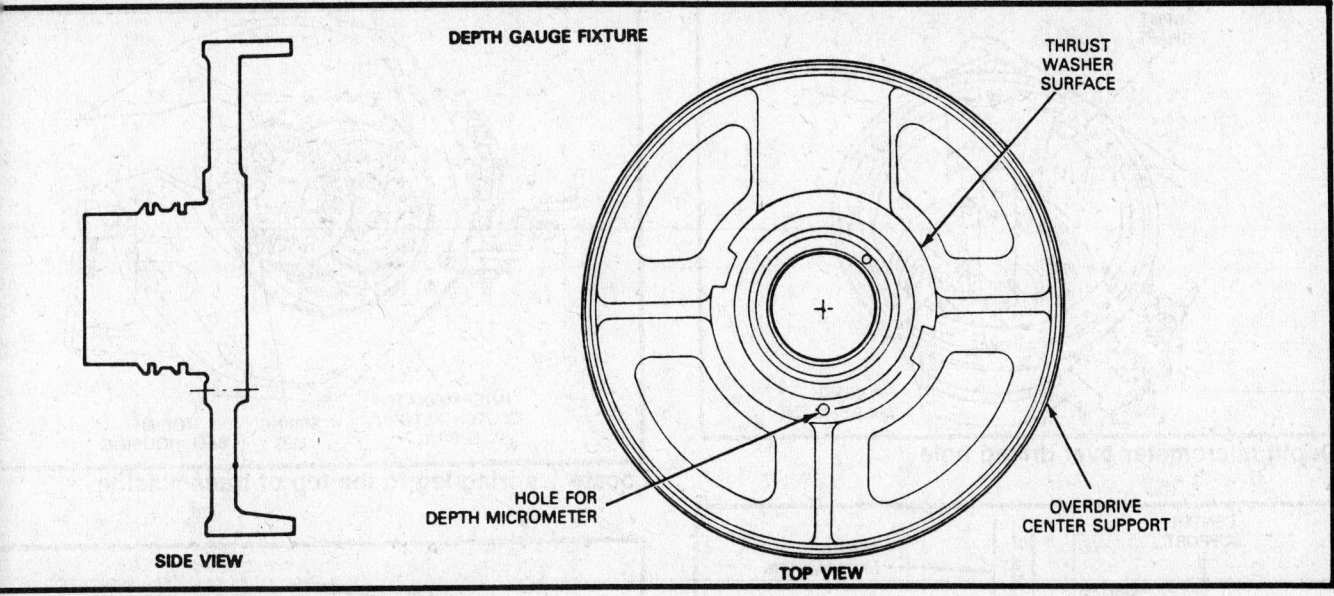

Installing micrometer to check endplay

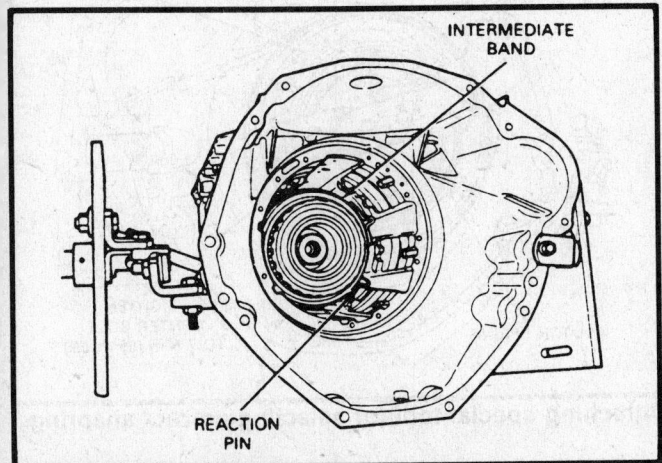

Installing intermediate band

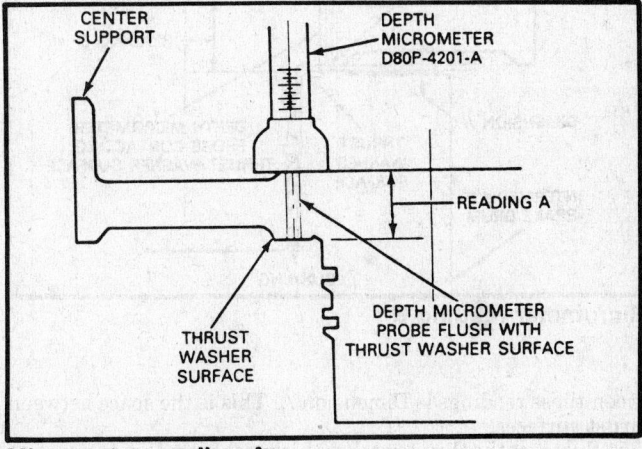

Micrometer reading A

thrust washer surfaces of the center support and the intermediate brake drum 0.081–0.032 in. (2.06–8.1mm).

19. Use depth micrometer D80P–4201–A or equivalent to access the area between the thrust surfaces of the support and the intermeidate brake drum. Remove the cast iron seals from the center support to allow easy insertion into the intermediate brake drum.

20. Place depth micrometer D80P–4201–A or equivalent over the drilled hole in center support fixture. Extend the micrometer probe until it is flush with thrust washer surface. Record micrometer reading. This is reading A.

21. Install the center support into intermediate brake drum and gently wiggle the input shaft to allow center support fixture to slide into the intermediate brake drum using its own weight. Ensure it is fully seated in transmission case.

22. Place the depth micrometer over the drilled hole in the center support.

23. Continue the extending micrometer probe until it contacts thrust washer surface of intermediate brake drum. This is reading B.

24. Subtract reading A from reading B. The difference be-

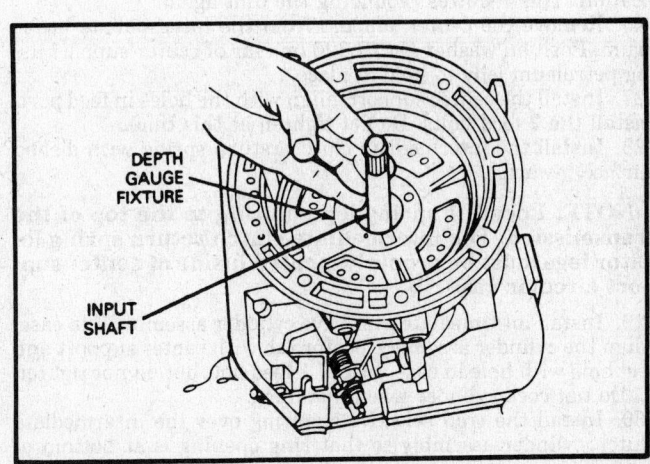

Installing center support

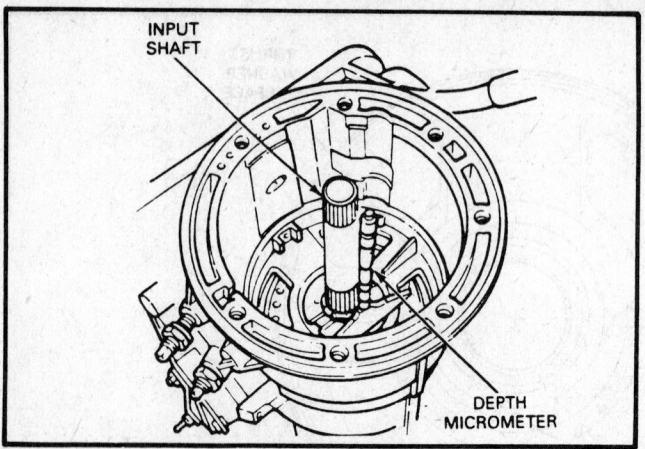

Depth micrometer over drilled hole

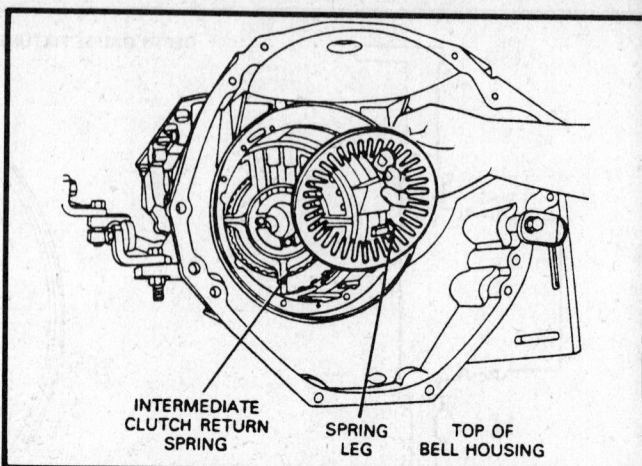

Locate 1 spring leg to the top of transmission

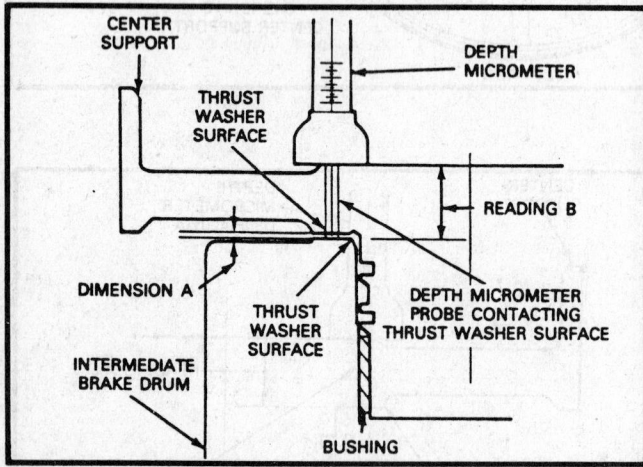

Micrometer reading B

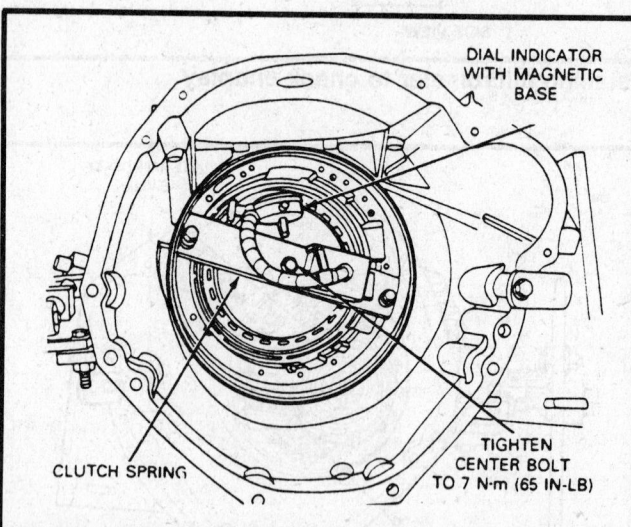

Attaching special tool for selecting correct snapring

tween these readings is Dimension A. This is the space between thrust surfaces.

25. Subtract the thrust washer thickness from Dimension A to determine final endplay. Specification is 0.081–0.032 in. (2.06–0.81mm). If the final dimension is outside specified limits, this indicates improper assembly, missing parts or parts out of specification. This requires rebuilding the unit again.

26. Remove the center support from the intermediate brake drum. Position washer No. 7L326 on rear of center support using petroleum jelly to hold in place.

27. Install the center support, align with the holes in feed port. Install the 2 feed bolts. Do not tighten at this time.

28. Install the intermediate clutch return spring with dished surface inward.

NOTE: Locate 1 spring leg pointing to the top of the transmission. The intermediate clutch return spring locator legs must be properly located inside of center support circular cast rib.

29. Install intermediate overdrive cylinder assembly into case. Align the cylinder assembly locator tab with center support and feel hole with hole in case. Install 1 feed bolt but do not tighten it. Do not cock cylinder when installing.

30. Install the trail selective snapring over the intermediate clutch cylinder assembly so that ring opening is at bottom of case for proper oil drainback. Place clutch spring compressor plate T89T–70010–F and intermediate clutch spring fixture

T89T–70010–C or equivalents onto the intermediate clutch cylinder assembly.

31. Tighten the center bolt to 65 inch lbs. Seat the selective snapring into the case ring groove.

32. Attach a dial indicator with magnetic base D78P–4201–B or equivalent or to bar. Place stylus onto the compressor plate T89T–70010–F or equivalent and zero the dial.

33. Release the torque on center bolt and record the reading on the indicator. If reading is not within specifications, repeat procedure using the correct selective snapring.
   Specifications:
   0.054–0.026 in. (1.37–0.67mm)
   Selective snaprings:
   0.061–0.057 in. (1.55–1.45mm)
   0.080–0.076 in. (2.05–1.95mm)
   0.100–0.098 in. (2.60–2.50mm)

34. Remove the clutch spring tool. Tighten the 3 (13mm) feed bolts into the intermediate overdrive cylinder assembly and the center support. Tighten the front feed bolt to 6–10 ft. lbs. and both rear feed bolts to 8–12 ft. lbs.

35. Using petroleum jelly to hold in place, postion needle bearing assembly No. 7G178 on the rear face of the center shaft. Install the center shaft, overdrive ring gear, overdrive planetary gearset and coast clutch cylinder as an assembly.

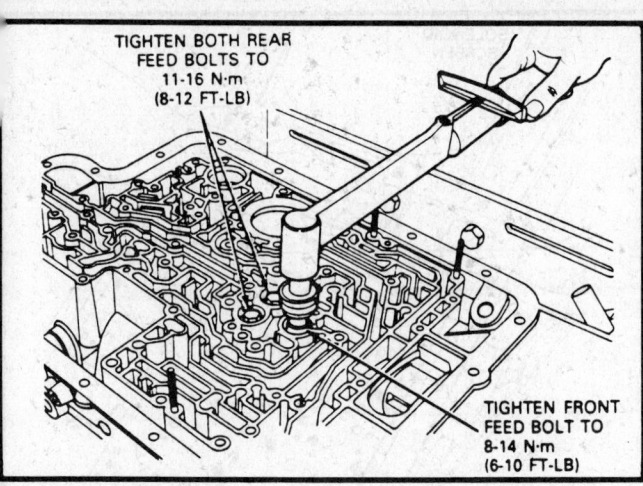

Tighten feed bolts

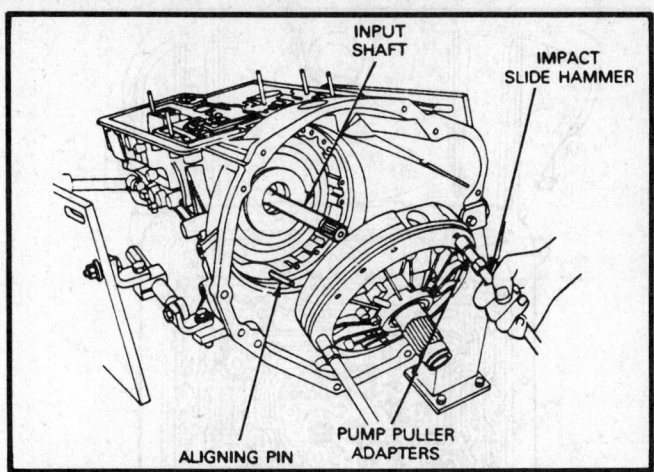

Installing pump onto case

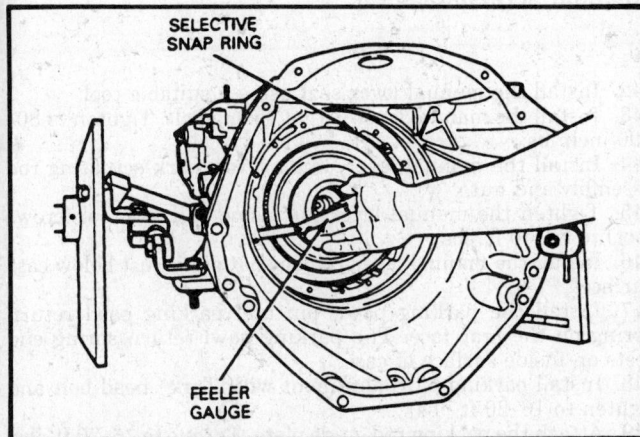

Measuring clearance of clutch pack

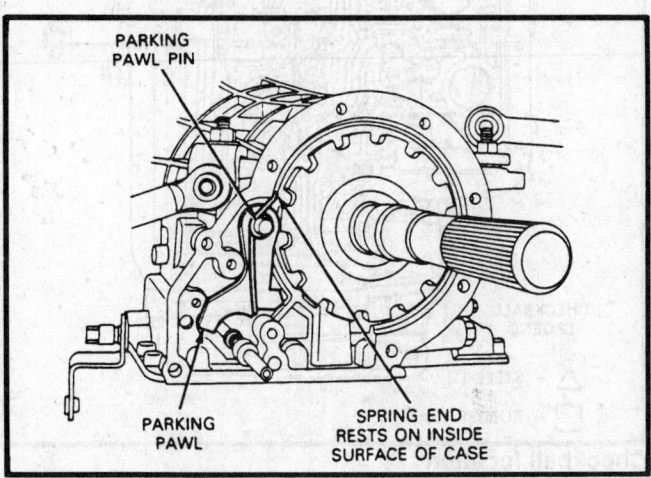

Parking pawl assembly

36. Install the overdrive clutch pack starting with a steel plate. Install pressure plate with dot facing outward and toward the top of the transmission. Install the trial selective snapring with opening at bottom of case.

37. Check the stack-up clearance using a feeler gauge. If not with specification, install correct selective snapring and recheck.

    Specification:
    0.047–0.022 in. (1.20–0.55mm)
    Selective Snaprings
    0.061–0.057 in. (1.55–1.45mm)
    0.80–0.076 in. (2.05–1.95mm)
    0.10–0.098 in. (2.60–2.50mm)
    0.12–0.118 in. (3.10–3.00mm)
    0.14–0.137 in. (3.60–3.50mm)

38. Install the pump gasket into the case. Screw the pump puller adapters T89T–70010–A or equivalent into pump threaded holes. Screw on impact slide hammers T59L–100–B or equivalent.

39. Install the thrust washer No. 7D014 and needle bearing assembly 7E486 onto pump. Use petroleum jelly to hold in place.

40. Install the input shaft (long splines end 1st) and alignment pin T89T–70010–B or equivalent into the case. Install the pump into the case. Position the filter inlet tube bore towards the valve body mounting surfaces.

41. Remove the old rubber coated washers from the 9 pump to case bolts. Install the new pump bolt washers. Remove aligning

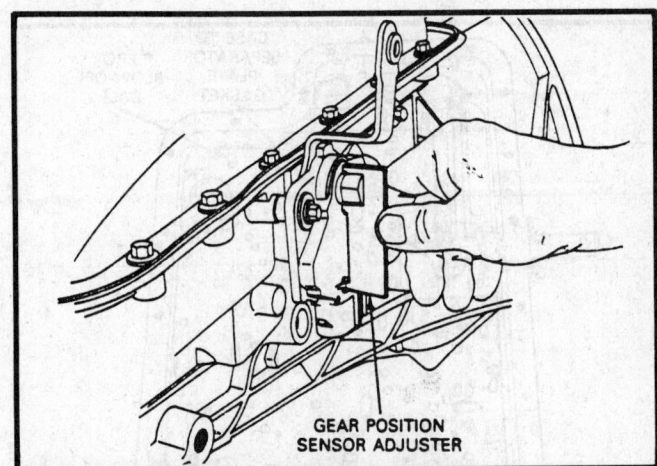

Adjustment of gear position sensor

pin T89T–70010–B or equivalent. Install the pump using 9 bolts. Torque to 18–23 ft. lbs.

NOTE: Draw the pump into the case assembly evenly, by tighten all bolts evenly, to avoid seal damage. Always remove the input shaft.

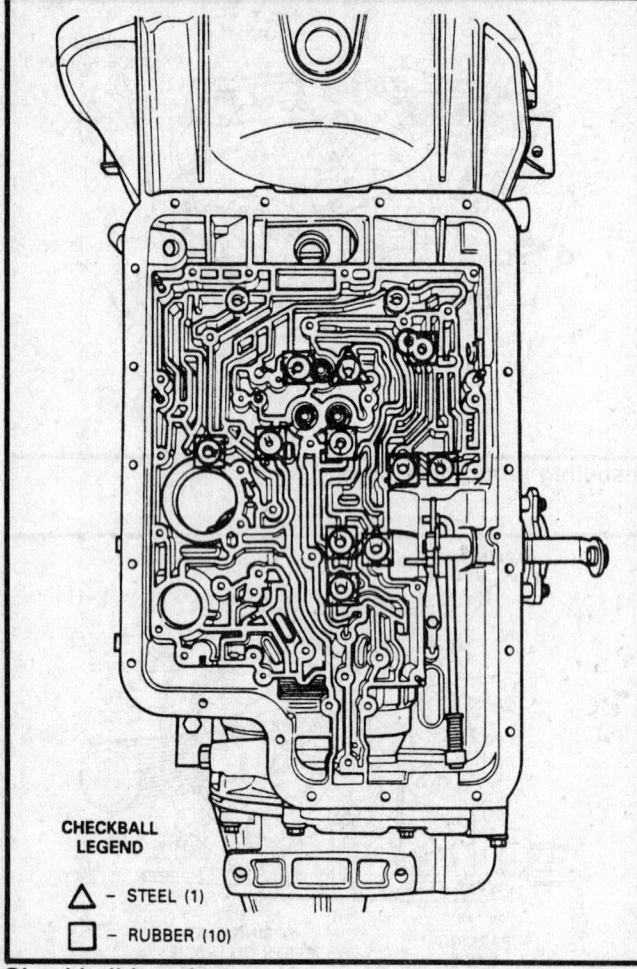

CHECKBALL LEGEND

△ – STEEL (1)

□ – RUBBER (10)

Checkball location

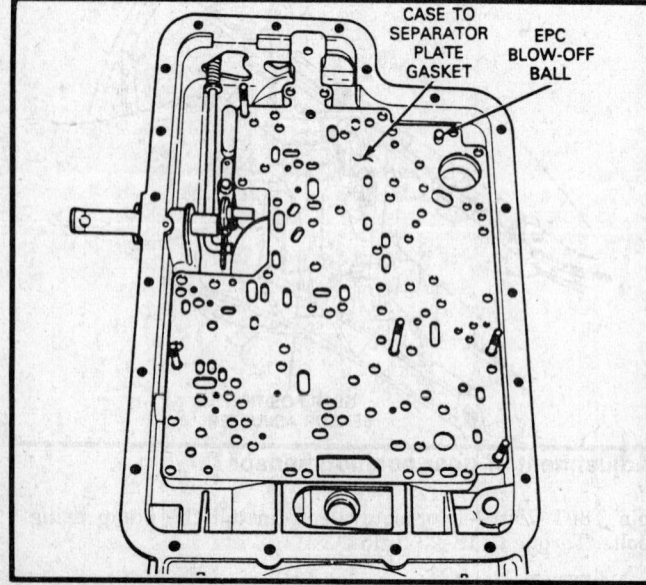

CASE TO SEPARATOR PLATE GASKET   EPC BLOW-OFF BALL

EPC ball location

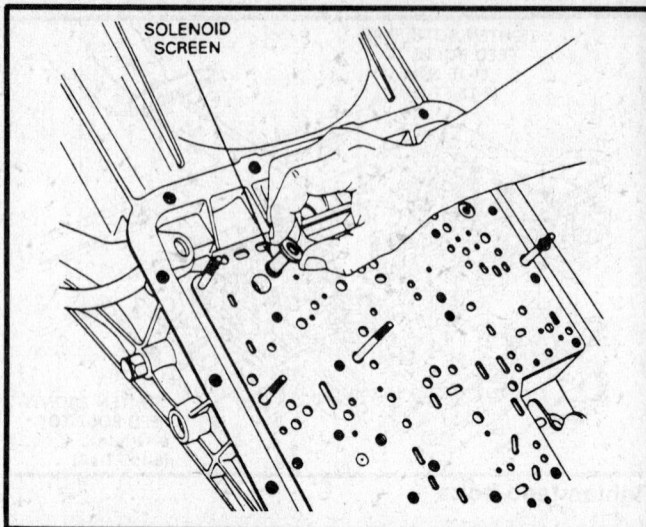

SOLENOID SCREEN

Solenoid screen location

42. Install the manual lever seal using a suitable tool.
43. Install the manual lever detent spring bolt. Tighten to 80–100 inch lbs.
44. Install the manual lever, inner lever, park actuating rod assembly and nut.
45. Tighten the manual lever nut using suitable tool (crows foot) to 30–40 ft. lbs).
46. Install the manual lever roll so that pin is just below case surface.
47. Install the parking pawl, pin and parking pawl return spring on the rear face. The parking pawl return spring end rests on inside surface of case.
48. Install parking pawl abutment with Torx® head bolt and tighten to 16–20 ft. lbs.
49. Attach the parking rod guide plate. Torque to 16–20 ft. lbs. Ensure the plate dimple is facing inward.
50. Install the manual lever position sensor. Do not tighten bolts at this time. Align manual lever position sensor for **N** gear position using gear position sensor adjuster T89T–70010–J or equivalent.
51. Tighten the (8mm) bolts to 55–75 inch lbs.
52. Using petroleum jelly to hold in place position gasket on the extension housing.
53. Install the extension housing and wiring bracket on rear of case. Tighten bolts to 20–29 ft lbs.

NOTE: The 2 bottom bolts are longer on 4WD vehicles.

54. Rotate the transmission so that pan is facing up. Install 1 steel and 10 rubber check balls, EPC blow off spring and ball into the case pockets. Make sure you install the check balls in the correct location.
55. Install the case to separator plate gasket.
56. Install the separator plate.
57. Attach the reinforcing plate with 3 (8mm) bolts with marking stamped **UP** facing up. Tighten to 80–100 in lbs. Check the placement of EPC blow off ball.
58. Install the new separator to the control gasket.
59. Install the solenoid screen into the separator plate. Turn and lock solenoid screen.
60. Install the accumulator body over studs and attach with 2 nuts and 11 bolt. Tighten to 80–100 inch lbs.
61. Lower the main control body over studs. Align manual valve with manual lever.
62. Attach the valve body with 2 nuts and 14 bolts. Tighten to 80–100 inch lbs.

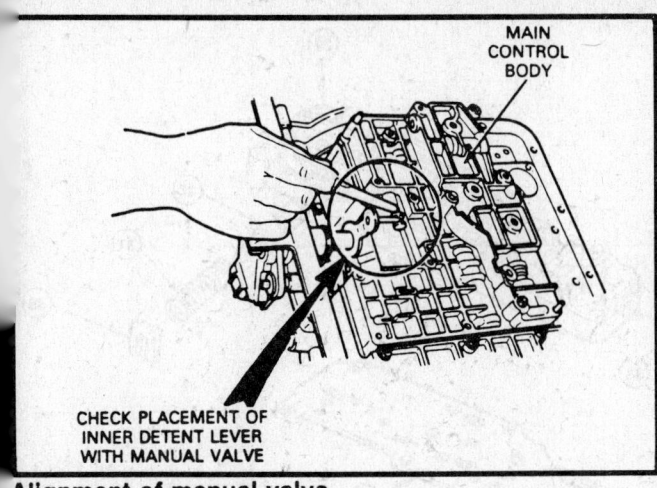

Alignment of manual valve

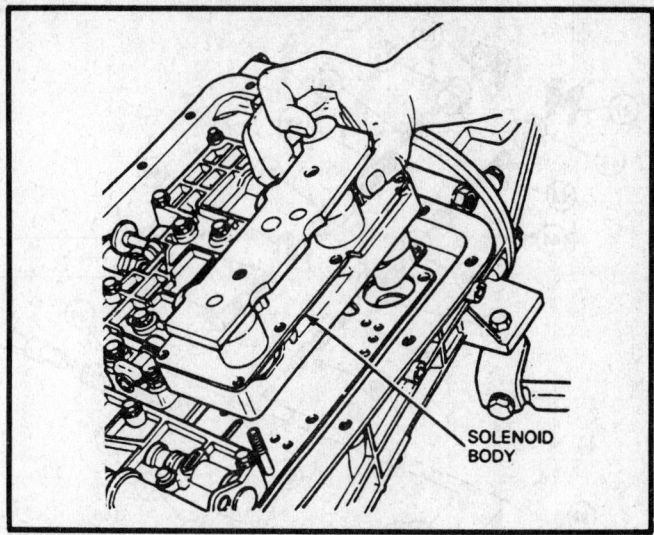

Installing solenoid body

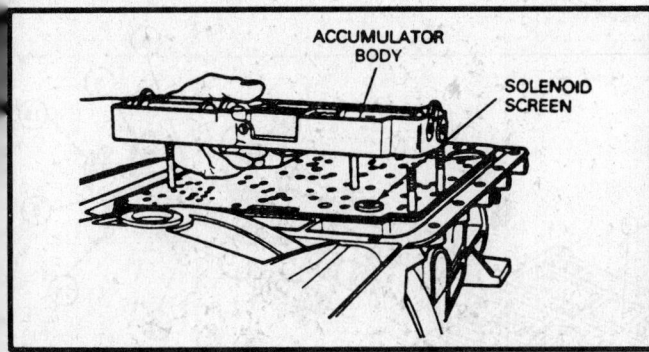

Installing accumlator body

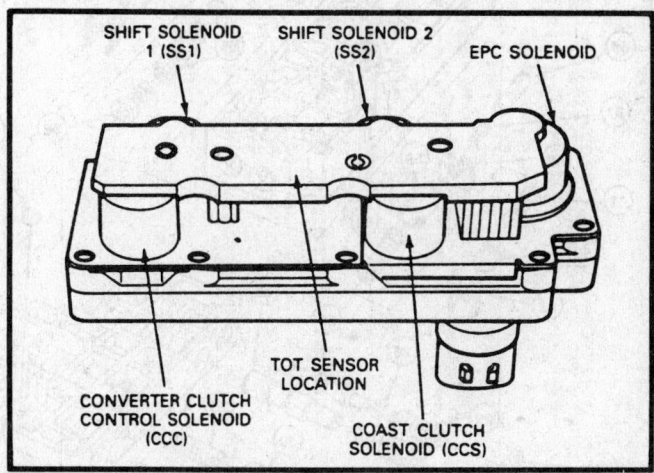

Shift solenoid body assembly

63. Install the solenoid body over stud and attach with 9 Torx® bolts and 1 nut. Tighten to 80–100 inch lbs. Prior to installing the solenoid body assembly, coast the case connector bore with M1C172–A grease or equivalent.

64. Install a new filter and seal assembly by lubricating the seal with transmission fluid and pressing the filter into place.

65. Place pan magnet on dimple in bottom of pan. Install new pan gasket.

66. Attach pan with 20 bolts. Tighten bolts to 10–12 ft. lbs.

67. If necessary, install the stub tube using suitable tool. Use the stripe on the side of tube for alignment. The stripe should be farthest outboard when installed.

68. Reinstall the input shaft, long splined end installed first.

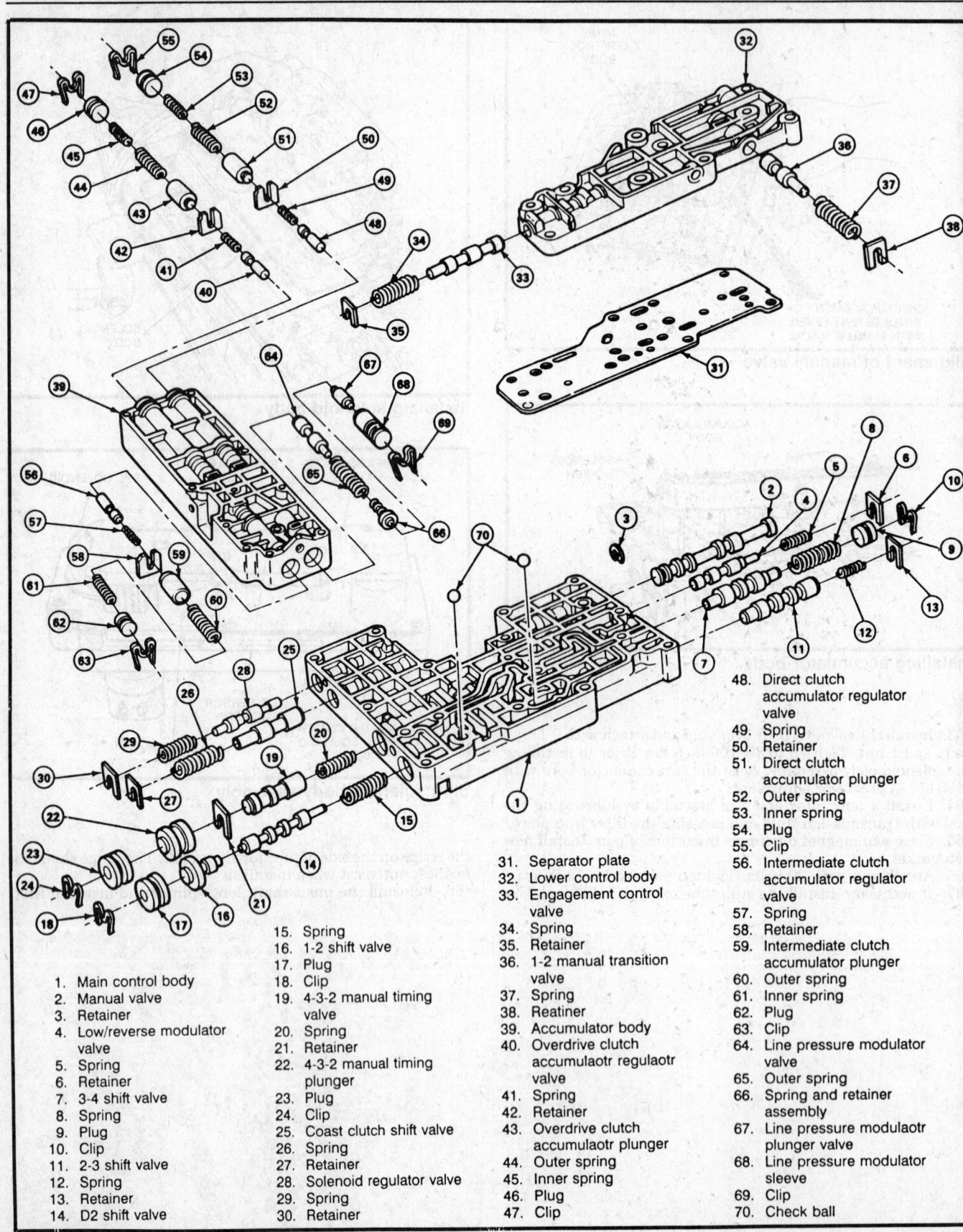

Exploded view of valve body

1. Main control body
2. Manual valve
3. Retainer
4. Low/reverse modulator valve
5. Spring
6. Retainer
7. 3-4 shift valve
8. Spring
9. Plug
10. Clip
11. 2-3 shift valve
12. Spring
13. Retainer
14. D2 shift valve
15. Spring
16. 1-2 shift valve
17. Plug
18. Clip
19. 4-3-2 manual timing valve
20. Spring
21. Retainer
22. 4-3-2 manual timing plunger
23. Plug
24. Clip
25. Coast clutch shift valve
26. Spring
27. Retainer
28. Solenoid regulator valve
29. Spring
30. Retainer
31. Separator plate
32. Lower control body
33. Engagement control valve
34. Spring
35. Retainer
36. 1-2 manual transition valve
37. Spring
38. Reatiner
39. Accumulator body
40. Overdrive clutch accumulaotr regulaotr valve
41. Spring
42. Retainer
43. Overdrive clutch accumulaotr plunger
44. Outer spring
45. Inner spring
46. Plug
47. Clip
48. Direct clutch accumulator regulator valve
49. Spring
50. Retainer
51. Direct clutch accumulator plunger
52. Outer spring
53. Inner spring
54. Plug
55. Clip
56. Intermediate clutch accumulator regulator valve
57. Spring
58. Retainer
59. Intermediate clutch accumulator plunger
60. Outer spring
61. Inner spring
62. Plug
63. Clip
64. Line pressure modulator valve
65. Outer spring
66. Spring and retainer assembly
67. Line pressure modulaotr plunger valve
68. Line pressure modulator sleeve
69. Clip
70. Check ball

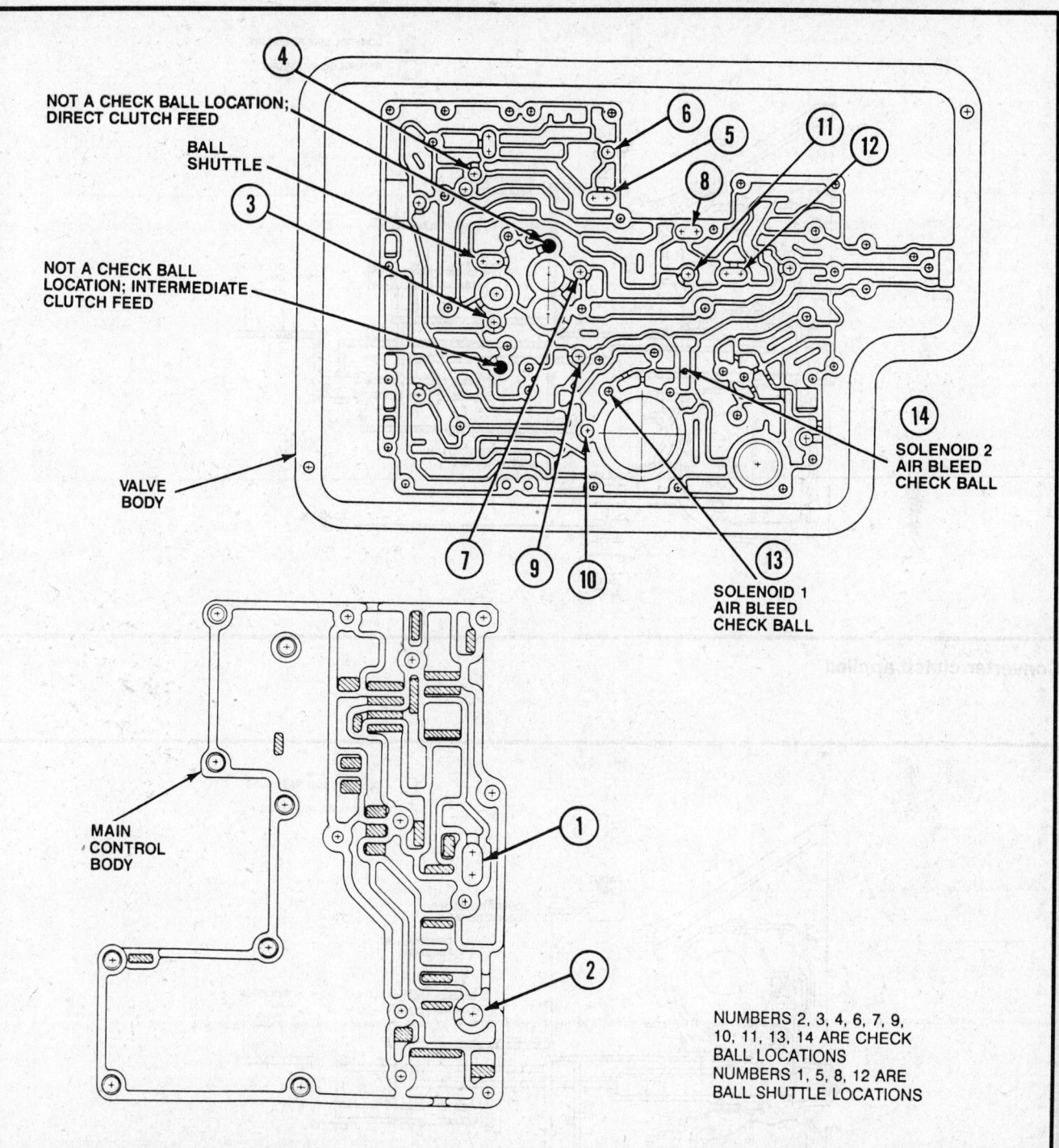

Check ball and ball shuttle locations

NUMBERS 2, 3, 4, 6, 7, 9, 10, 11, 13, 14 ARE CHECK BALL LOCATIONS
NUMBERS 1, 5, 8, 12 ARE BALL SHUTTLE LOCATIONS

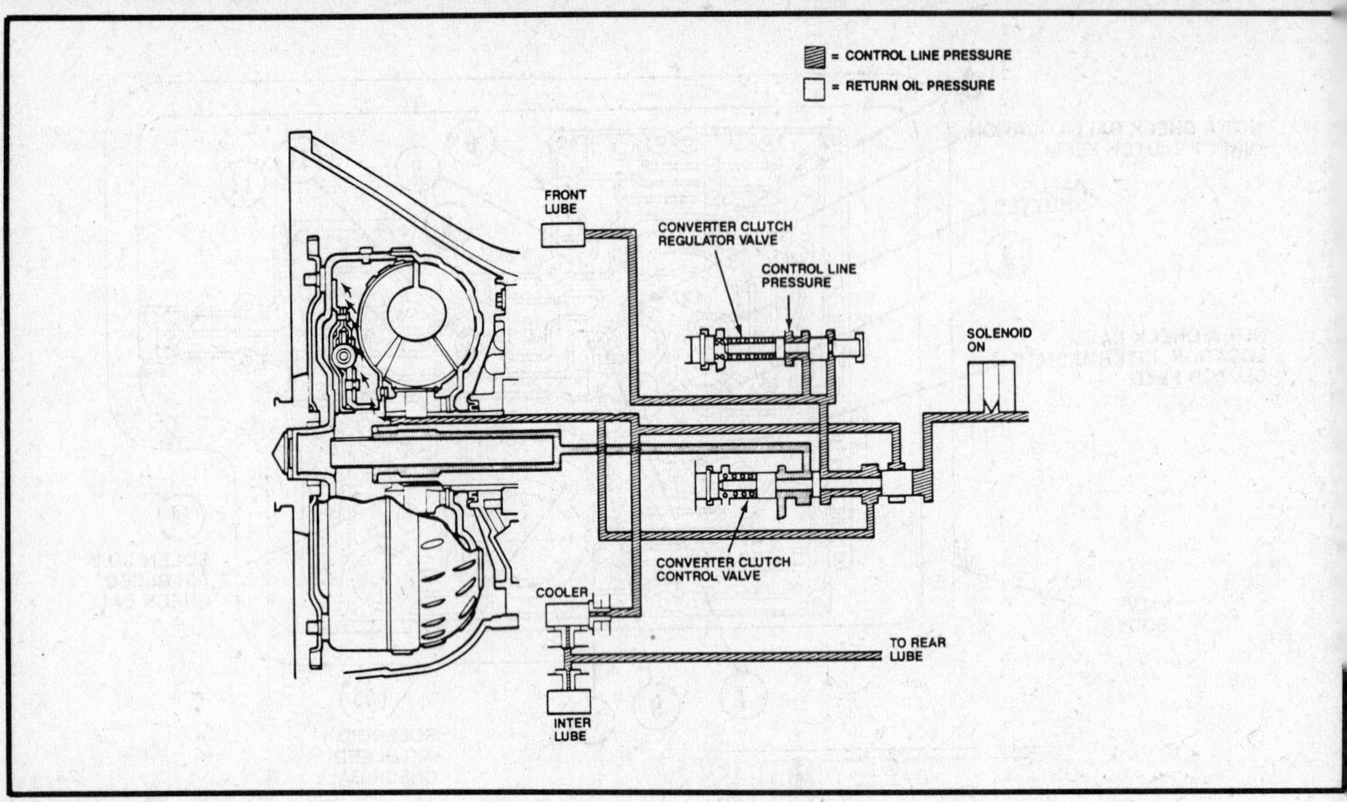

Converter clutch applied

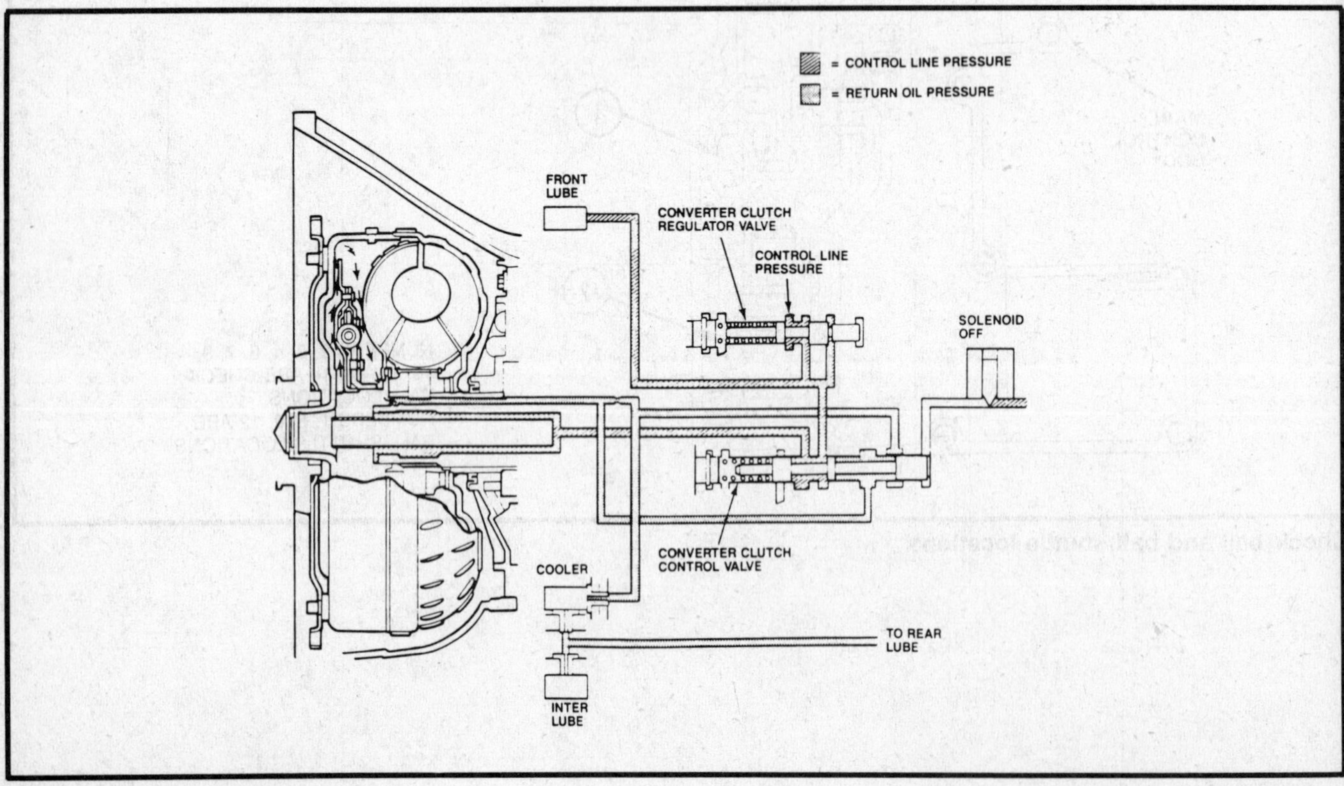

Converter clutch released

SPECIFICATIONS

TORQUE SPECIFICATIONS

Description	ft. lbs.	Nm	Description	ft. lbs.	Nm
Inner OWC race to case	18–25	24–34	Reinforcing plate to case	80–100 ①	9–11
Connector to case (fluid) cooler line	18–23	24–31	Main accumulator and solenoid body to case	80–100 ①	9–11
Plug line pressure case	6–12	8–16	Main and lower body to case	80–100 ①	9–11
Throttle pressure case plug	6–12	8–16	Lower body to main body	80–100 ①	9–11
Inner & outer lever to manual control shaft	30–40	40–54	Solenoid body to case	80–100 ①	9–11
Positive detent spring to case	80–100 ①	9–11	Park rod abutment to case	16–20	22–27
Parking rod guide plate to case	16–20	22–27	Control assembly to pump	18–23	24–31
Neutral switch assembly to case	55–75 ①	6–8	Oil pan to case	10–12	14–16
Center support to hub	80–120 ①	9–14	Converter drain plug	18–20	24–27
Center support fluid feed	8–12	11–16	Overdrive cylinder fluid feed	6–10	8–14
Extension housing to case	20–29	27–39	Stud—valve body to case short	80–100 ①	9–11
Extension housing to case (4x2)	20–29	27–39	Stud—valve body to case long	80–100 ①	9–11
Extension housing to case (4x4)	20–29	27–39	Nut—valve body to case	80–100 ①	9–11
Stator support to pump body	80–100 ①	9–11	Nut—manual detent lever	30–40	41–54
Oil pump body to case	18–23	24–31			

① inch lbs.

CLUTCH PLATE USAGE AND CLEARANCE SPECIFICATIONS

	Steel	Friction	Selective Snapring	
			Clearance in. (mm)	Thickness in. (mm)
Forward	4	4	(0.030–0.055) 0.76–1.40	(0.128–0.132) 3.25–3.35
				(0.110–0.114) 2.79–2.90
				(0.092–0.096) 2.34–2.44
				(0.074–0.078) 1.88–1.98
				(0.056–0.06) 1.42–1.52
Direct	4	4	(0.039–0.062) 0.99–1.57	(0.083–0.087) 2.11–2.21
				(0.074–0.078) 1.88–1.98
	3	3	(0.034–0.044) 0.86–1.12	(0.065–0.069) 1.65–1.75
Intermediate	3	3	(0.030–0.06) 0.76–1.52	(0.098–0.102) 2.49–2.59
				(0.077–0.081) 1.95–2.05
	2	2	(0.020–0.040) 0.51–1.02	(0.057–0.061) 1.45–1.55
Overdrive	3	3	(0.030–0.060) 0.76–1.52	(0.138–0.142) 3.5–3.6
				(0.118–0.122) 3.00–3.1
				(0.098–0.102) 2.49–2.59
				(0.077–0.081) 1.95–2.05
	2	2	(0.02–0.04) 0.51–1.02	(0.057–0.061) 1.45–1.55
Coast	2	2	(0.025–0.045) 0.635–1.140	(0.085–0.089) 2.15–2.26
				(0.069–0.073) 1.75–1.85
				(0.053–0.057) 1.35–1.45

SPECIAL TOOLS

Tool Number	Description
T50T-100-A	Impact slide hammer (use w/T89T-70010-A)
T59L-100-B	Impact slide hammer (use w/T89T-70010-A)
T58L-101-B	Puller
T77F-1102-A	Puller
T00L-1175-AC	Seal remover
T77F-1176-A	Clutch spring compressor
D79P-2100-T30	Torx® bit (T-30)
D79P-2100-T40	Torx® bit (T-40)
T78P-3504-N	Roll pin remover
T80T-4000-W	Handle (use w/PS88B800-10)
D78P-4201-B	Dial indicator with magnetic base
T00L-4201-C	Dial indicator with bracketry
T67P-7341-A	Shift linkage insulation tool
T84P-7341-A/B	Shift linkage grommet remover/replacer
T61L-7657-B	Extension housing seal replacer
T77L-7697-C	Extension housing bushing replacer
T77L-7697-D	Extension housing bushing remover
D89L-77000-A	Banding tool
T57L-77820-A	Pressure gauge
T80L-7902-A	Endplay checking tool
T81P-7902-C	Torque converter handles
T71P-19703-C	O-ring tool
T89T-70010-A	Pump puller adaptors

Tool Number	Description
T89T-70010-B	Aligning pin
T89T-70010-C	Clutch spring fixture
T89T-70010-E	Clutch remover/installer
T89T-70010-F	Clutch spring compressor plate
T89T-70010-G	Stub tube installer
T89T-70010-J	Gear position sensor adjuster
T88C-77000-AH2	Clutch spring compressor bar
T74P-77248-A	Seal remover
T80L-77405-A	Clutch spring compressor
T74P-77498-A	Shift lever seal replacer
T65L-77515-A	Clutch spring compressor
T77L-77548-A	Lip seal protector
T63L-77837-A	Pump seal replacer
T89T-70100-A	E4OD test harness
Not available at time of printing	Manual lever position sensor tester

ROTUNDA EQUIPMENT	
014-00028	Torque converter and oil cooler cleaner
014-00104	C-3 transmission adapter kit
014-00106	Rotunda twin post engine stand
021-00054	Torque converter leak test kit
014-00763	Transmission stand fixture

Section 5
Oil Flow Circuits

PARK — A500

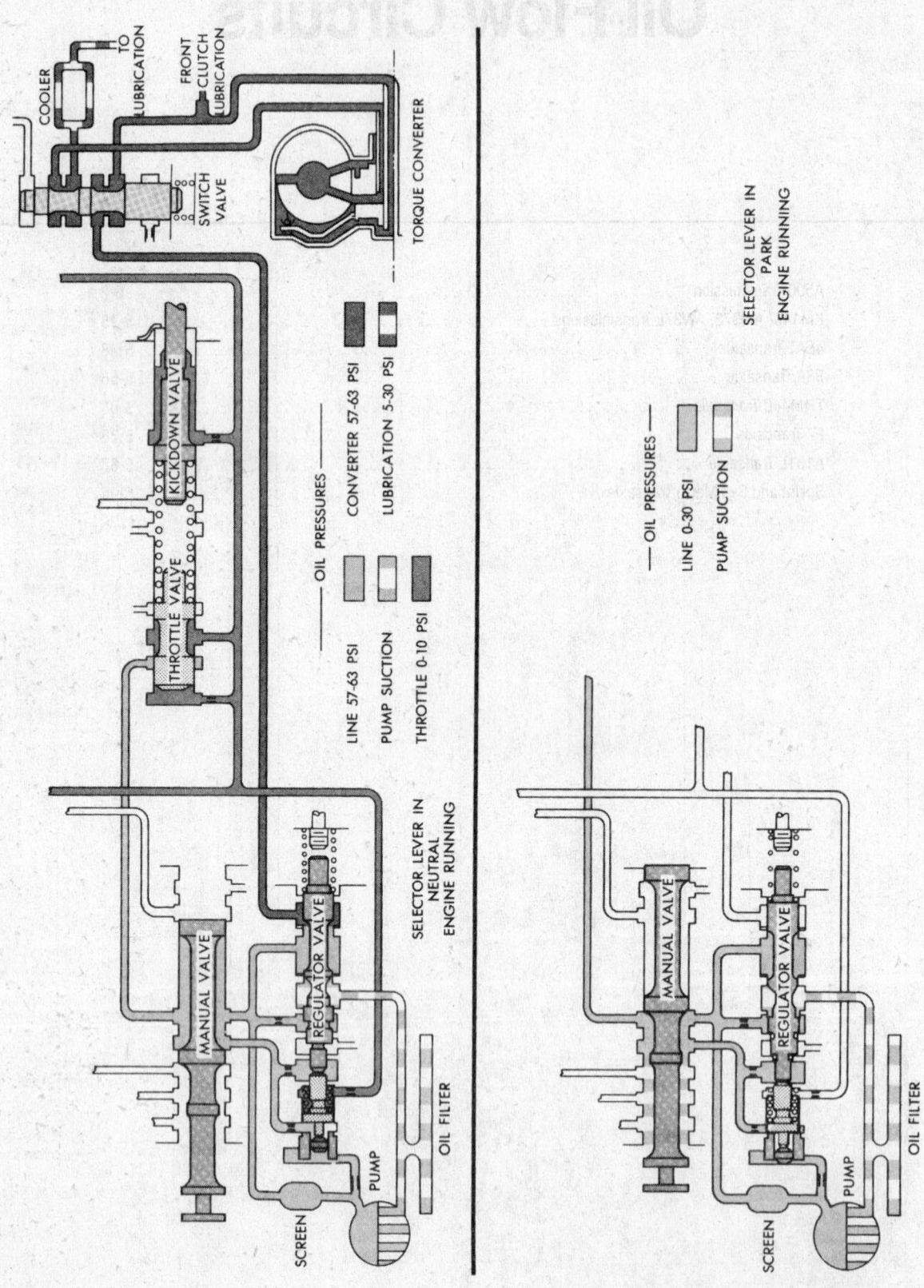

COOLER

TO LUBRICATION

FRONT CLUTCH LUBRICATION

SWITCH VALVE

TORQUE CONVERTER

KICKDOWN VALVE

THROTTLE VALVE

OIL PRESSURES

CONVERTER 57-63 PSI	
LUBRICATION 5-30 PSI	
LINE 57-63 PSI	
PUMP SUCTION	
THROTTLE 0-10 PSI	

MANUAL VALVE

REGULATOR VALVE

SELECTOR LEVER IN NEUTRAL ENGINE RUNNING

SCREEN

PUMP

OIL FILTER

OIL PRESSURES

LINE 0-30 PSI	
PUMP SUCTION	

SELECTOR LEVER IN PARK ENGINE RUNNING

MANUAL VALVE

REGULATOR VALVE

SCREEN

PUMP

OIL FILTER

DRIVE (BREAKAWAY) HALF THROTTLE—A500

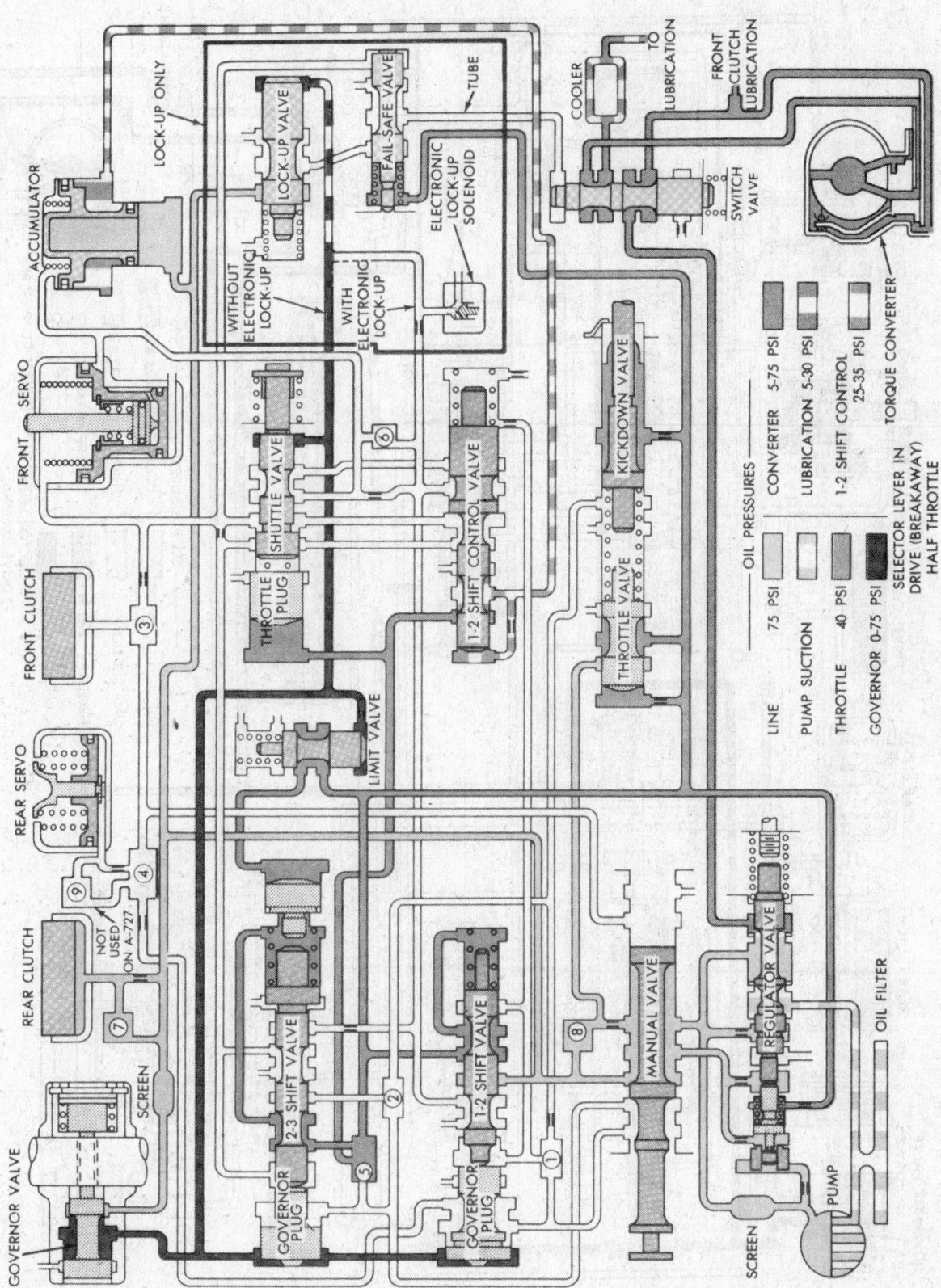

DRIVE (2ND) HALF THROTTLE—A500

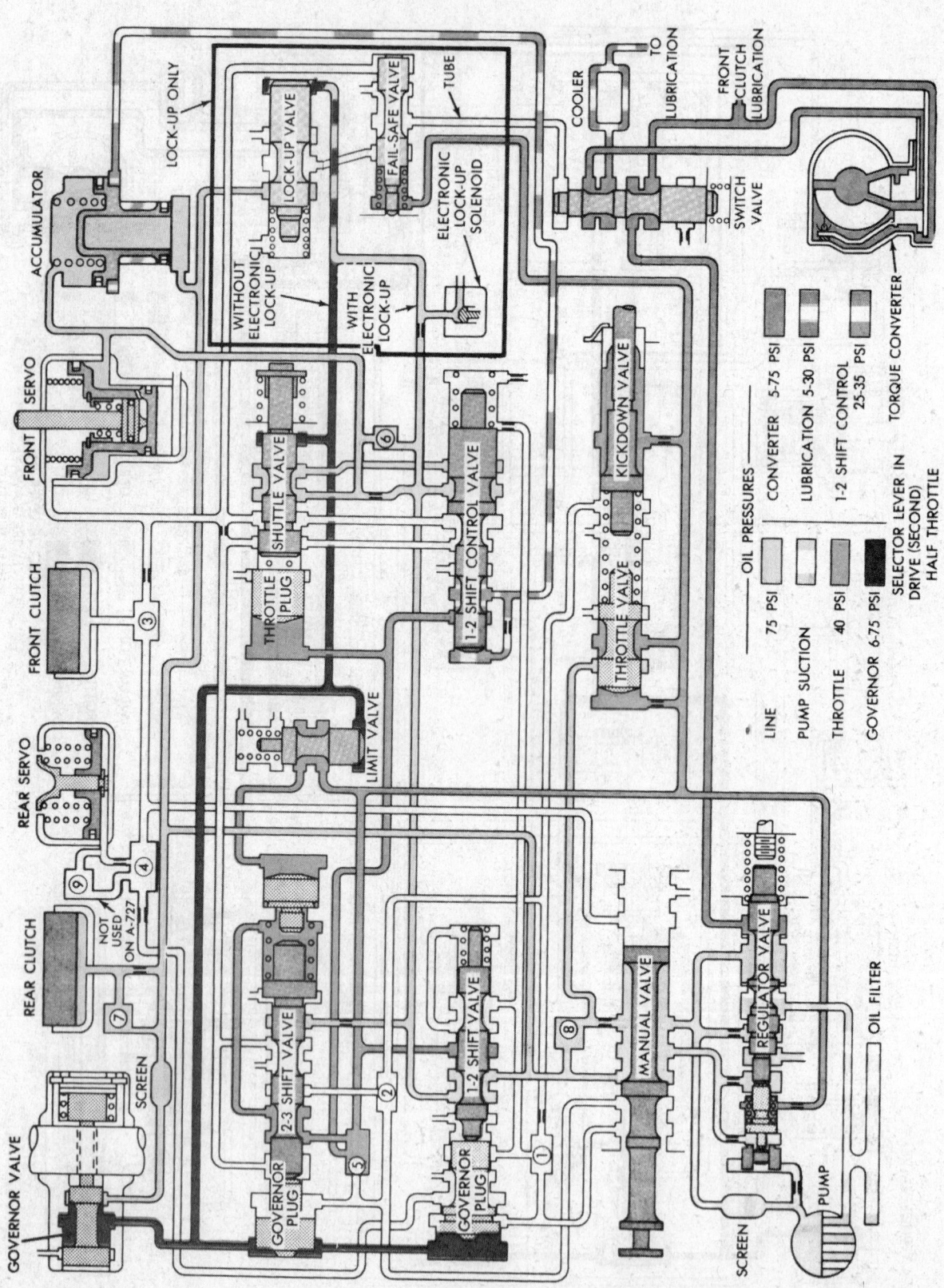

DRIVE (DIRECT) HALF THROTTLE—A500

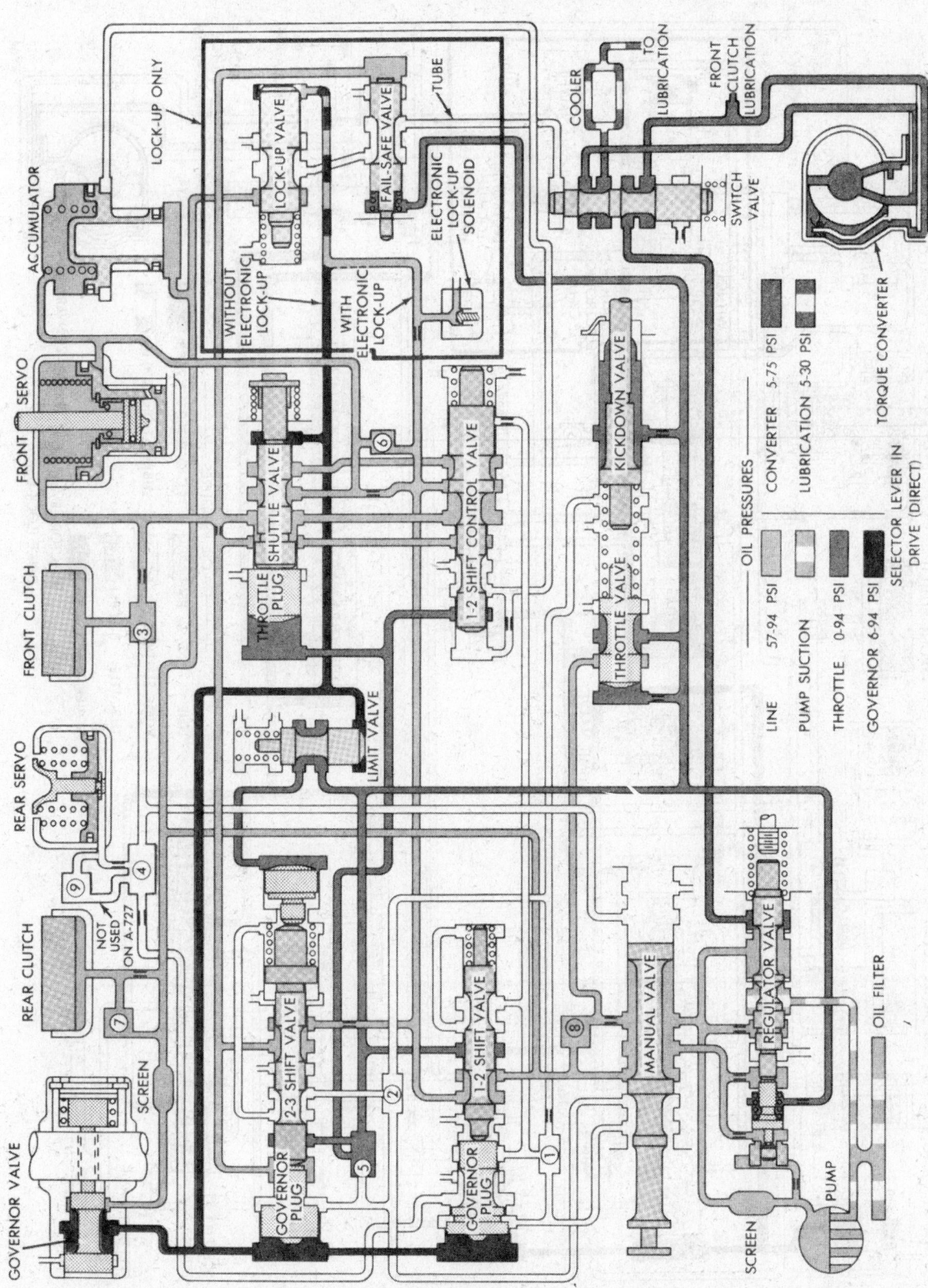

OIL PRESSURES

CONVERTER 5-75 PSI
LUBRICATION 5-30 PSI
TORQUE CONVERTER

LINE 57-94 PSI
PUMP SUCTION
THROTTLE 0-94 PSI
GOVERNOR 6-94 PSI
SELECTOR LEVER IN DRIVE (DIRECT)

DRIVE (LOCKUP) HALF THROTTLE — A500

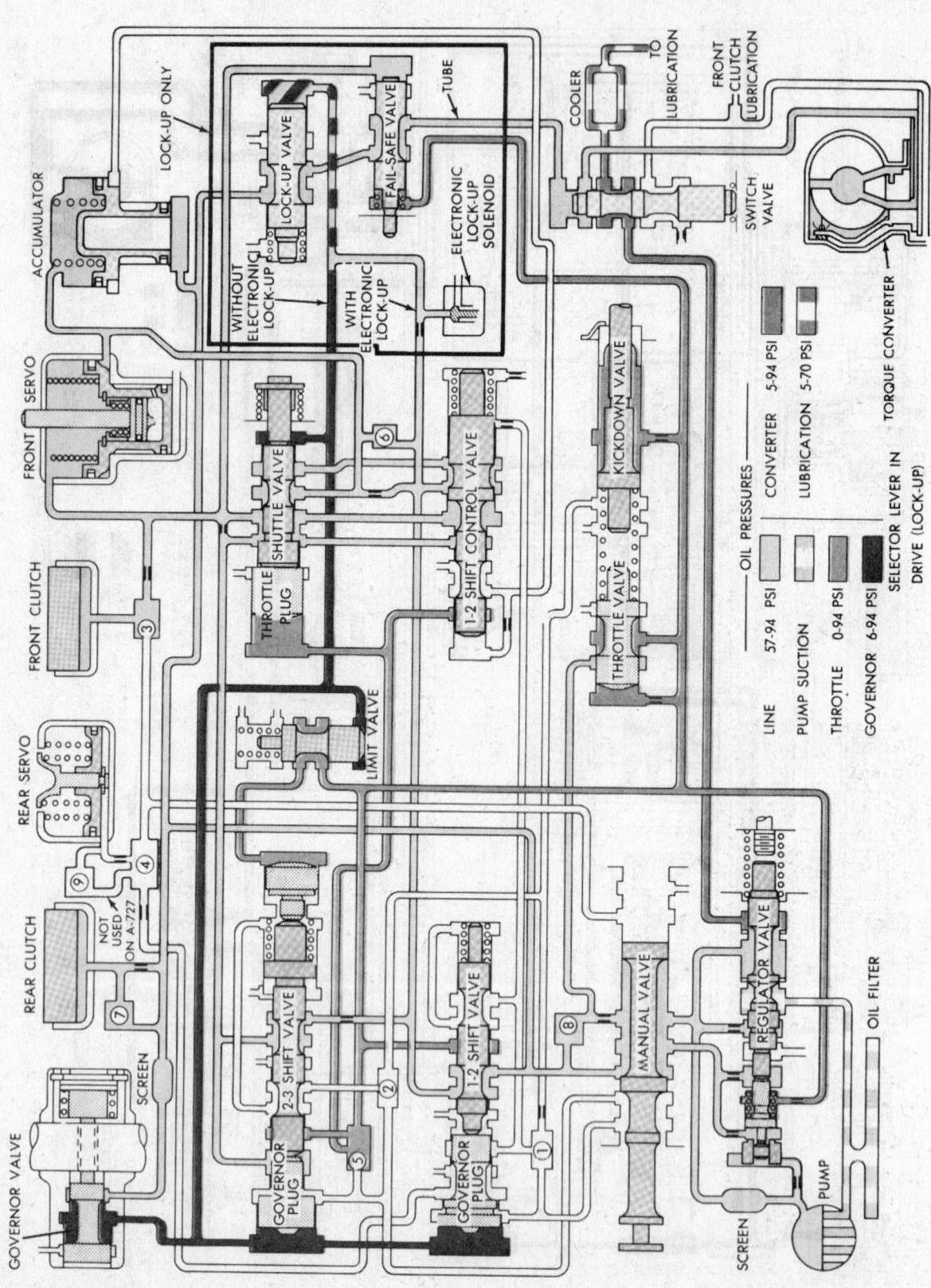

DRIVE (PART THROTTLE KICKDOWN) BELOW 40 MPH—A500

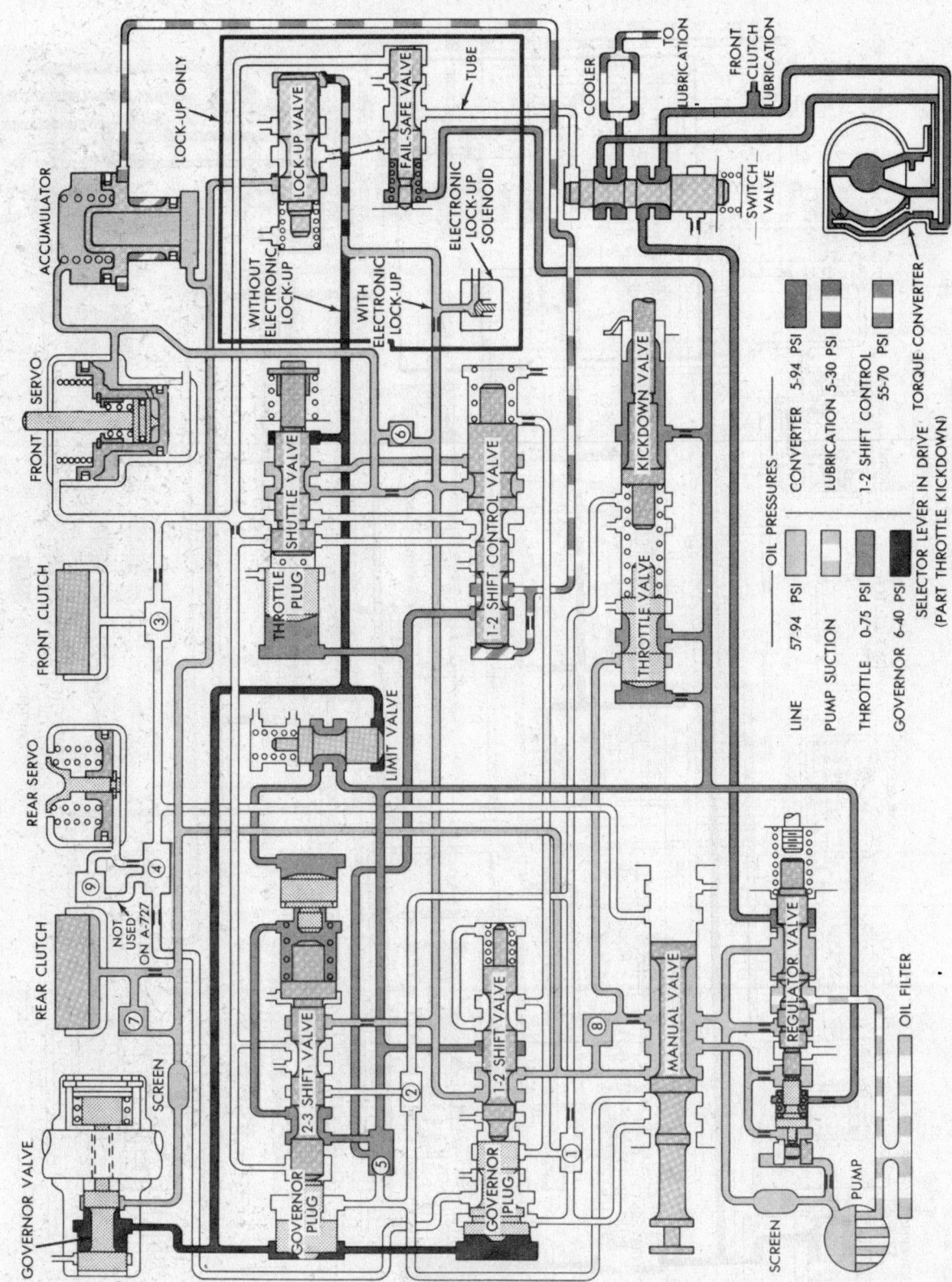

DRIVE (FULL THROTTLE KICKDOWN)—A500

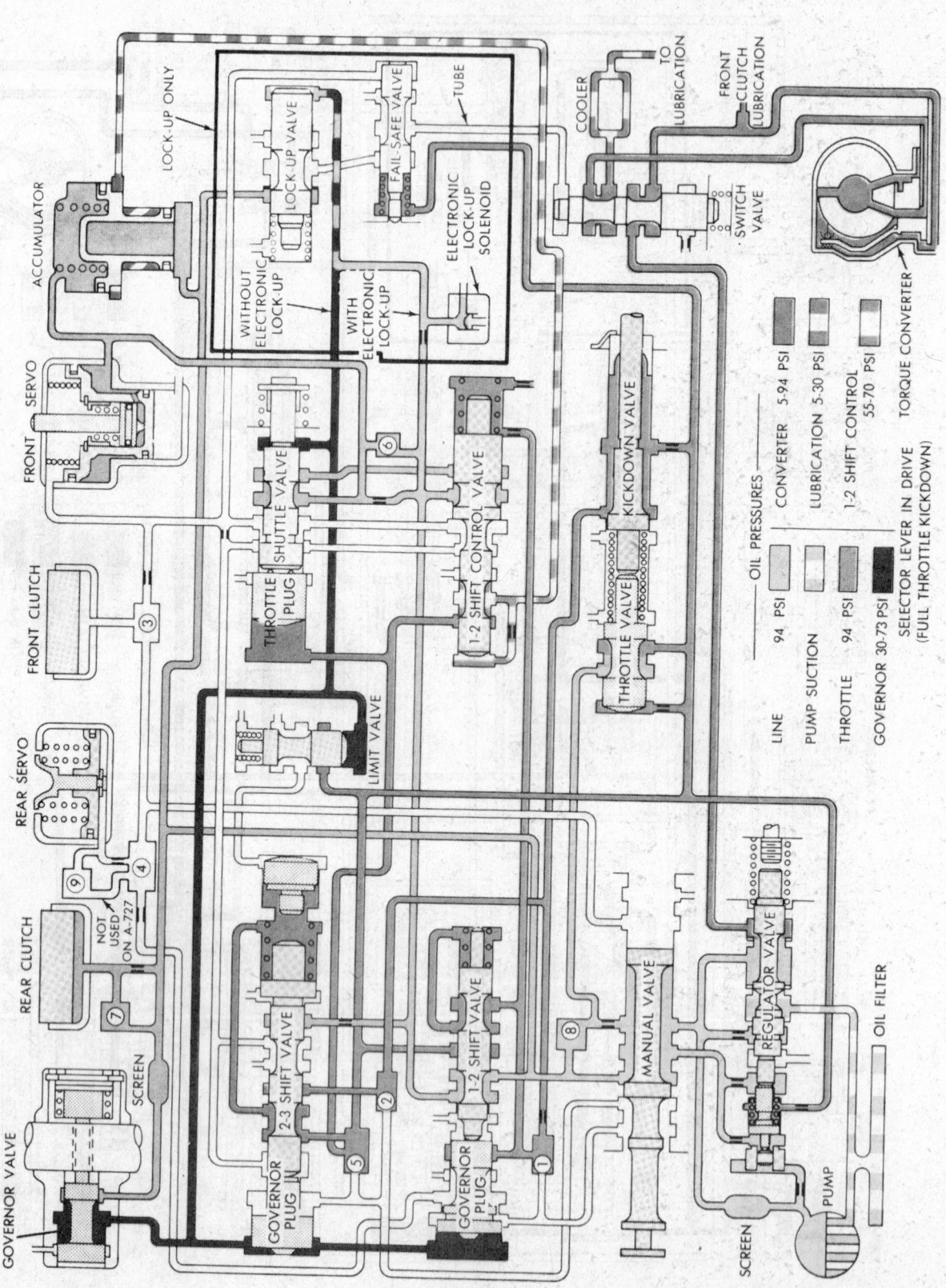

2—MANUAL 2ND (CLOSED THROTTLE)—A500

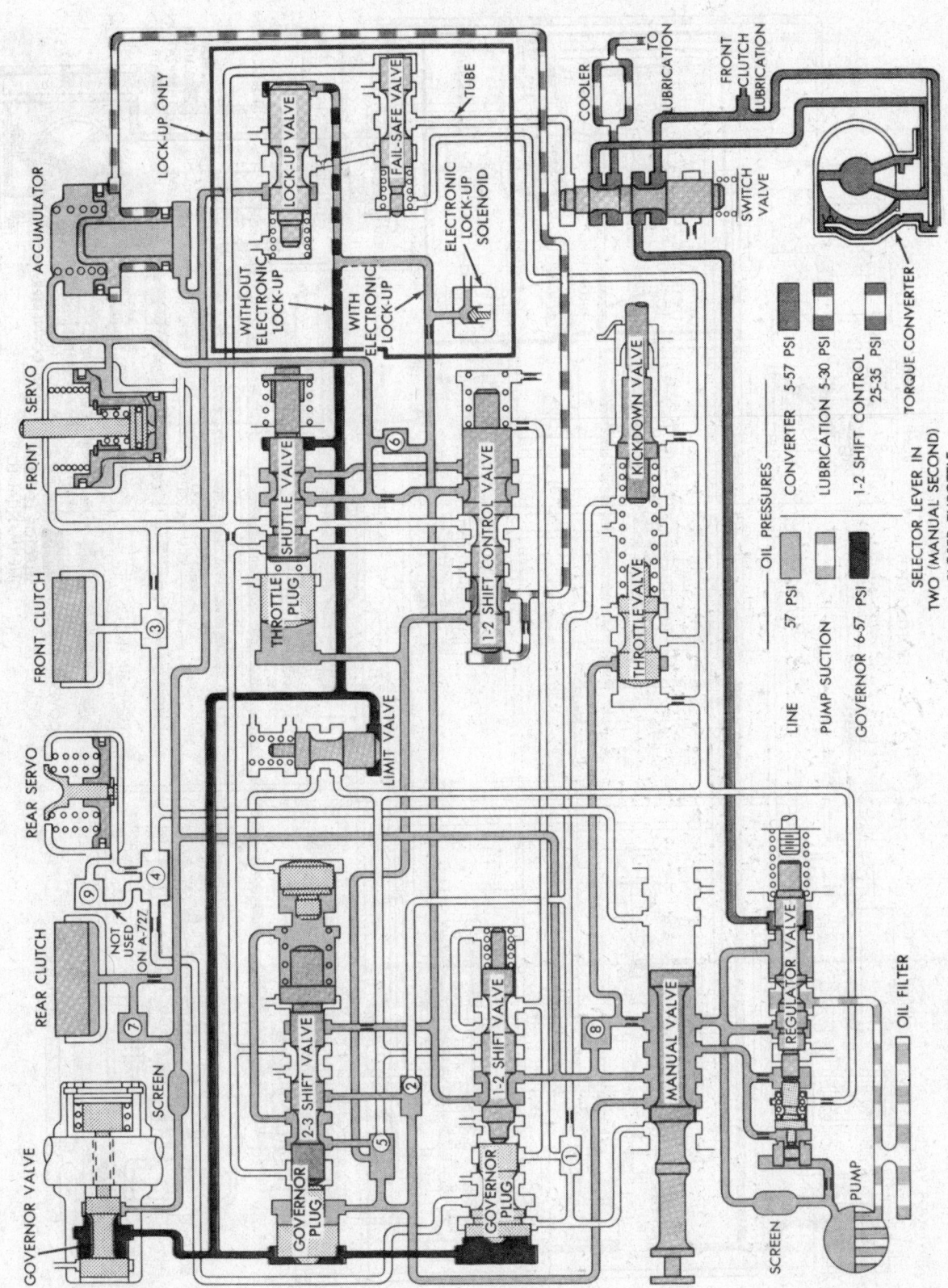

1 – MANUAL LOW (CLOSED THROTTLE) – A500

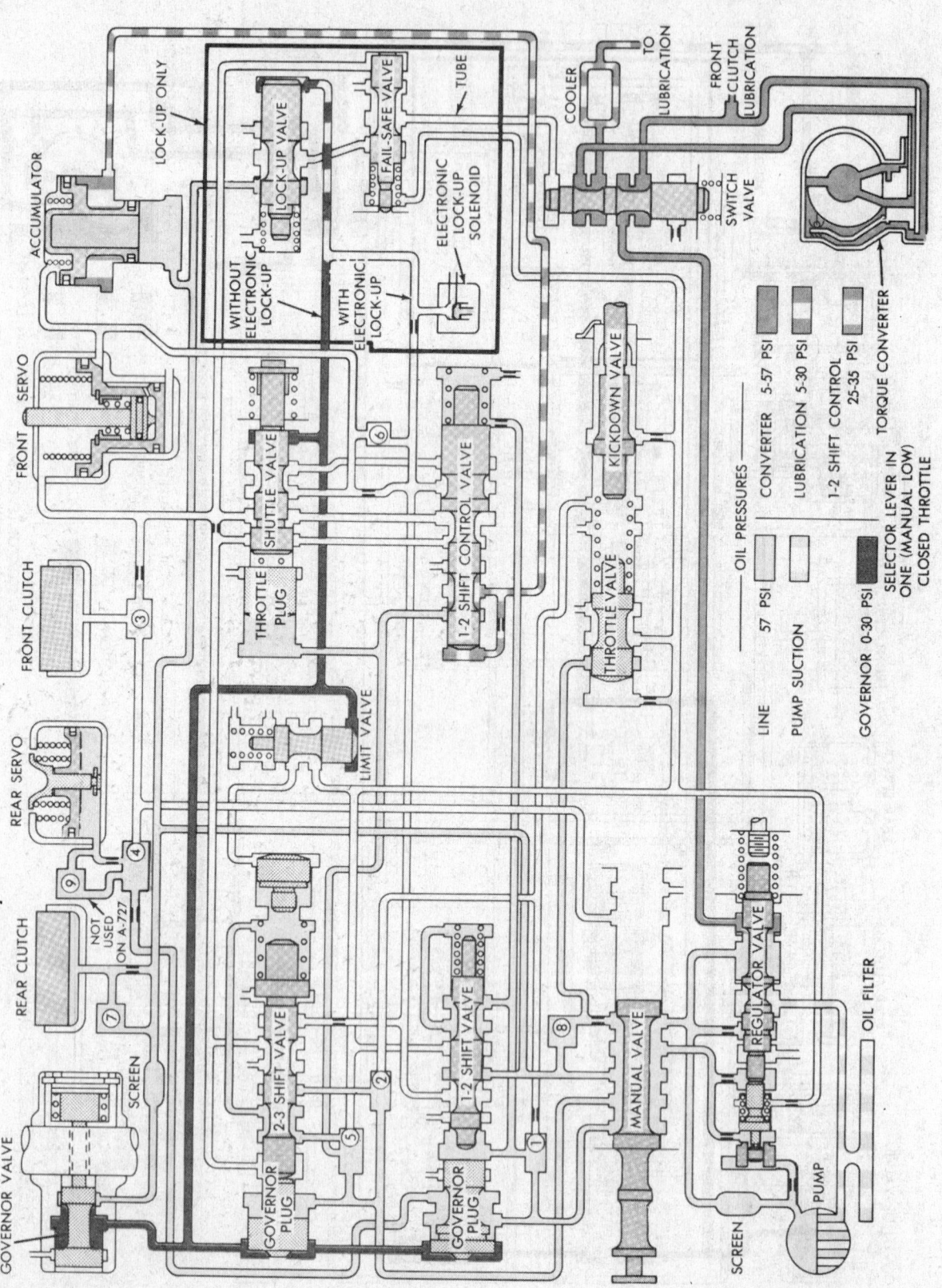

REVERSE — A500

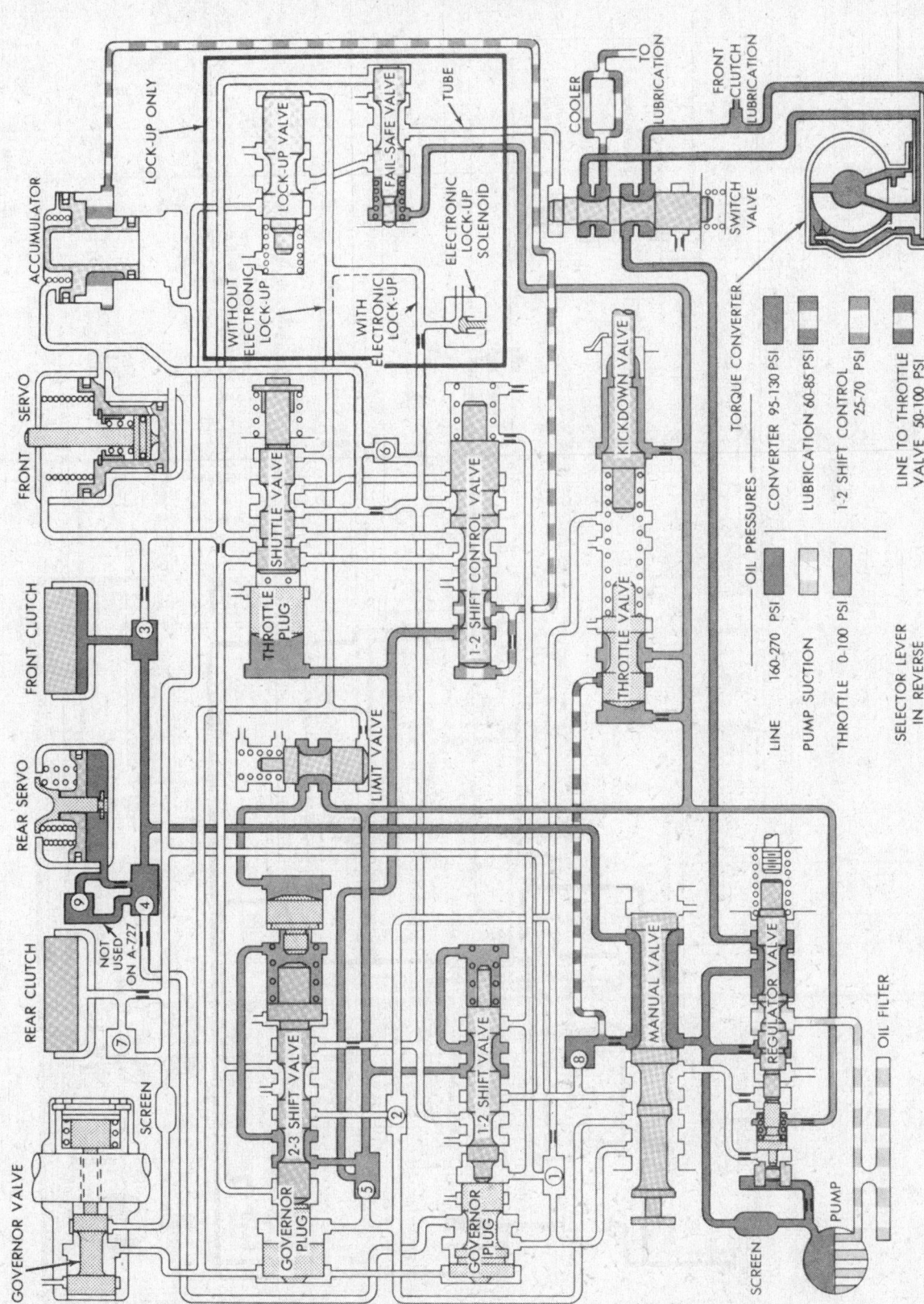

LOCK-UP ONLY

ACCUMULATOR

LOCK-UP VALVE

LOCK-UP VALVE

FAIL-SAFE VALVE

TUBE

WITHOUT ELECTRONIC LOCK-UP

WITH ELECTRONIC LOCK-UP

ELECTRONIC LOCK-UP SOLENOID

COOLER

TO LUBRICATION

FRONT CLUTCH LUBRICATION

SWITCH VALVE

TORQUE CONVERTER

FRONT SERVO

THROTTLE PLUG

SHUTTLE VALVE

1-2 SHIFT CONTROL VALVE

KICKDOWN VALVE

THROTTLE VALVE

FRONT CLUTCH

3

REAR SERVO

LIMIT VALVE

9
4

NOT USED ON A-727

REAR CLUTCH

7

GOVERNOR PLUG

2-3 SHIFT VALVE

2

6

5

GOVERNOR PLUG

1-2 SHIFT VALVE

1

8

MANUAL VALVE

REGULATOR VALVE

OIL FILTER

GOVERNOR VALVE

SCREEN

SCREEN

PUMP

OIL PRESSURES

CONVERTER 95-130 PSI

LUBRICATION 60-85 PSI

1-2 SHIFT CONTROL 25-70 PSI

LINE TO THROTTLE VALVE 50-100 PSI

LINE 160-270 PSI

PUMP SUCTION

THROTTLE 0-100 PSI

SELECTOR LEVER IN REVERSE

DRIVE (2ND) HALF THROTTLE COMPLETE WITH OVERDRIVE UNIT – A500

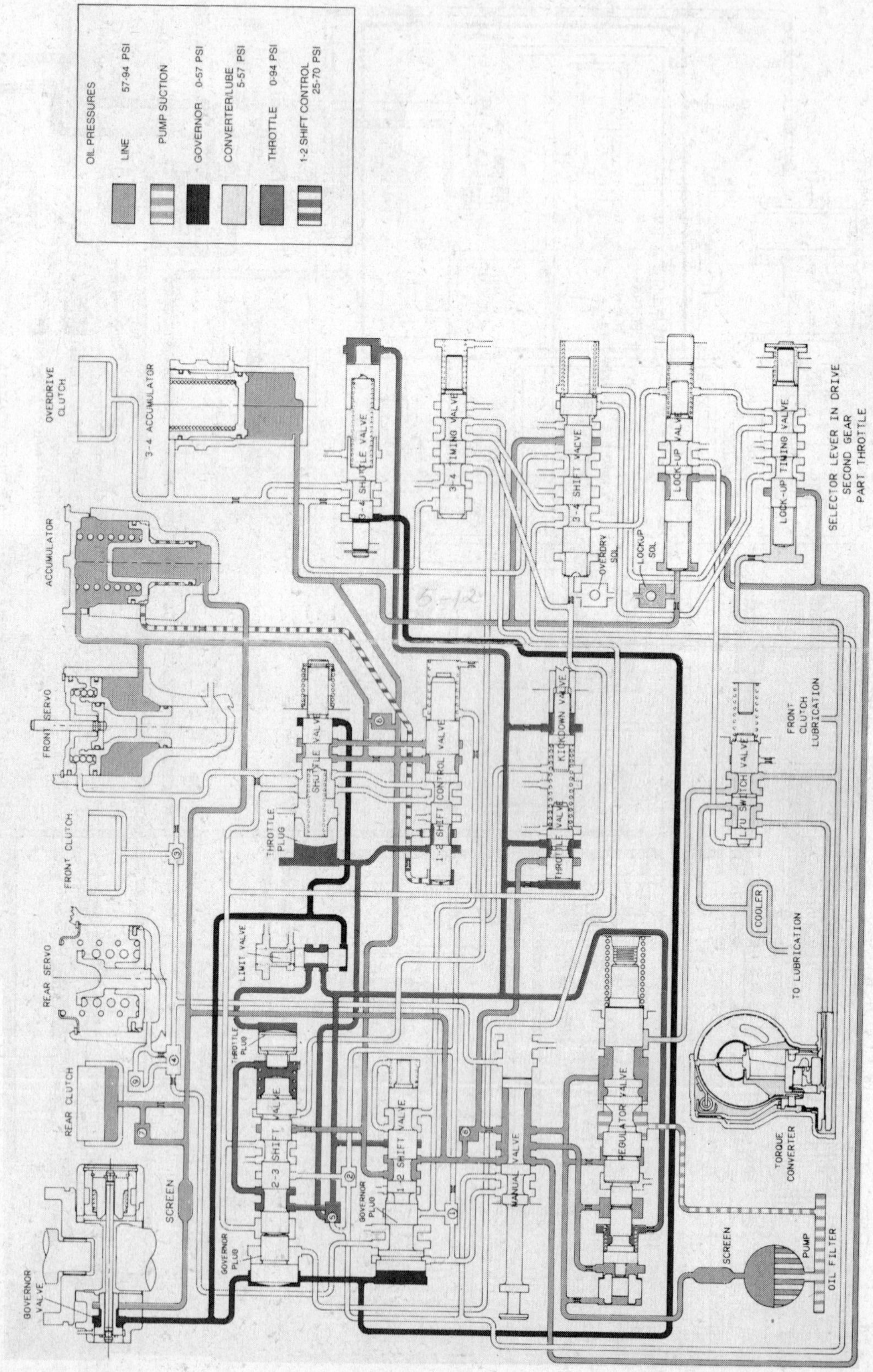

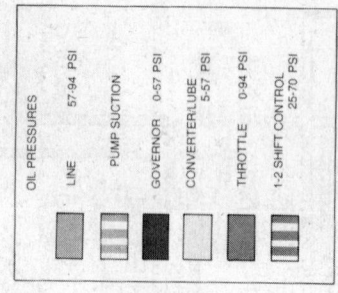

OIL PRESSURES

LINE	57-94 PSI
PUMP SUCTION	
GOVERNOR	0-57 PSI
CONVERTER/LUBE	5-57 PSI
THROTTLE	0-94 PSI
1-2 SHIFT CONTROL	25-70 PSI

DRIVE (DIRECT) COMPLETE WITH OVERDRIVE UNIT
AND TORQUE CONVERTER UNLOCKED—A500

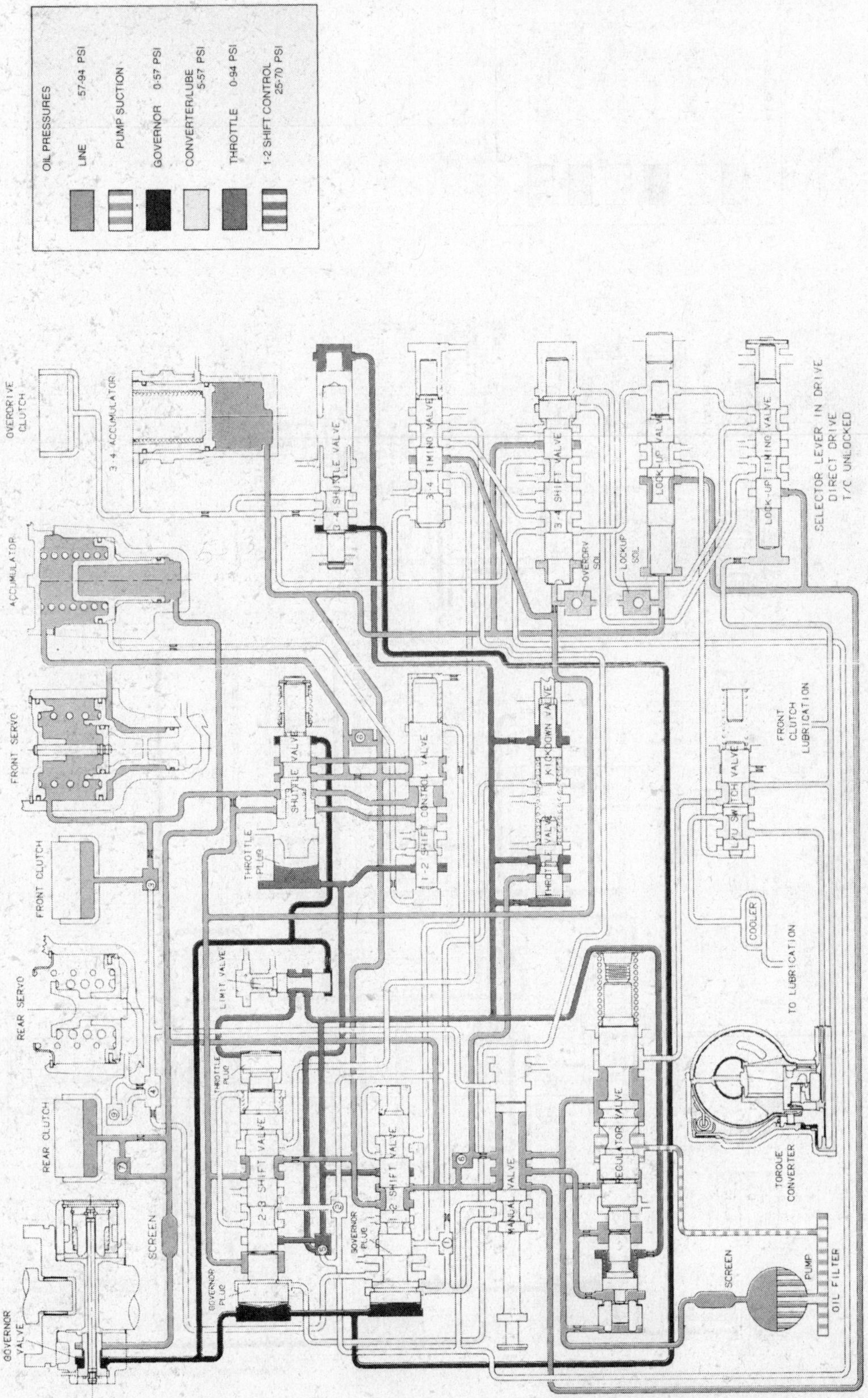

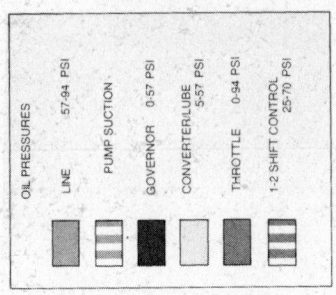

OIL PRESSURES

LINE	57-94 PSI
PUMP SUCTION	
GOVERNOR	0-57 PSI
CONVERTER-LUBE	5-57 PSI
THROTTLE	0-94 PSI
1-2 SHIFT CONTROL	25-70 PSI

DRIVE (OVERDRIVE GEAR) WITH TORQUE CONVERTER UNLOCKED — A500

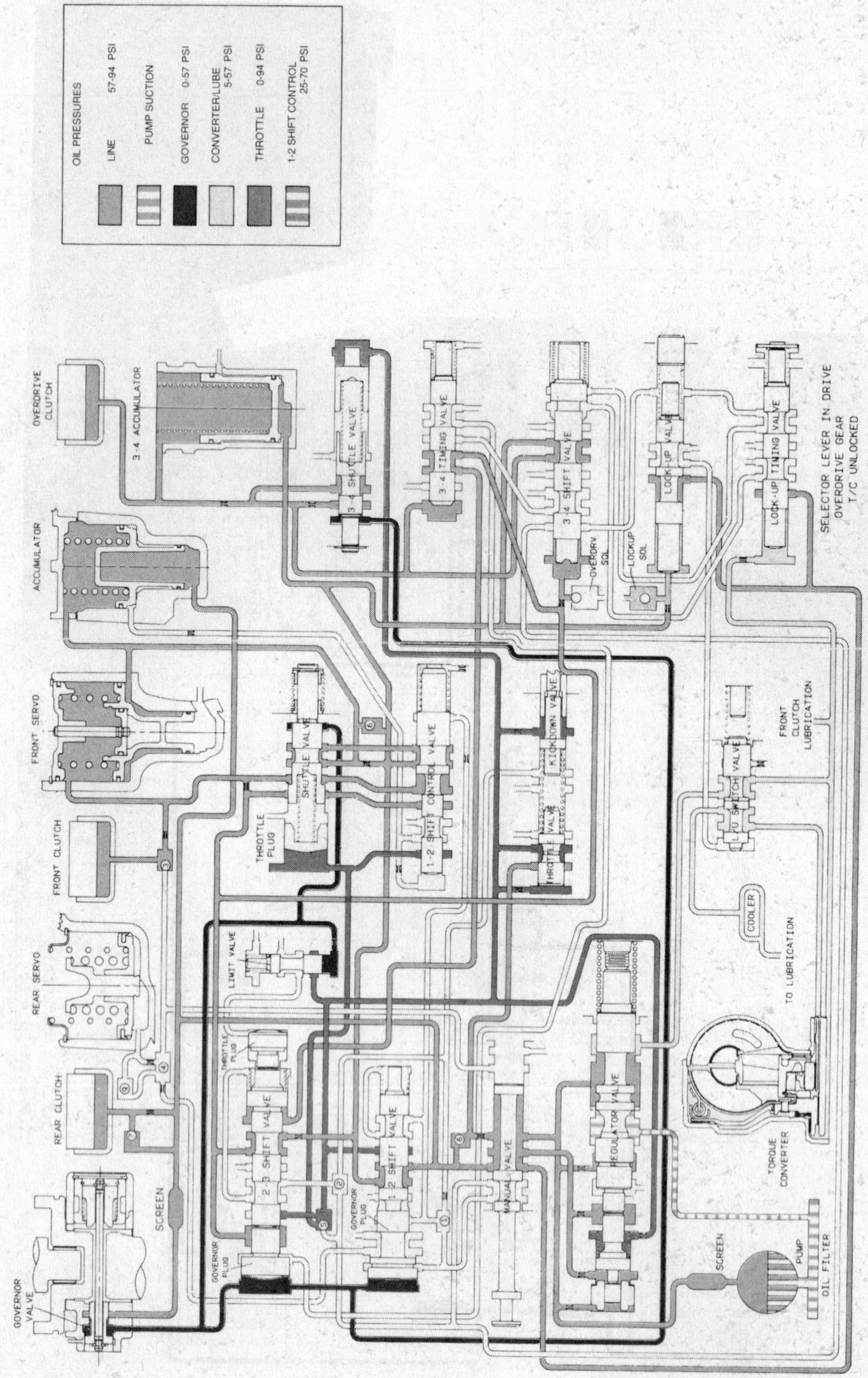

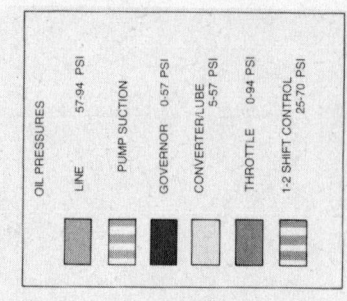

OIL PRESSURES	
LINE	57-94 PSI
PUMP SUCTION	
GOVERNOR	0-57 PSI
CONVERTER/LUBE	5-57 PSI
THROTTLE	0-94 PSI
1-2 SHIFT CONTROL	25-70 PSI

SELECTOR LEVER IN DRIVE
OVERDRIVE GEAR
T/C UNLOCKED

17

NEUTRAL—KM148 AND AW132

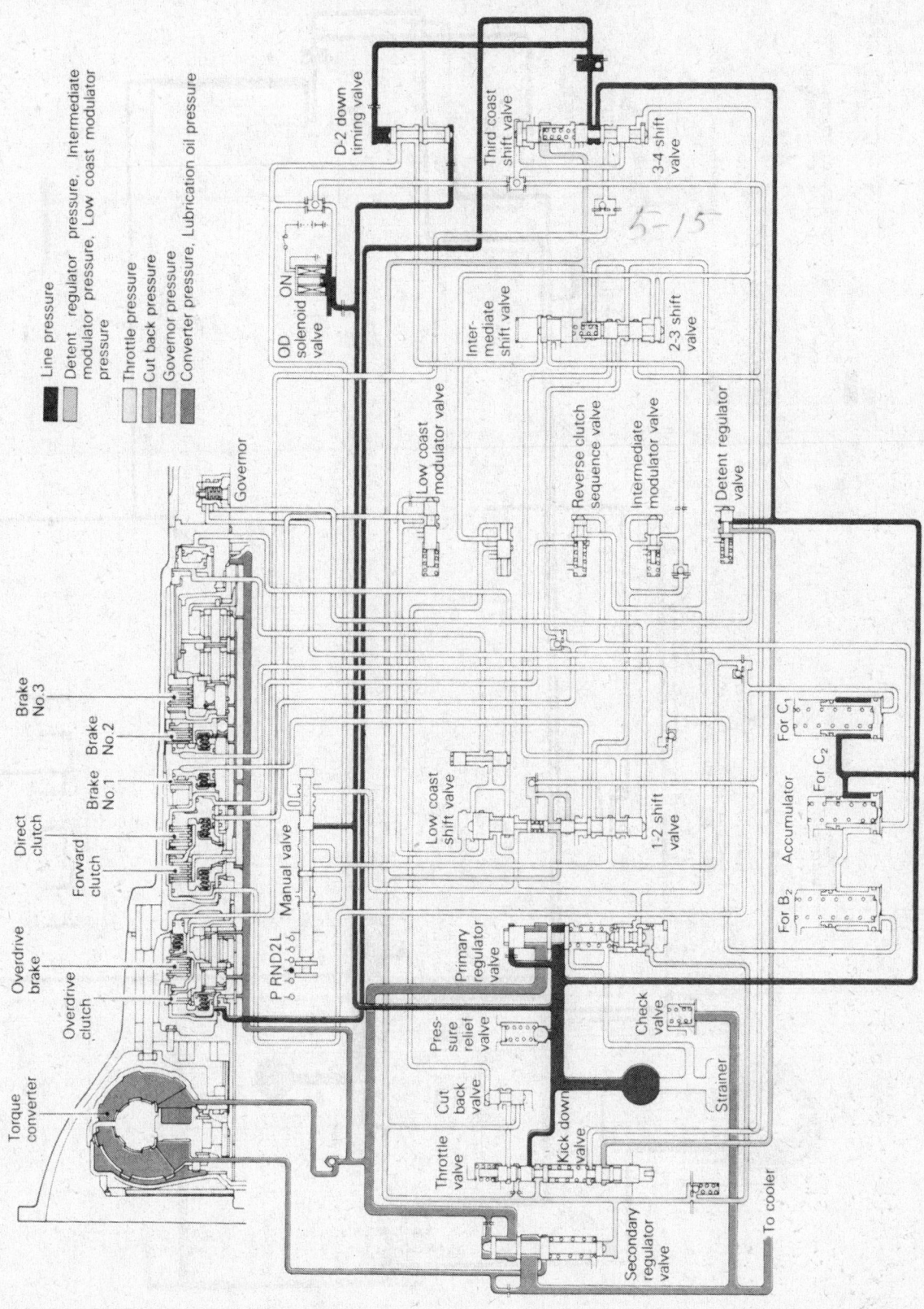

PARK—KM148 AND AW132

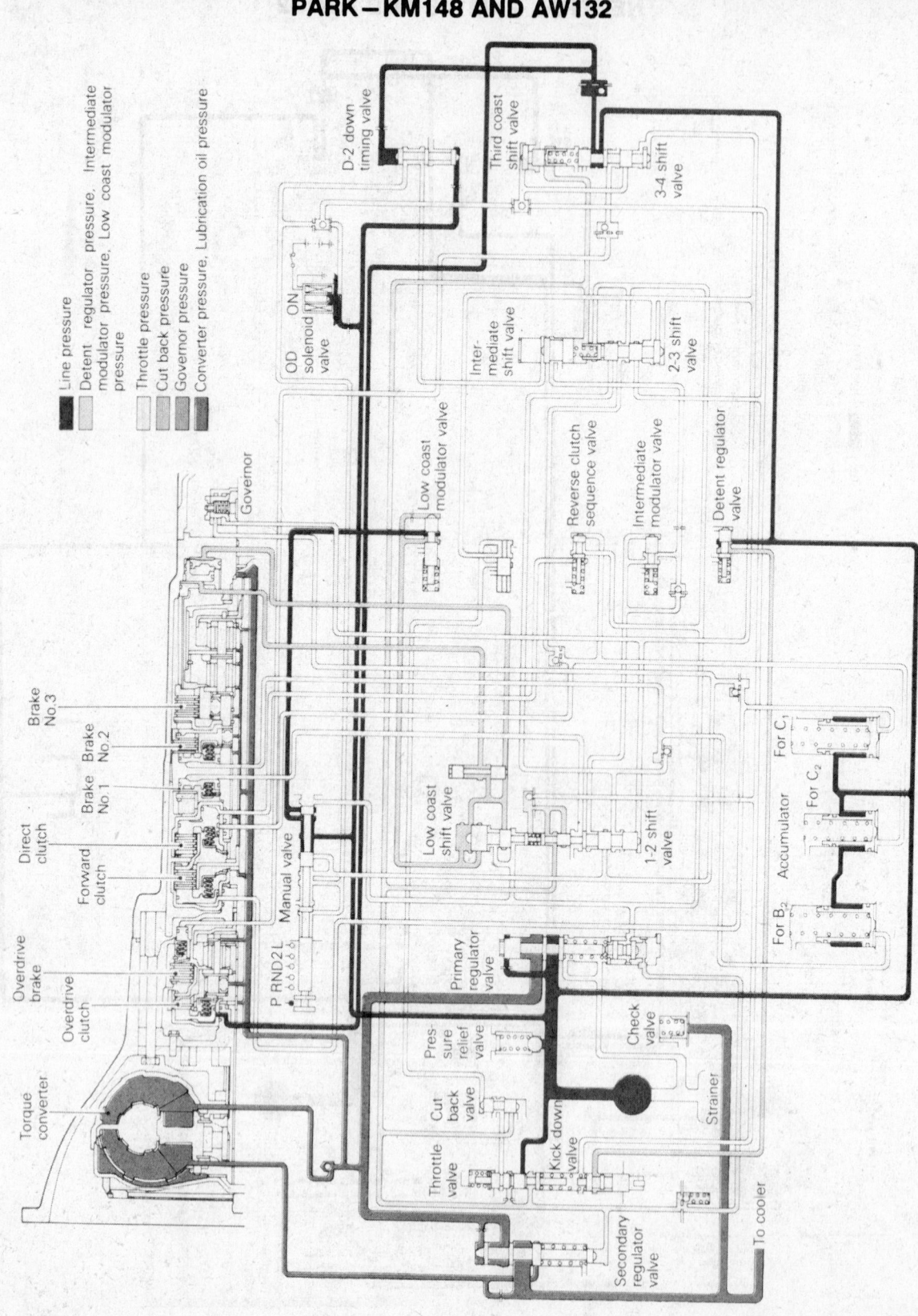

DRIVE—1ST GEAR—KM148 AND AW132

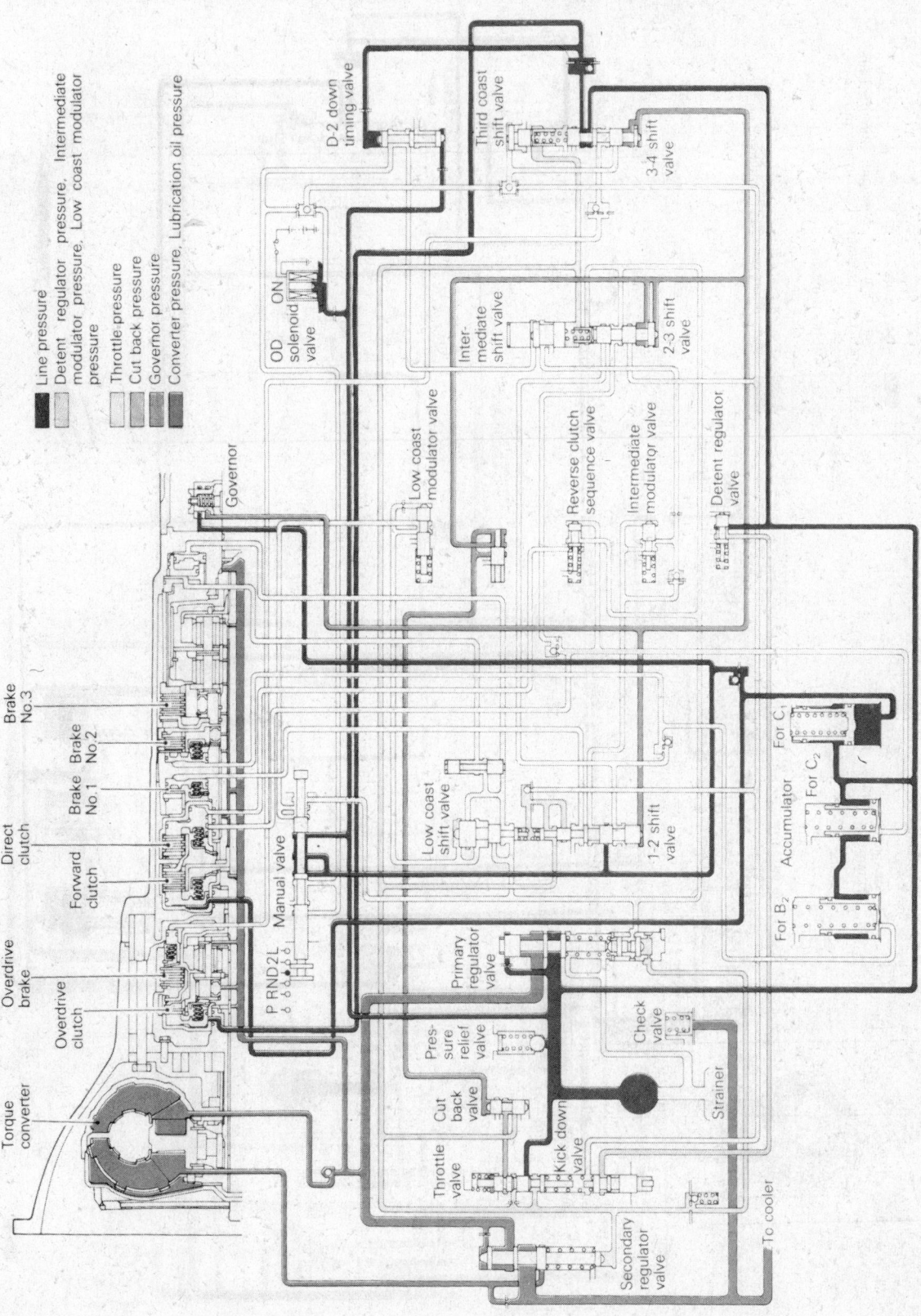

DRIVE – 2ND GEAR – KM148 AND AW132

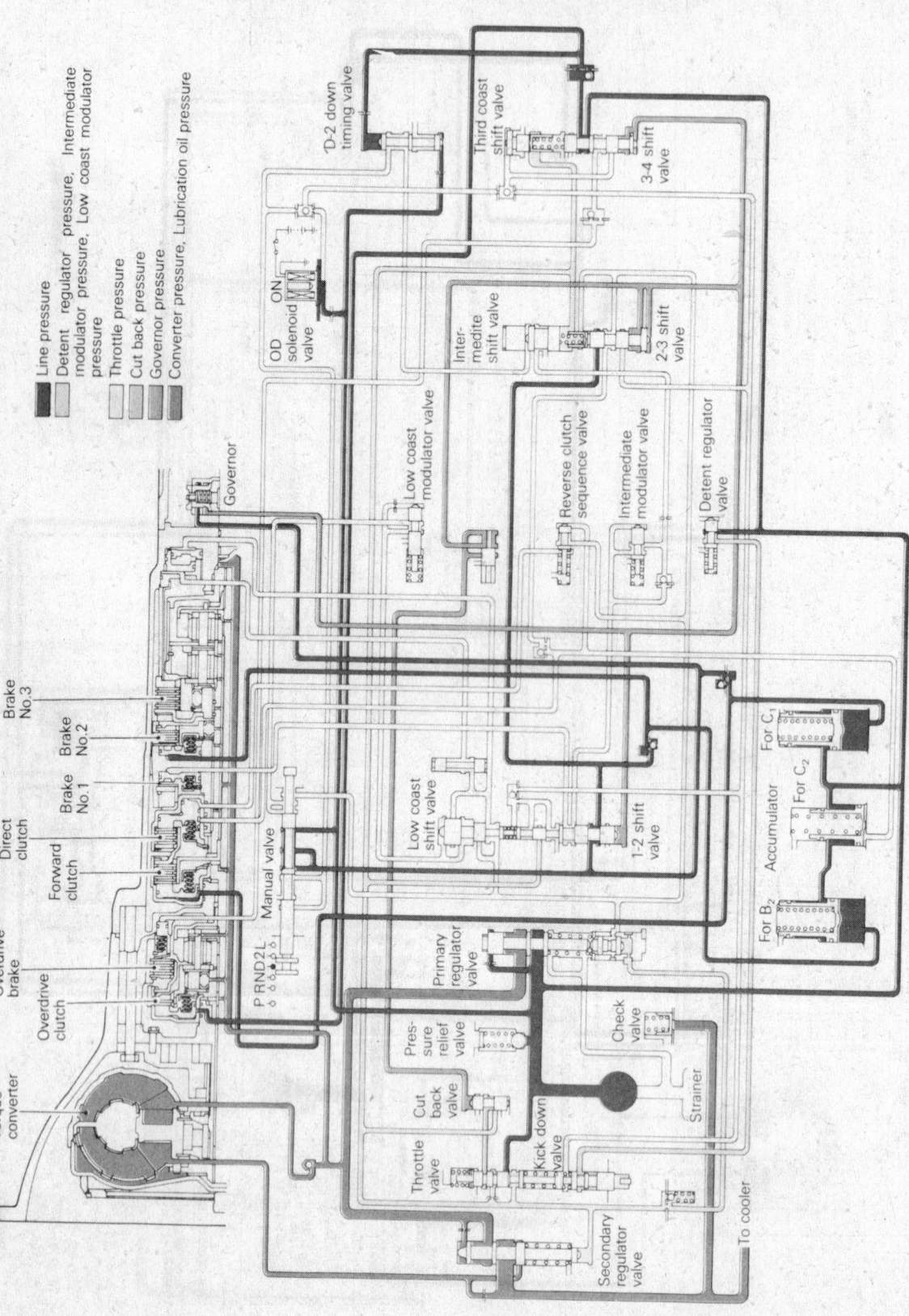

DRIVE – 3RD GEAR – KM148 AND AW132

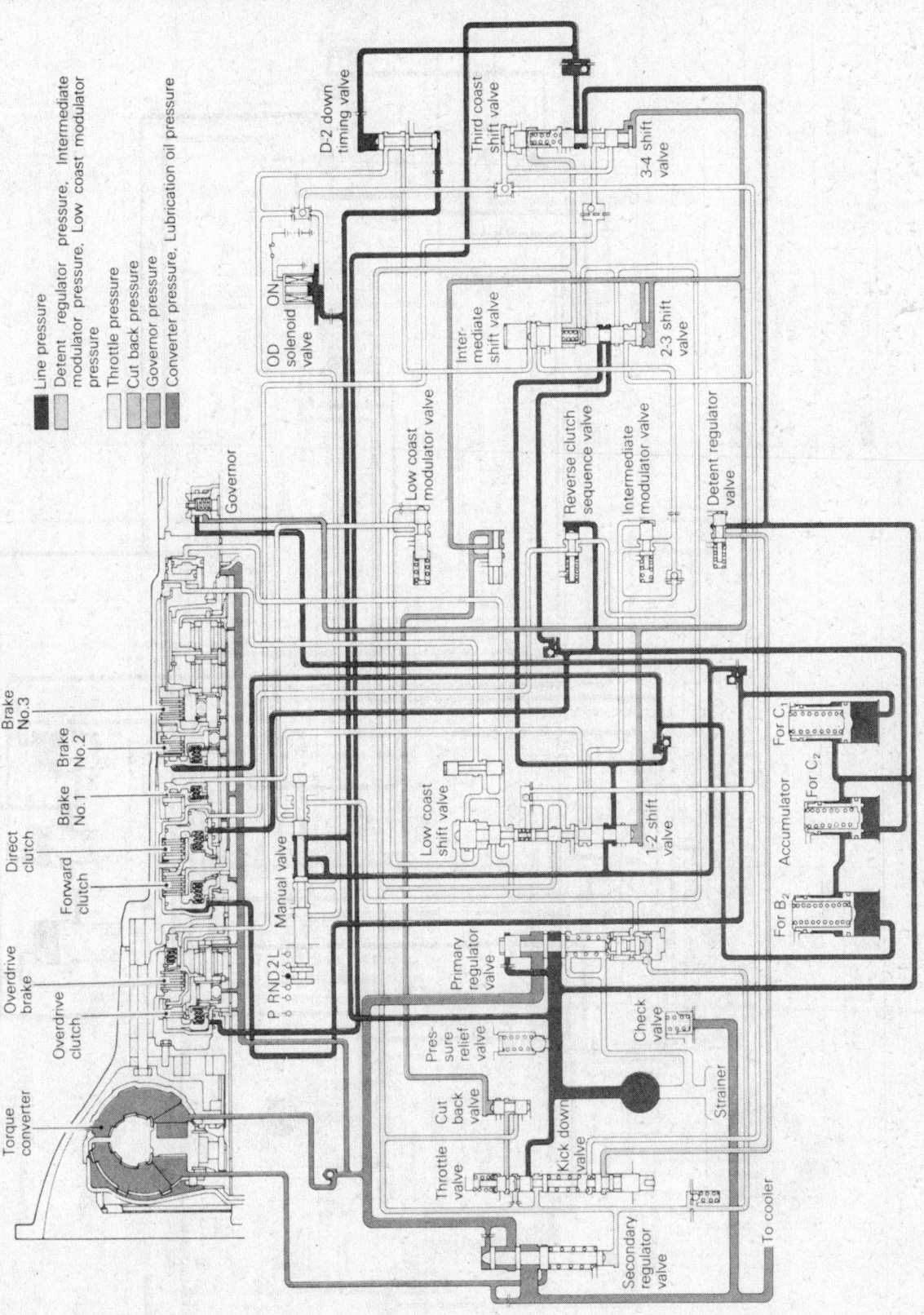

Legend:
- Line pressure
- Detent regulator pressure, Intermediate modulator pressure, Low coast modulator pressure
- Throttle pressure
- Cut back pressure
- Governor pressure
- Converter pressure, Lubrication oil pressure

Governor

Brake No.3
Brake No.2
Brake No.1
Direct clutch
Forward clutch
Overdrive brake
Overdrive clutch
Torque converter

Manual valve
P RND2L

D-2 down timing valve
Third coast shift valve
3-4 shift valve

OD ON
OD solenoid valve

Low coast modulator valve
Inter-mediate shift valve
2-3 shift valve

Reverse clutch sequence valve
Intermediate modulator valve
Detent regulator valve

Low coast shift valve
1-2 shift valve

For C₁
For C₂
Accumulator
For B₂

Primary regulator valve
Check valve

Pressure relief valve
Strainer

Throttle valve
Cut back valve
Kick down valve

Secondary regulator valve
To cooler

DRIVE — 3RD GEAR (OD SOLENOID VALVE OFF) — KM148 AND AW132

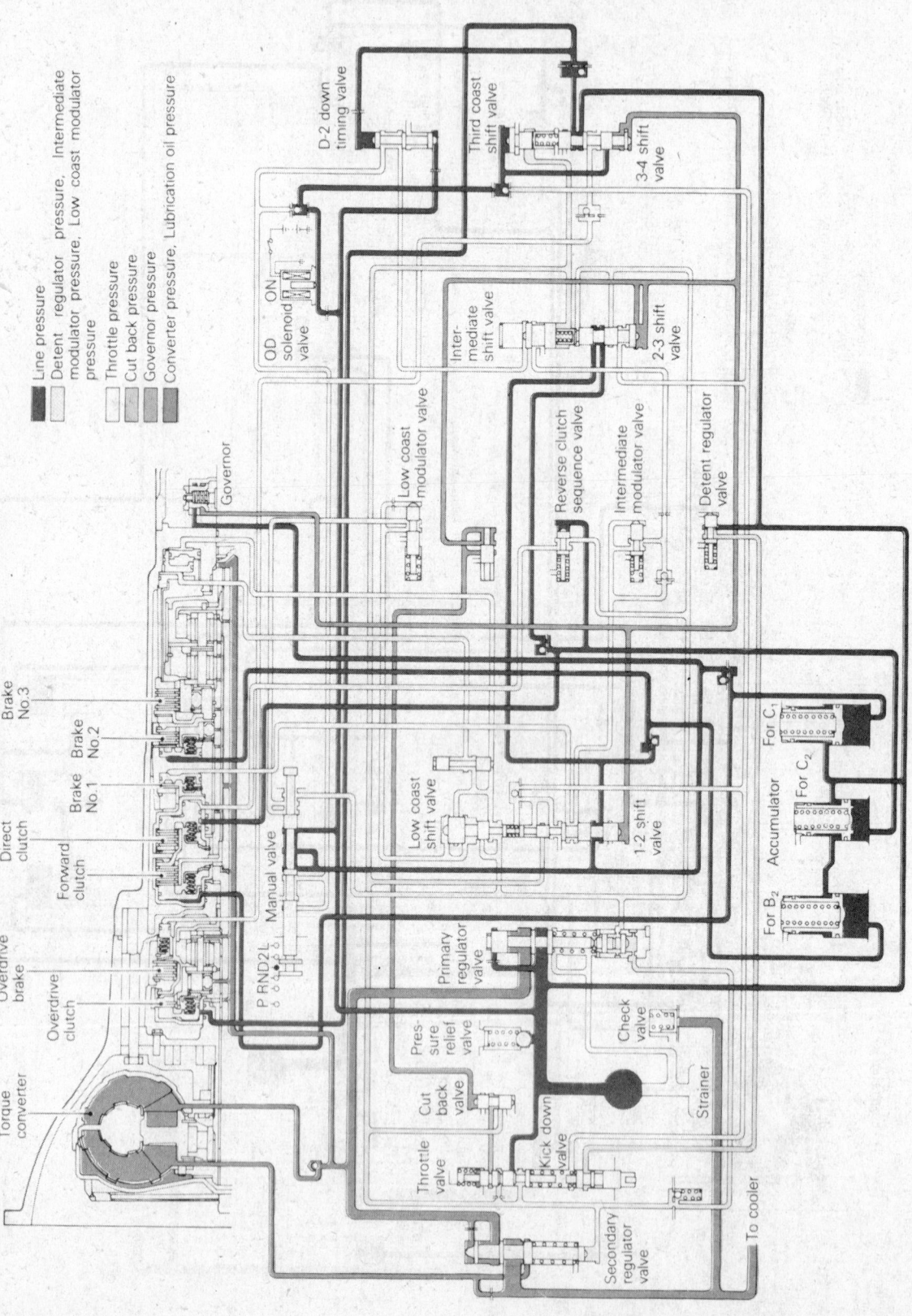

DRIVE–4TH GEAR–KM148 AND AW132

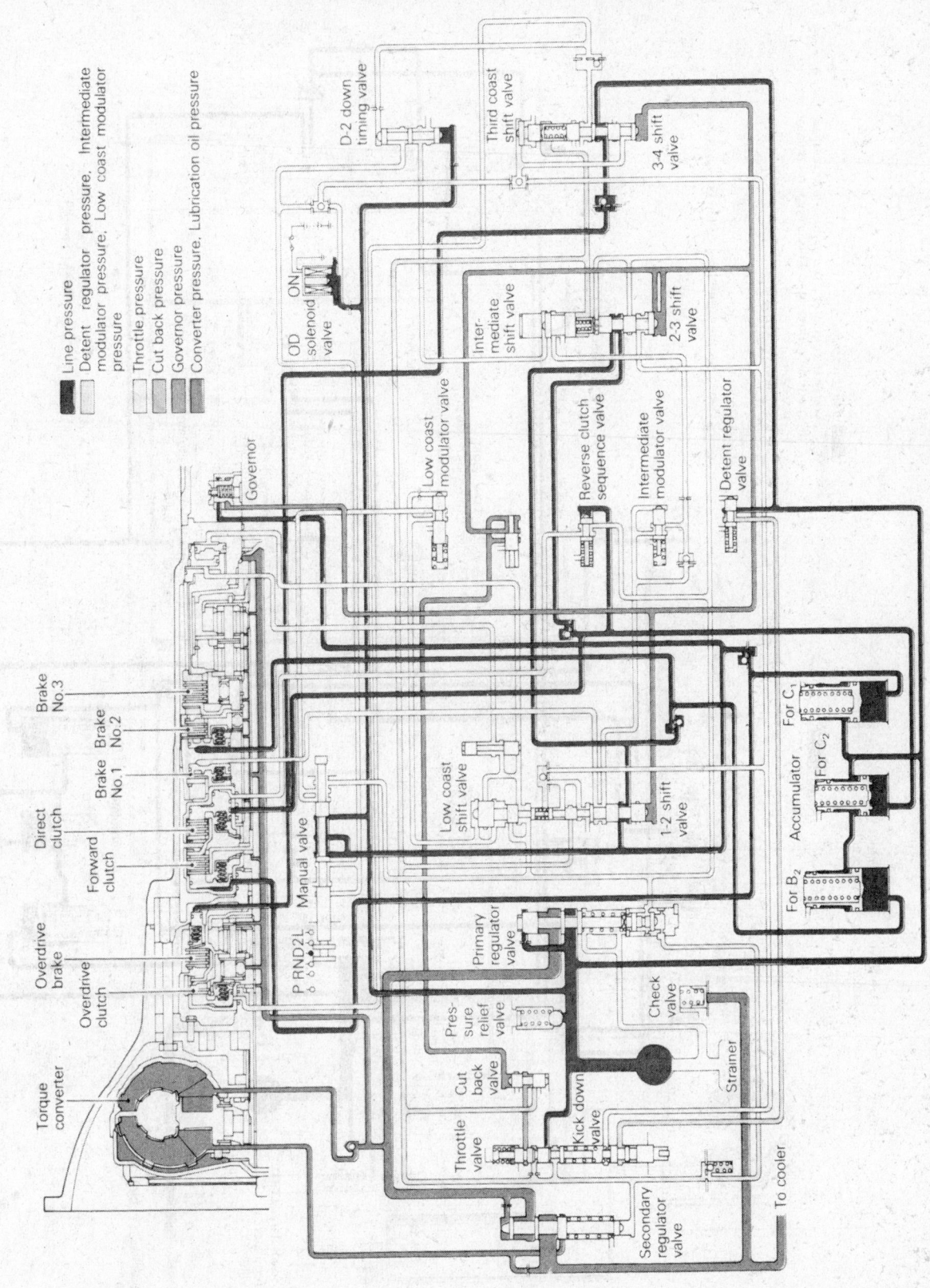

Line pressure

Detent regulator pressure, Intermediate modulator pressure, Low coast modulator pressure

Throttle pressure

Cut back pressure

Governor pressure

Converter pressure, Lubrication oil pressure

DRIVE – KICKDOWN GEAR (4TH TO 3RD) – KM148 AND AW132

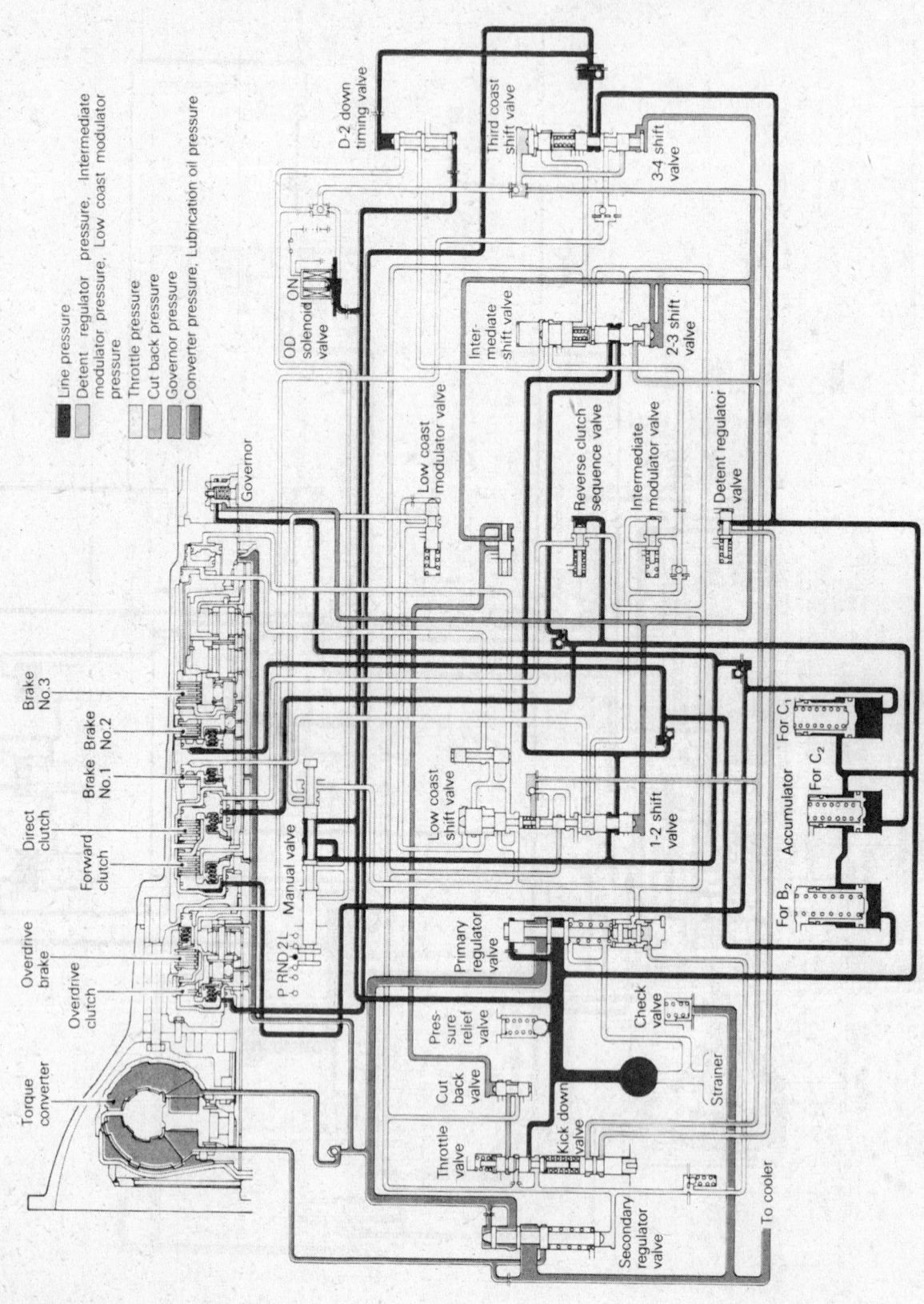

D2 — 2ND GEAR — KM148 AND AW132

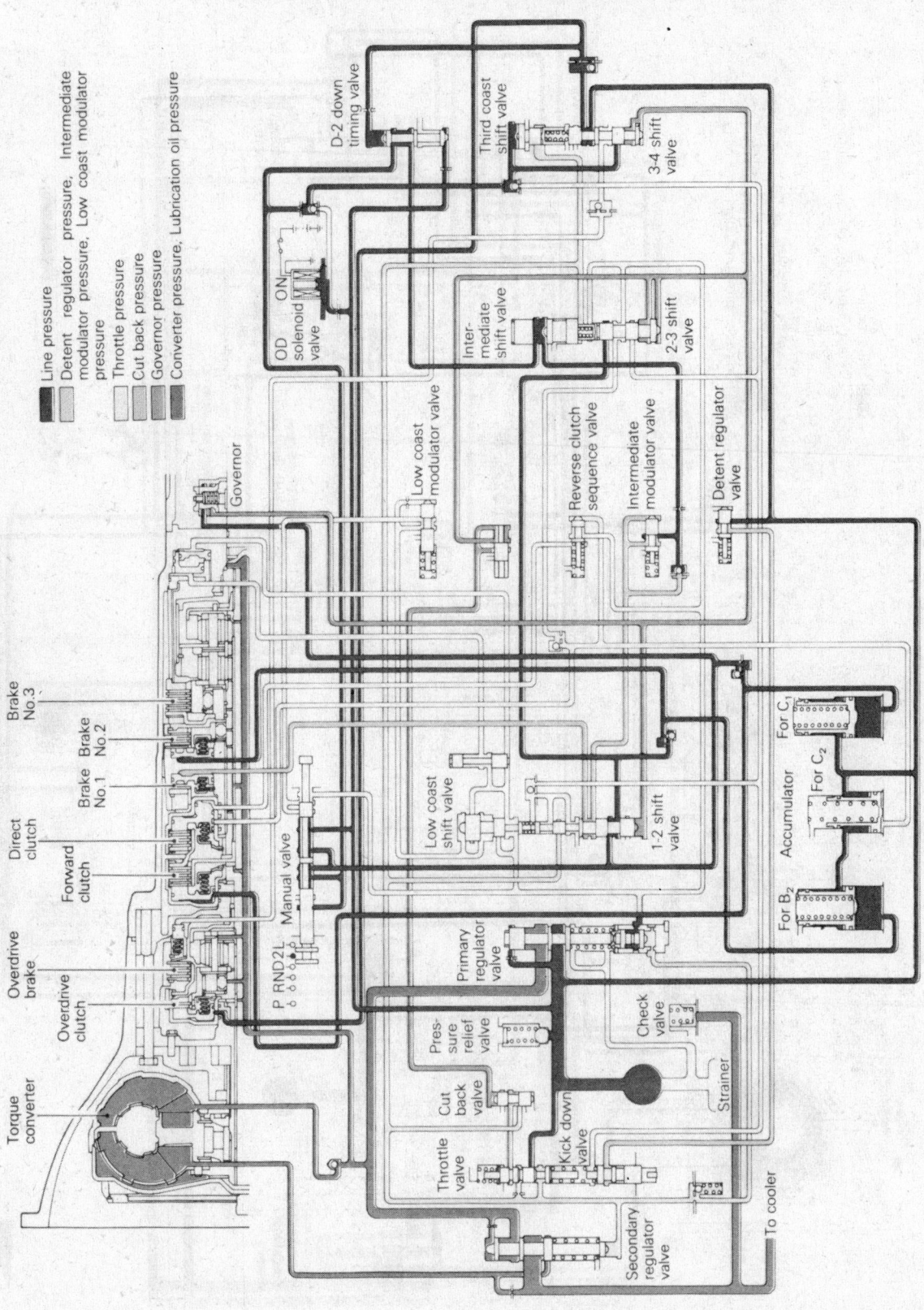

Line pressure

Detent regulator pressure, Intermediate modulator pressure, Low coast modulator pressure

Throttle pressure

Cut back pressure

Governor pressure

Converter pressure, Lubrication oil pressure

Governor

D-2 down timing valve

Third coast shift valve

3-4 shift valve

OD ON solenoid valve

Intermediate shift valve

2-3 shift valve

Low coast modulator valve

Reverse clutch sequence valve

Intermediate modulator valve

Detent regulator valve

Brake No.3

Brake No.2

Brake No.1

Direct clutch

Forward clutch

Overdrive brake

Overdrive clutch

Torque converter

Manual valve

P RND2L

Low coast shift valve

1-2 shift valve

For C₁

For C₂

Accumulator

For B₂

Primary regulator valve

Pressure relief valve

Check valve

Strainer

Cut back valve

Kick down valve

Throttle valve

Secondary regulator valve

To cooler

DRIVE—LOCKUP GEAR—KM148 AND AW132

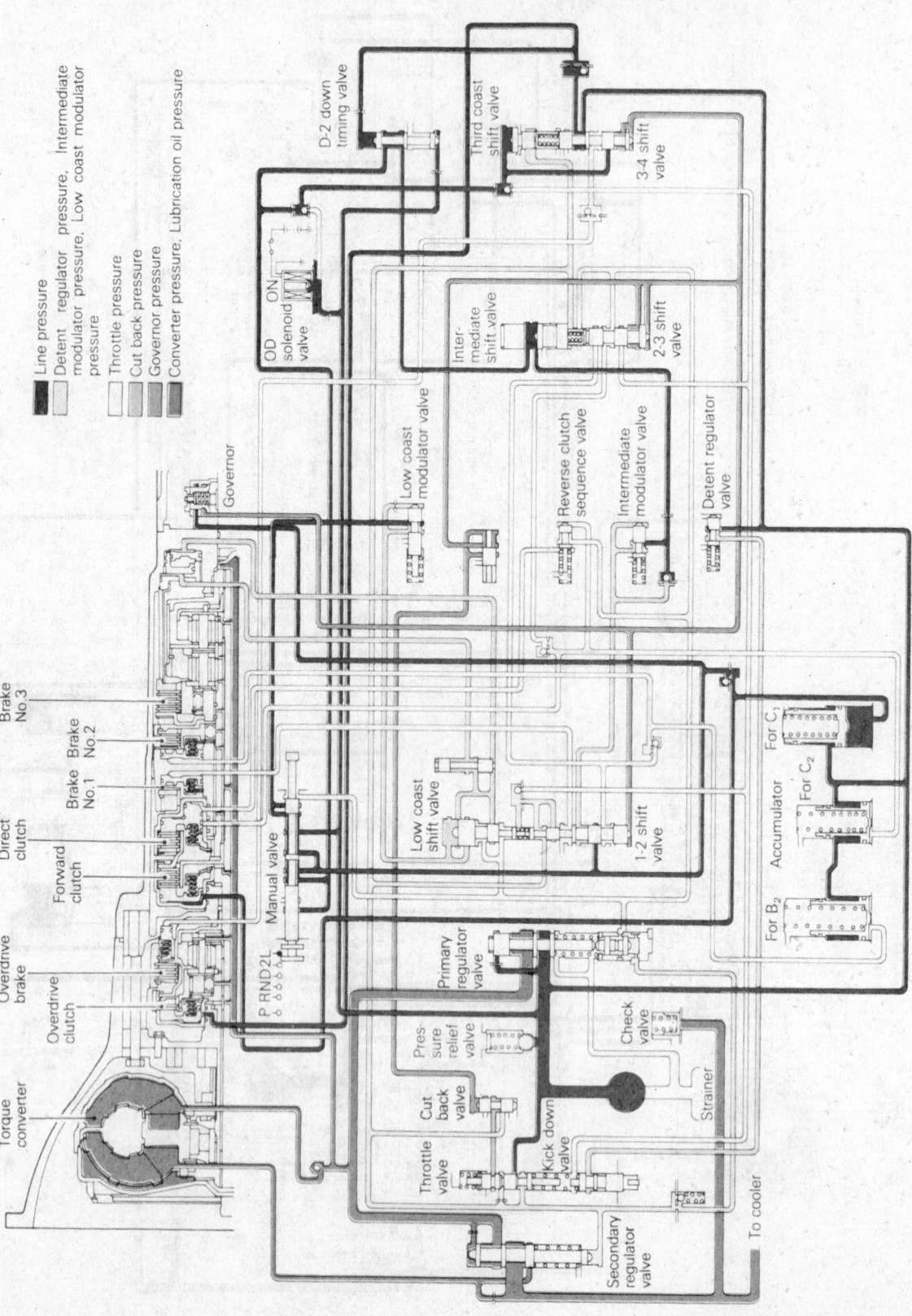

REVERSE—KM148 AND AW132

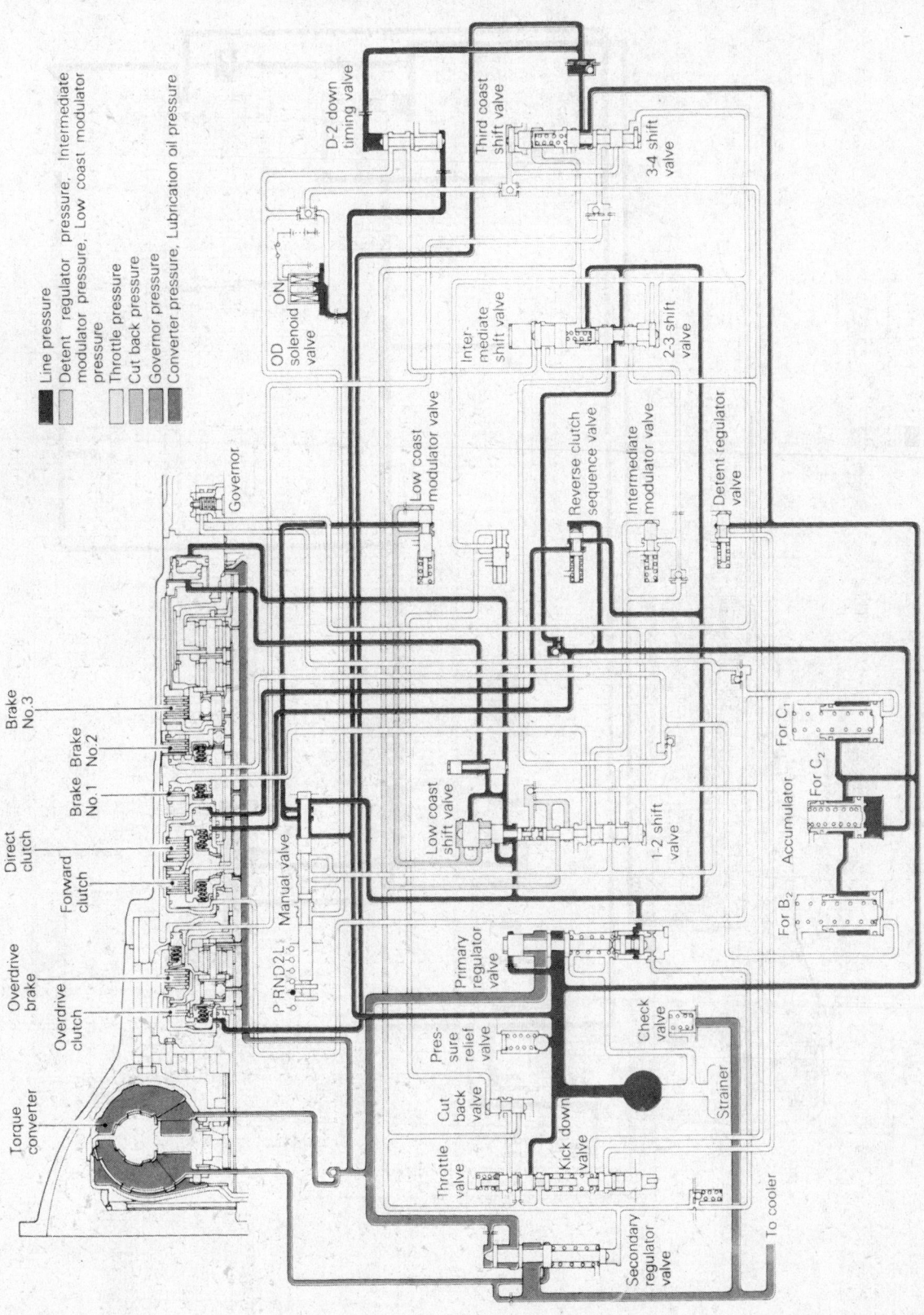

Line pressure
Detent regulator pressure, Intermediate modulator pressure, Low coast modulator pressure
Throttle pressure
Cut back pressure
Governor pressure
Converter pressure, Lubrication oil pressure

NEUTRAL GEAR – AW132L

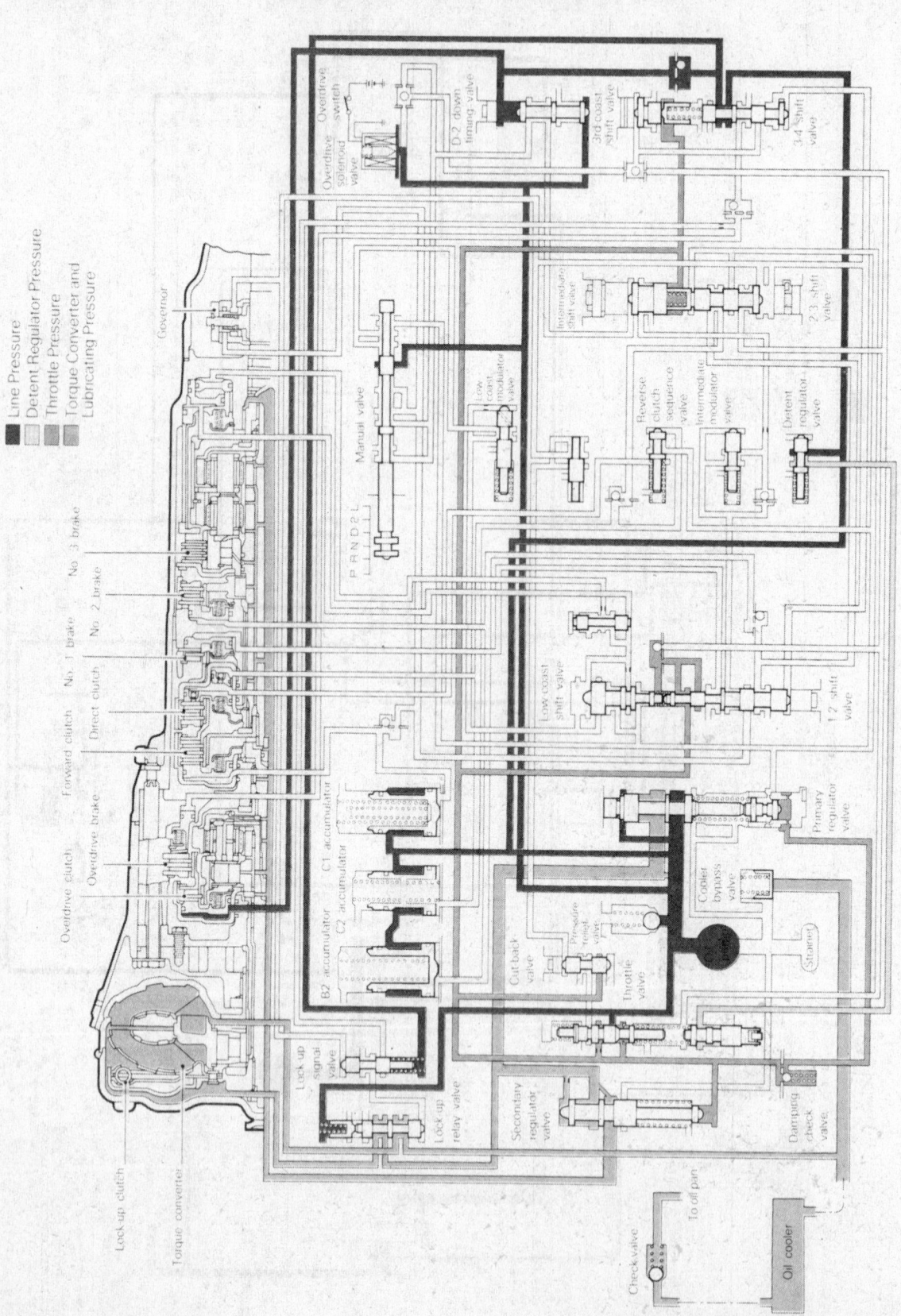

PARK — AW132L

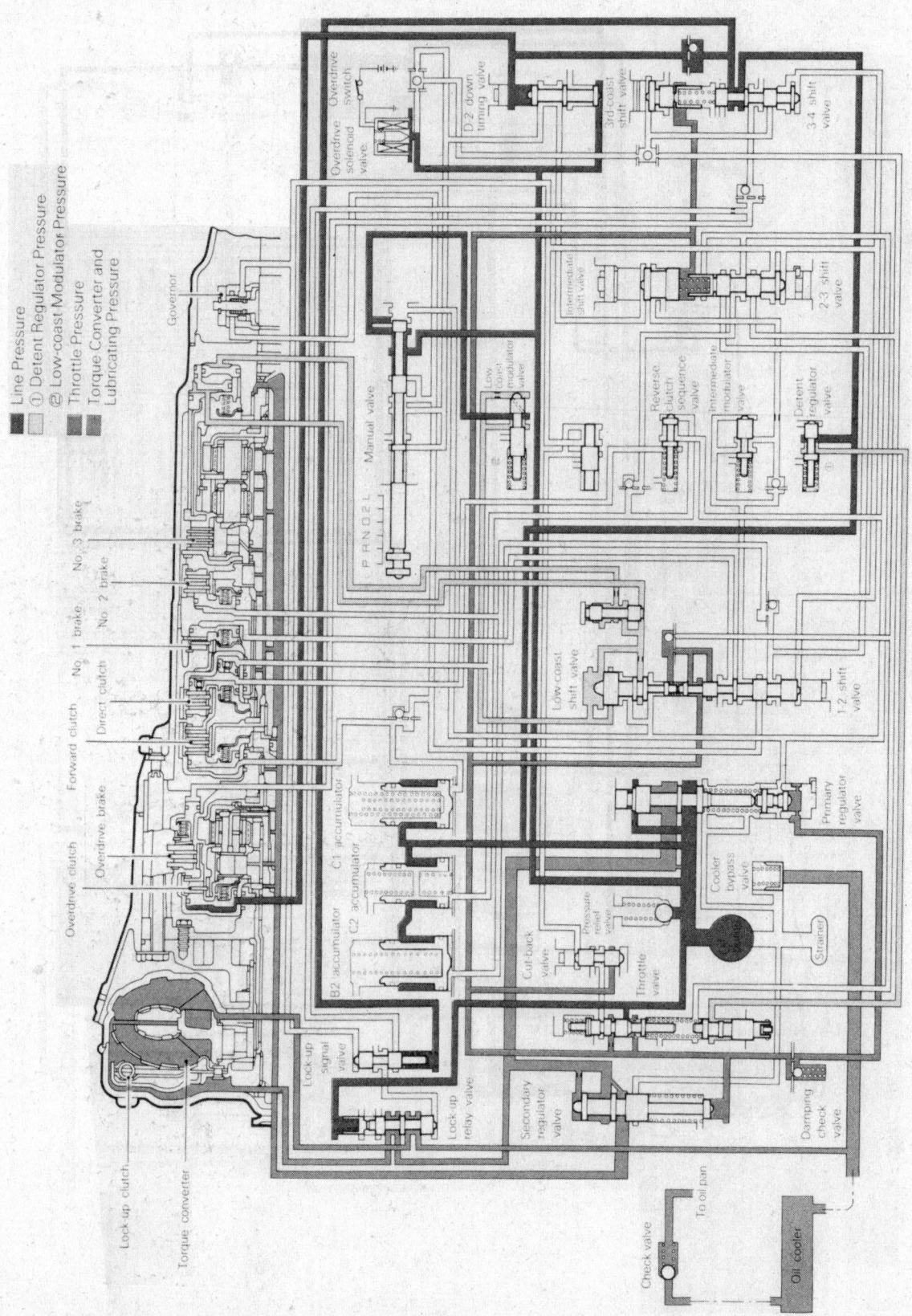

DRIVE—1ST GEAR—AW132L

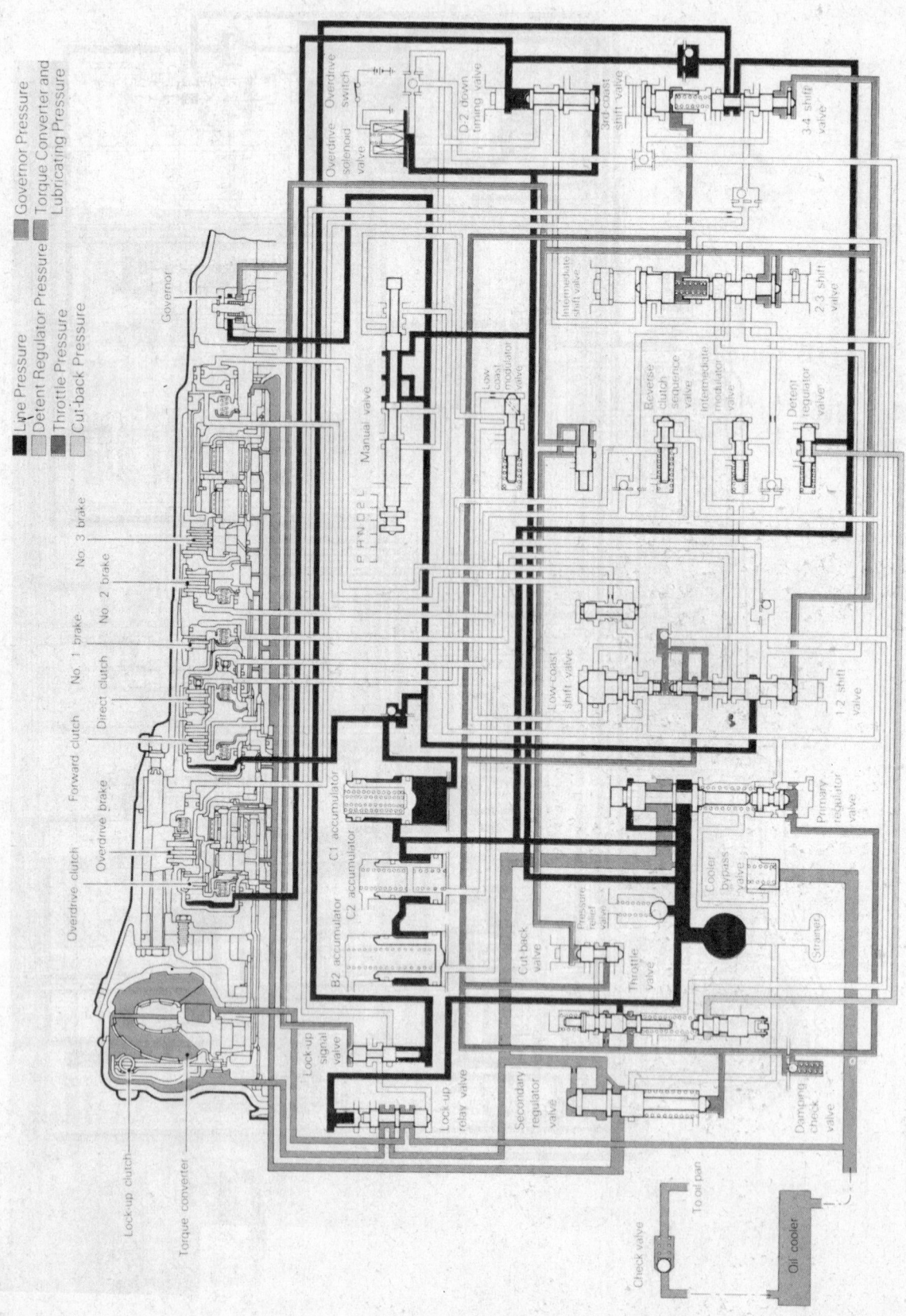

DRIVE – 2ND GEAR – AW132L

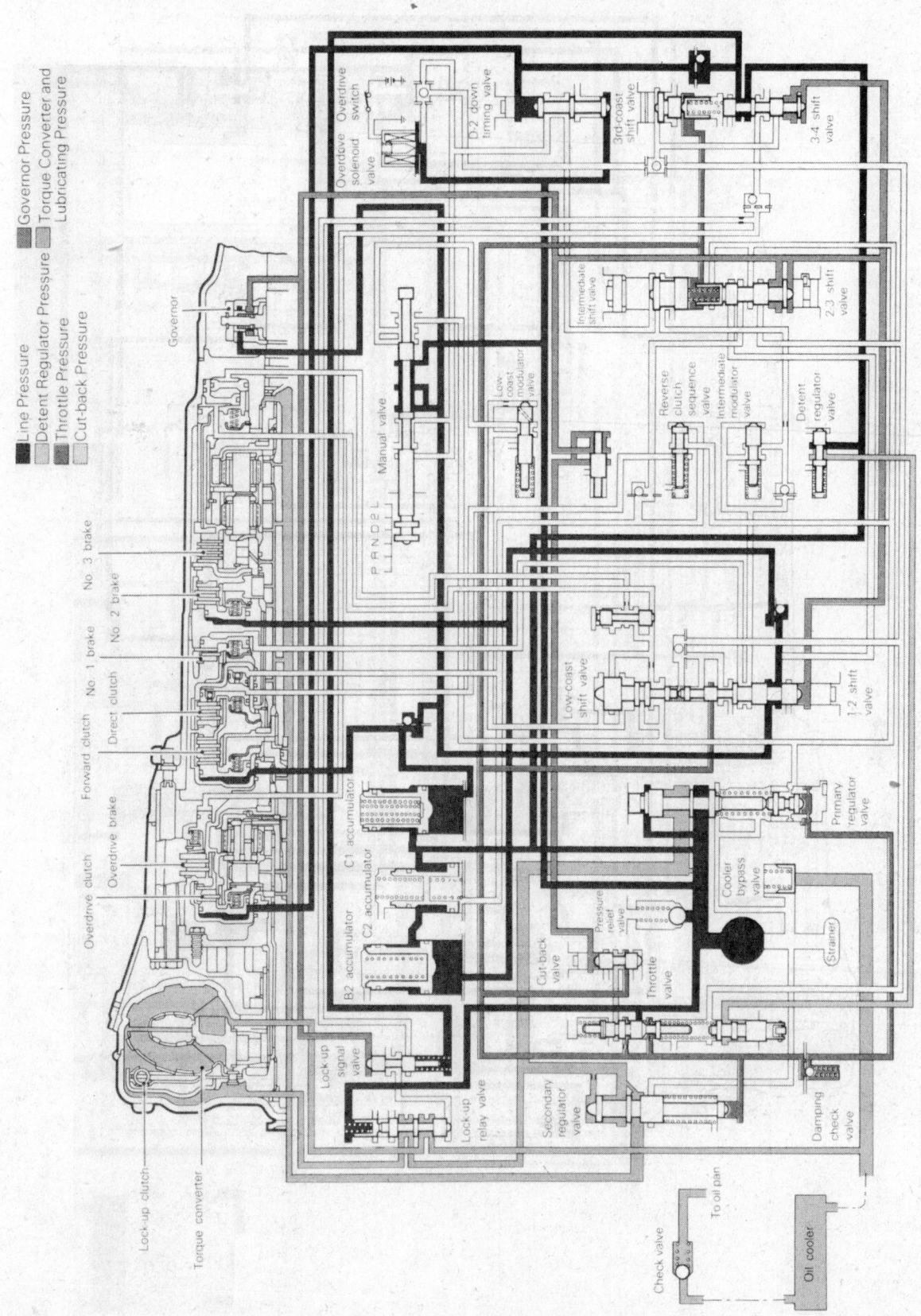

DRIVE — 3RD GEAR — AW132L

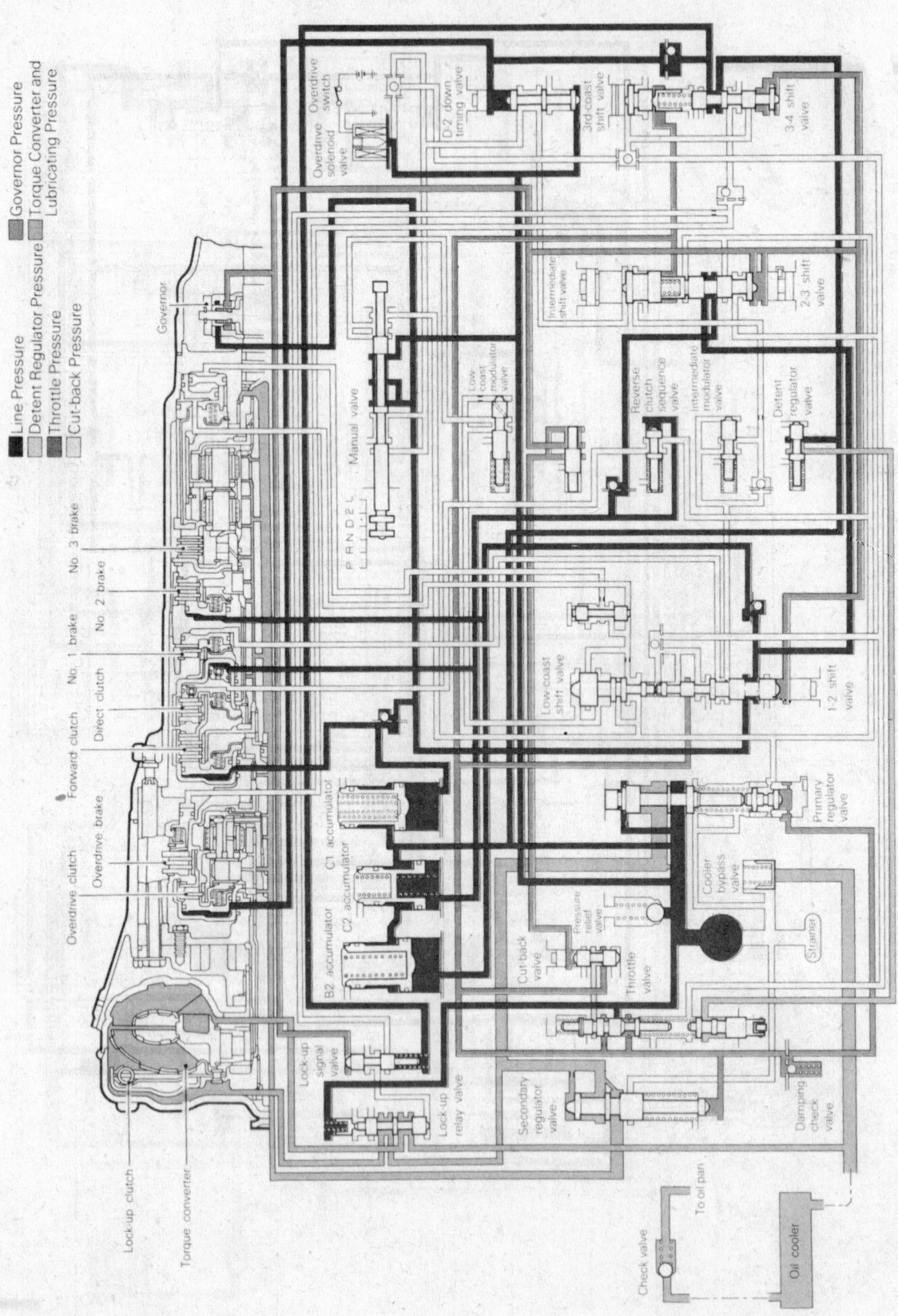

DRIVE—4TH GEAR (LOCKUP CLUTCH OFF)—AW132L

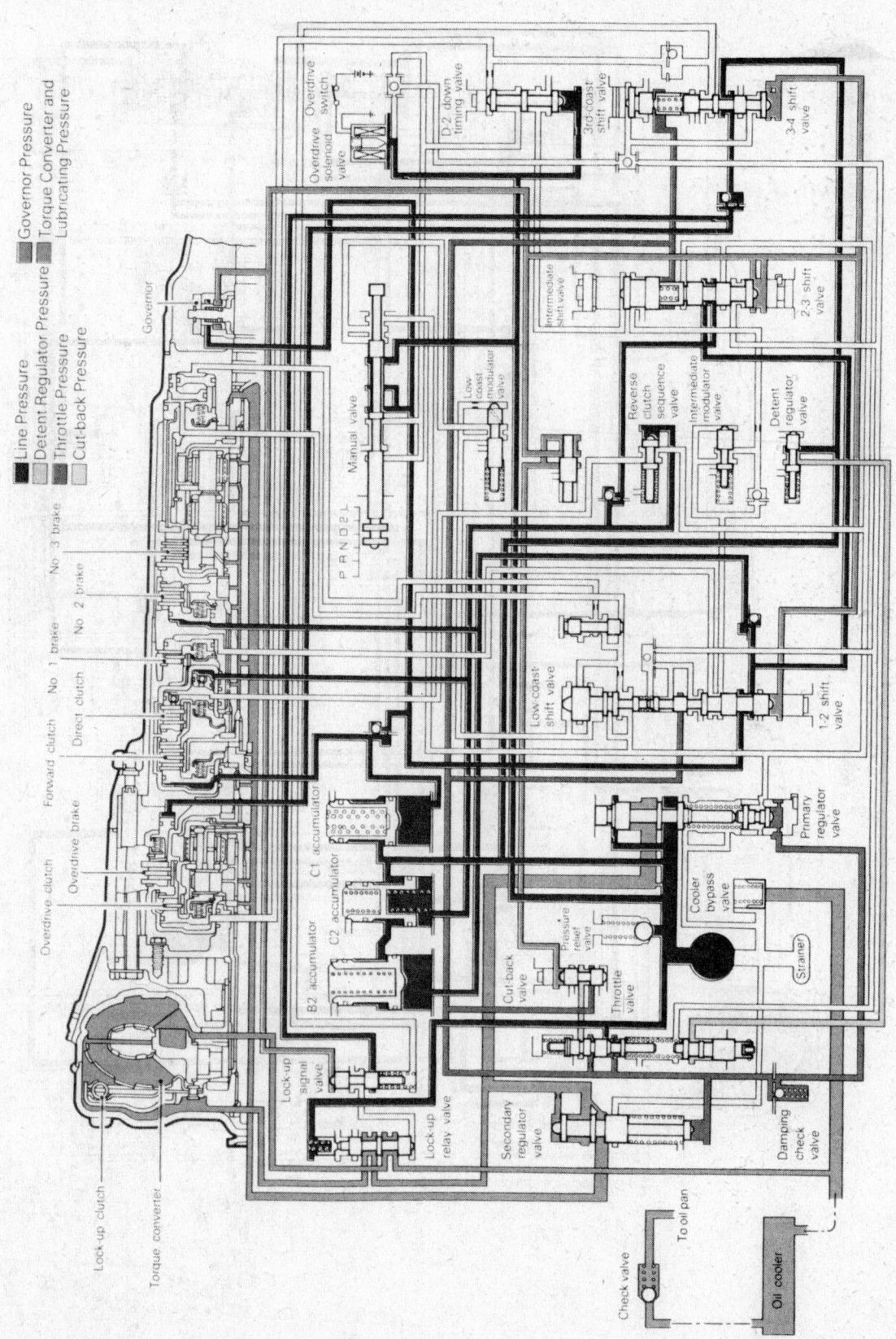

DRIVE — 4TH GEAR (LOCKUP CLUTCH ON) — AW132L

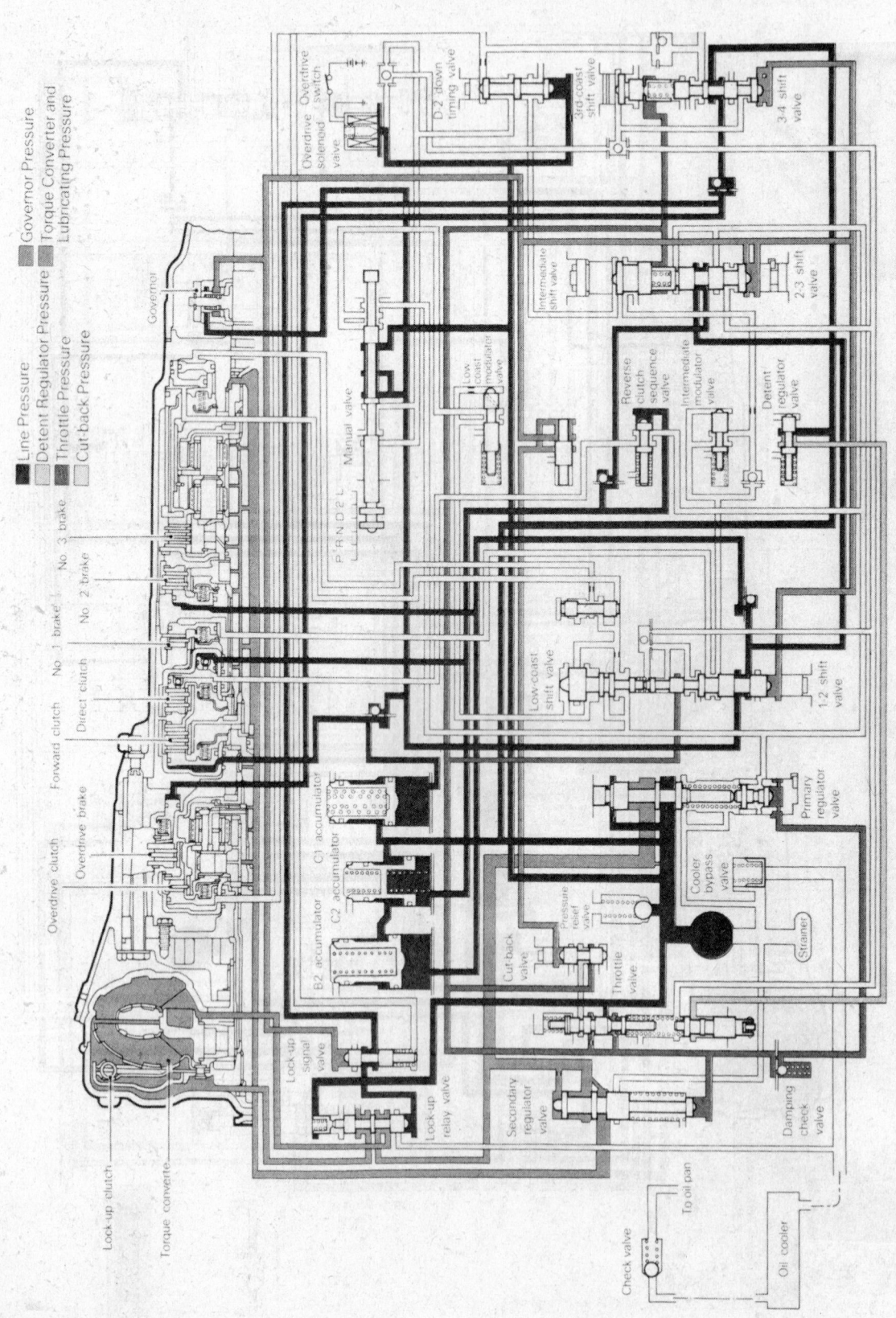

DRIVE—KICKDOWN GEAR (4TH TO 3RD)—AW132L

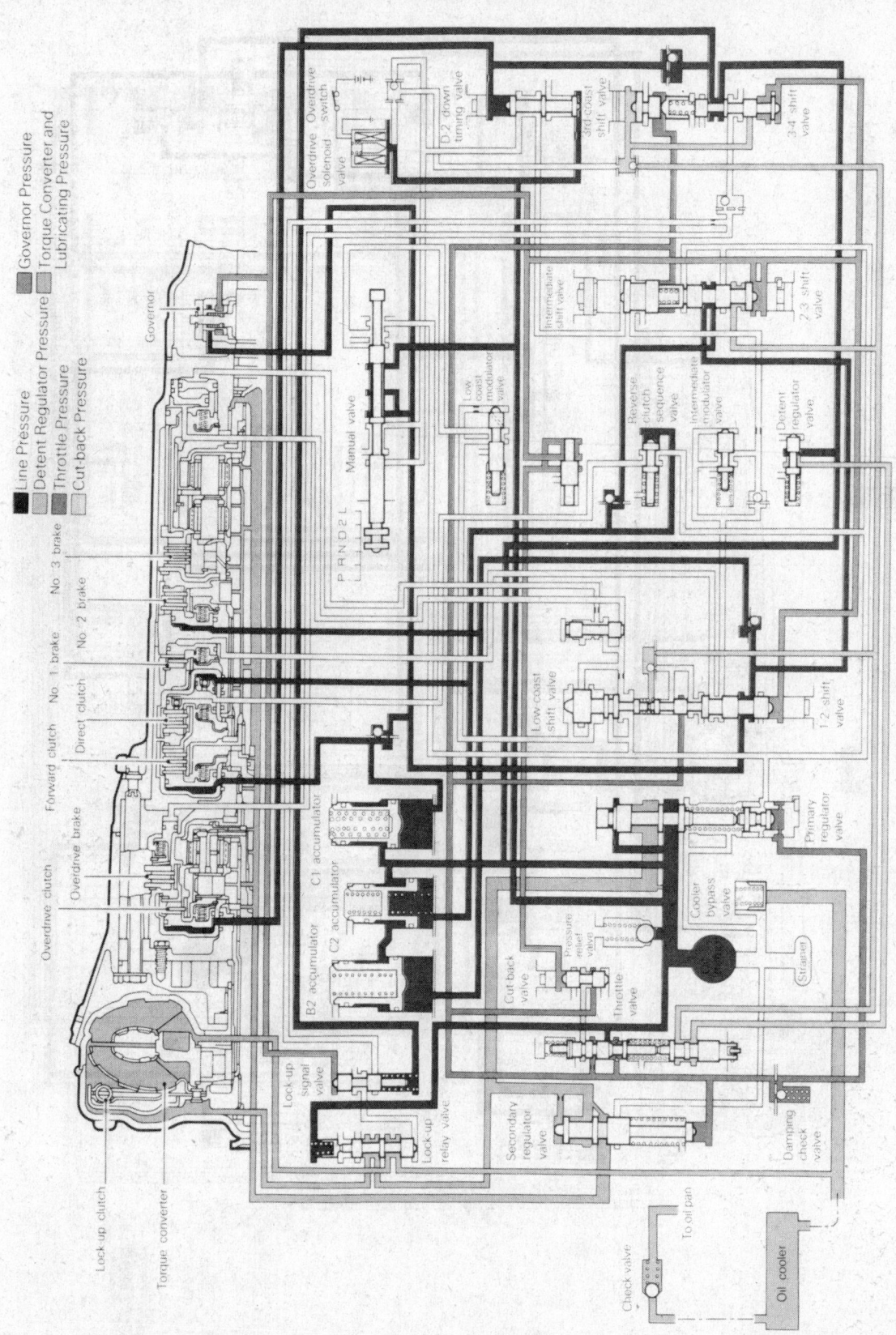

DRIVE – 3RD GEAR (OD SWITCH OFF) – AW132L

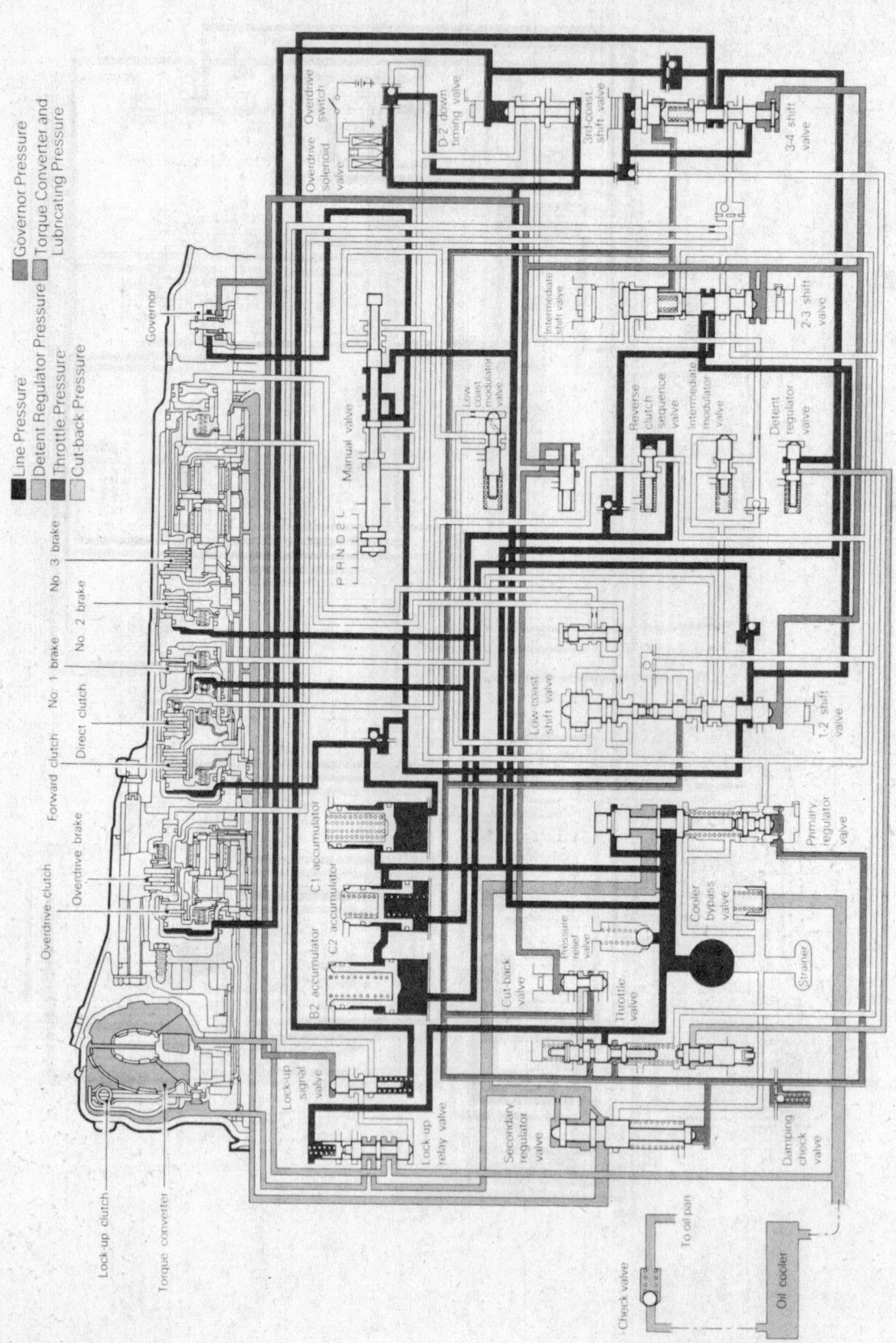

DRIVE – 2ND GEAR – AW132L

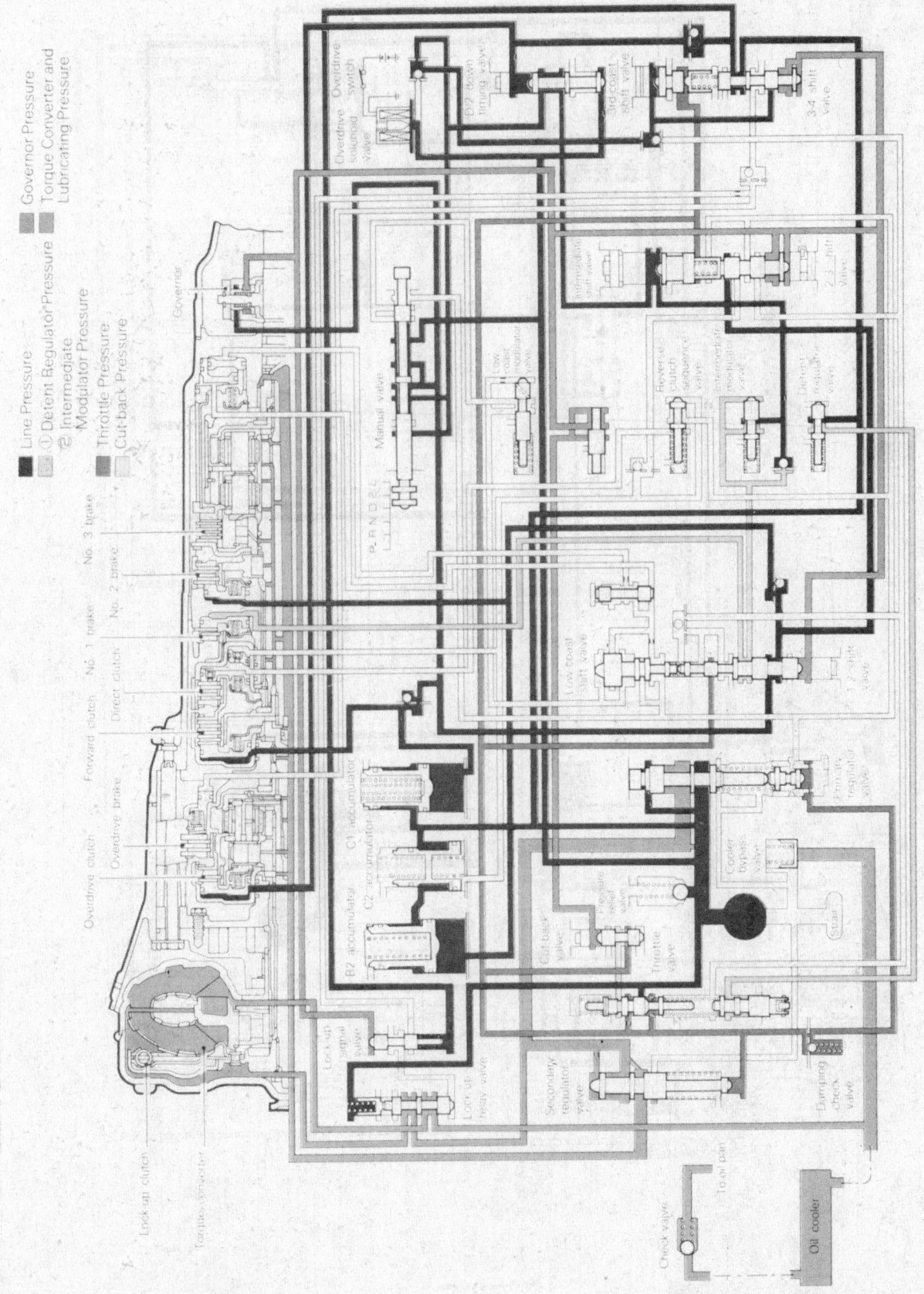

DRIVE – LOCKUP GEAR – AW132L

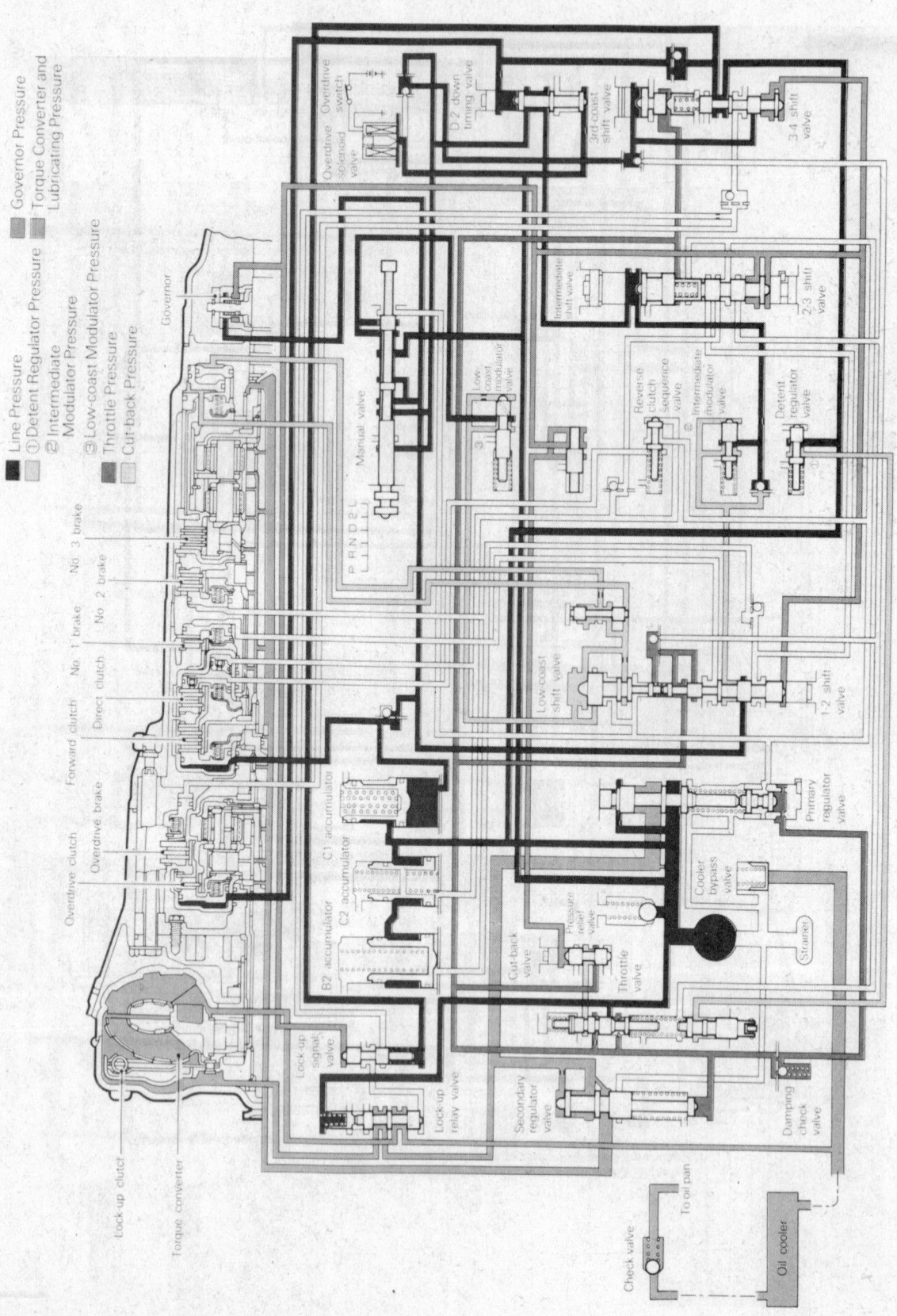

REVERSE – AW132L

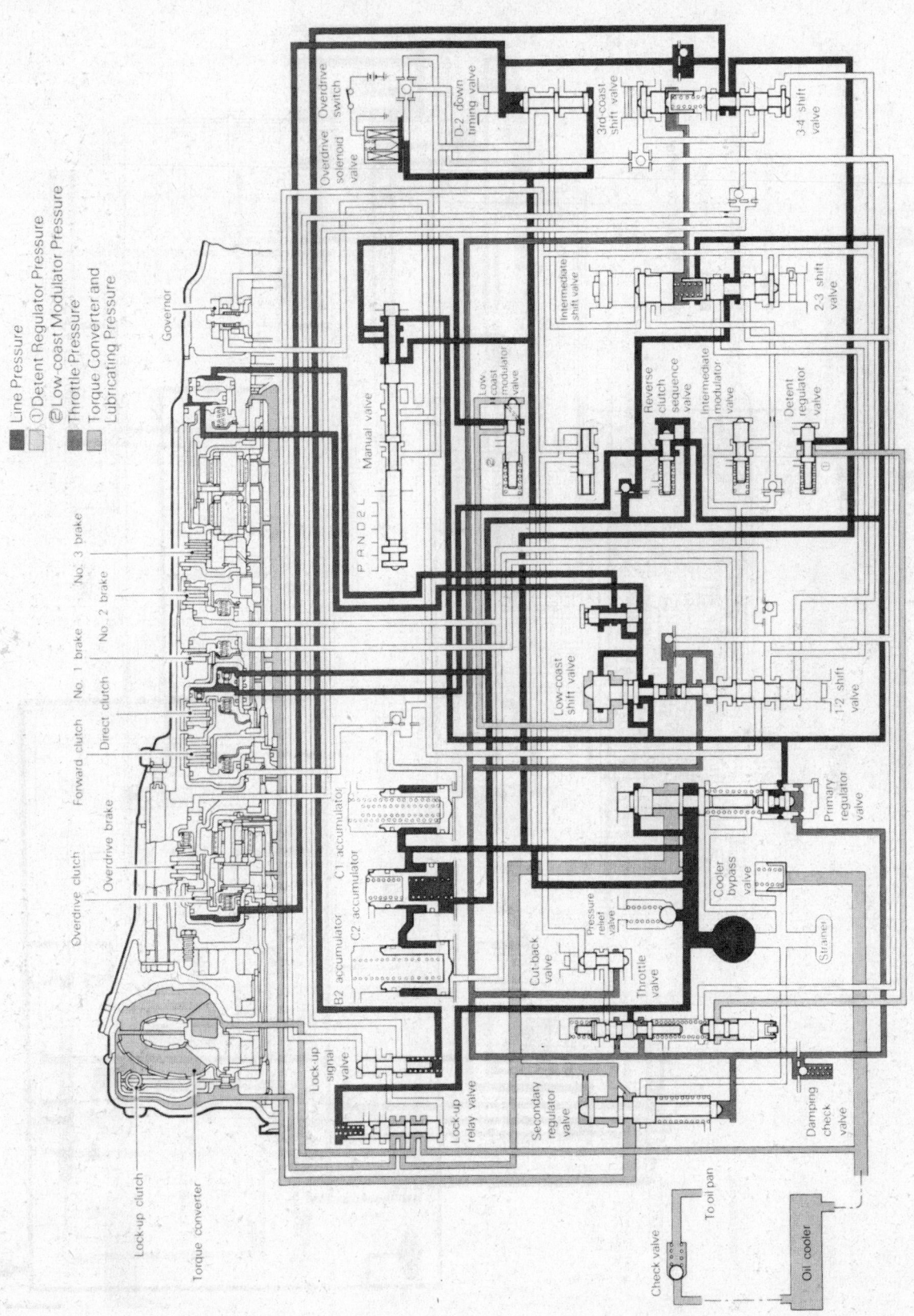

PARK—4EAT

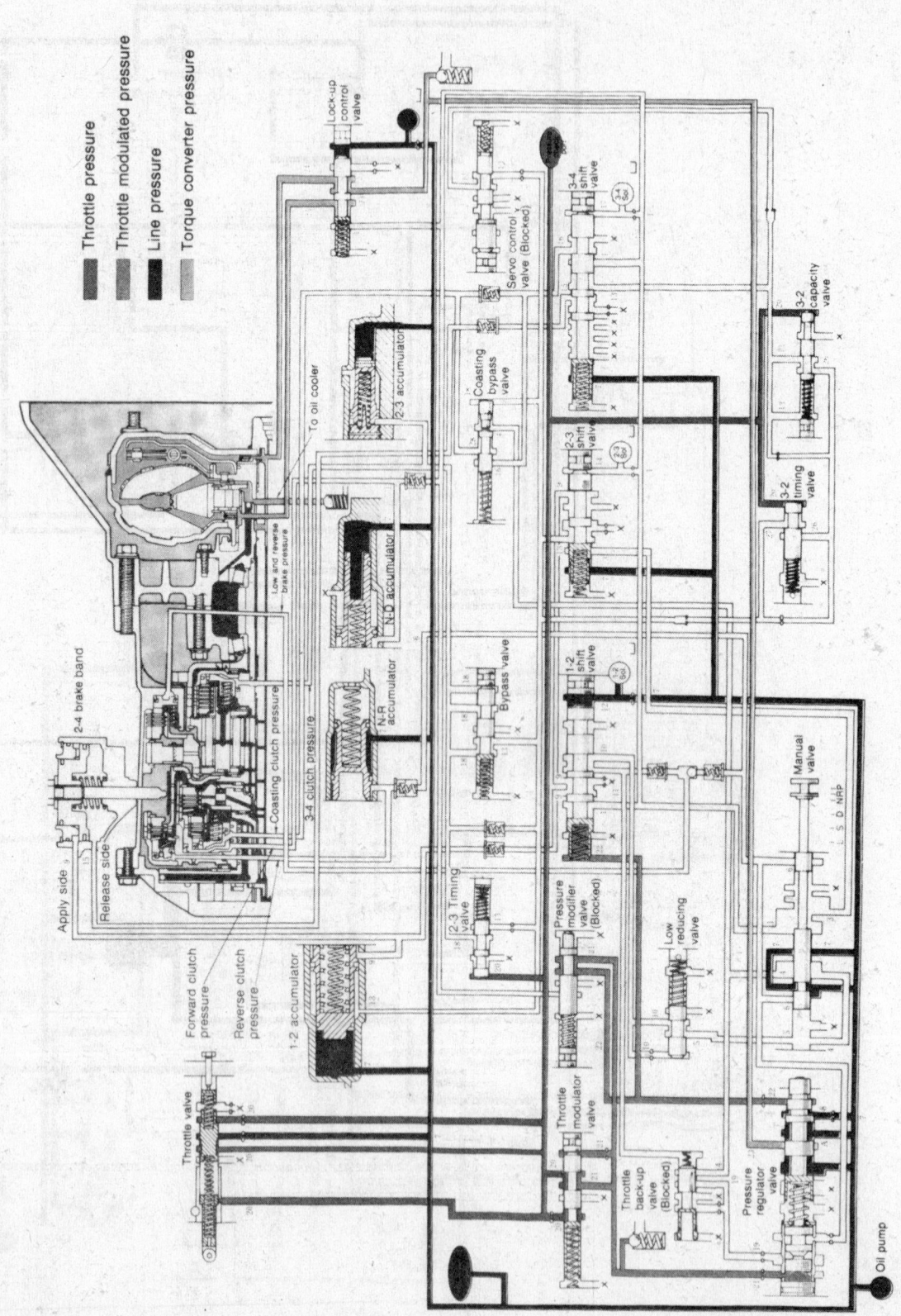

REVERSE—4EAT

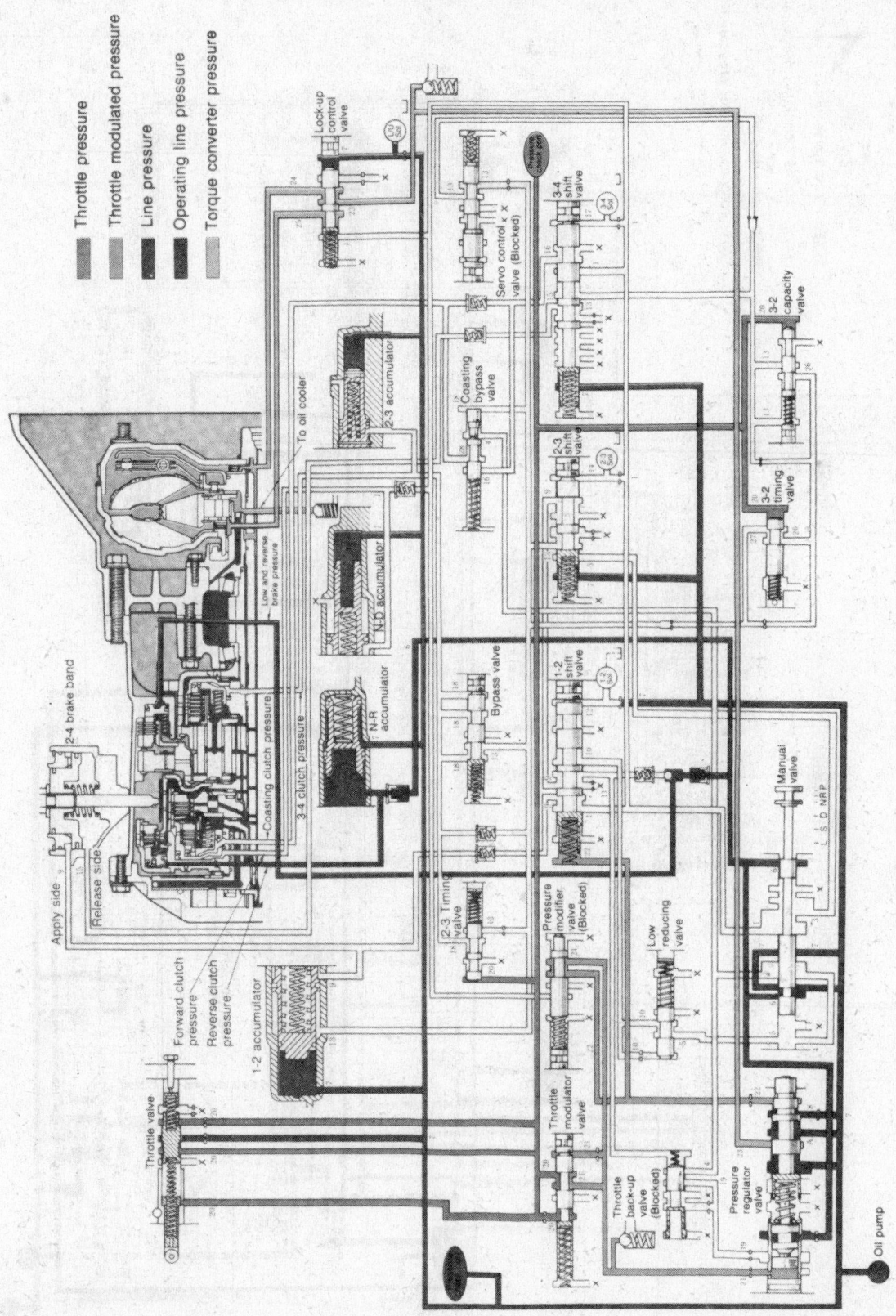

NEUTRAL BELOW 11 MPH—4EAT

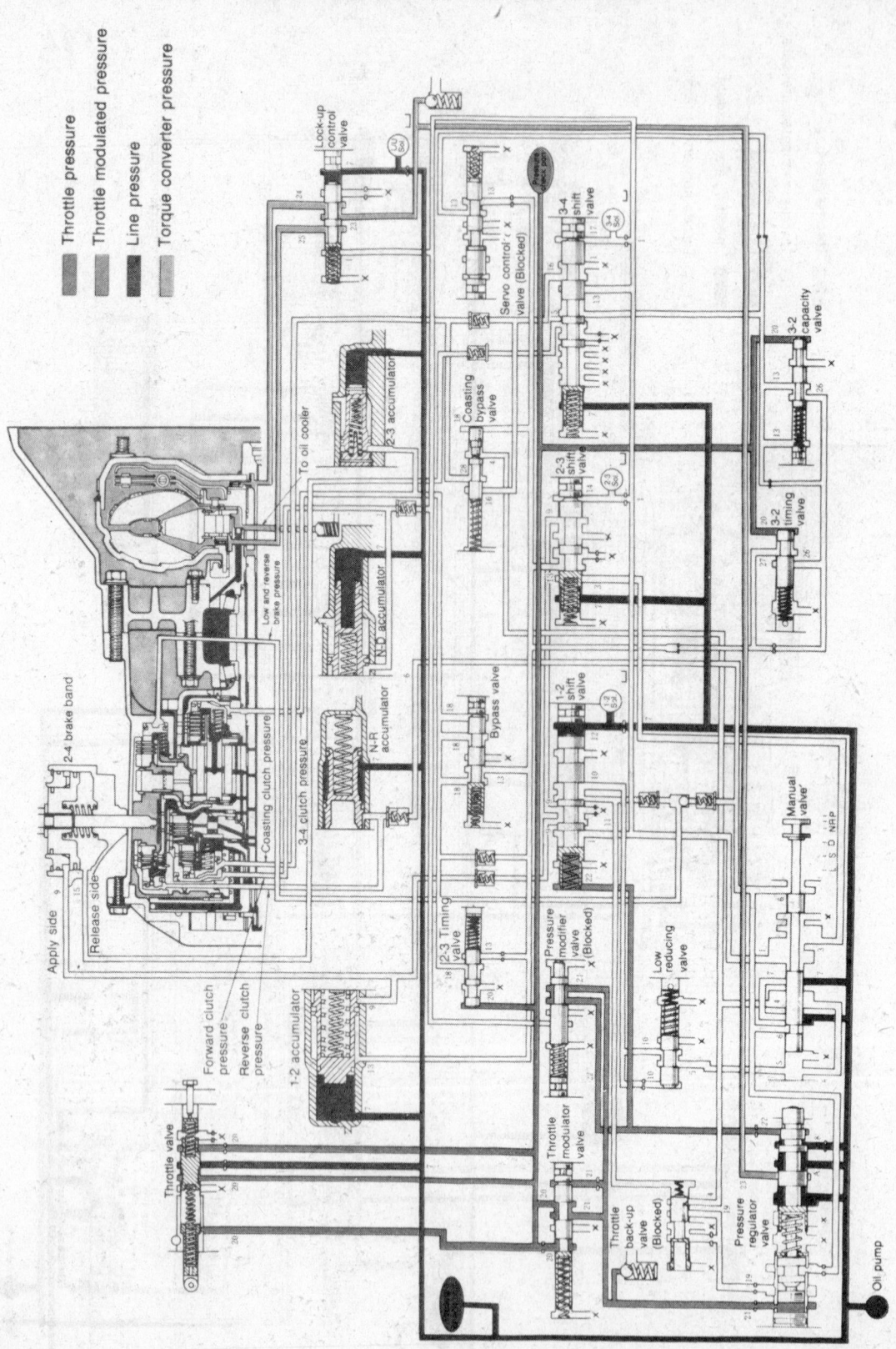

NEUTRAL ABOVE 11 MPH—4EAT

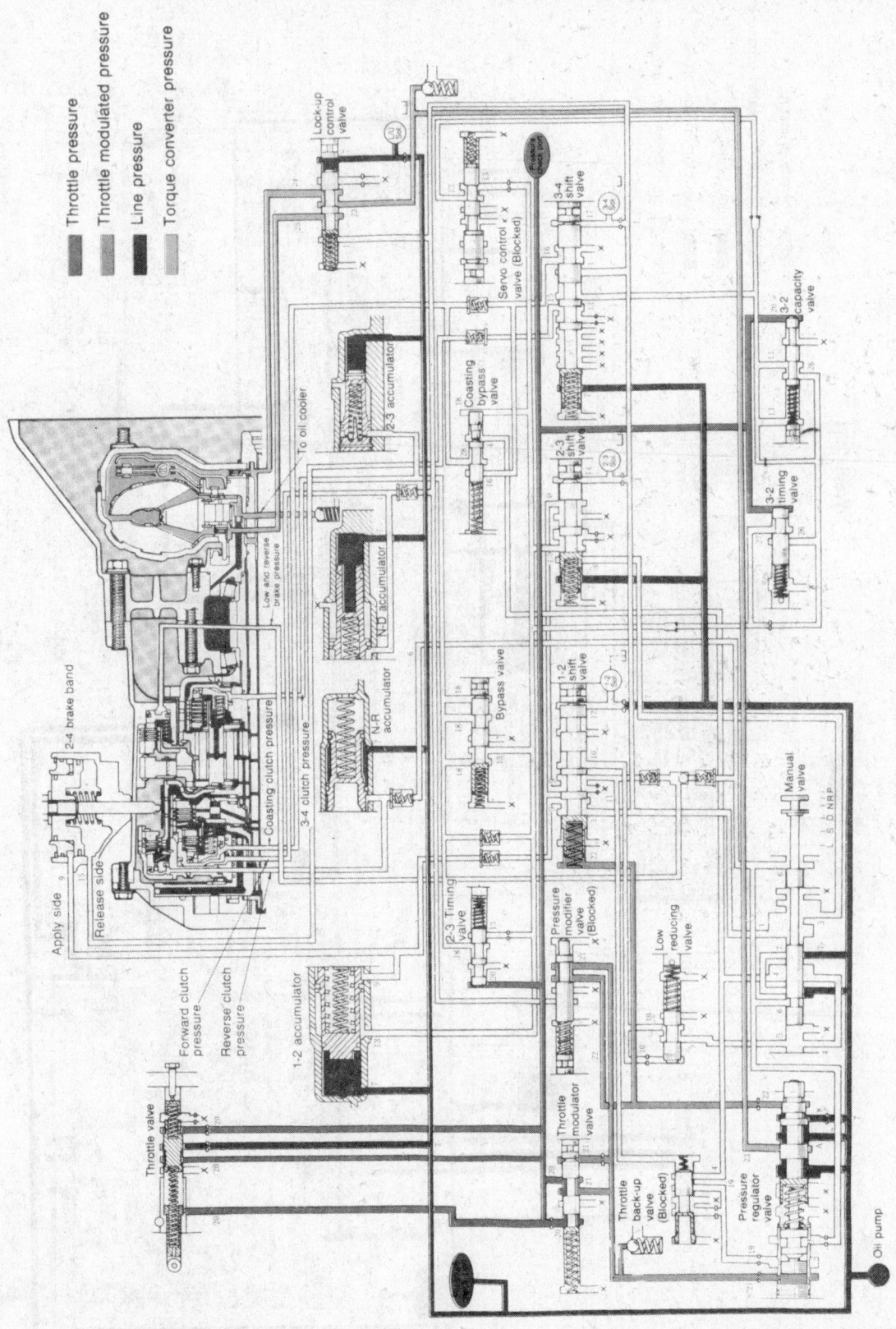

DRIVE—1ST GEAR—4EAT

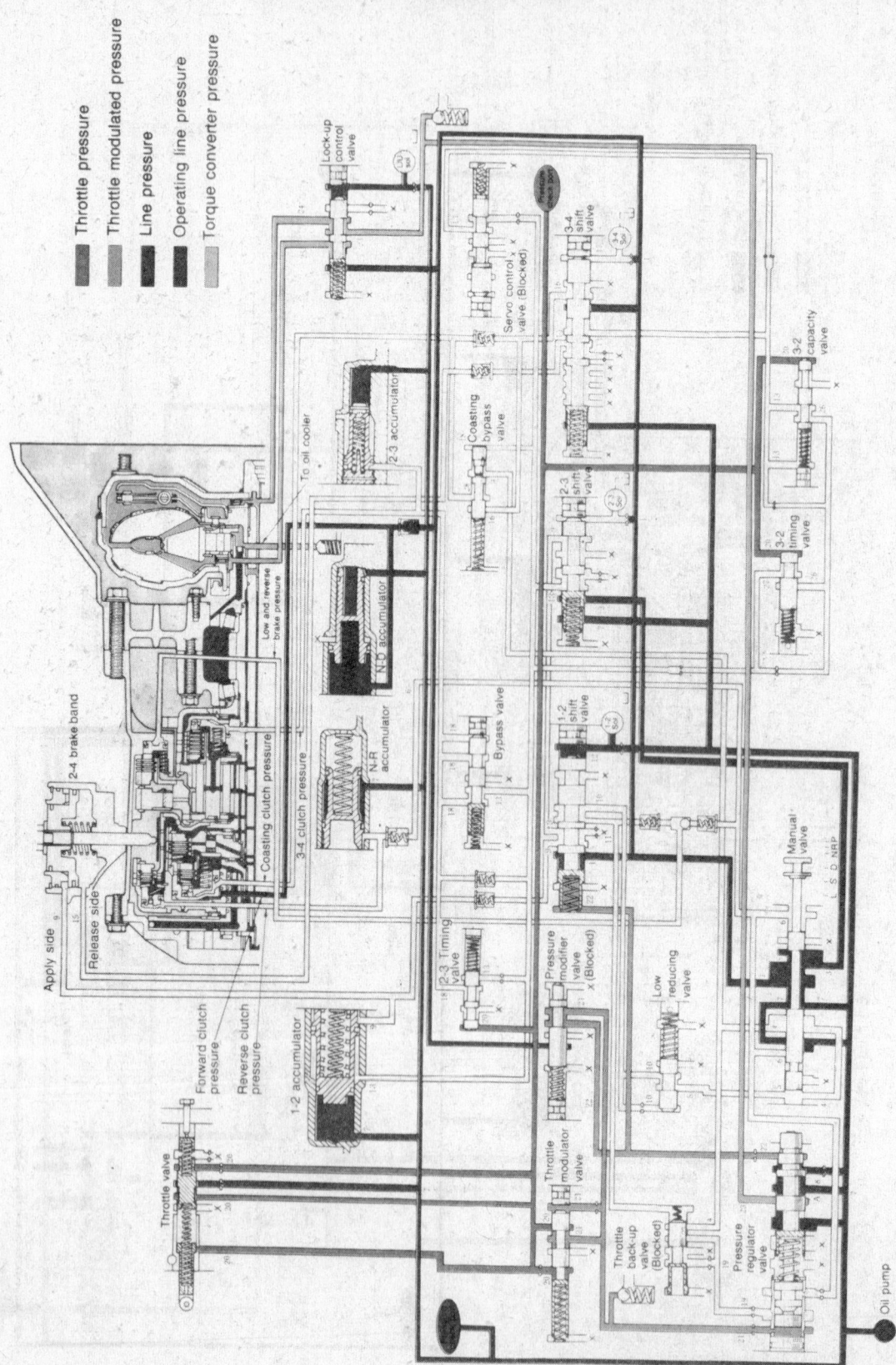

- Throttle pressure
- Throttle modulated pressure
- Line pressure
- Operating line pressure
- Torque converter pressure

DRIVE—2ND GEAR—4EAT

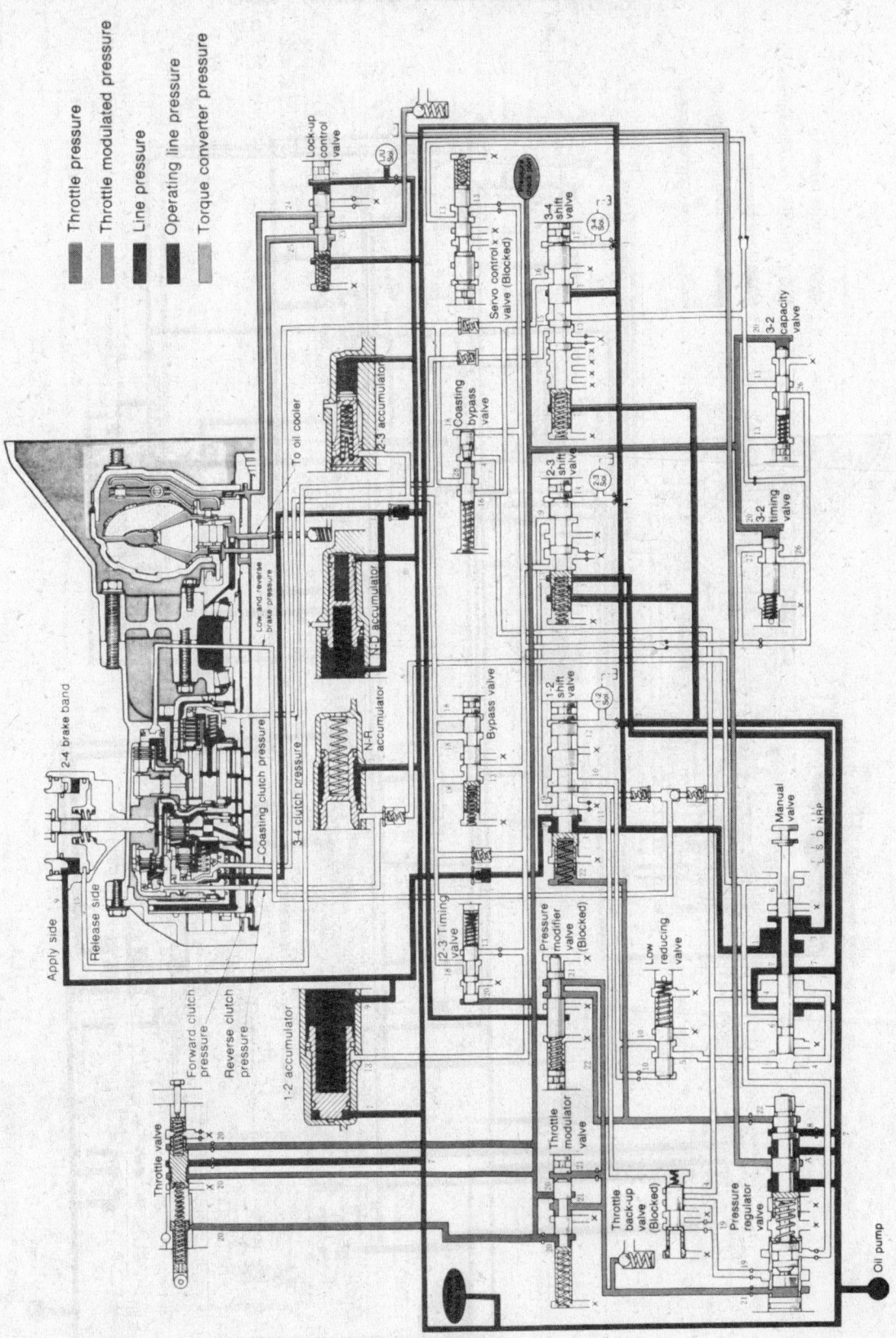

DRIVE—3RD GEAR BELOW 25 MPH—4EAT

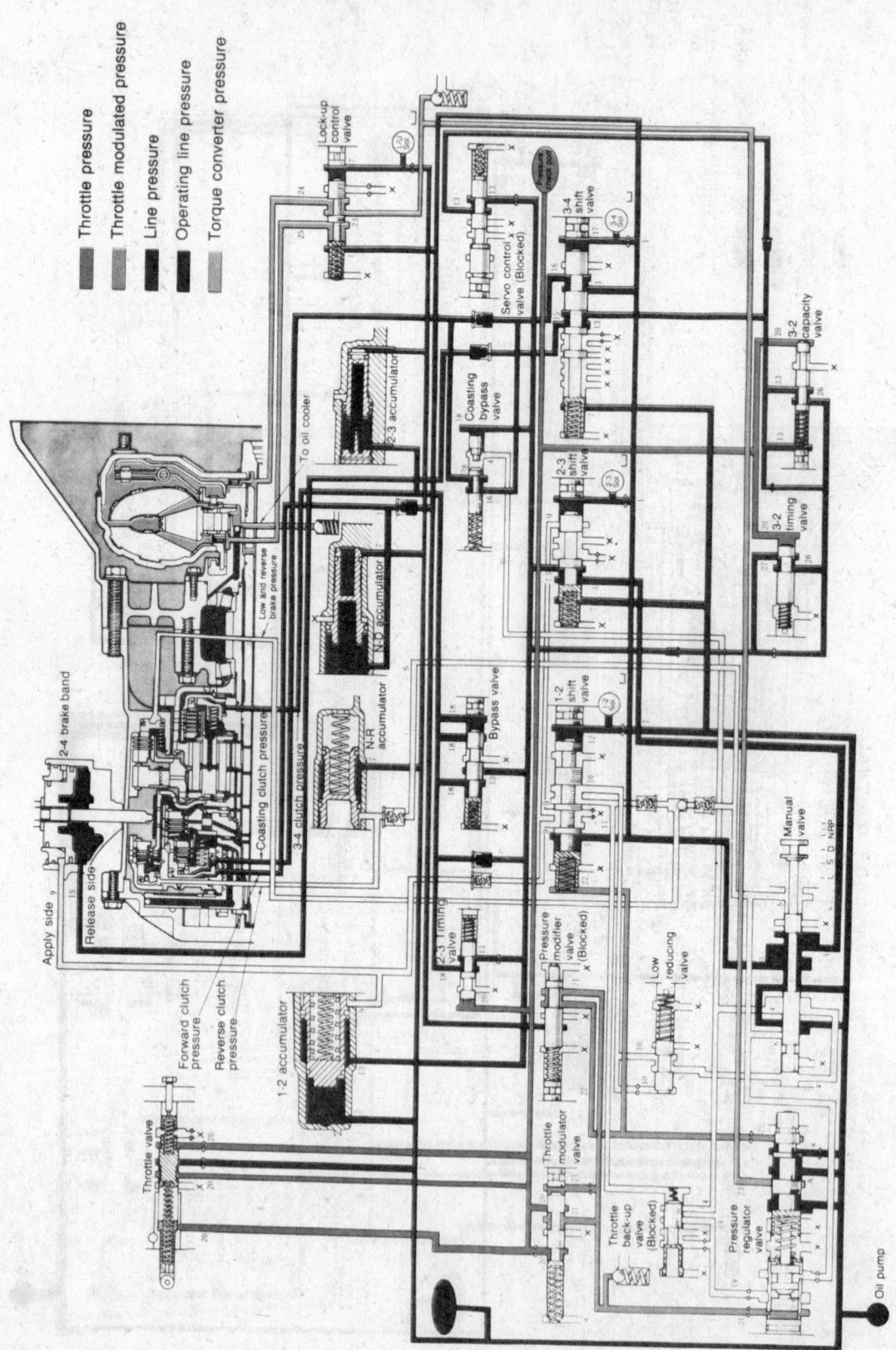

DRIVE—3RD GEAR ABOVE 25 MPH LOCKUP ON—4EAT

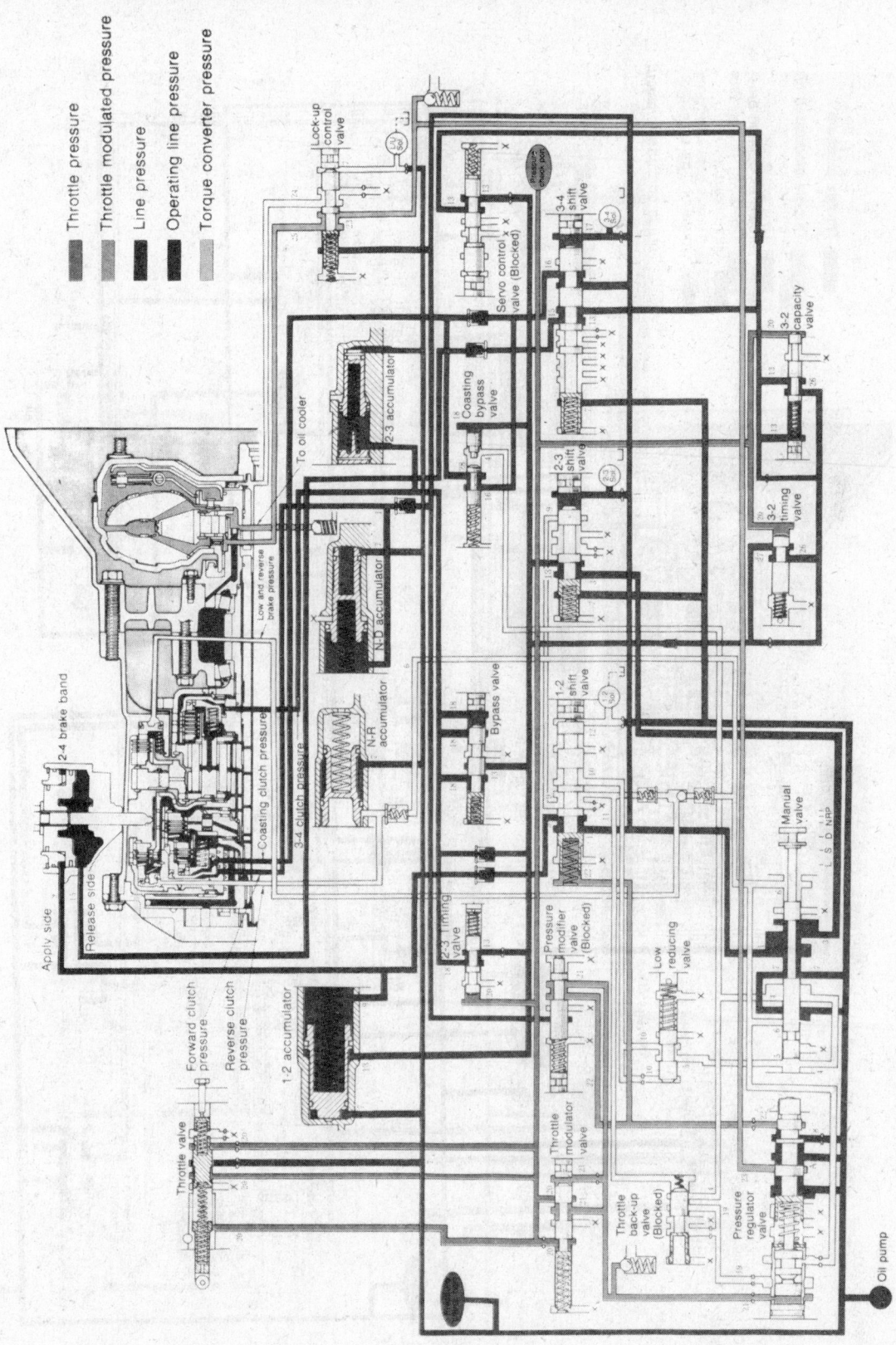

Throttle pressure
Throttle modulated pressure
Line pressure
Operating line pressure
Torque converter pressure

DRIVE—OVERDRIVE LOCKUP ON—4EAT

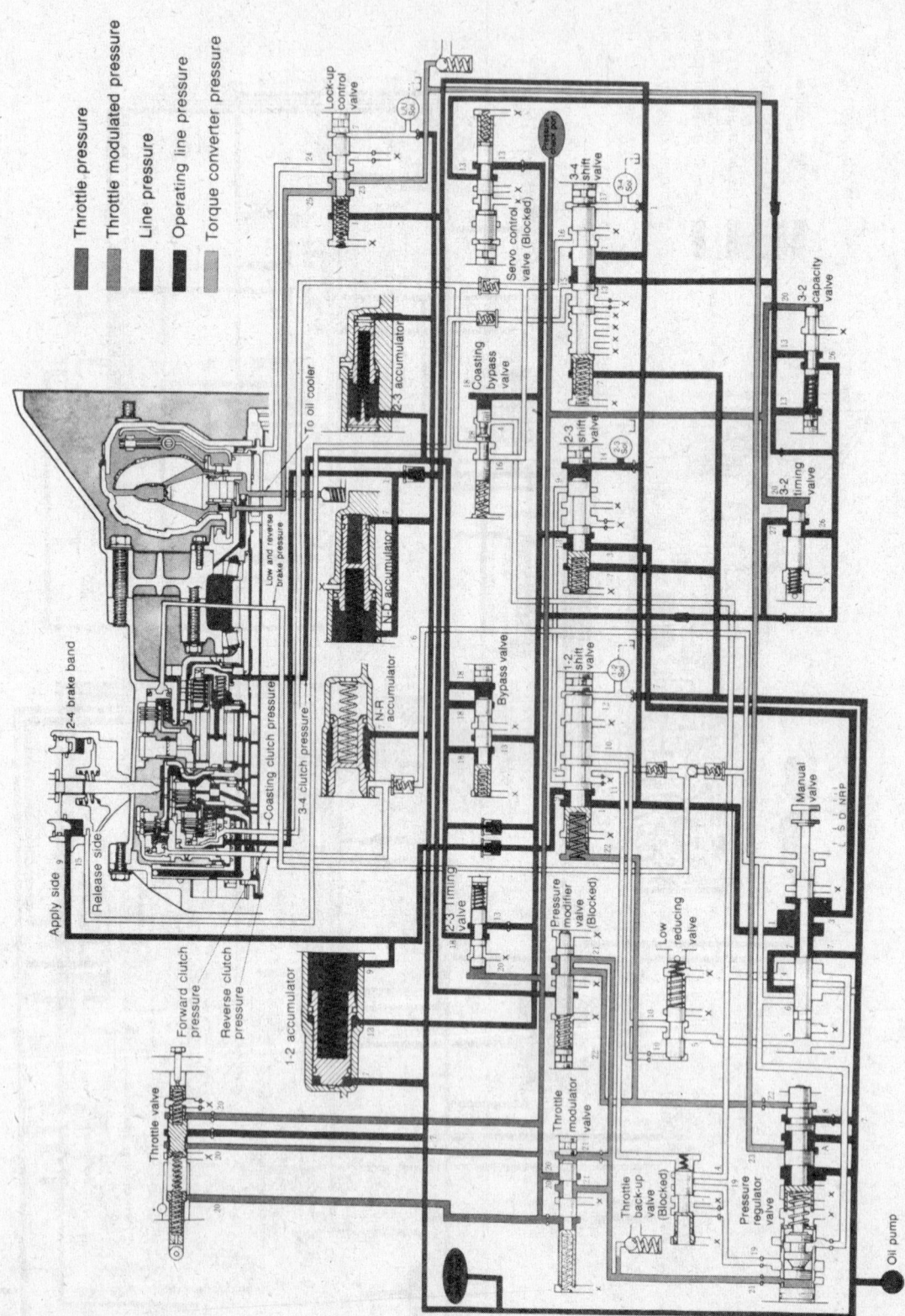

S—1ST GEAR—4EAT

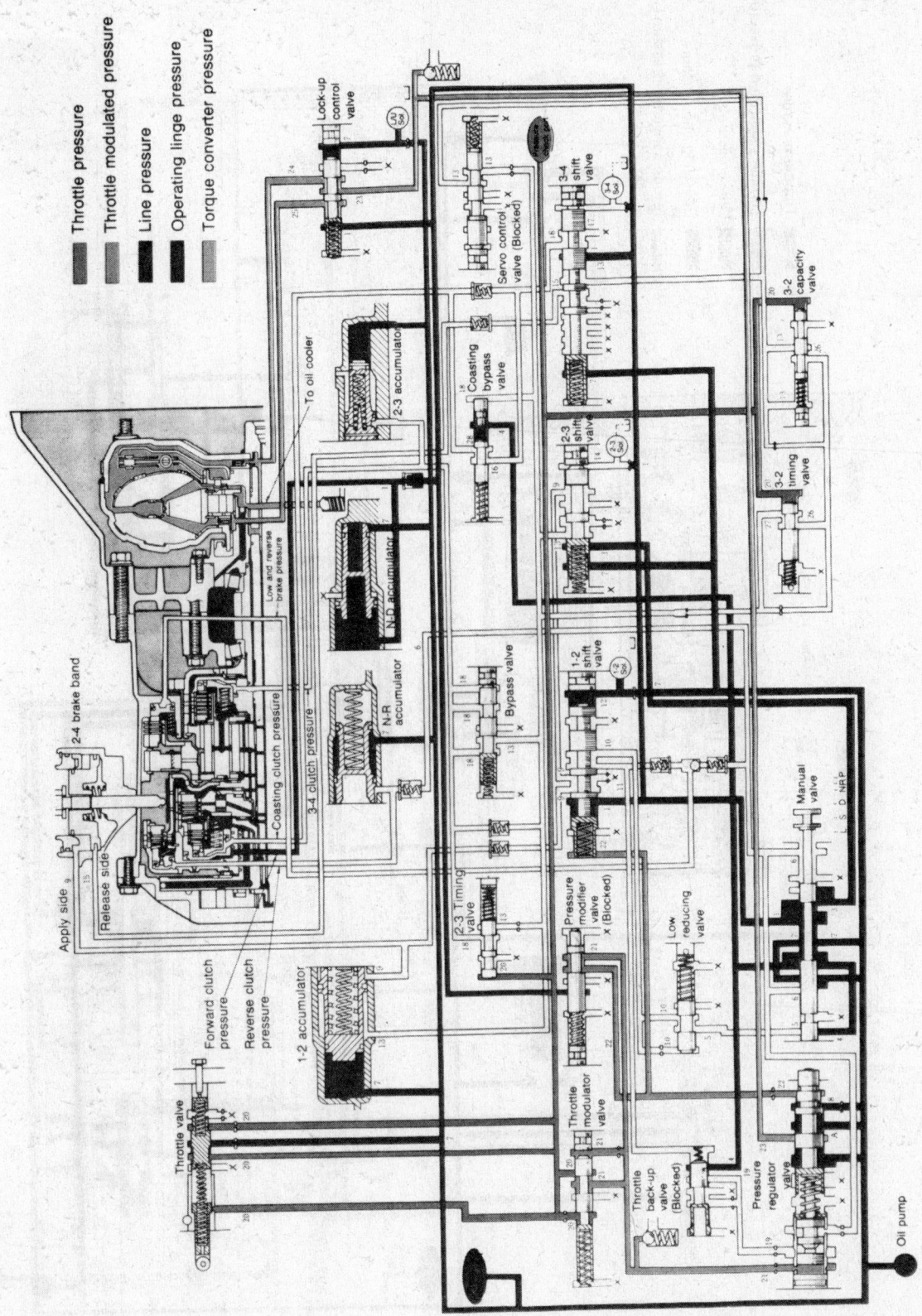

S − 2ND GEAR − 4EAT

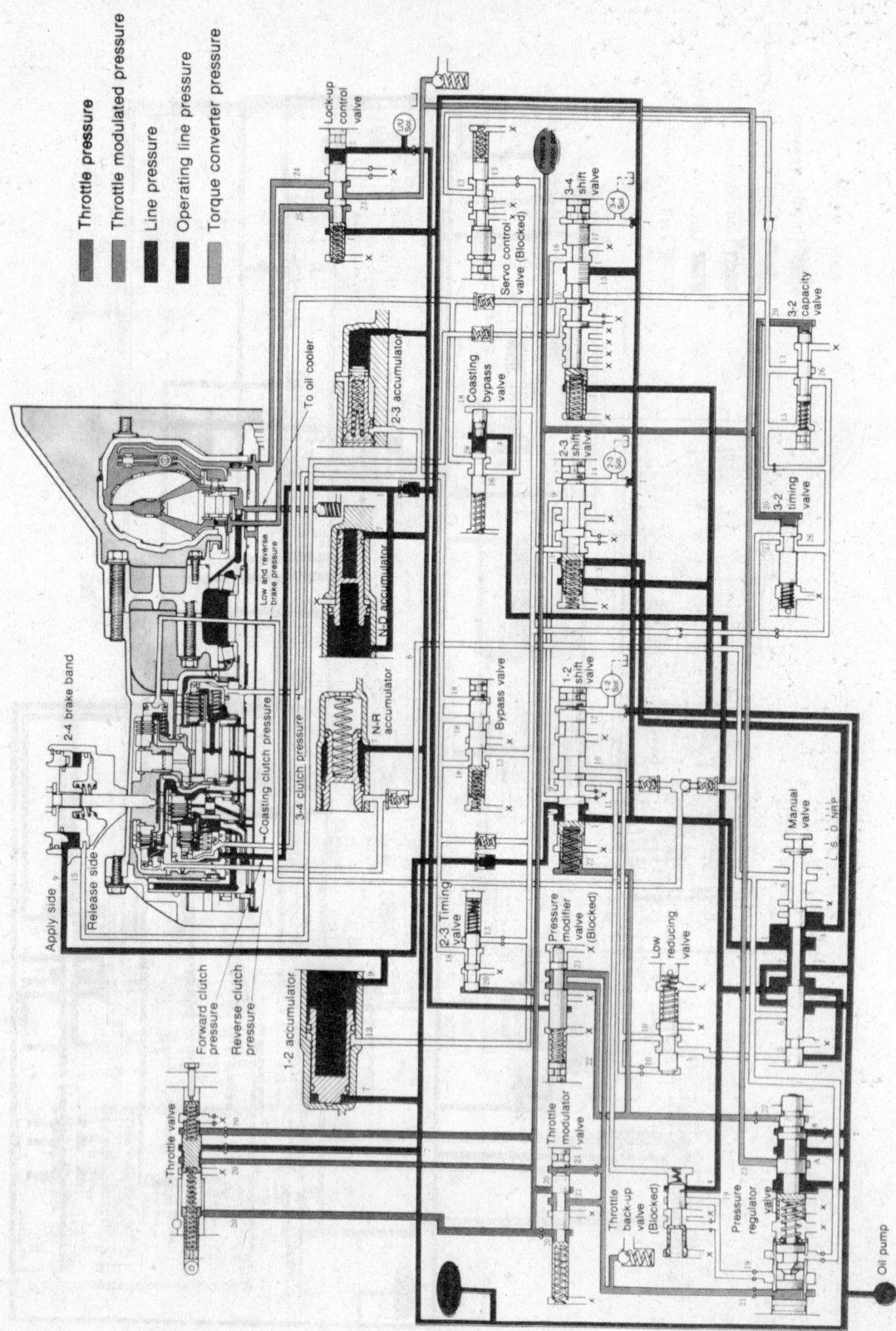

Throttle pressure

Throttle modulated pressure

Line pressure

Operating line pressure

Torque converter pressure

S—2ND GEAR HOLD—4EAT

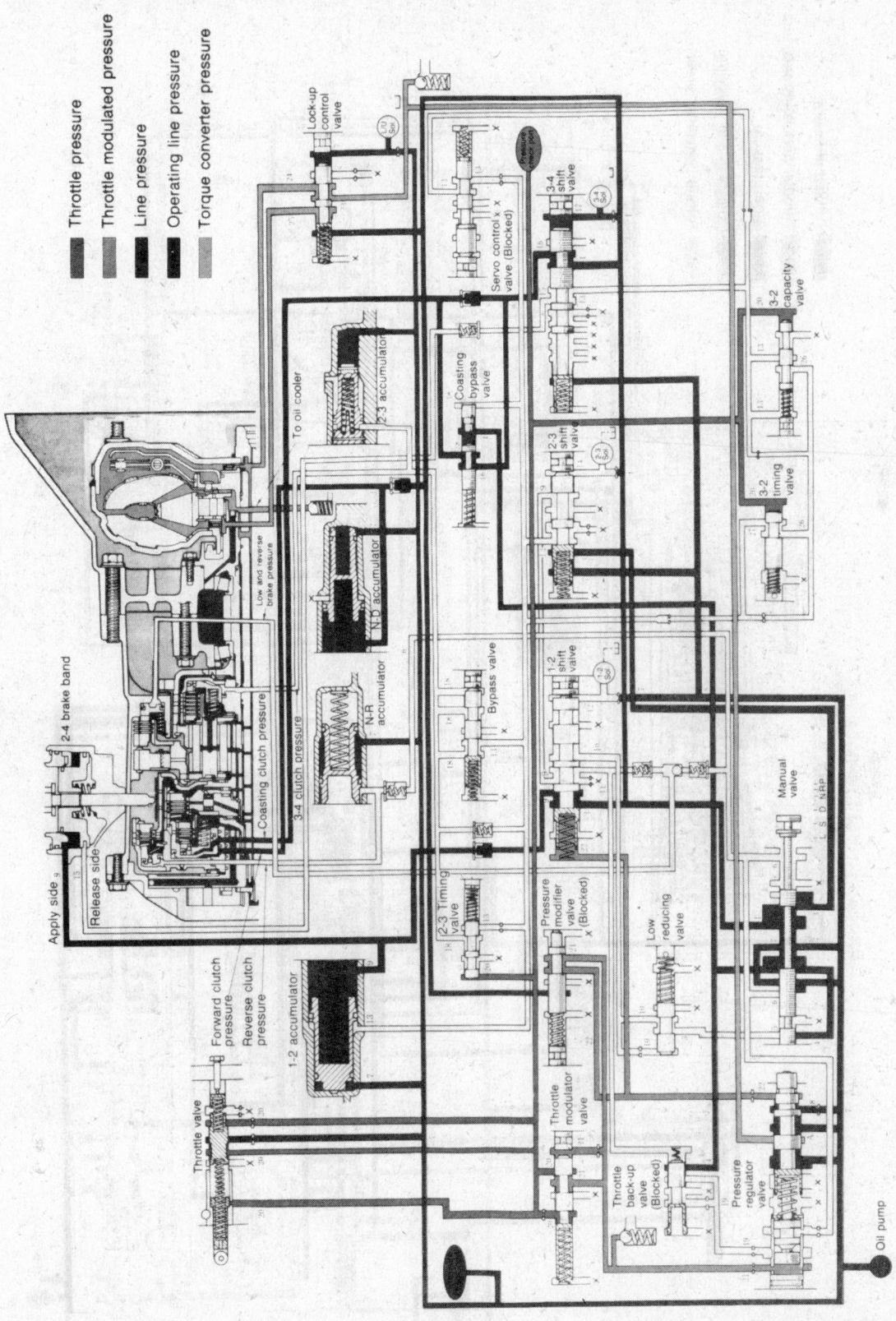

S—3RD GEAR BELOW 25 MPH—4EAT

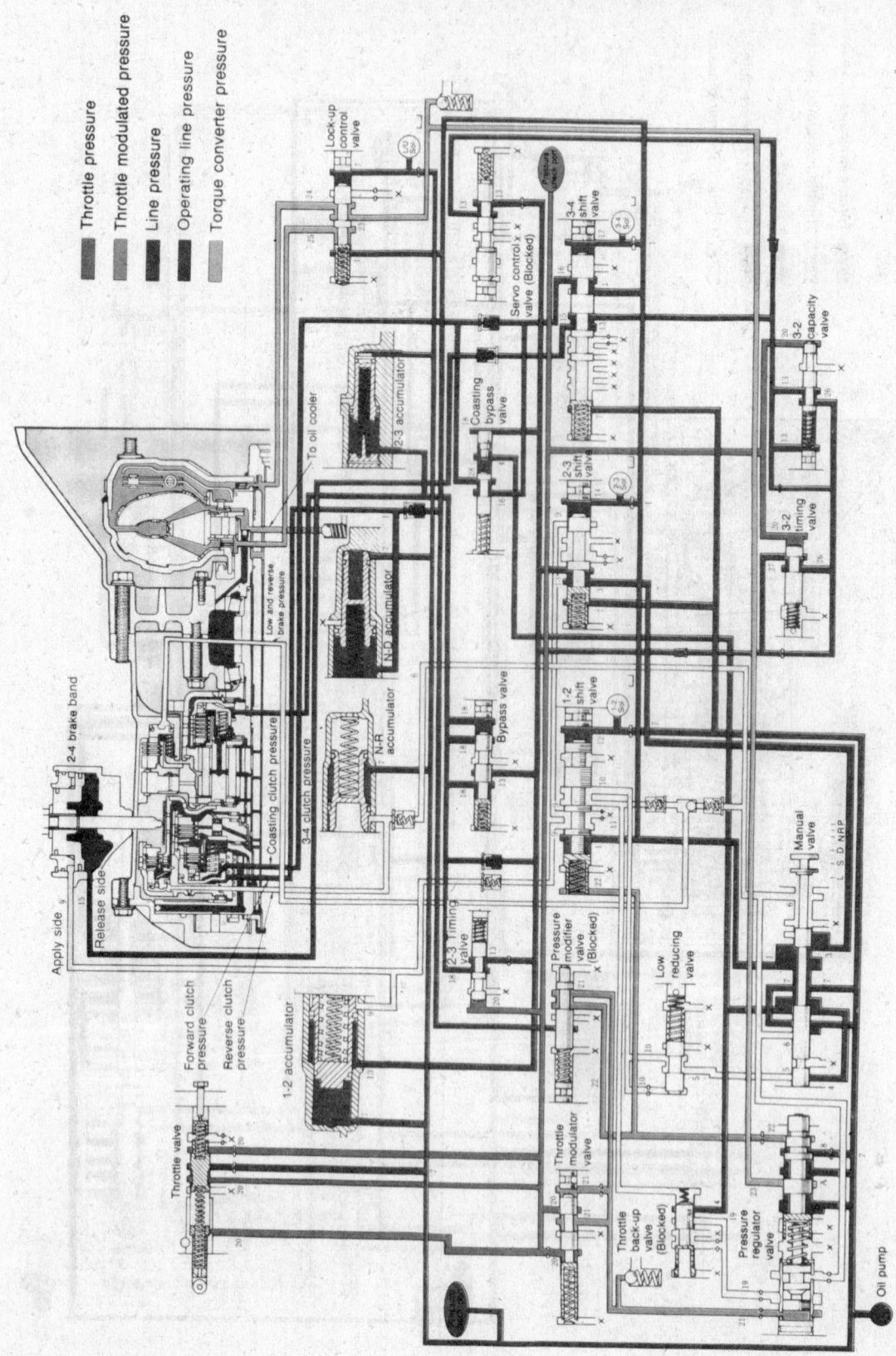

S—3RD GEAR ABOVE 25 MPH—4EAT

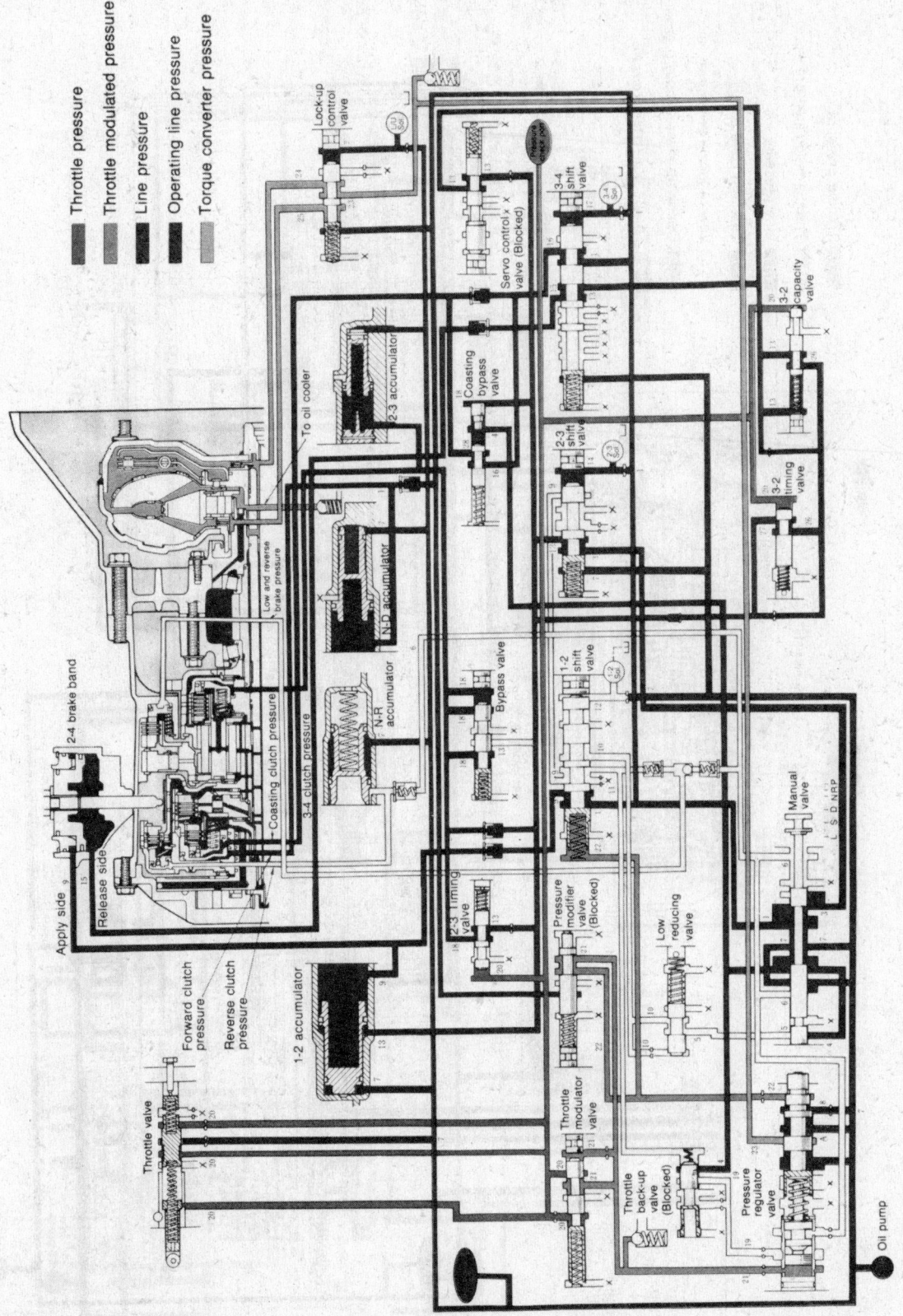

L—1ST GEAR—4EAT

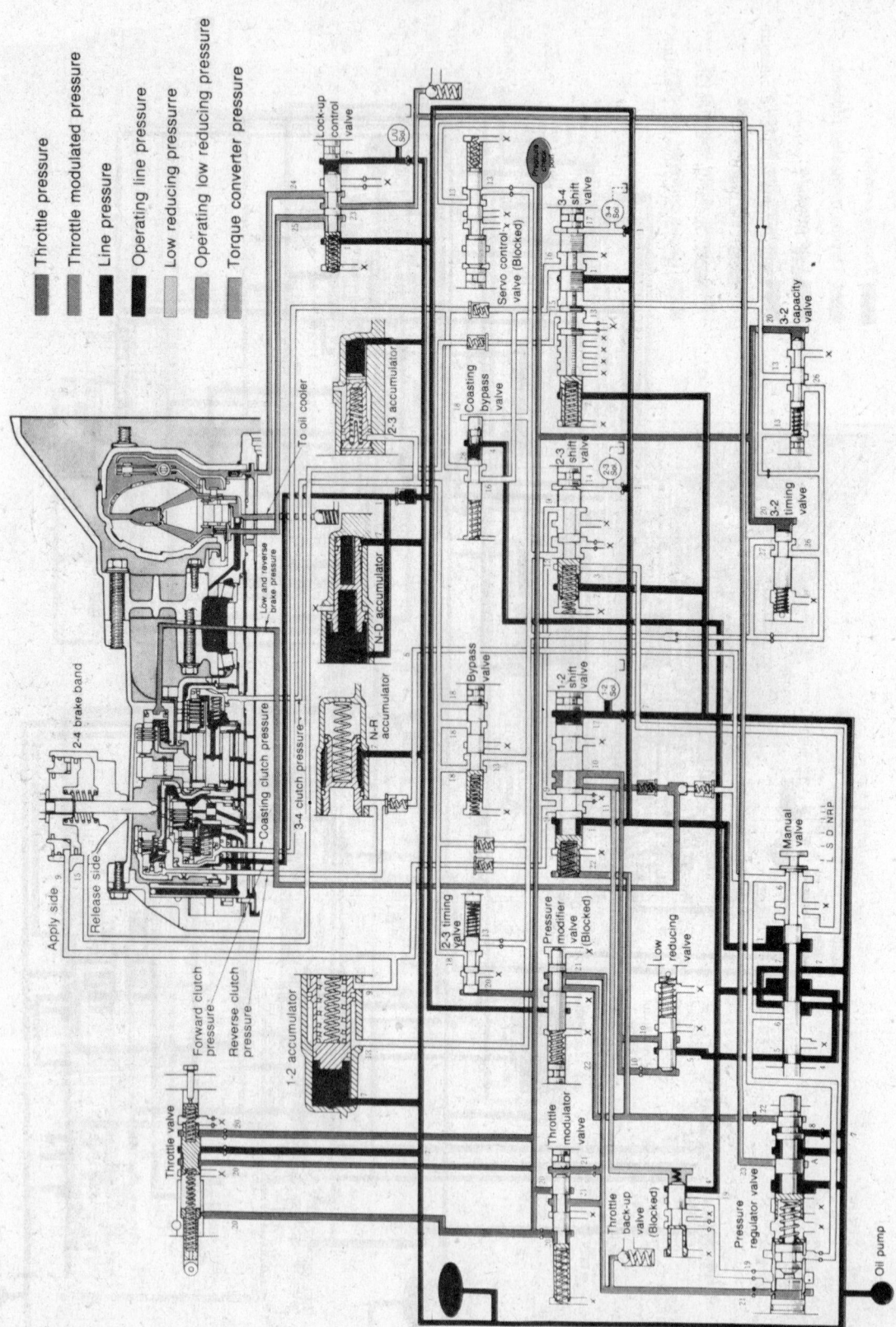

L—1ST GEAR HOLD—4EAT

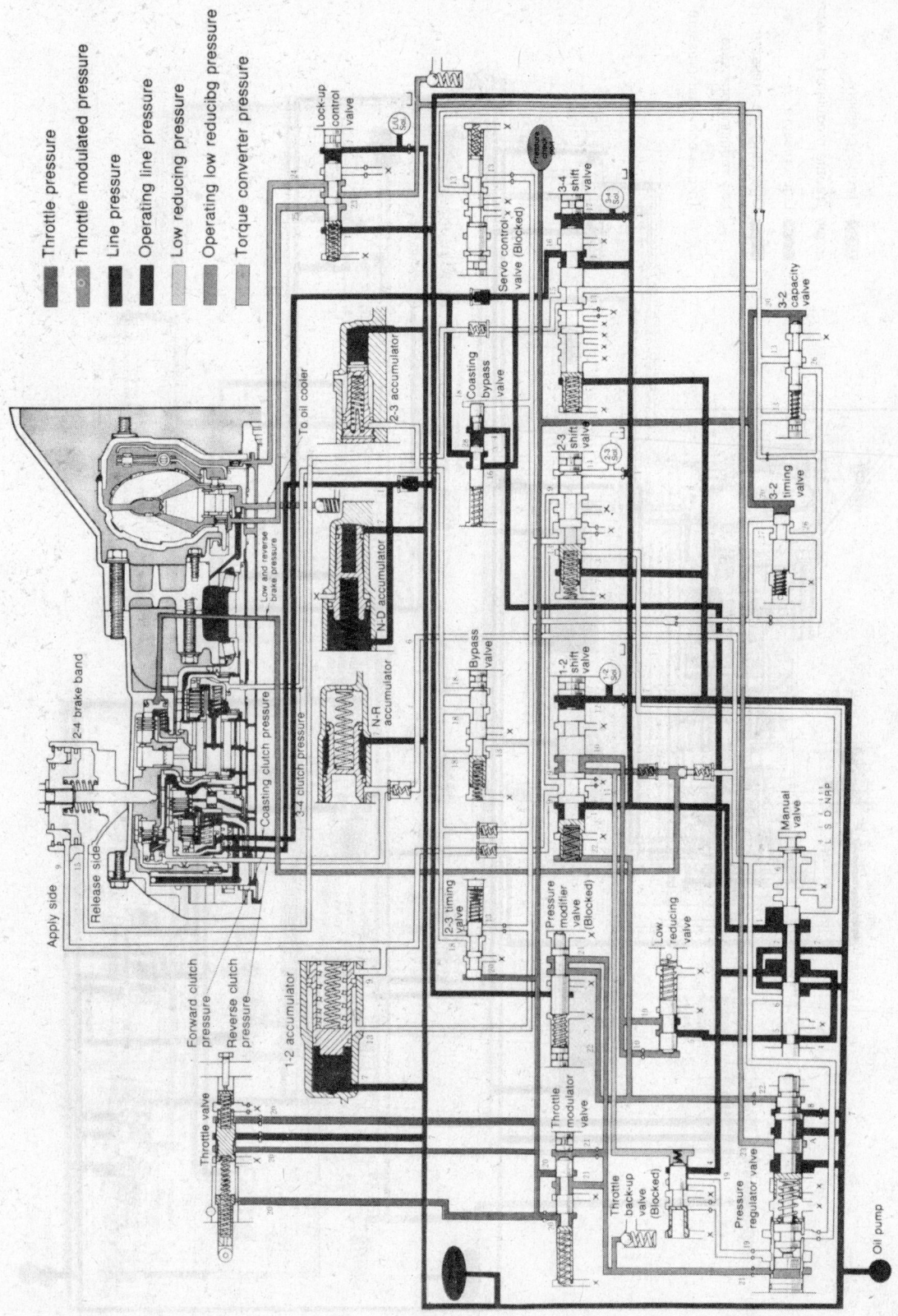

L—2ND GEAR BELOW 68 MPH—4EAT

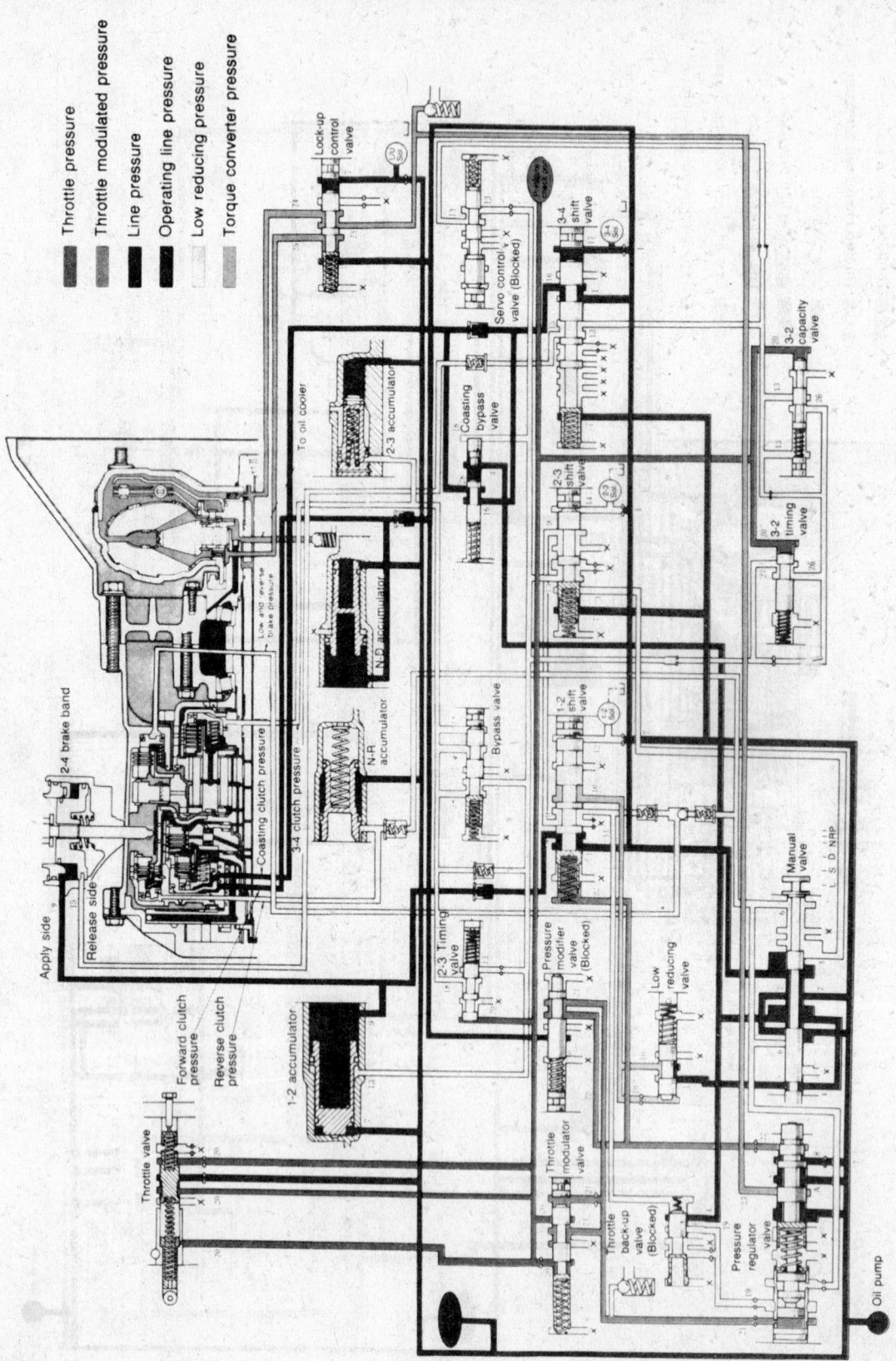

Throttle pressure
Throttle modulated pressure
Line pressure
Operating line pressure
Low reducing pressure
Torque converter pressure

L—2ND GEAR ABOVE 68 MPH—4EAT

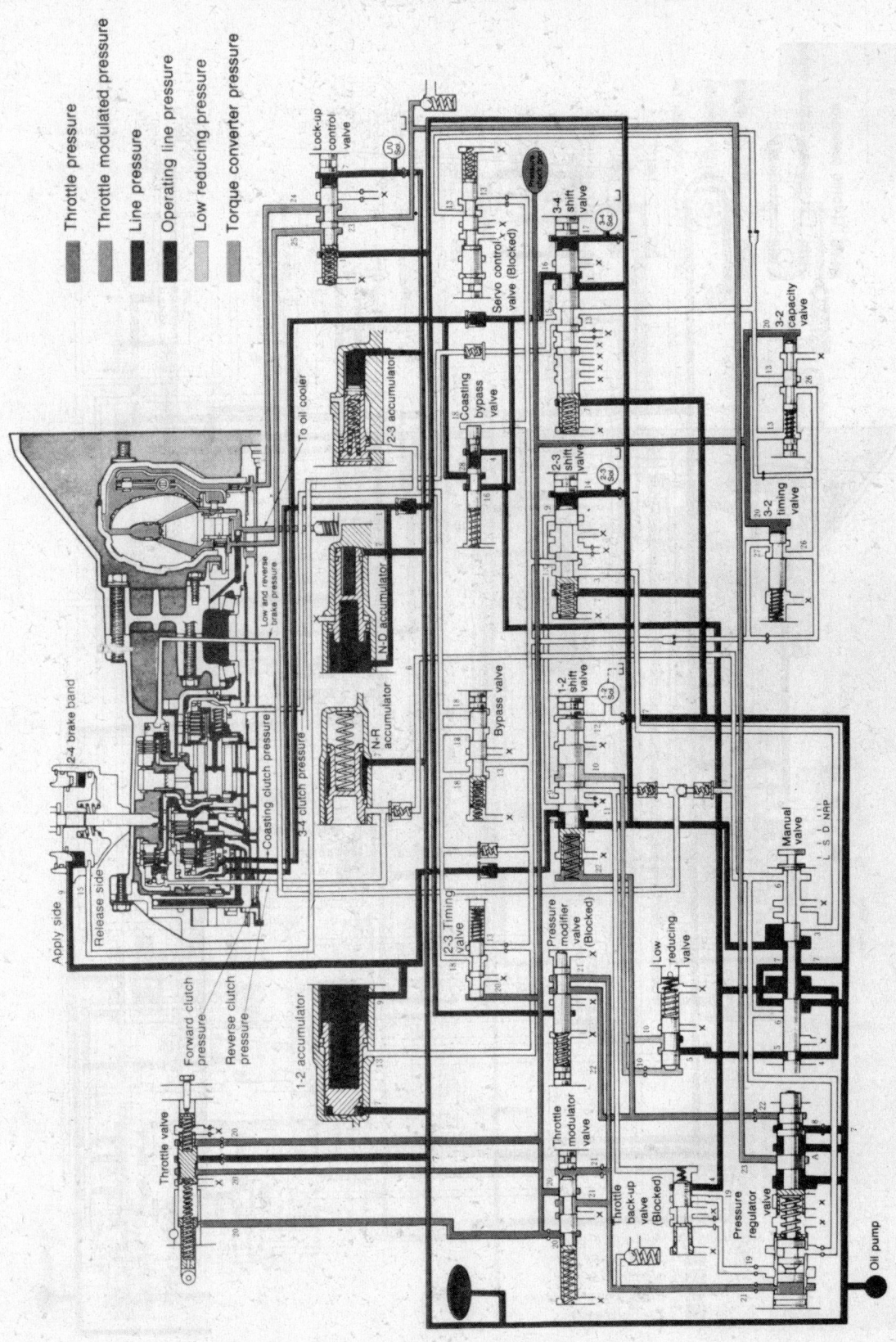

NEUTRAL—F3A

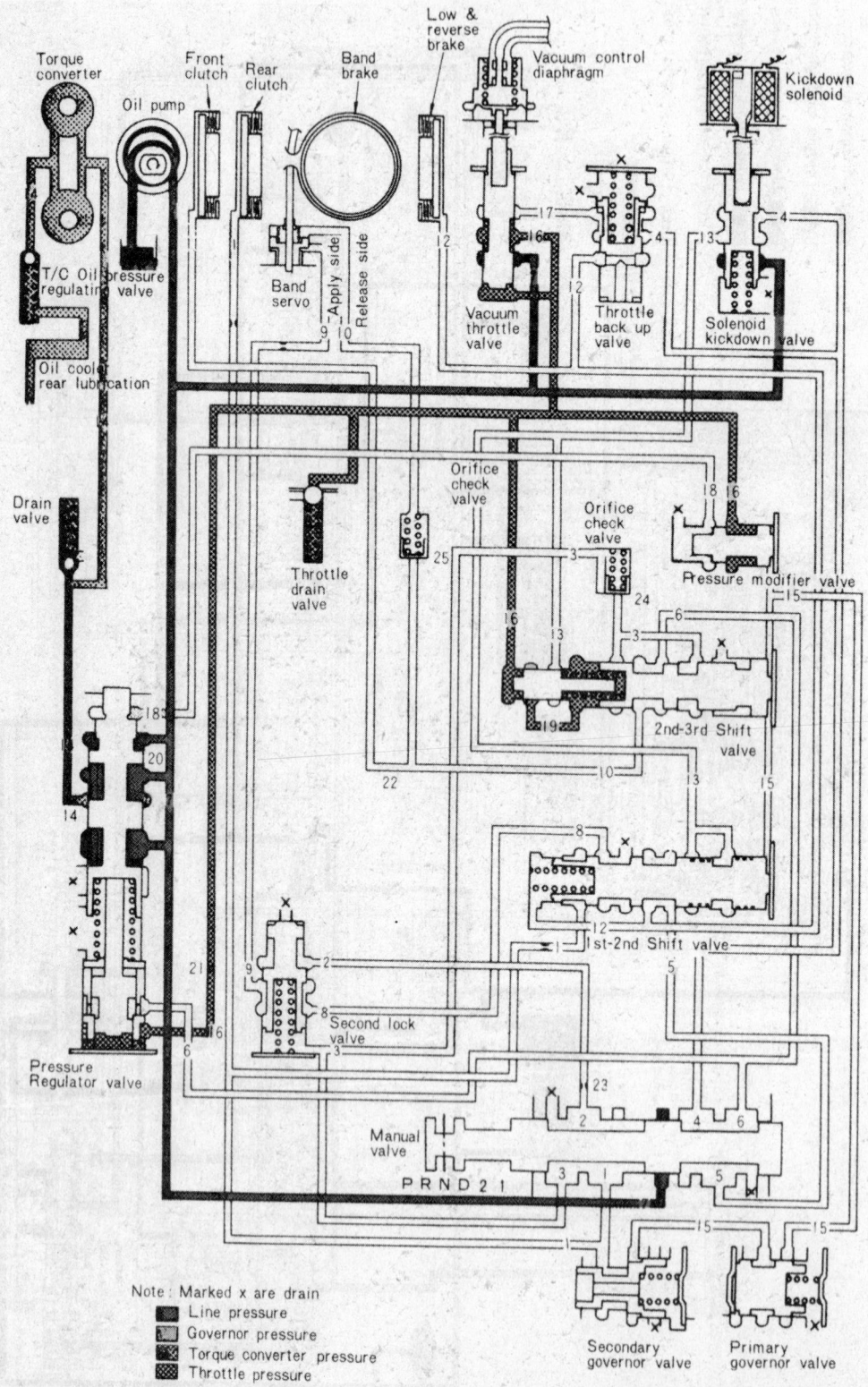

Torque converter

Front clutch

Rear clutch

Band brake

Low & reverse brake

Vacuum control diaphragm

Kickdown solenoid

Oil pump

T/C Oil pressure regulating valve

Oil cooler rear lubrication

Band servo

Apply side

Release side

Vacuum throttle valve

Throttle back up valve

Solenoid kickdown valve

Drain valve

Throttle drain valve

Orifice check valve

Orifice check valve

Pressure modifier valve

2nd-3rd Shift valve

1st-2nd Shift valve

Pressure Regulator valve

Second lock valve

Manual valve

P R N D 2 1

Secondary governor valve

Primary governor valve

Note : Marked x are drain
- Line pressure
- Governor pressure
- Torque converter pressure
- Throttle pressure

D1—1ST GEAR—F3A

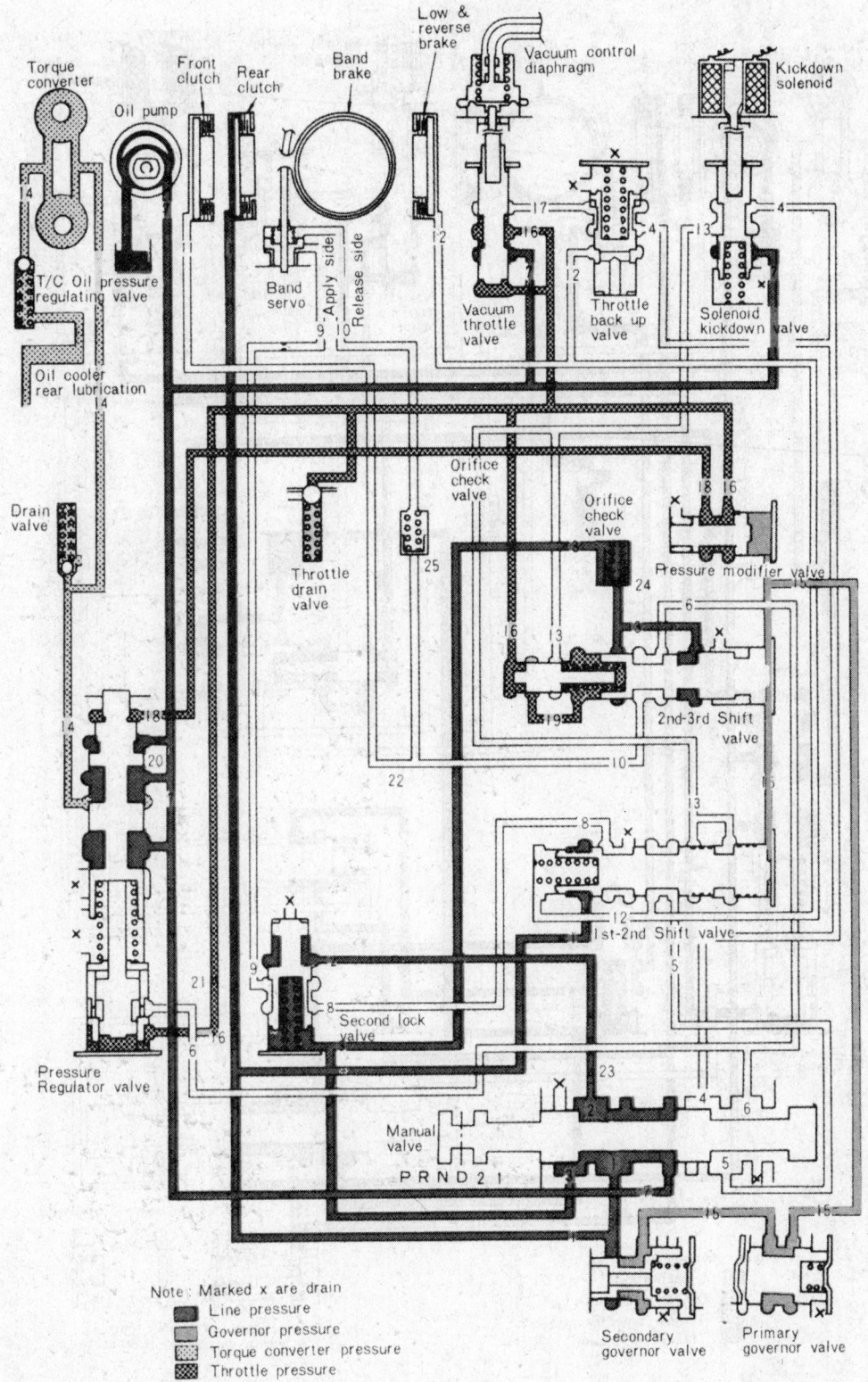

Torque converter
Oil pump
Front clutch
Rear clutch
Band brake
Low & reverse brake
Vacuum control diaphragm
Kickdown solenoid
T/C Oil pressure regulating valve
Band servo
Apply side
Release side
Vacuum throttle valve
Throttle back up valve
Solenoid kickdown valve
Oil cooler rear lubrication
Drain valve
Throttle drain valve
Orifice check valve
Orifice check valve
Pressure modifier valve
2nd-3rd Shift valve
1st-2nd Shift valve
Second lock valve
Pressure Regulator valve
Manual valve
P R N D 2 1
Secondary governor valve
Primary governor valve

Note: Marked x are drain
- Line pressure
- Governor pressure
- Torque converter pressure
- Throttle pressure

D2—2ND GEAR—F3A

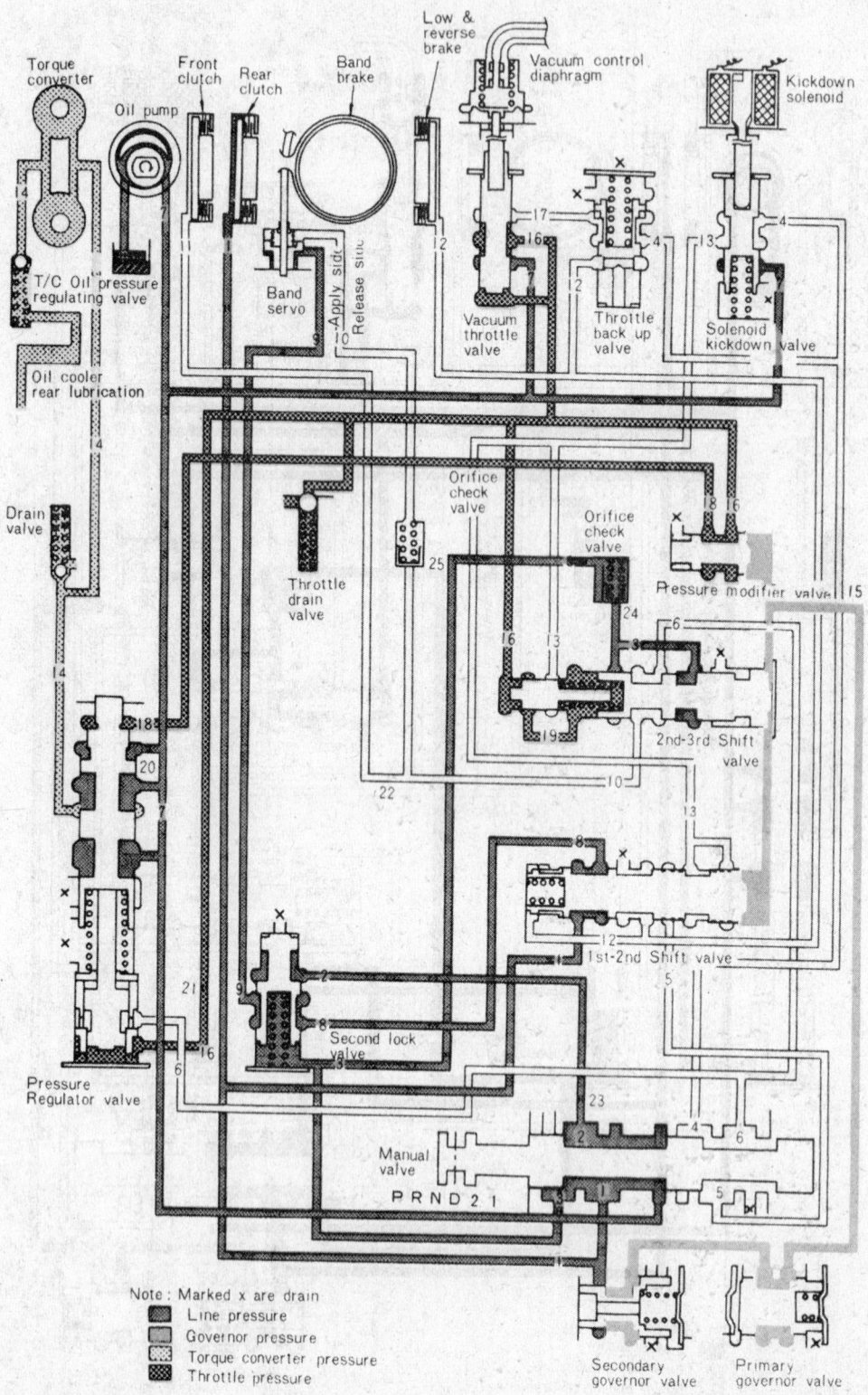

Torque converter

Oil pump

T/C Oil pressure regulating valve

Oil cooler rear lubrication

Drain valve

Front clutch

Rear clutch

Band brake

Band servo

Apply side

Release side

Low & reverse brake

Vacuum control diaphragm

Vacuum throttle valve

Throttle back up valve

Kickdown solenoid

Solenoid kickdown valve

Orifice check valve

Orifice check valve

Pressure modifier valve

Throttle drain valve

2nd-3rd Shift valve

1st-2nd Shift valve

Pressure Regulator valve

Second lock valve

Manual valve

P R N D 2 1

Secondary governor valve

Primary governor valve

Note : Marked x are drain
- Line pressure
- Governor pressure
- Torque converter pressure
- Throttle pressure

D3—3RD GEAR—F3A

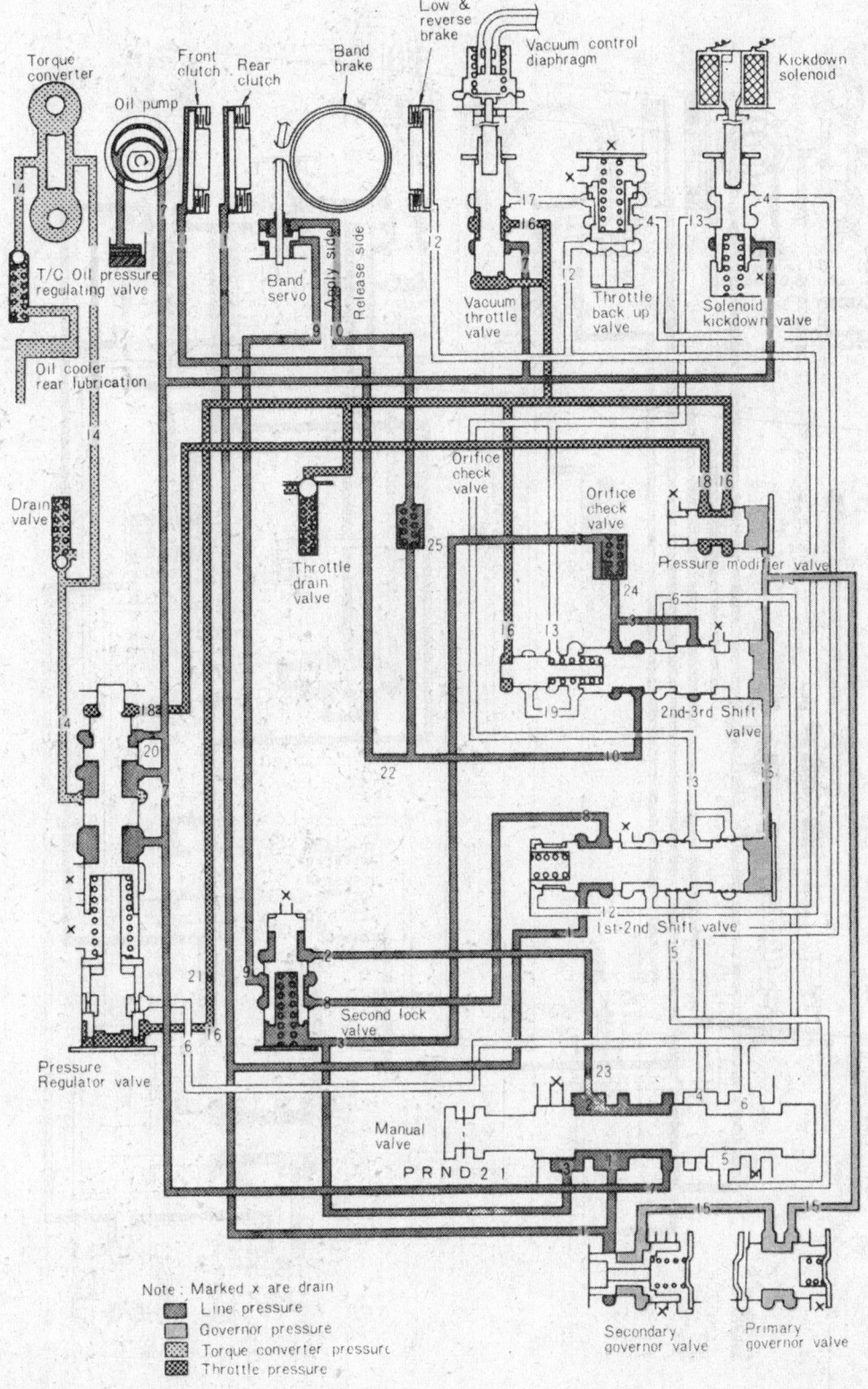

2–2ND GEAR—F3A

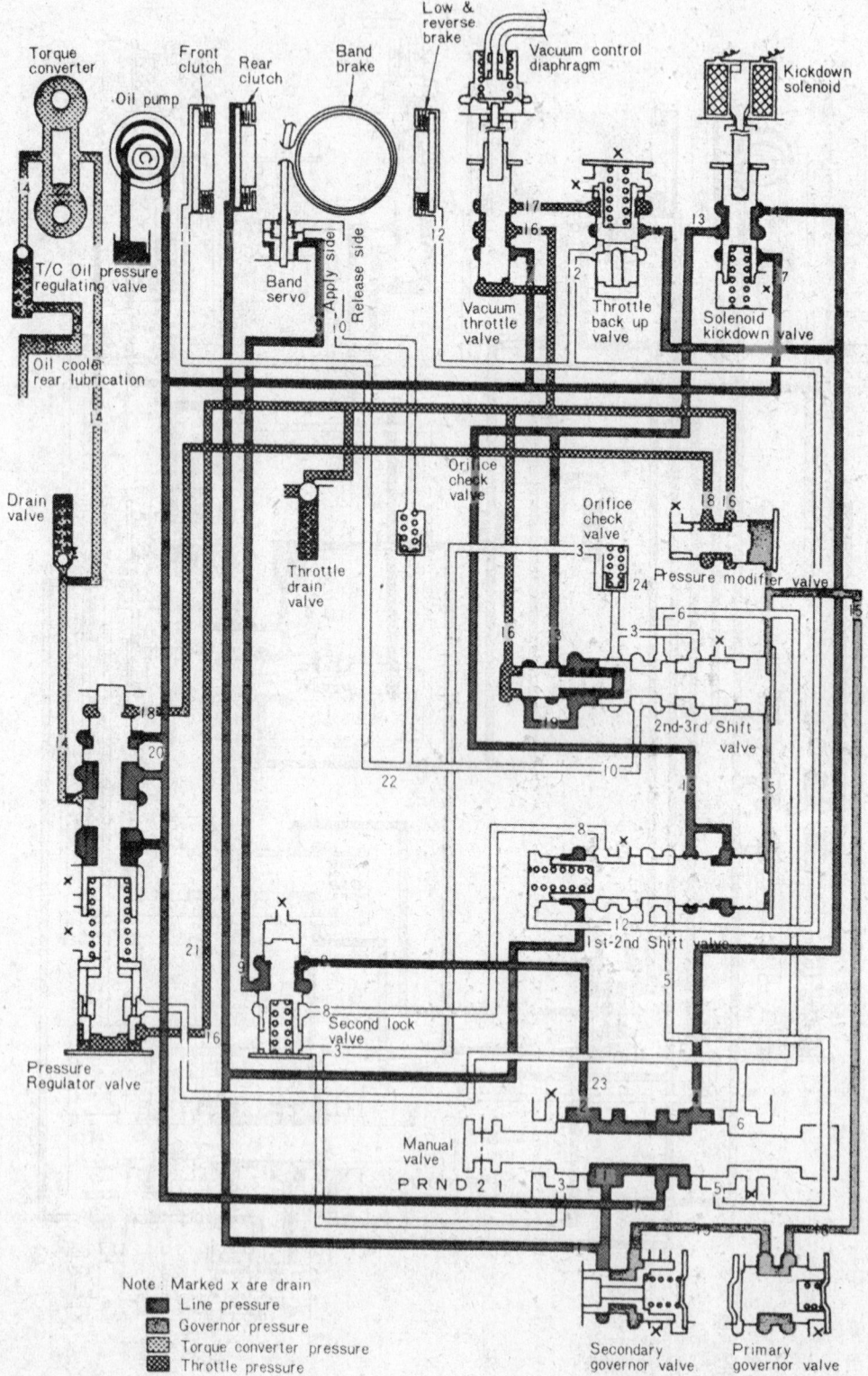

Torque converter

Front clutch

Rear clutch

Band brake

Low & reverse brake

Vacuum control diaphragm

Kickdown solenoid

Oil pump

T/C Oil pressure regulating valve

Band servo

Apply side

Release side

Vacuum throttle valve

Throttle back up valve

Solenoid kickdown valve

Oil cooler rear lubrication

Drain valve

Orifice check valve

Orifice check valve

Pressure modifier valve

Throttle drain valve

2nd-3rd Shift valve

1st-2nd Shift valve

Second lock valve

Pressure Regulator valve

Manual valve

P R N D 2 1

Secondary governor valve

Primary governor valve

Note : Marked x are drain
Line pressure
Governor pressure
Torque converter pressure
Throttle pressure

1—1ST GEAR—F3A

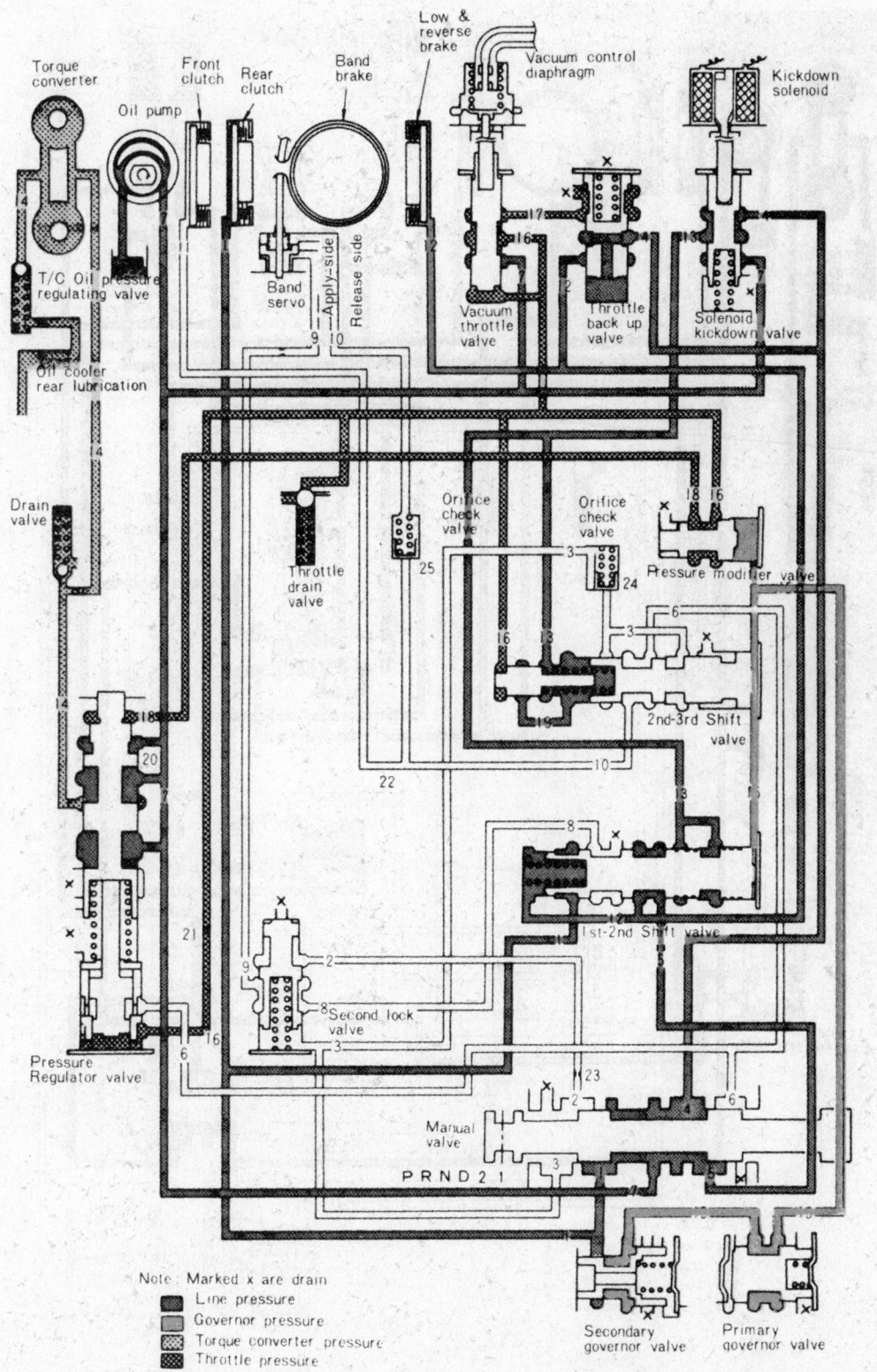

Torque converter

Oil pump

Front clutch

Rear clutch

Band brake

Low & reverse brake

Vacuum control diaphragm

Kickdown solenoid

T/C Oil pressure regulating valve

Band servo

Apply-side

Release side

Vacuum throttle valve

Throttle back up valve

Solenoid kickdown valve

Oil cooler rear lubrication

Drain valve

Throttle drain valve

Orifice check valve

Orifice check valve

Pressure modifier valve

2nd-3rd Shift valve

1st-2nd Shift valve

Second lock valve

Pressure Regulator valve

Manual valve

P R N D 2 1

Secondary governor valve

Primary governor valve

Note : Marked x are drain

■ Line pressure

▨ Governor pressure

▩ Torque converter pressure

■ Throttle pressure

REVERSE — F3A

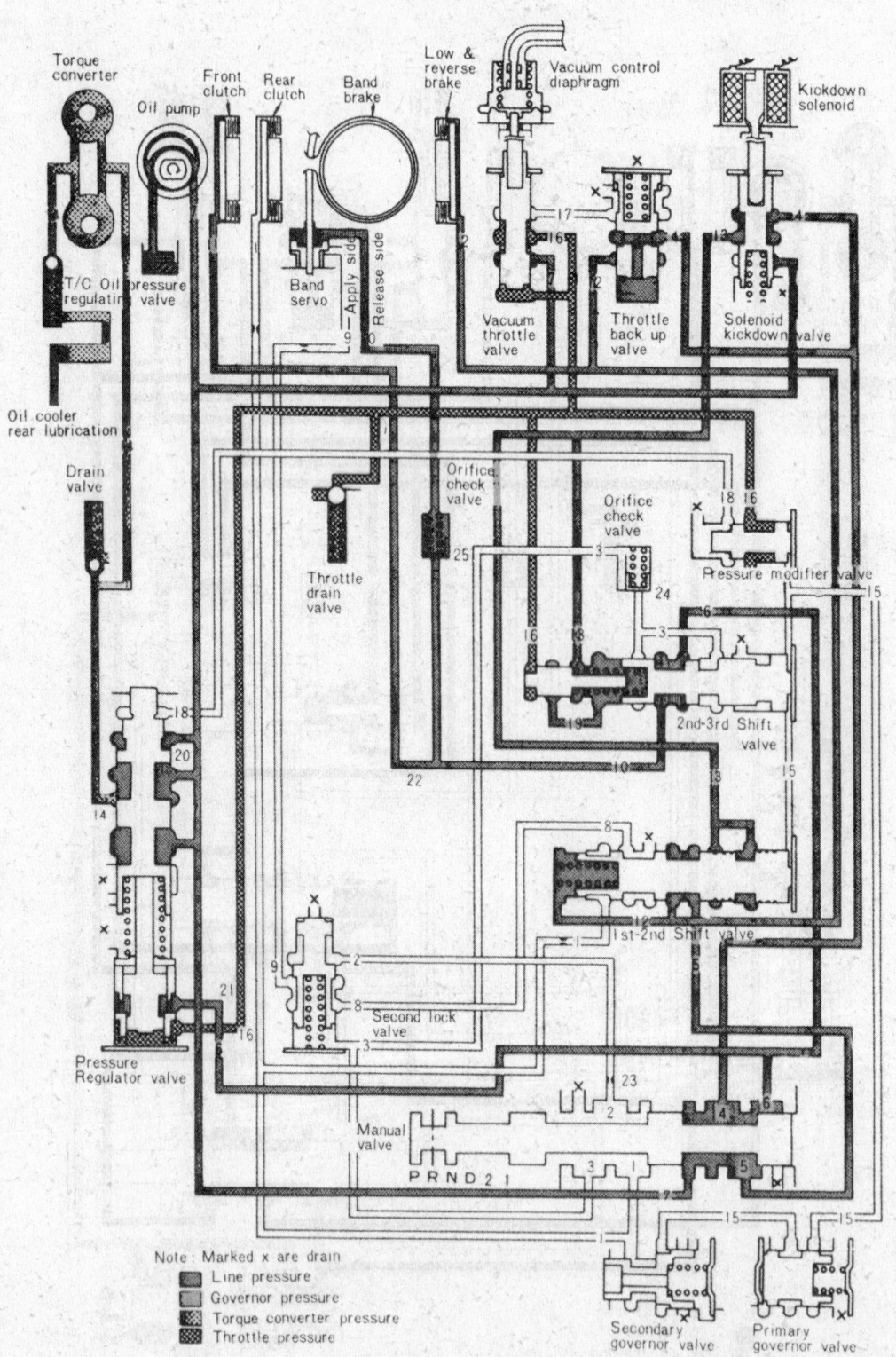

PARK–440–T4

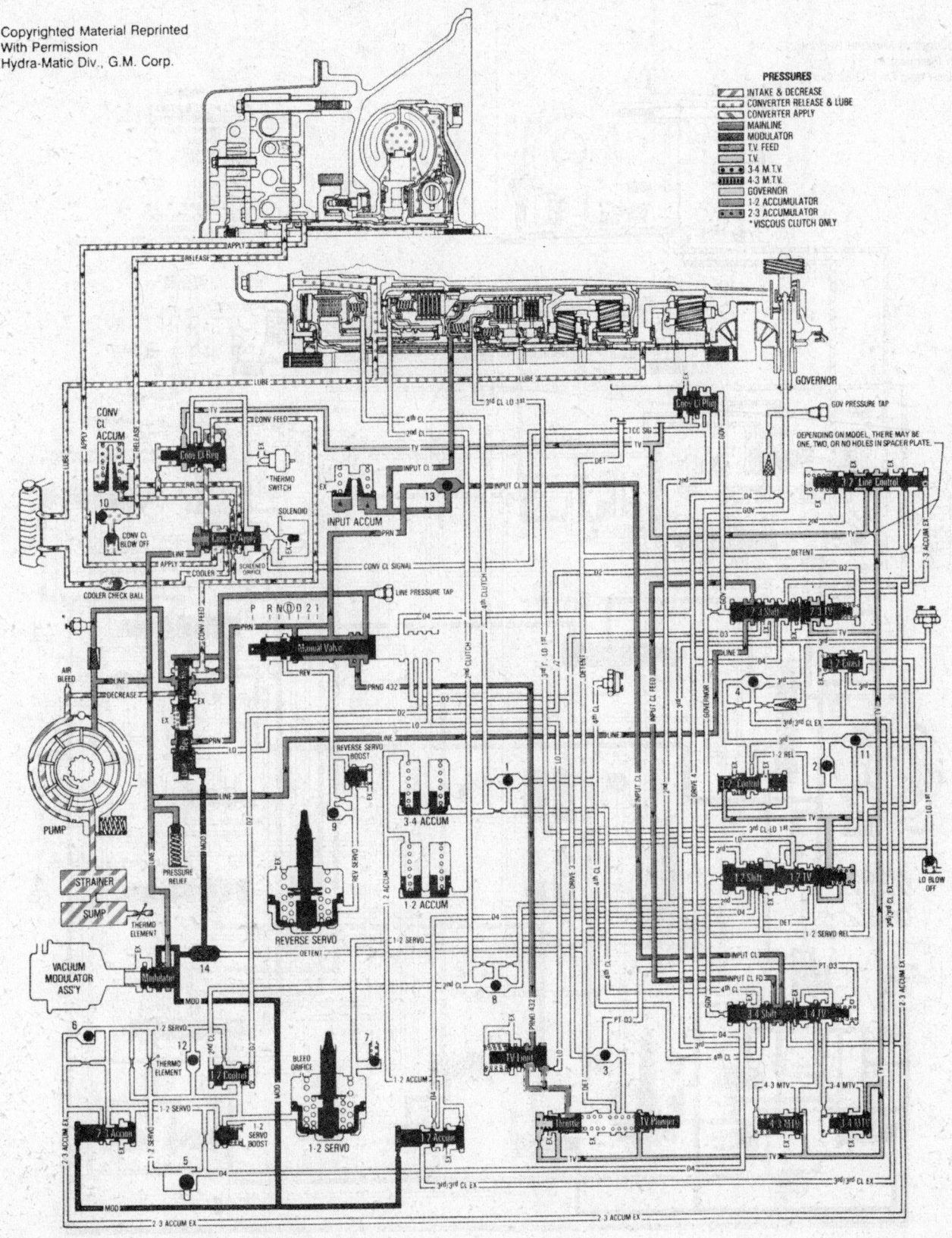

PRESSURES

- INTAKE & DECREASE
- CONVERTER RELEASE & LUBE
- CONVERTER APPLY
- MAINLINE
- MODULATOR
- T.V. FEED
- T.V.
- 3-4 M.T.V.
- 4-3 M.T.V.
- GOVERNOR
- 1-2 ACCUMULATOR
- 2-3 ACCUMULATOR
- *VISCOUS CLUTCH ONLY

DRIVE – 1ST GEAR – 440–T4

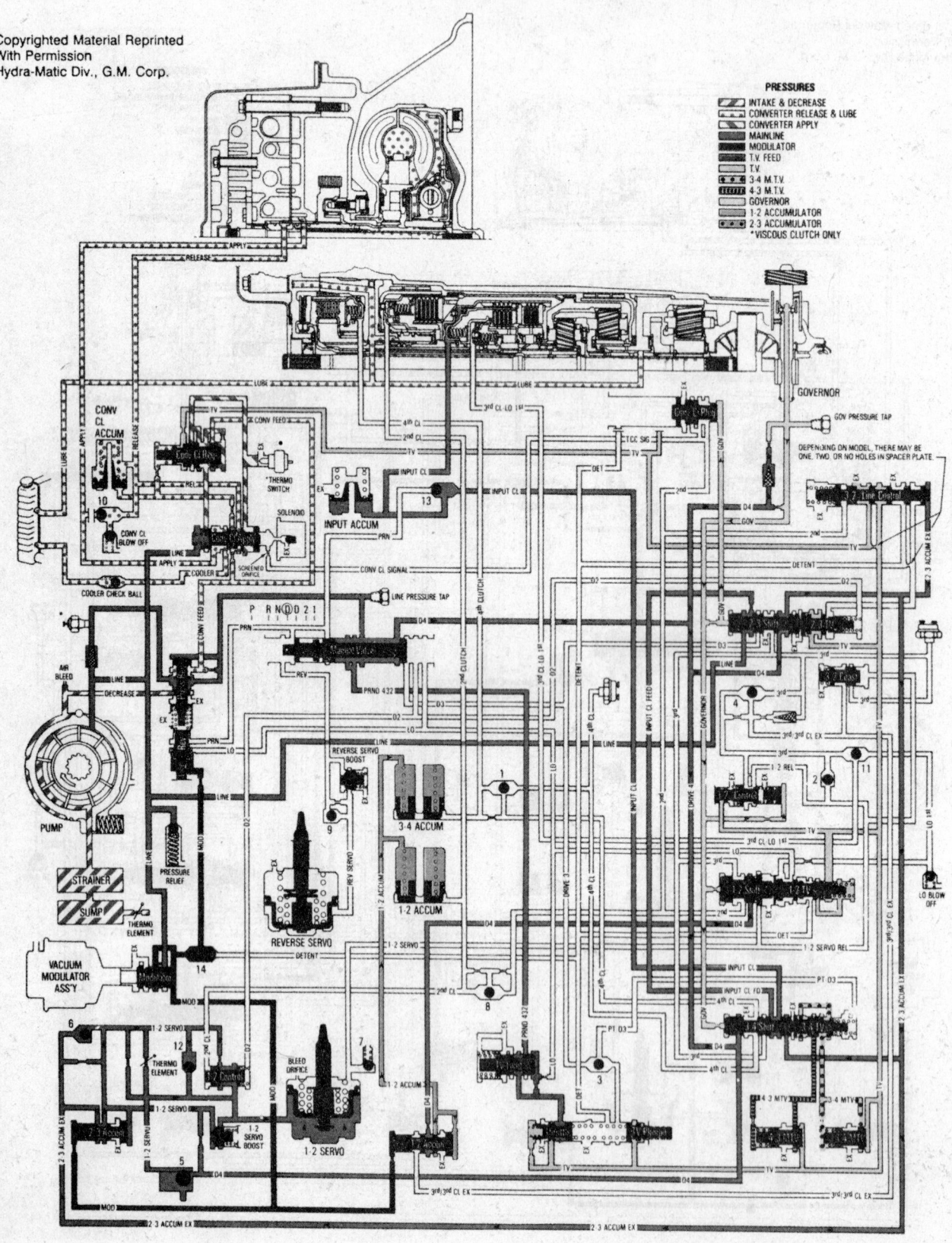

PRESSURES

- INTAKE & DECREASE
- CONVERTER RELEASE & LUBE
- CONVERTER APPLY
- MAINLINE
- MODULATOR
- T.V. FEED
- T.V.
- 3-4 M.T.V.
- 4-3 M.T.V.
- GOVERNOR
- 1-2 ACCUMULATOR
- 2-3 ACCUMULATOR
- *VISCOUS CLUTCH ONLY

DRIVE – 2ND GEAR – 440–T4

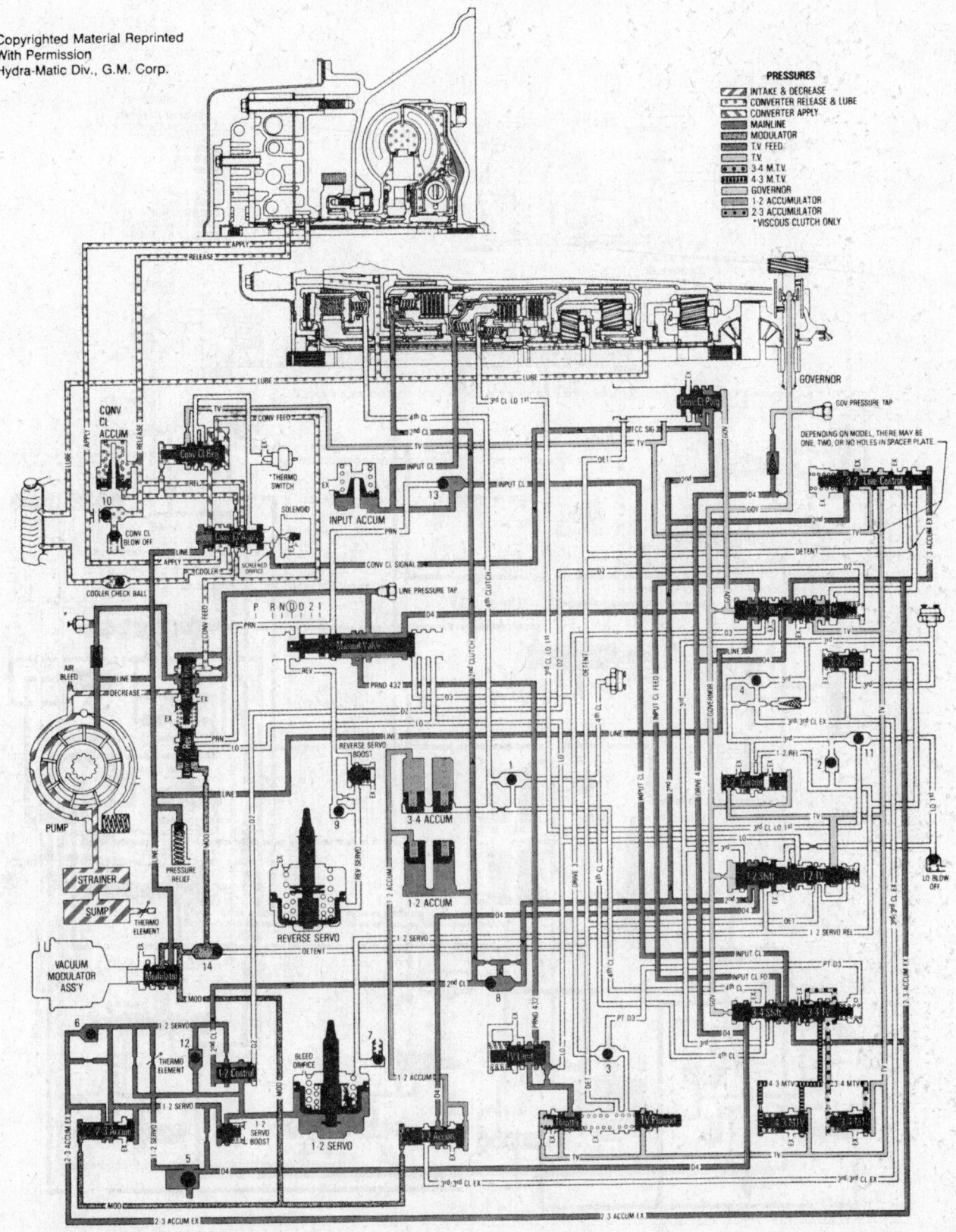

DRIVE – 3RD GEAR – 440-T4

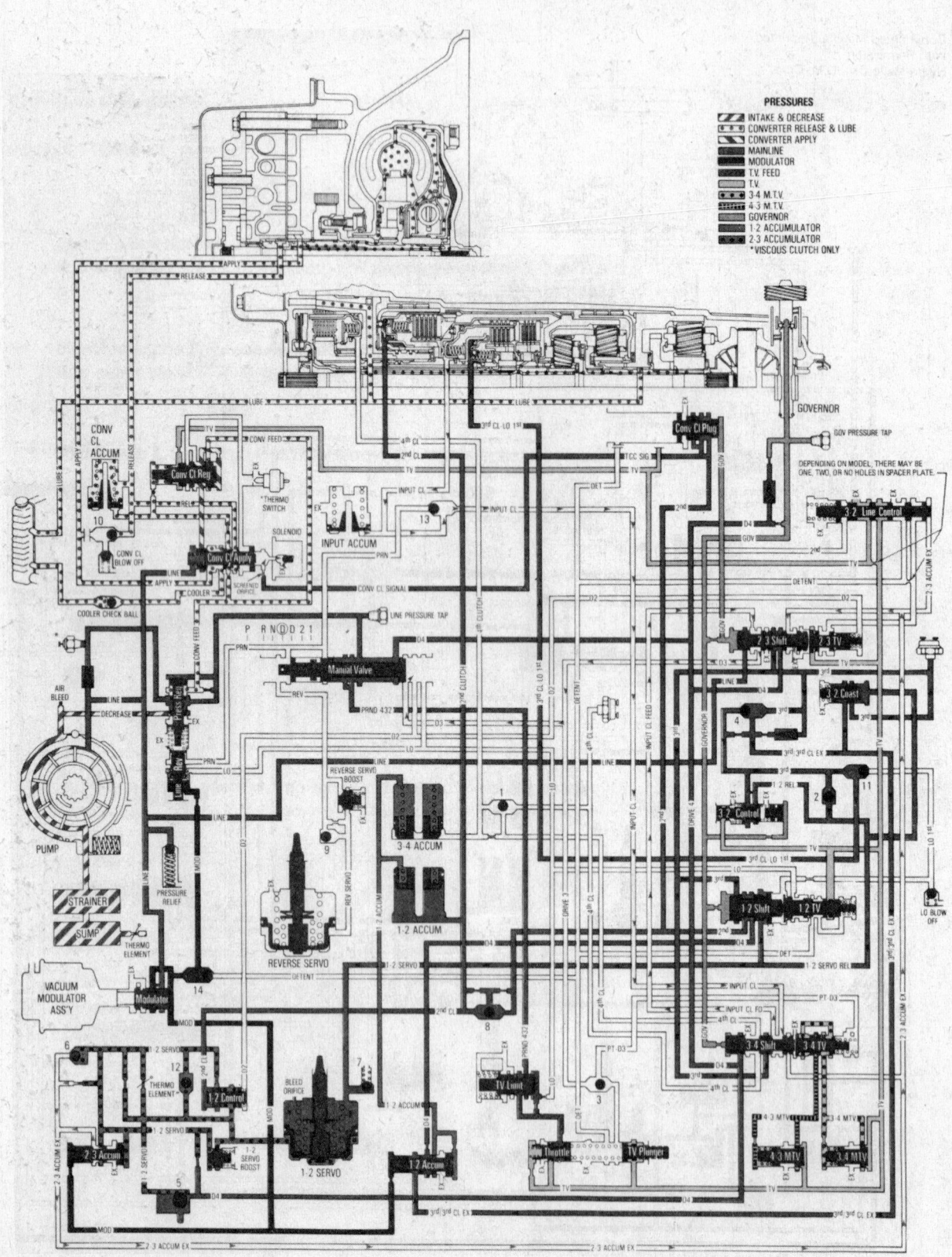

DRIVE–CONVERTER CLUTCH APPLY–440–T4

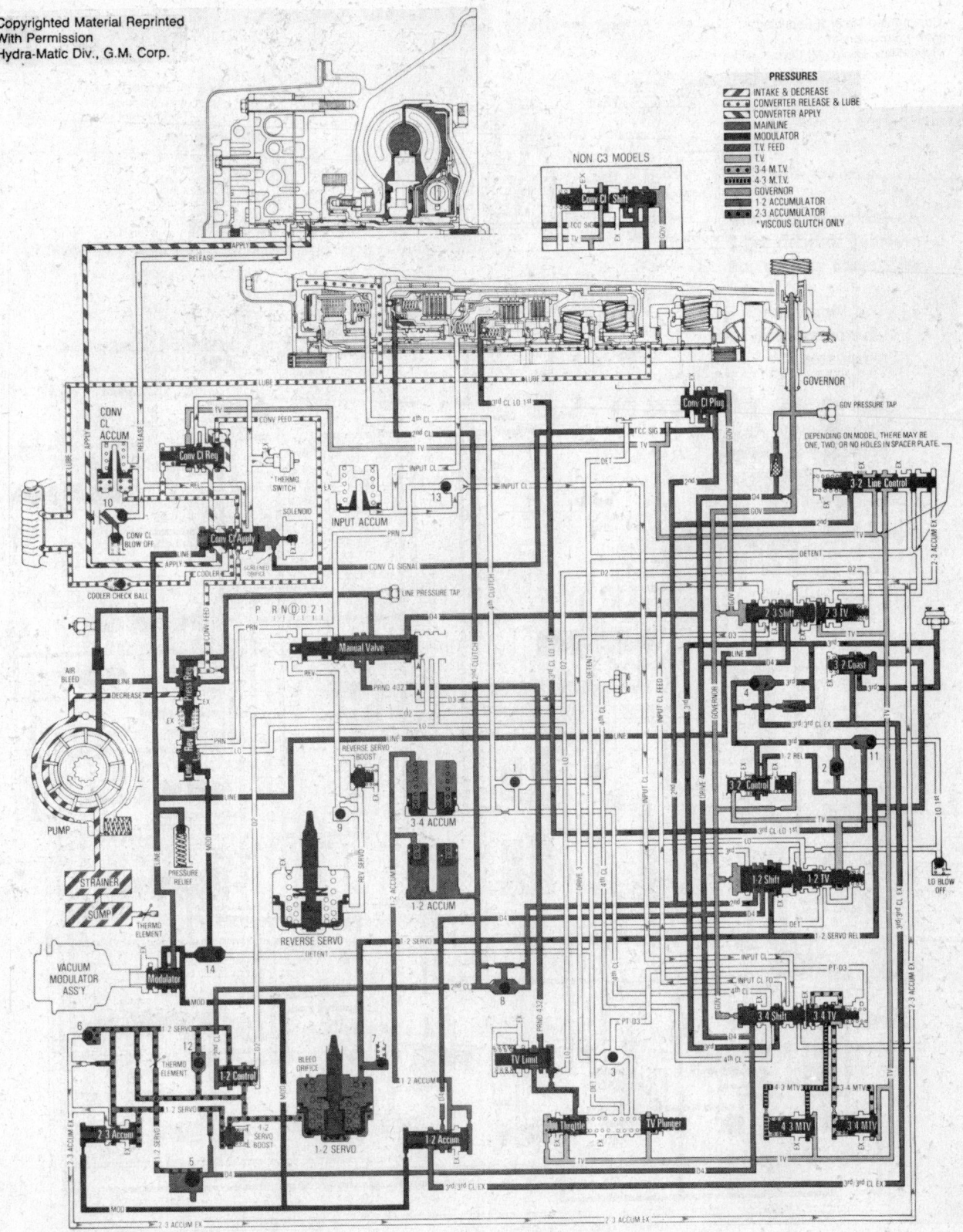

DRIVE–4TH GEAR–440–T4

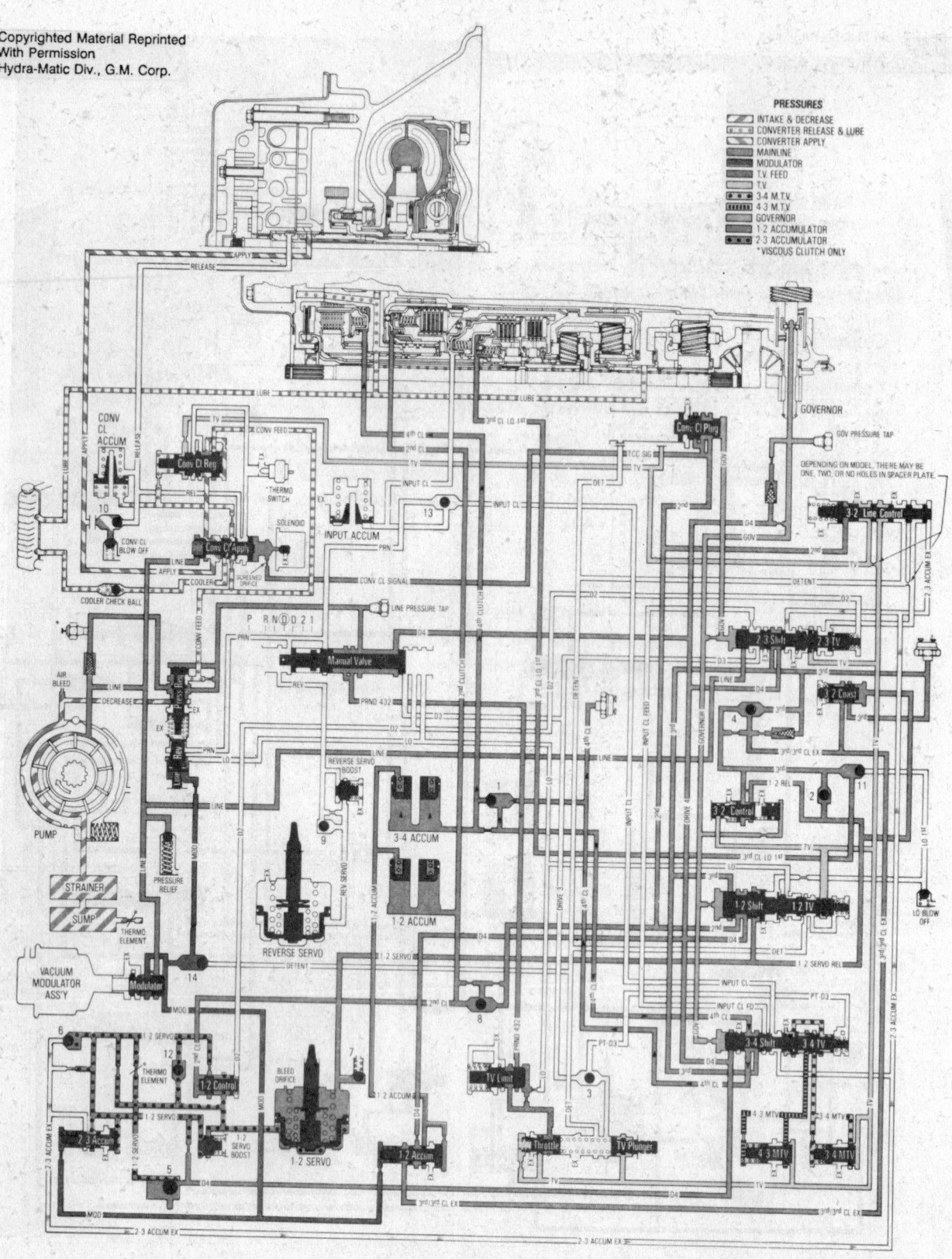

Copyrighted Material Reprinted
With Permission
Hydra-Matic Div., G.M. Corp.

PART THROTTLE 4–3 AND MODULATED DOWNSHIFT
(VALVES SHOWN IN 3RD GEAR POSITION) – 440–T4

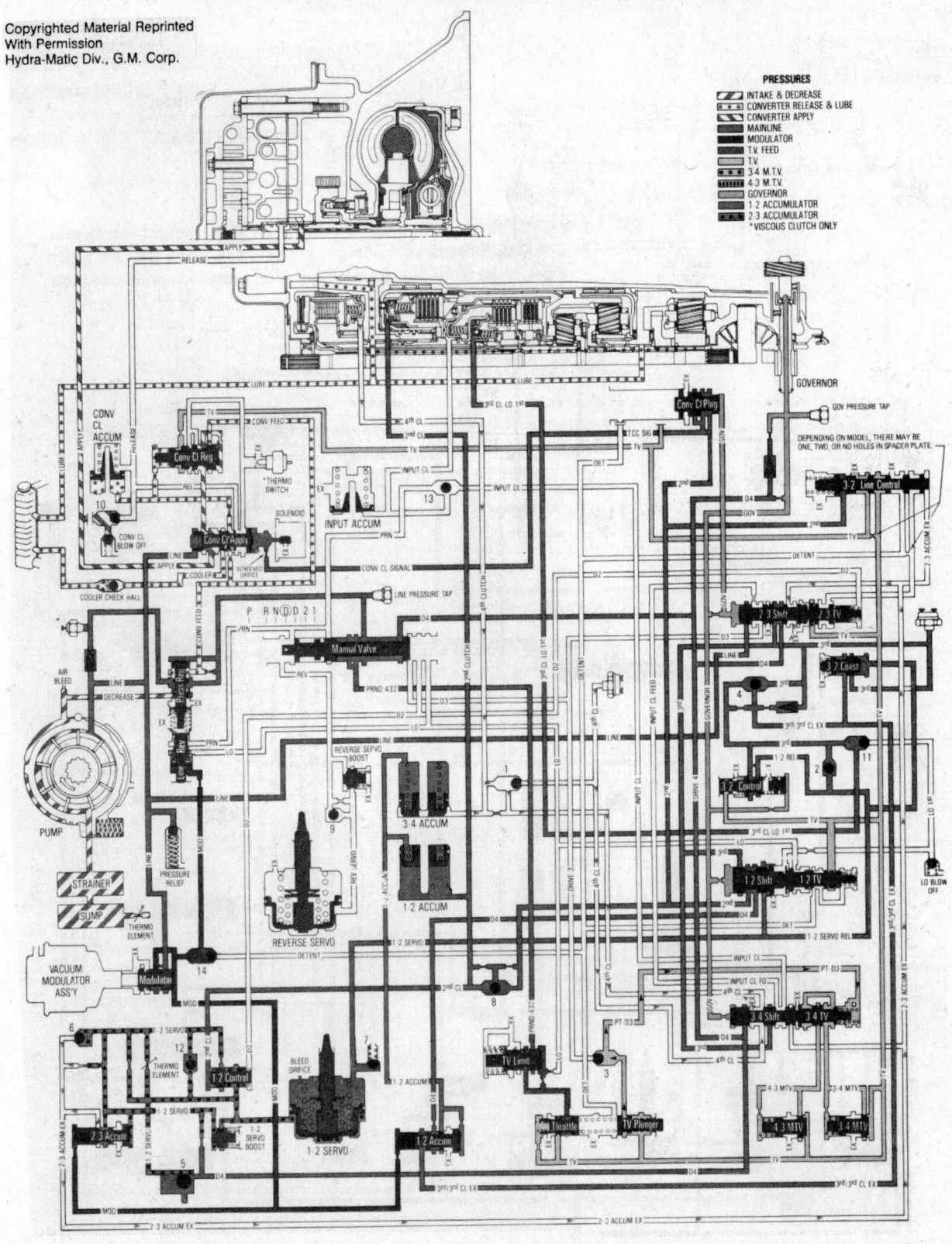

DETENT 3–2 DOWNSHIFT (VALVES SHOWN IN 2ND GEAR POSITION) 440–T4

NOTE: AT HIGH ALTITUDE (2000 FT. OR MORE ABOVE SEA LEVEL) NUMBER 14 CHECK BALL BLOCKS THE MODULATOR CIRCUIT TO ALLOW DETENT OIL TO BOOST LINE PRESSURE.

PRESSURES
INTAKE & DECREASE
CONVERTER RELEASE & LUBE
CONVERTER APPLY
MAINLINE
MODULATOR
T.V. FEED
T.V.
3-4 M.T.V.
4-3 M.T.V.
GOVERNOR
1-2 ACCUMULATOR
2-3 ACCUMULATOR
*VISCOUS CLUTCH ONLY

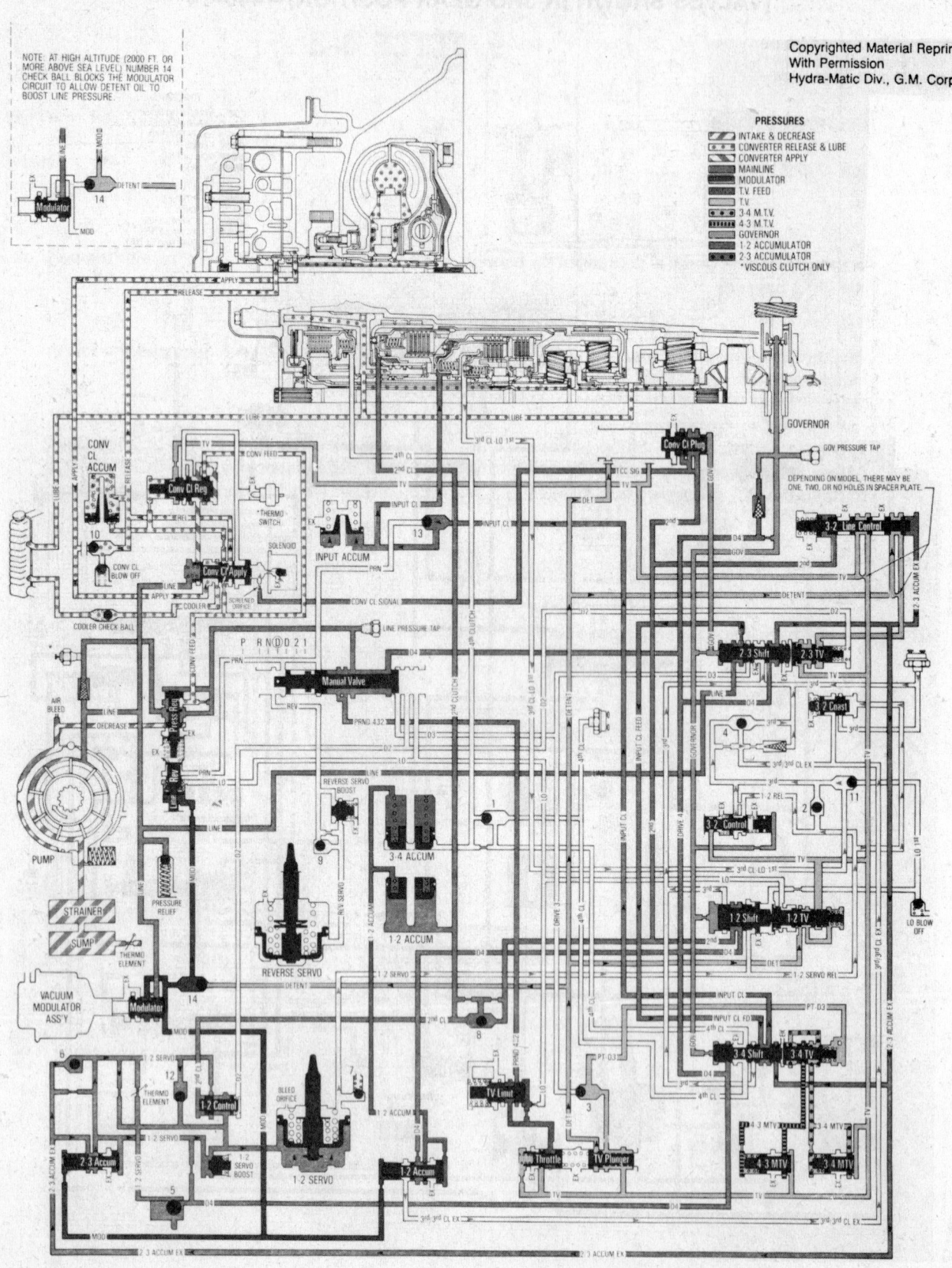

MANUAL 3RD – 440–T4

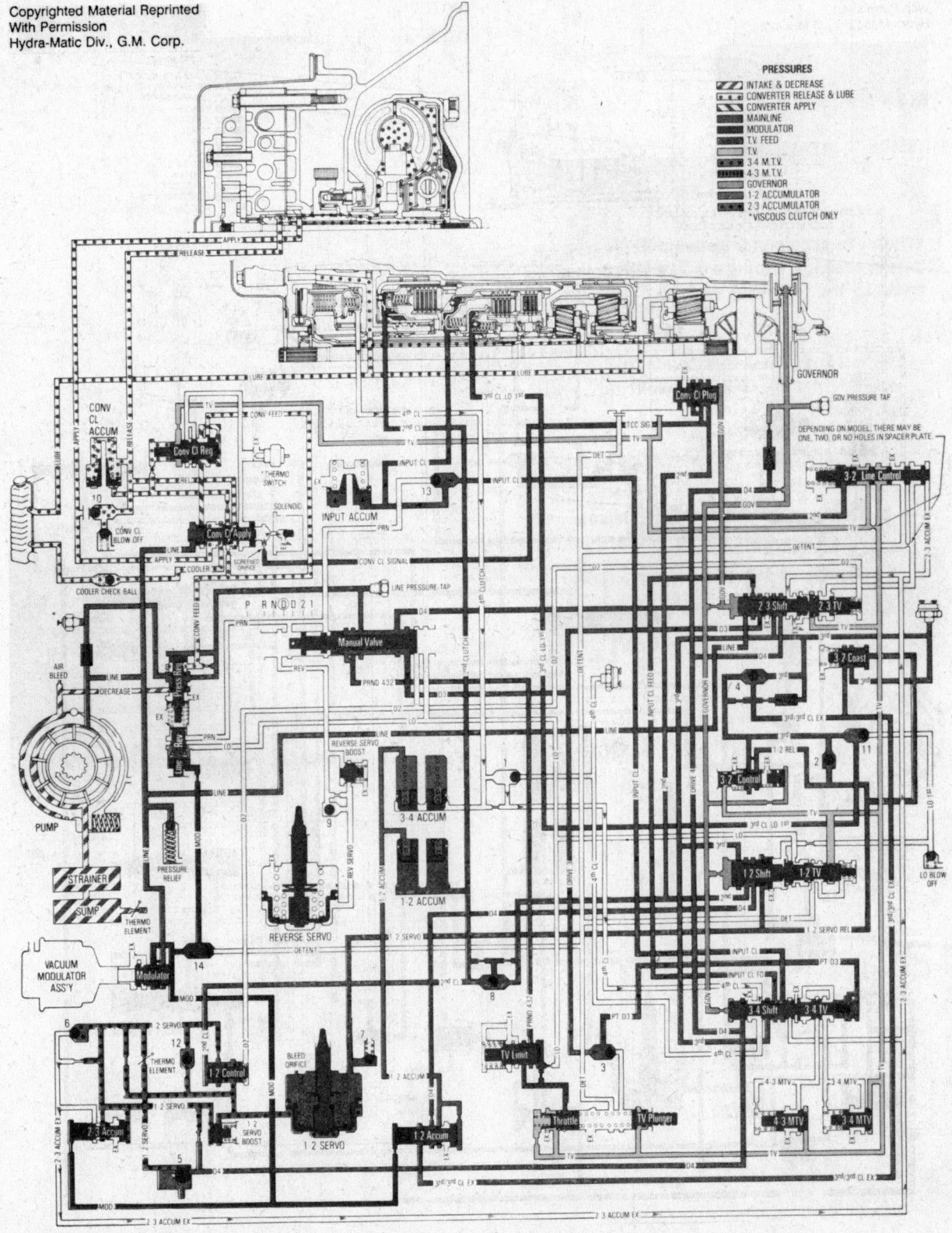

MANUAL 2ND – 440–T4

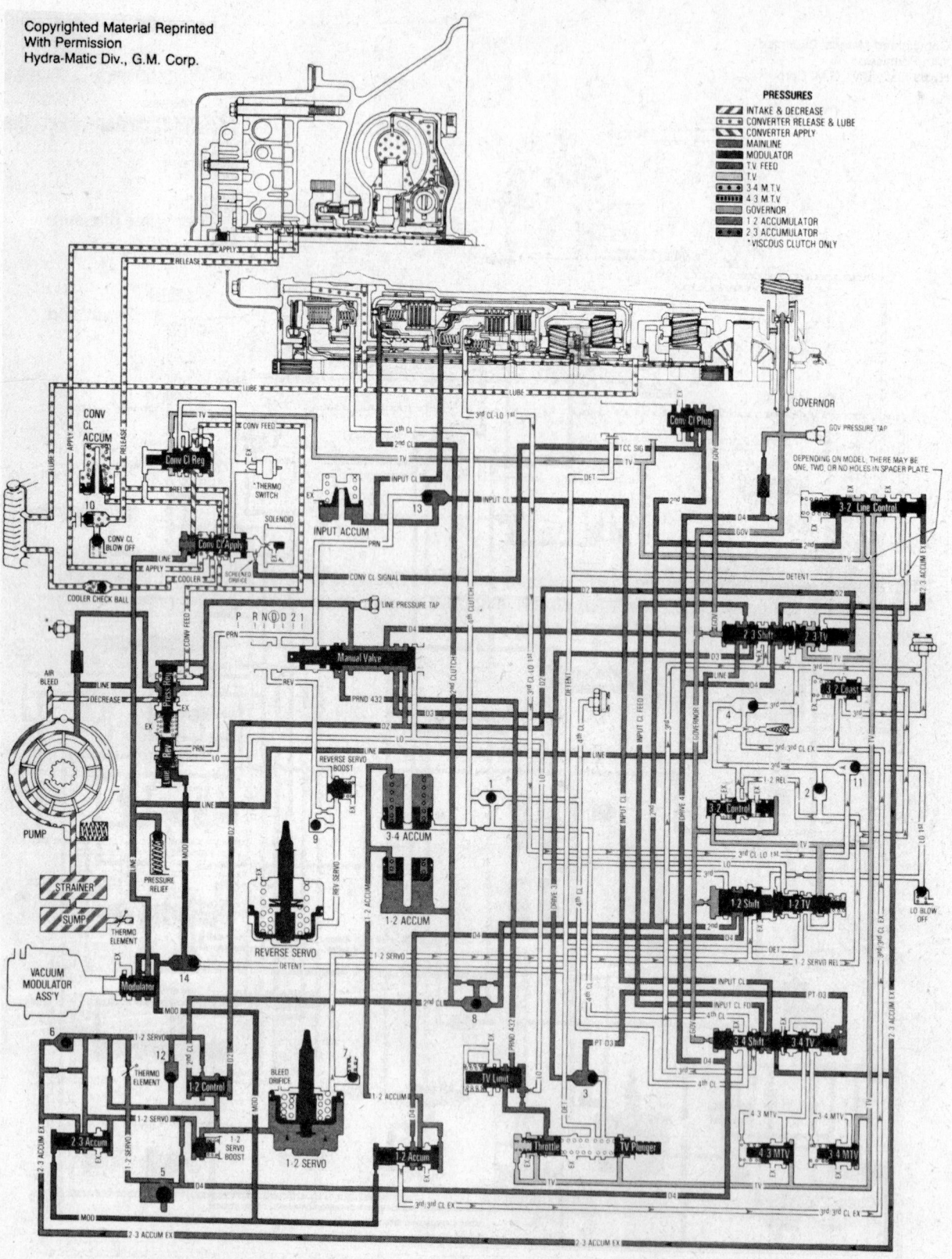

MANUAL LOW — 440–T4

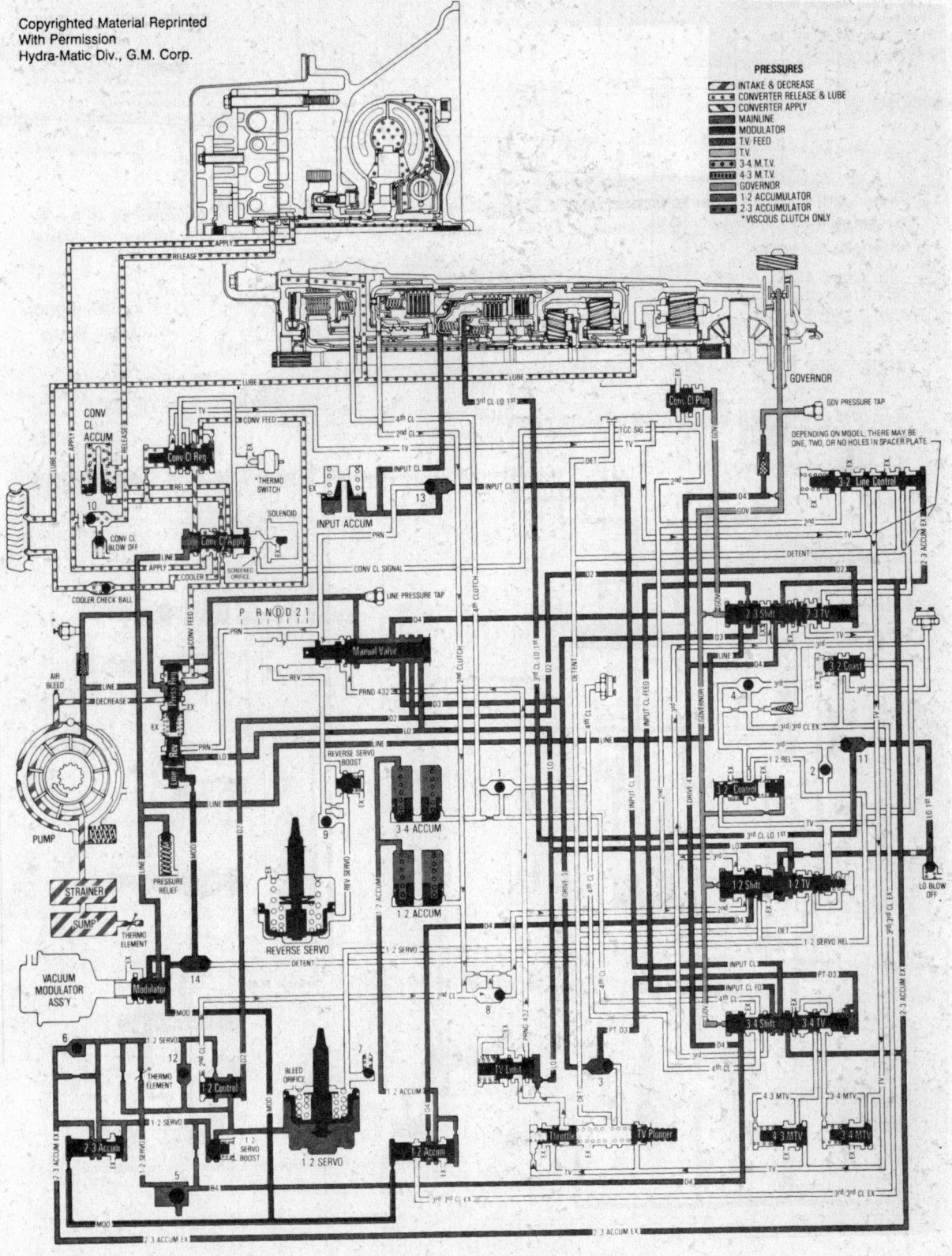

Copyrighted Material Reprinted
With Permission
Hydra-Matic Div., G.M. Corp.

PRESSURES

- INTAKE & DECREASE
- CONVERTER RELEASE & LUBE
- CONVERTER APPLY
- MAINLINE
- MODULATOR
- T.V. FEED
- T.V.
- 3-4 M.T.V.
- 4-3 M.T.V.
- GOVERNOR
- 1-2 ACCUMULATOR
- 2-3 ACCUMULATOR
- *VISCOUS CLUTCH ONLY

REVERSE – 440–T4

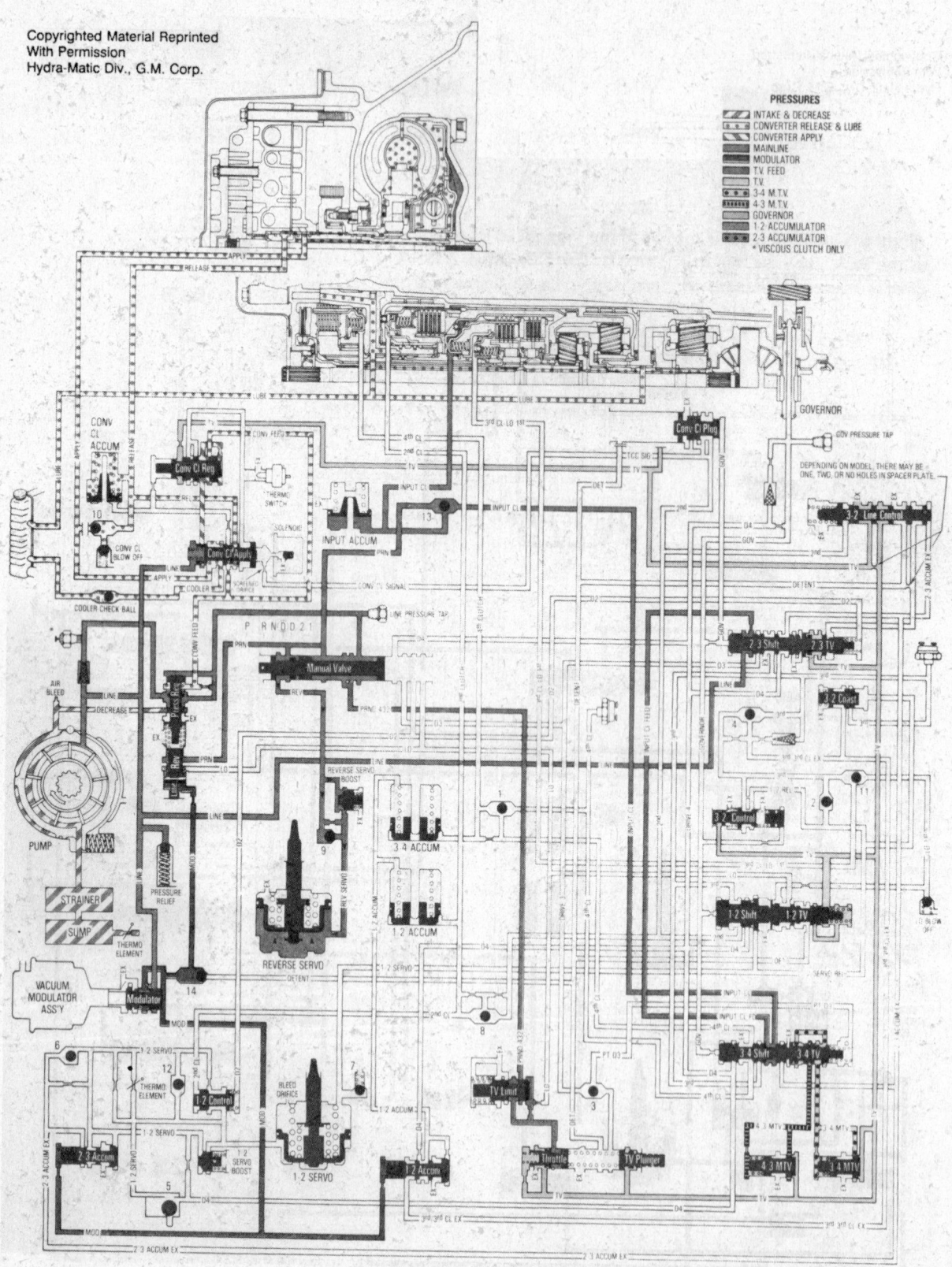

Copyrighted Material Reprinted
With Permission
Hydra-Matic Div., G.M. Corp.

PRESSURES
- INTAKE & DECREASE
- CONVERTER RELEASE & LUBE
- CONVERTER APPLY
- MAINLINE
- MODULATOR
- T.V. FEED
- T.V.
- 3-4 M.T.V.
- 4-3 M.T.V.
- GOVERNOR
- 1-2 ACCUMULATOR
- 2-3 ACCUMULATOR
- * VISCOUS CLUTCH ONLY

PARK — F7

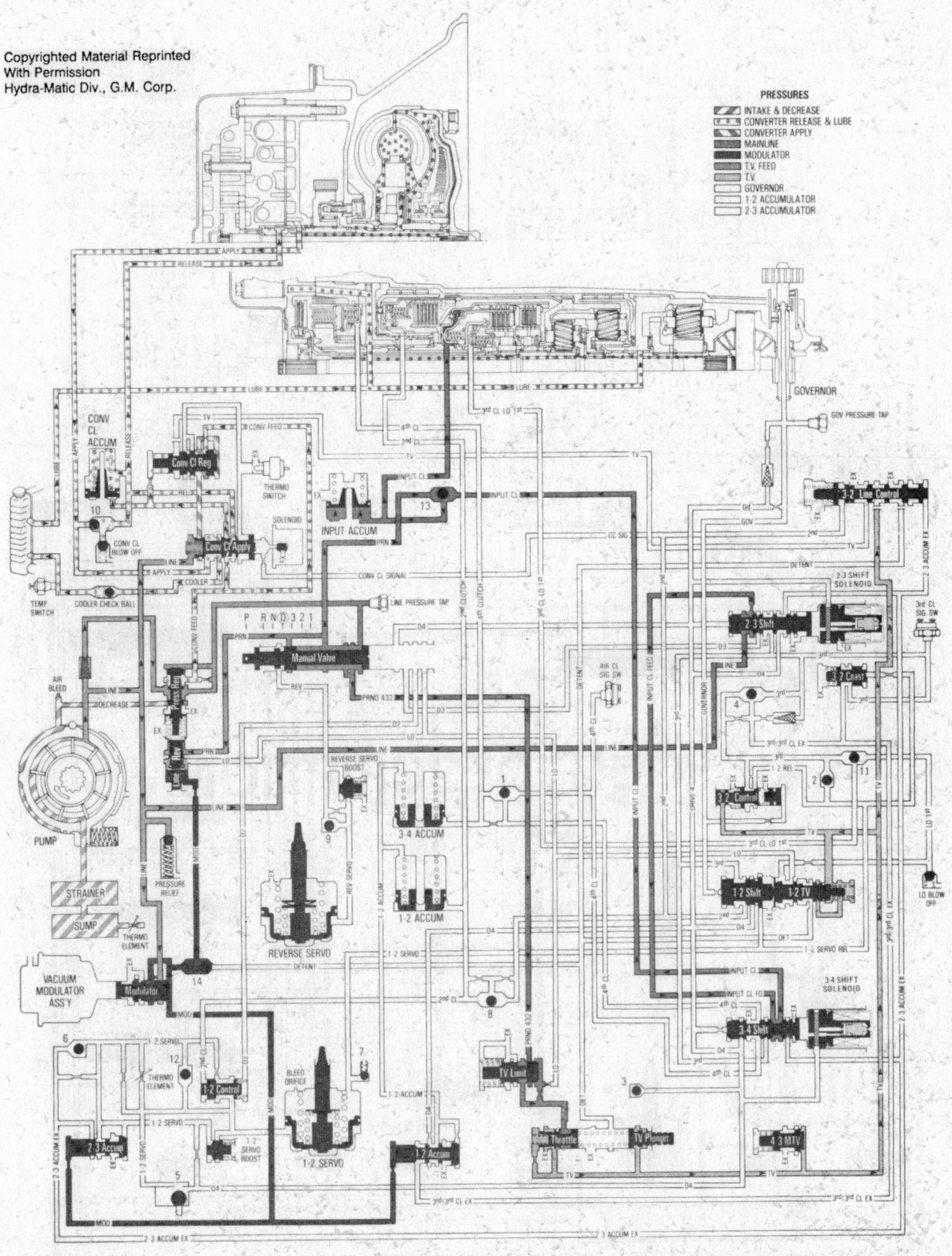

DRIVE RANGE – 1ST GEAR-F7

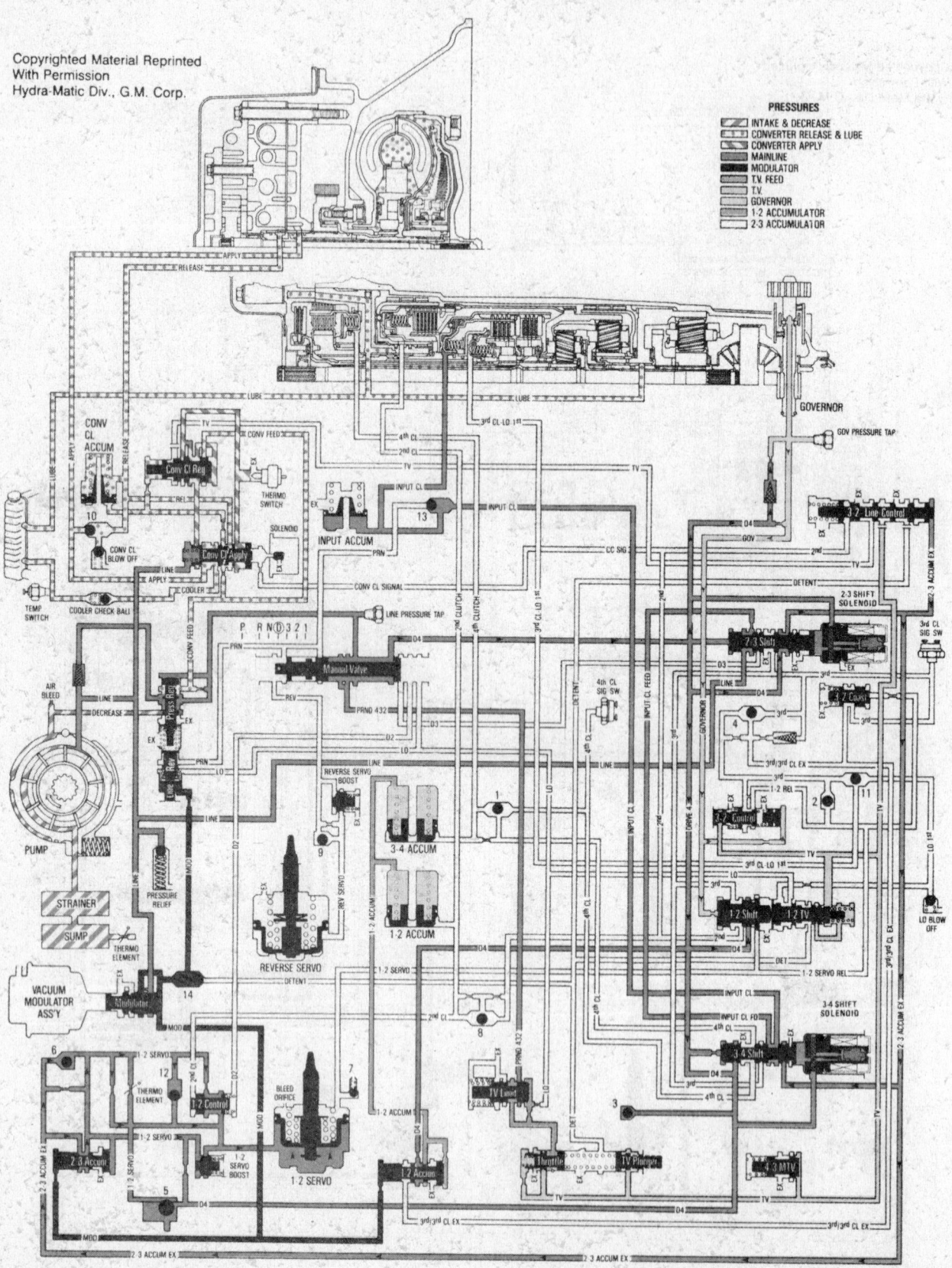

DRIVE RANGE—2ND GEAR—F7

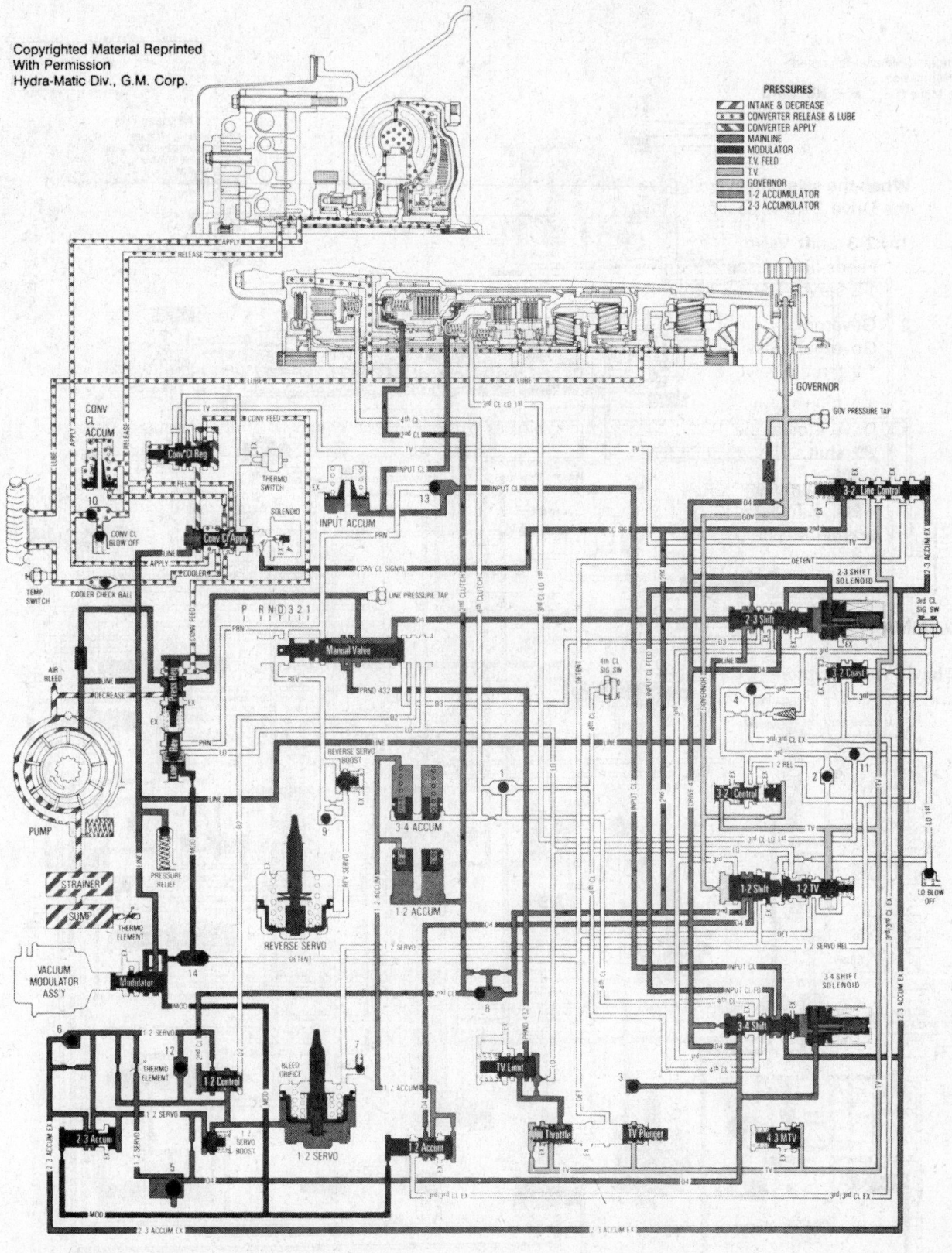

DRIVE RANGE – 3RD GEAR – F7

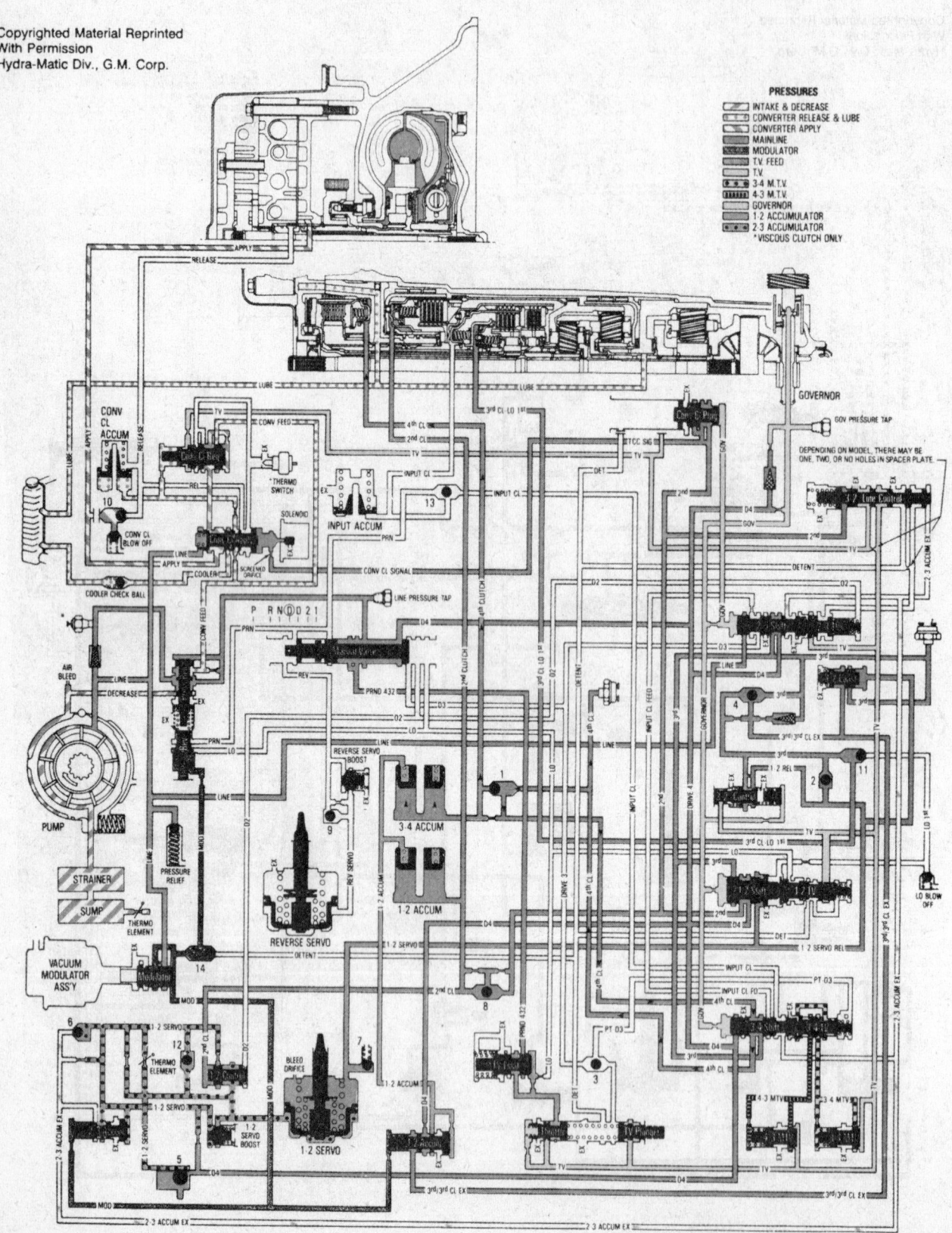

CONVERTER CLUTCH APPLIED – 3RD GEAR – F7

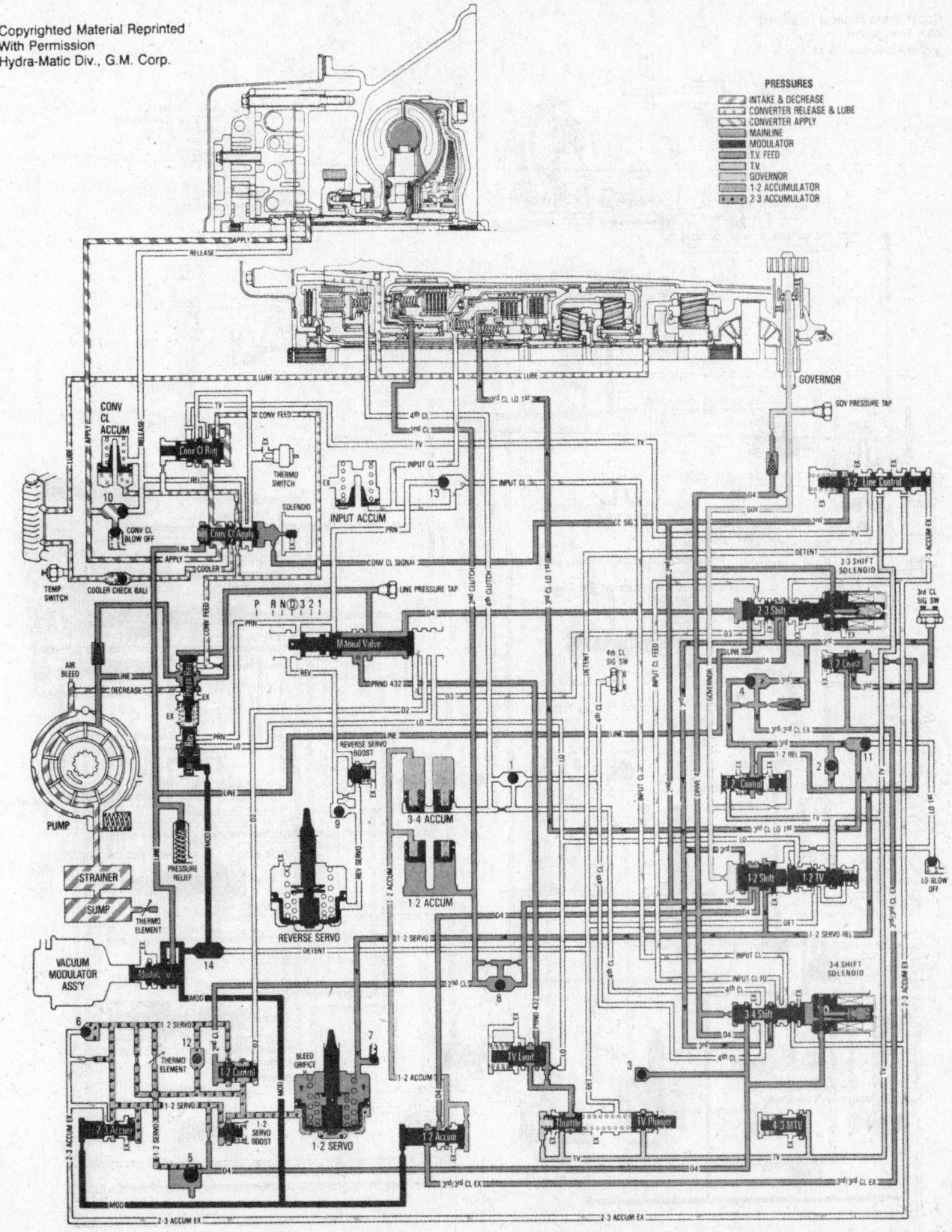

DRIVE RANGE – OVERDRIVE – 7

Copyrighted Material Reprinted
With Permission
Hydra-Matic Div., G.M. Corp.

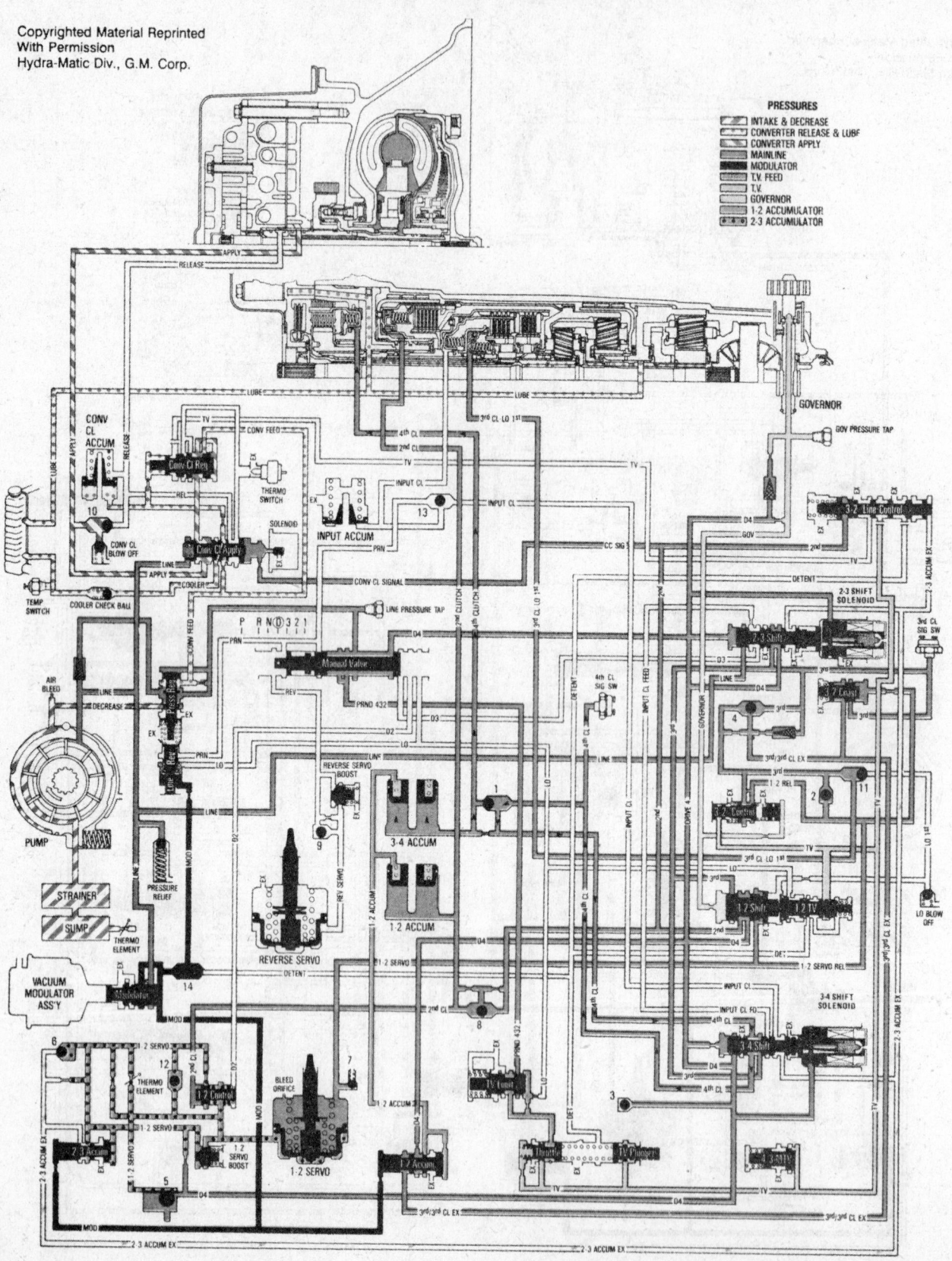

PRESSURES

- INTAKE & DECREASE
- CONVERTER RELEASE & LUBE
- CONVERTER APPLY
- MAINLINE
- MODULATOR
- T.V. FEED
- T.V.
- GOVERNOR
- 1-2 ACCUMULATOR
- 2-3 ACCUMULATOR

PART THROTTLE 4–3 AND MODULATED DOWNSHIFT
(VALVES SHOWN IN 3RD GEAR POSITION) – F7

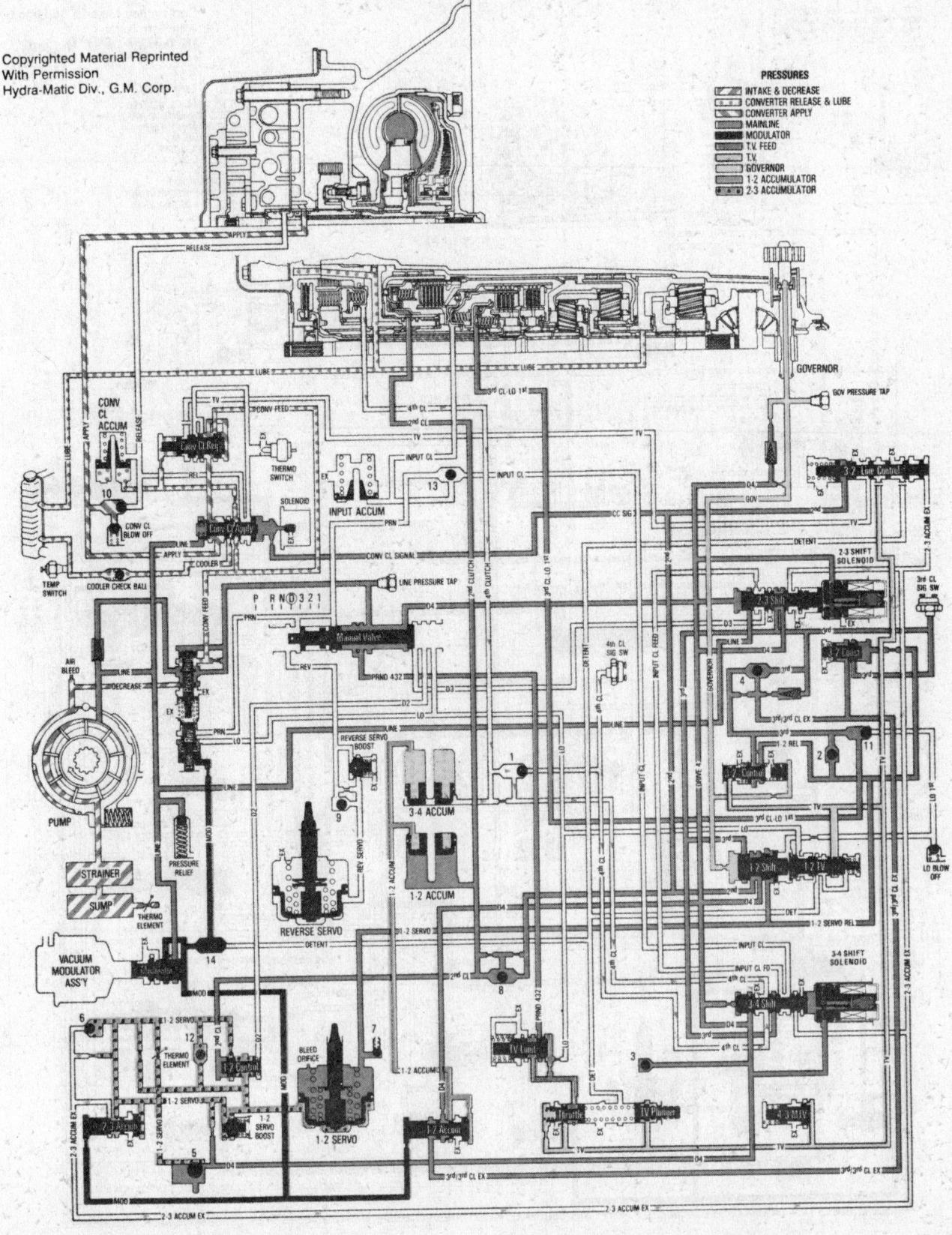

DETENT DOWNSHIFTS (VALVES SHOWN IN 2ND GEAR POSITION) – F7

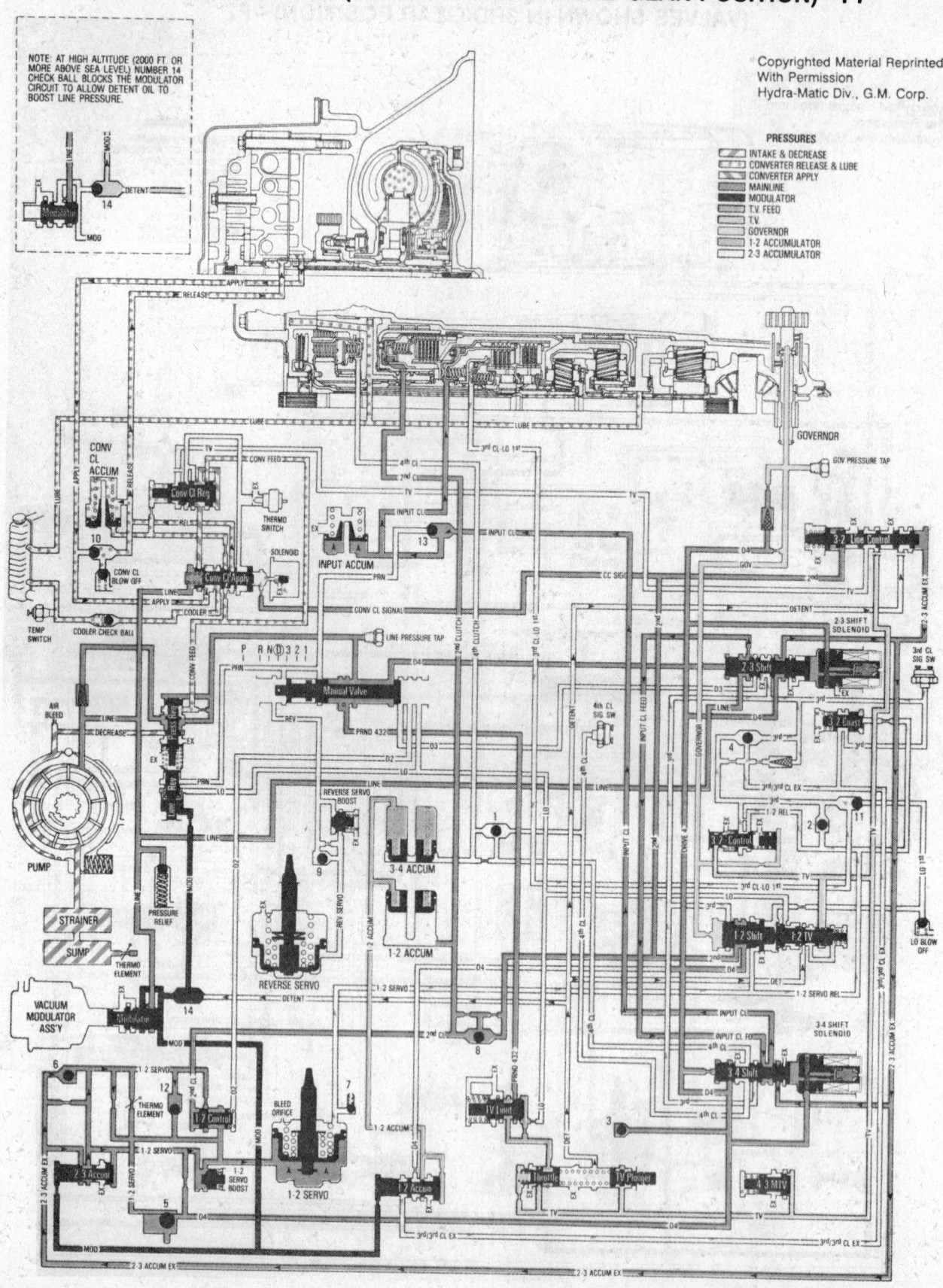

NOTE: AT HIGH ALTITUDE (2000 FT. OR MORE ABOVE SEA LEVEL) NUMBER 14 CHECK BALL BLOCKS THE MODULATOR CIRCUIT TO ALLOW DETENT OIL TO BOOST LINE PRESSURE.

PRESSURES

- INTAKE & DECREASE
- CONVERTER RELEASE & LUBE
- CONVERTER APPLY
- MAINLINE
- MODULATOR
- T.V. FEED
- T.V.
- GOVERNOR
- 1-2 ACCUMULATOR
- 2-3 ACCUMULATOR

MANUAL 3RD—F7

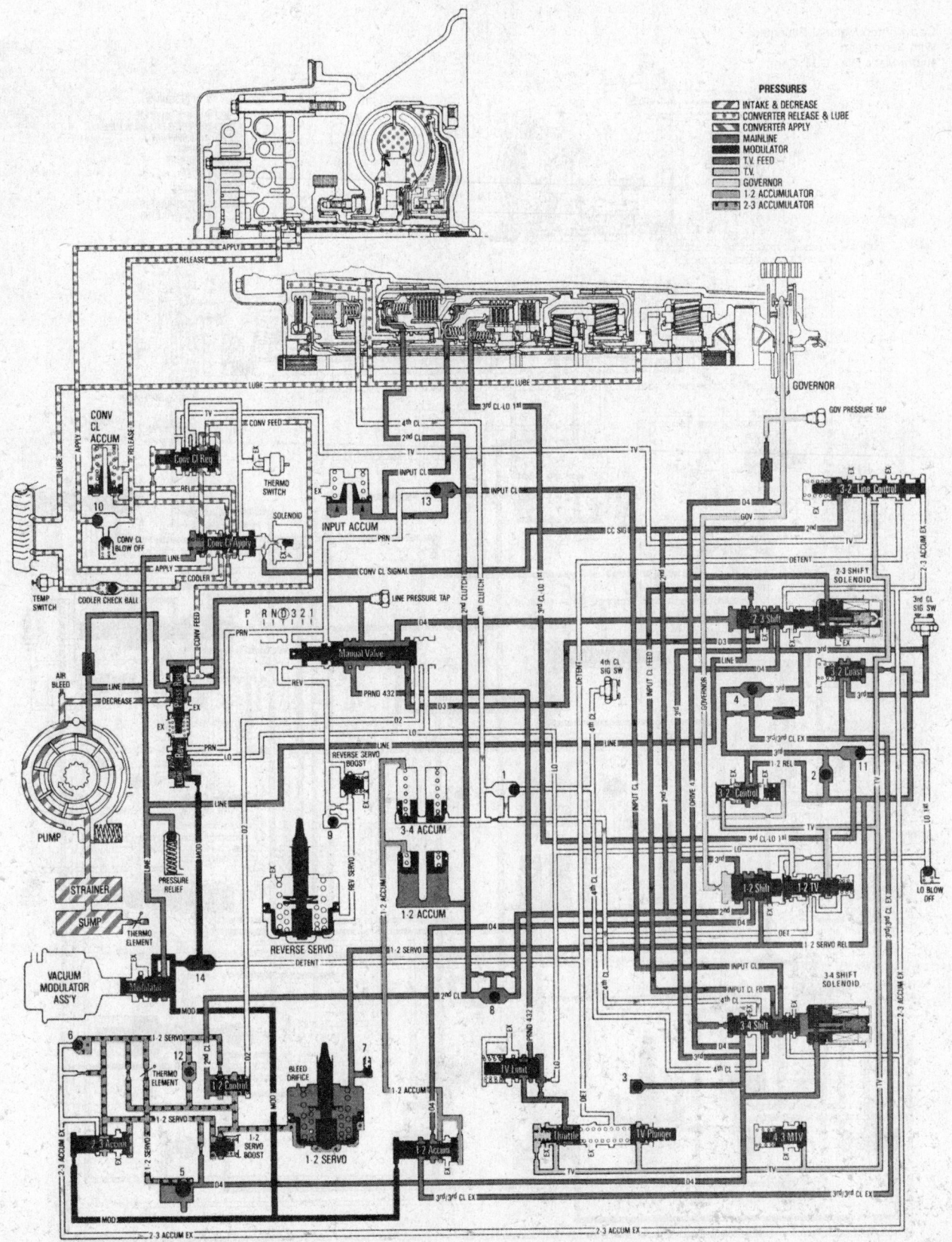

MANUAL 2ND – F7

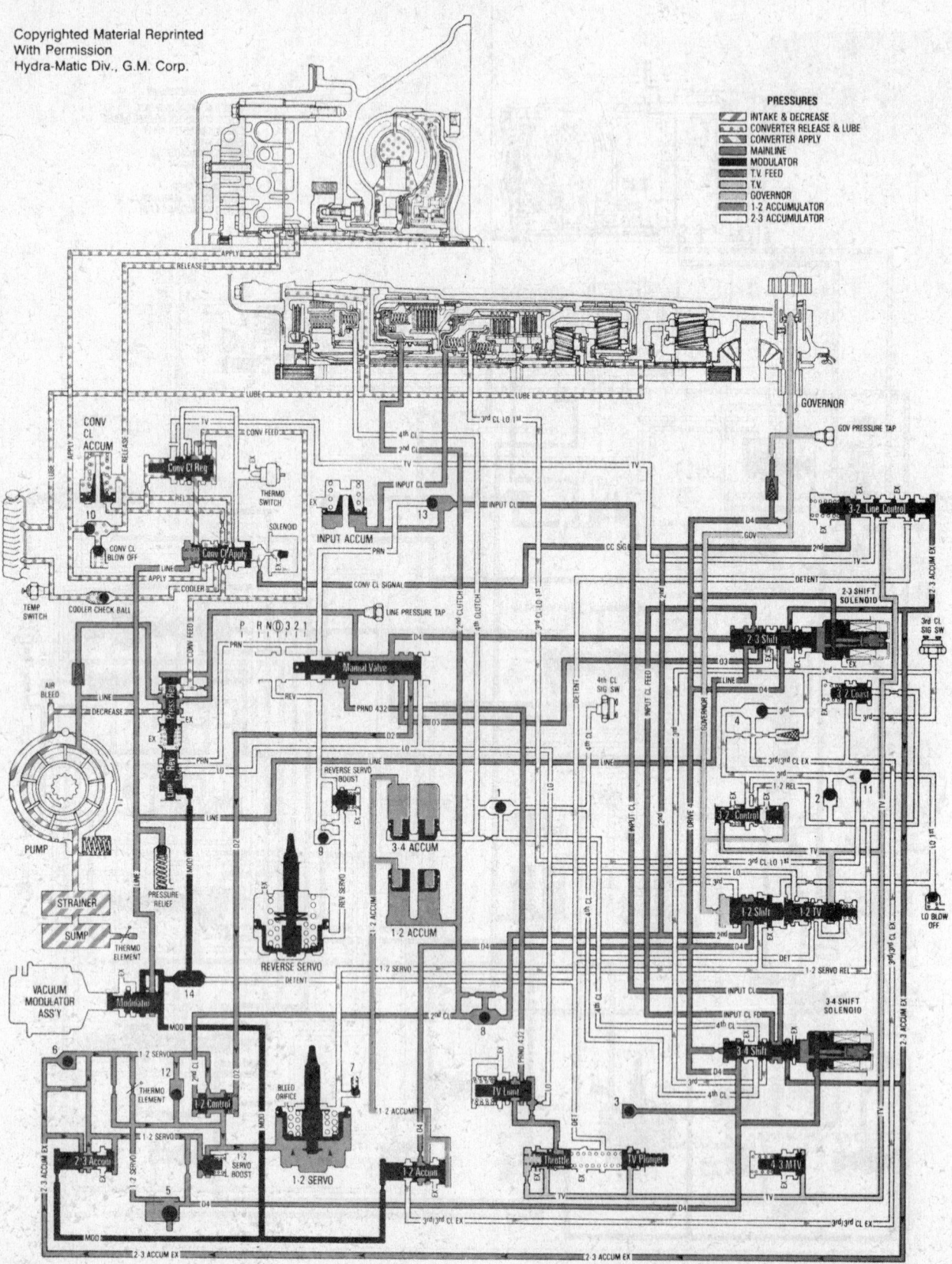

MANUAL LOW — F7

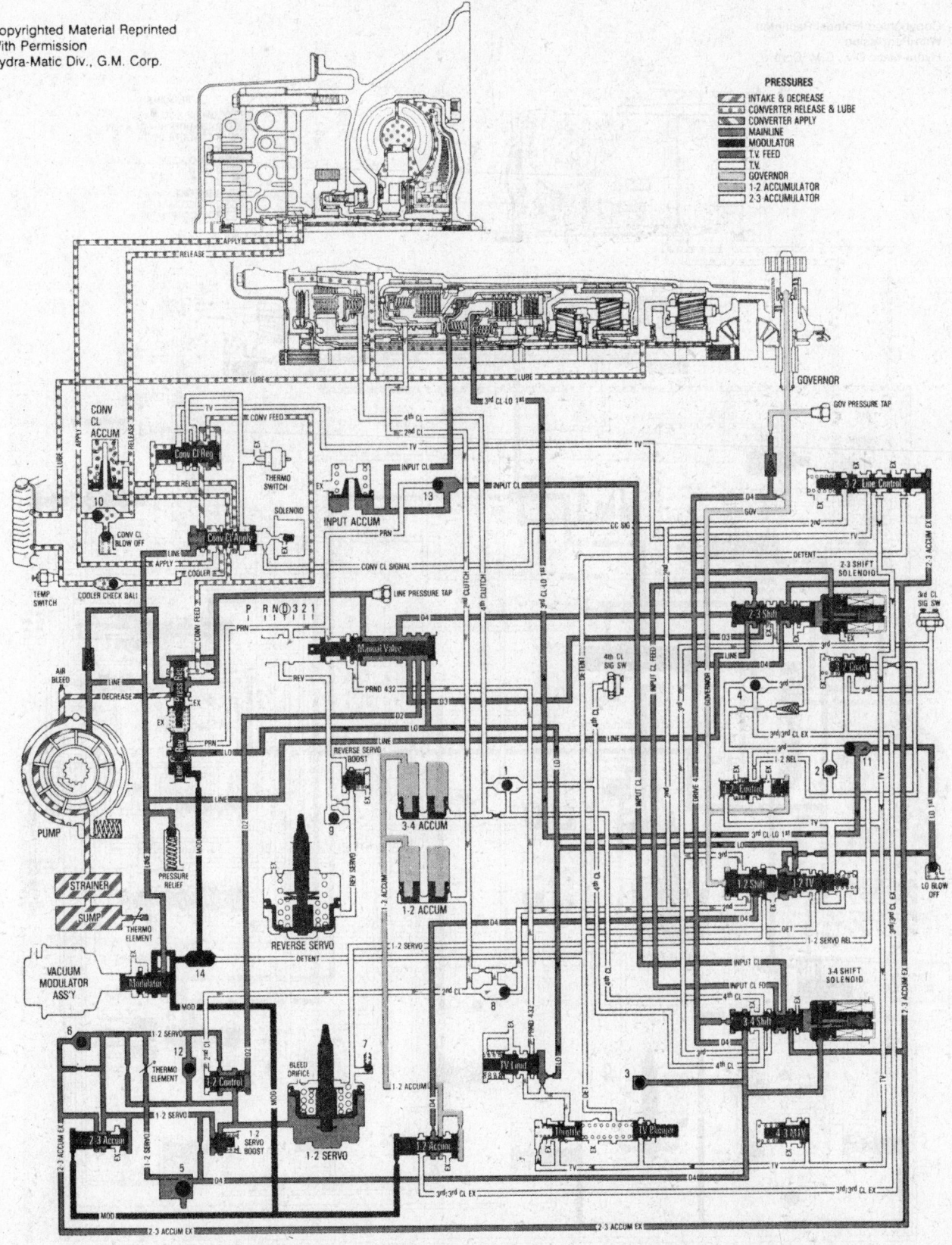

REVERSE – F7

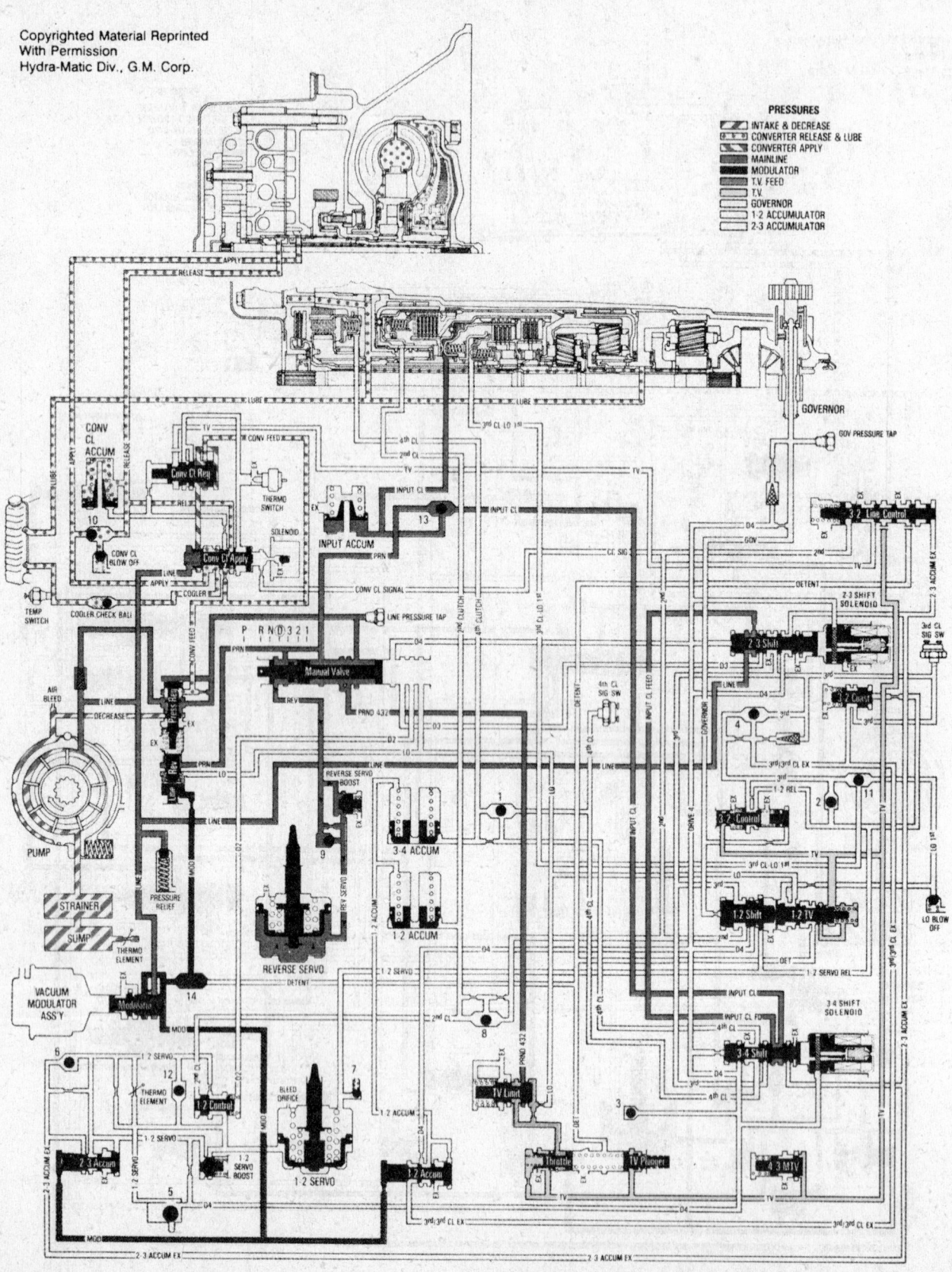

PARK OR NEUTRAL WITH ENGINE RUNNING—A131 L

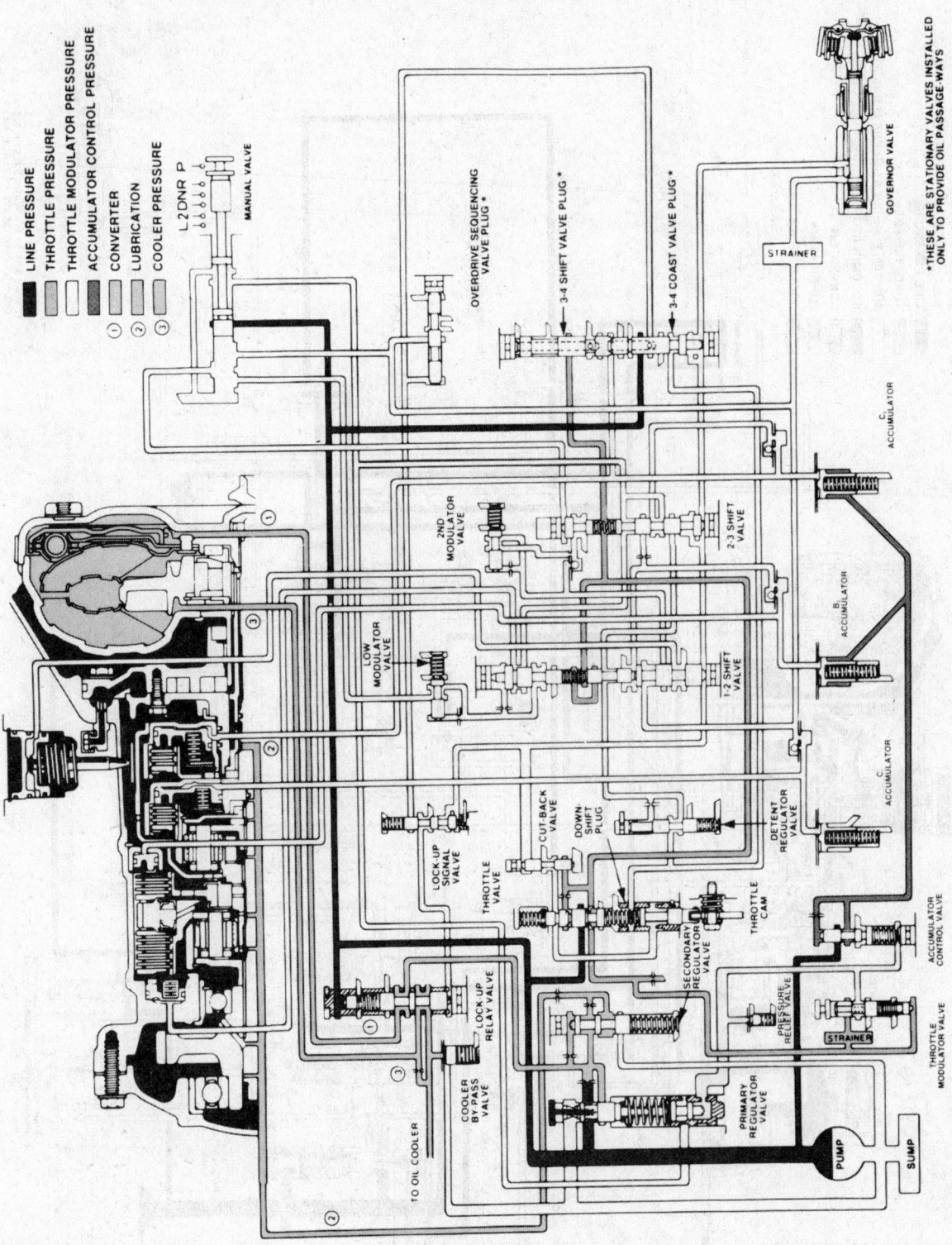

LINE PRESSURE
THROTTLE PRESSURE
THROTTLE MODULATOR PRESSURE
ACCUMULATOR CONTROL PRESSURE
CONVERTER
LUBRICATION
COOLER PRESSURE

MANUAL VALVE
L 2 DN R P

OVERDRIVE SEQUENCING VALVE PLUG *
3-4 SHIFT VALVE PLUG *
3-4 COAST VALVE PLUG *
GOVERNOR VALVE
STRAINER

* THESE ARE STATIONARY VALVES INSTALLED ONLY TO PROVIDE OIL PASSAGE-WAYS

C ACCUMULATOR
B ACCUMULATOR
C ACCUMULATOR

2ND MODULATOR VALVE
2-3 SHIFT VALVE
LOW MODULATOR VALVE
1-2 SHIFT VALVE

LOCK-UP SIGNAL VALVE
CUT-BACK VALVE
DOWN-SHIFT PLUG
DETENT REGULATOR VALVE

THROTTLE VALVE
THROTTLE CAM
SECONDARY REGULATOR VALVE
ACCUMULATOR CONTROL VALVE

LOCK UP RELAY VALVE
PRESSURE RELIEF VALVE
STRAINER
THROTTLE MODULATOR VALVE

TO OIL COOLER
COOLER BY PASS VALVE
PRIMARY REGULATOR VALVE
PUMP
SUMP

REVERSE—A131L

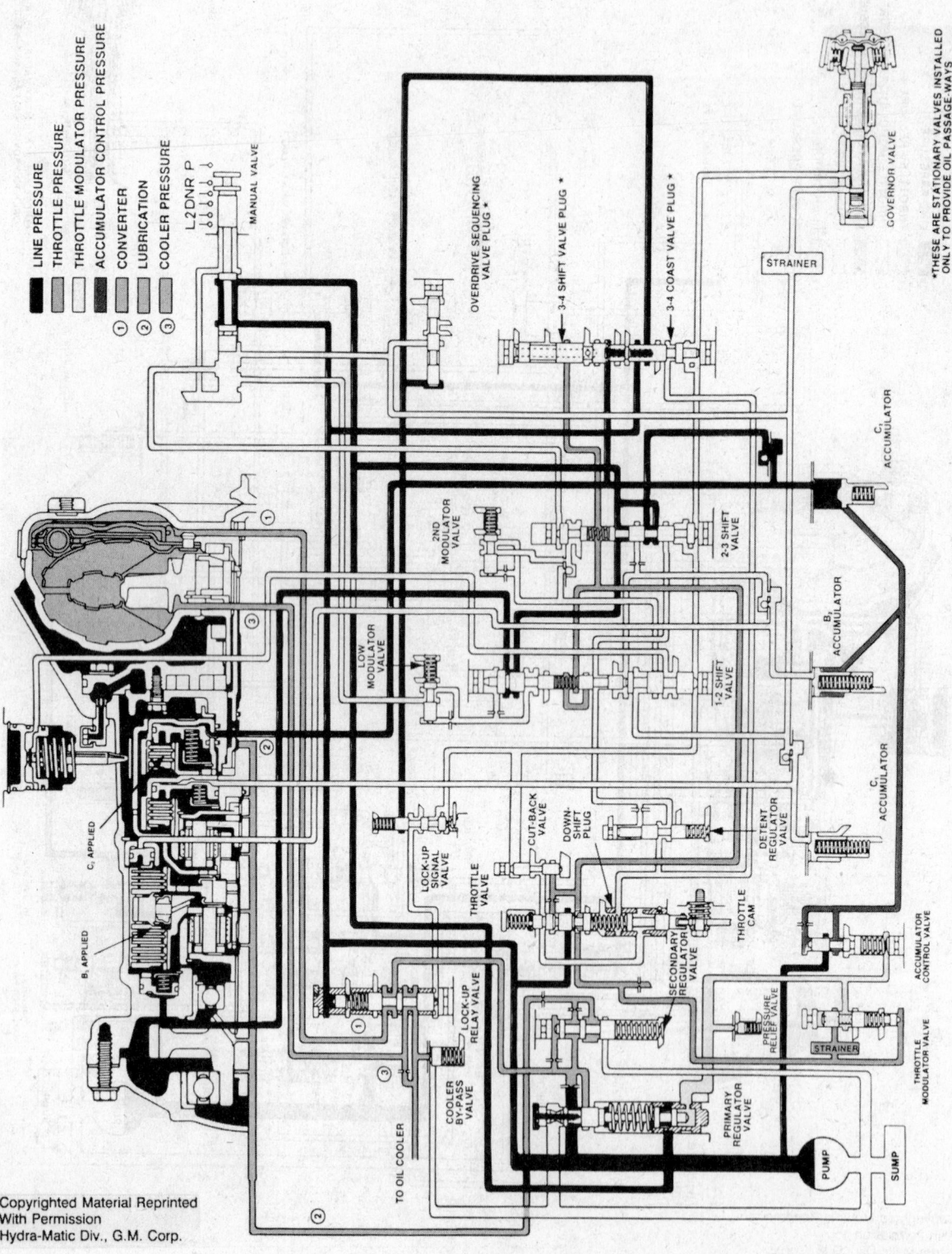

LINE PRESSURE
THROTTLE PRESSURE
THROTTLE MODULATOR PRESSURE
ACCUMULATOR CONTROL PRESSURE
CONVERTER
LUBRICATION
COOLER PRESSURE

*THESE ARE STATIONARY VALVES INSTALLED ONLY TO PROVIDE OIL PASSAGE-WAYS

DRIVE—1ST GEAR—A131L

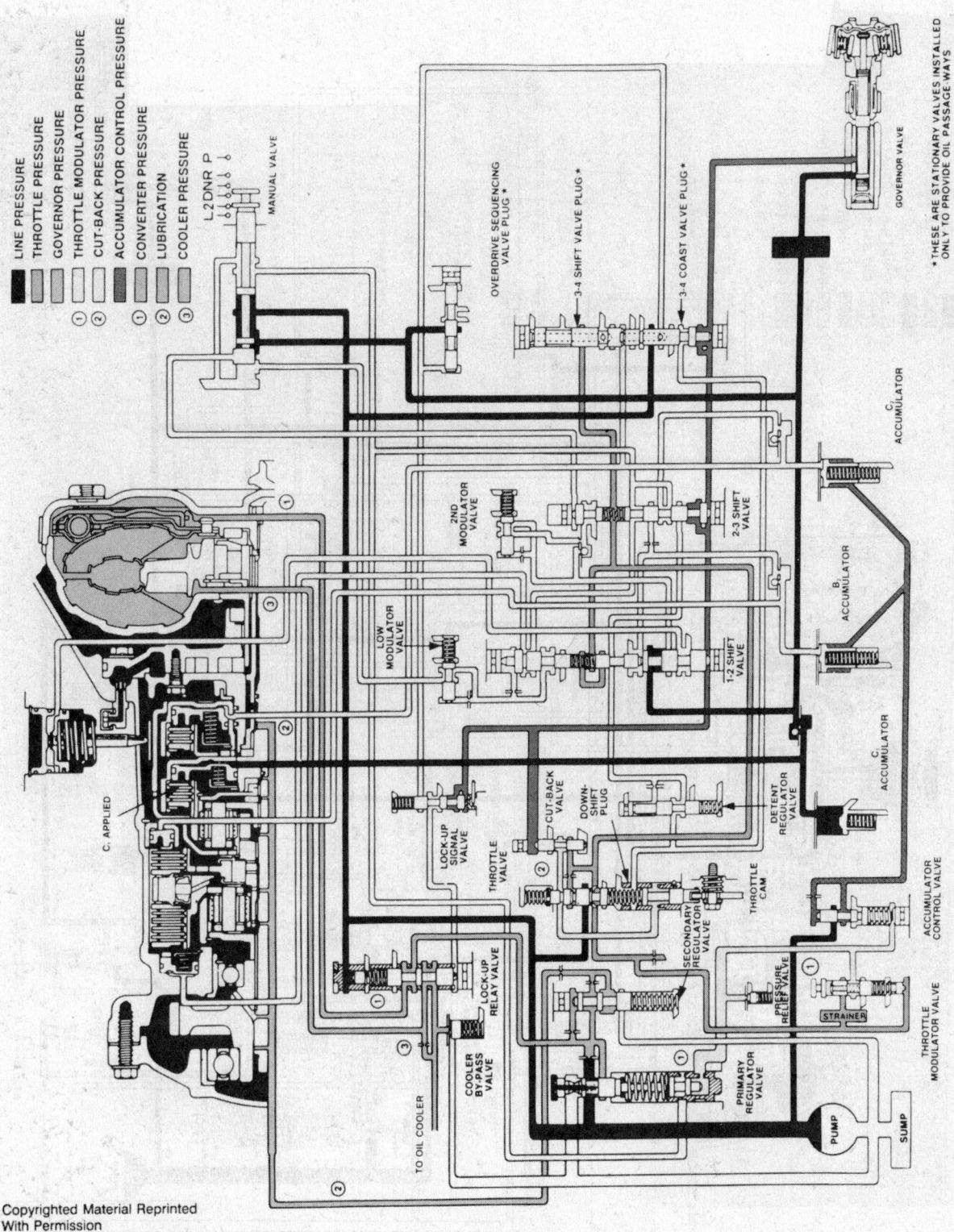

LINE PRESSURE
THROTTLE PRESSURE
GOVERNOR PRESSURE
THROTTLE MODULATOR PRESSURE
CUT-BACK PRESSURE
ACCUMULATOR CONTROL PRESSURE
CONVERTER PRESSURE
LUBRICATION
COOLER PRESSURE

* THESE ARE STATIONARY VALVES INSTALLED ONLY TO PROVIDE OIL PASSAGE WAYS

DRIVE—2ND GEAR—A131L

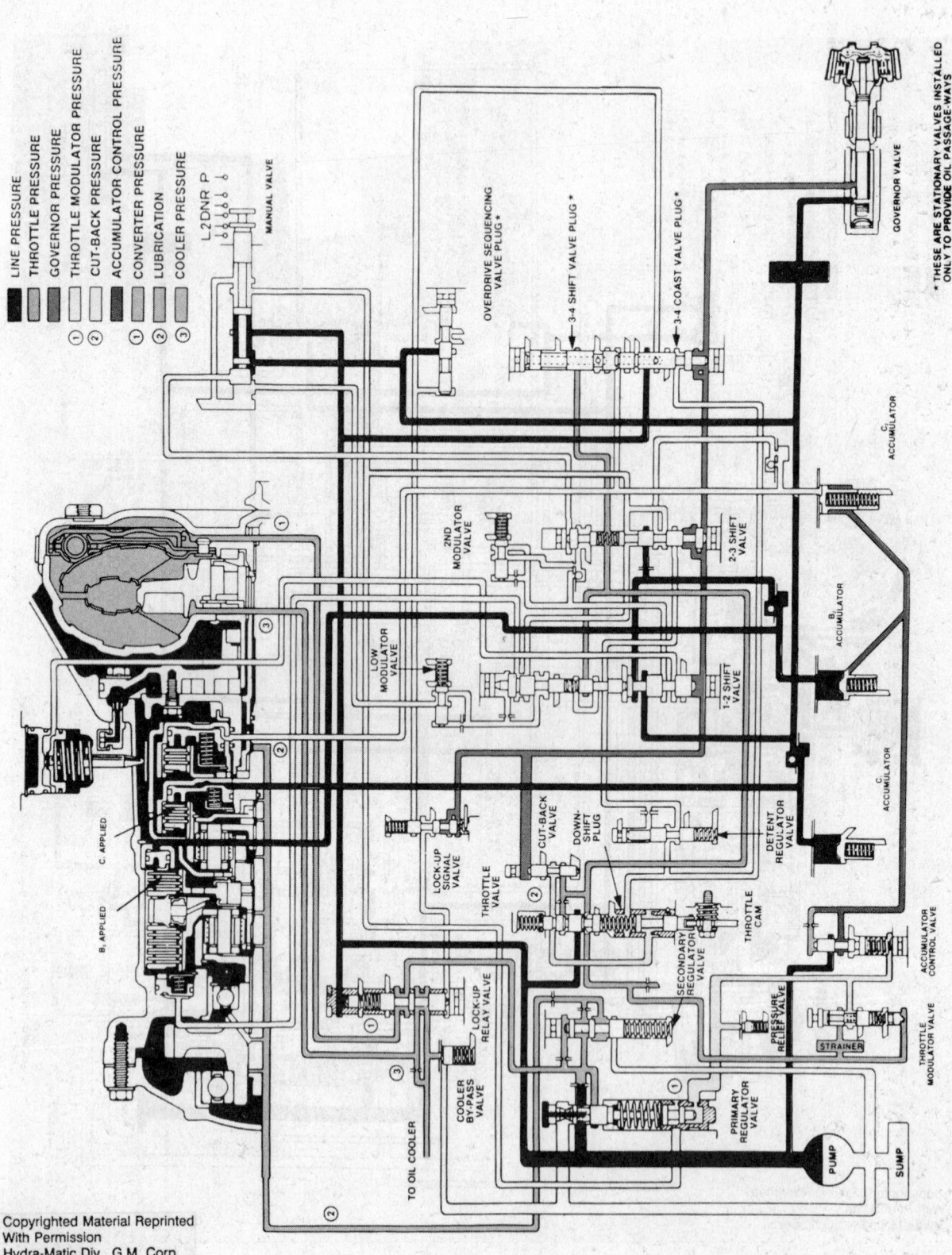

DRIVE – 3RD GEAR – A131L

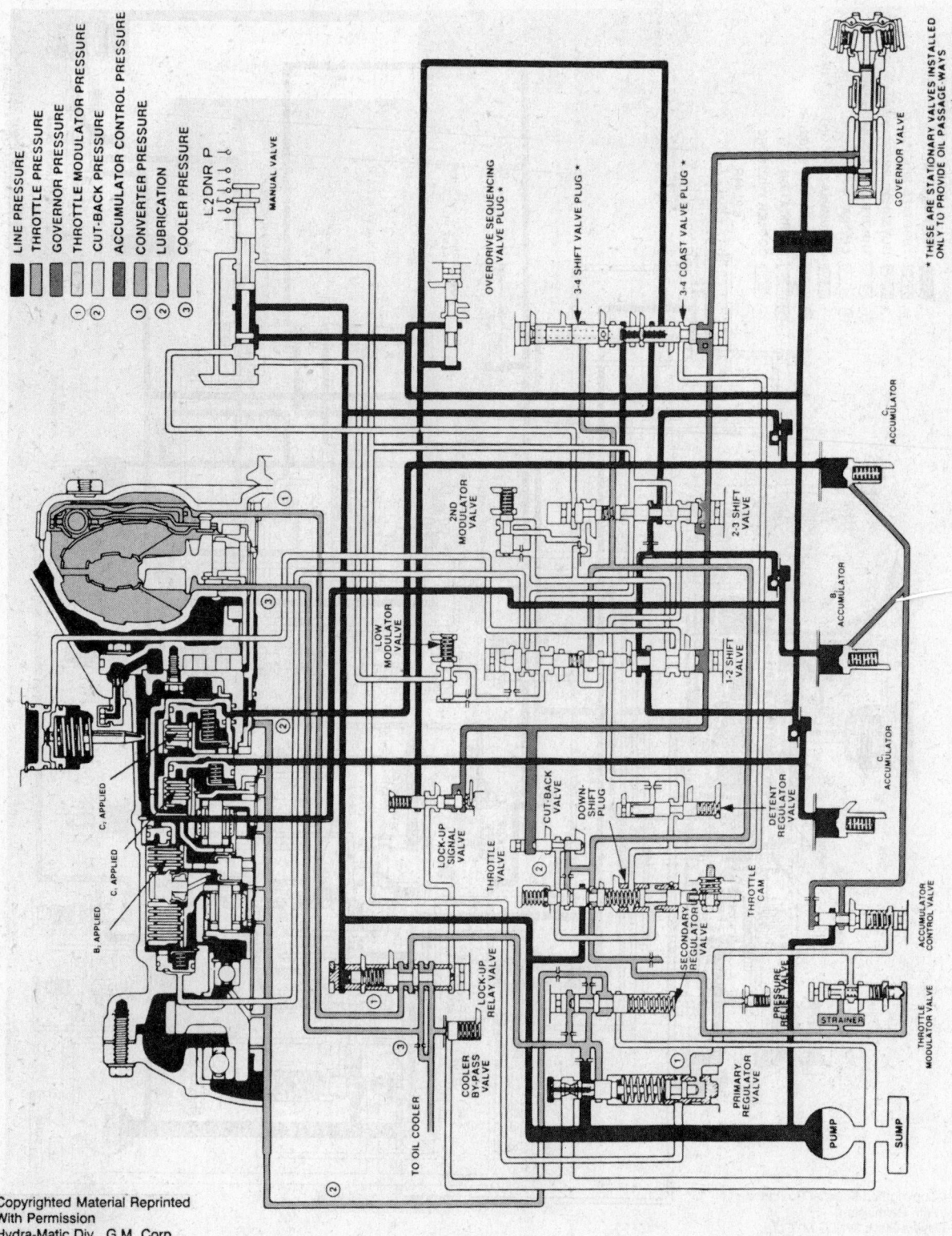

DRIVE—3RD GEAR (TCC APPLIED)—A131L

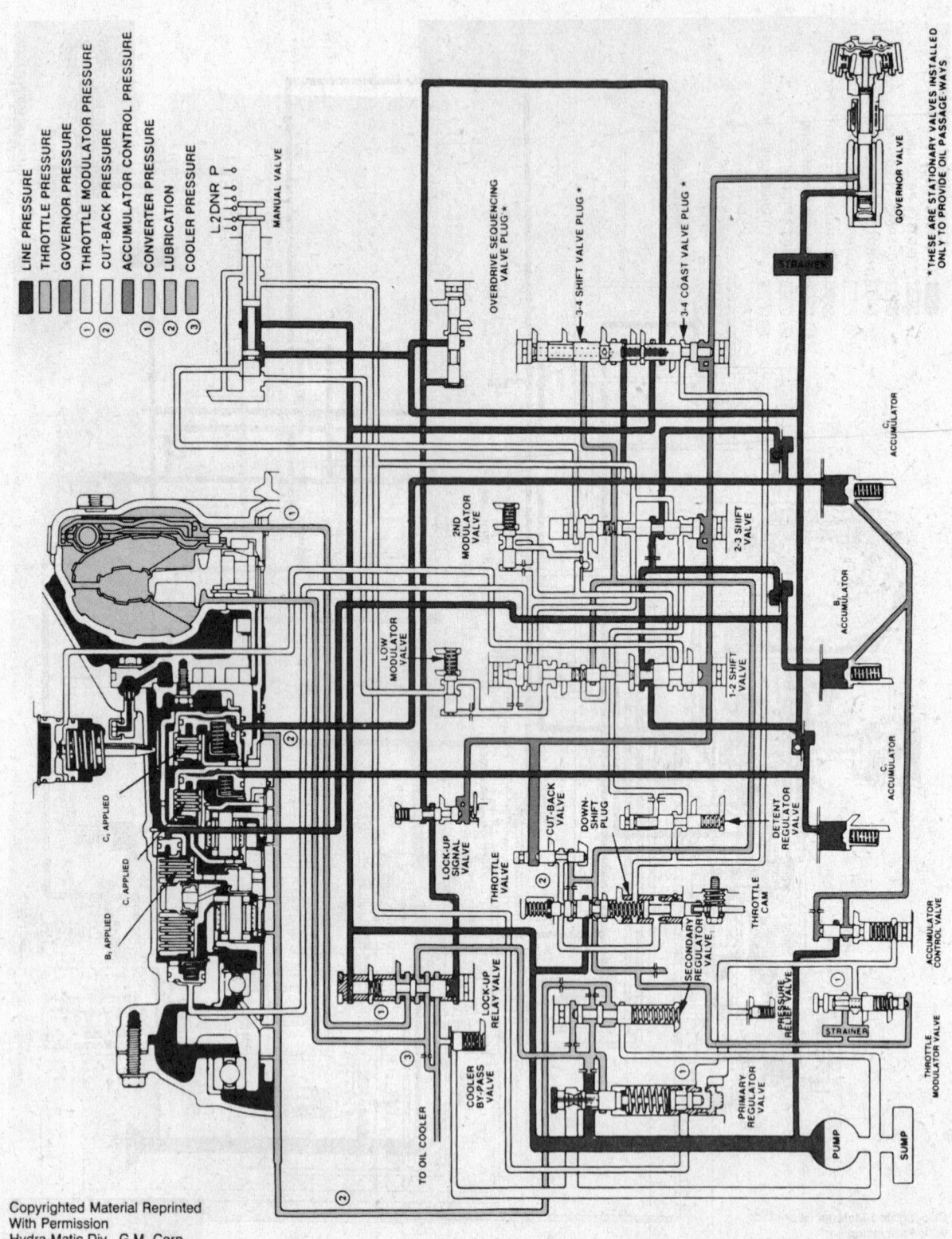

DRIVE—KICKDOWN—A131 L

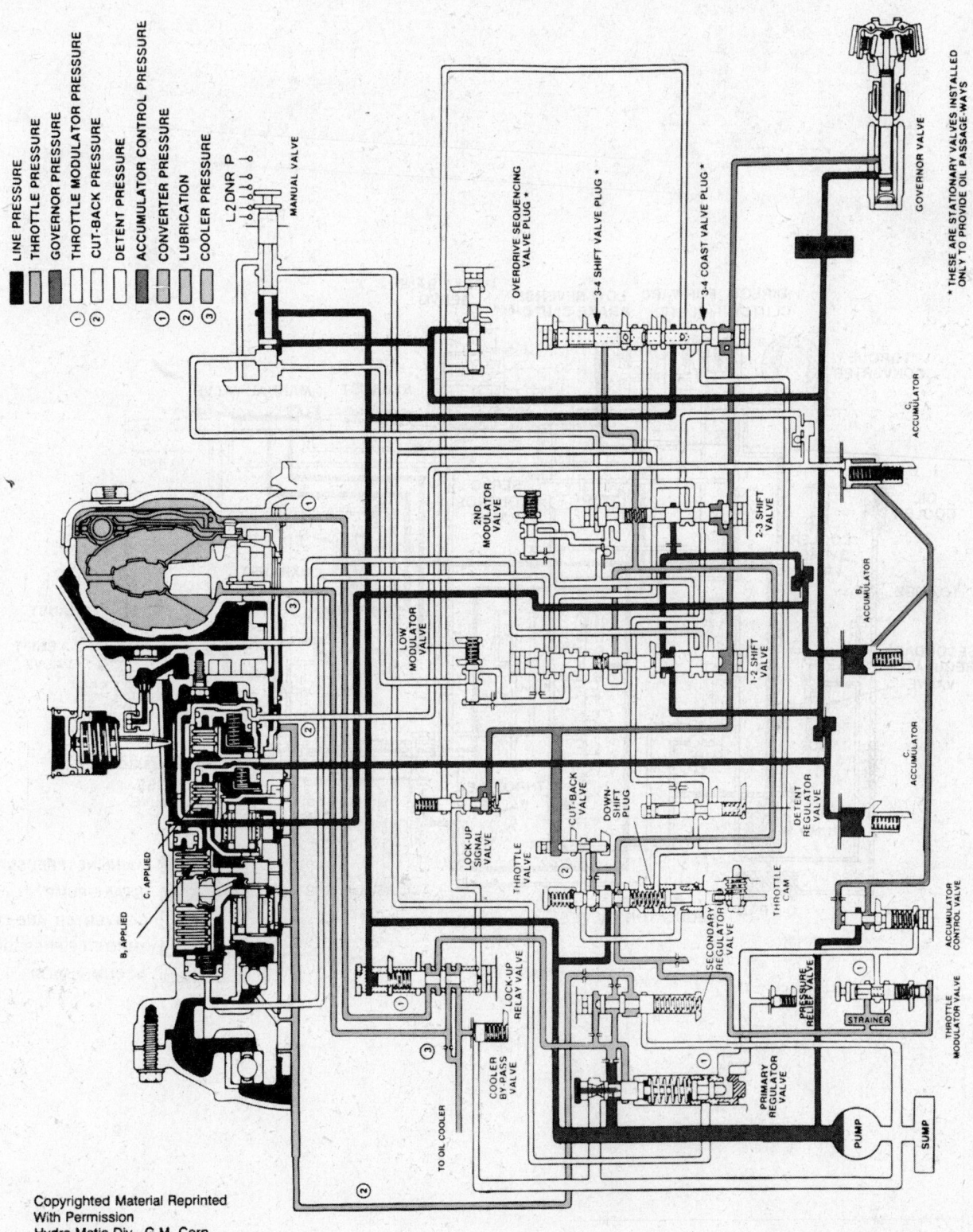

LINE PRESSURE
THROTTLE PRESSURE
GOVERNOR PRESSURE
THROTTLE MODULATOR PRESSURE
CUT-BACK PRESSURE
DETENT PRESSURE
ACCUMULATOR CONTROL PRESSURE
CONVERTER PRESSURE
LUBRICATION
COOLER PRESSURE

L 2 D N R P
MANUAL VALVE

OVERDRIVE SEQUENCING VALVE PLUG *
3-4 SHIFT VALVE PLUG *
3-4 COAST VALVE PLUG *
GOVERNOR VALVE

* THESE ARE STATIONARY VALVES INSTALLED ONLY TO PROVIDE OIL PASSAGE-WAYS

2ND MODULATOR VALVE
2-3 SHIFT VALVE
C₁ ACCUMULATOR
B₀ ACCUMULATOR
LOW MODULATOR VALVE
1-2 SHIFT VALVE
C₂ ACCUMULATOR
CUT-BACK VALVE
DOWN-SHIFT PLUG
DETENT REGULATOR VALVE
LOCK-UP SIGNAL VALVE
THROTTLE VALVE
THROTTLE CAM
ACCUMULATOR CONTROL VALVE
SECONDARY REGULATORY VALVE
PRESSURE RELIEF VALVE
STRAINER
THROTTLE MODULATOR VALVE
LOCK-UP RELAY VALVE
COOLER BY PASS VALVE
PRIMARY REGULATOR VALVE
PUMP
SUMP
TO OIL COOLER

C. APPLIED
B, APPLIED

PARK—SPRINT AND GEO

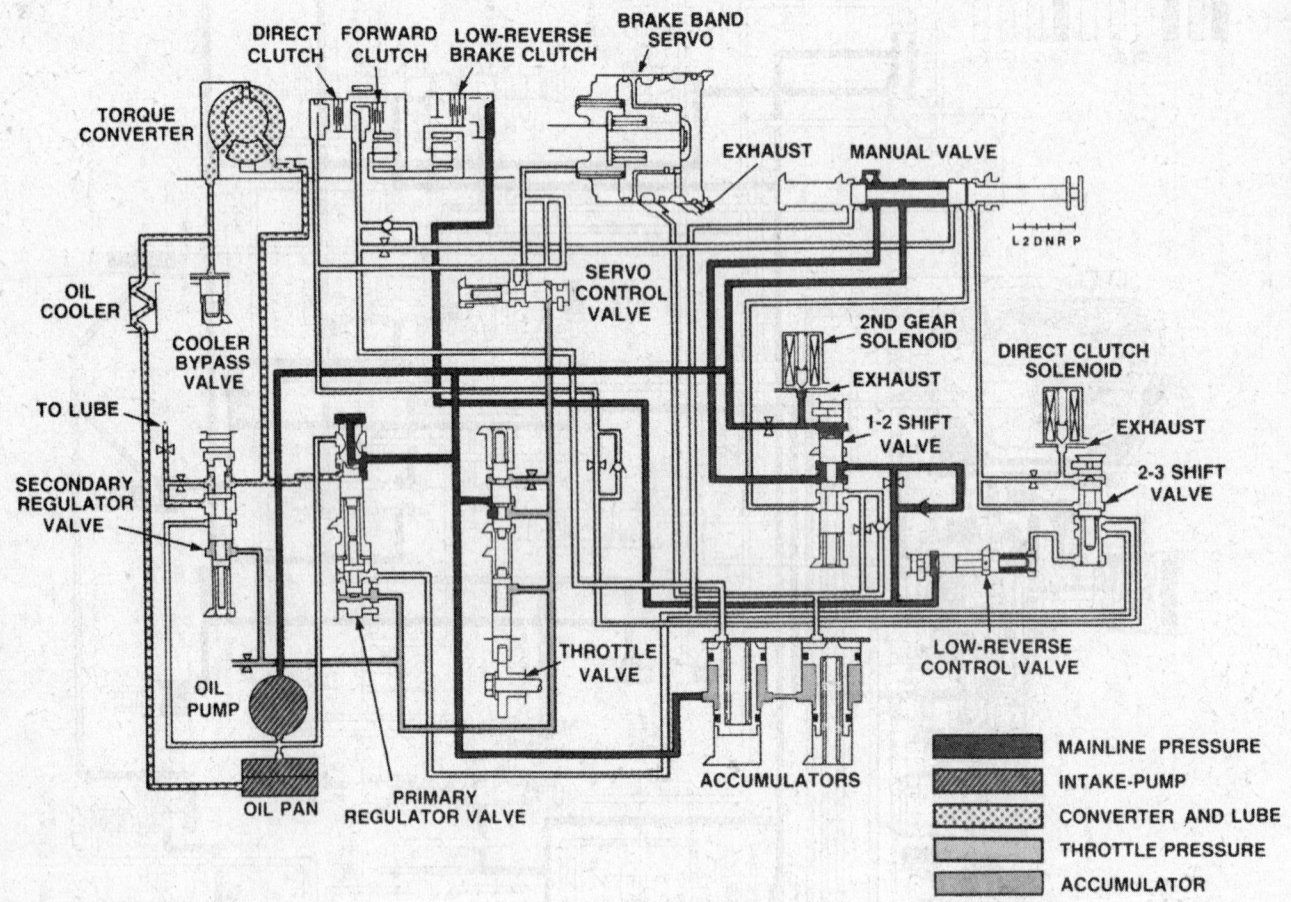

DIRECT CLUTCH · FORWARD CLUTCH · LOW-REVERSE BRAKE CLUTCH · BRAKE BAND SERVO · EXHAUST · MANUAL VALVE · TORQUE CONVERTER · OIL COOLER · COOLER BYPASS VALVE · TO LUBE · SECONDARY REGULATOR VALVE · OIL PUMP · OIL PAN · PRIMARY REGULATOR VALVE · THROTTLE VALVE · SERVO CONTROL VALVE · 2ND GEAR SOLENOID · EXHAUST · 1-2 SHIFT VALVE · DIRECT CLUTCH SOLENOID · EXHAUST · 2-3 SHIFT VALVE · LOW-REVERSE CONTROL VALVE · ACCUMULATORS · L 2 D N R P

MAINLINE PRESSURE
INTAKE-PUMP
CONVERTER AND LUBE
THROTTLE PRESSURE
ACCUMULATOR

NEUTRAL — SPRINT AND GEO

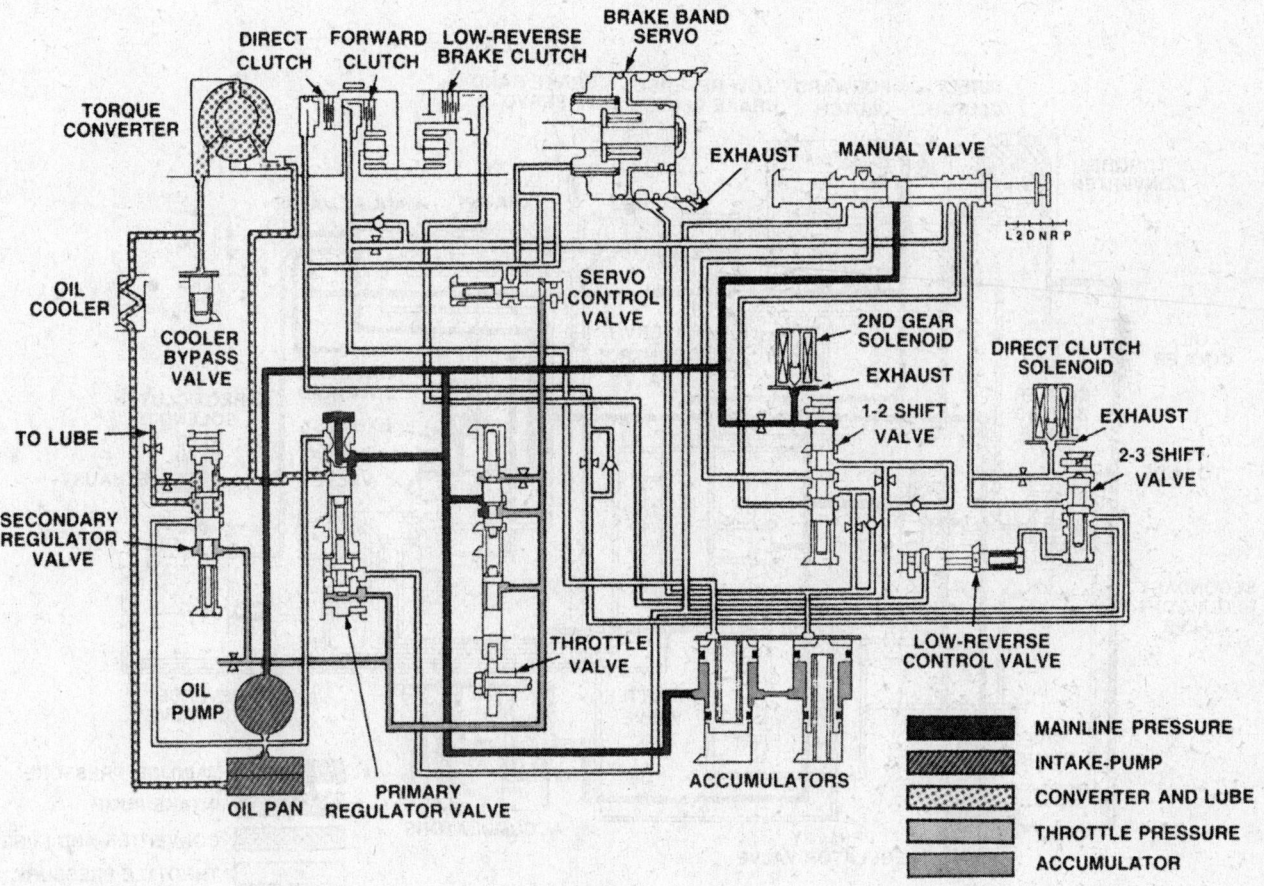

DRIVE OR 2ND RANGE – 1ST GEAR – SPRINT AND GEO

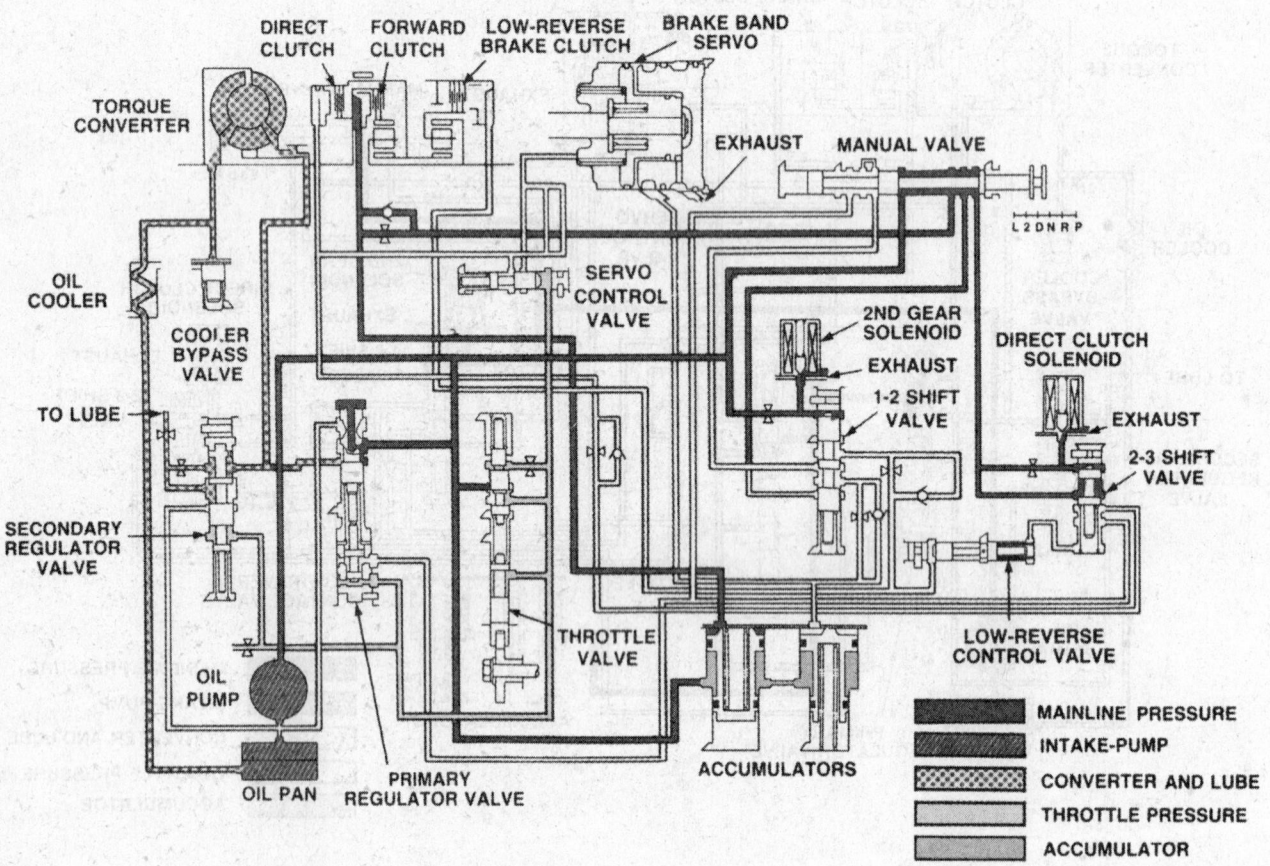

▓	MAINLINE PRESSURE
▨	INTAKE-PUMP
▒	CONVERTER AND LUBE
░	THROTTLE PRESSURE
▦	ACCUMULATOR

DRIVE OR 2ND RANGE–2ND GEAR–SPRINT AND GEO

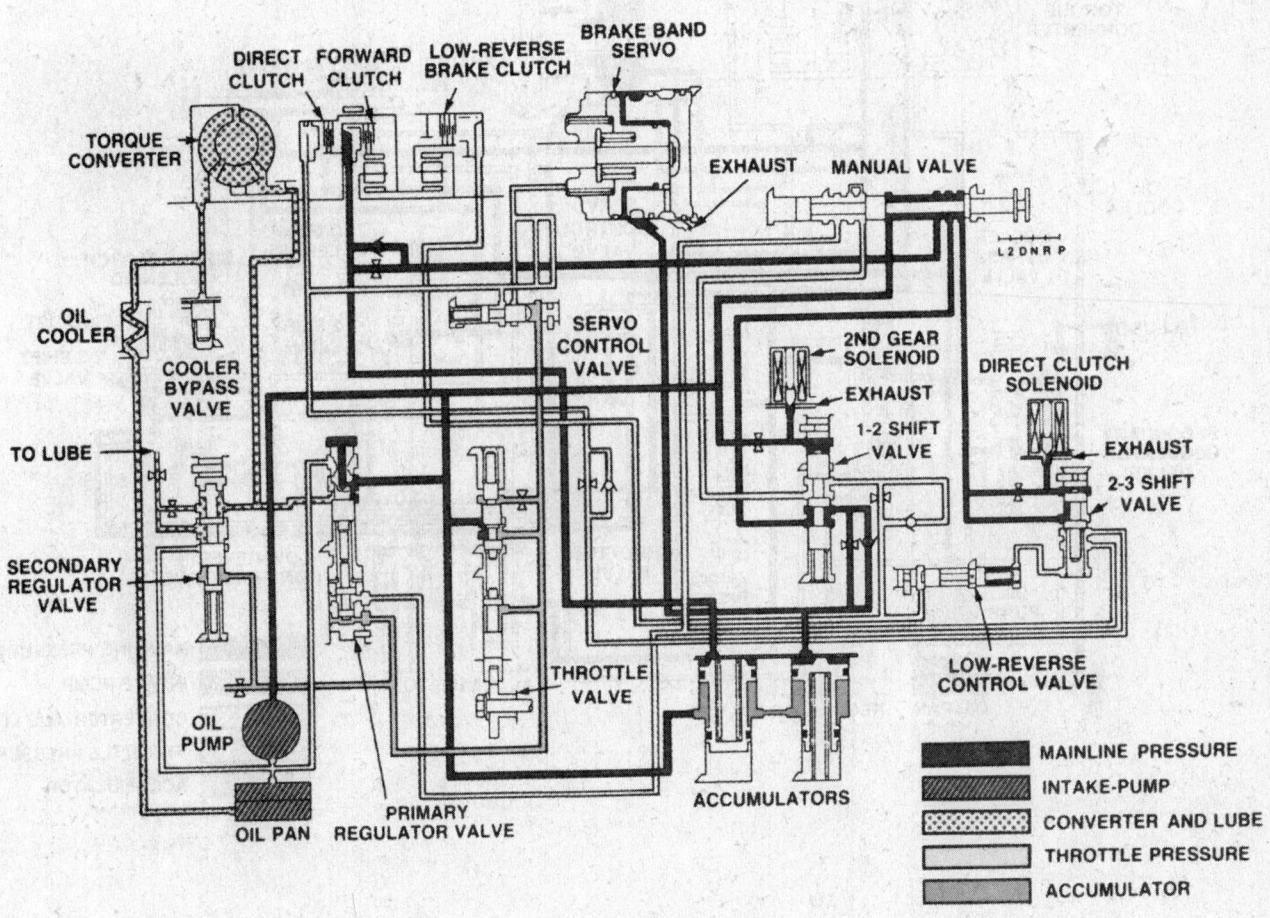

DIRECT CLUTCH

FORWARD CLUTCH

LOW-REVERSE BRAKE CLUTCH

BRAKE BAND SERVO

TORQUE CONVERTER

EXHAUST

MANUAL VALVE

L 2 D N R P

OIL COOLER

SERVO CONTROL VALVE

2ND GEAR SOLENOID

EXHAUST

DIRECT CLUTCH SOLENOID

COOLER BYPASS VALVE

1-2 SHIFT VALVE

EXHAUST

TO LUBE

2-3 SHIFT VALVE

SECONDARY REGULATOR VALVE

LOW-REVERSE CONTROL VALVE

THROTTLE VALVE

OIL PUMP

ACCUMULATORS

PRIMARY REGULATOR VALVE

OIL PAN

MAINLINE PRESSURE

INTAKE-PUMP

CONVERTER AND LUBE

THROTTLE PRESSURE

ACCUMULATOR

DRIVE RANGE – 3RD GEAR – SPRINT AND GEO

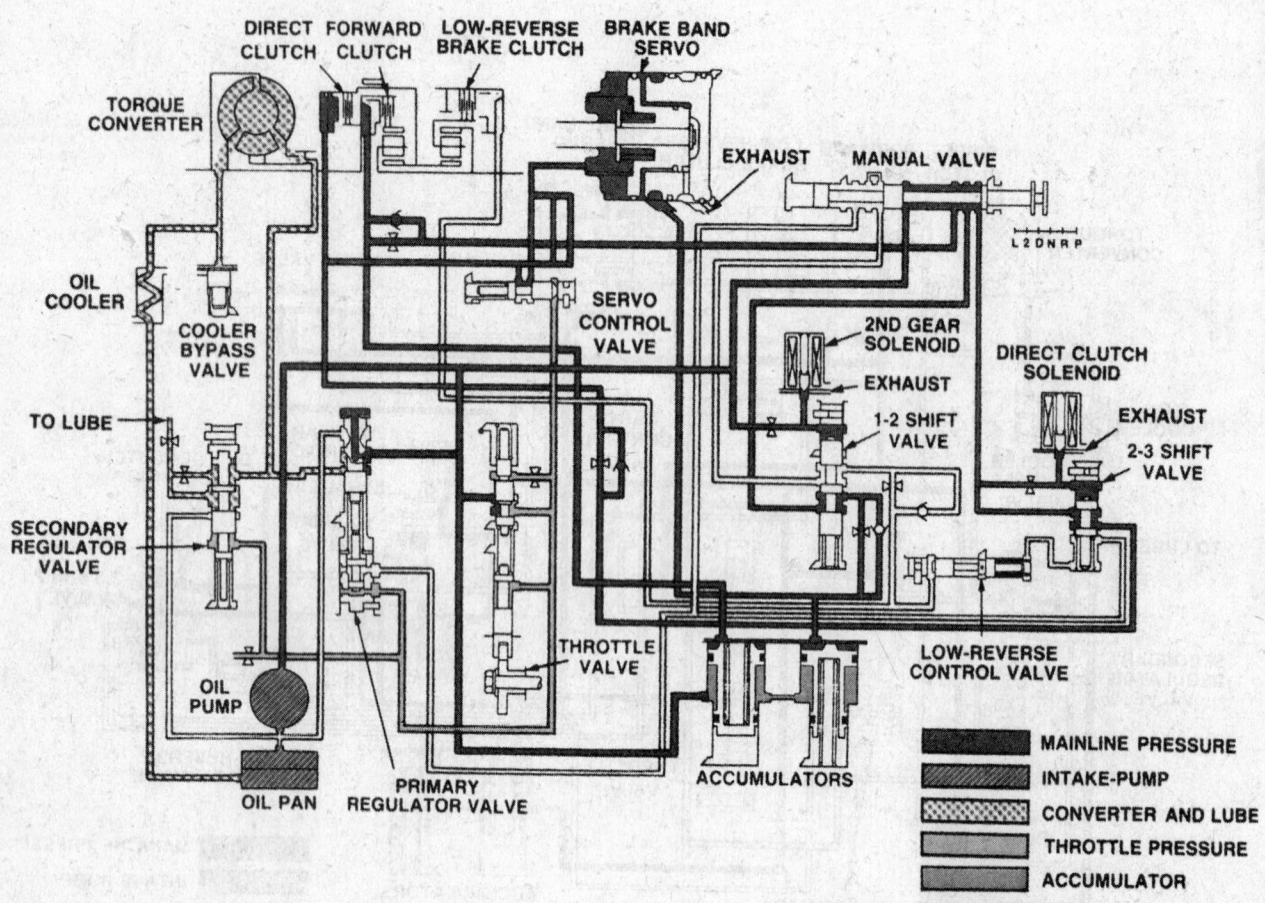